Tehillah le-Moshe

Moshe Greenberg

Tehillah le-Moshe

Biblical and Judaic Studies
in Honor of
Moshe Greenberg

Edited by

MORDECHAI COGAN
BARRY L. EICHLER
JEFFREY H. TIGAY

EISENBRAUNS
Winona Lake, Indiana
1997

Acknowledgments

The publication of this volume has been made possible by support from the Lucius N. Littauer Foundation, The University of Pennsylvania Research Foundation, The Hebrew University Internal Fund, The Seminary of Judaic Studies (Jerusalem), and The Jewish Theological Seminary of America.

Library of Congress Cataloging in Publication Data

Tehillah le-Moshe : biblical and Judaic studies in honor of Moshe Greenberg / edited by Mordechai Cogan, Barry L. Eichler, Jeffrey H. Tigay.
    p. cm.
  English and Hebrew.
  Includes bibliographical references and indexes.
  Added title page title: Tehilah le-Mosheh.
  ISBN 1-57506-027-2 (cloth : alk. paper)
  1. Bible. O.T.—Criticism, interpretation, etc. 2. Bible. O.T.—Criticism, interpretation, etc., Jewish. I. Greenberg, Moshe. II. Cogan, Mordechai. III. Eichler, Barry L. IV. Tigay, Jeffrey H. V. Title: Tehilah le-Mosheh
BS1171.2.T44 1997
296.1—dc21   97-25621
                                            CIP

Contents

PART 2
Historical, Thematic, and Methodological Studies

PART 3
Postbiblical and Rabbinic Studies

Hebrew Essays
PART 1
Biblical Studies

Part 2
Second Temple, Rabbinic, and Medieval Studies

Moshe Greenberg: An Appreciation

I

For nearly fifty years, Professor Moshe Greenberg has had an important impact on biblical scholarship through the content of his research, his teaching, and as a model of engaged scholarship. Moshe has summed up his lifelong goals as a scholar in the introduction to his *Studies in the Bible and Jewish Thought* (224). They are:

> to be true to the task of the classical Jewish Bible scholar: to enhance the Bible in the eyes of the faith/cultural community by (a) seeking to set forth existential values embodied in biblical narratives, laws and rituals; (b) pointing to the continuities and transformations of the biblical materials in later Jewish creativity. At the same time . . . to be true to the task of the critical scholar in (a) using historical, linguistic, and comparative methods that seek to understand the Bible in its ancient context; (b) presenting and dealing with material uncongenial to my predilections; (c) reviewing the goals and reflecting on the assumptions underlying the procedures of criticism (224, p. xv).

These goals mirror Moshe's ideal for Jewish biblical scholarship as consisting of academic-professional scholarship accompanied by

> Humility—that is, an openness to the new and the innovative, and to continuing debate that entails modesty and lack of dogmatism.
> Respect for the text, expressed in a systematic search for its "truth," in the universal-human sense as well as the particularistically Jewish; for the wealth of meanings, past and present, contained in it; and for its art of expression.
> Finally, and most important, a sense of responsibility toward a community whose members, the scholars' brethren, await their disclosure to them of the Scriptural message (224, p. 7).

II

Moshe has devoted most of his scholarly attention to the phenomenology of biblical religion and law, the theory and practice of interpreting biblical

Editors' note: Numbers in parentheses in this appreciation refer the reader to the numbered works in the "Bibliography of the Writings of Moshe Greenberg" (in this volume, pp. xxiii–xxxviii). Wherever possible, quotations are cited from item number 224.

texts, and the role of the Bible in Jewish thought (224, p. xv). His studies in the area of biblical religion include his magisterial survey of Israelite religion in the monarchic period (135), his article on prayer ("*Tĕfillâ*") in the *ʾEnṣîq-lôpedyâ Miqrāʾît* (154), and other essays on prayer and on the book of Job. In his study on the refinement of the conception of prayer in the Bible (121), he traces the development of petition and praise away from their roots in the conception that the deity literally needs to be informed of the plight of the worshiper and propitiated by flattery into "a vehicle of humility, an expression of un-selfsufficiency, which in biblical thought, is the proper stance of humans before God." Thus, "[i]n its highest reaches, biblical prayer remains still the embodiment of the awareness of creaturehood, as much a contrast to theurgic incantation as to the self-containedness of human-centered modernism" (224, p. 104).

In his monograph on biblical prose prayers (156), Moshe shows that these prayers reflect the piety of commoners, illustrating the popular conception of God as redresser of wrongs, constant, reliable, trustworthy, and fair. He reasons that the frequency of spontaneous prayer must have sustained a constant sense of God's presence and strengthened the egalitarian tendency of Israelite religion that led to the establishment of the synagogue. The fact that prayer was conceived as analogous to a social transaction between persons fostered an emphasis on sincerity and content, rather than formulation, and may lie at the root of the classical-prophetic view of worship as a gesture whose acceptance depends on the worshiper's adherence to the values of God.

In his "Reflections on Job's Theology" (140), Moshe observes that Job's experience of God's inexplicable enmity could not wipe out his knowledge of God's benignity gained from his earlier experience, and hence he became confused instead of simply rejecting God. Accordingly, the fact that the Bible retains Job as well as Proverbs reflects the capacity of the religious sensibility to affirm both experiences:

> One can see in individual as in collective life a moral causality (which the religious regard as divinely maintained . . .): evil recoils upon the evildoers . . . goodness brings blessings. At the same time, the manifestation of this causality can be so erratic or so delayed as to cast doubt on its validity as the single key to the destiny of people and nations. . . . No single key unlocks the mystery of destiny . . . but, for all that, the sober believer does not endorse nihilism. Wisdom, Torah, and Prophets continue to represent for him one aspect of causality in events which he can confirm in his own private experience. But one aspect only. The other stands beyond his moral judgment, though it is still under God: namely, the mysterious or preordained decree of God, toward which the proper attitude is "Though he slay me, yet will I trust in Him (Job 13.15, *qerê*)" (224, pp. 332–33).

The area of biblical law is well illuminated by Moshe's seminal studies of the postulates and social policies underlying biblical law. In his early study,

"Some Postulates of Biblical Criminal Law" (22), he argued that "the law [is] the expression of underlying postulates or values of culture" (224, p. 27) and that differences between biblical and ancient Near Eastern laws were not reflections of different stages of social development but of different underlying legal and religious principles. In "Biblical Attitudes toward Power" (202), he analyzed various economic, social, political, and religious laws in the Torah and showed that their thrust was to disperse authority and prestige throughout society and prevent the monopolization of prestige and political and economic power by narrow elite groups.

In his commentaries on the books of Exodus (70) and Ezekiel (157), and earlier studies leading up to them, Moshe has developed and exemplified his "holistic" method of exegesis. This method is beautifully explicated in the introduction to his commentary on Ezekiel. While building on the source-critical achievements of earlier scholarship, the holistic method redirects attention from the texts' "hypothetically reconstructed elements" to the biblical books as integral wholes, as the products of thoughtful and artistic design conveying messages of their own. "Details of this art . . . and design disclose themselves to the patient and receptive reader who divests himself of preconceptions regarding what an ancient prophet should have said and how he should have said it" (157, p. 26).[1] With this approach, Moshe has recalled scholarly attention to the "received text [which] is the only historically attested datum; it alone has had demonstrable effects; it alone is the undoubted product of Israelite creativity" (70, pp. 4–5). As Moshe showed, since midrashic and later precritical Jewish exegesis operated on the assumption of unitary authorship, they have many insights to offer the holistic commentator.

The recognition of the value of traditional Jewish sources for the holistic method is manifest in Moshe's recourse to postbiblical sources in explicating the biblical text and aspects of ancient Israelite culture. In his early study of Hebrew *sĕgullâ* and Akkadian *sikiltu* (3), he found the key to the meaning of both words in the Rabbinic Hebrew verb *siggel*. In other studies, he found that the release of the accidental killer from the city of refuge upon the death of the high priest is best clarified by the talmudic explanation that the priest's death constitutes a vicarious expiation of life by life (18); and he explained Ezekiel's dumbness (17) and Rachel's theft of Laban's *terāfîm* (27) on the basis of striking parallels from Second Temple times found in Josephus.

On the other hand, Moshe has remained true to his early recognition that the Bible is best understood in light of its ancient Near Eastern context as well as later Jewish tradition. Beginning with his doctoral work on the Ḥapiru through the study of biblical law in the light of ancient Near Eastern law, and now throughout his commentary on Ezekiel, Moshe has consistently shown how careful comparative use of the rich trove of texts and artifacts from the

---

1. This approach was already anticipated in "Some Postulates of Biblical Criminal Law" (22; see 224, pp. 26–27).

ancient Near East can recover the lost meaning of a Hebrew phrase or bring into sharp focus a uniquely Israelite idea.

Moshe's studies of Jewish thought include a masterful survey of the intellectual achievements of medieval Jewish exegesis[2] as well as investigations of rabbinic reflections on defying illegal orders (77), *biṭṭāḥôn* (224, pp. 63–74), and attitudes toward members of other religions (96, 228). He argues that a Scripture-based religion can and must avoid fundamentalism by being selective and critical in its reliance on tradition and by re-prioritizing values (see esp. 173, pp. 11–27, 49–67; 228, pp. 23–35). In his study of "Jewish Conceptions of the Human Factor in Biblical Prophecy" (196), Moshe shows that from the Talmud to the Renaissance, classical Jewish exegetes and thinkers who never doubted the divine inspiration and authorship of the Torah and other prophetic writings nevertheless acknowledged the literary evidence of human shaping of the text. They did so despite

> the great temptation to absolutize the authority of Scripture and silence the incessant challenges to its integrity and validity by categorically asserting that all is simply divine dictation. To modern Jewish critics they are a model of reverence toward the source of religion that does not entail blindness to the complexity of that source or the adoption of farfetched cloaking of that complexity. The tradition of honest and sober reasoning, accommodating articles of faith to (literary) facts, stands the critics in good stead as they confront a wave of simplistic dogmatic piety that seeks to impose itself on the entire community, stifling curiosity and independence of judgment (224, p. 416).

Underlying all of Moshe's scholarly contributions is the premise that scholarship is never to be viewed as an end in itself. Rather, it is a mirror of humanity's variegated intellectual and spiritual achievements, societal values, and cultural postulates, and remains incomplete and diminished unless it informs and enlightens the present reality. Moshe's most intimate and meaningful reality has always been Jewish peoplehood—a fact that not only determined his choice of academic study but that also was the decisive element in his settling in Israel. And yet his reality has never been parochial, for it encompasses all of humankind. Most telling of the humanistic outlook of his Jewish scholarship and identity is his statement in a public debate in the 1980s concerning a proposed cut in support of Israeli universities by the Ministry of Education. Departments of ancient Near Eastern studies were singled out as a luxury too expensive to maintain in a time of retrenchment. In defense of Assyriology, Moshe wrote:

> Contextual study of the Bible and Talmud (and even more so, our later literature whose dependence upon its surroundings is well known)—that is, inte-

---

2. "The Hebrew Bible and the Jewish Heritage," presented at a conference on "The Hebrew Bible: Sacred Text and Literature," sponsored by Wayne State University (Detroit), October 30, 1988. The article is not yet published.

grated study of the cultures of Sumer, Babylonia, Assyria, Hatti, Egypt, Persia, Greece and Rome—is of major importance in clarifying the commonality between us and the rest of humanity, as well as what distinguishes us from them. And we are in need of both clarifications. What is unique—which cannot be determined without knowing what we share with the nations—we will adopt as a substantive element of our identity. Our right of existence, upon which so many cast doubt, should be clear at least to us, if only we were cognizant of the unique values we contribute to the cultural trove of mankind. Observing what we share with the nations will help build bridges between us and them. Recognition of the commonality in the past will make it easier to achieve a proper balance in our relations with the nations in the present (172, p. 22).

Moshe's steadfast dedication to biblical scholarship and Jewish thought is surpassed only by his passionate devotion to teaching. He has always taken teaching seriously. Already known as an excellent teacher from his days on the staff at the Jewish Theological Seminary's Camp Ramah and JTS's high school department, in his first year on the Penn faculty he read Gilbert Highet's *The Art of Teaching* to help him meet the new challenges of teaching in a university. Imparting knowledge to others is a joyful affirmation of his very being, his most sublime raison d'être, whereby he creates an existential bond between himself and his fellow human being. In the classroom setting, Moshe is the consummate pedagogue who teaches by personal example. With beguiling simplicity, he reduces complex matters into their basic components and thus exposes fundamental issues, all the while allowing his students to be keenly aware of his analytical thought processes. With great patience, he prods his students to discover the unstated postulates and hypotheses underlying various scholarly positions so as to discern the true nature of the differing argumentations. With methodological rigor, sound judgment, and common sense, he trains his students to evaluate carefully the many types of evidence bearing on the issues, thereby enabling them to mature into independent critical thinkers. But to Moshe, scholarship is only a means to an end, and he is never content to grapple with methodological issues alone. He imbues his students with the broad humanistic significance of the ancient texts in the hope of creating thoughtful and caring scholars whose intellectual work will have relevance to the present.

Moshe's genuine love of teaching is also predicated on his concern for the well-being of others. For this reason, his teaching has always extended beyond the confines of the university classroom, encompassing every aspect of his inter-relationships with students, colleagues, acquaintances, and friends, in individual meetings or informal study circles at school and at home. His generosity with his time, the depth of his concern, and his eagerness to assist are hallmarks of his pedagogy, a pedagogy based not only on teaching a given subject matter but on offering guidance for life itself. His advice is always measured and thoughtful. Students and colleagues have benefited not only from his insights on ways to index one's dissertation prior to the advent of the computer, on the chairing of committees and departments, and on the art of teaching, but also on the art of living in all of its complexities. All who have spoken with Moshe can attest that even the most casual conversation with him is a personally edifying experience.

To be sure, Moshe's educational mission has never been confined to his students and acquaintances but has always extended to the public at large. His commitment to bringing the results of scholarship to the public has taken many forms: from penning popular articles in American Jewish newspapers and magazines to participating in the Jewish Publication Society's committee for translating *The Writings (Ketuvim)* (1966–82) and serving as the *Encyclopaedia Judaica*'s division editor for Law and Society in the Bible (1968–71); from preparing studies such as *Understanding Exodus* (1969) to assist educators in developing curricula based on the best of traditional and modern scholarship to publishing articles and lectures on teaching the Bible in schools (a subject to which no academic biblical scholar has devoted so much attention); from his efforts in his own Department of Bible at Hebrew University to train high school Bible teachers and his role as advisor to the Ministry of Education to his teaching at the Jewish Theological Seminary of America and at the Seminary for Judaic Studies in Jerusalem.

III

The experiences that Moshe has drawn upon in shaping his approach to scholarship are many and profound. Most formative was the nurturing influence of his parents and the home environment in which he was raised. He was born in Philadelphia on July 10, 1928 (22 Tammuz, 5688), to Rabbi Simon and Betty (Davis) Greenberg, who served the Conservative congregation Har Zion Temple. Their younger son, Daniel, was born in 1934. The Greenbergs' choice of Hebrew names for their sons in the English-speaking diaspora and their decision to raise them in a Hebrew-speaking home (each parent having spent time in Palestine to master spoken Hebrew) contributed greatly to Moshe's strong sense of Jewish identity. Rabbi and Mrs. Greenberg's passion for Judaic studies, Zionism, the Hebrew language, Jewish education, the ethical dimension of Judaism, and the harmony between Judaism and American democratic ideals were successfully transmitted to Moshe, and this passion formed the cornerstone of the commitments that would later manifest themselves in his activities and writings. Moshe's brother thinks of him as combining their father's philosophical depth and willingness to reexamine old conclusions with their mother's constant striving for excellence.

Moshe also benefited from the tutelage of excellent teachers who also served as advisors and mentors at important junctures in his life. The first of them was Samuel Leib Blank, a Hebrew author from Bessarabia living in Philadelphia.

Since there were no Conservative Jewish day schools in the city when Moshe was a youngster, his parents engaged Mr. Blank as a private tutor for his formal Jewish education. He came to the Greenbergs' home over a period of about eight years, twice a week, early in the morning, before Moshe left for public school. He taught Moshe Bible with Rashi, Mishna, Bialik's *Sefer hā-ʾAggādâ*, essays on Jewish national thought, literature, and grammar. He required Moshe to hand in a "written lecture" for critique at every session. In his critique, Mr. Blank would delete superfluous words so as to initiate Moshe in the "secret of conciseness" of Hebrew. This practice left its impact in the concise style that characterizes Moshe's writing to this day.

The Greenbergs and other parents who were devoted to the revival of Hebrew and spoke it with their children established a circle of Hebrew-speaking youth, called *ʾAḥăvâ*, so that their children would not feel isolated. This group, about a dozen strong, gathered from all parts of the city in each other's homes on Saturday nights and held discussions about culture and nationalism. In the early 1940s, Moshe as a young teenager was sent to the newly-opened summer camp "Massad," which was established for Hebrew-speaking youth. At Massad, he was exposed for the first time to hundreds of young Hebrew speakers like himself, most of them students at yeshivot in New York where their large numbers prevented them from feeling any strangeness in speaking Hebrew. There, life-long friendships were formed, many of which would be renewed later when Moshe settled in Israel, with people such as the linguist Haim Blanc, the pathologist David Meyer, and the poet T. Carmi.

As an undergraduate at the University of Pennsylvania, Moshe began a long association with one of the great biblical and ancient Near Eastern scholars of the generation, Ephraim Avigdor Speiser, who was to have a profound influence on Moshe's scholarly direction. During his final years of high school and his first years at Penn (which he entered in 1945), Moshe had become enamored of Spanish and Portuguese. He spent the summer of 1947 studying in Mexico to perfect his Spanish and roomed in the home of a Jewish woman. At her request, Moshe taught her son, who was approaching Bar Mitzvah age, the basic elements of Judaism. Upon Moshe's return to Penn in the fall, he consulted with Prof. George Seiver, Chair of the Romance Languages Department, seeking advice about majoring in Spanish. When Seiver asked why he wanted to do so, Moshe was taken by surprise; it was a question he had never thought through. So he improvised an answer based on his recent experience in Mexico: "Maybe one day I'll teach in a Hebrew school in South America." Prof. Seiver, surprised at the answer, asked Moshe to tell him something about his background. When he learned that Moshe spoke Hebrew fluently, he suggested that Moshe contact Penn's Department of Oriental Studies. He met with the chair of the department, Speiser, who described the department's offerings in the history of Hebrew, philological-historical study of the Bible, Akkadian, Sumerian, and Arabic—with every field presided over by a noted scholar:

besides Speiser, there were Zellig S. Harris in Hebrew linguistics, S. N. Kramer in Sumerian, and Georgio Levi Della Vida in Arabic. Speiser's description of the programs of study opened new horizons before Moshe's eyes and he was captivated. He registered in the department and so returned to his Hebrew roots.

Speiser became Moshe's primary instructor. Moshe would later cite him as one of "the two men who most profoundly shaped my understanding of the task and method of biblical scholarship . . . His pedagogy tempered rigorous discipline with unstinting consideration for his students, and set a standard for lifelong emulation" (157, p. ix).

Moshe's other scholarly model was the Hebrew University's Prof. Yehezkel Kaufmann. Kaufmann's tutelage was via his writings. While an undergraduate at Penn, Moshe came upon the first volume of Kaufmann's *Tôlĕdôt hā-ʾEmûnâ ha-Yisrĕʾēlît* in his father's library. He was enthralled by Kaufmann's conceptual, critical, and polemical power. When he realized that Kaufmann's work was unknown to the non-Hebrew world of biblical scholarship, he decided to make it known, starting with Speiser. He wrote his senior thesis on Kaufmann's treatment of the history of the Israelite priesthood, showing the superiority of Kaufmann's views over the views of others. Eventually, with Speiser's prodding and aided by Mr. Blank's earlier lessons in conciseness, he published a condensed version of his thesis as an article in *The Journal of the American Oriental Society* in 1950 (1). This was Moshe's first scholarly article and the first appearance of Kaufmann's views in English.

Moshe sent a letter with an offprint of the article to Kaufmann in Jerusalem and thus began a correspondence that continued until Kaufmann's death in 1963.[3] Kaufmann expressed the hope that all of his *Tôlĕdôt* would be translated into English. Moshe accepted the challenge, convinced that Kaufmann had advanced biblical scholarship but that as long as non-Hebrew-reading scholars were unfamiliar with the totality of his views and their rationale it would be necessary to present them repeatedly. He began by translating Kaufmann's article "The Bible and Mythological Polytheism" for the *Journal of Biblical Literature* (2) and his chapter "The Biblical Age" for Leo W. Schwarz's *Great Ages and Ideas of the Jewish People* (11) and eventually published his English abridgement of the first seven volumes of *Tôlĕdôt* as *The Religion of Israel: From Its Beginnings to the Babylonian Exile*, in 1960 (21).[4] When Moshe finally met Kaufmann in person in 1954, he was struck by the contrast between the intellectual power and polemical sharpness of Kaufmann the writer and his personal humility.

In 1949, Moshe received his B.A. from Pennsylvania (he was elected to Phi Beta Kappa a year earlier) and married his high-school sweetheart, Evelyn

---

3. Highlights of the correspondence are presented in Moshe's lecture "Yehezkel Kaufmann: Personal Impressions" (211, pp. 4–6).

4. Moshe describes the procedures he followed in abridging *Tôlĕdôt* in the preface to his English abridgement, *The Religion of Israel* (21).

Gelber. He continued in the Department of Oriental Studies as a doctoral student, working closely with Speiser. He devoted his dissertation to the subject of the Ḫapiru (or Ḫabiru), combining his interests in Bible, Assyriology, and Semitics. His fellow students included the Assyriologist J. J. Finkelstein, with whom Moshe would later edit a volume of Speiser's essays.

Since Moshe's studies at Penn covered the Bible only in the context of the ancient Near East, he decided in 1950 to enroll simultaneously at the Jewish Theological Seminary of America (where his father was then professor of education and would later become Vice-Chancellor) in New York, so as to satisfy the other half of his ambition, to study what later developed out of the Bible: the impression that it made on Jewish and world culture. The Chancellor of JTS, Louis Finkelstein, had foreseen that the post–World War II wave of sympathy for Judaism would lead to the establishment of chairs in Judaica in American universities. To prepare scholars qualified to occupy them, he created a program of special studies for students who were engaged in doctoral programs in pertinent fields at other institutions. At JTS they would receive intensive training in classical Judaica and be exempt from practical rabbinical courses. Moshe and his fellow students (Arthur Hyman, Fritz Rothschild, David Winston, and Arthur Cohen) studied Bible with H. L. Ginsberg, liturgy with Shalom Spiegel, Jewish thought with A. J. Heschel, and Talmud with Shraga Abramson and Saul Lieberman.

Moshe completed both programs in 1954, receiving his Ph.D. from Penn and rabbinical ordination from JTS. The Seminary offered him a stipend for postdoctoral research in Talmud, and Speiser offered him an appointment at the University of Pennsylvania to teach Hebrew of all periods. Drawn to the teaching of languages, Moshe chose Penn, and thus his academic career began. As the first Jewish biblical scholar appointed to a position in a secular university after World War II, his appointment was an important milestone in the development of Jewish Studies in American universities and in the realization of Louis Finkelstein's vision.

In the summer of 1954, Moshe visited Israel for the first time. He was invited to lecture in Jerusalem and Tel-Aviv about the Ḫapiru and the Hebrews and was astonished by the huge crowds that attended; he recognized for the first time the difference between the community of those interested in the Bible and its world in Israel and the community in America. The experiences of that summer planted the seed that eventuated, sixteen years later, in the Greenbergs' settling in Israel and Moshe's joining the faculty of the Hebrew University.

Moshe recalls his years on the faculty at Penn (1954–70), especially the first decade, as a period of "professional maturation and widening of horizons in the exotic and peaceful hothouse of the Oriental Studies Department."[5] He taught Hebrew language, Bible and biblical history, epigraphy, courses in

---

5. This comment is from Moshe's remarks at the Hebrew University's reception honoring him on the occasion of his retirement, June 6, 1996.

Judaica such as ʾ*aggādâ*, and tannaitic texts, and Jewish history. He began to publish articles, worked on his translation of Kaufmann, and wrote his innovative biblical Hebrew textbook, *Introduction to Hebrew*, that was published in 1965 (58). He edited the Journal of Biblical Literature Monograph Series from 1959 to 1966. The department attracted increasing numbers of graduate students, and Moshe exercised a profound personal as well as scholarly influence on many of them. The department's weekly faculty seminar on "Interconnections of Oriental Civilizations" and the Philadelphia Oriental Club, drawing together scholars of the Near East, India, and the Far East were an ongoing stimulus to intellectual breadth. Speiser fostered an atmosphere of intellectual independence to such an extent that when Moshe presented a paper dissenting from one of Speiser's cherished theories, it never occurred to Moshe to suppress his disagreement, and Speiser proudly cited this to students as a testimony to the freedom of expression that characterized the department (224, p. 270, note).

Recognition came to Moshe quickly. He became a full professor by 1961. The same year he was awarded a Guggenheim Fellowship and served as a visiting lecturer at the Hebrew University, where he found the intellectual collegiality to be both stimulating and rewarding. In 1965 he succeeded Speiser as A. M. Ellis Professor of Hebrew and Semitic Languages and Literatures. In the next few years, he served as Visiting Professor of Bible once a week at JTS (1966–70), was elected to membership in the Biblical Colloquium, and was elected a Fellow of the American Academy for Jewish Research. In 1968, he was a recipient of the Danforth Foundation's E. H. Harbison Award for Gifted Teaching, an award based on the teacher's concern for the student as an individual and his grasp of the art of teaching; it was presented to him in Washington, D.C., where the recipients were also received at the White House by President Lyndon B. Johnson.

Following Speiser's death in 1965, Moshe became increasingly involved in academic leadership and public affairs. He became the chairman of the department and the first director of Penn's Near East Center. He lectured and published articles, based on Jewish primary sources, addressing the great issues of the day: civil rights and the Vietnam War. He soon realized that his feelings of obligation to accept roles of academic leadership and to address the great issues that embroiled university campuses and the public at large had become a permanent feature of his life. He concluded that he would be more personally fulfilled if he could devote his energies and use these impulses on behalf of the Jewish people. To do so, he felt, he ought to accept a full-time position at JTS or at the Hebrew University. Following a year as Visiting Professor of Bible at the Hebrew University in 1968–69, Moshe and Evy decided that Israel was where their future and that of their family lay. In 1970, they settled in Israel.

In Jerusalem Moshe joined the Hebrew University of Jerusalem's distinguished Bible Department and set about trying to help advance the study of Bible within a society in which it is the most fundamental cultural asset, part of the curriculum in public as well as private schools, and the focus of on-going public debate. He exercised a substantial influence on the department both through his personal example and in his capacity as chairman for four years (1972–76), introducing new courses in such areas as biblical thought and theology and postbiblical Jewish exegesis. He made a concerted effort to train and encourage young students to enter the field of biblical scholarship and to prepare graduates well for teaching the Bible in high schools.

Outside the university Moshe served as an advisor to the Ministry of Education from 1971 to 1981, helping to bring the results of modern scholarship into the teaching of the Bible in public schools. Since 1984, he has served part-time as Professor of Bible at the Masorti (Conservative) Movement's Beit Midrash Seminary for Judaic Studies, which trains rabbis and educators for the non-Orthodox community in Israel. He also served as a member of the academic councils of the seminary (since 1983) and of the Israel Open University (1982–87) and as a member of the directorate of the World Union of Jewish Studies (1990–93). He chaired the Israel Academy of Sciences' committee for evaluating basic research in Bible (1986; see 182). As he did when he was in the United States, he has expressed himself forthrightly on burning public issues in Israel, always careful to base his positions on his scholarly understanding of Jewish values.

In his most far-reaching undertaking, since 1985, Moshe has been coediting (with Shmuel Aḥituv) *Miqrāʾ lĕ-Yisrāʾēl*, an Israeli commentary series on the Bible conceived in response to the fact that, for all of its distinction in modern biblical scholarship, Israel had rarely produced fully modern commentaries. *Miqrāʾ lĕ-Yisrāʾēl* is designed to fill that lacuna by presenting scholars, teachers, educated readers, and high school and university students with a Hebrew commentary, written in an accessible style, that draws on all of the resources of modern biblical scholarship in addition to traditional Jewish sources and also presents the Bible's reverberations in later Jewish and general culture.

Alongside all of his public service, Moshe's scholarship has continued unabated and has continued to attract admiration and recognition. The first part of his commentary on Ezekiel in the Anchor Bible series was published in 1983 (157) and received the Biblical Archeology Society Publication Award for "the best commentary on a book of the Old Testament." Moshe received an honorary degree from the Jewish Theological Seminary of America in 1986, was elected a Fellow of the American Academy of Arts and Sciences in 1987, and spent a year as a Fellow at the Hebrew University's Institute of Advanced Studies in 1988–89. He served as visiting professor at Berkeley (1981–82), Yale (1986–87), and the Russian State University of the Humanities (Moscow, 1991). In 1994, the State of Israel awarded him the Israel Prize in Bible, the highest prize awarded in Israel in recognition of personal achievement and public service. In recognition of his distinguished contributions to Jewish Studies when he was a member of the Penn faculty and since then, he was awarded a Moses

Aaron Dropsie Fellowship at the University of Pennsylvania's Center for Judaic Studies in 1994–95, and an honorary degree in 1996. In 1996, he was also awarded the Hebrew University's Samuel Rothberg Prize for Jewish Education, a prize that his father had received many years earlier. A Hebrew collection of his essays, *On the Bible and Judaism*, edited by Avraham Shapira, was published in 1984 (167), and an English collection, *Studies in the Bible and Jewish Thought*, was published in 1995 (224) by the Jewish Publication Society in its prestigious Scholar of Distinction Series.

IV

On a personal level, in addition to his parents' influence, the most profound influence in Moshe's life has been his lifelong companion and soulmate, Evy, and the wonderful family that they created. From the very outset of Moshe's academic life, Evy has been ever present as a sounding board, advisor, comforter, and constant source of encouragement. With her, he has shared his hopes and dreams, his frustrations and doubts, his joys and successes. Evy has devoted her life to Moshe and the accomplishment of his scholarly mission, sparing him many responsibilities so that his work could continue unabated. Over the years, she has graciously opened home and heart to Moshe's many students and colleagues, encouraging the meeting in their home of study groups and learning circles in which she often actively participates. Their sons, Joel, Raphael, and Eitan (born in 1955, 1958, and 1962, respectively) have always been a source of delight and wonder to their parents. Together Moshe and Evy created an environment for their family that would imbue their children with the values and ideals that they both hold dear. Evy supported Moshe's desire to raise their children speaking Hebrew and shared his exhilaration at living as a family in Israel. As their children grew, Moshe took an active role in their intellectual development, always learning with them and from them. Even when they were young, he considered their opinions seriously, and their insightful comments were always appreciated. Upon moving to Israel, as with every immigrant generation, the children began to take a more active part in educating Moshe and Evy about Israeli life. Through them they vicariously "grew up" in Israel, appreciating the forces and influences that shape Israeli youth, thus gaining insight and perspective on the nature of Israeli society. They are rightfully proud of the accomplishments of Joel, the journalist, Rafi, the archaeologist, and Eitan, the musician, and grateful for all they have shared with them.

V

In June of 1996, Moshe retired from full-time teaching at the Hebrew University. He continues to teach there and at the Seminary for Judaic Studies part-time. The second part of his commentary on Ezekiel (232), covering chapters

21–37, has just appeared in August, 1997, and he is now at work on the final volume. His retirement will also allow him vigorously to pursue his important editorial work on *Miqrā° lĕ-Yisrā°ēl.*

One appropriate way to characterize Moshe Greenberg's achievements would be to point out how well what he has written about Yehezkel Kaufmann applies to him: he has "elevated the discussion of biblical thought above ecclesiastical dogma and partisanship into the realm of the eternally significant ideas" (224, pp. 187–88). Further, he "embodie[s] a passionate commitment to grand ideas, combining the philosopher's power of analysis and generalization with the attention to detail of the philological exegete. His life-work is a demonstration that the study of ancient texts does not necessitate losing contact with the vital currents of the spirit and the intellect" (157, p. ix). To this we may add the following statement from the citation accompanying Moshe's Israel Prize: Moshe's "superb studies show that personal engagement, when controlled by a rigorous ability to criticize one's own theories, not only does not compromise scholarly research but, on the contrary, fructifies it."[6]

As Moshe continues to complete his current projects and to undertake new ones, we join together with all of his students, colleagues, friends, and admirers in wishing him many more years of scholarly creativity in good health and happiness, surrounded by all of his loved ones.[7]

---

6. *Pĕrāśê Yiśrā°ēl* (Israel Ministry of Science and Arts / Ministry of Education, Culture, and Sports, 1994) 7.

7. In addition to the sources cited, parts of the preceding are based on Moshe's autobiographical reflections at the Hebrew University's reception honoring him on the occasion of his retirement, June 6, 1996, on information kindly provided by Daniel and Hanna Greenberg, Judah Goldin, Shalom M. Paul, Emanuel Tov, and Yair Zakovitch, and on remarks Moshe has made to the editors over the years.

Bibliography of the Writings of
Moshe Greenberg

1950

1. "A New Approach to the History of the Israelite Priesthood." *Journal of the American Oriental Society* 70: 41–47.

1951

2. "The Bible and Mythological Polytheism," by Yehezkel Kaufmann. Translated from Hebrew by Moshe Greenberg. *Journal of Biblical Literature* 70: 179–97.

3. "Hebrew *sᵉgūllā*: Akkadian *sikiltu*." *Journal of the American Oriental Society* 71: 172–74. [See no. 224]

1953

4. "Biblical Criticism and Judaism." *Commentary* 15: 298–304.

1955

5. *The Ḫab/piru.* New Haven, Connecticut: American Oriental Society.

6. Review of *Ancient Israel*, by Harry M. Orlinsky. *The Reconstructionist* 21/13: 24–27.

7. Review of *The Jewish Commentary for Bible Readers: The Book of Kings* by Leo L. Honor. *The Reconstructionist* 21/11: 30–32.

8. ‏"לחקר בעית החׁברו (חפׁרו)." תרביץ כד (תשטׁו): 369–379.‏

1956

9. "Hebrew 'Alive' at the U. of P." *Women's League Outlook* 26/4: 6, 26.

10. "The Stabilization of the Text of the Hebrew Bible, Reviewed in the Light of the Biblical Materials from the Judean Desert." *Journal of the American Oriental Society* 76: 157–67. [See nos. 115, 224]

11. "The Biblical Age," by Yehezkel Kaufmann. Translated from Hebrew by Moshe Greenberg. Pp. 3–92 in *Great Ages and Ideas of the Jewish*

Editors' note: This bibliography contains additions and corrections to the bibliography in no. 224.

People. Edited by Leo W. Schwarz. New York: Modern Library (Random House).

12. Review of קדמוניות ארצנו: *The Antiquities of Israel*, by M. Avi-Yonah and S. Yeivin. *Journal of Biblical Literature* 75: 257–58.

13. Review of *The Bible: A Modern Jewish Approach*, by Bernard J. Bamberger. *Judaism* 5/1: 86–87.

1957

14. "Ezekiel 17 and the Policy of Psammetichus II." *Journal of Biblical Literature* 76: 304–9.

15. "The Hebrew Oath Particle *ḤAY/ḤĒ*." *Journal of Biblical Literature* 76: 34–39.

16. Review of *Israel and Revelation*, by Eric Voegelin. *American Political Science Review* 51: 1101–3.

1958

17. "On Ezekiel's Dumbness." *Journal of Biblical Literature* 77: 101–5.

1959

18. "The Biblical Conception of Asylum." *Journal of Biblical Literature* 78: 125–32. [See nos. 137, 224]

19. "On Teaching the Bible in Religious Schools." *Jewish Education* 29/3: 45–53. [See nos. 61, 167]

20. Review of *Rivers in the Desert: A History of the Negev*, by Nelson Glueck. *The JWB Circle—In Jewish Bookland*. New York: Jewish Book Council of America. May 1959: 1, 7.

1960

21. *The Religion of Israel: From Its Beginnings to the Babylonian Exile*, by Yehezkel Kaufmann. Translated and abridged by Moshe Greenberg. Chicago: University of Chicago Press. [See nos. 73, 105, 194]

22. "Some Postulates of Biblical Criminal Law." Pp. 5–28 in *Yehezkel Kaufmann Jubilee Volume*. Edited by Menahem Haran. Jerusalem: Magnes. [See nos. 78, 100, 138, 170, 209, 224]

23. "The Teaching of the Bible." Pp. 1–9 in *Proceedings [of the] Seventh Annual Pedagogic Conference*. Cleveland: Institute of Jewish Studies / Cleveland Bureau of Jewish Education.

24. "נסה in Exodus 20:20 and the Purpose of the Sinaitic Theophany." *Journal of Biblical Literature* 79: 273–76.

25. Review of הלשון והרקע הלשוני של מגילת ישעיהו השלמה ממגילות ים המלח
    The Language and Linguistic Background of the Isaiah Scroll, by Eduard
    Yechezkel Kutscher. *Journal of Biblical Literature* 79: 278–80.

1961

26. *Introduction to Hebrew.* Revised edition. Philadelphia: Department of Ori-
    ental Studies, University of Pennsylvania. [See no. 58]

1962

27. "Another Look at Rachel's Theft of the Teraphim." *Journal of Biblical
    Literature* 81: 239–48. [See no. 224]

28–41. Articles in *The Interpreter's Dictionary of the Bible.* Edited by Keith
    Crim. Nashville: Abingdon.

28. "Avenger of Blood." 1: 321.

29. "Banishment." 1: 346.

30. "Bloodguilt." 1: 449–50.

31. "Bribery." 1: 465.

32. "City of Refuge." 1: 638–39.

33. "Confiscation." 1: 669.

34. "Crimes and Punishments." 1: 733–44.

35. "Drunkenness." 1: 872.

36. "Hanging." 2: 522.

37. "Prison." 3: 891–92.

38. "Scourging." 4: 245–46.

39. "Stocks." 4: 443.

40. "Stoning." 4: 447.

41. "Witness." 4: 864.

42. Review of בימי בית ראשון: מלכויות ישראל ויהודה (*The Kingdoms of Israel
    and Judah*). Edited by A. Malamat. *Journal of Biblical Literature* 81:
    299–300.

1963

43. "The Bible: A New Translation." *Hadassah Magazine* 43/6: 6, 21.

44. "The New Torah Translation." *Judaism* 12: 225–37. [See no. 224]

45. "Reflections on a New Jewish Problem." *Jewish Exponent* September 13.

46–49. "Text and Tradition I–IV." *Jewish Exponent* February 1, 8, 15, 22.
[Four articles illustrating the Jewish Publication Society *The Torah: The
Five Books of Moses*]

50. "Yehezkel Kaufmann: In Memoriam." *Jewish Exponent* November 8.

51. Review of *The Torah: The Five Books of Moses. Philadelphia Inquirer*
January 27.

52. "לדמותו של שמואל ליב בלאנק המורה." שבילי החינוך 23/2 (תשכ״ג): 73–74.

1964

53. "Jewish Tradition vs. Prejudice." *Hadassah Magazine* 46/2: 6, 30.

54. "Kaufmann on the Bible: An Appreciation." *Judaism* 13/1: 77–89. [See
no. 224]

55. "Stocktaking 5725." *Jewish Exponent* September 11.

56. Review of *The Hebrew Scriptures: An Introduction to Their Literature and
Religious Ideas*, by Samuel Sandmel. *Jewish Quarterly Review* 54: 258–65.

57. "יחזקאל כ׳ והגלות הרוחנית." 433–442 בתוך: ע״ז לדוד. ירושלים: קרית ספר
(תשכ״ד).

1965

58. *Introduction to Hebrew.* Englewood, New Jersey: Prentice Hall. [Revised
edition of no. 26]

59. "Anthropopathism in Ezekiel." Pp. 1–10 in *Perspectives in Jewish Learning.* Edited by Monford Harris. Chicago: College of Jewish Studies.

60. "The Impact of the New Translation." *The JPS Bookmark.* [Philadelphia]:
Jewish Publication Society of America. 11/4: 4–6.

61. "On Teaching the Bible in Religious Schools." Pp. 79–88 in *Modern Jewish Educational Thought.* Edited by David Weinstein and Michael Yizhar.
Chicago: College of Jewish Studies. [See nos. 19, 167]

62. "Response to Roland de Vaux's 'Method in the Study of Early Hebrew
History.'" Pp. 37–43 in *The Bible in Modern Scholarship.* Edited by
J. Philip Hyatt. Nashville: Abingdon.

63. "The Unbroken Chain." *Jewish Exponent* February 5.

1967

64. "The Biblical Grounding of Human Value." Pp. 39–52 in *The Samuel
Friedland Lectures, 1960–1966.* New York: Jewish Theological Seminary
of America. [See nos. 74, 113, 167]

65. "The Thematic Unity of Exodus iii–xi." Pp. 151–55 in volume 1 of *Papers [of the] Fourth World Congress of Jewish Studies*. Jerusalem: World Union of Jewish Studies.

66. ‏"ח'ברו (ח'פרו)—עברים."‏ 95–102 ‏בתוך: ההיסטוריה של עם ישראל, כרך שני:‏ ‏האבות והשופטים, ערך בנימין מזר. תל־אביב: החברה להוצאת ההיסטוריה של‏ ‏עם ישראל והוצאת מסדה, תשכ"ז. [ראה מס' 75]‏

1968

67. "Liberation and Spoliation: A Passover Message." *Jewish Exponent* April 12: 25–26.

68. "Idealism and Practicality in Numbers 35:4–5 and Ezekiel 48." *Journal of the American Oriental Society* 88 (E. A. Speiser volume): 59–66. [See no. 224]

69. "In Memory of E. A. Speiser." *Journal of the American Oriental Society* 88 (E. A. Speiser volume): 1–2.

1969

70. *Understanding Exodus: Part I*. New York: Behrman.

71. ‏"על משמעות סיפור גן עדן ב'בראשית'." שדמות לג (תשכ"ט): 10–11. [ראה‏ ‏מס' 167]‏

72. ‏"תפקידה של התורה בחיי ישראל." 7–13 בתוך: פרקי בית המדרש. ירושלים: בית‏ ‏המדרש למורים העברי הממלכתי על שם דוד ילין (תשכ"ט). [ראה מס' 167]‏

1970

73. *Connaître la Bible*, by Yehezkel Kaufmann. Paris: Universitaires de France. [Unacknowledged, abridged translation of no. 21]

74. "El fundamento biblico del valor humano." *Libro Anual* [Lima, Peru] 4: 160–70. [Spanish translation of no. 64]

75. "Ḥab/piru and Hebrews." Pp. 188–200 in *The World History of the Jewish People*, volume 2: *Patriarchs*. Edited by B. Mazar. Tel-Aviv: Massada. [See no. 66]

76. "Prolegomenon." Pp. xi–xxxv in *Pseudo-Ezekiel and the Original Prophecy*, by Charles Cutler Torrey, and Critical Articles, by Shalom Spiegel and Charles Cutler Torrey. New York: Ktav.

77. "Rabbinic Reflections on Defying Illegal Orders: Amasa, Abner, and Joab." *Judaism* 19/1: 30–37. [See nos. 130, 145, 167, 224]

78. "Some Postulates of Biblical Criminal Law." Pp. 18–37 in *The Jewish Expression*. Edited by J. Goldin. New York: Bantam. [See no. 22]

79. Review of *Ezekiel's Prophecy on Tyre (Ez. 26,1–28,19): A New Approach*, by H. J. Van Dijk. *Journal of the American Oriental Society* 90: 536–40.

1971

80–95.   Articles in *Encyclopaedia Judaica*. Edited by Cecil Roth and Geoffrey Wigoder. Jerusalem: Keter.

80. "Decalogue." 5: 1435–46.

81. "Exodus, Book of." 6: 1050–67.

82. "Ezekiel." 6: 1078–95.

83. "Ginsberg, Harold Louis." 7: 580.

84. "Ḥerem." 8: 345–50.

85. "Labor." 10: 1320–21.

86. "Levitical Cities." 11: 136–38.

87. "Moses, Critical View." 12: 371, 378–88.

88. "Oath." 12: 1295–98.

89. "Plagues of Egypt." 13: 604–13.

90. "Resurrection: In the Bible." 14: 96–98.

91. "Sabbath." 14: 557–62.

92. "Sabbatical Year and Jubilee: Ancient Near Eastern Legal Background." 14: 577–78.

93. "Semites." 14: 1148–49.

94. "Speiser, Ephraim Avigdor." 15: 258–59.

95. "Urim and Thummim." 16: 8–9.

96. "Mankind, Israel and the Nations in the Hebraic Heritage." Pp. 15–40 in *No Man Is Alien: Essays on the Unity of Mankind*. Edited by J. Robert Nelson. Leiden: Brill. [See nos. 167, 224]

97. "The Redaction of the Plague Narrative in Exodus." Pp. 243–52 in *Near Eastern Studies in Honor of William Foxwell Albright*. Edited by Hans Goedicke. Baltimore: Johns Hopkins University Press. [See no. 107]

98. "Tribute (to W. F. Albright)." *Newsletter of the American Schools of Oriental Research* 6: [4–6].

99. Review of *A Rigid Scrutiny: Critical Essays on the Old Testament*, by Ivan Engnell. *Judaism* 20: 248–49.

100.   הנחות היסוד של החוק הפלילי המקראי: תורגם מאנגלית וללא כל שינוי מתוך
ספר היובל לי" קויפמן, ירושלים תשכ"א. פנימי, לתלמידי החוג למקרא. ירושלים:
האוניברסיטה העברית, הפקולטה למדעי הרוח—החוג למקרא (תשל"א). [ללא
עריכת המחבר]. [ראה מס׳ 22, 170]

101.   "חורבן וגאולה." שדמות מא (אביב תשל"א): 104–108. [ראה מס׳ 167]

102–3. ערכים בתוך: אנציקלופדיה מקראית, כרך ו, ערכו ב׳ מזר ואחרים. ירושלים: מוסד ביאליק (תשל״ב).

102. ״עברי, עברים.״ 48–51.

103. ״ערי מקלט.״ 384–388.

104. ״פרשת השבת בירמיהו.״ 27–37 בתוך: עיונים בספר ירמיהו, חלק ב, ערך ב״צ לוריא. [ירושלים]: החברה לחקר המקרא בישראל (תשל״ב).

1972

105. *The Religion of Israel: From Its Beginnings to the Babylonian Exile*, by Yehezkel Kaufmann. Translated and abridged by Moshe Greenberg. New York: Schocken. [Paperback edition of no. 21]

106. Review of *Ancient Israel's Criminal Law: A New Approach to the Decalogue*, by Anthony Philips. *Journal of Biblical Literature* 91: 535–38.

107. ״אמנות הסיפור והעריכה בפרשת המכות (שמות ז–יא).״ 65–75 בתוך: המקרא ותולדות ישראל: מחקרים לזכרו של יעקב ליור. תל־אביב: אוניברסיטת תל־אביב (תשל״ב). [ראה מס׳ 97]

108. ״המובאות בספר יחזקאל כרקע לנבואות.״ בית מקרא ג (נ) (תשל״ב): 273–278.

109. ״לשאלת היקפן ומידת גיבושן של התורה ומצוותיה.״ פתחים 20 (ניסן תשל״ב): 23–27. [ראה מס׳ 167]

1973

110. "Prophecy in Hebrew Scripture." Pp. 657–64 in volume 3 of *Dictionary of the History of Ideas*. Edited by Philip P. Wiener. New York: Scribner's.

111. Review of *Studies on the Bible and Ancient Orient, Volume 1: Biblical and Canaanite Literatures*, by U. Cassuto. *Ariel* 32: 205–7.

112. ״הרהורים על תפקידי המורה למקרא והכשרתו.״ 119–128 בתוך: הגות במקרא לזכר ישי רון. תל־אביב: עם עובד והחברה לחקר המקרא בישראל (תשל״ד). [ראה מס׳ 167]

113. ״ערך האדם במקרא.״ שדמות נ (תשנ״ד): 164–170. [עיבוד עברי של מס׳ 64]. [ראה מס׳ 167]

1974

114. "Biblical Judaism (20th–4th centuries BCE)." Pp. 303–10 in volume 10 of *Encyclopaedia Britannica: Macropaedia*. 15th ed. Chicago: Encyclopaedia Britannica.

115. "The Stabilization of the Text of the Hebrew Bible: Reviewed in the Light of the Biblical Materials from the Judean Desert." Pp. 298–326 in *The Canon and Masorah of the Hebrew Bible*. Edited by Sid Z. Leiman. New York: Ktav. [See no. 10]

116. "מתוך מכתב פרופ' מ' גרינברג לבנו בצבא 26 בנובמבר 1973." מידעון: עלון
לתלמידי בתי־הספר העל־יסודיים 3: 12–15. [ירושלים: משרד החינוך והתרבות,
תשל"ד]. [ראה מס' 167]

117. בקורת על: "הנסיון," מאת יעקב ליכט. פתחים 27 (טבת תשל"ב): 41–42.

1975

118. "Hope and Death." *Ariel* 39: 21–39. [See no. 167]

119. "המקרא ובן דורנו: הוראת המקרא באוניברסיטה—למי ולמה." שדמות נ"ז
(תשל"ה): 11–19. [ראה מס' 167]

1976

120. "On Sharing the Scriptures." Pp. 455–63 in *Magnalia Dei: The Mighty Acts of God—Essays on the Bible and Archaeology in Memory of G. Ernest Wright.* Edited by F. M. Cross, W. E. Lemke, and P. Miller. Garden City, New York: Doubleday.

121. "On the Refinement of the Conception of Prayer in Hebrew Scriptures." *AJS Review* 1: 57–92. [See nos. 123, 224]

122. "הזיקה בין העם והארץ על פי המקרא." הציונות: סמיניריון לקציני אוגדת סיני,
11–19.

123. "על עידון מושג התפילה במקרא." אשל באר שבע א (תשל"ו): 9–33. [ראה
מס' 121, 167]

124. ראיון עם פרופ' משה גרינברג [על ביקורת המקרא והאמונה]. קשת בענן 33
(תשל"ו). [ראה מס' 167]

1977

125. "Moses' Intercessory Prayer." *Tantur Yearbook* 1977–78: 21–36.

126. "*NHŠTK* (Ezek. 16:36): Another Hebrew Cognate of Akkadian *naḥāšu*." Pp. 85–86 in *Ancient Near Eastern Studies in Memory of J. J. Finkelstein.* Edited by Maria de Jong Ellis. Hamden, Connecticut: Archon.

127. "Two New Hunting Terms in Psalm 140:12." *Hebrew Annual Review* 1: 149–53.

128. "גישה להוראת המקרא בבית־הספר." פתחים 40 (אלול תשל"ז): 18–22. [ראה
מס' 167]

129. "חקר המקרא והמציאות הישראלית"—[חלק]. הארץ 23.9.77. [חלק] ב.
30.9.77. [קיצור של מס' 136]. [ראה מס' 167]

1978

130. "Rabbinic Reflections on Defying Illegal Orders: Amasa, Abner, and Joab." Pp. 211–20 in *Contemporary Jewish Ethics.* Edited by Menachem Marc Kellner. New York: Sanhedrin. [See nos. 77, 224]

1979

1980

157. *Ezekiel 1–20*. Anchor Bible 22. Garden City, New York: Doubleday.

158. פרשנות המקרא היהודית: פרקי מבוא, ערך משה גרינברג. ירושלים: מוסד ביאליק
(תשמ״ג) (ספריית האנציקלופדיה המקראית: סדרת ספרים על המקרא ועולמו
מיסודה של האנציקלופדיה המקראית, בעריכת ש׳ אחיטוב, א). מתוכו חיבר
״מבוא״ (2–1); ״פרשנות חז״ל״ (9–3); ״הפרשנות בתרגומים הארמיים״ (11–
13); ״פרשני צרפת״ (86–68); ״סוף דבר״ (138–137). [ראה מס׳ 153, 216]

159. "Can Modern Critical Bible Scholarship Have a Jewish Character?"
Immanuel 15: 7–12. [See nos. 164, 224]

160. "Ezekiel 17: A Holistic Interpretation." *Journal of the American Oriental Society* 103 (S. N. Kramer volume): 149–54. [See no. 171]

161. "Ezekiel's Vision: Literary and Iconographic Aspects." Pp. 159–68 in
History, Historiography and Interpretation: Studies in Biblical and Cuneiform Literatures. Edited by H. Tadmor and M. Weinfeld. Jerusalem: Magnes.

162. "MSRT HBRYT, 'The Obligation of the Covenant,' in Ezekiel 20:37."
Pp. 37–46 in *The Word of the Lord Shall Go Forth: Essays in Honor of David Noel Freedman in Celebration of His Sixtieth Birthday*. Edited by C. L. Meyers and M. O'Connor. Winona Lake, Indiana: Eisenbrauns.

163. Review of *Ezechiel*, by Bernhard Lang. *Journal of the American Oriental Society* 103: 472–73.

164. ״הייתכן מדע מקרא ביקורתי בעל אופי יהודי?״ 98–95 בתוך: דברי הקונגרס
העולמי השמיני למדעי היהדות (ירושלים: תשמ״ג): ישיבות מרכזיות, מקרא
ולשון עברית. [ראה מס׳ 159]

165. ״היחס בין פירוש רש״י לפירוש רשב״ם לתורה.״ 567–559 בתוך: ספר יצחק אריה
זליגמן, ערכו א׳ רופא וי׳ זקוביץ. ירושלים: אלחנן רובינשטיין (תשמ״ג).

166. ״מקומו ההיסטורי של יחזקאל בקהילת גולי בבל.״ 147–141 בתוך: ההיסטוריה
של עם ישראל: שיבת ציון—ימי שלטון פרס, ערך חיים תדמור. ירושלים ותל־אביב:
עם עובד (תשמ״ג).

1984

167. על המקרא ועל היהדות: קובץ כתבים, ערך אברהם שפירא. תל־אביב: עם עובד
(תשמ״ו). [מכיל: הדפסה חוזרת של מס׳ 71, 72, 101, 109, 112, 113, 116, 119,
122, 123, 124, 128, 133, 134, 136, 143, 145, 146, 148, 150]. [עיבוד עברי
של מס׳ 19, 96, 118]

168. "The Design and Themes of Ezekiel's Program of Restoration." *Interpretation* 38: 181–208.

169. ״ללמֹד וללמד.״ Pp. 183–92 in על זהות, תבונה ודת: *Studies in Jewish Education and Judaica in Honor of Louis Newman*. Edited by Alexander M. Shapiro and Burton I. Cohen. New York: Ktav. [Abridgement of no. 133]

170. "הנחות יסוד של החוק הפלילי במקרא." 13–37 בתוך: תורה נדרשת. מאת משה
גרינברג, יוחנן מופס וגרשון דוד כהן. ערך אברהם שפירא. תל־אביב: עם עובד
(תשמ"ד). [נוסח מתוקן של מס' 100]

171. "יחזקאל י"ז—אינטרפרטציה הוליסטית." מחקרי ירושלים בספרות עברית ד:
7–17. [ראה מס' 160]

172. "עצמאות וטפילות תרבותית או: הרהורים על אשורולוגיה כמותרות." ידיעות
אחרונות, 10 פברואר / ז' באדר א' תשמ"ד: 22. [ראה מס' 178]

1985

173. הסגולה והכוח. [תל־אביב]: הקיבוץ המאוחד / ספרית פועלים (תשמ"ו). [מכיל
גירסה עברית של מס' 186, 202]

174. Review of *Les écoles et la formation de la Bible dans l'ancien Israël*, by
André Lemaire. *Israel Exploration Journal* 35: 208–9.

175. "מסורת עשרת הדיברות בראי הביקורת." 67–94 בתוך: עשרת הדברות בראי
הדורות, ערך בן־ציון סגל. ירושלים: מאגנס (תשמ"ו). [ראה מס' 201]

176. "מפתח לחלק הראשון ('ל"ב נתיבות התרגום') של ספר 'אוהב גר' לשד"ל."
שנתון למקרא ולחקר המזרח הקדום ט (תשמ"ה): 83–94.

177. מקרא לישראל: פירוש מדעי למקרא. [פרוספקט עם דוגמת פירוש ליחזקאל לז,
א–יד]. תל־ אביב: עם עובד (תשמ"ה).

178. "עצמאות וטפילות תרבותית או: הרהורים על אשורולוגיה כמותרות." ידיעון
האיגוד העולמי למדעי היהדות 24: 5–8 (תשמ"ה). [ראה מס' 172]

1986

179. "More Reflections on Biblical Criminal Law." Pp. 1–17 in *Studies in Bible.*
Edited by Sara Japhet. Scripta Hierosolymitana 31. Jerusalem: Magnes.

180. "What Are Valid Criteria for Determining Inauthentic Matter in Ezekiel?" Pp. 123–35 in *Ezekiel and His Book.* Edited by J. Lust. Bibliotheca
Ephemeridum Theologicarum Lovaniensium 74. Leuven: Leuven University Press.

181. "חכמי ישראל וחכמה חיצונית." 117–126 בתוך: מחקרים במדעי היהדות, ערך
משה בר־אשר, ירושלים (תשמ"ו).

182. צרכי מדינת ישראל במחקר בסיסי: דין וחשבון של הוועדה להערכת המחקר
הבסיסי במקרא, ערך משה גרינברג. ירושלים: האקדמיה הלאומית הישראלית
למדעים (תשמ"ז).

1987

183. "Exegesis." Pp. 211–18 in *Contemporary Jewish Religious Thought.*
Edited by A. A. Cohen and P. Mendes-Flohr. New York: Scribner's. [See
no. 224]

184. "Ezekiel." Pp. 239–42 in volume 5 of *The Encyclopaedia of Religion.*
Edited by Mircea Eliade. New York: Macmillan.

185. "Ezekiel 16: A Panorama of Passions." Pp. 143–50 in *Love and Death in the Ancient Near East: Essays in Honor of Marvin H. Pope.* Edited by John H. Marks and Robert M. Good. Guilford, Connecticut: Four Quarters.

186. "Der Gebrauch der Bibel im heutigen Israel." Pp. 343–53 in *Mitte der Schrift? Ein jüdisch-christliches Gespräch: Texte de Berner Symposions vom 6.–12. Januar 1985.* Judaica et Christiana 11. Edited by Martin Klopfenstein et al. Bern: Lang. [See nos. 173, 222]

187. "Job." Pp. 283–304 in *The Literary Guide to the Bible.* Edited by Robert Alter and Frank Kermode. Cambridge: Harvard University Press. [See no. 224]

188. Review of *Biblical Interpretation in Ancient Israel,* by Michael Fishbane. *Numen* 34/1: 128–30.

189. Review of *The Pennsylvania Tradition of Semitics: A Century of Near Eastern and Biblical Studies at the University of Pennsylvania,* by Cyrus H. Gordon. *Jewish Quarterly Review* 77: 226–27.

190. Review of *Critique textuelle de L'Ancien Testament,* by Dominique Barthélemy. *Jewish Quarterly Review* 78: 137–40.

1988

191. Review of *Le livre de Jérémie,* edited by P.-M. Bogaert. *Jewish Quarterly Review* 79: 71–72.

192. Review of *Understanding Scripture: Exploration of Jewish and Christian Traditions of Interpretation,* edited by Clemens Thoma and Michael Wyschogrod. *Numen* 35/1: 154–56.

193.   ‏"מוסר יהודי במבחן השעה." עת לעשות 1 (תשמ״ט): 11–17.‏

1989

194. *A Religião de Israel,* by Yehezkel Kaufmann. São Paulo, Brazil: Perspectiva: Editora de Universidade de São Paulo: Associação Universitária de Cultura Judaica. [Portuguese translation of no. 21]

195. "Bible Interpretation As Exhibited in the First Book of Maimonides' Code." Pp. 29–56 in *The Judeo-Christian Tradition and the U.S. Constitution: Proceedings of a Conference at the Annenberg Research Institute, November 16–17.* Jewish Quarterly Review Supplement. [See no. 224]

196. "Jewish Conceptions of the Human Factor in Biblical Prophecy." Pp. 145–62 in *Justice and the Holy: Essays in Honor of Walter Harrelson.* Edited by D. A. Knight and P. J. Paris. Atlanta: Scholars Press. [See nos. 215, 224]

197. "Theological Reflections: Land, People and the State." Pp. 25–34 in *People, Land and State of Israel: Jewish and Christian Perspectives* (= *Immanuel* 22/23).

198. "השפעת המודרניות על הבנת העבר: מזווית ראייתו של מקראן." 13–19 בתוך:
     טורא: אסופת מאמרי הגות ומחקר במחשבת ישראל מוגשת לפרופ׳ שלמה
     (סיימון) גרינברג בשנות גבורותיו, ערך מאיר איילי. [חיפה תשמ״ט]: המרכז
     ללימודי יהדות באורנים והקיבוץ המאוחד.

199. "תפילה למען המדינה." ידיעון התנועה המסורתית בישראל, אביב (תשמ״ט).
     [ראה מס׳ 200]

200. "תפילה למען המדינה." שיח מישרים: כתב עת על חיי שעה וחיי עולם לישראל
     17: 11 (תשמ״ט). [ראה מס׳ 199]

1990

201. "The Decalogue Tradition Critically Examined." Pp. 83–119 in *The Ten
     Commandments in History and Tradition.* Edited by Gershon Levi. Jeru-
     salem: Magnes. [See nos. 175, 224]

202. "Biblical Attitudes toward Power: Ideal and Reality in Law and Proph-
     ets" and "Reply to the Comments of John Welch." Pp. 101–12 and 120–
     25 in *Religion and Law: Biblical-Judaic and Islamic Perspectives.* Edited
     by Edwin B. Firmage, B. G. Weiss, and J. W. Welch. Winona Lake, In-
     diana: Eisenbrauns. [See nos. 173, 224]

203. "On Teaching the Bible." Pp. 27–34 in volume 5 of *Studies in Jew-
     ish Education.* Edited by H. Deitcher and A. J. Tannenbaum. Jerusalem:
     Magnes.

204. "The Task of Masorti Judaism." Pp. 137–45 in *Deepening the Commit-
     ment: Zionism and the Conservative Movement.* Edited by J. S. Ruskay
     and D. Szonyi. New York: Jewish Theological Seminary of America.

205. "Three Conceptions of the Torah in Hebrew Scriptures." Pp. 365–78 in
     *Die Hebräische Bibel und ihre zweifache Nachgeschichte: Festschrift für
     Rolf Rendtorff zum 65. Geburtstag.* Edited by Erhard Blum, C. Macholz,
     and E. W. Stegemann. Neukirchen-Vluyn: Neukirchener Verlag. [See
     no. 224]

206. "To Whom and for What Should a Bible Commentator Be Respon-
     sible?" Pp. 29–38 in *Proceedings of the Tenth World Congress of Jewish
     Studies, Division A: The Bible and Its World.* [See no. 224]

207.   "שרה קמין ז״ל." מדעי היהדות 30 (תשנ״א): 114–115.

1991

208. "Nebuchadnezzar at the Parting of the Ways: Ezek. 21:26–27." Pp. 267–
     71 in *Ah, Assyria . . . : Studies in Assyrian History and Ancient Near
     Eastern Historiography Presented to Hayim Tadmor.* Edited by M. Cogan
     and I. Eph^cal. Scripta Hierosolymitana 33. Jerusalem: Magnes.

209. "Some Postulates of Biblical Criminal Law." Pp. 333–52 in *Essential
     Papers on Israel and the Ancient Near East.* Edited by Frederick E.
     Greenspahn. New York: New York University Press. [See no. 22]

210. Review of *Thinking Biblical Law*, edited by Dale Patrick. *Journal of the American Oriental Society* 111: 819–20.

211. "יחזקאל קויפמן—רשמים אישיים." איגרת האקדמיה הלאומית הישראלית למדעים 9 (שבט תשנ״א): [4–6]. [ראה מס׳ 213]

212. "ערך החיים במקרא." 109–141. בתוך: החיים: מהות וערך, ערכה לאה מזור. ירושלים: מאגנס (תשנ״א). [ראה מס׳ 217]

213. "רשמים אישיים על יחזקאל קויפמן." מדעי היהדות 31 (תשנ״א): 81–85. [ראה מס׳ 211]

1992

214. "איוב היה או לא היה: סוגיה בפרשנות ימי הביניים" Pp. 3*–11* in *Sha^carei Talmon: Studies in the Bible, Qumran, and the Ancient Near East Presented to Shemaryahu Talmon*. Edited by Michael Fishbane, Emanuel Tov, and W. W. Fields. Winona Lake, Indiana: Eisenbrauns.

215. "תפיסות יהודיות של הגורם האנושי בנבואה המקראית." 63–76 בתוך: ספר היובל לרב מרדכי ברויאר. ירושלים: אקדמון (תשנ״ב). [ראה מס׳ 196]

216. פרשנות המקרא היהודית: פרקי מבוא, ערך משה גרינברג. ירושלים: מוסד ביאליק (תשנ״ב). מהדורה שנייה, מורחבת (בתוספת מפתחות). [ראה מס׳ 158]

1993

217. "ערך החיים במקרא." 35–53 בתוך: קדושת החיים וחירוף נפש: קובץ מאמרים לזכרו של אמיר יקותיאל, בעריכת י׳ גפני וא׳ רביצקי. ירושלים: מרכז זלמן שזר. [קיצור מס׳ 212]

218. "Notes on the Influence of Tradition on Ezekiel." *Journal of the Ancient Near Eastern Society* 22 (Y. Muffs volume): 29–37.

1994

219. "היש הקבלה בתעודות מארי להחרמת (שלל־) האויב המקראית?" ארץ ישראל: מחקרים בידיעת הארץ ועתיקותיה 24 (ספר מלמט): 49–53. ירושלים: החברה לחקירת ארץ־ישראל ועתיקותיה (תשנ״ד).

220. "דרכה של שרה קמין במחקר." 20–26 בתוך: המקרא בראי מפרשיו: ספר זכרון לשרה קמין, בעריכת שרה יפת. ירושלים: מאגנס (תשנ״ד).

221. "Hittite Royal Prayers and Biblical Petitionary Psalms." Pp. 15–27 in *Neue Wege der Psalmenforschung* (W. Beyerlin volume). Edited by K. Seybold and E. Zenger. Freiburg: Herder.

1995

222. "On the Political Use of the Bible in Modern Israel: An Engaged Critique." Pp. 461–71 in *Pomegranates and Golden Bells: Studies in Biblical, Jewish, and Near Eastern Ritual, Law, and Literature in Honor of Jacob Milgrom*. Edited by D. P. Wright, D. N. Freedman, and A. Hurvitz. Winona Lake, Indiana: Eisenbrauns. [See nos. 173, 186]

223. "The Etymology of נִדָּה '(Menstrual) Impurity'." Pp. 69–77 in חִיִּים
ליונה—*Solving Riddles and Untying Knots: Biblical, Epigraphic, and
Semitic Studies in Honor of Jonas C. Greenfield.* Edited by Z. Zevit,
S. Gitin, and M. Sokoloff. Winona Lake, Indiana: Eisenbrauns.

224. *Studies in the Bible and Jewish Thought.* Philadelphia: Jewish Publication Society. [Includes reprints (those marked with + contain additional
notes) of nos. 3+, 10+, 18, 22+, 27+, 44+, 54+, 68+, 77+, 96+, 121+,
131+, 135+, 138, 140+, 159, 183+, 187+, 195, 196+, 201+, 202,
205+, 206]

225. Review of *Prayer in the Hebrew Bible*, by S. L. Balentine. *Journal of
the American Oriental Society* 115: 320–21.

226. "Permanence et actualité de l'élection." *Yerushalaïm* 8 (1995–96): 8–13.
Paris: Comité Oecuménique d'Unité Chrétienne pour la Repentance en-
vers le peuple juif. [Abridgement of no. 228]

1996

227. "Noisy and Yearning: The Semantics of שקק and Its Congeners." Pp. 339–
44 in *Texts, Temples, and Traditions: A Tribute to Menahem Haran.* Edited by M. V. Fox et al. Winona Lake, Indiana: Eisenbrauns.

228. "A Problematic Heritage: The Attitude toward the Gentile in the Jewish
Tradition—An Israel Perspective." *Conservative Judaism* 48/2: 23–35.
[See nos. 226, 229]

229. "בין ישראל לעמים: בעיה בהטמעת המורשת." טורא ד: אסופת מאמרי הגות
ומחקר במחשבת ישראל. תל־אביב (תשנ״ו), 9–17. [גרסה עברית של מס' 226]

230. Review of *The Law of the Temple in Ezekiel 40–48*, by Steven S. Tuell.
Israel Exploration Journal 46: 143–44.

231. "תועלת המחלוקת." יהדות והומניזם: סוגיות בהשתלמויות מורים. ירושלים:
משרד החינוך והתרבות (תשנ״ו), 4–9.

1997

232. *Ezekiel 21–37.* Anchor Bible 22A. New York: Doubleday.

In Press

233. "The Terms נפל and הפיל in the Context of Inheritance." In *Ki Baruch
Hu: Ancient Near Eastern, Biblical, and Judaic Studies in Honor of
Baruch A. Levine.* Edited by R. Chazan, W. W. Hallo, and L. H. Schiff-
man. Winona Lake, Indiana: Eisenbrauns.

234. "Ephraim Avigdor Speiser." In *Dictionary of Biblical Interpretation.*
Nashville; Westminster, John Knox.

235. "הערות על מושג הזכות (RIGHT) ומונחיו במקרא," בתוך ספר הזכרון ליעקב
ליכט.

Abbreviations

General

Ant.	Josephus. *Antiquities*
AO	Tablets in the collections of the Musée du Louvre
b.	Babylonian Talmud
BM	Tablets in the collections of the British Museum
E.T.	English translation
Kish	Tablets from Kish in the collection of the Ashmolean Museum, Oxford
KJV	King James Version
LXX	Septuagint
m.	Mishna
MT	Masoretic Text
ND	Field numbers of tablets excavated at Nimrud (Kalhu)
NEB	New English Bible
Ni	Tablets excavated at Nippur, in the collections of the Archaeological Museum of Istanbul
NJPSV	New Jewish Publication Society Version
NRSV	New Revised Standard Version
PAM	Palestine Archaeological Museum photograph number
REB	Revised English Bible (Revised NEB)
t.	Tosepta
Tg.	Targum
VAT	Tablets in the collections of the Staatliche Museen, Berlin
y.	Jerusalem Talmud

Reference Works

AASOR	Annual of the American Schools of Oriental Research
AB	Anchor Bible
ABD	*Anchor Bible Dictionary*
ABL	R. F. Harper. *Assyrian and Babylonian Letters*

AfO	*Archiv für Orientforschung*
AfO Beiheft	Archiv für Orientforschung Beiheft
AHw	W. von Soden. *Akkadisches Handwörterbuch*. 3 vols. Wiesbaden: Harrassowitz, 1965–81
AJBI	*Annual of the Japanese Biblical Institute*
AJSL	*American Journal of Semitic Languages and Literatures*
AJS Review	*Association for Jewish Studies Review*
ANET	J. B. Pritchard (ed.). *Ancient Near Eastern Texts Relating to the Old Testament*. 3d ed. Princeton: Princeton University Press, 1969
AnOr	Analecta Orientalia
ANRW	*Aufstieg und Niedergang der Römischen Welt*
AOAT	Alter Orient und Altes Testament
AOS	American Oriental Series
ARM	Archives royales de Mari
ATD	Das Alte Testament Deutsch
BA	*Biblical Archaeologist*
BaghMitt	*Baghdader Mitteilungen*
BASOR	*Bulletin of the American Schools of Oriental Research*
BHK	R. Kittel (ed.). *Biblia Hebraica*
BHS	*Biblia Hebraica Stuttgartensia*
Bib	*Biblica*
BibOr	Biblica et Orientalia
BibRev	*Bible Review*
BKAT	Biblischer Kommentar: Altes Testament
BM	*Beit Miqra*
BR	*Biblical Research*
BZAW	Beiheft zur *ZAW*
CAD	A. L. Oppenheim et al. (eds.). *The Assyrian Dictionary of the Oriental Institute of the University of Chicago*. Chicago: Oriental Institute of the University of Chicago, 1956–
CBQ	*Catholic Biblical Quarterly*
CBSC	Cambridge Bible for Schools and Colleges
CT	Cuneiform Texts from the British Museum
CTA	A. Herdner. *Corpus des tablettes en cunéiformes alphabétiques*
DJD	Discoveries in the Judaean Desert
EM	E. L. Sukenik et al. (eds.). *Encyclopaedia Miqra^ʾit* (*Encyclopaedia Biblica*). 9 vols. Jerusalem: Bialik, 1950–88
EncJud	Cecil Roth (ed.). *Encyclopaedia Judaica*. 16 vols. Jerusalem: Keter, 1972

ERE	*Encyclopaedia of Religion and Ethics*
ErIsr	*Eretz-Israel*
ExpTim	*Expository Times*
FOTL	Forms of the Old Testament Literature
GKC	E. Kautzsch (ed.) and A. E. Cowley (trans.). *Gesenius' Hebrew Grammar*. Corrected 2d ed. Oxford: Clarendon, 1946
HALAT	L. Koehler and W. Baumgartner et al. *Hebräisches und aramäisches Lexikon zum Alten Testament*. 4 vols. Leiden: Brill, 1967–90
HAR	*Hebrew Annual Review*
HAT	Handbuch zum Alten Testament
HBT	*Horizons in Biblical Theology*
HKAT	Handkommentar zum Alten Testament
HSM	Harvard Semitic Monographs
HSS	Harvard Semitic Studies
HTR	*Harvard Theological Review*
HUCA	*Hebrew Union College Annual*
ICC	International Critical Commentary
IDB	G. A. Buttrick (ed.). *Interpreter's Dictionary of the Bible*. 4 vols. Nashville: Abingdon, 1962
IEJ	*Israel Exploration Journal*
IOS	*Israel Oriental Studies*
ISET	S. N. Kramer et al., *Sumerian Literary Tablets and Fragments in the Archaeological Museum of Istanbul*
JA	*Journal asiatique*
JANES(CU)	*Journal of the Ancient Near Eastern Society (of Columbia University)*
JAOS	*Journal of the American Oriental Society*
JBL	*Journal of Biblical Literature*
JCS	*Journal of Cuneiform Studies*
JEOL	*Jaarbericht van het Vooraziatisch-Egyptisch Genootschap: Ex Oriente Lux*
JJS	*Journal of Jewish Studies*
JNES	*Journal of Near Eastern Studies*
JNSL	*Journal of Northwest Semitic Languages*
JPOS	*Journal of the Palestine Oriental Society*
JPS Torah Commentary	Jewish Publication Society Torah Commentary
JQR	*Jewish Quarterly Review*
JSJ	*Journal for the Study of Judaism*
JSOT	*Journal for the Study of the Old Testament*
JSOTSup	Journal for the Study of the Old Testament Supplement Series

JSS	*Journal of Semitic Studies*
JTS	*Journal of Theological Studies*
KAR	Keilschrifttexte aus Assur religiösen Inhalts
KAT	Kommentar zum Alten Testament
KHAT	Kurzer Hand-Commentar zum Alten Testament
KS	*Kirjath-Sepher*
LCL	Loeb Classical Library
Leš	*Lešonénu*
LSJ	H. G. Liddell and R. Scott. *A Greek-English Lexicon.* Rev. H. S. Jones. Oxford: Clarendon, 1968
MAD	Materials for the Assyrian Dictionary
MIO	Mitteilungen des Instituts für Orientforschung
NCB	New Century Bible
NTS	*New Testament Studies*
OBO	Orbis biblicus et orientalis
Or	*Orientalia*
OTL	Old Testament Library
OTS	*Oudtestamentische Studiën*
PAAJR	*Proceedings of the American Academy for Jewish Research*
PAPS	*Proceedings of the American Philosophical Society*
PEFQS	*Palestine Exploration Fund, Quarterly Statement*
PEQ	*Palestine Exploration Quarterly*
RA	*Revue d'assyriologie et d'archéologie orientale*
RB	*Revue biblique*
RevQ	*Revue de Qumran*
RHPR	*Revue d'histoire et de philosophie religieuses*
SAA	State Archives of Assyria
SANE	Sources from the Ancient Near East
SBLDS	Society of Biblical Literature Dissertation Series
SRT	E. Chiera. *Sumerian Religious Texts*
STT	O. R. Gurney and J. J. Finkelstein. *The Sultantepe Tablets I.* London: British Institute of Archaeology, 1957
TCL	Textes cunéiformes du Louvre. Paris: Geuthner, 1910–
TDNT	G. Kittel and G. Friedrich (eds.). *Theological Dictionary of the New Testament*
TDOT	G. J. Botterweck and H. Ringgren (eds.). *Theological Dictionary of the Old Testament.* 8 vols. Grand Rapids: Eerdmans, 1990–97
THAT	E. Jenni and C. Westermann (eds.). *Theologisches Handwörterbuch zum Alten Testament.* 2 vols. Munich: Kaiser / Zurich: Theologischer Verlag, 1971–76
TIM	Texts in the Iraq Museum

TWAT	G. J. Botterweck and H. Ringgren (eds.). *Theologisches Wörterbuch zum Alten Testament*
TZ	*Theologische Zeitschrift*
UET	Ur Excavations, Texts
UF	*Ugarit-Forschungen*
UT	C. H. Gordon. *Ugaritic Textbook*. AnOr 38. Rome: Pontifical Biblical Institute, 1965
VT	*Vetus Testamentum*
VTSup	Vetus Testamentum Supplements
WBC	Word Biblical Commentary
ZA	*Zeitschrift für Assyriologie*
ZAW	*Zeitschrift für die Alttestamentliche Wissenschaft*
ZDMG	*Zeitschrift der deutschen morgenländischen Gesellschaft*
ZDPV	*Zeitschrift des deutschen Palästina-Vereins*

PART 1

Exegetical and Literary Studies

Love of Zion:
A Literary Interpretation of Psalm 137

Jerusalem

Psalm 137 is one of the few psalms that have no heading. The Septuagint has supplied a heading that, following the example of many other psalms, ascribes the psalm to David. This ascription, however, does not accord with the psalm's indisputable historical setting—the Babylonian exile. The psalm may have been composed sometime after the exile ended, but in that case the poet projected himself into the past and painted a vivid picture of the exiles' state of mind.[1]

Attempts to classify the psalm according to conventional categories have met with considerable difficulty. In H. Gunkel's view, the psalm begins as though it were a song of lament, then considers whether it should not be a hymn, and finally turns to the curse genre.[2] H. Schmidt thinks that the poem cannot be identified with any of the other genres found in the psalms.[3] In his opinion it is a ballad, meaning a narrative poem, but it is only in the beginning that any narrative element can actually be detected. The psalm has features in common with the Songs of Zion (Psalms 46, 48, 76, and 87)[4] and with many of the Songs of Ascents, which appear just before it in the Book of Psalms (Psalms 120–34),[5]

---

1. C. A. Briggs holds that the psalm was written early in the Babylonian exile: see his *The Book of Psalms* (2 vols.; ICC; Edinburgh, 1907) 2:485. So also M. Buttenwieser, who writes that the psalm's tone and content leave no doubt that it was written among the captives in Babylonia (*The Psalms Chronologically Treated* [New York, 1969] 219). However, because of the past tense of the verbs in vv. 1–3 and the particle שׁם ('there'), most commentators think that it was composed a short time after the exile.

2. H. Gunkel, *Ausgewählte Psalmen* (Göttingen, 1904) 192–93; idem, *Die Psalmen* (HKAT; Göttingen, 1926) 580.

3. H. Schmidt, *Die Psalmen* (HAT; Tübingen, 1934) 242.

4. Similarity of construction has been pointed out by J. Jeremias, "Lade und Zion," in *Probleme biblischer Theologie: Festschrift G. von Rad* (ed. H. W. Wolff; Munich, 1971) 189–92.

5. In Psalms 125, 126, 128, 129, 132, 133, and 134, Zion is mentioned; in Psalms 122, 125, and 128, Jerusalem; and Psalms 127, 132, and 134 refer to the Temple. Cf. L. C. Allen, *Psalms 101–150* (WBC; Waco, Texas, 1983) 220.

but the differences are greater than the similarities.[6] The following pages, however, will not be devoted to matters of classification but to an analysis of the psalm's form and content.

The psalm is not characterized by clear metric regularity. Long verses and clauses alternate with short ones. There are only a few cases of (semantic) parallelism within the verses or between adjacent ones.

The psalm's structure is clear. As a starting point for exposing this structure, some grammatical phenomena will be pointed out. The form of the first four verses is first-person plural, the next two are first-person singular, and the last three verses use an imperative or exclamation. All three parts end with a phrase consisting of a preposition (על or אל) followed by one or two nouns. This division corresponds with the organization of the topics: vv. 1–4 reflect the sentiments of the exiles in Babylon; vv. 5–6 contain the vow always to remember Jerusalem; and vv. 7–9 have a wish for revenge on enemies as their subject.[7]

The first part (1–4) begins and ends with an adverbial phrase of place. Verses in the Bible usually begin with a subject or predicate and sometimes with an adverb of time. Only rarely does a verse begin with an adverb of place. By locating the adverb of place at the head of the verse and of the song as a whole, the place mentioned, Babylon, receives great emphasis, which is further reinforced by the (redundant) particle שם ('there'). At the end of the verse, another place is named, Zion. Consequently, Babylon and Zion are set opposite each other. This opposition will prove to be a central motif in the psalm.

More precisely, it is not Babylon that is mentioned at the beginning of the verse but the rivers of Babylon. Why the rivers? To this question the strangest answers have been given. According to Hupfeld, the exiles sat by the water, since there were no mountains. In the opinion of Hitzig, the exiles sat by the water in order to listen dreamily to the play of the waves and because their synagogues stood near the water in order to facilitate their purification. Hengstenberg thought that the exiles saw in the streams a symbol of their streams of tears. Duhm speculated that in the evenings after finishing their hard work, people would go to the water in order to relax, Briggs assumed that they used to retire there for solitary grief and reflection, and Kittel believed that they

---

6. Cf. U. Kellermann, "Psalm 137," *ZAW* 90 (1978) 50–51, who sees in our psalm a modified Song of Zion.

7. D. N. Freedman proposes a different division: vv. 1–2, introduction; v. 3, opening; vv. 4–6, central section; v. 7, closing; vv. 8–9, conclusion. See "The Structure of Psalm 137," in *Near Eastern Studies in Honor of William Foxwell Albright* (ed. H. Goedicke; Baltimore, 1971) 187–205. Briggs (*Book of Psalms*, 484), E. J. Kissane (*The Book of Psalms* [2 vols.; Dublin, 1954] 285), and A. Chakham (*The Book of Psalms, Books 3–5* [Jerusalem, 1981] 520 Hebrew]) divide the psalm into three parts of equal length: vv. 1–3, 4–6, and 7–9. The weakness of all of these divisions is that they separate v. 4 from v. 3, whereas the two verses clearly belong together, as shown by their vocabulary (the repetition of שיר), their grammatical form (first-person plural), and their content (v. 4 is the answer to the request of v. 3). Furthermore, v. 4 should not be joined to vv. 5–6, since it differs from them considerably, both in form and in content.

went to pray by the water in remembrance of the water that was found near the temple for personal cleansings.[8]

However, ישב does not mean 'to sit', in this case, but 'to dwell' (as in Jer 29:5: "Build houses and dwell therein"; and in Ezek 3:15: "And I came to the exiles in Tel Abib, who dwelled near the stream Kebar"). The word for rivers in the psalm is plural, and this indicates that the exiles had come to a land abounding in rivers and canals. This would have greatly impressed them, since they had left a country that had little water and was dependent on capricious winter rains, often suffering from periods of drought. The word *Zion* evokes dryness because of the similarity in sound between it and ציה ('dryness') and ציון ('dry land'). Thus, a contrast is created with "the rivers"[9] (see Isa 32:2, where ציון is contrasted with "streams of water," and Isa 41:18 and Ps 107:35, where ציה stands in opposition to "springs of water"). The poet of Psalm 137 is particularly sensitive to the sounds of words and their associations, as will be shown below.

Thus, from a material point of view, the exiles' condition had improved. They had settled in a country richer in water and more fertile than their own; they could build houses and plant fruit trees (Jer 29:5) and start a new life. But the material point of view is not the only one. Alongside the abundance of water was the memory of Zion, and it weighed more heavily.

Corresponding to the opposition between the beginning and the end of the first verse, the two halves of the central part embody a contrast that is expressed by similarity in sound and in grammatical structure: שם ישבנו—גם בכינו. The similarity in form draws attention to the difference in meaning: 'we dwelled by the water and yet we wept'.[10]

The structure of the verse as a whole is thus based on two pairs of contrasting components:

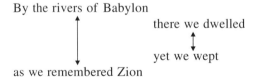

By the rivers of Babylon

there we dwelled

yet we wept

as we remembered Zion

Verse 2 begins with an adverbial phrase of place, just as v. 1 does. The trees that are mentioned, ערבים ('willows or poplars'), grow near water, and

8. H. Hupfeld, *Die Psalmen* (4 vols.; 2d ed.; Gotha, 1871) 4:365; F. Hitzig, *Die Psalmen* (Leipzig and Heidelberg, 1863) 405; E. W. Hengstenberg, *Commentar über die Psalmen* (4 vols.; 2d ed.; Berlin, 1852) 4:436; B. Duhm, *Die Psalmen* (KHAT; Freiburg, 1899) 283; Briggs, *Book of Psalms*, 485; R. Kittel, *Die Psalmen* (KAT; Leipzig, 1914) 466.

9. A. B. Ehrlich, *Die Psalmen* (Berlin, 1905) 355.

10. For this meaning of גם, see Ps 129:2: רבת צררוני מנעורי גם לא יכלו לי ('they have often assailed me from my youth on, yet they have never overcome me').

thus the beginning of v. 2 serves to illustrate the beginning of v. 1. The next word, בתוכה ('in her'), points back to Babylon, and תלינו כנרותינו ('we hung our lyres') gives a concrete picture of the exiles' distress and is therefore parallel to "we wept." The lyre is often mentioned in contexts of joy and thankfulness (for example, Gen 31:27: "I would have sent you with joy and songs, with tambourine and lyre") and its being silenced is considered to be an expression of grief (for example, Ezek 26:13: "And I will stop the tumult of your songs, and the sound of your lyres will be heard no more"). Verse 2 thus belongs to v. 1 and reinforces its content. But the final words of v. 1 have no counterpart in v. 2. The idea of remembering Zion is dealt with and elucidated separately in the succeeding verses.

Verses 3 and 4 also belong together. The opening word כי ('for') and the word שם ('there'), the repetition of which connects v. 3 to v. 1, make it clear that these verses contain the immediate reason that the exiles were in distress and had hung their lyres on the trees. Songs were as a rule accompanied by instruments, and the exiles did not want to sing and play for their captors. Five times the root שיר ('sing' or 'song') occurs. The request of the Babylonians is mentioned twice, first by the poet, then in direct speech by the Babylonians themselves, and thus is accorded special emphasis.

Another repetition is the ending נו- ('we, us, our'), which recurs in the first four verses no less than nine times. The first eight times it refers to the Judean exiles, whereas the ninth time it alludes to the Babylonians (לנו). But the songs belong to the Judeans not the Babylonians! So from here on the ending נו- is not used anymore until v. 8, where the word לנו returns but now refers to the Judeans.

The reply, in the form of a rhetorical question, is introduced by איך ('how'), a word characteristic of songs of lament. Since both the request and the reply are conveyed in direct speech, their wordings can be compared. What is striking here is that the exiles say "song of the Lord," whereas the Babylonians asked for "songs of Zion." This might indicate that "songs of Zion" were cultic songs and that the exiles' refusal to sing them sprang from their conviction that each god is attached to his land and therefore cannot be worshipped in a foreign country. This idea was current both in Israel (see 1 Sam 26:19, where causing David to flee from his country is equated with compelling him to worship other gods) and in other countries (see 2 Kgs 5:17, where Naaman, the commander in chief of Aram, asked for a load of earth from the land of Israel on which he would be able to worship the God of Israel in his home country). Yet this explanation seems unlikely, because songs of Zion does not necessarily refer to cultic songs. On the contrary, the fact that "words of song" and "joy" parallel each other in v. 3 means that what the Babylonians requested were probably songs of amusement. The victors wished to be amused, as did the Philistines who asked Samson to play for them (Judg 16:25). The exiles, however, were not in a mood for amusement, as is clear from v. 1, but they could not tell their captors the reason for their refusal. By mentioning a song of the Lord in their reply, they made it appear that all their songs were cultic ones and that their refusal was based on a religious concept.

Not only in the present does the memory of Zion (vv. 1–4) determine mood and behavior. In the following two verses (5 and 6), the psalmist takes an oath never to forget Jerusalem in the future. In these verses, the verbs change from plural to singular in number. Until now the psalmist has spoken as a representative of his community. Now, uttering an oath and in the form of a (conditional) curse aimed at himself (if I do not keep the oath, may this or that misfortune happen to me), he speaks in his own name. He pronounces the oath twice, using parallel sentences in which the parts of the condition and the misfortune appear in chiastic order, probably expressing the idea of talion.[11]

The nature of the misfortune mentioned by the poet is not quite clear. The phrase תשכח ימיני has been explained in various ways: the object of תשכח ('forget') has fallen out and must be supplied; תשכח should be vocalized תִּשָּׁכַח ('be forgotten', that is, become paralyzed and no longer felt); instead of תשכח, one should read תכחש ('grow thin'); the meaning of שכח is 'to waste away' (compare Ps 102:5 and Ugaritic *tkḥ*).[12] The words תדבק לשוני לחכי can also be interpreted in different ways: it can denote extreme thirst (see Lam 4:4: "The tongue of the suckling cleaves to its palate for thirst"), and it can be an expression for being mute (see Ezek 3:26: "And I will make your tongue cleave to your palate, and you shall be dumb"). Since תשכח ימיני and תדבק לשוני constitute a parallelism, tied together by alliteration, assonance, and rhyme, one would expect the ideas they represent to be similar. The meaning seems to be that the speaker will be unable to practice his profession because his right hand will not be capable of playing the lyre, and his tongue will be incapable of uttering songs. This interpretation makes it clear why the right hand is mentioned (see Ibn Ezra: "The reason for mentioning 'my right hand' is because of 'our lyres,' for the right hand plays the strings"), and it also fits in well with the preceding verses, where lyres and singing occupied a prominent place.

There is a twofold correspondence—one formal and one substantive— between the oath and the punishment for not keeping it. The formal correspondences between oath and punishment are that the hand raised in oath[13] will be unable to function and the tongue that uttered the oath will be unable

---

11. Cf. J. P. Fokkelman, *Narrative Art in Genesis* (Assen, 1975) 37.

12. Cf. W. F. Albright, "Anath and the Dragon," *BASOR* 84 (1941) 15 n. 3.

13. The custom of raising one's hand when swearing an oath is well attested in the Bible (compare Gen 14:22–23: "And Abram said to the king of Sodom, 'I lift up my hand unto the Lord, the Most High God, the possessor of heaven and earth, That I will not take so much as a thread or a shoestrap, and that I will not take anything that is yours'"; Exod 6:8: "And I will bring you to the land, concerning which I raised my hand to give it to Abraham, Isaac and Jacob"). Mouth and right hand are mentioned together in Ps 144:8, no doubt in connection with the taking of oaths: "whose mouth speaks lies and whose right hand is false."

to move. For similar correspondences, see 1 Kgs 13:4: "Jeroboam stretched out his arm above the altar and cried, 'Seize him!' But the arm that he stretched out against him became rigid and he could not draw it back"; and Job 31:21– 22: "If I raised my hand against the fatherless, looking to my supporters in the gate, May my arm drop off my shoulder, my forearm break off from its shaft."

The substantive correspondences between oath and punishment are that one who forgets Jerusalem will forget how to play, and one who does not mention[14] Jerusalem will not utter anything at all.

The ־ִי ending on the words לְחֻכִּי, לְשׁוֹנִי, and יְמִינִי, referring to the speaker, and on אַזְכְּרֵכִי, referring to Jerusalem, hints at the bond between the speaker and Jerusalem. Directly addressing Jerusalem gives a dramatic touch to the oath, which fits and reinforces its fierce content.

The end of v. 6, which means either "if I do not bring up (bring to mind) Jerusalem at (the time of) my highest joy" (compare with Jer 51:50: "remember the Lord from afar and bring Jerusalem to mind") or "if I do not let Jerusalem predominate over my highest joy" (compare with Deut 28:43: "the stranger in your midst will gain predominance over you"), parallels "if I do not remember thee" and also adds to it. It points back to v. 3, where the same word for 'joy' was used. In v. 6, however, it is not just 'joy' but 'highest joy', and even so, the feeling is subdued by the memory of Jerusalem. This verse, which began with parts of the head (tongue and palate), ends with the whole head (in the sense of highest point).

Verse 7 is addressed to God. Just as the exiles remember Jerusalem, so God is called upon to remember (the day of) Jerusalem. The intention is of course that God draw practical conclusions with respect to the Edomites. The day of Jerusalem is the fatal day[15] when the city was conquered by the Babylonians, and the Edomites took the side of the conquerors (see Ezek 35:5–15, Obadiah 10–16). The Judeans could not bear this, particularly from the Edomites, because they were a brother-people (compare Amos 1:11: "because he pursued his brother with the sword"; Obadiah 10: "your brother Jacob"; Obadiah 12: "the day of your brother").[16] Not surprisingly, no mention is made of the fact that the Edomites had lived under Judean occupation for centuries, so their joy over Judah's downfall is entirely understandable.

Just as were the Babylonians in v. 3, the Edomite collaborators are introduced by means of direct speech in v. 7. The quotation of their utterance shows how fervently and with what hatred they incited the Babylonians to destroy

---

14. In addition to 'to remember', זכר can also mean 'to mention'. This is well known from Medieval Hebrew but occurs in Biblical Hebrew as well (cf. 2 Sam 14:11; Jer 20:9, 23:36).

15. For this meaning of יום, see Ps 37:13 and Job 18:20.

16. Cf. J. R. Bartlett, *Edom and the Edomites* (JSOTSup 77; Sheffield, 1989) 180: "Edom is blamed for the perpetual enmity, and the idea of brotherhood is brought in to underline the enormity of the offence."

Jerusalem. This is brought out particularly by the repetition ערו ערו ('lay bare, lay bare').

The name *Jerusalem* consists of two elements: ירו (the verb ירה means 'to found'; compare with Job 38:6: "who founded its cornerstone") and שלם (the name of a Canaanite god). The proper name *Yeruel* is similar (2 Chr 20:16). The first element of the word *Jerusalem* is alluded to aurally by ערו (compare the spelling *Urusalim* in the El-Amarna letters and *Ursalimmu* in the inscription of Sennacherib) and semantically by יסוד ('foundation'). The second element of the word, שלם, recurs in the similar-sounding ישלם ('pays') in the next verse (see Ps 122:6–8 for another auditory association with the name *Jerusalem*, and see above, v. 1, for the auditory association with Zion). The Edomites shout: "Lay the 'founded' city bare unto its foundation" (see Hab 3:13, where the verb ערה is also combined with יסוד). But the psalmist hints that the city will repay those who do her evil.

Whereas the Edomites are named "sons of Edom" (v. 7), Babylon is designated "daughter of Babylon" (v. 8); in keeping with this, "your little ones" are mentioned in v. 9. Babylon is directly addressed in vv. 8–9, just as Jerusalem is in vv. 5–6—again, an expression of strong feelings. And just as v. 2 was an illustration of v. 1, both being introduced by על, so v. 9 is an example of v. 8, the wished-for retribution, both being introduced by אשרי. Here again, a sharp contrast is expressed: fortunate is he who brings misfortune over Babylon; happy he who executes the terrible vengeance.

Two verbs in succession in the last verse specify the cruel act. Dashing children was no exceptional phenomenon, being described in the Bible by the verb רטש (see 2 Kgs 8:12, Isa 13:16, Hos 14:1, Nah 3:10).[17] Why is the verb נפץ used here? It seems that it is connected with Jer 51:20–24, where the root נפץ (to shatter) occurs ten times in conspicuous positions (as anaphora) in relation to Babylon. The link with Psalm 137 strikes the eye: "And I shall pay to Babylon and to all inhabitants of Chaldea all the evil that they did in Zion before your eyes" (Jer 51:24).[18] The use of נפץ in the psalm suggests the idea of retaliation: just as Babylon shattered nations and kingdoms, man and woman, old and young (Jer 51:20, 22), so her little ones will be shattered in return.

The phrase "on the rock" at the end of the verse seems superfluous. Nowhere else in the Bible is it said where or how the dashing is carried out. Mentioning the rock of course intensifies the horror of the act, but it might have additional significance. The rock may signify that the blood is visible to all. This is the sense in Ezek 24:7–8: "For the blood she shed is still in her; she set it upon a bare rock; she did not pour it out on the ground to cover it with earth. She set her blood upon the bare rock so that it was not covered so that it may stir up my fury to take vengeance."

---

17. Dashing of little children is also mentioned in the Iliad (Homer *Il.* 22.63–64).

18. The affinity between Jeremiah 51 and Psalm 137 is evinced by additional words common to both: על לבבכם, שודדים, גמלות, שלם ישלם, ציה, ינהרו, זכרו, וירושלם תעלה.

It is more probable, however, that the rock serves to indicate dry, infertile land, as in Ezek 26:4, 14: "They shall destroy the walls of Tyre and demolish her towers; and I will scrape her soil off her and leave her a naked rock. I will make you a naked rock, you shall be a place for drying nets; you shall never be rebuilt." The rock at the end of the psalm thus functions as an antithesis to the waters at the beginning.[19] The psalm begins and ends with Babylon, but, whereas at the beginning Babylon was characterized by abundance of water, at the end it has become dry and barren (see Jer 51:36: "Therefore thus says the Lord . . . I will drain her sea and dry up her spring").

We are now in a position to view the psalm as a whole. In the first part (vv. 1–4), Babylon and Zion are placed in opposition to one another, and it is this bipolar opposition that creates the dramatic tension. The second part of the psalm (vv. 5–6) is devoted to the pole Jerusalem and the third (vv. 7–9) to the pole Babylon. Whereas in the first part Babylon and Zion are referred to in the third person, in the second and third parts they are addressed directly. In the first and third parts, Babylonians, Judeans, and Edomites enter the scene by means of direct speech, while in the central part the poet himself speaks in the first person.

The three parts differ to some degree in character and atmosphere, but they are firmly tied together by common elements. The central motif is remembrance: the roots זכר ('remember') and שכח ('forget') occur five times and in all three parts. Another motif, no less important, is Zion or Jerusalem, which is also mentioned five times.

Various terms allude to the occupation of the poet/singer/musician: lyre, song (the root שיר also occurring five times), right hand, and tongue. Moreover, the psalm evinces a strong sensitivity to sounds. It is poor in figurative language, but rich in auditory devices. In addition to the allusions deriving from the sounds of Zion and Jerusalem and the numerous repetitions of the ending *-nu*, mentioned before, several cases of alliteration can be detected. In vv. 3–4, the sound *š* occurs eight times at the beginning of words or syllables. In v. 7, four successive words end with the sound *m*. The first words of v. 8 begin with *b*, and so on (on the similarity in sound between תשכח ימיני / תדבק לשוני, see above).

It is usually impossible to determine the meaning of sounds with any degree of certainty. Interpretations of sound are culturally bound and dependent on personal associations.[20] In general, only this can be said: alliterations and other repetitions of sound draw attention to or accentuate the words in which

19. Compare the contrast of water flowing out of a rock, Num 20:7–11.

20. According to Freedman ("Structure of Psalm 137," 191–93), the sound effects in the psalm produce a mournful tone. The labials *b* and *m* in vv. 1–2 simulate the sound of the wind in the willows, resonating over the waters, while the keening note of the pronominal ending *nu* is sounded again and again in these verses. In addition, he says that the repetitions of the sibilants in v. 3 may reflect the stubborn silence of the exiles in the presence of their masters. These interpretations are unduly subjective and presumably based on personal impressions or associations.

they occur. In some cases they create connections between words or illuminate contrasts between them.

Psalm 137 is wholly devoted to the description of feelings. The first part depicts feelings of grief, the second of love and faithfulness, and the third of hatred and revenge. These feelings are given expression in the most passionate manner.

The unconcealed thirst for cruel revenge is understandable in the light of the historical circumstances. The Judeans had suffered heavily at the hands of the Babylonians, and in those times, revenge was not only wished for, as in our psalm, but its actual execution was the accepted rule. In the present case, the call for revenge, which ultimately derived from a sense of justice, was hardly more than an expression of powerlessness.[21]

In 1904, A. B. Ehrlich, commenting on our psalm, wrote that one should not apply the standard of our ethics, which is the result of the progress of so many centuries, to ancient writings.[22] Today we know better. We know that acts of revenge and atrocities are not only perpetrated but frequently justified and glorified in our time, even in "civilized" societies. Psalm 137 makes us aware of the regrettable fact that positive feelings of love for one's own group, people, or country are often accompanied by or manifested in negative feelings, sometimes understandable but never laudable, of hatred and enmity toward others.

---

21. The targum attributes the last three verses not to the psalmist but to the angels Michael and Gabriel.

22. Ehrlich, *Die Psalmen*, 359.

The Meaning of Amos's Third Vision
(Amos 7:7–9)

ALAN COOPER

Hebrew Union College

The Jewish Publication Society translation renders Amos 7:7:

> This is what he showed me: He was standing on a wall checked with
> a plumb line and He was holding a plumb line.

And when God explains the significance of the vision, in 7:8b, He says,

> . . . I am going to apply a plumb line to my people Israel; I will pardon
> them no more.

This fine translation, like most modern translations, perpetuates a medieval interpretation of the passage[1] that has been in disrepute for almost a century.[2]
But the translators can hardly be faulted, since none of the alternatives offered
by rabbinic, medieval, or modern scholarship has commanded assent.[3]

---

1. See the late ninth- or early tenth-century *Risāla* of Judah Ibn Quraysh (ed. Dan Becker;
Tel-Aviv: Tel-Aviv University, 1984) 232–35; Wilhelm Bacher, *Die hebräisch-arabische Sprach-
vergleichung des Abulwalid Merwan ibn Ganah (Rabbi Jona)* (Sitzungsberichte der Kaiserlichen
Akademie der Wissenschaften, Philosophisch-historische Classe 106; 1884) 35–36 n. 5.

2. Beginning with Albert Condamin, "Le prétendu 'fil à plomb' de la vision d'Amos," *RB* 9
(1900) 586–94; Wilhelm Riedel, *Alttestamentliche Untersuchungen* (Leipzig: Deichert, 1902) 1.27–
33; Arnold B. Ehrlich, מקרא כפשוטו (3 vols.; 2d ed.; New York: Ktav, 1969 [origin. 1901]). For a
good summary of the objections to the plumb-line interpretation, see C. van Leeuwen, "Quelques
problèmes de traduction dans les visions d'Amos chapitre 7," *Übersetzung und Deutung: Studien
zu dem Alten Testament und seiner Umwelt Alexander Reinhard Hulst gewidmet von Freunden und
Kollegen* (Nijkerk: Callenbach, 1977) 103–12, esp. 108–9.

3. Space limitations preclude a full review of the history of interpretation here. For surveys,
see Gilbert Brunet, "La vision de l'étain: Réinterprétation d'*Amos* vii 7–9," *VT* 16 (1966) 387–
95; Wilhelm Rudolph, *Joel-Amos-Obadja-Jona* (KAT 13/2; Gütersloh: Mohn, 1971) 234–37; Jean
Ouellette, "Le mur d'étain dans Amos, vii, 7–9," *RB* 80 (1973) 321–31; Walter Beyerlin, *Bleilot,*

Perhaps the most honest interpretation remains that of A. B. Ehrlich: "Those who interpret [חומת אנך] to be a wall built with a plumb line are, in my opinion, dreaming; their words have nothing to do with the meaning of the biblical text. . . . I do not know what a wall of אנך is, and I do not know what אנך itself is."[4] Ehrlich was not given to false reticence. His declaration of ignorance in this case serves as a useful warning: all interpretations of Amos 7:7–9 are fraught with difficulties. In the present paper, which I offer as a tribute to my revered teacher and mentor, I intend to revive an interpretation of the אנך-vision in Amos 7:7–9 that was first proposed in 1915 by Franz Prätorius.[5] I will come to that interpretation after a brief consideration of the vision's literary context.

Amos 7:1–8:3 consists of four visions, with the dramatic encounter between Amos and Amaziah, high priest of Bethel, between the third and the fourth.[6] The significance of the first two visions is clear (7:1–8), even if their details are not. Twice God symbolically portrays Israel's utter destruction, by insects and fire, respectively; twice Amos intercedes on Israel's behalf, and God relents. Thus far, the scene is reminiscent of Moses' acts of intercession on behalf of Israel.[7] In this case, however, God's relenting is not the end of the story.

Whatever the purport of Amos's third vision might be, the prophet's encounter with Amaziah (7:10–17) apparently effects a reversal of his position. Instead of pleading for mercy toward Israel, Amos prophesies exile and destruction (7:17). This reversal is reinforced by Amos's fourth vision: to the flat statement that "the end has come" (8:2), he offers no objection.

In the first two visions, Amos is Israel's defender; in the fourth, he participates in the announcement of the nation's destruction. The central block of material (7:7–17), comprising the third vision and the scene at Bethel, appears

---

Brecheisen oder Was Sonst? Revision einer Amos-Vision (OBO 81; Freiburg: Universitätsverlag, 1988); Meir Weiss, *The Book of Amos* (2 vols.; Jerusalem: Magnes, 1992) 1.219–22, 2.414–17 [Hebrew].

4. Ehrlich, מקרא כפשוטו, 3.414. The translation is mine.

5. Franz Prätorius, "Bemerkungen zu Amos," *ZAW* 35 (1915) 12–25, esp. 22–23; idem, *Die Gedichte des Amos: Metrische und textkritische Bemerkungen* (Halle: Niemeyer, 1924) 26.

6. The most comprehensive study of the vision sequence to date is Günter Bartczek, *Prophetie und Vermittlung: Zur literarischen Analyse und theologische Interpretation der Visionsberichte des Amos* (Europäische Hochschulschriften 23/120; Frankfurt a/M.: Lang, 1980). Some important studies that have appeared subsequent to Bartczek are: Susan Niditch, *The Symbolic Vision in Biblical Tradition* (HSM 30; Chico, Calif.: Scholars Press, 1983) 21–41; Robert Martin-Achard, *Amos: L'homme, le message, l'influence* (Geneva: Labor et Fides, 1984) 107–19; Francis Landy, "Vision and Poetic Speech in Amos," *HAR* 11 (1987) 223–46; Francis I. Andersen and David Noel Freedman, *Amos* (AB 24A; New York: Doubleday, 1989) 611–860; and Shalom Paul, *Amos* (Hermeneia; Minneapolis: Fortress, 1991) 222–55.

7. On the comparison of Amos with Moses, see Andersen and Freedman, *Amos*, 673–79.

to constitute a unified transition from the one role to the other.[8] The unity arises out of the fact that Amaziah's words represent a systematic and meaningful distortion of Amos's third vision, as indicated by the following parallels:

Amaziah (7:10–13)	Amos's Vision (7:8–9)
קשר עליך עמוס בקרב בית ישראל	הנני שם אנך בקרב עמי ישראל
כה אמר עמוס בחרב ימות ירבעם	ויאמר אדני . . . וקמתי על בית ירבעם בחרב
ובית אל לא תוסיף עוד להנבא	לא אוסיף עוד עבור לו

'Amos has conspired against you' קשר עליך עמוס, Amaziah tells Jeroboam. This statement contains a double irony: first, Amaziah ignores Amos's co-conspirator, God; second, the priest has no way of knowing that thus far, Amos's so-called conspiracy with God (in response to each of the first two visions) has actually saved Israel from destruction. According to Amaziah, the conspiracy has taken place 'in the midst of the house of Israel' בקרב בית ישראל (7:10), which naturally recalls 'in the midst of my people Israel' בקרב עמי ישראל in 7:8, substituting the impersonal (and royal) "house" for the emotionally charged "my people" of God's utterance.

All Amaziah sees standing before him is Amos, a man of flesh and blood; he fails to perceive the word of God in Israel's midst. The priest's terrible blindness is made plain by his next statement (7:11): כי כה אמר עמוס בחרב ימות ירבעם 'Thus said Amos: By the sword Jeroboam will perish' (compare 7:9, God speaking: וקמתי על בית ירבעם בחרב 'I will rise against the house of Jeroboam with the sword'). For Amaziah, these are the words of Amos and not the words of God. Note again the impersonal character of Amaziah's remark: he leaves out any mention of the agent (whether divine or human) of Jeroboam's death.

Finally—inevitably—the high priest of Bethel turns the prophet out of the sanctuary, saying (7:13), ובית אל לא תוסיף עוד להנבא 'do not prophesy at Bethel any more'. Once again we are reminded of 7:8, where God says, לא אוסיף עוד עבור לו 'I will not pardon/pass by it any more'.[9] In casting Amos out, Amaziah expels God from the place that is ironically called בית אל 'House of God'. As Amaziah concludes in one of the most pathetic moments in the Bible, Bethel is not a house of God, but מקדש מלך הוא ובית ממלכה הוא 'it is the *king's* sanctuary, and it is a *royal* house' (7:13).

Amaziah's corruption of Amos's third vision is a matter of simple substitution. In three instances, Amaziah transfers God's words and deeds to Amos.

---

8. So, rightly, Hans Walter Wolff, "The Irresistible Word (Amos)," *Currents in Theology and Mission* 10 (1983) 4–13; also, Lyle Eslinger, "The Education of Amos," *HAR* 11 (1987) 35–57.

9. On the ambiguity of עבר ל- in Amos 7:8, see Landy, "Vision and Poetic Speech," 229; Weiss, *Amos*, 1.222. Compare Amos 5:17, which shares with 7:8 both the verb עבר and the preposition בקרב, referring to Israel.

The second of the above-cited comparisons is the clearest: "The Lord said" in 7:8, as opposed to "Amos said" in 7:11. In the third pair of texts, Amaziah actualizes the divine threat of 7:8 by expelling Amos, and implicitly God, from the Bethel shrine.

The first pair of verses is the most important for the interpretation of the vision. These texts describe actions that take place "in the midst" of Israel. What Amaziah understands as Amos's "conspiracy" is the priest's interpretation of, or corruption of, God's placement of אנך in the midst of Israel. But how are we to understand that substitution?

The answer to this question must lie, in part, in Amos's response to Amaziah in 7:14, . . . לא נביא אנכי 'I am not a prophet. . . '. This statement represents a fourth point of contact between Amos's third vision and the Amos-Amaziah scene, because of the wordplay between its thrice-repeated אנכי and the אנך of the vision. The significance of the wordplay, unfortunately, is not clear. Perhaps Amos's words in 7:14 are not merely an autobiographical notice but are meant to correct Amaziah's fatal misapprehension: *God*, not Amos, is the author of all these things. As vv. 15–16 explain, the Lord Himself is responsible for the confrontation between the prophet and the priest and for the awful judgment against Israel.

God's reported instruction to Amos, לך הנבא 'go prophesy' (7:15), is a direct rebuke of Amaziah, whose advice was לך ברח 'go flee' (7:12). At first glance, there seems to be no mention of any such divine command to Amos to 'prophesy'. I suggest, however, that it is implicit in 7:8: at the very moment that God says, 'I am about to put אנך in the midst of my people Israel' (בקרב עמי ישראל), Amos turns up in Israel's royal shrine telling the high priest that he has been ordered to prophesy 'to my people Israel' (אל עמי ישראל). It seems, then, that the אנך that God places in the midst of Israel is none other than Amos the prophet,[10] who paradoxically insists that he is not a prophet. This paradox can be resolved, but only after further consideration of 7:7–9.

The basis for the interpretation of Amos's third vision was established independently by Max Löhr and Wilhelm Riedel,[11] who showed that the vision reports of 7:7–9 and 8:1–3 are structurally identical. Since the content of 8:1–3 is better understood and less controversial, it should aid in the interpretation of 7:7–9. The following diagram will facilitate comparison:

10. So, rightly, H. G. M. Williamson, "The Prophet and the Plumb-Line: A Redaction-Critical Study of Amos 7," *OTS* 26 (1990) 101–21 (reprinted in R. P. Gordon [ed.], *The Place Is Too Small for Us: The Israelite Prophets in Recent Scholarship* [Winona Lake, Ind.: Eisenbrauns, 1995] 453–77). As his title makes plain, however, Williamson adheres to the unlikely interpretation of אנך as 'plumb line'. I would like to thank Drs. David Marcus and Christoph Uehlinger for helping me to locate this article.

11. Max Löhr, *Untersuchungen zum Buch Amos* (BZAW 4; Giessen: Alfred Töpelmann, 1901) 25–26; Riedel, *Alttestamentliche Untersuchungen*, 29.

	8:1–3	7:7–9	
(a)		כה הראני	כה הראני אדני יהוה
(b)		והנה אדני נצב על חומת <u>אנך</u>	והנה כלוב <u>קיץ</u>
		ובידו <u>אנך</u>	
(c)		ויאמר יהוה אלי מה אתה ראה	ויאמר מה אתה ראה
		עמוס	עמוס
(d)		ואמר <u>אנך</u>	ואמר כלוב <u>קיץ</u>
(e)		ויאמר אדני הנני שם <u>אנך</u>	ויאמר יהוה אלי בא <u>הקץ</u>
		בקרב עמי ישראל	אל עמי ישראל
(f)		לא אוסיף עוד עבור לו	לא אוסיף עוד עבור לו
(g)		ונשמו במות ישחק . . .	והילילו שירות היכל . . .

Three points emerge from an examination of the parallel texts. First, in 8:1–3, the word that is underlined in line b (= d) is *not* identical to the underlined word in line e. The notion that there is no wordplay in 7:7–9,[12] in contrast to 8:1–3, is indefensible on literary grounds. Far preferable is Friedrich Horst's characterization of both texts as *Wortspielvisionen* 'wordplay visions'.[13]

Second, the underlined words in lines b (= d) and e, respectively, are most likely homonyms or near-homonyms in Israelite Hebrew. The Masoretic vocalization notwithstanding, the Israelite word for 'summer' was probably pronounced /qēṣ/. As many commentators have noted, that word is a homonym of the word for 'end'.[14]

Horst's suggestion that אנך in line e evokes the *Assonanzwort* אנחה 'groan'[15] is on the right track, but it is ultimately unsatisfactory. The wordplay in 7:7–8, like the one in 8:1–2, should not have to be inferred from the text (or produced by emendation); it should, rather, be brought out explicitly by the correct reading of line e. Riedel recognized this point, but his suggested reading of the word in line e as *ʾanakk*—an apocopated *Piel* form of the root נכה 'to smite'—is morphologically problematic, since the *Piel* of that root does not appear elsewhere in the Bible.[16]

---

12. So, e.g., Hans Walter Wolff, *Joel and Amos* (Hermeneia; Philadelphia: Fortress, 1977) 301; Beyerlin, *Bleilot*, 47.

13. Friedrich Horst, "Die Visionsschilderung der alttestamentlichen Propheten," *EvT* 20 (1960) 193–205, esp. 201.

14. See, e.g., Paul, *Amos*, 254. On the exegetical significance of the difference between the Israelite and Judahite pronunciations, see Al Wolters, "Wordplay and Dialect in Amos 8:1–2," *JETS* 31 (1988) 407–10.

15. Horst, "Visionsschilderung," 201; followed by Ouellette, "Le mur d'étain"; and, more recently, by H. Neil Richardson, "Amos's Four Visions: Of Judgment and Hope," *BibRev* 5/2 (1989) 16–21.

16. See the discussion of Riedel's proposal in Julian Morgenstern, *Amos Studies, Parts I, II, and III* (Cincinnati: Hebrew Union College, 1941) 83. Riedel was anticipated in relating אנך to נכה

The third observation that arises from a careful reading of 8:1–3 is that whatever symbolic significance a כלוב קיץ might have, the meaning of the image within the context of the vision is determined *only* by the wordplay.[17] It is not necessary to concoct an allegory about a basket of (rotten) summer fruit[18] in order to understand that the 'summer basket'[19] means that 'the end is coming'. Similarly, the חומת אנך and אנך of 7:7 need be nothing more or less than a 'tin wall' and 'tin', respectively, with no particular symbolic import.[20] Rather, the gist of the vision should be entailed by the wordplay.

Prätorius's solution to the problem of the 'tin wall' is to repoint *ʾănāk* in 7:8b (that is, line e of the diagram) as *ʾānōk*, a short form of אנכי,[21] the independent pronoun of the first person singular.[22] He translates the clause 'Siehe

---

by the first biblical lexicographer, Menachem ben Saruq. See his מחברת (ed. H. Filipowski; London: Filipowski, 1854) 28, 122; also the rejoinder by Menachem's adversary, Dunash ben Labrat, in ספר תשובות דונש בן לברט (ed. H. Filipowski; London: Filipowski, 1855) 12. The debate continued into the next generation. See ספר תשובות: תשובות תלמידי מנחם . . . [ו]תלמיד דונש (ed. S. G. Stern; 2 parts; Vienna: Self-published, 1870) 1.99, 2.36–37.

17. Or, rather, the wordplay is the outward literary manifestation of the prophet's (subconscious) free association of two unrelated terms. See Samuel E. Loewenstamm, כלוב קיץ: לטיפולוגיה של חזון הנבואה, *Tarbiz* 34 (1965) 319–22 (English translation in Loewenstamm's *From Babylon to Canaan: Studies in the Bible and Its Oriental Background* [Jerusalem: Magnes, 1992] 22–27).

18. This is the standard medieval Jewish interpretation (Rashi, Qara, and others), and it is followed by most modern commentators.

19. Or, rather, 'summer bird-trap', since כלוב, like Amarna Canaanite *kilūbu*, denotes not an ordinary basket but a trap or container for birds (compare Jer 5:27, Sir 11:28). So already Malbim, ad loc.

20. It makes no practical difference for interpretation, then, whether אנך means 'tin' or 'lead'. The fact that the former is almost certain, however, is a decisive blow to the plumb-line interpretation. See esp. Benno Landsberger, "Tin and Lead: The Adventures of Two Vocables," *JNES* 24 (1965) 285–96; William L. Holladay, "Once More, *ʾănak* = 'Tin', Amos vii 7–8," *VT* 20 (1970) 492–94; Harold R. (Chaim) Cohen, *Biblical Hapax Legomena in the Light of Akkadian and Ugaritic* (SBLDS 37; Missoula, Mont.: Scholars Press, 1978) 137; Paul, *Amos*, 233–34; Beyerlin, *Bleilot*, 18–22.

21. There is a great deal of evidence for this short form of the pronoun (without the final *i*-vowel), although its pronunciation is uncertain. First, the form is probably attested in Moabite, Phoenician, and Samalian by the spelling אנך; see, conveniently, W. Randall Garr, *Dialect Geography of Syria–Palestine, 1000–586 B.C.E.* (Philadelphia: University of Pennsylvania Press, 1985) 79. Second, the forms *anec* and *anech* are found in Latin transcriptions of Punic; see Stanislav Segert, *A Grammar of Phoenician and Punic* (Munich: Beck, 1976) 95. Third, the Greek transcription ανωχ is found in Origen's *Secunda* in Ps 46:11; E. A. Speiser suggests that it might correspond to the short Phoenician form of the pronoun ("The Pronunciation of Hebrew according to the Transliterations in the Hexapla," *JQR* n.s. 16 [1925–26] 359 n. 10). Fourth, the Tiberian Masorah may preserve a memory of the variant in the vacillation between penult and ultima stress of אנכי, not always related to pause. Finally, Coptic *anok* may be relevant here, although it is beyond my competence to judge.

22. I have suggested that the two words involved in the wordplay ought to be homonyms. To assert homonymy for the two forms of אנך would require special pleading, given our poor knowledge of ancient Hebrew pronunciation. The problem is compounded by the fact that אנך = 'tin' was

ich will das Ich mitten in mein Volk Israel stellen'.[23] Having threatened Israel with destruction by natural agents (locusts, 7:1–3, and fire, 7:4–6, God now moves against the people Himself. The prospect of such terrible divine action is a recurrent theme in Amos.[24]

To say that Prätorius's interpretation was not well received would be an understatement. Artur Weiser called it a "sonderbare Lesart,"[25] Julian Morgenstern termed it an "atrocity,"[26] and a number of commentators raised the obvious grammatical objection against the use of the independent personal pronoun

---

apparently unknown to postbiblical Hebrew until its recovery by medieval comparative philology (above, n. 1). It should be noted, however, that the cognate evidence does not support the Masoretic vocalization of *ʾănāk* for 'tin'. (For a convenient summary of that evidence, see Maximilian Ellenbogen, *Foreign Words in the Old Testament: Their Origin and Etymology* [London: Luzac, 1962] 31–32.) The medieval grammarian and exegete Abraham Ibn Ezra rightly described the Masoretic form as בלי משפחה 'unclassifiable' (שפה ברורה [ed. Gabriel Lippmann; Fürth: Müller, 1839] 4b). It does not correspond morphologically to any transcription of the Akkadian cognate, whether it be *anaku, annaku,* or *anāku.* And while the biblical form might, in theory, be an Aramaized rendering of **anāku,* it could not be a direct borrowing from Aramaic: all attested Aramaic forms (e.g., Syriac *ʾānkā* > Arabic *ʾānuk*) have long-*a* in the first syllable! If the Masoretic vocalization is not simply ad hoc, it has two possible sources: (1) analogy with other initial-*ʾalep* forms, such as אמם (Josh 15:26), אדר (Esth 3:7, etc.), and ארם (Gen 10:22, etc.); (2) the rare Rabbinic Hebrew word אנכה (*ʾănākâ*?) 'glaze' or 'overlay', evidently a Greek loan word, which appears in a difficult midrashic comment on Amos 7:8 (*Lev. Rab.* 33.2 [ed. Margaliyot, 759]):

ויאמר י״י אלי הנני שם אנך, אמר ר׳ יהודה בר סימון מה היורה הזו אין מעמידה אלא אנכה, כך
אמ׳ הקב״ה אונככם אני ביסורין בעולם הזה, אבל לעתיד לבא לא אוסיף עוד עבור לו.

The Lord said, "Now I am putting אנך." Rabbi Judah bar Simon said, Just as he keeps this wall standing only [by a metal] overlay, so the Holy One, Blessed Be He said, "I am overlaying you with torments in this world, but in the future, 'I shall no longer be furious (?) with him'."

For the interpretation of the text, see Margaliyot's notes and esp. Saul Lieberman, תוספת ראשונים (4 vols.; Jerusalem: Bamberger and Wahrmann, 1937–39) 3.32. Perhaps this very midrash provided the basis for the Masoretic vocalization of אנך, in which case the implicit interpretation of חומת אנך would be 'wall with a metal glaze'.

23. Prätorius, "Bemerkungen," 23. Closest to Prätorius among more recent commentators is Robert B. Coote, *Amos among the Prophets: Composition and Theology* (Philadelphia: Fortress, 1981) 92–93: "Whatever an *anak* (RSV, 'plumb line') is, the wordplay created probably means either 'I am about to set *myself* (*anoki*) in the midst of my people' (a reference to Yahweh's theophany at Bethel) or 'I am about to set you (implying an ungrammatical form with -*ennak*) in the midst of my people'." Coote's statement is unannotated. The former suggestion is Prätorius's; the latter is from an unpublished paper delivered at the 1976 Annual Meeting of the SBL by S. Dean McBride (summarized by David L. Petersen in *The Roles of Israel's Prophets* [JSOTSup 17; Sheffield: JSOT Press, 1981] 77–78). Another advocate of a wordplay between 'tin' and 'I' is Klaus Baltzer, "Bild und Wort: Erwägungen zu der Vision Amos in Am 7,7–9," *Text, Methode und Grammatik: Wolfgang Richter zum 65. Geburtstag* (St. Ottilien: EOS, 1991) 11–16. Baltzer adduces a parallel to the wordplay in an Akkadian hymn to Ishtar.

24. See especially Amos 4:12, 5:1, 5:17, 6:8.

25. Artur Weiser, *Die Profetie des Amos* (BZAW 53; Giessen: Alfred Töpelmann, 1929) 18.

26. Morgenstern, *Amos Studies,* 84.

in the oblique case.[27] Karl Budde went so far as to assert that if God wanted to place Himself in Israel's midst, He should have said, ‏הנני שם את נפשי בקרב‎* ‏עמי ישראל‎.[28]

The use of the independent personal pronoun in the accusative in the expression ‏הנני שם אנך‎ is certainly objectionable at first glance.[29] Even leaving aside an appeal to poetic license, however, a peculiarity of biblical style that was ignored by both Prätorius and his opponents counters the objection. As Moshe Greenberg has demonstrated, the independent personal pronouns of the first- and third-persons singular may be used as "surrogates for the Tetragram," particularly when employed by God when He takes an oath by Himself.[30] When it replaces the Tetragram, as in the oath formula ‏חי אנכי‎ 'by the life of I' = 'by my life', the pronoun is treated as a noun, and thus stands "solecistically" in the oblique case. In effect, ‏אנכי‎ is *not* a pronoun but a divine epithet. Such an apparent solecism with the pronominal surrogate for the divine name, I suggest, is precisely what we find in Amos 7:8b.

Amos 7:7–8 may be translated as follows: "Just then, [the Lord][31] showed me thus: the Lord standing on/over a tin wall with tin in his hand. The Lord said to me, 'What do you see, Amos?' I said, 'Tin'. The Lord said, 'Now I am putting I/myself in the midst of my people Israel. I will not pardon/pass by it any more'."

Amos's third vision expresses the irony that is the central theme of Amos's prophecies: because of Israel's iniquity, God's presence becomes a destructive, rather than a beneficent force for the nation. The crisis comes to a head in Amos's confrontation with Amaziah. The priest epitomizes Israel's stubborn refusal to acknowledge the divine presence in Israel. Amos personifies the transformation of that presence from beneficent to destructive. When God says, "I am putting myself in the midst of my people Israel," he means to put the physical manifestation of Himself—His divine word proclaimed by the prophet Amos—in the midst of the struggle.[32] And it is that divine presence which is cast out of the sanctuary.

Amos 7:14 represents a moment of absolute prophetic sympathy with God. Of course the man Amos is a prophet, but the 'I'—the ‏אנכי‎ who has entered the

---

27. So, e.g., Rudolph, *Joel-Amos-Obadja-Jona*, 235.

28. Karl Budde, "Zu Text und Auslegung des Buches Amos," *JBL* 44 (1925) 74.

29. A few exceptional cases adduced by Mitchell Dahood notwithstanding. See Dahood's article, "The Independent Personal Pronoun in the Oblique Case in Hebrew," *CBQ* 32 (1970) 86–90. The Amos text does not figure among his examples.

30. Moshe Greenberg, "The Hebrew Oath Particle ḥay/ḥē," *JBL* 76 (1957) 34–39.

31. Cf. Amos 7:1, 7:4, 8:1. I add the divine name here for clarity, not because I advocate any alteration of the text. Although many emendations have been proposed in this passage, none has been generally accepted. See the commentaries.

32. Cf. Petersen's suggestion (*Roles*, 77) that "Amos 7:7–8 can be appropriately interpreted as a wordplay vision, commissioning Amos for an active role as God's emissary to the North."

sanctuary at Bethel—is not the prophet; it is God manifest in the prophet. A perfect gloss on the situation is Hos 11:9: אל אנכי ולא איש בקרבך קדוש 'I am God and not man, Holiness in your midst'. Whatever else Amos might mean when he says, 'I am not a prophet', he must also be referring back to 7:8b, where אנך 'I' is an epithet of God.

Prätorius's interpretation of Amos 7:8b, with some modification and elaboration, makes both grammatical and exegetical sense in a way that no other interpretation does. It illuminates its immediate context, explaining why the encounter between Amos and Amaziah is interposed between the prophet's third and fourth visions, and it allows the full significance of Amos's rebuke of the high priest to emerge, perhaps even helping to solve the most notorious crux in the book (7:14).

On Reading Genesis 12:10–20

BARRY L. EICHLER
University of Pennsylvania

The biblical account of Abram's behavior in the face of the perceived danger of accompanying his beautiful wife Sarai, as a stranger in a foreign land, recorded in Gen 12:10–20 (with parallels in Gen 20:1–18 and 26:1–12),[1] has been interpreted in many ways: Some have condemned his stance as immoral;

Author's note: It is with deep gratitude and warm affection that I dedicate this article to a beloved teacher and dear friend, whose lifelong fascination with the meaning of the biblical text and the history of its exegesis has inspired the contemporary reader with an appreciation of the biblical message throughout the ages.

1. The patriarchal wife-sister episode is related twice with reference to Abraham and Sarah (Gen 12:10–20 and 20:1–18) and once with reference to Isaac and Rebekah (26:1–12). For a discussion of the relationship of these three passages to each other, with bibliography, see Claus Westermann, *Genesis 12–36: A Commentary* (trans. John J. Scullion; Minneapolis: Augsburg, 1985) 159ff., 316ff., and 420ff.; and M. E. Biddle, "The 'Endangered Ancestress' and Blessing for the Nations," *JBL* 109 (1990) 599–611. The majority of modern biblical scholarly opinion based on literary-critical considerations views these triple presentations as different portrayals of the same early folk narrative, with both Genesis 20 and 26 dependent on the earliest variant, Genesis 12. J. Van Seters (*Abraham in History and Tradition* [New Haven: Yale University Press, 1975] 167–91) presents a detailed study of the relationship of these three variants to each other and the nature of their structure within the literary sources. He concludes (p. 183) that Genesis 12 is the earliest version, with Genesis 20 clearly dependent upon it, and Genesis 26 exhibiting literary dependency on both (contra M. Noth, who views the Isaac traditions as older than those of Abraham, in his *Überlieferungsgeschichte des Pentateuchs* [Stuttgart: Kohlhammer, 1948] 114ff., especially p. 121). But as Van Seters and Westerman point out, the three presentations are more than different retellings of the same event. Genesis 20 is clearly an adaptation, presupposing knowledge of the original narrative, which addresses the moral questions of guilt and responsibility. Cf. Moshe Weinfeld, "Sarah and Abimelech (Genesis 20) against the Background of an Assyrian Law and the Genesis Apocryphon" (in *Mélanges bibliques et orientaux en l'honneur de M. Mathias Delcor* [AOAT 215; Neukirchener-Vluyn: Neukirchener Verlag, 1985] 431–36), where Weinfeld draws upon extrabiblical parallels, in which the paramour exonerates himself of guilt by swearing that he had no knowledge of the woman's married status and fulfills his legal obligation to compensate the husband, in order to underscore the message of the biblical passage. Van Seters considers Genesis 26 to be a literary conflation of the first two accounts, which is placed in the framework of chap. 26,

others have acknowledged a lack of chivalry in jeopardizing his wife's honor
or at least noted some measure of impropriety; while many have defended his
moral character, praising his steadfast belief. In raising the issue of textual determinacy in light of such a diverse history of interpretation, Robert B. Robertson has argued that the variation is largely determined not by the multifaceted
aspects of the textual elements, nor by the variability of the individual interpreter but by conventions shared by interpretive communities, which reflect
their interests.[2] Robertson explains that such interpretive conventions change
through time and thus are responsible for additional interpretative change. Even
the convention of realistic reading, which attempts to interpret the event as
depicted by the text, has undergone change. In premodern times, with the absence of fully developed critical conventions of interpretation, realistic reading
assumed the fundamental identity of the biblical world with that of the interpreter. This assumption allowed the interpreter to add details to the text uncriti-
cally from his own store of experience in order to understand the event. Now
modern conventions of realistic reading require greater critical control, based
on recently acquired knowledge of ancient Near Eastern history, archaeology,
and Semitic philology.[3]

A parade example of modern critical realistic reading of this biblical account has been E. A. Speiser's treatment of the wife-sister theme in the patriarchal narratives.[4] Based on his understanding of certain Nuzi marriage and
sistership adoption contracts, which he believed reflected an exclusively Hurrian sociolegal institution, Speiser concluded that within Hurrian society a
woman given in marriage by her brother became legally both her husband's
wife and sister. He further stated that such a juridical wife-sister status afforded the woman exceptional sociolegal protection, enjoyed only by women of
high social rank. Then, after having established a link between patriarchal custom and Hurrian practice by asserting that the West Semites of Haran and Na-

---

whose main purpose is to describe the life of Isaac as paralleling that of his father, Abraham (cf.
already *Pirqe R. El.* 61a and *Midr. Hagādôl* Gen 26:1). For different appreciations of the three
versions as three independent constructs, see U. Cassuto, *A Commentary on the Book of Genesis,
Part II: From Noah to Abraham* (trans. I. Abrahams; Jerusalem: Magnes, 1964) 337–43; C. A.
Keller, "'Die Gefährdung der Ahnfrau': Ein Beitrag zur gattungs- und motiv-geschichtlichen Er-
forschung alttestamentlicher Erzählungen," *ZAW* 66 (1954) 185ff.; D. L. Peterson, "A Thrice-Told
Tale: Genre, Theme and Motif," *BR* 18 (1973) 30–43; and S. Niditch, *Underdogs and Tricksters:
A Prelude to Biblical Folklore* (San Francisco: Harper & Row, 1987) 23–69.

2. R. B. Robertson, "Wife and Sister through the Ages: Textual Determinacy and the History
of Interpretation," *Semeia* 62 (1993) 103–28.

3. See Robertson's conclusions, ibid., 124–27.

4. E. A. Speiser, "The Wife-Sister Motif in the Patriarchal Narratives," in *Studies and Texts,
Volume I: Biblical and Other Studies* (ed. A. Altmann; Waltham, Mass.: Philip H. Lown Institute
of Advanced Judaic Studies, Brandeis University, 1963) 5–28; reprinted in *Oriental and Biblical
Studies: Collected Writings of E. A. Speiser* (ed. J. J. Finkelstein and M. Greenberg; Philadelphia:
University of Pennsylvania Press, 1967) 62–82.

hor lived in close cultural symbiosis with the Hurrian elements of that society, Speiser suggested that both Sarai and Rebekah were privileged with wife-sister status. The desire of tradition to underscore their exceptional, high status would thus account for the recurrence of the wife-sister theme in the patriarchal narratives. In his commentary on Genesis, Speiser asserted that although tradition retained the details of the wife-sister status, tradition misunderstood their import and reinterpreted them.[5] Thus, unbeknown to the redactor, the import of Abram's statement that Sarai was his sister was to protect her by emphasizing that Sarai enjoyed the highly respected status of wife-sister; the statement was not meant to serve as a ploy to save his own life. It was Speiser's belief that his knowledge of ancient Near Eastern legal contracts from the Hurrian site of Nuzi had enabled him to recover the original meaning of a patriarchal tradition that had been distorted through time.[6]

Because of Speiser's attempt to relate the Nuzi sistership documents to the patriarchal narratives, his interpretation of the Nuzi data gained widespread popularity. Critical remarks concerning the validity of Speiser's position,[7] however, necessitated a full-scale reexamination of the Nuzi sistership transaction. This investigation, based on almost twice the amount of documentation available to Speiser at the time of the writing of his article, revealed that Speiser's interpretation of the Nuzi texts could no longer be maintained.[8] The Nuzi texts indicate that, presumably in the absence of the father, a brother assumed certain rights and obligations over an unmarried sister, including the right to assign her in marriage or in adoption with her consent. Through adoption into sistership, a brother could transfer his rights over an unmarried sister to another, who was then empowered to assign his newly acquired "sister" to a third party in marriage and receive her bride-price. All of the Nuzi sistership adoption contracts thus involve the transfer of the privilege to negotiate the woman's marriage arrangements from the natural brother (or the woman herself) to the adoptive brother. With this transfer, the adoptive brother either gained the right to share in her future bride-price or obtained the sole right to her bride-price.

5. Speiser, *Genesis* (AB 1; Garden City, N.Y.: Doubleday, 1964) 92.

6. As Robertson duly noted ("Wife and Sister through the Ages," 118), Speiser's modern critical realistic reading assumes that the text does not correlate fully with the underlying event, and thus the text itself proves to be an unreliable guide to the event it reports.

7. D. Freedman, "A New Approach to the Nuzi Sistership Contracts," *JANES* 2 (1969) 77–85; C. J. Mullo Weir, "The Alleged Hurrian Wife-Sister Motif in Genesis," *Transactions of the Glasgow University Oriental Society* 22 (1967–68 [1970]) 14–25; T. L. Thompson, *The Historicity of the Patriarchal Narratives: The Quest for the Historical Abraham* (Berlin: de Gruyter, 1974) 234–48; J. Van Seters, *Abraham in History and Tradition* (New Haven: Yale University Press, 1975) 71–76; S. Greengus, "Sisterhood Adoption at Nuzi and the 'Wife–Sister' in Genesis," *HUCA* 46 (1975 [1976]) 5–31.

8. B. L. Eichler, "Another Look at the Nuzi Sistership Contracts," in *Essays on the Ancient Near East in Memory of Jacob Joel Finkelstein* (ed. M. de J. Ellis; Memoirs of the Connecticut Academy of Arts and Sciences 19; Hamden: Archon, 1977) 45–59.

It is clear that the woman or her natural brother must have been under severe socioeconomic pressure to enter into such a sistership arrangement; for it would have been more profitable for them to have negotiated the marriages on their own, rather than transferring the right of negotiation to an adoptive brother and thereby losing all or a part of the woman's bride-price. Thus, instead of reflecting high-ranking social behavior, it would seem that the sistership transaction was initiated either by brothers in need of raising immediate funds or by those who were financially incapable of supporting their sisters until the time when marriages could be arranged for them.[9] Furthermore, all textual evidence indicates that the rights of either the natural or adoptive brother terminated with the subsequent marriage of the sister to another party and that no sistership contract ever bestowed upon the adopted sister the concurrent status of sister and wife.

Since a reexamination of old evidence and additional data from more recently published documents have rendered Speiser's interpretation of the Nuzi sistership transactions untenable, no parallel can be drawn between this Nuzi practice and the wife-sister motif in the patriarchal narratives. At this juncture, having failed to illuminate the biblical text on the basis of ancient Near Eastern parallels, we would find it instructive to reread the text and review the major currents of exegetical narrative associated with a realistic reading of the biblical text.[10]

According to the NJPSV, Gen 12:10–20 reads:

> There was a famine in the land, and Abram went down to Egypt to sojourn there, for the famine was severe in the land. As he was about to enter Egypt, he said to his wife Sarai, "I know what a beautiful woman you are. If the Egyptians see you, and think 'She is his wife,' they will kill me and let you live. Please say that you are my sister, that it may go well with me because of you, and that I may remain alive thanks to you."
>
> When Abram entered Egypt, the Egyptians saw how very beautiful the woman was. Pharaoh's courtiers saw her and praised her to Pharaoh, and the woman was taken into Pharaoh's palace. And because of her, it went well with Abram; he acquired sheep, oxen, asses, male and female slaves, she-asses, and camels.

9. It is presumed that while the adopted sister is yet unmarried and resides in the adoptive brother's household, the adoptive brother is responsible for her support and maintenance in exchange for her services and handiwork.

10. Discussion will focus on the earliest version of the narrative, namely the Genesis 12 passage. It is uncertain whether this version of the narrative concludes with the end of the chapter division (v. 20) or whether the first four verses in Genesis 13 form the final sequel (cf. Cassuto, *A Commentary on the Book of Genesis, Part II*, 334). Note that the Masoretic Text lacks a paragraph break at the end of Genesis 12, and the Samaritan text has a paragraph break at the end of Gen 13:4.

But the Lord afflicted Pharaoh and his household with mighty plagues on account of Sarai, the wife of Abram. Pharaoh sent for Abram and said, "What is this you have done to me! Why did you not tell me that she was your wife? Why did you say 'She is my sister,' so that I took her as my wife? Now here is your wife; take her and begone!" And Pharaoh put men in charge of him, and they sent him off with his wife and all that he possessed.

As noted in Hugh C. White's analysis of this passage,[11] the biblical narrative begins by introducing the reader to the backdrop against which the subsequent plot will unfold: the vulnerability of Abram to the vicissitudes of nature and the whims of an alien society in which he unwillingly finds himself. The central conflict of the plot is then set forth by Abram's direct discourse, revealing his anticipated fears and disclosing the means by which he prepares to forestall the perceived life-threatening peril: a conspiracy to create the fiction of a sister-brother relationship between him and his wife. Abram's stratagem assumes societal behavior that condemns the more public act of seizing a married woman, while condoning the more covert act of killing her husband. It assumes a facade of morality beneath which lurks a hidden reality of compulsive sexual desire. The narration then describes the unfolding of Abram's anticipated fears. But while Abram's stratagem succeeds in preserving his life and enriching him, Sarai is abducted by Pharaoh. Abram's ultimate victory over Pharaoh is achieved only through divine intervention. Pharaoh's public response to his having been duped is again narrated in direct discourse, juxtaposed with the private fears of the vulnerable Abram, set forth in the initial direct discourse, as a series of astonished exclamations directed at Abram, which remain unanswered. The narrative ends with a final comment, indicating that Abram emerges as the victor in that he has succeeded in keeping his wife and wealth intact, while preserving his life.

This narrative confronts the reader with open ambiguity. The confrontation between Abram and Pharaoh does not end with the defeat of the wicked and the triumph of the upright. The central protagonists remain morally ambiguous. They are not unequivocally good or evil. Abram lies and compromises his wife to save his own life and gain wealth; Pharaoh protests his innocence, having nonetheless abducted Sarai in order to indulge his sexual appetite. As noted again by White, "this narrative achieves a state of openness and ambiguity which causes the story to live on in the reader as a source of continuing disturbance."[12] Pharaoh's accusatory questions remain unanswered, "and the absence of an answer from Abram sets the reader upon his own search."[13]

11. H. C. White, *Narration and Discourse in the Book of Genesis* (Cambridge: Cambridge University Press, 1991) 178–86.
12. Ibid., 184.
13. Ibid.

Within an interpretive community that views the patriarchs as paragons of virtue and their life-narratives as edifying instructions to future generations,[14] such ambiguity cannot be tolerated. Jewish and Christian exegetes[15] throughout the ages have focused most of their interpretive efforts on dispelling these ambiguities in their realistic reading of the text. Elements of the text are either emphasized or deemphasized in an effort to lessen the moral problematics.[16] The severity of the famine is stressed to minimize Abram's culpability in descending to Egypt; while the Egyptians' licentiousness is underscored to maximize the peril to Abram's life. Abram's deceptive claim of brothership is underplayed as justifiable in such life-threatening circumstances, with the possible consequence of Sarai's defilement remaining largely unspoken.[17] The

14. This function of the patriarchal narratives is clearly stated by Philo (*Philo VI* [trans. F. H. Colson; LCL; Cambridge: Harvard University Press, 1935] 7). More specifically, rabbinic exegesis views the narratives as presaging important events in the lives of the Israelites and thus affording instruction and inspiration to them in meeting future challenges. See *Midr. Tanḥuma*, Lekh-lekha 9; and especially *Gen. Rab.* 40:6, where this patriarchal narrative is viewed as a preenactment of the Exodus from Egypt (A. Mirkin [ed.], *Midrash Rabbah* [Tel-Aviv: Yavneh, 1971] 2.107–8. This theme was taken up by at least one important Jewish medieval exegete (see Nachmanides' commentary to vv. 6 and 10; my colleague, Edward Breuer, called my attention to A. Funkenstein's explanation of Nachmanides' use of prefiguration in "Nachmanides' Symbolical Reading of History," *Studies in Jewish Mysticism* [ed. J. Dan and F. Talmage; Cambridge, Mass.: Association for Jewish Studies, 1982] 129–50) and appears in modern treatments of the biblical narrative as literary typologies (cf. M. Z. Brettler, *The Creation of History in Ancient Israel* [London: Routledge, 1995] 52–55; and F. van Dijk-Hemmes, "Sarai's Exile: A Gender-Motivated Reading of Genesis 12.10–13.2," in *A Feminist Companion to Genesis* [The Feminist Companion to the Bible 2; ed. Athalya Brenner; Sheffield: Sheffield Academic Press, 1993] 233).

15. Although the Qurʾān does not incorporate or even allude to any of the patriarchal wife-sister narratives, Islamic exegetical literature contains many renditions of the Abraham and Sarah episode, which reduce to two slightly different versions. For detailed references, see R. Firestone, "Difficulties in Keeping a Beautiful Wife: The Legend of Abraham and Sarah in Jewish and Islamic Tradition," *JSS* 42 (1991) 198 n. 6 and 200–201. Neither of these two versions derives from scriptural exegesis, since the episode is not recorded in the Qurʾān.

16. For a convenient compilation of rabbinic aggadic exegesis with commentary, see M. M. Kasher, *Torah shelemah: Ve-hu ha-Torah shebi-khetav ʿim beʾur "Torah shebe-ʿal peh"* (New York: Shulzinger Brothers, 1948–49) 3.562–74. Selections from the major Jewish exegetical tradition of realistic readings of the narrative may be found in S. Kasher, *Peshuṭo shel Miqra* (Jerusalem: Mekhon Torah Shelemah, 1968) 2.212–23, with notations. For a study of the old versions and ancient Jewish literature on this passage, see A. Shinan and Y. Zakovitch, *Abram and Sarai in Egypt* (Research Projects of the Institute of Jewish Studies, Monograph Series 2; Jerusalem: The Hebrew University, 1983 [Hebrew]). Cf. also Philo, "On Abraham," *Philo VI*, 49ff. For a summary of the Islamic traditions, see Firestone, "Difficulties in Keeping a Beautiful Wife," 199–212. For an example of Catholic and Protestant readings in the writings of St. Augustine and Luther, see Robertson, "Wife and Sister through the Ages," 110–16.

17. There is some halachic discussion on this issue dealing with the relative severity of the sins of murder and adultery (M. Kasher, *Torah shelemah*, 565 with n. 145). However, Nachmanides (1195–1270) openly addresses this issue and disapprovingly states that "Abraham our father

issue of Abram's exploiting this deception for his own aggrandizement is handled through the indeterminacy of the text, reading "that it may go well with me because of you" as being explicated by the assumed parallel clause "that I may remain alive thanks to you" (v. 13). Accordingly, Abram is motivated only out of concern for his physical safety, with no thought of material gain. Further support for this position is marshaled from the subsequent narration, which states: "And because of her, he acquired (literally, he possessed) sheep, oxen, asses, male and female slaves, she-asses, and camels" (v. 16), that is, he was able to maintain his possessions and possibly acquire new ones despite his dependent alien status, the notion of gift-giving not being explicitly mentioned in the text.[18] Gaps in the narrative concerning the fabrication of Abram's claim of brothership and Sarai's possible defilement in the palace of Pharaoh are filled in by borrowing from the apologetically oriented account of Abraham's parallel encounter with Abimelech (Genesis 20), where Abraham

---

unintentionally committed a great sin by bringing his righteous wife to a stumbling-block of sin on account of his fear for his life" (*Ramban, Commentary on the Torah: Genesis* [translated and annotated by C. B. Chavel; New York: Shilo, 1971] 173) by requesting that she declare herself to be his sister. Even his decision to leave the land on account of the famine demonstrated a lack of faith in Providence and was also sinful. Nachmanides describes Sarah's role as purely passive. She remained silent and did not tell the Egyptians whether she was his wife or sister. It was Abraham himself who told them that she was his sister (ibid., 176). Nachmanides states that the episode with Abimelech was different from the episode in Egypt. Unlike the immoral Egyptians, the people of Gerar and their king were upright, but Abraham suspected them. Nachmanides is puzzled by Abraham's feeble explanation that Sarai was indeed his half-sister: "I know not sense of this apology. Even if it were true that she was his sister and his wife, nevertheless when they wanted to take her as a wife and he told them 'She is my sister,' in order to lead them astray, he already committed a sin towards them by bringing upon them a 'great sin' and it no longer mattered at all whether the thing was true or false!" (ibid., 263ff.) Thus Nachmanides is the first Jewish exegete to deviate from the traditional stance of viewing the patriarchs as paragons of virtue and morality by ascribing questionable behavior to Abraham in his treatment of Sarah both in Egypt and Gerar (Gen 12:10 and 20:12; cf. also his commentary on Gen 16:6, where he disapproves of both Sarah's and Abraham's treatment of Hagar). For a discussion of Nachmanides' significant but atypical exegesis against the backdrop of the polemical world of the Middle Ages, see D. Berger, "On the Morality of the Patriarchs in Jewish Polemic and Exegesis," in *Understanding Scripture: Explorations of Jewish and Christian Traditions of Interpretation* (ed. Clemens Thoma and Michael Wyschogrod; New York: Paulist Press, 1987) 49ff. The only medieval Jewish exegete to support Nachmanides' position is Bachya ben Asher (1263–1340), who brings a Talmudic statement (*b. Ned.* 32a) that Egyptian slavery was decreed upon Abraham's descendants because of his questioning God's promise in Gen 15:8 (*Rabbenu Bachya* [New York: Keter, 1945] 54). S. Kasher (*Peshuṭo shel Miqra*, 2.213 n. 7) cites the many commentators who take issue with Nachmanides' position.

18. This understanding of the purpose of Abram's ploy only to save his life and not to gain any material advantage from his claim of being Sarai's brother is found in the medieval commentaries of David Qimḥi (Radaq), Nissim ben Reuben Gerondi (Ran), and Isaac Abrabanel. In the modern period, U. Cassuto has most cogently argued this position (*A Commentary on the Book of Genesis, Part II*, 349ff.).

explains that "in truth she is my sister, my father's daughter though not my mother's" (v. 12),[19] and where it is explicitly stated that Sarah's chastity was protected by divine intervention (vv. 3–7).[20]

Other interpretive communities, not bound by the constraints of the faithful, will also utilize the conventions of realistic reading to render the above narrative less ambiguous by teasing out different insights from the text that suit their own communities. Distinct elements of the text are again either emphasized or deemphasized, and gaps in the text are again filled in. The Manichaean Faustus, in his anti-Christian stance, read the text as a moral indictment against Abram who, "acting from avarice and greed," profaned his sacred bond of marriage and endangered his wife in order to save his own life and procure great wealth.[21] Others, who are nonpolemical, are less harsh in interpreting the narrative's depictment of Abram. For example, H. Gunkel readily agreed that

19. Abraham's statement raises the problem of his being engaged in a forbidden incestuous relationship by marrying his half-sister. R. Firestone, in his "Prophethood, Marriageable Consanguinity, and Text: The Problem of Sarah's Kinship Relationship and the Response of Jewish and Islamic Exegesis" (*JQR* 83 [1993] 331–47), presents a detailed study of both rabbinic and Islamic exegetical responses to this issue. Although Rashi (Commentary to Gen 20:12) states that Abraham lived before the giving of the Torah and therefore was not bound by the laws of consanguinity detailed in Leviticus and Deuteronomy, rabbinic tradition often views the patriarchs as having observed all of the laws of the Torah. The explanations presented in rabbinic traditions are: (1) Sarah was not his genetic half-sister but rather his niece, the daughter of Haran (since grandchildren are referred to as children, Sarah could also be considered Terah's daughter and hence Abraham's half-sister; so *Tg. Ps.-J.* Gen 11:29, *b. Meg.* 14a, *b. Sanh.* 69b); (2) Sarah was Abraham's first cousin: "My father's brother's daughter, though not of my mother's family"; so *Tg. Ps.-J.* Gen 20:12. The wife-sister narrative is not found in the Qurʾān, but it is mentioned in the *ḥadith* reports attributed to Abu Hurayra, the earliest traditionist and contemporary of the Prophet Muhammad. Although the *ḥadith* enumerates it as one of the three times Abraham lied, Islamic exegetes attempt to explain the statement in the following ways: (1) Sarah was Abraham's spiritual sister, for they were the only two true believers in the world; (2) Sarah was the daughter of the king of Haran and was unrelated to Abraham; (3) Abraham and Sarah were first cousins (according to Islam and unlike Jewish law, union of uncle and niece is prohibited); (4) Sarah was Abraham's niece. On the basis of the above comparisons, Firestone argues for a shared realm of religious discourse between Muslim and Jewish scholars (Firestone, "Prophethood, Marriageable Consanguinity and Text," 343ff.).

20. Similarly, in Josephus' retelling of the Genesis 12 account, he borrows elements from the Abimelech account of Genesis 20, even though he will later relate the Abimelech version, where he again borrows elements from the first as suits his purposes. For a full discussion of his retelling of these accounts, see T. W. Franxman, *Genesis and the "Jewish Antiquities" of Flavius Josephus* (BibOr 35; Rome: Pontifical Biblical Institute Press, 1979) 127–32 and 147–49. Cf. Y. Zakovitch, "Assimilation in Biblical Narratives," in *Empirical Models for Biblical Criticism* (ed. Jeffrey H. Tigay; Philadelphia: University of Pennsylvania Press, 1985) 178ff.

21. Robinson, "Wife and Sister through the Ages," 111. The same negative reading may be found in the commentary of the modern German exegete, H. Holzinger, *Genesis* (KHAT 1; Freiburg: Mohr, 1898) 139: ". . . sodern wie Abraham in schmählicher selbst süchtiger Feigheit sein Weib der Lüsternheit eines fremden Fürsten preisgiebt und aus dem schmutzigen Handel noch Nutzen zieht."

the narrative does not depict Abram as a saint;[22] however, he not only excuses Abram's lie as necessary to save his life, but also views the narrative as extolling Abram's cunning: his artifice, with Sarai's self-sacrifice and with divine assistance, gains him the upper hand over his adversary.[23] To Gunkel, the form critic, such is the quality of the early patriarchal folk legends of Genesis, stemming from oral popular traditions.[24] More recently, feminist readings of the text have focused on Sarai.[25] F. van Dijk-Hemmes' sensitive reading[26] underscores Sarai's silence, the unspeakable personal experience of sexual violence, and societal repression of the telling of such violence. In the power struggle between men, Sarai is depicted as the helpless victim (sacrificed to save Abram's life and to satisfy Pharaoh's desire) who is passively taken to the palace. Only God hears her silent cry of desperation[27] and frees her from oppression.[28]

Over the ages, little interpretive energy in the realistic reading of the narrative has been devoted to a fuller understanding of the nature and intent of Abram's stratagem in claiming his wife as his sister. It seems that Jewish exegesis becomes sensitive to the issue of Abram's subordination of his wife's welfare to that of his own in the 13th–14th centuries C.E.[29] and addresses this issue by explaining that Abram's intent was to prevent the endangerment of both

---

22. H. Gunkel, *The Legends of Genesis: The Biblical Saga and History* (trans. W. H. Carruth; New York: Schocken, 1964) 113ff.

23. H. Gunkel, *Genesis, II* (Göttingen: Vandenhoeck & Ruprecht, 1964) 170.

24. Gunkel considers the other two tellings of the wife-sister legend (Gen 20:1–18 and 26:1–12) to be later than Genesis 12 because they exhibit signs of developing moral sensitivity and ethical judgments that are absent in early tales (*The Legends of Genesis*, 115).

25. For example, J. Otwell, *And Sarah Laughed* (Philadelphia: Westminster, 1977); S. J. Teubal, *Sarah the Priestess: The First Matriarch of Genesis* (Athens, Ohio: Swallow, 1984); and E. S. Campbell, "Listen to Her Voice: Six Speeches of Sarah—Gen. 11–23," a paper that was delivered at the SBL Conference in Anaheim, 1989.

26. Van Dijk-Hemmes, "Sarai's Exile," 222–34.

27. Van Dijk-Hemmes translates the phrase *ʿl dbr śry* as 'because of the word of Sarai', thus indicating that only to God did Sarai not remain speechless (ibid., 231). Her interpretation is in keeping with the motif of Sarai's prayer found in rabbinic midrashic literature (*Gen. Rab.* 41:2, 52:13; *Tanḥuma, Lekh-lekha* 5). Sarai's prayer also appears as an element in virtually all of the Islamic renditions of the legend (Firestone, "Difficulties in Keeping a Beautiful Wife," 206).

28. Van Dijk-Hemmes views Sarai's role as a prefiguration of the Israelites' experience of Egyptian oppression, their subsequent cry for help and their final liberation from bondage ("Sarai's Exile," 233). For interpretations of the narrative as a preenacted Exodus in rabbinic tradition, medieval Jewish exegesis and modern typological studies of the Bible, see above n. 14.

29. Sensitivity to this issue may have developed within the Jewish medieval exegetical community as a reaction to Nachmanides' indictment of Abram. This is clearly the case with Nissim ben Reuben Gerondi, who disputes Nachmanides' approach on the spot (see below, n. 32). This sensitivity also may have risen from an external polemical need to defend the morality of the patriarchs against Christian accusations. For evidence of such responses in the commentaries of the early French Jewish exegetes, see Abraham Grossman, *Ḥakhmey Ṣorfat ha-Rishonim* (Jerusalem: Magnes, 1995) 488ff.

of their lives. Textual support for Abram's concern not only for his life but for Sarai's well-being and his intention to safeguard her honor is sought in the narrative's formulation of Abram's anticipated fears: "they will kill me and let you live (i.e., for their sexual pleasures)." Both fears are to be allayed by his ruse.[30] Hezekiah ben Manoah (mid-13th-century French exegete), whose work is based chiefly on halakhic and aggadic midrashim and comments from another "20 books,"[31] understands Abram's behavior as a clever ploy designed to save his life and to protect Sarai's chastity. As her brother, he would remain alive and thus be able to deter Sarai's suitors by informing them that she is a married woman, whose husband is abroad.[32] Less naïve is the explanation of Nissim ben Reuben Gerondi (the RaN ?1310–?1375): Abram, as Sarai's brother, would be recognized as her legal guardian, who would thus be empowered to negotiate her marriage contract. In this ideal position, he would be in control of her destiny by warding off the lustful Egyptians with demands for an exorbitant bride-price and, should that fail, by protracting the negotiations, allowing time to escape from Egypt.[33] To this day, subsequent Jewish exegetes have adopted this explanation of Abram's stratagem with slight variations.[34]

New attention had been focused on this issue with the publication of E. A. Speiser's interpretation of the wife-sister motif in the patriarchal narratives. As mentioned above,[35] basing himself on a group of Nuzi documents, Speiser viewed the "wife-sister," title as conferring upon the woman high social rank. Accordingly, he explained that, although no longer understood by the redactor, Abram sought to protect Sarai by declaring her to be his "wife-sister," which thereby conferred upon her a highly privileged and protected status. The hope, however, that the original intent of Abram's statement could be recovered from

---

30. Note already Josephus *Ant.* 1.8.1: "He devised the following scheme: he pretended to be her brother and, telling her that *their* [italics mine] interest required it, instructed her to play her part accordingly" (H. St. J. Thackeray, *Josephus IV* [LCL; Cambridge: Harvard University Press, 1930] 81). An explanation about how Abraham's ruse would further their interests and accomplish his goal is not provided in Josephus' account.

31. See his "Introduction," published in *Torat Hayyim, Bereshit 1* (Jerusalem: Mossad Harav Kook, 1986) 20. Included in these twenty books are the commentaries of Solomon ben Isaac (Rashi), Samuel ben Meir (Rashbam), and Joseph ben Isaac (Bekhor Shor) and many midrashim that are no longer extant (*EncJud* 8.460).

32. See *Torat Hayyim, Bereshit 1*, 158.

33. *Perush ᶜal ha-Torah* (ed. L. A. Feldman; Jerusalem: Machon Shalem, 1968) 164.

34. For example, see Isaac Abrabanel (1437–1508), who cites Nissim ben Reuben Gerondi's interpretation in his commentary (*Perush ᶜal ha-Torah* [Jerusalem: Bnai Arbael, 1964] 1.194b); Obadiah Sforno (1470–1550) in *Torat Hayyim, Bereshit 1*, 157–58; Samuel David Luzzatto (1800–1865) in *Perush Shadal ᶜal Hamishah Humshay Torah* (Tel-Aviv: Devir, 1966) 62; Meir Loeb ben Yechiel Michael (Malbim, 1809–79) in *Sefer ha-Torah veha-Miṣvah* (Jerusalem: Pardes, 1956) 1.59–60; and in the 20th century, Cassuto, *A Commentary on the Book of Genesis, Part II*, 350 and N. M. Sarna, *Genesis* (JPS Torah Commentary; Philadelphia: Jewish Publication Society, 1989) 95.

35. See above, pp. 24–25.

the ancient past proved to be illusory when Speiser's interpretation could no longer be maintained. Therefore, it is appropriate to ask whether one's understanding of Abram's stratagem must depend once again solely on the subjectivity of the individual reader and the interests of one's interpretive community.

For a modern critical realistic reader, knowledge of the ancient sociolegal setting of the narrative remains crucial in navigating between the indeterminacy of the text and the necessity to fill in motives and gaps left unanswered by the narrator. In attempting to discern the import of Abram's conduct, we may find it helpful to examine the role of the brother vis-à-vis his sister in the ancient world.

Two biblical stories clearly reflect the importance of the brother in biblical society as protector of his unmarried sister and as her champion against overpowering forces. At the onset of the Rape of Dinah in Genesis 34,[36] the narrator describes Dinah as "the daughter of Jacob" (vv. 1, 2, 5, 7). This exclusive affiliation suddenly switches to "our sister" as the tale of the redress of Dinah's violation begins to unfold (vv. 13, 27, 31); and it is "two of Jacob's sons, Simeon and Levi, brothers of Dinah," who selflessly risk their lives to rescue their captive sister. These maternal brothers of Dinah are single-minded in their devotion to their sister and the attainment of her freedom. Unlike the other sons of Jacob, they take no part in the subsequent looting. (v. 27) Similarly, in the Rape of Tamar (2 Samuel 13), Tamar turns to her maternal brother, Absalom, and not to her father, David. After her defilement, Tamar seeks refuge with Absalom, remaining "in her brother Absalom's house, forlorn" (v. 20); and it is Absalom who eventually avenges his sister's wrong by slaying Amnon (v. 28).

In Mesopotamia, a woman's brother is most often documented in his capacity as the legal representative of his fatherless sister, who arranges for her marriage and receives her bride-price.[37] In his study of the authority of the brother, based on the Nuzi texts, A. Skaist concludes that at Nuzi there existed a "patrilocal extended family, patripotestal in authority and patrilineal in inheritance and descent," although there is "no patrilineal succession to the father's power over female children."[38] Hence the situation would be analogous to early Roman family structure, in which the female orphan was *sui juris* but

---

36. For a literary appreciation of this biblical narrative's persuasive art, see M. Sternberg, *The Poetics of Biblical Narrative: Ideological Literature and the Drama of Reading* (Bloomington: Indiana University Press, 1987) 445–81.

37. V. Korošeç, "Ehe," *Reallexikon der Assyriologie* (Berlin: de Gruyter, 1938) 2.287, 297; A. van Praag, *Droit matrimonial assyro-babylonien* (Archaeologisch-Historische Bijdragen 12; Amsterdam: Noord-Hollandsche Uitgevers Maatschappij, 1945) 77–78; J. M. Breneman, *Nuzi Marriage Tablets* (Ph.D. diss., Brandeis University, 1971) 20–21, 82, 127; M. Roth, "Age at Marriage and the Household: A Study of Neo-Babylonian and Neo-Assyrian Forms," *Comparative Studies in Society and History* 29 (1987) 724 with n. 20

38. Skaist, "The Authority of the Brother at Arrapha and Nuzi," *JAOS* 89 (1969) 16.

nevertheless was in need of a guardian. Skaist suggests that similarly, the authority of the brother in Nuzi was that of a guardian, whose authority over his sister was less than that of her father.[39] Other Mesopotamian documents from different geographical areas and chronological periods seem to conform to this pattern of limited fratriarchal authority over one's orphaned sister.[40] Unfortunately, there is little detailed evidence of a brother's responsibility for the well-being and protection of one's sister from Mesopotamian sources.[41] Most informative is a Nuzi deposition concerning a sistership adoption in which the woman states that her adoptive brother "will ward off her attackers and protect her possessions(?), treat her as a sister and come to her aid."[42] In Egypt, there is even scantier documentation concerning the role of a woman's brother. A passage from *The Eloquent Peasant*, however, in which the peasant appeals to the chief steward, seems clearly to attest to the brother's role as his sister's main support and protector. The passage reads: "For you are father to the orphan, Husband to the widow, Brother to the rejected woman, Apron to the motherless."[43] Thus it seems that, in ancient Egyptian society, it was to her brother that a divorced woman, rejected by her husband, would turn for help.

Anthropological research informs us that this special protective relationship between a brother and his sister is not unique to the ancient Near East.

39. An example of the lessened authority of the brother is the need for his sister's consent as prerequisite to the arrangement that he transacts for her.

40. See above, n. 37. Also cf. Middle Assyrian Law 48 (M. Roth, *Law Collections from Mesopotamia and Asia Minor* [Atlanta: Scholars Press, 1995] 173), which gives the brothers of an orphaned sister who has been residing in the house of her deceased father's creditor the right to redeem her prior to the creditor's giving her in marriage.

41. Bits and pieces of information may be gleaned from private correspondence, especially between brothers and sisters. For example, an Old Babylonian letter reports that a sister is residing in her brother's house (T. G. Pinches, *The Babylonian Tablets of the Berens Collection* [Asiatic Society Monographs 16; London, 1915] 99); and a Neo-Babylonian letter records a sister's request that her brother be mindful to redeem her children should they be taken prisoner, while chiding him for his lack of concern for her economic well-being and demanding an increase in his shipment of barley and dates to her (G. Contenau, *Contrats et lettres d'Assyrie et de Babylonie* [TCL 9; Paris: Geuthner, 1926] 141).

42. E. Chiera, *Excavations at Nuzi 1: Texts of Varied Contents* (HSS 5; Cambridge: Harvard University Press, 1929) Text 26, which is treated in Eichler, "Another Look at the Nuzi Sistership Contracts," 51 with n. 49.

43. M. Lichtheim, *Ancient Egyptian Literature, I: The Old and Middle Kingdoms* (Berkeley: University of California Press, 1975) 172. I would like to thank my colleague, Jeffrey H. Tigay, for calling this reference and the Herodotus passage below to my attention. A piquant observation with regard to Egyptian society is the custom of referring to one's wife (*ḥm.t*) as one's sister (*sn.t*), which is already attested in the Old Kingdom period but is especially documented from the 18th Dynasty onward (P. M. Pestman, *Marriage and Matrimonial Property in Ancient Egypt* [Leiden: Brill, 1961] 4 with n. 5; 11 with n. 3; and 12 with n. 2). Also cf. E. Lüddeckens, "Ehe," *Lexikon der Ägyptologie* (ed. W. Helck and E. Otto; Wiesbaden: Harrassowitz, 1975) 1.1170. Thus, for an Egyptian audience, Abram's calling Sarai his sister would not have precluded her being his wife. Accordingly, Abram's ploy would have been marred at the onset and Pharaoh's forcible seizure of Sarai could no longer have been construed as a totally innocent act.

E. E. Evans-Pritchard relates that, among the African Nuer, only a brother may interfere in the courting affairs of his sister, for her virtue is his responsibility. He keeps his eye on his sister and is aware of whoever is courting her. He will come between her and her lover only if he suspects that the suitor is not honorable.[44] As her brother, he also has rights in his sister's bride-wealth and in the part of her daughter's bride-wealth that is due her family.[45] His fraternal responsibility toward his sister extends to her children. This means that a man's greatest supporter is his maternal uncle, who, for his mother's sake, will always help him.[46] In the state of Gonja in West Africa, sibling bonds take on new importance in adulthood.[47] The adult brother bears responsibility for his sister's welfare. Upon marriage, a woman's husband is primarily responsible for her economic well-being and ritual assistance. However, even while his sister is married, the brother has certain duties and rights toward his sister and her children. These obligations include payment of his sister's debts and the provision of extra food. When she falls seriously ill, a sister takes up residence in her brother's home, where she benefits from his ritual intercession and knowledge of medicines.[48] When a woman becomes widowed or leaves her husband, her brothers are obligated to provide for her, and they become her primary source of support and shelter. Among the Polynesian Tokelau, brothers are also responsible for protecting and providing for their sisters and their sisters' children. Because of their "pule" (= secular authority), their strength and wisdom, brothers are called upon to safeguard their sisters, rescue them from adversity, and defend their rights against outsiders.[49] The brother-sister relationship takes precedence over that of husband-wife. This ideology is expressed in terms of a brother's being "from the same belly" as his sister and in terms of a brother's being "irreplaceable," in contrast to a spouse, whom it is possible to replace.[50] This great emphasis on the bond existing between a brother and his sister is also evident from the Tokelau folktales.[51]

---

44. E. E. Evans-Pritchard, *Kinship and Marriage among the Nuer* (New York: Oxford University Press, 1990) 53. The Nuer are primarily a cattle people, divided into a number of tribes, inhabiting the open savannah country near the Nile and its tributaries in the Sudan. Their smallest political unit is the village.

45. Ibid.

46. Ibid., 162–63.

47. E. Goody, *Contexts of Kinship: An Essay in the Family Sociology of the Gonja of Northern Ghana* (Cambridge Studies in Social Anthropology 7; London: Cambridge University Press, 1973) 224–25.

48. Ibid., 234.

49. J. Huntsman and A. Hooper, "Male and Female in Tokelau Culture," in *Women and Society: An Anthropological Reader* (ed. S. H. Tiffany; Montreal: Eden Press Women's Publications, 1979) 280–97, especially pp. 291–95, subheading "Brothers and Sisters" (this article was originally published in *Journal of Polynesian Society* 84 [1978] 415–30).

50. Ibid., 295.

51. Ibid., 293. Similar aspects of the brother-sister relationship are present in the folk literature of many different cultures. For detailed bibliography, see Stith Thompson, *Motif-Index of*

There is one last item of anthropological research that is most noteworthy. In the introduction to her anthropological study of life and customs in the Arab village of Artas, located a short distance south of Bethlehem, Hilma Granqvist presents a brief biographical sketch of her major informants. She relates that one of her informants, the widowed Hamdiye, had been married to a half-Bedouin. During World War I, hardship forced Hamdiye and her husband to leave the village. They lived in Transjordan among different Bedouin tribes and referred to each other as brother and sister. Her husband's behavior alienated him from the tribes and they thought of killing him. Granqvist further relates that "the Bedouin told Hamdiye: 'If it is thy husband, we will slay him, for he does not know how to behave to people.' And she heard them say: 'If he is her brother, good and well, and if he made brotherhood with her, it is good and well too, but if he is her husband we will slay him!'"[52] Granqvist then remarks in passing that ever since biblical times, people in Palestine had to leave their country during difficult periods and that Abraham and Isaac also referred to their wives as "sister" while residing in a foreign land.[53] Although Granqvist does draw the biblical parallel, she offers no explanation for such conduct.

It is suggested, in light of the above discussion, that the Bedouins' statements are to be understood as reflecting the great reverence in which Arab society views the role of the maternal brother as the protector of his sister. Basic to this reverence is the notion, expressed by the Arab villagers in Artas, that a woman can always find another husband, but a maternal brother is considered to be a divine gift from Allah, for which there is no substitute.[54] Therefore, despite their hatred toward Hamdiye's "brother," the Bedouin moral code prevented them from inflicting upon her an irreparable loss by bereaving her of her "brother."

The theme of the irreplaceable brother, common to such diverse cultures as Tokelau and Arabic, is also known from both Persian and Greek sources. Herodotus, in *The Persian Wars*, relates that Darius was touched with pity for the wife of the condemned Persian Intaphernes and sent a messenger to her saying:

> "Lady, king Darius gives you as a boon the life of one of your kinsmen—choose which you will of the prisoners." Then she pondered awhile before

---

Folk-Literature: A Classification of Narrative Elements in Folktales, Ballads, Myths, Fables, Mediaeval Romances, Exempla, Fabliaux, Jest-books, and Local Legends (Bloomington: Indiana University Press, 1955–58) 5.355 sub T131.1.1 = "brother's consent for sister's marriage needed"; and p. 159 sub P253.3 = "brother chosen rather than husband or son." Also cf. below, n. 54.

52. Hilma Granqvist, *Birth and Childhood among the Arabs: Studies in a Muhammadan Village in Palestine* (Helsingfors: Soderström, 1947) 24.

53. Ibid.

54. H. Granqvist, *Marriage Conditions in a Palestinian Village* (Helingfors: Soderström, 1935) 2.253. Also cf. Hasan M. El-Shamy, *Folk Traditions of the Arab World: A Guide to Motif Classification* (Bloomington: Indiana University Press, 1995) 1.300 sub P253.3 = "brother chosen rather than wife or son"; and p. 348 sub T131.1.1 = "brother's consent to sister's marriage needed."

she answered, "If the king grants me the life of one alone, I make choice of my brother." Darius, when he heard the reply was astonished, and sent again saying, "Lady, the king bids you tell him why it is that you pass by your husband and your children and prefer to have the life of your brother spared. He is not so near to you as your children, not so dear as your husband." She answered, "O king, if the gods will, I may have another husband and other children when these are gone. But as my father and mother are no more, it is impossible that I should have another brother. This was my thought when I asked to have my brother spared."[55]

Darius was pleased with her answer and gave her the life of her brother and also the life of her eldest son.

This sentiment has strong resemblance to Sophocles *Antigone* 909–912. Antigone, having been condemned to death for burying her brother, Polyneices, declares:

> One husband gone, I might have found another,
> or a child from a new man in first child's place,
> but with parents hid away in death,
> no brother, ever, could spring up for me.
> Such was the law by which I honored you.[56]

Now, with the help of the above-cited biblical and ancient Near Eastern materials and the supplementary anthropological data, the realistic reader is able to explore once again the purport of Abram's stratagem with greater critical control and less subjectivity. It is now clear that by assuming the status of Sarai's brother, Abram not only removes the threat to his life posed by being the husband of a beautiful woman in a foreign land but also enhances his chances for survival by being identified as her irreplaceable brother.[57] Furthermore, it is also clear now that, as her brother, Abram would be recognized as

---

55. *Herodotus: The Persian Wars* 3.119 (trans. G. Rawlinson; New York: Random, 1942) 269–70.

56. *Sophocles I: Antigone* (trans. Elizabeth Wyckoff; The Complete Greek Tragedies; ed. David Greene and Richmond Lattimore; Chicago: University of Chicago Press, 1954) 190. Although these lines were known to Aristotle in the following century (he cites them in his *Rhetoric* 3.16), classicists have debated their authenticity in this passage. Closely imitating the cited passage from Herodotus, some argue that they are illogical in context and inconsistent with other statements made by Antigone and that they were spuriously interpolated shortly after the poet's death (Andrew Brown, *Sophocles: Antigone* [Warminster, Wiltshire, England: Aris & Phillips, 1987] 199–200; James C. Hogan, *A Commentary on the Plays of Sophocles* [Carbondale: Southern University of Illinois Press, 1991] 162–64).

57. The verse "So when God made me wander from my father's house, I said to her, 'Let this be the kindness (*ḥesed*) that you shall do me: whatever place we come to, say there of me: He is my brother'" (Gen 20:13) now takes on added significance. For the term *ḥesed*, see S. Bendor, "The Meaning and Provenance of Biblical *Ḥesed*," *Shnaton: An Annual for Biblical and Ancient Near Eastern Studies* 10 (1986–89) 47–59.

the protector and legal guardian whom one would approach to negotiate Sarai's marriage.[58] Thus, based on evidence external to the narrative, the reader can now appreciate the twofold purpose of Abram's ploy: the preservation of his life and the protection of his wife. But alas, Abram never anticipated Pharaoh's swift abduction of Sarai, which suddenly rendered him so powerless.

The explanation of Abram's stratagem, however, represents only one element in the reading and appreciation of this patriarchal narrative, which is introduced just after Abram's identity and future become dependent on a divine promise (Gen 12:1–3). After such divine assurance, how will this man of faith now deal with the crises of life that have the potential to destroy him? The answer is found in this narrative, which continues to engage the modern reader with its open ambiguity and unresolved tension, thus marking its function as symbolic narrative.[59] H. C. White eloquently explicates:

> When the hero, the man of faith, whose life is founded upon a mere sign and not upon power, finds himself in a situation where his survival is at stake and conflict is unavoidable, he does not go like a lamb to the slaughter. He pays the price of entering into the moral ambiguities of a situation and follows a strategy which takes advantage of the blind subservience to desire of his more powerful opponents. . . . But the price paid for this successful strategy is that Abram and Sarai must lie, and so cast a shadow upon their own moral rectitude.[60]

But despite the fact that the man of faith acts to protect himself, his wife, and his possessions from his adversaries, it is evident from the narrative that the success of Abram's stratagem is ultimately dependent on divine assistance.[61]

---

58. This awareness now lends credence to the apologetic Jewish exegesis of the Medieval period that understood the concept of a brother's legal authority over his fatherless sister and his right to negotiate her marriage contract with her consent. Such a concept of the brother's legal authority is preserved in rabbinic law in the case of a fatherless minor sister: *m. Yebam.* 13:2, "Who is the minor that must exercise right of refusal? Any whose mother or brothers have with her consent given her in marriage" (H. Danby, *The Mishnah* [London: Oxford University Press, 1933] 237).

59. Narrative theory discerns three functional narrative types: representative, expressive, and symbolic. For a discussion of these narrative types and their characteristic features, see White, *Narration and Discourse in the Book of Genesis*, 65–91.

60. Ibid., 184–85. This reading of the narrative argues against the interpretations that view Abram's actions as a lack of faith in the divine assurances he had just received and Pharaoh's reproach as a shaming of Abram (Westermann, *Genesis 12–36*, 166ff.). Like White, G. W. Coats ("A Threat to the Host," in *Saga, Legend, Tale, Novella, Fable: Narrative Forms in Old Testament Literature* [ed. G. Coats; JSOTSup 35; Sheffield: JSOT Press, 1985] 72ff.) and Biddle ("The 'Endangered Ancestress,'" 599ff.) view the narrative as being intimately connected with the preceding divine promise to Abram (Gen 12:2–4), although to them the primary connection is with the "curse/blessing to the nations" element of the promise.

61. Cf. Peterson ("A Thrice-Told Tale," 30ff.), who views the contrast of Abram's scheme with the divine plan as the theme of the narrative.

Harvesting the Biblical Narrator's Scanty Plot of Ground: A Holistic Approach to Judges 16:4–22

J. CHERYL EXUM
University of Sheffield

> . . . and hence for me,
> In sundry moods, 'twas pastime to be bound
> Within the sonnet's scanty plot of ground;
> Pleased if some Souls (for such there needs must be)
> Who have felt the weight of too much liberty,
> should find brief solace there, as I have found.
>
> —William Wordsworth

For many years I've been fascinated by the artistry exhibited by the narrator of the story of Samson and Delilah in Judg 16:4–22, a tale as strictly repetitious as any in the biblical corpus, yet an engrossing and effectively suspenseful one in its manipulation of detail as it moves toward its denouement. In this brief analysis I would like to apply some of Moshe Greenberg's principles of holistic reading to Judg 16:4–22 in order to investigate the effect of minute, subtle alteration within a rigidly fixed form.[1]

It is perhaps presumptuous to apply the description *holistic approach* to a brief treatment of a few verses, so I should explain what I mean and how I see

---

1. My fascination with the artistic complexity of the Samson story goes back some 20 years (*Literary Patterns in the Samson Saga: An Investigation of Rhetorical Style in Biblical Prose*, Ph.D. dissertation, Columbia University, 1976) and has not diminished with time. Having read the story literally hundreds of times, I still find it fresh and suspenseful. Attention to many of the stylistic features of the material discussed below can also be found in a work by Yair Zakovitch, חיי שמשון (Jerusalem: Magnes, 1982); and, more recently, Jichan Kim, *The Structure of the Samson Cycle* (Kampen: Kok Pharos, 1993). In the interests of space, I have not reproduced the text; a helpful layout that highlights its repetitive features can be found in Zakovitch, חיי שמשון, 172–73.

my approach as Greenbergian. What I find most characteristic of Moshe Greenberg's approach to the biblical literature is his attentiveness to textual integrity, detail, and nuance, and his insistence that the interpreter's job is to illuminate the text as an organic whole on its own terms—as we have it before us, with all of its (for us) unfamiliar qualities and difficulties—and not some reconstructed version of the text that fits the modern interpreter's preconceived notions of unity, order, coherence, consistency, style, and so on. I confess to a certain unease in speaking of the text "on its own terms," as if the reader has no role in producing meaning, for I share Jonathan Culler's conviction that we can make anything signify. "We can always," as he observes, "make the meaningless meaningful by production of an appropriate context."[2] But it is equally true, as Culler discusses elsewhere, that we cannot tell the story of reading using the reader as the only protagonist.[3] I proceed from what I perceive to be givens in the text, from this particular sequence of signifiers and not another.

In this essay, I want to steer a middle course between text-bound and reader-bound approaches, and I hope that Moshe will view my stylistic analysis as an attempt to take seriously his proposition: "There is only one way that gives any hope of eliciting the innate conventions and literary formations of a piece of ancient literature, and that is by listening to it patiently and humbly."[4]

I have in mind an ideal reader not unlike Greenberg's:

> . . . each encounter with a fresh passage, a repetition, a variation on a phrase or theme will have affected him according to his growing experience of the book; on his second reading, these will have complexified as later elements now seemed foreshadowed, and as early elements resonated in later reminiscences. Our ideal reader will have been sensible of such resonances, echoes and allusions, and the holistic interpreter will attempt to reproduce his sensibilities.[5]

Following Greenberg's precept of inferring from the text itself the principles by which to interpret it, I also have in mind for Judg 16:4–22 an implied au-

---

2. Jonathan Culler, *Structuralist Poetics: Structuralism, Linguistics, and the Study of Literature* (Ithaca: Cornell University Press, 1975) 138. Culler is talking about the process of naturalization, an inevitable part of the reading process. " 'Naturalization' emphasizes the fact that the strange or deviant is brought within a discursive order and thus made to seem natural" (p. 137). Its opposite is what the Russian formalists called "defamiliarization." As I see it, Greenberg's approach aims not to naturalize but rather to make us aware of the unfamiliar and to make what is unfamiliar accessible.

3. Jonathan Culler, *On Deconstruction: Theory and Criticism after Structuralism* (London: Routledge & Kegan Paul, 1982) 64–83.

4. Moshe Greenberg, *Ezekiel, 1–20: A New Translation with Introduction and Commentary* (AB 22; Garden City, N.Y.: Doubleday, 1983) 21.

5. Moshe Greenberg, "The Vision of Jerusalem in Ezekiel 8–11: A Holistic Interpretation," in *The Divine Helmsman: Studies on God's Control of Human Events Presented to Lou H. Silberman* (ed. J. L. Crenshaw and S. Sandmel; New York: Ktav, 1980) 148. I am not imagining a first-time reader, since I believe the experience of the first-time reader is not recuperable (unless one were to keep a record while reading a text for the first time).

thor who is untroubled by the restrictions of the form he has imposed upon himself. This author (referred to below in his communicative function as "the biblical narrator"[6]) exploits the fact that within a framework of almost exact repetition, the slightest change will catch the reader's attention. He describes Delilah's four attempts to learn the secret of Samson's strength in formulaic language that follows a highly stylized pattern, relying on minor variations and controlled elaborations to build suspense, even as they lead the reader to a basic, but crucial theological insight. The situation seems to me not unlike that described by a later poet, William Wordsworth, who, in the sonnet from which my epigraph above is taken, defended the sonnet as a literary form that does not stifle creativity but rather rewards those who choose to work within its "scanty plot of ground."

My focus in this analysis will be on interconnections among the four attempt accounts (we might view them as interwoven accounts like the seven interwoven locks of Samson's hair) and, especially, on the subtle alterations and progressions that appear in the fourth, climactic account, where, in typical biblical fashion, expansion of the pattern takes place. The attempts are (1) vv. 6–9; (2) vv. 10–12; (3) vv. 13–14; (4) vv. 15–22. Verses 4–5 belong structurally with the first account, since they set the stage for the four attempts by providing background information: time; setting; the name of the woman (the fact that she, unlike the other women in the Samson story, is named hints that she will play a memorable role);[7] the facts that Samson loves her (again, a significant piece of information, since we know from 14:15–18 that love is Samson's Achilles' heel) and that the Philistines are behind Delilah's venture; the Philistines' motivation (to bind Samson in order to subdue or afflict him) and all we know of Delilah's motivation (the Philistines offer her money and she accepts their proposition, suggesting, in the absence of any other motive, that she could be bought). The Philistines' speech to Delilah (ויאמרו לה, v. 5) is followed by Delilah's speech (ותאמר דלילה v. 6)—not, however, in reply to their offer but rather as a direct address to Samson, which thrusts us immediately into the execution of her plan.

The basic pattern of the series of attempts is:

1. Delilah addresses Samson (ותאמר דלילה אל שמשון, vv. 6, 10, 13; ותאמר אליו, v. 15) and bids him to tell her (הגידה נא לי, vv. 6, 10; הגידה לי, v. 13; expressed negatively in v. 15 as ולא הגדת לי) by what means his strength is great (במה כחך גדול, vv. 6, 15) and/or how he might be bound (ובמה תאסר, vv. 6, 10, 13). In the second, third, and fourth attempts, she begins

---

6. For useful distinctions between *author*, *implied author*, and *narrator*, see Shlomith Rimmon-Kenan, *Narrative Fiction: Contemporary Poetics* (London: Methuen, 1983) 86–89.

7. As a result of this role, the name *Delilah* has become synonymous with treachery and deceit. Had she not been named, I doubt she could have become so infamous. On Delilah as cultural symbol of the *femme fatale*, see my *Plotted, Shot, and Painted: Cultural Representations of Biblical Women* (Sheffield: Sheffield Academic Press, 1996).

by chiding him for deceiving her (הנה התלת בי ותדבר אלי כזבים, v. 10;
עד הנה התלת בי ותדבר אלי כזבים, v. 13; התלת בי, v. 15).

2. Samson answers Delilah (ויאמר אליה שמשון, v. 7; ויאמר אליה, vv. 11, 13;
ויאמר לה, v. 17), replying that if (אם) she performs a certain procedure
(vv. 7, 11, 13, 17), he will become weak like any other human (וחליתי
והייתי כאחד האדם, vv. 7, 11, [13];[8] וחליתי והייתי ככל האדם, v. 17).

3. Delilah follows the procedure Samson has outlined (vv. 8, 12, 14, 19). She
tests the results by saying (ותאמר אליו, vv. 9, 12, 14; ותאמר, v. 20): "The
Philistines are upon you, Samson!" (פלשתים עליך שמשון, vv. 9, 12, 14, 20).

4. The first three times, Samson escapes; the last time, he is taken prisoner.

In its details, the second account most closely resembles the first, and the
third is most like the fourth. In addition, the first and final accounts share a
number of features not present in the middle two; this fact is not surprising,
since the first sets the stage, and the final account ties up loose ends in the plot,
bringing the story to a kind of closure.[9] The first two attempts set a pattern
based on the bonds with which Samson is secured: Delilah asks how he may
be bound (במה תאסר, vv. 6, 10), he replies that he may be bound (אם [אסור]
יאסר[ו]ני, vv. 7, 11) in a certain way, and she binds him (ותאסרהו בהם, vv. 8,
12) in the manner he has described. In each case, the bonds are special by virtue of something that has not been done to them (fresh, not having been dried,
v. 7; new and unused, v. 11); that is, they are in a pure or natural state. And in
each case, Samson's escape by snapping (נתק) his bonds is described through
simile (וינתקם מעל, v. 9; וינתק את היתרים כאשר ינתק פתיל הנערת בהריחו אש
זרעתיו כחוט, v. 12). Another feature that these two accounts have in common
is the ambushers who lie in wait for Samson (והארב ישב [לה] בחדר, vv. 9, 12).
By the third attempt, they are no longer there, and, in the fourth, Delilah has
to send for the Philistines to get them to come up to her, thus echoing the first
account, where they come to her, first with a promise of a reward, and then
with the ropes with which she binds Samson.

The third and fourth accounts are concerned with the seven locks (recalling the seven bowstrings of the first account) of Samson's hair (את שבע מחלפות
ראשי/ראשו, vv. 13, 19) and what happens to his hair between Samson's sleeping (ותישנהו, v. 19) and waking (וי[י]קץ משנתו, vv. 14, 20). The third account
presents a text-critical problem. We have two options: either to assume that
part of the text has been lost through homoeoteleuton and to restore it with the

---

8. The phrase is missing from the third account, unless we restore with the versions; see below.
9. Verses 21–22 are transitional and represent what Tzvetan Todorov (*The Poetics of Prose*
[trans. R. Howard; Ithaca: Cornell University Press, 1977] 76) describes as narrative embedding.
They contain "a supplement which remains outside the closed form produced by the development
of the plot. At the same time, and for this very reason, this something-more, proper to the narrative, is also something-less. The supplement is also a lack; in order to supply this lack created by
the supplement, another narrative is necessary."

help of the versions, or, following one of the principles of holistic interpretation, to take the text as it stands. Most commentators opt for restoring the text, arguing that the Hebrew does not make good sense as it stands, and I confess my agreement, not simply on text-critical grounds but primarily in view of the formulaic patterning the narrator has so carefully been following and which I really cannot believe he has abandoned here. In taking this position, I am making what Greenberg describes as a move "from 'simple' text-criticism to the study of style and literary conventions, where other criteria come into play."[10] The question remains, however, with what version should we restore, especially in view of minor variations among the LXX witnesses. In the interests of space, and because in the next paragraph I am going to consider what happens if we retain the MT, I refer the reader to Jichan Kim's discussion of the LXX witnesses and his convincing proposed retroversion based on the Lucianic and Old Latin.[11]

I would not want to go too far in basing a stylistic analysis on a restored text; fortunately, my concern here is not really with the patterning of the third account but rather with the artistry involved in adhering to a pattern and varying it in the fourth. I could, therefore, easily be led by my holistic approach to accept the text as it stands and, as a consequence, see in the third attempt a contraction of the pattern before its elaboration in the final, climactic attempt account. In this case, I still have to assume what the LXX and other ancient witnesses supply: that Delilah weaves Samson's hair into the web of her loom in the fashion he describes and that he is sleeping while she does it. As Culler points out in his discussion of convention and naturalization, we invariably put the actions of the text back into natural language: "if someone begins to laugh they will eventually stop laughing, if they set out on a journey they will either arrive or abandon the trip."[12] Similarly, Samson has to have been asleep in order to wake up in v. 14.

In the climactic last attempt account, the biblical narrator adheres to the established pattern, while at the same time introducing subtle changes that produce a suspenseful progression. The reader, who knows that Samson's strength

---

10. Greenberg, *Ezekiel, 1–20*, p. 20. Using Judg 16:13–14 as an example, Meir Sternberg (*The Poetics of Biblical Narrative: Ideological Literature and the Drama of Reading* [Bloomington: Indiana University Press, 1985] 372–73) criticizes such filling in of (missing) material on the grounds that it fails to appreciate the nature of biblical repetition. Whereas I agree, in principle, with his argument, I do not find it compelling in this case, where the patterning is the very stuff of the narrator's craft, functioning to highlight his variations. Far from trying to "stamp the Bible's structure of repetition as a formulaic scheme, with no room for play and meaning" (p. 373), I am arguing that the narrator of Judg 16:4–22 has found much room for "play and meaning" within a formulaic scheme.

11. Kim, *The Structure of the Samson Saga*, 161–63; see also the discussion of retroverting 16:13 in Emanuel Tov, *The Text-Critical Use of the Septuagint in Biblical Research* (Jerusalem: Simor, 1981) 107–9, 117; and his larger discussion of the method of retroversion, pp. 97–141.

12. Culler, *Structuralist Poetics*, 141.

lies in his hair, knows that the first two trials, in which Samson tells Delilah that special ropes can bind him, pose no threat to Samson. In the third account, however, when hair rather than bonds becomes the subject of the trial, the reader has reason to become alarmed, for Delilah is getting closer to the secret she seeks. In the fourth account, the narrator offers a further signal that Delilah is nearing her goal by introducing new material in the reproach. Before the expected charge of deception (התלת בי), an additional reproof appears: איך תאמר אהבתיך ולבך אין אתי. We know from v. 4 that Samson loves Delilah, and we also know from 14:16–17 that this reproof, coupled with another strategy that appears here in v. 16 (הציקה לו; cf. 14:17), has worked before. What was earlier a request, הגידה [נא] לי, now becomes a reproach: ולא הגדת לי. Delilah accuses Samson of deceiving her but not, as before, of telling her lies; speech (דבריה), however, will appear significantly in the next verse, as her means of breaking down his resistance.

The issues of strength, binding, and subduing are raised by the Philistines in their offer, and Delilah repeats all of them in her first attempt: she asks Samson about the source of his strength (כח) and how he might be bound (אסר) in order to afflict (ענה) him (cf. vv. 5 and 6). This ענה–אסר–כח triad does not appear again until the final, climactic account. In the second and third accounts, Delilah asks only how Samson might be bound. Binding (אסר), the theme in the first two attempts, plays little role in the third, where Delilah employs a different method of securing Samson, weaving his hair into the web rather than binding him. The secret of Samson's strength does not lie in a particular means of binding him but rather in God. Subtly and brilliantly the narrator brings home this point. For one thing, the question in the final account is not how Samson might be bound but, as at the beginning, by what means his strength is so great (במה כחך גדול, v. 15).

Before having Samson answer the question, however, the narrator builds suspense by slowing the pace. A temporal aside informs us of Delilah's persistence in questioning Samson כל הימים, until he is vexed "to death" (v. 16, למות is alarming foreshadowing) and tells her "all his heart."[13] In Samson's reply, between the usual "he told her" and אם, the narrator inserts a porten-

---

13. On the basis of the parallel in chap. 14, I take כל הימים to refer to a period of time during which Delilah seeks Samson's secret; *contra* Jack M. Sasson, "Who Cut Samson's Hair? (And Other Trifling Issues Raised by Judges 16)," *Prooftexts* 8 (1988) 335. Judges 14 offers a closer parallel than the ancient Near Eastern examples Sasson adduces, and the period of time the phrase covers does not detract from the unity of the episode. Nor am I convinced by Sasson's other argument, that presuming the presence of the three elements—"what makes you strong?" "what would bind you?" and "so that you could be weakened"—is "most natural if there is temporal unity to our scene." There are too many gaps in the attempt accounts to be bothered by a temporal gap. For example, how does Delilah manage to bind Samson in the first two attempt accounts? We have no reason to assume that he is sleeping, unless we naturalize the text on the basis of the next two accounts; see Zakovitch, חיי שמשון, 181–82 (following Radaq), who interprets the reference to sleeping in the third and fourth accounts as a "flashback," explaining how Delilah could have bound Samson.

tous explanation that links Samson's secret to his Nazirite status. Then, at last, we have what appears to be, but is not quite, the critical revelation—"if I am shaved, my strength (כחי) will turn from me." We know that, as before, Delilah will carry out the procedure Samson has outlined, but the narrator persists in holding us off: Delilah recognizes something new (v. 18). Between her charge, "your heart (לב) is not with me," in v. 15 and her execution of the procedure Samson describes for weakening him in v. 19, the narrator has introduced and developed a new motif: "he told her all his heart" (v. 17) becomes in v. 18 both a crucial recognition on Delilah's part and the reason she gives to persuade the Philistines to come again to her. (As in the first account, vv. 4–9, they come up to her, bringing her the money they had promised.)[14]

Here, as in the third account, Delilah lulls Samson to sleep. She then shaves him[15] and, indeed, his strength leaves him. But the narrator still has not reached the punch line, so to speak. It comes in v. 20, when Samson awakes from his sleep, thinking that he will escape as before, and does not know that God has left him. In vv. 17 and 19, the reference was to Samson's *strength* leaving him. By the simple substitution of יהוה for כח as the subject of סור, the narrator dramatically assures the reader that God has been the source of Samson's strength all along. A second member of the ענה–אסר–כח triad appears when Delilah begins to afflict Samson, and his strength leaves him (ותחל לענותו ויסר כחו מעליו, v. 19). The last occurs in v. 21, when, his secret having been revealed, his hair having been shorn, and God having left him, Samson is at last bound and taken prisoner: ויאסרוהו . . . בבית האסירים.

Through slight variations in the pattern, the narrator leads the reader to an awareness that more is at stake than binding (אסר), even more than strength (כח)—to a recognition that this is more than a story of a strong man enticed by a woman into revealing a secret that is his undoing.[16] It is that, of course, but

---

14. In the first account, the Philistines bring Delilah the ropes with which to bind Samson; in the second, she supplies them herself. As noted above, in the first and second accounts, there are ambushers in the chamber, but by the third they have disappeared, and in the fourth she has to summon the Philistine lords. Progressively she seems to have lost Philistine support until, assured of success, she summons them with the inducement that Samson has told her "all his heart"; see Sasson, "Who Cut Samson's Hair?" 337.

The Philistines' initial instruction to Delilah was to discover (ראי 'see') the secret of Samson's strength (v. 5); when Delilah recognizes (ותרא 'she saw', v. 18) that Samson has told her "all his heart," she has reached her goal and has the confidence to summon the Philistine lords.

15. The verb in 16:19 is third-person feminine singular. I am convinced by Sasson's proposal ("Who Cut Samson's Hair?" 336–38) that לאיש refers to Samson: "Bringing him to sleep on her lap, she called to the man [Samson], then began to cut the seven braids on his hair" (p. 338). Delilah calls to Samson to make sure he is deeply asleep. In all four attempt accounts, then, Delilah is the agent who carries out the procedures Samson outlines. There is thus no need (as in some of the versions, followed by most commentators) to supply a barber and have him shave Samson.

16. For parallels, see Hermann Gunkel, "Simson," in *Reden und Aufsätze* (Göttingen: Vandenhoeck & Ruprecht, 1913) 54–55; T. H. Gaster, *Myth, Legend, and Custom in the Old Testament* (2 vols.; Gloucester, Mass.: Smith, 1981) 2.436–39.

it is also the story of a man whose strength lies in his dedication to God. In addition to the shift from כח to יהוה as the subject of סור, with its profound theological implications, the narrator also underscores this point by means of the progressive variations that appear in the procedures Samson proposes to Delilah. In the first two accounts, in which Samson suggests that he will be robbed of his strength if only the right kinds of bonds are used, an indefinite subject of the binding tends to diminish the threat by dissociating it from Delilah ("if they bind me"). The third brings us closer to the fateful moment not only by having Samson mention his hair but also by having him make Delilah the subject of the action ("if you weave"). In the final account, however, where his hair is also concerned, the matter lies squarely with Samson: "if I am shaved." Also at stake is knowledge. At the end of Delilah's first, unsuccessful attempt to learn the source of Samson's great strength, we read, ולא נודע כחו. After Samson's hair has been cut and he seeks to escape the Philistine trap, we are told, והוא לא ידע כי יהוה סר מעליו. His enemies' lack of knowledge about the source of his strength prevented Samson's capture; his lack of knowledge about its true source enables it. His lack of knowledge replaces theirs, rendering him at last vulnerable.

Is Samson's lack of knowledge the source of false assurance? In v. 15, Delilah refers to the three times (זה שלש פעמים) she has tried unsuccessfully to learn Samson's secret. She recognizes that the fourth time is the right time and thus summons the Philistine lords: עלו הפעם (v. 18). Samson, however, thinks this time will be no different: ויאמר אצא כפעם בפעם ואנער (v. 20). The reader who knows that this is the fatal time, on the other hand, can only marvel at the way the narrator has prepared us, within such a carefully controlled framework, not only for the outcome that takes Samson unawares but for the theological insight it contains. In v. 22, with the mention of Samson's hair beginning to grow, the biblical narrator goes on to plant another clue, this time about the victory to come. One more reference to time will appear later, in v. 28, when Samson prays for strength אך הפעם הזה, and God responds by granting his prayer. This, however, leads us beyond vv. 4–22 and the scanty plot of ground that has been my focus here.

Judg 16:4–22 yields a rich harvest at each rereading. It exhibits a literary sophistication to which no one reading, including this one, can do justice, though I hope at least to have illustrated why it is I remain in awe of the virtuosity and genius of this ancient storyteller.

Proverbs 2 and 31:
A Study in Structural Complementarity

DAVID NOEL FREEDMAN

University of California, San Diego

The purpose of the essay that follows is to analyze and compare two poems, one near the beginning and the other at the end of the book of Proverbs. The latter is a striking example of an alphabetic acrostic poem, in which the letters of the alphabet in their normal sequence are used to organize and arrange the lines of the poem. In the case of this poem in praise of a virtuous woman, the design is quite simple: there are 22 lines, or bicola, each one beginning with a different letter of the alphabet, in the standard order (see table 1, p. 48).[1] Curiously enough, many examples of this basic pattern occur in the Hebrew Bible. Most of these alphabetic acrostic poems exhibit variations, elaborations, or adaptations of the simplest structure.[2] Some are shorter, with the letter of the alphabet introducing a half-line or single colon, some have a whole line (or bicolon), and still others have two- and three-line stanzas or, in an extreme case, eight-line stanzas for each letter.[3] More intricate deviations also turn up, showing that the poets of the Bible were not content to follow a simple pattern strictly.

Prov 31:10–31 also reflects the common metrical pattern for acrostic poems, which we may summarize or characterize as 8 + 8 = 16 syllables or 3:3 in accents, that is, a balanced rhythm, which is the dominant pattern of much of biblical poetry. Nevertheless, it is important to note that this is not the only meter available to or adopted by those who used the alphabetic acrostic system. The poems in Lamentations 1–4 have a distinctively different meter, with an average

---

1. The LXX reverses vv. 25 and 26, switching the pair ʿayin/pe to pe/ʿayin, an order we also find in the MT of Lamentations 2–4.

2. Cf. my "Acrostics and Metrics in Hebrew Poetry," *HTR* 65 (1972) 367–92, esp. p. 392.

3. Examples of half-line acrostics are: Psalms 111, 112; one-line: Psalms 25, 34; two-line: Psalms 9–10, 37; and Lamentations 4; 3-line: Lamentations 1–3; and above all, the eight-line acrostic: Psalm 119.

Table 1.   Proverbs 2 and 31

Syllable Count									
Proverbs 2				Proverbs 31					
verse	A	B			verse	A	B	C	
1	8	8	=	16	10	5	9		= 14
2	9	9	=	18	11	6	6		= 12
3	7	9	=	16	12	8	6		= 14
4	8	9	=	17	13	7	7		= 14
5	7	7	=	14	14	9	7		= 16
6	7	7	=	14	15	7	7	7	= 21
7	9	7	=	16	16	10	10		= 20
8	6	7	=	13	17	8	9		= 17
9	7	8	=	15	18	7	8		= 15
10	9	8	=	17	19	9	8		= 17
11	8	7	=	15	20	8	10		= 18
12	8	8	=	16	21	8	8		= 16
13	7	7	=	14	22	7	8		= 15
14	8	8	=	16	23	8	8		= 16
15	9	9	=	18	24	8	10		= 18
16	10	11	=	21	25	7	7		= 14
17	9	11	=	20	26	8	8		= 16
18	7	10	=	17	27	8	7		= 15
19	8	9	=	17	28	11	7		= 18
20	8	8	=	16	29	7	8		= 15
21	8	9	=	17	30	8	10		= 18
22	10	10	=	20	31	9	13		= 22
	177	186	= 363			173	181	7	= 361
Total:	363				Total:	361			
Average syllable count per colon: 8.13									

syllable count of 8 + 5 = 13 or a 3:2 accentual pattern. Overall, the difference between the two types is both measurable and sharp, even if the profiles of the individual lines tend to overlap. In the case of both types, or in fact all types of poetry, there is a great deal of variation and deviation from these theoretical or hypothetical norms, much more than is customarily allowed in the metrically controlled poetry of other language groups or cultures, whether ancient or modern. The range of variation, potential or actual, in Hebrew poetry is large

Table 1, cont'd.   Proverbs 2 and 31

Accent Count								
Proverbs 2				Proverbs 31				
verse	A	B		*verse*	A	B	C	
1	3	3	= 6	*10*	3	3		= 6
2	3	3	= 6	*11*	4	3		= 7
3	4	3	= 7	*12*	3	3		= 6
4	2	2	= 4	*13*	3	3		= 6
5	4	3	= 7	*14*	3	3		= 6
6	3	3	= 6	*15*	3	3	2	= 8
7	3	3	= 6	*16*	3	4		= 7
8	3	3	= 6	*17*	3	2		= 5
9	4	2	= 6	*18*	3	3		= 6
10	3	3	= 6	*19*	3	3		= 6
11	3	2	= 5	*20*	3	3		= 6
12	3	3	= 6	*21*	3	4		= 7
13	3	2	= 5	*22*	2	3		= 5
14	3	3	= 6	*23*	3	2		= 5
15	3	2	= 5	*24*	3	3		= 6
16	3	3	= 6	*25*	2	3		= 5
17	3	3	= 6	*26*	3	2		= 5
18	4	2	= 6	*27*	3	4		= 7
19	3	3	= 6	*28*	3	2		= 5
20	4	3	= 7	*29*	4	3		= 7
21	2	3	= 5	*30*	4	4		= 8
22	3	3	= 6	*31*	3	3		= 6
	69	60	= 129		67	66	2	= 135
Total:	129			*Total*:	135			
Average accent count per colon: 2.97								

enough to cast some doubt on the actual existence of any norms at all or on whether the poems have survived in pristine form in the Hebrew text (especially given the variant readings of ancient manuscripts and the early versions).

In spite of these legitimate concerns and doubts, I think it can be maintained that there is a clear quantitative component in Hebrew poetry and that its active presence can be shown by the fact that poems with the same structure are also of the same total length—meaning that the poet intentionally succeeded in balancing out deviations and variations to come up with identical or nearly identical totals, a coincidence that would not occur unless a recognized controlling factor were present from the beginning of the composition. In a word, the type of Hebrew poetry we are considering is not free verse. If we are right about these factors, then certain words of caution are in order.

(1) The degree and extent of variation will be greater than anything we normally encounter in the metrical poetry of other literary traditions, so the tendency to emend the existing Hebrew text to produce more regular or conformable lines is to be resisted. This is not to be understood as a blanket defense of the existing text, since it is clear on other grounds that not only differences but errors have crept into the surviving text. I am merely arguing that the Hebrew poets do not provide a strong enough standard or criterion by which to decide the validity or authenticity of a reading. Length alone cannot be used to judge and then change the text.

(2) For purposes of counting and determining the issue of quantity, it is necessary to use the existing text rather than an emended one. The danger of emending in the direction of the norm is too great to allow ourselves freedom in this regard. It is entirely permissible to make use of manuscript and versional evidence to determine the more original reading but not to venture into the realm of conjectural emendations, although on occasion these may well prove to be better than existing readings.

Turning our attention to the poem in Proverbs 2, we note that there are both similarities and differences in comparison with the poem in Proverbs 31. The major difference is that Proverbs 2 does not employ the alphabet as an organizing principle, whereas Prov 31:10–31 does. The major similarity is that both poems consist of 22 lines. In other words, Proverbs 2 has the same structure, but without the use of the alphabet. Such a class of poems has been recognized, the chief exemplar being Lamentations 5, which comes after four poems, all of which employ the alphabetic acrostic principle. The fact that Lamentations 5 has 22 lines or bicola shows that the poet consciously imitated the alphabetic acrostic structure but also quite deliberately avoided using the alphabet itself. Clearly such a pattern is an adaptation of or deviation from the alphabetic norm. The 22-line structure reflects a supposed alphabetic design, since there is no other explanation for the choice of this number. This class of poem is widespread in the Bible, more frequent and common than the alphabetic acrostic; in fact, the full number has yet to be determined, but already more of them have been located than the alphabetic type.

Another important similarity between both of the Proverbs poems is that they have the same meter: 8 + 8 = 16 syllables, 3 + 3 = 6 accents. In both poems, the distribution and variation in line length (and the number of accents) is roughly the same, and the total length is almost identical. Given the limitation in reproducing the exact vocalization of ancient Biblical Hebrew, we must allow ourselves a margin of error or legitimate variation (consider that poets in all countries and periods have exercised a certain license in fitting words to meter or meter around words). We can only reach approximate results, but these are close enough to warrant significant inferences and conclusions. So we must allow a margin of flexibility in our computations owing to the shortcomings of our position so far removed from the original poet and his/her composition. Nevertheless, the degree of precision and agreement is sufficiently impressive to suggest that the poet is operating within real norms and standards. The burden of proof is on those who would challenge or deny these findings.

A significant difference between the two poems is that while both consist of 22 lines (like Lamentations 5, which is as we should expect because of the alphabetic factor), Proverbs 31 has 45 cola, 21 bicola and one tricolon (31:15), while Proverbs 2 has the expected 44 (that is, 22 bicola, as is also the case with Lamentations 5). A question arises about the tricolon in 31:15. Is the third colon (*wḥq lnᶜrtyh*) part of the original composition, or is it an inadvertent add-on that should be excluded or deleted as a secondary addition or intrusion? The argument can go in either direction, but I hope to add a piece of evidence to help tilt the balance in the direction of authenticity or originality. I don't think there is anything in the phrase itself to indicate that it is or is not part of the original composition. The very fact that the extra colon is unique in the poem can be used to argue for and against its authenticity. My own contention is that only the poet himself/herself would have had the temerity to alter deliberately an established pattern, and, as I have shown elsewhere, there are numerous examples of such unique deviations from the established patterns.[4] It is hard to imagine that such deviations are invariably the result of accidental scribal mistakes. A case in point that I regard as particularly relevant is the fact that in chapters 1 and 2 of Lamentations, we have examples of the same kind of deviation that we have in Proverbs 31—namely, the addition of a line in one of the 22 stanzas of each poem.[5]

Most modern scholars emend away the extra lines (Lam 1:7 and 2:19) on the grounds that the one deviation from the established 3-line stanza in each poem is a mistake on the face of it (along with other arguments that can hardly be regarded as decisive or even valid), and the pattern shown for the rest of the poem rules out the one deviation. However, the more these deviations turn up, the more their cumulative weight argues against the assumption—which is all that it is—that the poet himself/herself could not have been responsible for the variation.

---

4. D. N. Freedman, "Deliberate Deviation from an Established Pattern of Repetition in Hebrew Poetry as a Rhetorical Device," *Proceedings of the Ninth World Congress of Jewish Studies*, Division A: *The Period of the Bible* (Jerusalem: Magnes, 1986) 45–52.

5. Freedman, "Acrostics and Metrics in Hebrew Poetry," 367–92.

There is yet another piece of evidence to be brought forward. Prov 31:10–31 has a total of approximately 360 syllables as it stands. The way I arrive at this total is by starting with the vocalization of the MT and then adjusting or modifying its total in the light of knowledge that we as modern scholars derive from early transcriptions of the Hebrew text that give pronunciations more contemporary with the time of composition than the MT—or in certain cases, using reconstructions of the vocalization based on structural analysis of the language and the help of early inscriptions.

Thus, I do not accept the Masoretic vocalization of segolate formations or the secondary vowels associated with laryngeals, or the so-called resolution of original diphthongs (for example, *mayim* for the older *maym*, *mawet* for *mawt*, or *bayit* for *bayt*). I do accept MT vocalization of 2d-singular forms of pronouns, verbs, and pronominal suffixes but reject, for the most part, the contracting and merging of syllables to which the MT is prone. Therefore, when the single-letter prepositions are prefixed to nominal forms, I add a syllable (for example, I would count *liq(ĕ)ṭol* as three syllables), and, in general, I add a syllable to masculine construct plural nouns (for example, I would count *ziqnê* of Prov 31:23 and *darkê* of Prov 2:13 as having three syllables each in the original poems).

Some of these points may well be disputed, but overall they do not affect the results, since we are dealing in large numbers. Furthermore, while seriously trying to recover the original poems, we cannot pretend to get back to the actual practice of the poet, who may have exercised as much freedom in counting syllables (and accents) as he/she did in composing lines and cola of radically different lengths, while remaining within certain norms and limits.

The standard number of syllables overall for an acrostic poem of 22 lines (44 bicola) in the balanced rhythm of most of the biblical poems (8 + 8 = 16 syllables, 3 + 3 = 6 accents) would be 352. The nonalphabetic acrostic poem in Lamentations 5 comes out as close to that number as one could wish (352). When we look at Prov 31:10–31, we note that it has the requisite 22 lines, but there is an extra colon, making a total of 45 instead of the expected 44 bicola. What should we look for as a total? Did the poet add syllables for the extra colon or fold the colon into the overall structure to bring the total into line with the normal or normative 352 syllables? In theory, the poet could have reasoned either way and come out with either total. In practice, the poem in Proverbs 31 consists of approximately 360 syllables, showing that the extra colon (v. 15c) is part of the original composition and that the total reflects the slightly altered structure. It is always possible that the extra colon is secondary, and if it were excised, the resulting poem would fit the standard pattern quite well (the 3d colon of v. 15 has 7 syllables, so the count would be slightly off, but the difference [1 syllable] is too small to affect the argument). My conclusion is that the extra colon is original and that the total and the norm for Prov 31:10–31 is in fact 360 syllables, not 352.

In counting syllables in Proverbs 31, I have followed resolutely the norms established and explained above—with allowances. There remain three places where a variation in counting is possible: vv. 12, 16, and 18.

1. In v. 12, MS L reads *ḥayyeyh* (2 syllables), whereas the normal reading would be *ḥayyeyha*. I regard the reading in L as a mistake and go with the longer reading.

2. In v. 16, the MT has *nṭ*^{c}, and the *Kethiv* probably was *nāṭōa*^{c}, whereas the *Qere* is *nāṭĕ*^{c}*â*, which would be quite normal. Again, the difference is one syllable. In this case, it is quite likely that the *Kethiv* is original, because it is clearly the more unusual and difficult, yet permissible, reading, and it is more likely that the *Qere* is a correction or improvement than the other way around.

3. In v. 18, the *Kethiv* is *blyl*, probably read as *ballayl* or *ballêl*, as against the *Qere*, which is the more normal *ballaylâ*. Again the difference would be one syllable. Thus, the counts in all three cases mentioned could vary by one syllable.

In the case of v. 12, I regard the reading in L as a scribal slip and will adopt the higher count and not deal further with it.

In the case of the other two, the variants can be shown as follows:

$$\text{v. 16:} \quad 10 + 9/10 = 19/20$$
$$\text{v. 18:} \quad 7 + 7/8 \;\; = 14/15$$

Counting both possibilities, that is, including both high and low numbers, we come out with a total for the poem of 359/361 syllables. If we go for the *Kethiv* in both cases, the total is 359. If we go with the *Qere* in both cases, we have 361. Perhaps the safest thing is to go both ways and, without deciding these cases, compromise and say we are about as close to 360 as we are ever likely to get. I think that the poet would be pleased to know that 2500 years after composing the poem, its metrical structure was clearly visible and quite precise.

Turning now to Proverbs 2, we find a poem of 22 lines or 44 cola. We might well expect a total of about 352 syllables, as is true of our model poem, the nonalphabetic acrostic in Lamentations 5. In Proverbs 2, however, we have a total that is considerably higher, closer to the total for Prov 31:10–31. In fact, the total is even higher than in Proverbs 31: 363. The difference, while slight, is nevertheless on the high side, showing that this poem's syllable count is closer to the total for its companion piece in Proverbs than it is to the supposed model, Lamentations 5. I believe this is what we should have expected, because the editor of Proverbs wished to unite the alphabetic acrostic at the end of the book with a nonalphabetic acrostic at or near the beginning of the book and wanted to show they belonged together by making them approximately the same length. That this isn't entirely ad hoc or arbitrary is shown by the fact that Ben Sira adopts an almost identical plan for his book (which is in many ways similar to and modeled on Proverbs).[6]

The poet may have added a colon to one line or another to achieve the same effect but preferred to follow a different method, of simply adding syllables here and there to accomplish it. That the visibility of such features is deliberately reduced in Proverbs 2 is shown by the elimination of the alphabetic acrostic and also by avoiding the addition of the 45th colon (as in Proverbs 31). If I am correct so far, then the evidence from Proverbs 2 concerning the number of syllables supports the view that the poem in Proverbs 31 had the extra colon and the full complement of 360 syllables when Proverbs 2 was composed and included in the Book. The simplest view is that the same poet was responsible for both poems.

In Proverbs 2, there is a single variant reading (*Kethiv* and *Qere*) that requires our attention. In v. 7 the *Kethiv* reads *wspn*, probably to be read as *wĕṣāpan* (3 syllables), whereas the *Qere* has *yiṣpōn* (2 syllables). All in all, the *Qere* is probably the superior reading (especially for poetry) and may be more original. The similarity of *yod* and *waw*, especially in the Herodian period, is notorious, so it is not difficult to infer that the *Kethiv* is secondary, inadvertently derived from the more original *yṣpn*. Therefore, the lower count is preferable, and the total for the poem would be 363. This is somewhat higher than the expected 360 (on the basis of Proverbs 31) and much higher than the normal or normative 352 for a 22-line, 44-colon acrostic poem. Because the total is high, it is possible to speculate that the poet himself indulged in a few contractions, one of which the MT already incorporates (*tĕbaqšennâ* [v. 4] for an earlier *tĕbaqqĕšennâ*), but which, according to our rules, we cannot adopt.

The conclusion of the matter is that these two poems are like bookends enclosing the book of Proverbs, with the alphabetic acrostic coming at the end to mark the completion of the book and the matching piece coming, not at, but close to, the beginning of the book, its function and role not being fully revealed until the end of the book. Almost the identical phenomena occur in the book of Ben Sira, which ends with an alphabetic acrostic (confirmed by the discovery of the chapter in the original Hebrew in the *Psalms Scroll* from Cave 11) and also has a nonalphabetic acrostic poem near the beginning of the book.

It is worth noting that the pattern exhibited by the two poems in Proverbs 2 and 31 is also shown in the sequence of chapters 1–3 of Lamentations. Lamentations 1–3 comprises a series of alphabetic acrostic poems with a structure different from the structure of Proverbs 2 and 31 (Proverbs 2 is a nonalphabetic acrostic and is closer in structure and pattern to Lamentations 5).

---

6. See P. W. Skehan and A. A. Dilella, *The Wisdom of Ben Sira* (New York: Doubleday, 1987) 74, 576.

The principal difference is that Lamentations 1–3 consist of 3-line stanzas, and the average line length is 13 syllables, whereas the poems in Proverbs 2 and 31 have single-line units with an average length of 16 syllables. Nevertheless, both sets exhibit a similar deviation feature. Thus, Proverbs 31 has an extra colon in v. 15, breaking with the standard pattern of bicola. In like manner, Lamentations 1 and 2 both have one four-line stanza that contrasts with the other 21 stanzas of 3 lines. We have observed that Proverbs 2, while containing the standard 22 lines or bicola without any deviation, still has the same total number of syllables as Proverbs 31. In other words, it matches the other poem in total length but does not imitate the deviation found in Proverbs 31. In like manner, Lamentations 3 (which has the same 3-line stanzas but modified by repeating the key letter of the alphabet at the beginning of each of the three lines instead of having it only at the beginning of the first line of each stanza) consists of the standard 22 stanzas of three lines each but without any deviant 4-line stanza such as the ones in Lamentations 1–2. However, chap. 3 is equal to the other two in total number of syllables, even though it is a line short.

Lamentations 1	67 lines	872 syllables
Lamentations 2	67 lines	868 syllables
Lamentations 3	66 lines	872 syllables

The norm for a poem of 66 lines at 13 syllables per line would be 858 syllables, whereas the norm for a poem of 67 lines would be $67 \times 13 = 871$. Since the three poems cluster around the higher number, the deviation in chaps. 1 and 2 was probably deliberate, and chap. 3 was probably designed to match the larger numbers in spite of its having fewer lines. As in the case of Proverbs 2, the difference is made up by extending or enlarging several lines, or, as in the case of Proverbs 31, by adding a colon here or there: vv. 40, 43 in Lamentations 3 as examples of enlargement and perhaps v. 56 as an example of the latter. These reciprocal phenomena strengthen the notion that the Hebrew poets were very much interested in achieving and maintaining symmetry in patterns and structure and in overall equivalence but arrived at these goals by different routes, using a variety of strategies and techniques.

Reading Rahab

TIKVA FRYMER-KENSKY
University of Chicago

As we study a biblical story, often simple on its surface, it opens like a rose to reveal complexities and significance unhinted at on the surface. I am delighted to dedicate this reading to Moshe Greenberg, who taught us to lift our eyes from the word and the verse and to look at biblical texts as coherent literary units.

The historical books of the Bible open with the story of Rahab, the prostitute who saved the Israelite spies trapped in Jericho. On the surface, this is a charming story of a familiar antitype in folklore, the prostitute-with-the-heart-of-gold. This biblical Suzie Wong is helpful to the spies, has close ties with her family, and faith in God's might. But the charm does not explain its prominence as the first of the conquest stories, strongly associated with the triumphal entry into the land. Its importance begins to become clearer as we take a careful look at the way the story is constructed. It begins and ends with a frame: the charge that Joshua gives the two men that he is sending on a reconnaissance mission and their report to him. He tells them to "go and see the land and Jericho" (Josh 2:1), and they return to declare, "God has given the land into our hands; all the inhabitants are melting away before us" (Josh 2:24).[1] Neither we nor the spies are given more information. Joshua doesn't charge the men to discover the defenses, and they do not gather any military information. In the next "spy story," when Joshua sends men to Ai (Josh 7:2–4), he makes it clear that the men are to 'spy', using the key word *rgl*, a technical term also used in the later story of the Danite spies at Laish (Judg 18:2–11). Yet another "spy story" in the Deuteronomistic History uses a separate technical term *tûr* 'to scout', the term used in one of the biblical stories that is a direct "intertext" to our story: Moses' sending of the spies to scout the land in Numbers 13.

---

1. *Gam* does not always mean 'and'; more often it means 'in return, in consequence of'.

The Rahab story is a masterpiece of allusive writing. It is set in the first five chapters of the book of Joshua, which contain numerous pentateuchal allusions designed to have readers keep in mind the activities of Moses as they read Joshua. The beginning of the book introduces Joshua as the second Moses when God announces to Joshua that he will be with him as he was with Moses (Josh 1:5). Events of these chapters then recapitulate events at the beginning of Moses' mission. An angel appears to Joshua with sword extended and tells him to remove his shoes because the ground on which he stands is holy ground (Josh 5:15); Moses at the burning bush (Exod 3:5) is the only other person told this. The burning bush theophany in Exodus is followed by a frightening scene: when Moses first heads to Egypt to begin the process of redemption, God attacks him and is only assuaged when Zipporah circumcises their son with a flint knife (Exodus 4); similarly, Joshua circumcises the Israelites with flint knives (Joshua 5).[2] The most striking parallel is the Israelite's miraculous crossing of the Jordan; Israel passes through the Red Sea on the way to the desert and through the Jordan on its way out of the desert. Both crossings are miraculous, and mention of them has major frightening impact on foreign nations. In this context, it is not surprising that the Rahab story, the first of the tales of the conquest, should contain a parallel to the story of Moses and the spies.

When Moses sends the twelve spies, one to a tribe, he gives them a specific charge: "you shall see what this land is and whether the people living there are weak or strong, few or numerous; whether this land is good or not good and whether the cities are open or fortified; whether the land is fat or thin, is wooded or not, and you shall be strong and bring back fruit" (Num 13:18–20). The spies are all choice men, great men of Israel, whose names are recorded. Nevertheless, despite their pedigree, these great men conclude that the land cannot be conquered. The nations are strong; the land can be lethal, and there are giants in the land, compared to whom the Israelites look and feel like grasshoppers (Num 13:30–33). Only two men, Joshua and Caleb, trust Israel can conquer the land. As a result, the entire generation stays in the wilderness until death overtakes them.

Now, in the book of Joshua, it is forty years later, and a new generation is poised to enter the land. This time, Joshua sends only two men.[3] They are not said to be prominent; on the contrary, the story gives the impression that

---

2. These parallels are seen by Robert Alter, who points out that the word *baderek* 'on the way' is used in both stories. In Exodus they are on the way to Egypt; in Joshua they were not circumcised on the way from Egypt (*The World of Biblical Literature* [New York: Basic Books, 1992] 117–21).

3. See Robert Culley, "Stories of the Conquest: Joshua 2, 6, 7, and 8," *HAR* 8 (1984) 25–44. See also Yair Zakovitch, who overplays the ordinariness of the women ("Humor and Theology or the Successful Failure of Israelite Intelligence: A Literary-Folkloric Approach to Joshua 2," in *Text and Tradition: The Hebrew Bible and Folklore* [ed. Susan Niditch; Atlanta: Scholars Press, 1990] 75–98).

Joshua picked any two men. The men are sent with no clear charge and not told what they should report. They are not special men and never give any impression of initiative or daring throughout the story.[4] However, this time, these two ordinary men come back with the report that only the exceptional Joshua and Caleb could give before: that God has given the land to Israel.

Within this framework of charge and response, the story of Rahab unfolds. In the next act, the men go directly to the house of Rahab the prostitute where they are almost caught, but she hides them, lies to the king's men, and then helps them escape. Hiding and lying is the way biblical women demonstrate their loyalty. For example, when Absalom is alerted that the sons of Zadok have gone to warn David, they quickly lower themselves into a well on the property of a man in Bahurim. The woman of the house spreads a cover over the well and then declares that the men had already returned to Jerusalem (2 Sam 17:17–22). The Canaanite General Sisera expects Yael to give him exactly this kind of protective deception, saying that he was not there (Judg 4:18–20).[5]

There is yet another subtle allusion to a biblical woman who hides: when Rahab hides the spies, the author uses the relatively rare word *ṣpn: watispĕnô 'and she hid him'. The knowledgeable reader will think immediately of the story of Moses' birth, when Moses' mother saved him by hiding him: watispĕnēhû 'and she hid him'. This phrase occurs only twice in the whole Bible, and the reader, alerted by the manifold allusions to Moses in Joshua 1–5, may catch the resonance: as the "hiding" of the infant Moses started the Exodus events, so Rahab's "hiding" of the representatives of the infant Israel begins the process of the conquest.

Rahab asks that she and her family be spared in the destruction, as a compassionate service ḥesed in return for the ḥesed she has shown them. The spies duly promise, and in Joshua 6 we hear that she was indeed saved. Once again, this story has a very close "narrative analogy." In the story of the conquest of Bethel in the first chapter of the book of Judges, the Josephites who are scouting Bethel see a man coming out of the city. They offer him ḥesed if he will reveal the entrance to his city (by sparing him when they defeat the city).[6] But the story of the man who revealed the entrance to this important city is told in four verses. In contrast, Rahab's story takes up a whole chapter and then still has to be finished in chap. 6.

The Rahab story is not longer because it contains details. On the contrary, the story is so sparse that scholars have speculated that chap. 2 is a vestige of

---

4. Zakovitch, "Humor and Theology." This should be read with Frank M. Cross, "Reply to Zakovitch," in *Text and Tradition*, 99–106.

5. She, of course, has other ideas; see the discussion below. Even Rahab's act of lowering the men out her window has a biblical parallel, for Saul's daughter Michal saves David by lowering him out the window and then lying about her reasons (1 Sam 19:9–17).

6. Judg 1:22–26. The importance of this analogy is noted by Robert G. Boling, *Joshua: A New Translation with Notes and Commentary* (Garden City, N.J.: Doubleday, 1982).

an originally longer tale.[7] Only the important narrative sequences are related, and the story is full of "gaps" that the readers must fill in by considering analogous texts and by imagination and speculation. Why did Joshua send the spies? There are clues in Numbers 13, but the narrators say nothing explicitly. Why did the spies go to Rahab's house? Is it because a prostitute's establishment is a good place to blend in unobserved and listen to people,[8] or is it because men who have been out in the wilderness all their lives immediately head to the bordello for soft beds and soft women? The narrator doesn't say; the reader can decide.[9] How did the king find out? Some suspicious readers have suggested that Rahab herself sent word so that she could demand *ḥesed*.[10] The story attains its length, not by narrative detail, but by the inclusion of three dialogues, each of which is vitally important in understanding the significance of this story to Israel.

The first dialogue is an interchange between Rahab and the king of Jericho. He assumes that the men are spies who have come "to investigate" the land[11] and demands that she bring them out. This is Rahab's moment of truth, and she chooses Israel, declaring, "The men came to me, but I didn't know from whence; and when the gate was about to close at dark, the men went out I know not whither" (Josh 2:4–5). Rahab is smart, proactive, tricky, and unafraid to disobey and deceive the king.[12] She reminds us of two other women who are portrayed in this way, the two midwives in Egypt who defy the Pharaoh's orders to slay the Hebrew children. Once again, the beginning of the conquest echoes the beginning of the Exodus.

---

7. J. Alberto Soggin, *Judges: A Commentary* (Philadelphia: Westminster, 1981) and Robert Culley, "Stories of the Conquest."

8. So Ann Engar, "Old Testament Women as Tricksters," *Mapping of the Biblical Terrain: The Bible as Text* (ed. Vincent Tollers and John Maier; Lewisburg, Pa.: Bucknell University Press, 1990) 143–57.

9. Josephus *Ant.* 6.2 fills in at this juncture by explaining that the spies first surveyed the city; only then did they go to Rahab's. In modern times, Ottosson suggests that the fact that the men went to Rahab's house suggests that she was associated with them either because she was originally a nomadic woman or because she belonged to asocial circles (Magnus Ottosson, "Rahab and the Spies," in *Dumu-é-dub-ba-a: Studies in Honor of Åke W. Sjöberg* (ed. Hermann Behrens, Darlene Loding, and Martha T. Roth; Philadelphia: Babylonian Section, University Museum, 1989). On the other hand, Zakovitch is extremely negative in his judgment of the men, whom he considers "first-class bunglers" (Zakovitch, "Humor and Theology").

10. Rahab has suffered greatly at the hands of some modern scholars. Once again, it is Zakovitch who is most extreme and suggests that it was Rahab herself who informed the king in order to make the men obligated to her (ibid., p. 85).

11. The king uses the word **ḥpr*, the very word that Deuteronomy 1 uses in referring to the spies that Moses sent.

12. The "trickery" of Rahab, like the trickery of other women in the Bible, has occasioned much disapproval and defense. See my *In the Wake of the Goddesses* (New York: Macmillan, 1992) 136–39, especially the discussion on Rivkah.

Rahab is also dominant in the third dialogue, between herself and the spies (2:16–21). When Rahab lowers them outside her window, she tells them to flee to the hills. This seemingly extraneous suggestion is a clue to yet another intertext, the story of Lot and the angels in Genesis 19, in which the angels tell Lot to "flee to the hills." The stories first seem very unlike each other, but they share a similar vocabulary[13] and similar plot sequence: two men enter and lodge in a city that is about to be destroyed; their host defies a demand to "bring out the men," the city is destroyed, the inhabitant who lodged them is saved and told to "flee to the hills," and the story ends with an etiological notice about the descendants of the host. A lexical allusion further reinforces the reference, for Rahab is said to have saved the 'envoys' *mal⁾ākîm*, the same Hebrew word that is also translated 'angels' (Josh 6:25)[14] and is used for the angels in Sodom. There are further parallels: both stories take place in the Jordan plain and may have originally been preserved as local legends, and in both cases the men lodge in the house of a character who is marginal to the city's social structure: Lot as an outsider, Rahab as a prostitute. However, Lot is hesitant and tentative as the angels save him; in Joshua, the visitors are saved by the assertive, proactive Rahab.[15]

The men adjure Rahab to gather her family into her house and to tie a scarlet cord in the window. The family must stay inside during the destruction; whoever ventures outside may be killed. Only those who stay inside the house marked with the scarlet cord will be safe from devastation. Once again, the alert reader, ancient and modern, catches the reference: on the night of the slaying of the first born of Egypt, the Israelites were to mark their doors with lamb's blood and stay inside in order to be safe from destruction.[16] Once again, the saved are to stay inside the house marked in red; Rahab's family is to be rescued from Jericho, as the Israelites were from Egypt.[17] This resourceful outsider, Rahab the trickster, is a new Israel.

The second discourse is the heart of the story. Rahab begins by acknowledging God's intentions: "I know that God has given you this land and that

13. F. Langlamet, "Josué, II, et les traditions de l'Héxateuque," *RB* 78 (1971) 5–17, 161–83, 321–54. Langlamet finds 17 lexical correspondences between Joshua 2 and Genesis 19.

14. For a study of these two texts together, see L. Daniel Hawk, "Strange Houseguest: Rahab, Lot and the Dynamics of Deliverance," *Reading between Texts: Intertextuality and the Hebrew Bible* (ed. Danna Nolan Fewell; Louisville, Ky.: Westminster/John Knox, 1992) 89–97. To his parallels, I would add the fact that they both happened in the same plain.

15. This is the conclusion reached by Hawk, ibid.

16. Exodus 12. For the allusion, see Engar, "Old Testament Women."

17. Verses 19–21 are sometimes considered a later addition in order to explain the scarlet cord. Taking another tack, Hawk suggests that the scarlet cord (*tiqwat ḥût ḥašānî*) may be nothing more than the 'hope' (*tiqwâ*) associated with the 'two' (*šnê*). However, the many references to the Exodus redemption throughout this story indicate that this episode is both original and a reminder of the saving of the firstborn.

dread of you has fallen upon us, and all the inhabitants of the land are melting before you" (2:9). This is clearly an exaggeration: if no one has the spirit to stand against Israel, what are the king of Jericho and his soldiers doing chasing these envoys? But it is an important message, and Rahab is the oracle who declares that God has given Israel the land. She is the first of the prophets who appear in the historical books to announce to Israel the paths of their history and the first of the women who declare and pronounce the will of God. The lines of women and prophets begin with Rahab and converge again at the end of 2 Kings and 2 Chronicles in the figure of Huldah the prophetess, who announces the destruction of Judah.

Rahab's speech is couched in language familiar to the readers in ancient Israel. The use of the special terms *ʾêmâ* 'dread' and *nāmōg* 'melt' introduce us to the vocabulary of the Holy War of the conquest of Canaan;[18] these particular phrases allude to the great song of Israel's sacred history, the Song of the Sea, preserved in Exodus 15: "All the dwellers of Canaan are aghast, terror and dread descend upon them."[19] The prediction made by the song is indeed coming true—the process of conquest has truly started.

Rahab acknowledges God with the words "I know," the very words with which Jethro pronounces his faith in God: "Now I know that the Lord is greater than all gods" (Exod 18:11) and with which the Syrian general, Naaman, declares God's greatness: "for I know that there is no such God in all the land" (2 Kgs 5:15). This phrase, *I know*, is a formula by which people from foreign nations come to acknowledge God. This literary use may have its origin in a rite of passage, a kind of proto-conversion, that may have been practiced in ancient Israel. In the historical books, Rahab is presented as the first of the inhabitants of the land to join God and Israel.[20]

In return for her demonstration of loyalty in saving the spies, Rahab asks for *ḥesed* from Israel. Her request for *ḥesed* is reminiscent of the request that Abimelech made of Abraham: "Do with me according to the *ḥesed* that I did to you" (Gen 21:23).[21] Abimelech sought a treaty with Abraham; Rahab seeks an arrangement with Israel. This doesn't mean that the finished text of the Genesis story was in the possession of the author of the Rahab story. On the contrary, the verbal correspondence between them comes from the fact that both use legal language, reflecting the juridical importance of this treaty transaction. Rahab's speech contains all the essential elements of the classic deu-

---

18. See Dennis McCarthy, "Some Holy War Vocabulary in Joshua 2," *CBQ* 33 (1971) 228–30.

19. Exod 15:15–16. The connection was noted by the ancient rabbis in *Mekilta Shirata* 9. Rahab reverses the order of these two sentences, as is the rule in biblical quotations (see Zakovitch, "Humor and Theology," 89).

20. See Gordon Mitchell, "Together in the Land: A Reading of the Book of Joshua," *JSOT* 134 (1993) 152–90.

21. Ottosson, "Rahab and the Spies."

teronomic form of covenants. The *preamble* and the *prologue*, in which Rahab confesses the greatness of God, are in vv. 9–11; Rahab's *stipulations* (salvation for family and sign of assurance) are in vv. 12–13, and the Israelite's *stipulations* (silence and staying within house) and the *sanctions* (salvation/death) are in vv. 18–20; the *oath* is in vv. 14 and 17; and the *sign* (the scarlet cord) is in vv. 18–21.[22] This request for *ḥesed* is a formal arrangement by which Rahab seeks to join Israel, and the oath and sign that the Israelites give is their acceptance of her and her family into this arrangement.

The denouement of the story comes in Joshua 6. When the Israelites conquer Jericho, Joshua sends the two men to Rahab's house, they bring out Rahab and her family, and she lives 'in the midst of Israel' *beqereb yisraʾel* "until this very day" (Josh 6:25). All has ended happily, Israel has been enriched by the family of a heroine, and the conquest has begun.

But is this the way the conquest is to proceed? Deuteronomy has very different ideas about how to treat the inhabitants of the land: "You must doom them to destruction, make no pacts with them, grant them no quarter."[23] The idea of *ḥerem*, total war, is an essential cornerstone of Deuteronomy's philosophy of history: the slaughter is necessary so that the inhabitants do not then introduce foreign ideas and foreign ways into Israel. The story of the conquest of Jericho in chap. 6 uses eleven variations of the verb *ḥrm*. Just before Joshua sends the spies to get Rahab, the narrator tells us, "They destroyed everything in the city, man and woman, youth and aged." In this context, it seems strange to see Rahab and her family joining Israel, and one might conclude that the first thing that the Israelites did on entering Canaan was to break the rule of the *ḥerem*.[24]

This saving of Rahab from the *ḥerem* seems even more problematic as we proceed to the next chapter in Joshua, which relates the Israelite defeat at Ai and its cause; Achan's violation of the *ḥerem* at Jericho. The two situations seem parallel, with parallel phrases: as Rahab is in the midst of Israel, Israel is warned that it must take away the *ḥerem* in its midst, the *ḥerem* being the Sumerian cloak that Achan took from Jericho. Achan and all that is his are killed just as Rahab and all that is hers are saved; the mound of stones that marked the spot stands in Israel "to this very day." Given the Deuteronomic explanation that the *ḥerem* is to prevent contamination by foreign ideas, it would seem that saving *people* from the *ḥerem* is a more serious violation than

---

22. K. M. Campbell, "Rahab's Covenant," *VT* 22 (1972) 243–45.

23. Deut 7:2, and see Deut 20:17.

24. For discussions of this issue, see Lyle Eslinger, *Into the Hands of the Living God* (Sheffield: Almond, 1989) 24–54. Polzin's theory that the story itself is a meditation on the issues of justice and mercy is unconvincing in that it requires him to make Rahab deserving of extermination and entirely undeserving of being saved (*Moses and the Deuteronomist: A Literary Study of the Deuteronomic History* [Bloomington: Indiana University Press, 1993]).

saving a cloak, and we might begin to suspect that there is a dark side to the
Rahab story. And yet—Achan's "liberation" of the cloak is punished by a defeat at Ai, whereas the men's promise to liberate Rahab is followed by a glorious victory. In fact, the conquest of Jericho is clearly a conquest by God, who
intervenes to perform a miracle of felling the walls, a clear mark that Israel
has *not* angered God by agreeing to save Rahab. The juxtaposition of the Rahab and Achan stories presents a discourse on the nature of the *ḥerem* and obedience to it. When Achan ignored the *ḥerem* for selfish reasons, all of Israel
was punished until he was found and executed; when the men of Israel ignored
the *ḥerem* as an act of *ḥesed* to repay *ḥesed*, then God reacted by miraculously
conquering Jericho. The *ḥerem*, this story would seem to imply, is not an absolute and should be superseded by issues of justice and mercy.[25]

The next group of stories in the book of Joshua also revolves around this
issue of the *ḥerem* and its application. After Ai, the book turns to the Gibeonites. Rahab states, "For we have heard how God dried up the Reed Sea before
you as you went out of Egypt and (we have heard) what you did to the two
Amorite kings of Transjordan, Sihon and Og, whom you utterly destroyed"
(2:10). With the same words, "for we have heard," the Gibeonites describe their
coming to believe in God: "for we have heard the reports of Him and all that
He did in Egypt and all that He did to Sihon king of Heshbon and to Og king
of the Bashan" (Josh 9:9–10). The name of God has grown great, the report
has gone out. The kings of the Amorites gather to fight, but the Gibeonites are
moved by this report to try to ally themselves with Israel. Knowing that Israel
is not to sign pacts with the local people,[26] they trick Israel into believing that
they come from far away.[27] They remain in Israel as hewers of wood and draw-
ers of water for both the community and for the altar of God. Once again, a
tricky outsider has escaped the *ḥerem* and joined Israel. And once again, when
the Gibeonites are attacked and Israel comes to their rescue, Israel wins by a
miracle. As the sun stands still, God has come visibly and directly to the aid
of Israel.

The Rahab and Gibeon stories in Joshua may indicate that Israel had a
tradition that told the story of the conquest as a process during which many
inhabitants of the land stayed and became aligned with and ultimately joined
Israel. This tradition understood the *ḥerem* to have applied only to those nations or kings who actively opposed Israel. The "Amorites" do not fight in Josh
5:1, and no battle is related; the Canaanite kings in 9:1–2 resolve to fight and
are defeated; the alliance under King Jabin fought, and Hazor was destroyed

---

25. See Mitchell, "Together in the Land."

26. They, like Rahab, seem to have studied Deuteronomy.

27. They pretend to be from far away by aging their clothes and equipment, patching their
sandals and bringing dry crumbly bread as they come to a people for whom God has performed the
miracle of not allowing their clothes and shoes to wear out during the forty years in the desert.

as a result (Joshua 11). In this view of the settlement of Canaan, the battles of conquest were "defensive," fought against those who sought to resist Israel. However, those who were convinced by the stories of God's might were assimilated rather than destroyed.[28] This view of the conquest as a process that included the amalgamation and incorporation of local inhabitants is strikingly like the account of the settlement of Israel that is currently accepted by archaeologists and historians.

Rahab and the Gibeonites refer to Egypt and to Sihon and Og; significantly, God "hardened Pharaoh's heart" and later did the same to Sihon and Og. In these cases, the stubbornness of the people served as the justification for conquering them, and their conquest followed a pattern of demoralization, hardening, and annihilation. One might ask why God "hardened" some people's hearts and not others'.[29] In the case of Pharaoh, Exodus tells us he hardened his own heart before God hardened it. This may also have been true of Sihon and Og. Since Sihon and Og wanted to fight Israel, God made their resolve even firmer. Rahab and the Gibeonites show that there was an alternative to fighting the Israelites and that those whose heart was moved to fear God did avoid destruction. On the other hand, Josh 11:19–20 declares that God hardened everyone's heart (except Gibeon) to fight so that they would be destroyed. In any event, God must have had God's own reasons for sparing these people.

The book of Joshua is part of the Deuteronomistic History, a reflection on Israel's history written at the time of the destruction, when the sky was falling, that attempts to make sense out of the fact that God has caused (or at least allowed) Israel to be destroyed. Deuteronomy does not trust foreign alliances or foreign women and couples its demand for the *ḥerem* with a prohibition of intermarriage with the local inhabitants.[30] To Deuteronomy, the very purpose of the *ḥerem* is to prevent intermingling and intermarriage and the subsequent introduction of "foreign" ideas into Israel.[31] Josh 23:13 and Judg 2:3 (both deuteronomic passages) explain why many inhabitants of the land are not eradicated: they are to be "a snare and a trap" for Israel "a scourge to your sides and thorns in your eyes" that will ultimately lead to Israel's loss of the land. From this perspective, the nations that remain are the source of evil danger, and Rahab, saved as an act of reciprocated *ḥesed*, is ultimately a stumbling block to Israel's survival. The rescue of Rahab is Israel's first act of apostasy, committed immediately after Israel's entry into the land. The Deuteronomist does

28. Lawson Stone, "Ethical and Apologetic Tendencies in the Redaction of the Book of Joshua," *CBQ* 53 (1991) 25–36.

29. Eslinger (*Into the Hands*, 24–54) attributes this to a "failing" by God, who did not perform the divine duty.

30. To the Deuteronomistic Historian, Solomon's one flaw was the fact that he loved foreign women, including the daughter of Pharaoh (1 Kgs 11:1–3).

31. Deut 7:1–5, 20:18.

not make any directly negative statements: the repeated use of the verb *ḥerem* in Joshua 6 reminds the reader of Deuteronomy and insinuates that the saving of Rahab contains the first seeds of the nation's destruction.

The very first words of the Rahab story inform us that Joshua was at Shittim when he sent out the spies. Whether this detail was original or added by a later hand, Shittim subtly cues us (the biblically-sophisticated readers) to the wider ramifications of the story in the underlying discourse about the permeability of Israel's boundaries. Shittim is the place where Israel angered God by going astray with the Moabite women in the incident of Baᶜal-peor in Numbers 25. During this incident, moreover, an Israelite man called Zimri brought a Midianite princess, Cozbi, into the Israelite camp and his chambers. Immediately, Phineas the priest stabbed them both. For this act, Numbers 25 records, Phineas was rewarded with a *brît shālôm* 'a pact of peace'. As we juxtapose these two Shittim stories, Rahab's position, profession, and name take on new significance. There is no hint of sex in the Rahab story, but Rahab is a professional prostitute, a *zōnâ*, the same word (*zānâ*) with which Israel is described as going astray at Shittim. Rahab's very name means 'wide, broad'. She is the 'broad of Jericho'—the wide-open woman who is the wide-open door to Canaan and maybe the open door to apostasy.[32] Cozbi, on the other hand, was a princess of Midian, and marriage with her might have facilitated alliances and peace with Midian. But Cozbi's name means 'deception', and she is killed immediately. She is not given any chance to profess her loyalty to God or Israel. To Phineas (and to the narrator of the story), the sight of a foreign woman being brought into Israel is such a danger that she must be eradicated immediately, she and the man who brought her to him. Had this same[33] Phineas been at Jericho, Rahab would have been killed rather than spared. The Cozbi story is clearly and unequivocally against intermerging; the Rahab story presents both voices to this long-standing Israelite dispute. Rahab the trickster-foreigner is a type of Israel, who survives by her wits and comes to God by her faith. Rahab the whore is the outsider's outsider; the most marginal of the marginal. She is the quintessential downtrodden from whom Israel comes and with whom Israel identifies.[34] Just as her pious behavior reverses expectations of how prostitutes act, so her elevation is a reversal of the normal expectations for a prostitute's future. Once again, as in choosing the younger sons and freeing the slaves, YHWH interrupts normative societal expectations by calling the

32. The most negative valuation is given by Lyle Eslinger, who states unequivocally, "Rahab is characterized as a whore precisely because she is the door, left open by the divine whoremonger, through which the Israelites are led to stray, 'a-whoring after other Gods'" (*Into the Hands*, 46).

33. We can assume that the Israelites at Jericho included Phineas the priest but not the same narrative character full of murderous zeal.

34. Phyllis A. Bird, "The Harlot as a Heroine: Narrative Art and Social Presupposition in Three Old Testament Texts," *Semeia* 46 (*Narrative Research on the Hebrew Bible*; 1989) 119–39.

poor and the downtrodden and raising them over others. The saving of Rahab the good Canaanite prostitute is part of and an example of God's nature and Israel's mission. Her name, Rahab the broad, is emblematic of God's inclusion of the many and of the permeable boundaries of the people of Israel. Phineas and the Deuteronomy see the open boundaries as danger; another reader may see them as opportunity.

In the end, it is the reader—both singly and in community—who must decide how to read Rahab. After the exile, some of Israel's prophets view the early remnant nations as signs of hope that Israel will survive;[35] they no longer share the deuteronomic view. Despite the fact that Ezra and Nehemiah demanded that the Israelites divorce their foreign wives and that intermarriage was prohibited in the Maccabean period, Christian and Jewish tradition both remember Rahab as an exemplary positive figure.[36] She is cited in the Second Testament as a model of faith[37] and as a second Abraham, justified by her deeds.[38] In Jewish tradition she is remembered as one of the great righteous proselytes.[39] In one major midrashic tradition, she marries Joshua[40] and becomes the ancestress of priests and prophets, including Jeremiah and Ezekiel.[41]

This righteous proselyte-prophet is listed in Matthew as the ancestor of Boaz and thus the ancestor of David. Jewish midrash also preserves such a tradition, pointing out the similarity between the "scarlet threaded cord" with which Rahab's house is marked and the "scarlet thread" that marked the firstborn son of Tamar, ancestress of David, and the many parallels between Rahab and Ruth.[42] Thus in both religious traditions, Rahab takes her place in the extraordinary genealogy of the Messiah.[43] These traditions have taken the choice offered by the story and have read Rahab, her contribution and her inclusion, in the most positive light possible.

35. See particularly the Philistines in Zech 9:7.

36. See Martinus Beek, "Rahab in the Light of Jewish Exegesis (Josh 2:1–24; 6:17, 22–23, 25)," *Von Kanaan bis Kerala: Festschrift für Prof. Mag. Dr. Dr. J. P. M. van der Ploeg* (ed. W. C. Delsman; Neukirchen-Vluyn: Neukirchener Verlag, 1982) 37–44.

37. See Heb 11:31.

38. Jas 2:25.

39. In *Midraš Tadše* 21, *Midraš Chronicles* iv 21, *Rabbah*, she is one of the righteous of the world and proof that God accepts sinners.

40. *b. Meg.* 14b.

41. *Ruth Rab.* 2:1; and cf. *Numbers Rab.* 8:9.

42. *Midraš Hagādôl Ḥayye Sarah* 94.

43. Even though some doubts have been expressed (Jerome Quinn, "Is Rachab in Matt 1:5 Rahab of Jericho," *Bib* 62 [1981] 225–28), there is general consensus that Rahab of Jericho is the Rahab in Matthew (Raymond Brown, "Rachab in Matt 1:5 Probably Is Rahab of Jericho," *Bib* 63 [1982] 79–80).

Psalm 8 on the Power and
Mystery of Speech

WALTER HARRELSON
Wake Forest University

Psalm 8 and Psalm 19 are both hymns of praise, the first praising God for the extraordinary place that the human self occupies in the cosmos and the second praising God for the splendor of the natural creation and for the gift of Torah. The two psalms have in common a theme that is clearly recognizable, but it may be that the theme as developed in Psalm 19 casts light on the interpretation of a difficult text in Psalm 8. The difficult text is Ps 8:3[8:2]. The theme is *speaking*, or more particularly, the power and mystery of *speech*, especially *speaking to God*, or *prayer*.

In Psalm 19, the dome of heaven and the heavenly bodies all utter silent praise to God their Creator as they do their appointed service. Such silent praise cannot be stilled, for the very being of these creatures calls attention to the divine glory, and the faithfulness with which they perform their appointed tasks is further testimony to the power of the Creator to have arranged the universe in such a way. Indeed, these creatures of God act as if they had consciousness of the glory of the Creator: God's creature Sun, for example, speeds across the heavens like a bridegroom coming from the bridal chamber with enthusiasm and energies to spare, eager to dash across the heavens, providing light and heat to every corner of the universe.

Even so, there is not a word uttered. This series of praises to God that regularly takes place during the day and during the night transpires in a palpable cosmic silence. Not a sound is heard. By contrast, Psalm 29 hears in the thunder and the roaring wind the very voice of God—even though it is God, not thunder or wind, who speaks. But who can deny that it is so: "The heavens declare the glory of God, / the sky proclaims His handiwork" (JPSV).

Author's note: It is a pleasure to present this study to my colleague and friend Moshe Greenberg, whose writings and lectures on prayer have been of great value to me.

By contrast, Psalm 8 points to the way in which the human self offers its praise to God. How does the human being praise God? No doubt also, as with the heavens and the sky, by being what God has appointed it to be, fulfilling its rounds as do the heavenly bodies, and even silently giving utterance to its praise through obedience to the divinely appointed responsibilities for earth's care. In this connection, the second half of Psalm 19, which deals with the glory of God's Torah, provides a further connection between the two psalms.

The human self's praise, however, centers in its use of the special gift of speech. Already in the refrain of Psalm 8, this point is suggested: it is the divine *name* that is glorious and majestic, a name that clearly is to be *spoken* throughout the universe. The creature appointed to utter that name is the human being.[1]

A contrast may be intended between vv. 2b and 3. Whereas God's splendor (*hwd*) covers the heavens (if this is how we read the difficult expression *ʾšr tnh*) as a feature of the creation itself, it is the human self, even in the attempts at speech by infants and sucklings, who can give voice to this praise, can speak, and therefore name God's name. Whether or not such a contrast is intended, v. 3, which is the crux of the interpretation offered here, is best understood as the psalmist's effort to probe the power and mystery of human speech, a theme well known from wisdom texts in the Hebrew and Christian scriptures.[2]

The point is not, or not primarily, that the babbling and gurgling speech of infants in itself praises God. Rather, in the sheer mystery of the gift of human speech lies what for this psalmist marks the human self as a distinct part of the creation. Viewed in this light, v. 3 then offers a literary anticipation of what follows. Through the mystery and the power of human speech, showing itself in the "speaking before speech" of infants, God has established or founded strength or a refuge[3] to deal with foes (Heb. root *ṣrr* II), silencing or bringing to an end (*šbt*) the enemy (*ʾōyēb*) and the avenger (*mitnaqqēm*).

Who are these foes, those hostile to God and to the praise of God, hostile also to the purposes of God and perhaps as well hostile to God's Torah (another possible connection of Psalm 8 with Psalm 19)? The same expression, 'enemy and avenger', occurs in the communal lament Ps 44:17, apparently of human foes but possibly also hinting at the hostility that the God of Israel seems to be directing at the people of God (see the following verses). No doubt the expression has its background in the mythic struggles among the divine powers that

---

1. The angels utter God's name in the heavenly assembly and sing the deity's praises, as we know from such texts as the hymns of the book of Revelation and the Qumran text 11QShir-Shabb, as well as from Psalm 29 and many other biblical parallels.

2. Prov 18:21, 25:15; Jas 3:1–12.

3. See *HALAT*, which offers this meaning for *ʿoz* II.

are features of West-Semitic religions,[4] but here the reference almost surely includes all foes, natural, human, and demonic. It is the gift of human speech that is being singled out as the chief bulwark or stronghold or protection against the enemies of God.

Once again, we can suspect that in the background of such an idea is the recognition of the power of the curse to effect damage to one's enemies and the power of the blessing to provide what it seeks. But our psalmist is unlikely to have in view the wonder-working power of human speech. Rather, the emphasis falls upon what is distinctive of the human being as such: human beings can speak, can name, can converse, can share life, and of course can communicate and miscommunicate, explain themselves and their ideas, and hide themselves and obscure their ideas—all with the gift of human speech.

In this setting, the remainder of the Psalm unfolds clearly. When the psalmist reflects on the power and majesty of the whole creation and turns from the cosmic scene to the human, how can the poet not ask, "What are human beings that you are mindful of them, mortals, that you care for them?" But the answer is ready at hand: the gift of speech, of capacity to name God's name, to share life with the deity, and in all these ways to have a hand at maintaining the order and share in the purpose of the creation—these place the human self in intimate relationship with the divine realm, making of earthbound selves little less than the angels of God (*ʾĕlōhîm*).

As is well known, Psalm 8 also has connections with the story of the creation of the universe in Genesis 1. In Genesis 1, the counterpart to the authority vested in human beings and capable of being exercised largely through the gift of speech (Psalm 8) is the creation of the human self, male and female, in the image (*ṣelem*) and likeness (*dĕmût*) of God (here also *ʾĕlōhîm*). Psalm 8 and Genesis 1 use different verbs to designate the exercise of human authority over the whole of the creation, but the basic import is clearly the same (as it is also in Ben Sira 17). The *fact* of the dominion of humankind over the creation, under the overarching authority of the Creator, is clear. But it is Psalm 8 alone that identifies the *means* by which human beings are to exercise that authority.

Since God called the world into being through speaking and naming—a theme found also in the Memphis theology of early Egypt[5]—it is not surprising perhaps that the only one created in the divine image and likeness should be singled out by the author of Psalm 8 as exercising creative rule through the power of speech. The differences, however, between the Creator's calling the world into being through speech and establishing its order and workings, on the one side, and the human being's using the gift of speech to exercise

---

4. See the brief but fine treatment in A. A. Anderson, *Psalms (1–72)* (NCB Commentary; Grand Rapids, Mich.: Eerdmans, 1972) 102.

5. See J. A. Wilson (trans.), "Egyptian Myths, Tales, and Mortuary Texts," *ANET*, 4–5.

authority over the world, thereby maintaining God's order, is no doubt very considerable indeed. What is the dividing line, according to our poet?

It must lie in the identification of some priority in the intended use of the gift of human speaking. Among all the features of speaking that the poet may have in mind, one stands out: the ability to speak and honor the divine *name*. Our poet believes, it seems probable, that the human community is charged first and foremost to use the capacity of speech to render praise and honor to God, to name God's name in prayer and praise, and in so doing actually to affirm the mystery and enhance the power of the divine name in the world.

Thus the poet reflects on the mystery of the place of the human self in the creation by calling attention to the fact that, from the time of the very birth of a human being, one human quality stands out: the capacity not only to make noises with the voice but (as the Memphite theology puts it) to coordinate heart and tongue, to begin to utter words that, in time, will join with the words of angels and of other human beings in declaring that God's name is glorious throughout the earth. Though God's glory is witnessed by the creation itself and by the heavenly bodies in particular, it is given its chief and most effective testimony as God's purposes are realized on earth through the praises and prayers of the human community.

Psalm 8 is of course a hymn of ancient Israel, created by a poet of Israel and preserved by the community of Israel. It will be used later by the author of the letter to the Hebrews in the New Testament as a witness to the Messiah of Christian faith, where the human self is seen as personified in Jesus, the archetypal human being. It is therefore a very particular religious text, with its meaning framed in different ways for the Jewish and the Christian communities. But the hymn itself clearly strives to portray the character of human selfhood as such, and the place of the human self in the universe. This place, according to the author, is as one who maintains the universe through the praise of its Creator. The use of human speech may thus stand as a metaphor for the capacity of human beings to take initiatives on behalf of others, for the sake of realizing purposes that lie beyond their own personal interest. It may be seen as a mark of what can be called self-transcendence. Speech is the human means not only of maintaining order in an existing creation but also of evoking or indeed calling into being a world, a universe of meaning, purpose, beauty, and completeness. But for the author of our Psalm, speech is fulfilling its fullest and most essential end when it is used as it is in the opening and closing refrain of the poem: "O LORD, our Lord, / How majestic is Your name throughout the earth!"

Two Aspects of the "Tent of Meeting"

ISRAEL KNOHL
The Hebrew University of Jerusalem

In the very heart of the priestly stratum of the Torah there lies the Tent of Meeting (אהל מועד). According to the priestly view, the Tent of Meeting was erected in the middle of the camp, and alongside of it were encamped the Aaronide priests, who alone had the right to enter the tent: around the tent were the Levites, who guarded the sanctity of the holy place, while in the outermost circle were the other tribes of Israel. One who did not belong to the priestly families and attempted to enter the Tent of Meeting was subject to the death penalty: "any outsider who encroaches shall be put to death" (Num 3:10, 38).

According to the priestly law-code, the tent located in the heart of the camp was first and foremost a place where the Glory of God was constantly present. God appeared in the cloud above the cherub covering that rested on the ark of the Pact: "for I appear in the cloud over the cover" (Lev 16:2). Consequently, the Tent of Meeting was called a tabernacle משכן (from the root שכנ 'to dwell'), because it was the fixed dwelling place of the Divine Glory. The constant presence of the Glory in the Tent is expressed in the cult of the fixed daily offering (תמיד), in whose framework the priests offered the daily burnt offering, burned the incense, lit the eternal light, and arranged the show-bread on the table. Only the perpetual presence of God's Glory within the Tent of Meeting can explain the complex of acts performed in the daily worship. However, the Tent was not only a cultic site but also a locus of revelation. Prior to the construction of the tabernacle, God said to Moses, "There I will meet with you, and I will impart to you—from above the cover, from between the two cherubim that are on top of the Ark of the Pact—all that I will command you concerning the Israelite people" (Exod 25:22). After it was set up, we read, "When Moses went into the Tent of Meeting to speak with Him, he would hear the voice addressing him from above the cover that was on top of the Ark of the Pact between the two cherubim: thus He spoke to him" (Num 7:89). God, who is seen above the cover (כפרת), meets Moses there and commands the children of Israel.

However, alongside this principal tradition, the Torah preserves fragments of another tradition that give a radically different image of the Tent of Meeting and its function. Fragments of this tradition are preserved in Exod 33:6–11, in Num 11:16–17 and 12:4–10, and in Deut 31:14–15. According to the viewpoint reflected in these texts, the Tent of Meeting was quite simply a site of prophetic revelation. The Tent was located outside of the camp, "Now Moses would take the Tent and pitch it outside the camp, at some distance from the camp. It was called the Tent of Meeting, and whoever sought the Lord would go out to the Tent of Meeting that was outside the camp" (Exod 33:7). God does not dwell within the Tent but descends in the pillar of cloud and stands at the entrance to the Tent for purposes of prophetic revelation: "And when Moses entered the Tent, the pillar of cloud would descend and stand at the entrance of the Tent, while He spoke with Moses" (38:9). From the story of the Kushite woman, which likewise belongs to this tradition, we learn that God departs from the Tent in His cloud at the conclusion of the revelation: "Still incensed with them, the Lord departed. As the cloud withdrew from the Tent . . ." (Num 12:9–10). In this Tent there is no Ark and, since it is not the constant dwelling place of God, it is clear that no regular cult, nor any other cultic act, is practiced there. If there is no cult, there is no need for cultic officials; therefore, the Tent is not reserved for priests but is open to "whoever sought the Lord."[1]

I wish to make note here of the profound theoretical and conceptual gap between the two concepts of the Tent of Meeting that have been preserved in the Torah. As stated, according to the priestly conception, the Tent of Meeting is a focus of sanctity in the heart of the camp of Israel. It is known that the area outside of the camp was perceived by the priesthood as an area of impurity to which impure people and the carcasses of sin-offerings that carried transgression were sent, where wild goats and satyrs danced, and which was desired by Azazel as a dwelling-place.[2] This contrast between the realm of holiness (the camp in whose heart is the Tent of Meeting) and the realm of impurity ("outside of the camp") is one of the cornerstones of priestly thinking.[3] In contrast, in the prophetic tradition the Tent of Meeting is specifically located outside of the camp!

One should mention that even according to the prophetic tradition of the Tent of Meeting, the area outside of the camp is a border area of questionable status. In chapter 12 of Numbers, which as mentioned, is also derived from

---

1. For the meaning of the expression מבקש ה׳, see Deut 4:29, Ps 27:8. For previous discussion of the two models, see M. Haran, *Temples and Temple-Service in Ancient Israel* (Oxford: Oxford University Press, 1978; reprinted Winona Lake, Ind.: Eisenbrauns, 1985) 260–75.

2. See Lev 4:12, 21; 9:11; 10:4–5; 13:46; 14:7, 53; 16:10, 22, 27; 17:5–7; 21:14; Num 5:2–4; 31:19.

3. See Y. Kaufmann, *The Religion of Israel* (trans. and abridg. M. Greenberg; Chicago: University of Chicago Press, 1960) 104–5 [Hebrew: Kaufmann, *Toledot ha-ʾEmunâ ha-Yiśrĕʾēlit*, 1.542–43].

this tradition, we read that Miriam was shut off outside of the camp for seven days when she became leprous (Num 12:14–15). That is to say, this tradition states that it is specifically in the border area, near the area to which the lepers and other impure people are banished, that "the Tent of Meeting," the site of God's appearance and prophetic revelation, is erected.

It seems to me that one may explain the dispute between the different views of the location of the Tent of Meeting in terms of differing models of the concept of holiness, as these have been described by scholars of religion in our generation. Mircea Eliade[4] states that the distinction between settled and unsettled areas is among the most striking hallmarks of traditional society. The settled area is that realm in whose center the holy is revealed, while the unsettled area, from which the sacred element is absent, is a chaotic region populated by spirits and demons. The sacred center in the heart of the settled area is the site of the cult in which contact takes place between the Divinity and man.[5] It seems that these distinctions are most apropos to the priestly approach, which as noted, stresses the distinction between the realm of settlement "within the camp," in whose center is the "Tent of Meeting," and the unsettled areas outside of the camp, populated by forces of impurity.

Another model of the holy place is presented in the various studies by Victor Turner. In his work on the subject of pilgrimage, Turner devotes attention to the holy places that are found in remote areas outside of the settled areas. The pilgrims leave the fixed and established social structures of the realm of settlement to go out to the sacred place, in which customary social barriers are broken down and differences in class are nullified (a phenomenon described by Turner as "anti-structure"). In the sacred place, there are created nonestablishment, egalitarian communities, which he designates *communitas*.[6] The prophetic Tent of Meeting may be explained by means of this model. It is found "outside the camp, at some distance from the camp" (Exod 33:7). The act of going out to it is open and voluntary and independent of any sort of pedigree or status: "and whoever sought the Lord would go out to the Tent of Meeting that was outside of the camp" (33:7). It is interesting in this respect to note the story in Numbers 11 of the seventy elders who are called upon to go out with Moses to the prophetic Tent of Meeting. God commands Moses, "Gather for Me seventy of Israel's elders of whom you have experience as elders and officers of the people, and bring them to the Tent of Meeting and let them take their place there with you. I will come down and speak with you there, and I will draw

4. M. Eliade, *The Sacred and the Profane* (New York: Harcourt Brace Jovanovich, 1959) 29ff.

5. It seems to me that Eliade's remarks, in the restrained form in which they appear here, remain valid even after the criticism of J. Z. Smith, *To Take Place* (Chicago: University of Chicago Press, 1987) 1–23.

6. V. Turner, *The Ritual Process* (Chicago: University of Chicago Press, 1969) 94–130; idem, "The Center out There: The Pilgrim Goal," *History of Religions* 12 (1973) 191–230; idem, *Dramas, Fields and Metaphors* (London, 1974) 166–230.

upon the spirit that is on you and put it upon them; they shall share the burden of the people with you, and you shall not bear it alone" (Num 11:16–17). There is an attempt here to exploit the unique prophetic qualities of the Tent of Meeting in order to establish the position of leadership. The wish here is to institutionalize prophetic revelation and to pass it on to a group of special individuals who are called by name. However, this attempt fails in the bud. God's spirit cannot be chained to a specific place or to a specific group of people. Surprisingly, it does not rest only upon the elders who went out to the tent but also upon Eldad and Medad, who remained in the camp and did not go out to the Tent of Meeting. Moses rejects Joshua's appeal, "My lord Moses, restrain them!" declaring, "Would that all the Lord's people were prophets, that the Lord put His spirit upon them!" (Num 11:28–29). The level of prophecy is open to all, and is not to be limited or restricted by place or status.

The tension between the two different pictures of the "Tent of Meeting" may therefore be described as a debate concerning the place of sanctity and the relationship between it and social structures. The priestly approach sees holiness and the holy place as constituting the central axis of Israelite society and of its cultic institutions, concentrated upon the priestly class. In contrast, the prophetic Tent of Meeting expresses the opposing view, which sees sanctity and the holy place as an element external to society and to its institutions, which even contains a certain anarchistic dimension. One could therefore speculate that the well-known tension between priesthood and prophecy lies at the basis of this conflict. This is not the place to attempt to fix these two pictures in a particular historical period;[7] my only concern here has been to define the ideological and religious dimensions of this controversy.

It is clear that both of these pictures of the Tent of Meeting also reflect different approaches regarding God's place in the world and the nature of his relation to Israel. The priestly tradition emphasizes the immanence of God. Religious certainty is attained by the fixed presence of God within Israel. The purpose of the complex cultic system practiced within the Tent of Meeting is to facilitate God's continued presence among His people. In contrast, the prophetic tradition claims that God's place is in the heavens, and that it is only for purposes of revelation that God descends in His cloud and momentarily reveals Himself at the entrance to the Tent of Meeting. At the conclusion of His revelation, he returns to his former place. Hence, the power of the religious experience in the prophetic revelation described here lies, not in its constancy, but in the intimacy of the fleeting encounter: "the Lord would speak to Moses face to face, as one man speaks to another" (Exod 33:11). It is important to stress that the opposition between God's immanence in the priestly tradition

---

7. I intend to deal with this issue elsewhere. See, meanwhile, what I wrote in my book, *The Sanctuary of Silence* (Minneapolis, 1995) 131 n. 24.

and His transcendence in the prophetic approach has no connection to the issue of abstraction and corporeality. On the contrary, as I have shown in my book,[8] it is precisely the priestly tradition, which stresses the Divine immanence, that reached heights of abstraction and distancing from anthropomorphism unparalleled in the Bible. The transcendent God of the prophetic tradition, in contrast, is described in terms of anthropomorphism and incarnation: "with him I speak mouth to mouth," and so forth (Num 12:8); "Still incensed with them, the Lord departed" (12:10), and other verses.

In several places in the Torah, one may see a desire to create a synthesis between these opposed images of the Tent of Meeting. Thus, for example, at the end of the priestly commands concerning the erection of the Tabernacle, we find a passage concerning the bringing of the permanent offering. The end of this passage states: ". . . a regular burnt offering throughout the generations, at the entrance of the Tent of Meeting before the Lord. For there I will meet with you, and there I will speak with you" (Exod 29:42). It would seem that this statement, which specifically fixes as the site of revelation the entrance to the Tent of Meeting rather than the Ark and the cover (כפרת) above it, reflects an attempt to combine the (prophetic) element of revelation at the entrance to the Tent of Meeting with the (priestly) cultic image of the Tent of Meeting. Another attempt, similar but in the opposite direction, appears in the story of the appointment of Joshua in Deut 31:11–15. In the Masoretic Text of v. 15, we read: "The Lord appeared in the Tent, in a pillar of cloud, the pillar of the cloud having come to rest at the entrance of the Tent." However, as noted by A. Rofé,[9] the text reflected in the Vatican MS of the Septuagint is different. Instead of "and God appeared (וירא) in the Tent in the pillar of cloud," as in the traditional version, the text known to the Septuagint evidently read, "and God descended (וירד) in a cloud and stood before the Tent of Meeting." Rofé's interpretation thus makes sense, namely, that the Masoretic Text of this passage reflects an attempt to paint the prophetic tradition of the Tent of Meeting, which speaks in its usual manner of God descending in a cloud to the entrance of the Tent of Meeting for purposes of prophetic revelation, in the colors of the priestly tradition of the Tent of Meeting, which states that God appears in a cloud within the tent! A similar synthetic tendency can be seen in a number of other passages in the Torah (such as Exod 16:10 and Num 17:7), which we have no space to discuss here in detail.[10]

---

8. Ibid., 128–37.

9. A. Rofé, "Textual Criticism in the Light of Historical Literary Criticism: Deuteronomy 31:14–15," *ErIsr* 16 (H. Orlinsky Volume; Jerusalem, 1982) 171–76.

10. In my opinion, all those passages in which this approach is expressed originated among writers and redactors belonging to the "Holiness School" (H). On the tendency of the Holiness School to mix popular and priestly traditions and the activity of this school in the editing of the Torah, see *The Sanctuary*, 101–3, 224.

The sages likewise sought to create a synthesis between these two opposing pictures. In *Midraš Siprê Zuṭâ* on Numbers, we read of the verse, "They shall be attached to you and discharge the duties of the Tent of Meeting, all the service of the tent" (Num 18:4), as follows: "Said R. Simeon: We have learned that there were two tents; the tent of service (אהל העבודות) and that of speaking (אהל הדברות)."[11] From the double appearance of the word *Tent* in this verse, ". . . the Tent of Meeting, all the service of the tent," R. Simeon b. Yohai inferred that there were two tents: (1) "the tent of speaking," that is, the site of revelation of the word of God; and (2) "the tent of service," that is, the cultic center. David Z. Hoffmann has already observed[12] that the aim of R. Simeon's remarks was to bridge between the two opposing traditions in the Torah regarding the nature and substance of the Tent of Meeting by assuming the simultaneous existence of two different tents. A similar midrashic approach is elaborated in a fragment from *Midraš Espa*[13] on the verse "and he gathered seventy people of the elders of Israel, and he made them stand around the Tent" (Num 11:24). The midrash comments: "In the tent of speaking, which is outside of the camp, they made two tents—a tent of service and a tent of speaking; . . . and the Levites served [at] each one." However, it is in fact difficult to accept the rabbis' attempt at harmonization. According to the priestly approach, the "Tent of Meeting" was, as mentioned, at one and the same time "the tent of speaking," that is, the place of God's revelation to Moses, and also "the tent of service," the cultic center. Thus, there is neither place nor need for an additional tent in this centralistic tradition.

A certain attempt to integrate the tradition of the two tents within the cultic reality of the Second Temple Period may be seen in the description of the Temple Mount in rabbinic sources. The Temple inherited the image of the "priestly Tent of Meeting" as a cultic center. Like the priestly Tent, it too was located in the heart of the sacred area, entrance into its inner parts being permitted to the priests alone (see *m. Kelim* 8–9). But at the margins of the holy area of the Temple Mount,[14] we find the "Chamber of Hewn Stone," which had some of the characteristics of the prophetic "Tent of Meeting": in the Chamber of Hewn Stone, the members of the High Court, the Sanhedrin, sit and conduct their deliberations. The members of the Sanhedrin are the heirs of the seventy elders

11. *Siprê Zuṭâ* (ed. H. S. Horovitz; Leipzig, 1917) 292. Cf. p. 257, line 4, and the redactor's notes there.

12. D. Hoffmann, *Die wichtigsten Instanzen gegen die Graf Wellhausen'sche Hypothese* (Berlin, 1906) 81 n. 1.

13. The passage is preserved in *Yalqut Šimᶜoni, Behaᶜalotekha*, sect. 737. On this midrash, see L. Zunz, *Die Gottesdienstlichen Vorträge der Juden* (Frankfurt, 1892) 292.

14. In the rabbis' opinion, the Chamber of Hewn Stone was located half within the holy precincts and half outside (see *b. Yoma* 25a). In this respect, one can see in an explicit way the quality of "liminality" that characterizes the model of the holy place in Turner (see his studies enumerated above, n. 6).

who, according to the description in Numbers 11, were gathered in the prophetic Tent of Meeting. This is made explicit in the Mishna: "The great Sanhedrin consisted of seventy-one [people]. . . . And from whence . . . that it consisted of seventy-one? As is said, 'Gather for me seventy of Israel's elders' [Num 11:16], and Moses was over them—hence seventy-one" (*m. Sanh.* 1:6).

It seems to me that, despite the various attempts at harmonization on the part of both the redactors of the Torah literature and the sages,[15] we would do well to note the essential tension between the two different images of the Tent of Meeting, embodying profound ideological and religious oppositions. Each of these images reflects a unique religious significance, and "both of these are the words of the living God."[16]

15. For a modern effort at harmonization, see R. de Vaux, *The Bible and the Ancient Near East* (New York, 1971) 140–51.

16. *B. ᶜErub.* 13b.

The Firstfruits Festivals of Grain and the Composition of Leviticus 23:9–21

JACOB MILGROM
University of California, Berkeley

I begin this investigation with a daring innovation: a new interpretation of the notorious crux *mimmāḥŏrat haššabbāt*, literally, 'from the day after the Sabbath'. It is well known that the four extant interpretations carved schismatic rifts into the world body of the Jewish people that lasted more than a millennium. It was variously defined as the day after the Sabbath falling during the Passover week (technically, during the Festival of Unleavened Bread, Exod 23:15, Lev 23:6, Num 28:17; for example, the Karaites), the day after the Sabbath falling immediately after the Passover week (for example, the Qumranites), the day after the first day of the Passover week (the rabbis), and the day after the seventh day of the Passover week (for example, the Falashas).

The two sabbatarian positions are justifiable by the plain meaning of the term *šabbāt*. But what may account for the festivalian position adopted by the rabbis? Since there is not the slightest hint in the sources,[1] I can only allow myself an unalloyed conjecture: The Pharisaic (and proto-Pharisaic) predecessors of the rabbis championed the lunar calendar.[2] Had they accepted the sabbatarian viewpoint, then in their calendar the Festival of the First Wheat offering would not always fall on the same date (see *b. Menaḥ.* 66a), since they held that this festival coincided with the Sinaitic revelation *bayyôm hazzeh* (Exod 19:1), that is, on a fixed day. Note that the sabbath day is independent of the lunar calendar. Counting fifty days starting with the day after the Sabbath

---

Author's note: I offer the prayer that the honoree, who motivated this farmer's firstfruit offerings, will enjoy many more years of productive labor in our field.

1. Ibn Ezra (on Lev 23:11) indeed claims that a festival can be called *šabbāt* (cf. Lev 23:24, 32, 39). All of his citations, however, use not the word *šabbāt* but *šabbātôn*, which has adjectival force, implying a less severe sabbath but in combination with *šabbāt* implies even more severe restrictions.

2. As opposed to *Jubilees* and Qumran, which had adopted a solar calendar.

would invariably lead to a different date each year for the Festival of the First Wheat. Thus, the pharisaic-rabbinic tradition had no choice but to tie the beginning of the fifty-day count to the Passover, which always fell on a fixed date in the lunar calendar.

I shall now offer a fifth interpretation, not in the hope of creating another sect, but to demonstrate that it may offer a key to unlocking the composition of this chapter. I propose 'the day after the sabbath-week'. My "day," in agreement with the sabbatarian positions, also is a Sunday, the day following the Sabbath (of creation). But it differs from them markedly, as will be shown below.

The phrase _mimmāḥŏrat haššabbāt_ occurs in three verses (Lev 23:11 and 15–16), each of which adds a critical element to my interpretation. The first two are in vv. 15–16 _ûsĕpartem lākem mimmāḥŏrat haššabbāt miyyôm hăbîʾăkem ʾet-ʿōmer hattĕnupâ šebaʿ šabbātôt tĕmîmōt tihyênâ ʿad mimmāḥŏrat haššabbāt haššĕbîʿît tispĕrû ḥămiššîm yôm_ 'and on[3] the day after the sabbath-week, from the day on which you bring the elevation offering of the sheaf, you shall count seven sabbath-weeks.[4] They must be complete. You shall count until the day after the seventh sabbath-week fifty days'. The second occurrence of sabbath, _šabbātôt_, unambiguously means sabbath-weeks. As discerned by H. L. Ginsberg,[5] would it not be incredible if _šabbāt in the same verse_ would mean two different things, particularly if both usages, as will be shown, were written by the same author? If, then, _šabbāt_ denotes the sabbath-week at the end of the verse (and again in the following one), it must also denote that in the phrase _mimmāḥŏrat haššabbāt_ in the first part of the verse.

The third occurrence of _mimmāḥŏrat haššabbāt_ is in v. 11 _wĕhēnîp ʾet-hāʿōmer lipnê YHWH lirṣōnĕkem mimmāḥŏrat haššabbāt yĕnîpennû hakkōhēn_ 'he shall elevate the sheaf before the Lord for acceptance on your behalf. On the day after the sabbath-week the priest shall elevate it' (literal translation). As I have remarked elsewhere,[6] the term _lirṣōnĕkem_ in H always begins the apodosis (for example, Lev 19:5, 22:9). But in this verse, this can only be achieved by deleting _mimmāḥŏrat haššabbāt_ and moving the _ʾatnāḥ_ to YHWH; thus the original position of _lirṣōnĕkem_ is restored, as follows: _wĕhēnîp ʾet-hāʿōmer lipnê YHWH / lirṣōnĕkem yĕnîpennû hakkōhēn_ 'he shall elevate the sheaf before the Lord; for acceptance on your behalf shall the priest elevate it' (literal rendering).

Moreover, what emerges is quintessential H style: the same verb is employed in both halves, the first time prefixed and the second suffixed, and a

---

3. The _mem_ and _beth_ are frequently interchangeable; see N. M. Sarna, "The Interchange of the Prepositions _Beth_ and _Mem_ in Biblical Hebrew," _JBL_ 78 (1959) 310–16.

4. Moving the _ʾathnaḥ_ from _hattēnûpâ_ to _šabbātôt_.

5. H. L. Ginsberg, "The Grain Harvest Laws of Lev. 23:9–22 and Num. 28:26–31," _PAAJR_ 46–47 (1979–80) 146 n. 12; _The Israelian Heritage of Judaism_ (New York: Jewish Theological Seminary, 1982) 74.

6. J. Milgrom, _Studies in Cultic Theology and Terminology_ (Leiden: Brill, 1983) 151 n. 37.

chiasm is created by reversing the position of the subject and object in the second half (for example, Lev 23:11, 15, 41; 25:22, 29).[7]

Thus *mimmāḥŏrat haššabbāt* is an interpolation, and if so, then the material into which is has been inserted must be older. I deduce it to be vv. 10aβγ, b; 11*; 14a; 15a*; 16aβ, b; 17*, as follows:

Barley and Wheat Firstfruits (Lev 23:10aβ–21)

[10]. . . kî-tābō²û ²el-hā²āreṣ ²ăšer ²ănî nōtēn lākem ûqĕṣartem ²et-qĕṣîrāh wĕhābē²tem ²et-ᶜōmer rē²šît qĕṣîrĕkem ²el-hakkōhēn [11]wĕhēnîp ²et-hāᶜōmer lipnê YHWH lirṣōnĕkem **mimmāḥŏrat haššabbāt** *yĕnîpennû hakkōhēn [12]wa*ᶜ*ăśîtem bĕyôm hănîpĕkem ²et-hāᶜōmer kebeś tāmîm ben-šĕnatô lĕᶜōlâ laYHWH. [13]ûminḥātô šĕnê ᶜeśrōnîm sōlet bĕlûlâ baššemen ²iššeh laYHWH rêaḥ nîḥōaḥ wĕniskōh[ôQ] yayin rĕbîᶜit hahîn [14]wĕleḥem wĕqālî wĕkarmel lō² tō²kĕlû ᶜad-ᶜeṣem hayyôm hazzeh ᶜad hăbî²ăkem ²et-qorban ²ĕlōhêkem* **ḥuqqat ᶜōlām lĕdōrōtêkem bĕkol mōšĕbōtêkem**

[15]ûsĕpartem lākem **mimmāḥŏrat haššabbāt** *miyyôm hăbî²ăkem ²et-ᶜōmer hattĕnûpâ* **šebaᶜ šabbātôt tĕmîmôt tihyênâ** *[16]ᶜad* **mimmāḥŏrat haššabbāt haššĕbîᶜît tispĕrû** *ḥămiššîm yôm wĕhiqrabtem minḥâ ḥădāšâ laYHWH. [17]mimmôšĕbōtêkem tabî²û leḥem tĕnûpâ štayim šnê ᶜeśrōnîm sōlet tihyênâ ḥāmēṣ tē²āpênâ bikkûrîm laYHWH. [18]wehiqrabtem ᶜal-haleḥem šibᶜat kĕbāśîm tĕmîmim bĕnê šānâ ûpar ben-bāqār ²eḥād wĕ²êlim šnāyim yihyû ᶜōlâ laYHWH uminḥātām wĕniskêkem ²iššēh rêaḥ-niḥōaḥ laYHWH. [19]wa*ᶜ*ăśîtem śĕᶜîr ᶜizzîm ²eḥād lĕḥaṭṭā²t ûšĕnê kĕbāśîm bĕnê šānâ lĕzebaḥ šĕlāmîm [20]wĕhēnîp hakkōhēn ²ōtām ᶜal leḥem habbikkûrîm tĕnûpâ lipnê YHWH ᶜal-šĕnê kĕbāśîm qōdeš yihyû laYHWH lakkōhēn. [21]ûqĕrā²tem bĕᶜeṣem hayyôm hazzeh miqrā²-qōdeš yihyeh lākem kol-mĕle²ket ᶜăbōdâ lō² taᶜăśû ḥuqqat ᶜōlām bĕkol-môšĕbōtêkem lĕdōrōtêkem.*

When you enter the land I am giving to you and you reap its harvest, you shall bring the first sheaf of your harvest to the priest. [11]He shall elevate the sheaf before the Lord. The priest shall elevate it *on the day after the sabbath-week* for acceptance on your behalf. *[12]On the day that you elevate the sheaf, you shall sacrifice an unblemished male lamb in its first year as a burnt offering to the Lord. [13]The accompanying cereal offering shall be two-tenths of an ephah of semolina mixed with oil, a food-gift of pleasing aroma to the Lord; and the accompanying libation shall be one fourth of a hin of wine.* [14]Do not

---

7. Cf. M. Paran, *Forms of the Priestly Style of the Pentateuch* (Jerusalem: Magnes, 1989) 56–73 [Hebrew].

partake (from the new crop) of any bread or parched or fresh grain until the very day you have brought your God's offering—*a law for all
time, throughout your generations, in all your settlements.*

[15]And **on the day after the sabbath-week** from the day on which
you bring the elevation offering of the sheaf, you shall count off **seven
sabbath-weeks. They must be complete:** *[16]**You shall count until the
day after the seventh sabbath-week*** fifty days. Then you shall present
a new cereal offering to the Lord. [17]You shall bring from your settlements as an elevation offering of bread two bread (loaves) comprising
two-tenths of an ephah of semolina and baked after leavening, as firstfruits for the Lord. *[18]With the bread you shall offer seven unblemished yearly lambs, one bull of the herd, and two rams; (they) shall
be a burnt offering to the Lord, and with their cereal offerings and
libations, a food-gift of pleasant aroma to the Lord. [19]You shall sacrifice one he-goat as a purification offering and two yearling lambs
as a sacrifice of well-being.* [20]And the priest shall elevate them *with
the bread of firstfruits* as an elevation offering to the Lord *with the
two lambs*; they shall be holy to the Lord for the priest. *[21]On that very
day you shall proclaim a sacred occasion; you must do no laborious
work—a law for all time, in all your settlements, throughout your
generations.*

This pericope, I submit, is composed of three layers, each representing a distinct contribution of the Holiness School. The earliest (II$_1$) is in regular type.
It ordains that each farmer shall bring his firstfruits of barley (an $^c\bar{o}mer$) and
wheat (two loaves), fifty days apart, to his local sanctuary. It should be apparent that this firstfruits barley offering has nothing to do with the approximately
concurrent Feast of Unleavened Bread. The farmer brings his offering whenever his grain ripens, a day that differs from one region to another and as much
as a month over the entire country. Fifty days later, he brings his firstfruits of
the wheat in the form of two loaves. These, being leavened, cannot be offered
on the altar (Lev 2:11) and, instead, are given to the priest.

I admit that I cannot fathom the purpose of the fifty-day counting, and the
literature I have consulted is of no help. But I have a visceral intuition that originally it was connected with some incantation recited each day to ward off the
demons of the weather.[8] With the triumph of Israelite monotheism, however,
the magical incantations were excised, and all that survives is the counting.

It is no accident that the Sirocco, the hot, dry Egyptian east wind, is called
in Arabic *el-ḥamsîn* (*el-ḥamāsîn*), a word related to Arabic *ḥamsûn* and He-

---

8. Perhaps by counting grain, J. G. Frazer, *Folklore in the Old Testament* (abridged ed.; New
York: Macmillan, 1927) 310; or by knots, W. J. Dilling, "Knots," *ERE* 7.747–51; G. Piccaluga,
"Knots," *Encyclopaedia of Religion* 8 (1987) 340–42; J. G. Frazer, *The Golden Bough*, vol. 3:
Taboo and the Perils of the Soul (3d ed.; London: Macmillan); abridged edition (1957) 314–21.

brew *ḥămiššîm* 'fifty'. The Sirocco blows for about fifty days between April and June, causing the temperatures to rise and the humidity to plummet, thereby withering and killing plants (Gen 41:6, 23; Isa 27:8; Ezek 17:10; 19:12; Hos 13:14; Jonah 4:8) and striking humans with weakness, heat stroke, and death (see 2 Kgs 4:18–20—during the grain harvest!).[9]

A silent yet significant witness to the perilousness of this season is the fact that Deuteronomy stresses the motif of rejoicing for the Festival of Weeks and Booths (Deut 16:11, 14–15) but omits it for the Festival of Unleavened Bread (vv. 1–8), even though the gathering of the nation at the central sanctuary would, presumably, be a prime occasion for family celebration. The beginning of a fifty-day period of unstable and precarious weather, which might fatally damage the year's crop, not to speak of human health, is no time for rejoicing (see *Yal.* 654). Nonetheless, echoes of this anxiety and trepidation during the fifty days following the spring festival continue to resound. They are reflected in the medieval prayerbook *Abudarham haššālēm*:

> Some explain it . . . on the ground that the world is anxious between Passover and Weeks about the crops and the fruit trees . . . Therefore God commanded to count these days, to keep the anxiety of the world in mind and to turn to him in wholehearted repentance, to plead with him to have mercy upon us, on mankind and on the land, so that the crops should turn out well, for they are our life.[10]

This period of anxiety and apprehension survives in the rabbinic laws of semi-mourning, which prohibit the solemnizing of marriages, haircutting, and the use of musical instruments during these fifty days, ostensibly alluding to a plague that decimated the disciples of R. Akiba during this period.[11]

Israel Knohl's doctoral thesis has, in my opinion, demonstrated beyond any doubt that H is both a later stratum and a redaction of P.[12] Leviticus 23, I submit, can prove decisive for his thesis. The formula *wĕhiqrabtem ʾiššeh laYHWH* 'you shall present a food-gift to the Lord' appears frequently throughout this chapter (vv. 25, 27, 36 *bis*, 37). It is H's "cf." But what is its referent? Since the formula refers to public sacrifices for festivals at the sanctuary, its only referent can be Numbers 28–29 (P). Of course, it can be argued that the antecedent source may not be in Scripture. However, that the public sacrifices alluded to in Leviticus 23 must be those of Numbers 28–29 can be demonstrated on other

---

9. Cf. G. Dalman, *Arbeit und Sitte in Palästina* (Gütersloh: Bertelsmann, 1928) 1/2.318–29, 460–61; O. Keel, "Erwägungen zum Sitz im Leben vormosäischen Pascha und zur Etymologie von *psḥ*," *ZAW* 84 (1972) 414–32.

10. Jerusalem edition (1959) 241, a reference I owe to our celebrant, Moshe Greenberg; see M. Greenberg, "Religion: Stability and Ferment," in *The Ages of the Monarchies: Culture and Society* (ed. A. Malamat; Jerusalem: Massada, 1979) 297 n. 22.

11. See *b. Yeb.* 62b [bar.]; *Shulḥan ʿArukh, ʾOraḥ Ḥayyim* 493:1–3.

12. I. Knohl, *The Sanctuary of Silence* (Jerusalem: Magnes, 1992) [Heb.].

grounds. It should be noticed that the only festivals in Leviticus 23 that do list public sacrifices are the grain offerings, the barley in vv. 12–13 and the wheat in vv. 18–19. The first, however, is entirely omitted in Numbers, and the second, the wheat offering, is in Numbers, but it differs in the amounts (compare Lev 23:18 with Num 28:27). Thus this chapter uses the formula *wĕhiqrabtem ᵓiššeh laYHWH* whenever it agrees with Numbers 28–29 (P), but it enumerates the sacrifices whenever it doesn't.

Finally, a logical consideration can clinch the argument. Nearly every critic has held, heretofore (under the assumption that P is later than H), that the calendar of Numbers 28–29 was composed subsequent to Leviticus 23 (H). Since in this allegedly later chapter H, takes pains to specify the sacrifices for the grain offerings, we would have to conclude that the category, species, and number of sacrifices unmentioned for the remaining festivals (Unleavened Bread, v. 8; Warning Blasts, v. 25; Purgation, v. 27; and Booths, v. 36 [2x]) would be left to the discretion (or whim) of the sanctuary! The absurdity of this deduction suffices, in itself, to demonstrate that Leviticus 23 is wholly dependent on an antecedent source, which can only be Numbers 28–29 (P). Thus Numbers 28–29 (P) must be prior to and the basis of Leviticus 23 (H), implying the possibility that H, in general, is the probable heir and redactor of P.

It should be noted that this *ᶜōmer*-day is neither a pilgrimage (*ḥag*) nor a fixed date nor a day of rest. This text therefore represents the pre-Hezekian firstfruits offering of the grain (labelled H₁), on which H₃, the main H strand, is based, as will be explained below.

An interpolator, H₂ (bold underlined), is the "Sunday Pentacostalist."[13] He sets the barley offering for the first Sunday after the week (ending with the Sabbath) during which the harvest has begun. His purpose is to provide a collective offering for farmers in a localized area (where the grain ripens at approximately the same time) and, thereby, create a celebratory event, a mini-*ḥag* (in the spirit of the wheat offering of Exod 23:16a), at the local sanctuary. The selection of Sunday was inevitable: it is the extension of the Sabbath. While in the celebratory mode of the Sabbath, the farmer and his family can easily and willingly make the short trip to their sanctuary before donning the clothes and woes of the working week. Again, it should be stressed that this firstfruit offering is independent of the approximately concurrent Festival of Unleavened Bread. Later interpreters, however, made this connection because they understood the word *šabbat* to mean the Sabbath day (rather than the sabbath-week), which they fixed either within or following the Passover week. These interpretations led to sectarian schools, mentioned above.[14]

---

13. The apt epithet coined by H. L. Ginsberg (oral communication).

14. It is of relevance to note that some Jewish sects (e.g., the Mesuri of Baalbeck and Boktan) began their pentacontad count on the first Sunday after the harvest began (cited by M. Haran, *Temples and Temple-Service in Ancient Israel* (Oxford: Clarendon, 1978; reprinted Winona Lake, Ind.: Eisenbrauns, 1985) 516.

Independently and, perhaps coevally, while presuming the existence of a barley offering (N.B., *minḥâ ḥădāšâ* 'a *new* cereal offering', Num 28:26a), P prescribes a *public* (sanctuary) firstfruits wheat offering (quantity unspecified) fifty days later (*běšābû^cōtêkem* 'in your Festival of *Weeks*', also 28:26a) at a *regional* sanctuary ('in *your* Festival of Weeks'), integrated into a series of fixed sacrifices (Num 28:27–30). The presumed barley offering was probably omitted from a list of public sacrifices in the calendar of Numbers 28–29 because it was brought by the individual farmer (see Exod 23:16a, Lev 2:14).[15] Possibly each sanctuary dedicated (by the *těnûpâ*) the collected sheaves on a fixed day, unaccompanied by other sacrifices, which then became the first day of the seven-week counting. No date is given because the grain may have ripened at different times among the various regional sanctuaries.[16] Neither the barley nor the wheat offering was declared an official *ḥag* (N.B. *ûběyôm* 'and on the day', not *ûběḥag* 'and on the pilgrimage', Num 28:26a). According to P, the offerers remained at home to tend to their harvest, while the sanctuary offered the requisite sacrifices on their behalf. H₂, however, by his interpolation of *mimmāḥŏrat haššabbāt*, tries to turn both grain festivals into mini-pilgrimages to the local sanctuary, an attempt that is vitiated by H₃.

H₃ (bold italic type) comprises the main strand of this chapter. It is the true H, the work of the school reflecting the sanctuary in Jerusalem.[17] It supplements the text by converting the individual's barley and wheat offerings into collective public sacrifices and integrating them into an array of fixed sacrifices, borrowed from Numbers 28–29 (P). This time, however, it cannot follow its customary "cf." notation *wěhiqrabtem ^ɔiššeh* (as in vv. 8, 25, 27, 36) because it prescribes a slightly different series of sacrifices for the wheat offering (vv. 18–19), and it innovates a public sacrifice for the barley offering (vv. 12–13). It also drops P's term for the pentacontad *běšābū^cōtêkem* 'in your Festival of Weeks', since it has no choice but to accept the text's (interpolated) term for weeks, *šabbātôt*. But it does borrow P's declaration that the day of the wheat offering must be observed as a sacred occasion requiring rest from laborious work (v. 21aβ; compare Num 28:26b), adding that the Israelites remain at home (*běkol-mōšěbōtêkem* 'in all your settlements', v. 21b), implying that this day is not a *ḥag*.

Furthermore, H₃ totally abolishes the individual farmer's offerings, as predicated by H₁ and H₂. Its grounds are purely pragmatic. Surely farmers cannot be expected to pilgrimage to a regional sanctuary together with their families and dependents (see Deut 16:11, 14). Instead, it ordains that, henceforth, it is the sanctuary's responsibility to supply both the barley and wheat firstfruit

15. Cf. J. Milgrom, *Leviticus 1–16* (AB 3; New York: Doubleday, 1991) 192–93.

16. As much as by a month; see S. Talmon, "Divergences in Calendar Reform in Ephraim and Judah," *VT* 8 (1958) 48–74; reprinted in "Jeroboam's Cultic Calendar Reform," *King, Cult and Calendar in Ancient Israel* (Jerusalem: Magnes, 1986) 113–39, esp. pp. 120–23.

17. See Knohl, *Sanctuary of Silence*, 185–208.

offerings.[18] The emphasis by both priestly sources, P and H, that the wheat offering is not a pilgrimage festival may also be an undisguised polemic opposing
the inclusion of this day among the required pilgrimage festivals (prescribed
by Exod 34:22a, 23; Deut 16:10, 16).

The parallel development of the grain offerings in the other cultic calen-
dars of the Bible has been illumined by H. L. Ginsberg.[19] He postulates that
the oldest rite is reflected in Exod 23:16a, 19a (E), which presumes that there
was a *ḥag* for the firstfruits of *barley* at the local sanctuary. Thus E would have
anticipated H_2's *ʿōmer* offering. Deut 16:9–11 (D) postpones the *ḥag* for seven
weeks to the end (*sic*) of the wheat harvest.[20] No firstfruits are required (they
can be brought any time, Deut 26:1–11), only a generous bounty from each
landowner that he and his family are willing to share with the underprivileged.

It has been proposed that Leviticus 23 comprises a three-layered development of the barley and wheat firstfruit offerings (vv. 9–21), as follows: (1) The

---

18. Contra Knohl, ibid., 209. H is not characterized by "its openness to the creative layers
of the people"—at least, not to judge by Leviticus 23. As demonstrated, H_3 has not only deprived
the individual farmer of his local sanctuary but also of the experiential joy of presenting his private offering to his God. But at least D substituted the pilgrimage and its attendant offerings for
the loss of local sanctuary. H, however, abolished (rather, declined to require) the pilgrimage to a
central sanctuary for the wheat offering. The Israelite farmers would have had a day of rest but no
worship and no religious joy.

19. Ginsberg, *Israelian Heritage*, 47–61.

20. Ginsberg's entire reconstruction is problematic, since seven weeks after the beginning of
the barley harvest only marks the *beginning* of the wheat harvest. (His opinion is held by many
scholars, for example, Haran, *Temples and Temple-Service*, 295; J. Licht, *EM* 7.492; and many
commentators, such as Kalisch, Dillmann, and Bertholet.) This notion is refuted by agricultural
realia, as noted by the rabbis: (1) "the beginning of the barley harvest till the end of the wheat
harvest is three months" (*Ruth Rab.* 5). But three months after Nisan 16 is Tammuz 16, not any
date in Sivan. (2) The rabbis knew of years when no wheat had ripened by the time of the festival
(*t. Menaḥ.* 10.33). Indeed Dalman (*Arbeit und Sitte*, 417) reports that on May 26, 1926, when the
Festival of Weeks was celebrated in Jerusalem, the wheat harvest had not yet begun. (3) "R. Akiba
said: The Torah has required to bring the *ʿōmer* of barley on Passover because it is the season of
barley, so that the wheat harvest would be blessed on its account. It required bringing firstfruits (of
wheat) on Pentecost because it is the season of wheat, so that on its account the produce of fruit-
bearing trees will be blessed" (*t. Suk.* 3.18). Thus the *ʿōmer* of barley and the firstfruits of the
wheat are to be brought at the *beginning* of their respective seasons.

One could object (as did the priestly schools H and P) that the beginning of the wheat harvest
is hardly a propitious time to undertake a pilgrimage. But my student David Stewart, an erstwhile
farmer, informs me on the basis of his experience and research (citing R. F. Peterson, *Wheat: Bot-
any, Cultivation, and Utilization* [London: Leonard Hill, 1965]; and E. J. M. Kirby, "Significant
Stages of Ear Development in Winter Wheat," in *Wheat Growing and Modelling* [ed. W. Day and
R. K. Atkin; New York: Plenum, 1984] 7–24) that of the final stages of ripeness, the "fully-ripe"
and the "dead-ripe," the early "fully-ripe" must be the firstfruits and that "while waiting for the
entire crop to be ready, i.e., waiting for 'dead-ripeness', one could take a break from farming
chores, take a pilgrimage to a nearby sanctuary bearing firstfruits and not miss the ideal moment
to begin the harvest in earnest." Thus D's establishment of the Feast of Weeks as a national *ḥag*
(Deut 16:10; compare Exod 34:22a) is not as irrational as it sounds.

earliest text (H_1) prescribes that each landowner bring his offerings, fifty days apart, to his individual sanctuary. (2) An interpolator (H_2), attempting to co-ordinate these offerings for a joint sanctuary rite on the same day at each sanc-tuary, fixed the date of the barley offering on the first Sunday following the week (ending in Sabbath) during which the harvest began, thereby assuring that the wheat offering, occurring (by tradition) fifty days later, would also fall on Sunday. (3) The final stage (H_3) represents the Hezekian period, reflecting the sanctuary in Jerusalem. In the throes of the harvest season, most Israelites could not take the time to present their firstfruits in person. Therefore, follow-ing the precedent of the cultic calendar of public sacrifices endorsed by prior regional sanctuaries (Numbers 28–29), H_3 converts the hitherto individual grain offerings into public sacrifices operated by Jerusalem, the main regional sanc-tuary, which are described in detail because they either differ with P (concern-ing the wheat) or fill in a lacuna of P (concerning the barley).

What Did Laban Demand of Jacob?
A New Reading of Genesis 31:50
and Exodus 21:10

JONATHAN PARADISE
University of Minnesota

I

Gen 31:44–54 contains the account of the pact concluded between Laban and Jacob. The episode follows on the heels of the dramatic description of Jacob's stealthy flight from Haran with his wives, family, and flocks. The flight culminates with Laban's unsuccessful search for his stolen *teraphim*. The denouement portrays Jacob venting his spleen for all the misery and toil he has endured during the previous twenty years and concludes with Laban suggesting that they make a covenant between them. The second half of that treaty is clear enough: it is a mutual nonaggression pact stipulating that neither party will cross the border with hostile intent against the other. But it is the first provision of the pact, contained in v. 50, that bears a reexamination and forms the subject of this study. The passage reads:

אִם תְּעַנֶּה אֶת בְּנֹתַי, וְאִם תִּקַּח נָשִׁים עַל בְּנֹתַי—אֵין אִישׁ עִמָּנוּ—רְאֵה אֱלֹהִים עֵד בֵּינִי וּבֵינֶךָ

Virtually all exegetical traditions[1] have translated the verse,

> If you ill-treat (or: mistreat) my daughters or take wives in addition to my daughters (beside my daughters), though no one else be with us, remember God himself will be witness between you and me.

---

1. For rabbinic treatment of ענה (as a "privative *Piel*") that differs from the standard translations, see *b. Ketub.* 47b and *Tosapot.*

The starting point of this discussion is the use of the verb תְּעַנֶּה. All have assumed as a matter of course that the verb[2] is to be rendered as a *Piel* used in
its common factitive[3] function. Accordingly, the verb, תְּעַנֶּה would mean 'to
make miserable, to afflict, mistreat'. This is the same verb that is used to describe the affliction imposed on the Hebrew slaves by the Egyptians, לְמַעַן עַנֹּתוֹ
בְּסִבְלֹתָם (Exod 1:11); as well as the violent rape (that is, forcible submission)
described in the Amnon-Tamar story, וַיְעַנֶּהָ וַיִּשְׁכַּב אֹתָהּ (2 Sam 13:14); and the
rape of Dinah by Shechem, וַיִּשְׁכַּב אֹתָהּ וַיְעַנֶּהָ (Gen 34:2). Similarly, in the
Samson-Delilah episode (Judg 16:5), this verb is used as Delilah tries to learn
the means whereby she may overpower Samson, בַּמֶּה נוּכַל לוֹ, וַאֲסַרְנֻהוּ לְעַנֹּתוֹ.

Are these translations signifying 'suffering and oppression' what the author has in mind in his wording of Laban's transfer of his daughters to Jacob?
I think not. In my view, Laban is not referring to any *physical* abuse of his
daughters. Rather, we are dealing with very practical, legal-economic matters,
such as might be found in a marriage contract.

I will argue further that תְּעַנֶּה, as used in this passage, should be taken as
an instance of a privative *Piel*. This use of the *Piel*, though far less commonly
attested, has the sense of 'taking away', 'removing' or 'depriving' of the substance designated by the **noun** that underlies a denominative *Piel*. Examples of
the *privative Piel* include: לְדַשְּׁנוֹ (דֶּשֶׁן) 'to clear the alter of fat' (Exod 27:3);
וְחִטְּאוֹ (חֵטְא) to remove the *sin-pollution*, hence 'purify' (Num 19:19); לְבַבְתִּנִי
(לֵבָב) אֲחֹתִי כַלָּה, לִבַּבְתִּנִי בְּאַחַד מֵעֵינַיִךְ 'You have taken away my heart' (Cant
4:9);[4] וְשֵׁרֶשְׁךָ מֵאֶרֶץ חַיִּים (שֶׁרֶשׁ) 'God will uproot you from the land of the living'
(Ps 52:7). Similarly in Job 31:12, כִּי אֵשׁ הִיא עַד־אֲבַדּוֹן תֹּאכֵל וּבְכָל־תְּבוּאָתִי תְשָׁרֵשׁ
'A fire burning down to Abaddon / Destroying the roots of all my increase'. No
doubt, the best-known example of the privative *Piel* is 'to stone' לְסַקֵּל[5] and 'to
remove stones' לְסַקֵּל.[6]

As an instance of a privative *Piel*, the verb תְּעַנֶּה assumes an underlying
noun ענה. This suggests that there is a connection between תְּעַנֶּה and the noun
עֹנָה—the same עֹנָה that appears as a technical term in Exod 21:10 as part of the

2. As is well known, the consonants ע-נ-ה represent a number of separate meanings and roots
that are attested in a large number of the Semitic languages. They include 'to be miserable, to turn
back, to change, to end, to turn (away from / toward) to take trouble with, take pains concerning,
to occupy one's self / be busy with, be concerned for'; cf. *HALAT*, p. 805.

3. See the discussion in Bruce K. Waltke and M. O'Connor, *An Introduction to Biblical Hebrew Syntax* (Winona Lake, Ind.: Eisenbrauns, 1990) 405.

4. Cant 4:9 gains in significance since it provides an example of the privative *Piel* where a
person is deprived of something.

5. Exod 17:4 and passim.

6. Isa 5:2, 62:10. English also provides examples of verbs indicating the removal or taking
away of a substance, for example: *to skin, to bone, to peel*. See Waltke and O'Connor, *Introduction*,
411–12. As they have noted, סָקַל does not rest on an attested noun, סקל 'stone'.

trio of items that a slave owner must provide a woman whom he has acquired,[7] should he subsequently acquire still another woman. In that event, he may not, according to Exod 21:10, diminish her עֹנָה (that is, the first woman's). Thus the Genesis narrative, according to my proposed reading, represents Laban as concerned that Jacob not deprive the two co-wives, Leah and Rachel, of their עֹנָה. Let us turn now to a consideration of this term.

II

Exod 21:7–11 reads:

⁷וְכִי־יִמְכֹּר אִישׁ אֶת־בִּתּוֹ לְאָמָה לֹא תֵצֵא כְּצֵאת הָעֲבָדִים: ⁸אִם־רָעָה בְּעֵינֵי אֲדֹנֶיהָ אֲשֶׁר־לֹא [לוֹ] יְעָדָהּ וְהֶפְדָּהּ לְעַם נָכְרִי לֹא־יִמְשֹׁל לְמָכְרָהּ בְּבִגְדוֹ־בָהּ: ⁹וְאִם־לִבְנוֹ יִיעָדֶנָּה כְּמִשְׁפַּט הַבָּנוֹת יַעֲשֶׂה־לָּהּ: ¹⁰אִם־אַחֶרֶת יִקַּח־לוֹ שְׁאֵרָהּ כְּסוּתָהּ וְעֹנָתָהּ לֹא יִגְרָע: ¹¹וְאִם־שְׁלָשׁ־אֵלֶּה לֹא יַעֲשֶׂה לָהּ וְיָצְאָה חִנָּם אֵין כָּסֶף:

When a man sells his daughter as a slave, she shall not be freed as male slaves are. If she proves to be displeasing to her master, who designated her for himself, he must let her be redeemed; he shall not have the right to sell her to outsiders, since he broke faith with her. And if he designated her for his son, he shall deal with her as is the practice with free maidens. If he marries another, he must not withhold[8] from this one her food, her clothing, or her conjugal rights. If he fails her in these three ways,[9] she shall go free, without payment.

Many commentators[10] have assumed that the word 'three', which appears in v. 11, refers to the three *items* that are mentioned in v. 10. However, this reading is difficult for two reasons. First, because of the operative verb יַעֲשֶׂה, which is best

---

7. That is, he has acquired her either in order to marry her himself or to give in marriage to his son.

8. Note the choice of words: אם אחרת יקח לו שארה כסותה וענתה לא יגרע. The NJPSV follows *Targum Onqelos*, לא ימנע, in translating 'withhold'. The NEB and REB opt for 'shall not *deprive*', which allows one to have it both ways. Most have translated 'he shall not *diminish*'. Despite a few biblical passages where גרע clearly does mean 'to take away, withdraw' (cf. Num 27:4, Job 36:7), most biblical instances of this verb are best rendered by 'reduce, diminish, restrict'. The NJPSV, in translating 'withhold', may have been unduly influenced by *Targum Onqelos* and hence chose to translate closer to the range of meanings of גרע = 'to shear off, shave', thus 'withhold'. But inasmuch as the verb in our passage governs clothing and *food* (in addition to עֹנָה), it would seem somewhat draconian if the master were to contemplate totally withholding these items.

9. See below for a discussion of what 'these three' refers to.

10. However, see Nahum M. Sarna, *Exodus* (The JPS Torah Commentary; Philadelphia: Jewish Publication Society, 1991) 121: "Any of the aforementioned possibilities: marriage to the master, or to his son, or allowing her to be redeemed." This is the interpretation presented already in *Mekilta de Rabbi Ishmael*, ad loc.

rendered 'to treat' (as indeed it is used in this pericope in v. 9), כְּמִשְׁפַּט הַבָּנוֹת יַעֲשֶׂה לָּהּ. This is precisely the sense of its Akkadian analogue *epēšu* in comparable legal contexts. If the writer had intended to refer to the *items* in v. 10, he would have used the verb יִתֵּן rather than יַעֲשֶׂה. But more importantly, the structure of the section suggests that the 'three' refers to the three alternate legal scenarios that were dealt with in the subsections of the legal situation introduced in v. 7. Each of the three alternate legal options is introduced with the word אִם.

Thus, if the girl is displeasing to the master and

1. he has her redeemed, then he may only sell her back to kin, not to outsiders (עם נכרי); or:

2. he assigns her to his son, then he must treat her as a free maiden, not as a slave girl; or:

3. he takes another maiden (who is more to his liking), then he must not diminish. . . .

And if he does not act on (any of) these three legal options, the maiden goes free without any payment.

The Hebrew עֹנָתָהּ rendered 'conjugal rights' in the NJPSV translation cited above uses the usual euphemism for sexual relations. According to this interpretation, the law assures the woman that her master may not diminish the frequency with which he visits her for the purpose of sexual intercourse.[11]

Nearly thirty years ago, Shalom M. Paul[12] took issue with this translation of עֹנָתָהּ, arguing that evidence from a variety of cuneiform documents—law collections and private documents—that spanned a broad chronological range shed light on the meaning of עֹנָה in the Covenant Code formulation. The cuneiform texts, according to Paul, show that there was an invariable formula that made up a wife's basic allotment: grain, oil/ointments, and clothing. These three items constituted a legal cliche. The terms are: (in Sumerian) ŠE.BA.Ì.BA SÍG.BA and (in Akkadian) *eprum, piššatum, lubuštum.*

Paul argued that, in view of the frequent and regular occurrence of this triad of commodities, they should be equated with the biblical שְׁאֵר, כְּסוּת, and עֹנָה. Thus שְׁאֵר was the biblical equivalent of *eprum* 'food', כְּסוּת was parallel to *lubuštum* 'clothing', and, perforce, עֹנָה was the functional equivalent of *pišša-*

---

11. What makes this passage a bit more interesting is that in postbiblical Jewish law, it is this verse that serves as *one* basis for defining the minimum annuity that every husband must provide his wife: food, clothing, and sex. Although all rabbinic authorities accept food, clothing, and sexual needs as constituting the husband's minimal obligation, the various legal opinions use the three terms, כְּסוּת, שְׁאֵר, and עֹנָה differently in order to arrive at the conclusion that these are the three items that must be provided. The most common explanation was that עֹנָה 'season' is to be understood as a euphemism for intercourse that occurs at regular intervals.

12. S. Paul, "Exodus 21:10: A Threefold Maintenance Clause," *JNES* 28 (1969) 48–53. (Paul follows the general view that the phrase אם שלש אלה refers to שארה כסותה וענתה; see p. 49.)

tum 'oil or ointment'. The attractiveness of Paul's suggestion lay in the parallel it drew between biblical and cuneiform legal practices and the light it shed on the long-standing difficulty in interpreting the meaning of עֹנָה.

However attractive this solution was, the question of the etymology of עֹנָה has remained a problem. For, although long-standing explanations existed for the figurative use of שְׁאֵר and the meaning of כְּסוּת[13] was clear, Paul was unable to supply an etymology for עֹנָה meaning 'ointments'. He therefore suggested that עֹנָה is a hapax legomenon with the meaning 'ointments'.

That the three commodities, food, clothing, and ointments, constituted a widespread formula in a variety of documents and periods cannot be denied. Nevertheless, there is another Akkadian term used in legal formulations pertaining to support and maintenance that may lead us closer to the plain sense of עֹנָה in Exod 21:10, while also pointing us toward a reasonable etymological derivation. At the same time, the Akkadian term will be a stepping-stone toward understanding what it was that concerned Laban in the pact with his son-in-law.

The first example is an Old Babylonian record of a court case from Sippar, dating to the reign of Sin-muballit.[14] ᶠHaliyatum had established ᶠAmat-Shamash as heir with the condition that she provide Haliyatum with maintenance. The document records that Amat-Shamash has not fulfilled the obligation, and thus her right to the legacy is being taken away.

(1) *aplūt Ḫaliyatum* (2) *ša ana* GEMÉ ᵈUTU DUMU.GAL *Yaqubi* (3) *iddinu* (4) *lubūšam piššatam* (5) *piqittaša ul iddimma.* . . . (9) *Ḫaliyatim* GEMÉ ᵈUTU *ina aplūtiša issuḫ.*

(1) (Regarding) the legacy of Haliyatum that she had bequeathed to Amat-Shamash, daughter of Yaqubi. (Subsequently) She (Amat-Shamash) did not give clothing, ointment, her maintenance . . . (9) Haliyatum took her legacy away from Amat-Shamash.

13. All three terms have provided grist for commentators' mills. Multiple occurrences of כְּסוּת in clear contexts indicated that 'clothing' was a reasonable translation. Cf. Exod 22:26; Deut 22:12; Isa 50:3; Job 24:7, 26:6, 31:19, 50:3. שְׁאֵר meaning 'meat/flesh' appears in Mic 3:2–3:

שֹׂנְאֵי טוֹב וְאֹהֲבֵי רָעָה [רָע] גֹּזְלֵי עוֹרָם מֵעֲלֵיהֶם וּשְׁאֵרָם מֵעַל עַצְמוֹתָם: וַאֲשֶׁר אָכְלוּ שְׁאֵר עַמִּי וְעוֹרָם מֵעֲלֵיהֶם הִפְשִׁיטוּ וְאֶת־עַצְמֹתֵיהֶם פִּצֵּחוּ וּפָרְשׂוּ כַּאֲשֶׁר בַּסִּיר וּכְבָשָׂר בְּתוֹךְ קַלָּחַת:

But you hate good and love evil. / You have devoured My people's flesh; / You have flayed the skin off them, / And their flesh off their bones. / And after tearing their skins off them, / And their flesh off their bones, / And breaking their bones to bits, / You have cut it up as into a pot, / Like meat in a caldron (syntax rearranged to follow the NJPSV).

In Ps 78:20, שְׁאֵר is paralleled by לֶחֶם, both meaning 'food' here:

הֲגַם לֶחֶם יוּכַל תֵּת, אִם יָכִין שְׁאֵר לְעַמּוֹ

But can He provide bread? Can He supply His people with meat?
14. CT 2 31.

Of particular interest is the term *piqittu* in the phrase in lines 4–5: *lubūšam piššatam piqittaša ul iddimma.* . . . 'She, (i.e, Amat-Shamash) did not give clothing, ointment—her maintenance'.

A similar context is furnished in CT 8 20a, lines 31ff. In this text, a man bequeaths an itemized list of property to his adopted daughter. Her inheritance will pass to Sin-shaduni, an adopted brother, who contracts to furnish her annually with 12 *qa* of oil and 5 (?) of another item (the tablet is broken) for as long as she lives. If Sin-shaduni fails to provide these to her, she may disinherit him: *lubūšam piššatam u piqittam ul idiššim* . . . 'If Sin-shadunni does not provide her with clothing, ointment, and maintenance, she may remove him from his legacy'.

The word *piqittu*, derived from the verbal stem *paqādu* and cognate with Hebrew פָּקַד, has several meanings, among them 'to care for, to provide'. The noun *piqittu* is simply 'care, maintenance'—items that are supplied or furnished. It is clear from the numerous texts where *piqittu* or its verbal cognate *paqādu* is used, that the usage is not restricted to a particular area of activity or to specific items. Rather a general meaning, amounting to 'what is required', is indicated.[15]

It seems likely that in the texts in which three categories are used and the third term is *piqittu*, the word *piqittu* does not represent a separate item but rather is a **comprehensive** term. This raises the possibility that in Exod 21:10, we are also dealing with a statement of two discrete items, followed by a general summarizing term, namely, 'her food, her clothing—that is her upkeep'. Significantly, what the use of *piqittu* illustrates is that we do not have a consistent and unvarying use of the triad 'food, clothing, and ointments'.

Akkadian has a number of ways of expressing the idea of maintaining support, or fulfilling a need or an obligation. An analysis of one of the most common, using the verb *apālu*, can point the way to understanding why the Hebrew root ענה is used in Exod 21:10 to express something furnished or supplied. At Alalakh, for example, we have an adoption agreement whose purpose is to secure old-age support for the adoptive father in exchange for property that will be given to the adopted son. The adoptee agrees to provide life-long satisfaction of his adoptive father's needs. *The Alalakh Tablets* (ed. D. J. Wiseman) No. 16 states:

(4) *adi bal(bal)ṭat* (5) *ittanappalšu* (6) *matimê* ¹*Tulpuri* (7) *imâtma minummê* ḪA.LA *zittašu* (9) *kala mimmašu* . . . (11) *ša* ¹*Tulpuri* (12) *ša Illimilimma.*

As long as he lives, he shall regularly satisfy him. When Tulpuri dies, all the property of Tulpuri shall belong to Illimilimma.

15. See, for example, CT 6 45: '1 *kur* 60 *qa* of grain, 240 *qa* of food (epru = ŠE.BA), 6 *qa* of oil (= Ì.BA), 1 shekel of silver for clothing—on six festivals she will furnish (*ipaqizi*): 10 *qa* of flour and 1 piece of meat in each year, as long as Amat-Shamash lives, 'Narubtum will give her' (Narubtum was the adopted daughter).

The verb *apālu* is widely used to indicate satisfying a need or fulfilling an obligation. It is also the common Akkadian verb for 'to answer'.[16] Moreover, like Hebrew ענה 'to answer', it also means 'to provide, take care of, attend to the needs of'. This use of ענה has long been noted in the Bible. For example: (1) Gen 41:16, אֱלֹהִים יַעֲנֶה אֶת שְׁלוֹם פַּרְעֹה 'God will see to Pharaoh's welfare'; (2) Qoh 10:19, וְהַכֶּסֶף יַעֲנֶה אֶת הַכֹּל 'Money satisfies every need' (takes care of everything); (3) finally, in Hos 2:23, we see a beautiful use of ענה with multiple nuances, 'to respond, to furnish, to satisfy':[17]

וְהָיָה בַּיּוֹם הַהוּא אֶעֱנֶה נְאֻם־יְהוָה אֶעֱנֶה אֶת־הַשָּׁמַיִם וְהֵם יַעֲנוּ אֶת־הָאָרֶץ:
וְהָאָרֶץ תַּעֲנֶה אֶת־הַדָּגָן וְאֶת־הַתִּירוֹשׁ וְאֶת־הַיִּצְהָר וְהֵם יַעֲנוּ אֶת־יִזְרְעֶאל:

On that day, I will respond—declares the Lord—I will respond to the sky, and it shall respond to the earth; And the earth shall furnish new grain, wine, and oil, and they shall satisfy Jezreel.

The Hebrew noun עִנְיָן, despite the lateness of its occurrence in the Bible (Qoh 2:26, 3:10, 4:8, and passim), should not be ignored. It means a 'care, concern'. Also noteworthy is the Arabic cognate *ʿana*, with its meanings 'to take care of, be concerned about', and in particular, in the III form, 'to see to it, to spend effort on, to be preoccupied with'.[18]

The biblical עֹנָה should thus be translated by the general term 'needs' rather than either of the specific notions, 'conjugal rights' or 'ointments'. It is possible that the *waw* of וְעֹנָתָהּ is best understood as an instance of the *waw explicativum*,[19] in which case, שְׁאֵר and כְּסֻת are *specific* items followed by a *general* resumptive statement: 'Her food, her clothing, i.e., her needs' וְעֹנָתָהּ.[20]

---

16. See CAD A/2 156ff. Note especially the many legal uses of the verb.

17. Ibn Ezra, in his comment on this Hosea passage, cites the Ecclesiastes verse והכסף יענה את הכל with the gloss, יַמְצִיא = 'furnish'.

18. To be sure, this meaning of ענה 'to take care of' is widespread in the Psalms and other passages where a petition to God is involved, as has long been recognized. Note also the form למען = 'for the sake/benefit of'.

19. Cf. GKC §154a.

20. Using the rabbinic terminology: an instance of פרט וכלל. Additional interesting light may be shed on this subject by the studies of marriage contracts from the Cairo Geniza by Mordecai Friedman, *Jewish Marriage in Palestine: A Cairo Geniza Study* (Tel Aviv and New York: Jewish Theological Seminary of America, 1980) 178. Friedman cites a marriage *ketubba* formula that reads *lazun lĕparnes ûlĕkasôt ʾôtâ* לזון לפרנס ולכסות אותה as reflecting the primary Palestinian formulation 'to provide food, to support the needs, and to provide cover'. Regarding the familiar formula: *wĕʿalay mĕzonaykî ûksutaykî wĕsipuqaykî ûmê ʿal ʿalakî kĕʾorah kol ʾar ʿa* 'I am obligated to provide your food, clothing and needs, and to come to you as the way of all the world', Friedman does not consider *sipuqaykî* as a euphemism for sexual intercourse, inasmuch as this notion is already expressed in the wording וּמֵעַל עַלִיכִי כְּאוֹרַח כָּל אַרְעָא The phrase is the equivalent of לבוא עליך כדרך כל הארץ. Friedman concludes, "Rather it refers to a certain sum that is given to the wife as a fixed allowance. This is a reflex of the statement in the Tractate *Ketubot*, chapter 5, section 9 'he gives her a *maʿah* of silver (a sixth of a dinar) each week for her needs', i.e., for small purchases."

Alternatively, as a specific, discrete item, עֹנָה may refer to a budgeted amount of money that a woman requires in order to fulfill her various and sundry needs.[21]

Returning, in conclusion, to the starting point of this discussion: Laban is concerned with protecting his daughters' marital status, their economic welfare, and the property rights of his grandchildren. Therefore, Jacob may not take any additional wives, since that would certainly alter their status and there would then be the risk that Laban's property could be willed to a child of the "outside" family; furthermore, Jacob must not deprive them of their maintenance or support. Thus Gen 31:50 should be translated:

> May the Lord watch between you and me, when we are out of sight of each other. If you remove my daughters' support, or take wives besides my daughters—though no one else be about, remember, God Himself will be witness between you and me.[22]

---

21. The word וְעֹנָתָהּ should probably be vocalized וַעֲנָתָהּ, similar to other nouns derived from the ל״ה/י verbs. For example, בכות (only in the name אלון הבכות), ראות עינים in Qoh 5:10, גלות (in Obad v. 20, it appears twice written without the *waw*: גָלֻת), פדות, שבות, כסות.

22. Rabbinic exegesis also saw a "privative *Piel*" in Gen 31:50. See above, n. 1. But in keeping with their understanding of ʿona as sexual intercourse, the rabbis explain that Jacob must agree to sleep with his wives on a regular basis. Similarly the rabbis (see *b. Yoma* 77a) derive the *halakic* prohibition against engaging in sexual activity on the Day of Atonement, Yom Kippur, from וְעִנִּיתֶם אֶת־נַפְשֹׁתֵיכֶם (Lev 16:31, 23:27, 32; Num 29:7). Compare NJPSV 'You shall practice self-denial'.

A Lover's Garden of Verse:
Literal and Metaphorical Imagery
in Ancient Near Eastern Love Poetry

SHALOM M. PAUL

The Hebrew University of Jerusalem

In love poetry, amatory allusions abound, and words, expressions, and images ofttimes bear deft erotic *double entendres*, both literal and metaphorical. Here,

Author's note: To Moshe, a fellow gardener in the orchard of Torah.

Abbreviations specific to this essay are:

ISET   S. N. Kramer, M. Çiğ, and H. Kizilyay, *Sumerian Literary Tablets and Fragments in the Archaeological Museum of Istanbul* (Ankara, 1969)

LH   Laws of Hammurabi

MAD 5   I. J. Gelb, *Sargonic Texts in the Ashmolean Museum* (Chicago, 1970)

MAL   Middle Assyrian Laws

Ni   Tablets excavated at Nippur in the Archaeological Museum of Istanbul

TCL 15   H. de Genouillac, *Textes religieux sumériens du Louvre* (Paris, 1930)

UET 6   C. J. Gadd and S. N. Kramer, *Literary and Religious Texts* (London, 1963)

For more information on love poetry in the ancient Near East, see: J. Goodnick Westenholz, "Metaphorical Language in the Poetry of Love in the Ancient Near East," in *La circulation des biens, des personnages et des idées dans le Proche-Orient ancien: XXXVIIIᵉ Rencontre assyriologique internationale* (Paris, 1992) 381–87; idem, "Love Lyrics from the Ancient Near East," in *Civilizations of the Ancient Near East* (ed. J. M. Sasson; New York, 1995) 4.2471–84; W. G. Lambert, "Devotion: The Languages of Religion and Love," in *Figurative Language in the Ancient Near East* (ed. M. Mindlen, M. J. Geller, and J. E. Wansbrough; London, 1987) 25–39; V. Afanasieva, "Zu den Metaphern in einem Lied der heiligen Hochzeit," in *Societies and Languages of the Ancient Near East: Studies in Honor of I. M. Diakonoff* (ed. M. A. Dandamayev; Warminster, 1982) 15–21; H.-P. Müller, *Vergleich und Metapher im Hohenlied* (Göttingen, 1984); O. Keel, *Deine Blicke sind Tauben: Zur Metaphorik des Hohen Liedes* (Stuttgarter Bibelstudien 114–15; Stuttgart, 1984). For other examples of the "complex interplay between literal and figurative rites and actions," see I. Pardes, *Countertraditions in the Bible: A Feminist Approach* (Cambridge, Mass., 1992) 118–43 and notes, pp. 172–76. See also R. Alter (*The Art of Biblical Poetry* [New York, 1985] 185–203) for his description of the "enchanting interfusions between the literal and metaphorical realms" (p. 202) throughout Canticles. I wish to thank both Y. Sefati, for allowing me to see in advance his study of Sumerian love poetry, *Love Songs in Sumerian Literature* (Ramat-Gan, 1997), and Jacob Klein, for his comments on these same love lyrics (written communication).

99

two very popular motifs from the realm of horticulture will be examined: the
garden/orchard and the vineyard.[1]

Garden/Orchard

The motif of the garden/orchard in Sumerian (^{giš}kiri$_6$), Akkadian (*kirû*),[2] Egyptian (*šnw, dd*), and Hebrew (גן)[3] love lyrics functions not only as a favorite
assignation (with its esthetic and sensual delights and hideaways) for lovers'
trysts and *afresco amour*, but may simultaneously allude to female sexuality
and fertility in general[4] and to the pudenda in particular.[5]

1. The same *double entendre* is present in the erotic metaphor of fruits and trees in general
and the apple and apple tree in particular. For fruits and trees as aphrodisiacs, see Lambert, "Devotion," 27–29; M. Held, "A Faithful Lover in an Old Babylonian Dialogue," *JCS* 15 (1961) 30. For
the apple and apple trees and the problem of whether *ḫašḫuru* refers to an apple or not, see Lambert,
"Devotion," 29–31; R. D. Biggs, *ŠÀ.ZI.GA.: Ancient Mesopotamian Potency Incantations* (Locust
Valley, N.Y., 1967) 70 (= KAR 61, lines 8–10), 74 (= KAR 69, lines 4–5), love incantations that
prescribe the sucking of the juice of an apple or pomegranate. For these two, see also the tale of
Enki and Ninhursag, T. Jacobsen, *The Harps that Once . . . : Sumerian Poetry in Translation* (New
Haven, 1987) 183–204; S. N. Kramer and J. Maier, *Myths of Enki, the Crafty God* (New York,
1989) 23–30. B. Alster, "Marriage and Love in the Sumerian Love Songs with Some Notes on the
Manchester Tammuz," in *The Tablet and the Scroll: Near Eastern Studies in Honor of William W.
Hallo* (ed. M. E. Cohen, D. C. Snell, and D. B. Weisberg; Bethesda, Md., 1993) 18 n. 33, 20 n. 43.
Alster follows this identification based on the study of M. A. Powell, "The Tree Section of ur$_5$ (=
ḪAR)-ra = *ḫubullu*," *Bulletin of Sumerian Agriculture* 3 (1987) 153–56. See also M. Civil, "Studies
on Early Dynastic Lexicography III," *Or* 56 (1987) 241; M. Pope, *Song of Songs* (AB 7c; Garden
City, N.Y., 1977) 663. For the possible appearance of the apple in Ebla (*du-bù-u*), see E. Zurro,
"Notes de lexicografía eblaíta: Nomres de árboles y plantas," *Aula Orientalia* 1 (1983) 268–69. For
fruit as designating sexual vigor in love poetry, see Gilgamesh VI 8, "Give me, O give me of
your fruits of love!" (see S. M. Paul, "The 'Plural of Ecstasy' in Mesopotamian and Biblical Love
Poetry," in *Solving Riddles and Untying Knots: Biblical, Epigraphic, and Semitic Studies in Honor
of Jonas C. Greenfield* [Winona Lake, Ind., 1995] 592). Compare also Maqlu III 8–10, "She robs
the handsome man of his vitality. She takes the pretty girl's fruit. With her glance, she steals her
sex appeal" (also lines 11–12; G. Meier, *Die assyrische Beschwörungssammlung Maqlû* [AfO
Beiheft 2: Berlin, 1937]). So, too, in an Old Babylonian text from Kish, B 472 i 7′: *muḫtanbū
inbūka* 'growing luxuriantly is your "fruit"'. See J. Goodnick Westenholz, "A Forgotten Love Song,"
in *Language, Literature and History: Philological and Historical Studies Presented to Erica Reiner*
(AOS 67; ed. F. Rochberg-Halton; New Haven, Conn., 1987) 415–25.

2. See Westenholz, "Love Lyrics," 2482; Lambert, "Devotion," 28; Alster, "Marriage and
Love," 7 n. 26; G. Leick, *Sex and Eroticism in Mesopotamian Literature* (London, 1994) 73–75. The
garden connected to the temple may even have served as the setting for the sacred marriage ritual.

3. So, too, פרדס, Cant 4:13.

4. For "love poetry as an expression of female sexuality," see J. S. Cooper, "Enki's Member:
Eros and Irrigation in Sumerian Literature," in *Dumu-e$_2$-dub-ba-a: Studies in Honor of Åke W.
Sjöberg* (Philadelphia, 1989) 88.

5. Lambert, "Devotion," 28; Westenholz, "Love Lyrics," 2477–78; Pope, *Song of Songs*, 324.
Greek κῆπος and Latin *hortus* also serve a dual function. For the Greek, see the reference to Diogenes Laertius 2.46, cited in H. G. Liddell and R. Scott, *A Greek-English Lexicon* (Oxford, 1940)

Sumerian[6]

The figurative erotic connotations of the garden are well attested in Sumerian Sacred Marriage songs:

a. CT 58 13[7]

24. "He (Dumuzi) made me (Inanna) enter, he made me enter,
25. (My) brother[8] [lit., 'the brother'] made me enter his garden.
26. Dumuzi made me enter his garden,
27. To lie with him at his standing tree;
28. He made me stand with him at his lying tree.[9]
29. By an apple tree,[10] I kneeled as is proper."

So, too, with the same arbor ardor:

b. Ni 4569 iii = *ISET*, I 119/61[11]

11. "The brother b[rought me] into his garden.
12. [Let] me raise his standing tree;
13. [Let] me lay down his lying tree."[12]

c. Ni 9602 = *ISET*, II, plate 16, col. iii[13]

7. "[At her rising from] the pure lap,[14]
8. The shoots and buds [rose up with her].

1.947–48, meaning III, *'pudenda muliebria'*. For the Latin, see the reference in Sir W. Smith (*A Latin-English Dictionary* [London, 1926] 508, meaning 3), who compares it to the Greek. See, too, J. Atkins, *Sex in Literature* (London, 1978) 3.222ff.

6. As is well known, Sumerian abounds with enigmatic difficulties and, as a result, the various translations at times differ greatly one from the other. A few of these divergencies will be noted; for the others, one should consult the bibliography appended to each song.

7. See Alster, "Marriage and Love," 21; S. N. Kramer, *The Sacred Marriage Rite* [hereafter *SMR*] (Bloomington, Ind., 1969) 101; idem, "BM 88318: The Ascension of Dumuzi to Heaven," in *Recueil de travaux de l'association des études du Proche-Orient Ancien* (Montreal, 1984) 2.5–9.

8. 'Brother' in these love lyrics serves as a term of endearment.

9. The 'standing' and 'lying' tree are metaphors for the male member.

10. See above, n. 1.

11. See Alster, "Marriage and Love," 21; Kramer, *SMR*, 101.

12. This is Alster's translation, ibid., 21. Sefati (*Love Songs*) translates, 'I stood with him among his standing trees. I lay down with him among his lying trees'. J. Klein suggests, in turn, another tentative translation: '[Let] me stand with him wherever he stands. [Let] me lie with him wherever he lies' (written communication).

13. Dumuzi-Inanna P. See S. N. Kramer, "Cuneiform Studies and the History of Literature: The Sumerian Sacred Marriage Texts," *PAPS* 107 (1963) 505–7; idem, *SMR*, 59; T. Jacobsen, *The Treasures of Darkness: A History of Mesopotamian Religion* (New Haven, 1976) 46. The present translation is based on a revised edition of the text by Sefati, *Love Songs*.

14. For Sum. úr, the lap or genital area of men or women, see Enlil and Ninhursag, lines 180, 182: "He embraced her; he lay in her lap" (*ANET*, 40). For "the bed of the sweet lap," CT 58 18–19, see W. H. P. Römer, *Sumerische 'Königshymnen' der Isin-Zeit* (Leiden, 1965) 191–92. For the equivalent Akkadian expression, *sūnu*, as a euphemism for sexual parts, see CAD S 387–88.

    9. At her rising from the king's lap,

  10. The flax rose up with her, the barley rose up with her.

  11. The plain has been filled (with abundance) with her like a
       blossoming garden."[15]

  d. TCL 15 20[16]

    1. "It sprouts, it sprouts, sprouts.
       It is the lettuce (i.e., pubic hair)[17] he watered.

    2. In the garden of deep shade, bending down his neck,
       My darling of his mother,

    3. My one who fills the grain in their furrows with beauty,
       It is the lettuce he watered/flooded.

    4. My apple tree (i.e., male member)[18] bearing fruit at its top (i.e.,
       seminal emission),[19]
       It is the garden he watered."

  e. Ni 4171; *ISET*, I, plate 24 (= p. 82)[20]

rev. 10. "My (?) sister (Inanna), I (King Šulgi) would go with you to my
       garden.

  11. My fair sister, I would go with you to my garden.

  12. My sister, I would go with you to my garden. . . .

  13. My sister, I would go with you to my apple tree.[21]

  14. May the . . . of the apple tree be in my hand.

  15. My sister, I would go with you to my pomegranate tree . . .

  17. My sister, I would go with you to my garden.

  18. Fair sister, I would go with you to my garden."

  f. *SRT* 31[22]

  27. "O my budding one, my budding one, sweet is your allure!

---

15. Here the garden is a simile for fertility.

16. Compare duplicates: *UET* 6/1, rev. 121; TIM IX 14; Ni 9846 (*ISET*, II, 87). See Alster, "Marriage and Love," 21; Kramer, "Cuneiform Studies," 508–9; idem, *SMR*, 95–96; Jacobsen, *Harps*, 94. Sefati's translation in *Love Songs* differs radically from the above. He renders: "(1) Growing, flourishing like well-watered lettuce, (2) My garden of the steppe, richly shaded with its blooming, favorite of his mother. (3) My barley full of allure in its furrows, like well-watered lettuce. (4) My choice apple-tree, bearing fruits, like well-watered lettuce." According to him, Inanna is describing her beloved's beauty. Leick (*Sex and Eroticism*, 121–23) interprets: " 'it' = the garden, as the vulva which 'swells' till it reaches an orgasmic climax."

17. Jacobsen, *Harps*, 94. For the symbolism of lettuce, see Leick, *Sex and Eroticism*, 123.

18. Ibid. For the apple tree, see also above, n. 1.

19. Idem, "Two *BAL-BAL-E* Dialogues," in *Love and Death in the Ancient Near East: Essays in Honor of Marvin H. Pope* (ed. J. H. Marks and R. M. Good; Guilford, Conn., 1987) 62 n. 29. See also A. Falkenstein, "Sumerische religiöse Texte," *ZA* 56 (1964) 116, 121–22, and corresponding notes.

20. S. N. Kramer, "Inanna and Šulgi: A Sumerian Fertility Song," *Iraq* 31 (1969) 18–23; idem, *SMR*, 100.

21. Once again the tree in the garden is a metaphor for sexual congress.

22. Jacobsen, "Two *BAL-BAL-E*," 61–62; idem, *Harps*, 98; Kramer, *SMR*, 104–6; B. Alster, "Sumerian Love Songs," *RA* 79 (1985) 146; Y. Sefati, "An Oath of Chastity in a Sumerian Love

28. My budding garden of the apple trees, sweet is your allure!
29. My fruitful garden of the *celtis*-trees, sweet is your allure!"

The metaphor of the garden symbolizing the female also appears in other love lyrics:

g. "The Message of Lú·dingir·ra"[23]

In the third of the five signs that Ludingira gives to a royal courier describing the charms and beauty of his mother, *Šāt Ištar*, he exclaims,

35. "O garden of delight (^{giš}kiri$_6$-la-la = Akk. *kirî lalê*), full of joy."

h. Gudea Cyl. B V 14–15[24]

14. "As she (the goddess Baba) sat down at the side of her, . . .
15. She was the mistress, the daughter of holy An,
    a charming garden (^{giš}kiri$_6$-nisi-ga), bearing fruit
    (kùrun íl-la-àm)."

Akkadian

The erotic nature of the "garden" is also a familiar theme in both Akkadian and Egyptian love poetry:

a. MAD 5:8[25]

6. ". . . , you two beautiful maidens,
7. Blooming are you.

Song (SRT 31)?" in *Bar Ilan Studies in Assyriology Dedicated to Pinḥas Artzi* (ed. J. Klein and A. Skaist; Ramat Gan, 1990) 45–63. Jacobsen, "Two BAL-BAL-E," 61 n. 29: "Lines 27–32 raptly contemplate, as noted, the growing sexual excitement of the customer. . . . Metaphor for the male member is here the apple tree (lines 28–29)." Compare also the ensuing lines, 31–32, in this poem—"O my clear pillar, my clear pillar, sweet are your charms! Pillar of alabaster set in lapis-lazuli, sweet are your charms" (where 'pillar of alabaster' and 'lapis-lazuli' serve as metaphors for the male and female genitalia)—with Cant 5:14b–15a: "His belly is a tablet of ivory adorned with sapphires. His legs are like marble pillars set in sockets of fine gold."

23. The text is known from four tablets of the Old Babylonian period and a couple of trilingual fragments (Sumerian-Akkadian-Hittite), one of which was found at Ugarit. See M. Civil, "The 'Message of Lú-dingir-ra to His Mother' and a Group of Akkado-Hittite 'Proverbs'," *JNES* 23 (1964) 1–11; J. Nougayrol, "Signalement Lyrique (R. S. 25.421)," *Ugaritica* 5 (1968) 313, 315. For additional bibliography, see Westenholz, "Metaphorical Language," 384 nn. 15–19.

24. M. Lambert and R. Tournay, "Le cylindre B de Gudéa," *RB* 55 (1948) 520–43; A. Falkenstein, *Sumerische und akkadische Hymnen und Gebete* (Zürich, 1953) 169–70; Jacobsen, *Harps*, 429 (translation in agreement with Falkenstein). See also Sefati, "Oath," 61. See now E. Jan Wilson, *The Cylinders of Judea* (Neukirchen-Vluyn, 1996) 142–43.

25. This late third-millennium Old Akkadian incantation for love-magic was published by I. J. Gelb, *Sargonic Texts in the Ashmolean Museum* (MAD 5; Oxford, 1970) 7–12. See also J. and Å. Westenholz, "Help for Rejected Suitors: The Old Akkadian Love Incantation MAD V 8," *Or* 46 (1977) 198–219; J. M. Sasson, "A Further Cuneiform Parallel to the Song of Songs?" *ZA* 85 (1973) 359–60. CAD K 413 follows Gelb in reading *ṭurdam* 'send'; J. and Å. Westenholz, on the other hand, favor *turdā*, the second personal dual of *warādu* 'go down'. For *ruḫti* (*ruʾtu*), see AHw 997, 'Speichel, Geifer'. Gelb translates 'spume'.

8. Send / go down to the garden,
9. Send / go down to the garden."

. . . .

17–18. "I leaped into the garden of Sin (*ašḫiṭ kirîš Suen*)"
(i.e., the moon-god, representing the crescent-shaped female
pubic triangle).[26]

b. TIM IX 54   A late Assyrian love lyric dialogue between Nabû and
Tašmētu[27]

13. "[Nabû], my lord, put an earring on me.
14. Let me give you pleasure in the garden (*qereb kirî lulallīka*).

. . . .

rev. 15. For what, for what are you adorned, my Tašmētu?
16. So that I may [go] to the garden with you, my Nabû.
17. Let me go to the garden, to the garden and [   ].
18. Let me go alone to the very beautiful garden (*ana kirî
banbanât*)."[28]

c. BM 41005 obv. ii[29]

9. "As I [went down] into the garden of your (fem.) love[30]

. . . .

13. Zarpānītum will go down to the garden."

('To go down to the garden', Akk. *ana kirî arādu* = Heb. לרדת אל הגנה
[see p. 107 for examples], is a further metaphor for the place and act
of lovemaking.)

d. KAR 158 VII (incipits from love poetry)[31]

---

26. See Jacobsen, "Two *BAL-BAL-E*," 63 n. 29.

27. TIM IX = A. Livingstone, *Court Poetry and Literary Miscellanea* (SAA 3; Helsinki, 1989)
36–37; E. Matsushima, "Le rituel hiérogamique de Nabû," *Acta Sumerologica* 9 (1987) 143–49.

28. The adjective, *banbanâtu*, which also appears in rev. line 24 and in Livingstone, *Court
Poetry*, 13, rev. line 1, is a rare variant of the adjective *babbanû*, fem. *babbanītu* 'of good quality,
beautiful, excellent' (for the latter, see CAD B 7). The reduplication here indicates intensification.
Compare Akk. *dandannu* 'almighty', *kaškaššu* 'overpowering'. See W. von Soden, *Grundriss der
Akkadischen Grammatik* (AnOr 33; Rome, 1952) 71, §57b. It would then be the interdialectal semantic equivalent of Heb. יְפֵה־פִּיָּה, Jer 46:20; יָפְיָפִית, Ps 45:3. See also Matsushima, "Le rituel
hiérogamique de Nabû," 173 n. 18.

29. W. G. Lambert, "The Problem of the Love Lyrics," in *Unity and Diversity* (ed. H. Goedicke
and J. J. M. Roberts; Baltimore, 1975) 104.

30. For the idiom 'to go down to the garden', see the examples cited by J. and Å. Westenholz,
"Help for Rejected Suitors," 212–13. As a metaphor for sexual congress, see Jacobsen, "Two *BAL-
BAL-E*," 62 n. 29; Leick, *Sex and Eroticism*, 191, 196. For its appearance in Hebrew, see the quo-
tations cited from Canticles in this article on p. 107.

31. See E. Ebeling, *Ein Hymnenkatalog aus Assur* (Berliner Beiträge zur Keilschriftforschung
1/3; Berlin, 1922).

26. "She seeks the beautiful garden of your (male) charms (*kirî lalīka*)."

28. "The king[32] goes down to the garden (*ārid kirî šarru*). . . ."

35. "The chief gardener of the pleasure garden[33] (*šandanak kirî ṣīḫāti*)."

Egyptian[34]

a. "I am headed to the 'Love Garden' (*dd*),
   My bosom full of persia (branches/fruits; i.e., allusion to her own fertility), my hair laden with balm."[35]

b. "The goose soars and alights,
   While the ordinary birds circle.
   He has disturbed the garden (*šnw*)."[36]

(The 'goose' = the young male lover; 'ordinary birds' = the other boys; the 'garden' = the young girl.)

c. "I am yours like the field,
   Planted with flowers and all sorts of fragrant plants.[37]

   . . . .

   A lovely place for strolling about,
   With your hand upon mine."[38]

Hebrew

In Cant 4:12–5:1, the female is referred to five times by the term 'garden':

a. 4:12. "A garden locked (גן נעול) is my sister, my bride, a fountain locked, a sealed-up spring." The 'locked garden' (as well as fountain and spring) symbolizes her virginity.[39] (In contrast,

---

32. For the use of 'king' as a term of endearment for a lover, see Paul, "Plural of Ecstasy," 595–96.

33. See Held, "A Faithful Lover," 20; CAD Š/1 374–75.

34. M. V. Fox, *The Song of Songs and the Ancient Egyptian Love Songs* (Madison, Wis., 1985) 283–84. On p. 283, Fox remarks on the theme of the garden/orchard as the setting of lovemaking: "This garden provides privacy and fresh, natural beauties that appropriately frame the lovemaking and are congruent with the lovers' state of mind." On pp. 285–86, he also discusses various motifs of the garden theme in Canticles.

35. Ibid., 15, song 8 and nn. *m* and *n*.

36. Ibid., 20–21, song 11. "The goose landing in a garden . . . represents the boy falling in love with the girl" (p. 21).

37. Cf. Cant 4:13–14.

38. Fox, *Song of Songs*, 26, song 18.

39. Ibid., 137, "The locked garden image both expresses the boy's desire for greater intimacy . . . and praises the girl's modesty and sexual exclusiveness." See also Kramer, *SMR*, 152 n. 17; Pope, *Song of Songs*, 488.

Heb. פתח פתוח 'an opened opening' [cf. *b. Ketub.* 9a–b, 10a, 36b]
and colloquial Arab. *maftûḥa(t)* 'opened' are euphemisms for a
deflowered virgin.[40]) In v. 13, she is compared to an exotic פדדס
'orchard'.

b. 4:15.   She, in turn, responds accordingly by reiterating his imagery:
"The spring in my garden ([ם]מעין גני) is a well of fresh water,
a rill of Lebanon," referring to her sexuality.[41]

c. 4:16.   And she then extends a delectable invitation to her lover to enter
her scented 'garden' and enjoy her sexual charms:

"Awake, O north wind! Come, O south wind!
Blow upon my garden (גני) that its perfumes may spread!
Let my lover come to his garden (גנו)
And eat[42] its luscious fruits."

d. 5:1.   He, in turn, immediately responds to her rapturous call for this
carnal encounter:

"I have come to my garden (גני), my sister, my bride,
I have plucked[43] my myrrh and spices,
Eaten[44] my honey and honeycomb,[45]
Drunk my wine and my milk."

40. See S. H. Stephan, "Modern Palestinian Parallels to the Song of Songs," *JPOS* 2 (1922) 214.

41. The final *mem* in גנים is enclitic. For this literary section, see J. S. Cooper, "New Cuneiform Parallels to the Song of Songs," *JBL* 90 (1971) 161–62.

42. For 'eating', see below, n. 44.

43. For the symbol of 'plucking', see the comment on Cant 6:2 in this article, p. 107.

44. For 'eating' (אכל) and 'drinking' (שתה) as erotic metaphors, compare Prov 5:15, 30:20. For the latter verse, see the comments of W. McKane, *Proverbs* (OTL; Philadelphia, 1970) 658. 'Eating' is also employed in a similar fashion in Rabbinic Hebrew. In *b. Ketub.* 65b, commenting on the Mishnah, 'She is to eat with him on the night of every Sabbath' (= every Friday night), R. Assi interprets 'eating' as לישנא מעליא 'a euphemism' for sexual intercourse and refers to Prov 30:20. For additional examples, see E. Z. Melamed, "Euphemisms and Textual Alterations of Expressions in Talmudic Literature," in *Benjamin de Vries Memorial Volume* (ed. E. Z. Melamed; Jerusalem, 1968) 140 n. 189 [Hebrew]; idem, "Euphemisms and Textual Alterations in the Mishnah," *Leš* 47 (1983) 8 [Hebrew]. So, too, in Mesopotamian poetry. Cf. Gilgamesh VI 68: "Let us eat (*i nīkul*) of your strength!" (also a euphemism for male potency). See Paul, "Plural of Ecstasy," 592 n. 27. See, too, the Seleucid astrological tablet, VAT 7847 + AO 6648, rev. C: "Pisces: Joy of heart. He should make love to his wife, eat fruit, his garden. . . ." F. Weidner, "Gestirnsdarstellung auf babylonischen Tafeln," *Sitzungsberichte ostereichischen Akademie der Wissenschaften* 254/2 (Graz, 1967) 32. Compare also T. Jacobsen's comments in *Toward the Image of Tammuz and Other Essays in Mesopotamian History and Culture* (ed. W. L. Moran; Cambridge, Mass., 1970) 79–80.

45. For the erotic connotations of honey (Sum. làl, Akk. *dišpu*), see Lambert, "Devotion," 21; Alster, "Marriage and Love," 16 n. 7, and p. 22, citing several examples in Sumerian; Kramer, *SMR*, 92–93, 96; Lambert, "Devotion," 21; idem, "Divine Love Lyrics from the Reign of Abi-ešuḫ," *MIO* 12 (1966) 48, 51. Lambert cites VAT 17347, lines 9–10: *duššupu dādūka dišpa išeb*[*bî*] [*kuzu*]*b rāmika* 'Passion for you is sweet; the [appeal] of your love is sat[ed] with honey'. For the expression

The rapid succession of verbs 'pluck', 'eat', 'drink' all allude to his sexual "culinary" enjoyment (cf. also Prov 5:15, 19; 3:20).

e. 6:2.   "My beloved has gone down into his garden (ירד לגנו)[46]
          to the bed of spices,
          To graze[47] in my garden ([ם]בגני),[48]
          and to pick lilies."[49]

Note the very same figure of speech, "going down into the garden,"
with the very same sexual overtones as in the Akkadian citations above,
2c, d. The erotic verbal metaphor of 'picking' (לקט) of lilies here and the
'plucking' (ארה) of spices (5:1) is also paralleled in an Akkadian love
lyric: 'May my (Tašmētu's) eyes behold the plucking of your (Nabû's)
fruit' (qatāpu ša inbīka),[50] where 'fruit'[51] represents the male's sexuality.

f. 6:11. "I went down to the nut garden (אל גנת אגוז ירדתי),[52]
          To see the budding of the vale,
          To see if the vines had blossomed,
          If the pomegranates were in bloom."

That "going down to the garden" (this time to a "nut grove") in order
to verify the vernal horticultural blossoming has sexual overtones becomes patently clear from the next verse (v. 12) where the lover falls
into an amorous ecstatic state.[53] Compare similarly 7:12–14.

g. 8:13. "O you, who linger in the garden (היושבת בגנים),
          Lovers are listening.
          Let me hear your voice!"

Here the garden serves as the preferred venue for the couple in love.

'to taste the honey plant' as an expression for intercourse, see Leick, *Sex and Eroticism*, 121, 123–
24. Compare also KAR 3:144 rev. 3–4; see E. Ebeling, "Beiträge zur Kenntnis der Beschwörungs-
serie Namburbi," *RA* 49 (1955) 182:3–4; H. Zimmern, "Der Schenkenliebeszauber," *ZA* 32 (1918–
19) 174–75, rev. 48–50: *šapātja lu lallāru qātāja lu kuzbu šapāt kipattija lu šapāt dišpi* 'May my
lips be white honey; may my hands be all charm; may the lips of my pudenda be lips of honey'.

    46. For 'going down to the garden' as a metaphor for sexual intercourse, see above, n. 30.
Compare also Cant 6:2, 11. See Westenholz and Westenholz, "Help for Rejected Suitors," 213.

    47. For 'grazing/browsing' as a metaphor for lovemaking, see Fox, *Song of Songs*, 143, 313.

    48. The final *mem* here, as in 4:15, is most likely enclitic. For other interpretations of the plu-
ral form, see ibid., 149.

    49. See R. Gordis (*The Song of Songs and Lamentations* [New York, 1974] 92), who com-
pares the "imagery of the garden as the symbol of the delights of love, which the lover would rather
not share with others," with a Viennese soldier's song, cited by T. Reik, *The Haunting Melody* (New
York, 1953) 83: "Was nutzet mir ein Rosengarten wenn and're drin spazieren gehen?" ('What use
to me a rose garden when others go walking in it?').

    50. Livingstone, *Court Poetry*, 37 (= TIM IX 54), rev. 20; see also rev. 30.

    51. For the metaphor of 'fruit', see above, n. 1.

    52. See Pope, *Song of Songs* (574–79), for the symbolism of 'nuts', which is also employed
as a figure for the female genitalia (p. 579). For this verse in Canticles, see also Müller, *Vergleich
und Metapher*, 40.

    53. S. M. Paul, "An Unrecognized Medical Idiom in Canticles 6, 12 and Job 8, 21," *Bib* 59
(1978) 545–47.

The motif of the garden becomes very predominant in medieval secular poetry, both Hebrew and Arabic.[54] And it also appears in Palestinian love songs.[55]

Compare, for example:

1. "The garden (*bistân*) of your beauty in its bloom
   Is fairer and more resplendent than a flower garden (*bistân*)."
2. "Your breast, O you, is like a pomegranate fruit,
   And your eyes have captured us,
   By God and (by) the Merciful One.
   Your cheek shines as it were a Damascene apple.
   How sweet to pluck it (*janâh*)[56] in the morning,
   And to open the garden (*il-bistân*; i.e., enjoy with you connubial bliss!)."

Vineyard[57]

Heb. כרם 'vineyard' also serves a dual role in the Song of Songs, both literally, as a delightful and appealing outdoor site for a rendezvous, and figuratively, as a symbol for female sexuality. Its literal meaning appears in:

1. 1:6b.   "My mother's sons quarreled with me. They made me guard the vineyards."[58]
2. 1:14.   "My beloved to me is a spray of henna blooms from the vineyards of En-gedi."
3. 8:11.   "Solomon has a vineyard in Baal-Hamon. He had to put guards in the vineyard."[59]

Its figurative erotic usage as a metaphor for female sexuality is present in:

1. 2:15.   The young woman's enigmatic yet provocative call,
            "Catch us the foxes,

54. M. Itzhaki, *Towards the Garden Beds: Hebrew Garden Poems in Medieval Spain* (Tel-Aviv, 1988) [Hebrew]; H. Peres, *La poésie andaluse en Arabe classique au XIème siècle* (Paris, 1953).

55. Stephan, "Modern Palestinian Parallels," 214. Both citations are educed by Pope, *Song of Songs*, 488.

56. For the image of 'plucking', see above, nn. 43, 50.

57. See Müller, *Vergleich und Metapher*, 47; Fox, *Song of Songs*, 102; O. Keel, *Das Hoheleid* (Zürcher Bibelkommentare, AT 18; Zürich, 1986) 56 on 1:6; p. 99 on 2:13; and p. 104 on 2:15.

58. For Ugar. *ngr krm* in a roster of royal personnel (UT 2011.12) and in a mythological fragment (UT 2000.2.1), see Pope, *Song of Songs*, 325.

59. Here one must also be sensitive to a *double entendre*, for the vineyards may also symbolize, as several commentators have noted, nubile women; see Fox, *Song of Songs*, 174–75; Pope, *Song of Songs*, 686, 689; Keel, *Das Hohelied*, 254; G. Gerleman, *Ruth: Das Hohelied* (BKAT 18/2–3; Neukirchen-Vluyn, 1965) 222; R. E. Murphy, *The Song of Songs* (Hermeneia; Minneapolis, 1990) 199. See also M. Falk, *Love Lyrics from the Bible* (Sheffield, 1992) 133.

> The little foxes that ruin vineyards,
> For our vineyard is in blossom!"

symbolizing her ripe bodily charms.[60]

2. 7:13   (which reminds one of the similar description of going down to
          the nut garden, 6:11) symbolizes the girl's budding sexuality as
          well as the site of excitement:

> "Let us go early to the vineyards.
> Let us see if the vine has flowered,
> If its blossoms have opened,
> If the pomegranates are in bloom.
> There I will give my love to you."[61]

3. 8:12. After its literal usage in the former verse (v. 12), the young girl
          contrasts Solomon's thousand vineyards (which may also be a
          sexual reference to a harem) to her very own, that is, her own
          body: "I have my very own vineyard. . . ."[62]

4. 1:6.   She explains that she was punished by her brothers, who made
          her guard their vineyards (literally), because, 'My own vineyard
          I did not guard' (כרמי שלי לא נטרתי)—where 'vineyard' serves as
          a metaphor for her pudenda.[63]

There is an additional nuance here that can be clarified in the light of Akkadian. The verb נטר, which is an Aramaism for Heb. נצר, is also the interdialectal etymological and semantic cognate of Akk. *naṣāru*, which likewise means 'to stand guard, watch' fields and gardens.[64] Compare, for example, *anāku eqlamma anaṣṣarma* 'I will guard the field'.[65] It is likewise employed in reference to taking care and protecting oneself (usually with *ramānu* or *pagru* as its object); compare, for example, *ramānka*[66]/*pagarka uṣur*[67] 'Take care of yourself!' But of particular significance is its employment, with or without an object, in connection with a woman guarding and preserving her chastity. Thus, LH 142:

---

60. See D. Lys, "Notes sur le Cantique," *Congress Volume: Rome, 1968* (VTSup 17; Leiden, 1969) 171–72; Fox, *Song of Songs*, 114; Keel, *Das Hohelied*, 104; W. Rudolph, *Das Hohe Lied* (KAT 27/1–3; Gütersloh, 1962) 135; Gerleman, *Ruth*, 127; Murphy, *The Song of Songs*, 141; Gordis, *The Song of Songs and Lamentations*, 83.
    61. See Fox, *Song of Songs*, 162; Pope, *Song of Songs*, 646.
    62. But see above, n. 59.
    63. See Pope, *Song of Songs*, 323–24, 326; Rudolph, *Das Hohe Lied*, 124; Gerleman, *Ruth*, 101; Keel, *Das Hohelied*, 56; Fox, *Song of Songs*, 102.
    64. CAD N/2 39.
    65. TCL 17 38 rev. 9. See also CAD N/2 35–36.
    66. TCL 18 94:7.
    67. ARM 10 7:11; 80:22; 107:10.

If a woman dislikes her husband and declares, "You shall not have me (sexually)," her case will be examined by her city ward, and if she has kept herself chaste (*naṣrat*) and is blameless, while her husband is philandering and treats her despicably, that woman shall suffer no punishment. She may take her dowry and go to her father's house.

Conversely, LH 143:

If she has not kept herself chaste (*la naṣrat*), but is wayward and squanders her property (and) treats her husband badly, they shall throw that woman into the water.[68]

Compare also LH 133:

If a man has been carried off as a captive, but there is sufficient food in his house. . . . If that woman (his wife) has not kept herself chaste (*pagarša la iṣṣurma*), but enters another man's house, they shall convict that woman and throw her into the water.[69]

So, too, MAL A 12:

If a man seizes another man's wife in the street and says to her, "Let me have intercourse with you," but she refuses and continues to be chaste (*tattanaṣṣar*),[70] but he takes her by force and has intercourse with her . . . , the man shall be put to death; for the woman there is no punishment.

It is also of interest to note that this very same Aramaic verb, נטר, is employed with identical meaning in the *b. Ketub.* 37a, in the course of the discussion concerning how long one must wait before having intercourse with a proselyte and a woman who had been a captive. The opinion of one of the sages is גיורת לא מנטרא נפשה, שבוייה מנטרא נפשה 'A proselyte does not remain chaste (lit., does not protect herself), while a captive woman does'.

Thus, returning to Cant 1:6, the young woman is employing 'vineyard', both figuratively (my bodily self, לא נטרתי 'I have not guarded', meaning 'I have not kept chaste') and literally (to explain the reason for the punishment inflicted upon her by her brothers).

---

68. For a discussion of this section, see G. R. Driver and J. C. Miles, *The Babylonian Laws* (Oxford, 1960) 1.299–303.

69. Ibid., 284–86.

70. For the iterative *tan*-form, see CAD N/2, 46. Cf. also AHw 756b, sub Gtn 3: elliptic, lit., 'she continues to guard (herself)'. Other translations lose the sense of chastity; cf. G. R. Driver and J. C. Miles, *The Assyrian Laws* (Oxford, 1975) 387, 'strenuously defends herself'; G. Cardascia, *Les lois assyriennes* (Paris, 1969) 115, 'se défend énergiquement'; T. Meek, *ANET*, 181, 'kept defending herself'.

Nehemiah 9: An Important Witness of Theological Reflection

ROLF RENDTORFF
University of Heidelberg

When I spent some months in Jerusalem in the severe winter after the Yom Kippur War, one of the highlights was the *shiᶜur* every Shabbat morning in Moshe Greenberg's home. We studied *Midraš Leviticus Rabba*, and for me it was a kind of opening of the door to the immeasurably wide field of classical Jewish literature. I am still close to the entrance, but the steps I took are connected with this valuable memory of study and friendship.

One of the important things I learned in the context of those studies was to be critical of the overestimation of diachronic views of biblical texts and instead to try to understand the texts' innerbiblical coherence. At the beginning of my studies almost fifty years ago, I was taught that a "late" biblical text is to be taken as less valuable and less important than an "early" or "old" one. One of the consequences of this kind of approach is a disregard for certain texts that should receive much more attention because of their theological importance.

In this brief essay I want to deal with one of these texts, which in my view has been badly neglected. My first encounter with the prayer in Nehemiah 9 was the observation by my teacher Gerhard von Rad that this text is the first time that Sinai is mentioned in a summary of Israel's *Heilsgeschichte*. This means, according to von Rad, that this element of tradition had been combined only "very late" with the older elements of the "historical creed."[1] It is obvious, indeed, that the author of Nehemiah 9 was familiar with the pentateuchal traditions in their final shape. But the more interesting question is what kind of theological consequences he himself drew from these traditions for his own situation and that of his people.

---

1. G. von Rad, *The Problem of the Hexateuch and Other Essays* (New York, 1966) 12.

There is still another remarkable peculiarity in Nehemiah 9: it is the only time in the Hebrew Bible that the verb בחר 'to elect' is used in reference to Abraham (v. 7). For the reader of Genesis, it is quite clear that God elected Abraham when he called him out of his familiar and local context and sent him into a new and unknown country (Gen 12:1–3). But the Hebrew term בחר with this meaning obviously was first used by Deuteronomy, and there it was only used for the election of Israel (Deut 7:6, and other places). These two examples show clearly that the author of the prayer in Nehemiah 9 employs an independent and sophisticated theological language. I want to examine this in a bit more detail.[2]

I

In its context, the prayer Neh 9:6–37 is part of the penitential liturgy of the 24th of Tishri. From the Hebrew text, it is not quite clear who is speaking. Ezra is not mentioned,[3] and the prayer of the Levites seems to have ended at v. 5. But this is not too important; nor is it greatly relevant whether this prayer had its "original" place elsewhere, within or outside of Ezra–Nehemiah. In any case, the prayer appears to be a more-or-less independent unit with a clear formal and theological structure.

Let us first of all view this structure. There are a number of structural signs throughout the prayer. It begins with אתה־הוא יהוה לבדך (v. 6) a phrase that is repeated in the phrase אתה־הוא יהוה האלהים (v. 7). With this formula, these two verses are connected to each other. They mark God's first two basic deeds: he created the world, and he elected Abram (whose name he immediately changed to Abraham, v. 7b). The main point of God's actions toward Abraham was the covenant (ברית, v. 8). These first two statements conclude with the emphatic formula כי צדיק אתה. It is quite obvious that this is of particular relevance. The formula is repeated only once in the last paragraph of the prayer in a quite different context: now (ועתה, v. 32) Israel is in great distress—but God is צדיק (v. 33). Here in v. 8 the formula closes the first unit of the chapter.

The prayer continues to recall God's deeds regarding Israel, jumping from Abraham to Israel's suffering in Egypt (v. 9). This story is told in such a way that it always mentions what God himself has done. The verbs are throughout

2. Among the commentaries, see in particular J. Blenkinsopp, *Ezra–Nehemiah: A Commentary* (OTL; Philadelphia, 1989). I am gratefully using his interpretation without quoting it in detail. See also the useful essay by H. G. M. Williamson, "Structure and Historiography in Nehemiah 9," in *Proceedings of the Ninth World Congress of Jewish Studies, Panel Sessions: Bible Studies and Ancient Near East* (Jerusalem: Magnes, 1988) 117–31.
3. The LXX adds: καὶ εἶπεν Ἔσρας (or: Εσδρας).

in the second-person singular: from Egypt through the Sea of Reeds, through the wilderness up to Sinai, where God gave his commandments to Israel, first of all the Shabbat (v. 14). Nothing is said about the behavior of the Israelites. In this second unit of the prayer (vv. 9–15), they seem just to be the happy recipients of all the good things God did for them.

But then the language changes. The verb appears in the third-person plural: והם ואבתנו 'but they, namely our fathers' (v. 16). Now we are told how the ancestors again and again counteracted God's mighty deeds. They refused to obey. But it is important to see how the text alternates between Israel's bad deeds and God's merciful reactions: seven times it is said that Israel acted badly (third-person plural), but then the language turns again (v. 17b), beginning with ואתה, followed by a series of epithets of the merciful God, and ending with the verbal 'you did not abandon them'. The same structure is repeated in vv. 18–19: Beginning with אף, the sin with the Golden Calf is mentioned and described with the words 'great contempt'.[4] But, again beginning with ואתה, God's mercy is set against their sin, by repetition of the words 'you did not abandon them'. This is widely explained by the divine guidance during the rest of the wandering in the wilderness (vv. 20–21). So vv. 16–21 are again a distinct unit, the third, speaking of the alternation between the bad actions of the fathers and God's merciful reactions.

Now Israel has reached the borders of the promised land, and the prayer continues with the record of its conquest, the settlement, and the enjoyment of its bounty (vv. 20–25). This decisive chapter of Israel's history is again depicted as a pure act of God's merciful guidance. From this point of view, the fourth unit stands in parallelism with the second one (vv. 9–15).

The next unit (vv. 26–28) begins according to the structure of vv. 16–17 and 18–19: the Israelites acted in disobedience, and God delivered them into the hands of their enemies; but then, when they cried to him, the language again changes, beginning with ואתה. In his great mercy, God listened to them from heaven and gave them saviors (v. 27b). The same is repeated in v. 28, the turning again indicated by ואתה. Here it is just briefly said that God rescued Israel. It is obvious that this fifth unit (vv. 26–28) stands parallel to the third one (vv. 16–19), showing both sides: Israel's bad behavior and God's merciful reactions, the latter always introduced by the emphatic ואתה.

However, the next unit begins differently. God warned the Israelites in order to bring them back to his *torah* (v. 29), 'but they' (והמה like והם in v. 16) refused to listen. Here the reaction of the Israelites follows on a particular warning. God warned them again and again, but they did not hear. This unit also ends differently from the earlier ones: God is still merciful, but this time it is only said that he would not make an end of them (v. 31). The tone is much less hopeful. So the sixth unit (vv. 29–31) leads up to the last unit.

---

4. According to the translation by J. Blenkinsopp.

This last unit begins with וְעַתָּה, expressing the idea that the current situation has been reached (v. 32). The language changes from reporting history to prayer and from third-person plural to first-person plural: אֱלֹהֵינוּ 'our God'. From now on, everything shifts to first-person plural, right up to the last word, אֲנַחְנוּ (v. 37). In this last unit of the prayer, a terrible tension can be felt: the situation seems to be hopeless, and the community, represented by the author of the prayer, is quite conscious that it is their own sin that brought about the present disastrous circumstances. But nevertheless, or even therefore, the first and most important thing is to praise God and to insist that he is not guilty, but on the contrary: וְאַתָּה צַדִּיק (v. 33). From the time that God elected Abraham, he has always acted in righteousness (v. 8) and kept his covenant (vv. 8 and 32), despite all of the misdeeds of Israel, above all those of its representatives, such as kings, princes, and priests. God's righteousness and faithfulness to his covenant are the only reason it is still possible to pray. Nevertheless, the final tone is not one of hope or even a call for God's help—just desperation: "we are now slaves in our own country, which you have given to our fathers—we are slaves" (v. 36).

II

The structure of the prayer as a whole is quite clear. In seven units, it gives an account of the creation of heaven and earth up to the present desolate situation of Israel under Persian rule. One of the most significant structuring elements is the word אַתָּה. The introductory first section (vv. 6–8) describes God's fundamental mighty deeds in creating the world and electing Abraham. It is marked by אַתָּה, twice at the respective beginnings of the two divine acts (vv. 6, 7) and a third time at the end of the whole unit (v. 8). The second and fourth units tell in narrative style about God's guidance of his people, first out of Egypt and up to Sinai (vv. 9–15), and then into the promised land (vv. 22–25). Here in the narrative framework, the word אַתָּה does not appear. But in the two units that interrupt and follow units two and four, that is, the third (vv. 16–21) and the fifth (vv. 26–28) units, the word וְאַתָּה always indicates the dramatic change from Israel's unfaithfulness and its consequences to God's acts of mercy (vv. 17b, 19, 27b, 28b). The sixth unit (vv. 29–31) then shows a fundamentally new situation: God warned Israel, but they did not obey. How bad Israel's behavior is considered becomes evident by the use of the word הֵזִידוּ 'they acted presumptuously' (v. 29; compare with v. 16), the same word that had been used to describe the behavior of the Egyptians against Israel, which had been the reason for God's acting against the Egyptians on behalf of Israel (v. 10). But then the last word of this unit is again אַתָּה, this time, however, אַתָּה does not introduce the report of a creative or merciful action of God but is part of the confession

כי אל־חנון ורחום אתה. This confession underlines the hope that God 'will not make an end' of Israel. But it remains to be seen how God will act to ensure this.

The seventh unit (vv. 32–37) begins with ועתה, which introduces an interesting contrast. In the Hebrew Bible, this expression often marks the beginning of a new chapter or view. In the following verses, nothing is said about God's help and nothing is expected. Nevertheless, the word אתה appears again, this time in a kind of repetition of what has been said in the first unit: ואתה צדיק (v. 33; compare with v. 8). It is very significant that this formulation appears at the beginning and at the end of the prayer (I will return to this point below).

III

The specific theological concept of the prayer is expressed in particular in the first unit. It begins with a praise of God the creator (v. 6). The language shows that the author knows all kinds of traditions, not only of the Pentateuch but also of other areas of biblical writings. Therefore it does not make sense to ask what "sources" or "redactions" or the like the prayer quotes. On the one hand, the "books," insofar as they existed at that time, would have been accessible to everybody interested. On the other hand, as in every religious community, there would have been a set of religious ideas and terms common to all, or at least to certain circles, from which the author could choose. Considering this, it is interesting that the prayer begins with creation, something that happens in very few texts that summarize history; among the psalms, only Psalm 136 does so. Another interesting detail might be that v. 6 combines the creation language of Genesis with an emphasis on the "monotheistic" aspect of God as creator in the expression לבדך 'you alone' (compare Isa 44:24).

The comparison with Psalm 136 highlights another characteristic of Nehemiah 9, the reference to Abraham (v. 7). Whereas Psalm 136 jumps from creation immediately to the exodus (vv. 9–10), Nehemiah 9 is particularly interested in Abraham. The reason for this becomes clear from the use of the word בחר. As mentioned above, this is the only text in the Hebrew Bible where this term is used for Abraham. The focus is on the election of Abraham. This is God's second great deed after creation, and its importance is specifically emphasized by structurally linking it to the first deed, as shown above. Abraham's election is then explicated step by step. First, God led him out of his homeland, Ur of the Chaldeans; at this point, the land where he should go is not yet mentioned. The next point is the changing of his name from Abram to Abraham. For those who know the traditions laid down in Genesis (as the readers or listeners of this prayer probably did), it is obvious that this means that God will make of Abraham a great nation (Gen 12:2), which is expressed

by giving him a new name indicating 'a multitude of nations' (Gen 17:5). Because of his reaction, Abraham's heart was found by God to be 'faithful' נאמן,
a word that is evocative of והאמן 'he believed' or 'he put his trust in the LORD'
(Gen 15:6). This is why God covenanted with him to give his descendants the
land that is now mentioned in detail. It is again one of the theological pecu-
liarities of Nehemiah 9 that these two very specific theological terms are combined with each other, בחר and ברית. Both of them have specific fields where
they are particularly used in the Hebrew Bible. In Nehemiah 9, their internal
relationship has been brought to the fore by putting them close to each other.
Again, it is Abraham who is God's partner in all of these fundamental, good
deeds. And it is most significant that all of this happened at the very beginning
of Israel's history.

There is only one other figure of Israel's history mentioned in the prayer:
Moses. Yet it is remarkable that he is not given as much prominence as Abraham. He is only mentioned at the end of the section on Sinai (v. 14b), after the
writer has explicitly reported the giving of the commandments (vv. 13, 14a),
including the commandment to keep the Sabbath holy, which is of particular
importance for our prayer. It is surprising that there is no reference to a covenant with Moses. According to this prayer, there is only one covenant God has
made with Israel, and he made it at the very beginning, with Abraham.

Because God has fulfilled his word and has done all of these things, the
first unit of the prayer concludes by stating, כי צדיק אתה. God's righteousness
is exactly that: doing what he has promised.[5]

IV

That God is צדיק is repeated at the end of the prayer but in a totally different
context. In v. 8, this fact was the copestone of the first and fundamental chapter of God's history with his people. In vv. 35–37, it contrasts with Israel's bad
behavior and miserable present situation. In v. 8, the fact that God is צדיק
confirmed and emphasized his great deeds; in vv. 32–37, it is voiced against all
appearances to the contrary and without explicitly expressed hopes. But even
if hopes are not expressed, the formula ואתה צדיק is like a cry that calls to

---

5. It should be mentioned that from the perspective of Nehemiah 9, there are good reasons for
understanding Gen 15:6 in this way: Abraham was נאמן—he trusted in God and reckoned God's
faithfulness to his word as God's צדקה. This interpretation was first expressed by Nachmanides.
Lloyd Gaston, who recently pled for this understanding, mentions Nehemiah 9 as "a text with dependence on, or at the very least clear affinity to, Gen 15:6" and therefore as a proof of at least one
possible later understanding of Gen 15:6 (L. Gaston, "Abraham and the Righteousness of God,"
HBT 2 [1980] 39–68; reprinted in L. Gaston, *Paul and the Torah* [Vancouver, 1987] 45–63; the
quotation is from p. 49 [in the reprint, p. 54]).

mind the beginning of the prayer and therefore carries implicit confidence that God will continue to stand by his promises in the future.

God is also called צדיק in related texts coming out of comparable situations. The closest parallel is Ezra 9:15. In a similar way, Ezra confesses Israel's guilt and God's merciful reactions, from the times of the patriarchs up to the present situation, when "none can stand in your presence" (9:6–15). Set against this statement is the statement צדיק אתה. In a similar prayer in the book of Daniel (9:4–19), God's righteousness is advanced twice in sharp contrast to Israel's sins (vv. 7, 14), although in this case, the prayer continues with explicit and urgent requests for God's help. Lam 1:18 also shows the situation of an individual or praying congregation confessing their sins and at the same moment calling God צדיק. Jer 12:1 provides an interesting parallel in which the prophet opens his prayer by the set phrase צדיק אתה יהוה before he begins to present charges against God. Finally, the Chronicler uses the formula צדיק יהוה by itself as a prayer of repentance that was heard by God (2 Chr 12:6). The formula seems to represent a prayer of this kind.

This group of prayers represents an important context for Nehemiah 9. The fact that God is צדיק was sometimes the only reason for the believing and praying congregation of postexilic Israel to continue to believe and to pray. At the same time, these texts show an intensive and independent use of the earlier religious traditions of Israel, shaping them into new impressive forms that became an integral and important part of our biblical heritage.[6]

---

6. The limited space of this essay does not allow me to study other important aspects of Nehemiah 9, such as the twice-appearing formula אל חנון ורחום with the unique variant סליחות אלוה and other elements of formulas connected to them, the expression that God "made a name for yourself," and so forth, all of them showing the independent and reflective use of the earlier traditions.

Naboth's Vineyard Revisited (1 Kings 21)

NAHUM M. SARNA

Brandeis University

King Ahab's unavailing attempt to acquire the vineyard[1] of a certain "Naboth the Jezreelite" and Queen Jezebel's infamous stratagem designed to ensure that her husband realize his desire are narrated at length in 1 Kings 21. This text preserves several noteworthy and perplexing features that have not been fully elucidated.

It is clear from the start that even in paganized Northern Israel, the monarch had no power, in the present instance simply to impose his will by force upon his subjects. He accepted the restraint of law. He offered to pay the full value of the property or even to exchange it for a superior parcel of land (vv. 1–3). Upon Naboth's refusal, he could only lie on his bed in a sullen mood, sulk, and reject food, but he could not confiscate the vineyard he so yearned to possess (v. 4).

Author's note: I am indebted to attorneys Sheila Mondshein, David Mofenson, and Professor Alan Field, as well as to Professor Marvin Fox, for their kind help.

1. 1 Kings 21 employs the word *kerem* ten times: vv. 1, 2 (2×), 6 (3×), 7, 15, 16, 18. However, 2 Kings 9 repeatedly designates the same property as *ḥelqah*: vv. 10, 21, 25, 26, 36, 37. A. Rofé (*The Prophetical Stories* [Jerusalem, 1988] 84) maintains that the object of Ahab's craving, according to 2 Kings 9, was "a plot—a field—not a vineyard" and that this is the original version of the story. Y. Zakovitch (in *The Bible from Within* [ed. M. Weiss; Jerusalem, 1984] 382) points out that Josephus's account also features "a field." However, it should be noted that while Josephus uses *ἀγρογείτων and *ἀγρόν in *Ant.* 8.355–56 (Loeb edition, p. 762), *ἀγρῷ in 8.407 (Loeb, p. 790) and 9.118 (Loeb, p. 62) and *ἀγρὸν in 9.119 (Loeb, p. 64), he also uses *ἀμπελῶνα 'vineyard' in 9.359–60 (Loeb, p. 760). Zakovitch (p. 382 n. 9) observes that *śādeh* and *kerem* are frequently paired, as in Exod 22:4; Num 20:17, 21:22; and 1 Sam 8:14, and that occasionally the two are parallel, as in Prov 24:30; also cf. Lev 19:19 with Deut 22:9. N. Liphschitz and G. Biger (*Beit Mikra* [1993] 119–21), through analysis of archaeological evidence from the Valley of Jezreel, conclude that Naboth's property was an olive grove and not a vineyard. The phrase *kerem zayit* indeed appears in Judg 15:5, but the targum, LXX, Vulgate, and Syriac and thus David Qimḥi, all treat this compound as asyndeton; so NJPSV, 'vineyard, [and] olive trees'; cf. *b. Ber.* 35a, *b. B. Meṣ.* 87b.

This remarkable limitation upon crown rights[2] is of particular interest in light of the contrasting arbitrary authority and personal privileges that kings could assert and enjoy in Israel's neighboring states. Akkadian legal and other documents from Ugarit and elsewhere have shown that Samuel's denunciation of the institution of kingship, as recorded in 1 Sam 8:9–17, is an authentic reflection of the contemporary state of affairs in the region.[3] The prophet's assertion that the king would seize his subjects' "choice fields, vineyards, and olive groves" and dispose of them at will (8:14) is in striking opposition to the situation in which Ahab now finds himself.

The impotence of the Israelite king, from a legal point of view, explains the diabolical measures to which Jezebel feels she must resort. As a Phoenician princess, accustomed to a different, Near Eastern conception of tyrannical kingship, in which monarchs can indulge their whims and exercise absolute, arbitrary power, Jezebel evinces undisguised contempt for Israelite limitations on royal authority (1 Kgs 21:7). Nevertheless, she realizes that if she is to secure the coveted property for her husband, her scheme must scrupulously preserve the appearance of legality, even though the substance of justice can be disregarded.[4] So she lays on a veneer of legitimacy by cloaking injustice in the robes of law. Wielding corrupt royal influence, she issues a writ in the king's name, recruits unprincipled, servile judges, and suborns two malevolent false witnesses (vv. 8–10).[5] On her orders, Naboth is unjustly charged with two capital crimes, blasphemy and treason. Of course, the victim is found guilty on both counts, is summarily executed, and his property is expropriated by the king (vv. 11–16).

The two offenses, blasphemy and treason, are listed in the pentateuchal legislation. Exod 22:27[28] prescribes:

> You shall not revile God,[6] nor put a curse upon a chieftain among your people.

---

2. Cf. Deut 17:14–20; cf. Ezek 45:8–9, 46:18.

3. I. Mendelsohn, "Samuel's Denunciation of Kingship in the Light of the Akkadian Documents from Ugarit," *BASOR* 143 (1956) 17–22. J. A. Thompson (*The Bible and Archaeology* [Grand Rapids, Mich., 1975] 12) draws attention to Canaanite mythology. He contrasts Jezebel's legal maneuvers to the violent means by which a goddess obtains a coveted bow in a Ugaritic text, which he feels reflects the values of Canaanite society. The reference is undoubtedly to the Anat and Aqhat myth, on which see C. Gordon, *Ugaritic Literature* (Rome, 1949) 84–103; H. L. Ginsberg, "The Tale of Aqhat," in *ANET*, 149–55; T. H. Gaster, *Thespis* (Garden City, N.Y., 1961) 316–29.

4. The observation of E. W. Nicholson (*Deuteronomy and Tradition* [Philadelphia, 1967] 68), that "Jezebel had evidently no difficulty in having the unfortunate Naboth removed," needs modification.

5. This accords with Deut 17:6 and 19:15.

6. See on this clause *b. Sanh.* 66a–b; *Mekilta de Rabbi Ishmael*, section 19 (ed. M. Friedmann, p. 97; ed. Horovitz and Rabin, p. 317; ed. Lauterbach, p. 151). These sources understand the word *ʾĕlōhîm* also to include a judge; see the targums, ad loc. This interpretation is probably based on the difference in style from the preceding and following verses, in which God, as the speaker, uses the first person.

While the Hebrew term *nāśîʾ*,[7] here rendered 'chieftain', is a designation for a tribal leader and reflects a premonarchic governmental administration, once the monarchy was established, its connotation of "ruler" would plainly be extended to include the king. The Covenant Code thus makes blasphemy and treason statutory offenses, but it specifies no penalty for infractions. However, Lev 24:15–16 is explicit regarding the punishment for blasphemy:

> And to the Israelite people, speak thus: Anyone who blasphemes his God shall bear his guilt; if he also pronounces the name LORD, he shall be put to death. The whole community shall stone him; stranger or citizen, if he has pronounced the Name, he shall be put to death.

Blasphemy appears to have been regarded everywhere as a capital offense, as a crime against public and social order, what in Roman law is termed *crimen publicum*.[8] The reason for this classification seems to have been the belief that the offense incurred the wrath of the insulted deity to the misfortune of the entire community. Hence the severity of the penalty and the involvement of the whole community in carrying out the punishment. The Middle Assyrian Laws, Tablet A 2, legislate that a woman who utters blasphemy "shall bear her liability; her husband, her sons, and her daughters shall not be touched."[9] The nature of the penalty is not specified, but as Driver points out, the explicit exclusion of her near relatives appears to be a revision of an earlier practice that seems to have entailed the punishment of the entire family. Some light on the lacuna in the Assyrian Laws is most likely shed by an inscription of Ashurbanipal (668–627 B.C.E.), which records the way in which two blasphemers were treated; their tongues were ripped out and they were skinned alive.[10]

As to the crime of reviling the king, no biblical legal text mentions the consequential punishment. However, since God and king are paired, implicitly

---

7. On the meaning of this title, see M. Noth (*Das System der zwölf Stämme Israels* [Stuttgart, 1930] 151ff.; and his *Commentary on Exodus* [Philadelphia, 1962] 187ff.), who takes *nāśîʾ* to refer to the tribal spokesman at the amphictyony. J. van der Ploeg ("Les chefs du peuple d'Israëls ets leurs titres," *RB* 57 [1950] 40–61) rejects this understanding and takes the term as a secular title for a leader. E. Speiser ("Background and Function of the Biblical *Nasiʾ*," *CBQ* 25 [1963] 111–17) takes it to mean simply a tribal leader.

8. On the offense of blasphemy, see G. D. Nokes, *A History of the Crime of Blasphemy* (London, 1928); L. W. Levy, *Treason against God: A History of the Offense of Blasphemy* (New York, 1981). For the rabbinic understanding of the offense, see *m. Sanh.* 7:5 and the gemara on it (pp. 55b, 60a), which lay down the precise conditions for execution by lapidation. The name *YOSY* used there is a surrogate for the Tetragrammaton, and the numerical value of the consonants equals that of *ʾĕlōhîm* 'God'.

9. G. R. Driver and John C. Miles, *The Assyrian Laws* (Oxford, 1935) 379, and the discussion on p. 20; T. J. Meek, "The Middle Assyrian Laws," *ANET*, 180. On Akk. *šillatu*, see CAD Š/2 445–47; S. Paul, "Daniel 3:29: A Case Study of Neglected Blasphemy," *JNES* 42 (1983) 291–94.

10. E. F. Weidner, "Assyrische Beschreibungen des Kriegs-Reliefs Aššurbanâplis," *AfO* 8 (1932) 184.

in Exod 22:27[28] and explicitly here in 1 Kgs 21:10, 13 and in Isa 8:21 (in reverse order), it is reasonable to assume that this offense was understood to be on the same level of high crime as blasphemy. It too was taken to be a grave threat to the established social order, a crime against the state, an act of treason meriting capital punishment. Quite likely, this conception is reflected in the desire of Abishai, son of Zeruiah, to slay Shimei ben Gera for "outrageously insulting" King David, as told in 2 Sam 16:5–13, 1 Kgs 2:8–9.

Ahab's expropriation of the vineyard is, on the surface, a puzzling detail in the narrative. After all, Ahab and Jezebel felt compelled to comply, however reluctantly and perversely, with the demands and forms of Israelite law and tradition. Hence, it is certain that the king's taking possession of the property immediately following the pretended trial and judicial murder of Naboth was legally sanctioned in the circumstances. If this were not the case, the biblical historiographer, who displays such intense antipathy toward the house of Omri and especially toward Ahab and his pagan spouse,[11] would assuredly have added the illegality of the royal acquisition to the inventory of heinous sins they committed. Elijah's condemnation "Would you murder and take possession?" is a judgment on the criminal, immoral nature of the entire conspiracy, not just on the specific act of royal acquisition. It cannot be that Jezebel simply confiscated the vineyard extrajudicially,[12] something neither she nor Ahab dared to do in the first place. If in the end the king would still have to act arbitrarily and *ultra vires*, why go through the motions of a trumped-up indictment and spurious judicial proceedings? It is most probable then that the act was seen as juridically acceptable. The forfeiture must have been merited in accordance with existing, recognized procedure and tradition. It may therefore be assumed that some formal, symbolic ritual that validated and effectuated the transfer of title from Naboth to Ahab lies behind the repeated use of the term 'take possession'.[13] Jezebel instructs her husband to "go take possession of the vineyard."

11. On Omri, see 1 Kgs 16:25–26; cf. Mic 6:16; on Ahab, see 1 Kgs 16:29–33; 18:13, 18; 2 Kgs 8:15–18; 9:7–10; 10:10; 21:3; on Ahaziah, see 1 Kgs 22:52–54[51–53]; on Jehoram, see 2 Kgs 3:1–3; 8:26–27; 9:22. As the text stands, Hos 1:4, "I will soon punish the House of Jehu for the bloody deeds at Jezreel," seems to refer to the massacre of the House of Ahab by Jehu (so Rashi, Ibn Ezra). Y. Kaufmann (*Tŏlĕdôt Hā-ʾEmûnâ Ha-Yisrĕʾelit* [Jerusalem, 1976] 3.97–99 and n. 7) emends "Jehu" to "Jehoram." The LXX here reads "Judah" in place of "Jehu"; see the NJPSV, ad loc., footnotes.

12. Hugo Grotius (1583–1645), cited with approval by J. A. Montgomery (*A Critical and Exegetical Commentary on the Book of Kings* [Edinburgh, 1951] 332), explains Ahab's act as exemplifying arbitrary royal power. J. Pedersen (*Israel: Its Life and Culture* [London and Copenhagen, reprint 1959] 69) similarly regards Ahab's act as "the arbitrariness of the despot" (cf. p. 125). R. de Vaux (*Ancient Israel: Its Life and Institutions* [New York, 1961] 55) likewise observes that Ahab's act may simply be an instance of arbitrary confiscation. F. I. Andersen ("The Socio-Juridical Background of the Naboth Incident," *JBL* 85 [1966] 46–47) notes that "interpreters have been at a loss to discover any legal grounds for Ahab's subsequent seizure of Naboth's vineyard." Andersen rejects both the suggestion that it was an arbitrary act and the claim that the property of certain criminals was forfeited to the crown. The first is indeed untenable, but the second can certainly be sustained.

13. This mode of legal acquisition is what is termed *ḥazaqah* in rabbinic parlance. This was noted by B. Uffenheimer, *Ancient Prophecy in Israel* (Jerusalem, 1973) 223–24 [Heb.]. On *ḥaza-*

The text tells us that "Ahab set out for the vineyard of Naboth the Jezreelite to take possession of it" (vv. 15–16). Similarly, the divine directive to Elijah to confront the king stresses, "He is now in Naboth's vineyard; he has gone down there to take possession of it" (v. 18).

Jezebel's effort to create a fictional impression of legality, her careful attention to the proper judicial formalities, albeit in order to accomplish an immoral objective, raises a basic question. The queen undoubtedly knew full well that the crimes of which Naboth was to be accused would be punishable by his execution and the consequent confiscation of his property, so that Ahab's possession of it would be assured. But on what legal grounds did the vineyard become forfeit and devolve to the crown? This basic question exercised the medieval Jewish exegetes Rashi, David Qimḥi, Gersonides, and Abrabanel. They all maintained that the "legal" justification for Ahab's final act was the existence of a law that the estate of a felon executed by royal degree escheated to the crown. This interpretation follows the majority view put forth in a debate among the tannaim of the second century C.E., as recorded in rabbinic sources,[14] although it is not clear whether the forfeiture was understood by these authorities to be a part of the penalty for the commission of high crime or a logical consequence of the punishment. The minority view held that Ahab received Naboth's estate by inheritance, since he was the deceased victim's first cousin and thus a rightful heir. This explanation is also cited by David Qimḥi. What is of special significance is that the sages on both sides of the debate, as well as the medieval exegetes, took it for granted that Ahab obtained the property on the basis of some established juridical principle applicable in the particular circumstances.

It is hardly likely that the minority view presented above rests on anything more than an attempt to counter the claim of the majority and to find an alternative reason why Ahab could inherit the estate. But what is behind the

---

qah, see M. Elon, *Jewish Law: History, Sources, Principles* (trans. from Hebrew, B. Auerbach and M. J. Sykes; Philadelphia, 1994) 1.79–80, 297–98; 2.580–87. In the Bible, Abraham's traversing the promised land, as told in Gen 13:17, is an example of such a legal ritual; cf. *Tg. Ps.-J.*, ad loc.; *y. Qidd.* 1:3 (60c); *t. Bab. Bat.* 2.11; *b. Bab. Bat.* 100a; *Gen. Rab.* 41:13; cf. Josh 24:3. According to E. R. Lacheman ("Note on Ruth 4:7–8," *JBL* 56 [1937] 53–56) it was the practice in Nuzi that, in order to enhance the validity of a real property transfer, the owner would "lift up his own foot from his property" and place the foot of the new owner on it. Some biblical passages relating to Israel's acquisition of its promised land, such as Deut 11:24 and Josh 1:3–4, may well be literary reflexes of this same symbolic gesture. See, however, J. M. Sasson, *Ruth* (Baltimore, 1979) 141–48.

14. See *b. Sanh.* 48b, *t. Sanh.* 4.6. Maimonides (*Yad, Hilkhot Evel* 1:9) codifies the law that the property of those executed by royal decree reverts to the crown. The same is repeated by him in *Hilkhot Melakhim* 4:9. However, in 4:10, he stipulates that this applies only when the royal actions are for purely idealistic reasons and are inspired by the noblest of causes. J. Weingreen ("The Case of the Daughters of Zelophehad," *VT* 16 [1996] 518–22) suggests that the protestation of innocence in Num 27:3 was a necessary part of the legal procedure and that it testifies to some ancient law, not recorded, about the property of a person convicted of treason.

majority view? Before dealing with this issue, we must note that a complicating factor appears in 2 Kgs 9:25–26.

In this text we are informed that when the rebel Jehu carries out his coup d'etat against Joram of Israel, the last of the Omrides, he has the body of the slain king dumped in "the field of Naboth the Jezreelite," and he cites a supposedly divine pronouncement, "I swear, I have taken note of the blood of Naboth and the blood of his sons yesterday. . . ." Surprisingly, the narrative of 1 Kings 21 makes no mention of Naboth's sons or of their execution.[15] The instructions sent by Jezebel to the judges contain not a word about them, nor are they referred to in the report of the fulfillment of her orders or in the announcement of the fulfillment to the queen, nor when she informs her husband, nor in the narration of the situation in v. 16. Indeed, had Jezebel really ordered the murder of the children, the narrator would surely have told of it as still one more example of the monstrous evil and the heinous crimes that characterized her reign. There would have been absolutely no reason to ignore or suppress the fact, and every reason to highlight it. The report of 2 Kgs 9:26 must derive from an independent, variant version of the Naboth affair.[16] At any rate, it is of interest that the above-mentioned rabbinic sources do not take the statement literally but treat it figuratively. That is, with the execution of Naboth the blood of his potential offspring was also shed, as it were, all of the generations now doomed never to be born.[17] Be that as it may, even if Naboth's children had been executed with him, we would still be without clear explanation for Ahab's lawful acquisition of the vineyard.

Although pentateuchal law features no such penalty as state forfeiture of a convicted criminal's property, the practice is attested over a long period of time and over a wide geographic and varied cultural area. In the Bible itself, Ezra (10:8) uses the threat of confiscation as a sanction to enforce obedience to an order to the returnees from the Babylonian exile. Moreover, the associ-

15. C. F. Keil and F. Delitzsch (*Commentary on the Old Testament* [Grand Rapids, Mich.; reprint, 1980] 3.342) cite J. D. Michaelis and H. G. A. Ewald that the omission of the murder of Naboth's sons is "because it was so usual a thing that the historian might leave it out as a matter of course." This, of course, is nonsensical.

16. J. Gray (*I & II Kings: A Commentary* [Philadelphia, 1963], on 1 Kgs 21:13 (p. 392), citing the case of Achan (Josh 7:22ff.), explains that Naboth's family was executed with him in "punctilious observance of Semitic custom." He gives no source for this assertion. As to Josh 7:25, the text is quite unclear about the fate of Achan's family. The LXX omits the last two clauses, and the Syriac and Vulgate omit the last clause. Rabbinic sources display conflicting interpretations; see L. Ginzberg, *The Legends of the Jews* (Philadelphia, 1946) 6.176 n. 31. On 2 Kgs 9:26 (*I & II Kings*, 494), Gray notes that the "passage belonged to different sources." A similar judgment is made by J. M. Miller ("The Fall of the House of Ahab," *VT* 8 [1967] 307–24); by J. A. Soggin, (*A History of Ancient Israel* [Philadelphia, 1984] 207), who notes that "additions have been made to the narrative"; and by J. T. Walsh ("Naboth," *ABD* 4.978), who notes that there seem "to have been several versions of the Naboth story in circulation."

17. Cf. *m. Sanh.* 4:5 for a similar interpretation of the plural form of 'blood' in Gen 4:10; and see the targums, ad loc.

ated admonition that the offender shall be "excluded from the congregation" amounts to the Roman concept of civil death. It is hardly likely that this device was Ezra's innovation, even though it is not otherwise clearly mentioned in a biblical text. But we note that when David, in flight from Absalom, learned that Mephibosheth, grandson of the deceased Saul, had stayed in Jerusalem in hope of gaining the crown, he immediately decreed the confiscation of the traitor's lawful inheritance and presented it to Ziba the informant (2 Sam 16:4).[18] These instances suggest that forfeiture of this kind was provided for in ancient Israelite customary law. Indeed, the strictures of Ezekiel (45:8, 46:18) against the confiscation of the people's land by "the prince" (Hebrew *nāśî*ʾ), that is, by the king, in the prophet's idealized description of the restoration of Israel after the exile, indicate that such practices were not uncommon in the monarchy period. In extrabiblical sources, an Akkadian legal tablet from Alalakh from the reign of King Niqmepa, bearing the seal impression of his father, King Idrimi, and deriving from the fifteenth century B.C.E., records that a certain Arpa had become a criminal, a *bēl mašikti*, a term that has been shown to carry the implication of treason. He was executed for his crime, and his estate escheated to the palace.[19] In Attic law, the penalty for treason (*prodosia*) was death, followed by confiscation of the condemned's property and a declaration of dishonor and deprivation of civil rights (*atimia*), which meant that his heirs too were disenfranchised.[20] This is what happened to the Athenian orator and politician Antiphon, who was executed in 411 B.C.E. after being convicted of high treason.[21] In ancient Rome, the property of a person convicted of a crime against the state (*crimen publicum*) became the property of the state (*res publica*).[22] According to the Hanafi school of Islamic law, the blasphemer is disenfranchised, and all claims to property or inheritance are voided.[23] In England, the famous and perhaps most crucial provision of the Magna Carta extracted from King John in 1215, clause 39, decreed that "no freeman shall be taken or

18. 2 Sam 16:4. The king later relented somewhat and divided the estate between Mephibosheth and Ziba (2 Sam 19:30).

19. D. J. Wiseman (*The Alalakh Tablets* [British Institute of Archaeology at Ankara, 1953] 40, no. 17) translated lines 7–8 'Apra has turned against a private enemy . . . '. B. Landsberger ("Assyrische Königsliste und Dunkles Zeitalter," *JCS* 8 [1954] 60 n. 129) corrects the translation of *bēl mašikti* to *Verbrecher* 'criminal'. S. E. Loewenstamm ("Notes on the Alalakh Tablets," *IEJ* 6 [1956] 224–25) accepts Landsberger's rendering and shows that the crime referred to was rebellion against the king. J. J. Finkelstein ("Documents from the Practice of Law," *ANET*, 546) similarly renders the Akkadian phrase 'committed treason'.

20. See W. J. Woodhouse, "ATIMIA," *ERE* 2.192–94, esp. p. 193a; D. M. MacDowell, *The Law in Classical Athens* (Ithaca, N.Y., 1978) 255–56; cf. pp. 73–75.

21. Ibid., 176, 178.

22. A. Berger, *Encyclopedic Dictionary of Roman Law* (American Philosophical Society, Transactions n.s. 43, part 2; Philadelphia, 195) 661.

23. C. W. Ernst, "BLASPHEMY: Islamic Concept," *The Encyclopedia of Religion* (New York, 1987) 2.243.

[and][24] imprisoned or disseised or exiled or in any way destroyed, . . . except by the lawful judgment of his peers or [and] by the law of the land."[25] It was aimed at preventing the arbitrary confiscation of property by the king; however, the law of the land did allow forfeiture of the property of a convicted criminal. English kings were still exercising this right in the seventeenth century.[26] The Statute of Treasons of 1352 specified that treason against the king entailed forfeiture of land and goods, and this law continued in force until the Forfeitures Abolition Act enacted in 1870, which abolished the whole law of escheat as a punishment for felony.[27]

The guiding principle that underlay the right of the state to impose forfeiture was the doctrine of "corruption of blood."[28] A convicted felon was deemed to be attainted; his blood was considered to be corrupt. The immediate consequence of this doctrine was the status of *civiliter mortuus*. In modern parlance, he became a "nonperson." "Civil death" operated retroactively and henceforth. It entailed automatic divestment of the rights of ownership. It extinguished the power to inherit, retain, and bequeath property. Descendants were thereby disinherited. Hence, the estate of the convicted felon, being now ownerless, belonged to the state.

The framers of the American Constitution took pains to nullify the doctrine of "corruption of blood." The second section of the second clause of Article III declared that "no attainder of treason shall work corruption of blood or forfeiture except during the life of the person attained." The legal implications of this clause have been explored several times in the courts, the most famous being the case of Avery v. Everett in the Court of Appeals of New York, October 2, 1888.[29]

The expression *corruption of blood* in the sense used in English law since feudal times has no counterpart in biblical Hebrew sources or in the cognate languages. But the concept, even if unarticulated, was implied in the recognized and accepted right of the monarch to take possession of the property of a felon convicted of blasphemy or treason, thereby disinheriting his heirs. Whether or not Naboth had heirs, Ahab was acting according to his legal rights in appropriating Naboth's vineyard following the unfortunate victim's condemnation on two capital charges, given the formal nature of the proceedings.

24. On the ambiguity of *vel* here, see W. S. McKechnie, *Magna Carta* (2d rev. ed.; Glasgow, 1914) 381–82 and n. 3.

25. On clause 39, see ibid., 375–95; J. C. Holt, *Magna Carta* (2d ed.; Cambridge, 1992) 9, 277, 463.

26. Ibid., 331; W. Holdsworth, *A History of English Law* (5th ed.; London, 1942; reprint 1966) 67ff.

27. Ibid., 70–71.

28. On this doctrine, see ibid., 67ff.; *The Dictionary of English Law* (London, 1959) 174, 505; *The Guide to American Law* (St. Paul, Minn., 1984) 1.360–61, 3.320; *Encyclopaedia of the American Constitution* (New York, 1986) 1.80.

29. *Avery v. Everett*, 110 NY 317, 18 NE 148. For a different interpretation of 1 Kings 21, see Tsafrirah ben Barak in *Proceedings of the Ninth World Congress of Jewish Studies*, Division A (Jerusalem, 1986) 15–20 [Heb.].

The "Aramean" of Deuteronomy 26:5:
Peshat and *Derash*

RICHARD C. STEINER
Yeshiva University

"The ideal reader treats the book as full of significance. . . . Ultimately, the holistic interpreter is animated by a respect for his cultural heritage that takes the form of a prejudice in favor of the ancient biblical author-editors and their transmitters. He requires more than a theoretical cause before discounting and disintegrating their products."[1] These are among the many methodological principles Moshe Greenberg attempted to impart to me as a student. May the Holy-One-Blessed-Be-He account it to him as if he had been successful.

The words ארמי אבד אבי at the beginning of the declaration of the first-fruits (Deut 26:5) have puzzled exegetes since ancient times. Who is the ארמי 'Aramean', and who is אבי 'my father'? What is the meaning of אבד? What is the subject and what is the predicate of the clause? How is it connected to the clauses that follow it: "He went down to Egypt and sojourned there with meager numbers, but there he became a great, mighty, and populous nation"?

Peshat

The reading of ארמי אבד אבי that is today considered its plain sense (אבי = subject; ארמי אבד = predicate noun phrase) is usually thought to have made its first unambiguous appearance in the commentaries of R. Abraham Ibn Ezra and

Author's note: I am indebted to Professors S. Abramson ל״ז, D. Berger, J. Blau, H. Z. Dimitrovsky, S. Friedman, S. Z. Leiman, Y. Maori, C. Milikovsky, S. Naeh, and R. White for their advice in matters pertaining to this article. I would also like to thank my students, P. Beltz Glaser and S. Isaacson, and my son-in-law, Rabbi M. Jacobowitz, for their detailed written comments on an earlier draft.

1. Moshe Greenberg, "The Vision of Jerusalem in Ezekiel 8–11: A Holistic Interpretation," *The Divine Helmsman* (ed. J. L. Crenshaw and S. Sandmel; New York: Ktav, 1980) 149.

Rashbam (12th century), but, in fact, it was proposed a generation earlier by R. Judah Ibn Bal^cam.[2] Ibn Bal^cam took it to mean 'a perishing Aramean was my father', a reference to Jacob's wretched condition in Aram.[3] In support of his interpretation of אבד, he cited Jer 50:6 and Ps 119:176 (see below), and for the theme of Israel's ascent from humble beginnings in Aram, he compared Hos 12:13–14.

Ibn Ezra and R. David Qimḥi[4] (and others) followed Ibn Bal^cam in identifying the "father" with Jacob, the former citing Prov 31:6–7, "give intoxicating drink to him who is perishing (לאובד) . . . , let him drink and forget his poverty (רישו)," as evidence that אבד could be used in the sense of 'destitute' and the latter citing Gen 31:40, "scorching heat consumed me by day and frost by night," as evidence of Jacob's suffering in Aram. Rashbam and R. Joseph Bekhor Shor,[5] on the other hand, identified the 'father' with Abraham, taking our phrase to mean 'a wandering (= emigrant)[6] Aramean was my father' on the

---

2. He presents it as a novel interpretation, superior to that of Onqelos and Saadia, here and in his commentary to Hos 12:13. At the same time, he hints at an innovative interpretation of *m. Pesaḥ.* 10:4, according to which the sentence "He begins with the negative and ends with the positive" is explained by the immediately following sentence: "And he expounds from ארמי אבד אבי until he finishes the entire portion." See Samuel Poznanski, "The Arabic Commentary of Abu Zakariya Yaḥya (Judah ben Samuel) Ibn Bal^cam on the Twelve Minor Prophets," *JQR* n.s. 15 (1924–25) 22–23; Ma^caravi Perez, פירוש לבמדבר ודברים (MA thesis, Bar-Ilan University, 1970) 60, 112, 182. (I am indebted to M. Linetsky for obtaining this thesis for our library and to Z. Erenyi for calling it to my attention.) For antecedents cited by Yefet b. ^cEli, see n. 24, below.

3. For Ibn Bal^cam and his followers, the phrase ארמי אבד is indivisible: Jacob, the scion of a wealthy Hebrew family, lived the life of a wretched Aramean for twenty years. Contrast J. Van Seters (*Abraham in History and Tradition* [New Haven: Yale University Press, 1975] 33) and J. Gerald Janzen ("The 'Wandering Aramean' Reconsidered," *VT* 44 [1994] 359–75), who also take it to mean 'perishing' but see it as a reference to Jacob's condition in *Canaan* during the famine ('starving'), which led him to descend to Egypt. For other advocates of 'perishing, destitute', see M. A. Beek, "Das Problem des aramäischen Stammvaters (Deut. XXVI 5)," *OTS* 8 (1951) 199–200, 211.

4. R. Abraham Ibn Ezra, פירושי התורה לרבינו אברהם אבן עזרא (ed. A. Weiser; Jerusalem: Mossad Harav Kook, 1976) 3.289; R. David Qimḥi, ספר השרשים (ed. J. H. R. Biesenthal and F. Lebrecht; Berlin: Bethge, 1847) 1, s.v. אבד.

5. Rashbam, פירוש התורה אשר כתב רשב״ם (ed. D. Rosin; Bratislava: Shottlender, 1881) 17–18 (Gen 20:13) 222; R. Joseph Bekhor Shor, פירושי רבי יוסף בכור שור על התורה (ed. Y. Nevo; Jerusalem: Mossad Harav Kook, 1994) 366.

6. Compare German *Auswanderer* 'emigrant'. Akkadian parallels favor a nuance closer to 'fugitive' or 'refugee'; see D. D. Luckenbill, "The 'Wandering Aramean,'" *AJSL* 36 (1920) 244–45; Alan R. Millard, "A Wandering Aramean," *JNES* 39 (1980) 153–55 and the studies cited there and in François Dreyfus, " 'L'Araméen voulait tuer mon père': L'actualisation de Dt 26,5 dans la tradition juive et la tradition chrétienne," in *De la Tôrah au Messie: Études d'exégèse et d'herméneutiques bibliques offertes à Henri Cazelles* (ed. M. Carrez, J. Doré, and P. Grelot; Paris: Desclée, 1981) 156 n. 4. *Papyrus Anastasi* I, from the end of the 13th century B.C.E., contains the verb אבד in a Canaanite sentence transcribed into hieratic syllabic script. According to some scholars, the sentence is a close parallel to Ps 119:176; see W. F. Albright, *The Vocalization of the Egyptian Syllabic Orthography* (New Haven: American Oriental Society, 1934) 33; *ANET*, 477; H-W. Fischer-Elfert, *Die satirische Streitschrift des Papyrus Anastasi I* (Ägyptologische Abhandlungen 44; Wiesbaden:

basis of Gen 12:1, "go forth from your land"; 20:13, "when God made me wander (התעו) from my father's house"; and (to prove אבד = תעה) Jer 50:6, "my people were lost (אבדות) sheep, their shepherds made them wander (התעום)"; and Ps 119:176, "I have wandered (תעיתי) like a lost sheep (אבד)."

Neither of these identifications is without its problems. Abraham "went down to Egypt" (Gen 12:10) but did not become a great nation there; he spent time in Aram, but it is not clear that his birthplace, Ur of the Chaldees, was located there. Jacob lived in Aram for twenty years, but Genesis seems to go out of its way to stress that he was not an Aramean (see Gen 31:20, 47).[7]

It was presumably such problems that led, in antiquity, to the rejection of these ethnically problematic interpretations in favor of linguistically problematic ones. Thus, we find renderings like Συρίαν ἀπέβαλεν ὁ πατήρ μου 'my father abandoned Syria' (LXX) and ܐܪܡ ܠܐܪܡ ܐܒܝ 'my father was taken to Aram' (Peshiṭta), featuring references to migration based more on the meaning of וירד מצרימה 'and he went down to Egypt'[8] than on the meaning of the words allegedly being translated. The standard Jewish interpretation, dealt with below, is also a response to these problems.[9]

In the modern period, the same problems have led some to conclude that the original meaning of the verse contradicts the Genesis narratives.[10] Others attempt to solve the problems by reinterpreting ארמי[11] or אבי. According to Mendelssohn's *Biur*, אבי refers to Abraham and Jacob together, since "all the patriarchs together were called אב, on account of their being . . . the root of the family and the nation."[12] We may add that the generic use of the singular is well attested in the Bible,[13] and examples of אב meaning 'ancestry, fathers' are perhaps to be found in Exod 3:6 ("the God of your father[s]—the God of Abraham, the God of Isaac, and the God of Jacob") and 15:2.[14]

Harrassowitz, 1986) 198–99; James E. Hoch, *Semitic Words in Egyptian Texts of the New Kingdom and Third Intermediate Period* (Princeton: Princeton University Press, 1994) 20–21.

7. See also Dreyfus, "L'Araméen," 152, and the literature cited there. Ibn Ezra was well aware of the problem: "Let no one object: 'How can he be called an Aramean?' It is like 'Ithra the Ishmaelite' (1 Chr 2:17), who was an Israelite, for so it is written (2 Sam 17:25)."

8. Yeshayahu Maori, תרגום הפשיטתא לתורה והפרשנות היהודית הקדומה (Jerusalem: Magnes, 1995) 274–76.

9. If the meaning 'Gentile, heathen' (attested for ארמי in Jewish and Christian dialects of Late Aramaic) developed early enough, the standard Jewish interpretation may have been a response to it, as well.

10. See Dreyfus, "L'Araméen," 153.

11. See the nonethnic interpretations of Luckenbill, Mazar, and Van Seters, rejected by Millard, "Wandering Aramean," 153–54, and those of Jacob and Junker cited by Beek, "Das Problem des aramäischen Stammvaters," 202–3.

12. Moses Mendelssohn, באור רמבמ"ן, in חומש מקור חיים (Berlin: Heinemann, 1833) 5.143.

13. P. Joüon and T. Muraoka, *A Grammar of Biblical Hebrew* (Rome: Pontifical Biblical Institute, 1991) §135c.

14. See the commentary of Nachmanides to Exod 3:6.

S. D. Luzzatto[15] expanded the referent of אבי further, to include all of the patriarchs. Luzzatto felt that his view was close to that of Rashbam, and he was probably right, for Bekhor Shor, who gives a fuller version of Rashbam's interpretation, indicates that it was Jacob who "went down to Egypt and sojourned there with meager numbers." Indeed, both Bekhor Shor and Luzzatto allude to 1 Chr 16:20, where all three patriarchs are described as wandering from nation to nation.

Can the referent of אבי be expanded still further to include Jacob's sons as well? All but one of the latter were born in Aram of Aramean mothers; Aramaic was presumably their native tongue. All of them were emigrés or fugitives[16] from Aram, and all of them went down to Egypt rather than perish from hunger.[17] The other capsule histories of Israelite origins mention their descent to Egypt together with their father (Josh 24:4) and even their children (Deut 10:22; cf. also Num 20:15). Thus, including them in the referent of אבי makes the aforementioned solution more compelling.

Derash

Onqelos translates ארמי אבד אבי in accordance with a very widespread *derasha*: לבן ארמאה בעא לאובדא ית אבא 'Laban the Aramean sought to destroy my father (= Jacob)'. The second half[18] of the following comment in *Sipre Deut.* 26:5 gives the same interpretation: ארמי אבד אבי, מלמד שלא ירד אבינו יעקב לארם אלא על מנת לאבד/לאובד[19] ומעלה על לבן הארמי כאילו איבדו 'It teaches that our father Jacob went down to Aram for no other purpose than to perish, and (nevertheless?) (Scripture) accounts it to Laban the Aramean as though he destroyed him'.[20] Many other *targumim* and *midrashim*, as well as the Passover

---

15. S. D. Luzzatto, פירוש שד״ל על חמשה חומשי תורה (ed. P. Schlesinger; Tel-Aviv: Dvir, 1965) 550.

16. See n. 6 above, and the works cited there, esp. Millard, "Wandering Aramean," 155. The verb 'flee' is used four times in the story of Jacob's departure from Aram with his family (Gen 31:20–22, 27).

17. See n. 3 above, and Gen 42:2, 43:8.

18. Maori (תרגום הפשיטתא, 178) accepts the claim of A. Geiger, D. Z. Hoffmann, and D. Goldschmidt that the *peshat* interpretation is implicit already in the first half of the *Sipre*'s comment; Dreyfus ("L'Araméen," 149, 153, 157 n. 16) rejects it.

19. This is a *qal* infinitive on the analogy of the imperfect (יאבד), as usual in Mishnaic Hebrew and, mutatis mutandis, Galilean Aramaic. Another initial-ᵓ*alep* infinitive with this spelling variation is לאכל/לאוכל/לוכל, found in a reliable manuscript of the Mishna; see Gideon Haneman, תורת הצורות של לשון המשנה (Tel-Aviv: Tel-Aviv University, 1980) 228. Cf. already יאכל/יאוכלו/יואכלו/יוכלו in the *Temple Scroll*.

20. *Sipre Deut.*, ספרי על ספר דברים (ed. L. Finkelstein; Berlin: Jüdischer Kulturbund in Deutschland, 1939) 319, §301. In מדרש תנאים לספר דברים [2 vols.; Berlin: Ittskovski, 1909] 172 n. 5), D. Z. Hoffmann claims that the words ומעלה על לבן הארמי כאילו איבדו are a later addition to the *Sipre*, but S. Friedman (personal communication) rejects this claim.

Haggada, reflect this interpretation,[21] which is believed to have originated in the Hasmonean period.[22]

This interpretation is far more midrashic than those of the LXX and Peshiṭta: in place of their extreme dependence on context, it exhibits supreme indifference to it.[23] And while it twists the meaning of fewer words than those interpretations, it nevertheless seems to stray quite far from the canons of Hebrew grammar. Most modern scholars accept the assumption of Ibn Balᶜam and Ibn Ezra that Onqelos's rendering and the second half of the *Sipre*'s comment are based on an ungrammatical interpretation of אֹבֵד as a transitive *Qal* participle meaning 'destroyer, destroying'.[24]

21. See Mauro Pesce, *Dio senza mediatori* (Brescia: Paideia, 1979) 123–24; S. T. Lachs, "Two Related Arameans: A Difficult Reading in the Passover Haggadah," *Journal for the Study of Judaism* 17 (1986) 65–69; Dreyfus, "L'Araméen," 148–49 and Maori, תרגום הפשיטתא; and add *Midraš Psalms* 30, cited below. The claim that the masoretic accents also reflect this interpretation seems reasonable; see M. Breuer, ת״אמ ספרי ובכ״א ספרים בכ״א המקרא טעמי (Jerusalem: Mikhlala, 1982) 370; S. Kogut, לפרשנות טעמים בין המקרא (Jerusalem: Magnes, 1994) 65. (I am indebted to M. Linetsky for the former reference and to J. Blau for the latter.) However, they are also compatible with the Peshiṭta's rendering.

22. See Louis Finkelstein, "The Oldest Midrash: Pre-Rabbinic Ideals and Teachings in the Passover Haggada," *HTR* 31 (1938) 299–300; and I. L. Seeligmann, *The Septuagint Version of Isaiah* (Leiden: Brill, 1948) 85–86. Seeligman's argument that it equates Laban, the Aramean, with Antiochus Epiphanes, the Syrian ruler, is a great improvement over Finkelstein's geopolitical arguments, but both of these scholars ignore the genuine exegetical problems that led to the rejection of the *peshat* by exegetes of all periods. Seeligmann, for example, writes that the "sovereign contempt of the grammatical possibilities of the Hebrew text," shown by the *derasha*, "is quite unjustified by either historical or homiletic necessity."

23. As Ibn Ezra notes (cf. also Dreyfus, "L'Araméen," 159 n. 37), it is difficult to find any direct connection between Laban attempting to destroy Jacob and Jacob going down to Egypt. The search for such a connection has been a favorite pursuit of commentators on the Passover *Haggada* through the centuries. As far as I know, it has not been noted that some late rabbinic sources solve the problem by making ארמי the subject not only of אבד but also of וירד. Thus *Tg. Ps.-J. Num.* 31:8 has Phinehas say to Balaam: "Are you not Laban the Aramean who sought to destroy Jacob our father and went down to Egypt to annihilate his offspring?" *Midr. Sekel Ṭob Gen.* 36:32 (cf. *Tg. Ps.-J. Num.* 22:5 and *Tg. 1 Chr.* 1:43) is similar: "In Edom, reigned Bela (בלע). This is Balaam the sorcerer, who wanted to destroy (בלע) the inheritance of the Lord, the offspring of his (own) daughters [= Leah and Rachel], as it is said, 'An Aramean [= Laban] wanted to destroy my father, and he went down to Egypt.' . . . And the name of the city was Dinhaba (הבה..). When he went down to Egypt to be an advisor to Pharaoh, he advised him to say to himself, 'Let (הבה) us deal shrewdly with them lest they increase.'" In other words, Laban (alias Balaam) continued his quest to destroy Jacob by going down to Egypt and joining forces with Pharaoh.

24. See, for example, Hermann L. Strack and Paul Billerbeck, *Kommentar zum Neuen Testament aus Talmud und Midrasch* (Munich: Beck, 1922–61) 4/2.644; Beek, "Das Problem des aramäischen Stammvaters," 194; contrast Kogut cited in n. 47 below. For a different formulation of the problem, see E. J. Revell, "ᵓObed (Deut 26:5) and the Function of the Participle in MT," *Sefarad* 48 (1988) 197–205. It is interesting to note that, in the two interpretations reported by Yefet ben Eli (MS London 275, f. 3a–b), אבד is taken as intransitive, despite the fact that the "Aramean" is identified as Laban. This is accomplished by making אבי (= Jacob) the subject of אבד and turning ארמי into a prepositional phrase: "with Laban, my father was destitute" or "at the hands of Laban (on Mt. Gilead), my father nearly perished."

According to the two Andalusians, the interpretation is ungrammatical because א-ב-ד in the *Qal* stem is always intransitive. But this is such an obvious defect that it can hardly have escaped the authors of the *Sipre*, who, in their own usage, carefully distinguished intransitive אובד (for example, ספינה אובדת 'a ship perishes')[25] from transitive מאבד (for example, מאבדים את העולם 'they destroy the world').[26] Moreover, in *Sipre Deut*. 11:17, we find א-ב-ד in the *Qal* stem paraphrased by the intransitive participle גולה 'going into exile',[27] precisely as in Rashbam's comment to our verse. Finally, *Sipre Numbers* contains, in two places, a question about Deut 30:3 that reveals that the rabbis were no less aware than Ibn Bal‘am and Ibn Ezra that some verbs in the *Qal* stem cannot take an object: וכשהם חוזרים שכינה חוזרת עמהם שנאמר ושב ה' אלהיך את־שבותך ורחמך והשיב לא נאמר אלא ושב... 'and when they return, the *Shekhina* will return with them, as it says, "the Lord your God will return with (את) your captivity." What it says is not והשיב but ושב.[28] This *derasha* rests on the assumption that since שב, unlike השיב, is intransitive, את must be the preposition 'with' rather than the accusative marker.

Ibn Bal‘am was no stranger to rabbinic hermeneutics[29]—indeed, he was known primarily as a halakist in his time[30]—and yet he seems to have been genuinely puzzled by this interpretation, asking: "What necessity (*ḍarūra*) led to the ousting of אבד from its true usage?" Of the many discussions of this problem since the Middle Ages, five seem worthy of note.

(1) R. Judah Loewe (Maharal) of Prague, in his defense of the midrashic interpretation, noted other cases of א-ב-ד in the *Qal* stem rendered by the targumists as if they were transitive: Deut 32:28, עם מאבדי עיצא = גוי אובד עצות 'a people destroying counsel', and Ps 2:12, ותהובדון אורחא = ותאבדו דרך 'and you shall destroy the way'.[31] Finding these parallels was a *tour de force*, but they do not shed as much light on our *derasha* as one might suppose, because the former renders a participle with a participle and the latter renders an imperfect with an imperfect. Accordingly, they fail to explain why Onqelos did not render the participle אֹבֵד with a participle, for example, בעא למהוי מובד 'sought to be the destroyer of' or בעי לאובדא 'was seeking to destroy', instead of בעא לאובדא 'sought to destroy'. We shall return to this point below (p. 136).

25. *Sipre Deut.*, 416, §354.

26. *Sipre Deut.*, 376, §324.

27. *Sipre Deut.*, 102, §43.

28. *Sipre Num.*, ספרי על ספר במדבר (ed. H. S. Horovitz; Leipzig: Gustav Fock, 1917) 83, §84; 223, §161.

29. Joshua Blau, "Ibn Bal‘am, Judah ben Samuel," *EncJud* 8, col. 1156.

30. M. Goshen-Gottstein (ed.), פירוש ר' יהודה אבן בלעם לספר ישעיהו (Ramat Gan: Bar-Ilan University Press, 1992) v.

31. R. Judah Loewe, ספר גבורות השם (London: Hachinuch, 1954) chap. 54, p. 237; see also גור אריה to Deut 26:5.

(2) R. Wolf Heidenheim, followed by R. Jacob Z. Mecklenburg, and many others,[32] claimed that the rabbis did not interpret אֹבֵד as a _Qal_ participle but rather, as the third masculine-singular perfect of a _binyan Poel_, the Hebrew counterpart[33] of the Arabic 3d form (_fāᶜala_). Verbs in that _binyan_ are transitive, he argued, and have the same meaning as their Arabic counterpart. Many modern Arabists believe that the 3d form has a conative sense—'attempt to, seek to'—which could not be closer to Onqelos's rendering with בעא ל- and the Passover _Haggada_'s paraphrase with בקש ל-. Heidenheim's own description of the meaning of Arabic _fāᶜala_—'seek constantly to'[34]—adds an aspectual component that is not mentioned in any of the standard Arabic handbooks and that detracts somewhat from his argument.

Heidenheim's theory is ingenious but problematic. There is not a shred of synchronic evidence that the Hebrew _Poel_ stem had a conative sense. The classical grammarians who debated the existence of this stem[35] never mention such a sense, nor does Gesenius, whose comparison of the Hebrew _Poel_ with the Arabic _fāᶜala_[36] appeared a few years before Heidenheim's. Heidenheim himself made no attempt to argue that any of the standard examples of his _binyan_ have that meaning. The same is true of Ewald, who applied labels like _ziel-stamm_ and _suche-stamm_ (alongside _angriff-stamm_ and _anpacke-stamm_) to the Hebrew

---

32. R. Wolf Heidenheim, מודע לבינה (Rödelheim: Heidenheim, 1818–21)—the comment appears in the supercommentary on Rashi, הבנת המקרא, printed in that work; R. Jacob Z. Mecklenburg, הכתב והקבלה (Frankfurt a/M: Kauffmann, 1880); see Dreyfus, "L'Araméen," 151 and 159 n. 39.

33. Rare except with hollow and geminate verbs.

34. ". . . [W]e also find it in the Arabic language, in which it is the third _binyan_. And according to the testimony of their linguists, its principal use is to refer to the constancy of the yearning of the agent to this action to the point where he seeks it perpetually." I am unable to determine the source of Heidenheim's description. The idea that the Arabic 3d form has conative meaning is generally believed to have been first proposed in G. H. A. Ewald, _Grammatica critica linguae Arabicae_ (Leipzig: Hahn, 1831–33) 97; see H. Fleisch, _Les verbes à allongement vocalique interne en sémitique_ (Paris: Institut d'ethnologie, 1944) 58. Fleisch (pp. 47–58) shows that it was completely unknown to the Arab grammarians and even to de Sacy, whose Arabic grammar Ewald praised (despite what he considered to be its excessive reliance on the native grammarians) in the prefaces to vols. 1 and 2 of his own book. Heidenheim could not have taken the idea from Ewald, who was only seventeen and still a student when the passage cited above was published. Indeed, it was only gradually that Ewald moved toward the view that the Arabic _fāᶜala_ equals the Hebrew _Poel_ as a _suche-stamm_. The idea is not very clear in his _Grammatica critica linguae Arabicae_, and it is completely absent in his _Kritische Grammatik der hebräischen Sprache_ (Leipzig: Hahn, 1827) 206–7. It appears fully developed in his _Ausführliches Lehrbuch der hebräischen Sprache des alten Bundes_ (8th ed.; Göttingen, 1870) 331–32, §125a.

35. See the works cited by William Chomsky, _David Ḳimḥi's Hebrew Grammar_ (New York: Bloch, 1952) 105 n. 159, esp. Abraham de Balmes, מקנה אברם (Venice, 1523) ב, טff., which surveys the debate, and add R. Moses Qimḥi, מהלך שבילי הדעת (Venice, 1546) ב, ג.

36. W. Gesenius, _Ausführliches grammatisch-kritisches Lehrgebäude der hebräischen Sprache mit Vergleichung der verwandten Dialekte_ (Leipzig: Vogel, 1817) 250–52.

Poel but ignored them when it came time to interpret individual examples.[37] A valiant attempt to practice what Ewald preached was made by Kautzsch, in his revision of Gesenius' grammar,[38] but even after excluding hollow and geminate verbs,[39] he was unable to impose a conative sense on more than thirty percent of the examples of *Poel* that he cited.

On the Arabic side, there are also many problems with Heidenheim's theory. According to Fleisch,[40] the only meaning for the 3d form given by Arab grammarians is *mušāraka*, implicit reciprocity.[41] In the words of Sibawaihi: "Know that when you say *fāʿaltuhu*, there comes from someone else to you the same as what goes from you to him."[42] Even modern scholars who hold that the 3d form is primarily conative frequently recognize reciprocity as an optional secondary component of the meaning.[43] And yet it is hardly likely that Onqelos meant that Jacob and Laban were attempting to destroy each other! Moreover, if the 3d form is conative at all, it is conative with respect to the 1st form, not the 2d form. Thus, if *ġālaba* really means 'attempt to overcome', as Wright says it does, it is the conative of *ġalaba* 'overcome'—not of *ġallaba* 'cause to overcome'.[44] The Arabic analogy, then, leads to the interpretation 'attempt to perish'[45] or 'attempt to perish together with', rather than 'attempt to destroy'.

(3) R. Meyuḥas b. Elijah,[46] a medieval exegete unknown to Heidenheim, was actually the first to analyze אִבֵּר as a *Poel* perfect: "*ʾŌbēd* like *ʾibbēd*, and it is a verb in the *Poel* form, as we wrote in *Seper ha-Middôt*." The causative interpretation of the *Poel* stem, recognized by Gesenius and cited by Kogut in

---

37. Ewald, *Ausführliches Lehrbuch*. Ewald's view was rejected by F. E. König, *Historisch-kritisches Lehrgebäude der hebräischen Sprache* (Leipzig: Hinrichs, 1881) 1.202: "Und für die Uebersetzung der obigen Stellen ist die Bedeutung des Einwirkungsstammes nicht gerade nöthig."

38. GKC¹ §55. Kautzsch's attempt was judged unsuccessful by Fleisch, *Les verbes*, 19: "L'examen des significations ne révèle pas une IIIᵉ forme, un Zielstamm comme le veut Kautzsch."

39. The need for this exclusion was cited as a weakness of Ewald's theory by König, *Historisch-kritisches Lehrgebäude*: "Dieselbe Form muss nach jener Ansicht bei den Verben, deren 2. u. 3. Stammconsonant gleich ist, anders als bei dem relgelmässigen Verb erklärt werden."

40. Fleisch, *Les verbes*, 47–57; idem, *Traité de philologie arabe* (Beirut: Dar el-Machreq, 1979) 2.288–90.

41. Both the 3d and the 6th forms express reciprocity or participation, that is, A and B doing something with each other. The difference is that the 3d-form verb takes A as its subject and B as its object, while the 6th-form verb takes A and B as its subject.

42. H. Derenbourg (ed.), *Le Livre de Sîbawaihi* (Paris: Imprimerie Nationale, 1885–89) 2.253, lines 13–14. I have followed Fleisch (*Les verbes*, 47) in omitting the last three words of the sentence.

43. E.g., W. Wright, *A Grammar of the Arabic Language* (3d ed.; Cambridge: Cambridge University Press, 1896) 1.32–33, §43.

44. Ibid.

45. Compare also Ethiopic *māsana* 'perish'; Thomas O. Lambdin, *Introduction to Classical Ethiopic* (Missoula, Mont.: Scholars Press, 1978) 225.

46. R. Meyuḥas ben Elijah, פירוש על ספר דברים (ed. M. Katz; Jerusalem: Mossad Harav Kook, 1968) 159.

connection with our problem,[47] is certainly easier to defend than the conative interpretation. The possibility that Onqelos and the *Sipre* interpreted אובד on the analogy of causatives like קומם and יודעתי (1 Sam 21:3) cannot be ruled out, but I still do not find this explanation convincing.

(4) A. B. Ehrlich[48] conjectured that Onqelos did not simply interpret our verb as being equivalent to the *Piel* perfect אִבַּד but actually read it that way. It is difficult to evaluate this claim in the absence of ancient manuscripts of Onqelos. Some manuscripts lead us to believe that Onqelos would have rendered a *Piel* form of א-ב-ד with an Aramaic *Pael* (לְאַבְּדָא; see Onqelos to Deut 12:2) rather than an *ʾApel* (לְאוֹבָדָא), but other, less consistent manuscripts do not.

Evidence for Ehrlich's hypothesis might be adduced from the traditional Samaritan reading of the word as a *Pi/ael* perfect, *abbəd*,[49] and from the *Sipre*'s paraphrase of אבד with איבד in our verse, but a comparison with Deut 32:28 shows how misleading this evidence is. There, too, the Samaritan tradition has *abbəd*[50] and the *Sipre* paraphrases אבד with a *Piel* perfect,[51] and yet this evidence hardly shows that the rendering מאבדי in Onqelos reflects a variant reading tradition.

(5) L. Finkelstein's claim that the compiler of the midrash in the Passover *Haggada* read אִבַּד[52] sounds the same as Ehrlich's, but he may have been referring to a midrashic revocalization rather than a variant reading tradition. However, neither the *Sipre* nor the other versions of the midrash contains statements like אל תקרי אובד אלא איבד[53] or כתיב איבד,[54] which would signal such a revocalization. Nor do any of the traditional commentators interpret the midrash that way. Indeed, *Hadar Zeqenim* asks a question (איבד היה לו לומר)[55] that presupposes the opposite view. And the version of the midrash in the *Leqaḥ Tob* has האביד instead of איבד.

47. Kogut, המקרא, 65. He too does not mention Meyuḥas.
48. A. B. Ehrlich, מקרא כפשוטו (Berlin: Poppelauer, 1899) 360.
49. Cited according to the transcription of Z. Ben-Ḥayyim, עברית וארמית נוסח שומרון (Jerusalem: Academy of the Hebrew Language, 1961) 3/1.142; Dreyfus, "L'araméen," 150; cf. also Pesce, *Dio senza mediatori*, 127 n. 84.
50. Ben-Ḥayyim, *Hebrew and Aramaic*, 160.
51. *Sipre Deut.*, p. 372, §322: איבדו ישראל עצה טובה.
52. Finkelstein, "The Oldest Midrash," 300.
53. For examples of this type of *derasha* in the *Sipre*, see Samuel Waldberg, דרכי השינויים (Lemberg: Menkes, 1870) 44a–b. For examples in rabbinic literature that alter the *binyan* of a verb, see ibid., 32b (*b. Šabb.* 114a, 119b), 34b (*b. Roš Haš.* 3a), 36b (*b. Soṭa* 10a), 37a (*b. Soṭa* 38b, *b. Qidd.* 9a [bis]), 37b (*b. B. Qam.* 10b), 39a (*b. Sanh.* 54b, 89a), 47a (*Gen. Rab.* §19). C. Milikowsky (personal communication) points out additional examples in *b. Sukk.* 52a (ישלם-ישלים), *b. Meg.* 28a (משנאי-משניאי), *b. B. Qam.* 10b (ישלמנה-ישלימנה).
54. For examples of this type of *derasha* in the Talmud that alter the *binyan* of a verb, see *b. B. Qam.* 36a (*b. Ketub.* 69b), 37b (*b. Qidd.* 59b), 39b (*b. Mak.* 7b).
55. See Jacob Gellis, תוספות השלם: הגדה של פסח (Jerusalem: Tosafot Hashalem, 1989) 61, §11.

A New Solution

I propose a new solution: that the rabbis interpreted the word אובד as though it were Aramaic.[56] In Aramaic, אוֹבֵד is not a *Qal* participle with the meaning 'perishing, wandering' but rather, a third masculine-singular *ʾApel* perfect with the meaning 'he destroyed'.[57] The initial א of the form is the marker of the *binyan* rather than the first radical; and the following *ō* is a reflex not of **ā* but of **aw*,[58] the root having been transferred from the initial-*ʾalep* class to the initial-*waw* class.[59] The *ʾApel* of this verb occurs, in fact, in Onqelos's rendering לבן ארמאה בעא לאובדא ית אבא; indeed, were it not for the insertion of בעא (compare בקש in the Passover *Haggada*), Onqelos's rendering would have been אוֹבֵד 'he destroyed', and there would never have been any question about the source of the *derasha*.

It should be noted that the proposed solution accounts not only for the targum's choice of *binyan* but also for the tense that it and the *Sipre* use. The interpretation of אֹבֵד as a past-tense verb was of crucial importance for the *Sipre*, since it is only this tense that would justify its underlying assumption that our verse presents Laban's intention to kill Jacob (at Mt. Gilead, according to Rashi) as though it had been realized.[60]

A clear example of a *derasha*'s equating intention with deed based on a past-tense verb is found in *Mek. Exod.* 12.28, ' "And they did" (ויעשו)—Did they (really) do (it) already (at this point)? (No), but as soon as they accepted the obligation to do (it), (Scripture) accounts it to them as though they had done (it)'. That the *derasha* on Deut 26:5 had a similar basis is clear from the similarity between the passage in the *Mekilta* and the following passage from

---

56. For the possibility of another bilingual pun underlying the rabbinic understanding of our verse (ארמי interpreted as a Greek word), see David Berger, "Three Typological Themes in Early Jewish Messianism: Messiah Son of Joseph, Rabbinic Calculations, and the Figure of Armilus," *AJS Review* 10 (1985) 161–62 n. 77.

57. Cf. *y. Qidd.* 3:12 64c, ואובדתא חיין דההוא גברא 'and you destroyed the life of "that man" '. The form אובד can also be a first-person singular *ʾApel* imperfect with the meaning 'I will destroy', as in *Tg. Onq. Lev.* 23:30. In Jewish dialects of Aramaic, the first syllable of these forms is *ʾo* rather than *ʾaw*.

58. It goes without saying that the rabbis did not consider the defective spelling of the *ō* in biblical אֹבֵד an obstacle to interpreting it as derived from **aw*; compare the midrashic interpretation of biblical תֹר 'turtledove' as 'ox' (< **tawr*), cited below.

59. Cf. G. Dalman, *Grammatik des jüdisch-palästinischen Aramäisch* (2d ed.; Leipzig: Hinrichs, 1905) 298, 302; T. Nöldeke, *Compendious Syriac Grammar* (London: Williams & Norgate, 1904) 118, §174E.

60. I owe this insight to S. Friedman (personal communication), who compares the midrash in *y. Peʾa* I,1 16b on Obad 9–10: מֶחֱמָס אָחִיךָ יַעֲקֹב: מְקַטֵּל 'Did he (really) kill him? (No), rather it teaches that he (= Esau) planned to kill him (= Jacob), and Scripture accounted it to him as if he had killed him'. Cf. also A. M. Silbermann, *Chumash with Targum Onqelos, Haphtaroth and Rashi's Commentary* (London: Shapiro Valentine, 1934) 5.125.

Midraš Psalms 30:[61] "R. Nehemiah says: 'If an idolater planned to transgress, even though he did not do it, the Holy-One-Blessed-Be-He counts it as if he had done it, for so it says: "The Aramean destroyed my father." Where did Laban destroy Jacob?[62] (Nowhere), but since he planned to do it, Scripture accounts it to him as though he had done (it)'."

It is perhaps not fortuitous that the rabbis chose to read this particular verb as Aramaic; after all, it describes an activity of an ארמי 'Aramean'. The Bible has a tendency to use Aramaisms in stories about Laban and other Arameans and in dialogue involving them.[63] An Aramaizing reading of ארמי אבד אבי would be nothing more than an extension of this tendency to the midrashic realm.

As a matter of fact, forms not unlike the Aramaic *ʾApel* of א-ב-ד are attested in dialectal contexts in the Bible. In Isa 63:3, in a passage about Edom, we find a causative with prefixed א- instead of ה-: אגאלתי. In Hos 11:4, the form אוכיל is, according to Rabin,[64] an example of Aramaic influence on the Hebrew of the Northern Kingdom: an initial-*ʾalep* verb treated as initial-*waw* in the H/*ʾ*-stem. It is precisely these two features which characterize the midrashic analysis of אֹבֵד as an Aramaic causative.

This would not be the only word in Deuteronomy identified as Aramaic by the *Sipre. Sipre Deut.* 33:2 tells us that the phrase ואתה מרבבת קדש is Aramaic, presumably on account of the word אתה "come"[65] and then proceeds to give the word a second Aramaic interpretation on the midrashic level.[66] The latter takes אָתָה as the Aramaic cognate of Hebrew אוֹת 'sign'—a noun in the emphatic state instead of a verb.[67]

---

61. Quoted here according to the Warsaw edition, p. 82a. Compare also Rashi's comment to Deut 26:5, which contains an interpolation based on this passage.

62. Buber's edition reads: 'Did Laban (really) destroy Jacob?'

63. See A. Hurvitz, "The Chronological Significance of 'Aramaisms' in Biblical Hebrew," *IEJ* 18 (1968) 236–37 and the works by Baumgartner and Kutscher cited there in n. 14; J. C. Greenfield, "Aramaic Studies and the Bible," in *Congress Volume: Vienna, 1980* (VTSup 32; ed. J. A. Emerton; Leiden: Brill, 1981) 129–30; S. A. Kaufman, "The Classification of the North West Semitic Dialects of the Biblical Period and Some Implications Thereof," in *Proceedings of the Ninth World Congress of Jewish Studies*, vol. 2: *Panel Sessions—Hebrew and Aramaic Languages* (ed. M. Bar-Asher; Jerusalem: Magnes, 1988) 55; A. Hurvitz, ‏"עברית וארמית בתקופת המקרא: סוגיית ה 'ארמאיזמים'‏" ‏(ed. M. Bar-Asher; Jerusalem: Bialik, 1996) 87. Examples involving Laban include Gen 30:34, הן‏ 'yes' rather than 'behold'; 31:16, הציל‏ 'took back' rather than 'rescued'; 31:28 -נטשת‏ 'you allowed' rather than 'you abandoned' (as though Laban were mistranslating שבקת‏); and, of course, 31:47, ‏יגר שהדותא. ‏מחקרים בלשון העברית ובלשונות היהודים מוגשים לשלמה מורג‏, in ‏במחקר העברית המקראית,‏

64. C. Rabin, ‏"עיונים בספר תרי־עשר‏," in ‏"לשונם של עמוס והושע‏ (ed. B. Z. Lurie; Jerusalem: Kiryat-Sepher, 1981) 125.

65. *Sipre Deut.*, p. 395, §343.

66. Ibid., p. 398.

67. The word is attested in Dan 3:32, 33; 6:28; it has the expected *ā* corresponding to Hebrew *ō*. In Galilean Aramaic, the emphatic ending is normally written with *h*.

There are, in fact, any number of midrashic Aramaisms scattered throughout rabbinic literature, without any special Aramean context to trigger them.[68] Occasionally, the interlingual[69] nature of the exegesis is acknowledged, as in the rabbinic interpretations of (1) Exod 12:4, תכסו, as 'you shall slaughter' instead of 'you shall apportion';[70] (2) Gen 15:9, תר, as 'ox' instead of 'turtle-dove';[71] (3) Hos 8:10, יתנו, as 'they recite' instead of 'they offer a harlot's wage';[72] and (4) Ps 136:13, לגזרים, as 'for the circumcised' instead of 'to pieces'.[73] In each of these *derashot*, there is an explicit reference to Aramaic (לשון ארמי/ ארמית/סורסי).[74]

The *derashot* considered here are part and parcel of the overall exegetical program of the rabbis, who were determined to ferret out every imaginable type of ambiguity in the biblical text: lexical and syntactic, homophonic and homographic,[75] synchronic and diachronic,[76] intralingual and interlingual. For them, each *derasha* was quite literally a "search"—a search for new manifestations of the omnisignificance of Scripture.

68. For a small collection, see L. Zunz, *Die gottesdienstlichen Vorträge der Juden historisch entwickelt* (Frankfurt: Kauffmann, 1892) 339 note *h*. See also R. C. Steiner, "המלים 'מאה' ו'מאתין' ומאתין" "בדרשות שנתיסדו על ניבים עממיים של הארמית, *Tarbiz* 65 (1996) 33–37. We are speaking here about wordplays, that is, intentional deviations from *peshat*. It goes without saying that the interpretation of Hebrew words based on the uncritical use of Aramaic homophones sometimes resulted in unintentional deviations from *peshat*. A well-known example of this type is the mistranslation of מואב סיר רחצי as 'Moab, the basin of my hope' instead of 'Moab is my washbasin' in LXX to Ps 60[59]:10 and 108[107]:10. For this and other examples, see J. Barr, *Comparative Philology and the Text of the Old Testament* (Oxford: Clarendon, 1968) 54–55 and the references cited there.

69. For a discussion of the interaction of Aramaic and Hebrew in rabbinic texts, see Daniel Boyarin, "Bilingualism and Meaning in Rabbinic Literature: An Example," in *Fucus: A Semitic/ Afrasian Gathering in Remembrance of Albert Ehrman* (ed. Y. L. Arbeitman; Amsterdam: Benjamins, 1987) 141–52. For the theological and historical background of the interlingual *derasha* and additional examples, see J. Fraenkel, דרכי האגדה והמדרש (Tel-Aviv: Modan, 1996) 115–18, and the literature cited there.

70. *Mekilta, Pisḥa* 3.

71. פרקי דרבי אליעזר, מהדורה מדעית (Jerusalem: Makor, 1972) 28a, 93.

72. *b. B. Bat.* 8a. I am indebted to S. Abramson ז״ל for this example.

73. *Tanḥuma Buber, Bešallaḥ* §12.

74. Unfortunately, none of these *derashot* involves Hebrew verbal forms with morphologically different Aramaic verbal homophones. The first explicit discussion of this type of interlingual homophony (e.g., שְׁלַח: Hebrew imperative but Aramaic perfect; אָמַר, יָדַע: Hebrew perfects but Aramaic participles) comes in the eleventh century, in *al-Kitāb al-Muštamil* of Abū l-Faraj Hārūn, but awareness of the phenomenon can be detected earlier, in *Kitāb jāmiᶜ al-Alfāẓ* of David ben Abraham al-Fāsī and in the *Masorah parva* of *Codex Leningrad* B19a to 2 Sam 24:10; see Aharon Maman, השוואת אוצר המלים של העברית ולארמית לערבית למן רס״ג ועד אבן ברון (Ph.D. diss., Hebrew University, 1984) 107, 240; A. Dotan, "De la Massora à la grammaire: Les débuts de la pensée grammaticale dans l'hébreu," *JA* 278 (1990) 23.

75. That is, the orthographic ambiguities inherent in the unpointed consonantal skeleton of the Masoretic Text. The most common are *derashot* substituting one vowel for another and שׂ for שׁ.

76. That is, *derashot* based on Mishnaic Hebrew usage.

"He Begot a Son in His Likeness after His Image" (Genesis 5:3)

JEFFREY H. TIGAY
University of Pennsylvania

The statement in Gen 5:3 that "When Adam had lived for 130 years, he begot a son in his likeness after his image" has elicited relatively little comment. Nachmanides observed that although it is obvious that all offspring of living creatures are in the likeness and image of their progenitors, the text specifies this in the case of Adam's son (Seth) because Adam was created in God's likeness and image (1:26–27, 5:1), and this exalted him.[1] Most commentators state that the verse means that Adam passed on the divine image to his descendants.[2] This is syllogistically correct, but if it were the main point the text

Author's note: This article is affectionately dedicated to my dear teacher and friend, Moshe Greenberg, in appreciation for his scholarly, pedagogic, and personal inspiration, although it is impossible fully to express my indebtedness to him. I am grateful to Martin Ostwald, Joseph Farrell, Barry Eichler, and Tsvi Abush for advice on several passages discussed here.

1. For the subject of man being created in the image of God, see E. M. Curtis, *Man as the Image of God in Genesis in the Light of Ancient Near Eastern Parallels* (Ph.D. dissertation, University of Pennsylvania, 1984); J. H. Tigay, "The Image of God and the Flood: Some New Developments," in *Studies in Jewish Education and Judaica in Honor of Louis Newman* (ed. A. M. Shapiro and B. Cohen; New York: KTAV, 1984) 169–82.

2. Nachmanides; D. Z. Hoffmann; J. Skinner; S. R. Driver; A. Dillmann; U. Cassuto (at 5:1); G. von Rad; N. M. Sarna; M. Weinfeld, in *Ḥămišâ Ḥumšê Tôrâ ʿim Pêrûš Ḥadaš . . . mēʾēt Š. L. Gôrdôn*, vol. 1: *Sēper Běrēšît* (newly revised; Tel Aviv: S. L. Gordon, 1972) 26; Westermann (at 5:1); cf. Keil and Delitzsch.

As Weinfeld notes, there is a similarity between our verse and *Enuma Eliš* I 16, "Anu begot his likeness (*tamšilašu*) Nudimmud (Ea)." What this passage might imply about Gen 5:3 is uncertain. Although it could mean that Nudimmud looked like Anu, the context does not favor this interpretation. *Enuma Eliš* I 12–20 contains a series of comparisons indicating whether successive generations of the gods were equal or superior to their predecessors. In this context, line 16 more likely means that Nudimmud was Anu's equal (cf. line 15, "Anshar made Anu, his firstborn, equal [*umaššil-ma*]"). For further discussion, see A. L. Oppenheim, "Mesopotamian Mythology 1," *Or* n.s. 16 (1947) 208–9; for another view, see J. V. Kinnier-Wilson, "The Epic of Creation," in *Documents from Old Testament Times* (ed. D. Winton Thomas; New York: Harper and Row, 1961) 14.

wished to emphasize, the text would have underscored it by saying that 'Adam begot a son in *God's* likeness, after *His* image' (*bidĕmût ʾĕlōhîm ukĕṣalmô*), rather than 'Adam begot a son in *his* likeness, after *his* image'. The wording of the text stresses Seth's resemblance to Adam, not to God.

What is the point of stressing what to Nachmanides seemed obvious? The third-generation Palestinian Amora R. Jeremiah b. Elazar inferred that begetting offspring in one's own image was *not* inevitable, and that prior to his 130th year, Adam had in fact begotten children who did not resemble him:

> All those years that the first man was under the ban (*bĕniddui*, shunned by God)[3] he begot spirits, *šēd*-demons, and *lîl*-demons,[4] as it is said: "When Adam had lived for 130 years, he begot a son in his likeness, after his image." This implies that until that time he begot offspring that were not after his image (*b. ʿErub.* 18b).[5]

The inference that, as a consequence of God's curse for having sinned in the Garden of Eden, Adam begot offspring unlike himself, namely spirits and demons, was fleshed out by R. David Qimḥi (Narbonne, Provence, 1160?–1235?), building on observations by R. Sherira Gaon (906–1006, Gaon of Pumbedita 968–1006):[6]

ויחי אדם, ואחרי שהיה שלשים ומאת שנה הוליד בדמותו בצלמו [sic], ופירושו כמו
שפירשנו בצלמינו כדמותנו, כי אדם טוב ושלם היה זה אחר שעשה תשובה. ואפשר שיהיה
פירוש בדמותו, על דמות גופני שהיה דומה לו בצורתו, ופירוש כצלמו, בדעתו ובשכלו,
כי אדם אף על פי שחטא בתחילה אחר ששב בתשובה והתחרט על חטאו היה שלם
בשכלו . . . וכתב הרב רבינו נסים בשם רבינו שרירא ז״ל פירוש דבר זה, דלטייה
הקב״ה לאדם נתן בו אות שלא היו ילדיו דומין לו וכמו נשים שיולדות בריות משונות
כאלו דאמור רבנן, אמר רב יהודה אמר שמואל המפלת דמות לילית אמו טמאה לידה,
ולד הוא אלא אלא שהוא בעל כנפים. וכשהיה אדם הראשון בקללה לא היה מוליד אלא
בריות משונות דומות שדין ולילין בכיעור פניהם וגביהם והם רוחות רעות, כדרך
שהיתה רוחו של אדם רוח רעה בשעה שהיה מקולל, יצאו ממנו רוחות רעות שיש
בהן רעה ואין בהן טובה, וכן דרך בני אדם לקרוא למכוערי הדמות ולאנשים רעים
שדים, וכשחפץ הקב״ה והסיר קללתו של אדם הראשון הוליד בנים שדומים לו במראה
נאה ורוח טובה והוא שנאמר: וילד בדמותו כצלמו.

3. B. Epstein, *Tôrâ Tĕmîmâ*, ad loc.

4. *Midr. Hagādôl* adds monkeys to the list of offspring. This reading may be influenced by Maimonides, *Guide to the Perplexed* 1:7, or by a passage like the one listing "monkeys and spirits and *šēd*-demons and *lîl*-demons" in another context, *b. Sanh.* 109a. Cf. M. M. Kasher, *Torah Shelemah* (New York: American Biblical Encyclopedia Society, 1949) 1.351 no. 33.

5. *Tg. Ps-J.* likewise holds that Adam previously begot offspring unlike himself but takes this to refer to Cain; cf. *Pirqe R. El.* chap. 22. See also Jacob al-Kirkisani, cited by M. Zucker, *Saadya's Commentary on Genesis* (New York: Jewish Theological Seminary of America, 1984) n. 189 [Heb.].

6. For the text of Qimḥi, see M. L. Katzenellenbogen (ed.), *Tôrat Ḥayyîm, Bĕrēʾšît*, part 1 (Jerusalem: Mossad Harav Kook, 1986) 81–82. Qimḥi cites Sherira from the works of R. Nissim Gaon of Kairouan, Tunisia (990–1062).

After Adam had lived for 130 years he begot offspring in his likeness after his image . . . for Adam was good and perfect after he repented. The interpretation of 'in his likeness' possibly refers to his bodily likeness, meaning that he resembled him in form, while 'his image' refers to his mind and intellect, for although Adam sinned at first, after he repented and regretted his sin he was perfect in his intellect. . . .

Qimḥi goes on to quote R. Jeremiah b. Elazar's comment from *b. ʿErub.* 18b and then quotes the explanation of Sherira:

The Holy One, Blessed be He, cursed Adam and placed on him a sign such that his offspring did not resemble him, like women who bear (*yolĕdôt*) strange creatures such as those mentioned by our [Talmudic] rabbis [in *b. Nid.* 24b], "R. Judah, citing Samuel, stated: 'If a woman aborted a fetus in the likeness (*dĕmût*) of Lilith, its mother is unclean by reason of the birth [as stated in Leviticus 12], for it is a child though it has wings.'" And while the first man was under a curse he begot only strange creatures resembling *šēd*-demons and *lîl*-demons in the ugliness of their faces and backs, and they were evil spirits, just as Adam's spirit was an evil spirit at the time he was accursed and there came forth from him evil spirits in which there is evil and no good. Similarly, it is people's custom to call people of ugly likeness and evil people demons (*šēdîm*). But when the Holy One, Blessed be He, was pleased to remove the first man's curse, he bore children who resembled him in comely appearance and good spirit, and that is what is meant when it is said: 'He begot in his likeness after his image' (Gen 5:3).

What is behind the assumption that the opposite of begetting offspring who resemble their parents is begetting grotesque, malformed offspring? The answer is found in a curse formula that appears in Greek compacts.[7] According to Aeschines, the members of the Delphis Amphictiony attacking Cirrha in 590 B.C.E. swore that:

If anyone should violate this, whether city, or private man, or tribe, let him be under the curse (*enagēs*) . . . that their land bear no fruit, nor may their wives bear children resembling their parents (*goneusin eoikota*), but monsters (*terata*), nor may the flocks beget offspring according to nature (*kata physin*). . . .[8]

Similarly, at Plataea in 479 B.C.E., the Greeks, before battle with the Persians, are reported to have sworn

---

7. I first learned of these blessings and curses from M. Weinfeld, "The Emergence of the Deuteronomic Movement: The Historical Antecedents," in *Das Deuteronomium* (ed. N. Lohfink; Leuven: Leuven University Press, 1985) 80.

8. Aeschines *Against Ctesiphon* 3.110–11, in C. D. Adams, *The Speeches of Aeschines* (LCL; Cambridge: Harvard University Press / London: Heinemann, 1938) 392–95.

> If I observe what is written in the oath . . . my (land) shall bear fruits—if not, it shall be barren; and (if I observe the oath) the women shall bear children resembling the parents (*en eoikota goneusin*)—if not, they shall bear monsters (*terata*); and (if I observe the oath) the flock shall bear resembling (*eoikota*) the flock—if not, monsters (*terata*).[9]

In these curses, 'resembling' (*eoikota*) parents refers to physical resemblance, as it does in Aristotle's discussion of children looking like their parents.[10] 'Monsters' (*terata*) is used in the sense of anomalies, that is, congenitally malformed persons or animals, as the term is used by Plato and Aristotle in discussing such phenomena as humans producing offspring that resemble animals or animals of one species producing offspring that resemble another.[11] Some other curses, instead of saying "nor may their wives bear children resembling their parents, but monsters," say that "the women shall not give birth according to nature" (*mēte . . . kata physin*, the phrase used of flocks in the oath against Cirrha), which means the same thing.[12]

In these blessings and curses, then, looking like one's parents does not mean bearing a close resemblance to them but looking human rather than inhuman. The curse formula resembles the comments of Jeremiah b. Elazar, Sherira, and

---

9. P. Siewert, *Der Eid von Plataiai* (Munich: Beck, 1972) 6–8, lines 39–46, and p. 98. Hesiod's *Works and Days*, line 235 states that in a city governed by justice, "the women bear children who resemble (*eoikota*) their parents," which probably means the same thing. See discussion by M. L. West, *Hesiod: Works and Days* (Oxford: Clarendon, 1978) 215–16; A. N. Athanassakis, *Hesiod: Theogony, Works and Days, Shield* (Baltimore: Johns Hopkins University Press, 1983) 95; W. J. Verdenius, *A Commentary on Hesiod: Works and Days, vv. 1–382* (Leiden: Brill, 1985) 133–34; and M. Delcourt, *Stérilités mystérieuses et naissances maléfiques dans l'antiquité classique* (Bibliothèque de la Faculté de Philosophie et Lettres de l'Université de Liège 83; Liège: Faculté de Philosophie et Lettres, 1938) 11 n. 3. As Delcourt observes, the fact that the children are said to resemble their 'parents' (*goneusin*) rather than their 'fathers' argues against the point's being that their paternity is not in doubt. (Contrary to Athanassakis [*Hesiod*, 71], *Works and Days* 1.182 is not pertinent to our subject; see Verdenius, *Commentary on Hesiod*, 109; West, *Hesiod*, 199; and the translations of West, *Theogony and Works and Days* [Oxford: Oxford University Press, 1988] 42, and H. G. Evelyn-White, *Hesiod, the Homeric Hymns and Homerica* [LCL; London: Heinemann/ Cambridge: Harvard University Press, 1959] 21.)

10. Aristotle *Generation of Animals* 767a.36–37.

11. LSJ, s.v. *teras*. See Plato *Cratylus* 393b, 394a; Aristotle *Generation of Animals* 767b.6, 8; 769b.10, 30; 773a.32, etc. The word is used in this sense in English derivatives, such as 'teratology', "the branch of medicine and of developmental biology which deals with congenital defects and abnormal formations" (L. Brown [ed.], *The New Shorter Oxford English Dictionary* [Oxford: Clarendon, 1993], s.v.).

12. See J. Pouilloux, *Choix d'inscriptions grecques* (Paris: Société d'Édition les Belles Lettres, 1960) no. 52, line 7; G. Dittenberger, *Sylloge inscriptionum graecarum* (4th ed.; Hildesheim: Olms, 1960) 1.773, no. 527, lines 85ff.; M. Guarducci, *Inscriptiones creticae* (Rome: La Libreria dello stato, 1942) 3.50, lines 24–25. For the usage, see Plato (*Cratylus* 393bc), who uses the phrase to illustrate the concept of monsters: "I am not speaking of monsters (*teras*). . . . If a horse, contrary to nature (*para physin*), should bring forth a calf . . . or if any offspring that is not human should be born from a human. . . ."

Qimḥi about Gen 5:3 in three respects: it describes a curse, comparable to the "ban" that Adam was under after his expulsion from Eden; it refers to children who do not resemble their parents; and it describes them as unnatural or grotesque. Although the exegetical traditions speak of spirits, not monsters, these two descriptions are not incompatible, since *šēd-* and *lîl-*demons were thought to be monstrous or grotesque in appearance.[13] In fact, in *b. Nid.* 24b (cited by Sherira), one type of malformed fetus, which looks like a human with wings, is called a *lîlît* (the feminine form of *lîl-*demon), and in the Babylonian birthomen collection *Šumma Izbu,* one type of malformed baby is called a LAMMA, the Sumerogram for a *lamassatu-* or *lamassu-*demon (*Šumma Izbu* II 67′).[14]

Underlying these blessings and curses is the concern about severely malformed babies that is reflected in the attention given to the subject in ancient literature. Talmudic sources mention the birth of a two-headed human (*b. Menaḥ.* 33a)[15] and discuss hermaphrodites a number of times (e.g., *m. Bik.* 4; *t. Bik.* 2).[16] Usually Talmudic sources deal with malformations when discussing the halakhic obligations of women after aborting a fetus, depending on whether the fetus has a human form (*ṣûrat [hā]ʾādām*) or looks like a *lîlît*-demoness or, wholly or partly, like an animal (*m. Nid.* 3:2; *m. Ker.* 1:3, 5; *b. Nid.* 22b–24b).[17] Since the Talmud refers to these only as aborted fetuses rather than live births (probably because such serious malformations are more common in aborted fetuses than in live births), its discussion, and R. Sherira's citation of it, are not strictly

13. See, for example, the descriptions in midrashic texts of the *šēd-*demon Qeṭeb: his head resembles that of a calf, with a single horn emerging from his forehead, and he rolls like a jar or ball; he is covered with scales, hair, and eyes; and a single eye is set on his chest (*Num. Rab.* 12:3; *Lam. Rab.* 1:3 [ed. Buber, p. 63]; *Midr. Ps.* 91:3 [ed. Buber, p. 397]). Pazuzu, the Mesopotamian "king of the evil lilû-demons" has four wings, a grotesque face, long horns, lion's claws, bird's talons as hind feet, and a scorpion's sting (see W. G. Lambert, "Inscribed Pazuzu Heads from Babylon," *Forschungen und Berichte* [Berlin: Akademie, 1970] 12.42:1; H. W. Haussig [ed.], *Wörterbuch der Mythologie,* 1: *Götter und Mythen im Vorderen Orient* [Stuttgart: Ernst Klett, 1965] 48).

14. E. V. Leichty, *The Omen Series Šumma Izbu* (Locust Valley, N.Y.: Augustin, 1970) 52.

15. See S. Lieberman, "*Tannāʾ hêkāʾ qāʾê,*" in *Studies in Memory of Moses Schorr, 1874–1941 (Qôbeṣ maddāʿi lĕ-zekher Mošeh Šôr)* (ed. L. Ginzberg and A. Weiss; New York: Hôtsāʾat Vaʿadat Zikhrôn Mošeh Šôr, 1944) 185. References to anomalous human births in post-Talmudic sources of the twelfth and nineteenth centuries are cited by I. Jakobovits, *Jewish Medical Ethics* (New York: Bloch, 1975) 379 n. 194. The earliest explicit reference in Jewish sources is 2 Esdr 5:8, "women in their uncleanness will give birth to monsters (*prodigia*)," part of a prediction of disasters. I know of no clear reference to the subject in the Bible. Mephibosheth's lameness, even if congenital, is not a birth defect of the same order. Exod 2:2, "When she saw that he was good," could mean that Moses' mother saw that he was normal, but the alternative was not necessarily a severe malformation.

16. B. M. Lerner, "Androgynus," *EncJud* 2.950.

17. Examples are fish, locusts, insects, creeping things, beasts, wild animals, birds, sea monsters (*tannîn*), and snakes (*nāḥāš*); in some cases the fetus has the body of a goat and the face of a human or vice versa, the face of a human but one eye of a beast; in other cases the fetuses lack or have extra bodily parts or have partly indistinguishable parts and features.

relevant to the subject. A Babylonian list of portents lists an incident when a woman gave birth to a child that ."had tusks(?) like (those) of an elephant."[18] The Babylonian omen series *Šumma Izbu* lists the predictive significance of women giving birth to children with a wide variety of malformations, including excess eyes, heads, and limbs, animal-like and demon-like features, and other types of malformation like those of the fetuses mentioned in Tractate *Niddah.*[19] The subject is also common in classical literature. Apart from the discussion by Aristotle and the reference by Plato, mentioned above, classical sources mention the birth of monsters that are half man and half beast, a pig with hawk's talons, as well as "hermaphrodites, two-headed animals and children, . . . excess limbs, misplaced body parts, missing limbs or other body parts, appearance like various animals. . . ."[20]

Malformations of these sorts are unfortunately well known even in modern times. "There are human beings with one eye in the forehead, without nose, or with 'flippers' in place of limbs, . . . children covered by a scaly integument that . . . resembles that of a fish, . . . double-headed, four limbed creatures, . . . mouthless individuals."[21] In 1991, surgeons in Tampa, Florida, performed plastic surgery on a baby who was born with Apert Syndrome. She had "a stovepipe-shaped head, bulging eyes, a concave face, gaping mouth and cleft palate. [Her] hands were grotesque mittens, two lumps of flesh with no fingers and only a stub of a thumb. A bone protruded from the bottoms of the infant's toeless, twisted feet." According to the story about the operation in *The St. Petersburg* [Florida] *Times*, "Apert is one of a cluster of syndromes that causes facial deformity and webbing of the hands and feet." It occurs once in every 160,000 births and afflicts all races and both genders.[22] A year earlier, sur-

---

18. CT 29 49:23, cited in CAD A/1 290a.

19. Aristotle's comment is relevant to Babylonian omens: when people say that an animal has the head of another animal, they do not mean it literally but are referring only to resemblance (Aristotle *Generation of Animals* 769b, 14ff. [LCL, pp. 417–19]). The malformations mentioned in *Šumma Izbu* include: looking like a lion, wolf, dog, pig, bull, elephant, ass, ram, cat, snake, tortoise, roe, bird, tigrilu monster, the head of various animals; children with two heads, with animal-like eyes, face, ears, beak, horns, or feet, or a single eye on the forehead; children with conjoined feet or more than two feet or with a beard or grey hair. *Šumma Izbu* uses the verb 'give birth' (*alādu*) rather than 'miscarry' (*ša libbiša nadû*). However, in some cases, where the women give birth to bodily parts, it, too, must have miscarriages in mind (see Leichty, *Omen Series*, 17, end).

20. Ibid., 14–16; Delcourt, *Sterilités mysterieuses*; Lieberman, "*Tannāʾ hêkāʾ qāʾê*," n. 11. See, for example, Herodotus 1.84; Livy 41.21.12; Tacitus *Annals* 12.64; *Scriptores Historiae Augustae*, Ant. Pius 9.3; Ammianus Marcellinus 19.12.19 (all cited by Lieberman).

21. F. Gonzalez-Crussi, "Teratology," in *Notes of an Anatomist* (London: Picador, 1986) 94, cited by L. Holden, *Forms of Deformity* (JSOTSup 131; Sheffield: JSOT Press, 1991) 14.

22. C. Gentry, "Doctors Rebuilt a Face, Life," *The St. Petersburg* [Florida] *Times*, July 7, 1991, City Edition, p. 1A. There are approximately 25 children born with Apert Syndrome in the United States each year (C. S. Vass, "Doctors Offer Baby Daryl Hope as Series of Operations Begins," *Chattanooga Free Press*, October 9, 1996, editorial section, p. A1).

geons at the same hospital reconstructed the face of an 18-year-old boy who "had no nose. His right eye socket was just above his ear. A large hole in the bone of his forehead left his brain protected only by a flap of wrinkled skin." According to the chief surgeon, when the boy first arrived at the hospital, "he was what you call a monstrosity." When he left, his mother said that he "does not look like an animal—he is human now."[23] Reports of two-headed babies, though rare, appear regularly, one as recently as July 28, 1996, in Tijuana, Mexico.[24]

The attention devoted to this subject in antiquity probably stems from at least two factors: such births were not only heart-breaking, but were regarded as portentous (hence their use as omens), and they were probably more frequent than they are today. According to E. V. Leichty:

> [W]e can be quite certain that the rate of abnormal birth was much greater in ancient times. Women in the ancient Near East must have conceived much more often than modern women because of high infant mortality and the lack of any type of birth control. In addition, the lack of medicine and prenatal controls can be assumed to have resulted in a much higher proportion of miscarriages. Since the probability of anomalies is increased after the fifth or sixth pregnancy, this in itself would increase considerably the ratio of malformations to births.[25]

To this we may add the likelihood that cases of Apert Syndrome, now the second most common craniofacial deformity, were probably more common in ancient and polygamous societies, in which wives often died in childbirth and men remarried or continued to marry and father children in their older years, since "men in their 50s have more than 20 times the risk of fathering Apert's syndrome children than men in their 20s."[26]

---

23. *The Daily Pennsylvanian*, September 28, 1990, from the Associated Press. More accessible, though less detailed, reports are available on-line on NEXIS (Library: News, Current News): K. Ovack, "Teen with New Face Leaves for Home," *The St. Petersburg Times*, September 28, 1990, City Edition, Tampa Bay and State section, p. 7B; and B. Port and B. Duryea, "Teen in Fair Condition after Facial Surgery," *The St. Petersburg Times*, August 18, 1990, City Edition, Tampa Bay and State; Metro Report section, p. 3B.

24. Reuters North American Wire, August 5, 1996, Monday, BC Cycle; this and several other cases are accessible on NEXIS (Library: News, Current News) sub "two-headed baby." Six cases from the Middle Ages through the nineteenth century are reported by B. C. Hirst and G. A. Piersol, *Human Monstrosities* (Philadelphia: Lea Bothers, 1891–93) 4.157 (cited by Lieberman, "*Tannāʾ hêkāʾ qāʾê*," 185).

25. Leichty, *Omen Series*, 17.

26. Geneticist Andrew Wilkie of the Institute of Molecular Medicine in Oxford, England, cited by R. Nowack, "Annual Genetics Meeting: Some Puzzles, Some Answers—1995 American Society of Human Genetics Meeting," in *Science* 270/5239 (November 17, 1995) 1120–21, available on-line on NEXIS (Library: News, Current News). Cf. D. J. David et al., *Craniofacial Deformities* (New York: Springer, 1990) 35.

The resemblance of the Greek curses to the comments of R. Jeremiah b. Elazar, Sherira and Qimḥi is striking; it is, in fact, more striking than their resemblance to Gen 5:3 itself. As noted above, the rabbinic comments all refer to a curse or a ban, they refer to children who do not resemble their parents, and they describe them as unnatural or grotesque. These similarities make one wonder whether the curse motif of bearing monstrous offspring—known to me only from the Greek world, not from the Near East—had made its way to Palestine, with so many other aspects of Greek culture, by R. Jeremiah's time (cf. 2 Esdr 5:8, cited in n. 15), and from there to tenth-century Babylonia either as curses or in some expanded version of R. Jeremiah's comment. Their resemblance to Gen 5:3 itself is less explicit. Perhaps this is simply because the verse describes a normal birth; like the Greek blessing that is a counterpart of the curse, it need not spell out that this is a blessing or state that the normal birth is non-monstrous.

It is natural to wonder whether the biblical verse reflects, or is reacting to, a mythological theme. Does it aim to counter some myth according to which the first humans gave birth to malformed, monstrous offspring? Mesopotamian and Greek myths refer to monsters in primordial times, but they are born *before* the human race comes into existence.[27] A Sumerian myth tells how, some time after Enki created humanity, he and Ninmah created eight humans with bodily defects (blind, crippled, incontinent, sexless, etc.). In the myth, however, they are not the offspring of humans, though they are obviously forerunners of various types of handicapped people who will be born to humans later.[28] Seth, the son of the first couple, is not the antithesis of any of the above. Closer to what we are looking for is Oannes, the name used by Berossus for the first of the seven antediluvian sages—known as *apkallus* in Akkadian—who taught mankind the arts and sciences of civilization.[29] According to Berossus, Oannes emerged from the Persian Gulf in the reign of the first human king. He had the body of a fish but had a human head growing beneath his fish-head and human feet growing from his fish-tail. In fact, cuneiform sources say that all seven of

27. In Hesiod's *Theogony* the offspring of Earth and Sky include the three Cyclopes who, though "in all other respects they were like gods (*theois enaligkioi*)," had one round eye in the middle of their foreheads, and three other sons who each had 100 arms and 50 heads (lines 139–52). In *Enuma Eliš*, Tiamat bears 11 monsters to battle Marduk, and Marduk himself has 4 eyes and 4 ears (I 95, 132–46). In Berossus's retelling of *Enuma Eliš*, these offspring of Tiamat are called monster-like (*teratōdē*) "men"; they have 2 or 4 wings and 2 faces, one body, and 2 heads, and both male and female sexual organs; others are men with horns and legs or feet of animals, or as composite animals (S. M. Burstein, *The Babyloniaca of Berossus* [SANE 1/5; Malibu, Calif.; Undena, 1978] 14–15; for the Greek text, see F. Jacoby, *Die Fragmente der griechischen Historiker* 3C [Leiden: Brill, 1958] 369–71).

28. See T. Jacobsen, *The Harps That Once . . . Sumerian Poetry in Translation* (New Haven: Yale University Press, 1987) 151–66.

29. Burstein, *The Babyloniaca of Berossus*, 13–14.

these sages were "pure *purādu*-fish of the sea."[30] In the opinion of Anne D. Kilmer, anomalous births are "exactly the perception that lies behind the *purādu*-fishmen *apkallu* mythology which no doubt originated in folkloric speculations based on observations of foetal development."[31] Scholars agree that one of these sages, probably Oannes, is the figure known as Adapa in Akkadian sources.[32] Now in the older myth of Adapa, Adapa is described as the son of the god Ea (*Adapa* B, 12), but he is also said to be mortal (A, 4) and 'human offspring' (*zēr amīlūti*, D, 12). Conceivably, then, Genesis, with its naturalistic conception of the origins of civilization,[33] is reacting to a tradition that civilization was founded by anomalous offspring of the first humans. However, nothing else is presently known of Adapa or of Seth to suggest that they are counterparts of each other and that Gen 5:3 is part of this reaction.[34]

In any case, it seems that the view of R. Jeremiah b. Elazar, Sherira, and Qimḥi may well be correct. The facts that "begetting children who resemble their parents" refers to normal rather than malformed, inhuman-looking off-spring; that anomalous births were relatively more common in antiquity; and that the subject received considerable attention in ancient literature lend color to their view that Gen 5:3 means that Adam fathered a normal child with a human appearance. These facts do not support the further, aggadic, inference that Adam previously begot demons or monsters. But they also suggest, since birth anomalies were usually considered ominous, that the birth of a normal child to Adam was a sign of blessing, in fulfillment of God's blessing in v. 2.

30. E. Reiner, "The Etiological Myth of the 'Seven Sages,'" *Or* 30 (1961) 2, 4; S. Dalley, *Myths from Mesopotamia* (Oxford: Oxford University Press, 1991) 182–83.

31. A. D. Kilmer, "The Mesopotamian Counterparts of the Biblical *něpîlîm*," *Perspectives on Language and Text: Essays and Poems in Honor of Francis I. Andersen's Sixtieth Birthday, July 28, 1985* (Winona Lake, Ind.: Eisenbrauns, 1987) 43 n. 14. The main point of Kilmer's article is to suggest that the *apkallus* are the counterparts of the *něpîlîm*. If that were the case, one might argue that the point of Gen 5:3 is to contrast Seth with the *něpîlîm*, but since one lacks evidence that the *něpîlîm* were thought of as culture founders, their identification with the *apkallus* is hard to sustain.

32. Dalley, *Myths from Mesopotamia*, 182–83; see the evidence cited by S. A. Picchioni, *Il Poemetto di Adapa* (Assyriologia 6; ed. G. Komoróczy; Budapest: Eötvös Loránd Tudományeg-yetem, 1981) 47–49 (citing the views of Hallo, Lambert, van Dijk, and Reiner). A. D. Kilmer, in contrast, holds that Adapa is the seventh sage, Utuabzu ("The Mesopotamian Counterparts of the Biblical *něpîlîm*," 40).

33. See N. M. Sarna, *Genesis* (The JPS Torah Commentary; Philadelphia: Jewish Publication Society, 1989) 35–36.

34. In postbiblical lore, Seth and his descendants do play a role analogous to that of the culture-bearing Babylonian *apkallus*, but that may well be due to the adoption of the motif from Berossus, whose work was known to Josephus (*Ant.* 1.93, etc.). See Josephus, *Ant.* 1.69–71, *Gen. Rab.* 26:5, and other sources cited by L. Ginzberg, *The Legends of the Jews* (Philadelphia: Jewish Publication Society, 1909–38) 1.121–22 and 5.149–50 n. 53. For the relationship between the Babylonian myth of the seven sages and Genesis 4 and 5, see W. W. Hallo, *Origins: The Ancient Near Eastern Background of Some Modern Western Institutions* (Leiden: Brill, 1996) 1–15.

Different Editions of the Song of Hannah and of Its Narrative Framework

EMANUEL TOV

The Hebrew University of Jerusalem

Introduction

The differences between the MT (with which the Targum,[1] Peshiṭta, and Vulgate more or less agree) and the LXX[2] in the Song of Hannah are mentioned in the commentaries and in several monographs.[3] The sources differ in many small details, as well as in major ones in 1 Sam 2:1, 2, 6, 9, 10. These major discrepancies consist of differences, omissions, and additions (when using these terms, the MT is taken as a point of departure without taking a stand regarding

Author's note: This paper was presented first at a workshop on Qumran studies held at the Institute for Advanced Studies of the Hebrew University in July 1994. The author is grateful to E. D. Herbert, who shared with him some valuable insights regarding 4QSam^a and N. Leiter ל"ז, who made several helpful suggestions.

1. See D. J. Harrington, "The Apocalypse of Hannah: Targum Jonathan of 1 Samuel 2:1–10," in *"Working with No Data": Semitic and Egyptian Studies Presented to Thomas O. Lambdin* (ed. D. M. Golomb; Winona Lake, Ind., 1987) 147–52.

2. The Old Latin version of the LXX is more or less identical with the LXX. See in detail P. A. H. de Boer, "Confirmatum est cor meum: Remarks on the Old Latin Text of the Song of Hannah 1 Samuel ii 1–10," *OTS* 13 (1963) 173–213; idem, "Once Again the Old Latin Text of Hannah's Song," *OTS* 14 (1965) 206–13.

3. P. Dhorme, "Le Cantique d'Anne (I Sam. II, 1–10)," *RB* 16 (1907) 386–97; G. Bressan, "Il cantico di Anna (1 Sam 2,1–10)," *Bib* 32 (1951) 503–21; 33 (1952) 67–89; J. T. Willis, "The Song of Hannah and Psalm 113," *CBQ* 35 (1973) 139–54; M. Philonenko, "Une paraphrase du cantique d'Anne," *RHPR* 42 (1962) 157–68; H. J. Stoebe, *Das erste Buch Samuelis* (KAT; Gütersloh, 1973) 100–107; P. A. H. de Boer, "Einige Bemerkungen und Gedanken zum Lied in 1 Samuel 2,1–10," in *Beiträge zur alttestamentlichen Theologie: Festschrift für Walther Zimmerli zum 70. Geburtstag* (Göttingen, 1977) 53–59; D. N. Freedman, "Psalm 113 and the Song of Hannah," *ErIsr* 14 (1978) 56*–69*; R. Tournay, "Le Cantique d'Anne I Samuel II.1–10," in *Mélanges Dominique Barthélemy: Études bibliques offertes à l'occasion de son 60e anniversaire* (OBO 38; Fribourg/Göttingen, 1981) 553–76. Additional monographs are mentioned in the most recent article on the Song of Hannah: T. J. Lewis, "The Textual History of the Song of Hannah: 1 Samuel II 1–10," *VT* 44 (1994) 18–46.

the originality of the readings of that text). As far as I know, the differences between the MT and the ancient versions of the Song of Hannah and its narrative framework have not been discussed in a monographic treatment,[4] with the exception of an article by Walters (on the relation between the MT and LXX);[5] nor have the differences between the MT and 4QSam[a] been discussed. When deviating from the MT, this scroll partially agrees with the LXX.[6] The differences between the Qumran scroll and the MT have been known for some time. They have been put forward in an article by F. M. Cross that presented the first edition of the Samuel scroll,[7] a monograph by Ulrich,[8] the notes of BHS, which in Samuel are more extensive and more cautious than in most other books in that edition,[9] the textual notes on the New American Bible,[10] and the commentary of P. K. McCarter.[11] What has not been sufficiently recognized is that the three different texts of the Song of Hannah do not merely reflect scribal differences such as are created in the course of the transmission of any text but reflect three different editions (recensions) of the Song and its narrative framework. That this is the case was, however, suggested long ago. Wellhausen referred to the different position of the Song of Hannah in the MT and LXX,[12] Driver to the MT and LXX of 1:28 and 2:11,[13] and Barthélemy referred to 2:8–9.[14] The difference between scribal and editorial activity is difficult to de-

---

4. Interestingly enough, these details are not discussed by S. Pisano, *Additions or Omissions in the Books of Samuel* (OBO 57; Fribourg/Göttingen, 1984).

5. S. D. Walters, "Hannah and Anna: The Greek and Hebrew Texts of 1 Samuel 1," *JBL* 107 (1988) 385–412. Even though I disagree with Walters's main contention, his article is well written and very stimulating.

6. The agreements between the LXX and the scroll should not be exaggerated, and a distinction should be made between the agreements of 4QSam[a] with the main tradition of the LXX and those with the Lucianic manuscripts. These agreements in the LXX and the Lucianic manuscripts pertain to many major details to be discussed below, as well as to many minor ones. For the problems in evaluating these data, see my article "The Contribution of the Qumran Scrolls to the Understanding of the LXX," in *Septuagint, Scrolls and Cognate Writings: Papers Presented at the International Symposium on the Septuagint and Its Relations to the Dead Sea Scrolls and Other Writings (Manchester, 1990)* (ed. G. J. Brooke and B. Lindars; Septuagint and Cognate Studies 33; Atlanta, 1992) 11–47 (including references to earlier discussions).

7. F. M. Cross, "A New Qumran Fragment Relating to the Original Hebrew Underlying the Septuagint," *BASOR* 132 (1953) 15–26.

8. E. C. Ulrich, *The Qumran Text of Samuel and Josephus* (HSM 19; Missoula, Mont., 1978).

9. The books of Samuel were prepared for publication by P. A. H. de Boer.

10. *The Holy Bible, II: Samuel to Maccabees—New American Bible* (1968); cf. also: *Textual Notes on the New American Bible* (Patterson, N.J. [n.d.]).

11. P. K. McCarter, *I Samuel: A New Translation with Introduction and Commentary* (AB 8; Garden City, N.Y., 1980).

12. J. Wellhausen, *Der Text der Bücher Samuelis untersucht* (Göttingen, 1871) 42.

13. S. R. Driver, *Notes on the Hebrew Text and the Topography of the Books of Samuel* (Oxford, 1913) 22.

14. D. Barthélemy, *Critique textuelle de l'Ancien Testament* (OBO 50/1; Fribourg/Göttingen, 1982) 1.144–45.

fine, and even scholars who agree in principle that there is a category of editorial differences do not always agree with regard to individual readings. When using the terms *editorial* and *recensional*, we refer to readings that presumably were created before a final form of the composition was accepted. In other words, we believe that when these readings were created, the biblical composition was still fluid, so that generations of editors allowed themselves to make major changes in the contents of its composition. What we mean by these editorial readings will become clear from the analysis. The main focus of this article is the Song of Hannah and the surrounding verses, but in a way, the history of this Song cannot be separated from the history of the surrounding chapters in Samuel. If different editions of the Song of Hannah are assumed, evidence for them should also be visible in other chapters in the book of Samuel.

An Analysis of the Major Differences

The view that different editions of the Song of Hannah are reflected in the textual witnesses is based on an analysis of the textual data.

The Position of the Song of Hannah (1 Samuel 1:28, 2:11)

The Song of Hannah is placed in a slightly different location in the three textual traditions, as shown by a comparison of the verses before and after the Song in 1 Sam 1:28 and 2:11.

1 Sam 1:28

LXX	4QSam[a]	MT
>	ותעזב]הו שם ותשתחו[ן]/ליהוה[15]	וישתחו שם ליהוה

1 Sam 2:11a

LXX	4QSam[a]	MT
ותעזבהו שם לפני יהוה	> ?	וילך אלקנה הרמתה על ביתו
ותלך הרמתה		

καὶ κατέλιπεν[16] αὐτὸν
ἐκεῖ ἐνώπιον κυρίου
καὶ ἀπῆλθεν εἰς Αρμαθαιμ

15. An alternative reconstruction would be ותנה[הו], as suggested by Wellhausen (*Der Text der Bücher Samuelis*, 42) for the LXX of 2:11.

16. For this verb as well as for ἀπῆλθεν, I follow (against Rahlfs) the text of B and a few other sources, disregarding the main evidence of the Greek tradition, which has plural forms (κατέλ(ε)ιπον, ἀπῆλθον). The slight difference between the two readings is scribal and cannot be ascribed to revisional tendencies relating to the MT, since there is no equivalent for these words in the MT. For the evaluation of the inner-Greek differentiation between the two textual traditions, the principle of the *lectio difficilior* is invoked. Since Hannah and Elkanah were together in Shiloh

The main actions described in 1:28 and 2:11, leaving Samuel at the temple and bowing before the Lord, are ascribed to different persons in the various textual traditions or are not mentioned at all (the bowing before the Lord in the LXX), as will be discussed in the next section. At this point in the analysis, it should be stressed that these actions take place at different points in the story. According to the MT, an unidentified person bows before the Lord prior to Hannah's Song. In a similar way, according to 4QSamᵃ, Hannah prostrates herself before the Lord before the Song, and at that point she leaves Samuel at the temple. On the other hand, according to the LXX, Hannah leaves Samuel at the temple *after* the Song. Since the actions themselves are more or less identical, the data could also be presented as the insertion of the Song at two different positions, according to 4QSamᵃ after Hannah's actions, and according to the LXX before exactly the same actions. The MT resembles the scroll inasmuch as it describes an action before Hannah's Song, but it differs from the LXX and 4QSamᵃ since it ascribes the actions to Elkanah. The insertion of the Song at two different locations in the context may indicate that it was added late in the history of the growth of the first chapters of Samuel. After all, the Song did not belong to the first layer of the text. When it was inserted into the text in the existing manuscripts, it was inserted in a slightly different place in each manuscript. A similar explanation applies to the different place in the textual traditions of the Song of the Ark (MT: Num 10:34–36), the pericope on the building of the altar (MT: Josh 8:30–35), Solomon's benediction for the dedication of the temple (MT: 1 Kgs 8:12–13), the story of Naboth (MT: 1 Kings 20–21), and the oracles against the foreign nations in Jeremiah (MT: chaps. 46–51).[17]

The evidence of 4QSamᵃ is only partly known. As mentioned above, in 1:28b before the Song of Hannah, the scroll mentions the same actions that appear in the LXX after the Song. Although the verses after the Song have not been preserved in 4QSamᵃ, a calculation of the available space easily enables the inclusion of v. 11a.[18]

---

during their second visit (see below), it is more logical to ascribe this action to both of them, meaning that the plural form of the majority of the Greek tradition should be taken as an inner-Greek correction. The more difficult singular form in the LXX of 2:11 is assumed to be original, and it is this form that agrees with the text of both the MT and 4QSamᵃ in 1:28.

17. Thus briefly Wellhausen, *Der Text der Bücher Samuelis*, 42. See further my article "Some Sequence Differences between the MT and LXX and Their Ramifications for the Literary Criticism of the Bible," *JNSL* 13 (1987) 151–60.

18. On the basis of the columns containing the text of chaps. 3, 4, and 5 of 2 Samuel (see photograph PAM 43.115), the column length of this scroll may be calculated at 43–44 lines (in the case of the column starting with 2 Sam 3:23, the lines average 40–45 spaces). The first almost completely preserved column on photograph 43.115 preserves the top margin as well as remnants of 34 lines containing the text of 2 Sam 3:23 until 4:4. Since the next column also preserves a top margin immediately followed by the text of 2 Sam 4:9, the bottom of the first column must have contained the text of vv. 5–9. This text is reconstructed as an additional 9–10 lines, bringing the

1 Samuel 1:24, 25, 28; 2:11: The Dramatis Persona(e)
during the Third Visit to Shiloh

There are major differences between the textual sources regarding the conception of the dramatis persona(e) during the third visit to Shiloh.[19] The analysis of these differences is hampered by textual complications in the MT, the difficulty of reconstructing the *Vorlage* of the LXX, and the fragmentary state of preservation of the Qumran scroll. Nevertheless the main facts are clear.

According to the MT, Hannah is the main person acting in 1:24–28. The first words of v. 24 (ותעלהו עמה) make it clear that she came up to Shiloh with Samuel but seemingly without Elkanah, and it is she who acts in vv. 24–28. However, an unidentified male person is mentioned at the end of the chapter in v. 28b וישתחו שם ליהוה 'and he bowed there before the Lord'. From the immediate context it is not clear who is referred to, although on the basis of the earlier verses (cf. v. 21) it is likely that Elkanah is meant.[20] That this is indeed the case becomes clear from the first verse occurring immediately after the Song of Hannah, 2:11, "and Elkanah went to his home to Rama." If according to this verse, which appears immediately after the Song of Hannah, Elkanah returned to his home, he must have been away from his home, in Shiloh, so that the subject of the verb in 1:28 has to be Elkanah, even if he has not been properly introduced, so to speak, in the account of the third visit to Shiloh (see n. 20). The reason for the lack of explicit reference to Elkanah in 1:28 becomes clear from an analysis of the preceding verses, in which apparently a textual mishap has occurred.[21] Whatever the background of the phrase in the

---

total number of lines for the column to 43–44. By the same token, col. II of the scroll would have contained an additional 7–8 lines after its 36 partially preserved lines. The next column, col. III, starts with 1 Sam 2:16 and continues with vv. 13b, 14, 17ff. It is therefore difficult to assess the exact evidence of the scroll, but it seems that the unusual text at the beginning of this column, which is in the nature of a duplication with changes, should be disregarded in the present analysis. Thus at the end of col. II there was ample room for v. 11a, more precisely for 1 Sam 2:11–16, partly duplicated at the beginning of col. III. For col. III, ll. 43–44 lines should also be reconstructed.

19. The first visit is described in 1:3–18, the second one in 1:21–23, and the third one in 1:24–2:11. At the end of the first and third visits, Elkanah and/or Hannah return to their home (1:19, 1:28, and 2:11), while a similar formal statement is lacking at the end of the second visit. If the second and third visit are regarded as one event, some of the problems described here are resolved, since in that case Elkanah is mentioned explicitly, though at a great distance from v. 23. This assumption is difficult, however, since it implies that Elkanah waited a very long period in Shiloh, about which nothing is said in the text. The argumentation below is not affected by this assumption.

20. On the other hand, according to McCarter (*I Samuel*, 58), the MT refers to Eli. Walters ("Hannah and Anna," 401) thinks of Samuel. Because of the unclear context, a case can be made for both of these persons, but in view of 2:11 (see below) and of the text omitted from the MT in 1:24 (see below), only Elkanah can have been intended here.

21. It is not likely that Elkanah's name has been omitted on purpose as part of a narrative technique (Walters, "Hannah and Anna," 400).

MT in 1:28 was, the text of the MT is problematic, since its subject is not disclosed. The Peshiṭta and the Vulgate have a plural form (compare v. 19 in the various witnesses), but in these translations this form probably reflects a contextual harmonization.[22] However, the difficulty in v. 28b is not created by a textual problem of conflicting verbal forms but is part of a discrepancy between different editions of the Song, now reflected in the various textual witnesses.[23]

What exactly happened in the MT at this place is not clear, but 1 Sam 2:11 describes Elkanah as being present in Shiloh at the time of the third visit to Shiloh, while these words are not represented in the LXX. These elements probably form part of the original design of the edition reflected in the MT, as becomes clear from an analysis of a section that appears before the last word of v. 24 in the LXX and 4QSamᵃ. This section is lacking in the MT and was probably omitted erroneously from that text through a special[24] type of homoioteleuton (הנער—והנער). The very fragmentarily transmitted text of 4QSamᵃ can be reconstructed well in accordance with the LXX, with which it agrees:

καὶ τὸ παιδάριον μετ' αὐτῶν καὶ προσήγαγον ἐνώπιον κυρίου καὶ ἔσφαξεν ὁ πατὴρ αὐτοῦ τὴν θυσίαν ἣν ἐποίει ἐξ ἡμερῶν εἰς ἡμέρας τῷ κυρίῳ. καὶ προσήγαγεν τὸ παιδάριον

והנער [עמם ויבאו לפני יהוה וישחט אביו את] הזבן[ח כ]א̇שׁ̇ר [יעשה מימים ימימה ליהוה ויבא את הנער]

Beyond the textual argument in favor of the assumption of homoioteleuton, there is no reason to assume an intentional omission of this phrase in the MT.[25] Besides, the information in the plus of 4QSamᵃ and the LXX is needed for the understanding of the surrounding verses in the MT, so it must have been omitted erroneously from that text. This plus mentions Elkanah, so he necessarily is the subject of the verbs in the singular in v. 28. It is he who brings the lad to Eli (this action runs parallel to Hannah's leaving the lad in the temple in 1:28 in 4QSamᵃ and in 2:11 in the LXX), and it is he who acts in the beginning of the next verse ("and he slaughtered"). When the information in this plus is taken into consideration, v. 28b in the MT is no longer strange: the verb in that verse now becomes understandable, since Elkanah had been introduced in v. 24, which was lost by a textual mishap. Further, Elkanah was also mentioned in the reconstructed original text of the first words of v. 24 (see below).[26]

22. Likewise the NJPSV, 'And they bowed low'. A textual note in this translation refers to *b. Ber.* 61a, implying that Elkanah was there.

23. Compare further the *Kethiv* in Gen 43:28, where וישתחו represents a plural form.

24. The two identical words are both contained in the MT.

25. Pace Walters, "Hannah and Anna," 403–4.

26. After the textual mishap in vv. 24–25 (homoioteleuton), "and he slaughtered" (thus the LXX and the reconstructed text of 4QSamᵃ), referring to Elkanah, was not understandable anymore

When the text omitted by homoioteleuton is restored to its proper place in vv. 24–25, the MT is understandable, but not all problems are solved. Hannah went to Shiloh together with her husband Elkanah and her son Samuel. It is she who is the main actor at this stage of the story. It is she who brings her vow to completion, and it is she who presents her Song. But there are two elements that remain unclear in the story in the MT. Even though we now understand that it is Elkanah who bows to the Lord in 1:28b, it is not clear why he should be singled out for mention, thus omitting reference to his wife and son. It does not suffice to point to the central place of men in worship. It is even more strange that the story ends with 2:11, referring to Elkanah's returning home and Samuel's serving the Lord. What happened to Hannah, and why was she not mentioned at the end of this episode in the same way she was in the beginning and middle of the story? To this issue we shall return below.

The LXX presents a different picture of 1:28 and 2:11, partly shared with 4QSam[a]. That the Greek translation does not reflect the translator's exegesis is demonstrated by the similar evidence of the Hebrew scroll, even though some of the words found in 2:11 in the LXX appear in the scroll at a different location, 1:28. The picture reflected in the LXX differs from the MT, since the statement of the MT in 1:28 (see above and below) is lacking in the LXX, and in the similar statement in that translation in 2:11, it is Hannah who acts, not Elkanah. In fact, more or less the same actions as are ascribed in the MT to Elkanah are ascribed to Hannah in the LXX and 4QSam[a] (with internal differences): an action connected with the Lord (prostration to the Lord in the MT and 4QSam[a] and the entrusting of Samuel to the service of the Lord in the LXX and 4QSam[a]) and returning home to Ramah at the end of the action.

Furthermore, although similar actions are described in the different versions, it should be noted that according to the LXX and 4QSam[a], it is Hannah who leaves Samuel behind in the temple for temple service. The entrusting of Samuel to the temple is not mentioned explicitly in the MT, although it is implied by 2:11b.

In sum, the relation between the texts is now clear: the main difference between the MT on the one hand and the LXX and 4QSam[a] on the other is that in certain episodes in the latter two texts, Hannah acts as the main character, while in the MT there are two main characters, Hannah and Elkanah. These two versions of the story are not parallel original versions, as suggested by Walters.[27] Rather, they are genetically related. Either the MT ascribed actions

---

and was made into a plural form in the MT. On the other hand, according to Wellhausen (*Der Text der Bücher Samuelis*, 41) and Driver (*Notes on the Hebrew Text*, 21), unmentioned "persons who slaughter" are the subject of the plural verb, reflecting a possibly original reading.

27. Within the scope of the present article, there is no room for an extensive discussion of the abstract concepts behind Walters's view, which center around the question of the original text and the transmission of the biblical books. For the latest formulation of my own views, see my *Textual*

to Elkanah which in an earlier version had been ascribed to Hannah, or vice versa.[28] I opt for the first possibility[29] because of the contextual difficulties in 1:28 and 2:11 in the MT. Especially difficult is 2:11 in the MT: since at this juncture Hannah should be considered the main person, it is strange that nothing is said in this verse about her movements. It is thus likely that the statements about Elkanah replaced the earlier story. The earlier version (the LXX and 4QSam[a]) ascribed certain actions to Hannah that have been removed in the MT, while similar statements were inserted about Elkanah. The impression is created that the MT did not wish to assign these actions to Hannah since she was a woman, and it would not be appropriate that a woman should play such a central role in the story.

This assumption is supported by two other verses in the story in which a similar tendency of suppressing Hannah's actions is visible:

(i) 1 Sam 1:23   MT   אך יקם יהוה את דברו   (= Targum, Vulgate)
                         May the Lord fulfill His word.
                4QSam[a] [אך יקם יהו]ה היוצא מפיך   (= LXX)
                         [May the Lo]rd [fulfill] that which comes
                         out of your mouth.

The two formulations differ in context, since the MT refers to the word of the Lord, while 4QSam[a] = LXX refer to Hannah's vow. It is difficult to decide between these two readings, and, therefore, to all appearances the two readings are alternative and could be equally original. In fact, on the basis of Num 30:3, which deals with vows, both readings are equally possible in this context: לא יחל דברו ככל היצא מפיו יעשה 'he must not break his word, but must carry out all that has crossed his lips (literally: came out of his mouth)'. According to a

---

Criticism of the Hebrew Bible (Minneapolis/Assen-Maastricht, 1992) 164–80. In Walters's detailed description of the differences between the versions, the Qumran evidence is not sufficiently taken into consideration, and in my view, Walters does not distinguish between the translator's exegesis (which is not relevant in the present context) and his deviations based on a reconstructed *Vorlage* differing from the MT. The translator's problems when encountering difficult words are also not taken into consideration. For example, Walters tabulated major differences between the two texts in v. 6 in parallel columns, but a great part of these differences derives from the translator's understanding of his *Vorlage*. According to Walters (p. 394), "M's story describes Hannah's difficult situation objectively. . . . But B's [that is MS B of the LXX] story, containing no *provocatrice*, describes the situation entirely in terms of Anna's subjective responses: she suffered *thlipsis* and *athymia*, distress and depression." However, the difference between the two texts derives partly from the translator's misunderstanding of צרתה 'co-wife', which he took as "her distress." In the wake of analyses of this type, Walters concludes (p. 392): "Both by its omission of Hannah's deferential reply and by the character of her first direct speech, M portrays Hannah more positively than B, giving to her person—both words and actions—a more substantive importance." This characterization is questionable.

28. Thus Driver, *Notes on the Hebrew Text*, 22: "LXX . . . an addition to MT, which looks like a various recension of the words not expressed by them in 1, 28[b]."

29. Wellhausen (*Der Text der Bücher Samuelis*, 42) also prefers the reading of the LXX, arguing that it would not make sense for the Greek text to suppress the involvement of Elkanah, which has been mentioned in detail in v. 24.

different train of thought, however, only one reading was original, while the other one reflects a later correction. It is possible that the reading of the MT reflects a correction of the text of 4QSam[a] = LXX: the mentioning of the "word" of God in the MT reflects more reverence toward God than the vow of a mere mortal, Hannah.[30] The MT thus did not mention Hannah's vow explicitly.

(ii) 1 Sam 1:25   MT   את הנער אל עלי   וישחטו את הפר ויביאו
                    LXX   הנער אל עלי   וישחט את הפר ותבא חנה אם

καὶ ἔσφαξεν τὸν μόσχον καὶ προσήγαγεν Αννα
ἡ μήτηρ τοῦ παιδαρίου πρὸς Ηλι

According to the MT, unmentioned persons bring the lad to Eli, while according to the LXX, "Hannah, the mother of the lad," comes to Eli. The connection in the MT is strange, since v. 26, referring to Hannah's conversation with Eli, is not connected with the previous verse, while the LXX presents a more logical context. It is not impossible that the original wording was changed in the MT in order to avoid mentioning another one of Hannah's actions.

1 Samuel 2:1

The Song of Hannah in the MT starts with ותתפלל חנה ותאמר, while the LXX, which does not give the first two words, merely reads: καὶ εἶπεν. The evidence of 4QSam[a] is not clear because of its fragmentary status; the first two words could have occurred in the lacuna but could also have been lacking. Most probably in the earlier text form (that is, the LXX), Hannah's Song was not referred to as a "prayer."[31] Probably the prayer element was added in the introduction to the Song on the basis of 1 Sam 1:26, since the Song is not written in the form of a prayer. Rather, it is a song of thanksgiving of the individual, referring to a personal calamity experienced by the psalmist, and most likely the Song was added to the story secondarily. The textual evidence thus testifies two stages in the editing of the Song of Hannah.

1 Samuel 2:2

LXX[32]	4QSam[a]	MT	
אין קדוש כיהוה	אין קדוש כיה[וה]	אין קדוש כיהוה	a
ואין צור* כאלהינו	[ ]		
אין קדוש* בלתך	[כי* אין קדוש* בלת]ך	כי אין בלתך	b
	ואין צור כאלהינו	ואין צור כאלהינו	c

30. It is also possible that the reading of the MT was corrected toward the text of 4QSam[a] and the LXX, possibly since the "word" of the Lord was not mentioned earlier in the text. For a comparative analysis of these readings, see my *Textual Criticism*, 176.

31. See the laconic statement of H. P. Smith, *The Books of Samuel* (ICC; Edinburgh, 1899) 15: "𝔊[B] has simply καὶ εἶπεν, which is enough."

32. Problematic elements in the reconstruction of the LXX and the Qumran scroll have been indicated with an asterisk.

צור] At first sight, it seems as though δίκαιος in the second stich of the LXX points to a *Vorlage* different from MT צור, but the Greek rendering should be seen in the light of the different renderings of צור elsewhere in the LXX.[33] The various Greek translation equivalents of this word reflect an avoidance of a literal rendering of צור as a designation of God.[34] This tendency may also be assumed in this verse. It is thus methodologically questionable to reconstruct צדיק here and to assume a graphic similarity between the two Hebrew words.

קדוש] ἅγιος in the third stich of the LXX may reflect קדוש, which could also have been contained in the lacuna in 4QSam[a], but it may also reflect a free addition of the LXX to the otherwise unusual[35] phrase כי אין בלתך.

The differences among the three witnesses pertain to major details, but not all of them can be analyzed because of the uncertainty of the reconstruction of the *Vorlage* of the LXX and the fragmentary status of the Qumran scroll. However, at least this is clear:

1. A calculation of the length of the lines in 4QSam[a] makes it likely that the scroll contained additional text, probably a stich, after אין קדוש כיה[וה]. This stich has been reconstructed by some scholars[36] as ואין צדיק כאלהינו on the basis of the LXX. However, the reconstruction of δίκαιος as צדיק is far from certain (see above), and furthermore it is not at all clear which text would have been included in the lacuna in the scroll.

2. The internal sequence of at least two of the witnesses differs. If the three stichs in the MT are taken as a point of departure for the description and are therefore denoted as *abc*, the sequence of the LXX is represented as *acb*; if the LXX reflects different readings, as presented above, this sequence should be represented as *ac'b'*. The sequence of the Qumran fragment is represented as *a[x]bc*, in which *x* represents either *a'*, *b'*, or *c'*, or a different

33. Thus also Stoebe, *Das erste Buch Samuelis*, 101.

34. Cf. A. Wiegand, "Der Gottesname צור und seine Deutung in dem Sinne Bildner und Schöpfer in den alten jüdischen Literatur," *ZAW* 10 (1890) 85–96; A. Passioni dell' Acqua, "La metafora biblica di Dio Roccia e la sua soppressione nelle antiche versioni," *Ephemerides Liturgicae* 91 (1977) 417–53 (non vidi).

35. The only comparable passages are 2 Sam 7:22 and 1 Chr 17:20, where the Hebrew (and Greek) text has an element describing the preposition: כי אין כמוך ואין אלהים זולתך.

36. Thus Cross, "New Qumran Fragment," 26; and Ulrich, *Qumran Text of Samuel and Josephus*, 121. In an article published after the manuscript of this article was completed, A. L. Warren argues that the plus in the LXX, and independently the plus in 4QSam[a], reflect liturgical expansions: "A Trisagion Inserted in the 4QSam[a] Version of the Song of Hannah, 1 Sam. 2:1–10," *JJS* 45 (1994) 278–85 (". . . LXX has been subject to liturgical adaptation for the autumn *Rosh Ha-Shanah* festival, probably on the basis that Elkanah's annual pilgrimages were also at this time of the year," p. 281). This article elaborates on H. St. J. Thackeray, "The Song of Hannah and Other Lessons and Psalms for the Jewish New Year's Day," *JTS* 16 (1914) 177–204. See further below, n. 63.

stich (*d*). According to this description, the three witnesses reflect different versions (editions) of the biblical verse.

It is hard to know which arrangement is preferable. The difficulties inherent in the sequence of the MT have often been pointed out, since stich *b* in the MT starts with כי, even though it does not explain the previous one.

1 Samuel 2:8

MT   a. מקים מעפר דל מאשפת ירים אביון
      b. להושיב עם נדיבים וכסא כבוד ינחלם
      c. כי ליהוה מצקי ארץ וישת עליהם תבל

     a. He raises the poor from the dust, lifts up the needy from the dunghill,
     b. seating them with nobles, granting them seats of honor,
     c. For the pillars of the earth are the Lord's, He has set the world upon them.[37]

The three textual witnesses for the third segment of this verse run as follows:

MT   כי ליהוה מצקי ארץ וישת עליהם תבל
4QSam[a]   כי ליהוה מצקי ארץ וישת] עליהם תֹבֹ[ל]
LXX   >

This third part of v. 8 is not represented in the LXX. According to our working hypothesis, v. 8c was lacking in the *Vorlage* of that translation, and was added in a different and later edition,[38] represented by the MT and 4QSam[a]. There are no literal parallels for this verse elsewhere in the Bible,[39] and it would probably have originated within the tradition of the Song of Hannah during one of the stages of its growth. It represents a causal clause, supposedly explaining the previous ones, although in actuality it does not provide an explanation or background for them.

The background of v. 8c should be understood in the light of its relation to the surrounding verses. The first two segments of v. 8, as well as the next verse, 9, deal with the fate of individuals, while v. 8c, the added clause of the MT and 4QSam[a], deals with God's cosmic powers. What all verses in this context have in common is that they stress God's power in determining the fate of the individual. But, while vv. 4–9 (with the exception of 8c) deal with God's ability to determine the fate of individuals, 8c mentions God's cosmic powers.[40]

---

37. The translation of this verse, as well as all other ones, follows the NJPSV.

38. Thus Wellhausen, *Der Text der Bücher Samuelis*, 43; and Smith, *Books of Samuel*, 16. Neither scholar uses a term such as *edition* or *interpolation*.

39. For a similar idea, see Ps 75:3–4, according to which God's giving judgment equitably is paralleled with His keeping the pillars of the earth firm. Other parallels are mentioned by Tournay, "Cantique d'Anne," 563.

40. This was recognized by Dhorme, "Cantique d'Anne," 391.

Verse 8c is phrased as an explanation of the preceding verses, but since it mentions God's cosmic power, it fails to do so. When faced with texts that either contain (MT and 4QSam[a]) or lack v. 8c (LXX), one should probably consider the text that does contain v. 8c as secondary. The cosmic power of God is mentioned again in v. 10, but in this verse the description of this type of cosmic power fits the description of God's overpowering his enemies. The juxtaposition of a description of the personal fate of individuals and God's greatness in the universe is also found in Psalm 113, which in many ways resembles the Song of Hannah, but this fact cannot be used as an argument in favor of the originality of v. 8c of the MT.

The presentation of 8c in the different versions is somehow related to v. 9a. This verse also is not represented in the LXX, which presents a different verse in its stead. However, vv. 8c and 9a should be dealt with separately because of their different structure. Verse 8c supposedly explains the preceding clauses, 8a–b, while 9a contains a new idea, for which 9b forms an explanation.[41]

The LXX stands alone in the nonrepresentation of v. 8c, against the MT and 4QSam[a], in which it is found. Likewise, the LXX is alone in not representing v. 9a. In other deviations from the MT, the LXX is joined by 4QSam[a], as shown below.

1 Samuel 2:9

MT	a.	רגלי חסידו ישמר ורשעים בחשך ידמו
		He guards the steps of His faithful, but the wicked perish in darkness,
	a′.	>
	b.	כי לא בכח יגבר איש
		for not by strength shall man prevail.
LXX	a.	>
	a′.	נתן נדר לנודר ויברך שני/שנות צדיק
	b.	כי לא בכח יגבר איש
		διδοὺς εὐχὴν τῷ εὐχομένῳ καὶ εὐλόγησεν ἔτη δικαίου ὅτι οὐκ ἐν ἰσχύι δυνατὸς ἀνήρ
		He gives the vower his vow and blesses the years of the just, for not by strength shall man prevail.
4QSam[a]	a.	ודרך ח̇[ו]סידיו ישמר ורשעים בחשך ידמו]
		[He guards] the way of [His] fa[ithful, but the wicked perish in darkness,]

---

41. It is unfortunate that de Boer in BHS did not provide the text of the LXX, for the note "𝔊 alit" underestimates the importance of that evidence. It is somewhat misleading that the evidence of 4QSam[a] relating to v. 9a is listed in a note to v. 8c.

a′. נתן נדר [לנוד]רֹ וֹיברך שֹ[ני/שנות צדיק

He gives [the vow]er his vow and blesses the y[ears of the just]

b. [כי לא בכח יגבר איש ?]

[for not by strength shall man prevail (?)].

In my view, the earlier text of vv. 8–9 consisted of only 8ab and 9b. This text was revised in different ways in the MT and the *Vorlage* of the LXX. 4QSam[a] represents a hybrid version.

Verse 9a of the MT and 4QSam[a][42] is not represented in the LXX. In a way, the idea of v. 9a (in the MT: רגלי חסידו ישמר ורשעים בחשך ידמו; 4QSam[a] presents a slightly different formulation[43]) fits the Song of Hannah. The Song mentions in vv. 4–5 unexpected changes for the better and the worse in the fate of individuals. Likewise in vv. 6–8, the Song mentions God's power to change the personal fate of individuals. The implication of these two groups of verses is that the unexpected change in condition (for example, the strong whose power fails, in v. 4a) is due to God, who can bring about these changes, just as He can make the poor rich and the rich poor (v. 7). The descriptions in vv. 4–8 serve as examples of God's power mentioned in v. 3, and they are in line with the general praise of God in vv. 1–3. This idea of God's almighty power underlies all textual traditions of the Song and is also behind v. 9b (כי לא בכח יגבר איש) but is made more specific in the MT and 4QSam[a] in v. 9a. The implication of vv. 1–3 and 6–8 for vv. 4–5 is that God's power is behind the changes in the fate of the individual mentioned in those verses as well. Verses 4–8 are therefore understandable as they are. The main idea of these verses is that changes will occur if God wants them to occur. However, in two textual traditions, the MT and 4QSam[a], this idea has been elaborated upon and made more specific. One might say that the original ideas have been given a theological slant. The presumably earlier stage in which the original idea of the Song was represented has not been preserved. The existence of an earlier stage reflecting a shorter text is reconstructed, although it is supported by the LXX. The support is only partial, since the LXX itself has expanded the originally shorter text. It is suggested here that the originally short version of the Song, lacking vv. 8c and 9a, was expanded in one direction in the MT and in another one in the *Vorlage* of the LXX. 4QSam[a] contains a hybrid text.

It is suggested here that the text common to the MT and 4QSam[a] in v. 9a, and lacking in the LXX, represents a theological elaboration on the main theme of the Song of Hannah. This addition to the original text reinterprets the

---

42. Only the first word of v. 9a has been preserved in 4QSam[a]; the remainder would have been contained in the lacuna.

43. For the reading of 4QSam[a], see Prov 2:8.

examples of the changes in the fate of the individual given in vv. 4–8 in a certain way. According to this reinterpretation, the sudden changes described in those verses do not exemplify the strength of God but the power of loyalty to God. It is the person who is loyal to God who will experience a change for the better, and it is the wicked (that is, the ones who are not loyal to God) who will experience a change for the worse. This reinterpretation found in the MT and 4QSam[a] of v. 9a was probably added to the Song.[44] It was the intention of the person who added v. 9a that the contents of this verse would be applied to vv. 4–8.

A different revision[45] of the earlier shorter text is found in the LXX, which (together with 4QSam[a]) contains a completely different text, v. 9a'. On the special status of the Qumran scroll, see below.

The verse that is found in the LXX and 4QSam[a] (וֹיברך [לנוד]ר נתן נדר שׁ[ני/שנות צדיק]) and not in the MT is secondary because of its content and position. After mentioning the various categories of change from worse to better and from better to worse, and after mentioning God's power in bringing about these changes,[46] it is somewhat anticlimactic to mention in v. 9a' God's granting the vow to the person who vows. God's power is reflected in so many categories that the granting of the vow[47] seems to be a mere detail presented as an afterthought. Since v. 9a' is not found in the MT, it may be suspected as secondary, since it reflects the special situation of Hannah. This verse clearly reflects an attempt to accommodate the Song more closely to Hannah's situation.[48]

The second phrase of the LXX, καὶ εὐλόγησεν ἔτη δικαίου = 4QSam[a] וֹיברך שׁ[ני/שנות צדיק], probably does not refer to the righteous in general but mentions them only in conjunction with the person who makes a vow. The mention of the righteous in the LXX = 4QSam[a] thus runs parallel to the mention of the persons who are loyal to God in v. 9a in the MT. The phrase of the LXX may be taken to imply that the persons who witness a change in their personal fate, as mentioned in vv. 4–5, are the righteous. In this case, the reinterpretation reflected in the LXX and 4QSam[a] runs parallel to that of the MT.

Verse 9b, כי לא בכח יגבר איש,[49] is common to the MT and LXX and probably to 4QSam[a], and its meaning in the different contexts of these witnesses

---

44. For the understanding of the background of this verse, it is important to note that the specific meaning of רשע 'wicked' as persons who are disloyal to God occurs mainly in Ezekiel, Psalms, and the Wisdom literature.

45. Thus already Stoebe, *Das erste Buch Samuelis*, 102, with reference to the LXX: ". . . Rezension, die noch stärker die Situation berücksichtigt."

46. This analysis is based only on the text of the LXX and disregards the pluses of the MT.

47. The exact phrase of God's "granting the vow to the person who vows" is not known from other verses but is not intrinsically difficult.

48. Driver, *Notes on the Hebrew Text*, 26. According to Wellhausen (*Der Text der Bücher Samuelis*, 42), the attempt is not successful, since the Song presents God as granting more than his worshipers expect, while according to v. 9a' God fulfills the wishes of the worshipers exactly.

49. For the idea and words, see Zech 4:6, Job 21:7.

needs to be discussed next. In the MT this sentence connects well with the two preceding ones.[50] Physical force does not give strength to people. The idea of this stich could continue v. 9a, according to which the righteous as well as the wicked will be judged according to their loyalty to God; physical power (that is, of the wicked) will not help them. But within v. 9 it appears to be an after-thought, since the main idea was already expressed by v. 9a. There is no good connection between this stich and its context in the LXX and 4QSam[a]. In these two sources, the third stich, mentioning the ineffectiveness of physical power, should explain the two preceding stichs. In the words of the LXX: (a′) διδοὺς εὐχὴν τῷ εὐχομένῳ καὶ εὐλόγησεν ἔτη δικαίου (b) ὅτι οὐκ ἐν ἰσχύι δυνατὸς ἀνήρ. In my view, there is no necessary connection between the ideas of a′ and b. This lack of connection may indicate that 9a′ of the LXX and 4QSam[a], lacking in the MT, contains an editorial insertion into the text.

The contextual appropriateness of 9b in the reconstructed original text of the Song of Hannah needs to be discussed next. In the reconstructed text, which lacked v. 8c and 9a of the MT, 9b immediately followed after 8b. The reference to the ineffectiveness of physical power in v. 9b connects well with v. 8b.

If the above analysis is correct, the MT and LXX = 4QSam[a] reflect two different and independent reinterpretations of the main ideas of an earlier form of the Song of Hannah.

When the different forms of this verse are compared, we are confronted with three different versions, which may be represented schematically as

MT	ab
4QSam[a]	aa′c
LXX	a′b

In this web of relations between the versions, 4QSam[a] holds a peculiar position. The text of the scroll is closely related with the LXX against the MT, since it contains the secondary verse about God's "granting the vow to the person who vows" (9a′). However, the scroll also agrees with the MT against the LXX in preserving another secondary addition, namely, v. 9a of the MT. According to my analysis, the additions of the MT and LXX present two different types of reinterpretation and contextual adaptation of the Song of Hannah, so that their juxtaposition in 4QSam[a] is very peculiar. In my view, since 9a of the MT and 9a′ of the LXX are contextually secondary, their combination in 4QSam[a] should be considered secondary as well. The juxtaposition probably represents a textual mishap[51] or a scribe's wish to present both versions. Ulrich

---

50. According to Tournay ("Cantique d'Anne," 564), v. 9b is connected with the next verse (10) in spite of the verse division of the MT. Stoebe (*Das erste Buch Samuelis*, 102), following others, considers v. 9b to be a secondary addition.

51. Thus Barthélemy, *Critique textuelle de l'Ancien Testament*, 145.

and McCarter[52] suggest a different type of solution, according to which the text of 4QSam[a] reflects an original text from which the other two texts developed because of a textual mishap, namely haplography by these scholars.[53] However, such a presumed development does not explain the text of the LXX. Besides, the methodological argument mentioned above is even stronger: the juxtaposition in 4QSam[a] of two intrinsically secondary verses should be regarded as nonoriginal.

On the basis of the aforementioned considerations relating to three textual witnesses, the following stages in the development of v. 9 are reconstructed:

stage 1:   9b כי לא בכח יגבר איש (all witnesses; connected with 8a–b)
stage 2a: addition in MT of 9a רגלי חסידו ישמר ורשעים בחשך ידמו before 9b
stage 2b: addition in the *Vorlage* of the LXX of 9a′ נתן נדר לנודר ויברך שני/שנות צדיק before 9b
stage 3:   combination of texts reflecting stages 2a and 2b in 4QSam[a]:

a.   [ודרך ח]סידו ישמר ורשעים בחשך ידמו]
a′.   [נתן נד]ר לנוד]ר ויברך ש]ני/שנות צדיק]
b.   [כי לא בכח יגבר איש   ?   ]

There is room in this reconstruction[54] for v. 9b, but it is not clear whether the sentence was included in the scroll. It would have appeared at the end of a line, but instead, the remainder of the line could also have been empty ("open section"). The latter assumption is unlikely, since this would be the only paragraph marker in the Song of Hannah.

1 Samuel 2:10

1 Sam 2:10 in the LXX and 4QSam[a] differs completely from the MT. Both texts add a long section after the first segment which they have in common with MT (יהוה יחתו מריבו in MT and a slightly different form in 4QSam[a] and LXX). In this case MT contains the earlier form, while the LXX reflects a long exegetical plus which is in the nature of an afterthought. The contents of the plus in the Qumran scroll, preserved fragmentarily, cannot be identified easily, but it is found in the same position as the plus in the LXX and possibly it has one phrase in common with the LXX (מי ק]דוש; see below). The addition of the LXX, which is presented here together with the surrounding verses, runs as follows in Greek and in its reconstructed *Vorlage*:[55]

---

52. Ulrich, *Qumran Text of Samuel and Josephus*, 120; and McCarter, *I Samuel*, 70.
53. It is not clear what kind of haplography one should have in mind. The only haplography (or rather homoioarchton or homoioteleuton) that comes to mind is between כי ליהוה at the beginning of v. 8c and כי לא at the beginning of v. 9b.
54. This reconstruction does not follow the layout of 4QSam[a].
55. Stars indicate especially problematic reconstructions.

1 Sam 2:10 MT	reconstructed *Vorlage*	LXX
יהוה יחתו מריבו	יהוה[56]יחת* מריבו	κύριος ἀσθενῆ ποιήσει ἀντίδικον αὐτοῦ
	יהוה[57] קדוש	κύριος ἅγιος
	אל יתהלל חכם בחכמתו	μὴ καυχάσθω ὁ φρόνιμος ἐν τῇ φρονήσει αὐτοῦ
	ואל יתהלל גבור בגבורתו	καὶ μὴ καυχάσθω ὁ δυνατός ἐν τῇ δυνάμει αὐτοῦ
	ואל יתהלל עשיר בעשרו	καὶ μὴ καυχάσθω ὁ πλούσιος ἐν τῷ πλούτῳ αὐτοῦ
	כי אם בזאת יתהלל המתהלל	ἀλλ᾽ ἢ ἐν τούτῳ καυχάσθω ὁ καυχώμενος
	השכל וידע את יהוה	συνίειν καὶ γινώσκειν τὸν κύριον
	ועשה משפט וצדקה *בארץ	καὶ ποιεῖν κρίμα καὶ δικαιοσύνην ἐν μέσῳ τῆς γῆς
עלו בשמים ירעם	עלה*⁵⁸ בשמים* ירעם*	κύριος ἀνέβη εἰς οὐρανοὺς καὶ ἐβρόντησεν
יהוה ידין אפסי ארץ	יהוה* ידין אפסי ארץ	αὐτὸς κρινεῖ ἄκρα γῆς
ויתן עז למלכו	ויתן עז למלכו*	καὶ δίδωσιν ἰσχὺν τοῖς βασιλεῦσιν ἡμῶν
וירם קרן משיחו	וירם קרן משיחו	καὶ ὑψώσει κέρας χριστοῦ αὐτοῦ

With a few differences the plus of the LXX reflects the MT of Jer 9:22–23 which is presented below together with the Greek text of 1 Sam 2:10 and its reconstructed *Vorlage*:

MT of Jer 9:22–23	reconstructed *Vorlage* of LXX of Samuel	LXX of Samuel
אל יתהלל חכם בחכמתו	אל יתהלל חכם בחכמתו	μὴ καυχάσθω ὁ φρόνιμος ἐν τῇ φρονήσει αὐτοῦ
ואל יתהלל הגבור בגבורתו	ואל יתהלל *גבור בגבורתו	καὶ μὴ καυχάσθω ὁ δυνατός ἐν τῇ δυνάμει αὐτοῦ

---

56. Thus also 4QSam[a]: יחת.

57. See the discussion below of a possible equivalent of this Greek plus in 4QSam[a].

58. The reconstructed Hebrew *Vorlage* of the LXX is contextually unusual, not only because of its awkward position in the context, but also since it refers to God's going up to heaven. This idea is not unprecedented, however (see Ps 69:19 in the MT and LXX [68:19]). Since God is the subject of other verses in the context, it was logical that in the LXX he was made the subject of עלה (by the contextual addition of κύριος), after עליו=עלו was misread as עלה. This change brought about another contextual adaptation: since God's name was already mentioned, the translator read יהוה as הוא. On the difficulties of the MT and suggested emendations, see Tournay, "Cantique d'Anne," 565.

ואל יתהלל עשיר בעשרו	ואל יתהלל עשיר בעשרו	καὶ μὴ καυχάσθω ὁ πλούσιος ἐν τῷ πλούτῳ αὐτοῦ
כי אם בזאת יתהלל	כי אם בזאת יתהלל	ἀλλ᾿ ἢ ἐν τούτῳ καυχάσθω ὁ
המתהלל	המתהלל	καυχώμενος
השכל וידע אותי ...	השכל וידע את י(הוה)	συνίειν καὶ γινώσκειν τὸν κύριον
עשה ... משפט וצדקה	ועשָׂה משפט וצדקה	καὶ ποιεῖν κρίμα καὶ δικαιοσύνην ἐν μέσῳ
בארץ	בארץ	τῆς γῆς

The differences between the MT of Jeremiah and the reconstructed *Vorlage* of the LXX of Samuel are indicated above with a larger font. The additional words of the MT of Jeremiah are indicated by ellipsis dots.

The added verses in the Greek translation of Samuel have not been transferred from the Greek translation of Jeremiah since they differ in several details, as indicated below, reflecting either different translation equivalents or differences in Hebrew *Vorlagen*.[59]

LXX of Jeremiah	LXX of Samuel
μὴ καυχάσθω ὁ **σοφός** ἐν τῇ **σοφίᾳ** αὐτοῦ	μὴ καυχάσθω ὁ **φρόνιμος** ἐν τῇ **φρονήσει** αὐτοῦ
καὶ μὴ καυχάσθω ὁ **ἰσχυρός** ἐν τῇ **ἰσχύι** αὐτοῦ	καὶ μὴ καυχάσθω ὁ **δυνατός** ἐν τῇ **δυνάμει** αὐτοῦ

---

59. The word ποιῶν in the LXX of Jeremiah reflects the participle עֹשֶׂה also found in the MT, while καὶ ποιεῖν of the LXX of Samuel points to an infinitive reflecting a different reading of the same consonants, namely עָשֹׂה. Likewise τὸν κύριον of Samuel reflects a Hebrew reading different from the MT of Samuel, probably את י׳ (the abbreviated Tetragrammaton), which is closely related to אֹתִי of the MT of that book. I. L. Seeligmann (*Studies in Biblical Literature* [ed. A. Hurvitz et al.; Jerusalem, 1992] 325–26) rightly considers the Hebrew reading behind the Greek translation of Samuel to represent the original meaning of the context in Jeremiah and not the MT *ad locum*. The Samuel text speaks about two desirable actions for mankind, knowing God and acting with justice, while the Jeremiah text speaks of man's knowing God and God's acting with justice. These two readings have to be evaluated in the light of the meaning of the context. The context creates a certain opposition between the boasting of men about certain qualities and possessions on the one hand and religious virtues on the other. Within this framework the clearly defined opposition between the actions and views of humans, as in the addition in Samuel, is more natural than in Jeremiah. It is, moreover, unusual that the text in Jeremiah stresses in a somewhat tautological formulation the fact that God acts with justice. "Is it appropriate that the God of the universe claims that He acts with kindness, justice and equity in the world, for in these He delights?" (Seeligmann, ibid., 326). According to Seeligmann, God is depicted here as an arbitrary ruler, doing only what He wants. It so happens that the formulation preserved in Samuel is contextually more appropriate to Jeremiah and also better reflects the terminology of that book (see Jer 22:15–16). Probably the text that is now only preserved in Samuel once served as the original text of Jeremiah; it was slightly corrupted by a misreading of an abbreviated Tetragrammaton, and this misreading caused a series of contextual adaptations in the text of Jeremiah.

καὶ μὴ καυχάσθω ὁ πλούσιος ἐν τῷ
πλούτῳ αὐτοῦ
ἀλλ᾽ ἢ ἐν τούτῳ καυχάσθω ὁ
καυχώμενος
συνίειν καὶ γινώσκειν **ὅτι ἐγώ εἰμι
κύριος**
ποιῶν ἔλεος καὶ κρίμα καὶ
δικαιοσύνην **ἐπὶ** τῆς γῆς

καὶ μὴ καυχάσθω ὁ πλούσιος ἐν τῷ
πλούτῳ αὐτοῦ
ἀλλ᾽ ἢ ἐν τούτῳ καυχάσθω ὁ
καυχώμενος
συνίειν καὶ γινώσκειν **τὸν κύριον**
καὶ ποιεῖν κρίμα καὶ δικαιοσύνην ἐν
μέσῳ τῆς γῆς

Since the Greek plus in Samuel did not derive from the Greek translation of
Jeremiah, it was most likely based on a Hebrew plus, such as reconstructed
above. This addition has contextual relevance, though not necessarily in its
present place, where it occurs after the first clause in the translation of v. 10,
representing יהוה יחתו מריבו of the MT. However, the plus of the LXX is actually connected with כי לא בכח יגבר איש, that is, the last words of v. 9. It
also refers back to v. 3, אל תרבו תדברו גבהה גבהה, which in the Greek translation is represented by the same Greek verb representing אל יתהלל, namely
μὴ καυχᾶσθε . . . (influence on the Greek level, however, has been discarded
above).

On the one hand, it is hard to imagine a running Hebrew text that would
be worded like the Hebrew text reconstructed from the LXX because the addition based on Jer 9:22–23 is located inappropriately between two phrases of
the Hebrew that are closely related to each other, namely, after יהוה יחתו מריבו
and before עלו בשמים ירעם. On the other hand, 4QSamᵃ has an equally long
addition at exactly the same point, meaning that this addition or a similar one
indeed formed part of a Hebrew text. This assumption may be strengthened by
two elements of the addition that did not derive from the Jeremiah context but
that are also found in 4QSamᵃ: the words immediately preceding the quotation
from Jeremiah in v. 10, κύριος ἅγιος, probably represent יהוה קדוש, and they
stand in exactly the same place as a plus in 4QSamᵃ line 29: מי ק], probably to
be reconstructed as מי ק]דוש.

The plus of 4QSamᵃ found at exactly the same point as the long plus in the
LXX cannot be identified, due to its fragmentary nature. In whatever way the
last letter of the one complete word in the first line of the plus is reconstructed,
it is difficult to know what it means.[60] In any event, the few preserved letters
cannot be correlated to the plus of the LXX, which is based on Jeremiah 9:

[   ]   [○○קֹם בשׁלמֹךְ/הֹ]   [
[   ]   רֹגֹלֹיֹ חֹ]סִידֹו ישׁמר[[
[   ]   מֹיֹ ○[[

60. Lewis ("Textual History of the Song of Hannah," 43) suggests that בשׁלמֹךְהֹ, or in his
reading בשׁלמי, is derived from the root שׁלם, signifying 'paying one's vows', for which see the
vow mentioned earlier in the context. For the reconstruction of the second line, see Prov 2:8. A

Little can be said about the location of the two additions in the LXX and 4QSam^a. The addition of the LXX seems to be out of place. The small addition κύριος ἅγιος is not at all connected with its context. Rather, it harks back to v. 2, where the same words occur. The long addition is inappropriately located between two phrases of the Hebrew (see above). The flow of the text is logical in the MT but not in the LXX. While the assumption of marginal notations must be reduced to a minimum,[61] it seems that this is a case of a marginal note or possibly two notes, originally placed in the margin and afterwards wrongly inserted into the text itself. This marginal note is not in the nature of a gloss or an interpolation[62] but rather a reader's remark.[63]

According to the above analysis, the short text of the MT is original in this place, while the plus(es) reflected in the LXX and 4QSam^a represent (a) contextual afterthought(s).

Conclusions

The three versions of the Song of Hannah differ in many small details, which have not been discussed here, as well as in the major details discussed above. In its original form, the so-called Song of Hannah reflects a thanksgiving hymn by an individual,[64] referring to various situations in which this individual was saved from a calamity. The psalm stresses the special power that enables God to bring about changes, especially changes for the better or for the worse.[65] The major stress in this psalm is on a change for the better, and the psalmist thanks and praises God for this change in his fate.

---

completely different reading of that line, if correct, would bring the addition of the scroll into close contact with the LXX. Cross, whose reading is quoted by Lewis, reads [ל]ל[ה]ת[י אל, which would be identical with the text of Jer 9:22 quoted above. However, while my own reading previously quoted in the scholarly literature by others is problematic, the reading suggested by Cross (if based on PAM 43.122) is even more problematic: between the first letter (read by Cross as an ^ɔ*alep*) and the next letter, read as a *lamed*, there is a clear remnant of another letter (which I read as a *gimel*). Further, the speck of ink that is read as a *lamed* in ל[ה]ת[י is positioned at the place where a *he* is expected, and if this were indeed a remnant of a *lamed*, probably a greater part of it would have been preserved.

61. See my article "Glosses, Interpolations, and Other Types of Scribal Additions in the Text of the Hebrew Bible," in *Language, Theology, and the Bible: Essays in Honour of James Barr* (ed. S. E. Balentine and J. Barton; Oxford, 1994) 40–66.

62. For a definition of these terms, see the article mentioned in the preceding note.

63. Thackeray suggested long ago that the addition in the LXX was based on Jer 9:22–23, read as a short *haphṭarah* together with the longer *haphṭarah* of the Song of Hannah on New Year's day (see H. St. J. Thackeray, "Song of Hannah," esp. p. 190).

64. For a different characterization, see Willis, "Song of Hannah and Psalm 113."

65. In this regard, Hannah's Song is very similar to the Magnificat in Luke 1:46–55, both in general ideas and in wording.

The main idea of the reconstructed original form of the Song has been reinterpreted in two directions in the preserved texts, which therefore are in the nature of different *editions* of the Song and its narrative framework. These changes are evidenced in the three main textual sources that have been preserved, either in individual witnesses or in groups of two, without any consistency. Sometimes the change is evidenced in the MT and sometimes in the LXX, and either one is sometimes joined by 4QSam[a]. In this regard, 4QSam[a] is rather peculiar, but in any event it is through the evidence of this scroll that the real nature of the two other texts comes to light. Each of these witnesses makes the Song of Hannah more relevant to its context or to certain trends in biblical theology. Furthermore, the MT replaces the role of Hannah in the story of the third visit to Shiloh with actions by Elkanah.

The "original" form of the Song cannot be reconstructed, but presumably it was shorter than the text now transmitted in the three witnesses. It is not impossible that that original form was even shorter than implied by the above discussion, since v. 10, with its description of God's cosmic powers and the messianic ending may have been added to the original Song,[66] even though this view is not supported by any textual evidence.

The differences among the three sources may be summarized as follows:

a. The Song of Hannah is located in two slightly different positions in the MT on the one hand and the LXX and 4QSam[a] on the other.

b. The three texts present different concepts of the events occurring before and after the Song (**1:28, 2:11**). The LXX and 4QSam[a] seem to present a more original and internally consistent version. The MT reflects a revision that shifts to Elkanah a role that was originally ascribed to Hannah.

c. The original form of **2:1** has been preserved in the shorter version of the LXX. The edition of the MT adapted the Song to the context by an addition that makes the Song into a prayer.

d. **2:2** has been preserved in three different editorial forms. The possible stages in the editing of this verse cannot be reconstructed.

e. **2:8c**, lacking in the LXX, was added in the MT and 4QSam[a] in order to stress the cosmic power of God not mentioned in the earlier edition. This cosmic power is also referred to in v. 10, where it suits the context.

f. The reconstructed earlier text of **2:8–9** consisted of 8ab and 9b only. This short text was interpreted in two different ways in the MT and the *Vorlage* of the LXX. 4QSam[a] represents a hybrid version of both reworkings and thus represents a secondary development.

---

66. Thus O. Loretz, "Psalmenstudien (II)," *UF* 5 (1973) 214. For a discussion, see Tournay, "Cantique d'Anne," 565.

2:9a, common to the MT and 4QSamᵃ and lacking in the LXX, represents a theological reinterpretation of the main theme of the Song of Hannah. According to this verse, the person who is loyal to God will witness a change for the better, and the wicked (that is, the ones who are not loyal to God) will witness a change for the worse.

The counterpart to **2:9a** in the LXX, v. 9a′, reflects an attempt to accommodate the Song more closely to Hannah's position by adding a reference to God's granting the vow to the person who vows.

g. **2:10** in the MT differs completely from the LXX and 4QSamᵃ. The latter two texts add a long plus after the first segment, which they have in common with the MT (יהוה יחתו מריבו in the MT and a slightly different form in 4QSamᵃ and the LXX). The MT contains the earlier form, while the LXX reflects a long exegetical remark that is in the nature of an afterthought. This afterthought was inappropriately added between the components of v. 10. The contents of the plus in the Qumran scroll have been preserved only fragmentarily, but the scroll may have reflected the same plus as the LXX.

The analysis of the aforementioned differences is relevant to the history of the biblical text as a whole, but within the scope of this paper, this issue cannot be discussed at length. One may view editorial differences between the textual witnesses as deriving from several irreducible pristine versions of the biblical text. This has been suggested by various scholars and has been spelled out in detail by Walters for the first chapters of Samuel.[67] In my view, however, almost all instances of variation can be explained as revisions of some kind of an earlier text,[68] so that in spite of the major differences between the textual witnesses, an *Urtext* of some kind can still be assumed. The main objective of this paper is to show that the Song of Hannah circulated in antiquity in different recensions. These data are instructive for our understanding of one stage in the development of the text of the Bible, in which different recensions were extant. At the same time, these assumptions need not bring about a change in our thinking about the earlier stages of the biblical text. There is still room in our thinking for an *Urtext*, the nature of which needs to be formulated carefully.

67. Walters, "Hannah and Anna."
68. The readings of 4QSamᵃ and the LXX in 2:10, however, are described as marginal notes.

PART 2

Historical, Thematic, and Methodological Studies

On the Use of Traditional Jewish Exegesis in the Modern Literary Study of the Bible

ADELE BERLIN

University of Maryland at College Park

In this essay, I will begin with a look at the role, or lack of role, that traditional Jewish exegesis has played in modern biblical scholarship. Then I would like to move to the question of whether traditional Jewish exegesis employs a literary approach. (The answer is yes, no, and maybe!) Finally, I want to present some possibilities for the use of traditional exegesis in the literary study of the Bible. I do not refer here to the study of traditional exegesis per se, or to the literary analysis of traditional commentaries (both worthy goals in their own right) but rather to the contribution that traditional exegesis may make to a modern literary approach to the Bible. Throughout this paper, I am lumping rabbinic and medieval exegesis together, without taking into account the major differences between midrash and the rational approach that arose in the Middle Ages or the wide divergences among individual exegetes. I do this for the sake of making broad comparisons between the traditional and the modern and because there is a certain thread of continuity running through traditional Jewish exegesis.

For most of the twentieth century, traditional Jewish exegesis has had little or no place in academic biblical scholarship because it did not appear to contribute to the scientific understanding of the Bible. Medieval Jewish commentaries and the vast body of midrashic literature were studied almost exclusively in Jewish religious schools and rabbinical seminaries, where they were valued for their parochial and/or traditional nature. In secular Jewish circles where Bible was studied, and even more so in non-Jewish circles, traditional Jewish exegesis was often ignored or ridiculed.

Author's note: It is an honor and a pleasure to dedicate this paper to my teacher, Moshe Greenberg. It was written, at his invitation, for the Eleventh World Congress of Jewish Studies, Jerusalem, 1993. I thank Sara Japhet, Baruch Schwartz, Moshe Bernstein, and Michael Fox for their useful comments and Barry Eichler and Jeff Tigay for their editorial suggestions.

The reasons for this are understandable, although not laudable. The modern academic study of the Bible has been largely a Christian enterprise, although increasing numbers of Jews have found positions as professors of Bible in North American universities (see Sperling 1992), and Bible faculties in Israeli universities are composed almost exclusively of Jews. Nevertheless, in many non-Israeli universities, the study of Bible has meant the study of the Christian scriptures, and even when "Old Testament" was taught in departments of Semitics or ancient Near Eastern studies, it was usually taught by Christians, of whom a significant number had received training and possibly ordination in Christian seminaries. Now the anti-Semitic elements in Christian Bible scholarship are well known (see Klein 1978) and not to be minimized, but by the middle of the twentieth century the slighting of traditional Jewish exegesis was not, I think, as much a result of prejudice as of ignorance. There were simply few Christian Hebraists; few Christian Bible scholars had the knowledge or skills to read Medieval Hebrew or Aramaic. Nor could one assume that Jews, even Jews in Israel, were equipped to draw on texts in these languages.

In addition, there were several other factors that worked to devalue traditional Jewish exegesis, even in the eyes of those who had expertise in this area. First and foremost was the nature of the academic study of the Bible. It was philological, historical, and comparative. To most scholars, interpreting the Bible meant finding the one correct meaning that the text had had for its author or original audience. Scholars sought the meaning of the words through the study of Biblical Hebrew and comparative Semitics, and they sought the meaning of the literary structures, the historical references, and the religious concepts through a comparison with other ancient Near Eastern texts. The historical and sociological backgrounds were clarified through the ever-more-detailed and presumably more accurate reconstruction of the history of ancient Israel, itself aided by the proliferation and growing sophistication of archaeological excavations and by the information provided by newly unearthed documents. By the middle of the twentieth century, the study of Bible, even when it was located in religion departments or divinity schools, could no longer ignore ancient Near Eastern studies.[1] Israeli scholars especially, living in situ, as it were, were natu-

---

1. I would add as an aside that the relationship between ancient Near Eastern studies and biblical studies is an interesting one that deserves more thought. As time progressed, the balance in the relationship seems to have shifted. It began with the Bible as mistress and ancient Near Eastern studies as its handmaiden. The vast riches of the Fertile Crescent were put in the service of proving the accuracy of the Bible, or at least shedding more light on it—*ex oriente lux*. But by now, due to growth and specialization, ancient Near Eastern studies have taken on a life of their own. Bible is now at best one of a number of subspecialties and is often thought of by assyriologists and egyptologists as a soft one, at that. I would argue that the gradual diminution of the status of Bible within ancient Near Eastern studies and the lessening of interest in and support for all premodern studies (at least in North American universities: witness the troubles besetting classics departments and medieval studies) means that if Bible is to continue to flourish in academic institutions, it must find a new place for itself. For a variety of reasons, this new place is often in a literature department or in a Jewish studies program.

rally attracted to this approach. Already speakers of one Semitic language, they could learn others with relative ease; and they lived in the land where it all happened and where archaeology was a national pastime. Moreover, studying the Bible in its ancient context accorded well with the needs of the secular Israeli psyche, which saw the Bible as the national epic and emphasized periods in Jewish history in which the nation was autonomous in its land—that is, ancient Israel. To introduce rabbinic and medieval Jewish commentary would have been to interject both a religious and a diaspora mentality—something to be avoided on both counts.

As long as Bible was a part of ancient Near Eastern studies, with its emphasis on philology and history (of the text and of the ancient Near East), traditional Jewish exegesis had no role to play. Midrash is notoriously a-chronistic; one need not keep to the chronological sequence of events when interpreting midrashically: Abraham would be expected to know the laws that Moses would give in the future, as they were understood by the rabbis. Medieval Jewish commentary does not primarily concern itself with historical questions, and even when it does, it does not look to extrabiblical sources.[2] Furthermore, though the medieval scholars do show a high degree of linguistic astuteness, even relying at times on comparative philology, Rashi did not know Akkadian or Ugaritic.[3] In short, the kinds of knowledge considered necessary and the kinds of questions to be answered by modern scholars are quite different from those found in traditional commentaries.[4] Traditional exegesis, Jewish and Christian, did not address the needs of the modern scholar. It was simply not considered scientific because it did not make use of the latest scientific data and methods.

Moreover, traditional Jewish exegesis made no pretense of being academically objective and religiously neutral. Its religious chauvinism and its frequently moralizing tone undermined whatever exegetical value it might have had in the eyes of modern scientific scholars.

Finally, although the history of ancient Israel was important, the history of biblical interpretation was not. Unlike nineteenth and early twentieth-century commentaries, which often included a sampling of interpretations going back

2. B. Barry Levy notes a few exceptions (in Sperling 1992: 193 nn. 5–6).

3. The medieval witness used Aramaic and Arabic, languages that postdated Biblical Hebrew, as the basis for their comparative Semitic discussions, not languages that predated or were contemporary with Biblical Hebrew. So their linguistic knowledge, like their historical and archaeological knowledge, was not drawn from contemporaneous extrabiblical sources.

4. B. Barry Levy notes that "many other issues that seem to differentiate modern Bible study from its pre-modern antecedents including skepticism about God's role in the composition of the Bible, commitment to the application of literary-critical principles, awareness of contradictions between different Biblical passages, freedom of the individual reader to challenge the authority of, and to deviate from, traditional interpretation, and doubts about the accuracy of the transmitted text—have important analogues in ancient and medieval writings. Contemporary interpretation often emphasizes them and ignores matters of faith and application, but *archeology and historical perspective, not rational thinking, are the primary differences between modern writers and many of their pre-modern counterparts*" (Sperling 1992: 160 [emphasis mine]).

to the Church Fathers, most mid- and late–20th-century commentaries act as if
all meaningful discussion began no more than a generation or two before the
date of publication. (A noteworthy exception is Marvin Pope's *Song of Songs*,
which contains such a wealth of earlier exegesis that reviewers did not know
what to make of it.) Just as natural scientists saw no place for the history of
science in their own domains, relegating it to the history department, so scientific biblical scholars saw no place for the history of biblical exegesis.

All of these factors—the ignorance of traditional Jewish exegesis, the ir-
relevance of it, and the psychological discomfort with it—acted in tandem to
reduce or eliminate the presence of traditional Jewish exegesis from the academic study of the Bible. There are, of course, a few exceptions. Modern orthodox institutions, such as Bar Ilan University and Yeshiva University, have
(within their theological limitations) combined both worlds, joining traditional
exegesis with current historical, archaeological, and linguistic information, as
has the דעת מקרא series published by Mosad Harav Kook. A few individuals located in secular universities have also done so. I single out for example
Moshe Greenberg, who, perhaps more than anyone else, has made a conscious
and sustained effort to introduce traditional Jewish exegesis into mainstream
biblical studies.[5]

In recent years, however, the picture has begun to change, and now reference to Jewish interpretation is more prominent in secular publications and
courses, both in Israel[6] and elsewhere. The factors that earlier conspired against
it are gradually disappearing. For one thing, the texts that once were available
only in old tomes, minuscule print, and Rashi script have been reprinted in
handsome editions and translated into English and other European languages.
Furthermore, the rise of Jewish studies programs in secular universities has
promoted the critical study of rabbinic and medieval Jewish texts and has made
the study of these texts academically respectable. In addition, a greater openness to religious diversity has made Christian Bible scholars more receptive to
Jewish exegesis.[7] Finally, and I think most important (at least in the United
States), certain movements within academia have changed the nature of what

---

5. Also to be noted are Meir Weiss, Nahum Sarna, and Uriel Simon. Nehama Liebowitz occupies a peculiar position in this picture. She taught traditional Jewish commentaries to several
generations of secular and observant students and readers, under the auspices of the Hebrew University's program for overseas students and elsewhere. Yet, she was never considered a member of
the academic guild of biblical scholars. Even though her writings have been translated into English,
they have had little impact on the field of biblical studies.

6. The prime example is the new commentary series Miqraᵓ Leyisraᵓel, edited by Moshe
Greenberg and Shmuel Aḥituv, a modern Hebrew Bible commentary designed for the Israeli public at large, which incorporates both secular and traditional Jewish exegesis.

7. The increased acceptance of Jewish sensitivities and point of view is seen in the growing
use, even by non-Jewish scholars, of terms like *b.c.e.*, *Hebrew Bible*, *Tanakh*, and *Torah*. This is,
of course, part of the self-conscious use of preferred ethnic designations.

is to be studied and how it is to be studied. The hegemony of the historical-philological model has crumbled and with it the notion that this was the only way to study Bible. In fact, the model of objective knowledge as defined by the Western scientific tradition now has a serious competitor in an alternate model that promotes multiple viewpoints and subjectivity. In terms of biblical studies, this means that a verse need not have one objective meaning but many subjective ones and that different ways of construing meaning—whether the medieval Jewish way, the Latin American Liberation Theology way, or the feminist way—all have validity. Whatever one may think of these developments, it seems obvious that traditional Jewish exegesis is more likely to be accepted into this new academic world order than it was into the old.

Much of the impetus for change originated in literature departments, and it is in literary theory and criticism that one most clearly sees a change in approach. This change manifests itself in the glorification of textual ambiguity or indeterminacy, misreadings, and interpretive playfulness. Literary theorists renounce the quest for the "original" meaning and substitute for it the meaning(s) perceived by the reader of the moment. They also show a preference for global, expansive discourse, instead of line-by-line commentary. Now midrash (as opposed to *peshat*), also evidences these traits: it excels at playfulness, is concerned with the readers of its own times and not biblical times, and brings together all manner of extraneous material, thereby creating its own story to rival the Bible's. It is not surprising, therefore, that many literary interpreters of the Bible embrace rabbinic midrash and engage in midrash-like strategies.[8] Examples abound; I will note here only one small instance. Just as the Midrash often supplies names for anonymous biblical characters, so Mieke Bal calls Jephthah's daughter "Bath" and the concubine in Judges 19 "Beth."[9] Note the similarity to the Midrash's name for Pharaoh's daughter in Exodus 2, "Bithiah."

8. In fact, literary critics in general have been attracted to midrash (see, for example, Hartman and Budick 1986; Handelman 1982). J. Kugel (1981) broadly criticized the literary approach to the Bible as nothing more than modern midrash (he meant this derogatorily).

9. I should stress that the motivations for the assigning of proper names to anonymous characters are quite different in the case of the Midrash and the case of Mieke Bal. The Midrash assigns names, I assume, to fill in the gap in the story formed by the omission of the name and perhaps also to make the characters more memorable in the mind of the reader.

Bal, a feminist interpreter wrestling with what she considers the patriarchal ideology of the text, explains her naming of "Bath" as follows:

> So far, I have referred to the victim of the only fully explicit human sacrifice in the Bible as Jephthah's daughter. . . . To name this nameless character is to violate the biblical text. Not to name her is to violate her with the text, endorsing the text's ideological position. I feel it is not only acceptable, but necessary, to take some critical distance from the alienating anonymity of the character without, however, losing site of the structure of subjectivity that it signifies. Therefore, I will give this woman a name, but a name which stresses her dependence and her state. In order to make her speakable, I will call her what she most basically is: Jephthah's daughter, Bath-Jephthah, or, briefer, *Bath* (Bal 1988: 43).

This new openness to midrash and other forms of Jewish exegesis brings with it both benefits and dangers. One danger is that the modern literary plundering of rabbinic and medieval works will wrench them out of context and distort their meaning and purpose. This undermines the integrity of the exegetical tradition and is not likely to be met with approval by serious students of rabbinic and medieval exegesis. By way of example, I cite Phyllis Trible's interpretation of Gen 3:3. On the woman's addition of "you shall not touch it" to the original command against eating from the tree, Trible comments: "Thus the woman 'builds a fence around the Torah', a procedure that her rabbinical successors developed fully to protect the law of God and to insure obedience to it" (Trible 1978: 110). What is going on here? Trible is an apologist feminist interpreter; she is concerned with recouping female characters and with showing the Bible to be positive in its portrayal of women. Thus, rather than blaming the woman, Trible praises her added words as evidence of the "hermeneutical skills of the woman" and proof that "she can also interpret it [meaning God's command] faithfully." By using such words, Trible makes the woman into a postbiblical exegete. More serious, by invoking the rabbinic principle of "building a fence around the Torah" in connection with the woman's added phrase, she misleads us by suggesting that the rabbinic tradition interpreted Gen 3:3 the way she herself does. This is not the case. The rabbis were certainly not feminists, and the majority of rabbinic and medieval exegetes who comment on the woman's addition see it as detracting from God's commandment, not enhancing it.[10] Trible has misapplied a rabbinic principle, has extended it beyond rabbinic usage, and by so doing has misrepresented her source. In a sense, she has imitated the woman in Genesis 3.

On the other hand, the benefits of opening up the world of traditional exegesis to literary interpreters of the Bible may outweigh the dangers. It can increase serious study of the exegetical tradition and expand the possibility of

---

Bal's naming of the concubine in Judges 19 is explained as follows:

> Like Bath, she comes to the story nameless. . . . The term that describes her in the text, *pilegesh*, means something like "patrilocal wife": a wife living in the house of the father, a wife who remains a daughter. Playing on the word "house," the motif that becomes so crucial in her story, on the word "daughter" as well as on her place of origin—Bethlehem, "the house of bread"—this woman, who is defined by the location of her married life, will be given the name *Beth*, which is a form of the word *house* (Bal 1988: 89–90).

10. Cf. *b. Sanh.* 29a; Rashi on Gen 3:3. These sources do not consider the addition to be "a fence around the Torah" but rather an example of how one detracts from God's command by adding to it. Prov 30:6 is their prooftext. There is some evidence that the rabbis wrestled with the question of why this is not to be interpreted as building a fence around the Torah, but this is quite different from what Trible has done.

ʾAbot R. Nat. A and B, chapter 1 (Schechter 1967: 4) does consider the addition to be "a fence around the Torah" but credits it to Adam, assuming that Adam was the first to say it and that the woman is merely repeating it (despite the fact that the woman's statement is the only one recorded in the text).

literary insights deriving from the tradition. In order to accomplish the latter, we must first understand the similarities and the differences between traditional exegesis and modern literary interpretation.[11]

Modern literary interpretation of the Bible and traditional Jewish exegesis emerged from two very different worlds, with different needs. Yet they can both be termed *literary approaches* insofar as they share certain assumptions and interpretive strategies, as opposed to the assumptions and strategies of historical criticism.

1. A focus on the text for the purpose of extracting meaning from it. The interpretation is an end in itself, not a means to reconstruct history or to reconstruct a former text.

2. The text is viewed as a coherent unity. Apparent discrepancies, repetitions, and contradictions are interpreted as part of the artistry of the text and as significant in understanding its meaning. The text can be understood as self-referential, an intertext. A phrase in one passage may echo or allude to a phrase in another passage. Similarities in structures or phraseology are hermeneutically significant.

3. The wording is to be taken seriously. Lexical and grammatical choices are not random but are fraught with meaning.

4. There is a greater awareness of the process of interpretation than in the historical-critical school, for the finding or making of meaning is the name of the game. Hermeneutical rules exist, whether or not they are clearly defined.

5. The interpreter is aware of different levels of meaning and different ways that the text can be construed. Metaphorical, allegorical, and symbolic readings take their place alongside literal readings. Multiple meanings are easily tolerated.

Having said this, I hasten to add that traditional and modern literary exegesis are not identical. They differ in significant ways. Although traditional exegetes may have employed a literary methodology, they did not view the Bible as an aesthetic object per se. Words were not chosen because they sounded good, nor were structures arranged for their aesthetic appeal. Rather, the Bible was divine revelation, conveyed in the only words possible. In times when there was a high degree of literary awareness in the culture in which Jews lived, Jews labored to show that the Bible had as much literary merit, if not more, than other literary works; but much of this discussion was overtly chauvinistic, and, by and large, it did not affect the actual exegesis of the text. Traditional exegesis remained focused on halakhic matters, on moral lessons and the promotion of certain values, and on connecting the verse under scrutiny with the body

11. For an earlier discussion of some of the similarities and differences, see Rozik (1976).

of mainstream Jewish texts (the rest of the Bible and rabbinic literature). In other words, traditional Jewish exegesis viewed the Bible as a Jewish text, even as the modern literary school views it as a literary text and the historical school views it as an ancient Near Eastern text.

There are, then, crucial differences in the purposes of traditional exegetes and modern literary scholars but major similarities in the ways that they work with the biblical text. This suggests that traditional exegesis can be of special benefit to literary interpreters, although modern literary exegesis will not be traditional in outlook or content. How can literary interpreters use traditional Jewish exegesis?

The most obvious contribution that the traditional commentaries make is their treasure of lexical and grammatical observations. Beyond this, there are relatively few fully-formed literary interpretations that can be lifted whole from the tradition, but there is an unlimited supply of raw material that lends itself to modern literary use.

Traditional exegetes often note points of literary interest, even though they may not draw literary conclusions from them. This may be the observation of an unusual phrase, a verbal or thematic connection, or the ordering of peri-copes. The Midrash loves to fill in gaps and spin fanciful tales about characters and situations. These may seem overly imaginative at times, but often they stimulate our own interpretive creativity.

The techniques of traditional exegesis can be imitated or adapted for liter-ary purposes. This is a tricky matter, because the techniques, even when simi-lar, may not be applied in the same manner;[12] and not all traditional techniques would be accepted by modern interpreters. Moreover, the modern results may differ from the traditional ones,[13] may vary from one interpreter to another, and can only be judged subjectively. Here I should note that there are two classes of literary interpreters of the Bible. One class still sees the Bible as an ancient text, to be understood in its original context, albeit as a literary work accessible through literary analysis. The other class reads the Bible as a contemporary text, using all the reading strategies in the postmodern arsenal. For the former class, at least, the label *midrashic* is definitely not a compliment, for it implies homiletics rather than a search for the plain sense. Yet this division into two classes does not mean that the first group will be attracted only to traditional *peshat* and the second group to *derash*, for it is possible to find intimations of the *peshat* in the Midrash. The hallmarks of both classes of modern literary exegetes—attending to repetitions and echoes, noting changes in wording, fill-ing in gaps, and discussions of characterization—are also the hallmarks of both *peshat* and *derash*. Seeing how these were used as interpretive tools in the past may teach us something about how they can be used in the present.

12. See Rozik (1976) on the use of "key-words."

13. See, for example, the interpretation that the Midrash ascribes to repeated terms as opposed to the interpretation that modern literary critics would give (Berlin 1994: 17–18).

I want to advocate a literary application of traditional Jewish exegesis. That is, while understanding that the aims of the tradition were not the same as our literary aims, we can use traditional exegesis for our own literary purposes. We can do this, I hope, without distorting the tradition; in fact, the process may give us a keener grasp of the tradition and at the same time a greater awareness of our own exegetical strategies.

I will demonstrate with a few observations on the book of Ruth. To modern critics, Ruth is the Bible's literary piece par excellence. Labels such as *idyll, novella,* and *pastoral* were applied to it even before the rise of sophisticated literary interpretation. Now there is no reason to suggest that Jewish tradition saw this book as any more literary than the rest of the Bible, yet a number of traditional comments on it can provide a stimulus for literary exegesis.

Ruth opens with "It was in the days when the judges judged." In some ways this is a typical narrative opening, yet if we attend to the comments of the Midrash and the medieval commentaries, we realize that it is untypical. *Ruth Rabbah,* Proem, VII, notes that the phrase *it was in the days of* occurs in four other places (Gen 14:1, Isa 7:1, Jer 1:3, Esth 1:1), and it finds a common link with misfortune in all. A modern literary use of this observation might note something slightly different: namely, that in all cases except Ruth, the name of a specific king is mentioned. We do not have the name of a specific judge in Ruth, a fact that led the rabbis to suggest a number of candidates and most medieval exegetes to follow the view in *b. B. Bat.* 91a that the judge was Ibṣan.[14] By filling in this gap and tying the story of Ruth to a more spe-cific historical context, these comments indirectly hint that the first verse of Ruth is anomalous—conventional in form but not in content. What does this mean? That Ruth is less historical—that is, more fictive—than other narratives? That an author who lumped together an entire period is obviously writing after that period? The conclusions that we draw will not be traditional ones, but the points made by traditional exegetes can open our eyes to new exegetical possibilities.

The phrase *Naomi's husband* in Ruth 1:3 is somewhat unusual and is explained by Rashi as emphasizing the husband-wife relationship and thereby signifying the heavy loss felt by Naomi at the death of her husband. As the rabbis said: אין איש מת אלא לאשתו 'A man is not dead except to his wife' (*b. Sanh.* 22b). While this explanation has not found favor among modern critics, they also feel the need, from a literary perspective, to explain a phrase in which a man is named in relation to his wife (reversing the usual practice of naming women in relation to men). I view the reference to Elimelech as "Naomi's husband" as part of a larger pattern of "naming" in the book of Ruth. As I have suggested elsewhere (Berlin 1994: 83–84), all of the characters in this book

---

14. See Meltzer 1990: 1 n. 4. Meltzer also points out that the grammatical construction of Ruth 1:1 differs in that it is the only time that the construct form 'in the days of' is followed by a gerund. *B. B. Bat.* 91a apparently liked the phonetic equivalence between בועז and אבצן.

are named in relation to Naomi, beginning with Elimelech in 1:3 and culmi-
nating in "a son is born to Naomi" in 4:17.

One could cite many other examples of traditional observations upon
which modern literary insights may be built. And, indeed, sensitive critics who
are familiar with traditional exegesis often call upon the tradition to help shape
their own interpretation. This generally requires insight into the problem perceived by the tradition, rather than an acceptance of the solution offered. The
traditional exegetes were exquisitely close readers of the text, and it is this,
more than anything else, that we can learn from them.

A famous dictum in *Ruth Rab.* 2.15 is:

אמר ר' זעירה מגילה זו אין בה לא טומאה ולא טהרה ולא איסור ולא היתר ולמה
נכתבה? ללמדך כמה שכר טוב לגומלי חסדים.

> Rav Zeira said: This scroll is not concerned with impurity or purity, or with
> the forbidden or the permitted. Why then was it written? To teach you how
> good is the reward of those who act with *ḥesed.*

First of all, the Midrash has hit upon an important theme in the book, *ḥesed*
'kindness and loyalty', which informs the relationship between the main characters. It is one of the central themes that many modern literary scholars find
in Ruth. Second, the comment implicitly cautions about the dangers of getting
bogged down in the legal aspects of the story (the levirate, the redemption of
land, the status of a Moabitess in Israel). These legal practices remain problematic but should not overshadow the main thrust of the work. Finally, although the rabbis were vitally concerned with *halakha*, they were aware that
many parts of the Bible were nonhalakhic (see Rashi on Gen 1:1) and also
nonhistorical or nonliteral (for example, that Job was not a real person but a
mashal). *Ruth Rabbah* is seeking to derive moral instruction, an example of
gemilut ḥasadim—an eternal value that the reader should derive from Ruth.
Although we might be tempted to write this off as parochial piety, we do with
great literature essentially what the rabbis did with the Bible: we look to it for
a lesson about life, the human condition, the way the world is or ought to be.
In that sense it is perhaps not wrong to declare that traditional Jewish exegetes
saw the Bible as literature.

Bibliography

Bal, Mieke
  1988   *Death and Dissymmetry*. Chicago: University of Chicago Press.
Berlin, Adele
  1994   *Poetics and Interpretation of Biblical Narrative*. Bible and Literature Series
          9. Sheffield: Almond, 1983. Reprinted Winona Lake, Indiana: Eisenbrauns,
          1994.

Handelman, Susan A.
  1982   *The Slayers of Moses.* Albany: State University of New York Press.
Hartman, Geoffrey H., and Budick, Sanford
  1986   *Midrash and Literature.* New Haven: Yale University Press.
Klein, Charlotte
  1978   *Anti-Judaism in Christian Theology.* Philadelphia: Fortress.
Kugel, James L.
  1981   On the Bible and Literary Criticism. *Prooftexts* 1:217–36.
Meltzer, F.
  1990   Ruth. In *Ḥamesh Megillot.* Jerusalem: Mossad Harav Kook.
Rozik, Sarah
  1976   מדרכי המדרש ומדרכי הספרות בפרשנות המקרא. *Beth Mikra* 64 [21]:71–78.
Schechter, Solomon
  1967   *Aboth De Rabbi Nathan.* New York: Feldheim.
Sperling, S. David
  1992   *Students of the Covenant.* Atlanta: Scholars.
Trible, Phyllis
  1978   *God and the Rhetoric of Sexuality.* Philadelphia: Fortress.
Würthwein, Ernst
  1979   *The Text of the Old Testament.* Grand Rapids: Eerdmans.

The Genre of the Biblical Commentary as Problem and Challenge

BREVARD S. CHILDS
Yale University

Many persons outside the field of Bible often regard the predominant role of the biblical commentary with both surprise and suspicion. Surely other important bodies of literature, both ancient and modern, are handled by the scholarly guild without the need of such commentary. Yet from the earliest period, first in Judaism and later in Christianity, the commentary provided the classic form by which Scripture was both studied and interpreted. Even in moments when a traditional understanding of the Bible was being challenged or a new model proposed, the genre of the commentary continued as a vehicle of change.

Traditional Rationale for the Commentary

Upon reflection, I find that the choice of the form of commentary has not been accidental. Of course, the study of the Bible has called forth other forms as well, such as the paraphrase, historical tractate, and philological treatise. Nevertheless, the commentary has remained dominant, both in periods of interpretive stability and of change. Several reasons come to mind that explain, in part, the choice:

1. Very early in the history of literary stabilization, the biblical text was assigned a privileged status. Even though the form of a targum was sanctioned and assigned a role within a specific historical context, basically text and interpretation were sharply distinguished.

2. The concern to follow the sequence of the biblical story was thought important rather than rearranging the text into more orderly topics. The commentary form best lent itself to this approach.

3. Because the Bible was traditionally understood as containing the very oracles of God, no word was regarded as superfluous. It was, therefore,

thoroughly rational to argue that if Genesis needed only one chapter for the creation of the heavens and the earth but Exodus needed thirteen to describe the tabernacle, the Exodus chapters must contain multitudes of hidden mysteries calling for the most detailed commentary.

4. Finally, because the Bible, which was to regulate the life of the nation, often contained problems of unclear interpretation, the need of help from learned scholars was often expressed. These difficulties involved linguistic, historical, and literary issues. The fact that each generation asked new questions also accounts for the continuing demand for commentaries and even super-commentaries.

The Modern Commentary in a Secular Context

An issue more difficult to explain is why the form of the commentary has continued "alive and well," even when many of the traditional assumptions regarding the nature of the Bible are no longer shared by the modern academic culture. Perhaps the most obvious reason is that the commentary form has proven itself to be a highly useful vehicle for incorporating the development of newer approaches to biblical texts, even though at times the traditional form has been strained to the breaking point.

One of the most dramatic examples of adapting the traditional commentary form to very new and different purposes has been thoroughly documented by Arnold Williams,[1] who studied the great Renaissance commentaries on the book of Genesis from 1527–1633. These industrious scholars of the Renaissance sought to incorporate into the framework of the six days of creation the sum total of scientific knowledge concerning the universe that had exploded in the fields of geology, astronomy, physics, chemistry, and zoology, to name but a few. The effect in the case of Benedictus Pererius was to produce a set of four monstrous folio volumes that relentlessly pursued the correlation between the text of Genesis and ancient, medieval, and Renaissance science, but in the end succeeded in smothering the Bible with the sheer mass of tangential learning.

The early nineteenth century saw a powerful reaction set in against this uncritical assembly of undigested material by which commentaries were expanded. In 1821, W. Gesenius,[2] the great semitic philologist from Halle, prepared a two-volume commentary on the book of Isaiah that consciously limited the choice of material to a precise new translation and to fresh philological, text-critical, and historical observations. Still, even in the case of Gesenius, the

---

1. Arnold Williams, *The Common Expositor: An Account of the Commentaries on Genesis 1521–1633* (Chapel Hill, N.C., 1948).

2. F. H. W. Gesenius, *Der Prophet Jesaia: Übersetzt und mit einem vollständigen philologisch-kritischen und historischen Commentar begleitet* (Leipzig, 1821).

force of the traditional format caused him occasionally to venture comments on theology and ethics. Later in the nineteenth century, scholars such as Thenius[3] and Cornill[4] felt free to focus much of their energy on text-critical problems, even when continuing to use the commentary format. In his own inimical way, Wellhausen[5] was more consistent when treating the text-critical problems of Samuel to abandon the pretense of writing a commentary in order to focus all his energy on the one issue of text criticism. Yet even in the case of text criticism, S. R. Driver's commentary on Samuel,[6] while undoubtedly less brilliant than Wellhausen's treatment, probably has served a wider circle of scholars over the years by staying closer to the commentary form and including philological, syntactical, and geographical notes in addition to offering his text-critical reconstructions.

It is significant to observe the influence of Driver, among others, who produced the famous English-language series, The International Critical Commentary. Driver established the format of the series in his initial volume on Deuteronomy in 1895. The series laid great stress on textual and philological problems and thereby broke fresh ground in departing from the earlier English homiletical tradition. However, the series was also "user friendly" when compared to the German series of that period, such as the *Kurzgefasstes exegetisches Handbuch* or the *Kurzer Hand-Commentar*, edited by Marti, and as a result allowed large sections to be read by the nonprofessional biblical student. The ICC commentaries offered a broad introduction to the major critical problems of the book and often rehearsed the history of interpretation. Moreover, it was expected that the religious dimension of the book be addressed in some fashion, as an obvious appeal to the needs of the clergy.

During the nineteenth century, new tensions developed in the use of the traditional commentary form with the explosion of new literary and historical-critical theories regarding the Bible's composition. In terms of making use of developing source-critical theories, there was the growing problem of retaining a sequential treatment of the text of Genesis when the historical order of the sources diverged radically from the biblical text's own order. At first, moderate and conservative commentators, like Dillmann,[7] sought to maintain the biblical sequence by means of unobtrusive signs to designate the alleged sources, but very shortly, in the commentaries of Gunkel[8] and Procksch,[9] the interest in tracing the development of the Genesis traditions forced the different sources to be printed separately or at least with a distinctive font.

---

3. O. Thenius, *Die Bücher der Könige* (2d ed.; Leipzig, 1873).

4. C. H. Cornill, *Das Buch Jeremia* (Leipzig, 1905).

5. J. Wellhausen, *Der Text der Bücher Samuel untersucht* (Göttingen, 1871).

6. S. R. Driver, *Notes on the Hebrew Text and the Topography of the Books of Samuel* (2d ed.; Oxford, 1913).

7. A. Dillmann, *Die Genesis* (6th ed.; Leipzig, 1892).

8. H. Gunkel, *Genesis* (4th ed.; Göttingen, 1917).

9. O. Procksch, *Die Genesis* (Leipzig, 1913).

With the rise of the form-critical commentary in the twentieth century, another problem for the traditional commentary form emerged, namely the fragmentation of the larger unity of the literature into endless minor genres. Because the Psalter lent itself remarkably well to Gunkel's categories, at least on one level, the issue of fragmentation was not as obvious. However, when the method was applied to the Pentateuch or the Prophets, the difficulties became acute. The editors of the form-critically oriented series Biblischer Kommentar: Altes Testament apparently sensed the problem when they sought to conclude each section with a paragraph entitled *Ziel*. However, with rare exceptions, this final section turned out to be an abstract expression of the writer's theology or piety without an integral connection to the prior analytical analysis. Zimmerli's commentary on Ezekiel[10] revealed a different attempt to overcome the fragmentation inherent in the form-critical method. He spoke of a *Fortschreibung* by later disciples who extended the primary level of tradition. Actually this move represented an early turn toward redactional criticism, although Zimmerli himself appeared largely unconscious of his shift from the classic form criticism of his teachers and colleagues.

Then again, the commentary has also been widely used in presenting a new literary construal of a given biblical book. Certainly one of the most influential formulations of a new understanding of a prophet was offered by Duhm[11] in his brilliant Isaiah commentary. For Duhm, the goal of exegesis was critically to recover the *ipsissima verba* of the original oracles as the avenue back to the creative personality of the prophet himself. He could radically eliminate whole sections of a book with impunity as "inauthentic" because secondary additions were viewed as only blurring the pristine profile of the original figure. In Duhm's understanding, the part was better than the whole. More recently, the very opposite literary concept was defended by Muilenburg,[12] who placed his emphasis on the consistent structure of the entire poem of Isaiah 40–66, which he thought to reconstruct into a harmonious poetic composition by an appeal to literary, rhetorical devices. What is particularly striking in the contrast between Duhm and Muilenburg is the diverse assumptions regarding the nature of the prophet that both authors brought to bear in their reconstructions. The obvious danger involved in such strong readings is that passages which do not easily conform to the larger theory are frequently bent into conformity.

Finally, a very common form of the modern critical commentary has laid its stress on interpreting the text in direct reference to a reconstructed ancient Near Eastern historical milieu. No one can doubt that modern historical research has provided a rich tapestry against which to view the Bible. One only

10. W. Zimmerli, *Ezechiel* (2 vols.; Neukirchen-Vluyn, 1969).

11. B. Duhm, *Das Buch Jesaia* (Göttingen, 1892).

12. James Muilenburg, *The Interpreter's Bible*, vol. 5: *The Book of Isaiah* (Nashville, 1956) 381–773.

has to compare a modern critical-historical commentary with the vague and fanciful stories of early Oriental travelers who once provided the historical *realia* of exegesis. However, a consistent appeal to reconstructed historical reference also entails major threats to the basic strengths of exegesis done according to the commentary form. The problem arises when the verbal sense of the text has become subordinated to a historical reconstruction of a level lying behind the text itself and assumed to be the key to the text's real meaning. Thus, for example, in his Jeremiah commentary, John Bright[13] frequently felt constrained to reorder the sequence of the prophetic text to accord with his understanding of historical reality. This exegetical move is particularly unfortunate if one holds to the very opposite hermeneutical position that the biblical text has its own internal integrity and that its meaning is not necessarily dependent on an exact correlation with a reconstruction of ancient Near Eastern historical events.

To summarize, the traditional form of the commentary has continued to be a useful vehicle for developing new theories regarding biblical books. However, it can be argued that the traditional commentary form can also function as a critical judgment on exegetical theories when the tension becomes unbearable between a new reading and the very integrity of the commentary form itself.

The Problem of an Audience: Technical or Popular

There is another aspect to the function of commentaries that turns on the problem of the specific audience to whom a commentary is directed. Obviously, the choice of the reader determines in large measure the level on which the interpretation is pitched. It should be stated at the outset that a quality of excellence can be achieved on almost every level, whether highly technical or very popular. Conversely there are many examples of exceedingly poor commentaries, regardless of the level of technicality.

A common problem results when a commentary is badly misdirected in its selection of an audience. This situation usually occurs when the explicit intention of a series is at variance with the goals of a specific author. Few knowledgeable scholars would question that M. Dahood's commentary on the Psalms[14] in the Anchor Bible series has made a genuine contribution to the field in spite of the heated controversy that his handling of the Hebrew text has evoked. Nevertheless, it is a valid criticism of his commentary that it has appeared unfortunately in a series that is directed to a semipopular audience that lacks the critical skills to evaluate Dahood's philological reconstructions.

In order properly to determine the significance of a given commentary, it is necessary to acknowledge that commentaries, especially in the modern

13. J. Bright, *Jeremiah* (AB 21; Garden City, N.Y., 1965).
14. M. Dahood, *Psalms I–III* (AB 16–17A; Garden City, N.Y., 1966–70).

period, perform very diverse functions. Unquestionably German scholarship has excelled in producing the finest quality of critical and highly technical commentaries for at least two centuries. Conversely, it is sad to admit that the English-speaking world has produced very few nonderivative commentaries that have broken fresh critical ground. Fortunately there are a few exceptions, such as M. Greenberg's brilliant Ezekiel commentary. The effect of this situation is that many of the commentaries most widely used in Britain and in North America reflect a very poor literary quality of "translation English."

Some commentaries written in a semipopular style have performed just as valuable a function as the technical commentary in communicating in a lucid manner a holistic view of a book to a wide audience. One thinks of the impact on the English-speaking world of George Adam Smith's popular Isaiah commentary.[15] His florid Victorian prose and brilliant imagery opened up the prophet's preaching in a way that T. K. Cheyne's many technical volumes never succeeded in doing. Similarly it can be argued that von Rad's semipopular Genesis commentary[16] has exercised a far greater influence on several generations of readers than, say, Westermann's exhaustive but tedious commentary.[17]

The commentaries that have emerged through continual usage as enduring classics are characterized by the authors' ability to work successfully on many different levels and to address several audiences. If one compare the contribution of Rashi, for example, with Ibn Ezra or Rashbam, Rashi's genius as a commentator shines forth as something quite unique. He was able to point interpretation in a new direction by his careful contextual handling of the plain sense, while at the same time critically retaining elements of traditional midrash that enriched, rather than competed with, the literal rendering.[18] Or again, B. Jacob's Genesis commentary[19] wove such a thick tapestry on so many different levels of interpretation that the commentary has retained its value, even though few would now agree with Jacob's running battle with the source-critical hypothesis.

The Increasing Complexity of the Hermeneutical Problem

One of the major issues that the modern biblical discipline is facing arises from the sheer complexity of the enterprise of interpretation. The problem does not

---

15. G. A. Smith, *The Book of Isaiah* (2 vols.; London, 1888–90).

16. G. von Rad, *Genesis* (Göttingen, 1949; E.T., rev. ed., Philadelphia, 1972).

17. C. Westermann, *Genesis* (3 vols.; Neukirchen-Vluyn, 1974–82).

18. Cf. S. Kamin, *Rashi's Exegetical Categorization in Respect to the Distinction between* Peshat *and* Derash (Jerusalem, 1986) [Hebrew].

19. B. Jacob, *Der erste Buch der Tora: Genesis* (Berlin, 1934).

lie simply in the difficulty of the task but in the fact that the field is being devoured by endless methodological controversies, which have seldom resulted in a more profound handling of the Scriptures. One of the major hermeneutical convictions of the sixteenth-century Protestant Reformers lay in the understanding of the Bible as "perspicuous." This technical term did not imply that Scripture was without its exegetical problems, which were readily admitted, but rather that the Bible as a whole spoke plainly about God to a community of faith and practice and was written in a straightforward style that generally could be understood. In other words, the Bible was not an esoteric collection of hidden Gnostic symbols, available only to the initiate, but rather, it spoke of God in a language that was grounded in the ordinary human experience of a historical people.

This common precritical understanding of the Bible was severely damaged in the eyes of the learned academy with the coming of the Enlightenment. Regardless of the subsequent weaknesses that have surfaced in respect to the Enlightenment's own program, the movement's critical perceptions have made a return to the innocence of the past quite impossible. Today no one can write a successful commentary on the Bible without being aware of the subtle relationship between the biblical text and authorial intent, between the interaction of the synchronic and diachronic dimensions of a book, and of the role of the interpreter in establishing sense and meaning.

However, the major point to be made is that hermeneutics and exegesis are not the same. An excellent theoretical grasp of a problem does not guarantee an illuminating and profound exegesis of the passage, which is the essence of a good commentary. Most biblical scholars would agree that both a synchronic and a diachronic dimension are required in biblical interpretation. It is simply not enough to assert: this is my own personal reading! However, there are not clear and obvious rules on precisely how these two dimensions of the enterprise interact. The challenge of writing a commentary is that the form itself forces the author to make innumerable exegetical decisions, the success of which tests the adequacy of his or her hermeneutical theories.

Finally, it is in this context that a commentary's attention to the history of interpretation—indeed, its *Wirkungsgeschichte*—plays such a crucial role. Serious attention to the history of interpretation serves as a constant reminder that no one comes to the biblical text *de novo*, but one stands in a long line of interpreters. Again, this aspect of a commentator's task continually calls to mind that every interpretation, both past and present, is culturally conditioned. There is no one purely objective interpretation that forever settles the issue, but both text and interpreter remain in considerable flux. The quality of excellence is seen when a highly concrete reading breaks open the text in such a way that true insight remains in spite of ongoing shifts in culture. Moreover, knowledge of the history of interpretation challenges the modern interpreter with the perception of long-neglected skills from the past. One tends to forget that the medieval rabbis knew by heart the Hebrew Bible, which allowed for an understanding of intertextuality that is impossible to recover simply through the use of a concordance.

Criteria for Evaluating a Commentary's Excellence

In the preface to his Romans commentary, John Calvin offered two criteria by which to judge excellence in biblical interpretation, namely, lucid brevity. Perhaps it would be helpful after 400 years to expand his list in the form of a series of questions.

1. Does the commentator do justice to the coercion of the biblical text, or does the author's private agenda overshadow the text itself?

2. Does the creative imagination of the commentator lead the reader back to the biblical text or away from it?

3. Does the interpretation deal seriously with the profoundest dimension of the biblical text without being diverted by clever, even brilliant, speculation?

4. Does the commentator reflect the needed patience and empathy to wrestle with the elements of the Bible that at first seem strange, distant, and even offensive to modern sensibilities?

5. Has the commentator learned enough from the history of interpretation to retain a sense of modesty regarding his or her efforts and a critical respect for those who have illuminated the way in the past?

David's Jerusalem: Notes and Reflections

MORDECHAI COGAN
The Hebrew University of Jerusalem

Jerusalem's special place in Israelite thought over the millennia owes much to the viewpoint expressed in the writings of the Deuteronomistic circle, which exalted Jerusalem as "the city which the Lord had chosen out of all the tribes of Israel to put his name there" (e.g., 1 Kgs 14:21). Many events contributed to cultivating the idea of the city's chosenness, but none competes in kind with that initial move during the early reign of David that raised Jerusalem out of its relative anonymity onto the world's stage. A combination of political events and ideological struggle under unique historical circumstances transformed this city on a mountain byway for all times. Yet despite countless attempts to fathom the enigmas of the pivotal text of 2 Samuel 5, scholarly consensus has not been reached. The present stocktaking, undertaken during the celebrations ostensibly marking 3000 years of David's entry into the city,[1] is offered in honor and esteem to Moshe Greenberg, scholar and teacher, who through his personal example has given new meaning to Isaiah's lofty vision for Jerusalem's future: כִּי מִצִּיּוֹן תֵּצֵא תוֹרָה.

The Date of the City's Capture

The date of David's conquest of Jerusalem cannot be fixed with any surety. Other than the note in 2 Sam 5:5 that David moved to Jerusalem after seven and one-half years in Hebron, no other data are available. Historians are

---

1. Records show that the government of the new State of Israel considered holding a 3000-year celebration in the early 1950s, during the first debate over international recognition of Jerusalem as the capital; on these plans and their subsequent shelving, see N. Brug, *Ha'aretz Daily Newspaper*, May 26, 1995, p. B5. Also note N. Alterman's witty critique of those planned festivities reprinted in the collection of his journalistic writings, *The Seventh Column* (Tel-Aviv: Davar, 1954) 2.142–44 [Hebrew]. Whether political considerations were behind the fixing of the recent festivities to 1995–96 will have to be left to future historians to determine.

divided over the issue whether the conquest took place at the start of his reign in Hebron or after his battles with the Philistines in the Rephaim Valley and at Baal-perazim. Those who argue for an early date, like the late Benjamin Mazar, claim that "it would have been impossible for David to organize a defensive front against the Philistines without having control of the Fortress of Zion, the main base in the heart of his state."[2] Seven years later, after winning over the Northern tribes through guile and force and having pushed the Philistines back to the coastal plain, David moved from Hebron to Jerusalem.

But this scenario seems somewhat flawed. One wonders whether David, at so early a juncture, would have risked antagonizing his Philistine overlords by an attack on the Jebusite city. Account should be taken of the Philistines entrenched in the central mountain range at least as far south as Bethlehem (2 Sam 23:14), making the approach to Jebus all but unnegotiable. Moreover, the Philistines might have put up with David as ruler of a petty kingdom in Hebron and the nearby Shephelah, but it is likely that they would have seen an attack on Jerusalem as a hostile move by an upstart vassal.[3]

According to 2 Sam 5:17, it was David's nomination as king of both Judah and Israel (2 Sam 5:1–3) that showed him to be the rebel he surely was. This instigated the Philistines to do battle with him (v. 17).[4] Only after the Philistines had been driven from all of the mountain regions (v. 25) was David free to move against the Jebusite enclave located midway between the two constituent parts of his kingdom (vv. 6–9). With Jerusalem in his hands, he did not wait long to move there from Hebron.[5]

---

2. B. Mazar, "David's Reign in Hebron and the Conquest of Jerusalem," *In the Time of Harvest: Essays in Honor of Abba Hillel Silver* (ed. D. J. Silver; New York: Macmillan, 1963) 235–44 (= *Biblical Israel: State and People* [Jerusalem: Magnes and Israel Exploration Society, 1992] 78–87). Aharoni also sees the taking of Jerusalem as an early act of David, prior to his battles with the Philistines; see Y. Aharoni, *The Land of the Bible* (2d ed.; Philadelphia: Westminster, 1979) 292, 318 n.12.

3. According to C. E. Hauer's reasoning, it was this very move that roused the Philistines against David ("Jerusalem, the Stronghold and Rephaim," *CBQ* 32 [1970] 571–78).

4. G. W. Ahlström speculates that once David upset the political balance in the area, the Philistines "might have forged an alliance with Jerusalem" against him (*The History of Ancient Palestine from the Paleolithic Period to Alexander's Conquest* [JSOTSup 146; Sheffield: Sheffield Academic Press, 1993] 466). If so, the fact that the Philistines did not come to the aid of Jerusalem when attacked by David also points to the priority of his battles with them.

5. S. Yeiven argued for maintaining the chronological sequence of the literary elements in 2 Samuel 5: David's taking Jerusalem was a sign to the Philistines that he was up to no good, and they set out to bring him in line (Yeiven, "The Military Campaigns of David," *The Military History of the Land of Israel in Biblical Times* [ed. J. Liver; Tel-Aviv: Maarachot, 1964] 150–56 [Hebrew]). Yeiven did, however, opt for all of this to have occurred at the close of David's stay in Hebron. J. Bright adopts the sequence suggested here but is less sanguine about the date: "after a few years of rule in Hebron" (*A History of Israel* [3d ed.; Philadelphia: Westminster, 1981] 200); cf. also M. Noth, *The History of Israel* (2d ed.; New York: Harper, 1960) 187–90.

The Capture of the City

The story of David's capture of Jerusalem has come down to us in two versions, 2 Sam 5:6–9 and 1 Chr 11:4–7. Both texts are rather opaque, the Chronicles version being basically a reworking of 2 Samuel, interpreting it from the distance of many centuries.[6] This is not to claim that the Samuel text is a contemporary record, free of later interpolation and interpretation, for even its editor may not fully have comprehended the course of events he transcribed and glossed. The words of the Jebusites to David, who had set to attacking Jerusalem—" 'You will not come in here, even the blind and the lame will turn you back,' thinking, 'David cannot come in here' " (NRSV to 2 Sam 5:6)—look like the scornful boasting of the city's defenders, who felt that they could withstand any attack, and in that confidence claimed that even the blind and the lame among them could be stationed on the walls as the front line of defense.[7] This taunt and David's rancor are now seen as the ground for the exclusion of persons with bodily infirmities from the Temple.[8] Regarding the battle itself, there are no details. The item in 1 Chr 11:6 about Joab's bravery, "Joab son of Zeruiah went up first," is more an etiology than it is a description of how the city was taken; it justifies Joab's first-rank position among David's men.

Most distressing is the lack of consensus about the meaning of the key phrase וְיִגַּע בַּצִּנּוֹר in David's remark (now very much cut short) to his fighting men.[9] The צִנּוֹר has been interpreted as some type of weapon,[10] as a tower or a fortification of sorts,[11] a vital part of the body (neck or throat, joint,

---

6. Following the latest discussion of S. Japhet, *I & II Chronicles* (OTL; Louisville: Westminster/John Knox, 1993) 239.

7. So already Josephus *Ant* 7.61. Other understandings of the verse seem less convincing to me: for example, that the words were an aspersion on the makeup of David's force—they were just a bunch of weaklings, that is, blind and lame (H. J. Stoebe, "Die Einnahme Jerusalems," *ZDPV* 73 [1957] 73–99); or Yadin's oft-cited reference to a Hittite oath ritual involving the blind and the lame (*The Art of Warfare in Biblical Lands* [New York: McGraw Hill, 1963] 267–70). P. K. McCarter, Jr. adopted a difficult Qumran reading against the MT (*2 Samuel* [AB 9; Garden City, N.Y.: Doubleday, 1984] 135–38); this needs further study.

8. Cf. M. Weinfeld, "Traces of Hittite Cult in Shiloh, Bethel and in Jerusalem," *Religionsgeschichtliche Beziehungen zwischen Kleinasien, Nordsyrien und dem Alten Testament* (OBO 129; Fribourg: Editions Universitaires / Göttingen: Vandenhoeck & Ruprecht, 1993) 458.

9. For a thorough review of the scholarly discussion, see G. Bressan, "L'espugnazione di Sion in 2 Sam 5,6–8 // I Cron 11,4–6 e il Problema del 'Sinnor,'" *Bib* 25 (1944) 346–81; cf. also, G. Brunet, "David et le sinnor," *Studies in the Historical Books of the Old Testament* (VTSup 30; Leiden: Brill, 1979) 73–86; C. Schäfer-Lichtenberger, "David und Jerusalem: Ein Kapitel biblischer Historiographie," *ErIsr* 24 (Malamat Volume; 1994) 197*–211*.

10. So the LXX. E. L. Sukenik proposed 'pitch-fork' ("The Account of David's Capture of Jerusalem," *JPOS* 8 [1928] 1–16); cf. NEB: 'grappling-iron'.

11. So many of the medieval commentators; cf. , e.g., Rashi, Qimḥi, ad loc.

phallus),[12] and most frequently, as a water conduit. It was L. H. Vincent, in particular, who popularized the identification made earlier by William Birch,[13] of the צִנּוֹר with the water project of the Gihon Spring that had been discovered by Charles Warren in 1867.[14] It was inferred that the residents of Jerusalem drew water from the Gihon through a system of tunnels and channels, the vertical shaft at the end of tunnel dug in the mountainside ("Warren's Shaft") that descended some 15 meters to the water level being identified as the צנור. According to Vincent, Joab and his men forced their way into the city through the shaft and in an act of outstanding bravery took Jerusalem. But as inviting as this suggestion is, following recent investigations on the spot, it no longer seems as plausible as it once did. Ascent through the shaft is virtually impossible; Yigal Shiloh, who directed the latest excavation in the area, had to engage mountain climbers to scale the top. Furthermore, Shiloh suggested that the construction of the entire water project was likely of early Israelite date.[15] Still, if the Hebrew צִנּוֹר is indeed connected with streaming water, as is suggested by the context of its only other occurrence, in Ps 42:8,[16] then perhaps David's words refer to cutting off the water supply to Jerusalem as part of the siege, which was meant to break the resistance of the well-protected Jebusites.[17]

Jerusalem's Position Prior to Its Capture

Pre-Israelite Jerusalem sat astride the low sloping hill west of the Kidron Valley, some distance from the main traffic arteries of the hill country, and it can only have been the ready supply of water from the Gihon Spring that drew the first and all future settlers to this insular site. The early Jerusalemites over-

12. The most recent commentator to adopt this tack was McCarter, *2 Samuel*, 139–40: "Whoever strikes a Jebusite, therefore, must strike at the windpipe or throat and, therefore, deliver a fatal blow."

13. W. B. Birch, "Zion, the City of David," *PEFQS* 11 (1878) 184–85.

14. L. H. Vincent, *Jérusalem sous terre* (London: Horace Cox, 1911) 33–53.

15. Y. Shiloh, *Excavations at the City of David I* (Qedem 19; Jerusalem: Israel Exploration Society, 1984) 21–22. G. Dalman had already remarked that the shaft was unscalable and thus set aside Vincent's identification ("Zion, die Burg Jerusalems," *Palästina-Jahrbuch* 11 [1915] 67); cf. Vincent's retort, *RB* 33 (1924) 365.

16. All modern translations adopt the LXX *katarraktōn* 'waterfall, cataract' of Ps 42:8[41:8], as apparently had been done by the Vulgate. Gersonides (Levi ben Gershon) glossed: 'a gutter from which the water flowed'.

17. J. Simons, in his vast compendium *Jerusalem in the Old Testament* (Leiden: Brill, 1952), argued the case for this interpretation of the events (pp. 168–74). See also, more recently, S. Holm-Nielson, "Did Joab Climb 'Warren's Shaft'?" *History and Traditions of Early Israel: Studies Presented to Eduard Nielsen* (ed. A. Lemaire and B. Otzen; VTSup 50; Leiden: Brill, 1993) 38–49; G. J. Wightman, *The Walls of Jerusalem: From the Canaanites to the Mamluks* (Mediterranean Archaeological Supplement 4; Sydney: Miditarch, The University of Sydney, 1993) 26–27.

came these "negative topographical and geographical features,"[18] and by the fourteenth century B.C.E., the Amarna Age, Jerusalem most likely supported urban functions, including a physical infrastructure for the city-state ruled by Abdi-Hepa. The somewhat later Jebusite city of the Early Iron Age has yet to yield its secrets to the archaeologist's spade. Despite the extensive excavations on the eastern slope of the City of David, archaeologists are far from agreement on the interpretation of the finds, for example, whether the remains of the "Stepped Stone Structure" and the terrace system supporting it are those of the Jebusite city or not.[19] But rather than conclude, as a few scholars have recently done,[20] that the city that David took was not the Jerusalem of later history, one should consider the possibility that the settled area of this period was further uphill, in an area still to be excavated.

Traditions now associated with the period of the Israelite settlement speak of Jerusalem as an autonomous enclave outside of the Israelite domain, isolated from both the Joseph tribes and Judah. The historical value of the two brief notices in Judges 1 concerning battles that were waged over the city is very problematic. The first tells of the tribe of Judah fighting against Jerusalem, capturing it, and burning it to the ground (Judg 1:8); the second describes the inability of the tribe of Benjamin to dispossess the "the Jebusites who dwell in Jerusalem" and who continue to live there "until this day" (v. 21). The editor of these notices preferred Judah over Benjamin and so passed over the contradictory tradition found in the book of Joshua (15:63), where it is Judah rather than Benjamin who could not oust the Jebusites from the city. Such tendentiousness coupled with vague writing diminish the usefulness of these notices.[21]

The city's continued autonomy down to the time of David probably indicates that Jerusalem was not very troublesome to the Benjaminite or Judean families in the area (note the uninterrupted passage of the threesome past Jebus in Judg 19:10–12). Yet the two tribes seem to have competed over rights to the

18. See Y. Karmon, "The Mountains Round About Jerusalem," in *Jerusalem through the Ages: The Twenty-Fifth Archaeological Convention* (Jerusalem: Israel Exploration Society, 1969) 96–108, esp. 108 [Hebrew].

19. See M. Steiner, "The Jebusite Ramp of Jerusalem: The Evidence from the Macalister, Kenyon and Shiloh Excavations," *Biblical Archaeology Today, 1990: Proceedings of the Second International Congress on Biblical Archaeology* (Jerusalem: Israel Exploration Society, 1993) 585–88; J. M. Cahill and D. Tarler, in ibid., 625–26; idem, *ABD* 2.55; M. Steiner, "Re-dating the Terraces of Jerusalem," *IEJ* 44 (1994) 13–20.

20. E.g., M. Steiner, in a paper delivered at the SBL Twelfth International Meeting (Louvain, August 1994).

21. Mazar ("David's Reign," 80 n.4) conjectured that the Judean attack on Jerusalem took place during the period when it was under Amorite control, after which it became a Jebusite enclave. J. Gray interpreted the verses in harmonistic fashion: the battle was over the outlying lands in the Rephaim Valley, so that the fortified city itself was not captured (*Joshua, Judges and Ruth* [NCB; Grand Rapids: Eerdmans / London: Marshall Morgan & Scott, 1977] 112). The wording of the text, however, makes this view unacceptable.

city, if only in theory, their rival claims having left their footprints in the historical writ. The Benjaminite claim to Jerusalem is expressly set forth in the territorial map in Joshua (18:28), where Jerusalem is included within the tribal inheritance of Benjamin. Premonarchic conditions would explain their demand, for after the city was captured by David and became inextricably linked with the Davidic dynasty, it is hard to imagine a later age when such a contestation could have been waged.[22]

David's Activities in Jerusalem

In an act of supreme political wisdom, David united his realm around Jerusalem, turning the Jebusite city into the capital of the united monarchy. A. Alt put it cogently: "The personal plan of one person, his determination and activity" were the main factors at play.[23] The traditions concerning David's activities in Jerusalem have been collected in 2 Samuel 5–6 and are retold in a different order in 1 Chronicles 11–15. According to the Chronicler's account, immediately after taking up residence in the city, David transferred the Ark of the Covenant to Jerusalem, and by this act, demonstrated his concern for cultic matters that took precedent over other affairs, such as the construction of a palace. As in other cases in the Chronicler's history, this is an example of ideological-historiographic chronology, unreliable for reconstructing the sequence of events as they were actually played out.[24] But neither can the order of events as they appear in 2 Samuel be used as is, considering the priority given by the editor to matters concerning Jerusalem over other affairs of state, which is reflected particularly in the severance of 2 Sam 5:17 from its natural antecedent in v. 3.

Setting the question of date aside, we are still able to observe the early stages by which Jerusalem became the religious center for the entire kingdom. After its recovery from Philistine captivity during the days of Samuel (cf. 1 Sam 5–7:1), "the Ark of the Lord over which the name of the Lord of Hosts

---

22. Kallai posits that Jerusalem's inclusion in Benjamin was part of the effort of David and Solomon "to tighten the nexus of the land of Benjamin to Judah" (*Historical Geography of the Bible* [Jerusalem: Magnes, 1986] 283–84). S. Aḥituv also dates this tradition to the period of the united monarchy but without explanation (*Joshua* [Miqra Leyisrael; Jerusalem: Magnes / Tel-Aviv: Am Oved, 1996] 300 [Hebrew]). As argued above, both positions are untenable.

23. See A. Alt, "Jerusalems Aufsteig," *ZDMG* 79 (1925) 1–19 (= *Kleine Schriften zur Geschichte des Volkes Israel* [Munich: Beck, 1968] 3.243–57).

24. For this feature of the Chronicler's editorial procedure, see the discussion of M. Cogan, "The Chronicler's Use of Chronology as Illuminated by Neo-Assyrian Royal Inscriptions," in *Empirical Models for Biblical Criticism* (ed. J. H. Tigay; Philadelphia: University of Pennsylvania Press, 1985) 197–209; also D. Glatt, "The Two First Acts of King David," *Beth Miqra* 137 (1994) 156–63 [Hebrew].

who dwells above the cherubim had been proclaimed" stayed at the House of Abinadab in Gibeah (7:1; 2 Sam 6:3); though no particular information concerning the ark is available from the reign of Saul, perhaps this Gibeah was the town that had served as Saul's capital.[25] The holy ark, associated with the nation's distant past, had been at home among the tribes of the house of Joseph (not Judah) and had moved about their cities. By transferring the ark to Jerusalem to the "tent which he had prepared for it" (6:17), David sought to secure for his capital the status of a holy city, a site of pilgrimage, similar to the status enjoyed by Shiloh, the major priestly city where the ark had sojourned in premonarchic days.[26] Moreover, by displaying his high esteem for the ark, David went a considerable way toward mollifying the house of Joseph, who might have otherwise resented its removal to Jerusalem.

Now the transfer of a holy palladium could surely not have been undertaken without divine approval, and though the text in 2 Samuel 6 lacks reference to a formal inquiry of the deity's wishes, such oracle-taking is implied by the reprise found in Ps 132:11–14: "The Lord swore to David, a firm oath that He will not renounce. . . . For the Lord has chosen Zion; He desired it for His seat. 'This is my resting-place for all time; here I will dwell, for I desire it.'"[27] Finally, David's personal participation in the cultic affairs served as a precedent for future kings of Jerusalem, so that they too would take an active role in decisions on cultic matters (compare, for example, the reform acts of Joash [2 Kings 12], Hezekiah [2 Kgs 18:4], and Josiah [2 Kings 22–23]), or would be officiants in Temple ceremonies (as was Solomon [1 Kgs 8:63–64]), even offering sacrifices at the altar (Ahaz [2 Kgs 16:12–13])![28]

Construction in Jerusalem during the reign of David consisted of the standard maintenance projects necessary from time to time, as, for example, in the Millo, the filled-in area of the eastern slope of the City of David, built on a system of terraced retaining walls, parts of which may have been damaged during the capture of the city.[29] Beyond this, David had plans to construct a palace and a royal sanctuary, two buildings essential to a capital city worthy of the name. The palace was constructed with the aid of David's ally, Hiram of Tyre, who

25. Yamada has recently reinvestigated the positive place the ark held in Saul's kingdom, written out by the Judean editors of the book of Samuel; see K. Yamada, *A Study of the History of the Ark of God . . . History and Historiography* (M.A. Thesis, Hebrew University, 1994) [Hebrew].

26. See the analysis of the anachronistic image of the Shiloh sanctuary by M. Haran, "Shiloh and Jerusalem: The Origin of the Priestly Tradition in the Pentateuch," *JBL* 81 (1962) 14–24.

27. See J. J. M. Roberts, "Zion in the Theology of the Davidic-Solomonic Empire," *Studies in the Period of David and Solomon and Other Essays: Papers Read at the International Symposium for Biblical Studies, Tokyo, 5–7 December, 1979* (ed. T. Ishida; Tokyo: Yamakawa-Shuppansha, 1982) 93–108, esp. 105.

28. See M. Noth, "Jerusalem and the Israelite Tradition," in *The Laws of the Pentateuch and Other Studies* (Philadelphia: Fortress, 1967) 132–44, esp. 134.

29. As originally proposed by K. Kenyon, *Royal Cities of the Old Testament* (New York: Shocken, 1971) 33–35; cf. also Shiloh, *Excavations at the City of David I*, 26.

sent materials and workers for the project (2 Sam 5:11); and though it is not explicitly stated in any text, one may suppose that this support was offered at a
negotiated price, as it was in the days of Solomon.[30] The king's residence was
likely located in the Ophel, the high ground just north of the City of David, below the height that was to serve as the Temple Mount; the distinct physical advantages of the Ophel recommended it as the location of the city's citadel.[31]
But the other project, that of a sanctuary to replace the portable tabernacle with
a permanent structure (2 Sam 7:2), did not get off the ground.

That David was unable to carry out his plan is rationalized in the divine
address delivered by the prophet Nathan: "From the day that I brought the Israelites out of Egypt to this day I have not dwelt in a house, but have moved
about in Tent and Tabernacle. As I moved about wherever the Israelites went,
did I ever reproach any of the tribal leaders whom I appointed to care for My
people Israel: 'Why have you not built Me a house of cedar?'" (2 Sam 7:6–7).
Behind these words one can still hear the religious conservatism of those distant days, stemming, it would seem, from the priesthood, which was entrusted
with the care of the ark and its cult, to whose mind the building of a temple
would have been a radical break with ancient Israelite tradition.[32]

---

30. According to Tyrian chronology, accessible in the works of Josephus, Hiram took the
throne seven years earlier than Solomon, which would then date the building of David's palace to
the last decade of his reign. See H. J. Katzenstein, *The History of Tyre* (Jerusalem: Shocken, 1973)
77–97.

31. Shiloh took *Ophel* to be "an urban architectural term denoting the outstanding site of the
citadel or acropolis" (*Excavations at the City of David I*, 27); for the Ophel at Samaria, see 2 Kgs
5:24; for the one at Dibon in Moab, see the Mesha Inscription, lines 21–22. Recent excavations in
the Ophel found that in the 9th century B.C.E., the Temple Mount was joined to the City of David
by a defense line; the southern quarter of the Ophel was "closed in" during Solomon's reign (cf.
1 Kgs. 11:27); see E. Mazar and B. Mazar, *Excavations in the South of the Temple Mount: The
Ophel of Biblical Jerusalem* (Qedem 29; Jerusalem: Israel Exploration Society, 1989) 58.

32. See R. de Vaux, "Jerusalem and the Prophets," *The Goldenson Lectures* (Cincinnati: Hebrew Union College, 1969) 279–81; idem, "Jérusalem et les prophètes," *RB* 73 (1966) 485–88; and
the analysis of F. K. Kumaki, "The Deuteronomistic Theology of the Temple—as Crystallized in
2 Sam 7, 1 Kgs 8," *AJBI* 7 (1981)16–52.

Several late biblical writers were constrained to defend Solomon's actions where David had
failed. The Deuteronomistic historians have Solomon explain to Hiram that it was "because of the
war that surrounded him" that David could not build a house for the name of the Lord his God
(1 Kgs 5:17–18), and only now had the prescribed time of "rest and possession" arrived. These
same writers edited Nathan's prophecy to include the promise that "your offspring after you . . .
shall build a house for My name" (2 Sam 7:12–13). The Chronicler was even more explicit, reinforcing the Solomonic propaganda: it was not because of the rigors of war that the construction of
the Temple had been postponed; rather, it was David's personal unfitness: "You have shed much
blood and fought great battles; you shall not build a House for My name." As a man of peace
(שלום), Solomon (שלמה) would build it (cf. 1 Chr 22:7–10). Considering these persistent attempts
to explain away David's rebuff by Nathan, F. M. Cross's skepticism with regard to the historicity of
the intended replacement of the tent by a temple seems overstated (*Canaanite Myth and Hebrew
Epic* [Cambridge: Harvard University Press, 1973] 231).

In only one matter can success in cultic construction be ascribed to David, the erecting of an altar to the Lord on the threshing floor he purchased "at full price"[33] from the last Jebusite king (?) Araunah[34] (2 Sam 24:18–25), this perhaps due to the tradition that identified the site with the Temple Mount. It remains a puzzle why this identification is not mentioned in any of the sources from the monarchic period; moreover, the very source that promoted Jerusalem's selection studiously avoided associating the threshing floor with Solomon's Temple. Only one biblical text, 2 Chr 3:1, relates that it was "Mount Moriah where (the Lord) had appeared to his father David, at the place which David had designated, at the threshing floor of Ornan the Jebusite." Many scholars consider this identification to be a late midrash without any basis in fact, the creation of the Chronicler, which was meant to grant legitimacy to the Second Temple built during the Persian period.[35] But the question of the historical accuracy of the identification is secondary; what is of primary significance is that Jerusalem was given a firm foothold in Israelite tradition, pointing up its early sanctity. It can be argued that this process of legitimation had begun as early as the days of the united monarchy, and certainly was underway after the division of the kingdom.[36] The Temple city in Judah had to compete with other time-honored cult sites for the nation's devotion; sites such as Bethel and Dan claimed ancient pedigrees (cf. Gen 28:10–19; Judg 18:30) that were not to be slighted. Their survival and, moreover, their renewed floruit after the dissolution of the united kingdom, challenged Jerusalem's claims at centrality. It was to counter such assertions that those partisan to Jerusalem answered with the identification of the Temple Mount as Mount Moriah. Thus, pilgrims to Jerusalem could identify with Abraham and David in the hope that they, too, would benefit from the Lord's grace, which He had revealed to their ancestors at His holy site.[37]

---

33. The present version of the story is certainly etiological, a *hieros logos*, explaining how the threshing floor became an Israelite cult site; recording the details of the purchase confirms Israel's legal ownership of the site for all time. See Y. Zakovitch, "The Purpose of Narrations in Scripture Stories concerning Purchase of Possessions," *Beth Miqra* 76 (1979) 17–21 [Hebrew].

34. Onomastic investigation of the name *Araunah* suggests that it may have been, in actuality, a foreign title, derived from the Hurrian *ewri* 'lord'. See B. Mazar, "King David's Scribe and the High Officialdom of the United Monarchy of Israel," *The Early Biblical Period: Historical Essays* (Jerusalem: Magnes and Israel Exploration Society,1986) 136–37; also G. Ahlström, "Der Prophet Nathan und der Tempelbau," *VT* 11 (1961)115–17.

35. So, e.g., M. Noth, *Überlieferungsgeschichte des Pentateuch* (2d ed.; Stuttgart: Kohlhammer, 1948) 126 n. 328; idem, *Überlieferungsgeschichtliche Studien* (Tübingen: Max Niemeyer, 1967) 171 n. 1.

36. See the author's extended discussion in "'The City That I Chose': The Deuteronomistic View of Jerusalem," *Tarbiz* 55 (1986) 301–9 [Hebrew]. For another view, see I. Kalimi, "The Land of Moriah, Mount Moriah, and the Site of Solomon's Temple in Biblical Historiography," *HTR* 83 (1990) 345–62.

37. S. Spiegel, *The Last Trial* (Philadelphia: Jewish Publication Society, 1967) 93–108.

The *Bĕrît* 'Covenant':
Its Nature and Ceremonial Background

MENAHEM HARAN

The Hebrew University of Jerusalem

I

The study of the concept of *covenant* in the Hebrew Bible and the ancient Near East proceeded by leaps and bounds after the discovery of parallels between the Hittite and biblical treaty formulas. Later on, parallels to the Bible were also found in Aramaic treaties from Sefîre, in treaties that Esarhaddon and Ashurbanipal made with their subordinate states, and in similar texts of the ancient Near East. The greatest impetus to the study of these parallels followed upon the conjecture that the covenant pattern might serve to explain the unique nature of the ancient Israelite religion, so different from all contemporary religions in the ancient Near East. It was assumed that the unique character of the Israelite religion was founded not necessarily on the reproaches of the prophets (as Wellhausen had claimed) but on a covenant of suzerainty that was believed to have been made between Yahweh and the people of Israel, as a religious

Author's note: It is a pleasure to dedicate these observations to Moshe Greenberg, a friend and colleague of long standing. The following abbreviations are used in the notes below: Baltzer, *Formular* = K. Baltzer, *Das Bundesformular* (2d ed.; Neukirchen-Vluyn, 1964). Driver, *Samuel* = S. R. Driver, *Notes on the . . . Books of Samuel* (2d ed.; Oxford, 1913). Fitzmyer, *Sefîre* = J. A. Fitzmyer, *The Aramaic Inscriptions of Sefîre* (Rome, 1967). Haran, *Temples* = M. Haran, *Temples and Temple-Service in Ancient Israel* (Oxford: Clarendon, 1978; repr. Winona Lake, Ind.: Eisenbrauns, 1985). Korošec, *Verträge* = V. Korošec, *Hethitische Staatsverträge* (Leipzig, 1931). McCarthy, *Treaty* = D. J. McCarthy, *Treaty and Covenant: A Study in Form in the Ancient Oriental Documents and in the Old Testament* (2d ed.; Rome, 1981). Mendenhall, "Covenant" = G. E. Mendenhall, "Covenant Forms in Israelite Traditions," *BA* 17 (1954) 50–76. Tadmor, "Oath" = H. Tadmor, "Treaty and Oath in the Ancient Near East," *Humanizing America's Iconic Book* (ed. G. M. Tucker and D. A. Knight; Chico, Calif., 1982) 127–52. Weinfeld, *Deuteronomy* = M. Weinfeld, *Deuteronomy and the Deuteronomic School* (Oxford, 1972; repr. Winona Lake, Ind.: Eisenbrauns, 1992).

group comprising different ethnic factions. Exigent in the terms of this covenant was complete obedience on the part of the faithful toward their divine overlord.[1] Study of the parallels was wholly based on the analysis of the covenant formulations—the structure and component parts of their texts, their motifs, notions, and conventional stylistic usage.[2] At the same time, there could be no doubt about the existence of ceremonial acts underlying these texts, and it was these acts that should have been meant to endow the contract between the two parties with its binding force. The text of the covenant certainly took center stage in the ceremonial proceedings, but in itself it could not possibly endow the agreement between the two parties with compelling authority. Occasionally, scholars would give consideration to some of the acts underlying the covenant but only to the extent that they were made explicit in the covenant text itself. These details, which would be referred to in the document of the covenant and were of significance, were the statement that the document should be deposited in the temple and the oath of loyalty sworn to by the vassal (as distinct from the curses in the closing part of the covenant text). Since the covenant text itself meant to highlight mainly the terms binding the two parties, every discussion of the subject reverted, of necessity, to treatment of the covenant formulas and verbal clichés.[3] To be sure, mention was made of certain gestures of magical significance that might have accompanied the oath of loyalty by a vassal to the king of Assyria, and it was also conjectured that the covenant text was read aloud before the vassals while details from the text were acted

---

1. Korošec (*Verträge*, 12–14), the prominent exponent of Hittite covenants, defined their formal structure. E. Bickerman ("Couper une alliance," *Studies in Jewish and Christian History* [Leiden, 1976] 1.23, 26–27) was the first to sense, albeit only generally, the possible similarity between them and the biblical material. Mendenhall ("Covenant," 50–70) drew on the covenant pattern to explain the uniqueness of biblical religion. Tadmor ("Oath," esp. p. 142) is somewhat skeptical on this score.

2. Suffice it to pay heed to the full titles of Baltzer's *Formular* and McCarthy's *Treaty* (both books being major works in this field) to realize that their main interest is the literary-formal study of covenants. See also McCarthy's frequent assertions that he is interested in the document's "form" (*Treaty*, 1, 3, 9–10 et al.; esp. p. 13). Mendenhall also made such remarks ("Covenant," 56–67), emphasizing the word *text*. This is also observable in Weinfeld's *Deuteronomy*, the central chapter (pp. 59–157) of its first part ("The Typology of Deuteronomic Composition") being wholly devoted to "Treaty Form [i.e., literary form] and Phraseology" (cf. Tadmor, "Oath," 128–29, and the references there).

3. Korošec, as a dyed-in-the wool linguist and jurist, saw fit to describe the covenants from the formal aspect as "literary" documents (*Verträge*, 11–17) and analyze them from the conceptual and juridical points of view (pp. 18–36 especially, and in other chapters). However, anyone discussing the role of the covenant in the *life* of ancient Israel had better attend to the ceremonial background as it is described, or alluded to, in biblical sources as well. For some brief remarks that have been made about the ceremonial background outside of what is indicated in the covenant texts themselves, see McCarthy, *Treaty*, 19–20; Weinfeld, *Deuteronomy*, 101–5 (assembling the entire community, "old and young alike," is a prologue to the ceremony, not a part of it). See also below, n. 24, on the vassal's oath in the covenant ceremony.

out.[4] But this still did not adequately cover up the deficiency of specification of the ceremonial background.

I will be less concerned here with the covenant formulas and will deal chiefly with the ceremonial background of the covenant. The Bible supplies clear evidence of this background, which, taken as a whole, yields a certain schema, founded, no doubt, on an ancient Near Eastern model. The biblical evidence concerning the covenant ceremony is mostly woven into the narrative frameworks surrounding the covenants, rather than occurring in the covenant texts themselves (aside from the covenant texts of Sinai/Horeb and "the Land of Moab" [see Deut 28:69], the Bible barely contains any texts of covenants). For the most part, the ceremonial schema is simple, though at times ancillary factors are added for the sake of ornamentation. At the same time, the biblical attestations refer to different periods, in which the ceremonial background of the covenants changes due to varying historical circumstances. In order to simplify the discussion, I will preface it with some remarks on certain essential aspects of the concept of *covenant* as such.

Without entering into the proliferation of shadings and nuances already suggested regarding the concept of *covenant* in research,[5] let us say that its principal, practical meaning is a commitment undertaken by two parties, each toward the other, to perform a certain deed (positive in nature) or to follow a particular course of action (positive in nature). As a rule, in biblical terms, a *běrît* 'covenant' (contrary to what some scholars believe) always includes two parties, whether equal ("covenant of brothers," parity treaty) or unequal. In general, each of the two sides makes a commitment to the other. In a treaty between unequal parties, however, and in that case only, the sovereign can impose upon his vassal the obligation to perform a certain act not necessarily toward the sovereign himself but towards a third party, and this too will be termed a *běrît* 'covenant'. Continuous cyclical change is a *běrît* 'covenant' that God laid upon night and day (Jer 33:20, 25), apparently, not for His own sake. Job made a *běrît* 'covenant' with his eyes, obliging them not to gaze on a maiden (Job 31:1), and Zedekiah made a covenant with the inhabitants of Jerusalem, requiring them to free their Hebrew slaves (Jer 34:8–22). After all, any act that the suzerain bids his subordinates to do, even if the act itself concerns a third party, is a commitment to the suzerain himself. The mutuality of the covenantal relationship, then, is not canceled, even if the act is not carried out toward the suzerain himself.

---

4. See R. Frankena, "The Vassal-Treaties of Esarhaddon," *OTS* 14 (1965) 138–39. It should be noted that Frankena (pp. 150–54) rightly sensed the need also to touch on the historical reality underlying the literary parallels in order to explain the literary parallels themselves.

5. For summaries, see E. Kutsch, *TAAT* (4th ed.) 1.339–51; M. Weinfeld, *TDOT* 2.253–79; see also the most extensive bibliography in McCarthy, *Treaty*, 309–42. For conjectures concerning the etymology of *běrît*, see Tadmor, "Oath," 137–38.

II

In the Bible, three covenants are referred to, in which it would seem that the suzerain, God in these cases, takes upon Himself a unilateral commitment, in which He alone is bound to his vassal. However, a mutual relationship is in fact implicit in these covenants as well. These are the covenants that God made with Abraham, David, and Phinehas—with them and their descendants. According to Genesis 15, God promised Abraham numerous offspring (Gen 15:1–6) and promised that they would inherit the land (7–21), and only the second promise in this narrative is labeled a *běrît* 'covenant' (v. 18). In the first promise, it is merely said that "Abram put his faith in the Lord," implying that he did not request a formal commitment and was content to trust, as a result of which God "reckoned it to him as righteousness" (v. 6). To David, God made the promise of "a house" (2 Sam 7:11), that is, a royal dynasty, although the adjunct "forever" (7:13, 16) apparently belongs to the deuteronomistic expansion. But in two psalms (Ps 89:4, 29 et al.; 132:12), as well as in Jer 33:21, this promise is termed *běrît*, and "an everlasting *běrît*" that God made with David is mentioned in an old piece of poetry (2 Sam 23:5). Phinehas was granted by God "a *běrît* of peace," "a *běrît* of priesthood for all time" (Num 25:12–13), that is, a divine promise that his descendants would never be deposed from the priesthood. In these three covenants, then, it would seem that the recipients of the promises are the passive party, while the party making the promise and committing itself is God alone.

No wonder it has been claimed that what we have in Gen 15:7–21 is not really a covenant but only an "oath," a unilateral promise made by God, recast into a narrative.[6] To this supposition I would briefly reply that the narrative is made up of two interlocking scenes. The two promises made to Abraham, of numerous offspring and of inheriting the land, are from the very beginning interconnected, just as in J's narrative (Gen 12:2, 7; 13:15–16; 26:3–4; 28:14) and P's descriptions (Gen 17:4–8, 28:3–4, 48:4), the two promises to the Patriarchs, as a rule, intertwine with each other. Now God's assurance to Abraham in Gen 15:1, "I am a shield to you; your reward shall be very great," is based on the assumption that Abraham is rewarded for his loyalty to his God. God's reward to Abraham, according to this (E's) narrative, parallels the words of

---

6. See especially N. Lohfink, *Die Landverheissung als Eid* (Stuttgart, 1967) 101–13; C. Westermann, *Die Verheissungen an die Väter* (Göttingen, 1976) 133–34. I am not unaware that ever since J. Wellhausen (*Die Composition des Hexateuchs* [3d ed.; Berlin, 1963] 21–22), it is customary to divide Genesis 15 into two distinct units (vv. 1–6 and 7–21), unconnected with each other, since "the classical division into sources is here . . . impossible," whereas the attempts to divide the chapter into layers have not resulted in consent (C. Westermann, *Genesis 12–36* [BKAT; Neukirchen-Vluyn: Neukirchener Verlag, 1981] 253). However, it is my profound conviction that there is a connection between the two parts, both of which are of E; yet, this is not the place to expand on this matter.

God about Abraham in the J narrative, "For I have singled him out, so that he may charge his sons and his posterity to keep the way of the Lord by doing what is just and right," the continuation of which is, "in order that the Lord fulfills for Abraham what He has promised him" (Gen 18:19; cf. 26:5). It follows that the implementation of God's promises to Abraham presupposes that he and his posterity will follow "the way of the Lord."[7] Abraham's reward is conditioned by his loyalty to his God, and it is also a direct outcome of his loyalty. Abraham's loyalty is the fulfillment of his part in the mutual relationship between the two parties.

However, in the same way that Abraham displays loyalty to God, David also exhibits exemplary devotion to Him (2 Sam 7:5–7, Ps 132:3–5), becoming a model of perfection in this respect (1 Kgs 3:6, 11:11–13, 15:5 et al.). Phinehas brandishes his passion in God's cause and thus saves Israel (Num 25:10–13). See also the praises accorded to the priestly tribe as a whole in Deut 33:9 and Mal 2:6.[8] These merits of loyalty and devotion to God as displayed by Abraham, David, and Phinehas lie at the root of the exclusive covenants that God made with them and afford a counterweight to God's promises.[9] Consequently,

---

7. It should be noted that J assumes a mutual relationship between God and the patriarchs without calling it a *bĕrît* (see G. E. Mendenhall, *IDB* 1.715b: "there are numerous references to covenants and covenant relationships where this term [*bĕrît*] does not occur"). E assumes the same type of relationship but only uses the word 'covenant' to refer to the promise of the land. P also assumes a mutual relationship, but in his language the term *bĕrît* refers to the commitments of both parties: the two promises God made to Abraham, as well as Abraham's commitment to perform circumcision (Gen 17:3–14).

8. M. Weinfeld ("The Covenant of Grant in the Old Testament and in the Ancient Near East," *JAOS* 90 [1970] 184–203) defined the three previously mentioned covenants as "covenants of grant." In fact, however, all the references adduced from Mesopotamia for this purpose speak of a simple "grant," that is, transferring property from one person to another, with no mention of a covenant. Alternatively, they refer to the concept of *covenant* (whose Akkadian parallels are *riksu* and *māmitu*) with no connection to *grant*. The terms *grant* and *covenant* are not of the same register and do not interact. The two relate (the grant of necessity, the covenant optionally) to transfer of property or rights from one to another but differ in essence in their inherent nature and place on the temporal axis: a grant is a one-time *act*, whereas a covenant is a legal *condition* of long-term duration (until it is revoked). A grant may be given within the framework of a covenant (an act that does not endow the covenant with any special status) and may also be given outside of that framework. Any attempt to conflate the two terms creates an unnatural hybrid.

9. It has already been established (F. C. Fensham, "Covenant, Promise and Expectation in the Bible," *TZ* 23 [1967] 307–8; cf. Korošec, *Verträge*, 89–91) that clear promissory elements (such as promises to a vassal that his dynasty will endure, that he will continue to possess his land, that "the great king" will protect him from his enemies) appear in the Hittite suzerainty treaties. This, however, cannot possibly turn those covenants into "covenants of grant" (*pace* Weinfeld, "Covenant of Grant," 184). The promise, in itself, is also a commitment. It has also already been noted (Fensham, "Covenant, Promise and Expectation," 310–11) that the Hittite covenants and those with Abraham and David bear some resemblance in this regard. Moreover, it has been remarked (Fensham, ibid., 308; cf. Korošec, *Verträge*, 66–67) that the vassal's fealty to his patron constitutes an absolute condition for the patron's promises (let me add: just as this is an absolute condition in the Bible).

all three of these covenants are founded on a mutual relationship, and a mutual commitment is implied in them, as in any suzerainty treaty.

III

In order to describe correctly the ceremonial background of covenants in the biblical milieu, it should first of all be borne in mind that the biblical evidence on this matter is for the most part elliptic in character. Quite often the biblical account will make do with the mention of only a few details from the cere- mony in its entirety, and at times only one detail is brought out. The phrase *KRT běrît* ('cut a covenant'), or similar wording, already entails in itself the de- tails of ceremonial activity without any further need to highlight them explic- itly. However, while the covenants referred to in the Bible frequently merely imply what need not be spelled out, it would seem that every one of them was, in fact, founded on a ceremony, by which it was endowed with its binding force. It is not in vain that one of the parties to a covenant, as related in Gene- sis, claims: "though no one else be about, remember, God will be the witness between us" (Gen 31:50). God's "witnessing" requires, of necessity, some cer- emonial expression. There are those who make a distinction between a "secu- lar" covenant, carried out between human beings, and a sacred covenant, in which God is the superior party.[10] This distinction may be valid enough, if only it does not blur the sanctity that must have been ascribed to any covenant, even when both of the partners were human beings. If there was no divine presence in so-called "secular" covenants, it is incomprehensible what would compel the parties to obey the terms of the agreement.

In joining together data related to the covenant ceremony, we must make a distinction between two main periods, and we should take care not to draw con- clusions from one and apply them to the other. The Bible itself differentiates between the period of the patriarchs, prior to the settlement, and the "historical" period, marked throughout by sedentary conditions in the land of Canaan fol- lowing its conquest. The living conditions in the two periods are represented as having a marked impact on the ceremonial background of the covenants. Since the patriarchs are depicted as nomadic, or seminomadic, tent-dwellers (Gen 12:8; 13:3, 5, 12; 18:6, 9–10 et al.) who in fact never set foot in a city, temples had no place in their life. These "houses of God" made their appear-

---

10. D. J. McCarthy ("*Běrît* and Covenant in the Deuteronomistic History," *Studies in the Re- ligion of Ancient Israel* [VTSup 23; Leiden: Brill, 1972] 65–67; cf. Weinfeld, *TDOT* 2.265, 270) believes that, essentially, the concept of *covenant* is secular in character, while at the outset it was only secular. McCarthy (p. 66, note), to be sure, did sense the limited applicability of this distinc- tion and attempted to qualify it.

ance in ancient Israel only after the settlement.[11] Indeed, all the cultic activity of the patriarchs takes place beside sacred objects of the open-area type: altars, pillars, sacred trees. The divine promises to the patriarchs, which J does not call *covenants* but which in content and subject matter are identical to covenants (see above, n. 7), all took place in open sacred sites, where the patriarchs are said to have built altars (Gen 12:7–8; 13:4, 18; 26:25; cf. 22:9 et al.).[12] The ceremonial character of covenants involving only human parties during the time of the patriarchs can be inferred from the site where the covenant took place, such as the cultic sites of Beer Sheba (Gen 21:22–32, 26:26–32) or Mizpah of Gilead (Gen 31:48–54), especially in instances where offerings are explicitly stated as having followed the making of the covenant (Gen 31:54). The only covenant that E records between God and one of the patriarchs is the one in Gen 15:7–21. While the place is not specified, it cannot be claimed that the place in question was, of necessity, a noncultic site (see also below, section VI). According to P, however, the covenants between God and the patriarchs could not possibly have all been accompanied by cultic acts, since the tabernacle had not as yet been established.

After the possession of the land, open cultic sites were replaced by houses of God as evidently being the appropriate places for making covenants. The descriptions of the "historical," that is postpatriarchal, covenants, like descriptions of covenants in the Bible in general, are limited and elliptic, yet their testimony is sufficient to conclude that the place suitable for conducting a covenant was within one of the "houses of God." Thus, David makes a *běrît* with the tribes of Israel in Hebron "before the Lord" (2 Sam 5:3), a technical term for any activity carried out in the temple premises.[13] Moreover, David also says of his covenant with Jonathan, "For you have brought your servant

---

11. A complete list of "houses of God" that the Bible alludes to (the largest and most important of them being, of course, the one in Jerusalem) can be found in my *Temples*, 26–39. On cultic open-areas, see there, pp. 48–57.

12. Gen 26:2–5, which deals with the two divine promises to Isaac of a multitude of descendants and the possession of the land, is considered by many critics to be an expansion or later addition. According to the context before us, these promises were given in Gerar, and the passage is undeniably not in its proper place (v. 6 is the continuation of v. 1). It would seem that the authentic connection of this passage is with Beer-sheba, after v. 23. Note that the opening "the Lord appeared to him and said" presents itself first in v. 2 and recurs in v. 24. The content of vv. 2–5 (with the reference to Abraham's merit that seems suspicious to some scholars) is reported again in a summarized form in v. 24. It thus seems that during the process of transmission, whether oral or written, these verses were moved from their proper location in the narrative.

13. On the technical meaning of the term "before the Lord," implying before the ark or in the outer sanctum before the Holy of Holies and the ark or in the temple court before them, and in practice indicating any temple activity (in Jerusalem or elsewhere), see my *Temples*, especially p. 26 et passim. Hebron was one of the temple cities (p. 34). Likewise, it is said of Josiah and Zedekiah: '[he] entered into a covenant before the Lord' (2 Kgs 23:3); 'you [pl.] made a covenant before Me in the House which bears My name' (Jer 34:15).

into *a covenant of the Lord* with you" (1 Sam 20:8), while elsewhere it is said of the two of them that "they made a covenant *before the Lord*" (23:18). It thus transpires that this covenant, or each of the two covenants (if indeed there were two), was not made in the same narrative context where it is mentioned but at some earlier or later time: not when David was in Saul's home (1 Sam 18:3, 20:8) or at Horesh in the wilderness of Ziph (23:14–18); rather, the two made their way to an appropriate place in which to conclude a covenant. The writer, however, for his part, was content with mentioning only the gist of the incident.[14] The same is true of the request of the inhabitants of Jabesh-Gilead for Nahash the Ammonite to make a covenant with them (1 Sam 11:1–2), of the treaty concluded between Solomon and Hiram, king of Tyre (1 Kgs 5:26), and of the treaty Ahab made with Ben-Hadad before dismissing him (1 Kgs 5:26), and of the treaty Ahab made with Ben-Hadad before dismissing him (1 Kgs 20:34). In all these cases, the biblical writer employs brief language, contenting himself with only a reference to the treaty itself.[15] However, if as a rule covenants had to be performed "before the Lord," it is unlikely that they were not concluded with an affirmation of respect and humility before God, in whose house and presence the covenant was made.

In the postpatriarchal period, crucial importance is given to the covenant documents, in which the terms of the bond between the two parties are inscribed. But the patriarchal period—the prehistoric period of Israel—was preliterary in its nature, and no use of writing is mentioned then. In P's view, the absence of documents of the covenants God made with various figures since the time of Creation is circumvented with the aid of a special system of "signs," which remind the two parties of the terms of agreement, without the necessity of inscribing them (see Gen 9:12–17, 17:9–14; Exod 31:12–17). Outside of P, this system is mentioned, for instance, in the *bĕrît* between Abraham and Abimelech (Gen 21:27–30; see also below, section VI). In this respect, the figure of Moses marks the transitional point between the two periods. Along with the Sabbath given to the Israelites as a sign of their covenant with God (Exod 31:12–17), Moses also receives "stone tablets written with the finger of God" (Exod 31:18), and he himself writes down the commands God has given to him (Exod 24:4, 34:27; Deut 31:9, 24; see also Exod 17:14). These are the first

---

14. For 1 Sam 20:14–16, the LXX has the preferred reading; see Driver, *Samuel*, 164–66. The simple meaning of this passage would indicate that an oath is referred to (cf. 2 Sam 21:7), not a covenant (see below and n. 17).

15. The words "and I shall let you go with a covenant" [read: *bibĕrît*] (1 Kgs 20:34) should be Ahab's, the 'covenant' being the one mentioned at the end of the verse. Since Wellhausen, however, many have emended the text to read: 'and I' [*waᵓănî*, that is, 'as for me', to stress the contrast], *bibĕrît tĕšalḥēnî* 'with a covenant you shall let me go'. At the same time, it would be odd to assume that Ahab made a treaty with Ben-Hadad while sitting in the chariot. In fact, the text refers to what followed: "So he made a treaty with him [that is, later on, after the conversation] and let him go [after the treaty or because he decided to make a treaty with him]."

references to writing in biblical tradition, and they are at the core of the ceremonial background of covenants.

Another quality that, contrary to the previous characteristics, is present in the patriarchal and "historic" periods alike, and at the same time has left a marked impression on the ceremonial background of covenants, is the special affinity between a covenant and an oath. An oath (*šĕbuᶜāh* or *ʾālāh*) is frequently mentioned as accompanying a covenant, and the two terms may appear in conjunction or interchange with each other.[16] To be sure, in the case of Jonathan and David (1 Sam 20:17, 42; 2 Sam 21:7), the oath may have been distinct from the covenant.[17] Nevertheless, the frequent coupling of the two terms may indicate that the oath was the primary nucleus of the covenant, though oaths could be made outside of the covenant framework as well. The basic connection between the two concepts seems to be a general phenomenon of the ancient Near East. In Akkadian, the concept of covenant was expressed by combining the nouns *riksu* ('an agreement, commitment', on the sovereign's part) and *māmītu* ('an oath', on the subject's part). Toward the middle of the first millennium B.C.E., the term *adê* became widespread, designating commitment 'solemnly imposed in the presence of divine witnesses by a suzerain upon an individual or people who have no option but acceptance of the terms'; it implies a 'solemn charge or undertaking an oath'.[18] A parity treaty was accompanied by an oath taken by both parties (see Gen 21:31). In the case of a suzerainty treaty, in the Bible the oath is frequently ascribed to the ruler as the one announcing the terms. But the vassal also undoubtedly had to make a commitment, whether by oath or otherwise, both in Israel and elsewhere, and it is clear

---

16. See Gen 21:24–31; 26:28; 31:44, 53; 2 Kgs 11:4; Ezek 17:13, 16, 19; Ps 89:4; 105:9; cf. E. Kutsch, "Gesetz und Gnade," *ZAW* 79 (1967) 23–26. Against the story of the covenant that Joshua made with the Gibeonites (Josh 9:6, 7, 11 et al.) is the other, priestly narrative, speaking of the *oath* sworn by the chieftains of the community (Josh 9:15, 18–20). Similarly, in D we find the combination "the *bĕrît* that He *swore* to [= made an oath with] your fathers" (Deut 4:31, 7:12, 8:18), though the usual way in D's style is to speak of God's oath to the fathers without mentioning *bĕrît* (1:8, 35; 6:10, 18, 23; 7:8 et al.).

17. Only an oath is spoken of in 1 Sam 20:12–16: in vv. 12–13, Jonathan swears to David that he will sound out his father and disclose his intention to David; in vv. 14–16, he makes David swear that upon ascending the throne he will not harm Jonathan's offspring (see above, n. 14). In v. 17, the LXX and the MT differ once again in their versions: according to the LXX, these words refer back to vv. 12–13 (cf. Driver, *Samuel*, 166), not to 1 Sam 18:3–4 (as was suggested by McCarthy, "*Bĕrît* and Covenant," 72). According to the MT, these words could refer back to vv. 14–16.

18. D. J. Wiseman, *The Vassal-Treaties of Esarhaddon* (London, 1958) 81; cf. *CAD* A/1, s.v. *adû* A. The substantive עדי, meaning 'covenant', appears also in the Aramaic Sefîre inscriptions and is apparently identical to the Akkadian *adê* (Fitzmyer, *Sefîre*, 23–24). On *adû*, see also Tadmor, "Oath," 142–43; on its use in Assyrian sources and the uncertainty concerning its exact meaning, ibid., 142–50. On the basic affinity between covenant and oath and the role of the "oath of the vassal" (and the commitment of the sovereign) in the Hittite covenant ceremony and in the Akkadian language, see Korošec, *Verträge*, 92–100; McCarthy, *Treaty*, 141–44.

that his commitment was an important factor in the ceremonial background of
the covenant, as we shall see.

IV

In five or six covenants, the Hebrew Bible provides important details of the
ceremonial background, and despite their incomplete nature, the features of the
ceremony recur in these covenants in a fixed pattern, and their combination creates a certain unity. These are all suzerainty treaties from the "historical" period,
said to have been sealed with written documents, on stone or in a book scroll.

1. The major and most striking covenant in the Bible is the one God made
   with Israel on Mount Horeb, and its document is the Decalogue inscribed
   in stone (Exod 20:1–17, Deut 5:6–18). The two sources E and D provide
   a wealth of ceremonial detail for this covenant, though E does not designate it a *běrît*, because the purpose of this ceremony for this source was no
   more than to instill reverence for God in the people of Israel (Exod 19:9a,
   20:20).[19] Several verses describing the revelation on Mount Sinai occur in
   J, but the stories of the tablets and of the Decalogue are missing in this
   source. In P, the entire account of the tablets and the decalogue is implied
   only by the term *ʿēdût* 'testimony' (Exod 16:34; 25:16, 21; 27:21 et al.)
   and the construct state, "tablets of *hāʿēdût*, the testimony" (Exod 31:18,
   34:29; cf. 32:15), which are customary in the priestly style.

2. According to E, the covenant God made with Israel at Horeb is not based
   on the tablets but on the code of laws (Exod 20:22–23:33), designated
   "the Book of the Covenant" in the text itself (Exod 24:4, 7). J also tells of
   the covenant that God made with the people of Israel at Mount Sinai and
   bases the covenant not on the tablets but on a legal code, the short code
   (Exod 34:11–26), known as the "Minor Book of the Covenant." However,
   no description of the ceremony is found in J, since the main part of the
   narrative is missing in this source.[20]

19. The assumption that awe of God should be deeply rooted in the hearts of the Israelites
because they heard the voice of God from Mount Horeb is also assimilated in D (Deut 4:10; 5:5,
25–26). However, D alone sees the announcement of the commandments in God's voice as constituting a covenant between God and his people (Deut 4:13, 5:2; cf. 4:23, 17:2–3, 28:69).

20. On the "Book of the Covenant" and the "Minor Book of the Covenant," see my observations in *Encyclopaedia Miqraʾît* 5.1087–91 (and ibid., p. 1090, for an explanation of Exod 34:1,
4, 28: these verses belong to E and were interposed here in J's narrative; their parallels appear in
Deut 10:1–4 one after the other [along with mention of the ark, which is not included in E's Exodus passages]). A reminder of the covenant at Sinai, according to J, occurs in Exod 34:27: "for in
accordance with these words I make a *běrît* with you and with Israel" (cf. Exod 34:10: "He said
[LXX: The Lord said to Moses], I hereby make a *běrît*"). The words "keep My covenant" in Exod
19:5 refer to the "Book of the Covenant" (Exod 24:3–8), not to the ten commandments (see below,
section V).

3. In Shechem, Joshua made a covenant between God and Israel (Josh 24:1–27), and he also wrote down the terms of the covenant in "a book of the law of God" (Josh 24:26).

4. Samuel anointed Saul as king of Israel in a special ceremony divided into two parts, which is in fact two ceremonies stitched together, one following immediately upon the other: the first in Mizpah of Benjamin (1 Sam 10:17–27), where Samuel wrote down "the rules of the kingdom" in a book, and the other at Gilgal on Mount Ephraim (11:14–12:25). In neither ceremony is the term *bĕrît* 'covenant' mentioned, but both exhibit marked features of covenant ceremonies (and both appear in one continuous narrative belonging to the same source).

5. In D we find several allusions to the ceremonial background of the covenant, which presumably served as the framework for this source (Deut 31:9, 24–26; see below). The speech made by Moses is called "the terms *dĕbārîm* of the covenant . . . in the land of Moab" (Deut 28:69; compare 1:5: ". . . in the land of Moab").

Like David's anointment as king in Hebron (2 Sam 5:3), Saul's investiture by Samuel occurred in Mizpah (1 Sam 10:19–24) and in Gilgal (11:15; cf. 12:7) "before the Lord," because houses of God were located there. Likewise, it is said that the Israelites 'presented themselves before God' for the covenant made by Joshua at Shechem (Josh 24:1), and several additional details of temple imagery are discernible in the description of this covenant. However, in this narrative, temple imagery was imposed on a cultic site that, in historical reality, was of the open-area type, with the result that a kind of short-circuit took place in the narrative.[21] No such short-circuit is to be felt in the description of the revelation at Horeb, fusing together as it does the two covenants of the Decalogue and the "Book of the Covenant." The technical term 'before the Lord' does not appear there; indeed, according to the view typical of the non-priestly sources (J, E, and D), there is no possibility, except by way of anachronistic projection, of using such a term for the Sinai/Horeb revelation, since no temples existed among the Israelites at that time. In fact, there was no need to use figures of speech pertaining to the temple for that event, since God Himself appeared "in person," though clouded, on the mountain, and Moses "brought the people out of the camp toward God" (Exod 19:17). Even so, there should be no doubt that the actual descriptions of the covenants at Horeb, and all the more so the covenants made at Shechem, Mizpah, and Gilgal, are patterned after a ceremony that prevailed in a court of a house of God. In the descriptions of these covenants, the fixed components of the ceremony are clearly observable in an established order, though it is not necessarily a strictly punctilious

---

21. On the site of the covenant Joshua made in Shechem (Josh 24:1–27), which was a cultic open-area outside the city, see my *Temples*, 49–51.

order, since certain internal expansions of minor or appreciable proportions are liable to occur in it.

V

The *first* component of the covenant ceremony is a spoken declaration, made by the sovereign or his representative, of the "terms" of the pact. The "terms" can be a single categorical statement, a short series of decrees, or a collection of laws, that the sovereign imposes on his protégés. In E's and D's descriptions, God Himself speaks the Decalogue aloud (Exod 20:1) "with a mighty voice" (Deut 5:19). In all other divine covenants with the Israelites, He is represented by a prophet: Joshua in Shechem and Samuel at Gilgal, in their parting speeches before their respective deaths (Josh 24:14–15; 1 Sam 12:14–15), demand that the Israelites worship God alone. In addition, Joshua "draws up statutes and ordinances" for the people in Shechem (Josh 24:25).[22] Samuel, in his speeches at Mizpah and Gilgal, expresses disappointment and resignation at the people's will to be ruled by a king. The choice of Saul as king in Mizpah and its "renewal" at Gilgal take place under Samuel's patronage, while in Mizpah he also tells "the people the rules of the kingdom" (1 Sam 10:18–25, 12:7–15).[23] In E's account of the covenant at Horeb, Moses announces to the people "all the words of the Lord and all the laws" (Exod 24:3), that is, all the commandments God told him out of "the dark cloud" on the mountain (Exod 20:21). In this case, Moses repeats the laws aloud to the people, reading them after they are written down in the book (24:7). Moreover, before this ceremony, he sets the people a prior condition, one might even say, an inducement of sorts, for making the covenant with God (19:5). It is quite clear that these elements are merely ornamental expansions, tagged on to the ceremony, taking the form of repeating its components. In D's main part, however, we have Moses' live speech, which presumably included the laws of Deuteronomy 12–26 (plus chap. 28) and constituted the first phase of making "the covenant in the land of Moab" (Deut 1:5, 28:69).

The *second* component is the immediate expression of consent on the part of the people to the covenant terms. Hearing the Decalogue, the people are startled and demonstrate their awe of God (Exod 19:9, 20:19–20; Deut 5:21–26). Their response to the laws of the Book of the Covenant, before and after

---

22. The nouns *ḥōq û-mišpaṭ* seem to be employed here in the collective sense (see GKC §123*b*).

23. The status of the prophet as the authority charged with choosing a king and the choice itself, implemented by casting lots and consulting God, tell us that the covenant is in fact between God and the people and that kingship among the Israelites was conceived of as divine grace (not divine in its inherent character).

they were committed to writing, and to the prior condition communicated to them by Moses, is "all that the Lord had spoken we will do and obey" (Exod 19:8 [LXX]; 24:3 [LXX], 7). The three expressions of agreement are balanced against the ornamentational highlighting of the first component in this ceremony. In response to the words of Joshua in Shechem, the people immediately decide "we also will serve the Lord for He is our God" (Josh 24:18). In response to Samuel's words in Gilgal, they express regret for requesting a king (1 Sam 12:19), and upon learning of the choice of Saul as king in Mizpah, they acclaim him, "Long live the king" (1 Sam 10:24). These two components, the first and the second, appear in the model of the treaty of suzerainty in the ancient Near East. There also the sovereign would announce the terms of commitment, and the vassal's oath seems mostly to have taken the form of agreement to the words uttered by the ruler.[24] The response of agreement may have evolved in the course of time from the oath.

In any case, it would seem that the response is the equivalent of the oath in this model of covenant (see the end of section III). In D, no mention is made of the cries of acceptance on the part of the people to Moses' words, but we find in it Deut 26:16–19, which appears at the end of the collection of laws. No law is referred to in this passage, and its language echoes a mutual commitment of the covenant type. It appears that its wording is of the same category as the "oath of the vassals" of the ancient Near East, which could at times be pronounced in a form of mutuality.[25]

In order for the commitment between the two parties to be binding, it requires still a *third* component: presenting a witness that will serve to remind the two parties, vassal as well as sovereign, of their commitment, and the witness has to relate to God. Witness can be provided even by inanimate objects in the open air, such as the altar "opposite the land of Canaan, in the region of the Jordan" that is "witness" to the commitment and to the right of the Transjordanian tribes to worship the God of Israel (Josh 22:27–28, 34). But only divine witness may impart the quality of a *běrît* to a commitment made by two parties. In the "historical" period, when writing was used, the simplest and most natural way to impart divine sanction to a pact was to write the terms in a document that would be placed before God. This is indeed what we find: after the oral declaration of the covenant and immediately after the people voice

---

24. See McCarthy, *Treaty*, 142. Korošec had a slightly different premise for this point. In his words: "Über die technische Durchführung der Beschwörung der Verträge sind wir leider nicht informiert." He supposes that the vassal would repeat the formulas of curses and blessings that the sovereign announced to him (*Verträge*, 96). Regarding the biblical testimony, the previous possibility is more likely.

25. Several commentators on Deuteronomy have already sensed the connection of this passage with the terms of the covenant. See, for instance, G. von Rad, *Deuteronomy* (OTL; London, 1966) 161–62; and especially McCarthy, *Treaty*, 182–84.

their acceptance, the sovereign or his representative writes down the terms. God inscribes the Decalogue with "the finger of God" on tablets of stone (Exod 24:12, 31:18, 32:15–16).[26] The inscription on stone attests, of course, both to ancient origins and to monumentality. In the other covenants as well, those who write are those who have spoken beforehand, but they are the representatives of the sovereign and they write records: Moses writes down "the Book of the Covenant" (Exod 24:4 [cf. v. 7]; likewise 34:27), Joshua writes a "book of the law of God" (Josh 24:26), which should contain the "statutes and ordinances" that Joshua previously made known to the people (Josh 24:25), and Samuel writes down "the rules of the kingdom" (1 Sam 10:25).

However, putting the terms of the covenant in writing, in itself, even when done by "the finger of God," has no binding force. It is rather unclear why it was done, unless the act is understood in light of the purpose of placing them as a testimony before God. In the case of the two inscribed stone tablets, this purpose is made especially clear, because they are deposited in the ark (Deut 10:1, 5) and ultimately brought to the Holy of Holies in the Temple in Jerusalem, where they are placed "beneath the wings of the cherubim" (1 Kgs 8:6). In the symbolic system of the Jerusalem Temple, the ark represents God's footstool. Depositing the tablets in this ark derives from the ancient Near Eastern practice of placing legal documents, such as covenant deeds, at the feet of the gods in the temples, to lie there as testimony.[27] This practice is probably presupposed when it is said of Samuel that he deposited the document containing the rules of the kingdom "before the Lord" in Mizpah (1 Sam 10:25). It is also implied in the story of Joshua, who wrote the "book of the law of God" in the Lord's *miqdāš* ('sanctuary' or 'sacred precinct') in Shechem (Josh 24:26), though (as has been stated above, section III) this narrative has a certain ambiguity in that the concept of the house of God is here projected onto a cultic site of the open-area type. No explicit reference is made to the final whereabouts of the "Book (or books) of the Covenant" written by Moses (Exod 24:4–7 [E]; 34:27 [J]), which contained the law codes of the E and J sources. But it cannot be doubted that, according to the conceptual view of these sources and also in historical reality, these were also lying in a conspicuous Israelite house, or houses, of God. Putting the words of the covenant in writing is therefore only the inevitable prologue to depositing the "record of the covenant" beside the god, in his temple, as testimony. The act of writing, after the speech, and the act of depositing the record in the temple are, essentially, a single proceeding, because

26. The subject of "and He [the h should be capitalized] wrote down" in Exod 34:28 (the parallel of Deut 10:4) is God, not Moses. Exod 34:1 (the parallel of Deut 10:1) explicitly reads: "and *I* [i.e., God] shall write upon the tablets the words that were on the first tablets," etc. See above, n. 20.

27. On this custom and the symbolic meaning of the ark as the "footstool" of the throne, see my *Temples*, 254–56. This practice is made explicit in the texts of several covenants as well as in other documents (see Korošec, *Verträge*, 100–101 [and the references there]; also n. 28 below).

one cannot exist independently of the other, even if a brief or prolonged hiatus separates the two.

Examination of the conventional form of suzerainty treaties of the ancient Near East has shown that it usually followed a fixed, six-part pattern.[28] Without denying the likelihood of this insight, it should be pointed out that, from the *ceremonial* point of view, the making of a covenant comprised only the three elements: the declaration of the terms of the covenant in a speech by the sovereign; the agreement (tantamount to an oath) by the vassal; and ratification of the agreement by putting it at god's feet, as testimony. These three components are also called for by the covenant's inherent nature, and it would be difficult to tag still another component onto them that could be considered a fundamental part of the ceremony.

VI

For the sake of precision, let us add that in the patriarchal period, in which writing is nonexistent, the content of covenants is portrayed as an agreement to which inanimate objects in the open can serve as witness (much like what the priestly language terms the "sign of the covenant"; see above, section III). Just as the altar in "the region of the Jordan" serves as witness to the fact that the Transjordanian tribes are part of the people of Israel (Josh 22:27–28), so also the mound and the pillar at Mizpah of Gilead serve as reminders to the Arameans and Israelites of the covenant made between their forefathers not to cross to each other's side "with hostile intent" (Gen 31:52). In addition, Laban and Jacob invoke God as a "witness" between them (Gen 31:50), thus bestowing their agreement with the stamp of a covenant (see above, section III). The mound and the pillar are witnesses to the *terms* of the covenant, not to the presence of God at the covenant, since in the absence of a house of God in that place, and with no written form, there is no symbolic representation of God's presence.

The noteworthy detail here is that preliterary suppositions and practices continued for some time into the historical period and coexisted with the use of "records." Thus we find that in the narrative of the renewal of Saul's kingship at Gilgal "before the Lord" (1 Sam 11:15), Samuel announces: "The Lord is witness among you, and His anointed is witness this day" (1 Sam 12:5).[29]

---

28. The six parts are: introduction, historical survey, declaration of terms, the decision to deposit the document of the covenant in the temple and to read it, invocation of the gods to be witnesses, curses and blessings. This division was first stated by Korošec (*Verträge*, 12–14), and other scholars followed in his path (with minor deviations). See: Mendenhall, "Covenant," 58–60; McCarthy, *Treaty*, 1–2; Baltzer, *Formular*, 20–25; Weinfeld, *Deuteronomy*, 61–65 (changing the order).

29. See Driver's notes (*Samuel*, 90–92). The progression is: "*wayyoᵓmer* (*Sevirin* [Masorah version]: *wayyoᵓmrû*, i.e., '*they* said'), *ᶜēd*, witness [He is]." Further on: "Samuel said to the people (LXX: + witness [is]) the Lord, who appointed *ᶜāśāh* Moses and Aaron," etc. (1 Sam 12:5–6).

No hint is found in this narrative of depositing any "record" in the temple at Gilgal, in contradistinction to the report of Saul's investiture as king at Mizpah, where Samuel places the rules of the kingdom "before the Lord." But in Shechem, Joshua makes the *people* "witnesses," and he raises a great stone to serve as a "witness against" them to the effect that they have taken upon themselves to serve God alone after He spoke to them (Josh 24:22, 27). Likewise, of the song in Deuteronomy 32, God says that it will serve as His "witness against the people of Israel" and "shall confront them as a witness" (Deut 31:19, 21), to the effect that He has warned them in advance against idolatry. In these two cases, then, the order is reversed and the testimony is given to the vassal, not to the sovereign, so that the vassal can possess it as a reminder of his commitment to the sovereign. At the same time, it goes without saying that invoking *God* as witness is not, in itself, dependent on a covenant proceeding. The emigrants going to Egypt say to Jeremiah, "Let the Lord be a true and faithful witness against us" (Jer 42:5), though no covenant or mutual commitments bind them to the prophet, and there is certainly no house of God.

Allow me to mention still another component, one that is optional and because it does not intrinsically belong to the covenant ceremony, serves as a kind of ornamental addition. This component might be a gesture toward the god, a gesture of basically cultic character that is directed to the god because the temple is his home, and all who enter the temple court are his guests. It may also be an act of basically magical-symbolic character (though, since it takes place in the temple precincts, it would be imbued with sanctity). A cultic act of the highest rank is the offering of a sacrifice following the covenant ceremony (see Exod 24:5, 1 Sam 11:15, Ps 50:5). However, dashing the sacrificial blood during the covenant ceremony at Horeb, half on the altar (that is, to God) and half on the people (Exod 24:6–8), is not a cultic act, although the blood is sacrificial. In fact, this is a magical-symbolic expression of the link between the two parties of the covenant. A similar link is suggested by the reference to "the blood of your covenant" in Zech 9:11.[30] Communal partaking of the sacrifice is also a symbol of unity (see Gen 31:54, Ps 50:5), as may be the joint consumption of salt (Lev 2:13, Num 18:19).

Passing between cut-up animal pieces, as mentioned in the cases of Abraham (Gen 15:9–18) and Zedekiah (Jer 34:18–19), is likewise a symbolic gesture. However, this gesture seems to have become so widespread and common that it may have turned into a kind of prevalent supplement to a covenant ceremony. The combination *KRT běrît* that frequently describes the making of a covenant may derive from the same gesture.[31] The idea that the cut-up animal

---

30. See S. R. Driver, *The Book of Exodus* (Cambridge, 1911; reprinted, 1953) 253.

31. The first to submit a possible connection between the combination *KRT běrît* and the practice of passing between cut-up animal pieces was C. H. Cornill, *Das Buch Jeremia* (Leipzig, 1905) 382. Several dictionaries (Brown-Driver-Briggs, Köhler-Baumgartner, and others) tried to relate

pieces (between which only the sovereign party making the promise and commitment can pass) are a sacrifice should be totally rejected.[32] Passing between parts of animals, which of necessity was done beyond the confines of the altar, could not render any animal or fowl a sacrifice. It would be mistaken to assume that the covenant of Abraham according to E and the covenant of Zedekiah entailed no other elements than passage between the parts of the animals. We should not wonder, however, at the fact that only this act was extracted from the entire ceremonial panoply to be mentioned, given its colorful drama and riveting power. In the case of Abraham an additional cause is present: the birds of prey descending on the carcasses were an ill omen, an allusion to the oppression in Egypt (Gen 15:11–14). This also was reason to put the act of passage between the cut-up pieces of animals at the center of the narrative.

---

this phrase to the obligation of the parties making a covenant to bring a sacrifice as a supplement to the covenant ceremony (rather than to the cutting up of animals that were not for consumption, as I believe). The comparison of passage between the cut-up animals to the Sefîre inscription IA, line 40 (in a series of curses), is inappropriate and improbable (see Fitzmyer, *Sefîre*, 14, 56–57). Likewise, notwithstanding the assumption of various scholars, no mention is made of passing between the cut-up pieces of a slaughtered animal in the Mari texts (ARM 2 35 et al.). Passing between cut-up animal pieces really occurs in a Hittite text (J. M. Sasson, "Isaiah lxvi," *VT* 26 [1976] 204–5; W. W. Hallo, *The Book of the People* [Atlanta, 1991] 130, no. 13), though it has to do with a defeated army.

32. Ramban (commentary) assumed that it was intimated to Abraham "that from these [the cut-up animals and fowl] all sacrifices of animal and fowl shall be made." He did not claim that they themselves were a sacrifice. Several moderns, however, adopted the idea that the cut-up animals and fowl in the Genesis 15 covenant are a sacrifice. S. E. Loewenstamm ("Zur Traditionsgeschichte des Bundes zwischen den Stücken," *VT* 18 [1968] 500–506) accepted this idea, concluding that the ceremony of passing between the pieces is a later expansion of the tradition. Weinfeld concurs that it is a sacrifice and makes claims for its antiquity ("Covenant of Grant," 197).

Prophecy and Soothsaying

Yair Hoffman
Tel-Aviv University

"One who foretells future events, especially under divine inspiration; a revealer or interpreter of the divine will . . ." is a common definition of *prophet* in a standard English dictionary.[1] The verb *prophesy* in the same dictionary is defined: "To predict, to foretell; to herald. . . ." Thus, about 2500 years after the last Hebrew prophets, 2000 years after Jesus, more than 1300 years since Mohammed, and after 2000 years of biblical exegesis, theological studies, and biblical research, prophecy is primarily conceived as "soothsaying" or "future-telling." How legitimate is this definition? The answer depends on the vantage point. It is quite right if one refers to the colloquial use of the word *prophet.* It is absolutely wrong if it is based on conceptions of scholars such as Buber, Kaufmann, and Heschel.[2] For them the essence of classical prophecy is moral commitment, monotheistic ethics, human sensitivity reduced to compulsive educational desire to improve man and society. Between these two conceptions exists a wide gap. The first conception is basically deterministic: the future events are there, and it is only for the prophet to reveal them. The second one is as anti-deterministic as any educational concept could be: it is the task of the prophet to change reality, to call for repentance, in order to shape a better future. I would like to examine the term *prophecy* from a third angle—the book of Jeremiah. The question is whether the rule of thumb that identifies a prophet with a soothsayer is correct based on the evidence of the book of Jeremiah. My focus is the book of Jeremiah, not mere semantics; however, the common dictionary definition is a point of departure for this study and is more than a rhetorical gimmick, as I will show toward the conclusion.

---

1. *Cassell's English Dictionary* (4th ed.; London: Cassell, 1968) 912.

2. See, e.g., M. Buber, *Torat ha-Neviʾim* (The prophets) (2d ed.; Tel-Aviv, 1961 [Heb.]); Y. Kaufmann, *Tôlĕdôt Hāʾemûnâ Ha-Yisrĕʾelît* (Tel-Aviv, 1960), 1.720–37, 3.1–10, and more; A. Heschel, *The Prophets* (New York: Harper & Row, 1962), e.g., pp. 3–26.

The two polar aspects of prophecy are sometimes referred to as "absolute" and "conditional," the first being to some extent a euphemism for "soothsaying." I also will employ this terminology, but for the sake of clarity, I will mainly use the noneuphemistic terms *seer* and *soothsayer* when I refer to the future-telling, deterministic aspects of the prophetic personality. I will use *prophecy* for the call for change. Since the Bible uses נביא for both meanings (which is not insignificant), I also will use it in due time. I begin by discussing the relevant laws in Deuteronomy, since I have found them very useful for a better presentation of the book of Jeremiah.

Introduction: The Laws of the Prophet in Deuteronomy

Two laws in the deuteronomic code refer to the prophet: Deut 13:2–6 and 18:9–22. Deuteronomy, "the most 'theological' book in the Old Testament,"[3] expresses its concern in theoretical terms of religion, as well as through its laws. What idea of prophecy, then, do these two laws reveal?

(1) Deuteronomy 13:2–6. Deut 13:2–6 refers to an Israelite "prophet or a dreamer of dreams." In his attempts to persuade people to worship "other gods,"[4] he might succeed in giving signs and doing miracles to support his claim. Yet such success should not mislead the people: it is God who is testing them by letting the enticer appear successful. Clearly this law indirectly implies that a real נביא could cause future events to happen, besides knowing them in advance. He is therefore a seer, rather than a prophet. However, the נביא here, whether a heathen or an Israelite,[5] is definitely not typical of the other prophets, which lessens the relevance of this law for our study.

(2) Deuteronomy 18:9–22. "Your God will raise up for you a prophet like me . . ." (v. 15). Is this promised, ideal נביא depicted as a seer or as a prophet?

3. H. G. Reventlow, *Problems of Old Testament Theology in the Twentieth Century* (Philadelphia: Fortress, 1985) 131.

4. For the term אלהים אחרים, see Y. Hoffman, "The Concept of 'Other Gods' in Deuteronomistic Literature," *IOS* 14 (1994) 103–18.

5. The word בקרבך is ambiguous. It could be understood either as one of your own or as one who appeared 'among you', such as a Canaanite. Ibn-Ezra insisted on the first option: "the reason for בקרבך is that there can be no נביא but from Israel." Nachmanides, on the other hand, did not insist on the Israelite origin of the enticing נביא, since "in the souls of some persons a prophetic power exists, by which they know the future." The word קרבך is also used in the second law of the prophet, 18:15 (and 18), where the meaning is unmistakably *an Israelite*, but this unequivocalness is conveyed by the sequence מקרבך מאחיך כמוני (not בקרבך). The Septuagint, the Samaritan version, and the Samaritan Aramaic Targum (A. Tal, *The Samaritan Targum II* [Tel-Aviv University, 1981] 355) read מקרב אחיך in chap. 13, as well as in 17:15.

The law itself is introduced by a denunciation of heathen mantic practices (vv. 9–12); then comes an interlude (vv. 13–14), which is concluded with the words "but as for you, your God has not given you [things] like this." The law therefore implies that the נביא is supposed to be a substitute for the heathen seers, namely, he is to function as a soothsayer. The conclusion of the law expresses this concept even more clearly when it gives a criterion to distinguish between a real and a false נביא. To the possible dilemma "how may we know the word that the Lord has not spoken" (v. 21), the answer is "if the word of the נביא . . . does not come to pass and come true . . . , the נביא has spoken it presumptuously" (v. 22). Therefore, a prophet equals a soothsayer, since the criterion of fulfillment is the only way to test him, not by the content or the message of his prophecy. However, this conclusion does not correspond to the depiction of this prophet in vv. 15–18. The main idea there is that the future prophet will be כמוך ,כמוני (vv. 15, 18), that is, like Moses himself, whose characteristics are certainly not of a fortune-teller. The idea that the future prophet, just like Moses, would be a replacement of a direct theophany, as at Sinai (v. 16), definitely indicates that this law did not envision a seer when it spoke of a נביא. The inconsistency between the two aspects of a prophet here is so pronounced that it raises the possibility of the existence of two layers in the law. Yet, the uprooting of vv. 15–18 would leave the rest of the law meaningless. Any more meticulous deletion of words[6] to reach a homogeneous, apparently original version is highly speculative, though unrefutable. However, the present version reflects a deep tension between two aspects of prophecy that neither the author nor the (posited) editor has obliterated. To this conclusion we will presently return.

Soothsaying Elements in Jeremiah

Jeremiah 1

Which characteristics of Jeremiah's prophetic personality did the author of the call narrative want to emphasize? I will try to show that the answer is the characteristics of a soothsayer.[7]

The premise of the call vision in its present edition is that it took place in the thirteenth year of King Josiah, that is, 627 B.C.E. The author expected the vision to be considered an authentic autobiographical account of the event that occurred in that year. However, this view can be adopted only if one accepts

---

6. For example, deletion of כמוני in v. 15 and vv. 16–18.

7. See B. Renaud, "Jérémie 1: Structure et théologie de la rédaction," in *Le livre de Jérémie* (ed. P. M. Bogaert; Leuven: Leuven University Press, 1981) 177–96. He emphasizes the importance of the theology of the Word (*parol*), that is, the unconditional aspects of prophecy. He ascribes this theology to the deuteronomistic redaction of the call narrative. On this issue, see below.

the religious axioms of prophecy, while a critical, nonaxiomatic approach un-
avoidably makes it suspect. According to the latter concept, a prophet's claim
of hearing the actual words of God (whose knowledge is not limited to the
actual present) might be a subjective truth but not an objective truth. Therefore,
the prophet's competence to foresee social, political, and moral developments
is always anchored in the prophet's own time, derived from his personal, practical observation. This secular, academic approach regards prophecy as a personal religious experience and therefore emphasizes the human factors of the
phenomenon—the time, style, place and personality of the prophet. The existence of the human factor by itself does not contradict the religious concept,
which admits the unique personality of each prophet.[8] Yet, the religious attitude finds the human factor mainly in idiosyncrasies of style, while the secular
approach considers a prophet's humanness to be the main, if not the only factor
that determines his interest, subject, content, and ideas. Hence, each prophecy
should reflect in one way or another the contemporary problems, fears, and expectations of the prophet and his social environment. In this sense, one could
expect Jeremiah's call narrative to reflect his personality and the Judean reality
of 627 B.C.E. But it does not. I intend to argue that the vision is retrospective and
thus emphasizes the soothsaying elements in the prophetic profile of Jeremiah.

(3) *Jeremiah 1:5.* The nomination of Jeremiah as נביא לגוים (1:5) is
unique and peculiar.[9] With no previous tradition of such a definition for any
prophet, there would have been no reason during this period for a young country boy from Anathoth, filled with religious, social, or national fervor, to perceive that God had chosen him to be a prophet to nations and not to his own
people. The escalated disintegration of the Assyrian Empire raised new national hopes within Judah[10] and paved the way for the religious and social
ideology of Deuteronomy, which culminated in the cultic reform. This background would normally have stimulated young Jeremiah to fulfill a national

    8. For a very interesting presentation of the traditional Jewish views on this subject, see
M. Greenberg, "Jewish Conception of the Human Factor in Biblical Prophecy," in *Justice and The
Holy: Essays in Honor of Walter Harrelson* (ed. D. A. Knight and P. J. Paris; Atlanta: Scholars
Press, 1989) 145–62.
    9. See Rashi, who quotes *Sipre*: "How could I account for נביא לגוים נתתיך? These are the
children of Israel who behave like Gentiles." A few Septuagint manuscripts have the singular form
(εθνος). B. Stade has even suggested emending the MT to לגויי (Stade, "Emendations," *ZAW* 22
[1902] 328).
    10. See, e.g., E. W. Nicholson, *Deuteronomy and Tradition* (Philadelphia: Fortress, 1967) 12ff.
N. P. Lemche, *Ancient Israel* (Sheffield: JSOT Press, 1988) 169. Some scholars deny the notion of
a restorative national movement in Judah during the beginning of King Josiah's reign. See N. Naʾaman, "The City List of Judah and Benjamin and the Kingdom of Judah in Josiah's Time," *Zion* 54
(1989) 17–71, esp. pp. 53–71 [Heb.]. But even they would agree that under those circumstances
it is reasonable to assume that the prophet and his audience were interested in national rather than
international problems. For a recent review of the Assyrian yoke, see M. Cogan, "Judah under Assyrian Hegemony," *JBL* 112 (1933) 403–14.

mission rather than to regard himself as God's prophet to the nations. Yet, retrospectively, this title has proven correct. No other prophet was as involved in "foreign affairs" as Jeremiah. He advised foreign nations about their practical policy;[11] more than any other prophet, he made the genre of "prophecies against foreign nations" a vehicle to carry political messages to other peoples.[12] It is therefore reasonable to assume that the concept of Jeremiah's being nominated a "prophet to the nations" is retrospective. It was formulated only after a long period of prophetic activity. This retrospection has been concealed by the claim that Jeremiah knew from the very beginning that he would be a נביא לגוים.

(4) Jeremiah 1:14. מצפון תפתח הרעה על כל יושבי הארץ. Many scholars have expressed doubt about the existence of this motif in the call narrative. What danger from the north could Jeremiah have envisaged in 627 B.C.E. that was important enough to be mentioned in a call vision? He could not possibly have had in mind either (1) the collapsing empire of Assyria or (2) Babylon, which was not yet recognized as a potential danger. The theory that he meant the Scytheans has already been totally rejected by most scholars.[13] This lack of certainty has led some scholars to claim that Jeremiah began his prophetic activity not in the thirteenth year of Josiah (627 B.C.E.) but years later, when Babylon had already become a world power (around 605 B.C.E.).[14] Additional arguments adduced are the lack of prophecies from the time of Josiah and the absence of Jeremiah in the story of the Josianic reform (2 Kings 22–23). There is no need for me to take a position on this controversy, since I am not

11. See Jeremiah 27–28.

12. Mainly in the prophecies against Egypt (chap. 46), the Philistines (chap. 47), Kedar (49:28–33) and Elam (49:34–38). For this and other matters concerning the prophecies against foreign nations mentioned below, see Y. Hoffman, *The Prophecies against Foreign Nations* (Tel-Aviv, 1977) 110–31.

13. A detailed survey of the Enemy-from-the-North problem would diverge us from our main subject. For a short review, see W. Holladay, *Jeremiah* (Philadelphia: Fortress, 1986) 1.42–43. For bibliography, see pp. 19–20. For a discussion about the identification of the enemy from the north with the Scythians or the Umanmanda, see H. Cazelles, "La vie de Jérémie," in *Le livre de Jérémie* (ed. P. M. Bogaert; Leuven: Leuven University Press, 1981) 21–39, esp. pp. 25–28.

14. For example, C. F. Whitly has suggested dating the call vision to 605 B.C.E., in "The Date of Jeremiah's Call," *VT* 14 (1964) 467–83 (reprinted in: *A Prophet to the Nations: Essays in Jeremiah Studies* [ed. L. G. Perdue and B. W. Kovacs; Winona Lake, Ind.: Eisenbrauns, 1984] 73–87). J. P. Hyatt believes "that his [Whitley's] date is four years too late" ("The Beginning of Jeremiah's Prophecy," *ZAW* 78 [1966] 204–14 [reprinted in *Prophet to the Nations*, 63–72; the quotation is from p. 64]). Other scholars have suggested that the thirteenth year of Josiah was Jeremiah's birthday. See F. Horst, "Die Anfänge des Propheten Jeremia," *ZAW* 41 (1923) 94–153; Holladay (*Jeremiah*, 2.25–26) sees ". . . seven arguments in favour of lower chronology." He explains that since Jeremiah was appointed a prophet from birth, his birthday and his call date are considered the same. On the other hand, some other scholars still support the idea that in 627, Jeremiah was already a young man, נער, and this was the date of his call (see Cazelles, "La vie de Jérémie"; J. Scharbert, "Jeremia und die Reform des Joschija," in *Le livre de Jérémie* [ed. P. M. Bogaert; Leuven: Leuven University Press, 1981] 40–57).

interested here in the actual biography of Jeremiah. The only relevant point is that the call narrative insists that already in 627 B.C.E. Jeremiah had foreseen the danger from the north that materialized about 22 years later.[15] In other words, the idea that Jeremiah anticipated the northern danger in his call vision is also retrospective. Carroll, who mainly treats the biographical elements in the book as mere fiction, has raised the question: "If nothing in [chapters] 2–20 necessitates a date in the time of Josiah, what is to be made of the editorial introduction setting Jeremiah in the period 627–587?"[16] His answer is "the conventionality of the forty-years motif."[17] Without commenting on the protasis of his question, I am suggesting another, not necessarily alternative, answer as the apodosis. The editors (and, as will be argued later, the author of the call narrative as well) meant to emphasize the soothsaying virtues of Jeremiah: he had anticipated very accurately what would happen, and all his prophecies indeed came true.

(5) Jeremiah 1:19. ונלחמו אליך ולא יוכלו לך. Verses 17–19 imply that already in his first call, Jeremiah expected opposition from kings and ministers, priests and laymen, who would not overcome him, "For I am with you, says the Lord, to deliver you" (v. 19). Such an anticipation is also unique in prophetic call narratives. A motif of unfavorable response toward prophetic preaching is found in the call visions of Moses (Exod 4:1–9), Isaiah (Isa 6:10), and Ezekiel (Ezek 2:3–7, 3:4–9), but only here is a real threat to the prophet's life insinuated. The subsequent passages that confirm this anticipation (1:18–23, 17:15–18, and chaps. 20, 26, and 36–38), sometimes even by quoting phrases from the call narrative (15:20, 39:17–18), attest to the retrospective character of the threat motif.

(6) Jeremiah 1:12. כי שוקד אני על דברי לעשותו. The almond vision is a kind of test, aiming to convince Jeremiah of his prophetic competence. The test refers to the ability to see visions, comprehend their meaning, and give them accurate verbal expression. Having succeeded in all of this, he is praised by God: "You have seen well." He saw a stick, recognized it as an almond (and not an apple, for example),[18] and knew to focus his verbal response on the most relevant element in the vision. Jeremiah's report of the vision reflects

---

15. I thus discard the notion that the text in 1:2 is mistaken and should be amended from בשנת שלש עשרה to בשנת עשרים ושלש (see T. C. Gordon, "A New Date for Jeremiah," *ExpTim* 44 [1932–33] 562–65).

16. R. P. Carroll, *Jeremiah* (OTL; London: SCM, 1986) 91–92.

17. By this he means that Jeremiah was depicted as having periods of activity similar to Moses' and David's (ibid., 90). Compare this to Rashi's commentary on 1:4: ". . . it was you that I meant when I said to Moses 'a prophet I will raise to them like you' (Deut 18:15); he reproached them and he reproached them, he prophesied forty years and he prophesied forty years."

18. The word is מקל 'a dry stick' (e.g., Num 22:27), not ענף 'branch', which is more easily identifiable botanically. This is what Jeremiah is praised for (היטבת לראות). His intuition is accurate, and it enables him to convey the message through the pun שקד-שוקד.

deep concern about the fulfillment of his prophecies, a concern that is not a conventional element in call narratives. It reflects the anxiety of a prophet who has not (yet) seen the fulfillment of his prophecies. Such apprehension seems to fit an experienced prophet or an editor speaking retrospectively, rather than a young idealist who feels that his destiny is to utter the message of God. However, the importance of this passage lies in the idea expressed by the almond vision, not in whether it is authentic or retrospective. Its significance is at the core of our discussion, the direct connection between a prophecy and its fulfillment. The message here is unmistakable: God's promise to keep his word (שׁוקד, participle, to express constant truth) is unconditional, a message that emphasizes the fact that prophecy is the utterance of God's words, which will be fulfilled. By implication, a prophet is one whose words are destined to be fulfilled. The expression of this idea in a call narrative amplifies its principal theological importance.

(7) Jeremiah 1:9–10.   The tendency to emphasize soothsaying's elements in the call narrative is most explicitly mirrored in vv. 9–10. Having said to Jeremiah, "Behold, I have put my words in your mouth," God appoints him "over the nations and over kingdoms to pluck up and to break down, to destroy and to overthrow, to build and to plant." The meaning of this appointment is clear: he should utter the words of God proclaiming the nations' future. Nothing in his mission refers to preaching, trying to improve the nation's misconduct, warning in order to prevent destruction. This amazing feature is another unique characteristic of Jeremiah's call narrative. Moses is given an executive mission—to deliver Israel from Egypt. Isaiah is appointed to influence his people.[19] Ezekiel's instruction is to preach to his people, "whether they listen [i.e., 'obey'] or not" (Ezek 2:7); God orders him to act as a "lookout"[20] (3:16), whose task is to warn Israel, not to proclaim their future. The unique presentation of Jeremiah's prophetic mission reveals the reason for the concealed retrospective character of the call narrative. It illuminates the inclination to emphasize the soothsaying features in Jeremiah's profile. To summarize, an innocent reading of the call narrative (that is, without questioning its authenticity) would lead the reader to consider Jeremiah an outstanding soothsayer.

Incidents from the Prophet's Life

Two narratives depict the struggle of Jeremiah against the people (chap. 26) and a false prophet (chap. 28).[21] Organizing the plot around confrontations is

---

19. "Make the heart of this people fat and make their ears heavy and shut their eyes . . ." (Isa 6:10). The verse is ambiguous, and this is not the right place to discuss it. Yet it is clear that the prophet should influence the behavior of Israel in one way or another.

20. Greenberg's translation of צופה, commonly translated 'watchman'. See M. Greenberg, *Ezekiel 1–20* (AB 22; New York, 1983).

21. For a discussion of these two narratives, see G. Brin, *The Prophet in His Struggles* (Tel-Aviv, 1983) 33–93 [Heb.]. On Jeremiah 26, see pp. 34–82.

a literary device aiming at a sharp delineation of the prophetic profile of Jeremiah and is therefore important to our study.

(8) Jeremiah 26. In chap. 26, "the priests, the prophets, and all the people" (v. 7) demand a death sentence for Jeremiah, because he has "prophesied in the name of God, saying, 'This house shall be like Shiloh and the city shall be desolate, without inhabitant'" (v. 9). Following this demand, the people establish a quasi court, where the contenders present their arguments. Some participants act as "prosecutors," others as "defenders," yet a clear formal accusation is missing, and commentators are divided regarding its identification. Some have suggested that the complaint was the impudence of proclaiming the destruction of the temple,[22] others define the charge as blasphemy against God,[23] and still others speculate that Jeremiah was accused of prophesying falsely.[24]

I support the third view for the following reasons: (1) When pleading not guilty, Jeremiah does not refer at all to a charge of blasphemy. On the other hand, he clearly rejects the accusation of prophesying falsely. He opens his address to the accusers by saying, "God sent me to prophesy against this house and this city all the words you have heard" (v. 12) and concludes by stressing once again, "for in truth God sent me to you to speak . . ." (v. 15). (2) The prophet's defenders repeat this declaration, "This man does not deserve the sentence of death, for he has spoken to us in the name of our God" (v. 16). (3) Scholars who advocate the blasphemy option refer to Exod 22:27 and Lev 24:10–16, "the punishment for blasphemy is death."[25] However, Exod 22:27 does not mention a death penalty, and the incident in Lev 24:16 is not mere blasphemy but literally cursing (ונקב שם ה') God's name, which is definitely not what occurs in our story. On the other hand, death is indicated as the punishment of false prophets in Deut 13:6, 18:20. (4) False prophecy is the common denominator of the whole context, Jeremiah 26–29.

One has to wonder why the author did not clearly explicate the accusation. I speculate that the omission is actually intentional paralepsis,[26] used to focus the reader's attention on the reason that Jeremiah's opponents have derived such an absurdity from his prophecy.[27] The reason, as implied by Jeremiah's words

---

22. For example, Qimḥi (לפי שהיה מתנבא רע), Malbim. See also the discussion in J. Skinner, *Prophecy and Religion* (Cambridge: Cambridge University Press, 1922) 171–74.

23. E.g., C. H. Cornill, *Das Buch Jeremia* (Leipzig, 1905) 300; W. Rudolph, *Jeremia* (HAT; Tübingen: Mohr, 1963) 170; Carroll, *Jeremiah*, 516 (he suggests another possible accusation— treason, "as vv. 20–23 seem to imply," p. 520); Holladay, *Jeremiah*, 2.107.

24. E.g., Abarbanel; Metzudat David; J. Bright, *Jeremiah* (AB 21; Garden City, N.Y.: Doubleday, 1965) 172.

25. Quoted from Holladay, *Jeremiah*, 2.107.

26. "A rhetorical figure by which a speaker pretends to omit mention of what at the same time he really calls attention to" (*Cassell's Dictionary*).

27. For the use of this narrative device for a similar purpose in Jeremiah 36, see Y. Hoffman, "And Many Similar Words Were Added to Them," in *Teuda: In Memory of J. Licht* (ed. Y. Hoffman and F. Polak; Tel-Aviv: Tel-Aviv University and Bialik Institute, in press) [Heb.].

in 26:13 and by the legal precedent of Micah (vv. 18–19), was that they erroneously considered a prophecy to be an irreversible prediction of the future.
They dogmatically believed in the immanent, unconditional holiness of the
temple and therefore its indestructibility. Hence, they deduced that whoever
prophesied otherwise was necessarily a false prophet, since his prophecy would
never come true and he would fail the test of fulfillment. It is clear that the author expressed the opposite view through the words of Jeremiah, ". . . correct
your ways and your doings and obey . . . and [the Lord] will repent of the evil
which he has pronounced against you" (v. 13). Here the "test of fulfillment"
was principally rejected as irrelevant, and the distinction between prophecy and
soothsaying was emphasized. Nevertheless, the expression of this concept of
prophecy in our story was not unequivocal. Having written his story from an
exilic perspective,[28] the author (and his potential readers) knew that Jeremiah's
prophecy had come true and that Jeremiah had passed the "test of fulfillment."
Thus, the narrative successfully "burned the candle at both ends": the postu-
late that a prophet is not necessarily a seer is expressed, and in any event, Jeremiah's virtue as a soothsayer has been confirmed. The conclusion of the story
regarding our subject is therefore: theoretically a prophet's soothsaying ability
could be disproved without diminishing his reputation as a true messenger of
God; practically, however, Jeremiah has proved his virtue as a soothsayer.[29]

(9) Jeremiah 28. Chapter 28 deals with the question of prophecy and
soothsaying more explicitly. Not only does it focus on two opposite person-
alities, Hananiah and Jeremiah, both repeatedly called נביא,[30] it also presents an

28. See Hoffman, ibid.; idem, "Aetiology, Redaction and Historicity in Jeremiah XXXVI,"
VT 46 (1996) 179–89.

29. This conclusion is valid even if one accepts the opinion of those who deny the integrity
of chap. 26 and regard some verses as later additions. The most vulnerable verses are 20–23 (e.g.,
Volz, Hyatt, Weiser, Carroll) and to a lesser extent, vv. 17–19 (e.g., Carroll). According to Hossfeld and Meyer, the original text is vv. 2a, 4a, 6, 7, 8b, 10–12, and 14–16, while the rest are deuteronomistic additions. See F. L. Hossfeld and I. Meyer, "Der Prophet vor dem Tribunal," *ZAW* 86
(1974) 30–50. Carroll has suggested that Micah was mentioned in the story in order to save his
reputation as a prophet, since his prophecy that Jerusalem would be ruined had not been fulfilled.
Therefore, the claim that Hezekiah saved the city by his repentance was an attempt "to deal with
the problem of Micah's unfulfilled prediction . . . a good example of response to dissonance" (see
R. P. Carroll, "Prophecy, Dissonance, and Jeremiah XXVI," in *A Prophet to the Nations: Essays in
Jeremiah Studies* [ed. L. G. Perdue and B. W. Kovacs; Winona Lake, Ind.: Eisenbrauns, 1984] 381–
91). However, the tension between the conditional and absolute elements is built into vv. 1–16, on
whose integrity there is a wide consensus. The precedent of Micah in vv. 17–19 only emphasizes
the conditional-prophetic elements that were already raised in v. 13. The episode of Uriah, vv. 20–
23, is irrelevant to our issue.

30. Hananiah: vv. 1, 5, 10, 12, 15, and 17; Jeremiah: vv. 5, 6, 10, 11, 12, and 15. Three times
Hananiah is mentioned without the epithet "the prophet": vv. 11, 13, 15 (שמע נא חנניה is not
represented in the Septuagint). This would have been reason for literary speculation if it were not
for v. 12, in which Jeremiah also is mentioned without the epithet. In the Septuagint, the epithet
הנביא is not represented, either for Jeremiah or for Hananiah (except for v. 1, where the epithet is
ψευδοπροφητες). Carroll has indicated that the later edition of the book, represented by the MT,

abstract formula to distinguish between the two types (vv. 8–9). The story depicts Hananiah as a soothsayer, and his conflict with Jeremiah could suggest that Jeremiah represents the opposite type—the prophet. This would be erroneous, however, as an analysis of the story's plot and theoretical statements will demonstrate.

The pivotal point of the plot is the question: which of the two contenders delivering contradictory messages in the name of God will prove his genuineness as a real נביא? The fact that only Jeremiah's prophecy came true provides an unequivocal answer to this question: (a) he proclaimed the death of Hananiah, and this was exactly what happened (v. 17); (b) he announced that God had appointed Nebuchadnezzar to dominate the world for a long period and that therefore Jehoiachin's deportees and the temple's vessels would not return to Jerusalem within two years. This prophecy also came true, as any reader of our narrative well knew. The bottom line of the plot is, therefore, that Jeremiah has fully proved his soothsaying abilities.

Verses 8–9 supply the theoretical rationale of the plot, which is unmistakably related to the law of the prophet in Deuteronomy 18. Both passages insist on the test of fulfillment as the only valid criterion for the genuineness of a prophet, but Jeremiah confines the test to deliverance prophets only (v. 9, הנביא אשר ינבא לשלום). Having done so, he releases himself from the test, since he has prophesied doom. This diminishes the importance of the fulfillment test by limiting its validity, while strengthening the element of contingency in the concept of prophecy. If judged retrospectively from an exilic vantage point, it also conveys a clear message of consolation to the people. Jeremiah uttered some very harsh prophecies that could easily have been interpreted as predicting the unconditional termination of the national existence of Israel.[31] By nullifying the test of fulfillment for doom prophecies, he automatically conditionalized all of them. Thus, room for repentance and deliverance has been opened without diminishing Jeremiah's reputation as a true prophet.[32]

Hence, the messages of the story regarding the prophetic qualifications of Jeremiah are complementary. The plot establishes his standing as a soothsayer,

---

uses the formula ירמיהו הנביא 26 times, while the Septuagint, representing a previous shorter edition, uses it 4 times only. He considers it part of the tendency of the later edition to emphasize the prophetic features in Jeremiah's personality. See Carroll, *Jeremiah*, 53, 61. In Jeremiah 28, however, this difference between the MT and the Septuagint refers not only to Jeremiah but to Hananiah as well. The notion that the longer MT edition represents a later stage in the growth of the book of Jeremiah compared to the shorter edition of the Septuagint has been advocated mainly by Jansen and Tov and has been widely accepted (see J. G. Janzen, *Studies in the Text of Jeremiah* [Cambridge: Cambridge University Press, 1973]; E. Tov, "Some Aspects of the Textual and Literary History of the Book of Jeremiah," in *Le livre de Jeremie* [ed. P. M. Bogaert; Leuven: Leuven University Press, 1981] 145–67). The opposite view has been suggested by S. Soderlund, *The Greek Text of Jeremiah* (Sheffield: JSOT Press, 1985).

31. See, e.g., 9:9–21, 10:20–22, 15:5–9, and 18:13–17. This is a random list of sections, with no intention to claim that they represent delineated prophetic units.

32. The tendency to soften this kind of prophecy is also recognized in some editorial remarks, such as וכלה לא אעשה (4:27, 5:18).

by emphasizing the fact that he has passed the test of fulfillment. The maxim in vv. 7–9 unfetters him from the necessity of being subjected to the doom-prophecy test and thus emphasizes his educational-prophetic qualities. Therefore, it would be wrong to judge the revision of the fulfillment test as being in direct opposition to the law of Deuteronomy 18. Since the principle of fulfillment as such is not disputed in our narrative, it would be more accurate to assume that its author has offered what seemed to him a legitimate interpretation of the law.

One can detect such an interpretive initiative in two other difficulties: (1) The core of the law is the obligation to obey the prophet and disobey the false prophet. Yet, this demand is problematic, since the criterion for distinguishing between the two—the fulfillment of the prophecy—is valid only retrospectively. It is impossible to employ this criterion for immediate decisions.[33] (b) The punishment of the false prophet in Deut 18:20 is: "that prophet shall die" (ומת הנביא ההוא). Should he be sentenced to death,[34] or will God cause his death?[35] The conclusion of the story suggests a solution to both difficulties—the information about the death of Hananiah (v. 17). This is an obvious answer to the second difficulty: God killed Hananiah, as proclaimed by Jeremiah and (by implication) as determined by the law of the prophet. The indication that Hananiah died in the seventh month, in other words, less than two full months after the whole incident (v. 1), solves the first difficulty. By indicating the proximity of the death, the author has interpreted the phrase ומת הנביא ההוא as "he will be killed by God."[36]

---

33. ". . . In setting up criterion the preacher is probably making things too easy for himself. If a serious matter arose, could the question of the genuine authority of the prophet be left in suspense until it has at last appeared that his message had come true?" (G. von Rad, *Deuteronomy* [OTL; London: SCM, 1966] 125). Uffenheimer has resolved this problem by suggesting that the legislator, when establishing this criterion, had in mind a mantic prophet, a seer, or advising people about domestic short-term issues. His genuineness could therefore be judged within a short period of time. This notion, however, does not accord with the main concept of the law, which compares the future prophet with Moses (כמוך), the national prophet, who is never depicted as a domestic seer (see B. Uffenheimer, *Ancient Prophecy in Israel* [Jerusalem: Magnes, 1973] 284–85 [Heb.]; "Jeremiah's Struggle with the False Prophets," *Neiger Book* [Jerusalem: Kiryat-Sefer, 1959] 96–111 [Heb.]).

34. So Rashi, quoting the Talmud. See *b. Sanh.* 89a, which mentions three types of false prophets that should be put to death (. . . שלשה מיתתן בידי אדם). Nachmanides is more hesitant about this.

35. So Ibn Ezra, on v. 19 (מיתתו בידי שמים).

36. Rofé has proposed that this is a mistaken exegesis of the deuteronomic law. If so, it was definitely not an innocent mistake but a well-calculated interpretation (see A. Rofé, *Introduction to Deuteronomy* [Jerusalem: Akademon, 1988] 308–9 [Heb.]).

The book of Jonah might be considered a narrative that demonstrates and interprets the limited rule of fulfillment defined in Jeremiah 28. It is thus another link in the interpretive chain of the deuteronomic law. The story demonstrates the case of a true prophet of God whose doom prophecy has not come true. However, it does not allow for true deliverance prophecies to be refuted similarly. The interpretive element in the story of Jonah refers to the central theme of the book, the motif of repentance (Jonah 3:1–4:2), which provides a theological explanation for the revised rule of fulfillment. This element is entirely missing in Jeremiah 28, which is quite odd. I suggest that

(10) Jeremiah 36.   In the "fourth year of Jehoiakim" (605 B.C.E.), God
orders Jeremiah to write a scroll of prophecies containing "all the words that
I have spoken to you . . . from the day I spoke to you, from the days of Josiah,
until today" (v. 2).[37] The purpose is to warn the people of "all the evil that I
intend to do to them so that every one may turn from his evil way and that I
may forgive their iniquity and their sin" (v. 3). This is the sole instance in the
story of a clear expression of the nonabsolute, conditional aspect of prophecy.
The soothsaying aspect, on the other hand, is one of the theoretical grids of the
whole narrative.

   The author tells us that the scroll was read in the ninth month of the fifth
year (v. 9),[38] and this date is repeated in v. 22. The repetition is obviously an
emphatic device,[39] used to indicate the importance of the date. The annals of
Nebuchadnezzar reveal the reason for this emphasis by mentioning the conquest of Ashkelon in his first year (604 B.C.E.), during that very month.[40] In
other words, when Jehoiakim is said to have read that the king of Babylon
would come and destroy the land (v. 29), Nebuchadnezzar was already there.
Yet Jehoiakim ignored the warning of Jeremiah and burned his scroll. This is
why the author emphasized the ninth month of Jehoiakim's fifth year. But why
did he indicate that the scroll was written in the fourth year of Jehoiakim (v. 1)?
The juxtaposition of vv. 1 and 9 raises the possibility that the author wanted
to show that at least 9 (and up to 21) months passed after Baruch wrote the
scroll before he read it to the people. Thus, Jeremiah's unconditional prediction of Nebuchadnezzar's arrival had been written (not just spoken!) "from the
mouth of Jeremiah" (vv. 4, 6, 17, 18, 27) a long time before the event materialized. In other words, the dates in the story testify to the veracity of the
soothsaying of Jeremiah. One can derive the same prophetic profile from the

this lack has to do with the latent tendency of Jeremiah 28 to nurture hopes for deliverance among
the exiles. Mentioning repentance as a precondition for possible deliverance might weaken national
hopes and is therefore avoided. For a recent discussion of the idea of repentance in the book of
Jonah, see U. Simon, *Jonah: Introduction and Commentary* (Miqra Leyisraᵓel [A Bible commentary for Israel]; ed. M. Greenberg and S. Ahituv; Jerusalem, 1992) 3–9 [Heb.]).

   37. The historicity of the story is irrelevant to the present discussion. It is the prophetic profile
of Jeremiah that we are interested in, and this is conveyed by the way the story is told, no matter
how accurate the details are. The historicity and other aspects of the story are dealt with in the
commentaries and in many articles. Some recent ones include: R. L. Hicks, "*Delet* and *Megillah*:
A Fresh Approach to Jeremiah 36," *VT* 33 (1983) 46–66; G. Brin, *Prophet in His Struggle*, 105–
49 [Heb.]; Y. Hoffman, "Aetiology, Redaction and Historicity in Jeremiah XXXVI."

   38. This is also the version of Codex Alexandrinus of the Septuagint, while the Codex Vati-
canus version has "the eighth year."

   39. The words בחדש התשיעי are not represented in the Septuagint. Their addition to the *Vorlage* of the MT reflects the importance of the date in the eyes of the editor. By adding it, he simply
overemphasized the already-existing intent of the original author, as will be explained below.

   40. D. J. Wiseman, *Chronicles of Chaldaean Kings* (London, 1956) 68–69: *a-na (al) is?-qi?-
il-lu-nu illik-ma ina (araḫ) Kislimi. . . .*

concluding prophecy, vv. 29–31. If reduced to a formula, its message to Je-hoiakim would be: "the already fulfilled prediction of Jeremiah certifies the veracity of his present one." To any potential exilic or postexilic reader of the story, the message is even more pointed: Jeremiah's doom predictions before and after 605 B.C.E. have been proved right.[41]

Thus, an idea of conditional prophecy (v. 2) is embedded in a context ex-pressing the opposite concept. Is v. 2 authentic, or is it a later insertion? Neither the style nor the ancient versions prove the latter speculation.[42] We may there-fore conclude that the two opposite concepts of prophecy coexisted originally in our story.

Prophecies against Foreign Nations

The following examples are from editorial headings or postscripts found in the block of prophecies against foreign nations, none of which is an integral part of a prophecy.

(11) Jeremiah 46:13. Jer 46:13 is an editorial introduction to a prophecy whose core is the defeat of the Egyptian king and army. The prophecy encour-ages "the daughter of Egypt" to prepare herself for exile (v. 19). While the prophecy does not identify the king who will invade Egypt, the introduction does: Nebuchadnezzar.[43] The historical background of the prophecy probably reflects the period between 605–601, following the defeat of Egypt at Carche-mish, when an invasion of Egypt might have been expected.[44] However, it did

41. It could be argued that such a retrospective reading does not compromise the prediction that Jehoiakim's corpse would "be cast out to the heat by day and the frost by night" (v. 30; see also 22:18–19). The Jeremiah passage seems to contradict 2 Kgs 24:6, which claims that "Jehoia-kim rested with his fathers." Kaufmann has even referred to this contradiction to support his claim that the book of Jeremiah was not updated and revised after Jeremiah's death (Kaufmann, *Toledot Haʾemunah Hayisraʾelit*, 3.407). This argument, however, is not convincing. The data seem to sug-gest that there were different traditions about Jehoiakim's death (another one is transmitted in 2 Chr 36:6: he was exiled to Babylon; see J. A. Montgomery, *The Book of Kings* [ICC; Edinburgh: T. & T. Clark, 1951] 553). The phrase וישכב יהויקים עם אבתיו does not necessarily imply that he was bur-ied peacefully. It may even be an intentional reconciliation of שכב\בוא\אסף\מות בשלום עם אבותיו (Gen 15:15, 2 Kgs 22:20, 2 Chr 34:28), avoiding a direct clash between the different traditions.

42. The only variant between the MT and the Septuagint refers to the words על ישראל, rep-resented in the Septuagint by επι Ιερουσαλημ (see Carroll, *Jeremiah*, 658).

43. The syntax of the phrase לבוא נבוכדראצר מלך בבל להכות את ארץ מצרים is not clear enough. The words לבוא, etc., might be translated either 'that Nebuchadrezzar would come' or 'about the coming of Nebuchadrezzar'. In both cases, the idea is that Jeremiah had predicted an in-vasion of Egypt.

44. Thus Rudolph, *Jeremia*, 271 (605); Bright, *Jeremiah*, 308 (604); M. Haran, Response to A. Malamat, "Jeremiah according to the Bible and External Documents," in *Studies in the Book of Jeremiah* (2 vols.; ed. B. Z. Luria; Givataim: The Israel Society for Biblical Research, 1971) 1.24–25 [Heb.]. I do not agree with Holladay (*Jeremiah*, 2.327–28), who suggests the year 588. His date is based on the speculation that 'Pharaoh' in v. 17 is a pun on the name (of the Egyptian king) 'Hophra'.

not materialize until 568/567,[45] which should therefore be considered a *terminus a quo* for the editorial heading. Thus, edited after the first prophecy on Egypt (46:2–12), this editorial comment implies that Jeremiah not only described *post factum* the Egyptian defeat in Carchemish but also predicted the invasion of Egypt by Nebuchadnezzar. Such a retrospective editorial, post-568 comment highlights the soothsaying faculties of Jeremiah.

(12) Jeremiah 47:1.   Jer 47:1 offers a similar case, where the retrospection is even more perceptible. To the shorter version of the editorial heading "On/To the Philistines" (compare with 48:1; 49:1, 7, 23, 28), represented by the Septuagint, a later editor has added the words "The word of the Lord that came to Jeremiah the prophet . . . before Pharaoh smote Gaza." This is the only case of an editor explicitly indicating that he wrote his heading retrospectively.[46] Here too, the effect of the heading is clear and reveals its primary purpose: to portray Jeremiah as a soothsayer.

(13–16) Jeremiah 46:26, 48:47, 49:6, and 49:39.   Short formulas promising future restoration are appended to the prophecies against Egypt (46:26), Moab (48:47), Ammon (49:6), and Elam (49:39). Their literary character is definitely editorial: nothing in the prophecies themselves leads to these predictions, and some prophecies even contradict them. For example, the prophecies say that "Moab will be annihilated from being a nation" (48:42); Elam will be persecuted "until I have consumed them" (49:37). The fact that two of these prophecies use the expression באחרית הימים (48:47, 49:39) has raised the possibility that their intent was eschatological—a depiction of a future universe of peace and tranquility.[47] I do not share this view. First, the expression באחרית הימים is not eschatological in this case. Only in a few biblical contexts does it have an eschatological meaning, while in others it refers to a relative, not an absolute future.[48] The fact that the other two prophecies mentioned above use a different expression, ואחרי כן, which is definitely noneschatological, supports this interpretation. Second, the restoration formulas are appended to only four out of nine prophecies on foreign nations, which eliminates the possibility that the editor wanted to depict a universal state of peace during the *eschaton*. I therefore suggest that these formulas are retrospective accretions, added after Egypt, Moab, Ammon, and Elam had already been liberated from the Babylo-

45. Bright, *Jeremiah*, 265.
46. For a discussion of this heading, see Y. Elizur, "Before Pharaoh Smote Gaza," in *Studies in the Book of Jeremiah* (2 vols.; ed. B. Z. Luria; Givataim: Israel Society for Biblical Research, [undated]) 1.173–88.
47. See Kaufmann, *Tôlĕdôt Hā᾿emûnâ Ha-Yisrĕ᾿elît*, 3.474.
48. See Y. Hoffman, "ביום ההוא and אחרית הימים: Their Relation to Eschatological Passages in the Bible," *Beth Miqra* 71 (1978) 435–44 [Heb.]. For the relative meaning of the expression, see also M. Weinfeld, *Deuteronomy 1–11* (AB 5; Doubleday, N.Y., 1991) 210.

nian yoke. The purpose of the additions was to emphasize that their restoration did not contradict Jeremiah's prophecies; rather, their restoration was the fulfillment of the prophecies. In other words: they reaffirm Jeremiah's soothsaying capabilities.

The Seventy-Years Motif[49]

(17–19) Jeremiah 25:11–12, 27:7, and 29:10. Twice in Jeremiah the phrase *70 years* is mentioned to indicate the predetermined period of the Babylonian imperial rule: 25:11–12, 29:10. Another verse, 27:7, assumes a similar period, saying that "all the nations shall serve him and his son and the son of his son until the time of his own land comes." Calculating a generation as 25 years, one may recognize the 3-generations pattern as a variant of the 70-years motif. Such an accurate dating of future events is very unusual in biblical prophecy, and this is one of the reasons that most scholars suspect the authenticity of these prophecies. Scholars correctly consider them to be later additions, inserted into the text after the conquest of Babylon by Cyrus in 540. The exact "fulfillment" of the "70-years" prophecies can only lead to the conclusion that we have here a clear case of *vaticinium ex eventu.* If the year 540 is considered the target date of the 70-years prediction, then the implied utterance date of these prophecies should have been 610. However, 70 is a well-known typological number,[50] and therefore any other proximate date might have been intended by the author, such as 609 (the death of Josiah and the beginning of Jehoiakim's reign), 605 (Nebuchadnezzar's first year),[51] or, in fact, any date up

49. This subject is too complicated to be discussed fully here. See, e.g., W. E. Lemke, "Nebuchadrezzar, My Servant," *CBQ* 28 (1966) 45–50; P. R. Ackroyd, "Two Old Testament Historical Problems of the Early Persian Period," *JNES* 17 (1958) 13–27; Carroll, *Jeremiah*, 493–96.

50. The number 70 has a wide variety of typological meanings. It is considered the average span of the human lifetime (Gen 5:12–14 [70 and 70×12], Ps 90:10). It expresses the idea of the entirety of a family (Deut 10:22), defeated kings (Judg 1:7), descendants (Judg 9:56, 2 Kgs 10:7), or any ad hoc group (Jer 41:5–9). The biblical passage most relevant to our discussion is Isa 23:15–18, when (probably also a later editorial insertion) God will 'visit' (יפקד) Tyre. Post-Jeremianic use of the motif will be discussed below. Weinfeld has indicated that the motif was "a conventional numerical typology . . . employed by Mesopotamian scribes" (M. Weinfeld, *Deuteronomy and the Deuteronomic School* [Oxford: Clarendon, 1972; reprinted Winona Lake, Ind.: Eisenbrauns, 1992] 146). He refers to the so-called "Black Stone" of Esarhaddon, mentioning a 70-year desolation of Babylon, until Marduk shows his grace to her. The typological status of 70 may be adduced in support of the Jeremianic authenticity of the motif by claiming that Jeremiah used it as a convention, but it accidentally proved true. This seems to me a remote possibility, especially since the Jeremianic authorship of chaps. 25, 27, and 29:10 has been questioned on other grounds, which will be mentioned below.

51. This is the date in 25:1, opening the first prophecy that mentions 70 years. The MT to 27:1 (the entire verse is not attested in the Septuagint) is בראשית ממלכת יהויקם בן יאושיהו, which does not accord with the subsequent story, which refers to Zedekiah. It is plausible that behind this scribal mistake was the 3-generations pattern in v. 7 (also missing in the Septuagint!), which erroneously led an incautious scribe to think of Jehoiakim's first year, 609.

to 587.[52] Be that as it may, the post-540 B.C.E. insertion of these prophecies has contributed considerably in reinforcing the soothsaying aspects in the book of Jeremiah.

Contra Soothsaying

(20) Jeremiah 18:7–10.   The nineteen passages discussed above share a similar, positive view of soothsaying. They all consider it an important, if not the most important category of real prophecy. This notion is unequivocally opposed by 18:7–10,[53] in which, just as in 28:8–9, the author has formulated a theoretical principle. Yet, while 28:8–9 advocates the (limited) rule of fulfillment, related to the soothsaying aspect of prophecy, 18:7–10 denies it entirely. Basic to these verses is the notion that God's plans are always contingent, determined by human behavior. Compared to the message of the book of Jonah, the rule here is more definitive and systematically congruous. The book of Jonah does not express explicit agreement even with the limited rule of fulfillment, that is, the notion that the conditionality of God's proclamations refers only to one aspect: human repentance followed by divine forgiveness. However, since people not only repent but also regress from their good behavior and "do evil . . . not listening to my voice" (18:10), God may also "repent of the good." The "contingency formula" should also take into account this element. In this sense—the clear and unequivocal denial of a necessary linkage between true prophecy and its fulfillment—Jer 18:7–10 is unique in the book of Jeremiah. A comparison with the previously discussed nineteen references might suggest that this section was written as a polemic against them, or their "subversive

52. Chapter 29 is dated after Jehoiachin's exile (v. 2), 588, yet this is not the date from which the reader is supposed to calculate the 70 years mentioned in v. 10. It is meant to be understood as a quotation from a previous prophecy of Jeremiah. For a discussion of redactional problems in this chapter, see my "Some Editorial Methods in Jeremiah," in *Dor Le-Dor: Joshua Ephron Jubilee Book* (ed. A. Kasher and A. Oppenheimer; Tel-Aviv: Tel-Aviv University, 1995) 57–72 [Heb.].

53. In all of the present versions these verses are an integral part of the unit 18:1–12, yet they may be a secondary accretion. In vv. 1–6, God orders Jeremiah to go to the potter's house, where he realizes that the potter is free to do anything he wishes with his clay. The analogous conclusion about the relationship between God and Israel is: "like the clay in the potter's hand, so are you in my hand" (v. 6). The natural inference of this metaphor is that Israel (= the clay vessel) cannot influence the acts of God (= the potter). This conclusion diametrically opposes the idea of vv. 7–10, whose essence is that nations determine God's reactions. This discrepancy has led many scholars to dispute the original integrity of 18:1–12 (see Carroll, *Jeremiah*, 371–74; McKane, *Jeremiah*, 420–28; W. Thiel, *Die deuteronomistische Redaktion von Jeremia 1–25* (WMANT 41; Neukirchen-Vluyn: Neukirchener Verlag, 1973) 210–18; C. Brekelmans, "Jeremiah 18:1–12 and Its Redaction," in *Le livre de Jeremie* (ed. P. M. Bogaert; Leuven: Leuven University Press, 1981) 343–50. The authentic integrity of 18:1–12 is maintained by Bright, *Jeremiah* 125–26; Holladay, *Jeremiah*, 1.513–14. This dispute is irrelevant to our discussion. I refer only to vv. 7–10 because there our subject is epitomized.

interpretation." This is best attested by the way vv. 7 and 9 paraphrase, nearly quote, 1:10. The formula לנתוש לנתוץ ולהאביד ולהרוס לבנות ולנטוע is breached by the contingency formula (vv. 8, 10) and thus reinterpreted not as an absolute message but as an open option.

Synopsis and Conclusions

The twenty passages examined above share two common denominators.

(1) The first, which has been demonstrated throughout this paper, is their relevance to the bipolarity of the concept of prophecy. However, their stance is not unanimous and is expressed in different manners—directly and implicitly, unambiguously and hesitantly. The book of Jeremiah expresses only one pole unequivocally as an authoritative dogma, the conditional concept of prophecy, in 18:7–10 (no. 20). Its closest, yet not perfect antithesis are the laws of the prophet in Deuteronomy (nos. 1–2). As we have seen, these laws are based on the rule of fulfillment, but the ideological premise of this rule is assumed, not phrased as an explicit theoretical dogma, unlike Jer 18:7–10. This is not an accident but a true reflection of an awareness of the nonsoothsaying aspects of the Israelite concept of prophecy. Thus the law of the prophet (no. 2) is straddling, sitting on the fence: it neither gives up the soothsaying aspect nor bridges it and the Mosaic aspect. Such unresolved tension is perceptible in the prophetic narratives as well (nos. 8–10), whose attachment to the deuteronomic law of the prophet (no. 2) is undisputed. The term *tension* better reflects the mental attitude embedded in these texts toward the bipolarity of "prophecy" than the word *contradiction*. In other words, the mere existence of conceptual discrepancy in a given passage does not mean that critical treatment is required—unless there is correlating philological evidence. This evidence has not been found in passages no. 2, 8, 9, or 10.

If such discrepancies originally coexisted within single units, there is no reason to assume that other units, which express only one aspect of prophecy, meant to reject the opposite aspect. Hence, the preoccupation of the call vision with the soothsaying pole (nos. 3–8) does not imply its dissent with the other aspect. The same holds true in examples 9–19. All of them transmit soothsaying messages, but none implies a rejection of the prophetic pole. The coexistence of the two contradictory concepts might be logically absurd but not necessarily a practical contradiction, since paradoxes are built-in elements of religious thinking. As long as inconsistent conceptions serve the requirements of a given society, it will adopt and adapt them and interpret them as complementary rather than contradictory in order to maintain their coexistence. This empirical truth is valid also for the relationship between Jer 18:7–10 (no. 20) and the rest of our examples.

This same conclusion may be transferred to other texts in which one identifies tension between the absolute and the conditional aspects of prophecy. This
is true in the case of the famous "temple sermon" in Jer 7:1–15, whose relation
to chap. 26 is widely recognized. Here one could easily identify absolute (vv. 14–
15) and conditional elements (vv. 3–7). This has led scholars to deny the original
unity of the sermon by demarcating the phases that correspond to its absolute
and conditional aspects.[54] This division can be dismissed once the idea of tension, a possible built-in paradox, is accepted. I suggest applying the same conclusion to other prose sermons, such as 11:1–14.[55]

(2) The second common denominator may be phrased in two different ways.
In technical terms, all of the twenty passages are prose. This statement will probably be undisputed, unless one principally invalidates the distinction between
prose and poetry in the Hebrew Bible.[56] Another, less technical and therefore
more contestable formulation of the second common denominator is that none of
the twenty passages is authentically Jeremianic. For some scholars, this latter formulation is a mere tautology, since they deny the Jeremianic authenticity of any
prose passage in the book.[57] However, my claim that none of the discussed
passages is Jeremianic is totally independent of this generalizing judgment.

Examples 1–2 are evidently non-Jeremianic. Numbers 8–10 belong to the
so-called biographical layer, whose non-Jeremianic origin is unanimously accepted by all scholars.[58] Numbers 11–16 are, generally speaking, editorial re-

54. See, e.g., Skinner, *Prophecy and Religion*, 170–84; Thiel, *Die deuteronomistische Redaktion von Jeremia*, 116–17; Carroll, *Jeremiah*, 211; McKane, *Jeremiah*, 165. Holladay, *Jeremiah*,
1.238 defends the integrity of vv. 1–12, while suggesting that vv. 13–15 "are evidently an appendix
added for the second scroll."

55. See Carroll, *Jeremiah*, 267–71.

56. See J. F. Kugel, *The Idea of Biblical Poetry* (New Haven: Yale University Press, 1981).
Holladay does not deny the principal distinction between prose and poetry in the book of Jeremiah,
but his criteria for poetic passages are wide and flexible. Accordingly he emphasizes metrical elements in the call vision, although he still uses the term *narrative* when referring to this vision (Holladay, *Jeremiah*, 1.25–26). For his theoretical arguments, see, e.g., "Prototype and Copies: A New
Approach in the Poetry-Prose Problem in the Book of Jeremiah," *JBL* 79 (1960) 335–67; idem,
"The Recovery of Poetic Passages of Jeremiah," *JBL* 85 (1966) 401–35. The only contestable passage is chap. 1 (examples 3–8). Some scholars have detected here a few poetic colons (e.g., vv. 5,
7–10). However, most of chap. 1 is prose (see Holladay, *Jeremiah*; McKane, *Jeremiah*, 6).

57. Following Duhm, *Jeremia*, x–xiv; and Mowinckel. Mowinckel's distinction of three
major layers in the book of Jeremiah is widely accepted today, though with variations. The three
layers are (A) Jeremianic poetry, (B) biographical narratives, (C) deuteronomistic prose sermons;
only A is considered authentic Jeremianic (see S. Mowinckel, *Zur Komposition des Buches Jeremia* [Kristiania, 1914]).

58. The only dispute is whether it was Baruch who composed them (Duhm, *Jeremia*, xiv–xvi;
Cornill, *Jeremia*, xlii–xliii; Kaufmann, *Tôlĕdôt Hāʾĕmûnâ Ha-Yisrĕʾelît* 3.410–11; Rudolph, *Jeremia*, xv–xvi; Holladay, *Jeremiah*, 2.13–14, 22–23) or someone else, not necessarily a contemporary
of Jeremiah (Mowinckel, *Zur Komposition des Buches Jeremia*, 30; G. Wanke, *Untersuchungen zur
sogenannten Baruchschrift* [BZAW 122; Berlin, 1971]; H. Graf Reventlow, "Gattung und Überlie-
ferung in der 'Tempelrede Jeremias,'" *ZAW* 81 [1969] 315–52, esp. p. 322; Carroll, *Jeremiah*, 44–46).

marks, and there is no reason to ascribe them to Jeremiah. Numbers 17–19 are, as I have argued above, post-Jeremianic *vaticinia post eventu.*

The scholarly consensus about the non-Jeremianic authorship of the remaining examples is more limited. Examples 3–7 refer to the call narrative, chap. 1. The authenticity of this narrative, told in an autobiographical style (vv. 4, 6, 7, 9, 11–14, etc.) is denied either partially or entirely by many scholars.[59] Some of their reasons relate to the retrospection of the call narrative, demonstrated above, but this alone does not refute the Jeremianic authorship. There is nothing in the call narrative that necessitates its post-586 dating, and therefore its retrospective view might go back to Jeremiah himself. However, scholars have set forth other arguments to justify the notion that chap. 1 is not authentic Jeremianic.[60] This is the theory of the Dtr (= the Deuteronomic School + its successors) style in the call narrative.[61] Another argument refers to its literary character: (a) The conventional pattern of "call narrative" is so transparent that it can hardly express an authentic experience. (b) Judged from the perspective of the whole book, one should recognize chap. 1 as a prologue written at one of the latest stages in the gradual growth of the book. Thus, obvious allusions to the call narrative are spread all over the book, mainly in prosaic passages.[62] I share the notion that chap. 1 in its present rendition is best defined "non-Jeremianic."

Once we grant that chap. 1 belongs to a relatively late layer of the book, granting the non-Jeremianic authorship of 18:7–10 (no. 20) is a logical deduction, since, as we have seen, it reinterprets 1:10.

The negative common denominator *non-Jeremianic* could be phrased positively as *deuteronomistic* if Thiel's view of the "deuteronomistische Redaktion von Jeremia" is accepted.[63] This view, however, seems too sweeping. In some cases the Dtr origin of a passage is more assumed than proven (yet it

---

59. E.g., Bright, *Jeremiah*, 6–7; Rudolph, *Jeremia*, 7–10; and Holladay, *Jeremiah*, 1.26–32 defend the authenticity of the call narrative. Scholars who deny the Jeremianic authenticity of the call narrative in its present form include: H. G. Reventlow, *Liturgie und prophetisches: Ich bei Jeremia* (Gütersloher Verlagshaus, 1963) 24–77; Thiel, *Die deuteronomistische Redaktion von Jeremia 1–25*, 62–72; E. W. Nicholson, *Preaching to the Exiles* (New York: Schocken, 1971) 113–15; McKane, *Jeremiah*, 11–14. Carroll's denial of the call narrative is *ex-hypothesi*, since he doubts the very existence of a historical Jeremiah who composed prophecies (see Carroll, *Jeremiah*, 62–64 and more). See also Renaud, "Jérémie 1: Structure et théologie de la rédation."

60. It is not my purpose to prove this notion here but only to provide some arguments for it.

61. See, e.g., Kaufmann, *Tôlĕdôt Hā^ʾemûnâ Ha-Yisrĕ^ʾelît*, 3.613–14; Weinfeld, *Deuteronomy and the Deuteronomic School*, 321, 324, 353, 359 ("The influence of Deuteronomy upon genuine Jeremiah"). Thiel has tried to distinguish between authentic elements and deuteronomistic redactional accretions all over the book (see Thiel, *Deuteronomistische Redaktion*, 52). In chap. 1, however, his identification of the redactional layer does not fully correlate with the deuteronomistic elements. This has been correctly criticized by Weippert, as indicated by McKane, *Jeremiah*, 13; see H. Weippert, *Die Prosareden des Jeremiabuches* (BZAW 132; Berlin: de Gruyter, 1973) 193–202.

62. Cf. 12:14–17, 18:7–10, 19:5–7, 31:27–28, 32:10, 45:4. For this argument, see Nicholson, *Preaching to the Exiles*, 115.

63. Thiel, *Deuteronomistische Redaktion.*

may be unrefutable as well, nos. 11–16); in other cases the definition *redaction* is dubious [nos. 8–10]. Generally speaking, the attempt to reduce the gradual process of the growth of the book of Jeremiah to the formula "kernel + deuteronomistic redaction" is too simplistic. I therefore think that "Dtr passage" (not "redaction") is a more applicable term for most (not all) of our examples. This umbrella would cover examples 1–2 (it is self-evident that they are from Deuteronomy), 3–10, and 17–20. Examples 3–7 refer to the call vision, whose Dtr features have been indicated above. The same holds true for nos. 8–10. Dtr style in the so-called "biographical narratives" (source B) has been clearly identified. A recent study has shown that the stylistic proximity between these narratives and the Dtr prose sermons (source C) undermines the legitimacy of a source separation between the two.[64] Jer 18:1–12 (no. 20), 25:1–14, 27:7, and 29:10 (nos. 17–19) have been recognized as Dtr (source C) since Mowinckel.[65]

Is it plausible that the Deuteronomist advocated both contradictory concepts of prophecy? The positive answer is clear. If the two polaric concepts could coexist in one and the same unit (see above), they could definitely be pronounced in different Dtr passages.

Given the well-known educational, homiletic orientation of Dtr, one might wonder at its promotion of the soothsaying elements of prophecy.[66] Yet this aspect is one of the most important factors in the theory of Dtr historiography: the theology of "Prophecy and Fulfillment"![67] Indeed, this theology, used retrospectively to decipher the causality of the past, is successful in explaining the past with the idea of repentance: the people had not repented, and therefore the doom prophecies came true. But this solution does not remove the logical contradiction between the two aspects of prophecy, which nevertheless coexist peacefully in Dtr. We have to realize that the "absolute-conditional" tension is part of the very essence of the Deuteronomists' theology. To this, one should add another speculation regarding Dtr: my Dtr theory does not conjecture a single person but a whole school. An exploration of the literary product of this school reveals that, except for one idea—the centralization of the cult—it was not very dogmatic but, rather, polyphonic and gave voice to various views.[68]

64. M. J. Williams, "An Investigation of the Legitimacy of Source Distinctions for the Prose Material in Jeremiah," *JBL* 112 (1993) 193–210.

65. Mowinckel, *Zur Komposition des Buches Jeremia*, 31. In addition to the various commentaries and Thiel, *Die deuteronomistische Redaktion*, 210–18, see also L. Stulman, *The Prose Sermons of the Book of Jeremiah* (Atlanta: Scholars Press, 1986) 73–76, 86–94.

66. See R. P. Carroll, "Prophecy, Dissonance, and Jeremiah xxvi," in *A Prophet to the Nations: Essays in Jeremiah Studies* (ed. G. Perdue and B. W. Kovacs; Winona Lake, Ind.: Eisenbrauns, 1984) 381–91. Speaking of the two strands of chap. 7, Carroll suggests that the "conditional element is more in keeping with the Deuteronomic view of history which permits repentance to save Hezekiah" (referring to Jer 26:19; p. 389).

67. See, e.g., G. von Rad, *Studies in Deuteronomy* (London: SCM, 1953) 78–82.

68. See Y. Hoffman, "The Deuteronomist and the Exile," in *Pomegranates and Golden Bells: Studies in Biblical, Jewish, and Near Eastern Ritual, Law, and Literature in Honor of Jacob Milgrom* (ed. D. P. Wright, D. N. Freedman, and A. Hurvitz; Winona Lake, Ind.: Eisenbrauns, 1995)

(3) The abundance of soothsaying elements in the book of Jeremiah is unique in prophetic literature and cannot be accidental. Consequently, the portrayal of Jeremiah as a peerless prophet, whose doom prophecies, and some of whose restoration prophecies (nos. 13–16), had already come true, must be intentional. What was the background of and what were the reasons for this portrayal? My answer to the first question is derived from the identification of most of the above passages as deuteronomistic: the background was the exilic period. In this, I agree with many of the scholars mentioned above, who have dated the so-called B and C sources to this period.[69] I find no reason to date the retrospective editorial formulas (nos. 11–16) to a later, postexilic period, although this may be a sound possibility.

Assuming this historical background, one should try to understand the reasons for the soothsaying infrastructure of the book. In this regard, a key passage is Jer 31:27–28. A prophecy of redemption (v. 27) is concluded with a comparative formula,[70] כן . . . כאשר: "and it shall come to pass that as I have watched over them to pluck up and break down, to overthrow, destroy, and bring evil, so I will watch over them to build and to plant, says the Lord" (v. 28). This paraphrase of Jeremiah's mission (1:10) clarifies the importance of his depiction as a prophet who has passed the fulfillment test: it guarantees the completion of his deliverance prophecies. In other words, Jeremiah's credibility as a soothsayer was strengthened in order to make his deliverance promises (for example, 31:2–22) trustworthy and comforting for the exilic community. On the basis of the limited rule of 28:8–9, one might even reach an *a minori ad majus* kind of deduction: if Jeremiah's doom prophecies have come true (which is not a necessary condition for a prophet), then certainly his deliverance prophecies will also be fulfilled.[71] Once the credibility of Jeremiah's redemption prophecies had been established, it was only natural that some non-Jeremianic comforting prophecies and statements were ascribed to him, because this increased their credibility and hence their effectiveness (e.g., 3:14–18, 5:18–19, 30:11, 31:38–40, 32:36–44). Another phase in this process was the later addition *post eventu*

659–75. The distinctive character of the deuteronomistic portrayal of Jeremiah can be illuminated by a comparison to Jeremiah's self-portrait, mainly in chap. 23. When denouncing the false prophets (vv. 13–32), he distinguishes them from the real prophets using the criteria of conscientious, moral conduct, sincerity, true religious feelings, and so on. Nothing is said about the fulfillment criterion, either for them or for Jeremiah.

69. Thiel, Rudolph, Bright, Nicholson, Carroll, McKane, and Wanke. Nicholson has specifically emphasized the message of the prose tradition in the book of Jeremiah for the exilic community. For a more recent study, see C. R. Seitz, *Theology in Conflict: Reaction to the Exile in the Book of Jeremiah* (Berlin: de Gruyter, 1989).

70. E.g., Gen 41:13, 50:12; Exod 27:8, 39:43, and more. See also Jer 32:42, where the formula is used exactly in the same manner.

71. An inverted example of this formula is ascribed to Moses in Deut 28:63: "And it shall come to pass that as the Lord took delight in doing you good and multiplying you, so the Lord will take delight in bringing ruin upon you and destroying you. . . ."

of the 70-years motive and its attribution to Jeremiah. I speculate that this was initiated by two factors: (a) the wish to intensify Jeremiah's soothsaying credibility, and (b) the conviction (following the deuteronomistic concept mentioned above) that a historical event such as the downfall of Babylon could not possibly have occurred unless Jeremiah had anticipated it.

This didactic, synthetic presentation of the process might create the wrong impression that the suggested explanation presupposes either a neat, systematic, gradual growth or a well-calculated plan. Neither possibility, of course, is assumed because both are too simplistic to describe such socioreligious dynamics. It is most likely that all of the suggested factors functioned reciprocally with no detectable diachronic sequence, and probably with no premeditated plan, to depict Jeremiah as a soothsayer. The pragmatic exigencies of the exiled community can be reduced to an urgent need for comfort and hence a need to cultivate credible hopefulness. This social need determined the convergence of the factors mentioned above to produce the process that has culminated in the canonization of the book of Jeremiah. How could a prophecy like Jer 18:7–10 (no. 20) be fit into this framework? Does it not undermine the whole structure of Jeremiah's soothsaying, which nourished the national faith for a better future? Indeed it does, because it invalidates the absoluteness of the deliverance prophecies. Yet it counterbalances the shortsighted pragmatic needs by introducing a religious-educational category. The importance of the latter is not only theological (that is, abstract) but in the long term, also practical. It vaccinates against a possible national crisis that might occur (and probably did occur in the beginning of *shivat Zion*, the return from Babylon to Jerusalem) when the absolute promises of complete deliverance are refuted.

A naive, positivistic approach might tempt one to delineate a diachronic development from a "primitive" concept of prophecy as soothsaying toward a purely nonabsolute concept. The biblical data, however, utterly refute such a thesis. Jeremiah's soothsaying reputation is indicated in late postexilic books such as Ezra (1:1), 2 Chronicles (36:21–22), and Daniel (9:2). In Deutero-Isaiah, one of the most significant proofs of the uniqueness of God is based on the prophetic ability to tell the future—the motif of ראשונות ואחרונות.[72] The portrayal of Jesus in the New Testament as a completion of previous biblical prophecies[73] is another manifestation of the same concept. These and many

---

72. Isa 41:4, 22–24, 26; 42:9; 43:9–13; 44:7; 45:19–22; 46:8–11. See M. Haran, *Between Rishonot (Former Prophecies) and Hadashot (New Prophecies)* (Jerusalem: Magnes, 1963) 23–32, int. al. Rofé has examined the question of prophecy and fulfillment in Isaiah 40–66. His conclusion is that the various views on this issue reflect the distinction between Deutero- and Trito-Isaiah (see A. Rofé, "How Is the Word Fulfilled?" in *Canon, Theology, and Old Testament Interpretation: Essays in Honor of B. S. Childs* (ed. G. M. Tucker, D. L. Petersen, and R. R. Wilson; Philadelphia: Fortress, 1988) 246–61.

73. E.g., Matt 1:22–23, 2:6, 2:17–18 ("Then was fulfilled what was spoken to Jeremiah the prophet . . ."), etc.

other examples annul any diachronic schema regarding the different concepts of prophecy. The soothsaying aspect is not limited to any specific period, primitive or advanced. Ideas change, crystallize, and purify, but man's psychological needs do not. The illusion that the future could be anticipated seems to be motivated by deeply rooted human psychological needs. It is so essential that no generation and no culture—religious or secular—could give it up, as exemplified by the dictionary entry quoted in the beginning of this paper. This ground, when fertilized by specific sociological circumstances such as the crisis of exile, germinated in the unique phenomenon of the book of Jeremiah: its preoccupation with soothsaying features, epitomized in the depiction of Jeremiah's prophetic profile.

The Next Phase in Jewish Religion:
The Land of Israel as Sacred Space

BARUCH A. LEVINE
New York University

In the ancient Near East of biblical times, one worshiped within sacred space and repaired to sacred precincts to perform other acts of religious significance. The operative premise in the concept of sacred space is that the "where" is a factor as important, if not more important, than the "what," "who," or "how." Actually, the "where" is often a prior condition governing the efficacy of the acts themselves. Simply put, the same act that is performed effectively in a designated, sacred space is not efficacious if performed outside of it.

Specifying that sacrificial worship must take place in sacred space is a way of saying that it must take place in the presence of the deity (or deities) in order to be efficacious. The consecration of space is realized by bringing the deity close to the human community and, ultimately, by bringing the human community close to the deity. So it has been that religious communities have promulgated set policies on sacred space, carefully instructing their members as to where worship is proper, and where it will be efficacious. In this respect, the Hebrew Bible is no exception, although identifying biblical statements of cultic policy requires methodical study.

It is clear in hindsight that since late antiquity, the monotheistic religions—Judaism, Christianity, and Islam—have differed significantly in their respective attitudes toward sacred space. Of the three, the religious civilization of Diaspora Jews has, ever since the destruction of the Second Temple of Jerusalem, placed the least emphasis on the function of sacred space. Of course, Jewish prayers speak dramatically of an earlier, ancient period, and of more blessed circumstances when the Temple stood in Jerusalem, and they express the eschatology of redemption that will bring with it cultic restoration. Such memories and hopes have had little to do, however, with the ongoing experience of

Author's note: Aspects of this study were discussed in an address inaugurating the Skirball Chair in Bible and Ancient Near Eastern Studies at New York University, in December, 1992.

Jewish religiosity in the Diaspora. In the traditional synagogue there is no cult of purity and no consecrated priesthood; any adult, male Jew may officiate.

To understand how this basic change came about requires studying a series of ancient decisions on religious policy by various waves of Israelite, and later, Jewish leaders. When the First Temple of Jerusalem was destroyed, prophets, priests, and civic leaders of the exilic communities faced real choices regarding the character of worship in foreign lands and subsequently, in Judea and Jerusalem restored. It is not to be taken for granted that they would opt to discontinue sacrificial worship of the God of Israel in Babylonia or elsewhere outside of Jerusalem. By the time the cult of the Second Temple of Jerusalem came to an end in the first Christian century, alternative forms of worship had greatly developed in Jewish religion.

One Temple and a Single Altar:
Deuteronomic Doctrine and the Edict of Josiah

This discussion begins in the monarchic period of biblical history and focuses on the historical relationship between two biblical sources: (1) the edicts of Josiah recorded in 2 Kings 22–23, aimed at terminating the *bāmôt* 'cult-platforms' and at centralizing all cultic worship of the God of Israel in the Temple of Jerusalem (these are dated by the biblical record to ca. 622 B.C.E.); (2) the legislation and doctrinal statements of Deuteronomy 12–18 on the restriction of all cultic activity to one, central temple, whose location is left unspecified. The essential connection between these two sources has been explored extensively but with varying conclusions since the beginnings of modern biblical research.[1]

The motivations and objectives of the movement to restrict sacred space, on which the Hebrew Bible reports, require renewed study, as do the important phenomenological factors associated with them. For now, it will suffice to examine aspects of the history of the movement. In my earlier review of H. L. Ginsberg's monograph *The Israelian Heritage of Judaism* (1982), I accepted the proposition that the policy restricting sacred space to a single, central temple is expressed, at least as a hidden agenda, in Hosea's strong opposition to the proliferation of royally-sponsored altars and cult places in Northern Israel.[2]

---

1. See R. Altmann, "Josiah," *ABD* 3.1015–18. The reader is directed to two chapters in *The Age of the Monarchies: Political History*, vol. 4/1: *World History of the Jewish People* (Jerusalem: Massada, 1979); H. Reviv, "The History of Judah from Hezekiah to Josiah" (chapter 9), 193–204, notes: pp. 344–48; and A. Malamat, "The Last Years of the Kingdom of Judah" (chapter 10), 205–21, notes: pp. 349–53. A bold reappraisal of the period of Josiah is provided by N. Naʾaman, "The Kingdom of Judah under Josiah," *Tel-Aviv* 18 (1991) 3–71, particularly the section entitled: "Summary: Josiah in Historiography and in Historical Reality," 55–59.

2. H. L. Ginsberg, *The Israelian Heritage of Judaism* (New York, 1982); B. A. Levine, "Review of Ginsberg," *AJS Review* 12 (1987) 143–57.

This opposition was voiced during the period preceding the Assyrian invasion, in the mid–eighth century B.C.E. It is likely that the delegitimation of *mĕqômôt* 'cult-sites' (the Northern Israelite term) ordained in Deuteronomy was not voiced for the first time in Judah of the mid-to-late–seventh century, when we read in the book of Kings that the *bāmôt* 'high places' were regarded as illegitimate, but rather at an earlier period and quite possibly in Northern Israel.

Religious ferment in Northern Israel in the mid–eighth century B.C.E. might explain Hezekiah's attempt to eliminate the *bāmôt* in Jerusalem and Judah at the end of the eighth century B.C.E. His policy, though probably abortive and surely short lived, would have constituted a response to Northern Israelite prophetic teaching. In and of itself, the historicity of the report of Hezekiah's effort to remove the *bāmôt*, preserved in 2 Kgs 18:4 and following, would be in doubt were it not for the speech subsequently attributed to the Assyrian Rabshakeh in 2 Kgs 18:19–35. Therein, the Assyrian commander taunted the citizens of Jerusalem on the subject of this very policy:

> And should you say to me: "Upon the LORD our God we rely"—Is He not the [very] one whose *bāmôt* and altars Hezekiah eliminated, saying to Judah and Jerusalem: "Before this altar alone shall you bow down, in Jerusalem"?

Expressed as part of a propagandistic statement and appealing to traditional notions of sacred space, the reference to Hezekiah's reform in 2 Kgs 18:22 sounds genuine and should not be taken merely as part of a noticeable tendency, *post hoc*, to credit otherwise virtuous kings with additional claims to religious correctness. In this light, we can also regard 2 Kgs 18:4 as a genuine report after all.

The radical shift of religious doctrine reflected in Deuteronomy 12–18 can be documented by comparing this source with Exod 20:19–23, the prologue to the Book of the Covenant, which should be regarded as an earlier statement. It is probable that both Exod 20:19–23 and Deuteronomy 12–18 are of Northern Israelite provenance, so that differentiating between their respective provisions can help to trace religious development within Northern Israel itself. The terms of reference employed in Exod 20:19–23 require careful elucidation:

> The LORD said to Moses: So shall you say to the Israelite people: You saw that from the very heavens I spoke with you. Do not fashion alongside Me gods of silver, nor fashion for yourselves gods of gold. Fashion for Me an altar of earth, and offer upon it your burnt offerings and your sacred gifts of greeting, your flocks and your large cattle; in every cult-place where I will pronounce My name (*bekol hammāqôm ᵓašer ᵓazkîr ᵓet šemî*) I will come to you and grant you blessings. And should you fashion for Me a stone altar, do not construct it of hewn stone, for by wielding your sword upon such you have rendered it unfit.

As a construction, *bekol hammāqôm* is unique in Scripture, but *kol hammāqôm*, minus the preposition, is elsewhere attested; thus, Deut 11:24: "Wherever (*kol hammāqôm*) your foot treads shall belong to you." This is resonated in Josh 1:3 as *kol māqôm*, without the definite article, showing that both constructions may share the same meaning.

I have translated the term *māqôm* as 'cult-place', which represents a specialized usage of a more general term. In Biblical Hebrew, *māqôm* is a highly nuanced term of reference, and serves as the *Leitmotif* of Jacob's theophany at Bethel (Genesis 28), also a Northern Israelite source. One immediately associates the statements of Jeremiah (7:12), concerning Shiloh in Northern Israel where *bayit* 'temple' and *maqom* 'cult-place' are equated:

> Just go to My 'cult-place' (*ʾel meqômî*) that is at Shiloh, where I formerly had my name installed (*ʾašer šikkantî ʾet šemî*), and see what I have done to it because of the wrongdoing of my people, Israel.

Continuing in Jer 7:14, we read:

> I shall do to the temple (*bayit*) over which My name is called (*ʾašer niqrāʾ šemî ʿālâw*) and to the cult-place (*welammāqôm*) that I have granted to you and to your ancestors what I did to Shiloh.

Exod 20:19–23 speaks of multiple, legitimate cult-sites, such as were in operation throughout the land of Israel at certain periods of preexilic history. This brief code of cultic practice insists only that such installations be constructed properly, and that the rites performed at them and the clergy officiating at them be proper. Although the Exodus statement is not explicit in prescribing these cultic regulations for Israel's governance in the Promised Land, rather than the wilderness, this undoubtedly should be assumed.

It is this very system of multiple cult-sites that is renounced in Deuteronomy 12 and following. Thus, instead of formulaic *bekol hammāqôm* 'in whichever cult-place', we read in Deut 12:13–14 of a restrictive doctrine, expressed in the very same language:

> Be careful not to offer your burnt offerings at whichever cult-place you see fit (*bekol māqôm ʾašer tirʾeh*). Rather in the cult-site (*bammāqôm*) that the LORD will select in one of your tribal territories, there shall you offer your burnt offerings. . . .

Or, earlier, in Deut 12:5:

> Rather to the cult-place (*ʾel hammāqôm*) that the LORD your God will select from all of your tribal territories to inscribe His name there (*lāśûm ʾet šemô šām*); you shall seek out his dwelling place and come there.

I take Exod 20:19–23 to represent the policy current in Northern Israel during the ninth-to-early–eighth centuries B.C.E., or even earlier; in other words, the pre-Deuteronomic cultic doctrine. If Ginsberg is correct, this doctrine was questioned in the Northern Kingdom later in the eighth century B.C.E., and a new policy was advocated, one aimed at restricting sacred space. It is core-Deuteronomy that formulates this new policy, one that was never implemented in Northern Israel, as far as we know.

After the fall of Samaria, writings and teachings from the temples and schools of Northern Israel were transmitted to Jerusalem and Judah. It was in this way that core-Deuteronomy, or parts of it, reached Jerusalem during the reign of Hezekiah, who actively endorsed the new doctrine of cult centralization and attempted to implement it. When he was followed by Manasseh, a king known for his heterodoxy, the Deuteronomic doctrine was abandoned, re-emerging in Judah only in the mid-to-late-seventh century. Ultimately, it was a version of this doctrine that informed Josiah's edict.

The originally unspecified site within the Northern Kingdom, probably intended as Shechem-Gerizim originally, was now reidentified as Jerusalem and its Temple. This reinterpretation is presupposed in any number of biblical sources, most notably in the deuteronomistic excurses of 1 Kgs 8:16–21, 11:29–39, 14:21–24, and most likely in Ps 78:67–72. In all of these sources, the verb *baḥar* 'to choose, select' is pivotal and resonates with deuteronomic diction.

Ginsberg provides a clue regarding the way this localization of the Northern Israelite doctrine was rationalized.[3] It may have been taught that since the Temple of Jerusalem was first erected by Solomon, son of David, a Judean, and since it had survived the downfall of Northern Israel, it was blessed and indeed represented "the cult-place that the LORD will choose."

2 Kings 22–23 emphatically endorse the restriction of sacred space ordained in Deuteronomy once we recognize that the venue chosen by God has become Jerusalem, the Judean capital. But 2 Kings 23 in particular shows considerable evidence of redactional activity, and this condition complicates the task of the historian. I take a more critical view than Ginsberg or even than Cogan and Tadmor in this instance and consider 2 Kgs 23:24–27, which assesses Josiah's activities as the fulfillment of 'teaching' (*tôrâ*), to be composed of exilic and possibly postexilic interpolations.[4]

Source-critical analysis allows us to read interpolations in 2 Kings 23 as evidence for the acceptance of Josiah's reforms by the exilic leadership and by the restored, postexilic community and brings into relief at least two sets of historical viewpoints: we have, first of all, a fairly contemporary record of Josiah's actual reforms in 2 Kings 23, and, in the second instance, we have, most notably in 2 Kgs 23:24–27, evidence of the later endorsement of these reforms.

---

3. See Ginsberg, *Israelian Heritage*, 34–38.
4. See ibid., 39–54; M. Cogan and H. Tadmor, "The Reign of Josiah: The Great Reform," *II Kings* (AB 11; New York: Doubleday, 1988) 277–302. Naʾaman, "Kingdom of Judah," 55–59.

Let us examine 2 Kgs 23:24–27 in particular detail:

(24) And further, Josiah removed (*bi^{c}ēr*) the necromancers and mediums, the idols and the fetishes—all the detestable objects that were to be seen in the land of Judah and Jerusalem. Thus he fulfilled the terms of the teaching (*hattôrâ*) recorded in the scroll that the priest Hilkiah had found in the Temple of the LORD.

(25) [And the likes of him (= Josiah) there never was before him; a king who turned back to the LORD (*$^{\jmath}$ašer šāb $^{\jmath}$el YHWH*) with all his heart and with all his being, and with all his resources (*bekol lebābô ûbekol napšô ûbekol me$^{\jmath}$ôdô*), according to all of the teaching of Moses (*kekol tôrat Môšeh*). And after him—the likes of him never arose again!]

(26) However, the LORD did not turn back (*lō$^{\jmath}$ šāb*) from His awesome wrath which blazed up against Judah because of all the things Menasseh had done to anger Him.

(27) The LORD said: I will also banish Judah from My presence, as I banished Israel; and I will reject the city of Jerusalem that I chose, and the Temple of which I declared: "My name shall abide there."

The redactional analysis of this passage should proceed in two phases: We should first present indications of the interpolation of vv. 24–27 within 2 Kings 23 and then, turning to v. 25 itself, show how it digresses from v. 24, which precedes it, and from vv. 26–27, which follow it.

2 Kgs 23:23 concludes the description of the celebration of the paschal sacrifice in Jerusalem, a major enactment of Josiah. 2 Kgs 23:28 and following resume the ongoing report of Josiah's activities. Within 2 Kings 23, adverbial *wegam* 'and also, further' occurs twice, in v. 19 and now, in v. 24. In both instances it most likely introduces an interpolation. Verse 19 extends Josiah's iconoclastic activities to the towns of Samaria, taking a cue from the reference to a prophet from Samaria in the preceding verse, v. 18. In v. 24, adverbial *wegam* introduces further iconoclastic activities by Josiah in Jerusalem and Judah. It is worth noting, however, that whereas 2 Kgs 23:21 tells how Josiah proclaimed celebration of the paschal sacrifice in Jerusalem in compliance with 'what was written on this scroll of the covenant' (*kakkātûb ^{c}al šēper habberît hazzeh*), v. 24 speaks of 'the terms of the teaching that were written on the scroll' (*dibrê hattôrâ hakketûbîm ^{c}al haśśēper*). The language has clearly changed. Subsequently, vv. 26–27 add the dire qualification that, notwithstanding Josiah's devoted efforts, the LORD 'did not turn back (*lō$^{\jmath}$ šāb*) from his great wrath' and brought about the destruction and exile. Verses 26–27 thus proceed logically from v. 24.

The language of v. 24 and of vv. 26–27 is picked up and amplified in v. 25, where we read that Josiah acted 'according to all the teaching of Moses' (*kekol tôrat Môšeh*), a distinctly postexilic designation. This designation (like the kindred *bĕsēper tôrat Môšeh* 'in the scroll of Moses' teaching') is characteristic of postexilic biblical statements (Mal 3:22; Neh 8:1; Dan 9:11, 13; Ezra 3:2, 7:6; and 2 Chr 23:18, 30:1, 16) and of late glosses in Joshua (8:31–32, 23:6).

What is perhaps most telling is that v. 26 says of the LORD that 'He did not turn back' (*lō' šāb*) from His wrath, and in v. 25 it is said of Josiah that he did, in fact, 'turn back to the LORD' (*šāb 'el YHWH*), wholeheartedly. The interpolated v. 25 is "braided" into the fabric of vv. 24 and 26–27 by echoing their language.

In effect, the passage including 2 Kgs 23:24, 26–27 endorses Josiah's reforms, adding further detail to his iconoclastic activities. At the same time, it concedes, with the awareness of hindsight, that even Josiah's iconoclasm and his restoration of cultic purity did not save Judah and Jerusalem from God's wrath over the sins of Manasseh. 2 Kgs 23:25, ensconced within this passage, may represent an even later gloss, parenthetically extolling Josiah as a repentant king. Read historically, the interpolations in 2 Kgs 23:24 [25] 26–27 anticipate the acceptance of Josiah's restriction of sacred space to the Temple of Jerusalem by the exilic community in Babylonia, who, quite significantly, understood that restriction to apply to them. Ultimately, this doctrine was endorsed by the restored Judean community under Persian rule.

Further Responses to the Edict of Josiah

It is difficult to assess the effectiveness of Josiah's edict during the period between 622 B.C.E. and the final destruction of 586 B.C.E., and opinions vary as to the extent of its enforcement and acceptance in this time frame when the situation in Judah was rapidly deteriorating. Yohanan Aharoni thought he had found evidence at Arad of the enforcement of Josiah's edicts aimed at the termination of local and regional cult-places.[5] Stratum VII at Arad, dating from the latter years of Manasseh (ca. 687–642 B.C.E.) and into the reign of Josiah (ca. 640–609 B.C.E.), was destroyed at the end of the seventh century. Aharoni is of the view that this destruction occurred in the process of enforcing Josiah's edict. Stratum VI, of the period from Jehoiakin to Zedekiah (from 608–586 B.C.E.), was destroyed at the time of the fall of Jerusalem early in the sixth century B.C.E.

Now, the sanctuary at Arad was part of a royal, military installation on the southern Judean border, and there is every reason to conclude that it had served

---

5. See M. Aharoni, "Arad: The Israelite Citadels," in *The New Encyclopaedia of Archaeological Excavations in the Holy Land* (ed. E. Stern; Jerusalem: Israel Exploration Society, 1993) 1.81–87; A. F. Rainey, "Arad in the Latter Days of the Judean Monarchy," *Cathedra* 42 (1986) 16–25 [Heb.].

as a proper, Yahwistic sanctuary ever since its initial construction in the tenth century on the site of an earlier, twelfth-to-eleventh–century B.C.E. *bāmâ*. The measurements of the altar and orientation of the sanctuary further express its legitimacy. Throughout this period, the sanctuary contained at least one, perhaps two cultic stelae (*maṣṣēbôt*), and sacrifices were offered to the God of Israel on its main altar.

Did the destruction of stratum VII at Arad result from the implementation of royal edicts, or was it also the result of attacks by foreign forces? Whether correct or not, Aharoni's interpretation of the archaeological evidence at least focuses on the likelihood that the movement to restrict sacrificial worship to the Temple of Jerusalem had as one of its objectives the elimination of sacrificial worship at such sites as Arad.

It has been argued, however, that even if there was an initial enforcement of Josiah's edict at royally sponsored cult-places like Arad, it is far from evident that such enforcement extended to many local and regional cult-places, which may not have been under direct, royal administration. Furthermore, there is the possibility of a relapse after the untimely death of Josiah, a reversion to previous practice in the last decades of Judean sovereignty. The prophetic tirades of Jeremiah and Ezekiel are replete with condemnations of all sorts of heterodoxy associated with cult-places, even with the Temple of Jerusalem itself. The realism of these prophetic statements, has, however, been heatedly debated. It must be conceded that at the present time we cannot determine how effective Josiah's edict was in the near-exilic period.

Of considerable significance, therefore, are the policies adopted by the exilic communities in Egypt and Babylonian on the matter of sacred space. What do we know of such decisions and of their long-range effect on the character of Jewish worship?[6] We know of two Jewish temples in Egypt, separated by time, and of radically diverse character. The Elephantine Jewish temple, where a sacrificial cult was practiced, operated throughout most of the fifth century B.C.E. under Persian rule, after which it was destroyed. There is no evidence that it had any impact on Egyptian Jewry of later times, although continuity from the Persian to the Hellenistic periods should not be summarily discounted. Contemporary leaders of the Jewish mercenary community at Elephantine were in contact with Jerusalem and its priesthood. We know that these Jews observed the Sabbath and the Passover festival at the very least, although their religious orientation shows evidence of syncretism. Since it is not known exactly when this temple was founded and by whom, it is uncertain whether its founders would have known of Josiah's edict in the first place.[7]

6. For a view that has deeply influenced scholarship, see Y. Kaufmann, *Toledot Ha²emunah Ha-Yisra²elit* (Jerusalem: Bialik, 1955) 1.81–112 and 2.268–75 [Heb.]. Also see M. Greenberg, "Religion: Stability and Ferment," in *The Age of the Monarchies: Religion and Culture*, vol. 4/2: *World History of the Jewish People* (Jerusalem: Massada, 1979) 79–123, notes pp. 297–303.

7. For a recent review, see B. Porten, "Elephantine Papyri," *ABD* 2.445–55.

The Onias temple in Leontopolis was erected ca. 160 B.C.E., after Onias IV had fled to Egypt. Its origin can be traced to a rift in the ranks of the Jerusalem priesthood and attributed to the initiative of a leading priest of Jerusalem seeking to reestablish himself in the Egyptian Jewish diaspora. The Onias temple was modeled after the Temple of Jerusalem, and Zadokite priests officiated at its sacrificial cult, for which there is archaeological evidence. The Jewish community of Leontopolis maintained fairly close relations with Jerusalem. Even the later rulings of the Mishnah, *m. Menāḥ.* 13:10, do not condemn the Jewish cult of Leontopolis as illegitimate in all respects. Considering that the Onias temple lasted for more than 200 years, until 73 C.E., when it was torn down by order of Vespasian, one would have to conclude that during the Hellenistic Period there was receptivity within Egyptian Jewry to a sacrificial cult.[8]

These two, differing Jewish temples of Egypt, both with active sacrificial cults, could be regarded as evidence that the Deuteronomic doctrine expressed in Josiah's edict had not been given uniform endorsement. This would be true, however, only if we were to conclude that Josiah's edict initially envisioned Diaspora communities and was not directed solely at the kings and people of the kingdom of Judah within the land of Israel. It seems, however, that neither core Deuteronomy, nor what we would regard as primary sources in 2 Kings shows concern with policy outside the land, in what were to become exilic communities. In fact, the dire prophecy interpreted by the prophetess Huldah (2 Kgs 22:16–20) speaks explicitly about the destruction to come 'upon this place' (*ᶜal hammāqôm hazzeh*), never mentioning exile or deportation as such. This suggests that those who subsequently understood the restrictions as prohibiting the sacrificial worship of the God of Israel in the lands of exile and whose views we see reflected in the interpolations of 2 Kgs 23:24–27 were applying this doctrine to their own situations, interpreting it to mean that no place on the face of the earth is sacred except the site of the Temple in Jerusalem. Consequently, at a time when no Temple stood in Jerusalem, as was the reality from 586 until 516 B.C.E., there would be no opportunity to persist in the sacrificial worship of the God of Israel elsewhere, either within the land of Israel or outside of it.

It would be of great value to have evidence of policy-making by the Jewish community in Babylonia during the actual period of the exile. It was Shalom Spiegel who first directed my attention to Ezekiel 20, which he viewed as a cryptic record of Ezekiel's instruction to the elders of the exilic community not to build altars or offer sacrifice in exile. A similar interpretation of the inquiry of the elders and of the substance of Ezekiel's oracle had been put

---

8. On Onias IV and the Jewish temple at Leontopolis, see U. Rapaport, "Onias (Person)," *ABD* 5.23–24; and A. Shalit, "Onias, Temple of," *EncJud* 12.1404–5. The main source of our limited knowledge is Josephus *Ant.* 13.62–72.

forward by M. Friedmann in the late-nineteenth century, and it was subsequently adopted with modifications by several other scholars.[9]

With the exception of probable interpolations, Ezekiel 20 is dated to 591 B.C.E., several years after the first deportations under Jehoiachin.

We read in Ezek 20:1–3 that the elders of the exilic community in Babylonia approached the prophet to seek oracular guidance but were rebuffed. They were told that they would receive no response from God, leaving unspecified what the subject of their inquiry was to begin with. The prophet is simply instructed to indict the people for their abominations, an act conveyed by the verb *šāpaṭ* in v. 3. We would have to infer the subject of the elders' inquiry from the content of the elaborate prophecies that follow, in Ezek 20:4–44.

The main question is whether Ezekiel 20 is talking about the specific problem of sacrificial worship in Babylonia, against the background of the Josianic reform, or in more general terms about the potential attraction of the Judean exiles to idolatrous cults they would encounter there and the resulting abandonment of God's commandments. After all, it is a theme of admonition and prophecy, most notably of the Deuteronomic school, that in exile the people of Israel will worship foreign gods (Deut 4:25–28; 28:36, 63–64; Jer 16:13). In fact, reference in Ezek 20:32 to worship of 'wood and stone' ($^c\bar{e}ṣ$ $w\bar{a}^{\,}eben$) in the lands of exile is particularly reminiscent of similar characterizations of idolatry (2 Kgs 19:18; Isa 37:19; Jer 2:27, 3:9).

Moshe Greenberg is of the view that once the inquiry of the elders, as reported in Ezek 20:1–3, had been rebuffed categorically, it would be illogical to regard the oracle (or oracles) contained in the rest of chapter 20 as responsive to the subject of the original inquiry, whatever it was.[10]

Greenberg explains the dynamics of inquiry and response by referring to Ezekiel 14, which also begins with an inquiry by the elders of Israel that is repeatedly rebuffed. There, the prophet explicitly clarifies why the community could not be afforded the oracular services of the prophet and would receive no response to their inquiries from God. Israelites who flaunted their fetishes could hardly expect divine guidance! So too in Ezekiel 20, the refusal of God to respond to the inquiries of the exilic community is followed by a denunciation of *gillûlîm* 'fetishes' and *šiqqûṣîm* 'detestable things'.

The situation in Ezekiel 20 is somewhat special, nonetheless. I would follow Moshe Greenberg in regard to Ezek 20:4–26, 30–31, which I consider to

---

9. See M. Friedmann (Meir Ish-Shalom), *Hassiyyun, That Is, A Commentary on the Prophecy of Ezekiel, Chapter 20* (Vienna, 1888) [Heb.]; A. Menes, "Tempel und Synagoge," *ZAW* 50 (1932) 268–76; J. A. Bewer, "Bietrage zur Exegese des Buches Ezechiel," *ZAW* 63 (1952) 193–201.

10. See M. Greenberg, *Ezekiel 1–20* (AB 22; New York: Doubleday, 1983) 360–88 on Ezekiel 20; and ibid., 155–57 for a comment on Ezek 7:26; ibid., "Structure and Themes," 251–55 on Ezekiel 14. Also see W. Zimmerli, *Ezekiel 1* (trans. R. Clements; Hermeneia; Philadelphia: Fortress, 1979) 399–418.

be the primary oracle, but I would insist that in contrast, Ezek 20:27–29 represents an interpolation and that it contains an explicit reference to *bāmâ* worship in Ezek 20:29a. Furthermore, the oracle that follows and that is contained in Ezek 20:32–44, allows for the interpretation that the issue of sacrificial worship in Babylonia was on the prophet's mind. Whether by the author of Ezek 20:1–26, 30–31, or by a different hand, Ezek 20:32–44 may be understood as a commentary on the primary oracle.

Let us first take up the interpolation of Ezek 20:27–29, which can be shown to refer to the issue of the *bāmôt*:

> By this, as well, your fathers affronted Me and committed trespass against Me. When I brought them to the land I had sworn to give them, and they saw any high hill and any leafy tree, they slaughtered their sacrifices there and presented their angering offerings (*ka^cas qorbānām*) there; there they produced their pleasing odors and poured out their libations. Then I said to them: What is this *bāmâ* which you visit? [It's name has been called *Ba-mâ* until this very day.]

The first observation to be made about Ezek 20:27–29 is that the rhetoric of condemnation has changed. There is no explicit reference to idolatry, to *gillûlîm* 'fetishes', for instance. The operative category is *ma^cal*, a term known best in priestly literature, where it connotes sacrilege. Furthermore, Ezek 20:29a explicitly denounces the fathers of the exiles, the Judeans of near-exilic times, for building cult-platforms and in that way offending God. This recalls 2 Kgs 17:11, where we read:

> They offered sacrifices there, on all [kinds of] *bāmôt*, like the Gentiles whom YHWH had driven out from before them, and they did evil things to anger YHWH (*lehak^cîs ^ɔet YHWH*).

Use of the *Hiphil hik^cîs* recalls the unique locution *ka^cas qorbānām* 'their angering offerings' in Ezek 20:28. It would make sense, therefore, to interpret the probable interpolation in Ezek 20:27–29 as expressing a viewpoint on the *bāmâ* question similar to that of the redactor (or one of the redactors) of Kings.

It is difficult to determine the comprehensive agenda of Ezek 20:32–44. Ezek 20:32, the opening statement of the second oracle, recalls 2 Kgs 17:11 in its reference to what the Gentiles do in the course of their worship of foreign gods. What the exiles are considering doing and what the author of the second oracle is telling them will never be countenanced is to act like the Gentiles! Can we be more specific as to what this tendency was perceived to mean?

Reference to the worship of objects of wood and stone begins in the near-exilic period as a derisive way of characterizing idolatry (2 Kgs 19:18; Isa 37:19; and Jer 2:27, 3:9). In Ezek 20:32, the idiom in question has been altered to *lešārēt ʿēṣ wāʾeben*, using a verb of ambiguous connotation that may mean both 'to worship' and 'to minister to' wood and stone, rather than *ʿābad*, which decidedly connotes worship. But the general intent may have remained the same. It can be argued that Ezek 30:32–44 is simply speaking of idolatry in exile, comparable to the idolatry for which the Israelites of the wilderness period were punished in their time (Ezek 20:36), and that this passage is not addressing the issue of sacrifice in exile at all.

And yet some modulation may have occurred. It may be the intent of the author of Ezek 20:32–44 to compare sacrifice at *bāmôt* in Babylonia to idolatry. What we may have in Ezek 20:32–44 and in the Deuteronomistic excurses in 1 and 2 Kings is the modulation of traditional denunciations of idolatry and their application to the new doctrine of cult-centralization. With this application, later authors were saying, in effect, that the worship of the God of Israel at *bāmôt* was henceforth tantamount to idolatry. If correctly analyzed, this would represent a major example of innerbiblical exegesis.

Ezek 20:39–40 is formulated as if in response to a question:

> As for you, O House of Israel, thus said the Lord, YHWH: Go, every one of you, and worship his fetishes, and continue [to do so], if you will not obey Me; but do not profane My holy name any more with your idolatrous gifts. For only on My holy mountain, on the lofty mountain of Israel—declares the Lord, YHWH; there, in the land, the entire House of Israel, all of it, shall worship Me. There I will accept them and there I will take note of your contributions and the choicest offerings of all your sacred things.

Would it be reading too much into this prophecy to say that the issue informing it is the unacceptability of sacrificial worship in the lands of exile, awaiting restoration to the land of Israel? The contrast between the thrice-emphasized *šām* 'there', namely, on God's mountain, and the exilic venue would support this reading. One could say that on the authority of Ezek 20:27–29, 32–44, sacrificial worship of the God of Israel was illicit in Babylonia.

The Restoration to Zion and Religious Fulfillment: A Hypothetical Reflection

The restoration of the Temple in Jerusalem was indispensable to the program of national repatriation. We can hypothesize that if religious fulfillment had been possible in the Diaspora, if the leadership of the exilic community in Babylonia had decided to erect Jewish temples there, sacred sites where the sacrificial worship of the God of Israel would have been legitimate, the drive toward a return to Zion would have been considerably weakened. Prophecies of the end of exile might have gone largely unheeded. This is to suggest that the decision to limit sacred space to the Temple of Jerusalem, taken in the near-exilic period for a particular set of contemporary reasons, gained new poignancy during the exile, when it was interpreted by at least some leaders of the exilic community in Babylonia to apply, as well, to foreign lands.

The elaborate repertoire of biblical ideas current during the near-exilic and exilic periods assumes a curious configuration. Alongside prophetic notions of universalism, which held that the loss of one's land did not mean the defeat or demise of one's God, the restriction of sacred space to the Temple of Jerusalem left the Babylonian community religiously deprived. Alongside the liberation of religion from territory, a departure in the history of religious ideas that enabled the communities of the Diaspora to retain an identity, the prophecies of restoration attained greater acceptance by holding forth the prospect of religious fulfillment. The restriction of sacred space to the Temple of Jerusalem ultimately stimulated alternative forms of worship, while at the same time withholding cultic sanctity from foreign spaces. In turn, this tension virtually necessitated that an exiled people would remain linked to its homeland.

For almost twenty centuries most of the Jewish people have been living out their religious life without sacred space. Even those small groups of Jews who have inhabited the Holy Land down through the centuries and the dribbling of arriving pilgrims had a very limited experience of sacred space. Not only were ancient buildings in ruin and consecrated sites abandoned, but the people of Israel were distant from its land. After all, the sanctification of space is realized by vital communities, acting out of a need and a want to experience *qirbat ᵓelōhîm* 'the nearness of God' (Isa 58:2). As the sages put it in their laconic succinctness: "If there are no flocks, there is no Shepherd."

In our own day, both the Jewish society of modern Israel, representing about 30% of world Jewry, and the rest of the Jewish people face a new opportunity and a new challenge. There are indications that the next phase in Jewish religion will be characterized by the return of sacred space, albeit in ways modulated by new concepts of sanctity and by new modes of religious expression. The land of Israel has been rebuilt by fellow Jews. It is they who lend sanctity to its space; they are the flocks who assure that the Shepherd is near.

The Methods of Late Biblical Scribes as Evidenced by the Septuagint Compared with the Other Textual Witnesses

Alexander Rofé

The Hebrew University of Jerusalem

The historian who studies Israel, from its beginnings down to the end of the Second Commonwealth, is interested in the divergences between the various textual witnesses from two perspectives: the recovery of primary texts in many passages and the perception of the motives that brought about the formation of secondary readings.

Naturally it is the former task, the recovery of primary readings, that has attracted more attention—after all, this is the traditional direction of textual criticism. Besides, the quest for beginnings has always fascinated the historian; he is at all times tempted to try and reach back beyond the extant sources to forgotten phases of culture. In our case he asks what the religion of Israel was at the outset. The divergent texts of Gen 32:2–3 have something to say about this. The Hebrew, translated into English, runs:

> And Jacob went on his way and the angels of God met him. And Jacob said when he saw them: "This is God's camp." And he called the name of that place 'the two camps' (מחנים).

But the LXX[A] reads instead in v. 2:

> Καὶ Ιακωβ ἀπῆλθεν εἰς τὴν ἑαυτοῦ ὁδόν, καὶ ἀναβλέψας τοῖς ὀφθαλμοῖς ἴδεν παρεμβολὴν θεοῦ παρεμβεβληκυῖαν, καὶ συνήντησαν αὐτῷ οἱ ἄγγελοι τοῦ θεοῦ.

Author's note: A first draft of this paper was offered at a meeting of the Septuagint Research Team, at the École Normale Supérieure, Paris, in January 1994. My thanks go to the audience for their stimulating reactions.

In English:

> And Jacob went on his way and lifting the eyes he saw a camp of God camping and the angels of God met him.

Most plausibly, in my opinion, what we find in the LXX is a doublet, containing the primary as well as the secondary reading. There are some good reasons, including literary ones,[1] to restore the Hebrew text of vv. 2–3 as follows:

ויעקב הלך לדרכו, וישא את עיניו וירא מחנה אלהים חֹנה; ויאמר יעקב כאשר ראם: מחנה אלהים זה. ויקרא שם המקום ההוא מחנים.

> And Jacob went on his way and lifting his eyes[2] he saw a camp of Gods camping. And Jacob said when he saw them: "This is a camp of Gods." And he called the name of that place 'the two camps'.

This fragmentary text would thus join more famous ones, such as the end of the Song of Moses (Deut 32:43) in the LXX or the story of the sons of Gods and the daughters of Man (Gen 6:1–2, 4), to establish a primeval phase in Israelite religion when myths about subordinate divine beings constituted an integral part of its folk religion. It is only to be expected that early phases of religion, replaced by later ones, would leave their traces in literary remains or in secondary textual witnesses.

This paper, however, will be dedicated to the other perspective mentioned above, namely secondary readings in the Hebrew Bible and their significance for the history of religion and literature in the time of the Second Commonwealth, 539 B.C.E.–70 C.E. The Septuagint will serve here as our main textual witness, set against the other witnesses, mainly the MT and the scrolls from Qumran.

The Jewish community from the late Persian age (around 400 B.C.E.) on was held together by its faith and its law. The divine law, as contained in the Pentateuch and as explained and amplified by the scribes, now became the object of popular veneration; it was taught to the people in the provinces (2 Chr 17:7–9); it regulated public life (Neh 13:1–9, 14–28); it was the ideal that inspired the writing of new fiction (Judith, Tobit); and it permeated the rewriting of histories of old times (Chronicles, *Jubilees*). Thus it comes as no surprise that the legal principle, or as it is usually termed, the nomistic principle, guided those other scribes who copied the older biblical books. The nomistic

---

1. Cf. A. Rofé, *The Belief in Angels in the Bible* (Jerusalem, 1979) 86–87 [Heb.]; aliter M. Harl, *La Bible d'Alexandrie: La Genèse* (Paris, 1986) ad loc.

2. The possessive pronoun was not represented, here as elsewhere, in the Greek version; cf. R. Sollamo, *Repetition of the Possessive Pronouns in the Septuagint* (Septuagint and Cognate Studies 40; Atlanta, 1995).

correction was one of the means used by orthodox Jews from later Persian and Hellenistic times in their struggle against their anarchic past.

Let me give a few instances of what I have in mind, without repeating too much of the evidence presented in former papers.[3]

Old Israel had worshiped its only God, the Lord, in a plurality of sanctuaries: Hebron, Gilgal, Bethel, Shechem, Penuel, and so on. However, as early as 622 B.C.E., King Josiah of Judah abolished all other places of worship and unified the cult in one place: Jerusalem. Later legislation, biblical and postbiblical, retrojected the date of promulgation of this law to the times of Moses, the lawgiver, thus invalidating *a posteriori* all cultic sites that had not been sanctioned by the presence of the divine tabernacle erected by Moses himself. Thus a problem was created concerning righteous Israelites such as Joshua or Gideon, whenever older stories had represented them as worshiping in what came later to be considered illegitimate sanctuaries.

A case in point is Josh 24:1. The MT tells us that Joshua "assembled all the tribes of Israel at Shechem . . . and they presented themselves before God." The phrase "present oneself before God" implies a temple. But how could Joshua avail himself of such an illicit site? The problem was solved by a scribe whose work is reflected in the LXX. In the latter we read: Καὶ συνήγαγεν Ἰησοῦς πάσας φυλὰς Ισραηλ εἰς Σηλω κτλ. 'And Joshua assembled all the tribes of Israel to Shilo'. . . . This was an apt solution, because Shilo was the place of the divine tabernacle (Josh 18:1). That this was really the point of the corrector is made clear in v. 25 where the LXX reads:

καὶ ἔδωκεν αὐτῷ νόμον καὶ κρίσιν ἐν Σηλω ἐνώπιον τῆς σκηνῆς τοῦ θεοῦ Ισραηλ.

And he [Joshua] gave them [the people] law and judgment in Shilo, before the tabernacle of the God of Israel.

The MT, however, has a shorter text here: "and he gave them law and judgment in Shechem."

In accord with these divergencies, the MT in v. 26 mentions "the sanctuary of the Lord." The LXX has no sanctuary, just "before the Lord."

To sum up, the MT has Shechem and its sanctuary of the Lord; the LXX, on the other hand, has Shilo and the tabernacle. Thus in the LXX, Joshua's action is legitimized. The rationale motivating this legitimation is presented in

3. A. Rofé, "Methodological Aspects of the Study of Biblical Law," *Jewish Law Association Studies* (ed. B. S. Jackson; Atlanta, 1986) 2.1–16; idem, "The Nomistic Correction in Biblical Manuscripts and Its Occurrence in 4QSamª," *RevQ* 54 (1989) 247–54; and compare: L. Mazor, "A Nomistic Reworking of the Jericho-Conquest Narrative Reflected in the LXX to Joshua 6:1–20," *Textus* 18 (1995) 47–62.

the Mishna, *m. Zebaḥ.* 14:4–8, where the history of Israelite worship is expounded from the point of view of an adherent to Mosaic law, that is, from a nomistic point of view:

> ... After the tabernacle was set up, the high-places were permitted. ... When they came to Shilo, the high-places were forbidden ... and that was the Resting Place. ... When they came to Nob and Gibeon, the high-places were permitted. ... When they came to Jerusalem, the high-places were forbidden and were never permitted and that was the Inheritance. ...[4]

Therefore, these readings of the LXX in Joshua 24 appear to reflect a concern of scribes writing Hebrew in Palestine, not of Greek-speaking translators in Egypt. Plausibly, then, the Greek faithfully rendered a Hebrew Vorlage.

The scribes of the Second Commonwealth paid no less attention to the details of ritual in the sanctuary, that is, to whether or not it was performed according to the biblical Priestly law. Their concern can be detected in quite a number of readings in the book of Samuel, all dealing with the "legitimate" temple of Shilo. Besides the ones dealt with elsewhere,[5] I would like to point out three passages.

In 1 Sam 3:3 one reads: "... and Samuel was sleeping in the temple of the Lord where the Ark of God was." For an orthodox Jew, this is a rather peculiar assertion: how could Samuel, not a priest according to all authorities, lie in the innermost chamber of the temple, where even the high priest of the Second Temple would enter only once a year? Indeed, one need only check the Masoretic punctuation, the Targum, and the comment in the Talmud,[6] to see how the rabbis, having discerned this problem, sidestepped it. Now the Septuagint, codex B, translates this clause:

καὶ Σαμουηλ ἐκάθευδεν ἐν τῷ ναῷ, οὗ ἡ κιβωτὸς τοῦ θεοῦ

And Samuel was sleeping in the temple where the Ark of God was.

---

4. Tov follows Holmes in asserting "that the location of the covenant has been altered to Shilo in the wake of such verses as *Jos.* XVIII, 1ff.; XXI, 2; XXII, 9, 12"; see E. Tov, "Midrash-Type Exegesis in the LXX of Joshua," *RB* 85 (1978) 50–61, esp. p. 59; S. Holmes, *Joshua: The Hebrew and Greek Texts* (Cambridge, 1914) 8–9. However, the scribes' conceptions of the history of legitimate worship count much more than the attraction of passages of similar content.

5. See above, n. 2. Add now: Z. Talshir, "The Contribution of Diverging Traditions Preserved in the Septuagint to Literary Criticism of the Bible," *VII Congress of the International Organization for Septuagint and Cognate Studies, Paris 1992* (ed. L. Greenspoon and O. Munnich; Atlanta, 1995) 21–41, esp. pp. 25–28.

6. The Targum (ad loc.) runs: "... Samuel was lying in the court of the Levites and a voice was heard from the temple of the Lord where the ark of the Lord was." The *Babylonian Talmud, b. Qidd.* 78b, rephrases the verse this way: "The lamp of God had not yet gone out in the temple of the Lord and Samuel was lying in his place."

The absence of Κυρίου 'Lord' here may look casual. But it is more probable, in my opinion, that it has been left out because a late scribe found the flat declaration that Samuel was sleeping in the temple of the Lord offensive.

In favor of this explanation one should adduce the recently found 4QSam[a]. At this point, we are told, space considerations imply that the scroll ran,

And Samuel was sleeping in the palace,

using the word בהיכל, which can mean any palace. Samuel was sleeping in the *hêkāl*, nothing else. Neither the Lord nor His ark were mentioned in this verse.[7]

It is this kind of sensitivity that explains the divergencies between the MT and the LXX in 1 Sam 1:9, 14.[8] This time it is the LXX that presents the longer and, in my view, the primary text.

The MT reads in v. 9: "Hannah rose after the eating in Shilo and after the drinking." The LXX represents a plus: καὶ κατέστη ἐνώπιον κυρίου 'and stood before the Lord'. And in the MT v. 14, Eli says to Hannah: "remove your wine from you." In the LXX, it is the servant of Eli who says these words, and then comes a plus again: καὶ πορεύου/ἄπελθε ἐκ προσώπου κυρίου 'and go away from the presence of the Lord'.

The pluses of the LXX concur in telling us the same fact: Hannah stood in the presence of the Lord, which by implication means the inner chamber of the temple. This problematic assertion has been struck out by the scribes who produced the proto-Masoretic Text.

Let me now touch upon a distinct type of nomistic correction. Here again the LXX appears to witness the primary reading. The repugnance, even the abhorrence, of Jews toward swine is well known; it is first expressed in Deut 14:8 and Lev 11:7, which forbid eating pork along with other impure animals. Yet, one may doubt if this prohibition was practiced in ancient Israel.

In 3 Kgdms 20:19, the LXX reads:

Ἐν παντὶ τόπῳ, ᾧ ἔλειξαν αἱ ὕες καὶ οἱ κύνες τὸ αἷμα Ναβουθαι, ἐκεῖ λείξουσιν οἱ κύνες τὸ αἷμά σου

In every place where the swine and the dogs licked the blood of Naboth there shall the dogs lick your blood.

---

7. P. K. McCarter, *I Samuel* (AB 8; Garden City, N.Y., 1980) 95. Strangely enough, McCarter comments: "One is tempted to regard this shorter reading as superior."

8. The following readings are attested by both MS B and the Lucianic recension; cf. A. E. Brooke, N. McLean, and H. St. J. Thackeray, *The OT in Greek*, 2/1 (Cambridge, 1927) ad loc.; N. Fernández Marcos and J. R. Busto Saiz, *El Texto antioqueno de la Biblia griega*, vol. 1: *1–2 Samuel* (Madrid, 1989) ad loc.

In 3 Kgdms 22:38:

καὶ ἐξέλειξαν αἱ ὕες καὶ οἱ κύνες τὸ αἷμα.[9]

And the swine and the dogs licked up the blood.

In both places the MT does not mention swine, just dogs.

I consider it most plausible that the swine were omitted from the texts in the course of transmission, out of deference to past generations. It could not be admitted that even in the sinful city of Samaria pigs would be raised. The Jewish attitude of abhorrence seems to have developed in the Hasmonean period.[10] At the beginning of the period, in 167 B.C.E., and at its end, in 65 B.C.E., we hear about scandalous episodes of attempted pig sacrifices (1 Macc 1:47; 2 Macc 6:18–7:42; *b. Soṭa* 49b; *b. B. Qam.* 82b; *b. Menaḥ.* 64b). The talmudic *Baraita* connects the following with the second incident: "Cursed be the man who will grow pigs and cursed be the man who will teach his son Greek wisdom" (ibidem in the Talmud).

Taking this evidence into account, one additional divergence between the MT and the LXX might be elucidated. In, LXX[B] of 2 Sam 17:8, David is compared:

ὡς ἄρκος ἠτεκνωμένη ἐν ἀγρῷ καὶ ὡς ὗς τραχεῖα ἐν τῷ πεδίῳ

כדב שכול בשדה וכחזירה זועפת (?) בבקעה (?)

like a bereaved bear in the field and like a raging boar in the plain.

The second simile is not represented in the MT.[11] Was it omitted out of respect for David? A late Jewish copyist would shy away from a swine metaphor, all the more when applied to God's chosen king.

It is not only Jewish legal ideology and practice that influenced the transmission of biblical books; so did Jewish legendary reworking of the biblical stories, a direction developed in what is usually defined as Jewish Haggadah or Aggadah. The characteristics of Aggadah have repeatedly been studied in the last generation, by such authorities as Isaac Heinemann and Joseph Heinemann (not related), Jonah Fraenkel and Avigdor Shinan.[12] Here I shall content myself

---

9. Here again LXX[Luc] = MT; cf. N. Fernández Marcos and J. R. Busto Saiz, *El texto antioqueno de la Biblia griega*, vol. 2: *1–2 Reyes* (Madrid, 1992) ad loc.

10. For pre-Hellenistic times, see R. de Vaux, "Les sacrifices de porcs en Palestine et dans l'Ancien Orient," *Von Ugarit nach Qumran* (O. Eissfeldt Festschrift; BZAW 77; Berlin, 1958) 250–65.

11. Nor does it show in the Lucianic recension; see n. 8, above.

12. I. Heinemann, *The Methods of Aggadah* (2d ed.; Jerusalem, 1954) [Heb.]; J. Heinemann, *Aggadah and Its Development* (Jerusalem, 1974) [Heb.]; J. Fraenkel, *The Methods of Aggadah and Midrash* (Givataim, 1991) [Heb.]; A. Shinan, *The Biblical Story as Reflected in Its Aramaic Translations* (Tel Aviv, 1993) [Heb.].

with highlighting only three characteristics. These belong to secondary matters but nevertheless explain divergences between the MT and the LXX, thus helping us decide which text is primary and which secondary. To my knowledge, these features have not yet been treated in systematic scholarly discussion.

One of the trends that have been pointed out in Jewish Aggadah is the spurious identification of two biblical heroes who share the same name or the same patronym.[13] A well-known instance of this method is the identification of Obadiah, the steward of the palace of Ahab (mid–ninth century B.C.E.) mentioned in 1 Kings 18, with the prophet Obadiah, who prophesied against Edom after the fall of Jerusalem (first half of the sixth century B.C.E.), nearly 300 years later. The identification is made in *b. Sanh.* 39b, as follows:

> The vision of Obadiah. Thus says the Lord God concerning Edom (Obadiah, v. 1). Why particularly Obadiah against Edom? R. Isaac said: The Holy One, blessed be He, said: Let Obadiah, who has lived with two wicked persons [i.e., Ahab and Jezebel] and yet has not taken example from their deeds, come and prophesy against wicked Esau [i.e., Edom] who lived with two righteous persons [i.e., Isaac and Rebekah] and yet did not learn from their deeds.

The same Aggadic trend appears to have affected the transmission of biblical manuscripts. There are two prophets by a similar name: Micaiah, a prophet to Ahab, about 850 B.C.E., and Micah, titular of a book of prophecies, who flourished in Judah some 120 years later. Now at the end of the story about Micaiah in 1 Kgs 22:28a, one reads that he told the king:

> If you safely return home, the Lord has not spoken through me!

Then we read:

> And he said: "Listen, you peoples, all of you" (1 Kgs 22:28b).

What is the meaning of this last sentence? And who are the peoples referred to here? Could he refer in this way to Israel and Judah? And what is the need for this last call for attention right here? Now, if we take into account the fact that these very same words open the prophecy of Micah (Mic 1:2), then we are led to conjecture that it was some late scribe who tried to identify the Micaiah of 1 Kings 22 with Micah the Morashtite, whose book is part of the prophetic canon.[14]

What favors this conclusion, and what may be of special interest in the present context, is the fact that the previously mentioned sentence, "And he

---

13. Heinemann, *Methods of Aggadah*, 29–30.

14. This late scribe should not be identified with a Dtr author or redactor; pace E. Ball, "A Note in 1 Kings XXII,28," *JTS* n.s. 28 (1977) 90–94.

said: Listen, you peoples, all of you," is not represented by LXX[B] and the Lucianic manuscripts. Apparently it did not appear in the Hebrew Vorlage of the Old Greek.

Thus we reach a twofold conclusion: (1) Aggadic elements did sometimes penetrate biblical manuscripts, and (2) it is difficult to assume that the conservative archetype of the MT accepted such additions in late periods; most likely they belong to pre-Hasmonean times, that is, before 167 B.C.E. Hence a relatively early date for the origin of Jewish Aggadah is suggested.

One further characteristic of Jewish Aggadah is its tendency to reshape a biblical narrative by creating new roles in it. In this way the narrative's plot is either made livelier, because more action appears, or sometimes rationalized, since heroes are made to act in a more consistent way. The means for this remodeling of narratives are both the addition of new characters and the differentiation of actions by attributing distinct roles to the heroes of the biblical story.

The former means, the addition of new characters, is seen for instance in the *Genesis Apocryphon*, a Jewish legendary reworking of Genesis, dated by scholars to the first century B.C.E. In the biblical story of Abram and Sarai in Egypt, only two personae take an active part, Abram and Pharaoh; the third one, Sarai, is passive (Gen 12:10–20). The *Genesis Apocryphon*, unsatisfied with this sobriety, adds two more personae: Hyrqanus, a minister of Pharaoh, and Lot, Abram's nephew. Their exchange brings home to Pharaoh the reason for his predicament:

> Then Hyrqanos came to me and begged me to come and pray over the King and lay my hands upon him that he might be cured, for [he had seen me] in a dream. But Lot said to him: Abram my uncle cannot pray for the King, while his wife Sarai is with him. Now go tell the King. . . .[15]

This situation obtains in the Septuagint, in a passage already treated above, 1 Sam 1:14. The MT reads there:

And Eli said to her: how long will you be drunk . . . ?

But the LXX reads:

καὶ εἶπεν αὐτῇ τὸ παιδάριον Ηλι κτλ.

And the servant of Eli said to her. . . .

---

15. I have followed the translation of J. A. Fitzmyer, *The Genesis Apocryphon of Qumran Cave I* (BibOr 18A; 2d ed.; Rome, 1971) 65.

It seems to me that a late scribe considered it improper for Eli to misjudge the personality of Hannah in such a way. Therefore the mistake was attributed to his servant, a suitable character invented for this purpose.[16]

The second means, the attribution of distinct roles to already extant heroes, appears to be more widespread. A few instances only can be offered here for this category.

In the story of Genesis 14, one reads about the kings of Sodom and Gomorrah who, being defeated in battle, fled and fell into bitumen pits (Gen 14:10). The *Genesis Apocryphon* (xxi 32–33) endeavors to improve the tale: the king of Sodom was routed and fled, while the king of Gomorrah fell into the bitumen pits.[17] Plausibly, this differentiation of the lot of the two kings was brought about by the fact that the king of Sodom later reemerges in the story at the celebration of the victory of Abram by Melchizedek (Gen 14:17, 21, 22).

The Bible states that when Pharaoh caught up with the Israelites at the Reed Sea, they reacted with fear and complaint:

> Greatly frightened, the Israelites cried out to the Lord. And they said to Moses: Was it for want of graves in Egypt that you brought us to die in the wilderness? What have you done to us, taking us out of Egypt? Is this not the very thing we told you in Egypt, saying, "Let us be, and we will serve the Egyptians, for it is better for us to serve the Egyptians than to die in the wilderness"? (Exod 14:10–12).

Later Jewish legend created here three or four roles.[18] The Tannaitic Midrash *Mekilta de Rabbi Ishmael* commented:

> The Israelites at the Reed Sea were divided into four groups. One group said: "Let us throw ourselves into the sea." One said: "Let us return to Egypt." One said: "Let us fight them." And one said: "Let us cry out against them" (*Bešallaḥ: Wayeḥi,* §II, end).

---

16. Another possibility to be taken into account is the presence of secondary assimilation to an analogous biblical story. In this case, the servant of Eli would assume the role first attributed to Gehazi in the Shunnamite story, 2 Kgs 4:27; see Y. Zakovitch, "Assimilation in Biblical Narratives," in *Empirical Models for Biblical Criticism* (ed. J. H Tigay; Philadelphia, 1985) 175–96.

17. Fitzmyer, *Genesis Apocryphon,* 71. A similar diversification in contradistinction to Scripture is found in the Babylonian Talmud concerning the sons of Eli: Hophni sinned, Phinehas did not (*b. Šabb.* 55b). This Aggadah was probably imported from Palestine; cf. J. Heinemann, *Aggadah and Its Development,* 166–67; M. Beer, "The Sons of Eli in Rabbinic Legend," *Bar-Ilan: Annual of Bar-Ilan University* 14–15 (1977) 79–93, esp. pp. 91–92 [Heb.].

18. Cf. the discussion by Joseph Heinemann, *Aggadah and Its Development,* 92–93. He convincingly argues that there were originally three roles, the fourth being merely a duplication of the third. ·

Pseudo Philo's *Liber antiquitatum biblicarum* reads:

> Tunc considerantes metum temporis, filii Israel in tres divisiones con-
> siliorum diviserunt sententias suas. Nam tribus Ruben et tribus Ysa-
> char, et tribus Zabulon, et tribus Symeon dixerunt: Venite mittamus
> nos in mare. Melius est enim nos in aqua mori, quam ab inimicis
> concidi. Tribus autem Gad, et tribus Aser, et tribus Dan et tribus
> Neptalim dixerunt: Non, sed revertamur cum eis, et si voluerint do-
> nare nobis vitam serviamus eis. Nam tribus Levi et tribus Iuda, et
> Ioseph et Beniamin dixerunt: Non sic, sed accipientes arma nostra,
> pugnemus cum eis, et erit Deus nobiscum (10.3).[19]

In English:

> Then, as they considered the fear of the moment, the Israelites severed
> their decisions into three divisions of counsels. For the tribes of Reu-
> ben, Issachar, Zebulun and Simeon said: Come, let us cast ourselves
> into the sea, for it is better for us to die in the water than to be slain
> by enemies. And the tribes of Gad, Asher, Dan and Naphtali said: No,
> let us return with them, and if they grant us life, we serve them. But
> the tribes of Levi, Judah, Joseph and Benjamin said: Not so, but let us
> take our weapons and fight them, and God be with us.[20]

And the Samaritan *Memar Merqa* presented a similar homily:

> They were divided at the sea into three divisions. Each division made
> a statement and the great prophet made a reply corresponding to each
> statement. The first division said: "Let us . . . go back to Egypt and let
> us serve the Egyptians . . . for it would have been better for us . . . than
> to die in the wilderness." The great prophet Moses said: "You shall
> never see them again." The second division said: "Let us flee from
> the Egyptians into the desert." The great prophet Moses said to them:
> "Stand firm, and see the salvation of the Lord, which He will work for
> you today." The third division said: "Let us arise and fight against the
> Egyptians." The great prophet Moses said to them: "The Lord will
> fight for you, and you have only to be still."[21]

---

19. Cf. G. Kisch (ed.), *Pseudo-Philo's Liber Antiquitatum Biblicarum* (Notre Dame, Ind., 1949) ad loc.

20. In this rendering, I have deviated somewhat from M. R. James, *The Biblical Antiquities of Philo* (London, 1917) 104.

21. J. MacDonald, *Memar Marqah*, vol. 2: *The Translation* (BZAW 84; Berlin, 1963) 167; cf. Z. Ben-Ḥayyim, *Tibat Marqe* (Jerusalem, 1988) 274–75.

It is impressive that basically the same Aggadah appears in three utterly distinct sources. This wide dissemination indicates, in my opinion, that the core of the legend must have been relatively old, perhaps going back to Hasmonean times, when the question of how to behave when overtaken by the Seleucid army was a crucial one. In any case, there is no doubt that this diversification of roles, perpetrated by the Jewish Aggadah, lent vivacity to the biblical story.[22]

With this phenomenon in mind, we come to discuss the scene at the gate in Ruth 4. In vv. 9–10, Boaz addresses the elders and all the people: "You are witnesses today." . . . In v. 11, "all the people at the gate and the elders said: 'We are witnesses. May the Lord make the woman who is coming into your house like Rachel and Leah. . . .'"

The LXX reads v. 11 in a different way:

καὶ εἴποσαν πᾶς ὁ λαὸς οἱ ἐν τῇ πύλῃ Μάρτυρες, καὶ οἱ πρεσβύτεροι εἴποσαν Δῴη κύριος τὴν γυναῖκά σου κτλ.

All the people at the gate said: "We are witnesses." And the elders said: "May the Lord make your woman. . . ."

There has been disagreement among commentators whether the MT or the LXX should be preferred.[23] In favor of the former, one can summon the chiasm of v. 11 vis-à-vis v. 9: "Boaz said to the elders and all the people" (v. 9); "All the people and the elders said to Boaz" (v. 11) Chiasm is indeed a beloved figure of speech in ancient Hebrew diction! On the other hand, how appropriate the diversification of roles is according to the LXX: the people function as witnesses and the elders follow up by adding their blessing. However, now that we have identified the phenomenon of diversification of roles in biblical stories as being characteristic of Jewish Aggadah, there can be no doubt that the MT represents the primary text and the LXX the secondary.

Was there a Hebrew Vorlage before the reading of the LXX in Ruth 4:11? Two facts militate in favor of this hypothesis. (1) The diversification of roles in biblical stories characterizes Palestinian Jewish Aggadah, as pointed out above. (2) We have already noted how an Aggadic element crept into the MT in 1 Kgs 22:28. Further instances of this phenomenon are now attested in Qumran Hebrew manuscripts.[24]

---

22. Further instances of this characteristic of Jewish Midrash are quoted and discussed in my essay "The Septuagint to Ruth 4:11: A Midrashic Dramatization," *Texts, Temples, and Traditions: A Tribute to Menahem Haran* (ed. M. V. Fox et al.; Winona Lake, Ind., 1996) 119*–24* [Heb.].

23. Bibliographical references have been given in my article cited in the preceding note.

24. Cf. A. Rofé, "The Acts of Nahash according to 4QSam[a]," *IEJ* 32 (1982) 129–33; idem, "Moses' Mother and Her Maid according to an Exodus Scroll from Qumran (4QExod[b])," *BM* 40 (1994/95) 197–202 [Heb.].

The Greek translation of Ruth has been recognized as a late version originating in Palestine.[25] Indeed, it has points of contact with Aquila, such as the
translation of שדי as ἱκανός, and with proto-Theodotion, when rendering גם as
καί γε. Nevertheless, it seems to me possible, and even probable, that the deviation from the MT in Ruth 4:11 is not the work of the late translator, since
otherwise he is known to faithfully adhere to a proto-MT text; Ruth 4:11 reflects, in my view, a Hebrew variant that originated in Jewish lore in Hellenistic and Roman times.

25. Cf. M. Harl, G. Dorival, and O. Munnich, *La Bible grecque des Septante* ([Paris], 1988)
83–111. I have benefited from the advice of P. G. Borbone (Turin) on this point.

PART 3

Postbiblical and Rabbinic Studies

Rabbinic Mythmaking and Tradition: The Great Dragon Drama in *b. Baba Batra* 74b–75a

MICHAEL FISHBANE
University of Chicago

The "Great Dragon Drama" is an old story, widespread and varied throughout the scriptures and mythologies of the world. The episodes reported in *b. B. Bat.* 74b–75a are also old and evoke motifs known from ancient Canaan, Israel, and Mesopotamia—not to mention Hellenistic, Jewish, and Christian literatures. As a whole, these episodes are set within a series of (primarily) fantastic fish tales and equally wondrous speculations on the future estate of the righteous and Jerusalem (73a–75b), and this string of traditions itself interrupts a sober consideration of the legal sale and acquisition of ships (and their stores). There is thus an initial presumption that the dragon episodes are generically part of the tall tales that introduce them and with the same minimal coherence to be expected of mnemonic or thematic anthologies.[1] But presumptions are at best a first suspicion, to be carefully evaluated and examined. Moshe Greenberg is our teacher in this and other respects—advocating critical thinking of the highest order and urging simultaneous respect for the received text as a literary whole. His interest in materials spanning ancient Near Eastern and rabbinic literatures is well known, and it is therefore an honor to dedicate this study to him with unfailing respect and deep gratitude for our friendship.[2]

* * *

The collection of dragon traditions in *b. B. Bat.* 74b–75a begins with the citation of Gen 1:21, "Elohim created the great sea monsters (*tannînîm*)," and

---

1. Compare the collections in *b. Ketub.* 111b–112a and *Lev. Rab.* 22.4 (M. Margulies edition; Jerusalem: Wahrmann, 1972) 2.503–11.
2. The present essay is part of a larger work on "Biblical Myth and Rabbinic Mythmaking" near completion. I wish to thank Profs. Marc Hirshman and Erica Reiner for comments and observations.

offers two explanations of the term used for the water dragons, the first being an Aramaic rendering, the second an identification (by R. Yoḥanan) of the creatures with the Leviathans described in Isa 27:1 as "elusive" and "twisting" serpents.[3] There then follow eight groups of tradition subdivided into two triads and one pair. The two triads are each preceded by mnemonic markers indicating the sequence of (three) incipits in each group; the final pair has no such tag. The three units all contain named traditions, and each is formulated in a distinctive and patterned style. Interspersed throughout are characteristic rabbinic discussions of alternative interpretations; some of these are cited verbatim in the tradent's name, while others are the words of the (anonymous) editor.

The first triad reports three mythic traditions, each with the introit *ʾāmar R. Yĕhûdâ ʾāmar Rab* 'R. Yehudah said in the name of Rab'. The first (I) states that "everything that the Holy One, blessed be He, created was created male and female" and goes on to speak specifically of Leviathan (citing the double reference in Isa 27:1) and Behemoth (on the basis of Job 40:16). We learn that had these monsters mated with their kind, "the entire world" would have been "destroyed," and so God intervened. He castrated the male Leviathan and killed (and salted) the female; whereas with respect to the two Behemoths, the male was castrated and the female "cooled off."[4] In both cases, the female of the species was set aside "for the righteous for the world to come." But in the meantime, God sported with the male Leviathan (Ps 104:26).

Tradition I thus presents a primordial event in which the Creator maimed and killed sea and land monsters for the sake of the creation as a whole. No battle or resistence is mentioned. In contrast, the second myth of this group (II) states that when the Holy One "desired to create the world," he told the tutelary Prince of the Sea (whom R. Isaac identifies as the sea monster Rahab) to "swallow all the waters of the world." However, the latter rebelled and was duly killed (as mentioned in Job 26:12) and also drowned, so that the stench of his corpse would not befoul the earth. By further contrast, the third tradition (III) reported by Rav Yehudah gives a geographical account of the flow of the Jordan from its headwaters in the north down to "the Great Sea," whence it flows "into the mouth of Leviathan." This mythic conclusion is adduced on the basis of Job 40:23 ("He is confident because the Jordan rushes forth to his mouth"); but Rabba b. Ulla properly observed that the subject of scripture here

---

3. The terms *bārîaḥ* and *ʿăqallāṭôn* are an old crux, found first in Ugaritic myth (UT 67:I: 1–2 = CTA 5.1.1–2; and ʿnt III:38 = CTA 3.3.38); I have followed the NJPSV here (rendering 'elusive' and 'twisting', respectively). Many medievals interpreted the first term to mean 'stretching'; cf. Ibn Balʿam (citing Ibn Janah), Ibn Ezra, and Qimḥi. For the second term, compare Ibn Ezra and Metzudat David. R. Yoḥanan clearly understands the terms to refer to *two* serpents, not one with synonymous epithets (as the plain sense suggests).

4. I.e., the sexual urge was diminished; compare *Gen. Rab.* 87:4 (Theodor-Albeck edition; Jerusalem: Wahrmann, 1965) 3.1072–73, and *y. Hor.* 2:5 (46d).

is Behemoth.[5] He then offers a synthetic position (namely, that *"Behemoth* is confident because the Jordan rushes into the mouth of Leviathan"), and with this the matter rests.

The second triad of mythic traditions now follows, each with the same patterned introit: *kî ʾātāʾ R. Dîmî ʾāmar Rabbî Yôḥānān/Yônātān* 'When Rav Dimi came, he said in the name of Rabbi Yoḥanan/Yonatan'. In the printed edition of the Talmud, the first and third traditions are in the name of R. Yoḥanan, although other versions read either R. Yoḥanan or R. Yonatan throughout.[6] Presumably, two distinct chains of authority (or orthographically similar names) have been fused. Whatever the case, the content of the fourth tradition (IV) is a list of the seas and rivers "that surround the Land of Israel," including the Great Sea and the Jordan River. In this context, such information seems merely to provide geographical specificity to the prooftext "for He (God) has founded it upon the seas and established it upon the rivers" (Ps 24:2), where "it" is interpreted as referring to the land of Israel ("the land" in v. 1 being construed nationally). But the plain sense of scripture is otherwise: the "land" clearly means the "earth," and the verbs evoke primordial acts of creation. There is thus a mythic allusion embedded in the citation, long since metaphorized by poetic or geographical perspectives.

The ensuing two traditions are more manifestly mythic. The fifth (V) has Rav Dimi say (in R. Yonatan's name) that "in the future," the angel Gabriel will perform an animal hunt (*qĕnēgîʾā*) of Leviathan,[7] a gamesome challenge initiated by God's query, "Can you draw out Leviathan with a fish hook?" (Job 40:25), which the angel is not up to without divine aid (for "only his Maker can draw the sword after him," Job 40:19). This fantastic scene is followed by another tradition (VI) that dramatizes the awesome monstrosity of Leviathan and Behemoth. The Leviathan, when hungry, has such ferocious breath that "he makes the depths seethe like a cauldron" (Job 41:23a); whereas Behemoth, when thirsty, gulps huge quantities of water and leaves a furrow-like "path" in "his wake" (v. 24a). R. Dimi adds that Leviathan's breath is so odiferous that God put the beast's head among the perfumes of Eden, lest its stench overwhelm the world. Proof is found in a creative reading of Job 41:23b. R. Aḥa b.

---

5. For a modern argument that the recipient of the waters is Leviathan, see N. H. Tur-Sinai, *The Book of Job: A New Commentary* (Jerusalem: Kiryat-Sefer, 1967) 557–58 and 562–63 (comments on vv. 15, 23, and 25).

6. For R. Yoḥanan, see MS Hamburg 165 (19); for R. Yonatan, see *Midraš Hagādôl*, ad Gen 1:21; *Yalqut Shimʿoni*, Isaiah, #361; and R. N. Rabbinowicz, *Diqduqei Sopherim* (Munich, 1881) 12.234.

7. Compare Rashi, ad loc. (also citing *b. Ḥul.* 60b; *Arukh Ha-Shalem* (A. Kohut edition; Vienna, 1926) 7.132. The term is Greek *kunēgia* (compare this topos in *Sibiline Oracles* 3.805–7, with the term *kunegesia*). In *Pesiqta de-Rab Kahana*, Sup. 2 ([B. Mandelbaum edition; New York: Jewish Theological Seminary of America, 1962] 456), the event is a "war" waged by the angelic host.

Jacob showed corresponding ingenuity in adducing from v. 24b that Behemoth's rampages leave a "hoary" foam on the deep for 70 years (v. 24b)—"not less."

Following the two triads is a final pair of traditions dealing with sea monsters. Each begins with the formulaic introit *ʾāmar Rabbâ ʾāmar Rabbî Yôḥā-nān* 'Rabba said in the name of Rabbi Yoḥanan', and each goes on to say that "the Holy One, blessed be He, will in time to come make" something "for the righteous from the" body "of Leviathan." According to the first of these traditions (VII), that something is a "banquet" from the monster's "flesh." Job 40:30 is used to prove the point through a clever rereading of 'traders shall traffic in him' (*yikrû ʿālâv ḥabbārîm*) as '(the scholarly) companions (*ḥăbērîm*) shall eat of him'. The paired variant (VIII) announces that the righteous will also be tabernacled by the skin of Leviathan, through an equally astonishing exegesis of Job 40:31a (for once the "darts" of destruction are read as the *sukkôt*-tabernacles of the righteous, the aggressive image of the source yields the promise of eschatological reward). The lesser righteous enjoy lesser gifts, as various passages come to prove (from Job 40:31b and 29, respectively; and from Isa 60:3). As earlier, the rabbinic myths are linked to scripture in sundry ways.

* * *

But what manner of sea menagerie does our talmudic text contain here? A casual editorial eye may see nothing special in the foregoing Leviathan myths, and even observe that the sequence is preceded by an earlier reference to the luminous eyes of the monster and followed by a medley of traditions revealing the wonders that will accrue to the righteous "in time to come." Seen thus, the myths are merely part of a chain of traditions—thematically clustered, to be sure, but without any overall coherence. But such a perspective misinterprets the details.

Viewed formally, the foregoing materials are (as noted) distinguished by three clusters of patterned introits that, in the case of the first two, even have a fixed, mnemonic sequence. These traditions are thus clearly marked off from the less-patterned Rabbah bar Bar Ḥana fish tales on the one side and the thematic medley of heavenly rewards on the other. What is more, the beginning and end of the series have a thematic cohesion that distinguishes them from the whole setting: tradition I speaks of the preservation of the female Leviathan (and Behemoth) 'for the righteous for the future' (*laṣaddîqîm lĕʿātîd lābôʾ*);[8] and this is exactly what is fulfilled in traditions VII and VIII, where the flesh and skin of Leviathan are enjoyed by the righteous. The temporal sequence of the pericope thus has a mythic span—from Urzeit to Endzeit, where First things correspond to Last things.

Once this is noticed, the role of R. Yoḥanan's teaching *before* our collection is clear. It will be recalled that he interpreted Gen 1:21 ("Elohim created

8. The word *ṣaddîqîm* is missing in MS Hamburg 165 (19) and other MSS; but this does not affect the overall theme.

the great sea monsters") in the light of Isa 27:1, so that the primordial monsters (*tannînîm*) of the first text are identified with the "elusive" and "twisting" Leviathans mentioned in the other. Clearly, R. Yoḥanan interpreted two Leviathans here (and not one, with two synonymous epithets). This being so, his teaching serves as a prologue to I, which cites this very passage in order to prove that God created the primeval sea monsters (and all other living things) "male and female."[9] What is more: in relation to the succeeding pericope, virtually every element of Isa 27:1 has a proleptic function. Let us start with v. 1a: "On that day, YHWH will punish (*yipqōd*), with His fierce, great, and mighty sword, Leviathan the elusive serpent—(and) Leviathan the twisting serpent." According to the plain sense of the passage, "that day" is the future time when the Lord will "punish" or requite the monster(s). But why? The prophet Isaiah does not say, and if he knows some myth, we do not know it from scripture. The rabbis filled this mythic gap. For them, the passage was easily construed (midrashically) to mean that in the end of days God will 'remember' (*yipqōd*) the (female) monster that he had "appointed" or "accounted" for the righteous[10] and will kill her consort with 'his sword' (*ḥarbô*). This very thing is accomplished in tradition V, when the male Leviathan is killed by God with 'his sword' (*ḥarbô*) before the final banquet is enjoyed.

Isa 27:1b assumes an equally proleptic function in this editorial context. From R. Yoḥanan's exegetical perspective, it is precisely the whole of v. 1 that permits his identification of the *tannînîm* ('monsters') in Gen 1:21 with the Leviathans in Isa 27:1a, in that the phrase "He (God) will slay (*wĕhārag*) the Dragon (*tannîn*) in the sea" (v. 1b) occurs just after the punishment forecast against the Leviathans (in v. 1a). Indeed, this very conjunction suggests that the two phrases are really one prophecy (doubly rendered by synonymous parallelism, with no special significance to be attached to the different dragon terms). But mythic midrash had other insights. Disconnected from the first clause, the verb *wĕhārag* would no longer double *yipqōd* (with a future sense) but be a simple perfect referring to a past event when God "killed" the *tannîn*. This is precisely how Isa 27:1b is construed in tradition I, where it is cited as a separate phrase. From a redactional perspective, R. Yoḥanan's opening prooftext may thus be understood to anticipate both this (past) event and another yet to come.

* * *

9. This view differs from the one in *Gen. Rab.* 7:4 (Theodor-Albeck edition, 1.52), where R. Idi states that neither Leviathan nor Behemoth was paired; according to Resh Laqish, Behemoth had a mate but was without desire. In my view, Rav gives a novel interpretation to Gen 1:27b. Following v. 27a, which states that God "created him" (namely, the human) in His image, the ensuing clause that "male and female He created them" begs interpretation; Rav has presumably related it to *all* living things.

10. Namely, reading *yipqōd* to mean that God will 'appoint', 'account', or 'set aside' the monster for the righteous.

The patterning of traditions reviewed so far suggests that the overall scheme of the collection is temporal. This sense is reinforced by tradition II, which refers to a rebellion by the tutelary Prince of the Sea at the beginning of creation. This monster refused God's command to swallow the waters and was duly destroyed. The prooftext evokes an echo of this mythic death from elsewhere in scripture. Perhaps, at first glance, this explains the occurrence of the ensuing tradition (III) about Leviathan, who *does* swallow the waters. Viewed thus, the very next tradition (IV) seems merely to be a thematic doublet dealing with several streams of water. We shall reconsider this matter later on, but for now let us group traditions III and IV and observe the following overall sequence in our pericope: (I) the creation and mating of primordial monsters at the beginning of time, with one Leviathan killed and set aside for the future; (II) the primordial rebellion of the Prince of the Sea and his death; (III and IV seem merely to be parenthetical references to seas and rivers throughout the land of Israel); (V) the future hunt of Leviathan and his death; (VI provides parenthetical traditions about the monsters' gastric and gustatory vices); and (VII–VIII) portray the events dealing with the use of Leviathan's body by the righteous in the future to come.

Thus together with its movement from past to future, the pericope develops toward thematic fulfillment: the two Leviathans at the beginning are slain—the female, at the outset; the male in due time, after the *qĕnēgîʾā*. Given this sequence linking the initial and final traditions, the double sea references in traditions III and IV seem interruptive. But one will observe that they occur in the center of this overall development and that their conjunction is deliberate. Indeed, the mnemonic markers manifest a clear editorial intention to join the two before resuming the opening thematics. Further reflection on this arrangement reveals the following chiastic structure.

	A	(I)	*Urzeit*: a Leviathan prepared for the righteous
	B	(II)	Death to the Sea dragon, in the beginning (Sea buried under water because of its stench)
C		(III)	The Jordan River and its flow
C		(IV)	The seas and rivers of the land of Israel
	B	(V)	Death to a Leviathan, in the future (VI Leviathan's odiferous breath perfumed)
	A	(VII–VIII)	*Endzeit*: the righteous partake of Leviathan

The linguistic and thematic connections of the outer frame (A) were adduced earlier. We may now observe that the inner frame (B) is similarly related. First and foremost are the two battle scenes—against the rebellious Sea and the wily, hard-to-catch Leviathan. God slays both monsters: the first by

trampling it;[11] the second by the sword.[12] But there are subsidiary themes linking the units. For example, in the first part of II, we read that 'when' (*běšāᶜâ
še-*) God began to create the world, he commanded the Prince of the Sea to
'open your mouth' (*pĕtaḥ pîkā*) and swallow the waters. The monster refused,
was killed, and was left to rot. The second section adds that 'were it not'
(*wĕʾilmālēʾ*) that God buried it in the sea, 'no creature would have been able
to withstand its stench' (*ʾên kol bĕrîyâ yĕkôlâ laᶜămôd bĕrêḥô*). Correspond-
ingly at the other end, we read first in V about the *qĕnēgîʾā* and that 'were
it not' (*wĕʾilmālēʾ*) that God intervened, the appointed angelic slayer 'would
have been unable' (*ʾên yākôl lô*) to succeed. The ensuing tradition IV adds that
'when' (*běšāᶜā še-*) Leviathan is thirsty, he fumes a foul odor 'from his mouth',
and 'were it not' (*wĕʾilmālēʾ*) that God perfumed his breath with the spices
of Eden, 'no creature would have been able to withstand its stench' (*ʾen kol
bĕrîyâ yĕkôlâ laᶜămōd bĕrêḥô*). These terms and phrases are virtually restricted
to this frame, so much so, that the trace of some editorial hand seems assured.[13] Presumably, tradition VI is itself a fragment of the final battle between Leviathan and Behemoth known from other midrashic sources.[14] This
episode is omitted in our pericope, except for the characterization of some of
the vile features of the contenders. The Talmud has transmitted it here in language that echoes and balances II.

Before proceeding to consider the middlemost pair of the pericope, I
would offer a comment on the pattern of prooftexts. Quite remarkably, citations are drawn from Job 40:16 (a+b), 25, 29, 30 (a+b), 31 (a+b); and 41:23
(a+b), 24 (a+b). Evidently we have before us part of a lost midrash on Job 40–
41, reworked into a myth spanning *Urzeit* to *Endzeit*.[15] Taken together, the

---

11. The verb used is *bāᶜat*, though the prooftext from Job 26:12 is *rāgaᶜ* (presumably a variant of *raqaᶜ* 'beat down'). In Job 9:8, God 'treads' (*dôrēk*) on Yam, while other rabbinic myths of
origins state that God 'trampled' (*kābaš*) the ancient waters at the beginning. *Tanḥuma, Ḥuqqat*, 1
(and *Num. Rab.* 18:22) use all three terms. In a wonderful play, *Tanḥuma, Berešit*, 1 states that
God "conquered" or "suppressed" the Tehom (*kābaš ʾet hattĕhôm*) with the Torah. The full mythic
undertone emerges by comparison with *Enuma Elish* IV 129 (*ikbus-ma bēlum ša Tiamtum išidsa*
'The lord [Marduk] trod on the legs of Tiamat').

12. According to *Midraš Alpha Beitot*, *v″h d″g* (S. Wertheimer, *Batei Midrashot* [2d ed.;
Jerusalem: Ktav Va-Seper, 1968] 2.438), God slaughters the monster ritually. In contrast, *Pesiqta
de-Rab Kahana* has God direct a final battle between Leviathan and Behemoth; while in *Tanḥuma,
Shemini*, 7, this double-death is a mutual ritual slaughter.

13. The word *ʾilmālēʾ* occurs twice in part I but without the other key phrases that mark the
relationship between II and V.

14. See n. 7; and also J. Schirmann, "The Battle between Behemoth and Leviathan according to an Ancient Hebrew *Piyyut*," *Proceedings of the Israel Academy of Sciences and Humanities*
(Jerusalem: Israel Academy of Sciences and Humanities, 1970) 4.350–59.

15. *Pesiqta de-Rab Kahana* adds mythic interpretations to Job 41:8, 9, 18, 19, 20, 21. For a
mythic reading of v. 17, see *Gen. Rab.* 4:4.

traditions encompassed by these passages are I, III, V, VI, VII, and VIII. This too is notable, for it will readily be observed that only traditions II and IV are unmarked by a Joban phrase. Most likely this is because neither deals with a dragon called Leviathan. In addition, one may even suggest that the theomachy (against the Sea) in II is not required by the themes of this cycle and that the river geography in IV is redundant, given the immediately preceding tradition about the Jordan. What, then, might account for the inclusion of traditions II and IV in our Talmudic myth?

Two considerations suggest an answer: the first is that tradition II is a combat occurring between the initial tradition about the mating of primordial sea dragons and the account of the Jordan's flow throughout the land; the second is that tradition IV links its reference to a total of 11 seas and rivers to Ps 24:2 ("For He [YHWH] has established it [the earth] upon the seas . . ."). Now, in and of themselves, the foregoing thematics of II and IV seem merely to add two more "sea" traditions to a string of Leviathan myths. But a comparative perspective raises another possibility, namely, that the final redaction of our talmudic pericope has been influenced by structural and topical features known from Mesopotamian sources.

The Babylonian myth of *Enuma Elish* is most pertinent in this regard. The myth begins with the mating of the primordial sea-gods Apsu and Tiamat and later, Lahmu and Lahamu (I 1–10); the ensuing noisy commotion of the offspring led to a cycle of antagonisms and revenge that, in due course, pitted the divine Marduk against Tiamat and her horde (IV 20–32); the battle resulted in Marduk's victory (IV 33–120), and the splitting of Tiamat's watery hulk to establish the upper and lower realms, including the founding of water springs and releasing "the Tigris and Euphrates through her eyes" (V 54–55);[16] and finally, Marduk built a temple and convened a banquet for the gods (VI 67–75). By comparison, our talmudic traditions take on new coherence, for it is now evident that the sequence of mating waters, theomachy, and earthly order are part of an ancient mythic pattern. Indeed, in the light of the Babylonian myth, the placing of traditions about the waters that flow through the land *after* the slaying of the sea monster makes structural and thematic sense, and what is more, this very nexus explains the citation and use of Ps 24:2. No mere praise, the statement that "[YHWH] has founded [the earth] *upon* the seas and established it *upon* the rivers" is now redolent with mythic implications.[17] One

16. For the text, see B. Landsberger and J. V. Kinnier Wilson, "The Fifth Tablet of 'Enuma Elis'," *JNES* 20 (1961) 160–61 (I have also examined the critical edition being prepared at The University of Chicago, courtesy of Prof. W. Farber). The image of the rivers emerging from the monster's eyes also appears in a late commentary to the myth; see E. Ebeling, *Tod und Leben nach den Vorstellungen der Babylonier* (Berlin: de Gruyter, 1931), vol. 1, 35:3.

17. It seems to me that the prooftext *in this context* has activated a latent "biblical" myth, for were this mythologem altogether lacking, it is hard to imagine its invention from this verse. The sequence of Ps 89:11–12 (slaying Rahab and creating cosmic order) is suggestive in this regard;

may even ponder whether the geographical notice of 11 seas and rivers mentioned alongside this prooftext is a mere gratuitous detail, since this is precisely the number of monsters who fight alongside Tiamat.[18] In any case, the overall redactional result is that traditions I–IV (death and the world order) + VII–VIII (booths and banquet) conform in structure and content to a celebrated and long-enduring mythic pattern from the ancient Near East. The mnemonic markers in the Talmud are thus more than an *aide de mémoire*. Rather, they impose the invariance of a specific mythic sequence on all future tradents. The inclusion (and position) of II and IV were absolutely necessary to this end.

The tradents mentioned in the talmudic pericope allow us to suggest further possibilities about the mythic traditions and their redaction.[19] To begin with, it is notable that a preponderance of traditions reported here derives from Eretz Israel: R. Yoḥanan bar Nappaḥa (d. 279) was head of the academy in Tiberias in the mid–third century C.E., and R. Isaac II was his student. What is more, R. Dimi visited the west on several occasions, and was known as a *nĕḥûtā*ʾ who 'came (back) down' to Babylon with traditions from Eretz Israel. On the other hand, it is also striking to note that all of the traditions in our pericope are associated with sages active at the Babylonian Academy of Pumbeditha: Rav Yehudah (d. 299; a contemporary of R. Yoḥanan, with whom he consulted)[20] founded this school, and Rabbah (d. 330) was a subsequent director (and a tradent of R. Yoḥanan);[21] in addition, Rav Dimi was associated with this academy (reporting to Abayye; d. 339),[22] and R. Aha b. Jacob lived

---

so, too, is the midrash that "the world was created *on* Leviathan" (cited by Ibn Ezra in the introduction to his Torah commentary). This myth is developed in Zohar, *Bo*ʾ (II 34a–35b) in profound ways. I shall discuss it at length elsewhere (see n. 2 above).

18. See *Enuma Elish* I 133–46 (with parallels in II and III). According to W. Lambert, the number 11 is part of a mythic revision of Ninurta mythology (where 8 monsters occur); see his "Ninurta Mythology in the Babylonian Epic," *Keilschriftliche Literaturen: Ausgewählte Vorträge der XXII. Rencontre Assyriologique Internationale, 1985* (ed. K. Hecker and W. Sommerfeld; Berlin: Reimer, 1986) 56–57. For other cases of 11 monsters, see p. 57 n. 6.

19. I am fully cognizant of the difficulties posed by named traditions in rabbinic sources. For the present subject, see p. 275 and n. 6 above; and in general, see the discussion of S. Stern, "Attribution and Authorship in the Babylonian Talmud," *JJS* 45 (1994) 28–51 (with literature cited). Nevertheless, the clusters in our pericope suggest some real or constructed tradition that cannot be outright dismissed.

20. R. Yehudah even consulted with R. Yoḥanan on occasion; see *b. Qidd.* 39a.

21. On the basis of various textual and analytical considerations, D. Sperber ("Hāʾim ʿâlâ Rabbâ lĕʾereṣ yiśrāʾēl?" *Sinai* 71 [1972] 140–45) rejects the possibility that Rabbah actually sat before R. Yoḥanan (even though he followed the master's methods; see *b. Šeb.* 10b). Many manuscripts read Rabba bar Bar Ḥana (instead of Rabba, as tradent of R. Yoḥanan) in *b. B. Bat.* 75a, but this does not undermine my overall argument, since bar Ḥana was a student of R. Yoḥanan, spent time in Pumbeditha, and met with R. Yehudah (see *b. Šabb.* 148a; *b. Pesaḥ.* 53b).

22. See *b. Ber.* 50a, *b. Šabb.* 72a, and *b. Qidd.* 12a.

nearby (in Pafunya). Accordingly, while it is evident that features (and even clusters) of the previously mentioned Near Eastern mythic pattern may have (also) existed in the west,[23] both the diversity of materials in our talmudic pericope *and* the provenance of its various tradents strongly suggest that what we have is a (new) rabbinic reformulation of ancient mythic traditions done in Pumbeditha, using local but also western (especially Tiberian) traditions.

The redactor of our talmudic pericope has thus created a composite myth from a series of separate, asyndetic traditions. His voice appears first in each of the various subunits, in that he introduces the tradents in whose name(s) the myths and prooftexts are given (or contested). Indeed, his voice is the continuous coordinator of the complex talmudic chorus in the various units. In this way, the topics are aligned and emplotted in such a way that the (local) debates are subordinated to the (larger) narrative development. The work of rabbinic myth-making is thus inseparable here from the process of tradition-building so central to the Talmud overall and indeed to its construction of a hierarchy of authoritative teachings and values.

A quite different hierarchy governs the spatial components of the pericope. In ascending order, these are: sea, earth, and heaven; together with their corresponding inhabitants: monsters and tutelary powers; human beings; angelic agents and God. This hierarchy not only moves along a natural-supernatural axis (with humans in between) but reveals the central value of our rabbinic myth: obedience to divine authority. Thus potentially uncontrollable or clearly rebellious natural forces must be contained or killed, even as controllable or variously obedient natural elements and human beings are variously celebrated or rewarded.[24]

The value scale of obedience is concretized around the mouth and ingestion. Thus in tradition I, the instinctual (and thus inherently uncontrollable) female Leviathan is set aside as food for the righteous (who obey God); in

23. See the discussions on traditions II and IV, above. The themes of killing and cleaving the sea monster seem to have been combined in Ugaritic myth, as well; compare Ch. Virolleaud, *Le Palais Royale d'Ugarit* (Paris: Imprimérie Nationale, 1957) 2.12 (who links ᶜnt III:33–43 to UT 1003:3–10); and the discussion of S. Loewenstamm, "Mîtôs ḥayyām běkitvê ʾûgārît wěziqātô ʾel mîtôs ḥayyām bamiqrāʾ," *EI* 9 (1969) 99–100. On the combination of the motif of splitting the sea, divine kingship, and temple-building in ancient Israel, compare Exodus 15 and the comments of S. Loewenstamm, *Massoret Yeṣiʾat Miṣrayim Behištalšelutah* (Jerusalem: Magnes, 1965) 114–15.

Western aspects of the *Enuma Elish* have been pointed out by T. Jacobsen, "The Battle between Marduk and Tiamat," *JAOS* 88 (1968) 104–8. Given the shared traditions, it may not be accidental that the myths of creation in *Tanḥuma, Ḥuqqat,* 1 include reference to the "sweet" and "salt waters" and the matter of their intermingling. In the Babylonian tradition, these waters are personified by Apsu and Tiamat, respectively. On the verbs *kābaš / kabāsu*, see n. 11 above.

24. For example, in VIII the righteous benefit maximally from the skin of Leviathan, while others partake of smaller pieces in descending degrees, depending on merit. The nations of the world are lowest in the hierarchy and only benefit from the radiance of the skin, which serves as an eschatological beacon to Zion.

tradition II the Prince of the Sea is commanded by God to 'open your mouth' (*pîkā*) and is killed for his resistence; in tradition III, the Jordan flows into the mouth (*pîw*) of Leviathan (or Behemoth), thus serving in an orderly way the habitable earth; in tradition V, the resistent and over-playful male Leviathan cannot be hooked by "his tongue" and must be slain; in tradition VI, we learn that when the monster Leviathan is hungry, he emits a foul odor from 'his mouth' (*pîw*), which God must deodorize with the spices of Eden (Behemoth also swallows water in gross gulps); and finally, in tradition VII, the righteous eat from the flesh of Leviathan, as promised long before.

From another angle, this obedience/disobedience split reveals the even deeper tension between nature and culture in our myth. The two are most dichotomous at the outset (in tradition I), where primitive desire (the monsters) and cultivated virtue (the righteous) are completely differentiated. Nevertheless, these poles are ultimately integrated at the end (in traditions VII–VIII). Indeed, through their ingestion of the erstwhile creatures of instinct (sacrificed by God for the sake of the creation), the righteous dramatically represent the transformative potential and ultimate triumph of (rabbinic) culture. Seated at their banquet under the luminous skins of Leviathan, the righteous are the Adamic figures of this myth—glorified in an embryo of light.[25]

25. On the one hand, the enthronement of the righteous in tabernacles has a clear messianic connotation; on the other, the canopy of skins alludes to the mythic quality of Adam's tunic. According to Ḥizquni, the "garments of skin" in Gen 3:21 are "from the skin of the mate of Leviathan, which the Holy One, be He blessed, slaughtered and salted the remainder for the righteous for the future to come." This interpretation is found in *Seper Daʿat Zeqenim* (Livorno, 1783); in the commentary of the Rosh on the Torah, in *Seper Hadar Zeqenim* (Livorno, 1840); and in the pentateuchal glosses of R. Yehudah b. Eliezer and R. Obadiah mi-Bertinoro, in *Baʿalei Ha-Tosaphot ʿal Ḥamishah Ḥumshei Torah* (Warsaw, 1876)—all in the name of a (lost) "midrash."

A Law and Its Interpretation

JUDAH GOLDIN

University of Pennsylvania

Two things stand out immediately in the compilations of the exegetical mid-rashim. The first is the determination of the compilers to provide comment on every verse in the sequence adopted by the biblical text. (This customary manner of pedagogy appeals to the rabbis as it does to scholars of Homer.) There may be interior digressions or detours and these too will be interpreted, but the framework is not abandoned. The second is their biblical erudition, their ability to quote from every book of the Bible, back and forth—with utter indifference to what we may call anachronism or even to gender, to single or plural interchange—to support or defend the interpretation of the particular verse they are explaining. More than just learning is required, to be sure; but without that learning, interpretation might appear arbitrary. " 'As God said'; where did He say it?"[1]

Verses can have more than one meaning, the compilers tell us; *dābār ʾaḥēr* ('another interpretation'). One interpretation is not necessarily preferred above others—a verse is only a compendium of meanings (that is why written To-rah requires oral Torah). Multiplicity is natural when conjecture is inevitable and, of course, when there are many scholars and advanced students engaged in study, each with a view of his own; was it ever otherwise in *schools*? Therefore, if you want nothing lost, preserve as much as you can[2] or assemble examples or review periodically (see *ʾAbot R. Nat.*, 24, p. 78). Each component

---

Author's note: I have been asked why I always adopt the Lauterbach edition of the *Mekilta* rather than the Horovitz-Rabin edition (see J. Goldin *The Song at the Sea* [1971] xi). Of course I always check the latter because of its fuller (?) cross references and recording of variants (not necessarily the last word). On the positive estimate of Lauterbach, no comparison intended, see Lieberman in *Kiryat Sepher* 12 (54–65), now reprinted in *Meḥqārîm bě-Tôrat ʾEreṣ Yiśrāʾēl* (Studies in Palestinian Talmudic Literature) (ed. David Rosenthal; Jerusalem: Magnes, 1991) 540ff.

    1. See the long list (26 examples) in *Mekilta Pisḥa* 12 (ed. Lauterbach, I, 89–94).

    2. Foreshadowed already by Sir 24:23–29 and also 8:8–9. In this mood, see also *ʾAbot R. Nat.* 18, p. 68.

of a verse enjoys a kind of autonomy plus interrelationship: every letter, every word, and needless to say, every verse has a lesson to teach.[3] They all shed light on each other. And since the texts are unvocalized, the consonants can yield kinetic and not static messages. *ʿĂlāmôt* ('maidens') can be *ʿal môt* ('to the point of death').

Evidence also is piled up. For this rhetorical approach, there is likewise a formula: *ka-yôṣēʾ bô* ('similarly') or *wĕ-ken* [*wĕ-kāʾn*] *ʾattâ môṣēʾ* ('so too [here] you will find'). The ability to recognize associations and correspondence between teachings extends the outreach of the interpretation just proposed for a particular verse and thus prevents possible inconsistencies in instruction (despite the presence of argument: dissent is not an end in itself).

Now, it is this very objective—flight from inconsistency—that compels attention to a passage (slightly condensed here) in *Sipre Numbers* (115, ed. Horovitz, 127–29; but compare *Sipre Zuṭâ*, 290) where the *ṣîṣit* commandment is discussed.

The biblical command is recorded in Num 15:37–41, but comment is especially concentrated on vv. 40–41: "Thus you shall remember and carry out all My commandments, and be holy to your God. I the Lord am your God, who brought you out of the land of Egypt to be your God; I the Lord am your God."

1. The two verbs, *zkr* ('remember') and *ʿśh* ('carry out'), come together to teach that there is a relation between keeping-in-mind and conduct; the former is like the latter, says the Midrash. Presumably the idea is that conduct will be the result of what first is on our minds; hence responsibility for both.

2. "Be holy." Holiness is indeed associated with *all* of God's commands ("all My commandments," vv. 39–40), but in our passage, says Rabbi, it refers specifically to the *ṣîṣit* commandment. Indeed, fulfillment of the *ṣîṣit* command increases the sanctity of Israel.[4]

3. Why does the *ṣîṣit* text in Numbers make mention of the subject of the Exodus from Egypt? What connection is there between them? . . . [an explanation of the "blue cord" requirement, v. 38, follows] . . . Then appears "another interpretation" for the recollection of the Exodus theme in connection with commands. A parable will explain this.[5] The son of the king's favorite friend was once taken captive, and the king redeemed him and said to the son, "You are not being redeemed from captivity in order to become a free man but to be my slave." If the son is now ordered by the king

---

3. *Midraš Tannaim*, p. 205.

4. See Issi ben Akiba in *Mekilta Kaspa* 2, III, 157. Cf. *Shabbata* 1, III, 200.

5. On midrashic parables, see now the study by David Stern, *Parables in Midrash* (Cambridge: Harvard University Press, 1991). On the fact that sometimes a parable will not fit, see *ʾAbot R. Nat.* 1, p. 6, top.

to do something, he may not refuse. When the king and son reached the capital (after a long journey), the king said to him, "Tie my sandals and bring my garments to the bath house." The son refused to perform these services; the king reminded him that he had to obey all of his orders. So too God said to the offspring of Abraham, God's "favorite friend," "You are My slaves. I did not redeem you (from Egypt) to be free; you must do whatever I command."[6]

The tone of voice is grim enough, as though God never called Israel, "my sons."[7] "You are My slaves!" (although *slave* is not necessarily pejorative). But tone of voice is not the chief problem here. What is perplexing is the content of the order: "Tie my sandals and bring my garments to the bath house." But this, among other things, is precisely what is forbidden to the master of a Hebrew slave.[8] How can God issue the kind of order that He has Himself condemned?

In the *Sipre* there is no protest at all, not even a murmur of surprise, as though the demands were thoroughly appropriate. Instead, the slave's rebellion reminds the commentator-compiler of the confrontation of elders with the prophet Ezekiel,[9] and this association is interpreted as dialogue: "Since," say the elders, "God put us in captivity, we are now free of His dominion. Are not slaves sold by their master free of him?" The prophet does not deny this but declares that if he sold them on condition of recovering them, they are not released from his authority. Israel is therefore not free (hence their wish to be like all others will not be granted: disobedience will be severely punished, as the verses proclaim).

By association of the demand in Numbers with the account in Ezekiel, the commentator has attempted to justify the Master's orders. Not unreasonable. But truly, by what right does the master have permission to demand what the law specifically forbids in the relation of master to slave? "Tie my sandals and bring my garments to the bath house!"[10]

Since this question is not raised or answered by the *Sipre*, it is especially significant to note how the Midrash continues: R. Nathan says: There is no

6. On the other hand, compare *Mekilta Beshallaḥ* 2, I, 190 and *Mekilta Simeon* (ed. Epstein-Melamed), p. 48, lines 5–6.

7. Deut 14:1; and see R. Meir in *Sipre Deut.* 96, pp. 157 and 308, pp. 346–47. On non-pejorative ʿeved, see *Sipre Deut.* 27, pp. 42ff.

8. Cf. *Mekilta Nezikin* 1, III, 5–6 and *Midraš Tannaim* 85. These restrictions incidentally prevented the complete dehumanization of the Hebrew slave.

9. Ezekiel 20; and see Moshe Greenberg's excellent translation and commentary (*Ezekiel 1–20* [AB 22; New York: Doubleday, 1983] 373–78, 379–88). Cf. the Passover *Haggadah* (ed. Goldschmidt, p. 45).

10. One may demand this only of his son or disciple (*Midraš Tannaim*, p. 18). Note also R. Yoḥanan ben Zakkai's instructions to his personal attendant (*šammaš*) in *ʾAbot R. Nat.* 14, p. 58. On *šammaš* see also *ʾAbot R. Nat.* 26, p. 82, line 5 from bottom.

commandment without its accompanying reward. Proof? An anecdote[11] of experience, despite its few hyperbolical touches.

There was once a man particularly fastidious with the *ṣîṣit* commandment. He heard that overseas (not in the Holy Land!) there was a prostitute whose fee was 400 zuz.[12] He sent her the amount and fixed an appointment. Her residence was lavishly furnished and she had a maidservant who would announce the arrival of clients to her mistress. When the man finally arrived, he was admitted, and just as they were about to enact what he came for, the four *ṣîṣîyôt* of his garment flew up like admonishing witnesses and began to beat his face. He immediately slid down to the ground. So did she. She exclaimed: "By the Agape of Rome,[13] I will not let you go before you tell me what blemish you have found in me."

"By the Temple Service,"[14] he exclaimed in turn, "I've seen no blemish in you, for in the whole world there is no beauty like yours. But we have a light-weight (!) commandment (*miṣwâ qallâ*!) from the Lord our God and in connection with it He wrote, 'I am the Lord your God, I am the Lord your God' two times (once at the beginning of the verse and once at the end of it, Num 15:41), (that is to say,) 'I am the Lord your God to reward, I am the Lord your God to punish!'"

"By the Temple Service," she (now) exclaimed,[15] "I will not let you go before you write out your name for me, the name of your city, and the name of the school where you study Torah." So he complied and gave his master's name too.

Whereupon she gave away all her wealth, one-third to the kingdom, one-third to the poor, and one-third she took along with her (to contribute to the academy?). She came to the Bet Midrash of R. Ḥiyya and said to him, "Master, make me a Jewess."

He said to her, "Has your eye perhaps been attracted to one of the students?" She took out and showed what had been written down, and R. Ḥiyya said to that student, "Rise and profit from your purchase. The bed she laid out for you in prohibition, now let her lay out for you with permission. This is her reward[16] in this world; as for the world to come, I can't even imagine it." R. Nathan's teaching is confirmed.

---

11. See also *Midraš ha-Gadol, Numbers* (ed. Fisch, 371–72).

12. On the number 400, see J. Goldin, *Studies in Midrash and Related Literature* (ed. B. L. Eichler and J. H. Tigay; Philadelphia: University of Pennsylvania Press, 1988) 81. On the anecdote, see also *b. Menaḥ.* 44a and *Leqaḥ Tob, Num.* 113 a–b.

13. Note a pagan's natural exclamation. On *Agape* see Morton Smith, *Tannaitic Parallels to the Gospels* (Philadelphia: Society of Biblical Literature, 1951) 172; S. Lieberman, *Greek in Jewish Palestine* (New York: Jewish Theological Seminary of America, 1942) 140–41. *Overseas*, according to Lieberman, means *Caesarea*.

14. Note well the Jew's expression, to which he is accustomed. (On light-weight command, compare *Sipre Deut.* 79, p. 145 and parallels.)

15. Observe how she has suddenly adopted the Jew's language!

16. *Her* reward, that her conduct had led her to. But his *ṣîṣit* has rescued him.

The whole section has moved with its verses from commentary on keeping-in-mind to conduct to the imperative and effect of holiness to a parable that incorporated a command whose details conflict with the law. The parable led to association with a confrontation recorded by Ezekiel in the form of dialogue. Like the slave, the people now wish to be entirely free. This, the prophet responds, is out of the question. So Israel must carry out what they have been commanded, for they are not free, like the son of the king's favorite, whom the king freed from captivity. R. Nathan's anecdote then supplements the academic and scholastic discussion and simultaneously introduces the influential role of the rabbi (R. Ḥiyya).

The compiler, then, has deliberately united with commentary and parable an anecdote everyone would understand immediately. It served as a popular lesson because without it the Bet Midrash rhetoric was insufficiently effective.

What remains puzzling is the fact that the parable about the king is inconsistent with the Halakah. Parables and anecdotes are certainly no rarity in midrashic literature, exegetical or homiletical, but as a rule they conform with the traditions of the Halakah. There are, indeed, occasions when a sage will admit that he lacks a proper answer.[17] There are, furthermore, instances when at least for a while the real reason for an injunction will be withheld from the public.[18] But a downright contradiction, without apology, used as support, defeats one's own purposes.

The anecdote is not without its ironies. The limits of propriety vary from culture to culture and age to age. The rabbis are not embarrassed by many stories they know from schoolhouse or marketplace gossip.[19] And after all, neither the parable nor the dialogue with Ezekiel said anything specifically about ṣîṣit. But *that* is our concern! For the Midrash compiler, the anecdote accomplished what neither text-explication nor parable did. He knew his audience. What is more, he knew how an eyewitness (the prostitute) is affected by the sight of adherence to a miṣwâ. The man suddenly rediscovered what had become merely habitual, strictly-observed piety; he reverted from mere 'doing' (ᶜśh) to 'remembering' (zkr), and hence to 'being holy'. The woman beheld what amazing self-restraint his religion could inspire.

---

17. See the anecdote about Yoḥanan ben Zakkai in *Pesîqtāᵓ dĕ-Rab Kāhănāᵓ* (ed. Mandelbaum, p. 74). See also *Pesiq. R.* 99a, bottom.

18. See Lieberman, *Greek in Jewish Palestine*, 140–42.

19. Nor, for example, is R. Abbahu (at least according to *Tanḥuma Gen.*, ed. Buber, 87b top) reluctant to explain God's love for Israel in terms of and comparison with Shechem's passion for Dinah. Note also the words of Abraham to Sarah in *Gen. Rab.* 53, p. 564, line 2. Cf. J. A. Fitzmyer, *The Genesis Apocryphon of Qumran Cave I* (Rome: Pontifical Biblical Institute, 1966) 54–55, col. xx, line 4 (cf. p. 104). See also *Gen. Rab.* 85:4, p. 1037, on Er. On what "fantasies" (including gematria!) can lead you to, see *b. Šabb.* 149b, bottom.

Masorah and Halakhah: A Study in Conflict

Sid Z. Leiman
Brooklyn College

The recovery of the Aleppo Codex some 35 years ago, cause for much celebration in academic circles, has had a less than salutary effect in rabbinic
circles. Initially ignored by rabbinic scholars, its recent publication in a facsimile edition as well as the publication of several Hebrew Bibles based on its
text have led to vigorous, even acrimonious rabbinic debate. Replete with law-
suits and bans, this debate has involved leading rabbinic authorities in Jerusalem and Bnei Braq.[1] While the details of the current rabbinic conflict need
not detain us, it is but the latest manifestation of an age-old conflict between
the masoretic enterprise and the halakhah. Modern scholarship has taken little
note of this conflict and, more importantly, of its implications. In this study I
will attempt to delineate some of the contours of this conflict and to spell out
some of its implications for the history of the transmission of the biblical text.

Masoretic Bibles and the halakhah live in a permanent state of tension. The
origins of the ascendancy of Masoretic Bibles over and against halakhic teaching are shrouded in obscurity. Certainly with the appearance of Ben Asher manuscripts of the Hebrew Bible in the ninth century, the ascendancy was well on
its way. The Cairo Codex of the Prophets, for example, dated by its colophon
to 895, presents the following order of the prophetic books: Joshua, Judges,
Samuel, Kings, Isaiah, Jeremiah, Ezekiel, and the Twelve Minor Prophets.[2] The

---

Author's note: לכבוד מורי ורבי בחכמה ובמדות, whose profound impact on my life has been such that
if I had to periodize my own intellectual development, the only natural divisions would be "before"
and "after" I first met Professor Moshe Greenberg. For all he has given me, I am forever grateful
and offer this study as a מנחת עני—a token of appreciation.

1. See, e.g., D. Yizḥaqi, נביאי אמת וצדק (Bnei Braq, 1995); anonymous, קנאת סופרים (Jerusalem, 1995); and M. Davidovitz, קונטרס דעת תורה (Jerusalem, 1995).

2. Some scholars date the Cairo Codex to the eleventh century or later, claiming that its colophon was copied from an earlier biblical manuscript in order to enhance the value of the codex.
See, e.g., M. Glatzer, "מלאכת הספר של כתר ארם צובה והשלכותיה," *Sefunot* 19 (1989) 167–276, esp.
pp. 250–59.

Aleppo Codex reflects the same ordering of the prophetic books.[3] Yet a *ba-raita* in the Babylonian Talmud rules that the correct ordering of the latter Prophets is: Jeremiah, Ezekiel, Isaiah, and the Twelve Minor Prophets.[4] No dissenting view is preserved in rabbinic literature. Moreover, the standard codes of Jewish law—Maimonides' *Code*, R. Jacob b. Asher's *Ṭur*, and R. Joseph Karo's *Šulḥan ʿArukh*—all rule according to the ordering of the Babylonian Talmud.[5] Observant Jews claim that they scrupulously follow the rulings of these codes. Yet all printed Bibles, and the majority of extant manuscripts, follow the Masoretic ordering rather than the halakhah.[6]

An even more interesting manifestation of the tension between Masoretic Bibles and the halakhah relates to the text (rather than to the ordering of the books) of the Hebrew Bible, and to this issue I devote the remainder of this study. It is an established fact, historically and halakhically, that early rabbinic texts of the Hebrew Bible differed from the Masoretic texts that emerged in the medieval period. By "historically" I mean that biblical scholars, engaged in lower criticism, and rabbinic scholars, expert in *jüdische Wissenschaft*, have adduced considerable and compelling evidence in support of the claim just mentioned. Suffice it to note the studies of V. Aptowitzer, S. Lieberman, D. Rosenthal, and Y. Maori; and especially the Mifʿal ha-Miqra's critical edition of Isaiah under the direction of M. Goshen-Gottstein.[7] By "halakhically" I mean the numerous rabbinic authorities expert in halakhah who openly acknowledged הש״ס שלנו חולק על הספרים שלנו 'there are discrepancies between the biblical citations in our texts of the Talmud and our biblical manuscripts'. These include the Tosafists (who introduced the phrase just cited), R. Meir Abulafia (d. 1244), Rashba (d. ca. 1310), Riṭba (d. ca. 1330), R. Judah Mintz (d. 1506), and more

---

3. Ibid., 170.

4. *b. B. Bat.* 14b.

5. Maimonides, *Code*, הלכות ספר תורה, ספר אהבה 7:15; *Ṭur*, יורה דעה §283; and *Šulḥan ʿArukh*, יורה דעה §283:5.

6. Even more pronounced is the discrepancy between the Masoretic Bibles and the halakhah regarding the ordering of the books of the Writings. In general, see C. D. Ginsburg, *Introduction to the Massoretico-Critical Edition of the Hebrew Bible* (London: Trinitarian Bible Society, 1897; reprint: New York: Ktav, 1966) 1–8. Still another discrepancy between the Aleppo Codex (specifically) and halakhic teaching relates to the number of lines in the Song of Moses (Deut 32:1–43). The Aleppo Codex—and in its wake, Maimonides—allots it 67 lines, whereas classical halakhic teaching knows only of a 70-line Song of Moses. See the discussion in M. Goshen-Gottstein, "The Authenticity of the Aleppo Codex," *Textus* 1 (1960) 17–58.

7. V. Aptowitzer, *Das Schriftwort in der rabbinischen Literatur* (Vienna: Alfred Holder, 1906–15; reprint: New York: Ktav, 1970); S. Lieberman, *Hellenism in Jewish Palestine* (New York: Jewish Theological Seminary of America, 1962); D. Rosenthal, "על דרך טיפולם של חז״ל בחילופי" נוסח במקרא in ספר יצחק אריה זליגמן זליגמן (Jerusalem, 1983) 2.395–417; Y. Maori, "מדרשי חז״ל כעדות" לחילופי נוסח במקרא in עיוני מקרא ופרשנות (Ramat-Gan, 1993) 3.267–86; and M. Goshen-Gottstein (ed.), ספר ישעיהו (Jerusalem, 1995).

recently, R. Akiba Eger (d. 1837) and R. Moses Sofer (d. 1839).[8] If I bother to adduce these "historical" and "halakhic" witnesses at all, it is because a minority view, perhaps best exemplified in the twentieth century by R. Ḥayyim Heller (d. 1960), insists that the early rabbinic texts of the Hebrew Bible and the Masoretic Text (henceforth: MT) are one and the same.[9] The minority view maintains that many of the apparent differences are exegetical in nature and in no way reflect conflicting readings of the biblical texts themselves. Other apparent differences are explained away as scribal errors in the Talmud. As noted by Y. Maori, the minority view has served a useful purpose: it has forced all scholars to sharpen their methodological tools.[10] Nonetheless, it remains a minority view and rightly so.

Two witnesses, §§1 and 2,—both with halakhic import—support the majority view. Following each passage, I list the MT of the verses cited in it.

§1. *b. Baba Batra* 9a:

אמר רב הונא בודקין למזונות ואין בודקין לכסות. אי בעית אימא קרא ואי
בעית אימא סברא, אי בעית אימא סברא האי קא מבזי והאי לא קא מבזי, אי
בעית אימא קרא הלא פרוש לרעב לחמך בשי"ן כתיב, פרוש והדר הב ליה.

R. Huna said: Applicants for food are investigated but not applicants for clothes. This rule is based, if you like, on Scripture, or if you prefer, on common sense. "If you prefer, on common sense," for the applicant for clothes is suffering humiliation; not so the applicant for food. "If you like on Scripture," in the verse *Is it not to share your bread with the hungry* (Isa 58:7), the word *paros* is written with a *shin*, as if to say, investigate and then give it to him.

MT: הלוא פרס לרעב לחמך (Isa 58:7; with *samekh*)

§2. *b. Ḥullin* 65a:

אלא מעתה את כדר לעומר דפסק להו ספרא בתרי הכי נמי דתרתי שמי נינהו,
אמרי התם בשתי תיבות פסיק להו בשני שיטין לא פסיק להו, אבל הכא אפילו
בשני שיטין נמי פסיק להו.

8. Tosafot to *b. Šabb.* 55b; R. Meir Abulafia, מסורת סייג לתורה (Florence, 1750) 34a and 55a, and compare the Abulafia citation in M. Lonzano, שתי ידות (Venice, 1618), section אור תורה, 6b; Rashba and Riṭba (see below, §§7 and 9); R. Akiba Eger, גליון השׁ"ס to b. Šabb. 55b (printed in the margin of the Vilna editions of the Babylonian Talmud); R. Judah Mintz, שאלות ותשובות (Munkacz, 1898) §8; R. Moses Sofer, שו"ת חת"ם סופר (Jerusalem, 1982) 1.52. Cf. לקרטי שו"ת חת"ם סופר (London, 1965), יורה דעה §35.

9. Ḥ. Heller, על תרגום השבעים בקונקרדנציה היכל הקדש (New York, 1943) 54–67, and throughout his published writings.

10. Maori, "מדרשי חז"ל," 277.

But according to this, it follows that Chedar Laomer (Gen 14:1, 4, 5, 9, 17), since the scribe has divided it into two words, represents two distinct names? I reply, in the case of Chedar Laomer while he divided it into two words, he did not place them on separate lines, but in the case of Bat ha-Yaᶜanah he also placed them on separate lines.

MT: כדרלעמר (Gen 14:1, 4, 5, 9, 17; appears as one word)

The talmudic readings in both instances are impeccable, and although significant talmudic variants appear in some manuscripts and commentaries, Rashi and a host of other commentaries had the readings as printed above.[11] Moreover, various extant Masoretic manuscripts preserve precisely these spellings of the biblical words, that is, the same spellings as those that appear in present editions of the Talmud.[12] In the case of §1, a Babylonian Amora derived a halakhah from the spelling in Isa 58:7. In the case of §2, the Talmud itself issues no official ruling on the spelling of Chedarlaomer, but later authorities would derive a halakhah from this passage relating to the proper way of recording names in a divorce document.[13] Although the Talmud assumes that Chedarlaomer is properly written as two words, in all Torah scrolls today it is written as one word. It is at least interesting to note that according to the *Šulḥan ᶜArukh*, any two consecutive words appearing together as one render a Torah scroll unfit for public use.[14] If you like, from a talmudic perspective (given §2), all present Torah scrolls may be unfit for public use! In any event, the halakhic teaching of §1 is not normative; and §2 is largely informational, that is, it makes no specific halakhic claims. For these reasons, they are more interesting than problematic. Far more problematic are §§3–6, but a preliminary remark is in order before we list and analyze those passages.

The halakhic stake in establishing the correct text of the Hebrew Bible, and especially of the Torah, is enormous. According to *m. Menaḥ.* 3:7 and the ensuing discussion at *b. Menaḥ.* 30a, and according to all codes of Jewish law, a Torah scroll with a mistaken letter, or with an additional letter, or lacking a letter, is unfit for public use.[15]

---

11. For talmudic variants of §§1 and 2, see R. Rabbinowicz, דקדוקי סופרים (New York, 1960) ad *b. B. Bat.* 9a and *b. Ḥul.* 65a. Cf. R. Meir Abulafia, יד רמ״ה (New York, 1946) ad *b. B. Bat.* 9a. See also S. Abramson (ed.), תלמוד בבלי: מסכת בבא בתרא (Jerusalem, 1958) 13; S. Mirsky (ed.), שאילתות דרב אחאי (Jerusalem, 1964) 3.15 (= שאילתא §41); S. Lieberman, "הערות למאמרו של י." in Y. Kutscher (ed.), ערכי המילון החדש לספרות חז״ל (Ramat-Gan, 1972) 102; and the discussion in Maori, "מדרשי חז״ל," 282.

12. See, e.g., Ginsburg, *Introduction*, 200–205; and idem (ed.), תורה נביאים כתובים (London: British and Foreign Bible Society, 1926) to Gen 14:1 and Isa 58:7. Cf. Goshen-Gottstein (ed.), ספר ישעיהו, ad Isa 58:7.

13. *Šulḥan ᶜArukh*, אבן העזר §129:32.

14. יורה דעה §274:4.

15. See, e.g., *Šulḥan ᶜArukh*, יורה דעה §275:6. The unsettled state of the text of biblical manuscripts and Torah scrolls in the Medieval Period led to a partial softening of the rules governing

§3. *b. Sanhedrin* 4a:

דתנן בית שמאי אומרים כל הניתנין על מזבח החיצון שנתן במתנה אחת כיפר,
שנאמר ודם זבחיך ישפך, ובחטאת שתי מתנות. ובית הלל אומרים אף בחטאת
שנתן במתנה אחת כיפר. ואמר רב הונא מאי טעמא דבית שמאי, קרנות קרנות
קרנות הרי כאן שש, ארבע למצוה ושתים לעכב. ובית הלל אומרים קרנות
קרנת קרנת הרי כאן ארבע, ג׳ למצוה ואחת לעכב.

For we learned: Bet Shammai maintains if only one sprinkling of the
blood of sacrifices that is to be sprinkled on the outer altar was applied,
atonement is effected, as it is said: *the blood of your sacrifices shall be
poured out* (Deut 12:27). In the case of a sin offering, however, two
sprinklings are required. Bet Hillel maintains that even in the case of
a sin offering, one sprinkling effects atonement. And R. Huna said:
What is the reason for Bet Shammai's view? It is the three occurrences
of *qarnot* (horns) in the plural form, totalling six sprinklings, four of
which are required initially, but only two of which are indispensable.
Bet Hillel, however, maintains that *qarnot* occurs once in the *plene*
form, and twice defectively, totalling four sprinklings, three of which
are required initially, but only one of which is indispensable.

MT: קרנת (Lev 4:25); קרנת (Lev 4:30); קרנת (Lev 4:34) (all three are
written defectively)

§4. *b. Sanhedrin* 4b:

ודכולי עלמא יש אם למקרא, והתניא לטטפת לטטפת לטוטפות הרי כאן
ארבע, דברי רבי ישמעאל. רבי עקיבא אומר אינו צריך, טט בכתפי שתים פת
באפריקי שתים.

Do all then agree that the reading tradition is determinate? Has it not
been taught: *le-ṭoṭafot* (frontlets) occurs three times in the Torah, twice
defectively, and once *plene*, totalling four (sections that are to be inserted into the phylacteries), so R. Yishmael. But R. Akiba maintains
that there is no need for this derivation, for *ṭaṭ* means "two" in Coptic,
and *pat* means "two" in African, hence the four sections.

MT: ולטוטפת (Exod 13:16); לטטפת (Deut 6:8); לטוטפת (Deut 11:18)
(all three are written defectively)

---

plene and defective spellings. While an error in plene and defective spelling rendered a Torah scroll
unfit for public use *ab initio*, if the error was discovered during a public reading—and it did not
affect the meaning or pronunciation of the word in question—the Torah scroll did not have to be
replaced immediately. The error, however, would have to be corrected in due course by a scribe.
See, e.g., *Šulḥan ʿArukh*, אורח חיים §143:4.

§5. *b. Qiddušin* 66b:

בעל מום דעבודתו פסולה מנלן, אמר רב יהודה אמר שמואל דאמר קרא לכן
אמור הנני נותן לו את בריתי שלום, כשהוא שלם ולא כשהוא חסר. והא שלום
כתיב, אמר רב נחמן וי״ו דשלום קטיעה היא.

How do we know that the temple service of a priest with a blemish is
invalid? R. Judah said in Samuel's name: Because Scripture says: *Say,
therefore, "I grant him My pact of friendship"* (Num 25:12), only
when he is whole, not when he is blemished. But the text reads *šalom*
(friendship)! R. Nahman explained: The *waw* of *šalom* is truncated.

MT: Truncated *waw* in the word *šalom* (Num 25:12) was lacking in
most Torah scrolls and manuscripts of the medieval period.

§6. *b. Niddah* 33a:

אלא הנוגע בכל אשר יהיה הזב תחתיו, ומאי ניהו עליון של זב, והנושא נמי
יטמא, ומאי ניהו נישא, מאי מעמא, והנשא כתיב.

Rather, it must mean: Whoever touches anything the person with the
discharge was under. What is meant by that? The cover above the
person with the discharge. Then one who carries over a person with a
discharge should also be rendered impure! And what is meant by that?
That which is being carried. Why? Because the text reads *ve-hannoseʾ*
defectively (which can also be read *ve-hannissaʾ*, i.e., 'and that which
is carried').

MT: והנושא (Lev 15:10; written *plene*)

§§3–6 present instances where specific halakhot were derived from the
early rabbinic text of the Hebrew Bible, and these halakhot were declared
normative; nevertheless, the MT has rejected the early rabbinic readings. These
instances create the anomalous and paradoxical situation whereby the rabbis
derived a halakhah from a specific spelling of a word in the Torah, and the
halakhah remains operative, yet if a scribe writes a Torah today with that specific spelling, it is unfit for public use! The dilemma becomes even more pronounced when one examines the underpinning of the legitimacy of the MT
from a halakhic perspective. The MT, after all, differs not only from the early
rabbinic text of the Hebrew Bible; Masoretic texts differ from each other. What
the rabbis said was: In cases of doubt, follow the reading of the majority of
manuscripts.[16] Thus, even among the Masoretic texts, when in doubt, the major-

16. While no such rule is enunciated in the talmudic sources, the practice is attested. See, for
example, the sources cited in S. Talmon, "The Three Scrolls of the Law that Were Found in the
Temple Court," *Textus* 2 (1962) 14–27. For the enunciation of the rule in medieval sources, see
§§7, 11, and 15 below. Compare the commentary mistakenly ascribed to the Ran (d. ca. 1375) ad
b. Sanh. 4a, ד״ה קרנת קרנת קרנות, where the rule is ascribed to מסכת סופרים.

ity reading was halakhically decisive. But where the rabbis derived a halakhah from a specific spelling of the biblical text, by definition the text is not in doubt. On what grounds, then, could the MT reject the early rabbinic readings? We proceed to an examination of §§3–6.

§3 discusses the sprinkling of blood on the horns of the altar. At *m. Zebaḥ.* 4:1, the schools of Shammai and Hillel disagree regarding the minimum number of acts of sprinkling required when bringing a sin offering. At *b. Zebaḥ* 37b, Rav Huna explains that the dispute turns on the implications of the spelling of the word קרנות at Lev 4:25, 30, and 34. Note especially that the two schools agree concerning the spelling of the three words: two occurrences are defective, one occurrence is *plene*.[17] They disagree only with regard to the implications of the spelling. Now the Mishnah incorporates the ruling of Hillel's school, a halakhic ruling derived from the peculiar spelling of the three words. In the twelfth century, Maimonides codified this very law, favoring Hillel's school over Shammai's.[18] One would then expect the medieval manuscripts to reflect the spelling of קרנות as embodied in the Talmud. To our chagrin, we discover that the Masoretic manuscripts, as well as the Masoretic notes, overwhelmingly agree that the word קרנות in Lev 4:25, 30, and 34 is spelled defectively in all three instances.[19] Apparently the Masoretes were oblivious to the undisputed spelling of the three words in the Talmud, spellings that the Talmud itself puts forward as the basis of a normative halakhic ruling. In this instance, of course, the halakhah is operative only in theory, since sacrificial offerings were generally not offered after the destruction of the Second Temple.

§4 provides the underpinning, according to R. Yishmael, for the four sections that are inserted in phylacteries. The word טוטפות occurs three times in the Torah. The first two are defective; the third is plene. The occurrences spelled defectively, read as singular forms, count for one section apiece. The occurrence spelled plene, read as a plural form, counts for two sections, hence a total of four sections. Again, the Masoretic manuscripts and Masoretic notes are virtually unanimous: in all three instances, טוטפות is spelled defectively.[20] Yet the halakhah, of course, remains: phylacteries contain four sections.

---

17. In §3, when delineating the view of Bet Shammai, the Talmud spells all three words plene. Since Masoretic vocalization was not applied by the redactors of the Talmud to the Talmud, this was their way of indicating that for Bet Shammai the reading tradition (that is, all three words are read as plurals) was determinate. In fact, the redactors of the Talmud assume that Bet Shammai's spelling of the three words was precisely that of Bet Hillel; otherwise, they could not ascribe the disagreement between Bet Shammai and Bet Hillel to the issue of whether the reading or textual tradition was determinate. See, e.g., R. Meir Abulafia, יד רמ"ה ad *b. Sanh.* 4a, ד"ה ואמר רב הונא ד"ה.

18. Maimonides, *Code*, ספר עבודה, הלכות פסולי המוקדשין, 17:1.

19. See, e.g., the *masora parva* in BHS ad Lev 4:7. Cf. S. Frensdorff (ed.), *Die Massora Magna* (Hannover: Cohen and Risch, 1876; reprint: *The Massorah Magna* [New York: Ktav, 1968]) 171 sub קרן. So too M. Breuer (ed.), המסורה הגדולה לתורה (New York, 1992) 2.440.

20. See R. Jedidiah Solomon Norzi, מנחת שי (Vienna, 1814) ad Deut 11:18.

§5 informs us that the *waw* in the word שלום at Num 25:12 is truncated. Moreover, a halakhah is derived from the truncated *waw*, namely that temple service performed by a priest with a blemish is invalid. This is so even if it is only after the fact that the priest discovers that he was unfit when he performed the service. That there is a truncated *waw* in Num 25:12 is nowhere disputed in all of rabbinic literature. Yet it appears that the vast majority of Torah scrolls, at least in the medieval and early modern periods, did not contain a truncated *waw*. In the eighteenth century, for example, all the Torah scrolls in Jerusalem and Salonika (over 800 of them) were examined. In virtually every case, the *waw* in Num 25:12 did not differ from any other *waw* in the Torah.[21]

§6 rules that objects carried above a *zab* are rendered impure, even if not touched directly by the *zab*. This ruling is derived from Lev 15:10, where the word הנשא occurs defectively and, for the purpose of providing an underpinning for the halakhah, was understood by the rabbis as if it were vocalized הַנָּשָׂא. The MT, however, reads הנושא, that is, plene, thus pulling the rug out from under this halakhah.

Regarding §§3–6, it should be noted that the spellings of the biblical words contained in them are never disputed in the Talmud. While other Tannaim or Amoraim derive these same laws from other biblical verses or by various exegetical means, they never challenge the accuracy of the spellings recorded in §§3–6. Nonetheless, the Masoretes successfully ignored these spellings, and the MT continues to ignore them to this very day.

Nor does it help to argue that the Tannaim and Amoraim invented artificial justifications for traditional halakhot, and thus one need not take seriously the derivations from Scripture that they suggested. Even if one concedes that the justifications are imaginary, the fact remains that, at the very least, the talmudic discussions provide evidence for what the biblical text looked like at the close of the talmudic period, if not earlier. And for the purposes of the halakhah, this will do admirably.

What is even more remarkable is the fact that medieval and early modern halakhists made a concerted and sustained effort to render the talmudic spellings normative for all Torah scrolls. The call fell on deaf ears; indeed, it failed ignominiously. §§7–14, deliberately selected from an even larger group of candidates so that every century from the thirteenth through the eighteenth is represented, demonstrate the relentless effort of the halakhah to revise the MT in accord with talmudic spellings. These authorities demanded that, at the very least, new Torah scrolls be written in accord with the talmudic spellings that served as bases for halakhot. Some authorities unabashedly required that even Torah scrolls already in existence be corrected accordingly. That the war still

---

21. See R. Isaac ha-Kohen Rappaport, בתי כהונה (Salonika, 1714) 3:20; and R. Moses Amarillo, דבר משה (Salonika, 1750) 3:8.

needed to be waged in the eighteenth century proves that, for all intents and purposes, it was a lost cause. Considering the fact that the warriors were hardly halakhic lightweights (for example, Rashba, Riṭba, Meiri, Radbaz, and Azulai), the futility of their efforts demands explanation.

§7. Rashba (ca. 1235–1310), שו"ת הרשב"א המיוחסות לרמב"ן, §232:[22]

> ומכל מקום בכל מה שבא בתלמוד דרך עיקר דין כקרנת וכבסכת לטוטפת ובן
> אין לו ביו"ד, דרשינן עיין עליו מדלא כתיב בלא יו"ד כמו מאן בלעם, שעליו
> דנין עיקר ירושה שממשמשת והולכת, בזה ודאי מתקנין, וכן בכל מקום ומקום
> אפילו בחסרות ויתרות מתקנין המיעוט על פי הרוב, דמקרא מלא דבר הכתוב
> אחרי רבים להטות.

Nevertheless, wherever the Talmud derives a law from a biblical spelling such as *qarnot* (Lev 4:25, 30, 34), *ba-sukkot* (Lev 23:42), *le-ṭoṭafot* (Deut 6:8), *u-ben ʾeyn lo* (Num 27:8)—ʾeyn is expounded as if it read ʿayyen 'investigate the deceased (for descendants)', from which we derive the primary rule of inheritance, namely, that the line of inheritance extends from the deceased downwards and (if necessary) upwards indefinitely, since it is not spelled defectively without a *yod*, as for example, the word *me²en* in *me²en Bileʿam* (Num 22:14)—in all such cases one must correct Torah scrolls accordingly. So too in all cases of discrepancies, even regarding defective and *plene* spellings, we correct the minority according to the majority of readings. For Scripture says openly: *One must side with the majority* (Exod 23:2).

§8. Meiri (ca. 1249–1316) ad *b. Qiddušin* 30a:[23]

> וזה שאנו מוצאין תקונים ביד הסופרים שעל פיהם אנו סומכין בכתיבת ספר
> תורה, אינם אלא אלא כפי מה שמצאו בספרים המוחזקים כמדויקים, לא שיהא הדבר
> ברור כל כך . . . ואף ספרי המסרות אין לסמוך עליהם כל כך, ואף לא המדרשות,
> והרי מצינו מחלוקת בין המדרשות והמסרות במלת הפילגשים שדרשו בו
> פילגשם כתוב, וכן ואשימם בראשיכם, ואשמם כתוב, וכן ביום כלות-משה,
> כלת כתיב, ובספרי המסרה שלשתם שלמים. וכן קרנות קרנת מצינו במסרה
> הפך מה שדרשו בו חכמים, אלא שבזו הסכימו הגאונים שמאחר שבא בתלמוד
> בעיקר דין, כגון זה לטטפת וכגון בסכת בסכת וכגון שכת וכגון אין לו שדרשו בו בעקר
> דין עיין עליו, סומכין עליהם על התלמוד.

---

22. The text printed in the standard editions of Rashba, for example, שו"ת הרשב"א (Jerusalem, 1990) 7:232, is corrupt. The text presented here is an emended one, based on ample medieval testimony. See the discussion below and the references cited in nn. 38 and 39.

23. A. Schreiber (ed.), (Jerusalem, 1971). Compare the even more striking formulation in Meiri's קרית ספר (ed. Hirschler; Jerusalem, 1956) 1.57–58.

The existence of scribal manuals, which we rely upon for the writing
of Torah scrolls, only indicates that some texts are considered more
accurate than others, and not that the readings are established with certainty. . . . Neither can one rely very much on either Masoretic manuscripts or Midrashim. Indeed, we find discrepancies between Midrash
and Masorah regarding *ha-pilagšim* (Gen 25:6), which they expounded
as if written defectively. So too regarding *va-ʾasimem be-raʾšekhem*
(Deut 1:13), which they expounded as if written defectively. So too
be-yom kallot mošeh (Num 7:1), which they expounded as if written
defectively. In the Masoretic manuscripts, all three are written *plene*.
So too regarding *qarnot* (Lev 4:25, 30, 34), the reading of the Masoretic manuscripts presents the opposite of what the Sages expounded.
Regarding this last discrepancy, the authorities have ruled that wherever
the Talmud derives a law from a biblical spelling—as in this case—and
in the cases of *le-ṭoṭafot* (Deut 6:8), *ba-sukkot* (Lev 23:42), and *ʾeyn
lo* (Num 27:8)—from which they derived the law that "one must investigate the deceased (for descendants)"—one relies on the biblical
spelling as it appears in the Talmud.

§9. Riṭba (d. ca. 1330) ad *b. Qiddušin* 66b:[24]

וא״ו דשלום קטיעא היא. נראה פי׳ שכרות בנתים, דאי לא, הוה ליה למימר
זעירתא היא, ונפקא מינה לס״ת, ויש להגיה כל הספרים שלנו שכתובה כדרכו.

The *waw* of *šalom* is truncated: It appears that the sense is that it is
split in half. Otherwise (i.e., if it is missing the bottom half), he should
have said that it is a miniature *waw*. The practical difference relates
to how one writes this letter in a Torah scroll. All Torah scrolls that
exhibit an ordinary *waw* here, need to be corrected.

§10. R. Simeon b. Ẓemaḥ Duran (d. 1444), שו״ת תשב״ץ 3:160:[25]

אבל הפילגשים וביום כלות משה נמצאו מדרשות שהם חסרים, אבל כבר
כתב הרשב״א ז״ל בתשובה שאין סומכין על אלו המדרשות לתקן הספרים,
ומניחים אותם שלמים, אלא בדבר שיוצא ממנו דין כגון בסכת בסכת בסוכות
או קרנת קרנת קרנות וכיוצא בהן.

Regarding *ha-pilagšim* (Gen 25:6) and *be-yom kallot mošeh* (Num
7:1), there are Midrashic passages that expound these as if written defectively. But Rashba has already ruled in a responsum that we do not
rely on these Midrashic passages in order to correct biblical spellings.
We leave these spellings *plene*. We rely only on spellings from which

24. A. Dinin (ed.) (Jerusalem, 1985).
25. Lemberg, 1891.

laws are derived, such as *ba-sukkot* (Lev 23:42), *qarnot* (Lev 4:25, 30, 34), and the like.

§11. Radbaz (d. 1573), שו״ת רדב״ז 4:101:[26]

אלא עיקרן של דברים מה שאגיד לך שכל מלא וחסר שתלוי בו דין לפי מה שלמדו בגמרא כגון קרנות קרנת וכגון סוכת סכת וכגון ובן אין לו, עייין עליו, אלו וכיוצא בהן יש להגיה הספרים אם נמצאו היפך ממה שכתוב בגמרא. אבל כל מלא וחסר דלא נפקא מינה לעניין דינא אלא מדרש בעלמא, לא נגיה שום ספר על פי הדרשה ולא על פי המסרה אלא אזלינן בתר רובא, דלא עדיף מכל דיני התורה קלים וחמורים דאמרינן אחרי רבים להטות. יש לנו להגיה הספרים בתר רוב הספרים במלתא דלא תליא לעניין דינא.

The principle is as follows: Regarding every *plene* and defective spelling from which the Talmud derives a law, such as *qarnot* (Lev 4:25, 30, 34), *sukkot* (Lev 23:42), and *ben ʾeyn lo* (Num 27:8)—understood as "investigate the deceased (for descendants)"—in these and similar cases one corrects the biblical manuscripts which offer readings that differ from the Talmudic spellings. But regarding all *plene* and defective readings which have no import on law, but merely serve as the source of a Midrashic comment, no biblical manuscript may be corrected on the basis of such a Midrashic comment. Nor may a correction be based on a Masoretic tradition. Rather, the rule is we follow the majority of readings. The case here is no different than all other Torah laws, minor and major, regarding which we rule: We follow the majority. Regarding spellings which do not relate to laws, we correct manuscripts only according to the majority of readings.

§12. R. Ephraim ha-Kohen of Vilna (d. 1678), שו״ת שער אפרים, יורה דעה, §82:[27]

לכאורה היה נראה לומר דא״צ להוציא ס״ת אחרת, לפי שהוא מן חסרות ויתרות ואנן אינן בקיאים . . . אמנם זה אינו, שהרי דרשינן בגמרא דהזהב וחמשתיו יוסף עליו, חמישיות הרבה, והיינו הואיל ונכתב מלא ביו״ד האחרונה.

In theory, it seems appropriate to rule that one need not take out a second Torah scroll, for this is a case of defective and *plene* spellings, regarding which we are no longer expert. . . . But this is not a correct ruling, for the Talmud (*b. B. Meṣ.* 54b; cf. *b. B. Qam.* 108a) expounds the verse *and he shall add a fifth part (va-ḥamišitav) to it* (Lev 5:24) as referring to many fifths. This is because *va-ḥamišitav* is written *plene*, with a second *yod*.

26. Warsaw, 1882.
27. Lemberg, 1887.

§13. R. Jacob Poppers (d. 1740), שו״ת שב יעקב, 1:56:[28]

חסר או יתיר שנלמד ממנו בש״ס ותלוי בו דין יש להגיה הס״ת, משא״כ דרש
בעלמא שלא יצא ממנו דין י״ל שדרשו כן משום שמצאו ברוב ס״ת שלהם כך.

A defective or *plene* spelling from which a law is derived in the Talmud serves as a source for correcting a Torah scroll. Not so an ordinary Midrashic comment from which no law is derived. One can claim
that it (i.e., the ordinary Midrashic comment) was expounded on the
basis of the reading of the majority of Torah scrolls at that time.

§14. R. Ḥayyim Joseph David Azulai (d. 1806), לדוד אמת, 11:3:[29]

כל מלא וחסר שתלוי בו דין לפי הש״ס, כגון קרנת קרנות סוכות סכת ובן אין
לו, יש להגיה הספרים.

One corrects Torah scrolls on the basis of all *plene* and defective spellings from which a law is derived in the Talmud, e.g., *qarnot* (Lev 4:25,
30, 34), *sukkot* (Lev 23:42), and *ben ʾeyn lo* (Num 27:8).

The disparity between the MT and the halakhah, as reflected in these passages,
raises some serious issues that have largely been ignored by modern scholarship. How did the MT, a biblical text that in some ways differs substantively
from the text of Talmud, become the normative biblical text for halakhic Judaism?[30] Why, in the medieval period, when halakhah reigned supreme and repeated efforts were made in every generation, was it impossible to make even
a dent in the MT? Given our ignorance of the state of the Bible text and the
history of its transmission between 500 and 800 C.E., scholarship may never
be able to provide a definitive solution to the problems just raised. Nevertheless, the attempt must be made. Here, I wish to suggest several new directions

28. Frankfurt am Main, 1702. I have presented here the summary of Poppers responsum, as
printed in the margin of the published text. It is an accurate summation; much more, of course,
appears in the responsum itself.

29. Jerusalem, 1986 (p. 18).

30. A suggestive, even attractive solution to the tension between Masoretic Bibles and the
halakhah would be to identify the Masoretic enterprise as Karaite (as first suggested by S. Pinsker,
לקוטי קדמוניות [Vienna, 1860] 32). The Karaites, of course, would never have allowed rabbinic
halakhah to color their *textus receptus*; hence the continuing tension. But the solution is too neat.
Why would the medieval rabbis have allowed a Karaite ordering of the biblical books and *textus
receptus* to replace their own? Why, in all of the Karaite-Rabbanite polemical literature, does there
never appear a dispute concerning the consonantal text of the Hebrew Bible? Why didn't the Karaites proclaim openly that the Masoretic enterprise was theirs and that the Rabbanites were dependent on them for their biblical texts? Clearly, the Masoretic enterprise was not entirely Karaite,
any more than it was entirely Rabbanite. More importantly, the evidence for the Rabbanite identity of many of the Tiberian Masoretes, and particularly of the Ben Asher family, is persuasive.
See M. Zucker, "נגד מי כתב רב סעדיה גאון את הפיוט ׳אשא משלי׳?," *Tarbiz* 27 (1958) 61–82; and
A. Dotan, *Ben Asher's Creed: A Study of the History of the Controversy* (Missoula, Mont.: Scholars Press, 1977).

for research and list some factors that may prove useful in resolving these is-sues, to the extent that it is still possible to do so. It is essential that studies be made of all Masoretic-Halakhic treatises, such as R. Meir ha-Levi Abulafia's מסורת סייג לתורה, R. Menaḥem Meiri's קרית ספר, R. Menaḥem Lonzano's אור תורה, and R. Jedidiah Solomon Norzi's מנחת שי. Each needs to be analyzed and its impact on halakhic practice assessed.[31] Only then will we know to what ex-tent these treatises impacted on the acceptance of the MT over talmudic spell-ings. Such studies should enable us to place in perspective the impact of the invention of the printing press—and the appearance of the first printed He-brew Bibles—on establishing a fixed, permanent text of the Hebrew Bible.[32] They may enable us to weigh the significance of Jacob b. Ḥayyim Ibn Adoni-jah's *Introduction to the Rabbinic Bible*, where it is suggested in no uncertain terms that the MT always takes precedence over talmudic readings.[33] They may also shed light on the impact of the Kabbalah on the MT. R. Menaḥem Lon-zano, for example (and likewise the Gaon of Vilna), was clearly influenced by the teachings of the Zohar to the detriment of talmudic spellings and in sup-port of the MT.[34]

A factor that must loom large in our discussion, previously suggested by Yisrael Ta-Shma, is the role played by scribal guilds.[35] Scribes formed a guild in the medieval world (and earlier as well). They developed their own traditions and trained their own successors. As a rule, biblical books were copied by pro-fessional scribes, not by halakhists. Scribes, then, and not rabbis, were respon-sible for the textual transmission of the Hebrew Bible. Indeed, so powerful and conservative were the guilds, they could ignore rabbinic intervention, even as they ignored scribes who wished to introduce change. A parade example is R. Abraham Ḥasan (ca. 1465–1524), a professional scribe who attempted to

31. Particular attention needs to be paid to Abulafia and Meiri, who authored commentaries on the Talmud and wrote masoretic treatises. Interestingly, they tend to follow the plain sense of the Talmud (against the masoretic spellings) when commenting on the Talmud; and they tend to agree with the MT (against the talmudic spellings) when writing on masoretic matters (see, for ex-ample, their respective comments to *b. Sanh.* 4a–b; compare their treatments of the same biblical verses in their masoretic manuals). This literary-exegetical phenomenon, that is, the tendency to explicate and defend the text at hand, merits further exploration.

32. See M. Cohen, "קווי יסוד לדמותו העיצורית של הטקסט בכתבי יד מקראיים מימי הביניים" in עיוני מקרא ופרשנות (Ramat-Gan, 1980) 1.123–82, who views the invention of the printing press as the most potent factor in establishing a fixed and uniform MT. But the invention of the printing press, while certainly a contributing factor in fixing the text of the MT, occurred much too late in history to shed any real light on the issue raised in this study, namely, the dominance of Masorah over halakhah.

33. See C. D. Ginsburg (ed.), *Jacob ben Chajim Ibn Adonijah's Introduction to the Rabbinic Bible* (London: Longmans, Green, Reader, and Dyer, 1867; reprint: New York: Ktav, 1968) 57–66.

34. For Lonzano, see שתי ידות, section אור תורה, 6b, 13b, and 20a. For the Gaon of Vilna, see his commentary on the Zohar, יהל אור (Vilna, 1882) ad Zohar 3:254a.

35. Y. Ta-Shma, "יצירתו הספרותית של ר' מאיר הלוי אבולעפיה," *KS* 45 (1970) 119–26, esp. pp. 125–26; idem, "קורים לאופייה של ספרות ההלכה באשכנז במאות הי"ג–י"ד," *Alei Sefer* 4 (1977) 20–41; idem, הלכה מנהג ומציאות באשכנז (Jerusalem, 1996) 94–111.

introduce change in writing Torah scrolls. He got nowhere with his fellow scribes, and his attempt to create a rabbinic-scribal alliance of sorts against his colleagues ended in dismal failure.[36] Convention is a powerful force indeed, one not easily overcome.

Still another factor that led to the dominance of the MT over halakhah, incredible as it may seem, was a scribal error.

§15. R. Jedidiah Solomon Norẓi (d. 1616), מנחת שי ad Lev 4:34:

וכבר קדמתי לך כי בכל מקום שהגמרא או המדרש חולק על המסורת בחסרות
ויתירות אנו הולכים אחר המסורת, ולא מבעיא בדרשות של אגדה כגון פלגשם
כלת ואשמם, אלא אפילו היכא דנפיק מיניה דינה . . . ובשו״ת הרמב״ן ז״ל,
סימן רל״ב, נשאל נשאל על זה . . . והשיב לו הרמב״ן ז״ל דבכל מקום אפילו
בחסרות ויתרות מתקנים מיעוט ספרים על פי הרוב דמקרא מלא דבר הכתוב
אחרי רבים להטות.

I have already mentioned that wherever there is a dispute between the Talmud or Midrash and the Masorah regarding defective or *plene* spellings, we follow the Masorah. Not only do we do so in the case of Midrashic homilies, such as *pilagšim* (Gen 25:6), *kallot* (Num 7:1), and *va-ʾasimem* (Deut 1:13), but even in cases where a law is derived from a specific spelling. . . . In Naḥmanides' *Responsa*, §232, he was asked specifically about this issue. . . . Naḥmanides responded that in all cases, even regarding defective and *plene* spellings, we correct the minority according to the majority of readings. For Scripture says openly: *One must side with the majority* (Exod 23:2).

In §15, Norẓi reveals his source for deciding in favor of the MT over the Talmud, even when a halakhah is derived from the talmudic spelling of a biblical word. Surprisingly, it is §7 (see above; in the early printed editions, Rashba's responsum was mistakenly ascribed to Nachmanides), which rules precisely the opposite of what Norẓi claims, namely, that when a halakhah is dependent on the talmudic spelling of a biblical word, the Talmud is favored over the MT! Apparently, Norẓi was misled by an egregious scribal error that already appears in the first printed edition (Venice, 1519) of this responsum. Due to the scribal error, an extra word was inserted in the printed text that turned the entire responsum on its head.[37] The original version of the responsum distin-

---

36. M. Benayahu, "אגרת הסופר רבי אברהם חסן משאלוניקי," *Sefunot* 11 (1971–78) 189–229.

37. For the correct version, see §7 above. The incorrect version (Venice, 1519 on) adds the word המיעוט immediately after the phrase בזה ודאי מתקנין. It appears likely that the error crept into the text from the following line, where the word המיעוט correctly follows immediately after phrase בחסרות ויתרות מתקנין. To add to the confusion, an abridged version of this responsum, still circulating as late as the sixteenth century, omits mention of the notion that when a halakhah is derived from the talmudic spelling of a biblical word, one decides in favor of the Talmud over the MT (see Y. Maori, "מדרשי חז״ל," 284).

guishes between biblical spellings that serve as a source for a halakhah and those that serve as a source for Midrash, ruling that in the former case we correct the reading of even a majority of Torah scrolls according to a single talmudic spelling, whereas in the latter case we follow the reading of the majority of Torah scrolls, regardless of whether it agrees or disagrees with the spelling of the Midrash. Norẓi's version makes no such distinction, ruling instead that in all instances—regardless of whether a spelling serves as a source for a halakhah or for Midrash—"we correct the minority according to the majority of readings." Early halakhic authorities who could only have seen the responsum in manuscript form cite it correctly.[38] Despite a long list of later authorities who emended the obviously corrupt printed text,[39] Norẓi's reading and ruling were perpetuated by R. Solomon Ganzfried (d. 1886), in קסת הסופר, where (following a lengthy discussion of what to do when the MT and Talmud disagree) he wrote:

ולכן מחוורתא כמו שכתב המנחת שי דבעלי המסורה פליגי אגמרא והילכתא כבעלי המסורה.

In sum, the clearest account is that of *Minḥat Shay* (i.e., Norẓi) who wrote that the Masoretes disagree with the Talmud and that the halakhah is in accordance with the Masoretes.[40]

The ultimate triumph of the MT over the Talmud came when Ganzfried's קסת הסופר was canonized for all generations by R. Moses Sofer. In a striking letter of approbation to the first edition of קסת הסופר (Ofen, 1835), Sofer wrote that from now on anyone under his jurisdiction who wished to be licensed to serve as a professional scribe would first have to master Ganzfried's treatise. Moreover, Sofer testified that he read the book from beginning to end; it was halakhically flawless. The upshot of this testimony, coming from perhaps the most prominent halakhist of the last 200 years, is that all Torah scrolls written among Ashkenazic Jews are now uniform and reflect the triumph of the MT over the Talmud. Interestingly, the confluence of Norẓi's reliance on a scribal error and of Ganzfried's reliance on Norẓi is made even more fortuitous by the following facts. Ganzfried, who was a prolific author, was only 31 years old when he published his first book, קסת הסופר, in 1835.[41] Had he authored

---

38. See the evidence cited by J. Penkower, "Maimonides and the Aleppo Codex," *Textus* 9 (1981) 40 n. 3. Compare the additional evidence cited by S. Z. Havlin, "ספר תורה שכתב לעצמו רבינו," *Alei Sefer* 12 (1986) 22 n. 102. נסים מגירונדי"

39. Among them: R. Moses Amarillo, דבר משה, 3:8; R. Israel Jacob Algazi, נאות יעקב (Warsaw, 1899) 1:1, p. 5b; R. Isaac ha-Kohen Rappaport, בתי כהונה, 3:20; and R. Solomon Loniado, בית דינו של שלמה (Constantinople, 1775), יורה דעה §10.

40. Ganzfried, קסת הסופר (1st expanded ed.; Ungvar, 1871) 103a, note.

41. In general, see Y. Rubenstein, "תולדות הגאון רבי שלמה גאנצפריד זצ״ל וביבליוגרפיה של ספריו," *ha-Maᶜayan* 11 (1971) 3:1–13 and 4:61–78. Cf. N. Ben Menaḥem, "הערות והשלמות," *ha-Maᶜayan* 12 (1971) 1:39–42.

and published it 5 years later (and almost all of his books were published after 1840), it would not have carried a letter of approbation from R. Moses Sofer, who died in 1839. More importantly, in the first edition of קסת הסופר, the only one seen by Sofer, no mention is made of Norzi's ruling that the MT takes precedence over the halakhah, nor does Ganzfried ever rule (following Norzi) והילכתא כבעלי המסורה 'and the halakhah is in accordance with the Masoretes'. These appear only in the much expanded, later editions of קסת הסופר (Ungvar, 1871 on), published long after the death of R. Moses Sofer, but still with his letter of approbation from 1835. With the publication of the expanded edition of קסת הסופר together with Sofer's letter of approbation, no halakhist came forward again with the suggestion that a talmudic spelling of a biblical word take precedence over the Masorah. A process that began early in the Middle Ages, and perhaps even earlier, had run its course. The total hegemony of the MT was finally settled by the קסת הסופר, who ruled (following Norzi) והילכתא כבעלי המסורה 'and the halakhah is in accordance with the Masoretes'.[42]

42. I am deeply grateful to Professors Barry Eichler, Richard Steiner, and Jeffrey Tigay for their perceptive comments on an earlier draft of this study. The errors that remain are entirely mine.

The Akedah—and What to Remember

MICHAEL ROSENAK
The Hebrew University of Jerusalem

And Abraham said unto his young men,
"Stay you here with the donkey,
and I and the boy will go yonder;
and we shall worship and return to you."
(Gen 23:5)

The Seat of Mercy

The Talmudic sages knew what they were doing when they chose the story of the *Akedah* as a Torah reading for Rosh Hashanah, the "day of remembrance." On this festival, *Yom Hazikaron*, we remember God's promise, and therefore we dare pray for the time when "you shall reign over all Your creatures." Yet through the prism of the *Akedah*, we also see this "day of remembering" as *ʾayom v'kadosh*, terrible and holy, for us and *kivyakhol*, for God. It is holy because Abraham was ready to do everything for the God of holiness, and it is his merit we invoke as we stand in judgment. It is terrible or at least awe-inspiring because God too seems to have much to remember. Why would he ask for such a "gift" and impose such a test? Is this the way of a moral and merciful God? Why did Abraham agree to do it? And what made it possible for the patriarch in the midst of this unbearable ordeal to "see beyond it," to promise his "young men" that Isaac and he would "worship and return"?

On Yom Kippur, these Rosh Hashanah questions are, if possible, heightened. In the *selihot* of *Mussaf* we read of the *ʿaśarah harugai malkhut*, the ten sages tormented to death by the Romans. And then, startlingly, we turn to God to "look from behind your veil and remove blemishes, O God and King Who sits on the seat of mercy"! Is this, perhaps, what Abraham knew when he promised to worship and return, that God "sits on a seat of mercy"? But what about those who didn't return, such as the ten sages themselves? And Sarah who, one midrash tells us, died of shock and grief upon hearing where Abraham had taken her son? (*Gen. Rab.* 58:5).

307

Honesty and Pedagogy

Several years ago, during this *seliḥot* liturgy of real death and entreated mercy, my son turned to me with a provocative and pained question: What mercy of God are we talking about here? And immediately, as though still on that ancient story of the trapped: Why did God allow the Holocaust to happen? And the question: How can we worship a God of compassion in this terrible world? Would we put our trust in a human being who acted like that?

This shocking and honest question brought to mind the meditation of Asaph, who gave us Psalm 73. The psalmist introduces his meditation with the apparently confident exclamation, "But surely God is good to Israel," and then proceeds to examine what he means by this, even whether it means anything at all. He too must have been asked such questions. Clearly he was, and saw himself as, a teacher. He was probably a paragon of uprightness and piety, one who was expected to have the right answers, who, despite what he felt and saw, could be expected to open his educational presentations, even about evil and injustice, with such sentiments as "but surely God is good to Israel, to the pure of heart." He himself confesses that he hesitated to speak forthrightly about the indignities and suffering he saw all around him lest he "be faithless to the generation of Your children." Perhaps, like devoted educators in every generation, he saw himself charged with the task of "making good Jews" of the young, giving them "right" answers without probing too deeply himself.

Yet Asaph, genuine teacher that he was, ultimately did strive for honesty. The moral chaos in the world and in the silence of Providence troubled him deeply. So, he tells us, he went to the Temple where he was served up "answers." Of these he mentions: that the wicked rise only to fall and that justice will triumph. Though we are not told so, it is possible that, in the Temple, our author heard all of the answers, all of the theodicies, with which we are familiar. Possibly the priests, hearing that a prominent educator-psalmist was coming to them, seeking solutions to "existential problems," organized a "workshop" for him. There they perhaps explained to our teacher-thinker that God is still present through His commandments, that suffering is a consequence of old and new sins. Such a workshop may have featured one very far-sighted and sophisticated priest who argued that society and individuals could, through the proper application of human intelligence, escape the ills that befall the stupid and short-sighted, just what we may now read as "post-Holocaust thought," just what I could have rehearsed to my son on that Yom Kippur noon.

Asaph gives us an intimation that these answers, however true they may be, are inadequate. Perhaps while still meditating in the Temple, he turned from collective hopes for the future to his personal experience, past and present. And he discovered that God, Who inexplicably does not prevent his torments, still holds his hand while he undergoes them, that "the nearness of the Lord is good." He understood that the words, "God is good to Israel" are not only a promise for the latter days, but a key to that experience and that potentiality. To be "near" is not to be protected from history and inevitable suffering and death but to "see" in the midst of it, that "I am continually with You, You hold my right hand." It is those who are "distant" who shall perish; those who are near, despite trials and tribulations, "shall tell of God's works."

Our psalmist still speaks to us because the catastrophies and sorrows and traumas of all times and in all forms have crucial commonalities. The priests Asaph met in the Temple and modern theological writers share an assumption that we should seriously consider. Eliezer Berkovits has reminded us that Rabbi Akiva, who was flayed to death, and the doomed Jew of Europe who decides to die ᶜ*al kiddush hashem*, as one commanded, share both a fate and an understanding of how to respond to it.[1] While it is justified to think that the horrors and dimensions of the Holocaust are unprecedented and uniquely incomprehensible, we should also see evil and suffering as perennial problems. Hence, though far removed from his times and ills, we may together with the late Rabbi Judah Magnes find fault with Job for complaining only when he himself was struck. Surely, declares Magnes, Job knew even before being personally afflicted that not all was right with the world, that children were in pain and despots ruled the earth. Why didn't he complain and call God to account then?[2]

The commonalities of catastrophe are still with us, darkening the present, overhanging the future. Despite the unequaled horror of the Shoᵓah, there is also much unspeakable evil to remember, not only from the distant but also the immediate past. How shall we deal with this? What does the *Akedah* come to teach us? What, if anything, can help us learn from it?

Honing the Questions

Abraham, the Bible tells us, was God's friend, His beloved. The "nearness" of being together "hand in hand" as it were, of which the psalmist speaks, might well be describing him. What will illuminate this nearness of Abraham to God, even in a moment of indescribable sorrow and perhaps rage? What can we say about nearness in the face of our own afflictions and bereavements?

Philosophies and theodicies have limited usefulness here. It may indeed be true that the problem of evil and suffering has largely to do with human viciousness, freely chosen, and/or that God limits himself for the sake of human freedom. Perhaps God Himself is bound to "process" and hence, as the

1. Eliezer Berkovits, *Faith after the Holocaust* (New York: Ktav, 1973).
2. Judah L. Magnes, "The Conquest of Pessimism by Faith," in *Faith and Reason: An Introduction to Modern Jewish Thought* (ed. Samuel H. Bergman; Washington, D.C.: Bnai Brith Hillel, 1961) 142–51.

kabbalists tell us, is hampered as it were by present "fracture" and flaws. Yet, philosophical "solutions" might tempt us to accommodate ourselves, sadly yet comfortably, to distance. *Before* we deserve the serenity of philosophy, we need psalms, *piyyutim*, and *midrashim* to hone questions and make us see the point of nearness, that call it up for us and help us to remember it.

It is in this connection that the following midrash comes to mind:

> Light is sown for the righteous . . . (Ps 97:11) . . . The Holy One blessed be He . . . left not a thing in the world about which He did not charge Israel with some commandment. If an Israelite goes out to plough, then ⟨s/he is charged with the commandment⟩ "You shall not plough with an ox and an ass to-gether" (Deut 22:11); to sow: "You shall not sow your vineyard with two kinds of seeds" (v. 9); reap: "When you reap your harvest and have forgotten a sheaf . . . you shall not go back to fetch it" (24:19). . . . If s/he builds a house: "You shall make a parapet for your roof" (14:1) and then "shall write them [the passages of the *Šema^c* in the *mezzuzah*] on your doorposts" (v. 9); if he wraps himself in a cloak: "Say to them that they make themselves *tzitzit* (fringes)." . . . To what may this be compared? To the case of one who has been thrown into the water. The captain stretches out a rope and says: "Take hold of the rope with your hand and do not let go, for if you do you will lose your life." Similarly, the Holy One blessed be He said to Israel: As long as you adhere to the commandments then "You that cleave to the Lord your God are alive, every one of you to this day" (Deut 4:4). In the same vein it says: "Take fast hold of instruction, let her not go: keep her, for she is your life" (Prov 4:13) (*Tanḥuma, Shlach Lekha* 15).

The message here bears a kind of comfort, but the imagery is paradoxical and frightening. It intimates the distance from God, the pain of having been thrown into the water. And it is this pain, of being "far" from God and thus at the very edge of "betray(ing) the generation of Your children" that is so well illumi-nated by our psalmist and here, by the midrashic teacher. Light, he tells us, is sown for the righteous and (somehow!) the "straight of heart" shall have joy. What at first glance looks like a pietistic and even sentimental piece about "how many mitzvot are waiting to be done" becomes, at its end, a matter of life and death. And then we realize that what started with a seemingly comfortable idea is not what it appears to be. The thin and endearing threads of *tzitziot* are, in fact, heavy and rough ropes thrown to those shipwrecked in a raging and sin-ister sea.

Why should we believe it, and why should Abraham have believed it? Why, seeing the light buried or scattered about, shall we not assume that it is extinguished or slowly dying out? Isn't this the reality we see anew with every human atrocity, with every act of injustice and unfairness? So why affirm the reality of this light? If our lives are truly like those "thrown" into the water, why should we trust the captain who presumably cast us into the deep? Why should we think of the commandments as a rope thrown to us so that we do not drown? Does keeping them protect us from tragedy and death? Are those who observe them "alive, every one to this day"? Why, reading about Abraham in the act of binding his son on the altar or reciting the saga of the righteous tortured to death, should we think that there is a God Who sits on a seat of mercy?

Abraham is taking his son Isaac to Mount Moriah. What is going through his mind that makes it possible for him to move, step by step, to his destination? Why should he obey such an absurd commandment? Why should he trust God? And what is he saying when he tells the young men that "I and the lad will go thither, worship and return to you"? Was he lying? Soothing? Hoping? Or did he know that this was an absolute certainty? And if he knew it, wherein was the trial? And what about all those who sacrificed their sons—to Moloch or principles or maniacs—whose sons did not "come back" with them?

A Declaration of Faith—or a Lie

The captain and Abraham and all the things we must remember on *Yom Hazikaron* 'the day of remembering', which is also the first day of the year, of Creation itself, remind me of a story told by the sociologist Peter L. Berger, and a question he addresses to it:

> A child wakes up at night, perhaps from a bad dream, and finds himself surrounded by darkness, alone, beset by nameless threats. At such a moment the contours of trusted reality are blurred or invisible, and in the terror of incipient chaos the child cries out for his mother. It is hardly an exaggeration to say that, at this moment, the mother is being invoked as the high priestess of protective order. It is she (and in many cases, she alone) who has the power to banish the chaos and to restore the benign shape of the world. And, of course, any good mother will do just that.[3]

The mother will cradle the child, turn on a lamp that will cast reassuring light, perhaps sing or speak to him or her. "And the content of this communication will invariably be the same—'Don't be afraid—everything is in order, everything is all right.' If all goes well, the child will be reassured, his/her trust in reality recovered, and in this trust s/he will go back to sleep."[4]

Once again, this time with Berger, we must ask: *Is the mother lying to the child?* For, on the face of it, nothing is all right! The mother will die, and when her life ends, so will her protection and her order-restoring powers. Furthermore, "The world that the child is being asked to trust is the same world in which he will eventually die." And so, if there is no truth in the religious

---

3. Peter L. Berger, *A Rumour of Angels: Modern Society and the Rediscovery of the Supernatural* (Middlesex: Penguin, 1969) 72–73.

4. Ibid.

interpretation of human existence, she *is* lying, whether deviously or innocently, whether with fervently good intentions or in lazy routine. Unless we sense the religious understanding of human existence, the final truth about our existence cannot be love or light but only terror and darkness. In that case, "The nightmare of chaos, not the transitory safety of order, would be the final order of the human situation."

The world, says Berger, is filled with "rumours of angels," intimations of transcendence that invite the choice of faith. There is the sense of order and security articulated by the mother of the crying child, there is the determination of the sick and dying to carry out a project or an obligation and to accept death itself as not final. There is humor that puts things into a different and astonishing perspective. The present reality is real enough, but it is not all there is. Light is sown in order to give joy; this sounds absurdly paradoxical, but we are asked to "recall" our experience of it. We are bidden to remember, from the things we have known, the reality of what we believe. And what we remember is filtered through our own sense of order, sown within us. We are to recall our "right" (or wrong) response to the demands made upon us for love, our persistent urge for more decency, our ability to see things differently.

In theologies of liberal optimism, it would now be added, "and it all depends on you." To an extent, this must be so. God surely needs those who trust, who testify to order and the "other dimension" by being trustworthy, by persisting, and by laughing. Those who see "not a thing in the world" regarding which God did not give some commandment bear witness by their steadfastness to another dimension of life, intimated by acts of faith.

But after the Holocaust, which is, despite all commonalities, still different and worse than anything that preceded it, liberal optimism is out of place. Perhaps it was never enough. The God "Who sits on a throne of mercy" cannot be pictured as simply "throwing out a rope" to rescue those drowning from a watery death by which happily heroic persons pull themselves to safe shores. It seems implausible that if only everyone were decent and intelligent, all catastrophes could be avoided. Not everyone is, and not all horrors are human-made. So, for example, while it makes good political sense to accuse Jewish leaders in Europe of not seeing what was in store for their Jewries, it is subtly unfair.

Certainly if all people were righteous, everything would be much, much better. But "the young men" accompanying Abraham who are told "to stay here with the donkey," though exposed to an extraordinary household, are not on the level of Abraham and Sarah, and one never knows what mischief to expect from them. And these "young men" are most of us, most of the time. Indeed, there must have been many times when Abraham and Sarah also asked themselves how they could have done it differently, without the expulsion of Hagar and Ishmael, without recriminations, yet without loss of faithfulness.

But is there a different way that guarantees constant happiness and unruffled virtue? It is doubtful. And if all diseases were conquered, would death nor chart new paths to humanity? Moreover, even if the future were redemptively bright, the record of children throughout the ages who suffered from meningitis or were raped by conquering troops or were savagely treated by parents would still need to be stored and held in loving care before the throne of mercy unless the statement that "everything is all right" is a blatant falsehood. And all of the evil we know about we shall never understand even if, in the midst of our horror and and anger, we hear a reassuring "rumour of angels."

As we think about all of this and imagine our father Abraham proceeding to Mount Moriah, surely not understanding it completely either, we might return to a second reading of our midrash. Is the captain, throwing us a rope, thereby pulling us out of the water? Hardly, though the promise of future joy tempts us to such an interpretation. But no. At least for now, the commandments that give life are "located" in the murky, death-dealing waters. *Tzitzit* are a way to "remember" what is beyond the everyday, but they adorn a plain piece of clothing, worn by simple, sometimes perspiring mortals. The "captain" is not providing a way out but showing a way in which He turns to each person, a way in which He instructs with His presence.

And again we are returned to our psalmist. As he looks around at the world of the powerful and the wicked, his "flesh and heart fail." He laments that "all the day have I been plagued and my chastisement came every morning." Yet God is "the Rock of my heart." Despite everything, he can say that "I am continually with Thee." He doesn't understand what is incomprehensible, and he may be a stranger to systems. But he knows that "the nearness of God is my good; I have made the Lord God my refuge that I may tell of all Your works."

As already said, our psalm is attributed to Asaph, a contemporary of David who, judging from the psalms that claim his authorship, was indeed a pedagogical person. But it seems to me that it may have been Abraham himself, our first father and teacher, who first uttered these words during the three-day journey from Beersheva to Moriah. Perhaps these verses, intimating "nearness" even in the face of death and tragedy, made it possible for him to speak to "the young men" as he did. For in some mysterious way, yet on the basis of his experience with God, he knew that his prayerful words, expressed in faith but great uncertainty, were not a lie, even if (mis)understood by these young men as a simple statement of fact.

Centuries later, his descendant Asaph was to proclaim, "But surely God is good to Israel," as though it were a simple matter. Perhaps he "learned" to do this from Abraham, who fortified by God "who held his hand," was able to say: "We shall go and worship . . . and return." Abraham was a prophet, a beloved of God and close to Him. Yet surely, even as he spoke, he knew that the "light" that gave him the strength to speak was still "sown." At the moment of his speaking, he knew that the truth of it was still "buried" or flickering and that he stood only at the precarious edge of reassurance, waiting for the nearness of God to be his refuge.

English Abstracts of Hebrew Essays

The Countenance of YHWH

Shmuel Aḥituv

Twice the Pentateuch speaks about an angel that will lead the people to the Promised Land (Exod 23:20ff.; 33:1ff.). In Exodus 33 Moses asked the Lord to know who this messenger was, and the Lord answered him: "My countenance will go" (v. 14). The pericope proceeds with the episode of the revelation of YHWH to Moses in the crevice of the rock, in which Moses is told that he cannot see the countenance of YHWH but his back.

The meaning of the countenance of YHWH is illuminated by comparison to the Punic goddess Tinnit, whose full name and title is *Tnt-pn-Bᶜl* 'Tinnit the Countenance of Baal'.

It is argued that the countenance of YHWH became an angel in the Bible, the angel that led the people in the wilderness to the Promised Land. In postbiblical mystical literature this angel came to be known as "the angel of countenance." The book of *Enoch* even mentions four angels of countenance by name (40:2ff.). The Talmud and later Midrashic literature identified the angel who led the people in the wilderness with the archangel Metatron, who is "the angel of countenance."

Creation and the Calendar of Holiness

Yairah Amit

The seven-day Creation story, as formulated and placed at the beginning of the Pentateuch, is the product of editing on the part of the Holiness school (H) and not the Priestly school (P). The Holiness school was responsible for the important position of the Sabbath throughout history.

The claim put forward in the first part of the essay is that the Sabbath is not only an integral part of the seven-day Creation story or its conclusion but is, in fact, its climax. Therefore the author of Gen 2:1–3 is the one who is responsible for the whole story (Gen 1:1–2:4). In the second part, the essayist analyzes the ideological and stylistic characteristics of the Sabbath in the

315

Creation story and their relationship to the Holiness school. She also examines two editorial questions: why the term *Sabbath* is not mentioned in Gen 2:1–3, and why the author refrained from directly commanding Sabbath observance. The third and the last part is dedicated to the subject of why H took pains to emphasize the Sabbath in different ways and presented it as one of the foundations of Creation, representing a new and sacred concept of time. The answer given is based on the connection between the idea of holiness and the daily life of Israel after the destruction of the First Temple.

The Philistine Entity and the Origin of the Name "Palestine"

Israel Eph^cal

This article rejects the commonly held view that the Philistines, after their defeat by King David (10th century B.C.E.), disappeared and were assimilated into the Canaanite environment. Assyrian royal inscriptions and other epigraphic documents clearly indicate that in the 9th–7th centuries B.C.E. there were four kingdoms in the southern coastal region of Palestine (Gaza, Ashkelon, Ashdod, and Ekron); there was no political entity called *Philistia*. However, these sources refer to individuals and groups in Assyria known as *Philistines*. The designation *Philistines* apparently derived from an awareness of common origin, unconnected with the political reality of the Assyrian period.

Recently discovered alphabetical epigraphic documents of the 8th–6th centuries B.C.E. reveal the existence in Philistia of groups of people whose names have no Semitic etymology. One of these was Achish, son of Padi, king of Ekron, an inscription of whose was discovered at Tel Miqne. It is suggested that these names are to be associated with descendants of the Philistines, implying that a "Philistine entity" did exist at least up to the end of Assyrian domination in Palestine. If this is true, it is easy to explain the circumstances under which the Greek toponym *Palestine* emerged. The chronological gap between the available evidence for the existence of a Philistine entity and the emergence of the Greek term *Palestine*, first occurring in Herodotus, thus shrinks to some 150 years at most, compared to the 500 years or so between its emergence and the time of David and Solomon.

On the Borderline between Biblical Criticism and Hebrew Linguistics: The Emergence of the Term ספר־משה

Avi Hurvitz

The lexemes תורה and ספר, referring to the commandments and laws transmitted to Israel through Moses, occur repeatedly in biblical literature either alone or within set combinations. Compare תורת־משה, תורת־ה׳, ספר־התורה, התורה, ספר־משה, ספר־תורת־משה. The first five of these terms are commonly labeled "Deuteronomistic." The sixth (ספר־משה) does not belong to this category; it is attested three times in Chronicles and Nehemiah.

At first glance, one may tend to believe that ספר־משה is nothing more than a stylistic variation of the other combinations in which its components (ספר; משה) are employed in a slightly different form. However, a close examination of non–Biblical Hebrew sources dated to the Second Temple period (the Aramaic portion of Ezra; Dead Sea Scrolls; apocryphal literature; New Testament) reveals that ספר־משה is specifically a term that enjoyed wide circulation in the postexilic period; therefore, the late distribution pattern of ספר־משה within Biblical Hebrew is—linguistically—a clear hallmark of the language current during the Persian period.

The question to be addressed now is how, and to what extent, this observation—drawn from *the discipline of Hebrew linguistics*—may be exploited for the purposes of *the discipline of biblical criticism*. Since the specific semantic nuance of the lexeme תורה in various biblical writings is widely debated, it goes without saying that the exact meaning of ספר־משה cannot be definitely established either (the entire Pentateuch or only some parts of it? and if the entire Pentateuch, was it necessarily the Pentateuch in its exact canonical form? etc., etc.). All that biblical criticism may safely infer from the data provided by the linguistic analysis is, therefore, that there is a chronological gap between the postclassical ספר־משה and its classical counterparts ספר־תורה, תורת־משה, and so on. Also, it may be concluded that the emergence of ספר־משה on the biblical scene, whatever its exact interpretation, represents a postdeuteronomistic phase in the history of biblical literature. However, in order to determine the exact semantic meaning of ספר־משה, biblical criticism must apply other sets of considerations and criteria, which are not operable in purely linguistic procedures.

"A Psalm, a Song for the Sabbath Day"

Meir Weiss

A close reading of Psalm 92 reveals that the psalmist is praising the Lord because He gladdens him. The cause of his joy, and the inspiration for his hymn, emerges not only from the ending of the Psalm (v. 16) but also from its structure and texture. This cause is not the favorable lot of the author, in which his particular case exemplifies the rule. The joy of the psalmist, and subject of the hymn, derives from the justice of God's rule over the world: the lot of the just man is good, while that of the wicked, in reality, is bad, "attesting that the Lord is upright."

Fragments of an Ezekiel Scroll from Masada 1043–2220 (Ezekiel 35:11–38:14)

Shemaryahu Talmon

The largest written item in Hebrew found on Masada consists of more than fifty pieces of parchment which together contain the text of Ezek 35:11–38:14 in four columns. Reconstituted, these columns took up approximately 41.0 cm of the width of one sheet of parchment. With some minor exceptions, the text corresponds to the MT. Section markings (*parashot*) mostly parallel those of one or the other major MT manuscripts (Aleppo, Leningrad, Cairo, Sassoon) but do not fully accord with any one.

The scroll was written by an expert scribe, in an "early Herodian book-hand" or "formal script" in conformity with traditional scribal rules laid down by the Sages. It was evidently penned before 73 (or 74) C.E., the year of the capture of Masada by the Romans, which constitutes a definite terminus ante quem. The actual date can be substantially lowered since there is no reason for assuming that the scroll was penned on Masada; rather, it was brought there at some time before the fall of the fortress. Moreover, the fragments were discovered in one of the two pits under the floor of the "synagogue" (the other pit contained fragments of a Deuteronomy scroll) which according to Yadin served as a "Genizah," suggesting that because of its condition the scroll was stored there to take it out of circulation. This would imply that it had been in use for quite some time and would underpin its dating to the latter part of the first century B.C.E. or to early in the first century C.E.

New Mari Documents and the Prophecy of Ezekiel

Abraham Malamat

The author discusses three items related to prophecy in Ezekiel and in relatively recently published "prophetic" letters from Mari (ARM 26/1 and 2):

(a) *The power of God's Hand.* Here some examples refer, in contrast to the majority of instances in Mari and in the Bible, to a state of calamity. In Ezekiel, the expression "the hand of God" is mentioned more often than in any other prophetic book.

(b) '. . . *and make them into one stick*' (Ezek 37:19), compared to the Mari idiom 'and they became one finger'. This symbolic expression is used in both Mari and Ezekiel to describe the diplomatic practice with regard to state unification.

(c) *Prophesying in the Bible by means of eating a scroll and in Mari by drinking beverage.* Ezekiel swallows a scroll fed to him by God. Similarly,

God touches Jeremiah's mouth, and his seraphs touch Isaiah's lips. We may compare this figure with ARM 26/1, no. 207, where the queen of Mari writes to the king (Zimri-lim): "I gave drink to the signs for male and female. . . ." The drink may have been alcoholic. In spite of all differences between the two sources, the enigmatic practice in each of the instances acted as a stimulant to arouse prophetic powers.

The Origin and Development of Languages on Earth: The Sumerian versus the Biblical View

Jacob Klein

S. N. Kramer proposed, as early as 1943, that the so-called "Spell of Nudimmud," included in the Sumerian epic tale "Enmerkar and the Lord of Aratta" (lines 136–55), constitutes a parallel to the story of "The Tower of Babel" in Gen 11:1–9. According to his interpretation, the Sumerian source depicts man's golden age in the remote past, when all peoples spoke one language and worshiped Enlil, the head of the Sumerian pantheon, until Enki, the god of wisdom, confounded their speech and caused division and controversy among the different nations. Kramer's hypothesis has been challenged by several Sumerologists, who claim that the Sumerian source describes an ideal ("messianic") situation in the future, when Enki will take care that all humanity speaks one language and worships the Sumerian god, recognizing the superiority of Sumerian religion and culture. Thus, the Sumerian source was parallel to Zeph 3:9.

The present study confirms Kramer's interpretation of the relevant passage in the Sumerian epic tale. However, it is argued here that this passage does not constitute the spell of Nudimmud (Enki), but it is an etiological comment by the poet. Its aim is to explain to the audience how Enmerkar of Uruk was able to exchange messages with the Lord of Aratta, a country whose inhabitants spoke, in the author's time, a language entirely different from any of those spoken in Mesopotamia. In another etiological comment (lines 500–506), the poet ascribes the invention of cuneiform writing to Enmerkar.

"And if Given Strength—Eighty Years": The Terms for Longevity in Akkadian, Biblical Hebrew, and Mishnaic Hebrew

Hayim Tadmor

The *locus classicus* for longevity in the Hebrew Bible is Ps 90:10. On every other occasion *gĕbūrôt* refers to the miraculous acts of God and the military achievements of kings. How then could 'mighty acts' become a term for an extremely old age? The present paper seeks to elucidate the origin of this specific use of *gĕbūrôt* within the context of its Akkadian semantic equivalents *šibūtu* and *littūtu* (often used as a hendiadys).

In the numerical expression of the ages of human beings in a Neo-Assyrian tablet from Sultan-Tepe (*STT* II 400), *šibūtu* corresponds to 80 years and *littūtu* to 90 years. It is suggested that *littūtu*, an abstract analogous to *šibūtu*, from *šibu* 'old man', must derive from *ilittu* 'son', 'descendant', well attested from the Old Babylonian period onward (CAD I/J 72; *littu* C, CAD L 219). The alleged derivation from *littu* D 'old man' (CAD L 219 and AHw 557) cannot be accepted, since *littu* in that sense is merely a lexical back-formation from the abstract *littūtu*. The traditional translation of *littūtu* as 'progeny' is therefore preferable to 'an extremely old age', as it appears in the current dictionaries of Akkadian.

Regarding *gĕbūrôt* in Ps 90:10, the writer proposes that it should be viewed as a "creative borrowing" from Akkadian: *littūtu* became contaminated with *lītātu* (pl. of *lītu*) 'mighty acts', thus yielding *gĕbūrôt* as its lexical equivalent. It is also possible that in the bilingual milieu in which such borrowing took place, this new meaning of *gĕbūrôt* was enhanced by popular etymology: *littūtu* was interpreted as the ability of the male (*geber*) and of his immediate successors to procreate, thus ensuring continuous progeny.

דיק, עין, שכל: *A Semantic Analysis*

Moshe Weinfeld

The three terms שכל, עין, דיק/דקדק, which have much in common, are analyzed here in detail. It is demonstrated that the terms שכל, השכיל not only denote wisdom and understanding, as usually found in the Hebrew Bible dictionaries but, as shown by Ibn Ganaḥ, also express contemplation and insight, like הסתכל in Mishnaic Hebrew (see *m. ʾAbot* 2:11, *m. Ḥag.* 2:1).

The second term, עין, found only once (= hapax) in the Bible (1 Sam 18:9), is not to be translated 'hate' but 'watch carefully', as attested in the rabbinic sources: exactness in measure, reading, and expression.

The third term, דיק/דקדק, does not appear in Biblical Hebrew at all. It is very common in later Hebrew and replaces the biblical השקיף and הביט.

The essay aims to show that verbs for 'seeing' and 'looking' have developed following the wide spectrum of contemporaneous expressions available in the Aramaic vocabulary. By influence of the Aramaic, השכיל widened its scope of meaning to include 'contemplation' as well; the verb עין, found only once in the Bible, is used very often in later Hebrew, while the verbs דיק/דקדק, not attested in the Bible at all, are introduced in Rabbinic Hebrew and thus became an indispensable expression in postbiblical Hebrew.

"Was It Not at His Hand the Sun Stopped?" (Ben Sira 46:6): A Chapter in Literary Archaeology

Yair Zakovitch

The miracle of stopping the sun and moon in Josh 10:12–14 is one of the most magnificent biblical miracles. A careful study of the Joshua narrative and of other manifestations of the tradition, mostly in postbiblical literature, testifies to the mythical nature of the original tradition, in which Joshua himself stopped the sun (not the moon) with his own hand.

Israelite monotheism, intolerant of any sort of mythology, found different methods with which to cope with this problematic heroic tradition. This paper deals with the history of the tradition from its prebiblical existence to its post-biblical expressions and analyzes the various modes of covert polemics connected with it.

Tradition and Innovation in the Commentary of Rabbi Samuel ben Meir (Rashbam) on Job: The Hymn to Wisdom (Job 28)

Sara Japhet

The literal method of biblical exegesis in northern France reached its zenith during the twelfth century with the work of Rashbam. Rashbam represents the high point in the development of the northern French literal school because of his grasp of the fundamentals of this form of interpretation, his definition of its purpose (as the only way of eliciting the plain meaning of the text), and his achievements in this sphere. Nevertheless, although Rashbam states that his aim is to base his interpretations on the plain meaning of the text, he still relies systematically and consistently on the Talmudic sources and earlier commentators, foremost among them Rashi. The relationship between tradition and innovation in Rashbam's commentary presents us with a major problem when determining the main characteristics of his methodology and place in the history of Jewish exegesis.

The subject is examined here by means of an analysis of Rashbam's commentary on a single complete section: Job 28. The first critical edition of Rashbam's commentary on Job is due to be published shortly and a preliminary reading of one chapter of this edition is provided here. It is not intended to impose a super-commentary on Rashbam's text but to examine a number of important facets of his work. These include the literary sensitivity reflected in the structure of Rashbam's own composition and his feeling for the literary aspects of the biblical text. Among these, Rashbam regards hemistich parallelism as a main feature of biblical poetry as well as an essential aid in its elucidation. Further points of discussion are the dialectical tension inherent in Rashbam's approach to the Talmudic sources and Rashi, and the fundamental theological concepts of Rashbam's world concerning the deity and his cognizance, as revealed in his commentary on this chapter.

The Pre-70 C.E. Judean Synagogue:
Its Origins and Character Reexamined

Lee I. Levine

Much as been written about the origins of the Second Temple synagogue. Owing to the paucity of sources prior to the first century C.E., scholarly hypotheses in this regard have ranged over a period of approximately 900 years, from the tenth to the first centuries B.C.E. Common to most views are the twin assumptions that the synagogue was in essence a religious institution and that its beginnings were an outcome of a major upheaval in Jewish life: either the reformation of Josiah, the destruction of the First Temple, or the reforms of Ezra and Nehemiah, to name three of the most popular theories.

The writer suggests here a very different approach. Instead of speculating when such an institution might have appeared, he proposes starting at the other end of the time spectrum, from when we do in fact have information about the functioning of the synagogue, that is, the first century C.E. At that time, the institution served as the central Jewish public building in communities throughout Israel and the Diaspora, where the political, social, judicial, and religious needs of the communities throughout Israel and the Diaspora were served. The question, then, is where these functions took place earlier. Phrased thus, it becomes quite obvious that the forerunner of the synagogue was the city-gate, and it is to this end that a survey of its role in the biblical period is presented.

Archaeological evidence allows us to conclude that the gate ceased to function as the main public area of a city in the Hellenistic era. This transition as well as a number of Second Temple phenomena seemingly associated with such a setting are discussed. A final section treats the development of the synagogue in late antiquity as a distinctly religious institution.

Was Maimonides Influenced by Al-Ghazzālī?

Ḥava Lazarus-Yafeh

It is hard to imagine that Maimonides did not know the writings of Al-Ghazzālī (d. 1111), although he does not mention him. Some examples are quoted here from the Commentary to the Mishna and Mishne Torah to show that Maimonides might have been influenced to a certain extent by Al-Ghazzālī's theory of prophecy, his attitude to prayer, trust in God, repentance, and miracles, as well as by some general statements or literary parables. It is, however, very difficult to prove this because some of the above-mentioned topics were widely discussed issues in medieval Arabic Ṣūfī literature in general. Furthermore, Maimonides shows no linguistic or literary traces of Al-Ghazzālī's writings, and his general approach is, of course, very different from that of Al-Ghazzālī the mystic and antiphilosopher.

Peshat Exegesis of Biblical Historiography: Historicism, Dogmatism, and Medievalism

Uriel Simon

The article deals with the following question: to what extent were the *peshat* (that is, philological-contextual) exegetes of the Middle Ages (from Saᶜadiah Gaon through Isaac Avravanel) open to the biblical historical perspective, and to what extent was this perspective closed to them by their beliefs concerning the sanctity of Scripture on the one hand and by their medieval mentality on the other?

Ambivalence about the relevance of scriptural historiography in the absence of contemporary historiography. The conventional solution was to theologize and moralize the accounts in Genesis and biblical historiography in general. Only a few exegetes recognized the value, albeit secondary, of chronological, genealogical, and demographic data.

The plain meaning of the verses is incompatible with the ahistorical perspective of the sages. The Sages' commitment to the eternal status of the Jewish commandments and ethics is buttressed by midrashim (homiletical exegesis) that describe the Patriarchs as having observed all of the commandments. The image of Abraham as a talmudic scholar who observes both the written and oral Torah is paradoxically transformed (in the Spanish School but not in the northern French School) into that of a medieval scholar who observes all of the commandments that were revealed to him through his inquiry.

Medieval realism and its cost. Given the medieval view that history and science are quite static, the *peshat* exegetes had almost no hesitation about interpreting Scripture in the light of their own present.

From a temporal perspective within the text to a temporal perspective about the text. Responding to obvious biblical anachronisms, some exegetes reach a historical perspective regarding the time of the book's composition, the identity of its author, and even its internal evolution.

Additional Fragments of the "Rhymed Ben Sira"

Ezra Fleischer

The few fragments of the medieval rhymed adaptation of Ecclesiasticus, discovered in the Geniza as early as 1931, aroused a justified interest among Ben Sira scholars. The work, authored by an anonymous poet who apparently flourished in Babylon at the beginning of the 13th century, presents a rather simplified version of the ancient book. Though its being based on the Hebrew original of Ben Sira is beyond doubt, it also contains a rather great deal of additional material of unknown origin. The medieval versifier seems to have based himself on an extended, possibly popular, version of Ben Sira.

Only six pages of this work, all of them detached from one and the same codex, were found in the Geniza. The author of this essay has collected them in an appendix to his Hebrew book *The Proverbs of Saᶜid ben Babshad*, published by the Ben-Zvi Institute in 1990. Two additional consecutive pages from this work, preserved in the small Geniza collection of Hebrew Union College in Cincinnati, are presented here. They cover the closing parts of Ben Sira (51:1ff.) and do not faithfully follow the Hebrew original. Interestingly enough, the closing hymn of Ben Sira (51:21–35), which is missing from the non-Hebrew variants of Ecclesiasticus, is here replaced by a thoroughly rhymed adaptation of Psalm 136.

The texts are published, commented on, and analyzed in the present paper.

Midrashic Derivations regarding the Transformation of the Names Jacob and Israel according to Traditional Jewish Exegesis: Semantic and Syntactic Aspects

Simcha Kogut

This article deals with the notions conveyed by traditional Jewish exegesis regarding the transformation of the name *Jacob* to *Israel* and the semantic and syntactic grounds for the interpretations of the two names as they were explicitly and implicitly perceived in the Midrashic derivations.

Two main approaches to the phenomenon of the name transformation are reviewed. One interprets the name *Jacob* unfavorably according to the words of Hosea, "In the womb he took his brother by the heel" (Hos 12:4), which in that context refers not only to the meaning of עקב as 'hold by the heel' but also, and maybe even more, to the meaning of crookedness and deception.

The other approach, which seeks to preserve the old name along with the new, interprets the name *Jacob* favorably by describing Jacob as a 'perfect man' (תם, Gen 25:17). This approach relies on the hidden Midrashic derivation of the name *Jacob* from the noun עקב, indicating payment and reward.

The name *Israel* is also ambiguous, but since it was given by an angel or God Himself, all the Midrashic derivations proposed have a positive meaning. The explanation of the name according to the biblical narrative, "for you have striven with God . . . and have prevailed" (Gen 32:29), presents a structural-syntactical difficulty. In principle, theophoric names are constructed as a sentence in which God is the subject and the verb is the predicate. However, in the name *Israel*, God is the object of the verb, and someone else has striven with Him. This conception also reveals a theological difficulty by implying that God was defeated in a struggle with a human. Therefore, the component אל in the name ישראל is interpreted by the Midrash (*Megilla* 40a; *Gen Rab.* 98, 3) as referring to Jacob and consequently as the subject of the syntagm that composes the name.

Reading 'Israel' as 'Išrael' (neutralization of *ś-š*) created additional Midrashic derivations. The interpretation in *Gen. Rab.* 78, 3 of כי שרית עם אלהים (Gen 32:29) 'You are the one whose icon is engraved above' reads *sarita* as *šarita* from the root שרי in the sense of 'dwell', or from the root שור, meaning 'looking and seeing'. Other Midrashic interpretations derive the sense of seeing from the root ראי by pronouncing the name ישראל, meaning איש ראה אל 'a man whom God saw' (according to *Tanna Debe Eliyyahu Rabba* 27) or 'a man who saw God' (Philo). The reading 'Israel' also approximates this name to the title *Yešurun*, which appears four times in the Bible (Deut 32:15; 33:5, 26; Isa 44:2).

"Moses Had Written about Many Deeds . . . and David Came and Explained Them" (Exodus Rabbah 15:22)

Avigdor Shinan

The article includes a first publication (based on manuscripts) of a long passage in the form of a Proem from *Midrash Exodus Rabbah*. The passage understands Psalm 104 as a systematic explanation of the story of Genesis 1 and includes 13 parables. These parables are of two kinds: *antithetical parables*, in which God is contrasted to a human king ("a human king does so and so . . . , but God . . ."); and *comparative parables*, in which God is compared to human beings ("God is compared to a human king that . . ."). The author suggests an explanation for the different use of these parables. It seems that the parables that describe God's continuous and everlasting characteristics are *antithetical*, while those that describe the past events of creation are *comparative* in order to imply that the creation of the world was for God a common and uncomplicated enterprise.

Index of Authors

Classical and Premodern Authors and Authorities

References to ancient, medieval, and other premodern authors are listed here; citations of written works by these authors are included in the Index of Ancient and Premodern Sources under the appropriate category.

Index of Scripture

Hebrew Canon

The Hebrew Bible is indexed according to Hebrew chapter and verse divisions; where the English versification differs, English chapter and verse are supplied in brackets.

Apocrypha

New Testament

Index of Ancient and Premodern Sources

Ancient Near Eastern Sources

Classical Sources

Qumran Scrolls

Bible Translations and Manuscripts

Rabbinic Sources

Commentaries on the Talmud

Jewish Legal Sources

Medieval Grammarians

Traditional Jewish Bible Commentaries

Miscellaneous

תהלה למשה

מחקרים במקרא ובמדעי היהדות
מוגשים למשה גרינברג

תהלה למשה

מחקרים במקרא ובמדעי היהדות
מוגשים למשה גרינברג

עורכים

אליהו דב אייכלר   יעקב חיים טיגאי
מרדכי כוגן

אייזנבראונס
וינונה לייק, אינדיאנה תשנ"ז

פרסום ספר זה התאפשר בסיועם האדיב של:

קרן מאגר בסיסי של האוניברסיטה העברית בירושלים
בית המדרש ללימודי היהדות בירושלים ובית המדרש לרבנים באמריקה
קרן לוציוס נ' ליטאואר
הרשות למחקר של אוניברסיטת פנסילווניה, ארה"ב

עריכה לשונית: יגאל מולדבסקי
התקנה והבאה לדפוס: דניאל שפיצר
סדר ועימוד: פוזנר ובניו, ירושלים
Hebrew section typeset by Posner & Sons, Jerusalem

תוכן העניינים של החלק העברי

מחקרים במקרא

פני ה'

שמואל אחיטוב

אוניברסיטת בן-גוריון בנגב

לאחר הסיפור על התגלות ה' בסיני ופרשת המשפטים ששם משה לפני בני ישראל, בא קטע המפסיק
את הרצף ומפריד בין סיפור ההתגלות (שמ' יט-כ) ופרשת המשפטים (שמ' כא, א-כג, יט) לבין
טקס הברית (שמ' כד, א-יא) ועליית משה אל ההר לקבל את הלוחות (כב, יב-יח). פרשייה זו מדברת
בביאת הארץ וכיבושה, ובהזהרות שלא לכרות ברית ליושבי הארץ ולאלוהיהם (כג, כ-לג).
הפרשייה, הנראית כמשנה-תורתית בלשונותיה וברוחה,[1] פותחת בהודעה על המלאך שה' ישלח
לשמור על העם בדרך ולהביאו אל הארץ.

ההודעה על המלאך היא טובה שה' גומל לעמו. עם זאת ה' מזהיר את העם: 'השמר מפניו ושמע
בקלו אל תמֵר בו כי לא ישא לפשעכם כי שמי בקִרבו' (פס' כא). הרי שהמלאך כמוהו כאלוהים עצמו.
לא זו בלבד שבני ישראל נצטוו לשמוע בקולו של המלאך ולא להמרות את פיו, אלא שבכוחו גם
להעניש, וכאדוניו אף הוא קפדן 'כי לא ישא לפשעכם'. קפדנות זו מובנת לפי מה שכתוב 'כי שמי
בקִרבו'. יש במלאך ממהותו של האל, והוא נושא אותה בקרבו. השם הוא המהות, כמו שניתן ללמוד
מכתובים הרבה, השווה למשל לתיאורו של שם ה' ביש' ל, כז-כח, תיאור של האל הקוצף: 'הנה שֵם
ה' בא ממרחק בֹעֵר אפו וכֹבֶד מַשָׂאָה שפתיו מלאו זעם ולשונו כאש אֹכָלֶת' וגו'. בכתוב זה כמו
בכתובים אחרים אפשר להשמיט את המלה שֵם והכתוב לא יֵצא חסר. המלה שֵם לא באה אלא מפני
עידון תפיסת האלוהות והרחקת ההגשמה.[2]

פרשייה זו על המלאך שה' ישלח לישראל לנחותו בדרך מזכירה מקום אחר, סיפור חטא העגל
והתגלות האל למשה בנקרת הצור (שמ' לב-לג), שגם בו ה' מודיע למשה על מלאך שישלח לפני
העם. אלא שיש שיש הפרש גדול בין שתי הפרשיות ומגמתן. אף-על-פי-כן יש ביניהן קשר כפי שראו
כבר בעלי המדרש שדרשו את הכתוב 'הנה אנכי שולח מלאך' (שמ' כג, כ): 'אמר הקב"ה לישראל
אילו זכיתם אני בעצמי נעשיתי לכם שליח כדרך שעשיתי לכם במדבר, שנאמר "וה' הולך לפניהם

1   M. Noth, *Exodus* (OTL), London 1962, p. 192

2   קשה להגדיר במדויק את המשמעות של 'שם'. גזניוס תרגם את 'שם' כאן לא במלה הלטינית nomen, אלא
במושג numen. ראה: W. Gesenius, *Lexicon Manuale Hebraicum et Chaldaicum in Veteris*
Testamenti Libros, Lipsia 1833, p. 1017. המונח numen כללי ומעורפל. משמעו כוח מניע שבאדם, אל
או דומם כלשהו, ראה: H.J. Rose, *Religion in Greece and Rome*, New York 1959, pp. 161ff. ועוד ראה
להלן הע' 17.

יומם" וגו' (שמ' יג, כא). ועכשיו שלא זכיתם הריני מוסר אתכם לשליח שנאמר "הנה אנכי שולח מלאך". ואימתי נמסרו לשליח בשעה שעבדו עבודה זרה' וגו' (שמ"ר לב, ג).

לאחר חטא העגל והנקמה בעובדיו (שמ' לב, א-כט), התחנן משה על העם לפני ה' (פס' ל-לב). בתשובת ה' למשה שני חלקים: 'מי אשר חטא לי אמחנו מספרי' (פס' לג) – רק האשמים יֵענשו; והוראה למשה: 'ועתה לך נחֵה את העם אל אשר דברתי לך' (פס' לד), והוסיף לכך דברי חיזוק ועידוד: 'הנה מלאכי ילך לפניך' (שם).

בהמשך באו הדברים ביתר הרחבה. שם הכתובים מפרשים את מצוות ה' למשה להנחות את העם אל הארץ (לג, א) ומרחיבים בעניני המלאך (פס' ב).[3] בשני הכתובים ה' מבטיח למשה לשלוח מלאך, לחזק את משה למלא את המצווה להביא את העם אל הארץ. אין כאן שום נימה שלילית. בניגוד להודעה על המלאך בשמ' כג, גם אין כאן שום הזהרה לשמוע בקול המלאך ולהיזהר בו כבאדוניו.

אבל מיד מתהפכת נימת הכתוב מחיוב לשלילה: 'כי לא אעלה בקרבך כי עם קשה עורף אתה פן אֲכֶלְךָ בדרך' (פס' ג[א]). הסתלקותו של ה' מלהיעלות את העם בעצמו ושליחת המלאך מתפרשת כאמצעי של זהירות: 'פן אֲכֶלְךָ בדרך'. התנהגותו של העם מהווה סיכון לעצמם, שכן התנהגות זו עלולה להכעיס את האל. מציאותו של האל בסמיכות מיידית אל העם עלולה להביא עליו אסון כבד. צריך שיהיה מרחק בין האל לעם, מרחק מְמַתֵּן. לפיכך התרחקותו של ה' מן המחנה היא לטובת העם. כדי להדגים את הדבר ממהר הכתוב לספר על תגובתו השלילית של העם לדברי ה': 'וישמע העם את הדבר הרע הזה ויתאבלו ולא שתו איש עדיו עליו' (פס' ד), ועל זעמו של ה' עליהם: 'אתם עם קשה עורף' – בהתנהגותם: 'ויתאבלו ולא שתו איש עדיו עליו' (פס' ד), הוכיחו את צדקת ה' בהחלטתו שלא לעלות בקרב העם: 'רגע אחד אעלה בקרבך וכליתיך' (פס' ה[א]).

משה הסיק מסקנה מיידית ונטה את אוהל מועד 'מחוץ למחנה הרחק מן המחנה' (פס' ז). מאחר שה' נועד למשה באוהל מן הדין שהאוהל יהיה מחוץ למחנה. משה אינו מערער על גזרת ה'; העם הם שהתאבלו על החלטתו של ה' שלא לעלות בקרבם ושלוח מלאך.

לכאורה ניתן היה לסיים כאן את פרשת הסתלקותו של ה' מקרב המחנה ושליחת המלאך. אבל לאחר שהכתובים סיפרו בתגובתם הראשונה של משה ובנטיית אוהל מועד מחוץ למחנה מתוך הסכמה לגזירת ה', באה בקשת משה לדעת מי הוא המלאך-השליח: 'ראה אתה אֹמֵר אלי הַעַל את העם הזה ואתה לא הודעתני את אשר תשלח עמי' (פס' יב). בקשתו של משה נראית כמובנת מאליה, רק שבהמשכם הדברים קשים והם מהפרשיות הקשות והסבוכות שבתורה. בקשתו של משה לדעת מי הוא השליח אינה אלא פתיחה לבקשתו לדעת את ה' ואת דרכיו, וניסיון להניא את ה' מלבצע את גזירתו, ולהוסיף ולהתהלך בקרב עמו.

משה מקדים לבקשתו: 'ואתה אמרת ידעתיך בשם וגם מצאת חן בעיני' (פס' יב). הקדמה זו מציגה שוויון כביכול בין משה לקב"ה: 'ואתה אמרת ידעתיך בשם', אבל – אומר משה – אני איני יודע אותך: 'ועתה אם נא מצאתי חן בעיניך הודעני נא את דרכך ואדעך' (פס' יג). בדבריו אלה יש לפי הבנתנו העזה רבה. הם פותחים בתחינה: 'אם נא מצאתי חן בעיניך', ומסיימים בהתנצלות: 'למען

---

3 פס' ב נראה כמפריד בין פס' א לפס' ג[א], ומותיר את הפסוקית 'אל ארץ זבת חלב ודבש' (ג[א]) ללא הקשר סביר. אבל ספק בעיני אם יש לתפוס את פס' ב כתוספת שנתנחבה בין שני חלקיו של כתוב אחד. נראה יותר שהפסוקית 'אל ארץ זבת חלב ודבש' נוספה אחרי מניין עממי כנען. השווה שמ' ג, יז: 'ואמר אעלה אתכם ... אל ארץ הכנעני ... והיבוסי אל ארץ זבת חלב ודבש'.

אמצא חן בעיניך'. משה מבקש: איני מבקש לדעת את דרכיך אלא על מנת שאדע כיצד להתנהג
וכך למצוא חן בעיניך, וזאת כדי שאוכל למלא את מצוותך 'הַעַל את העם הזה' (פס' יב), ולפיכך
מיהר להזכיר את העם: 'וראה כי עמך הגוי הזה' (פס' יג).

בקשתו של משה אינה נענית. תשובת ה' אינה מן העניין. ה' אינו עונה לו על 'הוֹדִעֵנִי נא את דרכך
ואדעך'. תשובתו, 'פני יֵלֵכוּ וַהֲנִחֹתִי לָךְ' (פס' יד), עונה רק על הרישא של פס' יב: 'ואתה לא הודעתני
את אשר תשלח עמי'. אין בהם תשובה לבקשתו של משה לדעת את דרכי ה', כי אם סירוב מנומס:
'וַהֲנִחֹתִי לָךְ', די לך בזה ש'פני יֵלֵכוּ', ואינך צריך לדעת את דרכי.

פירוש 'וַהֲנִחֹתִי לך' קשה. רוב פרשנינו פירשוהו על כיבוש הארץ. כך למשל רשב"ם: 'אלך עמך
לכבוש את הארץ עד שאניח לך מכל אויביך מסביב, כדכתיב "עד אשר יניח ה' לאחיכם ככם" (דב'
ג, כ), "והיה בהניח ה' אלהיך לך מכל אויביך" וגו' (שם כה, יט)'. רשב"ם התווכח עם מי שפירשוהו
מלשון נחת רוח: 'והמפרש "וַהֲנִחֹתִי לָךְ" נחת רוח אעשה במה שאעשה בקשתך שטות הוא. וכי בכל
הדברים שהיה הקב"ה מתרצה לבקשת משה יאמר לו "והנחתי לך"'? אבל הפירוש על כיבוש הארץ
אינו פשוטו של מקרא, וקרוב יותר שהקב"ה בתשובתו ביקש לומר למשה, בכך שפני ילכו אניח לך
מדאגתך (למשמעות זו השווה יש' יד, ג: 'ביום הניח ה' לך מֵעָצְבְּךָ וּמֵרָגְזֶךָ')[4] בכך הקב"ה פטר את
עצמו מלהשיב על בקשת משה לדעת את דרכי ה'.

אבל תשובת ה' לא הניחה את דעתו של משה. הוא לא הסתפק בהבטחת ה' 'פני ילכו', וביקש
אישור כי 'פני ה'' אכן ילכו עמם, וכי הוא עצמו מצא חן בעיני ה': 'ויאמר אליו אם אין פניך הלכים
אל תַּעֲלֵנוּ מזה ובמה יָוָדַע אפוא כי מצאתי חן בעיניך אני ועמך הלוא בלכתך עמנו' (פס' טו-טז[א]).
חילופי הדברים בין ה' ומשה מחייבים בירור, מה הם הפנים הללו, פני ה'; שהרי בהמשך מסביר משה
כיצד ידע כי הוא והעם מצאו חן בעיני ה' 'הלא בלכתך עמנו'. מה פשר דרישתו של משה מאת ה'
שפניו ילכו, או שהוא עצמו ילך עם העם?

'פני ה'' נזכרים בכתובים רבים, ורובם דימויים ציוריים,[5] לכמה דימויים כאלה יש כנראה
פריהיסטוריה אנתרופומורפית, דוגמת הכתובים המדברים במצוות העלייה לרגל: 'שלש פעמים
בשנה יראה כל זכורך את פני האדן ה'' וגו' (שמ' לד,כג; דב' טז,טז), וכן 'בַּעֲלֹתְךָ לֵרָאוֹת את פני
ה' אלהיך' (שמ' לד, כד), 'ולא יֵרָאֶה את פני ה' ריקם' (דב' טז, טז). כך גם התפלל המשורר: 'מתי
אבוא וְאֵרָאֶה פני אלהים' (תה' מב, ג). חנה שנמנעה לעלות לשילה עם אלקנה אחרי לדתה את
שמואל אמרה לאישה: 'עד יִגָּמֵל הנער וַהֲבִאֹתִיו וְנִרְאָה את פני ה'' (שמ"א א, כב). בכל הכתובים
הללו אין 'את פני' אלא 'לפני'[6] כמו שמצינו בשמ' כג, יז: 'שלש פעמים בשנה יראה כל זכורך אל
פני האדן ה''.

ביסודו של שימוש הלשון לראות את פני האל – מעשה של ממש, התייצבות לפני האל במקדשו
כדרך אדם העומד לפני רבו. במקדשים של עבודה זרה אולי עמד לפני צלם האל, כדי שהאל יֵרָאֶה

---

4   בתרגום היהודי האנגלי החדש (NJPS): 'אקל מעליך'. אהרליך הציע לגרוס כאן 'והנחתיך', הפעיל משורש
     נח"ה (A.B. Ehrlich, *Randglossen zur hebräischen Bibel* 1, Leipzig 1908 [repr. Hildesheim 1968],
     p. 405. לא כן בספרו העברי: מקרא כפשוטו א, ברלין תרנ"ט [ד"צ ירושלים תשכ"ט], עמ' 202).

5   ברובם דנתי במאמרי 'פניך יעקב', בספר הזיכרון ליעקב ליכט (בדפוס).

6   למשמעות של 'את פני' בהוראת 'לפני' השווה שמ"א ב, יא: 'והנער היה משרת את ה' את פני עלי הכהן', וכן
     בפס' יח: 'ושמואל משרת את פני ה''. נראה שאף המקור של 'לפני' בפנים, לעמוד מול הפנים, להיות מול הפנים
     של אדם או חפץ. לראשונה כנראה בהוראת מקום ואחר-כך גם בהוראה של זמן.

את העומד לפניו, והוא יֵרָאֶה לאל. ואילו בכתובים אין שהכוונה שהמבקר במקדש יראה את פני האל ממש; הכתובים גורסים תמיד רא"ה בהפעיל או נפעל. הלשון לֵרָאוֹת לפני האל שבכתובים כבר יצא משימושו הקדמון הראשוני והפך לדפוס לשוני שמשמעו לבוא למקדש כדברי הנביא: 'כי תבאו לֵרָאוֹת פני מי בִּקֵשׁ זאת מידכם רמֹס חֲצֵרָי' (יש' א, יב). ראיית פני האל אף הפכה לדימוי פיוטי, כלשון המשורר: 'ואני בצדק אחזה פניך אשבעה בהקיץ תמונתך' (תה' יז, טו).

אחת ההוראות של פנים היא עצמיות, האיש עצמו, וזאת משום שהפנים הם האיבר המייחד אדם מזולתו, מבני-אדם אחרים. אדם ניכר בפניו. לפיכך פירוש חושי לאבשלום: 'ופניך הלכים בקרב' (שמ"ב יז, יא) הוא: אתה עצמך תצא בראש הצבא. כך יש לפרש גם את הכתוב בדב' ד, לז על יציאת מצרים: 'ויוֹצִאֲך בפניו בכחו הגדל', הקב"ה בכבודו ובעצמו הוציאם ממצרים ולא על ידי שליח.[7] נראה שבדרך זו יש לפרש גם את דברי המקונן: 'פני ה' חִלְּקָם לא יוסיף להביטם' (איכה ד, טז) – ה' עצמו חילקם והפיצם בגויים והסיר עיניו מהם.

האם ניתן להחיל פירוש זה גם על דברי ה' למשה 'פני ילכו והניחתי לך' (שמ' לג, יד)? אכן אילו היה הכתוב מנותק מהקשרו היה סובל פירוש זה. אבל לפי שהדברים באו לאחר הודעת ה' למשה שהוא עצמו לא יעלה את העם, רק ישלח שליח, לא ניתן לפרש שבאמרו 'פני ילכו' התכוון לומר 'אני עצמי אלך'. על כרחך יש לפרש את 'פני האל' מצד אחד בזיקה לפרשת המלאך בשמ' לג, א ואילך, ומצד שני בקשר להתגלות ה' למשה בצור ששם אמר לו, למשה: 'וראית את אחרי ופני לא יֵרָאוּ' (פס' כג).

פנים אינם כאן דימוי ציורי, אלא כלשונם. ה' הודיע למשה 'פני ילכו'. ומשה קיבל: 'אם אין פניך הולכים אל תעלנו מזה' (שמ' לג, יג-יד). בהמשך נאמר שמשה ביקש לראות את פני ה', אלא שדבר זה הוא מן הנמנע: 'לא תוכל לראות את פני כי לא יראני האדם וָחָי' (פס' כ), 'ופני לא יֵרָאוּ' (פס' כג). אבל משה לא ביקש בפירוש לראות את פני ה', דבריו מצוערפים בבקשה לראות את כבוד ה': 'הראני נא את כבדך' (פס' יח). מתשובת ה' נראה שאי-אפשר לו לאדם לראות את הכבוד: 'והיה בעבר כבדי ושמתיך בנקרת הצור ושכֹּתי כפי עליך עד עָבְרִי וַהֲסִרֹתִי את כפי וראית את אחרי ופני לא יֵרָאוּ' (פס' כב-כג). משה יסתתר בנקרת הצור עד שכבוד ה' יעבור; רק אחרי שה' יעבור ויסיר את כפו[8] המכסה על משה, יוכל משה לראות את אחורי השכינה.

לבקשתו של משה לראות את כבודו, ענה לו ה': 'אני אעביר כל טובי על פניך וקראתי בשם ה' לפניך וחנתי את אשר אחן ורחמתי את אשר ארחם' (פס' יט). אין כאן תשובה לבקשת משה. אכן, נראה שהכתוב אינו מגוף התשובה ה'מקורית'. יש בו הכנה לקראת פרשת המידות שבהמשך (לד, ה ואילך). תשובת ה' לבקשת משה לראות את פניו באה בפס' כ-כב: 'ויאמר לא תוכל לראות את פני ... וראית את אחרי ופני לא יֵרָאוּ'. ואין הכבוד אלא פני האל. החילופים בין פנים לכבוד מעידים על הנפתולים שנפתלו בעלי הפרשה כדי לצמצם את ההאנשה הגסה שבתיאור האלוהות. גם פס' יט שייך לניסיונות העידון של הפרשה. אף שהוא מהווה הקדמה לפרשת מידותיו של ה', יש לחלק[ו]

---

7   אונקלוס תרגם 'במימרה', להרחיק את ההגשמה. רשב"ם: '"ועברתי בארץ מצרים" (שמ' יב, יב), "וה' הולך לפניהם יומם" (שם יג, כא)'. אבל ראב"ע הביא פירושי אחרים: 'בכעס שכעס על מצרים (פירשו פנים כמו כעס, על דרך לתת פנים) ויש אומרים כמו "ומלאך פניו הושיעם" (יש' סג, ט), ולפי דעתי שהוא כמו "ופניך הולכים בקרב" (שמ' יז, יא)'.

8   הציור האנתרופומורפי הגס של כף ידו של הקב"ה המכסה את משה נתעדן בלשון הנביא ביש' מט, ב, המדבר בשליח ה': 'בצל ידו החביאני'; נא, טז: 'ובצל ידי כסיתיך', לא עוד יד האל עצמה אלא צלה של היד.

לשניים. הרישא מדברת בטובו של הקב"ה: 'אני אעביר כל טובי על פניך'. טובו של הקב"ה יעבור
לפני משה הטמון בנקרת הצור, ואין טובו של ה' אלא מה שפס' כב קורא 'כבוד'. לחלק השני של
הרישא 'וקראתי בשם ה' לפניך' לכאורה אין זיקה לעניין. אבל לא כן הוא: אף זו תשובה לבקשתו
של משה לדעת את ה'. מה ה' מכיר את משה היכרות אינטימית – יודעו בשם (פס' יב, יז), אף ה'
ניאות למשה ומודיעו את שמו: 'וקראתי בשם ה' לפניך'.

הסיפא 'וחנתי את אשר אחן ורחמתי את אשר ארחם' אינה עונה על בקשתו של משה לראות את
פני ה', את כבודו; היא מבשרת את פרשת שלוש-עשרה המידות הפותחות בתיבות 'ה' ה' אל רחום
וחנון' (לד, ו). אבל היא גם מהווה המשך לתשובת ה' לתחינת משה אחרי מעשה העגל. משה ביקש
'אם תשא חטאתם' וגו' (לב, לב), וה' ענהו: 'מי אשר חטא לי אמחנו מספרי ... וביום פקדי ופקדתי
עליהם חטאתם' (לב, לג-לד). אבל היכן נשיאת החטא והסליחה? בא הכתוב ואמר: 'וחנתי את אשר
אחן ורחמתי את אשר ארחם'.

הפרשה המסובכת והמפותלת כמו שהיא מצויה לפנינו היא שלב אחרון בהתגבשותה. שלב המעיד
על הנסיונות שעברה הפרשה הקשה כל כך לעיכול מבחינה תיאולוגית, עד שהתפיסה
האנתרופומורפית הראשונית נתעדנה, ובמהלך העיבוד נשתלבו בתוכה עניינים שונים.[9]

לאחר שכבר נתברר לנו למעלה כי 'פני ה'' האמורים כאן אינם דימוי ציורי אלא ממשות, ודברי
ה' 'פני ילכו' הם התשובה לטענת משה 'ואתה לא הודעתני את אשר תשלח עמי' (שמ' לג, יב), נודע
לנו כי 'פני ה'' הם המלאך-השליח של שמ' לב, לד ואילך. המסורת של כג, ב ואילך לא זיהתה את
המלאך, ואילו זו של לב, לד ואילך זיהתה אותו עם 'פני ה''.

כיצד תפסו הקדמונים את 'פני ה''? לפי שקשה ללמוד על תפיסתם מתוך הכתובים עצמם, שומה
עלינו להיעזר במקורות חוץ-מקראיים.

בכתובות כנעניות (פוניות) מצפון אפריקה נזכרת לרוב האלה תִנת. התואר הנפוץ שלה הוא 'פני
בעל'. המדובר בכתובות רבות שבהן חוזרת נוסחת ההקדשה 'לרבת לתנת פן בעל',[10] היינו: לגבירה
לתנת פני בעל. תנת שהיתה אחת האלוהויות החשובות בקרתחדשת ומושבותיה, כנראה האלה
הראשית,[11] נחשבה כהתגלמות (היפוסטזה) של בעל. היא התגלמותו של בעל שבה הוא מתקרב אל
בני-אדם. האל הרם עצמו כבר התרחק מעובדיו והטיל על תנת לייצגו, כשם שהמלך אינו נגיש לכל
נתיניו, רק לשריו, והם המתווכים בינו לבין הנתינים. כך נעשתה תנת לאלה המגינה, הנאמנה
והאהובה שכל הרואה אותה רואה את פני בעל.[12]

---

9   על מורכבותה של הפרשה עמדו רבים, ראה למשל בפירושיהם של דרייבר ונות על אתר (S.R. Driver, *The*
    Book of Exodus [CBSC], Cambridge 1911; Noth, *ibid.* [n. 1]). הניתוח למקורות, תוספות, כפיליות וכו'
    מעיד על הקשיים בנסיונות להתיר את הפקעת שנסתבכה במהלך הדורות שבהם נתגבשה הפרשה מרבדים שונים
    שנתרבדו בה.

10 ראה נ' סלושץ, אוצר הכתבות הפניקיות, תל-אביב וירושלים תש"ב, במפתח.

11 על תנת ראה F.O. Hvidberg-Hansen, *La Déesse TNT: Une étude sur la religion canaanéo-punique*
    1-2, Copenhagen 1979

12 כך מנסח את הדברים אייכרודט W. Eichrodt, *Theology of the Old Testament* 2, London 1967, p. 39
    כבר בשנת 1847 פירש די-סוסי את התואר 'פני בעל' כהופעה (manifestation) של בעל (F. de Saulcy, *Revue*
    archéologique 3 (1846), pp. 629ff. מצוטט על-פי: Ph. Berger, 'Tanit Pene Baal', *JA* [1877], pp.
    147ff.). אולברייט (W.F. Albright, *Yahweh and the Gods of Canaan*, London 1968, pp. 117-118)
    מפרש 'תנת פני בעל' כזוהר פני בעל.

אפשר ששמה של תנת אינו אלא שם־עצם כללי שהיה לשם אלוהות. אם נכונה הצעתו של
אולברייט,[13] ששמו של המלך הצידוני Tennes אינו אלא תבנת, ולפנינו תופעה של הבלעת הבי"ת
בנו"ן שנכפלה לתשלום הבי"ת, אפשר לקבל גם את השערתו שהשם תנת, המועתק בכתובות
לטיניות Tinnit וכיו"ב,[14] בהכפלת n, הוא צורה מכווצת של תבנת. אין 'תנת פן בעל' אלא תבנית
פני בעל, היינו צורת, תמונת, פני בעל. תנת לא היתה אלוהות עצמאית אלא חלק בלתי נפרד של
בעל, פרצופו הנראה לבני־אדם. במשך הזמן נשתכח המובן הראשוני של התיבה תנת, והיא הפכה
לשמה הפרטי של האלה החשובה ביותר אצל כנעני צפון אפריקה.

לתופעה דומה אנו עדים באשקלון. במטבעות אשקלון הרומאית מתוארת דמות של אלוהות
שלגופה כיתון ושריון ולראשה קובע. בימינה נבל ובשמאלה מגן עגול וכפת תמרים. זהותה של
אלוהות זו נודעה מכתובת המופיעה במטבע אשקלוני כזה מימי הדריינוס, ומזהה אותה כ'פני בעל'
(Phanebalos).[15] באשקלון של התקופה הרומאית נתפס 'פני בעל' כאלוהות עצמאית ולא כתואר
של אלוהות. נראה שיש לזהות אלוהות זו, הידועה רק בתקופה הרומאית, באלוהות הראשית של
אשקלון שאינה אלא עשתרת, כפי שלמדנו מעדותו של הרודוטוס (א 105), המספר על חורבן
מקדשה של אפרודיטי השמיימית (Aphrodite Urania) באשקלון בידי הסקיתים.

על זיהויה של עשתרת של אשקלון באפרודיטי של היוונים ראה למשל בכתובת דולשונית
מאתונה (CIS I 115). בנוסח הפיניקי נזכר 'שמ[ ] בן עבדעשתרת אשקלני', ובנוסח היווני הוא קרוי
Antipatros Aphrodisou Aska[lonites] (אנטיפטרוס עבד אפרודיטי האשקלוני).

שעשתרת נתפסה כהתגלמות של תכונה של בעל נודע כבר מכתבי אוגרית, והרי זו עדות מוצקה
לקדמותן של תפיסות כאלה. שם נאמר בעלילת כרת:

ויעני.כרת.ת'ע.	ויען כרת השוע:
ית'בר. חרן. יבן.	ישבור חורון, הוי בן,
ית'בר. חרן.ראשׁך.	ישבור חורון ראשך
עת'תרת.שם.בעל.קדקדך.	עשתרת־שם־בעל קדקדך[16]

עדות מאוחרת יותר באה בכתובת שעל ארונו של אשמנעזר ב' מלך צידון. שם מתפאר אשמנעזר
שבנה בתים לאלים ובהם 'בת לעשתרת שם בעל' (KAI 14:18), היינו: בית לעשתרת שם בעל.
בדומה לתנת שנתפסה כהתגלמות של פני בעל, נתפסה עשתרת כהתגלמות של שמו של בעל,
כלומר של מהותו של בעל, שהרי אין השם אלא מהותו של בעל השם ועצמיותו.[17] באשקלון חל

13 שם, עמ' 37–38, הע' 86.

14 ראה: W. Röllig, 'Tinnit', in: H.W. Haussig (ed.), *Götter und Mythen im Vorderen Orient*
(*Wörterbuch der Mythologie* I), Stuttgart 1965, p. 311

15 אולברייט (לעיל, הערה 12, עמ' 112–113) סבור שפנבלוס של אשקלון הוא התגלמות של האלה ענת. למטבעות
אשקלון המתארות את 'פניבעל' ראה: G. Finkelsztein, 'Phanebal, déesse d'Ascalon', *Studia*
Phoenicia 9 (1992), pp. 51-58, pls. xi-xii. ידידי פרופ' ח"י גרינפלד ז"ל הוא שהסב את תשומת לבי למאמרו
של פינקלשטיין.

16 C.H. Gordon, *Ugaritic Textbook*, Rome 1965, p. 194 (127:54-57 [CTA 16 {127}] vi 54-57

17 ראה לעיל, הערה 2. ב'עשתרת שם בעל' דן אולברייט (לעיל, הערה 12, עמ' 117), ופירש אותו 'זוהר שמו של
בעל'. לטענתו יש לפרש עשתרת–זוהר, אלא שפירושו מפותל ביותר ואני מסתפק בתקפותו. מן הראוי להזכיר

תהליך שונה. עשתרת, שבמקומות אחרים היתה התגלות של שם בעל, היתה באשקלון היפוסטזה
של פני בעל. בשלב לא ידוע – ככל הנראה מאוחר – ניתק התואר מהמתואר, מעשתרת, ונעשה
לאלוהות עצמאית.[18]

כשם שתנת ועשתרת נתפשו לבני קרתחדשת ואגפיה ולבני אשקלון כהתגלמויות של פני בעל,
של החלק המהותי והאופייני שלו, כך גם המלאך שהוליך את בני ישראל במדבר, שלוחו של האל,
אינו אלא התגלמות של פני ה'. באמצעות המלאך יכולים בני ישראל לקרב אל האל הנורא, שאי־
אפשר לראותו: 'כי לא יראני האדם וָחָי' (שמ' לג, כ).

לסיכום הטענה עד עכשיו: המלאך שה' הבטיח למשה שהוא יוליך את העם ויעלה אותו אל הארץ
הוא 'פני ה''. מאחר שאי־אפשר לראות את פני ה', לפי ששהותו של ה' בקרב העם מסוכנת ומסכנת
את העם, בא מלאך – פני ה' – מלאך הפנים לַמצע בין ה' לעמו.

מסתבר שגם שם המקום פנואל / פניאל, שהכתוב דורש אותו 'כי ראיתי אלהים פנים אל פנים'
(בר' לו, לא) שייך לענייננו. הסיפור המספר על היאבקותו של יעקב עם 'האיש' צופן בקרבו משהו
על פני ה'. מסתבר שהכתובים מטשטשים את הסיפור המקורי ומבקשים להימלט מהאנתרופו־
מורפיזם הגס שבו. הסיפור פותח ומספר 'ויאבק איש עמו' (בר' לב, ה). שה'איש' אינו בדיוק איש
ברור מהמשך. יעקב אינו מניח לו ללכת: 'ויאמר לא אשלחך כי אם ברכתני' (פס' כז). יעקב –
וכמוהו המספר – יודע שאין זה סתם איש. האיש קורא את שמו ישראל 'כי שָׂרית עם אלהים ואם
אנשים ותוכל' (פס' כט). והיכן שָׂרה עם אלהים – כאן. יעקב מבקש לדעת מי המברך שנאבק עמו:
'הגידה נא שמך', ואינו נענה: 'ויאמר למה זה תשאל לשמי' (פס' ל). הרי זה דומה למה שסופר בפרשת
התגלות המלאך להורי שמשון, למנוח ואשתו, שם אומר מנוח למלאך: 'מי שמך' וגו' (שופ' יג, יז),
והמלאך משתמט 'למה זה תשאל לשמי והוא פלאי' (פס' יח).

מסופו של הסיפור עולה שברור ליעקב שמי שנאבק עמו הוא מלאך אלהים: 'ויקרא יעקב שם
המקום פניאל כי ראיתי אלהים פנים אל פנים ותנצל נפשי' (פס' לא). הסיפור הוא סיפור אטיולוגי
על שמו של המקום והוא מגלה לי משהו על תפיסתם של הקדמונים על המלאך. מה ביסודו של
הסיפור על פניאל לא ברור לי. מה שכן ברור הוא, שיש בו משהו על מאבק במלאך, ואני יכול לשער
שמלאך זה הוא 'פני האל' אבל הסיפור אינו מניח לומר יותר מכך.

השקפה שמלאך פנים הוא שהוציא את ישראל ממצרים והוליכם במדבר נמצאת כנראה בנוסח

כאן את האלוהות אשמבית אל שמתעודות יב. לפי אולברייט אין אשם אלא שֵׁם W.F. Albright, *Archaeology*)
(*and the Religion of Israel*[4], Baltimore 1956, p. 174

18 לתופעה זו אפשר להשוות שתי אלות ממצרים שנתפסו כהתגלמויות של חפצים מקודשים: אסת (איסיס) נחשבה
להתגלמות של כס המלוכה (סת), ותוארה כאשה עם על ראשה הכיסא. שמה של חתחור נתפרש ונכתב כבית האל
חור (הורוס). בין שמקורן של אלות אלה אכן בהתגלמויות (אינקרנציה), בין שלפנינו פירוש לשמותיהן, הרי לנו
עדות לאמונת הקדמונים. וכמובן אין לשכוח את האלוהות ביתאל, אלוהות הידועה מהמקרא וממקורות חיצוניים.
בסיפור שיבתו של יעקב לכנען נגלה לו האל, ועודנו בארם: 'אנכי האל בית אל' (בר' לא, יג), ובבואו לבית אל
נאמר: 'ויבן שם מזבח ויקרא למקום אל בית אל' (בר' לה, ז). האל בית אל אינו אלא האלוהות ביתאל המוזכרת
בחוזה של אסרחדון מלך אשור עם בעל מלך צור (p. 534 ,[3]ANET). אבנים אלוהיות הנקראות Baetylos
מוזכרות אצל פילון מגבל (H.W. Attridge and R.A. Oden Jr., *Philo of Byblos: The Phoenician History*,
Washington 1981, p. 53). השם ביתאל בא כרכיב בשמות של אלוהיות המוזכרות בתעודות ארמיות מיב:
אשמביתאל, חרמביתאל וענתביתאל, המוזכר גם בחוזה הנ"ל של אסרחדון ובעל (A. Cowley, *Aramaic*
Papyri of the Fifth Century B.C., Oxford 1923, nos. 7:7; 22:124-125), וגם כרכיב תיאופורי בכמה שמות

המסורה של יש' סג, ט. הפרשה (פס' ז-ט) פותחת בסקירת חסדי ה' שגאל את ישראל ממצרים
והוליכם במדבר, ועוברת לתחינה נרגשת לגאולה. בתיאור הגאולה ממצרים אומר הנביא (פס' ט):
'בכל צרתם לא (כתיב, לו קרי)[19] צָר וּמַלְאַךְ פָּנָיו הוֹשִׁיעָם באהבתו ובחמלתו הוא גאלם וינטלם
וינשאם כל ימי עולם'. לעומת זאת תרגום השבעים גורס צִר (presbus) תחת צָר שבנוסח המסורה.
לפי הכתיב והשבעים יש לקרוא ולפרש: בכל צרתם, לא צָר וּמַלְאַךְ (אלא) פָּנָיו הוֹשִׁיעָם (לתקבולת
ציר//מלאך השווה מש' יג, יז)[20]. ונראה שגירסה זו עדיפה על גירסת נוסח המסורה ששם יש לקרוא
ולפרש: בכל צרתם לו צָר,[21] וּמַלְאַךְ פָּנָיו הוֹשִׁיעָם וגו'. גירסה המבוססת על תפיסה המכירה במלאך
הפָּנִים.

בספרות הסוד הבתר-מקראית נתפתחה הישות של פני ה' אל דמותו של מלאך הפָּנִים. בספר חנוך
האתיופי מסופר על המון המלאכים העומדים לפני האדון שראה חנוך 'ועל ארבעת אדון הרוחות
ראיתי ארבעה פנים שונים ... ואלמד את שמותיהם' (מ, ב). '... הראשון הוא מיכאל ... והשני ...
הוא רפאל והשלישי ... הוא גבריאל והרביעי ... פנואל שמו. אלה הם ארבעת מלאכי אדון הרוחות'
(שם, פס' ט-י; השווה שם, פרק עא, פס' ח-ט). נראה שארבעת מלאכי הפנים קשורים בתיאור החיות
מרובעות הפנים שבחזון המרכבה שראה יחזקאל (א, ו, ו ועוד).

חז"ל זיהו את המלאך המוליך את ישראל במדבר במטטרון שר הפנים. וכך נדרש בסנה' לח, ע"ב:
'כתיב "ואל משה אמר עלה אל ה'" (שמ' כד, א). עלה אלי מיבעי ליה. אמר ליה זהו מטטרון ששמו
כשם רבו כדכתיב "כי שמי בקרבו"' (שם, כג, א).

ובספר זרובבל אומר מטטרון (יש נוסחות הגורסות מיכאל, המזוהה במטטרון): 'אני הוא המלאך
שנהגתי את אברהם בכל ארץ כנען ... ואני הוא שנהגתי את ישראל במדבר ארבעים שנה בשם ה'
כי שם ה' בקרבי' (נוסח אחר: אני הוא ששמו כשם רבו).[22]

אכן, יש בספרות הסוד ששמו של מטטרון שר הפנים הוא יהואל, וגם יהוה הקטן, כמו שמצינו
בספרות ההיכלות: 'אמר ר' ישמעאל אמר לי מטטרון שר הפנים מתוך אהבה שאהב אותי הקב"ה
יותר מכל בני מרומים עשה לי לבוש של גיאות שכל מיני מאורות בו והלבישני בו ... וקראני ה'
הקטן בפני כל פמליא שלו במרום שנאמר "כי שמי בקרבו"' (שמ' כג, כא).[23]

לדיון במלאכי פנים יש הד גם מחוץ לישראל, וכנראה המדובר באותו קו מחשבה והלך רוח, מורשת
היהדות לנצרות הקדומה. באיגרת אל הקולוסיים נאמר כי ישו הוא איקונין (eikon) של האל הלא

פרטים כגון ביתאלנתן וביתאלעקב (5-18:4 ;12:9 .Cowley, ibid, nos). הרי זו עדות נחרצת שביתאל היה שם
אלוהות. ברור שאין האל ביתאל אלא התגלמות של משכנה של האלוהות, ממש כמו האלה התחתור אצל המצרים.

19   במגילת ישעיה א שממדבר יהודה כתוב 'לוא', כתיב העשוי לשקף את מלית השלילה 'לא' אבל גם מלית
     הקניין 'לו'.

20   ראה למשל: J. Skinner, Isaiah, Chapters XL-LXXVI (CBSC), Cambridge 1910, p. 200; J.L.
     McKenzie, Second Isaiah (AB), New York 1968, p. 118. לפי פירוש זה ראוי היה לנקד 'הוֹשִׁיעָם' שכן
     פניו תמיד בלשון רבים (חוץ מהכתוב החריג באיכה ד, טז: 'פני ה' חלקם לא יוסיף להביטם').

21   רד"ק: 'ופירוש הקרי "לו" לאל בצרתם על דרך "ותקצר נפשו בעמל ישראל" (שופ' י, טז)'. השווה לדברי
     המתפלל ולתחושתו שהאל נמצא עמו בכל עת: 'ואני תמיד עמָּךְ אחזת ביד ימיני בעצתך תנחני' וגו' (תה' עג,
     כג-כד).

22   מדרשי גאולה (מהדורת י' אבן-שמואל), ירושלים ותל-אביב תשי"ד, עמ' 73–74.

23   א' ילינק, בית המדרש, חדר שני, ליפסיא תרי"ג (ד"צ ירושלים תשכ"ז), עמ' 115.

נראה (א, טו). כך טען גם הגנוסטיקון תיאודוטוס המצוטט אצל קלמנס מאלכסנדריה (מת בשנת
215), כי ישו היה שר פנים, אחד משמונה ארכי־מלאכים.[24]

24 ראה מ' אידל, 'מטטרון – הערות על התפתחות המיתוס ביהדות', אצל: ח' פדיה (עורכת), המיתוס ביהדות (אשל
    באר־שבע ד), באר־שבע תשנ"ו, עמ' 39–40. גלגול מוזר של ישו כשר פנים נמצא בתפילת 'יהי רצון' שבין
    התקיעות של ראש השנה: יהי רצון לפניך ה' אלהי ואלהי אבותי שתקיעת תש"ת (=תקיעה–שברים–תקיעה)
    שאנחנו תוקעים היום תהי מרוקמת על היריעה על ידי הממונה טרטיא"ל ותקבלנה על יד אליהו זכור לטוב וישו"ע
    שר הפנים שר מטטרון. והמלא עלינו רחמים. ברוך אתה בעל הרחמים'. כיצד נתגלגל ישוע למחזור, ומי הגניבו
    פנימה חידה היא. ראה י' ליבס, 'מלאכי קול השופר וישוע שר הפנים', אצל: י' דן (עורך), המיסטיקה היהודית
    הקדומה (מחקרי ירושלים במחשבת ישראל ו/א–ב), ירושלים תשמ"ז, עמ' 171–195.

הבריאה ולוח הקדושה

יאירה אמית

אוניברסיטת תל-אביב

לשבעה ימים נדרש האל כדי להשלים את בריאת העולם. שישה ימים אמר, עשה וברא, וביום
השביעי כילה את מלאכתו ושבת מכל אשר ברא לעשות. סיפור זה (בר' א, א–ב, ד*), שמתאר את
מעשה הבריאה כיחידה של שבעה ימים, הוא ייחודי למסורת המקראית. מאז ימיו של ולהויזן
מסכימים רוב החוקרים כי לא זו בלבד שסיפור זה נמנה עם החיבור הכוהני שבתורה (P=), אלא
שהוא עדות מכרעת לתפיסה המעודנת של האל, ששלטה בבית-המדרש הכוהני, ולעיצוב השיטתי
והרציונאלי שהעניקו הכוהנים, ממשכילי החברה, למעשה הבריאה.[1]

מאמר זה מטרתו לשכנע את הקורא כי סיפור בריאה, המושתת על יחידת זמן של שבעה ימים,
שבסיומה האל שובת, מברך את היום השביעי ומקדש אותו, הוא סיפור שנכתב בבית-מדרשה של
אסכולת הקדושה (H=), שהיא כנראה גם האחראית לעריכתה הסופית של ספרות התורה.[2] אסכולת
הקדושה היא זו שהכריעה לפתוח את התורה כולה בהצגת השבת כחלק בלתי נפרד מן המעשה
הקוסמי של הבריאה. וזאת כדי להודיע על לוח קדושה, שמאפיינת אותו ספירה של שבע, משמע
קצב קבל של שבתות, והוא מנותק מספירה קוסמית, שמקורה במאורות שברקיע השמים. החיים על-פי
הדגם שקבע האל זוכים, מטבע הדברים, לממד של קדושה, שמקורו בקדושה שהוענקה ליום
השביעי. קדושה זו מייחדת ומבדלת את הבוחרים בלוח זה. לפיכך, הכתובים שבמרכזם רעיון

---

1 ראה .J. Wellhausen, *Prolegomena to the History of Ancient Israel*, New York 1957 [1883], pp
297-308, 112-116. סקירה תמציתית של תולדות המחקר של סיפור כוהני זה ראה אצל: ,C. Westermann
*Genesis 1-11: A Commentary*², tr. by J.J. Scullion, Minneapolis 1984 (1976), pp. 81-88 הנסמך על
שמידט. ביקורת על טענת חוקרי אסכולת ולהויזן, בדבר תפיסה דתית מופשטת של סיפור הבריאה, נמצאת
במאמרו של מ' ויינפלד, 'האל הבורא בבראשית א ובנבואות ישעיהו השני', בתוך: ליקוטי 'תרביץ' א, מקראה
בחקר המקרא, ירושלים תשמ"ט, עמ' 117–146 (=תרביץ לז [תשכ"ח], עמ' 105–132). לאחרונה מצא י' קנוהל
(מקדש הדממה: עיון ברובדי היצירה הכוהנית שבתורה, ירושלים תשנ"ג, עמ' 120–141) פתרון של פשרה
למתיחות זו באמצעות ההפרדה בין שתי תקופות עיקריות של התגלות האל באסכולה הכוהנית: תקופת בראשית
ותקופת משה. לשון אישית ותיאורים מאפיינים מאפיינים, לדעתו, את עידן בראשית, ואילו מגמת ההפשטה
שייכת לתיאורים של ימי משה.

2 סיכום תמציתי על ההבחנה בין H ל-P ותולדות המחקר בסוגיית H, דהיינו היקף היצירה ויחסה ל-P, ראה
לאחרונה אצל קנוהל, שם, עמ' 11–16. הוא טבע את המונח 'אסכולת הקדושה' (=אה"ק) ומחקרו מצביע על
היותה מאוחרת ל-P, ועל תפקידה בעריכת התורה.

הקדושה מטעימים כי קדושת העם אינה מתקיימת בלא שמירת הלוח האלוהי או לוח הקדושה, שהוא לוח שבתותיו, ככתוב: 'קדשים תהיו כי קדוש אני ה' אלהיכם... את שבתתי תשמרו' (וי' יט, ב-ג).

בחלקו הראשון של המאמר אראה כי השבת היא חלק בלתי נפרד מסיפור הבריאה, ויתרה מזאת – היא שיאו. לפיכך, מחברה של פיסקת השבת (=בר' ב, א-ג) הוא גם מי שאחראי לסיפור כולו. בחלק השני אתייחס לסממנים התמאטיים והסגנוניים, הקושרים בין פיסקת השבת (בר' ב, א-ג) לבין אסכולת הקדושה. בסיום אתעמק בשאלות מדוע ייחסה אסכולת הקדושה מקום כה מרכזי לשבת, עד כדי הצגתה כתשתית למעשה הבריאה והעמדתה בפתיחה לספרות התורה כולה; ומדוע נמנעה מלהביא את המונח 'שבת' ומלנקוט לשון מצוה.

1. תפקיד השבת בסיפור הבריאה

התבוננות בסיפור הבריאה מבחינת מבנהו מלמדת על חשיבות התיאור המוקדש ליום השביעי (פיסקת השבת: בר' ב, א-ג), שמשמש בו לא רק סיום של תהליך אלא גם שיאו, ולפיכך יש לראות בו חלק בלתי נפרד מן הקומפוזיציה שלו.

1.1 פיסקת השבת היא חלק אינטגרלי של סיפור הבריאה, והיא קשורה אליו בסוגים שונים של קשרים:

1.1.1 קשר של סיום – פיסקת השבת מציינת את המנוחה בתום העשייה, ולפיכך היא מהווה סיום תמאטי ועלילתי לחומרים שלפניה. מנוחה בהקשר של סיום בריאה – זהו מוטיב שחוזר ונשנה בדתות שונות.[3] לפי המסופר באנומה אליש, האדם נברא כדי לאפשר את מנוחת האלים.[4] נמצא כי הקישור בין בריאה למנוחה, ובמיוחד סמוך לבריאת האדם, הוא עתיק יומין. מצד שני, שיוך המנוחה ליום השביעי הוא חידוש ייחודי לסיפור הבריאה הישראלי.[5] לדעת רבים, היחידה המחזיקה חידוש זה, שמגמתו לייחס קדמות ולתת סמכות יתרה ליום השביעי, היא הוספה משנית, שמקנה לסיפור

---

3 R. Pettazzoni, 'Myths of Beginnings and Creation-Myths', in *Essays on the History* ראה דיונו של *of Religions*, Leiden 1967, pp. 24-36. בעמ' 32 הוא דן במונה *otiositas*, שמציין את היפוכה של היצירתיות והעשייה של מיתוס הבריאה.

4 ראה: עלילת הבריאה הבבלית – אנומה אליש, תרגום והערות מ' וינפלד, ירושלים [אקדמון] תשל"ג, לוח ו, שו' 8, וראה גם שו' 34. נציין שמקור זה אף קושר את מוטיב המנוחה לכניסת האלים למקדשם (שם, שו' 47-66). על הזיקה הקיימת בין השבת לבין המקדש ראה אצל מ' וינפלד, 'שבת ומקדש והמלכת ה': לבעיית בית היוצר של בראשית א, א – ב, ג', בית מקרא סט/ב (תשל"ז), עמ' 188-193. השווה גם להופעת מוטיב המנוחה לאחר בריאת האדם בעלילות אתרח'סס, לוח 1, שורות 240-249 (W.G. Lambert A.R. Millard, *Atra-ḥasis: The*) *Babylonian Story of the Flood*, Oxford 1969, pp. 59-61. גם פתח, אלוהי ממפיס, מתואר כמי שלאחר J.B. Pritchard (ed.), *Ancient* שהשלים את מלאכתו היה מרוצה, ויש מפרשים במקום זה לשון מנוחה, וראה *Near Eastern Texts Relating to the Old Testament*[2], Princeton, New Jersey 1955, p. 5 n. 19

5 החוקרים נוטים להדגיש, במינונים שונים, מחד גיסא את הזיקה הקיימת בין השבת לבין התרבות המסופוטמית, ומאידך גיסא את האופי הייחודי שניתן לה בתרבות הישראלית. ראה, למשל, אצל מ"ד קאסוטו, מאדם עד נח: פירוש על ספר בראשית[4], ירושלים תשכ"ה, עמ' 39-43; י' גתי, 'הנחות מוקדמות בחקר השבת', בית מקרא מה/ב (תשל"א), עמ' 171-180; י"ח טיגאי, הערך 'שבת', אנציקלופדיה מקראית ז, ירושלים תשל"ו, טור 509; ב' אופנהיימר, 'שבת-שמיטה-יובל', בית מקרא ק/א (תשמ"ה), עמ' 28-40, והביבליוגרפיה העשירה בנושא בכל אחד ממחקרים אלה.

משמעות איטיולוגית. כך למשל טוען זליגמן: 'ברור, שאין איטיולוגיה זו ראשונית כאן מבחינת
ההתפתחות הספרותית הפנימית: מעשי בראשית לא נכתבו מלכתחילה כדי להסביר את קדושת
השבת. בישראל כבבבל היו רווחים סיפורים על בריאת העולם, ולאחד מהם צורפה בשלב מסוים
תהילת השבת, המהווה כיום גולת כותרתו, ולכתחילה לא היתה קשורה קשר פנימי לסיפור
הבריאה'.[6] זליגמן מבחין בין מלאכת צירוף שנעשתה 'בשלב מסוים' לבין הסיפור 'כיום'. טענתו כי
מעשי בראשית לא נכתבו כדי להסביר את קדושת השבת – משכנעת, בראש וראשונה משום היעדר
מקבילות. עם זאת, אין ללמוד ממנה על יחסים של קדום ומאוחר בסיפור שלפנינו, משמע – על
היות הפיסקה הדנה בשבת תוספת איטיולוגית תניינית. גם לדעתי, בסיפור העכשווי השבת מהווה
לא רק חלק אינטגרלי מן הקומפוזיציה של הסיפור, אלא סיום טבעי להשתלשלות הדינמית של
המסופר, שהנו גולת הכותרת של הסיפור כולו. נמצא כי טענת האיטיולוגיה לא בהכרח מצביעה
על תניניניות בסיפור הקיים, אלא יש עמה להורות על מגמת עיבוד שחדרה בשלב כלשהו של
מסירתו. זליגמן אף מדגיש כי 'לאמיתו של דבר, הדינאמיקה הפנימית לעתים משכנעת יותר מכל
מטבע חיצוני הנחשב כאיטיולוגי'.[7] במלים אחרות, גם היעדרם של ניסוחים פורמליים, שמכוונים
לפירוש האיטיולוגי, כמו: 'על כן' או 'עד היום הזה', אינו נוטל מן המסופר את מהותו האיטיולוגית.
ולכן, העובדה שפיסקת השבת חסרה נוסחאות פורמליות, ובכל זאת הסיפור מתפרש כסיפור
איטיולוגי, תורמת להבלטת כוחה של הדינמיקה הפנימית בתפיסת השבת כחלק בלתי נפרד של
הסיפור. הקורא חש שהוא מתקדם בסדר הימים ולמד על פרטי הבריאה והגיונה. רק טבעי שדרך זו
תוביל אותו לשלב האחרון, שהוא שביתת היוצר עם תום שלבי העשייה. הכותב, או המעבד, בחר
אפוא את החומרים לבניית סיפורו החדש מתוך נוסחאות מזומנות שהיו במאגר המסורות שעמד
לפניו, או אפילו משירת עלילה קדומה שהיתה שגורה בפיו.[8] סיפור חדש זה נועד להודיע על מעין
בריאה נוספת, ישות הנקשרת עם היום השביעי, והיא – שביתה לאחר ששה ימי מלאכה. תפיסת
השביתה כסוג של יצירה עולה מן הניסוח: 'ויכל אלהים ביום השביעי', ולא ביום השישי.[9] נוסח

6 ראה למשל אצל י"א זליגמן, 'יסודות איטיולוגיים בהיסטוריוגראפיה המקראית', בתוך: מחקרים בספרות
   המקרא, בעריכת א' הורביץ, ע' טוב, ש' יפת, ירושלים תשנ"ב, עמ' 11–45 (=ציון כו [תשכ"א], עמ' 141–169).
   הציטטה לקוחה מעמ' 37.

7 זליגמן, שם, עמ' 29.

8 השווה קאסוטו (לעיל, הערה 5), עמ' 2–5; וראה מאמרו 'שירת העלילה בישראל', בתוך: ספרות מקראית וספרות
   כנענית: מחקרים במקרא ובמזרח הקדמון א, ירושלים תשל"ב, עמ' 62–90 (=כנסת ח [תש"ג/תש"ד], עמ'
   121–142). אמנם קאסוטו אינו מתייחס במפורש לפיסקת השבת, אך ניתן ללמוד על כך מהתייחסותו הכוללת,
   בעמ' 85, ל'פרשה הראשונה בספר בראשית'.

9 נוסח השומרוני, תרגום השבעים, תרגום אונקלוס והפשיטתא גורסים: ביום השישי. השווה גם לספר היובלים, ב 2, 16, וראה את
   נסיונות ההתמודדות של התלמוד והמדרש עם קושי זה באמצעות תיאור הקב"ה כמי ש'נכנס בו כחוט השערה'
   (מגילה ט, ע"א; ב"ר, י; וכן פירושו של רש"י). הגירסאות העתיקות, חז"ל והפרשנות שבאה בעקבותיהם,
   בניגוד לנה"מ, שוקלים בעיה מעשית-הלכתית של שמירת שבת, לכן אצלם ההקפדה על ההפרדה בין הימים לבין
   הנעשה בם היא מרכזית. דרך מקובלת להתמודד עם קושי זה היא פירוש הפועל 'ויכל' כעבר לפני עבר, וראה
   למשל קאסוטו (לעיל, הערה 5), עמ' 38–39. וכן G.J. Wenham, Genesis 1-15 (WBC 1), Waco, Texas
   1987, p. 35; N.M. Sarna, Genesis (The JPS Torah Commentary), Philadelphia, New-York,
   Jerusalem 1989, p. 14 ועוד. ביקורת על כיוון פרשני זה ראה כבר אצל א"ב אהרליך, מקרא כפשוטו, דברי
   תורה, ניו-יורק 1969, עמ' 4.

המסורה מכין אפוא את התשתית לצירוף האוקסימורוני של עשייה שהיא שביתה, וכך רומז ליצירת השבת, ישות חדשה, שהנה שביתה מכל מעשה מלאכה.

אמנם, היו שניסו לערער על התפיסה של פיסקת השבת כסיום טבעי, משום אי־ההתאמה שבין מעשי הבריאה לבין ימי הבריאה. לפי השקפה זו, לא ייתכן שסיפור, שהגביל עצמו לשישה ימי בריאה, יתאר בסופו של דבר שמונה מעשי בריאה, אם לא למעלה מזה.[10] ההנחה המסתתרת מאחורי טענה זו היא, שכל יום בריאה מאופיין במעשה אחד ויחיד, ולכן אין לחרוג ממסגרת של שישה מעשים.[11] אולם טענה זו אינה עומדת במבחן, מחד גיסא – משום אי־ההסכמה באשר למספר מעשי הבריאה, ומאידך גיסא – משום שהניסוח 'ויכל אלהים ביום השביעי' מותיר גם את האפשרות הפרשנית של עשייה כלשהי גם ביום השביעי. נראה אפוא כי דווקא ההקפדה על ארגון מעשי הבריאה במסגרת נוקשה של שישה ימים, והעיצוב של היום השביעי כסיום לתהליך שקדם לו, מלמדים על תכנית מוקדמת, שאינה מוכנה להתפשר עם שבעה או שמונה ימי בריאה, אלא רק עם תיאור שבבבסיסו שישה ימים ויום שביעי נוסף, שייחודו בעשיית שביתה ובמהות המקודשת שניתנה לו, ככתוב בשמ' לא, טז: 'ושמרו בני ישראל את השבת לעשות את השבת לדרתם ברית עולם'.

קשר הסיום מוטעם אף באמצעות העדפות לקסיקוגראפיות, שמתבטאות בחזרה על השורש כל"ה, המציין גמירה וסיום, ושילוב התיבה 'כל', בעלת התפקיד המסכם: 'ויכלו השמים והארץ וכל צבאם. ויכל אלהים ביום השביעי... מכל מלאכתו אשר עשה' (ב, א־ב). לשימוש החוזר בתיבה 'כל' לצד השורש כל"ה אפקט של לשון נופל על לשון, שמתחזק אף בעזרת יחסי המצלול עם התיבה 'מלאכתו'. כל אלה מעצימים את התחושה של סיום וסיכום לכל מה שקדם. אין תמה שווסטרמן פותח את פיסקת השבת בכותרת: 'סיכום של סיפור הבריאה', ובהמשך חוזר ומגדיר יחידה זו כ'פסוקי הסיכום'.[12]

1.1.2 קשר של זמן – הדיווח על יום שביעי מיד לאחר רצף של שישה ימים יוצר יחידת זמן אחת, סגורה ושלמה, של שבעה ימים, שהולמת את השימוש במספר השלמות – שבע. תקופות של שבעה ימים שכיחות במסורת המקראית ובמסורת הספרותית של המזרח הקדום. כך, למשל, באפוס האוגריתי, בניית ביתו של בעל נמשכה שישה ימים והסתיימה ביום השביעי (לוח IV 51, שו' 22–33). דנאל הצדיק, גיבור עלילת אקהת האוגריתית, פנה אל האלים כדי שיברכוהו בבן, האכיל אותם והשקה אותם במשך שבעה ימים (לוח אקהת ב: I, שו' 1–17). לאחר שנתבשר על הולדת בנו, הוא ערך משתה, שנמשך אף הוא שבעה ימים (לוח אקהת ב: II, שו' 30–40).[13] גם סערת המבול

---

10 ניתן להתאים את מעשי הבריאה לכמה מבנים מספריים. מקורה של שיטת השמונה בתיאור שתי בריאות ביום השלישי, שבו נאמר פעמיים 'כי טוב', ושתי בריאות ביום השישי, שבו נאמר גם 'כי טוב' (פס' כה) וגם 'והנה טוב מאד' (פס' לא). אולם שיטה זו מלכתחילה מכלילה את נבראי היום הרביעי, החמישי והשישי. במלים אחרות, האם השמש, הירח והכוכבים הם מעשה בריאה אחד? האם השרצים, העופות והלוויתן, או החיה, הבהמה והרמש הם בריאה אחת? הקביעה 'שבשלב קדום נסתיימו שמונה מעשי הבריאה במנוחת האלהים, ורק בשלב מאוחר יותר נכפתה על הסיפור חלוקה לשבעה ימים כדי להפוך את מנוחת האלהים לפירוש איטיולוגי של יום השבת' (ראה אצל טיגאי [לעיל, הערה 5], עמ' 509) הנה אפוא רק אחת מני רבות של אפשרויות של שחזור השלב הקדום. והשווה, דרך משל, לשיטת כ"ב המינים שבספר היובלים, ב, 1–15.

11 ראה הסיכום אצל ווסטרמן (לעיל, הערה 1), עמ' 88–90.

12 ווסטרמן, שם, עמ' 167.

13 צ' וש' רין, עלילות האלים: כל שירות אוגרית, ירושלים תשכ"ח, עמ' 166–167, 367, 376.

במסורת המסופוטמית נמשכה שבעה ימים (עלילת גילגמש, לוח יא, שו' 141–146), ועוד.[14] מן
המסורת המקראית עולה כי יחידות זמן של שבעה ימים ליוו אירועים שונים כמו: טומאת היולדת
(וי' יב, ב), משתה של כלולות (בר' כט, כז-כח; שופ' יד, יב), חגים (שמ' כג, טו; לד, יח; ועוד),
טקסי פולחן שונים כמו: קידוש כוהנים (שמ' כט, ל; וי' ח, לג-לה), קידוש המזבח (שמ' כט, לז),
וכן חנוכת בית-המקדש (מל"א ח, סה-סו), ימי אבל (בר' נ, י; איוב ב, יג), ועוד. השימוש החוזר
ונשנה ביחידות זמן של שבעה ימים טיפוסי אפוא למחשבה הקדומה והוא קשור, כנראה, במהות
המאגית וההמיסטית של מספר זה, שהילת שלמות נלוותה אליו.[15]

1.1.3 קשר של סגנון – קשה להציג את תיאור היום השביעי כהדבקה מלאכותית לחומרים
שקדמו לו, כי הוא קשור אליהם גם בקשר הדוק של סגנון. הצירוף: 'בר"א שמים וארץ', שחוזר
בראשית תיאור היום השביעי (ב, א), נקשר הן אל פתיחת הסיפור: 'בראשית ברא אלהים את השמים
ואת הארץ' (א, א) והן אל סיומו: 'אלה תולדות השמים והארץ בהבראם' (ב, דא).[16] השורשים בר"א
(ב, ג) ועש"ה (ב, בפעמיים; ב, ג), חוזרים גם לאורך תיאור ששת ימי הבריאה (בר"א: כא, כז שלוש
פעמים; ועש"ה: ז, טז, כה, כו, לא, וראה גם יא-יב). קשר הסגנון מתבטא אף בשימוש במספרים
סידוריים, שראשיתם בציון 'יום שני' ואחריתם בחזרה המשולשת על 'יום השביעי'.

1.1.4 קשר מוטיבי – מוטיב הברכה, שנזכר בקשר ליום השביעי: 'ויברך אלהים את יום
השביעי (ב, ג), חוזר אצל נבראי היום החמישי (א, כב) ואצל האדם (א, כח).

ניתן אפוא לסכם, כי מי שהיה מעוניין להציג את היום השביעי כיום מנוחה בסיומו של תהליך
הבריאה נאלץ להציג את הבריאה כולה כתהליך שנמשך שישה ימים, ולהכריע מה נברא בכל אחד
משֵשת הימים, ומה מאפייניו של היום השביעי. לכן, הוא עיצב את היום השביעי כך שישמש
בפונקציות של הקשרים הנזכרים לעיל (1.1.1–1.1.4) וחתם את הסיפור בקשר מעגלי שמעצים את
התחושה של יחידה עצמאית, סגורה ושלמה (ראה הקשרים בין א, א לבין ב, דא). נמצא כי צירוף
השבת למסורת הבריאה, ועיבוד המסורת לדגם הסיפורי שלפנינו, חייב עיצוב חדשני, שקול ומדוד
מבחינה סגנונית ועניינית, כדי שהבריאה כולה תשמש איטיולוגיה קוסמית לשבת. עיבוד לפני
ולפנים מסוג זה – שהדינמיקה הפנימית שלו מוליכה את הקורא להבין כי לפני כל סיפור שבא לייחס
קדמות וסמכות יתרה ליום השבת, גם מבלי שהשבת ומצוות שמירתה תיזכרנה במפורש – הוא

14   פריצ'רד (לעיל, הערה 4), עמ' 94. על התופעה עמד מ"ד קאסוטו במאמרו 'ספרות מקראית וספרות כנענית',
      בתוך: ספרות מקראית וספרות כנענית (לעיל, הערה 8), עמ' 20–54 ובמיוחד עמ' 33–34 (=תרביץ יג [תש"ב],
      עמ' 197–212 ובמיוחד עמ' 206–207). דוגמאות אלה ונוספות, וכן וריאציות של שימוש בדגם שבעת הימים,
      ראה במאמרו של ש' ליונשטם, 'יחידת שבעת הימים באפוס האוגריתי', תרביץ לא (תשכ"ב), עמ' 227–235.
      ליונשטם מטעים כי סופרי אוגרית שאלו את הדגם מן האפוס המסופוטמי.

15   דיון מפורט בסוגיה זו ראה אצל: J. Hehn, *Siebenzahl und Sabbath bei den Babyloniern und im Alten*
      Testament, Leipzig 1907

16   רוב הפרשנים קושרים איבר זה (ב, דא) עם הסיפור הכוהני שמקדים אותו. גם סקינר (J. Skinner, *A Critical*
      and Exegetical Commentary on Genesis[2] [ICC], Edinburgh 1963 [1930], pp. 39-41), שרואה בו
      תחיבת עריכה, אינו קושר אותו עם הפרשה הסמוכה לו (ב, ד[2]–ג, כד). דעה שונה לקאסוטו (ראה לעיל, הערה
      5, עמ' 62–64), הסובר כי נוסחה זו היא פתיחה לפרשה שבאה בעקבותיה ומסתיימת בפרק ג, פסוק כד. הנוסחה
      'אלה תולדות' מרבה להופיע כנוסחה פותחת; וראה, למשל, בר' ה, א; ו, ט; י, א; יא, י, ועוד. לכן, יש סוברים
      כי במקרה שלפנינו היא הועברה לסיום מן ההתחלה. ראה הדיון אצל סקינר, עמ' 40–41.

בבחינת מעשה יצירה כשהוא לעצמו.[17] את הקשר שבין פיסקת השבת לבין מסורת הבריאה שלפניה
לא ניתן אפוא לתאר כהדבקת עריכה, אלא כעיבוד של יצירה חדשה, שלא זו בלבד שהיא משקפת
המשך לצד התנתקות ממסורות הבריאה של המזרח התיכון הקדום, אלא שהיא מהווה חידוש
בהתייחסות לנושא הבריאה במסורת המקראית.[18] ולבסוף, סביר להניח כי העמדת יצירה חדשה,
ולא עיבודים קיימים אחרים של נושא הבריאה, בפתיחת ספר בראשית ובתורה כולה אינה מקרית
ויש בה כדי ללמדנו על תכנון וכוונה בהיקף רחב יותר.

1.2 שימוש בדגם העולה כאמצעי להקנות לסיום ממד של שיא

ההנחה שאין להפריד בין תוכן לצורה, ושבחירה בצורה מסוימת באה להודיע ולהדגיש צדדים
הקשורים בתוכן, מכוונת אותי לבדוק את מבנה הסיפור. סיפור הבריאה נאמן לדגם המספר העולה
שישה-שבעה (1+6).[19] לפיכך, טענתי היא כי הבחירה בדגם של מספר עולה באה ללמד כי השבת,
שהנה הרכיב הנוסף (1+), נתפסת אצל מי שעיצב את הסיפור כשיאו של תהליך.[20] גם בסיפורים
נוספים, שבהם הדגם משרת את ממד הזמן, הוא מצביע על שלב השיא. כך למשל, בהקפות יריחו
לפני נפילתה נאמר: '...הקף את העיר פעם אחת כה תעשה ששת ימים... וביום השביעי תסבו את
העיר שבע פעמים...' (יהו' ו, ג–ד, וכן יב ואילך). השיא של היום השביעי מתבטא הן במספר
הסיבובים והן בהשגת המטרה – נפילת העיר.[21] בדומה, בפרשת נתינת הלוחות למשה, הוא מצווה
לעלות אל האלוהים ההרה על-מנת לקבל את לוחות האבן: 'ויעל משה אל ההר ויכס הענן את ההר.
וישכן כבוד ה' על הר סיני ויכסהו הענן ששת ימים ויקרא אל משה ביום השביעי מתוך הענן' (שם,
טז–יז). ביום השביעי מתרחש אפוא השיא, שביטויו בפנייה הישירה של האל.[22] השימוש בדגם

---

17 על היצירתיות שבמעשה העריכה והקושי בהבחנה בין מחבר לעורך, ראה הפרק הראשון בספרי: ספר שופטים –
אמנות העריכה, ירושלים תשנ"ב, עמ' 3–24 ובמיוחד עמ' 16–18.

18 כך למשל, תה' קד מוכר כתיאור בריאה קרוב מאוד לספר בראשית, וראה מ' וייס, המקרא כדמותו: שיטת
האינטרפרטאציה הכוליית[3], ירושלים תשמ"ז, עמ' 88–92. עם זאת, אין בו רמז לשבת. במענה האלוהים שבאיוב
לח נזכר כוחו של האל בבריאה, ואין בו רמז לשבת, ועוד.

19 בהרכב זה נזכר הדגם במפורש בספרות החכמה: 'שש הנה שנא ה' ושבע תועבות נפשו...' (מש' ו, טז-יט); וכן:
'בשש צרות יצילך ובשבע לא יגע בך רע...' (איוב ה, יט). נוכחותו בולטת בכתובים נוספים שבהם היא משתמע
ואינו נזכר במפורש: מל"א יח, מג-מד; עמ' ג, ג-ו; יח' מו, ד; תה' עח, מד-נא; קה, כח-לו (בשמ' ז-יא מועדף
הדגם תשעה-עשרה); דה"ב ב, יג-טו (בשמ"א טז-יז מועדף הדגם שבעה-שמונה). מן הראוי לציין שבכל
הדוגמאות הנזכרות, אין הדגם משרת יחידות של זמן.

20 את ההצעה לאתר באמצעות דגם המספר המודרג את שלב השיא, או את המקרה החמור, העלה מ"ד קאסוטו
במאמרו: 'ספרות מקראית וספרות כנענית' (לעיל, הערה 14). י' זקוביץ ('הדגם הספרותי שלושה-ארבעה
במקרא', חיבור לשם קבלת תואר דוקטור לפילוסופיה, האוניברסיטה העברית, ירושלים תשל"ח), שחקר את
הדגם שלושה-ארבעה, עמד על שימושים נוספים כמו: מפנה וחריגות. על השבת כשיאו של סיפור הבריאה ראה
אצל א' טויג, 'בראשית א' והשבת', בית מקרא נ/ג (תשל"ג), עמ' 288–296. גם טויג למד על שלב השיא
באמצעות הפן הצורני, אך לדעתו החזרות משרתות בעת ובעונה אחת את הפן הליטורגי-פולחני. השווה גם
לפירושו של סרנה (לעיל, הערה 9), עמ' 14.

21 מקרים נוספים של שימוש משתמע בדגם ביחידות זמן המורכבת מימים נמצא ב: מל"א כ, כט; אס' א, ה, ט. יש
שהוא מופיע בהרכב של זמן שנים: מל"ב יא, ד וראה גם דה"ב כב, יב – כג, א. בהקשר זה ראוי אף להזכיר את
חוקי העבד והשמיטה, וכן מאמרו של ב' אופנהיימר, לעיל, הערה 5.

22 החוקרים טוענים כי היחידה בשמ' כד, טז-יח[א] הנה משל המקור הכוהני. כך כבר דרייבר S.R. Driver, The
(Book of Exodus[1] [CBSC], Cambridge 1953 [1911], p. 258, שרואה בקטע זה את המקבילה של P לסיפור

בהקשר של יחידות זמן מאופיין בקיום מכנה משותף לששת האיברים השונים ומפנה או שינוי באיבר
האחרון, שהוא המספר העולה (1+). בזכות השינוי מצטייר השלב האחרון כעיקרה או כשיאה של
היחידה כולה. סיפורנו מתאר שישה ימי בריאה מול יום שביתה, שהוא היפוכם של הימים שקדמו
לו. הבריאה היא אפוא המכנה המשותף התהליכי, וההגעה לשלב השביתה היא המפנה והפסגה.
הדמיון בין האיברים השונים והשוני מודגשים גם באמצעות הסגנון. כל אחד מששת ימי הבריאה
מסתיים בהודעה: 'ויהי ערב ויהי בוקר יום X' (א, ה, ח, יג, יט, כג, לא). רק תיאור היום השביעי
אינו מסתיים בנוסחה הנזכרת, אם כי חוזר בו שלוש פעמים השימוש במספר הסידורי: יום השביעי
(ב, בפעמ"ים, ג). יתר על כן, השימוש במספרים סידוריים אינו מצריך ידוע, ואילו בפיסקת השבת
המספר מיודע בשלוש היקרויותיו: 'יום השביעי'. מחקר הדגם מצביע גם על חשיבות האיבר שלפני
האחרון, כשלב מקדם לקראת האיבר האחרון.[24] בסיפורנו, תחושת הסיום עולה ממעשה הבריאה של
היום השישי, שגם לגביו מתקיים ידוע, הן משום תיאור בריאת האדם כרודה בנבראים שקדמו לו,
והן באמצעות תיאור ההתבוננות המסכמת של האל במעשה ידיו: 'וירא אלהים את כל אשר עשה
והנה טוב מאד' (א, לא). אולם הסיום האמיתי הוא רק ביום השביעי, שתיאורו נפתח במלים: 'ויכלו
השמים והארץ וכל צבאם' (ב, ב). השימוש בדגם המספר העולה תורם אפוא להבלטת מעמדה
המיוחד של השבת. כך הוסט שלב השיא, או הפואנטה, מבריאת האדם למעמד המקודש שניתן ליום
השביעי. בחירת מעצב הפרשה דווקא בדגם זה מכוונת אפוא לקראת הצגת השבת לא רק כסיום של
מפנה אלא גם כשיא. הבריאה הגיעה לשיאה ביום השביעי, שהמהות המאפיינת אותו היא שביתה.
וכיוון שהמהות (=שביתה או שבת) והמסגרת (=יום השביעי) קשורים זה בזה, זוכה בברכה היום
עצמו. השיא מודגש גם באמצעות העובדה שהאל אינו מסתפק בברכה, אלא מקדש את היום. כך
יוצא שייחוד היום השביעי אינו רק באי-העשייה האלוהית, אלא בעשייה הייחודית ליום זה –
הקדשתו.

1.3 העיסוק בשאלת המבנה מכוון אף להתייחס למבנה הכולל, דהיינו למקום שניתן לשבת בספרות
התורה כולה באמצעות הצגתה כחלק מפרשת הבריאה. השבת, שהנה סיומו ושיאו של תהליך
הבריאה, פותחת את ספרות התורה. במלים אחרות, חשיבותה ומרכזיותה מוטעמים מכוח הנושא

JE בפרק יט. וראה גם הסקירה של פרשנים מאוחרים יותר אצל J.I. Durham, *Exodus* (WBC 3), Waco,
Texas 1987, pp. 340-341. א' טויג (מתן תורה בסיני: המסורות על מתן תורה בסיני, גיבושן בשמות יט–כד
והשתלשלותן בספר התורה, ירושלים תשל"ז, עמ' 10, 79) מטעים את תפקיד היחידה כיחידת מעבר. הופעת
הדגם בסיפור זה יוצרת תחושה של גודש, משום קיומו של מספר טיפולוגי נוסף: ארבעים יום (שמ' כד, יח[3]).
ראוי אף לציין כי שימוש במספר שבע לצד ארבעים נמצא גם בעלילת המבול, שהינו סיפור מורכב (ראה בר' ז,
ד, ועוד). ייתכן שצירופן של הדגם שישה-שבעה בהקשר זה משרת את ההתייחסות העתידית להופעתו בעניין השבת:
שמ' לא, טו–יח; לה, ב. לדעת קנוהל (לעיל, הערה 1, עמ' 66–67) האסכולה הכוהנית ששיבצה אותו היא אסכולת
הקדושה, שלה הוא מייחס את כלל מרקם העריכה ורקמת הקישור של ספרות התורה.

באפוס האוגריתי (ראה לעיל, הערה 13) השינוי מודגש באמצעות העצמת התיבה 'מכ', שתרגומה: אך, והיא מקדימה את
היום השביעי (=אך ביום השביעי). וראה לוח IV 51 שו' 31–32 (רין, 167); עלילת אקהת ב: I שו' 16 (רין 367);
עלילת אקהת ב: II שו' 39 (רין 376); וראה גם בלוח 124, הנמנה עם לוחות הרפאים (רין 432), שו' 25–26; וכן
עלילת כרת שו' 107–108, 118–119 (רין 299). בעלילת כרת השינוי מוטעם גם באמצעים נוספים כמו:
התייחסות לשמש, הוספת מילים לפני היום השביעי וכן המרת התיבה 'אך' ב'והנה'.

ראה אצל זקוביץ (לעיל, הערה 20), עמ' 523–525.

ומכוח מקום שיבוצו. הקורא למד כי לוח של שבעה ימים שירת את האל במעשה הבריאה. אין תֶמַה,
שבדומה לפרטי הבריאה השונים, שמהווים כוחות פועלים ביקום, גם לוח זה מקבל תוקף של
מציאות. נמצא שמנקודת זמן זו ואילך, הלוח ששירת את האל מהווה חלק מחוקיות היקום ויכול
לשמש גם חיקוי לנבראים בצלם אלוהים. כך נוכח הקורא כי לבד מן המאורות ברקיע השמים,
שנועדו 'להבדיל בין היום ובין הלילה' ולשמש 'לאתת ולמועדים ולימים ושנים' (בר' א, יד), יש לוח
של זמן אלוהי, שבועי, והוא לוח הקדושה. בעקיפין גם נרמז הקורא כי השבת של לוח הקדושה אינה
היום השביעי ו'יום השבתו' (=יום החמישה־עשר), הנזכרים בקשר ללידת הירח בעלילת הבריאה
הבבלית (לוח 5, שו' 17–18).[25] העובדה שלוח זה פותח את ספרות התורה משפיעה על המשך תהליך
הקריאה. כל מפגש עם נושא השבת מושפע משלב ראשוני זה. כך ניתן לנמק מדוע דווקא השבת
מופיעה כמצווה הראשונה שעם ישראל נדרש לקיים (שמ' טז), מדוע היא חלק מעשרת הדיברות,
ומדוע למתחייבים בברית העונש על הפרתה הוא מיתה, ועוד.

2. השבת וספרות הקדושה

לשבת מקום מרכזי הן בספר הקדושה (וי' יז־כו) והן בחלק מסוים של הספרות הכוהנית, שמקיים,
כפי שנראה בהמשך, זיקה הדוקה עם ספר הקדושה (שמ' טז; לא, יב־יז; לה, א־ג, במ' טו, לב־לו).

2.1 השבת בספר הקדושה

שורה של ראיות מצביעות על מקומה המרכזי של השבת בספר הקדושה:

2.1.1 השבת מוצבת בראש רשימת המועדים של ספר הקדושה (וי' כג, ג), על אף ייתורה המקורי
במסגרת זו.[26] מפסוקי הסיום של הרשימה (שם, לז־לח) ניתן ללמוד כי הרשימה נועדה לעסוק
ב'מועדי ה' אשר תקראו אתם מקראי קדש להקריב אשה לה'... מלבד שבתת ה'...'. השבת חורגת
מן המועדים האחרים ברשימה משום שהיא אירוע חוזר ונשנה לאורך השנה. החוקרים אף הצביעו
על משניות שילובה באמצעות הניתוח הפילולוגי של פס' ב² ('מועדי ה' אשר תקראו אתם מקראי
קדש אלה הם מועדי'), שהוצע כפתיחה בעייתית, המנוסחת ברוח פס' ד ומשמשת חזרה מקשרת
למטרת שילוב חוקת מועד השבת (פס' ג). לשון אחר, טכניקת השילוב, באמצעות פתיחה חוזרת,
ושימוש יוצא דופן בגוף ראשון (מועדי), מצביעים על השילוב התנייני והמגמתי של השבת
במקומה. זאת בניגוד לרשימת המועדים של חוקת כוהנים (במ' כח־כט), שבה הצבת השבת בראש
הרשימה היא מקורית וקשורה בסדר הצגת הקרבנות המוספים (במ' כח, ט־י): למן השכיחים, שבת
וראש חודש, ועד למועדים, שחלים פעם בשנה. לאור נתונים אלה יש מקום להביא את שאלת חז"ל:
'מה עניין שבת אצל מועדות, ללמדך שכל המחלל את המועדות מעלין עליו כאלו חילל את השבתות
וכל המקים את המועדות מעלין עליו כאלו קיים את השבתות' (ספרא, קמד, קמ והשווה רש"י לוי' כג,

---

25 ראה לעיל, הערה 4.

26 קביעה זו מקובלת במחקר הביקורתי למן המאה שעברה ועד ימינו אנו. ראה, למשל, את הניסיון להפריכה אצל
ד"צ הופמן (ספר ויקרא² ב, ירושלים תשכ"ד, עמ' צה־צו) ואת קבלתה כהנחת עבודה אצל קנוהל (ראה לעיל,
הערה 1), עמ' 22, ושם ביבליוגרפיה נוספת.

ג).[27] תשובת המדרש מטעימה את חשיבות השבת בסדר המועדים, וניתן ללמוד ממנה על החשיבות שייחסו לה עורכי הלוח בספר הקדושה.[28]

2.1.2 חשיבות השבת בספר הקדושה עולה גם מאזכוריה החוזרים, מהעדפות הצמדתה, ומהצבתה בין שלוש המצוות הפותחות את פרשת 'קדושים תהיו'. הצו הוא בדבר שמירת שבת נזכר בין כיבוד אב ואם לבין איסור עבודת אלילים ומסכות (וי' יט, ג–ד). אין ספק שסדר זה מצביע על זיקה מובהקת לחמשת הדיברות הראשונים.[29] על חשיבות כיבוד ההורים למדים לא רק מהצבת הדרישה בראש רשימת הקדושה ולצד ההכרזה: 'קדושים תהיו כי קדוש אני ה' אלהיכם' (שם, פס' ב), אלא גם מהשימוש הנדיר בהקשר זה בפועל יר"א. פועל זה חוזר בספר הקדושה ארבע פעמים בהקשר ליראת האל (יט, יד, לב; כה, לו, מג) ופעמיים בהקשר ליראת המקדש, שהנו ייצוגו הפולחני של האל (יט, ל; כו, ב). בשתי ההיקרויות האחרונות מצוות שמירת השבת צמודה לדרישת יראת המקדש: 'את שבתתי תשמרו ומקדשי תיראו אני ה' (יט, ל והשווה ל–כו, ב). שורץ אף מצביע על פן נוסף של הממד הסטרוקטורלי, שהופעתעו עשויה ללמדנו על חשיבות השבת. השבת נזכרת בסוף פרק יט לצד כיבוד זקנים ואיסור פנייה לאובות וידעונים (פס' ל–לב), ובכך דומה אזכורה לפתיחת החטיבה. במלים אחרות, היא חלק מהמסגרת המהווה סיום מעין פתיחה.[30] יתרה מזאת, גם הופעתה בסוף ספר הקדושה – לצד איסור עבודת אלילים (כו, א–ב) והדגשת עוון שבתות הארץ (שם, פס' לד–מה) – מעידה, כדברי וויינפלד, 'על מרכזיות הנושא בתפיסת עולמו של המחבר'.[31]

2.1.3 חשיבות השבת בספר הקדושה עולה גם מן השימוש המטונימי שנעשה בה. שנת השמיטה מכונה 'שבת הארץ' (וי' כה, ו) והיא אף מקבלת את התוספת המדגישה 'שבתון': 'ובשנה השביעית שבת שבתון יהיה לארץ שבת לה'...' (וי' כה, ד–ה).[32] אי־שמירת שבת הארץ גוררת עונש כבד של גלות כללית ונמשכת, כדי שהארץ תוכל לרצות את עונש שנות השמיטה שבטלו ולשבות תקופה ממושכת: '...כל ימי השמה תשבת את אשר לא שבתה בשבתתיכם בשבתכם עליה" (וי' כו,

---

27 אין בכוונתי למנות את התשובות השונות שניתנו לשאלה זו, ואסתפק בהזכרת תשובתו של הרמב"ן, שמטעים את הצד ההלכתי וחולק על חז"ל, שפירשו ל'רמז לעבורים'. לדעתו, הכתוב בא להודיע כי 'השבת תשמרו לעשות אותה שבת שבתון מכל מלאכה שבעולם... גם בבואו באחת מן המועדים...'.

28 נות (M. Noth, *Leviticus: A Commentary* [OTL], London 1965 [1962], pp. 165-168) מדגיש כי תוספת זו משקפת את החשיבות שיוחסה לשבת לאחר הגלות.

29 בשני הנוסחים של עשרת הדיברות נמצאת השבת בין שלוש המצוות הדנות ביראת האל לבין כיבוד ההורים (שמ' כ, ב–יב; דב' ה, ו–טז). כך היא מתפרשת כנקודת מעבר בין המצוות שבין אדם למקום לבין המצוות שבין אדם לחברו. אין ספק בכך שארבע המצוות הראשונות, שהשבת אחת מהן, הן יהודיות לאמונה הישראלית. ווינפלד בעקבות שורץ ('עשרת הדיברות – ייחוד ומקומם במסורת ישראל', בתוך: עשרת הדיברות בראי הדורות, ערך ב"צ סגל, ירושלים תשמ"ו, עמ' 10) מנמק מן שינוי הסדר בפרשתנו כתוצאה של ציטוט כיאסטי, הגורם לכך שיראת אם ואב מקדימה את יראת השבת ואת יראת האל.

30 ב"י שורץ, 'שלושה פרקים מספר הקדושה: מחקר ספרותי על ויקרא יז–יט', חיבור לשם קבלת התואר דוקטור לפילוסופיה, האוניברסיטה העברית, ירושלים תשמ"ז, עמ' 120–122. ראוי לציין כי לשיטתו פסוקים לג–לו מתפרשים כנספחם.

31 ראה לעיל, הערה 29.

32 רש"י, בפירושו לשמ' לא, טו, למד מחומרת ההעצמה כי הכוונה ל'מנוחת מרגוע ולא מנוחת עראי (שבת שבתון: לכך כפלו הכתוב לומר שאסור בכל מלאכה אפילו אוכל נפש וכן יוה"כ [ויקרא כג] שבת שבתון היא לכם אסור בכל מלאכה אבל יום טוב לא נאמר בו כי אם ביום הראשון שבתון וביום השמיני שבתון [שם לט] אסורים בכל מלאכת עבודה ומותרים במלאכת אוכל נפש)'.

לד-לה). [33] החומרה היתרה שיוחסה לאי-קיום מצוות השבת (שמ' לא, יד-טו; במ' טו, לב-לו) הופכת בהקשר השמיטה להנמקה שמצדיקה את חורבן הארץ והפיכתה לשממה. אין ספק שהשימוש בשם שבת ככינוי לשנת השמיטה נובע מן הדמיון שבין שתי המצוות. עם זאת, חשוב לציין שביטויים והדגשות אלה אינם באים בכתובים אחרים שמתייחסים לשמיטה, אלא בספר הקדושה (השווה את וי' כה, ב-ז; כו, לד-לה, מג לשמ' כג, י-יא; דב' טו, א; יר' לד, יד-טז).

2.1.4 הרצון להעניק קדושה יתרה לימי מועד מסוימים נעשה באמצעות החלת קדושת השבת על אותו יום. כך לגבי היום הראשון והיום השמיני של חג הסוכות (וי' כג, לט וראה גם לה-לו), וכך לגבי ראש השנה, המתואר כיום שבתון (וי' כג, כד), ובמיוחד לגבי יום הכיפורים: 'שבת שבתון הוא לכם ועניתם את נפשתיכם בתשעה לחדש בערב מערב עד ערב תשבתו שבתכם' (שם, לב).

2.1.5 הופעת השבת בספר הקדושה צוברת חשיבות אף מהיותה ציון זמן, שמכריע לגבי קביעת המועד של אירועים נוספים. כך בציון 'ממחרת השבת', הקשור לטקס הנפת העומר (וי' כג, יא), ובקביעת מועד חג השבועות: 'וספרתם לכם ממחרת השבת מיום הביאכם את עמר התנופה שבע שבתות תמימת תהיינה...' (שם, טו-טז). [34]

מן המתואר לעיל עולה כי לשבת מקום מרכזי בספר הקדושה. עובדה זו תנחה אותנו בבדיקת מקראות נוספים, שהנם מחוץ לספר הקדושה ומקובל לייחסם לספרות הכוהנית.

2.2 השבת בספרות הכוהנית שמחוץ לספר הקדושה

2.2.1 התייחסות לנושא השבת בחומרים שנמנים עם הספרות הכוהנית שבתורה, חוץ מספר הקדושה, מעלה שש היקרויות. מטבע הדברים, סיכום זה כולל את סיפור הבריאה (בר' א, א – ב, דא); אולם כיוון שסיפור הבריאה הוא מושא בדיקתנו, נתעלם ממנו בשלב זה ונבדוק את חמש הפיסקאות האחרות, על-פי סדר הופעתן ברצף ספרות התורה.

הסיפור האחד הוא סיפור המן, שניתן לבני ישראל במדבר סין, והוא – בעריכה הסופית המונחת לפנינו – סיפור של ניסיון (שמ' טז). האל מתחייב להמטיר לעמו המתלוננן לחם מן השמים ולראות אם ילך בתורתו (שם, פס' ד), כאשר במכילתא דר"י (מהדורת האראוויטץ-רבין, עמ' 19): 'ויהי ביום השביעי יצאו מן העם ללקוט ולא מצאו אלו מחוסרי אמנה שבישראל'. והנה, במרכז הניסיון ניצבת השבת (פס' ה, טז-ל). לניסיון כתהליך חינוכי מגמה מובהקת העולה מן המתואר בסוף: 'וישבתו העם ביום השבעי' (פס' ל). בדיקת ההפרשה על-פי שיטת המקורות מעלה, כי מחד גיסא היא מעשה שילוב, ומאידך גיסא המקור הכוהני הוא הדומיננטי במעשה שילוב זה. [35] במילים אחרות, לפי שיטה זו, החיבור הדן בחינוך בני-ישראל לקיים את מצוות השבת הוא חיבור כוהני.

השבת נזכרת בשתי היקרויות נוספות, שבהן היא משמשת מסגרת לפרשיות ששולבו בתוך מעשה

33 חומרה זו אף עולה מן המקור המאוחר שבדה"ב לו, כא, המושפע מספר הקדושה, וכנראה מן האסכולה בכללה. וראה, למשל, R.B. Dillard, *2 Chronicles* (WBC 15), Waco, Texas 1987, pp. 301-302.

34 על הציון 'ממחרת השבת' והמחלוקת בדבר פירוש התיבה 'שבת' בצירוף זה, ראה סיכום אצל מ' הרן, הערך 'שבת, ממחרת השבת', אנציקלופדיה מקראית ז, ירושלים 1976, טורים 517–521.

35 הסיפור מחזיק גם חומרי J, אך אין זה מעניינו של חיבור זה להיכנס לנושא על פרטיו. ראה סיכום מפורט אצל: B.S. Childs, *Exodus: A Commentary*[5] (OTL), London 1984 (1974), pp. 274-283. ביקורת על שיטת צ'יילדס ראה אצל דורהם (לעיל, הערה 22), עמ' 223–224.

המשכן (שמ' כה–מ). כידוע הרצף של צו וביצוע בתיאור עשיית המשכן (שם, פרקים כה–לא +
לה–מ), שהוא מן החומרים הכוהניים המובהקים, נקטע על־ידי מובלעת שאינה נמנית עם המקור
הכוהני לב–לד).[36] והנה אזהרות בדבר שביתה ממלאכה ביום השבת משמשות מסגרת פותחת (לא,
יב–יז) ומסיימת (לה, א־ג) ליחידה הקוטעת. אזהרות אלה, שמקובל לשייכן למקור הכוהני,
משמשות אפוא בתפקיד של עריכה מצרפת וחזרה מקשרת.

הפעם הרביעית שהמקור הכוהני עוסק בשבת הוא בפרשת המקושש (במ' טו, לב־לו), שנידון
לסקילה משום חילול שבת.

ולבסוף, השבת נזכרת בסדר המועדים של תורת כוהנים (במ' כח, ט־י), משום קרבן המוסף
המועלה בה.

2.2.2 עיון מעמיק בתוכן ובצורה של חמש היקרויות אלה מעמידנו על העובדה, כי פיסקת השבת
ברשימת המוספים של תורת כוהנים שונה באופיה ובסגנונה מהאזכורים האחרים.

2.2.2.1 מבחינת התוכן, המכנה המשותף של ארבע הפיסקאות הראשונות הנו גישה עקרונית,
שמפליגה בחשיבות שמירת שבת. עובדה זו עולה הן מממדיניות השיבוץ הננקטת, הן מן הניסוחים,
והן מן התוצאות הצפויות למחלל השבת. בפרשיות אלה חוזר איסור מלאכה כללי (שמ' לא, יד־טו;
לה, ב) או מלאכות מסוימות האסורות בשבת, כמו ליקוט המן (שמ' טז, כו), איסור הבערת אש (שמ'
לה, ג), ואיסוף עצים (במ' טו, לב־לו). השבת מוצגת, לפי שמ' טז, כראשית לימוד התורה. היא
מקדימה את מעמד הר סיני והיא ההתנסות הראשונה שהעם חווה לאחר שניתן לו חוק ומשפט במרה
(שמ' טו, כב־כו). כמו־כן, היא נקשרת בסיפור זה לתופעה קיומית ובסיסית בחיי אדם, והיא המזון.
איסור ליקוט המן הוא אפוא סמל למערכת של איסורים הקשורה בדאגתו של האדם למזונו.[37] איסור
הבערת האש בשמ' לה, ג משלים את איסור ליקוט המן בדונו באמצעי להכנת מזון.[38] שתי האזהרות
הנוספות, הסמוכות לצווים על מלאכת המשכן, נתפרשו כבר בידי חז"ל ופרשני ימי הביניים כהוכחה
לכך שאין מלאכת המשכן דוחה שבת.[39] במלים אחרות, כבר הפרשנות הקדומה חשה בטכניקת
השיבוץ ובמגמתה להגביר את קדושת השבת ולהעמידה במעלה אחת עם קדושת המקדש. ויתרה
מזאת, שיבוץ שתי אזהרות אלה בין הצו לבין ביצוע של מלאכת עשיית המשכן, שאי־הקמתו אינה

---

36 על היות פרקים לב–לד מובלעות לא כוהניות, שמקורן ב־JE ועברו אפילו עריכה דויטרונומיסטית, ראה אצל
צ'ילדס, (לעיל, הערה 35), עמ' 557–558.

37 לדברי מ' גרינברג ('חוויית השבת', בתוך: על המקרא ועל היהדות, תל־אביב תשמ"ה, עמ' 175–176): 'מלוא
העומר מן, אשר נשמר כמצות משה בצנצנת בארון־הברית, נשמר לא רק לזכר מעשה הנס שעשה אלוהים לבני
ישראל במדבר בהורידו להם את המן, אלא גם כתזכורת לדורות, לפגישתם הראשונה של ישראל עם השבת'.

38 מ"ד קאסוטו (פירוש על ספר שמות, ירושלים תשי"ד, עמ' 317) סובר כי פשט הכתוב מתייחס לעבודות הקשורות
במלאכת המשכן, כמו התכת מתכות; אך ראה מסקנת רשב"ם בפירושו לשמ' לה, ג, בעקבות הדיון אצל חז"ל:
'לפי שבימים טובים כתיב אשר יאכל לכל נפש הוא לבדו יעשה לכם (לעיל יב, טז), שם הותרה הבערת אש לאפות
ולבשל, אבל בשבת כתיב את אשר תאפו אפו ואת אשר תבשלו בשלו (שם טז, כג), לכך מזהיר
כי בשבת לא תבערו אש למלאכת אוכל נפש וכל שכן שאר מלאכות שאסורים אפילו ביום טוב'. והשווה לראב"ע,
רמב"ן ורבים אחרים. ולא נראית לי דעת ויינפלד (לעיל, הערה 1), עמ' 142, הטוען כי 'האמת היא כי אין בעל
ס"כ בא ללמדנו דין זה בהקשר זה. ענין השבת לא הובא כאן אלא כדי ללמדנו שאין מלאכת המשכן דוחה שבת'.

39 כך במכילתא דרשב"י (מהדורת אפשטיין-מלמד, עמ' 222) וכן אצל רש"י, רשב"ם, ראב"ע וספורנו לשמ' לא,
יג. מסקנה זו מתגלה כפשט העריכה לא רק אצל מ"ד קאסוטו (לעיל, הערה 38), עמ' 282, אלא גם אצל פרשנים
ביקורתיים, וראה למשל צ'ילדס (לעיל, הערה 35), עמ' 541–542.

כרוכה בעונש מוות, מלמד כי העריכה תופסת את קדושת השבת כנעלה מזו של המשכן. פרשת המקושש, הנידון לסקילה (במ' טו, לב-לו), מדגימה באופן מעשי וחד-משמעי כיצד יש לנהוג במחלל שבת, ובכך היא מבהירה ומשלימה את האזהרות שקדמו לה. אזהרת השבת בשמ' לא, יד-טו מחזיקה הן את הביטוי 'מות יומת' והן לשון כרת: 'ונכרתה הנפש ההוא מקרב עמיה'. הניסוח השני, שקושר את הביצוע עם האל, יכול לעורר ספק לגבי אחריות החברה.[40] לפיכך באה פרשת המקושש ומדגימה כיצד על העדה לנהוג במי שקושש עצים להבערה, וכך מסירה כל שמץ של ספק בעניין התנהגות החברה. התבוננות בקטעים אלו מנקודת מבט מצטברת, השוקלת תרומת כל קטע לקודמים לו ואת האפקט של המכלול, מצביעה אפוא על כוונה מכוונת: להודיע על מידת קדושת השבת, משמע: על עריכה שמעניקה לשבת חשיבות עליונה.

סממנים לשוניים אף הם תורמים להדגשת החשיבות המיוחסת לשבת בקטעים אלה. ואזכיר את השימוש בצירוף המעצים 'שבת שבתון' (שמ' טז, כג; לא, טו; לה, ב), את החזרה על התואר 'קדש' (שמ' טז, כג; לא, יד, טו, וראה גם פס' יג; לה, ב) ועל הציון המיוחד 'יום השביעי' (שמ' טז, כו, כז, כט, ל; לא, טז, יז; לה, ב), וכן את הדרישה לשמור שבת, החוזרת שלוש פעמים באמצעות השורש שמ"ר (שמ' לא, יג, יד, טו). בהקשר זה ראוי לזכור גם את המוטיבים של שיוך השבת לה' (שמ' טז, כג, כה; לא, יג; לה, ב) והצגתה כמתת האל (שמ' טז, כט) או כאות עולם בינו לבין עמו (שמ' לא, יג, יז). מוטיבים משמעותיים נוספים הקושרים בין פיסקאות אלה לבין ספר הקדושה מוחדרים באמצעות הביטוי 'וידעתם כי אני ה' אלהיכם' (שמ' טז, יב), החוזר בווריאציות שש-עשרה פעמים בוי' יט, וכן באמצעות הביטוי 'כי אני ה' מקדשכם' (שמ' לא, יג), שמדגיש כי מקור הקדושה באל, ככתוב בפתיחה לוי' יט: 'קדשים תהיו כי קדוש אני ה' אלהיכם'.

עד כאן נוכל לסכם כי החשיבות המוקנית לשבת בקטעים אלו, לצד הסגנון והמוטיבים הננקטים בהם, כל אלה קושרים אותם עם ספר הקדושה ועם הטענה שהם משקפים אותו בית-יוצר.

2.2.2.2 מצד שני, פיסקת השבת בלוח המועדים של תורת כוהנים שונה תכלית שינוי מן המתואר לעיל. ביטויים כמו 'שבתון', 'קדש', 'יום השביעי', או ביטויים שמציינים את שיוך השבת לאל ואיסור עשיית כל מלאכה – חסרים בה. חשוב לציין שמבחינת העניין היה מקום להזכיר לפחות חלק מן הביטויים הנזכרים, כפי שניתן ללמוד מהופעתם בתיאור המוספים של מועדים אחרים. כך למשל, חמישה-עשר בניסן מצוין כ'מקרא קדש כל מלאכת עבדה לא תעשו' (במ' כה, יח) וכך בתיאור מועדים נוספים (ראה גם פס' כה, כו; כט, א, ז, יב, וכן פס' לה). ואילו השבת נזכרת אך ורק בקשר לקרבן מוסף. אין בה לא רמז לאיסור עשיית כל מלאכה ולא ציון שהיא מקרא קודש.

2.2.2.3 לאור כל האמור לעיל, נראה שיש לקבל את המסקנה כי בית היוצר שאחראי לקטע הדן בשבת בלוח המוספים של תורת כוהנים שונה מבית היוצר של הכתובים האחרים. בעוד הראשון אינו מייחס לשבת חשיבות מיוחדת, בעל הקולמוס השני מציג את השבת ושמירתה כנושא מרכזי במערכת היחסים שבין האל ועמו. ראינו כי לבד מן הפן התמאטי גם סממנים של סגנון ומוטיבים מצביעים על זיקה בין ארבעת הקטעים הראשונים (שמ' טז, טז-ל; לא, יב-יז; לה, א-ג; במ' טו, לב-לו) לספר הקדושה. בדיקה זו מלמדת, שיש לקבל את טענתו הכוללת של קנוהל 'שפרשיות

40   סיוע לפירושי ראה אצל ש"א ליונשטם (הערך 'כרת, הכרת', אנציקלופדיה מקראית ה, ירושלים תשכ"ג, טורים 330–332): 'איסור חילול השבת חמור ביותר לפי השקפתה של תורת הכהנים, וכמו בדין המעביר בנו למולך גם כאן הכוונה, שאם לא יומת בידי אדם, יבוא ענשו בידי שמים...' (שם, עמ' 331).

רבות מחוץ לסה"ק, שעד כה יוחסו ל-P', הן למעשה חלק מכתביה של אסכולת H, שאותה הוא מכנה 'אסכולת הקדושה'.[41]

אזכורי השבת במקור הכוהני, לבד מלוח המוספים, שייכים אפוא לאסכולת הקדושה.

2.3 סיפור הבריאה ואסכולת הקדושה

עד הנה ראינו כי מרבית אזכורי השבת בספרות השבת בספרות תורת כוהנים נמנים עם אסכולת הקדושה. מסקנה אחרונה זו מותירה את הצורך לברר מה מקומה של פיסקת השבת בסיפור הבריאה – האם היא חלק מתורת כוהנים או מאסכולת הקדושה.

2.3.1 אין ספק שהבדיקה במישור התמאטי, שהאירה את המרכזיות והחשיבות של השבת בסיפור הבריאה (סעיף 1.2 לעיל) תואמת את מעמדה של השבת בספר הקדושה, וממילא – באסכולת הקדושה. הקשר בין השבת בסיפור הבריאה לבין אסכולת הקדושה נסמך אף על הדגשות סגנוניות ומוטיביות. וכוונתי הן למוטיב הקדושה (בר' ב, ג) והן לחזרה על ביטויים שרומזים לשבת, כמו: החזרה המשולשת על הצירוף 'ביום השביעי' (ב, בפעמיים, ג), החזרה על השורש שב"ת ('וישבת ביום השביעי', 'כי בו שבת') וההיקרות המשולשת של ביטויים, המורכבים מהשם 'מלאכה' ומהשורש עש"ה ('מלאכתו אשר עשה', 'מכל מלאכתו אשר עשה', 'מכל מלאכתו אשר ברא אלהים לעשות'). יתרה מזאת, תיאור האל כמי שכילה מלאכת עשייה וכמי ששבת, רומז לפן האנתרופומורפי של התנהגותו בבריאה, שעולה גם מן התיאור בשמ' לא, יז: 'כי ששת ימים עשה ה' את השמים ואת הארץ וביום השביעי שבת וינפש'. הוספת השורש נפ"ש מדגישה את המנוחה, שלה נזקק האל עם תום העשייה.[42]

ממצא זה מביא אותי למסקנה שגם בר' ב, א-ג מעיד על קולמוסה של אסכולת הקדושה.

2.3.2 מצד שני, יש מקום להציג את שאלת האיפכא מסתברא: מדוע רכיבים שמאפיינים את אסכולת הקדושה לא מצאו את מקומם בפיסקת השבת של סיפור הבריאה? וכוונתי להיעדר השם 'שבת' ולהיעדר ניסוח שיטעים את איסור עשיית מלאכה. שני רכיבים אלו חוזרים ובאים בכל הפיסקאות העוסקות בשבת באסכולת הקדושה, ולפיכך היעדרם במקומנו מצריך מענה. מצד שני, חסרונם הוא בבחינת פער של שכל פרשן, למן הראשונים ועד האחרונים, משלים אותו. כך למשל, כל פרשנות של הסיפור כאיטיולוגי (סעיף 1.1.1 לעיל) מניחה שבאמצעות הנמקה קוסמית הוא בא להעניק סמכות לחוק השבת. קאסוטו אף קובע בוודאות כי 'הפועל שבת בא גם לרמוז לשמו של יום השבת.' כותב הפרשה העדיף, לדעתו, ניסוחים שאינם מיוחדים לישראל, אלא משותפים לאומות העולם, לכן הוא התעלם ביודעין מן התיבה שבת, הנזכרת בספרי התורה רק בקשר למצוות שמירת השבת שניתנה לישראל.[43]

---

41 קנוהל (לעיל, הערה 1), עמ' 15.

42 בשמ' כג, יב מופיעים השורש נו"ח והשורש נפ"ש בתקבולת צלעות. בשמ' כ, י מופיע רק השורש נו"ח. השורש נפ"ש בא בהקשר של מנוחה בשמ"ב טז, יד. על הפן האנתרופומורפי בסיפור הבריאה, ובמיוחד בקשר למנוחת האל, ראה אצל ויינפלד (לעיל, הערה 1), ובמיוחד עמ' 138, וכן לעיל, הערה 4. סרנה (לעיל, הערה 9, עמ' 15) לעומת זאת, סובר כי רעיון המנוחה הוא משני.

43 פתרון זה מנמק לדעתו גם את העדפת השם 'אלוהים' על שם ההוויה. ראה קאסוטו (לעיל, הערה 5), עמ' 39–40. הצעות נוספות ופחות משכנעות ראה אצל סרנה (לעיל, הערה 9) עמ' 14, שמטעים בלשון נחרצת כי הטקסט הנוכחי מספק את התשתית למוסד העתידי של השבת.

העדפת לשון מרמזת על לשון ישירה, הימנעות מאזכור מפורש של נושא ידוע כלשהו, ושימוש במגוון אמצעים עקיפים שמכוונים לאותו נושא, הם מסממניו של הפולמוס הסמוי.[44] המשתמשים בטכניקת עיצוב זו מעדיפים את הרטוריקה העקיפה מכתיבה ישירה, משום כוח חדירתה ויכולתה לא לעורר התנגדות אצל הקורא. והתוצאה, שמבלי שתתוכר השבת בשמה ומבלי שיוזכרו איסוריה הם משתמעים מן הכתוב, ואת מקום הלשון הקשה והמצווה תופסת הנחת imitatio dei. מטבע הדברים מסקנת קורא הסיפור היא, שבדומה לאל ששבת לאחר שישה ימי עשייה, ראוי לו לאדם, שנברא בצלמו, ללכת בדרכיו; ונדגים מסקנה זו על קריאתו הפרשנית של קאסוטו: 'ויש לשבות בו כדי להתנהג כהתנהגות הבורא ולהידבק במידותיו'.[45]

3. מדוע לשבת מעמד כה מרכזי באסכולת הקדושה?

בפרקים הקודמים ראינו כי לשבת מקום מרכזי באסכולת הקדושה. שיאה של מגמה זו מתבטא בעיבוד מסורת הבריאה לסיפור איטיולוגי, שמקנה לשבת מעמד קוסמי, שהנו גם אוניברסלי, ובהצבתה השבת בפתיחת ספרות התורה כולה. גם ציינתי כי המקום והקשרו משמשים משים תשתית מנמקת לכל אזכור נוסף של השבת בספרות התורה. לכן, השאלה הנשאלת היא: האם ניתן להצביע על מניע אידיאולוגי של אסכולת הקדושה בעיבוד ושיבוץ זה?

אחד המאפיינים של ספר הקדושה, ולכן גם של אסכולת הקדושה, הוא הקדושה הכוללת. תורת הקדושה, בניגוד לתורת כוהנים, אינה מגבילה את הקדושה לטקסי פולחן ולמתחם המקדשי. לשיטתה הקדושה מחלחלת, מתפשטת ומשתלטת על כל תחומי החיים. גם האספקט הקוסמי של השבת, על-פי סיפור הבריאה, מעיד על קדושה שיכולה להתרחב, להתפשט ולחול על כל מי שהולך בדרכי האל. מצד שני, תביעת ההתקדשות מעלה על נס את הקריאה החוזרת ונשנית להתבדל ולהתרחק ממנהגי הגויים ומתועבותיהם. כך הופכת השבת לתחום התפשטותה של הקדושה. אימוץ לוח האלוהי, השבועי, השבתי, שמנחה אותו רצף של שבתות, יוצר חיק בין נושאי הקדושה לבין האחרים.

ספק אם ניתן היה לחשוב על טכניקת התבדלות יעילה יותר מזו של השבת. באמצעות השבת ניתק אדם מישראל ממעגלי הזמן של סביבתו והוא דבק בתפיסת זמן חדשה, שניתן לכנותה זמן אלוהי, או לוח הקדושה. החיים על-פי הזמן האלוהי מכתיבים קצב חיים חדש ושונה ומעניקים מעמד משני לראשי החודשים ולימי הכסה, או לימי מועד נוספים הקשורים בצורת הלבנה.[46] לוח השבע הוא

---

44   על הסממנים הנוספים של הפולמוס הסמוי ראה במאמרי: Y. Amit, 'Hidden Polemic in the Conquest of Dan: Judges XVII–XVIII', *VT* LX (1990), pp. 3-20 (=)'פולמוס סמוי בסיפור כיבוש דן' [שופטים יז–יח]', בית מקרא קכו/ג (תשנ"א), עמ' 267–278); וכן במאמרי: 'פרשת פילגש בגבעה כפולמוס סמוי נגד מלכות שאול ואוהדיה (שופטים יט–כא)', בית מקרא קכט/ב (תשנ"ב), עמ' 109–118.

45   קאסוטו (לעיל, הערה 5), עמ' 40, וראה גם עמ' 43. והשווה לדיוניו של מ' גרינברג 'החג במקרא וזמן מקודש', בתוך: על המקרא ועל היהדות, תל-אביב תשמ"ה, עמ' 161–167. נראה לי, שעל-פי שיטת אלייזה, שהוא מיישמה, יש לכלול גם את השבת במסגרת הזמן המקודש.

46   השווה לאנומה אליש (ראה לעיל, הערה 4) לוח ה, שו' 18–22. על המחלוקת בין תפיסת יום הכסה כיום מליאת הלבנה או כיום היה היתה מכוסה ראה אצל נ"ה טור-סיני, הערך 'כסא, כסה', אנציקלופדיה מקראית ד, ירושלים תשכ"ג, טור 216. מכל מקום, גם אם השבת היתה שבועית, כתוב במקורות הקדומים (שמ' כג, יב; לד, כא), סביר להניח שבדומה למתואר באנומה אליש, היא היתה צמודה להתמלאות הלבנה והתמעטותה.

יצירת אפיק של חיי קדושה, מנותקים מלוחות קיימים, הקשורים בגרמי השמים וממשיכים את הזמן האלוהי, שראשיתו בשבוע הבריאה. אפיק ייחודי זה אינו מבטל את ראשי החודשים או מועדים שנקבעו ביום מילוי הלבנה, אך הוא מעניק להם מעמד משני לצד התשתית של לוח שבועי-בסיסי, שהנו לוח מקביל ועצמאי.

מאבקים שחורתים על דגלם את נושא הלוח, או מסתייעים בו, לצרכים של התנתקות והתבדלות אנו מוצאים מימי ירבעם בן נבט (מל״א יב, לב-לג),[47] ובעיקר בכתות של ימי הבית השני.[48] 'שהרי אין לך חיק ממשי ובר תוצאות כהבדל בחשבון הלוח. שינוי בתאריך מן התאריכים הקוצבים את מהלך השנה מביא בהכרח לידי פירוק של שותפות חיים, לידי הפרת התואם שבין מעשי אדם לחברו והוא מבטל אותה סינכרוניזציה במנהגים ובמעשים שהיא יסוד מוסד לסדרי חברה מתוקנים. העושה שבת לעצמו – בזה שאינו מקיים את מועדי השנה בעונה אחת עם הציבור שבתוכו הוא חי – מפקיע עצמו מן הכלל ופוסק להיות איבר מן הגוף החברתי שעליו נמנה לפני מכן'.[49] נראה אפוא שאסכולת הקדושה, הרואה את החברה כולה נגד עיניה, והיא אינה תורת סוד של כוהנים ספונים בסתרי המקדש, היתה מעוניינת בעיבוד מסורת הבריאה לסיפור שבא להמליץ על חיים על-פי זמן אלוהי. יתרונו של לוח הקדושה, שהוא מנותק משיטת לוח מסוימת, שמשית או ירחית או משולבת, וכל שיטה צריכה למצוא את מקומה לצדו.

תורת כוהנים, לעומת זאת, כמעט שהתעלמה מן השבת, כפי שהיתה נהוגה בימי בית ראשון, כדברי קויפמן: 'הנימוס הכוהני-המקדשי המיוחד לשבת אינו אלא קרבן המוסף [במ' כח, ט-י]. אבל "המיתוס" של היום אינו מוצא לו ביטוי בעבודת המקדש אלא בחיי העם'.[50] קויפמן מצביע על הפער שבין תחום המקדש לבין חיי העם, ולמד ממנו כי השבת של ימי הבית הראשון היא אחד מגופי יצירתה של הדת העממית. שורש קדושתה בטאבו עתיק, שטעמו מיתולוגי-מאגי ולכן שבירתו קשורה בעונש מוות. שיטתו קשה לאישוש, משום שאין די נתונים בידינו כדי להכריע מה היה אופיה של השבת בימי הבית הראשון. האם כבר אז היא היתה קשורה בבריאת העולם? האם כבר אז כרך

47　ראה סקירתו של אל-קירקיסאני, הפותחת בפילוג של ירבעם ועוברת לפורשים אחרים, אצל: L. Nemoy, 'Al-Qirqisani's Account of the Jewish Sects and Christianity', *HUCA* VII (1930), pp. 317-397; ראה עוד: S. Talmon, 'Divergences in Calendar Reckoning in Ephraim and Judah', *VT* 8 (1958), pp. 48-74

48　על בעיית הלוח ולוחות כיתתיים ראה דיון כללי וביבליוגרפיה אצל יב״צ סגל, הערך 'שנה', אנציקלופדיה מקראית ח, תשמ״ב, טורים 198–209 ובמיוחד 207–208. אל-קירקיסאני מטעים כי נושאים של לוח ומועדים שימשו עילת עימות, שם, עמ' 342–344, 362, 364. דיון בלוח כיתתי ראה, למשל, אצל: ש' טלמון, חשבון הלוח של כת מדבר יהודה, בתוך: מחקרים במגילות הגנוזות – ספר זכרון לאליעזר ליפא סוקניק ז״ל, בעריכת י' ידין וח' רבין, ירושלים תשכ״א, עמ' 77–105. לוח אנשי הכת, שהיה לוח שמשי, נשקף גם מספר היובלים, ו 29–38 ומחנוך א, עב–פב. מדברי פילון האלכסנדרוני על התרפוטים (בתוך: כתבים, כרך ראשון, הכתבים האפולוגטיים, על חיי העיון, ערכה ד' דניאל-נטף, ירושלים תשמ״ו, עמ' 196 ([65=])), ניתן להבין שבלוח של כת זו ניתנה חשיבות מיוחדת למחזוריות של 50 יום (ולא נראית טענת דניאל-נטף (שם, עמ' 177 ו-196 הע' 78), שאין מדובר במועד חדש בלוח. דוגמה למחלוקת כיתתית בעניין לוח הוא הדיון בסוגיה 'ממחרת השבת', וראה לעיל, הערה 34.

49　טלמון (לעיל, הערה 47), עמ' 78.

50　י' קויפמן, תולדות האמונה הישראלית מימי קדם עד סוף בית שני, ירושלים–תל-אביב תשט״ז, ספר שני, כרך שני, עמ' 491–492.

חילולה עונש מוות? האם היא היתה שבועית, או אולי ציינה את אמצע החודש? ועוד.[51] פתרון שנראה לי עדיף להנמקת הפער בין השבת המקדשית לבין השבת העממית הוא התבוננות בשבת משתי נקודות מבט כוהניות: תורת כוהנים ואסכולת הקדושה. בעוד תורת כוהנים כמעט שהתעלמה מהשבת, שלא עלתה בקנה אחד עם פעילות המקדש, אסכולת הקדושה ראתה בה מוסד שיכול לקדש את החברה כולה.

טענתי היא אפוא, כי מי שטרחה ליצור את המיתוס של היום ויצרה את לוח הקדושה, ומי שהקפידה על הפיכת לוח זה לאורח חיים מחייב – היא אסכולת הקדושה, כדברי קנוהל: 'הדגשת קדושתה של השבת, ההחמרה בעונש מחלליה והדיון בפרטי איסור המלאכה מקנים לשבת מאווירת הקדושה החמורה האופפת את המתחם הפולחני. לדעת אה"ק, השבת היא אות לקדושת ישראל [שמ' לא, יג] וישראל שומרי השבת הם בבחינת כוהנים המשרתים בקודש'.[52] במלים אחרות, מי שהפך את השבת ממנהג עממי ללוח מחייב ומבדל היא אסכולת הקדושה.

* * *

מסקנה אחרונה זו מעוררת שאלה נוספת, והיא: מתי פעלה אסכולת הקדושה? תשובה לשאלה זו נוגעת מטבע הדברים אף לסוגיית החיבור והעריכה של סיפור הבריאה. הניסיון להכריע בשאלה זו כרוך, לדעתי, בסוגיית ההתבדלות, שאחד מאמצעיה הוא הפעלת לוח שונה. השאלה המכרעת היא אפוא, מהי התקופה ההיסטורית שההתבדלות מעמי הארצות היתה בה אירוע מרכזי ומכריע בחיי העם. נראה שהנסיבות של גלות בבל ותקופת שיבת ציון, החיים בכמה מרכזים ותחת לוחות שונים, ההתמודדות עם חיים בלא מקדש ועם הרצון ליצור מתחם מקודש בסביבה טמאה, הם 'המושב בחיים' של הפיכת השבת ללוח מחייב, וכך – לאמצעי מבדל ומייחד ואף הנמקה לחורבן עצמו. לוח הקדושה הוא אפוא פרי מאבקה של אסכולת הקדושה, שערכה את ספרות התורה בראשית ימי הבית השני.[53] בד בבד, ראוי לציין כי הדרישה המחמירה לשמור שבת והצגת חילולה כחטא מרכזי של החברה מאפיין את נביאי החורבן והגלות ואת נביאי שיבת ציון (וראה יר' יז, יט־כז; יח' טז, כא; כ,

51 מן הכתובים שבהם נזכרת השבת בספרות ההיסטוריוגראפית ובספרות הנבואית, שמשתקפת את ימי הבית הראשון, ניתן ללמוד על קשר הדוק בין השבת והחודש: מל"ב ד, כג; יש' א, יג; הו' ב, יג; עמ' ח, ה. ה גם האזכורים הנוספים במל"ב יא, ה, ז, ט; טז, יח אינם מלמדים על היותה שבת שבועית. וראה דעת טור־סיני (לעיל, הערה 46).

52 קנוהל (לעיל, הערה 1), עמ' 183. מסקנתו מעידה על הבעייתיות בשיוך סיפור הבריאה לתורת כוהנים. נראה לי אפוא, שדווקא לאור מחקרו יש צורך לבדוק מחדש את היקף חותמה של אסכולת הקדושה בספרות התורה.

53 מסקנה זו אינה תואמת את שיטתו של קנוהל (שם, עמ' 190–197), שקושר את צמיחת האסכולה עם ימי אחז–חזקיהו. לעניין זה ראה גם דבריו של מ' גרינברג (לעיל, הערה 37 עמ' 171): 'אומר רק, שהשבת מילאה תפקיד נכבד בחיי ישראל גם לפני גלות בבל, אך נכון שבתקופת גלות בבל הוענקה לה משמעות חדשה ונודעה לה חשיבות שונה מזו שהיתה לה לפני־כן. משחרב בית־המקדש ואבדו אזורי הקודש, משנתמעטה הנבואה ונצטמצמו החיים הדתיים־הפוליטיים של בני ישראל נותרו השבת והמילה ביטויים עיקריים לזהות העצמית של הקהילה היהודית, ובגלות אכן נודעה להן חשיבות שלא היתה להן קודם'. וראה גם דבריו על חשיבות השבת אצל נביאי הגלות במאמרו: 'פרשת השבת בירמיהו', עיונים בספר ירמיהו ב, ערך ב"צ לוריא, גבעתיים [תשל"ג], עמ' 27–37. ראוי במיוחד לציין את מקומה של השבת בנבואת יחזקאל, שמקובל להצביע על הקשר בינה לבין H (וראה סיכום אצל מ"ד קאסוטו, הערך 'יחזקאל', ס' יחזקאל', אנציקלופדיה מקראית ג, ירושלים תשי"ח, טור 642): כ, יב־יג, יט־כ; כב, כו; כג, לח; מד, כד. למקום השבת מימי מנשה ובנבואות יחזקאל ראה גם: .M Greenberg, *Ezekiel 1-20* (AB 22), Garden City, New York 1983, pp. 366-367

יב־כד; כב, ח, כו; כג, ג, ח; מד, כד; מה, יז; מו, ד; ישע׳ נו, ב־ו, י, כג).[54] גם בתיאור מעשי
נחמיה ניתן לשבת מקום מרכזי. בתפילת הווידוי שהשמיעו הלויים, לאחר שנבדל זרע ישראל מכל
בני הנכר (נחמ׳ ט, ב), אין התייחסות לחוקים ספציפיים, לבד מן השבת: 'ועל הר סיני ירדת וַדַּבֵּר
עמהם משמים ותתן להם משפטים ישרים ותורות אמת חֻקים ומצות טובים. ואת שבת קדשך הודעת
להם ומצוות וחֻקים ותורה צוית להם ביד משה עבדך' (שם, ט, יג־יד). הקשר בין שבת לבין התבדלות
עולה אף מתקנות האמנה, שנפתחות בדרישה להימנע מנישואי תערובת וממסחר בשבת (שם, י,
לא־לג). שני נושאים אלה, תקנות לשמירת שבת ומאבק בנישואי תערובת, אף חותמים את ספר
נחמיה (יג, טו־ל).

השבת ולוח הקדושה הפכו לכוח מעצב בהיסטוריה של עם ישראל, כפי שניתן ללמוד, דרך משל,
מדבריו של הרמן כהן בביקורתו על תיאור היהדות אצל קנט, בספרו 'הדת בגבולות התבונה
הטהורה': 'עד היום נחלקים החכמים – לועגים הם לעצמם ואינם יודעים, מה סוף סוף עשוי היה
לקיים את היהודים בעולם. אינם רוצים להודות שיסוד עליון זה מצוי באמת של אלוה יחיד והם
מעדיפים לייחס יסוד זה לחוק, וסבורים הם שרשאים הם לבוז לחוק זה משום הפורמאליות התקנונית
שלו כנעדרת פנימיות. והנה השבת היא הנציגה הנאמנה והפנימית ביותר של החוק. ואמנם על־ידי
השבת שמר החוק על־פי מצוות אלוה יחיד, האוהב את בני־האדם, על קיומם של היהדות והיהודים
בעולם'.[55] למעמדה זו של השבת ולכוחה ההיסטורי אחראית לדעתי אסכולת הקדושה. אסכולה זו,
שערכה את כל ספרות התורה, טרחה להבליט את השבת לא רק באמצעות אזכורים לאורך הנדודים
במדבר, ולא רק באמצעות חקיקה של לוח מועדים, אלא בהציגה אותה כאחד מיסודות הבריאה
וכתפיסת זמן חדשה ומקודשה.

---

54 העדות החיצונית היחידה לשמירת שבת בימי בית ראשון היא מאוחרת – הרבע האחרון של המאה השביעית
לפסה״נ – ושנויה במחלוקת. ראה דיונו של ש׳ אחיטוב (אסופת כתבות עבריות מימי בית־ראשון וראשית ימי
בית־שני, ירושלים תשנ״ג, עמ׳ 96–100) במכתב התלונה ממצד חשביהו. הצירוף 'לפני שב[ת]', הנזכר בשו׳ 5,
אינו בהכרח שמיני.

55 הרמן כהן, דת התבונה ממקורות היהדות, ירושלים תשל״ב (1918), עמ׳ 194. דברים ברוח זו ובניסוח שהפך
שגור במעיונותינו כתב אחד העם במאמרו 'שבת וציונות': 'אפשר לומר בלי שום הפרזה, כי יותר מישישראל שמרו
את השבת שמרה השבת אותם...', בתוך: כל כתבי אחד העם, על פרשת דרכים, חלק שלישי, תל אביב תשי״ד,
עמ׳ רפו.

על היישות הפלשתית ומקור השם פלשתינה

ישראל אפעל
האוניברסיטה העברית בירושלים

[א]

במחקר נדונו בהרחבה יתרה ראשית הופעתם של הפלשתים ויחסיהם עם בני־ישראל בדורות הראשונים להימצאות שני העמים הללו בארץ. סממני התרבות החומרית שיוחסו לפלשתים ואפיינו אותם נמוגו ונעלמו במרוצת המאה העשירית לפסה"נ, ובקרב החוקרים מקובלת הדעה כי, למעשה, נטמעו הפלשתים ונבלעו בתוך האוכלוסיה הכנענית שישבו בתוכה.[1] אישוש לדעה זו נמצא בעובדה שרוב שמותיהם של מלכי פלשת הידועים מכתבותיהם של מלכי אשור, מן המחצית השנייה של המאה השמינית ועד שנות ה־60 של המאה השביעית לפסה"נ, וכן של אישים הקשורים למִנהל של ממלכת אשקלון הם שמיים־מערביים.[2] נסיבותיה של תופעה זו לא נחקרו באורח יסודי, ו'היעלמותם' של הפלשתים היא יותר עניין שבהסכמה מאשר תופעה שעמדה במבחן המחקר. ברשימה זו יש בכוונתי להצביע על קיומה של 'יישות פלשתית' מאות שנים אחרי ימי דוד ושלמה.

לפי המקרא, בדורות הראשונים לישיבתם בארץ היו הפלשתים מאורגנים במסגרת חמש ערים: עזה, אשקלון, אשדוד, עקרון וגת, שבראשן עמדו סרנים; ומן הכתובים משתמע לכאורה כי הן פעלו במשותף נגד בני ישראל.[3] המקורות ההיסטוריים שבידינו על הפלשתים אחרי מלכות דוד

---

1 עיין B. Mazar, 'The Philistines', *Biblical Israel: State and People*, Jerusalem 1992, pp. 22-41 (ושם ספרות נוספת).

2 המלכים ששמותיהם שמיים־מערביים הם חנון (עזה); מת(נ)ת, צדקא (אשקלון); עזור, אחימת, מת(נ)ת, אחימלך (אשדוד); פדי (עקרון). על זמנם של מלכים אלה ועל ממלכותיהם בתקופה הנדונה ראה H. Tadmor, 'Philistia Under Assyrian Rule', *BA* 29 (1966), pp. 86-102. על זיקה למערכת המִנהל של ממלכת אשקלון מעידים חותמו של 'עבדאלאב בן שבע עבד מת מת בן צדקא' (ראה A. Bergman [Biran], 'Two Hebrew Seals of the ʿEbed Class', *JBL* 55 [1936], pp. 224-226), ושמו של עבדאל 'השליש האשקלוני' ברשימת מס מקובצת, משנת 707 לפסה"נ, שנמצאה בכלח (ND 2451 שורה 20; ראה J.N. Postgate, *Taxation and Conscription in the Assyrian Empire*, Rome 1974, p. 377). על אלה ניתן להוסיף את שמותיהם של אדן מלך עקרון (?) ואגא מלך אשקלון בתחילת שלטונו של נבוכדנאצר מלך בבל בארץ־ישראל (604 לפסה"נ); ראה: B. Porten, 'The Identity of King Adon', *BA* 44 (1981) pp. 36-52; E.F. Weidner, 'Joiachin, König von Juda in babylonischen Keilschrifttexten', *Mélanges syriens offerts à R. Dussaud* II, Paris 1939, p. 928, בהתאמה.

3 בתקופה שבה היתה מקובלת במחקר השערת הארגון האמפיקטיוני של עם ישראל, מייסודו של מ' נות, היה מי

וראשית מלכות שלמה מועטים והם מצויים במקרא בלבד (הם מתמצים, בעצם, בידיעות על
מלחמות צבאה של ממלכת ישראל על גבתון אשר לפלשתים בשנת שלוש ובשנת עשרים ושבע
לאסא מלך יהודה; ראה מל"א טו, כז; טז, טו). לפיכך, פרק־הזמן שבין סוף המאה העשירית ואמצע
המאה השמינית לפסה"נ הוא בחינת 'תקופה עלומה' ככל שמדובר בתולדות הפלשתים וארצם. עם
התחדשות ידיעותינו על דרום הארץ, בעקבות השתלטותה של אשור על מערבו של 'הסהר הפורה'
והופעת צבאה בארץ־ישראל בימי תגלת־פלאסר השלישי, בשנת 734 לפסה"נ, אנו מוצאים בפלשת
ארבע ישויות פוליטיות (עזה, אשקלון, אשדוד ועקרון), שבראש כל אחת מהן עמד מלך. ממלכות
אלו התקיימו במשך כל תקופת השלטון האשורי.

מן המידע, המפורט למדי, המצוי בידינו על היחסים שבין אשור לממלכות פלשת ניתן לקבוע
שבמשך התקופה הנדונה לא ניכר שיתוף פעולה מדיני וצבאי בין ארבע הממלכות הללו.[4] ונראה
שבדרך כלל שאפה כל אחת מהן להיבנות מחולשת שכנותיה, כדרך שקורה לעתים קרובות בחבל־
ארץ קטן־מידות שמצויות בו יחידות מדיניות או אתניות אחדות. ככל שמדובר בענייני המדינה,
כמו נאמנות למלך אשור או מרידה בו, וכן בתשלום מסים למיניהם, נרשמו בכתבות המלכים
ובמסמכי המנהל האשוריים שמותיהן של ארבע ממלכות פלשת הנוגעות בדבר, ואין בהם עדות
לקיומה של מסגרת מדינית כוללת לממלכות אלו.[5] עם זאת, אנו מוצאים בתעודות האשוריות גם
את המושג 'פלשת', המכוון לתחום גיאוגרפי־מנהלי מוגדר, ואת הכינוי 'פלשתים', המציין קבוצות
אוכלוסין שנמצאו בארץ אשור, כדלקמן:

המושג 'פלשת' מופיע כבר בכתובת כלח של אדד־נררי השלישי (שנכתבה כשישים שנה לפני
הגעתו הראשונה של צבא אשור לדרום ארץ־ישראל);[6] בכרוניקון האפונימי צוינה '(ארץ) פלשת'
(kurPilišta)[7] כיעדו של צבא תגלת־פלאסר השלישי בשנת 734 לפסה"נ; ובחוזה שבין אסרחדון
לבעל מלך צור מוגדרת פלשת (kurPilištu) כאזור שמטענן של ספינות צוריות אשר תישברנה אל
חופי יעבור לרשותו של מלך אשור ואשר יוקצו בו מעגנים ומוצאי דרכים לשימושו של מלך צור.[8]

שטען כי אם אמנם היה קיים מבנה ארגוני כזה בארץ־ישראל, הרי יש לבקשו בקרב הפלשתים (ראה: B.D.
Rahtjen, 'Philistine and Hebrew Amphictionies', *JNES* 24 [1965], pp. 100-104, אולם, אפשרות
זו דחוקה למדי.

4   כך פעלו תגלת־פלאסר השלישי בשנת 734 וסרגון בשנת 720 לפסה"נ נגד חנון מלך עזה, שניסה להתנער
משלטון אשור; בשנת 733 מרד מתנת מלך אשקלון; צבא סרגון יצא נגד אשדוד בשנים 713 ו־712; ובשנת 701
עלה סנחריב על צדקא מלך אשקלון שמרד בו (בעוד שפדי מלך עקרון סירב להשתתף במרד זה והוסגר לידי
חזקיהו מלך יהודה, והלה החזיק במעצר בירושלים). לפירוט שמותיהן של ממלכות פלשת במסמכי מנהל
הקשורים להבאת מסים לאשור ראה, למשל, *SAA* I 29 rev. 22-23; 110 rev. 4-13 (S. Parpola, *The
Correspondence of Sargon II*, Part I: *Letters from Assyria and the West*, Helsinki 1987, pp. 29, 92,
respectively); ND 2672 (Postgate, above, n. 2, pp. 387-389)

5   בכתובת של סרגון שנמצאה בנינוה נאמר על אנשי אשדוד המורדים (או על יַמָני שעלה למלוכה עליהם) כי
שלח(ו) דברי שקר, רעות וזדונות נגד מלך אשור אל '[...] של פלשת, יהודה, אדום, מואב ויושבי (חבל) הים'
H. Winckler, *Die Keilschrifttexte Sargons nach den Papierabklatschen und Originalen neu
herausgegeben* I, Leipzig 1889, p. 188. בכתוב זה, 'פלשת' הוא שם האזור ולא שמה של יחידה פוליטית
מוגדרת.

6   ראה: H. Tadmor, 'The Historical Inscriptions of Adad-nirari III', *Iraq* 35 (1973), pp. 148-149

7   ראה: A. Ungnad, 'Eponymen', RLA II, Leipzig 1938, p. 431

8   ראה SAA II 5 iii 15'-19' (S. Parpola & K. Watanabe, *Neo-Assyrian Treaties and Loyalty Oaths*,

בכתובת של סנחריב שמדובר בה בקבוצות אוכלוסין שהוגלו לאשור והועסקו שם בעבודות בנייה ופיתוח, הוזכרו כשדים, ארמים, וכן בני מני, קוה, חֲלַךְ, פלשת וצור.[9]

בראשיתה של תקופת השלטון האשורי בפיניקיה הוטל איסור על תושבי צידון למכור עצי ארז לבנון למצרים ולפלשתים (kurPalaštaia);[10] ויחידה של חיילים 'פלשתים' חנתה ביישוב uruLuqaše (בקרבת העיר אֲרְבָּאל שבארץ אשור);[11] ובתיאור גבולותיה של נחלה שנמכרה בשנת 679 לפסה"נ ביישוב Hatta נאמר שהיא גובלת ב(חלקה) 'של הפלשתים'.[12] קיומה של פלשת כישות (אתנית או גיאוגרפית) מתברר גם מכינויו של אדם, mPilištaiu, היינו 'הפלשתי', הרשום כעד במסמך משפטי שנכתב בעיר אשור בשנת 655 לפסה"נ.[13] המונח 'הפלשתים' מופיע גם במכתב־שאלה לאל שַמַש מימי אסרחדון. בתעודה זו מנויים עמים וארצות ברחבי האימפריה האשורית עד קצה גבוליה, שלכאורה נשקפת מהם סכנה של מרידה ביורש־העצר אשורבניפל, לכשתגיע שעתו למלוך.[14] לא פורטו בה שמותיהן של הממלכות שהיו בדרומה של ארץ־ישראל, ויש לראות את המונח 'פלשתים' כשם־עצם קיבוצי לכלל תושבי האזור.

מכלל הנתונים הללו עולה שאין עדות לכך שהכינוי 'פלשתים' היתה לו אחיזה כלשהי במציאות הפוליטית של התקופה האשורית, ומסתבר שכל אחיזתו היתה נעוצה בתודעה של מוצא משותף.[15]

[ב]

בשנים האחרונות מתבררת והולכת הימצאותה בפלשת של קבוצת אנשים ממוצא לא־שמי. תעודות אפיגרפיות מן המאות השמינית־שביעית לפסה"נ שנתגלו בפלשת מכילות שמות פרטיים שאין להם אטימולוגיה שמית (להרש, בנכֹש, אדנש, אנש, שגש, שמאש, חמש, פפש, כליטבש, דרימש, קסריה, ברציה, וננת [כל אלה בתעודות שנתגלו בתל־גמה]; דגגרת [נתגלה באשדוד]).[16] שמו של אכיש בן פדי מלך עקרון, החקוק בכתובת אלפביתית שנחשפה לאחרונה בחפירות תל־מקנה, הוא

Helsinki 1988, p. 25

9   D.D. Luckenbill, *The Annals of Sennacherib*, Chicago 1924, p. 104:53

10   ראה (Postgate, above, n. 2, p. 391) ND 2715:23-29

11   ראה SAA I 155 (Parpola, above, n. 2, p. 123)

12   ראה SAA VI 268:6 (Th. Kwasman & S. Parpola, *Legal Transactions of the Royal Court of Nineveh*, Part I: *Tiglath-Pileser III through Esarhaddon*, Helsinki 1991, p. 215)

13   ראה. E. Weidner, 'Neuassyrische Rechtsurkunden aus Assur', *AfO* 21 (1966), p. 69 :ספק אם 'הפלשתי' הוא השם שקראו לו הוריו של האדם שבו מדובר. סביר יותר שזה השם שקראו לו רעיו, ראה י' נוה, 'אנשים ללא שמות?', ציון נד (תשמ"ט), עמ' 16–1.

14   SAA IV 142:11 (I. Starr, *Queries to the Sungod: Divination and Politics in Sargonid Assyria*, Helsinki 1990, p. 152)

15   למסורת בדבר מוצאם של הפלשתים, ללא הבחנה בין הקבוצות שנכללו במונח זה, ראה עמ' ט, ז; יר' מז, ד. במקרא מוזכרים הפלשתים בכתובים שהקשרם התוכני קודם לחורבן בית ראשון. בחיבורים ההיסטוריו־גרפיים המקראיים חל המונח 'פלשתים' על כל ארבע הממלכות ובעצם אי־אפשר ללמוד מהם על ההתנהגות הפוליטית של כל אחד מרכיביו. אפילו בנבואות שבהן פורשו שמותיהן של הערים הממלכות, במסגרת השם הקיבוצי 'פלשתים' (כגון, עמ' א, ו–ח; יר' מז), אין משתקפת ההתנהגות הפוליטית הנפרדת של כל אחת מהן.

16   ראה: J. Naveh, 'Writings and Scripts in Seventh-Century B.C.E. Philistia. The New Evidence from Tell Jemmeh', *IEJ* 35 (1985), pp. 8-21

כנראה מאותו סוג. משמו של מלך זה – Ikausu – כפי שנרשם בכתובות אסרחדון ואשורבניפל
מלכי אשור, ומן הצורה 'Aγχοuς שבה נכתב שמו של אכיש (מלך גת) בתרגום השבעים, ניתן לקבוע
שצורתו המקורית היתה אַכַיִש או אֲכַיִש.[17]

עד כה נתגלו השמות הלא־שמיים בתחומיהן של שלוש מתוך ארבע ממלכות פלשת: עקרון,
אשדוד ועזה (שתל־גמה נמצא בתחומה), וניתן אפוא לקבוע בתופעה שמדובר בתופעה נרחבת
למדי. בשעתו, עם פרסום השמות הלא־שמיים הנ"ל מתל־גמה, הוצע לראות בהם בני קבוצה של
גולים, שהובאו מהרי זגרוס לדרום־הארץ בפקודת סרגון השני מלך אשור, בעקבות מסעו נגד מדי
שנערך בשנת 716 לפסה"נ.[18] אולם העובדה שאכיש הוא מלך באחת מממלכות פלשת ושם אביו,
פדי (וכן שמות אבות־אבותיו), שמי־מערבי, מבטלת את האפשרות שמדובר בקבוצת גולים, שזה
מקרוב הגיעו לאזור.[19] במקום לשער שהשמות הנדונים הם של קבוצה, או קבוצות, שהוגלו לפלשת
בידי השלטון האשורי, האם לא עדיף לסבור שהם נמצאו שם מתקופה קדומה יותר וכי אינם, בעצם,
אלא צאצאי הפלשתים? אפשרות כזו כבר העלה אהרן קמפינסקי, שסבר (כמה שנים לפני שנתגלתה
הכתובת מתל־מקנה) כי השמות הלא־שמיים שבתעודות תל־גמה, כמו גם השם אכיש, הם
איגאיים/מערב־אנטוליים של אוכלוסין אשר הגיעו לדרום הארץ לפני תקופת השלטון האשורי.[20]
אם התשובה לשאלתנו היא חיובית, ניתן לדבר על 'ישות פלשתית' שהתקיימה לפחות עד סוף
השלטון האשורי בארץ־ישראל, היינו עד המחצית השנייה של המאה השביעית לפסה"נ.[21]

[ג]

דומה שבירור זה עשוי לסייע גם להבנתנו את הנסיבות שבהן נוצר המושג 'פלשתינה', הגזור משמם
של הפלשתים (ופלשת ארצם). כידוע, העדות הקדומה ביותר לקיומו מצויה בחיבורו של הרודוטוס,

17 ראה S. Gitin, T. Dothan, J. Naveh, 'A Royal Dedicatory Inscription from Ekron', IEJ
(forthcoming). אני מחזיק טובה מרובה לפרופ' נוה על שמסר לי את המאמר לקריאה קודם הופעתו בדפוס.

18 ראה N. Na'aman & R. Zadok, 'Sargon II's Deportations to Israel and Philistia (716-708 BC)',
JCS 40 (1988), pp. 36-46

19 נאמן וצדוק (שם, עמ' 37) ביססו את הצעתם על ההבחנה שבשמות הרשומים בתעודות תל־גמה ניתן להבחין
זוגות: הראשון שמי־מערבי והשני לא־שמי (למשל, בעלא חמש; נתן פפש), ועל ההנחה שהקרויים בשמות
השמיים היו בניהם של בעלי השמות הלא־שמיים. לטענתם, ניתן להסביר תופעה זו בהתנהגות האופיינית
לאנשים שבאו זה מקרוב, לקרוא לבניהם בשמות הנהוגים במקום מושבם החדש. ברם, מתברר שהבחנה זו נכונה
רק בחלקה, לפי שניתן להבחין גם בתופעה הפוכה בשמותיהם של דרימש (בן) אליקם (בחותם שנתגלה בתל גמה)
ושל אכיש בן פדי מלך עקרון.

20 ראה A. Kempinski, 'Some Philistine Names from the Kingdom of Gaza', IEJ 37 (1987), pp.:
20-24

21 זוהי ההזדמנות נאותה לחזור בי מקביעתי הקודמת כי 'חַלְבֵּש השומרוני' המוזכר בתעודה ABL 633+, קשור לבעלי
השמות הלא־שמיים מתל־גמה (ראה: I. Eph'al, '"The Samarian(s)" in the Assyrian Sources', in M.
Cogan & I. Eph'al (eds.), Ah, Assyria...: Studies in Assyrian History and Ancient Near Eastern
Historiography Presented to H. Tadmor), Jerusalem 1991, pp. 43-44. עתה ברור לי כי זהו שם לובי
המופיע בתעודות אכדית יחד עם שמות מצריים, ויש לטפל בו כמו שאנו מטפלים בשמם של חַרוּצ ה־hazannu
המוזכר בתעודה מגזר משנת 651 לפסה"נ (על פקיד זה ראה: R. Giveon, 'An Egyptian Official in
Gezer?' IEJ 22 [1972], pp. 143-144

שנכתב באמצע המאה החמישית לפסה"נ, היינו כ־120 שנה לפני שהובאו פלשת (וארץ־ישראל
בכללה) בתחום השליטה היוונית. בחיבור זה 'פלשתינה' הוא חבל־ארץ בסוריה שתושביו הם
'הסורים אשר ב(חבל הארץ הקרוי) פלשתינה'.[22] היקפה של פלשתינה אצל הרודוטוס אינו ברור די
הצורך. מבין אזכורי 'סוריה הפלשתינית' בחיבורו ראויים לתשומת־לב דבריו על העמים שלמדו את
מנהג המילה מן המצרים, ביניהם 'הפיניקים והסורים אשר בפלשתינה' (ב 104). בדברים אלה יש
משום עניין מיוחד לאור העובדה שבמקרא נחשבים הפלשתים ל'הערלים' בה"א הידיעה (שופ' יד,
ג; שמ"א יז, כו; שמ"ב א, כ ועוד).[23] קשה לשער שהמושג 'פלשתינה' היה יכול להיווצר בתודעה
הגיאוגרפית של היוונים אילו חדלה הישות הפלשתית להתקיים כבר במאה העשירית לפסה"נ. אם
נכונה סברתנו שישות כזו התקיימה לפחות עד סוף השלטון האשורי בארץ־ישראל, אזי יתקצר
הפער שבין העדויות שבידינו על קיום הישות הפלשתית (לא לפני סוף המאה השביעית) ובין
היווצרות השם פלשתינה (לא אחרי אמצע המאה החמישית) בשיעור ניכר. לפי השקפה זו, במצב
הנוכחי של ידיעותינו, הפער הוא בן 150 שנה, לכל היותר.

---

22 הרודוטוס א, 105; ב, 104, 106; ג, 5, 91; ד, 39; ז, 89.

23 לאפשרות שהרודוטוס התכוון כאן ליהודים (כפי שטוען יוסף בן־מתתיהו, קדמוניות ח, 262; נגד אפיון א,
168–171), או לערבים ששכנו במאה החמישית לפסה"נ בדרום הארץ, ראה M. Stern, *Greek and Latin*
Authors on Jews and Judaism I, Jerusalem 1976, pp. 3-4. מכל מקום, נראה שתחומם של 'הסורים אשר
בפלשתינה' המוזכרים כאן חורג מתחומי פלשת. על המושג המעורפל שהיה ליוונים באשר לתיחומו של חבל־
הארץ הנדון עשויים להעיד דברי אריסטו (במאה הרביעית לפסה"נ) על האגם המלוח אשר בפלשתינה שאין בו
דגים וכל הנזרק לתוכו, אפילו כשהוא כפות, צף על מימיו (*Meteorologica* II, 359a). ראה: H.D.P. Lee,
Aristotle, vol. VII. *Meteorologica*, London 1952, p. 158

על קו הגבול שבין חקר־הלשון לחקר־המקרא –
לתולדות צמיחתו של המונח 'ספר משה'

אבי הורביץ

האוניברסיטה העברית בירושלים

[א]

בספרות המקראית ניתן למצוא כמה וכמה מונחים הבאים לציין את אוסף המצוות והחוקים אשר
נמסרו על־ידי האלוהים למשה ואשר בני ישראל נצטוו לקיימם. דרך משל: 'התורה', 'ספר התורה',
'תורת ה''; וכן גם 'תורת משה', 'ספר תורת משה', ו'ספר משה' – משום שעל־פי התפיסה המסורתית
חיבורה של 'התורה'[1] מיוחס, כמובן, למשה. חמישה מתוך ששת המונחים הללו נחשבים לביטויים
דויטרונומיסטיים[2] – למעט הצירוף 'ספר משה', אשר תיעודו במקרא מוגבל לנחמיה ודברי הימים
בלבד. צירוף זה הוא שיעמוד כאן במרכז דיוננו.

שמח אני להביא דברים אלה, העוסקים בענייני מינוח, בספר המוקדש למשה גרינברג – אשר
רבים ממחקריו עוסקים בליבונם של מושגים ומונחים המשמשים ברבדיה השונים של הספרות
המקראית.

[ב]

ההבדל בין הביטויים 'תורת משה' ו'ספר תורת משה' מחד לבין 'ספר משה' מאידך איננו נראה ממבט
ראשון כהבדל מהותי אלא כווריאציה סגנונית גרידא. הסיבה לכך נעוצה בעובדה, שבכל שלושת
המקרים שלפנינו משמשת המלה 'משה' – מבחינה לשונית – כסומך לשמות העצם 'תורה' ו/או
'ספר', ושבכולם באה גם לידי ביטוי – מבחינה רעיונית – אותה תפיסה עצמה בדבר מרכזיותה של
דמות משה ככותב התורה. זוהי מן הסתם הסיבה לכך שחוקרים רבים הנזקקים לשאלת חיבורה של
התורה כורכים בדיוניהם את כל שלושת הביטויים הללו (ואף את 'ספר התורה' וכו') בנשימה אחת,

---

1   אמנם אין אנו יודעים מהו בדיוק טיבה – והיקפה – של 'התורה' הנזכרת בכתובים המקראיים השונים.

2   השווה M. Weinfeld, *Deuteronomy and the Deuteronomic School*, Oxford 1972, pp. 320-365. למותר
לציין כי השימוש בהם ממשיך – ולפעמים אף מתרחב – בספרי הבית השני (כגון דניאל, עזרא, נחמיה, דברי
הימים). קרוב להם גם הביטוי 'ספר תורת אלהים', המופיע ביהו' כד, כו, אלא שכתוב זה מיוחס למקור E; השווה
ויינפלד, שם, עמ' 165.

ללא שום הבחנה ביניהם.[3] אולם, כפי שננסה להראות בהמשך הדברים, מבחינה פילולוגית אין דינו של המונח 'ספר משה' כדינם של יתר המונחים הדומים לו אשר נזכרו לעיל; וזאת משום שלגבי צירופים כמו 'תורת משה' ו'ספר תורת משה' אין בידינו נתונים לשוניים־דיאכרוניים חד־משמעיים העשויים לסייע לנו לקבוע בצורה ברורה את רקעם ההיסטורי המשוער. מגבלה זו מחייבת, כמובן, את כל הנזקק לסוגיה זו לדון בקבוצת המונחים הנ"ל תוך זיקה הדוקה למכלול רחב יותר של בעיות, הקשורות בטבורן לתולדות האמונה הישראלית; והעיסוק הטרמינולוגי נסמך כאן אפוא במידה רבה על שיקולים רעיוניים. כנגד זה, בבירור עניין מעמדו הכרונולוגי של הביטוי 'ספר משה' מאפשרים לנו המקורות שבידינו לבצע את הבדיקה הנדרשת מנקודת־מבט בלעדית של תולדות העברית המקראית; היינו, לבסס את קו הטיעון שלנו על שיקולים בלשניים טהורים.

בדיקה מעין זו, המתבצעת כולה – באופן אוטונומי – במישור הלשוני, יש בה כדי להעניק לממצאים המתקבלים ממד מיוחד. מסקנותיה עומדות כולן ברשות עצמן, ועל כן מלכתחילה ניתן לנתקה לחלוטין מתלות בסוגיות מחקריות מורכבות, אשר הטיפול בהן שייך לתחומה המובהק של 'הביקורת הגבוהה' ואשר 'הביקורת הנמוכה' (במקרה זה, הדיסציפלינה הלשונית) פטורה מלנקוט כלפיהן עמדה מחייבת לכאן או לכאן.

[ג]

מהם הנתונים הלשוניים העומדים לרשותנו לצורך בירור טיבו של המונח 'ספר משה' ומיקומו הכרונולוגי בהיסטוריה הלשונית של העברית המקראית?[4]

(1) תפוצה[5]

'ספר משה' מופיע בספרות המקראית שלוש[6] פעמים בלבד – פעם אחת בספר נחמיה, ופעמיים בס' דברי הימים:

3   ראה, למשל, .R.H. Charles, *The Apocrypha and Pseudepigrapha*, I, Oxford 1913 (1978), p. 45; J.A. Soggin, *Introduction to the Old Testament*, London 1976, pp. 79-80; M. Fishbane, *Biblical Interpretation in Ancient Israel*, Oxford 1985, p. 106 (וכן גם הנ"ל, 'תורה', אנציקלופדיה מקראית, ח, ירושלים תשמ"ב, עמ' 478); D.F. Morgan, *Between Text and Community – The 'Writings' in Canonical Interpretation*, Minneapolis 1990, pp. 64-65

4   ראה M. Baillet, J.T. Milik and R. de Vaux, *Les 'Petites Grottes' de Qumran* (DJD III) I, Oxford 1962, p. 90; E. Qimron, *The Hebrew of the Dead Sea Scrolls* (HSS 29), Atlanta 1986, p. 93; E. Qimron and J. Strugnell, *Qumran Cave 4,V – Miqsat Maʿaśe Ha-Torah* (DJD X), Oxford 1994, pp. 93-94 (להלן: ממ"ת). והשווה גם D. Talshir, 'A Reinvestigation of the Linguistic Relationship between Chronicles and Ezra-Nehemiah', *VT* 38 (1988), p. 184

5   למונחים הנזכרים כאן – 'תפוצה'; 'הנגדה'; 'מקורות חיצוניים' – השווה א' הורביץ, 'הלשון העברית בתקופה הפרסית', בתוך: ב' מזר (עורך כללי), ההיסטוריה של עם ישראל, ו (=שיבת ציון – ימי שלטון פרס [עורך: ח' תדמור]), ירושלים תשמ"ג, עמ' 222. לנוסח מורחב ומעודכן יותר של הדברים ראה סקירתנו 'מוקד ומאוחר בלשון המקרא – טיבה ואופייה של העברית המקראית המאוחרת', ספר זכרון לשושנה בהט, ירושלים תשנ"ז, עמ' 15–29.

6   בקונקורדנציה החדשה של א' אבן־שושן (ירושלים תשמ"ה), נשמט בטעות הפסוק שבנחמיה מתוך רשימת ההיקרויות של 'ספר משה' הנזכרות בראש הערך 'ספר' (שם, כרך ב, עמ' 814).

נחמ' יג, א:	ביום ההוא נקרא בספר משה באזני העם ונמצא כתוב בו אשר...
דבה"ב כה, ד:	ואת בניהם לא המית כי ככתוב[7] בספר משה אשר צוה ה' לאמר...
דבה"ב לה, יג:	ויסירו העילה... להקריב לה' ככתוב בספר משה.

נתונים אלה אין בהם כמובן כשלעצמם משום הוכחה לאיחורו של המונח; אולם הם בהחלט מעלים
חשד כבד כי לפנינו חידוש לשוני בתר־קלאסי, אשר לא היה נוהג בעברית המקראית בתקופה
שקדמה לימי הבית השני.

(2) הנגדה

בתיאור פרשת מלכות אמציהו מלך יהודה, המופיעה ב'פרקים הסינופטיים' שבספר מלכים ובספר
דברי הימים, מוצאים אנו אזכור מפורש לדין מסוים הנזכר בחומש (דב' כד, טז: 'לא יומתו אבות
על בנים ובנים לא יומתו על אבות איש בחטאו יומתו'). אולם, בעוד שספר מלכים מציין כי
החוק המצוטט על־ידיו לקוח מ'ספר התורה', נוקט בעל דברי הימים בהקשר זה בכינוי 'ספר
משה':

מל"ב יד, ו:	ואת בני הַמַכִּים לא המית	ככתוב בספר תורת־משה
דבה"ב כה, ד:	ואת בניהם	לא המית כי ככתוב בתורה בספר משה

מל"ב:	אשר צוה ה' לאמר לא יומתו אבות על בנים...
דבה"ב:	אשר צוה ה' לאמר לא ימותו[8] אבות על בנים...

דוגמה זו היא בעלת עניין מיוחד לדיוננו, משום שבשני הפסוקים גם יחד מוצאים אנו את שלוש
מלות המפתח 'ספר', 'תורה' ו'משה'. העובדה שדווקא בדברי הימים מצטרפות 'ספר' ו'משה' לביטוי
אחד ('ספר משה') – תוך סטייה מפורשת מן המונח האקוויוולנטי המקובל ('תורת משה') המשמש
תחתיו במקבילה שבספר מלכים – היא עדות לחיותו ברורה של הביטוי 'ספר משה' ולהעדפת
השימוש בו בימיו של בעל דברי הימים.

(3) מקורות שמחוץ לעברית המקראית

השימוש במונח 'ספר משה', אשר היקרויותיו בספרי המקרא העבריים מוגבלות, כפי שראינו,
לכתבי הבית השני בלבד, מתועד גם מחוץ לעברית המקראית בשורה ארוכה של מקורות מאוחרים
המשקפים אף הם את העידן הבתר־קלאסי של הלשון. השווה בטקסטים הבאים:

7   הצירוף 'כי ככתוב' קשה; ראה לעניין זה הפירושים השונים לפסוק.

8   לחילוף 'יומתו'/'ימותו' השווה, S. Japhet, *I & II Chronicles – A Commentary* (OTL), Louisville 1993,
p. 861; הנ"ל, אמונות ודעות בספר דברי־הימים, ירושלים תשל"ו, עמ' 145–146.

א. חלקו הארמי של ס׳ עזרא

עז׳ ו, יח: והקימו כהניא בפלגּתהון ולויא במחלקתהון על עבידת אלהא די בירושלם כְּכְתָב[9] **ספר משה**[10]

[והעמידו את הכהנים בפלגותיהם ואת הלוים במחלקותיהם על עבודת האלהים אשר בירושלים ככתב ספר משה׳]

ב. מגילות קומראן

DJD III, עמ׳ 90: [כי] כן כתוב **בספר מוֹשֹ[ה]**

DJD X, עמ׳ 58, שורה 10: [כתב]נֿו אליכה שתבין **בספר מוֹשֹה** [ו]בֿספר[י הנ]בֿיאים ובדוי[ד].

ג. הספרים החיצוניים[11]

טוביה ו, יג: ...לא יוכל רעואל למנוע אותה ממך... חיב מיתה הוא על פי דין **ספר משה**[12]

ז, יב: ...והיא תנתן לך על פי משפט **ספר משה**

ז, יג: ...על פי התורה והמשפט הכתובה **בספר משה**

עזרא החיצוני א, י[יב][13]: ...להקריב לה׳ ככתוב **בספר משה**

ה, מח: ...להעלות עליו עלות ככתוב **בספר משה**

(לע׳ פס׳ נ[נא]: ...ככתוב בתורה[14])

---

9 ׳כְּתָב = ספר; כלומר, ׳כתב-ספר-משה׳ עשוי להתפרש כצירוף סמיכות טאוטולוגי. ראה לעניין זה י׳ אבישור, סמיכויות הנרדפים במליצה המקראית, ירושלים תשל"ז. והשווה גם א׳ הורביץ, ׳לתולדות צמיחתו של הביטוי "מגלת-ספר" – פרק בהתפתחות מינוח הכתיבה בתקופת המקרא׳, בתוך: א׳ הורביץ, א׳ הורוויץ ואחרים (עורכים), מקדש, מקרא, ומסרת – מנחה למנחם הרן, Winona Lake 1996, עמ׳ 43*, הערה 32 (׳כְּתָב הַגִּשְׁתָּון [ארמית מקראית]: כְּתָב-תְּקֵף [נבטית]).

10 ב-G[L] הגרסה היא ἐν βιβλίῳ νόμου...; היינו ׳ספר התורה׳. לחילופי נוסח אלה בין ׳תורת-משה׳ ל׳ספר-משה׳ ניתן להשוות חילופים דומים במגנחים נוספים אשר היו רווחים בתקופה זו ואשר גם בהם משמש ׳משה׳ כנסמך בתוך צירוף של סמיכות. השווה: ׳דת משה׳ (מ׳ כתוב׳ ז, ו) לעומת ׳דין מ[ושה]׳ (DJD II), עמ׳ 110, שורה 3 [מורבעאת]), [דין] מושה׳ ([1944] 44 IEJ), עמ׳ 78, שורה 5 [נחל חבר]); וראה הדיון ב-IEJ, שם, עמ׳ 85–87. השווה גם ׳כתב-משה׳ ו׳ספר-משה׳ אשר ככל הנראה נתלכדו לביטוי (הטאוטולוגי) ׳כתב-ספר-משה׳ (עז׳ ו, יח); ראה ההערה הקודמת. והשווה גם להלן, הערות 12, 14.

11 הנוסח העברי מובא כאן על-פי מהדורת א׳ כהנא, הספרים החיצונים[2], כרך ב, ספר ב, תל-אביב תשט"ז, עמ׳ שכח, שלא, בהתאמה.

12 κατὰ τὴν κρίσιν τῆς βίβλου Μωυσέως...; זהו ׳הנוסח הארוך׳ (S ״כ), לעומת ׳תורת משה׳ (κατὰ τὸν νόμον Μωσῆ ״כ V). חילופים מעין אלה מצויים גם ב-ז, יב, יג המובאים להלן; והשווה לעיל, הערה 10. שאלת יחסי הגומלין בין שתי המסורות של כתבי-היד היווניים (׳הארוכה׳ ו׳הקצרה׳) – וערכה הטקסטואלי של כל אחת מהן – מורכבת, ולא כאן המקום לדון בה. אולם מה שראוי לציון בהקשר זה היא העובדה המאלפת, שקטעי ספר טוביה מקומראן מצביעים על מעלתו היתירה של ׳הנוסח הארוך׳ (S) – אשר בו דוקא נשתמר המונה ׳ספר משה׳ בן התקופה! ראה J.A. Fitzmyer, ‘The Aramaic and Hebrew Fragments of Tobit from Qumran Cave 4’, CBQ 57 (1995), p. 672 (‘The Qumran texts now reveal that of the various Greek forms, S is the one to which one must reckon priority... S was the earliest Greek text...’)

13 במהדורת כהנא, שם, עמ׳ תקמב, תקמד, תקמה, תקמח, בהתאמה.

14 השווה לעיל, הערה 10.

ז, ו: ...על פי הכתוב בספר משה

ז, ט: ויעמדו הכהנים... על פי ספר משה

ד. הברית החדשה

מרקוס יב, כו: ועל דבר המתים שיקומו... הלא קראתם בספר משה.

[ד]

הנתונים אשר הובאו לעיל – הן מן המקרא הן מחוצה לו; הן בעברית הן במקורות לא־עבריים – מצדיקים, כפי שראינו, את המסקנה שהופעתו של המונח 'ספר משה' משקפת את פרק הזמן של ימי הבית השני; ועל כן בהחלט מן הראוי לסווגו, מבחינה מילונאית, כאלמנט המשתייך ל'עברית המקראית המאוחרת'.[15] השאלה המתבקשת עתה בהקשר זה לדיוננו היא באיזו מידה ניתן לנצל את הנתונים שהעלינו – מתחום המחקר של תולדות העברית המקראית – לצורך בדיקת התפתחותה ההיסטורית של הספרות המקראית; או ליתר דיוק, לבדיקת תולדות צמיחתו והיווצרותו של ספר התורה. במלים אחרות, האם עובדת היותו של המונח 'ספר משה' מיוחד – במישור הטרמינולוגי – ללשון הבית השני, יש בה גם כדי לשפוך אור – במישור הספרותי־היסטורי – על טיבו ומהותו של ספר התורה עצמו בתקופה ההיסטורית אשר בה נטבע המונח הנידון?

לפני שאנו באים לדון בשאלה זו, מן הראוי תחילה לסקור כאן בקצרה כמה נתוני יסוד המתייחסים לתיבה 'תורה'. דעה מקובלת במחקר קובעת, כי מובנה הראשוני של 'תורה' הוא 'הוראה',[16] וכי רק במרוצת השנים הופכת המלה למונח המציין באופן ספציפי את 'תורת ה''.[17] התפתחות סימנטית מעין זו היא תופעה רווחת בתולדות הלשון, ובצורה ברורה ניתן להמחישה אם נתרגם את שתי המשמעויות הנ"ל לאנגלית: 'a law' ← 'The Law'. מכל מקום, נראה כי בעיקרו של דבר עלינו להבחין כאן בשלושה שלבים עיקריים בהשתלשלותה ההיסטורית של התיבה העברית 'תורה':

(1) 'תורה' = 'instruction, law' במובן מוגבל ומצומצם; כגון, 'תורת המצרע' (וי' יד, ב);

---

15 ראה במיוחד קימרון, לעיל, הערה 4. נתון נוסף העשוי להצביע על איחורו של הצירוף 'ספר משה' הוא השתייכותו לקבוצת מונחים כוללת, אשר ביסודה מונחת תבנית הסמיכות של 'ספר' + 'שם עצם פרטי'. הביטוי 'ספר ישעיה הנביא', למשל, איננו מתועד במקרא אך מצוי בקומראן (השווה DJD V, עמ' 53, שורה 15; וראה שם [שורה 16] גם 'ספר יחזקאל הנביא' ו'ספר דניאל הנביא' [עמ' 54, שורה 4], כמקובל בספרות חז"ל. כותרתו של ספר ישעיהו במקרא היא 'חזון ישעיהו בן אמוץ' [ולא *'ספר ישעיהו בן אמוץ']; והשווה גם נחום א, א: 'ספר חזון נחום האלקשי' [ולא *'ספר נחום האלקשי'], וכן מל"א יא, מא: 'ספר דברי שלמה' [ולא *'ספר שלמה']; 'ספר בן סירא' מופיע בספרות התלמודית (השווה תוס' ידים ב יג ['ספרי בן סירא']; יר' ברכ' ז יא ב ['בסיפרא דבן סירא']; וכן מתועדת דרך אזכור זו בברית החדשה (השווה לוקס ד, יז [סורית]: 'ספרא דאשעיא נביא'). עמיתי פרופ' מ' ויינפלד מעיר – בצדק – כי בהקשר זה יש להזכיר כאן גם את הברייתא במסכת בבא בתרא יד ע"ב: 'משה כתב ספרו...'.

16 הן 'תורה' והן 'הוראה' – ואף 'מורה' – נגזרות כולן מאותו שורש עצמו (ירה√); ראה במילונים (שאלת הזיקה האטימולוגית בין ירה√ 'הוראה' לבין ירה√ שעניינו 'השלכה' אינה מעניינינו בדיון זה).

17 ראה, למשל, י"א זליגמן, 'הנחות לפרשנות המדרש', מחקרים בספרות המקרא, ירושלים תשנ"ב, עמ' 450–451; M. Weinfeld, *Deuteronomy 1-11* (AB), New York 1991, pp. 17-18; והשווה לעניין זה גם פישביין (לעיל, הערה 3).

(2) '(ה)תורה' = ספר דברים; כגון, 'התורה הזאת' (דב' כז, ג, ח; לא, יא-יב), 'ספר התורה' (מלכים ב כב, ח, יא);

(3) '(ה)תורה' = החומש כולו; כגון, ב'נוסחה המשולשת' המבחינה בין 'תורה/ נביאים/ כתובים'.[18]

אולם, על אף שכיוון ההתפתחות הכללי שמדובר בו ברור ומוסכם, במידה רבה, על הכול, אין אנו יודעים לשחזר בבטחון את כל החוליות ושלבי הביניים של התהליך הסימנטי האמור; ומשמעותה המדויקת של התיבה 'תורה' בכתובים המקראיים השונים שנויה במחלוקת[19] – במיוחד במעבר מן השלב השני לשלישי. כך למשל סבור חלק מן החוקרים שמונחים כמו 'ספר התורה', 'תורת ה'' או 'תורת משה', המופיעים בספרי נחמיה ודברי הימים, עשויים כבר לציין את החומש כולו – על כל פנים בצורה בה היה ידוע בימי עזרא ונחמיה (או בפרק הזמן הסמוך להם). כנגד זה סבורים חוקרים אחרים שגם בכתבים של תקופת שיבת־ציון מתייחס עדיין המונח 'תורה' רק לחלקים מסוימים מתוך ספר התורה שבידינו – ולא לתורה כולה – בצורתה הקנונית. ויש כמובן גם עמדות ביניים שונות, הממוקמות בין שתי התפיסות הקוטביות הללו; כגון, שמחברי נחמיה ודברי הימים אכן מתכוונים בדבריהם לספר התורה בצורתו המוגמרת – אלא שנוסח התורה לא היה עדיין בימיהם מגובש וקבוע על אותיותיו.[20]

כפי שכבר ציינו לעיל, העיון בשאלות אלה – המתמקד בניסיון לשחזר את תולדות התפתחותה של התיבה 'תורה' – מבוסס במידה רבה על שיקולים רעיוניים, ועל כן חורג הוא אל מֵעֵבר לגבולות הדיון הלשוני המונח ביסודו של מאמר זה. אולם פרשת צמיחתו של הכינוי 'ספר משה' והופעתו בספרות המקראית היא כאמור כבר עניין שונה לחלוטין. כאן אכן רשאים אנו לקבוע בבטחון כי לפנינו תופעה לשונית דיאכרונית, אשר התרחשה בשלהי התקופה המקראית; ועובדה זו היא שמביאה אותנו עתה לנסות ולבחון את ההשלכות המתבקשות מנתון זה לגבי 'קו־התפר' שבין חקר הלשון לבין חקר המקרא.

במונחים של חקר הלשון, ההבחנה שעמדנו עליה לעיל היא הבחנה בין שתי חטיבות לשוניות ('העברית המקראית הקלאסית' ו'העברית המקראית המאוחרת'). לעומת זאת, במונחים של חקר המקרא ההבחנה שאנו באים להתייחס אליה היא עתה בין שני גושים ספרותיים ('ההיסטוריוגרפיה הדויטרונומיסטית'[21] ו'ההיסטוריוגרפיה הכרוניסטית'[22]); והשאלה שיש להשיב

---

18 בצורתה המגובשת ביותר מוכרת לנו נוסחה זו מספרות חז"ל. נראה כי את רישומה הקדום ביותר ניתן לראות עתה במגילת ממ"ת; השווה קימרון (לעיל, הערה 4), עמ' 111–112 (הקטע הרלבנטי לענייננו מצוטט לעיל בעמ' 40*). לתולדות 'החלוקה המשולשת' של הקנון המקראי והטרמינולוגיה המתלווה לה ראה ,H.M. Orlinsky 'Some Terms in the Prologue to Ben Sira and the Hebrew Canon', *JBL* 110 (1991), pp. 483-490

19 השווה לעיל, הערה 1; וכן פישביין (לעיל, הערה 3).

20 לבירור כל הסוגיה הזאת המלווה בניתוח מדוקדק של המונחים השונים המשמשים בהקשרים אלה, ראה ש' יפת, אמונות ודעות (לעיל, הערה 8), עמ' 202–210. והשווה גם דבריו של י"א זליגמן, 'ניצני מדרש בספר דברי הימים', מחקרים בספרות המקרא (לעיל, הערה 17), עמ' 460–465.

21 כפי שהיא באה לידי ביטוי בספרי נביאים ראשונים.

22 כפי שהיא משתקפת מספר דברי הימים ומספרי עזרא–נחמיה. אנו משתמשים במונח זה ('ההיסטוריוגרפיה הכרוניסטית') בצורה פשטנית וכוללנית ביותר, מבלי להיכנס למחלוקת בשאלת הקשר הספרותי המשוער בין דברי הימים לבין ספרי עזרא–נחמיה. יש לזכור כי ענייננו בשלושת הספרים הללו מצטמצם כאן אך ורק לקרבה

עָלֶיהָ אֵפוֹא הִיא מַהִי מִדַּת הַקּוֹרֶלַצְיָה בֵּין שְׁתֵּי קְבוּצוֹת הַמּוּשָׂגִים הַלָּלוּ? בָּרוּר שֶׁאֵין מְדוּבָּר פֹּה בַּחֲפִיפָה מוּחְלֶטֶת, שֶׁהֲרֵי כָּל אַחַת מֵהֶן מְעוּגֶּנֶת בְּדִיסְצִיפְּלִינָה מֶחְקָרִית שׁוֹנָה, הַנִּסְמֶכֶת עַל מַעֲרֶכֶת שֶׁל שִׁיקּוּלִים וּנְימוּקִים מֻשְׁלָהּ. אוּלָם, יַחַד עִם זֹאת אֵין סָפֵק שֶׁבְּעִיקָרוֹ שֶׁל דָּבָר אָכֵן עָדִים אָנוּ כָּאן לְמִתְאָם מַרְחִיק לֶכֶת בְּהַעֲרֶכֶת הַחוֹמֶר הַמִּקְרָאִי וּבְדֶרֶךְ הַטִּיפּוּל בּוֹ: שְׁתֵּי הַדִּיסְצִיפְּלִינוֹת, הֵן זוֹ שֶׁל חֵקֶר הַמִּקְרָא הֵן זוֹ שֶׁל חֵקֶר הַלָּשׁוֹן, רוֹאוֹת בַּמֵּאָה הַשְּׁשִׁית לִפְנָ"ס (זְמַן גָּלוּת בָּבֶל וְשִׁיבַת־צִיּוֹן) – מִבְּחִינַת הַהִיסְטוֹרְיָה הַמִּקְרָאִית – אֶת קַו הַגְּבוּל הַמַּפְרִיד בֵּין 'הַתְּקוּפָה הַקְּדוּמָה' לְבֵין 'הַתְּקוּפָה הַמְאוּחֶרֶת'; וְעַל־פִּי שְׁתֵּיהֶן מוֹצֵאת הִתְפַּתְּחוּת הִיסְטוֹרִית זוֹ אֶת בִּיטּוּיָהּ הַמּוּבְהָק – מִבְּחִינַת הַסִּפְרוּת הַמִּקְרָאִית – בַּהַבְחָנָה שֶׁהֵן עוֹשׂוֹת בֵּין 'הַקּוֹרְפּוּס הַקָּדוּם' (נְבִיאִים רִאשׁוֹנִים) לְבֵין 'הַקּוֹרְפּוּס הַמְאוּחָר' (דִּבְרֵי הַיָּמִים וְעֶזְרָא–נְחֶמְיָה). אוּלָם, יֵשׁ לְהַטְעִים, נְקוּדָּה זוֹ, שֶׁבָּהּ נִפְגָּשִׁים חֵקֶר הַלָּשׁוֹן וְחֵקֶר הַמִּקְרָא בִּרְאִיָּיתָם הַמְשׁוּתֶּפֶת, הִיא גַּם הַנְּקוּדָּה הַקְּרִיטִית שֶׁבָּהּ נִפְרָדוֹת דַּרְכֵּיהֶם. הַסִּיבָּה לְכָךְ נְעוּצָה בָּעוּבְדָה, שֶׁהַנְּתוּנִים הַלְּשׁוֹנִיִּים הָעוֹמְדִים לִרְשׁוּתֵנוּ פֹּה אֵין בָּהֶם כְּדֵי לְהַכְרִיעַ בַּשְּׁאֵלָה אִם הַבִּיטּוּי הַמְאוּחָר 'סֵפֶר מֹשֶׁה' הוּא בְּבְחִינַת חִידּוּשׁ לְשׁוֹנִי גְּרֵידָא, אוֹ שֶׁמָּא מְשַׁקֵּף הוּא גַּם חִידּוּשׁ תַּכְנִי מַרְחִיק לֶכֶת; בְּמִלִּים אֲחֵרוֹת, הַאִם צְמִיחַת הַמּוּנָח הֶחָדָשׁ כְּרוּכָה גַּם בְּשִׁינּוּי שֶׁחָל בְּמַהוּתוֹ שֶׁל 'סֵפֶר הַתּוֹרָה' וְ/אוֹ בַּקּוֹנְצֶפְּצְיָה שֶׁל מוּשַׂג 'הַתּוֹרָה' (הַמִּתְקַשֵּׁר עִם סוּגְיַית הַקַּנוֹנִיזַצְיָה הַמִּקְרָאִית). לְצוֹרֶךְ בֵּירוּרָהּ שֶׁל סוּגְיָה זוֹ עוֹמְדִים, כַּמּוּבָן, לִרְשׁוּתוֹ שֶׁל אִישׁ הַמִּקְרָא שִׁיקּוּלִים וּנְתוּנִים נוֹסָפִים, מֵעֵבֶר לָעוּבְדוֹת הַלְּשׁוֹנִיּוֹת הַבְּסִיסִיּוֹת אֲשֶׁר נִדּוֹנוּ לְעֵיל; אֶלָּא שֶׁשִּׁיקּוּלִים וּנְתוּנִים אֵלֶּה מְצוּיִּים כְּבָר מִחוּץ לְזִירַת פְּעִילוּתוֹ שֶׁל אִישׁ הַלָּשׁוֹן.[23]

רַשָּׁאִים אָנוּ אֵפוֹא לוֹמַר לְסִיכּוּמוֹ שֶׁל דִּיּוּן זֶה, כִּי הוֹפָעָתוֹ שֶׁל הַמּוּנָח 'סֵפֶר מֹשֶׁה' בְּסִפְרֵי דִּבְרֵי הַיָּמִים וְעֶזְרָא–נְחֶמְיָה בַּוַּודַּאי מַצְבִּיעָה עַל חִידּוּשׁ בְּתוֹלְדוֹת הַמִּינוּחַ הַמִּקְרָאִי הַמִּתְיַיחֵס לְסֵפֶר הַתּוֹרָה. וְאַף זֹאת נִיתָּן לִקְבּוֹעַ עַל־פִּי הַנְּתוּנִים שֶׁבְּיָדֵינוּ, כִּי הַשִּׁימּוּשׁ בַּמּוּנָח 'סֵפֶר מֹשֶׁה' מְצַיֵּין פָּאזָה בָּתַר־דְּוִיטֶרוֹנוֹמִיסְטִית בְּתוֹלְדוֹתֶיהָ שֶׁל הַסִּפְרוּת הַמִּקְרָאִית. אוּלָם הַשְּׁאֵלָה אִם, וּבְאֵיזוֹ מִידָּה, מְשַׁקֵּף הַחִידּוּשׁ הַטֶּרְמִינוֹלוֹגִי הָאָמוּר שְׁלָבִים שׁוֹנִים בְּהִתְפַּתְּחוּתוֹ הַהִיסְטוֹרִית שֶׁל סֵפֶר הַתּוֹרָה עַצְמוֹ – אוֹ תְּמוּרוֹת וְשִׁינּוּיִים שֶׁחָלוּ בְּתַפְסַת עוֹלָמָם שֶׁל בְּנֵי תְּקוּפַת שִׁיבַת־צִיּוֹן בַּנּוֹשֵׂא 'הַתּוֹרָה' – הִיא עִנְיָין הַמַּצְרִיךְ בֵּירוּר נוֹסָף, אֲשֶׁר יֵשׁ לָדוּן בּוֹ בְּמִסְגֶּרֶת אַחֶרֶת.

הַלְּשׁוֹנִית שֶׁבֵּינֵיהֶם; וּבְקִיּוּמָהּ שֶׁל קִרְבָה זוֹ – הַמּוּכְתֶּבֶת, בְּעִיקָרוֹ שֶׁל דָּבָר, עַל־יְדֵי מַצָּעָם הַכְרוֹנוֹלוֹגִי הַמְשׁוּתָּף שֶׁל הַסְּפָרִים – מוֹדִים גַּם אֵלֶּה הַסְּבוּרִים שֶׁעֶזְרָא–נְחֶמְיָה נִתְחַבְּרוּ מִלְּכַתְּחִילָה כְּחִיבּוּרִים נִפְרָדִים וּבִלְתִּי תְּלוּיִים בְּסֵפֶר דִּבְרֵי הַיָּמִים: רְאֵה S. Japhet, 'The Supposed Common Authorship of Chronicles and Ezra-Nehemia Investigated Anew', *VT* 18 (1968), pp. 332-333 (וְכֵן בְּפֵירוּשָׁהּ לְסֵ' דִּבְרֵי הַיָּמִים [לְעֵיל, הֶעָרָה 8], עַמ' 25); וְהַשְׁוֵוה גַּם H.G.M. Williamson, *Israel in the Books of Chronicles*, Cambridge 1977, pp. 37-59

23 רְאֵה לְמָשָׁל (1978) J.A. Sanders, *Torah and Canon*, Philadelphia 1974; מ' וַיינְפֶלְד, מְהוֹשֻׁעַ וְעַד יֹאשִׁיָּהוּ, יְרוּשָׁלַיִם תשנ"ב; מ' הָרָן, הָאֲסוּפָּה הַמִּקְרָאִית – תַּהֲלִיכֵי הַגִּיבּוּשׁ עַד סוֹף יְמֵי בַּיִת שֵׁנִי וְשִׁינּוּיֵי הַצּוּרָה עַד מוֹצָאֵי יְמֵי הַבֵּינַיִם, יְרוּשָׁלַיִם תשנ"ו.

'מזמור שיר ליום השבת' – עיון בתהלים מזמור צב

מאיר וייס
האוניברסיטה העברית בירושלים

לפי כותרתו, תהלים צב הוא 'מזמור שיר ליום השבת'. מן המוסכמות בפרשנות הביקורתית, כי הכותרת אינה חלק מקורי של המזמור, שכן תוכנו אינו משקף כל קשר לשבת. בין אם הנוהג של אמירת המזמור בשבת גרר את יצירת הכותרת ובין אם הכותרת גרמה להכנסת המזמור לתפילת השבת, מן הסתם משהו בתוכן היה המניע ליצירת הזיקה בין המזמור לשבת.[1]

אשר לפירושי המזמור בדורנו, המכנה המשותף בהם שהוא שיר תודה על ההצלה המופלאה של חיי המתפלל[2] או על נצחונו של מלך.[3]

במאמר זה אנסה לעמוד על המעוצב במזמור ולתת ביטוי להערכתי, להוקרתי את אלופי, מיודעי, פרופ' מ' גרינברג; ביתר דיוק, את חברי משה נ"י לאיו"ש, שבשבילו ס' תהלים, כמו יתר ספרי המקרא, הוא תורה שבכתב (ולא פחות – תורת חיים).

*

[פס' ב] טוב להודות לה' – האחרונים כראשונים מייחסים בדרך כלל למלה 'טוב' את שימושה הרגיל במובן של נעים, מהנה.[4] רק יחידים סבורים שמשמעותה כאן: ראוי.[5] על־פי ההקשר נראה סביר למדי להניח, שהמלה 'טוב' שבפסוקנו דו־משמעית.[6] הפועל 'להודות' אינו מציין כאן הבעת תודה, כפירושו המקובל, אלא הגדת תהילה, כפי שמסתבר מעניינו של המזמור. רק המשפט הראשון, הנדון כאן, וכן המשפט האחרון, 'להגיד כי ישר ה'' וגו' (פס' טז), היינו משפטי המסגרת, מדברים על ה' בגוף שלישי, בעוד מה שביניהם הוא פנייה ישירה לה', דיבור אליו בגוף שני. אפשר שהמשפט הראשון הוא ביטוי לזירוז עצמי. בעל המזמור מזרז את עצמו 'להודות לה'', לפני שהוא פונה אליו.

1 על דעות החוקרים במחציתה השנייה של המאה הנוכחית על המניע להיווצרותה של זיקת המזמור לשבת, ראה טייט, עמ' 468–471.

2 כגון קראוס; טייט, עמ' 471.

3 זוהי דעת N.M. Sarna, 'The Psalm for the Sabbath Day (Ps. 92)', JBL 81 (1962), pp. 155-168; דאהוד; H. Eaton, Kingship and the Psalms, London 1976, pp. 58-59; טייט, שם.

4 לפי וייזר; א"ה פיש, שירת המקרא, עדות ופואטיקה [רמת־גן תשנ"ג], עמ' 130, המלה 'טוב' נרדפת ל'יפה'.

5 ארליך; חיות.

6 לשימושה הדו־משמעי של המלה 'טוב' ראה תה' קמז, א. שם מקבילות לה שתי המלים: 'נעים', 'נאוה'.

הראשון הוא ביטוי לזירוז עצמי. בעל המזמור מזרז את עצמו 'להודות לה'', לפני שהוא פונה אליו. במשפט האחרון הוא מסכם לעצמו את תהילתו לה'. אפשרות נוספת לביאור ייחודם זה של משפטי המסגרת היא, שבאלה בעל המזמור פונה אל הציבור קודם שהוא פונה אל ה', ולאחר שהוא מסיים את דבריו אליו, הוא מוסר לציבור את המסקנה המתבקשת ממה שאמר בתחילתו. בהמשך הפתיחה בפס' ב, במלים 'ולזמר לשמך עליון', מה שחשב בעל המזמור ואמר לעצמו או לציבור – מיד אומר הוא לה'. הוי''ו במלה 'ולזמר' היא וי''ו הביאור, ומשמעותה אפוא: כלומר.[7] הפועל 'לזמר' מבהיר את המכוון בפועל 'להודות' ומוסיף עליו, כי למלות התהילה תתלווה נגינה בכלי. המושא 'לה'' מובהר על־ידי המלים 'לשמך עליון', היינו: לך, בתורת מהותך, ישותך הנקבעת בשמך, בתוארך: 'עליון', העליון.

בשני הכתובים הבאים (פסוקים ג–ד) הולך בעל המזמור ומפרט את מה שאמר בכתוב הקודם: פסוק ג מבהיר, מרחיב את המכוון בפועל 'להודות'; פסוק ד – בפועל 'לזמר'.

[פס' ג] להגיד בבקר חסדך ואמונתך בלילות. וכן, 'להודות' כוונתו: 'להגיד', לומר דבר־מה. 'בקר' ו'לילות' – צמד מלים שאחד מאבריו הוא בלשון יחיד ואחד ברבוי.[8] כפי שהוכח, אין צורת תקבולת זו בחינת תופעה חריגה. 'לילות' – כמו 'לילה'.[9] 'בבקר... בלילות' – מריסמוס המבטא את רצונו, את תכניתו של בעל המזמור 'להגיד' את חסדו ואמונתו של ה' בתמידות, בלא הפסק. המושג 'להודות' לא רק מובהר אלא גם מועצם; 'להודות' – לא הפעם בלבד, לא פעם אלא אלא הרף. 'חסד' מציין יחס שלפנים משורת הדין.[10] 'אמונה' במקרא, בפסוקים הרבה, מורה 'על מושג אמונים ונאמנות'.[11] בכמה מקומות המלה נרדפת לגזורה אחרת משורשה (אמ''ן), ל'אמת'.[12] על־פי עניינו של מזמורנו, ניתן להניח במידה ניכרת של סבירות שגם כאן היא משמשת בהוראה זו, אולי גם בהוראה זו. דוגמת 'חסד' ו'אמת', 'חסד' ו'אמונה' – צמד כהנדיאדיס,[13] שמשמעו: חסד קבוע, או חסד אמיתי, או שניהם יחד, שנתפרק בתקבולת. אם כן, שיעור הפסוק: 'להגיד חסדך ואמונתך בבוקר ובלילות', היינו: כל היום, תמיד.

[פס' ד] עלי עשור ועלי נבל עלי הגיון בכנור. 'עלי עשור ועלי נבל', דהיינו על 'נבל עשור' (תה' לג, ב; קמד, ט). נבל הוא בעל עשרה מיתרים. 'הגיון' – כאן מונח מוסיקלי, 'כנראה קול המית נימי הכינור'.[14] כשם שפס' ג מבהיר את 'להודות', כך פסוקנו – 'לזמר': ללוות את התהילה בכלי־נגינה, ליתר דיוק, בצלילים של כלי־נגינה.

[פס' ה] כי שמחתני ה' בפעלך במעשי ידיך ארנן. הפסוק מנמק מדוע 'טוב' הנאמר בפסוקים הקודמים, 'להודות', 'ולזמר'. מן ההמשך נעלה מכל ספק כי 'פעלך' ו'מעשי ידיך' אינם מתכוונים לבריאת העולם, כפי שכלכל הנראה מבטא הקשר המשני של המזמור לשבת. הכוונה להנהגת העולם. פועלו זה של ה' משמח, שכן לא הרי ה' כהרי 'פעלי און', 'פעלי און' (פסוקים ח, י).

7   ראה W. Gesenius & E. Kautzsch, *Hebräische Grammatik*[27], Leipzig 1902, §154[16]

8   A. Berlin, 'Grammatical Aspects of Biblical Parallelism', *HUCA* 50 (1979), pp. 30-35

9   ברלין, שם, עמ' 40. פרשנים אחדים (כגון בריגס; דאהוד) מייחסים לצורת הריבוי משמעות מיוחדת.

10 אוצר לשון המקרא: 'חסד'.

11 י' היינמן, 'אמונה', אנציקלופדיה מקראית א, טור 426.

12 כגון 'אל אמונה ואין עול' (דב' לב, ד). ראה: 342-345 .pp ,*TWAT* I, 'אמת, אמן, אמונה, אמן' A. Jespen

13 י' אבישור, סמיכויות הנרדפים במליצה המקראית, ירושלים תשל''ו, עמ' 121.

14 אוצר לשון המקרא: 'הגיון'.

בניגוד להם, ה' פועל צדק, כפי שיתברר מהמשך התהילה. הפסוקים ב–ה מהווים את המבוא
לתהילה. בפסוקים ב–ד, בעל המזמור מוסר את כוונתו להלל את ה'; בפס' ה הוא מנמק אותה, ובפס'
ו מתחילה התהילה.

[פס' ו] מה גדלו מעשיך ה' מאד עמקו מחשבתיך. במעבר מן המבוא לתהילה גופה חוזר בעל המזמור
על המלה 'מעשה'. במבוא הוא מציין שבגלל מעשי ה', הגורמים לו שמחה, 'טוב להודות לה''. עתה
הוא מביע את התפעלותו מגודל מעשיו. מעשי ה' הם פועלו הנראה לעין; באלה אין למצות את
הנהגתו. זאת מתבטאת גם במחשבותיו, דהיינו בתכניותיו,[15] שהנן עמוקות מאוד, נסתרות מעין
האדם.

[פס' ז] איש בער לא ידע וכסיל לא יבין את זאת. השמות 'איש בער', 'חסר דעת', ו'כסיל' – מונחים
של ספרות החכמה המה. אין הם הגדרות אינטלקטואליות, אלא כינויים לאדם "הדוחה "ראשית
חכמה" שהיא "יראת ה'".[16] הוא אינו יודע, אינו מבין; אליבא דאמת, אינו רוצה לדעת, אינו רוצה
להבין 'את זאת'. הדעות חלוקות בדבר המכוון במלה 'זאת'. האם מתייחסת היא לנאמר בפס' ו,[17] או
לנאמר בפס' ח.[18] דומה שההתייחסות היא הן לפס' ו והן לפס' ח, שהרי פס' ח בתיאודיצאה שבו מפרש
את הסתום בפס' ו: מחשבותיו העמוקות של ה' מה הן?

[פס' ח] בפרח רשעים כמו עשב. 'כמו עשב' – נשוא המשפט. פריחת רשעים היא כצמיחת עשב.
הוא ציץ ברדת הגשם ומיד נובל בבוא אחריו החום והיובש. כה מהירה וקצרה, כצמיחת העשב, היא
הצלחת רשעים.[19] ויציצו כל פעלי און להשמדם עדי עד – מוצאים ציץ, פרח, כדי שייכרתו לנצח.
בהלל בעל המזמור את ה' על פועלו ומעשי ידיו, עולים במחשבתו הכופרים בהשגחה האלוהית,
בצדקת הנהגתו של ה' את העולם, מן הסתם בטענה כי רשע וטוב לו. ואולם אין הם טוענים כך אלא
בהיותם 'בער' ו'כסיל'. שכן, אפילו מצליח רשע, הצלחתו אך ורק ארעית,[20] וזאת כדי שהעונש,
הכיליון, יהיה חמור יותר, ברור יותר. אחר העמדת הדבר, גורל 'רשעים' ו'כל פעלי און', על דיוקו,
אומר בעל המזמור לה':

[פס' ט] ואתה מרום לעולם ה'. מלבד הַסֶבַּרָה של המלה 'מרום' כתוארו של ה',[21] היינו שהוא 'רם
ונשא', מוסברת היא גם בתפיסתה כ־acc. loci, היינו, במובן: 'במרום', ככינוי לשמים כמקום
משכנו של ה'.[22] לפי פירושים אלה, אומר המשפט אל ה' שהוא שליט, שופטו של העולם. השאלה
היא: אם אחד מפירושים אלה של המלה הוא משמעותה, כיצד משתלב הפסוק בהקשרו? מפרשים

15 השווה תה' לג, י; אס' ח, ג. ראה טייט, עמ' 466.

16 A.A. Anderson, *Psalms* II, London 1972, p. 662

17 זוהי בדרך כלל סברת האחרונים. למשל גונקל; קראוס; טייט.

18 רש"י; ראב"ע; ביאור; מלב"ים, וכן, למשל, חיות; דאהוד. כך סבר גם ארליך. לפי רד"ק, ההתייחסות יכולה
    להיות גם לפס' ו וגם לפס' ח.

19 עשב כמשל להצלחת רשע נמצא עוד בתה' לז, ב; לחיי אדם – בכמה כתובים, כגון יש' לז, כז; מ, ר-ח'; תה'
    צ, ה-ו; קב, ה, יב; קג, טו; איוב יד, ב; ועוד.

20 תיאודיצאה זו מובעת גם, למשל, בתה' לז, ב; עג, יז-יט; ועוד.

21 מן האחרונים כך מסבירים, למשל, דאהוד; מרום: L. Vigano, "Il titolo 'l'Eccelso'", *SBFLA* 24 (1974),
    pp. 188-201; איטן (לעיל, הערה 3); שם; י' אבישור, 'הקבלה מדומה והקבלה אמיתית בין ספרות אוגרית
    והמקרא', שנתון ז–ח (תשמ"ג), עמ' 157.

22 כגון קראוס; טייט.

אחדים מוצאים קשר בין פסוק זה ובין קודמו, לאמור: בעוד 'רשעים', 'פועלי און' מצליחים 'להשמדם עדי עד', 'אתה' 'מרומם או במרום 'לעולם'.[23] נצחיות כנגד נצחיות. אך הנגדה זאת זרה לגמרי לעניני של המזמור. אם זוהי משמעות הפסוק, אין לראות בו חלק אורגני של מזמורנו.[24]

לאור שימושו של הפועל הגזור משרשרו של השם 'מרום (רו"ם) בכתובים, כגון: 'תרום ימינך' (תה' פט, יד), 'ירום איבי עלי' (שם, יג, ג), 'מן קמי תרוממני' (שמ"ב כב, מט; תה' יח, מט), היינו לאור שימושו כמטאפורה למושג ניצחון, נדמה שראוי לשקול את האפשרות שזהו כאן שימושו של השם 'מרום'; דהיינו במשפט 'ואתה מרום לעלם ה'' אומר בעל המזמור לה': הרי אתה מנצח לעולם, ה'! במשמעות זו של 'מרום', הדוק, הגיוני קשרנו של פס' ח עם פס' ט. כהמשך לנקבע בפס' ח על סופם של 'רשעים' ו'כל פעלי און', מעניק פס' ט לקביעה זו הסבר תיאולוגי. והנה בפס' ט מתגלה המכוון ב'עליון' שבראש המזמור: הוא מנצח, משליט את צדקתו בעולם. מפס' י, שבו מתחילה חטיבה חדשה, הבאה להשלים ולחזק את הנאמר בפסוקים ח-ט, מסתברת הגדרת ה' כ'מנצח' לעולם.

[פס' י] כי הנה איביך ה' כי הנה איביך יאבדו יתפרדו כל פעלי און. על פסוק זה שוררת כיום ההסכמה במחקר, שיש לו זיקה לחרוז אוגריתי על מלחמתו של בעל נגד נצר של ים.[25] ואולם מסתבר שאין זו זיקה ישירה, אלא גלגול של מסורת ספרותית. בבוא הפסוק, כאמור, לחזק את הנאמר בפסוקים ח-ט, משמשת המלית 'כי' בראשו במובן: אכן, אמנם כן. המשפט השני בפסוק מבהיר כי אויבי ה', נושא המשפט הראשון, הם 'כל פעלי און', וגורלם 'יאבדו' הוא כי 'יתפרדו', היינו: ייעלמו – כפי שיש להבין את הפועל 'פרד' בהקבילו ל'אבד'.[26] ועל-ידי הפסוק ניתנת הבהרה מחמירה לנאמר בפס' ח על 'כל פעלי און' ועל גורלם הנקבע עליהם שם, בציינו כי הם איבי ה', ובהישמדם 'עדי עד' – 'יתפרדו', כלומר ייעלמו לעולם. פסוקנו ממשיך ממשיך את תפקידו של פס' ט, בהשלימו את ההסבר התיאולוגי הניתן בו. מנת חלקם של 'רשעים' ו'כל פעלי און', שלפי פס' ח מוסבר בפס' ט בעובדה כי ה' 'מרום', לפי הנחתי: מנצח 'לעלם'. מנצח כתואר ה' נמסר אחרי המובא בפס' י המובא, כאמור, לחיזוק הנאמר בפס' ח-ט, 'כל פעלי און' הם איבי ה', הוא נלחם בהם, ובגרמו להם תמיד ש'יאבדו', 'יתפרדו', הריהו מנצח, בלשון פס' ט: 'מרום לעלם'.

אחר שתיאורו הציורי של גורל 'רשעים' ו'כל פעלי און' (פס' ח) מומחש, מאושש בפס' י, מחוזק הוא על-ידי נסיונו האישי של בעל המזמור, הנמסר בלשון מטאפורית.

[פס' יא] ותרם כראים קרני. 'קרן' – סמל לכוח, לעוז.[27] הרים קרן – חיזק.[28] 'ראים', ראם – זיהויו אינו בטוח. נראית הסברה המזהה אותו עם שור-הבר. במיוחד מדובר ב'קרני ראם'.[29] בפועל 'ותרם'

23 חיות; קירקפטריק; בריגס.

24 ה"ה לפי המשמע שאביושר (לעיל, הערה 21, עמ' 157) מייחס לפסוק, היינו שהוא תיאור המצב שיהיה כשיתקים הנאמר בפס' י ('לאחר השמדת אויבי ה' יהא אלוהים מרומם במלכותו לעולם').

25 ראה אבישור, שם, עמ' 148–157.

26 ראה גם איוב ד, יא.

27 ראה HALAT, 'קרן' 6.

28 שם, שם.

29 דב' לג, יז; תה' כב, כב. השווה גם במ' כג, כב; כד, ח. ראה ח. 'ראם, ראאם, רים, רם', אנציקלופדיה מקראית ז, טורים 296–297. לפי פליקס (י' פליקס, 'דימויים מעולם החי והצומח בתהלים צ"ב', חלמיש 2 [תשמ"ה], עמ' 11), 'שור הבר החזק שבין הבהמות המקרינות'.

נרמז 'מרום' שבפס' ט.[30] ברמז זה מביע בעל המזמור את אמונתו שה' מדביק אותו במידתו. גם הוא מנצח, גובר.[31]

בלתי בשמן רענן. משמעות המשפט שנויה במחלוקת. לפי הפירוש המבוסס ביותר, ושרק על-פיו המשפט משתלב בהקשרו, 'בלתי' – מקור בקל עם כינוי מדבר מן הפועל 'בלה'.[32] גרסתו המדויקת אפוא: 'בְּלֹתִי', כמו 'אחרי בְלֹתִי' (ברא' יא, יב), ומשמעו: זקנתי.[33] 'בשמן רענן'. מן המכוון במשפט מסתבר שאות-היחס בי"ת משמשת כאן משימושיה לציון דמיון,[34] היינו ככ"ף.[35] 'כשמן', זאת אומרת כעץ שמן, כזית.[36] 'רענן'. במקרא פירוש המלה: ירוק-עד.[37] הזית בעל העלים המכסיפים, ירוקי העד, המניב פירות עד לזיקנה מופלגת.[38] במשפט זה אומר בעל המזמור בלשון מטאפורית מעין מה שאומר על צדיקים בפס' טו. גם בזיקה זו סמך לסבירות פירושו של המשפט.

בהיות בעל המזמור רב-כוח ורענן בזקנתו, לכן:

[פס' יב] ותבט עיני בשורי. 'הביט ב...' – כאן כמו 'ראה ב...' בכתובים אחדים, כשהמושא אויב וכדומה,[39] מציין ראיית מפלה.[40] 'בשורי'. לפי פרשנינו הראשונים – 'כמו "בשוררי"'.[41] זוהי הגרסה המהימנה לפי התפיסה הרווחת במחקר.[42] 'שורר', הגזור מן השורש שו"ר, לשון ראייה, האויב המביט אחר מישהו ואורב לו. המשפט מביא אפוא את עונשם של האויבים במידה כנגד מידה: על שמביטים אחרי לתקוף אותי, מביט אני בהם כנצול.

בקמים עלי מרעים תשמענה אזני – לשון הפסוק צריך עיון. בעל המזמור אומר: 'ותבט עיני... תשמענה אזני', מדוע אינו אומר כי הוא מביט, הוא שומע? האם בניסוח זה אין מתבטאת ההרגשה שבמקרה כזה הוא כשהוא לעצמו אינו פועל כלל וכלל; אפילו ראיית המקרה ושמיעתו של עינו ואוזניו הן? אם אמנם לא: כשם שאלוהים הוא המביא את ההצלה, הניצחון, הוא הוא המפעיל גם את העין ואת האוזן, כמאמר החכם: 'אזן שמעת ועין ראה ה' עשה גם שניהם' (משלי כ, יב).

בכתוב זה יצר בעל המזמור משוואה בין אויבי ה' (שנזכרו בפס' י) לבין אויביו שלו, הרשעים. המסקנה מניסיונו האישי הזה של בעל המזמור בנוגע לגורל הרשע, בהתאמה למציאות שבה הוא מצליח, נמסרה לעיל (פס' ח). בנוגע לגורל הצדיק היא נמסרה להלן, בחטיבה הבאה.

---

30   ראה כבר ראב"ע: 'אמר "ותרם" כנגד "ואתה מרום"'.

31   ראה פס' יב.

32   תפיסה זו גם משתקפת בתרגומי השבעים, וולגאטה וסומכוס של הפועל. – ראה, S.E. Loewenstamm, 'Balloti beᵉšämän raᶜanān', *UF* 10 (1978), p. 112

33   ליונשטם, שם, עמ' 112–113. מלבד החוקרים המוזכרים שם, זהו הפירוש של הביאור (לשון זקנה'), מלבי"ם, ועתה פליקס (לעיל, הערה 29), עמ' 12.

34   ראה אוצר לשון המקרא: 'ב...'.

35   כך התרגום בסומכוס. זוהי דעת ליונשטם, שם; טייט; פליקס, שם.

36   כך הוא בסומכוס, ת"י. בין החוקרים, זוהי בין היתר דעת ליונשטם, שם; טייט; פליקס, שם.

37   פליקס, שם.

38   פליקס, עמ' 13.

39   כגון יש' סו, כד; תה' נד, ט; נט, יא; קיב, ח; ועוד.

40   יש מייחסים לצירופם זה של שני הפעלים האלה את המשמעות: ראייה בשמחה לאיד. ראה: קוהלר-באומגרטנר (לעיל, הערה 27): 'נבט'; נבט; H. Ringgren, 'נבט nbṭ', *TWAT* V. p. 139

41   רש"י, ראב"ע, רד"ק. כך גם הביאור.

42   ראה: BHS

[פס' יג] **צדיק כתמר יפרח.** בפרח רשעים כמו עשב, ואילו ה'צדיק כתמר יפרח', כאילן המתנשא לגובה, עושה פירות. **כארז בלבנון ישגה.** 'הארז מפורסם בהדרו, בקומתו ובאריכות ימיו'.[43]

[פס' יד] **שתולים בבית ה', בחצרות אלהינו יפריחו.** על הנושא במשפטים אלה ובפסוק הבא חלוקות הדעות. יש הסבורים 'כי כאן המשך הדימוי לעצים, ואין הכוונה לנמשל – לצדיקים. המשורר רואה לנגד עיניו עצים המפארים את חצרות המקדש'.[44] ויש סבורים שהכתוב חוזר ומדבר על צדיקים. בהיות דיבורו בלי מעבר, המשך לדיבור על תמר וארז, מובן מבחינה פסיכולוגית שמדובר על צדיק לא כמו לפני כן בלשון יחיד אלא בלשון ריבוי. ברם, לפנינו עירוב מכוון של המשל והנמשל. בעל המזמור ממשיך בתמונת העצים, מתכוון לגורל הצדיקים, אך בהמשך גובר הנמשל על המשל. 'שתולים' – העצים, 'בבית ה'', 'בחצרות אלהינו', היינו בקרבת ה'[45] שרויים באופן קבוע, תמיד: הצדיקים. 'יפריחו' כמו: יפרחו. בהיות 'פרח' בין הפעלים המשמשים בהפעיל גם בהוראה כמו בקל.[46] אך גם ייתכן שבהבמחיש בעל המזמור את גורל הצדיקים 'בחצרות אלהינו' אין הוא רואה אותו עוד כפי שהוא, כמו בפס' יח: 'יפרח', אלא 'יפריחו', היינו לא רק מוציאים פרחים אלא גם גורמים לפריחה. – בגלל המבנה התחבירי של המשפט בפסוק, הבינוני משמש בראש המשפט, 'שתולים', במובן של בינוני עם כינוי זיקה, 'השתולים'.[47] המשפט 'שתולים בבית ה'' משועבד אפוא שעבוד נושאי.

[פס' טו] **עוד ינובון בשיבה דשנים ורעננים יהיו.** בפסוק זה ה'שתולים', הארז והתמר, אינם עוד שהרי לארז אין תנובה. 'שיבה' יש לאדם ולא לעצים. החידוש במשפט זה לעומת מה שנאמר עד כה הוא, שהצדיקים עושים פרי גם בזקנותם; ליתר דיוק, שבו מפורש הסתום במשל הצדיק ל'ארז בלבנון' (פס' יג). שכן, 'בלבנון מצויים יערות ארזים ובהם עצי ארז חסנים שאומדים את גילם באלף שנים ואף למעלה מזה'.[48]

[פס' טז] **להגיד כי ישר ה' צורי ולא עולתה [קרי]** בו. המלה 'צורי' אינה נשוא לה' דוגמת 'ישר',[49] וגם לא תמורה,[50] אלא נושא במשפט השני שבפסוק. הוי"ו במלה 'ולא' משמשת כפתיחה לנשוא במשפט שמני,[51] ובאה להבליט את הקשר ההדוק – כמעט זהה – שבין הנושא ובין הנשוא. בכינוי הקנייני של 'צורי' מתבטאת תחושת הקרבה שבעל המזמור חש לה'; תחושה שאליה הוא מגיע בסוף

43 ש"א ליונשטם, 'ארז', אנציקלופדיה מקראית א, טור 553.

44 פליקס, עמ' 6. זוהי דעת בריגס; גונקל; דאהוד; טייט ועוד. כך סבר גם בעל הביאור. לפי פירושו ופירושי בריגס; גונקל; דאהוד, העצים הם הנזכרים בפסוק הקודם, תמר וארז. ואילו פליקס (עמ' 6–7, 13) טוען: 'ודאי שלא היו אלה ארז ותמר'. על עצי הזית וארז מדובר כאן. טייט (עמ' 468) מניח שבפסוקים יג–יד נרמז הרעיון שחצרות המקדש הן כגן-עדן, כגן ה' שבו מים שופעים ועצים פורים מאוד.

45 שימוש מטאפורי זה של הביטוי 'בית ה'' מופיע במקרא עוד פעמים (תה' כג, ו; כז, ד). ראה גם הביטוי 'בית אלהים' (תה' נב, י) והמלה 'באהלך' (תה' סא, ה).

46 ראה גזניוס-קאוטש (לעיל, הערה 7).

47 כך תרגום המלה בפשיטתא ('דנציבין'). לפי גרץ, הגרסה המקורית היתה: 'השתולים'. הה"א של 'השתולים' נבלעה בה"א של 'ישגה' שלפניה.

48 ש"א ליונשטם, 'ארז', אנציקלופדיה מקראית א, טור 555. פליקס (לעיל, הערה 29) מעיר: 'לפי בדיקותינו אין גילם [של ארזים] עולה על אלף שנה' (שם, עמ' 13).

49 כפי שפירש, למשל, חיות.

50 כתפיסתם של דליטש; גונקל; קיטל; קראוס; טייט, ועוד.

51 כך סבר כבר אהרליך.

תהילתו. שכן במשך התהילה הוא מכנה את ה' שבע פעמים בשמו (פסוקים ב, ה, ו, ט, י, יד, טז),
פעם אחת בכינוי 'עליון' (פס' ב). פעם גם אומר 'אלהינו' (פס' יד), היינו עם כינוי הקניין, אך הכינוי
של מדברים אינו משקף קרבה באותה המידה המרבית כמו הכינוי של מדבר, זה כללי בעוד שההוא
פרטי. יתרה מזו. המלה 'אלהינו' מביעה קרבה למי שהוא האלוהים של עמנו, ואילו המלה 'צורי'
מביעה את הקרבה לא רק למי שהוא האלוהים שלי אלא למי שהוא גם מחסה העוז שלי.

פסוק זה אפשר להבינו כהמשך לפסוקים ח–טו. הנמסר בהם בא 'להגיד' וגו'. ואפשר להבינו
כמסקנה מן הנמסר בפסוקים ההם, הבאה כהשלמת פס' ג. 'להגיד בבקר' וגו', כלומר 'להגיד כי ישר
ה'' וגו'.

בסיום המזמור, אין בעל המזמור מדבר עוד אל ה' אלא על ה', כמו בפתיחתו. על־ידי כך, שני
הפסוקים, פס' ב' ופס' טז, מהווים מסגרת למזמור.

מקריאתו הצמודה של תה' צב נמצאנו למדים שבעל המזמור מהלל את ה' הואיל והוא משמח אותו.
אשר לגורם שמחתו, למניע תהילתו – דבר זה לא למד רק מסופו של המזמור (פס' טז) אלא הוא גם
מסתבר מבנ).ינו וממסכת אריגתו – הגורם אינו גורלו האישי הטוב; זה רק פרט הבא ללמד על הכלל.
שמחתו של בעל המזמור, עניינו של המזמור: הנהגת ה' את העולם בצדק; צדיק וטוב לו, רשע,
אליבא דאמת, ורע לו, 'להגיד כי ישר ה''.

רשימת הקיצורים המשמשים בהערות למאמר

A.B. Ehrlich, *Die Psalmen*, Berlin 1905	ארליך
C.A. Briggs, *The Book of Psalms* II (ICC), Edinburgh [1907]	בריגס
H. Gunkel, *Die Psalmen*[4] (HKAT), Göttingen 1926	גונקל
H. Graetz, *Kritischer Commentar zu den Psalmen* II, Breslau 1883	גרץ
M. Dahood, *Psalms* II (AB), Garden City (New York) 1968	דאהוד
F. Delitzsch, *Biblischer Kommentar über die Psalmen*[5], Leipzig 1904	דליטש
A. Weiser, *Die Psalmen*[6] (ATD), Göttingen 1963	וייזר
צ"פ חיות, ספר תהלים (א' כהנא, תורה נביאים וכתובים עם פירוש מדעי), זיטומיר תרס"ג.	חיות
M.E. Tate, *Psalms 51-100* (WBC XX), Dallas, Texas 1990	טייט
R. Kittel, *Die Psalmen*[5-6] (KAT), Leipzig 1929	קיטל
A.F. Kirkpatrick, *The Book of Psalms* (CBSC), Cambridge 1906	קירקפטריק
H.F. Kraus, *Psalmen*[5] II (BKAT), Neukirchen 1978	קראוס

קטעי מגילה של ספר יחזקאל ממצדה (יח' לה, יא–לח, יד):
MasEzek, מצדה 2220–1043

שמריהו טלמון

האוניברסיטה העברית בירושלים

בחפירות מצדה שבהנהלת יגאל ידין נתגלו שרידים של חמישה־עשר פריטים כתובים עברית, מהם
ארבעה־עשר בכתב המרובע, ואחד בכתב העברי הקדום, המכונה בפי חז"ל כתב דע"ץ, רע"ץ או
לבונאה. ידין ההדיר במלואם את הקטעים ששרדו ממגילה של משלי בן־סירא,[1] וכן פרסם יחד עם
ק' ניוסם קטע קטן של 'מגילת שירת עולת השבת',[2] אבל לא זכה לפרסם קטעים שהשתמרו משבעה
כתבי־יד של ספרים מן המקרא, ושל שישה פריטים קטנים ששרדו מחיבורים שאת זהותם אי־אפשר
לקבוע בוודאות.[3] ההדרת כל אלה הופקדה בידי, במסגרת הפרסום הכולל של תגליות מצדה. בין
קטעי כתבי־יד של ספרים מן המקרא השתמרו חלקי מגילה של ספר יחזקאל. ידין לא מנה פריט זה
בין 'המגילות והכתובות' בדו"ח של 'חפירות מצדה',[4] אלא הזכירו לראשונה בהרצאה שנשא בכינוס

---

1   י' ידין, מגילת בן־סירא ממצדה, ירושלים תשכ"ה.

2   ראה: C. Newsom and Y. Yadin, 'The Masadah Fragments of the Qumran Songs of the
Sabbath Sacrifice', *IEJ* 34 (1984), pp. 77-88. חיבור זה נודע מתגליות קומראן. ראה: J. Strugnell, 'The
Angelic Liturgy at Qumran – 4Q Serek Šîrôt 'Olat Haššabāt', VTSup 8 (1960), pp. 318-345;
C. Newsom, *Songs of the Sabbath Sacrifice. A Critical Edition*, Missoula 1985

3   פרסמתי פרסום ראשוני את הפריטים האלה: 'קטעי כתבים כתובים עברית ממצדה', ארץ־ישראל כ, ספר יגאל
ידין (בעריכת א' בן־תור, ח"י גרינפלד וא' מלמט), ירושלים תשמ"ט, עמ' 278–286; 'קטע ממגילה חיצונית
לספר יהושע ממצדה', שי לחיים רבין. אסופת מחקרי לשון לכבודו במלאת לו שבעים וחמש (בעריכת מ' גושן־
גוטשטיין, ש' מורג וש' קוגוט), ירושלים תשנ"ג, עמ' 147–157; 'Fragments of a Psalms Scroll From
Masada, MPs[b] (Masada1103-1742)', *Minhah le-Nahum. Biblical and Other Studies Presented to
Nahum M. Sarna in Honour of his 70th Birthday* (ed. M. Brettler and M. Fishbane, JSOTSup
154), Sheffield 1993, pp. 318-327; 'קטעי שתי מגילות של ספר ויקרא ממצדה', ארץ־ישראל כד, ספר
אברהם מלמט (בעריכת ש' אחיטוב וב"א לוין), ירושלים תשנ"ד, עמ' 99–110. פריט אחד (1043/1–4), שבו
שרדו שרידי טקסט של סוף ספר דברים (לג, ז–לד, ו) והמצא 160–1039, המחזיק קטעים של תה' פא, ב–פה,
ו יתפרסמו בקרוב בספר לכבוד כ"ה גורדון, ובכתב־העת *Dead Sea Discoveries*. בעיזבון של ידין נמצא
באחרונה פרגמנט לא־ממוספר, שמידותיו 2.4×5.6 ס"מ, המחזיק אותיות אחדות בשלוש שורות. לא יכולתי
עדיין לקבוע אם מוצאו ממצדה, מקומראן או אולי ממקום אחר. ראה עתה: תרביץ סו (תשנ"ז), עמ' 116–118.

4   ידיעות החברה לחקירת ארץ־ישראל ועתיקותיה כט (תשכ"ה), עמ' 115–118.

הכ"ב של החברה לידיעת הארץ.[5] לאחר מכן תיארו בקצרה בערך 'מצדה' באנציקלופדיה לחפירות ארכיאולוגיות בארץ־ישראל בזו הלשון:[6]

יחזקאל. קטעי מגילה זו נתגלו טמונים מתחת לרצפת בית־הכנסת.[7] נשתמרו חלקים ניכרים מפרקים לה–לח, ובכללם פרק ל"ז (חזון העצמות היבשות).[8] גם נוסח זה,[8] חוץ מכמה פרטים לא חשובים, שווה לנוסח המסורה.

במאמר זה אני בא להציג את שרידי המגילה של ספר יחזקאל ממצדה, לכבוד בעל הסוגיה.

תיאור MasEzek

המימצא מחזיק למעלה מחמישים קטעי גוויל, השמורים בהיכל הספר תחת רשת של משי ולוח זכוכית שמידותיו 41.0×29.5 ס"מ,[9] כשהם מסודרים בארבעה טורים בהתאם למיקום של חלקי הטקסט שהשתמרו בהם בנוסח של ספר יחזקאל.[10] בתצלומים חלקים של המימצא יכולנו לזהות שלושה קטעים קטנים נוספים שאינם כלולים במעשה ההרכבה שבלוח. אחד מהם מחזיק צירופי אותיות משורות 31–33 בטור ב'.[11] מסתבר כי שברי גוויל אלה כבר לא היו בנמצא שעה שהלוח הותקן.

פרגמנט גדול, שגובהו 6.5 ס"מ ורוחבו 13.5 ס"מ, מחזיק חלקים של שש השורות העליונות של שני הטורים הראשונים, יחד עם הגיליון שבראשם והגיליון המבדיל ביניהם. בפרגמנט גדול אחר, שמידותיו 8.2×9.5 ס"מ, השתמרו חלקי 14 שורות אמצעיות של שני הטורים האחרונים עם הגיליון שביניהם. על קטעים קטנים נראות קבוצות אותיות המתחברות פעמים למלים שלמות, ועל הקטנים יותר נותרו אותיות יחידות בלבד. על שברי גוויל אחדים אין סימני כתב כלל. הללו שרדו ככל הנראה מן הגיליון שבראשי הטורים שהשתמר בחלקו, מן הגיליון התחתון שממנו לא נותר שריד, או מן הגיליונות המפרידים בין הטורים.

הצבע של קטעי הגוויל מן החלק העליון של צד ימין של היריעה חום בהיר עד חום, והולך ומשחיר בחלקה השמאלי, עד שבקטעים של תחתית שני הטורים השמאליים הכתב שוב אינו קריא. כאן שוחזר הטקסט על יסוד תצלומים באינפרה־אדום, שהוכנו בעוד מועד.

מעשה הכתב

המגילה נכתבה בידי סופר מיומן, בכתב מפותח מעט יותר מזה של קטעי המגילה של ספר דברים ממצדה, והוא קרוב לכתב של קטעי המגילות של ספר ויקרא.[12] על־פי הסיווג שהציע פ"מ קרוס, אפשר להגדיר את כתב המגילה 'כתב סופרים הרודיאני קדום' או 'הרודיאני פורמלי'. לפיכך ניתן

---

5   'קומראן ומצדה', ידיעות החברה לחקירת ארץ־ישראל ועתיקותיה ל (תשכ"ו), עמ' 126.

6   אנציקלופדיה לחפירות ארכיאולוגיות בארץ־ישראל (בעריכת ב' מזר), ירושלים תשל"א, עמ' 388.

7   באותו מקום נמצאו גם קטעי המגילה של ספר דברים. ידין נטה לסברה כי מחילה זו שימשה מעין גניזה.

8   כלומר גם נוסח מגילה זו, כנוסח של קטעי המגילות של ויקרא ותהלים, שהזכירם בקצרה לפני כן.

9   פעמים לא ניתן להבחין בבירור בקווי האיחוי של קטעי המגילה, ומשום כך קשה לדייק במניינם.

10 קטעים קטנים אחדים לא נקבעו במקומם המדויק.

11 ראה להלן בשחזור.

12 ראה לעיל, הערה 3.

לתארך את כתיבתה במחצית השנייה של המאה האחרונה לפני הספירה.[13] במגילה לא סומנו קווים אופקיים ולא אנכיים להדרכת הסופר (dry rulings). חרף זאת ראשי האותיות מאוזנים, כאילו נתלו כמקובל מתחת קווים מדריכים כאלה, עד שרק ראשי האות האות למ"ד מתגבהים מעליהם. כיוצא בזה ראשיתן של שורות עוקבות שהשתמרו בצד ימין של טור מיושרות אנכית, כגון: טור ב', שו' 8–13 ושו' 27–30 (יח' לו, כא–כג; ל–לב); טור ג', שו' 17–20 (יח' לז, ט–יא); טור ד', שו' 15–22, 26–28 (יח' לז, כח–לח, ד; לח, ז–ח), מה שלא כן בסופי שורות. השורות מופרדות בתחילתן זו מזו במירווח כמעט אחיד של קרוב ל־3 מ"מ, ואילו באמצעיתן ובסופו המירווח נע בין 2–4 מ"מ.

מידות

מידות רוב האותיות בין 2×2 עד 3×3 מ"מ. יוצאות מכלל זה האותיות ו, ז, י, ן, שרוחבן כדי 1 מ"מ, והאותיות ל, ם, ק שהן גדולות עד כדי 5 מ"מ וחורגות מן השורות כלפי מעלה או כלפי מטה. מירווח של חלקיק של 1 מ"מ מפריד בין אות לאות. אולם יש ששתי אותיות ואף יותר נושקות זו לזו או שהן כאילו משתלבות, כגון 'ני' בתיבה 'אני' (טור א', שו' 8 = יח' לה, טו), 'בכם' בתיבה 'בקרבכם' (טור ב', שו' 21 = יח' לו, כז), 'נבאתי' בתיבה 'והנבאתי' (טור ג', שו' 17 = יח' לז, י).[14] התיבות נבדלות זו מזו במירווח של פחות מ־1 מ"מ. הסופר נאלץ לפעמים לצופף כמה וכמה תיבות בסופי שורות עד שהן מתאחות זו עם זו, משום שלא חישב כראוי את כושר הקיבול של השורה. כך למשל בטור א', סוף שו' 1: 'כ]אשראשפטרדי̇דעת' (יח' לה, יא–יב), טור ג', סוף שו' 11: 'כאשרצויתי' (יח' לז, ז).

מספר התיבות בשורה ומספר המירווחים שביניהן אינו אחיד. לפיכך גם אורך השורות הכתובות נתון לשינויים. בטורים א' וב' השורות השלמות, ושורות שאפשר להשלימן בבטחה, מחזיקות בין 27 ל־36 אותיות ועוד 5–8 מירווחים בין תיבות.[15] בטור ג' מספר האותיות בשורה נע בין 29 ל־36, וכיוצא בזה בשורות המשוחזרות בטור ד'. גם בכל אחת משורות אלה יש להוסיף 5–8 מירווחים בין תיבות.[16] יוצא כי בטורים א' וב' שורה אחת מחזיקה בממוצע 32 אותיות, ובטורים ג' וד' 33 אותיות, כשבכל אחת מהן יש להוסיף 5–8 מירווחים בין תיבות.

האורך המרבי של שורה בטור א' 8.2 ס"מ, בטור ב' 9.2 ס"מ, בטור ג' 8.8 ס"מ, ובטור ד' 8.6 ס"מ, על־פי האומדן של שורה (משוחזרת). על מידות אלה יש להוסיף את הגיליון מצד שמאל של הטור,[17] שרוחבו בין 1.5 ל־2.0 ס"מ, הכל לפי אורך השורה הכתובה. לפיכך הרוחב של טור א' מגיע לכדי 9.9 ס"מ, של טור ב' לכדי 10.7 ס"מ, ושל טור ג' לכדי 10.3 ס"מ. ואם צדקנו במיקום שבריר

‏13 ‏ראה: F.M. Cross, Jr., 'The Development of the Jewish Scripts', *The Bible and the Ancient Near East. Essays in Honor of W.F. Albright* (ed. G.E. Wright), Garden City, NY 1961 (repr. Winona Lake, IN 1979), p. 138, Figure 2, ll. 3 & 4

‏14 ‏שילובי אותיות מעין אלה, שכדוגמתם מצאנו גם בכתבי־יד אחרים ממצדה ובכתבי־יד מקומראן, עשויים להיות מקור של שיבושי נוסח. ראה: ר' וייס, 'שילובי אותיות במקרא', מחקרי מקרא, ירושלים תשמ"א, עמ' 3–19.

‏15 ‏בטור א', שו' 9 כתוב שם היה בלבד. השורה המקבילה בטור ב' מחזיקה 13 אותיות ועוד ארבעה מירווחים בין תיבות. בשני המקרים חלק השורה שנותר חָלָק מסמן 'פרשה', כמו לפני יח' לה, יד; לו, כב. לעניין זה ראה להלן.

‏16 ‏שו' 16 בטור ד' מחזיקה אך ורק את חמש האותיות של התיבה 'לע[ו]לם]. גם כאן החלק שנותר חָלָק מסמן 'פרשה', כמו לפני יח' לח, א.

‏17 ‏רוחב הגיליון בין טורים מצטרף תמיד לרוחב הטור שלפניו.

גוויל המחזיק את האותיות 'שׂי' של המלה 'לֹבֵשׂי' (יח' לח, ד) בקצה שו' 21 בטור ד', מסתבר כי שורה זו החזיקה 36 אותיות ושבעה מירווחים בין תיבות, ואורכה היה 10.0 ס"מ לערך. יוצא כי ארבעת הטורים יחד תפסו כ-41 ס"מ של רוחב היריעה.[18]

בכל טור 42 שורות ו-41 מירווחים ביניהן. גובה השורה כ-3 מ"מ. בין שורה לשורה מירווח של 3 מ"מ. גובה הטור הכתוב מגיע לכדי 25 ס"מ (83 × 3 מ"מ) בערך. על כך יש להוסיף גיליון ברוחב 3.0 ס"מ בראש היריעה, ומן הסתם גיליון (שלא השתמר) ברוחב דומה בתחתית הטור. יוצא כי גובה המגילה היה בין 30 ל-31 ס"מ.

על יסוד הנתונים הנ"ל נוכל לאמוד את אורך המגילה בהיותה שלמה. חישובים מחישובים שונים מלמדים כי חטיבת הטקסט של ספר יחזקאל שהשתמרה ב-MasEzek, דהיינו יח' לה, יא–לח, יד, תופסת את החלק החמישה-עשר בערך של הספר כולו. במהדורת דפוס של המקרא ללא אפראטים והערות, כמהדורת קורן או Snaith, חטיבת טקסט זו משתרעת על מעט יותר מחמישה עמודים, מן הסה"כ של 75–79 עמודים המחזיקים את נוסח הספר כולו. כיוצא בזה בעלי המסורה מנו בס' יחזקאל 1273 פסוקים, ש-85 מהם, דהיינו החלק החמישה-עשר, כלולים בארבעת הטורים של MasEzek. על-פי חישובים אלה נדרשו לסופר המגילה בערך 60 טורים כדי לפרנס בהם את הטקסט השלם של ספר יחזקאל. כאמור לעיל, רוחב ארבעת הטורים שהשתמרו חלקית עם הגליונות שביניהם מגיע לכדי 41 ס"מ. לפיכך נוכל לשער כי אורך המגילה המקורית על 60 טוריה היה בערך 6.00 מ' (41 × 15 ס"מ). אם חלק היריעה האחרונה נותר חָלָק ושימש כמעין מעטפת של הטורים הכתובים (handle sheet), היה אורכה 6.50 מ' בקירוב.

נוסח המגילה

כפי שקבע ידין על-פי עיון ראשון, הנוסח של MasEzek תואם את נוסח המסורה, חוץ מכמה פרטים לא-חשובים.[19] קביעה זו מתאששת מבדיקה מדוקדקת של הטקסט:

1. תיקוני טעויות שתוקנו מן הסתם בידי הסופר עצמו:
טור א', שו' 4: יו"ד הוספה בין השיטין מעל לתיבה 'על',[20] ומעל 'דברכם'. בכך הותאם נוסח המגילה לנוסח המסורה ביח' לה, יג: והעתרתם עלי דבריכם.

טור ב', שו' 18: האות מי"ם נרשמה מעל שתי האותיות הראשונות של 'טאותיכ[ם]' = יח' לו, כה: טמאותיכם.

טור ב', שו' 26: ו"ו נכתבה מעל הרווח בין האותיות 'נב' בתיבה 'ותנבת'. אפשר כי עניין לנו כאן בהתאמת כתיב חסר לכתיב המלא של נהמ"ס: ותנובת (יח' לו, ל).[21]

---

18 דרך כלל יריעה של מגילה החזיקה ארבעה או חמישה טורים. כך עולה מן המימצאים של מצדה ושל קומראן כאחד. אולם כיוון שב-MasEzek לא השתמר הגיליון מצד ימין של טור א' ולא הגיליון מצד שמאל של טור ד', לא נוכל לקבוע אם היריעה החזיקה טור נוסף או שמא אפילו טורים נוספים.

19 ראה לעיל, עמ' 54* והערה 8.

20 אולם אין לקבוע בוודאות אם אמנם באות יו"ד עסקינן או בכתם דיו.

21 ראה להלן.

טור ג', שו' 6: האות בי"ת הוספה בין השיטין מעל 'הנא' = יח' לז, ד: הנבא.

2. פעמיים הסופר שכח לתקן נוסח שגוי:

טור ג', שו' 12: והנה רעש תקרבו. כאן הושמטה כנראה ו'"ו לפני 'תקרבו'. יח' לז, ז: 'והנה־רעש ותקרבו[22] עצמות עצם אל עצמו'.

טור ג', שו' 22: כה א]מ]ר אמר. דיטוגרפיה. השווה יח' לז, יב: 'כה־אמר'.

3. לפרקים אפשר להבחין באותיות או חלקי אותיות בין השיטין שמשמעותן אינה ברורה:

טור ב', שו' 12: שלוש אותיות, כנראה ב–י–ת, נכתבו מעל המלים 'בגוים אשר' ביח' לו, כב: 'כי אם לשם קדשי אשר חללתם בגוים אשר באתם שם'. אם אמנם אפשר לקיים את הקריאה המוצעת, קרוב לשער כי סופר המגילה התחיל לכתוב 'בית ישראל' לפני התיבה 'בגוים' או בסוף הכתוב, אם על יסוד נוסח שהיה לפניו שנבדל מנוסח המסורה והתרגומים העתיקים, אם מחמת אשגרת מעתיקים (דיטוגרפיה אנכית), בהשפעת הפסוק שלפני כן: 'אשר חללוהו בית ישראל בגוים אשר באו שמה' (יח' לו, כא).

טור ב', שו' 22: אין להכריע אם האותיות 'וי' בראש התיבה 'וישבתם' נכתבו מעל לשורה או שמא במקום זה קטע המגילה לא הותקן כראוי בלוח.

טור ג', שו' 20: ספק אם מעל לאות אל"ף בתיבה 'האלה' נותר שריד של אות נוספת.

4. שני מקרים נותנים לחשוב כי בזמן כתיבת המגילה עדיין לא התייצב השימוש המובחן בצורות של מ"ם אמצעית ומ"ם סופית:[23]

טור ג', שו' 12: מ"ם סופית כתובה באמצע המלה 'ה]עצמות' (יח' לז, ז).

טור ב', שו' 7: דומה כי כאן באה מ"ם אמצעית בסוף מלה בסמיכות 'עמ־ה' (יח' לו, כ). צורת האות קרובה יותר למ"ם אמצעית בתיבה 'ומארצו' שבאותה שורה מאשר למ"ם סופית בתיבה 'להם'.

5. כמה וכמה פעמים נבדל נוסח המגילה מנהמ"ס בענייני כתיב מלא וחסר:

טור ב', שו' 2: אתה	יח' לו, יז: אותה
טור ב', שו' 8: חללהו	יח' לו, כא: חללוהו[24]
טור ג', שו' 18: ותבא	יח' לז, י: ותבוא
טור א', שו' 3: לואכלה	יח' לה, יב: לאכלה
טור ב', שו' 4: ובגלוליה[ם]	יח' לו, יח: ובגלוליהם[25]
טור ב', שו' 19: והסרותי	יח' לו, כו: והסרתי
טור ג', שו' 9: גדים והעלי[תי]	יח' לז, ו: גידים והעלתי[26]

22   סבירין: ויקרבו, השווה תרגום הע': καὶ προσήγαγε, וראה להלן.

23   לעניין זה ראה: נ"ה טור־סיני, 'מנצפ"ך צופים אמרום', הלשון והספר, א, ירושלים תש"ח, עמ' 10–31, וכן את הערותי ב'קטעי שתי מגילות של ס' ויקרא' (לעיל, הערה 3) עמ' 104.

24   מהד' Snaith: חללהו.

25   אין להביא ראיה מטור ב', שו' 18, שם השתמר החלק הסופי של התיבה: [גלול]יכם = יח' לו, כה.

26   מהד' Snaith: גידים. בטור ג', שו' 13 המגילה גורסת 'גדים' בכתיב חסר, כמו יח' לז, ח (Snaith, BHS).

כיוון שגם בנוסח המסורה השימוש בכתיב מלא וחסר אינו אחיד וקבוע, ההבדלים הנ"ל בין המגילה
ובין נהמ"ס אינם בבחינת שינויי גירסה.

6. הוא דין ההבדלים שלהלן בין נוסח המגילה לבין נוסח המסורה:

טור ב', שו' 9: אשר באו שם[27]   יח' לו, כא: אשר באו שמה.

החילוף 'שם/שמה' מבדיל לא־פעם בין נוסח המסורה לבין הנוסח השומרוני של התורה, בין נוסח
המסורה לבין מגילות של ספרי מקרא מקומראן, ואף בין כתבי־יד שונים של נוסח המסורה. דומה
כי במקרה דלן, סופר המגילה התאים את הנוסח ללשון הכתוב שלאחריו: 'אשר־באתם שם' (יח' לו,
כב – טור ב', שו' 12), אם במחשבה תחילה אם מחמת אשגרת מעתיקים.[28]

7. משקל רב מעט יותר יש לייחס לשתי סטיות של נוסח המגילה מנוסח המסורה, שבהן משתקף
אולי טקסט עברי המונח ביסוד תרגום הע':

בטור ג', שו' 12 נוסח המגילה: 'תקרבו עצמות' נבדל למראית עין מנוסח המסורה: 'ותקרבו
עצמות' (יח' לז, ז) אך ורק בחסרון ו'ו מחברת. אולם הפער הגדול מן המקובל של 0.3 ס"מ המפריד
בין שתי התיבות הנ"ל ב־MasEzek, מעין lacuna, נותן לחשוב כי אבדה בו אות אחת. והנה בע'
המלה 'עצמות' מיודעת: καὶ προσήγαγε τὰ ὀστᾶ, כפי שגם בשני אזכורים קודמים היא מיודעת
בנוסח המסורה: העצמות, ובע': τὰ ὀστᾶ, כאחד (יח' לז, ד־ה). ביח' לז, ג, ד, יא היא מיודעת
על־ידי כינוי רומז: 'העצמות האלה', τὰ ὀστᾶ ταῦτα; וביח' לו, יא על־ידי כינוי הקניין:
'עצמותינו', ὀστᾶ ἡμῶν, τὰ ὀστᾶ.[29] שמא יש להסיק מן השימוש הרווח בקונטקסט של 'עצמות' עם ידוע,
כי בפער הנ"ל בטור ג', שו' 12 יש להשלים ה"א ולגרוס: 'תקרבו העצמות', כמו בנוסח העברי שלפי
המשוער היה לפני המתרגם ליוונית.[30]

בטור א', קרוב לסוף שו' 5, נוכל להבחין בשריד קטנטן של אות שכנראה אבדה בין שתי המלים
הראשונות של הצירוף 'כשמֹחַ כל־הארץ' (יח' לה, יד), שהוא כמדומה שארית הרגל של הקו השמאלי
היורד של תי"ו. אם אמנם כן הוא מסתבר כי נוסח המגילה גרס 'כשמחת כל הארץ', בדומה לנוסח
הכתוב שלאחריו: 'כשמחתך' (יח' לה, טו).

הע' תרגמו את שני הכתובים יח' לה, יד־טו כככתוב אחד. משום כך הנוסח היווני קצר במידה
ניכרת מנהמ"ס τάδε λέγει κύριος Ἐν τῇ εὐφροσύνῃ πάσης τῆς γῆς ἔρημον ποιήσω σέ ἔρημον
ἔσῃ, ὄρος Σηιρ καὶ πᾶσα ἡ Ιδουμαία ἐξαναλωθήσεται καὶ γνώσῃ ὅτι ἐγώ εἰμι κύριος ὁ θεὸς
αὐτῶν.[31] דומה כי עניין לנו כאן ב־homoioarkton. עין הכותב או המתרגם, ושמא עין הסופר של

---

27   שארית השורה נותרה ריקה לסימון 'פרשה'. גם בנוסח המסורה מסומנת 'פרשה' לפני לו, כב. לעניין חלוקת
    הפרשיות ראה להלן.

28   השווה עוד: יח לו, כא (לית ב־MasEzek): 'אשר־הלכו שם'. דומה כי בכל שלוש ההיקרויות, גירסת ת"י:
    'לתמן' משקפת 'שמה'.

29   גם ביח' לז, א: 'והיא מלאה עצמות', תרג' הע' מביא תוספת מיידעת: ὀστέων ἀνθρωπίνων. ראה להלן.

30   צימרלי (W. Zimmerli, *Ezechiel 25-48* [BKAT XIII, 2], Neukirchen-Vluyn 1979, p. 887) שוקל את
    האפשרות כי ו'ו שבסוף התיבה 'תקרבו' אינה אלא שיבוש של ה"א שהיתה בראש התיבה 'עצמות'.

31   המתרגם קרא אולי 'כָּלָה' במקום 'כֻּלָּהּ' בנוסח המסורה.

כתב־היד העברי שהיה לפני המתרגם, דילגה מן הצירוף 'שממה אעשה־לך' בפס' יד אל הצירוף
הזֶהֶה כמעט בפס' טו 'שממה כן אעשה־לך', תוך כדי פסיחה על חלק המשפט שביניהם:

כשמֹחַ כל־הארץ   שממה אעשה־לך

כשמחתך לנחלת בית־ישראל על אשר <u>שממה כן אעשה־לך</u> שממה תהיה הר־שעיר.

האפשרות של דילוג מעין זה סבירה במיוחד בטקסט שגרס 'כשמחת כל הארץ' גם באזכור
הראשון של הצירוף הנ"ל, משום שבשתי ההיקרויות בא אחריו צמד האותיות כ–ל: 'כשמחת <u>כל</u>־
הארץ' ו־'שמחתך <u>ל</u>נחלת בית־ישראל'. הגירסה המשוערת של המגילה כאילו ממצעת בין נהמ"ס
ובין תרגום הע', ומאירה את אופן ההתהוות של שינוי הגירסה בטקסט היווני.

אבל ככלות הכל, אין בהבדלים שמנינו כדי לעמעם את התואם המשכנע שבין נוסח המגילה לבין
נוסח המסורה. תואם זה מתגלה ביתר שאת במקרים של סטייה אחד התרגומים העתיקים מנוסח
המסורה, בראש לכל בהוספות ובחסרים בע':[32]

8. הוספות

ע': + עליהם[33]	טור ב', שו' 8 = יח' לו, כא: ואחמל על שם קדשי
ע': + אדם[34]	טור ג', שו' 2 = יח' לז, א: עצמות

9. חסרים[35]

ע': > בם... בך[36]	טור א', שו' 1 = יח' לה, יא: משנאתיך בם ונודעתי <u>בם</u>
ע': >	טור א', שו' 4 = יח' לה, יג: והעתר[ת]ם עלי דבריכם
ע': > על	טור א', שו' 3 = יח' לה, יב: [על הר] ישראל
ע': >	טור א', שו' 27 = יח' לו, ז: כ[ה] אמר אדני ה'
ע' > תתנו... ישראל[37]	טור א', שו' 30 = יח' לו, ח: [ענפכם תתנו ופריכם תשאו לעמי] ישראל
ע': >	טור ב', שו' 3–4 = יח' לו, יח: על הדם... טְמאוּהָ
ע': >	טור ב', שו' 14 = יח' לו, כג: נאם אדני ה'
ע': > קול[38]	טור ג', שו' 12 = יח' לז, ז: ויה[י] קול [כהנבאי
ע': > הרוח[39]	טור ג', שו' 17 = יח' לז, ט: באי הרוח ופחי

---

32   הסטייה מנהמ"ס מתועדת לרוב באחת המשפחות העיקריות של תרג' הע', A או B, כשהאחרת משקפת את נוסח
המסורה.

33   καὶ ἐφεισάμην <u>αὐτῶν</u> διὰ τὸ ὄνομά μου τὸ ἅγιον

34   ὀστέων <u>ἀνθρωπίνων</u>, כמו ת"י: גרמי <u>אנשא</u>.

35   חסר בע' יסומן ע"י >.

36   ראה להלן.

37   τὴν σταφυλὴν καὶ καρπὸν ὑμῶν καταφάγεται ὁ λαός μου ואישראל'. בתרגום הפרפסטי אין תמורה לתיבות 'תתנו
ו־'ישראל'.

38   καὶ ἐγένετο ἐν τῷ ἐμὲ προφητεῦσαι

39   ἐλθὲ καὶ ἐμφύσησον

ע': > הִנֵּה[40]   טור ג', שו' 20 = יח' לז, יא: המ]ה הנה אמרים

                               טור ג', שו' 24 = יח' לז, יב: והעליתי אתכם

ע': > עמי (פ'=פ')   מק[ברותיכם] עמי

ע': > ואתה ,Yiὲ ἀνθρῶπου   טור ג', שו' 29 = יח' לז, טו: ואתה ב]ן אדם[41]

יש להצביע במיוחד על חסר חוזר ונשנה של כינוי האדנות בתרגום הע', המביא תכופות κύριος
בלבד כנגד 'אדני ה'' בנוסח המסורה וב־MasEzek.[42] המגילה מתעדת אפוא את קדמותו של כפל
הכינוי (טור א', שו' 5 = יח' לה, יד; טור ב', שו' 10 = לו, כב; טור ג', שו' 8 = לז, ה; טור ג' שו' 16
= לז, ט; טור ג', שו' 22 = לז, יב).[43]

10. התואם של MasEzek עם נוסח המסורה מוכח מווריאנטים בע', שלגביהם לא נוכל לקבוע אם
המתרגם סטה באקראי מנוסח המסורה או שינה את הטקסט במחשבה תחילה, ושמא יסודם בגירסה
עברית שהיתה לפניו:

ע': קוֹל = τῆς φωνῆς   יח' לה, יב = טור א', שו' 2: ש[מעתי א]ת כל נאצותיך

ע': לַנַחֲלָה = εἰς κατάσχεσιν   יח' לה, יב = טור א', שו' 3: לנו נתנו לא]ן[כלה]

ע': וידעת = καὶ γνώσῃ   יח' לה, טו = טור א', שו' 8: וידעו

ע': אל הרי = τοῖς ὄρεσιν   יח' לו, א = טור א', שו' 10: וא]מ]רת הרי ישר]אל

ע': רוח חיים = πνεῦμα ζωῆς   יח' לז, ה = טור ג', שו' 9: רוח וח]יי]תם

= καθὼς ἐνετείλατό μοι   יח' לז, ז = טור ג', שו' 11: כאשר צֻוֵּיתי
כאשר צֻוָּנִי[44]

ע': ואמרתי = καὶ εἶπὸν   יח' לז, ט = טור ג', שו' 15: ואמרת

בהבדלי הנוסח שלהלן סדר היחידות הסינטקטיות בתרגום הע' שונה מסדרן בנוסח המסורה:

τὰ περικύκλω ὑμῶν   ע'   יח' לו, ז = טור א', שו' 28: הגוים] אשר לכ]ם מס]ב]יב
יח' לז, ט = טור ג', שו' 15–16: ויאמר אל]י הנבא אל־הרוח] הנבא בן־אדם ואמרת אל־[הרוח]
ע': καὶ εἶπεν πρός με Προφήτευσον υἱὲ ἀνθρώπου προφήτευσον ἐπὶ τὸ
πνεῦμα = הנבא בן אדם הנבא אל הרוח.

ארחיב את הדיון בהבדל גירסה אחד שיש בו משום עניין כללי יותר:

40 καὶ αὐτοὶ λέγουσιν

41 ההשלמה בנוסח המגילה מתחייבת ממניין האותיות הדרושות כדי למלא שורה. השווה למשל טור א', שו' 3 = יח'
לה, יב; טור א', שו' 29 = יח' לו, ח; טור ב', שו' 30 = יח' לו, יד; טור ב', שו' 39 = יח' לו, לז.

42 לפי הסברה, השם הכפול הוא צירוף של קרי עם כתיב.

43 במקרים שלהלן, שבהם לא נשתמר נוסח המגילה, מתחייב השם הכפול שחזור השם הכפול על־פי חישובים של אורך השורה
ומניין אותיות: טור א', שו' 16 = לו, ד; טור א', שו' 17 = לו, ד; טור א', שו' 20 = לו, ה; טור א', שו' 25 = לו,
ו; טור א', שו' 37 = לו, יג; טור א', שו' 40 = לו, יד; טור ב', שו' 30 = לו, לב; טור ג', שו' 39 = לו, לב; טור ג',
שו' 5 = לז, ג.

44 אפשר כי עניין לנו כאן בהרמוניזציה עם יח' לז, י: כאשר צֻוָּנִי = טור ג', שו' 17–18.

יח' לה, יא = טור א', שו' 1: ונ[וד]עתי בם   ע': καὶ γνωστήσομαί σοι = בך.

אפשר כי המתרגם התאים את כינוי הגוף לכינויי נוכח הבאים בראשית הכתוב: 'כאפך וכקנאתך אשר עשיתה משנאתיך'. ואפשר כי החליף מ"ם בכ"ף[45], או שאותיות אלה כבר הוחלפו במקור העברי שהיה לפניו. בהשוואה בין נוסח המסורה לבין הע' מצאנו חילוף כ"ף/מ"ם למשל במל"א ד, י: לו שכה וכל ארץ חפר; ע' Λουσαμηνχα καὶ Ρησφαρα. המתרגם ציירף 'לו' אל שם העיר 'שכה' והעתיק כ"ף שבו ב־μ = מ"ם.

כ"ף ו־מ"ם עשויים להתחלף במיוחד בכתב העברי הקדום משום דמיונם הגראפי. בפירושו לספר יחזקאל, כבר הציע שד"ל לקרוא ביח' ג, 12: ברום כבוד ה' ממקומו, תחת נהמ"ס: בָּרוּךְ כבוד ה'. על דרך זו מתבארים הבדלי גירסה בפרשיות מקבילות בנוסח המסורה, כגון:

שופ' א, לא: את־ישבי עכו... ואת־אפיק ואת־רחֹב; יהו' יט, ל: וְעָמָה ואפֵק ורחֹב.

דה"א טז, יח־יט: לך אתן ארץ כנען חבל נחלתכם בהיותכם[46] מתי מספר, השוה תה' קה, יא־יב: לך[47] אתן את ארץ כנען חבל נחלתכם בהיותם[48] מתי מספר.

מסתבר כי בשני הכתובים הושמטה מ"ם אחרי כ"ף בתיבה 'לך' מחמת הפלוגרפיה, ומאותה סיבה הושמטה כ"ף לפני מ"ם בתיבה 'בהיותם' (תה' קה, יב).

תופעה זו מבדילה לפעמים בין קרי לכתיב או בין נוסח המסורה לעדים עבריים אחרים של נוסח המקרא:

מל"א א, מז, כתיב: יֵיטֵב אלהיך (=פ'), קרי: אלהים (כי"י רבים, ע', וולגטה)

יש' מ, יז, מס': מַאפס ותהו נחשבו לו :1QIsa[a]   וכאפס

יש' נח, יג, מס': אם תשיב מִשַּׁבָּת רגלָך עשות חפצך :1QIsa[a]   רגלך מעשות

יש' סו, ג, מס': שוחט השור מַכה איש :1QIsa[a]   כמכה איש[49]

השווה עוד:

שמ"א ב, כט: ותכבד את בניך ממני להבריאכם מראשית כל־מנחת עמי; ת"י: לאוכלותהון=להבריאם.

שמ"א טו, יח: ונלחמת בו עד כלותם אתם   ע', ת"י, פ': עד כלותך אתם

מל"ב כב, ד: ויַתֵּם את־הכסף המובא בית ה'; שמא צ"ל ויתֶּךְ (הש' כב, ט: התיכו עבדיך).

---

45   הסוגיה של חילופי עיצורים במסורת נוסח המקרא, ועמהם גם חילופים בין נוסח המסורה לבין תרגום הע', נדונה במחקרים הרבה. ראה בין היתר: F. Delitzsch, *Die Lese- und Schreibfehler im Alten Testament* etc., Berlin/Liepzig 1920; J. Kennedy, *An Aid to the Textual Amendment of the Old Testament*, Edinburgh 1928; F. Perles, *Analekten zur Textkritik des Alten Testaments*, Leipzig 1922, pp. 52-53 (Neue Folge, München 1958, pp. 30-31). ע' טוב הציג את התופעה בטבלאות סטטיסטיות, ראה: E. Tov, 'Interchanges of Consonants Between the Massoretic Text and the *Vorlage* of the Septuagint', *Sha'arei Talmon, Studies in the Bible, Qumran, and the Ancient Near East presented to Shemaryahu Talmon* (ed. M. Fishbane and E. Tov, with the assistance of W.W. Fields), Winona Lake, IN 1992, pp. 255-266

46   ע', וולגטה תרגמו: בהיותם, כמו בתה' קה, יב.

47   קרי: לכם.

48   כי"י רבים וביניהם כ"י קהיר (C) גורסים: בהיותכם. נוסח זה מונח ביסוד ת"י ופ'.

49   אין להכריע אם במקרים של הפלוגרפיה בנוסח המסורה עסקינן או של דיטוגרפיה ב־1QIsa[a].

11. מערכת הפרשיות[50]

שיטת הפיסקאות המסתמנת ב־MasEzek זֵהֶה בעיקרה לזו של בעלי המסורה, ומאששת את הסברה כי נוסח המגילה תואם את נוסח המסורה. אולם כפי שאין אחידות בקביעת הפיסקות בכתבי־היד של נוסח המסורה, כך גם מערכת הפיסקות שבמגילה אינה מתייישבת לחלוטין עם הפיסקות של כתב־יד זה או אחר.[51] נוכל להסתפק בהשוואות המימצא שבמגילה עם מערכת הפיסקות בארבעה כתבי־יד מובהקים של נוסח המסורה: כתר ארם־צובא (א), שעליו סמך הרמב"ם, כתב־יד קהיר של נביאים (ק), כתב־יד לנינגרד (ל), המונח ביסוד המהדורה הביקורתית של ביבליה הבראיקה (BH, BHS), וכתב־יד ששון (ש).

טבלה[52]

מגילה	(א)	(ק)	(ש)	(ל)	מגילה	יחזקאל
ס	ס	ס	ס	ס	א, 5	לה, יד
פ	פ	פ	ס	פ	א, 10	לו, א
—	—	ס	ס	ס	א, 20	לו, ה
?	ס	פ	ס	ס	א, 37	לו, יג
?	פ	פ	פ	ס	א, 42	לו, טז
פ	פ	פ	פ	ס	ב, 10	לו, כב
—	ס	ס	ס	ס	ב, 31	לו, לג
?	ס	ס	ס	ס	ב, 39	לו, לז
?	פ	פ	פ	ס	ב–ג	לז, א
—	ס פב"פ	—	—	—	ג, 16	לז, ט: כה אמר
—	—	—	—	ס	ג, 19	לז, יא
—	—	—	—	ס	ג, 24	לז, יג
פ	פ	פ	פ	פ	ג, 29	לז, טו
פ	פ	ס	פ	ס	ד, 17	לח, א
?	ס	ס	ס	ס	ד, 31	לח, י
?	ס	ס	ס	ס	ד, 40	לח, יד

50   לעניין שיטת הפיסקות במקרא, ראה: Ch. Perrot, 'Petuhot et Setumot: Étude sur les Alinéas du Pentateuque', *RB* 76 (1969), pp. 50-91; idem, *La lecture de la bible dans la synagogue: Les anciennes lectures palestiniennes du Shabbat et des fêtes*, Hildesheim 1973, pp. 100-127; J.M. Oesch, *Petucha und Setuma. Orbis Biblicus et Orientalis* 27, Fribourg-Göttingen 1979. השאלה נדונה מחדש לאור מסורת הנוסח של מגילות מספרי מקרא מקומראן. ראה: י' מאורי, 'מסורת ה"פסקאות" בכתבי־יד עבריים קדומים: מגילות מקרא ופשרים מספר ישעיהו מקומראן', טקסטוס 10 (1982), עמ' א–נ.

51   כל האמור כאן לגבי MasEzek תופס גם לגבי MLev[b]. ראה ש' טלמון, 'שתי מגילות' (לעיל, הערה 3), עמ' 104.

52   הטבלה מיוסדת על רשימה שהוכנה במפעל המקרא של האוניברסיטה העברית. פרשה פתוחה תסומן ע"י [פ], סתומה ע"י [ס]. פב"פ = פיסקה באמצע פסוק.

דרך כלל, המימצא במגילה תואם את מערכת הפרשיות בכתבי-יד העיקריים של נוסח המסורה. פיסקה המצוינת במגילה, אם [פ] ואם [ס], או שאפשר לשחזרה על-פי חישובים של אורך שורה ומספר האותיות שבה, תמיד חופפת פיסקה בנוסח המסורה. אולם פעמים אין במגילה סימון כלל לפרשיה הבאה בכתבי-היד שלעיל. אבל לא מצאנו ב-MasEzek סימון ברור של פיסקה שאין לה זכר באחד מהם. בעניין זה המגילה קרובה במיוחד ל-(א), (ק) ו-(ש), כפי שיצוין:

א. בכתובים שלהלן מסתמנת פיסקה במגילה, אם [פ] או [ס], כמו בכל ארבעת כתבי-היד:

טור א' שו' 5: מירווח של 7–8 אותיות מפריד בין 'אני] שמעתי' (יח' לה, יג) ו'[כה] אמר אדני' (יח' לה, יד) ומסמן [ס].

טור ג' שו' 27–29: הפער בין 'אני' (יח' לז, יד = שו' 27) ובין 'ב]ן אדם' (לז, טז = שו' 29) יכול להחזיק 53–55 אותיות ומירווחים בין תיבות. אולם הטקסט של יח' יד–טז, שלא השתמר ב-MasEzek, משם ההויה ועד 'ואתה', מחזיק רק 45 אותיות ומירווחים בין תיבות. לפיכך נותרה כמחצית שו' 28 בטור זה בהכרח חלקה לשם סימון של [פ].

טור א', שו' 9: השורה מחזיקה את שם ההויה בלבד. חלק השורה שנותר ריק מסמן [פ], כמו ב-(א), (ק) ו-(ל) ביח' לו, א, בעוד ש-(ש) מסמן [ס].

טור א', שו' 37: השלמת הטקסט בין המלים 'והחרבות' (שו' 33) ובין 'א]מר]ים' (שו' 38), שהשתמרו במגילה, נותנת לחשוב כי שו' 37 החזיקה 29 אותיות ורווחים. לפיכך סביר לשער כי בשורה זו נכללה [ס] לפני 'כה אמר' (יח' לו, יג), כמו ב-(א), (ל) ו-(ש), ואילו (ק) מסמן [פ].

ב. במקרים הבאים כלולה במגילה [פ] כמו ב-(א), (ק) ו-(ש), כנגד [ס] ב-(ל).

בטור ב', שו' 9: השורה מחזיקה רק את ארבע המלים 'בגוים אשר באו שם' (יח' לו, כא). כפי שמוכח מן השורה הבאה הפותחת במלים 'לכן אמר' (לו, כב). חלק השורה שנותר ריק מסמן [פ] כמו (א), ואילו (ל) מביא [ס].

בטור ד', שו' 16 החזיקה אך ורק את המלה 'לע]ו]לם]' (יח' לז, כח). יתרה נותר חלק, כפי שאפשר לקבוע על סמך מלים או חלקי מלים שהשתמרו בראש שו' 15: 'א]ני]', ושו' 17: 'ויהי'. מסתבר כי במגילה סומנה כאן [פ] כמו ב-(א) ו-(ש), בעוד (ל) מציג [ס].

טור ב'–ג': השלמת הטקסט בין המלים 'והנשמו]ת' (טור ב', שו' 36 = לו, לה) ובין 'היתה' (טור ג', שו' 1 = לז, א) מקרבת כי השורה התחתונה של טור ב' החזיקה 25 אותיות בלבד, ונותר בה חלק ריק כדי 8–9 אותיות לסימון [פ], כמו ב-(א), (ק) ו-(ש). ואילו (ל) מסמן כאן [ס].

ג. תואם המגילה עם (ל):

טור א' שו' 42: השלמת הטקסט בין '[לכ]ן אדם' (טור א', שו' 39 = לו, יד) ובין 'אד]ם' (טור ב', שו' 1 = לו, יז) מקרבת כי בטור א', שו' 42 היה פער ברוחב של 5–6 אותיות לשם סימון [ס], כמו ב-(ל). שלושת כתבי-היד האחרים מסמנים כאן [פ].

ד. בכתובים שלהלן לא צוינה במגילה פרשה המסומנת בלפחות אחד מארבעת כתבי-היד דלעיל:

טור א', שו' 20: הכתובים יח' לו, ד–ה באים במגילה בכתיבה רציפה ללא שום רווח ביניהם, כמו ב-(א). ואילו (ל) (ק) ו-(ש) מציינים כאן [ס].

טור ב', שו' 31: על־פי השלמת הטקסט שהוצעה אין במגילה מקום ל[ס] הקבועה בכל ארבעת כתבי־היד לפני יח' לו, לג.

טור ב', שו' 39: כיוצא בזה אין במגילה מקום לסימון [ס] המסומנת בכל ארבעת כתבי־היד לפני יח' לו, לז.

ה. בכתוב שלהלן לא צוינה במגילה פרשה שסומנה ב־(א) בלבד:

טור ג', שו' 16: אפשר לקבוע בוודאות כי לא במגילה ואף לא ב־(ל) באה פיסקה באמצע פסוק המסומנת ב־(א) אחר התיבה 'הרוח' (יח' לז, ט).

ו. שתי פרשיות [ס] המסומנות אך ורק ב־(ל) לא צוינו במגילה:

טור ג', שו' 19: הפסוקים לז, י־יא כתובים ברצף אחד ללא הפסק ביניהם, כמו ב־(א). ואילו ב־(ל) סומנה [ס] לפני 'ויאמר אלי' (יח' לז, יא).

טור ג', שו' 24: [ס] שב־(ל) לפני יח' לז, יג חסרה במגילה.

כללו של דבר, הדמיון הרב של פרשיות בעין בקטעי MasEzek או פרשיות שאפשר לשחזרן מלמד כי מערכת הפרשיות במגילה אכן היתה זֵהֵה מעיקרה עם מערכת הפרשיות של נוסח המסורה.[53]

53   אני מודה לעוזרי יונתן בן־דב, שסייעני בהבאת מאמר זה לדפוס.

טור א   1   מִשִּׂנְאָתֶיךָ בָם וְנוֹדַעְתִּי בָם כַּאֲשֶׁר אֶשְׁפָּטֵךְ וְיָדַעְתָּ

2   כִּי אֲנִי יהוה שָׁמַעְתִּי אֶת כָּל נָאֲצוֹתֶיךָ אֲשֶׁר אָמַרְתָּ

3   עַל הָרֵי יִשְׂרָאֵל לֵאמֹר שָׁמֵמָה לָנוּ נִתְּנוּ לְאָכְלָה

4   וַתַּגְדִּילוּ עָלַי בְּפִיכֶם וְהַעְתַּרְתֶּם עָלַי דִּבְרֵיכֶם אֲנִי

5   שָׁמָעְתִּי   כֹּה אָמַר אֲדֹנָי יהוה כִּשְׂמֹחַ כָּל

6   הָאָרֶץ שְׁמָמָה אֶעֱשֶׂה לָּךְ כְּשִׂמְחָתְךָ לְנַחֲלַת בֵּית

7   יִשְׂרָאֵל עַל אֲשֶׁר שָׁמֵמָה כֵּן אֶעֱשֶׂה לָּךְ שְׁמָמָה

8   תִהְיֶה הַר שֵׂעִיר וְכָל אֱדוֹם כֻּלָּה וְיָדְעוּ כִּי אֲנִי

9   יהוה

10   וְאַתָּה בֶן אָדָם הִנָּבֵא אֶל הָרֵי יִשְׂרָאֵל וְאָמַרְתָּ הָרֵי

11   יִשְׂרָאֵל שִׁמְעוּ דְּבַר יהוה כֹּה אָמַר אֲדֹנָי יהוה

12   יַעַן אָמַר הָאוֹיֵב עֲלֵיכֶם הֶאָח וּבָמוֹת עוֹלָם לְמוֹרָשָׁה

13   הָיְתָה לָּנוּ לָכֵן הִנָּבֵא וְאָמַרְתָּ כֹּה אָמַר אֲדֹנָי יהוה

14   יַעַן בְּיַעַן שַׁמּוֹת וְשָׁאֹף אֶתְכֶם מִסָּבִיב לִהְיוֹתְכֶם

15   מוֹרָשָׁה לִשְׁאֵרִית הַגּוֹיִם וַתֵּעֲלוּ עַל שְׂפַת לָשׁוֹן

16   וְדִבַּת עָם לָכֵן הָרֵי יִשְׂרָאֵל שִׁמְעוּ דְּבַר אֲדֹנָי יהוה

17   כֹּה אָמַר אֲדֹנָי יהוה לֶהָרִים וְלַגְּבָעוֹת לָאֲפִיקִים

18   וְלַגֵּאָיוֹת וְלֶחֳרָבוֹת הַשֹּׁמֵמוֹת וְלֶעָרִים הַנֶּעֱזָבוֹת

19   אֲשֶׁר הָיוּ לָבַז וּלְלַעַג לִשְׁאֵרִית הַגּוֹיִם אֲשֶׁר

20   מִסָּבִיב לָכֵן כֹּה אָמַר אֲדֹנָי יהוה אִם לֹא בְּאֵשׁ

21   קִנְאָתִי דִבַּרְתִּי עַל שְׁאֵרִית הַגּוֹיִם וְעַל אֱדוֹם כֻּלָּא

22   אֲשֶׁר נָתְנוּ אֶת אַרְצִי לָהֶם לְמוֹרָשָׁה בְּשִׂמְחַת

23   כָּל לֵבָב בִּשְׁאָט נֶפֶשׁ לְמַעַן מִגְרָשָׁהּ לָבַז לָכֵן

24   הִנָּבֵא עַל אַדְמַת יִשְׂרָאֵל וְאָמַרְתָּ לֶהָרִים וְלַגְּבָעוֹת

25   לָאֲפִיקִים וְלַגֵּאָיוֹת כֹּה אָמַר אֲדֹנָי יהוה הִנְנִי

26   בְקִנְאָתִי וּבַחֲמָתִי דִּבַּרְתִּי יַעַן כְּלִמַּת גּוֹיִם נְשָׂאתֶם לָכֵן

27   כֹּה אָמַר אֲדֹנָי יהוה אֲנִי נָשָׂאתִי אֶת יָדִי אִם לֹא

28   הַגּוֹיִם אֲשֶׁר לָכֶם מִסָּבִיב הֵמָּה כְּלִמָּתָם

29   יִשָּׂאוּ וְאַתֶּם הָרֵי יִשְׂרָאֵל עַנְפְּכֶם תִּתֵּנוּ וּפֶרְיְכֶם

30   תִּשְׂאוּ לְעַמִּי יִשְׂרָאֵל כִּי קֵרְבוּ לָבוֹא כִּי הִנְנִי אֲלֵיכֶם

31   וּפָנִיתִי אֲלֵיכֶם וְנֶעֱבַדְתֶּם וְנִזְרַעְתֶּם וְהִרְבֵּיתִי

32   עֲלֵיכֶם אָדָם כָּל בֵּית יִשְׂרָאֵל כֻּלֹּה וְנֹשְׁבוּ הֶעָרִים

33   וְהֶחֳרָבוֹת תִּבָּנֶינָה וְהִרְבֵּיתִי עֲלֵיכֶם אָדָם וּבְהֵמָה

34   וְרָבוּ וּפָרוּ וְהוֹשַׁבְתִּי אֶתְכֶם כְּקַדְמוֹתֵיכֶם וְהֵטִבֹתִי

35   מֵרָאשֹׁתֵיכֶם וִידַעְתֶּם כִּי אֲנִי יהוה וְהוֹלַכְתִּי עֲלֵיכֶם

36   אָדָם אֶת עַמִּי יִשְׂרָאֵל וִירֵשׁוּךָ וְהָיִיתָ לָהֶם לְנַחֲלָה

37   וְלֹא תוֹסִף עוֹד לְשַׁכְּלָם   כֹּה אָמַר אֲדֹנָי יהוה

יען אמרים לכם אכלת אדם אתי ומשכלת גויך היית 38

לכן אדם לא תאכלי עוד וגויך לא תכשלי עוד נאם 39

אדני יהוה ולא אשמיע אליך עוד כלמת הגוים וחרפת 40

עמים לא תשאי עוד וגויך לא תכשלי עוד נאם 41

אדני יהוה ויהי דבר יהוה אלי לאמר בן 42

טור ב   אדם בית ישראל ישבים על אדמתם ויטמאו 1

אתה בדרכם ובעלילותם כטמאת הנדה היתה 2

דרכם לפני ואשפך חמתי עליהם על הדם אשר 3

שפכו על הארץ ובגלוליהם טמאוה ואפיץ אתם 4

בגוים ויזרו בארצות כדרכם וכעלילותם שפטתים 5

ויבוא אל הגוים אשר באו שם ויחללו את שם 6

קדשי באמר להם עם יהוה אלה ומארצו יצאו 7

ואחמל על שם קדשי אשר חללהו בית ישראל 8

בגוים אשר באו שם 9

לכן אמר לבית ישראל כה אמר אדני יהוה לא 10

למענכם אני עשה בית ישראל כי אם לשם קדשי 11

אשר חללתם בגוים ב״ת אשר באתם שם וקדשתי 12

את שמי הגדול המחלל בגוים אשר חללתם 13

בתוכם וידעו הגוים כי אני יהוה נאם אדני יהוה 14

בהקדשי בכם לעיניהם ולקחתי אתכם מן הגוים 15

וקבצתי אתכם מכל הארצות והבאתי אתכם אל 16

אדמתכם וזרקתי עליכם מים טהורים וטהרתם 17

מכל ט״אותיכם ומכל גלוליכם אטהר אתכם ונתתי 18

לכם לב חדש ורוח חדשה אתן בקרבכם והסרותי 19

את לב האבן מבשרכם ונתתי לכם לב בשר ואת 20

רוחי אתן בקרבכם ועשיתי את אשר בחקי תלכו 21

ומשפטי תשמרו ועשיתם וישבתם בארץ אשר 22

נתתי לאבתיכם והייתם לי לעם ואנכי אהיה לכם 23

לאלהים והושעתי אתכם מכל טמאותיכם וקראתי 24

אל הדגן והרביתי אתו ולא אתן עליכם רעב 25

והרביתי את פרי העץ ותנובת השדה למען 26

אשר לא תקחו עוד חרפת רעב בגוים וזכרתם 27

את דרכיכם הרעים ומעלליכם אשר לא טובים 28

ונקטתם בפניכם על עונתיכם ועל תועבותיכם 29

לא למענכם אני עשה נאם אדני יהוה יודע לכם 30

בושו והכלמו מדרכיכם בית ישראל כה אמר אדני 31

יהוה ביום טהרי אתכם מכל עונותיכם והושבתי 32

33   את הערים ונבנו החרבות והארץ הנשמה תעבד

34   תחת אשר היתה שממה לעיני כל עובר ואמרו

35   הארץ הלזו הנשמה היתה כגן עדן והערים

36   החרבות והנשמות והנהרסות בצורות ישבו וידעו

37   הגוים אשר ישארו סביבותיכם כי אני יהוה בניתי

38   הנהרסות נטעתי הנשמה אני יהוה דברתי ועשיתי

39   כה אמר אדני יהוה עוד זאת אדרש לבית ישראל

40   לעשות להם ארבה אתם כצאן אדם כצאן קדשים

41   כצאן ירושלם במועדיה כן תהיינה הערים החרבות

42   מלאות צאן אדם וידעו כי אני יהוה

טור ג   1   היתה עלי יד יהוה ויוצאני ברוח יהוה ויניחני

2   בתוך הבקעה והיא מלאה עצמות והעבירני

3   עליהם סביב סביב והנה רבות מאד על פני הבקעה

4   והנה יבשות מאד ויאמר אלי בן אדם התחיינה

5   העצמות האלה ואמר אדני יהוה אתה ידעת

6   ויאמר אלי הנבא על העצמות האלה ואמרת

7   אליהם העצמות היבשות שמעו דבר יהוה כה

8   אמר אדני יהוה לעצמות האלה הנה אני מביא

9   בכם רוח וחייתם ונתתי עליכם גידים והעליתי

10   עליכם בשר וקרמתי עליכם עור ונתתי בכם רוח

11   וחייתם וידעתם כי אני יהוה ונבאתי כאשר צויתי

12   ויהי קול כהנבאי והנה רעש תקרבו העצמות

13   עצם אל עצמו וראיתי והנה עליהם גדים ובשר

14   עלה ויקרם עליהם עור מלמעלה ורוח אין בהם

15   ויאמר אלי הנבא אל הרוח הנבא בן אדם ואמרת

16   אל הרוח כה אמר אדני יהוה מארבע רוחות באי

17   הרוח ופחי בהרוגים האלה ויחיו והנבאתי כאשר

18   צוני ותבא בהם הרוח ויחיו ויעמדו על רגליהם

19   חיל גדול מאד מאד ויאמר אלי בן אדם העצמות

20   האלה כל בית ישראל המה הנה אמרים יבשו

21   עצמותינו ואבדה תקותנו נגזרנו לנו לכן הנבא

22   ואמרת אליהם כה אמר אדני יהוה הנה אני

23   פתח את קברותיכם והעליתי אתכם מקברותיכם

24   עמי והבאתי אתכם אל אדמת ישראל וידעתם

25   כי אני יהוה בפתחי את קברותיכם ובהעלותי

26   אתכם מקברותיכם עמי ונתתי רוחי בכם וחייתם

27   והנחתי אתכם על אדמתכם וידעתם כי אני יהוה

דברתי ועשׂיתי נאם יהוה | 28

ויהי דבר יהוה אלי לאמר ואתה בן **אדם** קח לך | 29

עץ אחד וכתב עליו ליהודה ולבנֵי **ישראל** חברו | 30

ולקח עץ אחד וכתוב עליו ליוסף **עץ אפֹּרים** | 31

וכל בית ישראל חברו וקרב אתם אחד אל אחד לך | 32

לעץ אחד והיו לאחדים בידך וכאשר יאמרו אליך | 33

בני עמך לאמר הלוא תגיד לנו מה אלה לך דבר | 34

אלהם כה אמר אדני יהוה הנה אני לקח את עץ | 35

יוסף אשר ביד אפרים ושבטי ישראל חברו ונתתי | 36

אותם עליו את עץ יהודה ועשיתים לעץ אחד והיו | 37

אחד בידי והיו העצים אשר תכתב עליהם בידך | 38

לעיניהם ודבר אליהם כה אמר אדני יהוה הנה | 39

אני לקח את בני ישראל מבין הגוים אשר הלכו | 40

שם וקבצתי אתם מסביב והבאתי אותם אל אדמתם | 41

ועשיתי אתם לגוי אחד בארץ בהרי ישראל ומלך | 42

טור ד אחד יהיה לכלם למלך ולא יהיה עוד לשני גוים | 1

ולא יחצו עוד לשתי ממלכות עוד ולא יטמאו | 2

עוד בגלוליהם ובשקוציהם ובכל פשעיהם | 3

והושעתי אתם מכל מושבתיהם אשֶׁר **חטׂאו** בהם | 4

וטהרתי אותם והיו לי לעם ואני אהֶיה להם | 5

לאלהים ועבדי דוד מלך עליהם ורועה אחד יהיה | 6

לכלם ובמשפטי ילכו וחקתי ישמרו ועשו אותם | 7

וישבו על הארץ אשר נתתי לעבדי ליעקב אשר | 8

ישבו בה אבותיכם וישבו עליה המה ובניהם | 9

ובני בניהם עד עולם ודוד עבדי נשיא להם | 10

לעולם וכרתי להם ברית שלום ברית עולם יהיה | 11

אותם ונתתים והרביתי אותם ונתתי את מקדשי | 12

בתוכם לעולם והיה משכני עליהם והייתי להם | 13

לאלהים והמה יהיו לי לעם וידעו הגוים כי | 14

אני יהוה מקדש את ישראל בהיות מקדשי בתוכם | 15

לעולם | 16

ויהי דׇבר יהוה אלי לאמר בן אדם שים פניך אל | 17

גוג אׇרץ המגוג נשיא ראש משך ותבל והנבא עליו | 18

ואמׇרת כה אמר אדני יהוה הנני אליך גוג נשיא | 19

רׂאש משך ותבל ושובבתיך ונתתי חחים בלחייך | 20

והוצאתי אותך ואת כל חילך סוסים ופרשים לבשי | 21

מכֹלול כלם קהל רב צנה ומגן תפשי חרבות כלם | 22

פרס כוש ופוט אתם כלם מגן וכובע גמר וכל אגפיה 23

בית תוגרמה ירכתי צפון ואת כל אגפיו עמים רבים 24

אתך הכן והכן לך אתה וכל קהלך הנקהלים עליך 25

והיית להם למשמר מימים רבים תפקד באחרית 26

השנים תבוא אל ארץ משובבת מחרב מקבצת 27

מעמים רבים על הרי ישראל אשר היו לחרבה 28

תמיד והיא מעמים הוצאה וישבו לבטח כלם 29

ועלית כשאה תבוא כענן לכסות הארץ תהיה אתה 30

וכל אגפיך ועמים רבים אותך   כה 31

אמר אדני יהוה והיה ביום ההוא יעלו דברים 32

על לבבך וחשבת מחשבת רעה ואמרת אעלה על ארץ 33

פרזות אבוא השקטים ישבי לבטח כלם ישבים באין 34

חומה ובריח ודלתים אין להם לשלל שלל ולבז בז 35

להשיב ידך על חרבות נושבת ואל עם מאסף מגוים 36

עשה מקנה וקנין ישבי על טבור הארץ שבא ודדן 37

וסחרי תרשיש וכל כפריה יאמרו לך הלשלל שלל 38

אתה בא הלבז בז הקהלת קהלך לשאת כסף וזהב 39

לקחת מקנה וקנין לשלל שלל גדול   לכן 40

הנבא בן אדם ואמרת לגוג כה אמר אדני יהוה 41

הלוא ביום ההוא בשבת עמי ישראל לבטח תדע 42

תעודות חדשות ממארי ונבואות ספר יחזקאל

אברהם מלמט
האוניברסיטה העברית בירושלים

אחד הנושאים המרכזיים במפעלו המדעי של ידידי משה גרינברג הוא פירושו לספר יחזקאל.[1] ברשימה זו אני מקדיש לבעל ספר היובל שלוש זוטות על ספר מקראי זה שלהן מקבילות או אנלוגיות בתעודות של ארכיוני העיר מארי (ובמקורות דומים). אנו נדרשים כאן בראש וראשונה לתעודות חדשות יחסית ממארי, שפורסמו בשנים האחרונות בכרכים כו 1 ו־כו 2 (ראה הערות 5 ו־6) שבסידרת הפרסומים של ארכיוני מארי. הזוטות דנות בתחום ההתנבאות הן במארי והן בספר יחזקאל.[2]

[א] פגיעת ידו של האל

תחילה נעסוק בחומר ממארי (הכתוב באכדית) ולאחר מכן בספר יחזקאל. הניב האכדי המקביל במקרא ל'היה' או ל'חזק' של 'יד ה'' הוא *qāt ilim* (או *ŠU ilim*) בציירוף פועל, והוא מצוי בספרות של מיסופוטמיה גם מחוץ למארי. בניגוד למרבית המובאות במקרא ובמארי, הניב בספרות האכדית מכוון בדרך כלל לציון אירוע שלילי, כגון פורענות כלשהי או מחלה.[3] הוראה זו מצויה גם במרחב השמי־מערבי, כגון בתעודות תל אל־רימה מתקופת מארי, שחוברו אף הן בלשון האכדית. אחת התעודות מתל אל־רימה מזכירה בזה אחר זה שני נערים, שיד האל פגעה בהם: 'הנה הנער (היינו הנער השני) – יד האל היתה עליו והוא חולה בתמידות' (מס' 65, שו' 16 ואילך).[4] הנער היה בלי ספק מתנבא, כפי שמוכיח המנהג של נטילת שער ראשו ושולי בגדו – מנהג שרווח במארי לגבי מתנבאים ומתנבאות (השווה לעניין נער המתנבא ולוקה במחלה, ארכיוני מארי עצמם, כרך יג, מס' 112). המחלה במקרים מסוימים היתה בוודאי כרוכה בחוויה האקסטטית שחווה המתנבא. בתעודות

---

* מחקר זה נתמך בידי הקרן הלאומית למדע בניהול האקדמיה הלאומית הישראלית למדעים.

1 ראה: M. Greenberg, *Ezekiel 1-20* (AB), Garden City 1983. הכרך השני של הפירוש נמצא בדפוס.
2 על נבואה מקבילה נוספת במארי וביחזקאל (פרק כא, יט־כג) עמדתי כבר בספר היובל המוקדש לי"א סוג'ין, ראה *Storia e Tradizioni di Israele. Scritti in Onore di J. Alberto Soggin*, Brescia 1991, p. 188ff.
3 CAD Q (1982), p. 186 s.v. *qātu, qāt ilim*
4 ראה S. Dalley et al., *The Old Babylonian Tablets from Tell al Rimah* (British School of Archaeology in Iraq, 1976), pp. 64-65, no. 65, ll. 14-19

החדשות ממארי, המכונסות בכרך כו,1,[5] נזכרת פגיעת יד האל בשישה מקרים (ומקרה נוסף מצוי בכרך כו,2), הן יד של אל ספציפי והן יד של אלוהות בסתם, ועל־פי רוב תוך מגמה חיובית – היינו בלא לגרום למחלה. להלן נציג מקרים אלו כסדרם באסופת התעודות:

1) בתעודה מס' 83 אמנם המגמה היא שלילית והכוונה לפורענות. אסקודום, המומחה הראשי בארמון מארי לתורת האותות, שולח איגרת לאדונו יַסמַח־אַד, שהיה שליט מארי באותם ימים, בזו הלשון: 'האורקולום אשר ערכתי (לאמור) "היד של עשתר של רַדָּן" של העיר אכַלאתום. האלה הטילה עליה (על האשה) לחץ... עד שלא הלכה (האשה) לעיר אכלאתום לא רפתה המחלה (של האשה, ששמה נזכר בראשית המכתב)' (שורות 9–16). כאן, כמו במקרים אחדים נוספים, יד האלוהות עשויה לגרום למחלה, עד אשר הניב 'יד האל' משמש, בין השאר, במשמעות נרדפת לחולי עצמו.

2) המתכתבים בתעודה מס' 84 זהים לאלה שבתעודה הקודמת. אך הפעם אין במגע 'יד האל' (qāt ilutim; לצורה התמוהה ראה הערה d בפירוש התעודה) כדי פגיעה לרעה או כדי גרימת מחלה.

3) תעודה מס' 136. הכותב מודיע ליסמח־אד כי ערך בדיקה של הקרביים (של כבש), פעם אחר פעם, למען החלמתה של גברת בֶלְתום (=בעלת), שהיתה הגבירה בארמון מארי באותם ימים והיא ככל הנראה אשת יסמח־אד, שמוצאה מן העיר קַטְנה שבמערב. מן האורקולום משתמע שמחלתה של הנסיכה לא נגרמה מפגיעת 'יד האל' אלא שחלתה בחום גבוה בסתם והכותב מעיר שאין נשקפת סכנה לחייה.

4) תעודה מס' 260. גם איגרת זו מופנית ליסמח־אד. בתחילתה בא קטע בדבר 'יד האל'. הפעם ה'יד' הלכה ונרגעה, והיא איננה בחזקת פגע אלא היא שלווה ורגועה. עתה ביום הפעלת היד איש לא מת מפני 'יד האל' ואילו קודם לכן השתוללה מגיפה ונפטרו ביום אחד עשרה אנשים וחמישה ילדים.

5) תעודה מס' 264. פקיד בכיר כותב לשליט מארי: 'ראה כיצד "יד האל" ש(הונחתה) על הארץ היתה מפויסת'; לאמור כאן 'יד האל' פעלה פעולה חיובית.

6) תעודה מס' 265. בסופו של המכתב הנדון מובא מובא ספה, שתוכנו הוא כי 'יד האל' רגועה ושלווה ולארמון מארי שלום.

7) ובנוסף לדוגמאות אלה מצוי הניב 'יד האל' בכרך כו,2, מס' 371, שורות 9–12.[6] מדובר במכתב 'נבואי' שנשלח למלך זימרי־לים, שבו מופיע מתנבא בתואר אפילום (āpilum[7]) – ה'עונה') של האל מַרדוך. הלה איננו מפסיק לזעוק לאמור: 'אשְׁמֵי־דגן לא ייצא מ"יד מרדוך"!'

האיגרות ממארי בדבר 'יד האל' מזכירות שתי קטגוריות: מחד גיסא היד גורמת לפורענות ואף למוות, ומאידך גיסא אין 'יד האל' גורמת נזק, אדרבא היא מיטיבה עם האנשים או עם הארץ. אפשר שהקטגוריה האחרונה איננה טיפוסית לתפיסת העולם האכדית אלא אופיינית למרחב התרבות המערבי (בין השאר למארי ולמקרא).

במקרא נזכר המטבע 'יד ה'' (ופעם 'יד אלוה'; איוב יט, כא) פעמים רבות ובפונקציות שונות, כגון בפרשת יציאת מצרים ובסיפור נדודי ארון הברית בספר שמואל א'. כאן נדון בניב זה רק בזיקה

J.M. Durand, ARM 26/1 = AEM I/1, Paris (Editions Recherche sur les Civilisations) 1988   5

D. Charpin, in: ARM 26/2, Paris (Editions Recherche sur les Civilisations) 1988, pp. 177-179   6

A. Malamat, *Mari and the Early Israelite Experience*, Oxford על המתנבא המכונה אפילום ראה באחרונה   7

1989, pp. 86-87; D. Charpin, 'Le contexte historique et geographique des prophétes... à Mari',

לנבואה ולציון התעוררות החזון הנבואי,[8] כעדותו של אחד השימושים של הניב באכדית. נתמקד
בספר יחזקאל, שבו בולט השימוש המרובה בניב זה (שבע פעמים), יותר מאשר בספרי הנבואה
האחרים.

בספר יחזקאל נזכרים, דרך כלל, שני פעלים שונים בזיקה ל'יד ה'' – 'היה' ו'חזק'. הפועל 'היה':
'ותהי עליו שם יד ה'' (א, ג); 'ותהי עלי שם יד ה'' (ג, כב); 'ויד ה' היתה אלי בערב' (לג, כב); 'היתה
עלי יד ה'' (לז, א; מ, א). הפועל האחר הוא 'חזק' ומתאר את התעצמות החיזיון הנבואי; ראה למשל:
'רוח נשאתני... ויד ה' עלי חזקה' (ג, יד). בהקשר זה יש לשים לב לכתוב בישעיהו ח, יא: 'כי כה
אמר ה' אלי בחזקת היד...'. הדברים מכוונים כאן ליד ה' שפעולתה נעשית 'חזקה'. רק פעם אחת
משמש בהקשר להתנבאות בספר יחזקאל הפועל 'נפל': 'ותפל (תרגום השבעים מתרגם גם כאן לשון
'היה') עלי שם יד אדני ה' [אלוהים]' (ח, א), והשווה יח' יג, ט.[9]

כללו של דבר, שלושה פעלים שונים משמשים את הנוסחה שבאה כפתיחה להתעוררות רוח
יחזקאל, ובדרך כלל היא גם באה כפרולוג ישיר לדברי הנבואה עצמם שנאמרים אחרי ההתעוררות.
הנוסחה של הפעלת יד ה' אוצרת בקרבה ציפייה לחזון נבואי או ציפייה לפעולה מצד הנביא.[10] באשר
לנביא עצמו אפשר שהתרחש כאן אירוע אקסטטי אך אין הדברים, ככל הנראה, אמורים באובדן
חושים מוחלט של הנביא ובבלבול העגה שבפיו.

כשם שבאכדית (בייחוד מעבר למארי) יד האל נועדה בעיקר לפורענות, כך הוא גם ביחס לכמה
מובאות במקרא, אלא שבנבואות המקרא גופה מגמה זו היא לכל היותר שולית. מוטיב הפורענות
מצוי בייחוד בספרים שמחוץ לנבואה המקראית; למשל: 'הנה יד ה' הויה במקנך' (שמ' ט, ג); 'יד
ה' היתה בם לרעה' (שופ' ב, טו); 'כי יד אלוה נגעה בי' (איוב יט, כא). כאמור, זהו המקום היחיד
במקרא שנזכרה בו אלוהות בסתם ולא שם ההווייה. בניגוד לכך במארי, כפי שראינו לעיל, פעולתה
של יד האל היא בדרך כלל חיובית ומביאה רגיעה ושלווה.

ההבדל חיצוני בין מארי ובין נבואות המקרא הוא בייעודה של הנוסחה הנדונה. במקרא, כאמור,
היא משמשת נוסחת פתיחה לעצם הנבואה ואיננה נזכרת בגוף דברי החזון עצמו, ואילו במארי
הנוסחה מצויה גם בתוך דברי ההתנבאות והיא למעשה בעלת שימוש מקיף יותר מאשר היותה נוסחה
טכנית מקדימה.

[ב] 'ועשיתם לעץ אחד' (יח' לז, יט)

הנבואה המובאת בספר יחזקאל מיד לאחר חזון העצמות היבשות מעלה מעשה סמלי בדבר שני גזרי
עץ או מטות עץ שעל הנביא לקחת. ה' מצווה על הנביא לחבר את העצים בתוך ידו לעץ אחד, מעשה

Bulletin of the Canadian Society for Mesopotamian Studies 23 (1992), pp. 21-22

8　על יד ה' במקרא בזיקה לנבואה ראה: J.J.M. Roberts, 'The Hand of Yahwe', *VT* 21 (1971), pp.
244-251; A.S. van der Woude, in: *THAT* I (1971), pp. 672-673; P. Ackroyd, in: *TWAT* III (1982),
pp. 448-449

9　ראה: מ' גרינברג (לעיל, הערה 1), עמ' 41–42, 166, 236–237; W. Zimmerli, *Ezechiel,* I (BKAT XIII),
Neukirchen 1959, pp. 47-50

10　השווה רוברטס (לעיל, הערה 8), עמ' 251 וכן המילונים התיאולוגיים הנזכרים בהערה 8.

שבא לסמל את האיחוד לעתיד לבוא של שני חלקי האומה – בית יהודה ובית יוסף (יח' לז, טו-כב).[11]
שני חלקי האומה שוכנים בגולה וישובו על־פי חזון הנביא לארץ ישראל. צירוף שני העצים מתואר
על־ידי מטפורה בזו הלשון: 'וקרב אתם אחד אל אחד לך לעץ אחד והיו לאחדים בידך... ועשיתם
לעץ אחד והיו אחד בידי' (שם, יז-יט). העצים מתחברים אפוא בתוך ידו של הנביא, מטפורה
שנודעת לה חשיבות הן לגבי הממצא המצרי והן לגבי ניבים אכדיים בתעודות מארי, כפי שנראה
מיד. הסיכום של הנביא הוא: 'ועשיתי אתם לגוי אחד... ולא יהיו עוד לשני גוים... ולא יחצו עוד
לשתי ממלכות עוד' (שם, כב).

לנבואה זו יש אנלוגיות באיורים מצריים, המתארים חיבור והידוק של צמחים וגבעוליהם כדי
לסמל את איחודם של מצרים העילית והתחתית.[12] וראה בהקשר זה גם את נבואת נפרתי בדבר
איחודם של שני חלקי מצרים.[13] אבל עתה ניתן להעלות מקבילה מאלפת גם בתעודות החדשות
ממארי, אם כי במבט ראשון הקרבה אינה ניכרת. במארי מצוי נוהג סמלי, שכנראה מושתת על מנהג
דיפלומטי ממשי, בנוגע לאיחוד מדיני באמצעות שילוב אצבעות כפות הידיים של נציגי שני
הצדדים. על שני הצדדים (אנשים או מקומות) לכרוך את האצבעות של איש באצבעות יד רעהו
'והיו לאצבע אחת' (אולי יש להבין ברוח זו גם את אחת ההוראות של המונח המקראי 'תקע כף').
תעודה אחת ממארי המתארת מנהג זה פורסמה כבר ב־1950 (ארכיוני מארי, כרך ב, מס' 21, שורות
11–12).[14] לדוגמה יחידה זו נוספו עתה בתעודות מארי שבכרך כו2 ארבעה מקרים דומים. נביאם
להלן כסדרם בכרך כו2 ממארי:

1) תעודה מס' 392, שורות 29–30: 'אם אַתַמרום (פקיד בכיר במארי) יעשה זאת, אז הוא ואנוכי
נישבע שבועה מכל הלב, נהיה שוב אצבע אחת';

2) תעודה מס' 438, שורה 22: 'מדוע תיחלק (או תיחצה כלשון יחזקאל) אצבע אחת לשתיים'
(היינו הדברים מרמזים להפרת ברית);

3) תעודה מס' 449, שורות 14–15: '...הערים מארי ובבל היו לבית אחד ולאצבע אחת';[15]

4) תעודה A.4206, שורות 11–12 (הלוח לא פורסם עדיין, אך הקטע הנדון הובא בכרך כו
על־ידי שרפין): פלוני ואלמוני 'הנה (הם) אצבע אחת'.[16]

6 ,5) על דוגמאות אלה יש להוסיף כעת את התעודה A.4026, שורה 12 ואת התעודה A.2326,
שורות 8–13: 'חנה (היינו הנוודים) וארץ אדַמַרַץ מאז ומתמיד הם (כמו) אצבע אחת ולב אחד. עתה,
מדוע תיחלק אצבע אחת לשניים?'[17] מאלף כאן הביטוי 'לב אחד' שאינו מצוי בהקשרים הנדונים

11 על נבואה זו ראה בייחוד צימרלי (לעיל, הערה 9), ב, עמ' 903–912.

12 ראה, דרך משל, B.J. Kemp, *Ancient Egypt,* London-New York 1991, p. 28, fig. 6, ושם תיאור של
קשירתם של פרח הלוטוס ועלה פפירוס.

13 לנבואת נפרתי השווה N. Shupak, 'Egyptian "Prophecy" and Biblical Prophecy...', *JEOL* 31
(1989-90), p. 32f.

14 Charpin et al., in: ARM 26/2, Paris 1988, no. 100. והשווה את הערתו של מורן W.L. Moran, *NABU* 1989/4,
הרושם את כל המובאות הנדונות ומניח בצדק שהכוונה היא לכריתת ברית.

15 ביטוי דומה לברית בין שתי ערים או ממלכות נתגלה במכתב מאֶרך מטעם המלך אנאם למלך סינמובליט, אביו
של חמורבי: 'אֶרך ובבל הם בית אחד'; ראה A. Falkenstein, *BaghMitt* 2 (1963), p. 56ff., col. II 2, III 25

16 למובאה עיין Charpin et al., in: ARM 26/2, p. 225, text, 392, n. g.

17 על תעודה A.4026 ראה J.M. Durand, *Mari* 6 (1990), p. 50; ועל A.2326 ראה D. Charpin, *Mari* 7
(1993), p. 175.

במארי, אבל הוא נמצא פעמים במקרא, אך בהוראה 'בדעה אחת'. ראה: 'לב אחד להמליך את דויד' (דה"א יב, לח); 'לתת להם לב אחד לעשות' (דה"ב ל, יב).

קרובה הסברה שבכל הדוגמאות שהבאנו מכוונת הפעולה הסמלית לקשר, לאיחוד או לברית בין שני צדדים על־ידי שילוב אצבעות כף היד וכריכתן באצבעות היד שמנגד. אצל יחזקאל לעומת זאת קשר מעין זה מסומל על־ידי איחודם של שני גזרי עץ בכף היד, בדומה לציורים המצריים.

[ג] התנבאות במקרא – באמצעות אכילת מגילה, והתנבאות במארי – באמצעות שתיית משקאות

יחזקאל הוא הנביא היחיד הזוכה לחזון נבואי באמצעות בליעת מגילה, הכתובה משני צדדיה. ה' מאכיל את יחזקאל: 'אכול אכול את המגלה הזאת ולך דבר אל בית ישראל... ויאכלני את המגלה הזאת...' (יח' ג, א ואילך, והשווה שם ב, ח־י). יש כאן תיאור תמוה כיצד הנביא מציית לצו האלוהי, בולע את המגילה והיא ממלאת את מעיו (שם ג, ג) ומתאמץ לעכל את הדברים הכתובים עליה, הם דברי אלוהים.[18] המגילה כוללת את הנבואות שהנביא עתיד לנבא לעמו. גם אצל ירמיהו נזכר פעם אחת החיזיון של אכילת דבר ה': 'נמצאו דבריך ואכלם...' (יר' טו, טז). שמא בשני הספרים המוטיב הוא אחד אלא שבירמיהו הוא סתמי ואיננו נזכר בהקדשת הנביא ואילו ביחזקאל הוא מפורש ונושא צביון פלסטי מובהק ומובא בסוף פרשת ההקדשה.

הן בהקדשתו של ירמיהו והן בהקדשתו של ישעיהו מועבר דבר ה' על־ידי מגע אלוהי בלבד. בירמיהו א, ט שולח ה' את ידו לפי הנביא, ואילו בישעיהו ו, ו־ז אחד השרפים של ה' נוגע על־פי הנביא, אך הפעם כדי להסיר את עוון הנביא וכדי לטהרו. אפשר שגם לנגיעה זו יש הקבלה בכמה נבואות חדשות ממארי, אלא ששם הביטוי האכדי לעניין זה הוא 'לגעת בסנטר',[19] נגיעה הכרוכה כנראה בתנועה סמלית לא רק של האלוהות אלא בעיקר של אדם.

כאשר אנו שבים לפרשת יחזקאל ולאכילת המגילה תוך השוואה לנבואות מארי, הרי פעם אחת ואולי פעמיים אנו נתקלים בהקשר להתנבאות במנהג התמוה להשקות פלוני ואלמוני בנוזל שטיבו לא פורש, כדי לעורר את האנשים השותים להשמיע דברי נבואה. התעודה הבולטת היא ארכיוני מארי, כרך כו1, מס' 207 (A.996).[20] מבלי להידרש לדיון בתעודה זו, שנודעת לה חשיבות לסוגיות אחרות, נביא את השורות הרלוונטיות לענייננו כלשונן. המלכה שיבתו (ויש המעדיפים לגרוס שיבטו או שיפטו), אשת זימרי־לים, מכריזה בנוגע למסע צבאי שערוך בעלה נגד אויביו: 'השקיתי את האותות לזכר ונקבה (או שמא הכוונה היא שהאיש והאשה עצמם משמשים כאותות, aš-qi) כדעת דו'ראן) וחקרתי בענין' (שורות 4–6). גם טיב המשקה מעורר מחלוקת בין החוקרים. דו'ראן

---

18 השווה מ' גרינברג (לעיל, הערה 1), עמ' 67–68; צימרלי (לעיל, הערה 9), עמ' 78–79.

19 suqtam ilput. השווה דו'ראן (לעיל, הערה 5), עמ' 281, 378 (ושם הערה 13), 433 (והשווה עתה: .M Guidard, NABU 3 [Paris 1994], p. 271). המחבר מביא שם ארבעה מקרים של נוהג זה, שלחלקם אין קשר לנבואה דווקא. עניין אחר הוא הנגיעה ב'גרון', המשמשת במארי, כידוע, לעניין כריתת בריתות.

20 ראה דו'ראן (שם), עמ' 435–436. התעודה נתפרסמה לראשונה בארכיוני מארי, כרך י, מס' 4; השווה .J.M Durand, RA 76 (1982), pp. 43-50; idem, MARI 3 (1984), pp. 150-156; C. Wilcke, RA 77 (1983), p. 93; J.M. Sasson, in: Mém. NABU 3, Paris 1994, p. 308

סבור, כנראה בצדק, שהכוונה ליין; ואכן נראה שהדברים אמורים במשקה אלכוהולי (למשל שיכר), כדי ליצור אווירה הולמת להתעוררות נבואית.

מקרה דומה מצוי בכרך כו,1, מס' 212.[21] כאן מובאת תשובת שיבתו לבעלה בדבר אורקולום לגבי חמורבי, מלך בבל. שיבתו מכריזה: 'בנוגע לבבל השקיתי את האותות וחקרתי בעניין. האיש הלה (חמורבי) זומם דברים רבים נגד ארץ זו, אך הוא לא יצלח' (שורות 1'–2'). אף כאן מדובר בהשקאת נוזל, שאפשר מכיל בתוכו את ה'אותות', היינו האירועים לעתיד לבוא, מבלי שפורטו נושאי הבשורה בניגוד לנבואה הקודמת.

עם כל ההבדלים שבין החזון בדבר האכלת המגילה מידי האל בספר יחזקאל ומצד אחר של השקאת גבר ואשה בידי בשר ודם בנבואות מארי, הרי בשני המקרים המעשים התמוהים משמשים כעין סטימולנטים להתעוררות נבואית.[22]

---

21   עמ' 41–440.

22   מאמר זה מכיל סוגיות 7–9 בנושא 'הנבואות החדשות ממארי ונבואת המקרא'. לסוגיות הקודמות עיין ספרי היובל לכבוד סוג'ין (לעיל, הערה 2); ז' הרמן (1991); אנדרסון (A. Malamat, in: Understanding Poets and Prophets, Essays in Honour of G.W. Anderson, ed. A.G. Auld [JSOTSup. 152, Sheffield 1993]; וכן (NABU, 1989, pp. 61-65, nos. 88, 89). מראי המקומות ראה בספר היובל לאנדרסון, עמ' 241.

התהוות הלשונות בעולם והתפתחותן: ההשקפה
השומרית וההשקפה המקראית

יעקב קליין

אוניברסיטת בר-אילן

'אכן רוח היא באנוש ונשמת שדי תבינם' (איוב לב, ח)

למשה, איש הרוח, מורה דרך לרבים בנתיבות המקרא והיהדות

1. התהוות הלשונות בעולם לפי ההשקפה המקראית (בר' יא, א־יא)

אחד הנסיונות העתיקים ביותר לבאר את התופעה של ריבוי הלשונות בעולם[1] מצוי בפרשת מגדל
בבל בספר בראשית (יא, א־ט). הפרשה פותחת בתיאור המצב בעולם לפני האירוע הזה:

'ויהי כל הארץ שפה אחת ודברים אחדים' (א). הואיל וכל בני האדם מוצאם מאדם הראשון
ומבני נח (פרק י), בימי קדם דיברו שפה אחת, כלומר לשון אחת.[2] אין הכתוב מפרש איזו
לשון הם דיברו. ידועה השקפת חז"ל כי כולם דיברו עברית.[3] אין השערה זו רחוקה מן
הפשט, ואפשר שהיא מרומזת באטימולוגיה העממית 'לזאת יקרא אשה כי מאיש לֻקֳחה זאת'

---

1   הבלשנות, לפי אחת ההגדרות האחרונות (ראה חיים רוזן, 'בלשנות,' האנציקלופדיה העברית, ח, 1956, טור 958
    ואילך), עוסקת בהכרתן, בזיהוין ובריישומן של לשונות, בין שהן עתיקות ומתות, בין שהן חיות. בעיית ההתהוות
    של לשון האדם, שאלת העדרה של לשון אחת לכל המין האנושי והופעת הריבוי של לשונות בתוכו – אינן
    מעניינה של הבלשנות. הסירוב לעסוק בהן מיוסד על ההנחה שאין לפתור בעיות אלו בדרך מדעית, מאחר
    שפתרונן מחייב מחיי ידיעות וחישובים שהם מחוץ לשדה הראייה של הכרתנו. ניצניה של הבלשנות הפרימיטיבית
    ניכרים דווקא בגלוטוכרונולוגיה (או 'גלוטוגוניה' בלשונו של רוזן), כגון הסיפור המקראי על מגדל בבל, שבא
    להסביר את ריבוי הלשונות. צורה עתיקה אחרת של הבלשנות היא ההתעסקות באטימולוגיה העממית, הכוללת
    בין השאר גם מדרשי שמות. יחסם של העמים הקדומים לענייני לשון היה יחס של 'עם סגולה', שראה בלשונו
    שלו את הלשון האנושית הטבעית, ואילו את לשונותיהם של העמים האחרים ראה כתופעות בלתי טבעיות.

2   מיעוטם של הפרשנים מוציאים את הביטוי 'שפה אחת' מפשוטו, ומפרשים אותו במובן מושאל: דעה אחת. כוונתם
    לאחדות דעות והרמוניה. יש הנוקטים פירוש מאולץ זה כדי להסביר את קיומן של האומות השונות לפני דור
    הפלגה (פרק י); אחרים מונעים על-ידי שיקולים פרשניים זרים, שאין להם אחיזה בכתוב (ראה להלן, הערה 21).

3   רש"י, דבה"מ 'שפה אחת': לשון הקודש. והשווה תרגום ירושלמי: 'בלישן קודשא הוו ממללין דבה אתברי עלמא
    מן שרויא'.

(בר' ב, כג)[4]; וכן במדרש השם 'ויקרא האדם שם אשתו חוה כי היא היתה אם כל חי' (ג, כ).[5]
לביטוי 'דברים אחדים' הוצעו פירושים שונים, רובם דחוקים.[6] שני הפירושים הנראים לי
קרובים ביותר אל הפשט הם: (א) באו בעצה אחת (רש"י) – היינו לא רק דיברו באותה שפה,
אלא היתה ביניהם אחדות דעות והשקפות גמורה. אולי אפשר למצוא רמז לפירוש זה בצפניה
(ג, ט), המנבא כי בניגוד למצב בהווה, שבו האומות מדברות שבעים לשון ושונות זו מזו
בדעותיהן, במנהגיהן, בדתן ובהשקפת עולמן, באחרית הימים יהיה המצב הפוך: 'כי אז
אהפך אל עמים שפה ברורה לקרא כלם בשם ה' לעבדו שכם אחד'.[7] (ב) לפי דעה אחרת
(קאסוטו ומפרשים אחרים), יש כאן תקבולת נרדפת: 'שפה אחת' – אותה לשון, 'ודברים
אחדים' – אותן מלים.[8]

'ויהי בנסעם מקדם וימצאו בקעה בארץ שנער' (ב). זירת ההתרחשות היא דרום מסופוטמיה,
מה שכונה בסוף האלף השלישי ובתחילת האלף השני לפני הספירה: שומר ואכד.[9]

'ונעשה לנו שם פן נפוץ על פני כל הארץ' (ד). בביטוי 'ונעשה לנו שם' הכוונה, כנראה,

---

4   רש"י: 'לשון נופל על לשון, מכאן שנברא העולם בלשון הקודש'. השווה ב"ר פי"ח ו: 'מכאן שניתנה תורה
בלה"ק. ר' פנחס ור' חלקיה בשם ר' סימון אמרי: כשם שניתנה תורה בלה"ק, כן נברא העולם בלה"ק'. שמעת
מימיך אומר: גיני – גינא, אנתרופי – אנתרופיא, גברא – גברתא? אלא איש ואישה. למה, שהלשון הזה נופל
על הלשון הזה'. לדיון בפסוק זה, ראה לאחרונה S.A. Meier, 'Linguistic Clues on the Date and Canaanite
Origin of Genesis 2:23-24', *CBQ* 53 (1991) pp. 18-24. אפשר שהצדק עם מאייר, הטוען שהאטימולוגיה
העממית, הקושרת 'איש' עם 'אשה', מקורה במסורת כנענית. אולם השערתו שסופית הנקבה (ֶ ה) נתפסה אצל
הקדמונים כה"א המגמה (he locale), אינה מתקבלת על הדעת; שהרי הצורה הכנענית ל'אשה' היא: אשת.

5   המקורות העיקריים במדרשים, הרואים בביטוי 'שפה אחת' את לשון הקודש, נאספו בידי לוי גינצבורג בספרו
אגדות היהודים; ראה מהדורה עברית בתרגום ובעריכת הרב מרדכי הכהן, רמת־גן תשכ"ו, עמ' 253. למובאות
מבראשית רבה, מתרגום ניאופיטי ומתרגום ירושלמי, ראה מאמרם של א' אשל ומ' סטון, 'לשון הקודש באחרית
הימים לאור קטע מקומראן', *תרביץ* סב (תשנ"ג), עמ' 169–177. השווה עוד ירושלמי, מגילה פ"א ה"יא, שם
נחלקים ר' לעזר ור' יוחנן בשאלה מהי 'שפה אחת': 'חד אמר שהיו מדברים בשבעים לשון, וחורנה אמר שהיו
מדברים בלשון יחידו של עולם, בלשון הקודש'.

6   לדעת הראב"ע, למשל, הביטוי מלמד כי דברי חכם וכסיל היו אחדים, כלומר: לא היו מֻשלבים שונים בלשון
אותו הדור. פירושים אחרים: 'שפה אחת' – מלים שוות, 'דברים אחדים' – ביטויים שווים, או אוצר מילים
מצומצם (אהרליך), ועוד.

7   אמנם, לדעת רוב המפרשים הביטוי 'שפה ברורה' בפי צפניה אינו מציין בפירוש שמדובר בשפה אחת, ושהיא
הלשון העברית. לפירושים השונים שניתנו לביטוי זה, ראה לאחרונה מ' בולה, ספר צפניה, תרי עשר ב (פירוש
'דעת מקרא'), ירושלים תשל"ז, עמ' כג; A. Berlin, *Zephaniah* (AB), Garden City NY 1994, p. 133. לאור
ההנחה הנפוצה כי מדובר בשפה בהירה, מובנת (השווה איוב לג, ג; ישעיה לג, יט; יח' ג, ה-ו), נראה לי הפירוש
שמביא ראב"ע בשם רבי משה: 'יתהפכו לעבוד ה' לבדו בשפה ברורה, שבה לבדה נקרא ה'
הנכבד'. וכך נתפרש פסוק זה גם בטקסט המקוטע מקומראן, Q464‏4, שפורסם בידי א' אשל ומ' סטון (ראה לעיל,
הערה 5). אם נכון שחזורם של המהדירים, הרי לדעת מחברו דיברה כל האנושות מיום בריאתה ועד אחרי המבול
'לשון הקודש'. בעקבות בלבול הלשונות בדור הפלגה, נשתכחה לשון הקודש מפי הבריות, וה' גילה לשון זו
מחדש לאברהם, כדי שילמדה לבניו. באחרית הימים, ה' יהפך לעמים 'שפה ברורה', וכולם ישובו לדבר בלשון
הקודש.

8   לתקבולת בין המושגים 'שפה', 'לשון' ו'דברים', השווה יח' ג, ו: 'עמים רבים עמקי שפה וכבדי לשון אשר לא
תשמע דבריהם'.

9   לא מן הנמנע כי 'שנער' הוא גלגול מאוחר של הביטוי השומרי Kengir, בכתב הברתי (r)-Ke-en-gi, באכדית
Šumeru(m), שבו ציינו השומרים את ארצם. לדעות השונות באשר למקור השם 'שנער', ראה לאחרונה פ' ארצי,
א"מ ח, טור 227–228; R.W. Nysse, ABD 5, p. 1220.

לפרסום. כל מפעל בנייה ענקי היה מביא לבוניו פרסום, תחושת גאווה לאומית־קיבוצית, והיה בו משום כוח מלכד ומאחד.[10] כך הם רצו להמרות את רצון ה' שיפוצו על פני כל הארץ. יש כאן רמז לאידיאולוגיה אימפריאליסטית – לשלטון מרכזי אחד על כל העולם. התורה, לעומת זאת, מחייבת עצמאות לעמים הקטנים, ודוגלת בארגון האומות בעולם במסגרות קטנות.[11]

'וירד ה' לראת את העיר ואת המגדל... הבה נרדה ונבלה שם שפתם אשר לא ישמעו איש שפת רעהו' (ה–ז). מוסכם על החוקרים כי הכפילות של הירידה ('וירד' ו'הבה נרדה') מצביעה על שני מקורות שונים שהסיפור מורכב מהם. לדעת קאסוטו, לעומת זאת, פסוק ה ('וירד ה' לראות...') מתאר את עצם הירידה, ואילו פסוקים ו–ז ('ויאמר ה'... הבה נרדה' וגו') מתארים את מחשבותיו של ה' בעת שירד למטה לבלבל את לשון בני האדם (ה).[12]

'ויפץ ה' אותם משם על פני כל הארץ' (ח). כתוצאה מבלבול הלשונות, נפוצו הגויים על פני כל הארץ.

'על כן קרא שמה בבל כי שם בלל ה' שפת כל הארץ ומשם הפיצם ה' על פני כל הארץ' (ט). זהו מדרש־שם עממי, הגוזר את השם 'בבל' מן השורש בל"ל; השווה למשל המדרש הגוזר את שמו של 'נח' מן השורש נח"ם (בר' ה, כט), או 'שמואל' מן השורש שא"ל (שמ"א א, כ).[13] שם העיר באכדית: Babili. הבבלים עצמם האמינו ששם עירם מורכב משתי מלים: Bāb-ili 'שער האל' או 'שער האלים'. אולם החוקרים משערים שכבר אטימולוגיה זו היא עממית ושגויה, וכי מקור השם לא ידוע, ואינו לא שוּמרי ולא שמי.[14]

דיון מפורט בסוגיות של מבנה הפרשה, מקורותיה, מקבילותיה, גלגולי התהוותה ותולדות הפרשנות בתוספת ביבליוגרפיה מקיפה – ניתן למצוא בפירושם המונומנטלי של וסטרמן על בראשית א–יא משנת 1974;[15] וכן במחקרו המקיף והחדיש של אהלינגר, שנתייחד כולו לפרשתנו

10   ראה פירושו של וסטרמן על בראשית C. Westermann, *Genesis* I, 1974 (BKAT I/1), p. 729ff. והשווה הביטוי השומרי mu-ḡar, והביטוי האכדי המקביל (ראה) *šuma(m) šakānu(m)* ;CAD Š/1, p. 143f.; Š/3, p. 293; AHw 1275a), מילולית: 'לשים/לייסד שם'. בספרות המסופוטמית, ביטויים אלה מתייחסים בדרך כלל למלכים אינדיווידואליים, שביקשו להנציח את שמם במפעלי בנייה גדולים. ראה לאחרונה אהלינגר .Ch Uehlinger, *Weltreich und 'eine Rede': eine neue Deutung der sogenannten Turmbauerzählung (Gen 11, 1-9)*, Orbis Biblicus et Orientalis 101, Freiburg 1990, pp. 386ff.; 448ff.

11   על כל פנים במה שנוגע לעם ישראל. ראה במיוחד דב' לב, ח–יב (עם גרסת השבעים לפס' ח: 'למספר בני אל' תמורת 'למספר בני ישראל'). גם אהלינגר סבור כי הפרשה ביסודה נכתבה כפולמוס אידיאולוגי נגד האימפריאליזם האשורי. עם זאת, אין להתעלם מן הרעיון המיתולוגי העתיק המשתקף בפרשה, שלפיו האל חושש מן האדם, המבקש להתחרות בו (ראה גם פס' ו 'ועתה לא יבצר מהם כל אשר יזמו לעשות').

12   מ"ד קאסוטו, מנח עד אברהם, ירושלים תשי"ט, עמ' 167–168.

13   למחקר מקיף של מדרשי השמות שבמקרא, ראה לאחרונה M. Garsiel, *Biblical Names: A Literary Study of Midrashic Derivations and Puns*, Ramat Gan 1991, עמ' 15; 18; 32. גרסיאל דן גם במשחק המילים על העיצורים בל"ל, נבל"ה, שבאמצעותם מביע הכתוב את הרעיון של מידה כנגד מידה, שעמדו עליו כבר קאסוטו ואחרים (ראה שם, עמ' 248–250). למדרש אחר על השם בבל במקרא, ראה יר' נא, מד (גרסיאל, שם, עמ' 77). למדרשים אחרים על הפסוק שלפנינו השווה סנהד' כד ע"א; קז ע"ב; איכה רבה פל"א ועוד.

14   לאטימולוגיה של השם Babili, ראה p. 333 ,2 *Reallexikon der Assyriologie*; א"ל אופנהיים, אנציקלופדיה מקראית ב, טור 10, הערך 'בבל'.   15   ראה: וסטרמן (לעיל, הערה 10), פפף 707–740.

ושהופיע בשנת 1990.[16] החוקרים שעסקו בניתוח הספרותי של הפרשה עמדו על המבנה הסימטרי שלה. הפרשה מתחלקת לשני חלקים שווים: מצד אחד מעשיהם ויוזמתם של בני האדם (פס' א–ד), ומצד שני תגובת ה' (פס' ה–ח) וההערה האטיולוגית על מקור השם בבל (פס' ט). כמו כן, הצביעו על המבנה הכיאסטי הכמעט מושלם של שני החלקים.[17] לאור ממצאים אלה, חוקרים אחדים, ביניהם קאסוטו, טוענים לאחדותה הספרותית של הפרשה. אולם, כבר גונקל ערער על אחדות זו וניסה להפריד את הפרשה לשני מקורות – מקור אחד שנושאו היה בניית עיר, ומקור שני שנושאו היה בניית המגדל, וחוקרים רבים הלכו בעקבותיו. קאסוטו, ספייזר ואחרים טוענים, לעומת זאת, כי העיר והמגדל הם הנדיאדיון, וכי במסופוטמיה שני המושגים קשורים זה בזה, ולכן אין להפרידם בפרשתנו. ווסטרמן אמנם מקבל גישה זו, אך הוא סבור כי פרשתנו עברה גלגולים רבים ועריכות ממושכות, ונשתמרו בה שלושה מוטיבים שונים ועצמאיים: (א) מוטיב בניית עיר ומגדל בידי בני האדם, במטרה לעלות לשמים – מעשה שנחשב למרד באל ושנסתיים בגירסה המקורית בהריסת המגדל בידי האל; (ב) מוטיב הפצת האנושות על פני הארץ, לגוייהם וללשונותם, הנזכר כבר בפרקים ט–י כסיום לפרשת המבול (השווה ט, יט; י, ה, יח, כ, כה, לב); (ג) מוטיב בלבול הלשונות. בעוד מוטיב בניית המגדל הענק הוא סיפור סגור בפני עצמו, הרי מוטיב הפצת האנושות ומוטיב בלבול הלשונות קשורים זה בזה קשר הדוק, ואין לדעת מה קדם למה. לפי פרקים ט–י, הפצת האנושות קדמה כנראה לבלבול הלשונות, והיא גולת הכותרת של סיפור המבול. לפי פרשתנו, לעומת זאת, בלבול הלשונות קדם, והוא שגרם להפצת בני האדם בעולם. לדעתי, ניתן לבאר סתירה זו על־פי הכלל של 'אין מוקדם ומאוחר בתורה': בפרק י צייר הכתוב את מפת תפוצת העמים בימיו, ובפרשת העיר והמגדל הוא מבאר את השתלשלות העניינים שהביאה למצב זה.

אשר לרקע המסופוטמי של הסיפור, נהגו לראות בו לעג לבבל או פולמוס נגדה. יש שראו בו פולמוס נגד אמונתם של הבבלים בחשיבותו, בנצחיותו של מקדש מרדוך בבבל, האסגילה (בשומרית é-saǧ-íla) שמשמעו 'בית־ירים־ראש'; ויש שראו בו לעג על מגדל הקודש (ziqqurratu) של בבל, הלא הוא האתמננכי (בשומרית é-temen-an-ki, 'בית־יסוד־שמים־וארץ'), אשר לפי דעה אחת בנה אותו נבוכדנאצר הראשון, במאה ה־י"ב לפני הספירה. ידוע כי בנייתו של מגדל זה הופסקה כמה פעמים, עד שהושלמה בידי נבוכדנאצר השני, במאה השישית לפני הספירה. אולם, אין כל ביטחון בכך שהאתמננכי כבר היה קיים בימי מחבר פרשתנו, שכן העדות העקיפה הראשונה לזיקורת זה מצוי באפוס של אירה, המתוארך למחצית השנייה של המאה השמינית,[18] ואילו לכל הדעות המקור המקראי נתחבר הרבה לפני תאריך זה.[19] ווסטרמן (עמ' 726), בעקבות ספייזר,[20] מניח כי הרקע לתיאור של בניין המגדל בפרשתנו הוא התיאור הספרותי של בניין מקדש האסגילה למרדוך, באנומה אליש (לוח שישי, שו' 64–57), ותיאורים דומים של בניין מקדשים במסופוטמיה. עם זאת, אין ווסטרמן מוציא מכלל אפשרות שהסיפור מבוסס לא רק על תיאורים

16 לעיל, הערה 10. לביקורת מעמיקה על מחקרו של אהלינגר ראה: A. van der Kooij, 'The Story of Genesis 11:1-9 and the Culture of Ancient Mesopotamia', OLZ 53 (1996), pp. 28-38

17 השווה לאחרונה ניתוחה המעולה של י' אבישור, אנציקלופדיה עולם התנ"ך, בראשית, תל־אביב תשמ"ב, עמ' 82.

18 לביקורת של בבל ראה לאחרונה Evelyn Klengel-Brandt, Der Turm von Babylon, Wien 1982, p. 87

19 לדעת ווסטרמן (לעיל, הערה 10), מקור J, שפרשתנו נובעת ממנו, נתחבר בסביבות המאה העשירית לפני הספירה.

20 ראה E.A. Speiser, Or 25 (1955), pp. 317-323; idem, Genesis (AB), Garden City 1964, pp. 75-76

ספרותיים של המגדלים במסופוטמיה, כי אם גם על תיאורים ריאליים של המונומנטים
המסופוטמיים, מפי עדי ראייה או עדי שמיעה.[21]

כאמור, החוקרים חיפשו ומצאו רקע מסופוטמי לפרשת בניין המגדל. אולם עבר זמן רב לפני
שעמדו על המקבילה המסופוטמית למוטיב של בלבול הלשונות. במקרה זה, קרמר הוא שהיה
בבחינת 'החלוץ היוצא לפני המחנה'. כבר בשנת 1943, כעשר שנים לפני שחזורו ופרסומו של
האפוס 'אֶנְמֶרְכַּר ואדון אַרַתָּה', הרגיש קרמר באינטואיציה כי 'הלחש של נודימוד', המצוטט בשורות
136 ואילך של אפוס זה, מתאר את 'תור הזהב של האנושות', התקופה שבה עדיין דיברו בני האדם
לשון אחת, וכי הלחש הזה מהווה מקבילה קרובה ביותר לבראשית יא, א-ט.[22] אולם, מפאת מצבו
המקוטע של הטקסט, ששוחזר במאמרו הנ"ל של קרמר, לא שמו לב חוקרי המקרא למקבילה זו
כלל.[23] רק בשנת 1968 נתגלה שבר הלוח מאוקספורד, אשר בעזרתו ניתן לשחזר את הסוף המקוטע
של הלחש הנדון, ובעקבות גילויו זה עלה בידו של קרמר להציע תרגום משוכלל של המקבילה
השומרית לפרשתנו.[24] ואמנם, וסטרמן, בפירושו שיצא לאור ב-1974, כבר מכיר בחשיבותה של
המקבילה הזו לפרשתנו, ומייחד לה דיון השוואתי קצר.[25]

מאז פרסום מאמרו המכריע של קרמר, בשנת 1968, הופיעו לא פחות מעשרה פירושים ותרגומים
חדשים של המקבילה השומרית הנ"ל.[26] מרביתם מאששים באופן כללי את תרגומו ופירושו של

---

21   מבין המחקרים החדשים העוסקים ברקע המסופוטמי של פרשתנו ראוי לציין במיוחד את אהלינגר (לעיל, הערה
      10). לדעתו (שם, עמ' 291 ואילך), הפרשה בנוסח שלפנינו היא תוצאה של שלוש עריכות ספרותיות. גרעין
      הסיפור הוא תגובה של סופר יהודאי למות סרגון השני בשדה הקרב, מוות שהשבית באופן פתאומי את בניית
      בירתו החדשה, Dūr-Šarrukīn, שנועדה לשמש בירה לאימפריה שתשלוט על כל העולם. המחבר ראה באירוע
      זה סיכול אלוהי של שאיפת האשורים לייסד ממלכה עולמית. בזמן מאוחר יותר, בעקבות מפעלי הבנייה הענקיים
      של נבוכדנאצר השני, הועתק הסיפור אל העיר בבל, והפך לסאטירה על בירתה של ממלכה זו. כמו כן, תוך
      שילובו בהיסטוריה הקדומה, הפך הסיפור לחלק מתולדות האנושות בימי קדם. לבסוף, עברה הפרשה עיבוד נוסף
      בתקופה הפרסית וקיבלה אופי של סיפור תיאולוגי-פוליטי: אטיולוגיה המסבירה את התהוות הסדר העולמי,
      המאופיין בריבוי עמים ולשונות. כדי להוכיח את התזה המורכבת הזו, מוציא אהלינגר את הביטוי 'שפה אחת'
      מפשוטו; הוא מוצא הקבלה בין הביטוי הזה לביטוי האכדי pû(m) ištēn, 'פה אחד', השכיח בכתובות מלכותיות
      ממסופוטמיה והמבטא אידיאולוגיה אימפריאליסטית (ראה לעיל, הערה 2). קונספציה פרשנית זו הוא מנסה
      לכפות גם על 'לחש נודימוד', שהוא המקבילה השומרית המובהקת ביותר למוטיב של בלבול הלשונות שבפרשתנו
      (ראה להלן). מחקר חדש ביותר של א"ר ג'ורג' על הטקסטים מאורוך העוסקים בתכנית ובמידות מקדשו של
      מרדוך בבבל, האסגילה (ראה A.R. George, 'The Bricks of E-sagil', Iraq 57 [1995], pp. 173-197),
      מוכיח כי מקדש זה נהנה מיוקרה גדולה ומפרסום רב עוד בתקופה הפרסית. לדעת ג'ורג', גיליון של טקסטים
      אלה באורוך מוכיח שכוהני עיר זו, בבקשם להאדיר את פולחנו של האל אנו ולבנות לו את 'מקדש הראש'
      (Bīt-rēš), בנו אותו על-פי התכנית והמידות של מקדש האסגילה בבבל.

22   S.N. Kramer, 'Man's Golden Age: A Sumerian Parallel to Genesis XI,1', JAOS 63 (1943), השווה
      pp. 191-194

23   קאסוטו (לעיל, הערה 12), למשל, כותב כי אף-על-פי שרקע הסיפור הוא מסופוטמי, אין לו הקבלה בספרות
      המסופוטמית (ראה שם, עמ' 155). גם ספייזר, שפירושו על בראשית יצא לאור ב-1964, מתעלם כליל מן
      המקבילה השומרית (ראה עמ' 74–76 בפירושו).

24   שבר הלוח נמצא ב-Ashmolean Museum וסימונו הוא Ash. 1924.475. השווה 'The "Babel of
      Tongues": A Sumerian Version', JAOS 88 (1968) (Essays in Memory of E.A. Speiser), pp. 108-111

25   ראה פירושו, עמ' 717–718.

26   להלן רשימת הפירושים והתרגומים, לפי סדר הופעתם: ג'סטן 1957 (R. Jestin, 'Le poème d'En-me-er-kar',
      Revue de l'histoire des religions 151 [1957], pp. 145-220); ון-דייק 1970 (J.A. van Dijk, 'La confusion'

קרמר לטקסט הזה, חוץ משלושה מהם: מחקריהם של אלסטר, קומורוצי וונסטיפהוט. הללו מפרשים
את הטקסט הנדון כך שאי־אפשר להקבילו לבר' יא, א–ט.[27]

הגם שקשה להסכים עם מסקנותיהם של אלסטר וונסטיפהוט בנוגע למקבילה הנ"ל, יש ערך
מה למאמריהם, באשר הם מצביעים על הקשיים הלשוניים והפרשניים העומדים בפני מי שמנסה
להבין את הטקסט השומרי הנדון. בכוונתי לדון להלן בקשיים אלה, ולהציע כמה פתרונות חדשים־
ישנים אשר, כך אני מקווה, יכריעו בין עמדתם של אלסטר וונסיטפהוט מזה לבין עמדתם של קרמר
והחוקרים האחרים מזה.

2. 'הלחש של נודימוד' ('אֶנְמֶרְכַּר ואדון אַרַתָּה', שו' 134–155)

להלן יובא המקור השומרי שיש בו משום מקבילה לבר' יא, א–ט, ואשר נוהגים לכנות 'הלחש של
נודימוד', ותרגומו לעברית. התרגום מבוסס על עבודותיהם של כל החוקרים שהקדימוני, בצירוף
תיקונים קלים משלי, תיקונים שאצביע עליהם בהערות. לאחר מכן אדון בבעיה העיקרית, והיא
המשמעות הכללית והמסר של הקטע הנדון. ההקשר שהקטע הזה משולב בו הוא כדלהלן: אנמרכר,
מלך ארך, עיר עתיקה ומרכזית בדרום שומר, מבקש לבנות מקדש מפואר לאלה אינַנּה, פטרונית
העיר ואהובתו בפולחן 'נישואי הקודש'. בעירו קיים קיים מחסור באבנים ובמתכות יקרות, הנחוצות
למפעל, וכן באומנים מונחים. אנמרכר מחליט לדרוש ממושל ארתה, עיר רחוקה בהרי עילם,
שזהותה אינה ידועה, להיכנע לו ולספק לו חינם את החומרים הנחוצים, וכן לשלוח לו אומנים (או
פועלים) שיבנו למענו את המקדש. לשם כך הוא משגר אל מושל ארתה ('אדון ארתה') שליח מיומן,
ומצווה עליו לאיים על המושל, שאם לא ייענה לדרישתו, הוא ייצא נגדו למלחמה ויחריב את עירו.
לחיזוק השליחות, ולמען תת תוקף לדבריו, הוא מצווה על השליח לומר באוזני מושל ארתה את
'הלחש של נודימוד', הוא אֶנְכִּי, אל החכמה והמאגיה, פטרון הלחשים וההשבעות. הפיסקה שבה
נזכר לחש זה מהווה, אפוא, את סוף דברי השליחות הראשונה, שאנמרכר צווה לשליחו למסור
למושל ארתה:[28]

S. Cohen, 'Enmerkar and the Lord of Aratta',) 1973 כהן ;(langues', *Or* 39 [1970], pp. 302-310

B. Alster, 'An Aspect of 'Enmerkar and the) 1973 אלסטר ;(Diss. Philadelphia 1973, pp. 70-71

O.E. Gurney, 'A Note on the Babel) 1977–1974 גורני ;(Lord of Aratta', *RA* 67 [1973], pp. 101-109

B. Alster, 'Dilmun, Bahrain, and the) 1983 אלסטר ;(of Tongues', *AfO* 25 [1977], pp. 170-171
Alleged Paradise in Sumerian Myth and Literature', in D.T. Potts (ed.), *Dilmun, New Studies in*
G. Komoróczy,) 1983 קומורוצי ;(the *Archaeology and Early History of Bahrain*, 1983, pp. 39-74

W.W. Hallo, *The*) 1991 הלו ;('Fénylö Olednek édes örömében...', Budapest 1983, pp. 132f.; 419

Th. Jacobsen, *The Harps that Once...: Sumerian*) 1987 יעקובסן ;(*Book of the People*, 1991, pp. 123-124

Idem, 'The Spell of) 1992 יעקובסן ;(*Poetry in Translation*, New Haven 1987, pp. 288-290
Nudimmud', in M. Fishbein et al. (eds.), *Studies in the Bible, Qumran and the Ancient Near East*

H.L.J. Vanstiphout, 'Another) 1994 וונסטיפהוט ;(*Presented to Shemaryahu Talmon*, 1992, pp. 403-416
ראה עוד אהלינגר (לעיל, הערה .Attempt at the "Spell of Nudimmud"', *RA* 88 [1994], pp. 135-154

10), עמ' 409–429, שם מובא דיון מפורט ב'לחש נודימוד' וביחסו אל פרשתנו.

27   ראה אלסטר 1973; הנ"ל 1983; קומורוצי 1983; וונסטיפהוט 1994.

28   למהדורה הראשונה של האפוס, ראה S.N. Kramer, *Enmerkar and the Lord of Aratta*, Philadelphia 1952.

134   agrun-agrun-ba šìr-kù nam-šub du_{12}-a-ba

135   nam-šub ^{d}nu-dím-mud-da-kam e-ne-ra dug_4-mu-na-ab

136   **u_4 ba** muš nu-ğál(-la)-àm ğír nu-ğál(-la)-àm

137   kir_4 nu-ğál(-la)-àm ur-maḫ nu-ğál(-la)-àm

138   $ur-gi_7$ ur-bar-ra nu-ğál(-la)-àm

139   ní-te-ğá(-e) su-zi-zi(-i) nu-ğál(-la)-àm

140   lú-u_{18}(-lu) gaba-šu-ğar nu-tuku(-àm)

141   **u_4-ba** kur šubur^{ki} ḫa-ma-zi^{ki}

142   eme-ḫa-mun ke-en-gi kur-gal me-nam-num-na-ka(m)

143   ki-uri kur me-te ğál-la(-àm)

144   kur mar-tu ú-sal-la ná-a

145   an-ki niğin-na un sağ sì-ga

146   ^{d}en-líl-ra eme dili-àm ḫé-en-na-da-ab-dug_4

147   **u_4-ba** a-da-en a-da-nun a-da-lugal-la

148   ^{d}en-ki a-da-en a-da-nun a-da-lugal-la

149   a-da-en-(n)e a-da-nun-n[e] a-da-lugal-la

150   ^{d}en-ki en ḫé-ğál-la ([e]n) du_{11}-ga zi(-da)

151   en $ğeštu_2$-ga igi-ğál kalam-ma-ke_4

152   mas-su diğir-re-e-ne-ke_4

153   $ğeštu_2$-ge pà-da en eridu^{ki}-ga-ke_4

154   ka-ba eme ì-kúr en-na mi-ni(-in)-ğar-ra

155   eme nam-lú-lu_7 dili ì-me-a (var. ì-me-⌜àm⌝)

---

134   'בכל מקדשיה (=של ארתה), שם ייאמרו שירי קודש, לחשים,

135   את 'לחש (האל) נודימוד' הגד לו!'[29]

למהדורה מתוקנת, ראה כהן 1973. לתרגומים חדישים של האפוס ראה קומורוצי 1983, עמ' 151–129; יעקובסן 1987, עמ' 275–319. למחקרים ולתרגומים השונים של הקטע שלפנינו, ראה לעיל, הערה 26. הטקסט ערוך להלן על־פי מבנהו הספרותי, הכולל: מבוא (שו' 135–134) ושלושה חלקים, שכל אחד מהם נפתח בפתיחה האחידה והבעייתית u_4-ba, 'בימים ההם' (שו' 136, 141, 147). אני מצטט את הטקסט בצורתו המקובצת, בלי ציון חילופי הגרסאות בין כתבי־היד, שאינם משמעותיים, לדעתי. הקורא יכול למצוא מהדורה חדישה של הטקסט, עם חילופי גרסאות, אצל יעקובסן 1992, עמ' 139–136; ופרטיטורה מלאה של העותקים אצל ונסטיפהוט 1994, עמ' 139–136. יש לציין כי המהדורה החלקית של ונסטיפהוט מבוססת על הגהות, והיא נותנת לנו את הטקסט המדויק ביותר של המקור (ראה עמ' 136, הערה 11 במאמרו).

29   השורות 135–134 הן לכל הדעות דברי אנמרכר לשליחו. תרגמתי אותן על־פי אלסטר. כהן מתרגם: 'את שיר הקודש, הלחש, אשר ייאמר במקדשיה, לחש נודימוד, הגד לו (לאמור):' יעקובסן (1987) מתרגם: 'בכל מקדשיה אמור שירי קודש ולחשים, הגד לו את לחש נודימוד:' הנ"ל (1992) מתרגם: 'וכאשר בכל מקדשיהם יאמרו שירי

136   בימים ההם, (כאשר) נחש לא היה, עקרב לא היה,

137   צבוע[30] לא היה, אריה לא היה,

138   כלב וזאב לא היו,[31]

139   פחד ואימה לא היו,

140   לא קם שטן לבני אנוש[32] –

141   בימים ההם, ארצות שובור וחַמַזי,[33]

142   שומֵר 'תאומת הלשון',[34] ארץ־חוקות־המלכות הגדולה,

143   אכד, הארץ מלאת ההדר,

144   וארץ האמורי, הרובצת (לבטח) בנאות דשא,

145   שמים וארץ יחדיו, כל יושבי תבל –

146   דברו אל (האל) אנליל בלשון אחת.

147   בימים ההם, האדון המתחרה, הנסיך המתחרה, המלך המתחרה,

148   (האל) אֶנכי, האדון המתחרה, הנסיך המתחרה, המלך המתחרה,

149   האדון המתחרה, הנסיך המתחרה, המלך המתחרה,[35]

קודש ולחשים, הגד לו לחש זה של נודי־למוד:' בניגוד לפיסוק הנוכחי, כל החוקרים, כולל אלסטר, שמים נקודתים אחר שו' 135, בהניחם כי 'לחש נודימוד' מצוטט בסמוך, בשו' 136–155.

30   המילה השומרית kir₄ מקבילה במילונים למילה האכדית *būṣu* 'צבוע', בשיכול אותיות (המונח העברי מופיע לראשונה בבן־סירה).

31   הכלב המבית נקרא בשומרית 'החיה האצילה' (ur-gi₇); הזאב – 'חית הבר' (ur-bar-ra), והאריה – "החיה הגדולה" (ur-maḫ). בשורות 137–138 יש אפוא משחק על המילה ur 'חיה'.

32   מילולית "לא לא היה לבני אנוש מתנגד".

33   אזורים הרריים מצפון לשומר. שובור – איזור הפרת עד כרכוך; חַמַזי – אזור ממזרח לחידקל, בין הזָב העליון והדיאלה.

34   הביטוי eme-ḫa-mun (שו' 142), שתרגומו האכדי במילונים ובטקסטים דו־לשוניים הוא צירוף הסמיכות: lišān
mithurti הוא דו־משמעי. הסומך *mithurti* נגזר מן הפועל *mithurum* (בניין Gt של *maḫārum*), שמשמעו 'לעמוד מול', ויכול להתפרש כעניין של התנגדות (לשון מנוגדת) או כעניין של הרמוניה ('לשון תואמת'). קרמר (1943) מסב את הביטוי על שומֵר, ומתרגם: 'harmony-tongued Sumer(?)'. הוא סובר כנראה, שהשומרים ראו את לשונם כלשון החלקה והברורה, כלומר כלשון 'עם סגולה'. אולם במהדורתו הראשונה של האפוס משנת 1952 (ראה לעיל, הערה 28), הוא תרגם 'שומר הרב־לשונית' (Many-tongued Sumer). אחרים מתלבטים אם הביטוי מוסב על הארצות הנזכרות לפניו (שובור וחַמַזי) או על הארצות הנזכרות אחריו (שומר, אכד וארץ האמורי); ואם הכוונה ל'לשון הרמונית' או ל'לשון דיסהרמונית' (ראה החוקרים הנזכרים בהערה 26 לעיל; השווה עוד A. Sjöberg, *The Collection of the Sumerian Temple Hymns*, Locust Valley 1969, p. 83; CAD
(M/2, 173, sub *mithurtu*). דומה שהראשון שעמד על המשמעות הנכונה של הביטוי eme-ḫa-mun היה הוא פון סודן. הוא מתרגם את הביטוי האכדי המקביל lišān *mithurti* במילונו (AHw 662) 'לשונות הרמוניות/תואמות/ תאומות', כשהכוונה לרשימות הלקסיקליות הדו־לשוניות, שכבר בזמן חיבור האפוס של אנמרכר היו קיימות ונפוצות בשומר. ואמנם, יעקובסן (1987, [לעיל, הערה 26]) מתרגם בשו' 142 פשוט 'bilingual Sumer', 'שומר הדו־לשונית' (שם, עמ' 289). וכך מתרגם גם ונסטיפהוט. בתרגומי 'שומר "תאומת הלשון"' אף אני מתכוון לדו־לשוניותה של שומר. כיוצא בזה, אני מציע לתרגם את הביטוי maš-maš eme-ḫa-mun (תואר של האל Ningublaga במזמורי מקדש שומריים, שו' 153): 'כהן משביע דו־לשוני', היינו היודע את שתי הלשונות: שומרית ואכדית.

35   הביטוי a-da, בשו' 147–149, הוא סתום. קרמר תרגם לראשונה 'אב' (כוואריאנט פונטי ל־ad-da), אך לאחר מכן חזר בו. אלסטר מתרגם את המילים החוזרות בכל שורה 'one who at the same time is lord, aristocrat

150 (האל) אָנְכִּי, אדון השפע, האדון (אשר) דִּבְּרוּ אמת,

151 אדון החכמה, נבון הארץ,

152 נשיא האלים,

153 המלא רוח חכמה, אדון (העיר) ארידו,

154 בלל לשונם בפיהם, כמספר (הלשונות) אשר יוסדו –

155 לשון בני האדם, אשר (לפנים) היתה אחת!

שורות 141–146 ו־154–155, שהן המפתח להבנת היחידה הספרותית שלפנינו ובהן דימו החוקרים למצוא את המקבילה למוטיב בלבול הלשונות שבתורה, קשות ביותר לתרגום, והחוקרים נחלקים במשמעותן. הבעיה העיקרית כאן היא, האם יש לתרגם את הפעלים בזמן עבר או בזמן עתיד. אלסטר, קומרוצי וונסטיפהוט מתרגמים את הפעלים בשורות אלה בעיקרון בלשון עתיד.[36] לדעתם, כל הקטע הנדון מתאר מצב באחרית הימים, כאשר האל אָנְכִּי, בחכמתו כי רבה, יהפוך אל עמים שפה אחת ויגרום לכך שכולם יעבדו את אנליל. לשם כך הם יצטרכו ללמוד לדבר שומרית ולקבל עליהם את הדת השומרית, שהיא עליונה על שלהם.[37] לדעת חוקרים אלה, מטרת הלחש הזה היא לשכנע את מושל ארתה שיקבל על עצמו את מרותה ועליונותה של התרבות השומרית ואת הדת השומרית, למען יספק לעיר ארך חומרים לבניין מקדשה של האלה איננה. לשם כך, הלחש מתאר את המצב המצוי בהווה (היינו את המצב של ריבוי הלשונות, הדתות והתרבויות), ומנבא מצב

ראה 1 n .104 .RA 67 (1973), p. יעקובסן מתרגם: 'אָנְכִּי, בהילחמו מלחמות רוזנים, בהילחמו
מלחמות נסיכים, בהילחמו מלחמות מלכים' וגו'. מן הסתם הוא מפרש a-da 'להתחרות'. תרגומנו הולך בעקבות
קרמר, המתרגם לאחרונה: 'מתחרה' (contestant, disputant; ראה 11 .Or 39 [1970], p); וכן מתרגם כהן,
אנמרכר 119; וראה ביאורו של כהן בעמ' 202–203.

36 ראה אלסטר 1973, עמ' 104 ואילך; קומורוצי 1983, עמ' 133–134; 419, הערה לשו' 155; ונסטיפהוט 1994,
עמ' 147 ואילך. יש לציין כי חוקרים אלה מתעלמים מכללי הדקדוק המקובלים במחקר הלשון השומרית. הפעלים
המופיעים בשורות 146 ו־154 ניתן לתרגמם בלשון עתיד רק בדוחק רב.

37 לדוגמה נצטט כאן את תרגומו של אלסטר לשורות מפתח אלה:

141 On that day the countries of Šubur and Ḥamazi,

142 whose languages (originally) were opposed to that of Sumer, the great country
with a culture of nobility,

143 – and Akkad, the distinguished country,

144 and the countries of the nomads who sleep on the wide plains,

145 – the whole world, as far as it is populated

146 speaks to Enlil in one langue.

את שתי השורות האחרונות של ה'לחש' מתרגם אלסטר כך:

154 (Enki) will have changed in their mouth all languages that existed:

155 The Language of all mankind is one.

בהתאם לשיטתו, היה אלסטר צריך לתרגם את הפועל בשורה 155 בלשון עתיד: 'The language of Mankind
will be one'. לפועל me 'היה' נטייה אחת בלבד, והיא אל־זמנית (ראה: M.-L. Thomsen, The Sumerian:
Language, Copenhagen 1984, p. 273ff). כמו כן, ראוי היה לו לתרגם בשו' 146: 'will speak to Enlil in
one language' הוא נמנע מכך, משום שצורת הפועל ḫé-en-na-da-ab-dug₄ היא עבר מודגש. אשר
לתרגומו של ונסטיפהוט לשורות אלה, הוא מפותל ומאוד לא תקין. ונסטיפהוט מנסה לדייק יותר מאלסטר בזמני
הפועל, אך חוסר התחשבותו בתחביר המסובך של היחידה, תחביר שהוא אופייני לסופרי השושלת השלישית של
אור מימי המלך שולגי, גורם לחספוס רב של לשון התרגום.

רצוי בעתיד, מצב שבו האל אֱנכי, אל החכמה והמאגיה, ישנה את לשון כל בני האדם ויאחד אותם. באחרית הימים, כל האנושות תדבר בלשון אחת, ותתפלל לאנליל בלשון אחת. לחש זה אמור אפוא להשפיע על מושל ארתה שייכנע לדרישות אנמרכר.[38]

לפי קרמר וההולכים בעקבותיו, לעומת זאת, לחש נודימוד (=אֱנכי) מתאר את המצב הרצוי בעבר הרחוק, כאשר בני האדם דיברו בשפה אחת, והתפללו לאל אנליל בלשון אחת. לימים, האל אֱנכי, הידוע כמתחרהו של אנליל וכמי שתמיד מפר את עצתו של זה,[39] בלל את שפתם והטיל בהם מחלוקת, פירוד ומרי. לפי קרמר ואחרים, לא נתברר מה מטרת הלחש הזה, וכיצד הוא אמור לשכנע את מושל ארתה שייכנע לאנמרכר. להפך, הלחש הזה רק יחזק את רוחו של המושל לדחות את האולטימטום! שהרי אם אֱנכי בעבר הרחוק בלל את שפת בני האדם והטיל בהם פירוד, יש על מי להסתמך בהתנגדות לקבלת המרות של השומרים, בני־חסותו של אנליל!

יעקובסן אכן היה מודע לקושי זה.[40] בתרגומו החדיש לאפוס הוא מעלה את ההשערה כי ללחש הנוכחי, שהשליח לא חזר עליו במסרו את שליחותו למושל ארתה, אין כל קשר הגיוני למצב המתואר באפוס. לפיכך הוא רואה בלחש תוספת של עורך מאוחר, הלקוח ממיתוס אחר. כוונת העורך היתה, לדעתו, למלא חלל ספרותי: לתת דוגמה של לחש, במקום שהמחבר המקורי לא פירש.[41]

יש לתמוה על שהפתרון הפשוט וההגיוני ביותר לבעיה הנדונה, שהציעו וון־דייק שנתיים בלבד אחרי שחזור השורות האחרונות של הטקסט שלפנינו בידי קרמר,[42] לא זכה לתשומת הלב הראויה לו ושל החוקרים התעלמו ממנו.[43] לדעת וון־דייק, אין כאן לחש של אֱנכי כל עיקר. הלחש של אֱנכי שהשליח נצטווה לקרוא באוזני מושל ארתה (שו' 134–135) איננו מפורש, כפי הנראה, באפוס כלל וכלל. לפי דעה זו, הקטע המספר על בלבול הלשונות בימי קדם (שו' 136–155) הוא מין הערת סוגריים מורחבת של מחבר האפוס לקוראיו, בני זמנו, מימי השושלת השלישית של אור. מטרת

38 השווה הנבואה האסכטולוגית של צפניה (ג, ט), שהזכרנו במבוא, עם הערה 7.

39 ראה להלן, הערה 56.

40 ראה יעקובסן 1987 (לעיל, הערה 26), עמ' 288, הערה 25.

41 תופעה זו אנו מכירים גם מן המקרא. ידוע כי בסיפורת המקראית שולבו מזמורים מאוחרים, כגון תפילת חנה (שמ"א ב, א־י) או תפילת יונה אל ה' במעי הדגה (יונה ב, ג־יא) – מזמורים שהוצאו מהקשרם המקורי ושובצו בסיפורים אלה שיבוץ מלאכותי כלשהו. מן הראוי לציין כי במאמרו האחרון משנת 1992 (לעיל, הערה 26), שינה יעקובסן את דעתו מן היסוד, וניסה למצוא קשר הגיוני בין הלחש ובין העלילה שהוא משובץ בה (ראה דיונו שם, עמ' 414–416). לדעתו, אֱנכי היטיב עם האנושות כאשר נתן בפיה לשון אחת שכן בדברם לשון אחת הם הרגיזו את אנליל והיו חשופים לסכנת השמדה. לפי השערה דחוקה זו מסתבר, שבעדר בלבול הלשונות במקרא הוא בבחינת עונש, במיתולוגיה המסופוטמית הוא בבחינת חסד לאדם. לא פחות דחוקה היא השערת אהלינגר (לעיל, הערה 10), הסבור כי ב'לחש נודימוד' לא מדובר כלל על לשון אחת, שכביכול דיברו בה בני האדם בימי קדם, כי אם בהרמוניה אידילית, שבה עבדו כולם את האל השומרי אנליל. אמנם, אֱנכי שינה מצב זה והטיל בבני האדם מחלוקת, אבל עצם תיאורו של מצב אידילי זה בעבר הרחוק, במסגרת לחש, היה בו כדי לשכנע את מושל ארתה שייכיר בעליונותו של אנמרכר השומרי (ראה שם, עמ' 420–429).

42 ראה וון־דייק (לעיל, הערה 26), עמ' 303–305.

43 אפשר שהשערתו של וון־דייק לא זכתה לתשומת לב משום שכל החוקרים דחו את קריאתו ותרגומו לשתי השורות האחרונות של הקטע הנדון (שו' 154–155), שהן שונות משל קרמר. הוא תרגם שורות אלה כך: 'עד אשר (אֱנכי) שם בפיהם לשון בלולה – לשון בני האדם היתה אחת' (ראה וון־דייק, שם, עמ' 303–304). גם אם קריאה זו אינה נכונה, אין היא פוגמת בהשערתו של המחבר בנוגע למהות הקטע הנדון ולמגמתו.

ההערה להסביר לקוראים או לשומעים, כיצד יכול היה מושלה של העיר השומרית, ארך, להחליף
שדרים עם מושלה של עיר רחוקה וזרה כמו אַרַתה (שבימי המחבר דיברו בה עילמית, חורית או שפה
זרה אחרת). המחבר מודיע לנו, כי העלילה התרחשה בימי קדם, ב'תור הזהב' של האנושות, כאשר
בני האדם עדיין דיברו בלשון אחת וסרו למרות האל העליון של הפנתיאון השומרי, אנליל. העובדה
שבהתהוות האנושות מפוזרת ומפורדת, ומדברת בליל של לשונות, מוסברת בכך שאָנכִּי, מתחרהו של
אנליל, בלל את לשונם והטיל בהם מחלוקת.

ואמנם, כשהשליח מגיע לארתה, הוא מוסר את השליחות מילה במילה, ומספר למושל ארתה
שנצטווה לקרוא באוזניו את הלחש של נודימוד-אָנכּי. אולם, בניגוד למצופה ביצירה זו, שהיא
מלאה חזרות אפיות, על הסיפור של בלבול הלשונות אין הוא חוזר. אפשר שאין הוא עושה זאת
משום שאין זה כלל הלחש של נודימוד, כי אם הערת סוגריים של מחבר האפוס! השווה דברי השליח
למושל ארתה:

206   'בכל מקדשיה (=של ארתה), שם ייאמרו שירי קודש, לחשים,

207   [את לחש] (האל) נודימוד הגד [לו] למעני'.[44]

208   כל אשר תאמר אלי, אחר אשר [דיברת] –

209   לזרע ילוד (האל), 'עטור-זקן-הספירים'...[45]

214   לאנמרכר בן (האל) אותו,

215   אגידה את הדברים ההם, דברי נועם, בהיכל האֶאַנַּה;

216   בדביר-קדשו, הנושא פירות כעץ מַיֵש רענן,

217   אשוב אספרם למלכי, אדון כולבה!

אולם, מושל ארתה מסרב להיכנע לדרישות אנמרכר (ראה שם, שו' 218–226). משמע, הלחש של
נודימוד-אָנכּי (שלא מפורש כנראה באפוס) לא פעל את פעולתו.

אם השערתנו נכונה, הרי מחבר האפוס הזה, מתוך התעניינות בבעיות הקשורות בהתהוות ערכי
התרבות של האנושות, מעיר הערת אגב 'היסטורית-אטיולוגית-מיתולוגית', המסבירה את התופעה
התרבותית של קיום עמים שונים, בעלי שפה ותרבות שונים זה מזה בעולמנו. ואין זו הדוגמה היחידה
להתעסקותו של המחבר בשאלות של מקורות התרבות. להלן, המחבר מייחס לזמנו של אנמרכר גם
את המצאתה כתב היתדות. הוא מספר לנו כי אחרי מספר שליחויות לארתה, שנכשלו, אנמרכר שולח
אליה מסר ארוך ומסובך, שהשליח לא יכול לזכרו בעל פה. לכן, אנמרכר ראה צורך לכתוב את דברי
השליחות על לוח טין, ומושל ארתה קרא את הדברים מתוך הלוח. להלן לשון המספר:[46]

---

44   בשו' 206–207, השליח מוסר את דברי אנמרכר אליו בציטוט ישיר. בשו' 208 ואילך, כיאה לשליח חכם וזריז,
    הוא מוסיף דברים משל עצמו. זו דעת רוב המתרגמים. אלסטר חולק על פירוש זה, ומתרגם שו' 207 כך: 'הגד
    לי את לחש נודימוד'. לדעתו, השליח מבקש ממושל ארתה לחזור באוזניו על לחש של נודימוד (=שו' 136–155),
    לאות כי הוא נכנע לדרישות אנמרכר. אך דוק: בניגוד למקובל באפוס זה ובאפוסים העתיקים בכלל, אין השליח
    חוזר על ה'לחש' המשוער באוזני המושל כלל וכלל! לפיכך, אין זה מתקבל על הדעת שהוא ביקש מן המושל
    לחזור על הלחש באוזניו.

45   כינוי מליצי למלך אנמרכר. שו' 210–213 שהושמטמו מכילות כינויי כבוד דומים של המלך.

46   לדיון מקיף ומעמיק במשמעות שורות 500–506, וכן שו' 537–541, המובאות להלן, ראה, H.L.J. Vanstiphout,
    Studies Å.W. Söjberg, Philadelphia 1989, pp. 515-524; idem, *NABU* 1993, pp. 9-10

500 דבריו היו רבים, פשרם סתום(?),[47]

501 שפתי השליח כבדים, לא יוכל לשוב־לספרם.

502 כי שפתי השליח כבדים, לא יוכל לשוב־לספרם,

503 אדון כולבה גיבל טיט בידיו, ואת המלים כתב עליו כמו על לוח

504 (לפני היום הזה, כתוב מלים על לוח לא יוסד;[48]

505 עתה, תחת השמש, ביום הזה, כה אכן היה,

506 אדון כולבה כתב את המלים על לוח, כה אכן היה!).

בהגיע השליח לארתה, הוא מראה את הלוח למושל, ומודיע לו:

524 אנמרכר בן אותו נתן לי לוח־טין;

525 אדון ארתה, אחר אשר תביט בלוח־הטין, אחר אשר תדע את פשר המלים,[49]

526 כל אשר תאמר אלי, אחר אשר דברת –

527 לזרע ילוד (האל), 'עטור־זקן־הספירים'...[50]

532 לאנמרכר בן (האל) אותו,

533 אגידה את הדברים ההם, דברי נועם, בהיכל הֵאֲאַנַה;

534 בדביר־קדשו, הנושא פירות כעץ מַיֵש רענן,

535 אשוב אספרם למלכי, אדון כולבה!"

כראות אדון ארתה את הלוח וכשמעו את דברי השליח, כך הוא מגיב עליהם:

537 אדון ארתה לקח בידיו

538 את לוח החשבונות(?)[51] אשר לשליח.

539 אדון ארתה הביט בלוח־הטין,

540 המלים הכתובות(?) (?) – יתדות(?)[52](?) המה; פניו קדרו;

541 אדון ארתה יביט בלוח החשבונות(?) אשר לו.

---

47 שומרית: šà-bi su-su-àm. כהן ונסטיפהוט מתרגמים: 'תכנו רב מדי'. אולם, המילה šà (מילולית: לב) משמעה, בהקשרים דומים, 'מובן, משמעות' (השווה הערה 49 להלן).

48 המילים 'כָּתַב' ו'כָּתוּב' הן תרגום חופשי של הפועל השומרי gub, מילולית: הֶעֱמִיד, הִצִּיב.

49 מילולית: 'אחר אשר תדע את "לב" המלים' (השווה לעיל, הערה 47).

50 ראה לעיל, הערה 45.

51 קראנו ותרגמנו את רצף הסימנים הבעייתי im-šu-niğin₂-na על־פי הצעתו של קומורוצי (ראה, G. Komoróczy, AoF 3 (1975), p. 21, n. 13; השווה עוד הנ"ל, A Sumer Irodalmi Hagyomány, Budapest 1979, pp. 85-96). קומורוצי סבור כי מדובר ב'לוח סיכומים', היינו בלוח שבו נרשמו כל הסחורות שדרש אנמרכר ממושל ארתה. לדעתו, מחבר האפוס סבור כי כתב היתדות הומצא לצורך המינהל הכלכלי של המקדשים והיכל המלך. ואמנם, הטקסטים הראשונים שנכתבו בכתב זה הן רשימות מינהליות של סחורות, הוצאות והכנסות. זו גם דעת רוב החוקרים באשר לשימוש הראשוני בכתב היתדות. סיווויל, כהן ונסטיפהוט קוראים את רצף הסימנים הנ"ל: im-durun-na – 'בתנור', 'באבוקה'. לדעת סיווויל, מדובר כאן בשרפת הלוח באש לשימורו. לדעת כהן, מדובר באבוקה אשר לאורה קרא מושל ארתה את הלוח (ראה דיון אצל ונסטיפהוט 1989, עמ' 517 ואילך).

52 התרגום המילולי של המילים הסתומות inim-dug₄-ga kak-àm הוא: 'המילים האמורות – יתד(ות) הן'. אפשר שאין המחבר מתכוון למילים הכתובות, כי אם למילים שקרא מושל ארתה באוזני השליח מן הלוח. מכל מקום,

בניגוד לתגובתו לדברי השליחות הראשונה, שהיתה שלילית לחלוטין, מושל ארתה עומד הפעם על
סף שבירה, והוא כבר מוכן להיכנע לדרישותיו של אנמרכר. אולם כאן חל מפנה מפתיע בעלילה:
אישכור, אל הסערה השומרי, שובר את הבצורת המתמשכת, מחולל סערה ומוריד גשם נדבות על
ארתה. כתוצאה מזה, אסמיה של הממלכה מתמלאים דגן, והרעב הכבד נפסק. שוב אין תושבי ארתה
זקוקים למשלוחי התבואה של ארך, ואנמרכר ייאלץ כנראה להתמודד עם מושל ארתה, באמצעות
דו־קרב בין שני גיבורים.[53]

יושם לב לכך ששתי הפסקאות שנדונו לעיל, האחת המזכירה את 'לחש נודימוד' (השליחות
הראשונה) והאחרת המספרת על השדר שנכתב בלוח־הטין (השליחות האחרונה), כתובות באותו
מבנה ממש, וחלק נכבד מן הפסקאות האלה חוזרות מילה במילה על דרך החזרה האפית (ראה טבלה
משווה בסמוך). ההבדל בין שתי הפסקאות הוא רק באורכן. מכאן ניתן להסיק, כי כשם ששורות
504–506 מתארות את התהוותו של אחד מיסודות הציוויליזציה על דרך האטיולוגיה, דהיינו את
המצאת כתב היתדות, כך גם שורות 136–155 אינן אלא הערה אטיולוגית על יסוד אחר מיסודות
הציוויליזציה, דהיינו תופעת ריבוי הלשונות בעולם.

	השליחות הראשונה		השליחות האחרונה
אנמרכר לשליח	השדר: 'לחש נודימוד' (134–135)		השדר: 'לוח החשבונות' (503–507)
הערה אטיולוגית של המספר	תופעת ריבוי הלשונות: בעבר, דיברו בכל העולם לשון אחת (נוסחת פתיחה: u4-ba, 'בימים ההם'); לימים בלבל אנכי את הלשונות (136–155)		תופעת כתב היתדות: לפנים לא היתה קיימת כתיבה על לוח (נוסחת פתיחה: u4-bi-ta, 'לפנים'); אנמרכר היה הראשון שכתב שדר על לוח (504–506)

הלכנו בעקבות קרמר וקומורוצי, המפרשים את המילה kak כרמז לצורת היתדות של הכתב. כהן מתרגם את
המשפט בדוחק: 'המילים האמורות – היו חריפות/חדות/נוקבות (כ?ח)'. ונסטיפהוט (1989, עמ' 519) דוחה,
בצדק, את תרגומו של כהן, ומקבל בעיקרון את תרגומנו. אולם לדעתו, הערת המספר על שאנמרכר המציא את
כתב היתדות אינה אטיולוגית, כי אם מהותית לעלילה של האפוס. הוא סבור כי אנמרכר ממציא את כתב היתדות
ושולח לוח כתוב בכתב זה למושל ארתה, כדי להעמידו לפני אתגר קשה, שאין ביכולתו להתגבר עליו: מושל
ארתה מביט בלוח, כדי לקרוא בו את השדר ששמע מפי השליח. הוא ציפה למצוא בלוח כתב פיקטוגרפי,
לוגוגרפי, שניתן לקרוא בו בכל השפות, בלא שימוש באלמנטים דקדוקיים כלשהם. להפתעתו ולאכזבתו ראה
שם רק יתדות, המייצגות את הכתב השומרי המפותח, שבו כתבו שומרית, ולא היה יכול לקרוא את הכתוב.
משום כך קדרו פניו. במעשה זה הצליח אנמרכר, לשיטת ונסטיפהוט, להביך ולנצח את מושל ארתה, ובה בעת
להוכיח את עליונותה של התרבות השומרית (ראה לאחרונה ונסטיפהוט 1994). הקושי לקבל הסבר מפותל זה
הוא שניתן למצוא רק בין השיטין. הנימוק המפורש להמצאת הכתב, שמביא המספר, הוא שהשדר האחרון היה
ארוך מדי ומסובך להבנה או לזיכרה, ולכן נאלצו לכתבו על הלוח (ראה שו' 500–502).

53 המאבק לעליונות בין שתי הערים, ארך וארתה, מתואר בשלושה אפוסים שומריים, ובכולם העלילה מסתיימת
בכך שידה של ארך היתה על העליונה. באפוס שלפנינו, המאבק הוכרע, כפי הנראה, באמצעות מלחמת חידות
או דו־קרב של שני גיבורים (כאן הטקסט נקטע, ואי־אפשר לקבוע בוודאות את מהלך העלילה בסוף האפוס).
באפוס 'אנמרכר ואנסוח/כשדנה', מתנהל המאבק באמצעות מכשף ומכשפה, במישור המאגי (ראה, A. Berlin
1979 Enmerkar and Ensuḫkešdanna, Philadelphia); ואילו באפוס 'לוגלבנדה ואנמרכר', המאבק הוכרע
בשדה הקרב (השווה C. Wilcke, Das Lugalbandaepos, Wiesbaden 1969).

	השליחות הראשונה	השליחות האחרונה
השליח למושל ארתה	מסירת השדר: 'לחש נודימוד' – תוכנו לא פורש (206–207)	מסירת השדר: 'לוח-הטין' – תוכנו לא פורש (524–525)
השליח למושל ארתה	תוספת השליח לשדר: ועתה, כל אשר תאמר לי אמסור בנאמנות לאנמרכר, מלכי. חזרה אפית (526–535 = 208–217)	תוספת השליח לשדר: ועתה, כל אשר תאמר לי אמסור בנאמנות לאנמרכר, מלכי. חזרה אפית (208–217 = 526–535)
המספר	משפט קישור נוסחתי: 'אך אמר לו כדברים האלה' (536 = 218)	משפט קישור נוסחתי: 'אך אמר לו כדברים האלה' (218 = 536)
תגובת מושל ארתה	שדר חוזר: סירוב מוחלט לקבל את מרותה של ארך (226–219)	מבוכה ושתיקה: המושל קורא בלוח. פניו קדרו (537–541)

3. המקור השומרי והמקור המקראי – השוואה

אם הפירוש שהצענו כאן לאפוס של אנמרכר, שורות 134–155, נכון, הרי נתברר כי למוטיב של בלבול הלשונות בפי בני האדם והתהוות השפות בעולם, בספר בראשית, קיימת מקבילה מסופוטמית קרובה למדי. מסתבר כי שני המקורות אינם באים להסביר את התהוות הדיבור האנושי בכללו, היינו כיצד נולדה הלשון הראשונה, הלשון שדיברו בה בני האדם הקדמונים. שני המקורות מניחים, כנראה, כי האדם למד לדבר מן האלוהות; שהרי האל במקרא מדבר עם אדם מיום הראשון מיום בריאתו.[54] מן הסתם עברית. איזו שפה? ואילו לפי התפיסה השומרית ברור שהאלים המסופוטמיים ידעו לדבר, שהרי גם בטרם בראו את האדם, הם נזקקו ליכולת הדיבור ולידיעת השפה, כדי לתקשר ביניהם לבין עצמם. באיזו שפה דיברו האלים המסופוטמיים? מן הסתם בשפה השומרית, ושפה זו גם הורו לבני האדם. או לחלופין, יכולת הדיבור וידיעת השפה (העברית/השומרית) היו טבועות באדם מיום בריאתו. שכן, לפי התורה, האדם נברא 'בצלם אלהים' (בר' א, כו–כז); ואילו לפי המיתוסים המסופוטמיים (במיוחד האכדיים) נברא האדם מטיט שנגבל בדמו של אחד האלים, ועקב כך הוא דומה לאלים הן בצורתו החיצונית והן בתבונתו וביכולת הדיבור שלו.[55]

אם כן, שני המקורות עוסקים בשאלה, כיצד זה קרה שהאנושות הפכה מחד־לשונית לרב־לשונית. לפי שני המקורות, האנושות היתה מאורגנת במסגרות של עמים שנוצרו ממשפחות ומשבטים (בר' י"א), או ערים־מדינות (המקורות המסופוטמיים). אלא שעמים/מדינות אלה דיברו בלשון אחת. עד כאן שווים שני המקורות בתפיסתם, ומכאן מתחיל ההבדל ביניהם: לפי המקור השומרי, התפצלות הלשונות היא תוצאה של יריבות בין שניים מן האלים הראשיים של הפנתיאון: בימי קדם, כל בני אנוש עבדו את אנליל, מלך האלים, האל הלאומי של השומרים, בלשון אחת (השומרית)

---

54   ראה לעיל, סעיף 1, עם הערות 3–7.

55   ראה אנומה אליש, לוח שישי, שו' 1–38; אתרח'סיס, לוח ראשון, שו' 204–243.

ועל־פי דת אחת (השומרית). לימים בא אֶנְכִּי, יריבו, שמשום מה קינא בו, ובלל את לשון בני האדם.
מכאן המצב הנוכחי, שיש בו ריבוי לשונות ומָגוון של תרבויות ואמונות.[56]

לפי התורה, המבוססת על האמונה באל אחד, בלבול הלשונות הוא תוצאה של עוד חטא שחטאו בני
האדם נגד האל. האל רצה להפיצם, כדי ליישב את כל חלקי העולם, והם מרדו בו ולא קיבלו את
מרותו. ועוד זאת: הם ביקשו להתפשט לגובה (להגיע השמימה) במקום לרוחב. בל נשכח שלפי
התפיסה של הקדמונים, לא היו השמים רחוקים מן האדם כלל ועיקר, ובהחלט היו בני השגה.[57] אם
כן, בלבול הלשונות בא למנוע אותם מלהשיג את מטרתם, פשוטו כמשמעו. עם זאת, אין להתעלם
מן המגמה הנוספת של הסיפור, אשר בא לשים ללעג ולקלס את האימפריה הבבלית, שהייתה אז
המרכז הפוליטי והדתי של האלילות.

ועוד יש לשים לב לעובדה המעניינת, ששני המקורות, המסופוטמי והמקראי, מסבירים את תופעת
ריבוי הלשונות על דרך האטיולוגיה. באפוס השומרי המחבר מעיר הערת אגב אטיולוגית, כדי להסביר
לקוראיו איך ייתכן שבימי קדם, שני עמים שונים ורחוקים זה מזה יכלו לתַקשר ביניהם בלי
מתורגמנים, בשעה שבזמנו של המחבר דיברו עמים אלה לשונות שונות. ואילו במקרא יש לנו
אטיולוגיה כפולה: הפרשה מבארת הן את התופעה של ריבויֵ הלשונות והעמים והן את מקור השם
'בבל'.

ראינו כי ביסוד שני המקורות, הן המסופוטמי והן המקראי, עומדת ההשקפה כי בלֵיל הלשונות
בעולם בלשון אחת. זוהי בעצם עד היום דרכם של רוב הלינגוויסטים בתיאור התפתחות
הלשונות. ההבדל הוא רק בתיאור התהליך: לפי אמונת הקדמונים, ההתפצלות וההסתעפות של
הלשונות אירעו מאוחר יחסית בתולדות האנושות, הן בגדר אירוע חד־פעמי, פתאומי, מעין פיצוץ
אוניברסלי, שתוצאותיו הונצחו, והמצב בהווה הוא לדידם סטטי, ואין בו עוד התפתחות. הלשונות
אמורות להישאר במצב שהונצח בימי קדם. ואילו לפי הדעה המקובלת בבלשנות המודרנית,
ההסתעפות וההתפצלות של הלשונות הן תהליך הדרגתי, שנמשך אלפי שנים – תהליך מתמשך,
שלעולם אינו נפסק. לשונות מתפצלות לדיאלקטים, וללשונות נפרדות לגמרי זו מזו. לאחרונה גיוונו
את התיאוריה הזו על־ידי הכנסת האלמנט של האיסוגלוסה, וכן מביאים בחשבון השפעות של סובסטרט
לשוני וכדומה. אך מניחים כי באופן כללי ההתפתחות היא בדרך של התפצלות והסתעפות לינארית.

לאחרונה קמו מערערים על תפיסה זו. דיון מאלֵף ומעניין בהקשר זה מצוי במאמרו של ג'
קומורוצי, שהופיע ב־1978.[58] קומורוצי טוען כי קיומן של לשונות מבודדות (insel Sprachen),

---

56   השווה לדוגמה סיפור המבול הבבלי, 'אתרח'סיס', שבו אֶנְכִּי מגלה לבן־חסותו את גזֵרת האלים, ובכך מסכל את
תכניתו של אנליל להכרית את האנושות במבול. באותו מיתוס, למעשה, אֶנְכִּי מסכל גם נסיונות קודמים של
אנליל לדלל את האנושות על־ידי מגפות ורעב (ראה: W.G. Lambert and A.R. Millard, ATRA-ḤASIS:
The Babylonian Story of the Flood, Oxford 1969, pp. 9ff. et passim ראה עוד לעניין זה S.N. Kramer,
על האל אֶנְכִּי בכלל, ראה 'Enki and his Inferiority Complex', Orientalia 39 (1970), pp. 103-110
לאחרונה S.N. Kramer and J. Maier, Myths of Enki the Crafty God, New York 1989

57   ראה המיתוס 'אתנה והנשר', המספר על מעופו של אתנה לשמים על כנפי Anzu, הנשר המיתולוגי (השווה
לחטאם של J.V. Kinnier Wilson, The Legend of Etana, 1985; C. Saporetti, Etana, Warminster 1990).
דור הפלגה, ראה לאחרונה, F.E. Greenspahn, 'A Mesopotamian Proverb and its Biblical
Reverberations', JAOS 114 (1994), pp. 33-38

58   ראה G. Komoróczy, 'Das Rätsel der sumerischen Sprache als Problem der Frühgeschichte
Vorderasiens', Festschrift Lubor Matouš I, Budapest, pp. 225-252

כמו השומרית למשל, אפשר לבארו רק אם אנו משתחררים מן התפיסה המסופוטמית־מקראית,
ומניחים כי באזורים שונים של המזרח הקדום צמחו ונוצרו לשונות שונות ונפרדות זו מזו, היינו
לשונות מבודדות. לדעתו, אף ניתן לעקוב אחר תהליכים הפוכים מן המקובל: לאחר מגע בין
לשונות שונות, הלשון העליונה מבחינה תרבותית או כלכלית, או מבחינת מספר הדוברים בה,
דוחקת ומכחידה את הלשונות המבודדות שבסביבתה, והופכת ל־*lingua franca* (לשון בינלאומית).

יש להניח כי האמת מצויה אי־שם באמצע: כפי הנראה, בהתפתחות הלשונות בעולם פועלים,
מקדמא דנא, שני תהליכים הפוכים: איחוד מזה והתפצלות מזה, וקשה לדעת מה קדם למה.

'...ואם בגבורת שמונים שנה'
למונחי אריכות־ימים באכדית, בלשון המקרא ובלשון חכמים

חיים תדמור
האוניברסיטה העברית בירושלים

[א]

תפיסת אריכות הימים במקרא ובספרות של המזרח הקדום נדונה במחקר בשנים האחרונות דיון שיש
בו עניין רב.[1] אחת הסיבות, אם לא העיקרית שבהן, לדיון המחודש היה פרסומה של תעודה מן
הארכיון שבסולטאן־טֶפֶּה, היא חרן העתיקה, מהתקופה הניאו־אשורית, שנמנים בה שלבי חייו של
האדם מגיל ארבעים ועד תשעים.[2] בדומה לחלוקה הנודעת שבפרקי אבות ה, כא, מוגדר בתעודה
זו כל עשור בחייו של האדם במונח מיוחד, וזה לשון המקור:

פסגת – *metlūtu* – 60 ;חיים קצרים – *ûmū kurūtu* – 50 ;מיטב החיים – *lalūtu* – 40
זיקנה – *littūtu* – 90 ;זיקנה – *šībūtu* – 80 ;אריכות ימים – *ûmū arkūtu* – 70 ;החיים
מופלגת.

אין ספק שהשוואה שבין מערכת גיליו של האדם בתעודה האשורית לבין זו שבפרקי אבות יש בה
עניין לחוקר המקרא והמזרח הקדום, אך אין היא עיקרו של דיוננו. ברשימה זו באים אנו לדון אך
ורק בצמד המונחים *šībūtu*־ו *littūtu*, שבסיומה של התעודה מסולטאן־טפה, מאחר שמצד המבנה
תואמים הם למונחים 'שיבה' ו'גבורה' כציון לאריכות הימים המופלגת בפרקי אבות ה, כא.
הצימוד *šībūtu*־ו *littūtu* כמבטא את אורך חייו המרבי של האדם רווח מאוד בספרות האכדית,
בעיקר באלף הראשון לפני הספירה. הוא מתועד ברובד הבבלית הספרותית, באשורית החדשה
ובבבלית החדשה כלשון ברכה במכתבים ובתפילות, בעיקר באלה של מלכים הפונים לאלוהיהם
בבקשה לאריכות ימים. עם שגזרונו של *šībūtu*, 'שיבה', *šību* מלשון, זיקנה, זקן, הוא גלוי

1   מ' ויינפלד, 'בן שבעים לשיבה, בן שמונים לגבורה', ספר ברוך בן־יהודה, מחקרים
במקרא ובמחשבת ישראל (עורך ב"צ לוריא), תל־אביב תשמ"א, עמ' 312–317; ,A. Malamat 'Longevity:
Biblical Concepts and Some Ancient Near Eastern Parallels', *Vorträge gehalten auf der 28*
Rencontre Assyrologique Internationale in Wien 6-10. Juli 1981, AfO Beiheft 19, 1982, pp.
215-224; א' מלמט, ישראל בתקופת המקרא, ירושלים 1983, עמ' 295–306; M. Weinfeld, 'The Phases
of Human Life in Mesopotamian and Jewish Sources', in *Priests, Prophets and Scribes, Essays*
in Honour of J.R. Blenkinsopp (ed. E. Ulrich, et. al.), Sheffield 1992, pp. 182-189
2   O.R. Gurney – P. Hulin, *The Sultantepe Tablets* II, London 1964, no. 400 rev., ll. 45-47

וברור,[3] מוקשה גזרונו של *littūtu*. במילונים החדשים של האכדית נמנעו מלתרגמו בדיוק והסתפקו בתרגום שהוא מעין פירוש: 'extreme old age',[4] או 'langes erfolgreiches Leben'.[5]

ברם, התרגום הזה של *littūtu* ('זיקנה מופלגת') הוא חדש יחסית. עד לפני כשלושים שנה היה מקובל לראות את המונח כשם-עצם מופשט של *ilittu/littu* – 'בן' 'צאצא', 'יליד' – הנגזרים מלשון *(w)alādu*, יל"ד. גזרון זה מופיע כבר במילונים הראשונים של האכדית, מראשית המאה.[6] התרגום 'צאצאים' (/'offspring', 'progeny', 'Nachkommenschaft') ל-*littūtu* היה נקוט אפוא בכל תרגומי הספרות האכדית לסוגיה.[7]

התמורה התרחשה משנודע תוכנו של אותו לוח מסולטאן-טפה, שבו פתחנו את דיוננו,[8] ובו מוגדר *littūtu* כשלב מרבי באורך חייו של האדם, מעבר לזיקנה, ומאז התפשט הנוהג לתרגמו כ'זיקנה מופלגת', 'extreme old age'.[9] מכאן ואילך ניתקו הלקסיקוגראפים החדשים את *littūtu* מלשון *(i)littu* 'צאצא', וביקשו להציע לו גזרון אחר. פון-זודן גזר אותו מ-*littu* IV 'זקן', 'מלה נדירה ביותר, המופיעה רק בסידרה מילונאית מאוחרת, שנדון בה בהמשך. הוא אף ביקש למצוא מלה זו בשני מכתבים מן התקופה הבבלית הקדומה.[10] גם עורכי ה-CAD הסמיכו את *littūtu* לאותה מלה נדירה,[11] אף כי דחו באורח משכנע את ההשערה בדבר הופעתה בשני המכתבים הבבליים שמביא פון-זודן.

נראה לי שיש להפוך את היוצרות בקשר לפירושה של *littūtu*, ושהצדק הוא עם החוקרים הראשונים, שראו בה את את צורת המופשט (כדוגמת *šībūtu*, הקודמת לה בתיעוד), הנגזרת מלשון *(i)littu*, 'בן', 'צאצא'.[12] זו האחרונה[13] מוכרת היטב מתעודות ספרותיות ושאינן ספרותיות למן

CAD Š, II, 390-391, 399-400   3   CAD L, 220   4

AHw, 557a   5

Fr. Delitzsch, *Assyrisches Handwörterbuch*, Leipzig 1896, p. 234; W. Muss-Arnolt, *Assyrisch-*   6
     English-Deutches Handwörterbuch, Berlin-London-New York, p. 181

M. Streck, *Assurbanipal und die lezten Assyrischen Könige*, I-III, Leipzig 1916, p. 506;   7
     L. Waterman, *Royal Correspondence of the Assyrian Empire*, I-II, Ann Arbor 1930, nos. 76, 204,
     353; R.H. Pfeiffer, *State Letters of Assyria*, New Haven 1935, nos. 296, 306, 334; A. Falkenstein
     – W. von Soden, *Sumerische und akkadische Hymnen und Gebete*, Zürich-Stuttgart 1953, 283 (a),
     284(c), 286 no. 29, 287 no. 33; C.J. Gadd, 'Inscribed Barrel Cylinder of Marduk-apla-iddina
     II', *Iraq* 15 (1953), pp. 123-134, p. 125, l. 31; R. Borger, *Die Inschriften Asarhaddons Königs von*
     Assyrien, *AfO* Beiheft 9, Graz 1956, p. 26, l.18; C.J. Gadd, 'The Harran Inscriptions of
     Nabonidus', *AnSt* 8 (1958), pp. 35-92, p. 50, l. 34

גרני (לעיל, הערה 2), מס' 400. 8

מסתבר שתוכנו של הלוח מסולטאן-טפה היה ידוע לעורכי המילון האשורי של שיקגו שנים אחדות לפני פרסומו. 9
כבר ב-CAD, A/I משנת 1964, בעמ' 316 (ערך *alāku*) בצירופו ל-*šībūtu* מתורגם *littūtu* כ'זיקנה מופלגת'.
לשון זהה ננקט ל' אופנהיים, עורכו הראשי של ה-CAD, בבואו לתרגם את האסטילה של אם נבונאיד, בכרך
המילואים ל-*ANET* (1968), עמ' 561.

AHw, 557   10

CAD L, *littu* D, 220   11

R. Labat, *Commentaries Assyro-Babyloniens sur les présagés*, (= CT 41, 27 בלוח לקסיקלי-פרשני   12
(Bordeux 1933, pp. 38-39, בקטע העוסק במונחים *banû* ו-*alādu*, יצ"ר, יל"ד, מופיע זיהוי מפורש בין
i-lit-tu לבין *lit-tu-tu*. ראה גם CAD I/J, 72

CAD L, *littu* C, 219; CAD I/J, *illittu* 72   13

התקופה הבבלית הקדומה, ואילו littu D, במשמעות 'זקן', נודעת אך ורק מסידרה לקסיגראפית
אחת, היא erimhuš = anantu, בהעתק מהתקופה הבבלית החדשה. המהדורה המדעית של סידרה
זו, שהוכנה לפני שנים רבות בידי ב' לנדסברגר, במסגרת עבודותיו על הלקסיקוגראפיה השומרו-
אכדית, ראתה אור בשנת 1985.[14] בלוח השישי בסידרה זו נמצא הקטע שנתייחד לשלושה מונחים
המציינים 'זקן' באכדית ולתרגומם המשוער לשומרית,[15] ואלה הם (בטור האכדי): littu, šību ו-
puršumu. המונח הראשון הוא הרגיל לציין 'זקן' באכדית, הן מצד הגיל ('שיבה') הן מצד המעמד
החברתי.[16] המונח האחרון, אף שבמקורות הוא רווח פחות מ-šību, גם הוא מתועד למדי, ומציין 'זקן
נושא תפקיד'.[17] לעומת זאת, המונח השני אינו מתועד בשום מקור באכדית לתקופותיה, וכאן בעצם
הזכרתו היחידאית. רשאים אנו אפוא ללמוד מכאן ש-littu, במשמעות 'זקן', היא תצורה משנית מלשון
littūtu, על-פי האנלוגיה šību < šībūtu. וראוי לזכור בהקשר זה, שהנוהג לרשום בקפדנות כל
מלה מוכרת – ובכלל זה גם מלים יחידאיות, שרבות מהן לא היו אלא תצורות-משנה מלאכותיות,
מעשי-ידיהם של בעלי-לשון קדמונים – היה נוהג מקובל בלקסיקוגראפיה המסופוטמית לדורותיה.

משבים אנו לדון ב-littūtu, שפתחנו בו תחילה, נראה לנו שמעיקרו בא המונח לבטא ריבוי
צאצאים, בנים ובני-בנים, שהוא פיסגה בחייו של אדם בשלב הזיקנה. אריכות הימים המופלגת באה
לידי ביטוי באכדית בשני היבטים: šībūtu – 'שיבה', 'זיקנה', ההיבט הפיסי; ו-littūtu – ריבוי
הצאצאים, הוא ההיבט המשפחתי-החברתי. אם כן, šībūtu ו-littūtu, הבאים לרוב כצמד, הם
למעשה 'שניים שהם אחד', hendiadys, המביעים אריכות ימים מופלגת. מאחלים לו לאדם שיזכה
ויגיע לזיקנה ויראה בנים ובני-בנים, בעודו זוכה לבריאות הגוף והנפש. במרוצת הזמן, כל אחד
משני מרכיבי הצימוד היה עשוי לציין את מלוא הברכה; וכך, למעשה, היו šībūtu ו-littūtu
למושגים חופפים. אולם כשבא הצורך, בלוח מסולטאן-טפה, לסווג במדויק את מערכת הביטויים
המבטאים גיל ביחידות של עשר שנים, נתפצל שוב הצימוד, ו-littūtu הפך לשמש הדרגה המרבית
בסולם אריכות הימים.

ב

מה אפוא גורלה של המקבילה העברית התואמת לצימוד šībūtu/littūtu? בפרקי אבות ה, כא, אלה
הן ה'שיבה' וה'גבורה'. אלא שההסכמה המספרית באבות קטנה בעשור אחד מזו שבתעודה האשורית.
אותו עניין מובע בלשון החכמים המאוחרת בצמד הביטויים 'שיבה' ו'גבורות'. כך למשל, 'שבעים
שיבה, שמונים גבורות' (מ"ק כח, א), או 'כמה שנותיו של אדם? שבעים שנה, ואם בגבורות,
שמונים שנה' (פסחים צא, ב). בהקשר אחר, הצמד מתקצר למונח אחד בלבד, והוא 'גבורות': 'הגיע
לגבורות, זוהי מיתת נשיקה' (מ"ק כח, א), או 'זקן שלא הגיע לגבורות' (גטין כח, א). אך למה ייחסו
את אריכות הימים המופלגת במונח 'גבורות'? דומני שאין חולקים על כך שמונח זה שבלשון חכמים
מקורו בכתוב היחידאי במקרא: 'ימי שנותינו בהם שבעים שנה ואם בגבֹרֹת שמונים שנה' (תה' צ,
י), והוא אפוא יעמוד במרכז עיונֵנו.

14   MSL XVII   15   שם, עמ' 87, שו' 228–230.
16   CAD Š II, 390-394; AHw 1228
17   AHw 881

גלוי וברור הדבר, שכבר הקדמונים התקשו במשמעותה של 'גבורות' בכתוב זה. הקושי הוא בכך
שהלשון 'גבורה', 'גבורות' במזמורי תהלים מוסבת אך ורק למעשי גבורותיו של האל, ולא של האדם
(כך למשל, תה' כ, ז; סו, ז; פט, יד; קו, ב, ולפי רוב הדעות – אף עא, טז). ברוח זו פירש רש"י:
'בגבורתו של מקום הוא חי ולא מרוב כוח שבו' (ב, ברכות טו, ע"א). השבעים והוולגאטה, לעומת
זאת תרגמו בכוחות', במאמצים' ('en dynasteiois', 'in potentabibus'), והפשיטטא 'למחסן',
היינו 'בקושי', 'לכל היותר' – תרגומים שהם מעין פירושו. באותה רוח ממשיכים תרגומי המקרא
החדשים, למן המאה השבע־עשרה – (KJV) 'and if by reason of strength': 'if our ועד ימינו
(NEB) 'strength holds', או (NJPSV) 'given the strength'. וכך גם גורסים מילוני המקרא
החדשים 'bei höchster Lebenskraft', [18] או 'bei starker Lebenskraft'. [19]

אפשר היה, כמובן, להסתפק בתרגומי פירוש אלה ודומיהם; אך סבורני שיש דרך אחרת להבין
את משמעותו של 'גבורות', והוא לראות את הביטוי מן הצימוד האכדי שנדון לעיל. מ'
ויינפלד, הראשון שהלך בדרך זו, [20] אכן הקביל 'שיבה וגבורות' שבלשון חכמים ו'גבורות' בתה' צ,
י לצמד šībūtu ו־littūtu. יתר על כן, הוא אף הציע ל־littūtu גזרון המקרב אותו ללשון 'גבורות'.
לדעתו, זוהי צורת הרבים מלשון lītu, 'כוח', 'גבורה'. ואם כך, הרי הלשון 'גבורות' מציינת זיקנה
מופלגת הן באכדית והן במקורות העבריים, היא בבחינת דגם לשוני־תרבותי משותף.

ואולם, אף שהדמיון בין המונחים לאריכות ימים באכדית ובעברית, שהצביעו עליו בשעתו
ויינפלד ומלמט (לעיל, א) אינו מוטל בספק, הרי ההסבר האטימולוגי המוצע ל־littūtu אינו מסתבר
כל־עיקר. אין שום זיקה אטימולוגית בין lītu, 'גבורה', ובלשון רבים (נקבה) litātu, לבין littūtu,
שהוא שם־עצם מופשט, בלשון זכר, הנגזר מן (i)littu), 'צאצא' (לעיל, א). ומכאן שאין דגם משותף
לאכדית ולעברית בהגדרת אריכות הימים המופלגת כלשון גבורה, 'גבורות.'

ג

דומני שהזיקה בין 'זיקנה/שיבה/שיבה' ו'גבורות' לבין šībūtu ו־littūtu ניתנת להתפרש בדרך אחרת. יש
מקום להציע שבזמן מן הזמנים, בשלהי תקופת המקרא, אולי בתחומיה של הגולה שבבבל, ומכל
מקום תוך כדי מגע הדוק של סופרים יהודים יודעי אכדית עם סופרים בבלים, הורגש הצורך להעתיק
לעברית את צמד הביטויים šībūtu, littūtu הרווח באכדית בלשון ברכה ותפילה. בעוד ש־šībūtu
התאימה לפי גזרונה ל'שיבה' ולפי עניינה ל'זיקנה', לא היה בעברית מונח תואם ל־littūtu כמציין
את הדרגה המרבית באריכות הימים. החידוש שהומצא בדרך של תרגום־שאילה, 'גבורות', בא
מכוחה של אטימולוגיה עממית, שפירשה את littūtu כאילו היתה litātu, אף כי אפשר מאוד
שהשואלים ידעו שאטימולוגיה זו מוטעית. אדרבה, לא מן הנמנע שהמונח העברי החדש היה מעין

18   HALAT, p. 165

19   Wilhelm Gesenius, *Hebräisches und aramäisches Handwörterbuch über das Alte Testament*, 18
     Auflage (eds. V. Rüterswörden, R. Meyer, H. Donner), Berlin–Heidelberg 1987, p. 193

20   ויינפלד, 'בן שבעים לשיבה' (לעיל, הערה 1); הנ"ל, 'The Phases of Human Life' (לעיל, הערה 1), עמ'
     184–186.

מדרש מלים יוצר [21] littūtu, במקורו 'ריבוי צאצאים', נתפרש כיכולתו המרבית של הגבר להעמיד
צאצאים. בתפיסת העולם של המקרא, אריכות הימים האידיאלית היא זו שאדם זוכה לראות את
צאצאיו עד דור שלישי ורביעי:[22] הגבר שזכה להגיע לאריכות ימים מופלגת זו, שהיא 'גבורות',
כאילו זכה למידה מופלגת של 'גבריות'. דומה שהתופעה שלפנינו היא מעין 'משנה-הוראה',
המוכרת מחקר לשון המקרא, ולאחרונה מעבודתו של מ' פארן המנוח.[23]

משנתקבל 'גבורות' ללשון המקרא, ניתן לו בתה' צ, י ערך מספרי של שמונים שנה, שהוא גבוה
בעשרת אחת ממשך החיים האופטימלי של האדם לפי מושגי אותו זמן: 'ונשכחת צור שבעים שנה
– כימי מלך אחד' (יש' כג, טו); 'ועבדו הגויים האלה את מלך בבל שבעים שנה' (יר' כה, יא) היא
תקופת הפורענות, שבה עתידים כל הגויים לעבוד את נבוכדנאצר, 'אותו... ואת בנו ואת בן בנו'
(שם, כו, ז).[24] לעומת זאת, הנתון בדבר שמונים שנה בא מממערכת מספרים אחרת, הידועה בעיקר
מן התורה ומספר שופטים, ולפיה ארבעים שנה הם דור אחד.[25] במסורת שהשתמשה במערכת
מספרית זו הוגבל עוד בשחר האנושות משך חייו של האדם והועמד על מאה ועשרים שנה בלבד
(בר' ו, ג).[26] בדורות שאחרי אבות האומה, רק משה בן עמרם זכה להגיע לגיל האידיאלי: 'ולא כהתה
עינו ולא נס לחו' (דב' לד, ז). לכל הבאים אחריו חסד מעין זה לא ניתן עוד.

במרוצת הזמן, אם מכוח המונה החדש עצמו ואם מכוחו של הכתוב בתה' צ, י, נתקבל 'גבורות'
בלשון חכמים הקדומה והמאוחרת, שובץ בסכמה המספרית לשלבים בחייו של אדם, והפך למטבע
לשון, היחיד למעשה בעברית לכל תקופותיה, המביע את מאווייו של האדם להגיע לאריכות ימים
מרבית כשכוחו, שהיא 'גבורתו', עדיין לא נס ליחם. אאחל אפוא לחברי בעל היובל שיגיע לגבורות
ושתקוים בו הברכה הקדומה: *šībūtu likšud lišbî littūtu*.

21   תופעות של מדרש מלים יוצר אינן נדירות במגע שבין לשונות, וניתן למצוא להן תקדימים אצל הבלשנים שעסקו
      בחקר תרגומי-שאילה לסוגיהם. ראה למשל: L. Bloomfield, *Language*, New York-Chicago 1964;
      Chapter XXV, §7; U. Weinreich, *Languages in Contact*, The Hague 1966, pp. 52-53

22   מלמט, ישראל בתקופת המקרא (לעיל, הערה 1), עמ' 298.

23   מ' פארן, 'למשנה הוראה במקרא', באר שבע א (1973), עמ' 150–161, ושם ספרות.

24   מלמט, שם (לעיל, הערה 1), עמ' 300, ושם ספרות.

25   ראה, למשל, ח' תדמור, 'כרונולוגיה', אנציקלופדיה מקראית ד, ירושלים 1962, טור 250. על משך הזמן של
      דור במקרא ראה לאחרונה ThWAT II, עמ' 185–186.

26   מ"ד קאסוטו, מאדם עד נח, ירושלים תשי"ג, עמ' 204. בטקסט שומרו-אכדי שנתגלו באֱמֶר שבצפון סוריה,
      ופורסם לאחרונה, מובעת ביקורת קשה על רצונו של האדם להגיע לאריכות ימים מעין זו. וזה לשון הנוסח האכדי
      שם: 'משך חיים של 120 שנה (הוא בבחינת) איסור חמור (ikkibu), 'תועבה') למין האנושי' (J. Klein, 'The
      "Bane" of Humanity: A Lifespan of One Hundred Twenty Years', *Acta Sumerologica* 12
      [1990], p. 64, n. 15).

מחקרים בתולדות בית־שני,
חז"ל וימי־הביניים

'שכל', 'עיון' ו'דיוק' – ניתוח סמנטי

משה ויינפלד
האוניברסיטה העברית בירושלים

[א] 'שכל'

היה זה ר' יונה אבן ג'נאח שהאיר עינינו בכתובים סתומים, הארה שעדיין לא הפכה לנחלת כלל הפרשנים. אני רוצה להתעכב כאן על פירושו לשורש 'שכל' ולפועל 'השכל', פירוש המאפשר לנו הבנה אמיתית ונכונה לא רק של הפועל 'השכיל' אלא גם של 'עיון' ו'דיק'/'דקדק' שבלשון חכמים. מסתבר מן העיון שמשמעותם הבסיסית של הפעלים 'השכיל', 'עיין' ו'דיק'/'דקדק' היא הסתכל היטב, התבונן.

כבר התרגומים תרגמו 'להשכיל' בכתוב שבבר' ג, ו: 'ותרא האשה כי טוב העץ למאכל וכי תאוה הוא לעינים ונחמד העץ להשכיל' כהסתכלות.[1] יש לזכור כי 'הסתכל' בלשון חז"ל פירושו קונוטטיבית: 'כל המסתכל בארבעה דברים ראוי לו כאלו לא בא לעולם: מה למעלה מה למטה, מה לפנים ומה לאחור' (משנה חגיגה ב, א); 'הסתכל בשלשה דברים ואין אתה בא לידי עבירה, דע מאין באת ולאן אתה הולך וגו' (משנה אבות ב, א). משמע זה של 'להשכיל' מתאשר מן הכתוב המקביל לכתוב בבר' ג, ו: 'ויצמח ה' אלהים מן האדמה כל עץ נחמד למראה' במקום 'נחמד להשכיל' (שם ב, ט). אנו מוצאים מקבילה מסופוטמית לעניין זה בתיאור הגן של סידורי (הפונדקאית), שגלגמש שואל בעצתה בקשר לחיי נצח. הגן הזה הוא מעין גן עדן, שמצויים בו עצי פרי וכן אבנים יקרות (השווה יח' כח, יג). אנו קוראים שם:

אשכולות ענבים תלויים, טוב להסתכל (ana dāgala ṭābat)
נושא פרי, נחמד למראה (ana amāri ṣajāḫ)[2]

ר' יונה אבן ג'נאח הביא את הכתובים בהם מופיע 'שכל'/'השכיל' במשמע הסתכלות לידי מכנה משותף, ובכך הפיץ אור על כתובים רבים:

1   וי"א וכך גם פירשו אהרליך (A.B. Ehrlich, *Randglossen zur hebräischen Bibel*, Leipzig 1908, ad loc.) זליגמאן, ('דעת ה' ותודעה ההיסטורית בעם ישראל בימי קדם', בתוך הנ"ל: מחקרים בספרות המקרא, ירושלים תשנ"ב, עמ' 157–158).

2   R.C. Thompson, *The Epic of Gilgamish*, Oxford 1930, p. 52, ll. 49, 51

1) 'ומצא חן ושכל טוב בעיני אלהים ואדם' (משלי ג, ד), כתוב שדנתי בו ובהשלכותיו.[3]
כך גם הכתוב המדבר באביגיל: 'והאשה טובת שכל ויפת תאר' (שמ"א כה, ג) אינו אלא
מטבע לשון המקביל ל'יפת תאר ויפת מראה' שמצאנו בבר' כט, יז ביחס לרחל, 'יפה תאר
ויפה מראה' אצל יוסף (בר' לח, ו), ובאסתר ב, ז: 'יפת תאר וטובת מראה'. אין זה מן
הנמנע שיש קשר בין 'שכל' כאן ל'שכל' בערבית, שמשמעו צורה, כפי שהציע פרלס,[4]
אף-על-פי שיש המתנגדים לפירוש זה.[5]

2) 'אשרי משכיל אל דל ביום רעה ימלטהו ה'' (תה' מא, ב) משמעו לפי ג'נאח: אשרי
המסתכל אל דל, שם לב עליו ואינו מתעלם ממנו. פירוש זה לא היה ידוע לפרשנים
נוצרים. כך למשל גונקל גורס: 'מסכין אל' (der vertraute Gottes),[6] תיקון-נוסח
שהוא גם פירוש, ושניהם בלתי משכנעים. ז'ואון[7] מבחין כאן בשתי כותרות: מזמור +
משכיל, וקורא 'אשרי הדל ואביון'.[8] רש"י לעוממתו קבע בצדק ש'דל' = חולה, על סמך
שמ"ב יג, ד: 'מדוע אתה ככה דל בן-המלך בבקר בבקר', והלא בהמשך מזמור מא אכן
מדובר באדם חולה שנזנח.

3) משלי כא, יב: 'משכיל צדיק לבית רשע' מתורגם: 'ומסתכל צדיקא בביתה דרשיעא',
ואכן 'משכיל אל ...' או 'משכיל ל...', משמעו מסתכל על, כפי שנראה להלן.

4) המאלף ביותר הוא הכתוב: 'הכל בכתב מיד ה' עלי השכיל כל מלאכות התבנית' בדה"א
כה, יט (השווה פס' יב). 'עלי' כאן בא במקום 'לי', כאילו אמר דוד: ה' הראה לי את
התבנית, בדומה למה שנאמר למשה ביחס לבניית המשכן: 'וראה ועשה בתבניתם אשר
אתה מראה בהר' (שמות כה, מ; השווה במ' ח, ד); 'ככל אשר אני מראה אותך את תבנית
המשכן ואת תבנית כל כליו' (שמות כה, ט); 'והקמת את המשכן כמשפטו אשר הראית
בהר' (שם כו, ל).[9]

'שכל' משמעו אמנם גם תבונה, אך יש לזכור כי גם השורש 'בין'/'הבין' משמעו ראייה והבנה כאחד.
'להתבונן' פירושו להביט, והגבול בין ראייה וידיעה/הבנה באמת דק מאוד.[10] נראה כי 'להשכיל אל
דברי התורה' בנח' ח, יג משמעו להבין, וכך גם יש להבין 'למען יראו... וישכילו' בישי' מא, כ.
נראה כי בפסוק 'ונחמד העץ להשכיל' (בר' ג, ו), וכן בכתוב בשמ"א כה, השתמש הסופר
בכוונה בפועל 'שכל' לבטא הבטה, כדי לרמוז גם למשמע השני של השורש, דהיינו לדעת ולהתבונה.

---

3 מ' ויינפלד, 'ומצא חן ושכל טוב בעיני אלהים ואדם – לגלגוליה של משאלה בישראל ובעמים', ארץ-ישראל טז
(ספר צבי מ' אורלינסקי), ירושלים תשמ"ב, עמ' 93–99.

4 F. Perles, 'A Misunderstood Hebrew Word', JQR n.s. 17 (1926-1927), p. 233

5 J. Barr, Comparative Philology and the Text of the Old Testament, Oxford 1968, pp. 244-245

6 H. Gunkel, Die Psalmen, Göttingen 1929, p. 175

7 P. Joüon, Beyrouth VI (1913), p. 189

8 לדעתו מילת 'ביום' היא שיבוש מ(א)ביון.

9 על מושג התבנית של המקדש בישראל ומחוצה לו ראה: V. Hurowitz, I have Built You an Exalted House:
Temple Building in the Bible in Light of Mesopotamian and Northwest Semitic Writings (JSOTSup
115), Sheffield 1992, pp. 168-170

10 ראה: זליגמן (לעיל, בהערה 1).

עץ הדעת מעניק דעת הוא גם נחמד למראה.[11] גם אביגיל היא 'טובת שכל', דהיינו היא נחנה
בחן ובדעת כאחד. נראה לי שגם את הכתוב בתה' לב, ח: 'אשכילך ואורך בדרך זו תלך איעצה עליך
עיני', יש לפרש 'אשכילך' להראותך את הדרך, כפי שמלמדת הצלע המקבילה, 'איעצה עליך עיני',
שיש לפרשה: איעצה עליך, אקרוץ לך, בדומה ל'עֹצֶה עיניו לחשוב תהפכות, קֹרץ שפתיו כלה רעה'
(משלי טז, ל).

[ב] 'עַיֵן'/'עִיֵן'

נעבור עתה לפועל 'עָיֵן'/'עִיֵן'/'עָיַן', שאף משמעו הוא הסתכלות ולא שנאה או הבטה בעין רעה כפי
שנוהגים לפרש. 'ויהי שאול עון (קרי עָיֵן) את דוד מהיום ההוא והלאה' בשמ"א יח, ט משמעו הביט
בו היטב, שם עליו עין לבל ימלט, כמו באנגלית (to watch him), ואכן בתרגום יונתן: 'והוה שאול
כמין לדוד' = היה אורב לו (לשמרו). וזאת לאחר שנתנו לו את הרבבות והיתה סכנה שישתלט על
ישראל.

על כל פנים אין הצדקה לפרש 'עיון' במשמע שונא, אלא במשמע הסתכלות קפדנית. וכך אנו
יכולים לפרש לשון חז"ל 'עיון תפילה' = דיוק בנוסח התפילה. כך מצאנו בשמו של ר' יוחנן: 'ששה
דברים אדם אוכל פירותיהם בעולם הזה והקרן קיימת לו לעולם הבא: בקור חולים, עיון תפלה
והשכמת בית המדרש וכו'' (שבת קכז ע"א). אין כוונת 'עיון' כאן, כפי שמשיע רש"י על אתר (וראה
להלן), כי אם דיוק/דקדוק = הסתכלות קפדנית. כנגד זאת מצאנו שוב בשמו של ר' יוחנן: 'כל
המאריך בתפלתו ומעיין בה סוף בא לידי כאב לב' (ברכות לב ע"ב). אין זו סתירה ל'עיון' שבדברי
ר' יוחנן שבשבת קכז ע"א, שכן המעיין בתפילה מצפה שייעשה בדיוק כפי שביקש וכשזה לא בא
– לבו כואב. התלמוד מביא שם מאמר אחר: 'כל המאריך בתפלתו אין תפלתו חוזרת ריקם' ומוצא
סתירה לאמרה קודמת. ומתרצת הגמרא: 'לא קשיא הא דמאריך ומעיין בה, הא דמאריך ולא מעיין
בה', כלומר אם מאריך ולא מדייק, דהיינו אינו עושה תפילתו נוסחת קבע (סטראוטיפ) – הרי זה
טוב, אך אם מאריך לפי נוסח קבוע זה שלילי.[12]

המפרשים כרש"י וכרשב"ם, 'עיון' = 'כוונה', אומרים שלאחר שהמתפלל כיוון בתפילתו הוא
בטוח שה' יעשה רצונו ובכך מנסה כביכול את ה', אך לפי דרכנו הכוונה לדיוק בתפילה המעורר
אצל המתפלל תקווה שבקשתו המנוסחת כהלכה תתמלא, אך לא תמיד רצונו ייעשה לו. פירושנו
יסביר גם את מאמרו של רב: 'שלש עבירות אין אדם ניצל מהן בכל יום: הרהור עבירה ועיון תפלה
ולשון הרע' (ב"ב קסד ע"ב). אדם שמתפלל לפי נוסח קבוע אינו מכוון בדרך כלל את לבו למה
שהוא אומר, שכן הנוסחאות נוקשות וסטראוטיפיות – וזוהי עבירה. קשה לפרש לפי מאמר זה לפי
רש"י, שעיון זו כוונה, שכן מה רע יש בכוונת לב בתפילה. לעומת זאת מי שעושה תפילתו
בנוסחאות הוא חוטא.

כיוצא בזה במאמר: 'ולא יהא מאריך פנים כנגד אחד ולא מעיין כנגד אחד' (תוספתא סנהדרין ו,
ב), רוצה לומר כי אל לו לאדם לנהוג בסלחנות כלפי אחד ובקפדנות כלפי אחר (ובקשר למשקלות

11   ראה: B. Jacob, *Genesis*, Berlin 1934, p. 107

12   לדיון בכל הסוגיה ראה: י' תא-שמע, 'עיון תפלה וראשית מעשה הפיוט', תרביץ נג (תשמ"ד), עמ' 285–288.
הצעתו כי 'עיון תפילה' הוא אמירת 'מעין' שמונה עשרה דחוקה.

ומידות מצאנו: 'מנין שאין מעיין במקום שמכריעין ולא יכריע במקום שמעיינין [ספרי דברים,
רצד]). 'עיון' כאן כדברי רש"י לב"ב פט ע"א: 'שקל עין בעין שהמידה תהיה מדוייקת'. [13] 'מעיין'
במשמעות שם עין, משגיח בקפדנות, נמצא בארמית שומרונית, כפי שהראה ז' בן חיים, וכן בתרגום
ניאופיטי לדב' לב, י: יצרנהו (כאישון עינו)' = 'ועייני יתהון', וכך גם בסורית וגם בתלמוד
ירושלמי. [14]

[ג] 'דיק'/'דקדק'

ועתה מגיעים אנו ל'דיק'/'דקדק', שבניבי הארמית. משמעותו היסודית של 'דיק' ו'דקדק' דומה לזו
של עין שדנו בו. 'דיק'/'דקדק' בדרך כלל מתרגם את 'השקיף' המקראי, וקביעתו של רש"י
לברייתא בבבלי ברכות כח ע"ב – כט ע"א, כי 'השקיף' פירושו: 'חשב לזכור, לשון סוכה
כדמתרגמינן וישקף: "ואסתכי"' (רש"י לבר' יט כח) אינה מדויקת. תרגום אונקלוס בלבד מתרגם
'אסתכי' ואילו פסידו-יונתן והניאופיטי מתרגמים 'השקיף' ב'אודיק'. מ' מורשת שגה אפוא באמרו:
'כי השקיף מתורגם בת"א ובת"י בשורש סכי (ואסתכי) כגון בר' כו, ח; יח, טז; שמות יד, כד; שמ"ב
כד, כז; מל"ב ט, ל'. [15] האמת היא כי רק באונקלוס מצאנו את השורש 'סכי' (ואסתכי), ואילו
בתרגום המיוחס ליונתן, וכן בת"י לנביאים וכתובים, מצאנו תרגום ל'אדק'/'אודיק' בלבד: בבר' יח,
טז: 'וישקפו על פני סדם', אנו מוצאים בת"י: 'ואודיקו' ובניאופיטי: 'ודיקו'; שם יט, כח: 'וישקף
על פני סדם ועמרה' התרגום הוא: 'ואודיק על אנפי סדום ועמורה'; שם כו, ח: 'וישקף אבימלך'
מתורגם ב'ואודיק אבימלך'; במ' כא, כ: 'ונשקפה על פני הישימון' מתורגם ל'דמדיקא כל קבל בית
ישימון'; שם כג, כח: 'הנשקף על פני הישימון' מתורגם ל'דמדיקא על אנפי בית ישימות'; דב' כו,
טו: 'השקיפה ממעון קדשך מן השמים', מתורגם ל'אודיק ממדור בית שכינת קודשך מן שמיא'. הוא
הדין בספרי נביאים וכתובים – בשופ' ה, כח: 'בעד החלון נשקפה' התרגום הוא: 'מן חרכא אסתכיאת
ומדיקא אמו'; ובכתובים: מש' ז, ו: 'נשקפתי' = 'אדקת'; תה' יד, ב: 'ה' משמים השקיף' – 'ה' משמיא
אודיק על בני נשא' (=נג, ד); ובתה' קב, כ: 'כי השקיף ממרום קדשו', התרגום הוא 'ארום אודיק
משמי מרומא'.

מעניין לציין כי הצירופים 'השקיף על', 'השקיף אל', 'השקיף בעד' לא חדרו ללשון בית שני (ראה
למשל 'ויבט', בדה"א כא, כא, הבא במקום 'וישקף' שבמקבילה בשמ"ב כד, כ). לעומת זאת מצאנו
בספרות חז"ל 'השקיף ב...', 'הנרדף ל'עיין ב...'. כך אנו קוראים בברייתא שבמסכת ברכות כח –
כט, א: 'תנו רבנן שמעון הפקולי הסדיר יח ברכות לפני רבן גמליאל על הסדר ביבנה. אמר להן רבן

---

13   על עיון במאזנים במדרש תנחומא כי תשא לד, ראה: מ' ברגמן, 'אין המאזנים מעויין', תרביץ נג (תשמ"ד), עמ'
     292–287. ברגמן מראה, על סמך בדיקות כתבי-יד של התנחומא, כי יש לקרוא: 'אין המאזנים מצויין'. אולם
     כפי שהראה מ"ע פרידמן (תרביץ נד [תשמ"ה], עמ' 149–147) 'מצויין' מתייחס רק לכת"י של מדרש תנחומא
     ואילו בשאר המקומות במדרשים מקומות הנוסחה 'מעויין'.

14   ז' בן-חיים, תרביץ י (תרצ"ט), עמ' 368–367. ראה: י' קוטשר, מחקרים בעברית וארמית, ירושלים תשל"ז, עמ'
     קעו, הערה 7; ועיין לאחרונה בערך 'עיני', בתוך: M. Sokoloff, A Dictionary of Jewish Palestinian
     Aramaic, Ramat-Gan 1990, p. 404

15   מ' מורשת, לקסיקון הפועל שנתחדש בלשון התנאים, רמת-גן תשמ"א, עמ' 78.

גמליאל לחכמים, כלום יש אדם שיודע לתקן ברכת המינים.[16] עמד שמואל קטן ותקנה. לשנה אחרת
שכחה והשקיף בה שתים ושלש שעות[17] ולא העלוהו' (=לא סילקוהו מהתיבה).

לסיכום: השתדלנו להראות כי מונחי ראייה והבטה בעברית התפתחו בעברית מאוחרת והודגש
הניואנס של דיוק בעקבות הארמית: (1) 'השכיל' המקראי, שבדרך כלל מורה על ראייה בלבד,
התרחב וכלל גם את הקונטמפלציה דהיינו ההסתכלות (ראה משנה אבות, י, יא; חגיגה ב, א);
(2) המונח השני, 'עין', המופיע פעם אחת ויחידה (hapax) במקרא (שמ"א יח, ט), אינו מבטא שנאה
דווקא, כמקובל, כי אם פקיחת עין קפדנית watch him/it באנגלית). ואמנם הפועל הזה מופיע
לעתים קרובות בלשון חכמים במובן 'שם עין' בשקילה, בנוסח והתבטאות; (3) המונח השלישי,
'דיק'/'דקדק', אינו מופיע במקרא כלל, אך הוא מופיע בעברית מאוחרת לרוב, כשהוא תופס את
מקומם של 'השקיף' ו'הביט', ותופס את מקומו בלשון המאוחרת במשמעות של דיוק קפדני.

---

16 ראה מאמרה של נעמי כהן, 'מה חידש שמואל הקטן בברכת המינים?', סיני (תשמ"ד), עמ' סד.
17 בירושלמי ברכות פ"ה ה"ג, ט ע"ג, נאמר: 'שמואל הקטן עבר קומי תיבותא ואשגר "מכניע זדים" בסופה, שרי
משקיף עליהן, אמרין ליה: לא שערו חכמים בך' (אשגר משמעו דילג אגב שטף – ראה לאחרונה: ש' נאה, 'בורא
ניב שפתים: פרק בפנומנולוגיה של התפילה על-פי משנה ברכות ד, ג; לה, ה, ה', תרביץ סג (תשנ"ד), עמ'
188–191). על כל פנים לא מדובר כאן בעיון־בנוסח כבבלי אלא בהסתכלות על החכמים, כיצד יגיבו להשמטה
זו דווקא, העלולה לעורר חשד שמא מין הוא ויסלקוהו מהתיבה. ענייננו כאן רק בסמנטיקה ולא בהשתלשלות
הנוסח של ברכת המינים ומשמעו. על כך ראה: כהן (לעיל, הערה 16), עמ' נג–ע; וכן לאחרונה: .R
Kimmelman, 'Birkat Haminim and the Lack of Evidence for an Anti-Christian Jewish Prayer
in Late Antiquity', *Jewish and Christian Self-Definition* 2: *Aspects of Judaism in the Graeco-Roman
Period* (ed. E.P. Sanders), Philadelphia 1981, pp. 229-244, 391-403

'הלא בידו עמד השמש' (בן־סירא מו, ו) – פרק בארכיאולוגיה ספרותית

יאיר זקוביץ

האוניברסיטה העברית בירושלים

[א]

נס עצירת השמש והירח (יהו' י, יב־יד) הוא מן המרהיבים בנסי המקרא. עיון בכתובים המספרים
בארוע זה, וכן בגילויים וגלגולים נוספים של המסורת – בעיקר בספרות הבתר־מקראית – מעיד,
לדעתי, כי בראשיתה היה למסורת אופי מיתי מובהק: האיש יהושע עצר בכוחו ובעצם ידו את גלגל
החמה ממהלכו (ודוק: את החמה לבדה, ולא את הלבנה!) בשעת המלחמה באמורי. אמונת הייחוד,
שאינה יכולה לדור בכפיפה אחת עם גילוייו של מיתוס, מצאה לה דרכים שונות ומגוונות להתמודד
עם סיפור גבורה בעייתי זה, בין על־ידי השתקתו ובין על־ידי שינויו באופן שיאפשר את בואו
בקהל. דבריי ייסובו אפוא אודות שלל ביטויי המסורת ונתיבי הפולמוס הסמוי עימה.

הפנייה אל גיבושיו הבתר־מקראיים של המעשה מוצדקת, באשר מסורות דחויות, שלא עלו על
הכתב בגוף המקרא, עשויות להמשיך את חייהן כמסורות שבעל־פה ולעלות על הכתב בחיבור
מאוחר. הסופר המאוחר כונס את המסורת אל חיבורו, בין משום שאין הוא חש בו עוד בחומר הנפץ
הטמון בה, ובין משום שבימיו ממילא כבר דהה עוקצה ואין היא מהווה איום על מערכת האמונות
והדעות שהוא מייצג.[1]

גילוי יסודות קדומים בחיבורים מאוחרים הוא בבחינת עיסוק ב'ארכיאולוגיה ספרותית'; בין
'ארכיאולוג ספרותי', משלח־יד שאני מבקש לאמץ לעצמי, לבין ארכיאולוג של ממש, הפרש
מהותי: האחרון – ככל שיעמיק לחפור כן יעלו באתו ממצאים קדומים יותר; הראשון עשוי למצוא
רמזים למסורות קדומות דווקא בשכבות צעירות.[2]

---

1 למאמרים על תופעת הפולמוס הסמוי, העושים שימוש בגלגולים מאוחרים של המסורת, ראה מ"ד קאסוטו, 'שירת
העלילה בישראל', ספרות מקראית וספרות כנענית, ירושלים תשל"ד, עמ' 62–90; הנ"ל, 'מעשה בני האלוהים
ובנות האדם', שם, עמ' 98–107; ש"א ליונשטם, 'מות משה', תרביץ כז (תשי"ח), עמ' 142–157; א' שנאן,
'מארטאפאנוס עד לספר הישר': לתולדותיה של אגדת משה בכוש', אשכולות תשל"ז–תשל"ח, חוברת
שנייה–שלישית, עמ' 53–67; י' זקוביץ, 'עקבת יעקב', ספר ד"ר ברוך בן יהודה (בעריכת ב"צ לוריא), תל־אביב
תשמ"א, עמ' 121–144.
2 על 'ארכיאולוגיה ספרותית' ראה מאמרי: 'היציאה מאור כשדים – פרק בארכיאולוגיה ספרותית', ספר היובל
לברוך לוין (בדפוס).

[ב]

מבט אל מקום הופעתה של המסורת בספר יהושע פרק י, מעיד כי הפסוקים יב-יד הם חלק מתחיבה בגוף הסיפור על מלחמת יהושע במלכי הדרום. פסוק טז הוא המשכו הישיר של פסוק י: פסוק י מספר אודות מפלת האויבים בגבעון ורדיפתם 'דרך מעלה בית חורון...עד עזקה ועד מקדה'. פסוק טז ממשיך מאותה נקודה ממש: 'וינסו חמשת המלכים האלה ויחבאו במערה במקדה'. הכתובים שבתווך משיבים אותנו אל מורד בית חורון (ותן דעתך לשינוי המינוח – מורד בית חורון, תחת מעלה בית חורון), עד עזקה (פס' יא), ואל עצירת גרמי השמים בשעת המערכה בגבעון (פס' יב ואילך). לפסוק טו, הסוגר את התחיבה, אין ייצוג בתרגום השבעים. כתוב זה, שהוא הכפלה של פסוק מג הנועל את המעשה, הובא לכאן אגב גררה יחד עם המלים המקדימות אותו 'כי ה'...נלחם לישראל' (ראה פס' מב). בעל התחיבה, ולשם דיוק מי שכתב את פסוק יד, סבר כי יש בכוח המלים 'כי ה' נלחם לישראל' כדי לשרת את תפיסתו בדבר ההתרחשויות הנסיות, ולפיכך ביקש להציבן בסיום התחיבה.

מדברי יוצא כי הפרק בגיבושו הראשוני בכתב לא ידע לא את נס האבנים שהשליך ה' מן השמים (פס' יא) ולא את נס עצירת המאורות (פס' יב-יד). דומה כי נס הברד נוסף לסיפור, בראש ובראשונה כדי להסביר את פשרה וטיבה של המהומה שהם אלוהי ישראל באויב: במקרים רבים במקרא מוסברת המהומה כאחד מאיתני הטבע שהטיל ה' באויב: עמוד אש וענן (שמ' יד, כד), ברק (שמ"ב כב, טו = תה' יח, טו; קמד, ו), או רעם (שמ"א ז, י). בפעמים אחרות לא נתפרש טבעה של המהומה (דב' ב, טו; שופ' ד, טו; דה"ב טו, ו), ולסוג זה נשתייך גם יהושע י קודם שילוב התוספת. בסיום ההתייחסות החגיגית לנס הברד מציין המספר: 'וימתו[3] רבים אשר מתו באבני הברד מאשר הרגו בני ישראל בחרב' (השווה שופ' טז, ל; שמ"ב יח, ח).[4]

ואשר לנס עצירת השמש והירח: בעל הנוסחה הראשונית של יהושע י ביקש להעלימה ולהשתיקה. מחבר מאוחר יותר, אשר ידע את המעשה ולא השלים עם הסתרת אירוע כה חשוב מעיני הקורא, שילבו בתחיבה המקנה לגיטימציה לעצירת המאורות, שהרי זו מוצגת – בעקבות השלכת האבנים – כנס נוסף שחולל ה': יהושע פנה לה' בתפילה, וזה עשה כבקשתו: 'אז ידבר[5] יהושע לה' ביום תת ה' את האמרי לפני בני ישראל ויאמר לעיני ישראל שמש בגבעון דום וירח בעמק אילון' (פס' יב). הכתוב אף מדגיש כי ה' הוא המנחיל ניצחון לעמו: 'ביום תת ה'...'. להדגשת חלקו של ה' בנס עצירת המאורות כשותף גם פסוק יד: 'ולא היה כיום ההוא לפניו ואחריו לשמע ה' בקול איש...'.[6] לא יהושע בכוחו עוצר את המאורות כי אם ה': גדולתו של יהושע מתבטאת בעובדה כי ה' שמע לקולו (השווה במ' כא, ג; שופ' יג, ט; מל"א יז, כב). סיומו של פסוק יד: 'כי ה' נלחם לישראל' הובא לכאן, כאמור

---

3   ובתרגום השבעים: 'ויהיו רבים אשר מתו...'. התבה 'ויהיו' נשתבשה ל'וימתו' (חילופין של שתי אותיות בלבד) בהשפעת המלה 'מתו' הבאה בהמשך, ואולי גם בהשפעת שופ' טז, שבו מופיע השורש מו"ת ארבע פעמים.

4   על כתובים אלה ראה מאמרי 'שופטים טז, ל ורישומיו בנביאים ראשונים', בית מקרא ג(10) (תשל"ו), עמ' 475–477.

5   ללשון פתיחה זו השווה שמ' טו, א; במ' כא, יז.

6   לחלוקת התפקידים אדם-אלוהים במעשה נס זה ראה ר' כשר, 'דפוסי הפעילות של עושי-הנפלאות במקרא', עיוני מקרא ופרשנות ב (בעריכת א' סימון), רמת-גן תשמ"ו, עמ' 166–167.

לעיל, מסוף הפרק, מפסוק מב, כחיזוק לתפיסה שהמלחמה והניצחון לה' המה ולא לאדם (וראה
לדוגמה שמ' יד, יד, כה; דב' א, ל; ג, כב; כ, ד).

אפשר שדברי יהושע גופם: 'שמש בגבעון דום וירח בעמק אילון' (פס' יב²) לא שימשו במסורת
המקורית כתפילה לה' אלא כציווי לשמש לעמוד מלכת.[7] ועוד, דומה בעיני אמנם כי אף בעצירת
השמש הכתוב מדבר, בעמידתה דום (השווה שמ"א יד, ט), כדי לאפשר את השמדת האויבים,
ואילו משמע הצלע השנייה, חסרת הפועל, 'וירח בעמק אילון' הוא שהירח יכול דווקא להמשיך
להלך במסלולו, להופיע בעמק אילון, שהרי מקום זה מצוי על גבול שדה המערכה ומסלול
הנסיגה, ומחוצה להם.

המשך השיר 'וידם השמש וירח עמד...' אינו חלק אורגני של דברי יהושע.[8] לא עוד בצו מדובר
כי אם בהגשמת הדברים. שורה זו גם מתייחסת לצו כאילו חל אף על עצירת הירח, כאילו הפועל
שבצלע הראשונה של הצו 'דום' נמשך משיכה קדמית גם אל הצלע השנייה (על דרך כתובים כגון
בר' ד, כג; תה' קיד', א־ב, ד, ז, ח).[9] פירוש הצו כמדובר בירח אינו תולדה של טעות, אלא פרי
המגמה לטשטש קשר מיוחד בין יהושע לבין השמש (כפי שיתברר עוד להלן). והנה, פסוק יג² חוזר
אל הצו שבפסוק יב² באשר הוא אכן מבין אותו כמדובר בעצירת השמש לבדה: 'ויעמד השמש בחצי
השמים ולא אץ לבוא כיום תמים'. השמש לא אץ, וזאת בניגוד לטבעו, וראה תהלים יט, ו: 'והוא
(=השמש) כחתן יצא מחפתו ישיש כגבור לרוץ ארח'.

ובאשר לספר הישר המצוין כמקור הספרותי שהשיר שאול ממנו (פס' יג): מעניין כי השמש,
והשמש דווקא, נזכרת בציטוט נוסף מספר זה – אף כי באותו מקור מופיע שם הספר בשיכול
אותיותיו – ספר השיר:[10] הכתובים מלכים א ח, יב־יג מופיעים בתרגום השבעים בשינוי ניכר,
לאחר פסוק נג. וולהאוזן יסד את הנוסח הבא לאחר שתיקן בו כמה שיבושים: 'אז אמר שלמה:
שמש הכין בשמים ה', אמר לשכן בערפל. בנה ביתי בית נוה לי לשבת עולמים. הלא היא כתובה
על ספר השיר'.[11]

[ג]

ראיות נוספות לכך שהמסורת המקורית אכן דיברה בעצירת השמש לבדה ניתן להביא מגילויים
מאוחרים יותר שלה: בן־סירא, המפאר את גבורת יהושע, גורס: 'הלא בידו עמד השמש, יום אחד
היה לשנים' (מו, ד). יהושע עוצר אפוא בידו את השמש ממהלכה כשם שבידו אף עשה, אליבא

7 אף שתפילה המבקשת על נס דומה מופיעה באליאס, ספר שני, שורות 412–419 – תפילת אגממנון לזאוס כי
   השמש לא ישקע טרם ישרוף את ביתו של פריאמוס; ראה למשל מ' ויינפלד, 'מלחמתו של האל בישראל ובמזרח
   הקדמון', מחקרים במקרא ובמזרח הקדמון א (ספר ש"א ליונשטם; ערכו י' אבישור, י' בלאו), ירושלים תשל"ח, ח,
   עמ' 181.

8 ראה, למשל, J. Blenkinsopp, *Gibeon and History*, Cambridge 1972, p. 45

9 ראה מ"צ סגל, מבוא המקרא א, ירושלים 1967, עמ' 66.

10 ואפשר ששמו המקורי של החיבור 'ספר שיר ה'', ונכתב ה'' כקיצור לשם הויה, ולא הובן והועבר לראש המלה.
   השווה 'אשירה לה'' (שמ' טו, א); 'אנכי לה' אנכי אשירה' (שופ' ה, ג) וכן רבים. הצירוף 'שיר ה'' מופיע פעם
   אחת ויחידה, בתהלים קלז, ד.

11 ראה: J. Wellhausen, *Die Composition des Hexateuchs und der historischen Bücher des Alten Testaments*³, Berlin 1899, p. 271

דבן-סירא, מעשה נפלא אחר: 'מה נהדר בנטותו יד בהניפו כידון על עיר'. אין זאת אלא כי בעיניו
אף פעולה זו היא נס שחולל יהושע, כתפיסת יהושע ח, כו – פסוק מוסף לפרשת כיבוש העי, שאין
לו מקביל בתרגום השבעים – וזאת בניגוד לתפיסת תפקידה של נטיית הכידון כסימן לאורב לתקוף,
שם בפסוקים יח-יט.[12]

בן-סירא מעביר את קריאת יהושע לעזרת ה' מתמונת עצירת המאורות לתמונה המתרחשת
אליבא דידֵיה לאחר עצירת השמש: 'כי קרא אל אל עליון כאכפה לֹ[ו אויבים מסביב], ויענהו אל
עליון באבני [ברד וא]לגביש...' (שם, פס' ז-ח).[13]

גם המדרש, כבן-סירא, מספר בעצירת השמש (אך עימה גם שאר המאורות) בנטיית ידו של
יהושע, הנתפסת כפעולה של השבעה: '...וראה יהושע בצרתן של ישראל שלא יחללו את השבת...
מה עשה? פשט ידו לאור השמש ולאור הירח ולאור הכוכבים והזכיר עליהם את השם ועמדו כל אחד
ואחד ל"ו שעות עד מוצאי שבת...' (פדר"א נב, וראה גם בפירוש הרד"ק).

הדגשת עצירתה של השמש בלבד עולה מכמה מסורות מדרשיות: '''אז ידבר יהושע לה'' וגו'',
"שמש בגבעון דום", ביקש יהושע לשתק את החמה, לא אמר לו שמש בגבעון עמוד אלא דום. למה
אמר דום, שכל שעה שהוא הולך הוא מקלס להקב"ה, וכל זמן שהוא מקלס יש בו כח להלך. לכך
אמר לו יהושע שישתוק, שנאמר "שמש בגבעון דום"' (תנחומא בובר, אחרי, לד ע"ב).[14]

ועוד: 'תנו רבנן: שמונים תלמידים היו לו להלל הזקן. שלושים מהן ראויים היו שתשרה עליהן
שכינה כמשה רבינו, ושלושים מהן ראויים שתעמוד להם חמה כיהושע בן נון, ועשרים בינונים...'
(סוכה כח ע"א).

מסורת מדרשית אחרת המקנאת לכבודו של משה אף קובעת שבניגוד ליהושע שהעמיד חמה פעם
אחת: 'חמה עמדה לו למשה שתי פעמים, ראשונה כשעשה מלחמה עם עמלק ופעם שנייה במלחמת
סיחון ועוג' (שוחר טוב יט, ח).[15] אפשר שדימויי כזה של משה ליהושע, בחינת 'מעשה בנים סימן
לאבות', משתקף במגילת קומראן המכונה במחקר 'מזמורי יהושע', בפרגמנט 4Q378 26 המדבר
במשה, וראה שורה 5 שם: '. .] מפתים גדולים ובחמה יעצר [.'.[16]

במזמור שבחבקוק ג הוסיפה יד זרה את סיומו של פסוק י וראשיתו של פסוק יא: 'רום ידיהו נשא.
שמש ירח עמד זבֻלה' (ויש לגרוס: זבלה; מין זכר יהלום את מינו של הפועל[17]). מלים אלה קוטעות
את הרצף – דברים אל ה' בגוף שני: 'ראוך יחילו הרים... (פס' י) לאור חציך יהלכו לנגה ברק

12   ראה י' אמית, 'כידונו של יהושע (יהו' ח, יח, כו)', שנתון למקרא ולחקר המזרח הקדום ה-ו (תשמ"א-תשמ"ב),
      עמ' 11–18.

13   דומה כי בן-סירא כורך בין התפילה לבין מעשה הטלת אבני הברד משום דברי ה' קודם השלכת האבנים: 'אל
      תירא מהם...' (פס' ח). לשון 'אל תירא' שבפי ה' נתפסת הן בתרגומים הארמיים (ראה, לדוגמה, התרגומים
      הארמיים השונים לבראשית טו, א [א' שנאן, מקרא אחד ותרגומים הרבה, תל-אביב תשנ"ג, עמ' 53–54]) והן
      במדרש (ראה לדוגמה ב"ר מד, ד) כהיענות לתפילה.

14   כאן מתבאר השורש דמ"ם לא כלשון עמידה אלא כלשון שתיקה, ראה לדוגמה עמ' ה, מ; איכה ב, י.

15   לניסיון דומה לגימוד דמותו של יהושע ראה בבא בתרא עה ע"א: 'זקנים שבאותו הדור אמרו פני משה כפני חמה,
      פני יהושע כפני לבנה'.

16   את החומר הציגה Carol A. Newsom בהרצאתה: 'Psalms 4Q378 26: Transcription and Translation
      of Joshuaᵃ' בקונגרס ה-SBL הבין-לאומי במינסטר, גרמניה, ב-28.7.93. ניוסום מבינה את המלים 'ובחמה
      יעצר' הבנה שונה – כאילו עצר משה את כעסו/חמתו: 'and he restrained his wrath'.

17   כך, למשל, גורס נ"ה טור-סיני, פשוטו של מקרא ג², ירושלים תשכ"ז, עמ' 523.

חניתך...' (פס' יא). זאת ועוד, השוואה בין רצף פסוקי המזמור לקטע מקביל בתהלים עז, יז־יט
מעידה כי אין מקום לקטע הזה שבתוך:

חבקוק ג, יא+יא־ג		תהלים עז, יז־יט	
ראוך יחילו הרים		ראוך מים אלהים ראוך מים יחילו	
		אף ירגזו תהמות	
זרם מים עבר נתן תהום קולו		זרמו מים עבות קול נתנו שחקים	
לאור חצים יהלכו לנגה ברק חניתך[18]		אף חצציך יתהלכו. קול רעמך בגלגל	
		האירו ברקים תבל...	

שילוב היסוד הזר גם מערב מין בשאינו מינו: אם ניצבים השמש והירח ברום השמים, בזבול,[19] מדוע
יהלכו ההולכים לאור החצים־הברקים?[20] דומה שבעל התוספת מצא לנכון לפאר את תמונת ה' היוצא
לישע עמו (ראה פס' יא) ברכיב השאוב מן המסורת הקדומה על יהושע וכך להוסיף אור לזירת הקרב.
בתוספת, ה' הוא המעמיד את המאורות על־ידי השבעתם: 'רום ידיהו נשא' (והשווה דב' לב, מ: 'כי
אשא אל שמים ידי ואמרתי...').

בזיקה בין חבקוק ליהושע חש תרגום יונתן לנביאים המבאר את הסיטואציה המזמורית על הנס
שנעשה ליהושע: 'אף במעבדך נסין ליהושע במישר גבעון שמשא וסיהרא קמו במדוריהון עמך
במימרך אתגברו בתקוף נצחן גבורתך'.[21]

לשון התוספת בחבקוק דומה במיוחד ללשון מסורת יהושע שבספר בן־סירא:

בן־סירא מו, ו		חבקוק ג, יא
הלא בידו עמד השמש		רום ידיהו נשא. שמש...ירח עמד...

לשון התוספת בחבקוק תמוהה: איבריו של הנושא הכולל – שמש, ירח – אינם חבורים. זאת ועוד,
הנשוא 'עמד' מתייחס לנושא יחיד, וכן אף המושא – מקום העמידה – 'זבלה'. לפיכך דומה איפוא
כי הכתוב המקורי גרס 'שמש עמד זבלה' ואילו המלה ירח אינה אלא תוספת על גב תוספת: קורא
אשר עמד על זיקת הכתוב בחבקוק ליהושע, והכיר את פסוקי יהושע ככתבם וכלשונם בספר, ראה
לנכון להשלים את נס עצירת השמש בעצירת הירח.

---

18 להשוואת הקטע בתהלים לכתוב בחבקוק ראה י' אבישור, עיונים בשירה המזמורית והאוגריתית, ירושלים
     תשמ"ט, עמ' 96.

19 להבנה זו של זבול ראה אבישור, שם, עמ' 124.

20 אבישור חש בזרות צירופן של שתי התמונות (שם, עמ' 97) אך לדידו הגיבוב הוא מידו של המחבר הראשון של
     המזמור.

21 ראה גם רש"י, רד"ק ואברבנאל בפירושם לכתוב בחבקוק.

[ד]

מסרת עצירת השמש – והשמש בלבד – על־ידי יהושע כרוכה במסורת אודות נחלתו ומקום קבורתו – תמנת חרס: 'וימת יהושע בן נון עבד ה' בן מאה ועשר שנים. ויקברו אותו בגבול נחלתו בתמנת חרס בהר אפרים מצפון להר געש' (שופ' ב, ח־ט). וחרס הוא שמש (שופ' יד, יח; איוב ט, ז). בהופיע אותו כתוב ממש על קבורת יהושע בחתימת ספרו נמסר שם העיר בשיכול אותיות: 'תמנת סרח' (כד, ל), וכך מופיע שם העיר גם קודם לכן, במסופר אודות נתינתה כנחלה ליהושע: 'על פי ה' נתנו לו את העיר אשר שאל את תמנת סרח (בנוסח וטיקנוס של תרגום השבעים משקף התעתיק את השם 'תמנת חרס'!) בהר אפרים ויבנה את העיר וישב בה' (יהו' יט, נ).

ברי כי השם שונה בכוונה תחילה בספר יהושע כדי לטשטש כל קשר בין יהושע לבין השמש. השינוי נערך במרכז (ספר יהושע), ובפריפריה, בספר שופטים, נשתמרה הצורה המקורית.[22]

על קברו של יהושע קיימת מסורת מעניינת בסיום ספר יהושע בתרגום השבעים: 'וישימו שם אתו אל הקבר אשר קברו אותו שם את חרבות הצורים אשר מל בהן את בני ישראל בהוציאו אותם ממצרים כאשר ציוהו ה' ויהיו שם עד היום הזה'. ועל חרבות הצורים מסופר בזיקה לנחלת יהושע גם בתוספת שבתרגום השבעים לפרק כא, מב: 'ויתנו בני ישראל נחלה ליהושע על־פי ה' ויתנו לו את העיר אשר שאל את תמנת סרח נתנו לו בהר אפרים. ויבן יהושע את העיר וישב בה. ויקח יהושע את חרבות הצורים אשר מל בהן את בני ישראל הנולדים בדרך במדבר וישם אותן בתמנת סרח'.[23]

מסורת זו על שרידים מקודשים (רליקוויה)[24] שהונחו בקברו של יהושע מתמיהה ולא רק בשל נועזותה – הודאתה בקיום נוהג של הנחת חפצים בקברו של אדם – אלא בעיקר משום אופים החריג של החפצים; כאשר המקרא מספר על חפצים מקודשים הרי אלה בבחינת זכר למעשה נסים – כך צנצנת המן שהונחה למשמרת לפני העדות (שמ' טז, לב־לד), מטהו הפורח של אהרן שאף הוא הונח לפני העדות (במ' יז, כה) וכן האבנים שהוצבו בגלגל לציון נס חציית הירדן (יהו' ד, ו־ז, כ־כג).[25]

דומה אפוא כי מסורת קבורתן של חרבות הצורים – שאין לה, כאמור, זכר בנוסח המסורה – לא באה לעולם אלא כדי להתמודד עם מסורת אחרת, על חפץ אחר אשר עמד אצל קברו של יהושע בתמנת חרס. המסורת הדוחה הדורשת את שני מרכיבי שמו של מקום הקבורה נשתמרה במדרש מאוחר, מדרש בראשית רבתי (מהדורת ח' אלבק, עמ' 100):

'...ויהי אחרי מות יהושע' (שופ' א, א), משל לאדם שירד ארי ונצחו. אחרי ימים מת, אמר הב"ה עשו על קבורתו צורת אריה והיו אומרים אוי לזה שנצח הארי והוא מוטל כאן. כך יהושע העמיד את השמש והוא מוטל כאן כאן שנאמר 'ויקברו אותו בגבול נחלתו בתמנת חרס' (שופ' ב, ט).

22 למגמתיות השינוי ראה למשל א, לה .C.F. Burney, *The Book of Judges*, Oxford 1918, p. 56. גם בשופ' א, לה שונה השם 'הר חרס' במהדורות תרגום השבעים (ראה ברני, שם, עמ' 32). ולהפך, תחת השם 'עיר ההרס' בישעיה יט, יח מופיעה במגילת ישעיה השלמה מקומראן הגרסה המקורית: 'עיר החרס'.

23 לתרגומי הקטעים לעברית ראה א' רופא, 'סיומו של ספר יהושע לפי תרגום השבעים', שנתון למקרא ולחקר המזרח הקדום ב (תשל"ז), עמ' 219, 226.

24 ראה רופא, שם, עמ' 221.

25 ולשרידים מקודשים נוספים ראה בספרי: על תפיסת הנס במקרא, תל־אביב תשמ"ז, עמ' 104–106.

המדרש נמנע מלאמור מפורשות כי על קברו של יהושע העמידו תמונת חרס, חמה, משום החשש
לספר בשריד מקודש, ועוד כזה הנושא אופי מיתולוגי־אלילי, אך המשל על האיש שהרג ארי יעיד.

לנוסח השלם של המדרש מתייחס רש"י בפירושו ליהושע כד, ל: '...ובמקום אחר הוא קורא
אותה תמנת חרס, על שם שהעמידו תמונת חמה על קברו לומר: זה הוא שהעמיד חמה. וכל העובר
עליה אומר חבל על זה שעשה דבר גדול כזה ומת' (דברים דומים כתב רש"י גם בפירושו לשופטים
ב, ט). ורד"ק בפירושו לכתוב ביהושע מעיר: 'ולמה קראה חרס? בשביל שנקבר שם יהושע
שהעמיד חמה לישראל'.[26]

[ה]

ועתה עוד מקצת משהו על חשש המקרא מפני מסורות מיתיות הכרוכות בשמש או בשליטה בה.
אפשר שגם תמנה/תמנתה אחרת, זו המתייחסת לפעמים על דן (יהו' יט, מג) ולפעמים על יהודה
(שם טו, י) ומקומה בין בית שמש לעקרון, נקראה 'תמנת חרס': בהיות שמשון (הנושא בשמו את
היסוד שמש, ועל כך להלן) שמה (יד, א;ואילך), הוא חד חידה למרעיו, שושביניו הפלשתים, שאותה
הם צריכים לפתור בתוך שבוע ימים. המספר דורש את שם המקום בדבריו על פתרון החידה ברגע
האחרון ממש: 'ויאמרו לו אנשי העיר ביום השביעי בטרם יבוא החרסה...' (שם פס' יח). מדרש שם
זה מקנה משמעות תמימה, בלתי מיתולוגית לשם המקום.

כדי להימלט מקושי חמור הכרוך בשמו של שמשון העדיף מספר תולדותיו שלא לדרוש את השם
בסיפור לידת הגיבור (שופ' יג, כד), שלא כדרך סיפורי לידה מעין אלה. חז"ל, אשר יראו מן
הוואקום, דרשו את השם תוך עיקור הממד המיתולוגי, וכרכו בין השמש לבין ה': 'וא"ר יוחנן:
שמשון על שמו של הקב"ה נקרא. שנאמר "כי שמש ומגן ה' אלהים" (תה' פד, יב)... מה הקב"ה
מגן על כל העולם אף שמשון מגן בדורו על כל ישראל' (סוטה י, ע"א).[27]

מסורת על עצירת החמה (או אף על השבתה אחרנית במסלולה) משתקפת בסיפור על האות שנתן
ישעיהו לחזקיהו בהשבת הצל במעלות אחז (מל"ב כ, ח־יא; יש' לח, ז־ח), וניכר כי אף מעשה זה
גרם למבוכה רבה. נוסחת ישעיה לפרק לח, ח משובשת אך מדברת אמנם בהחזרת השמש אחרנית
במסלולה: 'הנני משיב את צל המעלות אשר ירדה במעלות אחז בשמש אחרנית עשר מעלות ותשב
השמש עשר מעלות במעלות אשר ירדה'. נוסחת תרגום השבעים עדיפה: 'אשר ירדה השמש
במעלות אחז אחורנית'. גרסת מגילת ישעיה השלמה מקומוראן 'את השמש' תחת 'בשמש' משקפת
אולי שלב קדום עוד יותר במסורת הכתוב: אפשר שהמלים 'את השמש' עמדו בראשונה במקום בו
ניצבות עתה המלים 'את צל המעלות': הסיפור לא דיבר כלל על השבתת הצל אלא על השבתת השמש:

26   לולי דמסתפינא הייתי טוען שגם במסורת החלופית שבתרגום השבעים נעשה נסיון לדרוש את השם 'תמנת חרס'
      על דרך מדרשי השמות – בין גלויים ובין סמויים – המפצלים את יסודות השם בין מלים שונות, כגון מדרש השם
      רחבעם בבן־סירא מז, לה: 'רחב אולת וחסר בינה רחבעם הפריע בעצ[תו] עם', וכדרך מדרשו הסמוי של השם
      נבות במלים 'נחלת אבות' (מל"א כא, ג, ד): המלים 'חרבות צורים' משחקות במלה 'חרס' (וידוע החילוף החפשי
      בין ס–צ כגון בשרש 'עלצ'–'עלס').

27   על המשקע המיתולוגי – שמש בסיפור שמשון – ראה מה שכתבתי בספרי חיי שמשון, ירושלים תשמ"ב, עמ'
      236–239, ושם ספרות.

'הנני משיב את השמש אשר ירדה במעלות אחז אחרנית עשר מעלות. ותשב השמש עשר מעלות במעלות אשר ירדה'.

נוסחת מלכים ב כ כבר משקפת עיבוד עמוק יותר של המרת השמש בצל: הסיפור כולו מדבר בנטיית הצל, ורק ארבע מִלים בפסוק יא, המפריעות את רצף הכתוב, רומזות לנוסחת השמש: 'אשר ירדה (לשון נקבה!) במעלות אחז'. מִלים אלה (המצויות בנוסחת ישעיה) אינן מופיעות בתרגום השבעים למלכים![28]

[ו]

לסיכום, מסורת קדמונית על עצירת החמה בידי יהושע הושתקה ולא נכללה כלל במהדורה ראשונה של הספר. גם שֵׁם נחלתו ומקום קברו 'תמנת חרס' שובש, ובלבד שלא יוודע על זיקה בינו לבין השמש.

משנוספה המסורת לפרק על־ידי סופר שביקש לתת לה ביטוי, הוקהה עוקצה על־ידי התפנית שניתנה לה: ה' הוא שחולל את הנס בהיענותו לתפילת יהושע. ויתרה מזאת, עצירת הירח, הנוספת על עצירת השמש ומעצימה, לכאורה, את ממדיו של הנס, מטשטשת את הקשר המיוחד שבין יהושע לבין השמש.

המסורת המאוחרת – התוספת על דברי חבקוק, בן־סירא, מזמורי יהושע מקומראן, ספרות חז"ל, ואף מדרש בראשית רבתי שמצטט רש"י באופן שלם ונכון יותר, מעידים על הסיפור הקדום, המושתק. זאת ועוד, אפשר שדברי רש"י מאפשרים לשחזר שלב נוסף בגלגולי המסורות ולטעון כי מסורת תרגום השבעים על חרבות הצורים שנטמנו בקברו של יהושע – מסורת שהושתקה אף היא בזרם המרכזי של תולדות יהושע – אינה אלא תחליף למסורת המקורית על גלגל החמה שניצב על קברו, זכר לגבורתו. הרגישות למסורות גבורה ונס הכרוכות בשמש ובעצירתה אינה נחלת יהושע בלבד, והיא ניכרת בסיפורי שמשון ובסיפור השבת השמש אחרנית במעלות אחז. ביטויו של חשש זה, הנראים בגלוי מחוץ לגבולות יהושע, מאוששים את הטיעון בדבר גלגולי המסורות אודות יהושע אשר 'בידו עמד השמש', וטעמם.

---

28 על מתח בין מסורת החזרת השמש אחורנית למסורת החזרת הצל ראה ר' כשר, 'הנסים במלכים ב כ, ח־יא בהשוואה למקבילה בישעיהו לח, כ־כב', שנתון למקרא ולחקר המזרח הקדום ז–ח (תשמ"ג–תשמ"ד), עמ' 82–83. לבירורי הגרסאות של ישעיה לח, ראה S. Iwry, 'The Qumran Isaiah and the End of the Dial of Ahaz', BASOR 147 (1957), pp. 3-27

מסורת וחידוש בפירוש רשב"ם לספר איוב
איוב פרק כח

שרה יפת
האוניברסיטה העברית בירושלים

פרשנות הפשט בצפון צרפת מגיעה לשיאה במהלכה של המאה השתים־עשרה, במפעלו הפרשני
של רשב"ם. בעוד הגורמים לצמיחתה של אסכולת הפשט, שלביה הראשונים, ותרומתם המסוימת
של הפרשנים המשתייכים אליה עדיין נתונים במחלוקת,[1] קיימת תמימות דעים בין החוקרים בדבר
מקומו המרכזי של רשב"ם באסכולת הפשט באשכנז. הן מצד הבנת מהותו של הפשט, הן בהצגת
מטרת הפירוש כחתירה בלבדית אל הפשט, והן מצד ההישג, מייצג רשב"ם את נקודת השיא
בהתפתחותה של אסכולה זו, שיא שהקודמים לו מובילים אליו והבאים אחריו ניזונים ממנו ובה בעת
הולכים ומתרחקים ממנו.[2]

רשב"ם הציג את מטרת פעילותו הפרשנית באופן ברור וחד־משמעי: אין הוא בא לפרש אלא
בדרך הפשט. ואולם בה בעת מסתמך רשב"ם באורח שיטתי ועקיב הן על מקורות חז"ל – המשנה,
התלמוד והמדרשים – שהוא מצטט אותם ומסתייע בהם, והן על פרשנים שקדמו לו, ובראש
ובראשונה רש"י, שבדרך כלל אין הוא מזכירם בשמותיהם.[3] עובדה זו, שרשב"ם נזקק לאלו שקדמו
לו, מן הדין היה שתתקבל על פניה וללא סימני שאלה. שהרי אף פרשן אינו פועל בחלל ריק ואינו
מתחיל את פירושו ב'נקודת אפס' מוחלטת. כל עשייה נתונה במסגרת של הווייה תרבותית קיימת
ונזקקת מעצם טבעה – וגם מתוך עמדה של מחלוקת – לאותה מציאות תרבותית, ופרשנות המקרא

---

1. ראה א' טויטו, 'שיטתו הפרשנית של רשב"ם על רקע המציאות ההיסטורית של זמנו', י"ד גילת, ח"י לוין, צ"מ
   רבינוביץ (עורכים), עיונים בספרות חז"ל, במקרא ובתולדות ישראל, מוקדש לפרופ' עזרא ציון מלמד, רמת־גן
   תשמ"ב, עמ' 48–54.

2. ראה ש"א פוזננסקי, פירוש על יחזקאל ותרי עשר לרבי אליעזר מבלגנצי, ורשה תרע"ג, עמ' XLIII, XLIX; א'
   סימון, 'לדרכו הפרשנית של הראב"ע על פי שלושת ביאוריו לפסוק אחד', בר אילן ג (תשכ"ה), עמ' 137–138;
   מ' גרינברג, 'היחס בין פירוש רש"י לפירוש רשב"ם לתורה', י' זקוביץ, א' רופא (עורכים), ספר יצחק אריה
   זליגמן ב, ירושלים תשמ"ג, עמ' 566–567.

3. על האישים הנזכרים בפירושו לתורה, ראה ע"צ מלמד, מפרשי המקרא, דרכיהם ושיטותיהם, ירושלים תשל"ה,
   עמ' 483–484, 489, 490. בפירושו לקהלת לא הזכיר אף לא פרשן אחד (ראה ש' יפת, פירוש
   רבי שמואל בן מאיר (רשב"ם) לקהלת, ירושלים תשמ"ה, עמ' 50–51), ואילו בפירושו לאיוב הוא מזכיר פעמים
   אחדות את פירוש רש"י ומכנהו: הקונטרס (ראה לפי שעה: S. Japhet, 'The Commentary of Rabbi
   Samuel ben Meir (Rashbam) on the Book of Job', *Proceedings of the Colloquium: La culture juive
   en France du nord au moyen age* (December 1990) (forthcoming)

115*

אינה יוצאת מכלל זה. ואולם, כיוון שרשב"ם נוקט לא פעם סגנון פולמוסי, מתייחס בביקורת למה שקדם לו ומדגיש את החידוש בפירושיו,[4] נוצרת בקורא מעין ציפייה, מודעת או בלתי מודעת, שעבודתו תגלה ניתוק גמור מן המסורת.[5] ציפייה זו מתנפצת לאור העובדה שבמקומות רבים רשב"ם מתייחס אל המקורות המסורתיים התייחסות חיובית ומקבלת. יתר על כן, חוקרים אחדים מפנים את תשומת הלב לפירושים 'מדרשיים' המצויים בין פירושי רשב"ם, שהם רואים בהם 'מעידות' או 'כשלונות' בדרך להשגת מטרתו.[6] שאלת זיקתו של רשב"ם למסורות חז"ל ולפרשנות שקדמה לו, וכנגדה – החידוש בשיטתו ובפירושיו, הם נושא עיוננו זה. בחרנו לעסוק בו לא באמצעות הכרזותיו המתודולוגיות, שבהן הוא מציג את מטרת עבודתו במודע ובמפורש, אלא באמצעות בירורו של קטע אחד שלם, שיש בו כדי להעיד על שיטתו הלכה למעשה.

פירושו של רשב"ם לספר איוב נשתמר בשלמותו בכתב־יד אחד; חלק נכבד ממנו מצוי בכתב־יד נוסף, וכן מצויים קטעים ממנו בכתבי־יד נוספים. הפירוש השלם עדיין לא ראה אור, ואנחנו מקווים להוציאו לאור בעתיד הקרוב.[7] בפרק כה, שבחרנו בו, יש עניין מבחינות רבות, ולנוחות הקורא צירפנו בנספח את טקסט הפירוש.

כמו פירוש רש"י לאיוב,[8] פירושו של רשב"ם הוא קצר. רוב ההערות הפרשניות מנוסחות בקיצור, ולא כל הפרטים זוכים לביאור. אף־על־פי־כן ניתן לראות בפירושו לפרק כה פירוש שלם, מפני שנידונות בו הבעיות המרכזיות של הפרק ומצויות בו הערות פרשניות לגבי כל הפסוקים מלבד שלושה.[9] בבחירת הנושאים, בדרך הכתיבה, במינוח, בשיטת הפירוש ובתכניו, מייצג הפירוש

---

4   הדברים ידועים ואין צורך להאריך. ראה למשל דבריו לבר' א, א; לז, ב; מט, ה, טז; שמות ב, ו; יט, כג ועוד. ראה מלמד (לעיל, הערה 3), בעיקר עמ' 488–489.

5   וראה, למשל, ניסחו של גרינברג: 'להפגנת שיא של עצמאות מסמכותה של מסורת חז"ל הגיעה הפרשנות הצרפתית בפירושו לתורה של שמואל בר מאיר' (מ' גרינברג, פרשנות המקרא היהודית – פרקי מבוא, ירושלים 1983, עמ' 77), ופוזננסקי: 'הנה כי כן נראה אצלו יחוס אחר לדברי רז"ל ולדרשותיהם מאשר אצל ההולכים לפניו ובזה יבדל מהם' (לעיל, הערה 2, עמ' XLII). תגובה לתפיסות מעין אלה מצויה במאמרו של א' טויטו, 'על שיטתו של רשב"ם בפירושו לתורה', תרביץ מח (תשל"ט), עמ' 251–253.

6   ראה ע"צ מלמד (לעיל הערה 3), עמ' 454–455, וראה גם ש' יפת, 'פירוש רשב"ם לפרשת העקדה – פשוטו של מקרא או מדרשו', בתוך: ש' יפת (עורכת), המקרא בראי מפרשיו – ספר זכרון לשרה קמין, ירושלים 1994, עמ' 364.

7   הפירוש השלם נשתמר בכ"י לוצקי 778 בספריית בית־המדרש לרבנים בניו־יורק, והפירוש החלקי, הכולל את הפרקים לו, א – מב, יז, מצוי בכ"י מס' 2752 בספריית קזנטה (Ms. Sacerdote 53) ופורסם בחלקו בידי ברלינר אצל א"א הרכבי, מאסף נדחים ה, ו (1878), צולם מחדש: קדם, ירושלים 1970, עמ' 53–56, 69–75. ראה, לפי שעה, במאמרי הנזכר בהערה 3.

8   יש להבחין, כמובן, בין המהדורה המודפסת במקראות גדולות, שבה הוכנסו לטקסט הערות שוליים והרחבות מסוגים שונים, ובין עדותם של כתבי־היד הקדומים, שחלקם נקיים מכל תוספת ואחרים מכילים חלק זה או אחר מן התוספות. למשל, ביחס לתוספות המדרשיות שבפירוש רש"י לפרק כה, לפירוש רש"י לאיוב בכ"י לוצקי 778, אבל ארבע השלמות כאלה מצויות בשוליים, וכולן נכללו במהדורת מקראות גדולות. כתבי־יד נוספים שבהם השתמשנו הם אוקספורד בודלי 186, וינה 23, וינה 24 ומילנו אמברוזיאנה 22. פירוש רש"י לאיוב לא יצא עד היום במהדורה מדעית, וראה הערותיי של מ' סוקולוב 'לקביעת הנוסח של פירוש רש"י לספר איוב', Proceedings of the American Academy of Jewish Research, XLVIII (1981), pp. 19-35

9   הפסוקים שאין לגביהם כל פירוש הם ט, כ, כא, ומה פס' כ הוא חזרה כמעט מדויקת על פס' יב. כיוון שהפירוש מצוי בכתב־יד אחד ויחיד, לא נוכל לדעת אם מלכתחילה לא פירש רשב"ם פסוקים אלו, או שהדברים נשמטו

נאמנה את מחברו, וניתן לראות בו חיבור אופייני לרשב"ם.[10] אין בכוונתי להציע פירוש-על
לפירוש רשב"ם, באמצעות דיון מסודר בכל פרטיו וכלליו, ואתייחס רק לנקודות אחדות בעלות
חשיבות:

א.   מבנה הפירוש;
ב.   היבטים ספרותיים: (א) מבנה ורצף ספרותי; (ב) תקבולת הצלעות;
ג.   חידושי "פשט" ומשמעותם;
ד.   היחס למקורות חז"ל ולפירוש רש"י.

א. מבנה הפירוש

במבט ראשון נדמה שאין לפירוש מבנה, ושאין בו אלא רצף של הערות, קצרות יותר או פחות,
לפרטים שונים בפרק על-פי סדר הפסוקים והמלים;[11] ואולם עיון מעמיק יותר מגלה שהכתיבה
על-פי סדר הפסוקים אין בה כדי להסביר את הילוכו וחיבורו של הפירוש. הפירוש מגלה מתכונת
קומפוזיציונית שהוגדרה מראש, המגיבה לתפיסה מבנית של הטקסט המפורש ומתחשבת ביחידות
הספרותיות שהוא מורכב מהן. עמדתי על שיטה זו במקום אחר, ואתייחס אליה כאן ככל שהיא נוגעת
לפרק הנידון.[12]

הביטוי הברור ביותר לשיטת כתיבתו של הפירוש מצוי באותן יחידות שהיקפן עולה על פסוק
אחד ובהן ניכרת ביותר סטייתו של רשב"ם מסדר הפסוקים ומרצף המלים. בפרק כח מוצגות,
בדרכים שונות, שש יחידות כאלה – פס' א-ב; ג-ד; טז-יז; כב-כג; כד-כה; כו-כז; ונקודת המוצא
להבהרת השיטה תשמש היחידה השנייה, פס' ג-ד.

בפירוש פיסקה זו שישה דיבורים מתחילים, שבדרך כלל הם עוקבים אחר סדר המלים בפסוק;
רק במקום אחד הסדר שונה: 'הנשכחים מני רגל' מקדים את 'פרץ נחל מעם גר'. לכאורה מדגים
פירוש הפיסקה את הדעה המקובלת – שורה של הערות על-פי סדר המלים ותו לא, ואילו לאמתו
של דבר לא כך הוא. לדיבור המתחיל הראשון 'ולכל תכלית הוא חוקר' נסמך ביאור רחב, וזה לשונו:
'"ולכל תכלית הוא חוקר" – שׁשׁם תכלית וחקר לאנשי סדום שפרץ עליהם נחל אש וגפרית מנהר
דינור ממקום שהוא ניגר שם. אבל לחכמה אין לה חקר ותכלית'. בביאור זה שני עניינים: מסירה
שלמה של תוכנה ועניינה של הפיסקה כולה, ובירור זיקתה להקשר.

בגלל טעות סופרים. שתי התופעות אפשריות, אך יש לומר שגם ביתר חיבוריו לא כל הפסוקים זוכים להערות
פרשניות. פירוש רש"י לפרק כח כולל הערות פרשניות לכל הפסוקים מלבד פס' כ, ואילו בפירוש ראב"ע חסרות
הערות לפס' יב, טו, יח, כ, כא.

10   אין ברצוני להידרש לשאלת האותנטיות של הפירוש שהעלה מ' ארנד, 'פירוש רשב"ם לאיוב?', עלי ספר ה
(תשל"ח), עמ' 25–47. נגעתי בשאלה זו במקצת במאמר הנזכר בהערה 3, והנושא ראוי לדיון מפורט שאין מקומו
כאן. נראה לי כי הדיון שלהלן יש בו כדי לתרום גם לבירורה של שאלה זו.

11   זוהי התפיסה המקובלת ביחס לכלל עבודתו של רשב"ם, וכך סבור אפילו טויטו, היוצא כנגד 'תפיסה מוטעית'
של פעולתו של רשב"ם, אך עדיין מתאר את מבנה פירושו של רשב"ם לתורה כפירוש 'העוקב את הפסוק ואת
המלים בפסוק' (במאמר הנזכר לעיל בהערה 5, עמ' 249).

12   ראה ש' יפת, 'פירוש הרשב"ם על מגלת קהלת', תרביץ מד (תשל"ח), עמ' 78–79, 80–84, יפת–סולטרס (לעיל
הערה 3), עמ' 32–35.

במסירת תוכנה של הפיסקה ניתן לראות את הקשר ההדוק בין הטקסט המפורש ובין המשפט
המבואר, כך:

הטקסט	הפירוש
ולכל תכלית הוא חוקר (פס' ג)	ששם תכלית וחקר
הנשכחים מני רגל (פס' דᵇ)	לאנשי סדום
דלו מאנוש, נעו (פס' דᶢ)	
	שפרץ עליהם נחל אש וגפרית מנהר
פרץ נחל מעם גר (פס' דᴬ)	דינור ממקום שהוא ניגר שם

מתברר שהפירוש הנסמך לדיבור המתחיל הראשון כולל ביאור לפיסקה כולה, ובכך נקבע גם היקף
הפיסקה: פס' ג-ד. מהו, אם כך, תפקידם של יתר הביאורים, חמישה במספר, המובאים בהמשך?
ביאורים אלה חוזרים ומבארים את פרטי הטקסט המקראי:

הנשכחים מני רגל – שאין אדם עובר ושב עליהם

פרץ נחל   – שנ' 'וה' המטיר על סדום וגו''

דלו מאנוש   – מלה כפול' ... שאין אורחים מצויין ביניהם

נעו   – ועל כן היו מנוענעים מן העולם

ביאורים אלה הם הבסיס שעליו וממנו נבנה הביאור הרחב שהובא ראשונה. הם מספקים תשובה
לשאלה המרכזית: מניין שפס' ד מדבר באנשי סדום? מפני שכל אחד מאיברי הפסוק מכוון אליהם.
בתהליך החשיבה הפרשנית, שעה שרשב"ם בירר בינו לבינו את משמעותו של הטקסט, קדם
החלק השני לראשון. רק לאחר שהפרשן מבין את פרטי הטקסט יכול הוא להגיע לידי ניסוח סינטטי-
כוללני של משמעותו. אבל בשעה שכתב את החיבור הציג רשב"ם תחילה את הסינתזה, כשהיא
נסמכת לדיבור המתחיל הראשון, ורק אחר-כך הביא את הפרטים, אחד לאחד. מסקנת הדיון בפרטים
כבר נכללה בביאור המקיף הראשון.[13]

מבנה זה מסביר היטב את החילוף בסדר הדיבורים המתחילים שהזכרנוהו לעיל, שהרי קביעת
הסדר נעשתה לא על-פי רצף המלים בטקסט המפורש אלא על-פי מהלך הפירוש, ולשונו של זה
היא: 'אנשי סדום שפרץ עליהם נחל וגו'', ניסוח המחייב להקדים את פס' דᵇ-ᶢ לפס' דᴬ. רק דיבור
מתחיל אחד בתוך הפסוק עומד לעצמו ואינו משתלב בפירוש הסינטטי המקדים, וזהו הפירוש ל'אבן
אופל', המציג את משמעות הביטוי אך אינו קושר אותו לסביבתו.

---

13   מעניין לראות כיצד בחר פרשן מודרני ללכת בדיוק בדרך זאת, מבלי שידע, כמובן, שהוא הולך בדרך שנסללה
לפניו בידי פרשן שאותו כלל לא הכיר. 'I have most often tried to say near the beginning of the
comment on any verse what I think it is in general about and how I think it connects up with
what precedes it, and only then how that general sense is supported by the actual words in
their actual sequence'. [– – –] The Comment proper is in constant tension between the part
and the whole... I have had to be in movement all the time between the smallest detail and
the larger wholes. My normal method has been to set down first my understanding of the
larger unit... and then to support that interpretation with a more detailed treatment of the
individual sentences and words.' D.J.A. Clines, *Job 1-20* (WBC), Dallas 1989, pp. XI, XXXII

כפי שאמרנו לעיל, שיטת החיבור ניכרת לעין ביחידות הגדולות, המקיפות יותר מפסוק אחד, מפני שיחידת הפירוש אינה תואמת את החלוקה לפסוקים. ואולם, שיטה זו קיימת גם ביחידות קטנות יותר, בנות פסוק אחד או אף מחצית הפסוק; נדגים זאת באמצעות הפירוש לפס' ח ולפס' יא*.

הדיבור המתחיל הראשון בפס' ח הוא: 'לֹא הִדְרִיכֻהוּ בְנֵי שָׁחַץ' ופירושו: 'גם חיה רעה לא עברה בֵּינֵיהֶם'. הביאור הוא פרפרזה המפרשת את 'לא הדריכוהו' כ'לא עברה ביניהם' ואת 'בני שחץ' כ'חיה היה רעה'. ממה נובע פירוש זה? ההסבר מצוי בשני הביאורים הבאים: '"הדריכוהו" – לשון דרך וארחא; "לֹא עָדָה" – לשון כפול. עדה תרגומו של סר...'. הביטוי 'לשון כפול' מצֵיג את הצלע השנייה בפסוק כמקבילה לראשונה, ועל כן מצטרפים 'בני שחץ' ו'שחל' לכלל המייצג את שניהם: חיה רעה. ומכיוון ש'עדה' משמעו 'סר', ו'הדריכוהו' גזור מלשון 'דרך', מצטרפים גם הם לעניין אחד: עבר. כלומר: הדיון הפרטני הוא הבסיס וממנו נוצרת הפרפרזה הסינתטית, אלא שהביאור הפרפרסטי הכולל מובא תחילה, והדיון בפרטים מובא בסוף. מבנה זה מסביר גם את מידת החזרה הקיימת בפירוש על־אף קיצורו, ובפסוקנו חוזר רשב"ם ומספק ל'הדריכוהו' ביאור מיוחד לאחר שכבר הציג את משמעותו בביאור הראשון. מה שנראה אפוא מלכתחילה כפרפרזה לצלע הראשונה של הפסוק ותו לא, הרֵיהו למעשה ביאור לפסוק כולו, על בסיס ההבחנה שהפסוק בנוי בתקבולת צלעות ועל בסיס הפרטים: הדריכוהו – לשון דרך, עדה – סר.

את שתי צלעות פסוק יא 'מִבְּכִי נְהָרוֹת חִבֵּשׁ' (יא*) ו'תַעֲלֻמָה יֹצִא אוֹר' (יא²) מבין רשב"ם כשני עניינים נפרדים, ומבנה הפירוש הוא כדלקמן:

'מבכי. ממי נבך. מצולות תהום הארץ תיקן הנהרות.
חיבש. תיקן, כמו "וַיְחַבֵּשׁ לָהֶם מִגְבָּעוֹת" ותרגומו: וְאַתְקִין. כך פתר דונש'.[14]

בדיבור המתחיל הראשון כלולים שני עניינים: פירוש מילולי של 'בכי' (מי נבך) ופרפרזה המסבירה את הצלע כולה. פרפרזה זו מציגה קודם כל את התפיסה התחבירית של המשפט: חיבש = נושא + נשוא; נהרות = מושא; מבכי – תיאור מקום, 'חיבש נהרות מבכי'. נוסף על כך, מציגה הפרפרזה את משמעות המלים בפסוק: בכי – צולות תהום הארץ; חיבש – תיקן. ואולם, בעוד שאת המרכיב הראשון 'בכי' כבר ביאר בתחילת דבריו, אין ביסוס מקביל לו לפירושה של המלה 'חיבש'; פרט זה מובא, בהרחבה, בשלב שני. גם כאן, אפוא, הביאור המופיע ראשונה אינו מפרש אך ורק את המלה המוצגת בדיבור המתחיל אלא את היחידה כולה, וביאור זה כבר כולל בתוכו את מסקנות הדיון בדיבור המתחיל השני, הבא אחריו. רק לאחר סיום הדיון בפס' יא* בא הביאור נפרד ל־יא²: 'ותעלומה. ממקום תעלום שהוא נעלם מעיני כל חי מוציא אור'.[15]

---

14   פירוש זה נכלל בחיבור הקומפילטורי 'פירוש ר' יוסף קרא לאיוב', ושם טוען ארנד, שפרט זה אינו מצוי אצל דונש. מ' ארנד, פירוש ר' יוסף קרא לספר איוב, ירושלים 1988, עמ' פב, הערה 35. על אופיו של חיבור זה וזיקתו לפירוש רשב"ם ראה ש' יפת, 'פירוש רבי יוסף קרא לאיוב': לדמותם ולתפוצתם של פירושים קומפילטוריים בימי הביניים', עיוני מקרא ופרשנות ג – ספר זכרון למשה גושן־גוטשטיין (עורכים: מ' בר־אשר, מ' גרסיאל, ד' דימנט, י' מאורי), רמת־גן תשנ"ג, עמ' 195–216. מנחם כורך את עניין חבישת המגבעות, שהוא מביא משם עמ' כט, ט, עם 'מבכי נהרות חבש' בפרקנו, אך מפרש אותם לשון 'אזירה וחגירה'. ראה צ' פיליפובסקי, מחברת מנחם, לונדון ועדינבורג 1854, עמ' 85.

15   אף שרשב"ם אינו מציג את הפסוק כתקבולת ואינו מצרף את שני איבריו לעניין אחד (ר' להלן), בכל זאת הוא

שיטת חיבור דומה לזו, אבל שונה ממנה במידת מה, משמשת ביחידת הפסוקים כו–כז. תפיסת שני הפסוקים כיחידה ספרותית אחת איננה מתבטאת באמצעות הביאור אלא על-ידי הדיבור המתחיל עצמו. רשב"ם מציג את תחילת פס' כו ואת תחילת פס' כז ברצף אחד: 'בעשתו למטר חק וג' אז ראה ויספרה' – וזהו פירושו. כלומר, בניגוד לעמדתם של פרשנים אחרים[16] הוא משעבד את פס' כו לפס' כז כמשפט זמן. לאחר הצגת היחידה הספרותית באמצעות צירוף הדיבורים המתחילים, הוא מביא שלושה פרטים: 'חק' – ובו ביאור לכל הצלע הראשונה של פס' כו; 'חזי קולות', 'והכינה וגם חקרה'. מכל הנתונים האלה ניתן היה לנסח פירוש סינתטי של היחידה כולה[17] ולהעמידו בראש היחידה, אבל רשב"ם אינו רואה צורך לעשות זאת.

כפי שהזכרנו לעיל, בפירושו לפרק כח מוצגות עוד מספר 'יחידות גדולות', והן פס' טז–יז, כב–כג; כד–כה, אך הצגתן כ'יחידות גדולות' נעשית בדרכים אחרות. בפס' כב–כג, כד–כה מובא פירוש היחידה, כולו ברצף אחד, כשהוא נסמך למלים הראשונות של היחידה, תוך ציון מפורש של הקשר הקשר בין שני הפסוקים: 'אבדון ומות. (פס' כב) – אם ישאל השואל לשני דברים הללו... יענו ויאמרו: באזנינו שמענו שמע שלה, וזה הוא השמע: אלהים הבין דרכה' (פס' כג); ובאופן דומה ביחידה הבאה, בהצגת פס' כה כתכלית פס' כד: 'כי הוא לקצות... (כד) שהרי הוא הביט וראה... כדי לעשות משקל לרוח...' (פס' כה). ביחידה הראשונה נוסף לפירוש לפירוש הכללי גם פרט פרשני, שבו מסביר רשב"ם את המלים 'אבדון ומות', וכך מצויים בו שני דיבורים מתחילים שווים (וראה גם פס' א, ח, כו). כפי שהראינו לעיל, זהו כורח השיטה. בדיבור הראשון אין 'אבדון ומות' אלא בחזקת מראה מקום, שאליו נסמך ביאור היחידה הספרותית כולה, ואילו במקרה השני המלים 'אבדון ומות' הן הן מושא הפירוש.

שתי יחידות נוספות, פס' א–ב, טז–יז מוצגות כ'יחידות גדולות' באמצעות תקבולת הצלעות, ונדון בכך להלן.

ראינו אפוא, כח משמשת שיטת חיבור אחת, בגיוונים צורה אחדים, ביחידות פס' א–ב, ג–ד, ז, ח, יא, יג, כב–כג, כו–כז – כלומר ברוב-רובו של הפירוש לפרק. ואולם לא בכל מקום רואה רשב"ם צורך לבנות את הפירוש בדרך זאת. לעתים הוא מסתפק במסירה כללית של תוכן היחידה המפורשת מבלי לדון בפרטיה בנפרד (כגון פס' ה, ו[5], י, יד, יח[2], כד–כה, כח[3]), ולעתים הוא דן בפרטים אחדים מבלי למסור את תוכנה ופירושה של היחידה כולה (כגון פס' ו[5], יב, יג[4], טו, טז–יז, יט), וישנם פסוקים וחלקי פסוקים שאותם אינו מבאר כלל. אבל המסקנה מבירור זה נראית לנו חד-משמעית: הפירוש איננו אוסף של הערות שוליים, אלא חיבור פרשני המודע לעצמו. שני עניני מבנה באים בו לידי ביטוי: (1) הגדרת יחידות מבניות בתוך הטקסט באמצעות פירושן כיחידות

מבאר את יא[3] על-פי יא[4], ובעיקר את המלה 'ותעלומה'. בפירושו למלה זו מתייחס רשב"ם לשלושה היבטים שונים: תחילה בירור תחבירי: ותעלומה = מתעלומה, כלומר המלה משמשת כתיאור מקום ומקבילה ל: מבכי; אחר-כך בירור מורפולוגי: תעלומה = מקום תעלים, כלומר: תעלום + ה"א המקום; ולבסוף בירור סמנטי: שהוא נעלם מעיני כל חי, המקביל ל: 'צולות תהום הארץ'. לאחר הביאור המקיף של המלה, משלימות המלים 'יוציא אור' את הביאור הצלע כולה. לביאור זה ראה עוד להלן עמ' 20*–21*. על הפרפרזה כשיטה פרשנית אני מתכוונת להרחיב את הדיבור במקום אחר.

16   ראה למשל בפירוש רש"י, הקושר מצד רצף הענין את פס' כו לפס' כד–כה. הוא מציג את פס' כד–כה. בפני עצמו מצד אחר את הענין הוא ממשיך את פס' כג. גם ראב"ע קושר את פסוק כו למה שקדם לו, החל מפס' כב.

17   וראה עוד להלן, עמ' 18*.

שלמות שהיקפן משתנה – חצי פסוק, פסוק, שני פסוקים ויותר;[18] (2) כתיבת החיבור במתכונת קבועה על־פי מספר דגמים, שהבולט בהם הוא זה שבו מוצגת תחילה משמעות היחידה השלמה, ואחר־כך מובא הדיון בפרטים – דיון שתוצאותיו כבר נכללו בפירוש הראשון.

מן הראוי להדגיש שכל התופעות האלה מצויות גם בחיבוריו האחרים של רשב"ם, והם פירושיו לתורה ולקהלת, אבל אין הן כוללניות. לא בכל מקום מגדיר רשב"ם את המבנה הפנימי של הטקסט המפורש, ולא בכל מקום הוא משתמש בדגמי החיבור שהצגנו לעיל. הריהו בבחינת מורה־דרך, המציג לקורא קווים מנחים וסימני דרך ומשאיר בידיו את גילוי הדרך כולה, בבחינת 'ואידך זיל גמור'. אבל המודעות לבעיות מבנה הטקסט, כתיבת חיבורו במתכונת קבועה ומחושבת, והשימוש המכוון בדיבור המתחיל – כל אלו מאפיינים את תודעתו הפרשנית ואת שיטתו.

[ב] היבטים ספרותיים

אף שיש להבחין בבהירות בין המתכונת הספרותית של החיבור הפרשני ובין ההיבטים הספרותיים של הטקסט המפורש, ראינו לעיל כי כבר במבנה הפירוש ניתן ביטוי למבנה הטקסט, ושני אלו כרוכים זה בזה בשיטתו של רשב"ם. אולם בכך נגלה לעין רק היבט אחד ברגישותו של רשב"ם לעניינים ספרותיים, שהיא אחד הקווים המאפיינים והמייחדים את כלל עבודתו כפרשן.[19] בפירוש לפרק כח מתגלה רגישות זו בכמה פנים, ואתייחס כאן לשניים מהם: שאלות של מבנה ורצף ספרותי, ותופעת תקבולת הצלעות.

1. מבנה ורצף ספרותי

שאלת הרצף הספרותי – מקומן והקשרן של יחידות גדולות וקטנות – היא מן השאלות הקשות העומדות בפני פרשני ספר איוב: כיצד מתפתחת הטיעון ומהו יחס החלקים זה לזה?[20] רשב"ם מתייחס לשאלה זו פעמים רבות, ודן בכך אף בפרק כח. המונח שהוא נוהג להשתמש בו הוא 'מוסב על', אבל אין זה מונח נוקשה משתי בחינותיו: מחד גיסא שאלות של רצף ספרותי עשויות להידון גם במישור אחר או ללא מינוח כלל, ומאידך גיסא משמש מונח זה להיבטים נוספים של זיקה בין מקראות.[21]

בראש פירושו לפרק כח, בקטע הארוך ביותר בפרק, משיב רשב"ם בהרחבה לשאלה בלתי מפורשת: מה היחס בין פרק כח לפרק כז? כיצד מתקשרים שני החלקים של נאום איוב?[22] לדעת

18 ליחידות גדולות יותר ראה למשל פירושו לברא' יח, א־ה; לו, ב־ה; שמ' כד, א־טז, ועוד הרבה; פירושו לקהלת ב, ט־יא; ג, ב־ח; ז, טז־יח; ח, י־יג ועוד.

19 ראה[18] D. Rosin, R. Samuel ben Meir (רשב"ם) als Schrifterklärer, Breslau 1880, pp. 87-88; מלמד (לעיל הערה 3), עמ' 468–469; יפת־סולטרס (לעיל הערה 3), עמ' 31–33, 39–44; טויטו (לעיל, הערה 5), עמ' 254–267.

20 ראה, למשל: O. Eissfeldt, The Old Testament – An Introduction, Oxford 1966, pp. 456-466

21 בפירושו לאיוב, המונח מופיע למעלה מעשרים פעם (לאיוב ח, י, כא, כב; י, טז; טז; טו; כב; ב־ג, כה; כא, ד; כז, ט, י, יג ועוד. וכן ראה פירושו לקהלת ג, ט, כא; ז, ה, י, וכן פירושו לדב' לג, א. המונח עצמו מצוי כבר אצל רש"י, כגון בפירושו לאיוב ג, יג; כו. ראה י' אביגור, היכל רש"י[2] א, ירושלים תשל"ט, עמ' תתפד–תתפו.

22 שאלה זו העסיקה מאוד את חוקרי ספר איוב, ותשובה מקובלת היא שפרק כח, המכונה 'הלל לחכמה', הוא תוספת מאוחרת לספר. ראה למשל אייספלט (לעיל הערה 20), עמ' 458, 463; קליינס (לעיל הערה 13), עמ' LIX; R. Alter, The Art of Biblical Poetry, New York 1985, pp. 92-93

רשב"ם, '"כי יש לכסף מוצא" מוסב על "בצדקתי החזקתי" ונותן טעם לדבריו'. אמירה זו היא חזרה כמעט מילולית על דבריו בפירוש כז, ח: '"כי מה תקוות חנף" – נותן טעם לדבריו ומוסב על "בצדקתי החזקתי"'. שתי אמירות אלו בצירופו מציגות את מבנהו של נאום איוב בפרקים כז–כח. טענתו המרכזית של איוב היא: 'בצדקתי החזקתי' (כז, ב־ז) והיא מנומקת בשני טיעונים, האחד בפרק כז, ח־כג והשני בפרק כח, כך:

כז, ח – 'כי מה תקוות חנף... לומר: מדוע ארשע ולמה אתן רפיון לצדקתי? כי מה תקוות חנף באחריתו? ואילו לא הייתי יודע עונש מעשים של רשע וחניפות אז יהא דין עליכם לחושדני, אבל עכשו שאני מכיר ומבין רוע מעשים, למה זה הבל אתם מחזיקים בי חזקת רשע?'

כח, א – 'כי יש לכסף מוצא... למה אהיה רשע בוצע בצע? כל ממון זהב וכסף יכול אני למצוא כי יש להם מקום בעולם, אבל והחכמה מאין תמצא?[23] ... ועל כן החזקתי בצדקתי'.

על־פי ניתוח זה, הנאום בנוי משלושה חלקים:

    ההכרזה   –   בצדקתי החזקתי (כז, ב־ז)

הנימוק השלילי – כיוון שאני יודע את גורל הרשעים, למה לי להיות רשע? (כז, ח־כג)

הנימוק החיובי – העושר הוא ערך פחות, מפני שכסף וזהב קיימים וניתנים להשגה, ורק החכמה ראויה שיחתרו אליה, מפני שהשגתה קשה. על כן המטרה היא:

                   להיות צדיק לפני הק' ברוב חכמה ובינה (כח)

מן הראוי להזכיר שרשב"ם לא יצר פירוש זה 'יש מאין', אלא הרחיב והעמיק את פירוש רש"י. בפירושו לפרק כח, א אומר רש"י: 'גם זה טעם אחר לדבריו הראשון שאמר "בצדקתי החזקתי" כי למה אהיה רשע? אם בשביל כסף וזהב – לכל יש מוצא וסוף, אבל החכמה מאין תבוא? זה סוף הפרשה: היא יקרה מכל על כן כל ימי נתתי לבי עליה ללמוד'.

הדמיון בין פירוש רשב"ם לזה של רש"י הוא ברור וחד־משמעי, אך אין להתעלם מן ההבדלים: בפירוש רש"י זהו הביאור היחיד בפרקים כז–כח העוסק בשאלת הרצף הספרותי, ואילו אצל רשב"ם זהו חלק מתפיסה כוללת, המגדירה את מבנה החטיבה ואת היחס בין חלקיה.[24] הבדל זה מדגים היטב את היחס בין שני הפרשנים: גם רש"י ייחד תשומת לב מסוימת לשאלות של זיקה ספרותית ורצף ספרותי,[25] אך רשב"ם הרחיב עניין זה במידה ניכרת וייחד לו תשומת לב רבה יותר ושיטתית יותר.

שאלת הרצף הספרותי עולה בפרק כח גם בפירוש פס' ג־ד. לדעת רשב"ם, נושא הפסוקים ג-ח

23   מניסוח הדברים ניתן אולי להסיק שרשב"ם היה ער למשחק הלשון בין 'מוֹצָא' לבין 'תִּמָּצֵא', אף־על־פי שיש להם שני שורשים שונים (יצ"א, מצ"א).

24   הבדלים אחרים מצויים בפרטי הפירוש. לדעת רש"י איוב אינו מבקש כסף וזהב, כי 'לכל דבר יש מוצא וסוף', והוא חוזר על כך גם בדבריו לפס' יב: 'לכל דבר יש מוצא וסוף רק לחכמה לא מוצא לה אלא מפיו, ולא סוף עולמית'. כלומר, היחידה הראשונה מקיפה את הפסוקים א־ג. ואילו לדעת רשב"ם מהווים הפסוקים א־ב יחידה אחת, ופס' ג־ד יחידה נפרדת, והשאלה היא לא בגבולות החכמה אלא מקומה והימצאותה: הכסף והזהב 'יכול אני למצוא כי יש להם מקום בעולם', ואילו החכמה 'מאין תמצא'. על ההבדל בפירוש המושג חכמה, ראה להלן עמ' 13*–18*. ראה גם: R. E. Murphy, *Wisdom Literature* (FOTL XIII), Grand Rapids 1981, p. 37

25   וראה מלמד (לעיל הערה 3), עמ' 433–435. עניין זה עדיין דורש ניתוח יסודי יותר. ההתעניינות ברצף הטקסט מאפיינת את עבודתו של ר' יוסף קרא. ראה ארנד (לעיל, הערה 14), עמ' 13–15; B. Einstein, *R. Josef Kara* *und sein Commentar zu Kohelet*, Berlin 1886, pp. 43-44

הוא סדום, שהיתה 'ארץ ממנה יצא לחם' (פס' ה) 'ומקומה נהפך לאש' (הפירוש לפס' ה).[26] פירוש זה מעלה את שאלת ההקשר הספרותי: כיצד משתלב עניין סדום בטיעון המרכזי של הפרק: 'והחכמה מאין תמצא'? על כך עונה הפירוש לפס' ג–ד: 'ולכל תכלית הוא חוקר. ששם תכלית וחקר לאנשי סדום ... אבל לחכמה אין לה חקר ותכלית'. מבנה זה מעמיד את פס' ג–ח כניגוד לחכמה, בהמשך לפס' א–ב. בפס' א–ב הניגוד הוא ״הימצאות״ מול אי־השגה, ובפס' ג–ח – סופיות מול אי־סופיות.[27]

רשב״ם משקיע מחשבה רבה בניסיון לחשוף את מבנה הפרשה ואת הקשרים שבין חלקיה, ומאמץ זה נובע מהכרה עמוקה יותר, המדריכה את כלל פעילותו הפרשנית. מתבטאת כאן התנגדותו לאחד העקרונות החשובים ביותר של פרשנות המדרש והוא האטומיזציה של הטקסט – מתן אוטונומיה גמורה לכל יסוד של הטקסט, בכל רובד שהוא.[28] עמדתו של רשב״ם מהווה ניגוד קוטבי ליסוד היסודות של החשיבה המדרשית. לדידו, כל מרכיבי הטקסט וכל התופעות המתקיימות בו בכל מישוריו קשורים זה בזה ומשלימים זה את זה – ביטוי להווייה ספרותית אחת.

2. תקבולת הצלעות

התופעה של תקבולת הצלעות, על צורותיה ומשמעויותיה, היא אחד הנושאים שרשב״ם מרבה לעסוק בהם בכל חיבוריו. כבר בעבר הצביעו חוקרים שונים על התייחסותו של רשב״ם לתופעת התקבולת ועמדו על חלק מחידושיו, ובעיקר על התופעה של 'התקבולת המדורגת'.[29] ואולם על־אף חשיבותו לחקר פרשנות השירה המקראית, לא נדון הנושא בכל היקפו ולא הוצגו כל מסקנותיו.[30] הפירוש לספר איוב תורם תרומה חשובה ביותר לבירורו של עניין זה, מפני שיש בו למעלה ממאה התייחסויות מפורשות לתופעת תקבולת הצלעות, ועוד מספר רב של פירושים המיוסדים על עיקרון זה ללא הזכרתו. נושא זה מחייב בירור מקיף, בירור שלא נוכל להידרש לו כאן, אבל נברר את מקומו בפירושו של פרק כח.

רשב״ם מזכיר במפורש את תקבולת הצלעות שמונה פעמים, בשלושה מונחים שונים: לשון כפול (פס' א–ב, ח), או בקיצור, כפול (פס' א–ב), מלה כפולה (פס' ג–ד, יב, טז–יז) וכפל לשון (פס' ז, יט).[31] נוסף על כך הוא מחיל עיקרון זה גם בפירושו לפסוקים אחרים, ונעבור תחילה אל המקראות שבהם נזכר המונח במפורש.

בפירוש לפס' א–ב מציג רשב״ם את התקבולת בפירוט יוצא דופן:

26   לא לגמרי ברור אם גם פס' ט מתקשר לחטיבה זו, מפני שאין פירוש לפסוק זה. מפס' י בוודאי מתחילה יחידת
      מבנה חדשה. על הפירוש עצמו ראה להלן, עמ' 22*.

27   והשווה למשל את פירוש רש״י, שבו חוזר פס' י אל עניינו של הפיסקה הראשונה בפס' א–ג: 'חוזר לתחלת עניינו
      שאמר כי לכל דבר יש מוצא'. רש״י גם הוא מפרש את פס' ד–ט כמתייחסים לסדום, אך אין הוא מבהיר כל עיקר
      מה יחסם להקשר.

28   י' היינמן, דרכי האגדה, ירושלים תש״ל, עמ' 102–100.

29   ראה פוזננסקי (לעיל, הערה 2), עמ' XLV; מלמד (לעיל הערה 3), עמ' 466.

30   ראה בעיקר J.L. Kugel, The Idea of Biblical Poetry, New Haven 1981, pp. 174, 176-177 ברלין
      מייחדת (Adele Berlin, Biblical Poetry Through Medieval Jewish Eyes, Bloomington 1991, p. 10)
      לראב״ע ולרשב״ם יחד משפט אחד. על קווים אחדים של תופעה זו עמדנו במבוא לפירוש קהלת; ראה
      יפת–סולטרס (לעיל, הערה 3), עמ' 25–27, 32–33, 42.

31   בפירוש לאיוב משמשים גם מונחים אחרים, והם: כפל מלה, כופל מלתו, מקרא כפול, כופל לשונו. ראה לפי
      שעה יפת–סולטרס (לעיל, הערה 3), עמ' 25.

'ברזל מעפר יוקח. לשון כפול על "כי יש לכסף מוצא". לקיחה על לשון יציאה. ו"אבן יצוק
נחושה" כפול על "לזהב יזוקו". לשון יציקה על לשון שפיכה'.

לפי פירוש זה, פס' ב כולו מקביל לפס' א כולו, בᵃ ל־אᵃ, ו־בᵇ ל־אᵇ, כך:

(אᵇ) ומקום לזהב יזוקו	(אᵃ) כי יש לכסף מוצא
(בᵇ) ואבן יצוק נחושה	(בᵃ) ברזל מעפר יוקח

רשב"ם מציין במפורש שני עניינים: תקבולת בין צלעות הפסוקים, שאותן הוא מצטט במלואן,
ותקבולת בין הפעלים: יצא//לקח; יצק//זוקק. ואולם, אף שאין הוא מציין זאת במפורש, מתברר
שהוא רואה גם את יתר מרכיבי הפסוקים כמקבילים זה לזה. הביאור למלה 'מוצא' (פס' אᵃ) הוא
ש'מוציאין אותו מן הקרקע', ובו 'מן הקרקע' נלמד מפס' בᵃ המקביל לו: 'ברזל מעפר יוקח'. על־פי
הדרכים המקובלות היום לרישום התקבולת, יהיה המבנה שמציע רשב"ם אבג / ב:ג, כך:

ג	ב	א
מוצא	לכסף	כי יש
ג'	ב'	
מעפר יוקח	ברזל	וברזל

להבהרת המשמעות המדויקת של בᵇ ('אבן יצוק נחושה') מסתפק רשב"ם בהבאת כתוב נוסף: 'שנ'
ומהרריה תחצב נחשת' (דב' ח, ט). כתוב זה לא זו בלבד שהוא עוסק באותו נושא, אלא שהוא מציג
תקבולת לפסוקנו, המבהירה את תחבירו:

נחושה	יצוק	אבן
נחשת	תחצב	מהרריה

מה שמתואר ב־אᵇ במשפט סתמי אקטיבי: 'ומקום לזהב יזוקו' מתואר ב־בᵇ באורח פסיבי: 'ו[מ]אבן
יצוק נחושה'.

בשבעה מקומות נוספים בפרק מציין רשב"ם את קיומה של תקבולת צלעות; פעמים אחדות הוא
מוסיף או מקדים מלים אחדות של ביאור לציון זה (פס' ג־ד, ח, יג, טז־יז) ופעמים שאינו מעיר
מאומה מעבר לציון התקבולת (פס' ז, יב, יח). מה תפקידו של ציון זה ולשם מה הוא מובא?

ראינו כי בפס' א־ב מגדירה התקבולת את היקף היחידה הספרותית, וכך היא מוצגת גם בפס'
טז־יז. הקביעה: 'מלה כפולה על לא תסלה' (פס' טז) בדיבור המתחיל 'לא יערכנה' (פס' יז) מבטאת
תפיסה כזאת של היחידה:

בשהם יקר וספיר	(טז) לא תסלה בכתם אופיר
[ותמורתה כלי פז]	(יז) לא יערכנה זהב וזכוכית

עם זאת משמשת התקבולת להבהרת המלה הקשה 'תסלה', הבאה במקראֵרק כאן, בפס' טז־יט. בפס'
יט אומר רשב"ם: '"לא תסלה" – כפל לשון על "לא יערכנה"', וההבנה זו היא מקור הפירוש המצוי
כבר בפס' טז: '"לא תסלה" – לא יהיה דמים וערך, כמו "המסולאים בפז"'.[32] ציון התקבולת בפס' יט

_____

32 זהו גם פירוש ראב"ע. רש"י, לעומתו, אינו קושר בין 'תסלה' ובין 'יערכנה' ומפרש: 'לא תסלה: לא תשתבח,

מבהיר תכונה נוספת שלה, והיא שסדר האיברים המקבילים אינו אחיד ואינו קבוע. בעוד שבפס' א-ב ו-טז-יז הסדר הוא ישר (אבג / ב'ג'; אב / א'ב'), בפסוק יט הסדר הוא כיאסטי (אב / ב'א').

המטרה המרכזית של ציון התקבולת היא ללא ספק פרשנית, ונדגים זאת בשני מקראות נוספים. בפס' ז שני דיבורים מתחילים; לראשון בהם נסמך פירוש קצר: 'לא ידעו עיט: 'לא הכיר אותו עוף פורח לעשות שם רעה', ואילו לשני נסמך ציון התקבולת: 'ולא שזפתו. כפל לשון'. במבט שטחי נראה ציון התקבולת מיותר: מה מוסיפה לקורא האינפורמציה שהפסוק בנוי כתקבולת? אבל לאמתו של דבר הבחנה זו היא הבסיס שעליו נבנית הבנת הפסוק.

אם הפסוק הוא תקבולת, כי אז יהיו איבריו כדלקמן:

א   ב   א'   ב'

לא ידעו עיט // לא שזפתו עין איה

משמע: 'לא ידעו' ו'לא שזפתו' מצטרפים לעניין אחד, ומכאן פירושו: 'לא הכיר אותו' וביתר הרחבה: 'לא הכיר אותו ... לעשות שם רעה'. גם הצמד המקביל עיט/איה מצטרפים לעניין אחד שאותו מציג רשב"ם על-ידי 'עוף פורח'. נמצא שהביאור הפרפרסטי, הנסמך לדיבור המתחיל הראשון, 'לא הכיר אותו עוף פורח לעשות שם רעה', הוא פירוש לפסוק כולו, על שתי צלעותיו, והוא מבוסס על ההבחנה (המוצגת אחר-כך), ששני חלקי הפסוק מקבילים זה לזה.[33]

דוגמה מורכבת יותר מצויה בפס' יג, שבו שלושה דיבורים מתחילים:

ערכה. סדר שלה לקנות הימנה.

ולא תמצא. אינה מצווייה לימכר בשווקים. מלה כפולה היא.

בארץ החיים. אלו שווקים ...

ניטיב להבין את פירוש רשב"ם על-ידי השוואתו לזה של רש"י. רש"י אינו מבאר את הצלע הראשונה, ובפירוש הצלע השנייה הוא הולך בעקבות המדרש: 'לא תמצא בארץ החיים: במי שמחיה, אלא במי שממית עצמו עליה ביגיעה וברעבון'.[34] ביאור זה, המבוסס על ההנחה המקובלת ש'חכמה = תורה', אינו מחבר את שתי צלעות הפסוק. אמנם רש"י אינו מסביר את הצלע הראשונה, אבל נראה בעליל שלכל אחת מצלעות הפסוק מסר עצמאי.

פירושו של רשב"ם מבוסס על שתי הבחנות: ההבחנה הספרותית שהפסוק בנוי בתקבולת צלעות, וההבחנה הלקסיקולוגית שהצירוף 'ארץ החיים' משמעו שווקים. אין באפשרותנו לדעת איזו משתי הבחנות אלו קדמה לחברתה; האם הביאור 'שווקים' מודרך על-ידי התפיסה שהפסוק בנוי כתקבולת

<hr>

לשון "סלו לרוכב בערבות"... וכן "המסלאים בפז"'. ראה גם פירושו של רש"י לתה' סח, ה: 'סלו. לשון שבח. וכן "לא תסלה בכתם אופיר", "המסולאים בפז"'.

33   וראה לעומת זאת את פירוש רש"י: 'לא ידעו עיט. לא עבר עליו חיל של לסטין. לא שזפתו עין איה. לפי שהיא רואה יותר משאר עופות ולכך נקראת ראה. לא חפרוה מרגלים'. כלומר: לא תמצא בארץ החיים גם מדרש, והוא בוודאי משני. בכתב-יד לוצקי 778 המדרש רשום בשוליים; בכתבי-יד מילנו אמברוזיאנה 22, אוקספורד-בודלי 186, וינה 23, 24 המדרש חסר לגמרי.

34   המקור לפירוש זה הוא בדברי רב, בסנהדרין קיא, ע"א: 'ולא תמצא בארץ החיים ... לא תמצא תורה במי שמחיה עצמו עליה'.

ונובע ממנה, או שהוא בלתי תלוי בו. מכל מקום, תפיסת היסוד היא ששתי הצלעות מוסרות מסר מקביל ומשלים, והכרה זו מתבטאת כבר בפירוש לדיבור המתחיל הראשון.[35] הביאור: 'ערכה – סדר שלה' הוא פירוש מילוני, אבל התוספת 'לקנות הימנה' מבוססת על הנאמר בצלע השנייה ועל פירוש 'ארץ החיים' כ'שוקים'. ומכאן גם התוספת 'לימכר' בפירוש הצלע השנייה.

נראה אפוא, שרשב"ם ראה את התקבולת כך:

א	ב
לא ידע אנוש	ערכה
א'	ב'
ולא תמצא	בארץ החיים

הבאנו דוגמאות אחדות כדי להדגים את שיטתו של רשב"ם על־פי מקראות שבהם הוא מציין במפורש שהפסוק נבנה בצלעות מקבילות. אבל יש לומר שגם פסוקים נוספים בפרק מתפרשים על־פי אותם עקרונות ללא שימוש באחד המונחים שהזכרנו לעיל, או בדומים להם. בפרק כח מפורשים באותה שיטה הפסוקים ו, יד, כד ו־כח.

לאור דוגמאות אלו, נראה שרשב"ם מגדיר כ'לשון כפול' או כ'מלה כפולה' את התקבולת המכונה במחקר המדעי מאז ימי לות' 'תקבולת נרדפת',[36] אף־על־פי שהוא מכיר גם את תופעת התקבולת הניגודית.[37] אבל, על־אף חשיבותה הגדולה, אין רשב"ם רואה בה תופעה ספרותית גורפת: מבין הפסוקים בפרק כח שנתן את דעתו עליהם, לא פירש על דרך התקבולת את פס' ה, יא, כב, כז. קבוצה לעצמה קובעים הפסוקים שבהם מציאות התקבולת ברורה מאוד, אלא שרשב"ם לא פירש אותם כלל (פס' כא), או שהסתפק בביאור חלקי (פס' טו, יח, כג, כה), ולגבי פסוקים אלו לא נוכל אלא לשער את עמדתו.

לאור הממצא כולו, זה המפורש וזה שבשתיקה, ברור שרשב"ם ראה בתקבולת הצלעות עקרון יסוד של השירה המקראית, שיש לו השלכות פרשניות מרחיקות לכת. כמו יתר העקרונות הדקדוקיים, התחביריים והספרותיים – גם עיקרון זה מהווה היבט אחד של 'דרך המקראות', שהיא אחד מעמודי התווך של פירוש בדרך הפשט.[38] זהו אחד האמצעים לקביעת היקפה של היחידה הספרותית שיש לפרשה כשלמות אחת, והוא משמש ככלי פרשני המדריך את הפרשן בחיפושיו אחר פתרונות למקראות קשים – תוך התחשבות בלשון הטקסט כנתינתו. הוא מגונן על הפרשן מפני הנטייה – שבאה אליו במסורת רבת־שנים – לסגמנטציה ואטומיזציה של הטקסט, ובמיוחד של הטקסט הפיוטי, ומעמיד כנגדו את תפיסת האחדות, הלכידות והשלמות של הטקסט. הוא מסייע לפרשן בחתירתו הבלתי נלאית אל הפשט.

---

35 על עניינים אחרים הנוגעים לביאור פסוק זה, ראה להלן, עמ' 21*.

36 ראה קוגל (לעיל, הערה 30), עמ' 12, 57–58.

37 ראה יפת־סולטרס (לעיל, הערה 3), עמ' 42, והערה 138.

38 ראה טויטו (לעיל, הערה 5), עמ' 269–271.

[ג] חידושי 'פשוטו של מקרא' ומשמעותם

בין הביאורים שבעניינם פירטנו לעיל נמצאו ביאורים שבהם סטה רשב"ם מן המסורת שקדמה לו: ממדרשי חז"ל, מן התרגום הארמי, ומפירוש רש"י. ואולם סטייה זו לא סומנה בסימן חיצוני כלשהו; הביאורים נכתבו בלשון חיווי נייטרלי, ואנו לא הצבענו על השוני בעמדתו של רשב"ם אלא במקרים אחדים. ואולם בשני מקומות בפרק כה, בפס' יב ו־כז, סוטה רשב"ם מדרך זו ומציג את דבריו על דרך הפולמוס באמצעות הביטוי 'לפי פשוטו של מקרא'.[39] בניסוח החריף ביותר בספר מנוסח הפולמוס בפס' כז: 'אין לך בו רק פשוטו. לפי פשוטו של מקרא...', והניסוח הפסקני קובע שיש לפרש פסוק זה אך ורק לפי הפשט. נראה אפוא, שבשני אלו ראה רשב"ם את עיקר המחלוקת עם המסורת הפרשנית. מה משמעות הפולמוס? כלפי מה או כלפי מי הוא מכוון?

שני הפסוקים הנדונים עוסקים בחכמה. בפס' יב 'החכמה' היא נושא המשפט, ובפס' כז – מושאו:

פס' יב: 'והחכמה מאין תמצא ואי זה מקום בינה';

פס' כז: 'אז ראה ויספרה, הכינה וגם חקרה'.

על פניהם אין בפסוקים אלו כל קושי, ואין ויכוח על משמעותם. כך למשל בפירושו של ראב"ע לאיוב, פס' יב אינו זוכה לשום התייחסות, ואילו בפס' כז עומד ראב"ע רק על כך ש'ויספרה' אין משמעה לשון סיפור אלא לשון ספר, כלומר: 'היא כתובה אצלו', ותו לא. המסורת הפרשנית היהודית לגבי עניינם של פסוקים אלו היא חד־משמעית, כפי שהיא מבוטאת בקיצור מרבי בדברי רש"י לפס' יב: 'והחכמה. התורה'. זוהי מסורת פרשנית עתיקת־יומין, ששורשיה מגיעים עד שלהי התקופה המקראית עצמה. הביטוי הקדום ביותר לתפיסה זו מצוי בחכמת בן־סירא, שנכתב על־פי המקובל בתחילת המאה השנייה לפני הספירה, והריהו ממשיכה המובהק ביותר של ספרות החכמה המקראית.[40]

כמו הספרים משלי ואיוב, המעמידים את החכמה כערך עליון, גם בן־סירא שם בראש סולם ערכיו את ה'חכמה' ו'החכם'. אלא שבתפיסת עולמו, ה'חכמה' מזוהה עם התורה, והחכם – עם מי שהולך בדרכה ומקיים את מצוותיה.[41] מפורסמות ביותר אמירותיו המפורשות של בן־סירא, כגון:

'כל חכמה יראת ה' וכל חכמה עשות תורה' (יט, יז);

'כי ירא ה' יעשה זאת ותופש תורה ידריכנה' (יה, א);

ובעיקר בשיר ההלל לחכמה (כד, א–כג):

'החכמה תהלל נפשה ובתוך עמה תתפאר
אנכי מפי עליון יצאתי וכערפל כסיתי ארץ...

---

39 ביטוי זה חוזר בפירוש לאיוב שתים־עשרה פעמים (ב, י; ה, יט; ו, יז־יט; ז, ח; כב, טז; כד, טז, כא; כח, יב, כז; ל, יז; לו, ו; לט, כו), ובכולן יש לו משמעות פולמוסית.

40 לזמנו של בן סירא ולדמותו, ראה בין היתר, מ"צ סגל, ספר בן סירא השלם[3], ירושלים תשל"ב, עמ' 3–11.

41 ראה: J. Fichtner, *Die altorientalische Weisheit in ihrer israelitisch-jüdischen Ausprägung, eine Studie zur Nationalisierung der Weisheit in Israel* (BZAW 62), Giessen 1933, pp. 125-127 וכן היינמן (לעיל, הערה 28), עמ' 115–116.

כל אלה ספר ברית אל עליון
תורה צוה לנו משה מורשה קהלת יעקב'.

ההשקפה שהחכמה, שספרות החכמה המקראית מהללת אותה, היא התורה, או התלמיד־החכם
המייצג אותה, חוזרת במדרשים אין ספור בכל המקורות המדרשיים, הן במפורש והן מכללא.
כדוגמאות בלבד, אשר בהן משמשים פסוקים מאיוב כח, נביא מדרשים אחדים:

(א) שהש"ר ו, ה:[42] 'והחכמה מאין תמצא וגו', ונעלמה מעיני כל חי וגו', תהום אמר לא בי היא
וגו'. ארבעה דברים הן תשמישו של עולם וכולן אם אבדו יש להם חילופין ואלו הם: "כי יש לכסף
מוצא ומקום לזהב יזקו. ברזל מעפר יוקח ואבן יצוק נחושה" (איוב כח, א-ב). תלמיד חכם שמת אין
אנו מוצאים תמורתו'.

(ב) סוטה כא, ע"ב (יל"ש ב, תתקמ): 'אמר רבי יוחנן: אין דברי תורה מתקיימין אלא במי שממים
עצמו כמי שאינו. שנאמר: והחכמה מאין תמצא'.

(ג) תנחומא, שמות, פרשת שמות כה:[43] '"ירעם אל בקולו נפלאות עשה גדלות ולא נדע" (איוב
לז, ה) ... כשנתן הקב"ה את התורה בסיני, הראה בקולו לישראל פלאי פלאים. כיצד? היה הקב"ה
מדבר והיה הקול יוצא ומחזיר בכל העולם, וישראל שומעין את הקול בא להם מן הדרום והיו רצים
לדרום לקבל את הקול ומדרום נהפך להם מן הצפון ... ומצפון נהפך להם למזרח ... וממזרח נהפך
להם למערב ... והיו ישראל אומרים זה לזה, והחכמה מאין תמצא ואי־זה מקום בינה, תהום אמר
לא בי היא וים אמר אין עמדי וגו'.

(ד) שוחר טוב ג' (ב') (יל"ש ב' תרכה): 'לא ידע אנוש ערכה. אמר ר' אלעזר לא נתנו פרשיותיה
של תורה על הסדר, שאם נתנו על הסדר כל מי שהוא קורא בהם היה יכול להחיות מתים ולעשות
מופתים. לכך נתעלמה סדורה של תורה והוא גלוי לפני הקב"ה...'.

(ה) שבת פט ע"א (יל"ש ב' תקצד): 'כשירד משה עם התורה בא השטן אל הקב"ה לשאול היכן
היא. אמר לו אצל בן עמרם. בא אל משה. אמר לו בתהום היא. הלך לתהום. אמר לו: לא בי היא...'.

(ו) חגיגה טו, ע"א:[44] 'אמר רבי מאיר לא יערכנה זהב וזכוכית: אלו דברי תורה שקשה לקנותם
ככלי זהב ... ונוחים לאבדן ככלי זכוכית. אמר ר' עקיבא. כלי זהב וכלי זכוכית אעפ"י שנשברו יש
להם תקנה. אף תלמיד חכם, אעפ"י שסרח יש לו תקנה'.

(ז) שוחר טוב, ח (ב):[45] 'אמר רבי. מצינו בשלשה מקומות שהיו המלאכים מדיינין כנגד הקב"ה:
באדם, במתן תורה, ובמשכן ... וכן במתן תורה. כשבא הקב"ה ליתן תורה לישראל בסיני התחילו
המלאכים מדיינין לפני הקב"ה ... אמרו לפניו: רבונו של עולם נאה הוא לך שתתן תורה בשמים,
למה שאנו קדושים וטהורים והיא טהורה וקדושה ... מוטב שתהא אצלנו. אמר להם: אינה ראוייה
להמצא בעליונים, שנאמר: ולא תמצא בארץ החיים...'.

ההשקפה זו משמשת בסיס לפירושו של רש"י לספר משלי, ועיקרון דתי בעל משמעות כוללנית

---

42   ומקבילותיו בשינויי לשון: בר"ר צא, ט (תיאודור־אלבק, עמ' 1131); קה"ר ה, יז; יל"ש א, קמח ועוד.

43   וכן ראה שמות רבה ה, ט; יל"ש ב, תתקכא; תנחומא בובר, שמות כב.

44   ומקבילותיו: רות רבה ו, ה; יל"ש א, תעג; יל"ש ב, תקלב, תתקעד, תתקטז. וראה גם ספרי עקב, יא.

45   ומקבילותיו, ראה ויקרא רבה לא, ה; יל"ש ב, תקלט.

בפירושיו האחרים, ובהם גם פירושו לאיוב.[46] כדוגמה לעמדתו של רש"י נביא דברים אחדים מפתיחת פירושו לספר משלי.

א, ב: 'לדעת חכמה ומוסר להבין אמרי בינה – המשלים האלה אמר להודיע לבריות שיהיו עמלים בתורה, שהיא חכמה ומוסר ובינה'.

א, ו: 'להבין משל ומליצה דברי חכמים וחידותם – שיתנו לב להבין במקראות שתי הדרכים, המשל והמליצה ... דברי חכמים וחידותם – דורשי רשומות, מקרא מלא וחסר, רמז דמיון וחידה'.

א, ח: 'שמע בני מוסר אביך – מה שנתן הקב"ה למשה בכתב ועל פה. תורת אמך – והם דברי סופרים שחדשו והוסיפו ועשו סייגים לתורה'.

עליונות התורה, חשיבותה, מעלותיה וכד' הם יסוד מוסד במחשבה הדתית היהודית כולה, עיקרון שהוא ביסוד כל הדברים ונעלה מכל ערעור. מה ראה אפוא רשב"ם לצאת כנגד המסורת הפרשנית החד־משמעית? האם הניעה אותו השאיפה להתנגדות עקרונית לכל מה שהוא מדרש, או שהיו לו מניעים אחרים?

מקומו של הפולמוס בפירוש לפרק כח וניסוחו עשויים להעיד שהערותיו של רשב"ם אינן מכוונות כלפי מסורת חז"ל כולה, אלא באופן ישיר כלפי ביטויה המסוים בפירוש רש"י. שני הפסוקים שבהם מציג רשב"ם את דבריו הם גם אלו שעליהם מתעכב רש"י. ראינו את הערתו הקצרה והדוגמטית של רש"י לפס' יב, ואילו בפירושו לפס' כז הוא מאריך בדבריו ומציע את אחד הביאורים הארוכים ביותר בפרק. פירוש זה מתקשר לפסוקים הקודמים, ואנו נביא, לפי העניין, מדבריו לפס' כג־כז:[47]

(כג) 'כי אלקי' הבין דרכה. נסתכל בה וברא את העולם באותיותיה כסדרן ומשקלן. יצר כל הנוצרים כאשר כתו' בסוד ספר יצירה:'

(כד) 'כי הוא לקצות הארץ יביט. בה היאך יבנם ויבראם.
ותחת כל השמים. צורכי בריאתו ראה בה. ...'

(כז) 'אז ראה. נסתכל בה ובעצתה יעשה הכל:
ויספרה. ספר אותיותיה, כפולות ופשוטו' ... ראשונה ואמצעי' ואחרונה הוא אמת, חותמו של הקב"ה וכן בשאר סדרים ברא כל דבר ודבר, זה באותי' הללו, וזה באותיו' הללו, והכל מפו' בסו' ספר היצירה.
הכינה. זימנה ליצירה'.

לשם הבנת פירושו של רש"י, יש להבחין תחילה בין הבסיס הרעיוני הכללי שדבריו מבוססים עליו, ובין הניסוח המסוים וההשקפות המסוימות של ביאור זה. הבסיס הרעיוני הכללי קדום ביותר, ונובע גם הוא ממסורת ארוכת שנים, שלפיה קדמה התורה לבריאת העולם, ועוד יותר – בה נועץ הקב"ה כשברא את העולם.[48] המקור לרעיונות אלו גם הוא מצוי בספרות החכמה המקראית, שבה מוצגת החכמה כמי שבאמצעותה ברא האל את העולם: 'ה' בחכמה יסד ארץ כונן שמים בתבונה' (משלי

46 וראה למשל לאיוב יא, ו: 'תעלומות חכמה. ותדע כי כפלים לתושיה יש לתורה שלא קיימת'. או לטו, ז: 'הראשון אדם תולד... לאדם הנוצר מאדמה נולדת שידעת לקיים כל חכמת מצות הבורא?' וראה עוד להלן.
47 הנוסח, על־פי כ"י לוצקי 778.
48 ראה א"א אורבך, חז"ל, פרקי אמונות ודעות, ירושלים תשכ"ט, עמ' 254–255, ועמ' 175–179. ראה גם .W Harvey, 'Torah', EncJud 15, pp. 1236-1246

ג, יט). ואילו הטקסט הקובע הוא זה המתאר את החכמה בדרך של האנשה כמי שקדמה לבריאה: 'ה'
קנני ראשית דרכו קדם מפעליו מאז. מעולם נסכתי מראש מקדמי ארץ. באין תהמות חוללתי וגו''
(משלי ח, כב ואילך).

את המשוואה חכמה = תורה, שהצבענו עליה לעיל, פיתחו חז"ל בהרחבה רבה ולכיוונים שונים.
התורה נמנית עם אותם הדברים שבריאתם קדמה לבריאת העולם,[49] ור' עקיבא מתאר אותה כ'כלי'
שבו נברא העולם.[50] עניין זה מקבל תפנית מיוחדת בדבריו של האמורא ר' הושעיה, מן המאה
הרביעית: 'רבי הושעיא פתח ... ואהיה אצלו אמון ... התורה אומרת אני הייתי כלי אומנותו של
הקב"ה. בנוהג שבעולם מלך בשר ודם בונה פלטין אינו בונה אותה מדעת עצמו אלא מדעת אומן.
והאומן אינו בונה אותה מדעת עצמו אלא דיפתראות ופנקסאות יש לו. לדעת היאך הוא עושה
חדרים. היאך הוא עושה פשפשין. כך היה הקב"ה מביט בתורה ובורא את העולם'.[51]

דבריו של רש"י בפירושו לפס' כג-כז אינם נקשרים למסורות המנוסחות ניסוח כללי על קדימותה
של התורה ועל היותה 'כלי', אלא דווקא לרוח הדברים שאמר ר' הושעיה, ועוד יותר – לאחד
הביטויים המובהקים של הספרות המיסטית הקדומה, לספר יצירה.

כניסוחם, דומה שדברי רש"י מורכבים משלושה יסודות:

'יביט בה היאך יבנם ויבראם' – הם פרפרזה על דברי ר' הושעיה 'היה הקב"ה מביט בתורה ובונה
את העולם'.

'ראשונה, אמצעית ואחרונה, הוא אמת, חותמו של הקב"ה' – הם שינוי לשון מדברי הירושלמי:
'מהו חותמו של הקב"ה? רבי ביבי בשם רבי ראובן: אמת. מהו אמת? ... אמר ריש לקיש: אלף
רישיה דאלפא ביתא, מ"ם באמצעיתה ת"ו בסופה. לומר, אני ה' ראשון שלא קבלתי מאחר,
ומבלעדי אין אלוהים שאין לי שותף. ואת אחרונים אני הוא, שאיני עתיד למוסרה לאחר'.[52]

'נסתכל בה וברא את העולם באותיותיה כסדרן ומשקלן ... ספר אותיותיה כפולות ופשוטות ...
ברא כל דבר ודבר, זה באותיות הללו וזה באותיות הללו' – הן המינים והן הרעיונות הם מיסודותיו
של ספר יצירה.

דעה מקובלת היא, שרש"י לא עסק בעניינים מיסטיים. כך באופן כללי טוען מלמד;[53] ומחקרו
של דן – אף-על-פי שהוא מעיד על עצמו שאין זה אלא מחקר ראשוני – מאשר את דבריו.[54] ואולם,
עמדה כוללנית זו מועמדת בספק לאור פירושו של רש"י לאיוב כח, כג-כז. לא זו בלבד שבפסוקים

---

49 בר"ר א, ד (תיאודור-אלבק, עמ' 6), פסחים נד, ע"א, ועוד.

50 אבות ג, יד.

51 בר"ר א, א–ב (תיאודור-אלבק, עמ' 2). על היסודות הרעיוניים של דברי ר' הושעיה, ועל הוויכוח בשאלת הרקע
האפלטוני שלהם, ראה אורבך (לעיל, הערה 48), עמ' 175 הערה 68. על דמותו של ר' הושעיה, ראה .A
Heilewitz, 'Hoshaiah', EncJud 8, p. 1026

52 ירושלמי, סנהדרין, פרק א הלכה א (יח, ע"א), ומקבילותיו. ראה: בר"ר פ"א, ב; שהש"ר א, מה; דברים רבה,
א, ז ועוד.

53 לעיל, הערה 3, עמ' 396: 'כידוע אין רש"י עוסק בקבלה'.

54 J. Dan, 'Rashi and the Merkabah', in: Rashi 1040-1090, Hommage à Ephraim E. Urbach, ed.
Gabrielle Sed-Rajna, Paris 1993, pp. 259-264. 'At this time we have no proof that Rashi and
his school were aware of the details of the mystical endeavor of the ancient Jewish mystics
in Late Antiquity' (p. 264)

אלו, ובהם בלבד בכל מפעלו הפרשני, מזכיר רש"י במפורש את ספר יצירה,[55] אלא שניסוח דבריו
ובחירת המונחים מעידים שהוא מכיר את תוכנו של הספר ומקבל אותו. ועוד יותר: בשתי הפעמים
שהוא נזכר הוא מכנה אותו 'סוד ספר יצירה'; כלומר, הוא מודע בבהירות למהותו.

כדי לרדת לשורש דבריו של רש"י, מן הראוי להביא מפירושיו ל'טקסט הקובע' שבספר
משלי. כאן דווקא, בפסוקים המהווים בסיס ומסד לתפיסת חז"ל על קדמות התורה ותפקידה בבריאת
העולם, נשמעים דבריו של רש"י כמעט נייטרליים:

משלי ג, יט: ה' בחכמה יסד ארץ כונן שמים בתבונה – עפ"י התורה, והיא החכמה, והיא
התבונה והיא הדעת. ואחר שכל העולם נברא בהם, לכך: בדעתו תהומות
נבקעו.

משלי ח, כב: ה' קנני ראשית דרכו – קודם בריאתו של עולם.

משלי ח, ל: ואהיה אצלנו אמון – גדולה אצלו.
יום יום – אלפים שנה.

משלי ט, א: חכמות בנתה ביתה – בחכמה בנה הקב"ה את עולמו.
חצבה עמודיה שבעה – שבעת ימי בראשית. ד"א, שבעה ספרים שיש בתורה
וכו'.

ההשוואה בין פירושיו לספר משלי לבין פירושיו לאיוב כח, כג-כח מגלה בבהירות כיצד פירושיו
לספר משלי נשענים על מסורת חז"ל ואינם חורגים מניסוחיה, ואילו הפירוש לאיוב כח מגלה את
זיקתו הברורה מאוד דווקא ל'מעשה בראשית' שבספר יצירה ולא לדברי חז"ל. שאלה לעצמה היא,
אם יש לפרש את הניסוחים הסתמיים יחסית של הפירוש למשלי לאור פירושיו לס' איוב, כלומר –
האם יש לייחס את ידיעת ספר יצירה ואת הנחת השקפותיו גם בביאורים הבלתי מפורשים של ספר
משלי. אבל תהא אשר תהא תשובתנו לשאלה זו, דומה שאין כל אפשרות לדחות את השפעתו של
ספר יצירה על הפירוש לאיוב כח עצמו. הן בהתייחסות המפורשת אל הספר, הן בתוכן הדברים והן
במינוחם, נזקק רש"י לתורת הבריאה של ספר יצירה.

נתונים אלו מעוררים שאלות שיש להן השלכות רחבות על עולמה התרבותי של יהדות אשכנז
במאה האחת-עשרה והשתים-עשרה. 'ספר יצירה' הוא חיבור קוסמוגוני-מיסטי קדום,[56] שהיתה לו
ככל הנראה תפוצה ניכרת בקהילות היהודיות השונות בימי הביניים. אולם ביותר ידועה השפעתו
הגדולה על חסידות אשכנז, שפעלה באשכנז ובצפון צרפת במחצית השנייה של המאה השתים-
עשרה ובמאה השלוש-עשרה.[57] 'ספר יצירה' היה בבחינת 'נוכח' במציאות הרוחנית היהודית

55   מלמד מציין שרש"י מזכיר את ספר יצירה פעמיים, אך מראי המקום שהוא מביא (איוב כד, ג, כז) מוטעים, וצ"ל:
איוב כח, כג, כז (לעיל, הערה 3, עמ' 396).
56   על הספר, ראה G.G. Scholem, *Major Trends in Jewish Mysticism*, New York 1946, pp. 75-78. ג'
שלום, יצירה, ספר, האנציקלופדיה העברית כג, ירושלים תשל"א, טורים 192–196, ראה גם: S. Pines,
'Points of Similarity between the Exposition of the Doctrine of the Sefirot in the Sefer Yezira
and a Text of the Pseudo-Clementine Homilies', *Proceedings of the Israel Academy of Sciences
and Humanities*, VII/3, Jerusalem 1989, pp. 63-121
57   על מקומו של ספר יצירה ופירושיו כבסיס לתורת הסוד של חסידי אשכנז, ראה י' דן, תורת הסוד של חסידי
אשכנז, ירושלים תשכ"ח, עמ' 22–23, ועוד לאורך הספר (ראה מפתח).

באירופה במשך זמן רב, החל מהמאה העשירית, והשאלה היא מאימתי הפך אבן יסוד להשקפות
המיסטיות. או כפי שניסח את השאלה י' דן: 'ספר יצירה היה ... נושא לפירושים פילוסופיים,
מדעיים ורציונליסטיים בידיהם של החכמים הגדולים ביותר ביהדות אירופה, בעקבות המסורת
המזרחית שראשיתה בסעדיה גאון. המפעל הגדול של המיסטיקנים, שפירשו את ספר יצירה
והשתמשו בו היה הטרנספורמציה של חיבור זה מחיבור קוסמוגוני־מדעי לחיבור מיסטי'.[58]

השאלה נוגעת במישרין לרש"י: איך יש להסביר את זיקתו של רש"י אל ספר יצירה, המתגלה
לנו בפירושו לאיוב כח? כ'ספר קוסמוגוני־מדעי', או כ'חיבור מיסטי'? לפחות לפי שעה אין בידינו
עדויות מספיקות כדי לתת לשאלה זו תשובה חד־משמעית; ועם זאת יש לצרף לכאן את היגדיו של
רש"י בפירושו ליחזקאל א, כז ו־ח ב: 'לא נתן רשות להתבונן במקרא זה', 'אסור להתבונן במקרא
זה', ואת העובדה שרש"י מכנה את החיבור שהוא מתייחס אליו 'סוד ספר יצירה'. כל אלו מקרבים
אל הדעת שרש"י היה מודע לאופיו המיסטי של ספר יצירה, ומתוך מודעות זו הפנה אליו קוראיו
בפירושו לאיוב כח.

נתונים אלו הם הרקע הרוחני והספרותי לפירושו של רשב"ם. המאה השתים־עשרה, תקופת
פעולתו של רשב"ם, היא תקופת צמיחתה של חסידות אשכנז. אמנם ר' שמואל החסיד, שנחשב
למייסד התנועה, חי זמן מה אחריו,[59] אבל ראשיתה של ספרות־הסוד האשכנזית קדמה להופעתו של
ר' שמואל החסיד ונעוצה, כנראה, עוד לפני מחצית המאה השתים־עשרה, 'ובוודאי קדמה לה מסורת
ארוכה בעל פה'.[60]

רשב"ם מכוון את פולמוסו כנגד הבנה קוסמוגונית של הטקסט המקראי, והוא עושה זאת בדרך
ובשיטה המאפיינות את דרכו – על־ידי פירוש הטקסט המקראי והיצמדות ל'פשוטו של מקרא'.
הוויכוח של רשב"ם עם פירוש רש"י, ועוד יותר – עם הספרות הקוסמוגונית, איננו נעשה במונחים
תיאולוגיים. כמו במקומות אחרים[61] הוא בוחן את הפירוש המוצע ושואל אם אכן הדברים הולמים
את הכתוב בטקסט. הוא מעמיד למבחן את שני היסודות של פירוש רש"י: הזיהוי 'חכמה = תורה',
והביאור לפס' כג־כז, ובעיקר כז. לגבי הזיהוי 'חכמה = תורה' אומר רשב"ם, באותו קיצור אופייני
הממשיך את ניסוחו הקצר של רש"י: 'חכמה ממש לירא את הק' ולא תורה'. הבסיס לפירושו ברור,
מפני שהוא מצוי בפרק זה עצמו: 'הן יראת ה' היא חכמה וסור מרע בינה' (כח, כח). כנגד עמדתו
של רש"י, בעקבות המסורת הארוכה, ש'חכמה, תבונה ודעת' הם כולם כינויים לתורה (רש"י למשלי
ג, יט, ראה לעיל) מגייס רשב"ם את עדותו של הפרק הנידון עצמו, המעיד בבהירות כי 'חכמה =
יראת ה'' ו'בינה' הריהי 'מלה כפולה' (פירוש לפס' יב).

היסוד השני הוא בחינת הלשון בפירושו של רש"י. שהרי לפי רש"י לפס' כז 'הכינה – זימנה
ליצירה', כלומר 'הכין **באמצעותה** את העולם', או בפס' כג: 'ונסתכל **בה** וברא את העולם'. על כך
אומר רשב"ם את הדברים בפשטות: 'הכינה' משמעו 'הכין אותה'. ו'חקרה' – 'חקר בה', ואין בכל אלה
התייחסות לעולם או לבריאתו. בדומה לכך יש להבין גם את פירושו לפס' כד־כה, שבו לא רמז כלל

58   דן (במאמר הנזכר בהערה 54), עמ' 261.

59   זמנו המדויק אינו ידוע, אך מקובל שנולד בתחילת המאה השתים־עשרה. ראה: א' אפשטיין, 'ר' שמואל החסיד
     ב"ר קלונימוס הזקן', כתבי ר' אברהם אפשטיין, ירושלים תש"י, עמ' רמז־רנה.

60   דן (לעיל, הערה 57), עמ' 50.

61   ראה למשל יפת (לעיל, הערה 6), עמ' 349.

על כיוון פולמוסי: 'הוא הביט וראה לקצות הארץ ... כדי לעשות משקל לרוח', ולא, כרש"י: 'יביט
בה [בתורה] איך יברא את העולם'.

עמדתו האנטי-מיסטית ואנטי-קוסמוגונית של רשב"ם ידועה גם ממקורות אחרים, והמרכזי
שבהם הוא פירושו לקהלת. בפירוש המושג חכמה, שקהלת מרבה לדבר בו, מבחין רשב"ם בין שני
סוגים, או שתי דרגות של חכמה. החכמה הרגילה, 'שאין בה עומק, שהיא צריכה לעולם', ו'החכמה
העמוקה', 'שאין בני אדם צריכין לה ואין רגילין בה' (פירושו לקהלת ב, ג).[62] החכמה המיועדת לאדם
היא החכמה הרגילה, ש'אין בה עומק', ואילו 'החכמה העמוקה' אינה ניתנת להשגה והיא מקור לכאב
ולייסורים. 'חכמה עמוקה' זו היא הנוגעת לאל, לבריאת העולם ולהנהגתו: 'ראיתי מעשיו של הק'
שאין אדם יכול לעמוד על הבירור ולמצוא את מעשי העולם ולידע מדעותיו של הק' שהוא מודד
לבריות'.[63] כדוגמאות לעיסוק זה, שיש בו מכאוב ואין בו תועלת, מזכיר רשב"ם במפורש – בפעם
היחידה בכל חיבוריו המצויים בידינו – את 'מעשה מרכבה' ו'ספר יצירה': 'כל אודות דבר זה נסיתי
ברוב חכמתי שהרי אמרתי בלבי שאחכמה בחכמות עמוקות והיא אותה חכמה עמוקה רחוקה ממני
שאיני יכול להבין ולעמוד בה. רחוק מה שהיה. עמוקה שהיתה כבר כגון מעשה מרכבה וספר יצירה,
רחוקה היא ממני שאיני יכול לעמוד בה...',[64] ועוד: 'שמתוך שהוא מוסיף חכמה יתירה ... מחשב
ומעמיק במעשיו של הק' שהוא עושה בעולם על מה הוא עושה אותם שאינו יכול לעמוד עליהם.
ומתוך רוב מחשבות' כועס ומוסיף מכאוב'.[65]

מתוך אותה מגמה, המבקשת להתרחק מענייני האלוהות, הן בתחום הבריאה והן בתחום ההשגחה,
נכתב גם פירושו של רשב"ם לבראשית פרק א, שעיקרו: המתואר בפרק א אינננו סיפור הבריאה
אלא 'מלאכת ששת ימים', שבהם הפך העולם לארץ נושבת.[66]

הערותיו הפולמוסיות של רשב"ם, המנוסחות בקיצור ובמתינות, מעידות היטב על התפקיד
המרכזי שייעד רשב"ם ל'פשוטו של מקרא'. אין זו אף ורק 'דרך אחרת', או 'דרך נוספת' לבחון את
הטקסט המקראי, אלא הדרך הנכונה. כפי שהוא מעיד בניסוח החד-פעמי בפירושו לאיוב כח, כז,
'אין לך בו רק פשוטו'.[67] פירוש המקרא הוא עבורו פנייה אל היסודות, אל הבסיס שממנו נבנה עולמה
הרוחני של היהדות. הוא מבקש לעצב את דמותו של עולם זה, ואולי נכון יותר – לבחור במרכיבים
שמהם יורכב עולם זה – מתוך חזרה אל היסודות וביאורם כמשמעם. מול המדרש – שכשיטה
פרשנית ועל-פי עקרונותיו אין לו גבולות, הכל אפשרי, והכל ניתן להיעשות – מציג רשב"ם את

---

62 יפת-סולטרס (לעיל, הערה 3), עמ' 77, וראה גם עמ' 52–53.

63 פירושו לקה' ח, יז, שם, עמ' 109.

64 פירושו לקה' ז, כג-כד, שם, עמ' 103.

65 פירושו לקה' א, יח, שם, עמ' 75.

66 ראה בהרחבה, S. Kamin, 'Rashbam's Conception of the Creation in Light of the Intellectual
Currents of his Time', in: S. Japhet (ed.), *Studies in Bible (1986)*, Scripta Hierosolymitana 31,
Jerusalem 1986, pp. 91-132 (=שרה קמין, בין יהודים לנוצרים בפרשנות המקרא, ירושלים תשנ"ב, עמ'
27*–68*).

67 יש מקום לבחון את עמדתו כאן לאור דבריו המתונים יותר בפירושו לתורה, שלפיהם 'נכתב פשוטו של מקרא
בלשון שיכולין ללמוד מימנו עיקר הדרשה' (לבר' א, א), וכן 'כי מיתור המקראות נשמעין ההגדות וההלכות...
ואפע"כ ההלכות עיקר' (לשמ' כא, ב). למרות כל מה שנכתב על הבנת הפשט ומעמד הפשט אצל רשב"ם, נראה
לי שיש מקום לשוב ולהידרש לנושא זה. ראה ש' קמין, רש"י – פשוטו של מקרא ומדרשו של מקרא, ירושלים
תשמ"ו, עמ' 268–272.

הפשט, כלומר: הבנת טקסט שיש לה גבולות, והיא מאפשרת לקורא להבין את הטקסט בתוך התחום המוגבל בגבולות אלו.

[ד] היחס למקורות חז"ל ולפירוש רש"י

הדיון בסעיף הקודם, בפירושים שהם במוצהר על-פי 'פשוטו של מקרא', גילה את עמדתו הביקורתית של רשב"ם כלפי המסורות שקדמו לו, ודווקא בנושא שיש לו יוקרה ומעמד מיוחד בפרשנות חז"ל. ואולם דיון זה מגלה רק פן אחד ביחסו של רשב"ם למקורות חז"ל, ונשלים אותו בפנים נוספים, המתגלים בפירושו לפרק כח.

דחיית פירושי חז"ל ומדרשיהם מגיעה לידי ביטוי בדברי רשב"ם גם כאשר אין לדבר כל סימן חיצוני. עניינים שונים, המנוסחים בארח נייטרלי ובלשון חיווי בלתי-פולמוסית, מציגים עמדות המנוגדות למדרש. הקורא תוהה לעתים מה ראה רשב"ם להביא פירוש כלשהו הנראה על פניו כמובן מאליו. רק משהוא מגלה את מדרשי חז"ל או את פירוש רש"י מתברר לו הטעם הפולמוסי, מדוע הביא רשב"ם את הפירוש ומדוע פירש כפי שפירש. ואולם, בגלל אופיָם הבלתי מפורש של ביאורים אלו, אין אופיָם הפולמוסי נעלה מכל ספק, ואפשר שמניעים אחרים עמדו מאחורי ביאור זה או אחר. אף-על-פי-כן נביא להלן דוגמאות אחדות מפרק כח, שבהן נראים ביאורי רשב"ם כמעמידים את פשט הכתוב כנגד המדרש.

(א)   פס' ד'   –   אבן אפל וצלמות

רשב"ם: אבן אופל. אבן יש שמשם יוצא אופל.

המדרש: אמר ריש לקיש... אבן זה יצר הרע שהוא משול לאבן... הוי אבן אפל וצלמות. [68]

(ב)   פס' יא[א]   –   מבכי נהרות חִבֵּשׁ

רשב"ם: מבכי. ממי נבך. מצולות תהום הארץ תיקן הנהרות.

המדרש: א"ר ברכיה: לא פירשו המים העליונים מן התחתונים אלא בבכי. הכא הוא דאמר: מבכי נהרות חיבש. [69]

רש"י: מבכי נהרות חבש. בברִיית עולם. [70]

(ג)   פס' יא[ב]   –   ותעלמה יצא אור

רשב"ם: ממקום תעלום, שהוא נעלם מעיני כל חי, מוציא אור.

המדרש: בתקופת טבת... הולך וסובב... עד שהוא מגיע לחלון תעלומה שבו האור

---

68   תנחומא בובר, מקץ א (יל"ש ב, תתקטו), וראה גם בבר"ר ראש פרשה פט: 'קץ שם לחשך – זמן נתן לעולם כמה שנים יעשה באפילה. ומה טעם קץ שם לחשך וגו' אבן אפל וצלמות, שכל זמן שיצר הרע בעולם אופל וצלמות בעולם, נעקר יצר הרע מן העולם, עבר אופל וצלמות וצלמות מן העולם' (תיאודור-אלבק עמ' 1086 = יל"ש א, קמז). למדרשים אחרים ר' שוחר טוב, צב, ד, ועוד.

69   בר"ר ה, ד (תיאודור-אלבק עמ' 35–34) ומקבילותיו: יל"ש ב, תתמה, תתקטו.

70   זוהי הגירסה בכתבי היד ויגה 23, מילנו אמברוזיאנה 22, אוקספורד-בודלי 18. בכתב-יד לוצקי 778, הנוסח מורחב מאוד, ובאופן אחר במקראות גדולות. הפירוש 'בבריאת העולם' חוזר ונשנה אצל כולם.

יוצא, שנאמר: ותעלומה יוציא אור. בתקופת ניסן מתחיל מחלון תעלומה
שבו האור יוצא והולך אל קרן צפונית (פרקי דרבי אליעזר, פרק ו).

רש"י: ותעלומה יוציא אור. חלון יש בשמים ששמו תעלומה משם תולדות
השמש. בפרקי דר' אליעזר.[71]

(ד) פס' יב – והחכמה מאין תמצא

רשב"ם: מאין. מאיזה מקום.

המדרש: אמר רבי יוחנן. אין דברי תורה מתקיימין אלא במי שמשים עצמו כמי
שאינו. שנאמר: והחכמה מאין תמצא (סוטה כא, ע"ב).

(ה) פס' יג – לא תמצא בארץ החיים

רשב"ם: ולא תמצא. אינה מצווייה לימכר בשווקים. מלה כפולה היא. בארץ החיים.
אילו שווקים...

המדרש: (א) אמר רב... לא תמצא תורה במי שמחייה נפשו עליה (סנהדרין קיא,
ע"א).

רש"י: לא תמצא בארץ החיים. במי שמחיה עצמו אלא במי שממית עצמו עליה
ביגיעה וברעבון.

המדרש: (ב) אמרו לפניו [המלאכים] נאה הוא לך שתתן תורה בשמים... אמר להם:
אינה ראויה להתקיים בעליונים. שנאמר: ולא תמצא בארץ החיים.[72]

האם יש ללמוד מנתונים אלו, שעמדתו של רשב"ם כלפי מקורות חז"ל ופירוש רש"י היא בכל מקום
עמדה של ביקורת? מסקנה קיצונית כזאת תהיה בוודאי מוטעית. ישנם מקומות רבים שבהם רשב"ם
מקבל את דברי מקורותיו, הן את דברי חז"ל והן דברי רש"י, ולעתים הוא אף חוזר עליהם. לעמדה
כזאת של הסכמה יש בפירושו לפרק כח שתי דרכי ביטוי: במפורש ושלא במפורש. הביטוי המפורש,
שהוא גם המדויק ביותר, מצוי בביאור לפס' יג:

בארץ החיים. אילו שווקים שהם חיים לעולם כאשר פירשו רבותינו במסכת יומא אתהלך
לפני ה'[73] בארצות החיים אילו שווקים.

רשב"ם מקבל אפוא את המסורת הפרשנית כלשונה, מבלי לבדוק אותה ומבלי לספק לה הוכחה משל
עצמו. ניתן אפילו לשער שהוא מגייס את סמכות חז"ל כדי להעניק לביאור את מלוא המשקל, ודומה
שהוא נוקֵט דרך זאת כדי לצאת נגד השקפה אחרת, אף היא של חז"ל, שאותה אינו מקבל. את
הביטוי 'ארץ החיים' פירשו חז"ל כארצם של אלו המחיים עצמם על התורה (ראה לעיל), או
לחילופין, ארצם של המלאכים – השמים. כנגד תפיסות אלו מעמיד רשב"ם ביאור אחר, שמקורו
אף הוא בדברי חז"ל. דוגמה זו עשויה להוכיח שדחיית דברי חז"ל אינה באה לשם עצמה, אלא נובעת
מברירה קפדנית של החומרים. מה שראוי להתקבל – מתקבל.[74]

71 כ"י וינה 23, ויש שינויים קלים בעדויות האחרות.
72 שוחר טוב ח (ב) ומקבילותיו. ראה גם לעיל, עמ' *14, וראה גם דברים רבה ח, ב.
73 תה' קטז, ט.
74 לעמדה אחרת בדבר יחסו של רשב"ם למקורות התורה שבעל־פה ראה גרינברג (לעיל, הערה 2), עמ' 566.

יש לציין כי הפניה מפורשת זו לטקסט תלמודי היא יחידה היא בפירוש רשב"ם לאיוב, אך מצאנו הפניות כאלה לרוב בפירושו לתורה.[75]

ביטוי אחר לקבלת מסורת חז"ל היא הדרך הבלתי מפורשת, ואף לכך יש דוגמה מעניינת בפרק כח, בפירוש לפס' ג-ח. מסורת פרשנית ארוכה מפרשת פסוקים אלו כמתייחסים לעיר סדום. מצד המתודה ודרך החשיבה המדרשית פועלים כאן עקרונות ברורים של זיהוי, המחשה והפרטה, ואלה מביאים בקביעות להיסטוריזציה של הטקסטים הפיוטיים.[76] הבסיס הטקסטואלי להתייחסות לעיר סדום מצוי בפס' ה: 'ארץ ממנה יצא לחם ותחתיה נהפך כמו אש'. הניגוד בין החיוב ובין השלילה מזכיר את מה שעבר על סדום, שהיתה תחילה 'כלה משקה'... כגן ה' בארץ מצרים' (בר' יג, י), ובעקבות חטאה ה' 'המטיר על סדום ועל עמורה גפרית ואש... עלה קיטור הארץ כקיטור הכבשן' (שם, יט, כד-כח), והשימוש בשורש 'הפך', מתקשר אל המהפכה בה"א הידיעה, היא 'מהפכת סדום ועמורה' (דב' כט, כב; יש' יג, יט ועוד). בעקבות פס' ה פורשו גם יתר הפסוקים ביחידה זו, ובראש וראשונה פס' ד, כמתייחסים אל סדום. פירוש זה הפך למעין אקסיומה פרשנית, המשמשת נקודת מוצא למדרשים רבים, ונזכיר כדוגמה את דברי הספרי:

'שאין אדם מורד במקום אלא מתוך שובע... וכן אתה מוצא באנשי סדום שלא מרדו במקום אלא מתוך שובע. מה נאמר בהם, ארץ ממנה יצא לחם, מקום ספיר אבניה, נתיב לא ידעו עיט, לא הדריכוהו בני שחץ וגו', אמרו אנשי סדום הרי מזון אצלינו, הרי כסף וזהב אצלינו, נעמד ונשכח תורת הרגל מארצנו, אמר להם המקום: בטובה שהיטבתי לכם אתם מבקשים לשכח תורת הרגל מבינכם, אני משכח אתכם מן העולם. מה נאמר בהם? פרץ נחל מעם גר, לפיד בוז וגו'.[77]

רש"י מקבל את מסורת חז"ל בעניין זה ומתייחס אליה בפירושו לפס' ד, ולאור דבריו בפס' י 'חוזר לתחלת ענינו', ניתן להבין שהוא מפרש את פס' ד-ט כיחידה אחת שעניינה סדום. אצל רש"י יש בקבלה זו ביטוי מובהק לשיטתו בדרך כלל; לא זו בלבד שהוא מקבל מדברי חז"ל הרבה ככל האפשר, אלא שהוא שותף לחז"ל בדרך חשיבתו, והנטייה להיסטוריזציה מאפיינת את כלל פירושו לספר איוב. בעשרות מקומות בספר הוא מפרש את ההיגדים הפיוטיים הכלליים כמתייחסים לאירועים היסטוריים או לדמויות היסטוריות ובהם דור המבול, דור הפלגה, סדום, מצרים, סנחריב, ועוד.[78]

גם רשב"ם מקבל את עמדתם של חז"ל, ומפרש את הקטע הזה כמתייחס לסדום; הוא סוטה ממסורת חז"ל רק בפרטים, כגון בכך שהוא רואה את תחילת היחידה המדברת בסדום בפס' ג ולא בפס' ד.[79] גם מפירוש רש"י נבדל רשב"ם בפרטים, כגון בכך שאת הצלע 'הנשכחים מני רגל' מפרש רש"י בעקבות המדרש: 'אלו אנשי סדום ששכחו תורת רגל מארצם', ואילו רשב"ם מבאר: 'שאין אדם עובר ושב עליהם', תוך התחשבות בצורת הנפעל של 'נשכחים'. בביאור ל'פרץ נחל מעם גר' (פס' ד), 'ארץ ממנה יצא לחם' (פס' ה) שווה פירוש רשב"ם לזה של רש"י.[80]

75 כגון שמ' כו, יד; במ' טו, כ, ועוד; ראה מלמד (לעיל, הערה 3), עמ' 482–483.

76 על תופעות אלו ראה היינמן (לעיל הערה 28), עמ' 15–34.

77 ספרי לדב' יא, טו (פסקה מג, טז), ראה פינקלשטיין עמ' 92–93. למקבילות ראה סנהדרין קט, ע"א; תנחומא, אחרי מות; פסיקתא דרב כהנא, אחרי מות, ועוד הרבה.

78 ראה, בין היתר, פירושיו לאיוב ד, יא; ח, ה; ט, יג; יב, כג; טו, כג; כ, י, כא, כג, ובעיקר כו; לה, י; לו יט, ועוד.

79 על סיום היחידה, ראה הערה 26.

80 והשווה גם פירושי רש"י ורשב"ם לפס' א (לעיל, עמ' 122*), ל'פרץ נחל מעם גר' (פס' ד), 'מקום ספיר אבניה'

עמדתו של רשב"ם בעניין זה מעניינת במיוחד, מפני שלא כמו אצל רש"י, אין היא משתלבת
בשיטתו הפרשנית הכוללת אלא חורגת ממנה במובהק. בביאורו לאיוב כב, טז אומר רשב"ם: 'אין
לפרש בכל הספר על דור הפלגה ואנשי סדום אלא כאן, שנאמר "נהר יצוק יסודם"'.

בהיגד זה מבטא רשב"ם את הסתייגותו מן ההיסטוריזיציה היתרה של הטקסט הפיוטי, המתבטאת
דרך משל בפירושי רש"י. עם זאת אינו מבטל אפשרות פירוש זו כעיקרון, אלא רואה בה פירוש פשט
אפשרי כאשר הטקסט מחייב זאת. כשם שהבהסיס לפירוש כב, טז בדור המבול מבוסס על הבנת
הטקסט 'ונהר יצוק יסודם', כך גם פירוש כח, ד־ה, וראש לכל פס' ה, כמתייחסים לסדום נובע
מהבנת הטקסט. בביאורו לפס' ה הוא אומר: 'ארץ ממנה יצא לחם. שממציאה לחם לשובע, ומקומה
נהפך לאש שנ' גפרית ואש', וכן בפס' ד: 'פרץ נחל. שנ' וה' המטיר על סדום וגו''. כלומר: רשב"ם
רואה בפסוקים אלו התייחסות ספרותית מכוונת – זו שחוקרי הספרות בדורנו מכנים בשם 'אלוזיה'
– לבר' יט, כד: 'וה' המטיר על סדום ועל עמורה... גפרית ואש מן השמים', התייחסות שהשירה חוזרת
אליה פעמיים, בפס' ד ובפס' ה.

דומה שגם דוגמה זו מאשרת את אשר אמרנו קודם לכן: רשב"ם אינו דוחה את דברי חז"ל מכל
וכל, דחייה הבאה לשם עצמה. עמדתו של רשב"ם היא מתודולוגית: הוא דוחה את דרך המדרש
בהיבטיה השונים, ובוחן את הטקסט המקראי מן הפרספקטיבה של הפשט, וממנה בלבד. ואולם,
לפי הצורך, בזהירות, ומתוך ביקורת מתמדת, הוא משתמש בחומרים הלקוחים מדברי חז"ל.

שאלת יחסו של רשב"ם לפירוש רש"י היא מורכבת יותר. שהרי מלכתחילה רב מאוד הדמיון בין
שני אישים אלו. הם שייכים לאותה סביבה היסטורית ותרבותית – הזרם המרכזי, הרבני, של יהדות
צפון צרפת במאה האחת־עשרה–השתים־עשרה, ולא זו בלבד שרשב"ם היה נכדו של רש"י, בן בתו,
אלא היה אף תלמידו. דמיון כללי זה מתעמק בעיסוקם המשותף: שניהם בחרו לעסוק ב'פירוש' כסוג
ספרותי מוגדר, הן למקרא והן לתלמוד. עד כמה שידיעותינו מגיעות, לרש"י שמורה זכות הבכורה
בתחום התרבות של צרפת ואשכנז – העמדת פירוש שיטתי ומקיף לכל המקרא, ואילו רשב"ם היה
בוודאי ממשיכו המובהק ביותר. יתר על כן, משותפת לשניהם ההבחנה ב'פשוטו של מקרא' כדרך
של פירוש הטקסט, ושאיפה לממש דרך זו בפירושיהם.

ואולם, דווקא לאור דמיון מהותי זה בולט ההבדל בין שני האישים ומתחדדת ההבחנה ביניהם.
במהלך דיוננו לעיל הבאנו דוגמאות שונות להנחות ולעמדות מנוגדות של רש"י ורשב"ם, הן
בכללים והן בפרטים, במסגרת הנושאים הנבחרים שבהם עסקנו. אלא שלא טיפלנו בנושאים אחרים
הנוגעים לעניין זה, כגון בפולמוס המפורש של רשב"ם עם רש"י, או בהיבטים הלשוניים של
הפירוש, וכל אלו מחייבים השלמה במקום אחר. דברינו הבאים יהיו, אפוא, בבחינת סיכום והצעה
כאחד.

(פס' ו), חק (פס' כז). דמיון בין ביאורי רש"י ורשב"ם עשוי לא רק מכך שרשב"ם מקבל את פירושו של
רש"י, אלא גם – וזאת במקרים רבים מאוד – מכך שמעתיקים מאוחרים הכניסו את דברי רשב"ם לתוך דברי
רש"י. הדמיון המשמש בין השניים מעוות את דמותם וייחודם של הפרשנים ומשבש את ראייתנו ההיסטורית (ראה
למשל, א' טויט, 'עקבות פירוש רשב"ם בנוסח פירוש רש"י לתורה', דברי הקונגרס העולמי העשירי למדעי
היהדות, ירושלים תש"ן, עמ' 79–86; הנ"ל, 'האמנם משקף כתב־יד לייפציג 1 את הנוסח המקורי של פירוש
רש"י לתורה? [בעקבות מחקרו של אברהם גרוסמן]', תרביץ סא [תשנ"ב], עמ' 99–100). תופעה זו מתגלה
במידה מסוימת גם בפירוש רש"י לאיוב כח, על־פי גירסתו שבמקראות הגדולות, אבל אין לה ביטוי בנוסחאות
כתבי־היד שבהם השתמשנו, ובהיקפה הרחב היא חורגת מתחום עיוננו זה.

המוקד להבדל בין רשב"ם לרש"י הוא בהגדרת תפקידם כפרשנים – עניין שנדרשו לו כל
העוסקים במפעלם של אישים אלו. מול עמדתו של רש"י, המציעה שתי פנים לפירוש, 'פשוטו של
מקרא' ו'אגדה המישבת דברי המקרא דבר דבור על אופניו',[81] מציג רשב"ם עמדה 'מוניסטית' חד-
משמעית. אין הוא בא לפרש אלא בדרך הפשט. ההבדל זה משתמע, כמובן, שרשב"ם יסטה מפירוש
רש"י בכל מקום שבו יהיה סבור שרש"י בחר ללכת בדרך הדרש. ואולם, ביקורתו של רשב"ם כלפי
רש"י מופנית לאו דווקא, ואולי לא בעיקר, אל אלו מפירושיו שנכתבו ברוח המדרש ובדרכיו, אלא
דווקא כלפי אלו שנכתבו בדרך הפשט. ביקורת זו מיוסדת על מספר יסודות: ידיעה טובה יותר של
הלשון המקראית, על דקדוקה, תחבירה ומשמעותה, ומחויבות גמורה כלפיה; הבנה עמוקה יותר
של הטקסט כיצירה ספרותית, וראיית דרכי המבע הספרותי כהיבט מחייב של 'דרך המקראות';
ועמדה רציונלית ובלתי אידיאליסטית כלפי תוכנו של הטקסט המקראי, כלפי דמותם של גיבורי
המקרא וכלפי מציאות החיים המקראית. כל אלו מסתכמים בראייה מדוייקת ומפוכחת יותר של
הפשט כשיטה, שהיא היא חידושו וגדולתו של רשב"ם.

81   החוקרים נחלקו מאוד במשמען של הגדרות אלו, אך לגבי דידנו חשיבות העניין נעוצה בהגדרה הכפולה עצמה,
ובהכללת 'אגדה' כמרכיב לגיטימי בחיבור הפרשני. ראה בהרחבה קמין, לעיל הערה 67.

פירוש רשב"ם לאיוב, פרק כח

מועתק מכ"י לוצקי 778 המצוי בספריית בית המדרש לרבנים בניו־יורק

(א–ב)   **כי יש לכסף מוצא.** מוסב על 'בצדקתי החזקתי'[1] ונותן טעם לדבריו אחר 'כי מה
תקות חנף כי יבצע'[2] למה לומר למה לא אהיה רשע בוצע בצע כל ממון זהב וכסף
יכול אני למצוא כי יש להם מקום בעולם אבל 'והחכמה מאין תמצא'[3] להידבק בה
ולהיות צדיק לפני הק' ברוב חכמה ובינה ועל כן החזקתי בצדקתי:
מוצא. שמוציאין אותו מן הקרקע:
יזוקו.[4] כמו 'יזוקו'[5] מטר לאידו':[6]
ואבן יצוק נחושה. שנ' 'ומהרריה תחצב נחשת':[7]
ברזל מעפר יוקח.[8] לשון כפול על 'כי יש לכסף מוצא' לקיחה על לשון יציאה.
ו'אבן יצוק נחושה' כפול על 'לזהב יזוקו'[9] לשון יציקה על לשון שפיכה:

(ג–ד)   **ולכל תכלית הוא חוקר.** ששם תכלית וחקר לאנשי סדום שפרץ עליהם נחל אש
וגפרית מנהר דינור ממקום שהוא ניגר שם. אבל לחכמה אין לה חקר ותכלית:
אבן אופל.[10] אבן יש שמשם יוצא אופל:
הנשכחים מני רגל. שאין אדם עובר ושב עליהם:
פרץ נחל. שנ' 'וה'[11] המטיר על סדום וג'':[12]
דלו מאנוש. מלה כפול' שהיו דלים וחסירים מאנוש שאין אורחים מצויין ביניהם:
נעו. ועל כן היו מנוענעים מן העולם:

---

*   הטקסט מועתק מכתב־יד לוצקי 778 בספריית בית־המדרש לרבנים בניו־יורק. אני מודה לראשי בית־המדרש
על שהפקידו בידי את הזכות לפרסמו. כתב־היד נמסר בדיוקו: סימני הפיסוק – נקודה ונקודתיים – מצויים
בכתב־היד ולא הוספתי עליהם. הקיצורים נשמרו כצורתם, וגם הניקוד נמסר על־פי המצוי בכתב־היד. הערות
השוליים נמסרו בהערות. התוספות שהוספתי הן: סימון הדיבור המתחיל באות אחרת, שימוש בסימן מרכאות
לציון מובאות וציון מספרי הפסוקים לפני יחידות הפירוש.
פירוש הלעזים נעשה בידי מ' בנית ונלקח מתוך הנספח שהכין לפירוש הספר כולו.

1   איוב כז, ו.
2   איוב כז, ח.
3   איוב כח, יב.
4   נה"מ: יזקן.
5   נה"מ: יזקו.
6   איוב לו, כז. נה"מ: לאדו. בכתב־היד מצויר עיגול קטן מעל למלה 'אידו', המכוון להערת שוליים. בשוליים:
'שהוא כמו יצוקו'. כתב־היד של הערה זו שונה מזה של הפנים, ונראה שאין זו השלמת החסר מידי המעתיק אלא
תוספת מיד אחרת.
7   דב' ח, ט.
8   נה"מ: יֻקח.
9   נה"מ: יזקו.
10   נה"מ: אפל.
11   כתיבת השם המפורש בכתב־יד זה היא באמצעות שלושה יודי"ן היוצרים צורת משולש, שניים בתוך השורה
ואחד מעליה, כך: יּ'יּ. בכל המקומות האלה קבענו תמורתו את הקיצור המקובל היום: ה'.
12   בר' יט, כד. נה"מ: סדם.

שרה יפת

(ה) **ארץ ממנה יצא לחם.** שמוציאה לחם לשובע ומקומה נהפך לאש שנ' 'גפרית ואש':[13]

(ו) **אבניה.** של אותו מקום היו אבני ספיר:
לו. לאותו מקום שממנו מוציאין זהב:

(ז) **לא ידעו עיט.** לא הכיר אותו עוף פורח לעשות שם רעה.
ולא שזפתו. כפל לשון:

(ח) **לא הדרי' בני שחץ.** גם חיה[14] רעה לא עברה ביניהם:
הדריכוהו.[15] לשון דרך וארח.
לא עדה. לשון כפול. עדה תרגומו של סר דְשָׁטוֹלִיט בלעז:[16]

(י) **בצרות יאורים**[17] **בקע.** משם נהוגין מים לצאת כעניין שנ' 'ויך את הסלע ויצאו מים רבים':[18]

(יא) **מבכי. ממי נבך.**[19] מצולות תהום הארץ תיקן הנהרות.
חיבש.[20] תיקן כמו 'ויחבש להם מגבעות'[21] ותרגומו 'ואתקין'.[22] כך פתר דונש:[23]
ותעלומה.[24] ממקום תעלום שהוא נעלם מעיני כל חי מוציא אור:

(יב) **והחכמה.** חכמה ממש לירא את הק' ולא תורה לפי פשוטו של מקרא:
מאין. מאיזה מקום:[25]
ואיזה[26] **מקום בינה.** מלה כפולה:[27]

---

13 שם, שם.
14 בכתב־היד המלה כתובה פעמיים, אחת בסוף השורה ואחת בתחילת השורה הבאה.
15 נה"מ: הדריכהו.
16 dèstolit = סר מדרכו.
17 נה"מ: יארים.
18 במ', כ, יא. הציטטה מקוטעת, ובמקור: 'ויך את הסלע במטהו פעמים ויצאו מים רבים'.
19 המלים 'ממי נבך' כתובות בכתב־היד ברצף כמלה אחת, אך הסופר הפריד אותן על־ידי סימן של שתי נקודות: ממי:נבך.
20 נה"מ: חבש.
21 וי' ח, יג.
22 התרגום 'אתקין' לשורש 'חבש' מיוחד להקשר זה וחוזר עוד בשמ' כט, ט. בהיקרויותיו האחרות של השורש מציעים התרגומים הארמיים פעלים אחרים (זריז, תקף, ועוד).
23 הביאור אינו מופיע ב'תשובות דונש' שבידינו. כך כבר ארנד (ראה במאמר, הערה 14).
24 נה"מ: ותעלמה.
25 בכתב־היד שתי המלים מחוברות, ומופרדות על־ידי סימן שתי נקודות. ראה הערה 19.
26 נה"מ: ואי זה.
27 במקום זה יש הערת שוליים בצד שמאל, שבו השוליים צרים מאוד. ההערה דהויה מאוד, וזה לשונה: 'והחכמה מאין תמצא לשון כפול על כי יש לכסף מוצא וג'. למרות השימוש במונח 'לשון כפול' הרגיל בפירוש רשב"ם, נראה לי שזוהי הערה משנית, ואין זו השלמת החסר לפירוש רשב"ם.

(יג) **ערכה.** סדר שלה לקנות הימנה:

ולא תמצא. אינה מצוייה לימכר בשווקים. מלה כפולה היא:
בארץ החיים. אילו שווקים שהם חיים לעולם כאשר פירשו רבותינו במסכת יומא
'אתהלך לפני ה' בארצות החיים'[28] אילו שווקים:[29]

(יד) **תהום אמר.** אם ישאל השואל אל התהום איזה מקום החכמה והבינה יענה ויאמר
לא בי היא ולא ידעתי את מקומה. בתהום וים שהם שני דברים חשובים וגדולים
אשר בעולם אוחז לשונו בהם והוא הדין לכל השאר. לֹא נראֹה.[30]

(טו) **סגור.** זהב טוב ומשובח משאר מיני זהב ועל שם שהעשירים אוצרים
וסוגרים אותו במסגר באוצרות מפני שהוא מעולה נקרא סגור:

(טז–יז) **לא תסלה.** לא יהיה דמים וערך כמו 'המסולאים בפז':[31]
בכתם. קבוצת זהב ביחד. מַשִׁיץ בלעז:[32]
אופיר. הבא מאופיר.
לא יערכנה. מלה כפולה על 'לא תסלה':

(יח) **ומשך חכמה.** מקום שהיא נמשכת בו כנהר יקר הוא יותר מפנינים:

(יט) **בכתם טהור.** בכתם של זהב טהור:
לא תסלה. כפל לשון על 'לא יערכנה':

(כב–כג) **אבדון ומות.** אם ישאל השואל לשני דברים גדולים הללו אשר נבראו בעולם והוא
הדין אם ישאל לכל השאר יענו ויאמרו באזנינו שמענו שמע שלה וזה הוא השמע
'אלהים הבין דרכה'.
אבדון ומות. גיהנם ומלאך המות:

(כד–כה) **כי הוא לקצות.** שהרי הוא הביט וראה לקצות הארץ תחת כל השמים כדי לעשות
משקל לרוח ומים תכן במידה הכל נעשה בחכמה:

(כו–כז) **בעשתו למטר חק וג׳** אז ראה ויספרה.
חק. קוֹשְׁטוּמָא בלעז[33] כעניין שנ׳ 'אף ברי יטריח עב וג׳'.[34] כמה מטר להוריד על
כל מדינה ומדינה:

---

28 תהל' קטז, ט.
29 יומא עא, ע"א, בשם רב יהודה.
30 מלים אלה, המסומנות בכתב־היד, נוספו בידי הסופר, שהביע בכך את אי־שביעות רצונו מן ההסבר. בשוליים
נוספה הערה בכתב־ידו של הסופר, לאורך העמוד, וזה לשונה: 'לכך אחז המקרא ים ותהום לפי שאין אדם יכל
לחפש שם שלא יאמר אם איני יכל למצוא...'. שתי המלים האחרונות אינן ניתנות לקריאה. נראה שאלו דברי
הסופר, המסביר את 'ים ותהום' לא כ'שני דברים גדולים וחשובים' אלא 'לפי שאין אדם יכל לחפש שם'.
31 איכה ד, ד. נה"מ: המסֻלאים.
32 massiç = גושי זהב.
33 costuma = מנה קצובה.   34 איוב לז, יא.

לחזיז קולות.[35] לענן הבא מכמה קולות[36] טוֹנְיֵירֶשׁ בלעז:[37] הכינה וגם חקרה. אין לך בו רק פשוטו. לפי פשוטו של מקרא הכין אותה וחקר בה:

(כח)   **וסור מרע.** ולסור מרע זו היא בינה:

35   נה"מ: קלות.

36   המלים: 'לענן הבא מכמה קולות' כתובות מעל השורה, ונראה שהמעתיק השלים אותן לאחר שתחילה השמיט אותן מן הכתוב.

37   tonèyres = רעמים.

בית־הכנסת בארץ־ישראל: ראשיתו ואופיו בראייה מחודשת

ישראל לוין
האוניברסיטה העברית בירושלים

עם ישראל עבר שינויים רבים בתקופת בית שני, לא רק במאות האחרונות של התקופה, דהיינו ימי החשמונאים והורדוס שעליהם יש לנו ידיעות רבות, אלא גם במאות הראשונות שלה. 'המאה האילמת' של התקופה הפרסית המאוחרת (מסוף המאה החמישית עד סוף המאה הרביעית לפני הספירה), שלגביה אין לנו כמעט כל מקור, וכן מאה וחמישים השנים אשר קדמו לה ואשר באו אחריה, חזו גם הן תמורות חשובות,[1] כפי שניתן לראות בהשוואת החברה הישראלית בסוף תקופת בית ראשון עם זו בתקופת החשמונאים והורדוס. עם עלייית המסך בתולדות עמנו במאה השנייה לפני הספירה ואילך, בתקופה שבה מתרבים המקורות העומדים לרשותנו, אנו עדים לדפוסי הנהגה, מוסדות פוליטיים, סוגות ספרותיות ורעיונות דתיים שלא הכרנו קודם לכן. במאות אלו התגבשו מוסדות כגון הגרוסיה, תפיסות דתיות כגון תחיית המתים והתורה שבעל־פה (לפחות לגבי הפרושים), נהגים דתיים (למשל, הגיור), מנהגי קבורה, צורות ארגון כתתיות, ספרות אפוקליפטית, ועוד. בין ההתפתחויות החשובות בתקופה זו היתה גם התגבשותו של בית־הכנסת העתיק.

הניסיון לעקוב אחר התחלתו והתפתחותו הראשונית של בית־הכנסת מעמיד בפני המחקר המודרני אתגר קשה ביותר. כדרכם של מוסדות, תנועות או רעיונות מהפכניים, היו הכוחות שהולידו מוסדות חדשים אלה, כמו גם השלבים הראשונים בהתפתחותם, חבויים מתחת לפני השטח. שם הם צמחו והתגבשו, עד שהופיעו לפתע במקורותינו ההיסטוריים בצורה מפותחת יחסית. כך אמנם היה המצב לגבי בית־הכנסת העתיק. על־אף רצוננו להבין כיצד התגבש מוסד זה מראשיתו, אילו גורמים היו מרכזיים בהתפתחותו, מי היה אחראי עליו והיכן בדיוק כל זה אירע, אין המקורות שעומדים לרשותנו מתייחסים לשאלות אלו. ניתן לייחס התעלמות זו לעובדה הפשוטה שהמקורות אינם באים לתעד תהליכים היסטוריים, כפי שהיינו רוצים, או אולי ששלבים מוקדמים אלה בהתפתחותו של מוסד זה לא היו חשובים דיים כדי שיוזכרו במקורות.

נרחיב את הדיבור מעט על אפשרות אחרונה זו: לרוב אין רגע מסוים – בין שהוא שינוי דרמטי או חידוש מהפכני – המציין את השלבים הראשונים של תופעה חדשה. ייתכן מאוד שבית־הכנסת

---

1 ראה, למשל, את הערותיו של: P. Ackroyd, 'The Jewish Community in Palestine in the Persian Period', *The Cambridge History of Judaism*, eds. W.D. Davies & L. Finkelstein, Cambridge 1984, I, pp. 130-161, esp. pp. 135-136; L. Grabbe, *Judaism from Cyrus to Hadrian*, 2 vols., Minneapolis 1992, I, pp. 119-145

לא היה תוצאה של משבר מסוים או החלטה ספציפית של בן־אדם אחד או קהילה כלשהי שביקש
ליזום דבר חדש ונועז. ייתכן שמדובר בתהליך הדרגתי, שהתפתח במשך עשרות אם לא מאות שנים,
ובקצב שונה המשקף תנאים שונים בכל מקום ומקום. אולם רק בשלב מאוחר יותר, כשהגיע בית־
הכנסת לצורה מגובשת ומפותחת, רק אז נוכל לומר שאכן נוצר מוסד חדש וייחודי.

בבואם לדון בסוגיה זו, ניסו חוקרים להצביע על ההקשר ההיסטורי או על הנסיבות שהביאו
להופעתו של בית־הכנסת. לאור מצב מקורותינו, או ליתר דיוק, לאור היעדרה של כל עדות מוצקה,
הופכים מאמצים אלה לתרגילי ניחוש בלבד. כתוצאה מכך, קיימת שורה ארוכה של תיאוריות
בנושא, המשתרעות על פני קרוב ל־700 שנה![2] ישנם חוקרים המתארכים את ראשיתו של בית־
הכנסת לתקופת בית־המקדש הראשון, המאה השמינית או השביעית לפני הספירה, בהסתמכם על
פסוקים מן המקרא (מל"א ח, כז ואילך; מל"ב ד, כג) או על מאורע דרמטי כגון הרפורמות של יאשיה
(מל"ב כג). אולם עד הדור האחרון לפחות, מקובל למקם את ראשיתו של בית־הכנסת במאה
השישית, כתגובה לחורבן בית־המקדש, או, לחלופין, במאה החמישית, כחלק של הרפורמות של
עזרא ונחמיה ביהודה, וליתר דיוק בטקס קריאת התורה, שהגיע לשיאו בברית האמנה בין העם
לאלוהיו (נחמ' ח־י). ועוד מניחים שמוסד בית־הכנסת נוצר במאה הרביעית (גיבוש מסגרות
קהילתיות בארץ בתקופת שיבת ציון), במאה השלישית (עת הופעת האזכור הראשון על בית־כנסת
בכתובות ממצרים), ואפילו במאה השנייה או הראשונה (כתוצאה מהתפתחויות בארץ בתקופה
ההלניסטית־חשמונאית). קשת רחבה זו של דעות מתייחסת לא רק להבדלים בקביעה כרונולוגית
אלא גם להקשרים גיאוגרפיים שונים. ישנם חוקרים הממקמים את הופעתו הראשונה של בית־
הכנסת בהקשר בבלי, אחרים – בהקשר מצרי, ואילו אחרים – בארץ יהודה.[3]

לתיאוריות הנ"ל, כמעט ללא יוצאת מן הכלל, תכונה משותפת אחת. כולן מניחות שהמרכיב

2 לסקירות על התיאוריות השונות לגבי ראשיתו של בית־הכנסת: J. Weingreen, 'The Origin of the
Synagogue', *Hermathena* 98 (1964), pp. 68-84; H.H. Rowley, *Worship in Ancient Israel: Its Form
and Meaning*, Philadelphia 1967, pp. 213-245; K. Hruby, *Die Synagoge: Geschichtliche
Entwicklung einer Institution* (Schriften zur Judentumskunde 3), Zürich 1971, pp. 19-30; J.
Gutmann, 'The Origin of the Synagogue: The Current State of Research', *Archäologischen
Anzeiger* (1972), pp. 36-40; idem, 'Synagogue Origins: Theories and Facts', *Ancient
Synagogues: The State of Research*, ed. J. Gutmann, Chico 1981, pp. 1-6 ;ראה את מאמרי: בית־
הכנסת בתקופת בית שני – אופיו והתפתחותו', א' אופנהיימר ואחרים (עורכים), בתי־כנסת עתיקים – קובץ
מחקרים, ירושלים 1987, עמ' 12–14.

3 להצעות האחרונות שאינן כלולות בסקירות הנ"ל, ראה: M. Hengel, *Judaism and Hellenism*, 2 vols.,
Philadelphia 1974, I, pp. 9-82; J.G. Griffiths, 'Egypt and the Rise of the Synagogue', *JTS* 38
(1987), pp. 1-15; L. Grabbe, 'Synagogues in Pre-70 Palestine: A Re-assessment', *JTS* 39 (1988),
pp. 401-410; M. Weinfeld, *Deuteronomy and the Deuteronomic School*, Oxford 1972, p. 44 ראה;
גם: L. Landman, 'The Origin of the Synagogue', *Essays on the Occasion of the Seventieth
Anniversary of the Dropsie University – 1909-79*, eds. A. Katsh & L. Nemoy, Philadelphia 1979,
pp. 317-325; H. Eberhard von Waldow, 'The Origin of the Synagogue Reconsidered', *From
Faith to Faith* (Pittsburgh Theological Monograph Series 31), Pittsburgh 1979, pp. 269-284;
J.D. Levenson, 'From Temple to Synagogue: 1 Kings 8', *Traditions in Transformation*, eds. B.
Halpern & J.D. Levenson, Winona Lake 1981, pp. 143-166; S. Talmon, *The World of Qumran
from Within*, Jerusalem 1989, pp. 204-209

הדתי של בית־הכנסת העתיק היה העיקר, ושהנסיבות הדתיות הן אלו שנתנו תאוצה לראשיתו
של מוסד זה. ברוב התיאוריות הללו, ההנחה היסודית היא שפעילות ליטורגית כגון האזנה לדברי
ה' מפי נביא, אמירת תפילות או קריאה בתורה וכדומה, מילאה תפקיד מרכזי בעיצוב בית־הכנסת
הקדום.

בהתחשב באופי השרירותי של ההצעות האלו, ברצוננו להציע גישה נוספת. במקום לחפש רמזים
ושברי עדויות לגבי המקום והזמן שבהם נוצר בית־הכנסת, הצעתנו היא להתחיל מנקודה אחרת,
מהזמן שאכן קיימת עדות מוצקה על בית־הכנסת ותפקודו. אם יעלה בידינו לקבוע את תפקידיו
ומעמדו של בית־הכנסת במאה הראשונה לספירה, בתקופה שעבורה קיים תיעוד רב יחסית, אזי
נוכל לשאול היכן התנהלו אותן הפעולות קודם לכן. אם נתחיל במה שידוע לנו על בית־הכנסת
כשכבר עמד בצורתו המפותחת, אולי אז נוכל לעמוד על ראשיתו של אותו המוסד (ושל ה'פרוסויכה'
קודם לכן במצרים). על כן במקום לחפש תהפוכות דתיות שקידמו את פני הופעתו של בית־הכנסת
בעבר הרחוק, ברצוננו להציע היבט סוציולוגי ומוסדי שעשוי להסביר את תופעת בית־הכנסת.

העדויות הקדומות ביותר המתארות את אופי פעילותו של בית־הכנסת בארץ מתוארכות לתקופה
ההלניסטית והרומית הקדומה, ובמיוחד למאה הראשונה לספירה. ידיעות אלו הן מוגבלות למדי
במספרן אך בכל זאת משמעותיות לגבי התקופה. יוסף בן־מתתיהו ופילון מזכירים במפורש את
בית־הכנסת בהזדמנויות אחדות; ראויות לציון התעודות הרשמיות הכלולות בספרים י"ד וט"ז של
'קדמוניות היהודים' של יוסף, המזכירות פעילות קהילתית בתפוצות, לרבות הבניין שבו התקיימו.
עדות חז"ל לתקופת בית שני דלה ולעתים נושאת אופי אגדי, ואילו בברית החדשה – במיוחד
בלוקס ובמעשי השליחים – ישנן מספר מסורות חשובות לגבי בתי כנסת בארץ ובתפוצות.[4]

העדות הארכיאולוגית בנושא חלקית ביותר. המבנים בגמלא, במצדה ובהרודיון מזוהים בדרך
כלל כבתי־כנסת, אף־על־פי שהשניים האחרונים בעצם מתוארכים לסוף תקופה זו ממש, זאת
אומרת, לשנות המרד עצמו (66–74 לספירה).[5] המבנה בגמלא הוקם כמה דורות קודם לכן, כנראה
בראשית המאה הראשונה לספירה. אין ספק שכתובת תיאודוטוס מירושלים מן המאה הראשונה

4 ראה את מאמרי (לעיל, הערה 2), עמ' 11–29. לבחינה יסודית במקורות אלה, ראה את ספרי: בית־הכנסת העתיק
(בהכנה). ה' קי טען לאחרונה שבית־הכנסת לא התקיים כמוסד ציבורי עד לאחר שנת 70 H. Kee, 'The)
Transformation of the Synagogue after 70 C.E.: Its Import for Early Christianity', NTS 36
[1990], pp. 1-24; idem, 'Early Christianity in the Galilee: Reassessing the Evidence from the
Gospels', The Galilee in Late Antiquity, ed. L.I. Levine, New York 1992, p. 10 אין זה המקום).
להתפלמס עם טיעוניו; עבודה זו כבר נעשתה בצורה יסודית ומשכנעת בידי R.E. Oster, Jr., 'Supposed
Anachronism in Luke-Acts' Use of ΣΥΝΑΓΩΓΗ', NTS 39 (1993), pp. 178-208
5 לסיכומי הממצאים מבתי־כנסת אלה, ראה: האנציקלופדיה החדשה לחפירות אריכאולוגיות בארץ־ישראל, עורך
א' שטרן, ד כרכים, ירושלים 1992 (להלן: אנציקלופדיה חדשה לחפירות), ע"ע; F. Hüttenmeister & G.
Reeg, Die antiken Synagogen in Israel, 2 vols., Wiesbaden 1977, I, pp. 173-174, 314-315; M.
Chiat, Handbook of Synagogue Architecture, Chico 1982, pp. 204-207, 248-251, 282-284
למחקרים ספציפיים, ראה: G. Foerster, 'The Synagogues at Masada and Herodium', Ancient
Synagogues Revealed, ed. L.I. Levine, Jerusalem 1981, pp. 24-29; E. Netzer, Masada, Jerusalem
1991, III, pp. 402-413; S. Gutman, 'The Synagogue at Gamla', Ancient Synagogues Revealed,
pp. 30-34; Z. Ma'oz, 'The Synagogue of Gamla and the Typology of Second-Temple
Synagogues', Ancient Synagogues Revealed, pp. 35-41 ;הנ"ל, 'בית־הכנסת בתקופת הבית השני – קווים

לספירה היא מקור המידע החשוב ביותר מארץ־ישראל הרומית העומד לרשותנו בנושא,[6] בעוד
בתפוצות קיימים שרידי בניין בית־כנסת באי דֶלוס (המאה השנייה או הראשונה לפני הספירה) וכן
שלב קדום של בית־כנסת באוסטיה שבאיטליה.[7] אולם העדות מהתפוצות בעלת הערך הרב ביותר
לענייננו הוא החומר האפיגראפי (וממצרים, גם חומר פפירולוגי), הכולל כתריסר כתובות ממצרים
המזכירות proseuche ו־synagoge,[8] שלוש כתובות מקירני,[9] כתובות אחדות מהקטקומבות ברומא
וממלכת בוספורוס[10] ולפחות כתובת משמעותית אחת מאסיה הקטנה של המאה הראשונה.[11] עד
סוף תקופת הבית השני היה בית־הכנסת ללא ספק המוסד המקומי הראשי של קהילות ישראל ברחבי
העולם – בין בארץ ובין בתפוצות, בין במזרח ובין במערב, בין בעיר ובין בכפר.[12]

מידה גדולה של שונות אפיינה בתי־כנסת אלה – תכניתם, מבניהם הארכיטקטוניים ומיקומם.
השונות ניכרת לא רק בהשוואת המבנים בארץ ובתפוצות, אלא גם אלה הנמצאים בארץ־ישראל

לדמותו הארכיטקטונית והחברתית', ארץ־ישראל כג (תשנ"ג), עמ' 331–344; ראה גם: M. Chiat, 'First Century Synagogue Architecture: Methodological Problems', *Ancient Synagogues: The State of Research*, pp. 49-60. ישנם חילוקי דעות בשאלה אם שלושת המבנים הללו היו בתי־כנסת. המבנה בהרודיון מזוהה כבית־כנסת רק בגלל קווים דומים לאלה שבמצדה – אותו פרק הזמן, אותו סוג של תושבים, אותם השינויים שנעשו במבנה ההרודיאני הקודם. המבנה במצדה הוא קרוב לוודאי בית־כנסת, בגלל שרידי טקסטים מן המקרא וכן בגלל האוסטרקונים (המתייחסים ככל הנראה לתרומות וכד') שנמצאו בו (ראה נצר לעיל). זיהוי המבנה במצדה נסמך על היותו הבניין הציבורי היחיד במקום שבו נמצאו מספר גדול של תושבים בעלי אידיאולוגיה לאומית־דתית קיצונית. אין לכלול כאן שני אתרים נוספים, שפעם זוהו כבתי־כנסת. בראשית המאה, זיהה הארכיאולוג אורי בניין שני בכורזין (מלבד הבניין הרומי המאוחר ששרידיו עומדים היום) כבית־כנסת מלפני שנת 70; אולם סקרים מאוחרים יותר באתר לא איתרו את הבניין האמור. ראה: G. Foerster, 'The Synagogues at Masada and Herodion', *Jounal of Jewish Art* 3-4 (1977), pp. 8-9. הפרנציסקאנים שחפרו במגדל, מצפון לטבריה, טענו שגילו בית־כנסת מן המאה הראשונה P.V.C. Corbo, 'Scavi Archaeologici a Magdala', *Liber Annuus* 24 [1974], pp. 19-28; אולם נצר הוכיח שהמבנה היה למעשה 'בית המעיין' או נימפיאום (א' נצר, 'האם שימש בית המעיין במגדלא כבית־כנסת?', בתי־כנסת עתיקים – קובץ מחקרים, עמ' 165–172.

6 ל' רוט־גרסון, הכתובות היווניות מבתי־הכנסת בארץ־ישראל, ירושלים 1987, עמ' 67–68; B. Lifshitz, *Donateurs et fondateurs dans les synagogues juives*, Paris 1967, pp. 70-71

7 P. Bruneau, 'Les Israélites de Délos et la juiverie Délienne', *Bulletin de Correspondence Hellénistique* 100 (1982), pp. 465-504; A.T. Kraabel, 'The Diaspora Synagogue: Archeological and Epigraphic Evidence since Sukenik', *ANRW* II, 19.1 (1979), pp. 491-494; L.M. White, *Building God's House in the Roman World*, Baltimore 1990, pp. 69-71

8 V. Tcherikover, A. Fuks & M. Stern, *Corpus Papyrorum Judaicarum*, 3 vols., Cambridge 1957-1964, III, pp. 139-144; E. Schürer, *The History of the Jewish People in the Age of Jesus Christ*, revised ed., 3 vols., Edinburgh 1973-1987, II, pp. 425-426, note 5; W. Horbury & D. Noy, *Jewish Inscriptions of Graeco-Roman Egypt*, Cambridge 1992, p. 276 passim על בתי־כנסת במצרים, ראה: P.E. Dion, 'Synagogues et temples dans l'Egypt hellénistique', *Science et Esprit* 29 (1977), pp. 45-75; גריפיתwatt (לעיל, הערה 3), עמ' 1–15.

9 G. Lüderitz, *Corpus jüdischer Zeugnisse aus der Cyrenaika*, Wiesbaden 1983, pp. 147-159

10 H. Leon, *The Jews of Ancient Rome*, Philadelphia 1960, pp. 135-166; ב' ליפשיץ, 'תולדות היהודים בממלכת הבוספורוס', מ' שטרן (עורך), הפזורה היהודית בעולם ההלניסטי־רומי, היסטוריה של עם ישראל, ירושלים תשמ"ג, עמ' 125–133.

11 P. Trebilco, *Jewish Communities in Asia Minor*, Cambridge 1991, pp. 58-60

12 שירר (לעיל, הערה 8), ב, עמ' 423–447.

הרומית עצמה. בתי־הכנסת נתכנו בשמות רבים במאה הראשונה: לרוב נקרא המקום συναγωγή
(מקום התכנסות) או ή προσευχή (מקום תפילה);[13] אולם הם נקראו גם בשמות הבאים: τὸ ἱερόν
(מקדש),[14] εὐχεῖον (מקום תפילה), σαββατεῖ[15] (מקום מיפגש בשבת), διδασκαλεῖον[16] (מקום
הוראה), templum[17] ואמפיתיאטרון.[18] סביר להניח שריבוי השמות מצביע על מגוון תפיסות לגבי
מהותו ותפקודו של מוסד זה; ייתכן שהוא שימש מטרות שונות במקצת ממקום למקום. ראוי לציין,
שכל השמות הללו נזכרים לגבי המוסד בתפוצות, כאשר המונח 'פרוסויכה' מופיע בתדירות הגבוהה
ביותר; לגבי ארץ־ישראל, מלבד יוצא מן הכלל אחד, שם הוא תמיד מופיע בשם synagoge.[20]

שני הכינויים השכיחים ביותר – 'פרוסויכה' ו'סינגוגה' – משקפים אולי שני דגשים שונים. ככל
הנראה הודגש יותר בתפוצות הממד הדתי, ואולי אפילו הודגשה מידה של קדושה, עקב מקומו
המרוחק של בית־הכנסת מן המקדש בירושלים ועקב הדגמים הדתיים הפגאניים שמסביבו. ייתכן
שהדגש על הממד הדתי בא כתוצאה מהצורך של יהודי התפוצות להגדיר את עצמם במונחים של
קהילה ודת לעומת סביבתם הפגאנית.[21] אולם נראה שהמצב בארץ־ישראל היה שונה, לא רק בגלל
השימוש הכמעט בלעדי במונח 'סינגוגה' אלא גם בגלל היות מונח זה נטול כל משמעות דתית.
ה'סינגוגה' היה, פשוטו כמשמעו, מקום התכנסות, מוסד קהילתי שבו התנהלה קשת רחבה של
פעילויות.

אם אמנם היתה שונות ניכרת בין בתי־הכנסת של המאה הראשונה, האם בכל זאת היו ביניהם
קווים משותפים? מה היו האפיונים והפעילויות הבסיסיים שאיחדו אותם? התשובה היא, בראש
ובראשונה, שבית־הכנסת סיפק את מלוא צרכיה של הקהילה. מקורות בני המאה הראשונה מצביעים
על העובדה שבתי־הכנסת בארץ שימש מסגרת לכל פעילות קהילתית שהיא – אסיפות פוליטיות,
מפגשים חברתיים, בתי־דין, בתי־ספר, אכסניות, קופות צדקה, סעודות קהילתיות, שחרור עבדים,
כמו גם פעילות דתית־ליטורגית.[22]

הגדרת בית־הכנסת בארץ־ישראל כמוסד קהילתי בעיקרו מבוססת על כמה עובדות: בראש
ובראשונה, כאמור, העובדה שפעולות קהילתיות רבות במקום מתועדות יפה. אפילו כשהמבנה

13 TDNT VIII, pp. 807-808

14 יוסף בן־מתתיהו, מלחמה ז, ג, ג, 45; ד, ז, ב, 408; ז, ה, ה, 144; ספר המכבים ג ב, כח.

15 צ'ריקובר (לעיל, הערה 8), ב, עמ' 223.

16 יוסף בן־מתתיהו, קדמוניות טז, ו, ב, 164.

17 פילון, חוקים מיוחדים ב, 62.

18 טקיטוס, דברי הימים ה, ה, ד; M. Stern, *Greek and Latin Authors on Jews and Judaism*, 3 vols., Jerusalem 1974-1984, II, p. 43

19 לדריך (לעיל, הערה 9), עמ' 151–155, מס' 71.

20 טברייה: יוסף בן־מתתיהו, חיי יוסף 54, 277 ו־280; 56, 293.

21 לוין (לעיל, הערה 2), עמ' 20–23.

22 ראה: לוין (לעיל, הערה 2), עמ' 18–19; TDNT VIII, pp. 821-828; השווה גם: ז' ספראי, 'התפקידים הקהילתיים של בית־הכנסת בארץ־ישראל בתקופת המשנה והתלמוד', ז' ספראי (עורך), בית־הכנסת בתקופת המשנה והתלמוד, ירושלים תשמ"ו, עמ' 105–123. על האופי הקהילתי ה'חילוני' של בית־הכנסת באסיה הקטנה לעומת 'ספרי הקודש' ו'כספי ההקדש' המופקדים בתוכו, ראה: יוסף בן־מתתיהו, קדמוניות טז, ו, ב, 164. על שחרור עבדים בבית־הכנסת, ראה: Corpus Inscriptionum Regni Bosporani, Leningrad 1965, nos. 70, 1127, 1123, 73, 71; שירר (לעיל, הערה 8), א, עמ' 105–106.

עצמו אינו נזכר במפורש במקורות, ניתן להניח שאמנם התקיימו פעולות כגון אלו בבית־הכנסת. לא נזכר במקורות כל בניין או מוסד אחר שהיה יכול למלא תפקיד דומה. כאמור, המילה: 'סינגוגה', על־פי מובנה הפשוט, מצביעה על כך שהבניין שימש בעיקר מקום התכנסות ומילא מגוון רחב של צרכים. המקום בעצם היווה מוקד לכל הקהילה היהודית; ואכן, יהודים ולא יהודים כאחד הכירו בו ככזה. כשפגאנים ביקשו לתקוף יהודים או מוסד יהודי, הם כילו את זעמם על בניין בית־הכנסת. כך היה המצב בדור, באלכסנדריה ובקיסריה במהלך המאה הראשונה לספירה.[23]

גם השרידים הארכיאולוגיים מצביעים על כך שבית־הכנסת בארץ היה במהותו מרכז קהילתי. הבניין הכיל ספסלים לאורך ארבעת קירותיו, כשמוקדו היה במרכז האולם, בדומה לכמה וכמה בניינים קהילתיים הלניסטיים ורומיים.[24] כל התופעות שבאו לאפיין את ממדו הדתי של בית־הכנסת בתקופת התלמוד היו חסרות בבניין זה: לא היתה לו אוריינטציה ברורה כלפי ירושלים, לא היה בו מקום קבוע לארון הקודש, לא היו בו עיטורים אמנותיים בעלי משמעות דתית ולא היתה בו כל כתובת הקדשה המציינת את מעמדו המיוחד של המבנה.

אולם על־אף האמור לעיל, אין לדחות את העובדה שבית־הכנסת בארץ בתקופת בית שני גם מילא תפקיד חשוב בחיי הרוח של הקהילה. הדבר מודגש כמעט בכל מקור שברשותנו. בעוד בתי־ הכנסת בתפוצות גם כללו תפילות במסגרת פעילותם, עמדו במרכז הפולחן בבתי־הכנסת בארץ ובתפוצות קריאת התורה ופעילויותיה הנלוות – קריאה בנביאים (ההפטרה), קריאת התרגום לתורה ומתן דרשות. ואף שכל המקורות מדגישים את הממד הדתי של בית־הכנסת, דגש זה משקף יותר את סדר היום של אותו מקור ולא דווקא את המציאות ההיסטורית. פילון ויוסף בן־מתתיהו, הברית החדשה וספרות חז"ל – כולם ביקשו לתאר את בית־הכנסת כמוסד יהודי ייחודי; ברוב המקרים פירושו של דגש זה הוא התמקדות בממד הדתי־ליטורגי של המוסד.

וכן במסגרת הממד הדתי, נוטים מקורותינו להדגיש את הפעילות הייחודית ביותר למסגרת זו, דהיינו הקריאה הקבועה של התורה בציבור. ככל הנראה זאת הסיבה לכך שנזכרים לעתים תכופות קריאת התורה ולימודה הן לגבי בית־הכנסת בתפוצות והן לגבי בית־הכנסת בארץ.[25] למחברי מקורותינו מן המאה הראשונה, המאפיין הייחודי של העבודה בבית־הכנסת לא היה אמירת תפילות או תהלים (פעולות אלו היו ידועות במסגרות דתיות פגאניות גם כן) אלא הקריאה של כתבי־הקודש ברבים ופירשונתם. לכן נטו מחברים אלה להתמקד בהיבט הדתי הייחודי של בית־הכנסת, מאפיין שתיארו החוקר מומיליאנו כ'שלב חדש בחיי הדת של העולם הקלאסי'.[26]

23 דור: יוסף בן־מתתיהו, קדמוניות יט, ו, ג, 299–310; קיסריה: הנ"ל, מלחמה ב, יד, ד–ה, 285–292; אלכסנדריה: פילון, גאיוס כ, 132 ואילך.

24 Y. Yadin, 'The Excavation of Masada', IEJ 15 (1965), pp. 78-79; N. Avigad, 'The "Galilean" Synagogue and Its Predecessors', Ancient Synagogues Revealed, pp. 42-44. הוצעו הצעות המקשרות בניינים אלה לדורא אירופוס ולאלכסנדריה (דרך ירושלים) בידי ג' פרסטר, 'מצדה והרודיון' (לעיל, הערה 5), עמ' 28; וצ' מעוז, 'Synagogue in the Second Temple Period' (לעיל, הערה 5), עמ' 334–337; וכן: הנ"ל, 'The Synagogue in the Second Temple Period as a Reflection of Alexandrine Architecture', Bulletin of the Israeli Academic Center in Cairo 18 (1994), pp. 5-12; השווה: לוין (לעיל, הערה 2), עמ' 16–17; צ'יאט (לעיל, הערה 5), עמ' 55–56.

25 לוין (לעיל, הערה 2), עמ' 20–23.

26 A. Momigliano, On Pagans, Jews and Christians, Middleton 1987, p. 90; A.I. Baumgarten, 'The Torah as a Public Document in Judaism', Studies in Religion 14 (1985), pp. 17-24

לפיכך, בקבענו כי בית־הכנסת שימש במאה הראשונה לספירה מרכז קהילתי לכל מיני פעילויות, לרבות פעילות דתית, ניתן עתה לחפש את המסגרת או את המוסד ששימש אותן המטרות (או דומיהן) במאות קודם לכן. כאשר הבעיה מוצגת בצורה זו, הפתרון כמעט מתבקש מאליו. ההקשר לרוב הפעילויות, אם לא לכולן, בתקופות שקדמו להופעת בית־הכנסת היה שער העיר – המקום המרכזי בחיי הקהילה בתקופת בית ראשון ובתקופה הפרסית.[27]

תפקידו של שער העיר כמוקד לפעילות קהילתית מתועד יפה בספרות המקראית והחוץ־מקראית.[28] בו נמצא השוק (מל"ב ז, א)[29] ובו ערך השליט משפט ונשאו הנביאים את נאומיהם (מל"א כב, י; יר' לח, ז).[30] שער העיר היה מקום התכנסות פופולרי לאסיפות־עם. למשל, חזקיהו המלך נתן 'שרי מלחמות על העם ויקבצם אליו אל רחוב שער העיר וידבר על לבבם...' (דה"ב לב, ו).[31] באי שער העיר עלו מקרב החברה הרחבה (רות ג, יא) וגם מבין הזקנים והמנהיגים. המשא ומתן בין אברהם לעפרון החתי התנהל בשער העיר (בר' כג, י, יח), וכמה תעודות משפטיות מנוזי מסתיימות בנוסחה: 'הלוח נכתב אחרי ההצהרה בשער'.[32] ההכרזה על יישוב סכסוך או על עריכת הסכם דווקא

---

27 הצעה זו העלה לראשונה מ' סילבר בעבודת הדוקטורט שלו, אשר סיכום ממנה יצא לאור בחוברת: *The Origin* *of the Synagogue*, New Orleans 1915. אולם סילבר תיארך את המעבר בין שער העיר לבית־הכנסת לתקופת שלמה והגיע למסקנה שבית־הכנסת בראשיתו היה חילוני באופיו, ורק לאחר דורות קיבל אופי דתי. לאחר מכן, אומץ רעיון שער העיר בידי: S. Hoenig, 'The Ancient City-Square: The Forerunner of the Synagogue', *ANRW*, II, 19.1, pp. 448-476. אולם הגיג בלבל את רחבת העיר של התקופה היוונית־רומית עם שער העיר במזרח הקרוב בעת העתיקה (ראה על כך: J.B. Ward-Perkins, *Cities of Ancient Greece and Italy: Planning in Classical Antiquity*, New York 1974, p. 12), והוא עשה בספרות חז"ל המאוחרת שימוש חופשי מדי כדי להשלים את המעט הידוע על הנושא בתקופה שלפני שנת 70. יתר על כן, טעינתו נחלשת בגלל קריאתו השגויה 'רחוב העיר' במקום 'חבר העיר', הרווח בספרות חז"ל. השווה גם: L. Löw, *Gesammelte Schriften*, 5 vols., Szegedin 1889-1900, IV, p. 5ff. על שער העיר בתקופת המקרא, ראה אנציקלופדיה מקראית ח, טור 231; R. de Vaux, *Ancient Israel*, London 1961, pp. 152-153; L. Köhler, *Der hebräischen Mensch*, Tübingen 1953, pp. 143-171

28 CAD, A/1, Chicago 1964, pp. 82-88, s.v. abullu; *ibid.*, B, Chicago 1965, pp. 19-20, s.v. babu; מקקאון; F.S. Frick, *The City in Ancient Israel*, Missoula 1977, pp. 83-84, 114-127 (C.C. McCown, IDB, p. 634). מסכנה את התופעה כהלן: 'לעברי הקדום, שער העיר היה יותר מאשר דרך כניסה ויציאה, יותר מאשר חלק חשוב במנגנון ההגנה של העיר. הוא היה גם ה"מרכז" (על אף שהיה בצד אחד) של ענייני החברה, הכלכלה והמשפט של העיר'. ראה גם: מ' כוגן, 'שער', אנציקלופדיה מקראית ח, טורים 236–232. חומר רב־ערך נושא נאסף בידי: G. Evans, '"Gates" and "Streets": Urban Institutions in Old Testament Times', *The Journal of Religious History* 2 (1962), pp. 1-12. 'סקירה של הטקסטים שבהם הם מופיעים מצביע בבירור על כך שהשער, יחד עם הרחוב שהיה מאחוריו, בין חומות העיר, היה מרכז של פעילות פוליטית ומשפטית, כמו גם של מסחר... השער היה הזירה של פעילויות רבות, שבעיר מערבית התנהלו ברחבה מרכזית' (עמ' 1).

29 I. Eph'al & J. Naveh, 'The Jar of the Gate', *BASOR*: ראה, על המשמעות הקהילתית של שער העיר, 289 (1993), pp. 59-65

30 להפניות אחרות על נזיפה בעם בשערים, ראה: יש' כט, כא; עמוס ה, י.

31 על גילוי רחבה כזאת באתר המקראי תל דן, ראה: A. Biran, 'Tel Dan: Five Years Later', *BA* 13 (1980), p. 177; הנ"ל, אנציקלופדיה חדשה לחפירות ב, עמ' 435.

32 ראה, למשל: R.H. Pfeiffer & E.A. Speiser, 'One Hundred New Selected Nuzi Texts', *AASOR* 16 (1935-36), p. 115; R. de Vaux, 'Les patriarches hébreux et les découvertes modernes', *RB* 56 (1949), p. 25 and note 1

בשער העיר השיגו את ההכרה המרבית בציבור כמו גם את אישורה של הקהילה כולה. גם פעילות נבואית התמקדה במסגרת זו, במטרה שדברי הנביא יגיעו למספר הגדול ביותר של שומעים (יש' כט, כא; עמוס ה, י).

אחד התפקידים העיקריים של שער העיר היה קשור בתחום המשפטי.[33] זקני העיר התכנסו שם כדי לערוך משפט: 'ותפשו בו אביו ואמו והוציאו אתו אל זקני עירו ואל שער מקמו' (דב' כא, יט, כב, ה; ראה גם תה' סט, יג), והנביא עמוס יעץ: 'שנאו רע ואהבו טוב והציגו בשער משפט' (ה, טו). חשיבותו של שער העיר כמקום ליישוב סכסוכים אישיים בנוכחות הקהילה משתקפת ברות ד, א–ב: 'ובעז עלה השער וישב שם, והנה הגאל עבר אשר דבר בעז ויאמר: סורה, שבה פה פלני אלמני. ויסר וישב, ויקח עשרה אנשים מזקני העיר ויאמר: שבו פה, וישבו'.[34]

ככל הנראה, זקני העיר (המכונים 'אבות העיר' בפי שפייזר) התכנסו במקום באופן קבוע לשמש דיינים, בוררים ועדים לעיסקות מסחריות.[35] הם היו בית-דין אזרחי – לעומת בית-דין של כוהנים בבית-המקדש בירושלים או במקדשים מקומיים אחרים.[36]

משמעות השער כלב לבה של העיר משתקפת בנוהג של קביעת כס הכובש במקום כאות של כניעה. כך עשו שרי המלך נבוכדנצר (יר' לט, ג) ובכך קיימו את נבואתו של הנביא (שם, א, טו–טז):

'כי הנני קרא לכל משפחות ממלכות צפונה, נאם ה'. ובאו ונתנו איש כסאו פתח שערי ירושלם ועל כל חומתיה סביב ועל כל ערי יהודה. ודברתי משפטי אותם על כל רעתם אשר עזבוני, ויקטרו לאלהים אחרים וישתחוו למעשי ידיהם'.[37]

המלך ישב בשער העיר כדי לאפשר לנתיניו לשטוח לפניו את תלונותיהם. כך, למשל, ביקש יואב מדוד שיפסיק להתאבל על מותו של אבשלום ועודדו לשבת בשער: 'ויבא כל העם לפני המלך' (שמ"ב יט, ח–ט), וכאשר אחאב מלך ישראל ויהושפט מלך יהודה נועדו בפתח שער שומרון כדי לקבוע את האסטרטגיה שלהם לגבי הקרב המתוכנן בעבר הירדן, הם קראו לנביאים לבשר להם שם על גורלם (מל"א כב, י). כמו כן, על-פי דה"ב לב, ו, קיבץ המלך חזקיהו את העם בשער העיר כדי לעודדם בפני התקפתו של סנחריב; כמאה שנים לאחר מכן אנו שומעים על המלך צדקיהו שישב גם הוא בשער העיר, שער בנימין, כדי לדבר אל העם (יר' לח, ז).

33 ראה: D.A. McKenzie, 'Judicial Procedure at the Town Gate', VT 14 (1964), pp. 100-104. לפירושי החכמים לפסוקים מן התנ"ך אודות הליכים משפטיים בשער העיר, ראה: D. HaLivni (Weiss), 'The Location of the Bet Din in the Early Tannaitic Period', PAAJR 29 (1960-1961), pp. 181-191

34 המושג 'עשרה' כמספר של מניין כלשהו מופיע בתיאור של יוסף בן-מתתיהו לגבי האסיים (מלחמה ב, 146 ובקומוראן (14 ,10 ;6, 7 ;6, 3 ;6, 1 CD 13; QS), וכמובן לאחר דורות – בספרות חז"ל (למשל, משנה, מגילה ד, ג).

35 בדומה לסיפור של אברהם ועפרון בבר' כג. ראה: E.A. Speiser, '"Coming" and "Going" at the City Gate', BASOR 144 (1956), pp. 20-23; H. Reviv, 'Early Elements and Late Terminology in the Descriptions of Non-Israelite Cities in the Bible', IEJ 27 (1977), pp. 190-191; וגם את דעתו הנוגדת של: G. Evans, '"Coming" and "Going" at the City Gate – A Discussion of Professor Speiser's Paper', BASOR 150 (1958), pp. 28-33

36 וינפלד (לעיל, הערה 3), עמ' 235. אחד משערי ירושלים נקרא על-שם יהושע, שר העיר בימי שלטונו של יאשיה (מל"ב כג, ח).

37 על עונש כוללני נגד העיר בכלל, ראה דב' יג, יז.

לבסוף, שימש שער העיר גם מקום לעריכת טקסים דתיים. בעת העתיקה התכנסו עמים בשער
העיר כדי לעבוד אלילים, וכראיה לכך נמצאו כלי פולחן ליד השערים במגידו Vא, בבאר שבע IV
ובתל דן.[38] לגבי האתר האחרון, מציין אברהם בירן, בעקבות ריצ'רד ברנט, ששער העיר שם שימש
אולי מקום לעריכת תהלוכות דתיות בעת העתיקה:

...אנו יכולים לראות בו גם מסלול לתהלוכות. ייתכן שדבר זה יהיה תלוי במידה מסוימת
בפירוש של המבנה היחידאי שנמצא ברחבה שבין השער החיצוני לשער הראשי. מבנה זה
הוא בצורת מלבן ובו שטח פתוח, שהוא המקום שבו הונח כס מלכות או מסד. שני בסיסי
עמודים מעוטרים נמצאו באתרם. בסיס שלישי נמצא במפולת, ומהבסיס הרביעי נותר רק
טביעה... שחזורנו המוצע מראה מבנה עם חופה ששימש את המלך כשהוא יושב בשער
(למשל, מל"ב כב, י) או ייתכן ששימש כבסיס לפסל של אליל.[39]

עדות מקראית מפורשת לכך נמצאת במל"ב כג, ח, המתייחסת לרפורמות של יאשיה בשנת 621
לפני הספירה:

ויבא את כל הכהנים מערי יהודה ויטמא את הבמות אשר קטרו שמה הכהנים מגבע עד באר
שבע ונתץ את במות השערים אשר פתח שער יהושע שר העיר אשר על שמאול איש בשער
העיר.

בתקופת שיבת ציון ניצלו עזרא ונחמיה את שטח שער העיר למטרה נוספת: 'ויאספו כל העם כאיש
אחד אל הרחוב אשר לפני שער המים ויאמרו לעזרא הסופר להביא את ספר תורת משה אשר צוה ה'
את ישראל' (נחמ' ח, א).

העדות הארכיאולוגית מוסיפה ומתארת את שער העיר כמקום מרכזי לפעילות קהילתית בתקופת
המקרא, דהיינו, בתקופת הברזל. לעומת השערים שעמדו בראשית תקופת הברונזה התיכונה ב'
(MBII) שכנראה מילאו תפקיד הגנתי בלבד, שונה באופן משמעותי המבנה של כעשרים מכלולי
השער שנתגלו מתקופת הברזל ב' (1000–580 לפני הספירה בערך).[40] בעוד בשערים מהאלף השני
לפני הספירה שימשו החדרים המסופחים לשער יחידות עצמאיות (שנפרדו בדרך כלל זו מזו בחומה),
חדרי השער מתקופת הברזל ב' נפתחו אל המעבר הראשי של השער. לכל שער היו שניים, ארבעה

38   ראה אנציקלופדיה חדשה לחפירות א, עמ' 139 (באר שבע); ב, עמ' 441–443 (תל דן); על מגידו, ראה: .Z
Herzog, *Das Staattor in Israel und in den Nachbarländern*, Mainz am Rhein 1986, p. 164. על נושא
זה בכלל, ראה: W. Dever, *Recent Archaeological Discoveries and Biblical Research*, Seattle 1990, p.
128ff.

39   A. Biran, 'To the God who is in Dan', *Temples and High Places Places in Biblical Times*, Jerusalem
1981, p. 143; R.D. Barnett, 'Bringing the God into the Temple', *ibid.*, pp. 10-20 .ולאחרונה :A
Biran, *Biblical Dan*, Jerusalem 1994, pp. 238-245. ייתכן מאוד שמקומו של שער העיר בתהלוכות דתיות
ובפולחן משתקף במילים 'שאו שערים... ויבא מלך הכבוד' (תה' כד, ז, ט).

40   הנושא נדון בעשרות השנים האחרונות בידי ז' הרצוג, שער העיר בארץ־ישראל ושכנותיה, תל־אביב תשל"ו;
ולאחרונה בצורה תקצירית: 'תכנון היישובים והביצורים בתקופת הברזל', ח' כצנשטיין ואחרים (עורכים),
האדריכלות בארץ־ישראל בימי קדם, ירושלים תשמ"ו, עמ' 195–231. השווה גם: א' שטרן, 'חצור, דור ומגידו
בימי אחאב והתקופה האשורית', ארץ־ישראל כ (תשמ"ט), עמ' 233–248.

או שישה חדרים כאלה,[41] והם היו גדולים למדי (אחד מהם הגיע עד תשעה מ' באורכו) והכילו
ספסלים (לעתים מטויחים) ואגני מים מאבן. יחד עם המרחבים הפתוחים הסמוכים, שהיו בדרך כלל
בתוך השער אך לפעמים מחוצה לו (ובמקרה כזה היתה בדרך כלל עוד חומה מקיפה), מילאו חדרים
אלה תפקידים רבים, כפי שציינו לעיל.[42] דוגמה מרשימה של מערך כזה נמצאת בתל דן, ובו שלושה
שערים (חיצוני, ראשי ועליון), שלפניהם עמדו, בסדר הבא, רחבה מרוצפת, חצר ותוואי לתהלוכות
מלכותיות. לכל אחד משני השערים האחרונים היו ארבעה חדרי שמירה. המערך כולו נבנה במאה
התשיעית לפני הספירה, כנראה בידי אחאב.[43]

על־סמך הנאמר לעיל, ברור למדי שרוב הפעילויות שמצאנו ביטוי בבית־הכנסת של סוף תקופת
בית שני כבר מתועדות ביחס לשער העיר בתקופת המקרא. לא ידוע מתי בדיוק הועברו פעילויות
אלה משער העיר או מהרחבה הסמוכה אל תוך בניין שְׁלֵמִים נקרא בית־הכנסת. ככל הנראה, אירע
המעבר אימתי בתקופה ההלניסטית, כאשר פעילויות רבות שנערכו קודם לכן תחת כיפת השמים
הועברו לבניינים (ראה להלן). לא בכדי, דווקא בתקופה זו השתנתה הארכיטקטורה של שער העיר;
ממרכז של פעילות עירונית הפך השער למקום פונקציונלי, ששימש לכניסה לעיר וליציאה ממנה.

העדות הארכיאולוגית מחזקת את השערתנו לגבי מעבר זה. מסורות שהתקיימו מאות בשנים
עתה החלו להשתנות, עקב מגע אינטנסיבי וממושך עם העולם ההלניסטי.[44] על אף הנתונים הדלים
העומדים לרשותנו, ברור שבתקופה ההלניסטית היה השער, כפי שנאמר, פשוט ופונקציונלי
באופיו, בלי רחבה פתוחה ובלי חדרים סמוכים אליו.[45] במקום זאת, עמדו לצידיו מגדלים עגולים
או מרובעים, הקבועים במרווחים קבועים זה מזה. השער עצמו היה לכל היותר מעבר בין המגדלים
האלה. ייתכן שהסיבה לשינויים אלה היתה ההתפתחויות במערכות ביצור יווניות בכלל, אשר היו
ככל הנראה תוצאה של התפתחויות בלוחמה הטכנולוגית בת התקופה, כגון השימוש בבליסטראות
ובמכונות מצור.[46]

41 שערים בעלי שישה חדרים נתגלו במגידו, בחצור, בגזר, בלכיש ובאשדוד. שערים בעלי ארבעה חדרים נחשפו
באשדוד, בתל דן, בבאר שבע, במגידו (בתקופה אחרת) ובדור, ואילו שערים בעלי שני חדרים נחפרו בדור
ובמגידו. באשר לשאלה, אם ישנן השלכות כרונולוגיות למספרים השונים של חדרים, ראה לעיל, הערה 40. על
     השער המסופוטמי הקדום יותר והתפתחותו באלף השלישי־הראשונה לפני הספירה, ראה: M.S.B. Damerji,
     The Development of the Architecture of Doors and Gates in Ancient Mesopotamia, Tokyo 1987, pp.
     181-198

42 אנציקלופדיה מקראית ח, טורים 237–243; 10,000-586 ;A. Mazar, Archaeology of the Land of the Bible
     B.C.E., New York 1990, pp. 467-470

43 בירן, Biblical Dan (לעיל, הערה 39), עמ' 235–253.

44 E. Stern, 'The Excavations at Tell Mevorakh and the Late Phoenician Elements in the
     Architecture of Palestine', BASOR 225 (1977), pp. 17-27; הנ"ל, 'חומות דור', ארץ־ישראל יט
     (תשמ"ז), עמ' 153–159; א' שרון, 'ביצורה של דור והמעבר מתפיסת ההגנה הישראלית־סורית לתפיסה היוונית',
     קדמוניות כד/95–96 (תשנ"א), עמ' 105–113; ראה גם: הנ"ל, 'מסורות מקומיות ותהליכי הלניזציה בדור –
     היבטים ארכיטקטוניים', הקונגרס הארכיאולוגי העשרים בישראל, ירושלים תשנ"ד, עמ' 5. ראה גם: G. & O.
     van Beek, 'Canaanite-Phoenician Architecture: The Development and Distribution of Two
     Styles', Eretz Israel 15 (1981), pp. 70*-77*

45 R. Arav, Hellenistic Palestine: Settlement Patterns and City Planning, 337-31 B.C.E. (B.A.R.
     International Series 485), Oxford 1989, p. 159

46 ראה: א' שצמן, 'אבני בליסטרה מתל דור והארטילריה של העולם היווני־רומי', קדמוניות כד/95–96 (תשנ"א),

בעוד במאה השלישית לפני הספירה היו לעיר מרישה שבשפלה רחבה ובניינים מסביבה בסמוך
לשער (שטח שיועד ככל הנראה לפעולות שונות – דתיות, מינהליות וצבאיות),[47] משקף אזור השער
באתרים אחרים את השינויים הללו. בדור, למשל, השתנו פני השער שינוי דרמטי מחומת סגרים,
שהיתה בשימוש במשך חמש מאות שנה, לשער פשוט בעל סגנון הלניסטי, שאין בו חדרים או
בניינים נפרדים. גם טכניקות בנייה הלניסטיות מופיעות בדור בתקופה זו,[48] והן מתועדות יפה גם
בשכבה ההלניסטית של שומרון–סבסטיה.[49] במאה הראשונה לפני הספירה, אימץ הורדוס המלך את
הסגנון ההלניסטי המוכר של שער בין שני מגדלים גם בסבסטיה[50] וגם בקיסריה.[51] על אף השתמרותו
הגרועה, ייתכן ששער 'גינת' בירושלים, שנתגלה בידי אביגד, משקף גם הוא דגם רווח בתקופה
ההלניסטית.[52]

דוגמה מאלפת, המצביעה על מעבר זה, נמצאת בבניין בית־הכנסת בגמלא, שהוא הקדום ביותר
מסוגו הידוע לנו בארץ, המתוארך למאה הראשונה לספירה. הבניין מוקם לא במרכז העיר ולא
במקום גבוה במיוחד, כפי שהיה נהוג במאות מאוחרות יותר, אחרי חורבן בית־המקדש, אלא בקצה
המזרחי של העיר, ליד חומת העיר ובין שני רחובות ראשיים, במקום שבו היתה אמורה להיות רחבת
שער העיר לו נצמדה העיר לתכנית־עיר מקראית.[53] על כן ייתכן שהמבנה בגמלא הינו דוגמה של
המעבר הזה משער־עיר לבניין בית־כנסת, ושהפעילות שהתנהלה בו היתה בעצם המשך של אותן
הפעילויות שהתנהלו בשער העיר בזמנו.

על־פי הצעתנו, אם כן, לא צמח בית־הכנסת כמענה למאורע דרמטי או למשבר מסוים; הוא היה
תוצאה של תהליך הדרגתי, שאופיין בהמשכיות ובשלבי השתלשלות, ולא בשינויים מהפכניים. על
כן אין טעם לנסות לנקוב בתאריך מדויק להופעתו זו. רק ניתן לומר שזה היה תהליך הדרגתי –
במקומות שונים ובזמנים שונים – שאירע בין המאה השלישית למאה הראשונה לפני הספירה.

נראה שטקס קריאת התורה, שהיה כאמור הפעילות המרכזית בעבודת ה' בבית־הכנסת בתקופת
בית שני, התקיים מראשיתו בשער העיר. לא ידוע מתי החל מנהג זה במישור המקומי. קשה להניח
שראשיתו היתה בימי עזרא; אולם אין בידינו לנקוט עמדה ברורה בנדון. אף מחבר יווני מהתקופה

עמ' 94–104; שרון, 'ביצורה של דור' (לעיל, הערה 44), עמ' 105–113; ובכלל: F.E. Winter, *Greek*
Fortifications, London 1971, pp. 222-223, 324-332

47   מ' אבי־יונה, 'מרישה', אנציקלופדיה חדשה לחפירות ג, עמ' 1015–1017. לשאלת אופי המעבר של מרישה
ההלניסטית – עם דגש חזק על מרכיביה המזרחיים, הקדם־הלניסטיים, ראה: G. Horowitz, 'Town
Planning of Hellenistic Marisa: A Reappraisal of the Excavations after Eighty Years', *PEQ*
112 (1980), pp. 93-111

48   שטרן, 'חומות דור' (לעיל, הערה 44), עמ' 153–159; שרון, 'ביצורה של דור' (לעיל, הערה 44), עמ' 105–113;
הנ"ל, 'מסורות מקומיות' (לעיל, הערה 44), עמ' 5.

49   J.W. Crowfoot, K.M. Kenyon & E.L. Sukenik, *The Buildings at Samaria*, London 1942, pp.
24-27

50   שם, עמ' 31, 39, 39–41; נ' אביגד, 'שומרון (העיר)', אנציקלופדיה חדשה לחפירות ד, עמ' 1500. על מגדל עגול
הלניסטי בעכו, דומה לזה שנמצא בשומרון, ראה: מ' דותן, 'ביצורי עכו', קדמוניות ט/34–35 (תשל"ו), עמ'
71–74.

51   A. Frova (ed.), *Scavi di Caesarea Maritima*, Rome 1966, pp. 249-271

52   נ' אביגד, העיר העליונה של ירושלים, ירושלים 1980, עמ' 50, 69; ראה גם: ערב (לעיל, הערה 45), עמ' 159.

53   גוטמן, 'The Synagogue at Gamla' (לעיל, הערה 5), עמ' 30–34; הנ"ל, 'גמלא', אנציקלופדיה חדשה
לחפירות א, עמ' 343–348.

ההלניסטית שהתייחס לחברה הישראלית ולדפוסיה אינו מזכיר מנהג כזה, וכן אין המעמד נזכר בספרים החיצוניים של המאות האחרונות לפני הספירה. ועם זאת, ערכה של טענה הנובעת מתוך שתיקת המקורות מוגבל ביותר. ככלל, אין התייחסות רבה למנהגים במוסדות שונים – אפילו לאלה במקדש בירושלים – בתקופה הפרסית וההלניסטית, ועל כן אין סיבה מיוחדת לכך שמנהג מקומי של קריאת התורה בשער העיר היה זוכה להתייחסות כלשהי.

יש מספר לא מבוטל של פסוקים בתורה שהיו עשויים להשפיע על התפתחותו של מנהג קריאת התורה (למשל, דב' ו, ז; לא, ט-יג), או שהיו יכולים להצדיק מנהג זה לאחר מעשה. פעם ראו החוקרים בראשיתו של טקס קריאת התורה פולמוס נגד השפעות זרות (השומרונים[54] או ההלניזם[55]) או, על-פי ספר דברים, פעולה ציבורית לשם תלמוד תורה ולימוד מסורת אבות.[56] כמו כן, הוצע לאחרונה שהחשיפה לעולם היווני ולדגמים יווניים מילאה תפקיד בגיבוש או, לחלופין, בחיזוק טקס קריאת התורה הקהילתי (כפי שאולי קרה בקרב יהודי התפוצות).[57]

רוב החוקרים רואים בטקס קריאת התורה תחליף לעבודה בבית המקדש שאומץ מתפוצות בבל.[58] אולם ייתכן שהתפתחותו היתה מקבילה, ולא בניגוד, לפולחן הקורבנות ובעצם היוותה ביטוי להשתתפות קהילתית מוגברת. ואמנם, ההתייחסות הקדומה ביותר שבידינו לטקס קריאת התורה המקומי היא זו של המעמדות, טקס מקומי שנערך באיזור מסוים כשכוהניו (ונציגים לא-מקצועיים אחרים) שירתו בקודש בבית המקדש בשבוע המיועד.[59] על-פי המשנה – מקור מאוחר מדי למטרותינו אך המקורה להלן מאלף לגבי הנוהג בימי בית שני – קטע מן התורה נקרא בציבור בעיירה או בכפר בכל יום של אותו שבוע: '...וישראל שבאותו המשמר מתכנסין לעריהן וקוראין במעשה בראשית' (בר' א–ב, ד).[60]

מקור זה חשוב לענייננו משלוש בחינות: (1) הוא מעיד על הנוהג לקרוא בתורה במסגרת מקומית כבר בתקופה קדומה;[61] (2) הקריאה נעשתה בפי אלה שנבצר מהם מלהשתתף בעבודת ה' בבית-המקדש בירושלים; (3) בית-הכנסת עצמו אינו נזכר, אולם הפעולה של התקהלות ב'עיירות' נרמזת. למרות שגרסאות מאוחרות של מסורת זו, וכן רוב הפרשנים, מניחים שהקריאה בתורה התנהלה

54 A. Büchler, 'The Reading of the Law and Prophets in a Triennial Cycle', *JQR* 5 (1893), p. 424. כמו כן, טוען ביכלר שההכרזות ההלניסטיות שיוסף בן-מתתיהו מזכירן משקפות את העימות היהודי-שומרוני של תקופת בית שני; ראה: הנ"ל, *Die Tobiaden und Oniaden im II.Makkabäerbuche und in der verwandten jüdisch-hellenistischen Literatur*, Vienna 1899, pp. 143-171

55 R. Leszynsky, *Die Sadduzäer*, Berlin 1912, p. 133ff.

56 J. Mann, *The Bible as Read and Preached in the Old Synagogue*, reprint, New York 1971, I, p. 4

57 J. Kugel & R. Greer, *Early Biblical Interpretation*, Philadelphia 1986, p. 56

58 M. Fishbane, *Biblical Interpretation in Ancient Israel*, Oxford 1985, p. 113

59 על החלוקה לכ"ד מעמדות של כוהנים, לוויים וישראלים, ראה: שירר (לעיל, הערה 8), ב, עמ' 245 ואילך; ש' ספראי, העלייה ברגל בתקופת בית שני, תל אביב תשכ"ה, עמ' 217–220; שפרבר (להלן, הערה 61), עמ' 89–93. על תקופת עיצובו של מוסד זה, ראה: י' ליוור, *פרקים בתולדות הכוהנים והלוויים*, ירושלים תשכ"ח, עמ' 33–52, ובמיוחד עמ' 49–52.

60 משנה, תענית ד, ב והערותיו של ח' אלבק, *שישה סדרי משנה*, ו כרכים, תל-אביב תשי"ח, ב, עמ' 495–496.

61 החלוקה למעמדות כבר היתה ידועה למחבר דברי הימים במאה הרביעית לפני הספירה (דה"א כד, ז-יח), וייתכן שהמנהגים המתוארים במשנה גובשו בתקופה קדומה זו. על מוסד זה בכלל, ראה: ד' שפרבר, 'משמרות ומעמדות', אנציקלופדיה מקראית ח, טורים 89–93; שירר (לעיל, הערה 8), ב, עמ' 245–250.

בבית־הכנסת המקומי, [62] אין כל יסוד לפירושים אלה. המשנה מזכירה 'עיירות' ותו לא, וככל הנראה
מקום התרחשותה של קריאה זו היה באזור שער העיר. אם נכון הסבר זה, אזי ברור הוא שלפחות
בחלק מתקופת בית שני המשיך שער העיר למלא תפקיד מרכזי בחיי הדת והקהילה של העיירה.
סביר להניח שבתקופה זו התקיים טקס קבוע של קריאת התורה בשבת ובחגים בשער העיר, אולם
אין הדבר ניתן להוכחה. [63]

עובדה מעניינת במקור הנ"ל היא, שטקס קריאת התורה המקומי של 'המעמד' היה בבירור פעולה
מקבילה לפולחן שהתנהל במקדש, מעין תחליף עבור אלה שלא יכלו להגיע לירושלים. בעבר, ראו
רבים בראשית הופעתו של בית־הכנסת ובהתפתחותו בתקופת בית שני תופעה מתחרה, ולא
מקבילה, לבית המקדש בירושלים. יתר על כן, רבים אפיינו את בית־הכנסת כמוסד 'פרושי', שצמח
בתגובה לעבודת המקדש בידי הצדוקים. [64] אולם לאמיתו של דבר, לא היה לפרושים כל קשר לבית־
הכנסת הקדום; אין כל מקור המעיד על קשר כלשהו. הפרושים הקדומים ('הזוגות') אינם נזכרים
ביחס לבית־הכנסת, ואין בליטורגיה הקדומה של בית־הכנסת (דהיינו, קריאת התורה והדרשה) דבר
המאפיין אותה כפרושית דווקא. בית־הכנסת פעל כמוסד ששירת את האוכלוסייה המקומית,
ולעתים אף אוכלוסיות ספציפיות שהתארגנו על־בסיס ארצות מוצא, מקצועות וכד' (מעשי שליחים
ו, ט; תוספתא, מגילה ב, יז), והפעילות הדתית שהתנהלה בו השלימה את זו במקדש.

כמו כן, אין כל יסוד להנחה שבית־הכנסת היה בדרך כלשהי מוסד המתחרה בבית־המקדש. עד
סוף תקופה זו לא הוענקה לבית־הכנסת, בארץ־ישראל לפחות, מידה כלשהי של קדושה או של
מעמד הלכתי. [65] בנוסף, ישנם כמה מקורות המצביעים על מרכזיותם של הכוהנים בבית־הכנסת. [66]

62   כך, למשל, בבלי, תענית כז ע"ב. ראה גם: אלבק, משנה, ב, עמ' 341; שירר (לעיל, הערה 8), ב, עמ' 293.
63   חוקרים רבים ראו בטקס המעמדות את המסגרת שבה התפתח בית־הכנסת. ראה, למשל: הרובי (לעיל, הערה
     עמ' 17–16; (25), J. Bowker, *The Targums and Rabbinic Literature*, Cambridge, MA 1969, pp. 9-10;
     S. Zeitlin, *The Rise and Fall of the Judaean State*, 3 vols., Philadelphia 1962-78, I, p. 179; J.
     Petuchowski, 'The Liturgy of the Synagogue', *The Lord's Prayer and Jewish Liturgy*, eds. J.J.
     Petuchowski & M. Brocke, New York 1978, p. 46. ייתכן שהמסורת הקדומה במשנה, ביכורים ג, ב,
     שם מתואר טקס הבאת הביכורים לבית־המקדש, השפיעה על מעמדו של אזור שער העיר בתקופת בית שני:
     'כיצד מעלין את הביכורים? כל העיירות שבמעמד מתכנסות לעירו שלמעמד, ולנין ברחובה שלעיר, ולא היו
     נכנסין לבתים. ולמשכים היה הממונה אומר: "קומו ונעלה ציון אל (בית) ה' אלהינו"' (יר' לא, ה).
64   רשימת החוקרים הטוענים כך היא ארוכה. לדוגמה, ראה: R.T. Herford, *The Pharisees*, reprint, Boston:
     1962, pp. 88-109; R.M. Grant, *A Historical Introduction to the New Testament*, New York 1963,
     pp. 274-275; P. Hanson, *The People Called: The Growth of Community in the Bible*, San Francisco
     1986, p. 353. הנגל (לעיל, הערה 3), א, עמ' 82; הנ"ל; *The Pre-Christian Paul*, London 1991, p. 57;
     גוטמן, 'Synagogue Origins' (לעיל, הערה 2), עמ' 4. אולם ראה: A. Saldarini, *Pharisees, Scribes and*
     Sadducees in Palestinian Society, Wilmington 1988, pp. 52-53; גראבה (לעיל, הערה 3), עמ' 408–409.
     גישה שונה לגמרי אימץ פ' פלשר, התומך בחלוקה בין בית־המקדש לבין בית־הכנסת, בדומה לתומכי הפרושים
     לעיל, אולם מזווית ראייה שונה; ראה: P.V.M. Flesher, 'Palestinian Synagogues before 70 C.E.: A
     Review of the Evidence', *Approaches to Ancient Judaism*, eds. J. Neusner & E.S. Frerichs,
     Atlanta 1989, pp. 67-81
65   S.J.D. Cohen, 'The Temple and the Synagogue', *The Temple in Antiquity*, ed. T. Madsen, Provo
     1984, pp. 151-174
66   E.P. Sanders, *Judaism: Practice and Belief – 66 BCE-66 CE*, London 1992, pp. 170-182

על כן, סביר יותר להניח שלא היה היה עימות כלשהו בין מוסדות אלה, אלא שהשתתפות ומנהיגות כוהנית בבית־הכנסת שיקפו את תפקידם הכללי כמנהיגים דתיים וקהילתיים באותם הימים.

עדות קדומה, המקשרת את התהליך המשפטי בשער העיר עם בית־הכנסת, נמצאת בספר שושנה. מוקד העלילה בו הוא אסיפת־עם בעיירה, בהשתתפות הזקנים והעם כאחד, לשם עריכת משפט; על־פי תרגום השבעים, התקיימה האסיפה בבית הכנסת (ἤ συναγωγή), ואילו הגרסה המתוקנת של תיאודוסיוס מזכירה פשוט ש'העם התאסף'.[67] חוקרים רואים בדרך כלל בתרגום השבעים את המסורת הקדומה יותר, ומניחים שהיו לו מודל שמי ומוצא ארץ־ישראלי ושהוא חובר אולי בתקופה הפרסית, או סביר יותר שחובר בתקופה ההלניסטית.[68] על כן ייתכן שיש לנו כאן עדות קדומה למונח 'בית־כנסת', שכוונתו היתה לבניין נפרד או לאזור שער העיר, ששימש מסגרת לפעילות קהילתית מרכזית.[69]

ניתן יהיה אולי למצוא סימוכין עקיפין להצעה לתארך את המעבר משער עיר לבניין בית־כנסת לתקופה ההלניסטית גם במקורות ספרותיים אחרים. טענתנו כאן – לצערנו, אבל מתוך הכרח – נשענת חזק על שתיקת המקורות. אילו היה בניין בית־הכנסת דבר ידוע ומוכר בחיי היהודים בארץ־ ישראל, היינו מצפים לכך שיוזכר בחיבורים רבים במאה השלישית והשנייה לפני הספירה.[70] על־אף האזכורים השונים של מנהיגים ומוסדות יהודיים בזמנו, אין בן־סירא מזכיר כלל את בית־הכנסת. היינו מצפים שספרי המקבים א' וב' יציינו את השפעתן של רדיפות אנטיוכוס על תפקודו של בית־ הכנסת, אילו היה קיים תפקוד כגון זה, אולם הם אינם עושים כן; טהרה, ברית מילה, השבת, חגים וכשרות, וכמובן בית־המקדש עצמו נזכרים כולם; ומאידך אין מילה או חצי־מילה על מוסד בית־ הכנסת.[71] השווה זאת לפרעות ולתקריות האנטי־יהודיות של המאה הראשונה לספירה, שבהן תפס בית־הכנסת מקום מרכזי בכתבי פילון ויוסף בן־מתתיהו.

אותה שתיקה קיימת גם בספרים טוביה, היובלים, איגרת אריסטיאס, צוואות שנים־עשר השבטים, חנוך ועוד. ציון בית־הכנסת כמקום לעבודת ה' או כמוסד מרכזי בחיים היהודיים אינו בנמצא. גם סופרים לא־יהודים המתארים את חיי היהודים, ובמיוחד את המרכיב הדתי, במאה השלישית והשנייה לפני הספירה אינם מתייחסים למוסד כזה.[72] כאשר המילה 'בית־כנסת' אכן

67 R.H. Charles, *Apocrypha and Pseudepigrapha of the Old Testament*, reprint, 2 vols., Oxford 1963, I, p. 649; C.A. Moore, *Daniel, Esther and Jeremiah: The Additions* (Anchor Bible 44), New York 1977, pp. 101-104

68 G.W.E. Nickelsburg, *Jewish Literature between the Bible and the Mishnah*, London 1981, pp. 25-26; מור (לעיל, הערה 67), עמ' 91–92.

69 ההפניה במתי ו, ה לאלה 'המתפללים בעומדם בבתי הכנסיות ובפינות השווקים' מרתקת. השימוש בבית־הכנסת או, לחלופין, בפינת השוק כמקום תפילה משקף אולי שלב־ביניים בהתפתחות שבין תקופת שער העיר וזו של מקומות תפילה מאורגנים, מתחת לקורת גג, כאשר שתי המסגרות היו בשימוש. אולם ייתכן גם שהפסוק מתייחס לתפילת־יחיד.

70 לספרות המתוארכת לתקופה זו, ראה: ניקלסבורג (לעיל, הערה 68), עמ' 71–160; הנגל (לעיל, הערה 3), א, עמ' 110 ואילך; M. Stone (ed.), *Jewish Writings of the Second Temple Period* (Compendia Rerum Judaicarum ad Novum Testamentum 2), Assen 1984

71 מכבים א א, מא־סד; מכבים ב ו.

72 זוהי נקודה שהועלתה בכמה הזדמנויות במשך 200 השנים האחרונות, לכל הפחות מאז זמנו של: G.L. Bauer, *Beschreibung der gottesdienstlichen Verfassung der alten Hebräer*, 2 vols., Leipzig 1805-1806, II,

מופיעה בחיבורים מן המאה השנייה המאוחרת לפני הספירה, הכוונה לרוב היא להתכנסות אנשים, 'אסיפת קהל־חסידים' (συναγωγὴ Ασιδαίων – מכבים א ב, מב), אסיפת 'קהילת־סופרים' (συναγωγὴ γραμματέων – מכבים א ז, יב), או ל'קהל גדול (ἐπὶ συναγωγῆς μεγάλης) של כוהנים ועם וראשי אומה וזקני הארץ', שהתכנסה להכרזת עלייתו לשלטון של שמעון המכבי בשנת 141 לפני הספירה (מכבים א יד, כח). המונח בתרגום השבעים מתייחס לקהילה עצמה ולא למקום התכנסות.[73]

על כן, על־פי הצעתנו בית־הכנסת במובן של מוסד התגבש בזכות שינוי מהותי בתכנית העיר. המסגרת הקודמת של התפקידים השונים של מוסד זה היתה מושרשרת היטב בחברה בתקופת המקרא. שערי עיר, על פעולותיהם הרבות, התקיימו שנים רבות, אם לא אלפי שנים או יותר, ברחבי ארץ־ישראל ובהקשרים אחרים במזרח הקרוב, ועל ידי כך המשיכו היהודים את הדגם הקיים. המעבר המאוחר יותר לתוך בניין, במקום מסגרת שער העיר תחת כיפת השמים, גם היה תופעה מוכרת מהעולם מסביב, הפעם מהעולם ההלניסטי. מעבר זה בקרב החברה היהודית היווה את ראשיתו של המוסד הקרוי בית־הכנסת.

ייתכן שהמעבר משער העיר למסגרת בתוך העיר כמרכז של פעולות שונות השפיע גם על העיר ירושלים ועל בית המקדש. אחד ההיבטים המיוחדים של בית המקדש במאה הראשונה הוא העובדה שהוא הפך למרכז פעילות עבור אלה המתגוררים בתוך העיר במיוחד, ובמובן מסוים עבור כל היהודים ברחבי יהודה ומעבר לה. ליתר דיוק, תחום הר הבית – השטח שהורחב בצורה ניכרת על ידי הורדוס – היה המקום שבו התנהלו מיגוון רחב של פעולות חברתיות, פוליטיות, דתיות, משפטיות וכלכליות.[74] שטח הר הבית לא תיפקד בצורה כה מקיפה קודם לכן. כבר ראינו שבתקופת המקרא, שערי העיר של ירושלים היו המוקד לרבות מפעולות אלו, כולל טקס קריאת התורה שאורגן על־ידי עזרא ונחמיה במאה החמישית לפני הספירה.

מתי עברו תפקידים אלה לתחום הר הבית? גם זה אירע כנראה בתקופה ההלניסטית, או אולי אף בראשית התקופה הרומית, עם העלמותו של אזור שער העיר מצד אחד, והאדרתו הבו־זמנית של אזור המקדש מצד שני. אין ספק שהשיפוצים שבוצעו בידי החשמונאים על הר הבית, וכמובן הרחבת השטח על ידי הורדוס לכפליים גודלו הקודם, נעשו לא רק על־מנת להגביר את מספר עולי הרגל ולספק את שאיפותיהן האישיות לגדולה במפעלי הבנייה שלהם, אלא גם כדי לשרת את תפקידיו החדשים של הר הבית. כשהורדוס תיכנן שטח זה מבחינה ארכיטקטונית כתחום מקודש (temenos) מצד אחד, וכאחותה של האגורה היוונית או הפורום הרומי מאידך, הוא בעצם ביקש לכנס למקום אחד את כל אותן הפעולות שפעם נערכו בחלקי העיר הציבוריים השונים, ובעיקר באזור שער העיר.

---

p. 125ff. הפירוש לתהלים עד, ח ('שרפו כל מועדי אל') כהתייחסות להשחתת בתי־כנסת בעת רדיפות אנטיוכוס (ראה לאחרונה :J. Goldstein, *I Maccabees* [Anchor Bible 41] New York 1976, p. 138, note 208) אינו מקובל היום.

73   ראה: *TDNT* VIII, p. 805, s.v. *Synagogue*. דווקא בגלל הסיבה הזאת, דהיינו הרמז בספרות תקופת בית שני במילה 'בית־כנסת' ל'קהילה', נראה שהמילה נקשרה לבניין שבתוכו התנהלו פעולות קהילתיות. ישנה עדות מפורשת בספרות חז"ל הקדומה לכך שבית־הכנסת היה שייך לקהילה בכלל; ראה להלן, הערה 79, וכן: תוספתא, בבא מציעא יא, כג, מהד' ליברמן, עמ' 125–126; הנ"ל, תוספתא כפשוטה, י כרכים, ניו־יורק תשט"ו–תשמ"ה, ט, עמ' 320.

74   J. Jeremias, *Jerusalem in the Time of Jesus*, London 1969, pp. 40, 54-57

התפתחות זו בירושלים כנראה התנגשה עם מיקומן מחדש של אותן הפעולות שנערכו באזור שער העיר במסגרות אחרות, כפי שקרה במקומות רבים ברחבי המזרח ההלניסטי.

אם יש לקבל תיאוריה זו, דהיינו, ששטח הר הבית ירש רבות מן הפעולות שנערכו פעם בשער העיר בירושלים, בדומה לבית־הכנסת שהופיע בעיירות ובכפרים רבים בארץ־ישראל ובתפוצות בגין סיבות דומות, אז אולי ניתן יהיה להסביר מספר תופעות שלא היו מובנות קודם לכן, דוגמת טקס קריאת התורה בתחום המקדש. טקס זה היה הפעולה הליטורגית הפורמלית היחידה שלא היתה קשורה לקורבנות (בדומה לשירות ההלל של הלויים). כל שנה, ביום הכיפורים, כמו גם בסוף כל שנת שמיטה, הכוהן הגדול היה קורא בציבור מן התורה (ההקהל, על־פי דב' לא).[75] פעולה זו היתה בבירור בעדיפות משנית בסדר היום העיקרי של בית המקדש, ובתור שכזה, היא נוהלה בעזרת הנשים ולא בעזרת הכוהנים. היה ברור שהפעולה נועדה לכל העם שהתקהל בתחום המקדש. האם זה היה המשך הנוהג בשער העיר?

כמו כן, אולי ניתן יהיה להסביר את האזכור המוזר לכאורה לשני מנהיגים שהיו קשורים לטקסים אלה – 'ראש הכנסת' ו'חזן הכנסת'. ספרות חז"ל מזכיר במפורש את שני המנהיגים האלה בקשר עם טקס קריאת התורה בבית־הכנסת במאות הראשונות לספירה.[76] ייתכן שהם נשאו תפקידים מרכזיים קודם לכן בפעולות בשער העיר, כולל פעולות דתיות, ולאחר מכן תפקידים אלו הועתקו לבית המקדש ולבית־הכנסת.

הצעתנו לגבי ראשית בית־הכנסת בשער העיר גם היתה מסבירה את ההתפתחות של ה'פרוסויכה' היהודי הקדום במצרים וכמה ממאפייניו החשובים, כולל ההשפעה הניכרת של דגמים תלמיים. ליהודים שהתיישבו במצרים ובמקומות אחרים לא היתה כל מסגרת רשמית ומוכרת לפעולותיהם הקהילתיות, לאותן הפעולות שנערכו ליד שער העיר בארץ יהודה. על כן, על־מנת להסתגל לסביבתם החדשה וכדי למצוא מסגרת לקיים את פעולותיהם הקהילתיות, חיפשו יהודי מצרים והתפוצות דגמים הולמים בתרבויות הסובבות אותם.[77] אין תועלת בוויכוח על מקום ראשיתו של בית־הכנסת – בארץ יהודה או בתפוצות. הוא התפתח בשני המקומות פחות או יותר באותו זמן, אך כתוצאה מסיבות שונות לחלוטין: היהודים בארץ־ישראל חיפשו מסגרת חליפית לאיזור שער העיר ההולכת ונעלמת; היהודים בתפוצות של התקופה ההלניסטית והרומית סירבו להשתמש בשער העיר של הפגאנים (אם אכן הוא עדיין היה קיים בצורתו הקדומה כיעד לפעילות קהילתית), ועל כן מן ההכרח היה עליהם ליצור מסגרת שתשמור על, ושתתן ביטוי, לזהותם הקהילתית בסביבה זרה. בנסיבות אלו נולדו בית־הכנסת והפרוסויכה.

75 משנה, יומא ז, א; משנה, סוטה ז, ח; ראה גם משנה, תמיד ה, ג.

76 תוספתא, מגילה ג, כא, מהד' ליברמן, עמ' 359; תוספתא, סוכה ד, ו, מהד' ליברמן, עמ' 273. במגנגנון בית המקדש, החזן וראש הכנסת כאחד היו כפופים לכוהונה; בבית הכנסת ההולך ומתפתח, תפקידים אלה נועדו להיות מרכזיים. על החזן במזרח הקרוב בעת העתיקה, ראה: D. Weisberg, *Guild Structure and Political Allegiance in Early Achaemenid Mesopotamia*, New Haven 1967, p. 93; S. Kaufman, *The Akkadian Influences on Aramaic* (Assyriological Studies 19), Chicago 1974, p. 55; B. Menzel, *Assyrische Tempel*, 2 vols., Rome 1981, I, p. 289; II, p. 232, notes 3864-3865. ראה ערך *ḥazzanu*, בתוך: CAD, H, Chicago 1956, pp. 163-165. לדוגמה של הממד הדתי של השימוש במונח, ראה: L. Waterman, *Royal Correspondence of the Assyrian Empire*, 4 vols., Ann Arbor 1930, I, pp. 254-255 (Letter 366)

77 כנגד פלשר (לעיל, הערה 64), עמ' 27–39. טיעוניו אינם עומדים במבחן; התיזה שלו, הגורסת התנגשות יסודית בין שני המוסדות, בעייתית מדי בכדי לקבל כמהימנה.

אחרית דבר: מֶעֶבַר לשנת 70 לספירה – המשך ושינוי

היו חוקרים שטָעֲנו שהיה בית־הכנסת הקדום תופעה של השנים שלאחר שנת 70.[78] לכאורה אין טענה זו סבירה, במיוחד לאור הנתונים שהבאנו לעיל. אולם אם בכל זאת קיים בה גרעין כלשהו של אמת, הריהו בגלל העובדה שבשנים שלאחר החורבן אכן עבר בית־הכנסת כמה וכמה שינויים משמעותיים. מצד אחד המשיך המוסד לתפקד כקודמו בתקופת בית שני, ומצד שני הוא התפתח בכיוונים שונים וחדשים.

בית־הכנסת המשיך לתפקד כמוסד קהילתי, כפי שמתועד בספרות חז"ל. המוסד בעצם היה שייך לקהילה; בני העיר ניהלו את ענייניו (רכישת הבניין, מכירתו וכד') וגם דאגו להעסקת פקידיו ולפיטוריהם.[79] הפעילויות שהתנהלו בו (לימוד, בית־דין, סעודות, צדקה, אכסניה וכד') היו דומות לאלו שהתנהלו בבית־הכנסת לפני שנת 70.[80] בית־הכנסת המשיך לשמש מקום הן להתכנסות הקהילה לדיון בנושאים דחופים[81] והן להתכנסויות קבועות בשבתות ובחגים לשיחה בנושאים שונים בפורום ציבורי.[82]

אולם לאחר שנת 70 הלכה והתפתחה הליטורגיה של בית־הכנסת בקצב מהיר. בעוד עבודת ה' בבית־הכנסת המשיכה להתנהל כמקודם, דהיינו המוקד היה קריאת התורה וההפטרה ודרשות,[83] אירעה גם התפתחות דרמטית בגיבוש תפילה בציבור. שאלת נוסח התפילה שנקבע בתקופת יבנה – שיכלול את שני החלקים המרכזיים, העמידה וה'שמע' וברכותיה – מעסיקה חוקרים מאז המאה התשע־עשרה. רוב החוקרים מאמצים עמדת־ביניים, דהיינו שתפילה בציבור התקיימה קודם לכן בצורה כלשהי ושרבן גמליאל וחוגו הוסיפו חומר בעת תהליך העריכה. אין תמימות דעים לגבי אופין

78 ראה: S. Zeitlin, 'The Tefillah, the Shemoneh Esreh: An Historical Study of the First Canonization of the Hebrew Liturgy', *JQR* 54 (1963-64), pp. 208-249; S. Hoenig, 'The Suppositious Temple Synagogue', ק', *JQR* 54 (1963-64), pp. 115-131 (לעיל, הערה 4); הנ"ל, 'Early Christianity' (לעיל, הערה 4). ראה גם: אוסטר (לעיל, הערה 4).

79 משנה, נדרים ה, ה; תוספתא, בבא מציעא יא, כג, מהד' ליברמן, עמ' 125; ירושלמי, מגילה פ"ג ה"ב, עד ע"ג; פ"ד ה"ד, עה ע"א; ירושלמי, יבמות פי"ב, יג ע"א; בראשית רבה פא, א, מהד' תיאודור־אלבק, עמ' 969–972.

80 ראה את ספרי: בית־הכנסת העתיק (בהקדמה); וכן: ספראי (לעיל, הערה 22), עמ' 105–123.

81 תוספתא, אהלות ד, ב, מהד' צוקרמנדל, עמ' 600.

82 בבלי, שבת קנ ע"א.

83 פעולה אחת שקשה יותר לעמוד עליה בהקשר לתקופה שלפני שנת 70 היא אמירת התרגום. אין ספק שהתרגום היה מרכזי לטקס קריאת התורה במאה השנייה, לפי עדותן של המשנה והתוספתא, וסביר להניח שפעולה זו היתה המשך של מה שהתנהל לפני החורבן. לאמיתו של דבר, אין לנו מקורות ברורים ומפורשים לקיומם של תרגומים כאלה במסגרת בית־הכנסת מלפני החורבן, אולם קשה להאמין שכל החוקים והתקנות המופיעים בספרות התנאית נובעים רק מן המאה השנייה. לכן יש להניח שהתרגום לתורה מצא את ביטויו במסגרת בית־הכנסת בעוד עמד בית־המקדש על תלו. ראה: M. McNamara, 'Targums', IDBSup, Nashville 1976, pp. 856-861; A.D. York, 'The Dating of Targumic Literature', *JSJ* 5 (1974), pp. 49-62; idem, 'The Targum in the Synagogue and in the School', *JSJ* 10 (1979), pp. 74-86; L. Smolar et al. (eds.), *Studies in Targum Jonathan to the Prophets*, New York 1983, pp. XII-XIX; R. le Déaut, 'The Targumim', *Cambridge History of Judaism*, 2 vols., Cambridge 1984-1989, II, p. 563ff.; P.S. Alexander, 'Jewish Aramaic Translation of Hebrew Scriptures', *Mikra*, ed. J.J. Mulder, Assen 1988, p. 247ff.

של תפילות אלו לפני כן וגם לגבי מה שהשיגו רבן גמליאל ועמיתיו ביבנה.[84] בעשרות השנים
האחרונות מקובלת התיאוריה, בעקבות היינימן, הופמן, רייף ואחרים, שקביעת נוסח התפילה
לטקסט אחיד יחסית היתה תהליך ארוך ומורכב, שהגיע לסיומו רק בשלהי העת העתיקה או בראשית
ימי הביניים.[85]

תכונה נוספת של בית-הכנסת שלאחר שנת 70 היתה אופיו הדתי ההולך וגובר. כפי שצוין, היה
בית-הכנסת בשלביו הראשוניים מוסד קהילתי בעיקרו; הפעילות הליטורגית שהתנהלה בו היתה
משנית. אולם בתקופה שלאחר שנת 70 חלו שינויים בממד הדתי.[86] מקורות חז"ל אחדים מן המאה
השנייה לספירה רומזים לקדושת בית-הכנסת על-ידי השוואתו, בין היתר, למקדש בירושלים;[87]
עדות נוספת לתופעה זו משתקפת באדריכלות בית-הכנסת מן המאה השלישית ואילך, שהתבטאה
באוריינטציה מכוונת כלפי ירושלים[88] ובמקרים רבים בהופעת ארון הקודש, שהכיל את ספרי התורה
המקודשים.[89] בית-הכנסת החל להיתפס אז כמקום קדוש, ולראיה: (א) כתובות המתייחסות לבניין
בית-הכנסת כמקום קדוש – 'אתרא קדישא' (בית שאן, טבריה, כפר חנניה ונערן),[90] ἅγιος τόπος

84 ראה: י' אלבוגן, התפילה בישראל, תל-אביב תשל"ב, עמ' 32 ואילך, 177 ואילך; י' היינימן, התפילה בתקופת
התנאים והאמוראים, ירושלים תשכ"ד. לאחרונה דנו בנושא: נ' כהן, ''שמעון הפקולי הסדיר י"ח ברכות'',
תרביץ נב (תשמ"ג), עמ' 547–556; ע' פליישר, 'לקדמוניות תפילות החובה בישראל', תרביץ נט (תש"ן), עמ'
T. Zahavy, *Studies in Jewish Prayer*, Lantham 1990; S. Reif, *Judaism and Hebrew Prayer*, ;441–397
Cambridge 1993, pp. 53-87; ולבסוף: ע' פליישר, 'מענה (בשולי השגותיו של ש"ק רייף)', תרביץ ס
(תשנ"א), עמ' 685.

85 ראה לעיל, הערה 84; וכן: Notre Dame :L. Hoffman, *The Canonization of the Synagogue Service*
1979, p. 107

86 ראה את מאמרי: 'The Sages and the Synagogue in Late Antiquity: The Evidence of the Galilee',
The Galilee in Late Antiquity, pp. 201-221; וכן: הנ"ל, 'מרכז קהילתי למקדש מעט: ריהוט ופנים בית
הכנסת העתיק', קתדרה 60 (תשנ"א), עמ' 79–84; Z. Safrai, 'From the Synagogue to "Little
Temple"', *Proceedings of the Tenth World Congress of Jewish Studies*, B/II, Jerusalem 1990, pp.
23-28

87 השווה, למשל: משנה, מגילה ג, ב. J. Branham, 'Sacred Space under Erasure in Ancient
Synagogues and Churches', *The Art Bulletin* 74 (1992), pp. 375-394; idem, 'Vicarious
Sacrality: Temple Space in Ancient Synagogues', *New Perspectives on Ancient Synagogues*,
eds. P. Flesher & D. Urman, Leiden 1994, pp. 1-27

88 F. Landsberger, 'The Sacred Direction in Synagogue and Church', *HUCA* 28 (1959), pp.
181-203

89 לעדות R. Hachlili, *Ancient Jewish Art and Archaeology in the Land of Israel*, Leiden 1988, p. 141ff.
בספרות על התפתחויות אלו, ראה, למשל: משנה, מגילה ג, א–ג; תוספתא, ברכות ג, טו–טז; ליברמן,
עמ' 15–16. ככל הנראה קיבלו בתי-הכנסת בתפוצות ממד קדוש זה בתקופה קדומה יותר, אפילו לפני שנת 70.
ראה, למשל, לגבי מצרים ההלניסטית: א' כשר, 'בתי-הכנסת כ"בתי-תפילה" ו"מקומות קדושים" בחי הקהילות
היהודיות במצרים ההלניסטית והרומאית', בתי-כנסת עתיקים – קובץ מחקרים, עמ' 119–132; ייתכן שבית-
הכנסת בתפוצות, שכבר השיג מעמד של קדושה ושכבר שיקע את המרכיב של תפילה בציבור לתוך הליטורגיה
שלו (ולראיה, השם *proseuche*), השפיע בצורה זו או אחרת על המוסד האח בארץ-ישראל. ראה, למשל: יוסף
בן-מתתיהו, מלחמה ז, 45; קדמוניות יד, 258; טז, 164; פילון, נגד פלאקום 48; תוספתא, סוכה ד, ה, מהד'
ליברמן, עמ' 173.

90 י' נוה, על פסיפס ואבן, ירושלים תשל"ח, עמ' 34, 48, 77, 95.

(אשקלון ועזה)[91] או ἁγιο[τάτος] τόπος (גרש),[92] ו(ב) תיאורים ברצפות פסיפס של תשמישי
קדושה, כמו המנורה, ארון הקודש, השופר, הלולב והאתרוג, או דמויות ותיאורים מסיפורי המקרא,
כגון עקידת יצחק.[93] תרגום יונתן, אשר קובץ בחלקו הגדול בסוף העת העתיקה, משתמש בביטוי
'לישנא דבי קודשא', המתייחס ככל הנראה לבית־הכנסת.[94] יתר על כן, המילה 'מקדשיכון' בתרגום
יונתן לויק' כו, ב, מתפרשת בדרך כלל כ'בתי־הכנסת שלכם'.[95]

כחלק מן התהליך הזה, במהלך העת העתיקה, הלך ונקשר מוסד בית־הכנסת לבית־המקדש
בירושלים; הוא הפך ל'מקדש מעט', כפי שכינהו ר' יצחק במאה השלישית.[96] יתר על כן, במהלך
המאות השלישית עד השביעית אומצו מנהגים להנצחת זכרו של בית־המקדש.[97]
מה גרם לשינויים אלה במעמדו של בית־הכנסת? ללא ספק היתה לאירועי שנת 70 – חורבן

91   רוט־גרסון (לעיל, הערה 6), עמ' 25, 101.

92   שם, עמ' 46. ראה גם האזכורים של 'קהילה קדישא' ביריחו ובסוסיה (נוה [לעיל, הערה 90, עמ' 104, [123]) או
של 'חבורתה קדישתא' בבית שאן (שם, עמ' 77); 'האחרון מתייחס ככל הנראה לחוג של חכמים. ראה: מ' בר, על
החבורה בארץ־ישראל בימי האמוראים', ציון מז (תשמ"ב), עמ' 185–178; הנ"ל, 'על החבורייא – מעולמן של
הישיבות בארץ־ישראל במאות השלישית והרביעית', שנתון בר־אילן כ–כא (תשמ"ג), עמ' 76–95.

93   חכלילי (לעיל, הערה 93), עמ' 234 ואילך.

94   A. Shinan, 'The Aramaic Targum as a Mirror of Galilean Jewry', *The Galilee in Late Antiquity*,
pp. 248-250; הנ"ל, תרגום ואגדה בו (האגדה בתרגום התורה הארמי המיוחס ליונתן בן עוזיאל), ירושלים
תשנ"ג, עמ' 113–115.

95   לוין (לעיל, הערה 95), עמ' 217 וההפניות שם. בית־הכנסת גם זכה למעמד של מוסד דתי ומוכר על־פי הממשל
הרומי של המאה הרביעית. בחקיקה משנת 370 לספירה בערך, שהוצהרה בידי ולנטיאנוס הא', יוחס התואר
religionum loca לבתי־הכנסת, ועל כן היה אסור לחיילים הרומיים להחזיק בו או לקחת את הנכסים שבו; ראה:
א' לינדר, היהודים והיהדות בחוקי הקיסרות הרומית, ירושלים תשמ"ג, עמ' 116–118.

96   בבלי, מגילה כט ע"א.

97   כבר הזכרנו את הדגש על האוריינטציה של בית־הכנסת כלפי ירושלים בכל סוגי בתי־הכנסת מן המאה השלישית
ואילך. המתפללים בבית־הכנסת גם זכרו את ירושלים ואת בית־המקדש תוך כדי קריאת המפטיר לחגים מסדר
הקורבנות, כפי שכתוב בספר במד' כח–כט; קריאת סדר העבודה (של יום הכיפורים במקדש) וכן תפילות המוסף
בשבת ובחגים מתקדמות בקורבנות שפעם הוקרבו בימים אלה. ראה: אלבוגן (לעיל, הערה 84), עמ' 88; .J
Hoffman, 'The Surprising History of the Musaf "Amida"', *Conservative Judaism* 42 (1989),
pp. 41-45

זכרונות של עבודת הכהנים בבית־המקדש נשרדו על לוחות אבן שנקבעו בקירות בית־הכנסת. בשברי לוחות
כאלה, שנתגלו באשקלון, בקיסריה, בכיסופים, בתימן, ברחוב, ולאחרונה בנצרת, רשומים כ"ד משמרות
הכהונה שפעם שירתו במקדש, כמו גם מקומות המגורים של משפחותיהם בגליל. ראה: אשקלון – א"ל סוקניק,
'שלוש כתובות יהודיות עתיקות מארץ־ישראל', הוספה לציון, א (תרפ"ו), עמ' 16–17; פריי (לעיל, הערה 45),
ב, מס' 962; קיסריה – מ' אבי־יונה, 'כתובת מקיסריה על כ"ד משמרות הכוהנים', ארץ־ישראל ז (תשכ"ד),
עמ' 24–38; כיסופים – צ' אילן, 'שבר לוח כ"ד משמרות הכוהנים מסביבות כיסופים', תרביץ מג (תשל"ד),
עמ' 225–226; תימן – ר' דיגן, 'כתובת מתימן על כ"ד משמרות־הכוהנים', תרביץ, מב (תשל"ג), עמ'
302–304; ובכלל: נוה (לעיל, הערה 90), עמ' 87–92, 140–143; רחוב – אנציקלופדיה חדשה לחפירות ד,
עמ' 1458; נצרת – ח' אשל, 'שבר כתובה של כ"ד משמרות מנצרת?', תרביץ סא (תשנ"ב), עמ' 159–161.
באותה עת, כתבו פייטנים קדומים על בית־המקדש ועל עבודת הכוהנים בחיבורים שהוכנו לקריאה בבית־הכנסת
בט' באב. ראה, למשל: צ"מ רבינוביץ, מחזור פיוטי רבי יניי (ב כרכים, ירושלים תשמ"ז, ב, עמ' 300–342; ע'
פליישר, 'לעניין משמרות בפיוטים', סיני סב (תשכ"ח), עמ' 142 ואילך; הנ"ל, שירת־הקודש העברית בימי
הביניים, ירושלים 1975, עמ' 202–206.

בית־המקדש והחלל שנוצר בעקבותיו – השפעה של ממש על מעמד בית־הכנסת בחיי היהודים.[98]
אולם ייתכן שגם עליית הנצרות וחדירתה לארץ־ישראל במאה הרביעית, לרבות שימת הדגש על
קדושת הכנסייה, הניעו גם יהודים רבים להגדיר את מקום התכנסותם ותפילתם כמקום 'קדוש',
כ'מקדש מעט'. בהדגישם את קדושת מוסדם, ייתכן שהיהודים אימצו מונחים ורעיונות נפוצים מן
העולם הנוצרי הביזאנטי, כפי שעשו באותו זמן לגבי המרכיבים הארכיטקטוניים והאמנותיים של
בית־הכנסת.[99]

בסיכום, גם לאחר שנת 70 נשאר הממד הקהילתי של בית־הכנסת מרכזי ובסיסי, אף שחלו
שינויים משמעותיים במרכיב הדתי. שינויים אלה היו ככל הנראה חלק מתהליך ארוך והדרגתי.
למרות שהתפתחויות במעמדו של בית־הכנסת כבר ניכרו אצל החכמים מדור יבנה ומדור אושא
לפחות (זאת אומרת, בסוף המאה הראשונה ובמאה השנייה), יש למצוא טביעה חזקה עוד יותר של
קדושת המקום ויצירת קשר ברור בין המקדש לבית־הכנסת רק מן המאה השלישית ואילך. תופעות
אלו עלו על פני השטח בעיקר כאשר התחיל היישוב היהודי בארץ־ישראל להיחשף לכנסייה
הנוצרית שהיתה בעלייה: העם היהודי מצא בזכרונותיו על בית־המקדש – במנהגיו, בסמליו
ובנבניהגיו – חיזוקים דתיים, לאומיים ופסיכולוגיים שנזקק להם על־מנת להתמודד עם מציאות
חדשה זו.

---

98 ראה את הערותי במאמר: 'ממרכז קהילתי למקדש מעט' (לעיל, הערה 86), עמ' 79–84. הנושא הוא המוקד של
עבודת הדוקטור של תלמידי, סטיבן פיין, *Synagogue and Sanctity: The Late-Antique Palestinian*
Synagogue as a Holy Place (האוניברסיטה העברית בירושלים, תשנ"ד).

99 R.A. Markus, 'How on Earth Could Places Become Holy? Origins of the Christian Idea of
Holy Places', *Journal of Early Christian Studies* 2 (1994), pp. 257-271. השפעות הכנסייה הביזאנטית
על בית־הכנסת הן נושא הדיון אצל: Y. Tsafrir, 'The Byzantine Setting and Its Influence on Ancient
Synagogues', *The Synagogue in Late Antiquity*, pp. 147-157; הנ"ל, ארץ־ישראל מחורבן בית שני ועד
הכיבוש המוסלמי ב: המימצא הארכיאולוגי והאמנותי, ירושלים תשמ"ה, עמ' 165–189, 285–300; חכלילי
(לעיל, הערה 89), עמ' 143–192. ראה גם: א' עובדיה, 'השפעות גומלין בין בתי־כנסת וכנסיות בארץ־ישראל
בתקופה הביזאנטית', מ' ברושי (עורך), בין חרמון לסיני, ירושלים תשל"ו, עמ' 163–170. השווה גם:
G. Stroumsa, 'Religious Contacts in Byzantine Palestine', *Numen* 36 (1989), pp. 21ff.

האם הושפע הרמב"ם מאלגזאלי?

חוה לצרוס־יפה
האוניברסיטה העברית בירושלים

הרמב"ם איננו מזכיר את אלגזאלי בכתביו; אולם אין בכך משום ראיה שלא הכיר את כתביו או שלא
קרא בהם.[1] קשה להניח ששמו של סופר מוסלמי גדול זה, שמת כמאה שנה לפניו (בשנת 1111) והיה
ידוע היטב במזרח המוסלמי כבמערב, לא הגיע אל הרמב"ם. עוד יותר קשה להניח שלא קרא משהו
מיצירתו הענפה של אלגזאלי, העוסקת רובה ככולה בשאלות הגדולות של האמונה ושל כל דת.
ואכן, חוקרים אחדים הניחו כמובן מאליו שהרמב"ם הכיר את כתבי אלגזאלי, ויש גם מי שהציע
שמקור השם 'מורה נבוכים' ('דלאלת אלחאירין') מצוי בכתבי אלגזאלי.[2] אנו יודעים שהוגי־דעות
וסופרים יהודים – ובראשם ר' יהודה הלוי[3] – הושפעו עמוקות מאלגזאלי גם כשלא הזכירוהו בשם,
תירגמו מכתביו לעברית ואף תיעתקו אותם בערבית לאותיות עבריות. ייתכן מאוד שגם ר' אברהם,
בנו של הרמב"ם, הלך שבי אחריו.[4] כלום ייתכן להניח שכל זה נעלם מעיני זה 'הנשר הגדול' או שלא

---

1   ראה 29 .n ,S. Harvey, 'Maimonides' Letter to Ibn Tibbon', *JQR* 83 (1992), p. 60, n. 29. וראה ש' פינס,
    במבוא לתרגום האנגלי של מורה הנבוכים, הסעיף על הכלאם (פינס מתייחס במיוחד ל'מפלת הפילוסופים' של
    אלגזאלי): *Moses Maimonides – Guide of the Perplexed*, Translated with an Introduction and
    Notes by S. Pines, With an Introductory Essay by L. Strauss, Chicago 1963, pp. cxxviiff. ראה.
    גם באופן כללי יותר על הכרת הרמב"ם את הספרות הערבית־מוסלמית מבלי שיצטטה במפורש: י' קרמר,
    'השפעת המשפט המוסלמי על הרמב"ם, אלאחכאם אלח'מסה', אלאחכאם אלח'מסה', תעודה י, מחקרים במדעי היהדות בעריכת מ"ע
    פרידמן, תל־אביב תשנ"ו, עמ' 225–244; י' שיפמן, 'עוד על הרמב"ם ואבן סינא', תרביץ סד (תשנ"ה), עמ'
    523–534; מ"ע פרידמן, 'רשימות תלמיד בבית מדרש הרמב"ם באמונות ודעות ובהלכה', תרביץ סב (תשנ"ג),
    עמ' 546, 550; Hava Lazarus-Yafeh, 'Taḥrīf and Thirteen Torah Scrolls', *Jerusalem Studies in*
    Arabic and Islam 19 (1995), pp. 81-89 ועיין גם H. Kreisel, 'Juda Halevi's Influence on
    Maimonides', *Maimonidean Studies* II, ed. A. Hyman, New-York 1992, pp. 95-121 (esp. p. 98);
    H.A. Davidson, *Proofs for Eternity, Creation and the Existence of God in Medieval Islamic and*
    Jewish Philosophy, Oxford 1987, pp. 194-201 ובמיוחד עמ' 199 שם. תודה לידידי י' קרמר על מראה מקום
    זה.
2   ראה A. Gileadi, 'A Short Note on the Possible Origin of the Title "Moreh Ha-Nevukhim"',
    Le Muséon 97 (1984), pp. 159-161; F. Rosenthal, *Knowledge Triumphant*, Leiden 1970 ועיין גם
    שם, עמ' 96.
3   ראה ד"צ בנעט, 'ר' יהודה הלוי ואלגזאלי', כנסת ז (תשי"ב), עמ' 311–329.
4   ראה א' שוסמן, 'שאלת המקורות המוסלמים לחיבורו של ר' אברהם בן הרמב"ם "כתאב כפאית אלעאבדין"',
    תרביץ נה (תשמ"ו), עמ' 229–251.

עורר בו עניין לקרוא בכתביו של אלגזאלי, שכמותו ביקש 'להחיות' את דת אבותיו וכמותו הרגיש
ששליחות זאת הוטלה עליו מפני שרק הוא יכול לקיימה כראוי?

במאמר קצר זה ברצוני להצביע על כמה מקבילות בין דברי אלגזאלי לדברי הרמב"ם (נוסף על
אחרות שכבר הצביעו עליהן אחרים – כגון ש' פינס), ועל הקשיים המתודולוגיים המתלווים לכל
ניסיון לקבוע שאכן היתה כאן השפעה ישירה. אחדות מן הדוגמאות שלהלן תהיינה לקוחות מ'שמונה
פרקים', שקראנו אותם ב'חוג ללימוד מדרש', המתקיים זה שנים רבות מדי שבת בשבתו בביתם של
ידידי משה וחוה גרינברג. לימוד 'שמונה פרקים' בחוג זה היה בבחינת היוצא מן הכלל המעיד על
הכלל, שכן זאת היתה הפעם היחידה שחרגנו בה ממנהגנו ללמוד מדרש דווקא. בכל מפגשי החוג
למדתי רבות, ופירות הלימוד הזה מוגשים בזה, בברכה ובהוקרה, למורי וידידי משה.

* * *

א. בסוף המבוא ל'שמונה פרקים' מציין הרמב"ם שיביא עניינים שונים מפי חז"ל ומדברי הפילוסופים
ו'מחיבורי הרבה בני-אדם', ומוסיף: 'ושמע האמת מפי מי שאמרה'. הוא מוסיף שלא יציין את שמות
המצוטטים, בשל האריכות חסרת התועלת הכרוכה בכך וכן משום ש'אפשר שיהיה שם זכרון שם
האיש ההוא לחשוב מי שאין לו חן: שהדבר נפסד ובתוכו רוע שלא יבינהו'.[5] הפירוש המקובל של
דברים אלה, הן על חכמים בינימיים והן על החוקרים כיום, הוא שהרמב"ם חשש שציטוט הוגים
מוסלמים או אחרים שאינם בני-ברית לא יכשר בעיני הקוראים היהודים בני דורו, והם עלולים
לדחות מיד את הדברים מבלי לנסות כלל לעמוד על אמיתתם. אולם ייתכן אף ייתכן שכוונתו של
הרמב"ם היתה כללית יותר ותואמת את דבריו של אלגזאלי על אותם אנשים הדוחים דברי נבואה
ודברי צופים-'מיסטיקאים אך ורק משום שמצאו אותם בתוך ספרי הפילוסופים, שאינם מקובלים
עליהם (בניגוד גמור לעמדת הרמב"ם וגם לעמדת אלגזאלי עצמו):

> כמה מעוטי דעת אומרים שדברים אלה, הואיל והם מצויים בדברי הבליהם (של הפילוסופים)
> – חובה להתעלם מהם ולא להזכירם, וכל המזכיר אותם חובה לסתור את דבריו, וכל כך משום
> שהם שמעו תחילה דברים אלה מפי הפילוסופים ועל כן עלה במוחם החלוש הרעיון שהדברים
> שקר הם כי דובריהם דוברי שקר... אכן זו דרכו של רפויי השכל: הם מכירים את האמת
> על-פי בני-האדם, אך לא את בני-האדם על-פי האמת. אך הנבון ילך בעקבותיו של אדון כל
> החכמים עלי, ירצהו אללה, אשר אמר: 'אל תדע את האמת על-פי האדם. הכר את האמת –
> ותכיר את דובריה'. אכן הנבון מכיר את האמת. הוא יעמיק חקור בכל דבר שנאמר, ואם
> יווכח כי דבר אמת הוא – יקבלנו, בין אם הדובר מרבה כזב ובין אם דובר אמת הוא. ויש
> אשר ישאף הנבון את האמת מתוך דברי התועים, כי הוא יודע כי מחצבי הזהב בעפר הארץ.[6]

5   ראה ההקדמה לשמונה פרקים, בתוך: הקדמות לפירוש המשנה, ערוכות ומבוארות על-ידי מ"ד רבינוביץ,
ירושלים תשל"ב, עמ' קנה. במהדורה של המקור הערבי מאת מ' וולף (ליפציג 1863), אין הקדמה זאת מצויה.
עיין גם בתרגום לאנגלית של I. Gorfinkle, ניו-יורק 1912, עמ' 36.

6   ראה אבו אבו אחמד אלגזאלי, הפודה מן התעייה והטעות, תירגמה ח' לצרוס-יפה, תל-אביב תשל"ה, עמ' 40, וראה
גם עמ' 41 והמשלים שם. השווה H. Malter, 'Shem-Tov ben Joseph Palaquera', JQR n.s. I (1910/11),
pp. 168-169, n. 31. תודתי לעמיתי וידידי ז' הרוי על מראה מקום זה ואחרים, ועל הערותיו המאלפות.

ב. באותו מבוא, כעמוד קודם לכן, הרמב"ם מציין שחסידות מביאה לידי נבואה, בהתאם למאמר
במשנה מפי ר' פינחס בן יאיר (הרמב"ם מביא רק את סוף דבריו): 'זריזות מביאה לידי נקיות ונקיות
לידי טהרה וטהרה לידי פרישות ופרישות לידי קדושה וקדושה לידי ענוה וענוה לידי יראת החטא
ויראת החטא לידי חסידות וחסידות לידי רוח הקודש' (סוטה ט, טו). הוא קובע שלדעת חז"ל 'קיום
מאמרי מסכת זאת (כלומר פרקי אבות) מביא ליא לידי נבואה'.[7]

מבלי להיכנס לתורת הנבואה של הרמב"ם אפשר לומר שמאמר נועז זה יש לו מקבילות ברורות
בכתבי אלגזאלי. במקומות רבים עומד אלגזאלי על כך שרק פרישות מוחלטת מהבלי העולם יכולה
להכין אדם לריכוז גמור ברצון האל ובאהבתו, ורק אלה יביאוהו לקליטת אורות האמת השופעים
ממעל, שהיא היא עיקר ההתגלות הנבואית. בדרך כלל אלגזאלי מדבר על הקדושים המקורבים
('אוליא'), אך הללו הם שלב מעבר בעיניו לנביאים, והם כמי שטעמו את טעם הנבואה ('ד'וק')
בחוויותיהם. בכך מניחים גם אלגזאלי וגם הרמב"ם את ההנחה הנועזת, שכל חסיד ופרוש עשוי
לזכות בהתגלות נבואית, ואולי הם גם רומזים לאפשרות שהם עצמם זכו לטעום מטעמה של נבואה.[8]
אולם אלגזאלי עוסק בנושא זה, באחד מדיוניו בספר ה־21, ספר נפלאות הלב ('כתאב עג'אאב
אלקלב'), של 'אחיא עלום אלדין' בהקשר זר מאוד לרוחו של הרמב"ם: עדיפות הדרך המיסטית מן
הדרך השכלתנית־לימודית להכרת בורא עולם ולזכייה בחוויית ההתגלות הנבואית (גם מבחינה
לשונית אין כל דמיון בין השניים):

ואם יקבל האל את עניין הלב ויקרבנו – ישפיעו[9] עליו הרחמים ויאיר האור בלב וירחב החזה[10]
ויתגלה לו סוד (עולם) המלכות[11] ותיעקר מן הלב מחיצת הסתת הדעת בחסד הרחמים ויבהיקו
מתוכו אמיתות הדברים האלוהיים ('חקאיק אלאמור אלאלאהיה'). ואין על האדם אלא להכין
עצמו על־ידי טיהור בלבד ועל־ידי הכנת שאיפתו עם רצון אמת וצימאון מלא וציפייה
מתמדת כבמארב למה שאללה יגלה מרחמיו. הנביאים והקדושים נגלה להם העניין ושפע
עליהם האור לא בשל הלימוד וכתיבת ספרים אלא על־ידי פרישות מן העולם ('באלזהד פי
אלדניא') וההתנערות מקשריו וריקון הלב מעסקיו ופנייה ממעמקי השאיפה אל האל
יתעלה. ומי שהוא לאללה – אללה יהיה לו. ויש לחשוב שהדרך היא קודם כל ניתוק
גמור של כל קשרי העולם וריקון הלב ממנו וקטיעת כל שאיפה למען המשפחה והרכוש
והילדים ו(ניתוק מן) מקום המגורים ('וטן') ו(התנתקות) מן המדע והשלטון והיוקרה. לבו של
האדם (צריך) להגיע למצב שבו מציאות כל דבר והיעדרו יהיו שווים בעיניו... ואם ייתכן
הדבר (גילוי הנסתר והעתיד) לנביא – ייתכן לזולתו, שכן הנביא פירושו אדם שנגלו לו
אמיתות הדברים האלוהיים והוא עסוק בתיקון הבריות.[12]

---

7   הקדמות לפירוש המשנה (לעיל, הערה 5), עמ' קנד במבוא שם. וראה המשנה בסוטה ט, טו.

8   ראה א' העשל, 'ההאמין הרמב"ם שזכה לנבואה?', ספר היובל ללוי גינצבורג, חלק עברי, ניו־יורק תש"ו, עמ'
     קנט–קפח. תודתי למשה גרינברג על שהפנה אותי למאמר זה. ועיין בספרי Studies in Al-Ghazzali,
     Jerusalem 1975, עמ' 297 ואילך, ובייחוד עמ' 304–305.

9   כאן משתמש אלגזאלי בלשון הניאופלטונית של האצלה ('פאץ'). ראה על כך בספרי שם, עמ' 307 ואילך.

10   על משמעות הביטוי הקוראני הזה ('שרח אלצדר') בכתבי אלגזאלי ראה שם, עמ' 284–290.

11   על שלושת העולמות בקוסמולוגיה של אלגזאלי ראה שם, נספח ג, עמ' 503–515.

12   אחיא עלום אלדין, קהיר 1356 להג'רה, עמ' 1377 (המשפט האחרון לקוח מעמ' 1379). אלגזאלי משתמש בהמשך

ג. בפירוש המשנה לפסחים ד, י עומד הרמב"ם על כך שחזקיהו המלך 'גנז ספר רפואות והודו לו', ומסביר שפירשו לו זאת 'ששלמה חיבר ספר רפואות שאם חלה אדם באיזה מחלה שהיא פנה אליו ועשה כמו שהוא אומר ומתרפא. ראה חזקיהו שלא היו בני אדם בוטחים בה' במחלותיהם אלא על ספר הרפואות – עמד וגנזו'. הסיפור עורר את רוגזו של הרמב"ם בשל 'אפסות דבר זה ומה שיש בו מן ההזיות', ובעיקר בשל ההנחה המונחת ביסודו: 'הנה ייחסו לחזקיה ולסיעתו שהודו לו סכלות שאין לייחס אלא לגרועים שבהמון (רעאע אלעאמה)'. ולפי דמיונם המשובש והמטופש אם רעב אדם ופנה אל הלחם ואכלו שמתרפא מאותו הצער הגדול בלי ספק – האם נאמר שהסיר בטחונו מה'? הוי שוטים – ייאמר להם – כי כמו שאני מודה לה' בעד האוכל שהמציא לי... כך נודה לו על שהמציא רפואה המרפאה את מחלתי כשאשתמש בה'.

נושא זה, המובא אצל הרמב"ם כבדרך אגב, הוא נושא מרכזי בדיוני הצופים המוסלמים על הביטחון באל (תַוֻכֻּל) וגבולותיו, ואלגזאלי מפתח את הגישות הצופיות המתונות לכדי תורה מסודרת בספר ה-35, ספר ייחוד האל והביטחון בו (כתאב אלתוחיד ואלתַוֻכֻּל), של 'אחיא עלום אלדין'. הוא עומד בהרחבה על כך שאמונת ייחוד נכונה מביאה בהכרח להכרה שהאל לבדו מסובב המסיבות ואין כי סיבה אחרת בלתו. מנקודת מוצא זאת הוא דן בשאלות שעלו בהקשר הצופי הקיצוני, כגון: האם מותר לאדם להסתכן מתוך ביטחון באל ולהיכנס, למשל, למדבר ללא מים וצידה? האם יש לנעול דלתות בפני הגנבים והאם מותר לאגור צורכי מזון? או האם ראוי לקחת תרופות בעת מחלה? אלגזאלי כמיסטיקאי משאיר מקום גם לביטחון קיצוני ובלתי מקובל, שהרמב"ם בוודאי היה מסתייג ממנו. אך גם אלגזאלי משתדל להרחיק את כלל ה'בוטחים' ממעשים מוזרים ומרחיקי לכת ומדגיש יותר את הצד הנפשי-אמונתי של ה'בוטח'. הוא מלגלג על תפיסתם הפגומה של ה'בוטחים' הקיצוניים בדברי לעג וגנאי המזכירים את דברי הרמב"ם, אך מפורטים בהרבה מהם. הנה דוגמה קטנה:

אם יושם לפניך אוכל כשאתה רעב וזקוק לו, אך לא תושיט אליו יד באמרך 'אני בוטח באל ותנאי לביטחון הוא עזיבת כל עשייה – והושטת היד היא עשייה ותנועה וכך גם הלעיסה בשיניים והבליעה...' – הרי זה שיגעון גמור ואין זה לבין הביטחון באל מאומה. ואם אתה מצפה שהאל יברא בך שובע ללא לחם או יברא בלחם תנועה אליך או יטיל על מלאך ללעוס ולהגיעו אל קיבתך – הרי אינך יודע את דרכו של אללה יתעלה. וכך אם לא תזרע את האדמה ותצפה שאללה יצמיח לך (תבואה) ללא זרע או שאשתך תלד מבלי משגל, כמו שילדה מרים עליה השלום, הרי כל זה שיגעון.[13]

במקום אחר באותו ספר מביא אלגזאלי סיפור מפי 'חכמי בני ישראל' על משה שחלה במחלה וסירב להתרפא ממנה באמרו: 'לא אתרפא (בתרופות) עד שירפאני הוא (האל) ללא תרופה'. גם כשארכה

בביטויו החביב עליו לציון התגלות פתע של האמת בלבנו לרגע קצר מועד ('כאלברק אלח'אטף'). גם הרמב"ם מדבר על האמת העולה במוחנו כברק מבריק, אך בלשון שונה ('ילוח אלחק כברק אלברק'). תודתי לתלמידי אליהו שטרן על שהסב את תשומת לבי למקבילה זאת.

13 ראה אחיא עלום אלדין, שם, עמ' 2529. הנס של הולדת ישו מבתולה נתקבל בקוראן, כמו גם סיפורי הנסים שישו עצמו עשה, אף-על-פי שהקוראן דוחה לחלוטין את סיפור צליבתו וקומו לתחייה. ישו נחשב לנביא ושליח, והקוראן מדגיש שכל סיפורי הנסים המיוחסים לו נעשו אך בכוחו וחסדו של האל.

מחלתו והחכמים הסבירו לו שהם מנוסים בטיפול בה, עמד בסירובו. אז נגלה אליו דבר האל לאמור:
'נשבעתי בכבודי ובעוזי שלא ארפאך עד שתתרפא ב(תרופות) שהזכירו לך'. משה הסכים לטיפול,
אך לבו נתמלא הרהורים על כך. ושוב שמע את דברי אללה לאמור: 'רצית לבטל את חכמתי בשל
בטחונך בי, אך מי זולתי שם בצמחי המרפא את התועלת?!'[14] אלגזאלי גם מוסיף שהנביא מוחמד
נהג לקחת תרופות ולשמור על בריאותו באורח קבוע.[15] למרות הדמיון לתפיסת הרמב"ם בנושאים
אלה – אין גם כאן כל דמיון לשוני בין דברי אלגזאלי לדברי הרמב"ם.

ד. מן המפורסמות הוא, שבשעה שדן הרמב"ם בעניין הקרבנות שהאל השאיר על כנם 'משום
שאי אפשר לצאת מן ההפך אל ההפך פתאום' ו'אי אפשר לפי טבע האדם שיניח כל מה שהורגל בו
פתאום' – הוא קושר לנושא גם את התפילה ואומר: 'והיה דומה אז כאילו יבוא נביא בזמננו זה,
שיקרא לעבודת השם ויאמר: השם ציווה אתכם שלא תתפללו אליו ולא תצומו ולא תבקשו תשועתו
בעת צרה, אבל תהיה עבודתכם מחשבה בלי מעשה' ('פכרה דון עמל').[16] אכן, נראה שהרמב"ם
עצמו מעדיף 'עבודה במחשבה בלי מעשה' או 'עבודה שבלב', אך הוא ידע שרוב הבריות לא יעמדו
בכך. והנה גם אלגזאלי מגלה עמדה דומה, ושוב בהקשר אחר לגמרי. אלגזאלי מונה שלוש דרגות
של ביטחון באל: הראשונה שבה האדם סומך על האל כעל אפוטרופסו או סוכן ביתו; השנייה –
הגבוהה ממנה – שבה האדם סומך על האל כתינוק על אמו, כשאינו מכיר זולתה איש ואינו מודע
כלל לבטחונו זה והיא ממלאת כל צרכיו. הדרגה השלישית והעליונה היא כשהאדם מפקיד עצמו בידי
האל 'כמת ביד המטהר'. הבוטח בדרגה הזאת שונה מן התינוק בכך שאינו זועק אל אמו ממהר
להחזיק בשולי בגדיה או לבקש ממנה דבר. לדברי אלגזאלי, דרגה זו של ביטחון מצמיחה 'את עזיבת
התפילה והבקשה מן (האל) מתוך ביטחון בנדיבותו ובהשגחתו ו(הידיעה) שהוא ייתן מלכתחילה יותר
מאשר יבוקש ממנו, ומה רבים החסדים שהעניק (האל) מלכתחילה ומבלי היות (האדם) ראוי'.[17]

ה. משלים ודוגמאות הלקוחים מעולם הרפואה שכיחים במיוחד בספרות ימי-הביניים, ולא רק
אצל אותם סופרים והוגים שהיו גם רופאים, כרמב"ם עצמו. כך למשל אלגזאלי, שלא היה רופא,
אוהב מאוד משלים כאלה ומרבה להביא גם דוגמאות להבהרה מעולם הרפואה. במיוחד נפוצה
בספרות היהודית והמוסלמית כאחת המשלת הנביאים לרופאי הנפש, המשלת תורה ומצוות
לתרופות והמשלת ההליכה אחר יצרי הנפש למחלות. והנה ב'אגרת תימן' הרמב"ם משתמש במשל
זה, יחד עם משל העיוור הסומך על המוביל אותו בדרך, כדי להמחיש לקוראיו שעל האדם לקבל
את דברי התורה והנביאים בלא ערעור, כשם שהוא מקבל את הוראות רופאיו, משום שהוא אינו
מבין לא במחלות גופו ולא במחלות נפשו ואינו יכול לדעת מה טוב לבריאותו:

ודע כי כמו שיניח הסומא הנהגתו והליכתו ביד הרואה, בעבור שידע שאין לו עינים שיורוהו
הדרך, וכמו שישים החולה אשר לא ידע ברפואות הנהגתו ביד הרופא שינהיגהו, בעבור

14   אחיא עלום אלדין, שם, עמ' 2564. רעיונות דומים אפשר למצוא אצל בחיי אבן פקודה ור' אברהם בן הרמב"ם
בפרקיהם על הביטחון באל ('תַוַכֻּל').
15   'הרפואה הנבואית' ('אלטב אלנבוי') תופסת מקום חשוב הן בספרות המוסלמית הרפואית והן בספרות הענף על
נוהגי הנביא. גם בתחום זה מוחמד נחשב למקור חיקוי ואינפורמציה עיקרי.
16   מורה הנבוכים חלק ג, ראשית פרק לב. ראה גם שם, פרק נא ('עבודה שבלב').
17   אחיא עלום אלדין (לעיל, הערה 12) עמ' 2522. התפילה שאלגזאלי מזכיר בהקשר זה היא תפילת רשות וֶרבלית
('דֻעַא') הנאמרת בסוף התפילה, אך לא עצם תפילת החובה היומית, שעיקרה השתחוויה וסגידה.

שאינו יודע העניינים הממיתים והמצילים, ויקבל ממנו כל מה שיאמר לו, כן יאות (ראוי) להמון[18] שיסגירו הנהגתם אל הנביאים בעלי הראות האמתי ויחזיקו (ויסתפקו) במה שילמדום... שעצה פלונית בריאה (נכונה) ועצה פלונית חולה (בלתי נכונה)...[19]

והנה בדיוק כך מתאר אלגזאלי את הנביאים:

כללו של דבר: הנביאים הם רופאי מחלות הנפש ואילו שכלנו זה כוחו וזו תועלתו, שהוא מודיע ומעיד על האמת שבנבואה ועל חוסר האונים של עצמו באין לו יכולת לרדת לעומקם של הדברים הנתפשים בעין הנבואה. אותה שעה יאחז בידינו וימסור אותנו לידיה כדרך שנוהגים למסור עיוורים לידי מדריכים, וחולים נבוכים לידי רופאים רחמנים...[20]

האם מותר ללמוד מדוגמאות אלה (ורבות אחרות כמותן, שבוודאי ניתן למצוא בכתבי הרמב"ם) משהו על השפעתם של כתבי אלגזאלי על הרמב"ם? אף־על־פי שבחרתי בדוגמאות ייחודיות – נראה לי שהדברים עוד צריכים עיון. הנושאים הללו נידונו בהגות הערבית בימי הביניים, ובמיוחד אצל הצופים, וחותמו האישי של אלגזאלי ולשונו אינם ניכרים בניסוחי הרמב"ם שהבאתי. ואם בנושאים ייחודיים כך – קל וחומר בנושאים כלליים נפוצים יותר. כך, למשל, דומים מאוד דברי הרמב"ם בהלכות תשובה[21] לדברי אלגזאלי המרחיב בנושא על התשובה שב'אחיא עלום אלדין'.[22] ואולם הדין הזה רווח מאוד בספרות הערבית וביחוד הצופית, ועל כן אין ללמוד מן הדמיון בין השניים אלא שהרמב"ם הכיר את הספרות הערבית הדתית וכנראה גם הושפע ממנה. אולם דבר זה הוא מן המפורסמות שאינן צריכות ראיה.

הוא הדין ביחסו המסייג של הרמב"ם לנסים כראיה לאמיתות הנבואה, הדומה מאוד לעמדתו של אלגזאלי בעניין זה. במשנה תורה אומר הרמב"ם:

משה רבינו לא האמינו בו ישראל מפני האותות שעשה. שהמאמין על־פי האותות יש בלבו דופי שאפשר שיעשה האות בלט וכישוף. אלא כל האותות שעשה משה לפי הצורך עשאם. לא להביא ראיה על הנבואה היה צריך להשקיע את המצרים, קרע את הים והצלילן בתוכו... ובמה האמינו בו? במעמד הר סיני שעינינו ראו ולא זר ואזנינו שמעו ולא אחר האש והקולות והלפידים... ומנין שמעמד הר סיני לבדו היא הראיה לנבואתו שהיא אמת שאין בה דופי? שנאמר: הנה אנכי בא אליך בעב הענן בעבור ישמע העם בדברי עמך וגם בך יאמינו לעולם...[23]

18   'ג'מהור אלעאלמין' – הכוונה לכלל בני־האדם. קאפח מתרגם במקום זה:: 'המוני החכמים'. ראה ההסבר לדבריו
      בתוך: אגרות ותשובות מאת רבינו משה בן מימון (מקור ותרגום), תרגם לעברית, ביאר והכין עפ"י כתבי יד
      ודפוסים הרב יוסף בן דוד קאפח, ירושלים תשמ"ז, עמ' מה, הערה 77. דבריו אינם נראים לי נכונים.
19   ראה תרגום אבן חסדאי במהדורת הלקין, ניו־יורק תשי"ב, עמ' 74.
20   ראה הפודה מן התעייה והטעות (לעיל, הערה 6), עמ' 66, ועיין גם שם, עמ' 65.
21   ראה, למשל, משנה תורה, הלכות תשובה ב, א–ד.
22   אחיא עלום אלדין (לעיל, הערה 12), שם, כתאב אלתובה, חלק ד, ספר ד, רכן ראשון, עמ' 2078 ואילך. וראה:
      S.M. Stern, 'Al-Ghazzali, Maimonides and Ibn Paquda on Repentance – A Comparative
      Model', *Journal of the American Academy of Religion* XLVII/4 (1979), pp. 589-607
23   ראה משנה תורה, הלכות יסודי תורה ח, א.

הדברים הללו חוזרים גם במורה הנבוכים, ודברים דומים מופיעים גם באיגרת תימן.[24] והנה, גם
אלגזאלי נקט עמדה דומה מאוד ביחס לנסים בספרו האוטוביוגרפי הידוע, אם כי בספרים קדומים
ו'כבדים' יותר כמו 'תהאפת אלפלאספה' (מפלת הפילוסופים) הוא מדגיש בוויכוחו עם הפילוסופים
את חשיבותם של הנסים.[25] ואלה דבריו בפרק על 'אמיתות הנבואה והזדקקות כל הבריות אליה':

על כן בדרך זו (בחינת הליכות הנביא ואמרותיו) הוי מבקש את האמונה הוודאית בנבואה
ולא בדרך הפיכת המטה לנחש או בקיעת הירח.[26] אם אתה מסתכל בנסים בלבד ואינך מוסיף
עליהם את המסיבות הרבות המלוות אותם ושאין להם מנין – עלול אתה להרהר שאין כאן
אלא כישוף ואחיזת עינים או התעיה מצד אללה... אם לאמונתך משמשים יסוד מופתי הגיון
על כוחו המושכל של הנס – תתמוטט אמונתך כאשר יוטחו נגדך דברים ערוכים היטב על
הספק והסתום שבנס. יהיו נא, אפוא, נסים כגון אלה רק אחת הראיות והמסיבות המעצבות
את כלל השקפתך, עד אשר תרכוש ידיעת-ודאי הכרחית, שאין בידך עוד להביא לה
אסמכתא מדויקת.[27]

ייתכן שאפשר לשייך לנושאים נפוצים מסוג זה גם את הדיון בענייני לשון, השאלה ומשמעויות
שונות של מלה ושורש ('אסם מֻשתרכّ'), שהרמב"ם עוסק בו בהרחבה בחלק הראשון של מורה
הנבוכים ואלגזאלי חוזר אליו מדי פעם בכתביו,[28] וכן בנושא הסבוך של היחס בין אמונה למעשה,
שבו דן הרמב"ם לפעמים בצורה דומה לאלגזאלי.[29]

מכל מקום, גישתו של אלגזאלי ולשונו[30] אינם ניכרים בדברי הרמב"ם אפילו בדוגמאות
הייחודיות שהבאתי לעיל. גם נקודות המוצא של אלגזאלי ועמדתו הכללית שונות מאוד מאלו של
הרמב"ם. על כן יהיה עלינו למצוא דוגמאות נוספות ומשכנעות יותר מן המובאות כאן כדי להוכיח
השפעה ישירה מן המיסטיקאי האנטי-פילוסופי המוסלמי הגדול על הרמב"ם.

---

24 ראה מורה הנבוכים, חלק ג, פרק כד, שם הוא מזכיר את המשך דבריו בהלכות יסודי תורה ח, ג על נביא (שקר)
שעושה אותות ומופתים; וראה איגרת תימן, מהדורה הלקין, ניו-יורק תשי"ב, עמ' 54–55. ראה גם H.A.
Wolfson, 'The Veracity of Scripture', *Religious Philosophy, A Group of Essays*, New York 1965,
pp. 220-222 (במראה המקום שם ממשנה תורה חלה טעות).

25 ראה כל הפרטים הביבליוגרפים: Al-Gazel, *Tahafot Al-Falasifat*, texte arabe établi par Maurice
Bouyges, S.J., Beyrouth 1927 (Bibliotheca Arabica Scholasticorum, série arabe II), pp. 271-276

26 נס המיוחס לנביא מוחמד על סמך הפסוק הראשון בסורה נד – 'סורת הירח'.

27 הפודה מן הטעות והטעייה (לעיל, הערה 6), עמ' 64. וראה גם שם, עמ' 50–51.

28 ראה, למשל, פירוט הנושא בספר שכתב אלגזאלי בסוף ימיו ושמו 'אלגّאם אלعואם عن עלם אלכلאם' ('מניעת
פשוטי עם מלעסוק בכלام').

29 ראה בספריו על אלגזאלי (לעיל, הערה 8), פרק ו, על מקומן של המצוות בתורתו. עיין גם י' טברסקי, מבוא
למשנה תורה לרמב"ם, תרגם מ"ב לרנר, ירושלים תשנ"א, עמ' 272–273, והערה 15 שם.

30 שני אלה נראים לי תנאים הכרחיים לדיון בהשפעה אפשרית, אולם יש הסוברים אחרת. כך, למשל, מציע עמיתי
מ"ע פרידמן לדון ביחס שבין משל אלגזאלי על זיד זבית וכיו"ב לבין משל הארמון במורה הנבוכים ג, נא,
אף-על-פי שאין כל דמיון לשוני ביניהם. משל 'זיד זבית' נמצא באחיא עלום אלדין (לעיל, הערה 12), עמ'
1371–1372, ותרגום שלו מצוי בנספח ב בספריו על אלגזאלי (לעיל, הערה 8), עמ' 490–491. משל דומה יותר
למשל הארמון נמצא בספר פחות ידוע של אלגזאלי, הנושא את השם 'אלגّام עن עלם אל-עואم عن עלם אל-כלאם', והוא
כלול בקובץ מבחר מכתבי אלגזאלי שערך מחמد מצטפא אבו אל-עלא (קהיר חש"ד), עמ' 92–93.

הפרשנות הפשטית של ההיסטוריה המקראית –
בין היסטוריות, דוגמטיות ובינייميות*

אוניברסיטת בר-אילן

ברכת "לֵךְ בכוחך זה"
לחוקר מקרא אוהב תורה
המהין לגשת אל הערפל אשר שם האלוהים

המקרא כולו, מ'בראשית' ועד 'ויעל', נתון במסגרת ההיסטוריוגרפית, אשר משובצים בה גם קובצי
החוק וספרי הנבואה. רק ספרות החכמה ומרביתה של השירה המקראית אינן מעוגנות בזמן באורח
משמעותי. ההיסטוריות הזאת, המבליטה את חילופי העתים ושינויי הזמנים והמכירה מעצם טבעה
ביחסיות שהזמן גרמה, אינה מתיישבת בנקל עם מערכת של אמונות ודעות החותרת למוחלטות
על-זمنית. הדוגמטיקה היהודית לגבי קדושת המקרא ולגבי נצחיות המצוות עוצבה בידי חז"ל
באמצעות פרשנות מדרשית, שאיפשרה להם להפקיע את המקרא במידה רבה מן ההיסטוריות
המובהקת שלו.[1] אולם בימי הביניים, כאשר ביקשו פרשני הפשט להבין את המקרא כפשוטו תוך
קבלת סמכותם הדוגמטית של חז"ל, חזר ונתעצם המתח שבין היסטוריות לבין דוגמטיות. יתרה
מזאת: הרתיעה מן היחסיות שבהתהיג ההיסטורית מהותית לא רק למחשבת חז"ל, אלא גם
לרציונליزם הביניايمی לזרמיו, החותר אף הוא אחר המופשט, המוחלט והיציב. מן הראוי אפוא לברר
באיזו מידה נפתחו פרשני הפשט הבินייميים (מרב סעדיה גאون ועד דון יצחק אברבנאל) אל
הפרספקטיבה ההיסטורית של המקרא, ובאיזו מידה מנעו זאת בעדם האמונות והדעות המוחזקות
בידם מכאן ודרכי החשיבה הביניايمיות המקובלות עליהם מכאן.

פרק א: באין יצירה היסטוריוגרפית עכשווית –
תהיית המפרשים לגבי תכליתה של ההיסטוריוגרפיה המקראית

ר' משה אבן עזרא[2] תולה בתלאות הגלות שני מחדלים תרבותיים-רוחניים חמורים: האחד –

נוסח ראשון של מאמר זה נידון בכנס על 'גישות יהודיות כלפי ההיסטוריה', שהתקיים באוניברסיטת הרוורד
באוקטובר 1994.

[1] ראה משה דוד הר, 'תפיסת ההיסטוריה של חז"ל', דברי הקונגרס העולמי השישי למדעי היהדות, כרך ג, חטיבה
ג, ירושלים תשל"ה, עמ' 129–142.

[2] ספר העיונים והדיونים, ההדיר ותרגם לעברית אברהם שלמה הלקין, ירושלים תשל"ה, עמ' 49–53.

הזנחת הדיבור העברי, חקר הלשון והיצירה הספרותית, והשני – הזנחת הכתיבה ההיסטורית בישראל. רק שמירת 'מצוות התורה וחוקי הדת' החזיקה מעמד במצב המתמשך של אבדן הריבונות, פיזור בין העמים וטמיעה תרבותית מאונס ומרצון: 'ודבקה בקודמינו ובאבותינו ז"ל הרשלנות – לא, כי החטא – שלא דאגו להחזיק בשפתם ולהקפיד על עבריותם, ולא השכילו ללטוש את לשונם ולערוך את קורותיהם ולזכור את תולדותיהם ומסורותיהם'. טיעונו המפורט בזכות חידוש היצירה ההיסטוריוגרפית פותח בטענה, המתעלמת הקודמת מהאשמתו בדבר חיקוי דרכי העמים ואימון לשונותיהם: 'הלא ראו – ואין משיב ואין טוען נגדם – שכל האומות התאמצו לכתב את דברי ימיהם ולהצטיין בהם'. האמביוולנטיות שלו לגבי הצבת תרבות הגויים כמופת לישראל מחייבת אותו שלא להסתפק בכך ולהשתית את הדרישה הזאת על בסיס איתן בכתבי הקודש. ואלה ארבע ראיותיו:

1. מפי הגבורה נצטווינו כמה וכמה פעמים על כתיבה היסטורית: 'כתוב זאת זכרון' (שמ' יז, יד), 'עתה בא כָּתבה על לוח אתם ועל ספר חֻקה ותהי אחרון לָעַד עד עולם' (יש' ל, ח), 'ועתה כִּתבו לכם את השירה הזאת' (דב' לא, יט).

2. איוב התאווה לכתוב אוטוביוגרפיה מורליסטית: 'מי יתן אפוא ויכָּתבון מִלָּי' (איוב יט, כג).

3. הכתובים מוכיחים שתפקיד ההיסטוריוגרפיה הוא לשמר את קורות העבר בעבור הדורות הבאים: 'והודעתם לבניך ובני בניך' (דב' ד, ט), 'אשר שמענו ונדעם' (תה' עח, ג).

4. בתקופת המקרא עשו זאת מלכינו ('הלא הם כתובים על ספר דברי הימים למלכי יהודה ולמלכי ישראל' – מל"א טו, ז) ונביאינו ('הנם כתובים על דברי נתן הנביא' – דה"א כט, כט) וגם מלכי פרס ומדי (אס' י, ב).

אין בפיו טיעון מקביל לגבי ההזנחה האחרת, משום שהיא כבר באה על תיקונה כמה דורות לפני הרמב"ע, כאשר יהודי ספרד עשו גדולות בתחומי הלשון העברית ושירת הקודש והחול, באמצם בגלוי ובמפורש את הדגם הערבי. ואילו המחדל האחר עמד בעינו – עד לאחר הגירוש נמנעו היהודים מלכתוב היסטוריוגרפיה יהודית על דרך שעשו הערבים והנוצרים. יוצאות מכלל זה שתי כרוניקות תרבותיות – הראשונה מאת ר' משה אבן עזרא עצמו, שייחד את הפרק הבא בספרו זה (עמ' 54–87) לתולדות המשוררים העבריים בספרד מראשיתן בשנות השלושים של המאה העשירית ועד ימיו; והשנייה, כעשרים שנה לאחר מכן, מאת ר' אברהם אבן דאוד, שסקר ב'ספר הקבלה' את תולדות הרבנות בישראל ממשה רבנו ועד לחכמי ספרד וחצרניה שבימיו. שני החריגים האלה, שנועדו להעניק תוקף היסטורי להישגים התרבותיים, הרוחניים והחברתיים של יהדות ספרד, מחזקים על דרך הניגוד את אחד ההסברים הרווחים להיעדרה של היסטוריוגרפיה יהודית פנימית – לעם מפוזר ומפורד אין הישגים מדיניים, צבאיים וממלכתיים שהוא יכול להתפאר בהם ולהנחיל את זכרם לבניו. כמשקל-נגד להוויה הגלותית המתמשכת יכולים לשמש רק עברו המפואר, המונצח בהיסטוריוגרפיה המקראית, ועתידו הזוהר, המובטח בנבואה המקראית. כך מבצר המקרא בקרב 'העם המושפל' את תודעת היותו 'העם הנבחר'.[3]

---

3 היטיב לסכם כל זאת ארנלדו מומיליאנו: 'On the one hand the postbiblical Jews really thought they had in the Bible all the history that mattered: superevaluation of a certain type of history implied underevaluation of all other events. On the other hand the whole development of

לא ייפלא אפוא, שלא ראיתי בין בעלי הפשט מפרש שיבאר כמו משה אבן עזרא את הפסוקים
הרבים שהביאם כאסמכתות לחובה לכתוב היסטוריה בכל הזמנים. ואכן, מי שאינו מעמיד את
תקופת המקרא ואת תקופת הגלות על מישור עקרוני אחד לא יעלה על דעתו לבאר את 'כתב זאת
זכרון בספר' (שמ' יז, יד) כמצווה לדורות, אלא ייסב את הצו על הקשרו (מלחמת עמלק), כראוי
לבעל הפשט. והוא הדין לגבי שאר הכתובים.

יתר על כן, בקרב פרשני הפשט ניכרת מבוכה לגבי המשמעות הדתית של ההיסטוריה המקראית
גופה. הרלוונטיות של החוקים – שבהם היתה התורה צריכה להתחיל, לדברי המדרש שבו פותח
רש"י את פירושו – ברורה, שכן הם תקפים גם היום. הרלוונטיות של הנבואות על הגאולה העתידה
ברורה אף היא, שכן הן תתקיימנה מחר. אך הרלוונטיות של ספר בראשית ושל שאר הספרים
ההיסטוריים (ואף של הנבואות שכבר נתקיימו) טעונה הנמקה והצדקה באשר הם בחזקת עבר שחלף.
אמת, הספקות אינם מוסבים על עצם נחיצותו של הזיכרון ההיסטורי, שכן מצוות הזכירה חוזרת
ונשנית בכתוב לגבי מאורעות מכוננים כמו שעבוד מצרים, היציאה לחירות, ההליכה במדבר
וחציית הירדן, ואף לגבי מאורעות משניים שלקחם בצדם כמו מלחמת עמלק וצרעת מרים.[4] הקושי
הוא בהיסטוריה האישית של האבות והמלכים, וביתר שאת ברשימות יחסי של עמים אחרים, אשר
לגביהן אפשר, לכאורה, לומר 'מאי דהוה הוה' (יומא ה, ע"א; כתובות ג, ע"א).[5]

על דרך ההכללה ניתן לומר שהפתרון המקובל הוא תיאולוגיזציה ומורליזציה של סיפורי ספר
בראשית ושל ההיסטוריוגרפיה המקראית בכללה, תוך הקפדה שלא להיגרר למטפוריזציה,
המפקיעה אותן ממשמעותן ההיסטורית.[6] זו היתה דרכם של חז"ל במדרשיהם,[7] ואילו לבעלי הפשט

Judaism led to something unhistorical, eternal, the Law, the Torah. The significance which the
Jews came to attach to the Torah killed their interest in general historiography.' (Arnaldo
Momigliano, *The Classical Foundations of Modern Historiography*, Berkeley–Los Angeles–Oxford
1990, p. 23. וראה בהרחבה ובעמקות יוסף חיים ירושלמי, זכור – היסטוריה יהודית וזיכרון יהודי, תירגם
מאנגלית שמואל שביב, תל-אביב תשמ"ח, עמ' 21–60.

4   ראה את ההבחנה החשובה של ירושלמי (זכור, עמ' 27–30, 60–67) בין זיכרון היסטורי – הנשמר באמצעותם
     של חגים, טקסים ותפילות – לבין כתיבה היסטורית.

5   מאלפת עדותו של רד"ק בהקדמת פירושו לדברי הימים: 'ולפי שהספר הזה הוא ספור דברי הימים הוא הרגילו
     ללמדו, ולא ראיתי לאחד מן המפרשים שהשתדלו בפירושו. אלא שמצאתי הנה בנרבונ"א פירושים בזה הספר
     לא ידעתי שמות מחבריהם, וראיתי כי הם הולכים בדרך הדרש ברוב'.

6   כסייג בפני המטפוריזציה הקראית של מצוות מסוימות טוען רס"ג, שכשם שדרך ביאור רדיקלית זו עלולה
     להפקיע את תוקפן של המצוות המעשיות, כך היא עלולה גם להפקיע את הנסים ממשמעותם ההיסטורית (ראה:
     אמונות ודעות, ז, ב). בדרך דומה מגן גם ראב"ע על חלותן של המצוות ועל ההיסטוריות של סיפורי בראשית
     כנגד האליגוריזציה הנוצרית, המותירה לאלה ולאלה כאחד משמעות רוחנית נסתרת בלבד: '(הדרך) האחת, היא
     דרך חכמי הערלים / האומרים כי כל התורה חידות ומשלים / ככה כל הדברים / שהם בספר בראשית נאמרים /
     גם ככה כל המצות והחוקים הישרים' (הקדמת 'השיטה האחרת' לתורה, בתוך המקראות הגדולות תורת חיים א,
     ירושלים תשמ"ו, עמ' רצט). וכאשר הוא עצמו בא להציע ביאור אלגורי לסיפור גן עדן, הריהו מקדים ומכריז
     שאין בכך כדי לערער באיזו צורה שהיא את העובדתיות ההיסטורית של הסיפור: 'דע כי כל מה שמצאנו כתוב
     הוא אמת, וכן היה ואין בו ספק, ויש לו סוד' (הפירוש לבר' ג, כד).

7   טיפוסיות לכך הן התשובות שניתנו לקביעה הבוטה של ריש לקיש: 'הרבה מקראות שראויין לשרוף והן גופי
     תורה' (ראה: חולין ס, ע"ב) ול'הגדות של דופי' שיוחסו למנשה, הרשע שבמלכי יהודה: 'וכי לא היה לו למשה
     לכתוב אלא "ואחות לוטן תמנע, ותמנע היתה פלגש לאליפז" (בר' לו, יב)?' (ראה: סנהדרין צט, ע"ב).

התווה גם בזאת את הדרך רב סעדיה גאון.[8] בהקדמתו לפירוש הארוך לספר בראשית,[8] הוא קובע
שהמצוות הן אכן עיקרה של התורה, אולם לצורך ההשפעה החינוכית המרבית אין הן נמסרות באורח
מקובץ ומסודר, אלא מוקפות באזהרות ובהבטחות ובהמחשה סיפורית של מה שאירע
למקיימיהן ולמפיריהן מכאן.[9] בהתאם לכך שכיחה בגוף הפירוש מנייה ממוספרת של הלקחים
שצריך להפיק מן הסיפור (כגון בעמ' 225, 226, 236, 251, 277, 356, 390, 399), שיטה שהגיעה
לידי שכלול קיצוני ב'תועליות' הממוספרות של הרלב"ג, הממוינות לשלושה סוגים: 'תועלת
במצוות' (שהן עיקר תכליתה של התורה), 'תועלת במידות' (ר"ל הלקח המוסרי המומחש בסיפור)
ו'תועלת בדעות' (ר"ל דעת העולם ודעת הבורא המשוקעות בסיפור).[10] בניגוד גמור לכל אלה לא
נחה דעתו של ר' יהודה החסיד עד שהעמיד את התורה כולה על ההלכה בלבד, כפי שמעיד עליו
בנו: 'אבי היה מקשה: למה אנו מברכין על ג' פסוקים ברכת התורה, והלא כמה פסוקים יש שאין
בהם תורה (ר"ל הלכות!), והוא היה אומר שמבראשית ועד לעיני כל ישראל אין ג' פסוקים זה אצל
זה אם אין דין יוצא מהן או איסור והתר. והקשתי לו הרבה ותירץ הכל'.[11]

גם אותם המפרשים שלא תפסו כר' יהודה החסיד את המושג 'תורה' באורח הלכתי בלעדי, אלא כללו
בו גם הוראת דרך דתית-מוסרית ואף הרחבת דעת מדעית-פילוסופית, לא החשיבו את ידיעת
ההיסטוריה גופה כחלק ממה שהתורה באה ללמדנו. אף-על-פי-כן לא יכול היה רב סעדיה גאון
להתעלם מן האופי ההיסטורי המובהק של פרקים מסוימים בתורה, ותחת להידחק ולהוציאם מידי
פשוטם, הוא העז להסיק מהם שאכן יש בתורה מקום (אף כי משני) להרחבת-דעת היסטורית. וכך
הוא אומר בהמשך הקדמתו, שמצויים בתורה גם שלושה סוגי עניינים שהם בעליל 'במדרגה
תחתונה, אבל גם בהם יש תועלת, כי לא ייתכן שתכיל התורה דברים נטולי תועלת' (עמ' 175).
ואלה הם:

(1) כרונולוגיה ופריודיזציה – 'שישמחו בהם (בציוני הזמן) הבריות ויתעודדו בהכרת מספר
השנים שעברו מראשית בריאת העולם עד ימיהם הם. ויחד עם זאת הודיע לנו את חלקיהם ופרקיהם:
כך וכך שנים מדור פלוני עד דור פלוני, כדי שיהיה במחשבתנו כנר המאיר וכתחנה מחלק אחד של
הזמן לחלק שני, כמו שכל אחד מאנשי התורה מרגיש בנפשו' (עמ' 180).[12]

---

8   פירושי רב סעדיה גאון לבראשית, ההדיר ותירגם מערבית משה צוקר, ניו-יורק תשמ"ד, עמ' 171–175.

9   גם יפת בן עלי הקראי מוצא לנחוץ להדגיש בפירושו הערבי לבר' ג, א, שהחלק הסיפורי שבמקרא הוא בגדר
תורה שחייבים ללמדה ביסודיות: 'ואף על פי שאין (הכתוב מדבר על) מצוה, הרי חובה לדעת (גם) את הידיעות
(ההיסטוריות) [אכ'באר] שבמקרא לאמתן, ועתיד האדם לקבל שכר על יגיעתו בלימוד ובבירור הדעה (הנכונה)'
(מובא ע"י חגי בן-שמאי, 'שיטות המחשבה הדתית של אבו יעקוב אלקרקסאני ויפת בן עלי', עבודת דוקטור,
האוניברסיטה העברית, ירושלים תשל"ח, כרך ב, עמ' קיח–קכ, נספח ב/21; תרגום עברי: כרך א, עמ' 24).

10   גם ר' יוסף אבן כספי (בן ארצו של רלב"ג, המבוגר ממנו בשנים ספורות) מרבה לומר, שמן הסיפור יש להפיק
'תועלות גדולות ורבות'. אך לרוב אין זה הוא מפרט אלא את העיקרית שבהן. ראה: משנה כסף, מהדורה יצחק הלוי
לאסט, כרך א, פרסבורג תרס"ה (דפוס צילום: ירושלים תשל"ל), עמ' 95, 97, 100.

11   פרושי התורה לר' יהודה החסיד, מהדורה יצחק שמשון לנגה, ירושלים תשל"ה, עמ' 55.

12   לא זו בלבד שרס"ג עסק בכרונולוגיה מקראית ובתר-מקראית, אלא שהוא ראה בכך תיקון לחוסר ההתעניינות
בהיסטוריה מצד חכמי דורו. הוא מעיד על כך בקטע ששרד מן ההקדמה לספר הגלוי שאבד, ובה הוא סוקר את
תוכנם של שערי הספר: 'והשער השני [יכיל] חשבון השנים. כמה ארכה הנבואה [אצל] אומתנו. ובארתי שהיתה
אלף שנים. ולכמה שנים נגמר קבוץ המשנה. והודעתי שזה היה ת"ק [שנה] אחרי כן. ולכמה שנים נגמר

(2) גיניאלוגיה, אתנוגרפיה וגיאוגרפיה – 'שנמצא קורת רוח בידיעת היחוסים האלה, כי נפשנו דורשת מאתנו את ידיעתם, למען יהיה האדם (ר"ל האנושות) בעינינו כעץ שנטעו אלוהים בארץ, ויסתעפו ענפיו ויתפשטו מזרחה ומערבה, צפונה ונגבה בחלק המיושב של הארץ. וכדי שנראה את הרבים בדמות היחיד ואת היחיד בדמות הרבים (מסתבר שכוונתו לטיפולוגיה אתנית), ועם זה ישים האדם את דעתו גם לשמות הארצות והערים' (שם).

(3) דמוגרפיה – 'שתדע איך התרבה העם אחרי היותו מעט... ושנדע מה רב היה המון האנשים שראו את המופתים של השליח ושמעו את דברי אלוהים על ההר...' (שם). [13]

גם הרשב"ם, שלא הכיר את פירושי רס"ג הכתובים ערבית ושהשפעתו עליו היתה לכל היותר עקיפה, לא יכול היה להתעלם מן החשיבות שהמקרא מקנה למידע הכרונולוגי. על הפסוק 'ויהי כל ימי למך' (בר' ה, לא) הוא מקשה: 'למה לנו למנות שני רשעים הכתובים בפרשה?' ומתרץ:

דכך דרכן של נביאים: זה אחר זה כדי לידע מניין השנים מבריאת העולם עד ימיהם. כי מתוך השנים ומניינם הכתובים כאן, ומניין שנות הדורות הכתובים עד משה רבינו, ומניין שעבוד מצרים דכתיב 'ומושב בני ישראל אשר ישבו בארץ מצרים וגו'' (שמ' יב, מ) ומניין מ' [ר"ל ארבעים שנות הנדודים במדבר] למדנו מניין שנים אשר מבריאת עולם עד שנכנסו ישראל לארץ. וכבר מפורש בנביאים מניין השנים אשר מיציאת מצרים עד בנין בית ראשון (כוונתו למל"א ו, א), ומבנינו עד חרבנו. ומתוך דברי דניאל למדנו מניין השנים אשר מחרבן בית ראשון עד חרבן בית שני, וכתב על זה 'שבועים שבעים נחתך על עמך' (דנ' ט, כד) פי שבעים מגלות בבל, וד' מאות ועשרים שעמד בית שני, הרי כאן שבע פעמים שבעים שנה, וזהו 'שבועים שבעה' (וראה גם ביאורו לשמ' ו, טז).

ואילו ר' אברהם אבן עזרא, שהושפע מאוד מכתבי רס"ג, לא הלך בזאת בעקבותיו ולא הכיר בלגיטימיות הדתית–רוחנית של העניין האינטלקטואלי בהיסטוריה. לצורך ההבנה השלמה של

התלמוד. וכי כל אלה לא פסקו מלהיות נמסר בקבלה (ר"ל בעל-פה) עד העת שנכתבו. והסבה שהגיעה [אותי] לזה היא מפני שמצאתי כי [אנשים] הנקראים בשם הרבנים עתה לא יעמדו על זה ולא ילכו בדרך הקדמונים אשר יחיו בפיהם (הערת המתרגם: ר"ל אשר יזכירו אותם תמיד בפיהם) ואשר ממזונותיהם יתפרנסו' (אברהם אליהו הרכבי, השריד והפליט מספר האגרון וספר הגלוי [=זכרון לראשונים, מחברת חמישית], ס"ט פטרבורג תרנ"ב, עמ' קנב). הוא חוזר לעניין זה שנית תוך הבאת ראיה מן המקרא לחובה לחקור את העבר: 'והתבוננת אל מה שקדם מן הזמן וכמה שנים עברו כפי חשבון שנות המקרא והמשנה והתלמוד וחבורי האבות (הרכבי משער שהכוונה לספרות הבתר-תלמודית כגון המדרשים והמסכתות הקטנות). כמו שכתוב: "כי שאל נא לדור רישון וכונן לחקר אבותם" (איוב ח, ח)' (עמ' קס וראה גם עמ' קצד).

13 גם בהקדמת ספר הגלוי (הנזכר בהערה הקודמת) מציע רס"ג הסברים – בעיקר הלכתיים ומוסריים – להימצאותו של מידע סיפורי, היסטורי, גיניאלוגי וגיאוגרפי בתורה, אשר מאז ימי מנשה מלך יהודה ועד לימינו שלו משתמשים בו כדי לנגח את קדושת התורה (ראה עמ' קע-קעו). אך כמו בהקדמת התורה אין הוא חושש לומר שיש בתורה גם מידע גיאוגרפי הנחוץ לגופו, למשל כדי לזהות את השם העברי של הר עם השמות שבהם הוא קרוי בפי העמים השוכנים בקרבתו מעבר לגבול: 'ומהם מי שיאשים את הכתוב: צידונים יקראו לחרמון שריון והאמרי יקראו לו שניר' (דב' ג, ט). אולם זה [נכתב] להודיע להעם שמות אלה המקומות בלשונות שתי האומות הקרובות להם. מפני שאחורי ההר (ר"ל צדו שמעבר לגבול) [נקרא] בשם חרמון בעברית. אך לא נודע אלא בשמו הגלוי להקדמונים [השמות] המפורסמים לשתי האומות צידונים ואמורים' (עמ' קעו). והשווה לפירוש המדרשי הניתן על-ידי רש"י לכתוב הזה, ולביאורו של רמב"ן הקושר את הזיהוי הרב-לשוני עם הצדקת הכיבוש הישראלי שהיא הנושא של דב' ב-ג.

דברי הנביאים הוא אימץ באורח מתון ומבוקר את דרך הפירוש ההיסטוריסטי של ר' משה הכהן אבן
ג'קטילה, הקושרת את נבואות העתיד אל מאורעות היסטוריים ידועים או משוערים. הראב"ע מרבה
להביא ביאורים כאלה בשמו, וכאשר הוא מסתייג מהם, הסיבה היא תמיד פרשנית ולא עקרונית.
וכקודמו גם הוא איננו מהסס ללמוד מן הנבואה עצמה על עובדת התקיימותה, כשאין על כך ידיעה
היסטורית עצמאית (כגון בפירושיו ליש' יא, יא-יב; לה, ג-י).[14] המידע ההיסטורי מועיל במיוחד
להבנת נבואות לא-עתידיות (ר"ל שכבר התקיימו בעבר), שכן הוא מאפשר להבחין בבטחה ביניהן
לבין נבואות עתידיות, אשר בני הגלות הנוכחית רשאים לצפות למימושן הקרוב. אך כאשר מידע
כזה אינו מצוי בידינו, מוטב להודות על כך בגלוי (על דרך שהוא עושה בביאורו ל'כמספר הדדרמון
בבקעת מגדון' [זכ' יב, יא]: 'ואנחנו לא ידענו כל הקורות, ולהיותו רמז לאחאב ויאשיה – דרך דרש
הוא זה', והשווה לפירושו לבר' מט, יט). הראב"ע עושה זאת הן הכתרים בפני השלמתו המדרשית
של המידע החסר, והן כמענה לספקנים הנוטים לפקפק בתוקפן של נבואות קצרות-טווח שאין ראיה
מן הכתובים בדבר התקיימותם. ההסתייגות מזיהויים מדרשיים המקובלים בציבור כמבוססים על
הפשט באה, למשל, בביאוריו ליואל א, א ולעוב', פס' א; והתשובה ההחלטית לספקנים מצויה
בביאורו לחגי ב, כב, אשר בו הוא מודה, שאין לנו מידע לגבי ההתעוררות הבין-לאומית הכבירה,
שחגי חוזה מראש שתתרחש בימיהם של דריוש וארתחשסתא מלכי פרס ושל בן-זמנם זרובבל בן
שאלתיאל. והריהו מטעים, שהיעדר זה של עדות היסטורית (מקראית או בתר-מקראית) לא צריך
לערער את בטחוננו לגבי התקיימות דבר הנביא (על דרך שהוא אומר ביתר בהירות בפירושו לעמוס
ז, יא: 'אע"פ שלא מצאנו כתוב כי ירבעם מת בחרב, ידענו כי דבר השם אמת הוא...'). שכן חוסר
כל מידע לגבי מאורע מסוים אינו מוכיח בשום פנים שהוא לא התרחש, בעיקר לנוכח אבדנה של
הספרות ההיסטוריוגרפית הבתר-מקראית (המקביל לאבדן ספרי ההיסטוריוגרפיה החוץ-מקראית,
כמו 'ספר מלחמות ה'' ו'ספר הישר', שהוא מתייחס אליו בפירוש הארוך לשמ' יז, יד ובפירושו לבמ'
כא, יד). וכך הוא מנסח כל זאת בלשונו הקצרה:

> כי מלחמות רבות היו עתידות בימי הנביא (ר"ל בזמן שהוא התנבא על
> המלחמות היתה התקיימותן עדיין בגדר עתיד). וידענו כי כן היה, רק לא מצאנו ספרים
> לקדמונים (ר"ל מימי בית שני) לדעת המלחמות, שהיו בימי דריוש זה הפרסי (להוציא את
> דריוש המדי) ובימי ארתחשסתא המולך אחריו (להוציא את ארתחשסתא הראשון שקדמו).
> ובימיהם היה זרובבל הנשיא ליהודה, כי הוא ששבצר בראיות גמורות מן המקרא.[15]

מי שבטוח לחלוטין בכוחה של הנבואה לצפות מראש את מה שעתיד לבוא אינו זקוק לאישורה של
ההיסטוריוגרפיה שאכן כך הווה. לעומת זאת יכולה ההיסטוריוגרפיה לסייע בהבנת נבואות סתומות.
ואכן, בהקדמה הקצרה לספר זכריה דן הראב"ע בתועלת הפרשנית המוגבלת שניתן היה להפיק
להבנת נביאי שיבת ציון מן ההיסטוריוגרפיה האבודה של ימי הבית השני. בטרם ייגש לפרש את

14   על המקוריות והחלוציות של הפרשנות ההיסטוריסטית של ר' משה אבן ג'קטילה ועל מגבלותיה הבינ"ימיות
     המובהקות, וכן על עמדתו של ראב"ע כלפיו ראה: Uriel Simon, 'Ibn Ezra between Medievalism and
     Modernism: The Case of Isaiah xl-lxvi)', VTSup 36 (1985), pp. 257-265

15   הנוסח המוגה של דברי הראב"ע שבמבואה הזאת ובמובאה הבאה לקוח מתוך: אוריאל סימון, שני פירושי ר'
     אברהם אבן עזרא לתרי-עשר – מהדורה מדעית מבוארת, כרך ג (בהכנה).

הספר עליו להבהיר לקורא, עד כמה שונה ספר זכריה משאר ספרי הנביאים בגלל הידלדלות כוח
הנבואה בישראל. בימי הבית הראשון היתה הנבואה שופעת וכוח הקליטה של הנביאים רב, וכתוצאה
מכך היו הנבואות ברורות וגלויות, והנביא וקהל שומעיו כאחד הבינו על מי הן מוסבות. ואילו בזמן
הבית השני, שבו לא נתחדשו ימינו כקדם (כפי שהוא אומר גם בביאורו לזכ' יא, יב: 'שסר הכבוד
מעליהם בבית שני'), נתעמעמה הנבואה. דבר זה ניכר בספרי דניאל וזכריה, המתנבאים באמצעות
מראות לילה סתומות וחידתיים, אשר הם עצמם אינם מסוגלים לפענחם בלא עזרת מלאך. ומה
שהותיר המלאך ללא ביאור נותר סתום הן בעבור הנביא והן בעבור 'המשכילים' (ר"ל החכמים
שבקרב שומעיו ובקרב קוראיו עד היום הזה). בני הדורות הסמוכים לזמנו של הנביא, שחוו את
התממשות נבואותיו קצרות־הטווח, יכולים היו להבין את מראות זכריה לאור התקיימותם (על דרך
שהנבואה האסכטולוגית של דניאל עתידה להתפרש בימות המשיח: 'כי בגעת הקץ יבינו המשכילים
רמיזות המלאך' [הארוך לדנ' יב, ח־ט]). ואילו הפרשן המאוחר מנוע מזאת, משום שאין בידיו מקור
היסטורי לגבי מלחמות ישראל בימי הבית השני (שישלים את המעט הידוע מספרי עזרא ונחמיה
וממקורות חיצוניים כמו 'ספר יוסף בן גוריון' ו'ספר מלכי פרס', שהראב"ע מאזכרם בארוח
ספורדי[16]). יתרה מזאת, אף אילו שרד ספר כזה, עדיין היינו שרויים בחשכה, משום שהקישור שבין
הנבואה לבין המאורע המתועד במקור החיצוני יישאר בהכרח בגדר השערה. אמור מעתה: בגלל
אופיה העמום של הנבואה המאוחרת, ומשום שמראות זכריה מוסבים בעיקרם על מאורעות פוליטיים
וצבאיים שזכרם אבד, אין המפרש יכול להאיר את סתומותיו של הספר באותו שיעור כמו בספרי
הנבואה הקודמים. והרי דבריו בנוסח מוגה:

מעלות הנבואה הם רבות ואין דרך לספרם. כי כח הנשמו' ההגונות המקבלות כח רוח הקדש
להנבא אינינו על דרך אחת. ובהיות הכבוד עם ישראל בטרם שגלו, אין צורך לפרש הנבואה,
כמו 'הנה בן נולד לבית דוד יאשיהו שמו' (מל"א יג, ב), והיה הדבר מתבאר מעצמו. ואחר
הגלות הן 'מראות', וצריכות פירוש פירוש כמראות דניאל. כי לולי שהמלאך מפרש, לא היה דניאל

---

16 הוא מסתמך על 'ספר יוסף בן גוריון' בעיקר בבירורים כרונולוגיים ושושלתיים ובזיהויים גיאוגרפיים ואתניים
(ראה אזכורו ב'שיטה האחרת' לבר' י, ד, ובביאורו לחגי ב, ט; תה' קכ, ה; בפירוש הקצר לדנ', הנבואה השנייה
[מהד' אהרן מונדשיין, עמ' 26]; ובארוך לדנ' ב, לט) ופחות מכך לשם השלמת המידע ההיסטורי (ראה: יש' ב,
ב; הפירוש הקצר לדנ', הנבואה השלישית [שם, עמ' 58] ובארוך לדנ' יא, ד). בביאורו לבר' לז, כה הוא מצטט
מכלי שני את דעתו לגבי מהותו של הצורי, אך מעדיף לסמוך על הזיהוי של ר' ישמעאל (צ"ל ר' שמעון בן
גמליאל) במשנה (כריתות ו, א). הראב"ע קרא ב'ספר מלכי פרס' בהיותו על אדמת ספרד, עשרות שנים לפני
שחיבר את פירושיו (כפי שהוא מעיד בפירושו הארוך לדנ' ז, יד). שלושה עניינים נחרתו בזכרונו: (1) שאין בו
מידע אודות תקופת שלום ממושכת, שניגד לראותה כהתקיימות חזון השלום של ישעיה במחלוקת קשה (ראה פירושו ליש' ב,
ב); (2) מהו הסדר הנכון של מלכי פרס, הנשוי במחלוקת קשה (ראה: הקצר לדנ', הנבואה השנייה [שם, עמ'
25]; הארוך לדנ' ו, א; ז, יד; ט, כה; יא, ב); (3) נהגים שנהגו בארמון הפרסי, היכולים להאיר שני פסוקים
במגילת אסתר — א, ז, ח. שני הספרים האלה נחשבו בעיניו לאמינים, בחינת עדויות היסטוריות שנכתבו
בקרבת זמן למאורעות המתוארים בהם (ובכך דומה גישתו לזו של רש"י כלפי ספר יוסיפון, ראה ספר יוסיפון,
מהדורת דוד פלוסר, כרך ב [המבוא], ירושלים תשמ"א, עמ' 67–69). על כן לא חלה עליהם ההסתייגות
העקרונית שלו מספרי מדרש לא־היסטוריים: 'ואשר כתוב ב"דברי הימים דמשה" אל תאמין. וכלל אומר לך: כל
ספר שלא כתבוהו נביאים או חכמים מפי הקבלה (ר"ל חז"ל כאשר אינם מדברים בשם עצמם אלא מסתמכים על
מסורת היסטורית שבידם) אין לסמוך עליו, ואף כי (ר"ל על אחת כמה וכמה כאשר) יש בו דברים שמכחישים
הדעת הנכונה, וככה "ספר זרובבל" וגם "ס' אלדד הדני" והדומה להם (בארוך לשמ' ב, כב וראה גם: ד, כ).

יודעם ואף כי (ר"ל על אחת כמה וכמה) אחרים, וככה מראות זכריה. ואשר פירש המלאך
הדובר בו במראות הלילה הם ידועות, ואשר לא פירש הם סתומות ונעלמות מעיני
המשכילים. ואלו היינו מוצאים ספר קדמון, שהיה מספר מה שהתחדש בימים ההם ממלחמות,
היינו ממשמשים כעורים קיר לומר: אולי בעבור זאת הייתה הנבואה. ועתה אין לנו על
מה להשען.

הכרתו זאת במגבלות המעשיות והעקרוניות של הפרשנות ההיסטוריציסטית לא מנעה בעד הראב"ע
מלנסות להאחיז את הנבואות זכריה במעט שהיה ידוע לו מתולדות הבית השני (כגון ההתייחסות לימי
עזרא ונחמיה [בפירושו לזכ' ט, א; יא, ז] ולמלכות החשמונאים [שם, ט, ט, יא, יד, טו; י, א, ב,
יא, יב; יא, ב, ג, ד, ז]). עם זאת ברי שהעניין המוגבל והמסויג שהיה לו בהיסטוריה ככלל פרשני
לא הגיע לכדי ייחוס חשיבות עצמית לידיעות קורות העבר. הוא אומר זאת במפורש כשהוא מסביר
(בפירוש הארוך לדנ' יא, ד) מדוע הוא יסתפק בביאור לשוני ועניני של נבואת דניאל שכבר התקיימה,
אבל יתן ביאור מפורט של השתלשלות המאורעות המתוארת בנבואתו העתידה
להתקיים:

והנה אומר לך עתה כלל: כי מתחלת 'ויחזק מלך הנגב' (יא, ה) עד 'וזרעים ממנו יעמדו וחללו
המקדש המעוז' (יא, לא), שהוא בפירוש חרבן בית שני – מלחמות שעברו. ולזכור פרטיהן
(ר"ל למנות אותן אחת לאחת) ולחפש הספרים הקדמונים בספר 301 בודלי (כ"י: כספר) יוסף
בן גוריון – אילו היינו יודעין כל דבריו (ר"ל אפילו אם היינו מבינים כראוי את כל המסופר
בו), לא יועילנו עתה לדעת שעבר (ר"ל מה שעבר). ועל כן אפרש המלות והטעמים
בדרך כלל, ואחר חרבן הבית אפרש בדרך פרט עד 'וכעת קץ' (יא, מ; נוסח המסורה: 'ובעת',
וכך הגירסה גם בדפוס הראשון של הפירוש, ונציה רפ"ו) – כי משם הם העתידות שנשארו,
כאשר אפרש.

---

17 הרמב"ם, שלא היסס כידוע לשחזר על־פי ספרי הצאבה את טעמיהן הנשכחים של כמה מן המצוות, ביקש
    להסתייע גם במידע ההיסטורי הרמוז ברשימת מלכי אדום שבבר' לו, לא־לט, כדי להסביר את איסור המלכת
    מלך נכרי על ישראל (דב' יז, טו). בדומה לראב"ע הוא מודע היטב למיעוט הידיעות שבידינו, אך שלא כמוהו אין
    הוא מביע ספקנות מתודולוגיות לגבי יישומן הפרשני: 'כמו שהזכרתי לך מריחוק שיטתם ה"צאבה" ממנו היום,
    כך דברי ימי אותם הימים נעלמים ממנו היום. ואלו ידענום וידענו אותם המאורעות אשר אירעו באותם הימים,
    היו מתבארים לנו בפרטות הרבה ממה שנזכר בתורה' (מורה הנבוכים ג, נ).

18 הוא גם לא היה בטוח שיש בידיעת ההיסטוריה הפוליטית־ממלכתית תועלת מעשית, כפי שניכר מן ההתלבטויות
    שלו בין ביאור אסטרולוגי לביאור היסטורי של 'ידעי העתים' (אס' א, יג) ובין הסבר בידורי להסבר תועלתי
    לקריאת 'דברי הימים' באוזני המלך ששנתו נדדה (ו, א). לא כך לגבי ההיסטוריה התרבותית, שכן לדעתו אין
    להבין את סיפור מגדל בבל בארח מוסרני־תיאולוגי אלא בארח היסטורי. בלבול הלשונות אינו בגדר עונש על
    חטא, אלא תוצאה טבעית של הפיזור הגיאוגרפי: 'ויפץ ה' אותם – יש אומרים כי שכחו לשונם הראשון, ואין
    כתוב כך ככה, רק בלל לשונם – שהתחדש כל משפחה לשון בפני עצמו. ויתכן שהיה כן בשנה הראשונה, או ספר
    הכתוב מה שהיה באחרונה אחרי דורות רבות, וספר לנו זה שנדע למה אין לשון אחד לכל' (השיטה האחרת לבר'
    יא, ח).

19 טענה דומה בניסוחה ובתוכנה מעלה הראב"ע בביאורו לבר' ד, יט נגד הסבריו של רס"ג לשמות עצם פרטיים:
    'אל תשים לבך לשמוע אל דברי הגאון בשמות, כי אילו (ר"ל אף אילו) היינו יודעים כל לשון הקדש (ר"ל את
    העברית המקראית במלואה), מאין נוכל לדעת כל הקורות (ר"ל כל האירועים הביוגרפיים שאליהם מתייחסים
    השמות) כטעם משה וישׂשכר (כפי שאנו יודעים לגביהם)'.

אילו זכינו למצוא את פירושו האבוד של הראב"ע לנביאים ראשונים, יכולנו לראות כיצד הוא
מתמודד עם מידע היסטורי מובהק, שלקחו הדתי-המוסרי לא תמיד ברור ושישימושו להבנת התורה
והנבואה לא תמיד נחוץ. אך באין פירוש זה בידינו, עלינו להסתפק בהיגד קיצוני ביותר בעניין זה,
הבא בשער הראשון של ספרו יסוד מורא, והאמור אגב רתחת פולמוס נגד הקראים. הוא תוקף
אותם על אשר הם נמנעים מללמוד מן התורה שבעל-פה כיצד צריך לקיים את מצוות התורה
שבכתב, וכתחליף לכך מתיימרים ללמוד זאת מספרי נ"ך. הוא מוכן להודות שאכן יש בהם מידע
חיוני הדרוש להבנת המצוות, אך טוען שאין בכך כדי להצדיק את הילמוד האינטנסיבי של ספרי
נביאים ראשונים, אשר רב בהם החומר הגיאוגרפי, ההיסטורי והארכיטקטוני, ושל ספרי נביאים
אחרונים, אשר נבואותיהם בחלקן כבר התקיימו, חלקן כה מעורפלות עד שאי-אפשר להגיע לידי
הסכמה בדבר משמעותן, ורק חלקן הן בגדר 'עתידות' שאפשר ללמוד מהן בוודאות מה צפוי לנו.
גם ספרי אמ"ת, חמש המגילות וספרי עזרא ודניאל אינם עומדים במבחן התקיף של הקניית ידיעה
ודאית אודות הקץ ושל דעת מצווה המנחילה חיים בעולם הבא. והריהו מסיים באמירה המפתיעה,
אשר את מידת רצינותה קשה לאמוד, שלפיה ניתן להפיק לפחות דבר אחד בבטחה מלימודם של
ספרי נ"ך – שליטה מלאה בלשון הקודש, הדרושה להבנת התורה! ככל שנתחשב בהקשר הפולמוסי
שבו נאמרו הדברים האלה, אי-אפשר שלא לשמוע בהם הד למבוכה אמיתית לנוכח המשקל הגדול
שיש לידיעת העבר בהיסטוריוגרפיה ובנבואה כאחד. נביא בזה את עיקר דבריו, בצירוף מילות
הסבר בסוגריים:

גם טוב הוא לדעת המקרא (ר"ל ספרי נ"ך), כי מצות רבות נלמד מדברי המקרא, כמצות 'לא
תאכלו על הדם' (ויק' יט, כו) מדברי שאול (ראה שמ"א יד, לב-לה) ו'לא יומתו אבות על
בנים' (דב' כד, טז) מדברי אמציה (מל"ב יד, ה-ו). רק התעלת קטנה היא כנגד היגיעה לדעת
שמות ערי ישראל (מספר יהושע), ודברי השופטים והמלכים (מיתר ספרי נ"ר), ובנין הבית
הראשון והעתיד להיות (מתחילת ספר מל"א ומסוף ספר יחזקאל), ודברי הנבואות שעברו
קצתן, ויש מהן עתידות לחקרן ויש שנגשש כעורים קיר – זה אומר בכה וזה אומר
בכה. [...] על כן אמרו קדמונינו על למוד המקרא 'מדה ואינה מידה' (בבא מציעא לג, ע"א).
רק טוב הוא למשכיל שיתבונן סוד לשון הקדש מהמקרא, כי ממנו תוצאות חיים להבין יסוד
התורה וסוד המורא [...].[20]

אם בעבור הראב"ע (ור' יוסף אבן כספי בעקבותיו[21]) ההיסטוריה המקראית שבספרי נביאים וכתובים

20 הדברים מובאים על-פי הנוסח (האקלקטי) שבמהדורת ישראל לוין, בתוך: ילקוט אברהם אבן עזרא, תל-אביב
תשמ"ה, עמ' 316–318. דיון מפורט בסוגיה זו בא בספרי, ארבע גישות לספר תהילים – מרס"ג עד ראב"ע,
רמת-גן תשמ"ב, עמ' 183–197.

21 עמדתו באה לידי ביטוי בקביעתו הנחרצת שאין בתורה היסטוריוגרפיה כפי שיש בספרי נ"ך: "והנה כבר ידוע כי
תעו רבים בזה הסוג מתורתנו, רצוני ה"אמרה", כי חשבו שבכללו (ר"ל שכלולים בו) או יותר (ר"ל ייתורים) או
קליפות או מילי דבדיחותא, כספור דברי הימים למלכי ישראל או מדי ופרס, שיחשבו רבים כמו זאת המחשבה
בהגדות התלמוד [זהו אזכור של דברי ראב"ע על המדרשים בהקדמת פירושו הארוך לתורה, הדרך הרביעית],
וכבר נתפרסם מאמר מנשה הרשע. וכן אמר דוד "אמרת ה' צרופה מגן הוא וג'" (תה' יח, לא) ר"ל ככסף צרוף
שאין בו סיגים. ולכן אמר "מגן הוא לכל החוסים בו", וטעם "מגן" – מגין ועוזר לדחות נזקים רבים, אם נזקי
הגוף אם נזקי הנפש. ובכלל אין בתורתנו הקדושה ספור שלא יהיה תכליתו לשלימות השכל...' (טירת כסף,

היא – במידה שאין בה לקח אמוני, מוסרי או הלכתי – בגדר של 'מה שהיה היה', הרי בעבור הרמב"ן
יש לפחות לתולדות האבות מעמד של ההיסטוריה מכוננת, בחינת 'מה שהיה יהיה'. באמצעות
פרשנות טיפולוגית שיטתית הוא מבאר את מעשי האבות כקובעים מראש את מה שעתיד לקרות
לבניהם אחריהם, החל משעבוד מצרים וכלה בימות המשיח. בפירושו לבר' יב, ו (כלומר עם תחילת
קורות האבות בארץ כנען) מסביר הרמב"ן את דרך הפירוש הזאת, תוך הסמכתה על חז"ל, אך מבלי
למעט מממידת החידוש שבה:

אומר לך כלל תבין אותו בכל הפרשיות הבאות בענין אברהם, יצחק ויעקב. והוא ענין גדול
הזכירוהו רבותינו בדרך קצרה, ואמרו: כל מה שאירע לאבות – סימן לבנים. ולכן יאריכו
הכתובים בספור המסעות וחפירת הבארות ושאר המקרים. ויחשוב החושב בהם כאלו הם
דברים מיותרים אין בהם תועלת, וכולם באים ללמד על העתיד. כי כאשר יבא המקרה
לנביא משלשת האבות יתבונן ממנו הדבר הנגזר לבא לזרעו.[22]

גם דון יצחק אברבנאל הכיר בערכה העצמי של ההיסטוריה המקראית, אך לא כרמב"ן על לא שום
שהיא מכוננת את העתיד מכוחה של הגזירה המוקדמת הנסיית, אלא כרס"ג על שום שהיא נחוצה
להבנת ההווה באשר היא מקנה לנו פרספקטיבה לגבי מקומנו ברצף הזמנים. בהקדמה לפירושו
לנביאים ראשונים הוא מציב, בדומה לרמב"ע, את הכרונוגרפיה של עמי אירופה בתקופת הרנסאנס
כציר'דון על דרך קל־וחומר לנחיצותה של הכרונולוגיה המקראית. כל העמים לומדים את קורותיהם
כדי להעמיד מבנה כרונולוגי רציף, המחולק לתקופות, ועל אחת כמה וכמה שחייב בכך עם ישראל,
בעל ההיסטוריה המקראית והציפייה המשיחית. דת ישראל היא היסטורית במהותה, באשר היא
עומדת על האמונה שהעולם אינו קדמון אלא נברא בזמן מסוים, ושהמצב הנוכחי אינו נצחי אלא
עתיד להשתנות מעיקרו עם בוא המשיח. עם זאת הוא מטעים, ככל קודמיו, שהמטרה הראשונה
והעיקרית של ההיסטוריוגרפיה המקראית היא תיאולוגית ומוסרית:[23]

ואומר אני בענין התכלית, שהתכלית הראשון, הכולל לארבעת הספרים האלה, הוא ללמדנו
תועלות ולימודים מועילים בידיעת ההשגות האמיתיות ובלמוד המדות והתכונות
המשובחות, כפי מה שיורו ספוריהם. ותכלית אחר כולל להם הוא בידיעת ימות עולם שנות
דור ודור. כי אין לנו דרך לדעת מספר השנים אשר עברו כי אם משנות השופטים והמלכים
להיותם נמשכים זה אחר זה מבלי הפסק כמו שאבאר אחרי זה בספר שופטים בעזרת האל.
ואם מדינה ומדינה ככתבה ועם כלשונו השתדלו להקיף ולדעת שנות הראשונים וגבולי
הימים, דור אחרי דור, כדי לדעת תקופות הימים ומספר שנותיהם, אף כי בני ישראל,
המשרשים באמונת חדוש העולם הכללי הרצוני, שראוי שידעו ויבינו הסתעפות הדורות
מתחילת הבריאה עד גלות ירושלם ועד כי יבא שילה ולו יקהת עמים.

_____

        בתוך: משנה כסף, מהד' יצחק לאסט, חלק א, פסבורג תרס"ה, עמ' 2).

22   ראה על כך בהרחבה במאמרו מאיר העינים של עמוס פונקנשטיין, 'פרשנותו הטיפולוגית של הרמב"ן', ציון מה
     (תש"ן), עמ' 35–59 (נדפס שנית באסופת מאמריו, תדמית ותודעה היסטורית ביהדות ובסביבתה התרבותית,
     תל־אביב תשנ"א, עמ' 157–179).

23   דון יצחק אברבנאל, פירוש על נביאים ראשונים, יפו-ירושלים תשט"ו, עמ' ו.

ואף־על־פי שבניסוח התכלית הראשונה יש מעין של אימוץ של שיטת רלב"ג ואף של המינוח שלו,
מוצא אברבנאל לנחוץ להסתייג ממנה, בלשון המעידה כמה גדול היה חששו פן ירדדו המורליזציה
והתיאולוגיזציה את החיוניות הספרותית של סיפורי נביאים ראשונים: 'והנה לא נתעסקתי להוציא
תועלות מהסיפורים כדרך הרלב"ג, להיותו פועל בטל בעיני, כי דברי הנביאים הם עצמם
התועלות במדות ובדעות' (עמ' יג). מכוחם של חושי הספרותי והבנתו ההיסטורית לא נעלם
ממנו, כי לא בכדי העדיפו מחברי ספרי נביאים ראשונים לספר את קורות העם וגדוליו מאשר לנסח
אמיתות מופשטות, ושלפיכך הסיפור גופו אמיתי ועתיר משמעות יותר מאשר לקחו.

פרק ב: הכתובים כפשוטם אינם מתיישבים עם הראייה הא־היסטורית של חז"ל

המחויבות של חז"ל לנצחיותה, לשלמותה ולאחדותה של התורה (ובמידה רבה גם של כלל כתבי
הקודש) כרוכה בראייה א־היסטורית מובהקת. כך מבוצרת הנצחיות של המצוות, של המוסר ואף
של אורח החיים היהודי במדרשים המתארים את האבות כמקיימים את כל המצוות. כך מחוזקת
השלמות האינפורמציונית של התורה על־ידי מדרשים המשלימים עובדות־רקע שלא פורשו בכתוב
ומזהים דמויות אלמוניות על דרך 'ההיסטוריוגרפיה היוצרת'. וכך מחושקת האחדות המקפת של
המקרא (שכל דבריו 'נתנו מרועה אחד') במדרשים המצרפים כתובים מספרים רחוקים והמנתקים
את המאורע מזמנו ואת הנבואה מאומרה. בסוגיית נצחיותן של המצוות מצטרף למשקל הגדול שהיה
לסמכות הרוחנית והפרשנית של חז"ל הלחץ הפולמוסי לדבוק בקדמות המצוות בחינת מענה הולם
לטיעון הנוצרי והמוסלמי בדבר ה'ביטול' שלהן. ההיסטוריזציה של המצוות (הנסמכת בעיקרה על
הכתובים כפשוטם) והפריודיזציה של ההיסטוריה (המבחינה בעיקר בין העידן שקדם למתן התורה
לבין העידן שבא לאחריו) משרתות היטב את הזיקה של המשך־תוך־דחייה לשתי הדתות
המאוחרות כלפי קודמתן. לעומת זאת מקנה פרשנות מדרשית א־היסטורית יתרון תיאולוגי מובהק
ליהדות, שכן היא משמשת כתריס איתן בפני כל תביעה להכיר בכך שתוקפן של המצוות אינו
על־זמני באשר יש לו היסטוריה. ודומה שרק שכנוע עמוק בלגיטימיות של דרך הפשט ובאמיתות
של ממצאיה יוכל לגבור על הצירוף הזה של מסורת פרשנית איתנה עם צורכי שעה דוחקים.

העיקרון של שמירת מצוות התורה בידי האבות לפני מתן התורה בסיני שנוי במשנה (קידושין ד,
יד): 'מצינו שעשה אברהם אבינו את כל התורה כולה עד שלא נתנה, שנאמר: "עקב אשר שמע
אברהם בקולי וישמר משמרתי, מצותי, חוקותי ותורתי" (בר' כו, ה)'. והאמוראים (יומא כח, ע"ב)
מוסיפים על כך אף את שמירת התורה שבעל־פה: 'קיים אברהם אבינו אפילו עירובי תבשילין,
שנאמר "תורתי" – אחת תורה שבכתב ואחת תורה שבעל פה'. על סמך מקורות אלה ואחרים נתן
רש"י בפירושו לבר' כו, ה ביאור מקסימליסטי לכל רכיביו של הכתוב (לדוגמה: 'וישמר משמרתי –
גזרות [ר"ל סייגים שעשו חכמים] להרחקה על האזהרות שבתורה, כגון שניות לעריות ושבות
לשבת'). ומאז ועד היום בטוחים רוב לומדיו שאכן פשוטה של לשון הרבים 'תורתי' הוא 'להביא
תורה שבעל פה, הלכה למשה מסיני', כפי שאינם יכולים לשער בנפשם שהאבות, המשמשים
לישראל כדגם ומופת, לא למדו תורה ולא קידשו את המועדים.[24] ואכן, מכוחה של תפיסה

24   ניתוח מעמיק של גלגולי התפיסה הזאת, מראשיתה בספר היובלים (יב, כז) ועד לחסידות חב"ד, הכולל גם את

א־היסטורית זאת מסיק רש"י מן הצו להרבות בהמות טהורות בתיבה 'מכאן שלמד נח תורה' (ביאורו
לבר' ז, ב), כפי שברי לו שיעקב אבינו גלה למקום תורה בנעוריו: 'ישב אהלים – אהלו של שם
ואהלו של עבר' (פירושו לבר' כה, כז ורא גם לפס' כב ולפרק מה, כז), ושאפילו לוט קיים בסדום
את מצוות הפסח: 'ומצות אפה ויאכלו – פסח היה' (פירושו לבר' יט, ג, ורא גם לפרק יח, י).

ברם, בצידה של האידיאליזציה של תקופת האבות, המקדימה את שמירת התורה לנתינתה, מצינו
אצל חז"ל, ובעקבותיהם גם בפירוש רש"י למקרא, את ההבחנה ההלכתית העקרונית בין העידן
שלפני מתן תורה לבין זה שלאחריו: 'כל זמן שלא ניתנה תורה אף ישראל נקראו בני נח' (פירוש
רש"י, עבודה זרה נא, ע"א, ד"ה 'לבני נח'; ורא גם: חולין ז, ו; סנהדרין נו, ע"ב; ופירוש רש"י
לבר' ה, לב; יש"ה, ז; יר' ב, כא). על סמך הפריודיזציה הזאת אין מתקשים בכך שיעקב
נשא שתי אחיות בחייהן (רש"י אינו מעיר על כך דבר); אין חוששים לומר שבני יעקב לקחו להן
לנשים את אחיותיהם התאומות או נשים כנעניות (בר' רבה פד, כא ורש"י לבר' לז, לה; נ, יג); ואף
מפליגים לדרוש ששמעון גאל את דינה אחותו מחרפת האינוס על־ידי שלקחה לו לאשה (בר' רבה
פ, יא ורש"י לבר' מו, י). אולם אף־על־פי שבתור 'בן נח' רשאי היה גם אברם לשאת את אחותו,
אין הדעת סובלת זאת לגבי אבי האומה – 'ותסברא אחותו הואי? בת אחיו הואי!' (סנהדרין נח, ע"ב
ופירוש רש"י לבר' יא, כט; כ, יב).

קשה למדי להכיר בכך שיש פער בין פשוטם של המקראות לבין ההכרזה החגיגית, הנאמרת
בתפילת העמידה של מנחה בשבת, 'אברהם יגל, יצחק ירנן, יעקב ובניו ינוחו בו'. למרות זאת
התשובה הא־היסטורית של רש"י לשאלת קיום המצוות בידי האבות היא כמעט דעת יחיד בקרב
פרשני הפשט.[25] ראשון הנוטשים את התפיסה המדרשית היה ר ב סעדיה גאון. בפירושו הארוך
לבר' כו, ה (בתרגום של צוקר, עמ' 427) הוא מסב את רכיביו של הפסוק על המצוות שאברהם קיים
(כגון מילה ומעשר) ועל אלה שסביר להניח שקיים (כגון עריות וסייגים למצוות); ובתפסיר הוא
מתרגם־מפרש את 'וישמר משמרתי' במשמע של 'וישמר כל מה שצויתיו לשמור ממצוותי'.[26] את
עמדתו העקרונית בסוגיה זו, שהיתה שנויה במחלוקת קשה גם בין הקראים,[27] הוא מבהיר בפירושו
הארוך לבר' ד, ד (שם, עמ' 304–306), אגב הדיון בקרבנות של קין והבל. הוא פותח בקביעה, שאין
הוא רואה את עצמו חייב לקבל את דעת חז"ל לגבי קדמות המצוות. שכן העובדה שיש מחלוקת
חכמים בדבר מספר המצוות שניתנו בעשרים ושש הדורות שבין אדם הראשון לבין משה רבנו (ראה
סנהדרין נו, ע"א וחולין צב, ע"א) מעידה שלא היתה להם בזאת מסורת מחייבת. את ממצאיתו של
בדיקתו העצמית הוא מסווג בשלוש קטיגוריות:

(א) 'המצוות שמצאתי במפורש שניתנו להם' (כגון הבאת קורבנות המתוארת בפרק ד והפרשת
מעשרות – בפרק יד).

─────────
דרכי התמודדותה עם פרשנות הפשט, ניתן בספר: Arthur Green, *Devotion and Commandment – The Faith of Abraham in the Hasidic Imagination*, Cincinnati 1989

25 החריג היחיד הוא ר' יוסף בכור שור, האומר בפירושו לבר', יח, ח: 'חמאה וחלב ואחר כך בן הבקר, שלא לאכול
    החלב אחר הבשר, כי שומר מצות היה אברהם אבינו'.

26 יוסף קאפח, פירושי רבינו סעדיה גאון על התורה, ירושלים תשכ"ג, על אתר (נדפס מחדש במקראות הגדולות
    תורת חיים, ירושלים תשמ"ז).

27 ראה: משה צוקר, על תרגום רס"ג לתורה, ניו־יורק תשי"ט, עמ' 442–440, 448–449, 453, 483.

(ב) 'המצוות שמצאתי בהן במפורש שלא היו בידם' (כגון פסח, מצה וסוכה – המצוות ההיסטוריות!).

(ג) 'המצוות שלא מצאתי בהן לא זה ולא זה, כגון טומאת קרי וכלאים, אפשר שהיו בידם ואפשר שלא היו, ולא אחליט בהן שום דבר, וזאת היא הדעה הנכונה'.

הסתייגותו של רשב"ם מפירושו של רש"י לבר' כו, ה אמנם אינה אמורה במפורש ובמישרין, אך היא מבוטאת בבירור רב באמצעות האפיון המתודי, שבו הוא פותח את ביאורו למילים 'חוקותי ותורותי': 'לפי עיקר פשוטו...', ללמדנו שהפירוש המקובל, הנשען על סמכותם של חז"ל ויוקרתו של רש"י, אשר לפיו 'תורותי' מורה על שתי התורות, אינו אלא מדרשי. הפירוש החילופי, שהוא מציע לכל רכיביו של הפסוק, הינו לא רק היסטורי אלא גם פילולוגי – כולם מוסבים על מה שאברהם יכול היה לקיים בזמנו, ורובם מבוארים בעזרת ביטויים הבאים בסיפורי אברהם. נביא בזה את פירושו תוך הדגשת הקישורים הלשוניים האלה:

עקב אשר שמע שמע אברהם בקולי – על העקידה דכת' '**עקב אשר שמעת בקולי**' (בר' כב, יח).
וישמור משמרתי – כגון מילה דכת' בה 'ואתה את בריתי תשמור' (בר' יז, ט).
מצותי – כגון מצות שמונה ימים דכ' 'כאשר צוה אותו אלהים' (בר' כא, ד).
חוקותי ותורותי – לפי עיקר פשוטו: כל המצוות הניכרות (ר"ל השכליות במינוח של רס"ג), כגון גזל, ועריות, וחימוד, ודינין והכנסת אורחים, כולם היו נוהגין קודם מתן תורה, אלא שנתחדשו ונתפרש[ו] לישראל וכרתו ברית לקיימן (ר"ל במתן תורה הן ניתנו מחדש בצורה יותר מפורטת ובדרגת חיוב גבוהה יותר, כפי שאומרים חכמים לגבי מצוות בני נח – סנהדרין נט, ע"א).

את ביאורו זה של הרשב"ם אימץ חזקוני, והוא אף ביקש לשכללו על-ידי הבחנה בין 'חוקותי' ל'תורותי', המעוגנת בכתובים באותה שיטה פילולוגית. ואילו מחוץ לתחומה של צפון צרפת הוא לא נודע כלל, וכל הביאורים לפסוקנו שביארו פרשני ספרד ופרובאנס הם בגדר פיתוח מקביל של דרך הפשט. גם הביאור שהביא הראב"ע הוא היסטורי ופילולוגי; אך, כפי שיתברר בהמשך, ראייתו ההיסטורית את תקופת האבות שונה מאוד מזו של רשב"ם וחזקוני, וגם המתודה הפילולוגית הנקוטה בידו היא אחרת לגמרי. שכן הוא אינו מפענח, כמותם, את רכיבי הפסוק בשיטה סגנונית-הקשרית, אלא עושה זאת בשיטה סמנטית-קטיגוריאלית. וזו לשון פירושו לבר' כו, ה, בתוספת ביאורים בסוגריים:

וישמור משמרתי – שם כלל (הכולל) כל מה שהוא חייב לשמור ממצות וחקים ותורות (ר"ל אין זה סוג נפרד של חובה דתית, אלא קטיגוריה מקיפה, הכוללת את מה שאברהם היה חייב לקיים משלושת הסוגים הבאים בהמשך הפסוק). ויתכן **המצוה** – 'לך לך' (בר' יב, א) גם 'קח נא את בנך' (שם כב, ב; ר"ל שני צווים אישיים שאברהם נצטווה בהם במפורש). **והחקים** – הם חוקות השם שילך האדם אחרי מעשיו (ר"ל שיקיים מה שמתחייב ממעשי ה' בבריאה), כאשר אפרש בפסוק שעטנז (בפירושו לויק' יט, יח הוא מסביר זאת: 'גם לא תעשה לבהמה לשנות מעשה השם, על כן כתוב "את חקתי תשמרו" – לשמר כל מין שלא יתערב עם מין'). ואלה החוקות נטועות בלב (ר"ל מצוות שכליות, כפי שהוא מסביר בפירוש הארוך לשמ' כ,

א, ד"ה 'דבור הראשון אנכי': 'דע, כי כל המצות הם על שני דרכים, והדרך הראשון – מצות שהם נטועות מהשם בלב כל אנשי דעת. והם רבים, ואין בעשרת הדברים רק השבת לבדה שאינה בכלל שקול הדעת. על כן כל משכיל בכל עם ולשון מודים בהם כי הם נטועים בשקול הדעת, ועליהן אין להוסיף ולא לגרוע, והם ששמר אברהם עם מצות אחרות נוספות...'.).

והתורה – שמל עצמו, ובניו ועבדיו, ובפסוק 'והתורה והמצוה' (שמ' כד, יב) אבארם היטב (כוונתו להסבר, הניתן בפירושו הקצר שם: 'והתורה – בעבור שהיא דבר אחד כצרעת והטֻמאה', ר"ל בצד ההוראה המורחבת של השם 'תורה', המציינת את חמשת החומשים, יש גם הוראה מצומצמת המציינת דין ספציפי, כמו 'תורת נגע הצרעת' [ויק' יג, נט] ו"תורת הילדת" [שם יב, ז]).

מצד אחד, ברור לראב"ע שלא ייתכן שאברהם שמר את המצוות שעדיין לא נתגלו (כגון מצוות השבת), ושלא ייתכן שהוא עסק בתורה שעדיין לא ניתנה. ומצד שני, ברור לו שאברהם שמר את ה'חוקים' הרבים (תשעת הדברות האחרים!) שהאדם יכול לגלותם בכוחות עצמו; ושהוא שקד לגלותם באמצעות התבוננות מעמיקה בבריאה[28] (כולל באדם עצמו, שהוא בגדר 'עולם קטן') ובירור שיטתי של כל מה שמתחייב מ'שיקול הדעת' (ר"ל המושכלות הראשונים והכושר האינטואיטיבי להבחין בין הנכון והמוטעה ובין המותר והאסור[29]). בטחונו זה של הראב"ע לגבי הזיקה ההדדית ההכרחית שבין הידיעה השלמה לבין ההתנהגות המושלמת מתחייב מן הרציונליזם הדתי-מוסרי שדגל בו. בביאורו לפסוקנו הוא מסיק משלמות המעשה של אברהם – שעליה מעיד הכתוב – על שלמות דעתו, ובפירושו לויק' יט, יט (בהמשך דבריו על הרציונליות של איסורי כלאי בהמה, שהובאו לעיל) הוא אומר ששלמות הדעת של אברהם כללה בהכרח ממילא את שלמות המעשה: 'ופה ארמוז לך סוד: דע, כי השלם – שלם מאד, על כן כתוב באברהם: "וישמר משמרתי מצותי חקותי ותורתי"'. את לשונו הקצרה של הראב"ע מרחיב מפרשו, ר' יוסף בן אליעזר: 'דע, כי מי שיהיה שלם בשכלו יהיה שלם במעשיו בלי ספק. [...] ואם תמצא איש משכיל עושה מעשים רעים, דע כי איננו משכיל כי אם סכל וכסיל'.[30]

דמותו של אברהם כחכם תלמודי המקיים את שתי התורות מומרת בדמותו של אברהם כמלומד בינימי הבקיא בכל המדעים והמקיים (נוסף על המצוות המעטות שנצטווה בהן במפורש) את מכלול האיסרים והחובים שנתגלו לו בחקירתו. מנקודת הראות של תפיסתנו ההיסטורית את התפתחות המדעים אין הבדל של ממש בין ההשלכה של האידיאל התורני המסרתי על האבות לבין ההשלכה של האידיאל המדעי-הפילוסופי הספרדי על האבות. ואילו בעיני הראב"ע הראשונה אינה אלא מדרש אנכרוניסטי, שעה שאת השנייה הוא מציע כפשוטו של מקרא! וזאת משום שמצמת ראייתו

---

28   כך, למשל, ידעו האבות מן הקוסמולוגיה שהטבעת תודתם לאל צריכה להתבטא בהפרשת עשירית מרכושם: 'ומי שיש לו לב להבין סוד העולם אז ידע סוד הבכור והעשירי (כבל הנראה כוונתו לעשרת הגלגלים). והנה אברהם נתן המעשר, גם יעקב אבינו עליו השלום...' (פירושו לויק' כז, לד).

29   ראה: יוסף כהן, 'משנתו הפילוסופית-דתית של ר' אברהם אבן עזרא', עבודת דוקטור, אוניברסיטת בר-אילן, רמת-גן תשמ"ג, עמ' 101–102, 105.

30   יוסף בן אליעזר, צפנת פענח, מהדורת דוד הרצאג, כרך א: קרקא תר"ב; כרך ב: ברלין תר"ץ (דפוס צילום: חיפה תשכ"ה).

הא־היסטורית את המדע היווני־ערבי כקדום,[31] הוא הניח בבטחה שמה שלא כתוב במפורש אודות
היקף הדעת של האבות הוא בגדר מובן מאליו, ומשום שכל מה שהוא אומר בנידון אכן מתיישב לפי
מיטב שיפוטו הפילולוגי עם פשט הכתובים. מן המלכוד הזה היו בעלי הפשט שבצפון־צרפת פטורים
מחמת אי־ידיעת המדעים. ואכן, הפירוש הסגנוני־הקשרי של הרשב"ם סביר יותר מן הפירוש
הסמנטי־קטגוריאלי של הראב"ע, אם כי אין ביתרון יחסי זה כדי לערער את עצם הלגיטימיות של
פירוש הראב"ע. ואכן, דומה שההיסוס הקל שהראב"ע מביע באמצעות המלה 'ויתכן' אינו מוסב על
תקפותה של דרך הפירוש שננקט (ר"ל שכאן מנויים סוגים שונים של מצוות), אלא רק על מידת
הוודאות שניתן להגיע אליה בבירור המינוח המקראי של סוגי המצוות.[32]

בעל הפשט פטור, לכאורה, מלתרץ מדוע עברו האבות על אותם איסורים שנאסרו רק במתן
תורה, ואף־על־פי־כן ראה הראב"ע חובה לעצמו לעשות זאת לגבי האיסורים הנגזרים, לשיטתו,
מ'שיקול הדעת', כגון איסור לקיחת שתי אחיות בחייהן ואיסור נישואים עם דודה. שני אלה נאסרו
במפורש בספר ו' י"ח, י"ח, י"ב־י"ג, י"ח, אך לפי שבהמשך הפרשה נאמר שבגללן 'כל התועבות האל' (פס'
כז) הקיאה הארץ את הכנענים, ברי שגם יעקב ועמרם היו צריכים להבין מדעתם שאלה הן תועבות!
על כך משיב הראב"ע ביסוד מורא, ראש השער החמישי, בעזרת ההבחנה בין 'העריות הקרובות
מאד', שהדעת לא סובלתן, לבין עריות קלות יותר, שאינן נתעבות בעליל – 'כי אלו היה יודע אסור
כל העריות לא היה לוקח יעקב אבינו שתי אחיות יחד. על כן נפרש "כי את כל התועבות האל" –
על רֶבֶן'.[33] ברי שיעקב (והוא הדין לעמרם) לא יעשה שום תועבה, ומכאן שהוא לא ידע, וגם לא
יכול היה לדעת, שמה שהוא עושה עתיד להיאסר כמשהו מגונה. אך עדיין הפריע לראב"ע הממד

31   עד כמה בטח הראב"ע בקדמות המדעים תעיד העובדה שהוא קיבל כהיסטורית את המסורת (המוסלמית בעיקרה),
     המייחסת ספרי אסטרונומיה ואסטרולוגיה ל'חנוך הקדמון' או 'חנוך הראשון' (כפי שמכונה חנוך המקראי בספר
     העולם [מהד' י"ל פליישר, הומנא תרצ"ז, עמ' 14, 17] בניגוד ל'חנוך המצרי' [שם, עמ' 14]). על סמך זאת הוא
     מסביר את מדרש השמות האנכרוניסטי, לכאורה, שנאמר בשעת לידתו של נח – 'זה ינחמנו ממעשנו ומעצבון
     ידנו מן האדמה אשר אררה ה'' (בר' ה, כט) בעזרת ידיעת העתידות הנבואית או האסטרולוגית של חנוך אבי סבו,
     שעדיין היה חי באותה שעה: 'אולי חנוך ראה בדרך נבואה כי נח החיה העולם ועל ידו סרה הקללה מהאדמה [...].
     או ראה זה במזלו (ר"ל בהורוסקופ שלו), כי ספרים רבים חבר בחכמות רבות והם היום נמצאים [...].' ('השיטה
     האחרת' לבר' ה, כט). רק כאשר סתרו הדברים שבספרי חנוך את מסקנות המדע בן־זמנו, הפקיע הראב"ע אותם
     ממחבריהם: 'אמר אברהם: הקדמונים וחכמי דורנו כולם השתמשו בחשבונות (ר"ל הם מודעים את ההשפעה הבו־
     זמנית של כוכב הלכת מכאן ושל המזל המסוים מכאן על ההורוסקופ), והנה מצאנום במבטים שיש דברים שיש
     ראיות גמורות על בטולם [...]. ולפי דעתי, שהחנוך לא יאמר כזה' (ספר הטעמים, מהד' י"ל פליישר, ירושלים
     תשי"א, עמ' 84). חשיבה ביקורתית מובהקת יש כאן, אך היא נתונה בסד של תפיסה א־היסטורית של המדע,
     המעגנת את אמתו בקדמותו.

32   ואכן, קשה למצוא עקיבות ברורה במינוח הזה. כך, למשל, הוא מעדיף לבאר בפירושו לתה' פט, לב: 'חקתי –
     מצות לא תעשה', ואילו המונח המיוחד ההולם מבחינה גזרונית את המצוות הנטועות בלב הוא, לדעתו, 'פקודים'.
     הוא חוזר ואומר זאת בביאוריו לתה' יט', כיט, יא; קז, קטו, ד, טו, קד, ובצורה השלמה ביותר בספרו על המצוות
     יסוד מורא, ראש שער ה: 'המצות שהם עקרים, שאינם תלויות במקום או בזמן או בדבר אחר, הן הנטועות בלב
     הם ה"פקודים" – כמו פקדון שהוא נתון ביד אשר הפקד אתו; על כן אמר המלך דוד: "פקודי ה' ישרים משמחי
     לב" (תה' יט, ט). ואלה היו ידועים בשיקול הדעת לפני תת התורה ביד משה, והן רבות כעשרת הדברים – חוץ
     מהשבת והן נשׂשׂן על־ידי משה, ועל כאלה אמר: "וישמר משמרתי מצותי חקותי ותורתי" (בר' כו, ה).'

33   ביאור לא־דווקני של 'כל' שכיח בפירושיו, כגון הארוכׂ לשמ' ט, ו: 'וימת כל מקנה מצרים – רובו, כי הנה כתוב
     "שלח העז את מקנך" (להלן, פס' יט), וככה תמצא בברד "את כל עשב השדה" (פס' כה) והעד – מכת הארבה
     "ואכל את יתר הפליטה" (י, ה) וראה גם לבר' מא, מח.

האובייקטיבי של האיסור, והוא ראה צורך לטהר את יעקב ועמרם גם מן הטומאה הדבקה במי שעושה עבירה אף בבלי־דעת. וכך הוא אומר בביאורו ל'ו' יח, כו:

וטעם 'ולא תעשו מכל התועבות האלה' שנית (ר"ל סיבת החזרה על האזהרות שבאו לעיל בפס' ג–ה) – להכניס הגר (הנזכר בפסוקנו), כי זאת המצוה היא שוה לאזרח ולגר, בעבור שהוא דר בארץ ישראל. ואם יש לך לב תוכל להבין כי בימי יעקב שלקח שתי אחיות בחרן ואחריו עמרם שלקח דודתו במצרים לא נטמאו בהם.

לא כל המקומות שווים, כפי שמעידה הזיקה הברורה שבין חומרת האיסור לבין מקום חלותו – מצד אחד יחולו בארץ־ישראל כל איסורי הערווה אפילו על גר תושב, ומצד שני לא חלו בחוץ לארץ לפני מתן התורה איסורים מסוימים אפילו על יעקב ועמרם. הקורא הרגיל אמור להתרשם מן הזיקה הזאת ומהשלכותיה לגבי קדושת ארץ־ישראל מכאן ולגבי ניקוי קדמונינו מטומאת נישואים אסורים מכאן. אך כל עוד הוא 'חסר לב' (ר"ל שלא הגיע לידיעה מקפת בתורה ובמכלול המדעים) הוא מנוע מלהבין את הבסיס העיוני שעליו עומדת הזיקה הזאת. ואילו הקורא המשכיל כבר נרמז בסוף הוויכוח עם מפרש אלמוני, שביקש לנקות את יעקב מאיסור צרירת שתי אחיות בעזרת ההנחה המופלגת שרחל ולאה לא היו אחיות מלאות (לעיל פס' יח[34]), שהמפתח להבנת סוד זה מסודות התורה ניתן במקום אחר: 'ודעתי תדענה בפרשת "וילך משה"'. כוונתו בכך לדבריו – הסתומים והחתומים בפני כל קורא שאינו משכיל – על מובנו של הצירוף התמוה 'אלהי נכר הארץ' (דב' לא, טז):

ידענו כי השם כי השם האחד, והשנוי יבוא מהמקבלים. והשם לא ישנה מעשיו, כי כולם הם בחכמה. ומעבודת השם לשמור כח הקבול כפי המקום, על כן כתוב 'את משפט אלהי הארץ' (מל"ב יז, כו), על כן אמר יעקב 'הסירו את אלהי הנכר' (בר' לה, ב). והפך המקום הַדָּבֵק בעריות שהם שְׁאֵר. והמשכיל יבין.

מאחדותו ויחידותו של האל מתחייב שאמתו מוחלטת, נצחית ובלתי־משתנה. ואילו מוגבלותם של כל הברואים מתבטאת בכך שהם שונים זה מזה בהבדלי הטבעים (המתוארים ב'חוכמת התולדת' ו'חוכמת הנפש') וגם משתנים מכוח תנאי המקום (המתוארים בתורות האקלימים ובעיקר בתורת האצטגנינות). מן הפער הקיומי הזה שבין האל והעולם מתבקשות שתי מסקנות: האחת, שמעשי ה' בעולם מותאמים בהכרח למגבלות של ה'מקבלים', והשנית, שעבודת ה' חייבת להיות מותאמת לשינויים ברמת הקדושה של המקום. הראב"ע מביא לכך שתי ראיות מן הכתובים: העובדה שהכותים, אשר הושיב מלך אשור בערי שומרון, טרפום האריות על שלא התאימו את עצמם לדרישות המיוחדות של 'אלהי הארץ' (שלא חייבו אותם בחו"ל); והעובדה המקבילה שעם בואו של

---

34 דבריו שם דומים בעיקרם לדברים ביסוד מורא, שער חמישי, שנידונו לעיל. הוא נזקק לעניין זה גם בביאורו לדב' כה, ה, אגב דיון ביחס שבין מצוות ייבום לבין היבום הוולונטרי של בניו של יהודה. מהלך הטיעון שונה במקצת ממה שראינו עד כה, וזאת משום שהוא משמש את צרכיו של פולמוס עם הקראים. וזו לשונו: '...וכל איש דעת ידע כי המצוות שנתנו למשה, שהם מצוות לא תעשה, לא היו אסורות קודם לכן. ואילו היה אדם מונע עצמו מהן קודם משה, לא היה הדבר רע בעיני ה', אף כי (ר"ל מה עוד) שכתב "כי את כל התועבות האל עשו אנשי הארץ אשר לפניכם" (וי' יח, כז), ולא מצאנו נביא שהזהירם. והנה הכתוב אמר על אונן שלא נתן זרע לאחיו "וירע בעיני ה'" (בר' לח, י)'.

יעקב לארץ הוא דרש מאנשי ביתו להסיר את 'אלהי הנכר' (שלא היו אסורים עליהם בחו"ל[35]). אם
'אלהי הארץ' משמעו הכוח האסטרלי השולט בארץ, ואם 'אלהי נכר' משמעו הכוח האסטרלי השולט
בארצות הנכר, אזי משמעו של הביטוי המצורף 'אלהי נכר הארץ' הוא הכוח האסטרלי שהוא זר בארץ
באשר אינו שולט בה ומנוגד לטבעה.[36] והמסקנה המתבקשת מכל זאת לגבי נישואיו של יעקב עם
שתי אחיות – מה שהיה מותר לחלוטין בחרן עתיד להיאסר על בני ישראל ערב בואם ארצה, משום
שההידבקות הגופנית אפילו עם העריות הפחות חמורות המנויות בפרשת העריות מתחת לכותרת
'שְׁאֵר בְּשָׂרוֹ' (וי' יח, ו) מנוגדת ל'כוח הקיבול' המיוחד של המקום הזה (ראה פירושו לבר' כח,
טז-יז).[37]

ביאורו של הראב"ע ל"אלהי נכר הארץ" מסתיים במלים "והמשכיל יבין". מטרתן לציין שהוא
כתוב בצורה חידתית, באשר הוא מיועד אך ורק למי שקנה לעצמו את הידיעות האסטרולוגיות
הנחוצות (הניתנות על-ידי מפרשי הראב"ע בהתאם לשיטותיהם השונות) וגם הגיע לתחכום
התיאולוגי הדרוש כדי להבין שהרלטיביזציה הזאת של המצוות אינה מחלישה את תוקפן.[38]

---

35 דבר זה הוא מבהיר בהטעמה יתרה בביאורו לבר' לה, ב (שאף הוא מסתיים בהפניה לביאורו הנידון כאן): 'הסירו
את אלהי הנכר – חלילה חלילה שישכב הנביא עם עובדות אלהי נכר (ר"ל אין להעלות על הדעת שעד כה יעקב
טימא את עצמו על-ידי קרבת גוף לעבודות עבודה זרה ממש), ופי' תמצאנו בפ' "וילך משה" (דב' לא, טז)'.

36 בהמשך מציע הראב"ע שני ביאורים חלופים למבנה התחבירי של הפסוק. הביאור הראשון (המתעלם מכל מה
שאמר עד כה, ומכאן שהוא מיועד לקורא שלא ירד לסוף דעתו): 'וטעם "בקרבו" שב אל "נכר", כאילו אמר:
וזנה אחרי אלהי עם נכר שהם אלהי הארץ'. והביאור השני (התואם את דבריו עד כה, ושהוא מעדיפו גם מבחינה
תחבירית משום שהוא מחייב להשלים את מלת 'עם'): 'והקרוב כי "בקרבו" שב אל "הארץ", כי ימצא לשון
זכר כמו "ולא נשא אותם הארץ" (בר' יג, ו), "נעתם ארץ" (יש' ט, יח)'. הראב"ע סומך על הקורא המשכיל שיבין
את ביאורו גם מבלי שינסה למענו פרפראזה חלופית לפסוק, אך הרמב"ן (ההולך בעקבותיו הן לגבי עניינו של
הכתוב והן לגבי מבנהו, והמיטיב ממנו לחוש את צורכי הקוראים) משלים את החסר הזה: 'האלהים שהוא נכר
בארץ הזאת'. הפניה נוספת לכתוב זה (אף היא מעורפלת ומצוענפת עד מאוד) מצינו בפירוש הראב"ע לבמ' טז,
כח: '...ובני לוי הרגו עובדי העגל, ויש כאן שאלה ותשובתה בפ' "וילך משה"'. ר' שמואל צרצה הטיב לחשוף
הן את השאלה והן את תשובתה בסופרקומנטר שלו מקור חיים (על אתר): 'ונראה כי השאלה היא: אם כל זה היה
בעבור מעשה העגל, אם כן מה עשה הגל [...] האיך לא הוסר מכהונתו? ואם כן נראה שמשה נשא פנים
לאהרן לפי שהיה אחיו! והתשובה היא מה שכתב ז"ל בפרשת "וילך" על הפסוק "וזנה אחרי אלהי נכר הארץ"
[...] ודע שאהרן עשה העגל בעבור שהיו הולכים במדבר, מקום שמאדים שולט בו [...] וכונת אהרן היתה לשמור
כח הקבול, ר"ל לשמור מנזק מאדים ולא לשם ע"ז, חלילה חלילה, ולפיכך לא הוסר מכהונתו [...]'. לשון אחר:
עשיית עגל אסורה בארץ משום שכאן היא בגדר עבודה זרה (מל"א יב, כח-ל), ואילו במדבר, שבו שולט כוח
אסטרלי אחר, עשהו אהרן כסגולה אסטרולוגית להישמר מפניו.

37 הראב"ע אינו רומז שם שעם הכניסה לארץ נתברר ליעקב שנישואיו לשתי אחיות אסורים בה. אך בסוף השער
השביעי של יסוד מורא (שנכתב בכתירסר שנים אחרי פירושו הקצר לתורה) הוא טוען שיעקב פרש מהן למעשה,
שכן בבואו לבית אל הוא התמסר לעבודת ה' אינטנסיבית בקיימו את הנדר אשר נדר שם בשעתו 'והיה ה' לי
לאלהים' (בר' כח, כא): 'כי כאשר בא אל בית אל אמר: "הסירו את אלהי הנכר אשר בתככם" (לה, ב), והניח
הצאן, והתבודד לעבוד השם, ולא שכב עם אשה, כי רחל מתה, וחללה בלהה, ועבורו זה מאס באם ראובן
ובשפחתה (ר"ל בלאה ובזלפה). על כן כתוב בפסוק אחר (ר"ל בפסוק שאחרי מעשה ראובן) "ויהיו בני יעקב שנים
עשר" (לה, כג) – להודיע שלא שכב עם אשה אחרי כן, על כן לא הוליד עוד'.

38 לא כך סבור דב שוורץ, 'ארץ, מקום וכוכב – מעמדה של ארץ ישראל בתפיסתו של החוג הניאופלוטוני במאה
הי"ד', בתוך: מ' חלמיש וא' רביצקי (עורכים), ארץ ישראל בהגות היהודית בימי הביניים, ירושלים תשנ"א, עמ'
138-150. בסעיף 'ארץ ישראל והאנטנומיזם' (עמ' 146-150) הוא מביא את ביאוריהם של חמישה
סופרקומנטרים (מאת שלמה פרנקו, אבן צרצה, עזרא גטיניו, אבן שפרוט ואבן מאיור) על פירוש ראב"ע לדב'
לא, טז, ומראה שהם הסיקו מסקנות אנטינומיסטיות קיצוניות, בין השאר, מדברי אבן עזרא על התנאית התוקף

רש"י ביצר את על־הזמניות של התורה ואת המעמד של האבות כשומרי מצוותיה ושילם על כך מחיר פרשני – קבלת מדרשים רבים כפשוטו של מקרא. רשב"ם העדיף לדבוק בפשט הכתובים ושילם על כך מחיר תיאולוגי – הכרה ברלטיביזם ההיסטורי (מה שמותר היה לאבות נאסר על הבנים). ואילו ראב"ע ביקש לדבוק בפשט מבלי לוותר על הנצחיות של ההבחנה השכלית בין טוב ורע, ולשם כך היה עליו לדרוך במידה ניכרת את הרלטיביזם ההיסטורי,[39] ולהשלימו על־ידי רלטיביזם מקומי (מה שמותר היה בחו"ל נאסר בארץ). הרלטיביזם ההיסטורי של רשב"ם הוא 'מקראי', הן משום שאינו יונק ממקורות חיצוניים והן משום שהוא מונחה על־ידי מה שנאמר בגלוי ובמפורש בכתובים. ואילו הרלטיביזם המקומי של ראב"ע הוא ביניימי, משום שהוא מונחה על־ידי הביטחון הגמור בנצחיותן של ההכרות השכליות, משום שהוא מבוסס על תורת האקלימים והאסטרולוגיה, ומשום שהוא יכול להסתמך רק על רמזים המשוקעים בין השיטין. בטחונו הגמור בכך שנוסף על פניה הגלויים של התורה יש לה גם פנים מוסתרים, אשר הקורא המשכיל יכול לחשפם בכלים פילולוגיים מובהקים, הוא שאפשר לו לעשות כל זאת מבלי להיות מודע למחיר הפרשני שהוא משלם.

ר' דוד קמחי מרכך וממתן, כדרכו, את תפיסתו החדשנית של הראב"ע. בביאורו לבר' כו, ה הוא מאמץ את דרך הביאור הסמנטי־קטיגוריאלי של קודמו, תוך שהוא מוסיף ל'כל מצות השכל' את שבע מצוות בני נח בהגדרתן ההלכתית.[40] אך שלא כמוהו, אין הוא מתעלם ממדרש החכמים, ומנסה לגשר בינו לבין הפשט על־ידי עקירתו ממשמעו העובדתי והבנתו כהיגד מופשט:

ואמרו (יומא כח, ע"ב) כי כל התורה קיים אברהם ואפילו ערובי תבשילין, רצו לומר – זה מפני שאמר (הכתוב) 'משמרתי', וערובי תבשילין הם משמרת למלאכת יום טוב, כן עשה הוא דברים יתרים למשמרת המצות.

ראייתו זאת את אברהם כשומר מצוות מרובות מדעתו לא היתה כרוכה בעבורו בקשיים העקרוניים שהטרידו את הראב"ע. אדרבה, היא עזרה לו להקטין את הפער שבין ראייה אידיאלית־תורנית של האבות לבין ראיה שכלתנית־היסטורית שלהם. כפי שאברהם עשה סייגים שכלתניים למצוות השכלתניות, כך ייעד יעקב את לוי לעבוד את ה' יותר משאר אחיו, 'ולמדו יעקב בהתבודדו ומסר לו סודות החכמה והתורה' (בביאורו לבר' כח, כא–כב). ודוק: החכמה קודמת לתורה, שכן התורה היתה

של כמה ממצוות התורה במערכות השונות של הכוכבים. בלשון זהירה מייחס ד' שוורץ תפיסה זו לראב"ע עצמו, בהסתמכו על 'הרמיזות האנטינומיסטיות' (עמ' 150) שבדבריו. אולם לדעתי אין ברמיזות אלה כשהן לעצמן בסיס מספיק למסקנה זו, וצריך להיזהר מלהפנה אותן על סמך דבריהם של פרשני־ראב"ע – המפרש שהיה למפורש', בתוך: שרה יפת [עורכת], המקרא בראי מפרשיו – ספר זיכרון לשרה קמין, ירושלים תשנ"ד, עמ' 397–402).

39   ביטוי נוסף לכך יש בתירוץ א־היסטורי מובהק שהוא נותן בביאורו לבר' כח, יז לבעיית הקמת מצבה בידי יעקב: 'ורבים יתמהו איך הקים יעקב מצבה, והנה שכתוב כי י"ב מצבות הקים משה! והכתוב לא אסר לשום מצבה לשם, רק (ר"ל אלא) אמר "לא תקים לך מצבה אשר שנא" (דב' טז, כב) ובגנאי אל מקומו אפרשנו'. ושם הוא מפרש – ככל הנראה בעקבות התפסיר של רס"ג ('אשר שנא ה' אלהיך – באופן השנוי לפני ה'') ותוך התעלמות ממדרש חכמים (ספרי דברים, קמו, פיסקה 1) – שרק מצבה לעבודה זרה אסורה (והשווה פירושו להו' ג, ג–ד וביאורי על אתר).

40   גרין (בספרו הנזכר לעיל בהערה 24, עמ' 38) מעמיד על כך שרד"ק אינו מבין את 'חוקותי' כמצוות שכליות (כמו ראב"ע), אלא כמצוות שמעיות (כמו רש"י), על מנת לכלול בהן אותן מצוות בני נח – הרבעת בהמה, הרכבת אילן ואיבר מן החי – שטעמן נגלה, לדעתו, רק לחז"ל, ושבימי אברהם היו בלתי מובנות.

עדיין מצומצמת בהיקפה. בניגוד לראב"ע, אין הקמת מצבה בבית אל ולקיחת רחל ולאה בחייהן
מוקשות בעיניו, ואין הוא מוטרד מ"אלהי הנכר" שיעקב מצווה להסיר מביתו, משום שאין אלה אלא
צורות של עבודה זרה שהיו טבועות בגזמים ובמטבעות שנלקחו זה עתה שלל בשכם (ראה ביאורו
לבר' לה, ב). לנוכח אחיזתו הרופפת באידיאל השכלתנות הספרדית יכול היה להסתפק ברלטיביזם
ההיסטורי הגלוי, מבלי להיזקק לרלטיביזם המקומי האזוטרי.

גישה דומה, הן כלפי מדרשי חז"ל והן כלפי הפלגות של הראב"ע, מציגן אצלר' יוסף אבן כספי.
אמנם ב'מצרף לכסף'[41] לבר' כו, ה הוא מסתפק באמירה, שאין לקבל בפשטות את דברי חז"ל בעניין
זה: 'מה אומר אחרי רבותינו ז"ל בפירוש זה שאמרו "קיים אברהם כל התורה כולה"? פקח עיניך
וראה!'. אך ב'טירת כסף' (שהוא מעין מסה פרשנית-מתודולוגית, שלפיו הורואתיו צריכה ללוות את
קריאת 'מצרף לכסף') הוא מציב כנגדם – ועמהם גם כנגד דברי הראב"ע! – את סמכותה של
הפריודיזציה המקראית כפשוטה, שאין לעקור אותה ממשמעה מתוך הגנת-יתר על כבוד האבות:

ואני תמה מה הביא לרבותינו ז"ל וגם לאבן עזרא לנטות (ר"ל לסור מן הפשט), ואם שלא
רצו ליחס זה הגנאי לאברהם, רצוני שישא אחותו. הנה ידוע ליודעים שלא היה זה עון לו אז,
כמו שלא היה ליעקב בנשאו שתי אחיות. ואם בעבור כבוד זרעו (ר"ל התוצאות
ה'אובייקטיביות' של הנישואים האלה), מה נעשה לזרע יעקב (ר"ל למה לנו לדאוג לכבודם
של צאצאיו), ואין ספק שלא נמצא בנים נכבדים כבני עמרם מדודתו! אבל כל זה היה קודם
מתן תורה, לכן אינו נמנע אצלי היות ענין זה המאמר כמו שהוא כתוב (עמ' 96).

אין הוא חושש, אם כן, לומר בפירוש שיש להעדיף את הפשט ההיסטורי מן המדרש הא-היסטורי,
אך עם זאת הוא מנסה (בהקשר אחר) לחשוף את הראייה ההיסטורית הגבונה המובעת באמצעות
לשונו הציורית של המדרש הזה, ואף למצוא לה הוכחה בכתוב. כך הוא מפאר ומרומם את אברהם
על שלפני מתן תורה הוא דבק באשתו היחידה, ונמנע מריבוי נשים שהיה מקובל בזמנו ושהתורה
עתידה להתירו. את ההשתאות הזאת מגדולתו של אברהם המקדים את זמנו הוא מוצא במדרש
המפליג בשבחו של אברהם כשומר התורה:

ואשיב ואומר כי ידוע שמנהג הארץ ההיא לקחת איש אחד נשים רבות, עם שגם תורתנו
התירה זה לעמנו. ולכן היה מהפלגת קדושת אברהם, אע"פ שגדלה תשוקתו לבנים, שלא
נזדווג רק לאשתו הנכבדת, אשר הוא נעזר ממנה לכל עת לכל צורך, גם לא לשפחותיו הנמצאות
אותו בבית. ומה טוב מה שאמרו פלוסופי חכמינו 'קיים אברם כל התורה כלה'. ודי במה
שזכרנו מופת שהחמיר על עצמו אף במקום שהתירה אותו התורה העתידה להמסר לכלל עם
ישורון. והנה ביאר כי אברהם לא בקש זאת משרה, אבל שמע לקולה כאשר בקשה זה מאתו,
ובכלל זה שלום הבית ג"כ שהוא עיקר גדול לכל מבקש שלמות (עמ' 83).

יחיד ומיוחד היהר' משה בן נחמן בהעזתו לדבוק במדרשים בנאמנות לא פחות מאשר רש"י ולאחוז
בדרך הפשט במיומנות ובמצפוניות לא פחות מאשר ראב"ע, ובחתירתו לשכלל את דרכי קודמיו
ולהביא אותן לסינתזה אמיתית.[42] הוא מעיד על עצמו שזו אכן מטרתו בפתיחה החרוזה של הקדמת

41 בתוך: יוסף אבן כספי, משנה כסף, מהד' יצחק לאסט, חלק ב, קראקוב תרס"ו.
42 ראה את התיאור המעמיק וההערכה השקולה של גישת הרמב"ן לשני קודמיו במאמר: Bernard Septimus,

פירושו לתורה: 'אבל מה אעשה ונפשי חשקה בתורה / והיא בלבי כאש אוכלת בוערה / בכליותי
עצורה / לצאת בעקבי הראשונים, אריות שבחבורה / גאוני הדורות בעלי גבורה / להכנס עמהם
בעבי הקורה / לכתב כהם פשטים בכתובים ומדרשים במצות ואגדה, ערוכה בכל ושמורה'.
אף־על־פי שהרמב"ן עובר בשתיקה גמורה על כל הרמזים הביקורתיים שבפירוש ראב"ע לתורה (ככל
הנראה משום שלא יכול היה להידיין עמהם בלי לחשוף את סודם, ואולי גם בגלל הכבוד שרחש כלפי
כובד־הראש של בעליהם), הריהו תוקף אותו בחריפות רבה כאשר נראה לו שהוא מזלזל מתוך אי־
הבנה במעמדם הפרשני של מדרשי חז"ל. כך, למשל, הוא אומר בביאורו לבר' א, א, בסוף מענהו
לדברים הקשים שכתב הראב"ע (בהקדמת פירושו הרגיל לתורה, 'הדרך הרביעית') נגד ראיית
המדרשים כפשוטות: '...הזכרתי זה לבלום פי קטני אמנה מעוטי חכמה, המלעיגים על דברי רבותינו';
וכיוצא בזה הוא כותב בביאורו לבר' כד, א, בסוף תשובתו לפירוש הראב"ע, המשמיט את הבסיס
הלשוני מתחת למדרש 'בת היתה לו (לאברהם) ו"בכל" 'שמה': 'ואלו ידע זה המתהדר בסודותיו,
תאלמנה שפתיו מהלעיג על דברי רבותינו! ולכן כתבתי זה לסכור פי הדוברים על הצדיקים עתק'.[43]

הראב"ע לא התייחס כלל למדרשים המקסימליסטיים בדבר אברהם השומר מצוות, אך אף־על־פי
שהוא אינו מסתייג מהם בגלוי ובמפורש, ביאוריו בעניין זה מבוססים על הנחות שונות לגמרי.
הרמב"ן, על כל פנים, רואה את עצמו פטור מן הפולמוס בסוגיה זו, ובביאורו לבר' כו, ה הוא מתיר
לעצמו 'להכנס עמהם (ר"ל עם קודמיו) בעבי הקורה', כלומר לעסוק בגופו של עניין על סמך בחינה
ביקורתית אוהדת של הביאורים המנוגדים של רש"י וראב"ע, ולחפש מוצא מן הסתירה שבין העמדה
הא־היסטורית של הפרשנות המדרשית לבין התביעה העולה של מקרא להכיר בהיסטוריות
של המצוות.

נקודת המוצא של הרמב"ן היא ביאורו של רש"י ואחיזתו במדרשים הבנויים 'על דעת שהיה
אברהם מקיים ומשמר את התורה עד שלא נתנה'. על כך הוא מקשה מסטיותיהם הברורות של יעקב,
עמרם ומשה מכמה ממצוות התורה, אשר לפי דעה זאת אברהם לא רק קיימן אלא גם ציווה את
צאצאיו לשמרן:

ויש לשאול: אם כן, איך הקים יעקב מצבה ונשא שתי אחיות, וכדעת רבותינו – ארבע
(על־פי המדרש שגם הפילגשים היו בנות לבן), ועמרם נשא דודתו, ומשה רבינו הקים שתים
עשרה מצבה, והאיך אפשר שיהיו נוהגים היתר בתורה במה שאסר אברהם אבינו על עצמו
וקבע לו השם שכר על הדבר, והוא יצוה את בניו ואת ביתו אחריו ללכת בדרכיו (כאמור
בבר' יח, יט)?

'"Open Rebuke and Concealed Love": Nahmanides and Andalusian Tradition', in: Isadore
Twersky (ed.), *Rabbi Moses Naḥmanides (Ramban): Explorations in his Religious and Literary
Virtuosity*, Cambridge, Mass. 1983, pp. 16-21

43 הרמב"ן תובע את עלבונו של המדרש גם מידיו של רש"י, אך הוא עושה זאת ללא כל נימה פולמוסית ותוך הכרה
מלאה ברוחב בקיאותו במדרשי חכמים. בביאורו לבמ' לב, מב מביא רש"י מדרש מיסודו של ר' משה הדרשן
ומקשה עליו: 'ותמיהני מה ידרוש בשתי תיבות הדומות לה [...]'. על כך עונה לו הרמב"ן: 'והרי הרב אוצר בלום
לתורה, להלכות ולהגדות, ואשתמיטתיה זו שאמרו במדרש רות [...] וכן בגמרא של מסכת סנהדרין אמרו [...]'.
לעומת זאת, כאשר רש"י אינו בוחן את המדרש באמת המידה של הפשט, יש שעושה זאת הרמב"ן, תוך הסתמכות
על התקדים של רש"י עצמו: 'אבל כיוון שרש"י מדקדק במקומות אחר מדרשי ההגדות וטורח לבאר פשטי המקרא,
הרשה אותנו לעשות כן, כי שבעים פנים לתורה, ומדרשים רבים חלוקים בדברי החכמים' (פירושו לבר' ח, ד).

בפירוש רש"י לפסוקנו אי־אפשר למצוא שום מענה לקושיה זו, והוא הדין במדרשים הא־
היסטוריים המובהקים שהסתמך עליהם. אך לאמיתו של דבר לא התעלמו החכמים, ורש"י עצמו
בעקבותיהם, מייחודו של העידן שקדם למתן תורה, ואשר בו היו גם ישראל, מבחינה הלכתית,
בחזקת 'בני נח' (ראה לעיל, עמ' 182*). לפיכך רואה הרמב"ן את תפקידו להראות שבחינה שיטתית
של דברי חז"ל בהלכה ובאגדה לגבי סוגיה זאת מגלה שאכן יש בפיהם תשובה הולמת לקושייתו,
ושדרכם בביאור פסוקנו אחראית ומעוררת כבוד.

במהלך הפרשני הראשון (הפותח בלשון השערה – 'ואולי נאמר') הוא מציע ביאור הלכתי
מינימליסטי של פסוקנו. לפי ביאור זה, ארבעת סוגי המצוות המנויים בפסוק מוסבים כולם על אותן
מצוות שלפי שורת הדין אברהם היה חייב לקיימן בחינת 'בן נח'. ומכאן שאין צדקתו המיוחדת של
אבי האומה מתבטאת בהרחבתן הכמותית אלא בהעמקתן האיכותית: 'והוא השומר והעושה רצון
בוראו ומשמר אפילו דקדוקין וחומרות במצות שלהן, וכמו שהזכירו (עבודה זרה יד, ע"ב) "ע"ז של
אברהם אבינו ארבע מאות פרקי הוות" (ר"ל מסכת עבודה זרה שבה עסק היו בה ארבע מאות פרקים,
לעומת חמשת הפרקים שבמשנתנו). ודרשו ב"מאה שערים" שמדדוה למעשרות, כי היו האבות
נדיבים עמים...'. על גבי התשתית הזאת של פירוש פשטי מובהק, המשקף בנאמנות את מעמדם
ההלכתי של בני ישראל בעידן שלפני מתן תורה, מציע עתה הרמב"ן (במהלך הפרשני השני, הפותח
אף הוא בלשון זהירות – 'והנראה אלי') הסבר הגיוני לדרשות מרחיקות־הלכת המייחסות לאברהם
גם את שמירת התורה שבכתב והתורה שבעל־פה:

והנראה אלי מדעת רבותינו (המובעת במדרש האגדה), שלמד אברהם אבינו התורה כולה ברוח
הקדש, ועסק בה ובטעמי מצוותיה וסודותיה, ושמר אותה כולה כמי שאינו מצווה ועושה.

הרמב"ן מוצא, אם כן, מתאם מאלף בין ההבחנה המתודולוגית (בין פשוטו של הכתוב ומדרשו) לבין
ההבחנה ההלכתית (בין מצווה ועושה ואינו מצווה ועושה). לפי הבנתו זו את שיטת חז"ל, שמר
אברהם מבחינה עובדתית את כל המצוות, אך הוא היה חייב לשמור רק את המצוות שעל שמירתן
מספר פסוקנו בדרך הפשט, ואילו אלה ששמירתן נלמדת מפסוקנו בדרך הדרש אותן הוא קיים
מרצונו. בדרך זו משבץ הרמב"ן את מדרש האגדה (שהוא מאפיינו כהבעת־דעה של חכמים)
במסגרתה התקיפה של ההלכה, וגם מצמצם במידה ניכרת את ההפלגה הפרשנית שלו. וכפי
שלשיטת השכלתנים, דוגמת הראב"ע, למד אברהם מצוות רבות מדעתו, כך לשיטת רבותינו למד
אברהם את כל המצוות כולן ברוח הקודש.

ההבדל בין שתי השיטות נובע, אם כן, מחילוקי דעות לגבי מקור הידיעה האמיתית, ולא ממשיעור
שונה של סבירות היסטורית! הרמב"ן אמנם אינו עושה את ההשוואה הזאת במפורש, אך על רקע
קני־המידה של הראב"ע לגבי סבירות פרשנית נקל לשער שהרמב"ן יכול היה לומר
לעצמו: ולא תהא כוהנת כפונדקאית? ודוק: הרמב"ן נמנע מלומר שאברהם אבינו עסק בלימוד שתי
התורות, זו שבכתב וזו שבעל־פה, כפי שעולה לכאורה מלשון המדרש. תחת זאת הוא מתאר את
אברהם כלומד ברוח הקודש את התורה (מן הסתם כוונתו לזו שבכתב), ואילו עיסוקו הפרשני בה
ובמשמעות של מצוותיה (הכוללת כמובן גם את בירור דרך קיומן למעשה) היא היא, כמדומה,
התורה שבעל־פה שאליה כיוונו חכמים במדרשם.[44]

44   א' גרין (בספרו הנזכר לעיל בהערה 24, עמ' 40) קושר את הלימוד הזה של אברהם את התורה ברוח הקדש עם

לשיטתו של הרמב"ן, הגנה משכנעת על מדרש האגדה צריכה להראות לא רק שהוא עומד במבחן הכפול של סבירות פרשנית והתאמה הלכתית, אלא גם שהוא מתיישב עם מה שמשתמע מכתובים אחרים. ולכן הוא פונה עתה לתירוץ הקושיה שהוצבה בראש הדיון – אם אמנם ידע אברהם את כל התורה ושמר את כל מצוותיה, מדוע לא ניכרת עובדה זו בהתנהגות של צאצאיו הנאמנים? כדי להשיב על כך נזקק הרמב"ן, למרבה ההפתעה, לרלטיביזם המקומי מבית מדרשו של הראב"ע. שכן הוא טוען שהם עשו זאת לא מפני שלא ידעו שזה אסור, אלא מפני שמחוץ לגבולות הארץ זה אכן היה מותר:

ושמירתו אותה (ר"ל שמירת אברהם את כל התורה) היה בארץ בלבד, ויעקב בחוצה לארץ בלבד נשא שתי אחיות וכן עמרם. כי המצות 'משפט אלהי הארץ' (רמיזה למל"ב י"ז, כו) הם, אף־על־פי שהוזהרנו בחובת הגוף בכל מקום. וכבר רמזו רבותינו הסוד הזה, ואני אעירך בו בעזרת השם.

סוד היחס שבין קדושת הארץ לבין חלות המצוות בה הוא אבן פינה חשובה במשנת הרמב"ן, והוא חוזר ודן בו לפחות עוד ארבע פעמים: בביאוריו לבר' כד, ג; ו' יח, כה (מקום שם הוא מביא את ביאור הראב"ע לדב' לא, טז במלואו); דב' יא, יח; לא, טז. מכלל דבריו עולה שהסוד הזה עומד על שלושה עמודים איתנים: (א) הנתון הגיאוגרפי – מיקומה של ארץ־ישראל באמצע היישוב; (ב) הנתון האסטרולוגי – אין מזל לישראל; (ג) הנתון המיסטי – בית־המקדש של מעלה מכוון כנגד בית־המקדש של מטה. אין אפוא כל ספק שסוד זה, המובא כאן כסיוע למדרש האגדה, נחשב בעיניו (כבעיני הראב"ע) למעוגן היטב בפשוטו של מקרא. הרמב"ן אף מצא לו ראיה בקורות חייו של יעקב, כפי שהוא מסביר בהתפעלות רבה בביאורו ל־ו' יח, כה:

וזו היא מצות יעקב אבינו לביתו ולכל אשר עמו בשעת ביאתם לארץ 'הסירו את אלהי הנכר אשר בתוככם והטהרו' (בר' לה, ב). וה' לו לבדו נתכנו עלילות, שמתה רחל בדרך בתחילת בואם בארץ. כי בזכותה לא מתה בחוצה לארץ, ובזכותו לא ישב בארץ עם שתי אחיות, והיא היתה הנשאת באיסור האחוה. ונראה שנתעברה מבנימין קודם בואם בשכם, ולא נגע בה הארץ כלל מפני הענין שהזכירנו.

נישואי יעקב ורחל היו כשרים משום שנעשו בחרן, אך המשך קיום יחסי אישות בארץ היה פוגע בקדושתה הנצחית של הארץ. יעקב היה מודע לכך ולכן נמנע מלגעת ברחל מאז הגיעם לארץ (כפי שגם ציווה על בני ביתו להיטהר מטומאת אלוהי הנכר בשעת ביאתם לארץ). אך גם עצם המשך קיום הנישואים לשתי אחיות היתה בו גנות, ולכן מנע הקב"ה אותם מכך בזכות צדקתו של יעקב! הצירוף המופלא של הנסיבות – היותה של רחל האשה השנייה, אשר עליה חל האיסור, ומותה הפתאומי בלדתה את בנימין עם הכניסה לארץ – נראה לרמב"ן כהוכחה מובהקת לכך שמעלתם

דברי הרמב"ן בהקדמתו לתורה בדבר התורה הכתובה באש שחורה על גבי אש לבנה, שקדמה לבריאת העולם. הקישור הזה מקנה, אמנם, ממשות מיסטית למושג 'ברוח הקודש', אך ספק בעיני אם התכוון הרמב"ן באמרו 'טעמי מצוותיה וסודותיה' לייחס לחז"ל גם את ראיית אברהם כמקובל. על כל פנים, מביאורו לבר' ח, כא ברור שהוא מבחין בין התגלויות ספציפיות שקדמו למתן תורה לבין מה שנתגלה בתורה גופה 'ביום צוותו את משה בכתיבת התורה'.

הנמוכה של ארצות העמים היא ההסבר הנכון לכך שיעקב ועמרם לא שמרו על כל איסורי העריות
שבתורה. בטחונו זה במה שכינינו 'רלטיביזם מקומי' הוא כה רב, עד שבהמשך דבריו הוא רואה את
עצמו חייב לתרץ מדוע דרשו חכמים שיוסף 'היה משמר את השבת אפילו במצרים'. ותשובתו היא,
שלשיטתם שמר יוסף את השבת בחוץ לארץ אך ורק מטעמים חינוכיים מיוחדים: 'מפני שהיא
שקולה כנגד כל המצות, לפי שהיא עדות על חדוש העולם, והיה עושה כן ללמד את בניו אמונת
בריאת העולם להוציא מלבם כונת עבודה זרה ודעת המצרים, וזאת כונתם.'

לעומת זאת, ההסבר שלו להקמת המצבות – בידי יעקב בבית אל ובידי משה במדבר סיני – אינו
מקומי אלא זמני מובהק: 'והמצבה מצוה שנתחדשה בזמן ידוע היא, כמו שדרשו ב"אשר שנא ה'
אלהיך" (דב' טז, כב) ששנאה אחר היותה אהובה בימי האבות'. גם רש"י, בביאורו על אתר, מאמץ
את אבחנת הזמנים שבמדרש (ספרי דברים, פיסקה קמו), אשר לפיה נאסרה הקמת מצבה רק בזמן
מתן התורה, וזאת 'כי חק היתה לכנעניים'. והרמב"ן, בביאורו שם, מקבל הן את הנמקת האיסור (אשר
לפיה אין ה' שונא את המצבות לגופן אלא רק משום שהן משמשות בעבודה זרה) והן את הפריודיזציה
הנסמכת עליה, אך מוסיף עליה את הדיוק הבא: 'אבל בימי יעקב לא נאמר עדיין "ובחוקותיהם לא
תלכו" (וי' יח, ג), ולכך היה משתמש במצבה לשם שמים כמנהג העובדים (ר"ל הכנענים).'[45]

בזאת יושרו כל ההדורים. במהלך הראשון ניתן פירוש הלכתי לכל סוגי המצוות המנויים
בפסוקנו; במהלך השני הותאמו מדרשי האגדה לפריודיזציה ההלכתית (בעזרת הקטגוריה של 'אינו
מצווה ועושה') וגם הוכנסו למסגרת הגיונית (בעזרת ההנחה שכל המצוות נתגלו לאברהם ברוח
הקודש)[46]; ובמהלך השלישי יושבו הקושיות על מדרשי האגדה מהתנהגותם של יעקב, עמרם ומשה
בעזרת שילוב מרשים של הרלטיביזם הזמני המצומצם שמצינו אצל חז"ל עצמם עם הרלטיביזם
המקומי מיסודו של הראב"ע. למרבה ההפתעה, לא הושלמה בכך מלאכת הביאור. הרמב"ן ממשיך
במהלך רביעי, הנראה לקורא לא רק כמיותר אלא גם כבלתי-צפוי, הצעת ביאור פשטי לכתוב,
שאינו מתיישב בנקל עם ההגנה על המדרש. וזו לשונו:

ועל דרך הפשט תאמר שיהא משמרתי – אמונת האלהות, שהאמין בשם המיוחד ושמר
משמרת זו בלבו וחלק בה על עובדי עבודה זרה וקרא בשם ה' להשיב רבים לעבודתו (בר'
יב, ח). מצותי – ככל אשר צוהו ב'לך לך מארצך' (יב, א) ועולת בנו (כב, א) וגרישת האמה
ואת בנה (כא, יב). חקותי – ללכת בדרכי השם להיות חנון ורחום ועושה צדקה ומשפט
ולצות את בניו ואת ביתו בהם (יח, יח). ותורותי – המילה בעצמו ובניו ועבדיו (יז, י-יד),
ומצות בני נח כלן (ט, ד-ו), שהן 'תורה' להן.

מראי-המקום ששילבנו בדברי הרמב"ן ניכר שנקודת המוצא שלו כאן אינה הלכתית (כבמהלך
הראשון) אלא טקסטואלית – ארבעת סוגי המצוות שבפסוקנו מתועדים היטב בסיפורי אברהם

---

45   בהערה 39 לעיל נידונה עמדתם הא-היסטורית של רס"ג וראב"ע לגבי הקמת מצבה – מה שמותר היה בעבר
     (הקמת מצבה לה') מותר גם בהווה, ומה שאסור היה בעבר (הקמת מצבה לעבודה זרה) אסור גם בהווה.

46   הלגיטימיות של בירורים כאלה אינה מובנת מאליה, והרמב"ן ראה את עצמו כמי שממשיך (ומרחיב) את מה
     שעשה רש"י: 'אבל כיון שרש"י מדקדק במקומות (נ"א במקראות) אחר מדרשי האגדות וטורח לבאר פשטי
     המקרא, הרשה אותנו לעשות כן, כי שבעים פנים לתורה, ומדרשים רבים חלוקים בדברי חכמים' (ביאורו
     לבר' ח, ד).

(בתוספת 'מצוות בני נח כלן', ר"ל כפי שהוגדרו בביאור המרחיב של חז"ל). אמת, אין הוא מזהה את רכיבי הפסוק בשיטה סגנונית-הקשרית (שהיא הישגגו הפרשני הגדול של הרשב"ם), אלא רק בשיטה סמנטית-קטגוריאלית (כמו שעשה הראב"ע). ואכן ניתן לומר, שכפי שבשלושת מהלכיו הראשונים הוא מבהיר, מעמיק ומאשש את פירוש רש"י לפסוקנו, הרי הוא מציע במהלך הרביעי גרסה משופרת של פירוש הראב"ע, המותאמת לתפיסתו שלו.

בעוד הראב"ע ביאר את תיבת 'משמרתי' כשם הכולל את שלושת הסוגים המנויים אחריה, מעדיף הרמב"ן לבארה (ככל הנראה על סמך יהו' כב, ג וראה פירושו לבמ' ט, יט) במשמע ספציפי – הדבקות באמונת הייחוד וקריאתו הפומבית בשם ה'. את 'מצותי' הוא מבאר ממש כראב"ע, אך מוסיף על מצוות ההליכה לארץ והעקידה את מצות 'גרישת האמה ואת בנה'. לעומת זאת יש הבדל ניכר בהבנת 'חקותי' – לדעת הראב"ע הכוונה למכלול הגדול של 'חוקות [ה]נטועות בלב', ואילו הרמב"ן מעדיף פירוש הנשען על הכתוב בדבר מעלתו המוסרית של אברהם, ומעוגן בדברי חכמים על חיקוי מידותיו של הקב"ה כמקור התוקף של חובות מוסריות שאינן מפורשות בתורה. לגבי 'ותורותי' מסכים הרמב"ן לראב"ע, שהכוונה למצוות הכרוכות בברית המילה, אך הוא מוסיף עליהן את מצוות בני נח.

במישור ההיסטורי-עובדתי אין הפירושים של רש"י וראב"ע מתיישבים זה עם זה, והגרסה המשופרת שמציע הרמב"ן לשניהם לא נועדה להשלים ביניהם. לשיטת רש"י, מדרש הכתובים משמש מקור למידע בדבר היקף שמירת אברהם את המצוות, ולשיטת הראב"ע צריך לסמוך בזאת אך ורק על הפשט ועל 'הקבלה' (ר"ל מסורת היסטורית לא-פרשנית, במידה שזו נשתמרה בידי חז"ל, וראה ביאורו לבר' כב, ד). המינוח הנקוט בידי הרמב"ן וגם סדר הטיעון בפירושו לפסוקנו מעידים שהוא רואה ב'דרך הפשט' את הביאור העובדתי המינימלי, בעוד המדרשים מבטאים את 'דעת' חכמים בדבר דמותו ההיסטורית של אברהם (ר"ל אינם בגדר ביאור מחייב או בגדר מסורת היסטורית נאמנה שבידם). שלושת מהלכיו הראשונים באים להראות שבשום פנים אין הכתובים מכחישים את דעתם זו המקסימליסטית, ושהיא אכן אפשרית מבחינה היסטורית. ואילו במהלך הרביעי, שבו הוא חותם את פירושו, מבהיר הרמב"ן שעל-אף כל זאת אין דעה זו מוכחת מלשון הכתובים, ומכאן משתמע שדמותו המדרשית של אברהם סבירה פחות מבחינה היסטורית מדמותו הפשטית.

הרמב"ן היה, אם כן, שותף לראב"ע לא רק באמון בכוחה של 'דרך הפשט' לחשוף את אמת הכתוב, אלא גם בהכרה באמיתות הנצחית של המדעים, המחייבת לצמצם את חלותו של הרלטיביזם ההיסטורי מחמת על-זמניותו של הרלטיביזם המקומי. ואילו אברנבאל, המבאר את בר' כו, ה בעקבות הפשט ההיסטורי של ראב"ע, רד"ק ורמב"ן (בתוספת שינויים משניים שאין בהם חידוש עקרוני), ושגם הכיר בממד האסטרולוגי של בחירת ישראל ושל קדושת הארץ (ראה ביאורו לדב' לא, טז-יח), שולל מכל וכל את הרלטיביזציה המקומית של המצוות:

והראב"ע כתב שאיסור העריות היה מצד המקום. כי יעקב לקח שתי אחיות בחרן, ואחריו עמרם לקח את יוכבד דודתו במצרים, ולא נטמאו בהם, אבל היתה הטומאה בעריות בארץ כנען. ואין טעם בדבריו, כי הם לא נשמרו מזה, ר"ל יעקב ועמרם, לפי שעדין לא ניתנה תורה ולא נאסרו העריות. כי בלי ספק הטומאה ורוע המעשה כולל בחרן ובמצרים כמו

בארץ כנען. וגם בבית יעקב היתה מריבה וקטטה מפני נשיו לאה ורחל. והקב"ה כשרצה
לזכות ישראל הדריכם במעגלי צדק ודרכי יושר שלא שערו בו ראשונים! (סוף ביאורו
לפרשת 'אחרי מות').

לא זו בלבד שהרלטיביזם המקומי נשלל באשר הוא פוגם בתוקפן של מצוות התורה, אלא
שהרלטיביזם הזמני נתפס כמעצים את צדקתן ויושרן. הקטטה והמריבה שבבית יעקב נבעה מכך
שעדיין לא נאסר לקחת שתי אחיות בחייהן, ואף הראשונים (ר"ל האבות) לא יכלו לשער מדעתם
שאסור לעשותם זאת. אין לטשטש את העובדה שהאבות לא קיימו את המצוות, משום שהיא נחוצה
כרקע נאות לזכייה הגדולה שבמתן התורה. אין להתנצל על הפריודיזציה המקראית, אלא אדרבה,
יש להעלותה על נס – גדולתה של התורה הוא בחידושה! בעבור בעלי הפשט שקדמוהו, לא יצאה
ההיסטוריזציה של המצוות מגדר של כורח פרשני שיש להשלים עמו ברב או במעט, ואילו בעבור
אברבנאל היה האיחור היחסי של מתן התורה בתולדות ישראל ביטוי של רצון האל, אשר ללא הבנתו
לאשורו אי־אפשר להגיע להערכה שלמה של המצוות ולגילוי טעמן.

פרק ג: הריאליזם הביניימי ומחירו

ההתייחסות הריאליסטית אל תקופת המקרא מהותית לדרך הפשט. בעיני בעלי המדרש, התורה
כתובה בלשון קְדושה, על־אנושית ועל־טבעית, וקדושה זו חופפת גם על העבר המקראי, הנתפס
כתקופה מעין־מיתית, שגיבוריה הגדולים הם על־אנושיים והחוקיות השלטת בה היא במידה רבה
על־טבעית. ואילו בעיני בעלי הפשט התורה כתובה כלשון בני־אדם וגם המציאות המעוצבת בה
זהה בעיקרון לזו המוכרת לנו מהתנסותנו. התפיסה הראשונה היא א־היסטורית, באשר היא מותירה
את ימי הזוהר המקראיים כעידן נפרד הניצב בראשית ההיסטוריה אך אינו כלול בה. ואילו התפיסה
השנייה היא היסטורית, באשר היא מניחה שמאז הבריאה עולם כמנהגו נוהג, ושלפיכך גם בתקופת
המקרא אין נס אלא חריג אשר על התרחשותו מספר הכתוב בגלוי ובמפורש.[47]

רש"י הולך גם בזאת בבירור בדרכם של חז"ל, הן מבחינת התפיסה הבלתי־ריאליסטית והן
מבחינת המתודה הדרשית, המאפשרת להעגין את התפיסה הזאת בכתוב. כך, למשל, הוא מבסס
(בפירושו לבר' כה, כ) את היותה של רבקה בת שלוש שנים בזמן נישואיה ליצחק על חישוב
כרונולוגי מעין־פשטי, ומתייחס (בפירושו לבר' כד, יז) למדרש בדבר מי המעיין שעלו לקראתה
כאל עובדה ממשית. ואילו כל בעלי הפשט הבינו באורח מציאותי את פרשת שאיבת המים והשקיית
הגמלים בידי הנערה טובת המראה ונדיבת הלב. בתפיסה המדרשית משתאים מכך שהתינוקת
המתנהגת כצדקת מכל מה שמוכר לנו במציאות, ואילו בתפיסה הפשטית משתאים מכך
שהנערה שהגיעה לפרקה המתנהגת כצדקת עושה זאת בתוכי המציאות המוכרת לנו.[48]

---

47 הראב"ע היטיב לנסח תפיסה זאת בפירושו לבר' מו, כז: 'ובדרש כי יוכבד נולדה בין החומות, גם זה תמה למה
לא הזכיר הכתוב הפלא שנעשה עמה שהולידה משה והיא בת ק"ל שנה? ולמה הזכיר דבר שרה שהיתה בת
תשעים?', וכן בפירושו הארוך לשמ' כ, א: 'והנה זה הדבר הפלא ופלא, שהשם דבר "זכור" ו"שמור" בבת אחת,
והיה ראוי להיות זה כתוב ומפורש בתורה יותר מכל האותות והמופתים שנכתבו!'.

48 על דרך זו אין רש"י רואה את כבדות ידיו של משה כהתעייפות טבעית, ובעקבות המדרש הוא מסבירה כעונש
'בשביל שנתעצל במצוה ומנה אחר תחתיו נתייקרו ידיו' (ביאורו לשמ' יז, יב). כנגד זאת כותב הראב"ע בפירושו

בימי הביניים לא היו ידועים שום מקורות היסטוריים חוץ־מקראיים לגבי ימי בית ראשון, ולפיכך היה הריאליזם ההיסטורי של פרשני הפשט מנוע מלהסתייע במידע היסטורי חיצוני, וצריך היה להסתפק בהקשה מן הריאליה העכשווית (הקרויה בפי רשב"ם 'דרך ארץ'). ומאחר שבתפיסה הביניימית ההיסטוריה היא סטטית למדי ושינוי העיתים הוא מינימלי, הם לא חששו להשליך על העבר המקראי את הידוע להם מן ההווה. כך מספר הראב"ע בפירושו הארוך לשמ' יט, כג, שסעדיה גאון 'שנים רבות חשב בזה הפסוק ולא ידע טעמו (רוצה לומר, לא הבין מדוע משה אומר לה' רק עכשיו שהוא ביצע את מצוותו להזהיר את העם מלעלות להר) עד שראה בספר מוסְרֵי מלכי פרס, שאין רשות לשליח לומר למלך "עשיתי שליחותך" עד שיצוונו לעשות דבר אחר, אז יאמר לו'. בהמשך הראב"ע אמנם דוחה ביאור זה מסיבה פרשנית, אך ניכר מדבריו שהוא התרשם מניסיונו של רס"ג להשתמש במידע חיצוני על גינוני בית המלוכה הפרסי כדי להיטיב להבין את התנהגותו של משה בעומדו לפני המלך שבשמים.

בעניין זה היה לראב"ע יתרון יחסי על שאר בעלי הפשט. מחמת נדודיו מארצות האיסלם לארצות הנצרות, הוא נהיה מודע להבדלים הניכרים שבין שתי התרבויות האלה, והבין שאין לייַשם בפשיטות את הריאליה המקומית על ימי המקרא. בפירוש הארוך לשמ' יב, ז הוא מסתייע בשני מאפיינים של האדריכלות האיסלמית, כדי להוכיח שהדם הניתן על המשקוף ושתי המזוזות צריך לשמש 'סימן למשחית שיראנו', ולא נועד, כסברת רבים, להראות למצרים שישראל אינם חוששים עוד לשחוט את תועבת מצרים בפרהסיה. וראייתו – נתינת הדם נעשתה במקום מוצנע, שכן המשקוף אינם הקורה המחברת את המזוזות, אלא חלון הקבוע בחזית הבית, אשר אינו פונה לרשות הרבים, אלא לחצר מוקפת חומה. 'וככה מנהג כל ארץ ישמעאל, כי מנהג הערלים לא היה כמנהג המצרים (ר"ל מנהגי הנוצרים אינם המשך של מנהגי מצרים), ואפילו במאכליהן, כמו "פתות אותה פתים" (ויק' ב, ו; ר"ל הכתוב מעיד שבישראל אכלו פתיתים כנהוג בארצות ערב ולא פת שלמה כנוצרים). וככה תכשיטי הנשים לשום נזם באף ובאזן וכל אשר הזכיר ישעיה על בנות ציון (יש' ג, יח-כד)'. הריאליה האיסלמית היא המשקפת את הריאליה המקראית, משום שארצות הישמעאלים הן ארצות המקרא, ובכללן ארץ ישראל – 'וכבר הזכרתי לך כי מנהג ארץ ישראל ותכשיטיהם אינם כמנהג אלה המקומות' (הפירוש הארוך לשמ' כח, לו שנכתב בצפון צרפת).

ברם הראב"ע נזהר מלכוף על פשט הכתוב את ההנחה הסוחפת שבכל עניין ועניין נשתמרה בארצות ערב הרציפות התרבותית מימי קדם. בפירושו לבר' מט, לג הוא מעיר, שבניגוד למצופה היתה מיטתו של יעקב מוגבהת כמו המיטות בארצות הנוצרים: 'ויאסף רגליו אל המטה – כי בתחילה ישב על המטה ורגליו תלויות כמנהג ארץ אדום היום, ולא כן מטות הישמעאלים'. ובפירושו לב' מו, לד הוא אף מסביר שכדי להבין מדוע 'תועבת מצרים כל רעה צאן' חייבים להבחין בין המצרים הקדמונים לבין תושביה הנוכחיים של מצרים: 'לאות כי בימים ההם לא היו המצרים אוכלים בשר, ולא יעזבו (ר"ל יניחו) אדם שיזבח צאן, כאשר יעשו היום אנשי הודו. ומי שהוא רועה צאן תועבה

הקצר על אתר: 'וידיו היו זקנים (בכ"י: כבדים וכצ"ל) מהזקנה, גם אין בעולם גבור שיוכל להרים ידיו שתי שעות, ואף כי "עד בא השמש". ולמה זה (כך) ידוע מדבר התולדת (ר"ל מחכמת הטבע)'. גם הרמב"ן מבהיר שלפי הפשט צריך להסביר את חולשת משה באורח טבעי: 'על דרך הפשט – כאשר יניח ידו באונס מפני כובד ידיו...', וכך מבארים גם ר' אברהם בן הרמב"ם ואברבנאל. וראה גם את מחלוקת המפרשים לגבי 'לא אוכל עוד לצאת ולבוא' (דב' לא, ב) ולגבי 'לא כהתה עינו ולא נס לחה' (שם, לד, ז).

היא, שהוא שותה חלב. ואנשי הודו לא יאכלו ולא ישתו כל אשר יצא מחי מרגיש עד היום הזה'.
הזהירות ההיסטורית, הניזונה מן הידיעה שמצרים נכבשה בידי הערבים המוסלמים שאכילת בשר
מותרת להם, הולכת יד ביד עם הנאיביות האנתרופולוגית, שלפיה אפשר ללמוד מנוהגם של אנשי
הודו 'עד היום הזה' על מה שהיה במצרים העתיקה.[49] ואילו לגבי זיהויָם של כמה מכלי הנגינה
המקראיים גברה ידה של הזהירות: 'זה הכלל: אין דרך לדעת אלה כלי הנגונים, כי כלים לנגונים
הרבה ימצאו בארץ ישמעאל ואנשי אדום לא ראום, גם יש באדום לא שמעום חכמי ישמעאל'
(פירושו לתה' קן, ה). נדודיו אפשרו לראב"ע, יותר מלכל אדם אחר, להתרשם מן השוני הרב שבין
כלי הנגינה בתחומי התרבות השונים, והוא הסיק מן השפע המביך הזה כמה מופרכת עלולה להיות
ההקשה מן ההווה על העבר, ומארץ אחת על רעותה. אך הישג נדיר זה אינו חל על שאר תחומי
הריאליה, שבהם גם הראב"ע לא היה יכול לחרוג ממגבלות הריאליזם הביניימי.

דוגמה מובהקת לכך משמשת גישתו לפרשת בת יפתח. בעוד במדרשי חכמים אפשרה ההסתייגות
החריפה ממעשהו של יפתח להבין את העלאת בתו לעולה כמשמעה (ראה ס, ג; ויק' רבה
לז, ד; קה' רבה י, יז), מוציא הראב"ע הן את הכתוב והן את המדרשים ממשמעם: 'ואשר יחשבו כי
כל האוכל או השותה בשעת התקופה (ר"ל בזמן חילוף העונות) ינזק ויתנפח דרש הדורש הוא [...].
ודרש שנשחטו יצחק ובת יפתח (בשעת התקופה) ולכן צריך להימנע מאכילה ושתייה) יש לו סוד,
כי לא נשחטו כאשר פרשתי בספר (המהדיר מתקן על-פי שני כתבי-יד: בספרי).[50] גם בביאורו לדב'
כד, יט הוא מזכיר בקיצור את נדרו של יפתח בחינת ראיה לכך שבמקרא יש ו' החיבור
במשמע של 'או' (השווה לפירושים הארוך לשמ' מ, לח): 'וכמוהו: "והיה לה/ והעליתיהו עולה" (שופ'
יא, לא), כאשר פירשתיו'. שני ציונים אלה מתייחסים אל-נכון לפירושו לנביאים ראשונים (או

49   ר' יוסף אבן כספי, אשר בניגוד לראב"ע הגיע למצרים, עומד בספרו טירת כסף (עמ' 19–20) על החשיבות
     העקרונית של ידיעת הריאליה להבנת המקרא ועל היתרון הרב שיש למראה עיניים בנידון. הוא מדגיש זאת, בין
     השאר, על-ידי אישור ביאורו של אחד של הראב"ע והפרכת ביאור אחר. הוא נסע למצרים כדי ללמוד את משנת
     הרמב"ם מפי צאצאיו ובכך נתאכזב, והריהו מתנחם בתרומת הביקור לפרשנות המקרא: 'ונחמתי במה שאמר
     החכם "אין אחר ההשתדלות אשם", וגם במה שהשגתי מהרגש העניינים, לא הייתי משער בם לפנים ממנהג
     הארצות ההם, עד שיסודתנו הוא "דברה
     תורה כלשון ב"א (ברכות לא, ע"ב), ואין הכונה בלשון כל בני אדם, איש איש ללשונו וכמנהגו, אבל תחלה
     בלשון העברי, לשון ישראל, בני עבר וכמנהגם בארץ ההיא (ר"ל הריאליה של ארצות המקרא). וזה יתבאר עוד
     תמיד בהגיעי בפירוש הפרטים, אבל אזכור בזה משלים. הנה כתוב בתורה "וירכיבם על החמור" (שמ' ד, כ),
     וידוע מה שכתב ע"ז הרב חכם אבן עזרא (הכוונה לדבריו בפירושו הארוך על אתר: 'והוצרכו הזקנים [ר"ל בעלי
     תרגום השבעים] לתרגם "על החמור" – "על נושא האדם" בעבור שהוא דרך גרעון שתרכב אשת הנביא על חמור
     אחד היא ושני בניה [...] והחמורים שהם במצרים יקרים ונכבדים מהפרדים...'), ואני ראיתי כמו זה העניין פעמים
     רבות. אבל בלבול דבריו בפירוש "הנה יוצא המימה" (שמ' ז, טו) שזכר בו שתי דעות (שתי הדעות באות בפירוש
     הארוך, הראשונה על האתר: 'מנהג מלך מצרים עד היום לצאת בתמוז ואב, כי אז יגדל היאור, לראות כמה מעלות
     עלה...', והשנייה על ח, טז: 'מנהג המלכים לצאת בבקר אל הנהר, כי ראות המים טוב לעינים'), אין העניין,
     לפי דעתי, כאחד מהם. אבל העניין כי מלך מצרים לא יצא מפתח ביתו רק יום השלישי ויום השבת מהשבוע,
     שילך בכל אחד משני אלו הימים בבקר השכם אל מקום רחב ידים על או על שפת היאור לשחק שם בכדור הקטן
     עם פרשיו ושריו. וזהו אמרו "ונצבת לקראתו על שפת היאור", כי לפי דעתי משה בא אליו באניה קטנה דרך
     היאור ומדבר אליו דבריו, בהיות פרעה עומד על שפת היאור וכאשר כלה דבריו ישוב לו לדרכו...'). משמע אזניו
     של הראב"ע הם סביר יותר ממראה עיניו של אבן כספי, המשליך על הפרעונים הקדמונים את נוהגי בית המלוכה
     הערבי במאה הארבע-עשרה.

50   ספר העיבור, מהד' שזח"ה, ליק תרל"ד, דף ט, ע"א.

לספר אחר מספריו האבודים), אשר הרמב"ן מצטט ממנו במישרין או בעקיפין, בביאורו לויק' כז,
כט: 'ואל תהיה נפתה בהבלי ר"א האומר כי פירוש "והעליתיהו עולה", לומר: אם יהיה היוצא מדלתי
ביתי איש או אשה "והיה לה' קודש" – שיהיה פרוש מדרכי העולם לעמוד לשרת בשם ה' בתפלה
והודות לאלהים, ואם יהיה דבר ראוי ליקרב אעלנו עולה. ועשה בית לבתו מחוץ לעיר והתבודדה
שם וכלכלה כל ימיה ואיש לא ידעה והיתה בתו צרורה. ואלה דברי רוח...'. רד"ק (בפירושו לשופ'
יא, לא) מביא בשם אביו, הריק"ם, ביאור דומה מאוד, אם כי בניסוח שונה (ומסתבר שביאורו של
הראב"ע הגיע אל ריק"ם במסירה שבעל־פה). ביאור זה התקבל על דעתו של רד"ק ובעקבותיו גם
על דעת רלב"ג ואברבנאל. אין אנו יודעים מה הניע את הראב"ע לבאר את הנדר באופן כה דחוק,
אך ניתן לשער שהוא ושאר בעלי הפשט (פרט לרמב"ן) לא הסכינו עם הרעיון ששופט בישראל
ייתפס לקרבן אדם, והעדיפו לפרש שהוא הקדיש את בתו לחיי פרישות, כמקובל בארצות
הנוצרים.[51] אברבנאל אכן מגדיר את הבעיה בצורה דומה: 'השאלה החמישית [...] והנה זה היה
העברה על דת ונדר כזה לא היה נדר, ואיך עשה זה הפך הדין והתורה? ואיך לא גנהו על כך הכתוב?'
אברבנאל גם מעמידנו במפורש על ההשוואה עם מנזרי הנשים שבימיו: 'וכוונתי שמזה למדו אומת
אדום לעשות בתי פרישות (קליסט"ר) לנשים, שיכנסו שמה ולא יצאו משם כל ימיהם ולא יראו איש
בעוד בחיים חיותם'. הביקורת החריפה של הרמב"ן (בהמשך דבריו המובאים לעיל) על ביאורו של
הראב"ע היא בעיקרה מוסרית–דתית: '...ואם הדבר כן, היתה בתו הבוכה על בתוליה ורעותיה עמה
כוונתם לקלס אתנן, וחס ושלום שיהיה חוק בישראל לתתנות לבת יפתח ארבעה ימים בשנה מפני שלא
נישאת לבעל והיתה את ה' בטהרה!...' ודומה שגם מבין השיטין של דבריו נשמעת התייחסות
(אמנם ניגודית) להווייה הנוצרית – וכי יעלה על הדעת שבישראל התאבלו על אשה שהוקדשה
לעבוד את ה' בטהרה גמורה כאשר הנוצרים מפארים ומרוממים את המעשה הזה!?

הרמב"ן הבין את הקרבת הבת כמשמעה, אך טרח הרבה לשלב את טעותו הקשה של יפתח בדרך
החשיבה ההלכתית. גם רש"י ור' יוסף קרא הבינו את הסיפור כפשוטו, אך הם הגיעו לכך בפשטות
גמורה, מבלי להיות מוטרדים מן הפער שבין מעשהו של יפתח לבין ההנחות של חכמי ספרד
ופרובאנס לגבי ההתנהגות המצופה ממושיענו עמו. ואילו הראב"ע דחה את האפשרות שבת יפתח
נשחטה בידי אביה באותה ודאות שבה דחה את המדרש שלפיו יצחק נשחט בפרשת העקידה (ראה
בר' רבה נו, יא). הוא יכול היה לפרש כך רק משום שמצא בידר ביאור תחבירי לגיטימי (אם כי
דחוק), ומשום שמציאות החיים בארצות הנוצרים שיוותה לפירושו סבירות ריאליסטית. כך
מאפשרות, למרבה האירוניה, הפילולוגיה והריאליה, שתי המתודות הפשטיות המובהקות, לבעלי
הפשט השבויים בראיית העולם של תקופתם, לדבוק בבטחה רבה בפשט מדומה.

---

51 ההלכה דומה של ההווייה המנזרית על ישראל בתקופת המקרא יש בתפיסת ראב"ע את הנשים 'הצבאת אשר צבאו
פתח אהל מועד' (שמ' לח, ח). בעוד אונקלוס ראה בהן מתפללות ('דאתין לצלאה בתרע משכן זמנא'), מתאר
אותן ראב"ע כצבא של נשים פרושיות, החברות במעין מנזר ללא חומות: 'והנה היו בישראל נשים עובדות ה',
שסרו מתאוות זה העולם, ונתנו מראותיהן נדבה, כי אין להם (בכמה כת"י: להן) צורך עוד להתיפות, רק באות
יום יום אל פתח אהל מועד להתפלל ולשמוע דברי המצות. וזהו "אשר צבאו פתח אהל מועד" – כי היו רבות'
(הפירוש הארוך שם).

פרק ד: מפרספקטיבה זמנית בתוך הכתוב לפרספקטיבה זמנית לגבי הכתוב

ההבחנה בין ציוני־זמן המוסבים על מה שהיה לבין ציוני־זמן המוסבים על מה שיהיה היא משמעותית
רק בזיקה למקומו של הדובר על פני רצף הזמן. מאורע שהוא היום בגדר 'מחר' יהיה מחרתיים בגדר
'אתמול', ומה שהיה בגדר עתיד בעבור מחבר קדום יהיה בהכרח בגדר עבר בפיו של מחבר מאוחר.
דרך הפשט חייבת להיות מודעת לנקודת־הראות הזמנית של הכותב, משום שהיא מנועה מלבאר
את מה שמנוסח בבירור כמעשה שהיה כאילו הוא בגדר נבואה לעתיד (אלא אם כן ברי שהכתוב
נוקט 'עבר נבואי'). הרשב"ם מבהיר עניין זה בביאורו ל'הוא אבי מואב עד היום' (בר' יט, לז): 'עד
היום – בימי משה, וכן כל "עד היום" – עד ימי הסופר שכתב את הדבר'. ברם אם נחיל את הכלל
הזה על הפסוק 'אשר יאמר היום בהר ה' יראה' (בר' כב, יד), ניאלץ לומר שהמלה 'היום' אינה מוסבת
כאן על ימי משה, אלא על ימי שלמה, שבהם אכן ניתן להסב את 'יראה כל זכורך' (דב' טז, טז) על
המקדש שבירושלים.

רש"י, בפירושו לפסוק זה, הקדים פתרון לבעיה על־ידי ניסוחו של כלל הפוך, שלפיו כל
אנכרוניזם שבמקרא אינו אלא מדומה, משום שצריך להבינו כהגיד נבואי: 'היום – הימים העתידין,
כמו "עד היום הזה" שבכל המקרא, שכל הדורות הבאים הקוראים את המקרא הזה אומרים "עד היום
הזה" על היום שעומדים בו'. הפתרון הזה הגיוני לחלוטין, אך לאו דווקא סביר. מבחינה הגיונית אין
כל מניעה לכך שבספר נבואי כמו התורה ידובב הכתוב את בני הדורות העתידים. אך בעיני בעלי
הפשט הפתרון הזה איננו סביר, שכן אילו לכך התכוון הכתוב, היה נוקט לשון: אשר יאמר מחר.

הרשב"ם אכן נמנע בפירושו לפסוקנו מלחרוג מדרך הפשט, אך נאלץ לגמש אותה במידה יתרה.
פירושו מנוסח כפרפראזה מרחיקת־לכת של לשון הכתוב: 'אשר יאמר היום – ולמחר (השלמה נועזת
של לשון קצרה), בהר ה' יראה, בהר ה' נראה ה' לאברהם (הפיכת ההווה ההתמדי לעבר היסטורי
והשלמה נוספת של היגד מובלע)'.

לעומת זאת נקט הראב"ע דרך אחרת לגמרי, ככל הנראה משום שמחויבותו הדתית לפשוטו של
מקרא גברה על מחויבותו לאמונה המסורה בדבר היותו של משה מחברה של התורה כולה. וכך הוא
דבק בפשט האנכרוניסטי של פסוקנו, אך נאלץ לגמש את דברי החכמים לגבי שמונת הפסוקים
האחרונים של התורה שכתבם יהושע (בבא בתרא טו, ע"א). והריהו מרחיב את הפתח הזה וטוען,
בלשון רמזים מוסתרת בקפידה, שפסוקנו, בדומה לכמה פסוקים אנכרוניסטיים אחרים, שובץ
בתורה בידי נביא מאוחר (דבר זה מתברר כאשר קוראים במצורף את ביאוריו לבר' יב, ו; כב, יד;
דב' א, ב; לד, א, ו).[52]

---

52 ר' יוסף בן אליעזר חשף את סודו של הראב"ע בביאוריו ל'הכנעני אז בארץ' (צפנת פענח, חלק א, עמ' 91–93)
ול'ואם תבין סוד השנים עשר' (שם, חלק ב, עמ' 65–66). לפי מסירה שבעל־פה, המובאת בספר מושב זקנים
(כתב־יד פריז 260), איחר גם הרשב"ם פסוק אחד בתורה מחמת היותו אנכרוניסטי: 'ואלה המלכים (בר' לו, לא)
פרשב"ם שפרש' זו נכתבה בימי שופטים. וק[שה] אפש' ס"ת חסר ונקראת על שם משה רבי' כדמקשי' בספרי.
וע"ק (ר"ל ועוד קשה) שהרי יש כמה מקראות שכת' משה רבי' על שם העתיד כמו שפרש"י בפ' בראשית – כוש
ואשור ולא היו עדיין ונכת' במק' ע"ש העתיד. גמגו'[ם].' ראה יצחק לנגה, 'ס' מושב זקנים', המעין יב, גיליון ד
(תמוז תשל"ב), עמ' 83 [אני מודה לד"ר מרק שפירא על שהפנה אותי למובאה זו]. והשווה ישראל מ' תא־שמע,
'משהו על ביקורת המקרא באשכנז בימי־הביניים', בתוך: המקרא בראי מפרשיו – ספר זיכרון לשרה קמין,
בעריכת שרה יפת, ירושלים תשנ"ד, עמ' 453–459.

השפעתו של 'ספר הישר', פירוש הראב"ע לתורה, ניכרת היטב בפירושי התורה של ר' אברהם בן הרמב"ם, רד"ק, רמב"ן, ר' יוסף אבן כספי, רלב"ג ואברבנאל. אף־על־פי־כן אין הרמב"ן ואבן כספי מתייחסים כלל לקושי שבפסוקנו, וגם ארבעת האחרים נמנעים בבירור מללכת בעקבות הראב"ע בסוגיה זו, אל נכון משום שהגמישות הדוגמטית שלו לא היתה כשרה בעיניהם. והריהם מעדיפים לנקוט שיטה הדומה לשיטת הרשב"ם (שאת פירושו לא הכירו), ולגמש באורח קיצוני את דרך הפשט. הזהיר שבהם הוא ר' אברהם בן הרמב"ם, המבאר את 'אשר יאמר היום בהר ה' יראה' כהבטחה לאברהם, שלעתיד לבוא 'יֵראה העולֶה לחג' במקום העקידה. הוא מאשש תפיסה זו בעזרת העובדה שאברהם כבר קיבל שתי הבטחות בעבר (בר' יב, ב; טו, יח), ונמנע מלהסביר את התיבה הקשה 'היום', אך דומה שהוא מתכוון אליה באמרו בגילוי לב 'ובכל זה קשה לנו הדיבור כפי קוצר הבנתנו'.

כמו הרשב"ם, נזקק גם רד"ק באורח מופלג למידת לשון קצרה (שהיא אכן מידה פשטית מובהקת, אך שהמפריז בשימושה מאבד את אחיזתו בלשון הכתוב). הוא מבאר את הסיפא של פסוקנו כדברו של אברהם, המתנבא על אודות הזיקה שבין העקידה לבין בניית בית־המקדש בהר ההוא. כדי להבין את הכתוב כך אין רד"ק יכול לבאר את התיבה 'היום' כציון־זמן, העונה על השאלה 'מתי יאמר?', אלא נדחק לבארה כמושא, העונה על השאלה 'מה עתיד להיאמר?' בתשובה: [אירועי] היום [הזה], כלומר מעשה העקידה. כמו כן אין הוא יכול לבאר את הפסוקית 'בהר ה' יראה' בפשיטות כמשפט שעיקרי הכולל ציון־מקום, אלא נדחק לבארה כמשפט טפל מציין זמן, ולשם כך הריהו מסרס את סדר המלים כדי שיהיה אפשר להוסיף לנשוא מילת־זמן מובלעת – [כש]'יראה ה' בו. וזו לשון פירושו:

אשר יאמר היום – זה היום יסופר בהר כשיראה ה' בו, כשיבנה בו מזבח ובית המקדש, יאמר אז ויסופר היום הזה שהעליתי בני יצחק לעולה. כי זה נאמר לו בנבואה למה בחר בהר ההוא, כי עתידים בניו להקריב שם קרבנות.

בניגוד לרד"ק, ברור לרלב"ג שהסיפא של פסוקנו אינה דבר הגיבור (ר"ל אברהם) אלא דבר המספר (ר"ל משה). על כן הוא מסב את ציון־הזמן 'היום' 'על דור המדבר, אשר בו 'היו קוראים האנשים אותו ההר "הר ה' יראה"'. הם יכלו לעשות זאת לא משום שהתנבאו על מה שעתיד להיות בימי שלמה, אלא משום שידעו מה שאירע בימי אברהם, שכן ברישא של הפסוק מסופר 'שכבר קרא אברהם את השם למקום ההוא, להורות על מעלת המקום ההוא, ושהוא מוכן מאד אל שידבק בו השפע האלהי, וזה הר המוריה אשר שם היה בית המקדש'. הביאור הזה סביר לגמרי מבחינה לשונית וסגנונית, אך הוא קשה מבחינה תוכנית – מה רבותא יש בעובדה שלא רק אברהם קרא כך למקום העקידה, אלא גם דור המדבר?

אברבנאל מציע את הביאור הנועז ביותר מבחינת השיטה ומבחינת התוכן. לדעתו, במילים 'ויקרא אברהם שם המקום ההוא' לא מדובר על קריאת שם למקום העקידה, אלא על קריאה וזעקה אל האל, אשר אותו אברהם מכנה 'שם המקום ההוא'. כינוי זה אמור בלשון קצרה מאוד, שהקורא חייב להשלים את כל מה שהובלע בה: 'ויקרא אברהם [אל] [ה]שם [הנכבד] (כפי שקרוי האל בדב' כח, נח) [המשגיח והמשפיע ב]המקום ההוא'. נביא בזה את המהלך הראשון של הביאור כלשונו:

...כי הנה לא מצינו שנקרא המקום ההוא בשום זמן 'ה' יראה' ולא 'בהר ה' יראה'. ומפני זה

נ"ל לפרש 'ויקרא אברהם שם המקום ההוא' שאינו קריאת שם אבל הוא, כתרגומו, תפלה וצעקה, שקרא אברהם אל אלהיו, כי הוא השם הנכבד המשגיח והמשפיע במקום ההוא, רוצה לומר שהיה עתיד לתת שכינתו במקום ההוא.

עכשו באה בכתוב תפילת אברהם, אשר המלה 'היום' משמשת בה כציון־זמן המוסב על ימיו שלו, ואשר צריך להשלים בה את המלים המוקפות: 'ה' יראה (במשמע של 'יתן אל לבו' כפי שמצינו בספר שמ"ב טז, יב) [את] אשר יאמר היום (על־ידי כל בני האדם): "בהר ה' יראה" [שלא נעקד שם יצחק אלא איל]'. חסד מניעת ביצוע ההקרבה ייחשב לאברהם לגנות, ולכן מובלעת בדבריו הבקשה להתיר לו לעשות ביצחק כאשר נצטווה בתחילה:

והיתה תפלתו וצעקתו אחרי שהעלה את האיל: 'ה' יראה אשר יאמר היום בהר ה' יראה', רוצה לומר: ה' אלהים, יהי נא חסדך להורות מה שיאמרו היום הזה מכל בני אדם, והוא שלא עקדתי את בני, ושכל כוונתי היתה שוא ודבר כזב, ויביאו על זה ראיה באמרו 'בהר ה' יראה', כי לא נמצא שם נעקד כי אם איל לא אחד לא יצחק! והיה תכלית תפלתו ותחנתו שלא ימנעונו מהעלות את יצחק גם אחר האיל, כי לולי זה לא תאמן כונתו ורצונו בעבודתו. ומפני זה בא לו דבור שני מהמלאך, ואמר לו 'יען אשר עשית את הדבר הזה' [...] לכן בשכר זה נשבע ה' 'כי ברך אברכך' וגו'.

דומה שאברבנאל נתפס להגשמה כה מרחיקת־לכת של דרך הפשט משום שהיה עליו לפתור שתי בעיות מעיקות: האחת, להסיר מעל לסיפא של פסוקנו את צל האנכרוניזם (אשר הראב"ע רומז עליו ור' אברהם בן הרמב"ם מודה שלא מצא לו פתרון נאות); והשנייה, לתת מענה פשטי להתרסה של בעלי הפולמוס הנוצריים, הטוענים לעליונות הצליבה שמשמשה על העקידה שלא מומשה.[53] והריהו משליך בבטחה רבה את ההוויה הפולמוסית הספרדית על תקופת האבות, ומניח שאבי האומה חזה מראש את השימוש הפולמוסי שיעשו שיאבי עמו בהווה ולעתיד לבוא בביטול צו ההקרבה, והתחנן לפני ה' להרשות לו להעלות את יצחק לעולה, לא משום שהדבר מוטל עליו כחובה, אלא משום שהדבר דרוש לחיזוק האמונה של בניו לדורותיהם.

שונה לחלוטין גישת אברבנאל לאנכרוניזמים שבספרי נביאים ראשונים. בהקדמת פירושו לספר יהושע, הוא טוען שהביטוי 'עד היום הזה' (השכיח מאוד בספרי יהושע ושמואל) מעיד, בצד ראיות נוספות, שיהושע ושמואל לא כתבו את הספרים האלה. והריהו מבחין בין ספר התורה, שבו כתוב במפורש שמשה כתבו (דב' לא, ט, כד), ולפיכך אי־אפשר לאחר את זמן חיבורו, לבין ספרי יהושע ושמואל, שבהם לא נאמר מי כתבם. בעקבות ההבחנה הספרותית הזאת הוא משיב לטענתנו הצפויה של הקורא: 'ואל תתמה על אשר נטיתי מדעת חז"ל בזה (רוצה לומר בשאלת המחברות של ספרי נביאים ראשונים), כי גם בגמרא לא הסכימו בדברים האלה וחלקו שם, אם משה כתב ספר איוב ואם כתב יהושע שמונה פסוקים מהתורה. ואחרי שחז"ל ספקו בקצת המאמר, אינו מהבטל שגם אני אבחר בקצתו דרך יותר ישר ונאות, כפי טבע הפסוקים ויושרם'.

כבר במאה האחת־עשרה הגיע ר' יוסף קרא בצפון־צרפת למסקנה זו סמך על

53 על התשובות של בעלי המדרש ובעלי הפיוט ראה: שלום שפיגל, 'מאגדות העקדה', ספר היובל לאלכסנדר מארקס, ניו־יורק תש"י, עמ' תעא–תקמז.

הפרספקטיבה ההיסטורית לגבי השתלשלות המינוח הנבואי, הבאה בגוף הכתוב: 'לפנים בישראל
כה אמר האיש בלכתו לדרוש אלהים: לכו ונלכה עד הראה, כי לנביא היום יקרא לפנים הראה'
(שמ"א ט, ט). והריהו מסכם את חקירתו הפילולוגית-היסטורית בדברים הבאים:

מכלל שספר זה לא נכתב בימי שמואל, שכשתחזור על כל המקרא לא תמצא שנקרא נביא
'רואה' כי אם כאן, שהוא אומר 'אי זה בית הראה' (פס' יח). למדת שדורו של שמואל הוא
נקרא 'לפנים בישראל', ודור אחרון (רוצה לומר מאוחר) לשמואל, ועל אותו הדור הוא אומר
'כי לנביא היום וגו'. ורבותינו זכרוניהם ברכה אמרו ששמואל כתב ספרו, והמאיר לארץ
ישים מחשך לאור ומעקשים למישור (רוצה לומר יסייע בידנו ליישב את הסתירה שבין
הכתוב כפשוטו לבין דברי רז"ל).

כך הגיעו, באופן בלתי-תלוי זה בזה, שניים מבעלי הפשט מן הפרספקטיבה ההיסטורית המצויה
בכתוב עצמו – אל פרספקטיבה היסטורית לגבי זמן כתיבתו של הספר ומיהות מחברו. ואילו רש"י,
שעמד בבהירות על חומרת הבעיה, נמנע מלהסיק את המסקנה הזאת, בגלל שתי סיבות הכרוכות
זו בזו – נאמנות-יתר לדברי חכמים ודבקות-יתר בשיטתם הפרשנית. ואכן, בדרך הדרש אין כל
מניעה לפרש את שמ"א ט, ט כהגיד נבואי של מחברו של הספר, הנוקק את נקודת-הראות
הזמנית של בני דורות מאוחרים: 'הסופר כתב זאת, ואין זה מדברי נער שאול'.

רד"ק העדיף גם כאן לגמש את הפשט ולבאר את 'לפנים' (המבחין בין ימי הגיבור לימי המחבר)
כאילו כתוב 'מלפנים' (המבחין בין ימי הגיבור לתקופה שקדמה לו). וברי שהוא נקט דרך זו לא בגלל
אי-יכולת פילולוגית או אי-הבחנה היסטורית,[54] אלא אך ורק משום שנאמנותו לדברי חז"ל לא
התירה לו להישמע ל'טבע הפסוקים ויושרם'.

לא כך ר' יצחק אברבנאל. משהתיר לעצמו להחיל את דרכו של הראב"ע בתורה לגבי ספרי
נביאים וכתובים (כולל שיטת ההוספות המאוחרות[55]), נפתח לפניו פתח רחב ליישם לגביהם בכשרון
רב ותנופה גדולה את החשיבה ההיסטורית של הרנסנס.[56] בהמשך הקדמתו לספר יהושע (בקטע
הפותח במילים 'ואומר שהיתה צורת אלה הספרים נבואיית') הוא קובע, שהאופי הנבואי של הספרים
ההיסטוריים עומד על שלושה מאפיינים הכרחיים: (א) המחבר היה נביא; (ב) הספר נתחבר בצו
האל; (ג) יש בספר מידע עלום (כמו 'מחשבות האומות ומלכיהם' וכמו 'שינחם ה' על הרעה אשר
אמר לעשות'), אשר יכול היה להיוודע למחבר אך ורק בהתגלות. עם זאת, 'אופן כתיבת הספרים
הזה' היא אנושית-טבעית לחלוטין: אין כאן התגלות מילולית, אלא עיבוד נבואי של כתבים
חילוניים קיימים, העוברים ביקורת קפדנית ועריכה סלקטיבית, ושנוסף עליהם כל מה שנודע
למחבר בנבואה. והתוצאה – ההיסטוריוגרפיה מקראית, אשר בניגוד גמור לספרי ההיסטוריה
החילוניים, אמינותה העובדתית גמורה וסמכותה התיאולוגית מוחלטת.

---

54 ראה דוגמה נאה לביקורת היסטורית בביאורו לשו' י, ד.
55 דוגמה לכך משמשים דבריו בסוף ביאורו לשמ"א ט, ט: 'והפסוק הזה מורה, שלא כתב זה שמואל כי אם ירמיהו
    או נביא אחר שקם אחריו ימים רבים, ולזה ספר מנהג השמות ומנהגם בימים הראשונים ומנהגם בזמן שנכתב הספר, או
    נוסף הפסוק הזה מיד עזרא'.
56 השווה יצחק בער, 'דון יצחק אברבנאל ויחסו אל בעיות ההיסטוריה והמדינה', תרביץ ח (תרצ"ז), עמ' 245–248
    (נדפס מחדש באסופת מאמריו: מחקרים ומסות בתולדות עם ישראל ב, ירושלים תשמ"ו, עמ' 402–405).

כך הניבה פרשנות המקרא היהודית על סף הזמן החדש תפיסה קדם־מודרנית של מחבר־עורך
נבואי. אברבנאל הגיע לכך משום שהשכיל לצרף תודעה היסטורית עם רגישות ספרותית, ומשום
שדרך הפשט הנחתה אותו לפרש את ספרי נביאים ראשונים לא רק לאור המציאות הריאלית
שמסביבו אלא גם תוך השוואה להיסטוריוגרפיה בת־זמנו.

סיכומו של דבר: החקירה העלתה שבכל עניין ועניין שונה פירוש רש״י, מבחינה עניינית
ומתודית כאחת, מכל פרשני הפשט, ויש בכך אישור נוסף לדעה המתגבשת כיום, שאין לראותו
כחלוץ של פרשנות הפשט, אלא כמאסף של הפרשנות המדרשית. דרך הפשט היא רציונלית בה
במידה שהיא פילולוגית, וההסתמכות על שיקול־הדעת העצמי, יחד עם ההאזנה הקשובה לדברה
ולאופיה של ההיסטוריוגרפיה המקראית, הביאו את בעלי הפשט לשיעורים שונים של מודעות
היסטורית ושל חשיבה ביקורתית. אך בעוד שבצפון־צרפת לא ביקשו אלא להוסיף ממד פשטי לדרך
הלימוד המקובלת, נטו בבבל, בספרד ובפרובנאנס לשלול את התוקף הפרשני של הדרש. הגישה
הקורקטיבית המתונה של הראשונים אפשרה להם להודות בחידוש שבדרך הפשט ולהעמידה בצדו
של הדרש המקובל, ואילו אחיזתם הרדיקלית של האחרונים בפשט כפירוש האמיתי היחיד הניעה
אותם לראות את דרך הפשט, ואת החשיבה הרציונלית־מדעית בכללה, כקדמונית. כתוצאה מחוסר
זה של מודעות היסטורית לגבי התהליך הפרשני הם ייחסו את דרך הפשט לחז״ל, והשליכו את המדע
הביניימי על המקרא. כך היתה דבקות־יתר בפשט למכשול במיצויו.

קטעים חדשים מן הפרפרזה המחוזרת של ספר בן סירא

עזרא פליישר

האוניברסיטה העברית בירושלים

[א]

בין החיבורים העבריים ה'חריגים' שנכתבו בימי הביניים, מקום חשוב יאות ל'בן סירא המחוזר', ששרידיו נתגלו בגניזת קהיר לראשונה בראשית שנות השלושים של המאה הזאת.[1] לא הרבה נותר בידינו מן הספר הזה, אבל ממה שנותר ברור שהוא הכיל במקורו עיבוד מחוזר של כל בן סירא העברי, והיה אם כן חיבור רחב ממדים למדי.[2] מן הספר נחשפו עד כה בסך הכל שישה דפים, שנתגלו כולם מהעתקה אחת. ברור שהעיבוד לא עורר עניין רב בשעתו, ואין פלא רב בכך: המעבד היה חרזן לא מוכשר במיוחד ועל מלאכתו לא טרח טרחה יתרה: הוא פירק את פסוקי המקור העברי, פישט את לשונם ואת עניינותיהם, הוסיף עליהם חרוזים, ועיצב אותם בסטרופות דו־טוריות. שיטות עבודתו פשוטות היו, והן גלויות מקטעי החיבור שהגיעו לידינו.[3] אף־על־פי שנתכוון כנראה להיצמד אל החומר שעיבד, הוא דילג תכופות על פסוקים שלא מצא בהם עניין, שלא ידע את פירושם או שלא התאימו להשקפותיו. הוא גם הוסיף לפעמים פסוקים שאינם לפנינו במקורות הידועים של בן סירא. תוספות אלו לא נתברר מקורן: אפשר שהן עמדו לפניו במקור שעבד עליו, שהרי ידוע שספר בן סירא קלט טקסטים חיצוניים לרוב; אבל אפשר גם שהוסיף על מה שמצא במקורו דברים משל עצמו.[4] בין כך ובין כך לא הפליא האיש לעשות אף לא באחת משיטותיו. מי

---

1   קטעים ראשונים מן החיבור פורסמו בידי י' מרקוס, יחד עם חומר מבן סירא העברי, מכ"י אדלר שבספריית
    בית־המדרש לרבנים בניו־יורק. ראה: J. Marcus, 'A Fifth Ms. of Ben Sira', *JQR* n.s. 21 (1930-1931),
    pp. 238ff.

2   בדפים שנתגלו עד כה בא עיבוד של קטעים מפרקים כב, לד, לו, לט, ו־מב. קטעים מסיום הספר קלוטים בממצא
    המתפרסם להלן. אי־אפשר להניח שהסופר החל לעבד את החיבור מאמצעו. מראי המקום מספר בן סירא כאן וכן
    להלן יצוינו על־פי מהדורת מ"צ סגל, ספר בן סירא השלם‎[2], ירושלים תשל"ב (להלן: מהדורת סגל).

3   ראה על כך בספרי משלי סעיד בן באבשאד, ירושלים תש"ן, עמ' 43 ואילך.

4   בחומר שנתגלה עד כה הפסוקים שאין להם מקבילה בבן סירא העברי משולבים בפסוקים שמקורם בבן סירא אינו
    מוטל בספק. רק קטע אחד רצוף מנותק כולו מן המקור הידוע לנו של הספר הקדום (ראה בספרי, שם, עמ' 279
    ואילך, קטע ה). רוב התוספות נראות כהרחבות (על־פי רוב מיותרות) של הטקסט האותנטי. מגמת קטע א אינה
    מחוורת די הצורך, אבל עניינה לכאורה בתהייה על הנהגת הבורא בסדרי העולם. הואיל והקטע קצר, אין דרך
    לדעת אל איזו מסקנה ביקש המעבד להוביל את טיעונו. מקור הקטע הזה לוט בערפל: אפשר שהוא המצאה של
    המעבד, אך אפשר – וכך נראה – שקטע דומה עמד לפניו בנוסח ספר בן סירא שאותו עיבד.

שהכירו את בן סירא המקורי (ובימי המעבד יש להניח שרבים עוד הכירוהו) לא סביר שמצא עניין
רב בעיבוד הזה.

אבל גילוי החיבור בעת החדשה עורר עניין, ובצדק. שהרי גורל ספר בן סירא הוא מן המופלאים
בתולדות תרבותנו. מבין כל הספרים הרבים שנכתבו בימי בית שני, ספר זה הוא היחיד שמסורתה
ה'רשמית' של האומה דאגה למלטו מבין הריסות חורבן הבית ומרד בר כוכבא. הוא היחיד מבין
הספרים החיצוניים שהיה מוכר לחכמי התלמוד במקורו והיה בעל תפוצה ידועה גם בראשית תקופת
הגאונים ואף־על־פי שנמצאו בספרות חז"ל, בשוליים, התבטאויות שליליות
כלפיו – האופן שבו הוא נזכר במקורות מן הדין היה שיבטיח את קיומו הרצוף בתודעת הקוראים.[6]
היעלמו מעולמם של ישראל הוא בחינת חידה שצריך לתת עליה את הדעת. גילויו מחדש של
המקור העברי בין קטעי הגניזה הסעיר על כן את רוח החוקרים: לא רחוק הוא להניח שאלמלא
נשתמרובו בצרור הכתבים שהובאו מקהיר לפני כמאה שנה אל ש"ז שכטר בקיימבריידג' גם דפים מן
המקור העברי של הספר הזה – לא היתה הגניזה כולה זוכה לגילויה הרשמי, ופני חקר היהדות בימינו
אפשר שהיו שונים מחמת זה מן הקצה אל הקצה ממה שהם כעת.[7]

הסערה הקטנה שעורר במחקר 'בן סירא המחורז' ניזונה כמובן משיירי ההתלהבות של גילוי בן
סירא המקורי. על אף מיעוט החומר שנתגלגל לידי החוקרים הראשונים מן העיבוד המחורז הזה, לא
מיעט איש בחשיבותה הממשית עצמו. אמנם לחקר לשונותיו של בן סירא הקדמון לא יכול היה החיבור
המאוחר להביא תועלת רבה, שהרי המעבד שינה את נוסח המקור כאוות נפשו ואף פישט במקרים
רבים בכוונת מכוון את המליצות שעמדו לפניו;[8] אבל גדולה היתה בעיני החכמים חשיבות העיבוד
להבנת הרכבו של הטקסט המקורי בגלגוליו המאוחרים. חשיבות גדולה מזו נודעה לו להבנת מהותה
ואופיה של הספרות העברית בימי־הביניים לסוגיה וגווניה; שהרי עיבוד זה שהותקן כנראה במזרח
סביב המאה השלוש־עשרה, מדבר בשם סוג של סקרנות ספרותית שלא שיערנו את קיומה במרכז
הזה בעת הזאת.[9] הוא גם מעיד על קיומן כאן ובעת הזאת של אנרגיות ספרותיות יוצרות, שלא
העלינו על הדעת את צביונן. וגם באשר לטעם הספרותי של תקופת המעבד וסביבתו צפן החיבור
בין דפיו לימוד שראוי היה לתשומת לב.

5   ראה על זה במבוא שהקדים סגל למהדורתו, עמ' 47 ואילך. כידוע המקור העברי של בן סירא מצוטט במבוא
    הערבי של רב סעדיה גאון ל'ספר הגלוי', ראה: א"א הרכבי, השריד והפליט מספר האגרון וספר הגלוי, פטרבורג
    תרנ"ב, עמ' קעו ואילך. תפוצת ספר בן סירא במקורו מוכחת מריבוי ההעתקות ממנו שנתגלו בגניזה.
    בסך הכל נתגלו בגניזה קטעים מחמש העתקות של הספר. ראה מהדורת סגל, עמ' 49 ואילך. כל ההעתקות הללו
    מאוחרות כמובן לימיו של רס"ג.

6   על ספר בן סירא בספרות חז"ל ראה במבוא למהדורת סגל, עמ' 37 ואילך. רבים מחכמי צפון אפריקה ואירופה
    בימי הביניים נוקטים עמדה שלילית כלפי הספר, אך כפי שהראה סגל, איש מהם לא הכיר: רובם החליפו אותו
    עם 'הספר הקטן והמגואל אלפביתא דבן סירא' (שם, עמ' 47). על ספר זה ראה עוד להלן.

7   על התפקיד ששיחקו הדפים מבן סירא בהחלטתו של ש"ז שכטר להעביר את תכולת הגניזה לקיימבריידג' ראה
    למשל: .S.D. Goitein, *A Mediterranean Society* I, Berkeley-Los Angeles 1967, pp. 3ff

8   אף־על־פי־כן נזורו חוקרי בן סירא בפרפרזה המחורזת גם לצורך זה. ראה למשל מהדורת סגל, עמ' קלה ואילך.
    וראה גם: מ' קיסטר, 'בשולי ספר בן־סירא', לשוננו מז (תשמ"ג), עמ' 127 ואילך; הנ"ל, 'נוספות למאמר "בשולי
    ספר בן־סירא"', לשוננו נג (תשמ"ט), עמ' 36 ואילך.

9   ראה לזה בספרי (לעיל, הערה 3), עמ' 20 ואילך. על זמנו ומקומו של העיבוד ראה עוד להלן, סעיף ד.

[ב]

ששת דפי 'בן סירא המחורז' שהיו ידועים עד כה נתגלו ונדפסו במרחבי זמן גדולים:[10] הממצא זכה
לשתי הדפסות 'מסכמות', אחת מהן, על־פי ארבעה דפים ראשונים ממנו, ב'שירים חדשים מן הגניזה'
של ח' שירמן, ואחת מהן, על־פי כל ששת הדפים שנתגלו, בספרי 'משלי סעיד בן באבשאד'.[11]
כרגיל בחקר הגניזה, הסיכומים היו מוקדמים מדי: כעת עומדים לפנינו עוד שני דפים מן הספר, והם
מעשירים את ידיעתנו בו בפרטים נוספים.

שני הדפים נתגלו באוסף הקטן של קטעי גניזה השמור בהיברו יוניון קולג' בסינסינטי (HUC
[1088.106] [1301), והם שייכים כצפוי לעותק שממנו נשרו ששת הדפים שכבר ראו אור. הממצא
לקוי למרבה הצער; בעיקר הדף הראשון שלו ניזוק קשה, והוא חסר הרבה בשתי פינותיו החיצוניות,
העליונה והתחתונה כאחת. הדף השני שלם יותר. שני הדפים רצופים; הם היו לפי זה, בכרך המקורי,
גיליון פנימי של קונטרס.[12] הטקסט הכתוב אינו רב. הסופר שהתקין את הטומוס הזה היה בזבזן גדול:
הוא כתב באותיות גדולות למדי והשאיר רווחים בין השורות ובין הפסוקים. הוא גם ניקד את הטקסט
בשלמותו בניקוד שעורר בשעתו פליאה בעיני שירמן: בארבעת הדפים שהיו לפניו הוא מצא את
הסופר מחליף באופן פרוע, כמנהגם של נקדנים 'בבלים', פתח בסגול, אך גם צירה וצירה
בפתח ובקמץ, ומתעלם מן התנועות החטופות. הוא ציין את השינויים הללו בפרסומו בהבלטה.[13]
למרבה הפלא, בשני הדפים החדשים הניקוד מתוקן הרבה יותר, ורק במקרים נדירים ניכרים בו
חילופי פתח בסגול וכדומה. רק ההתעלמות מן החטפים מקוימת גם בממצא החדש. התופעה מעידה
כמובן לא רק על המוצא ה'בבלי' של המעתיק, אלא גם על זלזול מסוים שלו במלאכת העיצוב של
הספר. זלזול זה ניכר בכתב־היד גם מן הקו העקום לעתים של הטורים ומצורת האותיות. אולי אפשר
ללמוד מזה שהחיבור עצמו לא נחשב הרבה אפילו בעיני המעתיק. כתבי־יד קדומים המביאים
שרידים מספרות החכמה העתיקה מועתקים בדרך כלל בהידור רב.[14]

[ג]

הקטעים החדשים מעבדים את פרק הסיום של ספר בן סירא. בן סירא העברי נחתם כידוע בשלושה
קטעים שצורפו אל הספר אחרי חתימתו.[15] אחד מהם, שתחילתו 'אהללך אלהי ישעי' (בן סירא נא,

10   שלבי פרסום הקטעים נסקרים בספרי, שם, עמ' 43 ואילך. בחומר טיפולו, אחרי מרקוס, מ' זולאי, ח' שירמן ואני.
11   ראה ח' שירמן, שירים חדשים מן הגניזה, ירושלים תשכ"ו, עמ' 436 ואילך, וספרי, עמ' 264 ואילך. וראה גם
       במאמרי 'עיון חדש בספרות המשלים העברית הקדומה', ביקורת ופרשנות 12–11 (תשל"ח), עמ' 19 ואילך.
12   בין דפי הספר שנתגלו עד כה אין עוד זוג דפים רצוף. ממצא אחד (כ"י ט"ש ס"ח 108.43) הוא של שני דפים,
       אבל לא רצופים. שאר הדפים שהגיעו לידינו בודדים.
13   ראה שירמן (לעיל, הערה 11), עמ' 429. שירמן ציין את הניקוד כ'מוזר ומעניין'. את הסטיות מן הניקוד המקובל
       רשם בשולי הטקסטים שם, עמ' 436 ואילך. על אופיו הבבלי של הניקוד הזה העמיד כבר סגל על־פי פרסומו של
       מרקוס; ראה מהדורת סגל, עמ' קלה, הערה 2.
14   ראה בפקסימילים המובאים בסוף ספרי (לעיל, הערה 3). את האופי המרושל של כתב־היד הזה מציין גם שירמן,
       עמ' 429.
15   ראה מהדורת סגל, עמ' שנב ואילך, ובדבריו של המהדיר לשלושת הקטעים. גוף ספר בן סירא מסתיים

א־כ) הוא מעין שיר תודה של המחבר על חסדי האל עמו. השני, שתחילתו 'הודו לה' כי טוב' (שם, כא–לה) דומה במתכונתו להלל הגדול שבתהלים קלו: לשון פתיחתו כלשון פתיחת המזמור המקראי ממש, וכמו שם – גם כאן כל פסוק נחתם ב'כי לעולם חסדו'. אבל פסוקי הקטע בבן סירא פותחים כולם ב'הודו', ולשונם כמובן שונה.[16] הקטע הזה בבן סירא מפורסם מפני שנזכרים בו כמה לשונות הידועים לנו מחתימות הברכות בתפילת העמידה, ויש בו צירופים נוספים, לא מעטים, המזכירים מקבילות בתפילות קבע אחרות.[17] הפרק נזכר מפני זה הרבה בחקר קדמוניות נוסחי התפילה שלנו. הקטע השלישי החותם את ספר בן סירא הוא המנון אלפביתי שתחילתו 'אני נער הייתי' (שם, לו–נו): הוא מדבר בשבח החכמה ומביא דברי התפארות של המחבר ושידול לתלמידיו לבוא ולשמוע תורה מפיו.[18]

הממצא החדש בעיבוד המחורז של הקטע הראשון, אלא שאין תחילת הפרק נפקדת במה שלפנינו. כתב־היד מתחיל בחמישה פסוקים (לקיים ביותר) שאין להם מקבילה בבן סירא, אבל ממשיך אחר־כך בעיבוד רצוף למדי של פסוקים יד, יב, טו, יז, יח, יט בפרק נא;[19] פסוק כ שם מעובד בהמשך, אחרי שני פסוקי הרחבה. לאחר מכן באות עוד שלוש מחרוזות סיכום שאין להן מקבילה בספר העברי.

כאמור, הפסקה 'אהללך אלהי ישעי' היא שירת הודיה של בן סירא לאל על חסדיו, על שהושיעו מידי אויביו ומבקשי נפשו, ועל עזרתו המתמדת לו בכל שעת צורך. המשורר מנסח את דבריו בהתלהבות, ומפרט את סוגי הסכנות שאפפוהו ושרחמי האל הצילוהו מהן.[20] העיבוד המחורז שומר על האקלים הכללי של המקור – אם כי כרגיל לא על דחיסות לשונו וחריפות מבעו ומקוריות אוצר מילותיו. גם האופי הפרטיקולרי של המקור מטשטש בעיבוד המחורז, ופירוט הסכנות שארבו למחבר נשמט.[21] במקום זה מדגיש הדובר את בדידותו בעולם ואת היותו עקור ממשפחתו ונעזב

בסוף פרק נ, במעין קולופון של המחבר. את שלושת הקטעים הנדונים, הכלולים בפרק נא, מכנה סגל 'נספח'; הוא משער שהם נוספו על הספר בידי המחבר עצמו, אחרי חתימתו. באמת אין לקטעים הללו אופי של חיתום ממש.

16 לדעת סגל נועד הקטע לשמש 'לתפילה שבמקדש בדורו של בן סירא'. מכאן לדעתו מילת הפתיחה הקבועה של הפסוקים, 'הודו', וכן הרפרין 'כי לעולם חסדו' (ראה מהדורת סגל, עמ' שנו). גם תוכן הפסוקים, שהוא לאומי כללי, אפשר שמראה כן. מובן שאפשר לטעון כנגד זה שהמחבר עומד בשיר במסגרתה של קונבנציה ספרותית יוקרתית ושהוא כותב על־פיה בלי לחשוב על ייעוד מסוים של יצירתו. מכל מקום, בספר העברי מוקף ה'הלל' קטע שירה אישיים אינטימיים, והוא יוצא דופן בהקשרו ברטוריקה הדרמתית שלו.

17 את כולם מונה סגל בביאורו לקטע הזה. ההקבלות לחתימות ברכות העמידה ברורות לחלוטין. שאר המקבילות אפשר שהן מקריות.

18 סגל מכנה את הקטע 'שבח קנין החכמה' (עמ' שנז). האקרוסטיכון האלפביתי של הפסקה נשתבש במסירה שהגיעה לידינו אבל הוא ניכר בעליל בכמה מקומות.

19 להלל, פסוקים 6 ואילך. אחרי עיבוד פסוק יד באה מחרוזת תלושה החוזרת על מה שכבר נאמר בפסוק 5. הופעת עיבודו של פסוק יב אחרי עיבוד פסוק יד מופלאה. בעיבוד הרצוף של פסוקים טו–יט דילג המעבד על פסוק טז, שגם במקור אין לו עניין חשוב. דרכי העיבוד האלה מקוימות גם בשאר חלקי הספר שנתגלו עד כה.

20 לדעת סגל 'אין כל ספק שבשיר זה מדבר ב"ס על נסיונותיו בחייו הפרטיים שלו [...]. השיר מספר שהמחברו היה בסכנה גדולה, ושנידון למות מפני מלשינות שהלשינו עליו אויביו, ושאחר כן ניצל ממות בדרך נס' (שם, עמ' שנג). אין ספק שהדברים מתוארים בקטע כאירועים אמיתיים. אופיַם הלירי־האישי בולט.

21 מה שנותר מזה מסוכם בשני הפסוקים הכלליים 12–13: [.... ...] פְּדָאֵנִי / וּמְכָּל צָרוֹתֵי חִלְּצָנִי // [... ...] מוֹקֵשׁ הַצִּילָנִי / וּמִבּוֹר שָׁאוֹן הֶעֱלָנִי. יותר מזה בא, אמנם בעיבוד צמוד של הספר הקדמון (בן סירא לד, א ואילך) בקטע ב של העיבוד, ראה בספרי (לעיל, הערה 3), עמ' 269 ואילך.

מהוריו ובני ביתו. פסוקי הפתיחה של הקטע, שאין להם מקבילה במקור, מפליגים בעניין הזה
בפירוט גדול, לפעמים תוך שאיבה מפסוקים ידועים במקרא:[22] 'למשורר אין תומך בלעדי ה' שהתיך
אותו ברחם אמו והוציאו מבטן; לא אביו ולא אמו, לא אחיו ואחיותיו, לא אבותיו ולא מוריו היו
בעזרו בצר לו. מפני זה לבו מלא הודיה לבורא ושש הוא לשבחו ולהללו. אפשר כמובן שאין כאן
אלא רידוד מכליל של העניינים החדים הנאמרים במקור, במהלך המכוון לאפשר למעבד ריבוי
דברים בעלמא. אבל ייתכן שהדברים באים לרמוז לידיעה משותפת של המעבד ושל קהל קוראיו
על קורות חייו האגדיים של בן סירא, כלומר על לידתו המוזרה ועל יניקותו הפלאית, כמתואר
בפירוט באגדת 'אלפא ביתא דבן סירא'.[23] זיקה רמוזה זו של בן סירא המחורז אל 'אלפא ביתא דבן
סירא' יש בה ענייו רב, ועוד נאמר בה מילה להלן.

חשובה בממצא שלפנינו הופעתו של הקטע המעבד (כביכול) את ההלל הגדול שבבן סירא נא,
כא ואילך. קטע זה חסר כידוע מן התרגום היווני של בן סירא ומן הנוסח הסורי שלו, אבל הוא נתגלה
בגניזה בנוסחו העברי. הופעת עיבודו בבן סירא המחורז מוכיחה שוב שהקטע היה כלול בנוסח
המקורי של הספר הקדום. אמנם למעשה אין בממצא שלפנינו עיבוד של ההלל של בן סירא, אלא
נוסח מחורז של ההלל הגדול האמיתי שבתהלים קלו,[24] אבל אין להעלות על הדעת שכך היה בספר
בן סירא שבידי המעבד. ההפך מזה מוכח מן המאמץ שהשקיע לפתוח את פסוקי המחורזים במילת
קבע המקבילה למילת 'הודו' שבראש פסוקי בן סירא במקום הזה. אמנם הוא החליף את המילה
ב'אודה', שהתאימה יותר לאופי האישי-הלירי של הקטע כפי שעיצבו בעיבודו,[25] אבל התמיד
בהבאת תיבה זאת בראשי הפסוקים ככל יכולתו, ואף נדחק משום כך זה לניסוחים בלתי אפשריים.[26]
הוא נושא מזה, אין ברירה, רק באמצע הקטע. אבל הרעיון לבנות את הפסקה באופן זה בא לו לא
מן המזמור המקראי, ששם אין 'הודו' אלא בראש שלושת הפסוקים הראשונים (ובראש הפסוק
האחרון), אלא מבן סירא, ששם כל הפסוקים מתחילים כך.

למה החליף המעבד את דברי בן סירא המקוריים בתהלים קלו? אפשר היה לשער שדווקא קרבת
כמה מפסוקי הקטע הזה אל נוסח ברכות העמידה הפריעה לו, לפי שכבר הרגיל עצמו לראות
בצירופים הללו לשונות תפילה, ונתקשה כעת בנוסחם השונה לעתים ובסדרם השונה תמיד בספר

---

22 ראה על כך להלן, בביאור לקטע.

23 לפי המסופר ב'אלפא ביתא דבן סירא' – בן סירא נולד מזרע של סבו, הלא הוא ירמיהו הנביא, שנפלט לאונסו
      באמבטי ונקלט לאחר זמן ברחם בתו. בן סירא התחיל להוכיח (כביכול) את אמו וזרע ברגע שנולד. אם כן אב אמיתי
      לא היה לו ומאמו לא שבע נחת. 'אלפא ביתא דבן סירא' הופיע במהדורה מדעית מסכמת מאת ע' יסיף, ספורי בן
      סירא בימי הבינים, ירושלים תשמ"ה. וראה שם, עמ' 198 ואילך.

24 חסרים מן העיבוד רק פסוק יב ('ביד חזקה ובזרוע נטויה') ופסוק יז ('למכה מלכים גדולים').

25 מטעם זה ויתר גם על הרפרין 'כי לעולם חסדו', המשותף לבן סירא ולתה' קלו, ולא השאיר לו זכר בעיבודו מלבד
      בפסוק 26, ששם נסתייע לו לחרוז בו. וטבעי שכך נהג. מעניין שהמעבד העמיד בראש הקטע את הפסוק: 'אודה
      ה' מאד בפי ובתוך רבים אהללנו' (תה' קט, ל), אף-על-פי שהקטע, כפי שעובד בידיו, לא נועד להיאמר 'בתוך
      רבים'. וברור שבחר בפסוק מפני שהוא פותח במילת 'אודה', ולא דייק בתוכנו.

26 ראה פסוק 30: 'א<ודה> את השמש לממשלת ביום'. אבל אפשר שיש שם טעות של המעתיק מכוח מה שמצא
      באופן קבוע לפני כן.

הקדום.[27] אפשר גם כן שהזכרתם (לשבח) של 'בני צדוק' בקטע הזה[28] הציקה לו, אחרי שכבר למד
מספרות חז"ל להיות סולד מן הצדוקים. אבל ספק אם אפשר לתלות בסיבות אלו שינוי מופלג כל
כך אצל מי שממילא לא הלך בנאמנות בעקבות מקורו, וכבר הסכין לדלג על פסוקים בעייתיים, או
לשנות את לשונם או את סדרם. ונראה לי שהטעם האמיתי שבשבילו שינה מה ששינה הוא שנתקשה
לומר הודיה למקום, אפילו מפי הממשל הקדום, על חסדים שהמציאות ההיסטורית שבה חי סתרה
אותם בעליל. וכי איך יאמר יהודי בן זמנו 'אודה לגואל ישראל', או 'אודה למקבץ נדחי ישראל', או
'אודה לבונה עירו ומקדשו' או 'אודה למצמיח קרן לבית דויד' – כשאין לו על מה להודות בדברים
הללו. על כגון זה אפשר היה להתפלל בימיו, אבל לא לומר הלל.[29] והנה בספר בן סירא הדברים אכן
אינם תפילה לעתיד לבוא, אלא סיכום נלהב של הסקירה ההיסטורית הרחבה הבאה בספר לפני כן
(בן סירא מד, א ואילך):[30] הקטע קורא להודות לה' על חסדיו עם האומה למן שיבת ציון וייסוד בית
שני עד ימות הממשל ועד בכלל.[31] ממילא מובן שהמעבד העדיף את ההודיה לחסדי ה' שתוקפם לא
פג, ושעל-פיהם הוא נמצא משתבח בקביעות בתפילותיהם של ישראל.[32]

הממצא החדש מסתיים עם סוף עיבוד הלל הגדול. אין לנו דרך לדעת אם כך נסתיים בן סירא
המחורז או שמא חסרה לנו ממנו עוד פסקה, שעיבודה את הקטע 'אני נער הייתי'. עיבוד ההלל הגדול
מסתיים בכתב-היד בשולי עמוד, ואם כי אין שום שם רמז להמשך שבא בדפי הקונטרס הנותרים,
גם אין שם שום רמז שהספר תם במקום ההוא. אבל סביר להניח שהמעבד טיפל גם ב'אני נער הייתי',
שהרי קטע זה בא בכל נוסחי בן סירא הידועים לנו. לא רחוק הוא להניח, שהאופי האישי של קטע
הסיום הזה, המקביל לאופי (האישי גם כן) של הקטע 'אהללך אלהי ישעי' הפותח את פרק נא, גרם
למעבד לנסח את ההלל הגדול שלו בלשון יחיד של המדבר בעדו. אם נכונה השערתנו, הרי עדיין
אין סוף בן סירא המחורז בידינו.

---

27 מכל ברכות העמידה שהתחימותיהן נרמזות בבן סירא אין שתיים הבאות ברציפות במקור הקדמון, מלבד 'הודו
     לבונה עירו ומקדשו' ו'הודו למצמיח קרן לבית דוד' (פסוקים כז–כח). אבל לשון שתי הברכות שונה גם כאן מן
     המצוי בעמידה.

28 שם, פסוק כט: 'הודו לבוחר בבני צדוק לכהן'.

29 גם מטעם זה אי-אפשר לראות בפסוקיבעל הפסקה הזאת הד או בבואה לאיזו תפילה קבועה שהייתה נהוגה בימי בן
     סירא בפי הרבים (או היחיד), כסברת רבים מן החוקרים. ראה על כך במאמרי 'לקדמוניות תפילות החובה
     בישראל', תרביץ נט (תש"ן), עמ' 434 והערה 91.

30 הקטע הזה, הקרוי בספר עצמו 'שבח אבות העולם', סוקר את תולדות ישראל מראשיתם ועד ימי המחבר. הוא
     נחתם בשיר התהילה המפורסם לכבוד שמעון בן יוחנן כהן גדול. ההלל הגדול שבפרק נא נועד להוסיף על
     הסקירה ההיא, המתמקדת בגדולי האומה, ציבון דתי בולט יותר.

31 ב'קרן לבית דוד', שהקב"ה מתהלל על הצמחתה בפסוק כח, נרמז בהקשר הזה מן הסתם זרובבל בן שאלתיאל
     שהיה מבית דוד, ואולי מי מצאצאיו שהיה פרנסם של ישראל בימי בן סירא. זרובבל נזכר בין 'אבות העולם' (בבן
     סירא מט, טו. לדעת המפרשים, פסוקי ההלל בבן סירא מדברים בימות המשיח; ראה למשל: R. Smend, Die
     Weisheit des Jesus ben Sirach erklärt, Berlin 1906, p. 502. אבל ספק אם אפשר לחשוב שבן סירא ביקש
     משומעיו להודות לה' על מעשים שהוא עתיד לעשות באחרית הימים. מופלג לא פחות לחשוב שהממשל הקדום,
     שירושלים עמדה לעיניו בנויה לתלפיות, ביקש מקהלו להודות לה' על בניין ירושלים שלעתיד לבוא. אין ספק
     שגישה פרשנית זו מושפעת ממעמדן של המליצות מבן סירא בברכות האסכטולוגיות של עמידות החול. אבל
     הופעתן של הלשונות הללו בעמידה מאוחרת ומשנית. ראה על כך במאמרי (לעיל, הערה 29).

32 ראוי לזכור שגם בהלל הגדול שבתהלים נסבים העניינים על חסדים שלעבר.

[ד]

ראוי לייחד ההרהור לצביונו המקורי של הספר אשר ממנו שרדו הקטעים הגדונים כאן, גם אם מיעוטם
אינו מאפשר הערכה בטוחה. כפי שכבר צוין לעיל, אין ספק שהמעבד החזיק בידו עותק שלם של
בן סירא העברי, ועיצב אותו, מתחילתו ועד סופו, בחרוזים. צריך להניח שבימיו ובמקומו לא היה
המעבד הזה האיש היחיד שהחזיק בביתו העתקה של ספר בן סירא. מה טעם ראה אפוא בעבודתו
ומה נתכוון להשיג בה? אפשר כמובן שלא ביקש להשיג דבר מלבד ה'שיפור' (לדעתו) בצורת הספר.
בימיו, יצירה ספרותית היתה ראויה להיכתב בחרוזים, וכל שלא היו בו חרוזים נחות היה בעיני
קוראים אניני־טעם.[33] המעבד, שחיבב את הספר, כסבור היה שהוא מייפה אותו בחרוזיו ומעלה את
כבודו בעיני קוראיו. אבל הוא לא ניסה לטשטש את צביון החיבור: הוא לא ליקט ממנו את משלי
החכמה כדי לעשות ממנו ספר משלים אחיד. להפך, הוא שמר על המקור ואף הרחיב בו את פסקאות
התפילה ואת הקטעים המזמוריים הליריים, המקנים לספר גם במקורו פרצוף מגוון ולעתים מפתיע.
הוא אף הקפיד לדובב את המחבר בקטעי הסיום של הספר בגוף ראשון יחיד: הוא שם אותו תולה
את תהילותיו בקורות חייו, ומסמיך את הכרת הטובה שלו לבוראו על עזרתו לו ועל חסדים שגמל
עליו מינקותו. גיבור הספר, גם בעיבודו המחורז, ולכאורה אף יותר מאשר במקורו, הוא ה'אני'
הדובר, ולא דברי החכמה שהוא אומר. ניתן אולי להניח שעיקר כוונת המעבד היה לענג את
קוראיו בתיאור דמותו וקורותיו של הממשל הקדמון, ולאו דווקא ללמדם מוסר על־פי משלי
החכמה שלו.

מובן שאין כוונתנו לשייך את החיבור למעגלם של נוסחי ה'אלפא ביתא דבן סירא', שהרי ברור
שבעליו התבסס על בן סירא העברי המקורי ועיבד אותו בעקיבות, ומכל מה שעלה לפנינו עד כה
אין ניכרת אלא זיקה מועטת בינו ובין הסיפורים שבספר הנזכר.[34] אבל אפשר שהמעבד ראה בחיבורו
מעין תשובה ל'אלפא ביתא דבן סירא' ודומיו, תשובה מעודנת, גבוהה ומשכילית יותר, שנועדה
לספר מחדש את סיפור בן סירא בצורה ספרותית ראויה.

[ה]

אשר לזמן שבו נעשה העיבוד, אין בקטעים החדשים שום נקודת אחיזה חדשה. בדיון קודם בנושא
הזה שיערתי שמדובר 'ביוזמה מאוחרת יחסית של משורר מזרחי', שחי אולי במאה השתים־עשרה.[35]

---

33 משלי החכמה והמוסר נגמנו (על־פי המסורת העברית בספרד) עם סוגי הספרות היפה, אשר החרוז (ועל־פי הרוב
     גם המשקל) נחשב חובה בהם. בנקודה הזאת נבדלה הספרות העברית מן הערבית: למן תקופת ספרד ואילך כנראה
     לא עלה על על דעתם של מחברים עבריים לכתוב משלי מוסר בלתי מחורזים: וכבר סעיד בן באבשאד (בראשית
     המאה האחת־עשרה) חרז את ספר משליו בהשפעת משוררי ספרד, וכך עשה גם בעל 'מוסר השכל' המיוחס לרב
     האיי גאון. הלכה פסוקה קבע בעניין זה שמואל הנגיד ב'בן משלי' וב'בן קהלת'. הדחף להצמיד חרוזים לטקסטים
     ספרותיים שנכתבו במקורם בלי חרוז הוא דחף מובן בתקופות שחיבבו את החרוז. הוא ניכר גם בשירת הקודש;
     ראה לזה למשל: א' מירסקי, 'פיוטים מקבילים', בתוך: הנ"ל, הפיוט, ירושלים תש"ן, עמ' 102 ואילך. מן הגניזה
     עולים לפעמים גם קטעים מתפילות קבע קדומות בעיבוד מחורז.

34 ראה על כך לעיל, סעיף ג. על זיקה אפשרית של בן סירא המחורז ללשון ה'אלפא ביתא דבן סירא' ראה במאמרי
     (לעיל, הערה 11), עמ' 49 ואילך, ובספרי (לעיל, הערה 3), עמ' 277.

35 ראה בספרי, שם, עמ' 45.

הקטעים החדשים מחזקים את רושם איחורו של הטקסט, אבל אינם מאפשרים לקבוע בביטחון את זמנו. כעת נראה לי שגבולות הזמן של הספר מתחייבים כמו מאליהם מגבולות מקומו. אין ספק שהחיבור נכתב במזרח: צורתו המרושלת, לשונו הדלה והיעדר תפוצתו במערב מעידים בו שאינו ספרדי. גם שאר מרכזי היצירה המערביים אינם באים בחשבון מטעמים אלה. העובדה שעד עכשיו לא מצאנו בגניזה אלא העתקה אחת של הספר נראית מלמדת שהעותק לא הותקן במצרים או בסביבתה. ניקודו הבבלי הבוטה של כתב־היד נראה מעיד בו שהועתק בבבל, וקרוב להניח שאכן חיבור בבלי לפנינו. ממילא, כך נראה, משמע מזה שמלאכת העיבוד נעשתה בסוף המאה השתים־ עשרה או בראשית המאה השלוש־עשרה, תקופה שבה ידעה היצירה העברית החילונית שגשוג פתאומי וקצר בבבל. בתקופה זו, אגב, מתהווים מרכזי יצירה תוססים של שירה עברית חילונית בכמה מקומות נוספים מחוץ לספרד: בפרובאנס, בסיציליה, בסוריה ואולי גם בתימן. שפע מפתיע של יצירות, ושל עדויות חיצוניות על פעילות ספרותית יוצרת, הגיע אלינו מן העת הזאת מכל המרכזים האלה.[36] על חיי ספרות תוססים בבבל בעת הזאת אנו שומעים עדות עזה ביטוי מחיבוריו של ר' יהודה אלחריזי. הוא מזכיר הרבה משוררים שפעלו במרכז הזה, וגם אם דעתו על רמת יצירתם אינה מחמיאה, כמפורסם, הנה עצם קיומם אינו מוטל בספק.[37] בעת הזאת פועל בבבל גם ר' אלעזר בן יעקב הבבלי (1195–1250), החשוב, הפורה והמעניין מבין המשוררים ה'ספרדים' שפעלו מחוץ לספרד.[38] הדיואן שלו מתעד חיי תרבות צבעוניים בבבל של ימיו. על הפריחה הפתאומית והבו־ זמנית הזאת של שירה עברית צריך לתהות תהייה ראויה, ואת תנובת השיר שלה ראוי לבדוק לגופה, אך לעניינינו נראה נראה שאין זמן סביר יותר להתהוות בן סירא המחזור מן הזמן הזה. נראה לי אפוא שאפשר לייחס את החיבור למחבר בבלי שפעל במחצית הראשונה (אולי בשליש הראשון) של המאה השלוש־עשרה.[39]

והרי לשון הקטעים החדשים כהווייתם, על־פי כ"י HUC 1301:

36 בסוף המאה השתים־עשרה ובראשית המאה השלוש־עשרה פעלו כידוע ראשוני משוררי פרובאנס. על המרכז הפורח בסיציליה בזמן הזה נודע לנו מאוסף שיריו של אנטולי בר יוסף, מכותבו ומעריצו של הרמב"ם ולימים דיינה של אלכסנדריה; ראה על כך: S.M. Stern, 'A Twelfth-Century Circle of Hebrew Poets in Sicily', JJS 5 (1954), pp. 60ff., 110ff. בסוריה (ארם צובה) פעל בעת הזאת תלמידו החשוב של הרמב"ם, ר' יוסף בן יהודה אבן שמעון, יליד המגרב ומשורר בעל שיעור קומה. לדעת י' טובי זאת גם תקופת פעילותו של ר' אברהם בן חלפון בתימן; ראה: י' טובי, שירי אברהם בן חלפון, תל־אביב תשנ"א.

37 ראה: י' אלחריזי, ספר תחכמוני, מהדורת י' טופורובסקי, תל־אביב תשי"ב, שער יח, עמ' 191 ואילך; שער מו, עמ' 350 ואילך. וראה גם במקאמה הערבית שלו: H. Hirschfeld, 'Fragment of an Unknown Work by Judah Al Harizi', JQR o.s. 15 (1903), pp. 683ff.; י' רצהבי, 'מקאמה ערבית מעטו של אלחריזי', ביקורת ופרשנות 15 (תש"ם), עמ' 5 ואילך; הנ"ל, 'שריד מן המקאמה הערבית של אלחריזי', ביקורת ופרשנות 23 (תשמ"ח), עמ' 51 ואילך. וראה גם ח' שירמן, 'משה בר ששת, משורר עברי ספרדי בבבל', בתוך: צ' מלאכי (עורך), שי להימן (ספר היובל לכבוד א"מ הברמן), ירושלים תשל"ו, עמ' 323 ואילך. וראה גם: י' טובי, 'יצחק בן ישראל – פייטן בבלי בן המאה הי"ג', שם, עמ' 125 ואילך.

38 ראה דיואן רבי אלעזר בן יעקב הבבלי, מהדורת ח' בראדי, ירושלים תרצ"ה.

39 כך שיער גם שירמן (לעיל, הערה 11), עמ' 429.

— — —

1 *   וְאָשׁוּב בְּכָל לְבָבִי אֵלָיו
      וּבְ[... ... ...]

2   וְאֵדַע כִּ[י אֵן] לִי סוֹמֵךְ בִּלְתּוֹ
      [... ...] אֵן זוּלָתוֹ

3   כִּי הוּא בְרֶחֶם הִתִּיכַנִי
      וּבְמ[... ... ...]

4   וּמִבֶּטֶן הוֹצִיאַנִי
      וּכְדֵי מַחְסוֹרִי ח[...]

5   וְאָבִי וְאִמִּי לֹא הוֹעִילוּנִי
      וְאַחַי וְאַחְיוֹתַי לֹא הִצִּילוּנִי

6   וְאָרִים מֵאֶרֶץ קוֹלִי
      וּבִקַּשְׁתִּי בּוֹרְאִי בְּכָל יָכְלִי

7   כִּי רַחֲמָיו עֲזָרוּנִי מִנְּעוּרַי
      וְלֹא הוֹעִילוּנִי אֲבוֹתַי וּמוֹרַי

8   וְאֶזְכְּרָה אֶת רַחֲמָיו הָעֲצוּמִים
      וְטוֹבוֹתָיו הָרַבִּים וְהַקְּד[וּמ]ים

---

*   ביאור. עשרים ואחד הפסוקים הראשונים מקבילים לבן סירא נא, א–יט. אבל לחמשת הפסוקים הראשונים שלפנינו אין מקבילה צמודה בבן סירא, ולפסוקים א–יד של בן סירא אין מקבילה במה שלפנינו.

1   **ואשוב בכל לבבי**: השווה למשל דב' ל, ב: 'ושבת עד ה' אלהיך [...] בכל לבבך ובכל נפשׁו'. וראה גם: מל"א ח, מח; מל"ב כג, כה, ועוד. יש להגיח שבדברים שלפני כן הזכיר הדובר את עוונותיו ואת הפורעניות שבאו עליו מחמתם. אבל אין לזה מקבילה בבן סירא במקום הזה.

2   **אן**: כך, במקום 'אין', גם בקטע ה, 17 (ראה בספרי [לעיל, הערה 3], עמ' 281): 'כִּי אָפֵס אֵן נֶגְדּוֹ'.

3   **כי הוא** וכו': לרעיון השווה תה' עא, ו: 'עָלֶיךָ נִסְמַכְתִּי מִבֶּטֶן, מִמְּעֵי אִמִּי אַתָּה גוֹזִי, בְּךָ תְהִלָּתִי תָמִיד'. ללשון השווה איוב י, י: 'הֲלֹא כֶחָלָב תַּתִּיכֵנִי וְכַגְּבִנָּה תַּקְפִּיאֵנִי'. בטור השני יש אולי להשלים: 'וּבמ[עֵי אִמִּי הִקְפִּיאַנִי]' או כיו"ב.

4   **ומבטן** וכו': על־פי המקרא הנ"ל בתה' עא, ו, בפישוט הלשון.   **ח[..]**: יש להשלים: 'ח[נני]' או כיו"ב. האות חי"ת תלויה למעלה מן השיטה ואחריה קרע, ואפשר שהיא ה"א.

5   **ואבי** וכו': השווה תה' כז, י: 'כִּי אָבִי וְאִמִּי עֲזָבוּנִי וה' יַאַסְפֵנִי'.

6   **וארים** וכו': בן סירא נא, יד: 'וָאָרִים מֵאֶרֶץ קוֹלִי וּמִשַּׁעֲרֵי שְׁאוֹל שִׁוַּעְתִּי'. היווני מתרגם: 'קוֹלִי' – 'תחינתי'; המעבד מקיים את לשון המקור העברי. בטור השני ויתר המעבד על התקבולת והלך לפי עניינו.   **בוראי**: הפעגוח מפוקפק, אבל הוא מתאים למה שנאמר על ה' בפסוקים שלפני כן.   **יכלי**: יכולתי. כך גם להלן, פסוק 17.

7   **כי רחמיו** וכו': אין לפסוק מקבילה בבן סירא. המעבד מסכם את עניין הפסוקים שלפני כן וכולל בין מי שאכזבוהו בצר לו גם את מוריו. ספק אם הממשל הקדום היה אומר כך.

8   **ואזכרה** וכו': המעבד שב אל בן סירא נא, יב: 'וְאֶזְכְּרָה אֶת רַחֲמֵי ה' וַחֲסָדָיו אֲשֶׁר מֵעוֹלָם'.

וְאָרוֹמֵם אָב ה[... ...]
9
כִּי בֶאֱמֶת ו[... ...]

וְאֶזְכְּרֵהוּ בִת[פִלָּה ....]
10
[... ... ...]

[... ... ...] קוֹלִי
11
וַיַּעַן שׁוְעָתִי וּפְלוּלִי

[... ...]וֹת פְּדָאַנִי
12
וּמִכָּל צָרוֹתַי חִלְּצַנִי

[... ...]מוֹקֵשׁ הִצִּילַנִי
13
וּמִבּוֹר שָׁאוֹן הֶעֱלַנִי

וְלֹא נָתַן לַמּוֹט רַגְלִי
14
וְהָפַךְ מִסְפְּדִי לְמָחוֹל לִי

וַיְכוֹנֵן אֲשׁוּרַי בְּדֶרֶךְ יוֹשֶׁר
15
וַיִּתֵּן רַגְלַי בְּאָרְחוֹת כּוֹשֶׁר

וַיָּשֶׂם בְּפִי שִׁירִים לְהַלְלוֹ
16
וּלְהוֹדוֹת לוֹ כְּטוֹב פָּעֳלוֹ

---

9 **וארומם וכו':** שם נא, טו: 'וָאֲרוֹמֵם ה' אָבִי אָתָּה, כִּי אַתָּה גִבּוֹר יֶשַׁע'. התרגום היווני והסורי גורסים: 'וָאִקְרָא'; המעבד מאשר את נוסח המקור העברי.

10 **ואזכרהו בת[...]:** שם, יז: 'וַאֲהַלְלָה שִׁמְךָ תָּמִיד וָאֶזְכְּרֵךְ בִּתְפִלָּה'. לפי זה יש להשלים: 'בִת[פלה]'. אבל התרגום הסורי והיווני גורסים: 'בִתְהִילָה'. המעבד דילג על פסוק טז: 'אַל תַּרְפֵּנִי בְּיוֹם צָרָה, בְּיוֹם שׁוֹאָה וּמְשׁוֹאָה'; אפשר שהפריעה לו ההתייחסות ה'נקודתית' של התפילה, שהרי מהללו בשבח הבורא מכלילי ביותר.

11 **[...] קולי:** שם, יח: 'אָז שָׁמַע קוֹלִי ה', וַיַּאֲזֵן אֶל תַּחֲנוּנִי'.   **ופלולי:** המילה שגורה בלשון הפייטנים.

12 **[...]ות פדאני:** שם, יט: 'וַיִּפְדֵּנִי מִכָּל רָע וַיְמַלְּטֵנִי בְּיוֹם צָרָה'. לפי זה יש להשלים: '[מכל רע]וֹת פדאני'.

13 **[...]מוקש וכו':** כנראה הרחבה של מה שנאמר קודם לכן. ואולי יש להשלים: [מפח ו]מוקש. ואפשר שיש כאן היזכרות מאוחרת בבן סירא נא, ו: 'מִמּוֹקֵשׁ צוֹפֵי סָלָע וּמִיַּד מְבַקְּשֵׁי נַפְשִׁי'. הסורי מתרגם שם: 'ממוקש ואבדן הושעתני'.   **ומבור שאון:** הצירוף על-פי תה' מ, ג: 'יַעֲלֵנִי מִבּוֹר שָׁאוֹן, מִטִּיט הַיָּוֵן'. ומעין זה גם בקטע ב, 8 (בספרי [לעיל, הערה 3], עמ' 270] הצירוף 'בטחתי על אלוה והצילני, ומבור שיחים מלטני'.

14 **ולא נתן וכו':** הרחבה נוספת. הלשון על-פי תה' סו, ט: 'לֹא נָתַן לַמּוֹט רַגְלֵנוּ'.   **והפך וכו':** על-פי שם ל, יב.

15 **ויכונן וכו':** הרחבה נוספת, מטונימית. הצירוף 'ויכונן אשורי' על-פי תה' מ, ג, שכבר שימש את המעבד בפסוק 13: 'וַיָּקֶם עַל סֶלַע רַגְלַי כּוֹנֵן אֲשֻׁרָי'.   **דרך יושר:** סמיכות תיאור, על דרך הפייטנים. יש במקרא 'דֶּרֶךְ יָשָׁר' ו'דֶרֶךְ יְשָׁרָה'. השווה למשל תה' קז, ז: 'וַיַּדְרִיכֵם בְּדֶרֶךְ יְשָׁרָה'. ובמש' ד, יא: 'הִדְרַכְתִּיךָ בְּמַעְגְּלֵי יֹשֶׁר'.   **בארחות כושר:** בְאורחות כשרים, הגונים; סמיכות תיאור.

16 **וישם בפי וכו':** בן סירא נא, כ: 'עַל כֵּן הוֹדֵיתִי וַאֲהַלְלָה וַאֲבָרְכָה אֶת שֵׁם ה''. המעבד הקפיד להביא את שתי מילות המפתח מן המקור: 'הודיי' ו'אההללה'. הוא מפליא כלאחר יד, בשם בן-סירא, את כשרון השירה שבפיו.

17 אֲבָרְכָה שְׁמוֹ כִּיכֻלִי
    כִּי הוּא חֶלְקִי וְחַבְלִי

18 וְכִי הוּא מִנְּעוּרַי אִיּוִיתִי
    וְעַל רַחֲמָיו וְטוּבוֹ קִוִּיתִי

19 [... ... ...]אַחֲרָיו
    וְלָנֶצַח [... ... ...]

20 [...] הָמוּ וְרַ[..] בַּאֲמָרָיו
    [... ... ...]

21 יִמְתַּק לְפִי עֵת אָזְכְּרֶנּוּ
    וְרוּחִי וְנִשְׁמָתִי מְאֹד תַּחְמְדֶנּוּ

22 אוֹדֶה יְיָ מְאֹד בְּפִי וּבְתוֹךְ רַבִּים אֲהַלְלֶנּוּ

23 אוֹדֶה לוֹ בְּכָל הַתּוֹשְׁבָּחוֹת
    כִּי הוּא יוֹצֵר כָּל רוּחוֹת

24 א‹וֹדֶה› לֵאלֹהֵי הָאֱלֹהִים
    הַשּׁוֹכֵן מְרוֹמוֹת וּגְבוֹהִים

25 א‹וֹדֶה› לַאֲדֹנֵי הָאֲדֹנִים
    הַשָּׂם כִּסְאוֹ בַּמְּעוֹנִים

---

17 **אברכה וכו׳:** מעבד את הסיפא של נא, כ הנ״ל: ׳וַאֲבָרְכָה אֶת שֵׁם ה׳׳.   **כיכלי:** כיכולתי, כמידת יכולתי. ראה
    גם לעיל, פסוק 6.   **חלקי וחבלי:** מנתי וכוסי. השווה דב׳ לב, ט: ׳כי חלק ה׳ עמו יעקב חבל נחלתו׳.

18 **מנעורי:** פענוח המילה מפוקפק.   **איויתי:** נכספתי. וראוי היה: כי אותו מנעורי איויתי.

19–20 פסוקים אלה ניזוקו בצורה קשה ואין דרך לעמוד על תוכנם.

21 **ימתק וכו׳:** סיום השבח. הדברים מתקשרים אל פסוק 16: ה׳ שם דברים בפי המשורר והם מתוקים בפיו.   **ורוחי
    ונשמתי וכו׳:** הלשון עילגת, ואפשר שאחת משתי המילים נוספה שלא לצורך, שהרי הפועל הוא ביחיד; אבל
    ראה גם להלן, פסוק 36.   **תחמדנו:** תתאווה אליו.

22 **אודה יי וכו׳:** כותרת להודיה שבהמשך, והוא פסוק כצורתו בתה׳ קט, ל. נראה שהכותרת מושפעת מן הקטע הבא
    בבן סירא המקורי, שהרי כאמור הצירוף ׳בתוך רבים׳ אינו הולם את המשך העיבוד המחורז, שהוא אישי במובהק.

23 **אודה וכו׳:** מכאן מביא המעבד נוסח מחורז של תה׳ קלו. אבל בפסוק הזה עדיין הוא כרוך אחרי בן סירא המקורי,
    ששם פותח ההלל (נא, כב) בפסוק ׳הודו לְאֵל הַתִּשְׁבָּחוֹת כִּי לְעוֹלָם חַסְדּוֹ׳. וקרוב לומר שנרמז כאן גם פסוק כד
    שבמקור: ׳הוֹדוּ לְיוֹצֵר כָּל, כִּי לְעוֹלָם חַסְדּוֹ׳, שהמעבד שיקע אותו בטור השני של המחרוזת. ואפשר להניח על־פי
    זה ששני הפסוקים היו רצופים לפניו בבן סירא המקורי, כפי שמתחייב מן העניין, וכפי ששיערו החוקרים.
    התושבחות: בהשפעת הארמית, במקום התשבחות.   **יוצר כל רוחות:** השווה למשל: זכ׳ יב, א: ׳וְיֹצֵר רוּחַ אָדָם
    בְּקִרְבּוֹ׳ וכד׳.

26 א<וֹדֶה> לְעוֹשֵׂה נוֹרָאוֹת לְבַדּוֹ
כִּי לְעוֹלָם חַסְדּוֹ

27 א<וֹדֶה> לְעוֹשֵׂה הַשָּׁמַיִם בִּתְבוּנָה
וְהוּא נִפְרָד בַּחֲנִינָה

28 א<וֹדֶה> לְרוֹקַע הָאָרֶץ
וְשִׁכְנוֹ בְרוּם עֶרֶץ

29 א<וֹדֶה> לְעוֹשֵׂה אוֹרִים
וַיְשִׂימֵם לְמֶמְשֶׁלֶת וּמִן שָׂרִים

30 א<וֹדֶה> אֶת הַשֶּׁמֶשׁ לְמֶמְשֶׁלֶת
וְעַל הַיּוֹם הִיא מוֹשֶׁלֶת

31 אֶת הַיָּרֵחַ וְכוֹכָבִים לְ[מֶמְשְׁלוֹת] בַּלַּיְלָה
אוֹתוֹ תָמִיד אֲיַחֲלָה

32 א<וֹדֶה> לְמַכֵּה מִצְרַיִם בִּבְכוֹרֵיהֶם
וַיָּשֶׂם לְדָם כָּל אַגַ[מֵּ]יהֶם

33 וַיּוֹצִיא יִשְׂרָאֵל מִתּוֹכָם
וּבַאֲרָצוֹת רַבּוֹת הִדְרִיכָם

34 לְגוֹזֵר יַם סוּף לִגְזָרִים
וַיּוֹלִיכֵם בִּדְרָכִים יְשָׁרִים

35 וְהֶעֱבִיר יִשְׂרָאֵל בְּתוֹכוֹ
לָכֵן אֲהַלְלוֹ וַאֲבָרְכוֹ

36 וְנִעֵר פַּרְעֹה וְחֵלוֹ
וְנִתְבָּאֲרָה אוֹתוֹתָיו וּפָעֳלוֹ

26 **נוֹרָאוֹת**: במקרא: נפלאות גדולות.
27 **נִפְרָד**: מיוחד. **בַּחֲנִינָה**: בחן ובחסד.
28 **ברום ערץ**: בגובהי שמים. 'ערץ' – כינוי פייטני נפוץ לשמים.
29 **לְמֶמְשֶׁלֶת**: המ"ם השנייה תלויה בין השיטין. **וּמִן**: איני יודע לכוון. **שָׂרִים**: האות שי"ן מפוקפקת.
30 **א<וֹדֶה>**: המילה אינה נקשרת אל המשך הטור, ואולי הועתקה בטעות.
34 לפני מחרוזת זו דילג המעבד על תה' קלו, יב: 'ביד חזקה ובזרוע נטויה'. **בדרכים ישרים**: ראה לעיל, ביאור לפסוק 15.
36 **וְנִתְבָּאֲרָה**: ונתגלו, ונתפרסמו. וראוי היה: ונתבארו. וראה לעיל, ביאור לפסוק 21. ואולי לשון היחיד כאן בא בהשפעת הערבית.

37   לְמוֹלִיךְ עַמּוֹ בַּמִּדְבָּר
אֲהַלֵל בִּלְשׁוֹן וּפֶה בָּר

38   וַיַּהֲרוֹג מְלָכִים אַדִּירִים
לְעוֹלָם בְּשִׁבְחוֹתָיו קוֹלִי אָרִים

39   לְסִיחוֹן מֶלֶךְ הָאֱמוֹרִי
עַד אֲשֶׁר נִצְרַנִי וַעֲזָרִי

40   וּלְעוֹג מֶלֶךְ הַבָּשָׁן
עַד הִצִּילַנִי מֵאוֹר הַכִּבְשָׁן

41   וְנָתַן אַרְצָם לְנַחֲלָה
נַחֲלָה לְעַם סְגוּלָה

42   שֶׁבְּשִׁפְלֵנוּ זָכַר לָנוּ
וּלְעוֹלָם תָּמִיד אֲהַלְלֶנּוּ

43   וַיִּפְרְקֵנוּ מִצָּרֵנוּ
עַד עוֹלָמִים אֲיַחֲדֶנּוּ

44   נוֹתֵן [לֶחֶם] לְכָל בָּשָׂר
וְטוּבוֹ לָעַד לֹא יֶחְסָר

45   אוֹדֶה לְאֵל הַשָּׁמַיִם
יוֹצֵר אֵשׁ וְעָפָר [רו]חַ וָמָיִם

---

37   **בר**: טהור. אחרי המחרוזת הזאת דילג המעבד על תה' קלו, יז: 'למכה מלכים גדולים'.

39   **לסיחון וכו'**: קרי: ויהרוג לסיחון וכו'.   **עד וכו'**: כנראה: ולא חדל ממלחמתו עד אשר עזרני.

40   **עד וכו'**: ראה הביאור למחרוזת הקודמת.   **מאור הכבשן**: מן הפורענויות.

45   **אש ועפר וכו'**: ארבעת היסודות. אין חידוש בציונם בעת הזאת: הם כבר נזכרים, בהקשר יהודי, בכתבי ר' יצחק
       ישראלי ורס"ג.

מדרשי השם ל'יעקב' ול'ישראל' ותפיסת המרת השם
בפרשנות היהודית המסורתית: בחינות סמנטיות ותחביריות

שמחה קוגוט

האוניברסיטה העברית בירושלים

סיפור המרת השם יעקב בישראל מובא בספר בראשית בשתי מסורות מקבילות: מסורת אחת תולה
את הסבת השם במלאך, והיא מעוגנת בסיפור 'ויאבק איש עמו' (לב, כה־לג) – מאבק המתרחש
בפניאל = פנואל – ומסורת אחרת, התולה את הסבת השם באל ולא במלאך, מצויה בסיפור 'וירא
אלהים אל־יעקב עוד בבואו מפדן ארם ויברך אותו' (לה, ט־טו) – התגלות המתרחשת בבית־אל.[1]
הנוסחה הבסיסית של המרת השם דומה היא בשתי המסורות:

לא(1) X(2) יאמר(3) עוד(4) שמך(5), כי אם Y (לב, כט)

לא(1) יקרא(3) שמך(5) עוד(4) X(2), כי אם Y (לה, י)

חלקה הראשון של הנוסחה – הוא החלק המבטל את השם הישן – בא אמנם בסדר מרכיבים שונה
בכל אחת משתי המסורות הנזכרות, אך אין לראות בסדר המרכיבים השונה שינוי מהותי בנוסחה
עצמה. כנגד זאת מתעשרת הנוסחה שבמסורת הראשונה בתוספת מהותית, הנעדרת מן הנוסחה
שבמסורת השנייה. תוספת זו מעמידה מדרש שם, המוצג כהנמקה להענקת השם החדש: 'כי־שרית
עם־אלהים ועם־אנשים ותוכל' (לב, כט). המסורת השנייה אינה מכילה הנמקה גלויה כלשהי
להענקת השם החדש, אך אפשר שבמילים 'וירא אלהים אל־יעקב עוד' (לה, ט) מהדהדת הנמקה
סמויה לשם ישראל, הגזורה אותו מלשון 'ישור אל' או 'איש רואה אל'.[2] אם אמנם זוהי ההנמקה לשם
ישראל במסורת השנייה, הרי היא שונה מזו שבמסורת הראשונה, וזאת לא רק בדרך שבה היא
מובעת – הבעה רמוזה כנגד הבעה מפורשת – אלא אף בתוכנה. בהמשך מבקשים אנו לבדוק, האם
התלבטה גם הפרשנות היהודית המסורתית בבחירת ההנמקה לשם ישראל, ומהן התפיסות הסמנטיות
והתחביריות המונחות ביסוד מדרשי השם שהועמדו בפרשנות זו ליעקב ולישראל.

1 אין עניינגו כאן בשאלת העריכה של מחזור הסיפורים של יעקב, שאלה שתתוצאות לה אל הנושא הכללי של חיבור
ספרות התורה. שאלת האחדות הפנימית של מחזור סיפורי יעקב והזיקה שבין חוליותיו ומרכיביו נידונה בהרחבה
אצל: ז' ויסמן, מיעקב לישראל, ירושלים תשמ"ו.

2 מדרש השם ישראל מלשון ראייה – בין משורש שׁוּר בין משורש ראי – עולה מדרשתו של פילון האלכסנדרוני
במאמרו De mutatione nominum (על שינוי השמות) – שינוי 81. וראה על כך: מ' שטיין, פילון האלכסנדרוני,
ורשה תרצ"ז, עמ' 146; ח' שׁוּר, 'מדרשי השמות העבריים בפרשנות האלגורית של פילון', חיבור לשם קבלת
התואר דוקטור לפילוסופיה של אוניברסיטת תל־אביב, 1991, חלק א' עמ' 138. למדרש־שם זה נזדקק עוד
בהמשך דיוננו.

העובדה שלשם חדש הבא להמיר שם ישן נסמכת הנמקה אין בה כשלעצמה כדי הבטחה, שהשם החדש יגבר על הישן וידחה אותו מן השימוש. דחייה כזאת אפשרית לדעתנו, כשהשם החדש אינו אלא וריאציה של הישן, והדמיון הפונטי והסמנטי שבין שני השמות מקיים בשם החדש את זכרו של השם הישן. כזה הוא המצב בהמרת השמות 'אברם' ב'אברהם' (בר' יז, ה), 'שרי' ב'שרה' (שם, שם, טו) ו'הושע' ב'יהושע' (במ' יג, טז), ולכך כנראה מכוונים דבריו של ר' יוסף בכור שור,³ בהציגם את השם החדש כתיקון והשבחה של השם הישן. וזה לשונו בפירושו לבראשית יז, ה:

'ולא יקרא עוד את שמך אברם והיה שמך אברהם': תיקן את השם והשביחו, ולא זהו שם אחר, אלא אותו שם עצמו שהיה לו קודם, אלא שהשביחו. ולפיכך לא מצינו שנקרא עוד אברם, שלא היה כי אם שם אחד; אבל יעקב שאמר לו הקב"ה 'לא יקרא שמך עוד יעקב כי אם ישראל יהיה שמך' אין השני שייך בראשון כלל, אלא שֵם אחר שָם לו, ולפיכך שני שמות היו לו, ונקרא בזה ובזה.⁴

קביעתו של ר' יוסף בכור שור, שבהמרת השם יעקב ב‏ישראל 'אין השני שייך בראשון כלל', מצביעה למעשה על ריחוקם של שני השמות זה מזה מבחינה פונטית ומבחינה סמנטית, וריחוק זה הוא שעמד לשני השמות שיתקיימו זה בצד זה. ואמנם עובדה היא, ששניהם משמשים במקרא הן בנפרד הן בתקבולת; הן כמכוונים לאישיות אחת – אביה השלישי של האומה – הן כמציינים את האומה כולה, ודומה שהשימוש המגוון הזה מזמן מְנַה וּבֶה את ההכחשות המגוונות לכל הנסיונות להעמיד דיפרנציאציה שיטתית בין ההיקרויות של שני השמות במקרא.⁵ נמצא שמחברי ספרי המקרא לא ראו עצמם כבולים לאיסור המובא בשתי המסורות של הסיפור: 'לא יעקב יֵאָמֵר עוד שמך כי אם‫־‬ישראל' (לב, כט) / 'לֹא‫־‬יִקָּרֵא שמך עוד יעקב כי אם‫־‬ישראל יהיה שמך' (לה, י). יוצא מכלל זה הוא בעל ספר דברי‫־‬הימים, שהפליג במחויבותו לאיסור זה עד כדי הימנעות מאזכור המרת השם – שלא כדרכו ב'אברם הוא אברהם' (דה"א א, כז) – והציג את יעקב מלכתחילה בשם ישראל. כך מצינו: 'ויולד אברהם את‫־‬יצחק בני יצחק עשו ויִשְרָאֵל' (דה"א א, לד), וכן גם בהמשך: 'אלה בני ישראל ראובן שמעון לוי ויהודה ...' (שם, ב, א). מן הראוי לעמוד על שני חריגים בספר דברי‫־‬הימים, שבהם נזכר יעקב, ובשניהם בתקבולת ל‏ישראל. שני המקרים באים בסמוך, בדברי‫־‬הימים א, פרק טז:

'זרע ישראל עבדו / בני יעקב בחיריו' (פס' יג)

'ויעמידֶהָ ליעקב לחק / ל‏ישראל ברית עולם' (פס' יז).

3   ספר רבנו יוסף בכור שור, פירוש על התורה, מהדורה חדשה, על‫־‬פי העתקת כתב‫־‬יד מינכן 52 בהשגחת ר' רפאל נטע ראבינאוויץ, ירושלים תשמ"ג.

4   ראה גם פירושיו לבראשית יז, טו; לה, י.

5   למסקנה זו הגיע מ"צ סגל, לאחר שתיאר וביקר הן את הדעות שנאחזו בשיטת המקורות ופירשו על‫־‬פיה את החילופים שבין השמות, הן את הדעות שתלו את החילופים הללו בגורמים שבתוכן, כדעותיהם של גייגר, קאסוטו ובנו יעקב. ראה: מ"צ סגל, 'השמות יעקב וישראל בספר בראשית', תרביץ ט (תרצ"ח), עמ' 243–256 (=מ"צ סגל, מסורת ובקורת, אסופת מאמרים בחקר המקרא, ירושלים תשי"ז, עמ' 61–75). לנימוקיו של קאסוטו לשלילת הדעות שתלו את החילופים שבין שני השמות בדרכי הכתיבה של המקורות השונים, ולסיבות העדפתו את תליית החילופים האלה בעניינים שבתוכן ראה: מ"ד קאסוטו, ספר בראשית ומבנהו (תרגם מאיטלקית מ"ע הרטום) ירושלים תש"ן, עמ' 113–124; 243–251.

ודוק: שני האזכורים החריגים של יעקב מצויים בקטע (דה"א טז, ח–כב) שיש לו מקבילה בתהלים
(קה, א–טו), ואין אפוא לתלותם בבעל ספר דברי–הימים. יתר על כן: בצד כמה שינויים קלי ערך,
שבהם נבדלים שני הקטעים המקבילים זה מזה, מצוי הבדל משמעותי ביותר, העושה את ההשוואה
הבאה למאלפת:

'זרע **אברהם** עבדו / בני יעקב בחיריו' (תה' קה, ו)
'זרע **ישראל** עבדו / בני יעקב בחיריו' (דה"א טז, יג)

אי–אפשר שלא להבחין בשינוי המגמתי שהכניס בעל דברי–הימים בפסוק. המרת **אברהם בישראל**
מכוונת היא, ובעל דברי–הימים נזקק לה כדי לתקן למצער את 'המעוות' שבאזכור שֵם יעקב לבדו –
כפי שהוא בא בפסוק בתהלים – ולאפשר את הצבת השם **ישראל** בתקבולת ליעקב. ההנחה, שנוסח
הפסוק בדברי–הימים הוא תוצר של שינוי מגמתי, הנעוץ במניע שתיארנו, אומרת למעשה, שבעל
דברי–הימים נלחץ כאן לוותר על תפיסתו הרגילה את נוסחת המרת השם – תפיסה הדוחקת את השם
הישן מפני החדש – ולאמץ את התפיסה 'הסלחנית' כלפי השם הישן, המאפשרת את קיומו, בהבינה
את נוסחת ההמרה כך: 'לא–ייקרא שמך עוד יעקב [בלבד], כי אם [גם] ישראל יהיה שמך; ויקרא
את–שמו [גם] ישראל'. ויוער, כי על–פי תפיסה זו מתורגמת נוסחת ההמרה בשתי המסורות שלה
בתפסירו של רס"ג, וברוח זו היא מתפרשת גם בידי כמה מהמפרשים.[6] אולם דומה, שבעל דברי–
הימים הכניס את התפיסה 'הסלחנית' שתיארנו בסד מצמצם. אין הוא גורם שנוסחת ההמרה מאפשרת
לכל אחד משני השמות לעמוד לבדו, שהרי אילו גרס כך, היתה דעתו נוחה מנוסח הפסוק בתהלים –
'זרע **אברהם** עבדו / בני יעקב בחיריו'. לדידו מקנה נוסחת ההמרה זכות עמידה עצמאית רק לשם
החדש, ישראל, ואילו לשם הישן, יעקב, מקנה היא רשות להיזכר רק כשהוא מתלווה לשם החדש.
תפיסה זו הנחתה את בעל דברי–הימים לנקוט את הנוסח 'זרע **ישראל** עבדו / בני יעקב בחיריו'.
תפיסת בעל דברי–הימים תואמת ודאי את התפיסה העקרונית של חז"ל, המקנה מכל מקום מעמד
מועדף לאחד מהשמות על משנהו. במסגרת תפיסה עקרונית זו של חז"ל תמצא אמנם התלבטות
בשאלה, איזה משני השמות הוא בעל המעמד המועדף. מצד אחד נשמעת אצלם הדעה המעדיפה
את **יעקב**: 'ר' זכריה בשם ר' אחא: מכל מקום יעקב שמך! אלא: "כי אם ישראל יהיה שמך" – יעקב
עיקר וישראל מוסיף עליו' (בראשית רבה עח, ג); ומצד שני ניתן בספרורת ביטוי לקביעה המעדיפה
את **ישראל**: '"לא יקרא שמך עוד יעקב, כי אם ישראל יהיה שמך" – לא שֶׁיֵעָקֵר יעקב ממקומו,
אלא ישראל עיקר ויעקב טפל לו' (ברכות יב ע"ב – יג ע"א). ברור שנטייתו העקרונית של בעל
דברי–הימים לדחוק את השם הישן מפני החדש מזמינה מלכתחילה את 'תמיכתו' בבעלי הדעה
השנייה שבמחלוקת הנזכרת. בכל זאת דומה אני, שראוי להצביע על העובדה, שדעה זו בניסוחה
המילולי – 'לא שֶׁיֵעָקֵר יעקב ממקומו, אלא ישראל עיקר ויעקב טפל לו' – תואמת את התנהגותו
בפועל של בעל דברי–הימים, באשר לחותם הנוסח שהטביע על תה' קה, ו בדה"א טז, יז, ומהדהד
ממנה שיקול נוסף בעיצוב הנוסח המתוקן של הפסוק. ודוק: משלא נחה דעתו של בעל דברי–הימים
מנוסח הפסוק בתהלים – 'זרע **אברהם** עבדו / בני יעקב בחיריו' – המיר, כמצוין לעיל,

6   ראה למשל: רד"ק לבראשית לב, כט; לה, י; ראב"ע לבראשית לה, י; רבנו יוסף בכור שור לבראשית יז, ה. גם
רמב"ן מעלה אפשרות זו בסוף פירושו לבראשית לה, י.

את **אברהם בישראל**, ולא העלה על דעתו לעקור את יעקב ממקומו ולהציע את הנוסח: *'זרע **אברהם**
עבדו / בני **ישראל** בחיריו'. ומשגזר על עצמו שלא לעקור את יעקב ממקומו ולא היה יכול היה להסכים
עם נוסח המקיים את השם **יעקב**, שהוא בגדר 'טפל', מבלי שיתלווה אליו השם **ישראל**, שהוא בגדר
'עיקר', נאלץ לעקור את **אברהם** ממקומו ולשתול תחתיו את **ישראל**.

נקל להסביר את התפיסות המקנות עדיפות לשם **ישראל** על השם **יעקב**, בין שעדיפות זו מבקשת
'לעקור את יעקב ממקומו', בין שהיא מעניקה ל**ישראל** את הציון 'עיקר' ומעמידה את **יעקב** כ'טפל
לו'. בהעדפה זו מצדדים סיפור המרת השם ככלל ונוסחת ההמרה על־פי פשטה בפרט, התולים את
המרת השם בגורם שמיימי, בין שהוא מלאך – שליח האל – בין שהוא האל עצמו. ניתן אפוא לומר,
שמקורו השמיימי של השם החדש מעניק לו מלכתחילה עדיפות על השם הישן, שמקורו בגורם
ארצי. רעיון זה זכה לביטוי מפליג במקור החז"לי שלהלן: 'למה נשתנה שמו של אברהם ושמו של
יעקב; ושמו של יצחק לא נשתנה? אֵילו (=**אברהם ויעקב**) – אבותן קראו אותן בשמן; אבל יצחק –
הקב"ה קראו יצחק' (ירושלמי ברכות א, ו). מקור זה אינו מסתפק בהעדפת השם החדש בדיעבד,
היינו, לאחר שכבר ניתן, אלא רואה בהמרת שמותיהם של אברהם ויעקב צורך שמלכתחילה, שכך
יאה להם לאבות האומה שישאו שמות שניתנו להם בגושפנקא של מעלה. זאת ועוד: אף את הרשות
לקיים את השם **יעקב** לצד **ישראל** היו שתלו בגושפנקא כזאת, שאלמלא מצאוה לא היה הקורא
ליעקב יעקב נמלט מגדר חוטא: בין שהיה נחשב לעובר בלאו, המעוגן בחלקה הראשון של נוסחת
ההמרה, בין שהיה נחשב לעובר בעשה, המשתמע מחלקה השני של הנוסחה – 'כי אם־ישראל יהיה
שמך'. זיכויו מחטא של 'הקורא ליעקב יעקב' נעוץ לדידם בעובדה 'דהדר אהדריה קרא [=שחזר
והחזירו הכתוב, היינו: שקראו הקב"ה את עצמו שוב בשם **יעקב**] דכתיב: "ויאמר אלהים ל**ישראל**
במראות הלילה ויאמר **יעקב יעקב** ויאמר הנני"' (בר' מו, ב) (ברכות יג ע"א). כאן ניתן 'הכשר'
לשימוש בשם **יעקב**, אך אין בהכשר זה כדי לגרוע ממעמדו המועדף של השם החדש, **ישראל**, על
השם הישן **יעקב**. מעמד מועדף זה זוכה לביטוי מיוחד בקטע שלהלן,[7] ששובץ בתפילת השחר לפני
קריאת שמע הראשונה, זו שלפני סדר הקרבנות: 'אבל אנחנו עמך בני בריתך... עדת **יעקב**...
שמאהבתך שאהבת אותו ומשמחתך ששמחת בו קראת את שמו **ישראל** ו**יְשֻׁרוּן**'. קטע זה מציג את
השם **ישראל** (וכורך עמו את השם **ישורון**) כשם שקרא האל ל**יעקב** בשל אהבתו אותו ושמחתו בו,
ומשתמע מכאן אחת מן השתיים: או שאהבה זו ושמחה זו הולידו אצל הבורא אי־נחת מן השם
יעקב, הקושר את בעל השם עם תכונת ה**עָקֵב** – תכונה שאינה מתיישבת עם אהבת האל לבעל
השם – ובשל כך המיר האל שם זה בשמות **ישראל** ו**ישורון**, הנושאים קונוטציות חיוביות; או שאהבה
זו ושמחה זו הניעו את האל לעצם מעורבותו בבחירת שם האהוב. בין כך ובין כך, המרת שמו של
אדם בשם חדש נשענת על ההנחה, שיש בשמו של אדם כדי להצביע על מהותו, ומשחל שינוי
במהותו של אדם אין השם הישן יכול עוד להלום אותו, ומן הראוי ליתן לו שם חדש, שיבטא את
השינוי שחל בו.

<hr>

7   לא כאן המקום לדון במקורה של תפילה זו, הפותחת במלים: 'רבון כל העולמים... לא על צדקותינו אנחנו מפילים
     תחנונינו לפניך...'. הקטע שהובא כאן מופיע בנוסחים אחרים של מדרש 'תנא דבי אליהו רבה' – כגון במהדורה
     וורשא תרל"ד, פרק כא, עמ' 80 – ונעדר ממנוסחים אחרים שלו, המבליעים אותו, אולי, בתיבת הקיצור 'וגו'',
     הבאה אחרי 'מפילים תחנונינו לפניך'. כך הוא ב'סדר אליהו רבה' מהדורת מ' איש שלום (המושתתת על כת"י
     רומי, שלפי קביעת המהדיר היא משנת [ד' אלפים] תתל"ג [=1073]), ירושלים תש"ך, פרק יט, עמ' 118.

מן הראוי לציין כי את הזיקה שבין מהותו של אדם לבין שמו אפשר לתאר לא רק בסדר המעמיד
את השם כנגרר אחר המהות אלא אף בסדר הפוך, זה המציג את המהות כנגררת אחר השם. לפי סדר
זה, שמו של אדם עשוי לקבוע את מהותו או את מזלו, ופעמים מתבקש שינוי השם לצורך שינוי
המזל. ביטוי ברור לתפיסה זו במקורות חז"ל מצוי בדברי ר' הונא בשם ר' יוסף, שראה להוסיף על
קביעת ר' יודן בשם ר' אלעזר, ש'שלושה דברים מבטלים גזירות רעות, ואלו הן: תפילה וצדקה
ותשובה', גורמים נוספים: 'אף שינוי השם ומעשה טוב. שינוי השם – מאברהם: "ולא יקרא עוד את
שמך אברם" (בר' יז, ה)' (בראשית רבה מד, יב). על שינוי חיובי במזלם של אברהם ושרה משנשתנה
שמם מעמיד המדרש בדברים מפורשים: '"ויאמר אברם הן לי לא נתת זרע" (בר' טו, ג) – אמר ר'
שמואל בר רב יצחק: המזל דוחקני ואומר לי: אברם, אין אַתְּ מוליד! אמר לו הקב"ה: הן כדבריך;
אברם לא מוליד, אברהם מוליד. "שרי אשתך לא תקרא את שמה שרי" (שם, יז, טו) – שרי לא תלד,
שרה תלד' (בראשית רבה מד, י). [8]

מן התפיסה הקושרת את שמו של אדם למזלו או למהותו – בין שהמזל או המהות מושפעים מן
השם בין שהם משתקפים בו – עולה בבירור, שיש במשמעי השמות יעקב וישראל כדי להסביר את
'יחסי הכוחות' שביניהם. ברור שאליבא דכל השיטות נושא השם ישראל משמעות חיובית, וכל
מדרשי השם שהוצעו לו כיוונו לכך. אך לא כזה חֵלֶק יעקב: אלה שביקשו לעקור אותו ממקומו
דרשו את שמו לגנאי; ואלה שביקשו לקיימו לצד ישראל – כ'טפל לו' ועל אחת כמה וכמה
כ'עיקר'[9] – מסתמא ייחסו לשמו משמע חיובי. בירור המשמעים שיוחסו לשני השמות מתבקש עתה
מאליו, שכן אין הפירוש השקוף שניתן לכל אחד מהשמות בסיפור המקראי פירוש בלבדי, ויש ליתן
את הדעת גם לפירושים אחרים – שקופים פחות או אף סמויים – העומדים ברקעם של כתובים או
מדרשים.

הקשר של השם יעקב אל סיפור 'ואחריֿ־כן יצא אחיו וידו אחזת בעקב עשו ויקרא שמו יעקב' (בר'
כה, כו) שקוף הוא. קשר זה נשנה גם בדברי הושע: 'בבטן עָקַב אתֿ־אחיו' (הו' יב, ד), עלֿ־פי המשמע
הגלוי של הפועל עָקַב – אחז בעָקֵב. אולם אין ספק בכך שהנביא ייחס לפועל זה גם את המשמע של
עקמומיות ורמאות, משמע ההולם את ההקשר שבו מופיע המשפט הנדון. הנביא פותח בקביעה:
'וריב לה' עםֿ־יהודה ולפקֹד עלֿ־יעקב כדרכיו, כמעלליו ישיב לו' (שם, ג), ומסמיך לה את המשפט
'בבטן עָקַב אתֿ־אחיו'. וכבר אתה תוהה, אם לסיפור בעלמא נתכוון הנביא ולשון עָקֵב כאן, או לדברי
תוכחה נתכוון, כיוצא בהם בדברי ירמיהו: 'איש מרעהו השמרו ועלֿ־כלֿ־אח אל תבטחו, כי כלֿ־אח עָקוֹב
יַעְקֹב וכלֿ־רֵעַ רכיל יהלך' (יר' ט, ג). משמע זה – עקמומיות והעדר יושר – משתמע בבירור גם
ממדרש שמו של יעקב בלשונו של עשו: 'הכי קרא שמו יעקב ויעקבני זה פעמים: אתֿ־בכרתי לקח
והנה עתה לקח ברכתי' (בר' כז, לו), והוא נרמז עוד בפסוקי מקרא אחדים. [10] אולם דומה אני,
שהתנגדות למשמע זה נשמעת מן הכתוב המגדיר את יעקב – כבר בהצגתו הראשונה – כ'איש תם'

---

8   יצוין כי רש"י, המביא דברי מדרש אלה בפירושו לבראשית טו, ה, ראה להוסיף לדברים המיוחסים במדרש לה'
    את הקביעה המפורשת: 'אני קורא לכם שם אחר וישתנה המזל'.

9   ודוק! דברי ר' זכריה בשם ר' אחא, שהובאו לעיל – 'יעקב עיקר וישראל מוסיף עליו' (בראשית רבה עח, ג) –
    אינם מעמידים את ישראל כטפל, אלא כשם נוסף לשם העיקרי, ולשיטה זו נושאים שני השמות משמעות
    חיובית.

10 כגון מיכה ב, ז; יש' מח, א'־ב. ראה על כך י' זקוביץ, 'עקבת יעקב', ספר ברוך בןֿ־יהודה, תלֿ־אביב תשמ"א,
    עמ' 144–121.

(בר' כה, כז). הגדרה זו מבקשת – ולו ברמז – לעקור מן השם **יעקב** את זיקתו לתכונת העקב,
ולייחס לבעל השם דווקא את התכונה ההפוכה, תכונת היושר; שכן התואר 'תם' משמש במקרא
כנרדפו של 'ישר'.[11] ואמנם מצינו מדרשי חז"ל שהבינו כך את 'יעקב איש תם', כגון: 'יעקב לא
עשיתי לו נסים מעולם וכל ימיו היה ישר; **תם** מן הגזל מן העבירה מדבר מכוער' (תנא דבי אליהו
רבה ו). ודוק: הצגת יעקב כ**תם** בהוראת ישר משתלבת יפה עם תפיסת השם **ישראל** כבנוי על שורש
זה, תפיסה שנרחיב בה בהמשך.

בצד הוראה זו של **תם** = ישר משמשת גם ההוראה הקרובה של **תם** = שלם. להוראה זו מכוונים
כמה מן המקורות, כגון תרגום אונקלוס לבראשית כה, כז: 'ויעקב גבר **שלים**', והמדרש שלהלן,
שקשר את 'ויעקב איש תם' עם 'ויבא יעקב **שָׁלֵם**' (בר' לג, יח):

ר' חייא בר אבא פתח: 'אם זך וישר אתה כי עתה יעיר עליך ושׁׁלַם נְוַת צדקך' (איוב ח, ו):
'אם זך וישר אתה' – 'הַיִית' אין כתיב כאן אלא 'אתה'; הא לשעבר לא היית צדיק; 'כי עתה
יעיר עליך' – עתיד הקב"ה להתעורר עליך ולשלם לך כל צדקות שעשית. **ולפי שכתוב**
'ויעקב איש תם ...' (בר' כה, כז), **לפיכך: 'ויבא יעקב שָׁלֵם'** (בראשית רבה עט, ג).

מדרש זה מניח, שבלדד השוחי – האומר לאיוב 'אם זך וישר אתה כי עתה יעיר עליך ושלם נות
צדקך' – אינו מאמין בתומתו של איוב, ואינו יודע את הנאמר על איוב בפתח סיפור המסגרת: 'והיה
האיש ההוא **תם** וישר וירא אלהים וסר מרע' (איוב א, א). דברי בלדד לאיוב אינם מכוונים, לפי
המדרש, לצדקות איוב בעבר, אלא לצדקות שיעשה – אם ייטיב דרכו – בעתיד, ולגמול שיהא ראוי
לו בגין צדקות אלו. בניגוד לאיוב ראוי יעקב, לפי המדרש, לגמול על היותו 'איש תם יושב אהלים'
כבר מראשית חייו. מכל מקום, הזיקה שמעמיד המדרש בין התמימות לבין הגמול הראוי לה,
והקישור שהוא מציע בין הכתוב 'ויעקב איש תם' לבין הכתוב 'ויבא יעקב שלם' מרמזים אולי על
משמע נוסף לתיבה שָׁלֵם – ראוי ל**תשלום**, זכאי לגמול. זאת ועוד: ברקעו של מדרש זה עומד
מדרש-שם סמוי ל**יעקב**, הנשען על המשמע החיובי של השורש 'עקב', שעניינו גמול ושכר. במשמע
זה משמש שם-העצם 'עקב' בכמה כתובים במקרא, כגון: '... בשמרם עֵקֶב רב' (תה' יט, יב); 'עֵקֶב
ענוה יראת ה', עשׁר וכבוד וחיים' (מש' כב, ד).[12] ייחוס משמע חיובי זה לשם **יעקב** יש לו הצדקה
גם מעבר לגבולותיו של מדרש-שם שבדיעבד, שכן יש רגליים לסברה, שזהו משמעו המקורי של
השם. סברה זו עולה בקנה אחד עם נטיימם הטבעית של נותני שם לתינוק שנולד, המבקשים

---

11 שימוש זה בולט במיוחד בהופעת שני התארים בסינטגמה אחת – 'תם וישר' (איוב א, א, ח; ב, ג) – או בתקבולת:
'שׁמָר תָם וראֵה יָשָׁר' (תה' לז, לז).

12 שימושה של התיבה ' 'עֵקֶב' בפסוק זה בהוראת 'תוצאה, גמול' הולם את שני הפירושים האפשריים לפסוק. פירוש
א': הסמוך של 'עֵקֶב' הוא הצירוף 'ענוה יראת ה'', צירוף שיש לראותו כסינטגמה-של-איחוי אסינדטית, היינו:
'ענוה [ו]יראת ה''. כך הציע כבר ר' יונה אבן ג'נאח (ראה: 'ספר הרקמה', מהדיר מ' וילנסקי, מהדורה שנייה,
ירושלים תשכ"ד, א', עמ' ר"פ, שורה 26). פירוש זה רואה את נושא הפסוק בצירוף הסמיכות 'עקב ענוה יראת
ה'' ואת הנשוא בצירוף 'עשר וכבוד וחיים'. שיעור הכתוב לפי תפיסה זו הוא: הגמול לענוה ולירָאת ה' הוא עושר
וכבוד וחיים. פירוש ב': נושא הפסוק הוא צירוף הסמיכות 'עקב ענוה', וצירוף הסמיכות 'ירָאת ה'' שייך לחלק
הנשואי של הפסוק. שיעור הכתוב לפי תפיסה זו הוא: תוצאתה של הענוה והגמול לה היא ירָאת ה', ונוסף עליה
גם עושר וכבוד וחיים. ברוח זו פירשו רש"י (בפירושו הראשון לפסוק) והמיוחס לראב"ע.

להעניק ליילוד שם המזל הצלחה[13] ונרתעים מבחירת שם בעל קונוטציות שליליות. הסיפור
המקראי מציג אמנם את בחירת השם יעקב בזיקה לאירוע שהתרחש בשעת לידתו – 'וידו אחזת
בעקב עשו' (בר' כה, כו) – אך אין בכך משום קביעה, שהשם הומצא בעקבות האירוע הזה. סביר
הוא, שהאירוע הקשור בעקב הוליך באסוציאציה פונטית לבחירת השם יעקב מתוך מאגר שמות שהיה
קיים בסביבה באותה עת. ואמנם במאגר זה מצויים בכמה לשונות שמות המכילים את היסוד 'עקב'
או אף 'יעקב'. מבין אלה נציין במיוחד את השמות התיאופוריים 'יעקבאל' – ששימש במסופוטמיה
במאה השמונה-עשרה לפני הספירה – ו'עקבאלהא' – גלגולו הסורי של אותו השם.[14] יש להניח
שהשם המקראי יעקב אינו אלא שם מקוצר של שם תיאופורי מעין אלה. ודוק: היחס שבין 'יעקבאל'
או 'עקבאלהא' לבין 'יעקב' הוא כיחס שבין 'עקביה' לבין 'עקיבא', המשמשים שניהם בתקופת חז"ל
(גם בכתיב עקביא, עקיבא), ובנויים אף הם על השורש 'עקב'. שמות אלה – ווריאציות השונות
שלהם – מבטאים את התקווה שהאל יגן על נושאיהם ויגמול להם טוב. תקווה זו עומדת גם מאחורי
השם 'גמליאל' (במ' א, י, ועוד), המוכר גם בגרסותיו האכדיות Gamâl-ilim ו-Gamâl-
Shamash, ודומה שאף הוא זכה לגרסה מקוצרת במקרא: 'גמול' (דה"א כד, יז). שם נוסף המושתת
על רעיון הגמול הטוב הוא 'יששכר' (בר' ל, יח; דה"א כו, ה), ומדרש-השם הצמוד לו – 'נתן אלהים
שכרי' (בר' ל, יח) – מבטא יפה את האטימולוגיה שלו. השם 'שָׂכָר' (דה"א יא, לה) הוא ככל הנראה
גרסה מקוצרת של 'יששכר'.[15]

המשאלה המובעת במשמעו החיובי של השם יעקב, היינו שהאל יגן על בעל השם ויגמול לו טוב,
זוכה להתענות בהתגלות ה' ליעקב בחלום, התגלות שבמרכזה עומדת ההבטחה: 'והנה אנכי עמך
ושמרתיך בכל אשר-תלך והשבתיך אל-האדמה הזאת, כי לא אעזבך עד אשר אם-עשיתי את אשר-
דברתי לך' (בר' כח, טו). העובדה שהבטחה זו מתרחשת במקום שיעקב מסב את שמו ל'בית-אל'
(שם, פס' יט) אינה מקרית. צא ולמד: סביב שם המקום 'בית-אל' טווה המקרא שני סיפורי המרת-
שם, המתרחשים לאחר התגלות האל ליעקב. בסיפור אחד (זה המוצג כאן) מקום ההתגלות הוא
המושא של המרת השם (מלוז לבית-אל), ויעקב הוא ממיר השם; ובסיפור השני (בר' לה, ט-טו)
יעקב הוא המושא של המרת השם, האל הוא ממיר השם והאירוע מתרחש – לפי אחת ממסורות
הסיפור – בבית-אל. הספק שמלווה את הסיפור השני באשר לתפיסתו את המשמע של השם יעקב
אין לו מקום בסיפור הראשון, שאינו נזקק להמרת שם יעקב. ברקעו של סיפור זה עומדת משמעותו
החיובית של השם יעקב. משמעות זו משתקפת מבעד להבטחה שהועמדה בסיפור במקום המשאלה

---

13   וראה ב' קלואר, מחקרים ועיונים, תל-אביב תשי"ד, המציין – במאמר 'שמות בני ישראל' – 'כי 'אתה מוצא
    במקרא גם שמות המביעים בקשה ומשאלה לעתיד לבוא, שישקיף ה' ממעון קדשו מן השמים על הרך הנולד
    ויגן עליו כל ימי חייו ויחלצהו מכל צרה וישלח לו את ברכתו ממעל' (שם, עמ' 49). ובהמשך: 'השם יעקב,
    שנמצא במקורו בשלמותו: יעקבאל, פירושו לפי הנראה: ישלם אלהים שכר. ויש מפרשים גם את השם הזה
    מלשון מחסה ומגן' (שם, עמ' 50).

14   על מגוון שמות אלה ראה: מ"ד קאסוטו, הערך 'יעקב', אנציקלופדיה מקראית ג, ירושלים תשכ"ה, טור 717;
    י"מ גרינץ, ייחודו וקדמותו של ספר בראשית, ירושלים תשמ"ג, עמ' 30.

15   ברור שתופעת השמות המקוצרים, המשלימים את היסוד התיאופורי שלהם, אינה מיוחדת לשמות שבמרכזם שורש
    השייך לשדה הסמנטי של שכר וגמול. כך תמצא את 'יפתח-אל' (יה' יט, יד, כז) בצד 'יפתח' (יה' טו, מג), ואת
    'יבנאל' (יה' טו, יא) בצד 'יבנה' (דה"ב כו, ו) (בין שהשם המקוצר מכוון לאותו מקום שמקבילו הארוך מכוון לו,
    בין שהוא מכוון למקום אחר).

המובאת בשם. הסיפור המקראי מלמד גם על מימושה של הבטחת ההגנה והגמול. כך מסביר יעקב את יכולת עמידתו כנגד נכלותו של לבן במילים: 'ואלהי אבי היה עמדי' (בר' לא, ה); 'ולא־נתנו אלהים להרע עמדי' (שם, פס' ז); 'ויצל אלהים את־מקנה אביכם ויתן־לי' (שם, פס' ט); 'לולי אלהי אבי ... היה לי, כי עתה ריקם שלחתני' (שם, פס' מב). ודוק: לדברים המפורשים של יעקב במובאה האחרונה, המצביעים על האל כגמול טוב ליעקב, יש לצרף את הדברים העולים מהרמיזה שבמילים ריקם שלחתני. במילים אלו מהדהד דין המענק שבחוק שילוח העבד: 'וכי־תשלחנו חפשי מעמך, לא תשלחנו ריקם. העניק תעניק לו מצאנך ומגרנך ומיקבך, אשר ברכך ה' אלהיך תתן־לו' (דב' טו, יג-יד). יעקב מציין אפוא כי בסופו של דבר לא שולח ריקם, אך את 'המענק' והגמול העניק לו האל בברכתו.

עתה, משהעמדנו על המשמע החיובי של השם יעקב, יש מקום לתהות באשר למשמעם של דברי עשו: 'הכי קרא שמו יעקב ויעקבני זה פעמים; את־בכרתי לקח, והנה עתה לקח ברכתי' (בר' כז, לו). האם במדרש־שם זה מתפרש ויעקבני מלשון עקמומיות ורמיה דווקא – פירוש הנתמך בדברי יצחק 'בא אחיך במרמה' (שם, פס' לה) – או שמא ניתן לפרשו גם כפועל דינומינטיבי הגזור מעֵקב = גמול ושכר, ומציין את שלילת שם־העצם שממנו נגזר, כדרכם של פעלים דינומינטיביים פעמים הרבה.[16] שיעור הכתוב לפי האפשרות השנייה הוא: 'ויעקבני [=שלל ממני את העֵקב, את הגמול] זה פעמים: את־בכרתי לקח [תחילה] והנה עתה לקח ברכתי'.[17] לפי פירוש זה מציינות הבכורה וברכת האב את העֵקב שנשלל מעשו ביזמת יעקב, והרי עיקרן של אלה הוא בגמול שבצידן.

נמצאנו למדים: האסוציאציה הפונטית, העומדת בסיפור המקראי מאחורי בחירת השם יעקב כשמו של מי שאחז בעקב אחיו בעת לידתו, מנומקת היא הן ממשמעו המקורי החיובי של השם הן מן המשמע השלילי שנתלה בשם בדיעבד. מי שראה באור שלילי את התנהגותו של יעקב בפרשיות הבכורה והברכה דרש את השם באסוציאציה לעָקֵב מלשון רמייה, ומי שביקש ללמד זכות על אבי האומה תלה בו תכונות של איש תם (=ישר), שָׁלֵם, ראוי לגמול = עֵקֶב, בין שהיה מודע למשמעו המקורי של השם בין שלא היה מודע לו.

גם השם ישראל איננו חד־משמעי. הסיפור המקראי התכוון לשם זה פירוש שקוף, המוצג כהנמקה להמרת השם: 'לא יעקב יאמר עוד שמך, כי אם־ישראל, כי־שָׂרִיתָ עם־אלהים ועם־אנשים וַתּוּכָל' (בר' לב, כט). אך דא עקא: המבקש ללמוד על משמע השם ישראל ממשמע הפועל שָׂרִית, או ממשמע השורש 'שרי' שממנו נגזר הפועל, מגלה מיד שהוא נתון במעין מעגל קסמים. שכן אין לפעלים הגזורים משורש זה קיום עצמאי במקרא, וכל שימושם אינו אלא בזיקה למדרש השם ישראל. פעלים אלה מזדמנים בשתי היקרויות ברורות בלבד: האחת בבראשית לב, כט (שָׂרִית), בסיפור המרת השם שאנו דנים בו; והשנייה בהושע י"ב ד: 'בבטן עקב את־אחיו ובאונו

<hr />

16 השווה: לַדַּשֵּׁן = להוציא את הַדֶּשֶׁן; לזַנֵּב = להסיר את הזנב, היינו את הַעוֹמֵד בקצה; לשָׁרֵשׁ = לעקור את השורש.

17 ודוק: שלילת העֵקב, היינו הגמול – המצוינת, לפי פירוש זה, בתיבה ויעקבני – יש שהיא מושגת באמצעות תרמית גלויה, כלכֹּיחת הברכה מעשו בסיפורנו; אך אפשר גם שתהיה תוצר של מעשה שיש בו כיסוי חוקי, כקניית הבכורה מעשו, בהסכמה. לפיכך ניתן לראות כפל הוראה בפועל לקח שבדברי עשו: 'את בכרתי לקח [=קנה בדין], והשווה שימוש זה בלשונות המכירה: 'מכרה כיום את־בכרתך לי' (בר' כה, לא); 'ויֹמר את־ בכרתו ליעקב' (שם, לג) והנה עתה לקח [=נטל (שלא כדין, במרמה)] ברכתי'. על לקח בהוראת קנה ועל דוגמה נוספת לכפל הוראה בשורש זה במקרא ראה: ש' קוגוט, 'כפל הוראה בשורש "לקח" במקרא', לשוננו לד (תש"ל), עמ' 320.

שָׂרָה אֶת־הָאֱלֹהִים". לאלה יש להוסיף את הפועל וַיִּשַׂר, הבא שם בסמוך, בפסוק ה, והמתייחס לשורש שׂוּר/שָׂרַר, אחי שָׂרִי: וַיָּשַׂר אֶל מַלְאָךְ וַיֻּכָל'. בשתי ההיקרויות שבהושע מהדהד סיפורנו בבירור, ונמצא שפירושם של הפעלים שָׂרָה וַיִּשַׂר תלוי בעליל בפירושו של הפועל שָׂרִית. קשרו של פועל זה לסיפור 'ויאבק איש עמו' (בר' לב, כה) גרם לשורשים שָׂרִי/שָׂרַר שיתפרשו כמציינים מלחמה או מאבק. לפשט זה נזקק המדרש, בפרשו את 'כי־שָׂרִיתָ עִם־אֱלֹהִים ועם־אֲנָשִׁים וַתּוּכָל' – 'נתגוששת עם העליונים ויכלת להם ועם התחתונים ויכלת להם' (בראשית רבה עח, ג). אף־עַל־פִּי שעיקרו של מדרש זה הוא בהמשכו, המתמקד בזיהוי הדמויות שמאחורי אֱלֹהִים/העליונים ואֲנָשִׁים/התחתונים, ענייננו כאן הוא דווקא במה שהיה בגדר מובן מאליו לבעל המדרש, היינו בפירוש שָׂרִית = נתגוששת, העולה במדרש כבדרך אגב. ההקרנה ההדדית המתקיימת בין ההיקרויות של הפעלים הנזכרים משורש 'שָׂרַי/שָׂרַר' לבין השם **ישראל** הוליכה לפירוש השם **ישראל** כמורכב מן יָשַׂר (=שָׂרָה; עתיד יוסיבי בהוראת עבר) + **אֵל**, היינו: התגושש עם אל. שני מרכיבי השם מצויים בעליל בשתיים מתוך שלוש ההיקרויות שהזכרנו, כשאֱלֹהִים הוא משלימו המושאי של הפועל: 'שָׂרִית עִם־אֱלֹהִים'; ו'שָׂרָה אֶת־אֱלֹהִים'; ואילו בהיקרות השלישית, הצמודה לשנייה, גיוון הנביא את הלשון והמיר את אֱלֹהִים במַלְאָךְ. עם זאת, דומה אני, שהשימוש במלת היחס אֶל כמוצרכת לפועל וַיָּשַׂר בהיקרות זו דווקא – שלא כהצרכות בשתי ההיקרויות האחרות, 'שָׂרִיתָ עִם' ו'שָׂרָה אֶת' – איננה מקרית. משהעמיד הנביא את מַלְאָךְ כמשלימו של הפועל וַיָּשַׂר, נפגם מדרש־השם **ישראל** באחד ממרכיביו. פגם זה ביקש הנביא לתקן בהצמדת מלת היחס **אֶל** לפועל וַיָּשַׂר, ונמצא השם **ישראל** מהדהד מן הצירוף 'וַיָּשַׂר אֶל־מַלְאָךְ'.

התפיסה, שלפיה מצייר השם **ישראל** תמונה של התגוששות עם האל, מעלה שני קשיים: האחד – מבני־תחבירי, והשני – תיאולוגי. הקושי המבני־תחבירי: דרכם של השמות התיאופוריים שהם בנויים כמשפט, שבו האל משמש נושא והפועל נשוא. מבנה תחבירי זה מתקיים הן כשהסדר מרכיבי השם הוא נשוא – נושא, כגון ישמעֵאל; ירחמאֵל; עשהאֵל; עזרִיה; ישעיָה וכיו"ב, הן בסדר נושא־נשוא, כגון: אליעֶזר; אלקנה; אלידָע; אליסָף; יהוֹיָדָע; יהוֹנָתָן וכיו"ב. שונה מכל אלה הוא השם **ישראל**, שבו מועמד האל כמושא, ומישהו אחר – יעקב – שָׂרָה עמו. בתפיסה זו של מבנה השם נעוץ גם הקושי התיאולוגי, שכן עולה ממנה שהשם **ישראל** מנציח כביכול את כשלונו של האל במאבק עם אדם, בעוד שמנקודת ראות תיאולוגית היה מן הראוי ששם זה יביע את ההפך, היינו שהאל הוא השוֹרֶה עם אחרים ויכול להם.[18]

דומה, שהקושי התיאולוגי העולה מן הפסוק '... ובאונו שָׂרָה אֶת־אֱלֹהִים' (הו' יב, ד) ועוד יותר מן הפסוק 'כי־שָׂרִיתָ עִם־אֱלֹהִים... וַתּוּכָל' (בר' לב, כט), משתקף גם בנתיב המילוט שברר לו הושע בפסוק 'וַיָּשַׂר אֶל־מַלְאָךְ וַיֻּכָל' (הו' יב, ה), שבו הומר אֱלֹהִים בּמַלְאָךְ. ואולי אין זה מקרה שהכתיב וַיֻּכָל, המציינת את נצחונו של יעקב במאבק, לא באה בפסוק 'ובאונו שָׂרָה אֶת־הָאֱלֹהִים', אלא בפסוק המעמיד מַלְאָךְ כמי שהובס בידי יעקב. ודוק: הקשיים שהעלינו כאן הוליכו את חז"ל לבדוק, אם

---

18 והשווה לשם **ישראל** את השם יְרֻבַּעַל ואת מדרש השם המלווה אותו: 'וַיֹּאמֶר יוֹאָשׁ... הַאַתֶּם תְּרִיבוּן לַבַּעַל אִם־אַתֶּם תּוֹשִׁיעוּן אוֹתוֹ... אִם־אֱלֹהִים הוּא יָרֶב לוֹ... וַיִּקְרָא־לוֹ בַיּוֹם־הַהוּא יְרֻבַּעַל לֵאמֹר יָרֶב בּוֹ הַבַּעַל כִּי־נָתַץ אֶת־מִזְבְּחוֹ' (שופ' ו, לא–לב). בדומה לשם **ישראל** גם יְרֻבַּעַל הוא שם תיאופורי המבקש לתעד מלחמה בין גורם אלוהי לגורם אנושי, אך שלא כבמדרש השם **ישראל** מועמד הגורם האלוהי (בעל) בשם יְרֻבַּעַל כנושא ולא כמושא!

אין בלשון הכתובים דו־משמעות, המאפשרת להציג את יעקב כמי שהובס. כך עולה מן הדרשה שלהלן:

'וישר אל־מלאך וַיֻּכֶל בכה ויתחנן־לו' (הו' יב, ה) – איני יודע מי נעשה שר למי. כשהוא אומר 'כי־שָׂרִיתָ עם־אלהים [ועם־אנשים וַתּוּכֶל]' (בר' לב, כט) – הוי אומר: יעקב נעשה שר למלאך! 'בכה ויתחנן־לו' – איני יודע מי בכה למי. כשהוא אומר 'ויאמר שלחני' (בר' לב, כז) – הוי אומר: מלאך בכה ליעקב! (חולין צב ע"א).

דרשה זו רואה בשני המשפטים שבהושע יב, ה – (א) 'וישר אל־מלאך וַיֻכֶל'; (ב) 'בכה ויתחנן־לו' – דו־משמעות, הנעוצה בגוף השלישי, השולט במשפטים אלה והמאפשר להבין את הפעלים וַיֻכֶל, בכה, ויתחנן ואת כינוי הנסתר שבמלת־היחס לו כמכוונים הן למלאך הן ליעקב.[19] להכרעת דו־משמעי זו בדברי הושע נזקקת היא לפסוקים שהביאה מבראשית לב. הנושא החד־משמעי של הפעלים 'שָׂרִיתָ... ותוּכָל', הבאים בגוף שני ומכוונים בהכרח ליעקב, מלמד על נושאם הזהה של מקביליהם בהושע – 'וישר... וַיֻכֶל'. כן רואה הדרשה את המשאלה שלחני – המוצגת כפסוקית תוכן מושאית של הפועל ויאמר, שנושאו הוא המלאך – כמהדדת מן הפעלים בכה ויתחנן שבהושע. מעתה אין הדרשה יכולה עוד להתעלם מפשט הכתוב שבהושע, ששיעורו הוא: 'וישר [יעקב] אל־מלאך וַיֻכֶל [יעקב למלאך]; בכה [המלאך] ויתחנן [המלאך] לו [=ליעקב]'.

הקושי התיאולוגי להכיר באפשרות שאדם יגבר במאבק על 'העליונים' – אלהים, או אפילו מלאך – מנע מאונקלוס לתרגם את 'שָׂרִיתָ עם אלהים' ברוח המדרש שהובא לעיל, הגורס 'נתגוששת עם העליונים', והביאו לפרש את שָׂרִיתָ מלשון 'שר וגדול', פירוש המשתקף מלשון תרגומו: 'רַב אַתְּ קדם ה''. בעקבות אונקלוס פירש גם רש"י: 'לשון שר ונגיד'.

לפי שיטת אונקלוס ורש"י בפירושם ל'שָׂרִיתָ עם אלהים' ניתן לפרש את השם ישראל: 'יהיה שר וגדול לפני האל'. פירוש זה מסלק אמנם את הקושי התיאולוגי, אך מותיר עדיין את המבנה התחבירי של השם כהריג, שכן אין זה הוא מעמיד את התיבה אל כנושא הצירוף המרכיב את השם. אולם מצינו כמה מדרשים שהפליגו בגדולתו של יעקב=ישראל, ואף שלא תלו תפיסה זו בשם ישראל, הרי היא עשויה לפרש את השם על דרך המבנה התחבירי השכיח של השמות התיאופוריים, היינו כשהיסוד אל בשם מוסב ליעקב, והוא הוא הנושא בצירוף. את ייחוס הכינוי אל ליעקב מצינו במדרשים כגון אלה:

'הקבצו ושמעו בני יעקב ושמעו אֶל־ישראל אביכם' (בר' מט, ב) – ר' יודן ור' פנחס. ר' יודן

---

19 הפועל וישר – עם שאף הוא בא בגוף שלישי – הוא חד־משמעי באשר לנושאו, יעקב. פירוש רש"י לחולין צב
ע"א, ד"ה 'ויוכל', מעמיד גם את וישר וישר בדו־משמעות: '"ויוכל". איני יודע על אי זה מהם הוא אומר "ויוכל",
שנצח ונעשה שר: וישר אל יעקב קאמר, והכי קאמר: וישר יעקב אל מלאך ויוכל יעקב; או הכי קאמר: וישר אל
יעקב מלאך, כלומר: נשתרר לעומתו המלאך, ויוכל המלאך ונצחו. העמדת המלאך כנושא אפשרי של
וישר – כעולה מפירוש רש"י – מאולצת היא ומותירה את מלת־היחס אל מיותמת ממשלים כלשהו, היינו 'וישר
אל מלאך' = 'וישר מלאך אל [x]', או: 'וישר מלאך אליו'. תן דעתך: פירוש מאולץ זה אינו נצרך להבנת דברי התלמוד, שאף שהם נתלים לכאורה בתיבה
וישר – כמשתמע מן הלשון 'איני יודע מי נעשה שר למי' – הם נשענים לאמיתו של דבר על התיבה וַיֻכֶל, כפי
שהרגיש גם רש"י, האומר: 'איני יודע על אי זה מהם הוא אומר "ויוכל", שנצח ונעשה שר'.

אמר: שמעו לְאֵל ישראל אביכם (היינו: לקב"ה), ור' פנחס אמר: אֵל הוא ישראל אביכם (בראשית רבה צח, ג).

הן ר' יודן הן ר' פנחס מוציאים את הפסוק מפשוטו. ר' יודן דורש את הפסוק בשיטת 'מקרא נדרש לפניו ולאחריו',[20] וקורא את התיבה אל פעמים (בהתעלם מן הניקוד השונה), כך: '... ושמעו אֶל [אֶל] ישראל אביכם'. קריאת ר' יודן אינה מעניינינו כאן. דעתנו נתונה לדרשתו של ר' פנחס, המעמידה את מבנהו התחבירי של הפסוק כך: '... ושמעו: אֵל (בשינוי הניקוד!) [הוא] ישראל אביכם'.

<u>נושא</u>   <u>נשוא</u>

כיוצא בזה נדרש גם הפסוק: 'ויצב־שם מזבח וַיִּקְרָא־לֹו אֵל אֱלֹהֵי ישראל' (בר' לג, כ). הדרשה שלהלן מהפכת את מבנהו התחבירי של הפסוק, בהפקיעה ממנו את הצירוף 'אל אלהי x',[21] כדי לזכות את יעקב בתואר אֵל:

ואמר ר' אחא אמר ר' אלעזר: מנין שקְרָאוֹ הקב"ה ליעקב 'אֵל'? — שנאמר: 'ויקרא לו אֵל אלהי ישראל'. דאי סלקא דעתך למזבח קרא ליה יעקב 'אֵל' — 'ויקרא לו יעקב' מיבעי ליה! אלא: ויקרא לו, ליעקב, 'אֵל', ומי קראו 'אֵל'? — אלהי ישראל! (מגילה מ ע"א).

דרשה זו של ר' אחא, המיוסדת על שיקולים תיאולוגיים והמנוגדת לפשט הכתוב ולפיסוק הטעמים המשקף אותו,[22] עולה בקנה אחד עם דרשה אחרת של ר' אחא, המתייחסת לפסוק 'ויתן־לך האלהים מטל השמים...' (בר' כז, כח) — 'ר' אחא אמר: ויתן לך אלהותא' (בראשית רבה סו, ג). לפי דרשת ר' אחא מבטיח יצחק ליעקב בברכתו, שה' יאציל עליו כביכול מאלוהותו. ר' אחא קורא אפוא את הפסוק כך: 'ויתן לך [ה' (הנזכר בסוף הפסוק הקודם)][את] האלהים (=האלוהות)', או בקריאה כפולה של התיבה 'האלהים' (בשיטת מקרא נדרש לפניו ולאחריו', שהוזכרה לעיל), כך: 'ויתן לך האלהים [את] האלהים (=האלוהות)'. בהמשך הדרשה מפליג ר' אחא ומפרש את קריאת שמשון 'ה' אלהים זכרני נא וחזקני נא אך הפעם הזה, האלהים ואנקמה...' (שופ' טז, כח), כך: 'אמר לפניו: ריבון העולמים, הווי זוכר לי אותה הברכה שברכני אבא (היינו: יצחק): "ויתן לך אלהותא"'. אמור מעתה: לשיטת ר' פנחס ור' אחא בדרשות שהובאו כאן ניתן לפרש את השם ישראל כ'אל שׂוֹרֶה', כשאל — הנושא בצירוף המרכיב את השם — מתייחס ליעקב, ומציין כוח, איילות, שהאציל האל על יעקב ובכך הטביע בו מסגולות האלוהות. זאת ועוד: חותמן של דרשות אלה מוטבע בבירור בדרשה נוספת, המקבלת כנתון את ההנחה, שהתיבה אל עשויה לבוא כאנטונומזיה (antonomasia = המרת שם)[23] ליעקב. הנחה זו מאירה את הדרשה שלהלן, המזיקה לפסוק 'ארור אפם כי עז' (בר' מט, ז) את הפסוק 'מה אָקֹב לא קַבֹה אֵל' (במ' כג, ח):

---

20   על שיטת קריאה זו ראה: ש' קוגוט, '"מקרא נדרש לפניו ולאחריו" — בחינה לשונית של מדרשי קריאה כפולה וזיקתם לפיסוק הטעמים', ספר היובל לרב מרדכי ברויאר — אסופת מאמרים במדעי היהדות (בעריכת מ' בר־אשר ואחרים), ירושלים תשנ"ב, ב, עמ' 697—706.

21   צירוף זה מופיע גם בביטוי 'אל אלהי הרוחת' (במ' טז, כב).

22   וראה על כך בהרחבה: ש' קוגוט, המקרא בין טעמים לפרשנות, מהדורה שנייה, ירושלים תשנ"ו, עמ' 133–135.

23   על התופעה הסמנטית הקרויה אנטונומזיה, שהיא סוג מיוחד של הסִינֶקדּוֹכֵה, ראה: H. Lausberg, Elemente der literarischen Rhetorik, München 1949, §§ 202-206

לא קלל אלא אפם, וכן בלעם הרשע אומר: 'מה אקב לא קבה אֵל' (היינו: מה אקב את אשר
לא קבה יעקב, הנקרא 'אל') – ומה אם בשעת הכעס לא קלל אלא אפם, ואני בא לקללן?!
(בראשית רבה צט, ז).

דרשה זו, עם שהיא מכנה את בלעם 'בלעם הרשע', היא רואה בו כביכול תלמיד חכם, המכיר לא
רק את הפסוק 'ארור אפם כי עז...' (בר' מט, ז), אלא אף את דרשות חז"ל (מבראשית רבה צח, ג;
ממגילה יח ע"א ומבראשית רבה סו, ג) שהובאו כאן. בהשראתן של אלה הוא מפליג בשימוש שהוא
עושה בשם אל; ומעתה במקום שבלעם נזקק – לפי הדרשה הנידונה כאן (המתעלמת מן התקבולת
'...לא קַבֹּה אל / ...לא זעם ה') – לאזכר את אבי האומה, הוא מתיר לעצמו להתעלם הן מן השם
יעקב הן מן השם ישראל והוא מציב תחת אלה את השם אל.

מדרשי השם שהציגו את הרכיב אל בשם ישראל כמכוון ליעקב והעמידוהו כנושא בצירוף
המרכיב את השם הינם תולדה של מניע תיאולוגי, שניזון מן ההנחה, שהרכיב השני שבשם קשור
בשורש שׂרי/שׂרר. אולם זו אינה ההנחה הבלעדית שפרנסה את דורשי השם ישראל. הנחות אחרות,
שנביא להלן, אפשרו את תפיסת הרכיב אל שבשם כפשוטו, בין שהעמידוהו כנושא בצירוף המרכיב
את השם, בין שהעמידוהו כמושא. הנחות אלו טעונות בירור, בעיקר באשר לתפיסתן את משמעו
של הרכיב השני שבשם.

נתחקה עתה אחר המניעים הלשוניים המסתתרים מאחורי המדרש המוזר לכאורה לשם ישראל,
המובא לאחר המדרש שהבאנו לעיל – 'נתגוששת עם העליונים' – בלשון זו:

דבר אחר: 'כי שׂרית עם אלהים' – אַתְּ הוא שאיקונין שלך חקוקה למעלה (בראשית רבה עח,
ג).[24]

מהו הבסיס הלשוני שאפשר לדרשן לתלות בכתוב 'כי שׂרית עם אלהים' דרשה בדבר תמונתו של
יעקב החקוקה וקבועה לפני ה'? אין ספק, שבבסיסה של דרשה זו – כמו ביסודן של דרשות רבות
אחרות – עומדת תופעת הנטרול של שׂ–שׁ, בין שנטרול זה הוא פונטי בין שהוא גרפי.[25] נטרול זה
מבטל את ההבחנה שבין השורשים שׂרי/שׂרר, ומעמיד כביכול את הגרסה 'שָׂרִית עם אלהים',
המתפרשת: שָׂרוי אתה לפניו. זאת ועוד: דומה, שאין הדרשן מסתפק בהעמדת שורש שׂרי ביסוד
הצורה שָׂרִית/שָׂרִיתָ והוא פוזל גם אל שורש שׁוּר, שעניינו הבטה וראייה (אף ששורש זה מזמין את
הצורה שַׁרְתָּ ולא שָׂרִיתָ), ומכאן מגיע הוא אל האיקונין, היינו תמונת יעקב החקוקה למעלה לפני
ה'. אמור מעתה: דרשה זו מעמידה את ישראל כישׂראל (כפי שהוא בהגייה השומרונית), ומייחסת
לשם זה את המשמע: 'האל יָשׁוּר', היינו זה את המבט ישׁמור.[26]

24   ובדומה לזה: '... יעקב שאיקונין שלו קבועה בכסאי...' (שם, פב, ב). ואפשר שבניסוח זה – קבועה (ולא
     חקוקה) – ניכר רישומו של מטמיע ששיחק בו הדרשן: השורש עקב שבשם יעקב נתהפך לו לדרשן בשורש
     קבע.

25   לא כאן המקום לעמוד על הביצוע הפונטי והייצוג הגרפי של הפונימה שׂ (שׁ) וזיקתה לפונימות שׁ (שׁ) ו־s (ס)
     בתולדות העברית. סיכום תמציתי לעניינו זה – בזיקה לעברית של השומרונים, המקיימת רק שׁ אחת, בהגייה שׁ
     (שׁ) – תמצא אצל: ז' בן־חיים, עברית וארמית נוסח שומרון, ה, ירושלים תשל"ז, עמ' 23–24 (סע'
     1.1.6–1.1.6.1).

26   ודוק: הקשר הסמנטי שבין שדה הראייה לשדה השמירה בנוי על הקשר שבין האמצעי (ראייה) לתכלית (שמירה).

קריאת **ישראל** כישראה אל משמיע הראייה גם בדרך אחרת, העולה מן המדרש: 'אל תקרי **ישראל**, אלא **שראה אל** שכל מעשיהם מכוונים לפניו' (תנא דבי אליהו רבה כז).[27] מדרש זה בנוי על השורש ראי, המסתתר כביכול בצירוף המרכיב את השם **ישראל**, היינו: 'איש שראה (אותו) אל', וראה בהקשר זה מובנו: 'הכיר בו שהוא ראוי'. דומה, שמובן זה של השורש, המצוי אולי במקרא[28] ומוכר היטב מלשון חכמים,[29] מהדהד גם בהמשך הדרשה: 'שכל מעשיהם מכוונים (=טובים וראויים) לפניו'.[30]

הדרשה האחרונה מוליכה אותנו אל פרשנותו של פילון האלכסנדרוני לשם **ישראל** – 'איש שראה אל', כשלידו **איש הוא יעקב**, שראה את האל, המלאך, שעמו נאבק.[31] פרשנות זו מחזירה אותנו אל הפשט של סיפור המעשה שבבראשית ל"ב. כנגד מדרש השם **ישראל** שבפי האיש–המלאך – 'לא יעקב יאמר עוד שמך כי אם–ישראל, כי–שָׂרִיתָ עם–אלהים ועם–אנשים ותוכל' (פס' כט) – מצינו בהמשך בסמוך מדרש סמוי בדברי יעקב, הקורא שֵם למקום האירוע על–פי תפיסתו–הוא את האירוע, תפיסה המתמקדת בראיית האל ולא במאבק עמו: 'ויקרא יעקב שם המקום פניאל כי–ראיתי אלהים פנים אל–פנים ותנצל נפשי' (פס' לא). מסתבר אפוא שנטרול ש–ש עומד ברקעו של מדרש השם שבכתוב זה, בין שמדרש זה רואה בתשתית השם **ישראל** את השורש ראי, בין שהוא מניח ביסוד השם את השורש שׁוּר, היינו **ישראל** = ישור אל = הביט באל.[32]

דומה, ששני מדרשי השם **ישראל**, זה המושתת על שורש שׂרי וזה המושתת על אחד השורשים שׁוּר/ראה, מתרוצצים בנבואת הושע פרק יב. דברי הנביא 'ובאונו שרה את–אלהים' (פס' ד) – עם

את צירוף שני המשמעים הללו של השורש שׁוּר אתה מוצא בשם העצם שׁוּר = חומה, ובתיבה חומה עצמה, ששורשה – חמי – שכיח בארמית כפועל המציין ראייה. והשווה גם את הפועל הערבי נַظَرَ (=הביט) למקבילו האטימולוגיים נָצַר העברי ונְטַר הארמי. אף השורש שׁמר משמש במקרא גם בהוראה של הַבָּטָה, כך למשל: '... ועלי שֹׁמֵר אֶת־פִּיהֹ' (שמ"א א, יב).

27   כך במהדורת ווארשא תרל"ד, עמ' 95. במהדורת איש שלום (ראה לעיל, הע' 7), פרק כה, עמ' 138–139, הנוסח שונה במקצת: 'אל תקרי ישראל אלא איש ראה אל שכל מעשיו מכוונין לפניו'. גם נוסח זה יש להבינו, לדעתי, כנוסח מהדורות ווארשא, היינו איש = מושא, ולא נושא. ונעיר כי הבנה מוטעית של התיבה 'מכוונין' גרמה לתרגום שגוי של הטקסט אצל בראודה וקפשטיין, ראה: W.G. Braude and I.J. Kapstein, *Tanna Děbe* *Eliyyahu* (translated from the Hebrew), Philadelphia 1981, p. 342 ואכמ"ל.

28   כגון: '... כִּי־רָאִיתִי בְּבָנָיו לִי מֶלֶךְ' (שמ"א טז, א).

29   כגון בדגם: 'רואה אני את דברי פלוני מדברי אלמוני', הבא למשל באבות ב, ט.

30   אך אפשר שכאן מסתתר מדרש־שם אחר, שיידון בהמשך, הרואה ביסוד השם ישראל את השורש ישׁר, היינו: ישראל = ישׁר [לפני ה]אל, ומכאן: 'מעשיו מכוונים לפניו'.

31   ראה על כך הערה 2 לעיל. על נטרולן של ש–ש אצל פילון, כמו אצל כלל יהודי אלכסנדריה שבזמנו, שהגו את השם ישראל – ישראל, ראה י"ג גומפרץ, 'השי"ן', טלטוליה וגלגוליה', תרביץ יג (תש"ב), עמ' 107–115, ולענייננו עמ' 111.

32   לדעתי, התפיסה הכפולה של השם ישראל, כקשור לשורש שׂרי מחד גיסא ולשורש שׁור/ראי מאידך גיסא, תוצאות לה גם לדרשות חז"ל הקשורות בשָׂרָה. כך זוהתה יִסְכָּה (בר' יא, כט) עם שָׂרַי–שָׂרָה, כעולה מן הדרשה שלהלן: 'ואמר ר' יצחק, יסכה זו שרה. ולמה נקרא שמה יסכה? – שֶׁסָּכְתָה (=ראתה) ברוח הקודש. ...דבר אחר: יסכה – שהכל סוכין ביופיה' (מגילה יד, ע"א. וראה גם ספרי בהעלותך צ, ט; ילקוט שמעוני א, תרס"ו). זיהוי יסכה–שרה מקובל גם על יוסף בן מתתיהו (קדמוניות היהודים א, ו, ה). אמור מעתה: השם יסכה, שנתפרש לדרשן משורש סכי/שׂכי שעניינו לראות, נתייחס לשָׂרי גם (בנוסף לניקומים אפשריים אחרים) על יסוד הקריאה שָׂרָי (כקריאת השומרונים) – קריאה המקרבת את השם לשורש שׁור, בין ששרה–יסכה נתפסה כנושא פועל הראייה, בין שהיא נתפסת כמושאו של פועל זה, ואכמ"ל.

שהם מותירים את היסוד **אל** בשם ישראל בדו-משמעות, ועשויים להתפרש כמדרש-שם כפול,
מעין: יעקב, שהוא בעל און, הוא בבחינת **אל** (נושא) שׂוֹרָה (כשיטת ר' פנחס ור' אחא בדרשות
שהובאו לעיל) והוא שׂוֹרֶה את **אל** (מושא) – חד-משמעיים הם באשר למשמע הפועל שָׂרָה. כבר
הראינו לעיל כי מהדהד בהם בבירור המשפט 'כִּי־שָׂרִיתָ עִם־אֱלֹהִים' (בר' לב, כט), והתיבה **ובאונו**
(=**ובכחו**) מאירה את שָׂרִיתָ/שָׂרָה ומפרשת את הפועל בשתי היקרויותיו אלו מלשון מאבק.[33] ברור
הוא אפוא זיהויו של השורש שרי בפעלים שָׂרִיתָ/שָׂרָה הנזכרים, וראייה זו גרמה להשתקפותו של
שורש זה – או שׁוֹר/שׂרר הקרוב לו – גם בפסוק הסמוך בהושע: 'וַיָּשַׂר אֶל־מַלְאָךְ וַיֻּכָל' (פס' ה). אולם
אפשר מאד שהמשפט 'וישׂר אל־מלאך' אינו בגדר חזרה בעלמא על 'ובאונו שרה את־אלהים',
ומשתקף ממנו – בשינוי קריאת השי"ן – השורש שׁוּר, בבחינת אל תקרי 'וישׂר אל־מלאך' אלא
'וישׁר אל־מלאך ויכל', כלומר: ראה את איש האלהים ונותר בחיים. קריאה זו ומשמע זה מכוונים
לכתוב 'כִּי־רָאִיתִי אלהים פנים אל־פנים ותנצל נפשׁי' (בר' לב, לא); והתיבה **ויכל** מדגישה את
הניגוד שבין מה שאירע את יעקב לבין מה שעולה מן הכתוב 'לֹא תוכל לראות אֶת־פָּנַי, כי לֹא־יִרְאַנִי
הָאָדָם וָחָי' (שמ' לג, כ), ואכן מצינו חשש מוות מפני ראיית מלאך, בדברי מנוח אל
אשתו: 'מות נמות כי אלהים ראינו' (שופ' יג, כב). זאת ועוד: כבר צויין לעיל, שלא בכדי בחר
הנביא להשתמש במלת־היחס **אל** – ולא **את** – בצירוף 'וישׂר אל מלאך', שכן בשימוש זה מהדהד
השם ישראל מן הצירוף 'וישׂר אל מלאך'. לכך נוסיף עתה, כי מלת-יחס זו נבחרה גם – ואולי
בעיקר – משום שהיא מכוונת יותר לקריאה וישׁר, קריאה המעמידה מדרש-שם שני
לישראל-ישׁראל, לצד מדרש-השם הראשון, המושתת על 'ובאונו שרה את־אלהים'.

הקרנה ממדרש-השם הכפול שבנבואות הושע על הבנת הפסוק '...לֹא יעקב יאמר עוד שמך כי
אם־ישראל כי־שׂרית עם־אלהים... וַתּוּכָל' (בר' לב, כט) אתה מוצא ברמיזה אצל רש"י בפירושו
לפסוק האחרון, ד"ה 'לֹא יעקב': 'לֹא יאמר עוד שהברכות באו לך בעקבה וברמיה כי אם **בשׂררה
ובגלוי פנים** וסופך שהקב"ה נגלה אליך בבית־אל ומחליף את שמך ושם הוא מברכך... וזהו שכתוב:
"וישׂר אל מלאך ויוכל"...'. הרי כאן 'שׂררה' – היינו: גזירת ישראל משורש שׂרר – מחד גיסא;
ו'גלוי פנים' – המרומז לשורש שׁוּר/ראי כמונח ביסוד השם ישראל – מאידך גיסא.

קריאת ישראל כישׁראל מקרבת שם זה לכינויו נוסף של העם – יְשֻׁרוּן, הבא במקרא ארבע פעמים
בלבד (דב' לב, טו; לג, ה, כו; יש' מד, ב). תרגומי המקרא הארמיים לא ראו בו שם עצמאי שיש
לקיימו גם בתרגום, והתייחסו אליו כאל גרסה חלופית לשם ישראל. גישה זו מצאה את ביטויה
בהמרת השם יְשֻׁרוּן בכל היקרויותיו בשם ישראל.

יחס זה של התרגומים לשם יְשֻׁרוּן יש בו כדי להסביר את כריכת יְשֻׁרוּן עם ישראל בשורת הסיום
של הקטע מתפילת השחר שהובא לעיל: '...קראת את שמו **ישראל ויְשֻׁרוּן**'. הזהות בין שני השמות,
העולה מקטע זה ומן התרגומים הארמיים, מעוגנת במקרא, שכן מצינו את כל אחד מהשמות מוצב
בתקבולת ליעקב, בשתי תקבולות שהועמדו זו בצד זו, כך:

33　אין ענייננו כאן ברמיזה העולה מן השימוש בתיבה **ובאונו** לאזכור בית־**אל** בפסוק ה' הסמוך ('בית־אל ימצאנו')
　　– רמיזה המקשרת את דברי הושע כאן לדברי עמוס 'ובית־**אל** יהיה לְאָוֶן' (ה, ה). וראה על כך י' זקוביץ, מבוא
　　לפרשנות פנים מקראית, אבן־יהודה תשנ"ב, עמ' 15.

'ועתה שמע יעקב עבדי / וישראל בחרתי בו
              א   ב

... אל־תירא עבדי יעקב / וישֻׁרוּן בחרתי בו' (יש' מד, א־ב).
                ג   א

מתקבולת כפולה זו, הבנויה בסדר א/ב//א/ג, אתה למד על מעמד חלופי של האיברים [ב]ישראל /
[ג]ישֻׁרוּן. מכל מקום, השם יְשֻׁרוּן משקף פרשנות נוספת לשם ישראל, פרשנות הגוזרת אותו
משורש ישר. ניגודו הסמנטי של שורש עקב שביסוד השם יעקב. מעתה נתפסת המרת שם יעקב
בישראל וישֻׁרוּן כתיקון השם השלילי בניגודו החיובי, בבחינת 'והיה העקב למישור' (יש' מ, ד),
וכבר צוין לעיל, כי המרה זו תואמת את הרמיזה ליושרו של יעקב, המסתתרת מאחורי הקביעה
ש'יעקב איש תם' (בר' כה, כז).

אף על־פי שגזרונו של יְשֻׁרוּן משורש ישר הוא שקוף ביותר,[34] לא זכה גזרון זה לבלבדיות בפירוש
השם, שכן תפיסת יְשֻׁרוּן כשם נרדף לישראל גרמה גם ליְשֻׁרוּן שיתפרש כגזור משורש שׁוּר. כך
מעמיד ראב"ע על הזהות שבין שני השמות, ומציע את שתי הגזירות זו בצד זו: 'וישמן ישרון – ישראל;
ויתכן להיות מגזרת ישר... ויש אומרים שהוא מגזרת אשורנו (במ' כג, ט)...' (ראב"ע לדברים
לב, טו, ד"ה, 'וישמן ישרון'). כנגד ראב"ע המעדיף את הגזרון הראשון – 'והראשון הוא הישר בעיני'
– מציע ספורנו רק את הגזרון השני, ומפרש: 'והנה גם בעלי העיון שבהם, הנקראים "ישורון" –
מן "אשורנו ולא קרוב" (במ' כד, יז) – עשו כמו הבהמות הבועטות בבני אדם שנותנים להם מזון...'
(ספורנו, שם).

בין כך ובין כך, דומה שמאחורי הקבלתו של ישורון לישראל עומדת תפיסה שראתה את שני
השמות גזורים מאותו שורש – בין שהוא ישר, בין שהוא שׁוּר – ותפיסה זו נשענת על הגיית ישראל
בשי"ן ימנית.

מדרשי השם והפירושים לשמות יעקב וישראל משקפים מעקשי לשון שנתחבטו בהם הפרשנים
והדרשנים. אפשר שבמעקב אחריהם שָׁרִינו עמם; הארנו את העקוב וקרבנוהו למישור.

---

34   והשוה ליְשֻׁרוּן את יֶשֶׁר (דה"א ב, יח) – שם אחד מצאצאי חצרון נכד יהודה.

'הרבה מעשים כתב משה... ועמד דוד ופרשן'

(עיון במדרש שמות רבה טו, כב)

אביגדור שנאן
האוניברסיטה העברית בירושלים

מזמור קד, שתחילתו 'ברכי נפשי את ה' ... הוד והדר לבשת', עוסק בהרחבה בסיפור בריאת העולם
ועושה לשם כך שימוש במסורות רבות, ובכללן אלה המתועדות בפתיחת ספר בראשית.[1] בדבר זה
חשו גם המקורות היהודיים הבתר-מקראיים, ולא ייפלא אפוא על שגם הם – קרי: התרגומים
הארמיים[2] והמדרש – קושרים בדרכים שונות ומגוונות בין המזמור לבין סיפור הבריאה. להלן נעסוק
בטקסט אחד משל משל חז"ל, הסולל לו בעניין זה דרך משלו, בראותו מפורשות את דברי המזמור כביאור
שיטתי לדברי התורה: סיפור בראשית פרק א (הוא ה'מעשים שכתב משה') מוצג כיסוד לדבריו של
בעל המזמור ('ועמד דוד ופרשן'). אביא תחילה את דברי המדרש – הרואים כאן לראשונה את אור
הדפוס בנוסח מנופה ועל יסוד כתבי-יד – ואדון בעקבות זאת באחד ממאפייניהם הבולטים, לכבוד
מו"ר משה (גרינברג), שמעשים רבים עשה ופירושים הרבה כתב, וכולם הוד הם לו והדר.

[א]

וכך אנו קוראים בשמות רבה [=שמו"ר] טו, כב על-פי כתב-יד ירושלים:[3]

דבר אחר: 'החדש הזה לכם' (שמות יב, ב). הדא הוא דכתיב: 'עשה ירח
למועדים שמש ידע מבואו' (תהלים קד, יט). הרבה מעשים כתב משה

2 מעשים] דברים א"יבס

1 וראה, למשל, מ' וייס, 'ברכי נפשי', בתוך: מקראות ככוונתם – לקט מאמרים, ירושלים תשמ"ח, עמ' 214–251.

2 ראה מאמרי: 'התרגומים הארמיים לסיפור בריאת העולם ומזמור ק"ד', שנתון למקרא ולחקר המזרח הקדום ב,
    ירושלים 1977, עמ' 228–232.

3 הוא כ"י ירושלים 5977 24°, תוך תיקונו פה ושם על יסוד כתבי-יד אחדים. פירוש חלקי יובא רק לקטעים שיידונו
    להלן בנפרד. להלן יובאו חילופי גרסה נבחרים, שיש להם משמע/ של משמעות כלשהי לפירוש הדברים (סימני כתבי-היד
    הם אלה הנוהגים במהדורתי למדרש שמות רבה, פרשות א–יד, ירושלים תשמ"ד: ש – כ"י ירושלים שהובא
    בראש ההערה; א – כ"י אוקספורד בודליאנה 147.1; י – כ"י ירושלים 515 8°; נ – כ"י ניו-יורק, בית-המדרש
    לרבנים 5014*1672; ב – כ"י אוקספורד בודליאנה 2335; ס – כ"י ששון 920; פ – כ"י פריס, הספרייה הלאומית
    187/15; ד – דפוס ראשון, קושטא רע"ב. הכוכבית [*] מצביעה על תיקון שהכנסתי בכ"י ש על יסוד כתבי-יד
    אחרים. סימן הגרשיים ["] מצביע על הגהה הבאה בכתב היד).

בתורה סתומים ועמד דוד ופרשן. אנו מוצאין ממעשה בראשית שמשברא
שמים וארץ ברא הָאור, שנאמר: 'בראשית ברא אלהים [את השמים ואת
הארץ]' (בראשית א, א), ואחר כך: 'ויאמר אלהים יהי אור ויהי אור'
(שם, ג). ודוד פירש, מאחר שברא אור ברא שמים, שנאמר: 'עוטה אור
5 כשלמה נוטה שמים כיריעה' (תהלים שם, ב), הרי למדנו שמשברא האור
ברא שמים. ג' בריות קדמו לעולם: המים והרוח והאש. המים הרו
וילדו אפלה. האש הרה וילדה אור. הרוח הרה וילדה חכמה. ובשש
בריות הללו העולם מתנהג: ברוח ובחכמה באש ובאור במים ובחשך.
10 לכך דוד אומר: 'ברכי נפשי את ה' ה' אלהי גדלת מאד הוד והדר
לבשת' (שם, א). אדם רואה עמוד נאה אומר: ברוך המחצב שנחצב ממנו,
נאה העולם, ברוך המקום שחצבו ובראו בדבר, אשריך העולם שהקב"ה
מלך בך. מלך בשר ודם צר איקונין שלו על הטבלה של עץ, הטבלה
גדולה מצורתו. הקב"ה יתברך הוא גדול ואיקונין שלו גדולה והעולם
15 קטן והוא גדול מן העולם, שנאמר: 'כי ביה ה' צור עולמים'
(ישעיהו כו, ד). מה תלמוד לומר 'צור עולמים' – שני עולמים עליו
אינן חשובין לכלום. לכך נאמר: ה' אלהי גדלת מאד [הוד והדר
לבשת]. משעטף את האור חזר וברא את העולם, שנאמר: 'עוטה אור
20 כשלמה [נוטה שמים כיריעה]'. בשר ודם משהוא בונה את הבית בונה
את העלייה, והקב"ה אינו כן. משמתח מעזיבה בנה עלייה, ומשבנה
עלייה העמיד אותן על אויר העולם, על מה, ואחר כך התקין
מרכבותיו עננים ואחר כך האיסטיס שלו על סערה. מי מודיעך כל
הדברים הללו? דוד, שהוא פירש מעשה הקב"ה להודיע לבאי עולם
25 גבורתו, שנאמר: 'המקרה במים עליותיו השם עבים רכובו [המהלך על
כנפי רוח]' (תהלים שם, ג). לא בנחשת ולא בברזל אלא קורות וגזוזטראות
שלמים, ואחר כך בנה את העליות, לא באבן ולא בגזית אלא רכסים
בסיס שלמים על עליות שלמים, שנאמר: 'המקרה במים עליותיו'. מלך
בשר ודם עושה לו סרגלה שלו חזקה שתתשש כל משאו ועושה אותה בברזל
30 ובזהב ובכסף, והקב"ה יהי שמו מבורך העַנן אין בו ממש ועושה אותו
סרגולין שלו, שנאמר: 'השם עבים רכובו'. בשר ודם אם היה לפניו
דרך של שקיעה הוא הולך על האבנים שהם קשים. הקב"ה אינו כן, אלא
עוזב את העַנן שנראה ומהלך על הרוח שאינו נראה, שנאמר: 'המהלך
על כנפי רוח'. בשר ודם מכתיב לו סרטיוטין גבורים בריאים כדי
35 ללבוש קסידה ושריון וכלי זיין, והקב"ה מכתיב לו סרטיוטין שאינן

3 מוצאין*] מוציאין שפ   10 ובאור*] ובאור שא, באור ג   13 שחצבו*] שחוצבו שא   בדבר] בדיבר ב
15 הקב"ה] האלהים ד   (וכן להלן פעמים נוספות בנוסח ד!)   21 משמתח*] משפתח שאי   22 על מה] עלמה
ג, על למה פ, ועל בלי מה ד, נ"א בלימה נ"   23 האיסטיס] האיסטוס נ, האיסטים נ, האיסטיס פ, האסטיס ד   35 קסידה*]
קסירה שאן, קסוירה בפפ, קסדה ד

נראין, 'שנאמר: עושה מלאכיו רוחות' (שם, ד). הרוח יוצא והברק
יוצא אחריו, שנאמר: 'משרתיו אש לוהט' (שם). משברא רקיע ברא
מלאכים ביום השני, ובו ביום ברא גהינם, שאין כתיב בו 'כי טוב',
כגון בשר ודם שהוא קונה עבדים והוא אומר: עשו אספתין. אמרו לו:

40   למה כך? אמר להם: שאם ימרדו ישמעו אספיקולא. כך אמר הקב"ה:
יברא גהינם שאם חטאו בני אדם ירדו לתוכה. ומנין שנבראת גהינם
ביום השני? שכן הנביא אומר ומפרש: 'כי ערוך מאתמול תפתה'
(ישעיהו ל, לג), מן היום שיכול לומר 'אתמול'. ואימתי יכול לומר
'מאתמול'? ביום השני, שיום אחד בשבת לפניו. ואחר כך ברא יבשה

45   בשלישי בשבת, שנאמר: 'יסד ארץ על מכוניה' (תהלים שם, ה). אותה
שעה עשה אחד ערום ואחד לבוש, כגון בשר ודם שיש לו שני עבדים
והפשיט כסותו של אחד והלבישה לחבירו, כך אמר הקב"ה: 'יקוו המים
[מתחת השמים אל מקום אחד ותראה היבשה]' (בראשית שם, ט). גלה
הארץ וכסה התהום, וכן דוד אומר: 'תהום כלבוש כסיתו [על הרים

50   יעמדו מים] מן גערתך ינוסון' (תהלים שם, ו-ז). כגון בשר ודם
שראה גתו מלאה ענבים והכרם לבצור. אמרו לו: היאך אתה נותן שאר
ענבים, בשביל שהגת קטנה? אמר להם: אני עושה גת שתקלוט כל
הענבים שבכרם. מה עשה? רפס כל הענבים ובעט ראשון ראשון, ואחר
כך הביא ענבים שבכרם והחזיקה הגת כל הענבים. כך היה כל העולם

55   כלו מלא מים במים והארץ שקועה במים. אמר הקב"ה: 'תראה היבשה'.
אמרו המים: הרי כל העולם כולו אנו מלאים ועד עכשיו צר לנו,
להיכן אנו הולכים? יהי שמו מבורך בעט באוקיאנוס, שנאמר: 'בכחו
רגע הים [ובתבונתו מחץ רהב]' (איוב כו, יב). ואין 'מחץ' אלא לשון
הריגה, שנאמר: 'ומחצה וחלפה רקתו' (שופטים ה, כו). כשהרגן, יש

60   אומרים שהם בוכים עד היום הזה, שנאמר: 'הבאת עד נבכי ים' (איוב
לח, טז). ולמה הרג אותן? לפי שהבית המחזיק מאה בני אדם חיים
מחזיק אלף מתים. לכך נקרא אוקיאנוס ים המות, ועתיד הקב"ה
לרפאתו, שנאמר: 'אל הימה המוצאים ונרפאו המים' (יחזקאל מז, ח).
כיון שראו שאר המים שבעט הקב"ה באוקיאנוס, מקול צעקתו ברחו

65   חבריהן. כגון חמר בשר ודם שהוא מהלך והיו לפניו שני עבדים,
אותן הראשונות שבבבטגי רצין ובורחין. כך היו שאר המים שבעולם
בורחין מקול צעקתו של אוקיאנוס, שנאמר: 'מן גערתך ינוסון'. היו

40 שאם–הקב"ה*] ח' שאינב (והושלם א"נ")   41 יברא*] יביא ש, יבא א, יבא א'', אברא פ, בורא אני ד
גהינם'] נ' שאין כתוב בו כי טוב ד   46 ערום ואחד*] לאחד שי, ואחד א (ותוקן א"), אחד (והושלם נ"), עריס
ואחד פ   49 התהום] המקום ב   51 היאך] והיכן יבספד   52 קטנה] מלאה פ   57 באוקיאנוס] נ' והרגו נ"פ,
נ' והרגן ד   61 הרג*] הרגן ש   63 המוצאים*] היוצאים שאב   65 חמר] ח' נפ   66 שבבבטגי] שבטגי
ב, שבטגו ס, שבכם טגו פ, ח' ד

בורחין בעולם ולא היו יודעין להיכן ילכו, שנאמר: 'יעלו הרים
ירדו בקעות אל מקום זה יסדת להם' (תהלים שם, ח). כגון עבד בשר
70 ודם שאמר ליה רבו: המתן לי בשוק, ולא אמר ליה היכן ימתין.
התחיל העבד אומר: שמא אצל בסילקי אמר לי להמתינו, או שמא אצל
בית המרחץ אמר לי להמתינו או שמא בצד תיטרון אמר לי להמתינו.
עלה ומצאו, סטרו מסטר, אמר ליה: על שער פלטרין של אפרכוס
שלחתיך. כך היו המים חוזרין כששמעו שאמר להם 'יקוו המים מתחת
75 השמים אל מקום אחד [ותראה היבשה]' (בראשית א, ט). לא לצפון ולא לדרום, אלא
אמר להם: היו חוזרין – 'יעלו הרים ירדו בקעות'. סטרן הקב"ה
מסטר, אמר להם: למקומו של לויתן אמרתי לכם לילך. מנין? שכן
כתיב: 'אל מקום זה יסדת להם'. וזה מקומו של לויתן, שנאמר:
'[לויתן] זה יצרת לשחק בו' (תהלים שם, כו). ונאמר: 'גבול שמת בל
80 יעברון [בל ישובון לכסות הארץ] (שם, ט). כגון בשר ודם שהכניס
בהמתו ונעל המסגר לפניה כדי שלא תצא ותרעה התבואה. כך נעל
הקב"ה את הים בחול והשביעו כדי שלא יצא מן החול, שנאמר: 'אשר
שמתי חול גבול לים [חק עולם ולא יעברנהו]' (ירמיהו ה, כב).
'המשלח מעיינים בנחלים [בין הרים יהלכון]' (תהלים שם, י), כגון
85 בשר ודם שיש לו שני עקלים של זתים. כבש את הקורה זה על זה וירד
לו השמן למטה. כך ההר מכאן וההר מכאן כבושין על המעיינות והן
מקטעין ויוצאין מבין ההרים. לכך נאמר: 'המשלח מעיינים בנחלים
[בין הרים יהלכון]'. אחר כך מה דוד אומר: 'עשה ירח למועדים
[שמש ידע מבואו]' (שם, יט). שס"ה חלונות ברא הקב"ה ברקיע, קפ"ג
90 במזרח וקפ"ב במערב, מהן ברא לשמש ומהן ברא ללבנה, שיהא העולם
שט אחריו והוא מהלך כולן חוץ מאחת עשרה חלונות שאין הלבנה
נכנסת בהן, כגון אפרכוס ודוכוס שהיו נוטלין דונטיבה, אפרכוס
נוטל לפי כבודו ודוכוס לפי כבודו. כך השמש נקרא גדול והלבנה
נקרא קטן, לכך השמש יתר על הלבנה י"א יום, לכך ברא הקב"ה הלבנה
95 בשביל המועדות שיהו ישראל מרבין וממעטין כלבנה, ואינו רע לו
בעבור תקנת המועדות, שכל השנה מונה לשני העולם ולשנים של בני
אדם, והוא שיודע קצו של כל אדם ואדם כמה שנים יראה השמש. והכל
הימך לומר שבשביל אלו המועדות עשה את הירח. עמד דוד ופירש:
'עשה ירח למועדים'. אמרו לו לדוד: עד שאנו במצרים נטלנו חדש
100 לבנה, הדא הוא דכתיב: 'החדש הזה לכם'.

70 רבו] אדונו פד   73 אפרכוס*] אפרכיס שאי   79 ונאמר*] שנאמר שאינבס, ח' פד   81 בהמתו] נ'
לדיר ד   91 מהלך*]ח' ש   כולן*]כולו שאיס   92 דונטיבה*] דתריו טובה ש, דתדתיו טובה אב, רתרין
טובה ס   94 הלבנה*] לבנה ש (ותוקן ש").

קטע ארוך זה, שמקבילה כמעט מלאה שלו באה במדרש תנחומא (חיי שרה ג),[4] בנוי במתכונת
הפתיחתא,[5] והוא מתקשר בסופו אל עניין הלוח וקביעת ראשי חודשים שבפרשת 'החודש הזה לכם'.
תוך עיסוק בחלק מפסוקי המזמור על־פי סדרם (פסוקים א–י), ולאחר מכן פסוק יט – כולל דילוג
בולט לעין על פסוקים יא–יח) מראה הדרשן האנונימי[6] כיצד מן הראוי לנצל את המזמור לשם פענוח
סתימותיו, מילוי פעריו ודיבוב שתיקותיו של סיפור הבריאה הפותח את התורה. בעל הקטע קובע
מפורשות, כי הרבה עניינים שבתורה נכתבו מלכתחילה ובכוונת מכוון כשהם 'סתומים' (שו' 3),
והריהם נזקקים[7] לפירוש המוצע להם במזמורי תהלים. הסיפור הלקוני והמאורגן של בראשית פרק
א הוא אחד מאותם סיפורים 'סתומים', והוא זוכה במזמור, אליבא דדרשן, הן להבהרה הן להרחבה.
כדוגמה להבהרת סיפור הבריאה נזכיר את קביעת בעל הפתיחתא, כי בריאת האור קדמה לבריאת
השמים, בניגוד למה שניתן לכאורה להסיק מבראשית א, א־ג:

אנו מוצאין ממעשה בראשית [כמסירתו בראש התורה], שמשברא שמים וארץ ברא האור,
שנאמר: 'בראשית ברא אלהים [את השמים ואת הארץ]' (בראשית א, א), ואחר כך: 'ויאמר
אלהים יהי אור ויהי אור' (שם, ג). ודוד פירש: מאחר [היינו: לאחר] שברא אור ברא שמים,
שנאמר: 'עוטה אור כשלמה נוטה שמים כיריעה' (תהלים שם, ב), הרי למדנו שמשברא האור
ברא שמים (שו' 3–8, וראה עוד שו' 19–20).

אמנם ב'מעשה בראשית' מסופר על בריאת האור לאחר שנאמר כי 'בראשית ברא אלהים את השמים
ואת הארץ', אולם שורה של מקורות מדרשיים – שיסודה ככל הנראה ברעיונות מיתיים וגנוסטיים
או בפולמוס עמהם – סבורה כי 'האור נברא תחילה';[8] ודרשננו, ההולך בדרכם, קובע כי כך עולה
כבר מן המזמור. לשיטתו אין מוקדם ומאוחר בדברי התורה, ובפועל קדם האור (כמו גם המים והרוח)
לבריאת שמים וארץ. כיוון שבעל הפתיחתא ממהר להדגיש בהמשך (שו' 8), כי גם האור הוא אחד בין
הנבראים, אין בריעון זה משום פגיעה באמונה בבריאה ex nihilo. ואפשר שהבנתו זו של בעל
המדרש את סדר האירועים (קדימת האור לבריאת השמים והארץ) עולה מראיית הפסוק הפותח את
התורה כהקדמה כללית לסיפור הבריאה, כמעין מבוא שאין לקבוע את האירועים הנזכרים בו
כאירועים הראשונים בזמן דווקא.

כדוגמה להרחבה שמרחיב המזמור את סיפור התורה מן הראוי להצביע בעיקר על הצגת המסורות
השונות בדבר מאבקו של האל הבורא בכוחות שביקשו להכשיל את תכנית הבריאה:

4 לצורכי מאמר זה נבדק נוסח התנחומא גם בכ"י קולומביה X893 M 5843. את כתב־היד בדקה עבורי גב' תמר
קדרי, ותודתי הנכונה אמורה לה בזה גם על עזרתה בעניינים אחרים הקשורים בכתיבת מאמר זה.
5 על דגם זה ראה מאמרי: 'לתורת הפתיחתא', מחקרי ירושלים בספרות עברית א (תשמ"א), עמ' 133–143, ושם
ביבליוגרפיה נוספת.
6 ואין בפתיחתא שמות חכמים כלל, כמאפיין חלקים נכבדים מן העולם הספרותי של מדרשי תנחומא־ילמדנו.
7 הצירוף של שמות או פעלים מן השורשים סת"ם ופר"ש נראה להיות צירוף קבוע בספרות חז"ל. ראה, למשל,
'הדברים הללו סתומים כאן ומפורשים במקום אחר' (חלק מכתבי־היד לרות רבה ב, א [עמ' 46 במהדורת לרנר])
או 'ומה סתומות שלכם כך, מפורשות על אחת כמה וכמה' (חגיגה כב ע"ב).
8 זו דעתו של ר' יהודה (בראשית רבה ג, א [עמ' 18 במהדורת תיאודור־אלבק]) כנגד ר' נחמיה, הסבור כי 'העולם
נברא תחילה' (שם, 19). וראה עוד בראשית רבה א, ו (עמ' 4); א, ט (עמ' 8). על הרקע הגנוסטי והמיתי האפשרי
של הסוגיה ראה א"א אורבך, חז"ל – פרקי אמונות ודעות, ירושלים תשל"א, עמ' 168–169.

כך היה כל העולם כולו מלא מים במים והארץ שקועה במים. אמר הקב"ה: 'תראה היבשה'.
אמרו המים: הרי כל העולם כולו אנו מלאים ועד עכשיו צר לנו, להיכן אנו הולכים? יהי שמו
מבורך בעט באוקיאנוס, שנאמר: 'בכחו רגע הים [ובתבונתו מחץ רהב]' (איוב כו, יב) ...
כשהרגן [את רהב ואוקיאנוס?] יש אומרים שהם בוכים עד היום הזה ... כיון שראו שאר המים
שבעט הקב"ה באוקיאנוס, מקול צעקתו ברחו חבריהן. כגון חמר בשר ודם שהוא מהלך והיו
לפניו שני עבדים,[9] אותן הראשונות שבבטגי[10] רצין ובורחין. כך היו שאר המים שבעולם
בורחין מקול צעקתו של אוקיאנוס ... סטרן הקב"ה מסטר, אמר להם: למקומו של לויתן
אמרתי לכם לילך ... (שו' 54–77).

סירובם של המים להישמע לצו האל, הריגת אוקיאנוס בבעיטה וזעקתו המפחידה, הזכרת 'רהב'
ו'לויתן', הכאת המים וכיית, ועוד מוטיבים כיוצא באלה מעידים בבירור כי התהליך שהחל בו
כבר בעל המזמור צבר לו תנופה במדרשנו: מסורות סיפוריות עתיקות שלא מצאו את מקומן
בתורה[11] שבות ומבצבצות במזמור ועולות כפורחות בפתיחתא שלפנינו.

וכך ממשיך בעל הפתיחתא ומצביע – אמנם בשעה שהוא עוסק במזמור – על נושאים מגוונים
אחרים הכרוכים באירועים שזמנם קודם לבריאה ובמהלכה, תוך הצגה מוחשית של האל הבורא את
עולמו גם במעשה ידיו ובגופו ממש, ואגב טיפול בשאלות שונות של קוסמוגוניה וקוסמוגרפיה,
אנגלולוגיה ואסכטולוגיה.

[ב]

הקטע שפרסמנו כאן ראוי בוודאי לפירוש מלא ולטיפול גם מכיוונים אחרים,[12] אך כאן מבקש אני
לעסוק רק בכלי הספרותי המרכזי המשמש את בעל הפתיחתא לשם בניית דבריו: הדיבור על בורא
עולם תוך השוואה מפורשת בינו לבין (מלך) בשר ודם. זאת עושה הדרשן שלוש־עשרה פעמים,
באחת משתי דרכים: באמצעות משל המדמה אותם זה לזה, או באמצעות משל המעמת ביניהם.
תחילה יש לתת את הדעת לטיבם השונה של שני סוגי המשלים. המשל המדמה בין האל לבין מלך
בשר ודם, אדם רם־מעלה או סתם אדם מן השורה הוא, כידוע, מן הכלים המרכזיים שחז"ל עושים

---

9   משל זה קשה להבנה (ואפשר שבשל כך הוא נשמט מן המקבילה שבתנחומא). נראה שיש להבינו לא כמדבר
     בשני עבדים בלבד אלא בשתי שורות של עבדים ההולכים לפני הנוהג בחמורים. וראה בהערה הבאה.

10   על־פי הצעתו של פרופ' ד' שפרבר (במכתבו אלי מערב ראש השנה תשנ"ה) נראה לפרש תיבה זו (והשווה חילופי
     גרסה לשו' 66) כגלגול של המונה הצבאי ἄγημα שעניינו השורה הראשונה, החזית. וכוונת הדברים: גערת החמר
     בעבדים הקרובים אליו מביאה את הרחוקים ממנו למהר ולרוץ, כשם שצעקת האוקיאנוס הביאה לבריחת שאר
     מי העולם. וראה עוד להלן, הערה 17.

11   אי־אפשר שלא להפנות בהקשר זה אל מאמרו הקלאסי של מ"ד קאסוטו ('שירת העלילה בישראל', כנסת ח
     [תש"ג–תש"ד], עמ' 121–142) ואל ספרו של ש"א ליונשטם, מסורת יציאת מצרים בהשתלשלותה, ירושלים
     תשכ"ח, בעיקר פרק ז, 'קריעת ים סוף', עמ' 101–129. ראה עוד אורבך (לעיל, הערה 8), עמ' 170–174.

12   פירוש מלא יבוא אי"ה במהדורה לשמות רבה פרשיות טו–נב, שאני עוסק בהכנתה. כאן נראה לי רק להפנות
     את תשומת הלב לתיבת 'כגון', הפותחת בקטע שלפנינו את כל המשלים המדמים. תיבה זו נפקד מקומה בין
     'נוסחות הפתיחה למשלים בספרות חז"ל' שמנה ש' שרביט (בלשונות עברית 28–30 [תש"ן], עמ' 199–206).
     תודתי לפרופ' שרביט שאישר (במכתבו אלי מיום כה בניסן תשנ"ד) את נדירות השימוש בתיבה זו לתפקיד זה.
     וראה עוד להלן, הערה 24.

בהם שימוש לשם פרשנות הכתובים, בעיקר במהלך דיונים תיאולוגיים או תוך עיון בסוגיות של
מוסר, וכבר עסקו רבות בטעמו של משל זה ובצרכים שהוא מבקש למלא.[13] המשל המעמת,[14]
לעומת זאת, נפוץ הרבה פחות מן המשל המדמה, ועיקרו במבנה מחשבתי־לשוני קבוע זה: '(מלך
בשר ודם [כך וכך] ... אבל מלך מלכי המלכים [לא כך, אלא היפוכו המוחלט]'. פתיחתא דנן כוללת
בראשה מקבץ של חמישה משלים מעמתים (האיקונין והטבלה [שו' 14]; הבית והעלייה [שו' 20];
הסרגלה [שו' 29]; הדרך השוקעת [שו' 31]; גיוס אנשי הצבא [שו' 34]) ולאחריהם היא מביאה ברצף
שמונה משלים מדמים (הענשת עבדים [שו' 39]; הלבשת עבדים [שו' 46]; הגת והענבים [שו' 49];
החמר [שו' 64]; העבד בשוק [שו' 68]; הבהמה והמסגר [שו' 80]; כבישת זיתים [שו' 83]; שרי
המלך ומתנותיו [שו' 91]). הופעת שני סוגים משלים אלו במקבצים נפרדים, חמישה כאן ושמונה
כאן, יכולה לכאורה ללמד על מקורות נבדלים שעמדו בפני בעל הפתיחתא, אשר לקח תחילה מזה
ולאחר מכן מזה, אך דומה שהשימוש בסוגי המשלים השונים – מכל מקום בפתיחתא הנדונה כאן –
הוא מכוון ואינו פרי המקרה או תוצאה של איחוי מקורות.

נראה לי שיסודו של השימוש הנפרד בשני סוגי המשלים הוא במזמור עצמו, בעניינו ובלשונותיו.
בפסוקים א–ד מדבר המשורר באלוהים בלשון בינוני, היפה לכל זמן ועת: 'עטה אור כשלמה נוטה
שמים כיריעה ... המהלך על כנפי רוח ... עשה מלאכיו רוחות' וכיוצא בהם), ואילו בפסוק ה הוא
מתחיל בסיפור הבריאה החד־פעמי, דבר שהוא עושה – בפסוקים ה–י, שבהם עוסק מדרשנו –
בעיקרו בלשון עבר: 'יסד ארץ על מכוניה ... תהום כלבוש כסיתו ... גבול שמת בל יעברון' ועוד.
מסתבר כי תאריו ותכונותיו העל־זמניים של האל דרשו, לפי הבנת בעל הפתיחתא, להגיד בינו
לבין (מלך) בשר ודם, בעוד תיאור מעשה הבריאה הביאו דווקא לערוך השוואה בין זה לזה. את
ההסבר להחלטה (אינטואיטיבית?) זו של הדרשן אפשר היה לכאורה לתלות בעובדה שתארי האל
ותכונותיו אינם מגיעים לכלל סיפור, בניגוד למעשיו בשעת הבריאה, ועל כן אין מקום לעסוק בהם
על דרך המשל המדמה, שהוא בעיקרו סיפור מעשה בלשון עבר.[15] אך נראה שניתן להבין עניין זה
הבנה מלאה יותר, כפי שנעשה להלן, מתוך עיון במרכיביו של המשל, המזכיר אלוהים ואדם
בנשימה אחת ואף אינו חושש מעריכת השוואה ביניהם.

מחקר המדרש כבר עסק רבות במשל המדמה ובמשל המעמת בין אלוהים לבין אנשים; אך
במסגרת זו, חוקרי המשל ופרשניו נוהגים כמעט דרך כלל להתמקד במרכיב העל־אנושי של
המערכת משל/נמשל, היינו: בדמותו של האלוהים, והריהם דנים בהרחבה בשאלת הצרכים

---

13   לדברים חשובים אחרונים בנושא זה ראה: D. Boyarin, *Intertexuality and the Reading of Midrash*,
Bloomington 1990, pp. 80-92; D. Stern, *Parables in Midrash*, Cambrdige Mass 1991. השווה גם הפרק
על המשל אצל: י' פרנקל, דרכי האגדה והמדרש, גבעתיים 1991, א, עמ' 323–393. אינני יודע להסביר את
התעלמותו של פרנקל מדברים מרכזיים שנכתבו על המשל בעשרים השנים האחרונות.

14   כך נראה לי לכנות סוג זה של משלים. פרנקל (שם, עמ' 375–378) מכנה אותו בשם 'משל שלילי', אך כינויי טעון
זה איננו נראה לי. שטרן (שם, עמ' 23) מכנה אותו בשם 'antithetical mashal' (שם, עמ' 22–24 דיון נוסף)
ושרביט (שם [הערה 13], עמ' 203) מגדירו כ'משל שהנמשל שלו הוא על דרך הניגוד'. חשוב במיוחד לענייננו
הוא חיבורה הנאה והשיטתי של ט' תוריון־ורדי: Talia Thorion-Vardi, *Das Kontrastgleichnis in der
rabbinischen Literatur*, Frankfurt a.M. 1986. חיבור זה אינו עוסק בטקסט שלפנינו, להוציא אזכרה חטופה
שלו בעמ' 35. וכאן המקום להודות לידידתי פרופ' גלית חזן־רוקם על עזרתה הנדיבה בגיבוש הטיעון המרכזי
של מאמרי זה.

15   ראה שטרן, שם, עמ' 23–24.

הספרותיים־מחשבתיים המניעים את יצירת המשל, כאשר כל התשובות מתרכזות מדרך הטבע,
וכצפוי בספרות דתית־תיאוצנטרית, סביב דמות האל ודרכי ההתייחסות השונות אליה. אך דומה
שמן הראוי להסב את תשומת הלב ביתר שאת גם אל היסוד האנושי שבמשל. והנה, בעוד המשל
המעמת מגמד את הדמות האנושית ומקטין בערכה, מקנה לה המשל המדמה דווקא מעלה נוספת
ואף מגדיל את מעמדה, גם אם לא תמיד בכוונת מכוון, שהרי המלך ושאר בני־האדם המושווים
במשל זה אל האלוהים – ואפילו אם מטרתו היא לדבר באל ולא בהם – מצטיירים מעצם ההשוואה
באור נשגב יותר.

נשווה, לשם הדגמת האמור לעיל, שני משלים מן הפתיחתא שלפנינו, אחד מכל סוג:

מ ש ל   מ ע מ ת: בשר ודם אם היה לפניו דרך של שקיעה (=דרך בוצית, טובענית[16]) הוא הולך
על האבנים שהם קשים. הקב"ה אינו כן, אלא עוזב את הענן שנראה ומהלך על הרוח שאינו
נראה, שנאמר: 'המהלך על כנפי רוח'.

מ ש ל   מ ד מ ה: כגון עבד בשר ודם שאמר ליה רבו: המתן לי בשוק, ולא אמר ליה היכן ימתין.
התחיל העבד אומר: שמא אצל בסילקי[17] אמר לי להמתינו, או שמא אצל בית המרחץ אמר
לי להמתינו, או שמא בצד תיטרון אמר לי להמתינו? עלה [הרב] ומצאו, סטרו מסטר, אמר
ליה: על שער פלטרין של אפרכוס שלחתיך. כך היו המים חוזרין [=מסתובבים ממקום
למקום] כשנשמעו שאמר להם 'יקוו המים מתחת השמים אל מקום אחד'. ... 'יעלו הרים ירדו
בקעות'. סטרן הקב"ה מסטר, אמר להם: למקומו של לויתן אמרתי לכם לילך. מנין? שכן
כתיב: 'אל מקום זה[18] יסדת להם'. וזה מקומו של לויתן, שנאמר: '[לויתן] זה יצרת לשחק בו'.

המשל הראשון, המפאר את האלוהים, גם מצביע בבירור על נחיתותו היחסית של האדם, המודע
לחוסר יכולתו להילחם בכוחות הטבע הראשוניים והמחפש על כן דרך, תרתי משמע, כדי להתגבר
על המכשולים שמציב העולם בדרכו. המשל השני, לעומת זאת, מעניק להתנהגותו הגחמנית
והבלתי ברורה של האדון האנושי הצדקה כלשהי מעצם ההשוואה עם האל. האלוהים לא אמר
מפורשות למים לאן כי להיקוות, מתוך הנחה שיבינו בעצמם כי המלים 'יקוו המים אל מקום אחד'
מכוונים למקומו של לויתן, אך משלא ידעו לאן לילך והתחילו מתרוצצים מהר להר לבקעה, העמידם
האל בנזיפה במקומם המיועד להם. הוא הדין באדון השולח את עבדו אל השוק, בלי לנקוב במקום
המדויק שבו עליהם להיפגש. משהעבד מהסס ומתרוצץ ממקום למקום, סוטר לו האדון ומסביר
להיכן צריך היה ללכת. אם יכולות לחשוב שהתנהגות האדון במשל היא בלתי הוגנת, משונה קמעה
או אימפולסיבית, באה ההשוואה אל האלוהים ומעניקה לה טעם ותכלית. הדמות האנושית שבמשל
זה באה, כמובן, רק כדי לשבר את אוזנו של השומע במה שהיא יכולה לשמוע, אך מתברר שדמות
זו נמצאה (אולי מבלי דעת) גם נשכרת מהשוואה זו אל הנשגב והבלתי נתפס שבבמהויות.

---

16   ראה: מילון בן יהודה בערכו, עמ' 7430.

17   כפי שניכר לעין ממבט חטוף, הפתיחתא משופעת במלים יווניות־רומיות (איסטיס, אספטין, אספיקולא ועוד),
     חלקן נדירות (והשווה לעיל, הערה 10, ולהלן הערה 20), ויש לראות בשכיחותן הרבה אחת מן הראיות לקדמותו
     היחסית של הקטע, כאמור להלן בהערה 23. וכאן מבקש אני להודות מכל לב לפרופ' ד' שפרבר על העזרה
     שהושיט לי בחפץ לב בעניין המלים הזרות שבפתיחתא זו.

18   והולך הדרשן וגוזר גזירה שווה בין תיבת 'זה' לבין האמור בלויתן, 'לויתן זה יצרת'.

הוי אומר, מנקודת מבטו של המרכיב האנושי שבמשל, מעביר המשל המדמה שמץ מהוד המלכות
האלוהית אל הדמות האנושית (בין שהוא מלך ובין שהוא אדם מן השורה); המשל המעמעם, לעומת
זאת, מקטין בדמות האנושית ויוצר פער גדול ככל האפשר בינה לבין הדמות האלוהית. במקרה
שלנו, במשלים שעניינם תכונותיו הקבועות העל־זמניות של האלוהים, תכונות היפות לכל זמן
והמנוסחות בלשון בינוני, אין זה מן הראוי להשתמש במשל המדמה, שכן זה היה מעניק גם
לבשר ודם מעמד העשוי לסכן את תפיסת הייחוד האלוהי שבעולם; במשלים שעניינם אירועים שמן
העבר הרחוק, אירועים שכבר חלפו ועברו, סכנה זו נראית קטנה הרבה יותר (אף אם לא בלתי
מוחשת לחלוטין), וכאן ניתן בשעת הצורך להשוות את העל־אנושי לאנושי. ההפסד והסכנה
הכרוכים בהאדרת היסוד האנושי שבמשל יוצאים במקרים אלה בשכר המסר שמבקש הממשל
להעביר אל שומעיו.

ומה הוא אותו מסר בפתיחתא שלפנינו? דומה ששמונת המשלים המדמים – שעניינם בריאליה
המוכרת לכל נפש – מבקשים לומר כי בריאת העולם, הנראית לאדם כה נשגבת ומלאת הוד, לא
הייתה לידידו של האלוהים אלא מעשה פשוט וקל לביצוע, כהפשטת בגד מעל גופו של עבד, כדריכת
ענבים וככבישת זיתים או ככליאת בהמה מאחורי מסגר ובריח, וכיוצא בהם עניינים של יומיום.
אם כן הוא, נמצא שדמות האלוהים במזמורנו מוצגת במדרש בכפל פנים שאינו למעשה אלא דמות
מורכבת אחת: מצד תאריו ותכונותיו (כאמור במשלים המעמעמים) הריהו רחוק ככל האפשר מן
העולם האנושי, אך רישומו על מה שיכול האדם לקלוט בחושיו – רוצה לומר: העולם הגשמי –
איננו אלא ביטוי זעיר וכמעט לא נחשב לגדולה האלוהית.

השערתנו זו בדבר אופים ותפקידיהם השונים של המשל המעמעם ושל המשל המדמה שבפתיחתא
שלפנינו מתחזקת לאור שאלת גיבורם האנושי של המשלים: האם מלך (או אדם רם מעלה אחר) הוא
או שמא אדם ('בשר ודם') שמן היישוב? אמנם גם המלך הוא אחרי הכל רק בשר ודם, ובכל זאת יש
לנסות לברר אם ניתן למצוא היגיון כלשהו העומד מאחורי שימושים לשוניים מתחלפים אלה. והנה,
מתברר שבמשלים המדמים שלפנינו נמצא תמיד רק 'בשר ודם'[19] ואף לא פעם 'מלך (בשר ודם)',
בעוד מן המשלים המעמעמים עולה תמונה מורכבת יותר: בתנחומא הנדפס מופיע בהם דרך קבע
'מלך בשר ודם', ואילו בשמו'ר בא המלך בשני משלים שהם 'מלכותיים' בעליל – חקיקת דמות על
איקונין ובניית סרגלה, מרכבה[20] מכסף וזהב; ומאידך, בשני משלים שאין בהם כל יסוד מלכותי –
בניית בית פשוט[21] והליכה ברגל בדרך טובענית – נמצא 'בשר ודם' בלבד. (בעיה יוצר בהקשר זה
המשל החמישי, המזכיר 'בשר ודם'. כאן היינו מצפים להזכרת מלך, שהרי רק הוא יכול לגייס
אזרחים לצבאו[22] ורק הוא מעניק להם קסדה ושריון וכלי־נשק. בשל כך נראה שיש להעדיף במקום
זה את גרסת הדפוס של התנחומא.) בין כך ובין כך ברור, כי במשלים המעמעמים – המבקשים להגדיל
את דמות האל ולהקטין את היסוד האנושי העומד מולה – יש ויש מקום וטעם בהזכרת המלך, בעוד

<hr>

19   והוא הדין במקבילה שבתנחומא (בנדפס ובכתב־היד האמור לעיל בהערה 4).

20   על־פי היוונית σαράγαρον והלטינית sarraculum? ראה הערת נ"ה טור־סיני במילון בן יהודה בערכו, עמ' 4204.

21   אך בכי"י קולומביה של התנחומא נזכר במשל זה 'מלך בשר ודם'.

22   זה פירוש 'מכתיב' בהקשר זה. השווה, למשל, 'מי שהיה מוכתב באסטרטיא של מלך' (קידושין ד, ה), וכמוהו עוד הרבה.

המשלים המדמים – התורמים להאדרת־מה של היסוד האנושי שבנמשל – מקפידים שלא לעשות כן בשום מקרה, וזאת בשל חשש ברור מפולחן המלכות.

לבעל שמו"ר טו, כב יש אפוא תפיסה ברורה של תפקידי המשל המעמת והמשל המדמה ושל אופן עיצובם הספרותי. דומה שהופעתם המרובה של המשלים ביחידה הספרותית שעסקנו בה מן הראוי שתקנה לה מעמד של טקסט מרכזי לבחינת סוגיית המשל בספרות חז"ל.[23] אכן, 'הרבה מעשים כתב משה בתורה סתומים', עד ש'עמד דוד ופרשן', ו'אל יהי המשל קל בעיניך' ככלי להבנתו של המזמור, שהרי 'על־ידי המשל הזה אדם יכול לעמוד' הן על 'סודה של תורה' הן על 'דקדוקיו' של מזמור.[24]

---

23   בשל סימנים שונים שבפתיחתא (השימוש יוצא הדופן בתיבת 'כגון' [לעיל, הערה 12]), המלים הלועזיות הנדירות [לעיל, הערה 17] ועוד) נראית לי הפתיחתא האנונימית הזו כקדומה ביחס, וגם זו סיבה שבגינה היא ראויה למשנה עיון. על בעיית קדמותו של החומר שבספרות התנחומא־ילמדנו ראה: מ' ברגמן, 'ספרות תנחומא־ילמדנו – תיאור נוסחיה ועיונים בדרכי התהוותם', עבודה לשם קבלת תואר דוקטור, ירושלים תשנ"א, בעיקר עמ' 176–180.

24   השווה שיר השירים רבה א, ח.

מפתח מקורות לחלק העברי

DICTIONARY OF
VISUAL SCIENCE

DICTIONARY OF VISUAL SCIENCE

―――――― *SECOND EDITION* ――――――

A modern comprehensive dictionary covering the terminology of the visual sciences, including the fields of ocular anatomy, ocular physiology, ocular pathology, ocular embryology, neuro-ophthalmology, ocular histology, ocular genetics, comparative anatomy of the eye, ocular prosthetics, physiological optics, psychological optics, ophthalmic optics, geometrical optics, ocular refraction, orthoptics, visual training, dispensing, aniseikonia, perimetry, contact lenses, subnormal vision aids, occupational vision, and motorists' vision, and also including the phases of remedial reading, statistics, illumination, and physical optics that relate closely to vision.

Illustrated

EDITED BY

MAX SCHAPERO, B.S., O.D.   DAVID CLINE, B.S.
HENRY WILLIAM HOFSTETTER, B.S., M.S., Ph.D.

CHILTON BOOK COMPANY
Radnor, Pennsylvania

Collaborators and Contributors

First Edition

ABEL, CHARLES A., B.S., O.D.
> Dean and Professor of Optometry, Los Angeles College of Optometry. Special field: refraction and graphic analysis.

ALLEN, MERRILL JAMES, B.S., M.S., Ph.D.
> Professor of Optometry, Indiana University. Special field: accommodation; convergence; torsion.

ALPERN, MATHEW, O.D., B.M.E., M.S., Ph.D.
> Assistant Professor of Physiological Optics, University of Michigan. Special field: physiology of vision.

BABER, WILMA R., B.S.Ed., B.S.Opt., O.D.
> Wichita Falls, Texas. Special field: visual training and orthoptics.

BAGLIEN, JAMES W., B.S., O.D.
> Los Angeles. Special field: contact lenses.

BANNON, ROBERT E., B.S., D.O.S.
> Consultant, Ophthalmic Instrument Division, American Optical Company; Member, Editorial Board, *Quarterly Review of Ophthalmology;* Consultant, National Society for the Prevention of Blindness. Special field: aniseikonia.

BARTLEY, S. HOWARD, B.S., M.A., Ph.D.
> Professor of Psychology, Michigan State University. Special field: visual perception; neurophysiology of the visual pathway; fatigue.

BECHTOLD, EDWIN W., B.S., M.A.
> Consulting Optical Engineer. Special field: geometrical optics; optical engineering.

BLOOM, HARRY W., B.S., B.S.Opt., O.D.
> Professor of Pathology, Los Angeles College of Optometry. Special field: ocular pathology; retinal photography.

BORISH, IRVIN M., O.D., D.O.S.
> Clinical Associate, Division of Optometry, Indiana University. Special field: refraction.

BRAFF, SOLON M., A.B.
> Lecturer, Los Angeles College of Optometry. Special field: contact lenses.

CARTER, DARRELL B., A.B., B.S., O.D., M.S., Ph.D.
Associate Professor of Optometry, University of Houston. Special field: physiological optics; refraction; strabismus.

CLINE, DAVID, B.S.
Co-Editor, *Dictionary of Visual Science*. Special field: physiological optics; ophthalmic optics; dispensing.

D'ARCY, DANIEL L., B.S., D.O.S.
Sierra Madre, California. Special field: geometrical optics.

FINKELSTEIN, ISIDORE SIGMUND, B.S., Ph.D.
Physicist, Servo Corporation of America. Special field: contact lenses.

FISHER, EDWARD J., O.D., B.A., M.A.
Dean, College of Optometry, Toronto, Canada. Special field: refraction; contact lenses.

FLOM, MERTON CLYDE, B.S., M.Opt., Ph.D.
Instructor in Optometry, University of California. Special field: binocular vision and its anomalies; orthoptics.

FREEMAN, EUGENE, A.B., O.D., Ph.D., D.O.S.
Chicago. Special field: contact lenses; subnormal vision aids.

FRY, GLENN A., A.B., M.A., Ph.D., D.O.S.
Director, School of Optometry; Professor of Physiological Optics, The Ohio State University. Special field: physiological optics.

GRAHAM, ROBERT, A.B., B.S.
Director of Research, Armorlite Lens Co., Inc. Associate Professor of Optometry, Los Angeles College of Optometry. Lecturer in Physical Optics, College of Medical Evangelists. Special field: ophthalmic lenses; contact lenses.

GREEN, RALPH H., O.D., D.O.S., D.Sc.
Dean, Massachusetts College of Optometry. Special field: refraction; physiological optics.

GUTH, SYLVESTER K., B.S., E.E., D.O.S.
Manager, Radiant Energy Effects Laboratory, General Electric Company. Special field: psychological effects of light and lighting; illuminating engineering.

HAYNES, PHILLIP ROBERT, O.D.
Newark, Ohio. Special field: contact lenses; orthoptics.

HEATH, GORDON G., B.V.S., O.D., M.S., Ph.D.
Assistant Professor of Optometry, Indiana University. Special field: color vision; physiological optics.

HESTER, MARGARET, B.S., O.D.
Los Angeles. Special field: visual training and orthoptics; visual fields.

HIRSCH, MONROE JEROME, A.B., Ph.D.
Associate Editor, *American Journal of Optometry and Archives of American Academy of Optometry;* Clinical Instructor, University of California. Special field: physiological optics; myopia; depth perception; statistics.

HOFSTETTER, HENRY WM., B.S., M.S., Ph.D.
Professor and Director of Division of Optometry, Indiana University. Co-Editor, *Dictionary of Visual Science.* Special field: physiological optics; optometry; occupational vision.

HUTCHINSON, ERNEST A., O.D.
President Emeritus, Los Angeles College of Optometry. Special field: physiological optics; history of optometry.

JAMPOLSKY, ARTHUR, A.B., M.D.
Assistant Clinical Professor of Ophthalmology, Stanford University. Special field: ophthalmology.

JANKIEWICZ, HARRY A., A.B., Ph.D.
Professor of Anatomy and Physiology, Los Angeles College of Optometry. Special field: ocular genetics; ocular anatomy, physiology and neurology.

KEMENY, STUART S., O.D.
Los Angeles. Special field: ocular physiology.

KNOLL, HENRY A., B.S., M.S., Ph.D.
Assistant Research Biophysicist, University of California. Special field: physiological optics; geometrical optics.

KNOX, GEORGE W., B.A., B.S., M.A., O.D., Ph.D.
Associate Professor of Optometry, The Ohio State University. Special field: psychological optics; physiological optics.

KRATZ, J. DONALD, A.B., O.D.
Professor of Optometry, The Pennsylvania State College of Optometry. Special field: orthoptics and visual training.

LAUER, ALVHH R., B.M., A.B., M.A., M.S., Ph.D.
Professor of Psychology; Director, Driving Research Laboratory, Iowa State College. Special field: driving safety; driver education.

LEVY, O. ROBERT, B.S.
Los Angeles. Special field: ocular prosthetics; contact lenses.

MANAS, LEO, Ch.E., M.A., O.D., D.O.S.
Associate Professor of Optometry, Illinois College of Optometry. Special field: visual training and orthoptics.

MARGACH, CHARLES B., O.D., B.S., M.S.
Associate Professor of Optometry, Pacific University. Special field: refraction.

MESSIER, J. ARMAND, B.A.
Dean and Director of Studies, School of Optometry, University of Montreal. Special field: contact lenses.

MORGAN, MEREDITH WALTER, A.B., M.A., Ph.D.
Professor of Physiological Optics and Optometry, and Research Associate in Physiology, University of California. Special field: motor aspects of binocular vision.

NADELL, MELVIN CHARLES, B.A., M.A., O.D., Ph.D.
Assistant Professor of Optometry, Los Angeles College of Optometry. Special field: sociology; physiological optics; geometrical optics; myopia.

NELSON, IRVING K., O.D.
Gardena, California. Special field: ocular neurology.

NUGENT, MAURICE WILFRID, M.D.
Member of Ophthalmological Staff of Children's Hospital, Queen of Angels Hospital, St. Vincent's Hospital, and Los Angeles County General Hospital, at Los Angeles. Special field: ophthalmology.

NYE, ARTHUR W., B.S., M.E., Ph.D.
Professor Emeritus of Physics, University of Southern California; Professor of Physics, Los Angeles College of Optometry. Special field: light; acoustics; illumination.

PASCAL, JOSEPH I., B.S., O.D., M.A., M.D.
Late Director, Eye Clinic, Stuyvesant Polyclinic; Late Lecturer in Ophthalmology, New York Polyclinic Medical School and Hospital; Late Lecturer, Brooklyn Eye and Ear Hospital. Special field: ophthalmology.

RAFALKO, J. STANLEY, A.B., M.S., Ph.D.
Associate Professor of Anatomy, Indiana University School of Medicine and Division of Optometry. Special field: gross and microscopic anatomy.

ROSENBLOOM, ALFRED A., B.A., O.D., M.A., D.O.S.
Dean, Illinois College of Optometry; Director, Subnormal Vision and Contact Lens Clinics, Illinois College of Optometry; Consultant, Chicago Lighthouse for the Blind. Special field: contact lenses; subnormal vision aids; developmental and remedial reading.

SCHAPERO, MAX, B.S., O.D.

Professor of Optometry, Director, Visual Training, Contact Lens, and Aniseikonia Clinics, Los Angeles College of Optometry; Co-Editor, *Dictionary of Visual Science*. Special field: visual training and orthoptics; contact lenses; aniseikonia.

SCOWN, LESLIE W., O.D., D.O.S.

Professor Emeritus of Optometry, Los Angeles College of Optometry. Special field: refraction.

SHANEDLING, PHILIP D., B.S., M.D.

Member of Ophthalmological Staff of Cedars of Lebanon Hospital, Mount Sinai Hospital, Temple Hospital, and Midway Hospital. Special field: ophthalmology.

SHLAIFER, ARTHUR, B.S., M.S., Ph.D., O.D.

Associate Professor of Optometry and Ocular Pathology, The Pennsylvania State College of Optometry. Special field: ocular histopathology; physiological optics.

SIMMERMAN, HAROLD, O.D.

Professor of Ocular Pathology, The Pennsylvania State College of Optometry. Special field: visual fields; ocular pathology.

SINN, FREDERICK WM., O.D.

Professor of Physical and Geometrical Optics, The Pennsylvania State College of Optometry. Special field: optics.

SMITH, WILLIAM, O.D., D.O.S.

Consultant, Orthoptics and Visual Training; Corrective Optometry Editor, *Optometric World;* Contributor, *The Optical Journal and Review of Optometry;* Abstractor, *Journal of American Optometric Association*. Special field: visual training and orthoptics.

STEWART, CHARLES REESE, B.S., M.S., Ph.D.

Dean, College of Optometry, University of Houston. Special field: physiological optics.

STIMSON, RUSSELL L.

President, Superior Optical Supply Company. Special field: dispensing; subnormal vision aids.

TOWER, PAUL, M.D.

Ophthalmologist, Board of Education School Clinic, Los Angeles. Special field: ophthalmology.

WALTON, HOWARD N., O.D., M.S.

Associate Professor of Optometry, Los Angeles College of Optometry. Special field: visual training and orthoptics; developmental reading.

[ix]

WESTHEIMER, GERALD, A.S.T.C., F.S.T.C., B.S., Ph.D.
> Associate Professor of Physiological Optics, The Ohio State University. Special field: physiological optics; oculomotor responses.

WEYMOUTH, FRANK WALTER, A.B., A.M., Ph.D.
> Professor Emeritus, Stanford University; Professor of Physiological Optics, Los Angeles College of Optometry. Special field: physiology of the eye.

WOOLF, DANIEL, A.B., B.S., Ph.D.
> Chief of Orthoptic and Vision Training, Optometric Center of New York. Special field: visual training and orthoptics.

Contributors to the
Second Edition

ADAMS, ANTHONY J., B.App.Sc., L.O.Sc., Ph.D. candidate
Lecturer in Optometry, Division of Optometry, Indiana University. Special field: physiology and neurophysiology of vision; comparative vision; geometrical optics.

ALLEN, MERRILL JAMES, B.Sc., M.Sc., Ph.D.
Professor of Optometry, Indiana University. Special field: motorists' vision; instrumentation; ocular motility; visual perception.

BALDWIN, WILLIAM R., O.D., Ph.D.
Dean, College of Optometry, Pacific University. Special field: refractive status; optometric educational administration.

BANNON, ROBERT E., B.S., D.O.S.
Consultant, Ophthalmic Instrument Division, American Optical Company. Special field: refraction; physiological optics; aniseikonia.

BARTLETT, ROBERT E., M.D.
Clinical Assistant Professor of Surgery (Ophthalmology), Department of Surgery, University of California at Los Angeles. Special field: ophthalmology.

BARTLEY, S. HOWARD, B.S., M.A., Ph.D.
Professor of Psychology, Director, Laboratory for the Study of Vision and Related Sensory Processes, Michigan State University. Special field: sensory processes; visual perception; fatigue.

BENNETT, IRVING, O.D.
Consulting Editor, *Optometric Management*. Special field: optometry.

BORISH, IRVIN M., O.D., D.O.S.
Visiting Lecturer, Division of Optometry, Indiana University. Special field: refraction; contact lenses.

BRAFF, SOLON M., A.B., O.D.
Lecturer in Contact Lenses, Los Angeles College of Optometry. Special field: corneal and scleral contact lenses.

BRECHER, GERHARD A., M.D., Ph.D.
Distinguished Professor of the Medical Center, University of

Oklahoma. Special field: physiology of the eye; cardiovascular physiology.

CARTER, DARRELL B., A.B., O.D., M.S., Ph.D.

Associate Clinical Professor of Optometry, School of Optometry, University of California. Special field: clinical optometry; binocular vision.

CARTER, JOHN H., O.D., M.S., Ph.D.

Research Professor in Physiological Optics, The Pennsylvania College of Optometry. Special field: physiological optics.

CHASE, WALTER WILLIAM, B.Sc., M.O., M.S., Ph.D. candidate

Associate Professor of Optometry, Los Angeles College of Optometry. Special field: physiological optics.

CLINE, DAVID, B.S.

Co-Editor, *Dictionary of Visual Science*. Special field: physiological optics; ophthalmic optics; dispensing; pediatric optometry.

ESKRIDGE, JESS B., B.Sc., M.Opt., M.Sc., Ph.D.

Associate Professor in Optometry and Physiological Optics, The Ohio State University. Special field: binocular vision; ocular motility.

FISHER, EDWARD J., B.A., M.A.

Professor and Director, School of Optometry, University of Waterloo, Waterloo, Ontario, Canada. Special field: refraction; contact lenses.

FLOM, MERTON C., M.Opt., Ph.D.

Professor of Physiological Optics and Optometry, School of Optometry, University of California. Special field: binocular vision; visual resolution.

FRY, GLENN A., A.B., M.A., Ph.D., D.O.S.

Regents Professor, The Ohio State University. Special field: physiological optics; color vision; space perception; accommodative convergence relations; image forming mechanisms of the eye.

GRAHAM, ROBERT, A.B., B.Sc.

Lecturer in Optics, Loma Linda University. Special field: contact lenses; subnormal vision devices; hard resin lenses.

GUTH, SYLVESTER K., B.S., E.E., D.O.S.

Manager, Radiant Energy Effects Laboratory, General Electric Company. Special field: psychophysical and psychological effects of light and lighting; illuminating engineering.

HEATH, GORDON G., B.V.S., O.D., M.S., Ph.D.

Professor of Optometry, Division of Optometry, Indiana University. Special field: physiological optics; color vision.

HILL, RICHARD M., O.D., Ph.D.
> Associate Professor of Physiological Optics, The Ohio State University. Special field: corneal biophysics; neurophysiology of vision.

HIRSCH, MONROE J., O.D., Ph.D.
> Lecturer, School of Optometry, University of California; Editor, *American Journal of Optometry and Archives of American Academy of Optometry*. Special field: physiological optics; myopia; depth perception; statistics; optometric journalism.

HOFSTETTER, HENRY W., B.S., M.S., Ph.D.
> Professor and Director of Division of Optometry, Indiana University. Co-Editor, *Dictionary of Visual Science*. Special field: physiological optics; optometry; occupational vision.

JAMPOLSKY, ARTHUR, M.D.
> Director, Smith-Kettlewell Institute of Visual Sciences, Presbyterian Medical Center, San Francisco. Special field: ophthalmology; visual physiology; ocular motility.

JANKIEWICZ, HARRY A., D.O.S., Ph.D.
> Professor of Ocular Biology, College of Optometry, University of Houston. Special field: ocular genetics; ocular anatomy; ocular neurology; ocular parasitology.

JUNGSCHAFFER, OTTO H., M.D.
> Assistant Clinical Professor, Ophthalmology, Loma Linda University. Special field: ophthalmology.

KNOLL, HENRY A., B.S., M.S., Ph.D.
> Head of Biophysics Research and Development, Bausch & Lomb, Inc. Special field: physiological optics; geometrical optics; ophthalmic instrument design.

KORB, DONALD R., B.S., O.D.
> Lecturer, Contact Lenses, Massachusetts College of Optometry; Consultant, Polaroid Corporation. Special field: subnormal vision; contact lenses.

KRAMER, PAUL W., B.S., M.Opt., M.D.
> Resident, Neurological Surgery, Indiana University.

LEVENE, JOHN R., D.Phil., M.Sc.
> Associate Professor of Optometry, Division of Optometry, Indiana University. Special field: history of physiological optics; night myopia; keratoscopy.

LEVY, O. ROBERT, B.S.
> Los Angeles. Special field: ocular prosthetics; corneal and scleral contact lenses.

LYLE, WILLIAM M., O.D., M.S., Ph.D.
Associate Professor, School of Optometry, University of Waterloo, Waterloo, Ontario, Canada. Special field: ocular pathology; genetics; ocular side effects of drugs.

MANDELL, ROBERT B., O.D., M.S., Ph.D.
Assistant Professor of Physiological Optics and Optometry, School of Optometry, University of California. Special field: contact lenses.

MARG, ELWIN, A.B., Ph.D.
Professor of Physiological Optics and Optometry, School of Optometry, University of California. Special field: physiology and neurophysiology of the visual system; computerized optometry.

MARGACH, CHARLES B., B.S., M.S., O.D.
Professor of Optometry, College of Optometry, Pacific University. Special field: clinical optometry; subnormal vision.

MICHAELS, DAVID D., B.S., O.D., M.S., M.D.
Chairman, Department of Ophthalmology, San Pedro Community Hospital; Instructor in Ophthalmological Surgery, University of California at Los Angeles. Special field: ophthalmology.

MORGAN, MEREDITH W., A.B., M.A., Ph.D.
Dean, School of Optometry, University of California. Special field: binocular vision; optometric education.

NADELL, MELVIN CHARLES, B.A., M.A., O.D., Ph.D.
Special field: physiological optics; geometrical optics; statistics; sociology.

NICHOLAS, JOHN P., M.D.
Assistant Clinical Professor, Ophthalmology, University of Southern California. Special field: ophthalmology.

PHEIFFER, CHESTER H., A.B., M.S., O.D., Ph.D.
Professor and Dean, College of Optometry, University of Houston. Special field: caecanometry; analytical optometry; developmental optometry.

PIERCE, JOHN R., B.S., O.D., M.S., Ph.D. candidate
Assistant Professor, Division of Optometry, Indiana University. Special field: neuropsychology; physiological optics; orthoptics.

PITTS, DONALD GRAVES, O.D., M.S., Ph.D.
Research Optometrist, United States Air Force, School of Aerospace Medicine. Special field: bioastronautics; neurophysiology of vision.

RICHARDS, OSCAR W., Ph.D.
Chief Biologist, American Optical Company. Special field: human vision; microscopy.

ROSENBLOOM, ALFRED A., B.A., M.A., O.D., D.O.S.
Dean, Illinois College of Optometry. Special field: subnormal vision; contact lenses; developmental and remedial reading; pediatric optometry.

ROTH, NILES, O.D., Ph.D.
Assistant Research Biophysicist, Medical Center, Department of Surgery, Ophthalmology, University of California at Los Angeles. Special field: automatic recording techniques in the study of visual functions; visual optical instrumentation.

SCHAPERO, MAX, B.S., O.D.
Professor of Optometry, Director, Contact Lens and Aniseikonia Clinics, Los Angeles College of Optometry; Co-Editor, *Dictionary of Visual Science*. Special field: amblyopia; orthoptics; contact lenses; aniseikonia; physiological optics.

SCHMIDT, INGEBORG, M.D.
Professor of Ocular Pathology, Division of Optometry, Indiana University. Special field: physiological optics; aerospace medicine.

SCHUBERT, DELWYN G., B.S., M.S., Ph.D.
Professor of Education, Los Angeles State College. Special field: psychology of reading.

SHANEDLING, PHILIP D., M.D.
Chairman, Department of Ophthalmology, Mount Sinai Hospital, Los Angeles. Special field: ophthalmology.

SHLAIFER, ARTHUR, B.S., M.S., O.D., Ph.D.
Professor of Optometry and Ocular Pathology, The Pennsylvania College of Optometry. Special field: ocular pathology.

SIMMERMAN, HAROLD, O.D.
Professor of Ocular Pathology and Optometric Science, The Pennsylvania College of Optometry. Special field: visual fields; ocular pathology.

SLOAN, LOUISE L., Ph.D.
Associate Professor of Physiological Optics, School of Medicine, Department of Ophthalmology, Johns Hopkins University. Special field: physiological optics; color perception; perimetry; optical aids for subnormal vision; depth perception.

SMITH, WILLIAM, O.D., D.O.S.
Brookline, Mass. Special field: orthoptics; pleoptics; remedial reading; developmental vision; visual perception.

TENNANT, E. R., O.D., D.O.S.
Professor of Optometry, Illinois College of Optometry. Special field: geometrical optics.

WALTON, HOWARD N., M.S., O.D., D.O.S.

Associate Professor of Optometry, Los Angeles College of Optometry; Faculty Member, Culver City Adult School. Special field: orthoptics; visual perception; remedial and developmental reading.

WESTHEIMER, GERALD, B.Sc., Ph.D., A.S.T.C.

Professor of Physiological Optics, School of Optometry, University of California. Special field: physiological optics.

WILD, BRADFORD W., A.B., Sc.B., M.S., Ph.D.

Associate Professor, School of Optometry, The Ohio State University. Special field: physiological optics; geometrical optics; physical optics.

Preface to the First Edition

This volume represents an attempt to compile a modern, meaningful, and comprehensive dictionary covering all the fields relating to visual science. The breadth of material included as visual science subjects should make this dictionary a valuable and reliable reference for those directly concerned with vision, as well as for those concerned with the visual aspects of other fields of interest.

The various terms defined were obtained by searching the literature of all the fields, including textbooks, journals, syllabi, dictionaries, encyclopedias, and other publications. In a work of this scope, no doubt there are instances of inadvertent omissions of terms, and notification of such instances is welcomed.

Emphasis throughout has been placed on the essential definitions of terms rather than on their encyclopedic elaborations. The sequence of definitions of terms with several meanings does not represent any known order of acceptability, though, where a connotation of relatively minor acceptance was recognized, care was taken not to place the corresponding definition ahead of that for a connotation of obviously greater acceptance.

The editors are indebted to many for their co-operation and assistance in this endeavor. Grateful appreciation is expressed to the various collaborators, who participated in the preparation of initial definitions in broad areas of subject matter, and to the contributors, who participated in a similar manner in highly specialized areas in which their authoritative assistance was essential. Special appreciation is extended to our two Technical Assistants, Mrs. Grace Weiner and Mrs. Winifred Hirsch, whose remarkable qualifications and devotion enabled us to submit a properly typed, grammatically correct, self-pronouncing manuscript.

Deep gratitude is expressed to the Los Angeles College of Optometry, which largely has borne the financial cost of this work and has supplied clerical assistance, library facilities, and working and storage space. Sincere gratitude is also expressed to the American Optometric Foundation, to the American Academy of Optometry, and to the Southern California Chapter of the American Academy of Optometry for their grants-in-aid which were used to defray some of the secretarial expenses.

THE EDITORS, 1960

Preface to the Second Edition

With the acceleration in recent years of the accumulation of knowledge and the resulting flow of scientific reports and new textbooks, there inevitably follows new terminology and new concepts of existing terminology.

Even before the publication of the first edition of the *Dictionary of Visual Science,* it was apparent that it would be necessary to commence work immediately on a second edition to maintain an up-to-date coverage. To this end, the latest literature has been constantly scrutinized for new inclusions and the definitions in the first edition have been extensively reviewed and many revised. The second edition, therefore, represents a continuing effort to provide a modern, meaningful, and comprehensive dictionary covering all the fields relating to visual science.

Even though the stream of new terms and concepts is endless, there arrives a time when a reluctant halt must be called to collecting and defining, and attention devoted to manuscript preparation. Hence, some of the most recent terms may not be included. Despite meticulous efforts to the contrary, errors and inadvertent omissions may be found, and notification of such instances is welcomed.

The format of the second edition is the same as that of the first edition with emphasis throughout placed on the essential definitions of terms rather than on their encyclopedic elaborations.

Sincere appreciation is expressed to the contributors for their invaluable assistance in the preparation of initial definitions of terminology within their respective specialized fields. Grateful thanks is extended to the Los Angeles College of Optometry for its generous co-operation in providing clerical assistance, working and storage space, and for making available its indispensable library facilities.

THE EDITORS, 1968

Notes on Use of the Dictionary
and
Key to Pronunciation

In order to facilitate the use of this dictionary, all listings of terms of more than one word are by nouns rather than by the modifying adjectives. For example, *asymmetric convergence, fusional convergence,* and *proximal convergence* are all found as subentries under *convergence.* Similarly, eponymic terms are cross-filed to the nouns and are listed thus: *"Hall's test.* See under *test," "Hamilton slide.* See under *slide."* When the entry includes many terms, the instruction is to *See under the nouns.* Thus, *"Donders' experiment; law; line; method.* See under the nouns" indicates that the specific definitions will be found as subentries under *experiment, law, line,* and *method,* respectively. In instances where two adjectives modify a noun and the significant adjective is second, the term is listed with the first adjective inverted, as for example, *deep punctate keratitis* is listed under *keratitis* as *punctate k., deep.* Where three adjectives modify a noun and the significant adjective is third, the first adjective is listed last in parentheses, as for example, *anterior principal focal length* is listed under *length* as *focal l., principal (anterior).*

For certain phrases, it may be necessary to look under more than one listing. For example, a term may be variously designated a syndrome or a disease; a test or a method; a reaction or a reflex; etc. Grammatical identifications and etymology are not included unless particularly important in denoting the true connotation of a word, or for clarification.

Pronunciation

A phonetic respelling, enclosed in parentheses, follows those entries whose pronunciation is not readily apparent. If more than one pronunciation is in common usage, all are given. None is given for very simple English words or for most adjectives. The basic rule to indicate vowel sound is: a vowel, without a diacritical mark, is short if followed by a consonant within the same syllable, and an unmarked vowel ending a syllable is long. The letter *h* is added to a short vowel which comes at the end of a syllable to indicate the short sound. For example, in "**halometer** (ha-lom'eh-ter)" the *a* is long, the *o* is short, and both *e*'s are short.

No attempt has been made to indicate fine gradations of sound by diacritical marks. However, certain diacritical marks are used. The macron (¯) is used to indicate a long vowel when the vowel is followed by a consonant in the same syllable; for example, "**acetone** (as′e-tōn)." The breve (˘) is used to indicate the short sound of a vowel in cases where confusion might otherwise arise; for example, the initial *a* in the word "**acopia** (ă-ko′pe-ah)." The *h* is also used after *a* in certain syllables ending with a consonant to indicate a broad *a* sound; for example, "**far-sighted** (fahr-sīt′ed)."

A syllable followed by a hyphen is unstressed and the primary (′) and the secondary (″) accents are indicated in polysyllabic words as follows, "**platycoria** (plat″ih-ko′re-ah)."

DICTIONARY OF
VISUAL SCIENCE

A

A; Å. Symbol for *angstrom unit*.

a. Abbreviation for *accommodation*.

α. The Greek letter *alpha* used as a symbol for (1) *angle alpha;* (2) *alpha movement;* (3) *absorptance.*

A.A.O. American Academy of Optometry.

A.A.O.O. American Academy of Ophthalmology and Otolaryngology.

A case. See *case, type* A.

Abadie's sign (ah″bah-dēz′). See under *sign.*

abaxial (ab-ak′se-al). Situated out of, or directed away from, the axis.

abaxile (ab-ak′zīl). Abaxial.

Abbe's (ab′ēz) condition; eyepiece; number; prism; refractometer; theory. See under the nouns.

abducens (ab-du′senz). 1. External rectus muscle. 2. Sixth cranial nerve.

oculi, a. External rectus muscle.

abducent (ab-du′sent). Abducting.

abduct (ab-dukt′). To turn away from the midline, as in abduction.

abduction (ab-duk′shun). 1. The rotation, temporally, of an eye away from the midline. 2. The diverging of the eyes away from each other, especially as determined by clinical tests with prisms, measured in terms of one or more of the criteria establishing the divergence limits of binocular vision, such as blurring, diplopia, or recovery from diplopia. Clinically, the base-in prism limits of clear and single binocular vision.

abductor (ab-duk′tōr). A muscle which rotates the eye away from the medial plane (templeward). The lateral rectus muscle is primarily an abductor, the inferior and the superior oblique muscles secondarily so.

oculi, a. External rectus muscle.

aberration (ab″er-a′shun). Failure of the rays from a point source to form a perfect or single point image after traversing an optical system. Optical aberration may manifest itself in the formation of multiple images or in the formation of a single imperfectly defined image. In Seidel's formula, it is the deviations from the path of light prescribed by Gauss's theory.

chromatic a. Aberration produced by unequal refraction of different wavelengths or colors. The typical manifestation of chromatic aberration in a simple optical system is a colored fringe on the border of an image. Syn., *color aberration; Newtonian aberration.*

chromatic a., axial. Longitudinal chromatic aberration.

chromatic a., lateral. Chromatic aberration, manifested as a change in size of the image of a point formed by a lens or an optical system, due to differences of incident wavelengths. (See Fig. 1.)

chromatic a., longitudinal. Chromatic aberration, manifested as a displacement of the image formed by a lens or an optical system along the axis, due to differences of incident wavelengths. Syn., *axial chromatic aberration.*

color a. Chromatic aberration.

curvature a. 1. Aberration attributable to curvature characteristics of the refracting surfaces in an optical system. 2. Aberration manifesting itself in curvature of the image field. See *curvature of the field*.

dioptric a. Aberration peculiar to, or characteristic of, dioptric systems. Sometimes synonymous with *spherical aberration*.

distantial a. Blurredness or loss of definition attributable to factors related to distance of viewing, one factor being atmospheric haze.

lateral a. The amount of aberration expressed as the lateral deviation of a ray from a point of reference on the axis, ordinarily from an assumed or empirical focal point.

least circle of a. The circle representing the smallest cross section of a bundle of rays manifesting aberration, especially spherical aberration. Cf. *circle of least confusion*.

longitudinal a. 1. A displacement of the image, or of a series of images, formed by a fixed lens or optical system along its axis. Ex.: *longitudinal spherical aberration; longitudinal chromatic aberration*. 2. Aberration expressed in terms of the distance between the axial crossing point of an aberrant ray and a point

of reference on the axis, the point of reference ordinarily being a focal point.

marginal a. Aberration encountered in the use of the peripheral areas of a lens, frequently mentioned in reference to ophthalmic lenses.

meridional a. 1. Aberration produced in the plane of a single meridian of a lens. 2. Differences in type or amount of aberration in two different meridians of a lens.

monochromatic a. 1. A defect of image formation in a lens or an optical system for a constant index of refraction, i.e., a single wavelength of incident light. Ex.: *spherical aberration; oblique astigmatism; coma; curvature of the field; distortion.* 2. Aberration exclusive of chromatic aberration; aberration present when monochromatic light is used.

negative a. See *spherical aberration*.

Newtonian a. Chromatic aberration.

peripheral a. 1. Aberration encountered in image formation on the peripheral retina. 2. Marginal aberration.

positive a. See *spherical aberration*.

spherical a. A monochromatic aberration occurring in simple refraction at a spherical surface,

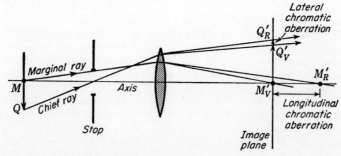

Fig. 1. Lateral and longitudinal chromatic aberration of a single lens. (From *Fundamentals of Optics*, ed. 3, Jenkins and White, McGraw-Hill, 1957)

characterized by peripheral and paraxial rays focusing at different points along the axis. In the Gauss theory, the focus of the system is identified with the paraxial rays, the peripheral rays being regarded as aberrant when they fail to intersect at the focal point of the paraxial rays.

spherical a., against the rule. Negative spherical aberration.

spherical a., lateral. Variation in size of an image of a point, formed by a lens or an optical system, due to spherical aberration.

spherical a., longitudinal. The difference measured along the axis between the distance from a lens or an optical system to the focus of peripheral rays and the distance to the focus of paraxial rays from an object point on the axis; commonly called *spherical aberration.*

spherical a., negative. Spherical aberration in which the paraxial rays show greater refraction than the peripheral rays. Syn., *against the rule spherical aberration.*

spherical a., positive. Spherical aberration in which the peripheral rays show greater refraction than the paraxial rays. Syn., *with the rule spherical aberration.*

spherical a., with the rule. Positive spherical aberration.

aberrometer (ab"er-om'eh-ter). An instrument for measuring aberration.

aberroscope (ab-er'o-skōp). An instrument for observing aberration. Especially, an instrument for observing aberrations in one's own eye.

Tscherning's a. An instrument constructed by Tscherning for measuring aberrations, consisting of a plano-convex lens mounted on a handle which has on its plano side a micrometer grid in the form of little squares.

abient (ab'e-ent). Tending to remove the organism from the source of stimulation.

abiotrophy (ab"ih-ot'ro-fe). A postnatal degeneration of an anatomical structure which was normal at the time of birth, as occurs in retinitis pigmentosa.

ablatio falciformis congenita (ab-la'she-o fal"se-fōr'mis kon-jen'ih-tah). A condition of the retina characterized by folds or ridges which project into the vitreous. They arise from the disk, involving the inner layer of the optic cup, and usually are found in the lower temporal quadrant of the retina. Syn., *congenital retinal septum.*

ablatio retinae (ab-la'she-o ret'ih-ne). Detachment of the retina.

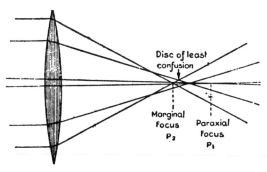

Fig. 2. Spherical aberration. (From *Text-book of Ophthalmology,* Vol. IV, Duke-Elder, Henry Kimpton, 1949)

[3]

ablation (ab-la'shun). Removal of a part by surgery.

ablepharia (ab''ble-fa're-ah). Ablephary.

ablepharon (ă-blef'ah-ron). Ablephary.

ablepharous (ă-blef'ah-rus). Without eyelids.

ablephary (ă-blef'ah-re). Congenital absence, complete or partial, of the eyelids. Syn., *ablepharia; ablepharon.*

  partial a. Eyelids of reduced size. Syn., *microblepharon.*

ablepsia (ă-blep'se-ah). Lack or loss of vision; blindness. Syn., *ablepsy.*

ablepsy (ă-blep'se). Ablepsia.

Abney's (ab'nēz) **colorimeter; effect; formula; law; phenomenon; photometer; sensitometer.** See under the nouns.

abnormal. Differing from the average, the typical, or the normal.

abrasio corneae (ab-ra'ze-o kōr'-ne-e). A scraping away of part of the surface of the cornea. It usually implies a superficial injury to the cornea by a physical agent, as differentiated from lacerations of the cornea extending deeper than Bowman's membrane.

abridgment of response. See under *response.*

abscess. A localized, circumscribed collection of pus.

  orbital a. Suppuration in the orbit.

  ring a. A yellow ring of purulent infiltration at the periphery of the cornea surrounding necrotic tissue and surrounded by about 1 mm. of clear cornea. Syn., *peripheral annular infiltration.*

  vitreous a. Accumulation of pus in the noncellular vitreous. True abscess should involve solid tissue.

abscissa (ab-sis'ah). The horizontal or the x axis of reference in a graph of rectilinear co-ordinates. See also *ordinate.*

abscissio bulbi (ab-sis'e-o bul'bi). Enucleation of the eyeball.

abscission, corneal (ab-sish'un). Surgical removal of the prominence of the cornea in staphyloma.

absolute impression; judgment. See under the nouns.

absorbance (ab-sōrb'ans). The logarithm of the reciprocal of spectral internal transmittance.

absorbancy (ab-sōrb'an-se). The logarithm of the reciprocal of transmittancy.

absorptance (ab-sōrp'tans). The ratio of absorbed radiant flux to incident radiant flux. Syn., *absorption factor.*

  spectral a. The ratio of the amount of light of a given wavelength absorbed by a medium to that incident upon it.

absorption (ab-sōrp'shun). The process in which radiant energy is converted into other forms, usually heat, by passage through, or reflection from, a medium. The absorbing of light by a blackbody or any light-absorbing substance. Absorbed light is that which is neither transmitted nor reflected in an optical system, but may be re-emitted as light of another wavelength, as in fluorescence or luminescence.

  band, a. See under *band.*

  factor, a. See under *factor.*

  general a. The reduction of intensity, in approximately the same amount, of all wavelengths of light entering a given medium.

  neutral a. The absorption of radiant energy uniformly throughout the spectrum.

  selective a. Absorption in selected or specific segments of the spectrum.

absorptivity (ab''sōrp-tiv'ih-te). 1. The absorption per unit thickness of an absorbing medium. Syn., *coefficient of absorption.* 2. The transmissivity of an absorbing medium subtracted from unity.

abtorsion (ab-tōr'shun). Extorsion.

abversion (ab-vur'zhun). Templeward rotation of the eye. A term used categorically to identify the rotation of the eye templeward irrespective of the mechanism or its association with other functions.

A.C.A. ratio. See under *ratio*.

acanthosis nigricans (ak"an-tho'sis nig're-kanz, ni'gre-kanz). A rare condition presenting numerous superficial, pigmented, papillomatous growths on many portions of the body and occasionally on the conjunctiva. A marked conjunctivitis occurs, characterized by a diffuse papillary hypertrophy; the palpebral conjunctiva, especially, may be heavily pigmented. Syn., *keratosis nigricans*.

acanthrocytosis (ah-kan"thro-si-to'sis). A rare, simple recessive hereditary disease characterized by malformation of the erythrocytes, faulty absorption of fat in the intestines, neuromuscular degeneration, and atypical retinitis pigmentosa.

acatamathesia (a-kat"ah-mah-the'ze-ah). 1. The inability to comprehend conversation. 2. Mental deterioration of the senses, as in psychic blindness.

acc. Abbreviation for *accommodation* or *accommodative*.

accommodation (ă-kom"o-da'shun). Specifically, the dioptric adjustment of the eye (to attain maximal sharpness of retinal imagery for an object of regard) referring to the ability, to the mechanism, or to the process. The effecting of refractive changes by changes in shape of the crystalline lens. Loosely, ocular adjustments for vision at various distances.

absolute a. 1. Accommodation specified with reference to, or measured from, the zero level of accommodation. 2. The accommodation of either eye separately; hence, the accommodation elic-

ited independently of the inhibitory or facilitative influence of convergence or binocular vision.

amplitude of a. See under *amplitude*.

apparent a. A semblance of accommodation by virtue of ability to accomplish usable, clear vision through a considerable range of distances, the clear vision being a matter of depth of focus rather than dioptric change. Applied especially to apparent accommodation in aphakia.

astigmatic a. Unequal accommodation in different meridians of the eye, ordinarily exclusive of differences in optical effectivity dependent on choice of a reference plane. Typically applied to differential changes in curvature of the surfaces of the crystalline lens in different meridians. Syn., *meridional accommodation*.

astigmatic a., innervational. Accommodation resulting in an astigmatic surface of the crystalline lens caused by meridional or sectional differences in innervation to the accommodative musculature.

attention, a. of. Psychology: The adjustment or readjustment of the individual which is essential for the maximal clearness of an impression.

available a. 1. Amplitude of accommodation. 2. Reserve accommodation.

binocular a. 1. Accommodation in the two eyes regarded as a single unitary response. Clinically, the accommodative response when both eyes receive the dioptric stimulus. 2. Rarely, the convergence response of the eyes to a binocular fixation object.

breadth of a. Range of accommodation.

center of a. See under *center*.

consensual a. Simultaneous accommodation in the two eyes occurring in accordance with Hering's law of equal innervation to the two eyes. Accommodation in one eye occurring as a correlated response with the accommodation of the other eye, especially when only one eye receives the dioptric stimulus.

convergence a. Accommodation changes induced by, or associated with, changes in convergence.

deficiency of a. Absence of, or reduced, ability to accommodate. Cf. *insufficiency of accommodation.*

distal a. Distant accommodation.

distant a. Active accommodation for distant fixation, distinguished from the concept of relaxation of accommodation for distant fixation, with the implication or assumption of an effector mechanism for accomplishing this. Syn., *negative accommodation.*

excessive a. 1. Accommodation in excess of the amount required for sharpest imagery of the stimulus object. 2. The tendency to maintain or sustain accommodation in the absence of a dioptric stimulus.

far point of a. The conjugate focus of the retina (fovea) when the accommodation is relaxed or at its minimum. In emmetropia, the far point is said to be at infinity; in myopia, it is at some finite distance in front of the eye; in hyperopia, it is at some finite (virtual) distance behind the eye. Syn., *punctum remotum of accommodation.*

focus a. 1. Accommodation in response to the desire for clear imagery. 2. Negative relative accommodation. 3. Retinal accommodation. 4. Accommodation changes necessary for clear imagery after convergence for a finite point has taken place, with the assumption that convergence reflexly stimulates accommodation.

ill-sustained a. Weakened or fluctuating accommodation resulting from prolonged use or due to extreme dioptric demand.

inertia of a. Slow or difficult accommodative response to dioptric change in stimulus; especially, sluggish accommodative response to changes in fixation distance.

inhibition of a. See under *inhibition.*

insufficiency of a. 1. Insufficient amplitude of accommodation to afford clear imagery of a stimulus object at a specified distance, usually the normal or desired reading distance. 2. One of several theoretical clinical types of cases identified by a syndrome of refractive findings. Definitions vary. 3. Less accommodative ability than expected for the patient's age.

lag of a. 1. The extent to which the accommodative response is less than the dioptric stimulus to accommodation. The failure to accommodate the full amount demanded for the sharpest imagery of the stimulus object. The phenomenon is quite general and often referred to as the *lazy lag of accommodation.* 2. In binocular fixation, the failure to accommodate for the full amount of the dioptric stimulus when the convergence response is normal. Hence, called the *lag of accommodation behind convergence.* 3. The additional lag sometimes induced by dissociating the two eyes. *Rare.* 4. *Optometric Extension Program:* By special definition, an index, expressed in diopter units, obtained by application of a formula using numerical values of several clinical findings. These formulas vary. Most commonly, "that amount of accommodation free of association with convergence as determined by the net of the unfused and fused cross-cylinder findings."

latent a. 1. That accommodation not manifested, elicited, or demonstrated by tests of the amplitude of accommodation. Accommodation in excess of the apparent near point of accommodation. The term also applies to the accommodation in play when all subjective attempts have been put forth to relax accommodation. 2. Neuromuscular accommodative action not eliciting a dioptric change in the crystalline lens, theoretically occurring beyond the limits of functional flexibility of the crystalline lens.

lazy lag of a. See *lag of accommodation.*

lenticular a. Accommodation attributable to dioptric changes in the crystalline lens of the eye, to be distinguished from other theoretical mechanisms of accommodation, such as corneal, axial, etc.

line of a. See under *line.*

manifest a. That accommodation measurable by conventional clinical tests or by demonstrable changes in the dioptric mechanism; distinguished from *latent accommodation.*

meridional a. Astigmatic accommodation.

monocular a. 1. Accommodation measured in one eye without regard to that occurring in the other eye. 2. Accommodation elicited when the stimulus is presented to one eye only. 3. Accommodation elicited when convergence factors are eliminated by clinical dissociation techniques.

muscle, a. Ciliary muscle.

near point of a. The point representing the maximum dioptric stimulus to which the eye can accommodate. Hence, usually the nearest point anteriorly on which the eye can focus. In absolute hyperopia, it may be a virtual point represented schematically as posterior to the eye.

near point of a., absolute. The conjugate focus of the retina (fovea) under maximum accommodation; clinically, the nearest point of clear vision.

near point of a., relative. The conjugate focus of the retina (fovea) under maximum accommodation attainable with a given amount of convergence; conventionally, measured by the maximum amount of minus lenses (or minimum plus) permitting clear vision at a fixed convergence distance, usually 33 or 40 cm.

negative a. 1. Negative relative accommodation. 2. Relaxation of accommodation below apparent zero level obtained by conventional clinical techniques, or below that level of accommodation manifested in the absence of any positive visual stimulus. 3. That reduction in accommodation accomplished by denervation, shock, or tonus-reducing experimental techniques. 4. Distant accommodation.

optical a. Physical accommodation.

painful a. of Donders. Accommodative spasms associated with hysteria, or as a hysterical manifestation.

paralysis of a. See under *paralysis.*

physical a. Accommodation changes as manifested in the lenticular body. Syn., *optical accommodation.*

physiological a. Accommodation referred to as a myologic function concerned with the innervation of the ciliary muscle and its contraction without regard to concomitant lenticular changes.

positive a. 1. Accommodative response normally associated with a positive dioptric stimulus. 2. Normal accommodation, distinguished only from the phenomenon of negative accommodation.

posture of a. The state of accommodation under specified stimulus or test conditions. Quantitative specifications may be in terms of diopters of accommodation, lag of accommodation, or the given clinical test finding itself.

power of a. Amplitude of accommodation.

proximal a. Accommodation induced by the apparent nearness, or awareness of nearness, of the fixation object, independent of the actual dioptric stimulus. Syn., *psychic accommodation.*

psychic a. Proximal accommodation.

range of a. The linear distance from the nearest point of accommodation or clear vision to the farthest point of accommodation or clear vision. Syn., *breadth of accommodation.*

 range of a., absolute. An expression employed by Donders to represent the maximum monocular amplitude of accommodation.

 range of a., binocular. The range or amplitude of accommodation that can be elicited with binocular fixation of the test object.

 range of a., relative. The dioptric range of change in accommodation that can be elicited with convergence held constant; clinically, measured binocularly with minus or plus lenses to the limit of clear vision, with convergence held at a specified point, usually 33 or 40 cm.

reflex a. 1. Accommodation changes occurring in direct response to reduced quality, or to blurredness, of the perceived image. 2. Accommodation induced reflexly by convergence or any other physiologically associated function.

region of a. Donders' term for *range of accommodation.*

relative a. Changes in accommodation that can be elicited with convergence held constant.

 relative a., negative. Relaxation or reduction of accommodation below that normally demanded for a given binocular fixation distance, with convergence fixed; clinically, measured subjectively by the maximum amount of plus lens power permitting clear, single, binocular vision at a given distance, usually 33 or 40 cm., or objectively by dynamic retinoscopic techniques.

 relative a., positive. Increase of accommodation in excess of that normally demanded for a given binocular fixation distance, with convergence fixed; clinically, measured subjectively by the maximum amount of minus lens power permitting clear, single, binocular vision at a given distance, usually 33 or 40 cm.

reserve a. The amplitude of accommodation minus the amount of accommodation needed for clear imagery at a given fixation distance.

 reserve a., negative. Negative relative accommodation.

 reserve a., negative fusional. Accommodation changes induced by changes in fusional divergence.

 reserve a., negative relative. Negative relative accommodation.

 reserve a., positive. Positive relative accommodation.

 reserve a., positive fusional. Accommodation changes induced by changes in positive fusional convergence.

 reserve a., positive relative. Positive relative accommodation.

resting state of a. The state of accommodation under the influence of normal muscle tonus, in the absence of any stimulus to accommodation and convergence.

retinal a. Accommodation reflexly induced by an out-of-focus retinal image.

sectional a. Astigmatic accommodation.

spasm of a. See under *spasm.*

static a. Zero level of accommodation.

time, a. See under *time.*

tonic a. Accommodation attributable to the normal tonus of the ciliary muscle.

unequal a. Unequal simultaneous accommodation in the two eyes, or unequal accommodation in two meridians of the same eye.

voluntary a. Accommodation induced by voluntary effort.

    voluntary a., negative. Accommodation reduced or relaxed through voluntary control.

    voluntary a., positive. Voluntary accommodation.

zero level of a. Clinically, the state of accommodation in the absence of any accommodative effort or stimulus to accommodation; relaxed accommodation, identified as that obtained in the subjective or objective determination of the distance correction or refractive error. Experimentally, the state of accommodation with third cranial nerve denervation or cycloplegia. Syn., *static accommodation.*

accommodative (a-kom'o-da"tiv). Pertaining to accommodation.

convergence, a. See under *convergence.*

reflex, a. See under *reflex.*

rock, a. An accommodative exercise consisting of a series of accommodative responses to alternate monocular increases and decreases in dioptric stimulus to accommodation. Clinically performed by having the right and the left eye alternately view a target through lenses which present different dioptric stimuli to each of the two eyes.

    rock, inhibitory phase of a. The phase of accommodative rock corresponding to decrease of dioptric stimulus.

    rock, stimulatory phase of a. The phase of accommodative rock corresponding to increase of dioptric stimulus.

accommodometer (ă-kom"o-dom'eh-ter). An instrument to measure ability or facility to accommodate.

acetazolamide (ah-set"ah-zōl-am'ĭd). A generic name for 2-acetylamino-1,3,4-thiadiazole-5-sulfonamide, a carbonic anhydrase inhibitor, supplied under the trade name *Diamox.* It is a diuretic used to control fluid retention in certain systemic conditions and also to reduce intraocular pressure in the treatment of glaucoma.

acetone (as'e-tōn). A liquid ketone, CH_3COCH_3, also called dimethyl ketone and propanone, used as a solvent for many organic compounds and, frequently, for glazing or repairing plastic spectacle frames.

acetylcholine (as"e-til-ko'lin). A chemical substance with excitatory properties, formed by cholinergic nerve fibers at synaptic and neuro-effector junctions during the transmission of nerve impulses. Fibers producing acetylcholine include all autonomic preganglionics, most parasympathetic postganglionics, motor fibers to skeletal muscle, and probably the neurons of the central nervous system. Acetylcholine is synthesized and liberated by action of the enzyme choline acetylase and normally exists only momentarily after formation, being rapidly hydrolyzed by the enzyme cholinesterase which is present in high concentration in surrounding tissues.

achievement, visual. 1. *Optometric Extension Program:* The ability to get meaning out of the external world through vision. 2. Improvement in performance of a visual task or tasks.

achloroblepsia (a"klo-ro-blep'se-ah, ak"lor-). Green blindness.

achloropsia (a″klo-rop′se-ah, ak″-
lor-). Green blindness.
achroma (a-kro′mah). 1. Lack of
color. 2. Lack of normal pigmentation, as in albinism.
　congenital a. Albinism.
achromasia (ak″ro-ma′se-ah). 1. Absence of pigment, as in albinism
or vitiligo. 2. Total color blindness.
　atypical a. Achromasia that is acquired and not inherited.
　typical a. Achromasia that is inherited as a simple recessive, not
sex-linked.
achromasy (a-kro′mah-se). Achromatism.
achromat (ak′ro-mat). An acromatic
lens.
achromate (ak′ro-māt). One who is
totally color blind, perceiving
colors as black, white, and grays.
achromatic (ak″ro-mat′ik). 1. Pertaining to a lens or an optical system corrected for, or free from,
chromatic aberration. 2. Pertaining to a totally color-blind individual. 3. Colorless.
achromaticity (a-kro″mah-tis′ih-te).
The state, quality, or degree of
being achromatic.
achromatism (a-kro′mah-tizm). 1.
The condition of a lens or an optical system corrected for, or free
from, chromatic aberration. 2.
The condition of being totally
color blind. 3. The condition of
being colorless.
　actinic a. The condition of a lens
or an optical system corrected for
chromatic aberration of actinic
wavelengths for photographic
purposes.
　optical a. The condition of a lens
or an optical system corrected
for, or free from, chromatic aberration of the visible wavelengths.
achromatize (a-kro′mah-tīz). To render achromatic.
achromatope (a-kro′mah-tōp). One
having achromatopsia.
achromatopsia (a-kro″mah-top′se-
ah). Total color blindness.

　cone a. Cone monochromatism.
　rod a. Rod monochromatism.
achromatosis (a-kro″mah-to′sis). A
deficiency of pigmentation in the
tissues, as in the iris.
achromatous (a-kro′mah-tus). Colorless.
achromia (a-kro′me-ah). Achroma.
achromic (a-kro′mik). Colorless.
achromoderma (a-kro″mo-der′-mah).
Albinism.
achromodermia (a-kro″mo-der′me-
ah). Albinism.
achromous (a-kro′mus). Colorless.
achroous (ak′ro-us). Achromatic.
achropsia (a-krop′se-ah). Color blindness.
acid, ascorbic. A water-soluble vitamin found in citrus fruits, toma-
toes, salad greens, apples, and
new potatoes necessary in the
maturation and maintenance of
teeth, bone, and vascular walls.
A severe deficiency in the diet is
a cause of scurvy with the symptoms of spongy gums, extreme
weakness, swollen joints, and
petechial hemorrhages of the skin
and mucous membranes and of
ocular structures. Syn., *vitamin
C.*
acid, nicotinic. Niacin.
acinesia (as″ih-ne′ze-ah). Akinesia.
aclastic (a-klas′tik). Nonrefracting.
acne (ak′ne). An affection of the skin,
especially of the face, the back,
and the chest, due to chronic inflammation of the sebaceous
glands and the hair follicles,
forming either papules, pustules,
or nodules.
　ciliary a. Inflammation or infection
of the glands of the margins of
the eyelids.
　mentagra, a. An inflammatory disease of the hair follicles characterized by papules or pustules
that are perforated by the hairs
and surrounded by infiltrated
skin. It may affect the eyebrows
or the margins of the eyelids.
Syn., *sycosis vulgaris.*
　rosacea, a. A chronic inflammatory

disease affecting the skin of the nose, the cheeks, the forehead, and, occasionally, the cornea and the conjunctiva. It is characterized by a red coloration of the skin due to dilatation of the capillaries and the presence of acnelike pustules; it is common in alcoholics.

tarsi, a. An inflammatory affection of the Meibomian glands.

acopia (ă-ko′pe-ah). The inability to copy written material.

acorea (ak″o-re′ah). Absence of the pupil.

Acoustic Localizer. A visual training instrument designed by Bangerter to teach spatial localization with the assistance of auditory clues, in the preliminary treatment of amblyopia ex anopsia. It consists essentially of a plate containing a series of holes which may be individually illuminated. A hand-held electrically connected stylus is used to locate and touch the illuminated hole and is guided by a humming sound which increases as the target is approached and ceases when the target is contacted.

acquired. Developed after birth; not congenital.

acritochromacy (ă-krit″o-kro′mah-se). Total color blindness.

acrocephalosyndactyly (ak″ro-sef″-ah-lo-sin-dak′til-e). Congenital malformation of the skull, tower-shaped anteriorly and shortened anteroposteriorly, in association with complete or partial webbing of the fingers and toes. Eye symptoms include strabismus, reduced visual acuity, exophthalmos, and ophthalmoplegia. Syn., *acrosphenosyndactylia; Apert's syndrome.*

acrodermatitis chronica atrophica (ak″ro-der″mah-ti′tis kron′ih-kah a-tro′fih-kah). A rare disease characterized by a thinning of the skin causing the venous network to stand out prominently; associated with scar formation in the conjunctiva.

acroisa (ă-croy′sah). Blindness.

acrosphenosyndactylia (ak″ro-sfe″-no-sin″dak-til′e-ah). Acrocephalosyndactyly.

acrylic (ah-kril′ik). The generic name for the family of transparent thermoplastic resins made by polymerizing esters of acrylic or methacrylic acid.

actinic (ak-tin′ik). Pertaining to wavelengths of radiant energy which produce chemical changes, especially those beyond the violet end of the spectrum.

actinism (ak′tin-izm). The property of radiant energy (especially ultraviolet) which produces chemical changes.

actinograph (ak-tin′o-graf). An instrument for measuring the actinic or chemical influence of solar rays.

actinology (ak″tin-ol′o-je). That branch of science which investigates the chemical action of light.

actinometer (ak″tin-om′eh-ter). An instrument for measuring the intensity of the sun's heat rays.

actinometry (ak″tin-om′eh-tre). The measurement of the intensity of solar radiation.

actinophthalmic (ak-tin″of-thal′-mik). Having eyes with a highly reflective tapetum lucidum, as in cats.

activity, optical. The property of certain substances to rotate the plane of polarization. Substances which rotate the plane (looking against the oncoming light) to the right are called dextrorotatory, and those which rotate to the left are called levorotatory. Syn., *optical rotation.*

acuity (ă-ku′ih-te). Clearness, distinctness, sharpness, or acuteness.

visual a. Acuteness or clearness of vision (especially of form vision) which is dependent on the sharpness of the retinal focus, the sensitivity of the nervous elements, and the interpretative faculty of the brain. Involved are the minimum visible (light sense), the minimum separable (resolving power), and psychological interpretations. Visual acuity varies with the region of the retina stimulated, the state of light adaptation of the eye, general illumination, background contrast, the size and the color of the object, the effect of the refraction of the eye on the size and the character of the retinal image, and the time of the exposure. Clinically, it is usually measured with a Snellen chart in terms of the Snellen fraction, and, occasionally, with the Landolt broken ring chart. Both methods are calibrated on a standard resolution threshold of 1 minute of arc.

visual a., absolute. Visual acuity as measured in an ametropic eye when accommodation is completely relaxed and the refractive error is corrected by a spectacle lens situated at the anterior focal point of the eye. It is expressed as the angle subtended at the anterior focal point of the corrected eye by the detail of the letter recognized. *Gullstrand.*

visual a., angular. Visual acuity measured in a manner such that the identification of the target is free from influence of neighboring contours and is thus considered to be solely dependent on the subtense of the visual angle. Clinically, it is usually determined with single, isolated targets. Cf. *cortical visual acuity.* Syn., *letter visual acuity.*

visual a., apparent. Relative visual acuity.

visual a., binocular. 1. Visual acuity as measured with both eyes viewing the test target simultaneously. 2. Stereoscopic visual acuity.

visual a., contour. Vernier visual acuity.

visual a., cortical. Visual acuity measured in a manner such that the identification of targets may be influenced by the contours of neighboring targets. Clinically, it is usually determined by the simultaneous presentation of grouped targets, such as a line of letters on a Snellen chart. Cf. *angular visual acuity.* Syn., *line visual acuity; morphoscopic visual acuity; separation visual acuity.*

visual a., darkness. Visual acuity of the dark-adapted eye.

visual a., decimal. Visual acuity expressed as a decimal derived by reducing the Snellen fraction, e.g., 20/40 = 0.5.

visual a., displacement threshold. Vernier visual acuity.

visual a., dynamic. Visual acuity as determined for test targets in motion. Syn., *kinetic visual acuity.*

visual a., grating. Visual acuity based on the ability to resolve fine parallel lines in a test object.

visual a., kinetic. Dynamic visual acuity.

visual a., letter. Visual acuity measured by the presentation of single isolated letter or equivalent targets free from influence of neighboring contours. Cf. *line visual acuity.* Syn., *angular visual acuity.*

visual a., line. Visual acuity measured by the simultaneous presentation of one or more lines of targets such that identification may be influenced by the proximity of contours of neighboring targets. Cf. *letter visual acuity.* Syn., *cortical visual acuity; morphoscopic visual acuity; separation visual acuity.*

visual a., minimal. Visual acuity based on the ability to distinguish form under the condition of threshold illumination.

visual a., minimum separable. Resolution visual acuity.

visual a., morphoscopic. Cortical visual acuity.

visual a., naked. Unaided visual acuity.

visual a., natural. 1. Unaided visual acuity. 2. The visual acuity of an eye not corrected by a spectacle lens, expressed as the angle subtended at the anterior principal point of the eye by the detail of the letter recognized with the object at the punctum remotum in myopia, at infinity in emmetropia, and with accommodation active in hypermetropia. *Gullstrand.* Syn., *true visual acuity.*

visual a., peripheral. Visual acuity of the extrafoveal or the peripheral regions of the retina.

visual a., primary. Visual acuity based solely on the resolving power of the eye, exclusive of psychological factors. Cf. *secondary visual acuity.*

visual a., relative. Visual acuity as measured in an ametropic eye when accommodation is completely relaxed and the refractive error is corrected by a spectacle lens which is not situated at the anterior focal point of the eye. It is expressed as the angle subtended at the anterior principal point of the correcting lens by the detail of the letter recognized. *Gullstrand.* Syn., *apparent visual acuity.*

visual a., resolution. Visual acuity based on the ability to distinguish two parallel lines or two points as two, and not as a single line or one point.

visual a., secondary. Visual acuity based on the minimum cognoscible, including the influence of the higher brain centers and, especially, such psycho-logical factors as experience and judgment. Cf. *primary visual acuity.*

visual a., separation. Visual acuity measured in a manner such that the identification of test targets is influenced by the contours of neighboring targets, being related to the distance between the targets.

visual a., Snellen. Visual acuity as measured with Snellen test letters.

visual a., stereoscopic. The smallest difference in distance of two objects, perceivable by stereopis cues, ordinarily specified as *angle of stereopis.*

visual a., true. Natural visual acuity.

visual a., unaided. Visual acuity as measured without a spectacle lens or any other corrective device before the eye. Syn., *naked visual acuity.*

visual a., vernier. Visual acuity based on the ability to detect the alignment or the nonalignment of two lines, as in the reading of a vernier scale. Syn., *displacement threshold visual acuity.*

acutance (ah-ku'tans). The sharpness of the optical or photographic image gradient for an object intensity step function, as by a knife edge, expressed quantitatively as the mean of the squares of the ratios of intensity or density differences to corresponding differences in distances across the edge function.

acutometer (ak"u-tom'eh-ter). An instrument for measuring visual acuity.

acyanoblepsia (a-si"ah-no-blep'se-ah, ă-si"-). Acyanopsia.

acyanopsia (a-si"ah-nop'se-ah, ă-si"-). The inability to distinguish blue tints. Syn., *acyanoblepsia.*

adacrya (a-dak're-ah, ă-dak'-). Deficiency or absence of tears.

Adair-Dighton syndrome (ă-dār′ di′ton). Van der Hoeve's syndrome.

Adams' (ad′amz) **diagram; theory.** See under the nouns.

adaptation. 1. Any adjustment of an organism to the conditions of its environment. 2. The change in sensitivity to continuous or repeated sensory stimulation.

alpha a. A term devised by Schouten to designate the neuroelectrical reaction of the retina to a light stimulus which results in almost instantaneous light adaptation, or reduced light sensitivity, of the entire retina (although it is more marked at the site of stimulation). Cf. *beta adaptation.*

amplitude of a. See under *amplitude.*

beta a. A term devised by Schouten to designate the local photochemical reaction of the retina to a light stimulus which results in very rapid light adaptation, or reduced light sensitivity, only in the stimulated area of the retina. Cf. *alpha adaptation.*

chromatic a. An altered sensitivity to color which produces apparent changes in hue or saturation. It may be induced, for example, by varying levels of illumination or by prolonged exposure to a specific color.

    chromatic a., general. Adaptation in viewing objects through a colored filter so that these objects seem of normal or true color, i.e., as if the colored filter were not placed before the eye.

    chromatic a., special. The apparent loss of saturation, hence of hue, in a color stimulus which is fixated steadily.

dark a. The adjustment occurring under reduced illumination in which the sensitivity to light is greatly increased or the light threshold is greatly reduced. The process is slower than light adaptation. Syn., *scotopic adaptation.*

lateral a. The effect of a specific, sharply defined retinal stimulus on adjoining areas of the retina, a factor in simultaneous color contrast.

light a. The adjustment occurring under increased illumination in which the sensitivity to light is reduced or the light threshold is increased. Syn., *photopic adaptation.*

    light a., direct. The decrease in sensitivity to light of a region of the retina previously stimulated by light.

    light a., indirect. The decrease in sensitivity to light of one, usually more central, region of the retina when another region, usually more peripheral, has been just previously or simultaneously stimulated by light. The term was introduced by Schouten and Ornstein, who found that this effect varied with the angular separation of the two retinal regions and with retinal illuminances. It is closely related to direct light adaptation in that light striking a peripheral region of the retina may simultaneously strike the central region as a consequence of light scattering within the eye.

local a. Adaptation produced by a stimulus that has been confined to a specific, more or less sharply defined, region of the retina, involved in afterimages and successive color contrast.

photopic a. Light adaptation.

pupil a. Adjustment of pupil size to the intensity of light, the quality of light, and/or the level of accommodation and convergence.

retinal a. A process in which the light threshold of the retina is shifted in relation to the level of illumination to which the eye is exposed.

scotopic a. Dark adaptation.

visual a. Any alleviatory, escape, or avoidance adjustment or response of the visual apparatus to an anomaly, defect, or condition, e.g., horror fusionalis, amblyopia, or suppression in strabismus.

adaptometer (ad″ap-tom′eh-ter). An instrument for measuring the temporal course or degree of retinal adaptation in terms of change of light threshold. Most adaptometers are designed to investigate dark adaptation.

Crookes a. An adaptometer used in a dark room with or without a fixation point, consisting essentially of a transilluminated white field subtending 7° at a viewing distance of 2 feet, with luminance controlled in steps by neutral density filters, and with a rotatable, four-position arrow on the test field to be identified at each luminance level and the elapsed time recorded.

Della Casa a. An adaptometer designed primarily as a quick and easily operated screening instrument in a somewhat darkened room and consisting essentially of an interiorly illuminated cylinder 40 cm. long with a 13.0 × 2.5-cm. viewing aperture at one end, with a cloth cover for the subject's head, and a low contrast, variable position, Landolt ring on a slightly luminous disk at the inner surface of the opposite end. The elapsed times, following preadaptation, for successive detection of the disk, the ring, and the gap in the ring are compared to norms for classification into normal and deficient dark adaptation.

Feldman's a. A dark adaptometer consisting primarily of a luminous slot to be identified after a bright preadaptation field is turned off, the time indicating the quality of dark adaptation.

Goldmann-Weekers a. An instrument consisting essentially of an interiorly and variably illumi-nated sphere with an open sector which confronts the subject's face as he looks into the sphere, a fixation light and test objects of variable reflectance and pattern at the surface opposite the subject's face, a constant speed rotating drum with a perforating marker for recording response times, and various incidental controls and attachments. It is variously used for measuring, during dark adaptation following preadaptation, the absolute threshold of a selected part or whole of the retina, the brightness contrast threshold, or the visual acuity by various techniques.

Hecht-Shlaer a. An adaptometer with controlled variability of the duration and intensity of the preadapting field and of the brightness, retinal location, size, time of exposure, and color of the threshold test light.

Nagel's a. An instrument consisting essentially of a box 80.0 cm. long divided into three compartments in sequence, with a circular opal glass 10.0 cm. in diameter on the front end face to serve as the test object in a darkroom in combination with a red fixation light. A second opal glass and an adjacent variable square shutter aperture separate the front and middle compartments, and a blue glass plate with immediately adjacent changeable plates of different proportions of perforation separate the middle from the rear compartment in which are housed three incandescent light sources. The range of intensity of the resultant white test object luminance is from 1 to 80,000,000.

add. Abbreviation for *addition.*

Addison's disease (ad′ih-sunz). See under *disease.*

addition. The difference in spherical power between the distance and the near corrections in a bifocal or trifocal lens; usually referred to as the "add."

adducens (ă-du'senz). The branch of the third cranial nerve which supplies the internal rectus muscles.

oculi, a. Internal rectus muscle.

adducent (ă-du'sent). Performing adduction.

adduct (ă-dukt'). To turn toward the midline, as in adduction.

adduction (ă-duk'shun). 1. The rotation of an eye toward the midline (nasally). 2. The converging of the eyes toward each other, especially as determined by clinical tests with prisms, measured in terms of one or more of the criteria establishing the convergence limits of binocular vision such as blurring, diplopia, or recovery from diplopia. Clinically, the base-out prism limits of clear and single binocular vision.

true a. Optometric Extension Program: The base-out–prism-to-blur finding during binocular fixation of a test object at a distance of 6 m.

adductor (ă-duk'tor). A muscle which rotates the eye toward the medial plane (nasally). The medial rectus muscle is primarily an adductor, the superior and the inferior rectus muscles secondarily so.

adenocarcinoma (ad"en-o-kar"sin-o'mah). A malignant tumor of the epithelial cells of a gland which typically metastasizes by way of the lymphatics.

adenologaditis (ad"e-no-log"ah-di'-tis, -lo"gah-di'tis). 1. Inflammation of the conjunctiva and the glands of the eyes. 2. Ophthalmia neonatorum.

adenoma (ad"e-no'mah). A benign tumor originating from, or having the appearance of, glandular epithelium; of endocrine or exocrine origin.

adenophthalmia (ad"e-nof-thal'me-ah). Inflammation of the Meibomian glands.

adiactinic (ad"ih-ak-tin'ik, a"di-). Impervious to the actinic or chemical rays of light.

adiaphanous (ad"ih-af'ah-nus). Opaque.

Adie's pupil (a'dēz). Tonic pupil.

Adie's syndrome (a'dēz). See under *syndrome.*

aditus orbitae (ad'ih-tus or'bih-te). The orbital opening.

adjustment, absolute. The mechanical provision for adjusting the two oculars of a binocular instrument separately.

adjustment shift. See under *shift.*

Adler's test (ad'lerz). See under *test.*

adnexa bulbi (ad-nek'sah bul'bi). Adnexa oculi.

adnexa oculi (ad-nek'sah ok'u-li). The appendages of the eye, as the lacrimal apparatus, the eyelids, and the extraocular muscles.

A.D.O. Association of Dispensing Opticians.

adorbital (ad-ōr'bih-tal). Located in, or near, the orbit. *Rare.*

adrenalin (ad-ren'al-in). Epinephrine.

adtorsion (ad-tōr'shun). Intorsion.

advancement. A corrective surgical procedure for strabismus in which an extraocular muscle is severed from its scleral insertion and reattached to a more anterior position on the sclera within the same plane of action of that muscle. This has the effect of enhancing the mechanical action of the muscle and, theoretically, alters the arc of contact. It is seldom used as an isolated procedure, but more often is combined with a resection of the same muscle, although resection alone, utilizing natural insertion, is employed more commonly.

capsular a. The surgical attachment of a part of Tenon's capsule to an ocular muscle for the purpose of advancing the insertion of the muscle.

adventitious (ad″ven-tish′us). Nonhereditary, acquired, accidental, or abnormally located.

adversion (ad-vur′shun). The nasal rotation of the eye. A term used categorically to identify the rotation of the eye nasalward, irrespective of the mechanism or its association with other functions.

aegilops (e′jih-lops). Egilops.

aeluropsis (e″loo-rop′sis, el″u-). A nasal inclination of the eyelids or the palpebral fissure.

afferent (af′er-ent). Carrying toward a main structure, as a sensory neuron, or a lymphatic vessel approaching a lymph node.

afixation (a-fik-sa′shun). Absence of fixation, as seen in strabismus when the deviating eye fails to make any fixation movement upon occlusion of the normally fixating eye.

afocal (a-fo′kal). Pertaining to a lens or a lens system with zero focal power, or one in which rays entering parallel emerge parallel.

aftercataract (af′ter-kat′ah-rakt). Remains of the lens capsule following extracapsular cataract extraction which lie in the pupillary area and interfere with vision.

afterdischarge. 1. The persistence of effect or discharge of impulses in a nerve fiber or trunk after stimulation has ceased. As observed in optic nerve studies, the phenomenon is differentiated from the off-effect. 2. A discharge of impulses from a neural center after the removal of the stimulus.

aftereffect. In general, the experience that may follow the removal of the external stimulus. More specifically, it is a synonym for *afterimage* or *after-sensation*.

figural a. The effect of a previously viewed figure or pattern on the perception of a different, subsequently observed, figure or pattern; especially any one of several classic distortion and illusion effects produced by previewing specially designed geometric patterns. Certain varieties of this phenomenon are also called *visual satiety effects*.

afterimage. A persisting sensation or image perceived after the correlated physical stimulus has been removed. Visually, the afterimage may be the continued perception of the essential form, motion, brilliance, or color qualities of the removed stimulus, or the perception of qualities of form, motion, color, or brilliance having an apparent relationship to the original stimulus though notably dissimilar. Ordinarily, the primary image is not regarded as an afterimage even though it persists a short period following the discontinuation of the stimulus.

complementary a. An afterimage in which the color is complementary to the color of the original stimulus.

Hering's a. First positive afterimage.

Hess's a. Third positive afterimage.

homochromatic a. An afterimage in which the hue is the same as that of the original stimulus.

induced a. An afterimage of an original stimulus which has been modified by secondary light stimuli.

motion a. An illusion of movement of an observed stationary object in the opposite direction from a just previously observed moving object.

negative a. 1. An afterimage in which the areas corresponding to the light areas of the original stimulus appear dark, dark areas light, and colors complementary. 2. An afterimage that appears less bright than its surround, regardless of hue.

original a. Any of the afterimages resulting from a single light stimulus, no secondary variations in light stimulus being presented.

positive a. 1. An afterimage in which the areas corresponding to the light areas of the original stimulus appear light, dark areas dark, and colors remain similar. 2. An afterimage that appears brighter than its surround, regardless of hue.

positive a., first. The first afterimage following the primary image of a brief, single, light stimulus of moderate intensity. It is a bright image of less intensity than the original stimulus and of the same hue. Syn., *Hering afterimage.*

positive a., fourth. An afterimage which, after a long dark interval, may follow the third positive afterimage if the original light stimulus was of high intensity.

positive a., second. An afterimage which, after a dark interval, follows the first positive afterimage. It is less bright than the first, and its hue varies with the intensity of the stimulating light. It is generally considered to be a function of the scotopic mechanism since it is absent in the light-adapted eye. It is seen best with a green light stimulus, worst with red, and rarely with foveal stimulation. Syn., *Purkinje afterimage; Bidwell's ghost; following image of von Kries; pursuant image of von Kries; satellite of Hamaker.*

positive a., third. An afterimage which, after a long dark interval, follows the second positive afterimage. It is less bright than the second and of the same hue as the first. Syn., *Hess's afterimage.*

Purkinje a. Second positive afterimage.

pursuant a. Second positive afterimage.

satellite a. Second positive afterimage.

afternystagmus (af"ter-nis-tag'mus). A vestibular nystagmus manifest after the abrupt cessation of a rotation of the head, due to the tendency of the labyrinthine fluid to persist in its movement. Syn., *secondary nystagmus.*

optokinetic a. Nystagmus appearing with the eyes closed after a previously elicited optokinetic nystagmus.

aftervision (af'ter-vizh"un). Vision persisting after the exciting visual stimulus has been terminated. Syn., *persistent vision.*

Agamodistomum ophthalmobium (ag"ah-mo-dis'to-mum of"thal-mo'be-um). A trematode parasite occasionally found in the crystalline lens of the human eye.

age. 1. The time elapsed from the beginning or birth of an object or a being to any given time. 2. The latter part of life. 3. A measure of development of an individual in terms of the chronological age of an average individual of corresponding development.

achievement a. Proficiency in study expressed in terms of what an average child of that chronological age can perform, as determined by tests.

anatomical a. Age estimated by body developments.

Binet a. Mental age approximated by Binet tests.

chronological a. The time elapsed from birth to the present in a living individual, measured in years.

mental a. The degree of mental development measured in terms of the chronological age of the average individual of corresponding mental ability; usually determined by the score of an intelligence test.

physiological a. Age estimated by functional development.

reading a. Proficiency in reading

[18]

expressed in terms of what an average child of a given chronological age can achieve, as determined by tests.

aglaucopsia (a"glaw-kop'se-ah, ă"-glaw-). Green blindness.

aglaukopsia (a"glaw-kop'se-ah, ă"-glaw-). Green blindness.

aglia (ag'le-ah). A spot or speck on the sclera or the cornea.

agnea (ag-ne'ah). A condition in which objects or persons are not recognized.

agnosia (ag-no'se-ah). Total or partial loss of the perceptive faculty or of the ability to recognize or orientate objects or persons due to a disturbance in the cerebral associational areas, the sensory pathway and the receptor areas being intact. It is classified according to the sense affected, e.g., visual agnosia, auditory agnosia.

color a. Total or partial inability to recognize or appreciate colors, though the sensory pathway and the receptors are normal, due to a disturbance existing in the integrative cerebral centers. Syn., *amnesic color blindness.*

corporeal a. The inability of an individual to recognize the existence or the identity of parts of his own body or to appreciate defects of its functions.

music a. Note blindness.

spatial a. The inability to orientate oneself in space, usually accompanied by object visual agnosia.

    spatial a., visual. Spatial agnosia due primarily to an inability to appreciate visual clues. Syn., *space blindness.*

visual a. The inability to understand or interpret what is seen due to a disturbance in the cerebral associational areas, the retina, the sensory pathways, and the striate area being intact. Syn., *cerebral blindness; cortical psychic blindness; psychic blindness.*

visual a., object. The inability to recognize, by sight, objects previously known, although the objects are seen clearly. Syn., *object blindness.*

agonist (ag'o-nist). Any muscle yielding the desired movement; the opposite of *antagonist;* a prime mover or protagonist. Superior rectus and inferior oblique muscles are agonists when they both elevate the eye.

agrammatism (a-gram'ah-tizm). A form of aphasia in which one cannot utter words in their correct form and sequence.

agraphia (a-graf'e-ah, ă-graf'-). 1. That type of aphasia characterized by an inability to express meaning in written language. 2. A pathological lack or loss of the ability to write, usually resulting from a brain lesion.

absolute a. Agraphia characterized by the complete inability to write. Syn., *agraphia atactica.*

acoustic a. Agraphia characterized by the inability to write material which is dictated verbally.

amnemonic a. Agraphia in which one is able to write letters or words but cannot write complete or meaningful sentences.

atactica, a. Absolute agraphia.

cerebral a. Mental agraphia.

jargon a. Agraphia in which one can write only senseless combinations of letters.

literal a. Absolute agraphia.

mental a. Agraphia characterized by an inability to express thoughts in words. The individual can write, but cannot express his ideas in written form. Syn., *cerebral agraphia.*

motor a. Agraphia in which the inability to write is consequent on muscular in-co-ordination.

optic a. Visual agraphia.

verbal a. Agraphia in which one is able to write letters but not words.

visual a. Agraphia in which one can write from dictation but not from copy. Syn., *optic agraphia.*

Ahrens' (ah'renz) **polarizer; prism.** See under *prism.*

aim. The process of placing the axis of reference of an object in line with a point of fixation or intent.

Airy's disk (ār'ēz). See under *disk.*

akinesia (ak"ih-ne'se-ah). Lack of movement due to loss or impairment of motor function.

   iridis, a. Immobility or rigidity of the iris.

akinesis (ak"ih-ne'sis). Akinesia.

aknephascopia (ak"nef-ah-sko'pe-ah). Reduced visual acuity in low levels of illumination, such as in twilight or in inadequate artificial illumination. Syn., *twilight blindness; twilight vision.*

akyanoblepsia (a-ki"ah-no-blep'se-ah). Acyanopsia.

Alabaster's projectionometer (al'-ah-bas"terz). See under *projectionometer.*

alacrima (a-lak'ri-mah). Lack of secretion from the lacrimal gland.

albedo (al-be'do). 1. The whiteness of a surface. 2. The diffuse reflecting power of a surface.

   retinae, a. Edema of the retina.

Albers-Schönberg disease (al'berz-shun'berg). See under *disease.*

Albini's E test (al-be'nēz). See under *test.*

albinism (al'bin-izm). Congenital deficiency or absence of pigment in skin, hair, choroid, retina, and iris.

albinismus (al"bih-niz'mus). Albinism.

albino (al-bi'no, al-be'-). One affected with albinism.

albinoism (al-bi'no-izm, al-be'no-). Albinism.

Albright's (awl'brīts) **disease; syndrome.** See under the nouns.

Albright-McCune-Sternberg syndrome. Albright's syndrome.

albuginea oculi (al"bu-jin'e-ah ok'-u-li). The scleral coat of the eye.

albugineous (al"bu-jin'e-us). 1. Whitish. 2. Pertaining to or resembling the sclera.

albuginitis (al"bu-jin-i'tis). Inflammation of a tunica albuginea, as in the scleral coat of the eye.

albugo (al-bu'go). A white corneal opacity.

alexia (a-lek'se-ah). The inability to recognize or comprehend written or printed words. Syn., *optic aphasia; visual aphasia; word aphasia; word blindness.*

   cortical a. Alexia in which word blindness results from lesions of the left angular gyrus.

   motor a. Alexia in which written words can be comprehended but cannot be read aloud.

   subcortical a. Alexia in which word blindness results from an interruption in the connection between a visual center and the angular gyrus.

allachesthesia, visual (al"ă-kes-the'-ze-ah). Visual allesthesia.

allel (ă-lēl'). Allelomorph.

allele (ă-lēl'). Allelomorph.

allelomorph (ă-le'lo-mōrf, ă-lel'o-). One of two or more genes which occupy the same locus in a pair of chromosomes and affect the same parts of the body in regard to inheritance of a trait or traits. Syn., *allele.*

Allen's (al'enz) **gonioprism; implant; contact prism; theory.** See under the nouns.

Allen-Braley fundus lens. See under *lens.*

Allen-Gulden plunger retractor. See under *retractor.*

Allen-O'Brien contact lens. Allen's contact prism.

Allen-Thorpe gonioprism. See under *gonioprism.*

allesthesia, visual (al"es-the'ze-ah). A rare disorder in which images are transposed from one half of the visual field to the other, occasionally from the lower to the upper quadrant, or vice versa. Syn., *visual allachesthesia.*

allochroism (al″o-kro′izm). Variation or change in color.

allochromasia (al″o-kro-ma′ze-ah). 1. Change in color of skin or hair. 2. Color blindness. *Obs.*

alloesthesia, visual (al″o-es-the′ze-ah). Visual allesthesia.

allokeratoplasty (al″o-ker′ah-to-plas″te). The grafting to the cornea of foreign material.

allometropia (al″o-me-tro′pe-ah). The refraction of the eye along any secondary line of regard. It is equal in magnitude and opposite in sign to the lens or combination of lenses required to bring any extrafoveal region of the retina into conjugate focus with an infinitely distant object.

allophthalmia (al″of-thal′me-ah). Heterophthalmia.

allopsychosis (al″o-si-ko′sis). A psychosis characterized by hallucinations and illusions and caused by disorganization of the external perceptive powers without disorder of the motor powers.

allotransplant, corneal (al″o-trans′-plant). The replacement of opaque corneal tissue by a transparent prosthesis, usually acrylic. See also *autotransplant; heterotransplant; homotransplant.*

allowance. In general, the deduction from the gross finding obtained at the end of a given test in order to obtain the net finding. Ex.: 1. *Retinoscopy:* The value of the lens which must be deducted from the total lens power before the eye of the subject at the conclusion of the test in order to change the conjugate focus of the subject's eye lens system from the peephole of the retinoscope to infinity. 2. *Fused and unfused cross cylinder test:* The value to be deducted from the total lens power before the subject's eye at the conclusion of the cross cylinder test in order to determine the net near point finding. 3. *Ophthalmometry:* The deduction which must be made from the keratometric astigmatism in order to determine the total astigmatism of the eye.

all-*trans* retinene₁. An isomer of retinene₁.

Aloe (al′o) **distance unit; reading unit.** See under *unit.*

alpha [α] (al′fah). The Greek letter used as the symbol for (1) *angle alpha;* (2) *alpha movement;* (3) *absorptance.*

alpha-chymotrypsin (al″fah-ki″mo-trip′sin). See *chymotrypsin, alpha.*

Alport's syndrome (al′portz). See under *syndrome.*

alternation, figural. Retinal rivalry.

Alternator (awl′ter-na″ter). A device which controls the light-dark cycle of intermittent illumination, used in conjunction with Cüppers' afterimage method in the treatment of amblyopia and eccentric fixation. Syn., *Alternoscope.*

Alternoscope (awl-tern′o-skōp). Alternator.

alychne (ă-lik′ne). The locus of points on a color mixture diagram which have zero luminosity coefficients; hence the line $y = O$ in the C.I.E. chromaticity diagram.

alypin (al′ip-in). A local anesthetic similar to, but less toxic than, cocaine; not mydriatic when used in the eye.

am. Abbreviation for *ametropia.*

A.M.A. American Medical Association.

amacratic (am″ak-rat′ik). Amasthenic.

Amalric's syndrome (ah-mal′riks). See under *syndrome.*

amasthenic (am″as-then′ik). Serving to bring a bundle of rays to a point; distinguished from *collimating* (making parallel). Cameras are classified as amasthenic optical systems, whereas microscopes are of the collimating type. Syn., *amacratic.*

amaurosis (am″aw-ro′sis). 1. Partial or total blindness from any cause. 2. Blindness occurring without apparent change in the eye itself, as from cortical lesions.

albuminuric *a.* Amaurosis due to renal disease.

Burns's *a.* Amaurosis due to sexual excess.

central *a.* Amaurosis due to disease of the central nervous system.

cerebral *a.* Amaurosis due to brain disease.

congenital *a.* Amaurosis which exists from birth.

diabetic *a.* Amaurosis associated with diabetes.

epileptiform *a.* A sudden amaurosis characterized by dilation of the retinal veins; considered by some to be epileptic in nature.

fugax, *a.* 1. Sudden temporary amaurosis. 2. The blackout or temporary loss of vision resulting from sudden acceleration, as in aviation.

hysteric *a.* Amaurosis associated with hysteria.

intoxication *a.* Amaurosis caused by a systemic poison, such as alcohol or tobacco.

Leber's congenital *a.* A recessive hereditary disease characterized by partial or complete blindness occurring at birth or shortly thereafter. The fundus may appear normal in the first months of life, but diffuse pigmentation typically appears and may develop into the bone corpuscle type, the retinal vessels become attenuated, and the optic nerve becomes atrophic. Photophobia is the rule, and other ocular anomalies may be keratoglobuslike keratoconus, cataract, and night blindness (when some residual vision remains).

partialis fugax, *a.* A partial amaurosis, sudden and transitory, associated with headache, vertigo, and nausea.

reflex *a.* Amaurosis caused by reflex action of a remote irritation.

saburral *a.* Amaurosis occurring in an attack of acute gastritis.

sympathetic *a.* Amaurosis of one eye due to transmission of disease from the other eye.

tobacco *a.* A toxic amaurosis due to excessive use of tobacco.

toxic *a.* Amaurosis caused by the toxic effects of the products of metabolic change occurring in uremia or diabetes or by the intake of various endogenous poisons such as ethyl and methyl alcohol, tobacco, quinine, and lead.

traumatic *a.* Amaurosis due to trauma.

uremic *a.* Amaurosis due to the products of metabolic change in uremia.

amaurotic (am″aw-rot′ik). 1. Pertaining to blindness. 2. One suffering from amaurosis.

cat's eye, *a.* Blindness of one eye due to various intraocular conditions such as retinoblastoma, vitreous deposits, exudative choroiditis, etc., in which a bright reflection is observed at the pupil as it would appear from the tapetum lucidum of a cat.

family idiocy, *a.* A familial lipoid degeneration of ganglionic cells in the central nervous system occurring in three forms: 1. Early infantile, characterized ophthalmoscopically by a cherry red spot at the fovea surrounded by a white edematous macular area, atrophic changes of the disk, and normal surrounding retina. It occurs mainly in Jewish children, beginning at about the fourth month of life; accompanying symptoms are blindness, flaccid muscles, and convulsions. See also *Tay-Sachs disease.* 2. Late infantile, occurs usually in non-Jewish children at about 2 years of age where pigmentary changes in the macula may occur instead of the cherry red spot. Syn., *Bielschowsky-Jansky disease.* 3. Juvenile, begins between 5 and 12 years of age and is characterized by "salt and pepper" pigmentation of the macula, pallor of the disk, reduced vision, and retarded mental development. See also *Batten-Mayou disease.*

pupillary paralysis, a. See under *paralysis, pupillary.*

ambient (am'be-ent). Pertaining to surroundings, e.g., *ambient light.*

ambiocular (am"be-ok'u-lar). 1. With both eyes. Etymologically, "with both eyes together," and, hence, synonymous with *oculi uniter;* however, the clinical connotation has been "with either eye," that is, synonymous with *oculus uterque.* 2. Pertaining to the absence of ocular dominance.

ambiocularity (am"be-ok"u-lar'ih-te). 1. The faculty of ambiocular vision. 2. In strabismus, the use of either eye at will. 3. In strabismus, a phenomenon reported by Brock in which both eyes are used simultaneously but in which various portions of the image of each eye are utilized to form a single, composite percept without normal sensory fusion.

amblyope (am'ble-ōp). One who has amblyopia.

amblyopia (am"ble-o'pe-ah). Reduced visual acuity not correctable by refractive means and not attributable to obvious structural or pathological ocular anomalies. Generally, it is detected by the measurement of visual acuity after the correction of any refractive error which may be present. Clinically, amblyopia is said to exist if vision is 20/30 or less, or if the vision of an eye is less than that of its fellow.

alcohol a., ethyl. 1. Amblyopia associated with the prolonged intake of ethyl alcohol and attributed to concurrent nutritional deficiencies. See also *nutritional*

amblyopia. 2. A toxic amblyopia resulting from the ingestion of impure ethyl alcohol.

alcohol a., methyl. Reduced vision due to the toxic effects of methyl alcohol. The onset is usually sudden and severe after ingestion of the alcohol.

alternating a. The alternating inhibition or suppression of vision which occurs in alternating strabismus. The deviating eye exhibits the suppression.

ametropic a. Refractive amblyopia.

anisometropic a. Amblyopia ex anopsia attributed to uncorrected anisometropia, typically in the eye with the greater refractive error.

arrest, a. of. A type of amblyopia ex anopsia in which the reduced vision results from failure in normal development of visual acuity with maturation. Cf. *amblyopia of extinction.*

astigmatic a. Reduced vision resulting from an uncorrected error of astigmatism, generally of large amount.

central a. Reduced vision confined to the macular area.

color a. Partial or complete color blindness.

congenital a. Reduced vision existing since birth with or without any accompanying congenital anomaly. Attributed by various authorities to arrested development of the macular area, to absence of the fovea, or to a fault in the conducting visual pathways.

deficiency a. Nutritional amblyopia.

dental a. Amblyopia resulting from the toxic effects of a dental infection.

disuse a. Amblyopia ex anopsia.

ex anopsia, a. Amblyopia attributable to nonuse or prolonged suppression. It is usually associated with strabismus or anisometropia and vision may be partially or totally recoverable. Syn., *disuse amblyopia; obligatory amblyopia; suppresion amblyopia.*

extinction, a. of. A type of amblyopia ex anopsia in which vision is reduced from that previously attained, and, hence, is recoverable. Cf. *amblyopia of arrest.*

facultative a. Suppression or inhibition of vision in one eye in response to the use of the other eye.

functional a. Amblyopia attributable to functional disorders, the retinal receptors and visual pathways being anatomically intact and free from pathology, as, for example, amblyopia ex anopsia or hysterical amblyopia.

hysterical a. A psychic loss of vision due to a neurosis or a psychosis; often characterized by tubular visual fields.

malarial a. Loss of vision resulting from the toxic effects of malaria.

nicotine a. Tobacco amblyopia.

nocturnal a. Night blindness.

nutritional a. Amblyopia due to dietary insufficiencies or malnutrition, especially to lack of the B vitamins. The loss of vision is gradual and the visual fields typically show a bilateral, roughly symmetrical, central, paracentral, or centrocecal scotoma, larger for red than white. Prognosis is good if treatment is instituted early. Syn., *deficiency amblyopia.*

obligatory a. Amblyopia ex anopsia.

occlusion a. Amblyopia ex anopsia which develops in an eye that has been constantly occluded for a period of time.

organic a. Amblyopia attributable to anatomical or pathological anomalies in the retinal receptors or visual pathways.

postmarital a. Loss of vision due to sexual excess. Syn., *Burns's amaurosis.*

quinine a. Loss of vision from the toxic effects of quinine.

receptor a. Amblyopia attributed to an anomaly in position, density, or composition of the foveal receptors, as, for example, tilting of the foveal receptors, or to a disturbance in their photopigment molecules.

reflex a. Partial or total blindness due to irritation or other disturbances in distal parts of the body, principally in peripheral sensory nerves, and especially in the trigeminal, as in dental amblyopia. Priestly Smith advanced the hypothesis that the irritation causes stimulation to the sympathetic nerve which leads to a contraction of the choroidal blood vessels and thus to an interference with chorioretinal functions.

refractive a. Amblyopia associated with, or attributed to, high but equal refractive errors or significantly unequal refractive errors. Syn., *ametropic amblyopia.*

relative a. Amblyopia ex anopsia coexisting with an organic loss of central vision.

simulated a. A pretense at blindness of varying degree; visual malingering.

strabismic a. Amblyopia, usually unilateral, in association with strabismus and generally considered to be a sequel to the onset of strabismus.

suppression a. Amblyopia ex anopsia.

tobacco a. Amblyopia associated with, or attributed to, the prolonged or excessive use of tobacco and considered by some to be due to toxic substances in the tobacco and by others to be due to concurrent nutritional deficiencies. Typically, it occurs in males between the ages of forty and sixty and is characterized by bilateral juxtacecal or centrocecal scotomata which may be more advanced in one eye than the other. Prognosis is good if the use of tobacco is discontinued, the amblyopia is not of long standing, and the patient is in good health.

toxic a. Amblyopia due to exogenous poisons, such as alcohol, or to endogenous poisons, such as focal infections. The visual fields may show either a central or a peripheral loss, depending on the poisonous agent.

traumatic a. Amblyopia as a result of injury.

uremic a. Amblyopia resulting from toxic effects of uremia.

amblyopiatrics (am″ble-o″pe-at′-riks). The therapeutics, or treatment, of amblyopia.

amblyopic pupillary paresis (am″-ble-op′ik). See under *paresis.*

amblyoscope (am′ble-o-skōp). A reflecting mirror haploscopic device consisting essentially of two angled tubes, held in front of the eyes like opera glasses, which can be turned on a swivel to any degree of convergence or divergence. Originally designed by Claude Worth.

major a. A large, table-supported amblyoscope. Usually greater freedom for adjustments is incorporated in its design than in a simple amblyoscope.

Wheatstone a. An amblyoscope using mirrors to change the convergence stimulus. Syn., *Wheatstone stereoscope.*

Worth a. See *amblyoscope.*

Worth-Black a. A modified Worth amblyoscope providing vertical as well as horizontal adjustments.

amebiasis (am″e-bi′ah-sis). Infection with *Endamoeba histolytica,* sometimes producing conjunctivitis.

amentia, nevoid (a-men′she-ah). Sturge-Weber disease.

American Academy of Ophthalmology and Otolaryngology. A professional and scientific organization, formed in 1896 under the name of the Western Ophthalmic and Otolaryngologic Society. The name was changed to the present one in 1903. Its purpose is to serve the interests of Doctors of Medicine in these three specialties. At first the membership consisted chiefly of Midwesterners, but within recent years it has attracted to its fold most of the Eastern ophthalmologists. It now includes most of the specialists in diseases of the eye, ear, nose, and throat in the United States. It was the first medical society to institute instructional courses.

American Academy of Optometry. A professional and scientific organization originated in 1922 for the purpose of encouraging the development of optometric science and practice by providing opportunities for the presentation, discussion, and publication of clinical and research papers. The Academy also provides funds for optometric research and graduate fellowships. Membership is confined to practitioners, scientists, and teachers who meet high professional standards.

American Board of Opticianry. An association of opticians organized in 1947 to establish standards of education and training and to accredit training programs in opticianry, and to examine and certify individuals for membership.

American Foundation for the Blind. An organization founded in 1921 for the advancement of care for the blind and partially sighted through research, literature, films, lectures, and consultations, and by making available subnormal vision aids.

American Medical Association. An organization, formed in **1847,**

whose principal function is to represent the interests of the medical profession. It has a present membership of over 200,000 Doctors of Medicine. It has published the *Journal of the American Medical Association* since 1883. Its section on ophthalmology, established in 1888, offers an opportunity for the presentation of scientific programs in conjunction with American Medical Association conventions.

American Ophthalmological Society. An organization formed in 1869 as the first specialty medical society in America. It has high requirements for membership, including excellent professional performance and adherence to the highest ethical standards.

American Optometric Association. A national organization of optometrists incorporated under the laws of the state of Ohio. Its prime purpose is to unite optometrists into a nationally representative group for the betterment of the optometric profession. It is supported by voluntary membership of individual optometrists, but membership must be accompanied by membership in local and state associations. It publishes the monthly *Journal of the American Optometric Association.*

American Optometric Foundation. An organization incorporated in the state of New York and sponsored by optometrists for the advancement of visual care through research, literature, education, and other related activities. This is accomplished largely through grants-in-aid to individuals and institutions.

American Research Council of Optometry. An organization formed in Ord, Nebraska, by George A. Parkins and others and concerned with problems in reading as related to vision.

Ames room. See under *room.*

ametrometer (am″e-trom′eh-ter). An instrument used in the refraction of the eye and consisting essentially of a complete set of trial lenses mounted in several rotating disks.

ametrope (am′e-trōp). One who has ametropia.

ametropia (am″e-tro′pe-ah). The refractive condition in which, with accommodation relaxed, parallel rays do not focus on the retina; a condition representing the manifestation of a refractive error, specifically *myopia, hypermetropia,* or *astigmatism;* hence, a deviation from *emmetropia.*

axial a. 1. Myopia or hyperopia due primarily to a deviation from the average, or some other standard value, of the anteroposterior diameter of the globe. 2. In geometric optics, ametropia due to an axial length other than that of the schematic eye (Gullstrand value, 24.38 mm.).

curvature a. 1. Myopia or hyperopia due primarily to a deviation from the average, or some other standard value, of the radius of curvature of one or more of the refracting surfaces of the cornea or the crystalline lens. 2. In geometric optics, ametropia due to differences in the radius of one or more of the refracting surfaces from the values of the schematic eye. 3. Clinically, the anterior surface of the cornea is considered to be the most frequent cause of curvature ametropia of significant amounts; hence, the term frequently implies ametropia due to the deviation of the anterior radius of the cornea from a standard value (Gullstrand value, 7.7 mm.).

index a. 1. Myopia or hyperopia due primarily to a deviation from the average, or some other standard value, of the index of refraction of any of the refracting media of the eye. 2. Clinically, since the changes in index are rare or of small degree except in the crystalline lens, the term usually refers to ametropia consequent upon changes in the index of refraction of this body.

position a. Myopia or hyperopia due primarily to a deviation from the average, or some other standard value, of the crystalline lens position, i.e., distance from cornea and from fovea. In the schematic eye, if other things are equal, placing the lens farther back (large anterior chamber) will create hyperopia, while the reverse will cause myopia.

refractive a. 1. Myopia or hyperopia due primarily to a deviation from the average, or some other standard value, of the refractive power of the eye (cornea-aqueous-crystalline system). 2. In geometric optics, ametropia due to a total refracting power greater or less than that of the schematic eye (Gullstrand value, 58.64 D.).

simple a. Ametropia due only to refractive anomalies in an otherwise healthy eye.

ametropic (am″e-trop′ik). 1. Relating to ametropia. 2. Having ametropia.

Amici prism (ah-me′che). See under *prism.*

Amidei's syndrome (am′ah-dēz). See under *syndrome.*

amimia (ă-mim′e-ah). A sensory aphasia characterized by the loss of ability to communicate by gestures or signs.

Ammann's test (am′anz). Dark filter test.

von Ammon's posterior protrusion (fon am′onz). See *protrusion, posterior, of von Ammon.*

amnesia (am-ne′ze-ah). Partial or total loss of memory.

color a. The inability to retain memory of color perceptions or to name colors properly.

visual a. The partial or total loss of ability to recall or identify past visual experiences, as the failure to recognize written or printed words or objects previously seen.

amotio retinae (ă-mo′she-o ret′ihne). Detachment of the retina.

amphiblestritis (am″fih-bles-tri′tis). Inflammation of the retina.

amphiblestrodes (am″fih-bles-tro′dēz). Retina. *Obs.*

amphiblestroid apoplexia (am″fihbles′troid ap″o-plek′se-ah). Hemorrhage of the retina.

amphicrania (am″fih-kra′ne-ah). Headache occurring in both sides of the head.

amphodiplopia (am″fo-di-plo′peah). Double vision in both eyes.

amphoterodiplopia (am-foh″te-rodi-plo′pe-ah). Amphodiplopia.

amplification. Optically synonymous with *magnification.*

amplifier. Optically synonymous with *magnifier.*

amplitude. The range or the extent of a surface, a space, or a capacity.

accommodation, a. of. The difference expressed in diopters between the farthest point and the nearest point of accommodation with respect to the spectacle plane, the entrance pupil, or some other reference point of the eye.

accommodation, a. of (absolute). The amplitude of accommodation, but distinguished from amplitude of relative accommodation.

accommodation, a. of (binocular). The amplitude of accommodation measured with binocular fixation of the test stimulus.

accommodation, a. of (minus lens). The amplitude of accommodation measured by increasing the minus lens (or decreasing the plus lens) to the limit of clear vision while the distance of the test object is held constant.

accommodation, a. of (monocular). The amplitude of accommodation measured with the test stimulus presented to one eye, the other being absent, occluded, or fusionally dissociated from the first.

accommodation, a. of (negative). Negative relative amplitude of accommodation.

accommodation, a. of (positive). Positive relative amplitude of accommodation.

accommodation, a. of (push-up). The amplitude of accommodation as measured by a push-up test, i.e., moving the test object toward the eye or eyes to the nearest point of clear vision.

accommodation, a. of (relative). The total dioptric range of accommodation which can be elicited with convergence fixed.

accommodation, a. of (relative, negative). The decrease in accommodation that can be elicited, as by means of convex lenses, with the convergence fixed, usually at a normal reading distance..

accommodation, a. of (relative, positive). The increase in accommodation that can be elicited, as by means of concave lenses, with the convergence fixed, usually at a normal reading distance.

accommodation, a. of (reserve). The amplitude of accommodation minus the accommodation needed for clear vision at a given fixation distance, usually an assumed reading distance.

accommodation, a. of (usable). 1. That portion of the total amplitude of accommodation available for prolonged use without discomfort, usually considered to be from one half to two thirds of the total amplitude. 2. The accommodation changes possible during binocular fixation of an object at a given fixed distance. Syn., *relative accommodation.*

adaptation, a. of. The difference between the light sense threshold of a light-adapted eye and the light sense threshold of the same eye when dark-adapted.

convergence, a. of. Clinically, the angle of maximum convergence; the angular deviation of the lines of sight from parallelism in converging to the maximum; occasionally synonymous with *absolute amplitude of convergence.* Syn., *amplitude of triangulation.*

convergence, a. of (absolute). The amplitude of convergence measured from the maximum limit of divergence to the maximum limit of convergence. Clinically, it is the range in angular units from the prism base-in to break findings, accommodation relaxed, to the near point of convergence, maximum accommodation in force.

convergence, a. of (fusional). The amplitude of convergence measured from the limit of negative fusional convergence to the limit of positive fusional convergence, with accommodation held constant.

convergence, a. of (negative). Amplitude of negative relative convergence.

convergence, a. of (positive). Amplitude of positive relative convergence.

convergence, a. of (push-up). The amplitude of convergence measured by moving a test object in the median plane of the two eyes to the nearest point of single binocular vision.

convergence, a. of (relative). The total relative convergence which can be elicited; conventionally measured from the prism base-in limit to the prism base-out limit of clear, single, binocular vision at a fixed level of accommodation.

convergence, a. of (relative, negative). That part of the amplitude of relative convergence measured from the normal convergence demand for a given fixation distance to the prism base-in limit.

convergence, a. of (relative, positive). That part of the amplitude of relative convergence measured from the normal convergence demand for a given fixation distance to the prism base-out limit.

convergence, a. of (reserve). 1. Relative amplitude of convergence. 2. The total convergence ability of the eyes, minus the convergence in use.

cyclofusional a. The angle between the limits of excyclofusional and encyclofusional rotation of the eyes.

fusional a. The angle between the maximum convergence and the maximum divergence of the eyes that can be elicited in response to change in convergence stimulus while the accommodation stimulus, but not necessarily the accommodation, remains constant.

size a. In the measurement of aniseikonia, the range of magnifying power through which the patient sees no difference in the appearance of the eikonic test elements. One half of the size amplitude is known as the "sensitivity."

stereopsis, a. of. An expression designating the interval between the upper or maximum limit and the lower or minimal limit of retinal disparity producing stereopsis. Cf. *range of stereopsis.*

triangulation, a. of. Amplitude of convergence.

wave a. The maximum displacement of any particle in a wave from its equilibrium position. The energy or intensity is proportional to the square of the amplitude.

ampulla, lacrimal (am-pul'ah). A dilatation of the canaliculus at the junction of its vertical and horizontal portions about 2 mm. from the lacrimal punctum.

Amsler (amz'ler) **charts; grids.** See under *chart.*

Amsler-Huber test (amz'ler hu'ber). See under *test.*

amydriasis (am"ih-dri'ah-sis). Contraction of the pupil.

amyloidosis (am"ih-loi-do'sis). A disease of unknown etiology characterized by the abnormal deposition of amyloid, a translucent homogenous glycoprotein, in various organs and tissues of the body. In the eye, it may occur as a primary affection, may follow trachoma or other chronic infections, or may occur rarely as part of a systemic involvement. It may affect the bulbar or palpebral conjunctiva, tarsus, cornea, sclera, vitreous humor, optic nerve, or the levator palpebrae muscle, and it leads to tumor formation.

anacamptic (an"ah-kamp'tik). Pertaining to reflection of light or sound.

anacamptics (an"ah-kamp'tiks). The study of reflection of light or sound.

anaclasis (an-ak'lah-sis). Refraction or reflection of light or sound.

anaclastic (an"ah-klas'tik). Pertaining to reflection or refraction of light or sound.

anagenesis (an"ah-jen'e-sis). 1. Regeneration, reparation, or reproduction of tissue. 2. A photochemical regeneration of previously bleached or exhausted color elements, such as rhodopsin of the retina.

anaglyph (an'ah-glif). Two related photographs or drawings, superimposed and laterally displaced, each outlined in a color complementary to that of the other (usually in red and blue-green), to be viewed through filters of the same colors, one to each eye. If the corresponding parts of the drawings have been properly displaced, or the photographs are of a single scene taken from two directions, when properly fused the anaglyph will give rise to the percept of relief or stereopsis.

anaglyphoscope (an″ah-glif′o-skōp). Anaglyptoscope.

anaglyptoscope (an″ah-glip′to-skōp). An instrument used to demonstrate the effect of shadows in the interpretation of perspective by redirecting the light upon an object in relief to an opposite direction, resulting in an apparent reversal of perspective.

anagnosasthenia (an″ag-nōs″as-the′-ne-ah). 1. The inability to read although the printed words are distinguishable. 2. Distress at any attempt to read.

analysis, Fourier's. Resolution of a complex periodic wave form into a series of single components according to Fourier's theory.

analysis, graphic. 1. An analysis of image formation by ray tracing. 2. An analysis of the accommodation and convergence interrelationships by plotting clinical findings on a co-ordinate graph.

analysis, visual. The analysis of functional visual problems in terms of cause and correction.

analyzer (an′ah-li″zer). 1. A polarizing filter with which it is possible to determine the direction of polarization of a beam of light. 2. One of the two filters in a plane polariscope, the other being the polarizer.

anamnesis (an″am-ne′sis). 1. The faculty of memory. 2. Information obtained from both an individual and others about the past history of that individual's case.

anamorphoser (an″ah-mōr-fo′ser). A device (the simplest form of which is the Brewster prism unit) by which meridional magnifica-

tion without effective power for distance vision can be obtained. Two identical prisms are placed base to apex and hinged at the base of one and the apex of the other so that the angle between the prisms may be changed. The degree of meridional magnification which occurs in the base-apex meridian varies with the angle between the prisms.

anamorphosis (an″ah-mōr′fo-sis, an″-ah-mōr-fo′sis). A method by which a distorted image is corrected when viewed through a curved mirror or through a pyramidal glass.

catoptric a. The correction of a distorted image by means of a curved mirror.

dioptric a. The correction of a distorted image by means of a pyramidal glass.

anaphalantiasis (an″af-ah-lan-ti′ah-sis). Lack of eyebrows or eyelashes. *Obs.*

anaphoria (an″ah-fo′re-ah). A tendency of both eyes to turn upward above the horizontal plane in the absence of a stimulus eliciting fixation attention.

anastigmatic (an″as-tig-mat′ik, an-as″-). Without astigmatism; corrected for astigmatism.

anastomosis (ă-nas″to-mo′sis). 1. A natural intercommunication of blood vessels or nerves. 2. A surgical or pathological formation of a passage between two spaces or hollow organs.

anatropia (an″ah-tro′pe-ah). A persistent, abnormal upward turning of the visual axes above the horizontal plane.

anchylops (ang′ki-lops). An abscess at the inner canthus of the eye.

Andersen-Weymouth hypothesis (an′der-sen-wa′muth). See *hypothesis, Weymouth-Andersen.*

Andogsky's syndrome (an-dog′skēz). See under *syndrome.*

anemia (ă-ne′me-ah). A diminution of the normal blood volume, or a deficiency of the number of red cells, hemoglobin, or both.

glaucomatous a. A localized anemia in the limbal area, characterized by a dead white appearance; seen in cases of chronic glaucoma.

retinal a. Anemia characterized in the retina by a generalized pallor and, occasionally, superficial hemorrhages and slight engorgement of the veins.

sickle-cell a. Sickle-cell disease.

anerythroblepsia (an″e-rith″ro-blep′-se-ah). Protanopia.

anerythropsia (an″e-rith-rop′se-ah). The inability to perceive the color red; red blindness or protanopia.

anesthesia, optic (an″es-the′ze-ah). Temporary loss of vision.

anesthesia, retinal (an″es-the′ze-ah). Temporary amaurosis, usually due to hysteria.

aneurin (an′ūr-in). Vitamin B_1.

aneurism (an′u-rizm). Aneurysm.

aneurysm (an′u-rizm). A saclike dilatation of the walls of a blood vessel, usually an artery. It is filled with fluid or clotted blood, usually forming a pulsating tumor.

Leber's miliary a's. Telangiectases of the retinal vessels occurring in *Leber's retinal degeneration.*

Angelucci's syndrome (an″jeh-lu′-chēz). See under *syndrome.*

angioblastomatosis (an″je-o-blas″-to-mah-to′sis). Von Hippel-Lindau disease.

angiogliomatosis (an″je-o-gli″o-mah-to′sis). Von Hippel-Lindau disease.

angioid streaks (an′je-oid). See under *streak.*

angiokeratoma corporis diffusum (an″je-o-ker″ah-to′mah kor-por′is dih-fu′sum). Fabry's disease.

angioma (an″je-o′mah). A tumor composed of lymphatic or blood vessels.

angioma pigmentosum atrophicum (an″je-o′mah pig-men-to′sum

ă-tro′fik-um). Xeroderma pigmentosum.

angiomatosis, encephalocutaneous (an″je-o-mah-to′sis). Sturge-Weber disease.

angiomatosis, encephalotrigeminal (an″je-o-mah-to′sis). Sturge-Weber disease.

angiomatosis, meningocutaneous (an″je-o-mah-to′sis). Sturge-Weber disease.

angiomatosis retinae (an″je-o-mah-to′sis). Von Hippel's disease.

angiomegaly (an″je-o-meg′ah-le). Enlarged blood vessels occurring mainly in the eyelids.

angiopathia retinae traumatica of Purtscher (an″je-o-path′e-ah ret′-ih-ne traw-mat′ih-kah). Purtscher's disease.

angiopathia retinalis juvenalis (an″je-o-path′e-ah ret″ih-nal′is ju″veh-nal′is). Eales's disease.

angiopathica traumatica of Purtscher (an″je-o-path′ih-kah traw-mat′ih-kah). Purtscher's disease.

angioreticuloma (an″je-o-reh-tik″-u-lo′mah). A hemangioma of the retina or the brain. See also *von Hippel-Lindau disease.*

angioscotoma (an″je-o-sko-to′mah). A scotoma due to the blocking of incident light by the larger retinal vessels; characteristically, it is ribbon-shaped and extends from the normal blind spot.

angioscotometry (an″je-o-sko-tom′-eh-tre). The plotting of angioscotomata by the use of sufficiently small test objects and accurate fixation.

angiospasm, retinal (an′je-o-spazm″). A spasmodic segmental contraction of a blood vessel of the retina.

angle. 1. The figure formed by the meeting of two lines at a point, or the space bounded by two such lines. 2. The degrees of turning necessary to bring one line or plane parallel to, or coincident with, another. 3. The direction from which an object is viewed.

aberration, a. of. The angle between a refracted ray and the extension of the incident ray. Syn., *angle of deviation.*

adaptation, a. of. Angle of anomaly.

alpha, a. 1. The angle formed at the first nodal point by the intersection of the optic axis and the visual axis. 2. The angle between the visual axis and the line normal to the cornea at its geometric center. *Donders.* 3. The angle between the visual axis and the major axis of the corneal ellipse. *Landolt.*

    alpha, negative a. The angle formed by the intersection of the visual axis and the optic axis in such a way that the visual axis lies temporal to the optic axis in the plane of the cornea.

    alpha, positive a. The angle formed by the intersection of the visual axis and the optic axis in such a way that the visual axis lies nasal to the optic axis in the plane of the cornea.

altitude, a. of. Angle of elevation.

anomaly, a. of. The angle between the line of visual direction of the fovea and the line of visual direction of a retinal area in the same eye which has a common visual direction with the fovea of the other eye. Usually it is represented by the difference between the objective and the subjective angles of strabismus in anomalous retinal correspondence. Syn., *angle of adaptation.*

anterior chamber, a. of the. The angle at the periphery of the anterior chamber, formed by the uveal meshwork, the ciliary body, and the root of the iris.

aperture a. The angle subtended in an optical system by the radius of the entrance pupil or the exit pupil at the anterior focal point or the posterior focal point, respectively.

apical a. The dihedral angle formed by the meeting of the two plane faces of a prism at its edge. Syn., *angle beta; prism angle; refracting angle.*

azimuth, a. of. In a system for specifying the direction of regard in terms of elevation and azimuth, the angle of rotation (μ) of the line of sight right or left from its zero value in the primary position about an axis perpendicular to the primary plane of regard.

beta, a. 1. The angle between the fixation line and that normal to the cornea which goes through the geometric center of the cornea. *Helmholtz.* 2. Refracting angle of a prism.

biorbital a. The angle of about 45° formed by the intersection of the orbital axes of the paired bony orbits.

Brewster's a. Angle of polarization.

convergence, a. of. The laterally or horizontally oriented angle between the lines of sight of the two eyes. The angle is positive when the lines of sight intersect in front of the centers of rotation, negative when behind. Directional axes other than the lines of sight may be employed as a basis for specifying angle of convergence.

critical a. That angle of incidence which results in the refracted ray traveling along the surface between the two media. Any angle greater than the critical angle results in total reflection. Syn., *limiting angle.*

declination, a. of. The total angular difference between (1) the meridians of orientation of the corresponding retinal images in the two eyes which produce a stereoscopic vertical appearance of the fixation object or (2) the meridians of orientation of the same images which produce a given inclination of the perceived (fused) images. Cf. *angle of inclination.*

deviation, a. of. 1. In strabismus, the angle by which the visual axis, or foveal line of sight, of the deviating eye fails to intersect the object of fixation, usually subtended at the center of rotation of the deviating eye. 2. The angle through which a ray of light has been deviated by reflection or refraction.

deviation, a. of (chromatic). The angle through which a ray of specific wavelength has been deflected in passing through a refracting surface or prism.

deviation, a. of (minimum). The angle between the incident ray and the emergent ray of an optical prism, when the path of light traversing the prism is that producing the least deviation. This condition exists when the path of light traverses the prism symmetrically, when the (reduced) angles of incidence and emergence are equal, and when the ray which traverses the prism is perpendicular to a bisector of the refracting angle of the prism.

deviation, a. of (primary). In strabismus, the angle of deviation when the normally fixating eye is fixating.

deviation, a. of (secondary). In strabismus, the angle of deviation when the normally deviating eye is made to fixate.

deviation, a. of (true). In strabismus, the angle of deviation when it includes consideration of angle kappa.

direction, a. of. The angle between the optical axis of an optical system and the chief ray to some object of interest, as measured at the appropriate principal point of the system. In the case of the eye, the point of reference may also be (1) one of the nodal points, (2) the center of the entrance pupil, or (3) the center of rotation.

discrimination, a. of. Minimum separable angle.

displacement, a. of. The angle between the line of sight when the eye is in the primary position and the line of sight when the eye is in any secondary position.

distinctness, a. of. The smallest visual angle at which the form of objects can be distinguished; visual acuity expressed in terms of the angle subtended.

divergence, a. of. The angle between the lines of sight when they diverge from parallelism, especially laterally, although it may refer to vertical divergence. Directional axes other than the lines of sight may also be employed as a basis for specifying angle of divergence.

eccentricity, a. of. In a system for specifying the direction of regard in terms of eccentricity and meridional direction, an angle of rotation of the line of sight in a meridian plane containing the lines of sight in both the zero and the eccentric direction. This is the system used in the perimeter in which meridional direction pertains to the position of the arc of the perimeter and eccentricity to the position of the line of sight on the arc.

elevation, a. of. In a system for specifying the direction of regard in terms of elevation and azimuth, the angle of rotation (λ) of the line of sight up or down from its zero value in the primary position about an axis lying in the primary plane of regard. Syn., *angle of altitude.*

emergence, a. of. The angle formed between the emergent ray and the normal at the point of emergence.

epsilon, a. The angle between the macular axis and the papillary axis, as subtended at the second nodal point. This is equivalent to the angle between the point of fixation and the nasal edge of the blind spot, as subtended at the primary nodal point.

eta, a. The relative binocular parallactic angle or the angle of stereopsis.

external a. The angle formed by the eyelids at the outer canthus.

field of view, a. of. The angle subtended by the entrance port at the center of the entrance pupil.

filtration, a. of. The peripheral portion of the anterior chamber between the root of the iris, the front surface of the ciliary body, and the sclera; the part of the anterior chamber related to the trabecular spaces and the canal of Schlemm.

focal point a. The angle subtended by an object at the primary focal point of the eye.

Fuchs, a. of. A recess or space between the superficial and the deep layers of the anterior surface of the iris along the line of the collarette in the ciliary portion of the iris.

fusion a. In strabismus, the angle through which haploscopic targets must be moved from parallelism for fusion to occur, or the angular displacement of the fixation target by a measuring prism for fusion to occur.

gamma, a. The angle between the fixation axis and the optic axis of the eye.

great a. of the eye. The angle formed by the lid margins at the inner canthus of the eye.

half-field a. One half the angle of field of view.

half-shade a. The angle between the planes of polarization in the field of a polarimeter.

image a. The angle of displacement when a prism is placed between the eye and an object.

incidence, a. of. The angle formed between the incident ray and the normal at the point of incidence.

inclination, a. of. The angle represented by the fore or aft tilt (or reorientation) of a line of reference which intersects the visual plane at the point of fixation. It is measured from the stereoscopic vertical or from the perpendicular to the visual plane. The angle of inclination bears a simple geometric relationship to the angle of declination. The apparent inclination of the vertical meridian may be created by an oblique meridional aniseikonia or by rotating the vertical meridian of targets in a stereoscope in opposite directions about the axes of fixation.

iridocorneal a. The angle between the iris and the cornea at the periphery of the anterior chamber of the eye. Syn., *angle of the iris; angulus iridis.*

iris, a. of the. Iridocorneal angle.

kappa, a. The angle between the visual axis and the pupillary axis of the eye, measured at the nodal point.

    kappa, negative a. The angle between the visual axis and the pupillary axis when the visual axis is temporal to the pupillary axis. A negative angle kappa is anomalous; if present, the eyes may appear to converge.

    kappa, positive a. The angle between the visual axis and the pupillary axis when the visual axis is nasal to the pupillary axis; if abnormally large, the eyes may appear to diverge.

lambda, a. The angle subtended at the center of the entrance pupil of the eye by the intersection of the pupillary axis and the line of sight. It is this angle which is measured in routine clinical tests, although it is commonly designated *angle kappa.*

latitude, a. of. In a system for specifying the direction of regard in terms of longitude and latitude, the angle of rotation (ϕ) of the line of sight about an axis lying in the primary plane of regard at the center of rotation of the eye.

limiting a. Critical angle.

longitude, a. of. In a system for specifying the direction of regard in terms of longitude and latitude, the angle of rotation (θ) of the line of sight about an axis perpendicular to the primary plane of regard at the center of rotation of the eye.

meridional direction, a. of. In a system for specifying the direction of regard in terms of eccentricity and meridional direction, the specified angle (κ), clockwise from the subject's point of view, between the plane of regard and the meridian plane in which the angle of eccentricity is measured.

meter a. A unit of convergence; the angular amount of convergence required for binocular fixation of a point on the median line 1 m. from the centers of rotation of each eye. The magnitude of the angle varies with interpupillary distance and may be converted into prism diopters by multiplying the number of meter angles by the interpupillary distance in centimeters.

minimum a. of resolution. The minimum separable angle as determined by the identification of form targets and represented by the reciprocal of the Snellen fraction, e.g., 20/40 = 2 minutes of arc.

minimum separable a. The smallest angle subtended at the nodal point, the center of the entrance pupil, or other point of reference of the eye by two points or lines in order that they may be discriminated as separate; a measure of the threshold of form sense. Syn., *angle of discrimination; limiting visual angle; minimum visual angle.*

minimum visible a. The angle subtended at the anterior nodal point, the center of the entrance pupil, or other point of reference of the eye by rays from the extremities of the smallest areal extension of light which can be perceived. It varies with the region of the retina stimulated, the nature of the surround, the state of adaptation, and the duration and the intensity of the stimulus.

nasal a. The angle formed by the lid margins at the inner canthus of the eye.

nasomalar a. The angle of about 145° made by the intersection of lines, extending from the lateral orbital margins through the medial orbital margins.

ocular a. Palpebral angle.

ommatidial a. The angular extent of the visual field encompassed by each ommatidium of a compound eye.

optic a. The angle formed by two lines from the anterior nodal point of the eye to the extremities of the object of regard. Cf. *visual angle.*

orbital a. An angle of about 45° where the orbital axes meet. Syn., *biorbital angle.*

palpebral a. The angle formed by the eyelids at the external or internal canthus. Syn., *ocular angle.*

pantoscopic a. The angle between the plane of a spectacle lens and the frontal plane of the face when the superior margin of the lens is farther away from the frontal plane than the inferior margin. Cf. *retroscopic angle.*

parallactic a. The magnitude of parallax expressed as an angle with reference to the entrance pupils of the two eyes in binocular parallax, or with reference to the entrance pupil of one eye in two separate positions in monocular parallax.

parallactic a., binocular. The angular difference in direction of a viewed object with respect to the entrance pupils of the two eyes, represented by the angle between the lines connecting the entrance pupils of the two eyes with the object.

parallactic a., monocular. The angular change in direction of a viewed object with respect to the entrance pupil of the eye when the eye is moved from one location to another, represented by the angle between the lines connecting the center of the entrance pupil of the eye, in the two positions, with the object.

parallactic a., relative binocular. The angular change of the relative difference in direction of two objects with respect to the centers of the entrance pupils of each of the two eyes considered as viewing the object separately. It is derived by subtracting the binocular parallactic angle for the one object from that of the other. Syn., *angle eta.*

parallactic a., relative monocular. The angular change of the relative difference in direction of two objects with respect to the center of the entrance pupil of the eye, viewed with the eye first in one position and then in another. It is derived by subtracting the monocular parallactic angle for the one object from that of the other.

parallax, a. of. Parallactic angle.

physiological a. The angle formed by the corneal and the visual axes. Syn., *angle alpha.*

polarization, a. of. The angle of incidence at which the reflected light is all plane polarized. This occurs when the reflected light is at right angles to the refracted light. Syn., *Brewster's angle.* See also *Brewster's law.*

principal a. The angle between the two refracting surfaces of a prism. Syn., *angle beta; prism angle; refracting angle.*

principal point a. The angle subtended by an object at the primary principal point of the eye.

prism a. The dihedral angle between the sides of a prism. Syn., *angle beta; principal angle; refracting angle.*

projection, a. of. The extreme angle between rays emerging from an optical system.

projection, a. of false. The angle between the line drawn from the true position of an object through the center of the entrance pupil and the line drawn from the perceived position of the object. It is most apparent in past pointing exhibited by a recent paralytic squinter; also, it may be apparent in patients with anomalous fixation.

re-entering a. An angle with its apex toward the interior of the figure in which it occurs. Hence, in perimetry, a wedge-shaped sector defect with its acute angle within the seeing field and with the side opposite this angle extending to the limit of the field.

reflecting a. of prism. The angle through which a reflecting prism will turn a ray of light.

reflection, a. of. The angle between the incidence normal and the reflected ray.

refracting a. The dihedral angle between the faces of a prism. Syn., *angle beta; principal angle; prism angle.*

refraction, a. of. The angle, formed at the point of emergence, between the emergent ray and the normal.

retroscopic a. The angle between the plane of a spectacle lens and the frontal plane of the face when the superior margin of the lens is closer to the frontal plane than the inferior margin. Cf. *pantoscopic angle*.

rotation, a. of. The angle through which the plane of polarization is rotated by an optically active substance. See also *optical activity*.

slope a. The angle between a ray of light and the optical axis of a lens or a lens system.

stereopsis, a. of. The difference between the angles subtended, at the centers of the entrance pupils of the two eyes, by two points in space at different distances from the eyes. The binocular relative parallactic angle considered as a stereopsis cue during binocular fixation. Syn., *angle eta*.

strabismus, a. of. The objective angle of strabismus, or the subjective angle of strabismus if no anomalous retinal correspondence is present.

  strabismus, a. of (objective). The angle by which the line of sight or other axis of reference of the deviating eye in strabismus fails to intersect the object of fixation, subtended at the center of rotation of the deviating eye. Usually it is measured by an objective technique such as the corneal reflex method, or by the alternate occlusion test combined with measuring prisms. If measured with an amblyoscope or under infinity testing conditions, it may be considered the angle between the line of sight of the deviating eye and the line of sight of the fixating eye.

  strabismus, a. of (residual). The angle of deviation remaining after corrective surgery for strabismus.

  strabismus, a. of (subjective). The angle of separation between the image of the point of fixation as seen by the fixating

eye and the image of the point of fixation as seen by the deviating eye, subtended at the center of rotation of the deviating eye; the angle through which dissimilar targets in an amblyoscope must be moved from parallelism for superimposition to occur; the angle through which light to the nonfixating eye is deviated by measuring prisms for superimposition to occur. As related to the eye, it may be considered to be the angle of separation between the point on the retina of the nonfixating eye stimulated by the image of the point of fixation and the retinal site in the same eye which gives rise to a common visual direction with the fovea of the fixating eye, subtended at the center of rotation.

temporal a. The angle formed by the lids at the outer canthus.

torsion, a. of. The dihedral angle between the horizontal meridian of the eye and the plane of regard where they intersect at the line of sight, or line of fixation, depending on how the plane of regard is defined, or for what purpose.

  torsion, a. of (negative). The angle of torsion when the horizontal meridian of the eye is displaced counterclockwise with reference to the subject's view.

  torsion, a. of (positive). The angle of torsion when the horizontal meridian of the eye is displaced clockwise with reference to the subject's view.

triangulation, a. of. Angle of convergence.

V of Helmholtz, a. The angle between the apparent (subjective) vertical meridians of the two eyes.

visual a. The angle subtended by the extremities of an object at the entrance pupil or other point of reference of the eye. Cf. *optic angle.*

visual a., limiting. Minimum separable angle.

visual a., minimum. Minimum separable angle.

angling. Bending the endpiece of a spectacle frame or mounting to alter the angle between the temple and the plane of the lenses.

anglometer (an'glo-me"ter). An instrument using corneal reflection for measuring the primary and the secondary deviations of strabismus.

angstrom, Angstrom (ang'strum), **Ångström** (ōng'strum) **law; unit.** See under the nouns.

angular gyrus (ang'gu-lar ji'rus). See under *gyrus.*

angulus (ang'gu-lus). Latin for *angle.*

iridis, a. Iridocorneal angle.

oculi, a. Palpebral angle.

anianthinopsy (an"e-an'thi-nop"se). The inability to recognize violet tints.

aniridia (an"ir-id'e-ah, an"i-rid'-). Complete or partial absence of the iris, usually hereditary. Syn., *irideremia.*

aniseikometer (an"is-i-kom'eh-ter). An instrument for the measurement of aniseikonia; usually referred to as an *eikonometer.*

aniseikonia (an"ih-si-ko'ne-ah). A relative difference in size and/or shape of the ocular images. It may be measured by viewing haploscopically a pair of objects and determining the relative difference in the visual angles which causes the objects to appear equal in size, or equal in distance from the point of binocular fixation.

anatomical a. Aniseikonia due to an anatomical cause, such as unequal distribution of the retinal elements.

anomalous a. Aniseikonia which is clinically significant and which is correctable by clinical means (iseikonic lenses). It is usually referred to simply as aniseikonia, the prefix "anomalous" being used to differentiate it from physiological aniseikonia which is due to retinal disparity caused by lateral separation of the eyes.

asymmetrical a. Aniseikonia characterized by a progressive increase or decrease in size across the visual field, as may be produced by a flat prism in front of one eye.

axial a. Aniseikonia due to unequal axial lengths of the two eyes.

crossed-meridional a. Aniseikonia in which the required meridional correction is axis 90° in one eye and axis 180° in the other eye.

induced a. Aniseikonia induced by refractive or size lenses.

meridional a. Aniseikonia in which there is a symmetrical meridional difference between the size of the ocular images of the two eyes, so that the ocular image in the one meridian is larger or smaller than the corresponding meridian of the other eye.

natural a. Physiological aniseikonia.

optical a. Aniseikonia due to optical (dioptric) factors.

optical a., acquired. Aniseikonia due to the refractive (corrective) lenses worn; their power, position in front of the eyes, curvatures, thicknesses, etc., create the difference in image size.

optical a., inherent. Aniseikonia dependent on the dioptric characteristics of the eyes.

over-all a. Aniseikonia in which the image of one eye is symmetrically larger or smaller than that of the other eye, in all meridians.

over-all–meridional a. A combination of over-all and meridional aniseikonia.

physiological a. The normal relative difference in retinal image size due to image disparities introduced by the lateral separation of the eyes, asymmetrical convergence, or asymmetry of the field of vision. Syn., *natural aniseikonia.*

symmetrical a. Aniseikonia in which the difference in image size is symmetrical, as distinguished from asymmetrical aniseikonia.

anisoastigmatism (an-i″so-ah-stig′-mah-tizm). Compound astigmatic anisometropia.

aniso-accommodation (an-i″so-ah-kom″o-da′shun). Unequal simultaneous accommodation in the two eyes.

anisochromatic (an-i″so-kro-mat′ik). 1. Lacking in uniformity of color; not of the same color throughout. 2. Pertaining to two pigments used for testing color blindness which are distinguished by both the normal and the color-blind eye.

anisochromatopsia (an-i″so-kro″-mah-top′se-ah). Deficient color perception affecting only one eye or of an unequal character or severity in the two eyes.

anisochromia (an-i″so-kro′me-ah). Heterochromia iridis.

anisocoria (an-i″so-ko′re-ah). Pupils of unequal diameter; may be physiological, as in antimetropia, or pathological, as in Adie's syndrome or in unilateral Argyll Robertson's pupil.

dynamic a. Unequal pupils during reflex activity; typically pathological.

static a. Unequal pupils during a state of rest; may be physiological or pathological.

anisocycloplegia (an-i″so-si″klo-ple′-je-ah). A term used by Beach for a phenomenon of unequal response to cycloplegics by the two eyes.

anisohypermetropia (an-i″so-hi″per-me-tro′pe-ah). Compound hypermetropic anisometropia.

anisometrope (an-i″so-met′rōp). One who has anisometropia.

anisometropia (an-i″so-me-tro′pe-ah). A condition of unequal refractive state for the two eyes, one eye requiring a different lens correction from the other.

compound astigmatic a. Anisometropia in which both eyes are astigmatic, the degree of astigmatism in one exceeding that of the other. Syn., *anisoastigmatism.*

compound hypermetropic a. Anisometropia in which both eyes are hypermetropic, the degree of hypermetropia of one exceeding that of the other. Syn., *anisohypermetropia.*

compound myopic a. Anisometropia in which both eyes are myopic, the degree of myopia of one exceeding that of the other. Syn., *anisomyopia.*

mixed a. Anisometropia in which one eye is myopic, the other hyperopic, the degree of difference between them being clinically significant. Syn., *antimetropia.*

relative a. Anisometropia in which the total refractive states of each of the two eyes are nearly equal but the components (such as corneal power, axial length, or crystalline lens power) exhibit marked differences.

simple astigmatic a. The presence of astigmatism in one eye but not in the other.

simple hypermetropic a. The presence of hypermetropia in one eye with emmetropia in the other.

simple myopic a. The presence of myopia in one eye with emmetropia in the other.

vertical a. Anisometropia in which there is unequal refraction for the two eyes only in the vertical meridians.

anisometropic (an-i″so-me-trop′ik). Relating to or having anisometropia.

anisomyopia (an-i″so-mi-o′pe-ah). Compound myopic anisometropia.

aniso-oxyopia (an-i″so-ok″se-o′pe-ah). Unequal visual acuity in the two eyes.

anisophoria (an″i-so-fo′re-ah). Heterophoria in which the degree of the phoria varies with the direction of gaze.

essential a. Anisophoria due to paresis or spasm of one or more of the extraocular muscles.

optical a. Anisophoria induced by spectacle correction of anisometropia and caused by the varying prismatic effect as the eyes deviate from the optical axes of the spectacle lenses.

anisopia (an″i-so′pe-ah). Difference of vision of the two eyes.

anisosthenic (an″i-sos-then′ik). Unequal strength of paired muscles.

anisotropic (an″i-so-trop′ik). Doubly refracting; polarizing; birefringent; pertaining to an optical medium in which the index of refraction is not the same for all directions within that medium (not to be confused with inhomogeneous as applied to optical media, for this refers to a difference in index at different points within the medium). An incident ray will be divided within a uniaxial anisotropic medium into two refracted rays: an ordinary ray obeying the usual law of refraction and an extraordinary ray following a different law. A biaxial anisotropic medium produces two extraordinary rays whose wavefronts are more complex than that of the extraordinary ray of the uniaxial medium.

ankyloblepharon (ang″kil-o-blef′ar-on). Partial or total adhesion of the eyelids to each other along their margins. Syn., *blepharocleisis*.

adnatum, a. Congenital ankyloblepharon.

external a. Adhesion of the eyelid margins to each other in the region of the external canthus.

filiforme, a. Ankyloblepharon in which the upper and the lower eyelids are united by filamentous bands.

internal a. Adhesion of the eyelid margins to each other in the region of the internal canthus.

anlage (ahn′lah-geh). 1. The first group of cells which will form any distinct part or organ of the embryo. 2. The embryonic area in which these aggregations of cells first appear.

anneal (ă-nēl′). A regulated process of heating materials (glass and metals) and the subsequent slow, controlled cooling to eliminate strains.

annexa oculi (ă-nek′sah ok′u-li). Adnexa oculi.

annulus ciliaris (an′u-lus sil″e-ar′is). The superficial portion of the ciliary body between the iris and the choroid. Syn., *ciliary ring.*

annulus conjunctivae (an′u-lus konjunk′tih-ve). The dense, raised, limbal conjunctiva where the bulbar conjunctiva approaches the corneoscleral junction. Syn., *conjunctival ring.*

annulus iridis major (an′u-lus i′rid-is ma′jor). A circle composed of anastomosing arteries derived from two long posterior ciliary and seven anterior ciliary arteries, located in the ciliary body about the root of the iris. Syn., *greater arterial circle of the iris; circulus arteriosus iridis major.*

annulus iridis minor (an′u-lus i′rid-is mi′nor). A vascular circle containing both arteries and veins located at the junction of ciliary and pupillary portions of the iris. Branches from the major circle anastomose to form most of the circle. Syn., *lesser arterial circle* of the iris; minor vascular circle; circulus arteriosus iridis minor.

annulus tendineus communis (an'-u-lus ten-din'e-us kom-u'nis). Annulus of Zinn.

annulus tendinosus (an'u-lus ten''-dih-no'sus). 1. A rarely used term for the peripheral rim of Descemet's membrane near the limbus. 2. The annular ligament, a term also rarely used for the scleral spur.

annulus of Zinn (an'u-lus). The common tendon of the rectus group of muscles that, as a fibrous cone, surrounds the optic foramen and a portion of the superior orbital fissure, to the anterior margin of which it is attached at the spina recti lateralis. Syn., *annulus tendineus communis; ligament of Zinn; tendon of Zinn.*

anodynes, ophthalmic (an'o-dīnz). Ocular analgesics.

anomalopia (ă-nom''ah-lo'pe-ah). Anomalous color vision.

anomaloscope (ă-nom'ah-lo-skōp''). An instrument to test the color sense. It usually consists of a viewing tube with a circular bipartite field, one half of which is illuminated with yellow, the other with a mixture of green and red. The yellow half is not variable except for brightness, while the other may be varied continuously from red to green. The color sense is tested by mixing the colors of the variable color field until it subjectively matches the yellow field. A certain combination in the variable field is considered normal, and specific variations indicate the type or the degree of anomalous color vision present.

anomalous (ă-nom'ah-lus). Deviating from the usual; existing in an abnormal location, form, or structure; functioning in an abnormal manner.

anomalous (ă-nom'ah-lus) **retinal correspondence; deuteranopia; dichromatism; projection; trichromatism.** See under the nouns.

anomaly (ă-nom'ah-le). A deviation from the usual or norm.
Axenfeld's a. Axenfeld's syndrome.
Rieger's a. Rieger's disease.

anomia (ă-no'me-ah). Loss of ability to recognize names or to name objects. Syn., *nominal aphasia; dysnomia.*

anomoscope, Brock's (ă-nom'o-skōp). An instrument for differentiating anomalous and normal binocular projection.

anoopsia (an''o-op'se-ah). Hypertropia.

anophoria (an''o-fo're-ah). Anaphoria.

anophthalmia (an''of-thal'me-ah). Absence of an eye or eyes in the newborn, due to failure of development of the optic cup or to disappearance of the eyes after partial development. Most clinical cases actually represent extreme microphthalmia and rudimentary extrinsic muscles usually are present. Syn., *anophthalmos; anophthalmus.*
consecutive a. Anophthalmia resulting from atrophy or degeneration of the optic vesicle subsequent to its initial formation.
cyclopica, a. A condition in which the eye and the orbital contents are imperfectly developed.
primary a. Anophthalmia resulting from suppression of the optic primordium during the differentiation of the optic plate and after the formation of the rudiment of the forebrain. It tends to be bilateral and usually occurs without other deformities.
secondary a. Anophthalmia secondary to complete suppression or grossly abnormal development of the entire anterior portion of the neural tube. It is usually accompanied by numer-

ous other abnormalities and therefore usually occurs in a nonviable monster.

unilateral a. Monophthalmia.

anophthalmos (an″of-thal′mos). Anophthalmia.

anophthalmus (an″of-thal′mus). Anophthalmia.

anopia (an-o′pe-ah). 1. Absence of the eye. 2. A rudimentary condition of the eye.

anopsia (an-op′se-ah). A defect or loss of vision from failure to use the visual capacity; differentiated from *anoopsia.*

    quadrantic a. Lost or reduced vision in a quarter sector of the visual field of one eye. Syn., *quadrantanopsia.*

anopsis (an-op′sis). Blindness.

anorthopia (an″or-tho′pe-ah). 1. A perceptual anomaly in which objects appear distorted, straight lines do not appear straight, etc. 2. Strabismus. *Rare.*

anorthoscope (an-or′tho-skōp). An apparatus for producing a specific illusion, consisting of a distorted picture on a rotating disk which is seen as not distorted when viewed through a second slotted disk rotating at a different speed.

anosognosia (an-o″sog-no′se-ah, an-o″so-). Inability to recognize loss of function, disease, or defect in a part of one's own body.

    visual a. The inability to recognize the partial or total loss of one's own visual acuity, or the partial loss of one's own visual field.

anotropia (an″o-tro′pe-ah). Anatropia.

antagonism. The mutually opposing action between two forces, as in the paired extrinsic muscles of the eye.

antagonist. A muscle having opposite primary action to that of another; an opposing muscle. Ex.: The right medial rectus is the antagonist of the right lateral rectus.

contralateral a. A rarely used term indicating a muscle in the fellow eye which acts as an antagonist to the yoke muscle of the other eye. Ex.: The right superior rectus muscle is the contralateral antagonist of the left superior oblique.

anterior. In man, ventral; nearer to the front; the opposite of *posterior.*

anterior pigment layer of Fuchs. See under *layer*

antimetropia (an″tih-met-ro′pe-ah). Mixed anisometropia.

antimydriatic (an″tih-mid″re-at′ik). An agent or a drug which prevents dilatation of the pupil or reduces dilation.

antinode (an′tih-nōd). That point of a wave motion at which the particles undergo maximum displacement. It is midway between two adjacent nodes.

antirheoscope (an″tih-re′o-skōp.) An apparatus for producing a specific illusion, consisting of a board perpendicular to the line of sight covered with a pattern (usually horizontal stripes) and an endless belt of the same pattern which is seen moving vertically through a window in the board. When the real motion ceases, there is an illusion of movement in the opposite direction (the *waterfall illusion*).

antixerophthalmic (an″tih-ze″rof-thal′mik). Preventive of xerophthalmia, as vitamin A.

Anton's (an′tonz) **symptom; syndrome.** See under the nouns.

antophthalmic (ant″of-thal′mik). Relieving ophthalmia.

antorbital (ant-ōr′bih-tal). Anterior to, or in front of, the orbit.

antrophose (an′tro-fōz). A subjective sensation of light or color originating in the visual centers of the brain.

A.O.A. 1. American Optometric Association. 2. Australian Optometrical Association.

A.O.F. American Optometric Foundation.

A.O.P. Association of Optical Practitioners.

A.O.S. American Ophthalmological Society.

apanastema (a″pan-as′te-mah). A wartlike protuberance on the conjunctiva.

Apert's syndrome (a′pertz). Acrocephalosyndactyly.

apertor oculi (ap′er-tōr ok′u-li). Levator palpebrae superioris muscle.

aperture (ap′er-tūr). An opening or hole which admits light.

angular a. The extreme angle between incident rays traversing an optical system.

effective a. That part of the aperture of a lens actually used by the bundle of rays contributing to the formation of an image.

numerical a. An expression designating the light-gathering power of microscope objectives; the product of the index of refraction of the object space and the sine of the half-angle of the incident cone.

palpebral a. The opening formed by the margins of the eyelids.

relative a. The ratio of the diameter of the entrance pupil to the primary focal length of an optical system; the reciprocal of the f-number. Syn., *aperture ratio.*

aperture-stop. The stop of an optical system which, by virtue of its size and position with respect to the radiating object, is effective in limiting the bundle of light rays traversing the system.

apex. 1. The vertex of an angle, a cone, or a pyramid. 2. The extreme point of any anatomical structure resembling an angle, a cone, or a pyramid; or the extreme point of any anatomical structure being in any respect a spheroid, a conoid, an ellipsoid, or a combination thereof.

corneal a. The point of the cornea which is most anterior when the eye is in a straightforward or primary position.

prism, a. of. 1. The end of a prism at which the two faces intersect. 2. The direction along the base-apex line of a prism opposite the base, or the same direction along the base-apex line as the apparent displacement of the image.

aphacia (ă-fa′se-ah, -she-ah). Aphakia.

aphakia (ă-fa′ke-ah). 1. Absence of the crystalline lens of the eye; due most frequently to surgical removal, occasionally to a perforating wound or ulcer, rarely to a congenital anomaly. 2. Absence of the lens from the pupillary area, as in dislocation or luxation of the lens.

primary a. Congenital absence of the crystalline lens due to failure of development, usually in association with other congenital ocular abnormalities.

secondary a. Congenital absence of the crystalline lens, partial or complete, due to degeneration or extrusion of a previously formed lens. In the case of degeneration, the lens substance may be absorbed, leaving remnants of the capsule and fibrous tissue to form a membranous cataract (*pseudoaphakia*) or it may be invaded by vascularized mesodermal tissue (*pseudophakia*).

aphakic (ă-fa′kik). 1. One who has aphakia. 2. Pertaining to or having aphakia.

aphasia (ă-fa′ze-ah). The inability, because of a disturbance in the cerebral mechanism, (1) to express oneself in speech or in writing, (2) to comprehend either the spoken or the written word, or (3) to do any combination of these.

motor a. The inability to express oneself in speech or in writing.

nominal a. Anomia.

optic a. Alexia.

semantic a. The inability to appreciate or to give an account of the general significance of what is heard or read, although the meaning of individual words or sentences is understood.

sensory a. The inability to comprehend written or spoken words, or gestures, or any combination of these.

visual a. Alexia.

Wernicke's a. Sensory aphasia in which the comprehension of written and spoken words is lost, although articulation is retained.

word a. Alexia.

aphose (ă-fōz', a'fōz, af'ōz). A subjective shadow or dark spot in the visual field.

aphytria retinae (ă-fĭt're-ah ret'ih-ne). A condition in which there is a loss of retinal pigment. *Rare.*

aplanasia (ap"lah-na'ze-ah). Absence of spherical aberration and coma in an optical system. Syn., *aplanatism.*

aplanatic (ap"lah-nat'ik). Pertaining to an optical system free from spherical aberration and coma.

aplanatism (ă-plan'ah-tizm). Aplanasia.

aplasia, retinal (ă-pla'se-ah). See *dysplasia, retinal.*

apochromatic (ap"o-kro-mat'ik). A lens design or condition in which maximum correction has been attained for the spherical aberration of a maximum number of wavelengths.

apodization (ap'o-dih-za"shun). The process of reducing the intensity of, or eliminating the peripheral portions of, a diffraction pattern as may be accomplished by suitably shaped apertures or apertures with nonuniform absorption.

Apollonio lens (ap"ŏ-lo'ne-o). See under *lens.*

aponeurosis (ap"o-nu-ro'sis, a-pon"u-). A tendinous expansion consisting of a fibrous or membranous sheath which serves as a

fascia to enclose or bind a group of muscles, or as a means of attachment for muscles at their origin or insertion.

lid a. Septum orbitale.

orbito-ocularis, a. Tenon's capsule.

apoplexy, corneal (ap'o-plek"se). Migration of blood into the cornea.

apoplexy, retinal. Copious hemorrhage into the retina.

apostilb (ă-post'ilb). A unit of luminance equal to ¹⁄₁₀ millilambert. See also *footlambert.*

apparatus (ap"ah-ra'tus, -rat'us). 1. A system or group of organs, or parts of organs, which collectively perform a common function. 2. A collection of instruments, devices, or implements used for a given work, as an experiment or an operation.

accessory sense a. Those parts of a sense organ, other than the afferent nerve and the receptor cells, which are essential for the functioning of the organ. In the eye, this would include all structures other than the optic nerve and the rods and cones of the retina.

accommodative a. The structures of the eye which are related to accommodation; the ciliary apparatus and the crystalline lens.

ciliary a. The ciliary muscle and processes; the structures other than the crystalline lens which are related to accommodation; the ciliary body.

lacrimal a. The tear-forming and tear-conducting system, composed of lacrimal and accessory lacrimal glands, eyelid margins, conjunctival sac, lacrimal lake, lacrimal puncta, canaliculi or lacrimal ducts, common canaliculus or sinus of Maier, lacrimal sac, nasolacrimal duct, and Hasner's valve at the inferior meatus of the nose.

muscular a. The intraocular and the extraocular musculature of the eye considered collectively. See under *muscle* for the specific muscles involved.

nervous a. The sensory and the motor nerves of the eye and the orbit considered collectively. See under *nerve* for the specific nerves involved.

refractive a. Cornea, aqueous humor, crystalline lens, and vitreous humor considered collectively; the surfaces and the media traversed by light entering the eye and involved in the production of the retinal image.

visual a. The two eyes, their extrinsic muscles and other contents of the orbits, the nerves, the pathways, and the visual cortex, considered collectively. Syn., *visuum.*

apparent height; magnification; magnitude; movement; position; pupil; size; strabismus. See under the nouns.

apparition (ap″ah-rish′un). 1. A supernatural visual manifestation. 2. A visual hallucination.

appearance. 1. The distinctive characteristics or features of an object or an individual as noted by visual observation. 2. The originating of an experience, particularly visual. 3. An incorrect visual or other impression.

appendages of the eye (ăpen′dih-jez). The accessory structures or adnexa of the eye, including the lacrimal apparatus, the conjunctiva, the cilia, the supercilia, the eyelids, and sometimes the extraocular muscles.

apperception (ap″er-sep′shun). The action of past experience upon received sensory stimuli, resulting in individual differences of interpretation of the same sensory stimuli.

applanatio corneae (ap″lah-na′she-o kor′ne-e). A flattened cornea due to degenerative changes.

applanation (ap″lah-na′shun). An abnormal flattening of a convex surface, especially of the cornea or the crystalline lens.

apraxia (a-prak′se-ah, ă-prak′-). The inability to accomplish an intended or purposeful movement, the nature of which is

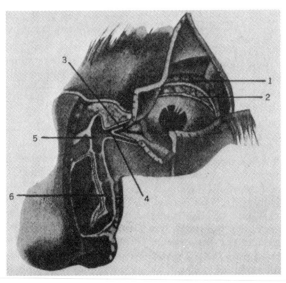

Fig. 3. The lacrimal apparatus. (1) Superior lobe and (2) inferior lobe of lacrimal gland. (3) Superior and (4) inferior canaliculus. (5) Lacrimal sac. (6) Nasolacrimal duct. (From *Text-book of Ophthalmology*, Vol. I, Duke-Elder, Henry Kimpton, 1942)

understood, in the absence of motor paralysis, sensory loss, or ataxia.

constructional a. Apraxia in which there is an inability to arrange objects into a desired pattern or formation.

ocular motor a. Apraxia in which there is an inability to perform intended or purposeful ocular movements.

optical a. Apraxia in which there is an inability to copy or spontaneously draw diagrams or drawings in their proper spatial orientation.

visual a. Optical apraxia.

aprosopia (ap″ro-so′pe-ah). Congenital absence of the eyelids in the newborn, usually occurring with other facial defects.

aqua oculi (ah′kwah, a′kwah ok′u-li). Aqueous humor.

aqueduct of Sylvius. A canal in the midbrain connecting the third and the fourth ventricles and containing cerebrospinal fluid. Syn., *cerebral aqueduct.*

aqueous (a′kwe-us, ak′we-) **chamber; flare; humor.** See under the nouns.

aquocapsulitis (a″kwo-kap″su-li′tis). Serous iritis.

arachnitis, chiasmal (ar″ak-ni′tis). Chiasmal arachnoiditis.

arachnodactylia (ă-rak″no-dak-til′e-ah). Arachnodactyly.

arachnodactyly (ă-rak″no-dak′til-e). 1. A hereditary, familial condition characterized by extreme length and thinness of bones. Syn., *dolichostenomelia; dystrophia mesodermalis congenita hypoplastica.* 2. Marfan's syndrome.

arachnoid (ă-rak′noid). The central, weblike member of the three meninges covering the brain, the spinal cord, and the optic nerve. It is separated from the pia mater by the subarachnoid space, but follows it into all of its folds, and is separated from the dura mater by the subdural space. From the optic nerve it becomes continuous with the sclera.

arachnoiditis, chiasmal (ă-rak″noid-i′tis). A localized inflammation at the base of the brain affecting the chiasma, the optic nerve, and the meninges surrounding them, and leading to a rapid loss of visual acuity and to primary optic nerve atrophy. Syn., *chiasmal arachnitis.*

Arago's spot (ar′ah-gōz). See under *spot.*

A.R.C. Abbreviation for *anomalous retinal correspondence.*

arc. A portion of a curved line, as that of a circle or an ellipse.

blue a's. An entoptic phenomenon elicited by a spot of light stimulating the temporal parafoveal area. The subjective sensation is of two bands of blue light arching from above and below the light toward the blind spot.

centune, a. The angle subtended by 1 cm. of arc whose radius is 1 m. Designated by the symbol ∇. Syn., *centrad.*

contact, a. of. That portion of an extrinsic muscle in actual contact with the surface of the eyeball, continually changing as the eye rotates.

visual reflex a. The complete anatomical pathway from the retinal receptors, including a centripetal pathway to the lower visual centers and to the cortex, the cortex itself, and a centrifugal pathway to the intrinsic and the extrinsic muscles of the eye and to the skeletal muscles of the body. See also *visual reflex.*

arcade. An anatomical structure composed of a series of arches, usually of blood vessels.

arterial a's., marginal. A group of anastomosing arteries at the margins of both the upper and the lower eyelids which supplies the lids and the conjunctiva. Syn., *tarsal arches.*

arterial a's., peripheral. A group of anastomosing arteries in the upper border of the tarsus of the upper eyelid (sometimes present in the lower eyelid), supplying the eyelid and the conjunctiva.

temporal a., superior. The supraorbital arch.

arch. An anatomical structure having a curved or bowlike shape.

orbital a. Supraorbital arch.

Salus' a. An arch in a retinal venule, above or below a sclerosed arteriole, due to deflection from its normal course by the arteriole. Syn., *Salus' sign.*

supraorbital a. The portion of the frontal bone forming the superior margin of the orbit. Syn., *superior temporal arcade; orbital arch; supraorbital margin.*

tarsal a's. Marginal arterial arcades.

Archambault's loop (ahr″shahm-bōz′). Meyer's loop.

arcus (ahr′kus). An arch or an arch-like structure.

arteriosus palpebrae, a. Marginal arterial arcades. *Rare.*

corneae, a. A white ring opacity in the periphery of the cornea due to a lipoid infiltration of the corneal stroma. See also *arcus juvenilis* and *arcus senilis.*

juvenilis, a. A white ring opacity in the periphery of the cornea, occurring in early or middle life, due to a lipoid infiltration of the corneal stroma; distinguished from arcus senilis, which occurs in later life. Syn., *anterior embryotoxon; arcus pre-senilis.*

lipoides, a. Any ring opacity in the periphery of the cornea due to a lipoid infiltration of the stroma, such as *arcus juvenilis* or *arcus senilis.*

marginale, a. A thickening of the periorbita at the orbital margin to which the orbital septum is attached.

marginalis, a. Arcus senilis.

pinguiculus, a. Arcus senilis.

pre-senilis, a. Arcus juvenilis.

senilis, a. A grayish-white ring opacity in the periphery of the cornea, occurring in the aged, due to a lipoid infiltration of the corneal stroma. It is separated from the limbus by a zone of clear cornea (lucid interval of Vogt). Syn., *arcus marginalis; arcus pinguiculus; gerontoxon.*

senilis lentis, a. A white ring opacity near the equator of the crystalline lens which sometimes occurs in the aged.

superciliaris, a. The superciliary ridge or arch on the frontal bone above the orbit. Syn., *supraorbital ridge.*

tarseus, a. Marginal arterial arcade.

Arcway (ahrk′wa). A trade name for a rimless spectacle mounting similar to the Numont.

area. 1. A limited space or extent of surface; a region. 2. A portion of the brain or the retina regarded as having a particular function.

anomalous associated a. In a strabismic with anomalous retinal correspondence, the peripheral retinal area in the one eye which corresponds in visual direction with the fovea of the other eye.

attraction to fusion, a. of. The area in a graphical representation of retinal disparity within which adequate or inadequate fusional movements of the eyes can be elicited in response to a given pair of disparate retinal stimuli; considered by some to bear a relationship to Panum's area and to stereopsis.

B17, a. Brodmann's area 17.

B18, a. Brodmann's area 18.

B19, a. Brodmann's area 19.

Brodmann's a's. Specific histological areas of the cerebral cortex located by Brodmann and numbered from 1 to over 44. Neurologists have found functional significance for each of these areas. Others, such as Vogt and von Economo, also numbered cortical areas, but they do not correspond to Brodmann's.

Brodmann's a. 3, 1, 2. The somesthetic or general sensory receptive area located in the parietal cortex, just posterior to the fissure of Rolando, and extending from the longitudinal sulcus to the Sylvian fissure.

Brodmann's a. 6, alpha. The region of the cerebral cortex used for voluntary mass movements of skeletal muscles, located between areas 4 and 8 in the posterior part of the frontal lobe. Also called the *precentral motor cortex* or *area 6*.

Brodmann's a. 6, alpha beta. The region of the cerebral cortex that controls the rotation of the head, the trunk, and the eyes to the opposite side, located in the posterior part of the frontal lobe, superior to the frontal eye fields in the superior frontal gyrus. Syn., *frontal adversive field*.

Brodmann's a. 8, alpha beta delta. The region of the cerebral cortex that controls voluntary conjugate movements of the eyes and affects the eyelids, the pupils, and the lacrimal glands; the frontal eye fields located in the posterior portion of both middle frontal convolutions in the premotor cortex. Also called *area 8, alpha beta*.

Brodmann's a. 8, gamma. The region of the cerebral cortex that affects the opening and the closing of the eyelids and inhibits mastication activity initiated by the motor cortex in the precentral gyrus, located in the posterior portion of the inferior gyrus, inferior to the frontal eye fields.

Brodmann's a. 17. The area striata on either side of the calcarine fissure, in the occipital lobe of each cerebral cortex.

Brodmann's a. 18. The parastriate area; the visual association area closely surrounding the area striata and located in the cuneus and the lingual gyrus of each occipital lobe.

Brodmann's a. 19. The peristriate area; the visual association area immediately surrounding the parastriate area in each occipital lobe.

caeca, a. Blind spot of Marriotte.

calcarine a. Brodmann's area 17 in the occipital lobe in and about the calcarine fissure. Syn., *area striata*.

centralis, a. 1. The portion of the retina with the greatest number of visual cells per unit area and with a more restricted hookup with ganglion cells. It is located just temporal to the optic disk, is about 6 mm. in diameter, and, according to Polyak, includes the fovea centralis and the parafoveal and the perifoveal regions. 2. The portion of the retina called the *macula lutea*, which contains a yellow pigment and has a diameter of about 5 mm.; the retina minus the periphery and the optic disk. 3. According to Chievitz, the region of the retina characterized by the fibers of Henle in the external molecular layer and by a rich number of ganglion cells. This roughly agrees with Polyak. (Until some compromises are made, a general disagreement exists as to size and restrictions of its included parts.)

comfort, a. of. Percival's term for the middle third of the range of relative convergence. For example, if, for a fixation distance of 40 cm., the base-out limit of relative convergence is 15 prism diopters and the base-in limit is 15 prism diopters, the total range is 30 prism diopters. The area of comfort then extends from 5 prism diopters base-out to 5 prism diopters base-in. If the convergence stimulus or demand falls within this range, comfort in convergence performance can be anticipated.

cone-pure a. Rod-free area.

confusion, a. of. An area of the visual field specified with reference to one eye, occurring especially in strabismus, in which objects are inaccurately or improperly localized.

critical definition, a. of. 1. The central portion of the visual field in which objects appear clearly defined. 2. That portion of any optical image in which detail is clearly defined.

dangerous a. The ciliary region of the eye, so called because the most serious results may follow injury to this area.

eight alpha beta delta, a. See *Brodmann's area 8, alpha beta delta.*

eight gamma, a. See *Brodmann's area 8, gamma.*

eye a. The frontal eye fields in the frontal lobes; the midportion of area 8 for voluntary conjugate movements of the eyes.

fusion a. Panum's area.

light a. 1. The entire illuminated area of the retinal image, whether of liminal or subliminal value. 2. The portion of the pupil illuminated by the retinoscopic reflex.

macular a. That portion of the retina containing a yellow pigment and including the rod-free area. Roughly, the portion of the retina that is used for central vision and that appears free of visible vessels when viewed with an ophthalmoscope. It is the part that contains Henle's oblique fibers.

Martegiani, a. of. The slightly dilated, posterior segment of the hyaloid canal in the vitreous humor at the optic disk.

mirror a. The reflecting surface of the crystalline lens and the cornea when viewed with the slit lamp.

opticomotor a. Portions of the cerebral cortex which affect the movements of the eyeballs. The voluntary opticomotor area is the frontal eye field located in each frontal cortex in the back of the middle frontal convolution. Also called *Brodmann's area 8, alpha beta delta.* The involuntary opticomotor area is the occipital eye field located in each occipital cortex, possibly in the peristriate or the parastriate area.

Panum's a. An area in the retina of one eye, any point of which, when stimulated simultaneously with a single specific point in the retina of the other eye, will give rise to a single fused percept. Syn., *fusion area; corresponding retinal area.*

parastriate a. Brodmann's area 18, a visual association area in each occipital lobe.

peristriate a. Brodmann's area 19, a visual association area surrounding area 18 in each occipital lobe.

psycho-optic a. Brodmann's areas 18 and 19 in each occipital lobe. Syn., *visual association areas.*

retinal a's., corresponding. 1. A pair of areas, one in each retina, which, when stimulated, gives rise to a percept of common visual direction. 2. Panum's areas.

rod-free a. The central portion of the fovea centralis, about 0.25 mm. to 0.5 mm. in diameter, containing only cone cells. Syn., *cone-pure area.*

sensitivity, a. of. That portion of the retinal image in which the intensity of illumination attains liminal or supraliminal value.

six alpha, a. Brodmann's area 6, alpha.

six alpha beta, a. Brodmann's area 6, alpha beta.

striata, a. Brodmann's area 17 in each occipital lobe, identified by the presence of the line of Gennari. Syn., *calcarine area; visual area; visual projection area; visuosensory area.*

suppression a. An area in the binocular field of vision in which the ocular image from one eye is not perceived in consciousness. This can be plotted in stereocampimetry and designated as a scotoma of one eye for a certain size target, when binocular vision is stimulated. The scotoma must be shown to be absent when the field of either eye is plotted separately.

three, one, two, a. Brodmann's area 3, 1, 2.

visual a. 1. Striate area. 2. Loosely, all parts of the occipital lobe and the angular gyrus related to visual function.

visual association a's. The parastriate and the peristriate areas, respectively numbered Brodmann's areas 18 and 19, in the occipital lobes that assist in interpreting the impulses received by area 17, the visual area. Syn., *psycho-optic areas; visuopsychic areas.*

visual projection a. Striate area.

visuopsychic a's. Visual association areas.

visuosensory a. Striate area.

Vogt's a. 8. A strip of cortex anterior to the precentral gyrus in the frontal lobe, containing in its central portion the frontal eye fields for voluntary conjugate eye movements. It also has suppressor action.

areola (ă-re'o-lah). 1. The part of the iris surrounding the pupil of the eye. 2. Any interstice or minute space in a tissue.

argamblyopia (ahr-gam″ble-o'pe-ah, ahr″gam-). Amblyopia ex anopsia.

argema (ahr'je-mah). A white ulcer of the cornea.

Argyll Robertson's (ahr'gĭl rob'ertsonz) **pupil; reflex; sign.** See under the nouns.

argyrosis oculi (ahr″jir-o'sis ok'u-li). Dusky gray or bluish pigmentation of the conjunctival and the corneal tissues, caused by granular deposition of silver from the prolonged use of preparations containing silver compounds.

arithmetic mean. See under *mean.*

Arlt's (ahrltz) **line; sinus; theory; trachoma.** See under the nouns.

arm, guard. That part or extension of a spectacle frame or mounting that connects the guard to the bridge or the front. Syn., *pad arm.*

arm, lens. A portion of a rimless or semirimless mounting, extending along the back upper edge of the lens from the endpiece to the strap.

arm, pad. Guard arm.

Armorlite (arm'or-līt). A trade name for hard resin lenses, made by casting pure, thermoset allyl diglycol carbonate.

Arneson Korector (ahrn'eh-sun). See under *Korector.*

Arnold's (ahr'nuldz) **fold; foramen; notch.** See under the nouns.

Arnold-Chiari syndrome (arn'ōld-ke-ar'e). See under *syndrome.*

Arroyo's sign (ar-roi'yōz). See under *sign.*

Arruga's implant (ă-ru'gaz). See under *implant.*

arteriolosclerosis (ahr-te″re-o″lo-skle-ro'sis). Thickening and loss of elasticity and contractility of the walls of arterioles, as manifested in the branches of the central retinal artery by increased tortuosity, a copper wire reflex, and A-V crossing defects.

arteriosclerosis (ahr-te″re-o-skle-ro'-sis). Thickening and loss of elasticity and contractility of the wall of an artery. A fibrous overgrowth, mainly of the inner coat of an artery, and degenerative change of the middle coat, usually associated with old age.

arteritis, brachycephalic (ar″teh-ri'-tis). Pulseless disease.

arteritis, temporal (ar″teh-ri'tis). A self-limiting disease of undetermined etiology occurring after the age of 50, in which there is widespread inflammation of the arteries, particularly the temporal arteries. Symptoms include malaise, fever, weight loss, severe headache, tinnitus, deafness, arthralgia, myalgia, and neuralgia. Vision may be mildly or severely impaired as a result of occlusion of the central retinal artery or one of its branches, and other ocular symptoms include ischemic papilledema or retrobulbar neuritis, ophthalmoplegia, pain behind the eye, and retinal hemorrhage.

artery (ahr'ter-e). A tubular vessel which conveys blood from the heart to the various parts of the body. Typically, its wall is composed of an outer fibrous and elastic coat (tunica adventitia), a middle muscular coat (tunica media), and an inner coat (tunica intima) of fibrous and elastic tissue lined with endothelium.

angular a. The terminal branch of the external maxillary artery located between the nose and the eye or the cheek, supplying eyelids, lacrimal sac, orbicularis oculi, and neighboring skin.

annular a. Annular vessel.

basilar a. A vessel formed by the union of paired vertebral arteries located on the ventral surface of the pons. Its terminal branches, the posterior cerebral arteries, enter the arterial circle of Willis.

calcarine a. A branch of the posterior cerebral artery found within the calcarine fissure. It supplies the optic radiations and the visual cortex together with the middle cerebral artery with which it forms an important anastomosis to allow for sparing of the macula from circulatory disturbances to the visual cortex.

carotid a., internal. An important branch of the common carotid artery that travels through the cavernous sinus. After giving rise

to the ophthalmic artery, it terminates in the anterior and the middle cerebral arteries.

central a. of optic nerve. A branch of the central retinal artery originating in the optic nerve and giving rise to an anterior branch which accompanies the central retinal artery and a posterior branch which is recurrent.

central retinal a. A direct or indirect branch of the ophthalmic artery which courses below the optic nerve, entering the center of the nerve and supplying it. In the vicinity of the optic disk it divides into superior and inferior branches, the nasal and the temporal branches of which course in the nerve fiber layer to supply capillaries feeding the bipolar and the ganglion cell layers of the retina. Except for a tiny anastomosis with the circle of Zinn or Haller, it is an end artery.

central retinal a's., collateral. Branches of the central retinal artery which originate within the optic nerve.

cerebral a., anterior. The terminal branch of the internal carotid artery distributed to cerebral hemispheres and basal ganglia. The left and the right arteries are connected by an anterior communicating artery to help form a portion of the arterial circle of Willis.

cerebral a., middle. A terminal branch of the internal carotid artery which supplies the lateral portion of the cortex, the optic chiasm, the optic tract, and the optic radiations. The macular portion of the visual cortex is supplied by it and the calcarine artery, the macula often being spared due to this double blood supply.

cerebral a's., posterior. Terminal branches of the basilar artery which, by the posterior communicating artery, connect with the internal carotid arteries, forming part of the circle of Willis. They supply parts of the forebrain and the midbrain, and the calcarine branch supplies the posterior portion of the visual pathway.

chiasmal a., central. A median branch of the anterior communicating artery that, together with the prechiasmal plexus from the anterior cerebral arteries, supplies the anterior optic chiasm.

chiasmal a., inferior. A medial branch of the internal carotid artery which supplies the inferior, lateral portion of the optic chiasm. Syn., *lateral chiasmal artery.*

chiasmal a., lateral. Inferior chiasmal artery.

chiasmal a., superior. A branch of the anterior cerebral artery which supplies the superior, anterior portion of the optic chiasm.

choroidal a., anterior. A branch of the internal carotid artery supplying the basal ganglia, the choroid plexus of the lateral ventricle, the lateral geniculate body, the chiasm, the optic tract, and the optic radiations.

choroidal a., posterior. A branch of the posterior cerebral artery to the choroid plexus of the third ventricle.

choroidal a., recurrent. Any of over a dozen branches of the major arterial circle of the iris, the anterior ciliary arteries, and the long posterior ciliary arteries, which supply the choriocapillaris from the ora serrata to the equator of the eye.

ciliary a's., anterior. Seven branches of the muscular arteries of the rectus muscles. They help form the major arterial circle of the iris, give off anterior conjunctival and episcleral arteries, and enter the eyeball at the anterior scleral apertures.

ciliary a., common. The embryological branch of the internal ophthalmic artery of an 18 mm. embryo.

ciliary a., nasal. An artery in an 18 mm. embryo which anastomoses with the common ciliary and helps form the nasal of the two long posterior ciliary arteries in the developed eye.

ciliary a's., posterior. Branches of the ophthalmic artery which yield the long and the short posterior ciliary arteries.

ciliary a's., posterior (long). Typically, two branches of the posterior ciliary artery or the ophthalmic artery which pierce the posterior sclera and course in the perichoroidal space. They supply the ciliary body and help form the major arterial circle of the iris.

ciliary a's., posterior (short). Approximately 12 branches of the two posterior ciliary arteries or of the ophthalmic artery which pierce the posterior sclera to supply the choriocapillaris, the optic disk, the circle of Zinn (Haller), the cilioretinal artery, and the episcleral artery.

ciliary a., temporal. An artery in an 18 mm. embryo which becomes the temporal of the two long posterior ciliary arteries in the developed eye.

cilioretinal a. A branch of the circle of Zinn or Haller around the optic nerve, posterior to the optic disk. It leaves the temporal side of the disk and supplies the bipolar and the ganglion cells between the macula and the disk. With this artery, cessation of circulation in the central retinal capillaries does not affect central vision. Roughly one fifth, or less, of human eyes possess one.

communicating a., anterior. An anterior unpaired artery of the circle of Willis that connects the anterior cerebral arteries and gives rise to the central chiasmal artery.

communicating a., posterior. A part of the circle of Willis that connects the internal carotid artery with the posterior cerebral artery of the same side.

conjunctival a's., anterior. Branches of the anterior ciliary artery or episcleral branch which supply the bulbar conjunctiva in the limbal area and do not move with the conjunctiva. They are involved in ciliary injection.

conjunctival a's., posterior. Ascending branches of the peripheral or marginal arcades formed by the palpebral artery. At the fornix they become the posterior conjunctival arteries of the bulbar conjunctiva.

copper wire a. A retinal artery exhibiting an increased brightness of the reflex, such that it resembles copper wire; a sign of sclerosis. Cf. *silver wire artery.*

episcleral a's. Branches of the anterior ciliary and the short posterior ciliary arteries which supply the outer layer of the sclera.

ethmoidal a., anterior. A branch of the ophthalmic artery that leaves the orbit through the anterior ethmoidal foramen to supply the ethmoidal air cells, the nasal cavity, the skin of the nose, and the frontal sinus.

ethmoidal a., posterior. A branch of the ophthalmic artery that leaves the orbit by the posterior ethmoidal foramen to supply the ethmoidal air cells, the dura mater, and the upper nasal cavity.

frontal a. The terminal branch of the ophthalmic artery which supplies the skin, the muscles, and the pericranium of the forehead.

Heubner's a. The recurrent branch of the anterior cerebral artery which supplies the anterior limb of the internal capsule. When obstructed, the frontopontine

tract degenerates and, rarely, the contralateral eyebrow cannot be lowered (frontal muscle) and the eyelids cannot be completely closed for a few days. Contralateral paralyses occur in the face below the eye, in the tongue, and in the arm.

hyaloid a. The fetal branch of the ophthalmic artery which divides in the vitreous humor and supplies the crystalline lens. It buds off retinal arteries, then degenerates down to this point, becoming the central retinal artery.

hyaloid a., persistent. Portions of the hyaloid artery which fail to fully degenerate and which remain in the vitreous, posterior to the crystalline lens or anterior to the optic disk.

hypophysial a., anterior superior. A branch of the internal carotid artery that supplies the inferior, posterior portion of the optic chiasm.

infraorbital a. A branch of the internal maxillary artery which enters the orbit through the inferior orbital fissure and leaves via the infraorbital canal. It supplies the inferior extrinsic muscles, the orbicularis oculi, the lacrimal sac, the maxillary sinus, and the upper teeth.

lacrimal a. A branch of the ophthalmic artery which supplies the lacrimal gland, the superior and the lateral rectus muscles, the eyelids, and the conjunctiva, and gives origin to the lateral palpebral arteries.

lenticulo-optic a. A branch of the middle cerebral artery which supplies the internal capsule, especially its posterior limb; when involved in cerebral hemorrhage, the resulting symptoms are the same as those from hemorrhage of the lenticulo-striate arteries.

lenticulo-striate a's. Branches of the middle cerebral artery which supply the internal capsule, especially its posterior limb, commonly involved in cerebral hemorrhage. If extensive, and the optic radiations become affected, the hemorrhage leads to contralateral homonymous hemianopsia, generally with partial recovery. Other symptoms are a transient deviation of the eyes to the ipsilateral side, contralateral weakness of the frontal and the orbicularis oculi muscles, and contralateral paralysis of the lower face, the tongue, the arm, and the leg.

macular a's. Branches of the temporal arteries of the central retinal system, or of a cilioretinal artery when present, which supply the macula lutea.

meningeal a., anterior. A recurrent branch of the ophthalmic artery that leaves the orbit through the superior orbital fissure to enter the middle cranial fossa.

meningeal a., middle. A branch of the internal maxillary artery which supplies the dura mater, V and VII cranial nerves, and, by orbital branches through the superior orbital fissure, anastomoses with the lacrimal or other branches of the ophthalmic artery.

meningeal a., recurrent. A branch of the lacrimal artery which leaves the orbit through the superior orbital fissure to anastomose with the middle meningeal artery. Rarely, it supplies the orbital branches that ordinarily come from the ophthalmic artery.

muscular a. 1. An artery to a skeletal muscle. 2. Muscular branches of the ophthalmic, the lacrimal, and the infraorbital arteries, and others which supply the extrinsic eye muscles.

nasal a. A terminal branch of the ophthalmic artery which supplies the side of the nose and anasto-

moses with the angular artery. Syn., *dorsalis nasi.*

nasofrontal a. That portion of the ophthalmic artery which gives rise to the two ethmoidal arteries and a few muscular branches and terminates by dividing into the frontal and the nasal arteries. *Obs.*

oculonuclear a. A small artery between the posterior cerebral and superior cerebellar arteries which helps supply the midbrain and pons in the region of the III, IV, and VI motor nuclei.

ophthalmic a. A branch of the internal carotid artery which enters the orbit through the optic canal. Typically, its branches are: central retinal, posterior ciliaries, lacrimal, recurrents, muscular, supraorbital, posterior and anterior ethmoidals, and medial palpebrals. It terminates by forming the nasal and the frontal arteries and supplies all the tunics of the eyeball, most of the structures in the orbit, the lacrimal sac, the paranasal sinuses, the dura mater, and the nose.

ophthalmic a., internal. An artery of a 16 mm. embryo which gives origin to the hyaloid, the common ciliary, and the nasal ciliary arteries.

ophthalmic a., primitive dorsal. A branch of the primitive internal carotid artery, appearing in the embryo at the 9 mm. stage, which, through its branches, is the principal blood supply to the developing eye.

ophthalmic a., primitive ventral. A branch of the primitive internal carotid artery, appearing in the embryo at about the 12 mm. stage, which supplies the ventral and medial portions of the plexus around the optic cup.

optic a., deep. A branch of the middle cerebral artery to the optic and the auditory radiations *opticociliary a.* An infrequent branch of the central retinal artery (or one of its branches in the region of the optic disk) that dips into the choroid. Syn., *retinociliary artery.*

palpebral a's., lateral. Superior and inferior branches of the lacrimal artery which anastomose with the medial palpebral arteries to supply the eyelids and the conjunctiva.

palpebral a's., medial. Superior and inferior branches of the ophthalmic artery which, with the lateral palpebral arteries, form the marginal and the peripheral (arterial) arcades and supply the eyelids, the conjunctiva, and the lacrimal sac.

prechiasmal a. A branch of the ophthalmic artery that supplies the region of the junction of the optic nerve with the optic chiasm.

recurrent a. An artery which turns back and runs in the opposite direction from its origin. The ophthalmic and the lacrimal arteries and the vessels that form the major arterial circle have such recurrents.

recurrent choroidal a. See *choroidal artery, recurrent.*

recurrent meningeal a. See *meningeal artery, recurrent.*

retinal a., central. A direct or indirect branch of the ophthalmic artery which courses below the optic nerve, entering the center of the nerve and supplying it. In the vicinity of the optic disk it divides into superior and inferior branches, the nasal and the temporal branches of which course in the nerve fiber layer to supply capillaries feeding the bipolar and the ganglion cell layers of the retina. Except for a tiny anastomosis with the circle of Zinn or Haller, it is an end artery.

retinociliary a. Opticociliary artery.

silver wire a. A retinal artery in which the whole thickness appears as a bright white reflex like a silver wire, a late sign of sclerosis. Cf. *copper wire artery.*

stapedial a. An artery arising from the primitive internal carotid artery which supplies the orbital tissues of the embryonic eye through its supraorbital division. In the 20 mm. embryo this division forms an anastomosis with the ophthalmic artery which eventually takes over its function.

striate a., lateral. A branch of the middle cerebral artery, superficial to the lentiform nucleus in the forebrain. It is a common site of cerebral hemorrhage.

striate a., medial. A branch of the middle cerebral artery which supplies the caudate and the lentiform nuclei of the forebrain.

supraorbital a. A branch of the ophthalmic artery to the levator muscle of the upper eyelid and the frontal bone, which, after leaving the orbit by the supraorbital notch (foramen), supplies the upper eyelid and the scalp.

Zinn's central a. Central retinal artery.

artiphakia (ar″tih-fa′ke-ah). The condition of an eye into which an artificial lens has been placed, following removal of the crystalline lens, in an attempt to duplicate a normal refractive state.

artiphakic (ar″tih-fa′kik). 1. One who has artiphakia. 2. Pertaining to or having artiphakia.

Arundel glass (ar′un-del). See under *glass.*

as. Abbreviation for *astigmatism.*

Ascher's (ash′erz) **outlets; glass rod phenomenon; syndrome.** See under the nouns.

Aschner's (ash′nerz) **phenomenon; reflex; sign.** See under the nouns.

A.S.C.O. Association of Schools and Colleges of Optometry.

asemasia (as"e-ma'ze-ah). Asemia.

asemia (ă-se'me-ah). Aphasia in which there is an inability to employ or understand writing, speech, or gestures as a means of communication. Syn., *asemasia; asymbolia; asymboly.*

Asher-Law stereoscope (ash'er-law'). See under *stereoscope.*

aspergillosis (as-per"jil-o'sis, as"-per-). An infectious disease caused by the *Aspergillus* fungus. In the eye, it is characterized by the development of a necrotic corneal ulcer, surrounded by a yellow line of demarcation, which results in an iridocyclitis and accompanying hypopyon. Orbital involvement is rare and is probably secondary to infection of the accessory nasal sinuses.

aspheric (a-sfer'ik). Not spherical.

aspherize (a'sfer-ize). A hand-polishing process by which various zones of one or both lens surfaces are given different curvatures to reduce spherical aberration.

assimilation. According to the Hering theory of color vision, the re-formation of the three primary substances in the retina by green, blue, and black; the reverse of *dissimilation.*

color a. The perceptual process by which a gray appears to be tinted by the color bordering it, as when a gray bordered by yellow appears to be a yellowish-gray, or the perceptual process by which the perceived saturation of a chromatic color is influenced positively by an achromatic border, as when a red appears to be a darker red when surrounded by black and a lighter red when surrounded by white.

association, corrective. A procedure advocated by the Optometric Extension Program to determine acceptable lens corrections for distance and near vision. The basic distance correction (No. 7) is determined by standard methods. The basic near correction is determined by the dynamic cross cylinder (14a or 14b) after a deduction (lag) depending on the phoria (15a or 15b) and the amplitude of accommodation (19). This basic near correction is called the *near net.* If either, or both, of the basic distance and the near net corrections indicates the use of convex lenses, comparisons of the ductions (break and recovery) of tests 10, 11, 16b, and 17b determine whether this convex lens power should be prescribed in full or reduced. The reduction may be from the basic distance correction only or from both distance and near. The amount of the reduction cannot be greater than 0.75 D. for each and is decided by a comparison of the blur points (16a, 17a, 20, and 21). The amount of reduction should modify these blur points so that their amounts will be closer to the published norms ("expecteds"), but should not reverse their relative values as compared to those obtained through the basic corrections. At no time should the final distance correction be more convex than the final near correction, although they may be equal.

Association for Research in Ophthalmology. A national society, organized in 1939, which admits to membership those with, or without, medical degrees who are interested mainly in ophthalmological research.

Association of Dispensing Opticians. A British organization which examines and issues diplomas of fellowship to qualified dispensing opticians.

Association of Optical Practitioners. A British association of ophthalmic opticians (optometrists) founded in 1946 to replace two older organizations, the Institute of Ophthalmic Opticians and the Joint Council of Qualified Opticians.

Association of Schools and Colleges of Optometry. An organization, founded in 1941, of the institutions teaching optometry in the United States and Canada, for the purpose of advancing the profession of optometry through development of its educational system.

ast. Abbreviation for *astigmatism.*

astaxanthin (as"tah-zan'thin). A derivative of β carotene present in the integument of lower animals and Euglena which makes phototactic responses possible.

asteroid hyalitis (as'ter-oid hi"ah-li'tis). Snowball-like bodies of calcium soaps occurring in a structurally intact vitreous body as an uncommon senile change. The condition is more frequent in males and is usually unilateral. These bodies do not signify inflammation, as "itis" would imply. It is often confused with the similar picture of synchysis scintillans, signifying degenerative changes which show numerous freely floating crystals of cholesterol in a fluid vitreous. Syn., *Benson's disease.*

asth. Abbreviation for *asthenopia.*

asthenocoria (as-then"o-ko're-ah, as'-the-no-). A condition in which the light reflex of the pupil is sluggish.

asthenope (as'then-ōp). One having asthenopia.

asthenopia (as"the-no'pe-ah). A term generally used to designate any subjective symptoms or distress arising from use of the eyes; eyestrain.

accommodative a. Asthenopia arising from the use of accommodation, as in uncorrected hypermetropia or low accommodative amplitude.

accommodative-convergence a. Asthenopia attributed to a high or low accommodative-convergence to accommodation ratio.

aniseikonic a. Asthenopia attributed to uncorrected aniseikonia.

anisometropic a. Asthenopia attributed to anisometropia.

aphakic a. Asthenopia attributed to aphakia, especially monocular aphakia.

astigmatic a. Asthenopia attributed to astigmatism.

cephalalgica, a. Asthenopia associated with headache.

cyclophoric a. Asthenopia attributed to cyclophoria.

dolens, a. Asthenopia associated with ocular pain.

heterophoric a. Asthenopia attributed to heterophoria.

hyperphoric a. Asthenopia attributed to hyperphoria.

hysterical a. Asthenopia associated with psychosis or neurosis.

integrative a. Asthenopia due to fusion difficulties, as in aniseikonia or anisometropia.

irritans, a. Asthenopia associated with ocular inflammation and irritation.

motor a. Asthenopia attributed to excessive lateral phoria, cyclophoria, hyperphoria, or deficiency of fusional reserve. Syn., *muscular asthenopia.*

muscular a. Motor asthenopia.

nervous a. 1. Hysterical asthenopia. 2. Asthenopia due to actual organic nervous disease.

neurasthenic a. 1. Asthenopia due to neurasthenia following a debilitating disease. 2. Hysterical asthenopia.

photogenous a. Asthenopia resulting from improper illumination.

presbyopic a. Asthenopia attributed to the low amplitude of accommodation in uncorrected presbyopia. See also *accommodative asthenopia.*

reflection a. Asthenopia attributed

to reflections from the surfaces of ophthalmic lenses.

reflex a. Asthenopia in which the exciting cause is remote from the eyes, as in sinusitis.

retinal a. Asthenopia attributed to actual fatigue or exhaustion of the nervous elements of the eyes.

tarsal a. Asthenopia attributed to pressure of the eyelids on the cornea.

asthenopic (as″the-nop′ik). Relating to, or suffering from, asthenopia.

astigmagraph (ă-stig′mah-graf). An instrument for showing or recording the astigmatism of an eye.

astigmatic (as″tig-mat′ik). Affected with, or pertaining to, astigmatism.

astigmatic chart; dial; interval. See under the nouns.

astigmatism (ă-stig′mah-tizm). A condition of refraction in which rays emanating from a single luminous point are not focused at a single point by an optical system, but instead are focused as two line images at different distances from the system, generally at right angles to each other. In the eye, a refractive anomaly due to unequal refraction of the incident light by the dioptric system, in different meridians. It is generally caused by a toroidal anterior surface of the cornea or, of less degree, by other ocular refracting surfaces or by the obliquity of incidence of the light entering the cornea or the crystalline lens.

accommodative a. Astigmatism induced by the act of the ciliary muscle in accommodation which causes either unequal curvatures of the surfaces of the crystalline lens or a tilt of the crystalline lens; changes in amount of astigmatism associated with changes in accommodation, exclusive of apparent changes in astigmatism due to meridional differences in optical effectivity.

acquired a. Astigmatism which appears after birth as a result of disease or injury, or of normal physiological changes.

against the rule a. Astigmatism in which the meridian of greatest refractive power of the eye is in, or within 30° of, the horizontal. Syn., *indirect astigmatism; inverse astigmatism; perverse astigmatism.*

asymmetrical a. Astigmatism in which the two weakest or the two strongest meridians of both eyes do not total 180° upon addition of their meridional locations. The meridians of greatest, or weakest, power in the two eyes are not located as mirror images of each other with respect to the midline.

bi-oblique a. Astigmatism in which the two principal meridians are not at right angles to each other.

complex a. Astigmatism present in both the cornea and the crystalline lens.

compound a. Astigmatism in which the two principal meridians of an eye are both either hypermetropic or myopic.

    compound hypermetropic a. Astigmatism in which the two principal meridians of an eye are both hypermetropic.

    compound myopic a. Astigmatism in which the two principal meridians of an eye are both myopic.

congenital a. Astigmatism present at birth.

corneal a. Astigmatism due to toroidal curvature of the cornea.

curvature a. Astigmatism due to unequal curvature in the two principal meridians of any surface of refraction.

direct a. With the rule astigmatism.

due to obliquity of the visual axis, a. Astigmatism induced by lack of coincidence of the optical axis of the eye and the foveal chief ray. Incident light therefore strikes the refracting surface obliquely and radial astigmatism results.

dynamic a. Astigmatism which becomes manifest during accommodation. See also *accommodative astigmatism*.

facultative a. Astigmatism attributed to the differential flattening of the cornea by the pull of the extrinsic ocular muscles.

heterologous a. Against the rule astigmatism with the corresponding cylinder axes in the two eyes symmetrical with each other.

heteronymous a. Astigmatism with the meridian of greatest power nearer the horizontal in one eye and with the meridian of greatest power nearer the vertical in the other eye.

homologous a. With the rule astigmatism with the corresponding cylinder axes in the two eyes symmetrical with each other.

homonymous a. Astigmatism in which the meridians of greatest power in the two eyes are within 30° of being parallel.

hypermetropic a. Astigmatism in which one principal meridian is hypermetropic and the other emmetropic, or in which both principal meridians are hypermetropic.

imbedded a. Optometric Extension Program: Astigmatism characterized by consistent and repeatable measurability and said to be "structured" or "fixed."

incidence a. Astigmatism caused by incident rays not being normal to a refracting surface. Cf. *radial astigmatism*.

index a. Lenticular astigmatism due to variation in the index of refraction in different areas of the crystalline lens.

indirect a. Against the rule astigmatism.

inverse a. Against the rule astigmatism.

irregular a. 1. Astigmatism in which the two principal meridians of the eye are not at right angles to each other. 2. Variations in refraction in a single meridian of the eye.

irregular a., abnormal. Irregular astigmatism due to abnormalities of the cornea caused by injury or disease.

irregular a., normal. Irregular astigmatism due to irregularities in the refracting power of the different sectors of the crystalline lens.

latent a. Astigmatism which is hidden or masked by the use of accommodation.

lenticular a. Astigmatism of the crystalline lens due to variations of curvature or to inequalities of refractive index.

lenticular a., dynamic. Dynamic astigmatism.

lenticular a., static. Lenticular astigmatism present when accommodation is not active.

manifest a. Astigmatism which can be measured in refraction.

marginal a. Radial astigmatism.

mixed a. Astigmatism in which one principal meridian is hypermetropic and the other myopic.

myopic a. Astigmatism in which one principal meridian is myopic and the other emmetropic, or in which both principal meridians are myopic.

near a. Accommodative astigmatism.

neutral a. An astigmatic refractive error having a mean spherical equivalent value of zero, such as that which would be produced artificially by placing a crossed cylinder lens before an emmetropic eye.

nonembedded a. Optometric Extension Program: Astigmatism which is characterized by lack of consistency and repeatability in its measurement and which varies in axis and power in different or repeated tests and which is said to be in process of becoming "imbedded."

nonneutral a. An astigmatic refractive error having a mean spherical equivalent value other than zero.

normal a. Physiological astigmatism.

oblique a. 1. Astigmatism in which the two principal meridians of an eye are oblique with respect to the horizontal or the vertical; nominally, between 30° to 60°, and 120° to 150°, on the spectacle axis scale. 2. Radial astigmatism.

pathological a. Astigmatism induced by a disease process, such as corneal disease, lenticular sclerosis, etc.

perverse a. Against the rule astigmatism.

physiological a. 1. Astigmatism of approximately 0.50 D. found in the normal eye when the cornea is spherical, or when the corneal astigmatism is neutralized, as with a contact lens. 2. The small amount of corneal astigmatism, usually up to 1.50 D., found frequently, as contrasted to pathological astigmatism, usually of greater magnitude.

postoperative a. Astigmatism created by an operation involving the cornea.

radial a. A monochromatic aberration of spherical surfaces, refracting or reflecting, as a result of small bundles of incident rays being oblique with reference to the optic axis, two line images of a point source being formed. Syn., *marginal astigmatism; oblique astigmatism.*

regular a. Astigmatism produced by normal refraction at a simple toroidal surface.

residual a. The difference between corneal and total astigmatism. Also called *physiological astigmatism.*

retinal a. Schlaer's retinal astigmatism.

Schlaer's retinal a. Apparent astigmatism demonstrated by the fact that resolution is better in certain meridians than in others even after optical astigmatism has been corrected. Described by Schlaer, although first described by Hering, and attributed to elliptical distribution of retinal receptors.

simple a. Astigmatism in which one principal meridian of the eye is emmetropic and the other either myopic or hypermetropic.

simple hypermetropic a. Astigmatism in which one principal meridian is hypermetropic and the other emmetropic.

simple myopic a. Astigmatism in which one principal meridian is myopic and the other emmetropic.

symmetrical a. Astigmatism in which the two weakest or the two strongest meridians of both eyes total 180° upon addition of their meridional locations. The principal meridians of the two eyes are as mirror images of each other with respect to the midline.

symmetrical a., heterologous. Against the rule astigmatism in which the total of the degrees representing the two weakest or the two strongest meridians for both eyes equals 180°.

symmetrical a., homologous. With the rule astigmatism in which the total of the degrees representing the two weakest or the two strongest meridians for both eyes equals 180°.

vitreal a. Irregular astigmatism attributed to variations in optical density in the vitreous humor.

with the rule a. Astigmatism in which the meridian of greatest refractive power is in, or within 30° of, the vertical. Syn., *direct astigmatism.*

astigmatizer (ă-stig′mah-ti″zer). Any device which brings a point of light into focus as lines; an astigmatic lens or lens combination.

astigmatometer (ă-stig″mah-tom′eh-ter, as″tig-). Astigmometer.

astigmatoscope (as″tig-mat′o-skōp). Astigmoscope.

astigmatoscopy (ă-stig″mah-tos′ko-pe). Astigmoscopy.

astigmia (as-tig′me-ah). Astigmatism.

astigmic (as-tig′mik). Astigmatic.

astigmism (as′tig-mizm). Astigmatism.

astigmometer (as″tig-mom′eh-ter). An instrument for measuring astigmatism. Syn., *astigmatometer.*

Lebensohn a. A test chart for determining the axis of astigmatism, consisting essentially of a rotatable white disk containing a centered black cross, with two short black lines set at 30° angles in arrowhead formation at the end of one line of the cross. The axis is located when the barbs of the arrowhead are equally blurred.

astigmometry (as″tig-mom′eh-tre). The measuring of astigmatism with the astigmometer.

astigmope (as′tig-mōp). One having astigmatism.

astigmoscope (ă-stig′mo-skōp). An instrument for observing and measuring the astigmatism of an eye. Syn., *astigmatoscope.*

astigmoscopy (as″tig-mos′ko-pe). The measuring of astigmatism with the astigmoscope. Syn., *astigmatoscopy.*

astrocyte (as′tro-sīt). A neuroglial cell of a macroglia type with many processes and perivascular feet, found in the central nervous system, the retina, and the optic nerve. Syn., *Cajal's cell; spider cell.*

astrocytoma (as″tro-si-to′mah). A tumor of the retina or of the central nervous system which is derived from astrocytic glial tissue. It does not recur or metastasize after removal. Syn., *glioma.*

astroglia (as-trog′le-ah). A type of neuroglia composed of astrocytes. Syn., *macroglia.*

asyllabia (as″ih-la′be-ah). A form of aphasia in which one cannot form syllables or words, although single letters are recognized.

asymbolia (as″im-bo′le-ah). Asemia.

asymboly (ă-sim′bo-le). Asemia.

asymmetropia (a″sih-met-ro′pe-ah). Anisometropia.

asymmetry (a-sim′eh-tre, ă-sim′-). 1. Lack of similarity in corresponding parts or organs on opposite sides of the body. 2. Lack of equal movement of two co-ordinated parts, as in asymmetrical convergence. 3. Lack of symmetry in the parts of an object or a geometric figure.

chromatic a. Difference in color in the irides of the two eyes.

monocular a. The perceiving of a line, bisected by a point which is monocularly fixated, as not being divided into two equal parts. The nature and the amount of the Hering-Hillebrand deviation result from the relationship between the asymmetries of the individual eyes.

monocular a., Kundt's. The more common form of monocular asymmetry in which the segment in the temporal field is underestimated, resulting in subjectively locating the midpoint too far nasalward; hence, the temporal segment is longer than the nasal. Syn., *partition of Kundt.*

monocular a., Münsterberg's. A less common form of monocular asymmetry, supposedly reported by Münsterberg, in which the segment in the temporal field is overestimated, resulting in subjectively locating the midpoint too far temporalward; hence, the nasal segment is longer than the temporal. Syn., *partition of Münsterberg.*

visual a. 1. A condition in which one eye converges more than the other, as occurs when the point of fixation is not in the median plane. 2. A condition in which one eye differs from its fellow in visual acuity, refractive error, or size or shape of the ocular image.

asynergia (as″ih-ner′je-ah). Asynergy.

asynergy (ă-sin′er-jē). Faulty co-ordination of skeletal muscles in their proper timing, or failure of a muscle to aid another when it would be normal for it to do so.

ataxia (ă-tak′se-ah). An inability to co-ordinate muscular movements.

Friedreich's spinal a. Friedreich's disease.

Marie's cerebellar a. Marie's disease.

Sanger-Brown a. A hereditary degeneration of the cells of the posterior column, Clark's column, and the spinocerebellar tracts, characterized by spasticity and lack of motor co-ordination of the arms and legs, optic atrophy, and usually ptosis and external and internal ophthalmoplegia. The onset is usually between the ages of 16 and 40 and the disease is slowly progressive, resulting in mental deterioration and helplessness.

telangiectatica, a. Louis-Bar syndrome.

atheroma of the eyelid (ath″er-o′-mah). Steatoma of the eyelid.

atherosclerosis (ath″er-o-skle-ro′sis). A lipoid deposition in the intima of arteries usually occurring as a senile change. Later it affects the deeper layers, producing plaques which obscure the vessel lumen. The ophthalmoscopic picture, according to Friedenwald, is of a narrowed arterial tree, arteries less tortuous than normal, and branches bifurcating at angles

more acute than normal. Others state that the arteries become more tortuous.

athetosis, pupillary (ath″e-to′sis). Hippus.

atopognosia (ă-top″og-no′se-ah). Loss of ability to localize a sensation accurately.

atopognosis (ă-top″og-no′sis). Atopognosia.

atresia iritis (ă-tre′ze-ah i-ri′tis). Closure or imperforation of the pupil.

atretoblepharia (ă-tre″to-bleh-fa′re-ah). Symblepharon.

atretopsia (ă″tre-top′se-ah). Imperforation of the pupil due to a persistent pupillary membrane.

atrophia bulborum hereditaria (ah-tro′fe-ah bul-bor′um her″ed-ih-ter′e-ah). Norrie's disease.

atrophoderma pigmentosum (at″-ro-fo-der′mah pig-men-to′sum). Xeroderma pigmentosum.

atrophy (at′ro-fe). An acquired wasting or decrease in size of a portion of the body, an organ, or a tissue due not to direct injury but rather to faulty nutrition or loss of nerve supply. It may occur physiologically or pathologically; and starvation, senile, disuse, pressure, endocrine, excessive overwork, and, possibly, toxic types exist.

essential progressive iris a. A progressive atrophy of the iris without accompanying inflammatory signs or an evident etiologic factor. It is typically unilateral, affects young adults, more commonly females, and is characterized initially by distortion and displacement of the pupil followed by multiple holes in the iris which may coalesce. Secondary glaucoma, which usually does not respond to treatment, gradually develops in the later stages, and the condition may terminate in enucleation.

gyrate a. of choroid and retina. A slowly progressive hereditary atrophy of the choroid and the retina producing irregularly shaped white areas which coalesce into bizarre forms as a result of pigment upset. Centripetal involvement is typical, with the macular area the last to be affected. The symptoms are night blindness (commencing in childhood) and disturbances of vision; etiology is unknown.

optic a. Degeneration of the optic nerve fibers, characterized by pallor of the optic nerve head which may appear grayish, yellowish, or white. Visual loss usually accompanies this condition.

optic a., ascending. Consecutive optic atrophy.

optic a., cavernous. Optic atrophy usually associated with glaucoma and characterized by the disappearance of optic nerve fibers and mucoid degeneration of the neuroglia, resulting in a riddling of the optic nerve with spaces filled with clear, mucoid material. Syn., *lacunar optic atrophy.*

optic a., choroiditic. Chorioretinitic optic atrophy.

optic a., chorioretinitic. Optic atrophy characterized by a waxy yellow color of the disk, which follows diffuse chorioretinal disease or degenerative processes, the prototype being optic atrophy as found in retinitis pigmentosa.

optic a., consecutive. 1. Optic atrophy associated with inflammatory or degenerative lesions of the retina and the choroid which have affected the ganglion cell layer of the retina. Syn., *ascending optic atrophy.* 2. Optic atrophy secondary to papilledema.

optic a., descending. Optic atrophy which results from a lesion in the intraorbital, intracanalicular, or intracranial portions of the nerve and progresses toward the retina to involve the optic nerve head.

optic a., Fuchs's. Optic atrophy associated with circumpapillary atrophy, presumably due to choroidal stretching and atrophy subsequent to high myopia.

optic a., glaucomatous. Optic atrophy secondary to glaucoma and characterized by a cupping or excavation of the nerve head which extends to the border of the disk. The retinal vessels are displaced toward the nasal border of the disk and bend sharply over the margins of the disk as they dip down into the excavation. The disk is pale and may be surrounded by an atrophic halo.

optic a., inflammatory. Optic atrophy due to local inflammation of the nerve head, intraocular inflammation, inflammation of the tissues surrounding the nerve fibers, systemic diseases, or diseases of the central nervous system. Syn., *secondary optic atrophy.*

optic a., lacunar. Cavernous optic atrophy.

optic a., Leber's. Optic atrophy, both bilateral and hereditary, of fairly rapid onset, usually in young adult males. As a rule, it involves the entire disk, but occasionally only the papillomacular bundle. It is an atrophy of the primary type, although there may be a papillitis at the onset of the disease.

optic a., noninflammatory. Optic atrophy due to causes other than inflammation, such as physical severance of the conduction path, pressure, or essential atrophy. Syn., *primary optic atrophy.*

optic a., postneuritic. Optic atrophy secondary to inflammation of the nerve head.

optic a., primary. Optic atrophy characterized by a sharply defined pale gray or white disk without excessive glial proliferation and, usually, with unobscured lamina cribrosa; typically seen in lesions affecting the conduction path posterior to the nerve head. Syn., *simple optic atrophy.*

optic a., retinitic. Chorioretinitic optic atrophy.

optic a., secondary. Optic atrophy characterized by a gray disk with obscured margins and glial proliferation filling the physiological cup; typically seen in lesions involving the nerve head directly.

optic a., simple. Primary optic atrophy.

optic a., temporal. Optic atrophy of the temporal portion of the optic disk. It results from involvement of the papillomacular bundle and occurs characteristically in multiple sclerosis.

optic a., vascular. Optic atrophy associated with extreme attenuation of the retinal vessels. It occurs characteristically from arteriosclerosis or embolus or thrombosis of the central retinal artery.

peripheral chorioretinal a. Paving-stone degeneration of the retina.

progressive choroidal a. Choroideremia.

progressive tapetochoroidal a. Choroideremia.

senile marginal a. Peripheral corneal ectasia.

traumatic macular a. Traumatic macular degeneration of Haab.

atropine (at′ro-pēn, -pin). A poisonous alkaloid derivative of belladonna. Its action is mydriatic, cycloplegic, antispasmodic, sedative, and narcotic. Atropine sulfate, used as a cycloplegic for therapeutic action and for refracting, paralyzes the pupillary sphincter and the ciliary muscle by preventing the action of acetylcholine at the parasympathetic nerve endings. Its action may persist for over 2 weeks after full cycloplegia.

atropinism (at′ro-pin-izm). Atropism.

atropinize (at′ro-pin-īz). 1. To bring under the influence of atropine. 2. To install atropine into the conjunctival sac.

atropism (at′ro-pizm). A condition produced by the use of atropine.

attensity (ă-ten′sih-te). Sensory clearness as distinguished from cognitive clearness; employed by Titchener.

attention. The focusing of conscious activity; conscious adjustment of the senses to facilitate optimal response.

fluctuation of a. The periodic variation of the degree of maximum clearness of the contents of consciousness, regardless of the change in content.

inertia of a. A lag or slowness of the normal shift of attention.

reflex, a. See under *reflex.*

span, a. See under *span.*

visual a. 1. Attention mediated by the visual sense. 2. The conscious or purposeful fixation of the eyes to an object of regard.

attolens oculi (at′ol-enz ok′u-li). Superior rectus muscle.

Aubert's (o-bārz′) **phenomenon; theory.** See under the nouns.

Aubert-Förster law (o-bār′fers′ter). See under *law.*

aura, visual (aw′rah). Visual sensations which precede an attack of epilepsy or migraine. These include flashes of light (photopsia), scintillating scotoma, fortification spectrum (teichopsia), or hallucinations.

Autocross, Matsuura. A phoroptor attachment for performing a crossed cylinder test for astigmatism, consisting essentially of a biprism doubling system and two crossed cylinder lenses, enabling the doubled image of the test object to be seen simultaneously through the two positions of the crossed cylinder lenses instead of sequentially.

Auto-disc, Nutt. An attachment used with the Projectoscope in the treatment of eccentric fixation, housing three graticules which are sequentially projected onto the fundus, the first being a green filter with a lighter green three degree central area, the second being clear with a centrally located three degree black spot, and the third, a green filter with a small central clear aperture. When connected to the control unit with the second graticule utilized, an intense light of preset duration illuminates the retina not shielded by the black spot. When the third graticule is in place, the control unit will automatically produce flashing light with preset light and dark phases.

autofundoscope (aw″to-fun′do-skōp). An instrument designed for the self-examination of the macular and the perimacular regions of the eye.

autokeratoplasty (aw-to-ker′ah-to-plas″te). Keratoplasty in which the transplanted tissue is obtained from the other eye of the patient or is rotated in the same eye. Cf. *homokeratoplasty.* Syn., *autogenous keratoplasty.*

autokinesis, visual (aw″to-kih-ne′sis). The apparent motion of a small, single, stationary spot of light when continuously observed in an otherwise dark field. Syn., *autokinetic visual illusion.*

auto-ophthalmoscope (aw″to-of-thal′mo-skōp). An instrument for examining one's own fundus.

auto-ophthalmoscopy (aw″to-of″-thal-mos′ko-pe). The examination of one's own fundus by means of an auto-ophthalmoscope or by means of entoptic imagery.

autoperimetry (aw″to-per-im′eh-tre). The examination of one's own field of vision.

autophthalmoscope (aw″tof-thal′-mo-skōp). Auto-ophthalmoscope.

autophacoscopy (aw″to-fa-kos′ko-pe). The viewing of the image of the interior of one's own eye. The apparatus consists of a lens to which adheres a drop of colorless viscous fluid on the outer surface. The lens is held before the eye in the same position as a spectacle lens, and the reflections from the interior of the eye are visible through the drop of fluid. The term is a misnomer, because only the movement of muscae volitantes is seen.

autophakoscopy (aw″to-fa-kos′ko-pe). Autophacoscopy.

autopsia (aw-top′se-ah). The apparent perception of an external object when no such object is present; a visual hallucination.

autorefraction (aw″to-re-frak′shun). A procedure of refraction in which the patient or subject controls or adjusts the lenses, knobs, or dials on the refractor.

autoscope (aw′to-skōp). An instrument for visually examining one's own organs, such as the eye or the larynx.

autoscopy (aw-tos′ko-pe). 1. Examination of one's own organs by means of an autoscope. 2. Examination of one's own eyes. 3. A vivid sense of one's own organs; a visualization of one's own organs.

autoskiascopy (aw″to-ski-as′ko-pe). Skiascopy of one's own eye by means of a mirror and the other eye.

autotransplant, corneal (aw″to-trans′plant). Transplantation of corneal tissue in which the tissue is obtained from the other eye of the patient or is rotated in the same eye. See also *allotransplant; heterotransplant; homotransplant.*

auxesis, visual (awk-ze′sis). 1. An increase in any specific visual sensibility while under the influence of the original stimulus. 2. Recovery from effects of what is conventionally spoken of as visual fatigue; the opposite of *visual minuthesis.*

auxiometer (awk″se-om′eh-ter). Auxometer.

auxometer (awks-om′eh-ter). An instrument for measuring the magnifying power of lenses.

auxoptician (oks-op-tish′an). One who uses his eyes to aid the blind by reading aloud, guiding, or helping generally by providing auxiliary vision.

A-V nicking. See under *nicking.*

average. Arithmetic mean.

aversion to fusion. Horror fusionis.

Aves's deviograph. See under *deviograph.*

avulsion (ă-vul′shun). The forcible separation, or tearing away, of a part or an organ.
>   *bulb, a. of the.* The forcible expulsion of the eyeball with tearing of the conjunctiva, the muscles, and the optic nerve.
>   *optic nerve, a. of the.* Traumatic separation of the optic nerve from its attachment to the eyeball.
>   *retina, a. of the.* The tearing of the retina away from the ora serrata boundary.

ax. Abbreviation for *axis* (of cylinder).

axanthopsia (ak″zan-thop′se-ah). An inability to distinguish yellow; yellow blindness.

Axenfeld's (ak′sen-feltz) **anomaly; accessory ganglion; intrascleral nerve loop; syndrome.** See under the nouns.

axicon (aks′ih-kon). A type of optic having the structural characteristic of being a figure of revolution and the property that a point source on its axis of revolution is imaged to a range of points along its axis.

axiometer (ak″se-om′eh-ter). A device for determining the axis of a cylindrical lens. It is a boxlike instrument emitting a luminous streak reflected on the lens and rotated until it is parallel with its reflected image.

axis. 1. An imaginary straight line passing through a body or a system with respect to which this body or system is symmetrical. 2. An imaginary straight line passing through a body or an object about which this body or object rotates. 3. A line of reference corresponding to a unique diametric dimension of a body or a system.
> *anteroposterior a.* Sagittal axis.
> *azimuthal a.* The axis about which azimuthal movements of the eye are made. It corresponds to the Z axis of Fick.
> *collineation, a. of.* 1. The intersection of all corresponding incident and refracted paraxial rays lying in a meridian plane of a single spherical refracting surface or of an infinitely thin lens. 2. A line perpendicular to the optic axis at the optical center of a thin lens, or at the vertex of a single refracting surface, and used to represent the lens or the surface itself in ray diagramming.
> *corneal a.* A variously defined axis to represent the anteroposterior orientation of the cornea as a discrete anatomical structure. Depending on the assumed or actual structural characteristics of the cornea, it has been variously named the axis of symmetry or the major axis of the corneal ellipsoid. The definitions sometimes stipulate that the axis must pass through the corneal apex or the center of curvature of the optical zone of the cornea.
> *cylindrical a.* 1. Mathematically, the axis of radial symmetry of a cylinder. 2. The meridian of least

refractive power or of longest radius of curvature on the toric surface of an astigmatic lens.

Fick, axes of. Primary axes of Fick.

fixation a. The line connecting the point of fixation to the center of rotation of the eyeball. Syn., *fixation line.*

frontal a. The line connecting the centers of rotation of the eyeballs. Syn., *x axis; base line.*

gaze, a. of. Visual axis.

geometrical a. The line passing through the anterior and the posterior poles of the eye. If the refractive surfaces are symmetrically located within the eye, then the geometrical axis coincides with the optic axis, which passes through the centers of curvature of the refracting surfaces.

 geometrical a., external. In a schematic topographical representation of the eye, the line joining the most anterior surface of the cornea to the most posterior surface of the episclera.

 geometrical a., internal. In a schematic topographical representation of the eye, the line joining the most anterior surface of the cornea to the most posterior point on the anterior surface of the retina.

horizontal a. Transverse axis.

lateral a. Transverse axis.

lens, a. of. 1. The straight line normal to both surfaces of the lens. Syn., *optical axis; principal axis.* 2. The cylindrical axis of a spectacle lens. 3. The line joining the anterior and the posterior poles of the crystalline lens.

Listing, axes of. Axes which lie in a plane (Listing's plane) passing through the center of rotation of the eye and perpendicular to the line of sight when the eye is in its primary position. Movements of the eyes are referred to these axes in the analysis of torsional movements.

macular a. The line joining the fovea to the second nodal point of the eye.

major a. The horizontal line at the maximum width of a spectacle lens; it may or may not fall on the datum line, depending on the lens shape.

marker, a. See under *marker.*

mechanical a. Datum line.

minor a. The perpendicular to the major axis at its midpoint.

oblique a. 1. An axis which is neither vertical nor horizontal. 2. In ophthalmic lenses, the axis of the cylindrical correction if it is not at 0° or 90° on the spectacle reference scale. 3. In ophthalmometry, the axis of the astigmatism if it lies between 30° and 60°, or between 120° and 150°, on the spectacle reference scale.

optic a. 1. In the eye, the line passing through the centers of curvature of all the optical elements (corneal and lens surfaces), or the best approximation of this line. 2. In doubly refracting crystals, such as calcite and quartz, the direction in which the ordinary and the extraordinary rays behave alike in all respects.

optic a. of Gullstrand. Pupillary axis.

optical a. 1. The straight line normal to both faces of a lens along whose path a ray will pass without being deflected. 2. The straight line joining the centers of curvature of all the refracting surfaces of a centered lens system.

orbital a. The line from the middle of the orbital opening to the center of the optic foramen. In an adult, the orbital axes make an angle of approximately 45° with each other.

papillary a. The line joining the temporal edge of the optic disk and the second nodal point.

primary a. The straight line normal

to the surfaces of a lens or a centered lens system which passes through the nodal points.

primary axes of Fick. A system of three mutually perpendicular coordinate axes which intersect at a point specified as the center of rotation of the eye and to which all positions of direction of the eye may be referred. These axes of reference were designated *x*, *y*, and *z* by Fick, and were defined with respect to the frontal plane of the head.

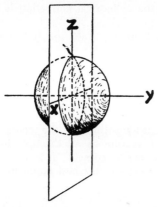

Fig. 4. Primary axes of Fick. (From *Text-book of Ophthalmology*, Vol. I, Duke-Elder, Harry Kimpton, 1942)

principal a. 1. A straight line which is normal to both surfaces of a lens. Syn., *optical axis.* 2. A straight line through the center of curvature of a spherical reflecting or refracting surface and through the center of the surface.

pupillary a. The line perpendicular to the cornea and passing through the center of the entrance pupil of the eye. It is the line by means of which the direction of a person's gaze is objectively determined. Syn., *optic axis of Gullstrand; pupillary line.*

rectilinear axes. Axes which are mutually perpendicular to each other.

refraction, a. of. The normal to a refracting surface at the point of incidence of a ray of light.

sagittal a. The line connecting the anterior and the posterior poles of the eye. Loosely, the visual axis or the y axis for true torsion or wheel rotation. Syn., *anteroposterior axis.*

secondary a. Any line not coincident with the primary axis which passes through the optical center of an infinitely thin lens or through the nodal points of a thick lens or of a lens system. Any ray not coincident with the primary axis which passes without deviation through an infinitely thin lens will be along a secondary axis. In the case of thick lenses, the path of such a ray will be a pair of parallel lines interconnected by the line connecting the two nodal points.

symmetry of the cornea, a. of. The line about which the cornea may be assumed to be symmetrical. The definition may variously be applied to the whole corneal structure or just to the optical zone. See also *corneal axis.*

transverse a. A line passing through the center of rotation of the eyeball, perpendicular to the anteroposterior axis and serving as the x axis for elevation or depression. Syn., *horizontal axis; lateral axis.*

vertical a. 1. A superior-inferior line through the center of rotation of the eyeball which serves as the z axis for abduction and adduction. 2. A line of reference for the whole body, extending from the head to the feet in the midsagittal plane.

visual a. 1. The line joining the point of fixation and the anterior nodal point. 2. The line connecting the fovea to the point of fixation and passing through the nodal points of the eye. Since it connects both nodal points, it is a broken, not a single, straight line. In practice, the two nodal points are regarded as coincident, in which case it is a straight line. Syn., *line of gaze; line of regard; line of vision; visual line.*

visual a., binocular. An arbitrary reference line connecting a binocularly fixated point and a reference point between the two eyes, ordinarily midway between the two eyes.

visual a., false. Any axis which, by reason of the method of determination, seems to be the visual axis but which is in fact not the true visual axis. It is occasionally incurred in subjective determinations in which an anomalously localized visual image of a foveally fixated object is used as a reference point instead of the real fixated point, or when an extrafoveal point is used for fixation.

working a. Datum line.

*x **axis.*** A line passing through the centers of rotation of the eyes; one of the primary axes of Fick. Syn., *frontal axis.*

*y **axis.*** A line passing through the anterior and the posterior poles and the center of rotation of the eye, perpendicular to the x and the z axes; one of the primary axes of Fick. Syn., *anteroposterior axis; sagittal axis.*

*z **axis.*** A vertical line passing through the center of rotation of the eye, perpendicular to the x and the y axes; one of the primary axes of Fick. Syn., *vertical axis.*

axometer (ak-som′eh-ter). 1. An instrument for determining the axis and the optical center of a lens. It is used especially to adjust a pair of spectacles to a patient so that the optical centers are properly placed with respect to the lines of sight of the eyes. 2. An instrument used in the subjective determination of the axis of astigmatism of the eye.

Ferree-Rand a. A visual testing instrument consisting essentially of three small, bright, transilluminated apertures in a row which, in astigmatism, are seen in streaked, meridional distortion and which may be made to coalesce by orientation of the instrument parallel or perpendicular to the axis of astigmatism.

axonometer (ak″so-nom′eh-ter). 1. An instrument for the determination of the axis of a cylindrical lens. 2. An instrument for locating the axis of astigmatism of the eye.

azimuth (az′ih-muth). The horizontal co-ordinate in a system of spherical co-ordinates, measured in a horizontal plane as an angular rotation about a fixed vertical axis.

B

B. Abbreviation for base (of prism).

B₁, B₂, etc., **case type.** See under *case.*

Babinet's (bah″be-nehz′) **compensator; principle.** See under the nouns.

Babinski-Froehlich syndrome (bahbin′skē-fra′lik). Froehlich's syndrome.

Babinski-Nageotte syndrome (bahbin′skē-nazh-yot′). See under *syndrome.*

Bach's (bahks) **test; theory.** See under the nouns.

back focus. See under *focus.*

background. Neutral surroundings and interstices of a figure; the framework in which a figure is suspended. It may be simple, amorphous, homogeneous, and localized behind the figure, and is characteristically less structured, less penetrating, less independent, and less meaningful than the figure.

backstroke. A specific series of afferent nerve impulses which originate in the sense organ and are of value in correcting for errors in the motor adjustments of the body.

Badal's optometer (bah-dalz′). See under *optometer.*

Bagolini's (bah′go-le″nēz) **striated glass; test.** See under the nouns.

Bailey's test (ba′lēz). See under *test.*

Baillarger's (bi″yar-zhāz′) **band; line; sign.** See under the nouns.

Bailliart's (bah′yartz) **test; tonometer.** See under the nouns.

balance, binocular. 1. The condition characterized by the two eyes being simultaneously in focus or equally out of focus. 2. The condition represented in the various ocular muscle functions providing for normal binocular fusion without stress, fatigue, discomfort, etc. E.g., orthophoria is said to indicate binocular balance. See also *muscle balance.*

balance, muscle. 1. Orthophoria, particularly when regarded as an indication of extraocular muscle function. 2. The status of extraocular muscle function as represented in phoria measurements.

Baldwin's (bawl′dwinz) **figure; illusion.** See under the nouns.

Balgrip (bal′grip). A trade name for a rimless spectacle mounting in which the lenses are held in place by tension instead of screws. Brackets, soldered to an arm, fit into notches cut on the nasal and the temporal sides of the lens.

Balint's syndrome (bah-lintz′). See under *syndrome.*

ball, Landolt's. A device designed by Landolt to demonstrate movements of the eyeball, consisting of a simple rubber ball on which are depicted cornea, anterior and posterior poles, horizontal and vertical meridians, etc.

Ballet's sign (bal-āz′). See under *sign.*

ballottement, ocular (bah″lotmawn′, bah-lot′ment). The falling of opaque particles in a fluid vitreous body, on movements of the eyeball.

Balopticon (bal-op′tih-kon). A trade name for an apparatus which projects enlarged images of

[70]

opaque objects onto a screen. See also *epidiascope; opaque projector.*

balsam, Canada (bawl'sam). A transparent substance used to cement glass, as in a cement bifocal. It is obtained from the sap of the North American balsam fir and is soluble in xylol. Its index varies, 1.54 being a typical value.

band. A flat strip, or a section of a surface having the appearance of a flat strip, separated from the adjacent areas by some differing characteristic, as color, texture, etc.

absorption b's. Regions of the spectrum absorbed by liquids or solids in contrast with gases which have absorption lines. The bands are generally continuous in character, fading off gradually at the ends. Salts of certain rare earth metals give narrow bands with fairly sharp limits.

astigmatic b. The band of light seen in the retinoscopic reflex of an astigmatic eye, especially on neutralization of only one of the principal meridians.

Baillarger's outer b. Baillarger's outer line.

Charpentier's b's. A series of alternating light and dark bands which are pulsations of sensation produced by the observation of a moving slit-shaped light stimulus in a dark visual field, e.g., a radial slit in a rotating disk, the center of which is constantly fixated. The magnitude of the effect depends on the intensity of the stimulus, the state of adaptation of the eye, and the region of the retina stimulated.

fusion b. of Langrange. A line horizontally traced, at eye level, on the three sides of a rectangular or square room to measure the horizontal field of binocular fixation, ruled into 5° intervals. With a red glass in front of one eye, the subject fixates a white light source target which is moved along the line until it no longer appears to be of such color as to indicate fusion of the red and white targets.

Gennari, b. of. Line of Gennari.

Haidinger's b's. Haidinger's fringes.

interference b. Black bands crossing the various orders of spectra produced when a diffraction grating is held in contact with a plane reflecting surface, due to the interference of the direct and reflected orders of the spectra.

Mach's b. Mach's ring.

neutral b. A band in the spectrum which, to a dichromat, is without hue, appearing as white or gray, and varies in location with the type of dichromat.

opacity, b. See *opacity, Haab's band.*

Talbot b's. Interference bands appearing in a prismatic spectrum when a thin glass plate is mounted in a spectroscope between the collimator and prism, or prism and telescope, so that half of the beam which is nearer the vertex of the prism passes through the glass.

trabecular b. A narrow band seen with the slit lamp or with the gonioscope which represents the meshwork of the angle of the anterior chamber. Syn., *trabecular zone.*

Vicq d'Azyr, b. of. Line of Gennari.

bandage, Borsch's. A bandage that covers both the diseased and the healthy eye.

Bangerter's occluders (bang'er-terz). See under *occluder.*

Bannon-Raubitschek chart (ban'-un-row'bih-shek). Paraboline chart.

bar. 1. A piece of material, usually rigid, which is proportionately greater in length than in breadth and thickness. 2. A strip, band, or broadline.

Galton b. An instrument for determining the accuracy of judgment of lengths, consisting of a horizontal bar to be bisected by an adjustable vertical line.

Koenig b's. A target used for visual acuity measurements, consisting of two parallel black bars of the same size and shape on a white background. The length of each bar is three times its width and the space between the bars is equal to the width of one bar. The smallest angular subtense (from the eye) for which the bars can be perceived as separate is a measure of the acuity.

prism b. A series of prisms of ascending powers arranged in a convenient barlike mount for rapid successive positioning in front of an eye.

pulley b. Falciform fold.

terminal b. A very thin opening or gap found at the posterior end of the intercellular borders between endothelial cells of the corneal mesothelium which is formed by a densification of neighboring cytoplasm in the terminal web.

bar reader. An appliance which provides for the placement of an opaque septum or bar between a printed page and the reader's eyes so as to occlude different areas of the page for each of the two eyes. Used for diagnosis and training of simultaneous binocular vision. Cf. *Javal's grid.*

bar reading. See *test, bar reading.*

Bar Trainer, Engelmann. A pair of slender vertical bars mounted on a horizontal piece with a central, downward-extending handle, the whole resembling a tuning fork in shape, to be held at given distances in front of the eyes with the plane of the two bars approximately in the median plane of the head. Alternate binocular fixation of test characters on the two bars provides tests and train-

ing for physiological diplopia, accommodation, and convergence.

bar-screen. A grid used in conjunction with a stereoscopic camera in order to produce a parallax stereogram so constructed that portions of the image blocked from one view are permitted to reach the film from the other view.

Bárány's (bah′rah-nēz) **chair; nystagmus.** See under the nouns.

Bard's sign (bardz). See under *sign.*

Bardet-Biedl syndrome (bar-da′-be′-del). Laurence-Moon-Biedl syndrome.

baring of the blind spot. See under *spot.*

Barkan (bar′kan) **Focal Illuminator; goniotomy lens; line; membrane.** See under the nouns.

Barlow's (bar′lōz) **disease; lens; method.** See under the nouns.

Barnet's theory (bar-netz′). See under *theory.*

Baron lens (bar′on). See under *lens.*

Barré's sign (bah-rāz′). See under *sign.*

Barré-Liéou syndrome (bar′a-le-a′-oo). See under *syndrome.*

Barrett subnormal vision monocular (bar′et). See under *monocular.*

Bartels' (bar-telz′) **nystagmus; spectacles.** See under the nouns.

Bartholin-Patau syndrome (bar′to-lin-pah′to). Trisomy 13-15 syndrome.

Bartley phenomenon. See *effect, Brücke-Bartley.*

base. 1. The lowest part of anything, considered as its support; a foundation. 2. The point or line from which actions or operations are performed or calculated. 3. The portion of an organ by which it is attached to a more central structure.

curve, b. See under *curve.*

line, b. The line joining the centers of rotation of the two eyes.

parallactic b. The separation between the optical centers of the two objective lenses in a stereoscopic camera, or the separation between the centers of the entrance pupils of the two eyes. Syn., *stereoscopic base.*

prism, b. of. 1. The edge of a prism at which the faces are separated a maximum distance. 2. The direction along the base-apex line of a prism opposite the apex, or the direction along the base-apex line opposite to the apparent displacement of the image.

stereoscopic b. Parallactic base.

vitreous b., Salzmann's. The portion of the peripheral anterior vitreous humor, about 1.5 mm. wide, which is attached to the ciliary epithelium in the area of the ora serrata.

Basedow's disease (bas'e-dōz). Exophthalmic goiter.

Basedow's triad (bas'e-dōz). See under *triad.*

basic. Cridland's term, prefixed to the phorias, to denote deviations measured at infinity under the condition of emmetropia.

basket, fiber (of Schultze). See under *fiber.*

Bassen-Kornzweig syndrome (bas'-en-korn'zwīg). See under *syndrome.*

batch. The mixture of raw materials from which glass is made.

Bates chart (bāts). See under *chart.*

bathomorphic (bath″o-mōr'fik). Having an eye of greater than average axial length; used in reference to a myopic eye.

Batten-Mayou disease (bat'en-ma'ō). See under *disease.*

Baumgardt-Segal experiment (bowm'gart-se'gul). See under *experiment.*

Baumgarten's glands (bowm'gar-tenz). See under *gland.*

Baumgartner reflectometer (bowm'-gart-ner). See under *reflectometer.*

Bayshore contact lens (ba'shōr). B.T. contact lens.

Beach test chart. See under *chart.*

Beal's conjunctivitis (bēlz). Acute follicular conjunctivitis of Beal. See under *conjunctivitis.*

beam of light. A family of light rays emanating from all points of a given area or source and proceeding to points within another given area, such as the total bundle of rays traversing an optical system from object plane to image plane, or from a projected source to a screen.

Bechterew's (bek-ter'yefs) **compensation; disease; nystagmus; reflex.** See under the nouns.

Bechterew-Mendel sign (bek-ter'-yef-men'del). See under *sign.*

Becker's (bek'erz) **chart; phenomenon; sign; test.** See under the nouns.

bedewing, corneal (be-du'ing). An edematous condition of the epithelium of the cornea characterized by irregular reflections from a multitude of droplets when viewed with the slit lamp.

Beer's law (bārz). See under *law.*

Begbie's disease (beg'bēz). See under *disease.*

Behçet's (beh-shets') **disease; symptom; syndrome.** See under the nouns.

Behr's (bārz) **disease; loupe; phenomenon; sign; syndrome; theory.** See under the nouns.

belladonna (bel″ah-don'ah). The plant *Atropa belladonna,* from the leaves and roots of which may be obtained the poisonous alkaloid precursors of various medically useful narcotics, chief among which is atropine.

Bell's occluder; palsy; paralysis; phenomenon; sign. See under the nouns.

belonoskiascopy (bel″o-no-ski-as'ko-pe). Determination of the refractive error by the elimination of perceived shadow movement when a slender bar or a needle is moved across the front of the eye while a distant point of light is fixated.

bench, optical. An elongated support usually consisting of a horizontal bar or pair of bars which rest on pedestals and on which sliding or clamped supports can be mounted for holding the components and auxiliary apparatus of an optical system or assembly such as lenses, mirrors, prisms, screens, light sources, and other objects. Frequently, the bars are graduated for measuring distances between components.

bend, Kohlrausch's. The transition point in the two segment curve of dark adaptation, representing a shift from cone adaptation to rod adaptation as the eye becomes increasingly dark adapted.

Bender's test (ben'derz). See under *test*.

Benedikt's syndrome (ben'e-dikts). See under *syndrome*.

Benham's (ben'amz) **disk; top.** See under *top*.

benign (be-nīn'). Applied to tumors; nonfatal unless in a vital organ; nonmalignant, innocent, tending to be localized or encapsulated.

Benson's disease (ben'sunz). Asteroid hyalosis.

Benton right-left discrimination test (ben'tun). See under *test*.

benzene ring schema. Any one of several mnemonics, invented by Pascal, and resembling the conventional benzene ring of chemistry, used to represent such functions as the interrelationships of the cardinal optical points, extraocular muscle actions, etc.

Béraud's valve (ba-rōz'). Valve of Krause.

Berens (ber'ens) **chart; test.** See under *chart*.

Berens-Tolman Ocular Hypertension Indicator (ber'ens-tōl'-man). See under *indicator*.

Berger's (ber'gerz) **loupe; sign; postlenticular space.** See under the nouns.

Bergmeister's papilla (berg'mi-stirz). See under *papilla*.

Berlin's (ber'linz) **disease; edema; opacity.** See under the nouns.

Bernard's syndrome (ber-narz'). See under *syndrome*.

Bernard-Horner syndrome (ber-nar'hōr'ner). Horner's syndrome.

Bernoulli distribution (bern-oul'e). Binomial frequency distribution.

Berry's circles (ber'ēz). See under *circle*.

besiclometer (bes-e-klom'eh-ter). An instrument for measuring the forehead to determine the proper width of spectacle frames.

Besnier-Boeck disease (bes-ne-a'-bek). Sarcoidosis.

Besnier-Boeck-Schaumann disease (bes-ne-a'-bek-shaw'man). Sarcoidosis.

Best's disease. See under *disease*.

beta (β) (ba'tah). The Greek letter used as the symbol for (1) *angle beta;* (2) *beta movement*.

Better Vision Institute. A nonprofit corporation supported by and representing subscribing ophthalmic manufacturers, distributors, ophthalmologists, optometrists, and dispensing opticians. Its main function is to provide speakers and educational literature, displays, movies, etc., concerning matters of eye care which are of direct interest to the public.

Betts's reading readiness charts. See under *chart*.

Betz's cells (betsz). See under *cell*.

bevel. 1. The V-shaped edge of a lens to be inserted in a frame. 2. To shape the edge of a lens to a V-shape. 3. The most peripheral curve on the posterior surface of a contact lens, usually narrow in width and of a radius considerably longer than that of the base curve. 4. A taper at the edge of a contact lens on the anterior surface to contour the edge and reduce its thickness. 5. To cut a taper or curve at the edge of a contact lens.

CN b. A taper at the periphery of the anterior surface of a contact lens to reduce edge thickness.

safety b. A slight flattening or rounding out of the otherwise sharp corners at the edge of a rimless spectacle lens.

bezel (bez'el). The grooved rim or flange of the spectacle frame or eye wire in which a lens is set.

Bezold spreading effect (ba'zold). See under *effect, spreading.*

Bezold-Brücke phenomenon (ba'-zold-bre'keh). See under *phenomenon.*

B.I. Abbreviation for *base-in (prism).*

Bianchi's valve (be-ang'kēz). Plica lacrimalis.

biastigmatism (bi"ah-stig'mah-tizm). A condition of the eye in which corneal and lenticular astigmatism coexist.

bicentric (bi-sen'trik). Pertaining to or having two optical centers.

biconcave (bi-kon'kāv). As applied to lenses, having two concave surfaces on opposite faces.

biconvex (bi-kon'veks). As applied to lenses, having two convex surfaces on opposite faces.

bicylinder (bi-sil'in-der). See *lens, bicylindrical.*

Bidwell's experiment (bid'welz). See under *experiment.*

Bidwell's ghost (bid'welz). Second positive afterimage.

Biedl's (be'dlz) **disease; syndrome.** See under the nouns.

Bielschowsky's (be-el-show'skēz) **heterophorometer; phenomenon; sign; test.** See under the nouns.

Bielschowsky-Jansky disease (be-el-show'ske-yan'ske). See under *disease.*

Biemond's syndrome (be'munz). Laurence-Moon-Biedl syndrome.

Bier contact lens (bēr). See under *lens, contact.*

Bietti's (be-et'ēz) **nodular corneal dystrophy; lens.** See under the nouns.

bifixation (bi"fik-sa'shun). The fixation of a single object by both eyes simultaneously so that the image on each retina is on the fovea.

bifocal (bi-fo'kal). 1. Pertaining to a lens system having two focal lengths. 2. A bifocal lens.

bilateral (bi-lat'er-al). Affecting or pertaining to both sides or halves of the body with reference to the midsagittal plane.

Billet's split lens (bil'ets). See under *lens.*

bimodal (bi-mo'dal). *Statistics:* A frequency distribution with two maxima, hence a distribution with two regions of high frequency.

Binkhorst (bink'hōrst) **implant; lens.** Iris clip lens.

Binkhorst - Weinstein - Troutman lens (bink'hōrst–wīn'stīn–trawt'-man). See under *lens.*

binocular (bin-ok'u-lar, bi-nok'u-). 1. Pertaining to both eyes. 2. The use of both eyes simultaneously in such a manner that each retinal image contributes to the final percept.

binocular balance; contrast; flicker; fusion; imbalance; instability; color mixture; parallax; rivalry; summation; vision. See under the nouns.

binoculars (bin-ok'u-larz, bi-nok'-). A double telescope, one for each eye; field glasses.

binoculus (bin-ok'u-lus). 1. Cyclopean eye. 2. A figure eight bandage covering both eyes. Syn., *oculus duplex.*

binophthalmoscope (bin"of-thal'-mo-skōp). Binocular ophthalmoscope.

binoscope (bin'o-skōp). A visual training instrument employed especially in correcting strabismus, in which both foveae may be simultaneously stimulated by one object.

bioluminescence (bi″o-lu″mih-nes′-ens). The emission of light by living organisms such as the firefly, certain mollusks, beetles, fish, bacteria, fungi, and protozoa.

biometrics (bi″o-met′riks). The elements of biometry.

biometry (bi-om′eh-tre). The branch of statistics which applies to biological data.

biomicroscope (bi″o-mi′kro-skōp). An instrument containing a magnifying lens system for examining living tissues of the body, as used with a slit lamp.

biophotogenesis (bi″o-fo″to-gen′e-sis). The production of bioluminescence.

biophotometer (bi″o-fo-tom′eh-ter). An instrument for measuring the rate and degree of dark adaptation.

Bioptic lens (bi-op′tik). See under *lens.*

Bioptor (bi-op′tor). A trade name for a Brewster type stereoscope for vision skills testing and training.

biphakia (bi-fa′ke-ah). A rare congenital anomaly in which two crystalline lenses are present in an eye.

biorbital (bi-ōr′bih-tal). Pertaining to or affecting both orbits.

biprism, Fresnel's (bi′prizm). An optical device for obtaining two virtual, coherent sources of light which are very close together, consisting of a piece of optical glass, about two inches square, optically flat on one side and ground and polished on the other side to form two prisms of very small refracting angle, set base to base. It is used to form interference fringes from monochromatic light coming from a narrow slit.

birefractive (bi″re-frak′tiv). Birefringent.

birefringence (bi″re-frin′jens). The property of nonisotropic media, such as crystals, whereby a single incident beam of light traverses the medium as two beams, each plane-polarized, the planes being at right angles to each other. One beam, the ordinary, obeys Snell's law; the other, the extraordinary, does not. Along the optical axis the two beams travel at the same speed; in other directions the extraordinary beam travels at different speeds. Syn., *double refraction.*

birefringent (bi″re-frin′jent). Having the property of birefringence. Syn., *birefractive.*

Birren's constant hue triangle (bēr′enz). See under *triangle.*

Bishop Harman (bish′up har′man) **magnifier; diaphragm test.** See under the nouns.

bispherical (bi-sfēr′ih-kal). As applied to lenses, spherical on both sides.

Bitot's spots (be′tōz). See under *spot.*

Bjerrum's screen (byer′oomz). Tangent screen.

Bjerrum's (byer′oomz) **scotoma; scotometer; sign; test types.** See under the nouns.

black. 1. An achromatic color of minimum lightness or maximum darkness representing one limit of the series of grays. The complement or opposite of white. 2. A visual sensation, arising from some portion of a luminous field which is of extremely low luminosity. Though typically a response to zero or minimal stimulation, black appears always to depend upon contrast.

Black bifocal contact lens. See under *lens, contact, bifocal.*

blackbody. A thermal source of radiant energy, or temperature radiator, whose radiant flux in all parts of the spectrum is the maximum obtainable from any such source at the same temperature.

Such a radiator is called a black-body because it will absorb all the radiant energy that falls on it. All other temperature radiators may be classed as nonblack-bodies. They radiate less in some or all wavelength intervals than a blackbody of the same size and the same temperature. Syn., *complete radiator; ideal radiator; Planckian radiator; standard radiator; total radiator.*

black-eye. Ecchymosis of the eyelid.

blackness. 1. A positive perceptual attribute of any surface or part thereof which has lower reflectance than its surroundings. Blackness is "induced" by the brighter surround. When the reflectance of a spot and surround differ sufficiently, the spot is accepted as "black." The color of any "dark" object has a content of blackness which leaves it if the object is spotlighted in a lightless surround. This converts the surface color to a film color having a brightness aspect but no light-ness-darkness aspect. Conversely, a patch of colored light projected on a screen is invaded by blackness and converted to an object color if the patch is surrounded by an annulus of white light much brighter than the patch. 2. The degree of approach to that extreme or limit of the series of grays known as *black*. 3. Suggesting *black,* e.g., the shade of a color.

blackout. Loss of central vision due to positive gravitational acceleration; attributed to restriction of blood supply to the eye. It occurs at 4.7 ± 0.8 g. to unprotected subjects seated upright. Cf. *grayout; redout.*

Blackowski's experiment (blah-kof'-skēz). See under *experiment.*

blank. 1. A piece of glass pressed, while hot, into its approximate finished shape and thickness so that it can be fabricated later into a lens, prism, or mirror. 2. A plastic disk, cut from a rod or flat sheet, from which a contact lens is fabricated.

dropped b. A glass blank shaped by heating it and allowing it to settle into a curved former.

fused b. A blank for the preparation of a fused multifocal lens at the stage when the contact surfaces have been ground and polished and fused together.

semifinished b. A blank, one side of which has been completely finished, that is, ground and polished to desired curvature specifications.

blanking, perceptual. The phenomenon of obliteration of the perception of tachistoscopically presented information by a subsequently presented brief flash of light.

blastomycosis (blas"to-mi-ko'sis). A fungus disease caused by yeast-like organisms that attack skin, eyelids, or lungs. Rarely, the uvea may be affected. Actually, the organism is a related *Monilia* yeast and not a true *Blastomyces.*

Blaxter's test (blax'ters). Bulbar pressure test.

blend, color. A color perceived as a composite of two adjacent colors in the color circle, e.g., purple is red-blue, or aquamarine is blue-green. Cf. *color fusion.*

blending. 1. A gradual or imperceptible change from one color to another. 2. The process of fusion, that is, the undifferentiated product of intermittent or multiple stimulation. 3. The removal of the sharp junction formed between curves of unlike radii on the surface of a contact lens, usually by polishing with a tool having an intermediate radius.

blennophthalmia (blen"of-thal'me-ah). Catarrhal conjunctivitis.

blennorrhagia ocularis (blen"o-ra'-je-ah ok'u-lar"is). 1. A particularly profuse blennorrhea. 2. Gonococcal conjunctivitis.

blennorrhea (blen″o-re′ah). A general term including any inflammatory process of the external eye which gives a mucoid discharge. More exactly, a discharge of mucus; popularly, purulent discharges from a variety of etiological factors, bacterial, allergic, and physical.

    inclusion b. A specific type of conjunctivitis, occurring chiefly in the newborn, caused by a virus which produces a follicular response of a hyperemic conjunctiva with intracellular inclusion bodies. Characteristically, it gives preauricular adenopathy and is supposedly transmitted via the genital system. In the adult it is usually called *swimming pool conjunctivitis.* Syn., *paratrachoma.*

    neonatorum, b. Any blennorrhea of the newborn; usually meant to describe ophthalmia neonatorum or gonorrheal neonatorum; often confused with *inclusion blennorrhea.*

blephar- (blef′ar-). A combining form denoting the eyelid.

blephara (blef′ah-rah). The eyelids.

blepharadenitis (blef″ar-ad″e-ni′tis). Inflammation of the glands of the eyelids. Although usually referring to involvement of the Meibomian gland, it may also apply to the marginal glands of Moll or Zeis.

blepharal (blef′ah-ral). Pertaining or relating to the eyelids.

blepharectomy (blef″ah-rek′to-me). Excision of all or part of an eyelid.

blepharedema (blef″ar-e-de′mah). An abnormal collection of excess watery fluid in the tissue spaces of the eyelid which produces a swelling and, often, a baggy appearance.

blepharelosis (blef″ah-rel-o′sis). Entropion.

blepharemphysema (blef′ar-em″fise″mah). An abnormal collection of air in the tissues of the eyelid which produces a crackling sensation of the eyelids when palpated, usually caused by a communication between the sinuses and the orbital tissues through a defect in the bone wall.

blepharis (blef′ah-ris). An eyelash. *Obs.*

blepharism (blef′ah-rizm). Rapid involuntary winking due to spasm of the orbicularis oculi muscle.

blepharitis (blef″ah-ri′tis). Any inflammation of the eyelid without reference to any particular part of the eyelid, but commonly meaning the margin. Syn., *blepharophlegmasia; palpebritis.*

    acaria, b. Inflammation of the eyelid margin caused by an acarid or a mite.

    angularis, b. Inflammation of the margins of the eyelids involving especially the canthi laterally, less so medially; it is caused by the diplobacillus of Morax-Axenfeld. A slight maceration sometimes extends over the skin of the lateral canthus.

    ciliaris, b. 1. Blepharitis marginalis. 2. Inflammation of the root of a cilium on the eyelid margin, producing a small abscess called a sty or a hordeolum.

    gangraenosa, b. A circumscribed, deep-seated, suppurative inflammation of the subcutaneous tissue of the eyelid discharging pus from several points.

    hypertrophic b. A condition in which the eyelid margins are hypertrophied, rounded, and thickened as a sequela to inflammation, and droop because of their own weight. Syn., *tylosis.*

    marginalis, b. A common chronic inflammation of the eyelid margin, usually bilateral and accompanied by crusts or scales, characteristically caused by a staphylococcus infection, although it may be due to various organisms or allergies. Syn., *blepharitis ciliaris; blepharitis simplex; psorophthalmia.*

mycotic b. Inflammation of the eyelid resulting from a fungus infection. Syn., *tinea tarsi.*

oleosa, b. A form of blepharitis squamosa in which a yellow, waxy crust forms about the bases of the cilia.

pediculosa, b. Inflammation of the eyelids due to infestation with pediculi or lice on the shafts of the cilia.

rosacea b. Inflammation and scaling of the eyelid margins, with frequent chalazia, occasionally accompanying acne rosacea of the skin of the face.

sicca, b. Blepharitis squamosa.

simplex, b. Blepharitis marginalis.

squamosa, b. A scaling or crusting of the eyelid margins commonly caused by a bacterial infection, usually staphylococcus or diplobacillus, but may be seborrheic. Removal of the scales does not leave, characteristically, an ulcerated base. Syn., *blepharitis sicca.*

sycotic b. Inflammation of the eyelid margins accompanied by an infection of the hair follicles of the eyelashes. The condition is usually recurrent and may result in permanent loss of the eyelashes.

ulcerative b. Inflammation of the eyelid margins producing numerous small ulcers which may be covered by crusts, generally caused by a staphylococcus infection.

blepharo- (blef'ah-ro). A combining form denoting the *eyelid.*

blepharo-adenitis (blef″ah-ro-ad″e-ni'tis). Blepharadenitis.

blepharo-adenoma (blef″ah-ro-ad″e-no'mah). Adenoma of the eyelid.

blepharo-atheroma (blef″ah-ro-ath″er-o'mah). An encysted tumor in the eyelid, such as a sebaceous cyst.

blepharoblennorrhea (blef″ah-ro-blen'o-re-ah). Conjunctivitis with a profuse purulent discharge.

blepharochalasis (blef″ah-ro-kal'-ah-sis). Atrophy of the skin of the upper eyelids, usually bilateral and equal, following chronic or recurrent edematous swellings of the upper eyelids; characterized in its later stages by loose folds of wrinkled and venuled skin overhanging the upper eyelid margin. Syn., *ptosis atrophica.*

blepharochromidrosis (blef″ah-ro-kro″mid-ro'sis). A condition in which colored sweat, usually bluish, is excreted from the eyelids.

blepharocleisis (blef″ah-ro-kli'sis). Ankyloblepharon.

blepharoclonus (blef″ah-ro-klo'nus). A spasm of the muscles that close the eye.

blepharocoloboma (blef″ah-ro-kol″o-bo'mah). A notch- or cleft-shaped coloboma of the eyelid.

blepharoconjunctivitis (blef″ah-ro-kon-junk″tih-vi'tis). Inflammation of both the conjunctiva and the eyelids.

rosacea, b. Inflammation of the eyelids and the conjunctiva occurring in most cases of ocular rosacea, characterized by a desquamation of the eyelid margins and either a diffuse hyperemia of the conjunctiva or a nodular conjunctivitis.

blepharodenitis (blef″ah-ro-de-ni'tis). Blepharadenitis.

blepharodermachalasis (blef″ah-ro-der″mah-kal'ah-sis). Blepharochalasis.

blepharodermatitis (blef″ah-ro-der″mah-ti'tis). Inflammation of the skin of the eyelids.

blepharodiastasis (blef″ah-ro-di-as'-tah-sis). 1. A condition in which the eyelids cannot be completely closed. 2. Excessive separation of the eyelids.

blepharodyschroia (blef″ah-ro-dis-kroy'ah). Discoloration of the eyelid, as from a nevus.

blepharoedema (blef″ah-ro-e-de′-mah). Blepharedema.

blepharolithiasis (blef″ah-ro-li-thi′-ah-sis). A condition in which chalky concretions are formed in or on the eyelid.

blepharomelasma (blef″ah-ro-me-las′mah). A condition of excessive secretion of the sebaceous glands of the eyelids, resulting in a dark, oily appearance.

blepharon (blef′ah-ron). The eyelid.

blepharoncus (blef-ah-rong′kus). A tumor of the eyelid.

blepharopachynsis (blef″ah-ro-pah-kin′sis). A pathological thickening of an eyelid.

blepharophimosis (blef″ah-ro-fi-mo′-sis). A condition in which the palpebral aperture is abnormally small.

blepharophlegmasia (blef″ah-ro-fleg-ma′zhe-ah). Blepharitis.

blepharophryplasty (blef″ah-rof′re-plas″te). Plastic surgery of the eyelid and/or eyebrow.

blepharophyma (blef″ah-ro-fi′mah). A tumor of the eyelid.

blepharoplasty (blef″ah-ro-plas′te). Plastic surgery of the eyelid.

blepharoplegia (blef″ah-ro-ple′je-ah). Paralysis of an eyelid.

blepharoptosis (blef″ah-ro-to′sis). Drooping of an upper eyelid. Syn., *ptosis.*

blepharopyorrhea (blef″ah-ro-pi″o-re′ah). A purulent discharge from the eyelid; purulent ophthalmia.

blepharorrhaphy (blef″ah-ror′ah-fe). 1. The suturing of a lacerated eyelid. 2. Tarsorrhaphy.

blepharorrhoea (blef″ah-roh-re′ah). Blepharopyorrhea.

blepharosis (blef″ar-o′sis). A degenerative condition of the eyelids, to be distinguished from blepharitis.

blepharospasm (blef′ah-ro-spazm″). Excessive winking; tonic or clonic spasm of the orbicularis oculi muscle.

clonic b. Blepharospasm in which

there is a twitching or vibratory movement within the eyelid.

essential b. Tonic blepharospasm occurring in the hysterical or the elderly.

symptomatic b. Tonic blepharospasm occurring in conjunction with ocular pathology (particularly that of the anterior portion of the eye), albinism, chorea, or tetanus.

tonic b. Blepharospasm in which there is a convulsive closure of the eyelids.

blepharosphincterectomy (blef″ah-ro-sfing″ter-ek′to-me). Surgical removal of fibers of the orbicularis oculi muscle, together with the overlying skin, to lessen the pressure of the upper eyelid on the cornea.

blepharostenosis (blef″ah-ro-ste-no′-sis). A pathological narrowing of the palpebral aperture.

blepharosymphysis (blef″ah-ro-sim′-fih-sis). Blepharosynechia.

blepharosynechia (blef″ah-ro-si-nek′-e-ah). An adhesion of the eyelids. Syn., *blepharosymphysis.*

blepharotomy (blef″ah-rot′o-me). Surgical incision of the eyelid.

blepsopathia (blep″so-path′e-ah). Eyestrain. *Obs.*

blepsopathy (blep-sop′ath-e). Eyestrain. *Obs.*

Blessig's (bles′igz) **cysts; groove.** See under the nouns.

blind. Wholly or partially unable to see; *amaurotic.*

blindness. The inability to see; absence or severe reduction of vision. Syn., *amaurosis.*

absolute b. Total blindness; complete amaurosis.

blue b. A form of partial color blindness or dichromatism characterized by the inability to distinguish the color blue; *tritanopia.*

blue-yellow b. A rare type of dichromatic vision about which detailed information is lacking, but in which the relative luminosity of blue stimuli is believed to be much less than normal, leading to confusion of blues with dark shades of other colors. Also, a neutral point occurs in the yellow region of the spectrum, leading to the confusion of yellow with other desaturated colors. See also *tritanopia* and *tetartanopsia*.

Bright's b. Partial or total loss of vision associated with uremia.

cerebral b. Visual agnosia.

color b. A misleading, but commonly used, term which includes all forms of defective color vision, however mild or severe. Usually a sex-linked hereditary defect, color blindness occurs in about 8% of all males and 3% of all females. See also *achromatism; deuteranomaly; deuteranopia; dichromatism; protanomaly; protanopia; anomalous trichromatism; tritanomaly; tritanopia*.

　color b., amnesic. Color agnosia.

　color b., partial. Any form of defective color vision except total color blindness, thus including the various types of dichromatism and anomalous trichromatism.

　color b., total. A rare form of defective vision, either congenital or acquired, characterized by total inability to discriminate any of the ordinarily differentiated hues. Presumably all hues are seen as varying shades of gray, black, or white. The condition is usually believed to be due to total absence, or inactivation, of the cones in the retina, since the photopic relative spectral sensitivity of affected individuals appears identical to that of the normal scotopic relative spectral sensitivity, no Purkinje shift is observable, and dark adaptation ordinarily shows no transitional change from cone to rod vision. The condition is typically accompanied by lowered visual acuity, nystagmus, and photopho-

bia. Syn., *achromatism; achromatopsia; monochromatism; achromatic vision*.

concussion b. Functional blindness caused by the shock of an explosion, as from a bomb or a shell.

congenital b. Absence of vision from the time of birth.

cortical b. Total loss of vision in all or part of the visual field due to a lesion in the striate area, characterized by the patient's subjective unawareness of his disability and the absence of cortical functions of vision, with the subcortical functions intact. Syn., *mind blindness*.

cortical psychic b. Visual agnosia.

Craik's b. A temporary loss of vision produced by external pressure on the eyeball.

day b. Reduced vision in daylight or in comparable illumination associated with normal, or relatively better, vision in dim light, variously synonymous with *nyctalopia* and *hemeralopia*.

desert b. Partial or complete loss of vision, usually temporary, caused by excessive exposure to brilliant sunlight reflected from the desert sands.

eclipse b. Partial or complete loss of central vision due to a foveal lesion caused by direct fixation of the sun, as in viewing a partial eclipse.

economic b. Industrial blindness.

educational b. A degree of blindness, specifically referring to school children, necessitating special teaching facilities and methods. That loss of vision defined by statutory, or other, provisions which is necessary for admittance to sight-saving or to similar special educational classes. Syn., *pedagogical blindness*.

electric light b. Dimness of vision due to prolonged exposure to intense electric illumination.

flash b. Visual loss during and following exposure to a light flash of extremely high intensity.

flight b. Amaurosis fugax.

functional b. Loss of vision not due to an organic cause; considered to be of psychogenic origin with the visual mechanism intact.

green b. A form of dichromatic vision in which the relative spectral luminosity does not differ noticeably from normal, but in which the only hues seen are blue and yellow (as reported by unilateral deuteranopes) and all colors can be matched by a mixture of blue and yellow stimuli. A neutral point occurs at about 497 mμ. Light of shorter wavelengths appears blue, of longer wavelengths, yellow, with saturation increasing to the ends of the spectrum. A sex-linked hereditary defect, it occurs in about 1% of all males and 0.01% of all females. Syn., *achloropsia; aglaucopsia; deuteranopia.*

hysterical b. Functional blindness associated with, or characterized by, hysteria.

industrial b. Loss of vision considered necessary to render a worker unable to compete or perform normally in industry. The degree of loss is usually defined by statute, industrial commissions, or insurance provisions, to be 20/200 or less, though various criteria apply. Cf. *educational, occupational,* and *vocational blindness;* also *visual efficiency.*

lactation b. Reduced vision of a mother during the time her child is a suckling.

legal b. Such degree or type of blindness as is defined in, or recognized by, the statutes to constitute blindness.

letter b. A type of aphasia in which individual letters are seen but have no meaning.

methyl-alcohol b. Loss of vision resulting from the consumption of methyl alcohol.

mind b. Cortical blindness.

moon b. Reduced vision, superstitiously said to be caused by exposure to the moon's rays during sleep.

negative b. Total loss of vision in all or part of the visual field which is not recognized subjectively by the affected individual. See also *cortical blindness.*

night b. Abnormal or complete loss of vision in dim light, characteristically associated with loss of rod function, variously synonymous with *nyctalopia* and *hemeralopia.*

note b. Alexia in which musical notes cannot be read.

object b. Object visual agnosia.

occupational b. Blindness resulting from occupational disease or as a result of injury from occupational hazards.

organic b. Absence of vision due to an organic cause; differentiated from *psychic* or *functional blindness.*

pedagogical b. Educational blindness.

psychic b. 1. Partial or total loss of vision due to a mental aberration. 2. Visual agnosia.

quinine b. Loss of vision, usually temporary, associated with excessive doses of quinine.

red b. A form of partial color blindness or dichromatism characterized by the inability to distinguish the color red; protanopia. Syn., *anerythropsia.*

red-green b. 1. A general term for the most common types of defective color vision; it includes *protanopia* and *deuteranopia* as well as *protanomaly* and *deuteranomaly,* since these are not differentially diagnosed by means of pseudo-isochromatic charts or the various yarn tests or their modifications. 2. According to the Hering theory of color vision, a form of partial color blindness in which red and green cannot be distinguished because of total or partial absence of the red-green photochemical substance in the retina.

simulated b. Feigned inability to see; a type of malingering.

snow b. Partial or complete loss of vision, usually temporary, caused by excessive exposure to brilliant sunlight reflected from snow.

soul b. Visual agnosia.

space b. Visual spatial agnosia.

sun b. Partial or total loss of vision, either temporary or permanent, due to overexposure to the rays of the sun.

total b. Complete inability to see; lack of the light sense.

twilight b. Abnormally reduced vision in low levels of illumination, as in twilight. Syn., *aknephascopia.*

violet b. Partial color blindness characterized by reduced sensitivity to violet or the confusion of violet with other hues; considered by some to be the same as *blue blindness* or *tritanopia*. Syn., *anianthinopsy.*

vocational b. Such degree or type of blindness as to prevent the continued pursuit of the vocation for which one is trained or otherwise qualified.

water b. Partial or complete loss of vision, usually temporary, caused by excessive exposure to brilliant sunlight reflected from water.

word b. A type of aphasia in which there is an inability to recognize or comprehend written or printed words. Syn., *alexia.*

yellow b. A rare type of dichromatic vision which occurs only as *blue-yellow blindness* (*tritanopia, tetartanopia*). A neutral point occurring in the yellow region of the spectrum in this form of dichromatism leads to confusion of yellows with light tints of other hues.

blind spot. See under *spot.*

blink. 1. A momentary closure of the upper and lower eyelids. 2. To close the eyelids momentarily.

blinking. 1. The brief closing of the eyelids; winking. Blinking usually applies binocularly; winking, monocularly. 2. Flashing (of a light) on and off.

Bloch's law (bloks). See under *law.*

Bloch-Sulzberger syndrome (blok-sulz′ber-ger). See under *syndrome.*

block. A tool, or part of a jig, usually a solid piece of iron, to which a lens (or lenses) is cemented or clamped during the grinding and polishing operations. Syn., *body.*

block, pupillary. A closure of the pupil which prevents the flow of aqueous humor from the posterior to the anterior chamber, as may occur in iridocyclitis from annular synechiae, in spherophakia from bulging forward of the small lens into the pupil, or in surgical aphakia from iridic adhesions to residual lens or capsule substance or to the vitreous.

blocking. The fastening or cementing of blanks or partially fabricated lenses to metal tools for grinding or polishing. The cementing agent is usually pitch.

blondel (blon-del′). A unit of luminance equal to $\frac{1}{10}$ millilambert; an apostilb.

Blondel-Ray law (blon-del′ra). See under *law.*

bloom. 1. An antireflection film. 2. A tarnish of a lens surface as a result of chemical action from exposure to the atmosphere.

blooming. The process of depositing a very thin film of a transparent substance on the surface of glass to create interference of light rays striking the surface, in order to prevent or reduce reflection. By varying the thickness of the film the reflection of specific wavelengths may be eliminated.

[83]

Lenses so treated are referred to as *coated.*

blue. 1. The hue attribute of visual sensations typically evoked by stimulation of the normal human eye with radiation of wavelengths approximately 476 mμ. 2. Any hue predominantly similar to that of the typical blue. 3. One of the psychologically unique colors. 4. The complement of yellow.

blue arc; spike. See under the nouns.

blue sclerotic (blu' skle-rot'ik). See under *sclerotic.*

blue-sighted. Displaying an abnormally high color sensitivity to blue. Congenital or acquired, the condition may occur alone or in combination with other defects of color vision (perhaps as a consequence of these other defects).

blur. 1. Diffuseness at the borders in any pattern involving lines, points, and areas, the transition across a given border being gradual instead of abrupt, resulting in a vague or indistinct appearance. 2. A form of degradation of an image formed by an optical system in which points, lines, and borders are less sharply or distinctly defined than in the original. It may result from lack of sharp focus, aberrations, diffusion by the scattering surfaces or media near the plane of the image, or by spread of the image in the retina or in a photographic film.

　spectacle b. Reduction in visual acuity experienced with spectacle lenses after the wearing of contact lenses and due to transient alterations in corneal curvature or index of refraction.

blur-image. An image of less than optimal quality for which the optically reproduced counterparts of sharp object borders are diffuse or gradientlike, variously due to out-of-focus conditions, refractive errors, vibrations, light scattering, diffraction, and optical aberrations.

blur-point. See under *point.*

B.O.A. British Optical Association.

Board, Posture, Brock's. See under *Posture Board.*

bobbing, ocular. A motor anomaly characterized by a periodic downward movement of the eyes of a comatose person with pontine disease.

Boberg-Ans (bo'berg-ans) **implant; sensibilitometer; test.** See under the nouns.

Bochdalek's valve (bok'dal-eks). See under *valve.*

Bochenek's (bo-hen'eks) **anterior accessory optic bundle; anterior accessory fasciculus; anterior accessory optic tract.** See *tract, optic, anterior accessory, of Bochenek.*

Bodal's test (bo'dalz). See under *test.*

Boder-Sedgwick syndrome (bo'der-sedj'wik). See under *syndrome.*

body. 1. A mass of matter distinct from other masses. 2. The physical structure of a man or an animal. 3. The largest and primarily central part of a structure. 4. A block used in lens grinding.

　amyloid b's. Microscopic, round, hyaline bodies occurring as a degenerate change in the prostate, meninges, lungs, and occasionally in the nerve fiber layer of the retina and the optic nerve head. Syn., *corpora amylacea.*

　asteroid b's. Small, discrete, disk-shaped or spherical bodies in the vitreous humor in asteroid hyalitis. Syn., *nivea; scintillatio albescens.*

　bigeminal b. The tectum of the midbrain in lower vertebrates receiving optic and spinotectal fibers and acting as a visual input and output center. In amphibia and in higher animals having hearing, it is replaced with a quadrigeminal body with superior and inferior colliculi.

ciliary b. The part of the uvea or vascular tunic, anterior to the ora serrata between the iris and the choroid, with the sclera outside and the vitreous and the posterior chamber inside. A longitudinal section is approximately the shape of a triangle, the outer side of which is formed by the ciliary muscle; the anterior portion of the inner side (pars plicata) includes the ciliary processes (corona ciliaris), and the posterior portion (pars plana or orbiculus ciliaris) is smooth.

colloid b's. Drusen.

cytoid b's. Sharply defined, shiny, white spots in the retina, due to localized degeneration of the nerve fibers.

Elschnig b's. Rounded or oval, transparent globules, each formed by a swollen and vacuolated epithelial cell, in the remains of the capsule of the crystalline lens following extracapsular cataract extraction. They usually occur in grapelike clusters. Syn., *globular cells of Elschnig; Elschnig pearls.*

geniculate b's., external. Ovoid protuberances lateral to the pulvinar of each thalamus in the diencephalon of the forebrain. They are one of the lower or primary visual centers, consisting of alternating white and gray areas. The white areas are formed by the medullated fibers of the optic tract, the gray areas are the nuclei in which these terminate and from which arises a new relay of visual fibers which form the optic radiations. The geniculate bodies also contain fibers which pass through without synapsing and go to the surface of the pulvinar and thence to the superior colliculus.

geniculate b's., internal. Bilateral protuberances below the pulvinar of the thalamus and medial to the lateral geniculate bodies in the diencephalon of the forebrain

which function as a relay station for the auditory pathway to the temporal lobes.

geniculate b's., lateral. External geniculate bodies.

geniculate b's., medial. Internal geniculate bodies.

Hassall-Henle b's. Rounded wart-like elevations of the posterior surface of Descemet's membrane at the periphery of the cornea which tend to increase in old age. Syn., *Hassall-Henle warts.*

Henle's b's. Hassall-Henle bodies.

hyaline b's. Drusen.

hyaloid b. Vitreous body.

pineal b. An unpaired protuberance from the roof of the diencephalon of the forebrain which suggests a rudimentary midsagittal eye. It is often listed with the endocrine system, but it forms no known hormone. Syn., *epiphysis cerebri.*

quadrigeminal b. Corpora quadrigemina.

vitreous b. A noncellular, transparent, colorless gel filling the posterior ⅘ of the eyeball between the retina and the crystalline lens. It is sphere-shaped with an anterior concave depression, the patellar fossa. The hyaloid canal, which in the fetus carries the hyaloid artery, traverses it centrally from the optic disk to the patellar fossa. It is adherent at the optic disk, more firmly to the ciliary epithelium adjacent to the ora serrata, less firmly to the capsule of the crystalline lens. Syn., *hyaloid body.*

Boeck's sarcoid (beks). Sarcoidosis.

Boettcher chart (bet'sher). See under *chart.*

bone. An element or an individual member of the skeleton or the material of which it is composed.

ethmoid b. An unpaired cranial bone which helps form the medial walls of the orbits and contains the ethmoidal air cells which drain into the nose.

frontal b. An unpaired cranial bone which forms the region of the forehead and the greater part of the roofs of the orbits and contains the frontal sinuses, which drain into the nose.

lacrimal b's. Paired facial bones in the medial walls of the orbits which help form the fossa for the lacrimal sac and the nasolacrimal canals.

malar b. Zygomatic bone.

maxillary b's. Paired facial bones which unite to form the upper jaw and help form the floor and medial wall of the orbits and the walls of the nasolacrimal duct. Each contains one of the two large maxillary sinuses.

nasal b's. Paired facial bones, located between the orbits, that form the upper part of the bridge of the nose.

palatine b's. Paired facial bones that help form the hard palate, lateral walls of the nose, and the floor of each orbit.

Soemmering's b. The marginal process of the zygomatic bone.

sphenoid b. An unpaired cranial bone with a body containing the sphenoid sinus and forming the posterior part of the medial walls of the orbits. It has paired great wings found in the lateral walls and paired small wings in the upper orbital walls.

zygomatic b's. Paired facial bones that help form the lateral and lower orbital walls. Syn., *malar bones.*

Bonnet's (bo-nāz') **capsule; syndrome.** See under the nouns.

Bonnevie-Ullrich (bon've-ul'rik) **status; syndrome.** See under *status.*

Bonvue (bon'vu). A trade name for a corrected curve series of lenses; also for a flat-top bifocal.

boopia (bo-o'pe-ah). A dazed, dull expression of the eyes in hysterical individuals; an oxlike eye.

border. 1. The outer part, the margin, or the edge of an area or a sur-

face. 2. The boundary between a figure and its background or between two figures in the perceptual field. Borders may interfere with and inhibit each other according to the organization of the perceptual field.

contrast, b. See under *contrast.*

posterior zonular b. A ridge, approximately 1.5 mm. anterior to the ora serrata on the pars plana of the ciliary body, that gives rise to thick and strong fibers of the suspensory ligaments of the crystalline lens.

tissue of Elschnig, b. See under *tissue.*

Bordier-Fränkel sign (bōr-dya'-freng'kel). See under *sign.*

Boston's sign (bos'tonz). See under *sign.*

Boström's (bost'remz) **charts; plates; test.** See under the nouns.

Boström-Kugelberg (bos'trem-kōō'-gel-berg) **charts; plates; test.** See under the nouns.

bothrion (both're-on). A deep ulcer of the cornea. *Obs.*

Bouguer's law (bōō-garz'). See under *law.*

bouquet of central cones of Rochon-Duvigneaud. The group of longest and thinnest cone cells, located in the center of the rod-free area of the fovea, which provide maximal visual acuity.

Bourdon's (bōōr'donz) **figure; illusion.** See under the nouns.

Bourneville's disease (boor'ne-vēz). See under *disease.*

Bouwers' optical system (bōō'werz). See under *system, optical.*

bow. The sidepiece or temple of a spectacle frame.

Bowen's disease (bo'enz). See under *disease.*

Bowman's (bo'manz) **lamina; layer; membrane; muscle; shadow; tubes.** See under the nouns.

box. A container with four sides, a bottom, and a top, or any similar structure.

Brock's scotoma b. A small optical

instrument for detecting a central scotoma, which, when properly strapped to the patient's head, maintains directly in front of the nonamblyopic eye a 2° transilluminated red disk with a central black fixation dot, the localization of which is adjusted by head movement to superimpose it on a small bright spot of white light seen by the other, amblyopic, eye in a dark room. Disappearance of the spot of light indicates a central scotoma. Syn., *projection box.*

Fles's b. A pseudoscope used to detect malingering, consisting of a box in which targets located inside the front corners are seen by reflection from two plane mirrors in the rear of the box, set at an obtuse angle with each other.

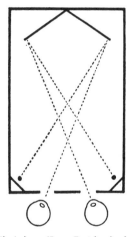

Fig. 5. Fles's box. (From *Text-book of Ophthalmology,* Vol. IV, Duke-Elder, Henry Kimpton, 1949)

Kühne's optical b. A schematic eye filled with water and having a cornea, an iris, and a crystalline lens of glass.

Maréchal's b. A pseudoscope used to detect malingering, consisting of a box in which targets on the inside front are seen by reflection from a plane mirror in the rear of the box.

Maxwell's color b. An instrument for the physical mixing of color, consisting essentially of an L-shaped box containing a mirror, prisms, a lens, three adjustable slits, and a viewing aperture. The three slits allow three different wavelengths to impinge upon the prisms, so that they are seen superimposed when viewed through the aperture and lens. A mixture of any three colors may be obtained by varying the position of the slits, and the intensity of each color can be varied by adjusting the width of the slits. White light is reflected by the mirror to an area adjacent to the color mixture for comparison.

Prato's b. A pseudoscope used to detect malingering, consisting of a box containing two viewing tubes which cross each other in an *x* pattern.

projection b. Brock's scotoma box.

smoke b. An airtight box with a glass side into which smoke is pumped. It is used to demonstrate the paths of light through lenses, prisms, apertures, and other optical elements.

Bozzi's foramen (bot'tsēz). Macula lutea. *Obs.*

brachium, superior (bra'ke-um). A bundle of nerve fibers connecting the optic tract to the superior colliculus for photostatic function and to the pretectal nuclei for pupillary reflex activity to light.

brachium tecti (bra'ke-um tek'ti). A bundle of nerve fibers from the ventral nucleus of the lateral geniculate body that synapses in the superior colliculus and may have a photostatic function.

brachydactylia (brak″e-dak-til′e-ah). Extremely short fingers and toes. In one syndrome, it may be inherited along with an abnormally small, spherical crystalline lens. Syn., *brachydactyly.*

brachydactyly (brak″e-dak-til′e). Brachydactylia.

brachymetropia (brak″e-met-ro′pe-ah). Myopia.

brachymetropic (brak″e-me-trop′ik). Myopic.

Bradley's method (brad′lēz). See under *method*.

bradyesthesia (brad″e-es-the′ze-ah). Abnormally slow perception.

bradylexia (brad″e-lek′se-ah). Abnormally slow reading.

bradypsychia (brad″e-si′ke-ah). Abnormally slow mental reaction.

Braid's strabismus (brādz). See under *strabismus*.

Braille (bra′il). A system of printing for blind persons, devised by Louis Braille, in which points raised above the surface of paper are used as symbols to designate the letter of the alphabet. Reading is accomplished through the sense of touch as the fingertips are moved over the points.

Brain's syndrome (brānz). See under *syndrome*.

Branchaud wand (bran′shōd). See under *wand*.

breadth of fusion. See under *fusion*.

break point. See under *point*.

brevissimus oculi (breh-vis′ih-mus ok′u-li). Inferior oblique muscle.

Brewster's angle (bru′sterz). Angle of polarization.

Brewster's (bru′sterz) fringes; law; prisms; stereoscope. See under the nouns.

bridge. That part of a spectacle front which connects the two eyewires, the lens arms, or the nasal straps. Its name stems from the early type of saddle bridge which rested on the bridge of the nose.

blanked b. A metal spectacle or eyeglass bridge stamped from flat stock.

form-fit b. A type of bridge used in plastic spectacle frames and shaped to fit the contour of the bridge of the nose.

high bar b. A type of bridge construction in which the bridge fastens near the top of the eyewires.

inset b. A saddle bridge having its apex behind the plane of the eyewires of the frame.

keyhole b. A type of bridge construction used in plastic spectacle frames, the outline as seen from the front resembling a keyhole. It differs from the saddle type in that only the sides touch the nose.

on-line b. A saddle bridge having its apex in the plane of the eyewires of the frame.

outset b. A saddle bridge having its apex in front of the plane of the eyewires of the frame.

pad b. A bridge of a spectacle frame to which pads are attached to act as the resting surface on the nose.

reversible b. An x-shaped bridge formed of two arches joined at their apices, used in reversible spectacle frames.

saddle b. A type of bridge construction used in metal and plastic spectacle frames without nose pads. It is a simple curved piece that conforms to and rests on the bridge of the nose.

  saddle b., modified. A saddle bridge on a plastic spectacle frame to which nose pads are attached to carry some of the weight.

wire b. A metal spectacle or eyeglass bridge stamped or drawn from wire stock.

Bright's blindness (brīts). See under *blindness*.

Bright's retinitis (brīts). Renal retinopathy.

bright. Said of light sensation or psychological light; having relatively high brightness; the opposite of *dim*. See also *light*.

brightness. The subjective attribute of any light sensation giving rise to the percept of luminous intensity, including the whole scale of qualities of being *bright, light, brilliant, dim* or *dark*. More popularly, brightness implies the higher intensities, dimness the lower. Cf. *luminance.*

contrast, b. See under *contrast.*

minimum field b. The brightness of an area or field which has been reduced in size so that it matches the brightness of a fixed comparison standard.

normal b. The brightness or luminance of a retinal image provided by an optical system when it is the same as that obtained without the optical system. This condition is met when the exit pupil of the optical system is not smaller than the entrance pupil of the eye.

photometric b. Luminance.

ratio, b. See under *ratio.*

specific b. The brightness value characteristic of a given hue.

brill (bril). A suggested unit of photometric brightness or luminance applying to the dark-adapted eye and for a 10° field. Luminance in brills = 10 $\log_{10}$ [(1000× luminance) +1], luminance being in footlamberts.

brilliance (bril'yans). 1. Brightness, especially as a subjective attribute of a light source; hence, differentiated from luminance. 2. The attribute of being *brilliant.*

brilliant (bril'yant). 1. Characterized by relatively high brightness. 2. Shining, glistening, lustrous, or sparkling.

brillmeter (bril'me-ter). An instrument to measure the luminance of a surface in brills.

Brinker-Katz method (brink'er-katz). See under *method.*

British Optical Association. An organization of ophthalmic opticians (optometrists) founded in London in 1895.

Broca's orbital index (bro'kahz). See under *index.*

Broca's plane (bro'kahz). Visual plane.

Broca-Sulzer (bro'kah-sul'zer) **curve; effect; phenomenon.** See under the nouns.

Brock's (broks) **projection box; scotoma box; method; Posture Board; rings; test.** See under the nouns.

brow. 1. The superciliary ridge and the eyebrow. 2. The forehead.

brown. 1. The hue attribute of visual sensations typically aroused by stimulation with radiation of wavelength approximately 593 mμ of relatively low luminance. 2. Any color which manifests a hue predominantly similar to that of brown, such as a mixture of red and dark yellow, or dark orange.

Brown's tendon sheath syndrome. See under *syndrome.*

Bruch's (brooks) **glands; layer; membrane.** See under the nouns.

Brücke's (bre'kez) **lens; loupe; muscle; theory.** See under the nouns.

Brücke-Bartley effect (bre'keh-bart'-le). See under *effect.*

Brungardt magnifier (brun'gart). See under *magnifier.*

Brunswik ratio (bruns'wik). See under *ratio.*

brushes, Haidinger's. A transient, entoptic phenomenon observed when polarized light, particularly blue light from a large homogeneous surface, is viewed. It consists of a pair of yellow, brushlike shapes which appear to radiate from the point of fixation; believed to be due to double refraction by the radially oriented fibers of Henle around the fovea.

Brushfield's spots (brush'feldz). See under *spot.*

Bückler's corneal dystrophy (bēk'-lerz). See under *dystrophy, corneal.*

buckling, scleral. A surgical procedure for the repair of detachment of the retina in which the deep sclera and choroid are indented in the region of the tear to impress them toward the retina, as by infolding a flap of superficial sclera, or by imbedding a silicone rod in the sclera.

Buerger's disease (ber'gerz). See under *disease.*

Buffon's theory (bu-fonz'). See under *theory.*

bulb. A rounded mass or structure, especially one at the end of a part.

end b. The end of a rod cell of the retina, located in the outer molecular layer, which synapses with bipolar and horizontal cells. Syn., *end knob; rod spherule.*

Krause, b's. of. End bulbs or corpuscles which act as cold receptors, formed by concentric layers spherically surrounding a sensory fiber, located in dermis, external genitalia, limbus corneae, and conjunctiva.

bulbus oculi (bul'bus ok'u-li). The eyeball.

bulbus quadratus (bul'bus kwodrat'us). Phthisis bulbi, in which the rectus muscles mold the shrunken eyeball into a mass of four segments.

Buller's shield (bul'erz). See under *shield.*

Bumke's (boom'kēz) **pupil; symptom.** See under the nouns.

bundle. A band, cluster, or group of relatively parallel lines or fibers, as of nerves or muscles; a fasciculus; a tract.

Druault's marginal b. In the 48 mm. embryo, a bundle of fibrils in the vitreous body, peripheral to the equator of the crystalline lens and somewhat parallel to the optic cup. It disappears when the iris and the zonule of Zinn develop. Syn., *faisceau isthmique.*

medial longitudinal b. One of a pair of medullated nerve fiber bundles on each side of the brain stem, extending from the midbrain to the cervical spinal cord, consisting of ascending and descending fibers contributed primarily by the superior vestibular nucleus of Bechterew, lateral vestibular nucleus of Deiter, third, fourth, and sixth cranial nerve nuclei, nucleus of Darkschewitsch, and interstitial nucleus of Cajal. It is involved in integrating the eye muscle nuclei with each other, with the facial nuclei, the vestibular nuclei (for maintaining equilibrium), and the head-turning nuclei. Syn., *medial longitudinal fasciculus; posterior longitudinal bundle.*

optic b., anterior accessory, of Bochenek. Anterior accessory optic tract of Bochenek.

papillomacular b. A well-defined, oval-shaped bundle of ganglionic axons in the nerve fiber layer of the retina, extending from the region of the macula lutea to the optic disk, entering it from the temporal side. All other temporal fibers course around this bundle as they approach the disk.

posterior longitudinal b. Medial longitudinal bundle.

rays, b. of. See under *ray.*

Spitzka's b. Nerve fibers from the cerebral cortex which pass through the cerebral peduncles to supply the contralateral oculomotor nuclei.

Bunsen's photometer (bun'sens). See under *photometer.*

Bunsen-Roscoe law (bun'sen-ros'ko). See under *law.*

buphthalmia (būf-thal'me-ah). Hydrophthalmos.

buphthalmos (būf-thal'mos). Hydrophthalmos.

buphthalmus (būf-thal'mus). Hydrophthalmos.

Burch interferometer (berch). See under *interferometer.*

Bürger-Grütz disease (bēr'ger-grētz). Essential familial hyperlipemia.

Burnham-Clark-Munsell color memory test. See under *test.*

Burton lamp. See under *lamp.*

Busacca's (bus-ah'kaz) **nodules; phenomenon.** See under the nouns.

butt. The anterior, thickened portion of a spectacle temple.

button. 1. In a multifocal lens, that component of a selected index of refraction which is fused to the main blank of another index and then partly ground away, the remainder forming the segment or segments for near seeing. In flat-top bifocal or trifocal constructions the button is made of two or more glasses of different re- fractive index which are fused together before being fused to the main blank. 2. A small disk of plastic from which a contact lens is fabricated.

butyn (bu'tin). A chemical compound which acts as a surface anesthetic when instilled in the eye.

B.V.I. Better Vision Institute.

C

C. Symbol for *coefficient of facility of aqueous outflow.*

c. Abbreviation for *cylinder.*

C case. See *case type C.*

cae- (se). For words begining thus, see also *ce-.*

caecanometer (se"kan-om'eh-ter). An instrument for plotting the blind spot of Mariotte. Its essential feature is the movement, over the indirect field of vision, of a metal ball by a concealed, manually controlled magnet.

Cajal's cell (ka-halz'). Astrocyte.

Cajal's interstitial nucleus (ka-halz'). See under *nucleus.*

calcar avis (kal'kar a'vis). A ridge in the posterior horn of the lateral ventricle of the brain formed by the anterior indentation of the calcarine fissure.

calcinosis oculi (kal"sih-no'sis ok'u-li). Deposits of calcium salts in tissues of the eye.

calcite (kal'sīt). Calcium carbonate ($CaCO_3$), a doubly refracting crystal found in a variety of forms, transparent to visible and ultraviolet radiation and used to produce polarized light.

calculator, Maddox torsion. A mechanical analog incorporating the system of axes of rotation of the eye and demonstrating the apparent torsion produced when conventional methods of specification of torsion are employed. It consists of a disk at whose center a rod protrudes perpendicular to the surface. A plumb line, attached to the rod, indicates the true vertical and its position is compared to the vertical meridian of the eye as it is diagrammed on the disk.

caligo (kah-li'go). Obscure vision.

corneae, c. Obscure vision due to corneal opacity.

lentis, c. Obscure vision due to cataract.

pupillae, c. Obscure vision due to an occluded pupil.

calisthenics, ocular. The exercising of the extraocular or intraocular muscle function for the purpose of developing strength, co-ordination, speed, or amplitude of action.

calorescence (kal"o-res'ens). Tyndall's term for the transference of heat radiations into visible radiations.

calyculus ophthalmicus (kah-lik'-u-lus of-thal'mih-kus). Optic cup.

camera. A chamber closed except for a relatively small aperture, through which light from external objects enters to form an image on an inner surface, usually one of light sensitive material. The aperture usually contains a lens, an adjustable diaphragm, and a shutter to time the exposure.

aquosa, c. The aqueous chamber of the eye.

fundus c. A camera with optics and an illumination system which permit photography of the ocular fundus.

lucida, c. An instrument, invented by Wollaston, consisting essentially of a prism or a mirror through which an object may be viewed so as to appear on a plane surface seen in direct view and on which the outline of the object may be traced. The direct view of the plane surface may be accomplished with the other eye, or with the same eye if the mirror or prism aperture is semitransparent, perforated, or divided so as to permit visual superimposition of the direct and indirect views.

obscura, c. A relatively dark chamber, on the interior surface of which is (invertedly) imaged a relatively luminous external scene by means of a stenopaic aperture or pinhole (sometimes provided with a lens); hence, a type of pinhole camera.

oculi, c. A chamber of the eye.

    oculi, anterior c. The anterior chamber of the eye.

    oculi, minor c. The posterior chamber of the eye.

    oculi, posterior c. The posterior chamber of the eye.

pinhole c. A camera having a pinhole aperture instead of a lens. See also *Abney's formula.*

Camp bifocal contact lens. See under *lens, contact, bifocal.*

campanula (kam-pan'u-lah). A ligamentous condensation of vitreous, of variable size and shape, attached to the crystalline lens of teleosts, considered by some to be involved in accommodation.

campimeter (kam-pim'eh-ter). Any one of several types of instruments for measurement of the field of vision, especially of the central or paracentral region. Ex.: *perimeter; tangent screen; stereocampimeter.*

campimetry (kam-pim'eh-tre). Investigation of the integrity of the field of vision with a campimeter.

black light c. Campimetry performed under ultraviolet light and with luminescent targets.

flicker fusion c. Determination of the integrity of the visual field by plotting of the critical fusion frequency (CFF) throughout its extent.

kinetic c. Exploration of the visual field with a moving test object of fixed luminance.

projection c. Campimetry performed with optically projected luminous targets.

static c. Exploration of the visual field in which test objects of various sizes, located at fixed positions, are gradually increased in luminance to the threshold of visibility.

Campos' ligament (kam'pos). See under *ligament.*

canal. A tubular channel or passageway; a duct.

central c. Hyaloid canal.

ciliary c. The spaces of Fontana in the pectinate ligament.

Cloquet's c. Hyaloid canal.

corneal c's. Channels that appear to connect lacunae which harbor the corneal corpuscles of the stroma.

ethmoidal c., anterior. A bony channel connecting the medial wall-roof junction of the orbit with the anterior cranial fossa of the cranial cavity and transmitting the nasal (anterior ethmoidal) nerve and the anterior ethmoidal artery and vein.

ethmoidal c., posterior. A bony channel extending from the region of the frontal-ethmoidal suture in the orbit to the anterior cranial fossa and transmitting the posterior ethmoidal artery and vein and the nerve of Luschka.

external c's. of Sondermann. Collector channels.

Ferrein's c. A channel formed by the margins of the closed eyelids, which conveys tears to the lacrimal puncta.

Fontana, c. of. The spaces of Fontana collectively.

Hannover's c. A circular channel about the equator of the crystalline lens between the anterior and posterior leaves of the zonule of Zinn that contains aqueous humor and zonular fibers. It is sometimes incorrectly called the *canal of Petit,* which is between the zonule of Zinn and the vitreous humor.

hyaloid c. A channel in the vitreous humor, between the optic disk and the postlenticular space of Berger, which harbors the hyaloid artery. This artery normally disappears prior to birth. Syn., *central canal; Cloquet's canal; Stilling's canal; tractus hyaloideus.*

hyaloid c., persistent. A conspicuous hyaloid canal seen with the ophthalmoscope as a gray tubular cord, which may contain a persistent hyaloid artery.

infraorbital c. A bony channel beginning at the infraorbital groove in the floor of the orbit and leading to the infraorbital foramen of the maxillary bone below the orbital margin. It harbors the nerve and artery of the same name. Syn., *suborbital canal.*

inner c's. of Sondermann. Endothelial lined passageways that drain aqueous humor from the trabecular spaces adjacent to the canal of Schlemm; they are believed to empty into this canal.

lacrimal c. Nasolacrimal canal.

nasolacrimal c. A bony passage beginning at the fossa for the lacrimal sac in the anterior, medial portion of the orbit and ending at the inferior meatus of the nasal cavity. It contains the nasolacrimal duct for tear drainage. Syn., *lacrimal canal.*

optic c. A bony channel from the middle cranial fossa to the optic foramen in the small wing of the sphenoid bone, transmitting the optic nerve and the ophthalmic artery.

orbital c., posterior internal. Posterior ethmoidal canal. *Obs.*

Petit, c. of. A circular space between the posterior leaf of the

zonule of Zinn and the anterior surface of the vitreous humor, located peripheral to the retrolenticular space of Berger.

pterygoid c. A canal in the sphenoid bone for the vidian nerve.

von Recklinghausen's c's. Artifacts in stained corneal sections originally thought to be spaces between the lamellae of the corneal stroma.

Schlemm, c. of. An annular vessel located just peripheral to and concentric with the posterior corneoscleral junction, anterior to the scleral spur, which receives aqueous humor from the meshwork of the angle of the anterior chamber and transmits it to the aqueous veins, deep scleral plexus, and efferent ciliary veins. It may bifurcate and unite again, has no proper wall of its own, and is lined with endothelium. Syn., *venous circle of Leber; sinus circularis iridis; scleral sinus of Rochon-Duvigneaud; sinus venosus sclerae.*

scleral c. The channel between the optic nerve and the choroid plus the deep one third of the sclera, bordered by the border tissue of Elschnig and the periphery of the lamina cribrosa.

Stilling, c. of. Hyaloid canal.

suborbital c. Infraorbital canal. *Rare.*

supraciliary c. A small bony channel in the frontal bone containing and transmitting a nutrient artery, diploic vein, and a nerve of Kobelt to the frontal sinus.

supraorbital c. A short passage in the frontal bone related to the supraorbital foramen or notch, transmitting the supraorbital nerve and vessels.

zygomatic c. A bony channel, transmitting the zygomatic nerve, which begins at the zygomatic foramen and bifurcates into the zygomaticofacial and zygomatico-temporal canals.

canaliculitis (kan″ah-lik″u-li′tis). Inflammation of a canaliculus.

canaliculodacryocystostomy (kan″-ah-lik′u-lo-dak″re-o-sis-tos′to-me). Surgical correction for a congenitally blocked tear duct in which the closed segment is excised and the open end is joined to the lacrimal sac.

canaliculus, lacrimal (kan″ah-lik′-u-lus). A membranous duct for tear drainage, leading from a lacrimal punctum at the eyelid margin and ending at the sinus of Maier or common canaliculus, or ending directly at the lacrimal sac. Each superior and inferior canaliculus has a vertical portion, an ampulla or dilated portion, and a horizontal portion.

cancellation, selective. Cancellation or suppression of monocularly observed objects in particular directions or areas within a binocular field.

candela (kan′deh-lah). The unit of luminous intensity in the C.I.E. photometric system. It is 1/60 of the luminous intensity of 1 sq. cm. of a blackbody radiator at the temperature of solidification of platinum. The term is intended by the C.I.E. to be used in place of *candle, international candle,* and *new candle.* Symbol cd.

candle. A former unit of luminous intensity now replaced by *candela.* It was a specified fraction of the average intensity of a group of 45 carbon filament lamps preserved at the United States Bureau of Standards.

international c. The unit of luminous intensity prior to January 1, 1948, now replaced by *candela.* By international agreement, it was the luminous intensity of the flame of a standard spermaceti candle of prescribed construction burning under prescribed conditions.

meter c. A unit of illumination equal to one lumen per sq. m. Originally, the normal incident illumination intensity produced by one candle at a distance of one meter. Syn., *lux.*

millimeter meter c. The retinal illumination produced by a magnesium oxide surface which is receiving one meter candle of illumination and is viewed through a pupil one square millimeter in area.

new c. The term formerly used instead of candela to emphasize the difference from candle. Syn., *candela.*

standard c. The secondary standard formerly used to determine the unit of luminous intensity. Weighing 1/6 lb., made of sperm wax to certain specifications, and burning 120 grains of wax per hour, the standard candle has a luminous intensity of one candle.

candlepower. Luminous intensity expressed in *candelas.*

apparent c. A term used in connection with extended sources of light (as distinguished from concentrated sources) and which must be specified as valid only at a definite distance. It is the candlepower of a point source which would produce the same illumination at a specified distance as is actually produced by the extended source.

beam c. A term of somewhat indefinite concept, usually referring to light from a lamp which has been concentrated in a narrow angle for spotlight or searchlight purposes. It is the maximum candlepower in the center of the beam and should be specified as having been measured at a certain distance because the source does not act as a point.

horizontal c. The average candlepower in the horizontal plane passing through the geometrical center of the luminous volume of the source (axis of symmetry assumed vertical).

spherical *c.* The average candlepower of a light source in all directions in space. It is equal to the total luminous flux, in lumens, divided by 4π.

Cantelli's sign (kahn-tel'ēz). Doll's head phenomenon.

canthal (kan'thal). Relating to the angles at the lateral and medial junctions of the eyelids.

canthectomy (kan-thek'to-me). Surgical removal of tissue at the junction of the upper and lower eyelids.

canthitis (kan-thi'tis). Inflammation of the eyelids in the region of the canthus.

cantholysis (kan-thol'is-is). Surgical division of a canthus of the eye.

canthoplasty (kan'tho-plas"te). Plastic surgery at a canthus of the eye.

canthorrhaphy (kan-thōr'ah-fe). Suturing at an outer canthus to shorten the palpebral fissure.

canthotomy (kan-thot'o-me). Surgical division of a canthus, usually the outer.

canthus (kan'thus). The angle formed at the nasal or temporal junction of the upper and lower eyelids. Syn., *palpebral angle.*

Cantonnet's (kan'ton-āz) **diploscope; test.** See under the nouns.

cap, corneal. Optic cap.

cap, optic. The anterior central area of the cornea within which the meridional curvature is maximum and relatively constant, not varying more than an arbitrary magnitude, such as 0.25 D. Syn., *corneal cap.*

capacity, rectifying. The influence of past experience on the interpretation of sensory stimuli such that the stimuli are modified by memories and the final percept does not correspond with the immediate stimuli, but conforms with past experience.

capsula (kap'su-lah). A capsule.

adiposa bulbi, c. Cellular fat tissue within the orbit which fills the spaces between other orbital structures.

bulbi, c. Tenon's capsule.

fibrosa, c. Sclera.

lentis, c. Capsule of the crystalline lens.

perilenticularis fibrosa, c. A condensation of the anterior surface of the primary vitreous which surrounds the posterior surface of the embryonic crystalline lens and contains terminal capillaries of the hyaloid artery. The tunica vasculosa lentis is derived from this structure.

capsule. 1. A structure enclosing an organ or a part. 2. A layer of white matter in the cerebrum.

adipose c. Capsula adiposa bulbi.

Bonnet's c. 1. Tenon's capsule. 2. That portion of Tenon's capsule posterior to the points where the rectus muscles pierce it.

crystalline lens c. The noncellular outer covering of the crystalline lens, secreted by the embryonic anterior and posterior epithelium, which receives the fibers of the zonule of Zinn and the hyaloideocapsular ligaments from the vitreous humor. Since the embryonic posterior epithelium disappears, the anterior epithelium forms the capsule for a longer period, resulting in a thicker anterior capsule than posterior. Syn., *capsula lentis; hyaline capsule.*

eyeball, c. of the. Tenon's capsule.

hyaline c. Capsule of the crystalline lens.

hyaloid c. Internal limiting layer of the retina. *Obs.*

internal c. White matter between the thalamus or caudate nucleus and the lenticular nucleus of the forebrain which contains sensory and motor tracts, including the optic radiations.

lens c. Capsule of the crystalline lens.

ocular c. Tenon's capsule.

optic c. Developmental tissue that forms the sclera.

perilenticular c. Concentric fibrils from the cone-shaped projections of the embryonic lens plate that are said to form the anterior limiting membrane of the vitreous and the base of the vitreous.

Tenon's c. The fibrous membrane surrounding the sclera which sends trabeculae to it and to the extraocular muscles. It is continuous with the dura mater of the optic nerve, episclera, and bulbar conjunctiva at the limbus. Syn., *capsula bulbi; Bonnet's capsule; capsule of the eyeball; ocular capsule; vaginal coat; bulbar fascia.*

capsulectomy (kap″su-lek′to-me). Surgical removal of a capsule, as of the crystalline lens.

capsulitis (kap″su-li′tis). So-called inflammation of the capsule of the crystalline lens.

capsulociliary (kap″su-lo-sil′e-er″e). Pertaining to the crystalline lens capsule, the zonule of Zinn, and the ciliary body epithelium.

capsulolenticular (kap″su-lo-len-tik′-u-lar). Pertaining to the crystalline lens and its capsule.

capsulopupillary (kap″su-lo-pu′pih-ler″e). Pertaining to the crystalline lens capsule and the pupil of the iris.

capsulotomy (kap-su-lot′o-me). The incision of a capsule, such as that of the crystalline lens in cataract operations.

carbachol (kar′bah-kol, -kal). Carbaminoylcholine.

carbaminoylcholine (kar-bam″in-o-il-ko′lin). A chloride salt which is a cholinergic parasympathetic stimulant and, when instilled into the eye in diluted solution, acts as a powerful miotic. See also *Carcholin* and *Doryl.* Syn., *carbachol.*

carcel (kar-sel′). A French photometric unit equal to 9½ candlepower. It is the light produced by a carcel lamp burning 42 gm. of oil an hour with a flame 40 mm. high. *Obs.*

Carcholin (kar′ko-lin). A trade name for a powdered form of carbaminoylcholine used in the preparation of ophthalmic solutions and ointments.

carcinoma (kar-sih-no′mah). A malignant tumor of epithelium which typically spreads via lymphatic vessels, but which may also spread via blood vessels.

cards, fusion. Cards used for testing and training fusion, usually in connection with a stereoscope or an amblyoscope. The term is often applied to sets which include cards for simultaneous binocular vision, stereopsis, and the like.

card, test. See *chart.*

carmine (kar′min, -mīn). A rich, purplish-red, intermediate between red and magenta; an extraspectral color corresponding to a mixture of long wavelength red and short wavelength blue or violet; the complement of a green of wavelength approximately 520 mμ.

Carmona y Valle's theory (kar-mōn′ah e vah′yes). See under *theory.*

carotene, beta (kar′o-tēn). A yellow photopigment synthesized by plants, a carotenoid of the formula $C_{40}H_{56}$, its chemical derivatives being found in photosensitive parts of plants, Euglena-like flagellates, and as vitamin A_1 and A_2 in the outer segments of visual cells.

carotenoids (kah-rot′eh-noids). Fat-soluble, highly unsaturated pigmented organic chemicals, varying in color from red to yellow, which act as photochemical and photosensitive agents in plants and animals.

Carter's test (kar'terz). See under *test*.

Cartesian ovals (kar-te'zhan, -te'zih-an). Aplanatic refractive surfaces named after René Descartes, who first investigated these surfaces.

cartilage (kar'tih-lij). A solid, white, tough, connective tissue consisting of a homogenous, translucent, intercellular substance in which are scattered nucleated cells lying in spaces called lacunae.

palpebral c. An incorrect term for the tarsal plates of the eyelids which actually contain no cartilage.

scleral c. Hyaline cartilage found in the inner portion of the posterior sclera in certain animal groups, e.g., nonbony fish, frogs, reptiles, birds, and Monotreme mammals, having nonspherical eyes or eyes not otherwise protected by skeletal structures.

tarsal c. An incorrect term for the tarsal plates of the eyelids.

caruncle, lacrimal (kar'ung-kl). A pink, fleshy mound of relatively isolated skin in the lacrimal lake at the medial canthus area adjacent to the plica semilunaris.

caruncle, supernumerary (kar'-ung-kl). A raised mass having all the structural characteristics of the normal lacrimal caruncle except that it is not isolated from the eyelid, being situated at the inner margin of the upper or lower eyelid; occurring as a rare congenital anomaly in addition to the normal caruncle.

case. 1. A particular instance of a visual condition or of a disease. 2. A container and/or its contents.

accommodative c. Any of several types of cases said to represent or result from deficient, anomalous, or abnormal accommodation, especially in relation to convergence, e.g., one having a high A.C.A. ratio.

convergence c. Any of several types of cases said to represent or result from deficient, anomalous, or abnormal convergence, especially in relation to accommodation, e.g., one having a low A.C.A. ratio.

degenerated c. Optometric Extension Program: A case said to have developed characteristic visual test responses from prolonged exposure to a visual demand to the extent that removal of the demand is in itself inadequate to alleviate the visual problem.

disorganized c. Optometric Extension Program: A case whose compensations to an existing visual problem are not considered to be habitually fixed, and, hence, are readily adjustable to changes in lens prescription. Syn., *nonimbedded case.*

imbedded c. Organized case.

nonimbedded c. Disorganized case.

organized c. Optometric Extension Program: A case considered to have made habitually fixed compensations to an existing visual problem; hence, the case is highly unresponsive to changes in lens prescription and/or visual training. Syn., *imbedded case.*

reversal c. Optometric Extension Program: A case considered to have maintained a prolonged inhibition of a particular function so that when the inhibition is released, an excessive reverse action occurs.

trial c. A set of trial lenses and supporting rack or container used for refracting the eye.

type, c. Optometric Extension Program: In general, any of several groups into which cases have been classified for diagnostic purposes, with the concept that all cases falling into a particular case type would respond to a common therapy or to common therapeutic principles. The classifying criteria are frequently other than the type of lenses needed for best distance visual acuity.

type A, c. *Optometric Extension Program:* Those cases in which static retinoscopy (No. 4), base-in prism to break and recover at 20 ft. (No. 11), phoria at 16 in. through the subjective finding (No. 13B), and base-in prism to break and recover at 16 in. (No. 17B) are concomitantly and quantitatively below the population mean. Also called "toxic interference case." Case type A is held to be characteristic of patients having systemic disturbances of nonvisual origin.

type B_1, c. *Optometric Extension Program:* A case type characterized by the base-out prism finding to break and recover at 16 in. (No. 16B) falling below the population mean, or similar standard. A few cases showing No. 16B "low" are classified as case type C (*q.v.*) on the basis of additional criteria, but in general No. 16B low is characteristic of case type B_1, also called the "accommodative problem" type of case. This syndrome is held by the Optometric Extension Program to be indicative of a need for extra convex lens power for both distant and near-point work. However, this basic therapeutic principle for this case type may be qualified as indicated by additional criteria. These additional criteria have been systematized by the Optometric Extension Program into subcase types called "degenerations" of the basic type. Two systems of identifying these degenerations have arisen. One of these labels the basic syndrome B_1-1 with the successive degenerations terminating in B_1-7. The other system starts with the basic syndrome labeled B_1-Simple and terminates in B_1-6. The latter

system of notation is utilized in the material on this subject which follows.

type B_1-Simple, c. *Optometric Extension Program:* A case type in which the following findings are concomitantly equal to, or in excess of, the population mean (or similar standard): dynamic retinoscopy (No. 5), base-out prism to break and recover at 20 ft. (No. 10), base-in prism to break and recover at 16 in. (No. 17B), dissociated cross-cylinder finding at 16 in. (No. 14A), base-out prism to blur-out at 16 in. (No. 16A), plus to blur-out at 16 in. (No. 21), and minus to first blur on reading material at 13 in. (No. 19). At the same time the following findings are concomitantly below the population mean (or similar standard): base-in prism to break and recover at 20 ft. (No. 11), base-out prism to break and recover at 16 in. (No. 16B), phoria at 16 in. through the dissociated cross-cylinder finding (No. 15A), base-in prism to blur-out at 16 in. (No. 20). This syndrome is said to be characteristic of those B_1 cases most readily amenable to convex lens therapy for both distant and near-point work.

type B_1-1, c. *Optometric Extension Program:* The first degeneration of the basic type characterized by the No. 14A finding dropping below its expected value. Other finding relationships of the basic type remain unchanged. This syndrome is said to indicate a lowering of the acceptance of convex lenses at the near point, below the tolerance of the B_1-Simple.

type B_1-2, c. *Optometric Extension Program:* The second degeneration of the basic type characterized by a rise of the No. 15A finding above its expected value, with the other finding relationships of the B_1-1 remaining constant. This case typing is said to show a further decrease in the ability to accept extra convex lens power for use at the near point.

type B_1-3, c. *Optometric Extension Program:* The third degeneration of the basic type characterized by some change (any change) in the relationships of the No. 16A, No. 17A, No. 20, and No. 21 findings from those expected in the B_1-Simple case, with the other relationships of the B_1-2 remaining constant, said to indicate increasing resistance to convex lens therapy from that of the B_1-2. Visual training procedures to increase convex lens acceptance may accordingly be necessary.

type B_1-4, c. *Optometric Extension Program:* The fourth degeneration of the basic B_1 type characterized by the dropping of the No. 19 finding below its expected value of 5 diopters. Cases falling in this type are said to show still greater resistance to convex lens application than the B_1-3's, with the increased likelihood that the patient will need visual training before the desired extra convex lens power can be tolerated.

type B_1-5, c. *Optometric Extension Program:* The fifth degeneration of the basic type characterized by the falling of the No. 10 finding below its expected value. This syndrome is said to indicate that the amount of convex lens power prescribed for both distant and near-point work be held to a minimum. Visual training is considered to be required in many instances.

type B_1-6, c. *Optometric Extension Program:* The sixth degeneration of the basic type characterized by the No. 5 finding falling below its expected value. This syndrome is said to indicate

that the amount of convex lens power prescribed for both distant and near-point work be held to a minimum. Visual training is almost always required. Those cases in which the No. 5, the No. 10, and the No. 16B are concomitantly below their expected value are to be considered carefully for possible assignment to the C case type category (*q.v.*).

type B_2, c. *Optometric Extension Program:* A case type characterized by the base-in prism finding to break and recover at 16 in. (No. 17B) falling below the population mean, or similar standard. The B_2 case differs from the B_1 case type in that in the former the No. 16B finding is above its expected value and the No. 17B finding is below its expected value. This reversal of these two findings is said to be characteristic of an increased demand for extra convex lens power for near-point work and a reduction in convex lens power for distant work. Also called the *Intensified Near-Point Problem* type of case. The B_2 case type has been subdivided into six degenerations from the basic type in a manner similar to the B_1.

type B_2-Simple, c. *Optometric Extension Program:* A case type with all finding relationships identical to the B_1-Simple (*q.v.*) except that the No. 16B and the No. 17B findings are reversed. The therapeutic significance of the B_2-Simple differs from that of the B_1-Simple in that the former is said to call more insistently for an increase in convex lens power at the near point than does the latter, while at the same time calling for a decrease in convex lens power at the far point.

type B_2-1, c. *Optometric Extension Program:* The B_2 counterpart of the B_1-1 with the No.

16B and the No. 17B of the latter transposed. The B_2-1 calls for the same type of modification of the basic B_2 therapy as does the B_1-1 of the basic B_1 therapy.

type B_2-2, c. *Optometric Extension Program:* The B_2 counterpart of the B_1-2 with the No. 16B and No. 17B of the latter reversed. The B_2-2 calls for the same modification of the basic B_2 therapy as does the B_1-2 of the basic B_1 therapy.

type B_2-3, c. *Optometric Exsion Program:* The B_2 counterpart of the B_1-3 with the No. 16B and No. 17B of the latter reversed. The B_2-3 calls for same modification of the basic B_2 therapy as does the B_1-3 of the basic B_1 therapy.

type B_2-4, c. *Optometric Extension Program:* The B_2 counterpart of the B_1-4 with the No. 16B and No. 17B of the latter reversed. The B_2-4 calls for the same modification of the basic B_2 therapy as does the B_1-4 of the basic B_1 therapy.

type B_2-5, c. *Optometric Extension Program:* The B_2 counterpart of the B_1-5 with the No. 16B and No. 17B of the latter reversed. The B_2-5 calls for the same modification of the basic B_2 therapy as does the B_1-5 of the basic B_1 therapy.

type B_2-6, c. *Optometric Extension Program:* The B_2 counterpart of the B_1-6 with the No. 16B and No. 17B of the latter reversed. The B_2-6 calls for same modification of the basic B_2 therapy as does the B_1-6 of the basic B_1 therapy. Since No. 17B rather than No. 16B is below its expected value, the B_2-6 can never be classified as a C type case.

type B_3, c. *Optometric Extension Program:* Originally said to be characterized by the No. 5, No. 9, and No. 14A being above

their expected values concomitantly with No. 10 and No. 16B low. Since it was not characterized by a distinctive therapy, this classification has fallen into disuse, and cases formerly included in it are now classified as B_1-5's. Also known as *Undeveloped Type, Accommodative Problem. Obs.*

type C, c. *Optometric Extension Program:* Those cases with the No. 5, No. 10, and No. 16B below their expected values (see *case type B_1-6*), in which, through the use of additional criteria, it is decided that the patient is not amenable to convex lenses, even through visual training. Also known as *Adductive Problem.* Formerly called case type C_1 before the dropping of the categories of C_2 and C_3 (*q.v.*).

type C_1, c. *Optometric Extension Program:* Same as case type C (*q.v.*). Originally devised to provide a label distinctive from C_2 and C_3. Since these latter categories have fallen into disuse, the C_1 label has been simplified to C. *Obs.*

type C_2, c. *Optometric Extension Program:* Originally said to be characterized by both the syndrome of the C case (No. 5, No. 10, and No. 16B low) and the syndrome of the A case (No. 4, No. 11, No. 13B, and No. 17B low). Since such cases were handled as A cases, no distinctive therapy resulted, and the classification was discarded eventually through disuse. Also called *Adductive Problem, Toxic Type. Obs.*

type C_3, c. *Optometric Extension Program:* Originally said to be characterized by No. 5, No. 10, No. 16B, and No. 19 concomitantly below their expected values. Also known as *Adductive Problem with Presbyopia.* Since this type of case is said to accept convex lenses for near-point work and can thus be handled as a B_1-5 case type, the C_3 was not characterized by a distinctive therapy and fell into disuse. *Obs.*

Caspar's opacity (kas'parz). See under *opacity*.

cast. A lay term for strabismus.

casting. A positive model of the anterior segment of the eye, for use in the preparation of a contact lens, made by filling the negative model or mold of the eye with a mastic which hardens to artificial stone.

catacaustic (kat"ah-kaws'tik). A caustic resulting from reflected light or produced by a reflecting optical surface or system.

catacleisis (kat"ah-kli'sis). Adhesive or spasmodic closure of the eyelids.

catadioptric (kat"ah-di-op'trik). Employing both reflecting and refracting optical systems.

catamysis (kat"ah-mi'sis). Closure of the eyelids.

cataphoria (kat"ah-fo're-ah). 1. A tendency of the visual axes of both eyes to deviate below the horizontal plane of the head in the absence of a stimulus eliciting fixation attention. 2. Rarely, hypophoria.

> *double c.* 1. Cataphoria. 2. Double hypophoria.

cataract (kat'ah-rakt). Partial or complete loss of transparency of the crystalline lens or its capsule; an opacity of the crystalline lens or its capsule.

> *aculeiform c.* Spear cataract.

> *adherent c.* A lenticular opacity in which the lens capsule is attached or adherent to the iris. Syn., *cataracta accreta.*

> *adolescent c.* A lenticular opacity which develops during youth.

> *aftercataract.* Secondary cataract.

> *amber c.* A mature senile cataract characterized by an amber-colored opacity. See also *black cataract.*

> *annular c.* Disk-shaped cataract.

> *anterior axial embryonic c.* A common congenital anomaly which does not affect vision, characterized by the presence of several small white dots in the region of the anterior Y-suture.

> *anterior capsular c.* A small, white, well-defined, centrally located opacity of the anterior lens capsule occurring in early life as a congenital anomaly or due to a perforating ulcer of the cornea.

> *anterior polar c.* A lenticular opacity situated at the anterior pole of the lens which affects the lens substance and capsule or, rarely, the capsule only. It is either congenital or the result of a perforating corneal ulcer.

> *anterior pyramidal c.* A type of anterior polar cataract shaped like a pyramid with the apex pointing anteriorly.

> *arborescent c.* A lenticular opacity which has the appearance of branching lines.

> *aridosiliculose c.* Siliculose cataract.

> *aridosiliquate c.* Siliculose cataract.

> *atopic c.* A lenticular opacity associated with atopic allergic dermatitis, usually bilateral and subcapsular, and appearing in either of two typical forms, as a radiating star-shaped opacity or as a dense, white, irregularly shaped plaque.

> *axial c.* A lenticular opacity situated along the anteroposterior axis of the crystalline lens.

> *axial fusiform c.* A congenital central lenticular opacity elongated anteroposteriorly and touching upon both poles of the lens. Syn., *fusiform cataract.*

> *axillary c.* Spindle cataract.

> *bipolar c.* Cataract involving both the anterior and the posterior poles of the crystalline lens.

> *black c.* A mature senile cataract in which the lens has a black

appearance. In the earlier sclerosing stages, the lens changes in color from yellow to amber (amber cataract) or gray (gray cataract), to reddish-brown, or, in a few cases, to black. Syn., *cataracta nigra.*

blood c. A blood clot anterior to the lens which obstructs the pupil, hence not actually a cataract. Syn., *sanguineous cataract.*

blue c. Blue dot cataract.

blue dot c. A developmental anomaly of the crystalline lens, found so frequently in adults as almost to be considered physiological, consisting of numerous small opacities in the adult cortex and nucleus seen only by oblique illumination as fine blue-white dots. Syn., *blue cataract; cerulean cataract; dotted cataract; punctate cataract; cataracta cerulea.*

bony c. Cataracta ossea.

bottle maker's c. Glass blower's cataract.

brown c. A mature, senile cataract characterized by a brown-colored opacity. See also *black cataract.* Syn., *cataracta brunescens.*

cachectic c. Binocular, rapidly maturing, lenticular opacities found associated with weakness and emaciation due to either acute toxic illness or starvation.

calcareous c. Chalky cataract.

capsular c. An opacity affecting the crystalline lens capsule only.

capsulolenticular c. An opacity involving both the capsule and the substance of the crystalline lens.

caseous c. Cheesy cataract.

central c. An opacity of the central area of the crystalline lens.

central pulverulent c. A rare type of nonprogressive, usually bilateral, centrally located, variably sized, lenticular opacity occurring with a familial tendency and composed of a group of small, discrete, white dots, each of which may be surrounded by a

halo. Ophthalmoscopically it appears as a sharply defined, circular disk which blocks the ordinary pupil, and with the slit lamp is seen to be in the fetal or embryonic nucleus. Syn., *Coppock cataract; discoid cataract; Doyne's cataract; Nettleship's cataract.*

cerulean c. Blue dot cataract.

chalky c. A hypermature cataract characterized by the presence of lime salt deposits. Syn., *calcareous cataract.*

cheesy c. A hypermature cataract in which the degenerated tissue has a cheesy appearance. Syn., *caseous cataract.*

cholesterin c. A hypermature cataract characterized by the presence of deposits of cholesterin.

choroidal c. A complicated cataract which follows inflammatory or degenerative processes in the posterior segment of the eye, the most frequent causes being high myopia and primary pigmentary degeneration of the retina.

complete c. An opacity which involves the entire crystalline lens.

complicated c. A lenticular opacity which accompanies or appears secondary to other intraocular disease. It is characterized initially by a polychromatic iridescence and a localized hazy opacity in the posterior subcapsular, usually polar, region. The opacity progresses, takes on a rosette shape, and continues to spread axially and peripherally to involve the entire lens. Syn., *cataracta complicata.*

concussion c. A type of traumatic cataract which results from an explosion or other form of concussion.

congenital c. A lenticular opacity present at birth.

contusion c. A type of traumatic cataract resulting from a bruising wound to the eyeball.

Coppock c. An old name for *central pulverulent cataract* (q.v.), from the Coppock family in which the anomaly was studied by Nettleship and Ogilvie.

coralliform c. A hereditary, congenital crystalline cataract occurring in the axial region of the lens, particularly in the fetal nucleus, in either of two forms. One radiates anteroposteriorly and is composed of amorphous, tubular, or discoid opacities. The other is made of masses of rectangular or rhomboid crystals lying in clusters.

coronary c. A series of opacities in a crown or ring formation at the periphery of the crystalline lens, the extreme periphery remaining clear; developmental in origin and common in occurrence. The opacities are usually club-shaped, with the rounded end pointing toward the center.

cortical c. A cataract in which the opacity lies in the cortex of the crystalline lens. According to the nature and position of the opacity, a number of types such as *cuneiform* and *cupuliform* are differentiated.

cretinous c. Lenticular opacity associated with cretinism.

crystalline c. Cataract characterized by random deposits of crystals in the axial region. They tend to be bilateral and hereditary, may impede vision if extensive, and are of various shapes but usually coralliform or needle-shaped.

cuneiform c. The most typical form of senile cortical cataract in which the opacities run from the periphery toward the center of the lens like spokes on a wheel.

cupuliform c. A form of senile cortical cataract consisting of many minute, yellow-appearing opacities lying in the posterior layers of the cortex directly beneath the capsule.

cystic c. Morgagnian cataract.

degenerative c. Any opacity of the normally developed crystalline lens which results from a degenerative change. One of the two major classifications of cataract (the other being *developmental cataract*) which includes senile cataracts, radiation cataracts, and others.

dermatogenous c. A lenticular opacity associated with general skin disease.

developmental c. A lenticular opacity due to interference with normal development of the crystalline lens. The cause may be heredity, malnutrition, or inflammation. One of the two major types of cataract, the other being *degenerative cataract.*

diabetic c. A rapidly forming bilateral cataract associated with diabetes mellitus. The senile form does not vary from the nondiabetic senile form, but the cataract in the young diabetic is typically the snowflake cataract.

dilacerated c. A type of juvenile cataract characterized by a delicate fretted structure, single or multiple, usually associated with some other type of opacity.

dinitrophenol c. A lenticular opacity due to the ingestion of dinitrophenol (DNP), a drug sometimes taken to reduce body weight.

disciform c. A type of congenital or developmental cataract consisting of a ring-shaped band opacity surrounding a central clear area.

discoid c. Cataracta centralis pulverulenta.

disk-shaped c. A congenital or developmental defect, usually bilateral, in which the lens nucleus is absent and is represented by a thin opaque membrane. A ring of lens fibers, of normal thickness, encircles this membrane, imparting to the lens the appearance of a lifebuoy, or in section that of a dumbbell. The surrounding lens fibers may be partially or completely opaque except at the extreme periphery, where they may remain clear. Syn., *annular cataract; lifebuoy cataract; umbilicated cataract.*

dotted c. Blue dot cataract.

Doyne's c. Cataracta centralis pulverulenta.

dry-shelled c. Siliculose cataract.

electric c. Cataract resulting from electric shock. Syn., *fulguration cataract.*

ergot c. Cataract due to ergot poisoning caused by the eating of rye cereals contaminated by a fungus. Syn., *cataracta raphanica.*

false c. False lenticonus.

fasciculiform c. Spear cataract.

fibrinous c. A condition in which exudate resulting from severe iridocyclitis is deposited on the lens capsule and obscures vision. A type of complicated cataract.

fibrous tissue c. Pseudophakia fibrosa.

floriform c. A type of developmental or congenital cataract in which the opacity takes the form of petals of a flower.

fluid c. A hypermature cataract which has degenerated into a milky fluid. Syn., *lacteal cataract; milky cataract.*

frosted c. Spear cataract.

fulguration c. Electric cataract.

fusiform c. Axial fusiform cataract.

galactosemic c. Cataract associated with galactosemia, a congenital disturbance of galactose metabolism. The opacities are bilateral and appear during the first three months of life. With prompt diagnosis and treatment, the prognosis for regression is good.

general c. A lenticular opacity of both lens cortex and nucleus. Syn., *mixed cataract.*

glass blower's c. A posterior cortical lens opacity found in glass blowers or steel puddlers and due to long exposure to intense heat and light. Syn., *bottle maker's cataract; heat-ray cataract.*

glaucomatous c. A type of complicated cataract occurring as a sequela of glaucoma.

gray c. A mature senile cataract characterized by a gray-colored opacity. See also *black cataract.*

green c. A green-gray pupil in advanced glaucoma, due to partial loss of transparency of the media; not a true cataract.

grumous c. An opacity due to hemorrhage into the cornea, aqueous, or vitreous; not a true cataract. *Obs.* Syn., *cataracta cruenta.*

gypseous c. A hypermature, white-appearing, lenticular opacity.

hard c. Cataract in which the lens nucleus has become hard, such as a nuclear cataract. Syn., *sclerocataracta.*

heat-ray c. Cataract due to long exposure to high temperatures. Syn., *glass blower's cataract.*

hedger's c. A corneal opacity due to a perforating wound caused by a thorn; so named because of its frequency in persons who trim hedges; not a true cataract. *Obs.*

heterochromic c. A complicated cataract secondary to heterochromic cyclitis.

hyaloid c. An opacity in the anterior portion of the vitreous; not a true cataract. *Obs.*

hypermature c. The fourth stage in the development of senile cataract, in which the lens becomes either dehydrated and flattened or liquid and soft. See also *incipient, immature,* and *mature cataract.* Syn., *overripe cataract.*

immature c. The second stage in the development of senile cataract, during which the lens absorbs fluid and swells considerably. See also *incipient, mature,* and *hypermature cataract.* Syn., *unripe cataract.*

incipient c. The first stage of senile cataract development which usually begins with the appearance of streaks similar to the spokes of a wheel or with an increased density of the nucleus. There is little loss of vision and frequently the cataract does not progress beyond this stage. See also *immature, mature,* and *hypermature cataract.*

infantile c. A lenticular opacity present in an infant or very young child.

infrared c. Cataract due to excessive exposure to infrared radiation.

intumescent c. A cataract characterized by an absorption of water and, consequently, a swollen lens.

irradiation c. A cataract caused by exposure to radium or x-ray radiation. It is sometimes synonymous with radiational cataract and, hence, due to overexposure to any form of radiant energy.

juvenile c. A congenital or developmental defect of the crystalline lens.

lacteal c. A hypermature senile cataract in which both the cortex and the nucleus have degenerated into a milky fluid. Syn., *cataracta lactea.*

lamellar c. Zonular cataract.

lenticular c. An opacity which appears in the crystalline lens but not in the capsule.

lifebuoy c. Disk-shaped cataract.

lightning c. 1. Cataract found in persons who have been struck by lightning. 2. A cataract attributed to a person's having observed flashes of lightning.

mature c. The third stage in the development of senile cataract. The lens has lost the fluid which was taken on in the preceding stage, has become completely opaque, and may be easily separated from the capsule. See also *incipient, immature,* and *hypermature cataract.* Syn., *ripe cataract.*

membranous c. A congenital condition in which the substance of the crystalline lens is absorbed, leaving the lens capsule collapsed upon itself in the form of a gray or chalky white membrane. The absorption may be complete at birth or become complete after birth. Syn., *pseudoaphakia.*

milky c. Fluid cataract.

mixed c. General cataract.

Mongolian c. A lenticular opacity associated with Mongolian idiocy.

Morgagnian c. A cataract in which the cortex has degenerated into a milky white fluid with the nucleus usually degenerated and at the bottom of the capsule. Syn., *cystic cataract.*

myotonic c. A cataract secondary to myotonic dystrophy and characterized by fine dustlike punctate opacities localized just beneath the capsule.

naphthalinic c. Cataract caused by the ingestion of naphthalene.

needle-shaped c. Spear cataract.

Nettleship's c. Cataracta centralis pulverulenta.

neutron c. Cataract due to neutron radiation from atomic explosion, characterized initially by posterior cortical opacities which may progress to involve the entire lens cortex.

nuclear c. An opacity of the central nucleus of the crystalline lens. Syn., *central cataract.*

overripe c. Hypermature cataract.

partial c. An opacity of only part of the crystalline lens.

perinuclear c. An opacity around the nucleus of the crystalline lens.

peripheral c. An opacity in the periphery, or away from the center, of the crystalline lens.

pigmented c. A type of traumatic cataract characterized by a deposition on the crystalline lens of pigment detached from the iris. See also *Vossius ring cataract.*

pisciform c. Rare congenital opacities in the axial region of the lens, characteristically curved, wider and rounder at one end and narrow and pointed at the other, simulating the shape of a fish.

poikilodermic c. Cataract occurring in association with the skin condition of poikiloderma.

polar c. An opacity at either pole of the crystalline lens. See also *anterior polar cataract; posterior polar cataract.*

posterior capsular c. A congenital anomaly in which the posterior capsule is affected.

posterior cortical c. Any lenticular opacity beginning in the posterior cortex, such as *radiational cataract.*

posterior polar c. An opacity at the posterior pole of the crystalline lens, usually due to remnants of the hyaloid artery or of the posterior fibrovascular sheath of the lens (not a true cataract). A true cataract sometimes develops as a result of degenerative changes of the lens fibers in this region.

primary c. A lenticular opacity not associated with any other ocular or general disease.

progressive c. A lenticular opacity which has passed, or will pass if not arrested, through the immature, mature, and hypermature stages.

punctate c. A cataract consisting of numerous small, discrete, dotlike opacities scattered throughout the crystalline lens.

pupillary c. A congenital iris defect in which the pupil is not formed; not a true cataract.

pyramidal c. An anterior polar cataract, conoidal in shape with the apex pointing forward. Sometimes this name is given to a congenital anterior polar cataract which protrudes into the anterior chamber as a laminated prominence.

radiational c. An opacity of the crystalline lens resulting from overexposure to any form of radiant energy. Wavelengths between 8,000 and 15,000 Å are believed to be particularly harmful. Such cataracts usually begin in the posterior cortex, occasionally in the anterior cortex, or in both simultaneously.

reduplicated c. A type of congenital anterior polar cataract characterized by an opaque area in the capsular region and another in the cortex, with a clear layer of lens substance between.

ripe c. Mature cataract.

rosette-shaped c. A star-shaped or leaf-shaped lenticular opacity resulting from trauma.

rubella c. Congenital cataract in which the mother has been infected with German measles during the first three months of pregnancy. It is more often bilateral and occurs either as a dense, pearly white, central opacity with a clear periphery, or as a total opacity.

sanguineous c. Blood cataract.

secondary c. An opacity of the lens capsule after the crystalline lens has been removed by an extracapsular operation. Syn., *aftercataract.*

sedimentary c. A soft cataract, the denser parts of which have moved downward, due to gravity.

senile c. A lenticular opacity in older persons. This is the most frequently seen type of cataract and its etiology presumably differs from those of others, such as *congenital, traumatic,* etc. The opacity is usually nuclear.

shrunken fibrous tissue c. A congenital posterior polar cataract in which fibrous tissue has invaded the lens substance, leaving the lens filled with shrunken, degenerated, fibrocellular material.

siliculose c. A cataract characterized by absorption and atrophy of the crystalline lens and calcareous deposit in the capsule. Syn., *aridosiliculose cataract; aridosiliquate cataract; dry-shelled cataract; siliquose cataract.*

siliquose c. Siliculose cataract.

snowflake c. 1. A familial, infantile, cortical cataract characterized by grayish or whitish flakelike opacities of irregular outline. The condition may be progressive and may occur in conjunction with stellate cataract. Syn., *cataracta nivea.* 2. A cataract characterized by numerous blue-white flakelike opacities. It is usually associated with severe diabetes and is the typical cataract in young diabetics.

soft c. Cataract in which the crystalline lens is of soft consistency and milky appearance, typified by congenital or juvenile cataract in which the lens nucleus has not hardened.

solar c. A cataract due to absorption of radiant energy from the sun. Wavelengths between 8,000 and 15,000 Å are believed to be particularly harmful.

spear c. A hereditary, congenital crystalline cataract in the axial region of the lens consisting of branching needle-shaped opacities, randomly arranged, and variously reported to be situated in the embryonic, fetal, or adult nucleus. Syn., *aculeiform cataract; fasciculiform cataract; frosted cataract; needle-shaped cataract; Vogt's cataract.*

spindle c. A spindle-shaped, lenticular opacity extending in an anteroposterior direction. Syn., *axillary cataract.*

spurious c. An opacity caused by adhesion of extraneous substance to the capsule of the crystalline lens, usually remnants of the hyaloid artery if on the posterior capsule, or of the pupillary membrane if on the anterior capsule; not a true cataract. Syn., *cataracta spuria.*

stationary c. A lenticular opacity which has not become more extensive over a considerable period of time.

stellate c. Sutural cataract.

steroid c. Cataract attributed to prolonged use of corticosteroids, characterized by discrete granular opacities in the posterior subcapsular polar region.

subcapsular c. A lenticular opacity situated beneath the capsule of the crystalline lens.

sunflower c. A sunflower-shaped opacity of the crystalline lens consequent upon the presence of copper, as in hepatolenticular degeneration. Syn., *chalcosis lentis.*

sutural c. An opacity developing about the time of birth and affecting the Y-shaped sutures of the fetal nucleus. Syn., *stellate cataract; triradiate cataract.*

tetany c. Cataract occurring in association with tetany, typically zonular when congenital or infantile, and subcapsular when occurring spontaneously in later life or following parathyroid damage or removal. Syn., *cataracta parathyropiva.*

total c. A cataract involving the entire lens substance.

toxic c. A lenticular opacity in individuals who have been exposed to certain drugs, such as paradichlorobenzene or dinitrophenol. See also *dinitrophenol cataract.*

traumatic c. The general term for any lenticular opacity resulting from injury to the crystalline lens, its capsule, or the eyeball itself. Traumatic is sometimes used when the wound is perforating; contusion, when nonperforating; and concussion, when resulting from an explosion.

tremulous c. A cataract associated with tremulous movement of the crystalline lens and iris upon the movement of the eyeball. Syn., *vacillating cataract.*

triradiate c. Sutural cataract.

true c. Lenticular cataract as opposed to other disorders such as *blood cataract* or *fibrinous cataract.*

umbilicated c. Disk-shaped cataract.

unripe c. Immature cataract.

vacillating c. Tremulous cataract.

vesicular c. A rare form of congenital cataract characterized by a few vesiclelike opacities scattered throughout the lens substance.

Vogt's c. Spear cataract.

Vossius ring c. A rare type of traumatic cataract consisting of an annulus 3 or 4 mm. in diameter at the center of the crystalline lens, believed to be composed of pigment from the posterior iris. Syn., *Vossius ring opacity; Vossius lenticular ring.*

x-ray c. A lenticular opacity due to prolonged exposure to roentgen rays.

zonular c. A lenticular opacity affecting one layer only, with clear lens substance on either side of the opaque zone or the lamella. Syn., *lamellar cataract.*

cataracta (kat″ah-rak′tah). Cataract.

accreta, c. The condition in which lens capsule and iris are adherent due to an iridocyclitic inflammation. Syn., *adherent cataract.*

acquisita, c. Any noncongenital lens opacity.

adiposa, c. Pseudophakia lipomatosa.

adnata, c. Congenital cataract.

adventitia, c. Any noncongenital, crystalline lens opacity.

arborescens, c. Arborescent cataract.

axialis, c. Axial cataract.

brunescens, c. Brown cataract.

centralis lentis, c. Nuclear cataract.

central pulverulent cataract. See *cataract.*

cerulea, c. Blue dot cataract.

complicata, c. Complicated cataract.

confirmata, c. Mature cataract.

congenita membranacea, c. A congenital membranous cataract.

congenita vasculosa, c. A congenital condition in which the crystalline lens has been invaded and replaced by vascularized mesodermal tissue.

consecutiva, c. Secondary cataract.

coronaria, c. Coronary cataract.

cruenta, c. Grumous cataract.

dermatogenes, c. Dermatogenous cataract.

elastica, c. Tremulous cataract.

fibrosa, c. Pseudophakia fibrosa.

fusca, c. A mature senile cataract in which the lens has a reddish-brown appearance.

gelatinosa, c. Soft cataract.

glauca, c. Green cataract.

glaucomatosa acuta, c. A cataract characterized by multiple, circumscribed, white spots beneath the anterior lens capsule. These are very white during an attack of glaucoma and less intense and more transparent when the intraocular pressure is reduced.

lactea, c. Lacteal cataract.

membranacea accreta, c. An aftercataract due to adherence of the anterior to the posterior capsule.

migrans, c. An opaque, dislocated, crystalline lens.

mollis, c. Soft cataract.

neurodermatica, c. The most common form of dermatogenous cataract.

nigra, c. Black cataract.

nivea, c. Snowflake cataract.

ossea, c. 1. Pseudophakia ossea. 2. A condition characterized by scar tissue and ossification of the crystalline lens. Syn., *bony cataract.*

parathyropiva, c. Tetany cataract.

raphanica, c. Ergot cataract.

scabrosa, c. Soft cataract.

spuria, c. Spurious cataract.

syndermotica, c. Dermatogenous cataract.

tenax, c. Hard cataract.

cataractous (kat″ah-rak′tus). Cataractlike; affected with cataract.

catarrh (kah-tahr′). Inflammation of a mucous membrane, accompanied by a mucus discharge.

atropine c. Atropine conjunctivitis.

dry c. Conjunctival hyperemia not consequent upon the presence of microorganisms. It is often caused by local irritants, may accompany nasal catarrh or hay fever, and may be associated with uncorrected errors of refraction.

Fruehjahr's c. Vernal conjunctivitis.

Saemisch c. Vernal conjunctivitis.

spring c. Vernal conjunctivitis.

vernal c. Vernal conjunctivitis.

catatropia (kat″ah-tro′pe-ah). 1. A strabismus characterized by the downward deviation of either eye while the other fixates. Syn., *alternating* or *double hypotropia.* 2. Alternating or double hypophoria.

cathodoluminescence (kath″o-do-lu″mih-nes′ens). Light resulting from bombardment by electrons.

catophoria (kat″o-fo′re-ah). Cataphoria.

catopter (kă-top′ter). A reflecting optical instrument; a mirror.

catoptric (kă-top′trik). Relating to a mirror or to reflected light; made by, or based on, reflection.

catoptrics (kă-top′triks). The branch of optics dealing with the behavior of light when it is reflected.

catoptry (kă-top′tre). The unit of reflective power of mirrors. A mirror that will reflect parallel rays of light to a point of focus at a distance of 1 m. from the mirror has a unit of reflective power of 1 catoptry.

catotropia (kat″o-tro′pe-ah). Catatropia.

caustic (kaws′tik). The focal concentration of light in the caustic

surface of a bundle of converging light rays.

cave, Meckel's. A cavity housing the Gasserian ganglion and located between the two layers of the dura mater near the apex of the petrous portion of the temporal bone. Syn., *Meckel's cavity; Meckel's space.*

caverns, Schnabel's. Schnabel's spaces.

cavity, Meckel's. Meckel's cave.

cavum lenticuli (ka′vum len-tik′u-li). A small fluid-filled vesicle located between the annular pad and crystalline lens in the eyes of some birds and reptiles; a remnant of the embryonic lens vesicle.

c.c. Abbreviation for *comfort cable* (*temple*).

cc. Abbreviation for *concave.*

cd. Abbreviation for *candela.*

cecity (se′sih-te). Blindness. *Obs.*

cedmatophthalmia (sed-mat″of-thal′me-ah). Inflammation of the eye secondary to rheumatism or gout.

cell. 1. Any of the minute masses of protoplasm containing a nucleus which make up organized tissue. 2. A rim or socket in a trial frame or an optical instrument into which a lens is mounted. 3. A compartment or small hollow receptacle.

absorption c., Pfund's. A device for measuring light absorption of gases and vapors consisting of a chamber containing the absorptive gas or vapor, at each end of which is a pair of centrally perforated and internally reflecting concave mirrors of equal curvature separated by their focal length on a common axis, whence a beam of light entering the chamber in focus at one of the mirror perforations reflects successively at each mirror, thereby traversing the length of the chamber three times, and exists in focus at the perforation of the other mirror.

absorption c., White's. An optical system used to measure the light absorption of gases or vapors in which three converging mirrors increase the optical path by eight times the length of the system.

amacrine c. 1. A neuron with cell body in the inner nuclear layer of the retina whose nerve fibers synapse with ganglion cells and centripetal bipolar cells. 2. A centrifugal bipolar cell which sends an ascending fiber (axon) to synapse with cone feet and possibly with rod spherules and receives impulses from centripetal bipolar cells, ganglion cells, and efferent fibers of the optic nerve. 3. A neuron without an axon. Proper staining has revealed an axon in most amacrines.

amacrine c., knotty. An amacrine cell, identified by Polyak, having its body deep in the inner nuclear layer and dendritic processes arborizing throughout the inner molecular layer; its synaptic relations are obscure.

amacrine c., tasselled. An amacrine cell, identified by Polyak, having its cell body deep in the inner nuclear layer and dendritic processes which arborize laterally immediately upon entering the inner molecular layer; its synaptic relations are obscure.

associational c's. 1. Neurons completely in the brain or the spinal cord which functionally synapse with other neurons. 2. Cells in the retina which synapse with retinal cells of the visual pathway, such as horizontal cells, amacrine cells, and centrifugal bipolar cells.

barrier-layer c. Photovoltaic cell.

basal c's., corneal. The row of corneal epithelial cells adjacent to the basement membrane. Having rounded outer surfaces

and flat inner surfaces, they undergo mitosis and are sloughed at the surface about a week after their origin.

Betz's c's. Giant pyramidal neurons located in the voluntary motor areas of the frontal cortex, with their cell bodies in layer 5 and their axons entering the corticobulbar and corticospinal tracts. They are the upper motor neurons that are under voluntary control when skeletal muscle, such as an extraocular muscle, is willfully contracted.

bipolar retinal c's. 1. Neurons whose cell bodies lie in the inner nuclear layer of the retina and connect rods or cones with the ganglionic cells. They are of two types: monosynaptic, connecting only a single cone to a single ganglion cell; and polysynaptic, connecting rods and/or cones to a ganglion cell. Both types are termed centripetal. 2. Neurons which receive impulses from efferent axons in the optic nerve and from ganglion cells and relay them to the visual cells. This type is termed centrifugal.

bipolar retinal c's., brush. Diffuse bipolar retinal cells characterized by a single main dendritic expansion which terminates in a series of brushlike filaments of equal length in the inner zone of the outer plexiform layer, and by an axon that synapses only with dendritic processes of ganglion cells and not with their cell bodies.

bipolar retinal c's., diffuse. Bipolar retinal cells that synapse with several rod or cone cells or with both; polysynaptic retinal bipolar cells. Cf. *midget bipolar retinal cells.*

bipolar retinal c's., flat-top. Diffuse bipolar retinal cells characterized by a single dendritic expansion which terminates in undulating lateral branches in the inner zone of the outer plexiform layer, and by an axon that synapses only with dendritic processes of ganglion cells and not with their cell bodies.

bipolar retinal c's., midget. Bipolar retinal cells characterized by a small cell body and thin, short, closely grouped dendritic ramifications which are smallest in the foveal area. They are monosynaptic in the central area, connecting one cone cell to one midget ganglion cell. Cf. *diffuse bipolar retinal cells.*

bipolar retinal c's., mop. Diffuse bipolar retinal cells characterized by a dendritic process which repetitively divides into a moplike group of terminal branches, synapsing with both cone and rod cells, and an axon which synapses mainly with cell bodies of ganglion cells, although some branches do synapse with dendrites.

Cajal's c. Astrocyte.

clump c. A round or oval cell which is found in the stroma of the iris especially near the sphincter muscle, without processes and containing melanin; a derivative of the distal end of the neural ectoderm of the optic cup.

cone c. 1. A type of photoreceptor cell in the retina, consisting of an outer and an inner member in the layer of rods and cones, a nucleus in the outer nuclear layer, and a cone fiber and cone foot in the outer plexiform layer. It synapses with a bipolar cell and is involved in color vision, high visual acuity, and photopic vision. There are about 6 or 7 million in each retina, the greatest proportion of which are located in the macular area. The cell is long, thin, and somewhat rodlike in the area of the fovea centralis, becoming shorter and more conical toward the periph-

ery. 2. The cone proper, consisting of the outer and inner members only.

corneal c. A specific form of fibroblast which has processes continuous with those of other corneal cells in the stroma of the cornea. Syn., *corneal corpuscle.*

dark c. of the corneal epithelium. Secretory cell of the corneal epithelium.

Dogiel's c. A ganglion cell of the retina, the cell body of which is located in the inner zone of the inner nuclear layer instead of in the ganglion cell layer.

ganglion c. 1. A retinal cell whose dendrites synapse with axons of bipolar and other cells in the inner plexiform layer and whose axons compose the nerve fiber layer from which they pass to the optic nerve to synapse in the lateral geniculate body, the pretectal area, or the superior colliculus. Its nucleus lies in the ganglion cell layer and both monosynaptic and polysynaptic types are found. 2. A large neuron in the central nervous system or in the sensory ganglia.

ganglion c., diffuse. A ganglion cell of the retina that synapses with numerous bipolar cells of all types; a polysynaptic ganglion cell.

ganglion c., garland. A diffuse ganglion cell characterized by a medium-sized body and by a few dendrites having thin, wavy, very long branches.

ganglion c., giant. A very large diffuse ganglion cell resembling the parasol or garland ganglion cell found in the periphery of the retina.

ganglion c., midget. A ganglion cell primarily located in the central area and characterized by a small body and a single dendritic process terminating in a series of closely grouped small branches which synapse with a single midget bipolar retinal cell. However, other synapses do occur with diffuse bipolar retinal cells.

ganglion c., parasol. A medium- to large-sized diffuse ganglion cell characterized by an approximately spherical body and single or multiple dendrites which repetitively divide into an umbrellalike formation.

ganglion c., shrub. A diffuse ganglion cell characterized by a small body and two or three dendrites in a shrublike formation.

ganglion c., small diffuse. A diffuse ganglion cell characterized by a small body and long filamentous dendritic branches that spread horizontally or obliquely.

globular c's. of Elschnig. Elschnig bodies.

goblet c. 1. A unicellular, mucin-producing gland located in a mucous membrane, such as the epithelium of the conjunctiva, intestine, or respiratory tract.

Golgi spider c. A small neuroglial or supporting cell with numerous processes in the vicinity of the ganglion cell layer of the retina. These cells are most numerous near the optic disk.

horizontal c. A neuron with a cell body in the inner nuclear layer of the retina which has dendrites connecting to one or to a few cone feet in the outer plexiform layer and an axon which synapses with a distant group of cone feet and rod spherules in the outer plexiform layer. Another type may also send a descending process into the inner plexiform layer.

Kerr c. A glass-walled cell containing two condenser plates in nitrobenzene, or other isotropic fluid, which becomes birefringent when subjected to an electrical field. See also *electrooptic shutter.*

Langerhans' c's. In the eye, star-shaped cells located between the cells of the corneal epithelium.

Mueller's c's. Neuroglial cells in the retina with nuclei in the inner nuclear layer and with fibers extending between the external and internal limiting layers and forming a dense network of interlacing trabeculae in the innermost layers. They are supportive to the retinal neurons and participate in their metabolism by storing glycogen and oxidative enzymes.

photoconductive c. A photoelectric cell containing a material, the electrical resistance of which varies as a function of the intensity of the light which falls upon it.

photoelectric c. A device for detecting and measuring light, such as a photoconductive cell, or photovoltaic cell.

photoemissive c. Photoelectric cell.

photomultiplier c. Photomultiplier.

photovoltaic c. A photocell consisting essentially of three layers, a thin semitransparent metal film (cathode), a semiconductor, and a supporting metal base plate. Incident light passes through the metal film into the semiconductor, and electrons are released, creating an electrical current which may be measured by an attached meter. It is commonly used in photographic exposure meters and portable illumination meters. Syn., *barrier-layer cell.*

Photronic c. Trade name for a type of photovoltaic cell.

prickle c. In the eye, protoplasmic processes which link the cells of the corneal epithelium.

pyramidal c's. of Meynert. Cells originating in the area striata and to a lesser extent in the parastriate area, whose axons enter the optic radiations, reach the superior colliculi, and make connections with nuclei that supply skeletal muscles. Syn., *solitary cells of Meynert.*

Remak's c's. Lemmocytes.

rod c. 1. A type of photoreceptor cell in the retina, consisting of an outer and an inner member in the layer of rods and cones, an outer rod fiber and cell body in the outer nuclear layer, and an inner rod fiber and end bulb in the outer plexiform layer. It synapses with a bipolar cell, contains rhodopsin in its outer member, and is involved in scotopic vision and detection of movement. About 130 million such cells exist in a human retina, exclusive of an area 300 to 400 microns in diameter, the fovea centralis. 2. The rod proper, consisting of the outer and inner member.

   rod c., green. A rod cell in the frog retina having a mesopic spectral sensitivity curve with a maximum in the blue region (400 to 440 mμ) instead of at about 500 mμ, the usual rod maximum. Such cells constitute 8% to 10% of the rods in the frog retina.

secretory c. of the corneal epithelium. A glandlike cell sparsely distributed on the basement membrane of the cornea, which supplies the membrane with secretory material. Syn., *dark cell of the corneal epithelium.*

solitary c's. of Meynert. The pyramidal cells of Meynert.

spider c. Astrocyte.

star c. A star-shaped cell; one with many filaments extending from the cell body in all directions. The term is particularly applied to a neuroglial cell of this description.

surface c's. of the cornea. Flat squamous cells which constitute the superficial layer of the corneal epithelium.

umbrella c. Wing cell of the cornea.

visual c's. 1. The rod and cone cells

of the retina. 2. Any of the neuroepithelial cells of the retina.

wing c's. of the cornea. The umbrella-shaped cells located between the basal columnar cells and the superficial squamous cells of the corneal epithelium. Syn., *umbrella cell.*

cellulitis, orbital (sel″u-li′tis). Inflammation of the connective or cellular tissue of the orbit, usually caused by nasal accessory sinus disease, especially ethmoidal, but may be from dental infection, dacryocystitis, etc. It is usually characterized by pain, swelling, edema of the eyelid and conjunctiva, impaired mobility of the eyeball, and proptosis and may be unilateral or bilateral, mild or severe, acute or chronic. Syn., *orbital phlegmon.*

cellulosa choroideae (sel″u-lo′sah ko-roi′de-e). The suprachoroidal layer of the choroid.

cement, optical. Any of several transparent adhesive substances, such as Canada balsam and certain thermosetting resins, used to join optical surfaces.

cement substance. See under *substance.*

center. 1. A collection of nerve cell bodies in the brain or spinal cord concerned with a particular function. 2. The middle point of a body or surface.

accommodation, c's. of. Brain centers subserving accommodation, consisting of higher, or cortical, centers, thought by some to be occipital, and paired lower centers in the Edinger-Westphal nuclei which relay impulses to the ciliary ganglia.

blinking c. 1. A center controlling voluntary blinking, located in the precentral gyrus of the frontal lobe. 2. A center involved in the dazzle reflex, probably located in the superior colliculus 3. A center involved in the menace reflex, located in the occip ·

tal lobe. 4. Two facial motor nuclei in the pons.

boxing c. In the boxing method of frame specification, the point at the center of the rectangle that encloses the lens.

ciliospinal c. A collection of preganglionic sympathetic cell bodies in the lateral gray matter of cervical segments 7 and 8 and thoracic segments 1, 2, and 3 of the spinal cord. Their axons synapse in the superior cervical ganglion and supply the dilator of the pupil. Syn., *pupillo-dilatator center.*

collineation, c. of. The point associated with a thin lens or a single refracting surface which is the center of perspective of object space and image space. It is the optical center of the thin lens or the center of the single refracting surface.

convergence c. 1. The portions of the paired oculomotor nuclei which control the medial rectus muscles. 2. A presumed, unknown, higher brain center, area, or complex which subserves the function of convergence and/or controls the paired oculomotor nuclei which control the medial rectus muscles.

curvature, c. of. The intersection of two perpendiculars to an arc of a circle or a spherical surface.

datum c. The midpoint of the datum line.

distance c. 1. The intersection of the line of sight and the spectacle lens when the eye is in a straightforward position or in any position otherwise defined to represent the eyes viewing a distant object. 2. The optical center or other point of reference of the portion of a multifocal lens used for distance seeing.

fusion c. An area assumed to exist in the cortex and in which sensory fusion is said to occur. This concept was introduced by Worth

to account for the apparent absence of fusion or a "fusion sense" in some strabismic individuals. The assumption was made that the center was lacking or had failed to develop properly.

geometrical c. 1. In an ophthalmic lens, the point of intersection of the horizontal and vertical meridians which mutually bisect each other. 2. The point midway between the two vertical tangents and midway between the two horizontal tangents of the edges of a lens.

Hitzig's c's. Frontal eye fields.

mechanical c. The center of rotation of a lens former. In the boxing method, it is identical with the boxing center.

motor c. for fusion. An area assumed to be located in the cortex, on or near Brodmann's area 19, which controls the motor adjustment of the extraocular muscles to facilitate fusion.

oculogyric c. The portion of Brodmann's area 8 found in the middle frontal gyrus which is involved in voluntary eye movements.

optic c's. Visual centers.

optical c. 1. That point on the optical axis of a lens through which a ray of light, or its projection, passes when its paths before and after refraction by the lens are in the same direction. 2. That point on the surface of a lens where the optical axis intersects the surface.

pattern c. In the boxing method, the point at the center of the rectangle that encloses the lens former. It is identical with the mechanical center.

pontile c. A postulated collection of neuron cell bodies serving as a supranuclear center for yoke movements of the eyes to left or right.

projection, c. of. A reference point from which objects in space are subjectively localized or projected; usually considered to lie about midway between, and slightly posterior to, the centers of rotation of the two eyes.

pupillo-constrictor c. A center located in the region of the third nerve nucleus, usually considered to be the Edinger-Westphal nuclei, which gives origin to preganglionic parasympathetic fibers for the constrictor pupillae and ciliary muscles of the eye.

pupillo-dilatator c. Ciliospinal center.

rotation, c. of. The point about which the eye rotates. It varies slightly with the direction of gaze, being fixed neither with respect to the eye nor to the head, and is approximated by the intersection of the lines of sight for different directions of gaze. Cf. *sighting intersect.*

    rotation, c. of (Mueller's). The geometric center of the sclera considered as a sphere.

    rotation, c. of (Volkmann's). The point of intersection of the lines of sight in different positions of gaze. Syn., *sighting intersect.*

sighting c. A schematic point, said to be fixed with respect to the head, representing the point of intersection of the extensions of the line of sight for various directions of fixation.

visual c's. Centers of the brain concerned with vision.

visual c's., basal. Lower visual centers.

visual c., of the cornea. The point of intersection of the line of sight with the cornea.

visual c's., cortical. Higher visual centers.

visual c's., higher. 1. Cortical centers or regions said to subserve the sensory visual pathways, such as the visual sensory area or the area striata and the parastriate and peristriate visual associational areas. 2. Cortical centers or regions said to subserve the oculomotor functions, such as the frontal and occipital eye fields and the higher occipital centers for convergence and accommodation. Syn., *cortical visual centers.*

visual c's., lower. Areas in which the ganglionic axons of the optic nerve terminate or synapse, namely: the lateral geniculate bodies which relay to the ipsilateral occipital cortex in the region of the calcarine fissure; the superior colliculi of the midbrain which relay to lower motor neurons supplying skeletal muscle; and the pretectal nuclei or areas which relay to both Edinger-Westphal nuclei for parasympathetic innervation of the sphincter pupillae muscle when light is flashed into an eye. Although some authorities list the pulvinar of the thalamus, it is doubtful if any ganglionic axons terminate here. Syn., *basal visual centers; subcortical visual centers.*

visual c's., subcortical. Lower visual centers.

winking c. A center controlling voluntary winking, probably located in the prefrontal convolution of the cortex, which sends impulses via the motor nuclei of the facial nerves to stimulate the orbicularis oculi muscle of one eye while inhibiting that of the other.

centering (sen'ter-ing). 1. Placing a lens so that its optical axis coincides with the mechanical axis of an instrument. 2. In ophthalmic lenses, placing the lens so that the line of sight will coincide with its optical axis. 3. Placing or mounting a lens so that its optical axis, optical center, or other point of reference coincides with the mechanical axis of a jig, as in a lens edging machine. 4. *Optometric Extension Program:* The total process by which a given stimulus in space is selected for special attention and localization. 5. Repositioning a corneal contact lens on the cornea after dislodgement onto the sclera.

centile rank (sen'til, -tīl). Percentile rank.

centrad (sen'trad). A unit of ophthalmic prism power equal to ¹⁄₁₀₀ of a radian and symbolized by an inverted delta (∇). See also *arc centune method*.

centrage (sen'trāj). The condition in which the centers of curvature of all the refracting and reflecting surfaces of an optical system lie on a single straight line.

central tendency. See under *tendency*.

centraphose (sen'trah-fōz). A sensation of darkness originating in the visual centers of the brain.

centroid, spectral (sen'troyd). The average wavelength of any light source computed by weighting each wavelength by its luminosity or brightness value.

Centrometer (sen-trom'eh-ter). An instrument with caliper points which can be inserted in the eyewire grooves of a spectacle frame to measure the distance between the nasal edges and the distance between the temporal edges of the eyewire grooves in accordance with the boxing system of dimensions.

Centrophore (sen'tro-fōr). An instrument devised by Bangerter for improving central fixation, subsequent to other pleoptic treatment, consisting essentially of a rotating spiral containing fixation letters at its center.

centrophose (sen'tro-fōz). A sensation of light originating in the visual centers of the brain.

centroptics (sen-trop'tiks). An orthoptic technique to improve central fixation and eliminate suppression in amblyopia ex anopsia by means of the *Centroscope*.

Centroscope (sen'tro-skōp). An instrument for successively producing vertical and horizontal after-images, both in the same eye or alternately in each eye, and consisting essentially of a long luminous filament lamp in a light tight box having a viewing slit with a small red filter at its center to serve as a fixation point.

cephalocele (sef'ah-lo-sēl", se-fal'-). 1. A hernia of the contents of the cranium. 2. A cyst at the root of the nose that extends into the orbit or eyebrow.

cephalopsin (sef-ah-lop'sin). A red photopigment found in the retina of the squid and other invertebrates and having absorptive characteristics similar to those of rhodopsin.

ceratitis (ser-ah-ti'tis). Keratitis.

cerato- (ser'ah-to-). See *kerato-*.

cerebro-ocular (ser"e-bro-ok'u-lar). Pertaining to the brain and eye.

cerebroscope (ser-e'bro-skōp). The ophthalmoscope when used to diagnose brain disease by examination of the eyeground.

cerebroscopy (ser-e-bros'ko-pe). The diagnosing of brain disease by examining the fundus with an ophthalmoscope.

Cestan's (ses-tanz') **sign; syndrome.** See under the nouns.

Cestan-Chenais syndrome (ses-tan'-shen-a'). See under *syndrome*.

c.f.f. Abbreviation for *critical flicker frequency* or *critical fusion frequency*.

Chagas' disease (chag'as). See under *disease*.

chain, diagnostic. *Optometric Extension Program:* An arrangement of clinical findings into high and low groups as compared to accepted norms. Characteristic patterns are considered diagnostic of specific visual problems.

chain, pathological. *Optometric Extension Program:* A diagnostic chain considered to indicate a visual problem due to pathological anomalies.

chain, physiological. *Optometric Extension Program:* A diagnostic chain considered to indicate a visual problem due to physiological anomalies.

chair, Bárány's. A chair in which a subject may be rotated rapidly and stopped suddenly, used to demonstrate and test for the presence or absence, direction, and degree of labyrinthine nystagmus.

chalazion (kă-la′ze-on, ka-la′-). A chronic inflammatory granuloma primarily resulting from the retention of the secretion of a Meibomian gland in the tarsus of an eyelid. Typically, it begins as a hard, painless tumor, increases slowly in size and bursts eventually on the conjunctival surface. However, it may be absorbed and disappear, remain of constant size, or suppurate on secondary infection. Syn., *Meibomian cyst; tarsal cyst.*

chalcitis (kal-si′tis). Chalcosis.

chalcosis (kal-ko′sis). A deposit of particles of copper in the tissues, particularly of the eye. Syn., *chalcitis; chalkitis.*

corneae, c. Copper deposition in the cornea, occurring in metal workers or after prolonged copper treatment for trachoma. The typical appearance in the cornea is of a brilliantly pigmented ring in the deep layers around the limbus.

lentis, c. Sunflower cataract.

ocular c. Inflammation of the tissues of the eye due to the effects of copper, characteristically seen in workers of this metal.

retinae, c. Deposits of copper in the retina due to diffusion from a foreign body in the posterior segment of the eye. They typically appear as shiny lustrous flecks located around the main arteries and veins.

chalkitis (kal-ki′tis). Chalcosis.

chamber. A compartment; an enclosed space or cavity.

anterior c. The space in the eye, filled with aqueous humor, bounded anteriorly by the cornea and a small portion of the sclera and posteriorly by a small portion of the ciliary body, the iris, and that portion of the crystalline lens which presents through the pupil.

aqueous c. The space in the eye, anterior to the zonule of Zinn and the crystalline lens, filled with aqueous humor and divided into anterior and posterior chambers by the iris.

eye, c's. of the. The anterior and posterior chambers, containing aqueous humor, and the vitreous chamber containing the vitreous humor.

posterior c. The space in the eye delimited by the posterior surface of the iris, the ciliary processes and the valleys between them, the zonule of Zinn, and the anterior surface of the crystalline lens; more extensively, it is also said to include the canal of Hannover, the canal of Petit, and the retrolental space of Berger.

vitreous c. The space within the ocular globe taken up by the vitreous humor, bounded by the retina, ciliary body, canal of Petit, and the retrolental space of Berger.

chamfer (cham′fer). A slight bevel on the edge of a rimless spectacle lens to prevent chipping. Syn., *safety bevel.*

chance. *Statistics:* An absence of selection, giving a random sample of a population.

Chandler's syndrome (chan′dlerz). See under *syndrome.*

channels, collector. Small vessels which transmit aqueous humor from the canal of Schlemm primarily to the deep scleral plexus of veins. Syn., *external canals of Sondermann; outlets of Ascher.*

Charcot's (shar'kōz) **disease; triad.** See under the nouns.

Charlin's syndrome (shar-lanz'). See under *syndrome.*

Charpentier's (shar-pan-tyāz') **bands; illusion; law; method.** See under the nouns.

chart. A sheet of paper, cardboard, etc., which contains test targets, a graphical representation, or tabulated information.

Amsler c's. A set of charts for detecting and measuring defects in the central visual field, each consisting of a black background on which is printed, in white, a 10 cm. square containing various patterns such as a grid of 5 mm. squares, parallel lines, or a central grid of 2.5 mm. squares in a grid of 5 mm. squares. A dot in the center of the pattern is fixated at a distance of 30 cm. from the eye, and a defect is demonstrated by the absence or irregularities of the lines. Syn., *Amsler grids.*

AO H-R-R c's. AO H-R-R plates.

arrow test c. A chart for subjectively determining the principal meridians of ocular astigmatism by means of an arrowlike pattern which may be rotated until the symmetrically arranged cuneiform lines or "feathers" appear equally clear or sharp.

astigmatic c. Any chart designed to determine the amount and axis of astigmatism. It usually consists of a series of radially arranged black lines.

Bannon-Raubitschek c. Paraboline chart.

Beach test c. A visual acuity test chart, consisting of letters, Landolt broken rings, and Maltese crosses of various sizes.

Becker's c. An astigmatism test chart consisting of sets of three parallel lines, each oriented in a different meridian.

Berens c. 1. A test chart with numbers, crosses, words, and tumbling E's, of various sizes, used for testing accommodation and near visual acuity. 2. A visual acuity chart containing tumbling E's and colored targets in the form of objects familiar to small children, scaled according to Snellen notation. 3. A chart for testing subnormal vision ranging from 20/500 to 20/40, containing large pictures and smaller tumbling E's on one side and large tumbling E's and smaller pictures on the other.

Betts's reading readiness c's. A series of stereoscope slides for determining reading rate and comprehension.

Boettcher c. A chart consisting of a series of geometrical figures for testing visual acuity.

Boström's c's. Boström's plates.

Boström-Kugelberg c's. Boström-Kugelberg plates.

clock dial c. An astigmatism test chart consisting of 12 sets of lines radially oriented to correspond with the positions of the hours on a clock face.

color c. 1. A chromaticity diagram. 2. A systematic arrangement of color samples mounted for convenient reference.

Cowan c. A visual acuity test chart with letters so constructed that the spaces within each letter subtend the same angles as the bars, stems, and arms of the letter.

Dennett c. A visual acuity test chart with differences in size of the various letters of the alphabet for any given test distance, so as to compensate for differences in inherent readability of the individual letters.

Duane's accommodation c. A test chart for determining the near point of accommodation, consisting of a card engraved with a single line, 0.2 mm. wide and 3 mm. long, at its center. The test card is brought toward the eyes until it appears blurred or doubled.

Dvorine animated fusion c's. A series of colored, line drawing stereograms designed to train fusion and fusional vergence. Some contain a rotatable disk on which are printed a series of pictures, one of which is exposed at a time through an aperture in the stereogram as the disk is turned.

Dvorine's color vision c's. Dvorine's plates.

Eastman c. A circular test target for subjective determination of the axis and amount of astigmatic correction, consisting of eight radially extending black test stripes, each having a width of one minute subtense at 6 meters and bordered on both sides by half as wide white stripes and surrounded throughout its corresponding 45° sector of the target by parallel, alternate, narrow black and white stripes of equal width which are too narrow to be resolved at a distance of 6 meters and hence appear as a uniform gray field. The test pattern and background are designed to have equal areas of black and white to result in equal average reflectance. Below the threshold of acuity the test stripes merge imperceptibly into the background instead of appearing blurred.

Edmond's picture c. A chart consisting of pictures of familiar objects for testing visual acuity of illiterates and children.

Ewing c. A visual acuity test chart for illiterates, in which the basic test pattern consists of three parallel bars separated by the width of a single bar, with variously located discontinuities or gaps in the middle bar, each gap

having the dimension of a bar width.

fan dial c. A chart or test pattern consisting of a semicircle of radially oriented lines (hence resembling a fan), used for determining the presence or the amount and meridional orientation of astigmatism. Syn., *sunburst chart.*

Fridenberg's c. A visual acuity test chart for illiterates, consisting of groups of dots or squares in various numbers separated by distances equal to their dimensions. The test consists of counting the number of dots or squares in each group. Syn., *stigmometric chart.*

Friedenwald c. An astigmatism test chart consisting of radially oriented lines upon a gray ground. The lines not corresponding to the axis of astigmatism become less visible than if on a white ground.

Gould's c. A chart for measuring visual acuity in which the test objects or letters are white and the background black.

Green's c. Any of a series of commercially available wall cabinet test charts with opaque test characters on a transilluminated field, astigmatic dial, and various other incidental test chart features.

Grow c. A visual acuity test chart consisting of a block of letters which can be masked for presenting in columns or rows to eliminate memorization.

Guibor c. A chart for determining visual acuity at a 14 in. test distance consisting of 10 graduated lines, each line containing the letter E oriented in various positions. A panel containing a small window slides over each line, exposing one letter at a time. The lines are designated in terms of Jaeger and Snellen visual acuity and in percentage of visual efficiency.

Guillery c. A visual acuity test chart consisting of a series of disks or dots of graduated sizes, each eccentrically located in a separated square. The test consists of identifying the location of the disk in each square.

Haitz c's. Charts designed for use in plotting central visual field defects with a stereoscope.

Hardy-Rand-Rittler c's. AO H-R-R plates.

Heppel muscle c. A test chart consisting of a central light source around which a pointer is pivoted and calibrated to show the distance and direction of displacement of a second image of the light source seen under dissociation when different colored lenses are placed in front of the two eyes.

Hertel's c's. Hertel's plates.

Hutchinson's c. A chart to test visual acuity at near and intermediate distances in the fitting of trifocals.

illiterate E c. A visual acuity test chart employing a graduated series of the Snellen letter *E* oriented in various directions for identification.

industrial motor field c. A chart for plotting the diplopia field and computing the binocular vision factor in the visual efficiency formula.

international c. Landolt's broken ring chart.

Ishihara c's. Ishihara plates.

iso-color c. A chromaticity chart divided into zones such that all stimuli represented by points lying within a given zone will appear identical when their brightnesses are equal. In dichromatism, the zones are strips extending from one side to the other of the chromaticity diagram, converging to the red corner of the diagram in protanopia and being approximately parallel to the long wavelength side of the diagram in deuteranopia.

Jaeger c. A chart for testing visual acuity at given reading distances, consisting of words and phrases in various sizes of ordinary printer's type.

Keeler c. A chart for testing visual acuity at a 25 cm. distance, containing capital letters, Landolt rings, and isolated words.

kindergarten test c. A visual acuity test chart consisting of designs familiar to young children and conforming, insofar as practicable, to the principle of design of the Snellen test letters.

Lancaster c. 1. A Snellen letter test chart in which each successive row of letters is 25% larger, e.g., 20/20, 20/25, 20/31.25, etc. 2. A chart for determining the axis and amount of astigmatism.

Lancaster-Regan c. An astigmatism test chart employing both a fixed set of radiating lines and a rotatable cross.

Landolt's broken ring c. A visual acuity test chart employing a

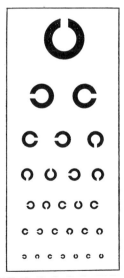

Fig. 6. Landolt's broken ring chart. (From *Practical Orthoptics in the Treatment of Squint,* ed. 4, T. Keith Lyle, H. K. Lewis & Co., 1953)

graduated series of incomplete rings with radial thickness and gaps equal to one fifth of their outer diameters. The test consists of identifying the radial orientation of the gap. Syn., *International chart; Landolt's C chart.*

Lebensohn c. 1. A chart employing the principle of the Grow chart. 2. A chart for testing visual acuity at a 14 in. test distance, containing capital letters, illiterate symbols, and isolated words.

Lutes near point c's. A set of three slides, each containing targets for vision testing at near, and a holder which attaches to the phoropter rod. The holder has a central aperture to expose only the desired target.

Maddox tangent scale c. Maddox cross.

Maddox V c. A test chart for determining the axis of astigmatism, consisting of a fan dial and a V which is moved along the circumference of the dial to the region of the radiating line seen blackest or most distinct. The position in this region in which both limbs of the V appear equally black or clear indicates the axis of the correcting cylindrical lens.

Newton's color c. Newton's color circle.

object c. A visual acuity test chart for illiterates, consisting of objects instead of letters.

orthops c. A subjective sight-testing chart, designed by Laurance, which includes a fan dial, Snellen test letters, and a red and green tangent scale.

Paraboline c. A rotatable test target with the parabolic curves of the Raubitschek chart in combination with a pair of broken, dashed lines of equal length, one along the axis of the funnel-form pattern and the other bisecting

the axis perpendicularly. It is used for determining the axis and the amount of the astigmatic correction. Syn., *Bannon-Raubitschek chart.*

Pray's astigmatic c. A chart for estimating the axis of astigmatism, consisting of letters constructed of short hatched lines in a specific meridian, the lines for each letter being oriented in a different meridian.

pseudoisochromatic c. A color vision test chart with varicolored dots composing both the pattern to be observed and the background, the colored dots being so arranged as to make the pattern unrecognizable to one who confuses certain colors.

Rabkin c's. A set of twenty pseudoisochromatic plates designed by Rabkin to detect color vision abnormalities and to classify them according to type and severity of deficiency.

Raubitschek c. A rotatable test target with two parabolic curves symmetrically arranged in a funnel-form pattern with the less curved ends forming the almost parallel small end of the funnel and the more curved ends diverging approximately 90° from each other. It is used for determining the axis and the amount of the astigmatic correction. See also *Raubitschek test.*

Reber's c. A chart for determining the visual acuity of very young children and illiterates, consisting of simple pictures of familiar objects.

von Reuss's color c. A color vision test chart consisting of colored letters printed on a colored background.

Robinson Cohen c. A commercially available instrument and projector slide for use with a projector in vision testing, its principal feature being a pair of rotating crossed lines projected in a field of red for astigmatic determination. See also *Robinson Cohen test.*

Seitz c. A chart for testing visual acuity of children and illiterates, consisting of pictures of animals and inanimate objects.

Sheard c. A phoria and duction testing chart having on one side a small black dot followed by "Read these words letter by letter" and on the reverse side a vertical row of letters arranged to read "Keep this row of letters single."

Sloan c's. 1. Two visual acuity test charts, one used at 20 feet and the other at 16 inches, each consisting of a set of ten capital letters graded in equal logarithmic steps and selected to be of comparable difficulty to each other and to the Landolt ring. 2. A set of nine reading cards providing samples of continuous text, used in the testing of subnormal vision to determine the magnification required to read newsprint. The letters range in size from a designation of 1.0 M to 10.0 M, 1.0 M approximating newsprint and subtending a visual angle of 5 minutes at 1 meter.

Snellen's c. A visual acuity test chart made up of Snellen test type.

stigmometric c. Fridenberg's chart.

Stilling's c's. Stilling's plates.

Stimson c's. 1. A series of charts for evaluating near visual acuity and for detecting central scotomata and malingering in persons with reduced visual acuity. Each chart contains groups of three disks, two neutral gray and one of concentric black and white circles of equal width and of varying angular subtense. 2. A reduced Snellen chart for determining visual acuity at a 35 mm. test distance in persons with subnormal vision. 3. A chart of words all composed of the same

seven letters, used to evaluate visual acuity and/or the efficacy of an optical aid at near, in persons with subnormal vision.

Streidinger c. A visual acuity test chart consisting of sets of dots notated with the distance at which they should be counted.

sunburst c. Fan dial chart.

Swann-Cole c's. A series of haploscope cards for determining the quality of fusion and stereoscopic vision.

Thomas' c. An astigmatic test chart consisting of a revolving cross, each arm of which contains three parallel lines.

Thorington c. A visual acuity test chart containing yellow Gothic letters on a black ground, so constructed as to subtend an angle of 4 minutes at specified test distances.

Vari-Test c. A reversible chart for near vision testing containing, on one side, an aperture exposing various test targets printed on a rotating disk, and on the other side, reading material of different type sizes for near and intermediate distances. It may be attached to a phoropter rod or be hand held.

Velhagen's c's. Velhagen's plates.

Verhoeff c. An astigmatic test chart consisting of a pair of rotating disks, one containing a series of concentric circles and 24 uniformly spaced radial lines, and the other a series of concentric squares with two lines transecting at right angles.

Walker's c. A chart for recording both perimeter and tangent screen findings with large radial dimension scales centrally, to permit greater detail, and successively smaller dimensional scales peripherally, whence the 0°–10° interval is twice the 80°–90° interval.

Wallace c. A visual acuity test chart consisting of Gothic letters which subtend an angle of 4 minutes at specified test distances.

Chavasse (shah-vahz') **lens; occluder; theory.** See under the nouns.

Chédiak-Higashi syndrome (cheh'-de-ak-hih-gash'e). See under *syndrome.*

cheiroscope (ki'ro-skōp). A haploscopic instrument designed for presenting a line drawing to the view of one eye to be projected visually and traced by means of a pencil or a crayon in the field of view of the other eye; a kind of binocular camera lucida.

chemiluminescence (kem"ih-lu"mih-nes'ens). The emission of light by a substance after excitation by chemical action.

chemosis (ke-mo'sis). Severe edema of the conjunctiva, least marked in the tarsal region.

chessboard of Helmholtz. A checkered pattern distorted into a non-rectilinear pattern as though stretched from the four corners, so designed that when viewed at a theoretically predetermined distance from the eye, the pattern will appear rectilinear. It was devised by Helmholtz to demonstrate subjectively the nonrectilinearity of peripheral vision.

chiaro-oscuro (kih-ah"ro-o-sku'ro). Chiaroscura.

chiaroscura (kih-ah"ro-sku'ro). The creation of apparent differences in distance in a two-dimensional picture through the use of shading.

chiasm, optic (ki'azm). A structure of nervous tissue formed by the junction and partial decussation of the optic nerves in the region above the pituitary body. The nasal fibers of each optic nerve decussate and enter the contralateral optic tract. Syn., *chiasma opticum.*

chiasma opticum (ki-az'mah op'tih-kum). Optic chiasm.

chiasmometer (ki"as-mom'eh-ter). An instrument designed by Landolt to measure the distance between the centers of rotation of the eyes. Two slits, each seen monocularly, are separated until they appear to be individually aligned with a single slit midway between the plane of the two slits and the eyes.

chiastometer (ki"as-tom'eh-ter). Chiasmometer.

Chievitz layer (che'witz). See under *layer.*

chionablepsia (ki"o-nah-blep'se-ah). Snow blindness.

chionablepsy (ki"o-nah-blep'se). Snow blindness.

chipping. The breaking away of excess glass with a special tool, for the purpose of roughly shaping a lens.

chiroscope (ki'ro-skōp). Cheiroscope.

chi square (ki, ke skwār). A number or measure which expresses: (1) The "goodness of fit" of observed data to expected results (the expected on the the basis of chance or of a hypothesis); (2) the "goodness of fit" of a line or curve to a series of points; (3) the degree of association or relationship between two variables for which only categorical information is available; the coefficient of contingency. Mathematical formula =

$$\chi^2 = \frac{(O - E)^2}{E}$$

where O = the observed, and
E = the expected on the basis of chance or hypothesis

chloasma (klo-az'mah). A skin discoloration due to pigmentary hypertrophy, occurring in patches of various sizes and shapes, usually light brown, but they may be yellow or black.

chlorolabe (klo'ro-lāb). The name proposed by W. A. H. Rushton for a retinal photopigment having its maximum absorption or maximum spectral sensitivity in the midspectral (green) region.

chloroma (klo-ro'mah). Multiple neoplasms usually occurring in or about the bones of the orbit; typically green in color and accompanied by a blood picture of leukemia.

chlorophane (klo'ro-fān). A yellowish-green pigment in the retinal cones of some animals but not of man.

chloropia (klo-ro'pe-ah). Chloropsia.

chloropsia (klo-rop'se-ah). A condition in which objects appear green, as may occur in digitalis poisoning; green vision.

choked disk. See under *disk.*

choline (ko'lēn, kol'ēn, ko'lin, kol'-in). A compound, $C_5H_{15}NO_2$, included in the vitamin B complex. It affects fat metabolism, helping to prevent fatty livers and "deficiency" hemorrhages in the eyes and kidneys and to develop appetite and growth. When used as a drug, it has an effect similar to that of parasympathetic stimulation.

chondrodystrophia calcificans congenita punctata (kon"dro-dis-tro'fe-ah kal-sif'ih-kanz kon-jen'-ih-tah punk-tah'tah). Stippled epiphyses.

chondrodystrophia fetalis hypoplastica (kon"dro-dis-tro'fe-ah fe-tal'is hi"po-plas'tih-kah). Stippled epiphyses.

chondrodystrophy, congenital calcareous (kon"dro-dis'tro-fe). Stippled epiphyses.

choriocapillaris (ko"re-o-kap"ih-la'-ris). A layer of the choroid between the lamina vitrea and Sattler's layer, consisting of a network of capillaries which supplies the outer 5 layers of the retina. The network is densest at the macula. Syn., *entochoroidea.*

choriocele (ko're-o-sēl). A protrusion or hernia of the choroid.

chorioid (ko're-oid). Choroid. (The etymologically more nearly correct spelling, *chorioid,* is becoming obsolete.)

choriopathy (ko"re-op'ah-the). 1. A morbid condition or disease of the choroid. 2. Noninflammatory disease of the choroid as distinguished from *choroiditis.*

   central angioneurotic c. A detachment of the retina in the macular area due to transudates from the choriocapillaris which accumulate behind the pigment epithelium or between the pigment epithelium and retina. When the fluid is situated between the pigment epithelium and the retina, it appears as a circumscribed, elevated, darkened area; when situated behind the pigment epithelium, it may simulate the appearance of a malignant melanoma of the choroid. Subjective symptoms may be reduced vision, micropsia, and metamorphopsia. The visual fields may reveal a central scotoma, often larger for blue than for red or white, which tends to be permanent. However, there may be an acquired hypermetropia with relatively good central vision.

chorioretinal (ko"re-o-ret'ih-nal). Pertaining to or involving the choroid and retina.

chorioretinitis (ko"re-o-ret"ih-ni'tis). Simultaneous inflammation of the choroid and retina.

   adhesiva c. A subacute chorioretinitis with destruction of the membrane of Bruch and resultant infiltration of fibrous tissue into the retina, so that the retina and choroid ultimately adhere into one continuous fibrous scar.

   centralis serosa, c. Central angiospastic chorioretinopathy.

   congenital syphilitic c. Chorioretinitis appearing in infancy in association with congenital syphilis and occurring in several classified clinical forms. Type 1.

Small reddish-yellow spots interspersed with pigment giving the fundus a salt and pepper appearance; Type 2. Large, round, confluent pigment patches in the periphery of the fundus together with patches of atrophic choroid; Type 3. Round, grayish or yellowish spots, extending from the periphery to the posterior pole, which may become confluent into stalactite shape formations. Pigmentation develops later and has a reticular appearance; Type 4. Atrophy of the retina and optic nerve with sclerotic choroidal vessels visible, small and large clumps or branching deposits of pigment resembling retinitis pigmentosa.

diffuse syphilitic c. Chorioretinitis appearing typically in the second stage of syphilis, characterized initially by dense dustlike vitreous opacities, retinal edema, and blurring of the margins of the optic disk without involvement of the nerve head itself. Exudates which may be few or numerous are sometimes found, especially around the macula, the veins are slightly engorged, the arteries normal, and the vessels may become sheathed. In the later stages the vessels are attenuated, the optic disk yellowish, the choroidal vessels sclerosed appearing white and readily visible, and atrophy of the pigment epithelium results in migration of pigment into small or large irregular deposits. The macular area may be spared with preservation of central vision.

toxoplasmic c. Chorioretinitis caused by infection with the protozoan parasite *Toxoplasma,* occurring in congenital or acquired forms. It is typically bilateral and appears as deep, heavily pigmented, necrotic lesions affecting both macular and peripheral areas. There is exten-

sive connective tissue proliferation from the lesions, the retina surrounding the lesions remains normal, and a secondary optic atrophy may occur.

chorioretinopathy (ko″re-o-ret″ih-nop′ah-the). 1. A morbid condition or disease of the choroid and retina. 2. Noninflammatory disease of the choroid and retina as distinguished from *chorioretinitis.*

central angiospastic c. A disease similar to central angiospastic retinopathy but more severe due to added involvement of the neighboring choroid. The elevation of the macular region is more pronounced, visual acuity is considerably reduced, proliferation of the pigment epithelium occurs in early stages, the refraction may become more hypermetropic, and the lesion is more diffusely distributed and contains silvery, irregularly shaped figures. The disease is recurring and prognosis is less favorable. It is attributed to coexisting extravasations from the retinal and choroidal vessels and may lead to circumscribed retinal detachment. Syn., *chorioretinitis centralis serosa; central serous chorioretinopathy; central serous choroiditis.*

central serous c. Central angiospastic chorioretinopathy.

choroid (ko′roid). The portion of the vascular tunic or uvea posterior to the ciliary body; the middle coat of the eye lying between the retina and sclera. It is composed of 5 main layers, the suprachoroid, Haller's layer, Sattler's layer, the choriocapillaris, and the lamina vitrea; its primary function is to nourish the retina. Syn., *chorioid; choroidea.*

detached c. A separation of the choroid from the sclera, usually caused by traction from within or by accumulation of fluid in the perichoroidal space.

choroidal (ko-roi'dal). Pertaining to the choroid.

choroidal cleft; fissure. Fetal fissure.

choroidea (ko-roi'de-ah). Choroid.

choroideremia (ko"roi-der-e'me-ah). A sex-linked hereditary degeneration of the pigment epithelium and choroid, usually detected in early life but may be present at birth. In males it is progressive, commences with pigment degeneration, providing a salt and pepper appearance to the peripheral fundus, and advances to complete atrophy with exposure of the white sclera. The earliest symptom is night blindness followed by constriction of the visual fields and eventual total blindness. In the female carrier it is benign and nonprogressive, with no visual complaints, and with the fundus having the salt and pepper appearance. Syn., *progressive choroidal atrophy; progressive tapetochoroidal atrophy; progressive tapetochoroidal dystrophy.*

choroiditis (ko-roid-i'tis). Inflammation of the choroid.

acute diffuse serous c. 1. A type of diffuse exudative choroiditis of sudden onset in adults, characterized by a diffuse, yellowish, edematous lesion of the entire fundus, retinal detachment, later retinal reattachment, and good prognosis for the return of vision lost during the disease process. 2. Harada's disease.

albuminuric c. Choroidal changes associated with advanced nephritis.

anterior c. Choroiditis limited to the anterior portion of the globe and, hence, to the periphery of the fundus.

areolar c. Choroiditis in which the first lesion occurs at the macula, with later lesions appearing at increasing distances from it. Un-

like other types of choroiditis, the single spots are initially pigmented, and depigmentation follows, proceeding from the center outward. Syn., *Förster's choroiditis; Förster's disease.*

central c. Choroiditis in the region of the macula. Syn., *macular choroiditis.*

central serous c. Central angiospastic chorioretinopathy.

circumpapillary c. Choroiditis near or around the optic disk.

circumscribed c. Exudative choroiditis in which the lesion occurs in one or more clearly defined patches, differentiated from *disseminated* and *diffuse choroiditis.*

conglomerate c. A rare form of choroiditis found in tubercular individuals, characterized by the presence of a conglomerate tubercle as a single irregular mass.

deep c. Choroiditis with lesions deep in the choroid.

diffuse c. Exudative choroiditis in which the lesion is large and diffuse, the result of the coalescing of numerous small, exudative plaques, as differentiated from *circumscribed* and *disseminated choroiditis.*

disseminated c. Exudative choroiditis with numerous isolated, inflammatory foci covering the fundus, as differentiated from *circumscribed* and *diffuse choroiditis.*

Doyne's familial honeycombed c. A primary familial degeneration of the choroid characterized by many colloid deposits in a ring-shaped formation in the area around the macula. In the late stages there is complete degeneration in the central region.

equatorial c. Paving-stone degeneration of the retina.

exudative c. Choroiditis in the exudative or active stage, a result of endogenous infection. The pathology consists of an inflammatory mononuclear infiltration followed by an atrophic stage with scarring and pigmentation in the destroyed spaces. The three major subdivisions are *diffuse, disseminated,* and *circumscribed choroiditis.*

Förster's c. Areolar choroiditis.

guttata senilis, c. Colloid bodies in the macular region; not a true choroiditis, but a degenerative change. Syn., *Hutchinson-Tay choroiditis; Tay's choroiditis; Tay's central guttate choroiditis.*

guttate c. A degenerative disorder characterized by the universal distribution of hyaline bodies or colloid excrescences beneath the retina.

histoplasmic c. Choroiditis due to infection with the fungus *Histoplasma capsulatum,* characterized by isolated, round, yellow-white nodules, of about ⅓ to ½ disk diameter in size, and diagnosed by specific tests for histoplasmosis.

Hutchinson-Tay c. Choroiditis guttata senilis.

hyperplastica, c. A subacute choroiditis with destruction of the lamina vitrea and resultant infiltration of fibrous tissue into the retina and vitreous.

Jensen's c. Jensen's disease.

juvenile exudative macular c. Juvenile disciform degeneration of the macula. See under *degeneration, disciform.*

juxtapapillary c. Jensen's disease.

macular c. Central choroiditis.

miliary c. Tuberculosis of the choroid associated with miliary tuberculosis, typically characterized by the presence of multiple, small, round, ill-defined, yellowish spots scattered over the fundus.

myopic c. 1. Chronic inflammation of the choroid attributed to myopia. 2. Degenerative choroidal changes accompanying myopia of high degree.

nonsuppurative c. Exudative choroiditis.

purulent c. Suppurative choroiditis.

senile macular exudative c. Senile disciform degeneration of the macula. See under *degeneration, disciform.*

serosa, c. Glaucoma.

superficial c. Choroiditis in which the lesions are located superficially in the choroid.

suppurative c. Choroiditis accompanied by the formation of pus. Syn., *purulent choroiditis.*

syphilitic c. Choroiditis attributable to the presence of syphilis.

Tay's c. Choroiditis guttata senilis.

tuberculous c. Choroiditis attributable to the presence of tuberculosis.

choroidocyclitis (ko-roi″do-sik-li′tis, -si-kli′tis). Inflammation involving both the choroid and the ciliary body.

choroido-iritis (ko-roi″do-i-ri′tis). Inflammation involving both the choroid and the iris.

choroidoretinitis (ko-roi″do-ret-ih-ni′tis). Inflammation involving both the choroid and the retina. Syn., *chorioretinitis.*

choroidoscopy (ko″roi-dos′ko-pe). Examination of the choroid, usually performed by transilluminating the eye and observing the fundus with an unilluminated ophthalmoscope.

choroidosis (ko″roi-do′sis). Noninflammatory degeneration of the choroid.

choroidotomy (ko″roi-dot′o-me). Surgical incision of the choroid.

Choyce implant (chois). See under *implant.*

Christian's disease (kris′chanz). Schüller-Christian-Hand disease.

Christian's syndrome (kris′chanz). Schüller-Christian-Hand syndrome.

chroma (kro′mah). 1. The dimension of the Munsell system of color which corresponds most closely to saturation. 2. Saturation; hue content. 3. Chromatic color. A visual quality manifesting hue and saturation.

chromaesthesia (kro″mah-es-the′ze-ah). Chromesthesia.

chromaphotometer (kro″mah-fotom′eh-ter). Chromophotometer.

chromaphotometry (kro″mah-fotom′eh-tre). Chromophotometry.

chromascope (kro′mah-skōp). Chromoscope.

chromasia (kro-ma′zhuh, -ze-uh). The coloring of an optical image, due to chromatic aberration in the optical system.

chromastereopsis (kro″mah-ste″re-op′sis). Chromostereopsis.

chromatelopia (kro″mat-el-o′pe-ah). Chromatelopsia.

chromatelopsia (kro″mah-tel-op′-se-ah). Color blindness; defective perception of colors. One of a number of rarely used or obsolete terms denoting defective color vision, such as *chromotelopsia, chromatodysopia, chromatometablepsia, chromatopseudopsis, chromatopseudoblepsia, dyschromatopia, dyschromatopsia.*

chromatelopsis (kro″mah-tel-op′sis). Chromatelopsia.

chromatherapy (kro″mah-ther′ah-pe). Treatment of disease by means of colored light; the real or supposed effects of such treatment. Syn., *chromotherapy.*

chromatic (kro-mat′ik). 1. Possessing the visual attribute of hue; colored; hued. 2. Perceptibly different in quality from a neutral gray of the same brightness value. 3. Pertaining to color or colors or to light from different regions of the visible spectrum.

audition, c. A form of synesthesia in which a subjective sensation of color is caused by sound, or the reverse (phonopsia). See also *chromesthesia.*

contrast, c. See under *contrast.*

dispersion, c. See under *dispersion.*

fading, c. The phenomenon of the sequence of colored afterimages which follows fixation of a white light or a white object. Syn., *flight of colors.*

chromaticity (kro″mah-tih′sih-te). 1. The color quality of a stimulus defined by its trichromatic (C.I.E.) specification or by specification of its dominant (or complementary) wavelength and purity. 2. Quality, as distinguished from quantity, of light. 3. The color quality of a stimulus, without reference to the luminance, as defined by two of the trichromatic coefficients (chromaticity co-ordinates) of the standard C.I.E. co-ordinate system (usually x and y).

chromaticness (kro-mat′ik-nes). The attributes of chromatic color sensation, *hue* and *saturation* collectively, as distinguished from *intensity.*

chromatics (kro-mat′iks). The science of color; that part of optics which treats of the properties of color. Syn., *chromatology.*

chromatism (kro′mah-tizm). 1. Chromatic aberration. 2. Color manifested in an optical image as a result of chromatic aberration.

lateral c. Lateral chromatic aberration.

longitudinal c. Longitudinal chromatic aberration.

chromatoblast (kro-mat′o-blast″). A cell that produces or synthesizes a pigment, such as melanin or a sensitizing visual pigment.

chromatodysopia (kro″mah-to-dis-o′-pe-ah). Color blindness. See also *chromatelopsia.*

chromatogenous (kro″mah-toj′e-nus). Producing color; causing pigmentation.

chromatology (kro″mah-tol′o-je). Chromatics.

chromatometablepsia (kro″mah-to-met″ah-blep′se-ah). Color blindness. See also *chromatelopsia.*

[129]

chromatometer (kro″mah-tom′eh-ter). Chromometer.

chromatometry (kro″mah-tom′eh-tre). Chromometry.

chromatophobia (kro″mah-to-fo′be-ah). 1. A morbid aversion to colors or to a particular color, e.g., erythrophobia, a hysterical fear of red. 2. An abnormal sensitivity of the eye to certain colors, resulting in a marked aversion to a particular color, e.g., the erythrophobia or intolerance to red which sometimes occurs after cataract operation. 3. Resistance to stains on the part of cells and tissues; the quality of staining poorly or not at all. Syn., *chromophobia.*

chromatophorotropin (kro″mah-to-for″o-tro′pin). A hormone which regulates concentration or dispersion of pigment in the retina or other pigment-containing structures.

chromatophotometer (kro″mah-to-fo-tom′eh-ter). Chromophotometer.

chromatopseudoblepsia (kro″mah-to-su″do-blep′se-ah). Color blindness. See also *chromatelopsia.*

chromatopseudopsis (kro″mah-to-su-dop′sis). Color blindness. See also *chromatelopsia.*

chromatopsia (kro″mah-top′se-ah). Colored vision; an abnormal condition in which all objects appear in a particular color or tinged with that color. The various chromatopsias are designated according to the color seen, as xanthopsia (yellow vision), erythropsia (red vision), chloropsia (green vision), and cyanopsia (blue vision). Colored vision may occur as an accompanying symptom in various illnesses and diseases, after cataract operation, and following prolonged exposure to dazzling light. Syn., *chromopia; chromopsia; chromopsy; chroopsia.*

toxic c. Colored vision induced by certain toxic drugs, infections, or certain diseases.

chromatopsy (kro′mah-top-se). Chromatopsia.

chromatoptometer (kro″mah-top-tom′eh-ter). Chromometer.

chromatoptometry (kro″mah-top-tom′eh-tre). Chromometry.

chromatoscope (kro-mat′o-skōp″). 1. Chromoscope. 2. A reflecting telescope for studying the scintillations of stars. Part of it may be rotated eccentrically to produce the image of a star as a ring instead of as a point.

chromatoscopy (kro″mah-tos′ko-pe). Chromoscopy.

chromatoskiameter (kro″mah-to-ski-am′eh-ter). A type of chromometer employing colored shadows.

chromatrope (kro′mah-trōp). 1. A device, usually used as a lantern slide, consisting of transparent colored disks with radiating designs, so arranged that by rotating them in opposite directions, one in front of the other, a kaleidoscopic effect is produced. 2. A disk so painted with different colors that when it is rotated on its central axis, streams of color appear to flow to or from the center.

chrome orthoptics (krōm or-thop′tiks). See under *orthoptics.*

chromesthesia (krōm-es-the′ze-ah). 1. A form of synesthesia in which colors are seen when certain sounds are heard or when certain smells or tastes are sensed. 2. The association of colors with various words, sounds, names, phrases, tastes, smells, or tactile sensations. 3. A condition in which another sensation, such as taste or smell, is excited by the perception of color. 4. The color sense.

chromheteropia (krōm″het-er-o′pe-ah). Heterochromia iridis.

chromic (kro′mik). 1. Pertaining to, having, or related to, color. 2. Of or pertaining to chromium.

chromodacryorrhea (kro″mo-dak″re-o-re′ah). The discharge of tears containing blood.

chromometer (kro-mom′eh-ter). An instrument or scale for doing chromometry. Syn., *chromatometer; chromatoptometer; chromoptometer.*

chromometry (kro-mom′eh-tre). Measurement (or testing) of color or color perception by matching or mixing procedures, or by direct measurement. Cf. *chromophotometry; chromoscopy; colorimetry.* Syn., *chromatometry; chromatoptometry.*

chromophane (kro′mo-fān). A retinal pigment; the coloring matter of the fat globules found in the retinal cones of birds.

chromophobia (kro″mo-fo′be-ah). Chromatophobia.

chromophose (kro′mo-fōz). A subjective sensation of color.

chromophotometer (kro″mo-fo-tom′-eh-ter). An instrument for doing chromophotometry.

chromophotometry (kro″mo-fo-tom′-eh-tre). Photometry of colors and colored light sources.

chromopia (kro-mo′pe-ah). Chromatopsia.

chromopsia (kro-mop′se-ah). Chromatopsia.

chromopsy (kro-mop′se). Chromatopsia.

chromoptometer (kro″mop-tom′eh-ter). Chromometer.

chromoretinography (kro″mo-ret′ih-nog″rah-fe). Color photography of the fundus of the eye.

chromoscope (kro′mo-skōp). An instrument or scale for doing chromoscopy.

chromoscopy (kro-mos′ko-pe). The observation, demonstration, or testing of color phenomena and color performances related to characteristics of color perception or to the optical properties of colored lights or pigments. Cf. *chromometry; chromophotometry; colorimetry.*

chromostereopsis (kro″mo-ster-e-op′-sis). Stereopsis resulting from differential prismatic effects in the eyes for different wavelengths of light when the pupils are eccentric with respect to the optical axes, whence, binocularly, a red object will normally appear closer than an equally distant green object. The effect may be eliminated, reversed, or accentuated by the proper placing of artificial pupils before the eyes.

chromostroboscope (kro″mo-stro′bo-skōp). A stroboscopic or kinetoscopic device employing color as an essential feature, or one used to demonstrate persistence of vision for various colors.

chromotalopsia (kro″mo-tah-lop′se-ah). Chromatelopsia.

chromotherapy (kro″mo-ther′ah-pe). Chromatherapy.

chromotrope (kro′mo-trōp). Chromatrope.

chronaxia (kro-nak′se-ah). Chronaxie.

chronaxie (kro′nak-se). The index of sensitivity of a tissue to electrical stimulation. It is the minimum time required to produce an effect with a constant current twice the rheobase.

chronaxy (kro′nak-se). Chronaxie.

chronoscope (kron′o-skōp). An instrument for measuring the duration of extremely short-lived exposures or flashes, utilizing a rapidly rotating mirror which projects the flash in an arc, the length or displacement of which corresponds to its duration.

chroopsia (kro-op′se-ah). Chromatopsia.

chrysiasis (krih-si′ah-sis). The permanent deposition of gold in the tissue following repeated parenteral administration of gold salts.

corneae, c. Chrysiasis of the subepithelial tissue of the cornea.

ocular c. Chrysiasis of the conjunctiva and/or cornea.

chrysopsin (kris-op′sin). A photosensitive pigment, "visual gold," found in the retinae of some deep sea fishes, of golden color because of high absorption of short wavelengths of light and relatively high reflectance of longer wavelengths.

chrysosis (kris-o′sis). Chrysiasis.

Chvostek's sign (vos′teks). See under *sign.*

chymotrypsin, *alpha* (ki″mo-trip′-sin). A proteolytic enzyme used in the procedure of zonulolysis to facilitate surgical removal of the crystalline lens. It is also used in the treatment of keratitis and corneal ulcers and in certain affections of the conjunctiva or sclera.

Ciaccio's gland (chah′chōz). See under *gland.*

C.I.E. Commission Internationale de l'Eclairage.

cilia (sil′e-ah). 1. The eyelashes. 2. Minute, lashlike processes.

ciliariscope (sil″e-ar′ih-skōp, si″le-). An instrument composed of a prism attached to an ophthalmoscope for examining the ciliary body of the eye.

ciliarotomy (sil″e-ar-ot′o-me). Surgical division of the ciliary zone in the treatment of glaucoma.

ciliary (sil′e-er″e). Pertaining to the eyelashes, the ciliary body, or to any hairlike processes.

ciliary body; canal; corona; folds; ganglion; injection; muscle; processes. See under the nouns.

ciliectomy (sil″e-ek′to-me). 1. Surgical removal of part of the ciliary body. 2. Surgical removal of part of a margin of an eyelid containing the roots of the eyelashes.

ciliogenesis (sil″e-o-jen′e-sis). The development and regeneration of eyelashes.

ciliometer (sih″le-om′eh-ter). Cilometer.

cilioretinal (sil″e-o-ret′ih-nal). 1. Pertaining to both the ciliary

body and the retina. 2. Pertaining to an arterial branch of the circle of Haller, which enters the retina on the temporal side of the optic disk; rarely to a vein that drains the macular region, emptying into a choroidal vein.

cilioscleral (sil″e-o-skle′ral). Pertaining to both the ciliary body and the sclera.

ciliosis (sil″e-o′sis). Cillosis.

ciliospinal (sil″e-o-spi′nal). Pertaining to the ciliospinal center.

ciliotomy (sil-e-ot′o-me). Surgical section of the ciliary nerves.

cilium (sil′e-um). 1. An eyelash. 2. A minute, hairlike process.

   inversum, c. A rare congenital anomaly in which an eyelash grows inward into the skin of the eyelid.

cillo (sil′o). Cillosis.

cillosis (sil-o′sis). Spasmodic twitching of the eyelids. Syn., *ciliosis; cillo.*

cilometer (sih-lom′eh-ter). An accommodation measuring instrument employing the Badal optometer system.

cinching (sinch′ing). Surgical dividing of an extraocular muscle tendon into several strands around which a cable of threads is wound and pulled taut, effecting a shortening of the tendon.

cinclisis (sin′klih-sis). Rapid winking.

Cinefro bifocal contact lens (sin′eh-fro). See under *lens, contact, bifocal.*

circle. 1. A closed curved line, all points of which are equidistant from a point within called the center. 2. A circular anastomosis of arteries or veins.

   arterial c. of the canal of Schlemm. An incomplete circle of arterioles which embraces the canal of Schlemm over most of its extent and which is derived from the anterior ciliary arteries.

   Berry's c's. Circles, used as a stereopsis test, which provide varying degrees of retinal disparity.

blur c. A cross section of a bundle of focused rays originating from a point source. Syn., *circle of confusion; diffusion circle; circle of dispersion.*

color c. A system of hues represented on a circle; the spectral colors in their original order arranged on a circle, with the purple hues connecting the extremes of the visible spectrum; a horizontal section of the color solid. Syn., *hue circle.*

    color c., Farnsworth double. A double-color circle in which the inner circle is a Munsell color circle modified to 85 hues and the outer is a circle showing the corresponding dominant spectral wavelengths.

    color c., Helmholtz'. A color chart with saturated colors on the circumference of a circle and with white in the center. The transitions from white to any saturated color at a point on the circumference of the circle lie along the radius drawn to this point. Syn., *Helmholtz' color table.*

    color c., Hering's. A psychologic color circle represented by an oval on two concentric circles such that it is tangent to the inner circle in the vertical meridian and to the outer circle in the horizontal meridian. The four crescent-shaped areas are labeled red and green at the top and bottom, respectively, and blue and yellow at the left and right, respectively, and the thickness of each crescent at any given meridian indicates the relative intensities of the primary ingredients in each color. The colors on opposite sides of the circle cannot be blended, while adjacent colors can be blended to form mixed hues.

    color c., Munsell. A color circle consisting of an orderly arrangement of 100 hues of constant Munsell value and chroma based on a just noticeable hue difference scale.

    color c., Newton's. A schema for mixing colors, consisting of Newton's colors arranged about a circle subtending distances proportional to the musical intervals of the octave, with white (gray) at the center. Syn., *Newton's color table.*

    color c., Ostwald. A diagram based on Hering's color circle divided into 24 numbered hues, based on eight principal color regions each divided into three sections. The eight principal color regions are derived from four primal colors and four in-between blends. Ostwald also published a similar color circle with 100 hue divisions.

    color c., psychologic. An orderly arrangement of the primal colors and their blends in a circle to demonstrate the continuous variation in hue from red to yellow to green to blue to red.

    color c., Southall's double. A pair of concentric circles with hues designated on the inner circle and the corresponding spectral wavelengths of the hues on the outer circle which is incomplete because purples are not present in the spectrum.

confusion, c. of. Blur circle.

corresponding c. of sensation. Panum's area.

diffusion c. Blur circle.

direction c's. The circles on the spherical field of fixation that pass through the occipital point. There are two sets of direction circles, i.e., the set that lies in a horizontal plane perpendicular to the vertical xz plane and the set that lies in a vertical plane perpendicular to the horizontal xy plane. The projection of each set of direction circles onto a plane perpendicular to the primary direction forms two families of hyperbolic arcs, the curves of which intersect orthogonally. *Helmholtz.*

dispersion, c. of. Blur circle.

greater arterial c. of the iris. A vascular circle, formed by anastomoses of 7 anterior ciliary arteries and 2 long posterior ciliary arteries, located about the root of the iris in the ciliary body. It supplies the ciliary body, anterior choroid, and the lesser arterial circle of the iris. Syn., *annulus iridis major; circulus arteriosus iridis major.*

Haller, c. of. An arterial circle about the optic nerve within the sclera, formed by anastomoses of a few short posterior ciliary arteries. Branches pass to the optic nerve, the pia mater, the optic nerve head, and the neighboring choroid and retina. The cilioretinal artery, when present, arises from it. Syn., *circle of Zinn; vascular circle of the optic nerve; Zinn's corona.*

Hovius, c. of. A network of veins in most mammals, other than man, located in the sclera posterior to the corneoscleral margin, which drains aqueous humor into the vortex veins. Syn., *circulus venosus hovii; Hovius' plexus; Leber's venous plexus.*

hue c. Color circle.

isogonal c., primary. The circle passing through the point of fixation and the centers of rotation of the two eyes. The plane of the circle contains the two visual axes and the two horizontal retinal meridians. See also *Vieth-Mueller circle, longitudinal horopter,* and *monoscopter.*

isogonal c., secondary. A circle passing through the centers of rotation of the two eyes and through any indirect point of view which lies above or below

the point of fixation at a distance equal to that of the point of fixation, this distance being measured from the midpoint of the line connecting the centers of rotation. For a given fixation distance there is an infinite number of secondary isogonal circles, the plane of each containing only indirect visual lines.

least aberration, c. of. Circle of least confusion.

least chromatic aberration, c. of. The circular image of a point source of heterochromatic light when the receiving screen lies approximately midway between the focal images of the extreme red and blue rays.

least confusion, c. of. 1. The circular section found intermediate between the two line images of the bundle of rays forming Sturm's conoid. 2. The smallest cross section of a circular (nonastigmatic) bundle of rays. Syn., *circle of least aberration; circle of least diffusion.*

least diffusion, c. of. Circle of least confusion.

Leber's venous c. Canal of Schlemm.

lesser arterial c. of the iris. An incomplete vascular circle formed by arterio-venous anastomoses in the region of the collarette, near the pupillary margin of the iris. It receives blood from the greater arterial circle of the iris and supplies the pupillary zone of the iris. Syn., *annulus iridis minor; minor vascular circle; circulus arteriosus iridis minor.*

lymphatic c. of Teichmann. Terminal lymphatic loops encircling the cornea, in the region of the limbus, which drain into the radial vessels of Teichmann.

Minsky's c's. A series of circles on clinical record cards for pictorially recording eye lesions, each circle representing one of a series of planes from the cornea to the retina. The circles are lettered *C* for *cornea*, *AC* for *anterior chamber*, *I* for *iris*, *L* for *lens*, *V* for *vitreous*, and *R* for *retina*. The layers are further divided, there being, e.g., 5 corneal layers labeled from C-1 to C-5. A lesion of the epithelial layer would be depicted in the circle labeled C-1.

minor vascular c. Lesser arterial circle of the iris.

Mueller's horopter c. Vieth-Mueller horopter.

optical c. In physics, a graduated circle fitted with the necessary appliances for illustrating the laws of refraction and reflection or, when accurately constructed, for measuring interfacial angles, refractive indices, etc.

Rowland's c. In a concave mirror diffraction grating, the locus of points where the spectrum is in focus.

Thompson's c's. An apparatus for producing motion afterimages; an apparatus for creating the illusion of motion in a stationary object after previous exposure to a stimulus in motion, similar to Plateau's spiral.

vascular c. of the optic nerve. Circle of Haller.

venous c. of Leber. Canal of Schlemm.

Verhoeff's c. A visual acuity test object consisting of two concentric rings of 1 minute of arc width separated by a space of the same width when viewed at a specified distance. Syn., *Verhoeff's rings*.

Vieth-Mueller c. Vieth-Mueller horopter.

Willis, c. of. An arterial ring surrounding the optic chiasm and hypothalamus, formed by the basilar, posterior cerebral, posterior communicating, internal carotid, anterior cerebral, and anterior communicating arteries.

Zinn, c. of. Circle of Haller.

circulus (ser'ku-lus). Circle.

arteriosus halleri, c. Circle of Haller.

arteriosus iridis major, c. Greater arterial circle of the iris.

arteriosus iridis minor, c. Lesser arterial circle of the iris.

arteriosus nervi optici, c. Circle of Haller.

senilis, c. An arcus senilis which completely surrounds the cornea.

vasculosus nervi optici, c. Circle of Haller.

venosus hovii, c. Circle of Hovius.

zinii, c. Circle of Haller.

circumbulbar (ser″kum-bul'bar). 1. Situated around the eyeball. 2. Situated around the hindbrain part of the brain stem.

circumcorneal (ser″kum-kōr'ne-al). Surrounding the cornea, as in circumcorneal injection.

circumlental (ser″kum-len'tal). Surrounding the crystalline lens at the equator, as does the canal of Hannover between the leaves of the zonule of Zinn.

circumocular (ser″kum-ok'u-lar). Surrounding the eyeball. Syn., *circumbulbar*.

circumorbital (ser″kum-ōr'bih-tal). Surrounding the bony orbit.

circumpapillary (ser″kum-pap'ih-ler″e). Surrounding the optic disk.

cirsophthalmia (ser″sof-thal'me-ah). 1. Conjunctivitis in which the vessels are in a varicose condition. 2. Corneal staphyloma in which the surface of the cornea and sclera have a bluish varicose appearance.

cistern, chiasmatic (sis'tern). A subarachnoid space between the pituitary body and the optic chiasm. Syn., *cisterna basalis*.

cisterna basalis (sis-tern'ah ba-sal'-is). Chiasmatic cistern.

Clason acuity meter (cla'son). See under *meter*.

Claude's syndrome (klodz). See under *syndrome*.

Claude Bernard's syndrome (klod ber-narz'). See *syndrome, Bernard's.*

clearness. A perceptual attribute of transparent and translucent materials, the opposite of *milkiness* or *cloudiness.* The quality of being clear, sharp, without blur.

cleft. A crevice, groove, or fissure.

choroidal c. Fetal fissure.

ciliary c. 1. In the avian eye, an opening between ciliary processes which provides passageway between the anterior and posterior chambers. 2. A triangular space between the outer scleral portion and the inner uveal portion of the anterior ciliary body in the region of the angle of the anterior chamber of lower animals such as rodents. In man and other primates it is replaced by tissue leaving only a remnant. Syn., *ciliary sinus.*

corneal c. The groove of the sclera into which the cornea fits.

fetal c. Fetal fissure.

Fuchs's c. A narrow space, seen at about the fifth fetal month, between the pupillary region of the iris and the pupillary membrane prior to its atrophy.

clinic. A place and organization for the examination, diagnosis, study, and treatment of physical and mental disorders.

clinical. 1. Pertaining to findings of a routine examination as opposed to findings obtained under controlled conditions for specific research purposes. 2. Pertaining to the observation of the symptoms and course of a disease. 3. Pertaining to a clinic.

clinometer (kli-nom'eh-ter). An apparatus for measuring ocular torsion.

Duane's c. An instrument for studying torsional movements of the eye.

clinoscope, Stevens' (kli'no-skōp). An instrument for measuring cyclophoria, consisting essentially of two tubes nearly 20 in. long, each mounted so that it may be rotated about its longitudinal axis.

clip-on. A lightweight frame without temples, for holding auxiliary lenses, which can be attached to regular spectacles by means of wire hooks. Syn., *fit-on; fit-over.*

clip-over. Clip-on.

clivus (kli'vus). The gently curved wall of the fovea.

clock, lens. Lens measure.

clock, Luer's. A cylindro-spherometer.

Cloquet's canal (klo-kāz'). See under *canal.*

closure. A perception of a single large unit rather than a number of apparently unrelated parts; collective configuration.

clouding, central corneal. A superficial diffuse edema of the cornea, usually circular, and associated with the wearing of contact lenses which either bear on the central epithelium or entrap tear fluid in this area. It is most easily seen without magnification with sclerotic scatter illumination from the beam of a slit lamp, appearing as a dull, gray area surrounded by clear cornea.

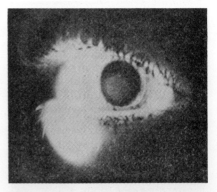

Fig. 7. Central corneal clouding as observed with the unaided eye and sclerotic scatter slit lamp illumination. (From *Corneal Contact Lenses,* ed. L. J. Girard, C. V. Mosby Co., 1964)

club, Landolt. A sclerally directed dendrite of a retinal bipolar cell which passes between the bodies of rods and cones to terminate in the vicinity of the external limiting membrane; of unknown synaptic relations and function.

clue, fusion. In a pair of haploscopic stimulus targets, the elements of the pattern which are presented to one eye only for the purpose of confirming that the eye is being used during binocular testing or training. Syn., *control.*

cm. Abbreviation for *centimeter.*

coagulation, light (ko-ag″u-la′-shun). Photocoagulation.

coat. 1. A layer of substance covering another. 2. A membrane covering or lining a part or an organ.

fibrous c. of eyeball. The cornea and sclera together.

nervous c. of eyeball. The retina.

uveal c. The vascular coat of the eyeball.

vaginal c. Tenon's capsule.

vascular c. of eyeball. The uvea, consisting of the choroid, ciliary body, and iris.

coating, lens. A thin deposit of a metallic salt, such as magnesium fluoride, about one fourth as thick as a wavelength of light, applied to the surfaces of a lens to reduce, by interference, the amount of light reflected, and, if combined with a coloring ingredient, to reduce light transmission also.

Coats's (kōts) **disease; retinitis; rings.** See under the nouns.

cocaine (ko-kān′, ko′kān, ko′kuh-ēn). An alkaloid derivative from coca leaves used as a local anesthetic, mydriatic, and narcotic. Its hydrochloride stimulates peripheral sympathetic nerve endings in the iris and causes moderate dilatation of the pupil with little effect on the ciliary muscle and hence on accommodation.

Cochet's test (ko-shāz′). See under *test.*

Cochet-Bonnet esthesiometer (ko′-sha-bo-na′). See under *esthesiometer.*

Cockayne's (kok′ānz) **disease; syndrome.** See under *disease.*

Coddington lens (kod′ing-tun). See under *lens.*

coefficient (ko″e-fish′ent). A number or a letter symbol which denotes any of a group of numbers. The coefficient or number may denote or express any of the following: (1) the amount by which a mathematical expression is to be multiplied; (2) the amount of change or the amount of effect due to change; (3) the amount or degree of a quality possessed; (4) a ratio.

absorption, c. of. The fraction of the incident intensity absorbed per unit thickness of a transmitting medium.

alienation, c. of. A number expressing the amount of lack of association or relationship between two variables. The mathematical expression is $\sqrt{1 - r^2}$, where r is the coefficient of correlation. Syn., *coefficient of nondetermination.*

association, c. of. A number within the range of -1.00 to $+1.00$ (similar in interpretation to the Pearsonian coefficient of correlation) describing the association of two variables, each of which is classed in two categories.

chroma-brilliance c. The ratio of the number of units of chromatic valence to the number of units of brightness in a sample visual stimulus.

colligation, c. of. A measure similar in interpretation and computation to the coefficient of association.

contingency, c. of. A number expressing the degree of association or relationship between two variables for which only categorical information is available. See also *chi square.*

correlation, c. of. 1. A number (mathematical symbol $= r$) which expresses (*a*) the degree of association or relationship between two variables; (*b*) the accuracy of predicting one variable if another associated variable is known. 2. The Pearsonian coefficient of correlation obtained from two variables, each of which forms a continuum. 3. Mathematically, *r* is the average of the cross products of the deviations from the means of the two variables divided by the product of the two standard deviations.

$$r = \frac{\Sigma xy}{NS_x S_y}$$

where x = a deviation from the mean of the *X*'s
    y = a deviation from the mean of the *Y*'s
    S_x = the standard deviation of the *X*'s
    S_y = the standard deviation of the *Y*'s
    N = the number of items

correlation, c. of (biserial). An estimate of the Pearsonian coefficient of correlation which may be obtained if one variable forms a continuum, while the other contains categorized information. (Symbol = r_b.)

correlation, c. of (partial). A number which describes the closeness of association of two variables or characteristics when one or more other variable is statistically held constant (partialed out). The scale is the same as that for the Pearsonian coefficient of correlation, *q.v.* See also *partial correlation.*

correlation, c. of (Pearsonian). A number which describes the closeness of association of two variables or characteristics. The Pearsonian coefficient of correlation (*r*) encompasses a range from −1.00 (complete inverse correlation) to +1.00 (complete direct correlation).

correlation, c. of (product

moment). Pearsonian coefficient of correlation.

correlation, c. of (rank). An estimate of the Pearsonian coefficient of correlation, *r*, which may be obtained if each variable is assigned a rank (first, second . . . tenth, etc.) instead of a place in a continuum. Symbol = ρ (*rho*).

Mathematically,

$$\rho = 1 - \frac{6\Sigma d^2}{N(N^2 - 1)}$$

where N = the number of cases, and
    d = the difference in rank of the two variables of the pair

correlation, c. of (tetrachoric). An estimate of the Pearsonian coefficient of correlation, *r*, which may be obtained if each variable yields dichotomized information only, rather than forming a continuum. (Symbol = r_t).

determination, c. of. 1. A measure expressing the variance in one characteristic that is explained by or associated with variance in the other value. 2. The Pearsonian coefficient of correlation squared, i.e., r^2 = coefficient of determination.

dichromatic c's. The relative intensities of the components (primary colors) of a two-color mixture required by a dichromat to match a sample color.

dispersion, c. of. A measure of variability free of units of measurement and obtained by dividing the measure of dispersion (standard deviation, average deviation, etc.) by a measure of central tendency (mean, median, etc.); hence, of value in comparing the variability of two characteristics with different units. Ex.: Is height or weight more variable?

facility of aqueous outflow, c. of. The change in tonometric scale

readings during prolonged tonometry in terms of units of intraocular fluid expelled, divided
by units of pressure change and
time; expressed by the ratio:

$$C = \frac{\Delta V}{T[average\ P_t - (P_0 + \Delta P_v)]}$$

in which C = coefficient of the
facility of aque-
ous outflow
ΔV = intraocular fluid
expelled
T = time
P_t = intraocular pres-
sure during to-
nometry
P_0 = intraocular pres-
sure just prior to
tonometry
ΔP_v = pressure change
in the episcleral
veins (approx.
1.25 mm. Hg.)

The P_0 values are those of the
1955 conversion scale for the
Schiötz tonometer.
Fresnel's dragging c. A coefficient
dealing with relative motion of
ether and light waves. It is ex-
pressed as a fraction $1 - \frac{1}{n^2}$, where
n is the index of refraction.
Friedenwald's c. A numerical
quantity representing the resistance of the ocular coats to distension, determined by Friedenwald by taking two readings with
the Schiötz tonometer, each with
a different weight, and relating
these measurements to the volume changes produced by these
weights. A high value indicates
a more rigid coat and a low value
a more pliable one.
heredity, c. of. The Pearsonian coefficient of correlation for a given
characteristic of a parent and
one of the offspring. Ex.: the coefficient of correlation between
the height of father and the
height of son.

light extinction, c. of. The relative amount or percentage of incident light of a given wavelength absorbed by a 1% solution
of a substance in a layer 1 cm.
thick.
luminosity c. The constants by
which the color mixture data for
any color must be multiplied so
that the sum of the three products is equal to the luminance of
the color. Syn., *visibility coefficient*.
nondetermination, c. of. Coefficient of alienation.
ocular rigidity, c. of. A numerical
value mathematically derived
from two tonometric readings
with different weights and said
to represent the resistance of the
ocular coats to distension, used in
calculating intraocular pressure.
Syn., *coefficient of scleral rigidity*.
reflection, c. of. The ratio of reflected flux to incident flux. Syn.,
reflectance.
refraction, c. of. Index of refraction. *Obs.*
regression, c. of. A number expressing the change in one variable for a unit change in the other.
In linear regression for two variables X and Y, the regression line
or curve is expressed as $Y =
a + bX$, where a is the Y inter-
cept and b is the coefficient of
regression.
reliability, c. of. 1. The coefficient
of correlation obtained from two
applications of the same test or
measurement. 2. The coefficient
of correlation for scores of the
same individuals on a test and
on a re-test. The range of coefficients is the same as for the
Pearsonian coefficient of correlation, i.e., +1.00 to −1.00.
scleral rigidity, c. of. Coefficient
of ocular rigidity.
skewness, c. of. Any one of a series
of measures of the degree of
asymmetry of a distribution.
transmission c. The fractional por-

tion of incident energy transmitted per unit thickness of the transmitting medium.

trichromatic c's. Chromaticity coordinates.

utilization, c. of. The ratio of luminous flux (lumens) received on the work plane to the rated lumens emitted by the lamps.

variation, c. of. One of the coefficients of dispersion; one hundred times the standard deviation divided by the mean; the coefficient of variation $= 100\frac{\sigma}{x}$.

visibility c. Luminosity coefficient.
Cogan's (ko'ganz) **implant; syndrome.** See under the nouns.
Cogan-Kinsey theory (ko'gan kin'-se). See *theory, osmotic pump.*
coherence (ko-hēr'ens). 1. A property of electromagnetic radiation from a source in which all the propagated energy is in phase, the maxima and minima of all waves being coincident; the energy being propagated from each point at the emitter is in phase with every other point. 2. In fiber optics, a point to point relationship between the two ends of the fiber bundle.

lateral c. Phase synchronism across a wavefront. Syn., *spatial coherence.*

longitudinal c. Temporal stability of phase in succeeding wavefronts of a wave train. Syn., *temporal coherence.*

spatial c. Lateral coherence.

temporal c. Longitudinal coherence.

Cohn's (kōnz) **test; theory.** See under the nouns.
Colenbrander's formula (ko'lenbrand"erz). See under *formula.*
collar. That part of a rimless spectacle mounting which fits against the edge of the lens and to which the straps are attached. Syn., *shoe.*
collarette (kol'er-et'). The line of junction between the pupillary

zone and the ciliary zone on the anterior surface of the iris. In the normal iris, it is an irregular circular line lying about 1.5 mm. from the pupillary border.

collective configuration. 1. The perception of a complete pattern, although parts of it are absent in the immediate stimulus, as in perceiving a straight line unbroken when it traverses the blind spot. 2. The tendency to perceive a complex pattern as a whole rather than as an assembly of its parts.

collectors. Very small ducts which transmit aqueous humor from the canal of Schlemm to the deep scleral plexus.

Collet's sign (kol-lets'). See under *sign.*

colliculus, inferior (kŏ-lik'u-lus). Either of the lower paired eminences of the dorsal midbrain, acting as relay centers for auditory reflexes.

colliculus, superior (kŏ-lik'u-lus). Either of the upper paired eminences of the dorsal midbrain, located near the pineal body, acting as relay centers for visual reflexes that affect skeletal muscle.

collimate (kol'ih-māt). 1. To render a bundle of rays parallel. 2. To adjust an optical instrument so that its mechanical and optical axes are coincident or parallel.

collimator (kol'ih-ma"tor). A device for producing parallel rays of light. Usually, an achromatic objective with a point source of light at one of its focal points.

collineation (kŏ-lin"e-a'shun). A point to point geometric correspondence between object and image space of an optical system.

central c. A method, by geometric construction, of locating images produced by the refraction of paraxial rays at a single spherical surface or through an infinitely thin lens.

Collins' glands; theory. See under the nouns.

collyria (kŏ-lir′e-ah). The plural of collyrium.

collyrium (kŏ-lir′e-um). An eyewash or a lotion for the eyes.

colmascope (kol′mah-skōp). An instrument which uses transmitted polarized light for determining stress and strain in glass.

coloboma (kol″o-bo′mah). 1. A congenital anomaly in which a portion of a structure of the eye (or eyelid) is absent. The majority are due to incomplete closure of the fetal fissure and are located inferiorly (typical coloboma). 2. Any defect in which a portion of a structure of an eye (or eyelid) is absent. It may be congenital, pathologic, or operative.

atypical c. A coloboma not located inferiorly in any part of the eye or not due to incomplete closure of the fetal fissure.

bridge c. A coloboma in which isolated areas of the fetal fissure fuse to form a bridge of tissue across the defect.

choroid, c. of the. A congenital absence of choroidal tissue in a portion of the fundus of the eye, typically located inferiorly and due to incomplete closure of the fetal fissure. The retina in the corresponding area is also absent, resulting in a scotoma in the visual field. The ophthalmoscopic picture is of a white area of exposed sclera with a sharply defined pigmented border.

ciliary body, c. of the. A congenital absence of tissue of the ciliary body which typically appears as an anterior indentation with a characteristic hyperplasia of the adjacent ciliary processes, forming large polypoid masses. The ciliary muscle is absent and the pigmented epithelium is incomplete in the region of the defect.

complete c. 1. A coloboma caused by failure of closure of the fetal

fissure along its entire length, thus involving the iris, ciliary body, choroid, retina, and optic disk. 2. A coloboma in which there is a local absence of both ectodermal and mesodermal layers.

eyelid, c. of the. A congenital notch or cleft in the upper or lower eyelid margin.

Fuchs's c. A congenital crescentic colobomatous defect of the choroid at the lower margin of the optic disk.

fundus, c. of the. A congenital absence of retinal and choroidal tissue in a portion of the fundus of the eye, typically located inferiorly and due to incomplete closure of the fetal fissure. The ophthalmoscopic picture is of a white area of exposed sclera with a sharply defined pigmented border.

    fundus, c. of the (bridge). A coloboma of the fundus which is divided into two or more sections by a strip of apparently normal tissue.

incomplete c. 1. Partial coloboma. 2. Coloboma in which there is a local absence of either the mesodermal or the ectodermal layer.

iris, c. of the. A congenital notch or cleft in the iris. It may be total, partial, simple, complete, incomplete, or notch coloboma.

    iris, c. of the (bridge). Coloboma of the iris in which mesodermal tissue derived from the pupillary membrane stretches across the defect.

    iris, c. of the (complete). Coloboma of the iris in which both mesodermal and ectodermal layers are absent. Cf. *incomplete coloboma of the iris.*

    iris, c. of the (incomplete). Coloboma of the iris in which either the mesodermal or the ectodermal layer is absent. Cf. *complete coloboma of the iris.* Syn., *pseudocoloboma.*

iris, c. of the (notch). A partial coloboma of the iris at the pupillary margin. It occurs typically in the lower sector of the iris and may be multiple.

iris, c. of the (partial). Coloboma of the iris not involving a whole sector up to the ciliary border. It may be in one of three forms: (1) a notch in the pupillary margin; (2) a hole in the iris substance (pseudopolycoria); (3) a peripheral defect near the ciliary margin (iridodiastasis).

iris, c. of the (simple). Coloboma occurring only in the iris in the presence of a normally closed fetal fissure.

iris, c. of the (total). Coloboma of the iris involving an entire sector of the iris up to the ciliary border.

lens, c. of the. A congenital notch or cleft at the margin of the crystalline lens, usually downward and with an associated defect of the zonule of Zinn in the same region.

macular c. A congenital defect in which there is an absence of choroidal tissue in the macular area.

notch c. A partial coloboma of the iris at the pupillary margin. It occurs typically in the lower sector of the iris and may be multiple.

optic disk, c. of the. A coloboma of the optic nerve head which may be part of a complete coloboma, be associated with coloboma of the fundus, or be limited to the region of the optic disk when only the proximal end of the fetal fissure fails to close. Ophthalmoscopically, it appears as a white area, usually considerably larger than the normal optic disk.

optic nerve, c. of the. A congenital defect in the formation of the optic nerve or its sheaths which characteristically appears as a craterlike excavation at the optic disk, surrounded by a hyperplasia of the adjacent retina.

palpebrale, c. A congenital notch or cleft of an eyelid at its margin.

partial c. A coloboma caused by failure of closure of part of the fetal fissure, thus involving only the iris, ciliary body, choroid, optic disk, or retina, but not all.

peripapillary c. Congenital failure of choroidal and retinal development immediately around a normal optic nerve.

retina, c. of the. A congenital notch or cleft of the retina, usually located inferiorly.

simple c. A coloboma occurring only in the iris in the presence of a normally closed fetal fissure.

total c. A coloboma of the iris involving an entire sector of the iris up to the ciliary border.

typical c. A coloboma due to an incomplete closure of the fetal cleft and located inferiorly.

vitreous, c. of the. A congenital indentation or separation of the vitreous body by persistent mesodermal tissue in the vitreous chamber. The ectodermal vitreous body is actually intact.

color. 1. A sensory or perceptual component of visual experience, characterized by the attributes of *hue, brightness,* and *saturation,* and usually arising from, or in response to, stimulation of the retina by radiation of wavelengths between about 380 and 760 mμ. Sensory components, such as white, gray, and black, which have neither hue nor saturation, are sometimes included with colors. Variously synonymous with *hue, tint,* or *shade.* 2. A stimulus or a visual object which evokes a chromatic response.

accidental c. A color percept resulting from an immediate preexposure to a nonneutral stimulus, as an afterimage effect.

achromatic c. Sensory or perceptual components possessing a brightness level but no hue or saturation. The achromatic colors are white, gray, and black.

amnesia, c. See under *amnesia*.

antagonistic c. Any of the colors paired in the Hering theory of color vision.

aperture c. A color perceived as filling an aperture. It may be seen close to the plane of the aperture or at some indefinite distance behind it. It is filmy and soft in character and is contrasted with a surface color, which is hard in appearance and exactly localized in space.

blend, c. See under *blend*.

blindness, c. See under *blindness*.

body c. Color perceived in an object by the reflection of light after it has penetrated the object a certain distance and has undergone selective absorption. The same color would thus be seen upon transmission of light through the substance of the object. It should be distinguished from *surface color*.

bulky c. Spatial color.

catoptrical c's. Iridescent colors. *Obs.*

chart, c. See under *chart*.

chromatic c. Color perceptions possessing hue and saturation in addition to the attribute of *brightness*, as red, green, blue, or yellow. Cf. *achromatic color*.

circle, c. See under *circle*.

complementary c's. 1. Any pair of colors in which the direct perception of one produces an afterimage of the other. 2. Any pair of colors in which the direct perception of one produces simultaneous contrast of the other. 3. Two colors which, when additively mixed, produce light gray or white. 4. Two colors which, when subtractively mixed, produce black or gray.

compound c's. Color sensations produced by additively mixing two or more primary colors, as, for example, purple or orange.

cone, c. A type of color solid.

confusion c. A color which appears the same as another color to a person who is color blind.

contrast, c. See under *contrast*.

cool c. A color said to give a psychological feeling of coolness, quietness, or lack of activity, as, for example, green or blue.

cycle, c. Color circle.

dark c. A color of relatively low brightness level. This may exist for any hue, depending on its luminance in relation to its background.

disk, c. See under *disk*.

equations, c. See under *equation*.

equilibrium c. A spectral hue which does not change with variations in intensity. See also *Bezold-Brücke effect*.

extraspectral c. A color, such as purple, which cannot be produced by any one wavelength of the spectrum.

Fechner's c's. Colored rings seen on a rotating disk which is marked out into black and white sectors.

fields, c. See under *field, visual*.

film c. A color seen as indefinitely localized and not belonging to any particular surface or object, as the color seen in the spectroscope.

flight, c. See under *flight*.

full c. A color sample in the Ostwald or Ridgway system which has maximum purity for a particular hue. See also *Ostwald semichrome*.

fundamental c's. 1. Any set of three colors, e.g., red, green, and blue, from which all other color sensations can be produced by additive mixing. Syn., *primary colors*. 2. The colors which subjectively seem pure, i.e., not psychologically composed of other colors. These are red, green, blue, and yellow. Syn., *primal colors.*

fusion, c. See under *fusion.*

glowing c. A color seen as an attribute of a glowing body. *Katz.*

hard c. 1. Color seen as an attribute of a hard or firm surface. 2. Certain colors classified by artists and psychologists as inherently hard or firm in appearance, as, for example, red or yellow. Cf. *soft color.*

harmonic c. One of a pair of complementary colors.

illuminant c. Color seen as glowing or as a light source either by virtue of its being an attribute of a light source, as in a neon light, or by possessing a high reflectance in relation to its background.

illumination c. A color seen as belonging to illumination distributed in space, as blue light flooding a stage.

impure c. Any color produced by a mixture of two or more wavelengths; opposite of *monochromatic color.*

induced c. A color appearing in a portion of the visual field, produced by simultaneous contrast from a neighboring portion of the field. Syn., *resulting color.*

inducing c. A color stimulus which induces or produces a color effect in the surrounding region of the visual field by simultaneous contrast.

induction, c. See under *induction.*

invariable c. Stable color.

iridescent c's. Rainbowlike colors produced by interference, as exhibited by soap bubbles or mother-of-pearl.

isomeric c's. Colors of identical spectrophotometric composition and tristimulus values. Syn., *isomeric pair.*

isovalent c's. In the Ostwald system, color of differing hue but having the same proportions of black and white content.

luminous c. A color having the appearance of being a light source. Syn., *illuminant color.*

luster c. A composite color which has the appearance of a color being situated behind and shining through another color, or a color in which bright areas seem to shift upon the surface.

matching, c. See under *matching.*

memory c. The color of an object as retained in one's memory.

metallic c. A color produced by selective reflection from semipolished metallic surfaces, or having the appearance of such colors, e.g., bronze.

metameric c's. Colors of different spectrophotometric composition which appear the same under given conditions. Syn., *metamers; metameric pair.*

mirrored c. Color having the appearance of being reflected in a mirror.

mixer, c. See under *mixer.*

mixing, c. Any process of combining two or more color stimuli, additively or subtractively, so as to produce a single resultant color, as by mixing pigments, superimposing colored lights, or presenting colored surfaces in rapid succession.

   mixing, additive c. The mixing of colors by summation of the wavelength composition of two or more color stimuli.

   mixing, binocular c. The subjective mixing of two color stimuli by viewing one color stimulus with one eye and another color stimulus with the corresponding retinal area of the other eye.

   mixing, subtractive c. The mixing of colors by subtraction of the wavelength composition of one color stimulus from that of another color stimulus, as in pigment mixing or in placing a selectively absorbing filter in front of a color stimulus.

mixture, c. See under *mixture.*

monochromatic c. A color produced by a single wavelength or by a narrow band of wavelengths of the spectrum.

Munsell c's. A series of about one thousand standard color samples, each designated by a letter-number system. The series represents various combinations of hue, saturation, and brightness and includes variations of brightness of the achromatic colors which have neither hue nor saturation.

neutral c. A color which has neither hue nor saturation, but which varies from other such colors in brightness only, as, for example, gray, black, or white.

Newton's c's. Seven principal colors (red, orange, yellow, green, blue, indigo, and violet) designated by Newton in his division of the visible spectrum into seven intervals of widths proportional to the intervals in the musical scale.

object c. 1. The color of light transmitted or reflected by an object illuminated by a standard light source such as illuminant A, B, or C. 2. A color perceived as an inherent attribute of an object resulting from characteristics of the object, and of the surround, viewing direction, and color adaptation of the eye.

Ostwald c's. A series of several hundred chromatic and achromatic color samples, designated by a letter-number system.

pale c. A color possessing a low degree of saturation.

pastel c. A color of low saturation and high lightness or brightness; a color containing a high proportion of white.

plane c. A color perception unassociated with any system of orientation or localization in space and, hence, regarded as the end result of complete color reduction. *Katz.*

plane transparent c. A plane color which appears transparent, such as that of colored glass. *Katz.*

primal c's. Four colors which psychologically do not contain component sensations of any other colors or of each other. They are red, green, blue, and yellow. Syn., *fundamental colors; psychological primary colors.*

primary c's. Any set of three colors, e.g., red, green, and blue, from which all other color sensations can be produced by additive mixing. Syn., *fundamental colors.*

prismatic c's. The colors produced from white light as it is reduced to its component parts by the dispersing action of a prism. They are often listed as red, orange, yellow, green, blue, indigo, and violet. *Newton.*

pure c. 1. A color stimulus which approaches the condition for maximum saturation. 2. Monochromatic color.

pyramid, c. A type of color solid.

reacting c. A color which by simultaneous contrast is altered to another color (induced color) from the effects of the inducing color.

reduced c. 1. Aperture color. 2. Plane color.

reduction, c. See under *reduction.*

reflected c. Color seen as though reflected from a perceived object.

resulting c. Induced color.

Ridgway c's. An early system of 1,115 combinations of hue, saturation, and brightness, varying in approximately equal, just noticeable difference, steps.

saturated c. A color of any given hue at its maximum possible degree of saturation.

secondary c. 1. A color produced by additive mixing of primary colors. 2. Any color not identified as a primary color.

sense, c. See under *sense.*

shadows, c. See under *shadow.*

[145]

soft c. 1. Any color stimulus appearing soft in texture. 2. Certain colors classified by artists and psychologists as inherently soft in appearance, as, for example, blue or green. Cf. *hard color.*

solid, c. See under *solid.*

spatial c. A color perceived in three dimensions, as having a space-filling attribute, or as being solid, such as is seen in colored liquids and transparent fogs. *Katz.* Syn., *bulky color; volume color.*

spectral c's. The colors visible in the spectrum.

spindle, c. A type of color solid.

stable c. Any hue which does not change with variations in brightness or with variations in the area of the retina stimulated. Syn., *invariable color.*

stereoscopy, c. See under *stereoscopy.*

strong c. A color of high saturation.

subjective c. The sensation of color derived from stimulation other than with chromatic stimuli, as may occur from intermittent exposure at low frequencies to achromatic stimuli or from exposure to dazzling lights.

　subjective c., binocular. Chromatic responses to intermittent achromatic stimuli (about 40 cycles per sec.) which are observed binocularly but not monocularly.

surface, c. See under *surface.*

surface c. A color perceived as belonging to the surface of an object and in the same plane.

　surface c., artificial. A color perceptually projected on the surface of an object to which it does not physically belong.

　surface c., transparent. A color perceived in a two-dimensional manner and possessing the property of transparency, whereby other objects can be seen through it.

table, c. See under *table.*

temperature, c. See under *temperature.*

tertiary c. A color with spectral composition more complex than a secondary color, i.e., consisting of more than the three primary wavelengths.

threshold, c. Chromatic threshold.

triangle, c. See under *triangle.*

true c. 1. The sensation of a hue as interpreted by an individual with normal color vision. 2. The color of an object as seen under ordinary conditions in normal diffuse daylight by the light-adapted eye. *Katz.*

unique c. A color which cannot be described in terms of any other color. Red, yellow, blue, green, white, black, and gray are considered to be the seven unique colors. Syn., *unitary color.*

unitary c. Unique color.

volume c. Spatial color.

warm c. A color said to give a psychological effect of warmth, as, for example, red or yellow.

weak c. A color of low saturation.

weakness, c. See under *weakness.*

zones, c. See under *zone.*

colorimeter (kul″or-im′eh-ter). A color-matching device used to designate an unknown colored stimulus by matching it with a known colored stimulus; a color comparator.

Abney's c. A colorimeter in which colors used in matching are isolated by three slits placed in the plane of a spectrum. The luminances of the components are varied by altering the widths of the slits. Syn., *Abney's sensitometer.*

Ives's c. A type of anomaloscope in which the colors used in matching are obtained from light passing through three adjustable slits for controlling the relative intensities of light through blue, green, and red glass filters.

Meisling's c. A type of colorimeter

in which the colors used in matching are produced by passing light through a system consisting of six quartz plates, of varying thickness, placed between two Nicol prisms. Any color used is specified in terms of the thickness of quartz plate and the angle between the Nicol prisms.

monochromatic c. A colorimeter calibrated to designate a particular color mixture in terms of the wavelength of monochromatic light which will produce the same hue sensation.

photoelectric c. A device employing a photoelectric detector to measure three quantities related by linear combination to the tristimulus values of any sample. Such devices usually employ either a single photocell and three color filters, or three separate photocells. Syn., *photocolorimeter.*

trichromatic c. A colorimeter calibrated to designate any particular hue in terms of the relative proportions of the three primary colors, red, green, and blue, whose mixture gives the same hue sensation.

Wright's c. A type of anomaloscope in which the colors used in matching are obtained by dispersing prisms and are focused directly into the observer's eye instead of projected onto a screen.

colorimetry (kul″or-im′eh-tre). The quantitative evaluation of color either in terms of such attributes as hue, saturation, and brightness or as equivalents or matches of fixed or known standards. Cf. *chromometry; chromophotometry; chromoscopy.*

direct c. Colorimetry in which the color of the sample is matched by varying combinations of known color stimuli, either visually or with light-sensitive instruments.

indirect c. Designation of a color in terms of colorimetric specifications computed from known color data.

colorless. Without color or chroma. The achromatic colors, white, gray, and black, are said to be "colors without color" since they lack hue and saturation. When white, gray, and black are considered as colors, then only transparent substances, such as water, are without color.

colytropia (ko″le-tro′pe-ah). A tropia due to paralytic or mechanical causes; nonconcomitant strabismus.

coma (ko′mah). An oblique monochromatic aberration of an optical system in which the image of a point off the optical axis appears comet-shaped, with the tail pointing toward the axis. It is a result of unequal magnification in different zones of the system and can be corrected by the sine condition or, if in Seidel's formulae, by S_1 and $S_2 = 0$.

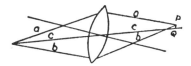

Fig. 8. Coma. (From *Text-book of Ophthalmology*, Vol. IV, Duke-Elder, Henry Kimpton, 1949)

negative c. Coma in which the magnification for the central rays is greater than that for the peripheral rays.

positive c. Coma in which the magnification for the peripheral rays is greater than that for the central rays.

Comberg (kōm′berg) **contact lens; method.** See under the nouns.

comedo (kom′e-do, ko-me′do). A plug of dried sebaceous material retained in an excretory duct of the skin, commonly called a blackhead.

comitance (kom'ih-tans). Concomitance.

comitancy (kom'ih-tan"se). Concomitance.

comitant (kom'ih-tant). Concomitant.

comma (ko'mah). A term used by Duke-Elder for coma.

Commission Internationale de l'Eclairage. An international organization devoted to studying and advancing the art and science of illumination. It is variously referred to as C.I.E., or I.C.I. from the English translation, International Commission on Illumination. Its membership is made up of national committees representing individual countries, and a limited number of local representatives from countries where there are no national committees. Individuals are members of the national committees and not of the C.I.E.

commissure (kom'ih-shūr). 1. The point or line of union between two parts, as that of the eyelids. 2. A band of nerve fibers connecting corresponding structures in the two sides of the brain or spinal cord.

arcuate c. Commissure of von Gudden.

basal c. Meynert's commissure.

Ganser, c. of. The most dorsal of the three supraoptic commissures; its composition is not fully known. It originates in part in the globus pallidus of the lentiform nucleus, conducts fibers to the ventromedial hypothalamic nuclei, and probably connects the hypothalamic regions of the two sides. Syn., *basal commissure; superior commissure; anterior hypothalamic decussation.*

von Gudden, c. of. A commissure connecting the medial geniculate body and inferior colliculus of one side to the opposite side by means of the medial portions of the optic tracts and the optic

chiasm. In man, such fibers are lacking, but some authorities still use this term for the same region of the human brain. Syn., *arcuate commissure; ventral supraoptic decussation.*

inferior c. Postoptic commissure.

lid c., lateral. 1. The juncture of the upper and lower eyelids at the lateral canthus. 2. Loosely, the lateral canthus.

lid c., medial. 1. The juncture of the upper and lower eyelids in the region of the medial canthus. 2. Loosely, the medial canthus.

Meynert's c. The largest of the three supraoptic commissures; it lies underneath the commissure of Ganser and is considered to be composed in part of fibers originating in the globus pallidus and ending in the lateral hypothalamic region and in part of autonomic fibers which leave the visual pathway to reach the supraoptic and tuberal nuclei. Syn., *superior commissure, dorsal supraoptic decussation.*

optic c. 1. Optic chiasm. 2. The nerve fibers from the left occipital lobe to the right occipital lobe which some authorities believe help to account for sparing of the macula.

posterior c. Myelinated nerve fibers connecting the opposite sides of the posterior parts of the diencephalon and of the superior colliculi. Some pupillary pathway fibers from the pretectal areas pass through to reach the contralateral Edinger-Westphal nucleus.

postoptic c. Nerve fibers connecting the left and right hypothalami via the floor of the third ventricle adjacent to the optic chiasm. Syn., *inferior commissure.*

superior c. Meynert's commissure.

supraoptic c's. In mammals, three fine bundles of transverse nerve fibers which cross dorsal to the optic chiasm, the commissures of von Gudden, Meynert, and Ganser (*q.v.*).

commotio retinae (ko-mo'she-o reh'-tih-ne). An edematous condition of the retina, particularly in the macular area, due to trauma. Syn., *Berlin's disease; Berlin's edema.*

comparator (kom-par'ah-tor). Any of several optical devices for the inspection of quality and the measurement of dimensions of an object by comparison to a standard or to a set of specifications, as, for example, a measuring magnifier used for contact lenses.

compensation. 1. The effect produced by rolling eye movements opposite to the direction of head movement to maintain stability of the visual field. 2. The effect of visual adaptation to varying levels of illumination. 3. The effect of amblyopia or suppression, when normal binocular vision is difficult to maintain. 4. The effect of head turning, or tilting, in strabismus or hyperphoria. 5. The effect of bifocal segment decentration to eliminate prismatic imbalances resulting from the distance prescription.

Bechterew's c. Compensation for the head and eye deviations which follow unilateral labyrinthectomy, such that removal of, or injury to, the other labyrinth gives rise to head and eye deviations as if the first labyrinth were intact. The head and eyes are deviated toward the operated side and a jerky nystagmus occurs with the slow phase toward this same side.

prism c. The equalization or neutralization, totally or in part, of prismatic effects at specified points of spectacle lenses by means of decentration, segment selection, or bicentric grinding.

compensator (kom'pen-sa"tor). A crystal plate of variable thickness used to produce or analyze elliptically polarized light.

Babinet c. A pair of quartz prisms arranged in sequence with axes perpendicular, for use in the study of elliptically polarized light phenomena.

Soleil c. A Babinet compensator adapted by means of a third prism to produce the same phase difference throughout a large field.

complement. One of a pair of two colors which, when mixed additively, produce white or gray, e.g., blue-green is the complement of red.

Compton effect (komp'tun). See under *effect.*

Compumatic Computer. A commercial name for a device for determining the back surface curvatures and optical zone diameter for the corneal contact lens which will provide a lacrimal layer of uniform thickness for a cornea of known curvatures. The data are obtained by matching graphic representations of lens curvatures to those of the cornea.

comus (ko'mus). A crescent-shaped, yellowish area seen near the optic disk in some high myopes.

con. Abbreviation for *convergence.*

concave (kon'kāv). Having a curved, depressed surface, as the inside of a sphere; opposed to *convex.*

concavoconcave (kon-ka"vo-kon'-kāv). Having concave surfaces on both sides, as a double concave lens.

concavoconvex (kon-ka"vo-kon'-veks). Having a concave surface on one side and a convex surface on the other.

concentric (kon-sen'trik). Having a common center of curvature or symmetry.

concession, visual. Adaptive loss of a visual skill.

conclination (kon"klin-a'shun). Intorsion.

concomitance (kon-kom′ih-tans). The condition in which the two eyes move as a unit, maintaining a constant or relatively constant angular relationship between the lines of sight for all directions of gaze, usually indicating absence of paresis or paralysis of the extraocular muscles. Syn., *comitance; comitancy; concomitancy.*

  secondary c. Concomitance following a period of noncomitance due to contracture and other compensating mechanisms.

concomitancy (kon-kom′ih-tan″se). Concomitance.

concomitant (kon-kom′ih-tant). Pertaining to or having concomitance. Syn., *comitant.*

concretions, conjunctiva (kon-kre′-shunz). Minute, hard, yellow masses found in the palpebral conjunctivae of elderly people, or following chronic conjunctivitis, composed of the products of cellular degeneration retained in the depressions and tubular recesses in the conjunctiva; incorrectly called *lithiasis conjunctivae.*

condenser (kon-den′ser). A large aperture, short focus lens or optical system used in microscopes and projectors, by means of which large angle cones of light are collected from a small source, transilluminating the whole object to be viewed or projected, and made to pass through the lens system. Syn., *condensing lens.*

condition. 1. A state essential to the appearance or occurrence of something else. 2. A mode or a state of being.

  Abbe's c. Sine condition.

  Gauss's c. A condition fulfilled by an optical system in which chromatic aberration is corrected for two colors.

  isoplanasie c. Isoplanatism.

  Petzval's c. A condition met by Petzval's formula necessary to eliminate curvature of the field in an optical system.

  sine c. The condition for eliminating distortion which is met when the magnification ratio in the various zones of a lens or optical system is equal to a constant representing the ratio of object to image size. Syn., *Abbe's condition.*

  tangent c. The optical condition in which the ratio of the tangents of the angles of the emergent and incident rays with the optical axis is constant. This condition must be met in order for the optical system to be free from distortion.

cone. 1. A solid body, with a circular base, tapering to a point. 2. A cone cell.

  color c. A type of color solid.

  crystalline c. A cone-shaped, light-collecting structure lying just beneath the corneal facet in an ommatidium of the compound eye of arthropods. Syn., *lens cone.*

  double c's. Cones of the retina which sometime occur in pairs in many fish, amphibians, birds, and marsupials, but are absent in higher mammals. They consist of a chief cone to which is attached an accessory cone. Syn., *twin cones.*

  fiber, c. See under *fiber.*

  foot, c. See under *foot.*

  granule, c. See under *granule.*

  lens c. Crystalline cone.

  light, c. of. A cone-shaped bundle of light rays defined by a point source (as the apex) and an entrance pupil of an optical system or eye (as the base), or a similar bundle defined by a point image and an exit pupil.

  muscle c. Muscular funnel.

  pedicle, c. Cone foot.

  proper, c. The outer and inner members of a cone cell; a cone cell in the restricted sense.

  retinal c. A cone cell.

  Roger's c. A glass cone which, when held in front of the eye, distorts a test source into a circle of light, hence, useful as a dissociation device in heterophoria determination.

Steinheil c. An optical element, used in some telescopic spectacles, consisting of a solid truncated cone of glass, convex at the base, and concave at the opposite surface, with the concave surface having the shorter radius of curvature.

twin c's. Double cones.

visual c. 1. The subtense of an area of regard with its apex at the nodal point of the reduced eye, considered as a cone. 2. The subtense of the entrance pupil of the eye with its apex at the point of regard, considered as a cone.

configuration. Form, pattern, structure, or Gestalt; an integrated whole, not a mere summation of units or parts.

confluence. The perceptual effect in which separate figures in space are perceived as a total single impression, as demonstrated by the Mueller-Lyer visual illusion.

confocal (kon-fo′kal). Having a common focus.

conformer. A device placed in the conjunctival sac to preserve the shape of the fornices after enucleation or evisceration, prior to insertion of an artificial eye. Syn., *stint.*

confusion. The common localization of two objects in space while perceptually aware of their physical separation, occurring especially in strabismus.

conjunctiva (kon″junk-ti′vah). A mucous membrane extending from the eyelid margin to the corneal limbus, forming the posterior layer of the eyelids (palpebral conjunctiva) and the anterior layer of the eyeball.

adnata, c. Bulbar conjunctiva.

arida, c. Xerosis of the conjunctiva.

bulbar c. The portion of the conjunctiva between the fornix and

the cornea proper, hence, the scleral and limbal conjunctivae. Some also include the corneal epithelium as part of the bulbar conjunctiva. Syn., *conjunctiva adnata; ocular conjunctiva.*

corneal c. The stratified squamous epithelium of the cornea and, according to comparative anatomists, also Bowman's membrane and the outer portion of the stroma.

fornix c. The loose, free conjunctiva connecting the palpebral with the bulbar conjunctiva. Syn., *cul-de-sac; retrotarsal fold.*

limbal c. The portion of the bulbar conjunctiva in the region of the limbus which is fused with the episclera and Tenon's capsule.

marginal c. The portion of the palpebral conjunctiva extending from the eyelid margin to the tarsal conjunctiva.

ocular c. The conjunctiva on the anterior portion of the eyeball including the scleral, the limbal, and, by many, the corneal conjunctiva. Syn., *bulbar conjunctiva.*

orbital c. The portion of the palpebral conjunctiva between the tarsal conjunctiva and the fornix.

palpebral c. The portion of the conjunctiva on the posterior surface of the eyelids consisting of the marginal, the tarsal, and the orbital conjunctivae.

scleral c. The portion of the bulbar conjunctiva on the sclera which is easily lifted by forceps, thus excluding the limbal conjunctiva.

tarsal c. The portion of the palpebral conjunctiva between the marginal and the orbital conjunctivae.

conjunctival (kon″junk-ti′val). Pertaining to the conjunctiva.

conjunctivitides (kon-junk″tih-vit′-ih-dēz). The plural for conjunctivitis; therefore, collectively, the various forms of conjunctivitis.

conjunctivitis (kon-junk″tih-vi′tis). Inflammation of the conjunctiva.

acne rosacea c. Inflammation of the conjunctiva, occasionally occurring with acne rosacea of the skin of the face, manifested in either of two forms: (1) a diffuse hyperemia characterized by an engorgement of the vessels of the tarsal and ocular conjunctiva; (2) a nodular form characterized by small, gray, highly vascularized nodules usually near the limbus on the interpalpebral area.

actinic c. Conjunctivitis resulting from exposure to ultraviolet rays, as from acetylene torches, therapeutic lamps, or klieg lights. Syn., *actinic ophthalmia.*

allergic c. Inflammation of the conjunctiva caused by hypersensitivity of the tissues to various allergens, not by a local organismal infection.

angular c. Subacute or chronic bilateral inflammation of the conjunctiva caused by the diplobacillus of Morax-Axenfeld, characterized by hyperemia in the area of the canthi, especially the outer, and extending into the skin at these regions. The discharge is grayish yellow, stringy, never abundant, adheres to the lashes, and accumulates especially at the angles. Syn., *diplobacillary conjunctivitis; Morax-Axenfeld conjunctivitis.*

arc-flash c. Actinic conjunctivitis caused by electric welding.

arida, c. Xerosis of the conjunctiva.

artefacta, c. Inflammation of the conjunctiva due to an irritant being purposely rubbed into the eye by a malingerer or by a hysterical or mentally unbalanced person.

artificial silk c. Inflammation of the conjunctiva common to workers in the artificial silk industry, probably caused by the acids used.

atopic c. Allergic conjunctivitis in persons with a familial history of hypersensitivity. It is of rapid onset and due to airborne substances such as dust or pollens, or to the ingestion of certain foods.

atropine c. Follicular inflammation of the conjunctiva from continued use of atropine in the eye.

bacillary dysentery c. Metastatic inflammation of the conjunctiva occurring in association with bacillary dysentery and urethritis; characterized by hyperemia and no discharge.

Beal's c. See *conjunctivitis, follicular, acute (of Beal).*

blennorrheal c. Gonococcal conjunctivitis.

calcareous c. Lithiasis conjunctivitis.

catarrhal c. Inflammation of the conjunctiva associated with cold or catarrhal irritation and marked by hyperemia and mucoid discharge, occurring in either acute, subacute, or chronic form. Syn., *blennophthalmia; catarrhal ophthalmia.*

catarrhal c., acute. Acute, infectious inflammation of the conjunctiva associated with cold or catarrhal irritation and characterized by a bright red hyperemia (most intense near the fornices), swelling, loss of translucency, and a mucoid or mucopurulent discharge.

catarrhal c., chronic. A mild, chronic inflammation of the conjunctiva with a slight hyperemia and mucoid discharge. Commonly, a sequel to acute catarrhal conjunctivitis, but may be due to a constant irritative element such as dust, glare, ingrowing lashes, exposure from ectropion, exophthalmos, or eyestrain.

catarrhalis aestiva, c. Vernal conjunctivitis.

chemical c. Inflammation of the conjunctiva due to exposure to chemical irritants.

contagious c., acute. Acute contagious inflammation of the conjunctiva caused by Koch-Weeks bacillus or pneumococcus infection. The disease starts approximately 36 hours after infection, with a feeling of smarting, is followed by all the symptoms of an acute catarrhal conjunctivitis, and intense hyperemia with a profuse mucopurulent discharge is typical. It occurs mainly in the spring, occasionally in the fall. Syn., *acute epidemic conjunctivitis; Koch-Weeks conjunctivitis; pink eye.*

croupous c. Pseudomembranous conjunctivitis.

diphtheritic c. Membranous conjunctivitis caused by the Klebs-Loeffler bacillus.

diphtheritic catarrhal c. A rare inflammation of the conjunctiva, usually found in the newborn, characterized by hyperemia of the conjunctiva and the skin of the eyelids and by a sticky yellow discharge which accumulates at the inner canthus and forms threads and flakes in the lower fornix. There is an associated rhinitis and swollen preauricular glands. The positive diagnosis is the presence of the Klebs-Loeffler bacillus, although the pneumococcus and staphylococcus may also be present.

diplobacillary c. Angular conjunctivitis.

eczematous c. Phlyctenular conjunctivitis.

Egyptian c. Trachoma.

epidemic c. Acute contagious conjunctivitis.

epidemic c., acute. Acute contagious conjunctivitis.

estival c. Vernal conjunctivitis.

exanthematous c. An infectious inflammation of the conjunctiva associated with an eruptive disease, as measles or scarlet fever, the symptoms usually being that of an acute catarrhal conjunctivitis.

flash c. Actinic conjunctivitis due to exposure to a high tension electric spark or arc, as from a welder's torch.

follicular c. Inflammation of the conjunctiva characterized by the formation of follicles, caused by chemical, toxic, or bacterial irritation.

follicular c., acute. An acute epidemic mucopurulent inflammation of the conjunctiva characterized by the appearance of small, round or oval, pinkish, translucent follicles, usually in the lower fornix, occasionally in the upper. It may easily be misdiagnosed as trachoma.

follicular c., acute (of Beal). A form of acute conjunctivitis characterized by rapid onset, swelling of the preauricular glands, mild symptoms, and rapid and complete recovery.

follicular c., chronic. A low grade catarrhal inflammation of the conjunctiva characterized by small, discrete follicles appearing especially in the lower fornix.

gonococcal c. A severe and acute inflammation of the conjunctiva caused by the gonococcus, characterized by a beefy-red, edematous, greatly swollen conjunctiva, swollen eyelids, and profuse purulent discharge. It is usually unilateral at onset, and corneal involvement may result in loss of the eye. It may occur in adults from self-contamination (gonorrheal ophthalmia) or in the newborn from passing through the birth canal of an infected mother (ophthalmia neonatorum).

gonococcal c., endogenous. Metastatic inflammation of the conjunctiva occurring bilaterally in association with a generalized gonococcal infection. Symptoms are those of an acute catarrhal conjunctivitis. Syn., *epibulbar gonorrheal subconjunctivitis.*

granular c. Trachoma.

herpetic c. Infection of the conjunctiva with the herpes virus which usually appears in an acute follicular form in association with preauricular lymphadenopathy.

ichthyotoxica, c. Acute, chemotic inflammation of the conjunctiva occurring in fishermen, caused by the blood of eels.

inclusion c. Follicular inflammation of the conjunctiva, caused by a filter-passing virus, characterized by slight discharge and extensive hyperemia and differentiated from trachoma by its slow onset, benign course, and the absence of corneal complications. The infantile form is called *inclusion blennorrhea* and the adult *swimming pool conjunctivitis.*

infective granulomatous c. Parinaud's conjunctivitis.

influenzal c. A rare form of conjunctival inflammation usually associated with influenza epidemics. Generally, the symptoms are of a chronic catarrhal conjunctivitis, although they last only about ten days.

interstitial c. Any type of conjunctival inflammation which involves the deeper connective tissue as well as the epithelial tissue.

klieg (or **kleig**) **c.** Actinic conjunctivitis caused by excessive exposure to klieg lights.

Koch-Weeks c. Acute contagious conjunctivitis.

lacrimal c. A chronic inflammation of the conjunctiva caused by infection and obstruction of the lacrimal passages.

larval c. Inflammation of the conjunctiva caused by the presence of larvae in the conjunctival sac.

leprous c. An inflammation of the conjunctiva occurring in leprotics which may manifest itself in

either of two forms: (1) anesthetic, in which the nerve supply to the cornea, conjunctiva, and eyelids is affected, causing loss of nutritional control, failure or diminution of the flow of tears, and exposure of the cornea and conjunctiva resulting in a diffuse catarrhal conjunctivitis with papillary hypertrophy; (2) nodular, in which nodules, either in crops or singly, appear on the conjunctiva.

leptotrichous c. Parinaud's conjunctivitis.

lithiasis c. A condition of the palpebral conjunctiva marked by the presence of minute, hard, yellow spots, consisting of products of cellular degeneration contained in Henle's glands or in glands of new formation. Only rarely are there calcareous deposits. Syn., *calcareous conjunctivitis; conjunctivitis petrificans; uratic conjunctivitis; lithiasis conjunctivae.*

lymphatic c. Phlyctenular conjunctivitis.

medicamentosa, c. An inflammation of the conjunctiva caused by the application of medicine in the eye.

meibomiana, c. A chronic inflammation of the Meibomian glands and adjacent conjunctiva, characterized by a swollen tarsal plate and a frothy seborrheic secretion.

membranous c. A severe inflammation of the conjunctiva caused, typically, by the Klebs-Loeffler bacillus, less commonly by the streptococcus or the pneumococcus, characterized by the formation of a grayish-yellow infiltrating membrane which cannot be removed without leaving a raw, bleeding surface. The membrane may occur in plaques or may involve the entire conjunctiva and is caused by the deposition of a profuse fibrinous exudate from the cul-de-sac on and into the epithelium. The preauricular glands are swollen and the eyelids are red, swollen, painful, and acquire a characteristic boardlike hardness. The usual results are a coagulative necrosis and subsequent cicatrization of the involved areas.

meningococcal c. An acute metastatic inflammation which infrequently accompanies epidemic meningitis, usually catarrhal in nature and benign.

microbilallergic c. Allergic conjunctivitis due to hypersensitivity to products of such microorganisms as bacteria, fungi, or parasites.

molluscum c. Inflammation of the conjunctiva due to molluscum contagiosum.

Morax-Axenfeld c. Angular conjunctivitis.

necrotic infectious c. A unilateral suppurative necrotic inflammation of the conjunctiva characterized by small, scattered, elevated, white spots in the fornices and palpebral portions and by an associated swelling of the preauricular, parotid, and submaxillary glands on the affected side. Syn., *Pascheff's conjunctivitis.*

Newcastle disease c. An acute follicular conjunctivitis, usually unilateral and of short duration, associated with preauricular adenopathy, due to a virus transmitted from fowls.

nodular c. An inflammation of the conjunctiva caused by irritation from the hairs of caterpillars or certain plants which have entered the cul-de-sac, characterized by nodules resembling those found in tuberculosis. Frequently associated are iridocyclitis and hypopyon. Syn., *pseudotubercular conjunctivitis; caterpillar hair ophthalmia; ophthalmia nodosa; pseudotrachoma.*

papillary c. An inflammation of the conjunctiva characterized by the appearance of papillae in the palpebral portion. Syn., *pseudofollicular conjunctivitis.*

papulosa, c. Granular syphilitic conjunctivitis.

Parinaud's c. An inflammation of the conjunctiva, usually unilateral, by a leptothrix infection and characterized by large polypoid granulations and swelling of the preauricular, parotid, submaxillary, and cervical glands. Syn., *infective granulomatous conjunctivitis; leptotrichous conjunctivitis.*

Pascheff's c. Necrotic infectious conjunctivitis.

petrificans, c. Lithiasis conjunctivitis.

phlyctenular c. A circumscribed inflammation of the bulbar conjunctiva characterized by the formation of one or more small elevations surrounded by a reddened area and due to allergic reaction to endogenous toxin. Syn., *eczematous conjunctivitis; lymphatic conjunctivitis; scrofulous conjunctivitis; eczematous ophthalmia; phlyctenular ophthalmia; scrofulous ophthalmia; strumous ophthalmia.*

plastic c. Pseudomembranous conjunctivitis.

pneumococcal c. Acute contagious conjunctivitis caused by pneumococcal infection.

prairie c. A chronic inflammation of the conjunctiva characterized by the appearance of white spots on the palpebral conjunctiva.

pseudofollicular c. Papillary conjunctivitis.

pseudomembranous c. Any inflammation of the conjunctiva characterized by the appearance upon, but not within, the conjunctiva of a coagulated fibrinous network which may be peeled off, leaving the epithelium intact. It may be due to infection, chemical irritants, or the wound-healing process. It is relatively rare and may be acute, subacute, chronic or recurrent, or circumscribed. Syn., *croupous conjunctivitis; plastic conjunctivitis.*

pseudotubercular c. Nodular conjunctivitis.

purulent c. 1. Any inflammation of the conjunctiva containing or forming pus. Syn., *purulent ophthalmia.* 2. Gonococcal conjunctivitis.

rheumy c. A chronic catarrhal conjunctivitis occurring in the aged and in alcoholics in which the eyes are watery and the lower eyelids sag.

rosacea c. Acne rosacea conjunctivitis.

Samoan c. An acute, purulent inflammation of the conjunctiva, endemic to the Samoan Islands, diagnosed by the presence in the discharge of a diplococcus similar to the gonococcus. Severe pains, marked photophobia, and a profuse purulent discharge are present, and corneal complications are common.

scrofulous c. Phlyctenular conjunctivitis.

shipyard c. Epidemic keratoconjunctivitis.

sicca, c. An inflammation of the conjunctiva usually accompanying keratitis sicca. See also *keratoconjunctivitis sicca.*

snow c. Actinic conjunctivitis caused by excessive solar glare from snow.

spring c. Vernal conjunctivitis.

squirrel plague c. Tularemic conjunctivitis.

superficial c. Any type of conjunctival inflammation which involves only the epithelial tissue and not the deeper connective tissue.

swimming pool c. The adult form of inclusion conjunctivitis.

syphilitic c. A general term for any inflammation of the conjunctiva accompanying syphilis.

syphilitic c., granular. An inflammation of the conjunctiva occurring in the secondary stage of syphilis, characterized by diffuse, rose-red, follicularlike formations on the tarsal conjunctiva of one or both eyelids, especially the upper. It may be accompanied by pannus and involvement of the preauricular glands. Syn., *conjunctivitis papulosa; syphilitic pseudotrachoma.*

syphilitic c., simple. An inflammation of the conjunctiva frequently occurring early in the secondary stage of syphilis, usually characterized by violent injection and chemosis and accompanied by other secondary manifestations of syphilis elsewhere in the skin and mucous membranes.

trachomatous c. Trachoma.

traumatic c. An inflammation of the conjunctiva caused by the action of irritant substances, such as dust, acids, vapors, or by excessive rubbing or by foreign bodies.

tuberculous c. An inflammation of the conjunctiva, caused by either a primary or a secondary infection with the tubercle bacillus, occurring generally in two forms: ulcerative, characterized by small miliary ulcers; or hyperplastic, characterized by yellow or gray subconjunctival nodules.

tularemic c. An infectious inflammation of the conjunctiva due to the bacterium *Pasteurella tularensis,* transmitted to human beings from rabbits or other rodents, characterized by chemosis, small yellow necrotic ulcers, and involvement of the preauricular, parotid, cervical, and submaxillary glands. Syn., *conjunctivitis tularensis.*

tularensis c. Tularemic conjunctivitis.

uratic c. Lithiasis conjunctivitis.

vaccinic c. An inflammation of the conjunctiva caused by accidental inoculation with smallpox vaccine, characterized by ulcers, usually in the palpebral portion, which are covered with a thick, gray, adherent membrane. The eyelids are red and greatly swollen, and, usually, the preauricular and postauricular glands are involved.

varicellic c. An inflammation of the conjunctiva which infrequently accompanies chickenpox, characterized by small pustules which may develop into ulcers with swollen, dark-red margins.

variolic c. A mild, catarrhal inflammation of the conjunctiva frequently accompanying smallpox and developing about the fifth day. Pustules rarely occur.

vernal c. A chronic, bilateral inflammation of the conjunctiva, of unknown etiology, which recurs seasonally during warm weather. It may take two forms: (1) the palpebral, characterized by hard, flattened papillae, separated by furrows, having a cobblestone appearance in the upper palpebral portion, with both upper and lower palpebral portions of a bluish-white color; (2) the bulbar or limbal, characterized by gelatinous-appearing nodules, sometimes slightly pigmented (Tranta's dots), adjacent to the limbus. The inflammation is accompanied by photophobia and intense itching. Syn., *Fruehjahr's catarrh; Saemisch catarrh; vernal catarrh; estival conjunctivitis; spring conjunctivitis; spring ophthalmia.*

welders' c. Actinic conjunctivitis caused by glare from acetylene or electric welding torches.

Widmark's c. An acute catarrhal inflammation of the conjunctiva, of unknown etiology, characterized by congestion and epithelial loss in the lower bulbar and tarsal portions.

conjunctivoanstrostomy (kon-junk″-tiv-o″an-stros′to-me). A surgical procedure for the treatment of epiphora in which an opening is made from the inferior conjunctival cul-de-sac into the maxillary sinus.

conjunctivochalasis (kon-junk″tiv-o″kah-lah′sis). An abnormal fold in the conjunctiva of the lower fornix.

conjunctivoma (kon-junk″tiv-o′mah). A tumor of conjunctival tissue occurring on the eyelid.

conjunctivoplasty (kon″junk-tiv′o-plas″te, -ti′vo-plas″te). Plastic surgery of the conjunctiva.

Con-Lish method (kon′lish). See under *method.*

conoid of Sturm (ko′noid). The astigmatic bundle of rays between the two mutually perpendicular focal line images of a point source. Cf. *interval of Sturm.*

conomyoidin (ko″no-mi-oi′din, -mi′-oi-din). Contractile protoplasmic material in the cones of the retina which reacts to light stimuli.

conophthalmus (kōn″of-thal′mus). Corneal staphyloma.

Conradi's syndrome (kon′rah-dēz). Stippled epiphyses.

consensual (kon-sen′shu-al). Excited by reflex stimulation; especially, the contraction of the contralateral pupil when the retina of only one eye is stimulated.

constancy. The relative apparent stability or lack of perceived change of certain object properties, despite a change in the stimulus characteristics which initiated the perception.

brightness c. A perceptual phenomenon wherein the perceived or subjectively attributed brightness of an object or a surface tends to remain fixed at a pre-perceived or attributed brightness level, rather than in direct ratio with the actual brightness, e.g., a piece of intensely illuminated coal may continue to seem black though actually brighter than an adjacent sheet of dimly illuminated white paper. Syn., *lightness constancy.*

color c. The relative apparent stability or lack of perceived change of the color of an object, despite a change in the spectral composition of incident light, or of adjacent surfaces, or of other related stimulus factors.

lightness c. Synonymous with *brightness constancy,* but preferred by some on the theory that the phenomenon is based on relative light reflectance, rather than on an attribute of brightness perception.

shape c. The relative apparent stability or lack of perceived change in the shape of an object, despite a change in the direction or angle of view.

size c. The relative apparent stability or lack of perceived change in the size of an object, despite a change in viewing distance, actual size, or other related stimulus factors.

constant. 1. Anything invariable, remaining unaltered, or not subject to change. 2. A magnitude or numerical quantity which retains the same value throughout an investigation, or during a stage of an investigation.

optic c's of the eye. Numerical values or measurements said or assumed to represent the optical dimensions and refractive properties of a typical or specially defined eye. Classic tables of such values include those of Helmholtz, Tscherning, Gullstrand, and others.

Planck's c. The universal constant for electromagnetic energy, equal to 6.624×10^{-27} erg sec.

statistical c. A value which characterizes a particular series of measurements or observations, e.g.,. a measure of central tendency such as the *mean* or *median,* or a measure of dispersion such

as the *standard deviation* or *average deviation.*

zonal c. A factor varying with zone size, by which the mean candlepower emitted by a source of light in a given angular zone is multiplied to obtain the lumens in the zone.

constringence, optical (kon-strin'-jens). The ν (nu) value of optical glass; the reciprocal of the dispersive power of the glass, denoted by the Greek letter ν.

$$\nu = \frac{N_D - 1}{N_F - N_C},$$

where N_D, N_F, and N_C are the refractive indices of the glass for the D, F, and C lines of the spectrum.

Con-Ta-Chek. An ophthalmometer attachment for measuring the curvature of a contact lens, containing a chamber filled with fluid on which the lens floats and a front surface mirror, inclined at 45°, which reflects the surface being measured into the instrument.

Contact Lens Manufacturers Association. An association of manufacturers of contact lenses organized in Chicago, Illinois, in 1963.

contact, optical. The effective optical elimination of the space between two optical surfaces, or the effective elimination of optical surfaces, usually accomplished by filling the intervening space with a substance of the same refractive index as that of one or both of the media whose surfaces bound that space.

Contactometer (kon"tak-tom'eh-ter). An ophthalmometer attachment for holding contact lenses during measurement of their surface curvatures and having one or more auxiliary reflecting surfaces of known curvatures for immediate calibration.

Contascope (kon'tah-skōp). An instrument for inspecting edge profiles and thickness, curvature characteristics, and surface integrity of contact lenses, consisting essentially of a light source, a stage for holding lenses, and a 20× optical system.

content, black. The difference between unity and the higher of the two reflectance values in the Ostwald system of specifying surface colors.

content, full color. The higher of the two reflectance values minus the lower in the Ostwald system of specifying surface colors.

content, white. The lower of the two reflectance values in the Ostwald system of specifying surface colors.

continuance (kon-tin'u-ans). The tendency to follow a linear pattern in the same direction and movement, despite conflicting interruptions by other linear patterns, as the tending to see a straight line in its continuation throughout a pattern. It may also apply to gradation of hues where the eye moves along the direction of the gradation.

contracture (kon-trak'tūr). 1. The temporary inability of a muscle to relax fully. 2. The state of rigidity of a contracted muscle. 3. Used incorrectly, a muscle in tetanus.

contraocular (kon''trah-ok'u-lar). Pertaining to the opposite eye.

contrast. The manifestation or perception of difference between two compared stimuli.

apparent c. The contrast of an object with its background as viewed from a specific direction and through a given distance of atmosphere which attenuates and/or scatters light.

binocular c. Induction effects on judgments, or sensitivity of an eye, produced by stimulation of the other eye.

border c. The enhanced contrast seen near the border between two juxtaposed fields. Syn., *marginal contrast.*

brightness c. 1. Luminance contrast. 2. Enhanced difference in the brightness of two fields owing to their proximity, juxtaposition, successive stimulation, or other related stimulus factors influencing brightness perception. Syn., *luminosity contrast.*

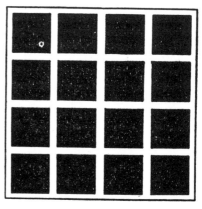

Fig. 9. Hermann's grid. A demonstration of brightness contrast effect. (From *Visual Illusions,* M. Luckiesh, Van Nostrand, 1922)

chromatic c. Color contrast.

color c. 1. The manifestation or perception of difference in color saturation or hue. 2. The enhanced contrast in the color (saturation or hue) of two stimuli owing to their proximity, juxtaposition, successive stimulation, or other related factors influencing color perception. 3. The change in hue or saturation of a color as a result of the proximity to, juxtaposition with, or successive stimulation by another color.

curvature c. A presumed perceptual attribute or phenomenon said to account for certain geometrical illusions involving curves.

depth c. Contrast between surfaces

at different distances or depth levels.

illusion, c. See under *illusion.*

inherent c. The actual contrast of an object with its background in a specific direction when it is unaltered by atmospheric attenuation or scatter or by the presence of a glare source in the field of view.

luminance c. The ratio or other numerical representation of the difference in luminance between two stimulus fields or surfaces. Syn., *brightness contrast.*

luminosity c. Brightness contrast.

marginal c. Border contrast.

phase c. Contrast produced in phase microscopy by translating into intensity differences the phase differences produced by unequal optical path lengths in a thin uniform section made up of elements having different indices of refraction.

phenomenon, c. See under *phenomenon.*

physical c. The relationship between the luminances of an object and its immediate background, equal to $\Delta B/B$, where ΔB is the luminance difference between the object and its background, and B is the luminance of the background.

physiological c. The relationship between the apparent or subjective brightness of two objects which are seen either at the same time (simultaneous contrast) or sequentially (successive contrast) against backgrounds which may or may not be identical.

simultaneous c. Contrast manifested or induced on simultaneous presentation of two stimulus fields.

successive c. Contrast manifested or induced on successive presentation of stimuli.

surface c. Contrast in brightness or color of two surfaces, usually juxtaposed.

control. 1. In a pair of haploscopic stimulus targets, the elements of the pattern which are presented to one eye only for the purpose of confirming that the eye is being used during binocular testing or training. Syn., *fusion clue.* 2. The portion of an experiment which is used to check or compare the results of another portion which involves some additional factor under investigation.

Controlled Reader. An instrument for training reading skills, by controlling the span and duration of fixation, consisting essentially of a 35 mm. film strip projector, providing a left to right presentation of groups of words at a rate of up to 1,000 words per minute.

contusio bulbi (kon-tu′ze-o bul′bi). Blunt injury of the eyeball.

conus (ko′nus). 1. A cone. 2. A large, circular, white patch around the optic disk due to the exposing of the sclera as a result of degenerative change or congenital abnormality in the choroid and retina. 3. Posterior staphyloma.

distraction c. A myopic crescent located adjacent to the temporal margin of the optic disk.

Fuchs's c. A small, crescentic, white area adjacent to the inferior edge of the optic disk.

myopic c. Conus due to degenerative changes associated with myopia.

opticohyaloid c. A rare congenital formation on the optic disk which extends into the vitreous.

papillaris, c. A pigmented, vascularized, conical protrusion from the optic nerve head into the vitreous of reptiles, functioning to nourish the inner layers of the retina.

supertraction c. A gray or yellowish ring at the nasal margin of the optic disk, sometimes occurring in myopic eyes, due to displacement of the retina over the optic disk.

conv. Abbreviation for *convergence.*

converge (kon-verj'). To tend toward a point. Visually, to turn the lines of sight inward toward each other. Optically, to turn light toward a point or focus.

convergence (kon-ver'jens). 1. The turning inward of the lines of sight toward each other. 2. The directional property of a bundle of light rays turned or bent toward a real image point; to be distinguished from the divergence property of a bundle of rays emanating from a point source.

accommodative c. Convergence changes physiologically induced by, related to, or associated with changes in accommodation, clinically measured by changes in phorias or changes in the convergence limits of clear, single, binocular vision with changes in accommodation. See also *convergence accommodation; gradient; A.C.A. ratio.* Syn., *associative convergence.*

active position of c. The state of convergence of the eyes during normal binocular fixation of a single object. Syn., *fixation position of convergence.*

amplitude of c. See under *amplitude.*

associative c. Accommodative convergence.

asymmetric c. Convergence of the eyes toward a point outside the plane perpendicular to and bisecting the interocular base line.

center of c. See under *center.*

directional c. Proximal convergence.

dynamic c. Convergence as a physiological function in the maintenance of bifoveal fixation, distinguished from *static convergence.* Cf. *fusional convergence; supplementary convergence.*

excess, c. 1. Esotropia or high esophoria in near vision in association with a relatively orthophoric condition in distance vision, a rel-

atively high increase in convergence being associated with an increase in accommodation. 2. The condition of esophoria or esotropia in near vision, esophoria or esotropia in distance vision being considered *divergence insufficiency.* 3. A condition in which esophoria or esotropia is greater at near than at distance.

far point of c. The point of intersection of the lines of sight when the eyes are in the position of maximum divergence or minimum convergence.

fixation position of c. The active position of convergence.

fusional c. Convergence induced by fusion stimuli without a manifest change in accommodation.

    fusional amplitude of c. See under *amplitude.*

    fusional reserve c. 1. The amount of available fusional convergence in excess of that required to overcome the heterophoria. 2. Relative convergence.

    fusional supplementary c. Supplementary convergence.

inhibition of c. See under *inhibition.*

initial c. The fusional convergence effecting a change from the phoria position to that of single binocular fixation of a distant object.

insufficiency, c. 1. Exotropia or high exophoria in near vision in association with a relatively orthophoric condition in distance vision, a relatively low increase in convergence being associated with an increase in accommodation. 2. The condition of exophoria or exotropia in near vision, exophoria or exotropia in distance vision being considered *divergence excess.* 3. A condition in which esophoria or esotropia is greater at far than at near. 4. Inability to converge the eyes to the average or normal near point of convergence.

insufficiency, absolute c. A limitation of total convergence ability to less than 30°. *Duke-Elder.*

insufficiency, relative c. A limitation of total convergence ability to less than three times the amount of convergence habitually required. *Duke-Elder*

lag of c. 1. Physiological exophoria. 2. A tendency or manifestation of convergence to be less than the amount necessary for single binocular vision, as indicated by an exophoria.

near point of c. The point of intersection of the lines of sight when the eyes are in the position of maximum convergence. Syn., *punctum convergens basalis.*

near point of c., absolute. The point of intersection of the lines of sight when the eyes are converged maximally.

near point of c., relative. The point of intersection of the lines of sight when the eyes are in the position of maximum convergence with accommodation fixed at a given level.

negative c. 1. Divergence. 2. Convergence measured in the negative or divergent direction from a given reference position of the eyes as, for example, the straightforward position or the position corresponding to the fusional demand.

negative fusional c. 1. Fusional divergence. 2. Fusional convergence measured from the phoria position of the eyes to the prism base-in limit of clear, single, binocular vision.

negative fusional reserve c. Fusional divergence in excess of that required to overcome the existing esophoria, clinically measured from the fusional demand point to the prism base-in limit of clear, single, binocular vision. Syn., *negative fusional reserve.*

negative relative c. Relative convergence measured negatively or in a divergent direction from the convergence position corresponding to the normal fusional demand. Clinically, the base-in prism range of clear, single, binocular vision. Syn., *negative relative reserve convergence; negative reserve convergence.*

negative relative reserve c. Negative relative convergence.

negative reserve c. Negative relative convergence.

paralysis, c. See under *paralysis.*

passive position of c. The relative position of the two eyes under dissociation.

perverted c. A convergence faculty regarded as a function of anomalous retinal correspondence and said to be responsible for maintaining a convergent squint persisting over many years.

positive c. Convergence measured in a positive or increasing direction from a given reference position of the eyes.

positive fusional c. Fusional convergence clinically measured in a positive or increasing direction from the phoria position of the eyes to the base-out prism limit of clear, single, binocular vision.

positive fusional reserve c. Fusional convergence in excess of that required to overcome the existing exophoria, clinically measured from the fusional demand point to the prism base-out limit of clear, single, binocular vision. Syn., *positive fusional reserve.*

positive relative c. Relative convergence measured positively or in a convergent direction from the position corresponding to the normal fusional demand. Clinically, the base-out prism range of clear, single, binocular vision. Syn., *positive relative reserve convergence; positive reserve convergence.*

positive relative reserve c.
Positive relative convergence.

positive reserve c. Positive relative convergence.

posture of c. The state of convergence of the eyes for a given set of stimulus conditions, distinguished from convergence as a movement or response.

proximal c. Convergence response attributed to the awareness or impression of nearness of a fixation object. Syn., *directional conversion; psychic convergence.*

psychic c. Proximal convergence.

range of c. The linearly specified distance between the far and near points of convergence.

reflex c. Any convergence response regarded as a part of a reflex action, as distinguished from *voluntary convergence.*

relative c. Fusional convergence measured and specified with reference to the position of the eyes corresponding to the normal fusional demand for the given testing distance. Clinically, the base-out and/or base-in fusion range to the limits of clear, single, binocular vision.

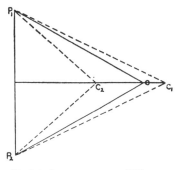

Fig. 10. Relative convergence. With accommodation for point O, OC_2 represents positive relative convergence and OC_1 represents negative relative convergence. The angular difference between $P_1C_2P_2$ and $P_1C_1P_2$ represents the amplitude of relative convergence. (From *Textbook of Orthoptics,* H. W. Gibson, Hatton Press Ltd., 1955)

reserve c. 1. Fusional convergence in excess of the amount needed

for normal binocular fixation, clinically measured by the amount of base-in or base-out prism which can be overcome without blur or diplopia. 2. Convergence ability in excess of the amount needed for normal binocular fixation, clinically measured by determining the near point of convergence.

static c. The state of convergence, or divergence, of the lines of sight when the eyes are said to be at rest, as in the absence of stimuli to accommodation and convergence in clinical phoria testing.

supplementary c. Fusional convergence which is used to compensate for the heterophoria in binocular fixation, hence, quantitatively equal to the heterophoria itself in persons with normal binocular vision.

tonal c. Tonic convergence.

tonic c. The continuous convergence response maintained by the extraocular muscle tonus, hence absent in paralysis and in death, and diminished during sleep or narcosis; the amount of convergence in effect when fixating a distant object with accommodational and fusional impulses absent. Syn., *tonal convergence.*

voluntary c. Convergence produced volitionally, as distinguished from *reflex convergence.*

Convergence Trainer. An instrument devised by Bangerter for improving convergence facility, consisting essentially of a chin rest fixed to one end of a rod on which targets slide to approach the eyes. The targets are either letters presented in rapid succession or a rotating spiral.

convergent (kon-ver'jent). Characterized by, associated with, or related to convergence.

convergiometer (kon-ver"je-om'eh-ter). An instrument for measuring phorias.

conversion, color (kon-ver'shun). Any perceived change in the characteristics of a color as a result of change in the viewing conditions.

convex (kon'veks). Having a curved, elevated surface, as the outside of a sphere.

convexoconcave (kon-vek"so-kon'kāv). Having a convex surface on one side and a concave surface on the other.

convexoconvex (kon-vek"so-kon'-veks). Having convex surfaces on both sides, as a double convex lens.

Cooke lens. See under *lens*.

co-ordinate. In plotting or graphic representation, one of a system of magnitudes used to fix the position of a point, a line, or a plane.

chromaticity c's. The ratios of each of the tristimulus values to the sum of the three. Symbols: x, y, z. Syn., *trichromatic coefficients*.

co-ordination, hand-eye. A relationship between visual and kinesthetic clues, resulting in accurate, manual, spatial localization.

Coordinator (ko-ōr'din-a"tor). An instrument for diagnosis and treatment of eccentric fixation designed by Cüppers and consisting essentially of a rotating transilluminated Polaroid filter which, when viewed through a blue filter, produces Haidinger brushes localized in relation to a fixation point mounted on the instrument.

copiopia (kop"e-o'pe-ah). Fatigue of vision; asthenopia.

copiopsia (kop"e-op'se-ah). Copiopia.

coquille (ko-kēl'). A deep, curved, blown or molded, glass lens commonly used in the most inexpensive sunglasses.

Cords' test (kōrdz). See under *test*.

core- (kōr'e). A combining form meaning the pupil.

coreclisis (kōr"e-kli'sis). Obliteration of the pupil.

corectasis (kōr-ek'tah-sis). A pathological dilatation of the pupil.

corectomedialysis (ko-rek"to-me-di-al'is-is). Excision of a small portion of the iris at its junction with the ciliary body to form an artificial pupil.

corectomy (kōr-ek'to-me). Any surgical cutting operation on the iris at the pupil.

corectopia (kōr-ek-to'pe-ah). A condition in which the pupil is not in the center of the iris. Syn., *ectopia pupillae*.

coredialysis (ko"re-di-al'is-is). Iridodialysis.

corediastasis (ko"re-di-as'tah-sis). A dilated state of the pupil.

corediastole (ko"re-di-as'to-le). Dilatation of the pupil.

coreitis (ko"re-i'tis). Keratitis.

corelysis (ko-rel'is-is). Surgical detachment of adhesions of the iris to the capsule of the crystalline lens or to the cornea.

coremetamorphosis (kōr"e-met"ah-mōr'fo-sis). The condition of an irregularly shaped pupil.

coremorphosis (kōr"e-mōr-fo'sis, -mōr'fo-sis). Surgical formation of an artificial pupil.

corenclisis (kōr"en-kli'sis). Iridencleisis.

coreometer (ko"re-om'eh-ter). An apparatus for measuring the size of the pupil of the eye. Syn., *pupillometer*.

coreometry (ko"re-om'eh-tre). Measurement of the size of the pupil of the eye.

coreoplasty (ko"re-o-plas'te). Coreplasty.

coreplasty (ko're-plas"te). Plastic surgery of the iris, usually for the formation of an artificial pupil.

corestenoma (ko"re-ste-no'mah). An anatomical partial closure of the pupil.

congenitum, c. A congenital partial closure of the pupil caused by outgrowths from the sphincter margins. These usually meet but leave several small openings.

coretomedialysis (ko″re-to-me″di-al′-is-is). Corectomedialysis.

coretomy (ko-ret′o-me). Corectomy.

cornea (kōr′ne-ah). The transparent anterior portion of the fibrous coat of the eye consisting of five layers, stratified squamous epithelium, Bowman's membrane, stroma, Descemet's membrane, and endothelium (mesenchymal epithelium), and serving as the first refracting medium of the eye. It is structurally continuous with the sclera, is avascular, receiving its nourishment by permeation through spaces between the lamellae, and is innervated by the ophthalmic division of the trigeminal nerve via the ciliary nerves and those of the surrounding conjunctiva which together form plexuses.

conical *c.* A cornea abnormally conoid in shape. Syn., *keratoconus.*

decentration of c. A condition in which the optical center of the cornea is not located at its geometric center.

ectasia of c. Corneal staphyloma.

farinata, c. A senile change, occurring bilaterally, in which the corneal stroma is marked with fine dustlike opacities, usually visible only with high magnification. Syn., *Vogt's floury cornea.*

globosa, c. Megalocornea.

guttata, c. Dystrophy of the endothelial cells of the cornea, characterized in its earliest stages by large black spherules and a golden hue on the posterior surface visible by indirect illumination. In later stages the posterior surface takes on a bronzed appearance. It is bilateral, though one eye may be affected more than the other, and vision is eventually reduced. Syn., *endothelial corneal dystrophy.*

opaca, c. Sclera.

plana, c. A congenital condition in which the cornea is flatter than normal.

sugar-loaf c. Keratoconus.

verticillata, c. Vortex corneal dystrophy.

Vogt's floury c. Cornea farinata.

corneal (kōr′ne-al). Pertaining to the cornea.

corneal allotransplant; autotransplant; bedewing; cap; basal cells; corpuscle; deturgescence; dystrophy; ectasia; facet; graft; image; lacunae; lens; mesothelium; radius; reflex; transplantation; ulcer. See under the nouns.

Cornealometer (kōr″ne-al-om′eh-ter). A type of ophthalmometer mounted to traverse an arc centered on the observed eye while the eye is fixating a stationary target, thus permitting direct readings of corneal curvature at any portion of the corneal surface.

corneascope (kōr′ne-ah-skōp″). An illuminating binocular loupe for viewing the cornea.

corneitis (kōr″ne-i′tis). Keratitis.

corneoblepharon (kōr″ne-o-blef′ah-ron). Adhesion of the eyelid to the cornea.

corneo-iritis (kōr″ne-o-i-ri′tis). Inflammation involving both the cornea and the iris.

corneosclera (kōr″ne-o-skle′rah). The sclera and the cornea when considered as forming one coat of the eyeball.

corneosclerectomy (kōr″ne-o-skle-rek′to-me). A surgical procedure for glaucoma in which trephining is performed at the superior corneolimbal junction into the anterior chamber under a conjunctival flap, followed by an iridectomy at the trephine hole.

Cornu (kōr-nu′) **prism; spiral.** See under the nouns.

Cornu-Jellet prism (kōr-nu′ jeh-la′). See under *prism.*

corocleisis (kōr″o-kli′sis). Coreclisis.

coroclisis (kōr″o-kli′sis). Coreclisis.

corodialysis (ko″ro-di-al′is-is). Iridodialysis.

corodiastasis (ko″ro-di-as′tah-sis). Corediastasis.

corona (ko-ro′nah). A crown or crownlike structure.

ciliaris, c. The ciliary processes considered as a single structure. Syn., *pars plicata.*

ciliary c. A large number of thin lines of light extending radially through the halo observed around a small bright light viewed in a dark room.

conjunctivae, c. The portion of the conjunctiva surrounding the cornea.

palpebrarum, c. The tarsus of the eyelid.

radiata, c. White matter containing fibers which pass to and from the internal capsule in the forebrain and which begin or end in the cerebral cortex, the optic radiations being in its posterior portion.

Zinn's c. Circle of Haller.

coroparelcysis (ko″ro-par-el′sih-sis). An operation to correct for partial opacity of the cornea, in which the pupil is drawn aside to bring it in line with a more transparent portion of the cornea.

corophthisis (ko-rof′thi-sis). Permanent contraction of the pupil resulting from an atrophy-producing disease of the eye.

coroplasty (ko′ro-plas″te). Coreplasty.

coroscopy (ko-ros′ko-pe). Retinoscopy.

corotomy (ko-rot′o-me). Corectomy.

corpora (kōr′po-rah). The plural of corpus.

amylacea, c. Amyloid bodies.

geniculata, c. The paired geniculate bodies in the diencephalon of the forebrain. Only the external geniculate bodies are visually important, serving as a relay center between the optic tract and the optic radiations.

nigra, c. Cystic protrusions of the pigmented retinal layers around the pupillary margin, characteristic of certain hoofed animals.

quadrigemina, c. (anterior). The paired superior colliculi in the tectum of the midbrain. As a lower visual center they receive ganglionic axons from the retina and reflexly connect with lower motor neurons that control skeletal muscles.

quadrigemina, c. (posterior). The paired inferior colliculi in the tectum of the midbrain which act as a relay center for reflex movements of the eyes in relation to sound.

corpus (kōr′pus). A relatively solid structure forming a part of an organ.

adiposum orbitae, c. The mass of fatty tissue in the orbit filling the interstices between the eyeball, the optic nerve, the extraocular muscles, the blood vessels, the nerves, and the lacrimal gland.

callosum, c. The great transverse commissure connecting the cerebral hemispheres consisting of a broad, arched band of white matter lying at the bottom of the longitudinal fissure. Its thickened posterior extremity, the splenium, is thought to be concerned with integration of opposite halves of the visual field and with the transmission of visual learning from one hemisphere to the other.

ciliare, c. Ciliary body.

ciliare choroideae, c. The iris and ciliary body, the term "choroideae" being used to mean "of the uvea." *Obs.*

ciliare hyaloideae, c. The vitreous humor in the region between the crystalline lens and the ora serrata. *Obs.*

ciliare retinae, c. The inner posterior portion of the ciliary body derived from the optic cup; it consists of a two-layered epithelium and the internal limiting membrane; the pars ciliaris retinae of present-day usage.

geniculatum, c. Geniculate body.

vitreum, c. Vitreous humor.

corpuscle (kōr'pus-l). 1. A small mass or body. 2. A sensory nerve end bulb. 3. A cell, especially that of the blood or the lymph.

conjunctival c. A tactile nerve ending of the conjunctiva.

corneal c. One of a number of fixed cells of connective tissue found between the lamellae of the substantia propria of the cornea. Each corpuscle is a flattened cell with a large flattened nucleus and branching processes which communicate with nearby corpuscles. Syn., *Toynbee's corpuscle; Virchow's corpuscle; keratocyte.*

Dogiel's c. A sensory end organ, somewhat resembling Krause's end bulbs, found in the mucous membranes of the eyes, the nose, the mouth, and the genitals.

Donders, c's. of. Cytoblasts of Henle.

hyaloid c. A vestige of the hyaloid artery remaining as a small white plaque just nasal to the posterior pole of the crystalline lens.

Krause's c's. Specialized end organs or nerve endings, ovoid in shape, acting as cold receptors. Primarily sensitive to decrements in temperature, they are found superficially in the skin and in large numbers in the mucous membranes of the mouth, nose, eyes, and genitals. Syn., *end bulbs of Krause.*

sclerotic c's. Connective tissue cells found in the lymph spaces of the sclera.

Toynbee's c. Corneal corpuscle.

Virchow's c. Corneal corpuscle.

corradiation (ko-ra"de-a'shun). Radiation to or from one point or focus.

Correct-Eye-Graph. A picture designed to be used in the Correct-Eye-Scope for cheiroscopic drawing.

Correct-Eye-Scope. A trade name for a Brewster type stereoscope mounted on an adjustable stand, so designed that it may also be used as a cheiroscope.

correction. A term applied to a lens prescription used to rectify a refractive error, a muscular imbalance of the eyes, or both.

corrective association. See under *association.*

Corrector. A visual training instrument designed by Bangerter to establish correct spatial localization, centric fixation, and normal visual acuity, in the treatment of amblyopia ex anopsia. It consists essentially of insulated line drawings on a metal plate which are traced with a hand-held metal stylus. Contact of the stylus with the metal plate completes an electric circuit, causing a light to flash or a buzzer to sound, which signifies that the stylus is off target.

correlation (kor"e-la'shun). The degree of association between two variables, usually expressed as a *coefficient of correlation.* Correlation should be differentiated from *regression.* It describes the closeness of the relationship, while regression enables values for one variable to be estimated if the other is known.

curvilinear c. The relationship between two variables characterized by regression lines which are not straight lines. Syn., *nonlinear correlation.*

linear c. The relationship between two variables characterized by straight line regression, that is, the relationship between the variables is linear. Syn., *rectilinear correlation.*

linear c., direct. Linear correlation in which the slopes of the regression lines are positive, that is, the higher one variable is, the higher the other. Syn., *positive correlation.*

linear c., inverse. Linear correlation in which the slopes of the regression lines are negative, i.e., the higher the one variable, the lower the other. Syn., *negative correlation*.

multiple c. Correlation involving more than one independent variable and a dependent variable. See also *multiple regression*.

negative c. Inverse linear correlation.

nonlinear c. Curvilinear correlation.

partial c. The relationship between two variables with the effect of one or more other variables ruled out. Ex.: Both height and weight are related to age. It is possible to determine statistically the relationship between height and weight with age partialed out. A similar result could be obtained by limiting the sample to individuals of the same age, but there are advantages to using an unrestricted sample and achieving the end statistically.

positive c. Direct linear correlation.

rank c. The relationship between two variables in which the data are arranged by rank rather than by score.

rectilinear c. Linear correlation.

simple c. The relationship between two variables, one of which is independent, the other dependent.

zero c. The absence of relationship between two variables, that is, the condition existing when one varies independently of the other.

correspondence. The state of being in accord or harmony; the relation or adaptation of things to each other.

motor c. The co-ordinated relationship of the extraocular muscle functions obtaining concomitant movements and bifoveal fixation.

motor c., secondary. The co-ordinated relationship of the extraocular muscle functions ob-taining concomitant movements in strabismus. *Chavasse.*

proprioceptive c., secondary. The condition in which the supposed proprioceptive impulses resulting from heterotropia are either suppressed (inhibitory) or altered (exhibitory). *Chavasse.*

proprioceptive c., secondary (exhibitory). The condition in which the supposed proprioceptive impulses resulting from heterotropia are interpreted by the mind as though the anomalous associated area of the deviating eye were a true fovea. *Chavasse.*

proprioceptive c., secondary (inhibitory). The condition in which the supposed proprioceptive impulses resulting from heterotropia are inhibited. *Chavasse.*

retinal c. The faculty of vision which gives rise to the unitary percept of a binocularly seen object or of a pair of objects viewed individually and separately by the two eyes, when the respective retinal images stimulate retinal receptors functioning co-ordinately to subserve this faculty. These receptors have common lines of direction and, thus, images stimulating them are interpreted as arising from the same direction or point in space.

retinal c., abnormal. Anomalous retinal correspondence.

retinal c., anomalous. A type of retinal correspondence, occurring frequently in strabismus, in which the foveae of the two eyes do not give rise to common visual directionalization, the fovea of one eye functioning directionally with an extrafoveal area of the other eye. Syn., *abnormal retinal correspondence; secondary retinal correspondence*.

retinal c., anomalous (anatomical). Anomalous retinal correspondence attributable to anatomical anomalies of the sensory mechanism, hence innate.

retinal c., anomalous (asymmetrical). Anomalous retinal correspondence in which the angle of anomaly is different when the right eye is fixating than when the left eye is fixating. *Chavasse.*

retinal c., anomalous (functional). Anomalous retinal correspondence learned or acquired as a functional response.

retinal c., anomalous (harmonious). A type of anomalous retinal correspondence in which the angle of anomaly is equal to the objective angle of strabismus.

retinal c., anomalous (inharmonious). Unharmonious anomalous retinal correspondence.

retinal c., anomalous (negative). Anomalous retinal correspondence in which the impulses from the retina of the deviating eye are inhibited. *Chavasse.*

retinal c., anomalous (negative central). Anomalous retinal correspondence in which there is inhibition of impulses from both the macula and the anomalous associated area of the deviating eye. *Chavasse.*

retinal c., anomalous (negative macular). Anomalous retinal correspondence in which there is an inhibition of impulses from the macula of the deviating eye. *Chavasse.*

retinal c., anomalous (negative macular and positive pseudomacular). Anomalous retinal correspondence in which there is an inhibition of impulses from the macula of the deviating eye and in which the impulses from the anomalous associated area of the deviating eye are interpreted as though originating in the macula. *Chavasse.*

retinal c., anomalous (negative subtotal). Anomalous retinal correspondence in which the inhibition of the impulses from

the macula is so slight (subtotal) that the subject can shift from anomalous correspondence to normal correspondence at will. *Chavasse.*

retinal c., anomalous (nonharmonious). Unharmonious anomalous retinal correspondence.

retinal c., anomalous (paradoxical). A type of anomalous retinal correspondence in which either the subjective angle of strabismus or the angle of anomaly exceeds the objective angle of strabismus. It is often manifested after corrective surgery in a strabismic in whom anomalous retinal correspondence previously existed.

retinal c., anomalous (positive). Anomalous retinal correspondence in which impulses from an anomalous associated area of the deviating eye are interpreted as though they originated at its fovea.

retinal c., anomalous (suppression). Anomalous retinal correspondence characterized by a suppression of one or the other of the two ocular images stimulating anomalously corresponding receptors, noted especially in clinical attempts to determine the subjective angle of strabismus.

retinal c., anomalous (symmetrical). Anomalous retinal correspondence in which the angle of anomaly is the same with either eye fixating. *Chavasse.*

retinal c., anomalous (unharmonious). A type of anomalous retinal correspondence in which the subjective angle of strabismus is less than the objective angle of strabismus but, in magnitude, lies between the objective angle and zero. Hence, the angle of anomaly is not equal to the objective angle. Syn., *inharmonious anomalous retinal correspondence; nonharmonious* *anomalous retinal correspondence.*

retinal c., normal. Retinal correspondence in which the two foveae and other binocularly paired extrafoveal receptor areas, having similar relative retinal localization with respect to the foveae, co-ordinate functionally as corresponding receptors to give rise to a unitary percept. Thus, the foveae of the two eyes have common lines of direction or a common local sign. Syn., *primary retinal correspondence.*

retinal c., primary. Normal retinal correspondence.

retinal c., secondary. Anomalous retinal correspondence.

retinal c., tertiary. Anomalous retinal correspondence, usually induced by surgical change of the angle of strabismus, differing from a previous anomalous correspondence. *Chavasse.* See also *paradoxical anomalous retinal correspondence.*

sensory c., secondary. Anomalous retinal correspondence. *Chavasse.*

cortex (kōr′teks). The outer or superficial part of an organ, situated beneath the capsule.

calcarine c. The superficial gray matter above and below the calcarine fissure. Syn., *Brodmann's area 17; area striata; visuo-sensory area.*

crystalline lens, c. of. The portion of the crystalline lens surrounding the nucleus and bounded anteriorly by the epithelium and posteriorly by the capsule. It contains lens fibers and amorphous, intercellular substance.

occipital c. The superficial gray matter on the posterior lobe of each cerebral hemisphere, composing Brodmann's areas 17, 18, and 19. It is thought to contain, also, centers for reflex fixation, pursuit movements, accommoda-

tion, convergence, and, probably, pupil size.

retinal c. The retina when considered as an extended portion of the cerebral cortex.

visual c. Area striata.

visuo-motor c. Parastriate area.

visuo-psychic c. Peristriate area.

visuo-sensory c. Area striata.

cortical (kōr′te-kal). Pertaining to the cortex of an organ.

coruscation (kōr″us-ka′shun). The subjective sensation of flashes of light.

Cotton effect. Circular dichroism.

Cotton-Mouton magneto-optic effect (kot′un moo′tun). See under *effect.*

couching (kowch′ing). Surgical displacement of the crystalline lens.

counter, photon. A device for the measurement of light at very low intensities by counting the number of photons incident upon its receiving surface per unit time.

Cowan chart (kow′an). See under *chart.*

Cowen's sign (ko′wenz). See under *sign.*

Craig Reader. See under *reader.*

Craik's blindness (krāks). See under *blindness.*

Cramer's theory (kra′merz). See under *theory.*

Crampton's muscle (kramp′tunz). See under *muscle.*

craniostenosis (kra″ne-o-ste-no′sis). Any congenital malformation of the cranium in which an abnormally shallow orbital cavity is present. In all, the embryonic or infantile type of orbit is retained.

Crédé's method (kra-dāz′). See under *method.*

crescent. A sickle-shaped structure, like a moon in the first quarter.

choroidal c. A mottled, lightly pigmented patch of exposed choroid around the optic disk, visible because the pigment epithelium of the retina stops short of the disk.

myopic c. A crescentic white patch, usually situated temporally about the optic disk, due to myopic degenerative change of the choroid and retina, allowing the sclera to become visible.

supertraction c. A gray or yellowish ring at the nasal margin of the optic disk, sometimes occurring in myopic eyes, due to pulling of the retina over the optic disk.

crest. A projection or ridge, especially on a bone.

anterior lacrimal c. A ridge on the maxillary bone which borders the fossa for the lacrimal sac.

posterior lacrimal c. A ridge on the lacrimal bone which borders the fossa for the lacrimal sac.

temporal c. A ridge that begins near the upper lateral orbital margin on the frontal bone and is continuous with the temporal lines on the parietal bone.

Creté's prism (kra-tāz'). See under *prism.*

cribra orbitalia (krib'rah ōr-bih-tah'-le-ah). Spongy-appearing bone in the orbital roof, especially in the region of the fossa for the lacrimal gland, containing small apertures through which pass veins from the orbital diploë.

cribriform plate (krib're-fōrm). See under *plate.*

Crichton-Browne sign (kri'ton brown). See under *sign.*

crisis. 1. The turning point of a disease, for better or for worse. 2. A sudden, striking change, or intensification, of a disease.

glaucomatocyclitic c. Recurring mild cyclitis associated with open angle glaucoma, usually limited to one and the same eye. Typically, pain is mild, the pupil is dilated, few keratic precipitates are present, vision is near normal, tension is elevated to 40 mm. Hg or higher, recovery is spontaneous in two weeks or less, and prognosis is good despite repeated attacks. Syn., *Posner-Schlossman syndrome.*

ocular c. A sudden attack of intense pain in the eyes accompanied by photophobia, lacrimation, and sometimes blurring of vision.

oculogyric c. A condition occurring in epidemic encephalitis in which the eyes are fixed in one position for minutes or hours.

Pel's c. A sudden attack of intense ocular pain, lacrimation, and photophobia, occurring in tabes dorsalis.

criterion. Clinically, a formula, a standard rule of thumb, or a syndrome serving as a basis for diagnosis, prognosis, or prescription.

balance plus and minus c. The criterion based on the assumption that asthenopia is not attributable to muscular imbalance when the positive and negative relative accommodation ranges are equal.

Judd c. A means of rating the diagnostic efficiency of a pseudo-isochromatic plate, based on its misclassification of normal and of color-deficient subjects by the formula $Q_n + Q_d$, Q_n being the proportion of normal who fail the plate and Q_d the proportion of color-deficient who pass it.

Percival c. The criterion based on the assumption that asthenopia is not attributable to muscular imbalance when the convergence demand or stimulus is in the middle third of the total fusional convergence range.

Rayleigh c. Two images are said to be just resolved when the central maximum in the diffraction pattern of one of the images is located at the first minimum in the diffraction pattern of the other.

Sheard c. The criterion based on the assumption that asthenopia is not attributable to muscular imbalance when the degree of heterophoria is less than half the opposing fusional convergence in reserve.

Sloan-Green c. A means of rating the diagnostic efficiency of a pseudoisochromatic plate, based on its misclassification of normal and of color-deficient subjects by the formula $(Q_n)^2 + (Q_d)^2$, Q_n being the proportion of normal who fail the plate and Q_d the proportion of color-deficient who pass it.

Strehl c. Strehl definition.

critical flicker frequency. See under *frequency.*

crocodile shagreen. See under *degeneration.*

Crookes' (krooks) **adaptometer; glass; radiometer.** See under the nouns.

Cross's (krosz) **method; stereoscope.** See under the nouns.

cross. A figure, mark, or structure formed by two intersecting straight limbs.

Maddox c. A scale for measuring vertical and lateral phorias or tropias, consisting of a graduated vertical line and a graduated horizontal line, in the form of a cross, and a light source placed at the point of intersection. Syn., *Maddox tangent scale chart; Maddox tangent scale.*

optical c. 1. A diagrammatic scheme for charting the axes and dioptric powers of the principal meridians of ophthalmic lenses, consisting of two lines crossing each other at right angles and oriented to represent the principal meridians. Each line is notated at one end with the degree and at the other end with the dioptric power. 2. The intersecting lines in the center of an optical protractor.

cross-disparity. A variation, found in Helmholtz' writings, of Hering's crossed disparity, and understood by him to represent any retinal disparity producing perception of stereopsis.

crossed cylinders. Crossed cylinder lens.

cross-eyed. The popular term for esotropic.

cross-hairs. A reticle of thin threads or wires stretched at right angles in the focal plane of the eyepiece of an optical instrument, for purposes of localization and focusing adjustments.

crossing, A-V. Arteriovenous crossing, referring to the crossing of arteries over veins, or vice versa, in the eyeground. See also *A-V nicking.*

Crouzon's disease (kroo-zonz'). Hereditary craniofacial dysostosis.

crowding. Crowding phenomenon.

Crowe's sign (krōz). See under *sign.*

Cruise stereoscope (krōōz). See under *stereoscope.*

crus cerebri (krus ser'e-bri). Cerebral peduncles.

crutch, ptosis. A spectacle frame attachment to support and elevate a ptotic eyelid. Syn., *ptosis prop.*

Cruveilhier's valve (kroo-vāl-yāz'). Plica lacrimalis.

cryoextraction (kri"o-eks-trak'shun). Intracapsular cataract extraction in which the lens is removed by a refrigerated instrument to which it adheres by freezing. Syn., *cryoprehensile extraction.*

cryoextractor (kri"o-eks-trak'tor). An instrument containing a refrigerant, used in cryoextraction. Syn., *cryophake.*

cryophake (kri'o-fāk). Cryoextractor.

crypt. 1. A small pitlike depression. 2. A glandular cavity.

conjunctival c's. Glands of Henle.

Fuchs, c's. of. Pitlike depressions, located near the collarette of the iris, serving as passageways for aqueous fluid. At these crypts the anterior endothelium and the anterior limiting layer are meager.

iris, c's. of. The crypts of Fuchs and also similar, but smaller, pits located near the root of the iris.

cryptophthalmia (krip"tof-thal'me-ah). Cryptophthalmos.

cryptophthalmos (krip″tof-thal′-mos). A congenital anomaly in which the eyelids are totally absent, with skin passing continuously from the forehead over a malformed or rudimentary eye, onto the cheek. The cornea and the conjunctiva are usually replaced by vascularized fibrous tissue adherent to the skin. Syn., *cryptophthalmia; cryptophthalmus.*

cryptophthalmus (krip″tof-thal′-mus). Cryptophthalmos.

crys. Abbreviation for *crystalline lens.*

crystal. A body having natural external plane faces and formed by a three-dimensional array of atoms, ions, or molecules, which is built up by some fundamental unit of structure which repeats regularly and indefinitely in the three dimensions.

anisotropic c. A crystal that exhibits different optical properties for light traveling through it in different directions; a crystal exhibiting double refraction.

biaxial c. A doubly refracting crystal that has two directions in which plane-polarized waves of light travel with the same velocity and without change in their state of polarization. In these two directions it acts as an isotropic crystal, in all other directions as an anisotropic crystal.

dichroic c. A doubly refracting crystal that unequally absorbs the ordinary and extraordinary rays, thereby producing linearly polarized light.

herapathite c. A synthetic dichroic crystal of iodoquinine sulfate which transmits one linearly polarized beam and absorbs the other; discovered by and named after W. B. Herapath, it served as the basis for the original Polaroid material.

isotropic c. A crystal the optical properties of which are identical in all directions.

left-handed c. An optically active crystal that rotates the plane of vibration of plane-polarized light in a counterclockwise direction as viewed by an observer looking toward the oncoming light.

negative c. A uniaxial anisotropic crystal in which the extraordinary ray is refracted away from the optic axis of the crystal.

optically active c. A crystal that rotates the plane of vibration of plane-polarized light that passes through it.

positive c. A uniaxial anisotropic crystal in which the extraordinary ray is refracted toward the optic axis of the crystal.

right-handed c. An optically active crystal that rotates the plane of vibration of plane-polarized light in a clockwise direction as viewed by an observer looking toward the oncoming light.

uniaxial c. A doubly refracting crystal in which there is one direction along which the two sets of refracted waves travel with the same velocity and without change in polarization. In this direction it acts as an isotropic crystal, in all other directions as an anisotropic crystal.

   uniaxial c., negative. A uniaxial crystal in which the index of refraction for the extraordinary ray is less than the index of refraction for the ordinary ray.

   uniaxial c., positive. A uniaxial crystal in which the index of refraction for the extraordinary ray is greater than the index of refraction for the ordinary ray.

crystalline, alpha. One of the three soluble protein fractions and antigens found in the crystalline lens and classified according to their precipitating properties, the other two being *beta* and *gamma crystalline.*

crystalline, beta. One of the three soluble protein fractions and antigens found in the crystalline lens and classified according to their precipitating characteristics, the other two being *alpha* and *gamma crystalline.*

crystalline, gamma. One of the three soluble protein fractions and antigens found in the crystalline lens and classified according to their precipitating characteristics, the other two being *alpha* and *beta crystalline.*

crystallitis (kris"tal-i'tis). Phacitis.

crystalloiditis (kris"tal-oi-di'tis). Phacitis.

crystalloluminescence (kris"tal-o-lu"mih-nes'ens). The emission of light by certain substances while they are crystallizing.

cube. A body of six equal square sides.

von Hornbostel c. A striking form of optical illusion named for the German psychologist. It consists of a skeleton wire cube which, when observed monocularly under proper conditions, will reverse as does the Necker cube. When perceived as reversed, rotations or tilting of the cube produce a visual perception of movement opposite to that felt by the hand moving it.

Inouye's c's. Two cubes, one containing Landolt C's of various sizes, the other Snellen E's of various sizes, used to train fixation by centering the doughnut-shaped negative afterimage on the test target, after stimulating the peripheral retina with bright light.

Lummer-Brodhun c. An optical device used in photometry consisting of two 45° by 90° prisms, one of which has on its hypotenuse face a convex spherical surface, except for a small central region which is flat and placed in apposition to the hypotenuse face of the other prism. Light normally incident from two comparison sources enters the cube from perpendicular directions.

The light incident on the prism having the spherical face will pass undeviated through the central flat region to form a disk of light, and light entering the prism having the flat hypotenuse will be totally reflected and deviated 90° in the peripheral region where the air space is present, to form an annulus of light surrounding the disk.

Necker c. A two-dimensional perspective drawing of the outlines of a cube, which, upon steady fixation, appears to turn ˙inside out, or to reverse perspective periodically.

Cuignet's (ke-ēn-yāz') **method; test.** See under the nouns.

cul-de-sac (kul'duh-sak'). The fornix of the conjunctiva.

cullet (kul'et, -it). Leftover glass from previous melts which is added to the raw materials of a new batch in the manufacture of optical glass.

cuneus (ku'ne-us). The portion of the medial surface of an occipital lobe above the calcarine fissure, containing the upper halves of both the higher visual centers and the visual association centers.

cup. A bowl-shaped drinking vessel, or any similar shaped structure.

cartilaginous c. A supporting structure of hyaline cartilage located in the sclera of the posterior hemispherical segment of the eyes of some birds.

glaucomatous c. A deep depression of the optic disk, seen in glaucoma and characterized by steep or overhanging walls over which the central retinal vessels may bend sharply to reappear faintly at the bottom of the depression.

ocular c. Optic cup.

optic c. A two-layered, cuplike structure, formed by invagination of the distal wall of the optic vesicle, which commences at

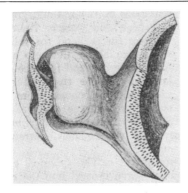

Fig. 11. Model of the optic cup of a 5.5 mm. human embryo, showing invagination of the optic vesicle to form the optic cup, and the deepening of the lens pit. (From *The Development of the Human Eye,* Ida Mann, British Medical Association, 1950)

about the fourth week of embryonic life and gives origin to the retina, the inner surfaces of the ciliary body and the iris, and the intrinsic muscles of the iris. Syn., *secondary optic vesicle.*

perilimbal suction c. A plastic, funnel-shaped device used in glaucoma testing to close the aqueous outflow channels for evaluating aqueous flow and outflow resistance. The narrow end is joined to a suction pump, and a flange of 15 mm. radius of curvature at its wide end is placed around the limbus. See also *perilimbal suction cup test.*

physiological c. A funnel-shaped depression at or near the center of the optic disk where the central retinal vessels leave or enter the retina; a normal physiological depression lined by the meniscus of Kuhnt.

Cüpper's (ke'perz) **afterimage method; test; theory.** See under the nouns.

curl. The portion of a riding bow temple which wraps around the base of the pinna.

current. A stream or flow of fluid, electricity, or gas in a certain direction, or the rate of such flow.

action c. The flow of electrons as a result of active portions of a tissue or cell being electrically negative to resting portions.

optic nerve c. An action current traveling in the optic nerve.

photoelectric c. A nerve current initiated by stimulation of receptors in the retina by wavelengths of the visible spectrum.

retinal c. A current in the retina initiated through stimulation of receptors by light waves. The stimulated cells are electronegative to the nerve fiber layer or optic nerve and form the basis for the electroretinogram.

curvature. The act of curving or the state of being curved; a bending from a rectilinear direction.

contrast, c. See under *contrast.*

field, c. of the. An aberration of refractive and reflective optics wherein a curved image surface results from a plane object, due to each object point being a different distance from the refracting or reflecting surface.

image, c. of the. Curvature of the field.

curve. 1. A bending or deviation without finite angles from a straight course; that which is bent or flexed. 2. A line, usually curved, representing graphically a variable element.

absorption c. A graphical representation of absorption as a function of some other factor, i.e., wavelength, temperature, or ion concentration.

base c. 1. In ophthalmic lenses, the standard or reference surface in a lens or series of lenses, classified by (varying) manufacturing nomenclature as having a given base curve. 2. In a toric surface, the curve of least power. 3. In multifocal lenses, the spherical curve on the segment side. 4. In single vision spherical ophthalmic lenses, the curve of the surface of lesser curvature. 5. In contact lenses, the curve of the posterior surface in the area corresponding to the optical zone.

bimodal c. Any curve characterized by two peaks. In statistics, usually the graphical representation of a bimodal frequency distribution.

blend c. A curved surface of narrow width on the posterior surface of a contact lens, designed to reduce the sharpness at the junction between two curves of unlike radii, usually produced by polishing with a tool having an intermediate radius. Syn., *transitional curve*.

Broca-Sulzer c. A curve showing changes in perceived brightness of light of constant illuminance with varied durations of flash, maximum values being obtained for intermediate durations.

caustic c. In optics, the cusp-tipped curve described by the intersections of consecutively adjacent pairs of rays in a longitudinal section through the axis of a bundle of converging rays, whence all rays in the section are tangent to the curve. If formed by reflection, it is termed *catacaustic*, by refraction, *diacaustic*.

cold c. In dichromatic vision, the sensation curve representing the color-mixing primary in the short (blue) wavelength region of the spectrum.

color c's., Maxwell's. The set of three curves representing the relative amounts of Maxwell's three primary colors needed to match visually each of the spectrum colors. Syn., *Maxwell's sensation curves*.

color mixture c. Curves representing the relative amounts of primary color required to match each part of the spectrum.

color valence c's., Hering's. Two interlacing curves, showing the variation in effectivity of spectral wavelengths in producing the sensations of (a) red and green, (b) blue and yellow. Relative valences for red and for yellow are shown above the zero axis, those for green and for blue below, to indicate that red and green are opponent pairs of colors, as are blue and yellow. Syn., *Hering valence diagram*.

corrected c. See *lens, corrected curve*.

countersink c. The spherical concave curve ground into the surface of a lens blank to which a segment will be fused in the manufacture of a multifocal lens.

cross c. The curve of greatest power of a toric surface, i.e., that lying in the meridian 90° from the base curve.

dichromatic coefficient c. A graphical representation, as a function of wavelength, of the proportions of suitable primary colors in a two-color mixture required by a dichromat to match a sample color.

dominator c., photopic. Granit's term for a spectral sensitivity curve, obtained by recording electrical responses of optic nerve fibers and ganglion cells, the maximum of which is at about 555 mμ. The curve is characteristic of light-adapted eyes having cone receptors. See also *dominator-modulator theory*.

dominator c., scotopic. Granit's term for a spectral sensitivity curve, obtained by recording electrical responses of optic nerve fibers and ganglion cells, the shape and maximum of which correspond closely to the absorption curve of visual purple, and said to be characteristic of dark-adapted eyes having rod receptors. See also *dominator-modulator theory*.

equal energy c. The spectral luminous efficiency curve, so named from the assumption that it is the luminous response curve of a hypothetical source with equal energy at all wavelengths.

frequency c. A curve representing graphically the occurrences of a number of samplings.

fundamental c. Base curve.

Gaussian c. Probability curve.

hue discrimination c. A graphic representation of the ability to discriminate differences in hue throughout the spectrum. Usually the wavelength difference threshold is plotted against wavelength. Syn., *sensibility for relative hue curve.*

learning c. The curve obtained by plotting a measure of success in some task as the ordinate and the amount of practice (trial number) as the abscissa. Syn., *practice curve.*

light distribution c. A curve showing the variation of luminous intensity of a lamp or a luminaire with the angle of emission.

logistic c. An exponential curve used to describe the growth of various biological populations.

luminosity c. Spectral luminous efficiency curve.

  luminosity c., photopic. Photopic spectral luminous efficiency curve.

  luminosity c., relative. Photopic spectral luminous efficiency curve.

  luminosity c., scotopic. Scotopic spectral luminous efficiency curve.

meter c. An arc of curvature having a radius of one meter; a basic unit in geometrical optics.

modulator c's. Granit's term for narrow spectral sensitivity curves derived from recordings of electrical activity of retinal ganglion cells and optic nerve fibers and considered by him to subserve the mechanism of color vision. See also *Granit's theory.*

normal distribution c. Probability curve.

Ostwalt c. The lower half of the

Tscherning ellipse representing the front surface curvature values providing minimum oblique astigmatism in ophthalmic lenses of various power.

persistency c. The curve obtained by plotting as ordinates the duration of sensation, measured by critical flicker frequency techniques, for different wavelengths plotted as abscissae.

Petzval c. The curved image field of an optical system corrected for oblique astigmatism.

photosensitivity c. Spectral luminous efficiency curve.

practice c. Learning curve.

primary c. The curve of the central posterior surface of a contact lens in the area corresponding to the optical zone. Syn., *base curve.*

probability c. 1. The bell-shaped symmetrical curve of infinite range described by the equation.

$$y = \frac{N}{\sigma \sqrt{2\pi}} e^{\frac{-x^2}{2\sigma^2}}$$

where x is any abscissa, and y is the corresponding ordinate. N is the number of cases in the distribution, and σ is the standard deviation. π and e are mathematical constants whose values are approximately 3.1416 and 2.7183, respectively. 2. A continuous distribution which is the limiting form of the discrete binomial distribution $(0.5 + 0.5)^n$ as n approaches infinity. 3. A curve whose ordinates represent relative frequency of an error in a large group of measurements or observations and whose abscissae represent the size of the error. Syn., *Gaussian curve; normal distribution curve.*

radiometric c. A curve showing radiant energy emitted by a given source at various wavelengths.

recovery c. A curve representing any of several aspects of recovery in retinal sensitivity of the eye following pre-exposure to an adapting stimulus of a given intensity.

regression c. The curve representing the change in one variable for different values of the other when correlation is nonlinear. For linear correlation, the curve is referred to as the *line of regression.*

secondary c. The curve on the posterior surface of a contact lens adjacent and peripheral to, and of longer radius than, the base curve.

sensation c's. Curves representing the amount of luminous energy from each of three selected primary colors required in an additive mixture to match each part of an equal energy spectrum.

 sensation c's., equal area. Sensation curves for three primaries, red, blue, and green, in which the ordinates of two of the curves have been multiplied by factors making the enclosed areas of all three curves equal.

 sensation c's., fundamental color. Sensation curves based on the three primary colors with actual luminosity values plotted against wavelength.

 sensation c's., Maxwell's. Maxwell's color curves.

sensibility for relative hue c. Hue discrimination curve.

spectral luminous efficiency c. A plot of spectral luminous efficiency values against wavelength. It usually pertains to photopic vision unless otherwise stated and indicates the relative capacity of radiant energy of various wavelengths to produce visual sensation. Syn., *luminosity curve; visibility curve.*

 spectral luminous efficiency c., photopic. A plot of spectral luminous efficiency values for photopic vision against wavelength, with unity at wavelength of maximum luminous efficacy (555 nanometers). Syn., *pho-*

topic luminosity curve; relative luminosity curve; relative visibility curve.

 spectral luminous efficiency c., scotopic. A plot of spectral luminous efficiency values for scotopic vision against wavelength, with unity at wavelength of maximum luminous efficacy (approximately 507 nanometers). Syn., *scotopic luminosity curve.*

spectral sensitivity c. A graph of sensitivity (usually the reciprocal of stimulus energy required to produce a threshold response) as a function of spectral wavelength or, less frequently, of spectral wave number or frequency. Often synonymous with *luminosity curve,* but usually restricted to threshold measurements rather than suprathreshold matches.

spectral transmission c. A curve showing the transmission of radiant energy of a filter at different wavelengths.

spectrophotometric c. A graphic representation of spectral transmittance, reflectance, absorbance, or relative spectral emittance as a function of wavelength.

spectroradiometric c. A graph of radiant energy versus wavelength, for a given radiant source.

tertiary c. The curve on the posterior surface of a contact lens adjacent and peripheral to, and of longer radius than, the secondary curve.

tonographic c. A graphic representation of the continuous changes in tonometer readings recorded during tonography.

transitional c. 1. Blend curve. 2. The curve of the intermediate zone between the corneal and scleral portions of a scleral contact lens.

transmission c. A curve formed by plotting the transmission factor against wavelength.

Tscherning c. Tscherning ellipse.

visibility c. Spectral luminous efficiency curve.

visibility c., relative. Photopic spectral luminous efficiency curve.

warm c. In dichromatic vision, the sensation curve representing the color-mixing primary in the long (red) wavelength region of the spectrum.

wavelength discrimination c. A curve representing the change in wavelength required at a given wavelength to elicit a just noticeable difference in hue.

Cushing's loop (koosh'ingz). Meyer's loop.

Cushing's syndrome (koosh'ingz). Chiasmal syndrome.

cushion, Soemmering's. Soemmering's ring.

Cushion lock. A trade name for a rimless spectacle mounting in which the shoes and straps are lined with a thin strip of rubber where they contact the lens.

Cutler's implant (kut'lerz). See under *implant.*

cutter. A machine for cutting ophthalmic lenses to desired sizes and shapes.

cutting line. See under *line.*

cx. Abbreviation for *convex.*

cyan (si'an). A bluish color normally corresponding to that produced by radiant energy of wavelength 494 mμ.

cyanocobalamin (si-an-o-ko-bal'ah-min). A vitamin which is the antianemia factor of liver considered necessary for the normal maturation of erythrocytes and used in the treatment of pernicious anemia. A deficiency of this and of other of the B vitamins may be a factor in nutritional amblyopia. Syn., *vitamin B$_{12}$.*

cyanolabe (si-an'o-lāb). The name proposed by W. A. H. Rushton for a blue-sensitive retinal photopigment, the existence of which is theoretical and has not yet been detected experimentally.

cyanophose (si-an'o-fōz, si'an-o-fōz"). A subjective sensation of blue light or color.

cyanopia (si-ah-no'pe-ah). A perversion of vision in which all objects appear blue. It may be a temporary condition following cataract extraction or may occur rarely with diseases of the retina or the choroid. Syn., *blue vision.*

cyanopsia (si-ah-nop'se-ah). Cyanopia.

cyanopsin (si"ah-nop'sin). A photosensitive synthesized carotenoid protein with an absorption maximum at 620 mμ and considered to have a spectral sensitivity similar to that of cone receptor cells of some animals.

cyanosis (si"ah-no'sis). A bluish discoloration of the skin and mucous membranes, due to insufficient oxygenation of the blood.

bulbi, c. Bluish discoloration of the sclera in cyanosis.

retina, c. of. A condition characterized by marked engorgement and tortuosity of the retinal veins, with a purplish coloration of the fundus, and occasional hemorrhages. It is part of a general cyanosis and is usually associated with congenital heart disease.

cycle. A complete course or round of regularly recurring events or phenomena with a return to the original state.

color c. Color circle.

Kühne c. The serial photoproducts formed in the breakdown and recomposition of visual purple, as depicted graphically by Kühne. The components of the cycle include *rhodopsin, visual yellow,* and *visual white.*

Lythgoe c. The serial photoproducts formed in the breakdown and recomposition of visual purple, as depicted graphically by Lythgoe. The components of the cycle include *rhodopsin, transient orange, indicator yellow,* and *visual white.*

Wald c. The serial photoproducts formed in the breakdown and recomposition of visual purple, as depicted graphically by Wald. The photoproducts include retinene and protein, and vitamin A and protein.

cyclectomy (si-klek'to-me, sik-lek'-). Excision of a portion of the ciliary body.

cyclicotomy (si"kle-kot'o-me, sik"le-). Cyclotomy.

cyclitis (si-kli'tis, sik-li'-). Inflammation of the ciliary body, usually accompanied by an inflammation of the iris (iridocyclitis). It occurs in three forms, plastic, purulent, and serous, and is characterized by circumcorneal injection fading toward the fornix (ciliary flush), normal intraocular tension, marked tenderness, dimming of vision, keratic precipitates, photophobia, lacrimation, and sometimes hypopyon.

> **herpetic c.** Inflammation of the ciliary body associated with herpes zoster of the cornea.

> **heterochromic c. of Fuchs.** Complicated heterochromia.

> **plastic c.** A severe inflammation of the ciliary body characterized by a copious plastic exudate, rich in fibrin, which accumulates in the anterior and posterior chambers and in the vitreous. The exudate may become organized and eventually consolidate into fibrous tissue and terminate in phthisis bulbi.

> **pure c.** Inflammation of the ciliary body without an accompanying iritis.

> **purulent c.** An acute inflammation of the ciliary body accompanied by a profuse discharge of pus. It usually involves the entire uveal tract constituting endophthalmitis.

> **serous c.** An inflammation of the ciliary body characterized by a relatively fluid exudate which travels into the anterior and posterior chambers and vitreous. Keratic precipitates are present on the posterior cornea, the iris, and sometimes the lens capsule, and aqueous flare is visible with the slit lamp.

> **sympathetic c.** An inflammation of the ciliary body associated with sympathetic ophthalmia.

> **traumatic c.** An inflammation of the ciliary body following ocular contusion.

cycloanemization (si"klo-an"e-mi-za'shun). Surgical obliteration of the long ciliary arteries in the treatment of glaucoma.

cycloaniseikonia (si"klo-an"ih-si-ko'ne-ah). Aniseikonia in which a difference in image size exists in oblique meridians of the two eyes but at perpendicular axes, e.g., right eye 1% axis 45°, left eye 1% axis 135°.

cycloceratitis (si"klo-ser"ah-ti'tis). Cyclokeratitis.

cyclochoroiditis (si"klo-ko"roid-i'tis, sik"lo-). An inflammation of both the ciliary body and the choroid.

cyclocryotherapy (si"klo-kri"o-ther'ah-pe). Local freezing of the ciliary body, used in the treatment of glaucoma.

cyclodamia (si"klo-da'me-ah). A noncycloplegic method of refraction employing a fogging technique for relaxing accommodation, especially one employing excessive amount of convex sphere to determine acuity-reduction gradients from which the refractive error may be estimated by extrapolation.

cyclodeviation (si"klo-de"ve-a'shun). 1. Cyclotropia or cyclophoria. 2. A rotation or rotary displacement of the eye about an anteroposterior axis.

cyclodialysis (si"klo-di-al'is-is). The operation, to reduce the intraocular pressure in glaucoma, which involves the detachment of the ciliary body from the sclera to form a communication between the suprachoroidal space and the anterior chamber.

cyclodiathermy (si″klo-di′ah-ther-me). A procedure for the treatment of glaucoma in which a portion of the ciliary body is destroyed by the heat generated from a high frequency alternating electric current passed through the tissue. The resulting decrease in aqueous humor production lowers the intraocular pressure.

cycloduction (si″klo-duk′shun). 1. Disjunctive torsional movements of the eyes to maintain single binocular vision, measured clinically by rotating oppositely a pair of straight lines, each seen by only one eye, until the limit of fusion is reached. 2. Cyclorotation.

cycloelectrolysis (si″klo-e-lek″trol′ih-sis). A procedure for the treatment of glaucoma in which a portion of the ciliary body is destroyed by the chemical action caused by a low frequency direct electric current passed through the tissue. The resulting decrease in aqueous humor production lowers the intraocular pressure.

cyclofusion (si″klo-fu′zhun). The relative rotation of the two eyes around their respective anteroposterior axes, in response to a cyclofusional stimulus, i.e., in response to retinal images meridionally disoriented, so as to necessitate the relative rotation of the eyes about their anteroposterior axes, to stimulate corresponding retinal areas.

cyclogoniotomy (si″klo-go-ne-ot′o-me). A surgical procedure for producing cyclodialysis, in which the ciliary body is cut from its attachment at the scleral spur under gonioscopic control.

Cyclogyl (si′klo-jil″). A trade name for *cyclopentolate hydrochloride.*

cyclokeratitis (si″klo-ker″ah-ti′tis). Inflammation of both the ciliary body and the cornea.

cycloparesis (si″klo-pah-re′sis, -par′e-sis). A weakened condition of the ciliary muscle.

cyclopentolate hydrochloride (si″-klo-pen′to-lāt hi″dro-klo′rīd). A parasympatholytic drug used in 0.5%, 1.0%, and 2.0% solutions as a short-acting mydriatic and cycloplegic.

cyclophoria (si″klo-fo′re-ah). The relative orientation of the two eyes about their respective lines of sight in the absence of cyclofusional stimuli, specified in terms of the deviation of the corresponding retinal meridians from parallelism.

anatomical c. Cyclophoria attributable to anomalies or variations in anatomical structure, usually involving the extraocular muscles.

asymmetrical c. Cyclophoria characterized by unequal cyclorotary deviations of the two eyes from a common reference plane, such as the median plane of the head or the perpendicular bisector of the interocular base line.

essential c. Cyclophoria attributable to anomalies or variations in anatomical or muscular structure or function.

intrinsic c. Cyclophoria inherently related to muscular anomalies, not related secondarily to innervation of convergence or other auxiliary functions.

minus c. Cyclophoria characterized by downward divergence of the corresponding vertical retinal meridians. Syn., *incyclophoria.*

myologic c. Cyclophoria attributable to anomalies or variations in muscular structure or function.

optical c. 1. Refractive cyclophoria. 2. Cyclophoria acquired through prolonged corrective torsion in compensation for meridional distortions due to uncorrected oblique astigmatism or to the prolonged wearing of oblique correcting cylinders.

paretic c. Cyclophoria attributable

to paresis, especially of the extraocular muscles.

plus c. Cyclophoria characterized by upward divergence of the corresponding vertical retinal meridians. Syn., *excyclophoria.*

refractive c. Apparent cyclophoria resulting from meridional differences in the refracting power of an ophthalmic lens being worn while the measurement is made. Syn., *optical cyclophoria.*

symmetrical c. Cyclophoria characterized by equal cyclorotary deviations of the two eyes from a common reference plane, such as the median plane of the head or the perpendicular bisector of the interocular base line.

cyclophorometer (si″klo-fo-rom′eh-ter). An instrument for measuring cyclophoria.

cyclopia (si-klo′pe-ah). Elements of the two eyes fused into one median eye in the center of the forehead of a fetal monster. Syn., *synophthalmia; synopsia.*

cycloplegia (si″klo-ple′je-ah). Paralysis of the ciliary muscle and the power of accommodation, usually accompanied by a dilated pupil. It may be pathological, or artificially induced.

cycloplegic (si″klo-ple′jik). 1. Pertaining to cycloplegia. 2. A drug which causes cycloplegia.

cycloposition (si″klo-po-zish′un). The position of the eye with reference to its rotation around an anteroposterior axis.

cyclops (si′klops). A developmental monster characterized by having only one eye.

cyclorotation (si″klo-ro-ta′shun). A wheel-like rotation of the eye around an anteroposterior axis. Syn., *torsion.*

cyclospasm (si′klo-spazm″). A spasm of the ciliary muscle.

cyclostasis (si″klo-sta′sis). The static position the covered eye assumes if it deviates in an incyclo- or

excyclodirection during a cover test. *Lancaster.*

cyclotomy (si-klot′o-me). Surgical incision of the ciliary body, usually for the relief of glaucoma. Syn., *cyclicotomy.*

cyclotorsion (si″klo-tōr′shun). A wheel-like rotation of an eye around an anteroposterior axis. Syn., *torsion.*

cyclotropia (si″klo-tro′pe-ah). A strabismic condition in which there is a meridional deviation around the anteroposterior axis of one eye with respect to the other.

cyclovergence (si″klo-ver′jens). A relative wheel-like rotation of the eyes around their respective anteroposterior axes, so that their vertical retinal meridians converge above (incyclovergence) or below (excyclovergence).

cycloversion (si″klo-ver′zhun). The meridional rotation of both eyes in the same direction around the anteroposterior axes.

negative c. Levocycloversion.

positive c. Dextrocycloversion.

cyl. Abbreviation for *cylinder* or *cylindrical.*

cylicotomy (sil″e-kot′o-me). Cyclotomy.

cylinder. 1. A surface traced by one side of a rectangle rotated around the parallel side as the axis, or a body of such form. 2. Cylindrical lens.

dielectric c. A cylinder of dielectric material such as glass, quartz, or optical plastic used in fiber optic devices.

rough c. Semifinished cylinder.

semifinished c. A glass lens blank with one surface unfinished and the other ground and polished into cylindrical or toric form. Syn., *rough cylinder.*

cylinder-prism. A lens which combines cylinder power with prism power.

cylindroma (sil″in-dro′mah). An epithelioma occurring in a benign form which affects the skin of the head or upper chest, and in a malignant form which affects mucous membranes. The malignant form is a type of carcinoma and is one of the most common of the tumors affecting the lacrimal gland.

cylindro-spherometer (sih-lin″dro-sfe-rom′eh-ter). An instrument for determining lens power or curvature in any given meridian by the sagittal depth method, which employs three aligned contact points, the center one of which controls an indicator needle on a calibrated dial face. Syn., *lens clock; Luer's clock; lens measure.*

cyst. A sac, especially one having a distinct membrane and containing fluid or semisolid matter.

Blessig's c's. Cystic spaces in the peripheral retina, near the ora serrata, first described by Blessig. See also *degeneration, cystic of retina.*

dermoid c. See *dermoid.*

Meibomian c. A chalazion.

prepapillary hyaloid c's. Single or multiple grayish bodies, anterior to the optic disk, representing cystic formations of hyaloid remnants, typically small and round and lying close to the disk, but may be elongated and project into the vitreous humor.

tarsal c. A chalazion.

cysticercus subretinalis (sis″tih-ser′-kus sub-ret″ih-nal′is). A parasitic infection beneath the retina which leads to retinal detachment and vitreous opacities.

cystinosis (sis″tin-o′sis). An inborn defect in which the renal tubules are defective and in which there is a disturbance of amino acid metabolism resulting in the deposition of cystine crystals in various tissues. In the eye, the crystals are found in the anterior corneal stroma and the superficial layers of the conjunctiva, giving the pathognomonic appearance of a myriad of scintillating, polychromatic, fine, refractile bodies.

cystitomy (sis-tit′o-me). Surgical incision of the capsule of the crystalline lens. Syn., *capsulotomy.*

cytoblasts of Henle (si′to-blasts). Cells of unknown origin and function in the peripheral portion of the vitreous body, situated close to the retina and more numerous near the pars plana. Syn., *corpuscles of Donders.*

Czermak's (chār′mahks) **experiment; phosphene.** See under the nouns.

D

D. Abbreviation for *diopter*.

Daae's color table (da'ēz). See under *table*.

dacrocystitis (dak″ro-sis-ti′tis). Dacryocystitis.

dacry- (dak′re). See *dacryo-*.

dacryadenoscirrhus (dak″re-ad-e-no-skir′us). A hardened tumor of the lacrimal gland.

dacryagog (dak′re-ah-gog″). Dacryagogue.

dacryagogatresia (dak″re-ag″o-ga-tre′ze-ah, dak″re-ah-gog″ah-). A closure or an obstruction of a tear duct.

dacryagogue (dak′re-ah-gog″). 1. Inducing a flow of tears. 2. A substance which induces a flow of tears.

dacrycystalgia (dak″re-sis-tal′je-ah). Pain localized in a lacrimal sac.

dacryelcosis (dak″re-el-ko′sis). Dacryohelcosis.

dacryhemorrhysis (dak″re-hem″o-ri′sis). Dacryohemorrhea.

dacryma (dak′re-mah″). Fluid secretion of the lacrimal gland; a tear.

dacryo- (dak′re-o). A combining form denoting relationship to tears or to the lacrimal apparatus.

dacryoadenalgia (dak″re-o-ad″e-nal′je-ah). Pain localized in a lacrimal gland.

dacryoadenectomy (dak″re-o-ad″e-nek′to-me). Surgical removal of a lacrimal gland.

dacryoadenitis (dak″re-o-ad″e-ni′tis). Inflammation of a lacrimal gland.

dacryoblennorrhea (dak″re-o-blen″o-re′ah). A chronic mucous discharge from a lacrimal sac.

dacryocanaliculitis (dak″re-o-kan″-al-ik″u-li′tis). Inflammation of a lacrimal canal.

dacryocele (dak′re-o-sēl). A pathologic swelling of a lacrimal sac.

dacryocyst (dak′re-o-sist″). A lacrimal sac. *Obs.*

dacryocystalgia (dak″re-o-sis-tal′je-ah). Dacrycystalgia.

dacryocystectasia (dak″re-o-sis-tek-ta′ze-ah). A dilatation of a lacrimal sac.

dacryocystectomy (dak″re-o-sis-tek′to-me). Surgical removal of a part of a lacrimal sac.

dacryocystenosis (dak″re-o-sis″ten-o′sis). Dacryocystostenosis.

dacryocystitis (dak″re-o-sis-ti′tis). Inflammation of a lacrimal sac.

blennorrheal d. A suppurative inflammation of a lacrimal sac. Syn., *dacryocystoblennorrhea.*

catarrhal d. A chronic catarrhal inflammation of the lacrimal sac, usually due to an obstruction in the nasolacrimal duct.

phlegmonous d. Inflammation of the lacrimal sac and the surrounding soft tissues.

dacryocystoblennorrhea (dak″re-o-sis″to-blen″o-re′ah). Blennorrheal dacryocystitis.

dacryocystocele (dak″re-o-sis′to-sēl). A swelling or protrusion of the lacrimal sac. Syn., *dacryocele.*

dacryocystogram (dak″re-o-sis′to-gram). An x-ray photograph of the lacrimal apparatus of the eye, made visible by radiopaque dyes.

dacryocystography (dak″re-o-sis-tog′rah-fe). Radiography of the lacrimal drainage apparatus of the

[184]

eye, made visible by radiopaque dyes.

dacryocystoptosis (dak″re-o-sis″top-to′sis). A downward displacement or prolapse of a lacrimal sac.

dacryocystorhinostenosis (dak″re-o-sis″to-ri″no-ste-no′sis). Constriction of the nasolacrimal duct.

dacryocystorhinostomy (dak″re-o-sis″to-ri-no′sto-me). An operation to restore the flow of tears into the nose from the lacrimal sac when the nasolacrimal duct does not function.

dacryocystorhinotomy (dak″re-o-sis″to-ri-not′o-me). Dacryorhinocystotomy.

dacryocystostenosis (dak″re-o-sis″to-ste-no′sis). Narrowing of a lacrimal sac.

dacryocystostomy (dak″re-o-sis-tos′to-me). Incision of a lacrimal sac, usually to promote drainage.

dacryocystotomy (dak″re-o-sis-tot′o-me). Incision of a lacrimal sac.

dacryogenic (dak″re-o-jen′ik). Causing a flow of tears.

dacryohelcosis (dak″re-o-hel-ko′sis). Ulceration of the lacrimal duct or of the lacrimal sac.

dacryohaemorrhoea (dak″re-o-hem″o-re′ah). Dacryohemorrhea.

dacryohemorrhea (dak″re-o-hem″o-re′ah). The discharge of bloody tears or of blood from the lacrimal sac.

dacryohemorrhysis (dak″re-o-hem″o-re′sis). Bloody tears. Syn., *lacrimae cruentae.*

dacryolin (dak′re-o-lin). An albuminous material found in tears.

dacryolite (dak′re-o-lit″). Dacryolith.

dacryolith (dak′re-o-lith″). A calcareous concretion in the lacrimal apparatus.

dacryolithiasis (dak″re-o-lih-thi′ah-sis). The presence or the formation of calcareous concretions in the lacrimal apparatus.

dacryoma (dak″re-o′mah). 1. A tumor of the lacrimal apparatus. 2.

A blockage of a lacrimal punctum, producing swelling.

dacryon (dak′re-on). A cranial point located at the junction of the lacrimomaxillary, frontolacrimal, and frontomaxillary sutures.

dacryopericystitis (dak″re-o-per″e-sis-ti′tis). Inflammation of the tissues adjacent to the lacrimal sac, usually secondary to a purulent dacryocystitis.

dacryops (dak′re-ops). 1. A watery condition of the eye. 2. A cyst of a tear duct of the lacrimal gland.

dacryoptosis (dak″re-op-to′sis). Dacryocystoptosis.

dacryopyorrhea (dak″re-o-pi-o-re′ah). A discharge of tears containing pus.

dacryopyosis (dak″re-o-pi-o′sis). Suppuration of the lacrimal passages.

dacryorhinocystotomy (dak″re-o-ri″no-sis-tot′o-me). The passing of a probe through the lacrimal sac into the nasal cavity.

dacryorrhea (dak″re-o-re′ah). An abnormally profuse flow of tears.

dacryosolen (dak′re-o-so″len). A lacrimal canal or duct.

dacryosolenitis (dak″re-o-so″le-ni′tis). Inflammation of a lacrimal canal or duct.

dacryostenosis (dak″re-o-ste-no′sis). A narrowing or a stricture of a lacrimal duct.

dacryosyrinx (dak″re-o-si′rinks, -sir′inks). 1. A lacrimal fistula. 2. A syringe used to irrigate lacrimal ducts.

dacryrrhea (dak-rir′e-ah). Dacryorrhea.

dadeleum (de-de′le-um). A stroboscopic apparatus devised by Horner.

daedeleum (de-de′le-um). Dadeleum.

Dalén's spots (da′lenz). See under *spot.*

Dalén-Fuchs nodule (da′len-fūks). See under *nodule.*

Dallos contact lens (dal′os). See under *lens.*

Dalrymple's (dal′rim-pelz) **disease; sign.** See under the nouns.

Daltonism (dawl′ton-izm). Color blindness. So named because John Dalton (1766–1844), who was partially color blind, published a description of his condition.

Daniel's spirals. See under *spiral.*

Dannheim (dan′hīm) **implant; lens.** See under *lens.*

dark. (*adj.*) 1. Pertaining to a color embodying a content of blackness induced by a brighter surround. 2. Pertaining to an area or a space devoid, or partially devoid, of light.

dark. (*n.*) An absence, or gross insufficiency, of light, usually connoting a percept of blackness.

darkness. The state or quality of being dark.

  total d. 1. Complete absence of light. 2. A luminance level below the human absolute threshold.

Darkschewitsch's (dark-sha′vich-ez) **nucleus; tract.** See under the nouns.

Dartnall's theory (dart′nalz). See under *theory.*

Davidson's reflex (da′vid-sunz). See under *reflex.*

day blindness. See under *blindness.*

daylight. A mixture of sunlight and skylight.

  artificial d. 1. Illumination produced by a source of artificial or controlled light matching the color quality of daylight obtained under standard conditions. 2. Illumination produced by a standard light source having a color temperature approximating expressed daylight conditions, such as C.I.E. Illuminant C.

  natural d. Light or illumination as received from the sun and sky combined without filtering, directional selection, or selective reflection. It varies in spectral character with the time of day, atmospheric conditions, or season of the year. Cf. *sunlight; skylight.*

day sight. See under *sight.*

dazzle. 1. To obscure or confuse vision by exposure to excessive or extraneous light, or moving lights. 2. To stimulate the peripheral retina with intense light while shielding the central retina, a procedure used in the pleoptic treatment of amblyopia ex anopsia to render the central area relatively more receptive to fixation stimuli.

D.B.C. Abbreviation for *distance between centers.*

D.B.L. Abbreviation for *distance between lenses.*

dcc. Abbreviation for *double concave,* as applied to an ophthalmic lens.

D.C.L.P. Diploma in Contact Lens Practice (British Optical Association).

dcx. Abbreviation for *double convex,* as applied to an ophthalmic lens.

D.D. Abbreviation for *disk diameter* of the optic nerve head.

dec. Abbreviation for *decenter* or *decentration,* as applied to ophthalmic lenses.

de Carle bifocal contact lens (deh-karl′). See under *lens, contact, bifocal.*

decenter. To displace, in the fabrication or the design of an ophthalmic lens, the optical center with respect to the geometric center or to some other mechanical point of reference.

decentration. The process of decentering, the decentered condition, or the amount of decentering. See also *decenter.*

  stereoscopic d. The relative, horizontal displacement between pairs of reference points in the two monocularly seen halves of a stereogram, vectogram, or other stereoscopic target, so as to produce retinal disparity.

decile (des′il). In statistics, any one of 9 points so situated with respect to a frequency distribution as to divide the distribution into 10 parts, each of which contains 10% of the total distribution. The position of any decile can be calculated by the formula $\frac{kN}{10}$, where k is a positive integer varying from 1 through 9 inclusive, according to which of the 9 decile points is being calculated, and N is a positive integer corresponding to the number of items in the total distribution.

declination (dek″lih-na′shun). 1. The amount of rotation of the eye about an anteroposterior axis: torsion, cyclophoria, cyclovergence. 2. The rotary deviation of retinal images in the two eyes from corresponding retinal meridians, produced by haploscopically viewing and fusing a pair of single line targets rotated in opposite directions from the true vertical. It is equal to the physical rotation of the targets minus the torsional deviation of the eyes from the vertical position. 3. Also called *declination error,* caused by a meridional aniseikonic error at an oblique axis and determined by the angle through which geared size lenses must be turned to correct any apparent inclination of the space eikonometer target about a horizontal axis. 4. Occasionally, excyclophoria, hence, synonymous with *disclination.*

minus d. Minus cyclophoria.

plus d. Plus cyclophoria.

declinator (dek′lih-na″tor). An instrument for measuring the torsion of the eyeball or the declination of the ocular meridians. Syn., *declinometer.*

declinograph (de-kli′no-graf). A recording declinator.

declinometer (dek″lih-nom′eh-ter). Declinator.

decoloration (de″kul-or-a′shun). 1. Lack or loss of color. 2. Bleaching or removal of color.

decolorize (de-kul′or-īz). To bleach; to remove color.

decomposition. The division or breaking down of a substance into its component parts, as in the decomposition of rhodopsin by light, or the dispersion of light by a prism or a grating.

decompression, orbital. Surgical relief of pressure behind the eyeball, as in exophthalmus, by the removal of bone from the orbit.

decussation (de-kus-a′shun). A crossing over, especially of nerve fibers crossing the midsagittal plane of the central nervous system and connecting with structures on the opposite side.

anterior hypothalamic d. Ganser's commissure.

dorsal supraoptic d. Meynert's commissure.

dorsal tegmental d. Fountain decussation of Meynert.

fountain d. of Meynert. The crossing over of nerve fibers from cells of the gray matter of the superior colliculi which, after decussation, connect with oculomotor nuclei. Syn., *dorsal tegmental decussation.*

optic d. In the visual pathway, the crossing over of the nerve fibers originating in the two nasal retinae to the opposite optic tracts; the optic chiasm.

ventral supraoptic d. Commissure of von Gudden.

defect. The absence, failure, or imperfection of a part or an organ.

arteriovenous crossing d. Any deviation of the crossings of retinal vessels from normal, as in A-V nicking.

hemianopic d. A blind area comprising approximately one half of the field of vision of one or both eyes and bounded by either horizontal or vertical diameters of the field.

optical d. Any physical or mechanical defect of an optical system that prevents the clear formation of an image, as in ametropia of the eye or aberrations of a lens system.

sector d. of visual field. A blind

portion of the visual field, roughly or exactly defined by two radii of the field, extending to and continuous with the peripheral limit.

definition. 1. The sharpness of imagery produced by an optical system. 2. In the eye, the maximum ability to discriminate between two points. See also *visual resolution; resolving power.*

    Strehl d. A criterion proposed by K. Strehl (1902) for evaluation of the imaging quality of optical systems. The ratio of the maximum intensity in the central part of a point-image formed by an actual optical system, to the corresponding intensity in the point-image formed by an aberration-free system of the same aperture and focal length. Syn., *Strehl criterion; Strehl intensity ratio.*

degeneratio (de-jen″er-a′she-o). Degeneration.

    cristallinea cornea hereditaria, d. Crystalline corneal dystrophy.

    hyaloideoretinalis, d. Vitreoretinal degeneration.

    punctata albescens, d. Retinitis punctata albescens.

    sine pigmento, d. Retinitis pigmentosa sine pigmento.

degeneration. Deterioration of an organ or a tissue resulting in diminished vitality, either by chemical change or by infiltration of abnormal matter.

    band-shaped d. of cornea. See under *dystrophy.*

    circinate d. Retinitis circinata.

    cobblestone d. of the retina. Paving-stone degeneration of the retina.

    colloid d. of retina. A degenerative disease involving the deposition of masses of hyaline material (drusen) on Bruch's membrane. It may occur under three sets of circumstances: (1) as a senile change commonly found in persons over 60 years of age, less frequently found in persons under this age; (2) as a degenera-

tion secondary to certain vascular, inflammatory, or neoplastic diseases of the retina or the choroid; and (3) in association with heredodegenerative diseases of the retina, such as retinitis pigmentosa or Doyne's familial honeycombed choroiditis.

    crocodile shagreen d. of cornea, deep. A very rare degeneration of Descemet's membrane of the cornea occurring in the axial region and giving the appearance of crocodile leather.

    crocodile shagreen d. of cornea, superficial. A rare degeneration of Bowman's membrane of the cornea characterized by a thin, central, disklike opacity, traversed by dark streaks attributed to tears in Bowman's membrane, and resembling crocodile leather.

    crystalline d. of cornea. See under *dystrophy.*

    cystic d. of the macula. A localized macular degeneration, resulting in edema and the formation of cystic spaces in the central area of the retina, which lead to a macular depression or to a complete macular hole. The etiology may be traumatic, toxic, or circulatory. Syn., *macular vesicular edema; honeycombed macula.*

    cystic d. of the retina. A secondary degeneration of the retina of varied etiology, in which gaps are formed within the tissue, usually at the macula or at the periphery, due to disintegration of neural elements. It usually arises in the outer and inner nuclear layers, rarely in other layers, and may be a cause of retinal detachment. Syn., *Iwanoff's cystic edema.*

    disciform d. of the macula, juvenile. A degeneration of the macula characterized by a subretinal exudative-type mass, probably caused by an extravasation, mainly of serum, between Bruch's membrane and the pigmentary epithelium, due to vascular disturbance in the choriocapillaris. It occurs in persons 20 to 40 years of age and is similar to a senile disciform degeneration of the macula, being differentiated by visual resolution, leaving little impairment of vision. Syn., *juvenile exudative macular choroiditis.*

disciform d. of the macula, senile. A rare disease characterized in the early stages either by a central subretinal hemorrhage or by a central grayish-white opacity, either varying in size from that of the optic disk to several times larger. Later the retina in the affected area becomes thickened into a sharply defined, raised mound, grayish-yellow in color, which projects for several diopters. The retinal vessels pass over the mound and may be seen to anastomose with choroidal vessels in the region of the lesion. Superficial and deep hemorrhages are present at the margin of the lesion and patches of exudate surround it. Other senile degenerative changes of the retina are usually present. The condition is permanent and central vision is completely or almost completely lost. It is attributed to transudation of plasma or blood from the choriocapillaris through a perforation in Bruch's membrane which, with reactive tissue formation, is organized into a fibroplastic mass. Syn., *senile macular exudative choroiditis; Kuhnt-Junius disease; disciform retinitis; exudative senile macular retinitis; central disk-shaped retinopathy.*

granular d. of the cornea. Granular corneal dystrophy.

Haab's d. 1. Latticelike corneal dystrophy. 2. Senile macular degeneration of Haab. 3. Traumatic macular degeneration of Haab.

hepatolenticular d. Wilson's disease.

hyaloideoretinal d. Vitreoretinal degeneration.

lattice d. of the cornea. Latticelike corneal dystrophy.

lattice d. of the retina. A thinning of the retina, at or anterior to the equator, resulting in a sharply demarcated circumferentially oriented lesion characterized by an arborizing network of fine white lines with some pigmentation. Usually it is bilateral, occurs in the superior temporal quadrant, and may progress to the formation of round holes and tears along the posterior margin of the lesion and to retinal detachment.

Leber's retinal d. A disease of the retina characterized by numerous sharply defined microaneurysms in a slightly elevated area of the fundus, considered to be an early stage of Coats's disease. Syn., *Leber's disease.*

lenticular progressive d. Wilson's disease.

macular congenital d. A bilateral congenital degeneration of the macula unaccompanied by other degenerative changes. Syn., *Best's disease.*

marginal d. of the cornea. Peripheral corneal ectasia.

paving-stone d. of the retina. A thinning and depigmentation of the retina typically located between the ora serrata and the equator and characterized by small, discrete, yellow-white areas which may have pigmented borders and may coalesce to form band-shaped lesions. It is of unknown etiology and may lead to detachment of the retina. Syn., *peripheral chorioretinal atrophy; equatorial choroiditis; cobblestone degeneration of the retina; punched-out chorioretinal degeneration.*

polymorphous d. of the cornea, deep. Hereditary deep corneal dystrophy.

punched-out chorioretinal d. Paving-stone degeneration of the retina.

reticular d. of the cornea. Latticelike corneal dystrophy.

senile macular d. of Haab. Macular degeneration in the aged characterized by fine pigmentary stippling which becomes denser as the disease progresses. It is attributed to arteriosclerosis of the choriocapillaris. Beginning unilaterally, it almost invariably becomes bilateral.

Sorsby's inflammatory d. of the macula. A dominant hereditary bilateral degeneration of the macula characterized initially by edema, hemorrhages, and exudates which progress to pigmented scar formation. In the later stages the peripheral choroidal vessels become exposed and sclerosed and eventually atrophy, leaving an exposed pigmented sclera. Typically, onset is at about age 40 with progression spreading over a 30-year period.

Stargardt's macular d. Stargardt's disease.

tapetoretinal d. A primary degeneration of the pigment epithelium layer of the retina, as occurs in retinitis pigmentosa, retinitis punctata albescens, etc.

traumatic macular d. of Haab. Degeneration of the macula following severe concussion or electric shock, characterized by pigmentary changes ranging from fine stippling to dense mottling or a heavily pigmented ring. Initially, the central area appears redder than normal, and small hemorrhages may be present. Syn., *traumatic macular atrophy; central traumatic retinitis.*

vitelline macular d. A hereditary macular degeneration occurring congenitally or in early life and characterized by reddish-orange lesions having the appearance of egg yolk.

vitreoretinal d. A rare familial condition characterized by a clear vitreous, except for preretinal filaments and veils which have been loosened from the retina, a dense hyaloid membrane which is perforated and detached, and masses of peripheral retinal pigmentation interspersed with areas of depigmentation. The visual fields are restricted, and detachment of the retina, cataract, optic atrophy, glaucoma, and atrophy of the iris, retina, and choroid are common complications. Syn., *hyaloideoretinal degeneration.*

Vogt's mosaic d. A rare degeneration of the cornea characterized by a central, thin, disklike opacity traversed by a mosaic of dark streaks and having the appearance of crocodile skin. It occurs in either of two forms, one affecting Bowman's membrane, the other Descemet's membrane.

degrees of fusion. See under *fusion.*

dehiscence, retinal (de-his'ens). A tearing of the retina from its attachment at the ora serrata. Syn., *dialysis retinae; retinal disinsertion; retinodialysis.*

Delacato Stereo-Reader (del-ah-kat'o). See under *Stereo-Reader.*

delacrimation (de"lak-re-ma'shun). An abnormally excessive flow of tears.

Delboeuf disk (del-buf'). See under *disk.*

Della Casa adaptometer. See under *adaptometer.*

delos (de'los). The ratio of the greatest distance at which an object of given dimension can be discerned for a given value of field luminance to the greatest distance at which the same object can be discerned under best field luminance conditions. (P. Moon and D. E. Spencer.)

delta (δ, Δ) (del'tah). The Greek letter used as a symbol for (1) *delta movement* (δ); (2) *prism diopter* (Δ); (3) a small increment (Δ); (4) the inverted delta (∇) is used to represent *centrad;* (5) *angle of declination* (δ).

demonstrator, halo. A light diffusing device held before the eye for looking at a bright light to simulate and demonstrate the halo seen in glaucoma.

Demours membrane (da-mūrz′). Descemet's membrane.

deneutralization (de-nu″tral-ih-za′-shun). A procedure for treatment of suppression and/or amblyopia, usually consisting of stimulation of the suppressing eye with strong light or a bright target, to induce simultaneous perception. See also *neutralization.*

Dennett's (den′its) **chart; method.** See under the nouns.

densitometer (den″sih-tom′eh-ter). An instrument for measuring optical density.

density. 1. The state or quality of being dense as opposed to rarity. 2. Quantity per unit area or volume. 3. The measure of the degree of opaqueness. 4. The measure of the degree of retardation of the speed of transmission.

luminous d. The quantity of light per unit volume, expressed in lumen-hours per cubic centimeter of the radiating substance.

luminous flux d. Luminous flux emitted or incident per unit area of surface. Cf. *luminous emittance* and *illumination.*

optical d. 1. The property possessed by bodies or by substances of resisting the speed of light. When compared to that of air or vacuum as a standard, it is termed the *index of refraction.* 2. The light-absorbing property of a translucent medium, usually expressed as the logarithm of the reciprocal of transmittance.

photographic film d. The logarithm of the ratio of incident to transmitted light. Cf. *opacity.*

radiant d. Radiant energy per unit volume, expressed in ergs per cubic centimeter of the radiating substance.

radiant flux d. Radiant flux emitted or incident on a surface, expressed in watts per unit area. Cf. *radiant emittance* and *irradiance.*

deorsumduction (de-ōr″sum-duk′-shun). Infraduction.

deorsumvergence (de-ōr″sum-ver′-jens). Infravergence.

deorsumversion (de-ōr″sum-ver′-zhun). Infraversion.

deplumation (de″plu-ma′shun). Loss of the eyelashes. *Obs.*

depolarization (de-po″lar-ih-za′-shun). The process or act of depolarizing.

depolarize (de-po′lar-īz″). 1. To deprive of polarity; to reduce to an unpolarized condition. 2. Occasionally, to change the direction of the polarization of light.

depolarizer (de-po′lar-i″zer). A reflecting or transmitting medium which depolarizes.

deposits, mutton-fat. Small masses of exudate which adhere to the posterior surface of the cornea, consisting of mononuclear leucocytes, fibrin, and serum, often found in iridocyclitis, especially of the tubercular types. Syn., *mutton-fat keratic precipitates.*

depression. Downward rotation of the line of sight.

depressor. A muscle which depresses; most frequently, the inferior rectus muscle; less frequently, the superior oblique muscle.

oculi, d. 1. Inferior rectus muscle. 2. The superior oblique muscle when used synergistically with the inferior rectus.

deprimens oculi (dep′re-menz ok′u-le). Inferior rectus muscle.

depth. 1. The perceived or actual, relative or absolute, difference in the distance of points in the visual field. 2. An attribute of color associated with increased saturation and decreased brightness.

criteria, d. The visual clues by

which an individual determines the relative or absolute difference in the distance of points in the visual field. They may be monocular, such as motion parallax, geometrical perspective, or binocular, such as convergence and stereopsis.

field, d. of. The variation in the object distance of a lens or an optical system which can be tolerated without incurring an objectionable lack of sharpness in focus. The greatest distance through which an object point can be moved and still produce a satisfactory image.

focus, d. of. The variation in image distance of a lens or of an optical system which can be tolerated without incurring an objectionable lack of sharpness in focus. Without objectionable blurring of the image, it is the greatest distance through which the image can be moved with relation to the image screen or receptoral surface, or the greatest distance through which the image screen or receptoral surface can be moved.

perception, d. See under *perception.*

sagittal d. The height or depth of a segment of a circle or a sphere; on an arc, AB, it is the perpendicular distance from the center of the cord, AB, to the arc. Thus, in the case of a planoconvex lens, the sagittal depth of the curved surface is the same as the center thickness of the lens, if the lens is ground to a knife edge. Syn., *sagitta.*

vertex d. The distance between the posterior pole (apex of the posterior concavity) of an ophthalmic lens and the plane containing the posterior edge of the lens.

depthoscope (dep'tho-skōp). An instrument for testing or training depth perception, consisting essentially of a rectangular, inte-

riorly illuminated box, about one half meter in length, containing movable targets. The subject views from one end of the box and adjusts the targets until they appear equidistant.

Derby's stereoscope (der'bēz). See under *stereoscope.*

deresolution (de"rez-o-lu'shun). The process, or the result of, deresolving.

deresolve (de-re-solv'). To modify an image so as to make it more difficult to resolve.

dermatitis herpetiformis (der"mah-ti'tis her-pet"e-fōrm'is). A recurring, inflammatory disease of the skin of unknown etiology, characterized by erythematous, papular, pustular, or vesicular lesions which tend to group and are accompanied by itching and burning. The conjunctiva is frequently affected with vesicles, erosions, pseudomembranous formations, xerosis, and keratinization which may lead to symblepharon and result in exposure keratitis. Syn., *Duhring's disease.*

dermatitis, spectacle (der"mah-ti'tis). A contact dermatitis due to sensitivity to the metal or the plastic materials in a spectacle frame or mounting.

dermatoconjunctivitis (der"mah-to-kon-junk"tih-vi'tis). Inflammation of the skin and the palpebral conjunctiva near the eyelid margins.

allergic d. Inflammation of the conjunctiva and eczema of the eyelids due to an allergic reaction to local contact with such agents as drugs, cosmetics, or chemicals. The allergic response is delayed, occurring 24 to 48 hours after contact.

dermato-ophthalmitis (der"mah-to-of"thal-mi'tis). Inflammation of the skin of the margin of the eyelid and of the cornea, the conjunctiva, or other anterior portions of the eye.

dermatopsia (der″mah-top′se-ah). Sensitivity to light in cells in the outer layer of some lower animals and subserving phototropic responses.

dermoid (der′moid). 1. A benign mixed tumor, usually congenital, containing teeth, hairs, skin glands, fibrous tissue, and other skin elements, rarely found in the limbal region of the eye and orbit. Syn., *dermoid cyst.* 2. Resembling skin.

dermolipoma (der″mo-lip-o′mah). A congenital, benign tumor, occurring in and under the bulbar conjunctiva at the external canthus as a fatty herniation covered by thick epidermal epithelium which may contain hair.

Descartes' law (da-karts′). The law of refraction.

Descemet's membrane (des-eh-māz′). See under *membrane.*

descemetitis (des″eh-meh-ti′tis). An apparent or a pseudo-inflammation of Descemet's membrane.

descemetocele (des-eh-met′o-sēl). A forward bulging of Descemet's membrane through a weakened or an absent corneal stroma, as a result of trauma or a deep corneal ulcer. Syn., *keratocele.*

Desmarre's law (da-marz′). See under *law.*

desmosomes (dez′mo-sōmz). Attachment bodies between cells, such as in the corneal epithelium, which possibly allow tonofibrils to pass from cell to cell and which can degenerate to allow cells to migrate to cover a denuded area.

desumvergence (de″sum-ver′jens). Infravergence.

detachment of retina. See *retina, detached.*

detachment of vitreous. See *vitreous, detached.*

deturgescence, corneal (de″ter-jes′ens). The state of relative dehydration maintained by the normal intact cornea which enables it to remain transparent.

deutan (du-tan′). One having deuteranomaly or deuteranopia; a deuteranomal or a deuteranope. Syn., *deuteranoid.*

deuteranoid (du′ter-an-oid″). 1. One having deuteranomaly or deuteranopia; a deuteranomal or a deuteranope. Syn., *deutan.* 2. Of, pertaining to, or having the characteristics of deuteranopia or deuteranomaly.

deuteranomal (du″ter-an′o-mal). One having deuteranomaly.

deuteranomalopia (du″ter-ah-nom″-ah-lo′pe-ah). Deuteranomaly.

deuteranomaly (du″ter-ah-nom′ah-le). A form of anomalous trichromatism in which an abnormally large proportion of green is required in a mixture of red and green light to match a given yellow. In the green to red region of the spectrum, hue discrimination is poor, and colors appear relatively more desaturated to the deuteranomal than they do to the normal trichromat, leading to confusion of light tints or of very dark shades of these colors. The degree of the defect covers a range from nearly normal to nearly deuteranopic. A sex-linked hereditary defect, it is the most common of all color vision deficiencies, occurring in about 5% of all males and 0.25% of all females. Syn., *deuteranomalopia; partial deuteranopia; deuteranomalous trichromatism; deuteranomalous vision; green-weakness.*

deuteranope (du′ter-an-ōp″). One having deuteranopia; a green-blind dichromat.

deuteranopia (du″ter-ah-no′pe-ah). A form of dichromatism in which relative spectral luminosity does not differ noticeably from normal, but in which all colors can be matched by mixtures of only two primary colors, one from the long wavelength portion of the spectrum (yellow, orange, or red), the other from the short wavelength portion (blue or violet). A neutral point (colorless or white) occurs at a wavelength of about 497 mμ, and it is in this region that hue discrimination is best. Light of shorter wavelengths appears blue; of longer wavelengths, yellow, with saturation increasing toward the ends of the spectrum. Thus, red, orange, yellow, and green cannot be differentiated when their brightness and saturations are made equal. Similarly, blue, violet, and blue-purple differ only in brightness and saturation, but not in hue. It is a sex-linked hereditary defect and occurs in about 1% of all males and only rarely in females. Syn., *green blindness; deuteranopic vision.*

anomalous d. A form of defective red-green color vision, with essentially normal relative spectral luminosity, in which the range of mixtures of red and green to match a given yellow, although principally of the deuteranomalous variety (requiring abnormally large proportions of green), is very much greater than the range of acceptable mixtures in deuteranomaly, yet not so great as the range in deuteranopia. A pure red (and, less frequently, a pure green) cannot be matched to yellow, and the normal observer's match (which is acceptable in deuteranopia) may be rejected. Disputed as representing a distinct type of defective color vision, it is also referred to as *deviant deuteranopia, incomplete deuteranopia,* or *extreme deuteranomaly.*

partial d. Deuteranomaly.
deuteranopic (du″ter-ah-nop′ik). Pertaining to or having deuteranopia.
deviation. 1. A departure from an expected or a normal course of

behavior. 2. A turning without change of vergence of a beam of light by an optical device or an optical system. In this sense, the concept of "deviation of light" is often used to account for a lateral difference in position between a real object and its virtual image as seen in an optical system. 3. A movement of one or both eyes, singly or jointly, from the median line, or from the original direction of fixation. 4. In strabismus, the departure of the foveal line of sight of one eye from the point of fixation. 5. In diplopia, the apparent difference in the position of the two images. 6. The departure of a value from a given point of reference.

average d. In statistics, one of the quantitative expressions of the dispersion of values within a frequency distribution about a measure of central tendency. It consists of the average of the deviations of the items in the distribution from their arithmetic mean or from their median, signs ignored. It is computed by totaling the deviations, signs ignored, of each value in the distribution from the chosen measure of central tendency, and dividing that sum by the number of items in the distribution. Syn., *mean deviation; mean variation.*

basic d. The fusion-free position of the eyes present in the straightforward position, with fixation at infinity and with natural or artificial emmetropia, i.e., accommodation at the zero level.

concomitant d. A strabismic deviation which is approximately constant for all directions of gaze; a characteristic of nonparalytic strabismus. The separation of double images resulting from such a deviation will remain relatively constant regardless of the direction of fixation.

conjugate d. The joint and approximately equal excursions of the two eyes, usually found as a physiological movement in certain conjugate palsies, in which there is inability to fixate objects in certain portions of the visual field. The term has been subdivided by certain writers into *parallel conjugate deviation, convergent deviation,* and *divergent deviation, q.v.*

conjugate d., parallel. The type of conjugate deviation in which both eyes move in equal amounts and in the same direction, found in the physiological form only when the gaze is shifted from one object to another equidistant object, or when the gaze pursues an object which moves at a constant distance. It is found in the pathological form when both eyes fail, in equal amounts and in the same direction, to fixate the object of regard. The gaze is often retained on the object by a compensating rotation or tilt of the head.

convergent d. 1. That type of conjugate deviation in which both eyes move nasally in equal amounts, demonstrated in the physiological form when the gaze is shifted from a distant to a near object on the median line. 2. Esotropia. 3. A nasalward turning of the occluded eye in the cover test.

divergent d. 1. That type of conjugate deviation in which both eyes move temporally in equal amounts, found in the physiological form when the gaze is shifted from an object on the median line to a farther object on the same line. 2. Exotropia. 3. A temporalward turning of the occluded eye in the cover test.

Hering-Hillebrand d. The deviation of the equidistant line of the horopter (often called the *frontoparallel plane*) from the Vieth-Mueller circle.

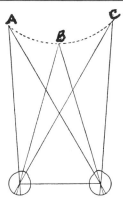

Fig. 12. Hering-Hillebrand deviation. Fixation point B beyond two meters. (From *Textbook of Orthoptics,* H. W. Gibson, Hatton Press Ltd., 1955)

latent d. 1. The deviation of an eye during occlusion, as in a cover test in a case of heterophoria. 2. The potential deviation in heterophoria or in intermittent or periodic strabismus.

lateral d. An inclusive term denoting either convergent deviation or divergent deviation of the occluded eye in the cover test or in strabismus.

manifest d. A deviation actually present and observable, as in strabismus.

mean d. Average deviation.

minimum d. The least change of direction of a bundle of light rays from its original path by a prism. This condition occurs when the angle of incidence is equal to the angle of emergence. See also *angle of minimum deviation.*

nonconcomitant d. A strabismic deviation which varies with the direction of gaze; a characteristic of paralytic strabismus. The separation of double images resulting from such a deviation will vary with the direction of fixation.

nonparalytic d. A concomitant deviation not attributable to paralysis or paresis of the extraocular muscles.

paralytic d. A nonconcomitant deviation attributable to paralysis or paresis of one or more of the extraocular muscles.

primary d. The deviation, in strabismus, of the nonfixating eye from the point of fixation when the normally fixating eye fixates.

quartile d. In statistics, one half the distance between the quartiles. This gives a measure of the average distance of each quartile from the median and is thus useful as a measure of dispersion of scores. Its formula is:

$$QD = \frac{Q_3 - Q_1}{2}$$

where QD = quartile deviation
      Q_3 = third quartile
      Q_1 = first quartile

secondary d. The deviation, in strabismus, of the normally fixating eye from the point of fixation when the normally deviating eye is made to fixate.

skew d. A spasmodic, disjunctive, binocular deviation in which the eyes move in equal amounts in opposite directions, usually vertically. See also *Magendie-Hertwig sign.*

standard d. In statistics, the degree of deviation of scores from the mean, computed by taking the quadratic mean of the individual deviations from the arithmetic mean of these values, thus the root-mean-square of the deviations from the arithmetic mean. It is denoted by σ and the formula for its computation is:

$$\sigma = \sqrt{\frac{\Sigma(x^2)}{N}}$$

where σ = standard deviation
      x = deviations from arithmetic mean
      N = total number of items

strabismic d. The deviation of the nonfixating eye from the point of fixation in strabismus.

vertical d. 1. That type of conjugate deviation in which both eyes move vertically in equal amounts, found in the physiological form when the gaze is shifted from an object on the median line to another object above or below it. 2. The type of deviation found in strabismus in which the deviating eye is turned upward or downward with respect to the fixating eye. 3. An upward or a downward turning of the occluded eye in the cover test.

Devic's disease (dev'iks). Neuromyelitis optica.

device, R-C. A lens system which is attached to the lens stop of a lensometer for the measurement of the base curve of a contact lens. It consists essentially of a standard lens of known curvature and thickness, and of an index of refraction equal to that of the contact lens to be measured. The contact lens is held to the standard lens by the surface tension of a thin film of fluid the index of refraction of which is the same as that of both lenses, thus neutralizing the refractive power of the front surface of the contact lens. Through provided tables, the reading of the lensometer and the thickness of the contact lens will indicate the radius of curvature of the base curve.

devioception (de've-o-sep"shun). Proprioception said to be derived from the deviating eye in strabismus.

deviograph, Aves's (de'vc-o-graf"). An instrument designed to permit the strabismic patient to record the apparent position of an object, presented in front of one eye, by a stylus seen only with the other eye. It consists of a chart holder set at 33 cm. from the patient's eyes, a target of 8 circles set in a rectangle calculated to include an area of the visual field subtending an angle of 20° laterally and 16° vertically, and the necessary chin and head rests, lens wells, and septum.

deviometer (de″ve-om′eh-ter). A device for measuring ocular deviation in strabismus.

Owen's d. A deviometer consisting essentially of a chin and head rest, a movable target, a prism bar, and an occluder.

Worth's d. A deviometer consisting of a series of fixation points on a graduated horizontal scale, to be fixated by one eye, and a fixed source of light over which the corneal reflex of the deviating eye is observed. The fixating eye is made to fixate successive points on the scale until the corneal reflex on the deviating eye is centered.

dextroclination (deks″tro-klin-a′-shun). Rotation of the top of the vertical meridian of an eye toward the right; intorsion of the left eye or extorsion of the right eye. Syn., *dextrocycloduction; dextrotorsion.*

dextrocular (deks-trok′u-lar). Pertaining to the right eye, or to the condition of dextrocularity.

dextrocularity (deks″trok-u-lar′ih-te). A condition in which better vision exists in the right eye, or in which the right eye is dominant.

dextrocycloduction (deks″tro-si″klo-duk′shun). Dextroclination.

dextrocycloversion (deks″tro-si″klo-ver′zhun). Rotation of the top of the vertical meridians of both eyes toward the subject's right. Syn., *positive cycloversion.*

dextroduction (deks″tro-duk′shun). Rotation of an eye toward the right.

dextrogyration (deks″tro-ji-ra′shun). A turning to the right; motion, especially rotatory, to the right; said of eye movements and of the plane of polarization.

dextrophoria (deks″tro-fo′re-ah). A phoria in which the nonfixating eye turns toward the right.

dextrorotatory (deks″tro-ro′tah-to″-re). 1. Turning of the plane of polarization toward the observer's right (looking against the oncoming light). 2. Bending rays of light toward the right. 3. Pertaining to dextroclination.

dextrotorsion (deks″tro-tōr′shun). Dextroclination.

dextroversion (deks″tro-ver′zhun). Conjugate rotation of both lines of sight to the right.

DFP. An abbreviation for the organic phosphate, di-isopropyl fluorophosphate, a powerful inhibitor of cholinesterase which in solution produces marked and prolonged miosis. It is used in the treatment of glaucoma and esotropia.

diacaustic (di″ah-kaws′tik). Denoting or pertaining to the *caustic curve* formed by refracted rays, as opposed to *catacaustic*, which denotes the caustic curve caused by reflected rays.

diactinic (di″ak-tin′ik). Having the property of transmitting actinic rays.

diagnosis. 1. The art or act of determining or distinguishing a disease. 2. In refraction, the determination of the refractive, muscular, or functional origin of the sources of visual discomfort or difficulty.

diagnostic chain. See under *chain.*

diagram. A chart or a graphic drawing demonstrating relative values, distributions, or relation of parts to the whole.

Adams' chromatic value d. A nonlinear transformation of the C.I.E. chromaticity diagram designed by Adams to provide greater uniformity in spacing of colors in relation to their perceived differences.

chromaticity d. A plane diagram, usually triangular, formed by plotting one of the three trichromatic coefficients against another, thus constituting a graphical representation of stimulus characteristics derived from color-mixture data. The colorimetric primaries are represented at the corners, and all other combinations of dominant wavelength and colorimetric purity are represented by points within the diagram. The most commonly used diagram at present, the C.I.E. (x, y) diagram, is essentially a right triangle plotted in rectangular co-ordinates (actually, a projection onto the x, y plane of an equilateral triangle whose corners lie on the x, y, and z axes of a three-dimensional co-ordinate system), representing hypothetical primaries and the entire chromaticity gamut of the C.I.E. standard observer. Another well known diagram is the Maxwell color triangle, plotted with oblique co-ordinates, having real primaries represented at the corners, thereby excluding portions of the chromaticity gamut for the normal observer. Syn., *color chart; color diagram; color table.*

color d. Chromaticity diagram.

Hering valence d. Hering's color valence curves.

isocandela d. A co-ordinate plot of one or more isocandela lines representing the locus or loci of directions in space around a source of light for which the candle-power is of a given value or of a series of given values.

isofootcandle d. Isolux diagram.

isolux d. A series of lines for various illumination values plotted on any appropriate co-ordinates, each representing the locus of points on a surface for which illumination is of equal value. Syn., *isofootcandle diagram.*

scatter d. A plot of statistical data as points on a system of co-ordinates (usually Cartesian). Each

point represents a pair of measurements, one of which is represented on one ordinate and one on the other. Syn., *scatter plot.*

Tschermak's d. A modification of Hering's color valence curves in which the individual curves have bell-shaped forms. It includes photopic and scotopic white valence (luminosity) curves in addition to the valence curves for red and green, blue and yellow.

dial, astigmatic. A chart or a pattern used for determining the presence or the amount and meridional orientation of astigmatism.

dial, fan. See *chart, fan dial.*

dial, sunburst. See *chart, fan dial.*

dialysis retinae (di-al'ih-sis ret'ih-ne). A tearing of the retina from its attachment at the ora serrata. Syn., *retinal dehiscence; retinal disinsertion, retinodialysis.*

diameter, disk. See under *disk.*

diameter, optical. The diameter of the optical zone of a contact lens.

Diamox (di'ah-moks). A trade name for acetazolamide.

diaphanometer (di″af-ah-nom'eh-ter). An instrument for measuring the transparency of substances such as gases or liquids.

diaphanosope (di-af'ah-no-skōp, di″-ah-fan'o-). An instrument for viewing a body cavity or tissue by transillumination.

diaphanoscopy (di″af-ah-nos'ko-pe). Examination with a diaphanoscope.

diaphragm (di'ah-fram). 1. A dividing membrane, a thin partition, or a septum. 2. A perforated plate or screen serving to limit the aperture or field of view of a lens or optical system; a stop.

condensing d. A diaphragm with an aperture containing lenses for the purpose of rendering the emergent light rays parallel or, in some cases, convergent.

iris d. A diaphragm with a central aperture of variable diameter, usually controlled by an annular arrangement of thin, movable plates or leaves whose medial edges intersect to approximate a circle.

lacrimal d. The posterior portion of the medial palpebral ligament and the lateral lacrimal fascia which act together to facilitate tear drainage in the lacrimal apparatus.

diaphragma sellae (di-ah-frag'mah sel'i). A circular layer of dura mater which forms the roof of the fossa for the pituitary body and is pierced by the stalk of the pituitary gland. Its posterior part usually lies below the optic chiasm.

diastereotest (di"ah-ster'e-o"-test). A hand-held test, ordinarily a modified flashlight, for determining the presence or absence of stereopsis in which the subject is asked to identify the nearest of three identical opaque disks, one of which is mounted slightly forward from a transilluminated diffusing surface, while the other two are directly in contact with the surface. Stereopsis threshold determinations may also be made with the same instrument by varying the test distance.

dichroic (di-kro'ik). Exhibiting, or pertaining to, dichroism.

dichroism (di'kro-izm). 1. The property of producing two different colors; associated with different directions of transmission of light, different directions of viewing, different thicknesses or concentrations of the transmitting substance, differences between color of transmitted and reflected light, etc. 2. The property of unequal absorption of the ordinary and extraordinary rays by certain doubly refracting substances.

circular d. The unequal absorption of two circularly polarized waves. Syn., *Cotton effect.*

linear d. The property of unequal absorption of two linearly polar-

ized beams by certain doubly refracting substances.

dichromasia (di"kro-ma'zhuh, -ze-ah). Dichromatism.

dichromasy (di-kro'mah-se). Dichromatism.

dichromat (di'kro-mat). One having dichromatism; a protanope, a deuteranope, a tritanope, or a tetartanope.

dichromatic (di"kro-mat'ik). Pertaining to or having dichromatism.

dichromatism (di-kro'mah-tizm). 1. A form of defective color vision requiring only two primary colors, mixed in various proportions, to match all other colors. The spectrum is seen as comprised of only two regions of different hue separated by an achromatic band. Dichromatism may occur as *protanopia, deuteranopia, tritanopia,* or some irregular form such as *tetartanopia.* Syn., *partial color blindness; dichromasia; dichromasy; dichromatopsia; dichromatic vision.* 2. Dichroism.

anomalous d. Color vision deficiency approaching dichromatism, although all colors cannot be matched by mixtures of only two primary colors. Since three primaries are required to match some colors, the condition is actually an extreme form of anomalous trichromatism, although hue discrimination is generally so poor that the condition more closely resembles dichromatism. See also *anomalous deuteranopia.*

dichromatopsia (di-kro"mah-top'se-ah). Dichromatism.

dicoria (di-ko're-ah). Two pupils in one eye. Syn., *diplocoria.*

dictyoma (dik"te-o'mah). Diktyoma.

Dieffenbach's theory (de'fen-bahks). See under *theory.*

Dietzel-Roelofs phenomenon. See under *phenomenon.*

difference. 1. The measure, state, or quality of being dissimilar or unlike. 2. That by which one thing is distinguished from another; a distinction.

just noticeable d. The smallest difference between two stimuli that, for a given individual, gives rise to a perceived difference in sensation. Abbreviation *j.n.d.* Syn., *differential limen; differential threshold.*

light d. Brightness difference threshold.

path d. The difference in length of the paths of light rays in passing through different parts of an optical system, as the difference in length of the paths of light rays in passing through the margin and the center of a lens.

phase d. The difference in the position and character of the wave of an oscillatory motion at two instances. In a wave motion, when two points on the wave have the same displacement and direction, they are said to be in phase. In a representation of the wave as a sine function, the wave repeats itself every 2 pi radians (360°); thus, any two points 360° apart will be in phase.

difficulty, dissociation. Crowding phenomenon.

difficulty, separation. Crowding phenomenon.

diffraction (dih-frak′shun). The tendency of light to deviate from a straight line path in an isotropic medium. In complete wavefronts, this tendency is canceled through mutual effects of the neighboring points on the wavefront. At the edge of a wavefront, as when a wavefront passes by an edge or through a slit, the canceling effects are eliminated on one side and the wavefront at that point bends in the direction of the removed portion of the wavefront.

figure, d. Diffraction pattern.

Fraunhofer d. Fraunhofer's diffraction phenomenon.

Fresnel d. Fresnel's diffraction phenomenon.

grating, d. See under *grating.*

pattern d. See under *pattern.*

Poisson d. Diffraction of light by a circular or spherical obstacle in the path of a light source, producing a bright spot in the center of the shadow having the same intensity as if no obstacle were present.

diffrangible (dih-fran′jih-bl). Capable of being diffracted.

diffusion (dih-fu′zhun). 1. The scattering of light in passing through a heterogeneous medium by a series of reflections. 2. The scattering of light by irregular reflection at a surface.

circle, d. Blur circle.

image, d. See under *image.*

Dighton-Adair syndrome (di′tun-ah-dār′). Van der Hoeve's syndrome.

diktyoma (dik″te-o′mah). An epithelial tumor of the pars ciliaris retinae which has the structure of an embryonic retina. It usually occurs in the young, developing slowly as a white flat lesion from the ciliary body and growing over the iris, the anterior surface of the crystalline lens, and the posterior surface of the cornea.

dilator iridis (di-la′tor ir′id-is). The dilator pupillae muscle.

dilator pupillae (di-la′tor pu′pih-le). The dilator pupillae muscle.

dim. Having relatively low brightness; the opposite of *bright.*

Dimitri's syndrome (dih-me′trēz). Sturge-Weber syndrome.

Dimmer's corneal dystrophy (dim′-erz). Latticelike corneal dystrophy.

dimness. The state or quality of being dim; the subjective attribute of any light sensation giving rise to the percept of relatively low luminous intensity. Cf. *brightness.*

dimples, corneal. Fuchs's dimples.

dimples, Fuchs's. Transient, superficial, dimplelike excavations on the cornea near the limbus, occurring as a senile change or due to interference with, or obliteration of, limbal vessels as may follow episcleral inflammation or cataract surgery.

dimpling. A cluster of small, round, discrete, concave depressions on the surface of the cornea, filled with air bubbles, sometimes found in association with the wearing of a corneal contact lens. It is associated with regions of entrapped tear fluid or with air bubbles entering beneath the edge of a lens which flares away from the cornea during blink.

dionin (di'o-nin). A derivative of morphine used in the eye as an analgesic in cases of iritis, iridocyclitis, or keratitis.

diopsimeter (di"op-sim'eh-ter). An instrument for measuring the extent of the visual field.

diopter (di-op'ter). 1. A unit proposed by Monoyer to designate the refractive power of a lens or an optical system, the number of diopters of power being equal to the reciprocal of the focal length in meters; thus, a 1 D. lens has a focal length of 1 m. 2. A unit of curvature, the number of diopters of curvature being equal to the reciprocal of the radius of curvature in meters.

    prism d. A unit proposed by Prentice to specify the amount of deviation of light by an ophthalmic prism, the number of prism diopters being equal to 100 times the tangent of the angle of deviation. Thus, a prism of 1 prism diopter will deviate light 1 cm. at a distance of 1 m. It is represented by the exponential symbol Δ. Syn., *tangent centune.* See also *Prentice's method.*

diopto-eikonometer (di-op"to-i"kon-om'eh-ter). An instrument de-signed to measure refractive power and magnification properties of ophthalmic lenses.

dioptometer (di"op-tom'eh-ter). An instrument used in the measurement of ocular refraction; an optometer.

dioptometry (di"op-tom'eh-tre). The measurement of ocular refraction by means of the dioptometer.

dioptoscopy (di"op-tos'ko-pe). Dioptroscopy.

dioptre (di-op'ter). Diopter.

dioptric (di-op'trik). 1. Of the nature of, or pertaining to, the diopter. 2. Pertaining to the refraction of light by transmission, as distinguished from *catoptric.*

dioptrics (di-op'triks). That branch of optics which deals with the refraction of light by transparent media.

dioptrometer (di"op-trom'eh-ter). Dioptometer.

dioptrometry (di"op-trom'eh-tre). Dioptometry.

dioptroscopy (di"op-tros'ko-pe). The measurement of the refraction of the eye by means of the ophthalmoscope.

dioptry (di-op'tre). Diopter.

dip. Abbreviation for *diplopia.*

diplegia, cerebral (di-ple'je-ah). Little's disease.

diplegia, congenital facial (di-ple'-je-ah). Moebius' syndrome.

Dipl. Opt. Optical Diploma (Association of Opticians, Ireland).

diplocoria (dip"lo-ko're-ah). The condition of an iris having two pupils.

diplometer (dih-plom'eh-ter, dip"lo-me'ter). An instrument designed to measure the distance between the two images in diplopia.

diplomometer (dip"lo-mom'eh-ter). Diplometer.

diplopia (dip-lo'pe-ah). The condition in which a single object, or the haploscopically presented equivalent of a single object, is perceived as two objects rather than as one; double vision.

binocular d. Diplopia in which one image is seen by one eye and the other image is seen by the other eye.

crossed d. Heteronymous diplopia.

direct d. Homonymous diplopia.

distal d. Physiological diplopia for objects beyond the point of binocular fixation.

dynamic d. The movement of diplopic images toward or away from each other as binocular fixation varies from one distance to another.

heterolocal d. Heterotopic diplopia.

heteronymous d. Diplopia in which the image seen by the right eye is to the left of the image seen by the left eye. Syn., *crossed diplopia.*

heterotopic d. Diplopia in which one object (or point) is seen in two directions at once, hence in two places at once, as distinguished from *homotopic diplopia.* Syn., *heterolocal diplopia.*

homolocal d. Homotopic diplopia.

homonymous d. Diplopia in which the image seen by the right eye is to the right of the image seen by the left eye. Syn., *uncrossed diplopia.*

homotopic d. In binocular vision, the perceiving of two different objects (or points) in one direction, as if superimposed or coincident in one place in space, as distinguished from *heterotopic diplopia.* Syn., *homolocal diplopia.*

horizontal d. Diplopia in which the two images appear at the same level.

incongruous d. Diplopia in which the two images do not conform to the laws of projection, for example, an exotrope experiencing homonymous diplopia. Syn., *paradoxical diplopia.*

introspective d. Physiological diplopia.

maculomacular d. A term em-

ployed by Worth to represent a form of diplopia present in strabismus, in which the image of a nonfixated object is not on the macula of either eye, resulting in a rivalry between the two maculae for fixation.

maculopseudomacular d. A term employed by Worth to represent a form of diplopia present in strabismus, in which the image of the object of regard is on the macula of the fixating eye and on a nonmacular area of the deviating eye.

monocular d. Diplopia identified with one eye only. It may be induced with a double prism, or it may occur either as a result of double imagery due to an optical defect in the eye, or as a result of simultaneous use of normal and anomalous retinal correspondence.

paradoxical d. 1. A form of diplopia present in individuals with anomalous retinal correspondence in which diplopic images do not conform to the laws of projection of normal retinal correspondence; for example, an esotrope experiencing heteronymous diplopia. Syn., *incongruous diplopia.* 2. A form of diplopia sometimes found in paralysis of the vertical rectus muscles. The diplopia occurs in the area of the visual field where the action of the affected muscle is least, that is, opposite in direction to the main field of action of the muscle.

pathological d. 1. Any diplopia resulting from a pathologic or anomalous condition of the visual mechanism, as in diplocoria, subluxation of the crystalline lens, or certain conditions of cataract. 2. Diplopia caused by the deviation of one eye in strabismus when the image of the fixated object falls on a nonmacular area of the deviating eye. Differentiated from *physiological diplopia.*

physiological d. Diplopia occurring in normal binocular vision for nonfixated objects whose images stimulate disparate points on the retinae outside of Panum's areas.

postoperative d. Diplopia occurring as a postsurgical symptom, as that following an extraocular muscle operation for strabismus.

proximal d. Physiological diplopia for objects nearer than the point of binocular fixation.

stereoscopic d. Physiological diplopia.

temporal d. Homonymous diplopia.

uncrossed d. Homonymous diplopia.

vertical d. Diplopia in which the two images do not lie at the same elevation in the visual field.

diplopiaphobia (dip-lo″pe-ah-fo′be-ah). An aversion to diplopia.

diplopiometer (dip″lo-pe-om′eh-ter). An instrument for measuring the distance between the two images in diplopia.

diploscope (dip′lo-skōp). Any of several instruments which test or train fusion or determine phorias and tropias.

Cantonnet's d. An instrument designed by Cantonnet for determining and measuring phorias or tropias. It consists of a tube fitted into the center of a plate perpendicular to the tube, a thin, transparent arrow indicator in the opening of the tube, two vertical slits in the plate, one on each side of the tube 60 mm. from the arrow, and holes at 1 cm. intervals lateral to each slit. The slits are marked zero and the holes are consecutively numbered. The instrument is used by placing the tube before one eye and directing it horizontally toward a light source. The hole to which the arrow appears to point indicates the type and approximate extent of the phoria or the tropia.

Rémy d. A diploscope consisting essentially of a bar with a target at one end which is viewed from the other end. Interposed between the target and the observer is a perforated screen through which letters on the target are seen.

direction. 1. The line or course in space in which an object is moving, aimed to move, or pointing. 2. The characteristic which differentiates two or more straight lines radiating from a common point.

absolute d. The direction of an object or an image with respect to a specified point of reference identified with the subject or subject's eye.

egocentric d. The perceived direction of an object or an image from a subjective point of reference thought of as the visual self; an absolute direction.

gaze, d. of (cardinal). The direction of gaze in the major field of action of any of the six extraocular muscles. There are six commonly recognized cardinal directions: right, left, left superiorally, right superiorally, left inferiorally, and right inferiorally.

motor d. The direction of an object from an observer, determined by the innervation to the extraocular muscles in moving the eyes to assume fixation of the object.

objective d. The direction of an object in space in relation to an observer, as physically determined; to be distinguished from *subjective direction.*

oculocentric d. The direction associated with a particular retinal point or area. It is independent of eye position and always maintains a fixed relationship to other oculocentric directions in that eye. It is a relative direction which contributes to the absolute direction (egocentric direction).

oculocentric d's., homologous. Directions from each eye as a center which are expressed as an angular measurement from the line of sight and which are identical for the two eyes. Thus, stimulation of corresponding retinal (or cortical) points arouses a percept for each eye, the two percepts lying in homologous oculocentric directions.

principal vibration d. The direction of wave vibration of plane-polarized light, as of either the ordinary or the extraordinary ray in double refraction.

relative d. The direction of an object or an image, or the direction associated with a retinal point or area, which is evaluated relative to the direction of another object, image, or retinal point or area. See also *oculocentric direction.*

subjective d. The absolute or relative direction of an object or an image as perceived in the visual space of a subject; to be distinguished from *objective direction.*

visual d. Relative direction in subjective visual space associated with a given retinal receptor element. The subjective correlate of the line of direction. See also *oculocentric direction.*

visual d., principal. The straight-ahead visual direction subjectively associated with the point of fixation, hence functionally associated with the center of the fovea, and serving as a direction of reference in relation to which all other visual directions are experienced.

disability, reading. Reading retardation in which achievement is significantly below the normal expectancy for the mental age. Generally a one-year retardation is considered significant in the primary grades.

disaggregation (dis″ag-re-ga′shun). In hysteria, the inability to integrate or co-ordinate visual perception with other sensory perceptions.

disassociation of the eyes (dis″ah-so″se-a′shun). The suspension of fusion in binocular vision, as may be accomplished by elimination of fusion stimuli. Syn., *dissociation.*

disc. See *disk.*

discharge. 1. A secretion, usually morbid. 2. An electrical manifestation in nerve tissue, particularly the transient electrical potentials in the axon (nerve fiber). In vivo, this is originated by the nerve cell body in the form of a series or train of nerve impulses and conducted along the fiber. In laboratory experiments, the discharge is often recorded from a nerve trunk consisting of a bundle of nerve fibers.

ganglion cell d. The discharge of the ganglion cells which constitute the final layer of the retina and whose axons make up the fibers of the optic nerve. This output of nerve impulses has been studied to determine the possible reorganization and elaboration of the initial discharge pattern of the sense cells themselves.

maintained d. On response.

off d. Off response.

on d. On response.

on-off d. On-off response.

optic nerve d. The electrical activity recorded from the optic nerve. The record is a picture of the temporal pattern of the discharge of impulses in the many fibers of the optic nerve. It is thus an over-all record.

X-type d. On response.

Y-type d. On-off response.

Z-type d. Off response.

dischromatopsia (dis″kro-mah-top′-se-ah). Dyschromatopsia.

dischromatopsy (dis-kro′mah-top″-se). Dyschromatopsia.

discission (dih-sish′un, -sizh′un). A surgical procedure for either soft cataract, in which the lens capsule is punctured to allow absorption of the lens substance, or aftercataract, in which capsular remnants in the pupillary area are cut. Syn., *needling*.

disclination (dis″klin-a′shun). Extorsion.

discoria (dis-ko′re-ah). Dyscoria.

discrimination. 1. The aspect of sensory response in which one feature of the stimulus is compared to another, that is, one area may be perceived as equal to, greater than, or less than another in brightness, area, linear dimension, hue, saturation, or orientation. 2. The principle of a response bearing some quantitative or qualitative relation to the stimulus and, thus, becoming less or different as the stimulus is physically reduced or changed and becoming greater or different as the stimulus is increased or otherwise changed. 3. The actual process of discriminating as described in definitions 1 and 2.

brightness d. Discrimination of the achromatic quality of color, usually specified in terms of energy or photometric units producing just noticeable differences in brightness.

color d. Discrimination of any of the several attributes of color, such as hue, saturation, or brightness, or of any combination of attributes of color, such as may be represented by linear distances on a color diagram or in a color solid.

hue d. Discrimination of the hue attribute of color. It is often measured by the wavelength change producing a just noticeable difference and, in this case, is synonymous with wavelength discrimination.

saturation d. Discrimination of the saturation attribute of color, usually measured by the number of barely distinguishable steps observable for a given hue.

spatial d. Discrimination involving any of several spatial attributes,

such as separation or resolution of two objects, direction, orientation, or geometric pattern.

two point d. The ability to experience two points as two. This term is applied most generally in cutaneous stimulation, but may refer also to two points of light. When either the contact or the visual stimuli are placed very close to each other, they tend to be experienced as a single area, rather than as two points.

visual d. The aspect of sensory response in which the stimulus features compared are perceived visually.

discus opticus (dis′kus op′tih-kus). Optic disk.

disease. An alteration of the state of the body, or of any of its organs or parts, which interrupts or disturbs the performance of the vital functions or of the mind; a specific type of such alteration, especially one having particular causes or symptoms. For diseases not listed, see under *syndrome*.

Addison's d. A systemic disease, usually fatal, due to hypofunction of the cortical portion of the adrenal gland, characterized by bronzed pigmentation of the skin, general weakness, low blood pressure, severe anemia, and digestive disturbances. Eye symptoms include enophthalmos and bronzed pigmentation of the skin of the eyelids.

Albers-Schönberg d. A rare anomaly of osteogenesis, of hereditary tendency, in which the bones become dense, sclerosed, and marblelike. It frequently affects the orbit and maxillary bone, resulting in progressive proptosis of the eyeball and optic atrophy. Syn., *osteopetrosis*.

Albright's d. Polyostotic fibrous dysplasia (*q.v.*) when associated with precocious puberty; primarily affecting girls.

Barlow's d. An acute systemic disease, often referred to as infantile scurvy, due to a deficiency of vitamin C and characterized by general weakness, spongy gums, a tendency to mucocutaneous hemorrhages, night blindness, and, rarely, retinal hemorrhages.

Basedow's d. Exophthalmic goiter.

Batten-Mayou d. The juvenile form of amaurotic family idiocy in which there is a widespread lipoid degeneration of the ganglion cells of the central nervous system and retina. It usually appears between the ages of 5 and 10, and defective vision is often the earliest symptom. This is followed by progressive mental deterioration, spasticity, epileptiform convulsions, disturbance of speech, blindness, and death between the ages of 14 and 18. The ophthalmoscopic picture varies, but characteristically the macula is pigmented, the optic disk is pale, the retinal vessels are narrowed, and in the later stages the peripheral retina is usually mottled with pigment. Syn., *Spielmeyer-Stock disease; Vogt-Spielmeyer disease.*

Bayle's d. In the insane, progressive general paralysis, including ocular structures.

Bechterew's d. Ankylosing spondylitis.

Begbie's d. Exophthalmic goiter, together with localized hysterical choreaform muscular twitchings.

Behçet's d. Aphthous ulcers in the mouth and on the genitalia, lesions of the conjunctiva and cornea, and iridocyclitis with hypopyon, tending to recur at intervals of from 1 to 2 months, with blindness usually resulting after 15 to 20 years. It primarily affects males under the age of 40. Uveitis and optic atrophy may be accompanying complications.

Behr's d. Macular degeneration in the adult at about the age of 20, believed to be caused by a primary degeneration of the tapeto-retinal type.

Benson's d. Asteroid hyalosis.

Berlin's d. Commotio retinae.

Besnier-Boeck d. Sarcoidosis.

Besnier-Boeck-Schaumann d. Sarcoidosis.

Best's d. Hereditary degeneration of the macula, occurring congenitally or during the first few years of life.

Biedl's d. An inherited disturbance of functions of some of the endocrine glands, e.g., the pituitary and/or other hypothalamic structures. The disease has physical and mental manifestations and is more commonly known as the *Laurence-Moon-Biedl syndrome.* The chief characteristics are obesity (of the "girdle" type), hypogenitalism, polydactyly or syndactyly, and mental retardation. The eyegrounds show a characteristic pigmentary degeneration of the retina.

Bielschowsky-Jansky d. The late infantile form of amaurotic family idiocy.

Bourneville's d. A rare congenital disease in which the essential pathology is the appearance of multiple tumors in the cerebrum and in other organs, such as the heart or the kidneys. It has a multitude of clinical symptoms, of which three are more or less characteristic, namely, mental deficiency, epilepsy, and adenoma sebaceum. The eyegrounds often show pathognomic tumor formations around the optic disk which are glistening gray and mulberry-like in structure. Syn., *epiloia; tuberous sclerosis.*

Bowen's d. Intraepithelial epithelioma affecting the skin and sometimes the mucous membranes. It may involve the cornea or the conjunctiva as a diffuse, slightly elevated, vascularized, gelatinous-appearing lesion, usually in the limbal region.

Buerger's d. A vascular disease, chiefly affecting young adult males, resulting in occlusion of arteries and veins, which impairs circulation, especially in the extremities. Ocular manifestations are recurrent hemorrhages in the retina and into the vitreous which are usually peripheral and spare the macula. The condition may partially clear up, but more often various complications supervene, such as glaucoma or retinitis proliferans, with detachment of the retina. Syn., *thromboangiitis obliterans*.

Bürger-Grütz d. Essential familial hyperlipemia.

Chagas' d. Infection with *Trypanosoma cruzi*, usually occurring in children. It is generally unilateral, and edema of the eyelids and conjunctiva is common. Dacryoadenitis may occur, but the infection rarely spreads to the eyeball or to the orbit.

Charcot's d. Multiple sclerosis. See also *Charcot's triad*.

Christian's d. Schüller-Christian-Hand disease.

Coats's d. Retinitis, typically occurring in young, apparently healthy males, characterized by large elevated masses of yellowish exudate, generally lying underneath the retinal vessels, chiefly in the posterior region near the optic disk or the macula. Multiple small aneurysms, present at the ends of the vessels, may burst to form hemorrhages, and the vessels often show caliber differences, sheathing, looping, and nodule formations. In the later stages, large retinal hemorrhages and retinal detachment may occur. Syn., *Coats's retinitis; retinitis exudativa externa; retinitis hemorrhagica externa; massive exudative retinitis.*

Cockayne's d. A progressive disease considered hereditary, commencing in the second year of life and characterized by dermatitis, mental retardation, dwarfism, maxillary prognathism, large hands and feet, prominent ears, carious teeth, microcephaly, loss of hearing, loss of fatty tissue in the face, optic atrophy, pigmentary degeneration of the retina of the salt and pepper type primarily in the macular area, and cataracts. Syn., *Cockayne's syndrome*.

Crouzon's d. Hereditary craniofacial dysostosis.

Dalrymple's d. Inflammation of the cornea and the ciliary body.

Devic's d. Neuromyelitis optica.

Duhring's d. Dermatitis herpetiformis.

Eales's d. Recurrent hemorrhages in the retina and the vitreous, found mainly in apparently healthy young males. The etiology may be latent tuberculosis. Syn., *angiopathia retinalis juvenalis*.

Eddowes' d. The familial condition of osteogenesis imperfecta associated with blue sclerae. Syn., *Lobstein's disease*.

Ehlers-Danlos d. Meekrin-Ehlers-Danlos syndrome.

Erb's d. Myasthenia gravis.

Erb-Goldflam d. Myasthenia gravis.

Fabry's d. A recessive, sex-linked, hereditary, metabolic disease in which glycolipid is deposited in the tissues of the body. It is characterized by small purple skin lesions in the region of the thighs, navel, buttocks and genitalia, especially in males, but usually absent in females. Typical ocular signs include: periorbital and retinal edema, tortuosity of the conjunctival and retinal blood vessels, filmy opacities of the corneal epithelium which radiate from the central cornea, and branching, spokelike, posterior capsular cataracts. Syn., *angiokeratoma corporis diffusum*.

Flajani's d. Exophthalmic goiter.

Förster's d. A localized choroiditis starting at the macula and gradually developing other patches peripherally. At first the spots are uniformly black, but later become depigmented in the center so that they appear as dark circles with white interiors. Syn., *areolar choroiditis.*

Friedreich's d. A hereditary progressive degeneration of various nerve tracts, particularly the spinocerebellar and corticospinal tracts, the posterior columns, and the posterior roots, occurring in childhood. The clinical symptoms are general impairment of coordination of movement, nystagmus, loss of tendon reflexes, and occasionally ptosis and external ophthalmoplegia. Syn., *Friedreich's spinal ataxia.*

Gaucher's d. A lipoid degeneration, often occurring in members of the same family, believed due to a congenital defect in metabolism, in which the cerebroside kerasin is deposited in the reticuloendothelial cells of the spleen, the liver, the lymph nodes, and the bone marrow. The spleen and the liver are enlarged, and there is pronounced microcytic anemia. In infants, the brain is involved; the findings are similar to those of amaurotic idiocy, and it is invariably fatal. In adults, it is chronic, the nervous system is not affected, the conjunctiva is brownish and may have a wedge-shaped thickening with the base near the limbus. Syn., *cerebroside lipoidosis.*

Gerlier's d. An epidemic disease, found in Switzerland and Japan, characterized by vertigo, ptosis, ophthalmoplegia, restricted visual fields, and dimness of vision. It is seasonal, beginning in the spring and lasting until fall, and is considered to be of infectious origin. Syn., *epidemic paralyzing vertigo.*

von Graefe's d. Progressive paralysis of all the ocular muscles.

Graves's d. Hyperthyroidism characterized by increased pulse rate, tremors, anxiety, loss of weight and sometimes diarrhea. Early eye signs are those of von Graefe, Dalrymple, Stellwag, Moebius, and Gifford, *q.v.* Exophthalmos may be an accompanying eye sign. Typically, it occurs between the ages of 15 and 50 and predominantly affects females. Syn., *Basedow's disease; Flajani's disease; March's disease; Parry's disease; Stokes's disease; thyrotoxicosis.*

Hand's d. Schüller-Christian-Hand disease.

Harada's d. A disease characterized by bilateral, acute, diffuse, exudative choroiditis, retinal detachment, headache, loss of appetite, nausea, vomiting, and sometimes temporary vitiligo, poliosis, and deafness. The retinae may reattach and the visual acuity improve. The disease is of undetermined etiology, but is thought to be due to a virus infection.

Hebra's d. Erythema multiforme exudativum.

Heerfordt's d. Uveoparotitis.

hepatolenticular d. A group of diseases, having in common degeneration of the liver and the lenticular nucleus, and characterized by attacks of jaundice, followed by difficulty in speaking, swallowing, and mastication. Eye symptoms include pigmentation of the cornea, which appears as a colored ring (red, yellow, or gray-green) on the posterior surface of the cornea (Kayser-Fleischer ring) and, occasionally, night blindness.

von Hippel's d. A rare, unilateral or bilateral disease, sometimes familial, in which hemangiomata occur in the retina, characterized ophthalmoscopically in the initial stage by one or more round or oval, elevated, reddish nodules, usually in the periphery, to each of which course from the optic disk an enormously dilated and tortuous artery and companion vein. Dense white exudates appear later and are followed by retinal detachment, iridocyclitis, glaucoma, and cataract. The course is slowly progressive, and many years may pass from the onset of the tumor to the complete loss of vision. Syn., *angiomatosis of the retina; Lagleyze-von Hippel disease; hemangioblastosis retinae; von Hippel's hemangiomatosis.*

von Hippel-Lindau d. Hemangioma of the retina associated with angiomatous cysts in the cerebellum, medulla, or spinal cord and similar cystic or angiomatous tumors in the pancreas, the liver, the kidneys, or other organs. See also *von Hippel's disease.* Syn., *angioblastomatosis; angiogliomatosis.*

Hurler's d. A congenital disease named after a German physician, Gertrude Hurler, who first described it as *lipochondrodystrophy,* characterized by dwarfism, crookedness of the spinal column, short fingers, stiff joints, and mental deficiency. Eye symptoms include large thickened eyelids, convergent strabismus, and increasing cloudiness of the cornea. Syn., *dysostosis multiplex; gargoylism; Hurler's syndrome.*

Hutchinson's d. Tay's choroiditis.

Jansky-Bielschowsky d. The late infantile form of amaurotic family idiocy.

Jensen's d. A localized choroiditis neighboring the optic disk which causes a sector-shaped defect in the visual field, characteristically extending farther toward the periphery than the actual lesion. The scotoma may reach the periphery and is sometimes found only in the periphery. The lesion is attributed to blockage of the deep vessels and consequent destruction of the neuroepithelium; because of its location the disease has been called *choroiditis juxtapapillaris.* The overlying retina may be involved only slightly, or it may be affected so very seriously that some have labeled it *retinochoroiditis juxtapapillaris.* Syn., *Jensen's choroiditis; Jensen's retinitis; juxtapapillary retinitis.*

Kalischer's d. Sturge-Weber disease.

Kaposi's d. Xeroderma pigmentosum.

Kayser's d. A systemic disease, the clinical manifestations of which include pigmentation of the skin of the body, greenish discoloration of the cornea, and intention tremor; usually associated with enlargement of the spleen and cirrhosis of the liver.

Kuhnt-Junius d. Senile disciform degeneration of the macula. See under *degeneration.*

Lagleyze-von Hippel d. Von Hippel's disease.

Leber's d. 1. A relatively rare disease occurring about the age of 20 in individuals who are otherwise apparently healthy, characterized by bilateral optic atrophy generally leading to marked bilateral reduction of vision. It is considered a sex-linked, recessive condition, and is found more commonly in males than in females. There may be some degree of visual improvement after the disease has run its course, and occasionally complete restoration of vision. 2. Leber's retinal degeneration.

Lindau's d. Angiomatosis of the central nervous system. See also *von Hippel's disease.*

Little's d. Congenital bilateral paralysis and rigidity or spasticity of the arms and legs, mental deficiency, and ocular signs which may include strabismus, optic atrophy, nystagmus, or cataract. Syn., *cerebral diplegia; congenital spastic paralysis.*

Lobstein's d. Eddowes' disease.

Manz's d. Retinitis proliferans.

March's d. Exophthalmic goiter.

Marie's d. A hereditary cerebellar ataxia in which palsies of the extraocular muscles, internal ophthalmoplegia, and optic atrophy are common, while nystagmus is rare. The onset is usually between the ages of 20 and 40, and it is slowly progressive, resulting in mental deterioration and helplessness. Syn., *Marie's cerebellar ataxia; Nonne-Marie syndrome.*

Ménière's d. Ménière's syndrome.

Mikulicz's d. A chronic, bilateral, noninflammatory, symmetrical enlargement of the lacrimal and the salivary glands, especially of the parotid and the submaxillary, with an associated swelling and drooping of the eyelids and a marked narrowing of the palpebral fissures, occurring in association with other disease, such as reticulosis, tuberculosis, sarcoidosis, and syphilis.

Moebius' d. Congenital paralysis of the sixth and seventh cranial nerves. The former involves the external rectus muscles, the latter involves the muscles of the face, giving it a masklike appearance. The internal recti may show slight weakness in lateral movements, but the function of convergence is intact.

Newcastle d. A virus disease of fowls which may be transmitted to man and cause an acute follicular conjunctivitis and enlargement of the preauricular nodes. It is usually unilateral and of short duration.

Niemann's d. Niemann-Pick disease.

Niemann-Pick d. A widespread, hereditary, lipoid degeneration, sometimes familial, affecting the reticuloendothelial and parenchymatous cells of the body, including the ganglion cell layer and the nuclear layer of the retina, usually affecting female Jewish infants. There is extreme enlargement of the liver and spleen, causing an enlarged abdomen, severe anemia, enlargement and hardening of the lymph nodes, usually a brownish pigmentation of the skin, and frequently a cherry-red spot at the macula surrounded by a white edematous area (as that found in Tay-Sachs disease). It usually commences between 3 and 6 months of age and terminates in death by the age of 2. It is differentiated from Tay-Sachs and Gaucher's diseases by its widespread involvement, gross enlargement of the liver and the spleen, and by the appearance of foam cells containing the lipids lecithin and sphingomyelin (phosphatides) in the affected organs. Syn., *essential lipoid histiocytosis; lipoid spleno-hepatomegaly.*

Nonne-Milroy-Meige d. A rare hereditary dysplasia of the lymphatics, resulting in lymphedema and hyperplasia of the subcutaneous tissue, which chiefly affects the lower extremities and may produce elephantiasis. It may be congenital or may appear as late as puberty. Ocular involvement may include conjunctival edema, blepharoptosis, buphthalmos, and strabismus.

Norrie's d. Congenital bilateral pseudotumor of the retina with recessive x-chromosomal inheritance. In the first few months of life the eyes appear of normal size with transparent corneae and crystalline lenses, behind which are dense retrolental membranes. With advancing age the corneae become opaque, the crystalline lenses cataractous, and the eyeballs become wasted and shrunken. Blindness is present from birth, and deafness and mental retardation are frequently present. Syn., *atrophia bulborum hereditaria.*

Oguchi's d. A form of congenital and hereditary night blindness, occurring mainly in Japan, in which visual acuity, visual fields, and the color sense are usually normal. The fundus has a grayish-white appearance, usually limited to the region of the papilla and the macula, but may extend to the periphery. After the eyes have been occluded for several hours, the fundi show a normal appearance.

Osler-Vaquez d. Vaquez' disease.

Paget's d. A hereditary systemic disorder of the skeletal system accompanied by a variety of ocular symptoms, the most common being retinal arteriosclerosis and central choroidal sclerosis. Other symptoms include brown corneal opacities, optic atrophy, retinitis pigmentosa, exophthalmos, or angioid streaks. Syn., *osteitis deformans.*

Parry's d. Exophthalmic goiter.

Pick's d. A form of retinitis seen in cases of advanced anemia and other wasting diseases and characterized by the appearance of multiple hemorrhages, exudates, and, occasionally, a macular "star." There is a progressive atrophy of the nerve fibers and extensive lipoid degeneration of the retinal substance. The cause is probably a toxic factor added to the anemia. Syn., *retinitis cachecticorum.*

pulseless d. A disease characterized by the absence of palpable arterial pulsation in the arms, the carotid arteries, and the superficial temporal arteries. Arteriovenous anastomoses occur around the optic nerve head, and the carotid sinus is hypersensitive.

Other signs may include cataract, absence of detectable blood pressure in the arms, slight enophthalmos, mydriasis, atrophy of the iris, retinal hemorrhages, dilated retinal vessels, and retinal detachment. Retinal and optic atrophy appear at a late stage. It usually commences during or after puberty, especially in females, is due to gradual occlusion of the aortic arch and its branches, and prognosis is poor. Syn., *brachycephalic arteritis; Takayasu's disease; Takayasu-Ohnishi disease; thrombo-obliterative aortic arch disease; aortic arch syndrome; Martorell's syndrome; pulseless syndrome.*

Purtscher's d. Angiopathy of the retina following severe skull trauma or compression injuries to the body, characterized by numerous large, white, blurred patches closely associated with the retinal veins and sometimes covering them, located in the area of the disk or the macula. Hemorrhages and retinal edema are usually present, and the retinal vessels may be dilated. The condition is usually transient and recovery complete. Syn., *angiopathia retinae traumatica of Purtscher; angiopathica traumatica of Purtscher; traumatic liporrhagia retinalis; traumatic lymphorrhagia retinalis; Purtscher's traumatic angiopathic retinopathy; retinal teletraumatism.*

Quincke's d. Angioneurotic edema.

Raynaud's d. A primary vascular disorder causing local and recurring interruption of the arterial circulation through the distal parts of the extremities. The principal eye manifestation is a spasm of the retinal vessels which, if it involves the central artery of the retina, causes almost complete loss of vision. The fundus picture resembles that seen in an embolus of the central retinal artery, namely, a cherry-red spot in the macula surrounded by a large white, opaque area. Sometimes there is a localized, complete anemia due to obliteration of the choroidal vessels which leads to destructive retinal lesions.

von Recklinghausen's d. A congenital disorder affecting various parts and organs of the body, characterized by the formation of multiple tumors, especially along the cranial and peripheral nerves but also involving the sympathetic system. There is pigmentation of the skin, small nodular growths often appear on the chest and extremities, and a tumor growth may be present in any of the structures of the eye or adnexa. Syn., *neurofibromatosis.*

Reiter's d. A systemic disease characterized by a triad of clinical manifestations: urethritis, conjunctivitis, and arthritis. The conjunctivitis is purulent and involves both eyes; keratitis and iritis may occur as complications.

Rendu-Osler d. A simple dominant hereditary disease, affecting both sexes equally, characterized by multiple telangiectases and hemorrhages of the skin and mucous membranes, including the conjunctiva. Similar vascular defects may occur in the retina. It usually does not become fully developed until late adolescent or adult life, but may occur in infancy or at birth.

Rieger's d. A dominant hereditary developmental anomaly of the cornea, iris, and the angle of the anterior chamber. It is characterized by a grayish-white translucent band opacity at the periphery of the cornea on its posterior surface, hypoplastic changes of the anterior stromal layer of the iris, and the presence of fibers connecting the iris and posterior cornea at the angle of the anterior chamber. Syn., *Rieger's*

anomaly; mesodermal dysgenesis of the cornea and iris; Rieger's syndrome.*

Romberg's d. Progressive atrophy of all structures of one side of the face, including skin, subcutaneous tissue, muscle, and bone. Of undetermined etiology, it frequently commences in the orbital region, resulting in thin eyelids, a sunken and retracted eyeball, whitening and/or loss of eyelashes, and sometimes anhidrosis. Syn., *facial hemiatrophy; Romberg's syndrome.*

Roth's d. A mild and benign condition of septic retinitis, usually associated with systemic infections, especially endocarditis, probably caused by an endotheliotoxin of relatively low virulence. There are round or oval white spots in the retina, usually near the disk, frequently surrounded by a hemorrhagic area so that the latter appears as if it had a white center (Roth's spots). Syn., *Roth's retinitis; retinitis septica of Roth.*

Rothmund's d. A rare, recessive, heredofamilial disease, occurring in early childhood, characterized by an atrophic, tightly stretched skin showing patches of depigmentation and hyperpigmentation, and telangiectasies, hypogonadism, and rapidly developing cataracts composed of discrete opacities.

Sachs's d. The infantile form of amaurotic family idiocy named after an American neurologist, Bernard Parnay Sachs (1858–1944); also known as Tay-Sachs disease because Tay later described the characteristic cherry-red spot in the macula. See *Tay-Sachs disease.*

St. Clair's d. A large group of eye diseases, of varied etiology and seriousness, generally classed under ophthalmia.

Sanders' d. Epidemic keratoconjunctivitis, first fully described by James Sanders, an English physician (1777–1843).

Schaumann's d. Sarcoidosis.

Schilder's d. A disease occurring mainly in infancy and childhood, characterized by massive demyelination of nerve fibers in the subcortical regions of the cerebrum and the cerebellum, resulting in apathy, convulsions, blindness, deafness, and spastic paralysis. Histological examination of the optic nerve may fail to reveal a single myelin sheath, the sheaths being replaced by dense glial tissue.

Schüller-Christian-Hand d. A lipoid degeneration affecting membraneous bones and other tissues, occurring primarily in male children, and characterized by exophthalmos, diabetes insipidus, and deposits of xanthomatous cells in the bones, especially of the skull. Other symptoms may include deafness, impairment of the sense of taste, ophthalmoplegia, xanthomatous tumors of the eyelids, bronze pigmentation of the skin, optic atrophy, and nystagmus. Syn., *dysostosis hypophysaria; lipoid granulomatosis.*

sickle-cell d. A hereditary anemia, affecting Negro and other dark-skinned peoples, in which the erythrocytes become sickle-shaped due to a defect in the hemoglobin molecule. Ocular manifestations include: retinal neovascularization, microaneurysms, hemorrhages and exudates, angioid streaks, papilledema, cataract, conjunctival telangiectasis and hemorrhage, glaucoma, and extraocular palsies. Syn., *sickle-cell anemia.*

Spielmeyer-Stock d. Batten-Mayou disease.

Spielmeyer-Vogt d. Batten-Mayou disease.

Stargardt's d. A heredofamilial, bilateral, macular degeneration oc-curring at puberty and not associated with degenerative changes in the central nervous system and not accompanied by any mental symptoms. Syn., *Stargardt's macular degeneration; Stargardt's foveal dystrophy.*

Steineri's d. Myotonic dystrophy.

Stevens-Johnson d. Stevens-Johnson syndrome.

Still's d. Juvenile polyarthritis.

Stokes's d. Exophthalmic goiter.

Strümpell-Lorrain d. Familial spasmodic paraplegia.

Strümpell-Marie d. Ankylosing spondylitis.

Sturge-Weber d. Malformation of the small vessels in various areas of the body, particularly of the skin, the brain, the pia mater, and the eye, characterized by cerebral symptoms, vascular nevi, epileptic convulsions, glaucoma, and calcification in the cortex of the brain. All of these changes are present in the complete syndrome, but each may occur alone. Syn., *nevoid amentia; encephalocutaneous angiomatosis; encephalotrigeminal angiomatosis; meningocutaneous angiomatosis; Kalischer's disease.*

Takayasu's d. Pulseless disease.

Tay's d. A senile colloid or hyaline degeneration of the choroid in the macular area, characterized ophthalmoscopically by small, oval, yellowish-white spots arranged around the macula. Syn., *choroiditis guttata senilis; Tay's choroiditis.*

Tay-Sachs d. The infantile form of amaurotic family idiocy in which there is widespread lipoid degeneration of the ganglion cells of the nervous system and the retina, confined principally in the latter to the ganglion cell layer. It primarily affects Jewish infants, mostly female, between 4 and 8 months of age, is of familial tendency, and is characterized by listlessness, flaccid muscles, rapid loss of vision, frequently progressing to blindness, mental deterioration, marked loss of weight, convulsions, and ophthalmoscopically by a cherry-red spot at the macula surrounded by a white area, due to edema and lipoid deposits, and pallor of the optic disk. The disease terminates in death, usually by the age of 2, and is differentiated from Niemann-Pick disease in that the liver and spleen are not enlarged, the nervous system is the primary site of involvement, and the affected cells contain a phosphorus-free lipoid.

Thomsen's d. A familial disease, characterized by delayed relaxation of the voluntary muscles but without wasting or atrophy, which commences during early life and is often associated with some mental defectiveness. The only definitely known ocular involvement is that a sudden closure of the eyelid may be followed by inability to open the eyes for several seconds. Lens changes similar to those always seen in myotonic dystrophy occur rarely in this condition. Syn., *myotonia congenita.*

thrombo-obliterative aortic arch d. Pulseless disease.

Vaquez' d. A disease of the blood-forming system, characterized by an enormous increase in the erythrocytes. The uveal vessels, especially the veins, are greatly dilated and are dark in color, so much so that the choroid may be thickened to several times its normal size. The color of the iris changes from a blue to a reddish-brown, and there may be an associated degeneration and scattering of the iris pigment. Syn., *Osler-Vaquez disease; erythremia; polycythemia rubra vera.*

Vogt-Spielmeyer d. Batten-Mayou disease.

Weil's d. A spirochete infection (*spirochetosis icterohemorrhagica*) characterized by jaundice, splenomegaly, hepatitis, and hemorrhages in almost every organ of the body. The eye involvement is occasionally iridocyclitis, usually associated with conjunctivitis. Syn., *leptospirosis.*

Wernicke's d. A disease characterized by bilateral, external ophthalmoplegia, prostration, delirium, excitement or stupor, and sometimes nystagmus, ptosis, pupillary abnormalities, and slight internal ophthalmoplegia, considered due to acute thiamine deficiency. Syn., *superior hemorrhagic polioencephalitis; Wernicke's syndrome.*

Wilson's d. A systemic disease of unknown etiology, characterized by degenerative changes in the lenticular nucleus and a mixed type of cirrhosis of the liver. General clinical symptoms are impairment of voluntary motion with rigidity, contractures, tremors, and chorealike movements. A prominent eye symptom is the appearance of a Kayser-Fleischer ring. Syn., *hepatolenticular degeneration; lenticular progressive degeneration; pseudosclerosis of Westphal.*

disinsertion, retinal (dis″in-ser′-shun). A detachment of the retina at the ora serrata. Syn., *dialysis retinae; retinal dehiscence; retinodialysis.*

disk. A circular or round flat structure.

Airy's d. The bright central disk, surrounded by concentric light and dark rings, in a diffraction pattern formed by plane waves from a point source passing through a circular aperture. Syn., *diffraction disk.*

anangioid d. An optic disk without blood vessels, due to congenital defects in vascularization.

Benham's d. Benham's top.

choked d. Noninflammatory edema of the optic nerve head, due to intracranial pressure. As observed ophthalmoscopically, the optic disk appears raised above the level of the retina and its margins are blurred. Accompanying changes are dilatation, tortuosity, and engorgement of the retinal veins, with retinal edema most pronounced in the area of the disk. Syn., *papilledema*.

color d. A disk composed of sectors of different colors which, when rapidly rotated, blend perceptually into a single color.

color d's., Walker's. Visual field test objects consisting of a thin rodlike handle, at each end of which is mounted a circular disk oriented at right angles to the disk at the opposite end. On each side of each disk is a different color; only one of the four colors is visible at a given time.

cupped d. An exaggerated depression of the optic disk, being larger and more basin-shaped than the normal physiological cup; commonly present in advanced glaucoma.

Delboeuf d. A device for determining the relationship of different brightnesses by the method of equal sensation intervals. It usually contains three concentric sectored rings which, when rapidly rotated, present three values of gray, the intermediate one of which is adjusted by the observer to appear midway between the brightness of the other two.

diameter, d. A unit of measurement equal to the diameter of the optic disk as seen with the ophthalmoscope, used for localizing retinal lesions, etc., in terms of the number of disk diameters away from the optic disk or other point of reference.

diffraction d. Airy's disk.

dragged d. An optic disk which appears to be displaced nasally from its normal position due to the temporal displacement of the retina and the emerging retinal vessels, caused by traction of temporal scar tissue formation in partially resolved retrolental fibroplasia.

Inouye's d. A home training device consisting of a flat, black, round metal disk, with a small central fixation dot, attached to a lamp to shield the macular area and provide light stimulation only to the peripheral retina. The resulting doughnut-shaped afterimage is used in fixation training by centering it around a fixation target.

Martius d. A color disk for determining the neutral brightness or gray-value of colors. A ring of the color being studied is placed on the disk between a central and a peripheral gray, each of which may be varied from black to white. The grays are adjusted until they are no longer darkened or lightened by the contrast-inducing action near the borders adjacent to the colored ring. When so adjusted, the brightness or the grayness of the variable rings is equal to the neutral brightness or gray-value of the color.

Mason's pupil d. An opaque disk with a movable slide containing several openings of different sizes which can be centered in front of the pupil in the trial frame, thus serving as an artificial pupil.

Masson d. A white disk with small, black, circularly sectioned sectors arranged in concentric order and of different sizes, used in determinations of brightness difference thresholds. When the disk is rapidly rotated, a series of neutral gray rings are seen, the brightness of each ring depending on the circumferential size of the black sectors composing the ring.

Maxwell's d. A color disk in which two or more differently colored disks are cut along a single radius and fitted together to overlap in any desired ratio of exposure.

Newton's d. A disk containing the seven colors of the spectrum which, when rotated rapidly, appears white or gray.

opaque d. A round opaque disk mounted in a trial lens rim and used in a trial frame as an occluder.

optic d. The portion of the optic nerve, seen in the fundus with the ophthalmoscope, which is formed by the meeting of all the retinal nerve fibers. It is insensitive to light, corresponds to the physiological blind spot, is pinkish in color, due to its many capillaries, and, normally, has a central depression, the physiological cup. Syn., *optic papilla.*

phase d. Phase plate.

pinhole d. An opaque disk mounted in a trial lens rim and containing a small (usually 2 mm. or less) perforation. It is frequently used to determine the maximum attainable visual acuity.

Placido's d. A form of keratoscope; a circular disk marked with concentric black and white rings and having a central opening through which the examiner observes the reflected image of the disk on the patient's cornea. It is used to determine the curvature characteristics of the anterior surface of the cornea.

Ramsden d. The exit pupil of a telescope.

Rekoss' d. A device consisting of two revolvable disks which may be turned independently about a common axis, each with a series of lenses of differing focal lengths mounted in openings around the periphery. By turning either disk, any one lens or combination of two lenses may be utilized. This device has found wide application in the construction of modern ophthalmoscopes and refracting units.

Scheiner's d. An opaque disk containing two small pinholes spaced to fall within the diameter of the pupil, used in demonstrations and investigations of the function of accommodation and of the refractive status of the eye.

Sherrington's d. A disk on which are constructed two narrow concentric rings, a semicircle of each of which is blue, with the other semicircle of each black. The smaller blue semicircle and the larger black semicircle are in the half of the disk having a yellow color or background, while the smaller black semicircle and the larger blue semicircle are in the other half of the disk having a black color or background. Although each ring is half black and half blue, the outer ring shows flicker at a higher rate of rotation.

stenopaic d. 1. An opaque disk mounted in a trial lens rim and containing a narrow opening or slit aperture, used in detecting and measuring astigmatism of the eye. Syn., *stenopaic slit.* 2. A pinhole disk.

straboscopic d. A lens or a disk used in visual testing to distort objects viewed through it.

stroboscopic d. 1. A disk with alternate open and closed sectors which, when revolving, gives successive instantaneous views of a moving object or a series of pictures. 2. A disk carrying a series of pictures showing the successive phases of a motion or a scene, as for use in the stroboscope.

Volkmann's d's. A pair of disks with a circle and a single radius drawn on each which, when viewed haploscopically, can be rotated so that the radial lines appear as a single diameter, thus indicating the angle between the apparently parallel meridians of the two eyes.

dislocation of the lens. A displacement of the crystalline lens from its normal position. Syn., *subluxation of the lens.*

Disontegrator (dih-son'teh-gra"tor). A trade name for a device which generates ultrasonic waves and transmits them through a tank containing a solution, for the purpose of cleaning small objects such as contact lenses.

disorganization, visual. *Optometric Extension Program:* A syndrome of refractive findings held to be characteristic of one who will adjust readily to changes in lens prescription, especially to increases in convex lens power.

disparation (dis"pah-ra'shun). 1. The apparent separation of the two images during diplopia. 2. Retinal disparity.

crossed d. Heteronymous diplopia.

uncrossed d. Homonymous diplopia.

disparator (dis'pah-ra"ter). A Brewster-type stereoscope with an attachment which introduces a continuous variation in the separation of corresponding points on split stereograms as the targets are moved from the infinity position to a near point position, so as to maintain a relatively constant relationship between accommodation and convergence stimuli. Syn., *stereodisparator.*

disparity (dis-par'ih-te). The state or condition of being distinct in respect to quality or character; inequality; dissimilarity.

conjugate d. The normal disparity or difference in the size or the location of the retinal images in the two eyes, created by asymmetrical convergence.

crossed d. 1. Retinal disparity induced by an object nearer than the longitudinal horopter. *Hering.* 2. Separation of diplopic images in which the right eye image is

seen to the left of the left eye image.

disjugate d. The normal disparity or difference in the size or location of any pair of extrafoveal images of a single object not on the longitudinal horopter. This creates the condition of physiological diplopia.

fixation d. A condition in which the images of a bifixated object do not stimulate exactly corresponding retinal points, but still fall within Panum's areas, the object thus being seen singly. It may be considered to be a slight over- or underconvergence, or vertical misalignment, of the eyes. Syn., *retinal slip.*

fixation d., negative. A small relative divergence or underconvergence of the eyes while maintaining single binocular vision for the point of fixation. Syn., *exodisparity.*

fixation d., positive. A small relative overconvergence of the eyes while maintaining single binocular vision for the point of fixation. Syn., *esodisparity.*

position d. Overconvergence or underconvergence of the eyes while fusion is maintained. The same as fixation disparity, but applicable also to the case where only peripheral stimuli are presented for fusion, i.e., when no central or foveal target for fixation is present.

retinal d. 1. Failure of the two retinal images of an object in the field of vision to fall on corresponding retinal points, as is obtained, for example, when the object lies outside the horopter, or when a pair of haploscopically viewed patterns are not identical. 2. Incongruities in anatomical and physiological aspects of the two retinae, such as lack of conformity of the various corresponding retinal elements, lack of confluence of the perceptual and anatomical vertical and horizontal meridians of each eye, and the difference in space values of the temporal and the nasal segments of each eye.

uncrossed d. 1. Retinal disparity induced by an object beyond the longitudinal horopter. *Hering.* 2. Separation of diplopic images in which the right eye image is seen to the right of the left eye image.

dispenser, ophthalmic. One who supplies and adapts prescribed ophthalmic products or appliances to the patient.

dispersion (dis-per'shun). 1. The act or state of being broken apart, scattered, or separated. 2. Chromatic dispersion. 3. *Statistics:* The variation of the scores or measures of a given sampling from one another or from some designated point, such as the mean.

angular d. The angular separation of the component rays of a pencil of light on passing through a refractive medium whose sides are not parallel to each other.

anomalous d. Dispersion produced by prisms of certain refractive media so that the spectral colors are not in their usual order. Such media are characterized by a high absorption band within the visible spectrum, a rapidly increasing index of refraction as the absorption band is approached from the red end, and a rapidly decreasing index as the band is approached from the blue end. Syn., *inverse dispersion.*

chromatic d. The splitting of a beam of white light into its component wavelengths or colors, as with a prism or a diffraction grating.

false internal d. In a medium, the internal scattering or refraction of light due to innumerable minute foreign particles, slight changes in structure, tiny fractures, etc., causing the medium to appear cloudy and self-luminous.

inverse d. Anomalous dispersion.

irrational d. Dispersion that is not a simple function of wavelength, occurring characteristically in a spectrum produced by a prism, in which the spectrum produced by one prism cannot be exactly reproduced by a prism of another substance.

linear d. The difference in distance to the red and blue image planes of an optical system.

mean d. The partial dispersion for the Fraunhofer C and F lines of the spectrum, designated by $(n_F - n_C)$, where n_F is the index of refraction for the wavelength of light of the F line (486.1 mμ), and n_C is the index for the C line (656.3 mμ).

normal d. Dispersion proportional to the wavelengths of the components of the light; the type of dispersion produced by a diffraction grating.

partial d. The difference in the index of refraction of a medium for two given wavelengths, especially wavelengths corresponding to prominent Fraunhofer lines.

prismatic d. The separation of white light into its component colors by passing through a prism.

reciprocal d. The reciprocal of the dispersive power of an optical medium, usually called the *nu*

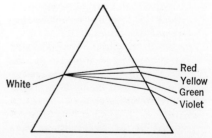

Fig. 13. Chromatic dispersion by a prism. (From *Vision and Visual Perception*, ed. by C. H. Graham, John Wiley and Sons, Inc., 1965)

(v) *value,* and represented by the formula:

$$v = \frac{n_D - 1}{n_F - n_C}$$

where n_D, n_F, and n_C represent the indices of refraction for three Fraunhofer lines corresponding to yellow, blue, and red, respectively. It is used in designing achromatic lenses, where the higher the nu value, the less the chromatic aberration.

relative d. The ratio of the mean dispersion to the mean deviation for a substance, usually termed *dispersive power* and designated by the formula:

$$\text{dispersive power} = \frac{n_F - n_C}{n_D - 1}$$

where n_F, n_C, and n_D are the indices of refraction for three Fraunhofer lines corresponding to blue, red, and yellow wavelengths, respectively. The higher the dispersive power, the more chromatic aberration a lens will have.

residual d. The chromatic aberration remaining in an optical system which has been rendered achromatic for two or more wavelengths.

rotatory d. The differential rotation of the plane of polarization of different wavelengths by an optically active substance. The amount of rotation differs with the wavelength of light and is approximately proportional to the inverse square of the wavelength.

true internal d. Fluorescence.

dissector, image. In fibers optics, a bundle of fibers which spatially rearranges the points in an image.

disseminated sclerosis (dih-sem'ih-na''ted skle-ro'sis). Multiple sclerosis.

dissimilation (dih-sim''ih-la'shun). According to the Hering theory of color vision, the breaking down of the three primary substances in the retina by red, yellow, and white light; the reverse of *assimilation.*

dissociation. The elimination of stimulus to fusion, usually by occlusion of one eye, gross distortion of the image seen by one eye, or by excessive displacement of the image seen by one eye.

sensory d. The absence of fusion because of a visual sensory pathway defect.

distance. The measure of space between two points of reference.

abathic d. The viewing distance at which the apparent frontoparallel plane, which varies in curvature with fixation distance, coincides with an actual frontoparallel plane.

between centers, d. 1. In the boxing method of frame specification, the distance between the boxing centers of the spectacle frame. Abbreviation *D.B.C.* Syn., *frame center distance.* 2. The distance between the geometric centers of a spectacle frame. Abbreviation *D.B.C.* Syn., *frame center distance.* 3. The distance between the optical centers of lenses mounted in a spectacle frame.

between lenses, d. 1. The shortest distance between the nasal edges of a pair of lenses; separation of the vertical tangents of lenses at the bridge. 2. Separation of lenses at the datum line. 3. Designation of the bridge width. Abbreviation *D.B.L.*

centration d. British: The distance between major reference points of lenses mounted in a spectacle frame.

conjugate d's. The object distance and the image distance with respect to an optical system.

distinct vision, d. of. An arbitrary projection distance used in the conventional formula for determining the magnifying power of an optical instrument, usually taken as 10 in. or 25 cm.

egoriginal d. The distance of an object from the ego or self.

equivalent d. Reduced distance.

eyewire d. The distance, along the line of sight, between the vertex of the cornea and the plane of the spectacle frame eyewire, with the eyes in the straightforward position.

focal d. The distance from an optical surface to a principal focal point, along the optical axis. In a compound optical system, it is the distance from a principal plane to the corresponding principal focal point, along the optical axis. Syn., *focal length.*

focal d., anterior. Primary focal distance.

focal d., back. Posterior vertex focal distance.

focal d's., conjugate. In a single surface optical system, the distances of conjugate focal points from the optical surface, along the optical axis. In a compound optical system, the distances of conjugate focal points from the respective principal planes.

focal d., front. Anterior vertex focal distance.

focal d., posterior. Secondary focal distance.

focal d., primary. The distance from an optical surface to the primary principal focal point, along the optical axis. In a compound optical system, it is the distance from the primary principal focal point, along the optical axis. Syn., *anterior focal distance; anterior principal focal distance; primary principal focal distance; anterior focal length; primary focal length.*

focal d., principal (anterior). Primary focal distance.

focal d., principal (posterior). Secondary focal distance.

focal d., principal (primary). Primary focal distance.

focal d., principal (secondary). Secondary focal distance.

focal d., secondary. The distance from an optical surface to the secondary principal focal point, along the optical axis. In a compound optical system, the distance from the secondary principal plane to the secondary principal focal point, along the optical axis. Syn., *posterior focal distance; posterior principal focal distance; secondary principal focal distance; posterior focal length; secondary focal length.*

focal d., vertex (anterior). In an optical system or lens, the distance along the optical axis from the anterior optical surface (first surface to the left) to the primary principal focal point. Syn., *front focal distance; anterior vertex focal length.*

focal d., vertex (posterior). In an optical system or a lens, the distance along the optical axis from the posterior optical surface (last surface to the right) to the secondary principal focal point. Syn., *back focal distance; posterior vertex focal length.*

frame center d. Distance between centers.

homologous d. The lateral distance between two corresponding objects in a stereogram.

hyperfocal d. The shortest distance for which a photographic lens may be focused to permit satisfactory image definition of an object at infinity.

hyperplastic d. The perceived distance of an image, especially from an optical instrument, when it is greater than the actual physical distance of the object.

hypoplastic d. The perceived distance of an image, especially from an optical instrument, when it is less than the actual physical distance of the object.

image d. The distance from the optical surface to the image. In a compound optical system, the distance from the secondary principal plane to the image. Symbol u'.

image d., extrafocal. The distance of an image formed by an optical system from the secondary focal point of the system.

image d., reduced. The image distance divided by the index of refraction of the medium in which the image lies, the reciprocal being the reduced image vergence.

infinite d. The distance from which light emanates to strike an optical surface with parallel rays. In vision testing, it is usually considered to approximate 20 ft., or 6 m.

interocular d. 1. The distance between the centers of rotation of the eyes; the length of the base line. 2. The distance between the optical centers of the two eyepieces of a binocular instrument.

interpupillary d. The distance between the centers of the pupils of the eyes. Unless otherwise specified, it refers to the distance when the eyes are fixed at infinity. Abbreviation *P.D.* Syn., *pupillary distance.*

motivator, d. Stereomotivator.

object d. In optics, the distance from the optical surface to the object. In compound optical systems, it is expressed as the distance from the primary principal plane to the object. Symbol u.

object d., extrafocal. The distance of an object from the primary focal point of an optical system.

object d., reduced. The object distance divided by the index of refraction of the medium in which the object lies. The reciprocal of this quantity is known as the reduced object vergence.

optical center d. The distance between the optical centers of a pair of mounted spectacle lenses without prescribed prism or with prescribed prism neutralized.

orthoplastic d. The perceived distance of an image, especially from an optical instrument, when it is equal to the actual physical distance of the object.

pupillary d. Interpupillary distance.

reduced d. The distance between any two points in an optical medium, divided by the index of refraction of the medium. It represents the distance that light would travel in the medium in the same time that it would travel the distance between the two points in air. Syn., *equivalent distance; reduced separation.*

sighting center d. The distance between the sighting center and the point of intersection of the line of sight with the anterior surface of the cornea.

stop d. The distance between the back vertex of a spectacle lens and the center of rotation of the eye, the latter being considered the field stop of the motile eye.

vertex d. 1. The distance, along the line of sight, from the posterior surface of a spectacle lens to the apex of the cornea, with the eye in the straightforward position. 2. The distance, along the line of sight, from the plane containing the center of the edge of a spectacle lens to the apex of the cornea, with the eye in a straightforward position.

working d. 1. In retinoscopy, the distance from the plane of the correcting lenses to the peephole of the retinoscope. 2. The distance at which the patient desires or is required to read or perform other essential functions. 3. In the use of microscopes and other optical devices, the distance from the objective lens to the object viewed.

distichia (dis-tik'e-ah). Distichiasis.
distichiasis (dis-tih-ki'ah-sis). An

anomalous condition in which there are two rows of eyelashes, one being normal, the other being on the inner lid border and turning in against the eye. The Meibomian glands are absent when this condition is present. Syn., *distichia.*

Distinguished Service Foundation of Optometry. An organization sponsoring optometric research; established in 1927 and incorporated in 1931 in Washington, D.C.

distometer (dis-tom'eh-ter). A device for determining the distance between the back surface of a spectacle lens and the apex of the cornea.

distortion. 1. An aberration as a result of unequal magnification of object points not on the optical axis of a lens system. 2. Any change in which the image does not conform to the shape of the object, such as when viewed through a cylindrical lens.

barrel-shaped d. Distortion resulting from decreasing magnification with increasing distance of object points from the axis of an optical system. As a result of this distortion, the corners of the image of a square would be closer to the center than expected, with a resulting barrel-shaped appearance. Syn., *positive distortion.*

Fig. 14. Barrel-shaped distortion. (From *Fundamentals of Optics*, ed. 3, Jenkins and White, McGraw-Hill, 1957)

negative d. Pincushion distortion.

pincushion d. Distortion resulting from increasing magnification with increasing distance of object points from the axis of an optical system. As a result of this distortion, the corners of the image of a square would be farther from the center than expected, with a resulting pincushion appearance. Syn., *negative distortion.*

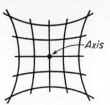

Fig. 15. Pincushion distortion. (From *Fundamentals of Optics*, ed. 3, Jenkins and White, McGraw-Hill, 1957)

positive d. Barrel-shaped distortion.

prism d. Differential magnification or differential displacement of objects in the field of view seen through a thin prism, resulting essentially in straight lines appearing curved.

distribution. The arrangement in space or time of things of any kind; the arrangement of values in a collection of data.

frequency d. In statistics, an ordered group of measurements or counts characterized by numbers of cases in each class range of sizes or counts. It may be presented as a table giving the frequency for each class, graphically as a histogram consisting of bars for each class of a height proportional to the number in that class, or by a continuous curve (frequency polygon) in which the frequency is represented by the height of an ordinate erected at the midpoint of the class.

frequency d., asymmetrical. Skew frequency distribution.

frequency d., Bernoulli. Binomial frequency distribution.

frequency d., bimodal. A frequency distribution showing two

modes or humps, suggesting, but not proving, that the sample was characterized by two types.

frequency d., binomial. A discrete or discontinuous frequency distribution, the mathematical form of which is derived from the expansion of the binomial $(p + q)^n$, in which p is the probability of the occurrence of an event and $q = (1 - p)$ is the probability of its nonoccurrence. Common examples of the binomial distribution are furnished by the tossing of pennies or the throwing of dice. As the number of classes is increased indefinitely, it approaches the normal curve. Syn., *Bernoulli frequency distribution.*

frequency d., Gaussian. Normal frequency distribution.

frequency d., normal. A continuous form of frequency distribution often encountered in biological or other data. It is symmetrical, the central classes are the most numerous, and a decrease in frequency is obtained toward both larger and smaller class values according to a relatively simple mathematical law. Syn., *Gaussian frequency distribution.*

frequency d., Poisson. A discrete or discontinuous frequency distribution in which the variates have the discrete values of 1, 2, 3, . . . n. If the probability of an event is very small, but enough independent cases are available to give adequate frequencies, the distribution will be of the Poisson type. Examples of this distribution are found in the counts of the types of corpuscles in diluted blood, or in the occurrence of scarce organisms in small areas or in small volumes of fluids.

frequency d., skew. An asymmetrical frequency distribution in which the two tails differ significantly and sometimes greatly in length. Syn., *asymmetrical frequency distribution.*

frequency d., symmetrical. A frequency distribution which is symmetrical about the central highest frequency, with the two tails not differing significantly in length. The normal frequency distribution is symmetrical.

frequency d., unimodal. A frequency distribution characterized by one mode or hump, suggesting, but not proving, that the sample is homogeneous. This is the more common type of distribution and the only one for which the mean, standard deviation, etc., have the proper significance.

light d., asymmetrical. Light distribution from a luminaire or a lamp, in which the distribution is not the same in all vertical planes.

light d., symmetrical. Light distribution from a luminaire or a lamp, in which the distribution is substantially the same in all vertical planes.

divergence (di-ver′jens). 1. Binocularly, a deviation or a relative movement of the lines of sight of the two eyes outward from parallelism, so that the lines of sight intersect behind the eyes, or from some other relative position of reference, so that the lines of sight intersect at a greater distance in front of the eyes or a lesser distance behind; negative convergence. 2. Monocularly, a deviation or a movement of the line of sight of an eye outward from a straightforward or other position of reference. 3. The directional property of a bundle of light rays, as when emanating from a point source; to be distinguished from the convergence property of a bundle of rays directed toward a real image point.

consecutive d. Exotropia occurring in a previously esotropic individual and attributed to development of marked amblyopia ex anopsia with a resultant loss of convergence function. Syn., *secondary divergence.*

excess, d. 1. Exotropia or high exophoria in distant vision associated with normal fixation in near vision. 2. Exophoria or exotropia in distant vision, exophoria or exotropia at near being considered as convergence insufficiency. 3. Exophoria or exotropia greater at distance than at near.

fusional d. Lateral divergence of the lines of sight of the two eyes in response to fusion stimuli, such as may be induced clinically by base-in prisms.

insufficiency, d. 1. Esotropia or high esophoria in distant vision associated with normal fixation in near vision. 2. Esophoria or esotropia in distant vision, esophoria or esotropia at near being considered convergence excess. 3. Esophoria or esotropia greater at distance than at near.

paralysis, d. See under *paralysis.*

secondary d. Consecutive divergence.

vertical d. Vertical deviation or relative vertical movement of the lines of sight of the two eyes from parallelism.

    vertical d., dissociated. Double hyperphoria.

    vertical d., negative. Vertical divergence in which the left eye deviates upward in relation to the right.

    vertical d., positive. Vertical divergence in which the right eye deviates upward in relation to the left.

Dixon's mirror telescope (dik'sunz). See under *telescope.*

Dixon Mann's sign (dik'sun manz'). Mann's sign.

D.L. Abbreviation for *difference limen.*

D.O. Diploma in Ophthalmology (United Kingdom).

Dobson's test (dob'sunz). See under *test.*

Dogiel's (do-zhe-elz') **cell; corpuscle.** See under the nouns.

dolichostenomelia (dol"ih-ko-sten"-o-me'le-ah). Arachnodactyly.

doll's eye sign. Doll's head phenomenon. See under *phenomenon.*

Döllinger's (del'ing-erz) **membrane; ring.** See under the nouns.

Dollond's objective (dŏl'ondz). See under *objective.*

Dolman's test (dŏl'manz). See under *test.*

dominance. The fact or state of having the prevailing or controlling influence.

cerebral phi movement d. A visual dominance demonstrated by the perception of apparent movement in either the left half or the right half of the visual field, in a test situation in which the center light of three lights is constantly fixated, either monocularly or binocularly, and the center light is flashed alternatingly with the two side lights. The two side lights may be two actual lights or, with binocular fixation, they may be diplopic images of a single light situated either nearer or farther from the subject than the fixated light. This visual dominance is attributed to a superiority of one half of the visual cortex over the other half.

crossed d. A condition in which the dominant eye and dominant hand are on opposite sides; right-handed and left-eyed, or vice versa.

eye d. Ocular dominance.

ocular d. 1. The superiority of one eye over the other in some perceptual or motor task. The term is usually applied to those superiorities in function which are not based on a difference in visual acuity between the two eyes, or on a dysfunction of the neuromuscular apparatus of one of the eyes. 2. Sighting ocular dominance.

ocular d., alternating. Mixed ocular dominance.

ocular d., mixed. A condition in which one eye is dominant in one function and the other eye is dominant in another function. Syn., *alternating ocular dominance.*

ocular d., motor. Ocular dominance based on a superiority of the neuromuscular apparatus of one eye over that of the other; said to be demonstrated by various sighting dominance tests, by the convergence test for ocular dominance, and by other motor tests.

ocular d., perceptual. Ocular dominance based on a sensory superiority of one eye over the other rather than on a motor difference between the two eyes. Types of perceptual ocular dominance include rivalry ocular dominance and the dominance demonstrated by the chromatic test.

ocular d., pseudosensory. An apparent ocular dominance resulting from a difference in visual acuity between the two eyes.

ocular d., rivalry. A perceptual ocular dominance in which the stimulus presented to one eye is perceived for a significantly greater percentage of the time than the stimulus simultaneously presented to the other eye, when rivalry is induced by a difference in the two stimuli.

ocular d., sighting. A type of motor ocular dominance in which the same eye is usually or always used in visual tasks requiring unilateral sighting. It is best demonstrated by tests made with the manoptoscope or the V-Scope in which a subject is not aware that he is being required to sight with only one eye. See also *preferred eye.*

visual d. 1. Ocular dominance. 2. A superiority of one member of a paired part of the visual mechanism over the other member of the pair. For example, a dominance of the left half of the visual cortex over the right half. See also *visual laterality.*

dominator, photopic. Granit's term for a retinal element exhibiting spectral sensitivity for a wide spectral band with a maximum corresponding to that of the light-adapted retina containing cones. See also *dominator-modulator theory.*

dominator, scotopic. Granit's term for a retinal element exhibiting spectral sensitivity for a wide spectral band with a maximum corresponding to the dark-adapted retina or to the absorption curve of visual purple. See also *dominator-modulator theory.*

D.O.M.S. Diploma in Ophthalmic Medicine and Surgery (United Kingdom).

Donders' (don'derz) **painful accommodation; corpuscles; experiment; reduced eye; glaucoma; law; line; method; wire optometer; patterns; rings; table; test; theories.** See under the nouns.

Doppler effect (dop'ler). See under *effect.*

D. Opt. Diploma in Ophthalmics (Institute of Optical Science).

dorsalis nasi (dōr-sa'lis na'zi). The nasal artery.

dorsum sellae (dōr'sum sel'i). A plate of bone which forms the posterior boundary of the sella turcica.

D. Orth. Diploma in Orthoptics (British Optical Association).

Doryl (do'ril). A trade name for carbaminoylcholine.

D.O.S. Abbreviation for *Doctor of Ocular Science* or *Doctor of Optometric Science.*

dot. 1. A small spot or a small round mark, such as may be made with a pen or a pencil. 2. Anything small and comparatively like a speck.

creek d's. Gunn's dots.

Gunn's d's. Small, white or yellowish nonpathological dots sometimes observed in the eyegrounds, usually in clusters. Syn., *creek dots.*

Mittendorf's d. A white dot seen, with the biomicroscope, 1 or 2 mm. nasal to the posterior pole of the crystalline lens. It appears to rest on the posterior lens surface and to serve as a place of attachment for one or several corkscrewlike white threads, remnants of the tunica vasculosa lentis, which hang down and float freely in the vitreous.

Nettleship's d's. Numerous small white dots in the peripheral retina, described by Nettleship, and said to be associated with familial pigment changes and night blindness.

Tay's d's. Yellowish colloid bodies occurring in or near the central region of the retina in Tay's choroiditis.

Trantas' d's. Small white dots in the limbal conjunctiva, described by Trantas, and said to be associated with vernal conjunctivitis.

doublet (dub'let). A fixed combination of two lenses, as in a telescope objective or a microscope eyepiece.

achromatic d. A combination of two lenses, usually a crown positive and a flint negative, which corrects for chromatic aberration.

orthoscopic d. A combination of two identical lenses with a stop midway between them, correcting for spherical aberration with respect to the entrance and exit pupils. This system is relatively free of distortion. Syn., *orthoscopic lenses; rectilinear lens.*

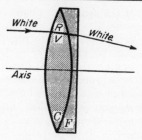

Fig. 16. Achromatic doublet. (From *Fundamentals of Optics*, ed. 3, Jenkins and White, McGraw-Hill, 1957)

separated d. An achromatic optical system employing two thin lenses made of the same glass and separated by a distance equal to half the sum of their focal lengths.

Troutman's air space d. A plastic anterior chamber implant consisting of a biconvex lens and a biconcave lens, separated by an air space, used in uniocular aphakia to correct ametropia and minimize aniseikonia.

Wollaston's d. A simple microscope consisting of a combination of two separated planoconvex lenses whose plane faces are both turned toward the object. The focal lengths of the lenses are in the ratio of 1:3, the stronger lens being the one nearer the object.

douzième (dōo-zyem'). A unit for designating lens thickness, equal to ¹⁄₁₂ of a ligne, or approximately 0.19 mm. *Obs.*

Dove prism. See under *prism.*

Doyne's (doinz) **cataract; choroiditis; occluder.** See under the nouns.

Draeger tonometer. See under *tonometer.*

Draper's law (dra'perz). See under *law.*

drill, lens. A machine with a revolving point, usually a diamond, used to bore holes in lenses to be fitted to rimless mountings.

Driver's test. See under *test.*

driving, alpha. Photic driving.

driving, photic. The stimulation of the eye with a flashing light at frequencies which induce an alteration in the normal alpha rhythm, as evidenced in electroencephalographic recordings of brain waves from the occipital cortex. Syn., *alpha driving.*

drop. 1. In a spectacle lens, the distance of the geometrical or mechanical center below the mounting line. 2. In a spectacle lens, the difference between the distance of the mounting line below the top of the lens and the distance of the mounting line above the bottom of the lens. *Rare.*

drops. A popular name for any solution instilled into the eyes.

dropsy, subchoroidal (drop′se). An accumulation of fluid between the retina and the choroid.

dropsy, subsclerotic (drop′se). An accumulation of fluid between the choroid and the sclera.

Druault's (dru′altz) **marginal bundle; theory.** See under the nouns.

drum, optokinetic. Optokinetoscope.

drusen (dru′sen). Small, sharply defined, circular, yellow or white dots lying below the level of the retinal vessels, either discrete or coalesced into larger masses, located throughout the fundus but tending to collect in the region of the macula, around the optic disk, or in the periphery. They may occur in adolescence, but generally do not appear until middle age or later, consist of hyaline material on the lamina vitrea of the choroid, are considered to be formed by secretions of cells of the pigment epithelium due to degenerative changes, and usually do not interfere with vision. Syn., *colloid bodies; hyaline bodies.*

optic disk, d. of the. Sharply defined, white or yellow masses of hyaline material on the optic disk, which may protrude over the disk margin and project into the vitreous in grapelike clusters.

They are attributed to degenerative changes in the glial cells and may become calcified.

Drysdale (drīz′dāl) **method; principle.** See under *method.*

Duane's (du-ānz′) **chart; clinometer; field; phenomenon; rule; screen; syndrome; table; test; theory.** See under the nouns.

duct. A tube or channel for conveying fluid.

lacrimal d. 1. Each of about a dozen ducts that receive the secretion of both lobes of a lacrimal gland and empty into the lateral superior fornix; one may empty into the lateral inferior fornix. 2. Incorrectly, the lacrimal canaliculus leading from the lacrimal punctum toward the lacrimal sac, or the nasolacrimal duct emptying into the inferior meatus of the nose.

nasolacrimal d. A membranous tube within the bony nasolacrimal canal, connecting the lacrimal sac to the inferior meatus of the nose, for the drainage of tears. This distal portion of the lacrimal apparatus has a mucous membrane lined by pseudostratified columnar epithelium with some goblet cells. Less accurately, the nasal duct.

tear d. 1. Nasolacrimal duct. 2. One of the dozen or so ducts of the lacrimal gland.

duction (duk′shun). 1. Under monocular conditions, the movement of an eye by the extraocular muscles. 2. The movement, or the test for movement, of the two eyes in opposite directions to maintain fusion through prisms, at a fixed testing distance; more correctly termed a *vergence.*

compensating d. Vergence used to overcome existing heterophoria.

jump d. A rapid change in convergence to maintain fusion induced by an instantaneous change in base-in or base-out prism effect.

lateral d. The movement, or the test for movement, of the two eyes in opposite directions to maintain fusion through base-in or base-out prism effect, at a fixed testing distance; more correctly termed *induced convergence* or *divergence.*

vertical d. The movement of the two eyes in opposite directions to maintain fusion through base-up or base-down prism effect at a fixed testing distance; more correctly termed *induced supravergence* or *infravergence.*

ductus nasolacrimalis (duk'tus na″-zo-lak″rih-mah'lis). Nasolacrimal duct.

Duddell's membrane (dud'elz). Descemet's membrane.

Duhring's disease (dūr'ingz). Dermatitis herpetiformis.

Duke-Elder lamp (dūk-el'der). See under *lamp.*

Dunnington-Berke test. See under *test.*

duochroism (du″o-kro'izm). The property of showing a different shade or hue by reflected light than by transmitted light.

dura mater (du'rah ma'ter). The outermost tough member of the three meninges covering the brain, the spinal cord, and the optic nerve. At the optic foramen it divides into two layers, the outer becoming continuous with the periorbita, the inner forming the dural covering of the optic nerve and becoming continuous with the sclera.

dural sheath (du'ral shēth). Dura mater.

duration of fixation. 1. The time interval between saccadic movements of the eyes, especially while reading. 2. The time of exposure of a tachistoscope.

Durham tonometer. See under *tonometer.*

Dutemps and Cestan sign (du-tahn' ses-tan'). See under *sign.*

Dvorine's (dvor'ēnz) **charts; plates; stereograms; pseudoisochromatic test.** See under the nouns.

dynamometer (di″nah-mom'eh-ter). 1. An instrument for estimating the magnifying power of lenses. 2. Landolt's ophthalmodynamometer. 3. An instrument for measuring and training relative convergence.

Dynascope (di″nah-skōp'). A small, manually controlled instrument, hand-held before the right eye, containing a pair of articulated plane mirrors which may be synchronously rotated to alter the direction of incident light. Light entering the front opening of the instrument is reflected by the first mirror onto the second mirror, which in turn reflects the light through the rear peephole. It is used for fusion and vergence training, and three-dimensional viewing. Syn., *Dynamic Stereoscope; Engelmann Stereoscope.*

dysadaptation (dis-ad″ap-ta'shun). Lack of, or defective, adjustment of the visual mechanism to variations in light intensity.

dysanagnosia (dis-an″ag-no'se-ah). A form of dyslexia in which there is an inability to recognize certain words.

dysantigraphia (dis-an″tih-graf'e-ah, -gra'fe-ah). The inability to copy writing although the words can be seen.

dysaptation (dis″ap-ta'shun). Dysadaptation.

dysautonomia (dis-aw″to-no'me-ah). Riley-Day syndrome.

dyscephaly, mandibulo-oculo-facial (dis-sef'ah-le). A combination of congenital malformations involving the face and eyes and including hypoplasia of the mandible, a beak-shaped nose giving the face a birdlike appearance, congenital cataracts, and usually microphthalmos. Other associated anomalies may include dwarfism, dental deformities, atrophy and hypotrichosis of the skin of the face, and strabismus. Syn., *dyscephalic mandibulo-oculo-facial syndrome; Hallerman-Streiff syndrome.*

dyschromasia (dis″kro-ma′ze-ah). Dyschromatopsia.

dyschromatope (dis-kro′mah-tōp″). One having dyschromatopsia.

dyschromatopia (dis″kro-mah-to′pe-ah). Dyschromatopsia.

dyschromatopsia (dis″kro-mah-top′-se-ah). Imperfect discrimination of colors; incomplete or partial color blindness. See also *chromatelopsia.* Syn., *dyschromasia.*

dyscoria (dis-ko′re-ah). Abnormality in the shape of the pupil.

dyserethesia (dis″er-e-the′ze-ah). A reduced sensibility to stimuli.

dysgenesis, mesodermal, of the cornea and iris (dis-jen′eh-sis). Rieger's disease.

dyskeratosis (dis″ker-ah-to′sis). A disturbance in normal keratinization, resulting, in the eye, in hornification of the epithelial layer of the cornea or conjunctiva.

   benign intraepithelial d. A hereditary dyskeratosis of the conjunctiva, resembling a pterygium, and of the mouth, resembling leukoplakia. The eye lesions may spread to cover the cornea and cause blindness.

dyslexia (dis-lek′se-ah). Partial alexia in which letters but not words may be read, or in which words may be read but not understood.

dysmegalopsia (dis″meg-ah-lop′se-ah). A condition in which the perceptual size of objects is abnormal, termed *micropsia* when smaller, and *macropsia* when larger.

dysmetropsia (dis″met-rop′se-ah). The inability to evaluate properly the measure or size of perceived objects; macropsia or micropsia.

dysmorphia, cervico-oculo-facial (dis-mor′fe-ah). Cervico-oculoacoustic syndrome.

dysnomia (dis-no′me-ah). Anomia.

Dyson interferometer (di′sun). See under *interferometer.*

dysopia (dis-o′pe-ah). Dysopsia.

dysopsia (dis-op′se-ah). Defective or uncomfortable vision.

dysostosis (dis″os-to′sis). Defective bone formation.

   craniofacial d., hereditary. A developmental cranial deformity characterized by a knoblike protuberance on the frontal bone, a hooked nose, protruding lower jaw and teeth, divergent strabismus, wide separation and proptosis of the eyes, and optic atrophy. It is familial and is fully developed in the first few months of life. Syn., *Crouzon's disease.*

   diabetic exophthalmic d. Schüller-Christian-Hand disease.

   hypophysaria, d. Schüller-Christian-Hand disease.

   mandibulofacial d. A rare congenital anomaly characterized by antimongoloid oblique palpebral fissures, coloboma of the lower eyelids (sometimes upper), hypoplasia of the facial bones, especially malar and mandible, malformations of the external ears and sometimes middle and inner ears, an abnormally large mouth with high palate and abnormal dentition, fistulae between the mouth and the ears, and tongue-shaped projections of the hairline onto the cheek. Syn., *Franceschetti syndrome; Franceschetti-Zwahlen syndrome; Treacher Collins syndrome.*

   multiplex, d. Hurler's disease.

dysphotia (dis-fo′te-ah). Myopia. *Obs.*

dysplasia (dis-pla′se-ah). Abnormal tissue development or growth occurring subsequent to the appearance of the primordial cells.

   encephalo-ophthalmic d. Bilateral congenital dysplasia of ocular tissue including the retina, choroid, and optic nerve, and of the central nervous system. The retina is detached and bunched into a mass fused with remnants of the tunica vasculosa lentis. Retinal hemorrhages are frequent and atrophy and gliosis are widespread. Associated ocular anomalies may include microphthalmus, colobomata, cataract, and glaucoma. Neurological symptoms include microcephalus or hydrocephalus and mental deficiency. Skeletal deformities and systemic anomalies may also be present. Syn., *retinal dysplasia; Krause's syndrome.*

epiphysialis punctata, d. Stippled epiphyses.

iridocorneal mesodermal d. Axenfeld's syndrome.

oculo-auricular d. Goldenhar's syndrome.

oculodentodigital d. Dysplasia of the extremities, such as campodactyly, syndactyly and polydactyly, of the teeth, and of the eyes, such as microphthalmus and coloboma. Syn., *oculodentodigital syndrome.*

oculovertebral d. A congenital syndrome consisting of malformations of the spine and ribs, unilateral dysplasia of the maxilla resulting in facial asymmetry and dental malocclusion, and unilateral microphthalmos, anophthalmos, or cryptophthalmos. Syn., *oculovertebral syndrome; Weyers-Thier syndrome.*

periosteal d. Osteogenesis imperfecta.

polyostotic fibrous d. A developmental skeletal anomaly characterized by replacement of the cancellous bone and marrow by solid fibrous tissue with a resulting widening of the affected bones. Endocrine dysfunction and skin pigmentation may occur. Involvement of the cranium may produce proptosis, papilledema, and optic atrophy. Syn., *disseminated osteitis fibrosa; fibrous osteodystrophy.*

posterior marginal d. of the cornea. Embryotoxon.

retinal d. 1. Any abnormal differentiation of retinal tissue occurring subsequent to the appearance of the primordial cells. 2. Encephalo-ophthalmic dysplasia.

dystrophia (dis-tro'fe-ah). Dystrophy.

adiposa corneae, d. A primary fatty degeneration of the cornea occurring physiologically as an arcus senilis. Only rarely is it pathological, affecting either the central or the peripheral area. Syn., *steatosis corneae; xanthomatosis corneae.*

adiposogenitalis, d. Froehlich's syndrome.

annularis, d. Ring-shaped corneal dystrophy.

calcarea corneae, d. A rare primary degeneration of the cornea in which deposits of calcium phosphate occur in its superficial layers.

corneae granulosa, d. Granular corneal dystrophy.

corneae maculosa, d. Macular corneal dystrophy.

corneae reticulata, d. Latticelike corneal dystrophy.

endothelialis corneae, d. Cornea guttata.

epithelialis corneae, d. Epithelial corneal dystrophy of Fuchs.

filiformis profunda corneae, d. A degeneration of the cornea characterized by fine, wavy, threadlike opacities deep in the stroma, just anterior to Descemet's membrane.

mesodermalis congenita hyperplastica, d. Marchesani's syndrome.

mesodermalis congenita hypoplastica, d. Arachnodactyly.

punctiformis profunda corneae, d. Deep punctiform corneal dystrophy.

uratica corneae, d. Keratitis urica.

urica, d. Keratitis urica.

dystrophy (dis'tro-fe). 1. Faulty or defective nutrition. 2. Abnormal or defective development. 3. Degeneration.

adiposogenital d. Froehlich's syndrome.

corneal d. Defective nutrition, abnormal development, or degeneration of the cornea.

corneal d., annular. Ring-shaped corneal dystrophy.

corneal d., band-shaped. A degeneration of the cornea characterized by the slow development of a horizontal gray band in the central area, first appearing as a slight turbidity at the level of Bowman's membrane in which are pathognomonic, small, dark, round holes. The most common form is secondary to iridocyclitis, a less common form is primary and occurs in the apparently normal eyes of the elderly, and the rarest form occurs in children, most of whom have rheumatism associated with a chronic iritis. It may also follow trauma due to exposure to irritants. Syn., *zonular corneal dystrophy; keratitis petrificans; band keratopathy; zonular keratopathy.*

corneal d., band-shaped nodular. Bietti's nodular corneal dystrophy.

corneal d., Bietti's nodular. A degeneration of the cornea characterized by elevated nodular opacities distributed in a horizontal band-shaped area within the palpebral fissure, usually bilateral and mainly found in hot arid regions. Syn., *band-shaped nodular corneal dystrophy.*

corneal d., Bückler's annular. A rare dominant progressive degeneration of the corneal epithelium and Bowman's membrane, commencing in childhood and characterized by thin, irregularly shaped, threadlike grayish opacities which gradually merge and obscure vision. The condition

occurs in episodes accompanied by pain, subsides at puberty, and reappears about two decades later in association with ulcers. Syn., *Bückler's corneal dystrophy type IV.*

corneal d., Bückler's type I. Granular corneal dystrophy.

corneal d., Bückler's type II. Macular corneal dystrophy.

corneal d., Bückler's type III. Latticelike corneal dystrophy.

corneal d., Bückler's type IV. Bückler's annular corneal dystrophy.

corneal d., crumblike. Granular corneal dystrophy.

corneal d., crystalline. A dominant, inherited, bilateral and symmetrical degeneration of the cornea occurring early in life and characterized by numerous fine needlelike opacities in the anterior stroma, often forming a central ring pattern. Syn., *Schnyder's corneal dystrophy.*

corneal d., deep filiform. Dystrophia filiformis profunda corneae.

corneal d., deep punctiform. A hereditary, bilateral, corneal dystrophy, described by Pillat, characterized by deep, grayish to bluish, fine punctate and short linear opacities in the central area, surrounded by a clear normal zone, and numerous, short, glassy, radial lines at the limbus peripheral to the clear area.

corneal d., Dimmer's. Latticelike corneal dystrophy.

corneal d., ectatic marginal. Peripheral corneal ectasia.

corneal d., endothelial. Cornea guttata.

corneal d., epithelial (of Fuchs). A degeneration of the cornea first described by Fuchs as an epithelial dystrophy, but later found to be dependent on a prior endothelial dystrophy. It occurs most commonly in females past the age of 50, the epithelial changes start with an edema consisting of vesicles which later become opacities, and after an extremely slow course, the cornea becomes opaque and insensitive.

corneal d., epithelial diffuse. A dominant familial degeneration of the corneal epithelium commencing in infancy and involving Bowman's membrane in the later stages. Repeated acute attacks leave scars and lead to reduced visual acuity.

corneal d., epithelial juvenile (of Kraupa). A degeneration of the cornea occurring early in life and involving the surface epithelium and, to a lesser extent, the corneal stroma.

corneal d., Fehr's spotted. Macular corneal dystrophy.

corneal d., fleck. François' speckled corneal dystrophy.

corneal d., Fleischer's whorllike. Vortex corneal dystrophy.

corneal d., François' cloudy central. A rare, inherited, familial, bilateral dystrophy of the corneal stroma characterized by numerous, small, grayish, snowflakelike opacities, primarily occurring in the pupillary area and the deep layers. It is unaccompanied by pain or inflammation, is essentially nonprogressive, and vision remains unimpaired.

corneal d., François' speckled. An autosomal, dominantly inherited, bilateral degeneration of the corneal stroma characterized by diffusely scattered dot opacities. It is either congenital or occurs in early life, is benign and nonprogressive, and vision is unimpaired.

corneal d., Fuchs'. See *dystrophy, corneal, epithelial (of Fuchs).*

corneal d., granular. A dominant inherited degeneration of the cornea with onset usually at about 5 years of age, in which, initially, small, superficial, and deep,

white dots occur in the center of the cornea or form radiating lines from the corneal center. The lesions gradually increase in size and have irregular shapes and patterns. Vision is at most only mildly affected. Syn., *Bückler's corneal dystrophy (type I); crumblike corneal dystrophy; Groenouw's nodular corneal dystrophy (type I).*

corneal d., Groenouw's macular (type II). Macular corneal dystrophy.

corneal d., Groenouw's nodular (type I). Granular corneal dystrophy.

corneal d., Haab-Dimmer. Latticelike corneal dystrophy.

corneal d., hereditary, deep. A rare, autosomal, dominantly inherited, bilateral degeneration of the cornea characterized by vesicularlike areas surrounded by gray polymorphous opacities in the corneal endothelium, in Descemet's membrane, and occasionally in the deep stroma. It is either congenital or occurs early in life, remains limited to the posterior cornea, and is essentially nonprogressive. Syn., *polymorphous deep degeneration of the cornea.*

corneal d., Koby's. A bilateral progressive degeneration of the corneal epithelium with formation of linear fissures in Bowman's membrane, occurring in middleaged, healthy persons without inflammation or discomfort. A faint opalescence bounded by a line of relief appears in the central region of the cornea, the underlying stroma is hazy, and vision deteriorates progressively.

corneal d., Kraupa's epithelial. See *dystrophy, corneal, epithelial juvenile (of Kraupa).*

corneal d., latticelike. A slowly progressive, dominant, familial degeneration of the superficial stroma of the cornea, beginning occasionally in infancy but usually at puberty, characterized by the deposit of fine lines of hyalinelike material in a cobweb, star-shaped, or crisscross formation. The lines increase in number and thickness into a diffuse opacification in later life, with vision mildly or severely affected. Syn., *Haab's degeneration; lattice degeneration of the cornea; reticular degeneration of the cornea; Bückler's corneal dystrophy (type III); Dimmer's corneal dystrophy; reticular corneal dystrophy; lattice keratitis; reticular keratitis.*

corneal d., lipid. Any of several corneal dystrophies in which lipoid deposits are found in the cornea.

corneal d., macular. A recessive familial degeneration initially affecting Bowman's membrane and then the surface epithelium and stroma. It commences in the first decade of life as a diffuse subepithelial opacification, with patches of greater density, and gradually increases in intensity, especially centrally, until, about the age of 30, little vision remains. Syn., *Bückler's corneal dystrophy (type II); Groenouw's macular corneal dystrophy (type II); Fehr's spotted corneal dystrophy.*

corneal d., marginal. Arcus senilis.

corneal d., Meesmann's. A dominant, hereditary, bilateral dystrophy involving only the corneal epithelium. It commences at about 18 months of age, with gradual progression, and is characterized by numerous small punctate opacities regularly distributed throughout the epithelium.

corneal d., nodular. Granular corneal dystrophy.

corneal d., reticular. Latticelike corneal dystrophy.

corneal d., ring-shaped. A bilateral, annular or ring-shaped degeneration, possibly dominant familial, affecting Bowman's membrane. The onset is early, acute attacks are frequent, and eventually poor vision results. In the late stage, the cornea has a moplike appearance. Syn., *dystrophia annularis; annular corneal dystrophy.*

corneal d., Salzmann's. An early hypertrophic and later degenerative change in the superficial corneal tissues, occurring in persons previously affected with phlyctenular keratitis. It is rare, noninflammatory, slowly progressive, and is characterized by the presence of several bluish-white nodules on the surface of the cornea. It is nonfamilial, usually unilateral, mainly affects females, and may appear at any age.

corneal d., Schnyder's. Crystalline corneal dystrophy.

corneal d., spotted. Macular corneal dystrophy.

corneal d., Terrien's marginal. Peripheral corneal ectasia. See under *ectasia, corneal.*

corneal d., total. Degeneration of the cornea involving all of its layers.

corneal d., uric. A rare corneal dystrophy commencing near the limbus and progressing centrally, characterized by the deposition of uric acid crystals in the stroma and epithelium. It is accompanied by corneal vascularization and frequently by recurring ulcers and anterior uveitis. Syn., *keratitis urica.*

corneal d., vortex. A rare, dominantly inherited, corneal dystrophy involving the superficial layers of the cornea and characterized by small brownish opacities on Bowman's membrane, arranged in a whirlpool-shaped line formation radiating out from the center of the cornea. Syn., *cornea verticillata; Fleischer's whorl-like corneal dystrophy; whorl-shaped opacity.*

corneal d., zonular. Band-shaped corneal dystrophy.

dermo-chondro-corneal d. A dystrophy due to a disturbance in the metabolism of polysaccharides and characterized by deformities of the hands commencing between the ages of 1 and 2, of the feet about the age of 5, xanthomata of the skin also about age 5, and bilateral corneal dystrophy, consisting of superficial and central opacities, appearing about age 8 or 9. The face, spine, and cranium are unaffected and intelligence is normal. Syn., *François' dermo-chondro-corneal dystrophy; osteochondral-dermal-corneal dystrophy.*

François' dermo-chondro-corneal d. Dermo-chondro-corneal dystrophy.

Laurence-Moon-Biedl d. Laurence-Moon-Biedl syndrome.

myotonic d. A heredofamilial disease characterized by a selective atrophy of muscles with lessened power to relax after contraction, baldness, atrophy of the gonads, premature senility, mental enfeeblement, and such ocular manifestations as fine punctate subcapsular lenticular opacities, low intraocular pressure, ptosis, enophthalmos, and occasionally lagophthalmos or blepharoconjunctivitis. Syn., *Steinert's disease.*

osteochondral-dermal-corneal d.

Dermo-chondro-corneal dystrophy.

progressive tapetochoroidal d. Choroideremia.

reticular d. of the retina. A rare progressive dystrophy of the pigment epithelium of the retina, characterized initially by the accumulation of pigment at the fovea; progresses to the formation of a cecocentral network of black pigmented lines with enlarged black spots at their junctions. In the later stages the network gradually disintegrates and fades, and small white areas appear in the deep retina. It is either congenital or occurs in early childhood and may be accompanied by deafmutism.

senile macular d. Macular degeneration occurring in the aged without apparent clinical cause and characterized by fine pigmentary stippling which becomes denser as the disease progresses, with a corresponding loss in vision. It typically commences unilaterally and eventually becomes bilateral.

Sorsby's macular d. A rare dominantly inherited dystrophy of the macula which is typically progressive and, in the elderly, is sometimes indistinguishable from senile macular degeneration. Vision is but slightly affected in childhood, except for color vision anomalies, but is significantly reduced in adult life.

Stargardt's foveal d. Stargardt's disease.

tapetoretinal d. Tapetoretinal degeneration.

E

E. Abbreviation for *emmetropia* or *esophoria*.

E. Symbol for (1) *illumination;* (2) *coefficient of ocular rigidity*.

Eales's disease (ēlz'es). See under *disease*.

Eames test (ēmz). See under *test*.

Eastman chart (ēst'man). See under *chart*.

Ebbecke's theory (eb'ek-ēz). See under *theory*.

Ebbinghaus' (eb'ing-hows) **figure; visual illusion; law.** See under the nouns.

ecblepharos (ek-blef'ah-rōs). A prosthesis mounted on the posterior side of a spectacle frame to simulate the appearance of an eye, usually consisting of a metal piece on which an eye and the surrounding structures are painted.

eccanthus (ek-kan'thus). A fleshy growth at the angle of the eyelids.

ecchymosis of the conjunctiva (ek"-ih-mo'sis). An extravasation of blood under the bulbar conjunctiva; a subconjunctival hemorrhage.

ecchymosis of the eyelid (ek"ih-mo'sis). An extravasation of blood into the loose areolar tissue of the eyelid, or the resulting discoloration of the skin. Syn., *black eye; suggilation of the eyelid*.

eccle rest (ek'l rest). A cork or zylonite pad attachable to the underside of a saddle bridge to distribute the weight of the frame over a larger area.

E.C.G. Abbreviation for *electrocorticogram*.

echelette (esh-eh-let'). A diffraction grating designed by R. W. Wood for the production of infrared spectra, made by ruling parallel V-shaped grooves in a polished metal plate.

echelle (esh-el'). A diffraction grating with a facet width of several hundred microns, hence intermediate between the narrow grooved grating with only a few microns and the echelon grating with thousands.

echelon (esh'eh-lon). A type of diffraction grating consisting of a number of rectangular blocks of glass all cut from a single plane-parallel plate of optical glass and arranged in the form of a flight of steps, each step forming a line of the grating.

echinophthalmia (e-kin"of-thal'me-ah). Inflammation of the eyelid margins with an accompanying bristlelike appearance of the lashes. *Obs.*

echogram, ocular. A recording of the reflection of ultrasonic waves from the structures of the eye, used to detect and locate intraocular tumors and to determine distances between intraocular structures.

echondroma (ek"on-dro'mah). A rare tumor of the eyelid occurring, usually, in the tarsal plate.

echophotony (ek"o-fot'o-ne). The association of certain colors with certain sounds.

ectasia (ek-ta'se-ah). Dilatation, or distention, of a hollow organ or a tubular vessel.

corneal e. A forward bulging of

the cornea as a result of intraocular pressure against corneal tissue which has been weakened by trauma, ulceration, atrophy, or inflammation.

corneal e., peripheral. Ectasia of the peripheral cornea resulting from idiopathic progressive degeneration of the marginal corneal tissue. The condition commences with an opacity resembling an arcus senilis, except that the clear zone between it and the sclera is vascularized. A gutterlike furrow appears in this area and is followed by the ectasia. Syn., *senile marginal atrophy; ectatic marginal corneal dystrophy; Terrien's marginal corneal dystrophy; peripheral furrow keratitis.*

scleral e. A bulging or distention of the sclera which may be total, as in buphthalmos, or partial, as in staphyloma.

scleral e., peripapillary. An ectasia of the peripapillary sclera resulting in an ophthalmoscopic picture of a deeply recessed optic disk.

ectiris (ek-ti′ris). The anterior endothelium of the iris.

ectochoroidea (ek″to-ko-roid′e-ah). The outer layer of the choroid; the suprachoroid.

ectocornea (ek″to-kōr′ne-ah). The anterior epithelium of the cornea.

ectodermosis erosiva pluriorificialis (ek″to-der-mo′sis). Stevens-Johnson syndrome.

ectopia (ek-to′pe-ah). Malposition or displacement of a part.

lentis, e. Displacement, subluxation, or malposition of the crystalline lens.

oculi, e. Displacement or malposition of the eyeball in the orbit.

pupillae, e. A marked displacement of the pupil from its normal position. Syn., *corectopia.*

tarsi, e. A congenital ectopia in which the tarsus is separated from the rest of the eyelid.

ectorbital (ekt′ōr-bih″tal). Situated upon or pertaining to the temporal portion of the orbit.

ectoretina (ek″to-ret′ih-nah). The pigment epithelium of the retina.

ectropion (ek-tro′pe-on). A rolling or turning outward (eversion) of the margin of an eyelid. Syn., *reflexio palpebrarum.*

atonic e. Ectropion due to loss of muscular tone, particularly of the orbicularis oculi muscle. Loss of skin tone may also contribute to the eversion.

cicatricial e. Ectropion due to scar tissue on the margins or the surrounding surfaces of the eyelids.

luxurians, e. Ectropion sarcomatosum.

mechanical e. Ectropion due to pressure from behind the eyelid. It may occur from a markedly thickened conjunctiva, as in trachoma, from tumors, or from an enlarged eyeball (buphthalmos).

paralytic e. Ectropion of the lower eyelid, due to facial paralysis involving the orbicularis oculi muscle.

sarcomatosum, e. A sequela to senile ectropion in which the conjunctiva, due to exposure, hypertrophies and produces granulation-like masses which accentuate the original ectropion. Syn., *ectropion luxurians.*

senile e. In the aged, ectropion of the lower eyelid due to atrophic changes in the eyelid structure, especially in the orbicularis oculi muscle and the lateral palpebral ligament.

spastic e. Ectropion due to contraction of the orbicularis oculi muscle together with other conditions, such as a swollen or thickened conjunctiva, staphyloma of the cornea, or a prominent or bulging eyeball. It may occur in either the upper or the lower eyelid, or in both.

uveae, e. A turning of the pigment

epithelium of the posterior iris over the pupillary margin to the anterior surface, seen as a narrow black rim of the pupil or, if extending further, as a black sector of the iris. It may occur as a congenital anomaly, or pathologically as in glaucoma or atrophy of the iris.

ectropium (ek-tro′pe-um). Ectropion.

Eddowes' (ed′ōz) **disease; syndrome.** See under the nouns.

edema (e-de′mah). Excessive amounts of fluid in the intercellular tissue spaces of the body.

angioneurotic e. A generalized, probably hereditary allergic reaction characterized by noninflammatory swelling of subcutaneous tissues and mucous membranes, with marked predilection for the face, especially the eyelids and lips, and for the viscera. It may subside in hours or remain for days, and may recur either frequently or infrequently. In the eye, it may affect the cornea, conjunctiva, or uvea. Syn., *Quincke's disease.*

Berlin's e. Commotio retinae.

Iwanoff's cystic e. Cystic degeneration of the retina.

macular vesicular e. Cystic degeneration of the macula.

preretinal e. of Guist. Central angiospastic retinopathy.

edge. 1. The border or circumferential surface of an ophthalmic lens, usually cut, ground, or polished parallel to the lens axis for mounting in a rimless frame, or to a bevel or roof-shaped surface for insertion in an eyewire or a plastic frame. 2. To grind the periphery of a lens to a desired shape and profile.

refracting e. The line of intersection of the two surface planes of a prism.

edger. A machine with a rotating, wet, abrasive stone for grinding the margins of an ophthalmic lens to a desired shape.

edging. The process of forming a lens to exact size and shape and of putting on the type of edge required for a particular mounting after it has been roughly cut to size and shape.

Edinger-Westphal nucleus (ed′ing-er-vest′fal). See under *nucleus.*

edipism (ed′ih-pizm). Intentional self-inflicted injury to the eye.

Edmond's chart (ed′mundz). See under *chart.*

Edridge-Green (ed′rij-grēn′) **lamp; test; theory.** See under the nouns.

E.E.G. Abbreviation for *electroencephalogram.*

effect. The consequence or result of an action.

Abney's e. Abney's phenomenon.

autokinetic e. Autokinetic visual illusion.

Bezold-Brücke e. Bezold-Brücke phenomenon.

Broca-Sulzer e. A change in perceived brightness of light of constant illumination with varied durations of flash, maximum values being obtained for intermediate durations. Syn., *Broca-Sulzer phenomenon.*

Brücke-Bartley e. The increased brightness of intermittent stimulation (illumination) over continuous illumination of the same intensity. The Brücke effect proper is the effect gained by using a revolving disk with dark and light sectors and comparing it to a solid surface similar to the light sector. The Bartley effect proper is produced by using a motionless surface intermittently illuminated and comparing it to a continuously illuminated one. See also *brightness enhancement.*

chartreuse e. A phenomenon of dichroism occurring in a liquid under varying conditions of volume or concentration. The name is derived from the chartreuse liqueur which appears deep ruby red in the flagon and brilliant emerald green when poured into a glass.

Compton e. The acquisition of energy and momentum by an electron at rest when a photon of energy collides with it. The photon flies off in a direction different from that of incidence and with a loss of energy. The energy imparted to the electron plus the energy lost by the photon equals the energy of the incident photon. The effect is demonstrated experimentally with x-rays or γ-rays and is considered to be evidence for the existence of photons.

Cotton e. Circular dichroism.

Cotton-Mouton magneto-optic e. The creation of double refraction in certain liquids when situated in a magnetic field.

dimming e. An enhancement or a recovery of either a chromatic or an achromatic afterimage when the field upon which the afterimage is projected is reduced in intensity.

Doppler e. A change in the frequency of waves, as of sound or light, which occurs when the distance between the source and an observer is changing. The wave frequency increases with decreasing distance and decreases with increasing distance; e.g., as a star recedes from or approaches the earth, its color is shifted toward red or violet, respectively.

end e. In a series of chromatic samples of the same dominant wavelength and luminance arranged on a neutral background in order of purity, the appearance of the end sample, the purest, being more saturated than it would be if followed by a still purer sample.

Faraday's e. The rotation of the plane of vibration of plane-polarized light as it passes through glass which has been made optically active by subjection to a strong magnetic field.

geometric size e. A rotatory displacement of the frontal plane horopter around the point of fixation, away from the eye whose ocular image is larger in the horizontal meridian, as in real or induced aniseikonia.

Helson-Judd e. For a given light adaptation level, objects having reflectances above that level arouse responses which tend to take on the hue produced by the illuminant, objects having reflectances below that level arouse responses that tend to take on the hue of the afterimage complementary, and objects of low purity relative to the weighted mean chromaticity of the field and having reflectances about equal to that of the adaptation level tend to appear as neutral or achromatic.

Hoefer e. With a fixated object, *F*, a second laterally adjustable object, *P*, in the same apparent frontoparallel plane, and a third object, *R*, beyond the frontoparallel plane and on the line of sight of one eye, *L*, but not visible to that eye, the object *P* must be more displaced laterally to make *R* and *P* and *F* and *R* appear to subtend the same angle with respect to the other eye when one eye, *L*, is occluded, than when both eyes are open.

induced size e. A rotation of the frontal plane horopter around the point of fixation toward the eye whose ocular image is larger in the vertical meridian. The effect is as if the horizontal meridian of the other ocular image were larger.

Kerr electro-optic e. The creation of double refraction in certain isotropic substances when situated in a strong electric field so that they behave optically as a uniaxial crystal with the optic axis parallel to the field direction.

Köllner e. The initial monetary appearance of a bipartite color field when a white surface is viewed through two different color filters, one before the right eye and the other before the left. The field to the right of the fixation point is of the color of the right filter, and the field to the left of the fixation point is of the color of the left filter. The effect is attributed to a fleeting binasal hemianopsia and is followed immediately by binocular rivalry or fusion.

Liebmann e. Loss of clarity and fading of a colored figure into its neutral background when the figure and ground are equally luminous and fixation is constant on the figure. Syn., *Liebmann phenomenon.*

off e. Off response.

on e. On response.

on-off e. On-off response.

photochemical e. A chemical change of a substance as a result of exposure to light, as in bleaching of the visual purple.

photoconductive e. An increase in electrical conductivity due to a change in resistance produced by absorption of radiation.

photoelectric e. The emission of electrons from a cathode plate as the result of incident light.

practice e. The effect of repetition on a perceptual or motor function. The nature and magnitude of the effect depends not only on the number of repetitions but also on the attitude and motivation of the subject, as well as the manner in which it is done.

prismatic e. The bending of a ray of light by a prism or as though by a prism; the prismatic equivalent of the bending of a ray of light traversing a lens peripheral to the optical center.

Pulfrich e. The apparently ellip-

soid or circular excursion of a pendulum actually swinging in a plane perpendicular to the direction of view when a light-absorbing filter is placed in front of one eye. Syn., *Pulfrich stereophenomenon.*

Purkinje's e. Purkinje's phenomenon.

Raman e. In certain substances, the occurrence of scattered light of wavelength differing slightly from that of the incident light. It differs from fluorescence in that the incident wavelength exhibiting the effect does not correspond to an absorption line or band of the substance, the intensity of the scattered light is much less, and the wavelength of the scattered light shifts with the wavelength of the incident light.

Roenne's e. Roenne's phenomenon.

spreading e. of Bezold. The appearance of a spot of color as being darker when surrounded by a black rim, and of being lighter when surrounded by a white rim. The black rim creates an apparent increase in saturation and the white rim an apparent decrease, an effect opposite to that expected on the basis of simultaneous contrast.

Stark e. The broadening and splitting of emission lines in a gaseous spectrum when subjected to a strong electric field.

Stiles-Crawford e. 1. *Of the first kind:* the difference in stimulus effectiveness (brightness) of two pencils of light incident on the same retinal point, one passing through the center of the pupil and the other passing through an eccentric part of the pupil, the central pencil producing a more intense response. 2. *Of the second kind:* the difference in perceived hue and saturation of two pencils of light of the same wavelength incident on the same retinal point, one passing through the center of the pupil and the other passing through an eccentric part of the pupil, the eccentric pencil appearing desaturated and shifted in hue slightly toward the red end of the spectrum, except for wavelengths near 526 mμ, which appear more saturated and shifted slightly toward the blue end of the spectrum.

Talbot e. The experience of continuous light from a rapidly intermittent source, but of an intensity equivalent to that produced if the total amount of light were equally distributed in time; the phenomenon giving rise to Talbot's law.

theta e. The apparent circulating movement of a spot of light seen through a red filter around the same spot seen by the other eye through a rotating prism.

Thomson e. A failure of two very small areas of the central visual field, which are matched precisely in hue for yellow wavelengths, to match either longer or shorter wavelengths. This effect is said to present evidence for the cluster hypothesis.

trace e's. The effects, left by a perception or an experience, which influence and modify the nature of a later perception or experience. Memory consists of the organization of trace effects. Learning consists of the influence of trace effects upon later perceptual and motor activities.

Troxler's e. Troxler's phenomenon.

Tyndall e. Scattering of light by small particles suspended in a liquid or a gas, thus rendering the particles visible. Syn., *Tyndall phenomenon.*

Voight e. Magnetic double refraction.

Zeeman e. The splitting of each line in a spectrum into three or more when the source is placed in a powerful magnetic field.

effectivity. The curvature of a wavefront at a given point of reference with respect to an optical system. For example, an ophthalmic lens may be said to produce a wavefront with a given effectivity at the cornea. Cf. *effective power.*

efficacy (ef'ih-kah-se). The power to produce an effect.

luminous e. of a light source. The quotient of the total luminous flux emitted by the source to the total power input to the source. In the case of an electric lamp, efficacy is expressed in lumens per watt.

luminous e. of radiant flux. The quotient of total luminous flux divided by total radiant flux, expressed in lumens per watt.

luminous e. of radiant flux, spectral. The quotient of the luminous flux at a given wavelength divided by the radiant flux at that wavelength, expressed in lumens per watt. Syn., *luminosity factor; visibility factor.*

efficiency. 1. The ability or capacity to produce desired results or to perform an action; competency. 2. The ratio of the output of energy or work, as from a machine or a storage battery, to the input of energy.

light source, e. of a. The ratio of the total luminous flux to the total power input, expressed in lumens per watt.

luminous e. Luminous efficacy of radiant flux. See under *efficacy.*

quantum e. A ratio indicating the number of molecules which will react per quantum of light energy absorbed, provided the quantum energy is sufficient to activate the molecule or molecules concerned. The ratio may be less than, equal to, or greater than unity.

spectral luminous e., photopic. Spectral luminous efficiency of radiant flux obtained with photopic vision; identical to the Y values of the spectral tristimulus values adopted by the C.I.E. in 1931.

spectral luminous e. of radiant flux. The ratio of the luminous efficacy for a given wavelength to the value at the wavelength of maximum luminous efficacy. Syn., *relative luminosity factor; relative visibility factor; relative luminosity.*

spectral luminous e., scotopic. Spectral luminous efficiency of radiant flux obtained by dark-adapted observers.

visual e. 1. The ability to perform visual tasks easily and comfortably. 2. A rating used in computing compensation for ocular injuries, based on a formula adopted by the American Medical Association and incorporating certain measurable functions of central acuity, field vision, and ocular motility. 3. The Snellen acuity fraction expressed in per cent.

visual e., industrial. A rating based on any of several scales, tables, or formulas adopted for computing or specifying visual competence or adequateness for industrial employment or for determining compensation in case of ocular injury. See also *visual efficiency.*

Egger's line (eg'erz). See under *line.*

egilops (e'jih-lops). An abscess at the inner canthus.

egocenter (e"go-sen'ter). A point of reference in, or identified with, the self, usually between the eyes, in relation to which absolute judgments of distance and direction of external objects are made.

Ehlers-Danlos syndrome (a'lerz-dan'los). Meekrin-Ehlers-Danlos syndrome.

Ehrlich-Türk line (ār'lik-tērk). Line of Türk.

eiconometer (i"ko-nom'eh-ter). Eikonometer.

eidetic imagery (i-det'ik im'ij-re). See under *imagery.*

eidetiker (i-det'ih-ker). One having the ability of eidetic imagery.

eidoptometry (i"dop-tom'eh-tre). The measurement of the acuteness of form vision.

eikonometer (i"ko-nom'eh-ter). Any instrument used for measuring aniseikonia.

space e. An instrument, designed for the measurement of aniseikonia, using a target, the parts of which are seen three-dimensionally in space. Introduction of magnification by means of adjustable optical systems causes the spatial relationship of the target elements to change.

standard e. An instrument designed for the measurement of aniseikonia and using a direct comparison target viewed through Polaroid plates so that some of the detail in the target is seen by both eyes, some by the right eye only, and some by the left eye only.

eikonometry (i"ko-nom'eh-tre). The measurement of aniseikonia.

Einstein's theory (īn'stīnz). See under *theory.*

E.I.R.G. Abbreviation for *internal electroretinogram.*

elastosis dystrophica (e"las-to'sis dis-trof'ih-kah). A degeneration of the membrane of Bruch resulting in angioid streaks.

electrocorticogram (e-lek"tro-kōr'tih-ko"gram). A graphic recording of the changes in electrical potential associated with the activity of the cerebral cortex, obtained by applying electrodes directly to the surface of the cortex and plotting voltage against time.

electrocortigography (e-lek"tro-kōr"tih-gog'raf-e). The production and study of the electrocorticogram.

electrodiaphake (e-lek″tro-di′ah-fāk). A diathermic instrument for removing the crystalline lens.

electroencephalogram (e-lek″tro-en-sef′ah-lo-gram). A graphic recording of the changes in electrical potential associated with the activity of the cerebral cortex, made with the electroencephalograph by means of electrodes applied either to the scalp or to the surface of the cortex, or placed within neural tissue of the brain; voltage is plotted against time. Abbreviation *E.E.G.*

electroencephalograph (e-lek″tro-en-sef′ah-lo-graf). An instrument for performing electroencephalography, i.e., for making electroencephalograms.

electroencephalography (e-lek″tro-en-sef-ah-log′rah-fe). The production and study of the electroencephalogram.

electroluminescence (e-lek″tro-lu″-mih-nes′ens). The emission of light from a high-frequency discharge through a gas, or from application of alternating current to a layer of phosphor.

electromyogram (e-lek″tro-mi′o-gram). The recorded electrical change in potential difference associated with muscular activity.

electromyography (e-lek″tro-mi-og′-rah-fe). The recording and study of the electromyogram.

electronystagmogram (e-lek″tro-nis-tag′mo-gram). An electro-oculogram which graphically depicts ocular movements in nystagmus.

electronystagmography (e-lek″tro-nis-tag-mog′rah-fe). The electrical recording of ocular movements in nystagmus. Abbreviated *E.N.G.*

vector e. Electronystagmography in which recordings are made simultaneously in more than one meridian in order to localize the positions of the eye by vector analysis.

electro-occipitogram, evoked (e-lek″-tro-ok-sip′ih-to″gram). A graphic record of changes in electrical potential, as measured by two midline scalp electrodes at the occiput when the eye is stimulated by light which is computer regulated to be of different frequency than the alpha ryhthm. Failure to record indicates blindness in the area of the retina stimulated by light. Abbreviation *E.V.O.G.*

electro-oculogram (e-lek″tro-ok′u-lo-gram). A record of eye position made by recording, during eye movement, the difference in electrical potential between two electrodes placed on the skin at either side of the eye. The potential difference is a function of eye position and changes in the potential difference are due to changes in alignment of the resting potential of the eye in reference to the electrodes. Abbreviated *E.O.G.* Syn., *electro-ophthalmogram.*

electro-oculography (e-lek″tro-ok″-u-log′rah-fe). The production and study of the electro-oculogram. Syn., *electro-ophthalmography.*

vector e. Electro-oculography in which recordings are made simultaneously in more than one meridian in order to localize the position of the eye by vector analysis.

electro-ophthalmogram (e-lek″tro-of-thal′mo-gram). Electro-oculogram.

electro-ophthalmography (e-lek″tro-of″thal-mog′rah-fe). Electro-oculography.

electro-optics (e-lek″tro-op′tiks). Various light phenomena wherein changes are brought about by strong electric fields.

electroperimetry (e-lek″tro-per-im′-eh-tre). Objective determination of the integrity of the visual field by recording changes in the electrical potential, as measured by two midline scalp electrodes at the occiput when the eye is stimulated by light which is computer regulated to be of different frequency than the alpha rhythm. Failure to record an evoked occipital potential indicates blindness for the retinal area stimulated.

electrophotoluminescence (e-lek″-tro-fo″to-lu-mih-nes′ens). Photoluminescence modified by means of an electrical input.

electroretinogram (e-lek″tro-ret′ih-no-gram). The electrical effect (action potential) recorded from the surface of the eyeball and originated by a pulse of light. It is usually recorded as a monophasic or a diphasic wave, but may be more complex. Abbreviated *E.R.G.* See also *E retina; I retina.*

internal e. A record of the electrical activity for a restricted region of the retina in response to a light stimulus near a retinal electrode at the level of the bipolar cells. The waveform is similar to that of the electroretinogram but of reverse polarity.

electroretinography (e-lek″tro-ret″-ih-nog′rah-fe). The production and study of the electroretinogram.

flicker e. Electroretinography in which the electroretinogram is elicited by a flickering light stimulus.

internal e. The production and study of the internal electroretinogram.

element, retinal. 1. *Anatomy:* One of the many anatomical elements of the retina, such as rods, cones, bipolar cells, amacrines, or Mueller's fibers; more usually used in connection with a rod or a cone. 2. An element of direction apparently associated with, or emanating from, some point on the retina. Each element or point is considered to have its own "local sign," direction in space, or visual direction.

elephantiasis neuromatosa (el″eh-fan-ti′ah-sis nu″ro-mah-to′sah). Neurofibromatosis of the eyelid. See also *von Recklinghausen's disease.*

elephantiasis oculi (el″eh-fan-ti′ah-sis ok′u-li). 1. Enlargement and protrusion of the eyelids due to lymphatic obstruction. 2. Extreme exophthalmia. *Obs.*

elevator. 1. A muscle which raises an eyelid. 2. A muscle which rotates the eye upward.

Elliot's (el′e-ots) **scotometer; sign.** See under the nouns.

ellipse (ĕ-lips′). A smooth symmetrical oval, each point of which has a constant sum of distances from two fixed points within it.

aniseikonic e. An elliptical diagram representing the aniseikonic ratio in all meridians.

Tscherning e. A graphical curve resulting from the plotting of front surface powers against total lens powers in best-form lenses, i.e., those forms which reduce marginal astigmatism and field curvature to a minimum.

Tscherning e., Ostwalt branch of. The lower portion of the Tscherning ellipse used in the designing of so-called corrected curve lenses.

Tscherning e., Wollaston branch of. The upper portion of the Tscherning ellipse.

ellipsoid, Fresnel's. The representation of the wavefront originating from a point source located within a birefringent substance as an ellipsoid for which the semiaxes are proportional to the principal indices of refraction of the substance.

ellipsoid, visual cell. The refractile outer portion of the inner member of a rod or cone cell located between the myoid and the outer member. It contains mitochondria for metabolic activity.

Ellis stereoscope. See under *stereoscope.*

Elschnig (elsh'n g) **bodies; globular cells; physiologic excavation; limiting membrane; pearls; spots; tissue.** See under the nouns.

em. Abbreviation for *emmetropia.*

embolism, retinal (em'bo-lizm). The blocking of a retinal artery or arteriole by an embolus which may result in atrophy and blindness of the portion of the retina affected. Obstruction of the central retinal artery presents a characteristic ophthalmoscopic picture in which all arteries are constricted and the fundus is milky white except for a cherry-red spot at the macula. Central vision may be spared when a cilioretinal artery is present.

embolus (em'bo-lus). A bit of foreign matter which enters the blood stream at one point and is carried until it is lodged or impacted in an artery and obstructs it. It may be a blood clot, an air bubble, fat or other tissue, or clumps of bacteria.

embryotoxon (em''bre-o-tok'son). A ring opacity of the periphery of the cornea, situated in its deep layers, distinguished from an arcus senilis in that it appears to be continuous with the sclera, having no clear zone at the limbus. It is a developmental anomaly due to an adhesion of the lamina capsulopupillaris to the cornea. Syn., *posterior marginal dysplasia of the cornea; post-corneal ring.*

   anterior e. Arcus juvenilis.

   posterior e. Embryotoxon.

emergence, grazing. The emergence of a refracted ray from a more dense to a less dense optical medium, such that it travels along the interface between the two media. It constitutes the limiting value of the angle of refraction.

emissivity (em''is-iv'ih-te). The ratio of the energy radiated by a non-

blackbody at any temperature to that radiated by a blackbody at the same temperature.

   spectral e. Emissivity for a specific wavelength.

   total e. Emissivity at all wavelengths.

emittance, luminous (e-mit'ans). The total luminous flux emitted per unit area of surface.

emittance, radiant (e-mit'ans). Radiant flux emitted per unit area of surface, expressed in watts.

Emmert's law (em'erts). See under *law.*

emmetrope (em'e-trōp). One having emmetropia.

emmetropia (em''e-tro'pe-ah). A visual condition identified by the location of the conjugate focus of the retina at infinity when accommodation is said to be relaxed; thus, the retina lies in the plane of the posterior principal focus of the dioptric system of the static eye. In emmetropia, an infinitely distant fixated object is imaged sharply on the retina without inducing an accommodative response.

emmetropic (em''e-trop'ik). Pertaining to or having emmetropia.

emmetropization (em''ĕ-tro''pih-za'-shun). A process presumed to be operative in producing a greater frequency of occurrence of emmetropia and near emmetropia than would be expected in terms of chance distribution, as may be explained by postulating that a mechanism co-ordinates the formation and development of the various components of the human eye which contribute to the total refractive power.

emphysema (em''fi-se'mah, -ze'mah). The abnormal presence of air or gas in the body tissues, as may occur in the eyelids through a fracture of the lamina papyracea of the ethmoid bone.

empiricism (em-pir'is-izm). 1. Generally, a theory that certain aspects of behavior or knowledge are dependent on accumulated experience or learning and are not innate. 2. The concept that spatial localization is a learned process based on experience and is not innate. Cf. *nativism*. 3. Empirical method or practice.

encanthis (en-kan'this). 1. A small neoplasm or tumor in the inner canthus of the eye. 2. A simple inflammatory hypertrophy of the lacrimal caruncle.

encanthoschisis (en-kan″tho-skih'-sis). Formation of a caruncle in two parts, or its division by a horizontal furrow.

encephalitis periaxialis diffusa (en″sef-ah-li'tis per″ih-aks-e-al'is dih-fu'sah). Schilder's disease.

encephalocele, orbital (en-sef'ah-lo-sēl″). A protrusion of a portion of the cerebral substance into the orbit, usually causing exophthalmos and lateral displacement of the eyeball.

encephalomyelitis optica (en-sef″ah-lo-mi″el-i'tis op'tih-kah). Neuromyelitis optica.

encephalopsy (en-sef'ah-lop″se). The association of certain colors with certain flavors, numbers, words, etc.

encyclophoria (en″si-klo-fo're-ah). Incyclophoria.

encyclotropia (en″si-klo-tro'pe-ah). Incyclotropia.

encyclovergence (en″si-klo-ver'jens). Incyclovergence.

end bulb. See under *bulb*.

end foot. The end of a cone cell, shaped like a pedicle, which synapses with a bipolar cell dendrite in the outer molecular layer of the retina. Syn., *cone foot; cone pedicle*

end knob. The end of a rod cell of the retina, located in the outer molecular layer of the retina, which synapses with bipolar and horizontal cells. Syn., *end bulb; rod spherule*.

endophlebitis, retinal (en″do-fle-bi'-tis). Venous thrombosis involving the retinal venules.

endophthalmitis (en-dof″thal-mi'-tis). Inflammation of the tissues of the internal structures of the eye. Syn., *entophthalmia*.

phacoallergica, e. Endophthalmitis phacoanaphylactica.

phacoanaphylactica, e. Inflammation of the uveal tract occurring after extracapsular cataract extraction or a needling operation, presumed to be an allergic reaction to one's own liberated lenticular proteins. Syn., *endophthalmitis phacoallergica; endophthalmitis phacogenetica*.

phacogenetica, e. Endophthalmitis phacoanaphylactica.

phacotoxic e. Endophthalmitis attributed to the toxic effect of liberated crystalline lens material, as that from a hypermature cataract.

suppurative e. Purulent inflammation of the uveal tract; a purulent uveitis.

endothelioma (en″do-the″le-o'mah). A malignant tumor derived from endothelium of the vascular system or the lining cells of body cavities. Reticulo-endothelial cells and cells of the tunica adventitia of vessels are claimed by some to yield endotheliomas.

endpiece. The part at the temporal end of a spectacle frame or mounting which contains the pivot for the temple.

energy. 1. The capacity for performing work. 2. Inherent power; the capacity of acting to produce an effect.

infrared e. Electromagnetic or radiant energy of wavelengths just longer than that which will ordinarily stimulate the eye, extending from approximately 760 mμ through several octaves of longer wavelengths.

luminous e. Visible radiant energy; light.

radiant e. Energy traveling in the form of electromagnetic waves considered as to its physical qualities and not as to its sensation-producing effect on the eye. It is measured in units of energy such as ergs or joules.

radiant e., spectral. Radiant energy with respect to a specified wavelength or narrow wavelength interval.

radiant e., visible. Radiant energy capable of eliciting the sensation of light when received on the retina, corresponding approximately to the wavelength range of 380 to 760 mμ.

spectral e. The radiant energy of the spectrum, referring either to the visible spectrum only or to the total electromagnetic spectrum.

ultraviolet e. Electromagnetic or radiant energy of wavelengths just shorter than that which will ordinarily stimulate the eye, extending from approximately 380 mμ through several octaves of shorter wavelengths.

Engel fundus lens (eng'el). See under *lens.*

Engelmann (eng'el-man) **Stereoscope; Bar Trainer.** See under the nouns.

Engström's accessory outer segment (eng'stremz). See under *segment.*

enhancement, brightness. 1. The increase in brightness resulting from making a stimulus intermittent. The rate of intermittency must lie materially below the critical flicker frequency and the photic pulses must not be feeble or enhancement will not occur. See also *Brücke-Bartley effect.* 2. The apparent increase of brightness of a surface when surrounded by a dark area as compared to when it is surrounded by a light area.

maximum brightness e. Maximum increase in the brightness of a target or other area intermittently illuminated, over one continuously illuminated. Under some conditions a maximum occurs when the stimulus rate is in the neighborhood of 8 to 10 pulses per sec., dropping with either higher or lower pulse frequencies. Under other conditions, enhancement increases continuously as pulse frequency decreases until the resulting flashes are so widely separated as not to be compared in brightness with continuous light.

enhancement, contrast. The apparent increase of brightness of a surface when it is surrounded by a dark area as compared to when it is surrounded by a light area.

Enoch's theory (e'noks). See under *theory.*

E.O.G. Abbreviation for *electro-oculogram.*

enophthalmia (en"of-thal'me-ah). Enophthalmos.

enophthalmos (en"of-thal'mos). Recession of the eyeball into the orbit.

enophthalmus (en"of-thal'mus). Enophthalmos.

enorthotrope (en-ōr'tho-trōp"). A form of zoetrope.

Enroth's sign (en'roths). See under *sign.*

enstrophe (en'stro-fe). Inversion of the eyelid margins.

entiris (en-ti'ris). The posterior pigment epithelium of the iris.

entochoroidea (en"to-ko-roi'de-ah). Choriocapillaris.

entocornea (en"to-kōr'ne-ah). 1. Descemet's membrane. 2. The posterior endothelium of the cornea.

entophthalmia (ent"of-thal'me-ah). Endophthalmitis.

entoptic (ent-op'tik). Arising from within the eye, pertaining especially to certain phenomena related to the optical or sensory effects of internal structures perceived illusorily, as in the external field of vision. Classic examples include muscae volitantes, Haidinger's brushes, and phosphene.

entoptoscope (en-top'to-skōp). An instrument for examining the media of the eye to determine their transparency.

entoptoscopy (ent"op-tos'ko-pe). The observation of the interior of the eye for determining transparency of the ocular media.

entorbital (ent-ōr'bih-tal). Pertaining to the inner portion of the orbit.

entoretina (en"to-ret'ih-nah). The inner five layers and the internal limiting membrane of the retina.

entrance port; pupil; window. See under the nouns.

entropion (en-tro'pe-on). A rolling or turning inward (inversion) of the margin of an eyelid. Syn., *blepharelosis.*

cicatricial e. Entropion due to scar tissue and subsequent contraction of the tarsus and conjunctiva.

contraction e. Entropion due to, or occurring with, contraction of the palpebral portion of the orbicularis oculi muscle.

mechanical e. Entropion due to lack of support to the eyelid, such as may occur in enophthalmos or lack of orbital fat.

organic e. Mechanical entropion.

senile e. Entropion occurring in the aged, usually due to loose, atrophied, and inelastic skin of the eyelids, together with normal tone of the palpebral portion of the orbicularis oculi muscle and a deep-set eye.

spastic e. Entropion due to spasm of the palpebral portion of the orbicularis oculi muscle.

superciliary e. A turning inward of the cilia of the eyebrow toward the eye; of pathological, traumatic, or congenital origin.

entropium (en-tro'pe-um). Entropion.

enucleate (e-nu'kle-āt). To remove a whole tumor or an entire organ, as in the removal of the eye from its socket.

enucleation (e-nu"kle-a'shun). The removal of a whole tumor or an entire organ, as in the removal of the eye from its socket.

ependyma (ep-en'dih-mah). Neuroglial-like cells lining the cavity of the neural tube of the central nervous system and bounding the cerebrospinal fluid of the canals and the ventricles. Visual cells are thought to develop from the ependyma of the embryo.

epiblepharon (ep"ih-blef'ah-ron). A rare developmental anomaly in which a fold of skin overlaps the eyelid margin, pressing the eyelashes inward.

epibulbar (ep"ih-bul'bar). Situated on the eyeball. Syn., *epiocular.*

epicanthus (ep"ih-kan'thus). A fold of skin partially covering the inner canthus, the caruncle, and the plica semilunaris. It is normal in the fetus, in some infants, and in Mongolians and other peoples characterized by low nasal bridges.

inversus, e. A condition in which a fold of skin from the lower eyelid runs crescentically upward, meeting the upper eyelid at the inner canthus. It is associated with a congenital ptosis.

lateralis, e. An acquired condition in which a fold of skin rides over the outer canthus.

palpebralis, e. Epicanthus in which the fold of skin originates above the tarsal fold of the upper eyelid.

supraciliaris, e. Epicanthus in which the fold of skin originates from the region of the eyebrows.

tarsalis, e. Epicanthus in which the fold originates from the skin of the tarsal fold of the upper eyelid.

epicauma (ep"ih-kaw'mah). Any superficial burn or ulcer of the eye.

epichoroid (ep″ih-ko′roid). The outer layer of the choroid adjacent to the sclera. Syn., *lamina fusca; suprachoroid.*

epicorneoscleritis (ep″ih-kor″ne-o-skle-ri′tis). Superficial inflammation of the cornea and the sclera.

epidermolysis bullosa (ep″e-der-mol′is-is bul′o-sah). A disease of the skin, usually hereditary, characterized by the development of vesicles and bullae on irritation or slight trauma of the skin. Vesicles resembling phlyctenules may appear in the conjunctiva and, when recurrent, may lead to superficial symblepharon. Affection of the conjunctiva is frequently accompanied by the corneal complications of blebs and ulcers.

epidiascope (ep″ih-di′ah-skōp″). An optical instrument for projecting opaque pictures onto a screen; an opaque projector.

epilation (ep″ih-la′shun). The removal of hair by the roots, as in the removal of misdirected eyelashes.

epiloia (ep-ih-loi′ah). Bourneville's disease.

epinephrine (ep′ih-nef′rin). A hormone of the adrenal medulla which, when instilled in the eye in dilute solution, constricts the conjunctival vessels, dilates the pupil by stimulating the sympathetic nerve endings of the dilator pupillae muscle, and reduces intraocular pressure. It is used to control conjunctival hemorrhages, to reduce conjunctival congestion, and to release recent iritic adhesions. It is also of value in acute glaucoma. Syn., *adrenalin.*

epiocular (ep″e-ok′u-lar). Epibulbar.

epipephysitis (ep″ih-pef″ih-si′tis). Conjunctivitis.

epiphora (e-pif′o-rah). An overflow of tears onto the cheek caused by excessive lacrimation, by obstruction of the lacrimal ducts, or by ectropion.

epiphysis cerebri (e-pif′ih-sis ser′e-bri). The pineal body in the forebrain which, in some low vertebrates, represents a median eye.

episclera (ep″ih-skle′rah). A loose structure of fibrous and elastic connective tissue on the outer surface of the sclera. It contains a large number of small blood vessels in contrast to the sclera proper, which is almost avascular.

episcleral (ep″ih-skle′ral). 1. Located on the outer surface of the sclera. 2. Pertaining to the episclera.

episcleritis (ep″ih-skle-ri′tis). Inflammation of the episclera and/or the outer layers of the sclera itself.

fugax, e. Episcleritis periodica fugax.

    fugax, partial e. Episcleritis periodica fugax.

nodular e. An inflammation of the episclera characterized by the appearance of localized purplish nodules, round or oval in shape and very sensitive to touch. The nodules are firmly attached to the sclera, but the conjunctiva moves freely over them. It occurs in adults, is benign, chronic, recurrent, of obscure etiology, and is differentiated from a phlyctenule by the mobility of the overlying conjunctiva.

periodica fugax, e. A transient and recurrent inflammation of a portion of the episclera, lasting from a few hours to a few days. It persistently recurs in different areas in the same eye or in the other eye, is fiery red, is sometimes painful, and usually does not affect vision or have serious sequelae. Syn., *episcleritis fugax; partial episcleritis fugax.*

rosacea, e. A rare inflammation of the episclera characterized by the appearance of transient, recurring, highly vascularized, small, gray nodules.

episclerotitis (ep″ih-skle″ro-ti′tis). Episcleritis.

episcotister (ep″ih-sko-tis′ter). A sectored disk which may be rotated in front of a light source to produce flashes of light. It is used in the study of the critical flicker frequency.

epitarsus (ep″ih-tar′sus). A congenital anomaly consisting of apronlike folds of conjunctiva attached to the inner tarsal surface of the eyelid. The edges of the folds are sufficiently free that a probe may be passed beneath. Syn., *congenital pterygium*.

epithelioma (ep″ih-the-le-o′mah). A tumor derived from epithelial tissue and composed primarily of epithelial cells which may be benign, e.g., *adenoma*, or malignant, e.g., *carcinoma*.

epsilon [ε] (ep′sih-lon). The Greek letter used as the symbol for (1) the *angle epsilon;* (2) the *dispersive power* of a light transmitting medium; (3) the *angle of deviation* of a refracted ray of light.

Epstein's (ep′stīnz) **implant; lens; symptom.** See under the nouns.

equate. In color vision, to combine colors to equal another color sensation.

equation. An expression of equality between two magnitudes.

    color e's. Equations representing the proportions of the primary colors needed in additive color mixing to match a particular hue.

    Rayleigh e. The proportion of red (usually 670 mμ) and green (usually 535 mμ) required in a mixture to match a given yellow (usually 589 mμ). It is used as a test to differentiate certain types of deficient color vision.

equator. A circle or a circular line which divides the surface of a body into two equal and symmetrical parts.

    crystalline lens, e. of. The outer zonular margin of the crystalline lens, lying in a vertical plane.

    eye, e. of the, (anatomical). The circumference of the eye representing a locus of points equidistant from the anterior and the posterior poles.

    eye, e. of the, (functional). A diagrammatic circle joining the arc of contact of the lateral rectus muscle (4 mm. behind the anatomical equator) and the arc of contact of the medial rectus muscle (4 mm. in front of the anatomical equator). It serves as a guide in strabismic surgery.

    eye, e. of the, (geometrical). The circumference of the eye in a plane perpendicular to and bisecting the anterior-posterior axis.

equilibrium, photochemical. The level of light or dark adaptation for which the rate of synthesis is equal to the rate of breakdown in the Wald cycle.

equivalent. That which is equal in value, force, significance, weight, worth, or size.

    spherical e. 1. A spherical lens whose focal point coincides with the circle of least confusion of a given spherocylindrical lens. 2. A lens differing in form from another lens, but including the same optical focal length from the posterior principal plane to the posterior principal focus; more correctly described as *equivalent power.* 3. A single lens whose effective power is equal to the sum total effective power of a combination of lenses.

    spherocylinder e. 1. A single lens or a combination of lenses with an effective power equivalent to that of a given combination of spheres and cylinders. 2. Any of the series of formulas obtained by transposition of the formula for a given spherocylinder combination.

Erb's disease; method. See under the nouns.

erector. An erecting prism.

E.O.G. Abbreviation for *electro-oculogram*.

E.R.G. Abbreviation for *electroretinogram*.

Erggelet's retrolental space (er'gehletz). See under *space, retrolental*.

ergograph (er'go-graf). An instrument for recording the value of work done by muscular contractions, primarily used in studies of muscular fatigue. The extent and duration of muscular contractions are recorded on a kymograph attached to the apparatus.

ophthalmic e. An instrument for studying fatigue of convergence and/or accommodation, consisting essentially of a movable target carrier which repeatedly approaches the eye of the observer and is connected to a kymograph for recording.

erisiphake (er-is'e-fāk). Erysiphake.

erisophake (er-is'o-fāk). Erysiphake.

error. The failure to achieve, or a deviation from, the right course or standard; a departure from truth or accuracy; a mistake.

average e. The average deviation of a series of attempts to make direct matches or measurements, used as a measure of threshold.

chromatic e. Chromatic aberration.

constant e. A factor contributing to a score of such nature as to affect all subjects or all settings in a similar manner and by a similar amount.

declination e. The apparent fore or aft deviation of vertical lines, specified in degrees, induced by oblique meridional magnification lenses or oblique meridional aniseikonia.

image shell e. The dioptric difference between the Petzval surface of a point-focal lens and the far point sphere of the eye, or near point sphere when appropriate, for a given oblique pencil of rays. Syn., *marginal spherical error*.

marginal spherical e. Image shell error.

mean oblique e. The mean dioptric power of a spherical lens for a given oblique ray minus its back vertex power.

oblique astigmatic e. The tangential dioptric vertex power of a spherical lens minus its sagittal dioptric vertex power for a given oblique ray.

probable e. A value equal to 0.6745 times the standard error. The use of this measure is discouraged by modern statisticians, since it yields no information not found in the more customary standard error.

refraction of the eye, e. of. The dioptric power of the correcting lens which, together with the dioptric system of the eye, converges parallel rays to focus on the retina, with accommodation fully relaxed. See also *ametropia*.

skew e. In a right angle reflecting prism, an error due to the edge of the 90° apex not being perpendicular to the long side of the hypotenuse face.

standard e. A measure of the dispersion or variability which any calculated statistical value would be expected to show in taking repeated samples of equal number from the same population or universe. It represents the abscissa value of the inflection point on either side of the normal distribution curve.

standard e. of the correlation coefficient. $S_r = \dfrac{1 - r^2}{\sqrt{N}}$, where r is the coefficient of correlation and N is the number of cases. See also *standard error of z*.

standard e. of estimate. The standard error of a regression coefficient. It is equal to the standard deviation of the dependent variable times the coefficient of alienation. $S_{y-x} = \sigma_y \sqrt{1 - r^2}$, where σ_y is the standard deviation of the dependent variable and r is the coefficient of correlation.

standard e. of the mean. $S_x = \dfrac{\sigma}{\sqrt{N}}$, where σ is the standard deviation of the sample and N is the number of cases.

standard e. of the median. $S_{MDN} = \dfrac{1.2533\sigma}{N}$, where σ is the standard deviation of the sample and N is the number of cases.

standard e. of the standard deviation. $S_\sigma = \dfrac{\sigma}{\sqrt{2N}}$, where σ is the standard deviation of the sample and N is the number of cases.

standard e. of z. $\sigma_z = \dfrac{1}{\sqrt{N-3}}$, where N is the number of cases. Cf. *standard error of the correlation coefficient.*

variable e. A cause of variation among data such that different subjects or different settings will be affected to different degrees. Cf. *constant error.*

erysipelas (er″ih-sip′eh-las, -lus). An acute, spreading, febrile disease characterized by inflammation of the skin, subcutaneous tissues, and mucous membranes, due to infection of the lymph spaces of the corium and underlying parts by *Streptococcus erysipelatis* (*S. pyogenes*). When the eye is involved, there is great swelling and redness, the eyelids are swollen shut, and this may be followed by abscess of the eyelids and sloughing of the skin. If the disease extends into the orbit, it may cause orbital cellulitis, thrombosis of retinal veins, optic neuritis, or optic atrophy.

erysiphake (er-is′ih-fāk). A surgical instrument for the removal of a

cataractous crystalline lens by suction. See also *phacoerisis.*

erythema exudativum multiforme (er″ih-the′mah eks-oo″da′tih-vum mul-tih-fōr′me). An eruption of the skin or the mucous membranes characterized by red patches of various shapes and associated with an edematous exudate. In the conjunctiva it may appear in three forms: mild catarrhal conjunctivitis, purulent conjunctivitis, or severe pseudomembranous conjunctivitis. Syn., *Hebra's disease.*

erythema nodosum (er″ih-the′mah no-do′sum). An eruption of the skin or the mucous membranes characterized by large nodular swellings, dark purple in the center and brighter red at the periphery. Occasionally, the subconjunctival tissues are affected with the appearance in the palpebral fissure of an edematous area containing vesicles or nodules.

erythremia (er″e-thre′me-ah). Vaquez' disease.

erythrochloropia (e-rith″ro-klo-ro′-pe-ah). A form of deficient color vision in which red and green are the only colors correctly perceived.

erythrochloropsia (e-rith″ro-klo-rop′-se-ah). Erythrochloropia.

erythrochloropy (e-rith″ro-klor′o-pe). Erythrochloropia.

erythrolabe (e-rith′ro-lāb). The name proposed by W. A. H. Rushton for a retinal photopigment more sensitive to long wavelength (red) radiation than are other retinal photopigments, although its maximum absorption and spectral sensitivity appear to be in the yellow-green, or perhaps the orange, portion of the spectrum rather than in the red.

erythrophane (e-rith′ro-fān). A red pigment found in the retinal receptor cells of some animals, but not of man.

erythrophobia (e-rith″ro-fo′be-ah). A fear of, or an aversion to, the color red.

erythrophose (e-rith′ro-fōz). A subjective sensation of red light or color.

erythropia (er″e-thro′pe-ah). Erythropsia.

erythropsia (er″e-throp′se-ah). A condition in which all objects are seen tinged with red. It may appear after overexposure to bright light, as in snow blindness, or following cataract extraction. Syn., *red vision.*

erythropsin (er″e-throp′sin). Rhodopsin.

escorcin (es-kōr′sin). A chemical compound which in solution imparts a red color to lesions of the cornea or the conjunctiva and is used for their observation.

eserine (es′er-in). A chemical compound used as a parasympathetic stimulant which, when instilled in the eye, constricts the pupil. Syn., *physostigmine.*

esocataphoria (es″o-kat″ah-fo′re-ah). The combined conditions of esophoria and cataphoria, the eyes tending to turn down and in.

esodeviation (es″o-de″ve-a′shun, e″so-). The deviation of the line of sight of the nonfixating eye from the point of fixation of the other eye, in esophoria with dissociation, or in esotropia.

esodisparity (es″o-dis-par′ih-te, e″so-). Fixation disparity in which the eyes overconverge slightly while single binocular vision is maintained for the point of fixation. Syn., *positive fixation disparity.*

esophoria (es″o-fo′re-ah, e″so-). The inward turning, or the amount of inward turning, of the two eyes relative to each other as manifested in the absence of a fusion stimulus, or when fusion is made impossible, such that the lines of sight cross at a point in front of and nearer to the eyes than a given point of reference, this point of reference usually being the point of binocular fixation prior to the phoria test or, more arbitrarily, at an infinite distance.

accommodative e. The manifestation of esophoria, or of that portion of total esophoria, resulting from accommodative convergence.

anatomical e. The manifestation of esophoria, or of that portion of total esophoria, attributable to structural (anatomical) anomalies or variations.

innervational e. The manifestation of esophoria, or of that portion of total esophoria, attributable to hypertonicity of the extraocular musculature subserving convergence. Syn., *tonic esophoria.*

intrinsic e. Esophoria attributable to primary structural, myologic, or neurological anomalies as distinguished from pseudoesophoria attributable to spurious manifestations of accommodative convergence.

monofixational e. See *phoria, monofixational.*

physiological e. Oversufficiency of accommodative convergence producing increased esophoria or decreased exophoria as the fixation object is brought nearer. It occurs when the A.C.A. ratio is greater than six.

relative e. 1. The amount by which the exophoria at near is less than the physiological exophoria, or the amount of esophoria at near plus the amount of the physiological exophoria. 2. The distance esophoria regarded as a finding different from the absolute value that would be obtained with tonic convergence eliminated. 3. The amount of esophoria expressed in relation to given test conditions and given points of reference for purposes of quantitative specification.

tonic e. Esophoria attributable to excess or anomalous tonicity of the extraocular musculature. Syn., *innervational esophoria.*

esophoric (es″o-fōr′ik, e″so-). Pertaining to or manifesting esophoria.

esostasis (es″o-sta′sis). An inward deviation of the eye from a straightforward position when all fixation stimuli and voluntary influences are eliminated.

esotropia (es″o-tro′pe-ah, e″so-). Convergent strabismus.

esotropic (es″o-trop′ik, e″so-). Pertaining to or manifesting esotropia.

esthesiometer (es-the″ze-om′eh-ter). An instrument for determining sensibility, especially one for tactile sensation.

Boberg-Ans e. Boberg-Ans corneal sensibilitometer.

Cochet-Bonnet e. A device used to evaluate corneal sensitivity consisting essentially of a nylon thread, 0.0113 mm.² in section, mounted in a handle so that its length may be varied, and calibrated in milligrams of weight necessary to bend a given length of the thread when pressed against the cornea. The criterion is the greatest thread length which causes a just noticeable sensation of pain.

Schirmer's e. A device used to evaluate corneal sensitivity consisting essentially of a small plastic disk attached to one end of a wire, the other end being connected to a spring mechanism giving readings in milligrams of force.

eta [η] (e′tah, a′tah). The Greek letter used as a symbol for the *angle of relative binocular parallax* or the *angle of stereopsis.*

etalon (et′ah-lon). Two parallel, optically plane, glass plates partially silvered on their inner surfaces and mounted at a fixed distance from each other, which produce circular interference fringes of high resolution in the light transmitted after it undergoes multiple reflections in the air space between the two plates.

ethmoiditis (eth″moid-i′tis). Inflammation of the ethmoid sinuses or of the ethmoid bone.

eucatropine (u-kat′ro-pēn, -pin). Euphthalmine.

euchromatopsia (u-kro″mah-top′se-ah). Normal color perception.

euchromatopsy (u-kro′mah-top″se). Euchromatopsia.

eucone (u′kōn). A separate refractive body called a crystalline cone, in the ommatidia of compound eyes in arthropods. It lies between the cornea and the retinal elements.

euphausiopsin (u″fah-u″sih-op′sin). A pigment of the vitamin A_1 group with a maximum absorption of 462 mμ, found in the photochemical system of the eyes of the shrimplike euphausiid crustaceans.

euphoropsia (u″fo-rop′se-ah). Comfortable or good vision; the absence of visual discomfort.

euphthalmine (ūf-thal′min). A derivative of eucaine which acts as a mydriatic of brief duration. Syn., *eucatropine.*

euryblepharon (u″re-blef′ah-ron). Large eyelids.

euryopia (u″re-o′pe-ah). Abnormally wide palpebral fissures.

euryphotic (u″re-fo′tik). Having the ability to see in any of a wide range of illumination intensities.

euscope (u′skōp). An instrument for projecting an enlarged image from a compound microscope on a screen.

euthyphoria (u″the-fo′re-ah). The absence of anaphoria or cataphoria, hence a tendency of the lines of sight to remain horizontal.

Euthyscope (u′the-skōp). An instrument used in treating amblyopia, consisting essentially of an ophthalmoscope containing a small opaque disk, in the center of the condensing lens, subtending a nonilluminated area of either 3° or 5°. The shadow is directed onto the macula, and the surrounding retinal area is illuminated with a 30° cone of intense light, rendering the macula relatively more sensitive for a short period.

evagination, optic (e-vaj″e-na′shun). The diverticulum in the forebrain of the embryo, from which the eyecup is developed.

Evans' test (ev′anz). See under *test.*

eversion of the eyelid (e-ver′zhun). The folding back of the eyelid on itself.

evisceration of the eye (e-vis″er-a′-shun). Surgical removal of the inner contents of the eye, the sclera being left intact.

evisceration of the orbit (e-vis″er-a′-shun). Surgical removal of the contents of the orbit including its periosteum.

evisceroneurotomy (e-vis″er-o-nu-rot′o-me). Evisceration of the eye with a resection of the optic nerve.

E.V.O.G. Abbreviation for *evoked electro-occipitogram.*

evulsio nervi optici (e-vul′se-o ner′vi op′tih-ki). Traumatic evulsion of the optic nerve from the eyeball.

Ewald's law (a′vahlts). See under *law.*

Ewing chart (u′ing). See under *chart.*

excavatio papillae nervi optici (eks″kah-va′she-o pah-pil′e ner′vi op′tih-ki). The physiological cup of the optic nerve head.

excavation. The act or process of forming a cavity or hollow, or the cavity or hollow itself.

atrophic e. A pathological cupping of the optic papilla due to atrophy of the optic nerve fibers.

glaucomatous e. Glaucomatous cup.

optic disk, e. of the. A physiological or pathological depression in the central area of the optic nerve head.

physiologic e. A funnel-shaped depression at or near the center of the optic disk where the central retinal vessels leave or enter the retina; a normal physiological depression lined by the meniscus of Kuhnt. Syn., *physiological cup.*

physiologic e., Elschnig's types. A classification of normal optic nerve head excavations into five types: Type I: Funnel-form. A small craterlike depréssion slightly lighter in color than the rest of the disk, located lateral to the central artery which rises in the center of the disk and branches on its surface. The central vein is formed at the apex of the funnel. Type II: Cylindric-form. The medial wall is steeper than the lateral, the lamina cribrosa is usually visible, the vessels are nasal, the central artery bifurcates on the disk surface, and the central vein is formed at the apex. Type III: Dish-form. The lamina cribrosa is very visible, the vessels are nasal, the central artery bifurcates on the floor or wall, and the central vein is formed within the excavation. Type IV: Gradually sloping lateral wall, as though derived from Type II or III by a bending outward of the lateral wall of the entrance canal. The lamina cribrosa is visible and conus formation is almost always present. Type V: Atypical form occurring in developmental anomalies such as coloboma of the choroid at the border of the optic nerve head. The excavation is almost always directed toward the greatest width of the usually associated conus formation.

excess, convergence. See under *convergence.*

excursion. 1. The path of movement of an eye in following a moving target. 2. Any movement of the eye.

excyclofusion (ek″si-klo-fu′zhun). The relative rotation of the two eyes around their respective anteroposterior axes in response to a cyclofusional stimulus, such that the upward extensions of their vertical meridians rotate templeward.

excyclophoria (ek″si-klo-fo′re-ah). The turning, or the amount of turning, of the two eyes relative to each other about their respective anteroposterior axes or lines of sight as manifested in the absence of a fusion stimulus, or when fusion is made impossible, such that their respective vertical meridians of reference diverge from each other superiorly and converge inferiorly. Syn., *plus cyclophoria.*

excyclotropia (ek″si-klo-tro′pe-ah). The turning, or the amount of turning, of the two eyes relative to each other about their respective anteroposterior axes or lines of sight so that their respective vertical meridians of reference diverge from each other superiorly and converge inferiorly. It is the same as excyclophoria except that the condition is continuous and unrelated to the presence or the absence of a fusion stimulus.

excyclovergence (ek″si-klo-ver′jens). The turning, or the amount of turning, of the two eyes with respect to each other about their respective anteroposterior axes so as to diverge the upward extensions of the vertical meridians of reference.

exenteration of the orbit (eks-en″-ter-a′shun). Surgical removal of the orbital contents.

exit port; pupil; window. See under the nouns.

Exner's theory (eks′nerz). See under *theory.*

exocataphoria (eks″o-kat″ah-fo′re-ah). Exophoria combined with cataphoria.

exocone (ek′so-kōn). A transparent ingrowth of the cornea which replaces the refractive crystalline cone in the ommatidia of compound eyes of arthropods.

exodeviation (eks″o-de″ve-a′shun). The deviation of the line of sight of the nonfixating eye from the point of fixation of the fixating eye, in exophoria with dissociation, or in exotropia.

exodisparity (eks″o-dis-par′ih-te). Fixation disparity in which the eyes underconverge slightly while single binocular vision is maintained for the point of fixation. Syn., *negative fixation disparity.*

exophoria (eks″o-fo′re-ah). The divergent turning, or the amount of divergent turning, of the two eyes relative to each other as manifested in the absence of a fusion stimulus, or when fusion is made impossible, such that the lines of sight cross at a point behind the eyes or at a point in front of the eyes beyond a given point of reference, this point of reference usually being the point of binocular fixation prior to the phoria test or, more arbitrarily, at an infinite distance.

accommodative e. The manifestation of exophoria, or that portion of the total exophoria, resulting from lack of accommodative convergence or from failure of accommodation with the concomitant lack of accommodative convergence in a testing situation in which a given amount of accommodation is a part of the test condition.

anatomical e. The manifestation of exophoria, or that portion of the total exophoria, attributable to structural (anatomical) anomalies or variance.

innervational e. The manifestation of exophoria, or that portion of the total exophoria, attributable to hypotonicity or lack of normal tonicity of the extraocular musculature subserving convergence.

intrinsic e. Exophoria attributable to primary structural, myologic, or neurological anomalies as distinguished from pseudoexophoria attributable to spurious manifestations, or failures of manifestation, of accommodative convergence.

monofixational e. See *phoria, monofixational.*

physiological e. 1. The mean exophoria at near for a given population and a given test procedure, usually considered to be about 5ᐃ or 6ᐃ exophoria for a 40 cm. distance. 2. The near phoria minus the distance phoria when exophoria is assigned positive value, and esophoria negative. 3. The portion of the exophoria in a near test corresponding to the amount of exophoria at distance.

relative e. 1. The amount of exophoria at near in excess of the physiological exophoria. 2. The distance exophoria regarded as a finding different from the absolute value that would be obtained with tonic convergence eliminated. 3. The phoria at near minus the phoria at distance, when exophoria is assigned positive value and esophoria negative value. 4. The amount of exophoria expressed in relation to given test conditions and given points of reference for purposes of quantitative specification.

exophoric (eks″o-fōr′ik). Pertaining to or manifesting exophoria.

exophthalmia (eks″of-thal′me-ah). Exophthalmos.

cachectica, e. Exophthalmic goiter.

fungosa, e. A late stage of retinoblastoma, in which the neoplasm perforates the cornea and protrudes from it.

exophthalmic (eks″of-thal′mik). Characterized by, or pertaining to, exophthalmos.

exophthalmic goiter; ophthalmoplegia. See under the nouns.

exophthalmometer (eks″of-thal-mom′eh-ter). An instrument for measuring the degree of exophthalmos. Syn., *ophthalmostatometer; proptometer; protometer.*

exophthalmometry (eks″of-thal-mom′eh-tre). The measurement of the degree of exophthalmos with the exophthalmometer. Syn., *ophthalmostatometry.*

exophthalmos (eks″of-thal′mos). An abnormal protrusion or proptosis of the eyeball from the orbit. Syn., *protrusio bulbi.*

endocrine e. Exophthalmos attributed to malfunction of the thyroid gland, the pituitary gland, or both. Syn., *hormonal exophthalmos.*

hormonal e. Endocrine exophthalmos.

intermittent e. An abnormal intermittent protrusion of the eyeball due to varicose veins in the orbit. Any condition which leads to stasis of blood in the head area, such as bending over or coughing, may cause this to occur if varicose veins are present.

malignant e. Exophthalmos, usually bilateral and marked, accompanied by severe edema of the eyelids, conjunctiva, and orbital fat and connective tissue; inflammation, degeneration, and increase in size of the extraocular muscles; and ophthalmoplegia. Although it may occur in association with either hyperthyroidism, hypothyroidism (as after thyroidectomy), or with a normal thyroid state, it has been considered by some to be an advanced or severe form of Graves's disease but more recently is attributed to overactivity of the anterior lobe of the pituitary gland and especially that of the thyrotrophic hormone. Typically occurring in middle age, it affects males and females equally except after thyroidectomy, in which case it affects males more frequently than females. The course and prognosis vary, with a tendency toward self-limitation. Syn., *progressive exophthalmos; thyrotropic exophthalmos, exophthalmic ophthalmoplegia.*

paralytic e. Exophthalmos caused by partial or total paralysis of the extrinsic muscles of the eye.

progressive e. Malignant exophthalmos.

pulsating e. Exophthalmos characterized by a pulsation of the eyeball which is synchronous with the heart beat, usually due to traumatic rupture of the internal carotid artery into the cavernous sinus.

thyrotoxic e. Exophthalmos present typically in hyperthyroidism; one of the early manifestations of exophthalmic goiter.

thyrotropic e. Malignant exophthalmos.

traumatic e. Exophthalmos resulting from injury involving scar tissue formation, hemorrhage in the orbit, callus formation of fractured bones, etc.

exophthalmus (eks″of-thal′mus). Exophthalmos.

exorbitism (eks-ōr′bit-izm). Exophthalmos.

exotropia (eks″o-tro′pe-ah). Divergent strabismus.

experiment. A trial, test, procedure, or special observation to discover some unknown effect or principle, to confirm or disprove a hypothesis or theory, or to illustrate a known truth.

Baumgardt-Segal e. The alternate presentation of two visual stimuli consisting of concentric circular spots of light of different size. When the spots are presented for 10 milliseconds each, with a 10 millisecond interval between, the large spot is seen with a brighter center. When the interval is increased to 50 milliseconds, a ring of light is seen with a black area the size of the small spot in the center.

Bidwell's e. The producing of the perception of the complement of a color stimulus, instead of the real color, by viewing it through an opening in a rotating disk which consists of three sectors, one black, one white, and one cut away to form the opening. The disk is rotated to present the stimuli in the sequence: black, color, and white.

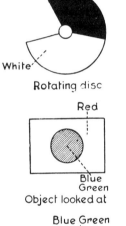

Fig. 17. Bidwell's experiment. (From *Text-book of Ophthalmology*, Vol. I, Duke-Elder, Henry Kimpton, 1942)

Blackowski's e. An experiment in brightness discrimination, in which a small white disk is surrounded by a larger annular area, the differential brightness limen between the two decreasing as the area of the annulus increases. That this is due to a shift in contours rather than an increase in area was shown by Fry and Bartley in a later experiment.

colored shadow e. The induction of a colored shadow by interposing an opaque object between a colored light source and a luminous white surface, the color of the shadow appearing complementary to the colored source although objectively achromatic.

Czermak's e. The observation of the apparent motion of an object, such as a thread, moved across a pinhole through which the eye is fixating a luminous surface, the pinhole being nearer the eye than the point of focus of the eye. When the object is between the eye and the pinhole, the apparent motion is opposite the real movement; when beyond the pinhole, the apparent motion is the same as the real movement.

Donders' e. The demonstration and/or measurement of relative convergence by the reading of print through prisms.

dropping e. Hering's dropping experiment.

Fechner's cloud e. The observation that a just noticeable difference in brightness of two adjacent cloud areas is still perceptible when viewed through a neutral filter which reduces the brightness of each proportionately.

Fizeau's e. The measurement of the velocity of light by the interval of interruption of light by means of a rotating toothed wheel, before and after traversing a long optical path reflected upon itself.

flicker e. Sherrington's flicker experiment.

Foucault's e. The measurement of the speed of light by the interval between reflections in a rotating plane mirror, before and after traversing a long optical path reflected upon itself.

Fresnel's biprism e. An experiment to produce interference fringes, without relying upon diffraction, by the use of Fresnel's biprism.

Fresnel's mirror e. A method of demonstrating interference by the use of a doubling mirror which splits incident light into two overlapping beams.

Hensen-Völckers e. A demonstration of the action of the ciliary muscle in accommodation by inserting needles through the sclera into the ciliary muscle. Stimulation of the muscle causes a backward movement of the free ends of the needles, indicating a forward movement of their points.

Hering's dropping e. A demonstration or test of depth perception, in which small beads viewed through a tubular aperture are dropped in front of or behind fine wires and are judged to be in front of or behind the plane of the wires.

Kravkov's e. A study of the relative effects of irradiation and brightness discrimination on visual acuity by determining the minimal separation of two black bars necessary for the perception of two when the brightness of the surround and the width of the bars are varied.

Lloyd's e. Lloyd's method.

Mariotte's e. An experiment demonstrating the existence of the physiological blind spot of the eye. The eye fixates a cross on a card which also contains a spot to the templeward side of the cross. The card is moved to and from the eye, and at a certain distance the spot will not be seen.

Meyer's e. A method of demonstrating simultaneous contrast. A narrow strip of gray paper is placed on a larger colored field, and the whole is covered with white tissue paper through which the gray strip appears as a complementary color to the surrounding field.

Molyneux e. An experiment suggested by Molyneux which consists of the showing of various objects to an adult, blind from birth but with vision just restored, to determine if the objects can be identified without tactile clues.

partition e. An experiment demonstrating the asymmetry of the two halves of the retina in which an individual, with constant monocular fixation, subjectively bisects a horizontal line. Underestimation of the temporal half of the line is termed *Kundt's monocular asymmetry*, while the reverse is termed *Münsterberg's monocular asymmetry*.

Ragona Scina e. A demonstration of color contrast in which an observer looks through a colored glass placed midway between two touching white screens set at right angles to each other, such that he sees, by reflection in the glass, one screen superimposed on the other. A black spot on the reflected screen will appear to be the same color as the glass, and one on the directly viewed screen will appear as its complement.

reversal e. The observation that a pin moved across a pinhole through which the eye is fixating appears to move in the opposite direction, providing the pinhole is nearer the eye than the point of focus and the pin is nearer than the pinhole.

Sachs's needle e. A demonstration of the action of the ciliary muscle in accommodation by inserting needles in the ciliary muscle of an eye through the sclera at varying distances from the equator of the eyeball. When the muscle contracts, the needle protruding from a certain portion remains motionless, the protruded part of the needle in front of this portion moves forward, and the

needle farther back moves backward.

Scheiner's e. A demonstration of the dioptric changes occurring during accommodation by observing a small object through a pair of laterally separated pinholes confined within the area of the pupil. The object appears double at all distances from the eye except the distance for which the eye is in focus.

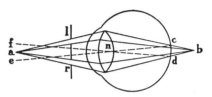

Fig. 18. Scheiner's experiment. (From *Physiological Optics*, ed. 3, W. D. Zoethout, Professional Press, 1939)

Sherrington's flicker e. An experiment to investigate binocular fusion of uniocular sensations produced by flickering lights with precisely controlled dark and light intervals, presented to each eye in a variety of sequences and frequencies and compared to summation effects obtained for both stimuli in one eye.

side-window e. A demonstration of binocular contrast in which the observer stands in profile to a window or other bright source so that one eye is strongly transilluminated from the side while the other eye is shaded. White objects will now appear greenish to the illuminated eye, reddish to the other eye.

Stratton's e. An experiment in which, by means of an optical inverting system, the visual directions are completely reversed for one eye for a long period of time, the other eye being occluded. Stratton learned to reach for an object which was visually to his right by moving his hand to his left. This learning, however, did not change the reversed perception of the location of objects in space.

Wundt's e. An experiment to determine the relative effects of accommodation and convergence on the judgment of distance.

Young's e. The first experiment to produce interference fringes performed by Thomas Young in 1802. Two coherent beams of light, produced by passing light from a pinhole in one screen through two pinholes in a second screen, come together to form interference fringes on a third screen.

exteriorization (eks-te″re-or-ih-za′-shun). A form of perception in which an object viewed monocularly appears as though seen through an opaque body placed in front of the other eye. The *hole-in-the-hand test* is an example.

external rectus (eks-ter′nal rek′tus). See under *muscle*.

extorsion (eks-tōr′shun). 1. The real, or apparent, turning of the two eyes relative to each other about their respective anteroposterior axes so that their respective vertical meridians of reference diverge from each other superiorly and converge inferiorly. 2. The real or apparent turning of an eye about an anteroposterior axis so that the upward extension of its vertical meridian of reference deviates temporally from the true vertical. Syn., *disclination*.

extort (eks-tōrt′). To turn toward a position of extorsion or away from a position of intorsion.

extraction (eks-trak′shun). The act or process of pulling or drawing out.

aspiration e. Surgical removal of congenital or other soft cataracts in which an incision is made into the anterior capsule of the crys-

talline lens and the lens mass evacuated by suction.

combined e. Surgical removal of a cataractous crystalline lens, together with iridectomy.

cryoprehensile e. Cryoextraction.

extracapsular e. Surgical removal of a cataractous crystalline lens by incising the anterior capsule of the lens and expressing the opaque lens.

intracapsular e. Surgical removal of a cataractous crystalline lens, together with its capsule.

linear e. Surgical treatment of soft or traumatic cataract in which an incision is made into the anterior capsule of the crystalline lens and the lens mass evacuated through the corneal wound by pressure or irrigation.

simple e. Surgical removal of a cataractous crystalline lens, without iridectomy.

extraocular (eks″trah-ok′u-lar). External to or outside of the eye.

extrarectus (eks″trah-rek′tus). External rectus muscle.

extravisual (eks″trah-vizh′u-al). Other than visual; outside of the field of vision, or beyond the visible spectrum.

eye. The organ of vision. In humans, it is a spheroid body approximately 1 in. in diameter, with the segment of a smaller sphere, the cornea, in front. It occurs in pairs, one in each of the bony orbits of the skull, and consists of an external coat of fibrous sclera and transparent cornea; a middle vascular coat, the uvea, composed of the iris, the ciliary body, and the choroid; and an internal nervous coat, the retina, which includes the sensory receptors for light. Within, it contains the anterior, the posterior, and the vitreous chambers, the aqueous humor, the vitreous body, the crystalline lens, the zonule of Zinn, and the intraocular portion of the optic nerve. Six extraocular muscles control its movements. Broader definitions sometimes include the conjunctiva, Tenon's capsule, and associated appendages.

acone e. A compound eye found in certain arthropods in which the region of each ommatidium normally containing the crystalline cone is cellular and nonrefractive.

aggregate e. A group of closely packed ocelli which resembles a compound eye, but differs in that each ocellus remains anatomically and functionally independent.

amaurotic cat's e. See under *amaurotic*.

aphakic e. An eye in which the crystalline lens is not present. See also *aphakia*.

appendages of e. The ocular adnexa, consisting of the eyelids, the eyebrows, the conjunctiva, lacrimal apparatus, Tenon's capsule, and the extrinsic ocular muscles. Some authorities omit the latter two.

apposition e. The typical compound eye in which both the crystalline cone and the retinule of each ommatidium is ensheathed by pigment cells so that light striking the corneal facet cannot reach or stimulate neighboring ommatidia. Hence, light from one corneal facet is incident upon only one rhabdome. Cf. *superposition eye.*

artificial e. A prosthesis made of glass, plastic, or similar material which simulates the anterior portion of an eye. It is placed in the socket after enucleation or evisceration or over the remnants of a nonfunctioning eye for cosmetic purposes.

artificial e., custom. An artificial eye expressly made to fit a patient's orbit. It is usually hand painted if made of plastic or, with a handmade iris if made of glass.

artificial e., semicustom. An artificial eye especially made to fit the patient's orbit but having a stock iris.

artificial e., stock. Any one of an assortment of ready-made artificial eyes from which a selection is made to fit a patient.

biunial e. Cyclopean eye.

black e. Ecchymosis of the eyelid.

blear e. An irritated or a watery-appearing eye.

bung e. A permanent swelling of the upper eyelid in association with onchocerciasis.

cerebral e. The eye of a vertebrate which has its retina derived from

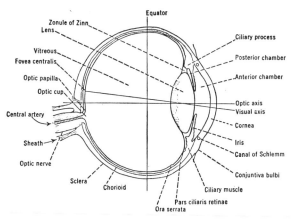

Fig. 19. Schematic cross section of the eye. (From *Ophthalmology,* Arno E. Town, Lea & Febiger, 1951)

the forebrain via an optic cup and not from the surface ectoderm as in many invertebrates.

chameleon e. Pronounced proptosis with downward, or downward and lateral, displacement of the eyeball, usually accompanied by impaired motility, chemosis, and eyelid edema, and resulting from an intraorbital tumor or invasion of the orbit by a tumor.

compound e. The eye of arthropods, such as insects, which consists of a grouping of structurally and functionally associated elements, ommatidia, whose surfaces collectively form a mosaic-patterned segment of a sphere.

congenital cystic e. A congenital cyst in the space normally occupied by the eyeball due to failure of the primary optic vesicle to involute.

controlling e. Predominant eye.

crossed e's. Convergent strabismus.

cupulate e. A type of simple eye composed of a group of contiguous light-sensitive epithelial cells which have invaginated to form a cup-shaped depression.

cyclopean e. An imaginary mental eye located between the two real eyes which serves as a center for directionalization. It represents a composite hypothetical visual perception area for the two eyes, with a macula, a center of rotation, a nodal point, and a principal point, all lying in a straight line in a medially located reference plane of the head. Syn., *biunial eye; mental eye.*

   cyclopean e., bimacular. The cyclopean eye in subjects with anomalous retinal correspondence. The apparent direction of a bifoveally perceived object differs for the right and the left eyes. This difference in direction can be represented by assuming that the imaginary cyclopean eye has two maculae instead of one.

   cyclopean e., macular. The

cyclopean eye in subjects with normal retinal correspondence.

dark-adapted e. An eye which has been sufficiently exposed to decreased illumination to bring about the chemical and physiologic changes necessary for maximum sensitivity to light. Such changes include dilation of the pupillary aperture, regeneration and advancement of rhodopsin in the rods of the retina, and dependence on peripheral retinal stimulation. See also *duplicity theory; scotopic vision.*

deviating e. The nonfixating eye in strabismus or under phoria testing conditions.

directing e. The dominant eye as established by criteria which are presumed to determine which eye primarily subserves the perception of direction or the function of guiding the orientation of the subject.

dominant e. 1. The eye that is dominant when ocular dominance exists. 2. The fixating eye in unilateral strabismus.

emmetropic e. An eye having the condition of emmetropia.

equidominant e's. Eyes equally dominant or failing to show dominance in reference to a specific type of ocular dominance.

eucone e. The typical compound eye of arthropods in which each ommatidium has a surface cuticular lenslike formation (corneal facet) and an underlying crystalline cone.

exciting e. In sympathetic ophthalmia, the eye which is originally injured and which seems to serve as a source of inflammation for the other eye. The term, *sympathogenic,* has also been suggested for this eye. Syn., *primary eye.*

exocone e. A compound eye found in certain arthropods in which the region of each ommatidium normally containing the crystalline cone is, instead, a conelike invagination of the surface corneal facet.

fixating e. 1. In strabismus, the eye which is directed toward the object of regard. 2. In cases of diplopia, natural or induced by testing devices, the eye which serves to locate correctly the object of regard in space; the eye which receives stimulation from the object at the fovea; the eye which serves as the organ of reference for the cyclopean eye. 3. The eye used for viewing through monocular instruments or small single apertures.

flat e. A type of simple eye composed of a few contiguous light-sensitive epithelial cells which, together, form a surface plaque.

fold, e. See under *fold.*

following e. In strabismus, the deviating eye.

gas e. An eye characterized by inflammation and photophobia and found among attendants of natural gas pumping stations.

hare's e. Lagophthalmos.

hop e. An eye with conjunctivitis caused by irritation from the hairs of the hop plant.

hyper e. An eye situated higher than its fellow in relation to an assumed horizontal plane of reference defined by one or another structural feature of the body, head, or face.

klieg e. An eye with conjunctivitis, photophobia, lacrimation, and edema, caused by exposure to the intense illumination from klieg lights.

lead e. 1. In strabismus, the fixating eye. 2. Predominant eye.

light-adapted e. An eye which has been sufficiently exposed to bright illumination to bring about the necessary physiological and photochemical changes for photopic or daylight vision. These changes include decreasing the pupil aperture, bleaching and retraction of the rhodopsin, and concentration on cone rather than rod vision. Color sensitivity is generally assumed to be associated with the light-adapted eye. See also *duplicity theory; photopic vision.*

master e. Dominant eye.

memory, e. Visual memory.

mental e. Cyclopean eye.

monochromatic e. An eye which perceives only one color.

optic constants of the e. See under *constant.*

phakic e. An eye in which the crystalline lens is present.

pineal e. A rudimentary median eye appearing in some lower forms of animal life.

pink e. 1. Acute contagious conjunctivitis. 2. (Vet. Med.) In livestock, infectious keratitis.

predominant e. The eye considered to control visual perception in binocular vision; to be differentiated from the sighting eye in sighting ocular dominance. Syn., *controlling eye; lead eye.*

preferred e. 1. The eye usually or always selected when unilateral viewing is required by some visual task. The term is best applicable when the subject is aware that only one eye can be used, as in the use of a monocular microscope. See also *sighting dominance.* 2. The eye which fixates the greater percentage of the time in alternating strabismus.

primary e. Exciting eye.

pseudocone e. A compound eye found in certain insects in which the ommatidium has a fluid substance instead of a crystalline cone.

reduced e. A mathematical concept (model) of the optical system of the eye as if it were a single ideal refracting surface with only one nodal point, principal point, and index of refraction.

reduced e., Donders'. A simplified concept of the optical constants of the eye in which the refracting portions are represented as a single spherical surface of which the radius of curvature is 5.73 mm., the index of refraction is 1.336, the refractive surface is 1.35 mm. behind the cornea, and the nodal point lies 7.08 mm. posterior to the cornea. Its anterior focal distance is 17.054 mm., and its posterior focal distance is 22.78 mm., both measured from the refracting surface of the reduced eye.

reduced e., Gullstrand's. A reduced eye which has a radius of curvature of 5.7 mm., an index of refraction of 1.33, and a length of 22.8 mm.

reduced e., Listing's. A reduced eye which has a radius of curvature of 5.1248 mm., an index of refraction of 1.35, and a length of 20.0 mm.

reform e., Snellen's. An artificial eye consisting of two convexoconcave laminae with an air space between them.

schematic e. 1. A diagrammatic representation of the optical system of an ideal normal eye based on a careful analysis of the dioptric systems of a number of emmetropic eyes. It includes constants for curvature, indices of refraction, and distances between the optical elements. 2. A simplified mechanical model of the human eye having a single refracting lens, a pupillary aperture, and a representation of the retina, used in the practice of retinoscopy and ophthalmoscopy. 3. An eye model, usually simplified and enlarged, to show the mechanical, optical, and anatomical features of the eye.

schematic e., Fisher's. A model eye designed with a single refracting lens, a variable pupil-lary aperture, and a means of varying the distance from the lens to the surface representing the retina, used for practice in ophthalmoscopy and retinoscopy.

schematic e., Gullstrand's. A representative or schematic eye computed from the average of a large number of human eye measurements by Allvar Gullstrand (1862–1930). Gullstrand gives values for the position of the principal, nodal, and focal points and thus defines the eye as an optical instrument.

schematic e., simplified. An approximation based on the schematic eye, in which calculations are carried out to fewer decimal places, and certain small values are considered negligible.

secondary e. Sympathizing eye.

shell e. An artificial eye consisting of a single thin layer. Cf. *Snellen's reform eye.*

shield, e. 1. A covering for the eye to protect it from light, infection, or injury. 2. An occluder.

shipyard e. Epidemic keratoconjunctivitis.

sighting e. The dominant eye in sighting ocular dominance.

simple e. An ocellus.

squinting e. The deviating eye in strabismus.

subdominant e. The eye considered to subserve the fellow (predominant) eye in binocular vision.

superposition e. A compound eye found in some nocturnal insects in which, in the dark-adapted state, the pigment is concentrated around the crystalline cones, leaving the retinules without insulation, so that light from several corneal facets may pass through several retinules to converge upon a single rhabdome. Cf. *apposition eye.*

sympathizing e. In sympathetic ophthalmia, the uninjured eye which is affected by an inflammation of the uveal tract following injury to the exciting eye. Syn., *secondary eye.*

trichromatic e. An eye with normal trichromatic color vision.

vesicular e. The most advanced type of simple eye composed of a group of contiguous light-sensitive epithelial cells which have invaginated to form a closed subepithelial globe.

eyeball. The globe or ball of the eye.

congenital cystic e. A large, bulging, tumorlike orbital mass existing from birth, due to failure of the optic vesicle to invaginate.

luxated e. An eyeball displaced forward from its normal position in the orbit.

eyebrow. 1. An appendage of the eye located in the region of the superciliary ridge of the frontal bone and consisting of skin with hairs (supercilia), subcutaneous tissue, three skeletal muscles, areolar connective tissue, and the cranial periosteum (pericranium). 2. The row of hairs (supercilia) between the upper eyelid and the forehead. Syn., *supercilium.*

eyecells. Postoperative shields made of black cup-shaped porcelain that fit over the eyelids.

eyecup. 1. The optic cup of the early embryo which gives rise to the retina and the inner portions of the ciliary body and the iris. 2. A vessel which may be filled with fluid and fitted to the orbital aperture to bathe or treat the area of the conjunctival sac.

eyecurrent. 1. The electrical effect that is recorded as the electroretinogram (E.R.G.). 2. The "current of rest," or the resting potential in the eye; an electrical potential from the eye when no light is involved, sometimes recorded when the eye is rendered neurally inactive. The effect is then due simply to ionic differ-

ences across membranes. The cornea is positive to the back of the eye.

eyedness. Ocular dominance.

eyeglass. 1. A monocle. 2. The eyepiece, or the ocular, of an optical instrument.

eyeglasses. 1. A pair of ophthalmic lenses together with the frame or the mounting; spectacles. 2. A pair of ophthalmic lenses supported in a frame or a mounting that is held on the nose by spring pressure without the aid of temples, as in a pince-nez or oxford.

eyeground. The fundus of the eye as seen with the ophthalmoscope.

eyelash. A cilium growing on the margin of the eyelid.

eyelids. A pair of protective coverings of the eye, consisting of a lower eyelid extending upward from the cheek and an upper eyelid extending downward from the eyebrow and more movable, due to the action of a levator muscle. Each eyelid consists of the following layers: skin, subcutaneous connective tissue, orbicularis oculi muscle, submuscular connective tissue, a fibrous layer made up of a tarsus with sebum-producing Meibomian glands and an orbital septum attached to the orbital margin, a smooth muscle of Mueller, and the palpebral conjunctiva.

fused e. 1. The normal epithelial joining of the eyelid folds present from about the ninth week until the seventh or eighth month of fetal life. 2. A congenital anomaly in which the eyelids remain joined. Syn., *ankyloblepharon.*

granulated eyelid. A lay term for chronic blepharitis, characterized by scaly desquamation.

third eyelid. Nictitating membrane.

tucked eyelid. A retraction of the upper eyelid, usually associated with ophthalmoplegia and occurring in lesions of the upper brain stem in the region of the posterior commissure.

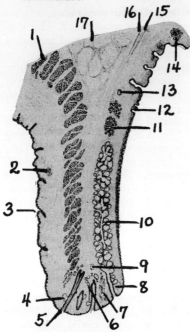

Fig. 20. Section through the upper eyelid. (1) Orbicularis oculi muscle. (2) Sweat gland. (3) Hair follicle. (4) Gland of Zeis. (5) Cilium. (6) Gland of Moll. (7) Pars ciliaris muscle. (8) Muscle of Riolan. (9) Inferior arterial arcade. (10) Meibomian gland. (11) Gland of Wolfring. (12) Conjunctival crypts. (13) Superior arterial arcade. (14) Gland of Krause. (15) Mueller's superior palpebral muscle. (16) Levator palpebrae superioris muscle. (17) Fat. (From *Text-book of Ophthalmology,* Vol. V, Duke-Elder, Henry Kimpton, 1952)

eyepiece. The lens or a combination of lenses in a telescope, microscope, or other optical instrument to which the human eye is applied in order to view the image formed by the objective system. Syn., *eye lens; ocular.*

Abbe's e. An orthoscopic eyepiece consisting of a triplet field lens and a planoconvex eye lens, designed to have a chromatic difference of magnification opposite to that of the objective and having a shorter focal length for red light than for blue light.

autocollimating e. Gauss eyepiece.

compensating e. An eyepiece in a lens system compensating for spherical or longitudinal aberration of the objective.

Gauss's e. An eyepiece in which the cross hairs or reticle can be illuminated from the side to serve as an object for an autocollimating telescope, as in a spectroscope. Syn., *autocollimating eyepiece.*

Huygens' e. An eyepiece, the most common on microscopes, designed by Huygens, a Dutch physicist (1629–1695), consisting of two planoconvex lenses, the convex side of each being directed toward the objective lens system. The first lens, the field lens, usually has a focal length three times that of the eye lens, and the separation is twice the focal length of the eye lens.

Kellner e. A modification of the Ramsden eyepiece, widely used in high power telescopes, gunsights, and, commonly, in prism binoculars, designed to reduce the amount of lateral chromatic aberration. The eye lens is an achromatic doublet made of dense barium crown glass and light flint glass.

negative e. An eyepiece in which a real image is formed between its lenses.

orthoscopic e. An eyepiece especially corrected for distortion, usually consisting of a triple field lens and a single eye lens, providing a wide field of view and high magnification; it is used on telescopes and range finders.

positive e. An eyepiece in which a real image is formed outside the eyepiece and which can be used as a magnifier.

Ramsden e. An eyepiece designed by Ramsden, an English optician, consisting of two planoconvex lenses, the convex side of each facing the other within the eyepiece. The lenses are often equal in focal length and separated by three fourths the focal length of either.

simple e. An eyepiece consisting of a single lens.

symmetrical e. An eyepiece consisting of two similar lenses, usually two symmetrical achromatic doublets, used primarily in telescopic sights on guns where the eye must be a distance from the eyepiece.

terrestrial e. An eyepiece which contains an erecting system in addition to its usual eyepiece lenses.

wide-field e. An eyepiece designed to give a wide field of view, as an orthoscopic eyepiece.

eyepoint. 1. The point in an optical system where a given point of reference of the observer's eye, such as the entrance pupil of the eye, should be placed; the exit pupil of a viewing system, e.g., of a telescope. 2. A reference point within the eye used in specifying angular magnification or distortion of an ophthalmic prism; usually the entrance pupil of the eye, the center of rotation of the eye, or a theoretical point that assumes that both the entrance pupil and the center of rotation are coincident.

eyesight. The sense of seeing; vision.

eyesize. The dimension of the eyewire of a spectacle frame. There are various methods of determining this dimension. It is specified by the Standards Committee of the American Optometric Association and the Technical Committee of the Optical Manufacturers Association as "the width of eye, length between vertical tangents to the ends of lens, 'boxed' length."

Eye-Span Trainer. A trade name for a manually operated tachistoscope used in flash recognition training of numbers, words, or phrases.

eyespot. A light-sensitive pigmented spot, found in unicellular organisms and in other invertebrates, which serves in phototaxis. Syn., *stigma.*

eyestrain. Discomfort or fatigue associated with the eyes or the use of the eyes and attributed to uncorrected errors of refraction, ocular muscle anomalies, prolonged use of the eyes, etc.

eye-vesicle (i-ves'i-k'l). Optic vesicle. *Obs.*

eyewash. Any fluid medication or cleanser applied to the eye. Syn., *collyrium.*

eyewire. The portion of a spectacle frame that conforms to the periphery of a lens and thereby retains the lens. It may be grooved to fit a beveled lens edge, or round (wire or nylon thread) to fit a grooved lens edge.

F

F. Symbol for (1) *rate of aqueous outflow;* (2) *visual field;* (3) *focal power.*

f. Symbol for *focal length.*

F.A.A.O. Fellow of the American Academy of Optometry.

Fabry's disease (fah-brēz'). See under *disease.*

Fabry-Pérot interferometer (fah-bre'peh-ro'). See under *interferometer.*

face tilt. A forward or a backward tilt of the head, especially as a postural symptom of an extraocular muscle paresis or paralysis.

face turn. Head rotation.

facet, corneal. 1. A small dip, or fossa, on the outer surface of the cornea, resulting from failure of the floor of an ulcer to fill in with tissue. 2. The surface lenslike structure, superficial to the crystalline cone, in the ommatidium of the compound eye of arthropods.

facial hemiatrophy (fa'shal hem"-ih-at'ro-fe). Romberg's disease.

facial hemiplegia, alternate (fa'-shal hem"ih-ple'je-ah). Millard-Gubler syndrome.

F.A.C.L.P. Fellow of the Association of Contact Lens Practitioners.

factor. 1. One of the circumstances, elements, or constituents contributing to produce a result. 2. Any of the quantities or elements that form a product when multiplied together; a quantity by which a magnitude must be divided or multiplied to express it in other terms. 3. A desirable or essential nutritional element. 4. A gene.

absorption f. 1. Absorptance. 2. In glass manufacture, the ingredient serving to make the glass absorptive.

discrimination f. The reciprocal, $B/\Delta B$, of the differential threshold in brightness discrimination, where ΔB equals the difference in luminance between the two parts of the test field and B equals the luminance of one of them. Syn., *discrimination index.*

luminosity f. Spectral luminous efficacy of radiant flux. See under *efficacy.*

luminosity f., relative. Spectral luminous efficiency of radiant flux. See under *efficiency.*

reduction f. The ratio of the mean spherical candlepower of a source of light to its mean horizontal candlepower. Syn., *spherical reduction factor.*

reflection f. The ratio of flux reflected from a surface to that incident on it. Syn., *reflectance.*

reflection f., diffuse. The ratio of flux diffusely reflected from a surface to that incident on it. Syn., *diffuse reflectance.*

reflection f., specular. The ratio of flux regularly reflected from a surface to that incident on it. Syn., *specular reflectance.*

reflection f., total. The ratio of flux reflected both diffusely and regularly from a surface to that incident on it. Syn., *total reflectance.*

room utilization f. The ratio of the luminous flux received on the workplane to that emitted by the luminaires.

[268]

transmission f. The ratio of radiant flux transmitted through a body to that incident on it. Syn., *transmittance*.

visibility f. 1. Spectral luminous efficacy of radiant flux. See under *efficacy*. 2. A coefficient obtained by any of several procedures or formulas to represent the extent to which glare affects visual acuity or brightness discrimination.

　visibility f., relative. Spectral luminous efficiency of radiant flux. See under *efficiency*.

faculty, fusion. 1. The ability to perceive with the two eyes a single, integrated, fused image of a pair of haploscopically presented objects or an object viewed binocularly, especially when characterized by the associated ability to maintain single, fused imagery through a finite range of changes in convergence stimulus. 2. The ability to perceive continuously uniform light when the stimulus is intermittent. *Rare*.

critical fusion f. The ability to appreciate intermittent visual stimulation as continuous when it reaches a certain frequency.

F.A.D.O. Fellow of the Association of Dispensing Opticians.

faisceau isthmique (fa-so' is'mēk). Druault's marginal bundle.

fallacia optica (fah-la'shih-ah op'tih-kah). A visual illusion or a visual hallucination.

Falls-Kurtesz syndrome (fals-kur'-tez). See under *syndrome*.

fan dial. See under *chart, fan dial*.

fantascopy (fan-tah'sko-pe). Retinoscopy.

fantasy. Imagination; the mental creation of nonexistent objects or images, or the so-created mental image itself.

far point of accommodation; convergence; fusion. See under the nouns.

Faraday's effect (far'ah-dāz). See under *effect*.

Farnsworth (fahrns'worth) **color circle; test.** See under the nouns.

Farnsworth-Munsell test (fahrns'-worth-mun-sel'). See under *test*.

farsighted. Hypermetropic.

farsightedness. Hypermetropia.

fascia (fash'e-ah). A layer or sheet of connective tissue covering, insheathing, partitioning, supporting, or binding together structures or internal parts of the body.

bulbar f. Tenon's capsule.

lacrimal f. The periosteum which encloses the lacrimal sac.

orbital f. A general term for all the fibrous membranes within the orbit, including the periorbita, the orbital septum, Tenon's capsule, intermuscular membranes, check ligaments, and others.

papebral f. Septum orbitale.

tarso-orbital f. Septum orbitale.

Tenon, f. of. Tenon's capsule.

fasciculus, anterior accessory, of Bochenek (fah-sik'u-lus). Anterior accessory optic tract of Bochenek.

fasciculus, medial longitudinal (fah-sik'u-lus). Medial longitudinal bundle.

fat, orbital. Fatty tissue which fills the interstices in the orbit in the regions of the optic nerve, the muscles, the lacrimal gland, the vessels, and the nerves.

fatigue. The condition of organs or cells in which the power or capacity to respond to stimulation is decreased or lost, due to excessive activity.

color f. 1. Chromatic adaptation, usually of such long duration or high intensity that all or most of the color has perceptually disappeared from the response. The observer perceives only a colorless, gray, or brown adapting light or stimulus surface. Perception of other colors, particularly colors complementary to the adapting color, may be heightened. 2. An excessively rapid perceptual fading of steadily observed colors.

retinal f. 1. The condition attributed to the retina when the sensory end result is impoverished as, for example, when a small, peripherally located target, initially seen, disappears after continued fixation of another target. 2. A condition postulated to explain negative afterimages, successive contrast, etc. Under the most recent view of fatigue and impairment, fatigue seems to be an ill-chosen term.

visual f. 1. A condition of improper or reduced function considered to accrue from the use of the eyes. It has been of concern as to where this fatigue takes place, whether in the eye, somewhere along the optic pathway, or elsewhere in the central nervous system. In the common view, there is no single set of signs or symptoms that indicates visual fatigue. Actually, some of the symptoms and signs pertain to nonvisual parts of the body. 2. A state of inadequacy of the individual attributable to the use of the visual apparatus. Under this view, visual fatigue, just as any other fatigue, pertains to the person as a whole, and differs from other forms primarily in the kind of task under which it develops. This view makes a distinction between fatigue and tissue impairment, and thus bypasses the need for distinguishing between mental and physical fatigue, except for the mode of production of the end result, fatigue itself.

favus (fa′vus, fah′vus). A skin disease due to a fungus infection, characterized by the presence of round, yellow, saucer-shaped crusts having a peculiar mousy odor. It mainly affects the scalp but may occur on the eyelids. Syn., *tinea favosa.*

F.B.O.A. Fellow of the British Optical Association.

feather. A feather-shaped defect in glass or other transparent materials which may be due to inhomogeneity, folds, or clusters of fine bubbles.

Fechner's (fek′nerz) **colors; experiment; fraction; law; paradox.** See under the nouns.

Fechner-Helmholtz law (fek′ner-helm′hōltz). Law of coefficients.

feeble-mindedness. 1. Mental inferiority or deficiency which is subdivided into three groups: *idiocy, imbecility,* and *moronity.* 2. Moronity.

Fehr's spotted corneal dystrophy (ferz). Macular corneal dystrophy.

Feinbloom contact lens (fīn′blūm). See under *lens, contact.*

Feincone contact lens (fīn′kōn). See under *lens, contact.*

Feldman's adaptometer. See under *adaptometer.*

feldspar (feld′spar). Fluorite.

fentoscopy (fen-tos′ko-pe). Observation, with the unaided eye, of the passage of the beam of a slit lamp through ocular structures.

Féréol-Graux's ocular palsy (fa-ra-ōl′grawz). See under *palsy.*

Fermat's (fer-māz′) **law; principle.** See under the nouns.

Ferree-Rand axometer (fer′e-rand). See under *axometer.*

Ferrein's canal (fer′inz). See under *canal.*

Ferry-Porter law (fer′e-pōr′ter). See under *law.*

Fery prism (fer′e). See under *prism.*

fever, pharyngoconjunctival. A triad of fever, pharyngitis, and acute follicular conjunctivitis caused by a virus infection, usually type 3 adenovirus. All three components are not always present, but the conjunctivitis is usually the chief complaint, lasting from a few days to a few weeks and always ending in full recovery. It is usually transmitted through swimming pools and mainly affects children.

fever, uveoparotid. Uveoparotitis.

fiber. A filament or a threadlike structure.

arcuate f's. The portion of the ganglionic axons in the nerve fiber layer of the retina which are temporal to the optic disk, and exclusive of the papillomacular bundle, traveling above and below this bundle in an arcuate course.

basket of Schultze, f. Fine extensions of the external limiting layer of the retina, or of the fibers of Mueller as some claim, which surround the inner members of the rods and the cones.

cilio-equatorial f's. The fibers of the suspensory ligament of the crystalline lens, originating in the area of the ciliary processes and inserting into the lens capsule at the equator.

cilioposterior f's. The fibers of the suspensory ligament of the crystalline lens, originating in the region of the ciliary processes and inserting into the posterior capsule of the lens, posterior to the equator.

cone f. A fiberlike extension of the retinal cone cell extending from the cell body or nuclear region to the inner member and the cone foot.

corticobulbar f's. Axons of pyramidal cells located in the cerebral cortex which enter the contralateral corticobulbar tract and synapse in the motor nuclei of cranial nerves located in the brain stem. See also *corticobulbar tract.*

Gratiolet, f's of. Axons in the optic radiations which leave the lateral geniculate body and end in the area striata.

Henle, f's of. Long S-shaped rod and cone fibers in the region of the macula lutea which enter the outer molecular layer of the ret-

ina and collectively form the fiber layer of Henle.

interretinal f's. Axons that supposedly leave one retina, enter the optic nerve, cross over in the chiasm, and enter the contralateral optic nerve and retina; commissural fibers between the two retinae.

Landolt, f's of. Processes of dendrites of cone bipolar neurons of the retina of certain fishes, amphibians, reptiles, and birds, which continue outward to the external limiting membrane.

lens f. An elongated protoplasmic unit, usually hexagonal in section, which is derived from an epithelial cell just within the capsule of the crystalline lens, and is attached to an anterior and to a posterior suture.

lens f's., primary. Fibers of the crystalline lens derived embryonically by the elongation of the posterior epithelium of the lens to fill in the cavity of the lens vesicle, present in the embryonic portion of the nucleus of the adult.

lens f's., secondary. Hexagonal fibers of the crystalline lens, formed at the periphery of the equator of the lens by the posterior portion of the anterior epithelium, which surround the few primary fibers at the very center of the nucleus, are produced throughout life, and eventually lose their nuclei.

longitudinal f's. 1. Smooth muscle fibers, comprising Brücke's muscle, that attach to the scleral spur and uveal meshwork, course through the length of the ciliary body, and attach to the suprachoroid at the equator. 2. The temporal ganglionic axons from the retina that do not decussate but enter the ipsilateral optic tract. 3. Any fiber oriented along the length of the structure of which it is a part.

medullated nerve f's. 1. Nerve fibers, axons, or dendrites which have myelin or fatty sheaths. 2. Ophthalmoscopically observable, anomalously medullated, ganglionic axons in the vicinity of the optic disk. Syn., *opaque nerve fibers.*

Meynert's f's. Axons in the tectobulbar tracts which leave the superior colliculus, synapse in the motor nuclei, and supply the extrinsic muscles of the eye.

Monakow's f's. Efferent pupillary fibers for the direct or consensual light reflexes. *Obs.*

Mueller's f's. Fibers of neuroglia in the retina, extending between the external and internal limiting layers, filling in the space between the conducting neurons and forming a dense network of interlacing trabeculae in the innermost layers. They are supportive to the retinal neurons and participate in their metabolism by storing glycogen and oxidative enzymes.

opaque nerve f's. Medullated nerve fibers.

orbiculoanterior f's. Fibers of the suspensory ligament of the crystalline lens that originate from the smoother posterior part of the ciliary body, just anterior to the ora serrata, and insert into the capsule of the lens, just anterior to the equator.

orbiculociliary f's. Accessory fibers of the suspensory ligament of the crystalline lens that run from the smoother posterior portion of the ciliary body to the ciliary processes, preventing the latter from moving forward.

orbiculoposterior f's. Fibers of the suspensory ligament of the crystalline lens which originate in the posterior smooth portion of the ciliary body and insert into the lens capsule just posterior to its equator.

papillomacular f's. Ganglionic axons from the macular region of the retina which comprise the papillomacular bundle in the nerve fiber layer and which enter the temporal portion of the optic disk and travel in the central portion of the optic nerve.

pupillary f's. 1. Ganglionic axons in the optic nerve that leave the optic tract via a brachium, reach the pretectal region anterior to the superior colliculus, and mediate the afferent impulses of the direct and consensual light pupillary constriction reflexes. 2. Fibers in the oculomotor nerve that synapse in the ciliary ganglion and mediate the efferent impulses of the direct and consensual light pupillary constriction reflexes.

retinomotor f's. 1. Efferent fibers in the optic nerves of lower vertebrates which supposedly control the movement of the outer members of the visual cells by contraction of the myoid elements or of the pigmented processes of the epithelium. If present in man, their function is unknown. 2. Efferent fibers that synapse with centrifugal bipolars of the retina and convey impulses to the cone feet.

Ritter's f's. Granulated fibrils located axially in inner rod segments.

rod f. A thin, delicate fiber extending from the inner member of a rod cell, through the external limiting membrane to the rod granule, and continuing to end in the outer molecular layer as a small end knob which is surrounded by the terminal arborizations of the bipolar cells.

Sappey's f's. Smooth muscle fibers found in check ligaments of the extrinsic eye muscles, near the orbital insertions of the ligaments.

sustentacular f's. The neuroglia or supporting cells of the retina, such as the fibers of Mueller, astrocytes, and others.

tectobulbar f's. Axons of neuron cell bodies, located in the superior and inferior colliculi of the midbrain, which enter the contralateral tectobulbar tract and synapse in the motor nuclei of cranial nerves located in the brain stem. See also *tectobulbar tract.*

trophic (in optic nerve) f's. Efferent fibers in the optic nerve that supposedly affect the nutrition of the retina. Such fibers have not been identified in humans.

visual f's. Axons from the ganglion cell layer of the retina that synapse in the lateral geniculate body and project back to the region of the calcarine fissure, conveying impulses for vision.

zonular f's. The noncellular fibers of the suspensory ligament of the crystalline lens which originate at the ciliary body and insert into the lens capsule near its equator.

    zonular f's., capsular. Fibers of the zonule of Zinn which insert into the capsule of the crystalline lens.

    zonular f's., coronal. Fibers of the zonule of Zinn which insert into the corona ciliaris.

    zonular f's., orbicular. Fibers of the zonule of Zinn which insert into the pars plana.

fiberscope (fi'ber-skōp). An optical device consisting essentially of a flexible bundle of transparent fibers which transmits an image, thus enabling the viewing of objects which cannot be seen directly, such as the interior of the stomach.

fibrodysplasia hyperelastica (fi″bro-dis-pla'se-ah hi″per-e-las'tih-kah). Meekren-Ehlers-Danlos syndrome.

fibroma (fi-bro'mah). A benign tumor, primarily consisting of masses of white, fibrous, connective tissue, which commonly appears on the conjunctiva or the eyelid as a result of inflammation or trauma, and may also occur on the sclera, the cornea, the choroid, or the optic nerve.

molluscum, f. The neurofibroma of von Recklinghausen's disease; a diffuse proliferation of the Schwann cells of the peripheral nerves which may involve any part of the eye or the adnexa.

fibroplasia, retrolental. Retinopathy of prematurity.

fibrosis, massive retinal (fi-bro'sis). An elevated grayish-white mass of glial tissue protruding from the retina, due to the organization of a massive retinal hemorrhage. In the newborn, it is primarily attributed to obstetrical trauma and is located near the optic disk or macula. In the adult, the affected eye often shows evidence of endophthalmitis, and the mass is usually at the ora serrata. Syn., *retinal pseudotumor.*

Fick's phenomenon; theory; tonometer. See under the nouns.

field. 1. An area, a region, or a space. 2. A range or sphere of activity.

curvature of the f. See under *curvature.*

depth of f. See under *depth.*

diplopia f. The portion or regions of the field of fixation in which diplopia occurs, a clinical finding used in the differential diagnosis of extraocular muscle paresis or paralysis.

    diplopia f., Duane's. A diplopia field plotted for various directions of gaze with a number of small, independently illuminated light sources in fixed positions on the test screen as fixation targets.

excursion, f. of. Field of fixation.

fixation, f. of. The total angular range of rotatory excursion of the eye, with the head fixed, represented by a plot of the limits of fixation on a tangent screen, or on a spherical surface concentric with the center of rotation of the eye. The approximate monocular limits specified from the straightforward position are: 45° outward, 50° inward, 35° upward, and 50° downward. Syn., *field of excursion; motor field; field of rotation.*

fixation, f. of (bifoveal). The total angular range or limits of excursion of the eyes under conditions of binocular fixation, with the head fixed, usually represented on a field of fixation diagram or plot.

fixation, f. of (practical). The field of fixation obtained with combined head and eye movements.

frontal adversive f. Brodmann's area 6, alpha beta.

frontal eye f. The posterior portion of the middle frontal gyrus of each frontal lobe, controlling voluntary contradirectional conjugate eye movements; Brodmann's area 8, alpha beta delta.

full illumination, f. of. In an optical system, the angular subtense of the entrance port when the sides of the enclosing angle are extended to the edges of the entrance pupil on the same side of the optical axis.

induced f. In simultaneous contrast, the portion of the visual field acted on and modified by the *inducing field.*

inducing f. In simultaneous contrast, the portion of the visual field acting on and modifying another portion of the visual field, the *induced field.*

motor f. Field of fixation.

occipital eye f. The reflex center in each occipital lobe, controlling pursuit and fixation ocular movements.

perceptual f., ambiocular. The region of space panoramically perceived in certain conditions of

strabismus. See also *ambiocularity.*

perceptual f., binocular. The region of space binocularly perceived with normal retinal correspondence.

perceptual f., monocular. The region of space perceived by a single eye.

phoria, f. of. In paralytic strabismus, the area in the field of fixation in which single binocular vision can be maintained. Cf. *field of tropia.*

receptor f. of optic nerve fiber. The retinal area whose visual receptors, via synapses with bipolar cells, are subserved by a single ganglion cell.

regard, f. of. The portion of the visual field dominant in consciousness at any given time.

retinal f. That portion of the retina containing visual sense cells; the anatomical correlate of the visual field.

rotation, f. of. Field of fixation.

sagittal f. The image surface formed by the sagittal foci of the points in an object surface perpendicular to the axis of the optical system.

schlieren f. The conjugate focal plane of the image plane for the objective lens of a schlieren optical system.

tilting f. A device used in demonstrating the effects of aniseikonia on spatial localization, usually consisting of a plane surface mounted on a universal pivot, on which objects designed to enhance stereoscopic clues are placed. When the observer sets the surface so that it appears level, the type and the amount of tilt indicate the kind and the degree of aniseikonia.

triangular f. of Wernicke. The portion of the posterior part of the posterior limb of the internal capsule of the corpus striatum which contains the general sensation pathway and the auditory and optic radiations.

tropia, f. of. In paralytic strabismus, the area in the field of fixation in which single binocular vision is not possible. Cf. *field of phoria.*

view, f. of. 1. The extent of the object plane visible through, or imaged by, an optical instrument. Syn., *absolute field of view.* 2. In an optical system, the angular subtense of the entrance port measured from the center of the entrance pupil. Cf. *field of full illumination; absolute field of view.*

view, f. of, absolute. In an optical system, the angular subtense of the entrance port when the sides of the enclosing angle are extended to the edges of the entrance pupil on the opposite side of the optical axis.

view, f. of, apparent. The angle subtended by the exit port of a visual aid at the center of the entrance pupil of the eye.

view, f. of, linear. The extent of object space imaged by an optical system, expressed as a linear distance in the object plane.

view, f. of, real. True field of view.

view, f. of, true. The angle subtended at the center of the entrance pupil of the eye by that part of the object plane visible to the eye through a visual aid. Syn., *real field of view.*

visual f. The area or extent of physical space visible to an eye in a given position. Its average extent is approximately 65° upward, 75° downward, 60° inward, and 95° outward, when the eye is in the straightforward position.

visual f., absolute. The visual field that would exist if the obstruction by the facial structures were eliminated so that the en-tire retina could be stimulated. It can be determined by using successively different positions of fixation other than the straightforward position. Cf. *relative visual field.* Syn., *maximum visual field; physiologic visual field.*

visual f., accordion. A visual field associated with hysteria and showing contraction in successively measured, alternate meridians so that the border of the plot looks like folds in a bellows.

visual f., anatomic. Relative visual field.

visual f's., antagonistic. Visual fields of the two eyes which cannot be integrated binocularly into a single composite percept, such as the two fields of vision normally seen by a strabismic individual, or those resulting from a pair of differing visual stimulus patterns presented haploscopically to the two eyes in a retinal rivalry test.

visual f., binocular. 1. The combined visual field. 2. The common visual field.

visual f., central. The area of the visual field corresponding to the fovea or the macula. Syn., *direct visual field.*

visual f., color. The portion of the visual field within which color can be perceived, the field for any given color being smaller than, and roughly concentric with, the visual field for white. In order of size of largest to smallest, the clinically obtained color fields are yellow, blue, red, green. The field for each color varies greatly with variation in such factors as target size, saturation, brightness, and contrast.

visual f., color (interlacing of). The interlacing of the borders of the plotted visual fields for two or more test objects of different color.

visual f., color (overlapping of). The extension of the visual field for a given color beyond the border of the visual field of another color normally expected to be larger.

visual f., combined. The extent of the visual field viewed with binocular fixation, including the extreme temporal regions visible to one eye only.

visual f., common. The extent of the visual field viewed with both eyes simultaneously during binocular fixation, i.e., not including the temporal regions visible to one eye only. Its vertical dimension is the same as the monocular visual field and its horizontal dimension is approximately 120°.

visual f's., congruent. Visual fields of the two eyes which have defects identical in size, shape, and position, so as to form a single defect of the binocular visual field.

visual f., cribriform. A visual field containing a number of isolated scotomata.

visual f., depressed. A visual field characterized by general or local reduction of sensitivity to stimuli within it. The isopters are smaller than normal or are missing, but an increase in intensity of the stimulation produces a field of normal extent.

visual f., direct. Central visual field.

visual f., dynamic. The composite of all visual fields, plotted for all possible positions of fixation, with the head fixed. Cf. *static visual field.*

visual f., exclusive left. The monocularly seen portion of the visual field to the left of the common visual field.

visual f., exclusive right. The monocularly seen portion of the visual field to the right of the common visual field.

visual f., exhaustion (of Wilbrand). A visual field associated with neurasthenia and characterized by apparently continuous shrinkage in any meridian as it is being plotted and replotted.

visual f., fixation. Field of fixation.

visual f., flicker fusion frequency. A visual field plotted by determining the critical fusion frequencies throughout its extent and comparing these frequencies to known norms.

visual f., form. The portion of the visual field within which form or shape can be recognized, varying greatly with such factors as target size, shape, brightness, and contrast.

visual f., heteronymous. The nasal or temporal half of the visual field of one eye with reference to the nasal or temporal half, respectively, of the visual field of the other eye.

visual f., homonymous. The nasal or temporal half of the visual field of one eye with reference to the temporal or nasal half, respectively, of the visual field of the other eye.

visual f., hysterical. Any of several visual field patterns resulting from hysterical responses during the testing, often including such anomalous characteristics as spiraling borders, successive contractions of the borders with repeated testing, fixed borders unrelated to the test distance (tubular visual field), and the reversal of color field borders.

visual f., indirect. Peripheral visual field.

visual f., maximum. Absolute visual field.

visual f., monocular. The visual field of an eye in a given position, especially in the straightforward position.

visual f., motion. The area or extent of the visual field in which motion can be detected.

visual f., neurasthenic. Any

of several visual field patterns associated with neurasthenia, usually characterized by continual changes as the field is being plotted.

visual f., oscillating. A visual field associated with hysteria and characterized by apparent concentric ring scotomata. The test target intermittently disappears and reappears as it is moved radially toward or away from the point of fixation.

visual f., overshot. A visual field in which there is a large scotomatous area approaching the macula, but not including it or its immediately adjacent area.

visual f., peripheral. The entire visual field exclusive of that corresponding to the fovea or the macula. Syn., *indirect visual field.*

visual f., physiologic. Absolute visual field.

visual f., recuperative extension (of von Reuss). A visual field associated with hysteria and neurasthenia, characterized by a marked increase in the size of an originally small field, following a purposive rest, or in response to the exhortations of the examiner.

visual f., relative. The visual field plotted with the eye in the straightforward position and including as limitations the restrictions produced by the nose, the brows, and the cheeks. Cf. *absolute visual field.* Syn., *anatomic visual field.*

visual f's., reversal of. A deviation in the normal order of size of the color fields, e.g., the blue field being smaller than the red field.

visual f., shifting (of Förster). A visual field associated with hysteria or neurasthenia, characterized by a large displacement in its limits when plotted, first, from the invisible to the visible (continuing to the invisible in each meridian) and,

second, by the same method in each meridian starting in the opposite direction.

visual f., spiral. A type of visual field pattern, usually attributed to neurasthenia or hysteria, in which there is a continuous progressive contraction as it is being plotted from meridian to meridian. A line connecting the limits of all the meridians has the shape of a spiral.

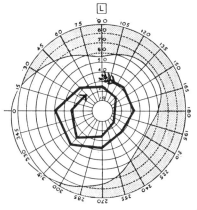

Fig. 21. Spiral visual field. (From *Text-book of Ophthalmology*, Vol. IV, Duke-Elder, Henry Kimpton, 1949)

visual f., static. 1. The visual field obtained by measuring the luminance threshold at a series of fixed locations by varying the luminance of stationary targets of various sizes while the eye remains fixed in the straightforward position. 2. The visual field obtained with the eye fixed in the straightforward position. Cf. *dynamic visual field.*

visual f., surplus. The portion of the visual field in incomplete hemianopsia which remains unaffected and extends beyond the point of fixation into the affected side.

visual f., tubular. A visual field pattern usually attributed to hysteria or malingering, characterized by concentric contraction and constancy of diameter, irrespective of the testing distance.

visual f., uncinate. A visual field pattern resulting from baring of the superior portion of the blind spot of Mariotte.

visual f., uncinate (inverted). A visual field pattern resulting from baring of the inferior portion of the blind spot of Mariotte.

field-stop. An opaque aperture rim which limits the field of view in an optical system.

Fiessinger-Leroy-Reiter syndrome. Oculo-uretero-synovial syndrome.

Fieuzel glass (fu-zel'). See under *glass*.

figure. That part of, or pattern in, the perceived visual field which has the perceptual attribute of completeness or definitiveness of form, distinct from other portions of the field perceptually appreciated as ground.

ambiguous f. A pattern or a drawing so structured as to be open to more than one interpretation.

Baldwin's f. A diagram consisting of a dot midway between two laterally separated circles of unequal size, giving rise to the illusion that the dot is nearer the larger circle.

Bourdon's f. A drawing consisting of two wedge-shaped areas joined at their apices, whose upper borders form a common, continuous, straight line, giving the illusion that the upper straight line is curved.

diffraction f. Diffraction pattern.

Ebbinghaus' f. A drawing consisting of two equal lines or demarcated spaces, one filled with a series of intersecting lines or narrow bands and the other left undifferentiated, and giving the illusion that the "filled" line or space is longer.

fortification f's. Fortification spectrum.

Hering's f. Any of several drawings consisting of a pair of parallel straight lines, intersected or met by a series of radiating lines, and giving the illusion that the parallel lines are bowed toward or away from each other.

Höfler's f. A drawing consisting of two arcs of equal length and radius, placed one above the other, and giving the illusion that the arc nearer the centers of curvature is longer.

Mach's f. A line drawing depicting a half-opened book which, when viewed continuously, alternately appears to be open toward and away from the observer.

Mueller-Lyer f. A diagram consisting of two parallel lines of equal length, one having arrow-like appendages and the other having quill-like appendages at their ends, and giving the illusion that the lines are of unequal length.

Poggendorff's f. A line drawing consisting of a bandlike rectangular area overlaying a diagonal line and giving the illusion that the two visible portions of the line, one on each side of the band, are not parts of a continuous straight line.

Purkinje's f's. Entoptically observable patterns formed by the shadows of the blood vessels in the eye when light is projected obliquely or grossly out of focus onto the retina. Syn., *Purkinje's shadows.*

reversible f. A geometric figure or pattern having two or more possible interpretations which are simultaneously incompatible and involve apparent differences in orientation, dimensional relationships, or perceptual interchanges of figure and ground.

Schroeder's f. A line drawing consisting of alternately parallel, steplike, line formations extending from the upper corner of a parallelogram to the lower opposite corner. Upon continuous viewing, the perspective changes from a staircase viewed from above to a staircase viewed from below, or vice versa. Syn., *Schroeder's staircase.*

Stifel's f. A black disk containing a central white spot, used as a test target for locating the physiological blind spot of the eye.

Thiéry's f. A line drawing consisting of a rectangular box to which is attached the side and base of another such box. Upon constant fixation, the perspective changes so that it appears to be two solid boxes, or one box with an extra side and base attached.

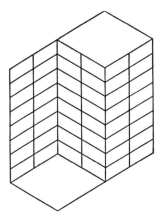

Fig. 22. Thiéry's figure. (From *Visual Illusions,* M. Luckiesh, Van Nostrand, 1922)

Wundt's f. A line drawing consisting of a pair of parallel straight lines crossed by lines radiating toward, and meeting, each other from two points, one on each side of the parallel lines, and giving the illusion that the parallel lines are bowed.

Zöllner's f. A line drawing consisting of long parallel lines, each crossed by a series of short diagonal lines which are parallel to each other, but which are angled opposite to those crossing the adjacent parallel lines, and giving rise to the illusion that the long

parallel lines converge toward, or diverge from, each other. Syn., *Zöllner's lines.*

figure-ground. The basic two-part nature of the perceived visual field, providing for perceptual differentiation of figure and ground.

filaments, basal. Hairlike projections of a cone foot at the regions of synapse with bipolar or horizontal cells.

Filaria loa (fih-la're-ah lo'ah). *Filaria oculi.*

Filaria oculi (fih-la're-ah ok'u-li). A parasitic, threadlike worm from one to two inches long, found in West Africa, which inhabits the subcutaneous connective tissue of the body, traversing it freely. It is seen especially about the orbit and even under the conjunctiva, rarely reported in the vitreous chamber. Syn., *Loa loa; Filaria loa.*

film, antireflection. A thin film of transparent material, such as magnesium fluoride, deposited on the surface of a lens which increases light transmission through the lens and reduces surface reflection. Syn., *lens coating.*

film, precorneal. The fluid covering the anterior surface of the cornea, approximately 10μ in thickness, which is composed of three sublayers, a superficial derived from the Meibomian glands, a middle derived from the lacrimal gland, and a deep mucoid derived from conjunctival glands. Syn., *lacrimal layer; tear layer.*

filoma (fih-lo'mah). A fibroma or benign connective tissue tumor of the sclera.

filter. A device or material which selectively or equally absorbs or transmits wavelengths of light.

actinic f. 1. A filter which selectively transmits actinic radiations. 2. A filter which absorbs actinic radiations.

birefringent f. A system of alternate quartz plates and polarizers for isolating a narrow spectral band of a few angstrom units. Syn., *polarization interference filter.*

blue f. A filter which selectively transmits only blue light, either by selective absorption or by interference.

blue-free f. Minus-blue filter.

cobalt blue f. A glass filter containing cobalt which transmits light primarily from the red and blue regions of the spectrum, absorbing the midspectral wavelengths.

conversion f. A filter used to change the color temperature of a radiator.

dichroic f. 1. A neutral filter or a color filter consisting of a doubly refracting medium which transmits only the ordinary or the extraordinary beam. 2. A light filter which permits only two colors to pass through. 3. A light filter which transmits a certain color when in a thin layer and a different color when in a thick layer.

gradient f. An optical filter whose transmission varies across the face of the filter. Syn., *optical wedge.*

green f. A filter which selectively transmits only green light, either by means of selective absorption, or by interference.

green-free f. Minus-green filter.

infrared f. 1. A filter which selectively transmits only infrared radiations. 2. A filter which does not transmit infrared radiations.

interference f. A light filter which usually consists of five layers, two outside glass, two intermediate evaporated metal films, and one central evaporated layer of transparent material. Multiple reflections cause destructive interference for all but one (approximately) wavelength, resulting in an emergent beam of one color.

minus-blue f. A filter which selec-

tively absorbs blue light. Syn., *blue-free filter.*

minus-green f. A filter which selectively absorbs green light. Syn., *green-free filter.*

minus-red f. A filter which selectively absorbs red light. Syn., *red-free filter.*

neutral f. A filter which transmits all visible wavelengths in approximately equal but reduced amounts.

polarization interference f. Birefringent filter.

Polaroid f. A patented product, usually in sheet form, made from minute crystals of a dichroic material embedded in a plastic, which transmits only plane-polarized light.

red f. A filter which selectively transmits only red light.

red-free f. Minus-red filter.

Tscherning's f's. A series of neutral filters for determining the light threshold and light adaptation of the eye, each successive filter in the series having an absorption factor ten times that of the preceding filter.

ultraviolet f. A filter which selectively transmits only ultraviolet radiations.

Wood's f. A glass filter containing nickel oxide which absorbs light of the visible spectrum and transmits ultraviolet radiation in the region near the visible spectrum. The light is used with certain dyes, such as fluorescein, to create fluorescence for diagnostic purposes, such as the detection of corneal abrasions or the evaluation of the fit of contact lenses. Syn., *Wood's glass.*

Wratten f's. A series of commercially available gelatin color filters manufactured to catalogued specifications of transmission characteristics.

yellow f. A filter which selectively transmits only yellow light.

Fincham's (fin'chamz) **coincidence optometer; theory.** See under the nouns.

finding. Data derived from an observation, an examination, or a test; that which is found.

equilibrium f's. Optometric Extension Program: Four blur points, clinically determined at a 40 cm. testing distance, representing the limits of positive and negative relative convergence and positive and negative relative accommodation.

gross f. In clinical testing, a direct numerical result or unmodified test score, usually implying that a net finding is to be computed from it.

net f. In clinical testing, a numerical result obtained by modifying the gross finding by some formula, rule, correction factor, or empirical allowance.

finger-piece. See under *frame.*

fining. The final lens surfacing process, prior to polishing, in which the smallest grain abrasive is used to smooth the surface.

Fink Near-Vision test. See under *test.*

F.I.O. Fellow of the Institute of Optometrists (Australia).

F.I.O.Sc. Fellow of the Institute of Ophthalmic Science.

firecrack. A shallow crack in or near the surface of a glass lens, due to overheating such as in grinding or polishing.

Firth test (furth). See under *test.*

Fisher's (fish'erz) **schematic eye; syndrome.** See under the nouns.

fissure (fish'ūr). A cleft or a groove. In the brain, it applies to the deepest clefts. See also *groove* and *sulcus.*

calcarine f. The sulcus on the medial aspect of the occipital lobe, between the cuneus and lingual gyrus. Its anterior limb is in front of the parieto-occipital fissure, and the longer posterior limb extends back to the occipital

pole region. Syn., *calcarine sulcus.*

central f. Fissure of Rolando.

choroidal f. Fetal fissure.

embryonic f. Fetal fissure.

fetal f. The incomplete portion or gap in the embryonic optic cup, ventrally, which normally disappears. If it remains, coloboma of the uveal tract occurs. Syn., *choroidal cleft; fetal cleft; choroidal fissure; embryonic fissure.*

optic cup, f. of the. The fetal fissure in the inferior portion of the optic cup.

optic stalk, f. of the. The fetal fissure in the inferior portion of the optic stalk, continuous with that of the optic cup.

orbital f., inferior. An elongated opening in the orbit, bounded posteriorly by the great wing of the sphenoid bone and anteriorly by the maxillary and the palatine bones, through which pass the maxillary-infraorbital nerve junction, the zygomatic nerve, the infraorbital artery, and an anastomosis between the inferior ophthalmic vein and the pterygoid venous plexus. The fissure commences below and lateral to the optic foramen and runs anteriorly and temporally for approximately 20 mm. Syn., *sphenomaxillary fissure.*

orbital f., superior. An elongated opening in the orbit, between the wings of the sphenoid bone. The portion within the annulus of Zinn is the oculomotor foramen. The fissure transmits the abducens, the frontal, the lacrimal, the nasociliary, the oculomotor, and the trochlear nerves, the sympathetic root to the ciliary ganglion, the superior ophthalmic vein, and recurrent arteries. Syn., *sphenoidal fissure.*

palpebral f. The region between the upper and lower eyelid margins within which can be seen, when the lids are open, the caruncle, the semilunar fold, the iris, the cornea, the sclera, the conjunctival and episcleral vessels, and other structures. Syn., *rima palpebrarum*.

Rolando, f. of. The sulcus or groove between the frontal and parietal lobes of the cerebral cortex. Syn., *central fissure*.

sphenoidal f. Superior orbital fissure.

sphenomaxillary f. Inferior orbital fissure.

fistula (fis'tu-lah). An abnormal passage from one hollow structure of the body to another, or from a hollow structure to the surface, formed by an abscess, disease process, incomplete closure of a wound, or by a congenital anomaly.

corneal f. A fistula extending from the anterior chamber through the cornea to the exterior of the eye. It usually develops in a weakened corneal scar and is usually lined by adherent iridic tissue or by a downward growth of corneal epithelium.

lacrimal f. A fistula, extending from a lacrimal sac or duct to the skin, which may develop after a severe dacrocystitis.

fit. The quality or state of being of the proper dimensions; adjustment; preparedness; adaptedness.

chemical f. The selection of a compatible solution to be used as a fluid filler in scleral contact lenses. Factors believed to control acceptability are chemical composition, hydrogen ion concentration, and relative osmotic pressure.

finished f. The alteration of an approximately fitted contact lens, as to size and shape, to the desired fit.

optical f. The determination of the dioptric power required in a contact lens to correct a patient's refractive error.

physical f. The adaptation or se-

lection of the dimensional elements of a contact lens to conform to the shape and the size of the eye, either by means of a molded impression of the eye or by trial-and-error fitting.

psychological f. The teaching of the techniques of inserting, removing, and caring for contact lenses and the implementing of the patient's confidence and motivation during the early stages of wear.

semifinished f. A stage in the mechanical fitting of a contact lens, prior to the finished fit, in which certain mechanical criteria of excellence of fit are met, but in which further alterations may be necessary to obtain maximum wearing comfort.

fit-on. Clip-on.

fit-over. Clip-over.

fixation (fik-sa'shun). The process, condition, or act of directing the eye toward the object of regard, causing, in a normal eye, the image of the object to be centered on the fovea.

anomalous f. 1. Eccentric fixation. 2. The apparent fixation by the deviating eye in strabismus with anomalous retinal correspondence. See also *facultative eccentric fixation*.

bifoveal f. Fixation in which the images of the object of fixation simultaneously fall upon the foveae of both eyes. Syn., *binocular fixation*.

binocular f. Bifoveal fixation.

central f. Centric fixation.

centric f. Fixation in which the image of the object of fixation falls upon the center of the fovea. Syn., *central fixation*.

contralateral f. The fixation of objects in the left half of the visual field with the right eye and objects in the right half of the visual field with the left eye, as may occur especially in esotropia or in paralysis of the lateral rectus muscles.

disparity, f. See under *disparity.*

eccentric f. Fixation not employing the central foveal area. Syn., *anomalous fixation; false fixation; pseudomacular fixation.*

    eccentric f., facultative. The apparent or functional fixation by the deviating eye in strabismus with anomalous retinal correspondence, in which the image of the object of fixation falls upon its anomalous associated area only under binocular conditions. Syn., *false associated fixation.*

    eccentric f., obligatory. The apparent or functional fixation by the deviating eye in strabismus with anomalous retinal correspondence, in which the image of the object of fixation falls upon its anomalous associated area both under binocular conditions and when the normally fixating eye is occluded.

    eccentric f., paradoxical. Eccentric fixation by the deviating eye in strabismus in which the retinal site used for fixation, under monocular conditions, is on the side of the fovea opposite to which the image of the object of fixation lies under binocular conditions, e.g., the temporal side in esotropia.

false f. Eccentric fixation.

false associated f. Facultative eccentric fixation.

field of f. See under *field.*

foveal f. Normal fixation in which the image of the object of fixation falls upon the fovea.

homolateral f. The fixation of objects in the right half of the visual field with the right eye and objects in the left half of the visual field with the left eye, as may occur especially in exotropia or in paralysis of the medial rectus muscles.

jump f. Saccadic fixation.

line of f. See under *line.*

lost f. 1. The absence of ability to fixate repeatedly or continuously with the same retinal area, normally the fovea, a condition associated with degeneration or destruction of the fovea or with amblyopia of high degree. 2. In reading, fixation which fails to provide or fails to be associated with adequate meaning of the words to be read, ordinarily resulting in a form of backtracking, termed *regression.*

monocular f. Fixation by one eye only, the vision in the other eye being absent, disregarded, suspended, or suppressed, as in conditions of monocular occlusion, monocular blindness, dissociation, or strabismus.

paradoxic f. Paradoxical eccentric fixation.

parafoveal f. Fixation utilizing a retinal area within the macula but not at the center of the fovea.

paramacular f. Fixation utilizing a retinal area near, but not within, the macula.

pause, f. The momentary cessation of eye movement occurring alternately with saccadic movement in reading or in a series of fixations by which an extended region is meaningfully scanned.

peripheral f. Fixation with a retinal area located in the peripheral retina, remote from the macular area.

persistent f. A prolonged staring fixation or fixation pause, ostensibly involuntary and often associated with hysteria, debilitation, fright, daydreaming, or paralysis of the extraocular muscles.

physiologic f. Normal centric fixation, the image of the fixated target stimulating the foveal center.

plane of f. See under *plane.*

point of f. See under *point.*

position of f. See under *position.*

pseudomacular f. Eccentric fixation. *Obs.*

pursuit f. 1. The continued fixation of a moving object, implying a dynamic movement of the eye, so as to keep the image of the object continuously on the fovea. 2. The repetitive fixation of a moving object, implying a series of corrective refixations, in response to the effort to keep the image of the object continuously on the fovea.

reflex f. Involuntary fixation such as may occur in response to peripheral retinal stimulation.

response, f. See under *response.*

response time, f. See under *time.*

saccadic f. 1. A rapid change of fixation from one point in the visual field to another. Syn., *jump fixation.* 2. The rapid phase of a nystagmoid cycle.

scanning f. A series of rapid fixations associated with an attempt to survey quickly the details of a view subtending a relatively large area of the visual field.

steady f. Continuous fixation of a nonmoving object for a given period of time.

time, f. See under *time.*

tracing f. A type of fixation occurring in response to an effort to move fixation along the path of a line drawing without the aid of a moving object, characterized by a series of saccadic movements.

voluntary f. Conscious and purposeful fixation as distinguished from reflex fixation.

wandering f. The absence of ability to fixate continuously with the same retinal area.

Fizeau's (fe-zōz') **experiment; method.** See under the nouns.

Flajani's disease (flah-jan'ēz). Exophthalmic goiter.

flakes, capsular. A type of congenital cataract consisting of white, oval or round, sharply circumscribed, dense opacities, up to 1 mm. in size, which are usually multiple and are found on the anterior sur-

face of the capsule of the crystalline lens.

flange, scleral. 1. The temporal spherical section of a Feincone contact lens. 2. The portion of a scleral type contact lens which covers the sclera.

flare. Light resulting from interreflection between refracting surfaces.

aqueous f. Tyndall's effect, or the scattering of light in a beam directed into the anterior chamber, occurring as a result of increased protein content of the aqueous humor, a sign of severe inflammation of the iris and/or the ciliary body

flash. A very short exposure of light, or the associated visual experience.

Flash Reader. A trade name for a hand-operated tachistoscopic device used for brief exposure of reading material.

Flatau's sign (flat-owz'). See under *sign.*

flattener, field. A fiber optics bundle with differential density of fibers to accomplish a flattening of the curved image field produced by an anastigmatic optical system.

Flechsig's (flek'sigz) **temporal knee; loop.** See under the nouns.

fleck, Foster-Fuchs. Fuchs's spot.

flecks, Michel's. Michel's spots.

Fleischer's (fli'sherz) **whirling corneal dystrophy; line; ring.** See under the nouns.

Fles's box (flez'ez). See under *box.*

flicker. Variations in brightness or hue perceived upon stimulation by intermittent or temporally nonuniform light.

binocular f. Flicker produced by alternate photic stimulation of the two eyes.

brightness f. Flicker produced by intermittent variations in brightness or illuminance. Cf. *chromatic flicker.* Syn., *illumination flicker.*

chromatic f. Variations in saturation or hue, perceived on alternately intermittent stimulation by light of two different colors but of constant brightness. Cf. *brightness flicker.*

contrast *f.* Flicker induced into a constantly illuminated field by flicker in a neighboring field.

field *f.* Flicker induced or observed in a dark or a constantly illuminated field which surrounds a target varying in intensity. Cf. *spot flicker.*

frequency, *f.* See under *frequency.*

illumination *f.* Brightness flicker.

marginal *f.* In critical fusion frequency experiments, the last trace of flicker observable in parts of the test field just before total fusion is obtained. Syn., *vestigial flicker.*

spot *f.* Flicker in the region of the field constituting the test target, as distinguished from the flicker in the visual field surounding the target. Cf. *field flicker.*

vestigial *f.* Marginal flicker.

Flieringa-Bonaccolto ring (flēr'ing-ah-bon-ah-kōl'to). See under *ring.*

Flieringa-Legrand ring (flēr'ing-ah-le'grahnd). See under *ring.*

flight of colors. The temporal succession of colors observed in an afterimage of a bright source.

float. To appear to remain suspended in space, as in the case of those elements of a fused stereogram, a vectogram, or an anaglyph that exhibit stereoscopic parallax relative to the perceived plane of the stereogram, the vectogram, or the anaglyph.

floaters. In the normally transparent vitreous, deposits of varying size, shape, consistency, refractive index, and motility, which may be of embryonic origin or acquired. If acquired, they may be an indication of degenerative changes of the retina or the vitreous humor. See also *muscae volitantes.*

flocculi (flok'u-li). Small, wool-like tufts or flakes.

cystic *f. of the iris.* Congenital, pigmented cysts occurring on the pupillary margin of the iris.

nodular *f. of the iris.* A congenital hyperplasia of the pigment epithelium of the iris resulting in grapelike clusters of small black nodules at the pupillary margin.

Flocks's pore tissue. Endothelial meshwork of Speakman.

Floropryl (flor'o-pril). A trade name for DFP in 0.10% solution dissolved in peanut oil.

fluid. A substance, such as a liquid or a gas, which alters in shape in response to any force, however small.

aqueous *f.* Aqueous humor.

intraocular *f.* All the fluid within the eye with the exception of that contained within the blood vessels. It includes the aqueous humor, the vitreous humor, and the tissue fluids of the eye.

    intraocular f., plasmoid. Intraocular fluid differing from the normal by more nearly approximating the composition of plasma, as may be produced by an increase in the permeability of the capillary walls following a sudden decrease in intraocular pressure, or due to a pathological process.

lacrimal *f.* The clear, salty, slightly alkaline fluid secret∼d by the lacrimal gland, constituting the major portion of the tear fluid.

Morgagnian *f.* 1. The amorphous material between the anterior epithelium of the crystalline lens and its anterior capsule. Syn., *Morgagni's humor; liquor Morgagni.* 2. A milky fluid consisting of the disintegrated cortex of the hypermature cataract and containing the nucleus of the crystalline lens.

vitreous *f.* Vitreous humor.

fluorescein (floo"o-res'e-in). A fluorescent, yellowish-red crystalline compound, $C_{20}H_{12}O_5$, whose sodium salt is used in dilute solution as a dye in determining the fit of contact lenses or in the detection of corneal abrasions, ulcers, etc., the affected areas staining a yellow-green.

fluorescence (floo″o-res′ens). The property of emitting radiation as the result of, and only during, the absorption of radiation from some other source, the emitted radiation being of longer wavelength; also, the emitted radiation. Cf. *phosphorescence.*

resonance f. Resonance radiation.

fluorite (floo′or-īt). A mineral composed of calcium fluoride and serving as a principal source of fluorine. It fluoresces under ultraviolet light and may phosphoresce upon heating or after exposure to ultraviolet light. It crystallizes in cubes or octahedrons and, in its clear colorless form of optical quality, is used for apochromatic lenses because of its low index of refraction and low dispersion. Syn., *feldspar.*

fluorochrome (floo″or-o-krōm′). Any of various fluorescent substances, such as sodium fluorescein.

fluorometry (floo″or-om′eh-tre). A method for estimating aqueous outflow in which the concentration of intravenously introduced fluorescein in the anterior chamber is determined at intervals by a slit lamp fluorometer and related to the concentration of fluorescein in the blood.

fluorophor (floo″or-o-fōr′). A substance which has the property of absorbing energy and releasing it again in the form of fluorescence.

flush, ciliary. A diffuse, rose-red coloration surrounding the cornea as a result of congestion of the branches of the anterior ciliary arteries, in cyclitis, iridocyclitis, or deep keratitis.

flux (fluks). The rate of flow of fluid or energy.

chromatic f's. Radiant fluxes expressed in arbitrary energy units,

in general different for the three primary colors, chosen to satisfy certain convenient relationships involving matches with other specified lights.

density f., luminous. See under *density.*

luminous f. The time rate of flow of light, usually designated in lumens.

radiant f. The time rate of flow of radiant energy expressed in watts or ergs per second.

   radiant f., spectral. Radiant flux with respect to a specified wavelength or narrow wavelength interval.

focal (fo′kal). Pertaining to or having a focus.

focal depth; distance; illumination; intercept; interval; length; line; plane; point; power; ratio. See under the nouns.

focimeter (fo-sim′eh-ter). A device for determining the vergence power of a lens.

focometer (fo-kom′eh-ter). An instrument for the determination of the vertex power of ophthalmic lenses; a variation of a focimeter.

focus (fo′kus). 1. The point at which a pencil of rays or their prolongations can be made to meet after reflection or refraction. 2. To adjust the elements of an optical system to achieve sharp imagery. 3. The center, the principal site, or the starting point of a disease process.

anterior f. Primary principal focus.

aplanatic f. The image point for which an optical system is corrected for spherical aberration and at which all zones of the system produce images of equal size.

back f. The secondary principal focal point of a lens or optical system located in reference to its distance from the posterior surface of the lens.

conjugate foci. Two points in an optical system such that rays originating at one are focused at the other, and vice versa.

depth of f. See under *depth.*

marginal f. The point at which the nonparaxial rays or their prolongations meet after refraction or reflection by an optical system.

meridional f. Tangential focus.

negative f. Virtual focus.

paraxial f. The point to which the central (paraxial) rays or their prolongations converge after refraction or reflection by an optical system.

posterior f. Secondary principal focus.

primary f. Primary principal focus.

primary f. in oblique astigmatism. Tangential focus.

principal f. 1. Either the anterior or the posterior principal focus of a lens or an optical system. 2. The virtual or real axial meeting point of rays, parallel to the optical axis on incidence, after reflection by a spherical surface.

   principal f., anterior. Primary principal focus.

   principal f., posterior. Secondary principal focus.

   principal f., primary. The axial point of an optical system from which rays diverge to become parallel after refraction by the system. Syn., *anterior focus; anterior principal focus; primary focus.*

   principal f., secondary. The axial meeting point of rays parallel to the optical axis on incidence, after refraction by a lens or an optical system. Syn., *posterior focus; posterior principal focus; secondary focus.*

radial f. Sagittal focus.

real f. The point at which a real image is formed by the meeting of convergent light rays.

sagittal f. The image formed by those rays contained in a sagittal (secondary) section of a homocentric bundle of rays obliquely incident on an optical system containing spherical surfaces. The sagittal (secondary) section is made up of two planes perpendicular to the tangential (primary) plane, one plane containing the incident rays, the other plane containing the emergent rays. The image of a point source will be a line perpendicular to the sagittal (secondary) section. Cf. *tangential focus.* Syn., *secondary focus in oblique astigmatism.*

secondary f. Secondary principal focus.

secondary f. in oblique astigmatism. Sagittal focus.

tangential f. The image formed by those rays contained in the tangential (primary) plane of a homocentric bundle of rays obliquely incident on an optical system containing spherical surfaces. The image of a point source will be a line perpendicular to the tangential (primary) plane. Cf., *sagittal focus.* Syn., *meridional focus; primary focus in oblique astigmatism.*

virtual f. The point at which a virtual image is formed by the intersection of the backward extensions of diverging light rays. Syn., *negative focus.*

focusing (fo′kus-ing). Adjusting the elements of an optical system, or the position of the image surface or screen, in order to create or obtain a clear and sharply defined image, or to obtain a desired relationship between object distance and image distance.

Fodéré's sign (fod-a-rāz′). See under *sign.*

fogging. The deliberate overcorrection of hypermetropia or the undercorrection of myopia for various purposes in the refraction of the eye. It is used in testing for astigmatism to reduce the tendency of the eye to accommodate during the test.

Foix's syndrome (fwahz). See under *syndrome*.

fold. A doubling; a turning of a part upon itself; a layer or a thickness.

Arnold's f. A fold of mucous membrane found in the lacrimal sac.

ciliary f's. Small ridges in the furrows between the ciliary processes. Syn., *plica ciliaris*.

conjunctival f. The part of the conjunctiva which joins the bulbar and the palpebral portions of the conjunctiva but is unattached to the eyelid and the eyeball. Syn., *cul-de-sac; palpebral fold; retrotarsal fold; fornix of the conjunctiva*.

contraction f's of Schwalbe. Contraction furrows of Schwalbe.

eye f. An upper eyelid skin fold which hangs over and partially covers the eyelashes.

falciform f. A thickening in the cleft between the tendon of an extraocular muscle and the eyeball, formed by the fusion of the muscle sheath and Tenon's capsule. Syn., *pulley bar*.

Hasner's f. Plica lacrimalis.

lacrimal f. Plica lacrimalis.

Lange, f. of. A forward projecting fold of the retina in the region of the ora serrata, in the eye of infants.

malar f. A vaguely defined furrow in the skin that runs downward and inward from the external canthus which, together with the nasojugal fold, indicates the junction of the tissue of the lower eyelid with that of the cheek.

median f. An uncommon type of eye fold which overhangs the medial part of the upper eyelid and leaves both canthi unobscured.

Mongoloid f. An eye fold which begins at the medial part of the upper eyelid and covers the lacrimal caruncle, or which, in its more complete form, obscures the lower edge of the upper eyelid

from the external to the internal canthus.

nasojugal f. A furrow in the skin extending inferiorly and laterally from the internal canthus which, together with the malar fold, indicates the junction of the tissue of the lower eyelid with that of the cheek.

Nordic f. An eye fold which begins at the medial part of the upper eyelid, laterally obscuring its margin and covering the external canthus.

orbital f. The loose protruding skin just above the upper tarsus of the eyelid, especially in the aged.

palpebral f. Conjunctival fold.

retinal f., congenital. Congenital retinal septum.

retrotarsal f. Conjunctival fold.

semilunar f. A fold of bulbar conjunctiva lateral to the caruncle in the region of the medial canthus and concentric with the limbus, representing a vestigial nictitating membrane or a rudimentary third eyelid.

structural f's of Schwalbe. Structural furrows of Schwalbe.

follicle (fol'ih-kl). 1. A small gland, crypt, or sac. 2. A small cavity or deep, narrow depression, as a hair follicle. 3. A small, localized aggregation of lymphocytes resembling a lymph node, occurring as a result of continued chronic irritation.

ciliary f's. Meibomian glands.

conjunctival f. A dense, localized, subepithelial infiltration of the conjunctiva by large, mononuclear lymphocyte, plasma, mast, and polymorphonuclear cells, occurring as the result of lymphatic tissue reaction to irritation and usually appearing as a small, round or oval, pinkish, translucent body.

palpebral f's. Meibomian glands.

folliculosis, conjunctival (fol-lik″u-lo′sis). A condition, frequently found in children, characterized by the presence of discrete follicles in the conjunctiva, mainly in the lower fornix. It is unaccompanied by inflammatory signs or secretions and runs a chronic, benign course with no sequelae.

Foltz's valve (fōltz′ez). See under *valve.*

Fontana's (fon-tah′naz) **canal; spaces.** See under the nouns.

foot, cone. The end of a cone cell that synapses with a centripetal, horizontal, or centrifugal bipolar cell in the outer molecular layer of the retina. Syn., *end foot; cone pedicle.*

foot, end. Cone foot.

footcandle. A unit of illumination equal to uniformly distributed flux of 1 lumen per sq. ft. Symbol: fc. Other units and conversion factors:

1 *lux* (*lumen/m²*) = 0.0929 fc.

1 *metercandle* = 0.0929 fc.

1 *phot* = 929 fc.

   apparent f. Footlambert.

   equivalent f. Footlambert.

footlambert. A unit of luminance equal to 1/π candela per sq. ft., or to the average luminance of a surface emitting or reflecting light at the rate of one lumen per sq. ft. The average luminance of any reflecting surface in footlamberts is the product of the illumination in footcandles and the reflectance of the surface. Symbol: fL. Other units and conversion factors:

1 *lambert* = 929 fL.

1 *millilambert* = 0.929 fL.

1 *stilb* (candela per cm.²) = 2919 fL.

1 *candela* per ft.² = 3.142 fL.

1 *candela* per in.² = 452 fL.

1 *nit* (candela per m.²) = 0.2919 fL.

1 *apostilb* = 0.0929 fL.

Syn., *apparent footcandle; equivalent footcandle.*

foramen (fo-ra′men). A natural hole or perforation, especially one in a bone.

   Arnold's f. Frontal foramen.

   Bozzi's f. Macula lutea. *Obs.*

   corneal f. Corneal interval.

   ethmoidal f., anterior. An opening into the anterior ethmoidal canal located in the fronto-ethmoidal suture, or in the frontal bone, which permits the anterior ethmoidal vessels and the nasal nerve to leave the orbit.

   ethmoidal f., posterior. An opening, a short distance behind the anterior ethmoidal foramen, which permits the posterior ethmoidal vessels and nerve (Luschka) to leave the orbit.

   frontal f. An opening in the frontal bone, sometimes present just medial to the supraorbital foramen on the medial superior orbital margin, which transmits medial branches of the supraorbital nerve, vein, and artery. If the bone is incomplete below, it is termed a *frontal notch.* Syn., *Arnold's foramen.*

   fronto-ethmoidal f. The anterior or posterior ethmoidal foramen.

   infraorbital f. The anterior opening of the infraorbital canal, slightly below the lower orbital margin, which transmits the infraorbital vessels and nerve. Syn., *suborbital foramen.*

   oculomotor f. That part of the superior orbital fissure, bounded by the annulus of Zinn, which transmits the sympathetic root of the ciliary ganglion and the naso-ciliary, oculomotor, and abducens nerves into the orbit.

   optic f. The opening of the optic canal into the orbit, located in the small wing of the sphenoid bone, transmitting the optic nerve and the ophthalmic artery with its carotid plexus of sympathetic nerve fibers.

   opticoscleral f. Posterior scleral foramen.

   ovale, f. 1. The opening in the great wing of the sphenoid in the cranium which serves as the exit of the mandibular division of the fifth cranial nerve and of the masticator nerve. 2. The opening in the interatrial septum which allows fetal blood to enter the left atrium and bypass the pulmonary circuit.

rotundum, f. The opening in the great wing of the sphenoid bone in the cranium, which permits the maxillary division of the fifth cranial nerve to enter the pterygo-palatine fossa before reaching the inferior orbital fissure.

scleral f., anterior. Corneal interval.

scleral f., posterior. The passageway in the posterior sclera which transmits the optic nerve. Syn., *opticoscleral foramen.*

Soemmering's f. Macula lutea. *Obs.*

suborbital f. Infraorbital foramen.

supraorbital f. An opening in the frontal bone at the upper and slightly medial margin of the orbit, serving as the exit of the supraorbital vessels and nerve. If the bone is incomplete below, it is termed a *supraorbital notch.*

zygomatic f. An opening in the lateral, anterior portion of the orbit which transmits the zygomatic nerve and vessels. Occasionally, the zygomatic nerve divides within the orbit and, in this case, a zygomaticofacial and a zygomaticotemporal foramen are found instead.

forceps; Feincone radius (fōr′seps). A plierlike instrument with contoured jaws which may be preheated for making peripheral shaping adjustments to plastic scleral contact lenses.

foriagraph (fo′re-ah-graf″). Phoriagraph.

former, lens. A master pattern, usually of metal, used to guide and control the lens shape in lens cutting and edging machines. Syn., *lens pattern.*

formula. 1. A principle or rule expressed in mathematical symbols.

2. A symbolic expression of the chemical composition of a substance. 3. A prescription.

Abney's f. The formula, $y = k\sqrt{x}$, for calculating the diameter (y) of the opening of a pinhole camera, in which k equals a constant 0.008 when x and y are in inches, or 0.01275 when x and y are in centimeters. x equals the distance of the pinhole from the plate.

apparent depth f. A formula giving the apparent depth of an object when seen through an interface separating two optical media of different indices of refraction.

Colenbrander's f. In subnormal vision, the dioptric power of the addition for reading ordinary newsprint is equal to the reciprocal of Snellen visual acuity, less one diopter, plus the normal reading addition.

cube root f. An expression, $A\sqrt[3]{I} = K$, intended to represent the interrelationship of the intensity (I) and the area (A) of the stimulus which produces a constant response (K).

displacement f. 1. A formula expressing the apparent lateral displacement of an object when seen obliquely through a plane-parallel plate. 2. Any formula expressing the relative position of an image as a function of the optical variables.

Fresnel's f. A formula for determining the loss of light by reflection in the case of perpendicular incidence on an interface between two transparent media. Expressed numerically, the reflection is equal to

$$\frac{(n_2 - n_1)^2}{(n_2 + n_1)^2}$$

n_1 being the index of refraction of the first medium and n_2 of the second.

Friedenwald's f. A formula devised by Friedenwald for calculating the intraocular pressure during tonometry (P_t) when employing the Schiötz tonometer: $P_t = \dfrac{W}{c_1 + c_2 R}$, where W = tonometer weight, R = tonometer scale reading, and c_1 and c_2 are constants.

Hofstetter's amplitude *f.* The formula, $A = 18.5 - 0.3Y$, in which A = average amplitude of accommodation and Y = age, based on a combined evaluation of Donders' and Duane's data and expressed with reference to the spectacle plane.

Hofstetter's practice appraisal *f.* The formula, $A = I + 0.11G$, for determining the median appraised value of an optometry practice in which A = appraised value, I = inventory value, and G = the sum of the gross incomes of the 24 preceding months.

Kestenbaum's *f.* In subnormal vision, the dioptric power of the addition for reading ordinary newsprint (Jaeger 5) is numerically equal to the reciprocal of Snellen visual acuity.

Magnus *f.* An empirical formula for estimating the earning ability of a worker who has sustained an injury affecting his vision, employing scaled values for central visual acuity, the visual field, extraocular muscle function, and the class of occupation. Syn., *Magnus-Würdemann formula.*

Newton's *f.* A formula expressing the relationship between the focal lengths of an optical system and the object and image distances as measured from the respective focal points.

Petzval *f.* The formula, $n_1 f_1 + n_2 f_2 = 0$, expressing the condition for eliminating the curvature of a stigmatic image produced by a system of two thin lenses, in contact or separated, in which n = index of refraction and f = focal length. Syn., *Petzval's condition.*

Seidel *f's.* Five formulas expressing mathematically the 5 monochromatic aberrations of optical systems. The aberrations treated are (1) *spherical aberration;* (2) *coma;* (3) *oblique astigmatism;* (4) *curvature of the field;* (5) *distortion.*

Smith-Helmholtz *f.* The formula expressing Lagrange's law, *q.v.*

Snellen *f.* The formula, $V = d/D$, in which V represents a simple numerical expression for visual acuity, d the testing distance, and D the distance at which the smallest readable Snellen letter subtends an angle of 5 minutes. See also *Snellen fraction.*

visual efficiency *f.* Any of several formulas using visual test scores as a basis for computing visual efficiency ratings, usually for purposes of compensation in occupational injury cases.

fornix of the conjunctiva (fôr'-niks). The part of the conjunctiva which joins the bulbar and the palpebral portions of the conjunctiva and which is unattached to the eyelid and the eyeball. Syn., *cul-de-sac; conjunctival fold; palpebral fold; retrotarsal fold.*

Förster's (fers'terz) **choroiditis; disease; shifting visual field; photometer; ring scotoma; theory; uveitis.** See under the nouns.

fossa (fos'ah). A cavity, depression, or pit.

accessory *f.* of Rochon-Duvigneaud. The posterior portion of the fossa for the lacrimal gland, containing mostly orbital fat.

hyaloid *f.* The anterior concavity of the vitreous body located just posterior to the retrolental space. Syn., *lenticular fossa; patellar fossa.*

hypophyseal *f.* A deep central depression in the floor of the sella turcica containing the pituitary body. Syn., *pituitary fossa.*

inferior oblique muscle, *f.* for

the. A small depression on the maxillary bone, on the anterior medial floor of the orbit, just lateral to the upper end of the nasolacrimal canal, which is the point of origin of the inferior oblique muscle.

lacrimal gland, *f. for the.* A large concavity of the frontal bone located in the upper wall of the orbit, lateral and posterior to the orbital margin, in which the orbital lobe of the lacrimal gland rests.

lacrimal sac, *f. for the.* A broad vertical groove in the anterior medial wall of the orbit, formed by the frontal process of the superior maxillary bone and the lacrimal bone, and bounded by the anterior and posterior lacrimal crests. It is approximately 14 mm. in height and 5 mm. deep inferiorly, becoming gradually more shallow as it extends superiorly, and contains the lacrimal sac.

lenticular *f.* Hyaloid fossa.

orbitalis, *f.* Orbit.

patellar *f.* Hyaloid fossa.

pituitary *f.* Hypophyseal fossa.

pterygopalatine *f.* The concavity between the pterygoid process of the sphenoid bone and the palatine and maxillary bones. As the maxillary nerve leaves the foramen rotundum in the cranium, it enters this fossa and lies near the infraorbital artery, the pterygoid plexus, and the sphenopalatine ganglion. Syn., *sphenomaxillary fossa.*

sphenomaxillary *f.* Pterygopalatine fossa.

trochlear *f.* A small depression, posterior to the medial upper margin of the orbit in the frontal bone, which contains the pulley of the superior oblique muscle. Syn., *trochlear fovea.*

fossette (foh-set'). A small and deep ulcer of the cornea.

Foster-Fuchs fleck (fos'ter-fooks). See under *fleck.*

Foster-Kennedy syndrome (fos'ter-ken'eh-de). Kennedy's syndrome.

Foucault's (foo-kōz') **experiment; prism; test.** See under the nouns.

Fourier's (foo-ryāz') **analysis; integral; series; theory.** See under the nouns.

fovea (fo've-ah). A small depression or pit.

centralis, *f.* An area approximately 1.5 mm. in diameter within the macula lutea where the retina thins out greatly because of the oblique shifting of all layers except the pigment epithelium layer and the members of the visual cells. It includes the sloping walls of the fovea (clivus) and contains a few rods in its periphery. In its center (foveola) are the cones most adapted to yield high visual acuity, each cone being connected to only one ganglion cell.

externa of Schäfer, *f.* The outer fovea.

false *f.* 1. A nonfoveal region of the retina functionally associated with the fovea of the other eye in anomalous retinal correspondence. Syn., *anomalous associated area.* 2. A nonfoveal region of the retina used for fixation.

inner *f.* Fovea centralis.

lentis, *f.* Lens pit.

outer *f.* An area in the retina, immediately external to the fovea centralis, where the external limiting membrane bulges slightly anteriorly due to the increased length of the slender outer and inner segments of the cones in this region. Syn., *fovea externa of Schäfer.*

trochlear *f.* Trochlear fossa.

foveola (fo-ve-o'lah). The base or bottom of the fovea centralis, not including the clivus.

Foville's (fo-vēlz') **paralysis; syndrome.** See under the nouns.

F.P. Abbreviation for *finger-piece.*

fraction. A part of the whole; the quotient of one expression divided by another.

Fechner f. Weber's fraction.

light-time f. 1. Pulse-to-cycle fraction. 2. In a repetitive, intermittent, light stimulus pattern, the light time in a cycle divided by the dark time in a cycle.

pulse-to-cycle f. In a repetitive, intermittent, light stimulus pattern, the light time divided by the total time of the light-dark cycle. Abbreviation *PCF.* Syn., *light-time fraction; light-dark ratio.*

Snellen f. An expression of visual acuity in the form of an unreduced fraction in which the numerator represents the testing distance, and the denominator represents the distance at which the smallest readable Snellen test type subtends an angle of 5 minutes.

Weber's f. A constant, $\Delta R/R$, derived from Weber's law, in which ΔR = the change in stimulus which produces a just noticeable difference and R = the value of the original stimulus. When applied to the smallest perceptible difference in brightness between two adjacent illuminated fields, it is a constant of about 1% for all but very high or very low brightnesses.

fragilitas ossium (frah-jil'ih-tas os'-e-um). Osteogenesis imperfecta.

frame. A structure for enclosing, containing, or supporting.

browline f. A spectacle frame with a plastic upper portion to which are fitted metal eyewires to retain the lenses.

eyeglass f. 1. A spectacle frame, without supporting temples, held by a spring or pinching grip at the root of the nose. Syn., *pince-nez.* 2. Any spectacle frame.

finger-piece f. An eyeglass frame held in position by a pinching grip on the sides of the narrow part of the nose by means of pad arms under tension of small coil springs, with small levers protruding anteriorly which may be grasped between the thumb and forefinger to release the tension to mount, reset, or remove the spectacles.

Ful-Vue f. A spectacle frame on which the endpieces are several millimeters higher than the datum line, so as not to obstruct the lateral view of the eyes.

innerrim f. A spectacle frame on which the metal eyewires are embedded in plastic. Syn., *Windsor frame.*

library f. A heavyweight spectacle frame, usually a plastic, suitable for reading lenses and characterized by straight or nearly straight temples to facilitate slipping the frame on or off the face.

Numont f. Numont mounting.

reversible f. A spectacle frame that presents either lens to either eye. It may have either an X-shaped bridge with straight temples, or an arc-shaped bridge with double-jointed endpieces.

rimless f. Rimless mounting.

rimway f. Rimway mounting.

shell f. Originally, a spectacle frame made from shell. In present usage, it includes all plastic spectacle frames.

spectacle f. A frame for supporting ophthalmic correcting lenses in front of the eyes. It rests on the nose and, usually, is supported by a pair of temples.

thermoplastic f. A spectacle frame made from any thermoplastic material, such as zylonite or Plexiglas.

trial f. A type of spectacle frame having variable adjustments for pupillary distance, temple length, bridge size, etc., and constructed to allow for the easy insertion and removal of trial lenses. It is commonly used in the refraction of the eyes.

Windsor f. Innerrim frame.

Franceschetti (fran"ses-chet'e) **sign; symptom; syndrome.** See under the nouns.

Franceschetti-Gernet syndrome (fran"ses-chet'e-gar'na). See under _syndrome._

Franceschetti-Zwahlen syndrome (fran"ses-chet'e-zvah'len). Mandibulofacial dysostosis.

François' (frahn-swahz') **corneal dystrophy; dermo-chondrocorneal dystrophy; syndrome.** See under the nouns.

Franklin bifocal lens; Reader; spectacles. See under the nouns.

Fraunhofer's (frown'hōf-erz) **diffraction grating; lines; diffraction phenomenon.** See under the nouns.

Freeman Near Vision Unit. See under _unit._

Frenzel (fren'zel) **goggles; nystagmus; spectacles.** See under the nouns.

frequency. 1. In harmonic motions, the number of cycles or vibrations per unit of time. 2. The number of occurrences of a given value or score falling into a specified class or population.

    flicker f. The rate of intermittency, alternation, or variation of the presentation of photic stimulation to the eye, usually expressed in cycles per second.

    flicker f., critical. Critical fusion frequency.

    flicker f., fusion. Critical fusion frequency.

    flicker f., subfusional. Flicker frequency below that required to produce uniform sensation. Syn., _subfusional pulse frequency._

    fusion f. Critical fusion frequency.

    fusion f., critical. The rate of presentation of intermittent, alternate, or discontinuous photic stimuli that just gives rise to a fully uniform and continuous sensation obliterating the flicker. Syn., _critical flicker frequency; fusion frequency; fusion flicker_

frequency; flicker fusion threshold.

    light wave, f. of. The rate of electromagnetic vibration of luminous flux. Designated ν (nu), it is equal to the quotient of the velocity of light (c) divided by the wavelength (λ); thus, $\nu = c/\lambda$. The frequency of visible light ranges from approximately 4.3×10^{14} to 7.5×10^{14} per sec.

    pulse f., subfusional. Subfusional flicker frequency.

Fresnel's (fra-nelz') **biprism; coefficient; ellipsoid; experiment; formula; integrals; law; lens; mirrors; phenomenon; rhomb; zone.** See under the nouns.

von Frey's hairs (fon-frīz'). See under _hairs._

Fridenberg's (frid'en-bergz) **chart; test.** See under the nouns.

Frieberg's theory (fre'bergz). See under _theory._

Friedenwald's (fre'den-walds) **chart; coefficient; formula.** See under the nouns.

Friedreich's (frēd'rīks) **spinal ataxia; disease.** Friedreich's disease.

frill, iris. The line of junction of the ciliary zone and the pupillary zone of the iris. Syn., _collarette._

frill, pigment. Pupillary ruff.

fringe. One of the dark or light bands produced by the diffraction or interference of light.

    Brewster's f's. White light fringes obtained by placing two Fabry-Perot interferometers in series so as to create a path difference of zero.

    circular f's. 1. Alternate circular bands of light and dark produced by interference of light from two coherent extended sources, as in the Michelson interferometer when the mirrors are optically parallel to each other, or by interference with a thin plane-parallel film. 2. The Haidinger's fringes, or fringes of constant inclination, observed with a thick plane-parallel plate or with the Fabry-

Perot interferometer. 3. The rings of a diffraction pattern produced by plane waves passing through a small circular aperture, or by diffraction of plane waves by a circular obstacle.

color f's. 1. A border of colors around images produced by a lens or an optical system not corrected for chromatic aberration. 2. Bands of color produced by interference or diffraction of white light.

constant inclination, f's of. Haidinger's fringes.

constant thickness, f's of. Interference fringes representing isothickness contours in thin films.

diffraction f's. A pattern of alternate dark and light bands produced by interference between the rays of diffracted light from a single narrow opening of finite width. The fringes occur, as with simple interference fringes, at points where the optical path differences of rays from points within the borders of the opening result in constructive or destructive interference, but the resultant pattern and the intensity distribution differ from the simple interference pattern in that the central band is very much brighter than other bands and its width is twice the separation of the minima (dark bands).

equal inclination, f's. of. Haidinger's fringes.

Haidinger's f's. Interference fringes observed when the separation between the reflecting surfaces is relatively large, as in the Fabry-Perot interferometer or with a thick plane-parallel plate, such as the Lummer-Gehrcke plate. In such cases, interference occurs between multiply reflected waves having the same inclination within the interspace between the reflecting surfaces, such interference being due to path differences arising from multiple crossings of the interspace by the reflected light. The observed pattern, then, is a result of differences of inclination of waves within the interspace, each individual fringe representing an isoinclination contour, hence also called *fringes of constant inclination.* For large separations of the reflecting surfaces, the fringes are always circular in form.

interference f's. A pattern of alternate light and dark bands produced by destructive and constructive interference between the propagation waves of two or more superposed beams of light from a coherent source, occurring as a result of a difference in the optical lengths of the paths of two or more beams of light (usually monochromatic) from a single source.

localized f's. Interference fringes observed with thin films or with the Michelson interferometer when the reflecting surfaces are not parallel to each other. Rays from a point on the source, reflected from the two surfaces and interfering to produce an interference fringe, are not parallel, but instead appear to diverge from a point near the surfaces. Hence, in order to observe the fringes clearly, the observer's eye must be focused approximately in the plane of the reflecting surfaces or in the plane in which the fringes appear to be localized. The fringes are usually nearly straight and parallel to the edge of the effective air wedge or film wedge between the reflecting surfaces.

moiré f's. Dark fringes produced when two diffraction gratings are placed in contact with each other such that the lines of the gratings intersect at a small angle.

white light f's. Interference fringes obtained in an interferometer when white light is used for the source, observed only when the path difference is of the order of a few wavelengths or less. In general, the central fringe is dark, while the other fringes have colored borders.

Froehlich's syndrome (fra'liks). See under *syndrome*.

Froment's sign (fro-mahnz'). See under *sign*.

front. The part of a spectacle frame, Numont, or rimway mounting, exclusive of the temple, i.e., the bridge and the eyewires or rims.

Frostig test (fros'tig). See under *test*.

frothing. An aggregation of numerous minute air bubbles under a contact lens, frequently due to intermittent and excessive flaring of the edge of the lens from the cornea.

Fruehjahr's catarrh (fru'hahrz, fru'-yahrz). Vernal conjunctivitis.

Fry's (frīz) **frame gauge; method.** See under the nouns.

F.S.A.O. Fellow of the Scottish Association of Opticians.

F.S.M.C. Freeman of the Spectacle Makers Company, or, more formally, Freeman of the Worshipful Company of Spectacle Makers of London.

Fuchs's (fooks'ez) **angle; optic atrophy; cleft; coloboma; conus; crypts; cyclitis; dimples; corneal dystrophy; heterochromia; heterochromic iridocyclitis; superficial punctate keratitis; lamella; anterior pigment layer; lines of clearing; phenomenon; sign; spot; spur; syndrome.** See under the nouns.

Fuller-Albright syndrome (ful'er-awl'brīt). See under *syndrome*.

Ful-Vue (ful'vu). 1. See under *frame* and *mounting*. 2. A trade name for one of several types of bifocal lenses having a reading segment with a slightly curved upper border.

function. 1. The special action which any tissue, organ, or system of the body performs. 2. Any fact or quality so related to another that it is dependent on and varies with it. 3. Either of two magnitudes so related that to values of one there correspond values of the other.

color-matching f's. The energy fluxes of the three chosen primary wavelengths required to match the unit energy flux of a given monochromatic test wavelength.

contrast transfer f. See *optical transfer function*.

edge spread f. A mathematical description of the distribution of light across the optical image of an edge, i.e., across the image of an extended target having a sharp change in luminance, or a luminance distribution described by a step function.

frequency response f. See *optical transfer function*.

line spread f. A mathematical description of the distribution of light across the image of an infinitesimally narrow bright-line object.

luminosity f. The relative brightness-producing capacity of light of different wavelengths measured by the reciprocals of the amounts of radiant flux required at each wavelength region to produce the same brightness. Syn., *photopic visibility function*.

modulation transfer f. See *optical transfer function*.

ocular rigidity f. A mathematical expression which relates intraocular pressure change to a change in intraocular volume, dP/dV, where P is the symbol for pressure and V is the symbol for volume.

optical transfer f. A mathematical expression of the relationship of the light distribution in an optical image to that in the object, hence an expression of the optical reproduction or optical transfer properties of the system, often in terms of the ratio of image contrast to object contrast as a function of spatial frequency (of a grating target), hence variously referred to as *contrast transfer function, modulation transfer function, frequency response function, spatial frequency transfer function, sine-wave response function,* etc. It is the Fourier transform of the spread function (see *line spread function, point spread function, edge spread function*).

photopic visibility f. Luminosity function.

point spread f. A mathematical description of the distribution of light in a cross section of the image of an infinitesimally small, bright, point object, hence a description of the point-imaging characteristics of an optical system.

sine-wave response f. See *optical transfer function.*

spatial frequency f. See *optical transfer function.*

fundus (fun'dus). The base of the internal surface of a hollow organ; the part farthest removed or opposite the aperture.

albinotic f. An ocular fundus characterized by partial or complete lack of pigmentation of the retinal and choroidal layers. Ophthalmoscopically, the choroidal and the retinal vessels are clearly visible against a light orange-red background.

albipunctatus, f. An inherited tapetoretinal degeneration, either congenital or occurring in early life, and characterized by numerous white dots scattered throughout an otherwise normal fundus and accompanied by night blindness in about two thirds of the affected. It may be either unilateral or bilateral, visual acuity is unaffected, the visual fields are normal or but slightly restricted, and the condition is non-

progressive. Some differentiate it from the progressive retinitis punctata albescens and others believe the two are transitional forms of the same entity.

lacrimal sac, f. of the. The superior portion of the lacrimal sac formed by its cul-de-sac and bounded inferiorly by the sinus of Maier.

leopard f. An ocular fundus of mottled appearance as a result of retinitis pigmentosa.

ocular f. The concave interior of the eye, consisting of the retina, the choroid, the sclera, the optic disk, and blood vessels, seen by means of the ophthalmoscope.

oculi, f. Ocular fundus.

salt and pepper f. The finely pigmented ocular fundus characteristic of hereditary syphilis; it consists of innumerable, small, bluish pigmented spots between which lie depigmented yellowish-red spots.

shot silk f. An ocular fundus, sometimes seen in young persons, which has an opalescent or shimmering appearance, due to retinal reflections of light from the ophthalmoscope.

tesselated f. A nonpathological ocular fundus to which a deeply pigmented choroid gives the ophthalmoscopic appearance of dark, polygonal-shaped areas between the choroidal vessels, noted especially in the periphery. Syn., *tigroid fundus.*

tigroid f. Tesselated fundus.

Funduscope (fun'dus-skōp). An ophthalmoscope.

funnel, muscular (fun'el). The four rectus muscles of the eye considered as a structural unit and so designated because of their resemblance to a cone or a funnel as they diverge from their common origin at the apex of the orbit and extend forward to their insertions on the eyeball. Syn., *muscle cone.*

funnel, vascular (fun'el). Physiological cup.

Furmethide (fur'meth-id). Furfuryl trimethyl-ammonium iodide, a parasympathomimetic drug used in the eye, usually in 10% solution, as a miotic.

furrow. A groove or narrow channel.

circular f's. Depressions of the posterior surface of the iris, concentric with the pupil and crossing the radial structural furrows at regular intervals, caused by a local thinning of the pigment epithelium.

contraction f's of Schwalbe. Shallow furrows near the pupillary margin of the posterior surface of the iris, extending radially for about 1 mm. and bending over the pupillary aperture, causing crenations on the pupillary margin. Syn., *contraction folds of Schwalbe.*

structural f's. of Schwalbe. Shallow furrows on the posterior surface of the iris, extending from the region of the sphincter pupillae muscle and becoming continuous with the valleys between the ciliary processes. Syn., *structural folds of Schwalbe.*

fuscin (fus'in, fu'sin). The melanin-like pigment found as granules or needles in the cytoplasm of the pigment epithelium layer of the retina, especially that pigment near the visual cells.

Fuse's nucleus (fu'zez). See under *nucleus.*

fusion. The act or process of blending, uniting, or cohering.

amplitude of f. See under *amplitude.*

attraction, f. The stimulus value of a pair of binocularly coexisting, disparate, retinal images which evokes a motor fusion response.

aversion, f. Horror fusionis.

binocular f. Sensory fusion.

breadth of f. The combined range of convergence and divergence of

the two eyes within which single binocular vision is maintained. Clinically, it is usually determined at a specific distance by the sum of the base-in and the base-out prism effects through which single binocular vision can be maintained.

cards, f. See under *card.*

center, f. See under *center.*

chiastopic f. Fusion obtained by voluntarily converging to fixate directly two fusible targets, laterally separated in space, such that the right eye directly fixates the left target and the left eye the right target.

clue, f. See under *clue.*

color f. 1. A type of sensory fusion wherein spectral stimulation which differs for the two eyes is combined or integrated into a unitary percept unlike either of the stimulating fields. 2. A unitary perception of color which bears no resemblance to any of the individual colors which form the composite. Cf. *color blend.*

critical f. Critical fusion frequency.

degrees of f. A classification by Worth of binocular vision into three divisions. First degree fusion: simultaneous, binocular perception of dissimilar objects which are projected in the same visual direction, as in the projection of a star seen by one eye into a circle seen by the other. Second degree fusion: single, simultaneous, binocular perception of identical, haploscopically viewed targets. Third degree fusion: stereopsis, requiring fusion of stereoscopic targets with a resultant third dimension percept.

faculty, f. See under *faculty.*

far point of f. The farthest distance at which single binocular vision is maintained. Hypothetically, it may be beyond infinity as measured by the maximum base-in prism effect through which single binocular vision can be maintained.

flat f. Sensory fusion in which the resultant percept is two-dimensional, that is, occupying a single plane, as may be induced by viewing a stereogram in a stereoscope in which the separation of all homologous points is identical.

foveal f. Sensory fusion in which only foveal images are considered.

frequency, f. See under *frequency.*

grades of f. An arbitrary division of fusional ability into four grades, determined with a white fixation target and a red lens before one eye. Grade A: immediate perception of one pink image. Grade B: immediate perception of one red and one white image, which subsequently merge into one pink image. Grade C: continuous perception of one red and one white image. Grade D: continuous perception of one image only, which is either red or white.

macular f. Sensory fusion in which only macular images are considered.

motor f. The relative movements of the two eyes in response to disparate retinal stimuli, to obtain or maintain simultaneous stimulation of corresponding retinal areas, so that sensory fusion may occur.

near point of f. The nearest distance at which single binocular vision is maintained. It may be determined by the push-up test for convergence, or by the maximum base-out prism effect through which single binocular vision can be maintained.

orthopic f. Fusion obtained by voluntarily diverging to directly fixate two fusible targets, laterally separated in space, such that the right eye directly fixates the right target and the left eye the left.

per cent of f. An arbitrary rating of fusional ability into per cent, one such rating being based on the smallest diameter of colored circular targets which can be fused when viewed haploscopically.

peripheral f. Sensory fusion in which the images in the peripheral portions of the retinae are considered, excluding the maculae.

quality of f. The degree of ability to maintain single, simultaneous, binocular vision. See also *grades of fusion* and *per cent of fusion.*

sensory f. 1. The process by which stimuli seen separately by the two eyes are combined, synthesized, or integrated into a unitary percept. Under normal binocular conditions, this occurs when corresponding retinal areas are stimulated by the same object, or objects of similar content. Syn., *binocular fusion.* 2. The combining of stimuli, presented intermittently or alternately, into a single constant sensation.

stereoscopic f. Sensory fusion of disparate retinal stimuli with a resultant third dimensional effect.

supplement, f. Fusional convergence.

temporal f. 1. The combining or integrating of stimuli presented intermittently or alternately at a specific temporal sequence into a single constant sensation. 2. Simulated sensory fusion presumed to occur as a result of the rapid alternating perception of the images of the two eyes in rapid alternating suppression.

torsional f. The component or type of motor fusion represented by torsional movements of the eyes.

fusional convergence; divergence; reserve. See under the nouns.

f-value. Focal ratio.

F.V.O.A. Fellow of the Victorian Optometrical Association (Australia).

G

Galassi's (gah-lahs'ēz) **phenomenon; reflex.** The orbicularis pupillary reflex.

galeropia (gal"eh-ro'pe-ah). A pathological condition in which objects appear abnormally light and clear.

galeropsia (gal"eh-rop'se-ah). Galeropia.

Galezowski's strabismometer (gal-eh-zow'skēz). See under *strabismometer.*

Galilean (gal"ih-le'an) **spectacle; telescope.** See under the nouns.

galloxanthin (gal-o-zan'thin). A pigment, isolated by Wald from the retina of a chicken, thought to assist in differentiating spectral radiation by absorbing violet.

Galton bar (gawl'ton). See under *bar.*

gamma [γ] (gam'ah). The Greek letter used as the symbol for (1) *angle gamma;* (2) *gamma movement.*

ganglion (gang'gle-un). An aggregation of nerve cell bodies located outside of the central nervous system.

accessory g. of Axenfeld. Episcleral ganglion.

cervical g., inferior. The lowest of three prominences of the paired sympathetic chains of vertebral ganglia in the region of the neck. Preganglionic and postganglionic nerve fibers synapse here, but the preganglionic axons relaying to the head pass through and synapse in the superior cervical ganglion.

cervical g., middle. The second of three prominences of the paired sympathetic chains of vertebral ganglia in the region of the neck. Preganglionic axons relaying to the head pass directly through and synapse in the superior cervical ganglion.

cervical g., superior. The highest of three prominences of the paired sympathetic chains of vertebral ganglia in the region of the neck. It is the relay station for thoracic sympathetic preganglionic neurons that supply the smooth muscles and glands in the head and orbit, and its destruction results in Horner's syndrome.

ciliary g. A terminal parasympathetic ganglion located within the orbit between the lateral rectus muscle and the optic nerve. By way of its short motor root, it receives preganglionic axons which synapse in the ganglion with postganglionic neurons supplying the sphincter pupillae and ciliary muscles. By way of its sympathetic root, it receives vasomotor postganglionic axons supplying the eyeball. Its long sensory root carries general sensory dendrites originating in the eyeball, and some sympathetic postganglionic axons going to the dilator pupillae muscle. It gives rise to six to ten short ciliary nerves which double in number, prior to piercing the posterior sclera, and carry the afferent and postganglionic fibers. Syn., *lenticular ganglion; ophthalmic ganglion; optic ganglion; Schacher's ganglion.*

episcleral g. A collection of postganglionic cell bodies in a terminal parasympathetic ganglion located adjacent to a ciliary nerve or the optic nerve, in or near the posterior episclera. It is the site of synapses in the near pupillary reflex pathway to the sphincter pupillae muscle. Syn., *accessory ganglion of Axenfeld.*

Gasserian g. A ganglion on the sensory root of the trigeminal nerve, located on the petrous portion of the temporal bone, which contains the unipolar cell bodies of the afferent neurons and to which are connected the ophthalmic, the maxillary, and the mandibular nerves. Syn., *semilunar ganglion; trigeminal ganglion.*

lenticular g. Ciliary ganglion.

Meckel's g. The parasympathetic terminal nodule in the pterygopalatine fossa which receives the vidian nerve and connects with the maxillary nerve. Vasodilator and secretory fibers for the lacrimal gland from the facial nerve synapse here, and sympathetic postganglionic axons for the lacrimal gland and for Mueller's orbital muscle pass through. Syn., *sphenopalatine ganglion.*

Mueller's intraocular g. Collectively, a group of sympathetic-type multipolar cells near the arterioles of the choroid which are associated with plexuses derived from the ciliary nerves and are thought to be of vasomotor function and to participate in the control of intraocular pressure.

oculomotor g. 1. Schwalbe's term for the ciliary ganglion. 2. Tiny nodules on the oculomotor nerve.

ophthalmic g. Ciliary ganglion.

optic g. 1. Any one of several structures, such as the superior colliculus, the pretectal nucleus, or the lateral geniculate body, and, less likely, the pulvinar of the thalamus, considered as a primary or lower optical center. 2. The ciliary ganglion. 3. A cluster of cell bodies within the tuber

cinereum of the diencephalon.

Schacher's g. Ciliary ganglion.

semilunar g. Gasserian ganglion.

sphenopalatine g. Meckel's ganglion.

thoracic g., superior. A ganglion on the sympathetic chain just below the inferior cervical ganglion, receiving preganglionic axons from the ciliospinal center of Budge which pass up the chain to the superior cervical ganglion, where they synapse with sympathetic neurons supplying the dilator pupillae muscle. It receives sympathetic fibers that originate in the upper thoracic cord and synapse in the superior cervical ganglion with neurons that supply the smooth muscles and glands in the head and the orbit. Syn., *first thoracic ganglion.*

trigeminal g. Gasserian ganglion.

Ganser's commissure (gahn'zerz). See under *commissure.*

gargoylism (gar'goil-izm). Hurler's disease.

Gasserian ganglion (gah-sēr'ih-an). See under *ganglion.*

Gát's schema (gahtz). See under *schema.*

Gaucher's disease (go-shāz'). See under *disease.*

gauge. An instrument for measuring dimension, curvature, or pressure, or for determining position.

douzième g. A caliper-type lens thickness gauge calibrated in douzièmes.

drop g. A device for determining the diameter of a contact lens, consisting essentially of a plate with a series of graduated apertures of various diameters. The smallest aperture through which the lens can pass indicates its diameter.

Duplex P-D g. An instrument for measuring the distance of the pupil of each eye from the center of the root of the nose, for the purpose of accurately positioning optical centers and/or bifocal segments of spectacle lenses. While the patient fixates successively the straight ahead images of his own eyes in a full-silvered mirror, the examiner notes the position of the root of the nose and each successively straightforward eye on a millimeter scale projected in the plane of the patient's pupils by a second (semisilvered) mirror.

Fry frame g. A device for measuring the dimensions of a spectacle frame according to the boxing method. It consists essentially of a ruled plastic plate, on which the frame is placed, and four single lines engraved on moveable transparent plastic strips, two vertical and two horizontal. Appropriate adjustment of the moveable lines indicates eyesize, DBL, major reference points, and multifocal segment positions.

interpupillary g. An instrument for measuring the distance between the centers of the pupils of the eyes.

lens g. Lens measure.

Livingston's binocular g. An instrument for determining the near point of either convergence or accommodation, consisting of a rule, 36 cm. long, with a track down its center for a movable vertical target. The near points are determined by placing one end of the rule against the face and moving the target toward the eyes until it blurs or doubles.

Obrig Radius Dial G. A trade name for a device used for measuring the base curve of a contact lens, consisting essentially of a shaft having a central plunger which protrudes from a rounded surface on one end and connects to a dial on the other end. When placed against the lens surface, the extent of protrusion of the plunger determines sagittal depth, which is converted to radius of curvature in millimeters on the dial.

strap g. A metal disk with calibrated notches along its periphery for measuring the edge thickness of spectacle lenses at the point of insertion into the strap.

surfacing g. A flat template, or one of a series of templates, with an edge of known curvature for checking the curvature of the surface of a lens or lap by inspection of its goodness of fit in contact with the surface.

thickness g. 1. A caliper used to measure spectacle lens thickness, especially during surface grinding. It may be calibrated in $\frac{1}{5}$ mm. or $\frac{1}{10}$ mm. as units, the $\frac{1}{5}$ mm. unit markings often being referred to as "points" in laboratory practice. 2. A device used to measure the center thickness of a contact lens, usually consisting of a stage on which the lens is centered while against the opposite surface of the lens is placed a spring-loaded plunger attached to a dial, usually calibrated in $\frac{1}{10}$ mm. units.

V g. A bar with a tapering slot calibrated in $\frac{1}{10}$ mm. units. The narrowest point in the slot into which a contact lens slides indicates its diameter.

Gaule's (gōlz) **pits; spots.** See under *spot.*

Gault's reflex (gōltz). Cochleopalpebral reflex.

Gauss's (gows'ez) **condition; eyepiece; theory.** See under the nouns.

Gaussian (gows'zhun) **curve; frequency distribution; optical system; points.** See under the nouns.

Gaviola's caustic test (gav″e-o′laz). See under *test.*

gaze. 1. To fixate steadily or continuously. 2. The act or the condition of gazing.

direction of g. See under *direction.*

position of g. See under *position.*

geisoma (gi-so'mah). The eyebrows or the supraorbital ridges.

geison (gi'son). Geisoma.

Gemminger's ossicle (jem'ing-erz). Os opticus.

General Optical Council. A representative corporate body created by Parliament (British) to carry out the provisions of the Opticians Act, 1958, which provides for the registration of optometrists and opticians and the regulation of certain related functions.

generator (jen'er-a-tor). A machine with cutting tools on arc-mounted jigs adjustable to selected curvilinear motions to grind lenses to desired thicknesses and surface curvatures.

geniculate body (je-nik'u-lāt). See under *body.*

Gennari's (jen-ah'rēz) **band; line; stria.** See under *line.*

genotype (jen'o-tīp). 1. A type determined by the common genetic characteristics of a group. 2. The hereditary characteristics of an organism, based on the genes which are postulated as occurring in its chromosomes.

Gerlach, muscle of (ger'lak). Anterior lacrimal muscle.

Gerlier's disease (zher-le-āz'). See under *disease.*

geromorphism (jer"o-mōr'fizm). A disease in which the skin becomes flaccid and wrinkled, resembling that of an aged person, occasionally affecting the upper eyelid and causing ptosis.

gerontopia (jer"on-to'pe-ah). Senopia.

gerontotoxon (jer-on"to-tok'son). Arcus senilis.

gerontoxon (jer"on-tok'son). Arcus senilis.

gerontoxon lentis (jer"on-tok'son len'tis). A surgical displacement of a cataractous crystalline lens in the aged.

Gerstmann's syndrome (garst'manz). See under *syndrome.*

ghost. 1. A phantom; a faint shadowy semblance. 2. An unwanted secondary image, as may be formed by internal reflection in a lens or an optical system, irregularity of spacing in a diffraction grating, or incomplete polarization by a polaroid filter.

Bidwell's g. Second positive afterimage.

Lyman's g's. Ghosts or faint line images produced by a diffraction grating having an error in the spacing of its lines involving two periods or a single short period.

Rowland's g's. Ghost or faint line images appearing symmetrically in spacing and intensity about the principal maxima, produced by a diffraction grating having a single periodic error in the spacing of its lines.

Swindle's g. An excessively long positive afterimage.

Gianelli's sign (jah-nel'lēz). Tournay's pupillary reflex.

Giantscope. A trade name for an ophthalmoscope manufactured by the American Optical Company.

Gibson's (gib'sunz) **method; theory.** See under the nouns.

Gifford's (gif'ordz) **reflex; sign.** See under the nouns.

gigantophthalmos (ji-gant"of-thal'mos). An anterior megalophthalmos in which the anterior segment of the eye is greatly enlarged.

Giles-Archer color perception unit (jīlz-ar'cher). See under *unit.*

Gillespie's syndrome (gih-les'pēz). See under *syndrome.*

girdle, limbus, of Vogt. A white, ragged-edged, subepithelial opacity of the cornea, located chiefly in the interpalpebral region and concentric with the limbus. It is differentiated into two types: in one the opacity is discontinuous, having gaps, and is separated from the limbus by a clear zone; in the other the opacity is unbroken, is continuous with the sclera, and has short projections extending toward the center of the cornea.

glabella (glah-bel′ah). 1. The region of the frontal bone between the eyebrows. 2. The skin, generally hairless, between the eyebrows.

gland. A cell or an organ which secretes or excretes a substance or substances.

Baumgarten's g's. Conjunctival glands located nasally in the eyelids of some animals but not man.

Bruch's g's. Lymph follicles in the conjunctiva of the eyelids.

Ciaccio, g's. of. Glands of Wolfring and Ciaccio.

ciliary g's. 1. Invaginations of the pigmented epithelium of the ciliary body, especially in the pars plana, thought by some to secrete aqueous humor. 2. Glands of Moll.

Collins, g's. of. Ciliary body glands in the region of the ciliary processes, formed by folds of the outer pigmented cells of the epithelium and thought by some to secrete aqueous humor.

conjunctival g. 1. Any gland, the duct of which empties into the conjunctiva, such as Meibomian, Krause, Wolfring and Ciaccio glands, or a goblet cell. Some include the lacrimal gland. 2. Any accessory lacrimal gland.

Harder, g. of. A mucosebaceous secreting gland in nonprimate vertebrates, found near the attachment of the nictitating membrane. It rapidly degenerates in the human fetal eye.

Henle, g's. of. Crypts of the palbebral conjunctiva between the tarsus and the fornix in both the upper and the lower eyelids, probably nonsecretory. Syn., *conjunctival crypts.*

infraorbital g. An accessory lacrimal gland located in the lower outer fornix of the conjunctiva, which is permanent in lower vertebrates and degenerates in the fetus of higher primates.

Krause, g's. of. Accessory lacrimal glands of the conjunctiva, most of which are located in the region of the superior fornix beneath the inferior lacrimal gland, with a few located just beneath the inferior fornix.

lacrimal g. A compound tubulo-alveolar gland which is divided into an orbital and a palpebral portion by the lateral horn of the aponeurosis of the levator palpebrae superioris muscle. The orbital lobe rests in a fossa of the frontal bone located laterally in the orbital roof, its ducts joining those of the palpebral lobe to form about twelve ducts which empty into the superior lateral fornix, although occasionally one empties into the inferior lateral fornix. The lacrimal gland forms the lacrimal fluid portion of the tears, to which mucin and sebum are added. Syn., *glandula orbitaria.*

lacrimal g's., accessory. Any of the conjunctival glands which secrete lacrimal fluid; the glands of Krause, or the glands of Wolfring and Ciaccio.

Manz, g's. of. Tiny, epithelial, cell-filled diverticula in the limbal conjunctiva of some domestic animals. Their presence in man is not established.

Meibomian g's. A series of simple, branched, alveolar, sebaceous glands, located in the tarsi of the eyelids, whose ducts empty into the eyelid margins in line with and lateral to the lacrimal puncta. Syn., *tarsal glands; tarsoconjunctival glands.*

Moll, g. of. A sweat gland located in the region of an eyelash.

Rosenmueller's g. The inferior or palpebral portion of the lacrimal gland.

tarsal g's. Meibomian glands.

tarsoconjunctival g's. Meibomian glands.

Waldeyer's g's. Modified sweat glands at the margin of the eyelid, near the border of the tarsus.

Wolfring and Ciaccio, g's. of. Accessory lacrimal glands in the upper eyelid, located in the region of the superior border of the tarsus, which empty into the palpebral conjunctiva.

Zeis, g's. of. Simple, branched, alveolar, sebum-forming glands attached directly to the follicles of the eyelashes.

glandula (glan'du-lah). A gland, especially a small gland.

concreta, g. The superior or orbital portion of the lacrimal gland.

lacrimalis, g. Lacrimal gland.

mucosa, g. Gland of Krause.

orbitaria, g. The lacrimal gland.

Glan-Foucault (glan-foo-ko') **polarizer; prism.** See under *prism.*

Glan-Thompson prism (glan-tom'son). See under *prism.*

glare. Relatively bright light, or the dazzling sensation of relatively bright light, which produces unpleasantness or discomfort, or which interferes with optimal vision.

accompaniment, g. Any of the sensory or motor end results, aside from the awareness or sensation of glare, elicited by glare-producing stimuli, such as the reduced ability to distinguish objects.

blinding g. Scotomatic glare.

central g. Glare as a result of intense light on the foveal or macular area of the retina, as occurs when directly viewing a small, bright light source. Syn., *direct glare.*

dazzling g. One of the three classes of glare designated by Bell, Troland, and Verhoeff. It is glare produced by adventitious light scattered in the ocular media so as not to form part of the retinal

image. Cf. *scotomatic glare; veiling glare.*

direct g. 1. Central glare. 2. Glare resulting from light sources or reflecting surfaces insufficiently shielded to prevent the direct entry of light into the observer's eye.

disability g. Glare which reduces visual performance and visibility, and may be accompanied by discomfort.

discomfort g. Glare which produces discomfort but does not necessarily interfere with visual performance or visibility.

eccentric g. Glare as a result of intense light falling on the peripheral retina. Syn., *indirect glare.*

indirect g. Eccentric glare.

reflected g. Glare resulting from specular reflections from polished or glossy surfaces.

scotomatic g. One of the three classes of glare designated by Bell, Troland, and Verhoeff. It is glare produced by light of sufficient intensity to reduce appreciably the sensitivity of the retina. Cf. *dazzling glare; veiling glare.* Syn., *blinding glare.*

total g. Glare in which excessive light falls on the whole retina.

veiling g. One of the three classes of glare designated by Bell, Troland, and Verhoeff. It is glare produced by excess light uniformly distributed over the visual field so as to cause reduced contrasts and, therefore, reduced visibility. Cf. *dazzling glare; scotomatic glare.*

glarometer (gla-rom'eh-ter). An instrument for measuring sensitivity to glare from the headlights of an approaching automobile.

glass. 1. A substance, ordinarily hard, brittle, and lustrous, produced by fusing sand (silica) with oxides of potassium or sodium and other ingredients, especially lead oxide, alumina, and lime. It is usually transparent, although it may be translucent, and even opaque, in certain forms. Special treatment of glass may cause it to change into tough fibers used in insulation and even in textiles. Glass may be produced in various colors by the addition of various chemicals. 2. A lens or a light filter.

absorption g. Glass which transmits only a portion of the light incident upon it, the remainder being absorbed and transformed into other forms of energy. The term is applied particularly to colored glass.

adhesive g. A contact lens.

alabaster g. A white, translucent glass used principally for vases, ornaments, and busts.

amethyst g. An absorptive glass, particularly useful in the absorption of ultraviolet rays inasmuch as it totally absorbs those below 3,000 Å. It is produced by the addition of manganese dioxide to the glass batch.

antique g. A glass in which bubbles, striae, etc., are intentionally introduced to produce a slight nonuniform diffusion.

Arundel g. A slightly pink, absorptive glass devised in 1872 by T. A. Wilson.

Bagolini's striated g. A lens on which fine parallel striations have been grooved. Visual acuity through the lens is only slightly or negligibly reduced, but a light source viewed through the lens appears as a streak of light oriented 90° from the striations (similar to a Maddox rod). Two such lenses mounted in front of the two eyes, with the striations oriented 90° apart, are used in the determination of suppression, anomalous correspondence, and fixation disparity.

barium-crown g. A type of ophthalmic glass used primarily in bifocal segments. It has an index of refraction ranging between 1.570 and 1.616, depending on

the ingredients, and a ν value between 55.0 and 57.0.

barium-flint g. A type of ophthalmic glass used primarily in multifocal segments and containing barium oxide, silica, lead oxide, and other elements. Its index of refraction ranges approximately between 1.58 and 1.62, depending on the proportion of ingredients, and its ν value approximately between 43.0 and 53.0.

blown g. Glass which has been blown to some predetermined form either by machine or by human breath. Glass blowing has been used in the manufacture of glass artificial eyes and glass contact lenses. Blown glass lenses are used in some inexpensive sunglasses.

cased g. A composite of two or more fused layers of different kinds of glass, usually one clear, transparent and another opal, opalescent, or colored.

cobalt-blue g. A cobalt-containing glass known for its property of transmitting light primarily from the red and blue ends of the spectrum. When used in refraction as a bichromatic filter for testing ametropia, it is sometimes called a *cobalt lens*.

configurated g. A nontransparent, diffusing glass having a patterned surface, such as pebbled or stippled glass.

Crookes g. Any of a series of commercially available absorptive glasses, ranging from pale amethyst to brownish gray or smoke in its usual forms, but also available in sage green, developed by Sir William Crookes about 1910, in association with the Chance Brothers, of Birmingham, England. It possesses the property of absorbing a large proportion of infrared rays and practically all ultraviolet rays. The transmission curve for Crookes A shows an over-all 10% reduction of light intensity in the visible range, with a sharp dip (up to 30% absorption) around the wavelength 5,800 Å. The transmission curve for Crookes 246 shows a reduction of light intensity in the visible range of more than 75%.

crown g. An optical, alkali-lime glass having a low dispersion (ν value 52.2) relative to the index of refraction ($n = 1.523$), commonly used in ophthalmic lenses. Cf. *flint glass.*

enameled g. A diffusing glass surfaced with enamel.

euphos g. A yellow-green, absorptive glass which does not transmit wavelengths shorter than 4,000 Å, developed in 1907 by Drs. Schauz and Stockhousen, of Dresden, Germany.

Fieuzel g. A yellow-green glass which absorbs a high percentage of both ultraviolet and infrared rays.

flint g. A lead-containing, optical glass having a high dispersion relative to its refractive index, as compared, e.g., to crown glass. It is softer and heavier than crown glass and is used in ophthalmic lenses required to be thin, and as bifocal segments in crown glass lenses.

ground g. Glass which has been surface ground with rough emery to make it translucent; especially used as an occluding lens.

Hallauer g. A smoky-green glass, produced in 1905 by Dr. O. Hallauer, of Switzerland, which absorbs ultraviolet radiations, totally absorbing those below 4,000 Å.

homogeneous g. A glass of uniform composition, as differentiated from cased glass, although striae or bubbles may still be present.

kalichrome g. A commercially available yellow glass which totally absorbs ultraviolet and large portions of the violet, blue, and infrared, hence, said to reduce blue haze effects; frequently pre-

scribed for spectacles used by marksmen and skeet shooters.

magnifying g. A simple converging lens or lens system, usually held in the hand and relatively near the object viewed, for magnifying apparent size without inversion.

mat-surface g. A highly diffusing glass having an etched, ground, or sandblasted surface.

Motex g. A trade name for glass of the same construction as Triplex glass.

noviol g. A yellow, absorptive glass, similar in type and purpose to kalichrome glass.

objective g. Objective lens.

opal g. A nearly white or milky, translucent diffusing glass.

opalescent g. A form of opal glass having selective properties of transmission which result in an iridescent appearance of transmitted light.

ophthalmic g. Optical glass meeting the specific requirements for ophthalmic lenses.

optical g. A form of glass meeting the specific requirements for use in optical systems with respect to transparency, homogeneity, bubbles, inclusions, striae, cloudiness, strain, refractive index, dispersive power, and chemical and physical stability.

Pfund's gold-plated g. A type of laminated absorptive glass consisting of a Crookes A glass to absorb ultraviolet, a very thin layer of gold to reflect infrared while transmitting visible light, and a crown glass to protect the layer of gold.

photochromic g. Transparent glass which darkens on exposure to light of high intensity and clears with reduced intensity.

plate g. Fine rolled, ground, and polished sheet glass.

polarizing g. Polarizing occluder.

prismatic g. A lenslike unit or assembly of transparent optical glass, molded or otherwise preformed so that different areas of the transmitting surface each have a prescribed prismatic effect to deflect light in a desired direction, thus to accomplish a distribution or a concentration of light suitable for special illumination purposes. Examples include horizontal sidewalk windows for illuminating basements, various luminaires, and automobile headlamp lenses.

red g. A glass transmitting red light more or less exclusively. When used monocularly in binocular clinical tests and training procedures, it is sometimes called a *red lens.*

safety g. 1. Nonshatterable, laminated glass consisting of a layer of transparent plastic between two layers of glass, commonly used in automobiles and goggles. 2. Glass, case-hardened by heat treatment, used in goggles and ophthalmic lenses.

Salvoc g. A trade name for a glass of the same construction as Triplex glass.

smoke g. A smoke-colored, absorptive glass transmitting the visible wavelengths more or less uniformly. Available commercially in various degrees of absorptiveness, it is useful for controlling illumination and brightness intensities.

transparent g. Glass through which objects can be seen clearly.

Triplex g. A trade name for a safety glass consisting of two layers of clear glass cemented together with a layer of cellulose acetate or zylonite. When broken, it cracks into fragments but does not splinter or fly.

window g. Glass used for windowpanes, usually manufactured in sheets by a rolling process and differing in characteristics from optical glass.

Wood's g. Wood's filter.

glasses. Spectacles.

glasses, field. Binoculars.

glaucoma (glaw-ko′mah). An ocular disease, occurring in many forms, having as its primary characteristic an unstable or a sustained increase in the intraocular pressure which the eye cannot withstand without damage to its structure or impairment of its function. The consequences of the increased pressure may be manifested in a variety of symptoms, depending upon type and severity, such as excavation of the optic disk, hardness of the eyeball, corneal anesthesia, reduced visual acuity, seeing of colored halos around lights, disturbed dark adaptation, visual field defects, and headaches.

absolute g. A final, hopeless stage of glaucoma in which vision is completely and permanently lost, intraocular pressure is increased, the optic disk is white and deeply excavated, and the pupil is usually widely dilated and immobile. Syn., *glaucoma consummatum.*

acute g. Acute congestive glaucoma.

air block g. A type of pupillary block glaucoma resulting from interruption or retardation of the flow of aqueous humor from the posterior to the anterior chamber by an air bubble, created by injection of air into the anterior chamber, following cataract extraction, goniopuncture, or cyclodialysis.

aphakic obstructive g. Glaucoma, following surgery for cataract, due to delayed re-formation of the anterior chamber.

apoplectic g. Hemorrhagic glaucoma.

auricular g. Glaucoma associated with increased intralabyrinthine pressure.

capsular g. Glaucoma due to clogging of the filtration angle with debris consisting of cellular flakes from exfoliation of the anterior lens capsule.

cerebri, g. A condition in which the diastolic pressure of the central retinal artery is increased while the intracranial pressure and that of the central retinal vein remain normal, causing prodromal glaucomatous symptoms, but without actual glaucoma.

closed angle g. Glaucoma in which the angle of the anterior chamber is blocked, such that aqueous humor cannot drain from the anterior chamber. It is usually associated with acute congestive glaucoma.

compensated g. Noncongestive glaucoma.

congenital g. Glaucoma caused by developmental anomalies in the region of the angle of the anterior chamber which present an obstruction to the drainage mechanism of the intraocular fluids. It usually results in a distended eyeball, an enlarged flattened cornea, a thinning of the sclera, a deep anterior chamber, and an excavation of the optic disk in the later stages. Syn., *buphthalmos; infantile glaucoma; hydrophthalmos.*

congestive g. Glaucoma characterized by obvious symptoms such as circumcorneal injection, corneal edema, or pain. It may occur either in a chronic or in an acute form and is a result of a relatively rapid increase in intraocular pressure. Syn., *incompensated glaucoma; inflammatory glaucoma; noncompensated glaucoma.*

congestive g., acute. Glaucoma characterized by a sudden violent elevation of the intraocular pressure which produces an excruciating eye pain radiating to the face, jaw, and head, accompanied by rapid loss of vision, intense ocular congestion, and constitutional disturbances. Usually, the cornea is hazy, the anterior chamber is shallow, the pupil is dilated and immobile, and pronounced circumcorneal injection is present. The majority of cases have prodromal attacks of less severity preceding the acute stage. Syn., *acute glaucoma; glaucoma evolutum.*

congestive g., chronic. Congestive glaucoma with symptoms similar to, but milder in intensity and slower in progress than, the acute form.

consummatum, g. Absolute glaucoma.

corticosteroid g. A type of open angle glaucoma attributed to the prolonged local or systemic use of corticosteroids.

developmental g. Glaucoma attributed to an abnormality of development of the angle of the anterior chamber.

dilatation g. Glaucoma induced in a predisposed eye by the instillation of a mydriatic.

Donders' g. Noncongestive glaucoma in an advanced stage.

evolutum, g. Acute congestive glaucoma.

fulminating g. Acute congestive glaucoma rapidly followed by blindness.

hemolytic g. Glaucoma attributed to obstruction of the outflow channels by erythrocytic debris and macrophages following intraocular hemorrhage.

hemorrhagic g. Glaucoma associated with retinal hemmorrhages. Syn., *apoplectic glaucoma.*

hypersecretion g. A type of open angle glaucoma attributed to an increased rate of aqueous humor secretion in the presence of a normal drainage mechanism.

incompensated g. Congestive glaucoma.

infantile g. Congenital glaucoma.

inflammatory g. Congestive glaucoma.

intermittent g. Glaucoma secondary to a low grade cyclitis which

has produced changes characteristic of glaucoma in the visual
field and in the fundus, but without manifesting a continued
raised intraocular pressure.

inverse g. Secondary glaucoma due
to a dislocation of the crystalline
lens into the anterior chamber,
or to the protrusion of the
rounded anterior surface of a microphakic or spherophakic lens
into the anterior chamber. A miotic substance raises the intraocular pressure and a mydriatic
substance lowers it.

iris blocked g. Glaucoma in which
the angle of the anterior chamber is closed by adhesions at the
root of the iris, blocking the outflow of aqueous humor.

juvenile g. Glaucoma occurring in
young persons, so named because
of the ordinary association of
glaucoma with advanced years.

low tension g. An ocular condition
or disease which does not manifest an increased intraocular pressure on prolonged observation,
but does manifest all other glaucomatous changes.

malignant g. A severe form of
glaucoma which rapidly leads to
blindness in spite of surgery or
other treatment.

mydriatic g. Glaucoma induced by
a mydriatic which, with dilation
of the pupil, increases the thickness of the iris tissue to form a
mechanical blockage of the angle
of the anterior chamber. It typically occurs in an eye which is
predisposed by having a shallow
anterior chamber with a narrow
angle.

narrow angle g. Glaucoma in
which the angle of the anterior
chamber is narrow.

neovascular g. Glaucoma attributed to neovascularization involving the angle of the anterior
chamber, as may occur in rubeosis
iridis.

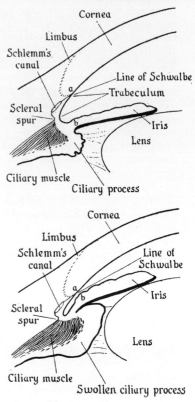

Fig. 23. (Top) Wide angle glaucoma showing
normal filtration angle; (bottom) narrow angle
glaucoma showing blockage of the filtration
angle. (From *Ophthalmology*, Arno E. Town,
Lea & Febiger, 1951)

noncompensated g. Congestive
glaucoma.

noncongestive g. A slowly, insidi-
ously developing glaucoma in
which subjective symptoms are
minimal, and in which clinical
signs of marked congestion are
absent. If the disease is long
standing, visual acuity is reduced,
visual field defects are present,
and the optic disk is excavated.
Syn., *compensated glaucoma;
noninflammatory glaucoma; quiet
glaucoma; simple glaucoma.*

noncongestive g., chronic.
Noncongestive glaucoma.

noninflammatory g. Noncongestive glaucoma.

open angle g. Glaucoma in which the angle of the anterior chamber is open and free of obstruction. It is usually associated with noncongestive glaucoma.

phacolytic g. Glaucoma secondary to hypermature cataract and due to permeation of liquefied cortical material through the lens capsule into the anterior chamber, with subsequent absorption by large mononuclear cells which swell, plug the trabecular spaces at the angle of the anterior chamber, and prevent the adequate escape of aqueous humor.

pigmentary g. Glaucoma associated with degeneration of the pigment epithelium of the iris and ciliary body, with marked deposition of pigment in the trabecular spaces at the filtration angle.

plethoric g. Glaucoma due to increased production of aqueous humor resulting from angiomatous changes in the ciliary body.

primary g. Glaucoma occurring without antecedent ocular disease in an otherwise apparently healthy eye.

pupillary block g. Glaucoma caused by interruption or retardation of the flow of aqueous humor from the posterior to the anterior chamber, due to the pupillary border being in contact with, or abnormally close to, the anterior capsule of the crystalline lens, or to the vitreous humor in aphakia. The resultant increased pressure in the posterior chamber causes the iris to bulge forward and block the filtration angle. It may occur as a primary glaucoma in narrow-angled eyes or be secondary to a swollen crystalline lens, posterior synechiae to the lens, lens dislocation, or posterior synechiae to the vitreous humor in aphakia.

quiet g. Noncongestive glaucoma.

secondary g. Glaucoma occurring as a result of a recognized preexisting ocular disease.

simple g. Noncongestive glaucoma.

sympathetic g. Glaucoma occurring in a formerly healthy eye following surgery on a glaucomatous eye.

trabecular g. Glaucoma due to blockage of the trabecular spaces at the angle of the anterior chamber, preventing adequate outflow of aqueous humor.

vitreous block g. A type of pupillary block glaucoma caused by adhesion of the iris to the hyaloid membrane of the vitreous humor in aphakia.

wide angle g. Glaucoma in which the angle of the anterior chamber is wide.

glaucomatous (glaw-ko'mah-tus). Pertaining to or resulting from glaucoma.

glaucosis (glaw-ko'sis). Blindness resulting from glaucoma.

glaze. 1. To insert lenses into spectacle frames or mountings. 2. To overlay with a thin surface consisting of, or resembling, glass. 3. To make glossy.

Glazebrook (glāz'brook) **polarizer; prism.** See under *prism.*

glia, retinal perivascular (gli'ah). Cells of unknown function which suround the retinal capillaries with a loose network formed by their processes.

glial mantle, peripheral (gli'al man'tl). See under *mantle.*

glioblastoma, retinal (gli"o-blas-to'-mah). Retinoblastoma.

glioma (gli-o'mah). A tumor derived from neuroglial cells or their antecedents.

endophytum, g. Retinoblastoma endophytum.

exophytum, g. Retinoblastoma exophytum.

retinal g. Generally, a congenital, malignant tumor arising from retinal neuroblasts, as a retinoblastoma or neuroepithelioma. Specifically, a tumor arising from neuroglial elements of the retina, i.e., an astrocytoma, or "true" glioma.

glioneuroma (gli″o-nu-ro′mah). A benign tumor composed essentially of mature glial and neuronal elements, occurring in the central nervous system or retina.

glitter. To gleam or shine with a brilliant and broken scintillating light.

globe (of eye). The eyeball.

globules, Morgagnian (glob′ūls). Drops of fluid which are formed in the spaces between lens fibers in early degenerative cataract. Syn., *Morgagnian spherules.*

glossiness. An attribute of the appearance of a surface dependent upon the type and the amount of reflection. Low glossiness is characteristic of rough diffusing surfaces and high glossiness of smooth surfaces that give a shiny or lustrous effect.

glossmeter (glos′me-ter). An instrument for determining the reflection factor of a surface or to determine the ratio of light regularly reflected from a surface to that diffusely reflected.

glossimeter (gloh-sim′eh-ter) Glossmeter.

glow. The perceived characteristic of a solid, self-luminous body in a relatively dark surround, as in the glow of an ember.

G.O.C. General Optical Council.

Godtfredsen's syndrome (gŏt′fred-senz). See under *syndrome.*

Goethe's theory (guh′tez). See under *theory.*

goggles. Spectacles, usually large, with auxiliary shields and padding, for protecting the eyes from wind, flying particles, intense light, and other external hazards. Some types may be worn over conventional corrective eye wear, and many types have a headband rather than temples.

diplopia g. Goggle-type spectacles with lenses of different color, usually red and green, to produce dissociation of a fixated spot or light source.

Frenzel g. Frenzel spectacles.

goiter, exophthalmic (goi′ter). A systemic disease characterized by increased basal metabolism, exophthalmos, a tendency to increased appetite, loss of weight, vomiting, diarrhea, profuse sweating, tremors, increased pulse rate, and psychic disturbances. Signs asociated with exophthalmic goiter are those of von Graefe, Dalrymple, Stellwag, Moebius, and Gifford, q.v. Syn., *Basedow's disease; Flajani's disease; Graves's disease; March's disease; Parry's disease; Stokes's disease; thyrotoxicosis.*

Goldenhar syndrome (gōld′en-har). See under *syndrome.*

Goldmann lens; tonometer. See under the nouns.

Goldmann-Weekers adaptometer. See under *adaptometer.*

goniolens, Troncoso (go′ne-o-lenz″). A hemispherical contact lens which fits beneath the eyelids, used in conjunction with a biomicroscope to view the filtration angle of the anterior chamber. Syn., *Troncoso contact lens.*

goniometer (go″ne-om′eh-ter). An instrument for measuring angles, such as those of crystals and prisms.

goniomyostomy (go″ne-o-mi-os′to-me). A cyclodialysis reinforced by interposing superior rectus muscle fibers, surgically inserted at a scleral incision anterior to the muscle attachment to the globe and pulled out through a second incision at the limbus.

goniophotography (go″ne-o-fo-tog′-rah-fe). Photography of the angle of the anterior chamber of the eye.

goniophotometer (go″ne-o-fo-tom′-eh-ter). Distribution photometer.

gonioplasty (go′ne-o-plas″te). A surgical procedure for glaucoma in which a plastic tube is implanted under the sclera to carry aqueous humor from the anterior chamber to subchoroidal and sub-Tenon's spaces.

gonioprism, Allen's (go′ne-o-prizm″). Allen's contact prism.

gonioprism, Allen-Thorpe (go′ne-o-prizm″). A prism in which the apex has been curved to fit against the cornea in gonioscopy. It is mounted on a handle held by the examiner, and all of its four sides are mirrored to afford an almost complete view of the filtration angle without its rotation.

goniopunciotomy (go″ne-o-punk″e-ot′o-me). A surgical procedure for congenital glaucoma in which goniopuncture is combined with goniotomy.

goniopuncture (gon″ne-o-pungk′-tūr). A surgical procedure for congenital glaucoma in which a puncture is made into the meshwork at the filtration angle, extending into the subconjunctival space, by means of a needle-knife inserted through the opposite limbus and carried across the anterior chamber, parallel to the iris. It is usually performed under the direct observation afforded by a gonioscope.

gonioscope (go′ne-o-skōp″). Any of several instruments, usually consisting of a biomicroscope used in conjunction with a prismatic contact lens, for viewing the filtration angle of the anterior chamber.

gonioscopy (go″ne-os′ko-pe). Observation of the filtration angle of the anterior chamber with the gonioscope.

direct image g. Observation of the virtual, upright image of the filtration angle of the anterior chamber as formed by a gonioscopic lens and viewed with an ophthalmoscope or biomicroscope.

indirect image g. Observation of the real, inverted, anteriorly located aerial image of the filtration angle of the anterior chamber as formed by a specially modified gonioscopic lens and viewed with an indirect opthalmoscope.

goniosynechiae (go″ne-o-sih-nek′e-e). Adhesions of iritic tissue to corneal or scleral tissue at the angle of the anterior chamber, usually associated with closed angle glaucoma.

goniotomy (go″ne-ot′o-me). A surgical procedure for congenital glaucoma in which a sweeping incision is made in the meshwork at the filtration angle by means of a knife-needle inserted through the opposite limbus and carried across the anterior chamber parallel to the iris. It is usually performed under direct observation afforded by a special contact lens. Syn., *goniotrabeculotomy*.

goniotrabeculotomy (go″ne-o-trah-bek″u-lot′o-me). Goniotomy.

goniotripsy (go″ne-o-trip′se). A surgical procedure for congenital glaucoma, used when lack of corneal transparency interferes with direct observation of the angle of the anterior chamber. A specially designed straight-handled knife, with a flat blade rounded at its tip, is inserted through a corneal incision near the limbus into the angle of the anterior chamber adjacent to the incision, rotated about the axis of the handle, and then moved laterally so as to scrape the angle rather than incise it.

Goppert's sign (gop′ertz). See under *sign*.

Göthlin's theory (guht′linz). See under *theory*.

Gougerot-Sjögren syndrome (gu-zher-o′-sye′gren). Sjögren's syndrome.

Gould's (gūldz) **chart; sign.** See under the nouns.

Gower's symptom (gow'erz). See under *symptom*.

Gower-Paton-Kennedy syndrome (gow'er-pat'en-ken'eh-de). Kennedy's syndrome.

gradation, Green's (gra-da'shun). A method for scaling the sizes of visual acuity test letters. Green proposed a series of 24 values bearing a constant ratio of 0.7937.

Gradenigo's syndrome (grah-den-e'-gōz). See under *syndrome*.

grades of fusion. See under *fusion*.

gradient. 1. The amount of change in phoria associated with a change of 1.0 D. of lens power at a given target distance; hence, a measure of the A.C.A. ratio. The routine clinical test is usually made at 40 cm. with the addition of 1.0 D. of convex lens power. 2. A measurable, uniform change in rate or magnitude.

contrast g. The rate of change of illumination in the transition zone of a contrast border, a sharp border having a high gradient and a blurred border having a low gradient.

filter, g. See under *filter*.

intensity g. A uniform variation of light intensity or luminance over a surface.

test, g. See under *test*.

Gradle tonometer (gra'dl). See under *tonometer*.

von Graefe's (fon gra'fēz) **disease; ophthalmoplegia; phenomenon; reaction; reflex; sign; spot; test; theory.** See under the nouns.

graft, corneal. Donor corneal tissue used in keratoplasty to replace removed opaque or diseased corneal tissue.

corneal g., mushroom. A mushroom-shaped corneal graft used in combined lamellar and penetrating keratoplasty, in which the superficial layers extend over most of the cornea, and the pedicle which includes the poste-

rior layers is fitted into the central perforation.

Granit's theory (grah-nētz'). See under *theory*.

Granit-Harper law (grah-nēt'-hahr'-per). See under *law*.

granule (gra'nūl). A small grain or particle.

cone g. The nucleus within the cell body of a cone cell, located in the outer nuclear layer of the retina and staining differently than a rod granule.

rod g. A round, densely staining portion of the rod cell, composed of a nucleus surrounded by an attenuated layer of protoplasm, located in the outer nuclear layer of the retina, and attached on either side to a rod fiber.

granuloma (gran"u-lo'mah). A nodule or neoplasm consisting essentially of granulation tissue, occurring as a result of localized inflammation.

iris, g. of the. A localized proliferation, within the iris, of inflammatory tissue containing lymphocytes. It is stimulated by the presence of a chronic irritative or infective agent such as an inorganic foreign body, tuberculosis, syphilis, actinomycosis, leprosy, or an attenuated form of pyogenic organism.

subconjunctival g. A firm, reddish, nonedematous, fleshy protrusion of the conjunctiva, forming a flat or rounded nodular mass ⅛ to ½ in. in extent, which may interfere with the closure of the eyelids.

graph. A visual form for the presentation of statistical or numerical data.

area g. A graph in which the distribution is described by the area under the curve.

arithmetic g. A graph in which both of the variables are presented in values in arithmetic progression.

bar g. A graph in which the frequency or the number of cases in each class interval is represented by the height of a bar. Syn., *histogram.*

histogram g. Bar graph.

logarithmic g. A graph in which both of the variables are presented in logarithmic progression.

semilogarithmic g. A graph in which one of the variables is presented in logarithmic form, the relative value of this variable being compared to the arithmetic value of the other. This type of graph is of considerable use in data on visual thresholds.

Grassmann's laws (gras'manz). See under *law.*

Gratama's tubes (grah-tah'maz). See under *tube.*

graticule (grat'ih-kūl). A very small, transparent scale, gratelike pattern, or system of lines in the front focal plane of the eyepiece of an optical instrument, for direct observation of the apparent image size or position in the field of view. In binocular instruments, the two graticules may be designed to produce a stereo or distance scale for measuring object distance, as in range finding. Syn., *cross-hairs; reticle; reticule.*

Linksz g. A target used in conjunction with the Projectoscope for the detection and measurement of eccentric fixation, consisting of an open center, four-pointed, star-shaped pattern surrounded by two concentric circles subtending angles of three and five degrees. The star pattern is fixated, and the location of the shadows of it and of the surrounding circles on the fundus, in reference to the foveal center, indicates the character of the fixation.

grating (grāt'ing). A latticework of parallel bars or crossbars.

diffraction g. A system of close, equidistant and parallel grooves, slits, lines, or bars, such as lines ruled on a polished surface, used for producing spectra by diffraction.

diffraction g., amplitude. A diffraction grating which modulates the amplitude across the emergent wavefront leaving the phase essentially unchanged; usually one composed of alternate clear and opaque strips.

diffraction g., concave. A reflecting diffraction grating, ruled on a concave, spherical, metallic surface, which diffracts and focuses light simultaneously without auxiliary lenses.

diffraction g., echelette. A diffraction grating in which the grooves are cut with one side very steep and the other inclined at a small angle to the surface of the grating, so that most of the reflected light will go to the spectrum lying in the direction in which the light is reflected from the less inclined sides of the grooves, or most of the transmitted light will go to the spectrum lying in the direction in which the light is refracted by the prismatic effect of the grooves.

diffraction g., echelle. A type of diffraction grating having a facet width, usually of several hundred microns, between that of the few microns of a narrow-grooved diffraction grating and the thousands of microns of an echelon diffraction grating.

diffraction g., echelon. A diffraction grating of high resolving power, devised by Michelson, consisting of rectangular plane-parallel plates of constant thickness stacked together with a constant offset of the edges, resembling a flight of stairs, each step forming a line of the grating.

diffraction g., Fraunhofer's. A diffraction grating consisting of regularly spaced, silver wires

wound around two parallel
screws.

diffraction g., phase. A diffraction grating which modulates
the phase across the emergent
wavefront, leaving the amplitude
essentially unchanged; usually
one composed of grooves. Most
diffraction gratings are of this
type.

diffraction g., piezoquartz. A
quartz plate between two condenser plates which, when in an
alternating electrical field, varies
the index of refraction of the
quartz differentially so that light
transmitted parallel to the plates
is retarded differentially and
emerges to produce phase difference diffraction spectra.

diffraction g., plane. A diffraction grating that is ruled on
a plane-parallel transmitting medium or on a plane-reflecting
surface.

diffraction g., reflection. A
diffraction grating which diffracts
light by reflection from a ruled,
polished surface.

diffraction g., replica. A diffraction grating produced by
making a cast of celluloid, col-
lodion, etc., of a grating ruled on
glass or metal. This cast is
mounted on or between glass for
protection.

diffraction g., Rowland's.
The original concave diffraction
grating.

diffraction g., transmission.
A grating which diffracts light by
transmission through a system of
slits.

sinusoidal g. A grating target or
pattern, usually black and white,
in which the variations in luminous intensity across the grating
lines conform to a sine wave function.

visual acuity g. 1. A diffraction
grating producing bands of variable separation for measuring vis-

ual acuity. 2. A system of parallel
lines or bars which can be presented to the eyes with variable
separation or at different distances, in continuous motion perpendicular to the lines of sight,
to induce optokinetic nystagmus.
The moving pattern induces nystagmus as long as the lines are
visually resolved.

visual acuity g., Ives's. An
apparatus consisting essentially of
two transilluminated line gratings, which are rotated opposi-
tively about a common axis corresponding to the line of sight of
the viewing eye, to produce,
when viewed from a distance in
excess of that permitting resolution of the component gratings, a
pattern of wide parallel lines of
covarying width and separation;
used for measuring visual acuity.

Gratiolet's (grah"te-o-lāz') **fibers;
optic radiations.** See under the
nouns.

Graux ocular palsy (grawz). Féréol-
Graux ocular palsy.

Graux-Féréol (graw-fa-ra-ōl) **ophthalmoplegia; paralysis.** Féréol-
Graux ocular palsy.

Graves's disease (grāv-ez). See under
disease.

gray. Any one of the series of colors
said to be achromatic or without
hue, ranging from white to black.

cool g. 1. A truly achromatic, neutral gray. 2. A neutral gray with a
slight trace of green or blue.

cortical g. A median gray whose
name is derived from the theory
that gray is a primary color process due to activity in the cerebral
cortex in the absence of retinal
stimulation.

Hering g's. A set of fifty neutral
gray papers ranging in lightness
from extreme white to extreme
black, in steps of equal, just noticeable difference units.

idioretinal g. The gray perceived
by the dark-adapted eye in the
total absence of light.

[316]

median **g.** A gray of lightness perceived as midway between the extremes of black and white.

retinal **g.** The gray perceived in the absence of visual stimulation, attributed to the normal, continuous, and spontaneous neuronal activity.

Gray oral reading test. See under *test.*

graybody. A thermal source of radiant energy or temperature radiation whose radiant flux at all wavelengths is less than that of a blackbody at the same temperature by a constant ratio. No known thermal source emits radiant flux in this manner throughout the ultraviolet, visible, and infrared regions. However, in the visible region, a carbon filament does so at a very nearly constant ratio and may be considered a practical approximation of a graybody. Syn., *incomplete radiator; nonselective radiator.*

grayout. Loss of peripheral vision due to positive gravitational acceleration, attributed to restriction of blood supply to the eye. It occurs at 4.1 ± 0.7 g. to unprotected subjects seated upright. Cf. *blackout.*

Greeff's vesicles (grēfs). See under *vesicle.*

green. 1. The hue attribute of visual sensations typically evoked by stimulation of the normal human eye with radiation of wavelengths approximately 515 mμ. 2. Any hue predominantly similar to that of a typical green. 3. One of the psychologically unique colors. 4. The complement of red-purple (magenta).

visual **g.** A green-colored pigment found in the retinal rod cells of frogs and some reptiles, having properties similar to those of visual purple in humans.

Green's chart. See under *chart.*

Greenough microscope (grēn'o). See under *microscope.*

green-weakness. Deuteranomaly.

Greig's hypertelorism (grēgz). See under *hypertelorism.*

grid. A network or pattern of perpendicularly intersecting lines.

Amsler **g's.** Amsler charts.

Haussmann multiple **g.** A pair of transilluminated, differentially rotatable, multiple stenopaic slits mounted one in front of the other so as to produce a grid pattern of variable dimensions according to the angle between the slits. It is used for testing subnormal visual acuity.

Hermann **g.** A grid of perpendicularly crossed white stripes in a black field, providing the qualitative appearance of darkened areas at the intersections, a contrast effect.

Javal's **g.** A form of bar reader consisting of five equally spaced parallel bars coupled together by two perpendicular bars and having a handle and two supporting legs.

Griffith's sign (grif'iths). See under *sign.*

grinding, multiple. A lens-grinding procedure in which more than one lens is surfaced in the same operation.

Groenouw's corneal dystrophy (gru'nōz). See under *dystrophy, corneal.*

Grönblad-Strandberg syndrome (grēn'blat-strand'berg). See under *syndrome.*

groove. A shallow furrow, channel, or linear depression. See also *fissure; sulcus.*

Blessig's **g.** The indentation of the embryonic and fetal eye, between the adult-forming retina and the blind part of the retina, which helps form the inner part of the ciliary body and iris; hence, the groove which becomes the ora serrata.

infraorbital **g.** A groove beneath the periorbita in the floor of the orbit, commencing at the inferior orbital fissure and extending anteriorly toward the infraorbital margin. It becomes roofed over to form the infraorbital canal, which dips beneath the margin to emerge anteriorly as the infraorbital foramen, and contains the infraorbital vein and artery. Syn., *infraorbital sulcus.*

lacrimal g. 1. The groove in the medial wall of the superior maxilla which forms a part of the nasolacrimal canal. 2. The fossa for the lacrimal sac.

Maddox g. A lens, named after E. E. Maddox, used in measuring heterophoria and heterotropia, and consisting of a long, narrow, concave, cylindrical groove which, when held in front of the eye, distorts a relatively distant light source into a long streak perpendicular to the axis of the groove.

optic g. A horizontal sulcus on the sphenoid bone, anterior to the pituitary fossa or sella turcica, leading from the regions of the paired optic canals. In about 5% of skulls, the optic chiasm rests in this groove, but in most it is posterior to it.

Stieda's g's. A series of shallow grooves separated by Stieda's plateaus and located in the palpebral conjunctiva, between the tarsus and the fornix.

supraorbital g. One of a few linear depressions on the frontal bone in the eyebrow region that leads into the supraorbital notch or foramen and to the notch or foramen of Arnold, if present. It contains a branch of a supraorbital nerve or a blood vessel.

zygomatic g. A groove on the lateral wall of the orbit which extends from the inferior orbital fissure to the zygomatic foramen and houses the zygomatic nerve and vessels.

Grotthus' law (grot′hus). Draper's law.

ground. 1. The relatively unstructured part of a figure-ground field. See also *background.* 2. The fundus, or the interior of the eye, as seen through the ophthalmoscope.

Grow chart (gro). See under *chart.*

Grünert's spur (grēn′ertz). See under *spur.*

guard. The part of a spectacle frame or mounting designed to support the spectacles by resting against either side of the nose; a nose pad.

arm, g. See under *arm.*

offset g. A guard mounted behind the spectacle lens plane to position the spectacle frame or mounting farther away from the eye than usual.

Gubler's paralysis (goob′lerz). Millard-Gubler syndrome.

von Gudden's (fon gūd′enz) **commissure; posterior accessory optic tract; transverse peduncular tract.** See under the nouns.

Guibor (gwe′bōr) **chart; test.** See under the nouns.

Guild of Prescription Opticians of America. An association of independent dispensing opticians organized to serve the general vocational, educational, and representational objectives of the membership.

Guillery chart (ge′yur-e). See under *chart.*

Guist's preretinal edema (gīstz). Central angiospastic retinopathy.

Guist's sign (gīstz). See under *sign.*

Gullstrand's (gul′strandz) **reduced eye; schematic eye; law.** See under the nouns.

Gunn's (gunz) **dots; phenomenon; sign; syndrome.** See under the nouns.

gyrospasm (ji′ro-spazm). Spasmus nutans.

gyrus (ji′rus). A convoluted ridge between the sulci, or grooves, on

the surface of the cerebral hemisphere.

angular g. A sharply bent, cortical
convolution about the posterior
end of the superior temporal
sulcus in the parietal lobe, included in visual associational
Brodmann's area 19 and visual
language areas.

lingual g. The medial portion of
the occipital lobe, below the calcarine fissure, containing the
lower portions of the area striata
and the visual associational areas.

H

H. 1. Abbreviation for *hypermetropia.* 2. Symbol for *irradiance.*

Haab's (hahbz) **degeneration; corneal dystrophy; band opacity; pupillometer; pupillary reflex; sign; striae.** See under the nouns.

de Haan's law (duh hahnz). See under *law.*

Haenel's sign (ha'nelz). See under *sign.*

Hague lamp (hāg). See under *lamp.*

Haidinger's (hi'ding-erz) **bands; brushes; fringes.** See under the nouns.

Haig's law. See under *law.*

hairs, von Frey. Hairs of various caliber and length used by von Frey to determine corneal sensitivity.

Haitz charts (hītz). See under *chart.*

halation (ha-la'shun). A spreading of light beyond its proper boundaries, such as may be reflected from the inner layers of the retina beyond the image border proper, and hence considered to be a cause of irradiation.

Hale telescope. See under *telescope.*

half-shade. A polarizing device, inserted in front of the polarizer of a polarimeter, which causes the transmitted light to vibrate in slightly different directions in the two halves of the sharply divided field of view. It is used to increase the accuracy of settings.

Hall's test (hawlz). See under *test.*

Hallauer glass (hal'ow-er). See under *glass.*

Halldén's (hawl-dānz') **method; test.** See under the nouns.

Haller's (hal'erz) **circle; layer; ratio; tunic.** See under the nouns.

Hallermann-Streiff syndrome (hal'-er-man-strīf). Mandibulo-oculofacial dyscephaly.

hallucination, visual (hah-lu''sih-na'-shun). Visual perception in the absence of a correlated physical stimulus. Cf. *illusion.*

cinematographic visual h. A formed visual hallucination consisting of a series of complex and integrated scenes.

formed visual h. A visual hallucination consisting of a formed figure or scene.

negative visual h. A form of functional blindness during which there is an inability to perceive objects in the visual field.

positive visual h. A visual hallucination in which the subject "sees" an object where none exists, as distinguished from negative visual hallucination.

unformed visual h. A visual hallucination without definite shape or form, as one merely of light or color.

halo. An annular flare of light surrounding a luminous body or image, occurring in optical imagery in varicolored patterns or as a brightness gradient, as a result of aberrations, internal reflections, diffraction, or scattering.

glaucomatous h. 1. Entoptically visible colored rings around lights, due to diffraction of droplets of fluid in the corneal epithelium in the presence of corneal edema, in glaucoma. 2. A white, halo-like ring of exposed sclera around the optic disk, due to the degeneration and migration of the retinal pigment epithelium, in glaucoma.

lenticular h. Entoptically visible colored rings around a bright light source caused by the action of the radial fibers of the crystalline lens as a diffraction grating.

macular h. A glittering ring of reflected light sometimes seen around the macula during ophthalmoscopy.

halometer (ha-lom'eh-ter). An instrument for measuring ocular halos.

halometry (ha-lom'eh-tre). The measurement of halos.

Hamaker's satellite (ha'māk-erz). Second positive afterimage.

Hamilton slide (ham'il-tun). See under *slide.*

hamulus (ham'u-lus). 1. The inferior portion of the posterior lacrimal crest of the lacrimal bone which articulates with the maxillary bone at the superior end of the nasolacrimal canal. 2. Any hooked-shaped bony process, as on the pterygoid process of the sphenoid bone.

Hand's (handz) **disease; syndrome.** See under the nouns.

hand-eye co-ordination. See under *co-ordination.*

Hand-Eye Co-ordinator, Leavell. A Brewster type stereoscope with a clip-board attachment to hold targets for tracing.

Hannover's canal (han'o-verz). See under *canal.*

haplopia (hap-lo'pe-ah). Single binocular vision, as opposed to binocular diplopia.

homolocal h. Normal single binocular vision in which the right and left ocular images of the same object are projected to the same spatial position. Cf. *heterotopic diplopia* and *homotopic diplopia.*

haploscope (hap'lo-skōp). An instrument for presenting separate fields of view to the two eyes so that they may be seen as one continuous, superimposed, integrated, or fused field, and hence useful for measuring or stimulating various binocular functions. Many specially designed experimental and clinical models provide for elaborate controls of the accommodation, convergence, and fusion stimuli, the color, brightness, and size of target and field, and stereo-producing disparity.

Hering h. A mirror haploscope designed by Hering and having the feature that the two fields of view are rotatable about separate vertical axes corresponding to the centers of rotation of the subject's eyes.

mirror h. A haploscope using mirrors to separate or displace the fields of view of the two eyes.

haploscopic (hap-lo-skop'ik). Pertaining to or of a haploscope.

haptic. The portion of a scleral contact lens which rests on the scleral conjunctiva; scleral flange.

Harada's (hah-rahd'az) **disease; syndrome.** See under the nouns.

Harder's gland (hahr'derz). See under *gland.*

Hardy-Rand-Rittler charts; plates; test. See under the nouns.

hare's eye (hārz i). Lagophthalmus.

Harlan's test (hahr'lanz). See under *test.*

Harman's test (hahr'manz). See under *test.*

Harms's method. See under *method.*

Harrington tonometer (har'ing-tun). See under *tonometer.*

Harrington-Flocks (har'ing-tun-floks) **visual field screener; test.** See under the nouns.

Harris' test; theory. See under the nouns.

Harting-Dove prism (hahrt'ing-duv). See under *prism.*

Hartline's stereoscope (hahrt'linz). See under *stereoscope.*

Hartmann (hahrt'mahn) **screen; test.** See under the nouns.

Hartridge's theory (hahrt'rijz). See under *theory.*

Hasner's (hahs'nerz) **fold; theory; valve.** See under the nouns.

Hassall-Henle (has'al-hen'le) **bodies; warts.** See under the nouns.

Haussmann multiple grid (haus'-mahn). See under grid.

Hawkins trifocal lens (haw'kinz). See under *lens, trifocal.*

haze. 1. The spatial attribute of smokiness or dustiness which interferes, or seems to interfere, with clear vision. 2. A meteorological classification of atmospheric visibility conditions between thin fog and clear. 3. As applied to nearly perfect transparencies, especially plastics, the ratio of diffuse to total transmittance of a beam of light.

head. 1. The anterior or upper extremity of the animal body containing the brains, eyes, ears, nose, and mouth. 2. The front or foremost part of an object. 3. A part or attachment of an instrument or apparatus that performs a chief function.

optic nerve h. Optic disk.

photometer h. The portion of a photometer which presents to the eye the two surfaces between which a comparison of brightness is to be made. Syn., *photoped.*

rotation, h. A deviation in position of the head about a vertical axis of reference and away from a straightforward position, especially as a clinical symptom. Cf. *head tilt; shoulder tipping.* Syn., *face turn; head turn.*

schlieren h. The lens and/or mirror system in the schlieren system which focuses the light beam "through" the schlieren field and for which the first and second knife edges are approximately conjugate foci.

tilt, h. 1. A deviation of the head from its upright position, especially as a clinical symptom. 2. A forward or a backward tilt of the head, as distinguished from *shoulder tipping.* Syn., *face tilt.*

turn, h. Head rotation.

hearing, color. A type of synesthesia in which certain sounds induce characteristic color sensations. Syn., *pseudochromesthesia.*

Hebra's disease (he'brahs). Erythema exudativum multiforme.

Hecht's theory (hekts). See under *theory.*

Hecht-Shlaer adaptometer. See under *adaptometer.*

hedger's cataract. See under *cataract.*

Heerfordt's (här'forts) **disease; syndrome.** See under the nouns.

height, apparent. The angular subtense of an object at a given distance, especially at a distance from which viewed or photographed.

Heine (hīn'e) **contact lens; retraction.** See under the nouns.

helcoma (hel-ko'mah). A corneal ulcer.

heliophobe (he'le-o-fōb). One who is neurotically afraid of being exposed to sunlight.

heliophobia (he''le-o-fo'be-ah). The neurotic fear of exposure to sunlight.

Helmholtz' (helm'hōltz) **chessboard; color circle; indicator; law; color table; telestereoscope; test; theories; color triangle.** See under the nouns.

Helson-Judd effect (hel'sun-jud). See under *effect.*

hemachromatosis corneae (he''mah-kro-mah-to'sis kōr'ne-e, hem''ah-). Bloodstaining of the cornea.

hemangioblastosis retinae (he-man''je-o-blas-to'sis ret'in-e). Von Hippel's disease.

hemangioma (he-man''je-o'mah). A tumor derived from blood vessels, usually as the result of aberrant development, but occasionally post-traumatic, ordinarily benign, and histologically consisting of endothelial-lined spaces containing red blood corpuscles, fibrinous coagula, or hyaline detritus. The stroma is cellular or fibrous and is richly vascular. There may be incorporation of other cellular elements, dependent upon the site of the tumor.

hemangiomatosis, von Hippel's (he-man''je-o-mah-to'sis). Von Hippel's disease.

hematoma, ocular (he''mah-to'mah). A tumorlike swelling due to sizable hemorrhage into the tissues of the eye.

hemeralope (hem'er-ah-lōp). One affected with hemeralopia.

hemeralopia (hem''er-ah-lo'pe-ah). A term used inconsistently to mean either *night blindness* or *day blindness;* synonymous or antonymous with *nyctalopia.*

hemiablepsia (hem''e-ah-blep'se-ah). Hemianopsia.

hemiachromatopsia (hem''e-ak-ro-mah-top'se-ah). Color blindness in one half of the visual field of one eye or of both eyes.

hemiakinesia, pupillary (hem''e-ah-kih-ne'se-ah). Constriction of the pupil in response to light stimulation of one half of the retina, and no pupillary response to light stimulation of the other half of the retina. Syn., *hemianopic pupillary paralysis.*

hemiamaurosis (hem''e-am''aw-ro'-sis). Hemianopsia.

hemiamblyopia (hem''e-am''ble-o'-pe-ah). Reduced vision in one half of the visual field of one or both eyes.

hemianopia (hem''e-an-o'pe-ah). Hemianopsia.

hemianopic (hem''e-an-op'ik). Pertaining to, or affected with, hemianopsia.

hemianopic pupillary paralysis. Pupillary hemiakinesia.

hemianopic pupillary reflex. See under *reflex.*

hemianopsia (hem''e-an-op'se-ah). Blindness in one half of the visual field of one or both eyes. Syn., *hemiablepsia; hemiamauro-*

sis; hemianopia; hemiopia; hemiscotosis.

absolute h. Hemianopsia in which the affected field is totally blind to all visual stimuli.

altitudinal h. Hemianopsia in either the upper or the lower half of the visual field of one or both eyes. Syn., *horizontal hemianopsia.*

  altitudinal h., crossed. Bilateral hemianopsia involving the upper half of the visual field of one eye and the lower half of the visual field of the other.

  altitudinal h., symmetrical. Bilateral hemianopsia involving either both upper halves or both lower halves of the visual fields.

bilateral h. Hemianopsia involving the visual fields of both eyes. Syn., *binocular hemianopsia.*

binasal h. Bilateral hemianopsia involving the nasal halves of the visual fields of both eyes.

  binasal h., crossed quadrant. Crossed binasal quadrantanopsia.

binocular h. Bilateral hemianopsia.

bitemporal h. Bilateral hemianopsia involving the temporal halves of the visual fields of both eyes.

  bitemporal h., crossed quadrant. Crossed bitemporal quadrantanopsia.

bitemporalis fugax, h. Transient bitemporal hemianopsia sometimes associated with syphilis.

complete h. Hemianopsia involving a full half of the visual field.

congruous h. Homonymous hemianopsia in which the defects in the two visual fields are identical in size, shape, and position, so as to form a single defect of the binocular field.

crossed h. Altitudinal hemianopsia involving the upper half of the visual field of one eye and the lower half of the visual field of the other eye.

heteronymous h. Hemianopsia involving either both nasal halves or both temporal halves of the visual fields.

homonymous h. Hemianopsia involving the nasal half of the visual field of one eye and the temporal half of the visual field of the other eye.

    homonymous h., left. Hemianopsia involving the temporal half of the visual field of the left eye and the nasal half of the visual field of the right eye.

    homonymous h., right. Hemianopsia involving the nasal half of the visual field of the left eye and the temporal half of the visual field of the right eye.

horizontal h. Altitudinal hemianopsia.

incomplete h. Hemianopsia not involving a full half of the visual field.

incongruous h. Hemianopsia in which the defects in the two visual fields differ in size, shape, or position.

lateral h. Vertical hemianopsia.

nonscotomatous h. Hemianopsia in which there is no central scotoma in the early field changes.

quadrantic h. Quadrantanopsia.

relative h. 1. Hemianopsia involving a loss of vision for form or color but not for light. 2. Hemianopsia present only when stimuli are presented simultaneously to both halves of the visual field, as may occur following injury or disease to one visual sensory cortical area. See also *Oppenheim's test.*

scotomatous h. Hemianopsia in which a central scotoma is one of the early field changes.

transient h. Hemianopsia of temporary duration, due to angiospasm, hemorrhage, edema, etc.

unilateral h. Hemianopsia affecting the visual field of only one eye.

vertical h. Hemianopsia involving the lateral (nasal or temporal) half of the visual field of one or

both eyes. Syn., *lateral hemianopsia.*

hemianoptic (hem″e-an-op′tik). Pertaining to or affected with hemianopsia.

hemichromatopsia (hem″e-kro″mah-top′se-ah). Hemiachromatopsia.

hemicrania (hem-e-kra′ne-ah). An ache or a pain in one side of the head, as in migraine.

hemikinesimeter (hem″e-kin″e-sim′-eh-ter). An instrument for detecting a hemianopic pupillary reflex consisting essentially of a chin and forehead rest and two light sources to emit pencils of light of equal intensity into the eye from two different angles.

hemimacropsia (hem″e-mah-krop′-se-ah). Macropsia in one half of the visual field.

hemimicropsia (hem″e-mi-krop′se-ah). Micropsia in one half of the visual field.

hemiopalgia (hem″e-op-al′je-ah). An ache or a pain in one side of the head and in one eye.

hemiopia (hem-e-o′pe-ah). Hemianopsia.

hemiopic (hem-e-op′ik). Pertaining to or affected with hemianopsia.

hemiplegia alternans facialis (hem″e-ple′je-ah awl′ter-nans fa″she-al′is). Millard-Gubler syndrome.

hemiscotosis (hem″e-sko-to′sis). Hemianopsia.

hemophthalmia (he-mof-thal′me-ah). A hemorrhage within the eye.

hemophthalmos (he-mof-thal′mos). Hemophthalmia.

hemorrhage (hem′or-ij). An extravasation of blood from the vessels.

flame-shaped h. A radially striated hemorrhage in the inner layers of the retina, especially in the nerve fiber layer.

petechial h. A minute, punctate extravasation of blood.

preretinal h. A large extravasation of blood from the retinal vessels between the vitreous and the retina, characteristically shaped like a *D* with the straight edge or fluid level uppermost. Syn., *subhyaloid hemorrhage*.

subhyaloid h. Preretinal hemorrhage.

hemosiderosis bulbi (he″mo-sid-eh-ro′sis bul′bi). Deposits of iron-staining compounds, derived from the hemoglobin of the blood, in the ocular tissues following hemorrhage.

Henderson's theory (hen′der-sonz). See under *theory*.

Henkes electroretinography lens (henk′ēz). See under *lens*.

Henle's (hen′lēz) **bodies; cytoblasts; fibers; glands; layer; membrane; notch; stratum nerveum; warts.** See under the nouns.

Hennebert's syndrome (en-barz′). See under *syndrome*.

Henschen's theory (hen′shenz). See under *theory*.

Hensen-Völckers experiment (hen′-sen-vel′kerz). See under *experiment*.

heptachromia (hep-tah-kro′me-ah). Normal color vision; perception of the total spectral scale of seven colors.

heptachromic (hep-tah-kro′mik). Having heptachromia, hence having normal color vision.

herapathite (her′ah-path″īt). A synthetic, dichroic, crystalline material which transmits one linearly polarized beam and absorbs the other; discovered by and named after W. B. Herapath, and served as the basis for the original Polaroid material.

Herbert's (her′berts) **pits; rosettes.** See under the nouns.

Hering's (her′ingz) **afterimage; color circle; color valence curves; valence diagram; experiment; figure; grays; haploscope; illusion; law; tests; theories; window.** See under the nouns.

Hering-Hillebrand (her′ing-hil′eh-brand) **deviation; horopter; phenomenon.** See under the nouns.

Hermann's grid (her′mahnz). See under *grid*.

hernia, iris (her′ne-ah). Protrusion of the iris through a corneal incision or wound, following surgery or trauma. Syn., *prolapse of the iris*.

herpes (her′pēz). An inflammatory disease of the skin or mucous membrane characterized by the formation of clusters of small vesicles.

corneae, h. Herpetic keratitis.

facialis, h. Herpes simplex of the face.

febrilis, h. See *herpes simplex*.

iridis, h. Herpetic iritis.

ophthalmicus, h. Herpes zoster ophthalmicus.

simplex, h. A superficial, epithelial, virus infection characterized by the presence of groups of small vesicles. It typically occurs on the borders of the lips, nostrils, or genitals and may occur on the eyelids, conjunctiva, cornea, or iris. See also *herpetic iritis; herpetic keratitis.*

zoster ophthalmicus, epidemic h. A virus infection of the Gasserian ganglion and its nerve branches, characterized by discrete areas of vesiculation of the epithelium of the forehead, the nose, the eyelids, and the cornea, together with subepithelial infiltration. It is limited to one half of the face, with a sharp demarcation in the midline of the forehead and nose.

zoster ophthalmicus, symptomatic h. A disease of the Gasserian ganglion and its nerve branches secondary to some infective, traumatic, or neoplastic disturbance, whose manifestations are identical to epidemic herpes zoster ophthalmicus.

Herschel prism (hur'shel). See under *prism.*

Hertel's chart; plates; test. See under the nouns.

de Hertogh's sign (dĕ-her'togz). See under *sign.*

Hertwig-Magendie sign (hert'vig-mah-zhan'de). Magendie-Hertwig sign.

hesperanopia (hes"per-an-o'pe-ah). Night blindness.

Hess's (hes'ez) **afterimage; screen; theory.** See under the nouns.

Hesse's (hes'ēz) **organs; test.** See under the nouns.

heterocentric (het"er-o-sen'trik). Pertaining to light rays that do not meet at a common focal point; the opposite of *homocentric.*

heteroception (het"er-o-sep'shun). Proprioception said to be related to the heterophoria overcome during binocular fixation. *Chavasse; Lyle.*

heterochromatic (het"er-o-kro-mat'-ik). Pertaining to or having more than one color or hue.

heterochromatosis (het"er-o-kro-mah-to'sis). Heterochromia.

heterochromia (het"er-o-kro'me-ah). A difference in the coloration of the parts of a structure or between two structures which are normally of the same coloration, as the iris or the irides. Syn., *heterochromatosis.*

  complicated h. A slow, chronic atrophy and depigmentation of the iris without associated inflammation or pain. The affected iris becomes thin, transparent, lighter in color than the other, and the usual iris markings are absent. It is frequently accompanied by cataract, corneal precipitates, vitreous opacities, and glaucoma. Syn., *heterochromic cyclitis of Fuchs.*

  Fuchs, h. of. Complicated heterochromia.

  iridis, h. A diversity of color in different parts of the same iris. Syn., *chromheteropia.*

  iridum, h. A difference in the color of the two irides.

  neurogenic h. Changes in the color of the iris due to a lesion, paralytic or irritative, of the sympathetic nervous system.

  partial h. A coloration in one sector of the iris different from that in the remaining portions.

  simple h. Heterochromia characterized by difference in color between the two irides, or by zones of different color in one iris, and not attributed to pathology.

  sympathetic h. Heterochromia due to dysfunction of the sympathetic nerves which affect development of the iris and its pigment.

heterochromous (het"er-o-kro'mus). Pertaining to or affected with heterochromia.

heterokeratoplasty (het"er-o-ker'-ah-to-plas-te). The transplantation of corneal tissue from an animal to a human eye, or from one type of animal to another.

heterometropia (het"er-o-meh-tro'-pe-ah). A condition in which the refractive errors of the two eyes differ. Syn., *anisometropia.*

heteronymous (het"er-on'ih-mus). 1. Pertaining to or designating crossed images of an object seen double, e.g., heteronymous diplopia. 2. Pertaining to or designating asymmetric halves of the visual fields, e.g., both temporal fields or both nasal fields.

heterophoralgia (het"er-o-fo-ral'je-ah). Asthenopia caused by heterophoria.

heterophoria (het"er-o-fo're-ah). The tendency of the lines of sight to deviate from the relative positions necessary to maintain single binocular vision for a given distance of fixation, this tendency being identified by the occurrence of an actual deviation in the absence of an adequate stimulus to fusion, and occurring in variously designated forms according to the relative direction or orientation of the deviation, as *excyclophoria, incyclophoria, esophoria, exophoria, hyperphoria, hypophoria.*

absolute h. Heterophoria present after one eye has been occluded for a period of time sufficient to eliminate factors associated with the use of binocular vision.

accommodational h. Kinetic heterophoria.

basic h. Heterophoria with accommodation relaxed and the fixation target at infinity.

essential h. Heterophoria characterized by its structural, static, and permanent nature and not of accommodative origin. Cf. *symptomatic heterophoria.*

kinetic h. Heterophoria attributed to the reflex effect of accommodation on convergence, e.g., esophoria due to uncorrected hypermetropia. Cf. *neurogenic heterophoria; static heterophoria.* Syn., *accommodational heterophoria.*

neurogenic h. Heterophoria resulting from a faulty central nervous system innervational pattern to, or a mild paretic or spastic condition of, one or more of the extraocular muscles. Cf. *kinetic heterophoria; static heterophoria.*

relative h. 1. Relative exophoria or relative esophoria. 2. Heterophoria expressed in relation to given test conditions and given points of reference for purposes of quantitative specification.

static h. Heterophoria attributed to the anatomical structure of the eyes, orbits, extraocular muscles, and other adnexa. Cf. *kinetic heterophoria; neurogenic heterophoria.*

symptomatic h. Heterophoria characterized by its functional, dynamic, and variable nature. Cf. *essential heterophoria.*

heterophoric (het″er-o-fo′rik). Pertaining to or affected with heterophoria.

heterophorometer, Bielschowsky's (het″er-o-fo-rom′eh-ter). A phorometer consisting of a fixation grid of vertical red lines with a green arrow above, all seen by one eye, while the other eye sees only the arrow, displaced and black, through a red filter and a dissociating prism.

heterophthalmia (het″er-of-thal me-ah). A difference in the appearance of the two eyes, as in heterochromia iridum.

heterophthalmos (het″er-of-thal′-mos). Heterophthalmia.

heterophthalmus (het″er-of-thal′-mus). Heterophthalmia.

heteropsia (het-er-op′se-ah). Unequal vision in the two eyes.

heteroptics (het-er-op′tiks). Visual hallucinations, illusions, perversions, or distortions.

heterorefraction (het″er-o-re-frak′-shun). The refraction of one's eyes by another person; the opposite of *autorefraction.*

heteroscope (het′er-o-skōp). An amblyoscope.

heterostereoscopy (het″er-o-ster″e-os′ko-pe). The viewing of a stereopsis-inducing pattern so as to perceive essentially the original scene, but not in true dimensional proportions. A type of distortion that may be induced, for example, by viewing a stereogram in a stereoscope different in focal length from that of the camera, by viewing a vectograph directly through Polaroid filters, or by making the lateral separation of the stereocamera lenses effectively different from that of the viewer's interpupillary distance. Cf. *orthostereoscopy.*

heterotopia, macular (het″er-o-to′-pe-ah). Displacement of the macula from its normal location, relative to the optic disk, which may be congenital and accompanied by other anomalies, or the result of a pathological process such as the traction of scar formation in retrolental fibroplasia. It is evidenced by an abnormal angle lambda, which may give the appearance of strabismus when none is present.

heterotransplant, corneal (het″er-o-trans′plant). Transplantation of corneal tissue from one species to another. See also *allotransplant; autotransplant; homotransplant.*

heterotrichosis superciliorum (het″-er-o-trik-o′sis su″per-sil′e-ōr-um). Heterochromic eyebrows.

heterotrichous (het-er-ot′rih-kus). Having eyelashes that are irregular in shape, size, or distribution.

heterotropia (het″er-o-tro′pe-ah). Strabismus.

Heubner's artery (hoyb′nerz). See under *artery.*

hexachromic (hek-sah-kro′mik). Pertaining to an individual who can perceive only six of the seven spectral colors, being unable to differentiate between violet and indigo.

Heyman's law (ha′manz). See under *law.*

high neutral. See under *neutral.*

von Hippel's disease (fon hip′elz). See under *disease.*

von Hippel-Lindau disease (fon hip′el-lin′dow). See under *disease.*

hippus (hip′us). Abnormal, rhythmic, irregular contraction and dilatation of the pupils. The oscillations occur within seconds, are of considerable excursion, reaching 2 mm. or more, are bilateral, and are independent of illumination, convergence, or psychosensory stimuli.

respiratory h. Contraction of the pupil during expiration, and dilation during inspiration.

Hirschberg's (hersh′bergz) **method; test.** See under the nouns.

His's marginal layer (his′ez). Marginal layer of the optic cup.

histamine (his′tah-min). An amine containing carbon, hydrogen, and nitrogen, which stimulates gastric secretion, dilates and increases the permeability of capillaries, and acts as a miotic on the eye.

histogram (his′to-gram). Bar graph.

Hitzig's center (hit′zigz). Frontal eye field.

Hl. Abbreviation for *latent hypermetropia.*

Hm. Abbreviation for *manifest hypermetropia.*

Hoefer effect (hōf′er). See under *effect.*

van der Hoeve's (van der hōvz) **scotoma; syndrome; theory.** See under the nouns.

van der Hoeve-Halbertsma-Waardenburg syndrome (van der he′-ve-hal′berts-mah-ward′en-burg). Waardenburg's syndrome.

Höfler's (hef′lerz) **figure; visual illusion.** See under the nouns.

Hofstetter's formulas (hof′stet-erz). See under *formula.*

hole in the macula. A condition in which the entire thickness of the retina, in the macular area, is lost as a result of trauma or degeneration, appearing ophthalmoscopically as a round, dark, red spot at the fovea. The edges are usually clearcut, and the hole has a depth of approximately 1.5 D.

Holm's theory (hōmz). See under *theory.*

Holmes's stereoscope (hōmz′ez). See under *stereoscope.*

Holmes-Adie syndrome (hōmz-a′de). Adie's syndrome.

Holmgren test (hōlm′gren). See under *test.*

holocaine (hol′o-kān, ho′lo-). A proprietary brand of phenacaine, a synthetic alkaloid. The hydrochloride of paradiethoxyethenyl-diphenylamidin, it occurs in the form of small, colorless, shiny crystals, or as a white powder, and is used as a local anesthetic in ophthalmic practice.

hologram (ho′lo-gram). A transparent photograph of interference patterns on light-sensitive film produced by an object when it is illuminated by, and reflects light to the film from, one beam of a coherent source, usually a laser, and the film receives light from another beam originating from the same source. Subsequent transillumination of the photograph by a coherent beam reconstructs an image of the original object in full dimension, seen as though the film were a window.

holography (ho-log′rah-fe). The technique or process of producing a hologram.

holophotometer (hol″o-fo-tom′ehter). A photometer, equipped with mirrors, for the measuring and comparing of intensities of light emitted at various angles from a light source.

holotrichous (hol-ot′rih-kus). Normal positioning and spacing of the eyelashes.

Holt's method (hōltz). See under *method.*

Holtzer tape (hōlt′zer). See under *tape.*

homatropine (ho-mat′ro-pin). Oxytoluyl-tropeine, a mydriatic alkaloid obtained by the condensation of tropine and mandelic acid, used in solution as a cycloplegic. It is milder in effect than atropine.

homocentric (ho-mo-sen′trik). Pertaining to light rays that meet at a common focal point; the opposite of *heterocentric.*

homofocal (ho-mo-fo′kal). Pertaining to light rays having a common focus.

homogeneous (ho″mo-je′ne-us). 1. Consisting of elements of like nature; of the same kind; of a uniform quality throughout. 2. Pertaining to radiant energy consist-

ing of only one wavelength, or radiant energy from so small a region of the spectrum as to include no perceptible differences of hue.

homokeratoplasty (ho-mo-ker′ah-to-plas″te). Keratoplasty in which the transplanted tissue is obtained from another individual. Cf. *autokeratoplasty.*

homonymous (ho-mon′ih-mus). 1. Pertaining to or designating uncrossed images of an object seen double, e.g., homonymous diplopia. 2. Pertaining to or designating symmetric halves of the visual fields, e.g., the nasal half of one field associated with the temporal half of the other.

homotransplant, corneal (ho″motrans′plant). Transplantation of corneal tissue obtained from the cornea of another human. See also *allotransplant; autotransplant; heterotransplant.*

Honi phenomenon (ho′ne). See under *phenomenon.*

hook-over. Clip-on.

hordeolum (hor-de′o-lum). A purulent infection of a sebaceous gland along the eyelid margin (external) or of a Meibomian gland on the conjunctival side of the eyelid (internal). It has the characteristic appearance of a markedly hyperemic, elevated area which increases in size and swelling and comes to a head with yellowish pus which breaks through and discharges.

external h. A purulent infection of a sebaceous gland along the eyelid margin. Syn., *sty.*

internal h. An acute purulent infection of a Meibomian gland on the conjunctival side of the eyelid. Syn., *Meibomian sty.*

horizon, retinal. The meridian of the retina which lies in a plane containing the x and the y axes and the horizontal meridian of the eye. It is the retinal meridian which coincides with the plane of fixation when the head is held erect and the two eyes look out in directions parallel to the median plane toward the far-off horizon.

von Hornbostel cube (fon hōrn′bostel). See under *cube*.

Horner's (hōr′nerz) **law; muscle; ptosis; syndrome**. See under the nouns.

Horner-Trantas points (hōr′nertran′tas). See under *point*.

Hornstein contact lens (hōrn′stīn). See under *lens, contact*.

horopter (ho-rop′ter). 1. The locus of object points in space simultaneously stimulating corresponding retinal points under given conditions of binocular fixation. 2. Any of several schematic representations of loci of object points in binocular space perception fulfilling specific criteria of singleness, position, alignment, direction, or distance, under given conditions of binocular fixation and presumed to represent manifestations of retinal correspondence.

circle, h. Vieth-Mueller horopter.

concave h. A horopter concave toward the observer.

convex h. A horopter convex toward the observer.

depth h. 1. The locus of points in the horizontal plane of regard which appear to be located at a distance from the observer equal to that of the fixation point, thus the empirical longitudinal horopter determined by the criterion of equidistance. See *equidistant horopter*. 2. An empirical longitudinal horopter, of doubted reliability, determined according to the criterion of maximal differential stereoscopic sensitivity, i.e., greatest awareness of small displacements of points toward or away from the observer. 3. An empirical horopter represented as having thickness corresponding to Panum's areas expressed in anteroposterior ranges of displacement of the test object.

empirical h. A horopter determined experimentally as opposed to a geometrical horopter or a theoretical horopter.

equal convergence, h. of. Vieth-Mueller horopter.

equidistant h. An empirical longitudinal horopter based on the criterion that all points appear at the same distance from the observer as the fixation point. Except in the extreme periphery, it differs little from the apparent frontoparallel plane horopter.

frontal plane h. Apparent frontoparallel plane horopter.

frontoparallel plane h., apparent. An empirical longitudinal horopter based on the criterion that all points appear to lie in the frontoparallel plane containing the fixation point. Syn., *frontal plane horopter; frontoparallel plane horopter.*

fusion h. The locus of longitudinal horopter points at which test objects do not induce fusional movements, i.e., points of zero retinal disparity, a theoretical criterion not yet demonstrated experimentally.

general h. The location of all object points in three-dimensional space simultaneously stimulating corresponding retinal points under given conditions of binocular fixation, especially the complex theoretical horopter form derived by Helmholtz from assumptions of the location of corresponding retinal points.

geometrical h. A horopter based on theoretical or geometrical concepts as opposed to an empirical horopter. See also *Vieth-Mueller horopter.*

haplopic h. An empirical horopter represented as having thickness corresponding to Panum's areas, expressed by the anteroposterior limits through which a nonfixated test object may be displaced and still be seen as single.

Hering-Hillebrand *h.* Hering-Hillebrand deviation.

longitudinal *h.* The horopter for corresponding horizontal meridians of the two eyes, or the horopter represented as contained in the plane of regard of the two eyes, the possible presence of small degrees of cyclophoria in the latter representation being disregarded during experimental determination by the use of vertically oriented linear test objects or bars which eliminate vertical disparity effects.

Mueller's *h.* Vieth-Mueller horopter.

nonius *h.* An empirical longitudinal horopter utilizing the criterion of identical primary subjective visual direction for the two eyes. In practice, a central vertical rod or line is bifixated while other, peripherally located, vertical rods or lines, whose upper halves are visible to one eye only while the lower halves are visible to the other eye only, are individually moved until the two halves appear aligned. Syn., *similo-directional horopter; vernier horopter.*

similo-directional *h.* Nonius horopter.

theoretical *h.* A horopter based on theoretical concepts as opposed to an empirical horopter.

vernier *h.* Nonius horopter.

Vieth-Mueller *h.* The circle defined by the fixation point and the anterior nodal points of the two eyes, hence having the property that any two points lying on the circle will subtend equal angles at the two nodal points. Syn., *Vieth-Mueller circle; horopter of equal convergence; Mueller's horopter.*

horopter-curve (ho-rop'ter-kurv). In the mathematical derivation by Helmholtz of a theoretical ho-

ropter, the complete spatial locus of all points whose projection will be simultaneously imaged on corresponding retinal points in the two eyes during a given condition of fixation. In the most general case, the horopter-curve is a curve of the third degree (one which pierces a plane in three points) formed by the intersection of two surfaces of the second degree (an hyperboloid and the surface of a cone or a cylinder), which passes through the point of fixation and the centers of the two eyes. In special cases of fixation (e.g., fixation in the median plane, or in the horizontal visual plane), the horopter-curve becomes a straight line joined to a conic section (circle or ellipse); or, in the case of fixation at infinity in the midline of the horizontal plane, it becomes a plane surface coinciding approximately with the floor plane upon which the observer stands. Thus, in general, the horopter-curve contains the entirety of the theoretical horopter (which may be defined as the visible portion of the horopter-curve, i.e., that portion which lies outside of the observer's head and body) plus the small portion which passes through and between the two eyes.

horror fusionalis (hor'ror fu-se-o-nal'is). Horror fusionis.

horror fusionis (hor'ror fu-se-ōn'is). The inability to obtain binocular fusion or superimposition of haploscopically presented targets, or the condition or phenomenon itself, occurring frequently as a characteristic in strabismus, in which case the targets approaching superimposition may seem to slide or jump past each other without apparent superimposition, fusion, or suppression. Syn., *fusion aversion.*

Houstoun's (hu'stonz) **tests; theory.** See under the nouns.

Hovius' (ho've-us) **circle; plexus.** Circle of Hovius.

Howard's stereomicrometer (how'-ardz). See under *stereomicrometer.*

Howard-Dolman test (how'ard-dōl'-man). See under *test.*

Hruby lens (hru'be). See under *lens.*

Ht. Abbreviation for *total hypermetropia.*

Hubbard-Kropf theory. See under *theory.*

Hudson's brown line (hud'sonz). Superficial senile line.

Hudson-Stähli line (hud'son-sta'le). Superficial senile line.

hue. The attribute of color sensation ordinarily correlated with wavelength or combinations of wavelengths of the visual stimulus and distinguished from the attributes *brightness* and *saturation.*

   extraspectral h. A hue sensation that cannot be matched by monochromatic light, but which can be matched by an additive mixture of wavelengths, e.g., the mixture of extreme ends of the visible spectrum to produce purple.

   invariable h. 1. A hue that remains constant for all luminances. There are considered to be four, one each in the red, yellow, green, and blue regions of the spectrum. 2. A hue that remains constant wherever it is seen in the visual field, i.e., regardless of the area of the retina stimulated.

   Munsell's h. Any one of the hue classifications in the system of Munsell color notations.

   Ostwald h. Any one of the 24 hue classifications in the Ostwald system.

   primary h's. 1. Any three hues, normally a red, a green, and a blue, so selected from the spectral scale as to enable one with normal color vision to match any other hue by their additive mixture in varying proportions; often called physical primary hues or colors, or the physical color primaries. 2. Four hues, red, green, blue, and yellow, which seem qualitatively individualistic or fundamental rather than mixed or composite; often called the psychological primary hues or colors, or the psychological color primaries. Syn., *unitary hues.*

   unitary h's. Primary hues.

Hueck's ligament (heks). Uveal meshwork.

Hughes test. Three-disk test.

humor (hu'mor, u'mor). Any normal fluid or semifluid of the body.

   aqueous h. The clear, watery fluid which fills the anterior and the posterior chambers of the eye. It has a refractive index lower than the crystalline lens, which it surrounds, and is involved in the metabolism of the cornea and the crystalline lens. Syn., *aqueous fluid.*

     aqueous h., plasmoid. The fluid that is rapidly formed after the normal aqueous humor is drained, or the modified aqueous that is formed following trauma or inflammation of the anterior segment of the eye. It contains a greater amount of protein than normal aqueous, approaching blood plasma in composition, and forms a diffuse cloud or aggregates into clumps. Syn., *secondary aqueous humor.*

     aqueous h., secondary. Plasmoid aqueous humor.

   crystalline h. Crystalline lens of the eye. *Obs.*

   Morgagni's h. Morgagnian fluid.

   ocular h. Either the aqueous or the vitreous humor of the eye, or both.

   vitreous h. 1. The gelatinous, colorless, transparent substance filling the vitreous chamber of the eye, i.e., the space between the crystalline lens, the ciliary body, and the retina. It is considered to be derived from the surrounding ectoderm, especially the retina, and has a chemical composition similar to that of the aqueous humor, with the exception of two proteins, peculiar to the vitreous, the mucoid and the vitrein. Syn., *vitreous body.* 2. The vitreous body minus the vitrein and the mucoid, thus a sol instead of a gel.

vitreous h., plasmoid. A modified vitreous humor formed following trauma or inflammation of the ciliary body, choroid, and/or retina. It contains a greater amount of protein than normal vitreous and forms a diffuse cloud or aggregates into clumps.

Humphriss's method (hum'fris-ez). See under *method.*

Hunt separator (hunt). See under *separator.*

Hunt-Giles test (hunt-jīls). See under *test.*

Hurler's (hoor'lerz) **disease; syndrome.** See under *disease.*

Hurvich-Jameson theory (hur'vik-ja'meh-son). See under *theory.*

Huschke's valve (hoosh'kēz). See under *valve.*

Husted tonometer (hu'sted). See under *tonometer.*

Hutchinson's (huch'in-sunz) **chart; disease; patch; pupil; sign; triad.** See under the nouns.

Hutchison's syndrome (huch'ih-sunz). See under *syndrome.*

Huygens' (hi'genz) **eyepiece; principle; theory.** See under the nouns.

hyaline (hi'ah-lin). Vitreous humor. *Obs.*

hyalitis (hi-ah-li'tis). Inflammatory involvement of the vitreous humor or the hyaloid membrane. Since the vitreous body is a clear homogeneous gel, is physiologically inert, and has no demonstrable metabolism, the term "hyalitis" for pathological reactions of the vitreous is currently avoided. The term has been employed to cover secondary disturbances of the vitreous as a result of diseases of adjacent structures which produce infiltration into the vitreous.

asteroid h. Asteroid hyalosis.

punctate h. A degeneration of the vitreous humor characterized by the formation of small opacities.

suppurative h. A purulent inflammation in the vitreous humor due to exudation of cells from surrounding pathologically involved structures, as occurs in panophthalmitis.

hyalocytes (hi-al'o-sīts). Cells in the vitreous body of mammals and birds, adjacent to the ciliary body and retina, which are considered to be connective tissue cells of the macrophage type.

hyalogen (hi-al'o-jen). An albuminous substance occurring in the vitreous humor and in other parts of the body.

hyaloid (hi'ah-loid) **artery; body; canal; cataract; cyst; fossa; membrane.** See under the nouns.

hyaloiditis (hi″ah-loid-i'tis). Hyalitis.

hyalomucoid (hi″ah-lo-mu'koid). A mucoid substance present in the vitreous humor.

hyalonyxis (hi″ah-lo-nik'sis). Surgical puncture of the vitreous body.

hyalosis (hi″ah-lo'sis). Degeneration of the vitreous humor.

asteroid h. The presence of numerous, small, discrete, spherical or oval-shaped bodies in the vitreous humor, occurring essentially as a senile phenomenon, more common in males than in females, and more frequently unilateral than bilateral. The asteroid bodies usually show no orderly arrangement, and, when viewed ophthalmoscopically, appear white and shiny. The vitreous humor retains its solidity, and vision is but little affected. Syn., *Benson's disease.*

hydatoid (hi'dah-toid). 1. Aqueous humor. 2. Hyaloid membrane. 3. Pertaining or relating to the aqueous humor.

hydranencephaly (hi"dran-en-sef'ah-le). A developmental anomaly of the cerebral hemispheres which are reduced, in whole or in part, to membranous sacs composed of meninges fused with glial cortical remnants and filled with cerebrospinal fluid. The head is of normal size or slightly enlarged, and the cranium, being filled with fluid, readily transilluminates. Frequent ocular signs include cortical blindness with retention of the pupillary light reflex, strabismus, and ocular motility disturbances.

hydrargyrophthalmia (hi-drar"ji-rof-thal'me-ah). Inflammation of the eye or the conjunctiva from mercury or a mercuric compound.

hydroblepharon (hi-dro-blef'ah-ron). Edema of the eyelid.

hydrodiascope (hi-dro-di'ah-skōp). A device consisting of a fluid-filled chamber, tightly taped over the eye, with an anterior glass window before which correcting lenses are placed. Its purpose is to neutralize the anterior refracting surface of the cornea and eliminate the aberrations of keratoconus, irregular astigmatism, etc.

hydrophthalmia (hi-drof-thal'me-ah). Hydrophthalmos.

hydrophthalmos (hi-drof-thal'mos). A condition in which congenital, structural abnormalities in the region of the angle of the anterior chamber offer an obstruction to the drainage mechanism of the intraocular fluids, so that the pressure of the eye is raised and a condition of congenital glaucoma results. The plasticity of the coats of the eye causes them to stretch under the increased pressure, and the whole eye en-

larges. The most striking changes are in the cornea, which is enlarged and becomes globular in shape, and thinned, especially at the periphery. The iris may appear atrophic and may be tremulous, owing to the lack of support from the crystalline lens, which is smaller than normal and usually displaced backward. There is generally a marked cupping of the optic disk, and vision is subnormal. Syn., *buphthalmos.*

hydrophthalmoscope (hi-drof-thal'mo-skōp). An instrument, used in ophthalmoscopy, which neutralizes the refractive power of the anterior surface of the cornea by means of a layer of water. It consists essentially of an eyecup with a flat glass bottom that serves as a viewing window.

hydrophthalmus (hi-drof-thal'mus). Hydrophthalmos.

hydrops, corneal (hi'drops). An accumulation of watery fluid, presumably aqueous humor, in the stroma of the cornea as a result of rupture of the posterior surface of the cornea involving the endothelium and Descemet's membrane.

hygroblepharon (hi-gro-blef'ar-on). An abnormally moist condition of an eyelid.

hyoscine (hi'o-sin). An alkaloid which, in its hydrobromide form, paralyzes the peripheral endings of the parasympathetic nerves, acting as a mydriatic, like atropine, but less powerfully. Syn., *scopolamine.*

hyperchromatopsia (hi"per-kro"-mah-top'se-ah). A defect of vision in which colorless objects appear colored.

hypercyclophoria (hi"per-si"klo-fo'-re-ah). Combined hyperphoria and cyclophoria.

hyperdacryosis (hi"per-dak"re-o'-sis). Abnormally profuse lacrimation.

hyperemia, retinal (hi″per-e′me-ah). Congestion of the retinal blood vessels, with some tortuosity, and increased redness and edema of the fundus, in whole or in part.

active retinal h. Congestion of the retinal arteries characterized by their fullness and tortuosity and by a pinkish color of the optic disk, due to capillary engorgement. It may occur from a systemic cause that raises the blood pressure, or from local inflammation.

passive retinal h. Congestion of the retinal veins due to some obstruction in the venous outflow.

hyperesophoria (hi″per-es″o-fo′re-ah, -ēs″o-fo′re-ah). Combined hyperphoria and esophoria.

hyperesthesia, optic (hi″per-es-the′ze-ah). Abnormal sensitivity of the eye to light.

hypereuryopia (hi″per-u-re-o′pe-ah). Abnormally large palpebral fissures.

hyperexophoria (hi″per-ek″so-fo′re-ah). Combined hyperphoria and exophoria.

hyperkeratosis (hi″per-ker-ah-to′sis). Hypertrophy of the cornea.

hyperkinesia (hi″per-kih-ne′ze-ah). Hyperkinesis.

hyperkinesis (hi″per-kih-ne′sis). Excessive muscular movement, as may be associated with spasm.

hyperlipemia, essential familial (hi″per-li-pe′me-ah). A familial disease, usually occurring in children, characterized by a milky blood serum (due to a rise in neutral fats), hepatosplenomegaly, and cutaneous xanthomatosis. Retinal lipemia and lipid keratopathy may also be present. Syn., *Bürger-Grütz disease; idiopathic hyperlipemia; essential hyperlipemic xanthomatosis.*

hyperlipemia, idiopathic. Essential familial hyperlipemia.

hypermetrope (hi″per-met′rōp). One who has hypermetropia.

hypermetropia (hi″per-me-tro′pe-ah). The refractive condition of the eye represented by the location of the conjugate focus of the retina behind the eye when accommodation is said to be relaxed, or the extent of that condition represented in the number of diopters of convex lens power required to compensate to the optical equivalent of emmetropia. The condition may also be represented as one in which parallel rays of light entering the eye, with accommodation relaxed, focus behind the retina. Syn., *farsightedness; hyperopia.*

absolute h. The portion of hypermetropia which cannot be compensated for by accommodation, hence present in those having a total hypermetropia greater than the amplitude of accommodation. Cf. *facultative hypermetropia.*

acquired h. Postnatal increase in hypermetropia, usually exclusive of the increase normally occurring in early infancy, and, more particularly, increases related to senility, surgery, and pathology.

atypical h. Hypermetropia resulting from congenital abnormalities, degenerative changes, trauma, or disease. Syn., *complicated hypermetropia.*

axial h. Hypermetropia attributed to shortness or decreases in the axial length of the eye.

benign h. Simple hypermetropia.

complicated h. Atypical hypermetropia.

congenital h. Hypermetropia existing since or at the time of birth.

curvature h. Hypermetropia attributed to excessive increases in the radius of curvature of one or more of the refractive surfaces of the eye, and especially of the radius of the corneal surface.

deformational h. Hypermetropia of high degree, attributable to extreme pathological or developmental anomalies, as in microphthalmos or an extremely flat cornea.

facultative h. The portion of hypermetropia which can be compensated for by accommodation. Cf. *absolute hypermetropia.*

high h. Hypermetropia of high degree, usually of 5.00 D. or more.

index h. Hypermetropia attributed to variations in the index of refraction of one or more of the ocular media.

latent h. The portion of the total hypermetropia compensated for by the tonicity of the ciliary muscle. It may be wholly or partially revealed by the use of a cycloplegic.

lenticular h. Hypermetropia attributed to a below average refractive power of the crystalline lens.

low h. Hypermetropia of a low degree, usually of 2.00 D. or less.

manifest h. The portion of the total hypermetropia which may be demonstrated or measured by the relaxation of accommodation occurring with the simple reduction in stimulus to accommodation, as in the increase of convex lenses in a routine refractive examination.

medium h. Hypermetropia of a medium degree, usually between 2.00 and 5.00 D.

pathological h. Hypermetropia resulting from pathological deformation of the eye; a type of atypical hypermetropia.

position h. Hypermetropia attributed to an excessive, or increase in, distance of the crystalline lens from the cornea.

refractive h. 1. Hypermetropia attributed to the condition of the refractive elements of the eye, including axial length, in distinction from deformational or pathological hypermetropia. 2. Hypermetropia attributed to the condition of the refracting elements of

the eye in distinction from axial hypermetropia.

relative h. Facultative hypermetropia which permits clear vision but induces overconvergence or convergent strabismus for the point of fixation.

simple h. 1. Hypermetropia uncomplicated by any associated condition, disease, trauma, or abnormality. Syn., *benign hypermetropia; typical hypermetropia.* 2. Hypermetropia occurring without an associated astigmatism.

total h. The sum of the manifest and the latent hypermetropia.

typical h. Simple hypermetropia.

hypermetropic (hi″per-me-trōp′ik, -trah′pik). Pertaining to or having hypermetropia. Syn., *hyperopic.*

hyperope (hi′per-ōp). Hypermetrope.

hyperopia (hi″per-o′pe-ah). Hypermetropia.

hyperopic (hi″per-op′ik). Hypermetropic.

hyperphoria (hi″per-fo′re-ah). The upward deviation, or the amount of upward deviation, of the line of sight of one eye with reference to that of the other eye, as manifested in the absence of an adequate fusion stimulus or when fusion is made impossible. The condition of hyperphoria may be designated as one of hypophoria when the opposite eye is used as a reference.

alternating h. Double hyperphoria.

alterocular h. Double hyperphoria.

anatomic h. The manifestation of hyperphoria or that portion of the total hyperphoria attributable to structural (anatomical) anomalies or variation.

concomitant h. Hyperphoria which does not vary in amount with direction of gaze. Syn., *static hyperphoria.*

dissociated h. Double hyperphoria.

double h. The condition in which, under dissociation, the line of sight of the right eye deviates upward when the left eye is fixating and the line of sight of the left eye deviates upward when the right eye is fixating. Syn., *alternating hyperphoria; alterocular hyperphoria; dissociated vertical divergence; alternating supraduction.*

innervational h. The manifestation of hyperphoria, or that part of the total hyperphoria, not attributable to structural (anatomical) anomalies or variation.

intrinsic h. Hyperphoria attributable to primary structural, myological, or neurological anomalies, distinguished from pseudohyperphoria attributable to spurious manifestations of neurological origin or to temporarily induced effects of lenses or prisms.

left h. Hyperphoria in which the line of sight of the left eye deviates upward with respect to that of the right eye.

nonconcomitant h. Hyperphoria varying in amount with changes in direction of gaze.

paretic h. Hyperphoria attributable to paresis of one or more of the extraocular muscles.

physiological h. Double hyperphoria which is considered to occur as a result of the nonfixating eye reverting toward the so-called position of rest assumed when both eyes are closed.

right h. Hyperphoria in which the line of sight of the right eye deviates upward with respect to that of the left eye.

spastic h. Hyperphoria attributable to overaction of one or both inferior oblique muscles, manifested pronouncedly with lateral fixation movements and presumed to be due to congenital check ligament deficiencies.

static h. Concomitant hyperphoria.

hyperphoric (hi″per-fōr′ik). Pertaining to or affected with hyperphoria.

hyperplasia (hi″per-pla′ze-ah). An abnormal increase in the number of normal cells in normal arrangement in a tissue. It is usually the response to continued irritation and may occur in pathology of the epithelium of the conjunctiva and the cornea.

hyperpresbyopia (hi″per-pres-be-o′-pe-ah). 1. Absolute presbyopia. 2. Hypermetropia. *Obs.*

hyperrhinoplaty, interocular (hi″-per-ri′no-plat-e). Ocular hypertelorism.

hyperstasis (hi″per-sta′sis). A term used by Lancaster to designate the static position of the covered eye during a cover test when its line of sight deviates upward.

hyperstereoscopy (hi″per-ster-e-os′-ko-pe). Exaggeration of apparent depth relationships by increasing the lateral separation of the stereocamera lens system.

hypertelorism, Greig's (hi″per-tel′-ōr-izm). Ocular hypertelorism.

hypertelorism, ocular (hi″per-tel′-ōr-izm). A congenital malformation of the skull characterized by an enlarged sphenoid bone, extremely wide bridge of the nose with great width between the eyes, exophthalmos, divergent strabismus, and optic atrophy. Syn., *Greig's hypertelorism.*

hypertension, arterial (hi″per-ten′-shun). See *retinopathy, hypertensive.*

hypertonia bulbi (hi″per-to′ne-ah bul′bi). The condition of consistently elevated intraocular pressure without associated destruction of the intraocular structures or the optic nerve.

hypertrichophrydia (hi″per-trik-of-rid′e-ah). Excessively long eyebrows

hypertrichosis (hi″per-trih-ko′sis). The condition in which the length and/or the number of the eye-lashes is increased.

hypertrophy (hi-per'tro-fe). An increase in the size of individual cells or fibers, without an increase in the number, resulting in enlargement of a tissue or an organ.

hypertropia (hi″per-tro'pe-ah). Strabismus characterized by the upward deviation of the line of sight of the nonfixating eye with reference to that of the fixating eye, hence similar to hyperphoria, except that the condition is continuous and unrelated to the presence or the absence of fusion stimuli.

alternating h. Double hypertropia.

double h. Strabismus characterized by the upward deviation of the line of sight of either eye while the other fixates. Syn., *alternating hypertropia.*

hyphema (hi-fe'mah). A sanguineous exudate in the anterior chamber of the eye: bloody hypopyon.

hyphemia (hi-fe'me-ah). Hemorrhage into the anterior chamber of the eye.

hypoblepharon (hi″po-blef'ah-ron). 1. A swelling beneath the eyelid. 2. An artificial eye.

hypocyclosis (hi″po-si-klo'sis). Deficient accommodation.

ciliary h. Deficient accommodation due to weakness of the ciliary muscle.

lenticular h. Deficient accommodation due to extreme rigidity of the crystalline lens.

hypoesophoria (hi″po-es″o-fo're-ah, -ēs″o-fo're-ah). Combined hypophoria and esophoria.

hypoexophoria (hi″po-ek″so-fo're-ah). Combined hypophoria and exophoria.

hypokinesia (hi″po-kih-ne'ze-ah). Hypokinesis.

hypokinesis (hi″po-kih-ne'sis). Decreased muscular movement, as of an extraocular muscle.

hypometropia (hi″po-me-tro'pe-ah). Myopia.

hypophasis (hi″po-fa'sis). Incomplete closure of the eyelids, leaving the sclera visible.

hypophoria (hi″po-fo're-ah). The downward deviation, or the amount of downward deviation, of the line of sight of one eye with reference to that of the other eye, as manifested in the absence of an adequate fusion stimulus or when fusion is made impossible. The condition of hypophoria may be designated as one of hyperphoria when the opposite eye is used as a reference.

alternating h. Double hypophoria.

double h. The condition in which, under dissociation, the line of sight of the right eye deviates downward when the left eye is fixating, and the line of sight of the left eye deviates downward when the right eye is fixating. Syn., *alternating hypophoria.*

hypoplasia (hi″po-pla'ze-ah). Defective or incomplete development of a tissue.

hypopyon (hi-po'pe-on). An accumulation of pus in the anterior chamber of the eye associated with infectious diseases of the cornea, the iris, and the ciliary body. The pus characteristically sinks to the bottom, filling the lower angle of the chamber, where it may be visible through the cornea.

recidivans, h. Iridocyclitis recidivans purulenta.

hyposcleral (hi″po-skler'al). Beneath the sclerotic coat of the eye.

hypostasis (hi″po-sta'sis). A term used by Lancaster to designate the static position of the covered eye during a cover test when its line of sight deviates downward.

hypostereoscopy (hi″po-ster-e-os'ko-pe). Diminution of apparent depth relationships by decreasing the lateral separation of the stereocamera lens systems.

hypotelorism (hi″po-tel'or-izm). A congenital malformation of the skull characterized by abnormal narrowness of the interorbital distance. Syn., *stenopia*.

hypothalamus (hi″po-thal′ah-mus). The portion of the diencephalon of the forebrain located in the floor of the third ventricle, consisting mainly of the posterior lobe and infundibulum of the pituitary gland, the optic chiasm, the tuber cinereum, and the paired mammillary bodies.

hypothesis (hi-poth′e-sis). An assumption, a supposition, or a conjecture; a tentative theory used provisionally to explain certain facts or to guide in the investigation of others.

cluster h. The hypothesis that color perception is due to specific retinal elements, grouped in clusters throughout the retina, which act as selective receptors to certain wavelengths of light. That is, one type of retinal cell acts in the perception of red, another in green, etc.

constancy h. The hypothesis that sensation is correlated directly with stimulation. That is, a given stimulus, if repeated, will produce the same sensation, providing the sense organ remains unchanged.

Ogata-Weymouth h. Night myopia is due in part to the greater axial length of the eye outside the outer fovea when parafoveal fixation occurs in dim light. Subsequent investigation indicates that it must be a minor factor.

Ségal's h. The retina contains light-sensitive structures other than the rods and cones, such as the synaptic terminals of rods and cones and the cells of the pigment epithelium layer.

three-channel h. Normal trichromatic color vision is mediated by three pathways, channels, or mechanisms which selectively transmit color information. They may be three photosensitive pigments in the retina, three types of retinal receptors, or three selective "filters" in the visual pathways.

two-quantum h. The absorption of two quanta, within a given time interval, by a single sensitive unit under optimum conditions is sufficient for sensory detection.

Weymouth-Andersen h. The subconal angular values of the thresholds of binocular stereopsis and vernier visual acuity, which decrease with an increase in the length of the lines, the result of a comparison of the percepts of average oculocentric position of the lines derived from the pattern of stimulation of many cones.

hypotonia oculi (hi-po-to′ne-ah ok′-u-li). Ocular hypotony .

hypotony, ocular (hi-pot′o-ne). Abnormally low ocular tension. Syn., *hypotonia oculi*.

hypotrichosis (hi″po-trih-ko′sis). A condition in which the eyelashes are underdeveloped or absent.

hypotropia (hi″po-tro′pe-ah). Strabismus characterized by the downward deviation of the line of sight of the nonfixating eye with reference to that of the fixating eye, hence similar to hypophoria, except that the condition is continuous and unrelated to the presence or absence of fusion stimuli.

alternating h. Double hypotropia.

double h. Strabismus characterized by the downward deviation of the line of sight of either eye while the other fixates. Syn., *alternating hypotropia*.

Hyrtl's valve (hĕr′tlz). See under *valve*.

hysterope (his′ter-ōp). One suffering from hysteropia.

hysteropia (his-ter-o′pe-ah). Disordered vision resulting from hys**teria.**

I

I. Symbol for *luminous intensity*.

I.A.B. Abbreviation for *International Association of Boards of Examiners in Optometry;* previously International Board of Boards, abbreviated *I.B.B.*

ianthinopsia (i-an″thin-op′se-ah). Ianthopsia.

ianthopsia (i-an-thop′se-ah). A very rarely reported perversion of color vision identified by the sensory attribution of the color violet to perceived objects.

I.C.I. International Commission on Illumination, the English translation for *Commission Internationale de l'Eclairage* (abbreviated *C.I.E.*)

ichthyosis (ik″the-o′sis). Hypertrophy of the corneous layer of the skin, usually congenital, in which the skin becomes dry, hard, and scaly, with an absence of secretion from the sweat and sebaceous glands. When affecting the eyelids, it may result in the loss of the eyelashes and in ectropion; when affecting the eye, it may result in chronic catarrhal conjunctivitis or keratosis of the cornea.

iconoscope (i-kon′o-skōp). An instrument devised by Javal for testing binocular perception of depth, designed to vary the binocular relative parallactic angle and thereby determine the threshold of stereopsis.

identification. *Optometric Extension Program:* The total process of cortically receiving impulses derived from the retinal image and integrating this input with other sensory information and past experience, with a resultant recognition and interpretation of the stimulus.

idiocy. The lowest of the three grades of mental deficiency, which describes those whose defectiveness is of such degree as to render them unable to guard themselves against common physical dangers. On the basis of intelligence tests, it includes those who have I.Q. scores of less than 25. Cf. *imbecility; moronity.*

amaurotic family i. See under *amaurotic.*

idiopathic (id″e-o-path′ik). Pertaining to a primary disease of unknow cause or origin.

idioretinal (id″e-o-ret′ih-nal). Pertaining to the retina alone, as in *idioretinal light.*

I.E.S. Illuminating Engineering Society.

illaqueation (il″ak-we-a′shun). A surgical operation in which a displaced or an ingrown eyelash is drawn into a correct position by use of a loop or a snare.

illuminance (ih-lu′mih-nans). Illumination.

illuminant (ih-lu′mih-nant). Any source of light or visible radiant energy, such as candle flame or fluorescent lamp.

A; B; C, i's. Light sources having specified spectral distributions, adopted by the C.I.E. in 1931 as international standards in colorimetry. A is a tungsten lamp operated at a color temperature of 2854° K and approximates a blackbody operating at that color

[340]

temperature. B is illuminant A in combination with a specified filter and approximates noon sunlight, having a color temperature of 4800° K or a blackbody operating at that color temperature. C is illuminant A in combination with a specified filter and approximates daylight provided by a combination of direct sunlight and clear sky, having a color temperature of approximately 6500° K.

illuminate (ih-lu′mih-nāt). To supply with light.

illumination (ih-lu″mih-na′shun). 1. The photometric term for the intensive property of the luminous flux passing through a cross section of a beam or falling on a surface; the density of luminous flux incident on a surface. It is the quotient of the luminous flux divided by the area of the surface when the flux is uniformly distributed. Symbol: E. Common units are lumen per sq. ft. (footcandle) or per sq. M. (lux, metercandle). Syn., *illuminance*. 2. The act or process by which light is made to be incident on a surface.

axial i. Illumination from light transmitted along the optical axis of a lens or a mirror.

contact i. Illumination of the interior of the eye by placing a light source directly on the conjunctiva or the cornea.

critical i. 1. The minimum amount of light which will provide optimal performance in terms of any one criterion. For example, the footcandle level which will permit the practical maximum rate of reading of a specific sample of printed matter. 2. In microscopy, illumination of the specimen by focusing the image of a diffuse light source directly on it by means of a condenser whose aperture size is equal to that of the microscope objective.

diffuse i. 1. Illumination by light sources having dimensions relatively large with respect to the distance from the point being illuminated and emitting or scattering light in all directions, or illumination by light incident from all directions. It is characterized by a relative lack of shadow if an object is interposed between the light source and the illuminated area. 2. In slit lamp biomicroscopy, illumination obtained with a wide slit and out of focus beam, to provide an over-all view of the surface being studied.

direct i. Illumination from a light source without being reflected from any surface. Cf. *indirect illumination.*

focal i. 1. Illumination by focusing the image of a light source on an object, by means of an optical system. 2. Illumination at the focal plane of an optical system. 3. In slit lamp biomicroscopy, illumination with beam and microscope both sharply focused on the structure being studied.

indirect i. 1. Illumination by means of reflected light. Cf. *direct illumination.* 2. Proximal illumination.

Kohler i. In microscopy, illumination of the specimen by collimated light obtained by imaging the light source at a diaphragm located at the primary principal focus of the condenser.

lateral i. Proximal illumination.

multidirectional i. Illumination produced by several separated light sources, characterized by the formation of multiple shadows when an object is interposed between the light sources and the illuminated area. Cf. *diffused illumination.*

oblique i. Illumination used with certain instruments, such as the slit lamp, in which the beam of light is incident from such an angle that it is not reflected into the objective lens of the viewing system.

oscillatory i. In slit lamp biomicroscopy, illumination in which the light beam is oscillated to provide alternate direct and indirect illumination.

parafocal i. Proximal illumination.

proximal i. In biomicroscopy, illumination of a structure by focusing a small beam of light on nontransparent, translucent tissue adjacent to the structure under observation. Syn., *indirect illumination; lateral illumination; parafocal illumination.*

retinal i. The luminous flux incident per unit area on the retina.

retro i. See *retro-illumination.*

sunset i. In biomicroscopy, illumination of a structure with an oblique tangential or surface grazing beam.

surround i. Illumination with respect to the area surrounding an object of reference.

through i. Transillumination.

unidirectional i. Illumination produced by a single light source of relatively small dimensions and characterized by the formation of a sharply defined shadow when a small object is interposed between the light source and the illuminated area.

illuminator (ih-lu′mih-na″ter). Any device which is used to illuminate a surface; that which illuminates.

Barkan Focal I. A hand-held lamp which provides a focused beam of light; used to examine the eye, as in gonioscopy.

Luckiesh-Moss i. An appliance for uniformly illuminating visual acuity test charts.

microscope i. A light source designed to illuminate the specimen being viewed in a microscope.

illuminometer (ih-lu″mih-nom′ehter). Photometer.

illusion, optical (ih-lu′zhun). 1. Visual illusion. 2. An apparent visual illusion induced by optical

design or optical circumstances unknown to the observer, as obtained with curved mirrors, trick projectors, or mirages.

illusion, visual (ih-lu′zhun). The visual perception of a pattern, a view, or a performance, which does not reflect, represent, or convey the actual physical characteristics of the stimulus conditions; or the pattern, the view, or the performance itself. Syn., *optical illusion.*

assimilative visual i. A visual illusion induced by nearby objects, suggestion, attitude, or past experience.

associative visual i. A type of contrast visual illusion in which the length of lines, or areas, is either overestimated or underestimated.

autokinetic visual i. The apparent motion of a small, single, stationary object when continuously observed in a surrounding dark environment. Syn., *visual autokinesis; autokinetic effect; Charpentier's visual illusion; autokinetic phenomenon.*

Baldwin's visual i. A visual illusion in which a dot, placed midway between a small circle and a large one, appears to be nearer the large one.

Bourdon's visual i. A geometrical visual illusion arising when viewing two wedge-shaped areas, joined at their apices, and whose upper borders form a common, continuous, straight line. The pattern appears curved, although the one line is straight.

cameo-intaglio visual i. The apparent reversal of normal depth relationships in a scene or an object, due to shadows which result from an unusual and unnoticed direction of illumination.

Charpentier's visual i. Autokinetic visual illusion.

chessboard visual i. The perception of straight, vertical, and horizontal rows of squares of equal width when viewing a figure, the chessboard of Helmholtz, at its center, from a specific distance. The figure actually does not consist of squares, as the rows are hyperbolic instead of straight. When the figure is viewed at its periphery, from the same distance, it has the appearance of a shallow bowl.

contrast visual i. A visual illusion due to the effects of the relationship of various components of a geometrical figure or pattern. Cf. *assimilative visual illusion.*

double interpretation visual i. Reversible visual illusion.

Ebbinghaus' visual i. The apparent increase in a linear dimension when it is "filled" rather than "empty," as illustrated when viewing two equal lines or spaces, one "filled" with a series of intersecting lines or narrow bands, and the other left "empty."

false reference visual i. A visual illusion leading to false aircraft orientation in which slanting clouds or aircraft are mistaken as horizontal, or in which stars are mistaken for ground lights, or vice versa, creating a false horizon.

geometrical visual i. A visual illusion dependent on the arrangement of lines, angles, and spaces, rather than on color, light, and shade.

Hering's visual i. A geometrical visual illusion in which a pair of parallel lines appear bowed, or abruptly bent, by the placement of diagonals on or adjacent to them, as when a number of radiating lines are crossed by two parallel lines on opposite sides of the point of radiation.

Höfler's visual i. A geometrical visual illusion arising when two curved bands or lines, each of equal length and radius, are placed one above the other, the band nearer the centers of curvature appearing longer.

horizontal-vertical visual i. A geometrical visual illusion arising when a horizontal line is near or touching a vertical line. When the bottom of the vertical line is placed at or near the midpoint of the horizontal, and the two lines are of equal length, the vertical appears to be longer. If the figure is rotated to any other position, the same line will still appear longer.

Jastrow visual i. A geometrical visual illusion arising when two curved bands of equal length and radii of curvature are placed one above the other, the band nearer the centers of curvature appearing longer.

Kundt's visual i. A geometrical visual illusion occurring when attempting to bisect a horizontal

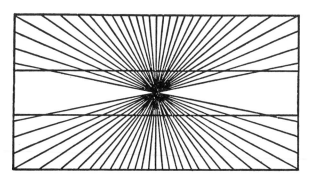

Fig. 24. Hering's visual illusion. (From *Visual Illusions,* M. Luckiesh, Van Nostrand, 1922)

line viewed by only one eye, the middle point being placed too far toward the nasal side.

linear surround visual i. The apparent motion of stationary vertical stripes adjacent to a rotating stimulus drum which is inducing horizontal optokinetic nystagmus.

Mach's visual i. A geometrical visual illusion in which a drawing, resembling a partially open book, first appears to open toward and then away from the observer, or vice versa, on continuous fixation.

moon visual i. A visual illusion in which the moon appears to be larger when viewed near the horizon than when viewed high in the sky.

Mueller-Lyer visual i. A geometrical visual illusion in which two lines of equal length do not appear equal when different appendages are placed at their ends, as when viewing two equal lines, one of which has arrowheads on both ends and the other has quills on both ends.

oculoagravic visual i. Apparent movements or displacement of an object in space associated with reduced gravity or weightlessness, as in aircraft maneuvers.

oculogravic visual i. The apparent rising of an observed object coincident with a sensation of tilting backward created by high acceleration, attributed to stimulation of the vestibular apparatus.

oculogyral visual i. The apparent movements of viewed objects subsequent to rotatory acceleration of the observer's head in one direction. The initially observed movement is opposite to the direction of rotation and is followed by movement in the same direction. Syn., *optogyral visual illusion.*

optogyral visual i. Oculogyral visual illusion.

Poggendorff's visual i. A geometrical visual illusion arising from viewing a bandlike rectangular area overlaying a diagonal line. The two visible portions of the line, one on each side of the band, do not appear to be parts of a continuous line.

Ponzo visual i. A geometrical visual illusion in which two parallel lines of equal length do not appear equal when viewed on a background of radiating straight lines emanating from a common point, the parallel line nearest the point of radiation appearing to be longer.

railroad visual i. The illusion of motion of one's own stationary vehicle when viewing another nearby parallel moving vehicle.

reverse optokinetic visual i. The apparent movement of a small stationary light, in a dark surround, in a direction opposite to the continuous movement of a previously viewed series of stripes oriented perpendicular to their movement, usually provided by means of a rotating striped drum.

reverse rotation visual i. The apparent movement of a stationary pattern of stripes in a direction opposite to that just previously observed when the stripes were in actual motion in a direction perpendicular to their orientation.

reversible visual i. The moment to moment variation in the interpretation of an ambiguous or a reversible figure. Syn., *double interpretation visual illusion.*

Schroeder's staircase visual i. A geometrical visual illusion arising from viewing a figure formed by parallel, steplike lines drawn from the upper corner of a parallelogram to the lower opposite corner. When observed continuously, the impression is, at one time, that one is viewing a staircase from underneath, and at another, that he is viewing the staircase from above.

stroboscopic visual i. The altered apparent speed of motion of a rotating, segmented pattern induced by rapid intermittent exposures, frequently observed when a revolving fan is illuminated by fluorescent light or when the spokes of a turning wheel are viewed in a motion picture. The segmented pattern may appear to move slowly, stand still, or to move in the opposite direction, depending on the relation of the amount of radial motion during each cycle of intermittency and the distance between the segments of the pattern.

Thiéry's visual i. A geometrical visual illusion in which a reversible perspective drawing first appears to be a solid rectangular box to which is attached the base and the side of another such box. Following fixation, the figure appears to change so that either two solid rectangular boxes are seen or the base and the side become a solid box and the solid box becomes the base and the side.

Tschermak-Seysenegg visual i. A geometrical visual illusion occurring in the attempt to bisect a vertical line, the inferior field being underestimated, resulting in subjectively locating the midpoint too far upward.

waterfall visual i. A visual illusion of motion induced as a temporary aftereffect of viewing an endlessly moving pattern, such as a waterfall or an endless belt. A subsequently viewed stationary object appears to move slowly in the opposite direction. Syn., *waterfall phenomenon.*

Wundt's visual i. A geometrical visual illusion in which a pair of parallel straight lines appear bowed when crossed by lines radiating toward, and meeting,

each other from two points, one on each side of the parallel lines.

Zöllner's visual i. A geometrical visual illusion in which a series of parallel lines appear to converge toward or diverge from each other when crossed by short diagonal lines. The diagonals on each line are parallel to each other, but are angled opposite to those of the adjacent line.

image. 1. In general, a likeness, a copy, a replica, a symbol, or a mental representation of an object. 2. The optical counterpart of an object produced by a lens, a mirror, or other optical system. 3. The perceived counterpart of a viewed object subjectively projected in visual space.

accidental i. An afterimage.

aerial i. 1. An image, especially a real image, formed by an optical system but perceived by alignment of the viewing eye with the path of light emerging from the optical system, instead of being focused first as an image on a receiving screen. Cf. *direct image.* 2. An image perceived in the air by reflection or refraction by strata of different atmospheric densities, as in a mirage.

after i. See *afterimage.*

apparent i. Virtual image.

catoptric i. An image formed by regular reflection, as from a mirror, or by reflection at refracting surfaces, as the Purkinje-Sanson images.

chemical i. The retinal image as represented by photochemical changes in the visual cells from light stimulation, as distinguished from *energy image.*

chiasmal i. A figurative image representing the pattern of impulses from a retinal image at a cross section of the optic chiasm.

congruous i's. 1. Ocular images having the same area representation in the visual cortex, as opposed to incongruous images present in aniseikonia. 2. Diplopic images seen under conditions of normal retinal correspondence.

corneal i. Either of the two catoptric images of an object or a light source, produced by reflection at one or the other surface of the cornea. See also *Purkinje-Sanson images.*

cortical i. The topographical representation of the image of external objects at the terminal region of the neurological visual pathway in the visual cortex. It is the representation in the brain of the nervous impulses originating with the retinal image and conditioned by the anatomy of the retina, the physiological processes involved in transmission, and the anatomy of the visual cortex. Syn., *ocular image.*

curvature of i. See *curvature of the field.*

cyclopic i. The single, fused image of one's eyes obtained when each eye fixates its own image in a mirror.

diffusion i. A blurred image of an object point, formed on a surface not located in the focal plane of a lens or an optical system; an out-of-focus image.

dioptric i. 1. An image formed by a refracting optical system, distinguished from a *catoptric image.* 2. The retinal image.

direct i. 1. A virtual image, such as the erect image seen in direct ophthalmoscopy. Cf. *indirect image.* 2. An image, especially a virtual image, formed by an optical system, but perceived by alignment of the viewing eye with the path of light emerging from the optical system, instead of being focused first as an image on a receiving screen. Cf. *aerial image.*

double i. A pair of images of a single object, obtained either perceptually, as in diplopia, or optically by a doubling system.

eidetic i. An extraordinarily experienced, mental picture based on the recall of a previous visual experience and characterized by its clearness, apparent realness, and accuracy of detail.

energy i. The retinal image as represented by the light energy received at the retina, as distinguished from *chemical image.*

erect i. An image that is not inverted with respect to the object, such as a virtual image produced by a concave lens or a convex mirror.

extraordinary i. The image formed by the extraordinary rays in double refraction.

false i. 1. The anomalously projected image in monocular diplopia or associated with the deviating eye in strabismus. 2. In physiological diplopia, the image which seems to be incorrectly localized in space when attempts are made to reach for it.

following i. of von Kries. Second positive afterimage.

foot-piece i. A figurative image representing the pattern of impulses from a retinal image at the foot pieces of the visual cells.

functional i. The image on the retina considered or analyzed in terms of the number of retinal elements (rods and cones) within it or stimulated by it.

ghost i. An unwanted secondary image, as may be formed by internal reflection in a lens or an optical system, irregularity of spacing in a diffraction grating, or incomplete polarization by a Polaroid filter. Syn., *ghost.*

half i. One of the two images present in diplopia. *Helmholtz.*

heteronymous i's. The images of an object, seen in physiological diplopia, when fixation is for a point farther than the object.

heterotopic i's. A pair of diplopic images separated in space. Cf. *homotopic images.*

homonymous i's. The images of an object, seen in physiological diplopia, when fixation is for a point nearer than the object.

homotopic i's. A pair of diplopic images, each arising from a different object, which are perceived at the same point in space, i.e., they are superimposed. Cf. *heterotopic images.*

incidental i. The bleached impression of an image remaining on the retina subsequent to the removal of the object. See also *optogram.*

incongruous i's. 1. Diplopic images seen under conditions of anomalous retinal correspondence. 2. Images which are not of the same size and/or shape, due either to aniseikonia or to the difference in direction of view created by the separation of the eyes in the head.

    incongruous i's., asymmetric. In aniseikonia, images which result from asymmetric magnification or minification in specific meridians. Syn., *irregular incongruous images.*

    incongruous i's., irregular. Asymmetric incongruous images.

    incongruous i's., regular. Symmetric incongruous images.

    incongruous i's., symmetric. In aniseikonia, images which result from symmetrical magnificacation or minification in specific meridians. Syn., *regular incongruous images.*

indirect i. A real image, such as the inverted image seen in indirect ophthalmoscopy. Cf. *direct image.*

inverted i. An optically formed image reversed in meridional orientation in relation to the object, i.e., upside down or right for left, usually implying reversal in all meridians unless otherwise qualified. Syn., *reversed image.*

leading i. The image seen by one eye in a direction farther from the primary position than the image seen by the other eye, in testing for paralysis or paresis of extraocular muscles.

line, i. See under *line.*

mental i. 1. A mental picture based on the recall of a previous visual experience. 2. A perceptual image. 3. A visual hallucination.

mirror i. 1. An image of an object formed by a mirror. 2. An object, or a part of an object, having the symmetrical attribute of replicating another object, or the other part of itself, as though it were its reflected image in a plane mirror.

negative i. 1. An image with features complementary to those of its correlated object in respect to luminance, color, or relief, as obtained, for example, in photographic negatives, negative afterimages, and contact lens molding processes, respectively. 2. A virtual image.

neural i. A pattern of neural activity represented at any specific point in the visual pathway as the correlate of a retinal image.

ocular i. 1. The cortical image. 2. The retinal image. 3. The image formed by the refracting system of the eye, the presence or the position of the retina being disregarded.

optical i. An image formed by the refraction or the reflection of light.

ordinary i. The image formed by the ordinary rays in double refraction.

orthoscopic i. An image exactly similar to its object in its entire extent, hence formed by an optical system corrected for distortions.

perceptual i. That which is perceived and interpreted as an object in the visual field; hence, an object in terms of its perceived attributes and localization rather than in terms of its physical attributes or location. Syn., *psychological image.*

pinhole i. An image formed by rays that have passed through a pinhole aperture.

pressure i. See *phosphene.*

primary i. The initial sensory effect of photic stimulation of the retina, distinguished from *afterimage.*

psychological i. Perceptual image.

Purkinje i's. Purkinje-Sanson images.

Purkinje-Sanson i's. The catoptric images of a light source, produced by reflection from the anterior and the posterior surfaces of the cornea and the crystalline lens.

pursuant i. of von Kries. Second positive afterimage.

real i. An optical image that can be received on a screen; one formed by the meeting of converging rays of light.

recurrent i's. A succession of afterimages following the primary image.

retinal i. The image formed on the retina by the refracting system of the eye.

reversed i. Inverted image.

satellite i. of Hamaker. Second positive afterimage.

schlieren i. The image formed by a schlieren optical system, consisting essentially of two components, one represented in the illumination of the field and the silhouette of opaque objects, and the other represented by intensity gradations resulting from refractive index gradients in the schlieren field.

shell i. See under *shell.*

space i. The image of an object perceived through a binocular instrument.

space i., homeomorphous. A space image which duplicates the object in shape but may differ in size.

space i., hyperplastic. A space image in which the depth dimensions are greater in proportion to the frontal dimensions than those of the object.

space i., hypoplastic. A space image in which the depth dimensions are less in proportion to the frontal dimensions than those of the object.

space i., orthoplastic. A space image in which the ratio between depth and frontal dimensions exactly duplicates that of the object.

space i., porrhallactic. A space image which does not duplicate the shape of the object.

space i., tautomorphous. A space image which exactly duplicates the real object in all dimensions when a pair of stereophotographs of the object are viewed in a stereoscope.

specular i. An image produced by regular reflection.

stereoscopic i. A single perceptual image resulting from sensory fusion of the two ocular images, so as to induce the attribute of depth, solidity, or the third dimension.

total i. The single image perceived in simultaneous binocular vision.

true i. The image associated with the normally fixating eye in strabismus.

virtual i. An optical image that cannot be received on a screen; one formed by the backward prolongation of diverging rays to the point of apparent origin. Syn., *apparent image.*

visual i. 1. A mental picture based on the recall of a previous visual experience. 2. A perceptual image. 3. A visual hallucination.

window i. The image of a window or other object formed by reflection from the surface of the cornea.

image plane. See under *plane.*

image point. See under *point.*

image ray. See under *ray.*

imagery (im'ij-re, -er-e). 1. The process of recalling actual past visual experiences. 2. Images taken collectively.

 eidetic i. The process of recalling actual past visual experiences with marked clearness, apparent realness, and accuracy of detail, often demonstrated or experienced by children.

imbalance. Lack of balance.

 binocular i. An inequality in some aspect of binocular vision, such as *anisometropia, aniseikonia, heterophoria,* or *strabismus.*

 muscular i. The condition of either heterophoria or strabismus.

  muscular i., compound. A combination of lateral and vertical muscular imbalance.

  muscular i., lateral. Esophoria, exophoria, or convergent or divergent strabismus.

  muscular i., vertical. Hyperphoria, hypophoria, hypertropia, or hypotropia.

 ocular i. Binocular imbalance.

imbecile (im'be-sil). A person who has imbecility.

imbecility (im″be-sil'ih-te). One of the three major grades of mental deficiency which describes those persons incapable of managing themselves or their affairs with ordinary prudence. On the basis of intelligence tests, it includes those persons who have I.Q. scores between 25 and 50. Cf. *idiocy; moronity.*

Imbert-Fick law (im'bert-fik). See under *law.*

imperception (im-per-sep'shun). Defective perception.

impingement. The energy reaching a sense organ, regardless of whether effective or not. A stimulus is an effective impingement.

implant. A material inserted or grafted into intact tissue, such as an inert filler placed in the eye socket in surgical enucleation, or in the scleral shell in evisceration, to replace the interior volume of the eyeball.

 Allen's i. A hollow, half-sphere, buried orbital implant with holes in each quadrant near its flat face to receive the four rectus muscles.

 anterior chamber i. A lens placed in the anterior chamber, at the pupillary aperture adjacent to the iris, to replace the crystalline lens following cataract surgery. Syn., *anterior chamber lens.*

 Arruga's i. An integrated orbital implant completely buried at the time of surgery with its one or two pegs at its summit covered by conjunctiva. Each peg erodes through the conjunctiva soon after surgery, at a site other than that of the original wound, and serves as an attachment for an artificial eye.

 attached i. An implant attached directly to the extraocular muscles, but not directly to the artificial eye.

 Binkhorst i. Iris clip lens.

 Boberg-Ans i. A form of the Strampelli lens in which the plate to which the lens is secured is modified in shape and fenestrated.

 buried i. An orbital implant which is completely covered with Tenon's capsule and conjunctiva.

 Choyce i. Any of several anterior chamber implants designed by Choyce.

 Cogan i. A modified form of the Strampelli lens in which the plate to which the lens is secured is fenestrated.

 corneal i. A lens made of transparent inert material which is placed in the cornea in lieu of tissue transplantation. Syn., *keratoprosthesis.*

  corneal i., mushroom. A small mushroom-shaped plastic lens used in combination with a lamellar corneal graft. The pedicle is placed through a central perforation of the cornea, its base extending into the anterior chamber, and the lamellar graft is sutured over its head.

Cutler's i. A semiburied implant consisting of a half-sphere of plastic surmounted with tantalum mesh, with a rectangular plastic peg protruding from its summit. The rectus muscles are attached to the mesh and covered with Tenon's capsule and conjunctiva, with the peg serving as attachment to the artificial eye.

Dannheim i. Dannheim lens.

Epstein i. Epstein lens.

external fixation i. An anterior chamber implant consisting of a convex lens held in position by loops of nylon filament which are passed through superior and inferior limbal incisions whereby it is fixed to the external surface of the sclera.

eyelid i. An acrylic or silicone implant placed in the upper eyelid to fill an area which is hollow due to surgery.

integrated i. An implant attached directly to both the artificial eye and the extraocular muscles.

intrascleral i. An implant inserted into the scleral cavity after evisceration of the eye.

Iowa i. A buried orbital implant having four mounds on its anterior face. The rectus muscles are sutured to the front of the implant with each muscle lying in a hollow between two mounds.

magnetic i. An orbital implant containing a magnet for holding the artificial eye.

mesh i. An orbital implant containing metal mesh to which the rectus muscles are sutured.

Mules's sphere i. A spherical implant with no direct attachment to either the artificial eye or the extraocular muscles.

orbital i. An inert filler placed in the eye socket in surgical enucleation, or in the scleral shell in evisceration, to replace the in-terior volume of the eyeball. Tenon's capsule and the conjunctiva are usually sutured over it.

posterior chamber i. A lens placed in the posterior chamber, between the iris and posterior lens capsule, in the approximate position of the removed crystalline lens, following cataract surgery. Syn., *posterior chamber lens.*

Roper-Hall i. A buried orbital implant in the shape of a hollow hemisphere with a magnet in its summit and a hole in each quadrant to receive the rectus muscles.

scleral i. A substance embedded into the sclera, usually for the purpose of impressing the choroid toward the retina for the repair of a retinal detachment.

semiburied i. An orbital implant, a portion of which is not covered with conjunctiva, thus affording a means of attachment to an artificial eye.

sponge i. A buried orbital implant consisting of polyvinyl sponge, on the front of which are sutured the rectus muscles.

Strampelli i. Strampelli lens.

subconjunctival i. An orbital implant completely covered by the conjunctiva; a buried orbital implant.

Torres-Ruiz i. Torres-Ruiz lens.

tunnel i. An orbital implant containing apertures through which the rectus muscles are placed.

vitreous i. A substance injected into the vitreous chamber to replace or supplement the vitreous humor.

impression. 1. A perceptor effect produced on the mind by sensory stimuli. 2. A mold.

absolute i. The perceived magnitude of one of the psychological dimensions (such as intensity) of a singly presented stimulus.

visual i. An impression activated by visual stimuli.

visual i., homeomorphous. Orthoplastic visual impression.

visual i., hyperplastic. An exaggerated or enhanced impression or percept of relief or relative distance.

visual i., hypoplastic. A diminished or reduced impression or percept of relief or relative distances.

visual i., orthoplastic. A quantitatively correct impression or percept of relief or relative distances. Syn., *homeomorphous visual impression.*

incandescence (in″kan-des′ens). The glowing or radiation of visible energy by a body, produced by heat.

inch. A unit of length.

Austrian i. A unit of length equal to 26.34 mm., used in the specification of focal length of early lenses.

English i. A unit of length equal to 25.4 mm.

Parisian i. A unit of length equal to 27.07 mm., used by Donders in specifying focal power.

Prussian i. A unit of length equal to 26.15 mm., used in the specification of focal length of early lenses.

incidence, grazing. The limiting direction of the incidence of a ray traveling from a less dense to a more dense optical medium along the interface between the two media, representing the largest angle of incidence from which a refracted ray will result.

inclinometer (in″klih-nom′eh-ter). An instrument for measuring or determining angles or inclinations, e.g., the axes of astigmatism.

incomitance (in-kom′ih-tans). Nonconcomitance.

incomitancy (in-kom-ih-tan′se). Nonconcomitance.

incomitant (in-kom′ih-tant). Nonconcomitant.

incongruity, retinal (in″kong-gru′ih-te). 1. The lack of correspondence, in the two retinae, of the anatomical positions of sensory receptors which do correspond in visual direction. 2. A normal condition in which the nasal and temporal halves of the retina do not contain the same number or distribution of receptor elements.

incontinentia pigmenti (in-kon″tih-nen′she-ah pig-men′ti). Infantile pigmentary dermatosis occurring in either of two forms, one characterized by slate-gray cutaneous pigmentation in reticular formation which occurs at about two years of age without ocular involvement, the other characterized by patches of wavy streaks of slate-gray cutaneous pigmentation and ocular anomalies in about one fourth of the cases (*Bloch-Sulzberger syndrome, q.v.*).

incyclofusion (in-si″klo-fu′zhun). Relative rotation of the two eyes around their respective anteroposterior axes in response to a cyclofusional stimulus, so that the upward extensions of the vertical meridians rotate nasalward.

incyclophoria (in-si″klo-fo′re-ah). The turning, or the amount of turning, of the two eyes relative to each other around their respective anteroposterior axes or lines of sight, as manifested in the absence of an adequate fusion stimulus, so that elongations of their respective vertical meridians of reference cross superiorly, i.e., above the horizontal plane of the eyes. Syn., *minus cyclophoria; encyclophoria.*

incyclotropia (in-si″klo-tro′pe-ah). The turning, or the amount of turning, of the two eyes relative to each other around their respective anteroposterior axes or lines of sight, as manifested in the presence or the absence of a fusion stimulus, so that elongations of their respective vertical meridians of reference cross superiorly, i.e., above the horizontal plane of the eyes. Syn., *encyclotropia*.

incyclovergence (in-si″klo-ver′jens). The turning, or the amount of turning, of the two eyes with respect to each other around their respective anteroposterior axes, so as to converge the upward extensions of the vertical meridians of reference. Syn., *encyclovergence*.

index. The ratio, or the formula expressing the ratio, of one measurement to another.

absorption, i. of. The constant κ (kappa) in the expression for the exponential reduction in intensity of light passing through an absorbing medium:

$$I = I_o e^{-\frac{4\pi n\kappa}{\lambda} x}$$

where *n* is the refractive index of the medium, and *x* is the distance traversed. The expression is more usually stated as

$$I = I_o e^{-ax}$$

where *a*, the *coefficient of absorption,* is defined as

$$a = \frac{4\pi n\kappa}{\lambda}$$

alpha i. The percentage of time the alpha rhythm shows on an electroencephalographic record.

blackout i. The time the brain is deprived of visual stimuli during a blink, divided by the frequency of occurrence of the blink. Normally, visual stimuli are absent 0.3 sec. each 2.8 sec. or 10.7% of the time.

    blackout i., modified. A blackout index which considers the periods of unreliable vision immediately before and after the blink, as well as the time the brain is deprived of visual stimuli during the blink. Normally this

period lasts 0.55 sec. each 2.8 sec. or 19.6% of the time.

blur, i. of. A measure of blur which can be applied to a line, point, or contrast border. As applied to the spread function for a border, it represents the ratio of the difference in luminance on the two sides of the border to the slope of the line connecting the points representing 25% and 75% of the difference between the two levels.

blurredness, i. of. The visual angle of the bar width of a test character for which increase of the bar width does not reduce the threshold visibility of the character.

Broca's orbital i. The ratio of the height to the breadth of the orbital entrance, multiplied by 100.

cephalic i. The ratio of the breadth to the length of the skull, multiplied by 100.

discrimination i. Discrimination factor.

extraordinary i. In a double refracting medium, the index of refraction for the extraordinary ray.

optical i. The index of refraction.

orbital i. Broca's orbital index.

orbitonasal i. The ratio of the sum of two lines each extending from the front point of the outer edge of one of the orbits to the lowest point on the root of the nose, to the direct distance between the two orbital points, multiplied by 100; hence, a ratio denoting the relative projection of the root of the nose anterior to the plane of the eye orbits.

reading efficiency i. The rate of words read per minute, multiplied by the percentage of comprehension.

refraction, i. of. The ratio of the speed of light in vacuum, air, or other medium of reference, to the speed of light in a given medium, obtained by Snell's law as the ratio of the sine of the angle of incidence to the sine of the angle of refraction, and usually designated by the letter *n*. Syn., *optical index.*

refraction, i. of (absolute). The ratio of the speed of light in vacuum to the speed of light in a given medium.

refraction, i. of (mean). The index of refraction determined for a line of the spectrum which lies midway between two spectral lines of reference.

refraction, i. of (relative). The ratio of the speed of light in a medium of reference other than vacuum to the speed of light in a given medium.

indicator. 1. An apparatus or a device which indicates or points out, such as a gauge or a dial. 2. A chemical substance which indicates, usually by color change, the condition, such as acid or alkaline, of a solution, or the end points of reactions.

Berens-Tolman Ocular Hypertension I. A tonometer designed for glaucoma screening which indicates ocular tension as being above or below 20 mm. Hg.

Helmholtz' i. An instrument for the detection and differentiation of palsies of the cyclomotor muscles, consisting of a vertical card marked with a horizontal line with a spot at its center and supported on a horizontal rod, the proximal end of which is held in the patient's teeth so that tilting movements of the head are communicated to the card. The relative tilt and displacement of the two images of the line seen in diplopia indicate the character of the palsy.

muscle i. An instrument designed by Savage to show the interrelationship of muscle action to monocular and binocular eye movements, consisting of a metal ring on which are mounted a pair of

mechanical schematic eyes with telescoping rods for visual axes which meet at a variable fixation point on the metal ring. The centers of rotation of the mechanical eyes are on the ring, and the ring can be tilted around a cord connecting the centers of rotation of the eyes.

Prentice's phoria i. A phoria measuring instrument consisting of a vertical row and a horizontal row of transilluminated green disks seen by one eye, and a single transilluminated red disk seen by the other eye through a red filter or a Maddox rod.

indigo (in'dih-go). 1. The hue attribute of visual sensation typically evoked by stimulation of the normal human eye with radiation of wavelengths approximately 436 mμ. 2. A color of the visible spectrum between the blue and the violet wavelengths.

induction (in-duk'shun). 1. The act or process of bringing in, initiating, or introducing. 2. Arousal by indirect stimulation.

color i. The modification of response to a color stimulus, due either to simultaneous perception of another color in a neighboring area or to a previous retinal excitation.

mutual i. The mutual modification of response to adjacent fields simultaneously stimulating the eye through the process of spatial induction.

spatial i. The modification of response to a part of the visual field, occasioned by simultaneous stimulation from another part of the visual field. Syn., *surface induction.*

successive i. Temporal induction.

surface i. Spatial induction.

temporal i. The modification of response to a stimulus, occasioned by a preceding stimulus. Syn., *successive induction.*

infiltration, peripheral annular (in-fil-tra'shun). A ring abscess.

infinity, optical (in-fin'ih-te). 1. The location of an optical image at infinity, so that rays emerging from a given point on the image are parallel. 2. Clinically, a test object distance great enough to be considered equivalent to infinity for certain test purposes, usually 20 ft. or 6 m.

informative sequence. *Optometric Extension Program:* A group of clinical visual test findings systematically tabulated in reference to norms or to each other, for purposes of diagnosing the visual condition.

infradextroversion (in″frah-deks-tro-ver'zhun). Conjugate rotation of the eyes, downward and to the right.

infraduction (in″frah-duk'shun). 1. The downward rotation of an eye. 2. In vertical divergence testing, the downward rotation of one eye with respect to the other in response to increases in base-up prism, or the equivalent. Syn., *deorsumduction; subduction.*

infralevoversion (in″frah-leh-vo-ver'zhun). Conjugate rotation of the eyes, downward and to the left.

infraorbital (in″frah-ōr'bih-tal). Situated beneath or on the floor of the orbit.

infrared (in-frah-red'). Radiant energy of wavelengths longer than light or visible radiant energy, generally including 770 mμ to more than 50 μ.

infravergence (in-frah-ver'jens). The downward rotation of an eye, the other eye remaining stationary. Syn., *deorsumvergence.*

infraversion (in-frah-ver'shun). Conjugate rotation of the eyes downward. Syn., *deorsumversion; subversion.*

infula (in'fu-lah). A horizontal band of specialized retina extending through the fovea of certain birds, such as winchats, geese, or swans, which provides acute vision.

inheritance. The acquisition or the reception of characteristics or qualities by transmission from parent to offspring.

autosomal i. The hereditary mechanism in which the genes are located in any pair of chromosomes other than the sex (X and Y) chromosomes.

polygenic i. The hereditary mechanism in which more than a single locus on a pair of chromosomes determines the trait. Two or more loci and two or more sets of genes are involved. Refractive errors and eye color are now believed to be so inherited.

sex-linked i. The hereditary mechanism in which the genes involved are located in the sex (X or Y) chromosomes.

inhibition. 1. The act of holding back, restraining, or hindering. 2. A stopping, restraining, or arrest of the action of an organ, a nerve reflex, a cell, or a chemical. 3. A restraining of one psychical activity by another.

accommodation, i. of. The reduction or prevention, or the effecting of reduction or prevention, of accommodation or of the stimulus to accommodation.

convergence, i. of. The reduction or prevention, or the effecting of reduction or prevention, of convergence or of the stimulus to convergence.

reciprocal i. The phase or portion of the reciprocal innervation pattern producing inhibition of the antagonist muscle.

retinal i. Inhibition of response (to visual stimuli) occurring as a function of, or in, the retina, as distinguished from inhibition at higher or more central levels.

Wedensky i. Failure of the lateral geniculate body to conduct more than six impulses when the optic nerve is subjected to a long train of electric shocks in the frequency range from 150 to 600 per second.

injection. Increased redness of an area due to dilatation and engorgement of the small blood vessels of the region, e.g., in conjunctivitis.

ciliary i. A pinkish area around the limbus of the eye caused by dilatation of small, deeply seated blood vessels which appear to radiate from the cornea, seen in diseases of the cornea, the iris, and the ciliary body. Syn., *circumcorneal injection.*

circumcorneal i. Ciliary injection.

conjunctival i. A diffuse, brick-red discoloration of the conjunctiva fading toward the limbus, due to congestion of the superficial conjunctival vessels.

scleral i. A diffuse, purplish redness of the sclera, sometimes localized, due to a congestion of the deep vessels.

innervation, reciprocal (in-er-va'-shun). Innervation which simultaneously stimulates an agonist and inhibits its antagonist.

Inouye's (in'oo-yēz) **cubes; disk.** See under the nouns.

insectorubin (in-sek-to'ru-bin). Pigments of unknown composition and function found in the eyes of insects.

insertion, foot-plate. An abnormal tendon insertion of an extraocular muscle extending posteriorly a greater distance than normal, although correctly positioned from the limbus both in distance and direction.

insertion, secondary. An abnormal tendon insertion of an extraocular muscle in which fibers leave the main tendon and attach farther back.

inset. The nasalward displacement of the segment of a multifocal lens with respect to the mechanical center or other reference point or line in the lens.

insistence. The power of a bright or highly saturated colored region of the visual field to gain attention and fixation. Cf. *target value.*

instability, binocular. Difficulty in the maintenance of clear, single, binocular vision, attributed to deficiencies in motor or sensory fusion.

instinct, binocular. A presumed inborn tendency to use the two eyes as a single unit for the attainment of single, binocular vision.

instrument, optical. A single mirror, prism, or lens, or a combination of such elements, together with the mountings, stops, and diaphragms, which refracts, reflects, or in some way alters the incident light or its path.

insufficiency. The state or quality of being incompetent, unfit, deficient, or inadequate.

accommodation, i. of. See under *accommodation.*

convergence, i. of. See under *convergence.*

divergence, i. of. See under *divergence.*

externi, i. of the. 1. Paralysis or paresis of the external rectus muscles. 2. Presumed relative insufficiency of the external rectus muscles in relation to the internal rectus muscles, in cases of esophoria or low divergence ability.

eyelids, i. of the. A condition in which a conscious effort is required to close the eyelids.

interni, i. of the. 1. Paralysis or paresis of the internal rectus muscles. 2. Presumed relative insufficiency of the internal rectus muscles in relation to the external rectus muscles, in cases of exophoria or low convergence ability.

integral, Fourier's. A mathematical expression for any arbitrary, nonperiodic, waveform in terms of the frequency distribution of the amplitude of component waves differing only by infinitesimal increments of wavelength.

integrals, Fresnel. Integrals, derived by Fresnel, which represent the x and y co-ordinates of Cornu's spiral.

integration, binocular. 1. Sensory fusion. 2. The organization of a binocular percept as a function of two monocular stimuli or percepts.

intensity. 1. The state, quality, or condition of being intense. 2. A specific measure of the effect of a physical agent such as light.

luminous i. In a given direction, the ratio of the luminous flux emitted by a source, or by an element of a source, in an infinitesimal cone containing this direction, to the solid angle of this cone; luminous flux per unit solid angle in a given direction. Symbol: I. Unit: *candela.*

radiant i. Radiant energy emitted per unit time, per unit solid angle about the direction considered, expressed in watts per steradian. Symbol: J.

specific i. Radiant intensity expressed for a specific source or element of a source.

interaction, contour (in″ter-ak′-shun). The phenomenon of decrease or enhancement in vision performance (such as visual acuity, brightness, or color) induced by the proximity or juxtaposition of one or more contours in the visual field.

intercept, focal (in′ter-sept). The focal length or the focal distance of a lens or lens system.

intercilium (in″ter-sil′e-um). The space between the eyebrows. Syn., *glabella.*

interface. A plane or surface forming a common boundary between two optical media.

interference. 1. The act or process of interposing or intervening. 2. The phenomenon of modification of light intensity due to the combined effect, or mutual action, of two or more coherent trains of light waves superposed at the same instant at the same point in space.

constructive i. Interference in which trains of light waves are superposed in such phase relationship that they mutually aid or enhance each other.

contour i. 1. The perceptual covering or overlapping of the contour or border of an object in space by a nearer object, or the simulation of this effect in a drawing or photograph; one of the clues to depth perception. 2. Border suppression.

destructive i. Interference in which the trains of light waves are superposed in such phase relationship that they partially or completely neutralize or destroy each other.

selective i. Interference in which specific wavelengths of light are enhanced or neutralized, producing a considerable variation in light intensity throughout the spectrum.

interferometer (in″ter-fĕr-om′eh-ter). An instrument providing for the adjustable superposition of two coherent beams of light for constructive and destructive interference, and thus useful in measuring wavelength of light, small distances and thicknesses, and optical surface quality.

Burch i. An interferometer used to test large aperture optical systems in which interference is produced by a pair of identical scattering plates of random surface structure, one of which is optically superimposed on the other at the center of curvature of the reflecting surface under test, or at one of the conjugate foci of a system. The image path of one plate suffers wave distortions by reflection or refraction at the test surfaces and recombines to form interference patterns with the undisturbed image path of the other plate.

Dyson i. An instrument used for testing optical systems in which birefringent crystals are used to produce two interfering beams polarized at right angles to each other and subsequently brought into coincidence with a quarter wave plate.

Fabry-Pérot i. An interferometer in which interference fringes are produced in the transmitted light after multiple reflection in the air film between two plane plates thinly silvered on the inner surfaces.

Jamin i. An interferometer for the measurement of the index of refraction of gases which utilizes interference fringes produced by reflection from two plane-parallel plates inclined at a slight angle to each other.

Lummer-Gehrcke i. An instrument used to study spectrum lines in which interference is produced by multiple reflections from a pair of parallel reflecting surfaces at a fixed separation, and where the angles of incidence are large enough to produce total internal reflection, thereby eliminating the need for reflection coatings.

Michelson's i. An interferometer in which light from an extended source is divided into two beams by partial reflection. The two beams travel in different directions and are recombined after reflection from plane mirrors, to form interference fringes.

Rayleigh i. An instrument for the measurement of index of refraction of gases, which uses two interference beams formed by a double slit placed in front of a collimating lens. A reference diffraction pattern from one beam is compared to the lateral shift in the other beam which passes through the gas medium.

Twyman and Green i. A modification of the Michelson interferometer in which the illumination is parallel monochromatic light produced by a point light source at the principal focus of a corrected lens. It is used for testing the perfection of prisms and lenses.

internal rectus (in-ter′nal rek′tus). See under *muscle.*

International Association of Boards of Examiners in Optometry. An association of boards of optometric examiners of the United States and Canada founded in

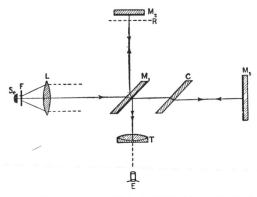

Fig. 25. Michelson's interferometer. (From *Light*, R. W. Ditchburn, Blackie & Son, Ltd., 1953)

1913 as the International Board of Boards and reorganized under the present title in 1919.

international candle. See under *candle.*

International Commission on Illumination. The English translation for *Commission Internationale de l'Eclairage.*

International Optical League. A co-operatively sustained organization representing member organizations of various nationally and regionally recognized groups of optometrists in many countries.

internus (in-ter'nus). Internal rectus muscle.

interocular (in"ter-ok'u-lar). Between the eyes.

interorbital (in"ter-ōr'bih-tal). Between the orbits.

interpalpebral (in"ter-pal'pe-bral). Between the eyelids.

interposition (in"ter-po-zish'un). The position of an object between another object and an observer, or the simulation of this effect in a drawing or a photograph so that contour interference results. Syn., *overlay.*

interpretation, visual. The involvement of meaning in a visually sensed situation.

interpupillary (in"ter-pu'pih-lār-e). Between the pupils.

interpupillary distance (in"ter-pu'-pih-lār-e dis'tans). See *distance, pupillary.*

intersect, sighting. The point of intersection of the lines of sight for various directions of gaze of an eye.

interval. 1. A period of time between two events or between the recurrence of similar states or conditions. 2. A space between objects or things. 3. A range or a gap between different states or qualities.

achromatic i. A range of low degrees of light intensity which produces visual sensation but not color sensation; the range between the absolute threshold for light perception and the threshold for hue. Syn., *colorless interval; photochromatic interval.*

astigmatic i. Interval of Sturm.

class i. In statistics, a range of continuous values considered as being in a single numerical class, e.g., ages 5 to 9 may be in one group, ages 10 to 14 in another, etc.

colorless i. Achromatic interval.

corneal i. The site of the cornea considered as an interruption of the most anterior portion of the scleral tissue. Syn., *anterior scleral foramen; corneal foramen; rima cornealis.*

focal i. 1. Interval of Sturm. 2. The distance from the anterior to the posterior principal focus of a lens or an optical system.

hyperfocal i. The linear distance between the focus of the paraxial rays and the focus of the peripheral rays of a lens or an optical system.

lucid i. of Vogt. The peripheral, clear zone of the cornea, located between the limbus and the circular opacity in arcus senilis.

photochromatic i. Achromatic interval.

Sturm, i. of. The linear distance between the two focal lines of an astigmatic eye or optical system. Syn., *astigmatic interval; focal interval.*

intorsion (in-tōr'shun). 1. The real or apparent turning of the two eyes relative to each other and around their respective anteroposterior axes, so that the upward extensions of their respective vertical meridians of reference converge toward each other. 2. The real or apparent turning of an eye around an anteroposterior axis, so that the upward extension of its vertical meridian of reference rotates nasally from the true vertical.

intort (in-tōrt'). To turn toward a position of intorsion or away from a position of extorsion.

intorter (in'tōr-ter). An extraocular muscle which acts to intort the eye.

intraciliary (in"trah-sil'e-er-e). Within the region of the ciliary body.

intraocular (in"trah-ok'u-lar). Within the eye.

intraocular (in"trah-ok'u-lar) **modification; pressure; tension.** See under the nouns.

intraorbital (in"tra-ōr'bih-tal). Within the orbit.

intraretinal (in"trah-ret'ih-nal). Within the retina.

intrascleral (in"trah-skler'al). Within the sclera.

intravitreous (in"trah-vit're-us). Within the vitreous humor.

invariant, optical (in-va'rih-ant). The product of the index of refraction and the angle between any ray and the normal.

inversion. 1. In an optical image, the reversal of orientation with respect to the conjugate object, i.e., upside down and left to right. 2. In space perception, the reversal of the perceived object with respect to its normal orientation, i.e., upside down and left to right, as when viewed through an inverting optical system. 3. The reversal of written characters, as in mirror writing. 4. The nasalward rotation of the eye.

inversion of the disk. A congenital anomaly in which the retinal vessels emerge from the temporal side of the optic disk and then course nasally.

invisible. 1. Incapable of being seen. 2. Visually indistinguishable from the surrounding field.

iodopsin (i-o-dop'sin). A photosensitive substance considered to be in the retinal cones which subserves photopic vision, as does rhodopsin in the retinal rods for scotopic vision. It has not been isolated from the human retina, but has been extracted from the retina of the chicken.

I.O.L. International Optical League.

ionophose (i'o-no-fōz"). A subjective sensation of violet light.

iontophoresis (i-on"to-fo-re'sis). The introduction of drugs in ionic form into superficial intact tissues by means of a low tension direct electric current. It may be accomplished on the eye by means of a nonconductive spectacle-type frame designed by Erlanger with a two-compartment eyecup, one compartment containing a dry cell and two electrodes and the other the dilute drug solution which contacts the cornea through an absorbent pad. One electrode leads to the drug solution and the other to the side of the head through the earpiece of the frame.

IOP. Intraocular pressure.

ipsilateral (ip"se-lat'er-al). Situated on the same side.

iralgia (i-ral'je-ah). Iridalgia.

iridal (i'rid-al, ir'id-). Pertaining to the iris.

iridalgia (ir"id-al'je-ah, i"rid-). Pain in the iris.

iridallochrosis (ir"ih-dal-o-kro'sis). A pathological change in the color of the iris. *Obs.*

iridauxesis (ir"id-awk-se'sis). A thickening or a swelling of the iris.

iridavulsion (ir"id-ah-vul'shun). Iridoavulsion.

iridectomesodialysis (ir"id-ek"to-me-so-di-al'is-is). A surgical procedure for the formation of an artificial pupil by detaching and excising a portion of the iris at its periphery.

iridectomize (ir"id-ek'to-mīz). To remove a part of the iris by surgery.

iridectomy (ir"ih-dek'to-me). Surgical removal of a part of the iris.

antiphlogistic i. Surgical removal of a part of the iris to reduce intraocular pressure in inflammatory conditions of the eye.

basal i. An iridectomy which includes the root of the iris.

complete i. Sector iridectomy.

optical i. Surgical removal of part of the iris to enlarge the existing pupil, or to form an artificial pupil, when the natural pupil is ineffectual.

peripheral i. Surgical removal of a portion of the iris in the region of its root, leaving the pupillary margin and sphincter pupillae muscle intact.

preliminary (preparatory) i. Surgical removal of part of the iris preceding cataract extraction.

sector i. Surgical removal of a complete radial section of the iris extending from the pupillary margin to the root of the iris. Syn., *complete iridectomy; total iridectomy.*

stenopeic i. Surgical removal of a narrow slit or a minute portion of the iris, leaving the sphincter pupillae muscle intact.

therapeutic i. Surgical removal of a portion of the iris for the cure or prevention of an ocular disease.

total i. Sector iridectomy.

iridectropium (ir″id-ek-tro′pe-um). Eversion of a portion of the iris.

iridelcosis (ir″ih-del′ko-sis). Ulceration of the iris. *Obs.*

iridemia (ir″id-e′me-ah, i″rid-). Hemorrhage from the iris.

iridencleisis (ir″ih-den-kli′sis). A surgical procedure for glaucoma, in which a portion of the iris is incised and incarcerated in a limbal incision.

iridentropium (ir″id-en-tro′pe-um). Inversion of a portion of the iris.

irideremia (ir″id-e-re′me-ah). Congenital absence of all or part of the iris.

irides (ir′id-ēz, i′rid-). The plural of iris.

iridescence (ir″ih-des′ens). The rainbowlike play of colors as in mother-of-pearl or soap bubbles.

iridescent (ir″ih-des′ent). Having or demonstrating iridescence.

iridesis (ir-id′e-sis, ir″ih-de′sis). A surgical procedure in which a portion of the iris is brought through and incarcerated in a corneal incision.

iridic (i-rid′ik, ir-id′-). Pertaining to the iris.

iriditis (ir″ih-di′tis). Iritis.

iridization (ir″id-ih-za′shun). The perception of a rainbow-colored halo around bright lights, in glaucoma.

irido- (ir′id-o, i′rid-do). A combining form denoting the iris.

iridoallochrosis (ir″id-o-al-o-kro′sis). Iridallochrosis.

iridoavulsion (ir″id-o-ah-vul′shun). Complete tearing away of the iris from its peripheral attachments.

iridocapsulitis (ir″id-o-kap″su-li′tis). Inflammation of the iris and the capsule of the crystalline lens.

iridocele (ih-rid′o-sēl, ir′id-o-). Hernial protrusion of a portion of the iris through a wound or ulcer in the cornea.

iridochisma (ir″id-o-kis′mah). Iridoschisis.

iridochoroiditis (ir″id-o-ko″roid-i′-tis). Inflammation of both the iris and the choroid.

iridocinesia (ir″id-o-sin-e′ze-ah). Iridokinesia.

iridocinesis (ir″id-o-sih-ne′sis). Iridokinesia.

iridocoloboma (ir″id-o-kol″o-bo′-mah). Coloboma of the iris.

iridoconstrictor (ir″id-o-con-strik′-tor). 1. Any of the elements of the short ciliary nerve fibers to the sphincter pupillae muscle. 2. Any chemical which causes constriction of the sphincter pupillae muscle. 3. The sphincter pupillae muscle.

iridocorneosclerectomy (ir″id-o-kōr″-ne-o-skler-ek′to-me). The surgical removal of a portion of the iris, the cornea, and the sclera.

iridocyclectomy (ir″id-o-si-klek′to-me). Surgical removal of the iris and the ciliary body.

iridocyclitis (ir″id-o-si-kli′tis, i-rid-o-). Inflammation of the iris and the ciliary body, usually characterized by ciliary flush, exudates into the anterior chamber, deposits on the posterior surface of the cornea and the anterior surface of the crystalline lens capsule, aqueous flare, constricted and sluggish pupil, discoloration of the iris, and the subjective symptoms of radiating pain, photophobia, lacrimation, and interference with vision.

heterochromic i. of Fuchs. Complicated heterochromia.

recidivans purulenta, i. A recurrent iridocyclitis with hypopyon, occurring usually in young adult males in association with systemic infectious diseases. Syn., *hypopyon recidivans; iridocyclitis septica; ophthalmia lenta.*

sarcoidal i. See *sarcoidosis.*

septica, i. Iridocyclitis recidivans purulenta.

syphilitic i. Iridocyclitis occurring in syphilis, especially that characterized by yellowish or pinkish nodules on the iris (roseola of the iris) or by fulminating exudates or hemorrhage.

tubercular i. Iridocyclitis occurring in tuberculosis in either of two forms: (1) the miliary form characterized by the absence of marked vascular engorgement, and the presence of mutton fat keratic precipitates and small nodules (Koeppe's nodules) on the iris; or (2) the conglomerate form characterized by a single, yellowish-gray mass on the ciliary zone of the iris with keratic precipitates.

iridocyclochoroiditis (ir″id-o-si″klo-ko-roid-i′tis). Inflammation of the iris, the ciliary body, and the choroid; uveitis.

iridocystectomy (ir″id-o-sis-tek′to-me). Surgical removal of a portion of the iris to form an artificial pupil.

iridodesis (ir″id-od′e-sis). Iridesis.

iridodiagnosis (ir″id-o-di″ag-no′sis). 1. Diagnosis of systemic disease by the appearance of the iris. 2. Determination of personality traits by examining the structure of the iris.

iridodialysis (ir″id-o-di-al′is-is). A localized separation or tearing away of the iris from its attachment to the ciliary body.

iridodiastasis (ir″id-o-di-as′tah-sis). A colobomatous defect of the iris at its ciliary border.

iridodilator (ir″id-o-di-la′tor). 1. Any of the elements of the sympathetic ciliary nerve fibers innervating the dilator pupillae muscle. 2. Any chemical which causes constriction of the dilator pupillae muscle. 3. The dilator pupillae muscle.

iridodonesis (ir″id-o-do-ne′sis). Tremulousness of the iris, as may occur when the crystalline lens is absent or subluxated.

iridokeratitis (ir″id-o-ker-ah-ti′tis). Inflammation of both the iris and the cornea.

iridokinesia (ir″id-o-kih-ne′ze-ah). The expansion and contraction of the iris, normal or otherwise.

iridokinesis (ir″id-o-kih-ne′sis). Iridokinesia.

iridokinetic (ir″id-o-kih-net′ik). Pertaining to the expansion and contraction of the iris.

iridoleptynsis (ir″id-o-lep-tin′sis). Attenuation or atrophy of the iris.

iridology (ir″ih-dol′o-je). The study of the structure, markings, and color of the iris for the purpose of iridodiagnosis.

iridomalacia (ir″id-o-mah-la′she-ah). Degeneration or softening of the iris as a result of disease.

iridomedialysis (ir″id-o-me-di-al′is-is). Iridomesodialysis.

iridomesodialysis (ir″id-o-me″so-di-al′is-is). The loosening of adhesions of the inner border of the iris.

iridomotor (ir″id-o-mo′tor.) Pertaining to movements of the iris.

iridoncosis (ir″ih-don-ko′sis). Swelling of the iris.

iridoncus (ir″ih-don′kus). Tumefaction of the iris.

iridonesis (ir″ih-don-e′sis). Iridodonesis.

iridoparalysis (ir″id-o-pah-ral′is-is). Paralysis of the iris; iridoplegia.

iridoparelkysis (ir″id-o-par-el′kis-is). An induced prolapse of the iris to displace the pupil artificially.

iridoparesis (ir″id-o-pah-re′sis, -par′-es-is). Partial paralysis of the iris.

iridoperiphakitis (ir″id-o-per″e-fah-ki′tis). Inflammation of the iris and the capsule of the crystalline lens.

iridoplania (ir″id-o-pla′ne-ah). Iridodonesis.

iridoplegia (ir″id-o-ple′je-ah). Partial or total immobility or rigidity of the iris.

    accommodative i. Failure of the sphincter pupillae muscle of the iris to contract in association with accommodation.

    complete i. Total paralysis of the iris; failure of the iris to respond to any stimulation.

    reflex i. Absence of the pupillary light reflex.

    sympathetic i. Failure of the pupil to dilate on irritation of the skin.

    traumatica, i. Paralysis of the iris as a result of trauma.

iridoptosis (ir″id-op-to′sis). Prolapse of the iris.

iridopupillary (ir″id-o-pu′pih-ler″e). Pertaining to the iris and the pupil.

iridorhexis (ir″id-o-rek′sis). 1. Rupture of the iris. 2. The tearing away of the iris from its attachment or from an adhesion.

iridoschisis (ir″id-os′ke-sis). Separation of the anterior layers of the iris from the posterior layers and multiple rupture of the iris fibers. Fibers, which remain attached only at the ciliary body and at the sphincter, bulge forward, and the ends of those torn in two float forward into the aqueous. The posterior layer is usually intact and the sphincter and dilator fibers function normally. It usually occurs in the lower half of the iris in those over 65 years of age, with senile atrophy considered a major cause.

iridoschisma (ir″id-o-skiz′mah). A simple coloboma occurring in the iris in the presence of a normally closed fetal fissure.

iridosclerectomy (ir″id-o-skle-rek′to-me). The surgical removal of a portion of the sclera and of a portion of the iris in the region of the limbus, for the treatment of glaucoma.

iridosclerotomy (ir″id-o-skle-rot′o-me). The surgical puncture of the sclera and the margin of the iris, in glaucoma.

iridoscope (ir″id′o-skōp). A type of ophthalmoscope.

iridosis (ir″ih-do′sis). Iridesis.

iridosteresis (ir″id-o-ste-re′sis). Loss or absence of all or a part of the iris.

iridotasis (ir″ih-dot′ah-sis). A surgical procedure for glaucoma in which the iris is stretched and drawn into a limbal incision, where it is incarcerated.

iridotomy (ir″ih-dot′o-me). An incision into the iris.

    peripheral i. An incision into the ciliary zone of the iris.

    radial i. A meridional incision into the iris.

iridotromos (ir″ih-dot′ro-mos). Iridodonesis.

iridovalosis (ir″id-o-val-o′sis). A condition in which the pupil is oval-shaped.

irin (i′rin). A chemical extracted from iris tissue which, when instilled into the eye, causes marked constriction of the iris which cannot be blocked by atropine or any other similarly acting drug. It is thought to be released by sensory nerve fiber endings in the iris through an axon reflex upon traumatizing the iris or the cornea, or stroking the trigeminal nerve.

irinic (i-rin'ik). Pertaining to or of the iris.

iris (i'ris). The most anterior portion of the uveal tract, consisting of a circular pigmented membrane, perforated to form the pupil, situated between the cornea and the crystalline lens and separating the anterior and posterior chambers. Its anterior surface is divided into two portions, a peripheral ciliary zone extending from its root at the anterior surface of the ciliary body to the collarette, and a pupillary zone extending from the collarette to the pupillary margin. The iris contains the sphincter pupillae muscle in the pupillary zone, which encircles the pupil, and the dilator pupillae muscle, whose fibers extend radially from the region of the sphincter pupillae muscle to the ciliary body. Its layers, anterior to posterior, are endothelium, the anterior border layer (both are absent at the crypts of Fuchs), the stroma, the region of the dilator pupillae muscle, and pigmented epithelium. The blood supply is from the anterior and long posterior ciliary arteries, which anastomose to form the greater arterial circle, from which branches anastomose to form the lesser arterial circle. The nerve supply consists of parasympathetic fibers via the third cranial nerve to the sphincter pupillae muscle, sympathetic fibers to the dilator pupillae muscle, and sensory fibers from the nasociliary branch of the ophthalmic nerve.

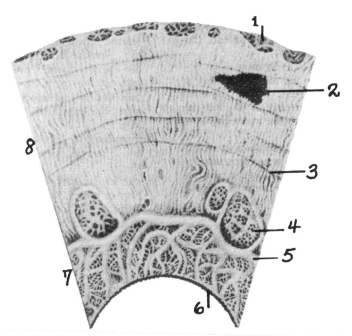

Fig. 26. The anterior surface of the iris. (1) Peripheral crypt. (2) Mole. (3) Contraction furrow. (4) Crypt. (5) Collarette. (6) Pigment frill. (7) Pupillary portion. (8) Ciliary portion. (From *The Anatomy of the Eye and Orbit*, ed. 4, Eugene Wolff, H. K. Lewis & Co., 1955)

bombé, i. A condition in which the iris is bulged forward by the pressure of aqueous humor contained in the posterior chamber by a total posterior synechia.

dehiscence, i. Accessory holes or slits in the iris in addition to the normal pupil.

detached i. An iris which is separated at its root from its junction with the ciliary body. See also *iridodialysis.*

diastasis, i. Small holes in the iris at its ciliary border, similar to that occurring in iridodialysis.

frill, i. The line of junction of the ciliary zone and the pupillary zone of the iris. Syn., *collarette.*

piebald i. An irregularly pigmented iris of spotted appearance. Syn., *variegated iris.*

plateau i. An abnormality of the iris in which its root inserts anteriorly into the ciliary body, lying in close apposition to the trabecular meshwork, with the iris having a less convex bulge than usual, tending to lie in a flat plane as it extends toward the crystalline lens.

prolapse of i. Protrusion of a portion of the iris into a perforating corneal wound. It may form an anterior synechia if the iris remains fixed in the wound by scar tissue.

tremulous i. A condition in which the iris shakes or quivers, usually caused by the absence of the crystalline lens from its normal position. Syn., *iridodonesis.*

umbrella i. Iris bombé.

variegated i. Piebald iris.

irisopsia (i-ris-op′se-ah). A defect of vision in which objects appear to be surrounded by rings of colored light.

iritic (i-rit′ik). Pertaining to or of the iris.

iritis (i-ri′tis). Inflammation of the iris usually characterized by circumcorneal injection (ciliary flush), aqueous flare, keratic precipitates, constricted and sluggish pupil, discoloration of the iris, and the subjective symptoms of radiating pain, photophobia, lacrimation, and interference with vision.

acne rosacea i. Neovascularization and swelling of the iris, especially in its ciliary zone, associated with acne rosacea of the face.

blennorrhagique à rechutes, i. Iritis with recurrent hypopyon.

catamenialis i. Iritis occurring before or during menstruation.

diabetic i. A mild plastic iritis occasionally occurring with diabetes, and sometimes accompanied by hypopyon or hemorrhage into the anterior chamber.

glaucomatosa, i. Increased intraocular pressure occurring in association with iritis or iridocyclitis, usually due to acute hyperemia and obstruction of the drainage channels by the inflammatory products.

gouty i. Iritis occurring with gout, characterized by sudden onset, intense injection of the conjunctiva, aqueous flare, steaminess of the cornea, keratic precipitates, and extreme pain. It is usually preceded by, or associated with, scleritis or episcleritis. Syn., *uratic iritis.*

hemorrhagic i. Iritis characterized by numerous petechial hemorrhages.

herpetic i. Iritis occurring with herpes zoster in either of two forms: (1) plastic iritis; (2) iritis characterized by swollen areas of acute vascular dilatation and hyphema, resulting in white atrophic scars (vitiligo iridis).

nodular i. Iritis due to a focal lesion and characterized by the presence of a nodule or nodules formed by aggregations of cells producing edema and tissue distortion.

obturans of Schieck, i. A low

grade, chronic iritis, occurring with tuberculosis, persisting over a period of years without serious symptoms other than a slight loss of vision.

plastic i. Iritis characterized by plastic exudates into the anterior chamber which consist essentially of fibrinous matter especially prone to the formation of synechiae and keratic precipitates.

purulent i. Iritis characterized by the presence of a pus discharge into the anterior chamber.

rheumatic i. A recurrent iritis associated with rheumatoid arthritis or muscular rheumatism. It is usually acute, with plastic exudates, keratic precipitates, synechiae, and pronounced subjective symptoms.

serous i. Iritis characterized by the presence of a serous discharge into the anterior chamber.

spongy i. Iritis characterized by the presence of a spongy mass of fibrinous exudates in the anterior chamber.

sympathetic i. See *sympathetic ophthalmitis.*

syphilitic i. See *syphilitic iridocyclitis.*

tubercular i. See *tubercular iridocyclitis.*

uratic i. Gouty iritis.

urica, i. Gouty iritis.

iritoectomy (ir″ih-to-ek′to-me, i-rih-to-). Surgical removal of the iritic deposits of aftercataract, together with a part of the iris, to form an artificial pupil.

iritomy (ir-it′o-me, i-rit′o-). Iridotomy.

irotomy (i-rot′o-me). Iridotomy.

irradiance (ir-ra′de-ans). Radiant flux incident per unit area, measured in watts per sq. cm. or per sq. m.

irradiation (ir-ra″de-a′shun). 1. The impact of radiant energy on a receiver. 2. A phenomenon in which bright areas or objects appear enlarged against a dark background, as demonstrated in the overestimation of the size of stars, incandescent cinders, narrow illuminated slits, and white objects on a black background, or the apparent displacement of a straight edge held in front of a bright light. 3. Exposure to or application of x-rays, radium rays, or other radiation, as for therapeutic purposes. 4. The dispersion of a nervous impulse beyond the immediate or normal path of conduction. 5. The spreading of light by reflections from particle to particle in a photographic emulsion, causing the developed image to be larger and more diffuse at the edges than the optical image. 6. Emission of a supposed influence or an immaterial fluid from the eyes. *Obs.*

irritation, sympathetic. Irritation of an organ secondary to irritation of its fellow, as in sympathetic ophthalmitis.

Irvine's method; syndrome; prism displacement test. See under the nouns.

I.S.C.C. Inter-Society Color Council.

ischemia of retina (is-ke′me-ah). A very pronounced anemia of the retina which may occur after profuse hemorrhage from any part of the body. A fixed, dilated pupil accompanies the condition, although the ophthalmoscopic picture varies.

iseiconia (īs″ih-ko′ne-ah). Iseikonia.

iseiconic (īs-ih-kon′ik). Iseikonic.

iseikonia (īs″ih-ko′ne-ah). A condition in which the size and the shape of the ocular images of the two eyes are equal.

iseikonic (īs-ih-kon′ik). Pertaining to or of the condition of iseikonia.

Ishihara (ish-e-hah′rah) **charts; plates; test.** See under the nouns.

isoametropia (i″so-am-e-tro′pe-ah). Ametropia in which the refractive error is similar in the two eyes. Cf. *anisometropia.*

isochromatic (i″so-kro-mat′ik). Possessing the same color throughout. Syn., *isochroous.*

isochroous (i-sok′ro-us). Isochromatic.

isochromes (i′so-krōmz). In the Ostwald color system, a series of surface color samples of approximately equal dominant wavelength and nearly constant purity, varying in luminous reflectance only, and arranged vertically in the Ostwald triangle parallel to the gray series. Syn., *shadow series.*

isoclinal (i″so-kli′nal). Isoclinic.

isoclinics (i″so-klin′iks). 1. Lines of equal inclination. Cf. *isotorsional lines.* Syn., *isoclinals.* 2. The lines of zero intensity, representing zero transmitted light, as may be observed in the examining of a material with a polariscope.

isocoria (i″so-ko′re-ah). Equality in size of the two pupils.

iso-**cyanopsin** (i″so-si-an-op′sin). A photosensitive pigment with λ max at 575 mμ, formed from the reaction of cis_2 retinene$_2$ with chicken cone opsin.

iso-iconia (i″so-i-ko′ne-ah). Iseikonia.

iso-ikonia (i″so-i-ko′ne-ah). Iseikonia.

iso-indicial (i″so-in-dish′al). Having the same index of refraction.

iso-**iodopsin** (i″so-i-o-dop′sin). A photosensitive pigment with λ max at 515 mμ, formed from the reaction of *iso-a* retinene$_1$ with chicken cone opsin.

isometropia (i″so-me-tro′pe-ah). Equal refractive states of kind and degree in the two eyes.

isomorphism (i″so-mōr′fizm). In gestalt psychology, the presumed or implied similarity of organization or pattern of conscious content, such as visual perception, and the simultaneously present cerebral cortex activity.

isophoria (i″so-fo′re-ah). 1. Lack of variation in phoria or muscular imbalance, with changes in the direction of gaze. Cf. *anisophoria.* 2. Vertical orthophoria.

isopia (i-so′pe-ah). Equality of visual acuity in the two eyes.

isoplanasie (i″so-plān′ah-se). Isoplanatism.

isoplanatism (i″so-plan′ah-tizm). The condition of an optical system free of spherical aberration and coma. Syn., *isoplanasie condition.*

iso-**porphyropsin** (i″so-por″fih-rop′-sin). An iso-pigment with maximum absorption at 507 mμ, obtained, by incubation with opsin, from the cis_2 fraction of a mixture of retinene$_2$ isomers.

isopter (i-sop′ter). In visual fields, a contour line representing the limits of retinal sensitivity to a specific test target, usually designated by a fraction, the denominator of which represents the testing distance and the numerator the diameter of the test target.

iso-**retinene**$_1$ (i″so-ret′ih-nēn). Either of two of the isomers of retinene$_1$ known as *iso-a* and *iso-b.*

iso-**rhodopsin** (i″so-ro-dop′sin). 1. An isomeric photosensitive pigment resulting from a combina- of *iso-a* retinene$_1$ with scotopsin having λ max at 487 mμ. 2. Regenerated rhodopsin derived from *neo-b*-retinene$_1$ and scotopsin.

isoscope (i′so-skōp). An apparatus for observing the effects of ocular torsional movements and cyclophoria subjectively, by comparison of the orientation of two parallel wires seen by one eye to a single wire seen by the other.

isotints (i′so-tints). In the Ostwald color system, the series of semichromes of constant white content.

isotones (i′so-tōnz). In the Ostwald color system, the series of semichromes of constant black content.

isotropic (i″so-trop-ik). Having uniform properties of refraction, or of radiation of light, in all directions.

Ivanoff's theory (i-van′ofs). See under *theory*.

Ives' colorimeter; gratings; test; theory. See under the nouns.

Iwanoff's edema (e-wan′ofs). Cystic degeneration of the retina.

J

J. 1. Symbol for *radiant intensity.* 2. Abbreviation for *Jaeger.*

Jackson's (jak'sunz) **crossed cylinder lens; test.** See under the nouns.

Jacob's (ja'kubz) **membrane; ulcer.** See under the nouns.

Jacobson's retinitis (ja'kub-sunz). Diffuse syphilitic neuroretinitis.

Jacod's triad (ja'kodz). See under *triad.*

Jaeger (ya'ger) **chart; ocular micrometer; test type.** See under the nouns.

Jahnke's syndrome (yahn'kēz). See under *syndrome.*

James's waterfall (jāmz'ez). See under *waterfall.*

Jamieson's occluder (ja'mih-sunz). See under *occluder.*

Jamin (zhah-min') **interferometer; refractometer.** See under the nouns.

Jansky-Bielschowsky disease (yan'-ske-be-el-show'ske). See under *disease.*

Jastrow visual illusion (jas'tro). See under *illusion, visual.*

Javal's (zhah-valz') **grid; method; rule; stereoscope; theory.** See under the nouns.

jaw-winking. An abnormal associated movement of the eyelid and the jaw in which a ptosed eyelid raises when the jaw is opened or is moved laterally. Syn., *Gunn's jaw-winking phenomenon; Marcus Gunn phenomenon; Gunn's jaw-winking sign; pterygoid-levator synkinesis; Gunn's jaw-winking syndrome.*

reverse j. An abnormal associated movement of the eyelid and the jaw in which a partially ptosed eyelid droops farther when the jaw is opened or moved laterally. Syn., *inverse jaw-winking phenomenon; reversed Marcus Gunn phenomenon; Marin Amat syndrome.*

Jellinek's sign (yel'in-eks). See under *sign.*

Jendrassik's sign (yen-drah'siks). See under *sign.*

Jenning's test (jen'ingz). See under *test.*

Jensen's (yen'senz) **choroiditis; disease; retinitis.** See under the nouns.

j.n.d. Just noticeable difference.

Joffroy's sign (zhof-rwahz'). See under *sign.*

judgment, absolute. Judgment of the magnitude or quality of a stimulus without reference to a comparison standard.

jugum sphenoidale (ju'gum sfe"noi-dal'e). The junction of the great and small wings of the sphenoid bone.

Judd criterion. See under *criterion.*

Juler scotometer (yu'ler). See under *scotometer.*

jump, prismatic. The apparent displacement of an object occurring in the transition of view across the borderline between the two lens powers of a bifocal or when the object is viewed alternately with and without a prism.

jump duction. See under *duction.*

junction, sclerocorneal. The union of the cornea and the sclera in the region of the limbus.

Jungschaffer contact lens (yung'-sha-fer). See under *lens, contact.*

just noticeable difference. The smallest difference between two stimuli that for a given individual gives rise to a perceived difference in sensation. Abbreviation *j.n.d.* Syn., *differential limen; differential threshold.*

K

K. Symbol for the central corneal curvature of longest radius, as measured by a keratometer.

Kagenaar prism (kag'en-ahr). See under *prism*.

kaleidoscope (kah-li'do-skōp). 1. A viewing instrument consisting of a pair of long plane mirrors, usually mounted inside a long tube at an angle of about 60° to each other, so that small colored beads or fragments loosely confined between two transparent plates at one end of the tube can be viewed through an opening at the other end as a striking, complex, symmetric pattern produced by multiple reflection in the mirrors and endlessly variegated in design by the rotation of the tube rearranging the beads or fragments. 2. A visual training instrument employing the kaleidoscopic principle or presenting kaleidoscopically produced views.

Kalischer's (kah'lish-erz) **disease; syndrome.** See under the nouns.

kalopsia (kal-op'se-ah). The perceptional attribution of beauty to anything seen.

Kalt's contact lens (kaltz). See under *lens, contact*.

Kant's theory (kahnts, kants). See *nativism*.

Kaposi's disease (ka-po'sēz). Xeroderma pigmentosum.

kappa (κ). The Greek letter used as the symbol for (1) *angle kappa;* (2) *angle of meridional direction*.

kataphoria (kat''ah-fo're-ah). Cataphoria.

katatropia (kat''ah-tro'pe-ah). Catatropia.

katophoria (kat''o-fo're-ah). Cataphoria.

katotropia (kat''o-tro'pe-ah). Catatropia.

Kayser's disease (ki'zerz). See under *disease*.

Kayser-Fleischer (ki'zer-flīsh'er) **ring; sign.** See under the nouns.

Kehrer's reflex (ker'erz). The aural blinking reflex.

Keiner's theory (ki'nerz). See under *theory*.

Keith's theory (kēthz). See under *theory*.

Kellner eyepiece (kel'ner). See under *eyepiece*.

Kelvin scale (kel'vin). See under *scale*.

Kennedy's syndrome (ken'eh-dēz). See under *syndrome*.

Kepler telescope (kep'ler). See under *telescope*.

keratalgia (ker''ah-tal'je-ah). Pain in the cornea.

keratectasia (ker''ah-tek-ta'ze-ah). A protrusion or forward bulging of the cornea due to pathological thinning or weakening of the corneal tissue. It differs from a corneal staphyloma in that it does not contain adherent uveal tissue. Syn., *kerectasis*.

keratectomy (ker''ah-tek'to-me). Surgical removal of a portion of the cornea. Syn., *kerectomy*.

keratic (ker-at'ik). 1. Pertaining to horny tissue. 2. Pertaining to or of the cornea.

keratic precipitates (ker-at'ik pre-sip'ih-tāts). See under *precipitates*.

keratitis (ker″ah-ti′tis). Inflammation of the cornea usually characterized by loss of transparency and dullness, due to cellular infiltration and vascularization from enlargement of limbal and anterior ciliary vessels. Keratitis is accompanied by circumcorneal injection, conjunctivitis, and the subjective symptoms of pain, lacrimation, photophobia, blepharospasm, and reduction of vision. If severe, ulceration and suppuration may result, and the iris and the ciliary body may become involved.

a frigore, k. Keratitis from exposure to cold.

acne rosacea k. Rosacea keratitis.

actinic k. Keratitis due to exposure to ultraviolet light.

alphabet k. Striate keratitis.

annular k. Keratitis in which plastic exudates are deposited on the posterior corneal surface in the form of a hazy ring, with the center and the periphery of the cornea relatively free, as may occur in syphilitic interstitial keratitis. Syn., *keratitis parenchymatosa annularis.*

arborescens, k. Dendritic keratitis.

artificial silk k. Keratitis occurring among workers in the artificial silk industry.

aspergillus k. Keratitis due to infection with the *Aspergillus* fungus and characterized by a corneal ulcer with a dull, dry surface, surrounded by a yellow line of demarcation. It may be accompanied by hypopyon and the ulcer may perforate.

band k. Band keratopathy.

bullous k. Bullous keratopathy.

catarrhal ulcerative k. A relatively benign ulceration of the cornea, usually near the limbus, which may occur secondarily to conjunctivitis, or in elderly or debilitated persons.

deep k. Interstitial keratitis.

deep pustular k. A dense suppu-

rative infiltration of the deeper corneal layers due to tuberculosis or syphilis, with an associated hypopyon, iritis, and periorbital pain, presumed to be due to an actual lodgment in the eye of the tubercle bacilli or of the treponema. Syn., *keratitis pustuliformis profunda.*

dendritic k. A form of herpetic keratitis characterized by the formation of small vesicles, which break down and coalesce to form recurring dendritic ulcers, characteristically irregular, linear, branching, and ending in knoblike extremities. Syn., *keratitis arborescens; furrow keratitis.*

desiccation k. Keratitis e lagophthalmo.

disciform k. A deep, localized, subacute, nonsuppurative keratitis, generally chronic and benign, characterized by a central discoid opacity and due to a virus infection or occurring as a sequel to trauma.

e lagophthalmo, k. Keratitis due to exposure and drying of the cornea from incomplete closure of the eyelids, characterized by a haziness and desiccation of the corneal epithelium which may result in fissures, exfoliation, and keratinization. Syn., *desiccation keratitis; exposure keratitis; lagophthalmic keratitis.*

electrica, k. A superficial punctate keratitis caused by exposure to an intense electric spark.

epithelial diffuse k. A rare, bilateral, superficial, punctate keratitis, usually associated with uveitis, and possibly vitamin B_2 deficiency, characterized by multiple, minute, epithelial flecks without vesiculation. Syn., *diffuse superficial keratitis.*

epithelial punctate k. Superficial punctate keratitis of Fuchs. See under *punctate keratitis.*

epithelialis marmorata, k. A rare, bilateral, mosaiclike, chronic, superficial, punctate keratitis involving the lower half of the corneal epithelium in the deep layers above Bowman's membrane. Vacuoles are present in the epithelium, and the surface layers are broken.

epithelialis vernalis, k. A corneal dystrophy, presumably due to disturbances of corneal nutrition, secondary to vernal conjunctivitis, in which dustlike, discrete, epithelial opacities develop, accompanied by edema and cystic subepithelial spaces. An extensive epithelial necrosis is found microscopically, and a peripheral degeneration in the interstitial tissue may also be present, causing an opaque white band resembling an arcus senilis.

epithelialis vesiculosa disseminata, k. A chronic, usually recurrent, form of punctate keratitis characterized by a relatively small number of opacities primarily in the area of the palpebral fissure, without vascularization. The superficial stroma is often infiltrated, although the condition is essentially epithelial.

exfoliative k. A corneal, epithelial denudation accompanied by corneal ulcers and degenerative interstitial keratitis, as may occur in a toxic, hypersensitive reaction to arsenic.

exposure k. Keratitis e lagophthalmo.

fascicular k. An inflammatory process secondary to phlyctenular keratitis, in which a limbal phlycten ulcerates and wanders toward the corneal apex, the periphery of the ulcer healing while the central margin remains active. A narrow band of neovascularization, extending from the limbus, follows in the furrow of the centrally advancing ulcer. The condition remains superficial, without perforation, and terminates in a linear opacity.

filamentary k. A corneal condition characterized by the occurrence of fine epithelial filaments, attached at one end to the cornea and having a bulbous extremity. It may occur idiopathically, following abrasions, in glaucoma, keratitis sicca, herpes, edema of the cornea, etc. Syn., *keratitis filiformis.*

filiformis, k. Filamentary keratitis.

furrow k. Dendritic keratitis.

herpetic k. 1. In herpes simplex: a superficial, epithelial, virus infection of the cornea characterized by the presence of groups of small vesicles which may break down and coalesce to form dendritic ulcers (dendritic keratitis). 2. In herpes zoster ophthalmicus: lesions in the subepithelial layers of the cornea, composed of minute dot opacities, which group together into large, well-defined, round areas. Usually epithelial vesicles appear over them, which may result in ulcers and secondary infection.

herpetic k., filamentary (superficial). A rare form of filamentary keratitis due to the herpes virus.

herpetic k., geographic. The late stage of superficial herpetic keratitis characterized by loss of epithelium between the branches of a dendritic ulcer, resulting in an irregularly shaped, sharply demarcated geographic ulcer.

herpetic k., punctate (superficial). Superficial punctate keratitis due to the herpes virus. See also *herpetic keratitis.*

herpetic k., striate (superficial). A rare form of herpetic keratitis characterized by numerous, minute, punctate opacities in linear formation.

herpetic k., vesicular (superficial). Vesicular keratitis due to the herpes virus.

hypopyon k. A purulent keratitis with accompanying hypopyon, as may result from a virulent corneal ulcer accompanied by quantities of leukocytes and fibrin which gravitate to the bottom of the anterior chamber to form the hypopyon.

infectious k. An acute, subacute, or chronic infectious keratoconjunctivitis of livestock. Syn., *pink eye; infectious ophthalmia.*

interstitial k. Any deep corneal inflammation primarily involving the substantia propria. See also *syphilitic keratitis.* Syn., *deep keratitis; parenchymatous keratitis.*

lagophthalmic k. Keratitis e lagophthalmo.

lattice k. Latticelike corneal dystrophy.

leprotic k. Keratitis associated with leprosy and occurring in three forms: keratitis punctata leprosa, leprotic pannus, and interstitial keratitis.

linearis migrans, k. A condition of obscure etiology in which a line of granular opacity slowly migrates from one portion of the cornea to another, as from limbus to limbus, from one layer to another, or both.

lipid k. Lipid keratopathy.

macular k. Superficial punctate keratitis of Fuchs. See under *punctate keratitis.*

marginalis miliaris, k. Keratitis characterized by a sudden onset of minute, subepithelial infiltrations which tend to occur in groups and seldom ulcerate.

marginalis profunda, k. An interstitial keratitis occurring rarely in elderly persons as a yellowish or gray infiltration, 1 to 2 mm. wide, continuous with the sclera, and usually in the superior cornea, although it may form a complete ring.

metaherpetica, k. A corneal ulceration which may follow the primary healing of a dendritic ulcer, consisting of single or confluent round ulcers of the epithelium and accompanied by slight congestion and pain.

mycotic k. Inflammation of the cornea caused by a fungus infection.

neuroparalytic k. A stippled and edematous corneal inflammation accompanied by conjunctival hyperemia and iritis and followed by vesiculation. It is marked by epithelial exfoliation, due to abnormal epithelial metabolism and inability to resist trauma, desiccation, and infection following loss of sensory nerve control in Vth nerve lesions. Syn., *neuroparalytic ophthalmia.*

neurotrophic k. Keratitis due to loss of sensory nerve supply to the cornea and the consequent loss of trophic influence.

nummular k. A slowly developing, benign keratitis characterized by disk-shaped infiltrates in the superficial substantia propria. It occurs mainly among young land workers, is usually unilateral, and the surface epithelium over the opacities eventually sinks, forming a pathognomonic, faceted depression. Ulceration is rare, but vascularization is common.

oyster-shuckers' k. A suppurative keratitis produced by pieces of oyster shell embedded in the cornea.

parenchymatosa annularis, k. Annular keratitis.

parenchymatous k. Interstitial keratitis.

petrificans, k. Band keratopathy.

peripheral furrow k. Peripheral corneal ectasia.

phlyctenular k. A primary corneal inflammation, or one secondary to phlyctenular conjunctivitis, in which gray nodules (phlyctens) occur on the corneal surface near the limbus. The epithelium may break down to form shallow ulcers, which may heal without opacification, or the ulcers may migrate centrally to form a fascicular keratitis. Syn., *scrofulous keratitis.*

profunda, k. An interstitial keratitis, usually unilateral, affecting adults, and associated with anterior uveitis. In the early stages, the cornea is edematous and stippled, and a deep interstitial haze develops. Keratic precipitates occur frequently, and deep vascularization is usually minimal. Etiology may be varied, but it is probably an allergic reaction to some mild, chronic infection.

punctata leprosa, k. The most common form of leprotic keratitis, consisting of scattered, irregular, minute, white spots in the substantia propria, extending downward from the superior margin of the cornea gradually to cover its upper half, the area involved being wedge-shaped in section with the base upward.

punctata profunda, k. Deep punctate keratitis.

punctata superficialis, k. Superficial punctate keratitis.

punctate k., deep. Keratitis which may occur with acquired or hereditary syphilitic iritis, characterized by small, sharply defined, punctate opacities in an otherwise clear cornea. There is no accompanying irritation or vascularization, and the opacities may quickly appear and disappear. Syn., *keratitis punctata profunda.*

punctate k., superficial. A group of corneal, inflammatory diseases characterized by discrete opacities in the superficial corneal layers.

punctate k., superficial (of Fuchs). An acute keratitis characterized by the appearance of small, sharply defined, punctiform infiltrates on either side of Bowman's membrane. No vesicles are present. It usually commences as a catarrhal conjunctivitis, is frequently associated with a respiratory infection, and may be of viral, bacterial, neurotrophic, or parasitic etiology. A similar condition may develop after ultraviolet light exposure. Syn., *epithelial punctate keratitis; macular keratitis; keratitis subepithelialis.*

pustuliformis profunda, k. Deep pustular keratitis.

reapers' k. A suppurative, corneal inflammation following wound of the cornea by a particle of grain.

reticular k. Latticelike corneal dystrophy.

rosacea k. The corneal involvement in ocular acne rosacea characterized initially by a superficial, marginal, loop-type vascularization in a zone of gray infiltration and followed by subepithelial infiltrates which at first are small, round or oval, delimited areas near the limbus and later become larger, less defined, and progress toward the center of the cornea. Ulceration may occur.

sclerosing k. Keratitis secondary to scleritis, characterized by hyperplasia and opacification of the substantia propria of the cornea.

scrofulous k. Phlyctenular keratitis

serpiginous k. A diffuse keratitis characterized by a disk-shaped ulcer with a tendency to travel in one direction in a serpentlike manner, associated with iridocyclitis, hypopyon, and posterior corneal abscess, and due to infection by the pneumococcus.

sicca, k. A chronic keratitis resulting from insufficient lacrimal secretion, characterized by punctate or linear opacities in the deeper layers of the cornea, mainly in its inferior portion, and usually associated with epithelial filaments and a slight viscid secretion. See also *keratoconjunctivitis sicca.*

stellate k. A form of dendritic keratitis characterized by a rosette or a star-shaped ulcer.

striate k. Any keratitis in which localized radial or intersecting linear formations are found in or on the cornea. Syn., *alphabet keratitis.*

subepithelialis, k. Superficial punctate keratitis of Fuchs. See under *punctate keratitis.*

superficial k. Keratitis primarily involving the superficial layers of the cornea.

　supercial k., diffuse. Epithelial diffuse keratitis.

　superficial k., disseminated. A type of superficial punctate keratitis, in which there are numerous widely scattered opacities.

　superficial k., linear. A keratitis associated with low intraocular pressure and characterized by folds in Bowman's membrane, the concavities of which are filled with fibrous tissue without vascularization. The lesion forms a linear pattern of gray ridges on the corneal surface, and nodes are found along the course of the ridges.

syphilitic k. 1. Interstitial keratitis due to inherited syphilis characterized by an early, localized, grayish infiltrate in the deep layers and by bedewing of the corneal epithelium. The infiltrate spreads to fill the entire stroma, deep brushlike vascularization appears, giving rise to yellowish-red discolorations (salmon patches), following which the cornea clears and vision improves, with the remnants of the vascularization remaining in the deep layers. It is usually bilateral, occurs between the ages of 5 and 15, and is part of a syndrome consisting of impaired hearing, notched teeth, saddle bridge nose, and rhagades at the corners of the mouth. 2. Interstitial keratitis, usually unilateral and affecting adults, due to acquired syphilis similar to the inherited

form but milder and much rarer.

trachomatous k. Keratitis appearing in trachoma, characterized by an early, avascular, superficial inflammation and later by vascular changes at the limbus, which result in the formation of a trachomatous pannus.

trophic k. Keratitis due to disturbance of the sensory nerve supply to the cornea, as may occur in neuroparalytic keratitis.

urica, k. An extremely rare, corneal dystrophy in which the corneal stroma becomes infiltrated with crystalline deposits of urea and sodium urate. A yellow opacity forms near the limbus and progresses centrally. Isolated punctate opacities may also be present. Syn., *dystrophia uratica corneae; dystrophia urica.*

varicellar k. A vesicular corneal inflammation frequently resulting in ulceration and interstitial inflammation, due to ocular involvement in chicken pox.

vasculonebulous k. Pannus.

vesicular k. Keratitis characterized by the development of small epithelial vesicles. It is generally neurotrophic in origin, but may occur in blind degenerated eyes or may result from inflammation or trauma.

　vesicular k., diffuse. A neurotrophic disturbance of the cornea resulting in epithelial vesiculation in the absence of concurrent inflammation or high intraocular pressure.

vesicularis neuralgica, k. A recurring, corneal vesiculation with exfoliation of the epithelium, frequently of traumatic origin.

xerotic, k. A corneal degeneration characterized by a dry, lusterless appearance of the cornea, due to deficient or disturbed metabolism. It may follow a debilitating disease or result from malnutrition with vitamin A deficiency, and usually develops into keratomalacia.

zonular k. Band keratopathy.

kerato- (ker'ah-to-). A combining form denoting the cornea.

keratocele (ker'ah-to-sēl). Hernia of Descemet's membrane of the cornea. Syn., *descemetocele; keratodermatocele.*

keratocentesis (ker"ah-to-sen-te'sis). Puncture of the cornea.

keratochromatosis (ker"ah-to-kro"-mah-to'sis). Discoloration of the cornea.

keratoconjunctivitis (ker"ah-to-konjunk"tih-vi'tis). Inflammation involving both the cornea and the conjunctiva. See also *conjunctivitis; keratitis.*

   eczematous k. Phlyctenular keratoconjunctivitis.

   epidemic k. An acute keratoconjunctivitis, highly contagious, characterized by edema of the eyelids and the conjunctiva, subepithelial corneal infiltration, petechial hemorrhages, hyperemia, and involvement of the regional lymph nodes, considered to be due to a virus. Syn., *shipyard conjunctivitis; Sanders' disease; shipyard keratoconjunctivitis; Sanders' syndrome; Sanders-Hogan syndrome.*

   garlandiform k. Keratitis characterized by wreathlike intraepithelial infiltrates within the palpebral fissure. It is considered to be of virus origin, is usually bilateral, and clears without leaving corneal scars.

   lymphatic k. Phlyctenular keratoconjunctivitis.

   phlyctenular k. Keratoconjunctivitis characterized by the appearance of small gray nodules (phlyctens) on the conjunctiva, the limbus, and the cornea. See also *phlyctenular conjunctivitis; phlyctenular keratitis.* Syn., *eczematous keratoconjunctivitis; lymphatic keratoconjunctivitis; scrofulous keratoconjunctivitis.*

   rosacea k. Acne rosacea involving both conjunctiva and cornea. See *acne rosacea conjunctivitis* and *rosacea keratitis.*

   scrofulous k. Phlyctenular keratoconjunctivitis.

   shipyard k. Epidemic keratoconjunctivitis.

   sicca, k. Keratoconjunctivitis characterized by insufficient lacrimal secretion, keratinization of the superficial epithelial cells, signs of chronic catarrhal conjunctivitis with dry mucoid secretion, and punctate or linear opacities of the cornea. Associated with the eye symptoms may be generalized dryness of the skin and of various mucous and synovial membranes, particularly the mucous membranes of the mouth. See also *keratitis sicca; Sjögren's syndrome.*

keratoconometer (ker"ah-to-ko-nom'-eh-ter). An instrument for determining the degree or condition of keratoconus.

keratoconus (ker"ah-to-ko'nus). A developmental or dystrophic deformity of the cornea in which it becomes cone-shaped, due to a thinning and stretching of the tissue in its central area. It usually manifests itself during puberty, is usually bilateral, and is more common in women than men. Syn., *conical cornea.*

   posticus, k. A rare deformity of the cornea in which the curvature of its posterior surface increases while the curvature of its anterior surface remains normal. The central area thus becomes abnormally thinner than the peripheral area.

     posticus circumscriptus, k. A localized keratoconus posticus.

     posticus totalis, k. Keratoconus posticus involving the entire posterior surface of the cornea.

keratocyte (ker'ah-to-sīt"). Corneal corpuscle.

keratodermatocele (ker″ah-to-der-mat′o-sēl). Keratocele.

keratoectasia (ker″ah-to-ek-ta′se-ah). Kerectasis.

keratoglobus (ker″ah-to-glo′bus). A bilateral developmental anomaly in which the cornea is greatly enlarged and protruded, intraocular pressure being normal. Syn., *cornea globosa; keratomegalia; megalocornea; anterior megalophthalmus.*

keratohelcosis (ker″ah-to-hel-ko′sis). Ulceration of the cornea.

keratohemia (ker″ah-to-he′me-ah). Blood deposits in the cornea.

keratoiditis (ker″ah-toid-i′tis). Inflammation of the cornea; keratitis.

kerato-iridocyclitis (ker″ah-to-ir″id-o-si-kli′tis). Inflammation involving the cornea, the iris, and the ciliary body.

kerato-iridoscope (ker″ah-to-ih-rid′-o-skōp, ker″ah-toir′id-). A microscope for examining the cornea and the iris.

kerato-iritis (ker″ah-to-i-ri′tis, ker″-ah-to-ih-ri′-). Inflammation involving both the cornea and the iris.

keratokeras (ker′ah-to-ker″as). A rare tumor of the cornea due to extreme epidermalization of the epithelium.

keratoleptynsis (ker″ah-to-lep-tin′-sis). A surgical procedure in which the anterior surface of the cornea is removed and replaced by bulbar conjunctiva for cosmetic reasons.

keratoleukoma (ker″ah-to-lu-ko′-mah). A dense white opacity of the cornea.

keratomalacia (ker″ah-to-mah-la′she-ah). A corneal degeneration characterized by early loss of luster, dryness, and reduced sensitivity, and later by infiltration, opacification, pannus, exfoliation of the epithelium, necrosis, ulceration, and often perforation, with an absence of inflammatory reaction. There is an accompanying xerosis epithelialis of the conjunctiva and usually degenerative changes in medullated nerves. It is part of a general systemic condition of deficient or disturbed metabolism following debilitating disease or resulting from malnutrition with vitamin A deficiency.

keratomegalia (ker″ah-to-meg-al′e-ah). Keratoglobus.

keratomeninx (ker″ah-to-me′ninks). The cornea. *Obs.*

keratometer (ker″ah-tom′eh-ter). An instrument for measuring the anterior curvatures of the cornea, consisting of a luminous pattern of mires whose images, produced by reflection on the cornea, are viewed through a telescope with which is combined a doubling and image-size measuring system. Syn., *ophthalmometer.*

keratometry (ker″ah-tom′eh-tre). Measurement of the anterior curvatures of the cornea with a keratometer. Syn., *ophthalmometry.*

keratomileusis (ker″ah-to-mih-lu′-sis). A surgical procedure for the reduction or elimination of myopia in which a thin segment of the cornea, sliced off with a microkeratome, is frozen, tooled with a lathe to alter its curvature, replaced on the cornea, and held in place by a contact lens temporarily sutured to the cornea.

keratomycosis (ker″ah-to-mi-ko′sis). A fungus infection of the cornea.

keratonosus (ker-ah-ton′o-sus). Any degenerative disease of the cornea.

keratonyxis (ker″ah-to-nik′sis). Surgical puncture of the cornea, especially in needling for soft cataract.

keratopathy (ker″ah-top′ah-the). 1. A morbid condition or disease of the cornea. 2. A noninflammatory disease of the cornea, as distinguished from *keratitis.* For types of, see *corneal dystrophy* and *keratitis*.

band k. A degenerative disorder of the cornea characterized by the slow development of a horizontal, gray, band-shaped opacity in the intrapalpebral part of the cornea, first appearing as a slight turbidity at the level of Bowman's membrane in which are small, dark, round, pathognomomic holes. The most common form is secondary to iridocyclitis, a less common form is primary and occurs in the apparently normal eyes of the elderly, and the rarest form occurs in children, most of whom have rheumatism associated with chronic iritis. It may also follow trauma due to exposure to irritants. Syn., *band-shaped corneal dystrophy; keratitis petrificans; zonular keratopathy*.

bullous k. A degenerative condition of the cornea characterized by the formation of recurring epithelial blebs or bullae, usually in the central area, which burst after a few days. It represents the advanced stage of a severe and prolonged epithelial edema consequent to ocular disease, such as glaucoma, iridocyclitis, or Fuchs's epithelial dystrophy.

lipid k. Any of several corneal diseases in which lipoid deposits are found in the cornea.

superficial polymorphic k. A degenerative change of the corneal epithelium occurring in advanced stages of starvation, characterized by hypesthesia of the cornea, variously shaped areas of granulation which may project above the corneal surface, and ulceration.

zonular k. Band keratopathy.

keratophakia (ker″ah-to-fa′ke-ah). A surgical procedure for the reduction or elimination of hypermetropia in which a suitably curved

lens is made from the tissue of a donor's cornea and implanted interlamellarly into the recipient's cornea.

keratoplasty (ker′ah-to-plas″te). Corneal grafting or plastic surgery of the cornea.

acrylic k. Keratoplasty in which a plastic lens is implanted in lieu of a tissue graft.

autogenous k. Autokeratoplasty.

circumscribed k. Partial keratoplasty.

lamellar k. A surgical procedure in which a section of superficial layer of an opaque cornea is removed and replaced by healthy corneal tissue.

optic k. Corneal transplantation for the purpose of improving vision.

partial k. A surgical procedure in which only a portion of the cornea is removed and replaced by healthy corneal tissue, forming a window. Cf. *total keratoplasty*. Syn., *circumscribed keratoplasty*.

penetrating k. A surgical procedure in which a section of the entire thickness of an opaque cornea is removed and replaced by transparent cornea.

refractive k. A surgical procedure for the reduction or elimination of ametropia in which a superficial layer of the central cornea is removed, mechanically reshaped to a desired curvature, and replaced.

rotating k. A surgical procedure in which a section of corneal tissue is removed, rotated so that transparent tissue is in the pupillary area with the opaque portion peripheral, and reinserted.

step k. A surgical procedure involving both lamellar and penetrating keratoplasty in which the central section of the graft involves the entire corneal thickness and is smaller in diameter than the superficial lamellar portion.

tectonic k. Corneal transplantation solely to replace lost tissue.

total k. A surgical procedure consisting of transplantation of the entire cornea, including some of the surrounding conjunctiva.

two-level k. Keratoplasty in which the graft has a different diameter for the anterior layer from that for the posterior layer.

keratopographometry (ker″ah-to-po″grah-fom′eh-tre). Measurement of corneal curvatures for the determination of corneal topography as may be performed by keratometry, photokeratoscopy, or profile photography.

keratopography (ker″ah-to-pog′rah-fe). Topography of the cornea.

keratoprosthesis (ker″ah-to-pros′the-sis). Corneal implant.

keratorhexis (ker″ah-to-rek′sis). Rupture of the cornea due to a perforating ulcer or to trauma.

keratoscleritis (ker″ah-to-skle-ri′tis). Inflammation involving both the cornea and the sclera.

keratoscope (ker′ah-to-skōp). An instrument for examining the curvature of the cornea, consisting of a pattern of alternately black and white concentric rings seen reflected on the cornea through a convex lens mounted in an aperture at the center of the pattern. Syn., *Placido's disk.*

Photo-Electronic K. See under *Photo-Electronic.*

keratoscopy (ker-ah-tos′ko-pe). 1. Examination of the anterior surface of the cornea with a keratoscope. 2. Originally used by Cuignet to mean *retinoscopy.*

photoelectric k. A method of investigating the corneal surface by scanning the cornea with a light beam and determining the changes in direction of the reflected beam by photoelectric detectors.

keratosis conjunctivae (ker″ah-to′sis kon-junk-ti′ve). Cornification of the conjunctival epithelium, occurring in various forms.

keratosis nigricans (ker″ah-to′sis nig′re-kanz, -ni′gre-). Acanthosis nigricans.

keratosis palmaris et plantaris. A marked, symmetrical thickening of the skin of the palms and soles, usually hereditary and sometimes congenital, which is frequently accompanied by ectropion, trachomalike lesions of the conjunctiva, and superficial and deep corneal vascularization.

keratotomy (ker-ah-tot′o-me). Surgical incision of the cornea.

delimiting k. Surgical incision into the cornea near the advancing border of a serpiginous corneal ulcer.

keratotorus (ker″ah-to-tōr′us). A rare corneal ectasia in which the bulging is eccentric and has a toric surface which creates against the rule astigmatism, with Descemet's membrane remaining intact.

keratouveitis (ker″ah-to-u″ve-i′tis). Simultaneous keratitis and uveitis.

kerectasis (ker-ek′tah-sis). A pathological protrusion or bulging of the cornea. Syn., *keratoectasia.*

kerectomy (ke-rek′to-me). Surgical removal of a portion of the cornea. Syn., *keratectomy.*

keroid (ker′oid). Resembling the cornea.

Kerr cell; effect; method; shutter. See under the nouns.

Kestenbaum's (kes′ten-baumz) **formula; sign; test.** See under nouns.

Kimmelstiel-Wilson syndrome (kim′el-stēl-wil-sun). See under *syndrome.*

kinephantom (kin″e-fan′tom). Perception of a moving visual object, such as a silhouette or shadow, as other than its actual direction or pattern.

kinephantoscope (kin″e-fan′to-skōp). A device for projecting shadows or other forms lending themselves to the perception of various movement patterns.

kinescope (kin′e-skōp). 1. An instrument for determining the refraction of the eye, in which the subject observes the apparent "with" or "against" movement of a test object through a stenopaic slit moved across the front of the eye. 2. An instrument for recording television programs by contact exposure of movie film on a television picture tube.

kinescopy (kin-es′ko-pe). The measurement of ocular refraction by use of the kinescope.

Kinsey-Cogan theory (kin′se-ko′-gan). See *theory, osmotic pump.*

Kirchhoff's law (kirk′hofs). See under *law.*

Kirschmann's law (kursh′manz). See under *law.*

Kisch's reflex (kish′ez). The aural blinking reflex.

Klein's syndrome. See under *syndrome.*

klieg (klēg) **conjunctivitis; light.** See under the nouns.

klinokinesis (kli″no-kih-ne′sis). A change in direction of movement of a motile organism in response to changes in the intensity of light stimulation but not in response to the direction of the light stimulation.

klinotaxis (kli-no-tak′sis). An irregular or wavy movement of a motile organism toward or away from light, which may be mediated by only one receptor organ that responds by comparing differences in light intensity of successive stimuli as the organism turns. See also *tropotaxis; telotaxis; menotaxis; mnemotaxis.*

Knapp's (naps) **law; streaks; striae.** See under the nouns.

knee, temporal, of Flechsig. Meyer's loop.

Knies's sign (k-nēz′ez). See under *sign.*

knob, end. End bulb.

Koby's corneal dystrophy (ko′bēz). See under *dystrophy.*

Koch-Weeks conjunctivitis (kōk-wēks). Acute contagious conjunctivitis.

Kocher's sign (kōk′erz). See under *sign.*

Koenig's (ke′nigz) **bars; theory; color triangle.** See under the nouns.

Koeppe's (kep′ēz) **gonioscopic lens; nodules.** See under the nouns.

Kohler illumination. See under *illumination.*

Kohlrausch's bend (kōl′rowsh-es). See under *bend.*

Kölliker's (kel′e-kerz) **layer; theory.** See under the nouns.

Kollmorgen contact lens (kōl′mōr-gen). See under *lens, contact.*

Köllner's (kel′nerz) **effect; law.** See under the nouns.

kopiopsia (kop″e-op′se-ah). Copiopia.

Koplik's spots (kop′liks). See under *spots.*

korectomia (kōr″ek-to′me-ah). Surgical formation of an artificial pupil.

korectopia (kōr″ek-to′pe-ah). Corectopia.

Korector, Arneson (kōr-ek′tor). An instrument used in visual training consisting of a large rotating disk on which is mounted an adjustable and removable fixation target to be observed through prisms, lenses, or both.

koroscopy (ko-ros′ko-pe). Retinoscopy.

Korte's laws (kōr′tēz). See under *law.*

Köster's (kes′terz) **prism; sign; test.** See under the nouns.

K.P. Abbreviation for *keratic precipitate.*

Kratoculator (kra-tok′u-la″tor). An instrument used in visual training, in conjunction with a Myoculator, which projects a fixation target onto a screen, the target being moved to various positions on the screen by a manual control.

Kratometer (kra-tom'eh-ter). An instrument used in visual training consisting essentially of batteries of prisms mounted in bars through which an observer fixates distant or near targets. The prism bars are moved through a holding slot, introducing increasing or decreasing prismatic power, in individual steps, before either eye. A Maddox rod and a red glass are included in each battery, and the instrument is provided with a chin rest and cells for trial case lenses.

Kraupa's dystrophy (krow'paz). See under *dystrophy, corneal, epithelial juvenile* (*of Kraupa*).

Krause's (krawz'ez) **bulbs; corpuscle; glands; syndrome; valve.** See under the nouns.

Kravkov's experiment (krahv'kovz). See under *experiment*.

von Kries (fon krēs) **law of coefficients; law of persistence; theory.** See under the nouns.

von Kries pursuant image (fon krēs). Second positive afterimage.

Krimsky's method (krim'skēz). See under *method*.

Kronfeld's test (krōn'feldz). See under *test*.

Krukenberg's spindle (kroo'kenbergz). See under *spindle*.

kryptok (krip'tok). See *lens, bifocal, kryptok*.

Kubelka-Munk method (ku-bel'kah-munk). See under *method*.

Kühne's (ke'nēz) **optical box; cycle.** See under the nouns.

Kuhnt's (koontz) **meniscus; intermediate tissue; post-central vein.** See under the nouns.

Kuhnt-Junius disease (koont-yun'e-us). Senile disciform degeneration of the macula. See under *degeneration*.

Kundt's (koondtz) **monocular asymmetry; illusion; partition; rule.** See under the nouns.

Kupfer's method (kup'ferz). See under *method*.

Kurova (koor-o'vah). A trade name for a series of corrected curve ophthalmic lenses.

kurtosis (kur-to'sis). The degree of peakedness of a frequency distribution. See also *leptokurtosis; mesokurtosis; platykurtosis*.

Kurz's syndrome (kurz'ez). See under *syndrome*.

kuttarosome (kut"ar'o-sōm). A series of parallel bars in the neck of a retinal cone cell, described by early microscopists.

kyanophane (ki'an-o-fān). A bluish pigment said to exist in oil globules of the retinal cones, probably absent in man.

kyanopsia (ki"ah-nop'se-ah). Cyanopsia.

L

L. Symbol for (1) *lambert;* (2) *luminance.*

lachry- (lak'rih-). For words beginning thus, see *lacri-.*

lacodacryostomy (lak"o-dak"re-os'-to-me). An operation to restore the flow of tears into the lacrimal sac from the lacrimal lake when the canaliculi are obstructed or obliterated.

Lacrilens (lak'rih-lenz). A trade name for a scleral contact lens with an inverted V-shaped opening in the inferior scleral portion to facilitate the flow of lacrimal fluid.

lacrima (lak'rih-mah). A tear.

lacrimae cruentae (lak'rih-me kruen'te). Bloody tears. Syn., *dacryohemorrhysis.*

lacrimal (lak'rih-mal). Pertaining to the tears, or to the structures conducting or secreting tears, or to the lacrimal bone.

lacrimal ampulla; apparatus; artery; bones; canal; canaliculus; caruncle; crest; diaphragm; duct; fluid; fossa; gland; lake; papilla; punctum; sac; tubercle. See under the nouns.

lacrimale (lak"rih-mal'e). The point of junction of the posterior lacrimal crest and the frontolacrimal suture.

lacrimalin (lak-rim'ah-lin). A chemical which causes tear production.

lacrimase (lak'rih-mās). An enzyme found in tears.

lacrimation (lak"rih-ma'shun). The secretion of tears, the common connotation being excessive secretion.

paradoxical l. Crocodile tears.

paroxysmal l. Excessive lacrimation occurring suddenly and periodically.

primary l. Lacrimation due to direct stimulation or to irritation of the lacrimal gland.

psychic l. Lacrimation associated with emotional states or physical pain.

reflex l. Lacrimation in response to neurogenic stimulation, such as irritation of the cornea or the conjunctiva, vomiting, or glare.

lacrimator (lak'rih-ma"tor). Any substance which stimulates the secretion of tears, usually through irritation of the conjunctiva.

lacrimonasal (lak"rih-mo-na'zal). Pertaining to, or in the region of, the lacrimal sac or duct and the nose.

lacrimotomy (lak"rih-mot'o-me). Surgical incision of the lacrimal sac, duct, or gland.

lacrymal. Lacrimal.

lacunae, corneal (lah-ku'ne). 1. Von Recklinghausen's canals. 2. Tiny spaces in the stroma of the cornea filled with tissue fluid.

lacus lacrimalus (la'kus lak"rih-mal'-is). Lacrimal lake.

Ladd-Franklin theory (lad-frangk'-lin). See under *theory.*

laevo- (le'vo-). For words beginning thus, see *levo-.*

lag. 1. Comparative or relative retardation or slowness in movement, function, or development. 2. The slippage or extent of slippage of a contact lens associated with gravity, blinking, or rotation of the eyes from the straightforward position.

[382]

accommodation, *l. of.* See under accommodation.

blink l. A downward movement of a contact lens following a blink.

convergence, l. of. See under convergence.

dynamic l. Optometric Extension Program: An empirical deduction from the gross dynamic retinoscopy finding to compensate for an estimated lag of accommodation.

excursion l. A slippage of a contact lens occurring during eye movement. Syn., *movement lag.*

globe l., of Means. Means's sign.

gravity l. A downward movement of a contact lens attributed to its weight or weight distribution.

movement l. Excursion lag.

Lagleyze-von Hippel disease (lah-glīz'fon hip'el). Von Hippel's disease.

lagophthalmia (lag"of-thal'me-ah). Lagophthalmos.

lagophthalmos (lag"of-thal'mos). Inability to close the eyelids completely. Syn., *hare's eye.*

l. in sopore. Failure of complete eyelid closure in profound sleep.

lagophthalmus (lag"of-thal'mus). Lagophthalmos.

Lagrange's law (lah-grahnz'ez). See under *law.*

lake, lacrimal. The accumulation of tears in the triangular-shaped region between the eyelids at the inner canthus prior to draining into the lacrimal puncta. Syn., *rivus lacrimalis.*

lambda (λ) (lam'dah). The Greek letter used as the symbol for (1) *wavelength;* (2) *angle of elevation* in the field of regard (*Fry*); (3) *angle lambda.*

lambert (lam'burt). A unit of luminance equal to $1/\pi$ candelas per sq. cm., or to the uniform luminance of a perfectly diffusing surface emitting or reflecting light at the rate of 1 lumen per sq. cm. Symbol: L. See also *footlambert.*

Lambert's law (lam'burts). See under *law.*

lamella (lă-mel'ah). 1. A thin leaf, plate, or layer. 2. A medicated gelatin disk for insertion under the eyelid.

iridis anterior, l. Anterior limiting layer of the iris.

posterior border l. of Fuchs. A layer of the iris containing the fibrils of the dilator pupillae muscle, exclusive of their cell bodies, located between the anterior pigment layer of Fuchs and the stroma. Syn., *Bruch's layer; Bruch's membrane; Henle's membrane; posterior membrane of the iris.*

posterior limiting l. Lamina vitrea of the choroid.

vitreous l. Lamina vitrea of the choroid. *Obs.*

zonular l. The superficial layer of the capsule of the crystalline lens.

lamina (lam'ih-nah). A layer; a thin plate.

basalis, l. Lamina vitrea of the choroid.

Bowman's l. Bowman's membrane.

capsulopupillaris, l. The lateral portion of the tunica vasculosa lentis, consisting of embryological vascular mesoderm, which normally unites with the pars iridica retinae to form the iris. In embryotoxon it adheres to the periphery of the cornea.

choriocapillary l. Choriocapillaris.

ciliaris retinae, l. The zonule of Zinn, derived from the pars ciliaris retinae of the optic cup.

cribrosa, l. A thin, sievelike membrane, composed of neuroglia and connective tissue, bridging the posterior scleral foramen and continuous with the choroid and the deepest third of the sclera. The fibers of the optic nerve and the central retinal vessels pass through its many openings. Syn., *cribriform plate.*

cribrosa sclerae, l. Lamina cribrosa.

cuticular l. 1. The portion of the lamina vitrea of the choroid secreted by the pigment epithelium of the retina, to which it is fused, and located internal to the lamina elastica. 2. The portion of the lamina vitrea of the ciliary body secreted by the pars ciliaris retinae and located internal to the avascular connective tissue which separates it from the lamina elastica.

elastica, l. 1. The portion of the lamina vitrea formed by the choroid, located external to the cuticular layer of the lamina vitrea and internal to the choriocapillaris. 2. The portion of the lamina vitrea of the ciliary body located external to the avascular connective tissue, which separates it from the cuticular lamina, and internal to the vascular layer of the ciliary body.

    elastica anterior, l. Bowman's membrane.

    elastica posterior, l. Descemet's membrane.

fusca, l. 1. The thin, brown, inner layer of the sclera containing melanin in chromatophores and fibrous elastic tissue. 2. The suprachoroid. 3. The external layer of the ciliary body, containing fibroblasts, chromatophores, and reticuloendothelial cells in its posterior portion, while anteriorly it becomes more of a serous space (suprachoroidal space). Syn., *membrana fusca.*

iridopupillaris, l. Embryological, vascular mesoderm from the tunica vasculosa lentis, of which the central portion forms the fetal pupillary membrane and the peripheral portion unites with the pars iridica retinae to form the iris.

medullary optic l. The large, fan-shaped group of projectional fibers in the optic radiations of the visual pathway, which leaves the lateral geniculate body and reaches the ipsilateral area striata or higher visual center.

papyracea, l. One of the thin, paired portions of the ethmoid bone which forms part of the medial wall of the orbit. Syn., *os planum.*

Sattler's l. Sattler's layer.

suprachoroidea, l. Suprachoroid.

vasculosa choroideae, l. The vessel layer of the choroid subdivided into Haller's layer of larger vessels and Sattler's layer of smaller vessels.

vitrea, l. 1. The inner layer of the choroid consisting of an innermost layer related to the pigment epithelium of the retina (cuticular lamina), a middle layer composed of a zone of elastin surrounded and interspersed by a collagenous meshwork, and an outermost basement membrane related to the endothelium of the choriocapillaris of the choroid, the latter two layers constituting the lamina elastica. Syn., *posterior limiting lamella; vitreous lamella; lamina basalis; Bruch's layer of the choroid; basement membrane of the choroid; Bruch's membrane of the choroid; Henle's membrane of the choroid.* 2. The layer of the ciliary body between its vascular layer and its epithelium. It is a forward continuation of the lamina vitrea of the choroid, but differs in that there is a layer of avascular connective tissue between the lamina elastica and the cuticular lamina. Syn., *Bruch's layer of the ciliary body; Bruch's membrane of the ciliary body.*

lamp. Any device for producing artificial light.

arc l. A lamp in which light is produced by an electrical discharge between two electrodes by raising the temperature of gaseous particles from the electrodes to incandescence.

argon l. A glow lamp filled with

[384]

an argon mixture radiating chiefly in the near ultraviolet region around 360 mμ, used clinically in conjunction with fluorescein in the fitting of contact lenses and for the detection of corneal abrasions.

Burton l. A viewing instrument consisting essentially of a magnifying lens in a rectangular frame that half shields a pair of tubular lamps which provide ultraviolet light at 360 mμ toward the object to be viewed through the lens. It is used primarily in conjunction with certain dyes, such as fluorescein, to create fluorescence for diagnostic purposes, such as in the evaluation of the fit of contact lenses.

carbon arc l. An arc lamp, consisting of carbon electrodes, which radiates light because of incandescence of the electrodes and luminescence of vaporized electrode material.

carcel l. A special type of oil lamp of standard size and construction which has been used as a photometric standard in France. See also *carcel*.

Duke-Elder l. A lamp which produces ultraviolet radiations for certain ophthalmologic therapy.

Edridge-Green l. A color perception test lamp containing color filters mounted in rotating disks for serial presentation.

electric discharge l. A lamp in which light is produced by the passing of electricity through a metallic vapor or gas contained in a bulb or a tube.

electric filament l. An electric incandescent lamp consisting of a glass bulb containing a filament which is heated to incandescence by an electric current.

electric incandescent l. Any lamp in which light is produced by electrically heating a material to incandescence, particularly an electric filament lamp.

fluorescent l. An electric discharge lamp in which the radiant energy from the electric discharge is absorbed by certain materials (phosphors) and re-emitted as light of longer wavelength. Typically, ultraviolet radiation is converted into visible radiation by a phosphor coating on the inside of a tube.

Hague cataract l. A portable luminaire providing ultraviolet light to fluoresce the crystalline lens for its inspection, and for use in examining the cornea and other ocular tissues stained with a fluorescent dye.

incandescent l. Any lamp in which light is produced by heating a material to incandescence. It includes combustion sources, such as gas mantles as well as electric incandescent lamps, but is commonly associated with the latter.

slit l. An instrument producing a slender beam of intense light for illuminating any reasonably transparent structure or medium (such as the cornea, the aqueous humor, the crystalline lens, or the anterior vitreous) in a sectionlike manner for oblique viewing, usually through a microscope.

Lancaster (lan'kas-ter) **chart; test.** See under the nouns.

Lancaster-Regan chart. See under *chart*.

lance, perceptual. The tridimensional spearhead-shaped representation of the visual acuity of the various regions of the retina, in which the point of the spearhead corresponds to the point of fixation and the spearhead base corresponds to the degree of eccentricity of retinal stimulation. The height of a line from a point on the base to the surface of the spearhead corresponds to the visual acuity obtainable for that point.

Land's theory. See under *theory*.

Landolt's (lahn'dolts) **ball; chart; club; fibers; prism; projectionometer; ring; stereoscope; tests; theory; test type.** See under the nouns.

Landström's muscle (lahnd'stremz). See under *muscle.*

Lange's fold (lang'ez). See under *fold.*

Langerhans' cells (lahng'er-hahnz). See under *cell.*

Langrange (lahn-grahnj') **fusion band; method.** See under the nouns.

Langworthy's theory (lang'wor-thēz). See under *theory.*

lap. A tool, or the face of a tool, used for grinding and polishing a refracting surface of a lens blank to the selected shape (curvature) of the face of the tool by means of sandlike abrasive and polishing compounds.

lapsus (lap'sus). The falling down or drooping of a part; ptosis.

palpebrae superioris, l. Ptosis or drooping of the upper eyelid.

lash. An eyelash.

laser (la'zer). An acronym for "light amplification by stimulated emission of radiation"; a device for producing an intense coherent beam of monochromatic light in a wavelength in or near the visible spectrum. Syn., *optical maser.*

Laser Refractor. An apparatus for the subjective determination of ametropia consisting of a slowly rotating drum on the surface of which is perceived a granular pattern resulting from illumination by a helium-neon gas laser beam. The grain of the pattern appears to move when the eye is not focused for the fixation distance; hence, the correcting lens which neutralizes the movement focuses the eye for the fixation distance.

laterality, visual. Any difference exhibited between the two eyes, the two halves of the binocular visual field, or the temporal and the nasal halves of the monocular visual field. See also *visual dominance.*

lateroduction (lat"er-o-duk'shun). Rotation of an eye or vergence of the eyes in the horizontal plane.

laterotorsion (lat"er-o-tōr'shun). Rotation of the eye about an anteroposterior axis.

lateroversion (lat"er-o-ver'zhun). Version of the eyes in the horizontal plane.

Laurence's (lah'ren-siz) **pupillometer; strabismometer.** See under the nouns.

Laurence-Moon-Biedl (lah'rens-moon-be'dl) **dystrophy; syndrome.** See under the nouns.

Laurent half-shade plate (lah-rent'). See under *plate.*

law. A statement of a sequence or an interrelation of phenomena which is invariable under the given conditions.

Abney's l. The luminosity of the combined spectrum is equal to the sum of the luminosities of its component parts.

absorption, l. of. 1. As light passes through a homogeneous substance of a given thickness, the same percentage of light is absorbed regardless of the intensity of the incident light. 2. The intensity of transmitted light varies as an exponential function of the length of the light path in the absorbing medium. Syn., *Bouguer's law; Lambert's law of absorption*

all or none l. The weakest stimulus capable of producing a response in cardiac muscle, fibers of striated muscle, or nerve fibers, produces a maximal response, i.e., if there is any response at all, it is maximum under the existing conditions.

Angström's l. The wavelengths absorbed by a substance are the same as those emitted by the substance when it is luminous.

Aubert-Förster l. An observation by Aubert and Förster that, peripheral to the foveal region, visual acuity is better for small letters and numbers at short distances than for large letters and numbers at greater distances, though they subtend the same visual angle.

Beer's l. The absorption of the intensity of radiant energy by a stable solution is an exponential function of the product of concentration and the length of path in the solution.

binocular projection, l. of. Images of an object or objects stimulating corresponding retinal points are perceptually localized as coming from the same direction and distance in space.

binocular rest and motion, l. of. The extrinsic muscles of normal eyes, under the control of brain centers, relate the two eyes so that their visual axes and horizontal retinal meridians always lie in the plane of the primary isogonal circle whether at rest or in motion, and so that the two visual axes will converge at some point on this circle, in the interest of both binocular single vision and correct orientation. *Savage.*

Bloch's l. The intensity of light required to produce a threshold response is inversely proportional to the duration of the stimulus, expressed by the formula: $Lt = C$ in which L = luminance of the stimulus, t = stimulus duration, C = a constant; valid only for short exposures.

Blondel-Rey l. A modification of Bloch's law for stimuli of long exposure. The intensity of light required to produce a response at threshold is inversely proportional to a function of the duration of the light, expressed by the formula: $Lt = L_\infty(t + t_0)$, in which L = luminance of the stimulus, L_∞ = luminance for an in-

definitely long exposure, t = stimulus duration, t_0 = a time constant varying with the subject and the experimental conditions. It does not apply after maximum time, t_2, beyond which summation does not occur.

Bouguer's l. The intensity of transmitted light varies as an exponential function of the length of the light path in the absorbing medium. Syn., *law of absorption; Lambert's law of absorption.*

Brewster's l. In a dielectric, such as glass, the angle of polarization is equal to the angle of incidence for which the reflected light is at right angles to the refracted light. Under this condition, the angle of polarization is equal to that angle of incidence whose tangent equals the refractive index of the medium.

Bunsen-Roscoe l. In photochemistry, for a reaction to a light stimulus of moderate intensity and short duration, the product of intensity and duration is a constant. Syn., *law of reciprocity.*

Charpentier's l. Ricco's law.

closedness, l. of. The tendency to see an incomplete form as complete, the process of completion being termed *closure.*

coefficients, l. of. A law expressed by von Kries and sometimes attributed to Helmholtz, Fechner, and Hering, which states that when two regions of the retina under conditions involving either the photopic or scotopic, but not mixed (mesopic), mechanism are differently adapted, the brightness matching results are the same as if all stimuli acting on one region were multiplied by a certain coefficient (of adaptation), whence the shape of the luminosity curve for either the photopic or scotopic mechanism remains the same for a range of intensities of the test standard. Cf. *law of persistence.*

conjugate planes, l. of. Conjugate planes are pairs of parallel planes perpendicular to the axis of an optical system, and any straight line drawn to one nodal point and continued as a parallel straight line from the other nodal point will pierce the conjugate planes in a pair of conjugate points.

constant orientation, l. of. Donders' law.

corresponding areas, l. of. When an object is seen singly under binocular conditions, the images of this object, one on each retina, fall on corresponding retinal areas.

cosine l. Lambert's cosine law.

cosine-cubed l. A mathematical extension of the law of illumination in which the illumination (E) of a surface is directly proportional to the luminous intensity (I) of a given point source and to the cosine cubed $(\cos^3)$ of the angle (θ) of incidence and inversely proportional to the square of the perpendicular distance (h) of the source from the plane of the surface in which the point of reference is located, expressed by the formula: $E \propto I \cos^3 \theta/h^2$.

decentration, l. of. Prentice's law.

Descartes' l. Law of refraction.

Desmarres' l. When a nonfixated object is beyond the crossing point of the visual axes, its diplopic images are uncrossed (homonymous diplopia); and when a nonfixated object is closer than the crossing point of the visual axes, its diplopic images are crossed (heteronymous diplopia).

disuse, l. of. When a neural pathway is not used for a period of time, its reaction to a stimulus is retarded.

Donders' l. For any determinate position of the line of fixation with respect to the head, there corresponds a definite and invariable angle of torsion, independent of the volition of the observer and independent of the manner in which the line of fixation has been brought to the position in question. Syn., *law of constant orientation.*

Draper's l. Only that portion of the spectrum which is absorbed by the medium it traverses exerts any effect on that medium. The effects may be thermal, photochemical, or the production of fluorescence. Syn., *Grotthus' law.*

Ebbinghaus' l. When luminosity alone is contrasted, the increase of brightness of a patch on a dark ground depends only on the relative difference of the two intensities and not on their absolute values.

effect, l. of. The linkage of a response to a stimulus is strengthened when the response is a success or satisfying and weakened when the response is a failure or unpleasant.

Emmert's l. A projected afterimage or an eidetic image is altered in size in proportion to the distance of the surface on which it is projected.

Ewald's l. When a semicircular canal, either horizontal or vertical, is maximally stimulated, it elicits a nystagmus with the quick phase toward its own side. Minimal stimulation causes a nystagmus with the quick phase toward the opposite side.

exercise, l. of. The exercise of a response to a given stimulus makes this response more precise, efficient, and stabilized.

Fechner's l. The intensity of a sensation varies as the logarithm of the intensity of the stimulus. For example, according to this law, brightness varies with the logarithm of luminance. Syn., *psychophysical law; Weber-Fechner law.*

Fechner-Helmholtz l. Law of coefficients.

Fermat's l. The actual path pursued by light in going from one point to another is that route which, under the given conditions, requires the least time.

Ferry-Porter l. The critical flicker frequency is directly proportional to the logarithm of the stimulus intensity.

frequency, l. of. Responses that are elicited frequently and repeatedly show more facile reaction to stimulation than those whose function is held in abeyance.

Fresnel's l. Fresnel's formula.

Granit-Harper l. In normal subjects, the critical fusion frequency increases logarithmically as the area of retinal stimulation increases.

Grassmann's l's. Laws of color mixture formulated by H. Grassmann (1853), but now stated in various forms, which hold true only within a prescribed set of conditions with respect to brightness level, adaptation of the observer, size of the field, etc. Essentially the laws are: (1) Any color, no matter how it is composed, can be matched in appearance by a mixture of three suitably chosen primary colors. (2) Any mixed color, no matter how it is composed, must have the same appearance as a mixture of a saturated (spectral) color with white. (3) If two different spots of light give the same color sensation, they continue to do so when the brightness of each is increased or decreased by the same factor. (4) When one of two kinds of light that are to be mixed together changes continuously, the appearance of the mixture changes continuously also. (5) Colors that look alike produce a mixture that looks like them. (6) The total light intensity of a mixture is the sum of the intensities of the mixed lights.

Grotthus' l. Draper's law.

Gullstrand's l. If, when a strabismic is made to turn his head while fixating a distant object, the corneal reflex from either eye moves in the direction in which the head is turning, it moves toward the weaker or paralyzed muscle

de Haan's l. The loss in visual acuity after the age of 30, expressed as a decimal, is equal to one tenth the increase in years of age. The law is now regarded as being fallacious.

Haig's l. The intensity of light required to produce a cone response at threshold is inversely proportional to the cross sectional area of cones stimulated, expressed by the formula: $L(s/a) = C$, in which L = luminance of the stimulus, a = area of retina stimulated, s = total cross sectional area of the cones in area a, C = a constant.

Helmholtz' l. of magnification. Lagrange's law.

Helmholtz' l. of torsion. The torsion of each eye is a function only of the angles of altitude and azimuth when the lines of fixation are parallel. Accordingly, the cyclophoria is constant in all directions of gaze as long as convergence is zero, confirming the theory that convergence movements are not identical to the otherwise similar fixational movements of the eye.

Hering's l. of equal innervation. Innervation to the extrinsic muscles of one eye is equal to that to the other eye, resulting in movements of the two eyes that are equal and symmetrical or parallel.

Hering's l. of ocular movements. Hering's law of equal innervation.

Hering's l. of sensation. The distinctness or the purity of a sensation is dependent on the proportion of its intensity to the total intensities of all simultaneous sensations.

Heyman's l. The threshold value of a visual stimulus is increased in proportion to the strength of a simultaneous inhibitory stimulus.

Horner's l. Color blindness is transmitted from males to males through unaffected females. (Recent research indicates that the female may be affected to a limited degree.)

identical visual directions, l. of. The stimulation of corresponding retinal points, either simultaneously or individually, will result in the same visual directionalization, i.e., objects will be localized in the same direction from the self.

illumination, l. of. The illumination (E) of a surface is directly proportional to the luminous intensity (I) of a given point source and to the cosine of the angle (θ) of incidence and inversely proportional to the square of the distance (d) between the point of reference on the surface and the source, expressed by the formula: $E \propto I \cos \theta/d^2$.

Imbert-Fick l. The external pressure required to flatten a given area of an infinitely thin spherical membrane filled with fluid is equal to the product of the internal pressure and the flattened area on which it acts; a principle applied to applanation tonometry.

inverse square l. The effective intensity of a freely irradiating source (i.e., not focused or otherwise confined in its path) is inversely proportional to the square of the distance between the source and the receiving surface.

Kirchhoff's l. At a given temperature, the ratio of radiant emittance to radiant absorptance for a given wavelength is the same for all bodies.

Kirschmann's l. The greatest contrast in color is seen when the luminosity difference is small.

Knapp's l. When a correcting lens is so placed before the eye that its second principal plane coincides with the anterior focal point of an axially ametropic eye, the size of the retinal image will be the same as though the eye were emmetropic.

Köllner's l. Lesions of the outer layers of the retina cause a yellow-blue color vision defect, and lesions of the inner retinal layers and of the optic nerve cause a red-green defect. For example, pigmentary degeneration of the retina causes a yellow-blue defect while retrobulbar neuritis causes a red-green defect.

Korte's l's. A series of formulas which express the optimal conditions for phi movement in terms of spatial, temporal, and intensity factors. They are: (1) With time interval constant, optimal distance varies directly with intensity. (2) With distance between stimuli constant, the optimal intensity varies indirectly with the time between the stimuli. (3) With the intensity constant, the optimal time between the stimuli varies directly with the distance between the stimuli.

von Kries l. of coefficients. See *law of coefficients.*

von Kries, l. of persistence. See *law of persistence.*

Lagrange's l. In paraxial optics, the product of the index of refraction of object space, object size, and slope angle for object space is equal to the product of the index of refraction of image space, image size, and slope angle for image space. See also *Abbe's sine condition.* Syn., *Helmholtz' law of magnification.*

Lambert's l. of absorption. Law of absorption.

Lambert's cosine l. The luminous flux emitted, reflected, or transmitted by a perfectly diffusing surface per unit solid angle is proportional to the cosine of the angle between the emitted, transmitted, or reflected ray and the normal to the surface. Syn., *cosine law.*

Listing's l. When the line of fixation is brought from its primary position to any other position, the torsional rotation of the eyeball in this second position will be the same as if the eye had been turned around a fixed axis perpendicular to the initial and final directions of the line of fixation.

Loeser's l. For foveal stimulation, the product of the square root of the threshold intensity of light stimulation and the angular diameter of the lighted retinal area is a constant.

Lorentz-Lorenz l. A relationship between the index of refraction, n, of a gaseous medium and its density, D, expressed by the formula:

$$\left(\frac{n^2 - 1}{n^2 + 2}\right)\frac{1}{D} = \text{constant}$$

Mach's l. A uniform movement has no effect in producing statokinetic reflexes, the only effective stimuli being the initiation of movement or the acceleration or retardation of movement.

Malus' l. The transmission of light through two consecutively placed polarizing media is proportional to the square of the cosine of the angle between their respective planes of polarization.

Malus-Dupin l. A bundle of rays normal to a surface, a so-called normal system, remains a normal system after refraction and reflection.

Maxwell's l. The dielectric constant for a transparent medium is equal to the square of its index of refraction as measured for very long waves only.

monocular projection, l. of. The monocular visual projection of a retinal stimulus is outward in the direction of that path of light incident toward the nodal point which would, after refraction, reach the locus of the retinal stimulus.

Mueller's l. of specific nerve energy. Each nerve of special sense, however excited, gives rise to its own peculiar sensation.

Nasse's l. In X-linked recessive traits, the daughters of a male case are carriers and pass the trait to one half of their sons, as in hemophilia.

Newton's l. of color mixture. Any one or a combination of the several rules of color mixing described by Newton. The following two are frequently cited: (1) If two color mixtures elicit the same sensation of light or color, the combination of the mixtures will arouse the same sensation. (2) The spectral nature of a color resulting from a mixture of two colors may be determined graphically in a schematic representation by dividing the line joining the two constituents inversely as to the quantities of each constituent in the mixture.

Newton-Mueller-Gudden l. In mammals, the relative number of uncrossed fibers in the optic chiasm is closely proportional to the degree of frontality of the eyes.

persistence, l. of. A law expressed by von Kries which states that, for either the photopic or scotopic, but not mixed (mesopic), mechanism, a match of two lights of different spectral composition remains a match at other levels of adaptation. Cf. *law of coefficients.*

Pieron's l. 1. For foveal images of moderate size, the luminance of the target at threshold is inversely related to the cube root of the retinal area stimulated, expressed by the formula: $L\sqrt[3]{A} = C$, in which L = luminance of the stimulus, A = area of the retinal image, and C = a constant. 2. A modification of the Blondel-Rey law. The intensity of light required to produce a response at threshold is inversely proportional to a nonlinear function of the duration of the light, expressed by the formula: $Lt^n = C$, in which L = luminance of the stimulus, t = stimulus duration, n = a value varying with retinal location, and C = a constant. It does not apply after maximum time t_2, beyond which summation does not occur.

Piper's l. For small images in peripheral vision, the product of intensity and the square root of the area stimulated is a constant for threshold effect, expressed by the formula: $L\sqrt{A} = C$, in which L = luminance of the stimulus, A = retinal area, and C = a constant.

Pitt's l. Differential wavelength discrimination in the color defective is best where saturation is poorest.

Planck's l. Energy distribution in the spectrum of a blackbody is expressed by the formula:

$$W\lambda = C_1\lambda^{-5}\left(\epsilon^{\frac{C_2}{\lambda T}} - 1\right)^{-1}$$

in which W_λ = watts radiated by a blackbody per sq. cm. of surface in each wavelength band, 1 μ wide, at wavelength λ; λ = wavelength in microns; T = absolute temperature; C_1 = 37,350 micron-degrees; C_2 = 14,380 micron-degrees; ϵ = 2.718+.

Prägnanz, l. of. There is a tendency to interpret the form of an object, seen in perspective, as being one of certain favored simple familiar forms, such as a circle, a square, or a rectangle.

Prentice's l. The deviation, expressed in prism diopters, at a point on a lens is equal to the product of the dioptric power of the lens and the distance, in centimeters, of the point from the optical center of the lens. Syn., *law of decentration.*

projection, l. of. Law of monocular projection.

proximity, l. of. Objects or forms that are adjacent or close together tend to be grouped visually, thus often becoming parts of a singly perceived object or pattern.

psychophysical l. Fechner's law.

Rayleigh l. In a transmitting medium whose heterogeneities have average dimensions which are small in comparison to the wavelength of the incident energy, the fraction of the incident flux scattered is inversely proportional to the fourth power of the wavelength.

reciprocity, l. of. Bunsen-Roscoe law.

rectilinear propagation of light, l. of. Light travels in straight lines in a homogeneous medium.

reflection, l. of. The angle of reflection is equal to the angle of incidence; the incident ray, the normal to the surface at the point of incidence, and the reflected ray lie in the same plane.

refraction, l. of. The ratio of the sine of the angle of incidence to the sine of the angle of refraction is a constant equal to the relative index of refraction; the incident ray, the normal to the surface at the point of incidence, and the refracted ray lie in the same plane. Syn., *Descartes' law; law of sines; Snell's law.*

Ricco's l. For small images on the fovea, the product of image area and light intensity is constant for threshold effect, expressed by the formula: $LA = C$, in which L =

luminance of the stimulus, $A =$ retinal area, and $C =$ a constant. Syn., *Charpentier's law.*

Schouten-Ornstein l. If any new brightness level is maintained indefinitely, the state of dark or light adaptation of the eye remains unchanged.

Sherrington's l. of reciprocal innervation. The contraction of each skeletal (including ocular) muscle is accompanied by a simultaneous and proportional relaxation of its antagonist.

similarity, l. of. Objects or forms which are similar, as in content or pattern, tend to be grouped visually.

sines, l. of. Law of refraction.

sine-squared l. The dioptric power in any meridian of a cylindrical lens is equal to the cylinder power multiplied by the square of the sine of the angle between that meridian and the axis of the cylinder.

size constancy, l. of. The perception of the size of an object remains constant, or nearly constant, although the object be moved farther from or nearer to the observer, subtending varying visual angles.

Snell's l. Law of refraction.

Stefan-Boltzmann l. The radiant emittance of a blackbody is proportional to the fourth power of its absolute temperature.

Stokes' l. In fluorescence, the wavelength of the emitted light is always greater than that of the exciting light; now known to have exceptions.

symmetry, l. of. The perceptual grouping of objects or forms into larger wholes is dependent on various features of geometrical symmetry.

Talbot's l. Talbot-Plateau law.

Talbot-Plateau l. The brightness of rapidly intermittent light perceived as continuous and unvarying is equal to that which would be produced by a constant light of intensity equal to the mean value of the intermittent stimuli.

use, l. of. The frequent use of a neural pathway facilitates its reaction to a stimulus.

Weber's l. The increase of stimulus which is necessary to produce a just noticeable difference in sensation bears a constant ratio to the stimulus from which the difference is noted.

Weber-Fechner l. Fechner's law or Weber's law, especially implying recognition of the identity of the two as can be shown by the mathematical derivation of one from the other when sensation is regarded as directly measurable in j.n.d. units, *q.v.*

Wien's displacement l. The wavelength for which spectral emittance is a maximum for complete radiators is inversely proportional to its absolute temperature.

Wien's radiation l. An empirical formula derived by Wien to represent the relationship between energy emission, wavelength, and the temperature of a radiator, similar to a more generally applicable radiation formula derived by Planck from quantum considerations. See also *Planck's law.*

Wundt-Lamanski l. The oblique fixational movements of the eye, as inferred from afterimage studies by Wundt and Lamanski, do not follow the shortest route, i.e., the afterimage tracing the path of movement is curved rather than straight.

Zeune's l. A theory that climate has much to do with blindness, whence it is stated that the proportion of blindness is least in the Temperate Zone and increases in the direction of the Frigid Zone and in the direction of the equator.

Lawford's syndrome. See under *syndrome.*

layer. A deposited substance of uniform, or nearly uniform, thickness; one thickness laid over or under another.

anterior border l. of the iris. Anterior limiting layer of the iris.

anterior limiting l. of the iris. The layer of the iris, between the anterior endothelium and the stroma, which is a condensation of the anterior stroma consisting of anastomosing and intertwining processes of connective tissue and pigment cells. Syn., *anterior border layer of the iris.*

anterior pigment l. of Fuchs. The anterior layer of the posterior pigmented epithelial layer of the iris containing myoepithelial, pigmented, spindle cell bodies. Their myofibrils constitute the dilator pupillae muscle. Syn., *layer of pigmented spindle cells.*

bacillary l. Layer of rods and cones.

Bowman's l. Bowman's membrane.

Bruch's l. 1. The lamina vitrea or innermost membrane of the choroid. 2. The lamina vitrea of the ciliary body. 3. The posterior border lamella of Fuchs.

cerebral l. of retina. One of two subdivisions of the retina which contains the inner nuclear, the inner molecular, the ganglion cell, and the nerve fiber layers and the internal limiting membrane, the other being the *neuroepithelial layer of the retina.*

Chievitz l. Transient fiber layer of Chievitz.

choriocapillary l. Choriocapillaris.

columnar l. Layer of rods and cones. *Obs.*

fiber l. of Henle. In the region of the macula lutea, the horizontally directed fibers of the rods and cones located in the outer molecular layer.

fiber l. of Mueller. Mueller's fibers.

ganglion cell l. The layer of the retina lying between the inner molecular and the nerve fiber layers and containing large cell bodies whose neurons send axons into the nerve fiber layer, into the ipsilateral optic nerve, and into both optic tracts to synapse in the lateral geniculate bodies, the pretectal areas, and the superior colliculi.

Haller's l. A layer of the choroid lying between the suprachoroid and Sattler's layer, composed of connective tissue and large blood vessels whose capillaries are located in the choriocapillaris.

Henle's l. Fiber layer of Henle.

inner granular l. Layer IV of the cerebral cortex which thickens in the region of the visual cortex to comprise its most voluminous layer. It is composed of three sublayers, an inner and an outer cellular lamina and a middle lamina containing the outer line of Baillarger.

Kölliker's fibrous l. The stroma of the iris.

lacrimal l. Precorneal film.

limiting l. of retina, external. The membrane of the retina lying between the layer of rods and cones and the outer nuclear layer, through which pass the processes of the rods and cones. It is thought to consist of the united ends of the fibers of Mueller or the remains of the original intercellular cement of the fetal retinal cells. Syn., *external limiting membrane of the retina.*

limiting l. of retina, internal. The membrane of the retina lying between the nerve fiber layer of the retina and the vitreous, forming the inner limit of the retina and the outer boundary of the vitreous, occasionally called the *hyaloid membrane of the vitreous.* It is continuous with the central meniscus of Kuhnt and is thought to be partially formed by the ends of the fibers of Mueller.

Syn., *internal limiting membrane of the retina.*

lipid l. of the cornea. The fatty layer of the basement membrane located between its reticular layer and the basal cells of the corneal epithelium.

marginal l. of His. Marginal layer of the optic cup.

marginal l. of the optic cup. The outer, nonnucleated layer of cells of the optic cup in the early embryo bounding the primitive layer of the optic cup. Syn., *marginal layer of His.*

molecular l., inner. The layer of the retina between the inner nuclear and the ganglion cell layers in which the neurons of these two layers synapse and in which amacrine cells synapse. Syn., *inner plexiform layer.*

molecular l., outer. The layer of the retina between the outer and the inner nuclear layers in which the neurons of these two layers synapse and in which horizontal cells synapse. Syn., *outer plexiform layer.*

nerve fiber l. The layer of the retina lying between the ganglion cell layer and the internal limiting membrane, containing axons of the ganglion cells and arterioles and venules of the central retinal vessels.

neuroblastic l. of optic cup, inner. The inner of two collections of nuclei in the embryonic retina which forms amacrine and ganglion cells.

neuroblastic l. of optic cup, outer. The outer of two collections of nuclei in the embryonic retina which forms visual, horizontal, and bipolar cells.

neuroepithelial l. of retina. One of two subdivisions of the retina which contains the layer of rods and cones, the external limiting membrane, the outer nuclear layer, and the outer molecular layer,

the other being the *cerebral layer of retina.*

nuclear l., inner. The layer of the retina lying between the inner and the outer molecular layers and containing amacrine, bipolar, and horizontal cell bodies, nuclei of the fibers of Mueller, and capillaries of the central retinal vessels. Syn., *membrana granulosa interna.*

nuclear l., outer. The layer of the retina lying between the external limiting membrane and the outer molecular layer containing the cell bodies of rods and cones. Syn., *membrana granulosa externa.*

pigment epithelium l. of retina. The layer of the retina lying between the lamina vitrea of the choroid and the layer of rods and cones of the retina, consisting of a single layer of hexagonal cells which contain the pigment fuscin and have processes that surround the outer segments of the rods and cones. One of its main functions is the transfer of oxygen and foods from the choriocapillaris to the rod and cone cells.

pigmented spindle cells, l. of. Anterior pigment layer of Fuchs.

plexiform l., inner. Inner molecular layer.

plexiform l., outer. Outer molecular layer.

primitive l. of optic cup. The innermost, nucleated layer of cells of the optic cup in the early embryo whose periphery is bounded by the marginal layer of the optic cup. It is the embryonic layer which differentiates into the *inner* and the *outer neuroblastic layers.*

proliferating l. of optic cup. The outermost layer of cells of the optic cup where cell division occurs in the early embryo. It gives rise to the visual cells, the fibers of Mueller, all neurons of the retina, and the pars caeca retinae.

reticular l. of the cornea. The layer of the basement membrane located between its lipid layer and Bowman's membrane which may be subdivided into three layers of reticular fibers, the anterior being most dense and the middle being the least.

retinal l's. The 10 layers of the retina: the pigment epithelium layer, the layer of rods and cones, the external limiting membrane, the outer nuclear layer, the outer molecular layer, the inner nuclear layer, the inner molecular layer, the ganglion cell layer, the nerve fiber layer, and the internal limiting membrane.

rods and cones, l. of. The layer of the retina containing the receptive portions of the rods and cones, excluding their nuclei. It is approximately 40 μ in thickness and is bounded posteriorly by the pigment epithelium layer and anteriorly by the external limiting membrane. Syn., *bacillary layer; Jacob's membrane.*

Sattler's l. The layer of the choroid, lying between Haller's layer and the choriocapillaris, containing the smaller arteries and veins. Syn., *Sattler's lamina.*

substantia propria l. The main connective tissue portion or stroma of a structure, as in the cornea, the sclera, the choroid, or the iris.

suprachoroid l. Suprachoroid.

tear l. Precorneal film.

transient fiber l. of Chievitz. The temporary layer which separates the primitive inner and the outer neuroblastic layers of the embryonic retina. It is a clear layer containing the inner processes of the fibers of Mueller.

Lazich's test (lăz'iks). See under *test.*

L.E. Abbreviation for *left eye.*

leaf room. See under *room.*

Leavell (leh-vel') **Hand-Eye Co-ordinator; tests.** See under the nouns.

Lebensohn (la'ben-sōn) **astigmometer; chart.** See under the nouns.

Leber's (la-berz') **congenital amaurosis; miliary aneurysms; venous circle; retinal degeneration; disease; plexus; theory.** See under the nouns.

Lederer lenses (led'er-er). See under *lens.*

LeGrand-Geblewics phenomenon (le-grahnd'geh-blev'iks). See under *phenomenon.*

leiomyoma (li″o-mi-o'mah). A tumor derived from smooth muscle characterized histologically by elongated spindle-shaped cells and myoglia fibrils. It is usually benign and may involve the iris and less frequently the ciliary body or orbit. When involving the iris it has a predilection for the pupillary margin, is lightly pigmented, and may be well localized but is more often diffuse

leiomyosarcoma (li″o-mi″o-sar-ko'-mah). A malignant tumor derived from smooth muscle which may involve the iris, ciliary body, or orbit.

leishmaniasis (lēsh-man-i'ah-sis). Ulceration of the face, eyelids, and cornea due to infection with the protozoan *Leishmania tropica.* The corneal lesions are deep and spread to involve the entire cornea.

lema (le'mah). The dried and hardened Meibomian secretion collected at the inner canthus of the eye.

Leman prism (le'man). See under *prism.*

lemmocytes (lem'o-sīts). Cells intimately connected with unmyelinated nerve fibers, representing the equivalent of the elements of the sheath of Schwann which surround myelinated nerve fibers. They are found in the peripheral nervous system and in the nerve fiber layer of the retina. Syn., *Remak's cells.*

lemniscus, optic (lem-nis′kus). Optic tract.

length. The number of units expressing the result of measurement of a distance in one direction.

focal l. The linear distance between a point of reference, usually a principal point, of an optical system and the corresponding primary or secondary focal point.

focal l., anterior. Primary focal length.

focal l., back. The linear distance between the back vertex of an optical system and the secondary focal point. Syn., *posterior vertex focal distance.*

focal l., equivalent. The linear distance between the secondary principal point of an optical system and the secondary focal point.

focal l., front. The linear distance between the front vertex of an optical system and the primary focal point. Syn., *anterior vertex focal distance.*

focal l., posterior. Secondary focal length.

focal l., primary. The linear distance from the primary principal point to the primary focal point of an optical system. Syn., *anterior focal length; anterior principal focal length; primary principal focal length.*

focal l., principal (anterior). Primary focal length.

focal l., principal (posterior). Secondary focal length.

focal l., principal (primary). Primary focal length.

focal l., principal (secondary). Secondary focal length.

focal l., secondary. The linear distance from the secondary principal point to the secondary focal point of an optical system. Syn., *posterior focal length; posterior principal focal length; secondary principal focal length.*

focal l., vertex. The focal length of an optical system as measured from the back or front vertex to the secondary or primary focal point, respectively.

optical l. The product of the length of the path of a ray in a medium and the index of refraction of the medium.

lens. A piece of glass or other transparent substance having two opposite regular surfaces, either plane or curved, and functioning as a part or all of an optical system. More generally, it may include opaque objects with regular reflecting surfaces (e.g., a mirror lens in a reflecting telescope) or an assembly of several individual lenses regarded as a single unit (e.g., a camera doublet or a multifocal spectacle lens).

absorption l. A lens which absorbs a portion of the incident light.

absorptive l. Absorption lens.

achromatic l. A compound lens designed to reduce or eliminate chromatic aberration. The most common form is a converging system consisting of a crown glass convex lens of low dispersive power combined with a flint glass concave lens of high dispersive power but of lower refractive power.

actinic l. An absorption lens which primarily absorbs ultraviolet radiation.

adherent l. Contact lens.

afocal l. A lens of zero focal power in which rays entering parallel emerge parallel.

Allen-Braley fundus l. A planoconcave plastic scleral contact lens mounted by means of spring wire supports in a plastic speculum for use in slit lamp examination of the deep vitreous and fundus.

anastigmatic l. A lens with spherical surfaces and therefore said to have no cylindrical component. Anastigmatic lenses are one of two categories of ophthalmic lenses, the other being *astigmatic lenses.* Syn., *stigmatic lens.*

aniseikonic l. Iseikonic lens.

anterior chamber l. Anterior chamber implant.

Aolite l. A trade name for one of a series of plastic lenses made in both single vision and multifocal form.

aphakic l. A convex spectacle lens of high dioptric power, so named because its principal use is in the correction of vision in aphakia. Syn., *cataract lens.*

aplanatic l. A lens designed to correct for spherical aberration and coma.

apochromatic l. A compound lens designed to correct for spherical and chromatic aberrations.

Apollonio l. A small, plastic lens placed in the anterior chamber of the eyeball to replace the crystalline lens, following cataract surgery. It is held in position by a three-pronged plastic mount.

armor plate l. Case-hardened lens.

aspherical l. A lens in which one or both surfaces in the central sagittal section do not describe a circle, usually conforming instead to a parabola or some similar curve systematically deviant from a circle from the center to the periphery of the lens, so designed to correct for or reduce certain types of aberrations.

astigmatic l. A lens with one or both surfaces toric or toroidal, and therefore said to have a cylindrical component and to produce two perpendicularly oriented focal lines in the principal meridians instead of a single focal point. Astigmatic lenses are one of two categories of ophthalmic lenses, the other being *anastigmatic lenses.*

Astikorrect l. A variable power, cylindrical lens system designed for use with the Raubitschek test consisting of two counterrotating +1.00 D. sph.−2.00 D. cyl.

lenses in a hand-held assembly. It provides powers ranging from plano to +2.00 D. sph.−4.00 D. cyl. with the spherical power at any position being half the cylindrical power and of opposite sign.

balance l. A spectacle lens of undesignated power serving only to balance the weight and the appearance of its mate in front of the other eye.

Barkan goniotomy l. A thick, convex, contact lens used to provide a magnified view of the iris and filtration angle during goniotomy.

Barlow l. A concave achromatic lens placed between the objective and eyepiece of a telescope to provide greater magnification of the image with only a slight increase in focal length.

Baron l. A rectangular, plastic lens placed in the anterior chamber of the eyeball to replace the crystalline lens, following cataract surgery. Being larger than other such lenses, it has no mount and is held in position by its own edges.

baseball l. A double bifocal lens in which the two reading segments are rounded so that the lens resembles the seamline of a baseball.

best-form l. A corrected curve lens.

bicentric l. A lens with two optical centers.

biconcave l. 1. A lens with both surfaces concave. 2. A double concave lens in which both surfaces are equal in curvature.

biconvex l. 1. A lens with both surfaces convex. 2. A double convex lens in which both surfaces are equal in curvature.

bicylindrical l. A lens with both surfaces toroidal. Syn., *bitoric lens.*

Bietti l. A small plastic lens placed in the anterior chamber of the eyeball to replace the crystalline lens, following cataract surgery.

The lens is held in position either by a four-pronged plastic mount or by a curved, rectangular, plastic plate into which the lens is secured.

bifocal l. A spectacle lens of two portions whose focal powers differ from each other. Usually the upper portion is larger and is for distant vision, and the lower portion is smaller and is for near vision.

bifocal l., baseball. See *lens, baseball.*

bifocal l., Bitex. An obsolete one-piece bifocal similar to the modern Ultex E bifocal lens.

bifocal l., blended. A one-piece bifocal lens in which there is a gradual transitional zone between the two curves of different radii instead of the line of demarcation contained in the conventional bifocal.

bifocal l., cement. A bifocal lens made by cementing a small wafer-thin lens to a larger lens.

bifocal l., C. V. (complete vision). An obsolete, monocentric multifocal lens designed by Andrew J. Cross. It consists of one piece of crown glass, ground on the inside surface into three different spherical curvatures, a large upper distance segment, a smaller lower reading segment, and two lateral areas of intermediate power.

bifocal l., depressed. An obsolete one-piece bifocal lens made by grinding the steeper curvature of the reading portion into the flatter surface required for the distance portion, causing the reading portion of the lens to be depressed and thinner.

bifocal l., double. A multifocal lens having two segments for near vision, one at the top and one at the bottom, with the portion for distant vision in between.

bifocal l., Executive. A mono-centric, one-piece bifocal lens with a straight, horizontal line of junction, between the two portions, extending across the entire lens.

bifocal l., Franklin. The original bifocal invented by Benjamin Franklin in 1784. It consists of two half lenses mounted together in the same frame, the upper half for distant vision and the lower for near vision.

bifocal l., Ful-Vue. A trade name for a fused bifocal lens with the optical center of the reading segment 4 mm. below its slightly curved top.

bifocal l., fused. A bifocal lens in which the added dioptric power required for near seeing is accomplished by countersinking into the surface of a crown glass lens a small lens, sometimes called a *button*, of barium crown, flint, or some other glass of higher index of refraction, and fusing the two types of glass in a high temperature oven for permanent adhesion.

bifocal l., Kryptok. A fused bifocal lens with a round flint glass reading segment, invented by John L. Borsch.

bifocal l., monaxial. An obsolete monocentric bifocal lens consisting of one piece of crown glass ground on the inside surface into three different spherical curvatures, similar in principle to the C. V. bifocal lens.

bifocal l., monocentric. A bifocal lens in which the optical centers of the two portions are coincident.

bifocal l., Nokrome. A trade name for a fused bifocal lens having a barium crown reading segment for the reduction of chromatic aberration.

bifocal l., one-piece. A bifocal lens consisting of a single piece of crown glass with two different curvatures ground on one surface.

bifocal l., Opifex. A cement bifocal lens having an extremely thin wafer reading segment.

bifocal l., Panoptik. A trade name for a fused bifocal lens with the optical center of the reading segment 3 mm. below its slightly curved top.

bifocal l., Perfection. A bifocal lens invented by August Morck, similar in principle to the Franklin bifocal lens. It was made by removing an arch-shaped portion from the lower half of the distance lens and fitting in a lens of different power for near vision.

bifocal l., RedeRite. A trade name for a one-piece bifocal lens featuring a major portion of the lens for near vision and a small segment in the upper portion for distant vision.

bifocal l., solid. A one-piece bifocal lens.

bifocal l., solid upcurve. An obsolete one-piece bifocal lens invented by Isaac Schnaitmann. The process of manufacture consisted of grinding the top portion of a reading glass to the distance prescription.

bifocal l., split. Franklin bifocal lens.

bifocal l., Turay. A trade name for a series of one-piece bifocal lenses.

bifocal l., Twinsite. A trade name for a series of one-piece bifocal lenses.

bifocal l., Ultex. A trade name for a series of one-piece bifocal lenses.

bifocal l., Unisite. An obsolete monocentric one-piece bifocal similar to the modern Ultex B bifocal lens.

bifocal l., Univis. A trade name for a series of fused bifocal lenses, most of which are char-

acterized by a straight top segment for near vision.

bifocal l., Widesite. A trade name for a series of fused bifocal lenses.

Billet's split l. Two halves of a convex lens divided along an axial plane and slightly separated to produce interference fringes in the overlapping images.

Binkhorst l. Iris clip lens.

Binkhorst-Weinstein-Troutman l. A lens placed in the pupillary opening following cataract surgery to render the eye emmetropic and to eliminate aniseikonia. It is a doublet consisting of an anterior concavoplano lens and a posterior convexoplano lens separated by an enclosed airspace, and is weightless in aqueous humor. Loops attached to the lens are fixed to the iris to hold it in position.

Bioptic telescopic l. A lens system used as a subnormal vision aid consisting of a small diameter Galilean telescope to magnify distant objects, mounted on the upper front surface of a plastic carrier lens having the patient's distance lens correction.

bispherical l. A lens that is spherical on both sides.

bitoric l. A lens having toroidal surfaces on both sides, used primarily in the correction of aniseikonia.

bitoric l., oblique. A bitoric lens in which the principal meridians of the two toroidal surfaces are not coincident, a type of lens used in the combined correction of a meridional aniseikonia and a cylindrical refractive error obliquely oriented with respect to each other.

blank, l. A molded piece of ophthalmic glass prior to grinding and polishing into a lens.

blended l. See *bifocal lens, blended.*

bloomed l. Coated lens.

Bonvue l. A trade name for a series of multibase curve lenses and for a series of fused bifocal and trifocal lenses.

Brücke's l. Brücke's loupe.

capsule, l. See under *capsule*.

Cartesian l. A lens proposed by Descartes to eliminate spherical aberration in which one surface is spherical and the other is ellipsoidal.

case-hardened l. A lens subjected to high temperature for superficial annealing of the glass to increase resistance to breakage by impact. Syn., *tempered lens.* Cf. *safety lens.*

cataract l. Aphakic lens.

Catmin l. A minifying spectacle lens consisting of a reversed Galilean telescope system of three glass lenses cemented together, designed to obtain equal binocular image size in the correction of monocular aphakia.

cement substance, l. The noncellular amorphous material secreted by the cells of the crystalline lens, found just within the lens capsule, posterior to the anterior epithelium, in the Y-sutures, in the more complicated lens stars, and between the individual lens fibers.

centered l. A lens whose optical center coincides with its geometrical center.

centering l. A plano lens having two etched lines, at right angles to each other, intersecting at its center, and used to align and center the cell of a trial frame with the center of the pupil.

Chavasse l. A spectacle lens with a rippled, multiple-facet back surface, designed by Chavasse to function as an occluder by its distortion of the retinal image, though still permitting the eye to be seen clearly through it.

Clear-Image l. A trade name for a magnifying telescopic spectacle lens designed and manufactured by Feinbloom.

clock, l. Lens measure.

coated l. A lens on whose surfaces is deposited a metallic salt, such as magnesium fluoride, about one fourth as thick as a wavelength of light, to reduce, by interference, the amount of light reflected, and, if combined with a coloring ingredient, to reduce light transmission also.

cobalt l. A plano ophthalmic test lens made of cobalt glass, characterized by its relatively selective transmission of the red and blue spectral colors, hence useful in the bichrome testing of ametropia.

Coddington l. A magnifying lens consisting essentially of a cylindrical section through a solid sphere of glass, its two refracting surfaces being segments of the surface of the sphere.

collimating l. A lens placed in such a manner that the source or object is located at one of its focal points; hence, the refracted rays from an object point will leave the lens parallel to each other.

compound l. 1. A spectacle lens which functions as a combination of a simple spherical lens and a simple cylindrical lens. 2. A lens system composed of two or more coaxially placed lenses.

concave l. Diverging lens.

concavoconcave l. A lens which is concave on both surfaces.

concavoconvex l. A converging meniscus lens. Cf. *convexoconcave lens.*

concentric l. A meniscus lens whose two surfaces have a common center of curvature.

condensing l. A condenser.

congeneric l. In relation to another lens of reference, one which is of the same sign or dioptric character, whence a pair of converging lenses or a pair of diverging lenses are said to be congeneric. Cf. *contrageneric lens.*

contact l. A small, shell-like, bowl-shaped glass or plastic lens that rests directly on the eye, in contact with the cornea or the sclera or both, serving as a new anterior surface of the eye and/or as a retainer for fluid between the cornea and the contact lens, ordinarily to correct for refractive errors of the eye.

contact l., A-B-C self-centering. A modification of the Feincone contact lens providing for minimum corneal clearance.

contact l., afocal. A contact lens whose optical section has no refractive power.

contact l., Akiyama. A narrow and approximately rectangular contact lens designed to rest on the lower portion of the cornea and to cover the pupil only when the eye rotates downward as in looking at a near object.

contact l., Allen-O'Brien. Allen's contact prism.

contact l., Bayshore. A type of palpebral contact lens fitted with a base curve significantly steeper than the flatter principal meridian of the cornea to provide constant and definite apical clearance, a secondary curve approximating the cornea on which it rests, and a narrow peripheral curve of 17.0 mm. radius to contain a reservoir of tear fluid at the rim. Syn., *B.T. contact lens.*

contact l., bicurve. A corneal contact lens having two curvatures on its posterior surface, one the central base curve forming the optic zone, and the other a flatter curve forming the annular peripheral zone.

contact l., Bier. Either the Contour contact lens or the Transcurve contact lens designed by Norman Bier.

contact l., bifocal. A contact lens having two portions of different focal powers, one for distant vision and one for near vision.

contact l., bifocal (alternating vision). A bifocal contact lens so designed that the pupillary area of the eye is effectively covered by either the reading zone or the distance zone, but not by both.

contact l., bifocal (annular). A bifocal contact lens having a central round zone for distance vision surrounded by an annular zone for near vision.

contact l., bifocal (Bicon). A monocentric, shifting, alternating vision, bifocal contact lens having two curvatures on its front surface, providing a central round zone for distance vision surrounded by an annular zone for near vision.

contact l., bifocal (Bi-Profile). An annular bifocal contact lens made from a single piece of plastic having four monocentric curvatures on its back surface, a central base curve, a slightly flatter secondary curve approximately 1.5 to 2.0 mm. wide, which provides up to +1.00 D. of additional power, and a flatter tertiary curve and bevel. A second peripheral curve commencing coincident with the margin of the central base curve is added to the front surface when more than a +1.00 D. addition is required.

contact l., bifocal (bivisual). A bifocal contact lens so designed that portions of the pupillary area of the eye are covered simultaneously by both the reading zone and the the distance zone, e.g., *deCarle bifocal contact lens.*

contact l., bifocal (Black). A shifting, alternating vision, bifocal contact lens made of a single piece of plastic with two different curvatures cut on the front surface to provide a reading portion below and a distance portion above, the junction line being a curve whose convexity is toward the bottom of the lens.

contact l., bifocal (Brucker). A prism ballast, alternating vision, bifocal contact lens having an optical zone for distance vision decentered upward and surrounded by the reading addition, the power of which is determined essentially by the radius of the secondary curve.

contact l., bifocal (Camp). A prism ballast bifocal contact lens, truncated at the base, having a round reading segment, of a plastic of higher index of refraction, fused into its posterior surface.

contact l., bifocal (Cinefro). A shifting, alternating vision, bifocal contact lens made of a single piece of plastic with two different curvatures cut on the front surface to provide a reading portion below and a distance portion above, the junction line being a curve whose convexity is toward the top of the lens.

contact l., bifocal (Contour Comfort). A truncated, prism ballast, alternating vision, fused, bifocal contact lens with a segment for near vision formed by pouring liquid plastic into a countersink cut on the back surface. The liquid plastic contains a dye which fluoresces under black light to facilitate its location.

contact l., bifocal (deCarle). A bivisual, monocentric, bifocal contact lens having two curvatures on its posterior surface, providing a central, small, round distance portion surrounded by an annular reading portion.

contact l., bifocal (fused). A bifocal contact lens constructed of two pieces of plastic, of different indices of refraction, fused together.

contact l., bifocal (Genevay). An alternating vision, bifocal contact lens made of one piece of plastic and having two curvatures on its posterior surface, providing a central round zone for distance

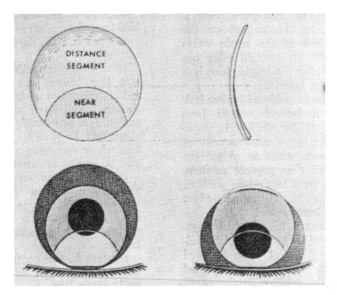

Fig. 27. Camp bifocal contact lens. (From *Corneal Contact Lenses*, ed. by L. J. Girard, C. V. Mosby Co., 1964)

vision surrounded by an annular zone for near vision.

contact l., bifocal (No-Jump). A prism ballast, alternating vision, bifocal contact lens, truncated at the base, made of a single piece of plastic having two curves on its front surface with a common center of curvature to eliminate prismatic jump. It provides a reading portion below and a distance portion above, the junction line being a curve whose convexity is toward the top of the lens.

contact l., bifocal (Paraseg K). An oval-shaped, alternating vision, bifocal contact lens made of a single piece of plastic having two curvatures on its posterior surface to provide a reading portion below and a distance portion above, the junction line being a curve whose convexity is toward the bottom of the lens.

contact l., bifocal (piggyback). A combination of a single vision contact lens and a half-moon-shaped lens which provides the additional power for near vision. The half-moon lens is placed by the patient on the lower half of the single vision lens with its straight edge upwards, after the single vision lens has been inserted.

contact l., bifocal (prism ballast). A bifocal contact lens, usually of the alternating vision type, having a small amount of base-down prism to weight the lens and thus prevent rotation, to provide a low riding position, and to assist the propping effect of the lower eyelid.

contact l., bifocal (shifting). A bifocal contact lens of the alternating vision type so designed that the lens will be displaced vertically, relative to the pupil, as the eye rotates upward or downward, so that the appro-

priate reading zone will effectively cover the pupil.

contact l., bifocal (target). A bifocal contact lens having a central round zone for distance vision surrounded by an annular zone for near vision, hence resembling a target.

contact l., bifocal (U.V.). An alternating vision, prism ballast, fused, bifocal contact lens having a circular reading segment in the lower portion of the lens impregnated with a dye which fluoresces under black light to facilitate its location.

contact l., bifocal (Wesley-Jessen). A prism ballast, alternating vision, fused, bifocal contact lens having a circular reading segment in the lower portion of the lens which has been impregnated with a fluorescing substance to facilitate its location with black light.

contact l., bitoric. A contact lens, both surfaces of which are toric, usually fabricated so that the steepest radius of each surface lies in the same meridian.

contact l., blown. A contact lens formed by glass blowing.

contact l., B.T. Bayshore contact lens.

contact l., channelled. A contact lens having one or more radial depressions on its posterior surface which serve as channels to facilitate tear circulation.

contact l., closed. A contact lens whose surface is continuous, that is, free of fenestrations.

contact l., Comberg. A contact lens containing radiopaque reference markings, used with x-ray photography for the localization of intraocular foreign bodies.

contact l., Concentra. Trade name for a type of bicurve corneal contact lens.

contact l., Continuous Curve. A corneal contact lens

having a spherical central base curve and an aspherical peripheral curve.

contact l., Contour. A corneal contact lens, approximately 9.5 mm. in diameter, which has a molded ocular surface of three different curvatures: a central curve conforming to the central corneal curve, a flatter peripheral curve, and a transitional curve blending the two.

contact l., control. Trial contact lens.

contact l., corneal. A contact lens which rests primarily on the cornea rather than on the sclera and requires no auxiliary fluid. Syn., *corneal lens.*

contact l., cosmetic. A contact lens designed to alter or enhance the appearance of the eye, as to conceal a disfigurement or to change its color. It may range from a tinted lens to a completely opaque lens with a painted pupil, iris, and sclera.

contact l., Cycon. The trade name for a corneal contact lens having a toric base curve. The peripheral curves of the posterior surface and the anterior lens surface may be either toric or spherical.

contact l., Dallos. 1. A glass scleral contact lens molded from a casting of the patient's eye, with its anterior corneal surface ground to prescription, originally designed by Dallos in 1932. 2. A glass scleral contact lens, more recently designed by Dallos, having a small perforating vent near the limbal area in the inferior temporal region.

contact l., diagnostic. 1. Trial contact lens. 2. A contact lens used in the diagnosis of ocular pathology, such as a goniolens.

contact l., facet (regular). A corneal contact lens with four slightly raised facets symmetrically distributed near the pe-

riphery of the otherwise spherical posterior surface.

contact l., facet (toric). A corneal contact lens with two slightly raised facets symmetrically placed in the meridian of greatest curvature near the periphery of the posterior toroidal surface.

contact l., Feinbloom. Any one of several types of contact lenses made and supplied by Feinbloom, including: (1) a molded, scleral contact lens, designed by Feinbloom in 1936, consisting of a transparent glass corneal section and a translucent plastic scleral section, used in conjunction with a fluid; (2) a prefabricated, scleral contact lens, designed by Feinbloom in 1939, consisting of a transparent glass corneal section, 12 mm. in diameter, and a translucent plastic scleral section 24 mm. in diameter, used in conjunction with a fluid; (3) the Feincone contact lens; and (4) the A-B-C self-centering contact lens.

contact l., Feincone. A prefabricated, plastic, scleral contact lens, designed by Feinbloom in 1945, consisting of a spherical corneal section, not in contact with the cornea or the limbus, a conical section extending from the corneal section in contact with the sclera, and a temporal spherical flange to prevent the lids from striking the edge of the cone. It is used in conjunction with a fluid. Syn., *tangent cone contact lens.*

contact l., fenestrated. A contact lens containing one or more perforations for the more rapid transfer of air and/or tears between the lens and cornea.

contact l., fitting. Trial contact lens.

contact l., fluid. A scleral contact lens in which the distance between the posterior optical surface and the anterior surface of the cornea is such that the addition of artificial tear fluid is required to fill the space between the two surfaces.

contact l., fluidless. Minimum clearance contact lens.

contact l., focal. A contact lens whose optical section has a measurable degree of refractive power.

contact l., formed. A contact lens made by thermoforming sheet acrylic plastic to a die or eye model.

contact l., gel. A contact lens made of hydrophilic plastic which is hard and brittle when dry, but becomes soft and flexible when hydrated, in which state it is worn.

contact l., ground. Any contact lens whose corneal section has been ground and polished.

contact l., haptic. Any contact lens having a section designed to rest on the sclera.

contact l., hard. A contact lens made of a substance which absorbs little or no water, thus remaining in a hard state when worn.

contact l., Heine afocal. A glass, scleral, afocal contact lens, designed by Heine in 1929, having a corneal section of a radius of curvature selected to provide a fluid lens of sufficient dioptric power to correct the ametropia.

contact l., Hornstein. A corneal contact lens designed to be fitted with a base curve steeper in curvature than the flattest central corneal curve, to provide definite central corneal clearance.

contact l., Imcor. A trade name for a corneal contact lens formed to a model of the cornea which, in turn, is made from a corneal impression. It may be used either as formed or with a central base curve cut with a lathe.

contact l., impression. A contact lens prepared from the casting of the eye to which it is to be fitted.

contact l., Jungschaffer. A diagnostic corneal contact lens of high concave dioptric power for examination of the vitreous and fundus in slit lamp biomicroscopy

contact l., Kalt's. One of the early corneal contact lenses constructed of glass and designed by E. Kalt in 1888.

contact l., Keraform. A microlens with four slightly raised facets symmetrically distributed near the periphery of the otherwise spherical posterior surface.

contact l., Kollmorgen. Any one of several types of contact lenses made and supplied by Kollmorgen, including: (1) a ground and polished glass, scleral contact lens having spherical corneal and scleral sections, used in conjunction with an auxiliary fluid; (2) a ground and polished glass, scleral contact lens having a spherical corneal and toroidal scleral section, used in conjunction with an auxiliary fluid; and (3) a molded glass, scleral contact lens used in conjunction with an auxiliary fluid.

contact l., lenticular. A corneal contact lens of high dioptric power with the prescription ground only in the central portion, permitting a reduced center thickness in convex lenses and a reduced edge thickness in concave lenses.

contact l., lenticular (tangential). A corneal contact lens of high convex dioptric power in which, to reduce central thickness, only the central portion contains the prescription, with the second curve being flatter and cut on the anterior surface, tangent to the central curve, in order to present a smooth and continuous transition.

contact l., LoVac. A series of plastic diagnostic contact lenses which are fixed to the eye by a low vacuum created by a rubber bulb connected to the lens by a polyvinyl-chloride tube. The series includes lenses for gonioscopy, for inspection of the fundus, for electroretinography, and for foreign body location.

contact l., LoVac fundus. A LoVac corneal contact lens having a flat anterior surface, used with the slit lamp biomicroscope for viewing the deep vitreous body and the region of the fundus of the eye central to the equator.

contact l., LoVac peripheral fundus. A LoVac contact lens having a flat anterior surface set at a 30° angle with the visual axis, used with the slit lamp biomicroscope for viewing the peripheral fundus of the eye.

contact l., Micro-V. A bicurve corneal contact lens having radial channels in the peripheral secondary curve portion to facilitate tear circulation.

contact l., minimum clearance. A scleral contact lens in which the posterior optical surface is in close approximation to the anterior surface of the cornea, the space between the two surfaces being filled with normal tear fluid, without requiring an auxiliary artificial tear fluid. Syn., *fluidless contact lens.*

contact l., molded. 1. A contact lens prepared from the casting of the eye to which it is to be fitted. Cf. *preformed contact lens.* 2. A contact lens prepared from dies, i.e., not cut by a machine.

contact l., monocurve. A corneal contact lens having a single

curvature on each surface, exclusive of edge bevels.

contact l., monticule. A contact lens having one or more small elevations on its posterior surface.

contact l., Mueller. 1. A blown glass contact lens, designed by F. E. Mueller in 1887, to protect the cornea from exposure. It is considered to be the first of the modern contact lenses. 2. A blown glass contact lens, designed by F. E. Mueller in 1909, having a transparent corneal section and a white opaque scleral section, for the correction of ametropia.

contact l., Mueller-Welt. Any one of several types of contact lenses developed by Mueller-Welt, including: (1) a spherical, afocal, blown glass, scleral contact lens, developed in 1924, used in conjunction with an auxiliary fluid, for correcting ametropia; (2) a spherical, blown glass, scleral contact lens, developed in 1933, having refractive power and used in conjunction with an auxiliary fluid; (3) a blown glass, scleral contact lens, developed in 1935, having refractive power and a parabolic scleral section and used in conjunction with an auxiliary fluid; (4) a prefabricated, plastic, scleral contact lens, developed in 1945, having refractive power and a parabolic scleral section, used in conjunction with an auxiliary fluid; (5) a type of prefabricated, fluidless, plastic scleral contact lens; and (6) corneal contact lenses.

contact l., multicurve. A corneal contact lens having two or more curvatures on its posterior surface.

contact l., offset. A preformed scleral contact lens in which the scleral section is aspherical and the centers of curvature of the radii do not coincide with the axis of symmetry of the corneal section.

contact l., open. A contact lens containing one or more fenestrations for the more rapid transfer of air and/or tears between the lens and cornea.

contact l., palpebral. A corneal contact lens usually of small diameter and designed to fit within the palpebral fissure, free of contact with the limbus and eyelid margins, except during blinking.

contact l., Para-Curve. A trade name for a type of corneal contact lens having an aspheric secondary curve.

contact l., pentacurve. A corneal contact lens in which the posterior optical zone is surrounded by four distinct and separate annuli, the surface of each being successively of less curvature.

contact l., peripheral angle. A corneal contact lens in which the peripheral portion of the posterior surface is shaped to a solid angle by means of a cone-shaped cutting tool.

contact l., piggy-back. A half-moon-shaped lens placed, straight edge upwards, by the wearer on the lower half of a regular single vision contact lens which has been inserted, in order to provide additional power for near vision.

contact l., prefabricated. Preformed contact lens.

contact l., preformed. A contact lens prepared from a stock model or die. Cf. *molded contact lens.* Syn., *prefabricated contact lens.*

contact l., prism ballast. A corneal contact lens having a small amount of prism to compensate for hyperphoria or to weight the lens in one meridional direction, either to effect a lower riding position or to aid in proper orientation of cylindrical corrections or bifocal segments.

contact l., scleral. A contact lens which fits over both the cornea and the surrounding sclera, used with or without an auxiliary fluid to fill the space between the lens and the cornea.

contact l., Scleroform. A fenestrated scleral lens having a small scleral section and therefore a small overall diameter, designed primarily for use in sports.

contact l., Soehnges Micro Pupil Multifocal. A multifocal corneal contact lens having a central zone for distance vision surrounded by a zone for near vision, in which the curvature on the anterior surface increases continuously toward the periphery to provide a continuously increasing addition.

contact l., soft. A contact lens made of a water-absorbing substance which, when worn, is soft and flexible.

contact l., Sphercon. A corneal contact lens, of approximately 9 mm. diameter and 0.2 mm. thickness, which has a secondary flatter curve or bevel at its periphery. Its central portion is fitted to conform closely to the central curves of the cornea.

contact l., Spherex. A trade name for a type of bicurve corneal contact lens.

contact l., spherical. 1. A corneal contact lens whose inside surface is spherical. Cf. *toric contact lens.* 2. A scleral contact lens whose corneal and scleral portions are segments of spheres.

contact l., Sphertan. A trade name for a type of tangential lenticular contact lens.

contact l., SpiroVent. A trade name for a corneal contact lens which has five curved tongue-shaped channels equally spaced in a spiral pattern, extending from the lens edge toward the optic zone, to promote tear circulation.

contact l., sports. A corneal contact lens made larger in diameter than customary, or with an added narrow scleral flange, to minimize its dislodgement in active sports.

contact l., tangent cone. Feincone contact lens.

contact l., Tangential Periphery (TP). A trade name for a type of tangential lenticular contact lens in which the peripheral portion of the anterior surface is conical and perpendicular to the radius of curvature of the central portion at their points of tangency.

contact l., Thorpe. 1. A contact lens containing radiopaque reference markings, used with x-ray photography for the localization of intraocular foreign bodies. 2. A diagnostic contact lens of high concave dioptric power, for examination of the fundus in slit lamp biomicroscopy.

contact l., Torcon. A trade name for a corneal contact lens having a toric curvature on its front surface for the correction of residual astigmatism.

contact l., toric. A corneal contact lens with a toroidal inside surface. Cf. *spherical contact lens.* 2. A scleral contact lens having a toroidal inside surface on its scleral section.

contact l., Transcurve. A trade name for a preformed, minimum clearance, ventilated, scleral contact lens consisting essentially of a corneal section and a scleral section separated by a transition zone approximately 1.5 mm. to 2.5 mm. wide and of a curvature midway between the corneal and scleral curvatures. It is fitted with two trial sets, one to determine the corneal

section dimensions and the other the scleral section dimensions.

contact l., trial. Any contact lens, usually one of a set of lenses having a range of specifications, used in preliminary fitting to determine the final specifications required to obtain a physical fit and the desired refractive power. Syn., *control contact lens; diagnostic contact lens; fitting contact lens.*

contact l., tricurve. A corneal contact lens in which the posterior optical zone is surrounded by two distinct and separate annuli, each of which is successively of less curvature.

contact l., Troncoso. Troncoso goniolens.

contact l., truncated. A corneal contact lens having one or more sections cut away so that it is no longer circular.

contact l., Tuohy. A monocurve corneal contact lens, with a narrow bevel of a curve flatter than the base curve, patented by Kevin M. Tuohy in 1948. In its original form it was approximately 11.5 mm. in diameter and was fitted with a base curve flatter than the flattest central corneal curve.

contact l., ventilated. Any contact lens containing an opening for the more rapid transfer of air and/or tears between the lens and the cornea. Examples are the Lacrilens and the Dallos contact lens.

contact l., wide angle. A preformed, minimum clearance, scleral contact lens having a flat, conical, transition zone between the corneal and scleral sections which is angled to be approximately tangent to the corneal section. The base of the transition zone is a constant of 16 mm. diameter, and the base of the corneal section is a constant of 11.5 mm. diameter.

Contour l. See under *lens, contact.*

contrageneric l. In relation to another lens of reference, one which is opposite in sign or dioptric character, whence a converging lens and a diverging lens are said to be a pair of contrageneric lenses. Cf. *congeneric lens.*

contrameniscus l. A concave meniscus lens. *Obs.*

converging l. A lens which converges light. Syn., *convex lens; plus lens; positive lens.*

convex l. Converging lens.

convexoconcave l. A diverging meniscus lens.

Cooke l. A triplet consisting of a biconcave lens between two convex lenses designed to minimize longitudinal chromatic aberration.

coquille l. A deep curve lens cut from a blown glass sphere, commonly used in inexpensive sunglasses.

corneal l. 1. The cornea of the eye when considered as a lens. 2. A corneal contact lens.

corrected curve l. 1. A spectacle lens with surface curvatures chosen to eliminate or reduce aberrations resulting from the use of the peripheral portions of the lens. 2. An ophthalmic trial case lens with surface powers chosen to make the power designation precisely correct for the spectacle plane or other plane of reference when inserted correctly in a properly designed trial frame.

correcting l. An ophthalmic lens which corrects the error of refraction of the eye.

cortex, l. See under *cortex.*

crossed l. A form of lens with surface curvatures selected to provide for minimum spherical aberration for an infinitely distant object. In the case of a lens with an index of refraction of 1.5, the ratio of the two radii of curvature is −6, whence the lens must be biconcave or biconvex.

crossed cylinder l. A compound lens in which the dioptric powers in the principal meridians are equal but opposite in sign, usually mounted on a rotating axis or handle midway between the principal meridians, commonly used in the clinical measurement of the power and the axis of astigmatism, and designated in terms of the powers in the two principal meridians.

    crossed cylinder l., homokonic. A modified crossed cylinder lens, devised by P. R. Haynes, which has the same magnification in all meridians to eliminate the rotary deviation and differential magnification present in the Jackson crossed cylinder lens.

crystalline l. The biconvex, normally transparent and resilient, lenticular body directly behind the pupil of the eye and nested in the patellar fossa of the vitreous body, having a relatively high index of refraction and an anterior surface whose convexity responds to ciliary muscle action. It consists of capsule, anterior epithelium, cortex, and nucleus, the latter two containing the lens fibers. It is supported by the fibers of the zonule of Zinn and the hyaloideocapsular ligament which are attached to its capsule.

cylindrical l. 1. A lens on which one surface is plane and the other cylindrical, or on which one surface is spherical and the other toroidal, such that one meridian has zero power and a meridian 90° to it has maximum power. 2. An astigmatic lens.

Dannheim l. A small, biconvex, plastic lens suspended in the anterior chamber by means of a double loop of thin resilient plastic thread passing through the peripheral body of the lens. It is used to replace the crystalline lens following cataract surgery or to correct ametropia. Syn., *Dannheim implant.*

decentered l. A lens so constructed that its optical center does not coincide with its geometrical center.

depth l. A 2.50 D. convex cylinder lens, axis 90°, used by artists to elicit perceptual depth in a realistic painting.

dispersing l. An inaccurate term for a diverging lens.

diverging l. A lens which diverges light. Syn., *concave lens; minus lens; negative lens.*

double concave l. A lens which is concave on both surfaces.

double convex l. A lens which is convex on both surfaces.

ectopic l. A crystalline lens which is displaced from its normal position.

eikonic l. Iseikonic lens.

Engel fundus l. A diagnostic contact lens of high concave dioptric power, with a flat or slightly convex anterior surface, for examination of the fundus and deep vitreous in slit lamp biomicroscopy.

Epstein collar-stud l. An intraocular lens in the shape of a double disk separated by a deep peripheral groove, resembling a collar button, which is positioned in the pupillary aperture, with the iris between its anterior and posterior disks, to replace the crystalline lens following cataract surgery. Syn., *Epstein collar-stud implant.*

Epstein Maltese Cross l. An intraocular lens which is positioned in the pupillary aperture following cataract surgery and is fixed in position by two solid limbs situated behind the iris and two fenestrated limbs, perpendicular to the solid limbs, situated in front of the iris. Syn., *Epstein Maltese Cross implant.*

equiconcave l. A double concave lens on which the two surfaces are equal in curvature.

equiconvex l. A double convex lens on which the two surfaces are equal in curvature.

equi-tint l. A lens with a uniform absorptive layer not affected by variations in lens thickness.

equivalent l. 1. A lens so located as to form on a screen the same size image as another lens or series of lenses. 2. A spherical lens equal in dioptric power to the mean spherical refracting power of an astigmatic lens. 3. Any one of two or more ophthalmic lenses having the same mean spherical refracting power.

Eventone l. A type of uniform density lens fabricated from glass.

eye l. The lens nearest the eye in an eyepiece which renders light from the objective or field lens parallel prior to entrance into the observer's eye.

fiber, l. See under *fiber.*

field l. The lens in an eyepiece nearest the objective lens, serving to increase the usable field of view in a telescopic or microscopic system over that obtained in using a single lens.

flat l. A biconvex, biconcave, planoconvex, or planoconcave ophthalmic lens, differentiated from a *meniscus lens.*

 flat l., plano-cylinder. A flat lens which is plane on one surface and cylindrical on the other.

 flat l., sphero-cylinder. A flat lens which is spherical on one surface and cylindrical on the other.

fluid l. 1. A lens consisting of liquid held between two transparent solid media. 2. Lacrimal lens.

fogging l. The ophthalmic lens or combination of lenses which constitute a slight overcorrection of plus lens in hyperopia or a slight undercorrection of minus lens in myopia for the purpose of inducing or maintaining relaxation of accommodation during certain types of vision testing, as for astigmatism with a fan dial chart, or to blur the vision in one eye, when attempting to force the use of an amblyopic eye.

fossette, l. The depression in the secondary eye vesicle of the human embryo.

Franklin l. Franklin bifocal lens.

Franklin gonioscopic l. A convex diagnostic contact lens fitted with a rubber scleral flange and handle, for viewing the filtration angle of the anterior chamber, usually in conjunction with a hand-held biomicroscope and focal illumination.

Franklin 3 mirror l. A contact lens in combination with three inclined mirrors in a plastic cone assembly, used with a slit lamp biomicroscope for viewing the fundus, the vitreous body, and the filtration angle of the anterior chamber.

Fresnel's l. A lens with a surface consisting of a concentric series of simple lens sections or zones of the same power, thereby effecting the optics of a simple, large diameter, short focal length lens without the incumbent thickness.

frosted l. An otherwise transparent lens made translucent by grinding or etching.

Goldmann fundus l. A diagnostic contact lens with a flat anterior surface, mounted in a plastic cone, for examination of the vitreous and fundus in slit lamp biomicroscopy.

Goldmann gonioscopy l. A diagnostic contact lens with a mirror attachment, mounted in a plastic cone, used in conjunction with a slit lamp biomicroscope for viewing the structures of the filtration angle of the anterior chamber.

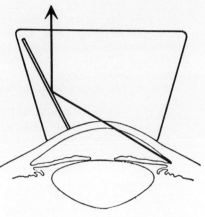

Fig. 28. Diagram of light rays emerging through a Goldmann lens. (From *Diagnosis and Therapy of the Glaucomas,* Becker and Shaffer, 2nd ed., C. V. Mosby Co., 1965)

Goldmann 3-mirror contact l. A contact lens in combination with three mirrors mounted in a plastic cone assembly and set at angles of 59°, 67°, and 73°, at 120° meridional intervals, used with a slit lamp biomicroscope for viewing the fundus, vitreous, and anterior chamber angle.

gonioscopic l. A thick convex or prismatic lens placed in contact with the eye for the purpose of viewing the structures of the filtration angle of the anterior chamber.

goniotomy l. A type of gonioscopic lens used in surgery of the filtration angle of the anterior chamber.

hardened l. Case-hardened lens.

Henkes electroretinography l. A diagnostic scleral-type contact lens used in electroretinography with or without a low vacuum retention attachment, and equipped with a limbal electrode and a protruding cone to hold the eyelids open, within which are mounted disks having various sized pupillary apertures.

Hruby l. A spherical diverging lens of 55.0 D. with a slightly convex anterior surface (+5.0 D.)

placed in front of the eye for the examination of its interior structures in conjunction with an ocular biomicroscope and slit lamp.

hyperchromatic l. A doublet lens having more chromatic aberration than a single lens of the same power.

Hyperocular l. A trade name for a plastic aspheric lens used in the correction of subnormal vision, available in 4×, 6×, and 8× magnifications.

intracorneal l. A small plastic lens placed between the layers of the cornea to substitute for the crystalline lens following cataract surgery.

iris clip l. An anterior chamber implant consisting of a biconvex lens positioned in front of the pupil and held to the iris by peripheral loops. Syn., *Binkhorst lens; Binkhorst implant; pupillary lens.*

iseikonic l. An ophthalmic lens designed to correct the image size difference between the two eyes in aniseikonia. Syn., *aniseikonic lens; eikonic lens.*

iseikonic l., bitoric. An ophthalmic lens having a toroidal curvature on each surface, for the correction of aniseikonia.

iseikonic l., doublet. A doublet consisting of two lenses separated by an air space, for the correction of aniseikonia.

isochromatic l. A tinted lens having the same absorption at all points, irrespective of variations in thickness.

Isokrystar l's. A trade name for a series of corrected curve lenses.

Jackson crossed cylinder l. Crossed cylinder lens.

Jungschaffer l. See under *lens, contact.*

Katral l's. A trade name for a series of lenses having an aspheric curvature on the inner surface with a spherical or spherocylindrical curvature on the other sur-

face. It is made in convex powers from 7.0 D. to 20.0 D. and is said to correct marginal aberration for a 60° field of vision.

Koeppe gonioscopic l. A hemispheric diagnostic contact lens for direct viewing of the filtration angle of the anterior chamber, usually employed with a portable microscope and focal illumination.

Kurova l's. A trade name for a series of corrected curve lenses.

lacrimal l. The layer of tears between a contact lens and the cornea.

laminated l. A protective, relatively shatter-proof lens consisting of a layer of clear plastic between two layers of glass.

Lederer l's. A series of convex lenses of high dioptric power, corrected for oblique astigmatism and curvature of the field, designed by Lederer for use in subnormal vision.

lenticular l. An ophthalmic or spectacle lens of high dioptric power with the prescription ground only in the central portion, the peripheral (usually afocal) portion of the lens serving only to give dimensions suitable for mounting in a spectacle or trial frame, permitting a reduced center thickness in the case of convex lenses and a reduced edge thickness in the case of concave lenses.

Lieb l. A small plastic lens suspended in the anterior chamber by means of a double loop of thin, resilient plastic thread fitted into peripheral grooves on either side of the lens. It is used to replace the crystalline lens following cataract surgery or to correct ametropia.

LoVac direct gonioscopic l. A Lo-Vac contact lens having a flat anterior surface set at a 45° angle with the visual axis, used with the slit lamp biomicroscope to provide a direct view of the filtration angle of the anterior chamber as well as of the iris and peripheral fundus.

LoVac six mirror gonioscopic l. A LoVac contact lens to which is attached a plastic cone containing six mirrors, all inclined at the same angle, to provide a composite view of the circumference of the filtration angle of the anterior chamber when directly viewed with a slit lamp biomicroscope.

Luboshez l. A lens designed so that the object point is at the center of curvature of the first surface and at the aplanatic point of the second surface.

luxated l. A crystalline lens that is completely displaced from the pupillary aperture, differentiated from a *subluxated lens,* which is displaced but remains in part within the pupillary aperture.

magnifying l. Any lens which will produce an apparent enlargement of an object viewed through it.

measure, l. See under *measure.*

meniscus l. 1. A lens having a spherical concave curve on one surface and a spherical convex curve on the other surface. 2. A deep curve spectacle lens as distinguished from a *flat* or *periscopic lens.* 3. A spectacle lens having a 6.0 D. base curve.

metallized l. A lens upon which a metallic film has been deposited to reduce the amount of light transmitted.

meter l. A converging lens of 1 m. focal length.

mi-coquille l. A lens cut from a blown glass sphere but of shallower curvature than a coquille lens.

microphakic l. See *microphakia.*

microscopic l. A magnifying spectacle lens, or a lens system, of short focal length for near viewing, designed to provide a flat field of view comparatively free from aberrations.

Micro-V l. See under *lens, contact.*

minifying l. Any lens which will produce reduction in the apparent size of an object viewed through it. Syn., *reducing lens.*

minus l. Diverging lens.

Motex l. A trade name for a laminated lens.

multifocal l. A composite spectacle lens with different dioptric powers in different segments, e.g., a bifocal or a trifocal lens.

Myo-disc l. A trade name for a lenticular lens used in the correction of high myopia, having a concave, central corrective area 20 to 30 mm. in diameter on the back surface, both the front surface and the peripheral area of the back surface usually being flat.

negative l. Diverging lens.

nonshatterable l. A term sometimes applied to laminated lenses.

objective l. The lens in a telescopic or microscopic system nearest the object, serving to converge light from points in the field of view. Syn., *objective glass; objective.*

occluding l. A spectacle lens for obscuring or preventing vision. It may be opaque, translucent, of irregular curvature, or of a dioptric power incompatible with the refractive state.

Omnifocal l. The trade name for a lens in which the dioptric power changes progressively from above to below to provide correction for variations from distance to near vision, usually used in the correction of presbyopia.

ophthalmic l. A lens used for correcting or measuring refractive errors of the eye and/or compensating for ocular muscle imbalances.

Orthogon l. A trade name for a series of corrected curve lenses.

orthoscopic l's. 1. A series of spectacle lenses designed by Tscherning to correct peripheral aberrations. 2. A symmetrical magnifying doublet, with a central aperture stop, which eliminates distortion, i.e., straight lines are reproduced as straight lines. Syn., *orthoscopic doublet; rectilinear lens.*

Ostwalt l. One of a series of corrected curve lenses based on the Ostwalt branch of the Tscherning ellipse, giving minimum marginal astigmatism and characteristically flatter than other corrected curve series.

pantoscopic l. A spectacle lens, for near vision only, approximating in shape only the lower half of a conventional spectacle lens, thus enabling the wearer to look over the top for distant seeing.

parabolic l. A lens having one or both surfaces of parabolic curvature.

pebble l. A spectacle lens made from quartz crystal; no longer in common use.

Percival l. Any of a series of lenses corrected for mean oblique astigmatic error, according to formulas by Percival.

periscopic l. 1. A lens with a 1.25 D. base curve. 2. One of a series of deep corrected curve lenses designed by Wollaston in 1804. Syn., *Wollaston lens.*

pit, l. See under *pit.*

plano l. A lens of zero focal power, in which light entering parallel will emerge parallel.

planoconcave l. A lens which is plane on one surface and concave on the other.

planoconvex l. A lens which is plane on one surface and convex on the other.

planocylindrical l. A lens on which one surface is plane and the other cylindrical, or on which one surface is spherical and the other toroidal, such that one meridian has zero power and the

meridian perpendicular to it has maximum power.

plastic l. A lens made of transparent plastic.

plate, l. See under *plate.*

plus l. A converging lens.

point-focal l. A corrected curve lens.

Polaroid l. A laminated lens containing a layer of Polaroid sheeting.

positive l. Converging lens.

posterior chamber l. Posterior chamber implant.

prismatic l. A lens with prism power. In a spectacle lens, one with prism power at the major reference point.

Punktal l. A trade name for a series of corrected curve lenses in which the curve for each power of lens is calculated independently to minimize aberrations.

pupillary l. 1. A lens placed in front of or in the pupillary opening to replace the crystalline lens following cataract surgery. 2. Iris clip lens.

rectilinear l. Orthoscopic lens.

red l. An ophthalmic filter primarily transmitting red light and used monocularly in binocular clinical tests and visual training procedures.

reducing l. 1. Minifying lens. 2. Diverging lens. *Rare.*

Richardson-Shaffer diagnostic l. A small version of the Koeppe gonioscopic lens for use on infant eyes.

Ridley l. A small plastic lens placed in the eyeball against the posterior wall of the capsule to replace the crystalline lens following extracapsular cataract surgery.

safety l. 1. A lens providing protection to the eyes, especially from injury due to impact. 2. A lens that meets standard specifications of construction and impact resistance, as determined by the *drop ball test.*

Sarwar l. A diagnostic contact lens of high divergent dioptric power for examination of the fundus and anterior chamber angle in slit lamp biomicroscopy.

Scharf l. A small plastic lens placed in the anterior chamber of the eyeball to replace the crystalline lens following cataract surgery. It is held in position by a four-pronged plastic mount.

Schreck l. A small plastic lens placed in the anterior chamber of the eyeball to replace the crystalline lens following cataract surgery. The lens is held in position by a curved plastic plate into which it is secured.

scleral l. Scleral contact lens.

simple l. A lens consisting of two spherical refracting surfaces.

single vision l. A spectacle lens having the same focal power (disregarding aberrations) throughout its useful area, thus distinguished from a *multifocal lens.*

size l. An iseikonic lens, usually implying one with zero verging power.

    size l., meridional. A size lens having different magnification in the various meridians, the meridians of maximum and minimum magnification being at right angles.

    size l., over-all. A size lens giving equal magnification in all meridians.

slab-off l. A lens on which one surface is ground and polished in two segments having the same curvatures, but with separated centers of curvature. The expression "slab-off" refers to the method of grinding, in which, in effect, a prismatic slab of glass is removed from one portion of the lens.

spectacle l. A lens used as a visual corrective aid and mounted a short distance in front of the eye, usually by means of a frame or attachment supported by the ears, the bridge of the nose, the cheeks, or the eyebrows. Specifically, a lens incorporated in a pair of spectacles, but, more generally, the term includes lenses used as monocles, pince-nez glasses, lorgnettes, etc.

Sphercon l. See under *lens, contact.*

spherical l. A lens in which all refracting surfaces are spherical.

spherocylindrical l. A lens which functions as a combination of a simple spherical lens and a simple cylindrical lens.

spherophakic l. The abnormally small and spherical crystalline lens characteristic of microphakia.

spheroprism l. A spherical lens eccentrically mounted or decentered to produce prismatic effect, or a combined spherical lens and prism.

stars, l. See under *star.*

Stigmagna l's. A series of convex lenses of high dioptric power, corrected to minimize oblique astigmatism and distortion, designed for use in subnormal vision.

stigmatic l. Anastigmatic lens.

Stokes's l. A combination of a planoconvex cylindrical lens and a planoconcave cylindrical lens of numerically equal power mounted with their flat surfaces almost in contact with each other in lens rings which are simultaneously but oppositely rotatable about their common axis, producing a maximum astigmatic resultant when the two lens power meridians are at right angles to each other, a minimum astigmatic resultant when the two lens power meridians are parallel, and intermediate astigmatic resultants for intermediate relative positions of the two lens power meridians.

Strampelli l. A small plastic lens placed in the anterior chamber of the eyeball to replace the crystalline lens following cataract surgery. The lens is held in position by a curved plastic plate into which it is secured. Syn., *Strampelli implant.*

subluxated l. A crystalline lens which is displaced from its normal position but remains in part within the pupillary aperture. Cf. *luxated lens.*

subluxated l., Vogt's. A spontaneous subluxation of the crystalline lens occurring in adults and considered to be due to a congenital abnormality of the zonule of Zinn.

symmetrical l's. A lens system consisting of two identical sets of thick lenses symmetrical about a stop placed between them.

tear l. Lacrimal lens.

telescopic l. A short, lightweight, wide angle, fixed focus Galilean telescope mounted in front of the eye as a magnifying spectacle lens

tempered l. Case-hardened lens.

thick l. A lens or a system of lenses in which the two or more refracting surfaces are regarded in their separate positions rather than as if coincident.

thin l. A lens or a combination of lenses in which the two or more refracting surfaces are regarded as if coincident rather than in their separate positions.

thin l., equivalent. The value (refractive power, or focal length) of a thin lens placed at the principal plane of a thick lens or lens system which will give the identical optical effect of the thick lens or lens system.

thinflint l. An ophthalmic lens made of dense flint glass, containing lead oxide, of relatively high refractive index. The lens is appreciably thinner than a crown glass lens of equal power, but is heavier and has more chromatic aberration.

Thinlite l. A trade name for a thinflint lens.

Tillyer l. A trade name for a series of corrected curve lenses.

tinted l. A lens with color absorption properties designed to reduce light transmission and/or selectively absorb undesirable incident radiations. In contact lenses, the color may be also for facilitating location.

toric l. 1. Any one of a series of meniscus cylindrical and spherocylindrical spectacle lenses characterized by a toric convex surface with a minimum curvature (base curve) of 6.00 D. refracting power. 2. A lens with a toric surface.

Torres-Ruiz l. A corneal implant consisting of a central glass cylinder, 3 mm. in diameter, convex anteriorly and concave posteriorly, 1.5 to 3.0 mm. long, surrounded by a metallic, annular, spherically curved flap, 6 mm. in diameter. The flap contains semicircular perforations through which the corneal tissue proliferates to hold the lens in position. Syn., *Torres-Ruiz implant.*

trial l. 1. Any of a set of lenses used to test vision or to correct temporarily ocular muscle imbalances, or refractive or aniseikonic errors. 2. A trial contact lens.

trifocal l. A multifocal lens of three portions whose focal powers differ from each other. Usually the top portion is the largest and is for distant vision, the middle for intermediate distances, and the bottom for near vision.

trifocal l., Hawkins. One of the original trifocal lenses designed by Hawkins, consisting of three separate portions of lenses mounted in one frame after the manner of a Franklin bifocal.

Trioptic telescopic l. A subnormal vision aid with three components, a plastic carrier lens having the wearer's distance correction, a small diameter Galilean telescope, to magnify distant objects, mounted on the upper front surface of the carrier, and a small microscopic lens, to magnify near objects, mounted on the lower front surface of the carrier.

Triplex l. A trade name for a laminated nonshatterable lens.

Troncoso gonioscopic l. Troncoso goniolens.

uncut l. A lens that is completely surfaced but has not been cut or edged to its final size and shape.

uniform density l. An absorptive lens whose color is distributed uniformly across the lens regardless of the power. This is achieved by making the body of the lens of clear glass or plastic, and applying the color in a thin layer to one or both surfaces. In glass lenses, this is done by fusing or cementing a thin plate of colored glass onto one surface or by depositing metallic oxides of the desired color onto the surfaces, and in plastic lenses by impregnating the lens surfaces with inorganic pigments.

variable focus l. 1. A lens system in which the focal length can be varied, usually by the differential moving of parts of the system along the axis. 2. A lens system mounted on a slide or rack, as in a projector, so as to permit variation of image distance by varying the distance of the lens unit from the object.

varifocal l. 1. A lens having a gradual and progressive change in dioptric power, either throughout its entire area or over a region intermediate between areas of uniform power, usually used in the correction of presbyopia. 2. Zoom lens.

Varilux l. Trade name for a multifocal lens consisting of an upper portion for distant vision, a lower portion for near vision, and a middle, aspheric portion in which the power gradually and progressively changes from that of the upper portion to that of the lower portion.

Volk conoid l. Any of a series of ten convex lenses of high dioptric power used as subnormal vision aids. Seven of the lenses each have one surface ellipsoidal and the other plano or spherical, while the other three, of highest power, have both surfaces hyperbolic.

wide-angle l. A corrected curve lens, so called because of the larger angle of field with reduced aberration.

Widesite l. A trade name for a series of corrected curve lenses and for a series of fused bifocal lenses.

Wollaston l. The original periscopic lens, a deep corrected curve lens, designed by Wollaston in 1804, based on the Wollaston branch of the Tscherning ellipse.

Worst's prismatic goniotomy l. A goniotomy lens having a flat anterior surface set at a 45° angle with the visual axis, a scleral rim containing four holes for suturing to the conjunctiva, a cannula through which saline solution is injected to eliminate air bubbles and obtain optical continuity between the lens and cornea, and an opening at the side of the lens for insertion of the goniotomy knife.

Worst's spherical goniotomy l. A hemispherical goniotomy lens of the Barkan type, modified by an added scleral rim containing four holes for suturing to the conjunctiva, a cannula through which saline solution is injected to eliminate air bubbles and obtain optical continuity between the lens and cornea, and an opening at the side of the lens for insertion of the goniotomy knife.

zero converging l. A lens for which the image position coincides with that of the object.

zero curvature, l. of. A converging meniscus lens in which the axial thickness is equal to the distance between the centers of curvature of the two surfaces and in which the radii of curvature are equal.

zoom l. A lens or a lens system providing continuously variable magnification without a change in object and image positions.

Lenscorometer (lenz-ko-rom′eh-ter). The trade name for a micrometer-like device for measuring the distance between the posterior surface of a spectacle lens and the anterior surface of the closed eyelid.

Lensmark. The trade name for a relatively durable black dye used for marking contact lenses.

Lensometer (lenz-om′eh-ter). A trade name for an instrument which determines the vertex refractive power, the cylinder axis, the optical center, and the prismatic effect of ophthalmic lenses.

lenticele (len′tih-sēl). Phacocele.

lenticonus (len″tih-ko′nus). 1. A rare congenital anomaly in which either the anterior or the posterior surface of the crystalline lens has a conical or spherical bulging, as a consequence of which refraction may be excessive (myopic) through the central pupillary area. Syn., *lentiglobus.* 2. A rare congenital anomaly in which either the anterior or the posterior surface of the crystalline lens, usually in its axial region, has a conical bulging, as opposed to a spherical bulging (*lentiglobus*).

false l. A condition of abnormally high refractive index in the axial portion of the crystalline lens, hence simulating the optical effects of lenticonus, and usually attributed to sclerosing of the crystalline lens nucleus in the

aged. Syn., *false cataract; pseudo-cataract.*

internal l. The condition of abnormally high convexity of the nucleus of the crystalline lens, hence simulating the optical effects of lenticonus.

lenticular (len-tik′u-lar). 1. Pertaining to, or resembling, a lens. 2. Pertaining to the crystalline lens of the eye. Syn., *lentiform.*

lentiform (len′tih-form). Lenticular.

lentiglobus (len″tih-glo′bus). 1. A rare congenital anomaly in which either the anterior or the posterior surface of the crystalline lens, usually in its axial region, has a spherical bulging, as opposed to a conical bulging (*lenticonus*). 2. Lenticonus.

lentitis (len-ti′tis). Inflammatory involvement of the crystalline lens. Syn., *phacitis; phakitis.*

lentoids (len′toidz). White or yellowish, opaque, round or oval, lenslike structures, about 0.1 to 0.2 mm. in diameter, consisting of newly formed lens tissue containing lens fibers and surrounded by a membrane resembling the lens capsule, appearing on the iris, posterior cornea, and in the vitreous following cataract surgery and in congenitally maldeveloped eyes.

lentoptosis (len″to-to′sis). Prolapse or hernia of the crystalline lens.

leprosy (lep′ro-se). A disease, common in tropical climates, caused by the *Mycobacterium leprae* and characterized by granulomatous lesions in the skin, the mucous membranes, and the peripheral nervous system. Two clinical types are recognized: (1) cutaneous or nodular; (2) neural or maculoanesthetic. The lesions may affect the structures of the eye or the eyelid and resultant interstitial keratitis and conjunctivitis are common.

leptokurtic (lep″to-kur′tik). Pertaining to or having leptokurtosis.

leptokurtosis (lep″to-kur-to′sis). The statistical attribute of having a distribution more peaked than normal. Cf. *mesokurtosis; platykurtosis.*

leptomeningitis (lep″to-men″in-ji′tis). Inflammation of the pia mater and the arachnoid of the brain, the spinal cord, or the optic nerve. Cf. *pachymeningitis.*

leptospirosis (lep″to-spi-ro′sis). Weil's disease.

Lesser's method (les′erz). See under *method.*

Lester's sign. See under *sign.*

letters, confusion. 1. Letters on visual acuity test charts which may easily be mistaken for each other because of their similarity, e.g., F and P. 2. Letters included in a visual acuity test in excess of the minimum variety intended to measure acuity, to prevent or discourage memorization or pure chance guessing.

letters, Snellen. Snellen test type.

Letter Separator. An instrument for the diagnosis and treatment of the crowding phenomenon in amblyopia ex anopsia, consisting of 25 randomly orientated letter E's mounted in radial slits on a flat vertical surface in a square formation, the distance between the E's being varied by a lever on the side of the instrument.

leucitis (lu-si′tis). Inflammation of the sclera. Syn., *scleritis.*

Leuckart's ratio (lūk′artz). See under *ratio.*

leukiridia (lu-kih-rid′e-ah). A condition in which the iris has whitish patches of depigmentation, as may occur in the secondary stage of syphilis.

leukokeratosis (lu″ko-ker″ah-to′sis). Leukoplakia.

leukokoria (lu″ko-kōr′e-ah). Any pathological condition, such as retrolental fibroplasia, which produces a white reflex from behind a clear crystalline lens.

leukoma (lu-ko′mah). A very dense, circumscribed, whitish opacity of the cornea. Cf. *macula; nebula.*

adherent l. A leukoma caused by scar tissue which encloses a prolapsed iris in a corneal wound.

leukophthalmos (lu″kof-thal′mos). A condition in which the sclera of the eye is unusually white.

leukoplakia (lu″ko-pla′ke-ah). A focal epithelial hyperplasia and keratinization affecting mucous membranes, especially of the mouth and occasionally of the conjunctiva. On the conjunctiva, it occurs most frequently in the limbal area, appears as a slightly elevated, white plaque and is considered to be the forerunner of an epithelioma. Syn., *leukokeratosis.*

leukopsin (lu-kop′sin). The colorless chemical end product resulting from the bleaching of rhodopsin by light and thought to be vitamin A plus a protein. Syn., *visual white.*

leukoscope (lu′ko-skōp). An instrument used by Hering to analyze the color mixture production of white, and later modified by Tschermak-Seysenegg for testing color vision by the mixture of colors to produce white.

levator palpebrae superioris (le-va′tor pal′pe-bre su-pe″re-ōr′is). See under *muscle.*

level. Character, degree, quality, standard, or rank.

illumination l. The amount of illumination on a surface, expressed in footcandles, metercandles, phots, etc.

reading capacity l. The highest level of difficulty at which a person can comprehend material read by, or to, him.

Talbot l. The level of brightness which results when intermittent stimuli are delivered at rates high enough to produce uniform sensation.

[420]

zero l. of accommodation. See *accommodation, zero level of.*

Levinsohn's theory (lev'in-sōnz). See under *theory.*

levoclination (le"vo-klih-na'shun). Levotorsion.

levocycloduction (le"vo-si"klo-duk'shun). Intorsion of the right eye or extorsion of the left eye.

levocycloversion (le"vo-si"klo-ver'zhun). Conjugate intorsion of the right eye and extorsion of the left eye. Syn., *negative cycloversion.*

levoduction (le"vo-duk'shun). Rotation of an eye to the left; abduction of the left eye or adduction of the right eye.

levophoria (le"vo-fo're-ah). A tendency of the eyes to turn toward the left, manifested in the absence of a fixation stimulus.

levorotatory (le"vo-ro'tah-to"re). 1. Turning of the plane of polarization toward the left (as seen by an observer looking toward the source of light). 2. Pertaining to levoclination. Syn., *sinistrorotatory.*

levotorsion (le"vo-tōr'shun). Intorsion of the right eye and/or extorsion of the left eye. Syn., *levoclination.*

levoversion (le"vo-ver'zhun). Conjugate rotation of the eyes to the left. Syn., *sinistroversion.*

Lhermitte's (lār'mitz) **ophthalmoplegia; syndrome.** See under the nouns.

lichen planus (li'ken pla'nus). A disease of the skin and the mucous membranes, of unknown etiology, characterized by purplish papules and white opalescent spots and striae, and accompanied by intense itching. The conjunctiva is rarely involved.

lid. The eyelid.

Lieb lens (lēb). See under *lens.*

Liebmann (lēb'man) **effect; phenomenon.** See under *effect.*

Liebreich's symptom (lēb'rīks). See under *symptom.*

ligament (lig'ah-ment). 1. A tough, flexible band of dense white, fibrous connective tissue which connects the articular ends of bones, or supports or retains an organ in its place. 2. Certain folds or processes of the pleura or peritoneum.

annular l. 1. Scleral spur. 2. A grouping of cells continuous with the corneal endothelium and extending to the anterior surface of the iris, filling the filtration angle of the anterior chamber, found in certain fishes, such as teleosteans, chondrosteans, cyclostomes, and holosteans.

Campos, l. of. Extensions of the vitreous humor between the ciliary processes to the ciliary valleys. They pass between the zonular fibers and attach to the internal limiting membrane of the ciliary body.

check l. A band of fibrous connective tissue, with a small amount of smooth muscle, which leaves the surface of the sheath of an extraocular muscle and attaches to the periorbita, the orbital septum, the conjunctival fornix, the sheath of another muscle, or some neighboring ocular structure, serving to limit the action of the muscle.

check l., extra. A check ligament arising parallel to the origin of the main check ligament of an extraocular muscle.

check l., fused. A series of several check ligaments forming a thick solid mass, especially observed to extend from the muscle sheath of the medial rectus to the orbital wall in congenital esotropes.

check l., posterior. A check ligament having its muscle sheath origin farther back than normal and inserting into a greater portion of the orbital wall.

Hueck's l. Uveal meshwork.

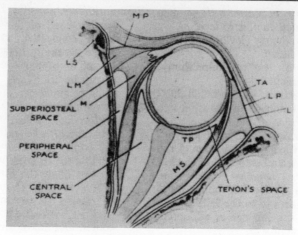

Fig. 29. Horizontal section through the orbit. (L) Lateral check ligament. (LM) Lacrimal portion of the orbicularis oculi muscle. (LP) Lateral palpebral ligament. (LS) Lacrimal sac. (M) Medial check ligament. (MP) Medial palpebral ligament. (MS) Muscle sheath. (TA) Anterior portion and (TP) posterior portion of Tenon's capsule. (From *Text-book of Ophthalmology,* Vol. V, Duke-Elder, Henry Kimpton, 1952)

hyaloideo-capsular l. Noncellular attachments of the anterior limiting layer of the vitreous to the posterior capsule of the lens in the form of a ring about 9 mm. in diameter. Syn., *ligament of Wieger.*

intermuscular l's. Connective tissue extensions between neighboring extraocular muscle sheaths which help bound the cone of muscles and separate the central adipose tissue from the peripheral adipose tissue of the orbit. Syn., *intermuscular membranes.*

intracapsular l's. Bands of fibers at the points of penetration of the extraocular muscles through Tenon's capsule, those of the superior rectus muscle being attached medially to the trochlea and laterally to the wall of the orbit, and those of the medial and lateral rectus muscles being attached inferiorly to the ligament of Lockwood; originally described by Lockwood but their presence has been denied by others.

Lockwood, l. of. A hammocklike structure extending beneath and supporting the eyeball, formed by the fusion of the sheaths of the inferior rectus and the inferior oblique muscles, blending with the sheaths of the medial and the lateral rectus muscles (thus in effect thickening the inferior portion of Tenon's capsule), and inserting medially on the lacrimal bone and laterally on the orbital tubercle of the zygomatic bone.

palpebral l., inferior. The septum orbitale of the lower eyelid.

palpebral l., lateral. A band of fibrous connective tissue formed by the fusion of the lateral extremities of the tarsal plates of the upper and the lower eyelids and inserting on the orbital tubercle of the zygomatic bone. Syn., *external tarsal ligament.*

papebral l., medial. A band of fibrous connective tissue formed by the fusion of the medial extremities of the tarsal plates of the upper and the lower eyelids and having two insertions, one superficially into the anterior lacrimal crest and the frontal process of the maxilla, and the other deep into the posterior lacrimal crest. Syn., *internal tarsal ligament.*

palpebral l., superior. The septum orbitale of the upper eyelid.

pectinate l. In lower mammals and birds, a group of large pigmented trabeculae stretching from the root of the iris to the cornea across the angle of the anterior chamber, forming the spaces of Fontana. In man, a vestigial structure after the sixth month of fetal life, the uveal meshwork. See also *meshwork of the angle of the anterior chamber.*

Soemmering's l. Trabeculae connecting the superior surface of the orbital portion of the lacrimal gland to the lacrimal fossa. Syn., *suspensory ligament of the lacrimal gland.*

suspensory l. Any ligament having as a principal function the support of another anatomical structure by suspension, e.g., the zonule of Zinn, the ligament of Lockwood, and Soemmering's ligament.

tarsal l., external. Lateral palpebral ligament.

tarsal l., internal. Medial palpebral ligament.

tarso-orbital l. Septum orbitale.

tenacular l. A ligament extending from the insertion of Brücke's muscle in the posterior region of the ciliary body to the sclera, found in the eyes of birds and reptiles.

transverse l. A condensation of the connective tissue running across the aponeurosis of the levator muscle of the upper eyelid and extending from the trochlea and the supraorbital notch to the lateral orbital margin. It probably checks excessive action of the levator muscle.

Wieger, l. of. Hyaloideocapsular ligament.

Zinn's l. Annulus of Zinn.

ligamentum pectinatum iridis (lig″-ah-men′tum pek″tin-a′tum ir′id-is). The pectinate ligament.

light (*v.*). To illuminate.

light (*adj.*). 1. Bright, luminous; in reference to colors of high or very high brightness. 2. Having light; not dark or obscure, as, the room was *light.* 3. Somewhat resembling white; pale in color, as a *light* complexion.

light (*n.*). 1. Radiant energy, approximately between 380 and 760 mμ, that gives rise to the sensation of vision on stimulating the retina. 2. The sensation of vision produced by stimulating the retina. 3. Radiant energy emitted at wavelengths in the ultraviolet, the visible, and the infrared bands of the electromagnetic grand spectrum. Syn., *physical light.* 4. A localized, usually named, source of illumination, e.g., a candlelight or windowlight.

accidental l. Stray light.

achromatic l. Light in which the quality of hue is absent. Syn., *neutral light.*

actinic l. Light capable of producing or serving to produce chemical changes.

adaptation, l. See under *adaptation.*

air l. Daylight scattered toward the observer along the path of sight, contributing to the apparent luminance of distant objects. Syn., *space light.*

ambient l. Light occurring in, and arising from, the surround of the object of regard.

area, l. See under *area.*

artificial l. Light produced by mechanical, electrical, thermal, and other man-made energy-transforming devices, in contrast to natural light received directly or by reflection from the sun and the sky.

axial l. Rays of light located on, or directly adjacent to, the axis of an optical system. Syn., *central light.*

beam, l. See under *beam.*

black l. Ultraviolet radiation near

the visible spectrum, approximately between wavelengths of 320 mμ and 400 mμ, used in conjunction with certain dyes, such as fluorescein, to create fluorescence for diagnostic purposes, such as in the detection of corneal abrasions or the evaluation of the fit of contact lenses.

central l. Axial light.

chaos, l. The irregular, usually minute, fluctuations occurring in the idioretinal light. Syn., *light dust*.

chromatic l. Light having the quality of hue.

coagulation, l. Photocoagulation.

coherent l. See *coherence*.

cold l. 1. Light emitted by any body whose temperature is below that of incandescence. See also *luminescence*. 2. Any visible light essentially free of infrared radiation.

colored l. Chromatic light.

compound l. Light composed of more than one wavelength.

convergent l. Light directed toward a common point.

dark l. Idioretinal light.

diascleral l. Light entering the eyeball through the sclera.

difference, l. See under *difference*.

diffuse l. Light characterized as coming apparently from a source of extensive area and having no predominant directional component

direct l. Light from a source falling directly on the eye or an object.

divergent l. Light directed away from a common point.

dust, l. Light chaos.

fluorescent l. Light emitted by a substance through the process of fluorescence.

flux, l. Luminous flux.

heterochromatic l. 1. Light composed of several noncontiguous wavelengths or of a spectral band broad enough so that it cannot be regarded as monochromatic light. 2. Light derived from a multiplicity of varicolored sources

presented in mosaic pattern or in sequence.

heterogeneous l. Heterochromatic light.

homogeneous l. Monochromatic light.

idioretinal l. A sensation of light occurring in the absence of any photic or other external physical stimulus and attributed to physiological processes within the brain or the retina. Syn., *dark light; intrinsic light; self light.* Cf. *idioretinal gray; light chaos.*

incandescent l. Light emitted by a substance through the process of incandescence; especially light emitted by electric incandescent lamps.

incident l. Light falling on a surface.

infrared l. Infrared energy.

intensity l. Luminous intensity.

intrinsic l. Idioretinal light.

klieg l. A flood lamp employing an incandescent filament to produce an intense light, used in film studios.

metameric l's. Metameric colors.

minimum, l. See under *minimum*.

monochromatic l. 1. Light consisting of a single wavelength, as obtained in isolated lines of line spectra. 2. Light composed of a spectral band so narrow, or a series of spectral lines so close together, as to serve as the practical equivalent of a single wavelength.

neutral l. Achromatic light.

objective l. Light regarded as a physical entity, exclusive of its sensation-producing property. Cf. *physical light.*

oblique l. Light incident on an object from a direction oblique in relation to a given direction, as a line or an axis of observation, or in relation to a plane of reference, as the receiving surface itself.

parallel l. Light whose component rays are parallel.

pencils, l. See *rays, pencil of*.

photometric l. Radiant energy evaluated as to its capacity to evoke the brightness aspect of visual sensation. Syn., *luminous energy.*

physical l. Radiant energy in the ultraviolet, the visible, and the infrared bands of the electromagnetic grand spectrum. Cf. *objective light.*

polarized l. Light for which the presumed transverse wave motion is not uniform in amplitude in all directions in a plane perpendicular to the direction of propagation.

    polarized l., circularly. Light consisting of two plane-polarized components of equal frequency, perpendicular to each other, with a phase difference such that the resultant vibration in a transverse plane is a circle.

    polarized l., elliptically. Light consisting of two plane-polarized components of equal frequency, perpendicular to each other, with a phase difference such that the resultant vibration in a transverse plane is an ellipse.

    polarized l., linearly. Plane-polarized light.

    polarized l., plane. Polarized light in which the transverse wave vibrations are parallel to a plane through the axis of the beam. Syn., *linearly polarized light.*

primary l. The initial or first phase of the light stimulus in the sequence leading to the formation of afterimages. It alters the retinal sensitivity to the secondary light stimulus. Syn., *tuning light.*

psychological l. The sensation of light as given by any stimulus effective on the retina or on the central visual pathways. Thus, both the viewing of a lamp and the direct electrical irritation of the visual cortex arouse psychological light. Syn., *subjective light.*

quantity of l. Luminous flux per unit of time.

ray, l. See under *ray.*

reacting l. Secondary light.

reflected l. Light turned back, bent, or "rebounded" by the surface of a second medium so that it continues to travel in the first medium, but in an altered direction.

refracted l. Light whose pathway is altered from its original direction as a result of passing from one medium to another of different refractive index.

secondary l. The second phase of the light stimulus in the sequence leading to the formation of a negative afterimage. The retinal response to this light is altered by the change in retinal sensitivity initiated by the primary light stimulus. Syn., *reacting light.*

self l. Idioretinal light.

solar l. Light from the sun, or light having the properties of light from the sun.

source, l. See under *source.*

space l. Air light.

stray l. Light reflected inside or passing through an optical system, but not involved in the formation of the image. Syn., *accidental light.*

subjective l. Psychological light.

transmitted l. Light which passes or has passed through a medium.

tuning l. Primary light.

Tyndall's l. Light from a transverse beam reflected or dispersed by small, otherwise invisible, particles in a transmitting medium, thus rendering these particles visible.

ultraviolet l. Ultraviolet energy.

wave, l. See under *wave.*

white l. 1. Achromatic light, or light perceived without the attribute of hue, such as may be obtained in proper mixtures of complementary hues, under conditions of scotopic vision, at the spectral neutral point of a dichromat, or under surround color conditions inducing the percept of white in a source. 2. Light produced by a source having an equal energy spectrum. 3. Light from any of several broadly heterochromatic sources adopted as standards for white light, such as sunlight and I.C.I. illuminants A, B, and C.

Wood's l. A lamp which emits ultraviolet radiation in the region near the visible spectrum, used with certain dyes, such as fluorescein, to create fluorescence for diagnostic purposes, such as the detection of corneal abrasions or the evaluation of the fit of contact lenses.

lighting. An artificial supply of light, or the apparatus supplying it.

diffused l. Lighting from a source of extensive area and having no predominant directional components.

direct l. Lighting in which light reaches the area to be illuminated directly from the luminaire or the lighting equipment.

directional l. Lighting from a specific direction, generally from a light source of relatively small dimensions, such as a spotlight.

general l. Lighting providing a substantially uniform level of illumination throughout an area, exclusive of any provision for special local requirements.

indirect l. Lightning in which light reaches the area to be illuminated after reflection from a ceiling or other object external to the luminaire or the light equipment.

local l. Lighting arranged to provide illumination to a relatively small area.

lightness. An attribute of object colors whereby they can be rated on an achromatic scale from black to white for surface colors, or from black to colorless for transparent spatial colors. It im-

plies a direction on the scale opposite to that implied by *darkness* and its physical correlate is *reflectance*.

limbal (lim'bal). Pertaining to, of, or situated near, the limbus corneae.

limbosclerectomy (lim''bo-skler-ek'-to-me). Limboscleral trephining.

limbus (lim'bus). A border.

corneae, l. An annular transitional zone, approximately 1 mm. wide, between the cornea and the bulbar conjunctiva and sclera. It is highly vascular and is involved in the metabolism of the cornea.

corneoscleral l. Limbus corneae.

luteus, l. Macula lutea.

palpebralis anterior, l. The anterior eyelid margin, in the region of the eyelashes, lined by skin.

palpebralis posterior, l. The posterior eyelid margin, lined by palpebral conjunctiva.

limen (li'men). Threshold.

liminal (lim'ih-nal). Pertaining to, or having the magnitude of, a limen or threshold.

limit of perception. Threshold of resolution.

limit of resolution. Resolving power.

limit, Rayleigh. A mathematical limit for the resolution of an optical system, without image deterioration from diffraction. The maximum difference in optical path distances for the rays meeting at the best focus is, as stated by Lord Rayleigh, a quarter of a wavelength of light.

limitation, eccentric. An irregular reduction in the limits of the visual field.

Lindau's disease (lin'dowz). See under *disease.*

Linder occluder. See under *occluder.*

Lindner's stenopaic spectacles; theory. See under the nouns.

line. 1. A narrow, distinct furrow, ridge, seam, or band; a long mark or threadlike formation; a mark of division or demarcation; a boundary. 2. A succession of ancestors or descendants of a given person.

absorption l's. Dark lines in a spectrum resulting from absorption of specific wavelengths of light by the substance through which it passes. Syn., *Fraunhofer lines.*

accommodation, l. of. The linear extent to which an object can be displaced toward and away from the eye in a given state of refraction without producing perceptible blurredness. Cf. *depth of focus.*

angular l. The collarette.

anti-Stokes's l's. New spectral lines occurring from a decrease in wavelength during scattering of monochromatic light. Cf. *Stokes's lines.*

arcuate l. A white crescentic line seen with the slit lamp in the posterior capsule of the crystalline lens, below the posterior pole in the region of the bifurcation of the posterior Y-suture. It encloses the area within which the vestiges of the hyaloid artery are found. Syn., *Vogt's line.*

Arlt's cicatricial l. A white line of scar tissue running horizontally across the tarsus in the region of the anastomosing of the terminal capillaries of the ascending and descending conjunctival vessels; the first indication of the cicatricial stage of trachoma.

Baillarger's outer l. The outer white band of myelinated nerve fibers in layer IV of the visual cortex which, in the area of the calcarine fissure, is known as the *line of Gennari.* Syn., *Baillarger's outer band.*

Barkan's white l. A white line observed in goniotomy following a circumferential incision of the root of the iris, representing the exposed scleral wall at the angle of the anterior chamber.

base l. The line joining the centers of rotation of the two eyes.

base-apex l. A line perpendicular to the intersection of two faces of a prism and bisecting the angle between the two faces.

cutting l. A horizontal line drawn on the 180° meridian of an uncut ophthalmic lens after the lens has been so placed that the cylinder axis and the optical center are in the desired position. It is the reference line for cutting and edging.

datum l. A line midway between the horizontal tangents of a spectacle lens shape at its highest and lowest points, used as a reference line in the cutting and edging of spectacle lenses. Under certain conditions it may coincide with the cutting line. Syn., *mechanical axis; working axis.*

demand l. In the graphical representation of accommodation and convergence in a two co-ordinate system, the locus of points representing, for a given lens or prism correction, the accommodation and convergence stimulus values of a fixation object varying in position on the midline from an infinite distance to the nearest point of binocular vision. Syn., *orthophoria line.*

direction, l. of. For a given point in space, the line connecting it with the anterior nodal point of the eye of reference.

direction, l. of (principal). The line joining the point of foveal fixation and the anterior nodal point of the eye; the visual axis.

direction, l. of (secondary). A line of direction other than the principal line of direction.

dividing l. The boundary line between two portions of a multifocal lens.

Donders' l. The demand line obtained with no lens or prism correction.

Egger's l. A line formed by the attachment of the hyaloideo-capsular ligament to the posterior capsule of the crystalline lens, in a ring of about 9 mm. diameter.

Ehrlich-Türk l. Line of Türk.

equidistant l. A type of horopter line characterized by the condition that all points on the line appear at the same distance as the fixation point. Syn., *iso-apostatic line.*

fixation l. Fixation axis.

Fleischer's l. Fleischer's ring.

focal l. A line image of a distant point source produced by an astigmatic optical system. Syn., *image line; Sturm's line.*

   focal l., anterior. The more anterior of the two focal lines of the conoid of Sturm.

   focal l., meridional. Tangential focal line.

   focal l., posterior. The more posterior of the two focal lines of the conoid of Sturm.

   focal l., radial. Sagittal focal line.

   focal l., sagittal. The line image of a point source perpendicular to the sagittal section of a homocentric bundle of rays obliquely incident on an optical system containing spherical surfaces. The sagittal section is made up of two planes perpendicular to the tangential plane, one plane containing incident rays, the other plane containing emergent rays. Syn., *radial focal line.*

   focal l., tangential. The line image of a point source, perpendicular to the tangential plane, formed by a homocentric bundle of rays obliquely incident on an optical system containing spherical surfaces. Syn., *meridional focal line.*

force, l. of. Line of traction.

Fraunhofer's l's. A series of dark lines in the solar spectrum due to the absorption of specific wavelengths by elements in the atmosphere of the sun and the earth. The chief ones have been desig-nated by the letters *A* through *K*, by Fraunhofer. Syn., *absorption lines.*

Fuchs's l's. of clearing. Clear lines occurring in various patterns in the midst of a corneal nebula or leukoma. They are associated with neovascularization of the cornea and follow the course of deep blood vessels.

gaze, l. of. Any of variously defined lines of reference intended to represent the direction in which the eye is looking, e.g., line of sight, line of fixation, and visual axis.

Gennari, l. of. A white line or stria formed in the middle of the fourth layer of the visual cortex or the area striata by the termination of the medullated fibers of the optic radiations. Syn., *outer band of Baillarger; band of Gennari; band of Vicq d'Azyr; stria of Gennari.*

Hudson's brown l. Superficial senile line.

Hudson-Stähli l. Superficial senile line.

image l. Focal line.

intermarginal l. A line of the margin of each eyelid corresponding to the anterior part of the tarsus and marking the union of the cutaneous and the tarsal portions of the eyelid.

iso-apostatic l. Equidistant line.

isocandela l. On any appropriate system of coordinates, the locus of points showing directions in space, with respect to an external light source, for which the candlepower is of a given and equal value.

isochromatic l's. Streaks or lines of the same color occurring when strains in photoelastic media are examined in polarized white light.

isofootcandle l. Isolux line.

isolux l. On a co-ordinate system representing a light-receiving surface, the locus of points for which the illumination is of a given and equal value. Syn., *isofootcandle line.*

isotorsional l's. In a fixation field plot, the contourlike lines representing the loci of points of equal degrees of ocular torsion.

keratoconus l's. Vertical lines in the corneal stroma which have the appearance of fibers of wood stretched apart, but still connected with each other at some points, seen with the slit lamp in keratoconus. Syn., *Vogt keratoconus stripes.*

least squares l. The line of best fit, for a series of values, determined by the *method of least squares.*

Lussi's l. A linear arrangement of leukocytes on the posterior corneal surface, found in normal eyes, usually of children, the pattern of distribution being attributed to thermal currents in the anterior chamber.

mounting l. of the face. A reference line for spectacle fitting, variously defined as one connecting the inner canthi, the outer canthi, or the centers of the pupils.

mounting l. of a frame. 1. In a metal rim or rimless type spectacle frame, the line which passes through the points on the eyewires or straps at which the guard arms are attached. 2. In a plastic spectacle frame: (*a*) the line which passes through the top points of attachment of the nose pads to the frame; (*b*) the line corresponding to the mounting line of the lens for which the frame is designed. 3. In a metal saddle bridge frame, the line which passes through the points at which the bridge is attached to the eyewires.

mounting l. of a lens. In an ophthalmic lens, a reference line parallel to the horizontal geometric axis at a vertical level de-

fined more or less arbitrarily by the manufacturer of the "former" or pattern from which the lens is shaped and specified in terms of the distance above the geometrical center.

orthophoria l. Demand line.

Paton's l's. Fine folds in the retina resulting from lateral displacement of the retina adjacent to the optic disk in papilledema, seen ophthalmoscopically as arcuate stripes concentric with the optic disk.

primary sagittal l. A line in the primary position of the plane of regard which bisects the base line.

pupillary l. Pupillary axis.

regard, l. of. A variously defined line intended to represent the direction of an object of either peripheral or central regard in relation to the eye or to a point of reference in the eye.

regression, l. of. The line describing one variable (y) in terms of the other (x), when the relationship between the two variables is linear. The general equation is $y = a + bx$ where y is the dependent variable, x the independent variable, b the coefficient of regression or slope, and a the x-intercept. See also *regression curve.*

rod l. The junction of the rod-free area in the fovea with the area of the retina containing rods.

Schwalbe's annular l. A gonioscopic landmark formed by the peripheral limit of Descemet's membrane of the cornea, indicating the anterior edge of the trabecular wall.

sight, l. of. The line connecting the point of fixation and the center of the entrance pupil of the fixating eye.

sighting l. 1. Line of sight. 2. A line passing through two or more visually aligned object points, such as the sights of a gun.

spectral l. Any of a series of lines in the solar or other spectra which form distribution patterns characteristic of individual chemical elements in the gaseous state, each line representing light of a specific wavelength. These lines appear bright when due to emission or dark when due to absorption.

Stähli's l. Superficial senile line.

Stocker's l. 1. A yellowish-brown line of pigmentation in the clear superficial cornea near the head of a pterygium, attributed to ruptures in Bowman's membrane caused by a flattening of the cornea produced by the pterygium. 2. A fine line of melanotic pigmentation extending across the cornea and located in its epithelium, found by Stocker in a case exhibiting a tuberculosislike lesion of the uvea and sclera with accompanying corneal vascularization and infiltration.

Stokes's l's. New spectral lines occurring from an increase in wavelength during scattering of monochromatic light.

Sturm's l. Focal line.

superficial senile l. A brown, yellow, or green line, occurring in the apparently normal corneae of the elderly, which characteristically runs horizontally slightly below the center of the cornea. Syn., *Hudson's brown line; Hudson-Stähli line; Stähli's line; linea corneae senilis.*

temporary atropic l. The line normal to the secondary axis plane.

traction, l. of. A line indicating the direction of force of an extraocular muscle on the eyeball on contraction. It extends from the origin to the point of tangential ocular contact of each of the extraocular muscles except the superior oblique, in which case it is from the trochlea to the point of tangential ocular contact. Syn., *line of force.*

Türk, l. of. 1. A deposit of leukocytes on the posterior corneal surface, observed with the slit lamp as a vertical line, normally present in children of ages 7 to 16. 2. Any similar vertical line formed on the posterior corneal surface by the deposition of pigment or precipitates.

vergence, l. See under *vergence.*

visual l. Visual axis.

visual direction, l. of. Line of direction.

Vogt's l. Arcuate line.

Zöllner's l's. Zöllner's figure.

linea corneae senilis (lin'e-ah kŏr'-ne-e sen-il'is). Superficial senile line.

Linksz graticule. See under *graticule.*

Linnér's test. See under *test.*

lipemia, retinal (lip-e'me-ah). A rare retinal condition due to abnormally high lipoid content of the blood. It occurs almost exclusively in association with diabetes mellitus and is characterized ophthalmoscopically by enlarged, flat, ribbonlike retinal arteries and veins which vary in color from salmon-pink to cream and are difficult to differentiate from each other.

lipoid granulomatosis (lip'oid gran"u-lo"mah-to'sis). Schüller-Christian-Hand disease.

lipoid histiocytosis, essential (lip'-oid his"te-o-si-to'sis). Niemann-Pick disease.

lipoid spleno-hepatomegaly (lip'-oid sple"no-hep"ah-to-meg'ah-le). Niemann-Pick disease.

lipoidosis, cerebroside (lip"oi-do'-sis). Gaucher's disease.

lipoma (lip-o'mah). A tumor composed of fat cells.

liporrhagia retinalis, traumatic (lip"o-ra'je-ah ret"ih-nal'is). Purtscher's disease.

lippitude (lip'ih-tūd). Marginal blepharitis.

lippitudo (lip″ih-tu′do). Marginal blepharitis.

liquor corneae (lik′er kōr′ne-e). The tissue fluid in the interstitial spaces of the cornea.

liquor Morgagni (lik′er mōr-gahn′-ye). Morgagnian fluid.

Listing's (lis′tingz) **reduced eye; law; pearl specks; plane.** See under the nouns.

lithiasis conjunctivae (lith-i′ah-sis con″junk-ti′ve). A condition of the palpebral conjunctiva marked by the presence of minute, hard, yellow spots consisting of products of cellular degeneration contained in Henle's glands or glands of new formation. Only rarely are there calcareous deposits. Syn., *calcareous conjunctivitis; conjunctivitis lithiasis; conjunctivitis petrificans; uratic conjunctivitis.*

Little's disease (lit′elz). See under *disease.*

Littrow prism (lit′ro). See under *prism.*

Livingston's (liv′ing-stunz) **gauge; test.** See under the nouns.

Lloyd's (loidz) **experiment; method; mirror.** See under the nouns.

loa loa (lo′ah lo′ah). Filaria oculi.

lobe. A rounded or partly rounded projection of an organ: a division of an organ separated by a fissure or constriction, as those of the brain or the lungs.

occipital l's. The portion of the cerebral hemispheres posterior to the parietal lobes containing the area striata, the visual associational areas, the occipital eye fields, and higher convergence and accommodative centers.

optic l's. The superior colliculi in the midbrains of birds and lower vertebrates which lack cortical visual centers.

orbital l. That portion of the frontal lobe which rests above the bony orbit.

Lobeck ocular micrometer (lo′bek). See under *micrometer.*

Lobstein's disease (lōb′stīnz). Eddowes' disease.

Lobstein's syndrome (lōb′stīnz). Eddowes' syndrome.

localization, spatial. The reference of a visual sensation to a definite locality in space.

absolute spatial l. The localization of an object in visual space with the observer as the center of reference.

anomalous spatial l. The reference of a visual sensation to a locality in space significantly different from its physical correlate.

egocentric spatial l. The localization of an object in visual space with the self as the center of reference.

partial spatial l. Localization of an object in visual space with reference only to direction and not to distance.

relative spatial l. The localization of an object in visual space with another object as the reference point.

similar spatial l. The localization of two or more objects to the same place in visual space.

Localizer. A visual training instrument designed by Bangerter to establish correct spatial localization, centric fixation, and normal visual acuity, in the treatment of amblyopia ex anopsia. Essentially it presents a series of various sized holes which are individually illuminated. With the nonamblyopic eye occluded, the amblyopic eye is made to fixate the illuminated hole such that the corneal reflex of the light source is properly positioned, that is, indicating centric fixation, and the patient is then instructed to touch the light source while maintaining his eye in this position.

Localizer-Corrector. A visual training instrument designed by Bangerter which incorporates the features of both the *Localizer* and the *Corrector.*

Lockwood's (lok'woodz) **ligament; tendon.** See under the nouns.

locus. 1. A place or locality in space. 2. The location of the plotted points on a co-ordinate chart or the path represented by a line joining these points.

   blackbody l. The locus of points on a chromaticity diagram which represents the chromaticities of blackbodies having various color temperatures. Syn., *Planckian locus.*

   egocentric l. The site or location of an object in visual space with reference to the self.

   Planckian l. Blackbody locus.

   spectrum l. The locus of points on a chromaticity diagram which represents the colors of the visible spectrum.

Loeser's law (lēs'erz). See under *law.*

Loewe's ring (leh'vēz). See under *ring.*

Loewi's sign (leh'vēz). See under *sign.*

logadectomy (log"ah-dek'to-me). Surgical removal of a portion of the conjunctiva.

logades (log-ah-dēz'). The "whites" of the eyes.

logaditis (log"ah-di'tis). Scleritis. *Obs.*

logadoblennorrhea (log"ah-do-blen"o-re'ah). Inclusion body blennorrhea.

logagnosia (log"ag-no'ze-ah). Alexia.

logagraphia (log"ah-graf'e-ah). A-graphia.

logamnesia (log"am-ne'ze-ah). The inability to comprehend either spoken or written words; sensory aphasia.

logaphasia (log"ah-fa'ze-ah). Motor aphasia.

Lomonosov's theory (lo-mon'o-sofs). See under *theory.*

long-sightedness. A lay term for hypermetropia.

look. 1. To direct one's visual attention, as in "*look* toward the ob-

ject." 2. To have resemblance, identity, or apparent quality, as in "to *look* new."

loop. A circular bend or fold in a cord or ribbonlike structure.

   Archambault's l. Meyer's loop.

   Axenfeld's intrascleral nerve l. A loop formed by a variation in the course of a long ciliary nerve. After traversing the perichoroidal space, the nerve pierces the sclera a few millimeters behind the limbus, turns back on itself, retraces the same path, and then enters the ciliary body.

   Cushing's l. Meyer's loop.

   Flechsig's l. Meyer's loop.

   Meyer's l. A loop of inferior fibers of the optic radiations which extends forward in the temporal lobe at a level with and external to the optic tract, sharply bends downward and passes backward through the temporal and the occipital lobes to terminate in the lingual gyrus below the calcarine fissure. Syn., *Archambault's loop; Cushing's loop; Flechsig's loop.*

Lorentz-Lorenz law (lo'rentz-lo'-renz). See under *law.*

lorgnette (lōrn-yet'). Opera glasses, especially with a long vertical (sometimes folding) handle for holding the glasses poisedly with one hand; or spectacles held in place in the same manner.

lorgnon (lōrn-yon'). 1. Lorgnette. 2. A single spectacle lens mounted on a handle.

L.O.Sc. Licentiateship in Optical Science (Australia).

Lotze's (lōt'zez) **sign; theory.** See under the nouns.

louchettes (loo-shets'). Goggles or similarly worn devices providing partial or total monocular occlusion as a treatment for strabismus.

Louis-Bar syndrome (loo-e'bahr). See under *syndrome.*

loupe (loop). Originally a simple convex lens for magnifying; now, any magnifying aid, monocular or binocular, held in the hand or mounted in front of the eye, for viewing very minute objects at very close range, but without image inversion as in a microscope.

Behr's l. A single or double lens magnifier held in front of one of the spectacle lenses by a clip attached to the temple of the spectacle frame.

Berger's l. A binocular loupe with the lenses mounted at the anterior end of a light-excluding chamber fitting over the eyes and held in place by an elastic headband.

Brücke's l. A loupe formerly used in dissecting, surgery, etc., essentially a Galilean telescope, which magnifies from 4 to 6 diameters and permits a working distance of from approximately 48 to 60 mm. Syn., *Brücke's lens.*

Wollaston l. A highly magnifying laminated lens consisting of two hemispherical lenses with a centrally perforated aperture stop cemented between.

LoVac contact lens; gonioscopic lens; goniotomy lens. See under *lens.*

Lowe's syndrome. See under *syndrome.*

Lowe-Terry-MacLachlan syndrome. Lowe's syndrome.

Lowenstein's (lo'en-stīnz) **climbing pupil; descending pupil.** See under the nouns.

low-neutral. See under *neutral.*

Loxit (loks'it). A trade name for a rimless spectacle mounting which is assembled to the lenses with solder pins instead of screws.

loxophthalmus (loks"of-thal'mus). Strabismus.

Luboshez lens (lu'bo-shāz). See under *lens.*

lucid interval of Vogt. See under *interval.*

luciferase (lu-sif'er-ās). The enzyme that allows the oxidation of luciferin to produce bioluminescence.

luciferin (lu-sif'er-in). An unidentified chemical of low molecular weight which, when oxidized by the aid of luciferase, emits light (*bioluminescence*).

lucifugal (lu-sif'u-gal). Avoiding bright light.

Lucite (lu'sīt). The commercial name of polymethyl methacrylate, produced by E. I. du Pont de Nemours and Company. A chemically identical form, marketed by Rohm & Haas Company, is called Plexiglas. Both are lustrous, water-white, lightweight, transparent thermoplastics used in making contact lenses, some spectacle frames, etc. They were formerly used in the U.S.A. in the manufacture of ophthalmic lenses, but have been largely replaced in this application by more abrasion-resistant, heat-hardened resins.

Luckiesh and Moss (lu'kēsh and maws) **illuminator; sensitometer.** See under the nouns.

Luckiesh-Taylor brightness meter (lu'kēsh-ta'lor). See under *meter.*

Luer's clock (lu'erz). A cylindro-spherometer.

Lumarith (lu'mah-rith). A trade name for a cellulose acetate material used in spectacle frames.

lumen (lu'men). The unit of luminous flux; the flux emitted within a unit solid angle (1 steradian) by a point source having a luminous intensity of 1 candela (1 candlepower). Symbol: *lm.*

lumen-hour (lu'men-our'). A unit of light; the quantity of light delivered in 1 hour by a flux of 1 lumen.

lumerg (lūm'erg). A unit of luminous energy representing that obtained from a radiant energy source of 1 erg with a luminous efficiency of 1 lumen per watt.

lumeter, holophane (lu'me-ter). A portable photometer for measuring luminance.

Lumi-Cote. The trade name for a coating applied to plastic contact lenses which renders them opaque to ultraviolet light without affecting the transmission of the visible spectrum.

Lumi-Mark. The trade name for a dye which is visible only when exposed to black light, used for reference markings on plastic contact lenses.

luminaire (lu′mih-nār). A complete lighting unit consisting of a light source, housing, supports, shields, etc.; a complete lighting fixture.

luminance (lu′mih-nans). The photometric term for the intensitive property of an emitting or reflecting surface; the luminous flux per unit of projected area per unit solid angle either leaving or arriving at a surface at a given point in a given direction; the luminous intensity in a given direction per unit of projected area of a surface as viewed from that direction. Previously termed *photometric brightness* and must be differentiated from *brightness,* the resulting visual effect. Symbol: *L.* Common units are *candela* per unit area, *stilb, footlambert, nit, lambert, apostilb,* and *millilambert.*

apparent l. The luminance of an object or its background as viewed from a specific direction and through a given distance of atmosphere which attenuates and/or scatters light. Cf. *inherent luminance.*

inherent l. The actual luminance of an object or its background in a specified direction when it is unaltered by atmospheric attenuation or scatter, or by the presence of a glare source in the field of view. Cf. *apparent luminance.*

lumination (lu″mih-na′shun). The emitting of light from a source.

luminator (lu′mih-na′tor). An emitter of light; a light source.

luminescence (lu″mih-nes′ens). Radiation which results primarily from the excitation of individual atoms, so scattered or arranged that each atom is free to act without much interference from its neighbors. As distinguished from radiation due to incandescence, it is not due to temperature; also, the radiation is apt to consist of discrete wavelengths, or colors, rather than forming a continuous spectrum. See also *bioluminescence; chemiluminescence; crystalloluminescence; electroluminescence; photoluminescence; thermoluminescence; triboluminescence.*

luminiferous (lu″mih-nif′er-us). Transmitting, producing, yielding, or conveying light.

luminophor (lu-min′o-fōr). A substance which has the property of absorbing energy and releasing it again in the form of luminescence, such as a fluorophor or phosphor.

luminosity (lu″mih-nos′ih-te). The luminous intensity or brightness sensation-producing attribute of radiant flux; brightness.

absolute l. Spectral luminous efficacy of radiant flux. See under *efficacy.*

contrast, l. See under *contrast.*

curve, l. See under *curve.*

factor, l. See under *factor.*

minimum-field l. Luminosity determined by reducing the size of the test object (hence the area or "field" of the test object) until it matches the brightness of a fixed comparison standard or fulfills some other comparable criterion for determining luminous equivalence, e.g., the level of hue extinction.

relative l. Spectral luminous efficiency of radiant flux. See under *efficiency.*

luminous (lu′mih-nus). 1. Emitting or reflecting light. 2. Having the property of exciting the visual receptors.

luminous dust. Light chaos.

luminous density; efficacy; efficiency; emittance; energy; flux; intensity. See under the nouns.

lumi-rhodopsin (lu'me-ro-dop'sin). An intermediate product in the chemical breakdown of rhodopsin by the action of light prior to the formation of meta-rhodopsin and then retinene.

Lumiwand. The trade name for a device used in visual field testing consisting essentially of a wand containing a 10.0 mm. electroluminescent light source at one end, a battery and switch in the handle at the other end, and a control to regulate luminance. Auxiliary caps with apertures ranging from 1.0 mm. to 5.0 mm. in diameter may be fitted over the light source to vary the size of the test stimulus.

Lummer-Brodhun (lum'er-brod'hun) **cube; photometer.** See under the nouns.

Lummer-Gehrcke interferometer (lum'er-gār'ke). See under *interferometer.*

Luneburg's theory (lūn'eh-burgz). See under *theory.*

lupus erythematosus conjunctivae (lu'pus er"e-them-ah-to'sus kon"-junk-ti've). A rare affection of the conjunctiva which almost invariably has spread from a neighboring lupus erythematosus of the eyelids. It commences with intense hyperemia and velvetlike edema and may be diffuse, limited to circumscribed patches, or scattered as dotted foci. The lesions later become bluish, then white and depressed as atrophy occurs. Symptoms include slight photophobia, itching, lacrimation, and mucoid discharge with little or no pain.

lupus pernio (lu'pus per'ne-o). Sarcoidosis.

Luschka's nerve (lush'kahz). The posterior ethmoidal nerve.

Lussi's line (lus'ēz). See under *line.*

luster. 1. The appearance of two different surface colors viewed haploscopically and superimposed, the resulting percept being characteristically unstable and aptly described as one surface being seen through the other; also called *binocular luster.* 2. A glossiness or sheen associated with metallic surfaces, sometimes called *metallic luster.*

　achromatic l. Luster obtained from two different achromatic colors, e.g., black and white, viewed haploscopically and superimposed.

　polychromatic l. Luster obtained by the haploscopic superimposition of two different hues.

Lutes near point chart (lūtz). See under *chart.*

lux. A unit of illumination equal to 1 lumen per sq. m. Syn., *metercandle.*

luxation of the eyeball. See under *eyeball.*

luxation of the lens. Complete dislocation of the crystalline lens from the pupillary aperture. Cf. *subluxation of the lens.*

luxometer (luks-om'eh-ter). A portable photometer by which an illuminated surface is compared with an area illuminated by a standard lamp contained within the instrument.

Lyle and Jackson's method (līl and jak'sunz). See under *method.*

Lyman's ghosts (li'manz). See under *ghost.*

lymphangiectasis, hemorrhagic, conjunctival (lim"fan-je-ek'tah-sis). A rare condition in which a conjunctival blood vessel becomes connected with a lymphatic vessel, resulting in intermittent or permanent filling of the lymphatic with blood.

lymphangiectasis, ocular (lim"fan-je-ek'tah-sis). Dilatation of the lymphatic vessels of the eye, characterized in the bulbar conjunctiva by single or multiple, small, transparent, pearl-like blebs or cysts.

lymphangioma (lim″fan-ge-o′mah). A congenital, benign, slowly progressing tumor of the lymph-vascular system which may affect the eyelids, conjunctiva, or orbit, and rarely the eyeball.

lymphatic (lim-fat′ik) **nodes; rings; spaces; vessels.** See under the nouns.

lymphogranulomatosis, benign (lim″fo - gran″u - lo - mah - to′sis). Sarcoidosis.

lymphogranulomatosis of Schaumann (lim″fo-gran″u-lo-mah-to′-sis). Sarcoidosis.

lymphoma (lim-fo′mah). Any tumor made up of lymphoid tissue.

lymphorrhagia retinalis traumatic (lim″fo-ra′je-ah ret-ih-nal′is). Purtscher's disease.

lymphosarcoma (lim″fo-sar-ko′mah). A form of malignant tumor of lymphatic tissue characterized by proliferation of masses of cells resembling lymphocytes and resulting in enlargement of lymph nodes and infiltration of other tissues. Of the malignant orbital tumors, it is one of the most common.

lysozyme (li′so-zīm). A bactericidal mucolytic enzyme present in tears (also in saliva, nasal secretions, egg white, and leukocytes).

Lythgoe (lith′go) **cycle; theory.** See under the nouns.

M

M. Abbreviation for *myopia* or *myopic.*

m. Abbreviation for *meter.*

M.A. Abbreviation for *meter angle.*

mμ. Symbol for *millimicron.*

Macbeth illuminometer; photometer. See under *illuminometer.*

McCarthy's reflex (mă-kar′thēz). Supraorbital reflex.

McCulloch's rule (mă-kul′oks). See under *rule.*

McDougall's theory (mak-du′galz). See under *theory.*

Mach's (mahks) **band; figure; visual illusion; law; ring.** See under the nouns.

Mackay-Marg Electronic Tonometer. See under *tonometer.*

Mackenzie's theory (mă-ken′zēz). See under *theory.*

macreikonic (mak″ri-kon′ic). Pertaining to the eye with the larger image, in aniseikonia.

macroblepharia (mak″ro-bleh-far′-e-ah; -fa′re-ah). An abnormally large eyelid.

macrocornea (mak″ro-kōr′ne-ah). An abnormally large cornea. Syn., *megalocornea.*

macroesthesia (mak″ro-es-the′ze-ah). Macropsia.

macroglia (mă-krog′le-ah). Astroglia.

macroglobulinemia (mak″ro-glob″-u-lin-e′me-ah). Waldenström's syndrome.

macrophthalmous (mak″rof-thal′-mus). An abnormally large eye.

macropia (mă-kro′pe-ah). Macropsia.

macropsia (mă-krop′se-ah). An anomaly of visual perception in which objects appear larger than they actually are. Syn., *megalopsia.*

accommodative m. Macropsia attributed to underaccommodation or reduced effort of accommodation in relation to the amount of accommodation normally required for the distance of the object in question.

retinal m. Macropsia resulting from a disturbance of the retina in which the visual receptor cells are crowded together. It may be due to a detachment, a tumor, exudative or inflammatory process, or cicatricial changes.

macropsy (mă-krop′se). Macropsia.

macula (mak′u-lah). 1. Any uniquely pigmented area such as the macula lutea of the retina. 2. A corneal macula.

corneal m. A moderately dense and circumscribed whitish opacity of the cornea. It is more dense than a *nebula* and less dense than a *leukoma.*

detached m. A detachment of the retina in the region of the macula lutea.

false m. In anomalous correspondence, the retinal area of the deviating eye corresponding in visual direction to the fovea of the fixating eye, hence appearing to exhibit certain projective attributes of the normal fovea. Syn., *anomalous associated area; pseudomacula.*

flava, m. Macula lutea.

heterotopia of m. See under *heterotopia.*

hole in m. See under *hole.*

honeycombed m. Cystic degeneration of the macula.

lutea, m. An oval area in the retina, 3 to 5 mm. in diameter, usually located temporal to the posterior pole of the eye and slightly below the level of the optic disk. It is characterized by the presence of a yellow pigment diffusely permeating the inner layers, contains the fovea centralis in its center, and provides the best photopic visual acuity. It is devoid of retinal blood vessels, except in its periphery, and receives nourishment from the choriocapillaris of the choroid. Rod and cone fibers from the visual cells in this area course obliquely to form the fiber layer of Henle. Syn., *limbus luteus; macula flava; punctum luteum; Soemmering's spot; yellow spot.*

sparing of m. The retaining of macular function in the presence of adjacent visual field losses, especially so identified in hemianopsia which circumvents the macula.

Macula Integrity Tester-Trainer. An instrument primarily for diagnosis and treatment of eccentric fixation, consisting essentially of a rotating transilluminated Polaroid filter which, when viewed through a blue filter, produces rotating Haidinger's brushes localized in relation to a fixation point mounted on the instrument.

madarosis (mad″ah-ro′sis). Loss of the eyelashes. Syn., *milphae; milphosis.*

Maddox (mad′oks) **calculator; chart; cross; groove; prism; prism verger; rod; tangent scale; strabismometer; tests; wing.** See under the nouns.

Magendie-Hertwig sign (mă″zhan″-de′-hert′vig). See under *sign.*

magenta (mă-jen′tah). 1. The hue attribute of visual sensation typically evoked by stimulation of the normal human eye by any combination of wavelengths which act as the complement of a wavelength of 515 mμ. 2. The hue at-

tribute produced by the additive mixture of red and blue.

magneto-optics (mag-ne″to-op′tiks; mag″net-o-). That area of optics which treats of the interaction of light with magnetic fields.

magnification (mag″nih-fih-ka′-shun). An increase in the apparent size, the perceived size, or the actual size of an object, or of its image in relation to the object.

angular m. Magnification expressed as a ratio of the angle subtended by the image to that subtended by the object with respect to a viewing point of reference, such as the entrance pupil of the eye.

apparent m. In an optical viewing instrument, the ratio of the apparent size of the image to the apparent size of the object at a standard or assumed distance, conventionally 25 cm. Syn., *magnifying power.*

axial m. The ratio of the distance between two axially located points in image space to the distance between the corresponding two axially located points in object space. Syn., *longitudinal magnification.*

chromatic difference of m. In an optical system with chromatic aberration, the difference in magnification produced by different wavelengths or colors.

effective m. Traditionally, the ratio of the apparent size of the image as seen through a lens or optical system to the apparent size of the object as it would appear at a distance of 25 cm., the so-called "distance of distinct vision." For a simple lens in front of the eye, this magnification is expressed by the formula: $M = F/4$, where $F =$ the dioptric power of the lens.

meridional m. Magnification, as produced by a meridional iseikonic lens, in which the image is magnified maximally in one meridian and minimally in a meridian at right angles to it.

normal m. The maximum magnification under which a microscope can provide a retinal image having the same brightness or luminance as that obtained without the microscope, called *normal brightness.* The limiting factor is the area of the exit pupil of the microscope in relation to the area of the entrance pupil of the eye.

objective m. The magnification attributed to the objective of a microscope. Syn., *initial magnification.*

over-all m. Magnification, as produced by an over-all iseikonic lens, in which the image is magnified equally in all meridians.

peripheral m. The magnification obtained when the eye fixates through a peripheral portion of a spectacle lens, usually differing from the normally obtained magnification through the center because of the greater distance of the periphery of the lens from the eye.

power m. Magnification resulting from the power of an ophthalmic lens, represented by the fraction $\dfrac{1}{1 - zF_v}$ in the formula

$$M = \left(\frac{1}{1 - cF_1}\right)\left(\frac{1}{1 - zF_v}\right)$$

where c = thickness divided by index of refraction, F_1 = refractive power of the front surface of the lens, z = distance from the back surface of the lens to the entrance pupil of the eye, and F_v = the effective power of the lens.

psychological m. The perceptual enlargement of an object not associated with an increase in size of the retinal image, e.g., the perceptual enlargement of the moon when seen at the horizon.

relative spectacle m. The ratio of the size of the retinal image in a corrected ametropic eye to that in the posterior focal plane of the same eye uncorrected.

shape m. Magnification resulting from the shape of an ophthalmic lens, represented by the fraction $\dfrac{1}{1 - cF_1}$ in the formula

$$M = \left(\frac{1}{1 - cF_1}\right)\left(\frac{1}{1 - zF_v}\right)$$

where c = thickness divided by index of refraction, F_1 = refractive power of the front surface of the lens, z = distance from the back surface of the lens to the entrance pupil of the eye, and F_v = the effective power of the lens.

spectacle m. The ratio between the size of the retinal image in an ametropic eye before and after correction.

transverse m. Lateral magnification.

magnifier. 1. An optical device or visual aid, usually for close viewing, producing apparent magnification. 2. Any optical system producing magnification.

binocular m. A binocular magnifying instrument, usually consisting of simple convex lenses, and sometimes prisms, supported before the eyes by an attachment to a spectacle frame or by a headband. Syn., *binocular loupe.*

Bishop Harman m. A binocular magnifying loupe consisting of two laterally adjustable, rectangular, convex, spheroprism lenses rigidly mounted anteriorly to a trial frame with single cells for auxiliary lenses.

Brungardt m. A 10× binocular lens assembly which can be attached to a focal illuminator for fitting and inspection of contact lenses and for locating foreign bodies.

Igard Hyperocular Spectacle M.
A plastic, aspherical, biconvex, lenticular lens mounted in a spectacle frame having two anterior posts acting as stops against which reading material is held. It is available in 4×, 6×, and 8× magnifications, for use in subnormal vision.

measuring m. A small, hand-held, magnifying viewer used in the inspection of contact lenses, consisting essentially of a convex lens eyepiece with a transparent scale at its object focal plane.

projection m. An instrument which projects a magnified image of printed matter onto a screen by reflecting light from the surface of the matter through a system of mirrors and lenses. A type used for subnormal vision contains both the optical system and a translucent screen on the back of which the image is focused to to be viewed from the front.

magnify. To produce magnification.

magnitude, apparent. 1. The perceived size of an object, or its image, when it is projected to, or identified with, a specific distance from the observer. 2. The size of an object, as measured by the plane angle which it subtends at the eye of the observer.

Magnocular (mag-nok'u-lar). A trade name for a binocular magnifying device consisting of two concave lenses mounted in a spectacle frame and two convex lenses anteriorly mounted on jointed arms.

Magnus (mag'nus) **formula; method.** See under the nouns.

Maier's sinus (mi'erz). See under *sinus.*

Maklakov's tonometer (mak'lah-kofs). See under *tonometer.*

malingering (mă-ling'er-ing). Feigning or deliberately giving false test responses, indicating illness or disability, to gain a desired award or compensation or to avoid doing a duty.

negative m. The opposite of malingering, hence feigning or deliberately giving false test responses, indicating the total or partial absence of illness, disability, or damage.

positive m. Malingering, distinguished from *negative malingering.*

malattia levantinese (mal-ah-te'ah leh-van'tih-nēz). A slowly progressive, dominant, inherited degeneration of the retina found among inhabitants of the Levantine valley in North Ticino, Switzerland. It is characterized in its later stages by numerous, closely grouped, round, yellowish spots of varying size in the region of the macula and optic disk, and results in a gradual loss of central vision.

malprojection (mal"pro-jek'shun). False projection.

Malus' law (mă-lūz). See under *law.*

Malus-Dupin law (mah-lu'-du-pen'). See under *law.*

mandrel (man'drel). A tapered hollow bar having a cross section

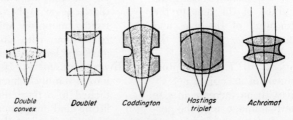

Double convex   Doublet   Coddington   Hastings triplet   Achromat

Fig. 30. Common types of magnifiers. (From *Fundamentals of Optics,* ed. 3, Jenkins and White, McGraw-Hill, 1957)

shape of a spectacle lens and used to stretch and shape the rims of plastic spectacle frames.

Mangin mirror. See under *mirror.*

Mann's sign (manz). See under *sign.*

manometer (mă-nom'eh-ter). An instrument for determining the intraocular pressure, by direct contact with the aqueous humor. It consists essentially of a cannula introduced into the anterior chamber and a U-shaped tube filled with mercury, saline, or some other fluid to register the pressure.

compensatory m. A manometer which has a compensating apparatus by which pressure may be applied or released to counterbalance any movement of fluid out of or into the eye during measurements.

manometry (mă-nom'eh-tre). Determination of intraocular pressure by means of a manometer.

manoptoscope (man-op'to-skōp). A hollow, truncated cone for testing ocular dominance on the principle of unilateral sighting. The subject holds the base of the cone against his face, covering both eyes, and views a distant object through the small end of the cone. Only one eye can fixate under these conditions, and that eye is considered to be the dominant eye. Syn., *manuscope.*

mantle, glial (peripheral). A layer of neuroglia located between the pia mater and the peripheral nerve fiber bundles of the optic nerve.

manuductor (man"u-duk'tor). An instrument used in visual training, based on the principle of the Brewster stereoscope, with large spheroprism lenses and a large target area especially adaptable for tracing, as in a cheiroscope, and for fusional convergence training.

manuscope (man'u-skōp). Manoptoscope.

Manz's (man'zez) **disease; gland; theory.** See under the nouns.

March's disease (mar'chez). Exophthalmic goiter.

Marchesani's syndrome (mahr"kesahn'ēz). See under *syndrome.*

Marcus Gunn phenomenon (mar'kus gun). Jaw-winking.

Maréchal's box (mar"a-shalz'). See under *box.*

Marfan's syndrome (mar-fahnz'). See under *syndrome.*

margin. A boundary, border, or edge.

ciliary m. The periphery of the root of the iris where it attaches to the ciliary body.

orbital m. The anterior rim of the bony orbit formed by the frontal, the zygomatic, the maxillary, and, according to some, the lacrimal bone.

pupillary m. The pigmented border of the iris that immediately surrounds the pupil.

supraorbital m. Supraorbital arch.

marginoplasty (mar'jin-o-plas"te). Plastic surgery of the eyelid margin.

margo palpebrae (mar'go pal'pebre, pal-pe'-). The margin of the eyelid.

Marie's disease (mar-ēz'). See under *disease.*

Marie-Guillan syndrome (mahr-e'ge-yān). Rubrothalamic syndrome.

Marin-Amat syndrome (mah-rin'ah-mat'). Reverse jaw-winking.

Marinesco-Sjögren syndrome (mar"ih-nes'ko-sye'gren). See under *syndrome.*

Mariotte's (mar-e-ots') **experiment; blind spot.** See under the nouns.

Mark diplopia test. See under *test.*

marker, axis. A device used to locate and mark the cylindrical axis and the optical center of a spectacle lens preparatory to cutting.

Marlow's (mar'lōz) **prolonged occlusion; test.** See under the nouns.

Martegiani, area of (mar-tej-ah'ne). See under *area.*

Martens photometer (mar'tenz). See under *photometer*.

Martius disk (mar'tih-us). See under *disk*.

Martorell's syndrome. Pulseless disease.

maser (ma'zer). An acronym for "microwave amplification by stimulated emission of radiation"; a device for producing coherent radiation at a frequency within the microwave band. Cf. *laser*.

optical m. Laser.

Mason's disk (ma'sunz). See under *disk*.

mass, ciliary (of Whitnall). A thickening at the lateral margin of the eyelid formed by the uniting of the connective tissue of the tarsus with that around the follicles of the eyelashes.

Masselon's spectacles (mas-eh-lawnz'). See under *spectacles*.

Masson disk (mah-son'). See under *disk*.

match, Rayleigh. Rayleigh equation.

matching, color. 1. The selection of colors possessing the same hue, saturation, or brightness from a group of colors varying in hue, saturation, and brightness. 2. The mixing of two or more colors on a spinning color wheel to match the hue, saturation, and brightness of a uniform surface.

Matsuura Autocross (mah"tsu-oor'-ah). See under *Autocross*.

Matthiessen's ratio. See under *ratio*.

Maurice's theory (mo're-sez). See under *theory*.

Mauthner's test (mout'nerz). See under *test*.

maxima, principal (mak'sih-mah). The brightest bands produced in interference phenomena by reinforcement of two or more separate wave trains.

maxima, secondary (mak'sih-mah). The bright bands produced in interference phenomena adjacent to the principal maxima.

Maxwell's (maks'welz) **box; color curves; disk; law; ring; spot;**
table; test; theory; top; color triangle. See under the nouns.

May's (māz) **ophthalmoscope; prism; sign.** See under the nouns.

Mazow pupilens (ma'zo). See under *pupilens*.

mean. A statistical measure of central tendency of a distribution.

arithmetic m. The average, obtained by summing the variables and dividing by the number of cases.

geometric m. The nth root of the product of the scores where n is the number of scores.

harmonic m. The reciprocal of the arithmetic mean of the reciprocals of the scores or values in a sample.

quadratic m. The square root of the arithmetic mean of the squared values in a sample.

Means' sign (mēnz). See under *sign*.

measure, lens. An instrument designed to measure the sagitta of a curve and so calibrated as to give this measurement in terms of diopters of refractive power for a given index of refraction, usually that of crown glass ($n = 1.523$ or 1.53). It is shaped like a pocket watch, with three prongs attached to the edge, the outer two being fixed and the center one varying in length with the curve of the lens surface. Syn., *lens clock; lens gauge*.

Mecholyl (mek'o-lil). A trade name for acetyl-beta-methyl-choline which, when instilled into the eye in diluted solution, acts as a powerful miotic through stimulation of the parasympathetic nervous system.

Meckel's (mek'elz) **cave; cavity; ganglion; space.** See under the nouns.

media (me'de-ah). Substances through which a force acts or an effect is transmitted.

anisotropic m. Optical media in

which the velocity of light is not constant for all directions.

isotropic m. Optical media in which the velocity of light is constant for all directions.

ocular m. The transparent substances of the eye through which light passes prior to stimulation of the retina. They include the tears, the cornea, the aqueous humor, the crystalline lens, and the vitreous humor.

optica, m. See *medium, optical.*

median (me′de-an). One of the statistical measures of central tendency of a distribution. It is the value of the middle case in an ordered series.

mediaometer (me″de-ah-om′eh-ter). An instrument for determining the dioptric powers of the ocular media.

medium, optical. Any material, substance, space, or surface regarded in terms of its optical properties.

medulloepithelioma (me-dul″o-ep″-ih-the″le-o′mah). A tumor of the retina or of the central nervous system which is derived from the primitive retinal epithelium or from the medullary epithelium of the primitive neural tube of the brain.

Meekren-Ehlers-Danlos syndrome (mēk′ren-a′lerz-dan′los). See under *syndrome.*

Meesmann's corneal dystrophy (mēz′mahnz). See under *dystrophy.*

megalocornea (meg″ah-lo-kōr′ne-ah). A bilateral developmental anomaly, in which the cornea is abnormally large in diameter in the presence of normal intraocular pressure. The cornea is otherwise normal, although there may be associated changes in the crystalline lens and the zonule of Zinn. Syn., *cornea globosa; keratoglobus; keratomegalia; anterior megalophthalmus.*

megalopapilla (meg″ah-lo-pah-pil′-ah). A congenital condition in which the optic disk is abnormally large, but otherwise of normal appearance.

megalophthalmos (meg″ah-lof-thal′-mus). Megalophthalmus.

megalophthalmus (meg″ah-lof-thal′-mus). The condition of abnormally large eyes, occurring as a developmental anomaly.

anterior m. Megalocornea with associated changes in the crystalline lens and the zonule of Zinn.

megalopia (meg″ah-lo′pe-ah). Macropsia.

megalopsia (meg″ah-lop′se-ah). Macropsia.

Megascope (meg′ah-skōp). A projection magnifier for use in subnormal vision which provides either 12× or 25× magnification.

megaseme (meg′ah-sēm). Having an orbital index greater than 89; characteristic of the yellow races. See also *mesoseme; microseme.*

megophthalmus (meg″of-thal′mus). Megalophthalmus.

Meibomian (mi-bo′me-an) **cyst; glands.** See under the nouns.

meibomianitis (mi-bo″me-ah-ni′tis). Inflammation of the Meibomian glands.

meibomitis (mi-bo-mi′tis). Meibomianitis.

Meisling's colorimeter (mīs′lingz). See under *colorimeter.*

Meissner's test (mīs′nerz). See under *test.*

melange (meh-lahnzh′). A multicomponent lubricant used in drilling lenses, commonly consisting of oil, turpentine, and camphor.

melanin (mel′ah-nin). A brown, black, or otherwise dark pigment derived from the metabolic activity of certain specialized cells and normally present in the skin, the hair, the choroid, the iris, the retina, the ciliary body, the cardiac tissue, the pia mater, and the substantia nigra of the brain. Melanin is found in melanoblasts, melanocytes, melanophages, and melanophores, is absent in true albinos, and its amount and distribution determine the color of the iris.

melanocataracta (mel''ah-no-kat-ah-rak'tah). Black cataract.

melanocytosis, ocular (mel''ah-no-si-to'sis). Melanosis bulbi.

melanocytosis, oculodermal (mel''-ah-no-si-to'sis). Oculocutaneous melanosis.

melanokeratosis, striate (mel''ah-no-ker''ah-to'sis). A condition occurring in Negroid eyes in which clear cornea is invaded by streaks of pigmented connective tissue growing from the limbus toward, and in response to, a corneal lesion.

melanoma (mel''ah-no'mah). A tumor arising from a pigmented nevus, as may occur in the conjunctiva, the choroid, the iris, the ciliary body, the optic nerve, etc.

melanosis (mel''ah-no'sis). A condition characterized by abnormal deposits of melanin.

bulbi, m. Melanosis of the eyeball especially affecting the iris, the ciliary body, the choroid, and the sclera.

corneae, m. A physiological or pathological deposition of melanin in the epithelial or endothelial layers of the cornea.

iridis, m. Melanosis of the iris.

lenticularis progressiva, m. Xeroderma pigmentosum.

oculi, m. Melanosis bulbi.

oculocutaneous m. A syndrome of ocular and cutaneous melanosis, usually congenital, in which the skin lesions commonly follow the branches of the fifth cranial nerve, especially the ophthalmic. Syn., *oculodermal melanocytosis; nevus of Ota.*

optic nerve, m. of the. A condition characterized by deposits of melanin in the optic nerve in the form of flecks, pigmented pits,

uniform pigmentation, or melanomata.

retinae, m. A congenital hyperplasia of melanin in the cells of the retinal epithelium. It is usually unilateral, nonprogressive, and characterized by a brown, sector-shaped area with its apex at the optic disk.

sclerae, m. A congenital condition characterized by flecks of melanin deposited in the sclera.

meliceris (mel''ih-se'ris). A chalazion.

Melkersson-Rosenthal syndrome. See under *syndrome.*

member, inner (of a rod or cone). The portion of a visual cell proper between the external limiting layer and the outer member of a visual cell in the retina. The thickness of an inner cone member is usually three to four times that of an inner rod member in the same region. Syn., *inner segment.*

member, outer (of a rod or cone). The portion of a visual cell proper between the inner member and the pigment epithelium layer of the retina. Rhodopsin is present in the outer member of a rod cell. Syn., *outer segment.*

membrana (mem-brah'nah). Latin for *membrane.*

capsularis, m. The hyaloid vascular network about the posterior pole of the embryonic crystalline lens or about a persistent hyaloid artery.

capsuli pupillaris, m. Capsulopupillary membrane.

coronae ciliaris, m. The suspensory ligament of the crystalline lens.

epipapillaris, m. Prepapillary membrane.

fusca, m. Lamina fusca.

granulosa externa, m. Outer nuclear layer of the retina.

granulosa interna, m. Inner nuclear layer of the retina.

hyaloidea plicata, m. Membrana plicata of Vogt.

limitans, m. Limiting membrane.

limitans perivascularis gliae, m. Perivascular limiting membrane.

nictitans, m. Nictitating membrane.

plicata m., of Vogt. A zone of vitreous condensation, appearing as a fine multifolded membrane, posterior to the capsule of the crystalline lens, which represents the anterior limit of the secondary vitreous, and bounds the anterior opening of the hyaloid canal. Syn., *tractus hyaloideus.*

ruyschiana, m. Ruyschian membrane.

vasculosa m. retinae. A dense network of blood vessels located in the vitreous, superficial to the retina, found in certain lower vertebrates.

membrane. A thin layer of tissue which covers a surface, surrounds a part, lines a cavity, separates adjacent cavities, or connects adjacent structures.

amphiblestroid m. The retina. *Obs.*

anterior basal m. Bowman's membrane.

anterior elastic m. Bowman's membrane.

arachnoid m. The spiderweblike tissue between the dura mater and the pia mater of the central nervous system and of the optic nerve. A subarachnoid space with cerebrospinal fluid is found between the arachnoid and the pia mater.

Barkan's m. A very thin membranous structure extending from Descemet's membrane to the iris and covering the filtration angle of the anterior chamber, said to be present in typical congenital glaucoma.

basal corneal m. Basement membrane of the corneal epithelium.

basement m. of choroid. Lamina vitrea.

basement m. of the corneal epithelium. The very thin noncellular layer of the corneal epithelium adjacent to Bowman's membrane, which is secreted by the basal cells and consists of two major layers, an anterior lipid and a posterior reticular layer. Syn., *basal corneal membrane.*

Bowman's m. The thin, noncellular, second layer of the cornea, located between the anterior stratified epithelium and the substantia propia. Syn., *lamina elastica anterior; Bowman's lamina; Bowman's layer; anterior basal membrane; anterior elastic membrane.*

Bruch's m. 1. The lamina vitrea of the choroid. 2. The lamina vitrea of the ciliary body. 3. The posterior border lamella of Fuchs.

capsulopupillary m. The lateral portion of the tunica vasculosa lentis of the embryonic crystalline lens, formed by the anastomoses of the intraocular and extraocular blood vessels.

choroid m. Choroid.

cyclitic m. A layer of fibrous tissue formed in the anterior vitreous during certain acute purulent inflammations of the ciliary body. It is developed from macrophages from the region of the pars plana which emigrate through the ciliary epithelium and transform into fibroblasts.

Demour's m. Descemet's membrane. *Obs.*

Descemet's m. The strong, resistant, thin, noncellular fourth layer of the cornea, located between the endothelium (from which it is secreted) and the stroma. Syn., *lamina elastica posterior; posterior basal membrane.*

Döllinger's m. Ruyschian membrane.

Duddell's m. Descemet's membrane. *Obs.*

epipapillary m. Prepapillary membrane.

glass m. of the iris. A transparent membrane on the surface of the iris, similar to Descemet's membrane, formed by proliferation of the corneal endothelium and found in degenerated eyes having extensive pathological changes.

Henle's m. 1. Posterior border lamella of Fuchs. 2. Lamina vitrea of the choroid. *Obs.*

hyaloid m. The condensed gel at the surface of the vitreous, at the interface between the primary and secondary vitreous, and at the boundaries of the hyaloid canal. Posteriorly it is inseparable from the internal limiting layer of the retina. Syn., *vitreous membrane.*

intermuscular m's. Intermuscular ligaments.

Jacob's m. Layer of rods and cones.

limiting m., accessory. A delicate sheath surrounding retinal capillaries, external to the retinal perivascular glia and internal to the perivascular limiting membrane.

limiting m. of Elschnig. A thin, glial sheath, interspersed with large oval nuclei, that lines the physiological cup of the optic disk. If the central depression of the physiological cup is deep, it may partly fill with a thicker layer of glial tissue known as the *meniscus of Kuhnt.*

limiting m., external (of the retina). External limiting layer of the retina.

limiting m., internal (of the ciliary body). A thin, homogeneous, structureless layer adjacent to the epithelium of the ciliary body. It is said to disappear both anteriorly and posteriorly.

limiting m., internal (of the iris). An extremely thin, homogeneous structure said to occur rarely on the posterior surface of the pigment epithelium of the iris.

limiting m., internal (of the ret-

ina). Internal limiting layer of the retina.

limiting m., intravitreal. The portion of the hyaloid membrane that separates the primary and secondary vitreous and forms the boundary of the hyaloid canal.

limiting m., perivascular. The external dense glial insulating sheath surrounding retinal capillaries. Syn., *membrana limitans perivascularis gliae.*

limiting m. of the vitreous. Hyaloid membrane.

limiting m. of the vitreous, anterior. Perilenticular capsule.

nictitating m. The third eyelid of lower vertebrates, supposedly represented in man by the vestigial plica semilunaris at the inner canthus.

periorbital m. The periosteum lining the bony orbit; the periorbita.

posterior basal m. Descemet's membrane.

posterior m. of the iris. The thin layer of the iris containing the dilator pupillae muscle fibers. Syn., *posterior border lamella of Fuchs.*

prepapillary m. A developmental anomaly consisting of remnants of embryonic tissue extending over or outward from the optic disk. Syn., *epipapillary membrane; prepapillary veil.*

pupillary m. The central thin portion of the lamina iridopupillaris of the fetus. Normally it degenerates during the seventh and eighth fetal month to form the pupil; at times strands of the membrane persist in the adult. Syn., *Wachendorf's membrane.*

pupillary m., persistent. Remnants of the fetal pupillary membrane which span the pupil or are adherent to the anterior lens capsule.

purpurogenous m. The pigment epithelium layer of the retina, so named because it was believed to form the visual purple.

Reichert's m. Bowman's membrane. *Obs.*

ruyschian m. The choriocapillary layer and lamina vitrea of the choroid combined with the layer of rods and cones and the pigment epithelium of the retina. Syn., *Döllinger's membrane.*

secondary m. Aftercataract.

superficial glial m. A delicate neuroglial sheath peripheral to the glial mantle of the optic nerve and over the surface of the central nervous system.

tarsal m. The tarsus or tarsal plate in the upper and lower eyelids.

Tenon's m. Tenon's capsule.

Verhoeff's m. The noncellular dense portion of the intercellular substance between cells of the pigment epithelium of the retina. In horizontal section it forms a net with hexagonal openings.

vitreous m. 1. Lamina vitrea of the choroid. 2. Descemet's membrane. 3. Hyaloid membrane.

Wachendorf's m. Pupillary membrane.

Zinn's m. The anterior surface of the iris. *Obs.*

memory, plastic. The tendency of certain thermoplastic materials to resume their original shape after forced deformation under heat, either gradually if kept warm, or more rapidly when reheated.

memory, visual. The ability to recall previous visual experiences.

men. Abbreviation for *meniscus.*

Mendel-Bechterew sign (men'del-bek-ter'yef). See under *sign.*

Ménière's (mān-e-ārz') **disease; syndrome.** See under the nouns.

meninges (me-nin'jēz). The three mesodermal coverings of the central nervous system and of the optic nerve: the dura mater, the arachnoid, and the pia mater.

meningioma (me-nin''je-o'mah). An essentially ectodermal nonmetastasizing neoplasm of the central nervous system thought to arise from the meningocytes of the arachnoid villi.

meningocele, orbital (me-nin'go-sēl). A congenital herniation of the meninges of the brain through the walls of the orbit, usually in the superior nasal region.

meniscus (me-nis'kus). A crescent-shaped structure.

Kuhnt, m. of. The thick deposit of neuroglia at the physiological cup of the optic disk, which is continuous at its periphery with the internal limiting membrane of the retina. Syn., *central connective tissue meniscus of Kuhnt.*

menotaxis. A phototactic movement of relatively high complexity of response in which the animal retains an impression of the distribution of the light stimulus over its retina and can orientate itself with respect to any selected part of its visual field. See also *klinotaxis; mnemotaxis; telotaxis; tropotaxis.*

mer. Abbreviation for *meridian.*

meramaurosis (mer''am-aw-ro'sis). Partial blindness.

meridian. The angular orientation of a great circle of the eye containing the line of sight or some other axis of reference and represented on an angular scale or protractor centered on and perpendicular to the axis of reference. In ophthalmic lens designations, the angular scale is considered parallel to the face plane with the 0°–180° meridian parallel to the base line or some other line of reference regarded as horizontal. See *axis scale.*

axis m. 1. The meridian of zero refractive power on a planocylindrical lens. 2. In a spherocylindrical lens, the meridian of zero power of the cylindrical component, whence it may be either principal meridian of the lens, depending on whether the designation is by minus or plus cylinder formula.

eye, m. of the (horizontal). The meridian of the eye which coincides with the plane of regard when the foveal line of sight is straight forward and the head is held with the base line horizontal and the face plane vertical.

eye, m. of the (vertical). The meridian of the eye which lies in a plane containing the foveal line of sight and which is perpendicular to the horizontal meridian of the eye.

iseikonic m's. The principal meridians of a meridional aniseikonic error or its correcting iseikonic lenses.

power m. 1. The meridian of greatest refractive power on a planocylindrical lens. 2. In a spherocylindrical lens, the meridian of greatest power of the cylindrical component, whence it may be either principal meridian of the lens, depending on whether the designation is by minus or plus cylinder formula.

principal m's. The meridians, normally located perpendicular to each other, of least and greatest curvature or refractive power of a toric surface or an optical system.

principal retinal m. The meridian of the retina which lies in a plane containing the y and z axes and the vertical meridian of the eye.

Merkel's (mer'kelz) **muscle; greater ring.** See under the nouns.

meropia (mer-o'pe-ah). Partial blindness or reduced vision.

Merseburg triad (mār-zeh-boorg). See under *triad*.

mesencephalon (mes"en-sef'ah-lon). The midbrain, consisting of a tectum dorsally, a cerebral aqueduct and paired cerebral peduncles ventrally. The tectum contains the superior colliculi, which are primary visual centers reflexly affecting skeletal muscle movements, and the cerebral

peduncles contain oculomotor and trochlear motor nuclei.

meshwork. Any system of fibers, lines, or channels which cross or interlace like the fabric of a net.

angle of the anterior chamber, m. of the. The meshwork of connective tissue located between the canal of Schlemm and the anterior chamber, containing spaces between intercrossing trabeculae which are involved in the drainage of aqueous humor. It is triangular on meridional section, the apex is attached to Descemet's membrane, and the base is continuous with the scleral spur, the anterior surface of the ciliary body, and the root of the iris. It is divided into three portions: uveal meshwork, corneoscleral meshwork, and endothelial meshwork.

corneoscleral m. The larger, anterior portion of the meshwork of the angle of the anterior chamber, consisting of a mass of trabecular tissue, each trabecula being a delicate flat band made of collagenous fibers, elastic fibers, hyaloid material, and endothelium. The corneoscleral meshwork lies between the canal of Schlemm and the uveal meshwork and extends from Descemet's membrane to the scleral spur. Syn., *corneal meshwork; scleral meshwork; corneoscleral trabeculum.*

endothelial m. of Speakman. A condensation of the trabecular meshwork of the angle of the anterior chamber which surrounds the canal of Schlemm. Syn., *pore tissue of Flocks.*

scleral m. Corneoscleral meshwork.

uveal m. The smaller, inner portion of the meshwork of the angle of the anterior chamber, consisting of a fine layer of loose connective tissue fibrils. It bounds the anterior chamber between Descemet's membrane and the root of the iris. Syn., *pectinate ligament; uveal trabeculum.*

mesiris (mes-i′ris). Substantia propria of the iris.

mesocornea (mes″o-kōr′ne-ah). Substantia propria of the cornea.

mesokurtic (mes″o-kur′tik). Pertaining to or having mesokurtosis.

mesokurtosis (mes″o-kur-to′sis). The kurtosis of normal distribution. Cf. *leptokurtosis; platykurtosis.*

mesophryon (mes-of′re-on). The glabella or its central point.

mesopia (mes′o-pe-ah). Mesopic vision.

mesopic (mes′op-ik). 1. Having the characteristics of mesopic vision or pertaining to levels of illumination between the photopic and scotopic ranges. 2. Having an orbitonasal index from 110 to 112.9 (or sometimes of 107.5 to 110). Cf. *platyopic; pro-opic.*

mesoropter (mes″o-rop′ter). 1. The normal position of the eyes when at rest. 2. The position of the line of sight of the eye when centered in its field of vision, as may be determined, e.g., by the orbital boundaries, spectacle rims, or an anterior field stop.

mesoseme (mes′o-sēm). Having an orbital index of 84 to 89; characteristic of the white race. See also *megaseme; microseme.*

mesothelium, corneal (mes″o-the′le-um). A single layer of flat hexagonal-shaped mesothelial cells lining the posterior surface of the cornea, more commonly termed *corneal endothelium.*

metacontrast (met″ah-kon′trast). The reduction in subjective brightness of a flash of light when it is followed closely by a second flash in a separate or an immediately adjacent portion of the visual field. Cf. *paracontrast.*

meta-**iodopsin** (met″ah-i-o-dop′sin). A form of cone pigment converted from iodopsin by irradiation with orange light and re-converted to iodopsin upon irradiation with blue light.

metamerism (me-tam′er-izm). The property of color perception which permits stimuli of different spectral composition to appear colorimetrically identical.

metamers (met′ah-merz). Metameric colors.

metamorphopsia (met″ah-mōr-fop′-se-ah). An anomaly of visual perception in which objects appear distorted or larger or smaller than their actual size.

retinal m. Metamorphopsia resulting from a displacement of the visual receptor cells of the retina. It may be due to detachment, tumor, exudative or inflammatory process, or cicatricial changes.

varians, m. Metamorphopsia in which the shape and/or size of an object appear to change while fixated.

meta-**rhodopsin** (met″ah-ro-dop′sin). An intermediate product in the chemical breakdown of rhodopsin by the action of light, after the formation of lumi-rhodopsin and prior to the formation of retinene.

metastereoscopy (met″ah-ster-e-os′-ko-pe). The viewing of a stereopsis-inducing pattern in which objects in a given plane are reproduced in natural proportions, whereas objects in other planes are not. Cf., *orthostereoscopy.*

Méténier's sign. See under *sign.*

meter. 1. The basis for measuring length by the metric system. It is equivalent to 39.371 in. 2. An apparatus for registering and measuring quantity.

acuity m. An apparatus for measuring visual acuity.

acuity m., Clason. An acuity-measuring instrument which projects test types of continuously variable size.

angle, m. See under *angle.*

candle, m. See under *candle.*

curve, m. See under *curve.*

footcandle m. Light meter.

illumination m. Light meter.

lambert, m. See under *lambert.*

light m. An instrument for measuring the illumination on a surface, by placing the meter in the plane of that surface, usually consisting of barrier layer cells connected to a scale calibrated in footcandles. Syn., *footcandle meter; illumination meter.*

Luckiesh-Taylor brightness m. A small portable, self-contained visual photometer for measuring luminance or illumination.

visibility m. An instrument for appraising the discernibleness of an object or a visual task in relation to that of a standard test object under a standard level of illumination.

metercandle. A unit of illumination equal to 1 lumen per sq. m. Syn., *lux.*

method. A set form of procedure for examination, operation, treatment, or instruction. See also *test.*

arc centune m. A method devised by Dennett for measuring the displacement or bending of light rays by a prism. The unit of measurement is the *centrad* (∇), representing the power of a prism which will deviate a ray of light 1 cm. along an arc of 1 m. radius at a distance of 1 m. from the incidence of light on the prism. Syn., *Dennett's method.*

average error m. A psychophysical method involving a series of repeated adjustments of a variable stimulus to subjective equality with a constant standard.

Barlow's m. A method by which eye movements are followed by observing the position of a tiny droplet of mercury placed on the surface of the cornea or sclera. The mercury acts as a small convex mirror and reflects light directed on it.

boxing m. A system of measurement and specification of eye size of spectacle frames based on the vertical and horizontal dimensions of the smallest horizontally oriented rectangle that can enclose the lens oriented in the position in which it is to be mounted. It is the approved system for manufacturers and dispensers of eyewear. Syn., *boxing system.*

Bradley's m. An astronomical method for measuring the velocity of light based on the telescopic observation that a star located in a direction perpendicular to the earth's orbit appears displaced in the direction of the earth's velocity.

Brinker-Katz m. A method for the treatment of eccentric fixation and amblyopia ex anopsia in which a deep red filter, such as a Kodak Wratten #92, is worn before the amblyopic eye, the other eye being totally occluded.

Brock's luster m. A method for eliciting a sense of fusion in which a small spot on a neutral background is monocularly fixated while a flashing light is held against the lid of the other, closed, eye. An attempt is made to perceive the glow from the light as if it were emanating from the background surrounding the fixation spot.

cascade comparison m. A method for determining the luminosity curve by direct and systematic, step-by-step, matching of the brightness of adjacent spectral segments of nondiscriminable hue difference.

Charpentier's m. A method for determining the objective angle of strabismus with the perimeter. The subject is placed so that the deviating eye is aligned with a light source in the center of the arc while the nondeviating eye fixates a distant point straight ahead. The examiner moves his eye along the arc of the perimeter until the reflection of the light appears to lie in the center of the pupil of the deviating eye. One half of the angle at this position, plus angle kappa in convergent and minus angle kappa in divergent strabismus, is the objective angle.

color mixing m., additive. The mixing or fusing of colors by any technique which produces a resultant color whose spectral composition represents a direct summation of the spectral components of the separate colors, as by direct superimposing of projected light sources of different color, by rapidly alternating exposures of different colors on a color wheel, or by the viewing of a closely interwoven pattern of different colors at a distance at which the separate colors are nondiscriminable.

color mixing m., physical. Color mixing so as to produce a single color stimulus having the physical or spectral attributes of an additively or subtractively produced combination.

color mixing m., physiological. The perceptual mixing of colors, by presenting them in rapidly alternating sequence or by presenting simultaneously one color to one eye and another to the other eye.

color mixing m., subtractive. The production of a resultant color whose spectral composition represents the remainder of the spectral components of an original source of illumination after selective absorption by one or more media of different color, as obtained in pigment mixing or by the superimposition of filters.

Comberg's m. A method of localizing an intraocular foreign body, consisting of making anteroposterior and lateral x-ray photographs of the eye with a contact lens in place to permit alignment of the anteroposterior views

on the major axis of the eye by centering with respect to four symmetrically located lead markers in the lens, and fore and aft positioning of the lateral view by reference to the plane of the four markers.

concentric m. An insertion method for making an eye impression in the fitting of molded contact lenses in which the molding shell does not have a handle, being placed on the eye in the same manner as a scleral contact lens.

Con-lish m. A method for contouring and polishing the edge of a contact lens, devised by Gilberto Cepero, in which the lens is placed with the concave surface first down, then up, for a specified number of seconds, on each of five angled polishing tools (40°, 60°, 90°, 140°, 180°) rotating at either 100 rpm or 500 rpm.

constant m. A psychophysical method in which each of a series of randomly varied stimuli is presented to be judged as "less than" or "more than" a fixed comparison stimulus. A third category response, "equal to" or "doubtful," also may be included. In the determination of an absolute threshold the two categories of response may be simply "observed" and "not observed," without reference to a fixed comparison stimulus.

corneal reflection m. Any method which utilizes the reflection of light from the cornea to determine the position or movement of the eye, as in measuring the objective angle of strabismus, photographing eye movements in reading, etc.

Crédé's m. The instillation of a few drops of dilute silver nitrate solution into the eyes of the newborn as a prophylactic measure against ophthalmia neonatorum.

critical frequency m. Any technique employing the critical flicker frequency of intermittent light as a criterion.

Cross's m. A method of retinoscopy, devised by Cross, in which the neutralizing lenses, obtained with the fixation target in the plane of the retinoscope at 1 m. or nearer, is considered to represent the refractive error.

cross cylinder m. The determination of the axis and the amount of astigmatism by the use of a low power crossed cylinder lens mounted on a handle 45° from its principal meridians to facilitate quick changes of resultant cylindrical power, or resultant cylinder axis, of the test lens combination in front of the eye for direct comparison of relative blurredness.

Cuignet's m. Retinoscopy.

Cüppers' afterimage m. A method of treating amblyopia in which all of the nonmacular area of the retina is stimulated with intense light with a Euthyscope to create an afterimage in the peripheral retina and to render the macular area relatively more sensitive. After the positive afterimage in the macula becomes white, the macula is stimulated with various targets.

datum m. A system of measurement and specification of spectacle frame dimensions based on the use of the datum line. Syn., *datum system.*

Dennett's m. Arc centune method.

direct m. See *ophthalmoscopy, direct.*

direct comparison m. 1. A method for measuring aniseikonia in which a target containing polarized horizontal and vertical lines is projected onto a screen and viewed through Polaroid filters. The relative positions of the lines, as seen individually by each eye, indicate the magnitude and kind of aniseikonia. 2. A method for determining a spectral luminous

efficiency curve by the direct matching of the brightness of each segment of the spectrum with a neutral standard.

.displacement m. The dissociation of the two eyes by means of a prism of sufficient power to break or prevent fusion for the purpose of measuring phorias.

distance motivation m. A type of training in which subthreshold Koenig bars or Snellen letters are repetitively moved from a 20 ft. distance toward the trainee until they become discriminable, with the objective of improving the visual acuity score by successively greater distances of discrimination or by the use of successively smaller test targets.

distortion m. The dissociation of the two eyes by the gross distortion of the imagery for one eye, as with a Maddox rod, for the purpose of measuring phorias.

Donders' m. The determination of false torsion by projecting afterimages, in different directions of gaze, onto a screen.

Drysdale m. A method for determining the radius of curvature of a short focal length mirror in which a light source in a modified microscope is placed in sharp focus at the mirror surface and at the center of curvature of the surface, the distance between the two being recorded on the instrument dial as the radius of curvature. This method is employed in the design of instruments for measuring the curvature of contact lenses. Syn., *Drysdale principle.*

duochrome m. The determination of the refractive correction of the eye by comparison of the sharpness of imagery formed by two different spectral wavelengths, as in comparing black letters on red and green backgrounds, or the image pattern of a small light source through a cobalt glass.

Syn., *bichrome refraction; duochrome refraction; bichrome test; duochrome test.*

Erb m. The deposition, by evaporation, of a thin transparent layer of titanium dioxide on the surface of a plastic contact lens to increase its wettability.

fan dial m. The determination of the axis and the amount of astigmatism with the aid of a fan dial chart.

Fizeau's m. A method for determining the velocity of light, devised by Fizeau in 1849, based on the interval of interruption of light by a rotating toothed wheel before and after traversing a long optical path reflected on itself.

flicker photometer m. In the photometric determination of the luminosity curve, the alternate presentation of the reference and test colors at a speed which just eliminates chromatic flicker, and the adjustment of the intensity of the test color until luminous flicker is abolished.

fogging m. The placement of more plus lens or less minus lens in front of the eye than is necessary to correct the refractive error, for the purpose of minimizing accommodative effects during tests for astigmatism, or as a means of forcing the use of an amblyopic eye by reducing the acuity of the nonamblyopic eye.

form emergence m. A method of visual training in which targets are projected out of focus onto a screen and gradually brought into focus while the subject attempts to identify them.

Fry's m. A method for eliciting normal retinal correspondence in a case of anomalous retinal correspondence, in which a small spot of light on a black background is fixated by one eye while a flashing ring of light on a black background is viewed by the other eye. The targets are presented in a major amblyoscope at the objective angle of strabismus, and an attempt is made to see the spot as being in the center of the ring.

geometrical m. Ophthalmoscopy by means of an instrument whose observation system and illumination system are conducted through separate portions of the pupil to eliminate the interference of corneal reflections.

Gibson's m. A method for eliminating suppression by attempting to obtain superimposition of two dissimilar, but superimposable, haploscopically presented targets, such as a bird and a cage.

GOMAC m. A method for specifying the dimensions of plastic spectacle frames, devised by a committee representing the countries of the European Common Market. It consists of four specifications: the maximum horizontal length of the lens; the minimum distance between the lenses; the distance between the midpoint of the datum line of one lens and the midpoint of the datum line of the other lens to the nearest millimeter; the width of bridge opening measured along the datum line to the nearest millimeter. Syn., *GOMAC standard.*

Halldén's m. A method for determining the objective angle, the subjective angle, and the angle of anomaly in strabismus, utilizing a semicircular filament for producing an afterimage, and a pair of projectors containing Polaroid filters such that each eye can see only one of the images projected onto the screen. The objective angle is measured by fixating a target on the screen with one eye and adjusting a projected target, seen only by the nonfixating eye, such that it appears to be centered in a semicircular afterimage previously provided to the nonfixating eye. The distance between the fixated target and the projected target indicates the objective angle. The subjective angle is measured by adjusting the two projected targets until they appear to be superimposed, the distance on the screen between the two projected targets indicating the subjective angle. The angle of anomaly is measured by fixating a target on the screen with one eye, and adjusting a projected target, seen only by the fixating eye, such that it appears to be centered in a semicircular afterimage previously provided to the other, the nonfixating, eye. The distance of the projected target from the fixated target indicates the angle of anomaly in the fixating eye.

Harms's m. A method of perimetry in which test objects of various sizes, located at fixed positions in the visual field, are gradually increased in luminance to the threshold of visibility.

heterodynamic m. A method of dynamic retinoscopy in which the fixation target is in a plane other than that of the retinoscope peephole.

Hirschberg's m. A method for approximating the objective angle of strabismus by noting the position of the reflex of a fixated light on the cornea of the deviating eye.

Holt's m. An empirical method for computing compensation for loss of vision, based on the assumption that the total loss of vision of one eye is an 18% loss of the total function of the body.

Humphriss's m. A method for treating amblyopia ex anopsia in which a red lens is placed before the nonamblyopic eye for periodic general wear.

hydrodiascopic m. A seldom used method of ophthalmoscopy in which the cornea is immersed in water to eliminate unwanted reflections from the cornea.

indirect m. See *ophthalmoscopy, indirect.*

injection m. A technique for making an eye impression for the fitting of molded contact lenses, in which the impression material is injected into the molding shell through a hollow handle after the shell has been placed upon the eye. Cf. *insertion method.*

insertion m. A technique for making an eye impression for the fitting of molded contact lenses in which the perforated molding shell is filled with impression material before being placed on the eye. Cf. *injection method.*

Irvine's m. Irvine's prism displacement test.

isodynamic m. A method of dynamic retinoscopy in which the fixation target is in the same plane as the retinoscope peephole.

Javal's m. A method for determining the objective angle of strabismus with the perimeter. The subject is so placed that the deviating eye is at the center of the arc while the nondeviating eye fixates a distant point straight ahead. The examiner moves a light source, with his eye directly

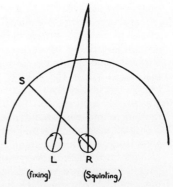

Fig. 31. Javal's method. (From *Text-book of Ophthalmology*, Vol. IV, Duke-Elder, Henry Kimpton, 1949)

above it, until the corneal reflex appears to lie in the center of the pupil of the deviating eye. The angle at this position, plus angle kappa in convergent and minus angle kappa in divergent strabismus, is the objective angle.

Kerr cell m. A method for determining the velocity of light, similar to Fizeau's method, except that the light is interrupted by a shutter instead of by a toothed wheel. The shutter is operated by an electrical and an optical system and can interrupt the beam at a rate of many millions of times per second.

Krimsky's m. A method for determining the objective angle of strabismus in which the examiner, with his eye directly above a light source fixated by the subject, observes the position of the corneal reflexes. Prisms are placed before the deviating eye until the reflex appears to occupy the same relative position as that in the fixating eye. A variation is to place prisms before the fixating eye, causing the eyes to turn, until the reflex is centered in the pupil of the deviating eye. Syn., *prism reflex test.*

Kubelka-Munk m. A method of analysis for the formulation of a colorant layer, such as in paper, textiles, and paint, which both reflects and transmits light, utilizing a general expression for the reflectance, R, of any colorant layer of known absorption and scattering coefficients, K and S, on a background of reflectance Rg, as a function of the thickness, X, of the layer.

Kupfer's m. A method for the treatment of eccentric fixation in which the patient is instructed in which direction to move his eye with respect to the light source of the ophthalmoscope until he learns the fixational position for which the light is observed to be centered on the fovea. He then observes, through a pinhole, the same light at several feet, and subsequently large letters, with the newly learned sense of fixation.

Langrange m. A method for determining the horizontal limits of the field of binocular fixation, employing the fusion band of Langrange. See under *band.*

least squares, m. of. The determination of a single straight line through a series of points, such that the sum of the squares of the deviation of the points from the line is the minimum obtainable.

Lesser's m. A method for determining a recommended near point prescription by deducting from the gross dynamic retinoscopic finding a dioptric value computed from the near phoria and the amplitude of accommodation.

limits, m. of. One of the psychophysical methods in which the test stimulus is adjusted to "just greater than" and "just less than" the comparison standard; the average of the two is taken as a measure of subjective equality while the difference between the two is a function of the threshold or sensitivity. Variations may include similar techniques for determining maxima or minima in which the variable is adjusted to obtain just noticeable decrements or increments on either side, as when a blind man locates the top of a hill.

Lloyd's m. A method of demonstrating the interference and the phase change of light on reflection at grazing incidence. Syn., *Lloyd's experiment.*

longitudinal horopter m. A method of determining aniseikonia in the horizontal meridian in which the magnitude of the rotation of the apparent frontal plane horopter about a vertical axis is measured.

Lyle and Jackson m. A method for eliciting normal retinal correspondence in a case of anomalous retinal correspondence by the rapid alternate fixation of two dissimilar targets haploscopically presented at an angle other than the subjective angle of strabismus and then gradually moved through the subjective angle to the objective angle.

Magnus m. A method for computing indemnification for loss of earning ability as a result of visual disability by the use of a formula which considers central visual acuity, the extent of the visual field, muscle function, and the ability to compete.

middle third m. The application of the clinical rule of thumb that visual discomfort is not induced as long as the convergence demand is in the middle third of the range of fusional convergence.

minus lens m., binocular. The determination of the amplitude of positive relative accommodation by the placing of consecutively stronger minus lenses binocularly before the eyes until the test type can no longer be seen clearly or until diplopia occurs; usually tested at a 16 or 13 in. distance.

minus lens m., monocular. The determination of the amplitude of accommodation by placing consecutively stronger minus lenses before an eye until the test type can no longer be seen clearly; usually tested at a 16 in. distance.

monocular diplopia m. A method for eliciting normal retinal correspondence, in a case of anomalous retinal correspondence, in which targets are presented in a major amblyoscope at the objective angle of strabismus and an attempt is made to obtain monocular diplopia which would indicate the simultaneous use of normal and anomalous correspondence.

mutiple pattern m. Harrington-Flocks test.

nonius m. Any method of utilizing vernier acuity as a criterion, as in measuring fixation disparity, plotting the nonius horopter, etc. (Nonius is the Latinized form of the name of Pedro Nunes, a Portuguese mathematician of the 17th century, a rediscoverer of the method of measuring first published by Vernier in 1631.)

Nott's m. A method of dynamic retinoscopy in which the fixation target is placed at a distance requiring 0.50 D. more accommodation than the distance of the retinoscope, e.g., the retinoscope at 40 cm. and the fixation target at 33.3 cm. This relationship is thought to compensate for the normal lag of accommodation.

Pascal's m. A method of dynamic retinoscopy in which a gross target is casually fixated in the plane of the retinoscope at a distance of 33 cm. The strongest convex lens power not giving an against motion (high neutral) is determined, and from this gross finding $+0.50$ D. is deducted to arrive at a near point correction.

Peckham's m. Peckham's test.

Pfund's m. A method for producing or analyzing polarized infrared rays in which light is reflected, at Brewster's angle, from the surfaces of selenium-coated glass mirrors.

polarization m. for ophthalmoscopy. Ophthalmoscopy in which Polaroid filters are used to eliminate unwanted reflections from the cornea.

Prentice's m. Tangent centune method.

Priestly Smith's m. A method for determining the objective angle of strabismus in which a fixation target is moved along a centimeter scale or tape, perpendicular to the midline and 1 m. from the subject, until the corneal reflex of a light source, at zero on the tape, is centered in the pupil of the deviating eye. The observer's eye remains directly above the light source.

psychophysical m's. The methods utilized in determining thresholds of relationship between stimulus and response. The methods include, among others, the *average error method,* the *method of limits,* and the *constant method.*

push-up m. 1. The determination of the near point of accommodation by moving a test object toward the eye or eyes until it blurs. 2. The determination of the near point of convergence by moving a fixation point toward the eyes, in the median plane, to the nearest point of binocular fixation.

Römer's m. The first successful method for determining the velocity of light, devised by Römer in 1676 and based on the time interval between eclipses of the satellites of the planet Jupiter.

rotating mirror m. A method for determining the velocity of light suggested by Arago and applied by Fizeau and Foucault independently in 1850. It consists essentially of measuring the deviation in the path of light reflected by a rotating plane mirror before and after traversing a long path to a fixed mirror and back.

Rushton's m. The locating of the posterior pole of the eye in situ by the visibility of a narrow transverse beam of x-rays when the eye is dark adapted, for the purpose of determining the axial length of the eyeball.

Ryer-Hotaling m. A method for determining the correcting cylindrical lens by finding a lens, placed at the wearing distance before the eye, through which

the ophthalmometer indicates 0.50 D. with the rule astigmatism. This lens rotated 90° represents the astigmatic correction.

Schapero's anomalous correspondence m. A visual training procedure for breaking down anomalous correspondence, in which superimposition or fusion targets in a major amblyoscope are simultaneously presented to the two eyes at the subjective angle. The patient is required to alternate fixation for the monocularly perceived target elements and is made aware of the necessary eye movements, even though both targets appear to lie in the same direction. Training is continued until superimposition is lost, and then carried on at the new subjective angle. The procedure is repeated until the subjective angle is the same as the objective angle.

Schapero's pupil measurement m. Determination of the diameter of the pupil in dim illumination by directing a black light source onto the eye while a distant target is fixated. The crystalline lens will fluoresce under these conditions and clearly define the pupillary limits, enabling easy measurement.

Scheiner's m. See *Scheiner's experiment.*

schlieren m. Photographic and/or observational use of a schlieren system.

screen parallax m. The determination and measurement of a phoria by the apparent movement of a fixated object when the eyes are alternately occluded and by the prism power necessary to eliminate the movement.

sensitometric m. of refraction. The determination of the ophthalmic lens correction producing the best scores on the Luckiesh-Moss Ophthalmic Sensitometer.

Sheard's m. A method of dynamic

retinoscopy in which a target is fixated in the plane of the retinoscope at a 40 cm. distance. The weakest convex lens power not giving a with motion (low neutral) is determined; from this gross finding a deduction, based on the patient's age, is made to arrive at a near point correction.

Sweet's m. A method of localizing an intraocular foreign body in which two objects of known position are used to create radiographic images to assist in plotting the location of the foreign body.

Swenson's m. A method for treating eccentric fixation and anomalous retinal correspondence associated with esotropia, in which the temporal portion of the spectacle lens before the deviating eye is occluded. The occluder is positioned with its edge bisecting the pupil as the dominant eye fixates a light source in the midplane at a 30 cm. distance.

Tait's m. A method of dynamic retinoscopy in which a target is fixated in the plane of the retinoscope at a 33 cm. distance through +3.00 D. fogging lenses. The lens power is reduced until a neutral point is reached. An allowance, dependent on the amount of accommodative convergence at this testing distance, is deducted from the gross finding to arrive at the distance correction.

Tajiri contacts-impression m. A method for examining the edge profile characteristics of a corneal contact lens in which a mold, made of a portion of the edge, is sectioned and studied under high magnification.

Tajiri custom-adjust m. A method for custom fitting plastic spectacle frames in which a soft plastic substance is fixed to the bridge and/or bends of the temples and allowed to harden while the frame is held firmly in the wearing position.

tangent centune m. A method devised by Prentice for measuring the displacement or bending of light rays by a prism. The unit of measurement is the *prism diopter* (Δ), which represents the power of a prism that will deviate a ray of light 1 cm. along a straight line perpendicular to the original path of the light at a distance of 1 m. Syn., *Prentice's method.*

telescopic ophthalmoscopy m. See under *ophthalmoscopy.*

timed resolution m. The distance motivation method employing an intermittently illuminated target.

Treleaven's m. A method of dynamic retinoscopy with the fixation target and retinoscope at 33 cm. and neutralization to high neutral, the results of which are used to recommend the power of the reading addition for 13 or 16 in. in accordance with a table formulated by Treleaven.

Updegrave's m. A method of visual training for increasing lens or prism acceptance in which intermittently illuminated reading material is fixated through the specific lens and/or prism power and an attempt is made to keep the print clear as the fixation distance is increased.

methyl methacrylate (meth″il methak′ril-āt). The chemical name of a liquid ester which, when polymerized, forms a light, strong, transparent, thermoplastic resin, widely used in contact lens manufacture, and known commercially as *Plexiglas* or *Lucite.*

metrec (me′trek). A unit of curvature representing the reciprocal of the radius in meters.

metronoscope (met-ron′o-skōp). An instrument used in visual training, consisting essentially of three rectangular shutters placed horizontally end to end, which expose phrases of reading material at a controlled rate, on a scroll moving beneath them at a controlled speed. The instrument also contains rotary prisms and cells for trial lenses.

Meyer's (mi'erz) **experiment; loop; phenomenon.** See under the nouns.

Meynert's (mi'nerts) **pyramidal cells; commissure; fibers; radiations.** See under the nouns.

Meyrowitz' test (mi'ro-vitz). See under *test*.

Michel's (mi'kelz) **flecks; spots.** See under the nouns.

Michelson's interferometer (mi'kel-sunz). See under *interferometer*.

micreikonic (mi''kri-kon'ic). Pertaining to the eye with the smaller image, in aniseikonia.

microblepharia (mi''kro-bleh-fa're-ah). Eyelids of abnormally short vertical dimension, a rare developmental anomaly.

microblepharism (mi''kro-blef'ah-rizm). Microblepharia.

microblepharon (mi''kro-blef'ah-ron). Microblepharia.

microblephary (mi''kro-blef'ah-re). Microblepharia.

microcoria (mi''kro-ko're-ah). Abnormally small pupils, usually congenital, and occurring with the absence of the dilator pupillae muscle.

microcornea (mi''kro-kōr'ne-ah). An abnormally small cornea. Syn., *anterior microphthalmus.*

microdensitometer (mi''kro-den''sih-tom'eh-ter). An instrument for measuring the transmission of light through an extremely small area of a photographic film, as needed, for example, for the determination of photographically recorded spectral line intensities. Syn., *microphotometer.*

microglia (mi-krog'le-ah). The phagocytic neuroglia of the central nervous system, the retina, and the optic nerve.

microgonioscope (mi''kro-go'ne-o-skōp). A magnifying gonioscope.

microinterferometer (mi''kro-in''ter-fēr-om'eh-ter). An instrument for the examination of very small optical components, such as the surface structure and cylindricity of glass fibers.

microlens (mi'kro-lenz). A plastic corneal contact lens characterized by its thinness (approximately 0.20 mm. center thickness) and by its small diameter (9 to 10 mm.).

microlentia (mi''kro-len'she-ah, -te-ah). Microphakia.

micromanometer (mi''kro-mah-nom'-eh-ter). A manometer with a closed system and with dimensions so small as to minimize errors. Usually it consists of a capillary tube closed at the top, filled with air both above and below a saline solution, and connected directly with a needle cannula.

micromegalopsia (mi''kro-meg''ah-lop'se-ah). The perception of objects smaller or larger than their true size, or alternately too small and too large.

micrometer (mi-krom'eh-ter). An instrument or attachment for measuring small distances or angles.

Jaeger's ocular m. A device designed for attachment to the Zeiss slit lamp biomicroscope for measurement of corneal thickness or anterior chamber depth. It produces two identical overlapping images, one of which is moved until the anterior limit of the distance being measured is aligned with the posterior limit on the other image, the micrometer giving a direct reading of the distance.

Lobeck's ocular m. A device designed for attachment to the Zeiss slit lamp biomicroscope for measurement of corneal thickness or anterior chamber depth. It splits the image into upper and lower halves, and the lower half is moved until the anterior limit of the distance being measured is aligned with the posterior limit on the upper half, the micrometer giving a direct reading of the distance.

tonometer m. A device for checking the accuracy of a Schiötz tonometer over the full scale range by controlling the plunger so that the scale reading associated with any degree of projection can be determined.

vertex m. A device for measuring the distance between the eye and the posterior surface of the lens.

micron (mi′kron). A unit of length equal to one thousandth of a millimeter. Symbol: μ

micronystagmus (mi″kro-nis-tag′mus). Minute oscillatory movements of the eye normally present on fixation.

micropapilla (mi′kro-pah-pil′ah). A congenital condition in which the optic disk is abnormally small, as may occur in such developmental disorders as cyclopia, anophthalmia, or microphthalmia.

microphakia (mi″kro-fa′ke-ah). A condition in which the crystalline lens is abnormally small and spherical. It is congenital and bilateral and may be complicated by glaucoma. Syn., *microlentia; spherophakia.*

microphotometer (mi″kro-fo-tom′eh-ter). Microdensitometer.

microphthalmia (mi″krof-thal′me-ah). Microphthalmus.

microphthalmos (mi″krof-thal′mus). Microphthalmus.

microphthalmoscope (mi″krof-thal′mo-skōp). An ophthalmoscope with high magnification.

microphthalmus (mi″krof-thal′mus). A rare developmental anomaly in which the eyeballs are abnormally small. When no other defects are associated, the condition is known as *nanophthalmos.*

anterior m. Microcornea.

micropia (mi-kro′pe-ah). Micropsia.

micropsia (mi-krop′se-ah). An anomaly of visual perception in which objects appear smaller than they actually are.

accommodative m. Micropsia resulting from an anomalous accommodative response, particularly from increased effort to accommodate, as in overcoming the effect of a partial cycloplegic.

paresis m. Micropsia resulting from the increased effort to converge, induced by paresis of the internal rectus muscles.

retinal m. Micropsia resulting from a disturbance of the retina in which the visual receptor cells are spread apart. It may be due to a detachment, a tumor, exudative or inflammatory process, or cicatricial changes.

microptic (mi-krop′tik). Affected by or pertaining to micropsia.

microscope (mi′kro-skōp). A magnifying optical instrument for viewing minute objects.

binocular m. 1. A microscope with a binocular body consisting of two eyepieces and a beam-splitting prism, making the objective image identically visible to both eyes. 2. A stereomicroscope, consisting of two complete microscope systems mounted in a single unit.

compound m. A microscope containing two or more lenses or lens systems, one, serving as the objective, to form an enlarged, inverted, real image of the object; the other, as the eyepiece, to form an enlarged, virtual image.

corneal m. A magnifying instrument, usually a stereomicroscope, for examining the anterior structures of the eye.

electron m. A microscope utilizing a beam of electrons instead of a beam of light. The beam is focused by means of an electric or a magnetic field onto a photographic plate or fluorescent screen. The magnification is 50 to 100 times that obtained with an optical microscope.

fluorescence m. A microscope used with a special light source and filters to observe fluorescent objects which may be naturally fluorescent or stained with a fluorescent dye.

Greenough m. A low power stereomicroscope with erecting prisms, used in dissecting, and with the slit lamp.

interference m. A microscope that reveals optical path detail within a transparent specimen, or on the surface of a reflective opaque specimen, by combining coherent light beams from the specimen and its surround.

phase-contrast m. A compound microscope having an annular diaphragm at the front focal plane of the substage condenser and an annular phase plate, corresponding in area to the image of the annular diaphragm, at the back focal plane of the objective. Variations of phase on the wavefront leaving the object are converted into variations of light intensity in the plane of the image. Syn., *phase-difference microscope.*

phase-difference m. Phase-contrast microscope.

polarizing m. A microscope equipped with a polarizer and an analyzer, used to enhance the view of objects by polarized light.

proton m. A microscope utilizing protons instead of electrons, otherwise similar to the electron microscope, and having a magnification of 600,000 diameters.

simple m. A converging lens placed between the object and the eye to provide a larger retinal image of the object. Syn., *magnifier.*

slit lamp m. See under *lamp.*

stereoscopic m. A stereomicroscope.

ultraviolet m. A microscope employing quartz lenses and prisms, used with ultraviolet light.

microscopy (mi-kros′ko-pe). Viewing or examination with the microscope; the use of the microscope.

bright field m. Microscopy in which the light from the transilluminating source is directed to go through the microscope unimpeded, except as prevented by the specimen.

dark field m. Microscopy in which the light striking or transilluminating the specimen does not enter the microscope objective except when scattered or reflected by the specimen itself.

phase-contrast m. Microscopy with the phase-contrast microscope.

microseme (mi′kro-sēm). Having an orbital index less than 84; characteristic of the black races. See also *megaseme; mesoseme.*

microspherometer (mi″kro-sfe-rom′-eh-ter). An instrument for measuring the curvature of a contact lens, having an optical system employing the Drysdale method.

microstimulation, retinal (mi″kro-stim″u-la′shun). 1. Photic stimulation of very small retinal areas by means of an optical reduction system providing the observer with direct control of such variable factors as position, size, distance, wavelength, and luminance of the test object, the fixation object, and the surround. 2. Stimulation of small portions of the retina by microelectrodes.

microstrabismus (mi″kro-strah-biz′-mus). Strabismus in which the deviation is so minute that it is either not detectable by customarily used tests or is concealed by a small angle eccentric fixation in the deviating eye which is equal in direction and magnitude to the deviation. Syn., *microtropia.*

microtropia (mi″kro-tro′pe-ah). Microstrabismus.

microwave (mi′kro-wāv). A very short electromagnetic wave, usually one less than 10 m., and especially one less than 1 m.

microzonuloscopy (mi″kro-zōn-ūl-os′ko-pe). Examination of the zonule of Zinn and adjacent structures with the slit lamp biomicroscope.

midbrain (mid′brān). The mesencephalon.

migraine (mi′grān, mih-grān′, me′-grān). A headache characteristically confined to one side of the head, usually intense and recurrent, and often associated with nausea, vomiting, and visual disturbances, such as scintillating scotomata.

ophthalmic (ocular) m. Migraine preceded or accompanied by characteristic visual sensory disturbances, especially peripheral scintillations and hemianopsia.

ophthalmoplegic m. Migraine accompanied by paralysis of the extraocular and possibly the intraocular muscles, characteristically temporary, though the ophthalmoplegia may become permanent with repeated recurrence.

mikro-. For words beginning thus, see *micro-*.

Mikulicz' (mik′u-lich) **disease; syndrome.** See under the nouns.

Miles A-B-C test (mīlz). See under *test*.

Millard-Gubler syndrome (me-har′-goob′ler). See under *syndrome*.

Miller's rule (mil′erz). See under *rule*.

Milles's syndrome. See under *syndrome*.

millilambert (mil″ih-lam′bert). A unit of luminance equal to ⅟₁₀₀₀ lambert, where 1 lambert is equal to 1/π candela per sq. cm. See also *footlambert*.

millimicron (mil″ih-mi′kron). A unit of length equal to one millionth of a millimeter. Symbol: mμ.

milliphot (mil′ih-fōt). A unit of illuminance equal to ⅟₁₀₀₀ lumen per sq. cm.

Mills's tests (milz′ez). See under *test*.

milphae (mil′fe). Milphosis.

milphosis (mil-fo′sis). 1. Loss of the eyelashes or eyebrows. Syn., *madarosis.* 2. Permanent reddening of the eyelids.

minification (min″ih-fih-ka′shun). A decrease in the apparent size, perceived size, or actual size of an object, or of its image in relation to the object.

minima (min′ih-mah). The darkest bands, or areas of minimum intensity, appearing in interference of two or more wave trains. The minima usually occur between the principal maxima and are due to a nullification of intensity by wavelets whose algebraic sum approximates zero.

minimum. The least or lowest intensity or level; the threshold.

cognoscible, m. The threshold for the identification of form.

distinguishable change of contour, m. The threshold of vernier visual acuity.

legible, m. The threshold for the identification of letters.

light m. The threshold for light perception. It varies with the state of dark adaptation, the location of the retinal area stimulated, the size of the stimulus, the spectral nature of the stimulus, etc., and is a measure of the light sense.

separable, m. The threshold of ability to resolve or perceive separately two small, nearly adjacent objects observed simultaneously; a measure of the sense of discrimination.

visible, m. The smallest perceivable areal extension of light. See *minimum visible angle.*

Minsky's circles (min′skēz). See under *circle.*

Mintacol (min′tah-kol). An anticholinesterase used in the eye, in concentrations of 1:5,000 to 1:10,000, as a miotic.

minus. The opposite of *plus* or *positive* in the designation of data, systems, or observations, the values of which may be represented on a continuous numerical scale from minus, through zero, to plus values, whence it may represent *divergence* as applied to lenses, *convergence* as applied to wavefronts. Syn., *negative.*

minuthesis, visual (min-u-the'sis). A reduction in any specific visual sensibility while under the influence of the original stimulus, often spoken of as visual fatigue; the opposite of *visual auxesis.*

miosis (mi-o'sis). 1. Reduction in pupil size. 2. The condition of having a very small pupil, i.e., approximately 2 mm. or less in diameter.

accommodative m. Miosis associated with accommodation.

irritative m. Spastic miosis.

paralytic m. Miosis resulting from paralysis of the dilator pupillae muscle, due to a paretic lesion of the sympathetic nervous system. See also *Horner's syndrome.*

spastic m. Miosis due to excessive contraction of the sphincter pupillae muscle. It may occur on sudden lowering of intraocular pressure, from irritative cerebral lesions, hysteria, pain, or action of drugs.

spinal m. Paralytic miosis resulting from lesions of the cervical sympathetic chain.

miotic (mi-ot'ik). 1. Pertaining to, affected with, characterized by, or producing miosis. 2. A drug which produces miosis.

mirage (mih-razh'). 1. An optical phenomenon produced by atmospheric strata of varying density through which the observer sees inverted or remarkably displaced images of distant objects. 2. Something illusory, like a mirage.

mire (mēr). One of the luminous objects on the ophthalmometer. Images of these objects formed by reflection at the cornea are used for determining curvature of the cornea in any meridian.

mirror (mir'or). 1. A specular, smooth, or polished surface, or a substance having such a surface, forming optical images by reflection. 2. To reflect, as in a mirror.

back surface m. A mirror which reflects from the back surface of a refracting layer, usually of glass. Ordinary household mirrors are common examples.

concave m. A mirror with a spherical concave surface forming erect, magnified, virtual images when the object distance is less than the focal distance and inverted real images when the object distance is greater than the focal distance.

convex m. A mirror with a spherical convex surface forming erect, virtual, and minified images.

Fresnel's m's. Two plane mirrors inclined at an angle of almost 180° so as to produce interference fringes from two reflected beams from a single slit light source.

front surface m. A mirror which reflects directly from its front surface, so that the reflected light does not penetrate the supporting medium. Examples are polished metal surfaces and glass with a reflecting coating on the front surface.

Lloyd's m. A front surface plane mirror used in conjunction with a slit light source in Lloyd's method for producing interference fringes.

Mangin m. A reflector consisting of a negative meniscus lens silvered on its convex surface and so designed that the reflected rays are corrected for spherical aberration by their incident and emergent refraction through the lens.

plane m. A mirror whose reflecting surface is plane.

spherical m. A mirror whose reflecting surface has a spherical curvature.

thick m. A reflecting optical system considered in terms of its equivalence to a simple mirror but consisting of a series of a mirror and one or more refracting surfaces as a unit, as obtains, e.g., in a back surface mirror or in a lens in which the front surface refracts and the back surface reflects.

thin m. 1. A front surface mirror. 2. A back surface mirror whose supporting refracting medium is so thin as to be considered negligible.

Wadsworth m. A plane mirror used in combination with a 60° prism to produce constant deviation of all wavelengths of incident light, used in spectroscopes and spectrometers.

Mirrorscope. A trade name for a magnifying telescopic spectacle lens containing a mirror system for gathering additional light, designed and manufactured by Feinbloom.

von Mises' marginal nerve plexus. See under *plexus*.

Mitchell's stability test. See under *test*.

Mittendorf's dot (mit'en-dorfs). See under *dot*.

mixer, color. Any device for combining two or more different color stimuli on the same area of the retina. The most common form is a rotating disk with colored sectors.

mixture, color. Two or more color stimuli combined by additive or subtractive methods to produce a single resultant color, as in superimposed colored lights, mixed pigments, colored surfaces presented in rapid succession, etc.

additive color m. Color mixture by the additive combination of lights of different color.

binocular color m. Color mixture by the perceptual fusion of a color stimulus seen by one eye with a different color stimulus seen by the other.

subtractive color m. Color mixture by the subtraction of wavelengths, usually by selective absorption, from the wavelength composition of the original source, as by placing a selectively absorbing filter before a color stimulus or by pigment mixing.

Mizukawa-Kamada test (me″zu-kah'wah-kah-mah'dah). See under *test*.

Mizuo's phenomenon (mih-zu'ōz). See under *phenomenon*.

mm. Abbreviation for *millimeter*.

Mnemoscope (ne'mo-skōp). An instrument designed by Bangerter which utilizes memory cues for the treatment of amblyopia ex anopsia. It projects individual targets of various sizes and complexities onto a stage where they are viewed by the amblyopic eye and copied, traced, or identified. The targets are presented in series, commencing with one large enough to be readily identified. Succeeding targets in the series are identical but successively smaller, the clue to identity being the memory of the previous larger target.

mnemotaxis. The movement or orientation of an animal, mediated in part by the memory of past experiences, as may be exemplified by navigational birds, and considered the most complex of five categories of motorial response to light. See also *klinotaxis; menotaxis; telotaxis; tropotaxis*.

modality. The property of a sensation which differentiates it from sensations of other sense organs; thus all visual sensations form a single modality.

mode. 1. The item or class, in a series of statistical data, which occurs most often, used as one of the statistical measures of central tendency. 2. A perceptual attribute or generalized characteristic of a specific sensation.

appearance, m. of. An incidental or secondary perceptual attribute or characteristic of a specific sensation, more or less independent of the primary quality of the sensation, tending to convey its form, structure, or identity in terms of another type of sensation, e.g., the attribute of luster, transparency, or bulkiness in color.

Modern Arc. The trade name for an instrument for the inspection of ophthalmic lenses consisting essentially of an intense light source which is passed through a small aperture, transilluminating a lens held before it, and casting a shadow of the lens onto a screen so as to reveal defects in its structure.

modification, intraocular. Any modification of a visual stimulus caused by the structural characteristics of an eye, e.g., selective absorption, refractive aberrations, or scattering of light.

modulator (mod″u-la′tor). Granit's term for a retinal element which is sensitive to a narrow spectral band and considered by him to provide the basis for color determination. See also *dominator-modulator theory.*

module (mod′ūl). In illumination, one of a series of identical or nearly identical lighting units designed to be used in varied multiples for lighting extensive areas.

Moebius' (me′be-us) **disease; sign; syndrome.** See under the nouns.

mold. 1. A negative form or replica of the anterior segment of the eye made by the introduction of a modeling material, usually a hydrocolloid, onto the eye. It is used for the preparation of positive models of the anterior segment of the eye, which, in turn, are used in the forming of contact lenses. Syn., *impression.* 2. A form for shaping a thermoplastic lens.

Moldent. The trade name for a solid material used on buffing wheels for rough polishing or small reductions in diameter of contact lenses.

Moldite. A trade name for an alginate hydrocolloid used in taking eye impressions for the fitting of impression contact lenses.

Moll's gland (molz). See under *gland.*

Moller test mark projector. See under *projector.*

molluscum contagiosum (mol-lus′-kum kon-ta-je-o′sum). A mildly contagious disease of the skin, thought to be due to virus infection, chiefly affecting the eyelids, characterized by one or more pearly nodules which vary in size from a pinhead to a small pea and usually have a central depression. The lesions contain ovoid, sharply defined bodies (molluscum bodies) which are considered to be forms of epithelial degeneration.

Molyneux experiment (mol′ih-nōoks). See under *experiment.*

moment. A constant for a statistical distribution. The first four moments about the mean may be used to calculate measures of central tendency, dispersion, skewness, and kurtosis. If x is the deviation of each score from the mean, and N is the number of cases, then the first four moments are respectively:

$$\frac{\Sigma x}{N}, \frac{\Sigma x^2}{N}, \frac{\Sigma x^3}{N}, \frac{\Sigma x^4}{N}$$

Monakow's (mon-ah′kovz) **fibers; syndrome.** See under the nouns.

monilethrix (mo-nil′eh-thriks). A sometimes hereditary and usually congenital condition in which hairs of the scalp, eyelashes, and eyebrows show alternate swellings and constrictions, giving them a beaded appearance. They are fragile, frequently break at the constrictions, and may be accompanied by abnormalities of the nails and teeth, cataract, and mental retardation.

monoblepsia (mon″o-blep′se-ah). A condition in which the visual acuity of one of the eyes is better than the binocular visual acuity. Syn., *monoblepsis.*

monoblepsis (mon″o-blep′sis). Monoblepsia.

monocentric (mon″o-sen′trik). 1. Pertaining to a bundle of light rays which meet or come to a focus at one point. 2. Pertaining to a lens with only one optical center or to a bifocal lens in which the optical centers of the two portions are coincident.

monochroic (mon″o-kro′ik). Monochromatic.

monochromasia (mon″o-kro-ma′se-ah). Monochromatism.

monochromasy (mon″o-kro′mah-se). Monochromatism.

monochromat (mon″o-kro′mat). One having the condition of monochromatism. Syn., *monochromate.*

cone m. A monochromat demonstrating a luminosity curve similar to the normal photopic luminosity curve, with normal visual acuity and dark adaptation and with no photophobia or nystagmus. Syn., *photopic monochromat.*

photopic m. Cone monochromat.

rod m. A monochromat demonstrating a luminosity curve similar to the normal scotopic luminosity curve under all intensities of light. He is usually affected with poor vision and photophobia and sometimes with nystagmus. Syn., *scotopic monochromat.*

scotopic m. Rod monochromat.

monochromate (mon″o-kro′māt). Monochromat.

monochromatic (mon″o-kro-mat′ik). 1. Pertaining to or having a hue produced by a very narrow band of the spectrum, or a single hue of the spectrum which may be produced by a wide band. Syn., *monochroic; monochromic.* 2. Pertaining to or affected with monochromatism.

monochromatism (mon″o-kro′mah-tizm). The condition of being unable to differentiate between the hues of the visible spectrum and in which all parts of the visible spectrum supposedly produce varying shades of gray. Syn., *achromatopsia; total color blindness; monochromasy; monochromatopia.*

cone m. A very rare atypical form of monochromatism in which the luminosity curve is similar to the normal photopic luminosity curve, and in which visual acuity and dark adaptation are normal with no photophobia or nystagmus. Syn., *cone achromatopsia.*

rod m. The typical form of monochromatism in which the luminosity curve is similar to the normal scotopic curve under all intensities of light, and with which reduced visual acuity, photophobia, and frequently nystagmus are associated. Syn., *rod achromatopsia.*

monochromatopia (mon″o-kro-mah-to′pe-ah). Monochromatism.

monochromator (mon″o-kro′mah-tor). A spectroscope provided with an exit slit for obtaining nearly monochromatic light.

monochromic (mon″o-kro′mik). Monochromatic.

monocle (mon′o-kl). A single ophthalmic lens which is worn by bracing it between the cheek and superciliary ridge.

monocular (mo-nok′u-lar). 1. Pertaining to or affecting one eye. 2. Pertaining to any optical instrument which is used with only one eye.

Barrett subnormal vision m. A Galilean-type telescope for use at near, having a +20.00 D. objective lens at one end of a tube and an eyepiece at the other end whose power is determined by trial and error. Accessory rectangular and round masks may be used to limit the aperture and assist in improving vision.

Sturman m. A simple telescopic magnifier for near vision designed to clip on to a spectacle frame.

monoculus (mo-nok′u-lus). 1. A monster with only one eye. 2. A bandage covering only one eye. Syn., *oculus simplex.*

monodiplopia (mon″o-dih-plo′pe-ah). Double vision with only one eye; monocular diplopia.

monophthalmia (mon″of-thal′me-ah). A rare developmental anomaly in which one eye is absent. The eye which is present is usually abnormal and microphthalmic. Syn., *unilateral anophthalmia.*

monophthalmos (mon″of-thal′mos). Monophthalmia.

monophthalmus (mon″of-thal′mus). Monophthalmia.

monops (mon′ops). Cyclops.

monopsia (mo-nop′se-ah). Cyclopia.

monoscopter (mon″o-skop′ter). Horopter.

Montes-Lasala syndrome. Maculolabyrinthine syndrome.

Moon-Bardet-Biedl syndrome. Laurence-Moon-Biedl syndrome.

Moore's lightning streaks. See under *streak.*

Mooren's ulcer (mōr′enz). Rodent corneal ulcer.

mope-eyed. Colloquial for *myopic.*

Morax-Axenfeld conjunctivitis (mōr′aks-ak′sen-felt). See under *conjunctivitis.*

Morgagni's (mōr-gahn′yēz) **humor; liquor.** See under the nouns.

Morgagnian (mōr-gahn′ye-an) **cataract; fluid; globules; spherules.** See under the nouns.

Morgan's theory (mōr′ganz). See under *theory.*

moronity. The highest of the three grades of mental deficiency which include those who may need care, supervision, or control for either their own or others' protection. On the basis of intelligence tests, this group includes those with I.Q. scores of between 50 and 70 or 75. Cf. *idiocy; imbecility.*

Morton's pupillometer (mōr′tonz). See under *pupillometer.*

mosaic, retinal (mo-za′ik). The pattern formed by the distribution of the retinal rods and cones and their interspaces.

Moskowskij's sign (mos-kof′skēz). See under *sign.*

motility, ocular. Capability or manifestation of spontaneous or induced movement of the eye or of its parts.

motion, apparent. See *movement, apparent.*

motor oculi (mo′tor ok′u-li). The third cranial or oculomotor nerve.

mouches volantes (moosh vo-lahnt′). Muscae volitantes.

mounting. 1. Any device which holds spectacle lenses before the eyes, particularly a rimless mounting. 2. The attaching of a pair of ophthalmic lenses to a rimless mounting.

finger-piece m. A mounting without temples and held by small spring clips to the bridge of the nose. The spring clips are applied or released by small levers grasped between the thumb and finger.

Ful-Vue m. A mounting on which the endpieces are several millimeters higher than the datum line, so as not to obstruct the lateral view of the eyes.

Numont m. A rimless mounting supported by metal arms following the contour of the upper posterior edges of the lenses to the temples and attached nasally to the bridge to which the lenses are attached at their nasal edges only.

rimless m. A device for holding spectacle lenses before the eyes, usually consisting of a pair of temples with endpieces and a bridge which are fastened to the lenses by cement, screws, or clamps but without supporting eyewires.

rimway m. A Numont-like mounting containing additional straps to secure the lenses to the metal arms at the temporal edges.

Wils-Edge m. A rimless mounting, similar to the Numont, in which the lenses are gripped across their entire tops by the arms of the mounting, the lenses being grooved and cemented into slots in the arms.

movement. Change or apparent change in position; the act of moving.

absolute m. The observed movement of an object when it is the sole object visible in a surrounding homogeneous field, i.e., its movement is not relative to any other object.

afterimage of m. The apparent movement of a fixated object in a direction opposite to that of the actual movement of an object just previously fixated. Ex.: *waterfall illusion.*

against m. 1. In retinoscopy, the movement of the light reflex in a direction opposite to the movement of the retinoscopic beam of light. 2. In parallactic movement, the apparent direction of movement of the nearer stationary object when the observer moves.

alpha m. The apparent movement produced by serial presentation of the parts of an optical illusion, the parts being physically the same dimension but perceptually unequal. There is growth or contraction according to which part is presented first. The alter-

nate presentation of the two "halves" of the Mueller-Lyer figures form a good example. Syn., S *movement.*

anorthoscopic m. 1. Illusory movements produced by an anorthoscope. 2. The movement corresponding to the illusory distortion of straight lines and other designs viewed in relation to or superimposed on conflicting, interrupting, delimiting, or contrasting patterns, e.g., the perceived displacement of the parallel lines in the Zöllner illusion.

apparent m. The perception of movement of a physically stationary object, hence illusory in nature. Syn., *illusory movement.*

associated m's. 1. Muscular movements which, though not necessarily dependent on each other, are somewhat instinctively performed simultaneously, e.g., the swinging of the arms when walking. 2. Ocular movements resulting from a combination of actions of more than one extrinsic muscle.

autokinetic m. The apparent movement of a stationary object of fixation, as occurs in steadily fixating a single, stationary spot of light in a dark surround, considered to be due to spontaneous and involuntary eye movements.

ballistic (ballistiform) m. A type of movement having the acceleration characteristics of a projectile, used to describe certain fixational and pursuit movements (rotations) of the eye.

beta m. The apparent movement perceived when two or more slightly separated objects are seen in rapid sequence. Thus, when two slightly separated lights are alternately flashed, they appear as a single light jumping back and forth.

binocular m's. Movements of the two eyes, either conjugate or disjunctive, regarded as single or unitary responses.

bow m. An apparent movement in which the displacement does not occur in a single plane or straight line but "bows" out into space, e.g., the end portions of the Mueller-Lyer figure appear to hinge fore and aft when the two halves are viewed alternately.

cardinal m. Movement of an eye from the primary position to a secondary position by rotation about the z axis or the x axis, i.e., either to the right, left, up, or down.

compensatory m. Any movement which functions to compensate for a change in stimulus or posture, e.g., the involuntary, rolling movement of the eyes in the opposite direction of a head movement; the involuntary, fixational movement of an eye when a prism is placed in its line of sight; the involuntary, oscillatory, corrective, fixational movement of an eye when the previous fixation is inexact; the turning or tilting movement of the head to compensate for an imbalance of the extraocular muscles.

conjugate m. Movement of the two eyes in the same direction. Syn., *version movement.*

convergent m. A disjugate movement in which the eyes turn toward each other, as in changing binocular fixation from a distant to a near object.

cyclofusional m. A torsional movement of one or both eyes in response to disparate cyclofusional stimuli.

    cyclofusional m., negative. A cyclofusional movement in which the top of the vertical meridian of one or both eyes rotates outward.

    cyclofusional m., positive. A cyclofusional movement in which the top of the vertical meridian of one or both eyes rotates inward.

cyclovergence m. Disjunctive torsional movement.

cycloversion m. Conjugate torsional movement.

delta m. That one of the several types or phases of apparent movement, induced in stationary lights presented alternately or serially, which appears in a direction opposite the stimulus sequence when the later stimulus is brighter.

depression m. Movement of one or both eyes downward from the primary position.

disjugate m. Disjunctive movement.

disjunctive m. Movement of the two eyes in opposite directions, as in convergence or divergence. Syn., *disjugate movement; vergence movement.*

divergent m. A disjunctive movement in which the eyes turn away from each other, as in changing binocular fixation from a near to a distant object.

eidotropic m. An apparent displacement of a portion of a pattern to an expected position on momentary exposure, such as may be observed in viewing a number of points arranged in a circle with one slightly out of place.

elevation m. Movement of one or both eyes upward from the primary position.

fixation m. The movement of an eye which functions to position the retina to receive the image of an object of regard on the fovea.

following m. Pursuit movement.

fusional m. A binocular movement, made in response to disparate retinal stimuli, for obtaining or maintaining single binocular vision.

    fusional m., peripheral. 1. A fusional movement made in the interest of obtaining or maintaining single vision of objects in the peripheral portion of the visual field. 2. A fusional movement made in response to disparate stimuli in the peripheral retinae.

gamma m. The apparent contraction or expansion, or alternately both, of an object when its luminance is suddenly lowered or raised, e.g., the apparent swelling and subsequent shrinking of a light source when it is turned on.

illusory m. Apparent movement.

interfixation m. The movement of the eye or eyes in changing fixation from one point to another.

lateral m. Movement of an eye in a horizontal direction by rotation about its z axis.

monocular m. 1. The movement of one eye without regard to the movement of the other, as when one eye is occluded. 2. Ocular movement manifested in only one eye.

nystagmoid m's. Involuntary, oscillatory movements of the eye or eyes, such as occurs in nystagmus.

oblique m. Movement of an eye in a direction diagonal to a cardinal movement.

optokinetic m. 1. The nystagmoid movement occurring in optokinetic nystagmus. 2. An autokinetic movement.

parallactic m. The apparent movement of a distant stationary object in relation to a near stationary object, or vice versa, when the observer is moving.

parallel m. Movement (rotation) of the two eyes equally in the same direction.

phi m. The apparent movement created by two or more stationary stimuli, separated in space by a relatively small distance, and presented to the eye alternately or successively in a specific temporal sequence. It is described as a perceptual "filling in" of the spaces between the stimuli and has been referred to as "pure" movement, in that it may be sensed even while the objects themselves are perceived to be stationary. Syn., *phi phenomenon.*

pursuit m. Movement of an eye fixating a moving object. Syn., *following movement.*

random m's. Wandering, ocular movements uninterrupted by fixations and apparently involuntary, as occur in the blind and the newborn.

real m. A perceived movement which correlates perceptually with the actual physical movement of the object of regard.

redress, m. of. Movement of an eye to recover fixation and fusion after the removal of the occluder in a cover test.

reflex m. 1. Movement of an eye induced by reflex innervation. 2. Movement of the retinoscopic reflex.

relative m. Perceived movement of an object relative to other moving or stationary objects in the field of vision.

reversal m. In retinoscopy, the change from against to with movement, or vice versa.

rolling m. Torsional movement.

rotatory m. Any movement of the eye about an axis through its center of rotation.

S movement. Alpha movement.

saccadic m. A quick, abrupt movement of the eye, as obtained in changing fixation from one point to another.

scanning m. One of a series of movements of the eye, characteristically saccadic, obtained in an attempt to scan or view an extensive object in systematic detail. Cf. *tracing movement.*

scissors m. 1. Simultaneous movement of the retinoscopic reflex in opposite directions in different portions of the pupil, hence resembling scissors blades, present in irregular astigmatism and keratoconus. 2. The apparent movement of a crossed line target when viewed through a rotating cylindrical lens.

screw m. A combined translatory and rotatory movement of the eye.

searching m. Involuntary, aimless excursions of an eye, as sometimes occur in the blind or the newborn.

split m. A form of apparent movement when a vertical line followed by a line perpendicular to it at its base is seen to divide and rotate both to the right and to the left to form the long horizontal line.

stroboscopic m. An apparent movement created by the presentation of a series of related motionless stimuli, each representing successive phases of a movement, as typically occurs in motion pictures. This movement may also be created by viewing an intermittently illuminated rotating object, wherein the movement may be made to appear to slow down, stop, or reverse by changing its speed of rotation or the frequency of the illumination.

synergic m. The harmonious action of two or more extraocular muscles to produce a movement of an eye or correlated movements of the two eyes.

torsional m. A rotational movement of an eye about an anteroposterior axis, such as the line of sight or the y axis. Syn., *rolling movement; wheel movement; torsional rotation; wheel rotation.*

   torsional m., conjugate. Simultaneous torsional movement of both eyes in the same direction. Syn., *cycloversion movement.*

   torsional m., disjunctive. Simultaneous torsional movement of the two eyes in opposite directions. Syn., *cyclovergence movement.*

tracing m. The movement of an eye occurring when attempts are made to fixate along the path of a continuous pattern, such as a line, characterized by a rapid series of fixational jumps.

translatory m. The movement of an eye in which all points of the eye move in the same direction, such as forward, backward, to the side, etc., in contrast to or as distinct from *rotatory movement.*

vergence m. Disjunctive movement.

version m. Conjugate movement.

vertical m. Movement of an eye up or down by rotation about a transverse axis, such as the x axis.

wheel m. Torsional movement.

with m. 1. In retinoscopy, the movement of the light reflex in the same direction as the movement of the retinoscopic beam of light. 2. In parallactic movement, the apparent direction of movement of the more distant stationary object when the observer moves.

M.R.P. Abbreviation for *major reference point.*

mu (μ). The Greek letter used as the symbol for (1) *micron;* (2) *angle of azimuth* in the field of regard (*Fry*).

mucin (mu'sin). Glycoprotein, produced by goblet cells of the conjunctiva, the mucous membranes, the synovial membranes, and the salivary glands, which forms the basis of mucus.

mucocele (mu'ko-sēl). A pathological swelling of a cavity due to an accumulation of mucoid material, such as occurs in dacryocystitis or sinusitis.

mucoids (mu'koids). A group of glycoproteins found in cartilage, the sclera, the vitreous humor, the cornea, and the crystalline lens, similar to mucin, but differing in solubility and precipitation properties.

mucoprotein (mu''ko-pro'te-in). A mucoid.

Mueller's (mūl'erz) **cells; center of rotation; fibers; ganglion; ho-**

ropter; law; fiber layer; contact lens; muscles; reticulum; spots; theories; Electronic tonometer. See under the nouns.

Mueller-Lyer (mŭl′er-li′er) **figure; illusion.** See under the nouns.

Mueller-Welt contact lens (mŭl′er-velt). See under *lens, contact*.

Mules's sphere implant (mŭlz′ez). See under *implant*.

multiple sclerosis. See under *sclerosis*.

Munsell's (mun-selz′) **colors; circle; hue; notation; power; renotation; system; top; value.** See under the nouns.

Munson's sign (mun′sunz). See under *sign*.

Münsterberg's monocular asymmetry; partition. See under *asymmetry*.

muscae volitantes (mus′se vol″ih-tan′tēz, mus′ke). Small floating spots, "flitting flies," entoptically observed on viewing a bright uniform field, such as the sky, and seen to flit away with attempted fixation. Their presence is normal and attributed to minute remnants of embryonic structures in the vitreous humor. Syn., *mouches volantes*.

muscle. A contractile organ whose special function is to produce motion; also, the tissues of which such an organ is composed, consisting of individual muscle fibers or muscle cells. Classified by structure as nonstriated or striated; by control as voluntary or involuntary; by location as skeletal, cardiac, or visceral.

abducens m. External rectus muscle.

abducens oculi m. External rectus muscle.

accessory m's. of accommodation. The frontal, pyramidal, corrugator supercilii, and the orbicularis oculi muscles, supplied by the facial nerve, which contract vicariously when an extreme effort is made to see.

adducens m. Internal rectus muscle.

adducens oculi m. Internal rectus muscle.

agonistic m. A muscle yielding the desired movement; a prime mover or protagonist; one opposed by an antagonistic muscle.

antagonistic m. A muscle that has the opposite function of the muscle engaged in the movement of a part. The antagonist of an abductor is an adductor; of an elevator, a depressor; of a flexor, an extensor; etc.

anterior lacrimal m. The fibers of the pars tarsalis portion of the orbicularis oculi muscle, lying anterior to the fascia which covers the lacrimal sac. Syn., *muscle of Gerlach*.

Bowman's m. Ciliary muscle.

Brücke's m. The meridional or longitudinal fibers of the ciliary muscle which attach in the scleral spur and uveal meshwork and extend to the choroid, where they usually end in branched stellate figures (muscle stars). Syn., *tensor choroideae muscle*.

bursalis m. In lizards, a muscle inserting into the posterior sclera near the optic nerve and encircled by the tendon of the nictitating membrane, which is drawn taut by its contraction.

capsulo-palpebralis m. Landström's muscle.

choanoid m. A retractor bulbi muscle found in land vertebrates but absent in the higher mammals. It pulls the eyeball into the orbit.

ciliary m. The intrinsic smooth muscle of the ciliary body. Its fibers course in three directions, meridionally (Brücke's muscle), radially, and circularly (Mueller's muscle). Innervation is from the ciliary nerves, and the blood supply from the anterior and posterior ciliary vessels. Its action, according to current theory, slackens the suspensory ligament of the crystalline lens, decreasing the tension on the capsule of the lens, permitting the lens to become more convex, as occurs in accommodation. Syn., *Bowman's muscle; musculus accommodatorius.*

contractor pupillae m. Sphincter pupillae muscle.

cornealis m. In lampreys, a large muscle arising outside of the orbit and inserting into the transparent dermal cornea, which acts to produce accommodation for distant objects by flattening the anterior eyeball on contraction and displacing the crystalline lens backwards to render the normally myopic eye emmetropic.

corrugator supercilii m. A small, striated muscle which arises at the medial end of the superciliary ridge, passes upward and outward, and inserts into the skin of the eyebrow at its middle. It draws the eyebrows toward the root of the nose, on contraction, as in frowning. Syn., *superciliary muscle.*

Crampton m. of. A muscle found in the eyes of birds and reptiles which arises from the inner peripheral surface of the cornea and inserts into the sclera in the ciliary region. It acts in accommodation by shortening the radius of curvature of the cornea.

dilator pupillae m. An intrinsic, smooth, radial muscle of the iris, located posteriorly in both the pupillary and ciliary portions and extending into the ciliary body. Its myoepithelial fibers constitute the *posterior border lamella of Fuchs* and its spindle cells the *anterior pigment layer of Fuchs.* Innervation by the sympathetic fibers in the long ciliary nerves results in enlargement of the pupil.

external rectus m. A striated, extrinsic muscle of the eyeball that originates from the annulus of Zinn and from the spina recti lateralis and inserts laterally into the sclera about 6.9 mm. from the limbus corneae. It is innervated by the abducens nerve and abducts the eyeball. Syn., *abducens oculi muscle; lateral rectus muscle.*

extraocular m's. The striated muscles, originating at the apex of the orbit or at the anterior medial portion of the orbit and inserting on the sclera, which rotate the eyeball. They are the extrinsic muscles of the eyeball and consist of the superior, inferior, internal, and external recti and the superior and inferior obliques. Syn., *oculorotary muscles.*

extrinsic m's. Muscles that have their origin outside of the structure under consideration but insert into that structure, such as the extraocular muscles.

frontalis m. A striated muscle which arises from the epicranial aponeurosis near the coronal suture and inserts vertically into the skin of the eyebrow. It is innervated by the facial nerve and causes horizontal wrinkling of the forehead as it lifts the eyebrows.

Horner's m. A thin layer of fibers that originates at the posterior lacrimal crest and passes outward and forward, dividing into two slips which surround the canaliculi, and becomes continuous with the pretarsal portion of the orbicularis oculi muscle and the muscle of Riolan. It affects tear drainage through action on the lacrimal sac and canaliculi. Syn., *pars lacrimalis muscle; tensor tarsi muscle.*

inferior oblique m. A striated, extrinsic muscle of the eyeball that originates from the anterior, medial portion of the orbital floor, passes beneath (external to) the inferior rectus and nasal to the external rectus to insert on the posterior, temporal portion of the eyeball, slightly below its horizontal meridian. It is innervated by the oculomotor nerve and elevates, abducts, and extorts the eyeball.

inferior rectus m. A striated, extrinsic muscle of the eyeball that originates from the annulus of Zinn and inserts inferiorly into the sclera about 6.5 mm. from the limbus corneae. It is innervated by the oculomotor nerve and adducts, depresses, and extorts the eyeball.

internal rectus m. A striated, extrinsic muscle of the eyeball that originates from the annulus of Zinn and inserts medially into the sclera about 5.5 mm. from the limbus corneae. It is innervated by the oculomotor nerve and adducts the eyeball. Syn., *adducens oculi muscle; medial rectus muscle*

intraocular m's. The smooth muscles within the eyeball. They are the intrinsic muscles of the eyeball and consist of the *ciliary, dilator pupillae,* and *sphincter pupillae muscles.*

intrinsic m's. Muscles that have both origin and insertion within the structure under consideration, as the intraocular muscles.

Landström's m. Smooth muscle fibers which extend from the orbital septum over the anterior portion of the eyeball and blend with fascial expansions of the extraocular muscles just back of their insertions. When innervated by the sympathetic, they tend to move the eyeball forward. Syn., *capsulo-palpebralis muscle.*

lateral rectus m. External rectus muscle.

levator bulbi m. In amphibians, a skeletal muscle derived from the jaw mesoderm and innervated by the trigeminal nerve, which, on contraction, pulls the eyeball forward after it has been displaced backward by the retractor bulbi muscle.

levator palpebrae superioris m. A striated muscle that arises at the apex of the orbit from the small wing of the sphenoid bone and inserts via an aponeurosis into the skin and tarsus of the upper lid, the lateral orbital tubercle, the medial palpebral ligament, and the superior fornix conjunctivae. It courses forward under the roof of the orbit, from its origin, on the superior rectus muscle to which it is adherent by fascial sheaths. It is innervated by the oculomotor nerve and elevates the upper eyelid.

medial rectus m. Internal rectus muscle.

Merkel's m. The portion of the pars septalis muscle that arises superficially from the anterior portion of the medial palpebral ligament and extends laterally and inferiorly to insert fanlike into the skin of the medial half of the lower eyelid.

Mueller's annular m. The circular fibers of the ciliary muscle located in the anterior inner portion of the ciliary body and which run parallel to the limbus. Absent in the newborn, it develops after birth.

Mueller's orbital m. The smooth muscle fibers which arise in the periorbita and extend fanlike over the floor of the orbit, bridging the inferior orbital fissure, to the cavernous sinus. It is innervated by the sympathetic via a branch from the sphenopalatine ganglion. Its function in man is doubtful, although it acts as a protruder of the eye in some lower animals. Syn., *musculus orbitalis.*

Mueller's palpebral m., inferior. A small sheath of smooth muscle fibers which originates from the fascial sheath of the inferior rectus muscle and from its expansion to the inferior oblique muscle. It extends upward and divides into two layers, one of which attaches in the bulbar conjunctiva and the other inserts into the lower margin of the tarsal plate of the lower eyelid. It is innervated by the sympathetic, assists in retracting the lower eyelid, and may tend to protrude the eyeball.

Mueller's palpebral m., superior. A small sheath of smooth muscle fibers which originates from the levator palpebrae superioris muscle and extends downward and forward to insert into the upper margin of the tarsal plate of the upper eyelid. It is innervated by the sympathetic, assists in raising the upper eyelid, and may tend to protrude the eyeball.

occipito-frontalis m. A striated muscle located on the upper part of the cranium and consisting of two occipital and two frontal muscles united by an aponeurosis. The occipital portions originate from the occipital bone and insert into the aponeurosis. The frontal portions originate from the aponeurosis and insert into the skin of the eyebrows. It is innervated by the facial nerve. The frontal portions act to draw the scalp forward and raise the eyebrows, and the occipital portions act to draw the scalp backward.

oculorotary m's. The extraocular muscles.

orbicularis oculi m. An oval sheet of striated muscle in the eyelid running concentrically around the palpebral fissure and spreading out into regions of the forehead and face around the orbital margin. It consists of two portions, the *pars orbitalis muscle* and the *pars palpebralis muscle,* is innervated by the facial nerve, and functions as the sphincter of the eyelid. Syn., *orbicularis palpebrarum muscle; musculus dormi-*

tator; *sphincter oculi; sphincter palpebrarum.*

orbicularis palpebrarum m. Orbicularis oculi muscle.

palpebral m's. 1. Mueller's inferior and superior palpebral muscles. 2. In aquatic mammals, striated muscular slips of the rectus muscles which insert into the eyelids.

pars ciliaris m. Muscle of Riolan.

pars lacrimalis m. Horner's muscle.

pars marginalis m. Muscle of Riolan.

pars orbitalis m. The peripheral portion of the orbicularis oculi muscle found in the eyebrow, the temple, and the cheek. The origin is from the inner orbital margin and the medial palpebral ligament. Its action is in forced or tight closure of the eyelids.

pars palpebralis m. That portion of the orbicularis oculi muscle present in the eyelids. It arises from the medial palpebral ligament and the adjacent bone and inserts in the lateral palpebral raphe, in the region of the external canthus. It consists of two parts, the *pars septalis muscle* and the *pars tarsalis muscle,* and acts in light or effortless closure or blinking of the eyelids.

pars septalis m. That portion of the pars palpebralis muscle which lies anterior to the septum orbitale. Syn., *preseptal muscle.*

pars subtarsalis m. Fibers of the muscle of Riolan which pass posteriorly to lie behind the openings of the ducts of the Meibomian glands.

pars tarsalis m. That portion of the pars palpebralis muscle which lies in the area of the tarsal plate. It consists of three parts, the *anterior lacrimal muscle, Horner's muscle,* and *muscle of Riolan.* Syn., *pretarsal muscle.*

preseptal m. Pars septalis muscle.

pretarsal m. Pars tarsalis muscle.

protractor lentis m. A smooth muscle found in fishes, amphibians, and reptiles which acts to draw forward the crystalline lens in accommodation.

pupillary m's. The sphincter and the dilator pupillae muscles.

retractor bulbi m. A skeletal muscle found in amphibians to mammals, probably derived from the lateral rectus muscle and innervated by the abducens nerve, which, on contraction, pulls the eyeball backward into the orbit.

retractor bursalis m. In lizards, a muscle slip extending upwards from the bursalis muscle and inserting in the sclera, acting to keep the bursalis muscle and the tendon of the nictitating membrane free of the optic nerve upon contraction.

retractor lentis m. In fishes, an ectodermal muscle that arises from the fetal cleft and courses in the falciform process to insert into the lens.

Riolan m. of. The portion of the orbicularis oculi muscle originating from the posterior lacrimal crest and encircling the eyelid margins between the tarsal glands and the eyelash follicles, with some fibers passing posteriorly to lie behind the openings of the ducts of the tarsal glands. It brings the eyelid margins together as the eyes are closed. Syn., *pars ciliaris muscle; pars marginalis muscle.*

sphincter iridis m. Sphincter pupillae muscle.

sphincter pupillae m. An intrinsic, smooth, circular muscle of the iris, approximately 0.8 mm. broad, located in the posterior stroma of the pupillary portion and forming a ring around the margin of the pupil. Innervation by parasympathetic fibers of the oculomotor nerve, which synapse in the ciliary or the episcleral ganglion, results in decreased diameter of the pupil. Syn., *sphincter iridis muscle.*

stars, m. Groups of smooth cell fibers arranged in star-shaped configurations, located in the suprachoroid in the region of the equator of the eyeball, where they are continuous with Brücke's muscle.

superciliary m. Corrugator supercilii muscle.

superior oblique m. A striated, extrinsic muscle of the eyeball that has its anatomical origin superior and medial to the optic foramen on the small wing of the sphenoid bone. It passes anteriorly and gives place to a rounded tendon about 1 cm. behind the trochlea. The tendon passes through the trochlea, then bends downward, backward, and outward at an angle of about 54°, passes beneath the superior rectus muscle, and inserts on the superior posterotemporal portion of the eyeball. It is innervated by the trochlear nerve and depresses, abducts, and intorts the eyeball. Syn., *musculus amatorius; musculus patheticus.*

superior rectus m. A striated, extrinsic muscle of the eyeball that originates from the upper part of the annulus of Zinn and from the sheath of the optic nerve. It passes anteriorly and laterally beneath the levator palpebrae superioris muscle and inserts superiorly into the sclera about 7.7 mm. from the limbus corneae. It is innervated by the oculomotor nerve, elevates, adducts, and intorts the eyeball and also assists in raising the upper eyelid. Syn., *musculus religiosus; musculus superbus.*

synergistic m's. Two or more muscles which act together to move a part, as the superior rectus and inferior oblique muscles in elevating the eyeball.

tensor choroideae m. Brücke's muscle.

tensor tarsi m. Horner's muscle.

tensor trochleae m. An abnormal slip of muscle extending from the levator palpebrae superioris muscle to the trochlea.

transverse m. In reptiles, a muscle derived from connective tissue between the ciliary body and sclera and inserting into the zonule of Zinn, thought to displace the crystalline lens nasally during accommodation.

yoke m's. Muscles of the two eyes which simultaneously contract to turn the eyes equally in the same direction, such as the right external rectus and the left internal rectus muscles in turning the eyes to the right.

musculus (mus'ku-lus). Latin for *muscle.*

accommodatorius, m. Ciliary muscle.

amatorius, m. Superior oblique muscle.

ciliaris, m. Ciliary muscle.

dormitator, m. Orbicularis oculi muscle.

orbitalis, m. Mueller's orbital muscle.

patheticus, m. Superior oblique muscle.

religiosus, m. Superior rectus muscle.

superbus, m. Superior rectus muscle.

tarsalis, m. The inferior or the superior palpebral muscle of Mueller.

mutton-fat deposits. See under *deposits.*

My. Abbreviation for *myopia.*

myasthenia gravis (mi"as-the'ne-ah grav'is). A disease of obscure etiology characterized by abnormal fatigue and exhaustion of striated muscles, sometimes leading to muscular paralysis. It may affect any muscle of the body, especially those of the head and the neck. Ocular symptoms include external ophthalmoplegia, ptosis, and diplopia. Syn., *Erb-*

Goldflam disease; asthenic bulbar paralysis; myasthenic pseudoparalysis.

myasthenia palpebralis (mi"as-the'-ne-ah pal"pe-brah'lis). A deficiency in function of the orbicularis oculi muscles.

mycophthalmia (mi"kof-thal'me-ah). A conjunctivitis due to a fungus.

mydesis (mi-de'sis). Purulent discharge from the eyelids.

Mydriacyl (mih-dri'ah-sil). A trade name for a parasympatholytic drug used as a cycloplegic and mydriatic.

mydriasis (mih-dri'ah-sis, mi-). 1. Increase in pupil size. 2. The condition of having an abnormally large pupil, i.e., approximately 5 mm. or greater in diameter.

alternating m. Mydriasis alternately affecting each of the two eyes, due to a disorder of the central nervous system. Syn., *bounding mydriasis; leaping mydriasis; springing mydriasis.*

amaurotic m. A condition in which the pupil of a blind eye is wider than that of its mate, the seeing eye.

bounding m. Alternating mydriasis.

leaping m. Alternating mydriasis.

paralytic m. Mydriasis due to paralysis of the sphincter pupillae muscle, as may result from lesions in the pupillary center of the midbrain or its efferent pathways, after contusions to the eyeball, or increased intraocular pressure affecting the long ciliary nerves or muscle itself.

psychic m. Mydriasis due to fright or violent emotion.

spasmodic m. Spastic mydriasis.

spastic m. Mydriasis due to irritation of the sympathetic pathway and spasm of the dilator pupillae muscle, accompanied by widening of the palpebral fissure and slight exophthalmos (Bernard's syndrome). The light and convergence pupillary reflexes are present, though limited, and the mydriasis is usually slight. Syn., *spasmodic mydriasis.*

spinal m. Mydriasis due to irritation of the ciliospinal center of the spinal cord.

springing m. Alternating mydriasis.

mydriatic (mid-rih-at′ik). 1. Pertaining to, affected with, characterized by, or producing mydriasis. 2. A drug or other agent which produces mydriasis.

myectomy (mi-ek′to-me). The excision of a portion of the belly of a muscle, sometimes done for the correction of strabismus.

myectopia (mi-ek-to′pe-ah). Abnormal placement of a muscle, either congenital or due to injury.

myectopy (mi-ek′to-pe). Myectopia.

myelinic dysgenesia (mi-el-in′ik dis-jen-e′ze-ah). A condition characterized by retardation or failure in the development of the myelin sheaths of nerve fibers of the central nervous system. Blindness, with little or no muscular co-ordination, is present at birth. Light perception and ocular fixations usually appear with postnatal development of the sheaths, but strabismus persists.

myelitis, neuro-optic (mi″eh-li′tis). Neuromyelitis optica.

Myerson's sign (mi′er-sonz). See under *sign.*

myiasis, ocular (mi′yah-sis). An infection of the conjunctival sac by maggots.

myiocephalon (mi″yo-sef′ah-lon). The protrusion of a minute portion of the iris through a perforation of the cornea; an iridocele.

myiodeopsia (mi″yo-de-op′se-ah). The perception of muscae volitantes.

myiodesopsia (mi″yo-des-op′se-ah). Myiodeopsia.

Myoculator (mi-ok′u-la-tor). An instrument used in visual training, consisting essentially of a motor-driven projector automatically controlled to move the projected fixation image meridionally or circularly under conditions of constant or intermittent illumination and often used in conjunction with a second manually controlled projector (Kratoculator).

myodeopsia (mi″o-de-op′se-ah). Myiodeopsia.

myodesopsia (mi″o-des-op′se-ah). Myiodeopsia.

myodiopter (mi″o-di-op′ter). The contractile force of the ciliary muscle necessary to increase the accommodation from zero to one diopter, said to be the unit of physiological accommodation.

myoid, visual cell (mi′oid). The nonrefractile inner portion of the inner member of a rod or cone cell located between the ellipsoid and the external limiting layer of the retina.

myokymia (mi″o-ki′me-ah, -kim′e-ah). Twitching or vibratory movements of individual muscle bundles, usually occurring in neurasthenics or following fatigue. In the eyelid, it is termed *clonic blepharospasm.*

myope (mi′ōp). One having myopia.

myopia (mi-o′pe-ah). The refractive condition of the eye represented by the location of the conjugate focus of the retina at some finite point in front of the eye, when accommodation is said to be relaxed, or the extent of that condition represented in the number of diopters of concave lens power required to compensate to the optical equivalent of emmetropia. The condition may also be represented as one in which parallel rays of light entering the eye, with accommodation relaxed, focus in front of the retina. Syn., *nearsightedness.*

acquired m. 1. Myopia which appears after infancy. 2. Myopia due to abnormal circumstances, such as a rise in blood sugar or a traumatic injury, wherein one suddenly becomes markedly more myopic than formerly.

acquired m., of maturity. Nonpathological myopia, typically of low or moderate amount, with onset after the attainment of physical maturity.

adventitious m. *Optometric Extension Program:* Myopia caused by near work.

apparent m. Hypertonic myopia.

associated m. A type of hypertonic myopia said to result from exophoria compensated for by accommodative convergence.

astigmatic m. 1. Myopia combined with astigmatism. 2. A type of hypertonic myopia said to result from accommodative efforts to compensate for uncorrected astigmatism.

atypical m. Malignant myopia.

axial m. Myopia attributed to excessive, or increase in, axial length of the eye.

benign m. Simple myopia.

complicated m. Malignant myopia.

curvature m. Myopia attributed to excessive, or increase in, curvature of one or more of the refractive surfaces of the eye, especially of the cornea.

degenerative m. Myopia due to degenerative changes in the eyeball. One of three major groups of myopia, according to the Harding classification, the others being *hypertonic* and *fibrillar myopia.* See also *pathological, progressive,* and *malignant myopia.*

diabetic m. Myopia due to change in refraction associated with variation in blood sugar.

dietetic m. Nutritional myopia.

empty field m. Sky myopia.

false m. Pseudomyopia.

fibrillar m. Myopia attributed to faulty development of the fibroblasts of the sclera and the consequent reaction of the sclera to the intraocular pressure during the period of growth. One of three major groups of myopia,

according to the Harding classification, the others being *hypertonic* and *degenerative myopia.*

functional m. Myopia attributed to a spasm of the ciliary muscle. Syn., *hypertonic myopia.*

gravis, m. High myopia.

healthy m. Simple myopia.

high m. Myopia of high degree, usually of 6.00 D. or more.

hypertonic m. The refractive condition of myopia attributable to spasm of the ciliary muscle or incomplete relaxation of accommodation. One of three major groups of myopia, according to the Harding classification, the others being *degenerative* and *fibrillar myopia.* Syn., *apparent myopia; functional myopia; pseudomyopia.*

hysterical m. Psychogenic myopia occurring in hysteria.

index m. Myopia attributed to variation in the index of refraction of one or more of the ocular media.

infantile pyretic m. Myopia which appears or increases following a childhood disease accompanied by high fever, such as measles or scarlet fever.

innervational m. Myopia attributable to innervational anomalies, as distinct from myopia attributable to structural or index anomalies, hence a hypertonic myopia.

inversa, m. A conus or atrophic choroidal area located on the nasal side of the optic disk; considered to be due to a coexisting high myopia.

lenticular m. Myopia attributed to excessive refractive power of the crystalline lens.

low m. Myopia of a low degree, usually of 3.00 D. or less.

malignant m. Myopia characterized by marked fundus changes, such as posterior staphylomata, and associated with a high refractive error and subnormal visual acuity after correction. See also *degenerative, pathological,* and *progressive myopia.* Syn., *atypical myopia; complicated myopia; pernicious myopia.*

medium m. Myopia of medium degree, usually between 3.00 and 6.00 D. Syn., *moderate myopia.*

moderate m. Medium myopia.

night m. Myopia or an increase in ocular refraction occurring in low levels of illumination, as in twilight or at night. Syn., *twilight myopia.*

nutritional m. Myopia attributed to nutritional deficiencies, as a lack of certain minerals or vitamins. Syn., *dietetic myopia.*

occupational m. Myopia occurring, or regarded as, an occupational disorder or attributed to the excessive visual demands of an occupation. Cf. *adventitious* and *school myopia.*

pathological m. Myopia attributable to pathological causes, or in which visual acuity is subnormal after correction. See also *degenerative, malignant,* and *progressive myopia.*

pernicious m. Malignant myopia.

position m. Myopia attributed to an excessively forward position of the crystalline lens, i.e., near the cornea.

primary m. Simple myopia.

prodromal m. The myopia which sometimes occurs in the early stage of lenticular cataract.

progressive m. Myopia which increases at an abnormally rapid rate or increases after maturity. See also *degenerative, malignant,* and *pathological myopia.*

pseudo m. Myopia due to spasm of the ciliary muscle. See *hypertonic myopia.*

psychogenic m. A hypertonic type of myopia of psychical origin, usually transitory, and ordinarily associated with other psychical phenomena or disorders.

refractive m. 1. Myopia attributed to the normal variation of the refractive elements of the eye, in-

cluding axial length, as distinguished from *degenerative* or *pathological myopia.* 2. Myopia attributed to the condition of the refractive elements of the eye as distinguished from *axial myopia.* Cf. *curvature* and *index myopia.*

school m. Myopia attributed to the use of the eyes for close work during the school years.

secondary m. Myopia due to degenerative or pathological changes in the structure of the eye.

simple m. 1. Myopia due to normal growth of a healthy eyeball or to a chance combination of the optical elements. Characteristically, it ceases to increase after maturity and is associated with normal visual acuity after correction. It is differentiated from *degenerative, progressive, malignant,* or *pathological myopia.* Syn., *benign myopia; healthy myopia; primary myopia; stationary myopia; typical myopia.* 2. Myopia occurring without an associated astigmatism.

sky m. An increase in the refractive state of the eye noted in the absence of optical stimuli to accommodation, as occurs in viewing a clear, cloudless sky. Syn., *empty field myopia; space myopia.*

space m. Sky myopia.

stationary m. Simple myopia.

sulfanilamide m. A transitory myopia which follows administration of sulfanilamide. Typically, the myopia appears a day or two after taking sulfa drugs in patients who, on a previous occasion, have taken the drug with no ensuing visual disturbance. The degree of myopia is approximately 5.00 to 10.00 D., and lasts for a period of a few hours to a few weeks, most frequently about a week.

transitory m. Myopia which appears suddenly, lasts for a period of time, and then disappears. In this group are included myopia due to trauma, high blood sugar level (hyperglycemia), sulfanilamide therapy, etc.

traumatic m. Myopia resulting from a blow to the eye. The myopia develops shortly after the trauma (usually within 48 hours) and lasts from a few days to many years.

true m. Myopia, or that part of the total myopia, not attributable to spasm of the ciliary muscle or unrelaxed accommodation.

twilight m. Night myopia.

typical m. Simple myopia.

very high m. Myopia of extreme degree, over 10.00 D. according to some authors, and over 15.00 D. according to others.

myopic (mi-op′ik). Pertaining to or having myopia.

myopic conus; crescent. See under the nouns.

myopiosis (mi″op-e-o′sis). Myopia.

myoporthosis (mi″o-por-tho′sis). The correction of myopia. *Obs.*

myopsis (mi-op′sis). Myiodeopsia.

Myoscope (mi′o-skōp). An instrument, similar to the Myoculator, used in visual training. It projects a circularly or meridionally moving target onto a screen.

myosis (mi-o′sis). Miosis.

myositis, orbital (mi-o-si′tis). 1. Inflammation of the extraocular muscles, either chronic or acute, which may be primary, but is usually secondary to other orbital inflammations, such as syphilis or tuberculosis. 2. A primary chronic inflammation of the extraocular muscles resulting in exophthalmos and external ophthalmoplegia, similar to that found in exophthalmic goiter. The condition is probably not a true inflammation.

myotic (mi-ot′ik). Miotic.

myotomy (mi-ot′o-me). Surgical division of muscle fibers, particularly in the belly of the muscle.

myotonia congenita (mi″o-to′ne-ah kon-jen′ih-tah). Thomsen's disease.

N

N. Symbol for *radiance.*

n. Symbol for (1) *nasal;* (2) *index of refraction;* (3) *normal.*

Nagel's (nah'gelz) **adaptometer; test; empiristic theory.** See under the nouns.

nahastigmatismus. The additional cylindrical correction needed in the spectacle plane for correcting the astigmatism for a near object as compared to that needed to correct the same astigmatic error for a distant object, due to differential lens effectively in the two principal meridians.

nanometer (nan-om'eh-ter). A unit of length equal to one millionth of a millimeter; millimicron. Symbol: *nm.*

nanophthalmos (nan-of-thal'mos). A rare developmental anomaly in which the eyeballs are abnormally small but are without other deformities. See also *microphthalmos.*

nasociliary (na"zo-sil'e-a-re). 1. Pertaining to or affecting the eyebrows and the bridge of the nose. 2. The nasociliary nerve.

nasolacrimal (na"zo-lak'rih-mal). Pertaining to the nasolacrimal duct.

Nasse's law (neh'sez). See under *law.*

National Society for the Prevention of Blindness. An incorporated, voluntary organization engaged in a program of eliminating preventable loss of sight through research, service, and education.

nativism. The theory, doctrine, or concept that certain aspects of behavior, knowledge, or perception are innate and independent of accumulated experience or learning. Cf. *empiricism.* Syn., *Kant's nativistic theory.*

Natural Environment Trainer. NET Orthoptor.

near point of accommodation; convergence; fusion. See under the nouns.

nearsight. Myopia.

nearsighted. Myopic.

nearsightedness. Myopia.

nebula (neb'u-lah). A faint or slightly misty corneal opacity. Cf. *leukoma; macula.*

Necker cube (nek'er). See under *cube.*

necroscleritis nodosa (nek"ro-skleri'tis no-dōs'ah). Nodular necrotizing scleritis.

necrosis (neh-kro'sis). The death of tissue or tissue cells, especially in a circumscribed portion of the body, as in gangrene, and/or the changes which take place in these cells after they have died.

needling. A surgical operation for aftercataract or soft cataract in which the lens capsule is punctured to allow absorption of the lens substance. Syn., *discission.*

Negocoll (neg'oh-kol). A compound, having agar as a base, and containing cotton fibers for binding and strength, used in making impressions of an eye for the fitting of molded contact lenses.

Negro's sign (na'grōz). See under *sign.*

Nela wools test (ne'lah). See under *test.*

neo-retinene$_1$ (ne″o-ret′ih-nēn). Either of two of the isomers of retinene$_1$ known as *neo-a* and *neo-b*.

neostigmine (ne″o-stig′min). Prostigmine.

Neosynephrine (ne″o-sin-ef′rin). A trade name for *phenylephrine hydrochloride*.

neosynoptophore (ne″o-sin-op′to-fōr). A type of major amblyoscope with accessory attachments for creating Haidinger's brushes and afterimages.

neotocophthalmia (ne″o-to-kof′thal-me-ah). Ophthalmia neonatorum.

nephelometer (nef″eh-lom′eh-ter). A device for comparing the light scattered from particles in an unknown suspension to that of a standard, for the purpose of determining the amount of material in suspension; used in chemical and bacterial analyses, and in measurements of atmospheric scatter.

nephelometry (nef″eh-lom′eh-tre). Determination of the amount of particles in suspension in a gas or liquid with a nephelometer.

nephelopia (nef-el-o′pe-ah). Reduced vision resulting from cloudiness of the cornea.

nerve. A cordlike structure of nervous tissue that connects parts of the nervous system with other tissues of the body and conveys nervous impulses to, or away from, these tissues. It is composed of bundles of nerve fibers, each bundle (funiculus) being surrounded by a connective tissue sheath (perineurium), and the whole is enclosed in a common sheath (epineurium).

abducens n. Cranial nerve VI. It has its deep origin from the abducens nucleus in the pons and its superficial origin from the pons-medulla junction, entering the orbit via the superior orbital fissure. It is the motor nerve innervating the ipsilateral external rectus muscle.

cervical sympathetic n. 1. Any sympathetic group of nerve fibers leaving the superior, inferior, or middle cervical ganglion. 2. In ocular neurology, any group of postganglionic axons leaving the superior cervical ganglion, the destruction of which yields Horner's syndrome.

ciliary n., long. One of a pair of nerves that leaves the nasociliary nerve, pierces a posterior aperture of the sclera, courses in the suprachoroidal space nasally or temporally, and carries sympathetic fibers for the dilator pupillae muscle and the sensory fibers to the iris, the cornea, and the ciliary body.

ciliary n., short. One of six to ten nerves which arise from the ciliary ganglion, double in number, pierce the posterior sclera in a ring around the optic nerve, travel in the suprachoroidal space, and innervate the sphincter pupillae muscle, the ciliary muscle, and the cornea.

ethmoidal n., anterior. A terminal branch of the nasociliary nerve that supplies the cartilaginous portions of the nose and leaves the orbit via the anterior ethmoidal foramen. Syn., *nasal nerve*.

ethmoidal n., posterior. A branch of the nasociliary nerve that supplies the sphenoidal and ethmoidal sinuses and leaves the orbit via the posterior ethmoidal foramen. Syn., *nerve of Luschka; spheno-ethmoid nerve*.

facial n. Cranial nerve VII, a mixed nerve arising from the pons-medulla junction. It is efferent to the muscles of facial expression, including the orbicularis oculi, and to the lacrimal, submaxillary, and sublingual glands. It carries taste fibers from the anterior two thirds of the tongue.

fifth cranial n. Trigeminal nerve.

fourth cranial n. Trochlear nerve.

frontal n. A sensory branch of the ophthalmic nerve which divides into the supraorbital and supratrochlear nerves. It enters the orbit via the superior orbital fissure.

glossopalatine n. Intermediate nerve of Wrisberg.

infraorbital n. The continuation of the maxillary nerve as it passes the inferior orbital fissure to enter the orbit. It leaves the orbit by the infraorbital canal and gives origin to the inferior palpebral nerve, the nasal nerve, and the labial nerve.

infratrochlear n. A terminal branch of the nasociliary nerve that is sensory for the caruncle, the lacrimal sac, the canaliculi, and the medial portions of the eyelid and the conjunctiva.

intermediate n. of Wrisberg. A root of the facial nerve arising from the sensory nucleus, lateral and posterior to the motor root, containing parasympathetic fibers coursing to the lacrimal gland via the great superficial petrosal nerve which synapses in the sphenopalatine ganglion. It also contains sensory (taste) fibers to the anterior two thirds of the tongue and parasympathetic fibers to the glands of the palate and the nose and to the submaxillary and the sublingual salivary glands. Syn., *glossopalatine nerve.*

lacrimal n. A sensory branch of the ophthalmic nerve that enters the orbit by way of the superior orbital fissure and courses laterally to reach the lacrimal gland. Its superior division is sensory to the lacrimal gland and gives origin to the lateral palpebral nerve of the upper eyelid. Its inferior division has an anastomosis with the zygomaticotemporal nerve to receive sympathetic and parasympathetic fibers for the lacrimal gland.

Luschka, n. of. Posterior ethmoidal nerve.

malar n. Zygomaticofacial nerve. *Obs.*

mandibular n. The third division of the trigeminal nerve consisting of two roots, a sensory root which comes from the Gasserian ganglion, and the motor root of the trigeminal. The two pass through the foramen ovale and join into one trunk. It is motor to the muscles of mastication and is sensory to the lower jaw region and the anterior two thirds of the tongue.

maxillary n. The second division of the trigeminal nerve which leaves the Gasserian ganglion, receives branches from the sphenopalatine ganglion, and then gives origin to the zygomatic nerve. After passing through the inferior orbital fissure into the orbit, it is known as the infraorbital nerve. It is sensory to the upper jaw and lower eyelid and contains autonomic fibers for the lacrimal gland.

maxillary n., superior. Maxillary nerve.

nasal n. 1. Anterior ethmoidal nerve. 2. A branch of the infraorbital nerve or of the sphenopalatine ganglion. 3. Nasociliary nerve.

nasociliary n. A branch of the ophthalmic nerve which receives most of the fibers of general sensation from the eyeball. It enters the orbit through the superior orbital fissure and gives origin to the anterior and posterior ethmoidal, the long ciliary, and the infratrochlear nerves and a sensory root to the ciliary ganglion.

oculomotor n. Cranial nerve III. It originates from the lower ventral surface of the midbrain and is classified as a motor nerve. Its superior and inferior divisions enter the orbit through the superior orbital fissure. The superior division supplies the levator palpebrae superioris muscle and the superior rectus muscle. The inferior division supplies the medial and inferior rectus muscles and the inferior oblique muscle and also has parasympathetic fibers for the ciliary muscle and the sphincter pupillae muscle via a branch to the ciliary ganglion.

ophthalmic n. The first division of the trigeminal nerve which leaves the Gasserian ganglion, receives twigs from the III, IV, and VI cranial nerves, and divides into the nasociliary, the frontal, and the lacrimal nerves. It is sensory for the upper eyelids, eyebrows, forehead, eyeball, nose, and the air sinuses above and medial to the orbit.

optic n. Anatomically, cranial nerve II of the peripheral nervous system, but embryologically and histologically a "tract" of the central nervous system since it is a derivative of the forebrain containing neuroglia. The optic nerve receives over 800,000 fibers from the ganglion cells of the retina and contains some efferent fibers that end in the retina. Classified as a nerve of special sense, it is divided into intraocular, intraorbital, intracanalicular, and prechiasmal or intracranial portions. It leaves the orbit through the optic canal to enter the cranial cavity where it forms the optic chiasma.

orbital n. 1. The branches of the sphenopalatine ganglion which enter the orbit through the inferior orbital fissure and supply the periorbita and the orbital muscle of Mueller. 2. The zygomatic nerve. *Obs.*

palpebral n., inferior. A branch of the infraorbital nerve which supplies the lower eyelid.

palpebral n's., superior. Branches of the lacrimal, the frontal, and the nasociliary nerves which supply the upper eyelid.

pathetic n. Trochlear nerve. *Obs.*

petrosal n., deep. Sympathetic fibers from the carotid plexus for the lacrimal gland. It unites with the great superficial petrosal nerve to form the vidian nerve of the pterygoid canal.

petrosal n., great superficial. A branch of the facial nerve that carries parasympathetic fibers for the lacrimal gland and fuses with the deep petrosal nerve to form the vidian nerve of the pterygoid canal.

pterygoid canal n. Vidian nerve.

second cranial n. Optic nerve.

seventh cranial n. Facial nerve.

sixth cranial n. Abducens nerve.

spheno-ethmoid n. Posterior ethmoidal nerve.

sphenopalatine n. Either of two branches that join the sphenopalatine ganglion to the maxillary nerve and contain autonomic fibers for the lacrimal gland.

supraorbital n. The branch of the frontal nerve that passes through the supraorbital notch or foramen and is sensory for the upper eyelid, the conjunctiva, the eyebrow, the forehead, and the scalp up to the occipital bone.

supratrochlear n. The branch of the frontal nerve which anastomoses with the infratrochlear nerve and supplies the medial portions of the upper eyelid, the conjunctiva, and the eyebrow.

temporomalar n. Zygomatic nerve. *Obs.*

tentorial n. A branch of the ophthalmic division of the trigeminal nerve which supplies the tentorium and the dura mater over the posterior cranial fossa, and which, when stimulated intracranially, is considered to refer pain to the eyes or forehead.

third cranial n. Oculomotor nerve.

Tiedemann's n. The sympathetic fibers from the carotid plexus which course on the surface of the central retinal artery on into the retina.

trifacial n. Trigeminal nerve. *Obs.*

trigeminal n. Cranial nerve V. It originates from the lateral surface of the pons by a motor and a larger sensory root. The latter leads to the Gasserian ganglion which connects with the three divisions of the nerve, viz., ophthalmic, maxillary, and mandibular. It is sensory for the eyeball, the conjunctiva, the eyebrow, the skin of face and scalp, the teeth, the mucous membranes in the mouth and nose, and is motor to the muscles of mastication. Syn., *trifacial nerve.*

trochlear n. Cranial nerve IV. It originates from the dorsal surface of the junction between the midbrain and the cerebellum and passes through the superior orbital fissure and is motor to the superior oblique muscle. Syn., *pathetic nerve.*

vidian n. The nerve of the pterygoid canal formed by the union of the deep petrosal and the great superficial petrosal nerves. It ends at the sphenopalatine ganglion and supplies parasympathetic and sympathetic fibers to the lacrimal gland. Syn., *pterygoid canal nerve.*

Wrisberg's n. See *nerve, intermediate of Wrisberg.*

zygomatic n. A branch of the maxillary nerve in the pterygopalatine fossa that enters the orbit by way of the inferior orbital fissure. It divides into the zygomaticofacial and zygomaticotemporal nerves and has sensory fibers for the skin of the cheek and the temple. It contains autonomic fibers for the lacrimal gland which enter a twig that leads to the lacrimal nerve. It leaves the orbit through the zygomatic foramen.

zygomaticofacial n. A terminal branch of the zygomatic nerve that supplies the skin just lateral to the eyelid and the skin of the cheek after passing through the zygomaticofacial canal.

zygomaticotemporal n. A terminal branch of the zygomatic nerve that passes through the zygomaticotemporal canal to enter the temporal fossa and supply the skin of the anterior temple and the forehead just above. The nerve may have a twig which conveys the autonomic fibers to the lacrimal nerve and gland. Syn., *malar nerve.*

nerve fiber. See under *fiber.*

nerve loop, intrascleral (of Axenfeld). A loop formed by a variation in the course of a long ciliary nerve. After traversing the perichoroidal space, the nerve pierces the sclera a few millimeters behind the limbus, turns back on itself, retraces the same path, and then enters the ciliary body.

NET Orthoptor. A device designed for visual training in the home for the improvement of fusion, accommodative facility, and visual acuity. It is clamped to a spectacle frame and consists essentially of two apertures, both containing Polaroid filters, a mirror system before the right eye, controlled by a lever at the top to alter the direction of incident light, and lens holders for auxiliary trial lenses or Polaroid filters. Syn., *Natural Environment Trainer.*

Neumueller's tables. See under *table.*

neurasthenia, optic (nu″ras-the′ne-ah). Neurasthenia accompanied by contraction of the visual fields. See also *neurasthenic visual field.*

neuritis (nu-ri′tis). Inflammation of a nerve or nerves.

optic n. Inflammation of the optic nerve that occurs in two principal forms, intraocular optic neuritis (papillitis) and retrobulbar optic neuritis.

optic n., axial. Optic neuritis in which there is a selective involvement of the papillomacular bundle in the optic nerve.

optic n., intraocular. Papillitis.

optic n., lactation. Optic neuritis occurring during the lactation period following childbirth.

optic n., orbital. Retrobulbar optic neuritis.

optic n., periaxial. Optic neuritis involving the peripheral interstitial tissues of the optic nerve, exclusive of the papillomacular bundle.

optic n., postocular. Retrobulbar optic neuritis.

optic n., pseudo. 1. A congenital abnormal elevation of the optic disk in which the nerve fibers are heaped and there is a neuroglial overgrowth. There are no accompanying hemorrhages or exudates and the vessels appear normal, although the disk margin may be ill-defined. 2. A mild hyperemia of the optic disk with slight blurring of its margins and some tortuosity and dilatation of the retinal vessels. The condition has been attributed to uncorrected errors of refraction, anemia, exposure to glare, or to congenital causes.

optic n., retrobulbar. Inflammation of the orbital portion of the optic nerve, usually without visible changes in the eyegrounds, and primarily occurring as an axial retrobulbar optic neuritis, although it may be periaxial or transverse. Characteristically there is a unilateral sudden loss of central vision with headache on the affected side, pain in the orbit, sluggishness of the pupil, and tenderness of the eyeball. The symptoms persist from two weeks to two months with gradual recovery, which is usually complete. The most common cause is multiple sclerosis, although it may be due to exogenous toxins and inflammatory general or local diseases. Syn., *orbital optic neuritis; postocular optic neuritis.*

optic n., spurious. Pseudo-optic neuritis.

optic n., transverse. Optic neuritis involving the entire cross section of the optic nerve.

papulosa, n. A rare disease, either unilateral or bilateral, occurring within the first two years of a syphilitic infection, characterized by a massive, sharply demarcated, grayish or yellowish exudate on the optic disk which protrudes into the vitreous and may extend onto adjacent retina. Vitreous opacities, patches of chorioretinitis, and hemorrhages, especially around the exudate, are also present. In the later stages the exudate becomes organized into connective tissue strands which extend from the disk and anchor in an atrophic patch of chorioretinitis. Vision is greatly reduced and may or may not be recovered.

postocular n. Retrobulbar optic neuritis.

retinae, n. Circumscribed exudative choroiditis.

neuroblastoma, retinal (nu″ro-blas-to′mah). Retinoblastoma.

neurochorioretinitis (nu″ro-ko″re-o-ret″ih-ni′tis). Inflammation of the optic nerve, the choroid, and the retina.

neurochoroiditis (nu″ro-ko″roid-i′-tis). Inflammation of the optic nerve and the choroid.

neurocytoma (nu″ro-si-to′mah). A tumor of the retina or the central nervous system composed primarily of neurocytes.

neurodeatrophia (nu″ro-de″ah-tro′-fe-ah). Atrophy of the retina.

neuroencephalomyelopathy (nu″-ro-en-sef″ah-lo-mi″eh-lop′ah-the). Neuromyelitis optica.

neuroepithelioma, retinal (nu″ro-ep″e-the″le-o′mah). A congenital, malignant, neuroectodermal tumor of the retina, characteristically containing retinoblasts and large columnar cells which tend to arrange radially around a central cavity to form rosettes; a type of retinoblastoma.

neuroepithelium (nu″ro-ep″e-the′-le-um). The epithelial structures containing receptor cells for special sense, as the neuroepithelial layer of the retina.

neurofibroma (nu″ro-fi-bro′mah). A fibrous tumor, usually benign, arising from the nerve sheath or the endoneurium. It occurs in either discrete or diffuse form (von Recklinghausen's disease) and in the eye may affect the choroid, the ciliary body, or the iris.

neurofibromatosis (nu″ro-fi-bro″-mah-to′sis). Von Recklinghausen's disease.

neuroglia (nu-rog′le-ah). The nonconducting supportive structures of the central nervous system, the retina, and the optic nerve, occurring in three types, *astroglia, microglia,* and *oligodendroglia.*

neuromyelitis optica of Devic (nu″ro-mi″eh-li′tis op′te-kah). A self-limiting, demyelinating disease of the optic nerves, the optic chiasm, and the spinal cord, characterized by bilateral retrobulbar neuritis, usually accompanied by papillitis and transverse myelitis. Onset is usually acute, with almost complete blindness. In favorable cases there is restoration of vision, although central scotomata and hemianopsia may persist. The disease differs from multiple sclerosis in that relapses do not occur, it is more extensive, and results in greater destruction of the axis cylinders. Syn., *Devic's disease; encephalomyelitis optica; neuro-optic myelitis; neuroen-*cephalomyelopathy; ophthalmoneuromyelitis.

neuro-ophthalmology (nu″ro-of″-thal-mol′o-je). The branch of ophthalmology which deals particularly with the nervous system associated with the eye.

neuropapillitis (nu″ro-pap″ih-li′tis). Papillitis.

neuroretinitis (nu″ro-ret″ih-ni′tis). Inflammation of the optic nerve head and adjacent retina.

descendens, n. Retinitis secondary to retrobulbar optic neuritis.

diffuse syphilitic n. Neuroretinitis appearing in the second stage of syphilis characterized by swelling of the retina around the optic nerve head and blurring of the margins of the disk. The entire retina becomes gray, cloudy, and opaque, and dense, dustlike, vitreous opacities are usually present. Hemorrhages are few and the veins are tortuous and engorged. As the condition subsides, the vessels, particularly arteries, reduce in size and show marked sheathing, the disk becomes atrophic, and a migration of pigment assumes a characteristic bone corpuscle appearance, particularly in the periphery. Syn., *Jacobson's retinitis.*

duplex, n. Bilateral neuroretinitis.

neuroretinopathy (nu″ro-ret″ih-nop′ah-the). A disease of the optic nerve head and the retina.

neurotomy, opticociliary (nu-rot′o-me). Surgical cutting of the optic and ciliary nerves of one eye in an attempt to prevent sympathetic ophthalmia.

neutral. 1. Pertaining to a color which has neither hue nor saturation, such as gray, black, or white. 2. The absence of, or the transition between, "with" and "against" movement in the retinoscopic reflex.

high n. In dynamic retinoscopy, the end point corresponding to the strongest convex or weakest concave lens in a range of dioptric values for which the reflex is neutral.

low n. In dynamic retinoscopy, the end point corresponding to the weakest convex or the strongest concave lens in a range of dioptric values for which the reflex is neutral.

neutralization. 1. Hand neutralization. 2. The process or result of suppressing the perception of one eye while the other is fixating.

absolute n. Constant involuntary neutralization as may occur in the deviating eye in strabismus. Syn., *suppression.*

hand n. The method of determining the power of a spectacle lens by combining it with test lenses of known power until the resultant power is zero, especially when done by observing the motion or displacement of the image of an object viewed through the combination as it is held in the hand and moved back and forth in a plane perpendicular to the line of view.

partial n. 1. Periodic involuntary neutralization. 2. Voluntary neutralization as may occur during the use of a monocular microscope. Syn., *suspenopsia; suspension.*

nevoxanthoendothelioma, intraocular (ne″vo-zan″tho-en-do-the″-le-o′mah). Nevoxanthoendotheliomatous involvement of the anterior uvea, and less frequently the epibulbar tissue, usually occurring in early life in association with skin lesions and characterized by yellowish-brown elevated lesions of the iris and ciliary body, spontaneous anterior chamber hemorrhages, and secondary glaucoma. Syn., *ocular juvenile xanthogranuloma.*

nevus (ne′vus). A circumscribed area of pigmentation or vascularization, usually in the form of a

congenital benign neoplasm occurring in the skin or in various ocular tissues, as the conjunctiva, the iris, the choroid, the ciliary body, or the optic nerve.

Ota, n. of. Oculocutaneous melanosis.

Newman's theory (nu′manz). See under *theory.*

Newton's (nu′tonz) **color circle; colors; disk; formula; law; rings; color scale; color table; ring test; theory.** See under the nouns.

Newton-Mueller-Gudden law. See under *law.*

niacin (ni′ah-sin). Pyridine-3-carboxylic acid, a water soluble vitamin found in yeasts, egg yolk, liver, cereals, fresh meats, and some leafy vegetables. Deficiency in the diet is a main cause of pellagra and such eye signs as edema, dermatitis, and alopecia of the eyelids, conjunctivitis, keratitis, dustlike crystalline lens opacities, and optic neuritis. Syn., *nicotinic acid.*

nicking, A-V. The depression of a retinal venule into the tissue of the retina, where it is crossed by an overlying arteriole, primarily as a result of the thickening of the wall of the arteriole and the adventitial coat. It is one of the signs of hypertensive and/or arteriosclerotic retinopathy.

Nicol (nik′ol) **polarizer; prism.** See under *prism.*

nictation (nik-ta′shun). Nictitation.

nictitatio (nik″tih-ta′she-o). A clonic spasm of the eyelid.

nictitation (nik″tih-ta′shun). Winking.

Niemann's disease (ne′manz). See under *disease.*

Niemann-Pick disease (ne′man-pik). See under *disease.*

night blindness. See under *blindness.*

night vision tester. A device for determining the lowest of eight scotopic levels of illumination at which an observer can discriminate the break in a large Landolt ring at a given test distance.

portable *n. v. t.* An instrument for measuring the threshold of dark adaptation at a testing distance of 15 in. It consists essentially of a black Landolt ring, subtending a visual angle of 2° on a background of self-luminous paint, the luminance of which can be controlled by a series of neutral density filters.

niphablepsia (nif″ah-blep′se-ah). Snow blindness. *Obs.*

niphotyphlosis (nif″o-tif-lo′sis). Snow blindness. *Obs.*

nit. A unit of luminance equal to 1 candela per sq. m. See also *foot-lambert.*

nivea (ni′ve-ah). Asteroid bodies.

node. 1. A knot, knob, protuberance, or swelling, or an organ or a structure of such appearance. 2. The point on a wave or in a vibrating body which is absolutely or relatively free from vibratory motion; the point which undergoes minimum displacement. See also *antinode.*

cervical lymph n's., deep. Numerous lymph glands of varying size, located along the internal jugular vein, which drain lymph from the parotid and submaxillary lymph nodes and empty into the jugular trunk.

cervical lymph n's., superficial. Small lymph glands located at the ramus of the mandible bone and along the external jugular vein. They receive some lymph directly from ocular structures, but more lymph indirectly from the parotid and preauricular group of lymph nodes.

parotid lymph n's., deep. Lymph glands, located anterior to the ear and deep to the parotid salivary gland, which receive lymph from the conjunctiva of the entire upper eyelid and the

lateral one third of the lower eyelid and drain into the deep cervical lymph nodes.

parotid lymph n's., superficial. Lymph glands, located anterior to the ear and superficial to the parotid salivary gland, which receive lymph from the lacrimal gland and the superficial structures of the lateral three quarters of the upper eyelid and the lateral one half of the lower eyelid. The glands drain into the superficial and deep cervical lymph nodes.

preauricular lymph n's. Superficial parotid lymph glands located anterior to the ear which receive lymph from the lacrimal gland.

submaxillary lymph n's. Four to six lymph glands, located between the lower jaw and the submandibular salivary gland, which receive lymph from the medial portions of the eyebrow, the eyelid, the conjunctiva, the caruncle, and the lacrimal drainage apparatus and drain into the deep cervical lymph nodes. Syn., *submandibular lymph nodes.*

nodule (nod′ūl). 1. A small, circumscribed, solid elevation. 2. A small node.

Bizzozero n's. Globular bodies arranged in regular rows between adjacent cellular membranes, found in the human corneal epithelium at the level of the basal and middle layers and considered to be related to, or a part of, the intercellular bridges (desmosomes).

Busacca's n's. Nodules frequently found in the iris of an eye affected with a low grade uveitis. They appear in the stroma as small, translucent, gray elevations and are formed by accumulations of epithelioid cells and lymphocytes, with no tissue loss. When appearing on the pupillary border, they are known as *Koeppe's nodules.*

Dalén-Fuchs n. A nodule found in isolated areas of the iris in eyes with sympathetic ophthalmia and caused by a swelling and proliferation of the cells of the pigment epithelium.

Koeppe's n's. Nodules frequently found in the iris of an eye affected with a low grade uveitis. They appear on the pupillary border as small, translucent, gray elevations and are formed by accumulations of epithelioid cells and lymphocytes, with no tissue loss. When appearing in the stroma of the iris, they are known as *Busacca's nodules.*

nomogram (nom'o-gram). Nomograph.

nomograph (nom'o-graf). A series of three or more co-ordinated scales representing the relationship of three or more variables to each other; a graph for finding, by inspection or with the aid of a straight edge, rather than by solving an equation, one variable when the others are known.

noncomitance (non-kom'ih-tans). Nonconcomitance.

noncomitancy (non-kom'ih-tan-se). Nonconcomitancy.

noncomitant (non-kom'ih-tant). Nonconcomitant.

nonconcomitance (non''kon-kom'ih-tans). The condition in which the angular relationship between the lines of sight of the two eyes is not constant, but varies with the direction of gaze, usually indicating paresis or paralysis of one or more extraocular muscles. Syn., *incomitance; incomitancy; noncomitance; noncomitancy.*

nonconcomitancy (non''kon-kom'ih-tan-se). Nonconcomitance.

nonconcomitant (non''kon-kom'ih-tant). Pertaining to or having nonconcomitance. Syn., *incomitant; noncomitant.*

Nonne-Marie syndrome (non'e-mar-e'). Marie's disease.

Nonne-Milroy-Meige disease (non'-e-mil'roy-mehzh). See under *disease.*

nonreader. A child who has failed to learn to read although instructed by normally successful methods.

norm. A standard or representative value; the usual or typical; the average value for a variable for a population; the expected.

normal. 1. Perpendicular to the tangent of a curve or surface at the point of tangency. 2. Having a statistical value that can best be regarded as within the range of natural or normal distribution about the mean. 3. Typical, average, or natural, or free from disorders, distortions, or disease.

Norrie's disease. See under *disease.*

Norris' theory (nōr'is). See under *theory.*

northlight. Daylight received only from northern sky areas. It is generally less variable in spectral quality than daylight received from other regions of the sky and the sun and has a bluish-white color.

No-scru. A type of rimless spectacle lens mounting employing a rivet and solder in place of a screw for holding the lenses in place.

nose glasses. See *spectacles, nose.*

nose pad. A guard.

nose piece. The bridge and guards of a spectacle frame or mounting.

notation. 1. The act, method, or process of representing by a system or a set of signs or figures. 2. Any system of signs, figures, or symbols used to express technical facts, quantities, etc.

Munsell n. Designation of hue, value, and chroma, in the 1,000 sample Munsell system. The original notation applies to the color samples of the 1929 Munsell *Book of Colors.* The Munsell renotation applies to a later method of designating the samples.

Ostwald n. Designation of the variables of the Ostwald system in the specification of a surface color. An arbitrary letter-number notation is used, the hue being designated by a number from 1 to 24, while the black content and the white content are indicated by arbitrary letters which are found by reference to charts of the system.

Snellen's n. See *fraction, Snellen's.*

Snell-Sterling n. The representation of visual efficiency as a function of visual acuity, according to the formula: $E = 0.836^{(1/s - 1)}$ where $s =$ the Snellen fraction. Syn., *Snell-Sterling visual efficiency scale.*

standard axis n. The spectacle lens axis scale for which the 0° is to the subject's left, 90° up, 180° to his right, adopted by an optical society in England in 1904, by the Technischer Ausschuss für Brillenoptik (TABO) in Germany in 1917, and by the Council of British Ophthalmologists in 1921. Syn., *TABO notation.* Cf. *axis scale.*

TABO n. Standard axis notation.

notch. An indentation or depression on the edge of a bone or other organ.

Arnold's n. Frontal notch.

frontal n. An indentation sometimes present just medial to the supraorbital notch on the medial superior orbital margin of the frontal bone which transmits medial branches of the supraorbital nerve, vein, and artery. Rarely, it becomes surrounded by bone to become the frontal foramen. Syn., *Arnold's notch; Henle's notch.*

Henle's n. Frontal notch.

supraorbital n. An indentation on the medial, superior, orbital margin of the frontal bone which transmits the supraorbital nerve,

vein, and artery. Occasionally, it becomes surrounded by bone to become the supraorbital foramen.

Nothnagel's syndrome (nōt'nah-gelz). See under *syndrome.*

Nott's method (nots). See under *method.*

nox (noks). One thousandth of a *lux.*

n.p.c. The near point of convergence.

nu (ν). The Greek letter used as a symbol for the reciprocal of the *dispersive power* of a light-transmitting medium.

nubecula (nu-bek'u-lah). A nebula.

Nuckolls' test (nuk'olz). See under *test.*

nucleus (nu'kle-us). 1. A collection of nerve cells in the central nervous system concerned with a common function. 2. A central mass, portion, or core.

abducens n. A collection of the cell bodies of lower motor neurons located in the floor of the fourth ventricle in the lower portion of the pons. The axons from the nucleus enter the ipsilateral abducens nerve and supply the external rectus muscle.

adult n. The outer portion of the nucleus of the crystalline lens between the infantile nucleus and the cortex, formed after puberty.

anteromedian n. A group of parasympathetic preganglionic cell bodies lying rostroventral to both Edinger-Westphal nuclei and considered by some to be a rostral continuation of these nuclei. It is part of the oculomotor nuclear complex.

basal optic n. Posterior optic tract nucleus.

bulbospinal n. A group name for the principal sensory and the spinal nuclei of the trigeminal nerve.

Cajal's n. Interstitial nucleus.

caudal central n. An unpaired nucleus, separate from the nucleus of Perlia, which is thought to supply both the levator palpebrae superioris muscles.

crystalline lens, n. of the. The central core of the crystalline lens, surrounded by the cortex, which contains the oldest, more sclerosed, and less translucent lens fibers. Its zones of optical discontinuity are subdivided into *embryonic, fetal, infantile,* and *adult nuclei.* Y-sutures occur in the fetal nucleus and more complex lens stars occur in the infantile and adult nuclei.

Darkschewitsch's n. A group of cells in the tegmentum of the mid-brain, dorsal to the red nucleus, in the central gray matter near the aqueduct of Sylvius. It sends fibers into the medial longitudinal fasciculus. Syn., *nucleus of the posterior commissure.*

dorsal n. 1. The main part of the external geniculate body, well developed in man and absent in lower vertebrates, which serves as a relay station for visual fibers in the optic tract. 2. A division of the lateral nucleus of the oculomotor nuclear complex.

Edinger-Westphal n. The portion of the oculomotor nucleus containing preganglionic parasympathetic cell bodies of neurons which, via the oculomotor nerve, reach the ciliary ganglion and the episcleral ganglion to synapse with ganglionic neurons supplying the sphincter pupillae and ciliary muscles. It is the lower center for accommodation and pupillary constriction.

embryonic n. The most central portion of the core of the crystalline lens formed during the first three months of intrauterine life and surrounded by the fetal nucleus. It contains the oldest lens fibers derived from the embryonic posterior epithelium of the lens.

facial n. A collection of lower motor neuron cell bodies, located in the floor of the fourth ventricle in the lower pons, which are motor to the muscles of facial expression, including the orbicularis oculi, frontal, and corrugator supercilii.

fetal n. The portion of the nucleus of the crystalline lens lying between the embryonic and infantile nuclei and formed from the third to the eighth month of intrauterine life. It contains the Y-sutures of the lens.

Fuse's n. A supranuclear center for the co-ordination of lateral eye movements, located at the pons-medulla junction.

infantile n. The portion of the nucleus of the crystalline lens lying between the fetal and adult nuclei and formed from the eighth fetal month until puberty.

interstitial n. of Cajal. A scattered group of cells in the cerebral peduncle of the midbrain, near the rostral end of the red nucleus, which extends dorsolaterally to send descending fibers into the medial longitudinal bundle. Fibers emerging from the superior colliculi and from the cortex, and going to the interstitial nucleus of Cajal, are considered to constitute pathways for cortical control of ocular movements.

lateral n. The portion of the oculomotor nucleus supplying the superior rectus, the inferior rectus, the internal rectus, and the inferior oblique muscles, and possibly the levator palpebrae superioris muscle.

mesencephalic n. of the trigeminal nerve. A group of unipolar cell bodies located lateral to the cerebral aqueduct of the midbrain, which gives origin to the fibers of the mesencephalic root of the trigeminal nerve. It is involved in relaying sensory impulses from the muscles of mastication and possibly from the extraocular muscles.

oculomotor n. The nucleus of the oculomotor nerve located ventral to the superior colliculus of the midbrain and subdivided into the *Edinger-Westphal nucleus,* the *nucleus of Perlia,* the *lateral nucleus,* and the *caudal central nucleus.*

Perlia's n. A single (unpaired) mass of cells lying between the ventral nucleus and the dorsal nucleus of the oculomotor nuclear complex, not always present in man and of undetermined function.

pontine n. 1. Any collection of cell bodies of neurons in the pons, as in the abducens or the facial nuclei. 2. A theoretical center for lateral gaze located near the abducens nucleus.

posterior accessory optic tract n. In quadrupeds, a group of cell bodies located ventrolaterally to the red nucleus, medial to the substantia nigra, and posterior to the mammillary body. It receives fibers from the posterior accessory optic tract and sends fibers to the substantia nigra, the oculomotor nucleus, the lateral reticular gray, and the interpeduncular nucleus. Syn., *basal optic nucleus; transverse peduncular tract nucleus.*

posterior commissure, n. of the. Darkschewitsch's nucleus.

pregeniculate n. A small elongated mass of cells located within the lateral division of the optic tract, anterior to the main (*dorsal*) nucleus of the external geniculate body but having no continuity with it. In lower vertebrates it represents the entire geniculate, but is vestigial in man, probably having only photostatic functions. Syn., *ventral nucleus of external geniculate body.*

pretectal n. An oval group of cells located at the dorsal surface of the tecto-thalamic junction and internal to the superior colliculus,

serving as a relay station for pupillary fibers.

principal sensory n. of the trigeminal nerve. A mass of cells located in the floor of the fourth ventricle, especially in the pons, where synapses occur with touch fibers in the sensory root of the trigeminal nerve.

spinal n. of the trigeminal nerve. The column of cells, extending from the lower pons to the middle of the cervical segments of the spinal cord, medially adjacent to the entire length of the spinal tract of the trigeminal nerve, in which the axons of the tract synapse. It is continuous with the principal sensory nucleus of the trigeminal nerve, courses through the medulla oblongata to end in the cervical cord, and is involved in relaying impulses for pain and temperature from the head region.

transverse peduncular tract n. Posterior accessory optic tract nucleus.

trochlear n. The collection of motor neuron cell bodies located in front of the inferior colliculus of the midbrain which supplies the contralateral superior oblique muscle.

ventral n. 1. A division of the lateral nucleus of the oculomotor nuclear complex. 2. Pregeniculate nucleus.

vestibular nuclei. A group of nuclei found in the region of the pons-medulla junction, named after Deiter, Bechterew, and Schwalbe, plus a descending spinal vestibular nucleus. They receive fibers from the vestibular nerve and send fibers into the medial longitudinal fasciculus to control the position of the eyes in relation to head position. The supranuclear center for lateral gaze may be located in this group.

number. A symbol or digit expressive of a specified quantity, of a certain value, or of a designated place in a series or sequence.

Abbe's n. The nu (ν) value.

blank n. A code number given to fused bifocal blanks which indicates the power of the reading addition of the finished lens for a specified base curve.

f n. The ratio of the focal length of an optical system to the diameter of the entrance pupil; reciprocal of the *relative aperture.*

index n. Statistics: A ratio, quotient, mean, or some other computational resultant combining two or more observations or measurements into a single numerical value convenient for classifying, cataloguing, rating, or statistical manipulation.

wave n. In light waves, the reciprocal of wavelength in centimeters; the number of waves per centimeter.

Numont. See *mounting, Numont.*

Nutt Auto-disc. See under *Auto-disc.*

N.V.V.O. Nederlandse Vakopleiding Voor Opticiens, an ophthalmic opticians' certifying organization.

nycotometer (nik″o-tom′eh-ter). An instrument for determining the threshold illumination for identifying form in the dark-adapted eye. It may also be used as an adaptometer.

nyctalope (nik′tah-lōp). An individual affected with nyctalopia.

nyctalopia (nik″tah-lo′pe-ah). A term used inconsistently to mean either night blindness or day blindness. Synonymous or autonymous with *hemeralopia.*

nyctotyphlosis (nik″to-tif-lo′sis). Nyctalopia.

Nyktometer (nik-tom′eh-ter). An instrument for testing visual acuity in the dark-adapted eye and changes in visual acuity upon sudden exposure to glare.

nystagmic (nis-tag′mik). Pertaining to or having nystagmus.

nystagmic time. See under *time.*

nystagmograph (nis-tag′mo-graf). An instrument for recording nystagmic movements of the eye.

nystagmography (nis″tag-mog′rah-fe). The study and recording of nystagmic movements of the eyes.

nystagmoid (nis-tag′moid). Resembling nystagmus.

nystagmus (nis-tag′mus). A regularly repetitive, usually rapid, and characteristically involuntary movement or rotation of the eye, either oscillatory or with slow and fast phases in alternate directions. Syn., *spasmus oculi; talantropia.*

after n. Secondary nystagmus.

amaurotic n. A jerky or pendular nystagmus sometimes occurring in those who have been blind for a considerable time.

amblyopic n. Nystagmus associated with, or attributed to, reduced central vision.

aspiration n. Nystagmus produced by the aspiration of air from the external auditory meatus.

asymmetric gaze n. A horizontal nystagmus without a rotatory component, occurring in lateral gaze and commencing nearer the straightforward position, and more intensely on one side than the other. It indicates a lesion within the pons varolii, affecting one medial longitudinal bundle.

ataxic n. A unilateral nystagmus associated with impaired lateral conjugate movements occurring in disseminated sclerosis. In lateral movements the inturning eye is restricted and the outturning eye shows a lateral, jerky nystagmus.

aural n. Labyrinthine nystagmus.

Bárány's n. Caloric nystagmus.

Bartels' cortical n. Nystagmus, reported by Bartels, due to paresis of conjugate ocular movements resulting from frontal lobe injury.

Bechterew's n. See *compensation, Bechterew's.*

caloric n. A vestibular nystagmus

induced by thermal stimulation of the labyrinth of the inner ear, usually by the introduction of either cold or hot water into the external auditory canal. When cold water is used, the slow phase of the movement is toward the stimulated side; when warm water is used, it is toward the opposite side. Syn., *Bárány's nystagmus; thermal nystagmus.*

central *n.* A jerky nystagmus resulting from a lesion in either the vestibular nerve in its intracranial course, the primary vestibular nuclei, or their secondary connections.

central labyrinthine *n.* Central nystagmus.

cerebral *n.* A pendular nystagmus resulting from a lesion or a tumor of the cerebrum or its meninges.

coarse *n.* Nystagmus in which the angular range of excursion is over 15°. See also *fine nystagmus; medium nystagmus.*

compression *n.* An induced, labyrinthine nystagmus resulting from unilateral changes of pressure in the semicircular canals.

conjugate *n.* Nystagmus in which there is symmetry of amplitude, type, and direction of movement in the two eyes.

convergence *n.* An intermittent, abrupt, spasmodic, convergence movement in which the eyes move rhythmically toward each other and then slowly return to the original position, usually due to a tumor of the anterior aqueduct of Sylvius, the third ventricle, or the midbrain.

deficiency of light *n.* An ocular nystagmus sometimes occurring in children raised in dark surroundings.

deviational *n.* End-position nystagmus.

disjunctive *n.* Nystagmus in which there is symmetry of amplitude and type of movement in the two eyes but in opposite directions.

dissociated *n.* Nystagmus in which the amplitude, type, and/or direction of movement in the two eyes are unrelated.

eccentric *n.* Nystagmus in which there is a position of gaze, usually eccentric, where the oscillatory movement is at a minimum and may be absent.

end-position *n.* A jerky, physiological nystagmus occurring in normal individuals when attempts are made to fixate a point at the limits of the field of fixation. Syn., *deviational nystagmus.*

essential *n.* Nystagmus occurring as a result of abnormal use of the eyes in certain occupations, such as *miners' nystagmus.*

fatigue *n.* Nystagmus as a result of fatigue caused by prolonged fixation at or near the limit of the field of fixation.

fine *n.* Nystagmus in which the angular range of excursion is less than 5°. See also *medium nystagmus; coarse nystagmus.*

first degree *n.* Nystagmus manifest only when fixation is in the direction of the quick component. See also *second degree nystagmus; third degree nystagmus.*

fixation *n.* 1. Nystagmus associated with attempts to fixate. 2. End-position nystagmus. 3. Ocular nystagmus.

Frenzel's hopping *n.* Nystagmus composed of two rapid phases with a short pause between, each phase starting and stopping abruptly.

galvanic *n.* A vestibular nystagmus induced by electrical stimulation of the labyrinth of the inner ear. When the anode is applied to one labyrinth, the slow phase of the movement is toward the stimulated side; when the cathode is used, it is toward the opposite side.

gaze-paretic *n.* Paretic nystagmus.

hereditary *n.* A hereditarily transmitted, pendular, horizontal nystagmus usually showing sex-linked, sometimes dominant, transmission, occurring only in males and frequently associated with partial albinism. Syn., *idiopathic nystagmus.*

horizontal *n.* Lateral nystagmus.

hysterical *n.* Nystagmus occurring in hysteria and other psychopathic conditions in which the movements are generally rapid, pendular, and lateral.

idiopathic *n.* Hereditary nystagmus.

irregular *n.* Nystagmus in which the movements are persistently unequal in duration, direction, and amplitude.

jelly *n.* A fine tremor of the eyes detectable only ophthalmoscopically by the rapid oscillation of the fundus structures. Syn., *quivering nystagmus.*

jerky *n.* Nystagmus characterized by a slow movement in one direction, followed by a rapid movement in the opposite direction to the original position. It is typical of vestibular nystagmus. Syn., *resilient nystagmus; rhythmic nystagmus; springing nystagmus.*

labyrinthine *n.* A vestibular nystagmus resulting from stimulation, injury, or disease of the labyrinth.

labyrinthine end-position *n.* A first degree nystagmus, mixed lateral and rotatory, occurring when looking to the side and associated with other symptoms of labyrinthine irritation, such as vertigo.

latent *n.* Nystagmus induced by covering either of the two eyes but otherwise absent.

lateral *n.* Nystagmus in which the movements are from side to side.

medium *n.* Nystagmus in which the angular range of excursion is between 5° and 15°. See also *fine nystagmus; coarse nystagmus.*

miners' *n.* A nystagmus, usually pendular, occurring in coal miners after many years of working in dark, cramped conditions. The more complicated cases may develop an accompanying blepharospasm, photophobia, vertigo, loss of vision, and psychoneurosis.

mixed *n.* 1. Nystagmus in which a vertical or lateral movement is combined with a cyclorotatory movement. 2. Nystagmus which is pendular in one position of gaze and jerky in another.

muscle-paretic *n.* Paretic nystagmus.

ocular *n.* Nystagmus manifest when conditions of fixation are difficult or impossible. It includes *visual, end-position, optokinetic, paretic, latent,* and *miners' nystagmus.*

optical rotatory *n.* Optokinetic nystagmus.

opticomotor *n.* Optokinetic nystagmus.

optokinetic *n.* A physiological ocular nystagmus induced by the attempt to fixate objects rapidly traversing the visual field. Syn., *optical rotatory nystagmus; opticomotor nystagmus.*

oscillating (oscillatory) *n.* Pendular nystagmus.

paretic *n.* A first degree nystagmus occurring only in particular directions of gaze due to extraocular muscle paresis.

pendular *n.* Nystagmus in which there is a smooth, undulatory movement of equal speed in each direction. Syn., *oscillating nystagmus; undulatory nystagmus; vibratory nystagmus.*

periodic alternating *n.* A rare form of central nystagmus which alternately occurs for a finite period, ceases, and recurs in the opposite direction. The duration of the periods is from 1 to 6 minutes with pauses of a few seconds between.

peripheral n. 1. Vestibular nystagmus. 2. End-position nystagmus.

physiological n. Nystagmus which may be induced in normal individuals, such as *end-position nystagmus* or *optokinetic nystagmus.*

positional n. Nystagmus manifest or more pronounced when the head is in specific positions.

protractorious, n. The protrusion and retraction of the eyeball accompanying the pulse beat and respiration due to a slight variation of the amount of blood in the orbital tissues. Physiologically the displacement is slight, a few hundredths of a millimeter; pathologically it is more pronounced.

pseudo n. Pseudonystagmus.

pupillary n. A dilatation and contraction of the pupils occurring synchronously with nystagmus.

quivering n. Jelly nystagmus.

radiary n. Symmetric gaze nystagmus occurring during oblique eye movements and in the same meridian as the eye movements. It is usually indicative of multiple sclerosis or other related diseases.

railroad n. Optokinetic nystagmus, so named because it is manifested during observation of the passing landscape while riding on a railroad car or other rapidly moving vehicle.

reflex acoustic n. Nystagmus induced by a loud noise.

reflex sensory n. Nystagmus induced by sensory stimulation of the skin in the region of the ear.

resilient n. Jerky nystagmus.

retraction n. Nystagmus retractorius.

retractorius, n. A central nystagmus accompanied by a saccadic jerk of the eyeball backward into the orbit with each oscillation. It characteristically occurs on certain ocular movements and is considered to be caused by tumors or inflammatory conditions in or near the oculomotor nuclei.

rhythmic n. Jerky nystagmus.

rotary n. Rotatory nystagmus.

rotation n. A vestibular nystagmus induced by rotation of the head around any axis, clinically demonstrated by rotating a subject in a revolving chair.

rotatory n. Nystagmus in which the movements are in more than one plane, being a partial rolling of the eyeball around the anterior-posterior axis.

second degree n. Nystagmus manifest when fixation is straight ahead as well as in the direction of the quick component. See also *first degree nystagmus; third degree nystagmus.*

secondary n. A vestibular nystagmus manifest after the abrupt cessation of a rotation of the head, due to the tendency of the labyrinthine fluid to persist in its movement. Syn., *after nystagmus.*

seesaw n. A rare form of vertical nystagmus in which the movements of the two eyes are in opposite directions.

springing n. Jerky nystagmus.

symmetric gaze n. A horizontal nystagmus without a rotatory component, occurring in lateral gaze and commencing before the end position, with equal movement to the right or left from the straightforward position and with equal intensity. It may be associated with nystagmus in upward gaze and is usually indicative of multiple sclerosis.

thermal n. Caloric nystagmus.

third degree n. Nystagmus constantly manifest regardless of the direction of fixation. See also *first degree nystagmus; second degree nystagmus.*

toxic n. Positional nystagmus induced by the ingestion of alcohol or of certain drugs such as barbiturates.

train n. Railroad nystagmus.

undulatory n. Pendular nystagmus.

unilateral n. 1. Nystagmus affecting only one eye. 2. Nystagmus manifest only when one eye is covered. See also *latent nystagmus.*

vertical n. Nystagmus in which the movements are up and down.

vestibular n. Nystagmus resulting from stimulation, injury, or disease of the labyrinth or of the vestibular nerves. It is typically jerky, fine, rapid, and of the latteral-rotatory type. Syn., *peripheral nystagmus.*

vibratory n. Pendular nystagmus.

visual n. An ocular nystagmus attributed to reduced central visual acuity.

voluntary n. Hysterical nystagmus.

nystagmus-myoclonus. Rare congenital nystagmus associated with abnormal involuntary body movements.

nystaxis (nis-tak′sis). Nystagmus.

O

O. Abbreviation for *oculus*.

obcecation (ob″se-ka′shun). Partial or incomplete blindness.

obfuscate (ob-fus′kāt). To darken, as by reducing illumination; to dim, as by reducing vision; to obscure, as by creating mental confusion.

object. 1. That which is experienced as having location, dimensions, and physical properties. 2. That which is regarded in terms of its visible or luminous attributes, as the origin of reference for an optically formed image.

distance, o. See under *distance*.

glass, o. See under *glass*.

plane, o. See under *plane*.

point, o. See under *point*.

ray, o. Incident ray.

regard, o. of. That object which is selectively receiving visual attention.

space, o. See under *space*.

test o. An object, pattern, or design used for vision testing.

objective. A single lens or doublet in a telescopic or microscopic system nearest the object, serving to converge light from points in the field of view.

Dollond's o. The first achromatic doublet, designed by Dollond in 1757, consisting of a double convex crown glass lens cemented to a double concave flint glass lens.

oblique (ob-lēk′, ob-līk′) **astigmatism; axis; illumination; muscles; ray.** See under the nouns.

obliquity of the lens (ob-lik′wih-te). A tilted position of a lens, especially of the crystalline lens, which produces astigmatism.

O'Brien test. See under *test*.

Obrig (o′brig) **Radius Dial Gauge.** See under *gauge*.

observer, standard I.C.I. A hypothetical observer whose color responses conform to those of a statistically computed mean derived from observers having normal color vision, as specified by the International Commission on Illumination.

occluder (ŏ-klūd′er). An opaque or translucent device placed before an eye to obscure or block vision.

aero o. A rubber, cuplike occluder which completely covers the eye from the nose to the temple, containing holes for ventilation.

Bangerter's graded o's. Adhesive plastic lens occluders of graded transparencies designed to reduce visual acuity in eight steps from 1.0 (20/20) to complete occlusion.

Bell's o. A cuplike occluder which clips onto the back of a spectacle frame and is shaped so that its edges rest against the brow, the cheek, and the temple to block vision completely.

Chavasse o. Chavasse lens.

clip-over o. A plastic disk with clips to attach it to the front of a spectacle frame.

Doyne o. A cuplike occluder which clips onto the back of a spectacle frame and to the temple. It is so shaped that its edges rest against the brow, the cheek, and the temple to block vision completely.

[500]

expansion shield o. An occluder for blocking peripheral vision or for protecting the eye against air, dust, or glare, consisting essentially of a side shield that fits onto the eyewires of a spectacle frame and does not occlude vision through the spectacle lens.

half o. A lens, one half of which is covered with an opaque or translucent material.

Jamieson's o. A cuplike occluder of pliable rubber attached to the posterior surface of a spectacle lens by means of a small suction cup and shaped so that its edges rest against the brow, the cheek, and the temple to block vision completely.

Linder o's. Either of two types of soft plastic occluders, flesh color on the outside and black inside, each having three adjustable metal tabs for attachment to a spectacle frame. One, a patch type, covers the front of the lens, and the other, the cup type, covers the back of the lens and has an added flange to block peripheral vision.

Pap o. A cuplike occluder with clips for attachment to the back of a spectacle frame and with a cushioned ventilated edge which conforms to the brow, cheek, and temple to block vision completely.

polarizing o. An occluder consisting of two Polaroid lenses, one behind the other, with one lens in a fixed position and the other rotatable so as to vary the amount of light entering the eye.

Pugh's o. One of a series of four neutral filters of various densities which clip on to the front of a spectacle frame. Syn., *Pugh's visual acuity reducer.*

scientype o. Chavasse lens.

Vaccluder o. A plastic occluder with edges shaped to fit closely to the brow and orbital bone structure and attachable to the back surface of a spectacle lens by means of a rubber suction cup.

occlusio pupillae (ŏ-klu′ze-o pu′-pil-e). Occlusion or covering of the pupil of the eye, as by a pathologically formed membrane.

occlusio pupillae lymphatica (ŏ-klu′ze-o pu′pil-e lim-fat′ik-ah). Occlusion or covering of the pupil of the eye by a pathologically formed membrane.

occlusion (ŏ-klu′zhun). 1. The act of obscuring or blocking vision with an occluder, or the resulting condition. 2. Closure or blockage of a blood vessel.

calibrated o. Graded occlusion.

graded o. Partial obscuring of vision with one of a series of occluders, such as Bangerter's graded occluders, designed to reduce vision an intended amount. Syn., *calibrated occlusion.*

inverse o. Occlusion of the amblyopic eye, a technique used in pleoptics before and between treatments for eccentric fixation.

Marlow's prolonged o. Occlusion of one eye for several days or weeks to determine more accurately the degree of heterophoria (especially vertical heterophoria) or to determine if symptoms of visual discomfort are due to binocular vision.

partial o. 1. The occlusion of a portion of the field of vision by covering part of the spectacle lens. 2. The reduction of vision, as with a neutral density filter. 3. Periodic or intermittent occlusion.

sneak o. A method used in the treatment of amblyopia in which a series of filters of increasing densities are placed before the nonamblyopic eye until it is totally occluded.

total o. 1. Occlusion in which both light and form vision are completely eliminated. 2. Constant occlusion.

ocellus (o-sel′us). A single light-sensitive cell or a group of such cells which function independently of each other, a primitive form of eye. Syn., *simple eye*.

composite o. A simple eye formed by the fusion of two or more ocelli.

ochronosis, ocular (o″kro-no′sis). Brownish pigmentation, usually bilateral, of the sclera in the intrapalpebral fissure in persons having an inherited inability to metabolize phenylalanine and tyrosine, resulting in the excretion of homogentisic acid in the urine (alkaptonuria). The pigmentation usually commences in middle age with patches or flecks which tend to merge into oval or triangular plaques. Pigmentation of the conjunctiva and cornea is a rare accompaniment.

octave, visible light (ok′tāv, -tiv). The visible spectrum regarded as a series of hues analogous in number to the tones in the musical octave, or as a spectral range fulfilling the condition that the longest wavelength is twice the shortest wavelength.

ocul- (ok′ūl). A combining form denoting the *eye* or *ocular*.

ocular (ok′u-lar). 1. An eyepiece. 2. Pertaining to or of the eye.

ocular ballottement; bobbing; dominance; echogram; motility; myiasis; rosacea; spectres; tension; torticollis. See under the nouns.

ocularist (ok-u-lar′ist). One who designs, fabricates, and fits artificial eyes.

oculentum (ok″u-len′tum). An ophthalmic ointment.

oculi (ok′u-li). The plural of oculus; the eyes.

marmarygodes, o. Metamorphopsia.

unitas, o. Oculi uniter.

uniter, o. The two eyes as a unit, i.e., considered together or simultaneously, not separately. Abbreviation *O.U.* Cf. *oculus uterque.*

uterque, o. Oculus uterque.

oculist (ok′u-list). A medical practitioner who limits his field to diseases and disorders of the eye and its appendages.

oculistics (ok-u-lis′tiks). The treatment of ocular diseases.

oculo- (ok′u-lo). A combining form denoting the *eye* or *ocular*.

oculodiagnostician (ok″u-lo-di″agnos-tish′an). One who practices iridodiagnosis.

oculofacial (ok″u-lo-fa′shal). Pertaining to both the eyes and the face.

oculofrontal (ok″u-lo-fron′tal). Pertaining to both the eyes and the forehead.

oculogyration (ok″u-lo-ji-ra′shun). Movement of the eyes.

oculogyric (ok″u-lo-ji′rik). Pertaining to or causing movements of the eyes. Syn., *ophthalmogyric*.

oculometer (ok″u-lom′eh-ter). Stigmatometer.

oculometroscope (ok″u-lo-met′ro-skōp). An instrument used in retinoscopy, consisting of a battery of trial lenses mounted on a wheel to permit successive placement in front of the eyes.

oculomotor (ok″u-lo-mo′tor). 1. Pertaining to movements of the eye. 2. Pertaining to the oculomotor nerve.

oculomotorius (ok″u-lo-mo-tōr′e-us). Oculomotor nerve.

oculomycosis (ok″u-lo-mi-ko′sis). Any disease of the eye caused by a fungus.

oculonasal (ok″u-lo-na′zal). Pertaining to both the eye and the nose.

oculophrenicorecurrent (ok″u-lo-fren″ih-ko-re-kur′ent). Pertaining to the recurrent laryngeal and phrenic nerves involved in Horner's syndrome.

oculopupillary (ok″u-lo-pu′pih-lār-e). Pertaining to the pupil of the eye.

oculoreaction (ok″u-lo-re-ak′shun). See *reaction, ophthalmic*.

oculozygomatic (ok″u-lo-zi″go-mat′-ik). Pertaining to both the eye and the zygomatic arch.

oculus (ok′u-lus) (pl. *oculi*). An eye.
  bovinus, o. Hydrophthalmos.
  bovis, o. Hydrophthalmos.
  bubulus, o. Hydrophthalmos.
  caesius, o. Glaucoma.
  dexter, o. The right eye. Abbreviation *O.D.*
  duplex, o. A figure eight bandage covering both eyes. Syn., *binoculus*.
  elephantinus, o. Hydrophthalmos.
  lacrimans, o. Epiphora.
  laevus, o. The left eye. Abbreviation *O.L.*
  leporinus, o. Lagophthalmos.
  purulentus, o. Hypopyon.
  simplex, o. A bandage covering only one eye. Syn., *monoculus*.
  sinister, o. The left eye. Abbreviation *O.S.*
  unitas, o. Oculi uniter.
  uterque, o. The two eyes, both the one and the other, i.e., each one considered individually and separately. Abbreviation *O.U.* Cf. *oculi uniter.*

O.D. Abbreviation for: (1) *oculus dexter;* (2) *Doctor of Optometry.*

O.E.P. Abbreviation for *Optometric Extension Program.*

off-effect. The positive wave in an electroretinogram which follows, after a short latent period, the shutting off of the stimulus light.

Oguchi's disease (o-gōō′chēz). See under *disease.*

O.I.C. Optical Information Council.

O.L. Abbreviation for *oculus laevus.*

oligodacrya (ol″ih-go-dak′re-ah). A deficiency of tears.

Oliver's test (ol′ih-verz). See under *test.*

O.M.A. Optical Manufacturers Association.

ommateum (om″ah-te′um). A compound eye, as in insects or crustaceans.

ommatidium (om″ah-tid′e-um). One of the group of functionally and structurally associated elements of the compound eye of arthropods. It consists of a surface corneal facet and an underlying crystalline cone which collect light and a retinule, the receptor cells arranged in tubular form.

ommatophore (ŏ-mat′o-fōr). A movable tentacle bearing a compound eye at the tip, as found in some mollusks, such as the snail.

ommochromes (om-o-krōmz′). Pigments of unknown composition and function found in the eyes and integument of arthropods.

Omnitrainer (om″nih-trān′er). A haploscopic orthoptic instrument patterned after the Brewster stereoscope, with rotatable lenses for variable separation of optical centers, using both opaque and trans-illuminated targets, and having a built-in mechanism for providing variably intermittent illumination.

onchocerciasis (ong″ko-ser-si′ah-sis, -ki′ah-sis). Parasitic infection with the *Onchocerca volvulus*, characterized by nodules on the skin when caused by the adult filaria and by such ocular complications as keratitis, iridocyclitis, or retrobulbar neuritis when caused by the immature filaria.

onyx (on′iks, o′niks). A gathering of pus behind the cornea, giving the appearance of a fingernail; hypopyon.

opacity (o-pas′ih-te). 1. A discrete or generalized portion of certain normally transparent tissues or structures of the eye which has lost its usual degree of transparency and hence has become relatively opaque. 2. In photographic film, the ratio of incident to transmitted light.
  Berlin's o. The milky white opacity resulting from edema, seen in the macular area in commotio retinae.
  Caspar's o. A ring or latticelike opacity of the cornea resulting from contusion.
  Haab's band o. A circular opac-

ity of the cornea characterized by the presence of bandlike stripes, which appear as glassy threads, on the posterior surface of the cornea. It is associated with buphthalmos and is due to tears in Descemet's membrane.

Schirmer's o. A threadlike opacity of the cornea resulting from contusion of the cornea.

Vossius ring o. Vossius ring cataract.

whorl-shaped o. Vortex corneal dystrophy.

opalescence (o″pal-es′ens). The milky iridescence seen in certain media, such as the opal.

opalescent (o″pal-es′ent). Pertaining to the property of opalescence.

opaque (o-pāk′). Impervious to light; not transparent or translucent.

operculum oculi (o-per′ku-lum ok′-u-li). The eyelid.

ophryitis (of″re-i′tis). Inflammation in the region of the eyebrow.

ophryosis (of″re-o′sis). Spasm in the region of the eyebrow.

ophryphtheiriasis (of″rif-thi-ri′ah-sis). Infestation of the eyebrows and the eyelashes with lice. Also spelled *ophryphthiriasis.*

ophrys (of′ris). The eyebrow.

ophthalmacrosis (of-thal″mah-kro′-sis). Enlargement of the eyeball.

ophthalmagra (of″thal-ma′grah, -mag′rah). Sudden pain in the eyeball.

ophthalmalacia (of″thal-mah-la′she-ah). Ophthalmomalacia.

ophthalmalgia (of″thal-mal′je-ah). Pain in the eyeball.

ophthalmatrophia (of″thal-mah-tro′-fe-ah). Atrophy of the eyeball; phthisis bulbi.

ophthalmecchymosis (of″thal-mek″-ih-mo′sis). An extravasation of blood into the tissue of the conjunctiva.

ophthalmectomy (of″thal-mek′to-me). Surgical removal of the eyeball; enucleation or excision of the eyeball.

ophthalmencephalon (of″thal-men-sef′ah-lon). The neural mechanism of vision: the retina, the optic nerves, the optic chiasm, the optic tracts, the optic radiations, the visual centers, etc.

ophthalmia (of-thal′me-ah). Inflammation of the eye, particularly one involving the conjunctiva; conjunctivitis.

actinic o. Actinic conjunctivitis.

ante-partum o. Inflammation of the fetal eye, prior to birth. Syn., *ophthalmia fetalis.*

arida, o. Xerosis of the conjunctiva; xerophthalmia.

Brazilian o. Xerosis of the conjunctiva resulting from malnutrition.

catarrhal o. Catarrhal conjunctivitis.

caterpillar hair o. Nodular conjunctivitis.

eczematous o. Phlyctenular conjunctivitis.

Egyptian o. Trachoma.

electric o. Conjunctivitis resulting from excessive exposure to a high tension electric spark or arc.

externa, o. Paralysis of the extraocular muscles.

fetalis, o. Ante-partum ophthalmia.

gonorrheal o. Gonococcal conjunctivitis.

granular o. Trachoma.

hepatica, o. Degenerative changes in the uveal tract and the retina and xerosis of the conjunctiva, associated with disease of the liver.

infectious o. Infectious keratitis.

lenta, o. Iridocyclitis recidivans purulenta.

migratoria, o. Sympathetic ophthalmia attributed to bacterial transmission via channels in the intervaginal spaces of the optic nerves and the chiasm.

military o. Trachoma.

neonatorum, o. Gonococcal conjunctivitis in the newborn.

neuroparalytic o. Neuroparalytic keratitis.

nivialis, o. Snow blindness.

nodosa, o. Nodular conjunctivitis.

phlyctenular o. Phlyctenular conjunctivitis.

purulent o. Purulent conjunctivitis.

pustular o. Phlyctenular conjunctivitis in which one or more phlyctenules have purulent contents.

scrofulous o. Phlyctenular conjunctivitis.

spring o. Vernal conjunctivitis.

strumous o. Phlyctenular conjunctivitis.

sympathetic o. Sympathetic ophthalmitis.

tarsi, o. Seborrheic meibomianitis.

varicose o. Conjunctivitis associated with varicosity of the conjunctival veins.

war o. Trachoma.

ophthalmiac (of-thal'me-ak). One affected with ophthalmia.

ophthalmiater (of-thal'me-a"ter, of-thal"me-a'ter). An ophthalmologist or an oculist. *Obs.*

ophthalmiatrics (of-thal"me-at'riks). Ophthalmology, especially with emphasis on medical treatment as distinct from the science itself. *Obs.*

ophthalmiatrist (of"thal-mi'ah-trist). One engaged in the medical treatment of the eye and its appendages. *Obs.* Syn., *ophthalmologist.*

ophthalmic (of-thal'mik). Pertaining to the eye or to related functions, services, or materials.

ophthalmic artery; ganglion; lens; nerve; optics; vein. See under the nouns.

ophthalmics (of-thal'miks). The science related to the testing, measurement, and treatment of the eye and its functions, especially in the nonmedical aspects.

ophthalmitic (of-thal-mit'ik). Pertaining to ophthalmitis.

ophthalmitis (of"thal-mi'tis). Inflammation of the eye.

sympathetic o. A bilateral inflammation of the uveal tracts following a uniocular perforating wound involving uveal tissue or the retention of a foreign body in an eyeball. The inflammation appears first in the injured eye (exciting eye) and follows in the other eye (sympathizing eye). It usually commences with an iridocyclitis and follows a progressive chronic course until all vision is lost, unless the exciting eye is enucleated. Syn., *sympathetic ophthalmia.*

ophthalmo- (of-thal'mo). A combining form denoting the *eye*.

ophthalmoblennorrhea (of-thal"mo-blen-o-re'ah). Purulent conjunctivitis.

ophthalmobrachytes (of-thal"mo-brah-kit'ēz). A myopic eye. *Obs.*

ophthalmocace (of"thal-mok'ah-se). Disease of the eye. *Obs.*

ophthalmocarcinoma (of-thal"mo-kar-sih-no'mah). Carcinoma of the eye.

ophthalmocele (of-thal'mo-sēl). Exophthalmos.

ophthalmocentesis (of-thal"mo-sen-te'sis). Surgical puncture of the eyeball.

ophthalmochromoscopy (of-thal"-mo-kro-mos'ko-pe). Ophthalmoscopy utilizing colored light.

ophthalmocopia (of-thal"mo-ko'pe-ah). Asthenopia.

ophthalmodiagnosis (of-thal"mo-di"-ag-no'sis). Diagnosis of an infectious disease, such as tuberculosis, by means of the sensitivity reaction of the conjunctiva to the instillation of a drop of a weak solution or suspension of the bacterial products, such as tuberculin.

ophthalmodiaphanoscope (of-thal"-mo-di"ah-fan'o-skōp). An instrument for viewing the interior of the eye by means of transillumination.

ophthalmodiaphanoscopy (of-thal"-mo-di"ah-fan-os'ko-pe). Examination of the interior of the eye by transillumination.

ophthalmodiastimeter (of-thal″mo-di″as-tim′eh-ter). An instrument for determining the separation of the lines of sight where they intersect the spectacle plane.

ophthalmodonesis (of-thal″mo-do-ne′sis). A trembling motion of the eye.

ophthalmodynamometer (of-thal″-mo-di″nah-mom′eh-ter). 1. An instrument for measuring blood pressure of the retinal vessels by determining the pressure necessary to collapse them. 2. An instrument devised by Landolt for determining the near point of convergence, consisting of a hollow cylinder containing a lamp and a tape marked in centimeters and in meter angles. A vertical, illuminated slit in the cylinder is moved toward the eyes until it appears double.

ophthalmodynamometry (of-thal″-mo-di″nah-mom′eh-tre). 1. Measurement of the blood pressure of the retinal vessels with the ophthalmodynamometer. 2. Determination of the near point of convergence with the ophthalmodynamometer.

ophthalmodynia (of-thal″mo-din′e-ah). Pain in the eye.

ophthalmo-eikonometer (of-thal″-mo-i-ko-nom′eh-ter). An instrument for measuring aniseikonia, the refractive error by stigmatoscopy, and the phoria.

ophthalmofluorescence (of-thal″mo-floo″o-res′ens). Fluorescence of tissues of the eye or its adnexa that have been stained with fluorescein or similarly acting solutions.

ophthalmofundoscope (of-thal″mo-fun′do-skōp). An apparatus for examining the fundus oculi under magnification; an ophthalmoscope.

Ophthalmograph (of-thal′mo-graf). An instrument which records eye movements during reading by photographing, on a moving strip of film, light reflected from the corneae.

ophthalmography (of″thal-mog′rah-fe). 1. Description of the anatomy of the eye. 2. Photography of eye movements with the Ophthalmograph.

ophthalmo-iconometer (of-thal″mo-i-ko-nom′eh-ter). Ophthalmo-eikonometer.

ophthalmokopia (of-thal″mo-ko′pe-ah). Asthenopia.

ophthalmoleukoscope (of-thal″mo-lu′ko-skōp). A color perception testing instrument in which the color intensities are controlled by polarizing filters to produce a white mixture.

ophthalmolith (of-thal′mo-lith″). A calculus of the lacrimal duct.

ophthalmologist (of″thal-mol′o-gist). A medical practitioner who is versed in and specializes in ophthalmology.

ophthalmology (of″thal-mol′o-je). 1. The profession or the professional services and applied science concerned with the medical and surgical care of the eye and its appendages. 2. The science which treats of the structure, the functions, and the disease of the eye and its appendages.

ophthalmoluminescence (of-thal″-mo-lu″mih-nes′ens). Luminescence of the tissues of the eye or its adnexa.

    primary o. The luminescence of tissues of the eye or its adnexa resulting from illumination with ultraviolet light, without the use of fluorescein or similarly acting solutions.

    secondary o. The luminescence of tissues of the eye or its adnexa that have been stained with fluorescein or a similarly acting solution.

ophthalmolyma (of-thal″mo-li′mah). Destruction of the eye.

ophthalmomacrosis (of-thal″mo-mah-kro′sis). Enlargement of the eyeball; buphthalmos. *Obs.*

ophthalmomalacia (of-thal″mo-mah-la′she-ah, -se-ah). Abnormally low intraocular pressure of the eye; hypotension.

ophthalmomanometer (of-thal″mo-mah-nom′eh-ter). An instrument for determining intraocular pressure, consisting essentially of a glass tube partially filled with colored water having a rubber diaphragm at one end and a branched rubber tube at the other. One branch is attached to a mercurial manometer and the other to a rubber bulb. The instrument is placed with its diaphragm against a plane surface and the level of the colored water is noted, then against the eye, and the rubber bulb is employed to supply air pressure to return the colored water to its original level. The pressure in millimeters of mercury is then read directly from the manometer.

ophthalmomelanoma (of-thal″mo-mel″ah-no′mah). A melanoma of the eye.

ophthalmomelanosis (of-thal″mo-mel″ah-no′sis). 1. Abnormal pigmentation of the eye by melanin. 2. The formation of an ophthalmomelanoma.

ophthalmometer (of″thal-mom′eh-ter). An instrument for measuring the anterior curvatures of the cornea, consisting of a luminous pattern of mires whose images, produced by reflection on the cornea, are viewed through a telescope with which is combined a doubling and image size measuring system. Syn., *keratometer*.

ophthalmometroscope (of-thal″mo-met′ro-skōp). An ophthalmoscope adapted or designed to determine the refraction of the eye.

ophthalmometry (of″thal-mom′eh-tre). The measurement of the curvature of the anterior surface of the cornea with the ophthalmometer. Syn., *keratometry*.

reflection point o. A method used in peripheral ophthalmometry enabling the region of the cornea being measured to be located in reference to its distance from the corneal intersection of the line of sight. A precalculated table indicates this location for a given radius of curvature of the cornea and for a given rotation of the line of sight from the optical axis of the instrument.

ophthalmomycosis (of-thal″mo-mi-ko′sis). Any fungus disease of the eye or its appendages.

ophthalmomyiasis (of-thal″mo-mi′-yah-sis, -mi-i′ah-sis). Invasion of the eye by the larvae of flies.

anterior o. Internal ophthalmomyiasis affecting the anterior chamber of the eye.

external o. Ophthalmomyiasis affecting the conjunctiva.

internal o. Ophthalmomyiasis affecting the interior of the eye.

posterior o. Internal ophthalmomyiasis affecting the posterior chamber of the eye.

ophthalmomyitis (of-thal″mo-mi-i′-tis). Inflammation of the extraocular muscles. Syn., *ophthalmomyositis*.

ophthalmomyositis (of-thal″mo-mi″-o-si′tis). Ophthalmomyitis.

ophthalmomyotomy (of-thal″mo-mi-ot′o-me). Myotomy of the extraocular muscles.

ophthalmoncus (of″thal-mon′kus). A tumor involving the eye. *Obs.*

ophthalmoneuritis (of-thal″mo-nu-ri′tis). Inflammation of the ophthalmic nerve.

ophthalmoneuromyelitis (of-thal″-mo-nu″ro-mi-el-i′tis). Neuromyelitis optica.

ophthalmonosology (of-thal″mo-no-sol′o-je). The science which treats of, or classifies, diseases of the eye.

ophthalmopathy (of″thal-mop′ah-the). Any disease of the eye.

external o. Any disease of the conjunctiva, the cornea, or the adnexa of the eye.

internal o. Any disease of the retina, the crystalline lens, or other internal structure of the eye.

ophthalmophacometer (of-thal"mo-fa-kom'eh-ter). A modification of the ophthalmometer, using the principle of the Purkinje images, for determining the curvatures and positions of the surfaces of the crystalline lens and the cornea.

ophthalmophacometry (of-thal"mo-fa-kom'eh-tre). The determination of the curvatures and positions of the surfaces of the crystalline lens and the cornea with the ophthalmophacometer.

ophthalmophantom (of-thal"mo-fan'tom). A model of the eye used for demonstration or for practicing surgery.

ophthalmophasmatoscopy (of-thal"-mo-fas"mah-tos'ko-pe). Ophthalmospectroscopy.

ophthalmophlebotomy (of-thal"mo-fle-bot'o-me). Surgical opening of a conjunctival vein to relieve congestion.

ophthalmophore (of-thal"mo-fōr'). Ophthalmotrope.

ophthalmophthisis (of"thal-mof'-thih-sis). 1. Phthisis bulbi. 2. Ophthalmomalacia.

ophthalmophyma (of-thal"mo-fi'-mah). A tumor of the eyeball. *Obs.*

ophthalmoplasty (of-thal'mo-plas"te). Reparative or plastic surgery of the eye or of its appendages.

ophthalmoplegia (of-thal"mo-ple'je-ah). Paralysis of one or more ocular muscles.

exophthalmic o. 1. Limitation of movement of the eyes occurring in exophthalmos. 2. Malignant exophthalmos.

external o. Paralysis of the extra-ocular muscles.

external o., hereditary. A hereditary and familial progressive external ophthalmoplegia, generally accompanied by ptosis, which usually develops in early life or is present at birth. Originally considered to be the result of degeneration of the nuclei of the nerves supplying the extra-ocular muscles, it is now thought to be a muscular dystrophy. Syn., *von Graefe's ophthalmoplegia; progressive nuclear opthalmoplegia.*

Féréol-Graux o. Féréol-Graux ocular palsy.

von Graefe's o. External hereditary ophthalmoplegia.

internal o. Paralysis of the intrinsic muscles of the eye, i.e., the dilator pupillae, the sphincter pupillae, and the ciliary muscles.

internuclear o., anterior. Paralysis of an internal rectus muscle for lateral conjugate movements, considered to be due to a lesion in contralateral ascending fibers of the medial longitudinal fasciculus. The external rectus muscle on the side of the lesion functions normally, and both internal rectus muscles contract normally in convergence. Syn., *Lhermitte's ophthalmoplegia; anterior internuclear palsy.*

internuclear o., posterior. Paralysis of an external rectus muscle for lateral conjugate movements, considered to be due to a lesion in homolateral descending fibers of the medial longitudinal fasciculus. Both internal rectus muscles function normally in convergence and in lateral conjugate movements. Syn., *posterior internuclear palsy.*

Lhermitte's o. Anterior internuclear ophthalmoplegia.

nuclear o. Ophthalmoplegia due to lesions in the nuclei of the motor nerves of the eye.

nuclear o., progressive. External hereditary ophthalmoplegia.

partial o. Ophthalmoplegia in which only some of the muscles are affected.

progressive congenital o. Progressive nuclear ophthalmoplegia present at birth.

Sauvineau's o. Ophthalmoplegia in which there is paralysis of the internal rectus muscle of one eye and spasm of the external rectus muscle of the other.

supranuclear o. Ophthalmoplegia due to lesions in the upper brain stem above the nuclei of the motor nerves of the eye.

total o. Ophthalmoplegia affecting all the muscles of the eye and resulting in immobility of the eyes, ptosis, immobility of the pupil, and paralysis of accommodation.

ophthalmoplegic (of-thal″mo-ple′-jik). Pertaining to paralysis of the ocular muscles (ophthalmoplegia).

ophthalmoplethysmography (of-thal″mo-pleth″iz-mog′rah-fe). Measurement of changes in the blood volume of the eye.

ophthalmoptosis (of-thal″mop-to′sis). Exophthalmos.

ophthalmo-reaction. See *reaction, ophthalmic.*

ophthalmorrhagia (of-thal″mo-ra′-je-ah). Hemorrhage of the eye.

ophthalmorrhea (of-thal″mo-re′ah). A discharge from the eye.

externa, o. A discharge from the eyelid.

interna, o. A discharge from the eyeball.

ophthalmorrhexis (of-thal″mo-rek′-sis). Rupture of the eyeball.

ophthalmos (of-thal′mos). The eye.

ophthalmoscope (of-thal′mo-skōp). An instrument for viewing the fundus and the interior of the eye, consisting essentially of: (1) a mirror, a prism, or other optical system used in conjunction with a light source for illuminating the interior; (2) a viewing aperture or optical system. More modern instruments have built-in illumination sources and auxiliary lens batteries for compensating for errors of refraction of the observer and patient, or for viewing anterior portions of the eye.

binocular o. A large, table model ophthalmoscope featuring a binocular viewing system permitting magnified, erect, stereoscopic observations of fundus structures. The optical paths of the two viewing systems and the optical path of the illuminating system penetrate the pupil in separate areas to prevent interference from corneal reflections. Syn., *stereoophthalmoscope.*

hand o. A simple ophthalmoscope which may be held in the observer's hand, usually consisting of a mirror or a reflecting prism to control the illumination and a peephole as the viewing system, though modern ones have attached sets of small lenses which may be revolved in front of the peephole, and built-in illumination systems in the handle and the body of the instrument.

luminous o. An ophthalmoscope with a built-in light source.

May o. A hand ophthalmoscope using a May prism.

nonluminous o. An ophthalmoscope which reflects light from a separate, external source.

polarizing o. An ophthalmoscope in which the light in the illuminating system and the light in the viewing system are made to pass through oppositely oriented polarizing media, thus eliminating the reflexes from the specular surfaces of the ocular media.

reflecting o. An ophthalmoscope which does not contain its own light source, reflecting light from an external source into the eye.

ophthalmoscopic (of-thal″mo-skop′-ik). Pertaining to or with the ophthalmoscope.

ophthalmoscopist (of″thal-mos′ko-pist). One who does ophthalmoscopy.

ophthalmoscopy (of″thal-mos′ko-pe). The examination of the interior of the eye with the ophthalmo-scope.

direct o. Direct ophthalmoscopic observation, at close range, of the virtual, upright, fundus image formed by the patient's eye in combination with whatever lenses are needed to correct for the refractive errors of the observer and patient; the technique normally employed with the hand ophthalmoscope.

indirect o. Ophthalmoscopic observation, usually at approximately arm's length, of the real, inverted, anteriorly located aerial image of the fundus as formed by the patient's eye itself in combination with whatever auxiliary lenses are needed to make the combination highly myopic, and ordinarily with the aid of a lens serving as a viewing eyepiece near the observer's eye. The conventional hand ophthalmoscope can be employed in this manner, and most table model ophthalmoscopes are designed on the principle of indirect ophthalmoscopy.

metric o. Ophthalmoscopy done as as a means of determining the refractive error.

red-free o. Ophthalmoscopic observation through a blue-green filter, rendering the nerve fiber structure more discernible, and blood vessels and hemorrhages more sharply outlined.

red light o. Ophthalmoscopic observation through a red filter, giving sharper contrast to the pigmentation and less contrast to blood vessels and hemorrhages.

telescopic o. Ophthalmoscopy employing a telescopic viewing system for virtual and erect magnification.

yellow-green light o. Ophthalmoscopic observation through a yellow-green filter rendering maximum definition and contrast to blood vessels and hemorrhages.

Retinal nerve fibers are discernible, but not as clearly defined as in red-free ophthalmoscopy.

ophthalmospasm (of-thal'mo-spazm). A spasm of an ocular muscle.

ophthalmospectroscopy (of-thal"mo-spek-tros'ko-pe). The ophthalmoscopic and spectroscopic examination of the interior of the eye. Syn., *ophthalmophasmatoscopy.*

ophthalmospintherism (of-thal"mo-spin'ther-izm). The visual sensation of luminous sparks without corresponding physical stimuli.

ophthalmostatometer (of-thal"mo-stah-tom'eh-ter). An exophthalmometer.

ophthalmostatometry (of-thal"mo-stah-tom'eh-tre). Exophthalmometry.

ophthalmosteresis (of-thal"mo-ste-re'sis). Absence or loss of one or both eyes. *Obs.*

ophthalmosynchysis (of-thal"mo-sin'kih-sis). 1. Effusion into the interior of the eye. *Obs.* 2. Mixing of the humors of the eye. *Obs.*

ophthalmothermometer (of-thal"-mo-ther-mom'eh-ter). An instrument for determining the local temperature of the eye.

ophthalmotomy (of"thal-mot'o-me). Incision, dissection, or enucleation of the eye. *Obs.*

ophthalmotonometer (of-thal"mo-to-nom'eh-ter). An instrument for determining ocular tension; a tonometer.

ophthalmotonometry (of-thal"mo-to-nom'eh-tre). Determination of ocular tension with the ophthalmotonometer.

ophthalmotrope (of-thal'mo-trōp). An apparatus for demonstrating the individual actions of the extraocular muscles, consisting essentially of a model eyeball to which are attached strings and pulleys to duplicate the lines of force of the muscles. Syn., *ophthalmophore.*

ophthalmotropia (of-thal″mo-tro′pe-ah). Strabismus.

ophthalmotropometer (of-thal″mo-tro-pom′eh-ter). Strabismometer.

ophthalmotropometry (of-thal″mo-tro-pom′eh-tre). Strabismometry.

ophthalmovascular (of-thal″mo-vas′-ku-lar). Pertaining to or of the blood vessels of the eye.

ophthalmoxerosis (of-thal″mo-ze-ro′-sis). Xerosis of the conjunctiva.

ophthalmula (of-thal′mu-lah). A scar of the eyeball.

ophthalmus (of-thal′mus). The eye.

ophthalmyalos (of″thal-mi′ah-los). Vitreous humor. *Obs.*

ophthalmyalus (of″thal-mi′ah-lus). Vitreous humor. *Obs.*

ophthoscope (of′tho-skōp). A device for determining sighting ocular dominance. It consists essentially of a double-faced mirror covered on each side with cardboard, with tubes inserted into a hole in the cardboard on each side of the mirror. The subject is asked to look into one of the tubes and to look for an eye. The eye used is considered to be the sighting dominant eye.

-opia (o′pe-ah). A combining form denoting *eye*, especially in relation to a condition or defect.

-opy (o′pe). A combining form denoting *eye*, especially in relation to a condition or defect.

opifex circumductionis (o′pe-fex ser″kum-duk′she-on-is). Superior oblique muscle. *Obs.*

opisthosynechia (o-pis″tho-sih-nek′-e-ah, -sih-ne′ke-ah). Posterior synechia. *Obs.*

Oppenheim's (op′en-hīmz) **reflex; test.** See under the nouns.

-ops. A combining form denoting the *eye.*

-opsia (op′se-ah). A combining form denoting *vision.*

opsin (op′sin). A protein formed, together with retinene, by the chemical breakdown of meta-rhodopsin

opsiometer (op″se-om′eh-ter). Optometer.

opsionosis (op″se-o-no′sis, -on′o-sis). Defective vision.

-opsis (op′sis). A combining form denoting *vision.*

opsoclonus (op-so-klo′nus). Irregular, nonrhythmic, rapid, noncontrollable conjugate movements of the eyes, in horizontal and vertical directions, as may occur as a sequel to nonepidemic encephalitis.

-opsy (op′se). A combining form denoting *vision.*

Opt. D. Abbreviation for *Doctor of Optometry. Obs.*

optepaphist (op-tep′ah-fist). One who is skilled in and practices optepaphy.

optepaphy (op-tep′ah-fe). The prescribing and adapting of corneal lenses to the human eye.

optesthesia (op″tes-the′ze-ah). Visual sensibility; the capacity to perceive visual stimuli.

optic (op′tik). Pertaining to or of vision, or the eye.

optic angle; atrophy; axis; bundle; canal; cap; capsule; center; chiasm; commissure; constants; cup; disk; foramen; ganglion; groove; lobes; nerve; neuritis; papilla; pedicle; peduncle; pits; plate; radiations; stalk; thalamus; tracts; ventricle; vesicle. See under the nouns.

optic pseudo-atrophy of the newborn. Papilla grisea.

optical (op′tih-kal). Pertaining to or of the science of optics, vision, the eye, or lenses.

optical activity; aphasia; axis; center; circle; constringence; contact; cross; density; diameter; glass; illusion; index; invariant; length; medium; path; rotation; surface; system; wedge; zone; zone of cornea. See under the nouns.

Optical Information Council. A public information disseminating agency sponsored by the optical industry of England.

Optical Society of America. An organization formed in 1916 to increase and diffuse the knowledge of optics in all its branches, pure and applied, to promote the mutual interest of investigators of optical problems, of designers, manufacturers, and users of optical instruments and apparatus of all kinds, and to encourage cooperation among them.

optically (op'tih-kal-le). With reference to optics; by optics or sight; by optical means.

optician (op-tish'an). 1. One whose vocation involves the design or manufacture of ophthalmic appliances or optical instruments or one who compounds and adapts ophthalmic prescriptions. 2. A dispensing optician. 3. An ophthalmic optician.

dispensing o. One who fits and adapts eyewear to the wearer, especially on prescription of the ophthalmologist or optometrist. Syn., *ophthalmic dispenser.*

laboratory o. Prescription optician.

manufacturing o. One employed in the manufacture of optical instruments or eyewear.

ophthalmic o. British designation, or equivalent, for *optometrist.*

prescription o. One employed in the fabrication or assembly of spectacles to prescription.

refracting o. Ophthalmic optician.

wholesale o. One engaged in the sale of optical supplies and products in varying quantities to ophthalmic dispensers, ophthalmologists, optical retailers, and optometrists.

opticianry (op-tish'an-re). The work of the optician as a vocation.

opticist (op'tih-sist). A person skilled in the science of optics.

opticochiasmic (op''tih-ko-ki-as'mik). Pertaining to or of both the optic nerve and the optic chiasm.

opticociliary (op''tih-ko-sil'e-ar''e). Pertaining to or of both the optic nerve and the ciliary nerves.

opticocinerea (op''tih-ko-sin-e're-ah). The gray matter of the optic tract.

opticomalacia (op''tih-ko-mah-la'she-ah). A degeneration of tissue in the optic nerve usually due to lack of normal circulation.

opticopupillary (op''tih-ko-pu'pih-lār''e). Pertaining to or of both the optic nerve and the pupil.

optics (op'tiks). 1. The science which treats of light, its nature, properties, origin, propagation, effects, and perception. 2. The elements and/or design of an optical system.

biological o. The branch of optics which deals with the effect of radiant energy on tissues, especially ocular tissues.

environmental o. The branch of optics concerned with environmental factors relating to vision and visually facilitated performance, especially as applied to groups and populations categorized by occupation or other behavioral identity.

fiber o. The branch of optics which deals with the conduction of light along a transparent dielectric cylinder such as a fiber of glass.

geometrical o. The branch of optics which deals with the geometric analysis of the paths of light in refraction and reflection.

mechanical o. Ophthalmic optics.

ophthalmic o. The branch of optics involving the design, manufacture, fabrication, assembly, and dispensing of spectacles.

physical o. The branch of optics which deals with the fundamental physical properties of light, especially in relation to its origin, propagation, spectrum, diffraction, interference, polarization, and velocity.

physiological o. The branch of optics concerned with visual perception; the science of vision.

psychological o. The branch of optics concerned with visual sensation and perception as psychological processes.

quantum o. The branch of optics which deals with the quantum theory of light emission.

opticus (op'tih-kus). Optic nerve.

optimeter (op-tim'eh-ter). Optometer.

optist (op'tist). Optometrist. *Obs.* A title proposed by Prentice before adoption of the title optometrist.

opto- (op'to). A combining form denoting *vision* or the *eye.*

optoblast (op'to-blast). A large ganglion cell in the ganglionic cell layer of the retina.

optogram (op'to-gram). The picture on the retina of a retinal image due to the bleaching of rhodopsin.

optokinetoscope (op"to-kih-net'o-skōp). An instrument to induce optokinetic nystagmus, consisting essentially of a revolving drum with alternate black and white vertical stripes parallel to the axis of rotation.

optomeninx (op"to-me'ninks). Retina.

optometer (op-tom'eh-ter). Any of several objective or subjective devices for measuring the refractive state of the eye. Syn., *opsiometer; optimeter; refractometer.*

Badal's o. A simple optometer mounted so that the focal point of the converging lens or lens system coincides with a variously specified point of reference of the eye, such as its anterior focal point, the entrance pupil, or the nodal point, for which a known fixed relationship between object and image size can be computed, and with reference to which point the dioptric stimulus to accommodation can be represented on a linear scale marking the distance from the test chart to the lens.

Cardell o. A subjective optometer containing miniature test types and astigmatic test charts scaled

to correspond to standard test distances.

coincidence o. of Fincham. An objective optometer which forms the image of a fine line target on the subject's retina to be viewed by the examiner through a telescope with an optical doubling and displacing system so that the resulting two half lines are out of alignment, and blurred, in relation to the ametropia. The adjustment of the dioptric stimulus value of the fine line target necessary to obtain sharpness and alignment of the two half lines gives a measure of the ametropia.

Donders' wire o. A small rectangular frame across which are stretched several fine black vertical wires, to be viewed against a white background and brought toward the eye to determine the nearest point of distinct vision. A small handle and measuring tape are attached. Syn., *hair optometer.*

hair o. Donders' wire optometer.

objective o. An optometer containing an optical system for determining the vergence of light reflected from the subject's retina.

prism o. Prisoptometer.

Schmidt-Rimpler o. An instrument consisting of a convex lens (+10.00 D.) mounted on a sliding carrier near the distal end of a graduated rod, the proximal end of which rests on the inferior orbital rim of the subject, and with a spring-wound measuring tape mounted on the sliding carrier and attached to a concave mirror ophthalmoscope which reflects the light from an externally located luminous grid through the convex lens into the the examinee's eye. When the examinee's retinal image of the luminous grid is seen distinctly by the examiner, the refraction may be computed from the positions of the convex lens and the mirror image of the luminous grid.

simple o. The combination of a simple plus lens and an independently movable test target for varying the dioptric stimulus and measuring the refractive state of the eye subjectively.

subjective o. An optometer employing the criterion of blurredness or sharpness of a test target.

Young's o. A simple optometer incorporating Scheiner's double pupillary aperture and a thread extended along the line of sight. The thread is seen double, crossing at the point for which the eye is focused.

Optometric Extension Program. An agency established in 1928 with offices in Duncan, Oklahoma, offering postgraduate educational material and programs to optometrists by subscription.

optometrist (op-tom′eh-trist). One who practices optometry.

optometry (op-tom′eh-tre). 1. The profession or the professional services and applied science concerned with vision and nonmedical visual care. 2. The use of an optometer.

optomyometer (op″to-mi-om′eh-ter). An instrument for measuring phorias or fusional convergence consisting essentially of 2 tubes, 20 in. long, one of which can be moved horizontally and the other vertically, and through which targets at the distal ends are viewed.

optophone (op′to-fōn). An instrument which converts light waves into sound waves, enabling the blind to discern between light and dark.

optophore (op′to-fōr). An instrument for the stimulation of an amblyopic eye, consisting essentially of a horizontal viewing tube, pivoted on a vertical axis, fitted at its distal end with a slide carrier containing two highly colored, illuminated, transparent targets which may be rotated in

opposite directions, producing a kaleidoscopic effect.

optostriate (op-to-stri′āt). Pertaining to the optic thalamus and the corpus striatum or, when these two structures are considered as one, the optostriate body.

optotype (op′to-tīp). Test type used for determining visual acuity. Snellen's original name for his test type.

ora serrata (o′rah seh-ra′tah). The serrated anterior border of the retina located approximately 8.5 mm. from the limbus and adjacent to the pars plana of the ciliary body. It is one of the sites of attachment of the retina to the choroid, the other being around the optic disk.

orange. A hue simulating that of an orange, corresponding to the spectral wavelength of approximately 600 mμ, and having the qualitative aspect of a red and yellow additive mixture.

transient o. An intermediate product of the decomposition of rhodopsin when exposed to light; an unstable carotenoid pigment which is transformed rapidly to xanthopsin and then to retinene.

orbicularis oculi (or″bik-u-la′ris ok′-u-li). See under *muscle.*

orbiculus ciliaris (or-bik′u-lus sil″e-ar′is). Pars plana.

orbit (or′bit). One of the two cavities in the skull which contains an eyeball, orbital fat, extraocular muscles, the optic nerve, etc. It is formed by parts of 7 bones: the maxillary, the palatine, the frontal, the sphenoid, the ethmoid, the lacrimal, and the zygomatic, and is shaped roughly like a quadrilateral pyramid.

orbita (or′bih-tah). The orbit.

orbital (or′bih-tal). Pertaining to or of the orbit.

orbital abscess; cellulitis; decompression; fascia; fat; fold; index; margin; periosteum; per-

iostitis; phlegmon; septum; tubercle. See under the nouns.

orbitale (or″bih-tah′le, -ta′le). The lowest point on the inferior margin of the orbit.

orbitonometer (or″bih-to-nom′eh-ter). An instrument for measurement of the compressibility of the orbital contents into the orbit.

orbitonometry (or″bih-to-nom′eh-tre). Measurement of the compressibility of the orbital contents into the orbit.

orbitopneumography (or″bih-to-nu-mog′rah-fe). X-ray photography of the orbit subsequent to the retrobulbar injection of air.

orbitopneumotomography (or″bih-to-nu″mo-to-mog′rah-fe). Sectional x-ray photography of the orbit subsequent to the retrobulbar injection of air.

orbitotomy (or″bih-tot′o-me). Surgical incision into the orbit.

ordinate (or′dih-nāt). 1. Any one of the scales of reference in a graphical system. 2. The vertical or y axis of reference in a graph of rectilinear co-ordinates. See also *abscissa*.

organs, accessory of the eye. The appendages or adnexa of the eye, consisting of the *lacrimal apparatus*, the *conjunctiva*, the *cilia*, the *supercilia*, the *eyelids*, the *extraocular muscles*, and *Tenon's capsule*.

organs of Hesse. Large photosensitive ganglion cells in the ventral and lateral portions of the posterior end of the nerve cord in *Amphioxus*, giving it directional ability. Each cell has a ciliated margin capped by a crescentic pigment mantle and has an issuing nerve fiber.

organelle, optic (or″gan-el′). An ellipsoidal, transparent hyalinelike structure in the photosensitive cells of worms and molluscs which is surrounded by a dense neurofibrillar network (retinella). Light striking this structure from any direction is brought to a focus on the retinella and initiates impulses to its nerve fiber.

organization, perceptual. The sensory attribution of one or another pattern of organization to a complex field, possibly in the interest of meaningfulness or economy of comprehension or retention, as in perceiving the digits 3825 as 38 and 25.

organon visus (or′gan-on vi′sus). The organ of vision; the eye.

orthochromatic (or″tho-kro-mat′ik). Pertaining to or of the reproduction of natural color, as in color photography.

Orthofusor (or″tho-fu′sor). An orthoptic training device consisting of a series of vectographic stereo pictures representing varying degrees of stimulus to convergence and divergence when viewed binocularly through a pair of Polaroid filters oppositely oriented in front of the two eyes.

Orthogon (or′tho-gon). A trade name for a series of corrected curve spectacle lenses.

orthokinesis (or″tho-kih-ne′sis). Acceleratory or deceleratory random movements of a motile organism in response to changes in the intensity of light stimulation but not in response to the direction of the light stimulation.

Ortholite (or′tho-līt). A trade name for an incandescent lamp, with a dark purple filter attachment, used in conjunction with fluorescein dye in the fitting of contact lenses and for the detection of corneal abrasions, or ulcers.

orthometer (or-thom′eh-ter). Exophthalmometer.

orthophoria (or″tho-fo′re-ah). The condition in which the lines of sight, in the absence of an adequate fusion stimulus, intersect at a given point of reference, this point of reference usually being the point of binocular fixation prior to the phoria test, or, more arbitrarily, at an infinite distance; the absence of heterophoria.

asthenic o. The condition of orthophoria in combination with low relative convergence reserves.

basic o. Orthophoria obtained with the test object at infinity and the eyes actually or artificially emmetropic, hence with accommodation relaxed.

relative o. Orthophoria with reference to a given fixation distance, said to be present when dissociation produces no deviation of convergence from that otherwise demanded for the fixation distance.

sthenic o. The condition of orthophoria in combination with normal relative convergence reserves.

orthophoric (or″tho-fōr′ik). Manifesting, or one who manifests, orthophoria.

orthophorization (or″tho-fo″rih-za′-shun). A process presumed to be operative in producing a greater frequency of occurrence of orthophoria, or only small amounts of heterophoria, than would be expected in terms of chance distribution, as may be explained by postulating a control of binocular co-ordination by higher visual centers.

orthopsia (or-thop′se-ah). The condition of having normal vision.

orthoptic (or-thop′tik). Pertaining to orthoptics, its procedures and instruments.

orthoptics (or-thop′tiks). 1. The teaching and training process for the improvement of visual perception and co-ordination of the two eyes for efficient and comfortable binocular vision. Syn., *visual training*. 2. The teaching and training process for the elimination of strabismus.

chrome o. Orthoptics based on the use and application of colored filters, usually with implications

of therapeutic value in the colors themselves.

orthoptist (or-thop′tist). One who practices, directs, or supervises orthoptic services.

orthoptoscope (or-thop′to-skōp). A type of amblyoscope.

Ortho-Rater (or″tho-ra′ter). A Brewster-type stereoscopic instrument for visual screening, with targets for measuring visual acuity, phorias, stereopsis, and color perception.

orthoscope (or′tho-skōp). 1. A device which neutralizes the refracting power of the cornea by means of a layer of water in a small glass container held in contact with the eye. 2. A Brewster-type stereoscope having an adjustment for interpupillary distance and a lens system designed to reduce aberrations. It is used primarily for visual screening and for testing aniseikonia.

orthoscopic (or-tho-skop′ik). 1. Affording a correct and undistorted view. 2. Pertaining to an orthoscope, orthoscopy, or an orthoscopic lens or optical system. 3. Pertaining to an optical system which produces an image free of distortion or aberration. 4. Pertaining to the condition of normal vision.

orthoscopy (or-thos′ko-pe). 1. Examination of the eye with an orthoscope. 2. That condition of an optical system which produces an image free of distortion or aberration.

orthostatic (or″tho-stat′ik). Pertaining to the condition of orthostasis.

orthostasis (or″tho-sta′sis). A term used by Lancaster to designate the static position of the covered eye, during a cover test, when orthophoria is present.

orthostereogram (or″tho-ster′e-o-gram″). A stereogram which fulfills the condition of orthostereoscopy.

orthostereoscopy (or"tho-ster"e-os'-ko-pe). The viewing of a stereopsis-inducing pattern so as to perceive the original scene in true dimensional proportions, both as to size and distance, the retinal images being identical to those from viewing the actual scene. This relief is produced when the focal length of the stereocamera is the same as that of the stereoscope, and the separation of the stereocamera lenses is the same as the viewer's interpupillary distance. Cf. *heterostereoscopy.*

Orthotrainer (or"tho-trān'er). A Brewster-type, stereoscopic, visual training instrument with carriers for transilluminated split targets and a rotor for providing various flash patterns. The separation of the split targets may be held constant for various viewing distances or may be varied by means of a disparator attachment.

orthotropia (or"tho-tro'pe-ah). 1. The absence of strabismus. 2. With respect to a given meridian of reference, a strabismus of zero angle of deviation, e.g., lateral orthotropia with right hypertropia.

O.S. Abbreviation for *oculus sinister;* the left eye.

O.S.A. Abbreviation for *Optical Society of America.*

os. A bone.
ethmoidale, o. Ethmoid bone.
frontale, o. Frontal bone.
lacrimale, o. Lacrimal bone.
o. opticus. A horseshoe-shaped formation of single or multiple pieces of bone in the cartilaginous cup surrounding the optic nerve head in some avian eyes. Syn., *ossicle of Gemminger.*
planum, o. The lamina papyracea of the ethmoid bone.
sphenoidale, o. Sphenoid bone.
unguis, o. Lacrimal bone.
zygomaticum, o. Zygomatic bone.

oscillopsia (os"ih-lop'se-ah). The condition in which viewed objects appear to oscillate; oscillating vision.

O'Shea's rule (o-shāz'). See under *rule.*

Osler-Vaquez disease (ōs-ler'-vak'-āz). Vaquez' disease.

ossicle of Gemminger (os'ih-kl). Os opticus.

ossicles, scleral (os'ih-klz). A ring of overlapping membranous bones which acts as a supporting structure at the centrally constricted area of the eyes of some birds and reptiles.

osteitis deformans (os"te-i'tis de-fōr'mans). Paget's disease.

osteitis fibrosa, disseminated (os"te-i'tis fi-bro'sah). Polyostotic fibrous dysplasia.

osteodystrophy, fibrous (os"te-o-dis'tro-fe). Polyostotic fibrous dysplasia.

osteogenesis imperfecta (os"te-o-jen'e-sis im-per-fek'tah). A familial disease characterized by brittle bones which fracture easily. It may be accompanied by blue sclerae and frequently by deafness. Syn., *periosteal dysplasia; fragilitas ossium; osteopsathyrosis.*

osteoma (os"te-o'mah). A slowly progressive benign neoplasm composed of osteoblastic connective tissue that forms new bone. It may occur in the choroid, sclera, or episclera, on the wall of the orbit, or it may invade the orbit from a neighboring sinus.

osteopetrosis (os"te-o-pe-tro'sis). A rare anomaly of osteogenesis, of hereditary tendency, in which the bones become dense, sclerosed, and marblelike. It frequently affects the orbit and maxillary bone, resulting in progressive proptosis of the eyeball and optic atrophy. Syn., *Albers-Schönberg disease.*

osteopsathyrosis (os"te-op-sath"ih-ro'sis, os"te-o-sath"-). Osteogenesis imperfecta.

Osterberg test; unit. See under the nouns.

ostium lacrimale (os'te-um lak-rih-mah'le). The inferior opening of the nasolacrimal duct, usually located on the lateral wall of the inferior meatus of the nose.

Ostwald (ost'valt) **colors; color circle; hue; notation; purity; semichrome; color solid; system; tints; tones; color triangle.** See under the nouns.

Ostwalt (ost'valt) **curve; lens.** See under the nouns.

Ota, nevus of. Oculocutaneous melanosis.

Otero theory (o-ther'o). See under *theory.*

O.U. Abbreviation for *oculus uterque* or *oculi uniter.*

outlets of Ascher. Collector channels.

overcorrection. 1. Ophthalmic lens power in excess of that necessary to correct or neutralize a refractive error. 2. An aberration of a lens or an optical system in which the marginal rays intersect the optical axis at a point farther from the lens than the paraxial rays. It is sometimes employed to neutralize spherical aberration in other elements of an optical system.

overlap, scleral. A surgical procedure for shortening the eyeball in the treatment of retinal detachment in which the sclera is incised and sutured so that it overlaps. It is performed in conjunction with diathermy.

overlay. Interposition.

Owen's deviometer (o'enz). See under *deviometer.*

oxford. A type of eyeglass frame without temples in which a straight or slightly curved spring joins the two lenses at the top. The frame is held on the bridge of the wearer's nose by tension of the spring. Some styles are of a folding type.

oxyblepsia (ok"se-blep'se-ah). Acute vision.

oxycephaly (ok"se-sef'ah-le). A condition in which the skull is conical in shape (tower skull), due to abnormal union of the cranial and the facial bones. The ocular signs are shallow orbits, wide separation of the eyes, divergent strabismus, exophthalmos, loss of vision, and sometimes ptosis and/or nystagmus.

oxyopia (ok"se-o'pe-ah). Acute vision.

oxyopsia (ok"se-op'se-ah). Acute vision.

oxyopter (ok"se-op'ter). A unit for measurement of visual acuity proposed by Blascovics. It is the reciprocal of the visual angle expressed in degrees.

P

P. Abbreviation for *pupil* or *papilla* (optic).

P **I.** One of the three separate potentials whose algebraic summation is considered responsible for the generation of the electroretinogram; the slow cornea positive component which, in Granit's analysis, is largely responsible for the *c* wave. See also *P II; P III.*

P **II.** One of the three separate potentials whose algebraic summation is considered responsible for the generation of the electroretinogram; the fast cornea positive component which, in Granit's analysis, is largely responsible for the *b* wave. See also *P I; P III.*

P **III.** One of the three separate potentials whose algebraic summation is considered responsible for the generation of the electroretinogram; the fast cornea negative component which, in Granit's analysis, is responsible for the initial *a* wave and at least part of the *d* wave. See also *P I; P II.*

P_o. Symbol for the intraocular pressure prevailing just prior to tonometric measurement; the starting point of tonography.

P_t. Symbol for the intraocular pressure during tonometry.

P_v. Symbol for the average pressure in the small episcleral veins or in the aqueous veins, near the limbus.

pachyblepharon (pak"e-blef'ah-ron). An abnormally thick eyelid. Syn., *pachytes.*

pachyblepharosis (pak"e-blef"ah-ro'-sis). Abnormal thickening of an eyelid.

pachymeningitis (pak"e-men"in-ji'-tis). Inflammation of the dura mater of the brain, the spinal cord, or the optic nerve. Cf. *leptomeningitis.*

pachytes (pak'ih-tēz). Pachyblepharon.

pad, annular. A broad radial outgrowth of the subcapsular epithelium in the equatorial region of the crystalline lens in some birds and reptiles; involved in the mechanism of accommodation through forces exerted by zonular fibers of the ciliary body attached to it.

pad arm. Guard arm.

pad, nose. One of the pair of attachments or protuberances of a spectacle frame or mounting designed to rest against the side of the nose. Syn., *guard.*

Paget's disease (paj'ets). See under *disease.*

pair, isomeric. Isomeric colors.

pair, metameric (pār). Metameric colors.

palisades (pal-ih-sādz'). Grayish-white, thin lines, about 1 mm. wide, that run radially from the sclera, at the limbus, to disappear in the clear cornea. Although not found in all eyes, they are frequently seen in slit lamp examination.

Palmer's theory. See under *theory.*

palpate (pal'pāt). To press the eyeball gently with the fingers to estimate ocular tension.

palpation (pal-pa'shun). The gentle pressing of the eyeball with the fingers to estimate ocular tension.

palpebra (pal'pe-brah, pal-pe'-). An eyelid.

frontalis, p. An upper eyelid.

inferior p. A lower eyelid.

malaris, p. A lower eyelid.

superior p. An upper eyelid.

tertia, p. Nictitating membrane.

palpebrae (pal-pe'bre). The eyelids.

palpebral (pal'pe-bral). Pertaining to or of an eyelid.

palpebralis (pal"pe-brah'lis). The levator palpebrae superioris muscle.

palpebrate (pal'pe-brāt). 1. To wink. 2. Possessing eyelids.

palpebration (pal"pe-bra'shun). The act of winking.

palpebritis (pal"pe-bri'tis). Blepharitis.

palsy (pawl'ze). Paralysis, especially in reference to special types. See also under *paralysis*.

abducens p. Palsy of the external rectus muscle resulting from involvement of the abducens nerve.

Bell's p. Paralysis of the upper and lower muscles of the face on one side, due to inflammation of the facial nerve within the stylomastoid foramen. The palpebral fissure is wider on the affected side and the eyelid on the affected side cannot be closed. Syn., *Bell's paralysis.*

conjugate p. The inability to move the two eyes simultaneously in the same direction, either laterally or vertically, due to involvement of cortical or subcortical oculomotor centers.

Féréol-Graux ocular p. An associated paralysis of the internal rectus muscle of one eye and the external rectus muscle of the other, affecting lateral conjugate movements. Syn., *Féréol-Graux ophthalmoplegia; Graux ocular palsy; Féréol-Graux paralysis.*

Graux ocular p. Féréol-Graux ocular palsy.

internuclear p., anterior. Anterior internuclear ophthalmoplegia.

internuclear p., posterior. Posterior internuclear ophthalmoplegia.

pseudobulbar p. Pseudobulbar paralysis.

trochlear p. Palsy of the superior oblique muscle resulting from involvement of the trochlear nerve.

panchromatization (pan"kro-mah-tih-za'shun). An evolutionary development making the original light-sensitive substance of the cones more sensitive to long waves, as postulated in the Schenck theory of color vision.

panmural fibrosis (pan-mu'ral fi-bro'sis). Hypopyon corneal ulcer.

pannus (pan'us). An abnormal, superficial vascularization of the cornea associated with a membranouslike infiltration of granulation tissue.

carnosus, p. Pannus in which the vascularization and infiltration of granulation tissue is thick, producing a dense opacity. Syn., *pannus crassus; pannus sarcomatosus; pannus vasculosis.*

crassus, p. Pannus carnosus.

degenerativus, p. Pannus occurring in blind, degenerated eyes following diseases such as iridocyclitis, glaucoma, or detachment of the retina, as a part of a general degeneration of ocular tissue.

eczematous p. Phlyctenular pannus.

glaucomatous p. A thin fibrous membrane formed between the corneal epithelium and Bowman's membrane in advanced glaucoma.

leprotic p. Pannus associated with leprotic keratitis and resembling phlyctenular pannus.

phlyctenular p. A thin and lightly vascularized pannus, extending completely around the periphery of the limbus toward phlyctens located in the cornea, commonly associated with phlyctenular keratitis. Syn., *eczematous pannus; scrofulous pannus.*

retrocorneal p. Pannus growing from the anterior surface of the iris over the posterior surface of the cornea, a rare condition which may occur as a sequela to traumatic iritis.

sarcomatosus, p. Pannus carnosus.

scrofulous p. Phlyctenular pannus.

siccus, p. Pannus whose surface appears dry and glossy.

tenuis, p. Pannus of recent origin characterized by few blood vessels and slight corneal cloudiness.

trachomatosus, p. Pannus occurring in the inflammatory stage of trachoma and characteristically extending from the superior limbus toward the central cornea.

vasculosis, p. Pannus carnosus.

panophthalmia (pan″of-thal′me-ah). Panophthalmitis.

panophthalmitis (pan″of-thal′mi-tis). Inflammation of the eyeball throughout all of its structures. Syn., *panophthalmia.*

Panoptik (pan-op′tik). See *lens, bifocal, Panoptik.*

panoramogram, parallax (pan″o-ram′u-gram). An autostereoscopic picture produced by photographing an object from continuously changing or discretely changed directions through a vertically gauged grid. It is viewed through a comparable grid, producing a parallactic movement with changes of position of the eye, or a stereoscopic effect when viewed binocularly. Prismatic furrows in the photographic emulsion may be substituted for the grid.

pantachromatic (pan″tah-kro-mat′-ik). Completely achromatic.

pantankyloblepharon (pan-tang″-kih-lo-blef′ah-ron). Complete ankyloblepharon.

Pantoscope (pan″to-skōp′). A trade name for an ophthalmoscope manufactured by Keeler Optical Products.

pantoscopic (pan″to-skop′ik). 1. Pertaining to or having a wide angle of view. 2. Pertaining to a lens which has foci for both distant and near objects; a bifocal lens. 3. Pertaining to the pantoscopic angle.

Panum's (pah′noomz) **area; phenomenon; fusional space.** See under the nouns.

papilla (pah-pil′ah). A small, nipple-shaped elevation.

Bergmeister's p. A cone-shaped mass of glial cells, at the center of the embryonic optic disk, which becomes vascularized by the hyaloid artery, its cells forming the sheaths of this vessel and its branches. Syn., *primitive epithelial papilla.*

conjunctival p. One of the finger-like extrusions of the substantia propria of the conjunctiva, the interspaces being filled with epithelium to form a flat surface; found near the limbus and the lid margin.

grisea, p. A gray optic disk seen in retarded development of the myelin sheaths of the optic nerve fibers. See also *myelinic dysgenesia.*

lacrimal p. A slight elevation, one on each eyelid margin, at the inner canthus, containing a lacrimal punctum.

leporina, p. An optic disk in which medullated nerve fibers are present at its surface and extend to the surrounding retina.

optic p. Optic disk.

primitive epithelial p. Bergmeister's papilla.

vascular choroidal papillae. Conical vascularized papillae in the fundus of fruit-bats and flying foxes which nourish the visual cells of the avascular retina covering its surface.

papillary diameter (pap′ih-ler″e). Disk diameter.

papilledema (pap″ih-le-de′mah). Noninflammatory edema of the optic nerve head, due to increased intracranial pressure, orbital tumor, blood dyscrasias, etc. As observed ophthalmoscopically, the optic disk appears raised above the level of the retina and its margins are blurred. Accompanying changes are dilatation, tortuosity, and engorgement of the retinal veins, with retinal edema most pronounced in the area of the disk. It is termed *choked disk* when due to increased intracranial pressure.

papillitis (pap″ih-li′tis). Inflammation of the optic nerve head characterized initially by partial or complete loss of vision, lowering of dark adaptation, failure to maintain pupillary contraction under bright illumination, pain in and behind the eye, headache, and nausea. Ophthalmoscopically, the optic nerve head is hyperemic, has blurred margins, and is slightly edematous. The blood vessels are dilated, hemorrhages and exudates may appear, and fine diffuse opacities are usually present in the posterior vitreous. The condition is transient in nature, usually of short duration, and recovery may be complete. Syn., *intraocular optic neuritis.*

papilloma (pap″ih-lo′mah). A benign epithelial neoplasm which may arise from the skin, mucous membranes, or glandular ducts. It may affect the canaliculus, the lacrimal sac, the eyelid, or the conjunctiva.

papillomacular (pap″ih-lo-mak′u-lar) **bundle; fibers.** See under the nouns.

papilloretinitis (pă-pil″o-ret″ih-ni′-tis). Inflammation of the optic disk and the retina. Syn., *neuro-retinitis.*

parablepsia (par″ah-blep′se-ah). False or perverted vision, such as

visual hallucination or illusion. Syn., *parablepsis; paropsia; paropsis.*

parablepsis (par″ah-blep′sis). Parablepsia.

paracentesis bulbi (par″ah-sen-te′-sis). Surgical puncture of the eyeball, usually into the anterior chamber for the drainage of aqueous humor or the removal of foreign matter.

paracentesis oculi (par″ah-sen-te′-sis). Paracentesis bulbi.

parachromatism (par″ah-kro′mah-tizm). Partial color blindness. Syn., *parachromatoblepsia; parachromatopsia.*

parachromatoblepsia (par″ah-kro″-mah-to-blep′se-ah). Parachromatism.

parachromatopsia (par″ah-kro″mah-top′se-ah). Parachromatism.

paracontrast (par″ah-con′trast). The reduction in subjective brightness of a flash of light when it is preceded by another flash in an adjacent region of the visual field. Cf., *metacontrast.*

paradox, Fechner's. A decrease in the binocularly perceived brightness of a surface occurring with the increase in luminance presented to one of the eyes from a very low intensity (as obtained by occlusion) to an intermediate intensity (as through a dark filter), while the stimulus to the other eye remains constant at a relatively high level of luminance.

parafovea (par″ah-fo′ve-ah). A band, approximately 0.5 mm. wide, immediately surrounding the fovea centralis and surrounded by the perifovea.

parafoveal (par″ah-fo′ve-al). Beside or near the fovea.

parakinesis (par″ah-kih-ne′sis, -kine′sis). Irregular action of an individual extraocular muscle.

paralexia (par″ah-lek′se-ah). A partial alexia in which words or syllables are substituted or transposed.

parallax (par′ah-laks). The apparent change in direction or lateral displacement of a viewed object when the eye is moved from one position to another, or when the object is viewed first with one eye and then with the other.

absolute p. The apparent difference in direction of an object from two points of view, either simultaneously or successively, and usually measured in angular units, e.g., the difference in direction of a star from two points on the earth.

binocular p. Parallax effected by viewing with the two eyes separately, or in succession, and in their respective positions, i.e., without head movements.

chromatic p. The differential, apparent, lateral displacement of two objects of different color when observed through a narrow vertical slit moved horizontally across the pupil of the eye.

crossed p. The perceived relative displacement of the two images of an object seen in crossed binocular diplopia, i.e., under dissociation, particularly when perceived as a sudden movement of the fixated object in alternate monocular occlusion, hence manifested for the condition of exophoria. Syn., *heteronymous parallax.*

entoptic p. Relative entoptic parallax.

heteronymous p. Crossed parallax.

homonymous p. Uncrossed parallax.

instantaneous p. The relative parallax value of one point with respect to another when the other point is fixated; hence the relative parallax of any point with respect to a given point of fixation. *Helmholtz.*

monocular p. Parallax effected by the movement or displacement of one eye.

motion p. Relative parallax resulting from the continuous motion of the observer and perceived as differences in speeds or direction of movement of objects at different distances, e.g., as may be observed in viewing the landscape from the window of a moving train.

relative p. The apparent relative displacement of one object with respect to another when seen from two points or directions, either simultaneously or successively, and usually measured in angular units representing the difference in angle subtended at the two points of view by the two objects.

    relative p., binocular. Relative parallax effected by viewing with each of the two eyes separately while they remain in their respective positions, i.e., without head movements.

    relative entoptic p. The motion of the projected image of the retinal shadow of an opacity in the ocular media, relative to the field of view, when the illuminating source is moved transversely with respect to the optical system of the eye.

    relative p., monocular. Relative parallax effected by the movement or displacement of the viewing eye.

stereoscopic p. The relative parallax effected or stimulated by a stereogram so as to induce stereopsis.

uncrossed p. The perceived relative displacement of the two images of an object seen in uncrossed binocular diplopia, i.e., under dissociation, in particular when perceived as a sudden movement of the fixated object in alternate monocular occlusion, hence manifested for the conditions of esophoria. Syn., *homonymous parallax.*

vertical p. The perceived, relative, vertical displacement of the two images of an object seen in binocular vertical diplopia, i.e., under dissociation, in particular when perceived as a sudden movement of the fixated object in alternate monocular occlusion of the two eyes, hence manifested for the condition of vertical heterophoria.

parallelepiped, corneal (par″ah-lel″e-pi′ped). The section of the cornea, transilluminated by the narrow beam of a slit lamp, having the geometrical shape of a curved parallelepiped when viewed obliquely.

paralysis (pă-ral′ih-sis). Loss or impairment of muscle function or sensation.

abducens p. Sixth nerve paralysis.

accommodation, p. of. Absence of accommodation due to paralysis of the ciliary muscle.

asthenic bulbar p. Myasthenia gravis.

basilar p. Ocular paralysis due to a peripheral lesion of the nerve before it enters the orbit.

Bell's p. Bell's palsy.

congenital oculofacial p. Moebius' syndrome.

congenital spastic p. Little's disease.

conjugate p. Paralysis resulting in the loss of one or more of the conjugate movements of the eyes.

convergence p. A pronounced limitation or absence of binocular convergence ability with monocular fixational eye movements intact. This clinical classification of paralysis implies or presumes a lesion involving the convergence control centers.

divergence p. The inability to diverge the eyes, characterized by a fixed state of convergence with monocular fixational eye movements intact.

Féréol-Graux p. Féréol-Graux ocular palsy.

fifth nerve p. Lack of sensation in the cornea, the conjunctiva, and parts of the face and head, and absence of the blink reflex, due to involvement of the ophthalmic branch of the fifth cranial nerve.

fourth nerve p. Paralysis of the superior oblique muscle due to involvement of the fourth cranial nerve. Syn., *trochlear paralysis.*

Foville's p. Conjugate paralysis of gaze with or without facial paralysis on one side, and contralateral paralysis of the arm and the leg, due to lesions of the pons varolii.

gaze, p. of. The inability to move the eyes conjugately, either laterally or vertically, due to involvement of cortical or subcortical oculomotor centers.

Gubler's p. Millard-Gubler syndrome.

irritative cervical sympathetic p. Horner's syndrome.

oculomotor p. Third nerve paralysis.

 oculomotor p., cyclic. Cyclic oculomotor spasm.

orbital p. Ocular paralysis due to a peripheral lesion of a nerve within the orbit.

pseudobulbar p. Progressive loss of voluntary eye movements, with reflex eye movements intact, due to bilateral involvement of the frontal cortex. Syn., *pseudobulbar palsy.*

pupillary p., absolute. Immobility of the pupil, regardless of stimulation, due to paralysis of both the sphincter and dilator pupillae muscles.

pupillary p., amaurotic. Loss of direct and consensual pupillary reactions to light on ipsilateral stimulation of an eye blind from a completely destructive lesion in the retina or the optic nerve, with retention of the consensual pupillary reaction by contralateral stimulation.

pupillary p., hemianopic. Pupillary hemiakinesia.

pupillary p., reflex. Absence of direct and indirect pupillary reflexes to light with retention of the near and orbicularis pupillary reflexes, due to a lesion in the efferent pupillomotor pathway between the point of departure of the pupillomotor fibers from the optic tract and the constrictor center. Miosis and anisocoria are frequent accompaniments.

sixth nerve p. Paralysis of the external rectus muscle due to involvement of the homolateral sixth cranial nerve. Syn., *abducens paralysis.*

tegmental mesencephalic p. Benedikt's syndrome.

third nerve p. Paralysis of the levator palpebrae superioris, the superior rectus, the internal rectus, the inferior oblique, the ciliary, and the sphincter pupillae muscles, due to involvement of the third cranial nerve and resulting in ptosis, cycloplegia, iridoplegia, and exotropia. Syn., *oculomotor paralysis.*

trochlear p. Fourth nerve paralysis.

Weber's p. Homolateral oculomotor paralysis and contralateral hemiplegia of the face and limbs, produced by a lesion in the region of the cerebral peduncle affecting the third cranial nerve. Syn., *Weber's syndrome.*

paramacular (par″ah-mak′u-lar). Beside or near the macula lutea.

paraphimosis oculi (par″ah-fi-mo′sis o′ku-li, -fih-mo′sis). Paraphimosis palpebrae.

paraphimosis orbicularis (par″ah-fi-mo′sis or-bik″u-lar′is, -fih-mo′sis). Paraphimosis palpebrae.

paraphimosis palpebrae (par″ah-fi-mo′sis pal-pe′bre, -fih-mo′sis). Ectropion resulting from spastic contraction of the palpebral portion of the orbicularis oculi muscle. Usually it is of short duration, affects the upper eyelid, and **is** due to birth trauma. Syn.,

paraphimosis oculi; paraphimosis orbicularis.

paraplegia, familial spasmodic (par″ah-ple′je-ah). Familial spasmodic hypotonic paresis of pyramidal origin, without ataxia, sensory disturbances, or muscular atrophy, usually appearing in the second decade. Ocular involvements may include extraocular muscle paralysis, strabismus, macular degeneration, pupillary defects, and optic atrophy. Syn., *Strümpell-Lorrain disease.*

parastereoscopy (par″ah-ster″e-os′-ko-pe). The viewing of a stereopsis-inducing pattern so as to perceive essentially the original scene but with diminished depth or distance, although the objects within the scene appear to have full natural relief. This relief is produced by increasing the focal length of the stereocamera lenses and by increasing the parallactic base in the same proportion.

paratrachoma (par″ah-trah-ko′mah). Inclusion blenorrhea.

paraxial (par-ak′sih-al). Pertaining to light rays or the space closely surrounding the axis of an optical system.

Paredrine (par-ed′rin). A trade mark for an adrenergic drug closely related to Benzedrine which, used in its hydrobromide form, is said to act as a mydriatic without producing cycloplegia. It is sometimes used in combination with atropine or homatropine to exert a synergistic action and heighten the cycloplegic effect.

paresis (pah-re′sis, par′e-sis). Incomplete or partial paralysis.

amblyopic p., pupillary. Diminished direct and consensual pupillary reactions to light on ipsilateral stimulation of an eye which is amblyopic due to an incomplete lesion in the retina or the optic nerve, with retention of the consensual pupillary reaction for contralateral stimulation.

parfocal (par-fo'kal). Pertaining to sets of eyepieces or objectives which may be interchanged on an optical instrument without varying the focus of the instrument.

Parinaud's (pah-rih-nōz') **conjunctivitis; syndrome; theory.** See under the nouns.

parophthalmia (par"of-thal'me-ah). Inflammation of the tissues around the eye.

parophthalmoncus (par"of-thal-mong'kus). A tumor near the eye.

paropsia (par-op'se-ah). Parablepsia.

paropsis (par-op'sis). Parablepsia.

glaucosis, p. Glaucoma. *Obs.*

longinqua, p. Presbyopia. *Obs.*

lucifuga, p. Day blindness. *Obs.*

noctifuga, p. Night blindness. *Obs.*

propinqua, p. Myopia. *Obs.*

paroptic (par-op'tik). Extraretinal.

parorasis (par"o-rah'sis). Any perversion of vision, such as color blindness or a visual hallucination.

Parrot's sign (par-ōz'). See under *sign.*

Parry's disease (par'ēz). Exophthalmic goiter.

pars (pahrz). A part.

caeca oculi, p. The optic nerve head.

caeca retinae, p. The parts of the retina which are not sensitive to light, i.e., the pars ciliaris retinae and the pars iridica retinae.

ciliaris retinae, p. The epithelium of the ciliary body which represents the forward continuation of the retina and is subdivided into the *pars plana* and the *pars plicata.*

iridica retinae, p. The posterior pigmented epithelium of the iris.

lacrimalis, p. Horner's muscle.

optica hypothalami, p. The portion of the optic chiasm and its surrounding area which lies in the optic recess of the hypothalamus.

optica retinae, p. The retina proper; the light-sensitive retina

extending from the optic disk to the ora serrata.

plana, p. The heavily pigmented, innermost portion of the ciliary body, composed of epithelial tissue, extending anteriorly from the ora serrata to the ciliary processes. It is approximately 3.6 to 4 mm. wide and appears smooth to the naked eye. However, under low magnification, slight dark ridges (striae ciliaris) are seen running parallel to each other from the ora serrata to the ciliary processes. Syn., *orbiculus ciliaris.*

planitis, p. A form of granulomatous uveitis occurring in the region of the pars plana.

plicata, p. Corona ciliaris.

Parson's test (par'sunz). Manoptoscope test.

partition of Kundt. Kundt's monocular asymmetry.

partition of Münsterberg. Münsterberg's monocular asymmetry.

Pascal's (pas-kalz') **method; schema.** See under the nouns.

Pascal-Raubitschek test (pas-kal'-row'bih-shek). See under *test.*

Pascheff's conjunctivitis (pas'shefs). See under *conjunctivitis.*

past pointing. Pointing too far in the direction of the displacement of an object of fixation presented monocularly in the field of action of a paretic extraocular muscle.

pastel (pas'tel). 1. Lightly tinted; of relatively high brightness and low hue saturation. A color with these characteristics. 2. A picture made with a crayon composed of paste and ground pigments. 3. A crayon composed of paste and ground pigments.

patch. A circumscribed area differing from the tissue surrounding it.

cotton-wool p's. White, fluffy-appearing patches occurring in edematous areas of the retina, as may occur in renal or hypertensive retinopathy. They are coagulated exudates of plasma and fibrin from the retinal capillaries. Syn., *cotton-wool spots.*

Hutchinson's p. A salmon-colored, localized area of the cornea seen in syphilitic interstitial keratitis, due to neovascularization of the deep corneal tissues. Syn., *salmon patch.*

Roth's p's. Roth's spots.

salmon p. Hutchinson's patch.

path difference. See under *difference.*

path, optical. The product of the length of path of a ray of light in a medium and the refractive index of that medium. It is equivalent to the distance that would be traversed by that ray in a vacuum in the same time taken to traverse the medium.

patheticus (pah-thet'ih-kus). 1. Trochlear nerve. 2. Superior oblique muscle.

pathological chain. See under *chain.*

pathology, ophthalmic (pă-thol'o-je). The branch of biological science which is concerned with the nature of disease of the eye and its surrounding structures and of the structural and functional changes which cause or are caused by such disease.

pathway. The course of the nerve structures, or the structures themselves, along which impulses are conducted.

centrifugal p. The motor pathway of the visual reflex arc; that portion of the visual pathway conducting impulses from the visual cerebral centers to the intrinsic and extrinsic muscles of the eye and to the skeletal muscles of the body.

centripetal p. The sensory pathway of the visual reflex arc; that portion of the visual pathway conducting impulses to the visual cerebral centers.

geniculocalcarine p. Geniculocalcarine tract.

visual p. The neural path of visual impulses starting in the retinae and ending in the visual cortex. The structures most commonly included are: the *retinae,* the *optic nerves,* the *optic chiasm,* the *optic tracts,* the *external geniculate bodies,* the *optic radiations,* and the *visual cortical areas.*

visual p., higher. The neural path of visual impulses starting at the external geniculate bodies and ending in the visual cortical areas. The pathway includes the *external geniculate bodies, optic radiations,* and the *visual cortical areas.*

visual p., lower. The neural path of visual impulses commencing in the retinae and ending at the external geniculate bodies. The pathway includes the *retinae,* the *optic nerves,* the *optic chiasm,* the *optic tracts,* and the *external geniculate bodies.*

patient. A person on whom a study is being made, or to whom treatment is being given, for any aberration of normal organization, particularly in matters of health.

Paton's lines; syndrome. See under the nouns.

pattern. A specific arrangement or interrelation of parts; a design; a model.

diffraction p. The alternate dark and light bands representing the distribution of light intensity due to diffraction of light at an aperture or an edge. See also *diffraction fringes.*

Donders' pseudoisochromatic p's. Patterns of colored threads wound in stripes around a piece of wood for detecting color blindness. See also *Donders' test for color blindness.*

equilibrium p. Optometric Extension Program: The relationships between the positive relative convergence finding (#16 A) and the negative relative convergence finding (#17 A) and between the positive relative accommodation finding (#20) and the negative relative accommodation finding (#21), in estimating the maximum amount of convex lens power (or minimum amount of concave lens power) which can be prescribed for the patient's near-point use.

interference p. The alternate light and dark bands representing the distribution of light as a result of interference phenomena. See also *interference fringes.*

lens p. A jig, usually of metal, which is attached to a lens cutting or edging machine to produce the desired shape of a lens.

receptor-type distribution p. The pattern of distribution of the rod and cone cells in the foveal area of the retina. Abbreviated *RDP.*

visual p. A characteristic or apparent interrelationship or consistency in a group of visual test data.

pause, fixation. See under *fixation.*

PCB. Abbreviation for *punctum convergens basalis;* the near point of convergence.

pcc. Abbreviation for *periscopic concave,* in reference to periscopic concave lenses.

pcx. Abbreviation for *periscopic convex,* in reference to periscopic convex lenses.

P.D. Abbreviation for *prism diopter* or *pupillary distance* (*interpupillary distance*).

P-D Scope. The trade name for an instrument for measuring interpupillary distance, the distance of each pupil from the center of the bridge of the nose, and the size of the pupil, cornea, or palpebral fissure

pearls, Elschnig. Elschnig bodies.

pearl specks of Listing. The bright spots seen entoptically as a result of vacuoles in the crystalline lens of the eye.

Pearsonian coefficient of correlation (pēr-son'e-an). See under *coefficient.*

pebble. Transparent and colorless quartz; rock crystal; a lens made of quartz or rock crystal.

Pechan prism (pek'an). See under *prism.*

Peckham's (pek'amz) **method; test.** See under *test.*

pecten (pek'ten). A black, heavily pigmented, typically pleated or vaned structure in avian eyes, composed primarily of small blood vessels projecting into the vitreous from the optic disk and functioning primarily to nourish the retina and inner eye.

pecten sclerae (pek'ten skler'e). The edge of the sclera surrounding the optic nerve.

pedicle (ped'ih-kul). A narrow supporting part; a stem or stalk.

cone p. Cone foot.

optic p. 1. The embryonic link between the optic vesicle or optic cup and the forebrain or diencephalon, which becomes the optic nerve. Syn., *optic stalk.* 2. In cartilaginous fish such as sharks or skates, a cartilaginous stalk extend'ng from the cranium into the orbit and terminating in an expanded concave head against which the eyeball rests and receives support.

peduncle (pe-dung'k'l). A narrow supporting part; a stem.

cerebral p's. Portions of the midbrain, ventral to the aqueduct of Sylvius, crossed by the optic tracts and connecting the cerebrum with the pons. Each is subdivided into a dorsal tegmentum, a substantia nigra, and a basis pedunculi; the dorsal tegmentum contains the oculomotor and trochlear nuclei. Syn., *crus cerebri.*

optic p. The fibers of the optic radiations as they leave the lateral geniculate bodies and enter the internal capsule prior to the formation of the fan-shaped medullary optic lamina.

P.E.K. Photo-Electronic Keratoscope.

Pel's crisis (pelz). See under *crisis*.

pelopsia (peh-lop'se-ah). A perversion of vision in which objects appear to be abnormally near.

pemphigus, ocular (pem'fih-gus). Bullous eruptions or ulcerations of the conjunctiva, usually associated with bullae on other mucous membranes and on the skin, with invasion of the conjunctiva by newly formed connective tissue, which subsequently contracts, resulting in shrinkage of the conjunctiva.

pencil of rays. See under *rays*.

penetration. The depth of focus of a lens or an optical system.

pentachromic (pen"tah-kro'mik). 1. Pertaining to partial color blindness in which only five colors can be distinguished. 2. Pertaining to, or of, five colors.

penumbra (pe-num'brah). The region of gradually diminishing darkness surrounding the region of complete darkness (umbra) in the shadow cast by an opaque object in the presence of an extensive light source.

percentile (per-sen'til, -tīl). One of 99 ordinarily designated points on a scale which divides a series into 100 equal parts.

percentile rank. The cardinally expressed percentile value indicating the per cent frequency of inferior values in the sampled population.

percept (per'sept). 1. The meaningful impression of an object obtained in response to sensory stimuli. 2. Formerly, the object perceived.

perceptible (per-sep'tih-b'l). Discernible; perceivable; apprehendable through the senses.

perception (per-sep'shun). 1. The appreciation of a physical situation through the mediation of one or more senses. 2. The process of discriminating between two or more stimulus presentations.

after p. 1. An afterimage. 2. An aftereffect.

albedo p. Perception of surface attributes as a function of diffuse reflection values rather than in terms of luminance.

ambiocular p. Perception as obtained in ambiocular strabismus.

binocular p. 1. Perception from simultaneous use of the two eyes. 2. Perception resulting from fusion of the images of the two eyes.

color p. Perception of hue.

depth p. Perception of relative or absolute difference in distance of objects from the observer; perception of the third dimension.

dermo-optical p. The perception or identification of reading material or colors through stimulation of the skin and exclusive of stimulation of the eyes, an unverified skill.

form p. Perception of shape or contour.

immediate p. Perception resulting only from direct sensation, i.e., not influenced by memory of previous experience.

light p. Perception of the brightness attribute of light.

selective p. Perception of some but not all of the exposed environment, presumably in relation to motivation and past experiences.

simultaneous p. Perception of the images of the two eyes simultaneously, with or without sensory fusion.

visual p. Perception through the sense of vision.

perceptivity (per"sep-tiv'ih-te). The ability to apprehend or perceive.

perceptual lance; organization; visual skill. See under the nouns.

Percival's (per'sih-valz) **criterion; lens; rule.** See under the nouns.

periarteritis, retinal (per"ih-ar"-ter-i'tis). Inflammation of the perivascular sheaths and adventitia of the retinal arterioles.

peribrosis (per″ih-bro′sis). Ulceration of the eyelid in the area of the canthus.

peribulbar (per″ih-bul′bar). Surrounding the eyeball.

perichoroid (per″ih-ko′roid). Perichoroidal.

perichoroidal (per″ih-ko-roi′dal). Surrounding the choroid.

periconchitis (per″ih-kong-ki′tis). Inflammation of the periorbita.

pericorneal (per″ih-kōr′ne-al). Surrounding the cornea.

pericranium (per″ih-kra′ne-um). The periosteum on the outer surface of the cranial bones; it is considered as the deepest layer of the eyebrow.

peridacryocystitis (per″ih-dak″re-o-sis-ti′tis). Infection in the area of the lacrimal sac, but not involving its interior or the lacrimal canals.

peridectomy (per″ih-dek′to-me). Surgical removal of a strip of conjunctival tissue from around the cornea for the relief of pannus. Syn., *perimitry; periotomy; peritectomy; peritomy; syndectomy.*

perifovea (per″ih-fo′ve-ah). A band, approximately 1.5 mm. wide, immediately surrounding the parafovea and representing the outer limit of the macular area.

perifoveal (per″ih-fo′ve-al). Around or encircling the fovea.

perikeratic (per″ih-ker-at′ik). Surrounding the cornea.

perilenticular (per″ih-len-tik′u-lar). Surrounding the crystalline lens.

perimeter (per-im′eh-ter). An instrument designed to determine the angular extent and characteristics of the visual field peripheral to the direction of fixation, or of the field of fixation peripheral to a forward direction of reference. Types of test targets, fixation controls, illumination, recording apparatus, head and chin rests, mechanical features, and auxiliary attachments vary.

  arc p. A perimeter employing an arc scale for peripheral angular specifications and the test object path, pivoted on an axis coinciding with the straightforward position of the line of sight of the eye being tested, the eye being located at the center of curvature of the arc. The pivot permits orientation of the measuring arc to coincide with any desired meridian of exploration.

  hand p. A simplified, lightweight perimeter held in position by the examiner instead of being mounted on a stand.

  hemispherical p. A perimeter consisting essentially of a large segment of a hollow sphere instead of a pivoting arc.

  projection p. A perimeter that has a projection system for target presentation and is typically controlled from behind the instrument, the location of the target being simultaneously indicated on a recording chart.

perimetric (per″ih-met′rik). 1. Pertaining to perimetry. 2. A trade designation of a spectacle lens shape.

perimetry (per-im′eh-tre). The determination of the extent of the visual field for various types and intensities of stimuli, usually for the purpose of diagnosing and localizing disturbances in the visual pathway.

  black light p. Perimetry performed under ultraviolet light and with luminescent test targets.

  electroencephalographic p. Objective perimetry in which alterations of the recorded alpha rhythm are used to determine the visual field while a narrow beam of light from a perimeter arc is projected through the pupil to various positions on the retina.

  flicker fusion p. Determination of the integrity of the visual field by plotting the critical fusion frequency (CFF) throughout its extent.

kinetic p. Exploration of the visual field with a moving test object of fixed luminance.

light sense p. Static perimetry.

projection p. Perimetry performed with an instrument that provides projected luminous targets which are typically controlled from behind the instrument with the location in the field being simultaneously indicated on a recording chart.

qualitative p. Perimetry performed with test targets of the same size but of different stimulus intensity.

quantitative p. Perimetry performed with test targets of various sizes but of the same content, to determine the smallest visual angle for which each retinal area is sensitive.

static p. Exploration of the visual field in which test objects of various sizes, located at fixed positions, are gradually increased in luminance to the threshold of visibility. Syn., *light sense perimetry.*

ultraviolet p. Black light perimetry.

perimitry (per-im′ih-tre). 1. Peritomy. 2. Peridectomy.

perineuritis, optic (per″ih-nu-ri′tis). Inflammation of the sheaths of the optic nerve, usually in association with involvement of the optic nerve itself. It is classified into two main types, *pachymeningitis*, affecting the dura mater, and *leptomeningitis*, affecting the pia mater and the arachnoid.

perineuritis, retrobulbar (per″ih-nu-ri′tis). Optic perineuritis affecting the sheaths of the orbital portion of the optic nerve.

periocular (per″ih-ok′u-lar). Surrounding the eyeball.

period. 1. The interval of time during which anything occurs. 2. The interval of time between regular occurrences in an ordered series.

action p. Action time.

base p. In a statistical or a graphical representation of a function in relation to time, a period of time used as a reference standard and for which the function is represented at 100%, or unity, and its value in any other period is represented in proportion.

latent p. The time interval between the application of a stimulus and the response to that stimulus. In vision, it varies with light intensity, wavelength, state of light adaption of the eye, and with location and size of the retinal area stimulated.

light wave, p. of. The time interval for one complete cycle of periodic motion of a light wave; the reciprocal of the wave frequency.

refractory p., absolute. A short interval of time following the excitation of a nerve or muscle fiber during which the application of a second stimulus is not effective in producing a response.

refractory p., relative. The interval of time, immediately following the absolute refractory period, during which a stimulus greater than threshold is necessary to produce a response.

periophthalmia (per″ih-of-thal′me-ah). Periophthalmitis.

periophthalmic (per″ih-of-thal′mik). Situated around the eyeball.

periophthalmitis (per″ih-of″thal-mi′tis). Inflammation of the tissues around the eye. Syn., *periophthalmia.*

perioptic (per″ih-op′tik). Situated around the eyeball.

perioptometry (per″ih-op-tom′eh-tre). The measurement of the limits of the visual field or of peripheral visual acuity.

periorbita (per″ih-ōr′bih-tah). The periosteum within the orbit. It is loosely attached to the bone, except at sutures, fossae, foramina, and the orbital margin where it is firmly attached. At the optic canal it is continuous with the dura mater of the optic nerve; at the orbital margin, where it is continuous with the periosteum of the face, it is thickened to form a ridge, the arcus marginale, to which the orbital septum is attached.

periorbital (per″ih-ōr′bih-tal). Situated around the orbit or pertaining to the periorbita.

periorbititis (per″ih-ōr″bih-ti′tis). Inflammation of the periorbita.

periosteum, orbital (per″ih-os′te-um). Periorbita.

periostitis, orbital (per″ih-os-ti′tis). Periorbititis.

periotomy (per″ih-ot′o-me). Peridectomy.

peripapillary (per″ih-pap′ih-ler-e). Situated around the optic disk.

periphacitis (per″ih-fah-si′tis). Presumed inflammation of the capsule of the crystalline lens.

periphakitis (per″ih-fah-ki′tis). Periphacitis.

periphakus (per″ih-fak′us, -fa′kus). The capsule of the crystalline lens.

peripheraphose (peh-rif′er-ah-fōz″). A perceived dark spot, shadow, or interruption of light, originating in the optic nerve or the eyeball.

peripherophose (peh-rif′er-o-fōz). A subjective sensation of light or color originating in the optic nerve or the eyeball.

periphlebitis, retinal (per″ih-fle-bi′-tis). Inflammation of the external walls and the surrounding tissues of the retinal venules.

periphoria (per″ih-fo′re-ah). Cyclophoria.

peripupillometer (per″ih-pu″pih-lom′eh-ter). An instrument for measuring the extent of the pupillomotor area of the retina by determining the extent of the visual field in which the pupillary reaction to light is elicited.

periscope (per′ih-skōp). An optical instrument enabling an observer to see around an obstruction in the line of view, or to obtain a view otherwise impossible for a given position of the observer's eye, used in submarines, tanks, trenches, and in other circumstances in which the observer may be recessed or hidden.

periscopic (per″ih-skop′ik). Pertaining to a periscopic lens or to a periscope.

peritectomy (per″ih-tek′to-me). Peridectomy.

peritomy (peh-rit′o-me). 1. The cutting of the conjunctiva at the limbus prior to enucleation or for the relief of pannus. Syn., *perimitry*. 2. Peridectomy.

perivasculitis, retinal (per″ih-vas″-ku-li′tis). Inflammation of the perivascular sheaths and adventia of the retinal vessels.

Perlia's (per′le-ahz) **nucleus; test.** See under the nouns.

perspective. The perceptual attribute of three-dimensional space, or its graphic representation on a plane or a curved surface.

  aerial p. 1. Perspective as influenced by the state of clarity of the atmosphere. In clear atmosphere contours remain sharp, colors are essentially unaltered, and objects appear nearer than in hazy atmosphere, in which contours are less distinct and colors altered. 2. Perspective in a painting effected by gradations of color and distinctness.

  ambiguous p. Perspective which changes or alternates, as that obtained in viewing an ambiguous figure.

  geometrical p. Perspective identified with the apparent converging of receding parallel lines. Syn., *linear perspective; mathematical perspective.*

  inverse p. Perspective as seen through a pseudoscope, in which near objects appear far, and far objects appear near.

  linear p. Geometrical perspective.

mathematical p. Geometrical perspective.

movement p. Apparent slowing of the motion of an object crossing the visual field, in proportion to its distance from the observer, i.e., the greater the distance the slower the apparent velocity.

reversible p. Perspective which reverses or alternates, as that obtained in viewing a reversible figure.

Petit's canal (ptēz). See under *canal.*

Pettit's test. See under *test.*

Petzval's (pets'valz) **condition; curve; formula; surface; theory.** See under the nouns.

Pfund's (fundz) **absorption cell; gold-plated glass; method.** See under the nouns.

phacentocele (fah-sen'to-sēl). Dislocation of the crystalline lens into the anterior chamber.

phacitis (fah-si'tis). Presumed inflammation of the crystalline lens. Syn., *crystallitis; phacoiditis.*

phaco- (fak'o-, fa'ko-). A combining form denoting a lens or the crystalline lens of the eye.

phaco-anaphylaxis (fak″o-an″ah-fih-lak'sis). Hypersensitivity to the protein of the crystalline lens, following extracapsular cataract surgery of one eye, so that breakage of the capsule of the other eye allows anaphylactic reaction.

phacocele (fak'o-sēl). Hernia of the crystalline lens, as when extruded out of the eyeball, through a rupture of the sclera near the limbus, to lodge beneath the conjunctiva. Syn., *lenticele.*

phacocyst (fak'o-sist). The capsule of the crystalline lens.

phacocystectomy (fak″o-sis-tek'to-me). Excision of a portion of the capsule of the crystalline lens.

phacocystitis (fak″o-sis-ti'tis). Presumed inflammation of the capsule of the crystalline lens.

phacodonesis (fak″o-do-ne'sis). Tremulousness of the crystalline lens.

phacoerisis (fak″o-er'ih-sis). Surgical removal of the crystalline lens in cataract by means of pneumatic forceps which adhere to the anterior surface of the lens by suction.

phacoerysis (fak″o-er'ih-sis, -er-e'-sis). Phacoerisis.

phacoglaucoma (fak″o-glaw-ko'-mah). Changes produced in the crystalline lens secondary to glaucoma.

phacohymenitis (fak″o-hi″men-i'-tis). Presumed inflammation of the capsule of the crystalline lens.

phacoiditis (fak″oid-i'tis). Phacitis.

phacoidoscope (fak-koi'do-skōp). Phacoscope.

phacolysin (fah-kol'ih-sin). An albumin used in the treatment of cataract.

phacolysis (fah-kol'ih-sis). 1. Dissolution of the crystalline lens. 2. Surgical discission of the crystalline lens.

phacolytic (fak″o-lit'ik). Pertaining to or causing dissolution of the crystalline lens.

phacoma (fah-ko'mah). A tumorlike swelling of the crystalline lens, due to an overgrowth of lens fibers.

phacomalacia (fak″o-mah-la'she-ah). Softening of the crystalline lens as may occur in hypermature cataract.

phacomatoses (fak″o-mah-to'sēz). A group of congenital and familial diseases characterized by the appearance of multiple tumors and cysts in various parts of the body, particularly in the retina and the central nervous system. Included in this group are *Bourneville's disease, von Hippel-Lindau disease, von Recklinghausen's disease,* and *Sturge-Weber disease.*

phacometachoresis (fak″o-met″ah-ko-re'sis). Luxation or subluxation of the crystalline lens.

phacometecesis (fak″o-met″eh-se'-sis). Displacement of the crystalline lens into the anterior chamber.

phacometer (fah-kom'eh-ter). Lensometer.

phacoplanesis (fak"o-plah-ne'sis). A wandering or free-floating crystalline lens.

phacosclerosis (fak"o-skle-ro'sis). Hardening of the crystalline lens.

phacoscope (fak'o-skōp). An instrument for observing the crystalline lens, especially its accommodative changes. Syn., *phacoidoscope*.

phacoscopy (fah-kos'ko-pe). Examination of the crystalline lens with the phacoscope.

phacoscotasmus (fak"o-sko-taz'mus). Darkening or clouding of the crystalline lens.

phacoscotoma (fak"o-sko-to'mah). A lenticular opacity or cataract.

phak-. For words beginning thus, see *phac-*.

phalangosis (fal"an-go'sis). An abnormality in which the eyelashes grow in multiple rows.

phantasmagoria (fan-taz"mah-go'-re-ah). 1. An optical effect whereby figures projected on a screen are made to appear to dwindle markedly into the distance, or to rush toward the observer with enormous increase of size. 2. A hallucination of a shifting succession of figures or objects.

phantasm (fan'tazm). A visual hallucination or illusion.

phantom. A phantasm.

phase difference. See under *difference*.

phase of light wave. A point or stage in the periodic changes of a light wave considered in relation to a point of reference in the periodic change of the same wave or of an interacting wave.

phenakistoscope (fe"nah-kis'to-skōp). A device consisting of a slotted disk containing a series of pictures representing the successive stages in the movement of objects or persons. It is held with the side containing the pictures facing a mirror and rotated while an observer on the other side of the disk sees the pictures, individually and instantaneously, in the mirror through the slots, obtaining the effect of animation. Syn., *stroboscopic disk*.

phengophobia (fen"go-fo'be-ah). A morbid dread of light.

phenomenon. 1. A remarkable or an unusual event or appearance, or one of unique significance. 2. A fact or an event which may be described or explained scientifically.

A p. A syndrome.

Abney's p. A hue change resulting from a change in purity or saturation. The hues of colors having a dominant wavelength near 488 mμ (blue-green) become increasingly different from the hue of 488 mμ with increase of purity, whereas the hues of colors having a dominant wavelength near 577 mμ (yellow) become increasingly like the hue of 577 mμ. Syn., *Abney's effect*.

anorthoscopic p. Anorthoscopic movement.

aqueous influx p. The filling of the laminary vein, which normally carries blood and aqueous, with aqueous when the junction of the aqueous vein and the recipient vein is partially occluded by pressure of a glass rod, indicating higher pressure within the aqueous vein than within the recipient vein. Syn., *Ascher's positive glass rod phenomenon*.

ascension p. The persistence of elevated position of the walls of Cloquet's canal instead of the normal immediate gravitational settling, seen with the biomicroscope after abrupt vertical movements of the eye. It is attributed to pathologic conditions which change the specific gravity of the components of the vitreous hu-

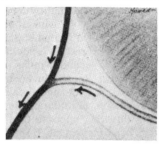
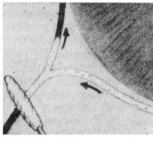

Fig. 32. Ascher's aqueous influx phenomenon. (From *The Glaucomas*, ed. 2, H. Saul Sugar, Hoeber, 1957)

mor. Syn., *Busacca's phenomenon.*

Ascher's negative glass rod p. Blood influx phenomenon.

Ascher's positive glass rod p. Aqueous influx phenomenon.

Aschner's p. Reduction of the pulse rate on exerting pressure on the eyeball, indicating cardiac vagus irritability. Syn., *oculocardiac reflex.*

Aubert's p. The apparent tilting in one direction of a bright vertical line, viewed in a dark room, when the head is slowly tilted in the opposite direction, due to the absence of compensatory postural changes.

autokinetic p. Autokinetic visual illusion.

Bartley p. See *Brücke-Bartley effect.*

Becker's p. Pulsation of the retinal arteries, associated with exophthalmic goiter.

Behr's abduction p. In syphilitic sixth nerve palsy, attempted conjugate movement of the eyes toward the affected side produces an inequality of size of the pupils, the abducting eye having the smaller pupil.

Behr's pupillary p. Anisocoria associated with hemianopsia wherein the pupil on the hemianopic side is larger than its fellow and reacts less markedly to light, considered to be due to a lesion in the contralateral optic tract.

Bell's p. The normal upward and outward rotation of the eyes on bilateral closure, or attempted closure, of the eyelids.

Bell's inverse p. Downward rotation of the eyes on bilateral closure, or attempted closure, of the eyelids.

Bell's paradoxical p. Absent or abnormal (downward or lateral) rotation of the eyes on bilateral closure, or attempted closure, of the eyelids.

Bell's perverse p. Lateral rotation of the eyes on bilateral closure, or attempted closure, of the eyelids.

Bezold-Brücke p. A change in perceived hue of some, but not all, spectral colors with change in intensity. Syn., *Bezold-Brücke effect.*

Bielschowsky's p. The downward movement of the nonfixating hypertropic eye in some strabismics on placing a dark lens or a filter before the fixating eye.

blood influx p. The filling of the laminary vein, which normally carries blood and aqueous, with blood when the junction of the aqueous vein and the recipient vein is partially occluded by pressure of a glass rod, indicating higher pressure within the recipient vein than within the aqueous vein. Syn., *Ascher's negative glass rod phenomenon.*

blue-arc p. An entoptic sensation of two bands of blue light arching toward the blind spot from above and below a spot of light stimulating the temporal parafoveal area.

Broca-Sulzer *p*. Broca-Sulzer effect.

Busacca's *p*. Ascension phenomenon.

chromatic dimming *p*. Loss of saturation of a colored surface on steady fixation.

colored shadow *p*. The tendency of shadows cast on a gray surface to appear complementary in color to the intercepted illuminant, e.g., when shadows are cast on a neutral screen by an opaque body from two equidistant light sources of equal intensity, one white and the other colored, the shadow cast by the white light appears to be the color of the colored light and the shadow cast by the colored light appears to be its complement.

constancy *p*. The tendency of an object to retain its associated perceptual attribute, such as hue, size, and shape, under conditions altering its correlated physical stimulus value.

contrast *p*. A form of interinfluence between different perceptual processes whereby one perception induces a characteristic opposite to itself in another perception. The phenomenon occurs in *successive contrast* (time) and in *simultaneous contrast* (space).

crowding *p*. The increased difficulty in identifying targets which are closely adjacent to other targets, as clinically demonstrated by poorer visual acuity when using closely grouped multiple targets instead of an isolated single target. It is a normal phenomenon but is more pronounced in amblyopia ex anopsia. Syn., *crowding; dissociation difficulty; separation difficulty*.

depth contrast *p*. The perceived backward inclination of a vertical line when viewed binocularly between a bilaterally displaced pair of lines inclined slightly forward.

Dietzel-Roelofs *p*. The apparent movement of a fixated stationary light in a direction opposite to that of a second similar light, both being located in an otherwise empty, dark field.

doll's head *p*. Rotation of the eyes in a direction opposite to a sudden head movement, through an angle equal to the head movement, with a subsequent return toward the original position, in a case of a destructive lesion of the central mechanism for voluntary eye movements when the lesion is above the pontine centers. Syn., *head turning reflex; Cantelli's sign; doll's eye sign*.

Duane's *p*. Duane's syndrome.

entoptic *p*. A visual sensation, such as muscae volitantes or phosphene, arising from stimuli within the eye and perceived illusorily as in the external visual field.

exhaustion *p*. Rapid decrease of the b potential in the electroretinogram following stimulation with repeated flashes of light when the retina is in a condition of anoxemia.

extinction *p*. Imperceptibility of a stimulus in one portion of the visual field, or extinction of sensation, evoked by simultaneous stimulation elsewhere in the visual field.

Fick's *p*. Sattler's veil.

flicker *p*. Rapid variation or wavering of perceived luminance or hue associated with intermittent, interrupted, or suddenly varying stimulus intensity or quality; flicker.

fluttering heart *p*. Apparent fluttering of a colored figure drawn on a background of a very different hue when the drawing is moved back and forth laterally at a certain rate.

Fraunhofer's diffraction phenomena. Diffraction phenomena in which both the light source and the screen on which the diffraction is observed are effectively at infinite distances from the aperture or edge causing the diffraction.

Fresnel's diffraction phenomena. Diffraction phenomena in which either the source of light, or the screen on which the phenomena are observed, or both, are at a finite distance from the aperture or the edge causing the diffraction.

Fuchs's p. Paradoxical retraction of a formerly ptotic eyelid associated with eye movements and occurring during the healing stage of oculomotor paralysis or paresis; usually indicative of aberrant regeneration of fibers of the oculomotor nerve.

Galassi's pupillary p. Orbicularis pupillary reflex.

glass rod p., negative. Blood influx phenomenon.

glass rod p., positive. Aqueous influx phenomenon.

von Graefe's pupillary p. Pupillary constriction, after a forced abduction movement, in the presence of absolute and reflex paralysis of the iris to light.

Gunn's arteriovenous p. Gunn's crossing sign.

Gunn's jaw-winking p. Jaw-winking.

Gunn's pupillary p. In unilateral disease of the retina or optic nerve, e.g., retrobulbar neuritis, minimal pupillary contraction of the affected eye followed by dilatation, on illumination of the affected eye with the sound eye simultaneously covered, due to an impaired direct reflex to light in the affected eye, with a dominant, consensual, darkness dilatation reflex from the covered sound eye. Syn., *Gunn's pupillary sign.*

Hering-Hillebrand p. A characteristic departure of the experimentally determined horopter from the Vieth-Mueller circle, explained by the asymmetry in the effective spatial positions of the corresponding elements in the two eyes. Syn., *Hering-Hillebrand deviation.*

Honi p. A failure of certain inductive visual environmental influences to produce an expected distortion of size or shape of a person with close emotional or sociological ties to the observer, named after the woman who first failed to report the usual perceived distortion of her husband seen in an Ames room.

inflection p. A perceived distortion of a straight contour toward the center of the physiological blind spot when the image of the contour falls on the edge of the blind spot.

interareal inhibitional p. Any of several demonstrations of the effect which stimulation of one retinal area may have on adjacent or remote retinal areas, including *border contrast, metacontrast,* and *paracontrast.*

jack-in-the-box p. Sudden appearance of an object when the eye shifts its fixation from the actual direction of the object through a peripheral portion of a strong convex spectacle lens, where the prismatic deviation renders it out of sight, to a more central direction, enabling the object rays to be received through the pupil.

jaw-winking p. Jaw-winking.

　jaw-winking p., inverse. Reverse jaw-winking.

LeGrand-Geblewics p. Perception of an indirectly observed colored flickering light (40–50 times per sec.) as a constant white light.

Liebmann p. Liebmann effect.

Marcus Gunn p. Jaw-winking.

　Marcus Gunn p., reversed. Reverse jaw-winking.

Meyer's iliac p. Transient, fixed, pupillary dilatation produced in psychotics or psychoneurotics by the exertion of pressure on the abdomen over McBurney's point.

Mizuo's p. In Oguchi's disease, characterized by a gray-colored fundus, the return of a normal red appearance to the fundus after several hours in the dark. Upon re-exposure of the eye to light, the fundus quickly returns to its former gray color.

on-off p. The alternate opening and closing of the filtration angle of the anterior chamber, during gonioscopic examination, as the illumination is alternately turned on and off.

orbicularis p. Orbicularis pupillary reflex.

Panum's p. The appearance of one line nearer than another line when a single vertical line presented haploscopically to one eye is fused with one of two vertical lines close together, presented haploscopically to the other eye.

paradoxical pupil p. Paradoxical pupillary reflex.

phi p. Phi movement.

Piltz-Westphal p. Orbicularis pupillar reflex.

pseudo-Graefe's p. Pseudo-Graefe's sign.

Pulfrich stereo p. Pulfrich effect.

Purkinje's p. The relatively greater brightness of blue and green in comparison with red on adaptation to low, scotopic levels of illumination, corresponding to a shift of the relative luminosity curve toward the shorter wave length during transition from light to dark adaptation. Syn., *Purkinje's effect; Purkinje's shift.*

Purkinje's pupillomotor p. Light from the green portion of the spectrum produces the maximal constriction of the pupil in the dark-adapted eye, instead of yellow, which produces the maximal constriction in the light-adapted eye.

Redlich's p. A transient, fixed, pupillary dilatation produced in psychotics or psychoneurotics by voluntary muscular effort, such as movement of the eyes in any direction or squeezing an object in the hand. Syn., *Redlich's symptom.*

Roenne's p. In viewing two isolated spots of light in the midsaggital plane, one nearer and one farther than the crossing point of the visual axes, also in the midsaggital plane, the resulting percept is two spots of light lying in a frontal plane, one to each side of the point of intersection of the visual axes.

Rosenbach's p. 1. Tremor of the upper eyelid on its gentle closure. 2. The inability to close the eyes on command in neurasthenia.

Scheerer's p. Entoptic appearance of red blood corpuscles circulating in the paramacular blood vessels on looking at a homogeneous blue field, such as the sky or a snowfield through a blue filter.

Schlesinger's p. Constriction of the pupil on forcible raising of the eyebrows, even in the absence of a normal reaction to light.

size constancy p. The relative apparent stability, or lack of perceived change, in the size of an object despite a change in viewing distance, actual size, or other related stimulus factors.

Troxler's p. Originally, the temporary and irregular fading or disappearance of a small object in the visual field during steady fixation, variously attributed to the presence of angioscotomata and receptor fatigue, and now identified with the same type of disappearance obtained when the image is stabilized on the retina so as to constantly stimulate the same retinal receptors. Syn., *Troxler's effect.*

Tyndall p. Tyndall effect.

V p. V syndrome.

waterfall p. Waterfall visual illusion.

Weber's p. The visibility of an incandescent body to the dark-adapted eye as a gray glow at about 400° C., at which temperature the glow is not yet visible to the light-adapted eye.

Westphal-Piltz p. Orbicularis pupillary reflex.

white with pressure p. A localized change of the normal orange-red choroidal color of the fundus into a translucent white or greenish-white color upon external scleral depression. It is attributed to pathology of the retina or overlying vitreous, such as retinal atrophy or vitreous traction. Syn., *white with pressure sign.*

Wilbrand's p. An abrupt refixation movement occurring in hemianopsia when prisms, to displace the images onto the blind sides of the retinae, are suddenly placed before the eyes while a small spot on a uniform background is fixated. According to Wilbrand, this movement indicates a cerebral lesion and its absence an optic tract lesion.

Wilson's p. Oculo-aural reflex.

winking-jaw p. Corneomandibular reflex.

phenotype (fe′no-tīp). A type determined by the common visible characteristics of a group rather than by genetic characteristics.

phenylephrine hydrochloride (fen″il-ef′rin hi″dro-klo′rīd). A synthetic sympathomimetic amine chemically differing from epinephrine in having only one instead of two hydroxyl groups on the benzene ring, and used ophthalmically as a mydriatic and vasoconstrictor.

phi (ϕ) (fi, fe) The Greek letter used as the symbol for (1) *phi phenomenon;* (2) the *angle of longitude* in the field of regard. Fry.

phimosis palpebrarum (fi-mo′sis pal″pe-brah′rum). Blepharophimosis.

phlebography, orbital (fle-bog′rah-fe). A method of localizing and diagnosing an intraorbital hemangioma in which a series of x-ray photographs are made immediately after injecting a roentgenopaque material into the angular vein.

phlegmon, orbital (fleg′mon). Orbital cellulitis.

phlycten (flik′ten). A nodular pustule or minute subepithelial abscess on the conjunctiva or cornea in phlyctenular conjunctivitis or keratitis. Syn., *phlyctena; phlyctenula; phlyctenule.*

phlyctena (flik-te′nah). Phlycten.

phlyctenula (flik-ten′u-lah). Phlycten.

phlyctenule (flik′ten-ūl). Phlycten.

phlyctenulosis (flik″ten-u-lo′sis). The presence of phlyctens, as in phlyctenular conjunctivitis or keratitis.

phobotaxis (fo-bo-tak′sis). Random trial and error light-avoiding movements of a motile organism.

phonism (fo′nizm). Synesthesia in which there is a sensation of sound created by the effect of sight, smell, taste, touch, or thought.

phonopsia (fo-nop′se-ah). Visual sensations, as of color, associated with, or induced by, the hearing of sounds.

phoria (fo′re-ah). The direction or orientation of one eye, its line of sight, or some other reference axis or meridian, in relation to the other eye, manifested in the absence of an adequate fusion stimulus, and variously specified with reference to parallelism of the lines of sight or with reference to the relative directions assumed by the eyes during binocular fixation of a given object. Cf. *anisophoria; cyclophoria; esophoria; exophoria; heterophoria; hyperphoria; hypophoria; orthophoria.*

habitual p. The phoria obtained through the patient's habitually worn lens prescription.

horizontal p. 1. Lateral phoria. 2. The phoria obtained with the fixation object in the horizontal visual plane.

induced p. 1. The phoria obtained through the subjectively determined lens correction. 2. A phoria obtained through any lens correction other than the one worn habitually.

lateral p. The phoria representing deviations in the plane of fixation.

monofixational p. A small angle strabismus, of about 1° to 4°, which persists after a greater deviation has been overcome to obtain peripheral fusion. It is of a greater magnitude than fixation disparity and is usually associated with central suppression of the deviating eye.

version p. 1. A tendency for both eyes to deviate in the same direction in the absence of a stimulus eliciting fixation attention, as in anaphoria or cataphoria. 2. Anisophoria.

vertical p. The phoria representing deviations perpendicular to the plane of fixation.

Phoriafractor, Smith (fo′re-ah-frak″-tor). A trade name for a device, interposed between a refractor and a near-point chart, consisting essentially of a metal plate with two rectangular apertures through which each eye sees half of the target.

phoriagraph, Rosen (fo′re-ah-graf″). A plastic rectangular chart of small numerals and letters with a centered transilluminated ruby-red aperture, to be viewed with a dark neutral or red filter in front of one eye and a light green filter in front of the other, making only the numerals and the letters visible to one eye and only the red spot to the other. The letter or the numeral on which the spot is seen superimposed gives a measure of the vertical and lateral phoria.

phoriascope (fo′re-ah-skōp). An instrument containing prisms for use in visual training.

Phoro-Lenscorometer (fo″ro-lenz-ko-rom′eh-ter). A device for determining the distance of a phoropter lens from the cornea, consisting essentially of a rule, scaled to compensate for the thickness of the instrument, which is placed through the open aperture of the phoropter against the closed eyelid to provide a direct reading.

phorometer (fo-rom′eh-ter). 1. Any instrument or device for determining the kind and extent of phoria. 2. An instrument containing rotary prisms, Maddox grooves, and lens cells for determining phorias and ductions.

reflecting p. A phorometer containing mirrors to reflect separate targets into the two eyes.

Stevens′ p. A phorometer consisting of two single, five prism diopter ophthalmic prisms, mounted one before each eye, so that the base-apex lines of the two prisms are parallel to each other but in opposite directions. The two prisms are so geared together that both rotate simultaneously in the same direction.

Wilson′s p. A phorometer in which a revolving disk containing fixed prisms for dissociation is before the right eye and a rotary (variable) prism for measuring phorias and ductions is before the left eye.

phorometry (fo-rom′eh-tre). Measurement of the kind and extent of phoria with a phorometer.

phoro-optometer (fōr″o-op-tom′eh-ter). An instrument for determining phorias, ductions, and the refractive state of the eye, consisting essentially of rotary prisms, Maddox grooves, and lens cells.

phoropter (fōr-op′ter). An instrument for determining the refractive state of the eye, phorias, ductions, amplitude of accommodation, etc., consisting essentially of a housing containing rotating disks with convex and concave spherical and cylindrical lenses, pinhole disks, occluders, and sometimes color filters and prisms. Attached to the front of the housing are crossed cylinder lenses, rotary prisms, and Maddox grooves.

phoroscope (fōr'o-skōp). 1. An instrument for reproducing an image, as of a photograph, conveyed by electric or other processes not necessarily optical, from a distance. 2. A variant of phorometer, sometimes applied to a trial frame with a bracket for attachment to a table.

phose (fōz). A subjective visual sensation, as of light or color.

phosgenic (fos-jen'ik). Light-producing.

phosis (fo'sis). Any condition of the eye, the optic nerve, or the brain, giving rise to a subjective visual sensation.

phosphene (fos'fēn). A subjective visual sensation of a luminous spot or an area in the external visual field, arising from mechanical or electrical stimulation of the eyeball.

accommodation p. A luminous border appearing around the visual field following a conscious sudden relaxation of accommodation. Syn., *Czermak's phosphene.*

Czermak's p. Accommodation phosphene.

electrical p. A phosphene arising from electrical stimulation of the eyeball.

flick p. A phosphene observed on sudden movement of a rested and dark-adapted eye, attributed by Nebel to instantaneous and transient deformation of the posterior surface of the vitreous.

movement p. A phosphene appearing in the portion of the visual field corresponding to the physiological blind spot, arising from sudden movements of the eyes in the dark.

pressure p. A phosphene which appears during local pressure on the eyeball in the sector of the visual field corresponding to the region of the retina receiving the pressure.

phosphor. A substance which has the property of absorbing energy and releasing it again in the form of phosphorescence.

phosphorescence (fos"fo-res'ens). 1. The property of emitting light, without any apparent rise in temperature, or the light so produced, due to absorption of radiation from some other source, and lasting after exposure has ceased. The emitted light differs in composition and color from the absorbed radiation. Cf. *fluorescence.* 2. The glow, as of phosphorus, decaying wood, or certain living organisms, resulting from a slow process of oxidation.

phosphorescent (fos"fo-res'ent). 1. Pertaining to or exhibiting phosphorescence. 2. A substance which exhibits phosphorescence.

phot. A unit of illumination equal to 1 lumen per sq. cm.

photalgia (fo-tal'je-ah). Pain produced by excessive light. Syn., *photodynia.*

photaugiaphobia (fo-taw"je-ah-fo'-be-ah). Abnormal intolerance of glare.

photerythron (fo"teh-rith'ron). A deuteranope.

photerythrous (fo"teh-rith'rus). Deuteranopic.

photesthesia (fo"tes-the'ze-ah). Sensitiveness to light.

photic (fo'tik). Pertaining to light or the production of light.

photics (fo'tiks). The branch of physics dealing with light, including ultraviolet and infrared radiation.

photism (fo'tizm). Visual sensation, as of light or color, induced by another sense, body temperature, or by thought.

photo- (fo'to). A combining form denoting *light*.

photoactinic (fo"to-ak-tin'ik). 1. Pertaining to or emitting both visible and actinic light. 2. Capable of producing actinic effects.

photoallergy (fo"to-al'er-je). Marked hypersensitivity to light.

photocampsis (fo"to-kamp'sis). Refraction of light.

photocatalysis (fo"to-kah-tal'ih-sis). The acceleration of a reaction by radiant energy, particularly light, either directly, or indirectly, through excitation of an intermediate substance.

photocell (fo'to-cel). A cell which produces electric current when radiant energy is incident upon it.

photoceptor (fo"to-sep'tor). A photoreceptor.

photochemical (fo"to-kem'ih-kal). Pertaining to, capable of, or resulting in chemical change by the action of light.

photochromatic (fo"to-kro-mat'ik). 1. Pertaining to colored light. 2. Of or pertaining to color photography.

photochromic (fo-to-kro'mic). Pertaining to substances which change in color and in light transmission properties upon exposure to a change of light intensity or to ultraviolet radiation. The change may, or may not, be reversible.

photocoagulation (fo"to-ko-ag"u-la'-shun). Coagulation of tissue by the heat generated at the focus of an intense beam of light. In the eye, it is used in the treatment of retinal detachments, retinal holes, aneurysms, hemorrhages, and malignant and benign neoplasms.

photocolorimeter (fo"to-kul"or-im'-eh-ter). A photoelectric colorimeter.

photoconductivity (fo"to-kon-duk-tiv'ih-te). Electrical conductivity of certain insulators and semi-conductors, such as selenium, induced by radiation of suitable wavelength.

photodrome (fo'to-drōm). An apparatus consisting essentially of a rotating disk containing various patterns and a regulated flashing light. By varying the frequency of the flashes, the disk may be made to appear stationary, rotating at a different speed, or rotating in the opposite direction.

photodynamics (fo"to-di-nam'iks). The effect of light on organisms, especially the phototropic effect in plants.

photodynia (fo"to-din'ih-ah). Photalgia.

photodysphoria (fo"to-dis-fo're-ah). Photophobia.

photoelectric (fo"to-e-lek'trik). 1. Pertaining to the emission of electrons from liquid, solid, or gaseous bodies on exposure to radiations of certain wavelengths. 2. Pertaining to the decrease in electrical resistance of certain substances on exposure to radiations of certain wavelengths.

photoelectricity (fo"to-e-lek"tris'ih-te). 1. Electricity produced by the effect of radiation of suitable wavelengths on certain metals. 2. A change in electric resistance of certain metals on exposure to radiations of suitable wavelengths.

photoelectroluminescence (fo"to-e-lek"tro-lu"mih-nes'ens). Electroluminescence in which the electric current is created by light or other electromagnetic energy; a means of light amplification.

photoelectron (fo"to-e-lek'tron). One of a stream of electrons emitted from certain substances on exposure to radiations of suitable wavelengths.

Photo-Electronic Keratoscope (fo"-to-e-lek-tron'ik). An instrument for evaluating corneal topography and determining corneal curvatures, consisting essentially of a target of black and white concentric rings of varying widths and a camera to photograph the reflected corneal image of the target. The photograph is analyzed with a densitometer.

photogene (fo'to-jēn). 1. A photograph. *Obs.* 2. An afterimage.

photogenesis (fo"to-jen'e-sis). The production or generation of light, as in certain bacteria or in the firefly; phosphorescence.

photogenic (fo"to-jen'ik). 1. Due to light; producing or generating light, as in certain bacteria or in the firefly; phosphorescent. 2. Pertaining to photography.

photogenous (fo-toj'e-nus). Photogenic.

photoisomerization (fo"to-i-som"er-i-za'shun). Isomerization from absorption of radiant energy, especially light.

photokeratograph (fo"to-ker'ah-to-graf). A photograph of the reflected corneal image of the target of a photokeratoscope, used to calculate corneal curvatures and evaluate corneal topography.

photokeratography (fo"to-ker"ah-tog'raf-e). Determination of corneal curvatures and topography by photographing and measuring the corneal image of the target of a photokeratoscope.

photokeratoscope (fo"to-ker'ah-to-skōp). An instrument consisting essentially of a Placido's disk and attachments for viewing or photographing the image of the disk on the cornea.

photokeratoscopy (fo"to-ker"ah-tos'-ko-pe). Determination of corneal curvatures and topography by observing or photographing the corneal image of the target of a photokeratoscope.

photokinesis (fo"to-kih-ne'sis). A movement or motion response of a motile organism to changes in intensity of light stimulation but not in response to the direction of the light stimulation.

photolabile (fo"to-la'bil). Affected by, or unstable in the presence of, radiant energy, especially visible radiant energy, as, for example, a photopigment which is converted by light to a different substance.

photology (fo-tol'o-je). The branch of physics which deals with light.

photoluminescence (fo"to-lu"mih-nes'ens). The emission of visible radiant energy by a substance on absorption of radiant energy of a different wavelength.

photolysis (fo-tol'ih-sis). Chemical decomposition by the action of light.

photoma (fo-to'mah). A visual hallucination consisting of sparks or flashes of light.

photometer (fo-tom'eh-ter). An instrument for measuring radiant energy in the ultraviolet, infrared, or visible regions of the electromagnetic spectrum. Syn., *illuminometer.*

Abney's p. A direct, heterochromatic, comparison photometer for determining luminosity in which one portion of a beam of light passes through a wavelength-selecting spectroscopic system and the other portion through an episcotister-controlled system to form adjacent patches of light for comparison and luminance matching.

acuity p. A photometer employing acuteness of vision as a measure of illuminance.

bar p. Bench photometer.

barrier-layer cell p. A photometer employing a barrier-layer cell which generates a current when exposed to light.

bench p. A device consisting of a photometer head fixed to an optical bench between reference and test sources which are mounted on independently sliding carriers. It provides for an illumination match by varying the relative distances of the sources from the head and computing according to the inverse square law. Syn., *bar photometer*.

Bunsen's p. A photometer employing a Bunsen disk, a translucent paraffined spot in the center of a substantially opaque white paper flanked by two mirrors forming an angle of 90° bisected by the paper, permitting a simultaneous view of both sides of the disk. When the spot disappears, the illumination on the two sides is equal. Syn., *grease spot photometer*.

cosine p. 1. A photometer in which the illumination on the comparison surface is varied by tilting it relative to the direction of the incident light. 2. A light meter corrected for the cosine error introduced by the angle of incidence of the light.

diaphragm p. A photometer employing a variable aperture for controlling the intensity of illumiation from the reference or test source.

distribution p. A photometer, used in conjunction with a goniometer, for determining the illumination of a light source in various directions. Syn., *goniophotometer*.

extinction p. A photometer employing the criterion of just invisible, the intensity of the test light usually being controlled by a calibrated neutral wedge filter.

flicker p. 1. A photometer employing the criterion of elimination of flicker when the test source and the reference standard are of equal luminance and alternately presented at a rate less than the critical flicker frequency for a given luminance difference, but greater than the critical flicker frequency for hue differences. 2. A photometer in which the critical flicker frequency for the alternate presentation of a test source and a reference standard

is considered an index of the luminance of the test source.

Förster's p. A photometer with an adjustable diaphragm, used to determine the least amount of light that renders an object visible. Syn., *photoptometer*.

grease spot p. Bunsen photometer.

integrating p. A photometer with an integrating sphere or equivalent attachment for measuring the total output of light from a source, independent of the variation of intensity with direction.

integrating sphere p. A photometer employing a hollow sphere coated internally with a perfectly diffusing material such that the luminance at all points is equal and proportional to the total emitted by the source. Hence a measurement of the illumination on any segment of the sphere indicates the total flux of the source.

Lummer-Brodhun p. A photometer with a Lummer-Brodhun cube or head, in which two adjacent or concentric portions of a comparison viewing screen are separately illuminated by the test source and the reference or measuring standard.

Macbeth p. A portable bar photometer using a Lummer-Brodhun cube, an eyepiece, and a movable comparison lamp illuminating a diffusing surface seen as an annulus by reflection within the cube. The portion of the object to be measured is seen through the cube as a luminous area within the annulus. The brightness of the annulus is then adjusted to match the brightness of the central spot. Syn., *Macbeth illuminometer*.

Martens p. A photometer which, by means of a Wollaston prism, produces perpendicularly polarized images of the reference and test surfaces which are equated in brightness by rotating an analyzing prism.

meridian *p.* A photometer with telescopic and reflecting mirror arrangements for the simultaneous comparison of two stars.

photoelectric *p.* A photometer employing a calibrated photoelectric cell instead of the human eye.

physical *p.* A photometer consisting essentially of a radiant energy-sensitive element, such as a photoemissive cell, barrier layer cell, or thermopile, and an intensity indicator.

polarization *p.* A photometer employing light-polarizing elements to control intensity.

Pritchard *p.* A precision, portable photometer for measuring luminance in a selected portion of the visual environment, the size of the measured field being regulated by an aperture ranging from six minutes to two degrees of arc. Light from the selected area, focused directly onto the aperture plate by an objective lens, activates a photomultiplier. A built-in radium plaque serves as a standard. Syn., *Spectra-Pritchard photometer.*

Pulfrich *p.* A photometer which makes use of the Pulfrich effect to determine an illumination match. Syn., *stereo photometer.*

radiometric *p.* Any photometer employing a device, such as a thermocouple or photoelectric tube, for converting incident radiant energy into another form of energy for purposes of measurement.

Ritchie *p.* A photometer consisting of a double diffuse reflecting viewing comparison screen, in the form of a wedge, arranged and housed to reflect separately from each surface the light from a reference source and a test source. Syn., *wedge photometer.*

Rumford *p.* A device for comparing two sources of light by placing a small opaque object or bar in front of a white screen and adjusting the distances of the two sources until the densities of the shadows cast by the object are equal. Syn., *shadow photometer.*

shadow *p.* Rumford photometer.

Simmance-Abady *p.* A pair of base-to-base, conical, diffuse reflecting surfaces rotated on an axis oblique to the apex-to-apex line and viewed through an aperture from a direction perpendicular to the axis of rotation so that the two conical surfaces, independently illuminated, one by a reference source and the other by a test source, are seen alternately, and hence flickering occurs if the separate illuminations are unequal.

Spectra-Pritchard *p.* Pritchard photometer.

stellar *p.* A photometer used in astronomy for measuring the luminance of a star, as by comparison with an artificial star of variable luminance.

stereo *p.* Pulfrich photometer.

thermopile *p.* A photometer employing a thermopile to measure intensity of illumination.

visual *p.* A photometer used to evaluate intensity in the visible spectrum and in which equality of brightness with a comparison standard is established through visual observation.

wedge *p.* Ritchie photometer.

photometry (fo-tom′eh-tre). The measurement of light; the use of a photometer.

flicker *p.* Light measurement by means of a flicker photometer.

heterochromatic *p.* The measurement of light intensities of sources of different hue.

visual *p.* Photometry by means of intensity judgments with the human eye.

photomotor (fo″to-mo′tor). Pertaining to the response of a muscle to light stimuli, as in the contracting of the pupil.

photomultiplier (fo″to-mul″tih-pli′-er). A photoelectric device in which electrons from the cathode of a photoelectric cell or tube are caused to impinge on a second cathode, which in turn emits secondary electrons more numerous than the incident electrons, thus amplifying the current.

photon (fo′ton). 1. The basic unit of radiant energy, given by the equation: $E = hv$, where $h =$ Planck's constant $(6.55 \times 10^{-27}$ erg sec.) and $v =$ frequency electromagnetic radiation concerned $(v = c/\lambda$, where $c =$ velocity of light, approximately 3×10^{10} cm. per sec., and $\lambda =$ wavelength of radiation); the quantum. 2. Troland.

photone (fo′tōn). A visual hallucination or a visualization of light.

photonosus (fo-ton′o-sus). A disease due to exposure to excessive light. Syn., *photopathy.*

photo-ophthalmia (fo″to-of-thal′me-ah). Photophthalmia.

photopathologic (fo″to-path″o-loj′-ik). Pertaining to a disease due to exposure to excessive light.

photopathy (fo-top′ah-the). Photonosus.

photoped (fo′to-ped). A photometer head.

photoperceptive (fo″to-per-sep′tiv). Capable of perceiving light.

photophobia (fo″to-fo′be-ah). An abnormal intolerance or fear of light.

photophobic (fo″to-fo′bik). Pertaining to or affected with photophobia.

photophore (fo′to-fōr). A simple or complex organ that produces bioluminescence, such as may be found in certain worms, arthropods, insects, and deep sea fishes.

photophthalmia (fo″tof-thal′me-ah). Inflammation of the eyes from exposure to intense light, as in snow blindness or from a welder's arc.

photopia (fo-to′pe-ah). Photopic vision.

photopic (fo-top′ik). Having the characteristics of photopic vision or referring to the levels of illumination at which the eye is light adapted.

photopigment (fo″to-pig′ment). A pigment which is affected by, or unstable in the presence of, radiant energy, especially visible radiant energy, such that its chemical composition is altered. In the eye, the breakdown of photopigments by light is the first stage in the visual process.

photopsia (fo-top′se-ah). An unformed hallucinatory perception of sparks, lights, or colors, frequently due to disease of the optic nerve, the retina, or the brain.

photopsins (fo-top′sinz). The photopigments in the retinal cones. Cf. *scotopsins.*

photopter (fo-top′ter). The unit of light transmission of Tscherning's filters designated by Tscherning to be $\frac{1}{10}$ of the incident light, hence 2 photopters represent a transmission of $(\frac{1}{10})^2$, or $\frac{1}{100}$, and x photopters represent a transmission of $(\frac{1}{10})^x$.

photoptic (fo-top′tik). Pertaining to photopsia.

photoptometer (fo″top-tom′eh-ter). An instrument for determining the light threshold which just permits objects to become visible or identifiable.

photoptometry (fo″top-tom′eh-tre). Determination of the light threshold which just permits objects to become visible or identifiable.

photoreceptive (fo″to-re-sep′tive). Capable of receiving and perceiving light; activated by light.

photoreceptor (fo″to-re-sep′tor). A receptor capable of being activated by light stimuli, as a rod or cone cell of the eye.

photoretinitis (fo″to-ret-ih-ni′tis). Inflammation of the retina due to exposure to intense light, as from viewing an eclipse or a welder's arc with insufficient protection. The condition results in a central scotoma, which may be temporary, and may be followed by pigmentary changes in the macular area.

photoscope (fo'to-skōp). 1. A statoscope. 2. A type of fluoroscope.

photoscopy (fo-tos'ko-pe). Retinoscopy. *Obs.*

photosensitive (fo″to-sen'sih-tiv). 1. Pertaining to the cells of an organ or an organism that are capable of being stimulated to activity by light. 2. Pertaining to certain chemicals which have the property of reacting to light.

photosensitivity (fo″to-sen″sih-tiv'ih-te). 1. The capacity of the cells of an organ or an organism to be stimulated to activity by light. 2. The property of certain chemicals to react to light.

photosensitize (fo″to-sen'sih-tīz). To sensitize a substance or the cells of an organ or an organism to light stimulation.

photosensory (fo″to-sen'so-re). Pertaining to the act or process by which an organ or an organism responds to light stimuli.

photoskiascopy (fo″to-ski-as'ko-pe). An objective method of determination of the refractive error based on the pattern of light and dark areas appearing in the pupil when illuminated by the light of a stationary ophthalmoscope, and its modification by neutralization with ophthalmic lenses.

photostatic (fo'to-stat-ik). Of, constituting, or relating to postural, orientation, or equilibrium reflexes initiated by light stimulation.

photostimulator (fo″to-stim″u-la'-tor). An instrument which generates light pulses (flashes) of variable frequency, duration, and intensity.

phototachometer (fo″to-tah-kom'eh-ter). A device for measuring the velocity of light by means of a rotating mirror.

phototaxis (fo″to-tak'sis). A purposive movement of a motile organism in response to the direction of light stimulation. It is positive when directed toward the light and negative when away from the light.

phototherapy (fo″to-ther'ah-pe). The treatment of a disease or condition by exposure to certain portions of the spectrum.

phototonus (fo-tot'o-nus). An irritable state of protoplasm to light stimulus; specifically applied to reciprocal co-ordination of muscle tone of certain symmetrical animals, when light is employed to induce motion.

phototopia (fo″to-to'pe-ah). A subjective light sensation.

phototrauma (fo″to-traw'mah). Injury from exposure to intense light, as in snow blindness.

phototropism (fo-tot'ro-pizm). The directional orientation of parts of sessile plants and animals toward (positive) or away from (negative) light stimulation.

phthiriasis ciliorum (thir-i'ah-sis sil-e-ōr'um). Infestation of the eyelashes or the eyelids with lice.

phthiriasis palpebrarum (thir-i'ah-sis pal-pe-brah'rum). Infestation of the lid margins by lice.

phthisis (thi'sis). A wasting away of tissue or of a part of the body.

   bulbi, p. Shrinking, wasting, and atrophy of the eyeball; the sequela of panophthalmitis, absolute glaucoma, etc. Vision is completely lost, and intraocular pressure is abnormally low.

   corneae, p. Shrinking, wasting, and atrophy of the cornea; the sequela of anterior staphyloma, etc.

   essential p. Ophthalmomalacia.

physostigmine (fi″so-stig'mēn, -min). Eserine.

pi (π). The Greek letter used as the symbol for the *angle of eccentricity* in the field of regard. *Fry.*

pia mater (pi"ah ma'ter). The innermost vascular member of the three meninges covering the brain, the spinal cord, and the optic nerve. It is closely attached to the central nervous system and all of its folds, and helps form the tela chorioidea or choroid plexus of each ventricle of the brain. From the optic nerve it becomes continuous for the most part with the sclera, but some fibers run into the choroid and some into the border tissue around the optic nerve.

Pick's (piks) **disease; vision.** See under the nouns.

Pickford test. See under *test.*

picture, retinal. The retinal image.

Pierce's test (pēr'sez). See under *test.*

Piéron's law; theory. See under the nouns.

piezometer (pi"e-zom'eh-ter). A type of orbitonometer in which the compressibility of the orbital contents is represented by the amount of depression produced by the addition of a 25 mg. weight on a foot-plate resting on a vertically directed anesthetized cornea.

Pigeon-Cantonnet stereoscope (pe'-je-ōn kan'ton-a). See under *stereoscope.*

pigment, photosensitive. Photopigment.

pigmentum nigrum (pig-men'tum ni'grum). The pigment of the stroma of the choroid.

pili torti (pi'li tōr'te). A dominant inherited condition in which the eyelashes, and sometimes eyebrows and head hair, are short, scanty, twisted, and brittle. Affected children are usually born bald and remain so for one or two years.

pilocarpine (pi"lo-kar'pēn, -pin). An alkaloid obtained from leaves of the South American shrubs *Pilocarpus jaborandi* and *P. microphyllus,* and used in salt form in a dilute solution as a miotic.

Piltz's reflex (piltz'ez). 1. Attention pupillary reflex. 2. Orbicularis pupillary reflex.

Piltz-Westphal (piltz-vest'fahl) **phenomenon; reaction; reflex.** Orbicularis pupillary reflex.

pimelopterygium (pim"eh-lo-teh-rij'-e-um). Pinguecula.

pince-nez (pans'na"). Eyeglasses, without supporting temples, held on the nose by tension from springs attached to the nose pads.

pinguecula (ping-gwek'u-lah). A small, slightly raised, yellowish, nonfatty thickening of the bulbar conjunctiva on either side of the cornea, usually the nasal side, essentially formed by hyaline degeneration and proliferation of elastic fibers of the substantia propria.

pinhole. A pinhole pupil.

pink. Typically, a hue approximately complementary to a blue-green of 493 mμ; a desaturated or pastel red, orange-red, or bluish-red.

pink eye. See under *eye.*

Piper's law (pi'perz). See under *law.*

pit. A surface depression, hollow, or indentation.

    foveal p. Fovea centralis.

    Gaule's p's. Gaule's spots.

    Herbert's p's. Facets in the cornea appearing in the chronic stage of trachoma, due to degeneration and sloughing of its superficial layer with subsequent filling by optically clear epithelium.

    lens p. A tiny depression formed by the invagination of the surface ectoderm or lens plate of the embryo, adjacent to the optic vesicle. It subsequently develops into the lens vesicle and the adult crystalline lens. Syn., *fovea lentis; lenticular sac.*

    optic p's. Paired pits formed by lateral depressions in the neural ectoderm of the forebrain during

[548]

the stage of closure of the neural groove, the earliest embryonic stage in the development of the optic cups.

optic disk, p. of the. A rare, congenital, craterlike depression in the optic nerve head, typically located in its inferior temporal quadrant near the disk edge and generally between ⅓ to ⅙ disk diameter in size, between 2 and 8 diopters in depth, and round or oval in shape. The visual field may show an arcuate scotoma continuous with an enlarged blind spot and a central angiospastic retinopathy may be an accompaniment.

pitch. 1. Any one of several materials of varying colors and sometimes transparent, characteristically sticky when warm, and hard or brittle at ordinary temperatures, used in ophthalmic laboratories for cementing a lens to a block, for impregnating polishing pads, and in molded form as a surfacing lap. 2. The distance between corresponding points in two adjacent threads of a screw, measured along the axis.

Pitt's law. See under *law.*

pityriasis rubra pilaris (pit″ih-ri′ah-sis). A chronic skin disease characterized by the formation of hard yellowish or reddish papules at the mouths of the hair follicles which may be accompanied by involvement of the conjunctiva and cornea. The conjunctiva may have a general thickening and may have typical mother-of-pearl papules on its bulbar portion, and the cornea may have a generalized epithelial thickening with pannus, ulceration, or interstitial keratitis.

placebo (plah-se′bo). A prescription or medicine given merely to satisfy a patient, irrespective of its corrective or therapeutic value.

Placido's disk (plah-si′dōz). See under *disk.*

placidoscope (plah-si′do-skōp). Placido's disk.

placode, lens (plak′ōd). Lens plate.

pladaroma (plad″ah-ro′mah). A soft tumor of the eyelid.

pladarosis (plad″ah-ro′sis). Pladaroma.

Planck's (planks) **constant; law; theory.** See under the nouns.

plane. A surface of zero curvature.

active p. The section of a cylindrical lens or prism in which the chief refraction occurs, as distinguished from the *passive plane,* perpendicular to this plane.

axial p. Muscle plane.

Broca's p. Visual plane.

cardinal p. Principal plane.

conjugate p's. The object plane and its corresponding image plane considered as a pair in the Gaussian representation of an optical system.

equatorial p. The plane, containing the transverse and vertical axes, which divides the eyeball into anterior and posterior halves.

face p. A plane taken to represent the geometric location and orientation of the face, such as one tangent to the two superciliary ridges and the point of the chin.

fixation, p. of. The plane containing the axes of fixation of the two eyes.

focal p. 1. A plane, perpendicular to the optical axis, passing through one of the focal points of an optical system. 2. Occasionally, any image plane in an optical system.

    focal p., anterior. Primary focal plane.

    focal p., posterior. Secondary focal plane.

    focal p., primary. A plane, perpendicular to the optical axis, passing through the primary focal point of an optical system. Syn., *anterior focal plane.*

    focal p., secondary. A plane, perpendicular to the optical axis, passing through the secondary focal point of an optical system. Syn., *posterior focal plane.*

frontal p. A plane through two points of reference representing the two eyes, such as the entrance pupils, the centers of rotation, the nodal points, or the sighting intersects, and perpendicular to a plane connecting the same two points of reference with the point of fixation.

frontoparallel p. Any plane parallel to a frontal plane.

    frontoparallel p., apparent. A surface containing the point of fixation and all other points judged by the observer to be equidistant from his frontal plane.

    frontoparallel p., objective. A surface containing the point of fixation and all other points which are equidistant from the frontal plane.

horizontal p. of the eye. The plane, containing sagittal and transverse axes, which divides the eyeball into superior and inferior halves.

image p. A plane, perpendicular to the optical axis, through the axial image point of an optical system.

incidence, p. of. The plane containing the incident light ray and the normal to the surface at the point of incidence.

Listing's p. A plane passing through the center of rotation perpendicular to the primary position of the line of sight. According to Listing, all fixational movements of the eye can be analyzed in terms of rotation of the line of sight about axes in this plane. Syn., *primary axis plane.*

median p. The plane, containing the sagittal and the vertical axes, which divides the eyeball into right and left halves.

meridional p. in oblique astigmatism. Tangential plane in oblique astigmatism.

muscle p. A plane containing the line of traction of an extraocular muscle and the center of rotation of the eyeball. Syn., *axial plane; plane of rotation; plane of traction.*

nodal p. A plane, perpendicular to the optical axis, passing through one of the nodal points of an optical system.

object p. A plane, perpendicular to the optical axis, through the axial object point of an optical system.

orbital p. 1. The plane approximating the surface of the maxillary bone which helps to form the floor of the orbit. 2. The visual plane.

passive p. The section of a cylindrical lens or prism in which no refraction occurs, as distinguished from the *active plane* perpendicular to this plane.

polarization, p. of. The plane which is perpendicular to the plane of vibration of the electric vector of linearly polarized light.

primary axis p. Listing's plane.

primary p. in oblique astigmatism. Tangential plane in oblique astigmatism.

principal p. A plane in an optical system, perpendicular to the optical axis, at which refraction of the incident or emergent light may be considered to take place. Syn., *cardinal plane; unit plane.*

    principal p., primary. The principal plane at which the total refraction with respect to the incident light may be considered to take place. It is located at the intersections of the incident rays from the primary focal point with the corresponding emergent parallel rays.

    principal p., secondary. The principal plane at which the total refraction with respect to the emergent light may be considered to take place. It is located at the intersections of the emergent rays converging to the secondary focal point with the corresponding incident parallel rays.

principal p. of extraordinary ray. A plane in a crystal containing the optical axis and the extraordinary ray.

principal p. of ordinary ray. A plane in a crystal containing the optical axis and the ordinary ray.

principal section p. The plane containing the optical axis and normal to a surface of a doubly refracting crystal.

refraction, p. of. The plane containing the refracted light ray and the normal to the surface at the point of refraction.

regard, p. of. A plane passing through the point of regard and two points of reference for the two eyes, such as the centers of the entrance pupils, the centers of rotation, the sighting intersects, or the nodal points.

rotation, p. of. Muscle plane.

sagittal p. in oblique astigmatism. A plane perpendicular to the tangential plane in oblique astigmatism. Syn., *secondary plane*.

secondary axis p. According to Listing's law, the plane containing the axes around which fixational rotations may occur when the eye is in a secondary position. It is described as a plane bisecting the angle made by the equatorial plane of the eye when it changes from the primary to the secondary direction of fixation.

secondary p. in oblique astigmatism. Sagittal plane in oblique astigmatism.

spectacle p. A plane taken to represent the geometric location and orientation of the spectacle lenses in relation to the eyes and usually considered to correspond with the posterior vertices of the two spectacle lenses and to lie from 12 to 15 mm. anterior to the two corneal apices.

symmetrical p's. Planes perpen-

dicular to the axis of an optical system and containing the symmetrical points.

tangent p. A modified Bjerrum's tangent screen having a black surface with a white fixation spot facing the patient with the reverse surface white and divided into squares or circles. The outlines of scotomata are shown on the white side by pins thrust through from the black surface.

tangential p. in oblique astigmatism. A plane containing the optical axis of the lens system and the off axis object point. Syn., *meridional plane; primary plane*.

tilting p. Tilting field.

traction, p. of. Muscle plane.

unit p. Principal plane.

vibration, p. of. The plane, perpendicular to the plane of polarization, indicating the direction of oscillation of the electric vector of linearly polarized radiation.

visual p. The plane containing the two visual axes. Syn., *Broca's plane; orbital plane*.

visual projection, p. of. The plane in which a visually perceived object is subjectively localized.

xy p. The horizontal plane of the eye containing both the x axis and the y axis. When the eye is in the primary position, this plane cuts a circle on the eyeball called by Helmholtz the retinal horizon.

xz p. The vertical plane of the eye containing both the x axis and the z axis.

yz p. The vertical plane of the eye containing both the y axis and the z axis. When the eye is in the primary position, this plane cuts a circle on the eyeball called by Helmholtz the principal retinal meridian.

plano (pla′no). Afocal; without dioptric power.

plano- (pla′no-). A combining form denoting that one surface is plane, e.g., planoconvex.

planoconcave (pla″no-kon′kāv). Pertaining to a lens that is flat on one surface and concave on the other.

planoconvex (pla″no-kon′veks). Pertaining to a lens that is flat on one surface and convex on the other.

plano-prism (pla′no-prizm). A prism with no dioptric power.

planum orbitale (pla′num ōr-bih-tal′e). Orbital plane.

plasmoma (plaz-mo′mah). A tumor consisting essentially of plasma cells, sometimes found on the conjunctiva in chronic inflammatory conditions such as trachoma.

plastic. 1. Pertaining to stereoscopic or third dimension effect, as in plastic relief. 2. Any of various materials showing plasticity, often used in lenses, spectacle frames, artificial eyes, etc.

plate. A flat, or nearly flat, structure or layer.

AO H-R-R p's. Pseudoisochromatic plates for testing color vision, each containing one or two variously located geometric figures (circle, cross, or triangle). Four plates are for demonstration; six are for screening into red-green deficient, blue-yellow deficient, and normal; ten are for further testing of the red-green deficient; and four are for further testing of the blue-yellow deficient.

Boström's p's. A series of 16 pseudoisochromatic plates for testing color vision, 12 containing digits, and 4 blank to detect malingering.

Boström-Kugelberg p's. A series of 20 pseudoisochromatic plates for testing color vision, 15 containing digits, 2 winding trails for illiterates, and 3 blank to detect malingering.

cribriform p. Lamina cribrosa.

Dvorine's p's. A series of pseudoisochromatic plates for testing color vision.

half-wave p. A thin sheet of crystalline material, such as mica or quartz, cut parallel to the optical axis and of such thickness as to produce a 180° phase difference between the ordinary and extraordinary ray vibrations. Its effect is to alter the direction of vibration of plane-polarized light.

Hardy-Rand-Rittler p's. AO H-R-R plates.

Hertel's p's. A series of 35 plates for testing color vision consisting of 2 for indoctrination and detection of malingering, 10 pseudoisochromatic plates (based on Stilling's plates) for the detection of red-green deficiencies, 6 pseudoisochromatic plates to differentiate protans from deutans, 4 plates incorporating marked brightness as well as color differences, 6 "selection" plates containing a random array of disks of similar hues, 3 plates to test the effect of adjacent stimuli on hue judgment, and 4 plates for the detection of yellow-blue deficiencies.

Ishihara p's. A series of pseudoisochromatic plates for testing color vision.

Laurent half-shade p. A semicircular half-wave plate of quartz or other crystal set between the polarizer and analyzer of an instrument to measure rotatory polarization.

lens, p. The thickened surface ectoderm in the embryo, peripheral to the primary optic vesicle which forms, by its invagination, the lens pit and subsequently the lens vesicle and adult crystalline lens. Syn., *lens placode.*

optic p. That portion of the neural ectoderm in the embryonic forebrain, located at the anterior extremity of the neural fold, which gives rise to the retina and the pars caeca retinae.

orbital p. The portion of any facial or cranial bone that forms a part of the orbit, such as the lamina papyracea, the process of the frontal bone, or the process of the superior maxillary bone.

orbital p., frontal. The portion of the frontal bone that forms most of the roof of the orbit.

orbital p., maxillary. The portion of the maxillary bone that forms the floor of the orbit anterior to the palatine bone.

orbital p., zygomatic. The portion of the malar or zygomatic bone that forms a portion of the lateral wall and floor of the orbit.

phase p. A layer of transparent material introduced into an optical system to advance or retard the direct light a fraction of a wavelength with respect to diffracted light originating from the same source. Syn., *phase disk.*

phase retardation p. A piece of doubly refracting material cut and polished so that it retards either the ordinary or extraordinary ray more than its companion ray, thereby changing the phase relationship between the two rays

pseudoisochromatic p. A chart for testing color vision on which are printed numerous small disks, varying in color and brightness,

some of which are oriented to form numbers, letters, or geometric figures so as to be perceived only by those with normal color vision and not by those with deficient color vision, or vice versa.

quarter-wave p. A thin sheet of crystalline material, such as mica or quartz, cut parallel to the optical axis and of such thickness as to produce a 90° phase difference between the ordinary and extraordinary ray vibrations. It is used to transform plane-polarized light into circularly or elliptically polarized light, or the reverse, or to analyze any form of polarized light.

Rabkin polychromatic p's. A set of 20 pseudoisochromatic charts designed by Rabkin to detect color vision abnormalities and to classify them according to type and severity of deficiency.

Savart p. A device consisting of two plane parallel plates of equal thickness, cut from a uniaxial crystal, such as quartz or calcite, such that the angle between the optic axis and the normal to the surface shall be the same for both. The two plates, shaped into squares, are mounted geo-

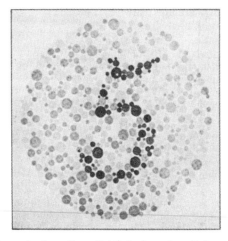

Fig. 33. A pseudoisochromatic plate. (From *Ophthalmology*, Arno E. Town, Lea & Febiger, 1951)

metrically parallel but with one optical axis turned 90° with respect to the other. It is used to detect linearly polarized light in a pencil of natural light, to study elliptically polarized light, and to alter phase differences.

Stilling's p's. A series of pseudoisochromatic plates for testing color vision.

tarsal p. Tarsus.

Velhagen's p's. A series of plates for testing color vision, of which some are pseudoisochromatic and others are based on color selection, color contrast, and brightness difference.

zone p. A screen consisting of a series of alternately opaque and transparent concentric rings whose common borders have radii successively proportional to the square roots of whole numbers. The rings will correspond to half-period zones for a given point of reference at which there will be a concentration of light from a source transmitting light through the screen.

Plateau's spiral (plah-tōz'). See under *spiral.*

plateau (plah-to'). 1. A leveling off or an interval of no increment in a curve otherwise showing continuous increase or growth, as, for example, in a learning curve. 2. A level elevated area.

Stieda's p's. A series of low elevations, separated by Stieda's grooves, located in the palpebral conjunctiva between the tarsus and the fornix.

platoscope (plat'o-skōp). Stereoscope. *Obs.*

platycoria (plat"e-ko're-ah). A dilated or large pupil.

platycoriasis (plat"e-ko-ri'ah-sis). The condition of having a dilated or large pupil.

platykurtic (plat"e-kur'tik). Having platykurtosis.

platykurtosis (plat"e-kur-to'sis). The statistical attribute of having a distribution less peaked than normal. Cf. *leptokurtosis; mesokurtosis.*

platymorphia (plate"e-mōr'fe-ah). A flatness in the shape of the eyeball, resulting in a short anteroposterior axis and hypermetropia.

platymorphic (plat"e-mōr'fik). Pertaining to the condition of platymorphia.

platyopic (plat"e-op'ik). Having an orbitonasal index below 110 (or 107.5). Cf. *mesopic; pro-opic.*

pleating, scleral. A surgical procedure for shortening the eyeball in the treatment of retinal detachment in which a fold is made in the sclera, at about the equator of the eyeball, and is fixed with a mattress suture. It is performed in conjunction with diathermy.

Pleopticon (ple'op-tih-kon). A device for the improvement of visual acuity and fixation in amblyopia, consisting essentially of a tube having a small circular aperture at ⌐ne end and an opaque disk of 5° subtense with a central fixation point at the other end. The opaque disk is viewed through the aperture and fixated while a bright light source illuminates the area surrounding the disk. The opaque disk shields the central area of the retina from light stimulation, creating a positive afterimage having a dark center and a light surround. It is followed by a negative afterimage which is then centered on fixation targets.

pleoptics (ple-op'tiks). A method of treating amblyopia ex anopsia in which concentrated and intensive stimulation is provided to the fovea of the amblyopic eye. One procedure involves intense light stimulation of the nonfoveal area to render the foveal area more receptive to fixation stimuli; other procedures involve association of touch, hearing, and memory with visual perception.

Pleoptiscope (ple″op-tih-skōp′). An instrument which creates Haidinger's brushes for the diagnosis and treatment of eccentric fixation and the improvement of visual acuity in amblyopia.

Pleoptophor (ple-op′to-fōr). A visual training instrument designed by Bangerter for the treatment of amblyopia ex anopsia and eccentric fixation. It consists essentially of a telescope with a 40 degree field of view providing continuous observation of the fundus during treatment, with 18× magnification. The treatment consists of first stimulating the peripheral retina with bright light while shielding the central area with an opaque disk (dazzling phase), then stimulating the central and peripheral areas while shielding the pericentral area with a doughnut-shaped opaque disk (stimulating phase), and last, briefly repeating the initial phase. The treatment is designed to enhance foveal fixation and is immediately followed by fixation training on other instruments.

plesiopia (ple″se-o′pe-ah, ples″e-). Myopia.

Plexiglas (plek′sih-glas). A trade name for polymethyl methacrylate, marketed by Rohm & Haas Company.

plexus (plek′sus). A network of nerves, blood vessels, or lymphatics.

annular p. Paramarginal plexus.

anterior ciliary p. A plexus of veins in the longitudinal or outer portion of the ciliary muscle that empties into the intrascleral and episcleral plexuses.

cavernous p. A network of nerve fibers derived from the internal carotid nerve and located on the medial side of the internal carotid artery in the cavernous sinus. It supplies sympathetic postganglionic axons to orbital effectors

and the eyeball via the superior orbital fissure.

ciliary p. 1. A network of thin vessels at the root of the ciliary processes, believed to serve in the absorption of aqueous humor. 2. Canal of Schlemm. *Obs.*

episcleral p. A plexus of veins in the anterior episclera which receives blood from the anterior ciliary, deep scleral, and superficial scleral plexuses and empties into the anterior ciliary veins.

episcleral limbal p. A network of branches of the episcleral arteries near the corneo-scleral junction which communicates with anterior conjunctival arteries.

Hovius′ p. Circle of Hovius.

infraorbital p. The embryonic veins below the optic vesicle or optic cup, which later differentiate into the inferior ophthalmic vein.

intersphincteric p. A network of capillaries located between the fibers of the sphincter pupillae muscle in the iris.

intraepithelial p. The network of very fine fibers in the epithelial layer of the cornea.

intrascleral p. The deep scleral plexus and superficial scleral plexus in combination.

Leber's venous p. Circle of Hovius.

marginal nerve p. of von Mises. A plexus of nerve fibers surrounding the follicles of the eyelashes.

ophthalmic p. The network of sympathetic nerve fibers about the ophthalmic artery which are vasoconstrictor in function.

paramarginal p. A superficial network of sensory nerve fibers, about 1.5 mm. wide, derived from subconjunctival and episcleral plexuses, located just beneath Bowman's membrane near the limbus, and terminating in receptors in the corneal epithelium. Syn., *annular plexus.*

pericorneal p. A network of vessels lying in a band around the limbus and formed by the anastomosing of conjunctival and anterior ciliary arteries. It lies superficially in the conjunctiva, where it is a branching network, and deeper in the episclera, where it follows a relatively straight course.

peripheral pericorneal p. Annular plexus.

posttarsal p. 1. A plexus of capillaries, running between the marginal and the peripheral arcades of the eyelid posterior to the tarsus, which supplies the conjunctiva. Syn., *retrotarsal plexus; subconjunctival plexus.* 2. The posttarsal lymphatic vessels.

pretarsal p. 1. A plexus of capillaries, running between the marginal and the peripheral arcades of the eyelid anterior to the tarsus, which supplies the tarsal glands and all structures anterior to the tarsus. 2. The pretarsal lymphatic vessels.

pterygoid p. The network of veins near the pterygopalatine fossa, which receives tributaries corresponding to the branches of the internal maxillary artery and the lower division of the inferior ophthalmic vein and communicates with the cavernous sinus and the anterior facial vein.

retrotarsal p. Posttarsal plexus.

scleral p., deep. A plexus of capillaries in the deep layers of the sclera, encircling the limbal area in close apposition to the canal of Schlemm, which receives aqueous humor from the canal of Schlemm via collectors and blood from the surrounding area. It drains into the superficial scleral plexus and anterior ciliary veins.

scleral p., superficial. A plexus of vessels, predominantly venous, in the anterior superficial sclera which receives blood from the deep scleral plexus and anterior ciliary plexus and communicates with the episcleral, Tenon's and anterior conjunctival plexuses.

stroma p. Superficial and deep networks of nerves in the substantia propria of the cornea.

subconjunctival p. Posttarsal plexus.

subepithelial p. The network of nerve fibers located immediately beneath Bowman's membrane of the cornea. It receives nerve fibers from the stratified epithelium and leads to the stroma plexus.

subsphincteric p. A network of capillaries located between the sphincter pupillae muscle and the pigment epithelium of the iris.

superficial marginal p. The network of small arteries and capillaries derived from the anterior ciliary arteries, located in the limbus of the cornea deep to the stratified epithelium.

supraorbital p. The embryonic veins above the optic vesicle or optic cup, which later differentiate into the superior ophthalmic vein.

plica (pli′kah). A fold or a folded structure.

centralis, p. A fold in the retina coursing between the fovea centralis and the optic disk, observed only in postmortem examination.

ciliarias, p. Ciliary fold.

iridis, p. One of the many minute folds on the posterior surface of the iris.

lacrimalis, p. A fold of mucous membrane at the entrance of the nasolacrimal duct into the inferior meatus of the nose. It represents the remains of the fetal septum. Syn., *Hasner's fold; lacrimal fold; Bianchi's valve; Cruveilhier's valve; Hasner's valve.*

lunata, p. Plica semilunaris.

semilunaris, p. The crescent-shaped conjunctival fold at the medial canthus lateral to the caruncle. It is a vestigial structure corresponding to the nictitating membrane of lower vertebrates. Syn., *plica lunata.*

pliers. A hand-held tool having two short handles and two grasping jaws working on a pivot, used for gripping, bending, or cutting.

angling p. 1. Pliers with jaws shaped to fit and hold the endpiece of a spectacle frame or mounting while the temples are angled. Syn., *endpiece pliers.* 2. Pliers with jaws shaped to fit and hold a saddle bridge while it is angled.

chipping p. Pliers with wide, flatfaced jaws used in chipping excess glass from the edge of a lens after it has been cut to approximate shape.

cutting p. Pliers with knife edge jaws used for removing the excess portions of screws of spectacle frames or mountings.

endpiece p. Angling pliers.

half-round p. Pliers with one round, tapered jaw and one flatfaced, tapered jaw, used in adjusting spectacle frames and mountings.

Numont arm p. Pliers with jaws that contain a small transverse groove for gripping the arm of a spectacle mounting, used for reshaping the arm or in angling the temple.

snipe nose p. Pliers with long, flatfaced jaws tapered to a point, used in adjusting spectacle frames and mountings.

strap p. Pliers with jaws designed for shaping the straps of spectacle mountings.

ploration (plo-ra'shun). Lacrimation. *Obs.*

plot, scatter. Scatter diagram.

plotter, ray. Any of a number of devices used to determine the path of a ray of light through optical media or an optical system.

plus. The opposite of *minus* or *negative* in the designation of data, systems, or observations, the values of which may be repre-

sented on a continuous numerical scale from plus, through zero, to minus values, whence it may represent *convergence* as applied to lenses, *divergence* as applied to wavefronts. Syn., *positive.*

plus acceptance. The acceptance, or the indication of acceptability, of convex sphere, or of an increased amount of convex sphere, as a dioptric correction either in a lens prescription or during a specific test or visual task, based on any one criterion or a combination of criteria related to blurredness, discomfort, and other clinical signs or symptoms.

pneumocele, orbital (nu'mo-sēl). An enclosed pocket of air in the orbit, usually caused either by forcible blowing of the nose or by trauma.

Poggendorff's (po'gen-dorfs) **figure; illusion.** See under the nouns.

point. 1. A place considered only as to its position, having definite location but no extent in space. 2. A condition or position attained; a step; a stage. 3. A unit of thickness of spectacle lenses equal to one fifth of a millimeter.

aplanatic p's. The object and image points as a pair in an optical system corrected for spherical aberration and satisfying the sine condition.

blur point. 1. Under a given set of test conditions, the point at which the fixation target appears blurred on the introduction of gradually increasing prism and/or lens power. 2. A point on a graph representing the limit of clear, single, binocular vision.

  blur p., accommodative. A blur point induced by the addition of concave or convex lens power at a fixed test distance.

  blur p., base-in. The point of blur obtained by gradually introducing base-in prism power or effect during binocular fixation at a fixed test distance.

blur p., base-out. The point of blur obtained by gradually introducing base-out prism power or effect during binocular fixation at a fixed test distance.

blur p., beginning. A just noticeable determination of a blur point. Cf. *blur-out point.*

blur p., convergence. 1. Base-out blur point. 2. Either base-in or base-out blur point.

blur p., minus lens. The point of blur obtained by gradually introducing minus lens power in front of one or both eyes at a fixed test distance.

blur p., plus lens. The point of blur obtained by gradually introducing plus lens power in front of one or both eyes at a fixed test distance.

blur-out p. The point at which a target becomes so blurred as to be illegible or unrecognizable. Cf. *beginning blur point.*

break p. The point at which diplopia occurs on gradually varying the prism or lens power during binocular fixation.

cardinal p's. Six points on the axis of an optical system, viz., the two principal foci, the two principal points, and the two nodal points. Cf. *Gaussian points.*

centration p. British equivalent to *major reference point.*

chief p. A point on the principal surface of an optical system corrected for coma where an incident ray intersects the surface.

conjugate p's. The object point and its corresponding image point considered as a pair in an optical system.

convergence, p. of. 1. The point of intersection of the lines of sight. 2. The point to which a pencil of light converges.

corresponding p's. Corresponding retinal points.

demand p. The point in a graphical co-ordinate system representing the stimulus to accommoda-

tion and the stimulus to convergence in a given test situation. It may or may not represent a single target point in space.

disparate p's. Noncorresponding retinal points.

divergence, p. of. 1. The point of intersection of diverging lines of sight. 2. The point from which a pencil of light diverges.

diving p's. Minute objects which approach the minimum visible threshold and appear to move or to disappear and reappear as stars do when constantly viewed.

entrance pupil p. The center of the entrance pupil.

equivalent p's. A pair of points on the axis of an optical system, corresponding simultaneously to the nodal and principal points, as when the object and image space have the same refractive index.

exit pupil p. The center of the exit pupil.

eye p. Eyepoint.

far p. of accommodation. See under *accommodation.*

far p. of convergence. See under *convergence.*

far p. of fusion. See under *fusion.*

fixation, p. of. 1. The point in space to which one or both eyes are consciously directed. In normal vision its image is on the fovea. 2. Point of regard.

fixation, p. of (primary). The point fixated when the eye is in the primary position.

focal p. The point of convergence or divergence of a pencil of light.

focal p., anterior. Primary focal point.

focal p., posterior. Secondary focal point.

focal p., primary. The point of convergence or divergence of a pencil of incident light rays which emerge parallel to the axis of an optical system. Syn., *anterior focal point; anterior principal* *focal point; primary principal focal point.*

focal p., principal (anterior). Primary focal point.

focal p., principal (posterior). Secondary focal point.

focal p., principal (primary). Primary focal point.

focal p., principal (secondary). Secondary focal point.

focal p., secondary. The point of convergence or divergence of a pencil of emergent light rays which are incident parallel to the axis of an optical system. Syn., *posterior focal point; posterior principal focal point; secondary principal focal point.*

Gaussian p's. The two principal foci and the two principal points on the axis of an optical system. Cf. *cardinal points.*

homologous p's. Two points, one on each half of a stereogram, which are of identical target content.

homonymous p's. Corresponding retinal points.

Horner-Trantas p's. White pinpoint projections visible on the conjunctiva in vernal conjunctivitis which represent circumscribed areas of epithelial cells undergoing rapid and progressive degeneration. They are first situated in the deeper layers of the epithelium, extending later toward and breaking through the surface.

identical p's. Corresponding retinal points.

image p. The point at which an object point is imaged by an optical system.

incidence, p. of. The point at which a ray of light is incident upon a refracting or reflecting surface.

infraorbital p. The lowest point on the margin of the orbit.

isosbestic p. A point on the spectral absorption curve of a photopigment that corresponds to the wavelength at which the optical density remains unchanged throughout the whole bleaching process, with increasing or decreasing densities at other points.

lacrimal p. Lacrimal punctum.

major reference p. The point of the front or back surface of a spectacle lens at which the prism power corresponds to that prescribed.

near p. of accommodation. See under *accommodation.*

near p. of convergence. See under *convergence.*

near p. of fusion. See under *fusion.*

neutral p. 1. In retinoscopy, the point at which the motion of the reflex cannot be detected, determined either by placing lenses before the eye or by moving the retinoscope to a point in space conjugate with the retina. 2. In certain types of color blindness, the point or points in the spectrum which appear colorless to an observer, or those spectral wavelengths which appear to match the chromaticity of a standard white.

nodal p's. A pair of points on the axis of an optical system which have the property that any incident ray directed toward the first, the anterior nodal point, leaves the system as though from the second, the posterior nodal point, and with its direction unchanged, i.e., parallel to the incident ray.

nodal p., anterior. See *nodal points.*

nodal p's., negative. A pair of points on the axis of an optical system which have the property that the angle made by an incident ray directed toward the first leaves the system as though from the second at an angle of the same size, but on the opposite side of the axis.

[559]

nodal p., posterior. See *nodal points.*

noncorresponding p's. Noncorresponding retinal points.

object p. A point at which the object is represented in relation to an optical system.

occipital p. 1. The pointed posterior extremity of the occipital lobe of the brain. 2. The most prominent point on the posterior protuberance of the occipital bone.

occipital p. of the field of fixation. A point behind the eye symmetrical to the point of fixation with respect to the center of rotation of the eye when the line of sight is in the primary position. *Helmholtz.*

ophthalmometric axial p. The point of intersection of the axis of the ophthalmometer with the cornea.

orthoscopic p's. The centers of the entrance and the exit pupils of an optical system free from aberration.

principal p. In an optical system, the point of intersection of a principal plane with the optical axis.

principal p., anterior. Primary principal point.

principal p's., negative. Conjugate points on the axis of an optical system, lying at twice the focal length on opposite sides of the system, for which the lateral magnification is unity and negative. An object located at one such point will have an inverted image of the same size at the other point. Syn., *symmetrical points.*

principal p., posterior. Secondary principal point.

principal p., primary. The point of intersection of the primary principal plane with the optical axis. Syn., *anterior principal point.*

principal p., secondary. The point of intersection of the secondary principal plane with the optical axis. Syn., *posterior principal point.*

quasi-corresponding p's. Quasi-corresponding retinal points.

recovery p. Under a given set of binocular test conditions, the point at which fusion is regained on gradual decrease of the prism or lens power which originally induced the diplopia.

reflection p. The point of incidence of a light ray on a surface from which it is reflected.

refraction p. The point of incidence of a light ray on a surface at which it is refracted.

regard, p. of. 1. A point in space to which visual attention is directed. It may be independent of the point of fixation, as in giving attention to a peripherally located object. 2. Point of fixation.

retinal p's., abathic. A pair of retinal points, one in each eye, which binocularly give rise to a single impression of a distance equal to that of both the fixation point and the actual frontoparallel plane.

retinal p's., corresponding. A pair of points, one in each retina, which, when stimulated, give rise to a percept of common visual direction. Syn., *homonymous points; identical points.*

retinal p's., disparate. Noncorresponding retinal points.

retinal p's., noncorresponding. A pair of points, one in the retina of each eye, which, when stimulated, do not give rise to a percept of common visual direction. Syn., *disparate retinal points.*

retinal p's., quasi-corresponding. Noncorresponding retinal points lying within Panum's areas.

reversal p. 1. In retinoscopy, the point at which the motion of the reflex changes from with to against motion, or vice versa. 2. Neutral point.

symmetrical p's. Negative principal points.

tangential p. The point of ocular contact of an extraocular muscle nearest its origin, at which the muscle action may be regarded as a tangential force on the eyeball.

visual p. The point of intersection of the line of sight with the back surface of a spectacle lens with the eyes either in the primary position (distance visual point) or in a given position for near vision (near visual point).

Poisson diffraction; spot. See under the nouns.

Polack's stereoscope (pol'aks). See under *stereoscope.*

polarimeter (po″lar-im'eh-ter). An instrument for determining the amount of polarization of light or the amount of rotation of the plane of polarization.

polarimetry (po″lar-im'eh-tre). The measurement of the amount of polarization of light or the amount of rotation of the plane of polarization with a polarimeter.

polariscope (po-lar'ih-skōp). An instrument for examining substances in, or for studying the properties of, polarized light, consisting essentially of a polarizer and an analyzer with their planes of polarization at right angles to each other. One of its uses is to detect stress in glass.

polariscopic (po″lar-ih-skop'ik). Pertaining to the polariscope or to polariscopy.

polariscopy (po″lar-is'ko-pe). The science or process of using the polariscope.

polarization (po″lar-ih-za'shun). The act, process, or result of altering the presumed transverse wave motion of radiant energy, such that it is not uniform in amplitude in all directions in a plane perpendicular to the direction of propagation. See also *polarized light.*

polarize (po'lar-īz). To induce or effect polarization.

polarizer (po'lar-īz″er). 1. An agent or a medium which induces or effects polarization. 2. In a polarimeter or a polariscope, the first of two polarizing elements in sequence, the second being called the *analyzer.*

Ahrens p. Ahrens prism.

Glan-Foucault p. Glan-Foucault prism.

Glazebrook p. Glazebrook prism.

Nicol p. Nicol prism.

Rochon p. Rochon prism.

Wollaston p. Wollaston prism.

Polaroid (po'lar-oid). A trade name for a manufactured polarizing medium available in sheet form, originally made of tiny iodoquinine sulfate crystals aligned and embedded in a cellulose film and now largely supplanted by a stretched sheet of polyvinyl alcohol containing polymeric iodine.

Polatest (po'lah-test). An instrument used in refraction and for investigating binocular functions which presents a series of vectograms to be viewed through Polaroid filters, for testing heterophoria, fixation disparity, aniseikonia, stereopsis, and visual acuity.

pole. 1. Either end of the axis of a body, farthest removed from its equator, as of the eyeball or the crystalline lens. 2. The point on a mirror or a lens at which the optical axis intercepts the surface.

anterior p. 1. Of the eyeball, the point on the anterior surface of the cornea corresponding to the intersection of an anteroposterior axis of reference of the eye, or of the pupillary axis. 2. Of the crystalline lens, the geometric center of its anterior surface, or the intersection of the optical axis of the lens with its anterior surface.

posterior p. 1. Of the eyeball, the point on the posterior surface of the sclera corresponding to the intersection of an anteroposterior axis of reference of the eye, located between the optic disk and the fovea centralis. 2. Of the crystalline lens, the geometric center of its posterior surface, or the intersection of the optical axis of the lens with its posterior surface.

polemophthalmia (pol″em-of-thal′-me-ah). Trachoma.

polioencephalitis, superior hemorrhagic (pol″i-o-en-ceph″a-li′tis). Wernicke's disease.

poliosis of the cilia (pol″e-o′sis). A condition in which there is a loss of pigment in the cilia, resulting in gray eyelashes.

polishing. The final stage in the process of lens surfacing in which the lens is made smooth to provide regular light transmission or specular reflection.

polus (po′lus). A pole.

anterior lentis, p. The anterior pole of the crystalline lens.

posterior lentis, p. The posterior pole of the crystalline lens.

Polyak's theory (pōl′yaks). See under *theory.*

polyarthritis, juvenile (pol″e-ar-thri′tis). Rheumatoid arthritis in infants and children accompanied by lymphadenopathy, splenomegaly, and sometimes keratouveitis. Syn., *Still's disease.*

polyblepharia (pol″e-blef′ah-re-ah). Polyblepharon.

polyblepharon (pol″e-blef′ah-ron). A congenital anomaly in which there is an extra eyelid. Syn., *polyblepharia; polyblephary.*

polyblephary (pol″e-blef′ah-re). Polyblepharon.

polychromatic (pol″e-kro-mat′ik). Pertaining to or exhibiting many colors.

polycoria (pol″e-ko′re-ah). An anomaly consisting of more than one pupil in a single iris.

spuria, p. Polycoria in which only one of the openings in the iris is a true pupil, having a sphincter pupillae muscle.

vera, p. Polycoria in which each

pupil has its own sphincter pupillae muscle.

polycythemia rubra vera (pol″e-si-the′me-ah). Vaquez' disease.

polydacrya (pol″e-dak′re-ah). Excessive lacrimation.

polygon, rectangular frequency (pol′e-gon). Bar graph.

polymethyl methacrylate (pol″e-meth′il meh-thak′ril-āt). Polymerized methyl methacrylate, a lightweight, transparent thermoplastic, used in the manufacture of contact lenses and spectacle frames. It was formerly used for opthalmic lenses but has been replaced by more abrasion-resistant, heat-hardened resins.

Polyophthalmoscope (pol″e-of-thal′-mo-skōp). An instrument with nine viewing tubes to allow simultaneous observation of the fundus and interior of the eye by nine observers.

polyopia (pol″e-o′pe-ah). A condition in which more than one image of a single object is perceived; multiple vision. Syn., *polyopsia; polyopy.*

monophthalmica, p. Monocular polyopia.

polyopsia (pol″e-op′se-ah). Polyopia.

polyopy (pol′e-o″pe). Polyopia.

polystichia (pol″e-stik′e-ah). An anomalous condition in which there are two or more rows of eyelashes on a single eyelid.

pons varolii (pons va-ro′le-i). A white eminence consisting of fibers and nuclei located in the hindbrain between the cerebral peduncles of the midbrain and the medulla oblongata, and acting in the relaying of impulses. It contains the abducens and facial motor nuclei that supply the lateral recti and the facial muscles of expression, the supranuclear center for lateral gaze, the parasympathetic lacrimal nucleus, and ascending and descending tracts important in ocular neurology.

pontocaine hydrochloride (pon'to-kān hi"dro-klo'rīd). A trade name for a local anesthetic, the base of which is related to procaine, applied in 0.5% solution to the eye, and in 2% solution to the nose and throat. For spinal anesthesia an injection is given of 1 to 2 cc. of a 1% solution.

Ponzo visual illusion. See under *illusion, visual.*

porphyria (por-fi're-ah). A disease due to abnormal metabolism of porphyrin and occurring in both a chronic and an acute form. The chronic form is inherited recessively, has an onset typically in infancy or early childhood, and affects twice as many males as females. It is characterized by a severe dermal sensitivity to sunlight resulting in bullous or vesicular lesions on exposed areas of the body which may mutilate the eyelids, conjunctiva, cornea, and sclera. The acute form appears in the third decade or later and is characterized by severe abdominal pain and nervous symptoms varying from peripheral neuropathy and mental disturbances to involvement of the autonomic nervous system. Ocular symptoms in the acute form include diplopia, ischemia of the retina, and exophthalmos.

porphyropsin (por"fih-rop'sin). A carotenoid protein, similar to rhodopsin, found in the retinal rods of some fresh water fish. Syn., *visual violet.*

Porro prism (pōr'o). See under *prism.*

port, entrance. In an optical system, the image of the field stop as formed in the object space. Syn., *entrance window.*

port, exit. In an optical system, the image of the field stop as formed in the image space. Syn., *exit window.*

porus opticus (po'rus op'tih-kus). The opening, in the lamina crib-rosa of the sclera, through which the central retinal artery passes.

Posey's theory (po'sēz). See under *theory.*

position. A place; a posture; a condition.

active p. The position of the eyes in binocular vision when attention is actively directed to an object and the oculomotor reflexes are operative. Syn., *functional binocular position.*

apparent p. The position at which a perceived object is mentally projected.

blind p. Physiological position of rest.

dissociated p. The position assumed by the eyes in relation to each other in the absence of adequate fusion stimuli. Syn., *fusion frustrated position; phoria position.*

fixation p. The position of the eyes in relation to each other during binocular fixation of a single object.

fixation-free p. The position of the eyes in relation to each other when under the influence of normal muscle tonus and postural reflexes and free from fixational and fusional reflexes. Syn., *static position.*

functional binocular p. Active position.

fusion-free p. The position assumed by the eyes in relation to each other when fusion is suspended and the oculomotor system is free from control of fusional impulses, but is affected by postural and fixational reflexes and by normal muscle tonus. Syn., *functional position of rest; passive position.*

fusion-frustrated p. Dissociated position.

gaze, p. of (primary). Primary position.

gaze, p. of (secondary). Secondary position.

gaze, p. of (tertiary). Tertiary position.

orthophoric p. 1. The position or distance from the eyes at which a fixation target may be placed so as to elicit no lateral heterophoria, i.e., a zero prism scale reading in a phoria test. 2. In a haploscope, the position of the stimulus targets corresponding to orthophoria.

passive p. Fusion-free position.

phoria p. Dissociated position.

primary p. 1. The position of the eye, in relation to the head, from which vertical and lateral fixational movements may be made unassociated with torsional movements; not necessarily identical with the straightforward position. 2. The straightforward position.

primatial p. A downward, inward, and intorted position of the eyes in the binocular fixation of a near point.

rest, p. of (absolute). Anatomical position of rest.

rest, p. (anatomical). The position of the eyes, in relation to each other, in the absence of neuromuscular control or innervation, as in death. Syn., *absolute position of rest.*

rest, p. of (comparative). Physiological position of rest.

rest, p. of (functional). Fusion-free position.

rest, p. of (physiological). The position of the eyes in relation to each other under the influence of normal muscle tonus and free from accommodation, fixation, and fusion reflexes. Syn., *comparative position of rest; relative position of rest.*

rest, p. of (relative). Physiological position of rest.

secondary p. Any position of the eye represented by a vertical or horizontal deviation of the line of sight from the primary position.

static p. Fixation-free position.

straightforward p. The position of the eye when the line of sight is perpendicular to the face plane. Cf. *primary position.*

tertiary p. Any position of the eye represented by an oblique, or a combination of vertical and horizontal, deviation of the line of sight from the primary position.

Posner-Schlossmann syndrome (pōs'ner-shlos'man). Glaucomatocyclitic crisis.

posterior. In man, dorsal; nearer to the back or toward the rear. The opposite of *anterior.*

posterior border lamella of Fuchs. See under *lamella.*

postocular (pōst-ok'u-lar). Situated or occurring posterior to the eye.

postopticus (pōst-op'tih-kus). Corpora quadrigemina.

postorbital (pōst-ōr'bih-tal). Situated or occurring posterior to the orbit.

Posture Board, Brock's. An instrument used for visual testing and training at a near fixation distance, consisting essentially of a transparent red plastic plate mounted parallel to a baseboard, such that a light source mounted on a wand can be placed between the two. It is used in conjunction with red-green complementary color filters so that any of a number of various targets clipped to the red plate are seen by one eye and the light source is seen by the other.

potential. The amount of work necessary to bring a unit positive charge from one point in an electrical field to another; strictly, a potential difference.

cone-receptor p. An electrical potential which is obtained in or at a region very close to the retinal cone receptors of the primate retina, and considered to account for the rapid cornea negative *a* wave and at least part of the *d* wave in the electroretinogram.

corneofundal p. Resting potential of the eye.

corneoretinal p. Resting potential of the eye.

dark p. of the eye. Resting potential of the eye.

focal p's. Intraretinal electrical potentials recorded in the frog retina and elicited only by illumination falling close to the recording electrode in the region of the bipolar cells; considered responsible for the generation of the internal electroretinogram.

oculorotary p. The electrical change in direct current potential resulting from rotation of the eye in the orbit, measured by electrodes placed on the skin at the eyelid margins or at the canthi.

resting p. of the eye. The direct current potential difference which exists between the anterior and posterior poles of the eye, the cornea being positive relative to the retina. It is of the order of several millivolts in humans. Syn., *corneofundal potential; corneoretinal potential; dark potential of the eye; standing potential of the eye; static potential of the eye; steady potential of the eye.*

Schubert's p. An electrical potential recorded in the human ciliary muscle and considered to be related to the state of accommodation.

standing p. of the eye. Resting potential of the eye.

static p. of the eye. Resting potential of the eye.

steady p. of the eye. Resting potential of the eye.

Potts-Maurice theory. Metabolic pump theory.

power. The ability to act or to produce effect.

air equivalent p. The designated power of a lens in air which would have the same vergence effect on light traveling in air as a lens of reference has on light traveling in another medium of reference.

aligning p. 1. Vernier visual acuity. 2. The ability to place two or more objects on a straight line passing through the entrance pupil of the eye, as in aiming a gun, the center of the images of the aligned objects falling at the same point on the retina.

approximate p. The sum of the powers of the two surfaces of an ophthalmic or spectacle lens, as commonly determined with a lens measure, without regard to the form and thickness of the lens.

back p. Back vertex power.

defining p. Definition.

dioptric p. The vergence power of a dioptric system.

dispersive p. In a given medium, the ratio of the difference in the index of refraction for two extreme spectral lines (usually Fraunhofer F and C) to the difference in index for an intermediate line (usually Fraunhofer D) and unity. Syn., *relative dispersion.*

effective p. 1. The vergence power of an optical system designated with respect to a point of reference other than the principal point. 2. In a lens, the back vertex power.

emissive p. The time rate of emission of radiant energy, in all directions, per unit surface area of a radiating body at a given temperature.

equivalent p. 1. The vergence power of an optical system expressed with reference to the principal point. Syn., *true power.* 2. The mean spherical power of a cylindrical or spherocylindrical lens, determined by adding half the power of the cylindrical component to the spherical component.

focal p. Vergence power.

front p. Front vertex power.

magnifying p. 1. The ratio of image size to object size. Syn., *magnification.* 2. With reference to a magnifying optical viewing aid, the ratio of the angle subtended by the image at the nodal point of the eye to the angle subtended by the object when at the least distance of distinct vision from the eye, this distance conventionally being assumed to be 10 in. or 25 cm. Syn., *apparent magnification.*

mean oblique *p.* The arithmetic mean of the tangential and sagittal oblique vertex sphere dioptric powers.

Munsell *p.* The product of Munsell value and Munsell chroma.

neutralizing *p.* The power of a spectacle lens as indicated by the power of a trial case lens which neutralizes it when placed so that the back vertex of the trial case lens contacts the front vertex of the spectacle lens, and hence the front vertex power of the spectacle lens if the power of the neutralizing lens is designated by its back vertex power.

prismatic *p.* The angular deviation of the direction of light propagation, produced by a prism or other optical system.

reading *p.* A ratio representing visual acuity for reading, expressed as a fraction in which the numerator is the maximum distance at which the reading material can be read, and the denominator is the distance at which the letters subtend an angle of 5 minutes.

refractive *p.* The vergence power of a refracting optical system.

resolving *p.* 1. In an optical system, the ability to form a clearly defined image; the least separation of two optically imaged luminous points discernible as two, usually evaluated in terms of the separation of the maximum and first minimum of the intensity distribution curve of the diffrac-

tion pattern of the image of one of the luminous points. Syn., *limit of resolution.* 2. In the eye, the threshold of resolution. 3. In a grating or a prism, the ability to separate two wavelengths close together into two spectrum lines, usually specified in terms of the change in wavelength necessary to shift the central intensity maximum into the position of the first intensity minimum for the diffraction image of a given wavelength.

sagittal oblique vertex sphere *p.* The reciprocal of the distance, in meters, from the vertex sphere to the sagittal focus, as measured along the chief ray of the pencil.

stereo *p.* In a pair of prism binoculars or similar instrument, the ratio of the distance between the optical axes of the objectives to the distance between the optical axes of the eyepieces, multiplied by the magnifying power.

surface *p.* The vergence power of a single refracting or reflecting surface.

tangential oblique vertex sphere *p.* The reciprocal of the distance, in meters, from the vertex sphere to the tangential focus, as measured along the chief ray of the pencil.

thin lens *p.* The sum of the dioptric powers of the two surfaces of a lens of negligible thickness.

true *p.* Equivalent power.

vergence *p.* The ability of an optical system to change the vergence of a pencil of rays, usually designated quantitatively by the reciprocal of the focal length of the system. Syn., *focal power.*

vertex *p., back.* The vergence power expressed with reference to the posterior surface, at the optical axis, of a lens or an optical system instead of to the secondary principal point. Syn., *back power.*

vertex *p., front.* The vergence power expressed with reference to the anterior surface, at the optical axis, of a lens or an optical system instead of to the anterior principal point. Syn., *front power*.

P.P. Abbreviation for *punctum proximum*.

P.R. Abbreviation for *punctum remotum*.

Pr. Abbreviation for *presbyopia* or *prism*.

pragmatagnosia, visual (prag″mat-ag-no′ze-ah). The inability to recognize by sight objects previously known, although the object is seen clearly. Syn., *object visual agnosia*.

pragmatamnesia, visual (prag″mat-am-ne′se-ah). The inability to recall the visual image of an object.

Prato's box (pra′tōz). See under *box*.

Pray's (prāz) **chart; test; test type.** See under the nouns.

precipitates, keratic (pre-sip′ih-tātz). Fibrinous and cellular deposits on the posterior surface of the cornea from exudates from the iris and the ciliary body into the anterior chamber, usually an accompaniment of iritis or iridocyclitis. Abbreviation *K.P.*

keratic p's., glass. Keratic precipitates which persist after the causative inflammation has ceased and which appear as translucent rings with opaque centers.

keratic p's., mutton-fat. Keratic precipitates which have coalesced, found in long standing, severe cases of iritis or iridocyclitis, typically in the tubercular types.

keratic p's., plastic. Keratic precipitates in mass, usually appearing in severe iridocyclitis.

keratic p's., star-map. Keratic precipitates in the form of round deposits connected by fine line deposits, producing geometrical patterns.

preglaucoma (pre″glaw-ko′mah). A condition in which clinical and gonioscopic evidence indicates potential glaucoma.

prelacrimal (pre-lak′rih-mal). Situated or occurring anterior to the lacrimal sac.

Prentice's (pren′tis-ez) **phoria indicator; law; method; rule.** See under the nouns.

prepresbyope (pre-pres′be-ōp). One who has not yet manifested presbyopia.

prepresbyopia (pre-pres″be-o′pe-ah). The period or condition prior to the onset of presbyopia.

preretinal (pre-ret′ih-nal). Situated or occurring anterior to the retina.

presbyope (pres′be-ōp). One who has presbyopia.

presbyopia (pres″be-o′pe-ah). A reduction in accommodative ability occurring normally with age and necessitating a plus lens addition for satisfactory seeing at near, sometimes quantitatively identified by the recession of the near point of accommodation beyond 20 cm.

absolute p. 1. Presbyopia in which accommodative ability is completely absent. 2. Presbyopia in which some convex lens power is necessary for reading small print. Cf. *incipient presbyopia*.

incipient p. Beginning presbyopia, sometimes described as the stage in which small print may be read without the addition of convex lens power, but with effort. Cf. *absolute presbyopia*.

nocturnal p. A reduction in the apparent amplitude of accommodation induced by the reduction of the intensity of illumination.

premature p. Presbyopia manifested at an early age, as before the age of 40 years.

presbyopic (pres″be-op′ik). Pertaining to or having presbyopia.

presbytia (pres-bish′e-ah). Presbyopia. *Obs.*

presbytism (pres′bih-tizm). Presbyopia *Obs.*

pressure, intraocular. The pressure of the intraocular fluid, measurable by means of a manometer. Cf. *ocular tension.*

normal intraocular p. Intraocular pressure within the range of values obtained in normal, healthy eyes, usually considered to represent an ocular tension of approximately 25 mm. of mercury.

normative intraocular p. Intraocular pressure which is compatible with normal health and function of the eye. Cf. *normal intraocular pressure.*

Prevost's sign (pra-vōz). See under *sign.*

prezonular (pre-zōn′u-lar). Situated or occurring in the posterior chamber of the eye, anterior to the zonule of Zinn.

Priestley Smith's (prēst′le smiths) **pupillometer; tape; test.** See under the nouns.

primochrome (pri-mo-krōm′). Weale's term for *chlorolabe.*

Prince's (prinsz) **rule; rule test.** See under the nouns.

principle. 1. A fundamental law, doctrine, or assumption; a general or fundamental truth. 2. A rule or basis of action.

Babinet's p. The principle that complementary sets of obstacles, for which one set has openings where the other set is opaque, provide for superposition of diffraction pattern amplitudes without zero summation.

Drysdale p. Drysdale method.

Fermat's p. of least time. Fermat's law.

Huygens′ p. Every point of any wavefront may be considered as the source of secondary spherical waves (wavelets) which, in combination with each other, constitute a new, further advanced, wavefront.

prism (prizm). 1. A transparent body bounded in part by two plane faces which are not parallel. 2.

An optical element or system, or the component of an optical system, which deviates the path of light as does a prism.

Abbe's p. Any of several prisms designed by Abbe. One is a constant deviation 30°–60°–90° prism with the internal reflecting face on the side opposite the 60° angle. Others include a modification of the Porro prism and a direct vision prism which invert and revert the image.

abducting p. An ophthalmic prism placed before a fixating eye with its base-apex line horizontal and its base nasal.

achromatic p. Two prisms, of different refractive indices, combined so that the dispersion of one is offset by the dispersion of the other, thus producing deviation without dispersion.

adducting p. An ophthalmic prism placed before a fixating eye with its base-apex line horizontal and its base temporal.

adverse p. An ophthalmic prism placed before the eye so as to produce a displacement of the image seen through the prism in a direction opposite to that which would compensate for the deviation, or tendency to deviation, of the viewing eye. Cf. *relieving prism.*

Ahrens′ p. A device, used in polarizing microscopes, consisting of three wedge-shaped prisms cemented together with Canada balsam to form a rectangular block which is coated black on its sides. Extraordinary rays pass straight through, while the ordinary rays undergo total internal reflection and are absorbed by the black coating. Syn., *Ahrens′ polarizer.*

Allen's contact p. A totally reflecting plastic prism attached to a contact lens, used in conjunction with a biomicroscope to view the filtration angle of the anterior chamber. Syn., *Allen's gonio-prism; Allen-O'Brien contact lens; contact prism.*

Amici *p.* Any one of several complex prisms designed by Amici. One, a roof prism, consists of a right-angled prism whose hypotenuse surface is replaced by an internally reflecting roof, so that a beam entering one of the other faces perpendicularly will be reflected successively at both surfaces of the roof and emerge from the last surface in a direction perpendicular to the incident path to form an inverted image. Another, a direct vision prism, consists of a prism of very dense flint glass cemented between two prisms of crown glass.

Barr and Stroud *p.* A very complex, ocular prism system used in fire control instruments, consisting of four single prisms and a cover, all cemented together.

base-in *p.* An ophthalmic prism placed before the eye with its base-apex line horizontal and its base nasalward.

base-out *p.* An ophthalmic prism placed before the eye with its base-apex line horizontal and its base templeward.

Brewster *p's.* Two identical prisms placed base to apex and hinged at the base of one and the apex of the other, so that the angle between the prisms may be changed. They are used to produce meridional magnification, without effective power for distance vision, the magnification occurring in the base-apex meridian and varying with the angle between the prisms.

Carl Zeiss *p.* Any of several very complex prism systems used in military fire control instruments.

combining *p.* Measuring prism.

compensating *p.* Relieving prism.

cone *p.* Quadrant prism.

constant deviation *p.* A prism unit with an internal or adjunct reflecting surface so constructed that, for each wavelength, the orientation of the unit which provides equal angles of entrance and emergence at the respective faces of the unit also provides for a constant total deviation of the emergent ray with respect to the entering ray.

contact *p.* Allen's contact prism.

Cornu *p.* A 60° prism consisting of one 30° right-handed quartz and one 30° left-handed quartz in contact, thus transmitting light at the minimum deviation position without double refraction because of the interchange in velocities at the interface.

Cornu-Jellet *p.* A Nicol prism modified by making a longitudinal cut, removing a small wedge, and cementing the cut surfaces together. It is used as an analyzer or polarizer in instruments for measuring rotatory polarization.

correcting *p.* Measuring prism.

Creté's *p.* A rotary prism, especially one designed with a sliding indicator on a long, radially protruding handle.

diopter, *p.* See under *diopter.*

direct vision *p.* 1. A combination of two (or more) prisms of different refractive indices, whose over-all effect is to produce spectral dispersion, but no deviation of the light corresponding to the D line, or other wavelength of reference. 2. Any prism for which the directions of propagation of the emerging and entering beams are the same.

dissociating *p.* A prism which, when placed before one of the eyes, so displaces the image of that eye that fusion is impossible and diplopia results.

double *p.* A pair of prisms, base to base, which serve to divide a beam of transmitted light into two separately deviated beams. When thin, it may be designed as a single, very obtuse prism with an apical angle of almost 180°, used with the incident light beam approaching normal to the base. See also *Fresnel biprism*.

double p., Dove. A combination of two Harting-Dove prisms, their reflecting surfaces silvered and cemented together.

double p., Maddox. Maddox prism.

double p., Thorington. An ophthalmic test lens of ruby red, cobalt blue, or colorless glass, in the shape of an obtuse truncated prism, which consists of two lateral thin prism portions with bases toward each other, separated by a plano central portion or strip. A small light viewed through this lens is seen in triplicate with the three images connected by a streak produced by refraction at the borders of the plano central portion.

double image p. 1. A combination of two prisms composed of doubly refracting media with their optical axes so arranged in relation to each other that the ordinary and extraordinary beams are widely separated, producing separate images. 2. A double prism.

Dove p. An isosceles prism designed to refract light entering one side so as to reflect it internally on the base surface and refract it again on the opposite, emerging side, thus inverting the resulting image. The unused apical portion of the prism may be removed or absent, forming a frustum (Harting-Dove prism).

erecting p. A prism interposed in a refracting or reflecting optical system for the purpose of rendering an inverted image erect. Specifically applied to a prism attached to the eyepiece of a microscope to correct the inversion of the image. Syn., *erector*.

Fery p. A type of reflecting prism

in which the surfaces of entrance and emergence are spherical curves.

Foucault p. A polarizing prism, similar in design to the Nicol prism, but employing an air film or space instead of balsam, thus to permit the transmission of ultraviolet light.

Frankford arsenal p. Any of several very complex prism systems used in military fire control instruments.

Fresnel's p. Fresnel's biprism.

Glan-Foucault p. A polarizing prism made of two wedge-shaped pieces of calcite, so cut that the geometrical axis of the prism is parallel to the optic axis, and mounted with a thin air gap between their hypotenuses. It is used primarily for the polarization of ultraviolet light and transmits only the extraordinary ray. Syn., *Glan-Foucault polarizer*.

Glan-Thompson p. A polarizing prism designed to give a wider field and more perfect plane polarization than the Nicol prism. It must be cut with the optical axis parallel to the end faces, using more calcite than the Nicol prism.

Glazebrook p. A polarizing prism equivalent to half of an Ahrens prism cut in a plane perpendicular to the optic axis and transmitting only the extraordinary rays. Syn., *Glazebrook polarizer*.

Harting-Dove p. A Dove prism with the unused apical portion of the prism removed.

Herschel p. A type of rotary prism.

horizontal p. An ophthalmic prism placed base-in or base-out before the eye with its base-apex line horizontal. Syn., *lateral prism*.

Kagenaar p. A pair of thick slabs of plane glass mounted edge to edge at an angle of about 150° so as to separate, by displacement, the two halves of a beam of transmitted light, used in early ophthalmometers to double the mire images.

Kösters p. An interferometer element made from a pair of nearly identical prisms cut from a single 30°–60°–90° prism. A semireflecting film of aluminum or silver is applied to the face opposite the 60° angle of one prism, and this face is then cemented to the corresponding face of the other prism in various relationships, depending upon its intended use.

Landolt p. Rotary prism.

lateral p. Horizontal prism.

Leman p. A complex, one-piece prism unit employing two flat internal reflecting surfaces and a reflecting roof. It inverts and reverts the transmitted beam without deviation, but with some displacement.

Littrow p. One of the halves of a Cornu prism, with the interface side silvered to reflect the light back out through the face of incidence, the reversed orientation of the vibrations on reflection nullifying the double refraction, as does the second half of the Cornu prism.

Maddox p. A double prism with an apical angle of about 170°, sometimes made in ruby red or cobalt blue glass, used in ophthalmic clinical testing.

May p. A small, one-piece optical unit in the head of the May ophthalmoscope, consisting of a lower convex surface, at which light enters from a small source in the instrument handle, a pair of internal reflecting surfaces, and an oblique refracting surface which directs the light beam out of the unit, near its upper prism edge. adjacent to the viewing aperture, so as to illuminate the eye under observation.

measuring p. A prism used for determining the amount of devia-

tion in heterophoria and **heterotropia**, distinguished from **the** dissociating prism. Syn., *combining prism; correcting prism.*

Nicol p. A polarizing prism made from an Iceland spar or a calcite crystal, cut diagonally in half, with the two halves cemented together with Canada balsam; it transmits the extraordinary ray but totally reflects the ordinary ray. Syn., *Nicol polarizer.*

Pechan p. A direct vision, two-piece prism assembly which provides for five internal reflections of the transmitted beam, similar in function to the Dove prism, but usable with either convergent or divergent light.

Pellin-Broca p. A one-piece, quadrilateral, constant deviation, dispersing prism producing a deviation of 90°

penta p. Any prism whose section is pentagonal. In particular, a prism with five faces, not including the end faces, in which light enters one face perpendicularly, reflects successively at two silvered faces, and emerges perpendicular from a fourth face at right angles to the first. The unused face results from the removal of a dihedral section between the two reflecting faces.

plano p. A prism of zero focal power.

polarizing p. A prism made of a doubly refracting material such as Iceland spar, calcite, or quartz, used for producing or analyzing polarized light.

Porro p. A triangular, totally reflecting prism with angles of 90°, 45°, and 45°, commonly used in pairs in telescopic systems such as prism binoculars. Light entering perpendicular to the hypotenuse surface is totally reflected in turn by the two opposite surfaces, to emerge from the hypotenuse surface parallel to the incident light.

Porro-Abbe p. A modification of the Porro prism, sometimes called a double right-angle prism, used successively in pairs to invert and revert an image.

quadrant p. An ophthalmic test lens in the shape of an obtuse pyramid with its apex at the center, through which an object is seen in quadruplicate. Syn., *cone prism; quadrilateral prism.*

quadrilateral p. Quadrant prism.

reflecting p. A prism in which the internally contained light is totally reflected at one or more of the plane surfaces before emerging. Syn., *total reflecting prism.*

   reflecting p., double. A prism in which the internally contained light is totally reflected in turn at two of the plane surfaces before emerging.

   reflecting p., single. A prism in which the internally contained light is totally reflected at one of the plane surfaces before emerging.

   reflecting p., total. Reflecting prism.

relieving p. An ophthalmic prism placed before the eye so as to produce a displacement of the image seen through the prism in a direction which would compensate for the deviation, or tendency to deviate, of the viewing eye. Cf. *adverse prism.* Syn., *compensating prism.*

rhomboidal p. A long, narrow, rhomboid-shaped piece of glass used to displace a beam of light without deviation, reversion, or inversion of the image. The light enters near one end of a long rectangular side, reflects internally at the two inclined end surfaces, and emerges near the other end of the other long rectangular side.

Risley p. A type of rotary prism.

Rochon p. A rectangular polarizing unit consisting of two right-angled calcite or quartz prisms cemented together by their hypotenuse faces with the optic axis of the first prism perpendicular to its front surface, and with the optic axis of the second prism perpendicular to that of the first prism and parallel to the interface, producing an emergent ordinary beam undeviated, achromatic, and polarized, and a deviated, emergent, extraordinary beam which may be screened off easily at some distance from the prism. Syn., *Rochon polarizer.*

roof p. A complex prism unit which includes a pair of internally reflecting surfaces perpendicular to each other, thus resembling a roof externally. One type is an Amici prism, another has the plane of bisection of the reflecting surfaces parallel to and bisecting the incident beam, serving to reverse the resulting image by translating and inverting the two halves of the transmitted beam.

rotary p. A pair of equal power, thin prisms mounted one in front of the other, so that they can be rotated in opposite directions at equal rates to give a resultant power in a single meridian, varying from zero when the apex of one coincides with the base of the other to a maximum when the two apices coincide.

Schmidt p. A complex, one-piece prism unit which reverts and inverts the image and deviates the transmitted beam through an angle of 45° by a series of internal reflections.

slab-off p. The prism represented in a lens as a result of the bicentric grinding of one of its spherical surfaces, i.e., grinding the surface in two portions having separate centers of (equal) curvature, to compensate for the unequal prismatic effect produced when looking through the lower portions of an anisometropic lens prescription.

subducting p. An ophthalmic prism placed base up before a fixating eye, causing the eye to rotate downward.

superducting p. An ophthalmic prism placed base down before a fixating eye, causing the eye to rotate upward.

tank p. A long 90°–45°–45° prism used in military tank periscopes.

thick p. A prism in which the refracting angle is great enough to introduce a significant error in the mathematical assumption that the angle of deviation is arithmetically proportional to the refracting angle.

thin p. A prism in which the refracting angle is small enough to permit, without significant error, the mathematical assumption that the angle of deviation is arithmetically proportional to the refracting angle.

Thollon p. Young-Thollon prism.

Thorington p. Thorington double prism.

variable p. A rotary prism.

verger, p. See under *verger.*

vertical p. An ophthalmic prism placed before the eye with its base-apex line vertical.

Wadsworth p. A constant deviation, dispersing prism employing an auxiliary, externally located mirror instead of an internal reflecting surface.

Wernicke p. A composite of three glass prisms, two right-angle prisms of identical glass positioned on their hypotenuse faces to a triangular-shaped prism of nearly the same index for yellow light, but of different dispersion. It is used to obtain high dispersion with high transmission.

Wollaston p. 1. A double image prism consisting of two right-angled quartz or calcite prisms cemented together by their hypotenuse faces to form a rectan-

gular unit, and with the optic axes of the two halves perpendicular to each other and to the direction of propagation of the incident light. The resulting two emerging beams are oppositely polarized and relatively free of dispersion. Syn., *Wollaston polarizer.* 2. A one-piece prism, with two internal reflecting surfaces, which will deviate a beam of light through an angle of 90° without inversion or reversion, and hence is useful in camera lucida systems.

Young-Thollon p's. A pair of 30° prisms, one of right-handed and one of left-handed quartz, arranged for additive dispersion in a spectrograph or monochromator, so that the incident light is normal to the first surface of the first prism and the emergent light is normal to the second surface of the second prism.

Zeiss p. Carl Zeiss prism.

Zenger p. A composite of two right-angle prisms, made of glass of nearly the same index for yellow light, but of different dispersion. The components are arranged hypotenuse to hypotenuse to form a right parallelepiped of glass. It is often used in direct vision spectroscopy.

Prism Reader. An attachment of rotary prisms to the *Controlled Reader* for developing fusional convergence and divergence.

prismatic (priz-mat'ik). Produced by, pertaining to, or resembling, a prism or its action or effect.

prisme mobile. Creté's prism.

prismoptometer (priz"mop-tom'eh-ter). Prisoptometer.

prismosphere (priz'mo-sfēr). A spherical lens eccentrically mounted or decentered to produce prismatic effect; a combined spherical lens and prism. Syn., *spheroprism.*

prism-vergence (prizm-ver'gens). Vergence induced by prism effect.

prisoptometer (priz″op-tom′eh-ter). An instrument for determining ametropia, consisting essentially of a glass prism, the apical portion of which covers half of a central aperture in a revolving diaphragm. The subject views a circle at a distance of 20 ft., monocularly, through the aperture, with resulting monocular diplopia. The relative position of the doubled circle indicates the type of refractive error and the correction required. Syn., *prism optometer; prismoptometer.*

Pritchard photometer. See under *photometer.*

probability. The likelihood of the occurrence or nonoccurrence of a particular form of event in relationship to the total number of forms of the event that can occur.

probability ratio. See under *ratio.*

probit (pro′bit). An arbitrary number assigned to a percentage value when dealing with an ogive resulting from accumulating the increments of a normal curve. The resulting curve is a straight line rather than an ogive, and one probit step corresponds to one standard deviation. The probit scale usually ranges from 2 to 8, with 5 the median value, and is particularly useful in psychophysical determinations of threshold, using the constant method.

procedure. See under *method, process,* or *test.*

process. 1. Any marked prominence or projecting part; an outgrowth or extension. 2. A course or method of procedure. 3. Any phenomenon which demonstrates a continuous change, such as an inflammatory process.

ciliary p's. Meridionally arranged projections, approximately 70 in number, extending from the ciliary body posterior to the iris, and forming collectively the corona ciliaris. Each process is a ridge about 2 mm. long and 0.5 mm.

high, is almost white in color, and consists essentially of blood vessels, being the most vascular region of the eye. The ciliary processes serve as attachments for fibers of the zonule of Zinn and are considered to be involved in the formation of aqueous humor.

descending p. The inferior projection of the lacrimal bone which unites with the lacrimal process of the inferior nasal concha or turbinate to help bound the nasolacrimal canal.

filling-in p. Perceiving of areas in the visual field which correspond to the blind spot of Mariotte and to Arago's spot as of the same brightness, color, and pattern as their surrounds and not as dark or void spots.

frontal p. The upper medial projection of the maxillary bone which forms the anterior portion of the medial wall of the orbit and contains the anterior lacrimal crest and the anterior portion of the fossa for the lacrimal sac.

maxillary p. of the embryo. An embryological mass of visceral mesoderm, posterior and inferior to the optic vesicle, which gives rise to the connective tissue of the lower eyelid and to the orbital portions of the maxillary and zygomatic bones.

orbital p. of the palatine bone. The projection, at the upper end of the perpendicular portion of the palatine bone, which extends to the posterior portion of the floor of the orbit.

orbital p. of the zygomatic bone. The projection of the zygomatic bone that extends above the infraorbital process at the lateral wall of the orbit to form the anterior boundary of the temporal fossa.

photoreceptive p. The photochemical reaction which occurs when light energy strikes rhodopsin, iodopsin, or some other light-sensitive pigment in the outer segments of rods or cones and which initiates action currents.

pterygoid p. of the sphenoid bone. A projection, on either side of the junction of the body with the great wing of the sphenoid bone, which extends downward behind the lateral part of the hard palate and the last molar socket, forming the posterior boundary of the pterygopalatine fossa.

retinal p's PI, PII, PIII. Two excitational processes symbolized as PI and PII and one inhibitional process, PIII, the algebraic sum of which yields the resultant potential which registers in an electroretinogram. PI is related to the *c* wave, PII to the *b* wave, and PIII to the *a* wave.

visual p. The total sequence of events involved in the act of seeing from the incidence of light on the cornea to the cortical activity which results in a percept.

   visual p., physiological. The portion of the total visual process involving the photochemical changes produced in the retina by light stimulation, the formation of an impulse, and its transmission to the brain.

   visual p., physical. The portion of the total visual process involving the transmission of light through the transparent media of the eye and its incidence upon the retina.

   visual p., psychological. The portion of the total visual process involving the cortical interpretation of visual impulses with the formation of a percept.

projection. 1. The referring or localization of sensations from sense organs to the apparent source or place of origin of the stimulus. 2. A part that juts out or extends, or the act of jutting out or extending. 3. The act of causing a light, shadow, or optical image to fall into space or on a surface, or the light, shadow, or optical image itself.

anomalous p. The spatial localization of a visual sensation different from that which would have been predicted from the application of the laws of projection and the theory of local retinal sign for a given physical stimulus correlate in a normal eye, as occurs in anomalous retinal correspondence.

binocular p. The spatial localization of a binocularly perceived visual sensation. Cf. *cyclopean projection.*

center of p. See under *center.*

cyclopean p. Spatial localization of a binocularly perceived visual sensation with reference to a hypothetical single eye having certain attributes peculiar to the condition of binocular vision and presumed to resemble a cyclopean eye.

direction of p., absolute. The direction in which a perceived image is seen or projected in relation to a line of reference established by a given structural or functional characteristic of the eye or the subject.

direction of p., relative. The direction in which a perceived image is seen or projected in relation to a line of reference established by a given external point or object.

eccentric p. 1. Anomalous projection. 2. The spatial localization of an extrafoveally initiated visual sensation. 3. The aspect of the concept of projection that is concerned with localization external to the body or the sense organ itself.

erroneous p. False projection.

false p. 1. The reference of a visual sensation to a locality in space significantly different from its physical correlate, such as occurs in past pointing, and associated

with extraocular muscle paresis.
2. Anomalous projection.

flash p. The optical projection of images onto a screen for brief exposures, i.e., tachistoscopically.

flicker p. The rapid and alternate projection of pictures viewed alternately by the two eyes through a device alternately occluding the eyes synchronously with the projector; used to create stereopsis.

minus p. *Optometric Extension Program:* A condition or syndrome represented by either the static retinoscopy finding being in minus lens power and the unaided distance visual acuity being 20/20 or better, or the net of near point crossed cylinder findings being in minus lens power and the unaided visual acuity at near being 20/20 or better.

monocular p. Spatial localization of a monocularly perceived visual sensation, especially in relation to the line of sight or other line of reference.

normal p. The spatial localization of a visual sensation in accordance with the laws of projection and the theory of local retinal sign.

optical p. Optical image formation on a surface or viewing screen, or the image so projected.

paradoxical p. Spatial localization represented in paradoxical diplopia, often manifested after corrective surgery on a strabismic in which anomalous retinal correspondence previously existed.

postural p. The aspect of visual projection associated with proprioceptive impulses from the neck muscles and labyrinth and possibly from the extraocular muscles. Syn., *proprioceptive projection.*

proprioceptive p. Postural projection.

retinal p. 1. The aspect of visual projection associated with retinal local sign. 2. Visual projection in

geometric reference to the retina. 3. Visual projection as influenced only by stimulation of the retina and exclusive of proprioceptive impulses.

visual p. Spatial localization identified with visual perception.

projectionometer, Alabaster's (pro-jek″shun-om′eh-ter). A device for the detection and measurement of false projection, consisting essentially of a platform extending out horizontally from the patient's face just below the eyes, supporting a peripheral metal railing on which a light is moved by the examiner. The patient with one eye occluded attempts to place a wooden ball, situated out of sight beneath the platform, underneath the light.

projectionometer, Landolt's (pro-jek″shun-om′eh-ter). A device for the detection and measurement of false projection, consisting essentially of a horizontal shelf above which a vertical fixation line is marked on a screen perpendicular to the shelf and below which is a continuation of the screen containing a tangent scale. The patient looks over the shelf, with one eye occluded, and places a finger on a point on the scale, out of sight beneath the shelf, which seems to be just below the fixation line.

Project-o-chart (pro-jek′to-chart). A trade name for an optical instrument that projects test types and other test targets onto a screen.

projector. An optical instrument for projecting an image on a screen.

acuity p. An optical instrument which projects targets used in the determination of visual acuity and in the refraction of the eyes.

Moller test mark p. A hand-held projector which produces colored or white spots of light, of various sizes, used as targets on a tangent screen.

opaque p. An instrument which

[576]

projects by reflection an enlarged image of an opaque object, such as printed material, on a screen.

Polamatic acuity p. A 35 mm. slide projector adapted for visual acuity testing and for refraction procedures which includes polarized slides for monocular testing while maintaining binocular fusion of peripheral contours.

spectrum p. An instrument which projects the spectrum on a viewing screen.

Projectoscope (pro-jek'to-skōp). A trade name for an ophthalmoscope having an assortment of graticules which are projected onto the fundus, including targets for the detection and treatment of eccentric fixation.

projicience (pro-jish'ens). The localization of a perceived sensation in the external environment.

prolapse of the iris (pro-laps'). Protrusion of the iris through a corneal wound.

prolapse of the lens (pro-laps'). A falling forward of the crystalline lens into a corneal wound.

prong, Snellen's. The letter *U* of various sizes and orientation, used as a test target for visual acuity.

pronouncedness. The perceptual, psychological, affective, or phenomenal attribute of quality or degree of "goodness" of a color perception, such as the whiteness of a white or the blueness of a blue.

pro-ophthalmus (pro-of-thal'mus). Exophthalmos.

pro-opic (pro-op'ik). Having an orbitonasal index above 113 (or 110). Cf. *mesopic; platyopic.*

prop, ptosis. Ptosis crutch.

proprioception (pro''pre-o-sep'shun). Awareness of posture, balance, and muscular adjustment through sensory organs or receptors located within muscles, tendons, tendon sheaths, joints, and the vestibular apparatus of the inner ear.

proprioceptor (pro''pre-o-sep'tor). A receptor or sense organ located within muscles, tendons, tendon sheaths, joints, or the vestibular apparatus of the inner ear, which provides awareness of posture, balance, and muscular adjustment.

proptometer (prop-tom'eh-ter). Exophthalmometer.

proptosis ocular (prop-to'sis). Exophthalmos.

pro-sensation (pro-sen-sa'shun). A hypothetical, sensory response, presumed to be a fundamental hue, aroused by stimulation of a single retinal receptor or receptor-type, which cannot be experienced alone but only after combination with, or modification by, other pro-sensations or sensory processes.

prosthesis, ocular (pros'the-sis). Specifically, an artificial eye or implant. More generally, all mechanical and/or optical devices worn as ocular or visual aids, e.g., ptosis crutches, spectacles, and occluders.

prosthokeratoplasty (pros''tho-ker'-ah-to-plas''te). A surgical procedure in which diseased or opaque corneal tissue is replaced by a transparent prosthesis, usually of acrylic.

prostigmine (pro-stig'min). A trade name for a synthetic alkaloid (neostigmine) available only in its salts. Prostigmine bromide instilled in the eye in diluted solution acts as a powerful miotic through its neutralizing effect on choline esterases, permitting the continued action of acetylcholine.

protan (pro'tan). Protanoid.

protanoid (pro'tah-noid). 1. Pertaining to, or having the properties of, protanopia or protanomalous trichromasy. 2. One whose color vision shows some or all of the characteristics of protanopia or protanomaly. Syn., *protan.*

protanomal (pro″tah-nom′al). One having protanomaly.

protanomalopia (pro″tah-nom″ah-lo′pe-ah). Protanomaly. *Obs.*

protanomaly (pro″tah-nom′ah-le). A condition characterized by relatively lowered luminosity for long wavelength lights and, concomitantly, by abnormal color matching mixtures in which an excess of the red primary is necessary. Syn., *protanomalous trichromatism; protanomalous vision.*

protanope (pro′tah-nōp). One having protanopia

protanopia (pro″tah-no′pe-ah). A form of dichromatism characterized by decreased luminosity for long wavelengths and an inability to differentiate the hues of red, orange, yellow, and green, or blue and violet, or blue-green and a neutral gray. A sex-linked, hereditary form of color blindness occurring in about 1% of the male population. Syn., *anerythropsia; red blindness.*

protanopic (pro″tah-nop′ik). Pertaining to or having protanopia.

prothesis (proth′e-sis). Prosthesis.

protometer (pro-tom′eh-ter). Exophthalmometer

protractor. *Ophthalmic:* A chart containing a circle sectioned into degrees for positioning the axis of cylindrical spectacle lenses, and scales for positioning the optical center of lenses and multifocal segments.

protrusio bulbi (pro-trōō′ze-o bul′-bi). Exophthalmos.

protrusion, posterior, of von Ammon. Scleral ectasia in the region of the posterior pole of the eyeball, due to an incomplete closure of the fetal cleft and found in conjunction with a coloboma of the choroid.

psammoma (sam-o′mah). A small, hard, fibrous tumor occurring in brain tissue and the optic nerve.

pseudagraphia (su″dah-graf′e-ah, -gra′fe-ah). Pseudoagraphia.

pseudo-accommodation (su″do-ah-kom″o-da′shun). Apparent accommmodation.

pseudoagraphia (su″do-ah-graf′e-ah, -gra′fe-ah). A condition in which written material can be correctly copied but in which meaningful original material cannot be written.

pseudoaphakia (su″do-ah-fa′ke-ah). Membranous cataract.

pseudoblepsia (su″do-blep′se-ah). Pseudoblepsis.

pseudoblepsis (su″do-blep′sis). A visual hallucination or illusion. Syn., *pseudopsia.*

pseudocataract (su″do-kat′ah-rakt). False lenticonus.

pseudochalazion (su″do-kal-la′ze-on). An eye lesion, such as a sarcomatous or syphilitic lesion, which resembles a chalazion.

pseudochromesthesia (su″do-kro″-mes-the′ze-ah). A type of synesthesia in which certain sounds induce characteristic color sensations. Syn., *color hearing; psychochromesthesia.*

pseudochromia (su″do-kro′me-ah). False perception of color.

pseudocoloboma (su″do-kol″o-bo′-mah). 1. A line or a scar on the iris resembling a coloboma. 2. Incomplete coloboma.

pseudocyclophoria (su″do-si″klo-fo′-re-ah). Optical cyclophoria.

pseudoesophoria (su″do-es″o-fo′ re-ah, su″do-e″so-). An apparent esophoria attributable to spurious manifestations of accommodative convergence or positive relative convergence, or to temporarily or inadvertently induced effects of lenses or prisms.

pseudoexfoliation, capsular (su″do-eks-fo-le-a′shun). A disease in which small, gray, fluffy particles are deposited on the crystalline lens, zonule of Zinn, iris, cornea, and in the filtration angle. It is of undetermined etiology and pathogenesis and is often confused with a true exfoliation of the capsule of the crystalline lens.

pseudoexophoria (su″do-eks″o-fo′-re-ah). An apparent exophoria attributable to spurious manifestations, or failures of manifestation, of accommodative convergence, or to temporarily or inadvertently induced effects of lenses or prisms.

pseudogeusesthesia (su″do-gu″es-the′se-ah, su″do-ju″-). 1. A type of synesthesia in which certain tastes induce characteristic color sensations. 2. A false sensation of taste.

pseudoglaucoma (su″do-glaw-ko′-mah). Any anomaly of the optic disk which may appear to be of glaucomatous origin, as, for example, a congenitally large and pale physiological cup, a branching of the central retinal artery posterior to the lamina cribrosa, a congenital coloboma of the optic disk, or an excessively oblique connection of the optic nerve with the eyeball.

pseudoglioma (su″do-gli-o′mah). 1. An organized exudate in the vitreous body, caused by endophthalmitis, which simulates the reflex from the interior of the eye seen in retinoblastoma. 2. Any condition which simulates retinoblastoma, as retrolental fibroplasia or retinal detachment.

pseudohyperphoria (su″do-hi″per-fo′re-ah). An apparent hyperphoria attributable to spurious manifestations of neurological origin or to temporarily or inadvertently induced effects of lenses or prisms.

pseudoisochromatic (su″do-i″so-kro-mat′ik). Pertaining to the different hues which appear alike to the color blind.

pseudomacula (su″do-mak′u-lah). False macula.

pseudomonochromasy (su″do-mon-o-kro′mah-se). A term introduced by König for a type of total color blindness with luminosity func-

tions corresponding to the known forms of congenital dichromasy but with normal visual acuity. Syn., *cone monochromatism*.

pseudomyopia (su″do-mi-o′pe-ah). Appearance of myopia due to spasm of the ciliary muscle or to failure of relaxation of accommodation. See also *hypertonic myopia*.

pseudoneuritis (su″do-nu-ri′tis). Pseudo optic neuritis.

pseudonystagmus (su″do-nis-tag′-mus). An accentuation of the normal oscillatory movements of the eyes occurring when fixation is changed from one point to another.

pseudo-ophthalmoplegia (su″do-of-thal″mo-ple′je-ah). Loss of voluntary eye movements, with reflex movements intact and possibly exaggerated, due to bilateral destructive lesions of the frontal cortex.

pseudopapilledema (su″do-pap″ih-le-de′mah). A condition of apparent papilledema, observed ophthalmoscopically, in the presence of normal visual acuity, normal size of the blind spot, and normal intracranial pressure.

pseudoparalysis, myasthenic (su″-do-pah-ral′ih-sis). Myasthenia gravis.

pseudophakia (su″do-fa′ke-ah). A congenital condition in which the crystalline lens has been invaded and replaced by mesodermal tissue.

    artificial p. An aphakic eye with an artificial lens implant. *Binkhorst.*

    fibrosa, p. Pseudophakia in which the invading mesodermal tissue undergoes fibrous degeneration. Syn., *fibrous tissue cataract; cataracta fibrosa.*

    lipomatosa, p. Pseudophakia in which the invading mesodermal tissue undergoes fatty degeneration. Syn., *cataracta adiposa.*

    ossea, p. Pseudophakia in which the invading mesodermal tissue undergoes osseous degeneration. Syn., *cataracta ossea.*

pseudophotesthesia (su″do-fo″tes-the′ze-ah). Color or light sensation or attribution, induced by stimuli or irritants abnormal for vision, such as sound, taste, smell, pressure, thought, or anger.

pseudopolycoria (su″do-pol″ih-ko′re-ah). Polycoria spuria.

pseudopsia (su-dop′se-ah). A visual hallucination or illusion. Syn., *pseudoblepsia.*

pseudopterygium (su″do-ter-ij′e-um). An adhesion of the conjunctiva to the cornea, as a result of an inflammatory process, which resembles a pterygium but which may occur at any part of the corneal margin and is attached only at its apex.

pseudoptosis (su″do-to′sis). A condition resembling ptosis, due to an abnormally small palpebral aperture (blepharophimosis), to lack of normal support to the upper eyelid by the eyeball, or to a fold of atrophic skin falling below the edge of the upper eyelid (blepharochalasis). Syn., *apparent ptosis; false ptosis; spurious ptosis.*

pseudoretinitis pigmentosa (su″do-ret″ih-ni′tis pig-men-to′sah). Any disease of the retina presenting the ophthalmoscopic picture of bone corpuscle pigmentation similar to that in retinitis pigmentosa, but without the other accompanying symptoms.

pseudoretinoblastoma (su″do-ret-ih-no-blas-to′mah). Any organized mass in the vitreous body which gives rise to a grayish-white pupillary reflex simulating that seen in retinoblastoma. Syn., *pseudoglioma.*

pseudosclerosis of Westphal (su″-do-skle-ro′sis). Wilson's disease.

pseudoscope (su″do-skōp). An instrument which transposes to the right eye the view normally seen by the left, and vice versa, usu-

ally by means of prisms and mirrors.

pseudoscopic (su″do-skop′ik). Seen in reversed stereoscopic relief, or pertaining to the effect obtained in, or tests done with, a pseudoscope.

pseudoscopy (su-dos′ko-pe). The viewing of targets in reverse stereoscopic relief, or in a pseudoscope.

pseudostereopsis (su″do-ster-e-op′sis). Binocular visual perception in reversed stereoscopic relief, as obtained in viewing a three-dimensional field in a stereoscope with the view for the two eyes transposed. Syn., *pseudoscopic vision.*

pseudostrabismus (su″do-strah-biz′mus). Apparent strabismus.

pseudotrachoma (su″do-trah-ko′mah). Nodular conjunctivitis.

　syphilitic p. Granular syphilitic conjunctivitis.

pseudotumor cerebri (su″do-tu′mor ser′e-bri). Increased intracranial pressure, without clinical evidence of tumor, which may be idiopathic or may occur following otitis media, upper respiratory infections, trauma, or thrombosis of the superior, sagittal, and lateral sinuses. The symptoms are primarily ocular and include blurring of vision, strabismus, diplopia, blindness, and papilledema.

pseudotumor, orbital (su″do-tu′mor). Orbital myositis.

pseudotumor, retinal (su″do-tu′mor). Retinal fibrosis.

pseudoxanthoma elasticum (su″do-zan-tho′mah e-las′tih-kum). A rare disease of the skin characterized by the appearance of elevated yellowish papules or plaques, particularly on the neck, chest, and abdomen, and infrequently on the eyelids. It is due to degeneration of dermal elastic tissue and is sometimes associated with angioid streaks (Grönblad-Strandberg syndrome).

psoriasis (so-ri'ah-sis). A disease of the skin of unknown etiology, characterized by sharply defined red patches covered with silvery scales which appear particularly in the regions of the elbows and knees, in the scalp, and rarely in the eyelids.

psorophthalmia (sōr″of-thal'me-ah). Blepharitis marginalis.

psychalia (si-ka'le-ah). A depressed mental state associated with visual and auditory hallucinations. *Obs.*

psychanopsia (si-kah-nop'se-ah). Visual agnosia.

psychochromesthesia (si″ko-kro″-mes-the'ze-ah). Pseudochromesthesia.

psycho-optic (si″ko-op'tik). Pertaining to the relations between mental and optical processes or functions.

psychophysics (si″ko-fiz'iks). The branch of science that deals with the interrelationships of physical stimuli and their mental or perceptual correlates.

psychophysiology (si″ko-fiz″e-ol'o-je). Physiological psychology; the branch of science which deals with the interrelationships between psychological and physiological processes.

pterygium (teh-rij'e-um). A horizontal, triangular growth of the bulbar conjunctiva, occupying the intrapalpebral fissure, with the apex extending toward the cornea. The base is typically at the internal canthus, rarely at the external canthus, and the pterygium is fixed to the conjunctiva along its entire length, so that a probe cannot be passed entirely beneath it. It is highly vascularized during growth, is considered to be due to a degenerative process caused by long continued irritation, as from exposure to wind and dust, and, if not treated surgically, may encroach on the cornea and destroy Bowman's membrane.

carnosum, p. Pterygium crassum.

cicatricial p. Pseudopterygium.

congenital p. Epitarsus.

crassum, p. A thick, fleshy, vascular pterygium. Syn., *pterygium carnosum; pterygium sarcomatosum; pterygium vasculosum.*

false p. Pseudopterygium.

membranaceum, p. Pterygium tenue.

sarcomatosum, p. Pterygium crassum.

tenue, p. A thin, tendinous, stationary pterygium. Syn., *pterygium membranaceum.*

vasculosum, p. Pterygium crassum.

pterygoid (ter'ih-goid) **canal; plexus.** See under the nouns.

ptilosis (tih-lo'sis). Pathological loss of the eyelashes.

ptosed (tōst). Affected with ptosis.

ptosis (to'sis). 1. Prolapse or falling down of an organ or a part. 2. Drooping of the upper eyelid below its normal position. Syn., *blepharoptosis.*

adiposa, p. Ptosis occurring in advanced stages of blepharochalasis, in which the atrophic upper eyelid tissue is weighted down by herniated orbital fat.

apparent p. Pseudoptosis.

artificial p. Ptosis produced by surgical section of nerves to the levator palpebrae superioris muscle for the protection of the eyeball, as in lagophthalmos.

atonica, p. 1. Ptosis occurring in later stages of blepharochalasis in which atrophic, wrinkled, discolored, and venuled skin overhangs the upper eyelid margin and in which the power to raise the lid is diminished. 2. Pseudoparalytic ptosis.

atrophica, p. Blepharochalasis.

crutch, p. See under *crutch.*

false p. Pseudoptosis.

functional p. Partial closure of the

[581]

eyelids to reduce the effective pupillary aperture.

Horner's p. Sympathetic ptosis present in Horner's syndrome.

hypertonic p. Ptosis associated with Parkinson's disease and due to increased tonicity of the opposing muscles, with a resulting rigidity and loss of voluntary movement.

iridis, p. Prolapse of the iris.

lipomatosis, p. Mechanical ptosis due to lipoma of the eyelid.

mechanical p. Ptosis due to edema or inflammation of the conjunctiva or eyelid, to hypertrophy or atrophy of the eyelid tissue, to herniation of orbital fat into the eyelid, etc., without involvement of the levator palpebrae superioris muscle or its nerve supply.

morning p. Waking ptosis.

myogenic p. Ptosis due to disease of the levator palpebrae superioris muscle.

paralytic p. Ptosis due to lesion in the pathway of the oculomotor nerve.

periodic p. The intermittent ptosis associated with cyclic oculomotor paralysis.

pseudoparalytic p. Ptosis due to loss of normal tonicity of the levator palpebrae superioris muscle as may occur in senility, after prolonged bandaging, or after continued blepharospasm. Syn., *ptosis atonica.*

relative p. An apparent ptosis of a normally positioned eyelid in comparison with a contralateral upper eyelid retraction, presumed to be suggested by the asymmetry, but which may occur in part as a binocular compensatory effect of the unilateral retraction.

senilis, p. Pseudoparalytic ptosis occurring in the aged.

simple p. Congenital ptosis due to impaired development of the levator palpebrae superioris muscle or to absent or incomplete innervation to the muscle. It may be associated with paresis of the homolateral superior rectus muscle, but is unaccompanied by any other defect.

spurious p. Pseudoptosis.

sympathetic p. Ptosis due to paresis of Mueller's muscle; its association with other signs of sympathetic paresis constitutes Horner's syndrome.

synkinetic p. Ptosis associated with movements of the eye or jaw, as in jaw-winking.

voluntary p. 1. Voluntary closure of one eyelid to avoid diplopia. 2. Partial closure of the eyelids to reduce the effective pupillary aperture. Syn., *functional ptosis.*

waking p. Temporary paralysis of the upper eyelid on awakening from sleep. Syn., *morning ptosis.*

ptotic (tot'ik). Pertaining to or affected with ptosis.

Pugh's (pūz) **occluder; visual acuity reducer.** See under the nouns.

Pulfrich (pul'frik) **effect; phenomenon; photometer; refractometer; stereoscope.** See under the nouns.

pulse, photic. A short duration of light, used in reference to a light stimulus and differentiated from a *flash,* the sensory correlate.

pulvinar (pul-vi'nar). The medial angular prominence of the posterior portion of the thalamus, thought to be associated with higher somatic functions, and with visual and auditory integration because of its connections with cortical areas adjacent to the primary cortical receptive areas for these types of impulses.

pump, lacrimal. The mechanism which acts to facilitate tear drainage in the lacrimal apparatus, primarily by action of the orbicularis oculi and Horner's muscles, initiated by blinking of the eyelids.

punctometer (punk-tom'eh-ter). 1. An instrument making use of the subjective appearance of a very small, in and out of focus, point of light for the determination of the conjugate focus of the retina and related refractive values. 2. A punctumeter.

punctometry (punk-tom'eh-tre). Measurement of the refractive state of the eye, or the status of accommodation, by use of an illuminated pinhole target subjectively adjusted in optical distance from the eye to appear maximally bright, most sharply defined, and of minimum size.

punctum (punk'tum). A point.

caecum, p. The blind spot of Mariotte.

convergens basalis, p. The near point of convergence, abbreviated P.C.B.

lacrimal p. The small, pointlike orifice in the lacrimal papilla which serves as the opening into the lacrimal canaliculus.

luteum, p. Macula lutea.

proximum of accommodation, p. Near point of accommodation.

proximum of convergence, p. Near point of convergence, abbreviated P.P.C.

remotum of accommodation, p. Far point of accommodation.

remotum of convergence, p. The far point of convergence, abbreviated P.R.C.

punctumeter (punk-tum'eh-ter). An instrument for determining the near and far points of accommodation.

Punktal (punk'tal). A trade name for a series of corrected curve ophthalmic lenses.

pupil (pu'pil). 1. The aperture in the iris, normally circular and contractile, through which the image-forming light enters the eye. 2. *Zoology:* The dark central spot of an ocellus.

Adie's p. Tonic pupil.

apparent p. The entrance pupil of the eye, hence the pupil as normally seen, i.e., through the cornea. It is slightly larger than,

and anterior to, the actual pupil.

Argyll Robertson's p. A pupil characterized by the loss of both direct and consensual reflexes to light, with normal contraction on accommodation and convergence and otherwise normal vision. Miosis may or may not be present. The condition usually indicates syphilis of the central nervous system. Syn., *Vincent's sign.*

artificial p. 1. A pupil made by iridectomy. 2. A perforation in a diaphragm or disk to be held or mounted in front of the eye to effect a small or constant pupil size.

bounding p. A pupil showing alternate dilations and contractions unassociated with illumination changes.

Bumke's p. A catatonic pupil found in neurotics.

cat's-eye p. A pupil with a narrow vertical aperture.

catatonic p. A pupil which transiently dilates and which may become inactive to light and convergence stimuli. The dilatation may persist for only a few seconds or for several days and is associated with catatonia and other psychotic states, hysteria, neuroses, syphilis, or alcoholism. Syn., *spasmus mobilis.*

climbing p. of Lowenstein. A pupil which contracts poorly to light and dilates in excess of the amount of original contraction and, upon repeated subsequent light stimulation, demonstrates a greater and greater dilatation.

cogwheel p. A pupil found in hysteria in which the contraction to light and the redilatation do not take place in a single continuous movement but in a series of steps, giving a cogged appearance to a continuous graphical recording of the pupillary diameter.

descending p. of Lowenstein. A pupil which contracts to light, does not demonstrate an equivalent redilatation on removal of the light stimulus, and, on repeated subsequent light stimulation, demonstrates a greater and greater contraction.

entrance p. The image of the aperture stop formed by the portion of an optical system on the object side of the stop.

exit p. The image of the aperture stop formed by the portion of an optical system on the image side of the stop.

fixed p. An immobile pupil, one which is inactive to all reflexes.

Hutchinson's p. An immobile, widely dilated pupil which is inactive to all reflexes, associated with intracranial hemorrhage, as may occur in fracture of the skull or with cranial neoplasm.

inverse Argyll Robertson's p. A pupil characterized by normal, direct, and consensual reflexes to light with loss of contraction on accommodation and convergence. It is due to a midbrain lesion of the connection of the convergence center with the constrictor center of the pupil.

keyhole p. A pupil shaped like a keyhole, due to coloboma, surgery, or trauma of the iris.

miotic p. 1. A pupil which is reduced in size, as one constricted in response to the instillation of a miosis-producing drug. 2. A very small pupil, i.e., approximately 2 mm. or less in diameter.

multiple p's. Polycoria.

mydriatic p. 1. A pupil which is increased in size, as one dilated in response to the instillation of a mydriasis-producing drug. 2. A very large pupil, i.e., approximately 5 mm. or greater in diameter.

myotic p. Miotic pupil.

myotonic p. Tonic pupil.

neurotonic p. A pupil which contracts slowly on stimulation by light and, when contracted, remains immobile for some time.

nonluetic Argyll Robertson's p. Tonic pupil.

paradoxical p. A pupil which dilates on stimulation of the retina by light or has any other action opposite to that normally expected.

pinhole p. 1. An extremely small pupil. 2. A pupil or an aperture small enough to make the effects of refraction negligible; a pinhole.

pseudo-Argyll Robertson's p. Tonic pupil.

reverse Argyll Robertson's p. A pupil characterized by the loss of constriction on convergence and accommodation, with retention of the normal light reflexes.

Robertson's p. Argyll Robertson's pupil.

springing p. A sudden momentary dilation of one pupil, followed, after a short interval, by sudden momentary dilation of the other, seen in tabes, general paralysis, neurasthenia, veronal poisoning, and sometimes in apparently normal persons.

tonic p. A pupil in which the reaction to light, both direct and consensual, is almost abolished, being elicited only after prolonged exposure to dark or light, and in which there is a delayed reaction to changes in accommodation and convergence. It usually occurs unilaterally, with the affected pupil being the larger, and reacts normally to mydriatics and certain miotics. Syn., *Adie's pupil; myotonic pupil; nonluetic Argyll Robertson pupil; pseudo-Argyll Robertson pupil; pupillotonia.*

pupilantoscope (pu″pih-lan′to-skōp). An instrument for examining one's own pupil, consisting essentially of a magnifying lens in front of a concave mirror, contained in a rim mounted on a handle.

pupilens, Mazow (pu′pih-lens). A corneal contact lens, opaque except for a small central aperture, giving the effect of a pinhole pupil, which increases the depth of focus of the eye and eliminates the necessity for a reading correction in presbyopia.

pupilla (pu-pil′ah). The pupil of the eye.

pupillary (pu′pih-lār-e). Pertaining to or of the pupil.

pupillary axis; block; distance; line; reaction; reflex; ruff. See under the nouns.

pupillography (pu″pih-log′rah-fe). 1. Photography of the pupil. 2. The recording of pupillary reactions.

pupillometer (pu″pih-lom′eh-ter). An instrument for measuring the diameter of the pupil. Syn., *coreometer.*

Haab's p. A series of graduated circles which are compared with the pupil for size.

Laurence's p. A caliper-type pupillometer.

Morton's p. A disk of graduated circles attached to Morton's ophthalmoscope for direct comparison with the pupil for size.

Priestley Smith's p. A millimeter scale engraved on a convex lens through which an observer at the focal point views the pupil to be measured.

projection p. A millimeter scale optically projected or mirrored in the plane of the pupil to be measured.

Schlösser's p. A series of short parallel lines of graduated length engraved on a transparent scale for direct comparison with the pupil diameter.

pupillometry (pu″pih-lom′eh-tre). The measurement of the size of the pupil of the eye. Syn., *coreometry.*

pupillomotor (pu″pih-lo-mo′tor). Pertaining to motor activity affecting pupil size.

pupilloplegia (pu″pih-lo-ple′je-ah). Complete or partial paralysis of the pupillary reflexes.

pupilloscope (pu-pil′o-skōp). 1. An instrument for observing the pupil or its reactions. 2. A retinoscope.

pupilloscopy (pu″pih-los′ko-pe). 1. Retinoscopy. 2. Observation of the pupil or its reactions with a pupilloscope.

pupillostatometer (pu-pil″o-stah-tom′eh-ter). An instrument for measuring the interpupillary distance.

pupillotonia (pu″pih-lo-to′ne-ah). Tonic pupil.

pupillotonic pseudotabes (pu″pih-lo-ton′ik su″do-ta′bēz). Adie's syndrome.

purity. 1. A measure of the degree of freedom of a color from achromatic content; or, the degree to which a color approaches the condition required for maximum saturation. Various purity scales are used, all of which can be expressed as some mathematical function of the ratio of the spectral to the achromatic components of a color mixture. 2. Excitation purity.

colorimetric p. The spectral purity of a color expressed as the ratio of the luminance of a monochromatic spectral component which, if mixed with an achromatic component, would match the color, to the luminance of the color itself. Syn., *luminance purity.*

excitation p. The ratio of the distance, on the C.I.E. standard chromaticity diagram, between the achromatic (white) point and the sample point to the distance in the same direction between the achromatic point and the point on the spectrum locus representing the dominant wavelength of the sample.

luminance p. Colorimetric purity.

Ostwald p. In the Ostwald system, the ratio of full color content to white content.

Purkinje's (pur-kin'jēz) **afterimage; effect; figures; images; phenomenon; shadows; shift.** See under the nouns.

Purkinje-Sanson images (pur-kin'je-san'son). See under *image*.

purple. 1. A mixture of blue and red, a nonspectral hue complementary to yellow-green of about 560 mμ. 2. One of a series of related hues ranging from blue to red on the nonspectral portion of the color scale.

retinal p. Rhodopsin.

visual p. Rhodopsin.

purpura (pur'pu-rah). A disease characterized by recurrent multiple hemorrhages in the skin, mucous membranes, serous membranes, and internal organs. The ocular manifestations may be hemorrhages into the eyelids, conjunctiva, iris, choroid, or retina, or palsies of the extraocular muscles due to hemorrhages in the brain.

hyperglobulinemic purpura. Waldenström's syndrome.

pursuitmeter (pur-sūt'me-ter). A device for indicating degree of eyehand co-ordination, utilizing an irregularly moving visual target that must be followed as accurately as possible by a hand-held stylus.

Purtscher's (poor'cherz) **disease; retinopathy.** See under the nouns.

purulent (pu'roo-lent). Consisting of, containing, associated with, or identified by the formation of pus.

pyophthalmia (pi"of-thal'me-ah). Purulent inflammation of the eye, especially of the conjunctiva. Syn., *pyophthalmitis.*

pyophthalmitis (pi"of-thal-mi'tis). Pyophthalmia.

pyramid, color. A type of color solid.

pyridoxine (pir"ih-dok'sin). A water-soluble vitamin present in yeast, cereals, and liver and thought to be associated with the metabolism of unsaturated fatty acids. A deficiency in the diet may be a factor in nutritional amblyopia. Syn., *vitamin B_6.*

pyron (pi'ron). A unit of radiation intensity equal to a gram calorie per square centimeter of receiving surface per minute when the receiving surface is perpendicular to the direction of radiation.

Q

quadra (kwod'rah). Having a pre-dominantly square or rectangu-lar shape; a British classification of spectacle lenses differentiated in outline from those predomi-nantly round or oval.

quadrantanopia (kwod-ran"tah-no'-pe-ah). Quadrantanopsia.

quadrantanopsia (kwod-ran"tah-nop'se-ah). Blindness or loss of vision in a quarter sector of the visual field of one eye. Syn., *quadrantic anopsia; tetranopsia.*

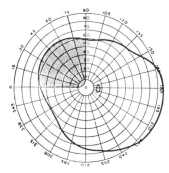

binasal q., crossed. Quadrantanop-sia involving the lower nasal quadrant of the visual field of one eye and the upper nasal quadrant of the visual field of the other eye.

bitemporal q., crossed. Quad-rantanopsia involving the lower temporal quadrant of the visual field of one eye and the upper temporal quadrant of the visual field of the other eye.

heteronymous q., lower. Quad-rantanopsia involving either both lower temporal quadrants of the visual fields or both lower nasal quadrants of the visual fields.

heteronymous q., upper. Quad-rantanopsia involving either both upper temporal or both upper nasal quadrants of the visual fields.

homonymous q., lower. Quad-rantanopsia involving the lower nasal quadrant of the visual field of one eye and the lower tem-poral quadrant of the visual field of the other eye. Syn., *lower te-tartanopsia.*

homonymous q., upper. Quad-rantanopsia involving the upper nasal quadrant of the visual field of one eye and the upper tem-poral quadrant of the visual field of the other eye. Syn., *upper te-tartanopsia.*

quadrantic anopsia (kwod-ran'tik an-op'se-ah). Quadrantanopsia.

quadrilopia (kwod"ril-o'pe-ah). The perception of a single object in quadruple, or double diplopia, as sometimes may occur with anom-alous retinal correspondence.

quality, spectral. The color char-acteristic of a light source or a lighted area, as represented by the relative amounts of luminous energy of different wavelengths.

quantum of light (kwon'tum). A quantity of light energy equal to the product of the frequency of the light and Planck's constant (6.624×10^{-27} erg. sec.).

quartile (kwor'til). 1. One of three specific points by which a serial distribution is divided into four groups of equal frequency. 2. One of the four groups so obtained.

deviation, q. See under *deviation.*

quartz. Silicon dioxide (SiO_2), a doubly refracting crystal, found in nature in a variety of forms, which is transparent to visible and ultraviolet radiation and is used in optics to produce polarized light.

amorphous q. Silicon dioxide (SiO_2) not in crystal formation; fused quartz.

quasi-correspondence, retinal (kwa'si-kōr"e-spon'dens). The faculty of vision which gives rise to the unitary percept of a binocularly seen object or of a pair of objects viewed haploscopically when the respective retinal images stimulate noncorresponding retinal receptors lying within Panum's areas.

Quincke's disease (kvink'ēz). Angioneurotic edema.

quizzing glass. Monocle.

quotient. A number obtained by dividing one number by another.

accomplishment q. The achievement age divided by the mental age.

achievement q. The achievement age divided by the chronological age.

intelligence q. The mental age multiplied by 100 and divided by the chronological age.

perversion q. The angle of anomaly divided by the objective angle of strabismus.

reading q. The reading age divided by the mental age.

R

r. Symbol for *radius of curvature.*

Rabkin charts; polychromatic plates; test. See under the nouns.

radiance (ra′de-ans). Radiant flux per unit solid angle per unit projected area of the source in a given direction. The usual unit is the watt per steradian per sq. cm. It is the radiant analog of *luminance* (photometric brightness). Symbol: *N.*

radiant. Transmitted or emitted by radiation.

radiant energy; flux; intensity. See under the nouns.

radiation. 1. The process by which radiant energy is emitted and transmitted. 2. A group of nerve fibers that diverge after leaving their place of origin.

> **beta r.** Radiation of negatively charged electrons which travel in a straight line at about the speed of light unless affected by a magnetic field. The electrons vary in penetrating power, travel about 9.0 to 10.0 cm. in air and up to 1.0 cm. in tissue. It may be derived from x-rays, radium, radon, radium D, or an isotope such as strontium 90, and, in the eye, is used for the treatment of rosacea keratitis, recurrent pterygia, and vernal conjunctivitis, and for the removal of corneal blood vessels prior to keratoplasty.

> **blackbody r.** The characteristic thermal radiation emitted by a heated blackbody; the radiation from a field in an enclosed cavity in thermal equilibrium with the matter surrounding it.

> **Meynert, r′s of.** A large number of coarse, medullated fibers in the deep area striata that represent the continuation of the projection system of the optic radiations.

> **optic r′s. of Gratiolet.** Geniculocalcarine tract.

> **resonance r.** Radiation emitted from a medium as the result of, and only during, the absorption of radiation from another source, the emitted radiation being of the same wavelengeh as that of the exciting radiation. Syn., *resonance fluorescence.*

radiator (ra′dih-a″tor). An emitter of radiant energy.

> **complete r.** Blackbody.

> **ideal r.** Blackbody.

> **incomplete r.** Graybody.

> **nonselective r.** 1. A radiator for which spectral emissivity is constant throughout the spectrum. 2. A graybody.

> **Planckian r.** Blackbody.

> **selective r.** A radiator for which spectral emissivity varies for different wavelengths.

> **standard r.** Blackbody

> **total r.** Blackbody.

radiometer (ra″dih-om′eh-ter). An instrument for detecting and measuring radiant energy.

> **Crookes' r.** An exhausted glass globe in which is mounted a freely rotating shaft with several vanes, black on one side and silvered on the other, which rotate in reaction to radiant energy, with the blackened side of the vanes retreating, the velocity being roughly proportional to the energy received.

radiometry (ra″dih-om′eh-tre). The measurement of radiant energy; the use of a radiometer.

radius. 1. The straight line extending from the center of a circle or a sphere to the curve or surface; the semidiameter of a circle or a sphere. 2. A circular limit defined by a fixed distance from an established point or center.

corneal r. The radius of curvature of the posterior surface of the corneal section of a contact lens.

scleral r. The radius of curvature of the posterior surface of the scleral section of a contact lens.

stereoscopic vision, r. of. Range of stereopsis.

Radiuscope (ra′de-us-skōp). The trade name for an instrument for measuring the curvature of a contact lens; it has an optical system employing the Drysdale method.

radix nervi optici (ra′diks ner′vi op′-tih-ki). Optic tract.

Raeder's syndrome (ra′derz). See under *syndrome.*

Ragona Scina experiment (rah-go′-nah she′nah). See under *experiment.*

Raman effect (rah′man). See under *effect.*

Ramsden (rams′den) **disk; eyepiece.** See under the nouns.

ramus ophthalmicus (ra′mus of-thal′-mih-kus). Ophthalmic nerve.

range. The difference between the least and the greatest values in a series of measurements or values.

accommodation, r. of. See under *accommodation.*

convergence, r. of. See under *convergence.*

haplopic r. In the haplopic horopter, the anteroposterior distance through which a nonfixated test object may be displaced and still be seen as single.

semi-interquartile r. Quartile deviation.

stereopsis, r. of. The linear distance from the eyes to the point

just noticeably nearer than infinity as determined by the retinal disparity cue; the distance beyond which stereoscopic vision is not possible. Syn., *radius of stereoscopic vision.*

vision, r. of. See under *vision.*

rank order. The arrangement and numerical designation in a serial order of magnitude.

raphe (ra′fe). A line of union or demarcation, resembling a seam, between two more or less symmetrical halves of an organ or a structure.

palpebralis, r. A thin horizontal band of connective tissue which extends from the external canthus to the lateral margin of the orbit.

retinal r. A horizontal raphe on the temporal side of the macula in the nerve fiber layer of the retina above and below which the nerve fibers follow an arcuate course to the optic disk.

Rasin's sign. Jellinek's sign.

rate of aqueous outflow. The speed of drainage of aqueous humor, generally expressed in cubic millimeters per minute as $F = C(P_o - P_v)$, in which C = coefficient of facility of aqueous outflow, P_o = intraocular pressure just before tonometry, and P_v = episcleral venous pressure.

rate, reading. The rate at which an individual can read and comprehend, usually represented as the number of words read silently per unit time with a comprehension level of at least 80 per cent.

Rateometer (rāt-om′eh-ter). The trade name for an instrument used in improving reading speed and comprehension, consisting essentially of a shutter which moves down over reading material at a preset speed, thus setting a pace for the reader.

ratio. A proportion; the quotient of one magnitude divided by another of the same kind.

A.C.A. (*A.C./A.*) *r.* The ratio

of accommodative convergence (A.C.) to accommodation (A.), usually expressed as the quotient of accommodative convergence in prism diopters divided by the accommodative response in diopters. Syn., *gradient*.

aniseikonic r. A ratio representing the difference between the sizes of the two images in aniseikonia as determined by plotting the apparent frontoparallel plane horopter. It is the ratio of the angle subtended at the nodal point of one eye by the point of fixation and a peripheral point on the horopter to the angle subtended at the nodal point of the other eye by the same two points.

A.V. r. The apparent ratio of arterial to venous diameter in the retinal blood vessels, typically about 3:4, as observed ophthalmoscopically.

aperture r. The ratio of the diameter of the aperture of an optical system to its focal length. Syn., *relative aperture*.

blank r. The ratio indicating the relationship of the index of refraction of the button of a multifocal lens to that of the carrier as expressed by the formula: $(n - 1)/(N - n)$ in which n = index of refraction of the carrier and N = index of refraction of the button.

brightness r. The ratio, expressed as a fraction, indicating the luminance (photometric brightness) relationship between two areas.

Brunswik r. The expression, $S - S'/L - S'$, in which L = luminance of an unshadowed object, S' = luminance of the same object in shadow, and S = luminance of an experimental match to the shadowed object. It is used in experiments for determining the color constancy of an object when placed in shadow.

contrast r. The ratio of the luminance of an object backed by black to that of the same object backed by white, and hence correlated with the transparency of the object.

critical r. A numerical measure representing the ratio of the deviation of the difference in means of two populations from zero to the standard deviation of the distribution of the differences of the means (based on successive samplings from the two populations). The size of the critical ratio is taken as a criterion for the acceptance or rejection of the null hypothesis, viz., that there is no difference between the means of the two populations.

focal r. The ratio of the focal length of an optical system to the linear diameter of its entrance pupil, usually written as follows: f/5, f/4.5, etc. Syn., *f-value*.

Haller's r. A generalization that the size of animal eyes varies inversely with the size of the body.

Leuckart's r. A generalization that the size of animal eyes varies directly with swiftness of movement.

light-dark r. 1. In a repetitive, intermittent, light stimulus pattern, the ratio of light time to dark time in a cycle. 2. In a repetitive, intermittent, light stimulus pattern, the ratio of light time to the total time of the light-dark cycle.

Matthiessen's r. The radius of the crystalline lens $\times$ 2.55 is equal to the distance from the center of the lens to the retina, a constant in fishes, according to Matthiessen.

off/on r. The ratio between the stimulus thresholds for off and on responses of cells in the retina.

probability r. The ratio of the number of ways a given event can occur to the entire number of possible events, assuming chance alone is operating.

Strehl intensity r. Strehl definition.

Thouless r. An alternate for the Brunswik ratio (*q.v.*), in which log luminances are substituted for luminances.

Raubitschek chart; test. See under the nouns.

ray. 1. A line representing the radiation or direction of the propagation of light, often regarded as an infinitesimally narrow pencil of light. 2. Light or radiant energy, especially in the sense of an element of light or radiant energy.

aberrant r. Stray light, or a ray of stray light.

actinic r. Radiant energy capable of producing or serving to produce chemical changes.

axial r. A ray coincident with the axis of an optical system.

bundle of r's. A cone or pencil of light.

　　bundle of r's., direct. A homocentric bundle of rays emanating from or directed toward a point on the axis of an optical system.

　　bundle of r's., homocentric. A bundle of rays which originate or meet at a common point. Syn., *monocentric bundle of rays.*

chief r. 1. An effective ray which passes through the center of the entrance pupil of an optical system. 2. A central or representative ray in a bundle of rays.

　　chief r., foveal. The ray or ray path represented in object space by the line connecting the point of fixation and the center of the entrance pupil, and, in image space, by the line connecting the center of the exit pupil and the fovea.

coherent r's. See *coherence.*

convergent r's. A pencil or a bundle of rays directed toward a common point.

divergent r's. A pencil or a bundle of rays directed away from a common point.

effective r's. Rays which emanate from an object point and com-pletely traverse an optical system.

emergent r. An effective ray in image space. Syn., *image ray.*

extraordinary r. In birefringence or double refraction, that ray which does not follow Snell's law; it is deviated even though the incident ray is normal to the surface.

grazing r. A ray which is presumed to travel along the interface between two media prior to incidence or after emergence. See also *grazing emergence; grazing incidence.*

Hertzian r's. Rays of radiant energy of wavelengths longer than infrared; used in radio and wireless transmission.

homocentric r's. Rays which originate or meet at a common point. Syn., *monocentric rays.*

image r. Emergent ray.

incident r. An effective ray in object space. Syn., *object ray.*

infrared r's. Rays of radiant energy in the region of the spectrum between the end of the visible red and the Hertzian rays, i.e., between 7,000 Å and 500,000 Å.

luminous r's. Rays from the visible region of the spectrum.

meridian r's. 1. Rays which lie in the plane containing the axis of the cylinder of a cylindrical refracting surface and the chief ray. 2. Tangential rays.

monocentric r's. Homocentric rays.

monochromatic r. A ray of monochromatic light.

normal r. A ray perpendicular to an optical surface.

object r. Incident ray.

oblique r. 1. A ray or one of a bundle of rays with a chief ray not parallel to the axis of the optical system. 2. A ray not perpendicular to a surface at the point of incidence.

ordinary r. In birefringence or double refraction, that ray which follows Snell's law; it is undeviated when the incident ray is normal to the surface.

parallel r's. 1. Rays parallel to each other. 2. Rays parallel to the axis of an optical system.

paraxial r. A ray which makes a very small angle with the axis of an optical system, lies close to the axis throughout the distance from object to image, and has a nearly normal incidence on the system.

pencil of r's. A narrow cone of rays coming from a point source or from one point of a broad source.

    pencil of r's., astigmatic. A nonhomocentric bundle of rays which has as a focus two mutually perpendicular lines, each centered along the chief ray and separated along this ray.

    pencil of r's., eccentric. A pencil of rays which is obliquely incident on a surface.

    pencil of r's., homocentric. A pencil of rays which have a common point of origin or which tend to meet at a common point.

reflected r. An image ray resulting from the impingement of an object ray on a reflecting surface.

refracted r. An effective ray after it has passed through an optical surface separating two transparent media of different indices of refraction.

residual r's. Rays of a narrow band of wavelengths which have been isolated by a series of reflections from selective reflection surfaces.

sagittal r's. 1. Rays which lie in the plane containing the chief ray and the perpendicular to the axis of the cylinder of a cylindrical refracting surface. 2. Rays of an oblique bundle which lie in the plane perpendicular to the plane of the tangential rays and containing the chief ray.

secondary r. A nonaxial, effective ray which passes through the primary nodal point or the optical center of an optical system.

Schumann r's. Rays of radiant energy in the ultraviolet region of the spectrum between 1,850 Å and 1,200 Å.

skew r's. Rays which are not in a plane containing the optical axis.

tangential r's. Rays which lie in the plane containing the axis of an optical system and the chief ray of the bundle. Cf. *meridian rays.*

tracing, r. See under *tracing.*

ultraviolet r's. Rays of radiant energy in the region of the spectrum between the end of the visible violet and the x-rays, i.e., between 4,000 Å and 136 Å.

Rayleigh (ra'le) **criterion; equation; interferometer; law; limit; match; refractometer; scattering; test; theory.** See under the nouns.

Raymond Cestan syndrome (ramon' ses-tan'). See under *syndrome.*

Raynaud's disease (ra-nōz'). See under *disease.*

RDP. Abbreviation for *receptor-type distribution pattern.*

R.E. Abbreviation for *right eye.*

reaction. A response to stimulation. For reactions not listed here, see under *reflex.*

light-compass r. A type of menotaxis in which the animal travels at a fixed angle, the orientation angle, to a light source, in either a straight or a circular direction. See also *telo-menotaxis; tropo-menotaxis.*

ophthalmic r. The reaction of the conjunctiva to toxins, as those of typhoid fever or tuberculosis, which have been instilled into the eye. The reaction is more severe in those affected with the disease.

ophthalmotonic r., consensual. Change in the intraocular pressure in one eye following or associated with change in intraocular pressure in the fellow eye.

time, r. See under *time.*

Reader, Craig. The trade name of an instrument for improving reading speed and comprehension, consisting essentially of a viewing screen on which reading material from film strips is projected and exposed sequentially at a controlled rate.

Reader, Franklin. The trade name of a projection magnifier for use in subnormal vision which provides either 3× or 5× magnification.

reader, retarded. An individual whose development of reading skills is below the normal performance for his age or grade placement.

readiness, reading. Capability of responding successfully to routine formal instruction in reading, especially in terms of maturational criteria.

Reading Accelerator. The trade name of an instrument for improving reading speed and comprehension, consisting essentially of an electrically controlled shutter which moves down over reading material at a preset speed, thus setting a pace for the reader.

reading, developmental. A program of instruction for improving reading rate and comprehension by training the component reading skills.

Reading Eye. A table model instrument which records eye movements during reading by photographing, on a moving film strip, light reflected from the corneae.

reading, mirror. Reading characterized by persistent left-right reversals and directional confusion of the printed symbols and word order.

Reading Pacer, Keystone. The trade name of an instrument for improving reading speed and comprehension, consisting essentially of an electrically controlled metal rod which moves down over reading material at a preset speed, thus setting a pace for the reader.

Reading Rate Controller. The trade name of an instrument for improving reading speed and comprehension, consisting essentially of a wide shutter which moves down over reading material at a preset speed, thus setting a pace for the reader.

reading, remedial. Systematic training for the development, improvement, or enhancement of reading ability.

Reading Trainer. The trade name of an instrument for improving reading speed and comprehension which rotates specially printed material past an opening at a controlled rate varying from 20 to 2,800 words per minute. The reverse side of the reading material has a comprehension test which is answered by pushing buttons on the instrument.

Reber's chart (ra′berz). See under *chart.*

receiver, photoelectric. A device in which electrical discharges are produced in response to incident radiant energy, as, for example, a photoelectric cell.

receptor, distance (re-sep′tor). A sense organ which responds to impressions from objects remote from the body. This would include such sense organs as the eyes, the ears, and the nose.

receptor, visual. A rod or a cone cell of the retina.

recess. A small groove, cleft, or cavity.
  optic r. 1. In the young embryo, the portion of the cavity of the forebrain where the lumina of the optic stalks open. Syn., *preoptic recess.* 2. In the older fetus and the adult, the recess in the ventral and medial portion of the hypothalamus, in the floor of the III ventricle, occupied by the optic chiasm.
  prelacrimal r. A groove on the medial wall of the maxillary sinus which forms a part of the bony passage for the nasolacrimal duct. Syn., *lacrimal groove.*
  premarginal r. A small osteo-

fibrous pocket containing adipose tissue in the region of the ascending portion of the zygomatic bone, between the orbital margin and the attachment of the septum orbitale to the periosteum a few millimeters below the margin.

recession (re-sesh'un). Surgical displacement of the insertion of an extraocular muscle posteriorly.

reciprocal (re-sip'ro-kal) **dispersion; inhibition; innervation; replacement.** See under the nouns.

von Recklinghausen's (fon rek'ling-how"zenz) **canals; disease.** See under the nouns.

reclinatio palpebrarum (rek"lih-na'-she-o pal"pe-brah'rum). Ectropion.

reclusor palpebrarum (re-klu'sor pal"pe-brah'rum). Levator palpebrae superioris muscle.

recombiner. The second basic component of an interferometer which superposes the two coherent beams of light.

recovery. The binocular response to a fusion stimulus which eliminates diplopia and results in single binocular fixation of the test target, usually represented quantitatively in terms of the maximum amount of prism or other dissociating unit through which the response is made.

involuntary r. A recovery response without voluntary effort on the part of the subject.

point, r. See under *point.*

voluntary r. A recovery response associated with or enhanced by voluntary effort on the part of the subject.

recruitment (re-kroot'ment). In neurophysiology, the gradual increase in response of a reflex when a given stimulus is repeatedly or consistently applied, believed to be due to the gradual increase in the number of motor units involved, additional ones being added during the stimulation.

rectangle, Tschermak's. A two dimensional arrangement of colors in which the four primals are located at the corners of a rectangle, with white at its center. The shorter sides of the rectangle represent colors between red and yellow and between blue and green, the longer sides colors between yellow and green and between red and blue.

rectifying capacity. See under *capacity.*

rectus muscles (rek'tus). See under *muscle.*

red. The hue attribute typically evoked by stimulation of the normal retina with a combination of long and short wavelength radiation which is complementary to a blue-green of about 493 mμ and listed as one of the psychologically unique colors. Thus pure red does not occur in the spectrum, but long wavelength light, from about 650 mμ to the end of the spectrum, though slightly yellowish, normally is scarcely distinguishable from the pure or elementary extraspectral red.

red, visual. According to Kühne, the initial product of the decomposition of rhodopsin when exposed to light; an unstable carotenoid pigment which is transformed rapidly to visual yellow.

Redlich's (red'likhs) **phenomenon; symptom.** See under the nouns.

redout. Reddening of vision resulting from negative acceleration and due to blood being forced to the head. Cf. *grayout; blackout.*

reduced distance; eye; vergence. See under the nouns.

reducer, Pugh's visual acuity. Pugh's occluder.

reduction, color. Change in the perceived hue of an object when all environmental accessories are removed, as may be approximated by viewing the surface of an object through a tube.

Reed-Van Osdal test (rēd-van oz′-dal). See under *test*.

refixation (re-fiks-a′shun). Fixation movement from one object to another, or one of the series of saccadic movements in fixational pursuit of a moving object.

　　active r. A volitional change of fixation from one object point to another.

　　compensatory r. Refixation due to postural changes.

　　passive r. Passive, nondeliberate reversion of fixation to an inconsequential object point on disappearance of, or discontinuation of attention to, a previously fixated object.

reflect. To turn, bend, send, or direct back within the same medium.

reflectance (re-flek′tans). The ratio of reflected flux to incident flux. Syn., *reflection factor*.

　　adaptation r. For a given discrete area within the total visual field, the reflectance value of a contained, spectrally nonselective surface above which it would tend toward the hue of the illuminant and below which it would tend toward the hue of the complementary color.

　　diffuse r. 1. The ratio of diffusely reflected flux to incident flux. 2. The reflectance of a sample relative to a perfectly diffusing, perfectly reflecting standard, with 45° incidence and perpendicular observation. Syn., *diffuse reflection factor*.

　　directional r. Reflectance of a surface as determined for specific directions of incidence and viewing.

　　spectral r. Reflectance in reference to a specific wavelength or to a narrow band of wavelengths.

　　specular r. The ratio of regularly reflected flux to corresponding incident flux. Syn., *specular reflection factor*.

　　total r. The ratio of the total flux reflected, both diffusely and regularly, to incident flux. Syn., *total reflection factor*.

reflecter. Reflector.

reflection. 1. A turning back, bending, or rebounding of light by the surface of a medium such that it continues to travel in the same medium but in an altered direction. 2. An image formed by a reflecting surface.

　　coefficient of r. See under *coefficient*.

　　dense-to-rare r. Internal reflection.

　　diffuse r. Reflection in which the light is scattered in many or all directions, due to irregularities or roughness of the reflecting surface. Cf. *specular reflection*.

　　direct r. Specular reflection.

　　external r. Reflection of light at the interface of two transparent media when the second medium is more dense (has a higher index of refraction) than the first. Syn., *rare-to-dense reflection*.

　　factor, r. See under *factor*.

　　internal r. Reflection of light at the interface of two transparent media when the second medium is less dense (has a lower index of refraction) than the first. Syn., *dense-to-rare reflection*.

　　　internal r., total. Internal reflection in which the angle of incidence is greater than the critical angle and in which no rays pass into the second (rarer) medium, but are all reflected at the interface.

　　irregular r. Diffuse reflection.

　　mixed r. A mixture of specular, diffuse, and preferential reflection; characteristic of glazed surfaces.

　　preferential r. Reflection characteristic of semipolished surfaces in which the light is not directly reflected but is distributed more in certain directions than in others. Syn., *spread reflection*.

　　rare-to-dense r. External reflection.

　　regular r. Specular reflection.

　　specular r. Reflection characteristic

of smooth surfaces in which there is no scatter and in which the angle of incidence is equal to the angle of reflection. Syn., *direct reflection; regular reflection.*

spread r. Preferential reflection.

veiling r. Reflection from an object which reduces its contrast with the surround and therefore reduces its visibility.

reflectivity (re″flek-tiv′ih-te). The property of a surface to return flux incident on it.

reflectometer (re″flek-tom′eh-ter). A device for measuring the percentage of light reflected by a surface.

Baumgartner r. A reflectometer consisting essentially of two spheres, one an integrating sphere photometer having two photovoltaic cells in its wall and an attached collimated light source which can be alternately directed toward the sphere wall and onto a reflecting test sample in a window for determining the reflectance of the sample, and the other sphere housing a light source and having an opening to the window of the first, at which a transmitting sample may be alternately placed and removed for determining its transmittance to the first sphere.

Taylor r. A reflectometer consisting essentially of an integrating sphere photometer employing a Macbeth illuminometer as the measuring element.

reflectometry (re″flek-tom′eh-tre). The measurement of reflectance with a reflectometer.

reflector. That which reflects; in particular, the structure or the medium with which the reflection is identified.

reflex. 1. A response to a stimulus without the necessary intervention of consciousness. 2. Pertaining to, or produced by, a stimulus without involving consciousness.

3. Reflected light or an image formed by reflection.

acceleratory r. Statokinetic reflex.

accommodation r. 1. Accommodative pupillary reflex. 2. The reflex initiated by an out-of-focus retinal image, as occurs when fixation is changed from far to near, resulting in increased convexity of the crystalline lenses. Syn., *ciliary reflex.*

accommodative r's. The reflexes initiated by an out-of-focus retinal image, as occurs when fixation is changed from far to near, resulting in constriction of the pupils, convergence of the eyes, and increased convexity of the crystalline lenses.

   accommodative r., frontal. See *occipital accommodative reflex.*

   accommodative r., harmonic. See *occipital accommodative reflex.*

   accommodative r., occipital. One of the three reflexes postulated for accommodation by Chavasse, the other two of which are the *harmonic* and the *frontal accommodative,* differentiated on theoretical neurological presumptions.

accommodative-convergence r. Convergence presumed to be induced reflexly by the act of accommodation.

acoustic r. 1. Cochleopalpebral reflex. 2. Audito-oculogyric reflex.

acoustic nystagmus r. Nystagmus in response to stimulation by a sudden loud noise.

annular r. A ringlike light reflex around the macula lutea, sometimes seen in ophthalmoscopy.

Argyll Robertson's r. Argyll Robertson's pupillary reflex.

Aschner's r. Oculocardiac reflex.

associational r's. Psycho-optical reflexes.

attention r. Attention pupillary reflex.

audito-oculogyric r. Reflex movement of the eyes toward the source of an unexpected loud sound. Syn., *acoustic reflex; auditory reflex; cochlear reflex.*

auditory r. 1. Cochleopalpebral reflex. 2. Audito-oculogyric reflex.

auriculopalpebral r. Cochleopalpebral reflex.

auropalpebral r., acoustic. Cochleopalpebral reflex.

auropalpebral r., caloric. Momentary reflex closure of the eyelid on thermal stimulation of the outer ear near the tympanic membrane.

auropalpebral r., tactile. Momentary reflex closure of the eyelid on mechanical stimulation of the outer ear near the tympanic membrane.

Bechterew's r. 1. A quiver, followed by contraction, of the orbicularis oculi muscles of both lower lids after percussion of the bones of the forehead, the zygoma, and the root of the nose. It is marked in cases of trigeminal irritation and lost in complete facial or trigeminal paralysis. 2. Bechterew's pupillary reflex.

binocular attention r. Oriental fixation reflex.

blinking r., aural. Blinking on thermal or mechanical stimulation of the outer ear, near the tympanic membrane, usually accompanied by lacrimation on the ipsilateral side. Syn., *external auditory meatus reflex; Kehrer's reflex; Kisch's reflex.*

blinking r., optical. Blinking in response to stimulation of the eyes by light, as occurs in the *dazzle reflex* or the *menace reflex.* It is normally developed between the ninth month and second year of life and occurs only in the higher mammals. Syn., *opticofacial reflex; visual blink reflex.*

blinking r., protective. Blinking to protect the eyes from threatened injury, as occurs in the

corneal, conjunctival, dazzle, and menace reflexes.

blinking r., sensory. Blinking in response to an irritative sensory stimulus of the eye, as occurs in the conjunctival and corneal reflexes.

caloric lacrimo-aural r. Bilateral lacrimation in response to thermal stimulation of the external auditory meatus, as by irrigating the ear with warm or cold water.

cat's eye r. A bright reflection observed at the pupil of the eye, as would appear from the tapetum lucidum of a cat, and due to such intraocular conditions as retinoblastoma or exudative choroiditis.

cerebral cortex r. Haab's pupillary reflex.

ciliary r. 1. Accommodative pupillary reflex. 2. Accommodation reflex.

ciliospinal r. Cutaneous pupillary reflex.

ciliovisceral r. Any vascular, respiratory, gastrointestinal, urinary or other visceral reflex that is initiated by pushing the eye into the orbit. See also *oculocardiac reflex; oculo-esophageal reflex; oculovisceral motor reflex.*

cochlear r. 1. Cochleopalpebral reflex. 2. Audito-oculogyric reflex.

cochleo-orbicular r. Cochleopalpebral reflex.

cochleopalpebral r. Momentary closure of the eyelid in response to an unexpected loud sound. Syn., *acoustic reflex; acoustic auropalpebral reflex; auditory reflex; auriculopalpebral reflex; cochlear reflex; cochleo-orbicular reflex; Gault's reflex.*

conjunctival r. 1. Blinking or winking in response to tactile stimulation of the conjunctiva. 2. Lacrimation in response to an irritation of the conjunctiva.

consensual light r. Consensual pupillary reflex.

convergence r. 1. Convergence

pupillary reflex. 2. Convergence providing single, binocular vision in response to disparate retinal stimuli.

corneal **r.** 1. Blinking or winking in response to tactile stimulation of the cornea. 2. Lacrimation in response to irritation of the cornea. 3. Reflection of light from the cornea.

corneomandibular **r.** Contralateral deviation of the lower jaw simultaneous with closure of the eyelids, occurring when the mouth is open and the cornea of one eye is touched. Syn., *winking-jaw phenomenon; corneopterygoid reflex; mandibuloconjunctival reflex; pterygocorneal reflex.*

corneopterygoid **r.** Corneomandibular reflex.

crossed **r.** Response on one side of the body induced by stimulation of the other side, such as the *consensual pupillary reflex.*

Davidson's **r.** Light seen through the pupil when a light source is held in the mouth.

dazzle **r.** Blinking of the eyelids in response to sudden stimulation by bright light.

direct light **r.** Direct pupillary reflex.

external auditory meatus **r.** Aural blinking reflex.

eye closure **r.** Blinking or closure of the eyelids in response to any of a variety of stimuli, such as pressure on the supraorbital nerve, touching the cornea or the conjunctiva, or exposure to bright light.

eyeball compression **r.** Any reflex initiated by compression of the eyeball, such as the *oculocardiac,* the *oculo-esophageal,* and the *oculovisceral motor reflexes.*

eyeball-heart **r.** Oculocardiac reflex.

fixation **r.** Fixation occurring in response to stimulation of an ex-

trafoveal retinal area. Syn., *visual fixation reflex.*

fixation **r., compensatory.** 1. Orientation of the eyes in response to proprioceptive impulses from the labyrinths and from muscles of the neck. Syn., *gravitational reflex.* 2. Movement of the eye to regain fixation when it is artificially disrupted, as by placing a prism before the eye.

fixation **r., conjugate.** A fixation reflex in which both eyes move in the same direction to assume binocular fixation. Syn., *version fixation reflex.*

fixation **r., disjunctive.** A fixation reflex in which the two eyes move in opposite directions, as in convergence or divergence, to assume binocular fixation. Syn., *vergence fixation reflex.*

fixation **r., oriental.** Conjugate movement of the eyes and the head of primitive and lower animals to maintain the object of regard in the center of the field of binocular vision; this reflex is also said by some to be demonstrable in the newborn. Syn., *binocular attention reflex.*

fixation **r., vergence.** Disjunctive fixation reflex.

fixation **r., version.** Conjugate fixation reflex.

foveolar **r.** The small, dotlike reflex of light from the foveola observed during ophthalmoscopy.

fundus **r.** Light reflected from the fundus that appears as a red glow in the plane of the pupil, as observed in retinoscopy, due to the reflected light having passed through the choroid. Syn., *red reflex.*

fusion **r.** Movement of the eyes, providing single, binocular vision in response to disparate retinal stimulation.

fusion **r., corrective.** Disjunctive movements, or myologic adaptations, of the eyes to compensate for a heterophoria or an artificial disorientation of binocular fixation, as by placing a prism in front of one eye, to provide fusion.

fusional convergence r. Convergence to provide single, binocular vision in response to disparate retinal stimulation.

Galassi's r. Orbicularis pupillary reflex.

Gault's r. Cochleopalpebral reflex.

Gifford's r. Orbicularis pupillary reflex.

von Graefe's r. Orbicularis pupillary reflex.

gravitational r. Compensatory fixation reflex.

gustolacrimal r. A profuse flow of tears from an eye on the affected side on tasting food, occurring during the stage of recovery from a facial palsy due to a lesion in the area of the geniculate ganglion.

Haab's r. Haab's pupillary reflex.

head turning r. Doll's head phenomenon.

indirect light r. Consensual pupillary reflex.

iris r. Pupillary reflex.

juvenile r. The glistening reflection of light from the fundus of young individuals, observed ophthalmoscopically.

Kehrer's r. Aural blinking reflex.

Kisch's r. Aural blinking reflex.

labyrinthine r. Any reflex originating from stimulation of the inner ear, such as the *tonic labyrinthine* or the *statokinetic reflexes.*

    labyrinthine r., tonic. Orientation of the head and the eyes from stimulation of the otolith apparatus, initiated by the position of the head in space. Syn., *otolith reflex.*

lacrimal r. Secretion of tears in response to irritation of the cornea or the conjunctiva and to other conditions or actions grossly identified with initiation of the reflex, such as eyestrain, glare,

laughing, vomiting, etc. Syn., *weeping reflex.*

lid r. Orbicularis pupillary reflex.

light r. 1. Constriction of the pupil in response to light stimulation of the retina, as occurs in the consensual and direct pupillary reflexes. Syn., *photo-pupil reflex; Whytt's reflex.* 2. Reflected light.

McCarthy's r. Supraorbital reflex.

mandibuloconjunctival r. Corneomandibular reflex.

menace r. Blinking of the eyelids in response to a suddenly and rapidly approaching object. Syn., *threat reflex.*

miral r. The image of the mires of an ophthalmometer as mirrored by the cornea.

myopic r. Weiss's reflex.

naso-ocular r. Hyperemia of the conjunctiva in response to irritation of the nasal mucosa.

nasolacrimal r. Profuse lacrimation in response to the touching of certain areas of the endonasal mucosa.

nasopalpebral r. Blinking of the eyelids in response to stimulation of the nasal mucosa. It is absent in facial paralysis and is marked in Parkinsonism.

near r. 1. Near pupillary reflex. 2. Accommodation, convergence, and pupillary constriction on fixation of a near object. 3. Proximal accommodation and proximal convergence initiated by the awareness of a near object.

oculo-aural r. Pulling backward of the external ear by contraction of the transversus auriculae muscle on looking forcibly to the side. Syn., *Wilson's phenomenon.*

oculocardiac r. Slowing down of the rate of the heart beat following compression of the eyeballs. Syn., *Aschner's phenomenon; Aschner's reflex; eyeball compression reflex; eyeball-heart reflex.*

oculocephalogyric r. The synkinetic or associated movements of the eye, the head, and the body in fixating an object.

oculo-esophageal **r.** A diminution of esophageal contraction following compression of the eyeball, as by firmly pressing a finger on the lid of the closed eye.

oculofrontal **r.** Elevation of the ipsilateral eyebrow and depression of the contralateral upon concomitant lateral eye movement, occurring as a congenital anomaly.

oculolingual **r.** Homolateral deviation of the tongue upon concomitant lateral eye movement, occurring as a congenital anomaly.

oculomandibular **r.** Contralateral protrusion of the lower jaw upon rapid concomitant lateral eye movement, occurring as a congenital anomaly.

oculonasal **r.** Dilatation of the nostrils upon concomitant lateral eye movement, occurring as a congenital anomaly.

oculopharyngeal **r.** Rapid swallowing movements and closure of the eyelids in response to irritative stimulation of the bulbar conjunctiva.

oculopupillary **r.** Oculosensory pupillary reflex.

oculosensory **r.** Oculosensory pupillary reflex.

oculostapedial **r.** Unilateral blepharospasm and buzzing in the ears upon concomitant lateral eye movement, occurring as a congenital anomaly.

oculovisceral motor **r.** Contraction of the abdominal wall, the bladder, and the colon following compression of the eyeball, as by firmly pressing a finger on the lid of the closed eye.

Oppenheim's corneal **r.** Impairment of corneal sensation on the contralateral side in supratentorial lesions and on the ipsilateral side in infratentorial lesions.

optical righting **r.** Visual righting reflex.

opticofacial **r.** Optical blinking reflex.

orbicularis **r.** Orbicularis pupillary reflex.

orbicularis oculi **r.** Sudden, bilateral contraction of the orbicularis oculi muscle in response to any of a variety of stimuli, such as loud noises or bright lights.

orbiculomandibular **r.** Protrusion of the lower jaw upon forcible contraction of the orbicularis oculi muscle, occurring as a congenital anomaly.

otolith **r.** Tonic labyrinthine reflex.

palatopalpebral **r.** Closure of the eyelids when the palate is touched.

photoglycemic **r.** Alteration of sugar metabolism initiated by photic stimulation of the eye.

photo-pupil **r.** Light reflex.

Piltz's **r.** 1. Attention pupillary reflex. 2. Orbicularis pupillary reflex.

Piltz-Westphal **r.** Orbicularis pupillary reflex.

platysma **r.** Cutaneous pupillary reflex.

postural **r.** Righting reflex.

proprioceptive **r.** Orientation of the body and its parts in response to proprioceptive impulses from the labyrinth and from muscles of the limbs, the trunk, and the neck.

proprioceptive head turning **r.** Doll's head phenomenon.

protective **r.** Any defensive response to a noxious stimulus, as occurs in the *menace reflex.*

psycho-optical **r's.** Reflexes involving the eye or the eyelids which are involuntary and are mediated by the occipital cortex. They include the *accommodation,* the *protective blinking,* the *convergence,* the *fixation,* and the *fusion reflexes.* Syn., *associational reflexes.*

psychosensory r. Psychosensory pupillary reflex.

pterygocorneal r. Corneomandibular reflex.

pupillary r. 1. Constriction of the pupil in response to light stimulation of the retina. 2. Any reflex involving the iris, with resultant alteration of the diameter of the pupil.

pupillary r., accommodative. Constriction of the pupils induced reflexly by the act of accommodation. Syn., *accommodation reflex; ciliary reflex.*

pupillary r., Argyll Robertson's. A pupillary reflex characterized by inactivity to light, both direct and consensual reflexes being absent, but with normal contraction on accommodation and convergence. See *Argyll Robertson's pupil.*

pupillary r., associated. Near pupillary reflex.

pupillary r., attention. Contraction of the pupil on sudden change of visual attention to an object. Syn., *Piltz's pupillary reflex.*

pupillary r., aurosensory. Pupillary dilation in response to stimulation of the middle ear by tactile or thermal means or by rapidly varying the air pressure.

pupillary r., Bechterew's. Dilatation of the pupils on exposure to light. Syn., *paradoxical pupillary reflex.*

pupillary r., cochlear. Bilateral, transitory, pupillary constriction followed by dilatation in response to intense sensory stimulation to the cochlea, as with a tuning fork. The effect is usually more pronounced on the pupil of the stimulated side.

pupillary r., cogwheel. Constriction of the pupil, in response to light, and subsequent redilatation, in a series of discrete steps instead of in the usual, single, continuous movement. Syn., *cogwheel pupillary reaction.*

pupillary r., consensual. Constriction of the pupil of one eye, in response to light stimulation of the retina of the other eye. Syn., *consensual light reflex; indirect light reflex; indirect pupillary reflex.*

pupillary r., convergence. Constriction of the pupils induced reflexly by convergence.

pupillary r., cutaneous. Dilatation of the pupils in response to scratching or pinching of the skin of the neck. Syn., *ciliospinal reflex; platysma reflex; skin pupillary reflex.*

pupillary r., direct. Constriction of the pupil of an eye in response to light stimulation of its retina. Syn., *direct light reflex.*

pupillary r., Galassi's. Orbicularis pupillary reflex.

pupillary r., Gifford's. Orbicularis pupillary reflex.

pupillary r., von Graefe's. Orbicularis pupillary reflex.

pupillary r., Haab's. Contraction of the pupils in a darkened room when attention is directed to a light source stimulating the peripheral retina without an ensuing eye movement. Syn., *cerebral cortex reflex; visuocortical reflex; Haab's sign.*

pupillary r., hemianopic. In hemianopsia, constriction of the pupil in response to light stimulation of the unaffected side of the retina and no pupillary response when light falls on the affected side. Syn., *hemianopic pupillary reaction; Wernicke's pupillary reflex; Wernicke's sign.*

pupillary r., indirect. Consensual pupillary reflex.

pupillary r., lid. Orbicularis pupillary reflex.

pupillary r., myotonic. A pupillary reflex in which the reaction to light, both direct and consensual, is almost abolished, being elicited only after prolonged exposure to dark or light and in which there is a delayed reaction to changes in accommodation and convergence. The condition usually occurs unilaterally, with the affected pupil being the larger, and the reaction to mydriatics and certain myotics is normal. It is usually associated with diminution or absence of tendon reflexes.

pupillary r., near. Constriction of the pupils induced by accommodation and/or convergence for a near object. Syn., *associated pupillary reflex.*

pupillary r., neurotonic. Delayed and slow constriction of the pupil in response to light, followed by delayed and slow dilatation. Syn., *neurotonic pupillary reaction.*

pupillary r., oculosensory. Bilateral, initial, slight dilatation of the pupils followed by sustained constriction in response to irritative sensory stimulation of the cornea, the ocular conjunctiva, or the eyelid. It is absent in the Argyll Robertson's pupil. Syn., *oculopupillary reflex; oculosensory reflex; trigeminal pupillary reflex.*

pupillary r., orbicularis. Unilateral constriction of the pupil when an effort is made to close eyelids which are forcibly held apart. Syn., *Galassi's pupillary phenomenon; orbicularis phenomenon; von Graefe's lid reaction; orbicularis pupillary reaction; Piltz-Westphal pupillary reaction; Gifford's pupillary reflex; Galassi's pupillary reflex; von Graefe's pupillary reflex; lid reflex; orbicularis reflex; Piltz's pupillary reflex; Piltz-Westphal pupillary reflex; Westphal's pupillary reflex; Westphal-Piltz pupillary reflex.*

pupillary r., pain. Dilatation of the pupil induced by pain.

pupillary r., paradoxical. 1. Reversed pupillary reflex. 2. Dilatation of the pupil on stimulation of the retina by light. Syn., *Bechterew's reflex.*

pupillary r., perverse. Dilatation of the pupil on converging the eyes to a near object.

pupillary r., Piltz's. 1. Attention pupillary reflex. 2. Orbicularis pupillary reflex.

pupillary r., Piltz-Westphal. Orbicularis pupillary reflex.

pupillary r., psychosensory. Dilatation of the pupil in response to stimulation of any sensory nerve other than those of the eye or its adnexa or in response to psychic stimuli, as emotion or fear.

pupillary r., reversed. An anomalous pupillary reflex in which the action is opposite to that normally expected, e.g., dilatation of the pupil on light stimulation of the retina or on converging the eyes to a near subject. Syn., *paradoxical pupillary reflex.*

pupillary r., Schlesinger's. Constriction of the pupil in response to forcible raising of the eyebrows. Syn., *Schlesinger's reaction.*

pupillary r., skin. Cutaneous pupillary reflex.

pupillary r., tonohaptic. An anomalous pupillary reaction to the onset and removal of a light stimulus, characterized by a long latent period preceding a short rapid constriction and a long latent period preceding a short rapid redilatation. Syn., *tonohaptic reaction.*

pupillary r., Tournay's. Inequality of the size of the pupils produced by extreme lateral conjugate movement of the eyes, the abducted eye having the larger pupil. Syn., *Tournay's reaction; Gianelli's sign; Tournay's sign.*

pupillary r., trigeminal. Oculosensory pupillary reflex.

pupillary r., vagotonic. Dilatation of the pupil in response to deep inspiration, and constriction in response to deep expiration.

pupillary r., vestibular. 1. Bilateral pupillary constriction followed by wide dilatation which passes into hippus, in response to thermal, rotation, or air compression stimulation of the labyrinth. Syn., *vestibulopupillary reaction.* 2. A pupillary constriction associated with the removal of the middle ear in rabbits.

pupillary r., visuocortical. Haab's pupillary reflex.

pupillary r., Wernicke's. Hemianopic pupillary reflex.

pupillary r., Westphal's. Orbicularis pupillary reflex.

pupillary r., Westphal-Piltz. Orbicularis pupillary reflex.

red r. Fundus reflex.

refixation r. See *refixation.*

retinal r. Light reflected from the fundus as observed with the retinoscope or the ophthalmoscope.

retinal accommodation r. Accommodation in response to an out-of-focus retinal image.

righting r. Any reflex which aids in maintaining the normal orientation of the body and its parts in space. Syn., *postural reflex.*

righting r., labyrinthine. Orientation of the head and the eyes from labyrinthine stimulation, as occurs in the *tonic labyrinthine* and the *statokinetic reflexes.*

righting r., neck. Tonic neck reflex.

righting r., visual. Orientation of the head in response to the perception of objects in the field of vision. Syn., *optical righting reflex.*

Robertson's r. Argyll Robertson's pupillary reflex.

Ruggeri's r. Quickening of the

pulse induced by extreme convergence of the eyes.

Schlesinger's r. Schlesinger's pupillary reflex.

scissors r. A bipartite, retinoscopic (skiascopic) reflex showing opposite movements in the two sectors of the pupil, resembling the relative movements of scissors blades.

secondary light r. Increased constriction on consensual light stimulation of a pupil already constricted by direct light stimulation, or increased constriction on direct light stimulation of a pupil already constricted by consensual light stimulation.

senile r. A gray reflex seen in the pupil of the aged, due to light reflected from the crystalline lens.

shot silk r. Watered silk reflex.

skin r. Cutaneous pupillary reflex.

specular r. An image formed by a regularly reflecting surface, especially one so produced by a glossy surface coincidentally superimposed or interspersed on an otherwise rough or diffusing surface, as obtained by reflection of a bright source in a smooth wood table top.

static r. A righting reflex initiated by the position or change of position of the head, as occurs in the *tonic labyrinthine* and the *tonic neck reflexes.*

statokinetic r. Orientation of the eyes from stimulation of the semicircular canals, caused by changes in head movement (initiation, acceleration, or deceleration). When the head movement persists, a labyrinthine nystagmus results. Syn., *acceleratory reflex.*

supraorbital r. A quiver, followed by contraction, of the orbicularis oculi muscles of both lower eyelids after a tap on the supraorbital nerve. It is marked in cases of trigeminal irritation and lost in complete facial or trigeminal paralysis. Syn., *McCarthy's reflex.*

threat r. Menace reflex.

tonic neck r. Orientation of the head and the eyes in response to proprioceptive impulses from muscles of the neck, initiated by the position of the head in relation to the trunk. Syn., *neck righting reflex.*

Tournay's r. Tournay's pupillary reflex.

trigeminal r. Oculosensory pupillary reflex.

trigemino-facial r. Twitching of the jaw muscles following compression of the eyeball, as by firmly pressing a finger on the lid of the closed eye.

vagotonic r. Vagotonic pupillary reflex.

vergence r. Disjunctive fixation reflex.

version r. Conjugate fixation reflex.

vestibulo-palpebral r. Involuntary closure of the eyelids following rapid rotation of the body, as with Bárány's chair.

vestibulo-pupillary r. Vestibular pupillary reflex.

vestibulo-retinal r. Papillary stasis and hypertension of the retinal arteries associated with labyrinthine hyperexcitability.

visual r. Any reflex commencing with a pattern of stimulation on the retina and involving the use of the visual reflex arc, the intrinsic and the extrinsic muscles of the eye, and the skeletal muscles of the body, with the projection of the resultant sensation into space.

visual blink r. Optical blinking reflex.

visual fixation r. Fixation reflex.

visual righting r. See *righting reflex, visual.*

visuocortical r. Haab's pupillary reflex.

watered silk r. Glistening, shimmering reflections of light from the fundus, observed ophthalmoscopically, especially in the young. Syn., *shot silk reflex.*

weeping r. Lacrimal reflex.

Weiss's r. A crescent-shaped reflection of light on the nasal side of the optic disk, described by Weiss and considered by him to be an ophthalmoscopic sign of early myopia. It is attributed to a reflection of light from the surface of a posteriorly detached vitreous and may also be observed on the temporal side of the optic disk or around the posterior pole by changing the position of the viewing instrument. It also appears in nonmyopic eyes. Syn., *myopic reflex; Weiss's sign.*

Wernicke's r. Hemianopic pupillary reflex.

Westphal's r. Orbicularis pupillary reflex.

Westphal-Piltz r. Orbicularis pupillary reflex.

Whytt's r. Constriction of the pupil in response to light stimulation of the retina, first deduced by Robert Whytt to be of reflex nature.

winking r. Closure of the eyelids in response to any of a variety of stimuli, such as pressure on the supraorbital nerve, touching the cornea or the conjunctiva, or exposure to bright light.

reflexio palpebrarum (re-fleks'ih-o pal"pe-brah'rum). Ectropion.

refract (re-frakt'). 1. To change the direction of light by refraction. 2. To determine the refractive and muscular state of the eyes.

refraction (re-frak'shun). 1. The altering of the pathway of light from its original direction as a result of passing obliquely from one medium to another of different index of refraction. 2. The refractive and muscular state of the eyes, or the act or process of determining and/or correcting it.

analytical r. 1. The specific routines and procedures for determination of the refractive correction as promulgated in the techniques and the papers of the Optometric Extension Program. 2. Any system or procedure for determination of the refractive correction not solely based on the subjective or retinoscopic examination but on supplementary testing of the visual functions.

angle of r. See under *angle.*

aplanatic r. Refraction in a system which meets the sine condition.

atmospheric r. Refraction due to varying density of the earth's atmosphere, which is greatest at the earth and decreases with increasing elevation, causing mirages and apparent displacement of heavenly bodies.

bichrome r. Duochrome refraction.

bicylindric r. A method of determining the error of refraction of the eye in which a cylindrical lens to correct the corneal astigmatism, as measured with the ophthalmometer, is first placed before the eye. The residual astigmatism is then determined by means of a fan dial and the spherocylindrical equivalent of the combination is considered to be the correcting lens.

coefficient of r. Index of refraction. *Obs.*

conical r. 1. External and internal conical refraction. 2. Refraction by means of axicons.

  conical r., external. An effect observed with biaxial crystals in which an external hollow cone of light is refracted into a narrow pencil of light inside the crystal.

  conical r., internal. An effect observed with biaxial crystals in which an unpolarized ray entering such a crystal will form a cone of light within it.

cross cylinder r. See *method, cross cylinder.*

cycloplegic r. 1. The refractive state of the eye when accommodation is totally or partially paralyzed by a cycloplegic. 2. The

process or act of determining the refractive state of the eye when accommodation is totally or partially paralyzed by a cycloplegic.

diffuse r. The scattering of light in many or all directions, due to irregularities or roughness of the refracting surface. Cf. *regular refraction.*

double r. The property of nonisotropic media, such as crystals, whereby a single incident beam of light traverses the medium as two beams, each plane-polarized, the planes being at right angles to each other. One beam, the ordinary, obeys Snell's law; the other, the extraordinary, does not. Along the optical axis the two beams travel at the same speed; in other directions the extraordinary beam travels at different speeds. Syn., *birefringence.*

  double r., electric. Double refraction which occurs when a strong transverse electric field is applied to a vapor through which light is passing.

  double r., magnetic. Double refraction which occurs when a strong magnetic field is applied to a vapor through which light is passing perpendicular to the field. Syn., *Voight effect.*

duochrome r. A method of determining the error of refraction of the eye in which a test chart of two colors, usually one half red and one half green, is used. Correcting lenses are placed before the eye until the test letters on both halves of the test chart can be seen equally clear. It is based on the chromatic aberration of the eye. Syn., *bichrome refraction.*

dynamic r. 1. The refractive state of the eye when accommodation is activated, as by fixating a near test target. 2. The act or process of determining the refractive state of the eye when accommodation is activated.

error of r. See under *error.*

eye, r. of the. 1. The process or act of determining the refractive state of the eye. 2. The refraction of light effected by the media of the eye. 3. The error of refraction of the eye.

index of r. See under *index.*

laser r. The subjective determination of ametropia with the Laser Refractor in which corrective lenses are placed before the eye to eliminate the perceived motion of a granular pattern created by projecting a helium-neon gas laser beam onto a rotating drum.

manifest r. 1. The refractive state of the eye when accommodation is at rest, as by fixating a target at infinity, but not paralyzed. 2. The act or process of determining the refractive state of the eye when accommodation is at rest, but not paralyzed.

oblique centric r. Astigmatism resulting from the passing of a pencil of light obliquely through a lens.

ocular r. Refraction of the eye.

principal point r. Refraction of the eye with respect to the anterior principal point of the eye.

regular r. Refraction at a regular, highly polished, smooth, nondiffusing surface. Cf. *diffuse refraction.*

sensitometric r. A method of determining the refractive error of the eye, in which the brightness and contrast of a test target of constant size are simultaneously varied by means of neutral filters and trial lenses until the smallest brightness difference between test target and background is recognized.

static r. 1. The refractive state of the eye when accommodation is at rest or paralyzed by a cycloplegic. 2. The process or act of determining the refractive state of the eye when accommodation is at rest.

stereo r. Refraction of the eyes performed while the patient is binocularly viewing a projected, colored stereo-inducing picture through Polaroid filters. The scene has a central blackened area on which polarized test targets are projected from a second instrument. The Polaroid filter on the acuity projector may be adjusted to provide central occlusion of one eye during monocular testing of the other eye.

subjective r. 1. The refractive state of the eye as determined by visual judgment of the patient. 2. The act or process of determining the refractive state of the eye utilizing the visual judgment of the patient.

vertex r. Vertex power.

refractionist (re-frak'shun-ist). One skilled in determining the refractive state of the eyes, the state of binocularity, and the proper corrective lenses.

refractionometer (re-frak"shun-om'-eh-ter). 1. Optometer. 2. An instrument which determines the vertex refractive power, the cylinder axis, the optical center, and the prismatic effect of ophthalmic lenses.

parallax r. An objective optometer, devised by Henker, consisting essentially of a Gullstrand ophthalmoscope modified by means of eccentric apertures in a test disk in the lens system to produce doubling of the test marks by parallactic displacement when the test disk is not focused precisely on the retina.

refractive (re-frak'tiv). Pertaining to refraction; capable of refracting.

refractivity (re"frak-tiv'ih-te). The ability to refract; the power of refraction; the quality of being refractive.

refractometer (re"frak-tom'eh-ter). 1. An instrument for determining the refractive index of a medium. 2. Optometer.

Abbe's r. An instrument designed to determine the index of refraction, based on measurement of the critical angle at the interface between the sample and a prism of known index of refraction. It contains two Amici compensating prisms which may be adjusted to neutralize chromatic dispersion of the unknown and thus permit the use of white light.

Jamin r. An instrument designed to determine the index of refraction of a gas, based on the production of interference fringes. A single beam of monochromatic light is broken into two parallel beams by reflection from the two parallel faces of a thick glass plate, one beam being passed through the sample and the other through a vacuum. The beams are recombined by a second thick glass plate to form the interference fringes.

Pulfrich r. An instrument designed to determine the index of refraction, based on measurement of the critical angle at the interface between the sample and a prism of known index of refraction. It is used in conjunction with a monochromatic light source.

Rayleigh r. An instrument designed to determine the index of refraction of a gas based on the production of interference fringes. A single beam of monochromatic light is made parallel by a lens and then split into two beams by a double slit, one beam being passed through the sample and the other through a vacuum. The beams are recombined by a lens to form the interference fringes.

Williams r. A modification of the Rayleigh refractometer which utilizes a prism instead of a double slit to split the collimated beam, thus enabling greater accuracy of measurement through increased intensity of the interference fringes.

refractometry (re″frak-tom′eh-tre). Determination of the refractive error of the eye or the index of refraction of a medium with a refractometer.

refractor (re-frak′tor). 1. An instrument containing spherical and cylindrical lenses, Maddox rods, rotary prisms, and other devices for measuring the refractive and muscular condition of the eyes. Syn., *phoropter.* 2. A refracting telescope.

Leland r. An instrument utilizing polarized light to achieve monocular refraction while maintaining binocular fusion of peripheral contours.

refrangibility (re-fran″jih-bil′ih-te). The capability of being refracted.

refrangible (re-fran′jih-bl). Capable of being refracted.

refringent (re-frin′jent). Refractive; refracting.

Refsum's syndrome (ref′soomz). See under *syndrome.*

regard, object of. See under *object.*

regard, plane of. See under *plane.*

regard, point of. See under *point.*

region. A part, a portion, an area, or a division.

accommodation, r. of. See under *accommodation.*

ciliary r. The portion of the eyeball just anterior to the ora serrata which includes the ciliary body, the ciliary processes, and neighboring structures.

pretectal r. The nuclei or area between the superior colliculi or tectum and the diencephalon; a primary or lower visual center for the pupillary light reflex.

regression. 1. *Statistics:* (*a*) The systematic change in a dependent variable as a function of differences in the value of the independent variable. The quantitative relationship between the two variables is usually expressed as an equation, either linear or curvilinear, depending on the nature of the relationship. (*b*) The fact that in a group with a pair of imperfectly correlated attributes, *x* and *y*, the mean of the *y* values corresponding to a given value of *x* will be nearer the mean of the whole group than the *y* value for which the mean of the corresponding *x* values would have equaled the given value of *x*. Thus, the average weight of a group of 6′4″ men will be 212 lbs., but a group of men weighing 212 lbs. each will average less than 6′4″ in height. 2. *Reading:* An eye movement to refixate words inadequately perceived at the first reading. 3. *Psychology:* A reversion to an earlier type of behavior no longer appropriate to the later situation.

multiple r. The mutual, quantitative interrelationships of three or more variables, expressed as the regression of one variable on two or more variables.

phenomenal r. The approach of a mental percept of a stimulus toward a midpoint between the sensation which would be expected if the response were entirely a function of the receptoral stimulus and the sensation which would be expected on the basis of previous conditioning of the response function by factors extrinsic to the objective stimulus situation.

Reichert's membrane (ri′kerts). Bowman's membrane. *Obs.*

reinforcement. The influence of one neurological activity on another, such as to increase the intensity of the latter activity.

Reiter's (ri′terz) **disease; syndrome.** See under the nouns.

Rekoss' disk (re′kos). See under *disk.*

reliability. The repeatability of a test or other measuring device. See also *coefficient of reliability.*

relief. 1. Projection of an object or parts of an object from the general plane or background in

which it lies. 2. Alleviation or removal of pain or distress.

plastic r. The effect of depth produced by stereopsis, as observed by viewing appropriate targets in a stereoscope.

stereoscopic r. The effect of depth produced by stereopsis.

religiosus (re-lij″e-o′sus). Superior rectus muscle. *Obs.*

relucency (re-loo′sen-se). The characteristic appearance of the cornea and crystalline lens in the beam of the slit lamp as created by the dispersion, irregular reflection, and scattering related to normal inhomogeneity of the tissue.

relucent (re-lu′sent). Radiant; reflecting light; shining.

Remak's cells (ra-maks′). Lemmocytes.

Rémy (ra′me) **diploscope; separator.** See under the nouns.

Rendu-Osler disease (ron-de′ōs′ler). See under *disease.*

renotation, Munsell (re-no-ta′shun). A revision of the Munsell notation based on further studies.

replacement. The act of replacing.

complementary r. Reciprocal replacement.

reciprocal r. A theory accounting for single image formation from binocular stimulation in which there is alternate, conscious acceptance of each of the pair of stimulated corresponding points, the other being mentally suppressed. See also *Verhoeff's theory.*

total unitary r. Reciprocal replacement.

resection (re-sek′shun). Removal of a segment of tissue. In extraocular muscle surgery, it involves detachment of the muscle at its insertion, excision of a segment, and reattachment of the remaining muscle at the original site of insertion.

reserve, fusional. 1. That part of the range of fusional vergence measured from the fusional demand point, or from the vergence stimulus value, to the limit of clear, single, binocular vision in the direction opposite that represented by the phoria, accommodation being held constant. Hence, the amount of available fusional vergence in excess of that needed to overcome the phoria, clinically measured by the amount of vergence-inducing prism which can be overcome without blur or diplopia. 2. Relative vergence.

negative fusional r. Negative fusional reserve convergence.

positive fusional r. Positive fusional reserve convergence.

vertical fusional r. 1. Fusional reserve in terms of the vertical deviation of one line of sight with respect to the other, as measured by the vertical duction in the direction opposite that represented by the vertical phoria. 2. Fusional reserve in terms of the vertical deviation of one line of sight with respect to the other in excess of that needed for normal binocular fixation, clinically measured by the amount of base-up or base-down prism which can be overcome without blur or diplopia.

resolution, spurious. The return of visibility, usually with reversed contrast, of a grating target after it has ceased to be resolvable as the grating is progressively reduced.

resolution, visual. The ability to perceive two target elements as two. Syn., *resolution visual acuity.*

resolve. To distinguish between, or render visible, separate parts or elements.

response. The activity or reaction of an organism or its parts which results from stimulation.

abridgment of r. The shortening of the process of performing an act as a result of practice.

cortical r. The complex electrical potential recordable in or on the cerebral cortex as a result of brief peripheral (e.g., visual) stimulation.

excitatory r. On response.

fixation r. Fixation movement.

inhibitory r. The decrease of firing frequency or the cessation of the spike activity of a neuron due to an inhibitory effect resulting from stimulation of another functionally related neuron.

off r. The burst of spike activity from a neuron immediately after cessation of stimulation; probably a post-inhibitory rebound phenomenon. Syn., *off discharge; Z-type discharge; off effect.*

on r. The commencement of spike activity from a neuron, or an increase in its firing frequency, in response to the onset of stimulation and continuing to cessation of stimulation. Syn., *maintained discharge; on discharge; X-type discharge; on effect; excitatory response.*

on-off r. The burst of spike activity from a neuron upon commencement and following termination of stimulation with no activity in between. Syn., *on-off discharge; Y-type discharge; on-off effect.*

photo-oculoclonic r. The spikes and slow waves in an electroencephalogram which are associated with photic stimulation.

pursuit r. Pursuit movement.

saccadic r. Saccadic movement.

reticle (ret′ih-k′l). Graticule.

reticule (ret′ih-kūl). Graticule.

reticulum of Mueller (re-tik′u-lum). A series of branched ridges on the surface of the cuticular lamina of the lamina vitrea of the ciliary body which fit into the depression of the pigment epithelium, helping to anchor it to withstand the traction of the zonule of Zinn.

retina (ret′ih-nah). The light receptive, innermost, nervous tunic of the eye which represents the terminal expansion of the optic nerve. It is a thin, transparent membrane lying between the vitreous body and the choroid and extending from the optic disk to the ciliary body, where it becomes continuous with the inner epithelium of the ciliary body. It is derived from the outer and the inner walls of the optic cup and consists essentially of nuclei and processes of three layers of nervous elements which synapse with each other, the visual cells (rods and cones), the bipolar cells, and the ganglion cells. The region providing best visual acuity is the macula lutea, near the posterior pole of the eye, containing in its center the fovea centralis. The inner layers receive blood from the central retinal artery and its branches and in some cases from the cilioretinal artery; the external layers and the fovea are nourished by the choriocapillaris. The retina is usually described as having 10 layers; from without to within they are: (1) the pigment epithelium layer; (2) the layer of rods and cones; (3) the external limiting membrane; (4) the outer nuclear layer; (5) the outer molecular layer; (6) the inner nuclear layer; (7) the inner molecular layer; (8) the ganglion cell layer; (9) the nerve fiber layer; (10) the internal limiting membrane.

anangiotic r. In the Leber classification of retinal vascularization in placentals, a retina which has no direct blood supply and is characteristic of primitive mammals including bats, sloths, armadillos, porcupines, chinchillas, beavers, and other rodents. Cf. *holangiotic retina; merangiotic retina; paurangiotic retina.*

anesthesia of r. Temporary reduction in vision and in the size of the visual field due to trauma of the eyeball.

caeca, r. The thin, double, pigmented epithelium extending from the ora serrata over the ciliary body as far as the pupillary margin of the iris.

central r. Macula lutea.

coarctate r. A funnel-shaped condition of the retina caused by effusion of fluid between the retina and the choroid.

converse r. Verted retina.

corrugated r. A retina, found in fruit-bats and flying foxes, having elevations and depressions due to underlying vascular choroidal papillae. Receptors at the tip of the papillae are considered to subserve distance vision, while those in the depressions to subserve near vision.

cortical r. 1. The representation of retinal points in the area striata. 2. The retina when considered to be a forward extension of the brain.

detached r. Separation of the retina from the pigment epithelium layer which generally stems from one of 4 main causes: (1) shrinkage of the vitreous; (2) effusion of fluid or a growth, such as a tumor, which pushes the retina forward; (3) degeneration of the retina in which holes or tears allow the vitreous to seep behind it; and (4) trauma. A detached retina is characterized ophthalmoscopically by being raised above the level of the surrounding retina, requiring more plus power to bring it into focus, and by appearing to be a grayish, uneven, tremulous surface on which the retinal vessels are seen as wavy black lines. Subjective symptoms include loss of vision in a portion of the visual field and prodromal sensations of flickering lights or color.

   detached r., flat. A detached retina in which the separated area is raised only slightly above the surrounding retina.

detached r., rhegmatogenous. A retina detached as a result of a retinal break or tear.

detached r., steep. A detached retina in which the separated area projects markedly from the surrounding area.

duplicated r. A U-shaped retina, found in the tubular eyes of some deep sea fishes, in which the base, being further from the lens, subserves near vision and the sides, being nearer the lens, subserve distance vision.

E r. A retina dominated by rod function, especially with reference to the electroretinographic reaction to intermittent light, where onset of the stimulus evokes an increase in E.R.G. potential followed by a decrease. This electrophysiological classification does not always correspond to the histological appearance of the retina, for E retinas (excitatory) are found in the rat, the mouse, the guinea pig, the rabbit, the dog, the cat, and in man.

holangiotic r. In the Leber classification of retinal vascularization in placentals, a retina which, except for the central fovea, receives direct blood supply from either a central retinal artery, cilioretinal arteries, or both. It is characteristic of primates and some insectivores, carnivores, and ungulates. Cf. *anangiotic retina; merangiotic retina; paurangiotic retina.*

I r. A retina dominated by cone function, especially with reference to the electroretinographic reaction to intermittent light, where onset of the stimulus evokes a decrease in E.R.G. potential followed by an increase. I retinas (inhibitory) are found not only in diurnal snakes, pigeons, and turtles, which have nearly pure cone retinas, but also in frogs and owls, which have a

plentiful number of retinal rods.

inverse r. Inverted retina.

inverted r. A retina typical of vertebrates and rare in invertebrates in which the visual cells are orientated so that their sensory ends are directed away from the incident light, whence light must traverse the cell bodies before reaching the end organs. See also *verted retina.* Syn., *inverse retina.*

ischemia of r. See under *ischemia.*

leopard r. Leopard fundus.

merangiotic r. In the Leber classification of retinal vascularization in placentals, a retina in which only the horizontal segment containing medullated nerve fibers receives a direct blood supply. It is characteristic of rabbits and hares. Cf. *anangiotic retina; holangiotic retina; paurangiotic retina.*

paurangiotic r. In the Leber classification of retinal vascularization in placentals, a retina in which the blood vessels are very small and extend only a short distance from the optic disk. It is characteristic of perissodactyla (horse, rhinoceros), elephants, hyracoidea, sirenia, and guinea pigs. Cf. *anangiotic retina; holangiotic retina; merangiotic retina.*

peripheral r. The portion of the retina extending from the macula lutea to and including the ora serrata.

ramp r. A retina found in some selachians and ungulates for which portions differ in distance from the crystalline lens. The lower retina, nearer the lens, subserves distance vision, and the upper retina, farther from the lens, subserves near vision.

shot silk r. Shot silk fundus.

tesselated r. Tesselated fundus.

tigroid r. Tesselated fundus.

verted r. A retina typical of invertebrates in which the visual cells are orientated so that their sensory ends are directed toward the incident light. See also *inverted retina.* Syn., *converse retina.*

retinaculum, lateral (of Hesser) (ret″ih-nak′u-lum). The joined attachments of the check ligament of the lateral rectus muscle, the ligament of Lockwood, the lateral palpebral ligament, and the aponeurosis of the levator palpebrae superioris muscle at the lateral orbital tubercle of the zygomatic bone.

retinal (ret′ih-nal). Pertaining to or of the retina.

retinal aplasia; correspondence; dehiscence; detachment; dysplasia; element; field; horizon; illuminance; image; incongruity; ischemia; principal meridian; picture; purple; reflex; rivalry; septum; slip; zones. See under the nouns.

retinella (ret-ih-nel′ah). A dense light-sensitive neurofibrillar network surrounding the optic organelle in the photosensitive cells of worms and molluscs.

retinene (ret′ih-nēn). A carotenoid pigment formed by the decomposition of rhodopsin on exposure to light, following the breakdown of xanthopsin and prior to the formation of vitamin A plus a protein. In aquatic vertebrates it is an intermediate product in the decomposition of porphyropsin and is designated as retinene$_2$ whereas in the decomposition of rhodopsin it is termed retinene$_1$.

reductase, r. An enzyme which reduces retinene to vitamin A and the visual protein, opsin.

retineum (reh-tin′e-um). That part of an invertebrate eye which contains light receptor cells.

retinitis (ret″ih-ni′tis). Inflammation of the retina.

actinic r. Retinitis resulting from exposure to ultraviolet rays, as from acetylene torches or therapeutic lamps.

albi punctatus, r. Retinitis punctata albescens.

albuminuric r. Liebreich's (1859) term for lesions of the fundus characterized by hemorrhages and exudates occurring in association with albumen in the urine. It is now differentiated into *arteriosclerotic retinopathy, hypertensive retinopathy,* and *renal retinopathy.*

apoplectic r. Retinal apoplexy.

arteriosclerotic r. Arteriosclerotic retinopathy.

arteriospastic r. Arteriospastic retinopathy.

atrophicans, r. A hole in the macula through the entire thickness of the retina, a sequela of cystic macular degeneration.

Bright's r. Renal retinopathy.

cachecticorum, r. Pick's disease.

central r. Retinitis involving the macular area.

central angioneurotic r. Central angiospastic retinopathy.

central angiospastic r. Central angiospastic retinopathy.

central punctate r. A type of diabetic retinopathy characterized by soapy- or waxy-appearing, sharply defined, punctate exudates distributed irregularly in the macular area or forming a rough circle around the macula; sometimes associated with hemorrhages which are deep and round rather than flame-shaped.

central recurrent syphilitic r. A rare, recurring disease of the retina in which there is slight clouding of the macular area with small, whitish or yellowish dots and a characteristic, positive, central ring scotoma. Micropsia and metamorphopsia are often present, and the disease is often bilateral.

central serous r. Central angiospastic retinopathy.

central traumatic r. Traumatic macular degeneration of Haab.

centralis annularis, r. Central angiospastic retinopathy.

circinata, r. A degeneration of the retina characterized by a girdle of white exudates in the deeper retinal layers at a short distance from and around the macula, which are sharply defined, of various sizes, and may coalesce to form large irregular patches. The macular area may appear grayish or yellowish and may contain hemorrhages. The girdle contains no pigmentation, and the retinal vessels pass over it undisturbed. The disease occurs typically, but not invariably, in advanced age and is usually bilateral.

circumpapillaris, r. Retinitis occurring in the early stage of diffuse syphilitic neuroretinitis, characterized by intense localized swelling around the optic nerve head which completely blurs the margins of the disk.

Coats's r. Coats's disease.

congenital syphilitic r. Congenital syphilitic chorioretinitis.

diabetic r. Diabetic retinopathy.

diffuse syphilitic r. Diffuse syphilitic chorioretinitis.

disciform r. Senile disciform degeneration of the macula. See under *degeneration.*

eclamptic r. Toxemic retinopathy of pregnancy.

electric r. Retinitis due to exposure to intense electric light, as in electric welding or in the flash from a short circuit. It is characterized subjectively by a central, positive scotoma which may not completely disappear. Pigment changes may subsequently appear at the macula with permanent reduction in vision.

exudativa externa, r. Coats's disease.

exudative senile macular r. Senile disciform degeneration of the macula. See under *degeneration.*

gravidarum, r. Toxemic retinopathy of pregnancy.

gravidic r. Toxemic retinopathy of pregnancy.

gummatous r. A syphilitic gumma of the fundus.

guttate r. Choroiditis guttata senilis.

hemorrhagica externa, r. Coats's disease.

hypertensive r. Hypertensive retinopathy.

Jacobson's r. Diffuse syphilitic neuroretinitis.

Jensen's r. Jensen's disease.

juxtapapillary r. Jensen's disease.

leukemic r. Leukemic retinopathy.

lipemic r. Lipemia retinalis.

massive exudative r. Coats's disease.

metastatic r. Purulent retinitis due to lodgment of infective emboli in the retinal vessels as a result of septicemia or pyemia. In the very early stages, fluffy white exudates and numerous hemorrhages can be seen, the optic disk margins are blurred, and the retinal veins are dilated and tortuous. Within a few days the vitreous becomes opaque, obscuring the fundus from view, the iris, the ciliary body, and the choroid become involved, and panophthalmitis often follows.

nephritic r. Renal retinopathy.

photo r. Solar retinitis.

pigmentosa, r. A primary degeneration of the neuroepithelium of the retina with subsequent migration of the retinal pigment. The ophthalmoscopic appearance is of individual clumps of black pigment peripherally located and shaped like bone corpuscles, attenuated retinal vessels, and a pale waxy optic disk. The main symptoms are night blindness and progressive contraction of the visual field. It is familial, of unknown etiology, and usually bilateral.

pigmentosa, inverse, r. Retinitis pigmentosa in which the pigmentation is either confined to, or commences in, the macular area.

pigmentosa, pseudo r. Pseudoretinitis pigmentosa.

pigmentosa sine pigmento, r. A rare disease presenting all the symptoms and characteristics of retinitis pigmentosa except that the bone corpuscle-shaped pigment deposits are not present. A few scattered pigment dots and flecks may be seen in the periphery, or pigment deposits may be completely absent. Syn., *degeneratio sine pigmento.*

proliferans, **r.** Connective tissue proliferation and neovascularization extending into the vitreous and over the retinal surface as a result of the organization of hemorrhage into the vitreous, usually arising from the optic disk. Syn., *Manz's disease.*

pseudonephritic **r.** Stellate retinopathy.

punctata albescens, **r.** A bilateral, familial, degenerative disease of the retina, either congenital or beginning in early life, characterized by numerous discrete white dots scattered throughout a tesselated fundus except at the macula, by night blindness, and frequently by constricted visual fields. The dots always remain small, lie in a plane beneath the retinal vessels, and may contain pigment in their centers. It is differentiated from retinitis pigmentosa by the absence of optic atrophy and the lack of marked narrowing of the retinal vessels. Syn., *degeneratio punctata albescens; retinitis albi punctatus.*

purulent **r.** Infection of the retina by pus-forming organisms which may be exogenous, as from perforating wounds of the eye, or endogenous, as from metastasis.

renal **r.** Renal retinopathy.

Roth's **r.** Roth's disease.

rubella **r.** Pigmentary changes in the retina as a result of rubella.

The pigment is typically deranged into small, irregularly round or filiform masses of a black or lead-gray color.

sclopetaria, **r.** Retinal disturbance of severe degree following trauma from the impact of a heavy foreign body, as a bullet.

septica of Roth, **r.** Roth's disease.

serous **r.** Retinitis characterized by serous infiltration, edema, and hyperemia, especially affecting the nerve fiber and the ganglion cell layers.

simple **r.** Serous retinitis.

solar **r.** Retinitis due to excessive exposure to sunlight, as from observing a solar eclipse without adequate protection or from sunlight reflected by snow. It is characterized subjectively by a central, positive scotoma which may not completely disappear. Pigment changes may subsequently appear at the macula with permanent reduction in vision. Syn., *photoretinitis.*

stellate **r.** Stellate retinopathy.

suppurative **r.** Purulent retinitis.

syphilitic **r.** Retinal inflammation as the result of syphilis, generally accompanied by choroidal and optic nerve involvement, which occurs in several clinical forms including: *congenital syphilitic chorioretinitis; diffuse syphilitic chorioretinitis; neuritis papulosa; diffuse syphilitic neuroretinitis;* and *central recurrent syphilitic retinitis.*

traumatic **r.** Inflammation of the retina due to injury; commotio retinae.

retinoblastoma (ret″ih-no-blas-to′-mah). A congenital malignant tumor, usually observed before the age of 5, composed of embryonic retinal cells arising from the nuclear layers, and having a tendency to multiple origins in one or both eyes. It may invade the choroid and the optic nerve, may extend beyond the confines of the eyeball, and causes exophthal-mos, cataract, and glaucoma. It is usually diagnosed initially by a yellowish or whitish reflex of light (cat's eye reflex) observed at the pupil, and the lesion characteristically appears in the vitreous as a pinkish-white mass with blood vessels extending over its surface or into its substance. Pathognomonic, pearly or chalky white, calcium deposits are usually present. Syn., *retinal glioma; retinal glioblastoma; retinal neuroblastoma; retinoma.*

endophytum, r. A retinoblastoma which extends into the vitreous chamber and does not cause retinal detachment.

exophytum, r. A retinoblastoma which grows in the subretinal space, detaches the retina, and in the early stages may not extend into the vitreous chamber. The ophthalmoscopic picture characteristically is of a funnel-shaped retinal detachment, some portions of which appear translucent and some opaque.

retinocele (ret″ih-no-sēl′). A congenital cyst of the retina typically located peripherally in the inferior temporal quadrant and giving a smooth bulbous appearance to the affected area. It may remain stationary or it may progress to cause retinoschisis or retinal detachment.

retinoception (ret″ih-no-sep′shun). The appreciation of the distance and direction of objects in space as a function of the stimulation of specific retinal receptors or of the rotation of the eye necessary to stimulate these receptors.

retinochoroidal (ret″ih-no-ko′roid-al). Pertaining to both the retina and the choroid.

retinochoroiditis (ret″ih-no-ko″roid-i′tis). Inflammation of both the retina and the choroid.

juxtapapillaris, r. Jensen's disease.

retinochoroidopathy (ret″ih-no-koroid-op′ah-the). Noninflammatory disease involving both retina and choroid.

retinodialysis (ret″ih-no-di-al′ih-sis). A tearing of the retina from its attachment at the ora serrata. Syn., *retinal dehiscence; dialysis retinae; retinal disinsertion.*

retinograph (ret′ih-no-graf). A photograph of the retina or the fundus.

retinography (ret″ih-nog′rah-fe). Photography of the retina or the fundus.

retinoma (ret″ih-no′mah). Retinoblastoma.

retinomalacia (ret″ih-no-mah-la′she-ah). Retinosis.

retinomotor (ret″ih-no-mo′ter). Pertaining to the function of a retinal receptor in regulating the angular extent and direction of a fixational movement. See also *retinomotor value.*

retinopapillitis (ret″ih-no-pap″ih-li′tis). Inflammation of the optic nerve head and the retina; neuroretinitis.

retinopathy (ret″ih-nop′ah-the). 1. A morbid condition or disease of the retina. 2. Noninflammatory disease of the retina as distinguished from *retinitis.*

arteriosclerotic r. Sclerosis of the arterioles of the retina characterized ophthalmoscopically by widening of the light reflex resulting in a copper and silver wire appearance, increased tortuosity, arteriovenous crossing defects, perivascular sheathing, localized variations in caliber, and attenuation. Small, scattered hemorrhages and small, hard, sharply defined, white spots without surrounding edema may be seen. Syn., *arteriosclerotic retinitis.*

arteriospastic r. Retinopathy associated with persistent contraction of the retinal arterioles with reduction in the size of the lumen, as in renal and hypertensive retinopathy. Syn., *arteriospastic retinitis.*

central angiospastic r. A disease of the retina characterized by a round or oval, restricted, macular edema which causes the macula to be swollen and indistinct. Small, yellowish or grayish white dots are frequently found in this area, and a light reflex usually encircles the edge of the swelling. The visual field shows a central relative scotoma for form and color, which in some cases may be absolute. The disease is usually unilateral, affects the young and the middle-aged, and has a tendency to recur. Subjective symptoms are metamorphopsia, micropsia, and misty vision or a central black spot. It is considered by some to be a disturbance in the circulation of the arterioles and the capillaries; prognosis is favorable. Syn., *preretinal edema of Guist; central angioneurotic retinitis; retinitis centralis annularis; central serous retinopathy.*

central disk-shaped r. Senile disciform degeneration of the macula. See under *degeneration.*

central serous r. Central angiospastic retinopathy.

chloroquine r. Retinopathy associated with the prolonged ingestion of chloroquine, an antimalarial drug used also in the treatment of lupus erythematosus and rheumatoid arthritis. It is characterized by retinal edema, marked constriction of retinal arterioles, pigmentary degeneration resembling retinitis pigmentosa, paracentral scotomata, temporal field defects, and contraction of the peripheral fields.

circinate r. Retinitis circinata.

diabetic r. A disease of the retina associated with diabetes mellitus, characterized by small, punctate hemorrhages and numerous, smaller, round, red spots scat-

tered around the posterior pole which are microaneurysms in the inner nuclear layer of the retina. In this same area are hard, sharply defined, white or yellowish, soapy or waxy exudates which may be isolated or coalesced into larger masses in a circinate manner around the macula. The disease is frequently found in association with arteriosclerotic and hypertensive retinal changes. Preretinal hemorrhages may occur, causing a retinitis proliferans. Syn., *diabetic retinitis.*

diabetic r., proliferative. An infrequent type of retinopathy associated with diabetes mellitus, characterized by proliferation of connective tissue and the formation of new blood vessels in the retina, and by hemorrhages into the vitreous. Typically, those affected have diabetes which began in childhood.

dysoric r. Retinopathy occurring in the debilitated and emaciated which is characterized by snow-white nodules, about one-fourth to one-half disk diameter in size, in the area of the optic disk. The nodules may remain without change for several weeks but eventually break down and disappear.

glomerulonephritic r. See *renal retinopathy.*

gravidic r. Toxemic retinopathy of pregnancy.

hypertensive r. A disease of the retina associated with essential or malignant hypertension. It may be classified into 4 grades of severity by the ophthalmoscopic picture. Grade I: The caliber of the arterioles is reduced to three-quarters to one-half the caliber of the corresponding vein, an occasional focal constriction of an arteriole may be present, and no hemorrhages, cotton-wool patches, or edema residues are seen. Grade II: Further reduction in the caliber of the arterioles to one-half to one-third of the corresponding vein, several focal constrictions of arterioles may be present and no hemorrhages, edema residues, or cotton-wool patches are seen. Grade III: Added to the changes in arteriole constriction are flame-shaped hemorrhages and/or cotton-wool patches and edema residues. Grade IV: Increased severity of the previous changes with the onset of papilledema which may range from mild blurring of the optic disk margins to pronounced edema and elevation with a star figure of edema residues at the macula. Arteriolosclerotic changes may accompany any of the four grades.

leukemic r. A retinopathy found in all types of leukemia characterized by edema of the optic disk and the surrounding retina, marked engorgement, segmentation, and tortuosity of the veins, widely scattered superficial and deep hemorrhages of various sizes and shapes, some containing white centers, large, yellowish-white patches of exudate, and a yellowish-orange fundus. Syn., *leukemic retinitis.*

nephritic r. Renal retinopathy.

prematurity r. of. A bilateral retinal disease of premature infants, especially if placed in an abnormal oxygen environment, characterized by vascular proliferation and tortuosity, followed by intraocular hemorrhages, retinal edema and detachment, and finally by proliferation of fibrous tissue into the vitreous to form a dense retrolental mass. The cicatricial stage may terminate with only a small mass of opaque tissue in the peripheral retina, with useful vision, or it may progress to retrolental tissue covering the entire pupillary area, with no fundus reflex. Syn., *retrolental fibroplasia.*

Purtscher's traumatic angiopathic r. Purtscher's disease.

renal r. A disease of the retina associated with disease of the kidney (glomerulonephritis, nephrosclerosis, etc.) and hypertension, which presents the ophthalmoscopic picture of hypertensive retinopathy.

sickle-cell r. Retinopathy associated with sickle-cell disease or anemia, usually classified into four grades of severity. Grade I: increased tortuosity and dilatation of the retinal venules and mild ischemia in the peripheral fundus. Grade II: sheathing, neovascularization, microaneurysms, circumscribed narrowing, and telangiectasis of the peripheral venules. Grade III: the addition of retinal hemorrhages and exudates, and chorioretinal atrophy. Grade IV: retinitis proliferans, vitreous hemorrhages, cholesterol deposits, central artery or vein occlusion, and occasionally papilledema.

solar r. Retinopathy due to excessive exposure to sunlight, as from observing a solar eclipse without adequate protection or from sunlight reflected by snow. It is characterized subjectively by a central, positive scotoma which may not completely disappear. Pigment changes may subsequently appear at the macula with permanent reduction in vision. Syn., *photoretinitis.*

stellate r. A retinal disease resembling hypertensive retinopathy, but not as a component of renal, arteriosclerotic, or hypertensive disease, characterized by pronounced retinal edema, exudates, hemorrhages, a macular star, and blurring of the optic disk. It may occur as a result of trauma, obstruction of a retinal artery or vein, papilledema, toxemia, etc.

Syn., *pseudonephritic retinitis; stellate retinitis.*

thioridazine r. Retinopathy associated with the prolonged ingestion of large doses of thioridazine, a phenothiazine derivative used in psychotherapy. It is characterized by impairment of central vision, which may vary from slight and transient to severe and permanent, peripheral contraction of the visual fields with or without central scotomata, abnormal dark-adaptation curves, and pigmentary degeneration of the retina.

toxemic r. of pregnancy. A retinopathy associated with toxemia of pregnancy, characterized in the early stages by attenuation of the retinal arterioles, with a rise in diastolic blood pressure, occurring first in the nasal periphery, gradually spreading toward the optic disk, and becoming generalized. Local angiospasm may also appear. The later stages present the typical picture of advanced hypertensive retinopathy with exudates, hemorrhages, massive retinal edema, and possibly retinal detachment. The onset is acute and sudden, and restitution is equally rapid on the termination of pregnancy, with good prognosis for both vision and life. Syn., *eclamptic retinitis; retinitis gravidarum; gravidic retinitis; gravidic retinopathy.*

retinopexy (ret"ih-no-peks'se). Surgical reattachment of a separated or detached retina, usually implying the use of high frequency electrical current.

retinophore (ret'ih-no-fōr"). Vitrella.

retinophotoscopy (ret"ih-no-fo-tos'-ko-pe). Retinoscopy.

retinopiesis (ret"ih-no-pi-e'sis). The pressing of a detached retina back into its normal location, as by intravitreal silicone injection.

retinoschisis (ret"ih-no-skis'is). A splitting of the retina, usually at the outer plexiform layer, occurring as a slowly progressive hereditary disease, typically bilateral and affecting males. It appears ophthalmoscopically as a translucent veil-like membrane emanating from the retina and carrying the retinal vessels. It appears in the inferior temporal quadrant and spreads to involve the lower half of the fundus. Syn., *congenital vascular veils in the vitreous.*

retinoscope (ret'ih-no-skōp). An instrument for determining the conjugate focus of the retina, and hence the refractive state of the eye, consisting essentially of a transparent or perforated mirror which serves to reflect light on the retina from an external or contained light source and through which the observer views the light emerging through the subject's pupil from the retina and notes the apparent transverse motion of the emergent light in relation to the pupil and the motion of the source. Syn., *pupilloscope; skiascope.*

bi-vue r. An electric retinoscope having a plane mirror with two perforating apertures, 7 mm. and 3 mm. in diameter, either of which may be used.

concave mirror r. A retinoscope utilizing a concave mirror typically of short radius of curvature so that light entering the subject's eye diverges as though emanating from a point in front of the mirror and results in an "against" motion of the emerging light reflex in hypermetropia and a "with" motion in myopia, the opposite of that seen with a plane mirror retinoscope.

electric r. A retinoscope which contains an electric incandescent lamp as its light source, the current being supplied by batteries or through a transformer.

luminous r. Electric retinoscope.

nonluminous r. A retinoscope used with a separate source of light not contained in the instrument.

plane mirror r. A retinoscope utilizing a plane mirror so that light entering the subject's eye diverges as though emanating from a point behind the mirror and results in a "with" motion of the emerging light reflex in hypermetropia and an "against" motion in myopia.

spot r. A retinoscope which reflects a beam of light from a circular source into the patient's eye.

streak r. A retinoscope which reflects a beam of light from a transversely elongated or line source into the patient's eye. The beam is adjustable in width and is rotatable for meridional position.

V r. A streak retinoscope employing a light source with a right-angle-shaped filament, one leg of which provides the "streak" source for one principal meridian of measurement, and the other leg for the other principal meridian.

retinoscopy (ret″ih-nos′ko-pe). The determination of the conjugate focus of the retina, hence the objective measurement of the refractive state of the eye, with a retinoscope. The movement of the light reflex in the patient's pupil in relation to movement of the retinoscope and light source is noted and neutralized with suitable lenses. The power of the neutralizing lenses, less the dioptric equivalent of the working distance, is a measure of the refractive error of the eye. Syn., *koroscopy; pupilloscopy; retinoskiascopy; skiametry; skiascopy; shadow test; umbrascopy.*

book r. Retinoscopy performed while the subject is reading.

cylinder r. The secondary, confirmatory determination of the cylinder axis in retinoscopy by the rotation of the correcting cylinder axis away from its originally determined meridian, noting the reflex band, and redetermining the true axis by rotating the axis back until the band is eliminated.

dynamic r. Retinoscopy performed while the subject fixates a near object.

static r. Retinoscopy performed while the patient fixates a target at infinity or with accommodation otherwise relaxed.

retinosis (ret″ih-no′sis). Noninflammatory degeneration of the retina.

retinoskiascopy (ret″ih-no-ski-as′kope). Retinoscopy.

retinula (reh-tin′u-lah). A group of light receptor cells located at the base of an ommatidium. Syn., *retinule.*

retinule (ret′ih-nūl). Retinula.

retractio bulbi (re-trak′she-o bul′bi). Duane's syndrome.

retraction, relative, of Heine. In high myopia, a bending of optic nerve fibers from their normal course in the region of the temporal margin of the optic disk, due to a temporal displacement of the margin of the lamina vitrea to which the fibers are attached.

retractor, Allen-Gulden plunger. An accessory pin on the handle of a Schiötz type tonometer which engages the edge of the weight and holds up the plunger until after the tonometer footplate is placed on the cornea.

retrobulbar (ret″ro-bul′bar). Situated, located, or occurring behind the eyeball.

retrography (re-trog′rah-fe). Mirror writing.

retro-illumination (ret″ro-ih-lu″mih-na′shun). Illumination of transparent or semitransparent media by reflecting light from tissues situated more posteriorly, as in slit lamp biomicroscopy.

direct r. Retro-illumination in which the tissue observed is in

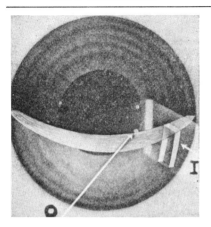

Fig. 35. Direct retro-illumination. The observer (O) views on opacity on the posterior corneal surface in the direction of rays reflected from the iris. The incident light (I) forms a corneal parallelpiped. (From *Biomicroscopy of the Eye*, Vol. I, M. L. Berliner, Hoeber, 1949)

the direct path of the reflected light.

indirect r. Retro-illumination in which the tissue observed is not in the direct path of the reflected light.

retro-iridian (ret″ro-ih-rid′e-an). Situated, located, or occurring behind the iris.

retrolental (ret″ro-len′tal). Situated, located, or occurring behind the crystalline lens.

retrolental fibroplasia (ret″ro-len′-tal fi″bro-pla′se-ah). See under *fibroplasia.*

retro-ocular (ret″ro-ok′u-lar). Situated, located, or occurring behind the eyeball.

retroscopic (ret″ro-skop′ik). Pertaining to the retroscopic angle.

retrotarsal (ret″ro-tar′sal). Situated or occurring behind the tarsus.

von Reuss's (von rois′ez) **chart; recuperative visual field.** See under the nouns.

Revilliod's sign (ra-ve-yōz′). Orbicularis sign.

rhabdom; rhabdome (rab′dom, -dōm). A rodlike refractile structure located along the central axis of an ommatidium and formed

by the limiting membranes of the receptor cells.

rhabdomere (rab′dom-ēr). A subdivision of a rhabdome.

rhabdomyoma (rab″do-mi-o′mah). A benign tumor involving, and composed of, skeletal muscle tissue which appears rarely in the orbit.

rhabdomyosarcoma (rab″do-mi-o-sar-ko′mah). A malignant tumor of mesenchymal origin which in the orbit is one of the most common types and generally affects children in the first decade of life.

rhagades of eyelids (rag′ah-dēz). Cracks, fissures, or linear excoriations of the skin of the eyelids.

rhanter (ran′ter). Internal canthus.

rheobase (re′o-bās). The minimal electric current of indefinite duration which will produce an effect on tissue. Cf. *chronaxie.*

rheum (rōōm). A thin serous or catarrhal discharge from the eye. *Obs.*

rhinodacryolith (ri″no-dak′re-o-lith). A concretion or stony formation in the nasolacrimal duct.

rhinommectomy (re″nom-mek′to-me). Surgical removal of a portion of the internal canthus.

rhinopsia (ri-nop′se-ah). Convergent strabismus. *Obs.*

rhitidosis (rit″ih-do′sis). Rhytidosis.

rho [ρ] (rō). The Greek letter used as the symbol for (1) the *angle of torsion;* (2) the *coefficient of rank correlation.*

rhodogenesis (ro″do-jen′e-sis). The anabolism of rhodopsin.

rhodophane (ro′do-fān). A red pigment, or chromophane, in the retinal cones of birds and fishes.

rhodophylactic (ro″do-fi-lak′tik). Pertaining to rhodophylaxis.

rhodophylaxis (ro″do-fi-lak′sis). The property of the pigment epithelium of the retina to regenerate rhodopsin.

rhodopsin (ro-dop′sin). A purplish carotenoid protein in the outer segment of the rod cells of the retina which, on stimulation by light, bleaches and breaks down into transient orange, xanthopsin, and finally retinene and opsin. It is re-formed by the recombining of retinene and opsin. Syn., *visual purple.*

rhomb, Fresnel's. A crown glass block, rhomboidal in shape, which produces circularly or elliptically polarized light from plane-polarized light which is incident at a specific angle and then undergoes two internal reflections.

rhythm, alpha. In electroencephalography, rhythmic oscillations in electrical potential in the cortex of the human brain, normally occurring at a rate of from 8 to 13 cycles per second and best recorded in the occipital region. Syn., *alpha wave.*

rhytidosis (rit″ih-do′sis). A wrinkling, especially of the cornea.

riboflavin (ri″bo-fla′vin). A water-soluble yellow crystalline powder present in milk, eggs, cheese, leafy vegetables, liver, kidney, and heart. It is necessary in cellular oxidation, and a deficiency in the diet results in lesions of the lips, cheilosis, glossitis, and seborrheic dermatitis. Eye signs include photophobia, blepharitis, peripheral vascularization of the cornea, and corneal opacities. Syn., *vitamin G.*

Ricco's law (re′kōz). See under *law.*

Richardson-Shaffer diagnostic lens. See under *lens.*

Riddoch's syndrome (rid′oks). See under *syndrome.*

riders, lenticular. V-shaped opacities which project from the surface of a zonular cataract like the spokes of a wheel, one limb of the V extending over the anterior surface of the main opacity and the other over the posterior surface.

ridge, superciliary. Arcus superciliaris.

ridge, supraorbital. Arcus superciliaris.

Ridgeway colors (rij′wa). See under *color.*

Ridley lens (rid′le). See under *lens.*

Rieger's (re′gerz) **anomaly; disease; syndrome.** See under the nouns.

Riesman's sign (rēs′manz). See under *sign.*

rigidity, ocular. The resistance of the coats of the eye to distension; the summation of all factors in the eyeball and its adnexae, other than fluid pressure, which resists indentation. Its effect is considered in indentation tonometry. Syn., *scleral rigidity.*

rigidity, scleral. Ocular rigidity.

rima cornealis (ri′mah kor″ne-al′is). Corneal interval.

rima palpebrarum (ri′mah pal″pe-brah′rum). The palpebral fissure.

ring. Any circular or continuous round structure, line, or object; a circular or round arrangement of parts of a structure, a line, or an object.

anterior border r. of Schwalbe. A circularly arranged bundle of collagenous and elastic fibers located near the posterior surface of the cornea at the termination of Descemet's membrane. It gives rise to the scleral meshwork or corneoscleral trabeculae. A gonioscopic landmark. Syn., *Schwalbe's ring.*

benzene r. Benzene ring schema.

Brock's r's. Two complementary, colored rings viewed directly, or by projection onto a screen, through complementary colored filters, so that each ring is seen by only one eye. They are used in various visual training techniques, especially for the training of peripheral stereopsis.

Coats's r. A small, whitish-gray, ring opacity in the cornea, usually near the periphery, seen with the biomicroscope as a delicate, white, dotted circle, composed of lipoid deposits in Bowman's zone. It is variously considered to be hereditary, due to a disturbance in fat metabolism, or secondary to trauma or intraocular disease.

choroidal r. 1. A mottled, lightly pigmented ring around the optic papilla which is exposed choroid due to failure of the pigment epithelium of the retina to reach the disk. 2. An improperly used term for *pigmented ring.*

ciliary r. Annulus ciliaris.

conjunctival r. Annulus conjunctivae.

Döllinger's r. A thickening of Descemet's membrane in the region of the limbus.

Donders' r's. Rainbowlike halos seen around lights in glaucoma.

Fleischer's r. A thin, brownish or greenish, usually incomplete ring of pigment around the base of the cone in keratoconus, situated in the region of the basal epithelium and Bowman's membrane. It usually is visible only with the slit lamp. Syn., *Fleischer's line.*

Flieringa-Bonaccolto r. A thin stainless steel ring which is sutured to the sclera, between the limbus and the equator, to prevent vitreous loss in cataract extraction. It holds the sclera rigid and acts to prevent collapse of the anterior chamber and forward movement of the vitreous humor.

Flieringa-Legrand r. A device consisting of two concentric rings with four equally spaced, interconnecting, radial arms which is sutured to the anterior sclera as a supporting structure to prevent collapse of the anterior chamber during surgery, as in keratoplasty.

glaucomatous r. A light yellowish, circumpapillary ring of choroidal atrophy seen in the late stage of glaucoma.

greater r. of the iris. Ciliary zone.

greater r. of Merkel. Ciliary zone.

Kayser-Fleischer r. A pigmented ring in the periphery of the cornea, observed in Wilson's disease. It is about 1 to 3 mm. wide, starts close to the limbus in a sharp border, and fades toward the center of the cornea. Characteristically it is brown or grayish-green to the unaided eye and golden brown or reddish with the slit lamp and may be interspersed with any of the spectral colors. The pigment consists of fine, dense granules, believed to be deposits of copper, located in the deepest layers of the cornea.

Landolt r. An incomplete ring, similar to the letter *C* in appearance, used as a test object for visual acuity, especially in children and illiterates. The width of the ring and the break in its continuity are each one fifth of its over-all diameter. The break or gap is placed in different meridional positions with its location to be identified by the observer as evidence of its perception. The visual angle is represented by the subtense of the gap at the eye.

Lesser r's. Metal rings of various diameters with attached metal rod handles, used in visual training, especially for the elimination of suppression. The patient circles, with one of the rings, an area on one half of a haploscopically viewed stereogram corresponding to a target located on the other half.

lesser r. of the iris. Pupillary zone.

lesser r. of Merkel. Pupillary zone.

Loewe's r. A bright halo entoptically perceived surrounding Maxwell's spot when the eye is exposed to intermittent, uniformly diffused, blue or purplish light.

lymphatic r., pericorneal. An incomplete ring formed by two subconjunctival lymph collector channels located about 7 mm. from the limbus and running circumferentially above and below it. It receives lymph from the limbal area and eventually drains into the preauricular nodes temporally and submaxillary nodes nasally.

Mach's r. A relatively bright or dark band perceived in a zone of brightness transition where the rate or gradient of change of brightness increases or decreases suddenly or rapidly, commonly referred to as Mach's ring because the phenomenon is usually demonstrated on rotating disks on which the brightness gradient is controlled by the proportions of black and white sectors at various distances from the center. Syn., *Mach's band.*

Maxwell's r. Maxwell's spot.

myopic r. A circular white area surrounding the optic papilla due to myopic degenerative changes of the choroid and the retina allowing the sclera to become visible.

Newton's r's. Concentric colored rings or interference fringes, produced when two glass lenses or plates are pressed together, due to interference of light in the thin film of air of varying thickness between the adjacent surfaces. See also *Newton ring test.*

pigmented r. A dark ring of pigment epithelium of the retina concentrated around the optic papilla.

postcorneal r. Embryotoxon.

posterior border r. of Schwalbe. The scleral spur, as observed gonioscopically.

Root red-green fusion r's. A target for testing and training sensory fusion consisting essentially of a pair of overlapping, complementary colored, red and green, oval rings encircling a smaller pair of similarly colored, overlapping, oval rings, which in turn encircle a white oval ring, all on a black background. When viewed through colored filters, and fused, the rings appear in stereoscopic relief.

Schwalbe's r. Anterior border ring of Schwalbe.

Schwalbe's posterior r. The scleral spur, as observed gonioscopically.

scleral r. A small, circular, white patch around the optic papilla which is the exposed sclera visible because both the pigment epithelium of the retina and the choroid stop short of the disk.

Soemmering's r. A doughnut-shaped ring of clear crystalline lens covered by a capsule, occurring as a result of physical destruction of the lens cortex and the nucleus, with the capsule and the subcapsular epithelium remaining intact. The central part, occupying the pupillary aperture, usually consists of a membrane composed of posterior capsule and fibrous tissue. Syn., *Soemmering's cushion.*

von Szily's r. Ring sinus of von Szily. See under *sinus.*

Verhoeff's r's. Verhoeff's circles.

Vossius lenticular r. Vossius ring cataract.

Wallach's r's. A two dimensional figure consisting of a series of four or five eccentric, but nonintersecting, rings placed one inside another, which, when rotated about an axis perpendicular to the plane of the figure, produces a three dimensional effect; used as a target in visual training.

Riolan's muscle (re″o-lanz′). See under *muscle.*

Ripault's sign (re-pōz′). See under *sign.*

Risley prism (riz′le). See under *prism.*

Ritchie photometer (rich′e). See under *photometer.*

Ritter's fibers (rit′erz). See under *fiber.*

rivalry. A competition or antagonism; a vying for supremacy.

binocular r. Retinal rivalry.

border r. Contour rivalry.

color r. A form of retinal rivalry, or a sequence of alternate sensations, when the two eyes are separately but simultaneously exposed to different colors.

contour r. A form of retinal rivalry or alternation of sensations, when the two eyes are separately but simultaneously exposed to differently oriented contours which superimpose each other. Instead of an integrated pattern of contours, the borders of different orientation are alternately and intermittently suppressed. Syn., *border rivalry.*

retinal r. Alternation of perception of portions of the visual field when the two eyes are simultaneously and separately exposed to targets containing dissimilar colors or differently oriented borders. Syn., *figural alternation; binocular rivalry; strife rivalry.*

 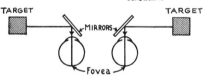

Fig. 36. Retinal rivalry resulting from simultaneous binocular stimulation with differently oriented borders. (From *Strabismic Ophthalmic Symposium II*, ed. J. H. Allen, C. V. Mosby Co., 1958)

strife r. Retinal rivalry.

visual fields, r. of. Retinal rivalry.

rivus lacrimalis (ri'vus lak"rih-mal'-is). Lacrimal lake.

Roaf's theory (rōfs). See under *theory.*

Robbins rock. See under *rock.*

Roberts Tachistoscreener. See under *Tachistoscreener.*

Robertson's (rob'ert-sunz) **pupil; reflex; sign.** See under the nouns.

Robin's syndrome. See under *syndrome.*

Robinson Cohen (rob'in-sun ko'en) **chart; slide; test.** See under the nouns.

Rochester's sign (roch'es-terz). See under *sign.*

Rochon (ro-shon') **polarizer; prism.** See under *prism.*

Rochon-Duvigneaud (ro-shon'-du-ve-nyo') **bouquet of central cones; accessory fossa; scleral sinus.** See under the nouns.

rock, accommodative. An accommodative exercise consisting of a series of accommodative responses to alternate monocular increases and decreases in dioptric stimulus to accommodation. It is usually performed clinically by having the right and the left eye alternately view a target through lenses which present different dioptric stimuli to each of the two eyes.

rock, Robbins. A training procedure for improving the facility of accommodative response in which a reduced Snellen chart is viewed at a 16" distance through a phoropter and through a vertical dissociating prism. Fixation is alternated between the two images with lenses of different power placed before the two eyes, and the difference is increased in 0.25 D steps as the successive clearing of vision is demonstrated in each.

rod. A straight slender structure.

fiber, r. See under *fiber.*

granule, r. See under *granule.*

Maddox r. A cylindrical glass rod used in measuring a phoria or heterotropia which, when placed in front of the eye, distorts the image of a light source into a long streak perpendicular to the axis of the rod.

proper, r. The outer and the inner members of a rod cell; a rod cell in the restricted sense.

retinal r. A rod cell.

Roenne's (ren'ēz) **effect; phenomenon; nasal step.** See under the nouns.

Roger's cone (roj'erz). See under *cone.*

Rolando's fissure (ro-lan'dōz). See under *fissure.*

Romaña's sign (ro-mahn'yahz). See under *sign.*

Romberg's (rom'bergz) **disease; sign; syndrome.** See under the nouns.

Römer's method (re'merz). See under *method.*

Ronchi's theory (ron'kēz). See under *theory.*

Rönne. See *Roenne.*

room, Ames. A room with trapeziform sides, or a miniature facsimile, designed so that all of the visible features on its walls, ceiling, and floor subtend, from a single point of reference, angles which are identical to those that would be subtended by a rectangular room with rectangular features with respect to the same point, whence it is perceived as a rectangular room when viewed monocularly with the eye at the predesigned point of observation, and normal-sized objects discretely placed in the room are simultaneously seen tilted and distorted in size and shape.

room, leaf. A room about 7 feet square, open at one end, set exactly level and' with true right angles, the interior sides of which are covered with artificial leaves to reduce monocular depth clues so that depth judgment depends on the appreciation of binocular retinal disparity (stereopsis). It is used to demonstrate, detect, and measure spatial distortions resulting from aniseikonia.

root. 1. The portion of an organ by which it is attached. 2. The portion of a nerve adjacent to the center with which it is connected; in spinal and cranial nerves, the

bundle of fibers connecting them with their respective nuclei and gray columns.

ciliary ganglion r's. See *ganglion, ciliary.*

iris, r. of the. The portion of the iris attached to the ciliary body.

mesencephalic r. of the trigeminal nerve. Dendrites of unipolar neurons originating in the mesencephalic nucleus of the trigeminus located in the lateral gray matter about the aqueduct of Sylvius. The root descends from the midbrain to the pons, and its fibers leave the brain to enter the motor root of the trigeminus. It carries proprioceptive impulses from the muscles of mastication and possibly from the extraocular muscles.

sensory r. of the trigeminal nerve. The thickest portion of the fifth cranial nerve extending from the pons to the Gasserian ganglion. It contains the axons of general sensory neurons which course in the ophthalmic, the maxillary, and the mandibular divisions.

Root red-green fusion rings. See under *ring.*

Roper-Hall implant. See under *implant.*

Roque's sign (roks). See under *sign.*

rosacea, ocular (ro-za'se-ah). Acne rosacea involving the eye or its adnexa. See *rosacea blepharoconjunctivitis; rosacea episcleritis; rosacea keratitis.*

Rosen phoriagraph (ro'zen). See under *phoriagraph.*

Rosenbach's (ro'zen-bahks) **phenomenon; sign; test.** See under the nouns.

Rosenmueller's (ro'zen-me"lerz) **gland; valve.** See under the nouns.

rosettes, Herbert's (ro-zets'). Slightly elevated, translucent nodules surrounded by a fine capillary network, appearing in the superior cornea or the limbus, in the early stages of trachoma.

rotation. The act or process of turning about an axis, as rotation of the eye.

cardinal r. Rotation of the eye in the major field of action of any of the six extraocular muscles, i.e., to the right, the left, the left superiorly, the right superiorly, the left inferiorly, or the right inferiorly.

center of r. See under *center.*

excyclofusional r. Relative rotation of the two eyes around their respective anteroposterior axes in response to a cyclofusional stimulus, such that the upward extensions of their vertical meridians rotate templeward.

head r. A deviation in position of the head about a vertical axis of reference and away from a straightforward position, especially as a clinical symptom. Cf. *head tilt; shoulder tipping.* Syn., *head turn; face turn.*

incyclofusional r. Relative rotation of the two eyes around their respective anteroposterior axes in response to a cyclofusional stimulus, such that the upward extensions of their vertical meridians rotate nasalward.

optical r. 1. Optical activity. 2. The angular rotation of the plane of polarization by an optically active substance.

specific r. The angular rotation of a beam of plane-polarized light when passing through a solid medium of specified thickness or through a liquid medium of specified thickness and concentration.

torsional r. Wheel rotation.

wheel r. Rotation of an eye about an anteroposterior axis of reference, as the line of sight. Syn., *torsional movement; wheel movement; torsional rotation.*

Roth's (rōts) **disease; patches; retinitis; spots.** See under the nouns.

Rothmund's (rōt'mundz) **disease; syndrome.** See under the nouns.

Rothschild's sign (roths'chīldz). See under *sign.*

Rotoscope (ro'to-skōp). A trade name for a visual training instrument which consists essentially of a modified Brewster stereoscope, a lighting system with rheostat controls, a flashing mechanism, and a motor for moving the target holders in a circular course. The target holders are separate for each eye, and the speed and the diameter of the excursion of the targets and the horizontal distance between them and their vertical alignment can be altered by manual controls.

Rototrainer (ro'to-trān"er). The trade name for an instrument consisting essentially of a manually or motor-activated rotating disk with interchangeable fixation targets mounted on it for viewing as a visual training exercise.

rouge. 1. A red powder consisting of ferric oxide, usually prepared by calcining ferrous sulphate, used in polishing glass, metal, and gems. 2. Any powdery substance used for polishing lenses.

roughing. The grinding of a lens to its approximate curvature and thickness with a coarse abrasive.

Rowland's (ro'landz) **circle; ghosts; diffraction grating.** See under the nouns.

rubeosis diabetica (ru"be-o'sis di"ah-bet'ih-kah). Rubeosis iridis.

rubeosis iridis (ru"be-o'sis i'rid-is). Noninflammatory neovascularization of the iris occurring in diabetes mellitus, characterized by numerous, small, intertwining blood vessels which anastomose near the sphincter region to give the appearance of a reddish ring near the border of the pupil. The vessels may extend from the root of the iris to the filtration angle to cause peripheral vascular synechiae and secondary glaucoma. Syn., *rubeosis diabetica.*

Rubin's vase (roo'binz). See under *vase.*

Rubino-Corrazza syndrome. Uveo-meningitic syndrome.

ruff, pupillary. The fringe of black pigment at the pupillary margin of the iris representing the anterior termination of the pigmented layer lining the posterior surface of the iris. Syn., *pigment frill.*

Ruggeri's reflex (ru-ja'rēz). See under *reflex.*

rule. 1. A prescribed guide for action or procedure. 2. The usual, expected, or normal case or condition. 3. A graduated measuring instrument.

Duane's accommodation r. A device for determining the near point and the amplitude of accommodation, consisting of a flat wooden ruler calibrated on the top and sides in centimeters and diopters, with the calibration commencing 14 mm. in front of the cornea. It is grooved at one end to fit the bridge of the nose and a test chart is moved along the rule, toward the eyes, until a blur is noticed.

Foster near point r. An aluminum rule for measuring the near point of accommodation calibrated in centimeters, diopters, and the mean near points of accommodation for various ages. It is provided with a double-sided sliding test card.

Gulden accommodation r. An opaque white plastic rod calibrated in centimeters, inches, diopters, and the mean near points of accommodation for various ages, used to measure the near point of accommodation by utilizing a sliding carrier with small test objects.

Javal's r. The total astigmatic correction of the eye approximates the ophthalmometrically determined astigmatism multiplied by

1.25 and combined with −0.50 cyl. axis 90°.

Kundt's r. 1. Divided or graduated distances appear greater than physically equal nongraduated distances. 2. In attempting to bisect a horizontal line with monocular vision, there is a tendency to place the middle point too far toward the nasal side.

McCulloch's r. The total astigmatic correction of the eye approximates the ophthalmometrically determined astigmatism increased by one eighth of itself and combined with −0.75 cyl. axis 90°.

Miller accommodation r. A device for determining the near point and the amplitude of accommodation, consisting of a light metal tubular rod, ½ in. in diameter and 35 cm. long, scaled in inches and millimeters. One end of the tube is curved to fit against the nose, and an attached occluder may be rotated in front of either eye. Test charts mounted on a holder are moved along the tube, toward the eye, until a blur is noticed.

O'Shea's r. The total astigmatic and spherical correction of the eye approximates the ophthalmometrically determined astigmatism combined with −0.50 cyl. axis 90°, added to a spherical "corneal equivalent" ametropia, and further modified by a calculated table for effectivity at 15 mm. from the cornea.

P.D. r. A ruler calibrated in millimeters, used for measuring interpupillary distance.

Percival's r. Lateral imbalance should not be considered a source of discomfort beyond 33 cm. when the binocular demand point is in the middle third of the range of relative convergence.

Prentice's r. Prentice's law.

Prince's r. A device for determining the near point and the amplitude of accommodation, consisting of a steel tape scaled in diopters on one side and in millimeters on the other. One end of the tape is held against the lower orbital margin, and a test chart is moved along the tape, toward the eye, until a blur is noticed.

R.A.F. near point r. A device for measuring the near points of accommodation and convergence consisting essentially of a sliding four-sided rotatable target holder mounted on a rod calibrated in centimeters, diopters, the mean near points of accommodation for various ages, and a convergence scale rated "normal," "reduced," and "defective."

Ryer-Hotaling r. The correcting cylindrical lens is the lens placed at the wearing distance before the eye, through which the ophthalmometer indicates 0.50 D. with the rule astigmatism when rotated 90°.

Sinclair's r. A rule used to set the distance of the patient from a tangent screen and to determine the position and the extent of a plotted scotoma. It consists of a flat wooden ruler, 25 mm. wide and 1 m. long, scaled on one side in degrees for a one meter testing distance and on the other side with degrees for a 2 m. testing distance.

Sutcliffe's r. An empirical rule for estimating the total astigmatic correction of the eye: For with the rule astigmatism, using minus cylinders, add one-half the amount of the corneal astigmatism to itself and deduct 1 D. For against the rule astigmatism, using minus cylinders, add one-third to the astigmatism indicated by the ophthalmometer.

Rumford photometer (rum'ford). See under *photometer.*

Rushton's method (rush'tonz). See under *method.*

Rydberg's theory. See under *theory.*

Ryer-Hotaling (ri'er-ho'tah-ling) **method; rule; spectacles.** See under the nouns.

rytidosis (rit"ih-do'sis). Rhytidosis.

S

S.A.A.O. South African Association of Optometrists.

sac. A baglike structure.

    conjunctival s. A continuous mucous membrane which begins at the posterior lid margins, lines the inner surface of the eyelids, and is reflected at the fornix to cover the sclera.

    lacrimal s. The membranous, saclike structure which receives tears from the canaliculi, via the sinus of Maier, and conveys them into the nasolacrimal duct. It is situated in the lower, anterior, medial wall of the orbit, in the lacrimal fossa, and is surrounded by periosteum (the lacrimal fascia). The upper portion, above the entrance of the sinus of Maier, is closed superiorally, forming the fundus of the sac and the lower portion is continuous with the nasolacrimal duct.

    lenticular s. Lens pit.

    tear s. Lacrimal sac.

saccade (sah-kād'). An abrupt voluntary shift in fixation from one point to another, as occurs in reading.

saccadic (să-kad'ik) **fixation; movement; speed.** See under the nouns.

sacculus lacrimalis (sak'u-lus lak"-rih-mal'is). Lacrimal sac.

saccus lacrimalis (sak'us lak"rih-mal'is). Lacrimal sac.

Sachs's (saks'ez) **disease; experiment.** See under the nouns.

Saemisch's corneal ulcer (sa'mish-ez). Serpiginous corneal ulcer.

Saenger's (zeng'erz) **sign; syndrome.** See under the nouns.

sag. Abbreviation for *sagitta* or *sagittal depth.*

sagitta (să-jit'ah). Sagittal depth.

St. Clair's disease (sānt klārz'). See under *disease.*

Sainton's sign (san-tonz'). See under *sign.*

Salmon's sign (sam'onz). See under *sign.*

Salus' (sal'uz) **arch; sign.** See under the nouns.

Salzmann's (salz'manz) **vitreous base; corneal dystrophy.** See under the nouns.

sample. A limited number of cases taken from a larger population for statistical treatment or analysis.

    purposive s. A selected group of cases from a larger population chosen in deliberate fashion to yield a cross section representation of the larger population.

    random s. A number of cases taken from a larger population without preference or regard to any characteristic and so chosen that each case has an equal chance of being included.

Sanders' (san'derz) **disease; syndrome.** Epidemic keratoconjunctivitis.

Sanders-Hogan syndrome (san'derz-ho'gan). Epidemic keratoconjunctivitis.

Sanger-Brown ataxia. See under *ataxia.*

S.A.O. Scottish Association of Opticians.

S.A.O.A. South African Optical Association.

Sappey's fibers (sap'ēz). See under *fiber.*

sarcoid, Boeck's (sahr′koid). Sarcoidosis.

sarcoidosis (sahr-koi-do′sis). A disease of unknown etiology characterized by tuberclelike, granulomatous nodules which may affect the skin, the lungs, the lymph nodes, the bones of the distal extremities, the conjunctiva, the lacrimal gland, the retina, and the uveal tract. The nodules are differentiated from true tubercles in that caseation or necrosis rarely occurs. It is a chronic, recurring, and relatively benign disease except when affecting the uveal tract. Syn., *Besnier-Boeck disease; Besnier-Boeck-Schaumann disease; lupus pernio; benign lymphogranulomatosis; lymphogranulomatosis of Schaumann; Boeck's sarcoid; Schaumann's syndrome.*

sarcoma (sahr-ko′mah). A malignant tumor arising from any nonepithelial, mesodermal tissue, such as fibrous, mucoid, fatty, osseous, cartilaginous, synovial, lymphoid, hemopoietic, vascular, muscular, or meningeal. Each form is specified by an appropriate combining form: fibro-, lipo-, osteo-, etc. In the eye, it may occur in the eyelid, the conjunctiva, the lacrimal gland, the choroid, etc.

Sarwar lens. See under *lens.*

satellite of Hamaker (sat′eh-līt). Second positive afterimage.

satiation (sa″she-a′shun). An alteration of a medium, as the visual cortex, through which impulses have been passing, as from fixating a figure, evidenced by a perceived displacement effect on figures or patterns subsequently imaged on the same area of the retina, or by a change in percept of a constantly fixated figure. Syn., *satiety.*

satiety (să-ti′eh-te). Satiation.

Sattler's (sat′lerz) **lamina; layer; veil.** See under the nouns.

saturation (sat″u-ra′shun). The quality of visual perception which permits a judgment of different purities of any one dominant wavelength; the degree to which a chromatic color differs from a gray of the same brightness.

Sauvineau's ophthalmoplegia (so′-vin-ōz). See under *ophthalmoplegia.*

Savart plate. See under *plate.*

scale. 1. A graduated instrument used for measuring. 2. A system of graduations for measuring.

axis s. A protractorlike representation of the meridians of the eye for designating cylinder axis orientation in spectacle lenses. In the United States the 0° is to the subject's left, 90° up, 180° to his right, etc. In Europe two systems prevail, one as above, the other having 0° nasalward and 180° temporalward. Cf. *standard axis notation.*

Kelvin s. An absolute scale of temperature in which zero is equal to $-273°$ C. or $-459.4°$ F. This scale is used to designate the temperature at which a blackbody yields a hue matching that of a given sample of radiant energy.

Newton's color s. 1. The sequence of interference colors observed in thin films with increasing optical path difference. It often is used to judge the magnitude of optical path differences semi-quantitatively. 2. Newton's division of the visible spectrum into seven intervals of widths corresponding to the intervals in the musical scale, thus giving seven principal colors: red, orange, yellow, green, blue, indigo, and violet.

saturation s. A graduated series of colors of constant hue and brightness which appear to vary by uniform steps of saturation from a neutral gray to the maximum attainable saturation for that hue.

Snell-Sterling visual efficiency s. Snell-Sterling notation.

spectral chroma s. A color scale or a color series consisting of equally bright spectral colors arranged in uniform steps of just noticeable, or equally perceptible, differences in chromaticity; a scale of wavelength discrimination in a spectrum of uniform brightness.

tangent s., Maddox. Maddox cross.

tangent s., orthops. A calibrated horizontal scale for measuring lateral phorias or tropias.

Ziegler prism s. A combined horizontal and vertical scale used to measure the deviation in centimeters of a prism placed at a distance of 1 m.

scanner, cathode ray tube. In fiber optics, a bundle of short fibers, one end of which is placed against the face of a cathode ray tube and the other against a photographic plate.

Scarpa's staphyloma (skahr'pahz). Staphyloma posticum of Scarpa.

scatter, sclerotic. A method of illumination used in examination of the cornea with the slit lamp, in which the beam of light is focused on the corneoscleral limbus to create internal reflection through the cornea. The light will pass through normal tissue unimpeded and unobserved, but will be scattered by any disturbance of transparency (nebula, keratocele, etc.), rendering it visible.

scattering. Diffusion or deviation of light in all directions by irregular reflection, as may be produced by particles in the medium through which the light passes.

Rayleigh s. The scattering of light by molecules and other particles small in comparison to the wavelength, the intensity occurring as a function of the fourth power of the frequency of the incident light, whence the resulting color

of the scattered light is typically blue, as in the blue sky.

Schacher's ganglion (shah'kerz). Ciliary ganglion.

Schäfer's (sha'ferz) **fovea externa; syndrome.** See under the nouns.

Schapero's method. See under *method.*

Scharf lens (sharf). See under *lens.*

Schaumann's (shaw'manz) **disease; lymphogranulomatosis; syndrome.** Sarcoidosis.

Scheiner's (shi'nerz) **disk; experiment; method; test.** See under the nouns.

schema, Gát's (ske'mah). A full circle graduated schematic, serving as a reference guide for designating the angular location of the insertions of the four rectus muscles for the right eye between 80°–103°, 169°–190°, 257°–282°, and 351°–13°, and for the left eye at symmetrically corresponding positions, on a scale for which 0° is at 3:00 o'clock, 90° at 12:00, etc.

schema, Pascal's benzene ring (ske'-mah). Any one of several mnemonics, invented by Pascal, resembling the conventional benzene ring of chemistry, used to represent such functions as the

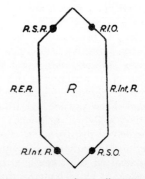

Fig. 37. Benzene ring schema, illustrating action of the extraocular muscles by the position of the limb (principal action), the position of each dot in relation to the adjacent vertical limb, and the slant of the limb (secondary actions). (From *Textbook of Orthoptics*, H. W. Gibson, Hatton Press Ltd., 1955)

interrelationships of the cardinal optical points, the extraocular muscle actions, etc.

schemograph (ske'mo-graf). An instrument for tracing the limits of the visual field as determined with the perimeter.

Schenck's theory (shenks). See under *theory.*

Scherer cataract spectacles (shēr'er). See under *spectacles.*

scheroma (ske-ro'mah). Xerosis of the conjunctiva.

Schieck's iritis (shēks). Iritis obturans of Schieck.

Schilder's (shil'derz) **disease; test.** See under the nouns.

Schiötz tonometer (shuts). See under *tonometer.*

Schirmer's (shir'merz) **esthesiometer; opacity; syndrome; test.** See under the nouns.

schistoscope (skis'to-skōp). An early form of colorimeter employing a combination of Rochon prism, polarizing nicol, and cleavage plates of mica for producing variations in color.

schizoblepharia (skiz″o-bleh-fa're-ah). A cleft or fissure of the eyelid.

Schlemm's canal (shlemz). See under *canal.*

Schlesinger's (shla'zing-erz) **phenomenon; reaction; pupillary reflex.** See under the nouns.

schlieren (shle'ren). Streaks or optical inhomogeneities, especially in glass, negatives, and optical images. *German.*

schlieren (shle'ren) **field; head; optical system.** See under the nouns.

Schlösser's pupillometer (schles'-erz). See under *pupillometer.*

Schmidt's (shmitz) **prism; sign; telescope.** See under the nouns.

Schmidt-Rimpler (shmit-rimp'ler) **optometer; test; theory.** See under the nouns.

Schnabel's (shnab'elz) **caverns; spaces.** See under the nouns.

Schnyder's corneal dystrophy (shni'-derz). Crystalline corneal dystrophy.

Schober's theory (sho'berz). See under *theory.*

Schoen's theory (shānz). See under *theory.*

Schöler's theory (sha'lerz). See under *theory.*

Schouten-Ornstein law (shu'ten-orn'stīn). See under *law.*

Schreck lens (shrek). See under *lens.*

Schroeder's (shra'derz) **figure; visual illusion; staircase.** See under the nouns.

Schubert's potential. See under *potential.*

Schüller's disease (shil'erz). Schüller-Christian-Hand disease.

Schüller's syndrome (shil'erz). Schüller-Christian-Hand syndrome.

Schüller-Christian-Hand (shil'er-kris'chan-hand) **disease; syndrome.** See under the nouns.

Schultze's fiber basket (shoolt'sez). See under *fiber basket.*

Schwalbe's (shval'bēz) **contraction folds; structural folds; contraction furrows; structural furrows; annular line; ring; space.** See under the nouns.

sciascopia (si″as-ko'pe-ah). Retinoscopy.

sciascopy (si-as'ko-pe). Retinoscopy.

sciascotometry (si″ah-sko-tom'eh-tre). Skiascotometry.

science, visual. The aggregate of knowledge considered to be particularly essential and pertinent to the understanding of the phenomena, processes, and functions of vision as a sense modality.

scieropia (si-er-o'pe-ah). An anomaly of vision in which objects appear shaded, darkened, or in a shadow.

scintillatio albescens (sin″tih-lah'-te-o al-beh'sens). Asteroid bodies.

scintillatio nivea (sin″tih-lah'te-o niv'e-ah). The shiny white bodies of calcium salts of fatty acids seen in asteroid hyalitis.

scintillation (sin″tih-la′shun). 1. A subjective visual sensation of sparks or quivering flashes of light. 2. An emission of sparks or a twinkling, as of stars.

scirrhencanthus (skir″en-kan′thus). A hard carcinoma of the lacrimal gland.

scirrhoblepharoncus (skir″o-blef″-ah-rong′kus). A hard carcinoma of the eyelid.

sclera (skle′rah). The white, opaque, fibrous, outer tunic of the eyeball, covering it entirely excepting the segment covered anteriorly by the cornea. It is surrounded by the capsule of Tenon and the conjunctiva, to which it is connected by the episclera; its inner, brown, pigmented surface (lamina fusca) forms the outer wall of the suprachoroidal space. It is essentially avascular and contains anterior apertures for the anterior ciliary vessels and the perivascular lymphatics, middle apertures for the venae vorticosae, posterior apertures for the long and the short posterior ciliary vessels and nerves, and a posterior foramen, which is traversed by the lamina cribrosa, for the optic nerve and the retinal vessels. It receives the tendons of insertion of the extraocular muscles and at the corneoscleral junction contains the canal of Schlemm.

blue **s.** A sclera which appears bluish, due to the color of the blood and the pigment in the underlying ciliary body and the choroid, and which may occur normally, as in infants, or pathologically, as in Eddowe's disease.

scleral (skle′ral) **flange; radius; ring; spur; sulcus.** See under the nouns.

scleratitis (skle″rah-ti′tis). Scleritis.

sclerectasia (skle″rek-ta′ze-ah). A localized protrusion or outward bulging of the sclera.

sclerectasis (skle-rek′tah-sis). Sclerectasia.

sclerecto-iridectomy (skle-rek″to-ir″-ih-dek′to-me). Surgical removal of a portion of the sclera and of the iris, as for glaucoma.

sclerecto-iridodialysis (skle-rek″to-ir″id-o-di-al′ih-sis). Surgical removal of a portion of the sclera and a localized separation of the iris from its attachment to the ciliary body, as for glaucoma.

sclerectomy (skle-rek′to-me). Surgical removal of a portion of the sclera.

scleriasis (skle-ri′ah-sis). Sclerosis of an eyelid.

scleriritomy (skle″rih-rit′o-me). Incision of the sclera and the iris.

scleritis (skle-ri′tis). Inflammation of the sclera. It may occur in conjunction with an episcleritis, keratitis, uveitis, or tenonitis, or alone.

annular **s.** Anterior scleritis which extends entirely around the cornea. The sclera is deeply injected with dark violet vessels and small whitish nodules may appear. Its course is protracted, it is extremely resistant to treatment, and there is an accompanying uveitis and keratitis.

anterior **s.** Scleritis of the anterior portion of the eyeball which usually appears as a dark red or bluish swelling. More than one nodular area may appear, and they may fuse with each other.

brawny **s.** A chronic, slowly progressive, virulent form of diffuse annular scleritis, occurring more commonly in the elderly, characterized by a gelatinous-appearing swelling of the episcleral tissue around the cornea. The affected area extends backward as the disease progresses, and keratitis and uveitis are an accompaniment. Syn., *gelatinous scleritis.*

gelatinous **s.** Brawny scleritis.

herpetic **s.** Herpes zoster involving the sclera, characterized by round nodules covered by glossy, smooth, hyperemic conjunctiva. The condition is painful, remains active for several months, and the lesions gradually heal, leaving permanent, slate-colored scars.

metastatic s. A pyogenic scleritis resulting from the lodgment of a bacterial embolus in a scleral vessel.

necroticans, s. Scleromalacia perforans.

nodular necrotizing s. A localized necrosis of the sclera characterized by the formation of nodules which break down and heal slowly to leave a thin sclera. Syn., *necroscleritis nodosa.*

posterior s. Inflammation of the posterior sclera and Tenon's capsule. It is diagnosed by the presence of ocular pain, edema of the eyelids, slight protrusion and immobility of the eyeball, and chemosis of the conjunctiva. Syn., *sclerotenonitis.*

pyogenic s. Scleritis resulting from the lodgment of a bacterial embolus in a scleral vessel, giving rise to the formation of an abscess.

suppurative s. Pyogenic scleritis.

sclero- (skle′ro-, skler′o-). 1. A combining form denoting *hardness*. 2. A combining form denoting the *sclera* or pertaining to the *sclera*.

sclerocataracta (skle″ro-kat″ah-rak′-tah). Hard cataract.

sclerochoroiditis (skle″ro-ko″roid-i′-tis). Inflammation of both the sclera and the choroid.

posterior s. Sclerochoroiditis occurring in malignant or pathological myopia together with posterior staphyloma.

sclerocleisis (skle″ro-kli′sis). A surgical procedure for glaucoma in which a flap of the sclera, ·approximately 3 mm. wide and 6 mm. long, based at the limbus, is inserted into the anterior chamber through an incision just anterior to the base.

scleroconjunctival (skle″ro-kon″-junk-ti′val). Pertaining to both the sclera and the conjunctiva.

scleroconjunctivitis (skle″ro-kon-junk″tih-vi′tis). Inflammation of both the sclera and the conjunctiva.

syphilitic s. A lesion of the secondary stage of syphilis, occurring in the conjunctival and the scleral tissues, characterized by a thickening of these tissues, which have a smooth, moist, waxy appearance like pink coral and are raised above to overlap the corneal margin and occasionally invade the cornea.

sclerocornea (skle″ro-kōr′ne-ah). The sclera and the cornea considered as a single structure.

sclerocorneal (skle″ro-kōr′ne-al). Pertaining to both the sclera and the cornea.

sclerocyclodialysis (skle″ro-si″klo-di-al′ih-sis). Cyclodialysis in which a scleral flap is inserted into the channel formed between the ciliary body and the sclera.

sclero-iridectomy (skle″ro-ir″ih-dek′-to-me). Sclerocleisis combined with a broad iridectomy.

sclero-iridencleisis (skle″ro-ir″ih-den-kli′sis). Sclerocleisis together with a radial incision of the iris and incarceration of the incised portion with the scleral flap.

sclero-iridotasis (skle″ro-ir″ih-dot′ah-sis). Sclerocleisis together with pulling the iris upward, out of the sclerocorneal incision, to be incarcerated with the scleral flap.

sclero-iritis (skle″ro-i-ri′tis). Inflammation of both the sclera and the iris.

sclerokeratitis (skle″ro-ker″ah-ti′tis). Inflammation of both the sclera and the cornea.

sclerokeratoiritis (skle″ro-ker″ah-to-i-ri′tis). Simultaneous inflammation of the sclera, the cornea, and the iris.

scleromalacia (skle″ro-mah-la′she-ah, -se-ah). Degenerative softening of the sclera.

  perforans, s. A slowly progressing degeneration of the sclera occurring in the elderly, usually in females and in association with rheumatoid arthritis. It is characterized by localized atrophy and necrosis, without inflammation, resulting in perforation of the sclera. The lesions vary in number, may coalesce, and usually affect the anterior sclera. Syn., *scleritis necroticans.*

scleronyxis (skle″ro-nik′sis). Surgical perforation of the sclera.

sclero-optic (skle″ro-op′tik). Pertaining to both the sclera and the optic nerve.

scleroperikeratitis (skle″ro-per″ih-ker″ah-ti′tis). Inflammation of the sclera and the peripheral cornea.

sclerophthalmia (skle″rof-thal′me-ah). A rare condition in which scleral tissue has encroached on the cornea, leaving only the central area clear.

scleroplasty (skle′ro-plas″te). Plastic surgery of the sclera.

sclerosis, disseminated (skle-ro′sis). Multiple sclerosis.

sclerosis, multiple (skle-ro′sis). An idiopathic disease in which there are disseminated areas of demyelinization and sclerosis of the spinal cord, the optic nerves, and white and gray matter of the brain. It is characterized by spastic paraplegia, nystagmus, speech defects, and frequently by retrobulbar neuritis, and diplopia due to involvements of the extraocular muscles. Syn., *Charcot's disease; disseminated sclerosis.*

sclerosis, tuberous (skle-ro′sis). Bourneville's disease.

sclerostomy (skle-ros′to-me). Surgical perforation of the sclera, as for the relief of glaucoma.

sclerotenonitis (skle″ro-ten″o-ni′tis). Posterior scleritis.

sclerotic (skle-rot′ik). 1. Pertaining to the outer coat of the eye; the sclera. 2. Hard, indurated, or sclerosed.

  blue s. One who is afflicted with a congenital, hereditary anomaly characterized by light blue sclerae. Fragility of the bones and deafness frequently are found concomitantly.

  scatter, s. See under *scatter.*

sclerotica (skle-rot′ih-kah). Sclera.

scleroticectomy (skle-rot″ih-sek′to-me). Surgical removal of a portion of the sclera.

sclerotico- (skle-rot′ih-ko-). For words beginning thus, see *sclero-.*

sclerotitis (skle″ro-ti′tis). Scleritis.

sclerotomy (skle-rot′o-me). Surgical incision of the sclera.

  anterior s. Surgical incision through the sclera into the anterior chamber of the eye, as for glaucoma.

  posterior s. Surgical incision through the sclera into the vitreous chamber of the eye.

sclerotonyxis (skle″ro-to-nik′sis). An obsolete operation for cataract in which the crystalline lens is depressed into the vitreous humor by a broad needle introduced through the sclera.

sclero-uveitis (skle″ro-u″ve-i′tis). Inflammation of both the sclera and the uvea.

scopolamine (sko-pol′ah-min, sko″-po-lam′in). Hyoscine.

scoterythrous (sko″teh-rith′rus). Protanopic. *Obs.*

scotodinia (sko″to-din′e-ah). Vertigo and headache with a dimming of vision or black spots before the eyes.

scotoma (sko-to′mah). An isolated area of absent vision or depressed sensitivity in the visual field, surrounded by an area of normal vision or of less depressed sensitivity.

  absolute s. A scotoma in which vision is entirely absent, i.e., light perception is not present.

  annular s. A circular scotoma,

either a partial or complete ring, characteristically around the fixation area in the visual field.

arcuate s. A scotoma which arches from the normal blind spot into the nasal field and follows the course of the retinal nerve fibers. A double arcuate scotoma extending both inferiorly and superiorly from the blind spot may form a ring scotoma. Syn., *comet scotoma; scimitar scotoma.*

Bjerrum's s. A comet-shaped, arcuate scotoma, occurring in glaucoma, which extends from the superior or the inferior margin of the physiological blind spot into the nasal field, around the fixation area. It is usually located between the 10° and 20° circles and becomes wider as it leaves the blind spot.

cecocentral s. A scotoma involving the physiological blind spot, the area corresponding to the macula lutea, and the area between. Syn., *centrocecal scotoma.*

central s. A scotoma involving the area of the visual field corresponding to the macula lutea.

centrocecal s. Cecocentral scotoma.

color s. An area in the visual field for which color vision is absent or deficient.

comet s. Arcuate scotoma.

congruous scotomata. Scotomata of equal size, shape, and intensity in both eyes and homonymous in position so that they superimpose in the binocular visual field.

cuneate s. A wedge-shaped scotoma which characteristically extends from the physiological blind spot into the temporal visual field with its apex toward the blind spot.

eclipse s. A small central scotoma resulting from observation of an eclipse of the sun without adequate protection.

facultative s. A scotoma considered to be due to suppression.

false s. A scotoma due to opacities

obstructing the light from the retina, as in disease of, or hemorrhage into, the ocular media.

fleeting s. Wandering scotoma.

flimmer s. Scintillating scotoma.

flittering s. Scintillating scotoma.

Förster's ring s. A ring-shaped scotoma around the fixation area due to involvement of the nerve fiber layer of the retina in the acute stage of syphilitic chorioretinitis.

hemianopic s. A scotoma involving half of the central visual field. Cf. *hemianopsia.*

van der Hoeve's s. Enlargement of the physiological blind spot attributed to paranasal sinusitis. Syn., *van der Hoeve's sign.*

incongruous scotomata. Scotomata in both eyes of unequal size, shape, or intensity, but homonymous in position.

junction s. A defect in the visual field due to a lesion at the junction of the optic nerve with the chiasm, in the region where the nasal fibers of the contralateral optic nerve loop into the ipsilateral optic nerve before coursing into the body of the chiasm. Characteristically, it is manifested either as a superior temporal quadrantanopsia or as a temporal hemianopic scotoma in the field of the contralateral eye, usually in association with a defect in the peripheral field of the ipsilateral eye.

juxtacecal s. A scotoma adjacent to the physiological blind spot. Syn., *paracecal scotoma.*

motile s. A false scotoma of varying location due to a floating opacity of the vitreous humor.

negative s. A scotoma not perceived as such by the afflicted, i.e., one of which he is not aware except on demonstration of absence of vision in the involved area.

paracecal s. Juxtacecal scotoma.

paracentral s. A scotoma adjacent

to the area corresponding to the macula lutea.

pericecal s. A scotoma surrounding the physiological blind spot. Syn., *peripapillary scotoma.*

pericentral s. A scotoma surrounding the area corresponding to the macula lutea. Syn., *perimacular scotoma.*

perimacular s. Pericentral scotoma.

peripapillary s. Pericecal scotoma.

peripheral s. A scotoma which does not involve the central or the fixation area.

physiological s. A negative scotoma corresponding to the site of the optic disk; the blind spot of Mariotte.

positive s. A scotoma directly perceivable by the afflicted, i.e., one of which he is continuously aware without proof of absence of vision in the involved area, usually seen entoptically as a black or a gray area.

quadrantic s. A scotoma involving the apex of one quadrant of the visual field.

relative s. 1. A scotoma of depressed sensitivity, or one blind to certain types and intensities of visual stimuli but not to others. 2. An area of depressed sensitivity in the visual field in which one or more colors cannot be recognized but in which achromatic stimuli are seen.

ring s. A circular scotoma around the fixation area in the visual field. It may be formed by two arcuate scotomata extending superiorly and inferiorly from the physiological blind spot.

roving ring s. A circular restriction in the peripheral field of view, due to the prismatic effect at the edge of a strong convex spectacle lens, which expands upon eye movement away from the center of the lens.

scimitar s. Arcuate scotoma.

scintillating s. A transient, shimmering, peripherally expanding scotoma with brightly colored, serrated edges which usually occurs as a prodromal symptom of migraine. Syn., *flimmer scotoma; flittering scotoma; spectrum scotoma.* See also *fortification spectrum.*

Seidel's s. A sickle-shaped scotoma appearing as an upward or downward prolongation of the physiological blind spot, found in glaucoma.

space s. In space physiology, the portion of visual space traversed by flight motion between the presentation and the perceptual awareness of a visual stimulus.

spectrum s. Scintillating scotoma.

suppression s. A unilateral scotoma found only when testing under binocular conditions, i.e., not present monocularly.

wandering s. A scotoma which changes its shape, position, size, or intensity in a relatively short period of time. Syn., *fleeting scotoma.*

zonular s. A curved scotoma which does not emerge from the blind spot and does not follow the lines of the nerve fibers. Its concavity is always toward the fixation area, it may occupy any part of the visual field, and is considered to be vascular in origin.

scotomagraph (sko-to′mah-graf). An instrument for recording the size, the shape, and the position of a scotoma.

scotomameter (sko″to-mam′eh-ter). Scotometer.

scotomata (sko-to′mah-tah). Plural of *scotoma.*

scotomatous (sko-tom′ah-tus). Pertaining to or affected with a scotoma.

scotometer (sko-tom′eh-ter). An instrument such as a tangent screen, a perimeter, or a stereocampimeter, for detecting, measuring, and plotting scotomata.

Bjerrum's s. Tangent screen.

Elliot's s. A large black disk rotatable about a central fixation object with a movable, white, test bead on a black cord extending from center to periphery, used for plotting scotomata.

Juler s. A device for projecting a circular patch of light of various diameters and colors onto a tangent screen to serve as a test target in plotting visual field defects.

scotometry (sko-tom'eh-tre). The detecting and plotting of scotomata with a scotometer.

scotopia (sko-to'pe-ah). Scotopic vision.

scotopic (sko-top'ik). Having the characteristics of scotopic vision or referring to the levels of illumination at which the eye is dark adapted.

scotopsins (sko-top'sinz). The photopigments in the retinal rods. Cf. *photopsins.*

scotoscopy (sko-tos'ko-pe). Retinoscopy.

scotosis (sko-to'sis). Scotoma.

scototaxis (sko-to-tak'sis). A purposive movement of a motile organism toward darkness and away from light; a negative phototaxis.

screen. A material, such as cloth, which affords a surface for receiving projected images or for plotting the visual fields.

apodizing s. An aperture of suitable shape and with non-uniform absorption which is placed in an optical system to reduce the intensity of, or eliminate, the peripheral portions of a diffraction pattern.

Bjerrum's s. Tangent screen.

Duane's s. A dull black tangent screen with small, light source, fixation targets placed in several positions on it, used to test the state of motility of the extraocular muscles in various directions of gaze. The test is performed in a darkened room with a red lens

before one eye to create diplopia for the fixated light source. The patient locates with a pointer the positions of the diplopic images for each direction of gaze, first with one eye fixating, and then with the other eye fixating.

Hartmann s. A diaphragm consisting of a series of small holes, usually lying in a single meridian, which is used in the Hartmann test (*q.v.*) to confine the light striking the optical system to a series of narrow beams.

Hess s. A black cloth tangent screen for testing extraocular muscle function, calibrated both horizontally and vertically into 5° intervals by red lines, with red dots at the intersections of the 0°, 15°, and 30° lines. Two of three radially oriented, short, green threads of common origin are continuous with two black thread extensions leading to counterbalances attached to the upper corners of the screen. The patient, while wearing a red lens in front of one eye and a green lens in front of the other, attempts to superimpose the com-

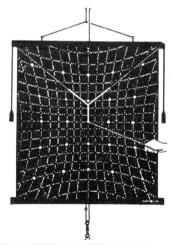

Fig. 38. Hess screen. (From *Text-book of Ophthalmology*, Vol. IV, Duke-Elder, Henry Kimpton, 1949)

mon origin of the green threads on each of the 25 red dots by means of a pointer attached to the third green thread.

tangent s. A large plane surface of black cloth or other material mounted so as to be perpendicular to the straightforward direction of view of the subject and at a convenient distance, usually 1 m., and typically calibrated in degrees of subtense from the eye with reference to a central point of fixation. It is used for plotting the physiological blind spot, scotomata, and other visual and fixational field restrictions. Syn., *Bjerrum's scotometer; Bjerrum's screen.*

screener, Harrington-Flocks visual field. A visual field screening instrument having a series of 20 large spiral-bound cards on which are printed patterns of dots and crosses visible only when illuminated under ultraviolet radiation. A chin rest, occluder, rack to support the targets, and an automatic timer for a one-quarter second flash exposure are provided. The serial presentation of the 20 card patterns systematically tests the integrity of all major sectors of the visual field.

screw tap. A device for rethreading the screw receptacles in ophthalmic frames or mountings.

S.D. Abbreviation for *standard deviation.*

S.D.O.N.Z. State Diploma in Optometry, New Zealand.

seam, pigment. The fringe of pigment epithelium at the pupillary margin of the iris. Syn., *pupillary ruff.*

seborrhea nigricans (seb″o-re′ah ni′-grih-kans). Seborrhea of the eyelids and adjacent skin in which they appear greasy and dark colored.

sebum palpebrale (se′bum pal″pe-brah′le). The secretion of the Meibomian glands of the eyelids.

seclusio pupillae (se-kloo′se-o pu′-pil-e). A complete blocking of the anterior chamber from the posterior chamber by a posterior annular synechia.

section, optic. In slit lamp biomicroscopy, the sagittal section of tissue illuminated by a very narrow focused beam of the slit lamp for the observation and localization of structural defects.

section, principal. A section lying in a plane perpendicular to the refracting edge of a prism.

sector defect. See under *defect.*

secundochrome (se-kun′do-krōm). Weale's term for *erythrolabe.*

see. 1. To perceive by the sense of sight. 2. To behold, as if with the eye, in imagination, dreams, hallucinations, or illusions. 3. To discern.

seeing. The using, or the act of using, the sense of sight; vision; sight; having the faculty of sight.

Seeligmueller's sign (za′lik-mil″erz). See under *sign.*

seg. Abbreviation for *segment,* as of a bifocal.

Ségal's hypothesis (sa-gahlz′). See under *hypothesis.*

segment. Any of the parts or portions into which an object is divided, naturally separated, or demarcated.

accessory outer s. of Engström. A ciliumlike structure lying beside the outer member of a visual receptor cell and originating from basal granules at the distal end of the inner member.

bifocal s. The smaller of the two dioptrically different portions of a bifocal lens.

inner s. (of a rod or cone). Inner member (of a rod or cone).

outer s. (of a rod or cone). Outer member (of a rod or cone).

Seidel's (si′delz) **formulas; scotoma; sign; test.** See under the nouns.

Seitz chart (sītz). See under *chart.*

Selectachart. The trade name for an attachment to an American Optical Co. acuity projector which permits remote control selection of target content.

selective cancellation. See under *cancellation.*

self-light. Idioretinal light.

sella turcica (sel'ah tur'sih-kah). The upper surface of the body of the sphenoid bone. On rare occasions the optic chiasm rests in its optic groove.

semichrome, Ostwald (sem'ih-krōm). An ideal Ostwald color having zero black content and zero white content, hence having a full color content of unity; thus a surface color with the maximum colorfulness which is theoretically possible. In terms of the theoretical ideal surface of the Ostwald system, this would be achieved by (1) complete absorption below a wavelength which has no spectral complement and complete reflectance for longer wavelengths, or vice versa, or (2) complete absorption in a band extending from one wavelength to its complementary wavelength and complete reflection of wavelengths outside this band, or vice versa. Syn., *full color.*

senopia (se-no'pe-ah). Unexpected, unaided improvement of vision, especially of near vision in the aged, regarded as a sign of incipient cataract. Syn., *gerontopia; second sight.*

sensation. 1. The apprehension of features of the external environment or bodily condition through the mediation of sense organs. 2. The afferent output of any sense organ. 3. Perception.

  accommodative s. A sensation which indicates changes in ocular accommodation. A sensory attribute of the act of accommodating.

  after s. 1. Afterimage. 2. A sensation lasting or occurring after the exciting stimulus has ceased to operate.

  autokinetic s. The sensation of apparent motion of a fixated stationary object, as occurs in the autokinetic visual illusion.

  color s. A visual sensation exhibiting hue, usually dependent on the selective use of portions of the spectrum as stimuli.

  glass s. A visual sensation of a transparent solid which appears different from empty space, i.e., as if filled with substance.

  light s. Any sensation whose proper stimulus is radiant energy between about 380 and 760 mμ, and mediated by the eye.

  psychovisual s. A sensation having the perceived attributes of visual sensation but not mediated by the retinal cells.

  visual s. A sensation produced by the sense of sight.

    visual s., toned. A visual sensation evoked by stimulation with a chromatic color.

    visual s., untoned. A visual sensation evoked by stimulation with an achromatic color.

sense. 1. Any of the faculties by which some aspect of the environment, or of body condition, may be apprehended, as that of sight, hearing, touch, smell, taste, hunger, or thirst. 2. The experiences or other end reactions from stimulation of sensory faculties. 3. To apprehend some aspect of the environment, or some bodily condition, through the use of a sense organ.

  color s. The faculty by which hues are perceived and distinguished.

  direction, s. of. The faculty enabling the orienting of each of the various object points in external space to some direction in the visual field, either in reference to the self or to other object points.

  discrimination s. 1. The faculty by which slightly separated objects in space are perceived as separate; the resolving power of the eye. 2. The faculty by which slightly differing stimuli are perceived as different, such as distinguishing between nearly equal spectral wavelengths.

distance s. The faculty of appreciating the spatial separation between the self and objects in the visual field or between two objects in the visual field. Cf. *stereopsis.*

form s. The faculty enabling one to distinguish the shapes of objects in the visual field.

fusion s. 1. The faculty of perceiving with the two eyes a single, integrated, fused image of a pair of haploscopically presented objects or an object viewed binocularly. 2. The faculty of perceiving continuously uniform light when the stimulus is intermittent.

light s. The faculty by which light (approximately 380 to 760 mμ) is perceived and by which gradations in its intensity are appreciated.

position s. The faculty enabling one to localize each of the various object points in external space either in reference to the self or to other object points. Syn., *space sense.*

space s. Position sense.

stereognostic s. The faculty by which objects in the visual field are perceived as solid, i.e., having three dimensions.

sensibilitometer, corneal. An instrument for determining the sensitivity thresholds of the cornea for touch, pain, or friction.

corneal s., Boberg-Ans. A device consisting of a nylon thread mounted in a handle such that its exposed length may be varied. Corneal sensitivity is measured by the greatest thread length which, when pressed against the

cornea, causes a just noticeable sensation of pain.

sensitivity. 1. The capability of responding to stimulation or to receive sensations therefrom. 2. In psychophysical measurements, the reciprocal of the threshold.

contrast s. The ability to detect border contrast; the reciprocal of the minimum perceptible contrast.

sensitometer (sen"sih-tom'eh-ter). An instrument for measuring sensitivity, as of the human eye.

Abney's s. Abney's colorimeter.

Luckiesh-Moss ophthalmic s. An instrument using brightness contrast threshold instead of acuity threshold for the subjective determination of the dioptric power producing maximum visibility. It consists essentially of a pair of neutral, graded density filters, one in front of each eye, a white target containing a vaguely defined vertical band of diffused light with a central gap in which a small, horizontal, black line is located. While the vertical band serves as a binocular fusion stimulus, a +2.50 D. cylinder, axis horizontal, is placed before one eye to obliterate the horizontal black line, and the neutral filters are rotated before the eyes until the black horizontal line is just visible. Lenses of various power are placed before the other eye until the lens power is found which provides visibility of the test target through the greatest filter density.

sensitometry (sen"sih-tom'eh-tre). Determination of the ophthalmic lens correction producing the best scores on the Luckiesh-Moss ophthalmic sensitometer.

separation difficulty. See under *difficulty.*

separation, reduced. Reduced distance.

separation, retinal. Separation of the retina from its pigment epithelium layer, commonly called *detachment of the retina.*

Separation Trainer. An instrument for the diagnosis and treatment of the crowding phenomenon in amblyopia ex anopsia, consisting of 25 randomly orientated letter *E*'s mounted in radial tracks on a flat vertical surface in a square formation, the distance between the *E*'s being varied by a lever on the side of the instrument.

separator (sep'ah-ra"tor). An instrument for separating the fields of vision of the eyes.

Hunt s. An instrument consisting of a drawing board divided by a perpendicularly mounted septum. The forehead is rested on the septum edge so that the field of vision of the two eyes is separated, a line drawing is placed on one side of the septum, and an attempt is made to copy it on the other side.

Rémy s. An instrument consisting of a vertical septum, with a handle below, which is attached to and bisects a target holder at one end. The other end of the septum is placed on the nose so that a target on either side of the septum is seen by only one eye and an attempt is made to fuse or superimpose them by voluntary effort.

septum (sep'tum). A dividing wall or partition, especially one which separates tissue, fluids, or two cavities.

orbitale, s. A thin membrane, containing collagenous and elastic fibers, which is attached to the arcus marginale at the orbital margin and extends to the tarsus of the upper and the lower eyelids. In the upper eyelid it fuses with the sheath of the levator palpebrae superioris muscle. Syn., *lid aponeurosis; palpebral fascia;* *tarso-orbital fascia; tarso-orbital ligament; orbital septum.*

retinal s., congenital. A congenital condition characterized by gross folds or ridges of undifferentiated neural elements of the retina which arise from the optic disk and project into the vitreous. It is considered to arise from the inner layer of the embryonic optic cup and most often occupies the lower temporal quadrant of the retina. Syn., *ablatio falciformis congenita; congenital retinal fold.*

serial reproduction. A visual training procedure in which a line drawing is flashed onto a screen and an attempt is made to reproduce the pattern. The procedure is repeated a number of times, and each time an attempt is made to improve without referring to the previous drawings.

series. A group of happenings or things in succeeding or progressing order.

continuous s. A type of representation of statistical data in frequency distributions employing continuous gradation values, such as rank order. Cf. *discrete series.*

dark clear s. In the Ostwald system, a series of surface color samples of decreasing luminous reflectance and purity which are arranged along the lower side of the Ostwald triangle.

discrete s. A type of representation of statistical data in frequency distributions employing gradation values representing discrete steps, as in grouped values. Cf. *continuous series.*

Fourier's s. The components of a complex periodic wave form as resolved by Fourier's analysis.

light clear s. In the Ostwald system, a series of surface color samples of decreasing purity and increasing luminous reflectance which are arranged along the upper side of the Ostwald triangle.

shadow s. In the Ostwald system, a series of surface color samples of approximately equal dominant wavelength and nearly constant purity, varying in luminous reflectance only, and arranged vertically in the Ostwald triangle, parallel to the gray series. Syn., *isochromes.*

shade. 1. A device used to diminish or intercept light from a lamp or other source to prevent full illumination in certain directions from the source. 2. The relative darkness of that side of an object which is turned away from a source of light, as distinguished from the shadow cast by the object. 3. Shadow, or the dimness or the relative darkness of or within a shadow. 4. A general term often used to designate a color not greatly different from another particular color. A gradation of color, or a slight variation of a color from a reference standard. 5. A mixture of black with a color. Thus, the antonym of *tint.* 6. Any color darker than median gray. 7. A term descriptive of a difference in hue only, as, "a redder shade than orange." 8. A variation in saturation or chroma only, when hue and lightness remain constant, as, "a paler shade of blue." Thus, synonymous with *tint.* 9. A variation in the lightness or brightness of a color. A darker shade of a color is one that has the same hue and saturation but a lower lightness. 10. A general term often used as a synonym for *color.* 11. To shield from light. To dim illumination by partially blocking light, as with a screen. 12. To create shadows. 13. To tone a drawing by increasing the thickness or the darkness of certain lines or portions of outlines. 14. To blend, as from one color to another.

Shado-Spector (shad'o-spek-tor). The trade name for an instrument that projects a 50× magnified image of a contact lens onto a calibrated viewing screen for the purpose of inspection.

Shado-Spectorette (shad'o-spek-to-ret"). The trade name for an instrument that projects a 25× magnified image of a contact lens onto a calibrated viewing screen for the purpose of inspection.

shadow. An obscure or darkened area from which rays from a source of light are cut off by an interposed opaque body.

Bowman's s. The dark appearance, when viewed in profile, of the portion of the cornea which has become conical in advanced keratoconus.

color s's. Shadows cast on a neutral screen by an opaque body from two equidistant light sources of equal intensity, one white and the other colored. The shadow cast by the white light appears to be the color of the colored light and the shadow cast by the colored light appears to be its complement.

iris s. A shadow cast by the iris on the crystalline lens in oblique illumination, used as a guide to the depth of opacity in the lens. When the shadow on a cataractous lens can no longer be seen, the cataract is considered to be ripe.

Purkinje's s's. Purkinje's figures.

shadowscope (shad'o-skōp). An instrument consisting essentially of an intense light source which is passed through a small aperture, transilluminating a lens positioned before it, and casting a shadow of the lens onto a screen for the purpose of inspection of the lens.

Shadowscope Reading Pacer. The trade name for an instrument used in improving reading speed and comprehension in which a rectangular band of light illuminates the material to be read, moving down over the reading material at a preset speed and thus setting a pace for the reader.

shagreen of the crystalline lens (shah-grēn'). The granular leatherlike (shagreen leather) or pounded metal appearance of the anterior and posterior surface of the capsule of the crystalline lens when viewed with the biomicroscope under specularly reflected light.

shank. On a spectacle frame, that part of a metal saddle bridge connecting the strap or the eyewire to the crest of the bridge.

Shaxby's theory (shaks'bēz). See under *theory*.

Sheard's (shērdz) **chart; criterion; method.** See under the nouns.

sheath. A covering and/or supporting structure, usually one of connective tissue.

arachnoidean s. The middle of the three meninges that cover the middle and the distal portions of the optic nerve. It consists of collagenous fibers and endothelium and connects through the subdural space with the dural sheath and by way of trabeculae through the larger subarachnoid space with the pial sheath.

dural s. The outer of the three meninges that cover the optic nerve; blends with the sclera. It contains a thick collection of collagenous fibers, is lined with endothelium, and forms a tough protective layer around the nerve.

fascial s. of eyeball. Capsule of Tenon.

glial s. A sheath of neuroglial cells that protrudes from the optic disk of the fetus and encircles the proximal third of the hyaloid artery. It is an extension of Bergmeister's papilla and degen-

erates as the physiological cup is formed.

pial s. The inner of the three meninges that cover the optic nerve. It is lined with the glial mantle, contains elastic and collagenous fibers, and carries capillaries into the nerve.

shell. An outside covering, exterior, husk, or any similar hollow, usually frail, structure.

cosmetic s. A plastic shell placed over a disfigured eye and colored with opaque dyes to conceal the disfigurement and match the color of the fellow eye. It may have a clear or opaque scleral portion and does not possess any optical properties.

image s. The curved surface containing either all the sagittal, or all the tangential, foci of a homocentric bundle of rays obliquely incident upon an optical system containing spherical surfaces.

molding s. A shell of plastic, glass, or hard rubber, used to hold molding material while taking an impression or mold of the anterior segment of an eye in contact lens fitting. It consists of a small cup, curved to conform approximately to the anterior segment of the eye, is usually perforated, and often has a small handle affixed to the center of its convex side.

Walser s. A thin plastic shell, resembling the scleral portion of a scleral contact lens, which is placed on the bulbar conjunctiva to separate it from the palpebral conjunctiva to promote healing and to prevent adhesions of wounds, such as from burns.

shelves, lens. The intercellular cement substance in the Y-sutures of the crystalline lens or in the more complex lens stars which receive the ends of lens fibers.

Sherrington's (sher'ing-tonz) **disk; experiment; law; theory.** See under the nouns.

shield, Buller's. A watch glass in a frame of adhesive tape secured over the nonaffected eye to protect it from infection from the other eye.

shield, eye. 1. A covering for the eye to protect it from light, infection, or injury. 2. An occluder.

shift, adjustment. A type of binocular vision present in some strabismics with harmonious, anomalous, retinal correspondence in which the perceived binocular field of vision is made up of portions of each uniocular field of vision. *Brock.*

shift, Purkinje's. Purkinje's phenomenon.

shoe. The part of a rimless spectacle bridge or endpiece which rests against the end of the lens.

short pointing. The kinesthetic directionalization of a gross object of fixation, presented monocularly in the field of action of an extraocular muscle affected with spasm, to a point nearer than it actually is.

shortsightedness. Myopia.

shoulder. The transitional zone between the corneal and the scleral sections on the inner surface of a scleral contact lens.

shoulder tipping. A tilting of the head toward one shoulder, especially as a clinical symptom.

Shtremel's test (shtrem'elz). See under *test.*

shutter, electro-optic. A device which provides a nonmechanical method of interrupting or modulating a light beam. It consists of a Kerr cell placed between crossed polarizing filters and transmits light only when subjected to an electric field.

shutter, Kerr. See *electro-optic shutter.*

siderophone (sid'er-o-fōn″). An instrument for detecting and locating iron particles in the eyeball

by the electrical production of sound.

sideroscope (sid'er-o-skōp″). An instrument for detecting and locating iron particles in the eyeball.

sideroscopy (sid″er-os′ko-pe). The detection and location of iron particles in the eyeball.

siderosis (sid″er-o′sis). A deposit of iron in a tissue.

bulbi, s. Pigmentary and degenerative changes in the eyeball resulting from the prolonged presence of an iron foreign body in the ocular tissue. The changes may be localized to the immediate vicinity of the foreign particle, or they may be generalized and occur throughout the ocular structures. The typical clinical picture includes a rusty discoloration, together with the pigmentary and degenerative changes.

conjunctivae, s. Rusty discoloration in the conjunctiva and the sclera resulting from the prolonged presence of an iron foreign body.

Siegrist's (se′grists) **spots; streaks.** See under the nouns.

Siemens' (se′menz) **star; syndrome.** See under the nouns.

Siezel-Fusor. The trade name for a home training device utilizing the anaglyph principle to eliminate suppression, consisting of a special checkerboard with blue and black squares, reversible red and blue filters, and three sets of various-sized red and black checkers. The red and black checkers, but not the squares, can be seen through the red filter. The squares can be seen through the blue filter, with all the checkers appearing black.

sight. 1. The special sense by which objects, their form, color, position, etc., in the external environment are perceived, the exciting stimulus being light from the objects striking the retina of the eye; the act, function, process, or power of seeing; vision. 2. That which is seen. 3. A device to aid the eye in aiming. 4. To look at; to see.

aging s. The lay term for presbyopia.

day s. Vision in higher levels of illumination, implying reduced vision in lower levels, or night blindness.

far s. Hypermetropia.

line of s. See under *line*.

long s. The lay term for hypermetropia.

near s. Myopia.

night s. Vision in lower levels of illumination, implying reduced or less than normal vision in higher levels, or day blindness.

old s. The lay term for presbyopia.

second s. Unexpected, unaided improvement of near vision in the elderly, resulting from swelling of the crystalline lens in incipient cataract. Syn., *gerontopia; senopia.*

short s. The lay term for myopia.

weak s. The lay term for reduced visual acuity or for asthenopia.

Sight Screener, American Optical. A Brewster-type stereoscopic instrument for visual screening, with targets for measuring visual acuity, phorias, stereopsis, and color perception.

sigma (sig'mah). The Greek letter used in capital form (Σ) as a symbol for the *sum of,* and in lower case form (σ) as a symbol for *standard deviation.*

sign. Objective evidence of a disease. See also *phenomenon; reflex; symptom; syndrome.*

Abadie's s. A spasm of the levator palpebrae superioris muscle in exophthalmic goiter.

Argyll Robertson's s. The Argyll Robertson pupil, indicating syphilis of the central nervous system.

Arroyo's s. Asthenocoria, as seen in hypoadrenia.

Aschner's s. The oculocardiac reflex, indicating cardiac vagus irritability.

Baillarger's s. Unequal size of the pupils in syphilitic meningoencephalitis.

Ballet's s. Partial or complete external ophthalmoplegia without internal ophthalmoplegia in exophthalmic goiter.

Bard's s. Increase of the oscillations of the eye in organic nystagmus in reflexly fixating a moving target and cessation of the oscillations under the same conditions in congenital nystagmus, as described by Bard.

Barré's s. Retarded contraction of the iris in mental deterioration.

Bechterew-Mendel s. Mendel-Bechterew sign.

Becker's s. Pulsation of the retinal arteries in exophthalmic goiter.

Behr's s. Paralysis of upward gaze associated with loss of the pupillary reflex to light, with slightly dilated pupils and with retention of convergence, considered to be due to a lesion of the midbrain.

Bell's s. Outward and upward rotation of the eyeball on the affected side on attempt to close the eyelids in Bell's palsy. Syn., *Bordier-Fränkel sign.*

Berger's s. An elliptical or irregularly shaped pupil in the early stages of syphilis of the central nervous system.

Bielschowsky's s. Involuntary upward rotation of an eye when the head is forcibly tilted toward the shoulder on the same side as the eye, indicating a paretic superior oblique muscle of that eye.

Bjerrum's s. A comet-shaped, arcuate scotoma which extends from the superior or the inferior margin of the physiological blind spot into the nasal field, around the fixation area, indicating glaucoma. It is usually located between the 10° and 20° circles and becomes wider as it leaves the blind spot.

Bordier-Fränkel s. Bell's sign.

Boston's s. Spasmodic lowering of the upper eyelid on downward rotation of the eye, indicating exophthalmic goiter.

bowed head s. Gould's sign.

Cantelli's s. Doll's head phenomenon.

Cestan's s. Dutemps and Cestan sign.

Chvostek's s. A spasm of the facial muscles, including the orbicularis oculi, elicited by tapping the terminus of the seventh nerve in front of the ear, indicating tetany, hysteria, or chlorosis.

Collet's s. The opening of the lid of one eye more quickly and more widely than the other on rapid, repeated, effortless opening and closing of the eyelids, indicating beginning paralysis of the orbicularis oculi muscle of that eye.

conjunctival s. Multiple, isolated, saccular dilations of capillaries in the bulbar conjunctiva, seen with the slit lamp biomicroscope and attributed to vascular stasis, an indication of sickle-cell disease.

Cowen's s. A jerky, consensual, pupillary reflex to light in exophthalmic goiter.

Crichton-Browne s. Twitching of the outer corners of the eyes and the lips indicating syphilitic meningoencephalitis.

Crowe's s. Bilateral engorgement of the retinal veins on compression of the jugular vein on the healthy side, an indication of unilateral cavernous sinus thrombosis.

Dalrymple's s. Abnormal wideness of the palpebral fissures in exophthalmic goiter.

Dixon Mann's s. Mann's sign.

doll's eye s. Doll's head phenomenon.

Dutemps and Cestan s. A slight upward movement of the upper eyelid of one eye on attempted slow closure of the eyelids while looking straight ahead, indicating involvement of the orbicularis oculi muscle of that eye in peripheral facial paralysis.

Elliot's s. A jagged, irregular extension of the margin of the physiological blind spot, as plotted with an Elliot scotometer, consisting of several isolated scotomata, indicating glaucoma.

Enroth's s. Edematous swelling of the eyelids, especially the upper eyelids near the supraorbital margin, in exophthalmic goiter.

Flatau's s. Rapid mydriasis on gentle irritation of the skin, such as a scratch by the fingernail, in epidemic cerebrospinal meningitis.

Fodéré's s. Edema of the lower eyelids, indicating kidney malfunction.

Franceschetti's digital-ocular s. Franceschetti's digital-ocular symptom.

Froment's s. On closure of the eyelids while looking upward, one eye is closed imperfectly, indicating beginning paralysis of the orbicularis oculi muscle of that eye.

Gianelli's s. Tournay's pupillary reflex.

Gifford's s. Difficulty of eversion of the upper eyelid in exophthalmic goiter.

Goppert's s. Mydriasis produced on passive stretching of the neck muscles by bending the head backward, in epidemic cerebrospinal meningitis.

Gould's s. Turning of the head downward in walking to bring the image of the ground on the functioning portion of the retina, in destructive disease of the peripheral retina. Syn., *bowed head sign.*

von Graefe's s. Immobility or lagging of the upper eyelid on downward rotation of the eye, indicating exophthalmic goiter.

Griffith's s. Lag of the lower eyelid

on upward gaze in exophthalmic goiter.

Guist's s. Tortuosity of the retinal veins, especially of the smaller venules, an early sign of arteriosclerosis.

Gunn's crossing s. The compression of a retinal venule into the tissue of the retina, where it is crossed by an overlying arteriole so that it appears tapered and/or disconnected; one of the signs of hypertensive and/or arteriolosclerotic retinopathy. Syn., *Gunn's arteriovenous phenomenon.*

Gunn's jaw-winking s. Jaw-winking.

Gunn's pupillary s. Gunn's pupillary phenomenon.

Haab's s. Haab's pupillary reflex.

Haenel's s. Decrease in the sensation of pain on firm tactile pressure on the eyeball in tabes dorsalis.

de Hertogh's s. Absence of the lateral portion of the eyebrows, occurring in certain hereditary anomalies of the skin.

Hertwig-Magendie s. Magendie-Hertwig sign.

van der Hoeve's s. Enlargement of the physiological blind spot in paranasal sinusitis.

Hutchinson's s. 1. Hutchinson's triad: interstitial keratitis, notched teeth, and deafness occurring together in congenital syphilis. 2. Hutchinson's triad, together with rhagades at the corners of the mouth and a saddle-shaped bridge of the nose.

Jellinek's s. Abnormal pigmentation of the skin of the eyelids, in exophthalmic goiter. Syn., *Rasin's sign; Tellais' sign.*

Jendrassik's s. Apparent paralysis of the extraocular muscles, in exophthalmic goiter.

Joffroy's s. Absence of the normal wrinkles in the forehead on looking upward with the head bent down, a sign of exophthalmic goiter.

Kayser-Fleischer s. The Kayser-Fleischer ring, indicating Wilson's disease.

Kestenbaum's s. In unilateral amblyopia, marked anisocoria with dilatation of the pupil of the affected eye, when it fixates a light source with the normal eye covered, and little or no anisocoria, when the normal eye fixates with the affected eye covered, indicating an organic lesion of the macula or the optic nerve in differentiation from a functional visual loss.

Knies's s. Unequal dilatation of the pupils in exophthalmic goiter.

Kocher's s. 1. Spasmodic retraction of the upper eyelid on attentive fixation in exophthalmic goiter. 2. Means's sign.

Koster's s. Failure of the upper eyelid to elevate, or ability to elevate only slightly, upon the administration of cocaine, indicating absence of the levator palpebrae superioris muscle in congenital ptosis.

Lester's s. Hyperpigmentation of the iris in a clover-leaf pattern.

Loewi's s. Ready dilatation of the pupil with instillation of adrenalin into the cul-de-sac, in exophthalmic goiter.

Lotze's local s. The subjective identification of a specific spatial direction from the self for each retinal element stimulated; a characteristic assumed to be inherent and present for any sensory receptor.

Magendie-Hertwig s. Spasmodic deviation of the eyes in opposite directions, in acute cerebellar lesions. It persists for all directions of gaze. Thus, if one eye looks down and in, the other eye will turn upward and outward. Syn., *skew deviation.*

Mann's s. The appearance of one eye being higher than its fellow, in exophthalmic goiter.

May's s. Ready dilatation of the

pupil on instillation of adrenalin into the cul-de-sac, in glaucoma.

Means's s. Movement of the upper eyelids faster than the eyeballs on looking upward, thus exposing the sclera above the cornea, in exophthalmic goiter. Syn., *globe lag.*

Mendel-Bechterew s. Dilatation of the pupils on exposure to light (the paradoxical pupillary reflex) in cerebral syphilis, tabes dorsalis, or general paralysis.

Méténier's s. Spontaneous eversion of the upper eyelid upon upward pulling of the skin of the upper eyelid, occurring when the skin is loose, thin, and elastic.

Moebius' s. Convergence weakness in exophthalmic goiter.

Moskowskij's s. Anisocoria, with dilatation of the pupil of the right eye, in acute abdominal disease, such as appendicitis, cholecystitis, or colitis.

Munson's s. A cone-shaped bulging of the margin of the lower lid when looking downward, such that the lower lid margin bisects the cornea, indicating keratoconus.

Myerson's s. A series of blinking movements in response to a tap on the forehead or to a sudden thrust toward the eyes, frequently seen in Parkinson's disease.

Negro's s. Overshooting of the eye on the more severely affected side on looking upward, in peripheral facial paralysis.

objective s. A sign apparent to the observer.

optokinetic nystagmus s., negative. Symmetric, horizontal, nystagmoid movements to both sides, as normally occur in optokinetic nystagmus. When present with homonymous hemianopsia, it is indicative of a lesion involving the optic tract, lateral geniculate body, the most anterior optic radiations in the temporal lobe,

or the occipital cortex. Cf. *positive optokinetic nystagmus sign.*

optokinetic nystagmus s., positive. Horizontal optokinetic nystagmus less pronounced, or absent, to one side as compared to the other. When occurring with homonymous hemianopsia, it is indicative of a lesion involving the middle or posterior optic radiations. Cf. *negative optokinetic nystagmus sign.*

orbicularis s. Forced closure of the eyelids on the unaffected side on closure of the eyelids on the affected side, in hemiplegia. Syn., *Revilliod's sign.*

Parrot's s. Pupillary dilatation on pinching the skin of the neck, in meningitis.

physical s. Objective sign.

Piltz's s. 1. Attention pupillary reflex. 2. Orbicularis pupillary reflex. 3. Delayed and slow reaction of the pupils to light followed by slow dilatation, in neurosis or psychosis.

Prevost's s. Turning the head and eyes toward the affected hemisphere and away from the palsied extremities, in hemiplegia.

pseudo-Graefe's s. Failure of the upper eyelid to follow the eyeball downward or the elevation of the upper eyelid when the eyeball turns downward, usually indicative of aberrant regeneration of fibers of the oculomotor nerve following paresis or paralysis. It is to be differentiated from *von Graefe's sign* in exophthalmic goiter. Syn., *pseudo-Graefe's phenomenon.*

Rasin's s. Jellinek's sign.

Revilliod's s. Orbicularis sign.

Riesman's s. 1. A decrease in ocular tension in diabetic coma. 2. A bruit heard stethoscopically over the closed eye, in exophthalmic goiter. Syn., *Snellen's sign.*

Ripault's s. A change in the shape of the pupil from external pressure on the eyeball, which is temporary during life and may be permanent after death.

Robertson's s. Failure to elicit pupillary dilatation on exerting pressure on an alleged painful area, an indication of malingering.

Rochester's s. The inability to maintain light closure of the eyelid on the affected side when the eyes are moved superiorly under lightly closed eyelids to a point beyond the limit of the field of fixation, an indication of beginning paresis of the seventh cranial nerve.

Romaña's s. Pronounced unilateral edema of the eyelids, with conjunctivitis and swelling of the regional lymph glands, an indication of Chaga's disease.

Romberg's s. Swaying of the body due to the inability to maintain equilibrium when standing with feet together and eyes closed, indicating tabes dorsalis.

Roque's s. Mydriasis of the left eye resulting from irritation of the cervical sympathetic chain, in exudative endocarditis.

Rosenbach's s. 1. Fine, rapid tremor of gently closed eyelids, an indication of exophthalmic goiter. 2. The inability to close the eyelids immediately on command, an indication of neurasthenia.

Rothschild's s. Sparseness of the outer third of the eyebrows, in hypothyroidism.

Saenger's s. The return of an absent pupillary light reflex after a short stay in the dark, indicating cerebral syphilis in differentiation from tabes dorsalis.

Sainton's s. Contraction of the frontalis muscle after the levator palpebrae superioris muscle has ceased to contract on looking upward, i.e., wrinkles in the forehead appear after the raising of the eyelids instead of during, an indication of exophthalmic goiter.

Salmon's s. Unilateral dilatation of the pupil in ruptured ectopic pregnancy.

Salus' s. An arch in a retinal venule, above or below a sclerosed anteriole, due to deflection from its normal course by the arteriole, an indication of hypertensive and/or arteriolosclerotic retinopathy. Syn., *Salus' arch.*

Schmidt's s. A sign of manifest heterozygosity in carriers of protanomaly and protanopia, consisting of abnormal luminosity functions intermediate between those of normals and those of protanomals and protanopes without any color-matching abnormalities. The sign is manifested in the relatively high brightness adjustment of a red light as compared to that of a blue light when she, the carrier, attempts to equate each of them to the brightness of green light.

Seeligmueller's s. Mydriasis on the affected side in facial neuralgia.

Seidel's s. A sickle-shaped scotoma appearing as an upward or downward prolongation of the physiological blind spot, indicating glaucoma.

Snellen's s. A bruit heard with a stethoscope placed over the closed eye, in exophthalmic goiter.

Stellwag's s. Infrequent and incomplete blinking, indicating exophthalmic goiter. Syn., *Stellwag's symptom.*

subjective s. A sign apparent only to the subject or the afflicted person.

Suker's s. The inability to maintain extreme lateral fixation of the eyes, indicating exophthalmic goiter.

Tay's s. The cherry-red spot in the region of the macula lutea of each eye in Tay-Sachs disease.

Tellais' s. Abnormal pigmentation of the skin of the eyelids in exophthalmic goiter. Syn., *Jellinek's sign; Rasin's sign.*

Terrien's s. Paralysis of downward gaze associated with loss of accommodation and convergence, considered to be due to a lesion of the midbrain.

Thies's s. Miosis occurring in lesions of the sigmoid flexure and the rectum.

Topalanski's s. Congestion of the pericorneal region of the eye in exophthalmic goiter.

Tournay's s. Tournay's pupillary reflex.

Uhthoff's s. The nystagmus associated with multiple sclerosis.

Vincent's s. Argyll Robertson pupil.

Vogt's s. Loss of the normal shagreen of the capsule of the crystalline lens in the affected area under slit lamp examination, indicating anterior capsular cataract.

Wartenberg's s. Reduced muscular control of the upper eyelid in facial paralysis.

Weber's s. Homolateral oculomotor paralysis and contralateral hemiplegia of the face and limbs, indicating a lesion in the region of the cerebral peduncle affecting the third cranial nerve. Syn., *Weber's paralysis; Weber's symptom; Weber's syndrome.*

Weiss's s. Weiss's reflex.

Wernicke's s. Hemianopic pupillary reflex.

Westphal's s. Dilated pupils which fail to contract to light in neurosis or psychosis.

white with pressure s. White with pressure phenomenon.

Wilder's s. A slight twitch of the eyeball on lateral movement, an indication of exophthalmic goiter.

Wood's s. Fixation of the eyeballs in a divergent position, and relaxation of the orbicularis oculi muscle in deep anesthesia.

significance, statistical. The statistically evaluated extent to which a given quantitative relationship may be considered due to chance or to the operation of those factors whose influence the experi-

mental procedure was designed to test.

silhouette (sil″ōō-et′). 1. A representation of the contour or the outline of an object or a person filled with a uniform color differing from the surrounding field. 2. To represent by a silhouette.

Simmance-Abady photometer (sim-mahnz′-ah′bah-de). See under *photometer.*

Sinclair's rule (sin-klārz). See under *rule.*

sine condition. See under *condition.*

sinistral (sin′is-tral). 1. Showing preference for the left eye, hand, or foot. 2. Pertaining to, or on, the left side.

sinistrality (sin″is-tral′ih-te). Left-eyedness or left-handedness.

sinistroclination (sin″is-tro-klih-na′-shun). Rotation of the top of the vertical meridian of an eye toward the left; extorsion of the left eye or intorsion of the right eye. Syn., *levocycloduction; levotorsion; sinistrotorsion; sinistrocycloduction.*

sinistrocular (sin″is-trok′u-lar). Pertaining to the left eye or the condition of sinistrocularity.

sinistrocularity (sin″is-trok″u-lar′ih-te). A condition in which better vision exists in the left eye, or in which the left eye is dominant.

sinistrocycloduction (sin″is-tro-si″-klo-duk′shun). Sinistroclination.

sinistrocycloversion (sin″is-tro-si″-klo-ver′zhun). Rotation of the top of the vertical meridians of both eyes toward the left. Syn., *negative cycloversion; levocycloversion.*

sinistroduction (sin″is-tro-duk′shun). Rotation of an eye toward the left. Syn., *levoduction.*

sinistrogyration (sin″is-tro-ji-ra′-shun). A turning to the left; motion, especially rotatory, to the left; said of eye movements and of the plane of polarization.

sinistrophoria (sin″is-tro-fo′re-ah). A phoria in which the nonfixating eye is turned toward the left. Syn., *levophoria.*

sinistrorotatory (sin"is-tro-ro'tah-to"re). 1. Turning of the plane of polarization toward the left. 2. Bending rays of light toward the left. 3. Pertaining to sinistroclination. Syn., *levorotatory.*

sinistrotorsion (sin"is-tro-tor'shun). Sinistroclination.

sinistroversion (sin"is-tro-ver'zhun). A conjugate rotation of both lines of sight to the left. Syn., *levoversion.*

sinus. A hollow space, cavity, or recess in the body.

anterior chamber, s. of the. The space within the angle of the anterior chamber.

Arlt, s. of. A small diverticulum sometimes found in the lower, lateral wall of the lacrimal sac.

cavernous s. One of the paired venous sinuses in the dura mater of the brain extending on each side of the pituitary body and the body of the sphenoid bone from the inner end of the superior orbital fissure to the petrous portion of the temporal bone. It receives blood from the superior and the inferior ophthalmic veins and the central retinal veins, empties into the superior and the inferior petrosal sinuses, and communicates with the pterygoid venous plexus. Its central spongy tissue contains the internal carotid artery with its sympathetic carotid plexus and the abducens nerve. Its lateral wall contains the oculomotor and the trochlear nerves and the first two divisions of the trigeminal nerve.

ciliary s. Ciliary cleft.

circular s. The venous ring around the pituitary gland formed by the two cavernous sinuses and the communicating anterior and posterior intercavernous sinuses.

circularis iridis, s. Canal of Schlemm.

intercavernous s's. Two sinuses in the dura mater of the brain which connect the two cavernous sinuses, one located anterior to and the other posterior to the pituitary body. Syn., *transverse sinuses.*

Maier, s. of. A small diverticulum from the middle lateral wall of the lacrimal sac into which the canaliculi drain.

marginal s. Ring sinus of von Szily.

ring s. of von Szily. A circular space between the two layers of the optic cup, at the extreme tip of the growing edge in the developing iris, which appears at the end of the third month and disappears by the seventh month of fetal life. Syn., *von Szily's ring; marginal sinus.*

scleral s. Canal of Schlemm.

scleral s. of Rochon-Duvigneaud. Canal of Schlemm.

subscleral s. In the lamprey, a venous sinus composing the external portion of the choroid which drains blood from the choroid and empties, by way of four apertures, into extraocular venous sinuses surrounding the sclera.

transverse s's. Intercavernous sinuses.

venosus sclerae, s. Canal of Schlemm.

situs inversus of the disk (si'tus inver'sus). A developmental abnormality in which the retinal vessels course nasally from the optic disk instead of temporally, giving the optic disk a reversed appearance.

size. Physical extent, bulk, or magnitude.

angular s. The size of an object expressed in terms of the angle subtended by it with respect to some point of reference, such as the nodal point of the eye or the center of the entrance pupil.

apparent s. 1. The size of an object represented by the angle or a trigonometric function of the angle it subtends at the eye. 2. The perceived size of an object, or the size attributed to the object, as distinguished from the actual size.

boxed lens s. Spectacle lens size specified in terms of the horizontal and vertical dimensions of the box which contains the lens.

constancy, s. The apparent relative stability or lack of perceived change in the size of an object despite a change in viewing distance, viewing angle, actual size, or other related stimulus factors.

datum lens s. Spectacle lense size specified in terms of the horizontal and vertical dimensions through the datum center.

diminution, s. The perceived relative decrease in size of elements in a stereopsis-inducing target which appear closer than other fused elements in the stereogram though they are the same actual size.

perceptual s. The perceived size of an object as distinguished from the actual size.

Sjögren's (syeh'grenz) **syndrome; test.** See under the nouns.

Sjögren-Larsson syndrome (syeh'-gren-lahr'son). See under *syndrome.*

skew deviation (sku de"ve-a'shun). See under *deviation.*

skewness (sku'nes). The extent of departure from symmetry of a normal frequency distribution.

skiakinescopy (ski"ah-kin-es'ko-pe). A method of determining the refractive state of the eye in which a pinhole is moved across the pupil while a distant light source is viewed through it. The light source appears stationary in emmetropia, appears to move in the same direction as the hole in myopia, and in the opposite direction in hypermetropia.

skiametry (ski-am'eh-tre). The determination of the refractive error by retinoscopy.

skiaporescopy (ski"ah-po-res'ko-pe). Retinoscopy.

skiascope (ski'ah-skōp). Retinoscope.

skiascopy (ski-as'ko-pe). Observation of the retinoscopic reflex.

skiascotometry (ski"ah-sko-tom'eh-tre). A method of measuring blind areas in the visual field in which test objects are moved automatically at a given rate of speed by means of an adaptation of the Goldmann perimeter.

skill, visual. The ability to perform a visual act, usually measured by psychophysical methods; the representation of a given aspect of a visual, ocular, or extraocular function as an attribute or a score.

motor visual s. A visual skill relating to the ability or function of the intrinsic and extrinsic muscles of the eye.

perceptual visual s. A visual skill relating to the perceptual aspect of vision, implying a more complex or higher level of interpretation than a sensory visual skill.

sensory visual s. A visual skill relating to the sensory aspect of vision, e.g., visual acuity or brightness discrimination.

Ski-optometer (ski-op-tom'eh-ter). An instrument for determining the refractive state of the eye, phorias, ductions, etc., consisting essentially of a pair of rotating disks containing convex and concave spherical lenses, cells for trial cylindrical lenses, rotary prisms, and Maddox grooves.

skot (skot). One one-thousandth of an *apostilb.*

skylight. 1. Sunlight scattered by the atmosphere. 2. A window in a roof or a ceiling.

slab-off. A slab-off lens.

slide. 1. A moving piece guided by the parts along which it slides. 2. A guiding surface or piece along which something slides. 3. A plate of transparent material on which is a picture to be projected.

Hamilton s. A slide containing letters, numerals, astigmatic dials, and other devices for vision testing, for use with the Clason acuity meter.

nodal s. An optical bench mount permitting adjustment of the perpendicular axis about which a lens or a lens system may be rotated to locate the nodal points.

Robinson Cohen s. A projector slide containing letters and other characters for vision testing and a rotatable astigmatic dial consisting of two broken black lines at right angles to each other on a red background, with an axis indicator on the control knob.

slip, retinal. Fixation disparity.

slip-on. Clip-on.

slip-over. Clip-on.

slit, stenopaic. Stenopaic disk.

slit lamp. See under *lamp.*

Slit-Lite. The trade name for a hand-held portable slit lamp used in conjunction with a magnifier for examination of the anterior structures of the eye.

Sloan charts; test. See under the nouns.

Sloan-Green criterion. See under *criterion.*

Sluder's syndrome (slu'derz). See under *syndrome.*

smoothing. Fining.

Sn. Abbreviation for *Snellen.*

Snell's law (snelz). Law of refraction.

Snellen's (snel'enz) **visual acuity; chart; eye; formula; fraction; notation; prong; sign; test; test types.** See under the nouns.

Snell-Sterling (snel-ster'ling) **notation; visual efficiency scale.** See under *notation.*

snow blindness. See under *blindness.*

Society of Ocularists. An association of persons who make and fit ocular prosthetics.

socket, eye. The bony orbit which contains the eye and adjacent structures.

Soehnges Micro Pupil Multifocal contact lens (sen'jēz). See under *lens, contact.*

Soemmering's (sem'er-ingz) **bone; cushion; foramen; ligaments; ring; spot.** See under the nouns.

Soleil compensator (so-leh'yeh). See under *compensator.*

solid, color. A representation in three dimensions of the quantitative or psychophysical relations of all possible colors with respect to their primary attributes of hue, brightness or lightness (value), and saturation (chroma). Brightness (lightness) is usually represented as the vertical axis of the solid, with hue and saturation represented as polar co-ordinates around this axis, the hues being arranged circumferentially and saturations radially. Although the boundaries of any such solid representation must necessarily be irregular because of the inequalities of maximal saturations of various hues, the solid is nevertheless represented variously as a cylinder, a sphere, a spindle, a double cone, or a double rectangular pyramid.

color s., Ostwald. A three dimensional representation in the form of two cones placed base to base with white represented at the upper apex, black at the lower, and full color circumferentially at the center. Mixtures of full color with white and with black are represented, respectively, above or below the central circle. See also *Ostwald color system.*

Sondermann, canals of (son'derman). See under *canal.*

Sorsby's degeneration; dystrophy; syndrome. See under the nouns.

soule (soo-la'). To cut from the lower nasal edge of a spectacle lens to give clearance for the nose.

source, light. Any source of visible radiant energy, such as a candle flame, incandescent lamp, or fluorescent lamp.

A; B; C light s's. A; B; C illuminants.

coherent light s's. Light sources which maintain a continual point-to-point phase relationship with each other.

cool light s. Luminescent light source.

luminescent light s. A light source which emits light without being heated, such as a fluorescent lamp. Syn., *cool light source.*

standard light s. A light source which has a specified spectral distribution and is used as a standard in colorimetry, such as illuminant A, B, or C (*q.v.*).

Souter's tonometer (sōō′terz). See under *tonometer.*

Southall's double color circle. See under *circle, color.*

space. 1. A potential or an actual cavity within the body. 2. A delimited area, region, or interval, usually three dimensional.

central s. of the orbit. The retrobulbar space lying within the cone formed by the rectus muscles. Syn., *muscle cone space.*

circumlental s. Zonular space.

corneal s's. Tiny spaces between the lamellae of the corneal stroma containing tissue fluid. Syn., *interlamellar spaces.*

epichoroidal s. Perichoroidal space.

episcleral s. Tenon's space.

Fontana, s's. of. In lower mammals and birds, large spaces formed by the trabeculae of the pectinate ligament. In man, smaller vestigial spaces, after the sixth month of fetal life, in the uveal meshwork of the angle of the anterior chamber, involved in the drainage of aqueous humor. Syn., *trabecular spaces; spatia anguli iridis; spatia iridis.*

image s. The space containing rays emanating from an object after

they have been refracted or reflected by an optical system.

interfascial s. Tenon's space.

interlamellar s's. Corneal spaces.

intermarginal s. The space on the surface of the eyelid margin.

intervaginal s's. The subarachnoid and the subdural spaces in the sheath of the optic nerve.

iridocorneal angle, s's. of. Trabecular spaces.

Meckel's s. Meckel's cave.

muscle cone s. Central space of the orbit.

object s. The space containing rays emanating from an object prior to refraction or reflection by an optical system.

Panum's fusional s. The space enclosed between the anteroposterior limits of the haplopic horopter and within which fusion of a nonfixated target can occur, its images stimulating retinal points within Panum's areas.

perichoroidal s. The potential space between the choroid and the sclera across which fine lamellae stretch to blend the superficial layer of the choroid with the lamina fusca of the sclera. It is traversed by branches of the posterior ciliary arteries, the short and long ciliary nerves, and extends from the scleral spur to the opticoscleral foramen. Syn., *epichoroidal space; suprachoroidal space.*

perilenticular s. Zonular space.

peripheral s. of the orbit. The space between the cone formed by the rectus muscles and the periorbita.

perivascular s. Fluid-filled spaces around the orbital vessels, considered to act as lymph channels.

postlenticular s. of Berger. Retrolental space of Berger.

preseptal s. 1. A space in the upper eyelid, containing submuscular areolar tissue, bounded anteriorly by the orbicularis oculi muscle,

[656]

posteriorly by the orbital septum and the fibers of the levator palpebrae superioris muscle, and superiorly by a preseptal cushion of fat. 2. A space in the lower eyelid, containing submuscular areolar tissue, bounded anteriorly by the orbicularis oculi muscle and posteriorly by the orbital septum.

pretarsal s. A space in the upper eyelid, containing submuscular areolar tissue, bounded anteriorly by the tendon of the levator palpebrae superioris muscle and posteriorly by the tarsus and the muscle of Mueller. It extends superiorly to the origin of the muscle of Mueller and inferiorly to the attachment of the fibers of the levator palpebrae superioris muscle to the tarsus.

prezonular s. The circular space between the iris and the anterior leaf of the zonule of Zinn, containing aqueous humor.

retrobulbar s. The area within the orbit outside Tenon's capsule, posterior to the conjunctiva, which contains orbital fat, extraocular muscles, vessels, and nerves.

retrolental s. of Berger. A potential space between the posterior surface of the crystalline lens and the hyaloid fossa of the vitreous body. Syn., *postlenticular space of Berger.*

retrolental s. of Erggelet. The optically empty space formed by the anterior expansion of the hyaloid canal.

retrozonular s. A circular space filled with aqueous humor, peripheral to the retrolental space of Berger, and bounded by the posterior leaf of the zonule of Zinn, the ciliary body, and the anterior surface of the vitreous humor. Syn., *canal of Petit.*

Schnabel's s's. Small spaces in the optic nerve, posterior to the

lamina cribrosa, resulting from degeneration or atrophy of nerve fibers, in glaucoma. According to Schnabel, their coalescence leads to glaucomatous cupping. Syn., *Schnabel's caverns.*

Schwalbe's s. Supravaginal space.

subarachnoid s. The space between the arachnoid and the pia mater which contains connective tissue trabeculae and is filled with cerebrospinal fluid. It is continuous from the cranium to the optic nerve and terminates in the region of the lamina cribrosa.

subdural s. A space between the dura mater and the arachnoid which is continuous from the cranium to the optic nerve where, unlike the corresponding space in the brain, it becomes very thin.

subperiosteal s. The potential space between the periosteum and the bony wall of the orbit.

suprachoroidal s. Perichoroidal space.

supraciliary s. The anterior portion of the perichoroidal space between the ciliary body and the sclera.

supravaginal s. A space, between the dura mater of the optic nerve and the orbital fat, described by Schwalbe and considered by him to contain lymph. Syn., *Schwalbe's space.*

Tenon's s. The space between Tenon's capsule and the sclera, containing interconnecting trabeculae. Syn., *episcleral space; interfascial space.*

trabecular s's. Small spaces between the intercrossing trabeculae of the meshwork of the angle of the anterior chamber, involved in the drainage of aqueous humor from the anterior chamber to the canal of Schlemm.

visual s. Space as perceived through the sense of vision, having dimensional and directional attributes similar to, but not necessarily commensurate with, physical space.

zonular *s.* The circumlental space between the equator of the crystalline lens and the ciliary processes, bounded by the anterior and posterior leaves of the zonule of Zinn, and containing aqueous humor. Syn., *Hannover's canal; circumlental space; perilenticular space.*

Space Coordinator. An instrument primarily for the treatment of eccentric fixation designed by Cüppers and containing interchangeable fixation targets and a rotating transilluminated Polaroid filter which, when viewed through a blue filter, produces Haidinger brushes localized in relation to the fixation target, both of which are projected to a more distant plane seen through the instrument.

Spache binocular reading test (spätch). See under *test.*

span. A limited interval of space or time, or the representation of that interval by its contents or circumstances.

attention *s.* The amount of material that is grasped or perceived and dealt with or mentally processed in a single, continuous, uninterrupted period of attention, or the duration of this period.

recognition, *s. of.* The number of words, symbols, or digits, or the size of the field in which they are contained, that can be correctly identified or perceived during a time exposure sufficiently brief to exclude eye movement.

sparganosis, ocular (spar″gah-no′-sis). Infestation of the eyelids, conjunctiva, episclera, or orbit with *Sparganum mansoni,* the larvae of tapeworms.

sparing of the macula. See under *macula.*

sparkle. To glitter, gleam, or shine with a brilliant and broken scintillating light.

spasm. An anomalous, involuntary muscular contraction.

accommodation, *s. of.* A spasm of the ciliary muscle, producing excess accommodation.

accommodation, s. of (clonic). Alternate spasm and relaxation of the ciliary muscle.

accommodation, s. of (tonic). Prolonged uniform spasm of the ciliary muscle.

convergence, *s. of.* A spasm of the extraocular muscles producing excess convergence.

cyclic oculomotor *s.* Alternating spasm and relaxation of the sphincter pupillae muscle with similar involvement of other muscles innervated by the third cranial nerve, and occasionally those innervated by the fourth and sixth cranial nerves. During the miotic phase the upper eyelid retracts, the eye converges, and accommodation undergoes a spasm, and during the mydriatic phase there is almost complete total ophthalmoplegia with ptosis. The onset is usually at birth or early in life, and it affects females more frequently than males. Syn., *cyclic oculomotor paralysis.*

nictitating *s.* Spasmus nictitans.

nodding *s.* Spasmus nutans.

oculogyral *s.* A spasm of the extraocular muscles occurring in oculogyric crisis.

winking *s.* Spasmus nictitans.

spasmus (spaz′mus). A spasm.

mobilis, s. Catatonic pupil.

nictitans, s. A clonic spasm of the orbicularis oculi muscle causing an increase in the rate of blinking and a prolongation of the phase of eyelid closure. Syn., *nictitating spasm; winking spasm.*

nutans, s. Head nodding associated with nystagmus and occasionally with torticollis, occurring usually in the first year of life.

Head nodding is usually the first symptom, is frequently transient and inconstant, bears no relationship to the movements of the eyes, and does not occur when the head is supported. The nystagmus is constant, pendular, rapid, of small amplitude, may be horizontal, vertical, or rotary, is usually bilateral, with one eye affected more than the other, and disappears during sleep. The condition is of unknown etiology, but is thought to be related to a dimly illuminated environment with poor fixation control; the prognosis is favorable. Syn., *gyrospasm; nodding spasm.*

oculi, s. Nystagmus.

spatium (spa'she-um). A space.

anguli iridis, spatia. Spaces of Fontana.

interfasciale, s. Tenon's space.

intervaginalia nervi optici, spatia. Intervaginal spaces.

iridis, spatia. Spaces of Fontana.

perichoroideale, s. Perichoroidal space.

zonularia, s. Zonular space.

Speakman's endothelial meshwork. See under *meshwork.*

spectacle, primary. A fixed transparent cutaneous structure constituting a dermal cornea underneath which the eye is free to rotate, found in cyclostomes, tadpoles, and adult aquatic amphibians.

spectacle, secondary. A transparent window in a moveable lower eyelid, or a fixed transparent structure formed by fusion of the two eyelids which have become transparent, found in reptiles and lizards.

spectacles. A pair of ophthalmic lenses together with the frame or mounting.

anisometropic s. Spectacles in which one lens is of a significantly different refractive power from the other, for the correction of anisometropia.

Bartels' s. Spectacles with lenses of high refractive power (as +20.00 or −20.00 D.) used to impair vision while inducing optokinetic nystagmus by rotating a subject who is wearing them.

clerical s. Pantoscopic spectacles.

crutch s. Spectacles with a ptosis crutch attachment. Syn., *Masselon's spectacles.*

diver's s. Spectacles usually in some form of headgear and inserted in such a manner as to render them airtight and watertight, to enable the wearer to see under water.

folding s. Spectacles that are hinged or otherwise especially constructed so that the two lenses can be placed in apposition when not worn.

Franklin s. Spectacles containing Franklin bifocal lenses.

Frenzel s. Plano spectacles with a built-in light source for the purpose of dazzling the eyes and preventing fixation, used in a darkened room for the clinical detection of nystagmus.

Galilean s. Spectacles containing Galilean telescopic lenses, usually used as a subnormal vision aid.

half-eye s. Spectacles having semicircular lenses for only the upper or only the lower part of the field of view, the other part of the field being seen by the unaided eye.

hemianopic s. Spectacles with a prism, of approximately 8△, affixed to one lens with its base toward the blind side of the visual field, used to increase the field of vision on the blind side in homonymous hemianopsia by reflecting light onto the seeing side of the retina.

industrial s. Spectacles made of frames and lenses designed with protective and other features (hardened or plastic lenses, side shields, etc.) especially suitable or necessary in certain types of hazardous industrial occupations.

Lindner s. A spectacle frame with

a single pinhole aperture for each eye.

Masselon's s. Crutch spectacles.

meshed s. Spectacles in which the lenses are etched with a number of fine lines at right angles to each other, used to obscure vision in experiments for determining effects of reduced vision on visual perception.

microscopic s. Spectacles containing lenses of relatively high convex power ($+10.00$ D. or higher), used as a subnormal vision aid at near.

nose s. Spectacles held on the nose by spring pressure without the aid of temples, as in a pince-nez or an oxford.

orthopedic s. Spectacles with an attachment for the relief of an anatomical deformity, for example, spectacles with a ptosis crutch.

orthoscopic s. Spectacles in which the lenses are of strong convex power with base-in prism, used in fine near tasks to magnify and to reduce convergence.

pantoscopic s. Spectacles used for reading, in which the top halves of the lenses are cut off so as not to affect distant vision. Syn., *clerical spectacles; pulpit spectacles.*

pinhole s. Spectacles having, in place of lenses, opaque disks with one or more small perforations, used as an aid in certain types of subnormal vision, or as protection from bright light or glare.

pulpit s. Pantoscopic spectacles.

recumbent s. Spectacles having right-angle prism lenses which enable the wearer to read or do other near work while recumbent.

reversible s. Spectacles that present either lens to either eye. It may have either an X-shaped bridge with straight temples, or an arc-shaped bridge with double-jointed endpieces.

rimless s. Spectacles in which the lenses are fastened to the frame by cement, screws, or clamps but without supporting eyewires, the lens edges being exposed.

Ryer-Hotaling cataract s. Spectacles having amber lenses with an untinted reading segment, for use with cataractous eyes.

Scherer cataract s. Spectacles in which the peripheral portion of the reading lens in front of the cataractous eye is covered with an opaque shield, leaving a 10 mm., central, circular aperture.

stenopaic s. Spectacles having, in place of lenses, opaque disks containing narrow slits or circular perforations, used as a subnormal vision aid or as protection against bright light or glare.

telescopic s. Spectacles containing telescopic lenses, usually used as a subnormal vision aid.

tubular s. Spectacles containing small tubes which shield the eyes from extraneous light, used as a subnormal vision aid in corneal or lenticular opacities.

Spectograph (spek′to-graf). The trade name for an instrument that projects a magnified image of a contact lens onto a calibrated viewing screen for the purpose of inspection.

spectrocolorimeter (spek″tro-kul″or-im′eh-ter). A colorimeter employing a spectral source of light.

spectrogram (spek′tro-gram). The picture, or other record, of radiations taken by a spectrograph.

spectrograph (spek′tro-graf). An instrument for producing and photographing spectra of substances, consisting essentially of a diffraction grating, prism, or crystals, to disperse the radiations, and a camera to photograph them.

spectrometer (spek-trom′eh-ter). An instrument for producing and making measurements of a spectrum, for purposes of determining the index of refraction and other optical properties of a medium or source.

spectrometry (spek-trom'eh-tre). The measurement of wavelengths with the spectrometer.

spectrophotometer (spek"tro-fo-tom'eh-ter). An instrument for measuring the photic intensities of the various lines or regions of a spectrum.

spectrophotometry (spek"tro-fo-tom'eh-tre). Measurement of the intensity of various lines or regions of a spectrum with a spectrophotometer.

spectroprojector (spek"tro-pro-jek'-tor). An apparatus for projecting a spectrum onto a screen for group observation.

spectroradiometer (spek"tro-ra-dih-om'eh-ter). An instrument for measuring the radiant intensities of the various lines or regions of a spectrum.

spectroscope (spek'tro-skōp). An instrument for producing and observing spectra, consisting essentially of a diffraction grating, prism, or crystals to disperse the radiations and an eyepiece to view them.

spectroscopy (spek-tros'ko-pe). Producing and observing spectra with the spectroscope; the study of spectra.

spectrum (spek'trum). 1. The spatial arrangement or series of the dispersed components of radiant energy, in order of their wavelengths, emitted, absorbed, or reflected by a substance. 2. A series or a phenomenon, especially visual, having some of the attributes of a spectrum.

absorptance s. A graphical representation of the radiant flux absorbed by a substance, plotted against wavelength.

absorption s. A spectrum formed by passing light, which normally gives a continuous spectrum, through a selectively absorbing medium. The wavelengths which

are absorbed give rise to dark lines or bands in specific positions in the spectrum, indicating the chemical structure of the medium. In the solar spectrum the dark lines are termed Fraunhofer lines. Cf. *emission spectrum.*

action s. A graphical representation of the relative energy required to produce a constant biological effect, such as frequency of discharge in optic nerve fibers, plotted against wavelength.

atomic s. Line spectrum.

band s. A spectrum containing a series of bands, each with a sharply demarcated edge on one side called the *head.* Spectra of this type are produced by molecules and are distinguished from line spectra, which are produced by atoms. Syn., *molecular spectrum.*

bleaching s. A graphical representation of the bleaching effectiveness of radiant flux on a photopigment, plotted against wavelength.

channeled s. A bandlike spectrum formed by passing parallel white light through a plate or a thin film, producing alternate maxima and minima by selective interference.

chemical s. The ultraviolet portion of the spectrum.

chromatic s. That portion of the entire spectrum which includes visible radiations.

continuous s. A spectrum ranging continuously, without lines or bands, from the long red wavelengths to the short blue wavelengths, characteristic of gases under high pressure or of hot solids.

difference s. In densitometry or spectrophotometry, the change in spectral transmittance, absorbance, or reflectance of a substance which occurs as a result of exposure to radiant flux, or a graphical representation of such change as a function of wavelength.

diffraction s. A spectrum formed by a diffraction grating. Syn., *grating spectrum.*

discontinuous s. A spectrum in which some wavelengths are not present, as in a line or band spectrum, characteristic of gases and vapors under low pressure.

electromagnetic s. The spectrum including all known radiations, i.e., cosmic rays, gamma rays, x-rays, ultraviolet rays, visible rays, infrared rays, and radio waves. Syn., *energy spectrum; physical spectrum.*

emission s. A spectrum formed of radiations given off directly from excited bodies, as by heat or electric discharge. Cf. *absorption spectrum.*

energy s. Electromagnetic spectrum.

equal energy s. A spectrum characterized by equal flux per unit wavelength interval, i.e., the same amount of energy at each wavelength.

fortification s. The gradually expanding zigzag of colored light which forms the boundary of a scintillating scotoma, associated with migraine. Syn., *fortification figures.*

grating s. A spectrum formed by a diffraction grating. Syn., *diffraction spectrum.*

invisible s. The portions of the entire spectrum which lie at wavelengths too long or too short to stimulate the retina, i.e., approximately outside of the range between 380 and 760 mμ.

irrational s. A spectrum whose dispersion is not uniformly proportional to the wavelength, as characteristically obtained by a prism.

line s. A spectrum consisting of a series of distinct lines which are monochromatic images of the slit of the spectroscope, each image being formed by light of a particular wavelength. Spectra of this type arise from single or uncombined atoms and are distinguished from band spectra, which arise from molecules. Syn., *atomic spectrum.*

molecular s. Band spectrum.

normal s. 1. A spectrum in which the dispersion is in direct proportion to the wavelengths, as in one produced by a diffraction grating. 2. Diffraction spectrum.

photopic s. The spectral range of wavelengths visible as colors, hence that included within the range of the photopic spectral luminous efficiency curve, and ordinarily represented as the array of spectral colors.

physical s. 1. Electromagnetic spectrum. 2. The visible spectrum, extending from red to violet and exclusive of the purples. Cf. *physiological spectrum.*

physiological s. A perceptual spectrum which contains all the hues perceived, i.e., the visible spectrum, extending from red to violet, with the addition of the purples. Cf. *physical spectrum.*

prismatic s. A spectrum formed by passing a beam of light through a prism.

rational s. A spectrum whose dispersion is uniformly proportional to the wavelength, as normally produced by a diffraction grating.

reversed s. A spectrum, or a portion of a spectrum, which has been reversed, as by reflection in a mirror, for superimposition on another spectrum, not reversed, for spectral color mixing.

scotopic s. The spectral range of wavelengths visible at scotopic levels of luminosity, hence that included within the range of the scotopic spectral luminous efficiency curve, and ordinarily represented as an array of grays of varying intensity.

secondary s. A small circular zone

of color about each image point, due to chromatic aberration of the optical system.

solar s. The spectrum formed from sunlight, normally characterized by numerous Fraunhofer absorption lines.

thermal s. The infrared portion of the spectrum.

visible s. The portion of the electromagnetic spectrum which contains wavelengths capable of stimulating the retina, approximately between 380 and 760 mμ.

speed of recognition. The time rate at which symbols, digits, or words of a specific angular subtense at the eye, can be correctly perceived or identified without eye movement. It is usually determined with the use of a tachistoscope.

speed, saccadic. The speed of movement of the eye in changing fixation from one point to another.

sph. Abbreviation for *sphere* or *spherical*.

sphere. 1. A body or a space bounded by a surface, all points of which are equidistant from a point within, termed its center. 2. A spherical lens.

color s. A spherical color solid; an orderly arrangement of all colors according to hue, value (brightness or lightness), and chroma (saturation), represented by position co-ordinates within a sphere. Black and white are represented at opposite poles, hues are arranged longitudinally around the circumference at the equator, and chroma or saturation is represented by the distance from the polar axis. See also *color tree*.

far point s. of the eye. The locus of the far points of accommodation for all directions of gaze.

Morgagnian s's. Morgagnian globules.

near point s. of the eye. The locus of the near points of accommodation for all directions of gaze.

vertex s. A surface, concentric with the center of rotation of the eye, on which the back vertex of the ophthalmic lens is situated.

spherocylinder (sfe″ro-sil′in-der). A spherocylindrical lens.

spherometer (sfe-rom′eh-ter). 1. An instrument for determining the curvature of a surface by measuring its sagittal depth, consisting essentially of three fixed legs in an equilateral triangle formation and a fourth adjustable central leg attached to a micrometer scale. 2. An instrument based on the Drysdale method for determining the curvature of a surface.

spherophakia (sfe″ro-fa′ke-ah). Microphakia.

spheroprism (sfe-ro-prizm′). A spherical lens eccentrically mounted or decentered to produce prismatic effect; a combined spherical lens and prism. Syn., *prismosphere*.

spherule (sfer′ūl). A small sphere.

Morgagnian s's. Morgagnian globules.

rod s. End bulb.

sphincter (sfingk′ter). A muscle which surrounds an orifice or opening and acts to close or reduce it.

iridis, s. Sphincter pupillae muscle.

oculi, s. Orbicularis oculi muscle.

palpebrarum, s. Orbicularis oculi muscle.

pupillae, s. Sphincter pupillae muscle.

sphincterectomy (sfingk″ter-ek′to-me). Excision of a sphincter muscle, such as the sphincter pupillae or orbicularis oculi.

sphincterolysis (sfingk″ter-ol′ih-sis). Surgical freeing of the iris from the cornea in anterior synechia.

sphincterotomy (sfingk″ter-ot′o-me). Surgical incision into the sphincter pupillae muscle of the iris.

Spielmeyer-Stock disease (spēl′ma-er-stok). Batten-Mayou disease.

Spielmeyer-Vogt disease (spēl′ma-er-fōgt). Batten-Mayou disease.

spike, blue. An entoptic phenomenon elicited by a spot of light stimulating the nasal parafoveal area. The subjective sensation is of a single strip of blue light running horizontally and downward to the blind spot.

spina (spi'nah). A spine.

recti lateralis, s. A small bony projection on the orbital plate of the great wing of the sphenoid bone, situated on the inferior margin of the superior orbital fissure at the junction of its wide and narrow portions. To it are attached the annulus of Zinn and a part of the lateral rectus muscle.

trochlearis, s. A small bony projection surmounting the trochlear fossa, in the anteromedial roof of the orbit, representing an ossification of the fibrocartilagenous attachment of the pulley for the superior oblique muscle.

spindle, color. A type of color solid.

spindle, Krukenberg's. A vertically oriented, spindle-shaped deposition of melanin pigment on the corneal endothelium in the region of the pupil, occurring bilaterally as a congenital or presenile pigmentation, or unilaterally as the result of uveitis.

spine, trochlear. The spina trochlearis.

spintherism (spin'ther-izm). Entoptic perception of sparks or flashes of light; photopsia. Syn., *spintheropia.*

spintheropia (spin"ther-o'pe-ah). Spintherism.

spiral, Cornu. A spiral of two oppositely coiled branches symmetrically located in opposite quadrants, each branch of which is the diagram of vector amplitudes corresponding to a half of a cylindrical wavefront.

spirals of Daniel. Simple or complex spirals of fibers of the oculomotor nerve encircling fibers of the extraocular muscles and con-

Fig. 39. Plateau's spiral. (From *Text-book of Ophthalmology*, Vol. I, Duke-Elder, Henry Kimpton, 1942)

sidered to subserve proprioception.

spiral, Plateau's. A circular white disk on which is painted a black spiral-like band with its origin at the center. When the disk is rotated and fixated at its center, the spiral band gives the illusion of moving forward or backward in a megaphonelike formation, with its small end toward or away from the observer, depending on the direction of rotation of the disk. Following exposure to the rotating disk, if another motionless object is fixated, it will appear to swell and come forward or shrink and move backward, the effect of this motion afterimage being opposite to the effect produced when fixating the rotating disk.

spiral of Tillaux. A diagrammatic spiral line connecting the points of insertion of the four recti muscles; used as a guide in approximating the distance of the insertions from the limbus.

Spitzka's bundle (spitz'kahz). See under *bundle.*

splitter. The first basic component of an interferometer which separates the incident light into two coherent beams.

spondylitis, ankylosing (spon"dih-li'tis). Rheumatoid arthritis of the spine occurring primarily in young males. Iridocyclitis is a frequent accompaniment. Syn., *Bechterew's disease; Strümpell-Marie disease; rhizomelic spondylosis.*

spondylosis, rhizomelic (spon"dih-lo'sis). Ankylosing spondylitis.

spongioneuroblastoma (spon"je-o-nu"ro-blas-to'mah). A malignant neoplasm composed of spongioblastic and neuronal components in different stages of maturity, occurring in the central nervous system, retina, and ciliary epithelium.

spot. A small, circumscribed area differing, as in color or content, from its ground.

Arago's s. 1. A physiological negative scotoma present in low levels of illumination corresponding to the rod-free area at the center of the fovea. 2. Poisson spot.

Bitot's s's. Small, white or gray, sharply defined spots appearing on dried areas of the palpebral conjunctiva in xerosis of the conjunctiva from vitamin A deficiency. They have a soapy appearance, as of dried foam, and are at first oval in shape and then triangular, with the base toward the limbus.

blind s., baring of. The condition in which contraction of the temporal peripheral visual field is so marked that the temporal limit of the visual field lies on, or nasal to, the blind spot of Mariotte. Cf. *inverted uncinate visual field; uncinate visual field.*

blind s. of Mariotte. A physiological negative scotoma in the visual field corresponding to the head of the optic nerve which is insensitive to light stimulation. It is typically oval in shape, approximately 7.5° along its vertical axis and 5.5° along its horizontal axis, and its center is located 15.5° to the temporal side and 1.5° below the point of fixation. Syn., *punctum caecum; physiological blind spot; Mariotte's spot.*

blind s., physiological. Blind spot of Mariotte.

Brushfield's s's. Small, white or light yellow flecks on the iris of infant Mongolian idiots.

cherry-red s. A red spot in the center of a white, edematous, and/or atrophic macular area appearing in the fundus in Tay-Sachs disease and in occlusion of the central retinal artery. It has the coloring of the normal fovea, due to choroidal circulation, but appears redder by contrast to the surrounding whitened retina.

corneal s. An opacity of the cornea, as a leukoma or a macula.

cotton-wool s's. White, fluffy-appearing patches, occurring in edematous areas of the retina, as may occur in hypertensive retinopathy. They are coagulated exudates of plasma and fibrin from the retinal capillaries distal to angiospastic arterioles. Syn., *cotton-wool patches.*

Dalén's s's. Small white spots, resembling drusen, which may occur in the fundus as an early sign of sympathetic ophthalmia, due to changes in the pigment epithelium layer of the retina.

Elschnig s's. Small bright red or yellow spots with isolated flecks of black pigment at their borders, appearing in the fundus in advanced hypertensive retinopathy.

eye s. Eyespot.

flame s's. Flame-shaped areas characteristic of hemorrhage into the nerve fiber layer of the retina.

Fuchs's s. A round and sharply defined black spot occasionally occupying the macular area, due to degenerative changes in high myopia. Syn., *Foster-Fuchs fleck.*

Gaule's s's. Sharply circumscribed areas of degenerated corneal epithelium, sometimes appearing in neuroparalytic keratitis. Syn., *Gaule's pits.*

glaucoma s's. Multiple, circumscribed, white spots beneath the anterior lens capsule, occurring in association with glaucoma. See also *cataracta glaucomatosa acuta.*

von Graefe's s's. Areas over the vertebrae or near the supraorbital foramen which, when pressed, result in relaxation of the orbicularis oculi muscle in blepharofacial spasm.

green s. A spot occupying the macular area, similar to Fuchs's spot, but of a greenish coloration, due to degenerative changes in high myopia.

Koplik's s's. Pale whitish spots appearing in the mucous membrane of the mouth, and sometimes in the conjunctiva, in the prodromal stage of measles.

Mariotte's s. Blind spot of Mariotte.

Maxwell's s. An entoptically seen, darkened spot in the visual field corresponding to the fovea, observed on fixating a diffusely illuminated field, especially a field of dark blue or purplish-blue color, used clinically to detect anomalous fixation or the integrity of the foveal area.

Michel's s's. An atrophic patch of the iris, with the posterior pigment epithelium visible, as may result from a tuberculomatous nodule. Syn., *Michel's flecks.*

Mueller's s's. Small, white, depigmented areas on the iris resulting from local circumscribed atrophy, as may occur after an attack of smallpox.

Poisson s. A bright spot in the center of a shadow created by a circular or spherical obstruction in the path of a light source, due to diffraction. It is as bright as if no obstruction were present.

Roth's s's. Small white spots, frequently surrounded by hemorrhage so that the latter appears to have a white center, occurring in the fundus near the optic disk in Roth's disease. Syn., *Roth's patches.*

Siegrist's s's. Chains of pigmented spots which course along the paths of sclerosed choroidal vessels, occurring in the fundus in advanced hypertensive retinopathy.

snow bank s's. Cotton-wool spots.

Soemmering's s. Macula lutea.

Tay's s. The cherry-red spot seen in the macular area in Tay-Sachs disease.

yellow s. Macula lutea.

S-potential. An intraretinal electrical potential assumed to be generated in the regions of the outer molecular or outer nuclear layers which has a square waveform whose amplitude remains nearly constant as long as the stimulus light is in effect. It is not considered to be a receptor potential nor to contribute directly to the ERG.

spur. A projecting structure or formation.

Fuchs, s. of. A spur of indented, iridic, posterior pigment epithelium into the posterior surface of the sphincter pupillae muscle, about midway along its length, associated with the junction of a few fibers of the dilator pupillae muscle.

Grünert's s. A spur of indented, iridic, posterior pigment epithelium at the junction of the iris and the ciliary body, marking the peripheral termination of the dilator pupillae muscle.

Michel's s. A spur of indented, iridic, posterior pigment epithelium marking the peripheral border of the sphincter pupillae muscle and its juncture with fibers of the dilator pupillae muscle.

scleral s. A dense mass of circularly arranged scleral fibers at the level of the limbus, interposed between the posterior portion of

Schlemm's canal and the anterior attachment of the ciliary muscle, terminating at the meshwork of the angle of the anterior chamber. Syn., *annular ligament; Schwalbe's posterior ring.*

Spurway's syndrome (spur'wāz). Eddowes' syndrome.

squint. Strabismus.

Squint Korector, Arneson. An orthoptic instrument consisting essentially of a large, circular, motor-rotated disk mounted vertically on a stand. On the surface of the disk are an E-shaped design in three colors and an eccentrically located, movable, small, ruby glass, fixation target.

Stähli's line (shta'lēz). Superficial senile line.

staining. The artificial coloration of tissue in order to facilitate its study.

ocular s. Staining of ocular tissue (cornea and conjunctiva) by instilling a dye into the conjunctival sac. The tissue which retains the dye is either abraded, dead, or degenerated.

surface s. The usual form of ocular staining in which a 1 or 2% solution of fluorescein or rose bengal is instilled only once so as to stain only the superficial layers.

vital s. A seldom used form of ocular staining in which a dye, such as a dilute solution of azure II, is instilled several times so as to stain debilitated living cells.

staircase, Schroeder's. Schroeder's figure.

stalk, lens. A pedicle of cells by which the newly formed lens vesicle in the embryo is still attached to the surface ectoderm. It atrophies, and the lens vesicle separates from the surface ectoderm at about the fourth or fifth week of embryonic life.

stalk, optic. Optic pedicle.

standard, GOMAC. GOMAC method.

standard deviation; error. See under the nouns.

Stanford stereoscope (stan'ford). See under *stereoscope.*

Stanloscope (stan'lo-skōp). An instrument used in visual training which doubles the image from a motion picture projector. Each of the doubled images is passed through a Polaroid or color filter and is viewed through a Polaroid or color filter, so that each eye sees only one of the images.

staphyloma (staf"ih-lo'mah). A bulging or protrusion of the cornea or the sclera, usually containing adherent uveal tissue.

annular s. Ring staphyloma.

anterior s. 1. Corneal staphyloma. 2. Staphyloma anterior to the equator of the eyeball.

anterior s., congenital. A corneal staphyloma existing since birth, characterized by a bulging opaque cornea lined on its posterior surface by an incarcerated iris.

ciliary s. Anterior scleral staphyloma occurring in the region of the ciliary body and lined with prolapsed tissue of the ciliary body.

corneae racemosum, s. Corneal staphyloma resulting from a number of corneal perforations in each of which is incarcerated iridic tissue.

corneal s. A bulging cicatrix of the cornea formed essentially by prolapsed iris partially converted into fibrous scar tissue. Syn., *anterior staphyloma.*

equatorial s. Scleral staphyloma occurring in the region of the equator of the eyeball, especially in the area of exit of the vortex veins.

intercalary s. Anterior scleral staphyloma occurring between the anterior extremity of the ciliary body and the iris and lined with tissue from the root of the iris.

posterior s. Scleral staphyloma occurring posterior to the equator of the eyeball, especially in the region of the posterior pole.

posterior s. of von Ammon. Posterior protrusion of von Ammon.

posticum of Scarpa, s. Posterior staphyloma occurring at the posterior pole of the eyeball, due to degenerative changes in high myopia. Syn., *Scarpa's staphyloma; staphyloma verum.*

ring s. An anterior scleral staphyloma around the cornea in the ciliary region formed by the confluence of smaller staphylomata. Syn., *annular staphyloma.*

Scarpa's s. Staphyloma posticum of Scarpa.

scleral s. A bulging or protrusion of a thin or weakened sclera, ordinarily lined with uveal tissue.

scleral s., anterior. Staphyloma of the sclera anterior to the equator of the eyeball, occurring either as a *ciliary staphyloma* or as an *intercalary staphyloma.*

verum, s. Staphyloma posticum of Scarpa.

staphylomatous (staf"ih-lom'ah-tus). Pertaining to, resembling, or affected with staphyloma.

staphylotomy (staf"ih-lot'o-me). Surgical incision of a staphyloma.

star. A figure having five or more points representing a star, or anything which is like or suggests a star or such a figure.

lens s's. The starlike formations, one in the anterior and one in the posterior portion of the crystalline lens, formed by the sutures of the lens fibers.

muscle s's. Groups of smooth cell fibers arranged in star-shaped configurations, located in the suprachoroid in the region of the equator of the eyeball, where they are continuous with Brücke's muscle.

Siemens' s. A target for testing the resolution of an optical system consisting of a circle containing alternate black and white wedge-shaped spokes of equal size whose apices all meet at a common point at the center of the circle. The resolution is determined by the diameter of the area of central blur resulting from lack of resolution of the spokes.

Winslow's s's. Whorls of capillaries in the choroid which drain into the vorticose veins. Syn., *stellulae vasculosae winslowii.*

stare. To gaze or look fixedly; a fixed gaze.

postbasic s. A stare characteristic of posterior basic meningitis in which the eyeballs are rotated downward and the upper eyelids are retracted.

Stargardt's (stahr'gahrtz) **disease; macula degeneration; foveal dystrophy.** See under *disease.*

Stark effect. See under *effect.*

stasis, papillary (sta'sis). Cessation of the flow of blood in the retinal vessels in the region of the optic disk, due to papilledema.

statistics. 1. The science of the collection, classification, and systematic compilation of data on the basis of the relative number or occurrence in a given group or population so as to analyze, describe, or infer certain basic relationships or tendencies. 2. Classified data showing the relative or actual number or frequency of occurrence in a given group or population.

statometer (stah-tom'eh-ter). An instrument for determining the degree of proptosis in exophthalmos.

statoscope (stat'o-skōp). An instrument consisting essentially of a tube in which a light source, a blue filter, a diaphragm, and a lens are so arranged that parallel light is reflected into one eye by a plane mirror, to be fixated while the other eye is being examined with a retinoscope. Syn., *photo-scope*.

status **Bonnevie-Ullrich.** Lymphatic edema of the hands and feet, pterygium colli, malformation of the ears, muscle defects (especially of the pectoralis), hypertelorism, epicanthus, syndactyly and other digital deformities, and paralyses of the third, sixth, seventh, and twelfth nerves; occurring as a hereditary congenital anomaly. Syn., *Bonnevie-Ullrich syndrome.*

steatoma of the eyelid (ste″ah-to′-mah). A sebaceous cyst or tumor, associated with the hairs of the eyelid, encapsulated by fibrous tissue and containing disintegrated epithelial cells, keratin, cholesterol crystals, and fatty granules. Syn., *atheroma of the eyelid.*

steatosis corneae (ste″ah-to′sis). Dystrophia adiposa corneae.

Stefan-Boltzmann law (shta′fahn-bōlts′mahn). See under *law.*

Steiger's theory. (sti′gerz). See under *theory.*

Steinert's disease (sti′nertz). Myotonic dystrophy.

Steinheil cone (stīn′hīl). See under *cone.*

stella (stel′ah). A star.

   lentis hyaloidea, s. The posterior pole of the crystalline lens of the eye.

   lentis iridica, s. The anterior pole of the crystalline lens of the eye.

stellulae vasculosae winslowii (stel′-u-le vas″ku-lo′se wins-lo′ih-i). Winslow's stars.

Stellwag's (stel′vagz) **sign; symptom.** See under the nouns.

stenochoria (sten″o-ko′re-ah). Stenosis, or narrowing, particularly of a lacrimal duct.

stenocoriasis (sten″o-ko-ri′ah-sis). Constriction of the pupil of the eye.

stenopaic (sten″o-pa′ik) **disk; slit.** See under the nouns.

stenopia (steh-no′pe-ah). Hypotelorism.

step, Roenne's nasal. A steplike defect in the nasal visual field, caused by asymmetrical involvement of the retinal nerve fibers on either side of the horizontal raphe, indicative of glaucoma.

stereo-acuity (ster″e-o-ah-ku′ih-te). The ability to perceive depth by the faculty of stereopsis, represented as a function of the threshold of stereopsis.

stereocampimeter (ster″e-o-kam-pim′eh-ter). A haploscopic type of instrument used for examination of the visual fields, especially the central fields, in which the fields of view of the two eyes are separated and in which the eyes fixate similar targets to be fused, thus enabling the plotting of the visual field of one eye under conditions of binocular fixation. One type is similar to a Brewster stereoscope and another type has a movable mirror to reflect the test target into one eye while the target of the other is directly viewed.

stereocomparator (ster″e-o-kom-par′-ah-ter). A variable pair or a graduated series of disparately fused fiducial lines or reticles incorporated in the optics of a binocular viewing instrument to serve as a stereoscopic reference for judging the distances of viewed objects; a binocular instrument incorporating this feature.

stereocryptogram (ster″e-o-krip′to-gram). A typewritten stereogram in which the words or letters, constituting an otherwise unnoticed message or legend, are displaced horizontally so that they appear to stand out or recede from the plane of reference of the binocularly fused stereogram.

stereodisparator (ster″e-o-dis′pah-ra″ter). Disparator.

stereogram (ster'e-o-gram"). A target composed of a pair of drawings or similar photographs side by side such that, when viewed in a stereoscope, the right eye sees only the right side drawing or photograph and the left eye only the left side. If the corresponding parts of the drawings have been properly decentered, or the photographs are of a single scene taken from two directions, the stereogram, when properly fused, will give rise to the percept of relief or stereopsis. Syn., *stereograph*.

Dvorine animated fusion s's. A series of stereograms, each of which contains an aperture on the one side so that a rotatable disk mounted on this side may present a variety of pictures to the one eye. Thus, e.g., one side of the stereogram may present a cage and the other side may present either a tiger, a lion, or a bear.

parallax s. A stereogram consisting of a composite photograph taken with a camera having two apertures and a grid interposed between the lens system and the film. The resultant photograph consists of alternate vertical parallel strips, each alternate strip being formed through one aperture. The stereogram is viewed through a screen of alternate opaque and transparent bands, so that the left eye is exposed to the portions of the photograph taken through the left aperture and the right eye through the right aperture.

rotating s. A stereogram in which the two pictures may be rotated simultaneously, by a central cogwheel, to produce variations in the stereoscopic effect.

split s. A stereogram in two separate halves to permit variable vertical and lateral separations in the stereoscope.

stereograph (ster'e-o-graf"). Stereogram.

stereography (ster"e-og'rah-fe). The representing or delineating of three dimensional attributes in a single plane, as in a stereogram; making a stereogram.

stereomicrocamera (ster"e-o-mi'kro-kam"er-ah). A stereocamera which magnifies as it photographs.

stereomicrography (ster"e-o-mi-krog'-rah-fe). Photography with a stereomicrocamera.

stereomicrometer, Howard's (ster"-e-o-mi-krom'eh-ter). A binocular instrument with micrometer control of the lateral position of one of four vertical wires in the focal plane of the eyepieces, two seen by each eye, to be fused stereoscopically and adjusted for stereo judgments.

stereomicroscope (ster"e-o-mi'kro-skōp). Two complete microscope systems mounted in a single unit to permit binocular viewing of the object or specimen. Cf. *binocular microscope*.

stereomonoscope (ster"e-o-mon'o-skōp). An instrument which, by means of two separate and differently oriented lens systems, projects onto the same portion of a ground glass plate two images which appear in relief when viewed binocularly from the proper direction and distance.

Stereomotivator (ster"e-o-mo"tih-va'-tor). A visual training instrument consisting of a target holder for a laminar series of three projector slides or transparencies, the top two of which are of red and green color composition and synchronously and laterally displaceable in opposite directions to produce stereoscopic and prismatic effects when viewed by transillumination or by projection on a screen while wearing a red filter before one eye and a green filter before the other eye.

stereo-ophthalmoscope (ster″e-o-of-thal′mo-skōp). A binocular ophthalmoscope.

Stereo-orthopter (ster″e-o-ōr-thop′-ter). A visual training instrument, similar to a Wheatstone stereoscope, consisting essentially of two front surface mirrors joined at an angle at one end to reflect targets, one into each eye, and eyepieces of spherical convex lens power to reduce or eliminate accommodative demands. The angular separation of the mirrors may be varied to alter prismatic effect and a built-in motor provides for lateral rotation of the mirrors about a point where they meet and for introducing various flash patterns.

stereoperception (ster″e-o-per-sep′-shun). Stereopsis.

stereophantoscope (ster″e-o-fan′to-skōp). A stereoscope in which, instead of still pictures, rotating stroboscopic disks are used to impart apparent motion to the views.

stereophenomenon, Pulfrich (ster″-e-o-fe-nom′e-non). Pulfrich effect.

stereophorometer (ster″e-o-fo-rom′-eh-ter). A phorometer with an attachment for the use of stereograms.

stereophoroscope (ster″e-o-fōr′o-skōp). An early instrument for producing a series of images in apparent motion and in relief, consisting essentially of a series of stereograms attached to a many-sided prism rotating about a horizontal axis, to be viewed in rapid sequence in a Brewster stereoscope.

stereophotogram (ster″e-o-fo′to-gram). Paired photographs of the same scene taken from two stations which, when viewed through an appropriate haploscopic optical system, give rise to a three-dimensional percept.

stereophotography (ster″e-o-fo-tog′-rah-fe). Photography to produce pictures which give rise to the percept of the third dimension when viewed through a device such as a stereoscope. Syn., *stereography*.

stereophotometry. (ster″e-o-fo-tom′eh-tre). Subjective photometry based on the Pulfrich effect, in which the apparent path of a laterally moving spot or pendulum bob is changed from an ellipse, when the background luminosity differs for the two eyes, to its true on-plane motion when the background luminosity is the same.

stereopsis (ster″e-op′sis). 1. Binocular visual perception of three dimensional space based on retinal disparity. 2. Visual perception of depth or three dimensional space.

amplitude of s. See under *amplitude*.

anteroscopic s. Stereopsis in which objects appear closer than the plane of the stereogram.

axial s. Central stereopsis.

binocular s. Stereopsis based on depth clues present only when both eyes are in use, such as retinal disparity.

central s. Stereopsis based on retinal disparity within the foveal or the macular areas. Syn., *axial stereopsis*.

chrome s. Chromostereopsis.

monocular s. Perception of the third dimension based on depth clues not dependent on binocular vision, such as shadows, aerial perspective, or contour interference. Such clues are not exclusive to monocular vision, but are usually more effective in the absence of conflicting binocular clues, as may be noted by viewing a photograph monocularly.

peripheral s. Stereopsis based on retinal disparity stimuli peripheral to the maculae.

range of s. See under *range*.

retroscopic s. Stereopsis in which objects appear farther away than the plane of the stereogram.

stereoptor, Verhoeff's (ster″e-op′-ter). A small, hand-size, trans-illuminated, black frame with three opaque, different-sized bars which can be presented in a variety of orders with one always being a fixed distance behind or in front of the other two; it is used to measure stereopsis by determining the maximum viewing distance at which the displaced bar can be identified.

stereoradiography (ster″e-o-ra″-de-og′rah-fe). Stereoroentgenography.

Stereo-Reader, Delacato (ster″e-o-re′der). A visual training instrument consisting essentially of a Brewster-type stereoscope with a flat platform on which target material is presented to either or both eyes. A reading guide attachment may be utilized before either eye.

stereorefraction (ster″e-o-re-frak′-shun). Refraction performed while the patient is binocularly viewing projected stereo-inducing targets through Polaroid filters. The usual procedure is to project a stereo picture or scene with a central clear area on which the polarized test targets are projected from a second instrument. Adjustments may be made for central occlusion of one eye during monocular testing of the other.

stereoroentgenography (ster″e-o-rent″gen-og′rah-fe). The making of a stereogram containing two roentgen ray photographs. Syn., *stereoradiography.*

stereoscope (ster′e-o-skōp″). An instrument which separates the field of view of the two eyes, either by tubes, a septum, or an arrangement of mirrors, so that only certain portions of stereogram targets viewed through it

are seen by one eye and other portions by the other eye to give rise to a combined binocular percept. Usually spheroprism eyepieces are used in conjunction with the septum or the tubes and spherical eyepieces with the mirrors.

Asher-Law s. A Brewster-type, hand stereoscope with a disparator attachment for use with split stereograms.

automatic s. A stereoscope with an attachment housing a number of stereograms, so that they may be successively viewed by manipulating a lever or turning a knob.

book s. A folding stereoscope.

Brewster's s. A pyramidal-shaped stereoscope consisting essentially of two tubes, acting to separate the fields of view of the two eyes, and containing double convex base-out spheroprism eyepieces of 6 in. focal length, which are adjustable for interpupillary distance and distance from the targets at the base of the instrument. Syn., *Brewster-Holmes stereoscope; lenticular stereoscope; prismatic stereoscope; refracting stereoscope.*

chain s. A Brewster-type stereoscope in which a series of stereograms are attached to a chain affixed to sprockets, so that the turning of a knob rotates successive stereograms into view.

Cross's s. A Brewster-type, hand stereoscope with a target holder consisting of a rotatable fourteen-sided drum, on each face of which is mounted a stereogram for individual viewing.

Cruise s. A Brewster-type, hand stereoscope in which the eyepieces may be rotated to provide variable prism power.

Derby's s. A Brewster-type stereoscope containing spheroprism eyepieces (+7.00 D. lenses combined with 5△ base-out) which are attached to a screw mounting for adjustment of the interpupillary distance, and a target holder marked off in square centimeters on which are attached small, circular, split targets.

Dynamic s. Dynascope.

Ellis s. A Brewster-type, hand stereoscope containing +4.00 D. spheroprism lenses, cells for use of auxiliary prisms or lenses, and a movable target carrier.

Engelmann s. Dynascope.

folding s. A simplified Brewster-type stereoscope in which the eyepieces are mounted in material which can be folded. It usually contains no target holder and is held manually before the eyes when viewing stereograms (usually those contained in books). Syn., *book stereoscope.*

Hartline's s. A Wheatstone-type stereoscope in which the angle between the two mirrors is adjustable.

Holmes's s. A Brewster-type, hand stereoscope with a movable target holder and eyepieces of +5.25 D. spheres so decentered as to produce about 8^Δ base-out before each eye.

Javal's s. 1. A Brewster-type stereoscope in which narrow split targets may be moved laterally or vertically in the plane of the target holder. 2. A Wheatstone-type stereoscope in which two plane mirrors are hinged together, each of which in turn has attached at its opposite end a target holder at a 45° angle, providing a view of each target by one eye, while the angle between the two mirrors may be adjusted to the desired convergence stimulus.

kinetic s. A Brewster-type stereoscope having a variable separation split-target holder mounted on a rotatable grooved arc mechanism, providing for variations in direction of fixation in all meridians independent of the convergence demand.

Landolt's s. A box stereoscope, 166 mm. long, in which the optical system consists of any pair of desired trial case lenses or prisms.

lens s. Lenticular stereoscope.

lenticular s. A stereoscope containing spheroprisms for eyepieces, together with a septum to separate the fields of view of the two eyes, as in the Brewster stereoscope. Syn., *lens stereoscope; prismatic stereoscope; refracting stereoscope.*

mirror s. A stereoscope in which mirrors separate the fields of view of the two eyes, as in the Wheatstone stereoscope. Syn., *reflecting stereoscope.*

phoro-optometer s. A phoro-optometer with a target holder for stereograms.

Pigeon-Cantonnet s. A visual training instrument consisting of three black, stiff, cardboard leaves, 31.5 x 23 cm., hinged together at one end, as in a book, with a small plane mirror placed on one face of the middle leaf, and targets or patterns on the inner faces of the two outer leaves. When the middle leaf is held to the nose as a septum, one target may be seen directly by one eye and the other by reflection in the mirror, and the convergence demand may be controlled by the angle between the outer leaves and the position of the targets on their inner faces.

Polack's s. A Brewster-type, hand stereoscope containing two rotary prisms for eyepieces which may be synchronously rotated to provide prism effects varying from 0° to 18°.

prismatic s. 1. Lenticular stereoscope. 2. A Wheatstone-type stereoscope containing reflecting prisms in place of plane mirrors.

Pulfrich s. A Wheatstone-type stereoscope containing two 90°

reflecting prisms for eyepieces.

reflecting s. Mirror stereoscope.

refracting s. Lenticular stereoscope.

Stanford s. A Wheatstone-type stereoscope for viewing roentgen ray stereograms.

Wheatstone s. A stereoscope consisting of two plane mirrors joined at one edge at a 90° angle and two target holders, one opposite one mirror and the other opposite the other, mounted on a screw base which, when turned, synchronously moves the targets toward or away from each other. Syn., *Wheatstone amblyoscope; reflecting stereoscope.*

Whittington s. A Brewster-type stereoscope designed primarily for cheiroscopic drawing.

stereoscopic (ster″e-o-skop′ik). Pertaining to or producing stereopsis.

relief, s. See under *relief.*

stereoscoptometer (ster″e-o-skoptom′eh-ter). An instrument for determining the threshold of depth perception.

stereoscopy (ster″e-os′ko-pe). 1. The science treating of stereoscopic effects and the methods of producing them. 2. Seeing in the third dimension.

color s. 1. Chromostereopsis. 2. Stereoscopic viewing accomplished by means of a red filter in front of one eye and a green filter in front of the other and a composite picture or pattern whose red detail represents the view of one eye and the green detail the view of the other.

irradiation s. The perception of stereoscopic relief in a flat target resulting from retinal images of a different effective size, produced by reducing the irradiation of one eye by means of a neutral filter, the difference in effective image size causing an apparent rotation of the frontoparallel plane about a vertical axis. It may be observed by binocularly fixating a point on either side of which are white squares in the frontoparallel plane, with a neutral filter before one eye.

stereostroboscope (ster″e-o-stro′bo-skōp). An apparatus for producing binocular relief effects by means of differential or asynchronous stroboscopic views presented separately but concurrently to the two eyes.

stereotest, Wirt (ster′e-o-test). Wirt test.

stereothreshold. Threshold of stereopsis.

Stevens' (ste′vens) **clinoscope; phorometer; test; tropometer.** See under the nouns.

Stevens-Johnson (ste′vens-jon′son) **disease; syndrome.** See under the nouns.

Stieda's (ste′dahz) **grooves; plateaus.** See under the nouns.

Stifel's figure (sti′felz). See under *figure.*

stigma. Eyespot.

stigmas, hysterical (stig′mahz). The specific symptoms of hysteria including reversal of the color visual fields, contraction of the visual field, and transient amblyopia.

stigmatic (stig-mat′ik). Affected with or pertaining to stigmatism.

stigmatism (stig′mah-tizm). The condition in which light from a point source is brought to a point focus by a lens or an optical system.

stigmatometer (stig″mah-tom′eh-ter). An instrument for measuring refractive error by the criterion of sharpness of appearance or imagery of a very small pointlike source of light. Syn., *oculometer.*

stigmatoscope (stig-mat′o-skōp). 1. An instrument for observing the character or pattern of a very small pointlike source of light in relation to the refractive error. 2. A stigmatometer.

stigmatoscopy (stig″mah-tos′ko-pe). Observation or measurement of the refractive state of the eye by means of a stigmatoscope.

objective s. A modified method of retinoscopy in which the observer moves his head instead of the light source or the mirror.

stilb (stil′b). A unit of luminance equal to 1 candela per sq. cm. See also *footlambert.*

Stiles theory. See under *theory.*

Stiles-Crawford effect (stīlz-kraw′-ford). See under *effect.*

Still's disease. Juvenile polyarthritis.

stillicidium lacrimarum (stil″ih-sid′-e-um lak-rih-mah′rum). Epiphoria. *Obs.*

Stilling's (stil′ingz) **canal; charts; plates; test; theory.** See under the nouns.

Stilling-Türk-Duane syndrome. Duane's syndrome.

Stimson charts. See under *chart.*

stimulation. The act or the effect of applying a stimulus.

biretinal kinetic s. Stimulation of the peripheral retinae by viewing in an amblyoscope superimposition targets which are locked at the objective angle of strabismus and then moved laterally back and forth while the eyes remain motionless in the straightforward position; a method designed to reestablish normal retinal correspondence by attempting to obtain peripheral superimposition.

peripheral s. In visual training, the haploscopic presentation of peripherally located patterns to one eye, while the other eye fixates a centrally located object, to break down suppression.

stimulus. Any agent, condition, or environmental change having the capability or property of influencing the activity of living protoplasm or of initiating or controlling a response, a percept, or a sensation, especially through the medium of a sense organ or receptor.

achromatic s. Neutral stimulus.

adequate s. 1. A stimulus of sufficient magnitude and/or of appropriate character to elicit, control, or influence a response, a percept, or a sensation, with respect to a given type of receptor mechanism. 2. A stimulus of a type for which the receptor is especially sensitive, such as wavelengths within the visible spectrum for the rods and cones.

cardinal stimuli. Four standard visual stimuli by means of which three reference stimuli and the basic stimulus of any trichromatic system may be defined. Light of wavelengths 700, 546.1 and 435.8 mμ and Illuminant B have been adopted by the C.I.E.

color s. A photic stimulus capable of eliciting the sensation of color.

equal-energy s. Photic radiation whose irradiance per unit wavelength is equal throughout the spectrum.

inadequate s. 1. A stimulus of insufficient magnitude or of inappropriate character or type to elicit, control, or influence a response, a percept, or a sensation, with respect to a given type of receptor mechanism. 2. A stimulus of a type for which the receptor is not especially sensitive but to which it may respond, such as pressure on the eyeball producing phosphene.

liminal s. A stimulus of the least energy value capable of evoking an overt response. Syn., *minimal stimulus; threshold stimulus.*

maximal s. The stimulus which evokes the greatest response capable for that type of stimulation.

minimal s. Liminal stimulus.

neutral s. Photic radiation that does not produce a chromatic experience. Syn., *achromatic stimulus.*

subliminal s. A stimulus of insufficient magnitude to evoke an overt response. Syn., *subminimal stimulus; subthreshold stimulus.*

subminimal s. Subliminal stimulus.

subthreshold s. Subliminal stimulus.

supraliminal s. A stimulus of greater magnitude than necessary to evoke an overt response; one of greater magnitude than a liminal stimulus. Syn., *supraminimal stimulus; suprathreshold stimulus.*

supramaximal s. A stimulus of greater energy value than necessary to produce the greatest response for that type of stimulation.

supraminimal s. Supraliminal stimulus.

suprathreshold s. Supraliminal stimulus.

threshold s. Liminal stimulus.

stint. Conformer.

stippled epiphyses (stip'ld e-pif'ih-sēs). A rare congenital condition characterized by enlargement of the epiphyses due to punctate calcium deposits with resulting deficient skeletal growth. The affected are short-limbed dwarfs with immobile joints, most of whom die by the age of three. Bilateral total cataract is frequently present. Syn., *chondrodystrophia calcificans congenita punctata; chondrodystrophia fetalis hypoplastica; congenital calcareous chondrodystrophy; dysplasia epiphysialis punctata; Conradi's syndrome.*

stippling (stip'pling). Pinpoint areas of discontinuous or devitalized corneal epithelium which, upon the application of fluorescein, will absorb the dye and be detected with the slit lamp biomicroscope as a series of discrete green dots.

Stocker's line. See under *line.*

Stokes's (stōks'ez) **disease; law; lens; lines.** See under the nouns.

stop. The material, opaque border of an aperture, or the border of an optical element in an optical system, which limits the number of rays traversing the system. Syn., *diaphragm.*

aperture s. The stop of an optical system which, by virtue of its size and position with respect to the radiating object, is effective in limiting the bundle of light rays traversing the system.

back s. A stop in an optical system located in the image space.

field s. The stop of an optical system which limits the extent of the field of view.

front s. A stop in an optical system located in the object space.

light s. A stop, a baffle plate, or a baffling ring located between the lenses of an optical system to cut out stray light derived from the body tube or the lens mounts.

telecentric s. A stop placed at one of the focal points of an optical system.

strabilismus (stra"bih-liz'mus, strab"-ih-). Strabismus. *Obs.*

strabism (stra'biz-um, strab'iz-um). Strabismus. *Obs.*

strabismal (strah-biz'mal). Pertaining to or affected with strabismus.

strabismic (strah-biz'mic). 1. Pertaining to or affected with strabismus. 2. One affected with strabismus.

strabismometer (strah"biz-mom'eh-ter). Any instrument for measuring the angle of strabismus. Syn., *ophthalmotropometer.*

Galezowski's s. A strabismometer consisting of a graduated horizontal bar to which are attached a nose rest, temples, and two adjustable, vertical needles, one on each side of the nose rest, which are aligned with the centers of the pupils, or some other reference point.

Laurence's s. A strabismometer consisting of a flat piece of ivory or metal with a concave graduated edge to fit against the lower eyelid to estimate the angle of strabismus.

Maddox' tangent s. Maddox cross.

strabismometry (strah"biz-mom'eh-tre). Measurement of the angle of strabismus. Syn., *ophthalmotropometry.*

angular s. Strabismometry in which the deviation is measured in degrees, as with a perimeter.

linear s. Strabismometry in which the deviation is estimated by means of a scale placed before the eyes, as with Laurence's strabismometer.

tangential s. Strabismometry in which the deviation is measured with a tangent scale.

strabismus (strah-biz'mus). The condition in which binocular fixation is not present under normal seeing conditions, i.e., the foveal line of sight of one eye fails to intersect the object of fixation. Syn., *heterotropia; ophthalmotropia; squint; tropia.*

absolute s. Constant strabismus.

accommodative s. 1. Strabismus resulting from abnormal demand on accommodation, such as convergent strabismus due to uncorrected hypermetropia or divergent strabismus due to uncorrected myopia. 2. Strabismus resulting from the act of accommodating in association with a high A.C.A. ratio.

adventitious s. Optometric Extension Program: Acquired strabismus considered to be an adaptation to the stress of convergence demands.

alternating s. Strabismus in which either eye can maintain fixation. Syn., *bilateral strabismus; binocular strabismus.*

    alternating s., accidental. Alternating strabismus in which either eye can maintain fixation, although one eye is preferred.

    alternating s., convergent isoametropic. A convergent alternating strabismus associated with high hypermetropia of equal amount in the two eyes.

    alternating s., convergent paretic. Convergent alternating strabismus associated with paresis of the external rectus muscles.

    alternating s., essential. Alternating strabismus in which either eye can maintain fixation with the same facility and in which either eye is used indiscriminately.

ambiocular s. Strabismus in which both eyes are used simultaneously but in which different portions of the image of each eye are utilized to form a single composite percept, said to occur in anomalous retinal correspondence.

anatomical s. Strabismus resulting from anatomical anomalies of the orbits, the eyeballs, or the extraocular muscles and their check ligaments.

apparent s. The appearance of strabismus as induced by an abnormally small or large angle lambda, extreme variation in the shape or placement of the eyelids, the breadth of the nose, or epicanthus. Syn., *pseudostrabismus.*

ascendens, s. Strabismus sursumvergens.

bilateral s. Alternating strabismus.

binocular s. Alternating strabismus.

Braid's s. A simultaneous upward and inward turning of the eyes; a requested response sometimes employed as a part of the procedure to induce hypnosis.

comitant s. Concomitant strabismus.

concomitant s. Strabismus in which the angle of deviation remains constant for all directions of gaze and with either eye fixating. Syn., *comitant strabismus.* Cf. *nonconcomitant strabismus.*

    concomitant s., primary. Concomitant strabismus not of paralytic origin.

    concomitant s., secondary. Concomitant strabismus which

follows a long standing nonconcomitant strabismus.

congenital s. Strabismus present or
existing since birth.

consecutive s. Strabismus in which
the deviation differs from that of
a pre-existing strabismus, as may
occur following surgery.

constant s. Strabismus present at
all times. Syn., *absolute strabis-*
mus; continuous strabismus; fixed
strabismus; permanent strabis-
mus.

continuous s. 1. Constant strabismus. 2. Strabismus which, when
present, occurs for all distances
and directions of fixation. 3. Strabismus in which the magnitude
of the deviation is the same for
all fixation distances.

convergens, s. Convergent strabismus.

    convergens deorso-adductor-
ius, s. Convergent strabismus in
which the deviating eye turns
downward on convergence.

    convergens surso-adductor-
ius, s. Convergent strabismus in
which the deviating eye turns upward on convergence.

convergent s. Strabismus in which
the deviating eye turns inward,
so that its foveal line of sight
crosses the line of sight of the
fixating eye at a point nearer than
the object of fixation. Syn., *eso-*
tropia; strabismus convergens;
internal strabismus.

cyclic s. Strabismus recurring at
regular time intervals.

deorsumvergens, s. Strabismus in
which the deviating eye turns
downward, so that its foveal line
of sight is below the object of
fixation. Syn., *hypotropia; stra-*
bismus descendens.

descendens, s. Strabismus deorsumvergens.

divergens, s. Divergent strabismus.

divergent s. Strabismus in which
the deviating eye turns templeward, so that its foveal line of
sight crosses the line of sight of

the fixating eye at a point farther
than the object of fixation or at a
hypothetical point behind the
eyes. Syn., *exotropia; strabismus*
divergens; external strabismus.

external s. Divergent strabismus.

fixed s. 1. Constant strabismus. 2.
Strabismus in which the magnitude of the deviation is the same
for all fixation distances. 3. Strabismus in which the magnitude
of the deviation is the same at all
times for the same fixation distance.

fixus, s. Congenital strabismus in
which both eyes are held in a
fixed adducted position by fi-
brotic and inelastic internal rectus
muscles, muscle foot plates, or
check ligaments.

hysterical s. Strabismus occurring
in hysteria, characterized by extreme inconstancy.

incipient s. Premonitory strabismus.

incomitant s. Nonconcomitant strabismus.

inconstant s. Intermittent strabismus.

infantile s. Spurious strabismus.

innervational s. Strabismus attributed to anomalous innervation to the extraocular muscles.

intermittent s. Strabismus which
is not present at all times. Syn.,
inconstant strabismus; occasional
strabismus; periodic strabismus;
recurrent strabismus; relative
strabismus.

internal s. Convergent strabismus.

kinetic s. Strabismus resulting
from a spasm of an extraocular
muscle due to an irritative lesion
in the central nervous system.
The onset is usually sudden and
the duration temporary.

latent s. Heterophoria.

lateral s. Strabismus in which the
deviating eye is turned either in
or out.

manifest s. Strabismus, as distinguished from *latent strabis-*
mus. Syn., *patent strabismus.*

mechanical s. Strabismus resulting from pressure or traction on the eyeball, as may occur from an orbital tumor.

monocular s. Unilateral strabismus.

monolateral s. Unilateral strabismus.

muscular s. Strabismus due to overdevelopment or underdevelopment of any of the extraocular muscles or to anomalies of their insertions or check ligaments.

nonaccommodative s. Strabismus not attributable to abnormal demands on accommodation.

noncomitant s. Nonconcomitant strabismus.

nonconcomitant s. Strabismus in which the angle of deviation varies with the direction of gaze and/or with the eye that fixates, due to paralysis or paresis of one or more extraocular muscles. Syn., *incomitant strabismus; noncomitant strabismus.* Cf. *concomitant strabismus.*

nonparalytic s. Strabismus not attributable to paresis or paralysis of extraocular muscles, characterized by concomitant eye movements and equal primary and secondary deviations.

occasional s. 1. Intermittent strabismus. 2. Spurious strabismus.

occlusion s. Strabismus manifested after prolonged occlusion of one eye.

optical s. Strabismus in which refractive error is considered a primary etiological factor, such as high hypermetropia or anisometropia.

paralytic s. Strabismus resulting from paralysis of extraocular muscles, often characterized by nonconcomitant eye movements, unequal primary and secondary deviations, limitation of eye movement, head tilt or turn, and diplopia.

paretic s. Strabismus resulting from paresis of extraocular muscles,

characterized by an overshooting of the nonaffected eye when the affected eye fixates in the field of action of the paretic muscle.

patent s. Manifest strabismus.

periodic s. 1. Strabismus present only at certain distances or directions of fixation. 2. Intermittent strabismus. 3. Strabismus in which the magnitude of the deviation varies with the fixation distance.

   periodic s., direct. Strabismus in which the deviation is greater at near fixation distances than at far fixation distances, as would obtain in esotropia with a high A.C.A. ratio or in exotropia with a low A.C.A. ratio. Cf. *inverse periodic strabismus.*

   periodic s., inverse. Strabismus in which the deviation is greater at far fixation distances than at near fixation distances. Cf. *direct periodic strabismus.*

permanent s. Constant strabismus.

physiological s. A class of strabismus identified with faulty extraocular muscle innervation, as distinct from anatomical and optical classes of strabismus.

premonitory s. Dissociations of the eyes of infants prior to the full development of binocular fixation, occurring relatively frequently and lasting a few minutes or more. Syn., *incipient strabismus.*

psychopathic s. Strabismus attributed to psychological or emotional causes.

purposive s. Strabismus in which the magnitude of the deviation is increased so that the stimulation of the deviating eye is more peripheral, thus to facilitate suppression.

recurrent s. Intermittent strabismus.

relative s. 1. Periodic strabismus. 2. Intermittent strabismus.

spasmodic s. Spastic strabismus.

spastic s. Strabismus resulting from

spasm of extraocular muscles which may be primary, of neurogenic or myogenic origin, or secondary to a paretic contralateral or ipsilateral synergist or an ipsilateral antagonist. Syn., *spasmodic strabismus.*

spurious s. The momentary, incoordinated dissociations of the eyes of normal infants prior to the full development of binocular fixation. Syn., *infantile strabismus; occasional strabismus.*

sursumvergens, s. Strabismus in which the deviating eye turns upward, so that its foveal line of sight is above the object of fixation. Syn., *hypertropia; strabismus ascendens.*

tonic s. Strabismus attributed to abnormal tonicity of the extraocular muscles.

unilateral s. Strabismus in which the same eye is always the deviating eye and the other eye is always the fixating eye. Syn., *monocular strabismus; monolateral strabismus; uniocular strabismus.*

uniocular s. Unilateral strabismus.

variable s. Strabismus in which the magnitude of the deviation is not constant.

vertical s. Strabismus in which the deviating eye is turned either up or down.

strabometer (strah-bom'eh-ter). Strabismometer.

strabometry (strah-bom'eh-tre). Strabismometry.

strabotic (strah-bot'ik). Strabismic.

strabotomy (strah-bot'o-me). An operation for the correction of strabismus.

strain. A deformation of, or an internal tension in, a solid elastic body resulting from stress. In ophthalmic glass it may be induced by annealing, from a nonuniform coefficient of expansion, or from external pressure at eyewire or mounting contact points, and results in birefringence detectable with a polariscope.

Strampelli (stram-pel'e) **implant; lens.** See under *lens.*

strap. That part of a rimless bridge or endpiece that extends from the shoe over the surface of the lens. It is usually one of a pair, the other strap being on the other surface of the lens, and the two are connected by a screw which passes through holes in the two straps and a hole in the lens.

Stratton's experiment (strat'onz). See under *experiment.*

stratum (stra'tum, strā'tum). A layer.

bacillorum, s. Layer of rods and cones of the retina.

cinereum, s. The thin layer of gray matter in the superior colliculus, between the stratum zonale and the stratum opticum, containing small multipolar cells which synapse with the optic and corticotectal fibers. Syn., *stratum griseum.*

ganglionare, s. Ganglion cell layer of the retina.

griseum, s. Stratum cinereum.

lemnisci, s. The deepest of four layers of the superior colliculus, composed of cell bodies and fibers from the stratum opticum, the spinotectal tract, and the medial lemniscus, and the fibers which either enter the fountain decussation of Meynert and connect with the nucleus of the oculomotor nerve, or enter into the tectobulbar and tectospinal tracts, or connect with the reticular formation.

nerveum of Henle, s. Fiber layer of Henle.

opticum, s. 1. Nerve fiber layer of the retina. 2. The third layer of the superior colliculus, between the stratum cinereum and the stratum lemnisci, composed of multipolar cells and fibers from the optic nerve and the lateral geniculate body which enter via the superior brachium and, for the most part, terminate in the stratum cinereum.

pigmenti bulbi oculi, s. The layer of pigmented epithelium, derived from the outer layer of the optic cup, which extends from the optic disk to the pupillary margin of the iris. It is collectively: the *stratum pigmenti retinae,* the *stratum pigmenti corporis ciliaris,* and the *stratum pigmenti iridis.*

pigmenti corporis ciliaris, s. Pigmented layer of the epithelium of the ciliary body.

pigmenti iridis, s. Posterior pigment epithelium of the iris.

pigmenti retinae, s. Pigment epithelium layer of the retina.

sagittal s., external. A layer of visual fibers of the optic radiations passing from the posterolateral extremity of the thalamus to the outer side of the posterior horn of the lateral ventricle.

sagittal s., extreme. A layer of nerve fibers just lateral to the optic radiation fibers in the external sagittal stratum, of uncertain function.

sagittal s., internal. A layer of nerve fibers probably from the visual association areas of an occipital cortex that terminates in the superior colliculus and elsewhere; located just external to the posterior horn of the lateral ventricle.

sagittal s., medial. A layer of nerve fibers between the posterior horn of the lateral ventricle and the internal sagittal stratum near the optic radiations. It contains commissural fibers from the two occipital cortices via the splenium of the corpus callosum.

zonale, s. The thin, white, superficial layer of the superior colliculus, consisting of nerve fibers, chiefly from the occipital cortex, which enter via the superior brachium.

Straub's theory (strawbz). See under *theory.*

streak. A stripe, a line, or a furrow.

angioid s's. A bilateral degenera-tive affection characterized by pigmented lines or streaks in the fundi of the eyes in a pattern similar to that of blood vessels, due to degeneration of the lamina vitrea of the choroid. The streaks anastomose around the optic disk and radiate toward the equator, rarely passing it. It may occur in association with *pseudoxanthoma elasticum* (Grönblad-Strandberg syndrome).

Knapp's s's. Pigmented lines resembling blood vessels which may appear following retinal hemorrhage. Syn., *Knapp's striae.*

Moore's lightning s's. Flashes of light upon eye movement, comparable to lightning, usually vertical, almost invariably referred to the temporal side of the field and either accompanied or followed by dark spots before the eyes. It is not considered to be a precursor of any serious fundus disease.

reflex s. A shining or glistening streak seen along the retinal vessels, in ophthalmoscopy, attributed to reflection of light from the surface of the blood column.

Siegrist's s's. Chains of pigmented spots coursing along the paths of white sclerosed choroidal vessels in advanced hypertensive retinopathy. Syn., *Siegrist's spots.*

Strehl criterion; definition; ratio. See under *definition.*

Streidinger chart (stri'din-jer). See under *chart.*

strephosymbolia (stref"o-sim-bo'le-ah). Partial alexia in which letters, such as *b* and *d*, and words, such as *no* and *on*, which form mirror images of each other, are confused.

stress. Tension, compression, or shear within a solid elastic body such as optical glass, which results in strain detectable with a polariscope.

stretcher, cone. A hollow, tapered, rigid metal tube having a cross section shape of a given spectacle lens and mounted over a heating element for stretching and shaping the rims of plastic spectacle frames.

stria (stri′ah). 1. A streak. 2. A streak in glass caused by a variation in the refractive index, due to an imperfect mixture of the ingredients or to contamination during manufacture.

ciliares, striae. Shallow dark grooves on the inner surface of the pars plana of the ciliary body extending from the ora serrata to the valleys between the ciliary processes. They are formed by the invagination of the pigment epithelium.

Gennari, s. of. Line of Gennari.

Haab's striae. Branched ruptures in Descemet's membrane, due to distension of the cornea in hydrophthalmos.

Knapp's striae. Knapp's streaks.

retinae, striae. White concentric lines in the retina formed following a retinal reattachment operation.

striate area (stri′āt). See under *area.*

stripes, Vogt keratoconus. Keratoconus lines.

Stroblite (strōb′līt). An argon lamp used in conjunction with fluorescein in the fitting of contact lenses and for the detection of corneal abrasions or ulcers.

stroboscope (stro′bo-skōp, strob′-). An instrument which presents, by means of intermittent illumination or shutters, a series of motionless pictures, each representing successive phases of a movement or successive instantaneous views of a moving object. See also *stroboscopic disk; stroboscopic movement.*

strobostereoscope (stro″bo-ster′e-o-skōp). Stereostroboscope.

stroma (stro′mah). The supporting framework of an organ or a structure, consisting primarily of connective tissue and blood vessels.

cornea, s. of the. The lamellated connective tissue constituting the thickest layer of the cornea, located between Bowman's and Descemet's membranes.

iridis, s. The iridal loose connective tissue in which the sphincter pupillae muscle, nerves, and pigment cells are contained, located between the anterior border layer and the region of the dilator pupillae muscle.

vitreum, s. The gossamerlike fibrillar structure within the vitreous body, especially as seen with the slit lamp.

stromectomy, lamellar corneal (stro-mek′to-me). A surgical procedure for the treatment of myopia in which a thin layer of corneal stroma is removed to reduce the convexity of the curvature of the cornea.

Strümpell-Lorrain disease (strim′-pel-lo-rān). Familial spasmodic paraplegia.

Strümpell-Marie disease (strim′pel-mar-e′). Ankylosing spondylitis.

Studt-Abel chart. See under *chart.*

Sturge-Weber (ster′je-web′er) **disease; syndrome.** See under the nouns.

Sturm's (sturmz) **conoid; interval; lines.** See under the nouns.

Sturman monocular. See under *monocular.*

sty. 1. External hordeolum. 2. A purulent infection of a gland of the eyelid.

Meibomian s. Internal hordeolum.

Zeisian s. Inflammation of a gland of Zeis

stye. Sty.

subcapsular (sub-kap′su-lar). Occurring or situated beneath the capsule of the crystalline lens.

subconjunctival (sub″kon-junk-ti′-val). Occurring or situated beneath the conjunctiva.

subconjunctivitis, epibulbar gonorrheal (sub″kon-junk″tih-vi′tis).

Endogenous gonococcal conjunctivitis.

subduction (sub-duk'shun). Infraduction.

subfusional (sub-fu'zhun-al). Pertaining to intermittent stimulation at a frequency too low to produce continuous uniform sensation.

subhyaloid (sub-hi'ah-loid). Occurring or situated beneath the hyaloid membrane.

subjective. Subjective refraction.

sublatio retinae (sub-la'she-o ret-ih-ne). Detachment of the retina.

subliminal (sub-lim'in-al). Below the threshold of sensation, as a subliminal stimulus.

subluxation of the lens (sub"luk-sa'-shun). Incomplete dislocation of the crystalline lens, so that it remains in part within the pupillary aperture. Cf. *luxation of the lens.*

subocular (sub-ok'u-lar). Occurring or situated beneath the eyeball.

suborbital (sub-ōr'bih-tal). Occurring or situated beneath the orbit.

subretinal (sub-ret'ih-nal). Occurring or situated between the retina and the choroid.

subscleral (sub-skle'ral). Occurring or situated beneath the sclera.

substance, cement. An amorphous substance in the crystalline lens which binds the individual lens fibers with each other and which is also found beneath the anterior and the posterior capsule, in back of the anterior epithelium, and in a central strand occupying the anteroposterior axis of the lens, extending out to form the Y lens sutures.

substantia lentis (sub-stan'she-ah len'tis). The substance of the crystalline lens contained within its capsule.

substantia propria (sub-stan'she-ah pro'prih-ah). The main connective tissue portion or stroma of a structure, as in the cornea, the sclera, the choroid, and the iris.

subtarsal (sub-tahr'sal). Occurring or situated beneath (posterior to) the tarsus of the eyelid.

subversion (sub-vur'zhun). Infraversion.

subvitrinal (sub-vit'rih-nal). Occurring or situated beneath the vitreous body.

subvolution (sub"vo-lu'shun). An operation for pterygium in which a flap is turned over and placed so that its outer surface is in contact with the raw dissected surface.

successive contrast; induction. See under the nouns.

Suda ocular compression test. See under *test.*

suggilation of the eyelid (sug"jih-la'shun). Ecchymosis of the eyelid.

Suker's sign (soo'kerz). See under *sign.*

sulcus (sul'kus). A furrow or groove as occurs on the surface of the brain or in bone. See also *fissure; groove.*

calcarine s. Calcarine fissure.

circularis corneae, s. The shallow circular groove at the margin of the posterior surface of the cornea at its junction with the sclera.

circum-marginal s. of Vogt. A circular furrow in the iris, near the pupillary margin, due to localized senile atrophic changes.

infraorbital s. Infraorbital groove.

infrapalpebral s. The furrow or crease in the skin below the lower eyelid.

lacrimal s. An infrequent extension of the tract of the nasolacrimal duct downward toward the floor of the nasal cavity, consisting of a groove sometimes bridged by a mucous membrane to form a blind tube.

lacrimalis maxillae, s. A vertical groove on the orbital surface of the frontal process of the maxillary bone which contributes to the formation of the fossa for the lacrimal sac.

lacrimalis ossis lacrimalis, s. A vertical groove in the lacrimal bone which contributes to the formation of the fossa for the lacrimal sac.

lateral calcarine s. A lateral prolongation of the posterior calcarine fissure at the posterior pole of the occipital lobe in the area striata.

lunate s. A groove often present on the outer surface of the occipital lobe, near the occipital pole, representing the anterior edge of the area striata.

oculomotor s. A longitudinal furrow on the medial side of the cerebral peduncle from which a series of rootlets of the oculomotor nerve emerge.

orbitopalpebral s., inferior. A sulcus in the skin of the lower eyelid extending along the inferior margin of the tarsus.

orbitopalpebral s., superior. A sulcus in the skin of the upper eyelid extending along the superior margin of the tarsus.

paracalcarine s., inferior. A groove in the lingual gyrus, inferior to the area striata, which separates that area from the surrounding cortex.

paracalcarine s., superior. A groove in the cuneus, superior to the area striata, which separates that area from the surrounding cortex.

scleral s., external. The shallow circular groove at the margin of the anterior surface of the sclera at its junction with the cornea.

scleral s., internal. The shallow circular groove on the margin of the posterior surface of the sclera at its junction with the cornea.

subtarsal s. A groove on the inner surface of the eyelid, near the eyelid margin and parallel to it, which marks the junction of the

marginal and the palpebral conjunctivae.

summation. The accumulative effect of stimuli presented simultaneously or successively.

binocular s. The accumulative effect of stimulating the two eyes simultaneously or alternately.

spatial s. The combining of the effect of two or more stimuli which impinge simultaneously on different retinal regions.

temporal s. The combining of the effect of two or more stimuli which impinge consecutively on the same retinal region.

sunglasses. Spectacles, or attachments to spectacles, which have absorptive lenses or otherwise reduce transmission of light to the eye.

sunlight. Light received directly from the sun. Cf. *daylight; skylight.*

superciliaris (su"per-sil"e-a′ris). Corrugator supercilli muscle.

superciliary (su"per-sil′e-ar-e). Pertaining to the region of the eyebrow.

supercilium (su"per-sil′e-um). An eyebrow.

superduction (su"per-duk′shun). Supraduction.

superimposition (su"per-im"po-zish′-un). The laying or imposing of one object, pattern, or form over another. In haploscopic viewing, the common localization of the images seen by the two eyes, as a bird seen by one eye in a cage seen by the other.

superposition (su"per-po-zish′un). Superimposition.

superversion (su"per-vur′zhun). Supraversion.

suppression. The lack or inability of perception of normally visible objects in all or part of the field of vision of one eye, occurring only on simultaneous stimulation of both eyes and attributed to cortical inhibition.

active s. Suppression occurring in the absence of binocular fixation, to avoid diplopia and confusion.

border s. 1. The reduction in perceptibility of a stimulus pattern in the perceptual region of a contrast border. 2. The suppression of perception of a pattern presented to one eye when a contrast border is viewed in the corresponding retinal area of the other eye.

central s. Suppression of images in the foveal or the macular area.

gross s. Suppression involving a large area of the visual field.

passive s. Suppression attributed to gross inequality of vision in the two eyes, as in uncorrected anisometropia.

peripheral s. Suppression of images in the peripheral retina.

suprachoroid (su″prah-ko′roid). 1. The outer layer of the choroid between Haller's layer and the perichoroidal space or the lamina fusca of the sclera, consisting of relatively nonvascular, loose, connective tissue containing fibroblasts, chromatophores, and reticuloendothelial cells. Syn., *epichoroid; lamina fusca of the choroid; lamina suprachoroidea; suprachoroid layer; suprachoroidea.* 2. The outer layer of the ciliary body.

suprachoroidea (su″prah-ko-roi′de-ah). Suprachoroid.

supraciliary (su″prah-sil′e-er″e). Superciliary.

supradextroversion (su″prah-deks″-tro-vur′zhun). Conjugate rotation of the eyes, upward and to the right.

supraduction (su″prah-duk′shun). 1. Upward rotation of an eye. 2. In vertical divergence testing, the upward rotation of one eye with respect to the other in response to increases in base-down prism, or the equivalent. Syn., *sursumduction.*

alternating s. Double hyperphoria.

supralevoversion (su″prah-lev″o-vur′zhun). Conjugate rotation of the eyes, upward and to the left.

supraliminal (su″prah-lim′ih-nal). Above the threshold of sensation or response, as a supraliminal stimulus.

supraobliquus (su″prah-ob-li′kwus). Superior oblique muscle.

supraorbital (su″prah-ōr′bih-tal). Occurring or situated above the orbit.

suprascleral (su″prah-skle′ral). Occurring or situated on the outer surface of the sclera.

supratrochlear (su″prah-trok′le-ar). Occurring or situated above the trochlea.

supravergence (su″prah-vur′jens). Upward rotation of an eye, the other eye remaining stationary. Syn., *sursumvergence.*

supraversion (su″prah-vur′zhun). Conjugate rotation of the eyes upward. Syn., *sursumversion.*

surface. 1. The outside or exterior of a body. 2. A two dimensional face of a body

abathic s. The surface of the objective frontoparallel plane horopter determined for a fixation distance at which it coincides with the apparent frontoparallel plane horopter.

aplanatic s. A refracting or reflecting surface of such shape that it brings all the rays emanating from a point source to a point image.

aspherical s. A surface which deviates from a spherical form, usually to conform to a parabola or similar curve, or to a systematically changing series of curves, often employed on a lens to correct for or to reduce certain types of aberration.

base s. In ophthalmic lenses, the standard or reference surface in a given series of lenses. Syn., *base curve.*

Cartesian s's. Cartesian ovals.

caustic s. The surface or form generated by the revolution of the caustic curve about the optical axis of the reflecting or refracting system converging the light rays; hence, the surface containing all the caustic curves.

color s. A plane section of a color solid representing all possible hue, saturation, and brightness variations at that level.

combining s. The surface of a lens on the side opposite to the base surface.

concave s. A curved surface depressed toward the center, as that of the inside of a sphere.

convex s. A curved surface elevated toward the center, as that of the outside of a sphere.

cylindrical s. 1. A surface forming either the inside or the outside of a cylinder. 2. In ophthalmic lenses, synonymous with *toric surface.*

diffusing s. A surface which scatters reflected light in all directions away from the surface. Syn., *mat surface*

diffusing s., perfect. A surface which reflects light in accordance with Lambert's cosine law, regardless of the angle of incidence.

emergent s. The last surface in an optical system; the surface from which the light leaves the optical system.

index s. A theoretical surface relating the indices of refraction for different directions in doubly refracting crystals, so called in analogy to the ray velocity surface from which it is derived.

induction, s. Spatial induction. See under *induction.*

isochromatic s. With respect to the point of origin of a group of in-phase waves in an anisotropic medium, the locus of all points for which the phase difference is a given constant.

isogonal s. The surface generated by the rotation of the Vieth-Mueller horopter about the two points of reference representing the eyes.

isoindicial s's. Surfaces corresponding to regions of the media having the same index of refraction, such as those delineating zones of the crystalline lens of the same index.

mat s. Diffusing surface.

normal velocity s. With respect to the point of origin of a group of in-phase waves in an anisotropic medium, the locus of points whose distances from the origin equal the phase velocities in the corresponding directions.

ocular s. The surface of a spectacle or contact lens worn toward the eye.

optical s. A surface at which specular reflection or uniform refraction occurs, especially one having the desired quality and designed for this purpose in an optical system.

Petzval s. A parabolic surface formed by point images of point objects, both on and off the axis, in an optical system corrected for spherical aberration, coma, and astigmatism.

plane s. A flat surface; a surface of zero curvature; one having an infinite radius of curvature.

principal s. A spherical surface, in an optical system corrected for coma, at which refraction of the emergent light may be considered to occur, its center of curvature being the secondary focal point of the system.

ray velocity s. Wave surface.

redirecting s. A surface which changes the direction of incident light, such as that of a mirror or a prism.

refracting s. A surface separating two isotropic media of different indices of refraction.

scattering s. A surface which redirects light into a multiplicity of separate, variously directed pencils.

spherical s. A surface that conforms to either the inside or the outside of a sphere; one having a single radius of curvature.

toric s. 1. A surface described by a circle rotating about a straight line in its own plane, especially about an off-center line. 2. An ophthalmic lens surface with meridians of least and greatest curvature located at right angles to each other.

wave s. 1. A wavefront. 2. The envelope of wavefronts in doubly refracting crystals representing the positions of the ordinary and the extraordinary waves at a given time, hence a surface of constant phase for waves spreading from a point source. Syn., *ray velocity surface.*

wave s., **extraordinary.** The wave surface in a doubly refracting substance corresponding to the loci of points of equal phase belonging to the extraordinary ray.

wave s., **ordinary.** The wave surface in a doubly refracting substance corresponding to the loci of points of equal phase belonging to the ordinary ray.

surfacing. Grinding and polishing of the surface of a lens to a specified curvature.

sursumduction (sur″sum-duk′shun). Supraduction.

sursumvergence (sur″sum-vur′jens). Supravergence.

sursumversion (sur″sum-vur′zhun). Supraversion.

suspenopsia (sus″pen-op′se-ah). 1. Voluntary ignoring of the objects in the field of vision of one eye when visual attention is directed to objects in the field of vision of the other eye, as occurs when using a monocular microscope with both eyes open. 2. Suppression.

suspension (sus-pen′shun). 1. Suppression. 2. Suspenopsia.

Sutcliffe's rule (sut′klifs). See under *rule.*

suture (su′tūr). 1. The line of junction between immovable bones, as those of the skull, or the junc-

tion itself. 2. The line of junction formed by the meeting of fibers of the crystalline lens. 3. The act, the process, or the method of stitching tissue, or the type of stitch so used. 4. The material used in stitching tissue.

ethmofrontal s. The suture between the frontal and the ethmoid bones in the orbit. Syn., *frontoethmoidal suture.*

ethmolacrimal s. The suture between the ethmoid and the lacrimal bones in the medial wall of the orbit.

ethmomaxillary s. The suture between the ethmoid bone and the orbital plate of the maxillary bone.

ethmopalatine s. The suture between the ethmoid and the palatine bones in the orbit.

ethmosphenoidal s. The suture between the ethmoid and the sphenoid bones in the orbit. Syn., *sphenoethmoidal suture.*

frontoethmoidal s. Ethmofrontal suture.

frontolacrimal s. The suture between the frontal and lacrimal bones.

frontomalar s. Frontozygomatic suture.

frontomaxillary s. The suture between the frontal process of the maxillary bone and the frontal bone. Syn., *maxillofrontal suture.*

frontonasal s. Nasofrontal suture.

frontosphenoidal s. The suture between the wings of the sphenoid bone and the frontal bone. Syn., *sphenofrontal suture.*

frontozygomatic s. The suture between the frontal and the zygomatic bones. Syn., *frontomalar suture; zygomaticofrontal suture.*

infraorbital s. The suture in the maxillary bone over the infraorbital canal.

lens s. One of the many radiating lines in the crystalline lens, formed by the meeting of systems of lens fibers.

lens s., anterior Y. The lens suture in the shape of an upright Y, formed anterior in the fetal nucleus.

lens s., posterior Y. The lens suture in the shape of an inverted Y, formed posterior in the fetal nucleus.

maxilloethmoidal s. Ethmomaxillary suture.

maxillofrontal s. Frontomaxillary suture.

maxillolacrimal s. The suture between the maxillary and the lacrimal bones, in the medial wall of the orbit.

maxillonasal s. Nasomaxillary suture.

maxillopalatine s. The suture between the orbital plate of the maxillary bone and the palatine bone, in the floor of the orbit.

maxillozygomatic s. The suture between the maxillary and the zygomatic bones. Syn., *zygomaticomaxillary suture.*

nasofrontal s. The suture between the frontal and the nasal bones. Syn., *frontonasal suture.*

nasomaxillary s. The suture between the nasal and the superior maxillary bones. Syn., *maxillonasal suture.*

sphenoethmoidal s. Ethmosphenoidal suture.

sphenofrontal s. Frontosphenoidal suture.

sphenomalar s. Sphenozygomatic suture.

sphenopalatine s. The suture between the sphenoid and the palatine bones in the orbit.

sphenozygomatic s. The suture between the great wing of the sphenoid bone and the zygomatic bone, in the lateral wall of the orbit. Syn., *sphenomalar suture.*

zygomaticofrontal s. Frontozygomatic suture.

zygomaticomaxillary s. Maxillozygomatic suture.

Swann's syndrome (swahnz). Blind spot syndrome.

Swann-Cole charts (swahn-kōl). See under *chart.*

Sweet's method. See under *method.*

Swenson's method. See under *method.*

Swindle's ghost (swin'd'lz). See under *ghost.*

sycosis palpebrae marginalis (si-ko'-sis pal-pe'bre mar-jih-nal'is). Sycotic blepharitis.

sycosis vulgaris (si-ko'sis vul-ga'ris). Acne mentagra.

Sylvian syndrome (sil've-an). See under *syndrome.*

symblepharon (sim-blef'ah-ron). A cicatricial attachment of the conjunctiva of the eyelid to the conjunctiva of the eyeball. Syn., *symblepharosis.*

anterior s. Symblepharon in which the tarsal or the marginal conjunctiva is attached to the conjunctiva of the eyeball but which does not involve the fornix.

posterior s. Symblepharon extending to and involving the fornix.

total s. Symblepharon forming a complete adhesion of the conjunctiva of the eyelid to the conjunctiva of the eyeball.

symblepharopterygium (sim-blef''-ah-ro-ter-ij'e-um). A symblepharon in which the cicatricial band resembles a pterygium.

symblepharosis (sim-blef''ah-ro'sis). Symblepharon.

symparalysis (sim''pah-ral'ih-sis). Simultaneous paralysis of synergistic extraocular muscles of an eye or of the yoke muscles of the eyes.

sympathetic ophthalmia (sim''pah-thet'ik of-thal'me-ah). See under *ophthalmia.*

sympathizer. A sympathizing eye.

symptom. An incidental or concomitant subjective indication of a disease, a disorder, or an anomaly. See also *phenomenon; reflex; sign; syndrome.*

Anton's s. Subjective unawareness of one's own visual disability in cortical blindness.

Behçet, triple s. complex of. Behçet's syndrome.

Bumke's s. Absence of normal pupillary dilatation to psychic stimuli, as fear or pain, in catatonia.

Epstein's s. Failure of the upper eyelid to move downward on downward movement of the eye, occurring in premature and nervous infants.

Franceschetti's digital-ocular s. Frequent pressing of the eyeballs with the fingers, occurring in association with such congenital deformities as coloboma of the eyelids or gargoylism.

Gower's s. Abrupt intermittent oscillation of the pupil on light stimulation of the eye, occurring in tabes dorsalis.

halo s. Colored circles seen around lights in glaucoma. Syn., *rainbow symptom.*

Liebreich's s. A symptom of red-green color blindness in which light areas are reported red while dark areas are reported green.

rainbow s. Halo symptom.

Redlich's s. Redlich's phenomenon.

Stellwag's s. Stellwag's sign.

Weber's s. Weber's sign.

Wernicke's s. Hemianopic pupillary reflex.

synaphymenitis (sin-af″ih-men-i′tis). Conjunctivitis.

syncanthus (sin-kan′thus). Adhesion of the eyeball to the orbital tissues or structures.

Synchro-haploscope (sin″kro-hap′lo-skōp). A motor-activated visual training haploscope, designed by Mason, with independent control of the vergence, version, and accommodative demands.

synchysis (sin′kih-sis). Liquefaction of the vitreous body, commonly occurring in senile or myopic degeneration and often in other inflammatory or degenerative states of the eye or after trauma. It is usually associated with the development of vitreous opacities, which may be ophthalmoscopi-cally visible, and which, when seen entoptically, move more freely than similar opacities seen when the elastic structure of the gel is maintained.

scintillans, s. The presence of numerous, bright, shiny particles in a fluid vitreous body, occurring secondarily to degenerative conditions of the eye. They appear as flat, angular, golden crystals and are considered to be composed of cholesterol. They may be hidden at the bottom of the vitreous when the eye is immobile and then suddenly float into sight when the eye is moved.

syndectomy (sin-dek′to-me). Peridectomy.

syndesmitis (sin″des-mi′tis). Conjunctivitis.

syndrome (sin′drōm). The aggregate signs and symptoms characteristic of a disease, a lesion, an anomaly, a type, or a classification. For syndromes not listed, see under *disease.*

A s. 1. Exotropia in which the deviation increases as the eyes rotate straight downward, or esotropia in which the deviation increases as the eyes rotate straight upward. Cf. *V syndrome.* Syn., *A phenomenon.* 2. Case type A.

A.C.L. s. Large hands and feet and protruding jaws as in acromegaly, a type of cutis verticis gyrata, and corneal leukoma.

Adair-Dighton s. Van der Hoeve's syndrome.

adenopharyngealconjunctival s. Acute contagious conjunctivitis and upper respiratory infection of viral origin. Syn., *APC syndrome.*

adherence s. A developmental abnormality of the extraocular muscles in which one becomes joined or adherent to another, resulting in a condition simulating paralysis or paresis.

Adie's s. Dilatation of the pupil, usually unilateral, with sluggish response to light, darkness, accommodation and convergence, together with absence of tendon reflexes, such as the knee jerk. It is usually found in women and is of unknown etiology. Syn., *Holmes-Adie syndrome.*

adiposogenital s. Froehlich's syndrome.

Albright's s. Pigmented nevi of the skin, precocious puberty, and polyostotic fibrous dysplasia which may lead to unilateral cranial thickening and optic atrophy. Syn., *Albright-McCune-Sternberg syndrome.*

Albright-McCune-Sternberg s. Albright's syndrome.

Alport's s. Hereditary progressive nephropathy with albuminuria and hematuria and progressive bilateral nerve deafness, mostly affecting males. Cataract, spherophakia, and lenticonus are sometimes present.

Amalric's s. Deaf-mutism associated with macular dystrophy without functional loss.

Amidei's s. Strabismus, stuttering, and left-handedness, of undetermined etiology.

Andogsky's s. Cataract associated with the late stage of an allergic dermatitis, occurring as a recessive heredofamilial trait.

Angelucci's s. Vasomotor instability, tachycardia, lymphoid hyperplasia, and sometimes vernal conjunctivitis, attributed to endocrine disturbance.

angio-encephalo-cutaneous s. Sturge-Weber syndrome.

anterior choroidal artery s. Monakow's syndrome.

Anton's s. Statements of visual experience although totally blind, with intellectual deterioration, especially of memory, a tendency to confabulate, and amnesic aphasia, due to bilateral destruction of cortical visual sensory area 17 or to a lesion affecting fibers from this area leading to the thalamus.

aortic arch s. Pulseless disease.

APC s. Adenopharyngealconjunctival syndrome.

Apert's s. Acrocephalosyndactyly.

apex s. Paresis of the third, fourth, fifth, and sixth cranial nerves and lesions of the optic nerve resulting in central scotomata, peripheral visual field defects, and sometimes papilledema, due to a large diffuse lesion at the base of the skull.

aqueduct of Sylvius s. Sylvian syndrome.

Arnold-Chiari s. Herniation of a portion of the cerebellum and medulla into the cervical portion of the spinal canal, often associated with spina bifida. Nystagmus is a usual accompaniment, typically horizontal on lateral gaze and vertical on upward gaze.

Ascher's s. Blepharochalasis, edema of the lips, and goiter without hyperthyroidism. Syn., *Laffer-Ascher syndrome.*

Axenfeld's s. Embryotoxon associated with adhesions of strands of iridic tissue to a prominent Schwalbe's line; an inherited anomaly usually associated with glaucoma occurring in adolescence or early adulthood. Syn., *iridocorneal mesodermal dysplasia.*

B s. Case type B.

Babinski-Froehlich s. Froehlich's syndrome.

Babinski-Nageotte s. Cerebellar hemiataxia, nystagmus, miosis, ptosis, and enophthalmos on the side of the lesion, with hemiparesis and sensibility disturbance on the contralateral side, due to involvement of the pyramidal tract, the median fillet, the inferior cerebellar peduncle, and the descending sympathetic fibers in the brain stem.

Balint's s. Ocular motor apraxia in which there is an inability to perform voluntarily fixational movements in the presence of normal reflex ocular movements, with specific inattention for visual stimuli, especially for objects in the peripheral field of vision.

Bardet-Biedl s. Laurence-Moon-Biedl syndrome.

Barré-Liéou s. Cervical spine abnormalities, cervical pain, tinnitus, vertigo, headache, and retrobulbar pain.

Bartholin-Patau s. Trisomy 13–15 syndrome.

Bassen-Kornzweig s. Crenated erythrocytes, celiac disease, ataxia of the Friedreich type, and atypical pigmentary degeneration of the retina; a rare recessive hereditary disease.

Behçet's s. Recurrent ulceration of the genitalia, aphthous ulcers of the mouth, and uveitis which may affect either the anterior or the posterior segment of the eye and usually results in hypopyon. It is of unknown etiology and is attributed by some to a virus or focal infection. Syn., *triple symptom complex of Behçet.*

Behr's s. Infantile optic atrophy, predominantly temporal and usually stabilizing after a few years, increased tendon reflexes usually with a positive Babinski sign, mild ataxia, mental deficiency, nystagmus, and weakness of the sphincter of the bladder with incontinence; occurring as a heredofamilial disease.

Benedikt's s. Ipsilateral oculomotor paralysis and contralateral tremor, spasm, or choreic movements of the face and the limbs, due to involvement of the red nucleus, oculomotor nerve, and the superior cerebellar peduncle. Syn., *tegmental mesencephalic paralysis; tegmental syndrome.*

Bernard's s. 1. Ipsilateral pupillary dilatation, widening of the palpebral fissure, and slight exophthalmos, with possible associated vaso-constriction, lowered

temperature, and excessive sweating of the face, due to irritation of the sympathetic pathway. 2. Horner's syndrome.

Bernard-Horner s. Horner's syndrome.

Biedl's s. Laurence-Moon-Biedl syndrome.

Biemond's s. Laurence-Moon-Biedl syndrome.

blind spot of Swann s. Esotropia in which the magnitude of the deviation is such that the image of the object of fixation falls on the optic disk of the deviating eye.

Bloch-Sulzberger s. A form of incontinentia pigmenti usually occurring either congenitally or in the first year of life, primarily affecting females, and characterized by patches of wavy streaks of slate-gray cutaneous pigmentation and other defects such as of teeth, hair, nails, and eyes. Ocular anomalies accompany about one-fourth of the cases and include pseudoglioma, cataract, strabismus, optic atrophy, nystagmus, uveitis, and chorioretinitis.

blue sclera s. Eddowes' syndrome.

Boder-Sedgwick s. Progressive cerebellar ataxia commencing in infancy, sinus and pulmonary infection, slow spasmodic eye movements, fixation nystagmus, slow labored indistinct speech, and telangiectasia of the bulbar conjunctiva, of the skin in the area of the bridge of the nose, and of the external ears, occurring as a disease of strong familial incidence.

Bonnet's s. Congenital tortuosity of the retinal vessels and vascular malformations in the midbrain.

Bonnevie-Ullrich s. Status Bonnevie-Ullrich.

van den Bosch s. Horizontal nystagmus, high myopia, choroideremia, mental deficiency, abnormal electroretinogram, and skeletal and skin anomalies; occurring as a heredofamilial disease.

Brain's s. Exophthalmos and external ophthalmoplegia in exophthalmic goiter.

Brown's tendon sheath s. An apparent paralysis of the inferior oblique muscle with an inability to elevate the eye above the horizontal plane in full adduction, limitation of movement of the affected eye in the forced duction test (*q.v.*) into the field of action of the inferior oblique muscle on abduction, elevation of the eye in a straight line from the inner canthus, widening of the palpebral fissure on adduction, and essentially normal motility in the temporal fields of gaze, due to a congenitally short anterior tendon sheath of the superior oblique muscle.

C s. Case type C.

carotid occlusion s. Transient monocular blindness, which may become permanent, and hemiplegia and hemianesthesia of the opposite side of the body, due to unilateral carotid artery occlusion. The most characteristic diagnostic sign is a significant difference in the retinal arterial pressure, the affected side being lower.

cavernous sinus s. Paralysis or paresis of the third, fourth, and sixth nerves and the first division of the fifth nerve, proptosis, and possibly edema of the eyelids and the conjunctiva, due to involvement of the cavernous sinus as from thrombosis, a tumor, or inflammatory conditions.

cerebellopontine angle s. Mixed nystagmus, falling and past pointing toward the affected side, marked vertigo, tinnitus and deafness, due to a lesion in the region of the cerebellopontine angle. Extension of the

lesion may involve the fifth and seventh nerves.

cervico-oculo-acoustic s. Retractio bulbi, vertebral synostosis, cervical spina bifida, labyrinthine deafness, and occasionally pterygium colli and/or torticollis; occurring congenitally as a dominant hereditary disease. Syn., *cervico-oculo-facial dysmorphia; cervico-oculo-muscular syndrome.*

cervico-oculo-muscular s. Cervico-oculo-acoustic syndrome.

Cestan's s. 1. Cestan-Chenais syndrome. 2. Raymond-Cestan syndrome.

Cestan-Chenais s. Cerebellar hemiataxia, nystagmus, miosis, ptosis, and enophthalmos on the side of the lesion, hemiparesis and sensibility disturbance on the contralateral side, ipsilateral paralysis of the soft palate and the vocal cords, due to involvement of the pyramidal tract, the median fillet, the inferior cerebellar peduncle, the nucleus ambiguus, and the descending sympathetic fibers in the brain stem.

Chandler's s. Dystrophy of the corneal endothelium, corneal edema, mild atrophy of the stroma of the iris, peripheral anterior synechiae, and glaucoma.

Charlin's s. Orbital and periorbital neuralgia, keratitis, iritis, rhinorrhea, and inflammation in the area of the nose, due to affection of the nasal, the nasociliary, and the anterior ethmoidal nerves.

Chédiak-Higashi s. Hematologic abnormalities including anomalous granulations in the polymorphonuclear leukocytes and lymphocytes, anemia, neutropenia, thrombopenia, lymphadenopathy, hepatosplenomegaly, low resistance to infection, and partial albinism with localized hyperpigmentation. Eye signs include pale fundi, photophobia, increased lacrimation, papilledema, and infiltration of ocular tissues with immature leukocytes. It is familial and results in death in childhood.

chiasmal s. Bitemporal, visual field defects and primary optic atrophy with apparently normal roentgenological findings in the sella turcica, due to involvement of the optic chiasm as by tumors or expanding aneurysms. Syn., *Cushing's syndrome.*

Christian's s. Schüller-Christian-Hand syndrome.

Claude's s. Ipsilateral, third nerve paralysis and contralateral, cerebellar ataxia or hemichorea, due to involvement of the red nucleus and the oculomotor nerve.

Claude Bernard's s. Bernard's syndrome.

clivus ridge s. Ipsilateral fixed mydriasis of the pupil, ipsilateral exotropia, and occasionally a slight ipsilateral ptosis, due to increased intracranial pressure on the oculomotor nerve in the region of the clivus ridge, caused by a space-taking lesion such as a tumor, abscess, or hemorrhage.

Cockayne's s. Cockayne's disease.

Cogan's s. A patchy granular type of posterior interstitial keratitis, usually bilateral, with daily variation in severity, accompanied by the vestibuloauditory symptoms of severe vertigo, nausea, vomiting, nystagmus, and finally deafness.

compression of the anterior angle of the chiasm s. of. Unilateral blindness with temporal hemianopsia of the other eye, usually indicative of a meningioma of the tuberculum sellae.

cone dysfunction s. Subnormal visual acuity, defective color vision, and absence of the photopic flicker electroretinogram, frequently accompanied by nystagmus and photophobia, due to a generalized disturbance of the cone system.

conjunctivoglandular s. of Parinaud. Granulomatous conjunctivitis characterized by red or yellowish growths (Parinaud's conjunctivitis), swollen hardened eyelids, and swelling of the lymph glands of the neck, especially the preauricular, due to a leptothrix infection.

Conradi's s. Stippled epiphyses.

crocodile tears s. Lacrimation reflexly induced by gustatory stimuli to the tongue, occurring in the stage of recovery of a facial nerve injury in or proximal to the geniculate ganglion, thought to be due to misdirected regeneration of fibers which proceed to the lacrimal gland instead of to the salivary glands.

Cushing's s. Chiasmal syndrome.

Dighton-Adair s. Van der Hoeve's syndrome.

Dimitri's s. Sturge-Weber syndrome.

Duane's s. Retraction of the eyeball into the orbit, associated with drooping of the upper eyelid on attempted adduction of the affected eye. Adduction is limited and, when attempted, the eye also moves upward or downward. Abduction is limited or abolished and, when attempted, the palpebral fissure may widen. It is usually unilateral, rarely affecting both eyes, and is considered to be due to congenital aberrant innervation to the lateral and medial rectus muscles which produces an anomalous co-contraction. Syn., *Duane's phenomenon; retractio bulbi; retraction syndrome; Stilling-Türk-Duane syndrome.*

dyscephalic mandibulo-oculo-facial s. Mandibulo-oculo-facial dyscephaly.

Eddowes' s. Blue sclerae associated with osteogenesis imperfecta. Syn., *blue sclera syn-*

drome; Lobstein's syndrome; Spurway's syndrome.

Ehlers-Danlos s. Meekrin-Ehlers-Danlos syndrome.

embryonic fixation s. Waardenburg's syndrome.

Falls-Kurtesz s. Distichiasis, chronic lymphatic edema of the lower extremities, pterygium colli, and ectropion of the lower eyelids; a dominant hereditary disease.

Fiessinger-Leroy-Reiter s. Oculo-uretero-synovial syndrome.

Fisher's s. Symmetrical ophthalmoplegia, ataxia, and absence of reflexes, due to cranial nerve neuropathy without an accompanying fever.

Foix's s. Paresis of third, fourth, fifth, and sixth cranial nerves, due to involvement of the external wall of the cavernous sinus by a neoplasm.

Foster Kennedy s. Kennedy's syndrome.

Foville's s. Ipsilateral palsy of the abducens nerve, loss of conjugate deviation of the eyes toward the affected side, ipsilateral facial paralysis, and contralateral paralysis of the limbs, due to a pontine lesion at or above the level of the sixth nerve nucleus.

Franceschetti s. Mandibulofacial dysostosis.

Franceschetti-Gernet s. Microphthalmia without microcornea, associated with macrophakia, high hypermetropia, tapetoretinal degeneration, disposition to glaucoma, and dental anomalies; occurring as a familial disease.

Franceschetti-Zwahlen s. Mandibulofacial dysostosis.

François' s. Dyscephalia with bird face, dental anomalies, dwarfism, hypotrichosis, cutaneous atrophy, bilateral microphthalmia, and congenital cataracts; a hereditary ectodermal dysplasia.

Froehlich's s. Adolescent obesity, especially around the shoulders and hips, soft hairless skin, genital hypoplasia, disturbed carbohydrate and fat metabolism, absence of secondary sex characteristics, and ocular signs of optic atrophy, bitemporal field defects, and delayed pupillary reaction to light, depending on the extent of the lesion. Diabetes insipidus and polyuria may also be present. The condition is due to involvement of the medial nuclei of the hypothalamus, the tuber cinereum, and neighboring structures. Syn., *dystrophia adiposogenitalis; adiposogenital dystrophy; adiposogenital syndrome; Babinski-Froehlich syndrome.*

Fuchs's s. Unilateral heterochromia of the iris, iridocyclitis with keratic precipitates, and cataract, occurring as a congenital, slowly progressive condition of unknown etiology.

Fuller-Albright s. A disease entity representing a generalized bone lesion (disseminated osteitis fibrosa) affecting the long bones, the pelvis, and the skull, and associated with patches of pigmentation on the skin. Ocular symptoms may involve a depression of the globe, pupillary dilation, occasional exophthalmos, and diplopia.

general fibrosis s. Bilateral ptosis and paralysis of all the extraocular muscles, due to a general congenital fibrosis.

Gerstmann's s. Visual agnosia, visual apraxia, dyslexia, loss of revisualization, acalculia, agraphia, finger agnosia, confusion of laterality, occasionally astereognosis, and possibly right-sided homonymous hemianopsia and loss of optokinetic nystagmus, due to a lesion at the occipitoparietal border involving the peristriate and the parastriate areas, the angular gyrus, and the interparietal sulcus area.

Gillespie's s. Aniridia, cerebellar ataxia, and oligophrenia, occurring as an autosomal recessive condition.

Godtfredsen's s. Ophthalmoplegia, trigeminal neuralgia, and twelfth nerve paralysis, resulting from involvement of the cavernous sinus and the neck lymphatics by a neoplasm.

Goldenhar's s. Subconjunctival dermoids near the limbus, accessory auricular appendages, and auricular fistula, occurring unilaterally and considered to be due to maldevelopment of the first branchial arch. Syn., *oculo-auricular dysplasia; oculo-auricular syndrome.*

Gougerot-Sjögren s. Sjögren's syndrome.

Gower-Paton-Kennedy s. Kennedy's syndrome.

Gradenigo's s. Ipsilateral pain in or about the eye, in the temple, or the side of the face, facial paralysis, photophobia, lacrimation, reduced corneal sensitivity, and paralysis of the sixth nerve, due to mastoiditis extending to the tip of the petrous bone and affecting the meninges in the epidural space and the adjacent sixth nerve, Gasserian ganglion, and seventh nerve.

Grönblad-Strandberg s. Pseudoxanthoma elasticum occurring in association with angioid streaks, due to degeneration of elastic tissue of the skin and the lamina vitrea of the choroid.

Gunn's jaw-winking s. Jaw-winking.

Hallermann-Streiff s. Mandibulo-oculo-facial dyscephaly.

Hand's s. Schüller-Christian-Hand syndrome.

Harada's s. Bilateral, acute, diffuse, exudative choroiditis, retinal detachment, headache, loss of appetite, nausea and vomiting, and sometimes temporary vitiligo, poliosis, and deafness, of undetermined origin, thought due to a virus infection.

Heerfordt's s. Bilateral parotitis, uveitis, and fever, often associated with paresis of the cranial nerves, especially the seventh, and considered to be a form of sarcoidosis. Syn., *Heerfordt's disease; uveoparotid fever; uveoparotitis.*

Hennebert's s. Attacks of spontaneous nystagmus and dizziness with exaggeration of the nystagmus when the column of air in the auditory meatus is compressed, due to a fistula in the labyrinth.

van der Hoeve's s. Blue sclerae, otosclerosis, and osteogenesis imperfecta. Syn., *Adair-Dighton syndrome.*

van der Hoeve-Halbertsma-Waardenburg s. Waardenburg's syndrome.

Holmes-Adie s. Adie's syndrome.

Horner's s. Unilateral miosis, slight ptosis, anhidrosis, slight enophthalmos, and flushing of the face, due to involvement of sympathetic fibers on that side. Syn., *Bernard-Horner syndrome.*

Hurler's s. Hurler's disease.

Hutchison's s. Neuroblastoma of the adrenal gland with metastases to the bones of the orbit and the skull, usually occurring in the first five years of life.

hypophyseo-sphenoidal s. Ophthalmoplegia, paresis of the sympathetic, and neuroparalytic keratitis, due to involvement of the trunks of the ocular cranial nerves in the region of the cavernous sinus by an infiltrating tumor.

inferior s. of the red nucleus. Rubro-ocular syndrome.

interoculo-irido-dermato-auditive s. Waardenburg's syndrome.

Irvine's s. Vitreous syndrome.

Jahnke's s. The Sturge-Weber syndrome but without glaucoma.

Kalischer s. Sturge-Weber syndrome.

Kennedy's s. Ipsilateral optic atrophy with contralateral papilledema, due to direct pressure on one optic nerve with the resultant forcing of cerebrospinal fluid into the sheath of the opposite optic nerve, most commonly caused by a tumor at the base of the frontal lobe. Syn., *Foster Kennedy syndrome; Gower-Paton-Kennedy syndrome; Paton's syndrome.*

Kimmelstiel-Wilson s. Renal edema, pronounced albuminuria, and frequently hypertension and diabetic retinopathy.

Klein's s. Hypertelorism, blepharophimosis, hypertrophy of the eyebrows, retrognathism, partial albinism and bilateral blue irides, high arched palate and dental anomalies, bilateral deafness, rigidities of the joints, amyoplasias, skeletal dysplasias, and syndactyly.

Krause's s. Encephalo-ophthalmic dysplasia.

Kurz's s. Partial or total blindness, enophthalmos, moderately dilated and fixed pupils, high hypermetropia, and progressive mental retardation.

labyrinthine s. Ménière's syndrome.

Laffer-Ascher s. Blepharochalasis, edema of the lips, and goiter without hyperthyroidism. Syn., *Ascher's syndrome.*

Laurence-Moon-Biedl s. Pigmentary degeneration of the retina, obesity, polydactylism, hypogenitalism, and mental retardation, considered due to inherited endocrine dysfunction. The condition is usually progressive, and night blindness and reduced visual acuity are primary symptoms. Syn., *Bardet-Biedl syndrome; Biedl's syndrome; Biemond's syndrome; Moon-Bardet-Biedl syndrome.*

Lawford's s. Vascular nevi of the face and scalp and glaucoma, occurring without neurologic signs or enlargement of the eyeballs.

Lhermitte's s. Paralysis of the internal rectus muscle for lateral conjugate gaze with normal function in convergence, due to a lesion in the posterior longitudinal bundle in the pons. Syn., *anterior internuclear ophthalmoplegia.*

Lobstein's s. Eddowes' syndrome.

Louis-Bar s. Cerebellar ataxia and telangiectases of the conjunctiva, face, and external ears. Bronchiectases was later added to the syndrome. It is a hereditary and developmental disease classified as one of the phacomatoses group. Syn., *ataxia telangiectatica.*

Lowe's s. Aminoaciduria, glycosuria, albuminuria, faulty ammonia metabolism, nephritis, renal dwarfism, mental deficiency, muscular hypotony, vitamin resistant renal rickets, congenital cataracts, and congenital glaucoma; considered to be a recessive sex-linked hereditary disease. Syn., *Lowe-Terry-MacLachlan syndrome; oculocerebrorenal syndrome.*

Lowe-Terry-MacLachlan s. Lowe's syndrome.

maculo-labyrinthine s. Recurrent central angiospastic retinopathy and Ménière's syndrome. Syn., *Montes-Lasala syndrome.*

Marchesani's s. Spherophakia, myopia, and glaucoma associated with brachydactyly and short stature. Syn., *dystrophia mesodermalis congenita hyperplastica; Weil-Marchesani syndrome.*

Marfan's s. Congenital, familial, bilateral, partial dislocation of the crystalline lens associated with arachnodactyly. It occurs more frequently in males, congenital miosis is usually present, and the pupils do not respond readily to atropine.

Marie-Guillan s. Rubrothalamic syndrome.

Marin Amat s. Reverse jaw-winking.

Marinesco-Sjögren s. Bilateral congenital cataracts, oligophrenia, and spinocerebellar ataxia; a hereditary disease.

Martorell's s. Pulseless disease.

Meekren-Ehlers-Danlos s. Hyperelastic and fragile skin, hyperflexible joints, and fragile blood vessels, with resulting hematomata which sometimes develop into pseudotumors. The condition has a hereditary tendency and often affects the skin of the eyelids. Syn., *fibrodysplasia hyperelastica*

Melkersson-Rosenthal s. Recurrent facial paralysis, recurrent edema of the face and lips, and furrows in the tongue. Associated eye signs may include swelling of the eyelids, epiphora, conjunctivitis, marginal corneal opacities, retrobulbar neuritis, or exophthalmos.

Ménière's s. Severe vertigo, nausea, nystagmus, falling toward the affected side, tinnitus, and deafness on the affected side, due to labyrinthine involvement, cerebellopontine angle tumors, otitis media, etc. Syn., *Ménière's disease; labyrinthine syndrome.*

Mikulicz' s. Chronic, bilateral, noninflammatory, symmetrical enlargement of the lacrimal glands, enlargement of the salivary glands, especially the parotid, and swelling and drooping of the eyelids with marked narrowing of the palpebral fissures, occurring in association with another disease, such as reticulosis, sarcoidosis, tuberculosis, or syphilis.

Millard-Gubler s. Ipsilateral abducens palsy and facial paralysis and contralateral hemiplegia of the limbs, due to a nuclear or

infranuclear lesion in the pons. Syn., *hemiplegia alternans facialis; Gubler's paralysis; Weber-Gubler syndrome.*

Milles's s. Vascular nevi of the face and scalp and angioma of the choroid, without glaucoma.

Moebius' s. Congenital, bilateral, abducens, and facial paresis due to a lesion in the brain stem. There also may be restricted adduction, deafness, webbed fingers or toes, or absence of induced vestibular nystagmus. Syn., *congenital facial diplegia; congenital oculofacial paralysis.*

Monakow's s. Contralateral hemiplegia, hemianesthesia, and homonymous hemianopsia, due to occlusion of the anterior choroidal artery. Syn., *anterior choroidal artery syndrome.*

Montes-Lasala s. Maculo-labyrinthine syndrome.

Moon-Bardet-Biedl s. Laurence-Moon-Biedl syndrome.

mucocutaneous s. Stevens-Johnson syndrome.

nondominant parietal lobe s. Spatial disorientation, confusion of laterality, dressing apraxia, hemianopsia, inability to maintain motor responses, and abnormal optokinetic responses, with intact language and mental functions; due to lesions involving the nondominant parietal lobe.

Nonne-Marie s. Marie's disease.

Nothnagel's s. Third nerve paralysis with contralateral cerebellar ataxia, due to a lesion of the superior cerebellar peduncle, red nucleus, and emerging oculomotor fibers.

oculo-auricular s. Goldenhar's syndrome.

oculocerebrorenal s. Lowe's syndrome.

oculodentodigital s. Oculodentodigital dysplasia.

oculoglandular s. of Parinaud.

Conjunctivoglandular syndrome of Parinaud.

oculo-uretero-synovial s. Initial diarrhea followed by urethritis, polyarthritis, and conjunctivitis, iridocyclitis, or keratitis; a rare condition of unknown etiology primarily affecting young adult males. Syn., *Fiessinger-Leroy-Reiter syndrome; Reiter's syndrome.*

oculovertebral s. Oculovertebral dysplasia.

orbital apex-sphenoidal fissure s. S-O syndrome.

paratrigeminal s. Raeder's syndrome.

Parinaud's s. 1. Paralysis of vertical conjugate movements of the eyes either for elevation or depression, or both, due to a lesion in the subthalamic or the upper peduncular region. Pupillary abnormalities, especially dilated pupils which fail to react to light, may be present, as may be ptosis, retraction of the upper eyelid, or paralysis of convergence. Bell's phenomenon is present. 2. Conjunctivoglandular syndrome.

Paton's s. Kennedy's syndrome.

pineal s. Sylvian syndrome.

Posner-Schlossman s. Glaucomatocyclitic crisis.

pulseless s. Pulseless disease.

Raeder's s. Involvement of the trigeminal nerve and one or more other cranial nerves, together with oculopupillary fibers, which varies with the site of the lesion. It may include ptosis, miosis, enophthalmos, and facial hyperesthesia. Severe unilateral head pain is typical and characteristically sweating is intact on the ipsilateral side. Syn., *paratrigeminal syndrome.*

Raymond's s. Ipsilateral abducens palsy and contralateral hemiplegia of the limbs, due to a lesion involving the pyramidal tract and sixth nerve nucleus.

Raymond Cestan s. Paralysis of the lateral rectus muscle for conjugate gaze, sometimes associated with contralateral hemiplegia, due to a lesion of the posterior longitudinal bundle in the pons and the lower midbrain.

Refsum's s. Cerebellar ataxia, chronic polyneuritis, atypical pigmentary degeneration of the retina, night blindness, and contraction of the visual fields; a recessive hereditary disease.

Reiter's s. Oculo-uretero-synovial syndrome.

retraction s. Duane's syndrome.

retraction s., vertical. Congenital paralysis of the superior and the inferior rectus muscles of the same eye, slight enophthalmos, and slight narrowing of the palpebral fissure, usually due to limiting fibrous bands in the vertical recti.

Riddoch's s. Loss of interest and attention in the homonymous half fields, due to interference in the corticothalamic connections with visual sensory area 17.

Rieger's s. Rieger's disease.

Riley-Day s. Crying without tears, corneal hypesthesia or anesthesia, sleeping with the eyelids partially open, and such dehydration symptoms as attacks of high fever, vomiting, diarrhea, broncho-pneumonia, profuse salivation, and sweating, occurring in young children. Corneal pathology may be present, especially in the lower portion, ranging from superficial involvement to severe deep keratitis. Syn., *dysautonomia; familial autonomic dysfunction.*

Robin's s. A congenital triad of temporary abnormal smallness of the chin (microgenia), abnormal smallness of the tongue with backward dislodgement, and cleft palate. Accompanying ocular anomalies may include glaucoma, retinal detachment, or high myopia.

Romberg's s. Romberg's disease.

Rothmund's s. Atrophy of the skin with patches of pigmentation and telangiectasis, hypogonadism, and rapidly developing cataracts, occurring in early childhood as a recessive heredofamilial trait.

Rubino-Corrazza s. Uveo-meningitic syndrome.

rubro-ocular s. Ipsilateral third nerve paralysis and contralateral cerebellar ataxia, due to involvement of the superior cerebellar peduncle and the inferior portion of the red nucleus. Syn. *Claude's syndrome; Nothnagel's syndrome; inferior syndrome of the red nucleus.*

rubrothalamic s. Contralateral cerebellar ataxia, nystagmus, and contralateral hemianesthesia due to involvement of the superior cerebellar peduncle and superior portion of the red nucleus. Syn., *Marie-Guillan syndrome; superior syndrome of the red nucleus.*

Saenger's s. Pupillary rigidity to light and delayed pupillary contraction in convergence which persists for a short period after the convergence movement has ceased.

Sanders' s. Epidemic keratoconjunctivitis.

Sanders-Hogan s. Epidemic keratoconjunctivitis.

Schäfer's s. Dyskeratosis of the palms of the hands and soles of the feet, hyperhidrosis, disseminated follicular hyperkeratosis, leukoplakia of the buccal mucosa, and congenital cataract; a dominant hereditary disease.

Schaumann's s. Sarcoidosis.

Schirmer's s. Vascular nevi of the face and scalp and hydrophthalmos.

Schüller's s. Schüller-Christian-Hand syndrome.

Schüller-Christian-Hand s. Exophthalmos, polyuria associated with diabetes insipidus, and lipoid deposits in the bones, occurring in Schüller-Christian-Hand disease. Syn., *Christian's syndrome; Hand's syndrome; Schüller's syndrome.*

Siemens' s. Congenital atrophy or hypoplasia of the skin, and congenital cataract; a simple recessive hereditary disease.

Sjögren's s. 1. Failure of lacrimal secretion, keratoconjunctivitis sicca, failure of secretion of the salivary glands and mucous glands of the upper respiratory tract, and polyarthritis, usually occurring in women after menopause, due to degeneration of the glandular parenchyma followed by fibrosis, of undetermined etiology. Syn., *Gougerot-Sjögren syndrome.* 2. Bilateral congenital cataracts and oligophrenia; a recessive hereditary disease.

Sjögren-Larsson s. Congenital ichthyosis, oligophrenia, spastic paraplegia, and occasionally bilateral macular degeneration.

Sluder's s. Orbital and periorbital neuralgia, accommodative asthenopia, and sensation of the eyeball being too large for the orbit, due to irritation of the ciliary ganglion.

S-O s. External and internal ophthalmoplegia of varying degree, ptosis, hyperesthesia or anesthesia of the upper eyelid, half of the forehead and the cornea, vasomotor disturbances, impairment of vision which may result in blindness, and constant radiating pain behind the eyeball, due to a traumatic, inflammatory, or neoplastic process involving the sphenoidal fissure and the optic canal which results in pressure on the structures passing through them. Syn., *orbital apex-sphenoidal fissure syndrome; sphenoidal fissure-optic canal syndrome.*

Sorsby's s. Absence or rudimentary presence of the terminal phalanges of the hands and feet and bilateral pigmented macular colobomata; a dominant familial disease.

sphenoidal fissure-optic canal s. S-O syndrome.

Spurway's s. Eddowes' syndrome.

Stevens-Johnson s. An acute purulent form of erythema multiforme exudativum in which vesicles appear on the mucous membranes of the conjunctiva, mouth, nose, genitourinary orifices, and anal canal, followed by similar eruptions on the skin. It may be of toxic origin or of unknown etiology. Syn., *Stevens-Johnson disease; ectodermosis erosiva pluriorificialis; mucocutaneous syndrome.*

Stilling-Türk-Duane s. Duane's syndrome.

Sturge-Weber s. Vascular nevi of the face and the scalp, epileptic convulsions, glaucoma, angioma of the brain and the meninges, calcification of the cortex of the brain, and sometimes hemiplegia, of undetermined etiology. Syn., *angio-encephalo-cutaneous syndrome; Sturge-Weber-Kalischer-Dimitri syndrome; vascular encephalotrigeminal syndrome; vascular neuro-oculo-cutaneous syndrome.*

superior oblique tendon sheath s. Brown's tendon sheath syndrome.

superior orbital fissure s. Ipsilateral motility disturbances of the extraocular muscles, hypesthesia of the ipsilateral cornea, ipsilateral exophthalmos, ipsilateral palpable swelling in the temporal region, partial or complete loss of the field of vision, ipsilateral disturbances of the pupillary reflexes, and frequently papilledema and edema of the eyelids and conjunctiva, usually caused by a meningioma of the sphenoid bone affecting nerves passing through the superior orbital fissure.

superior s. of the red nucleus. Rubrothalamic syndrome.

Swann's s. Blind spot syndrome.

Sylvian s. Nystagmus retractorius, palsy of ocular movement, especially of elevation, tonic spasms of convergence on the attempt to look upward, and attacks of clonic convergence movements, due to a neoplasm or inflammation in the region of the aqueduct of Sylvius. Syn., *aqueduct of Sylvius syndrome; pineal syndrome.*

tegmental s. Benedikt's syndrome.

temporal arteritis s. Temporal arteritis.

tendon sheath s. Brown's tendon sheath syndrome.

Terson's s. Subarachnoid hemorrhage and profuse bleeding into the vitreous.

Tolosa-Hunt s. Recurrent unilateral retro-orbital pain and extraocular muscle palsies, attributed to indolent inflammation of the cavernous sinus or superior orbital fissure.

Touraine-Solente-Golé s. Thickening of the skin, especially of the forehead, face, and eyelids, and enlargement of the extremities, particularly the hands; a hereditary mesenchymal disease commencing in the second decade of life.

Treacher Collins s. Mandibulofacial dysostosis.

trisomy D s. Trisomy 13–15 syndrome.

trisomy 13–15 s. A congenital condition in which an extra autosomal chromosome of the 13–15 (D group) is present, resulting in 47 chromosomes instead of the normal 46, and producing a variety of deformities, the most common of which are mental retardation, malformed ears, heart defects, cleft palate, deafness, polydactyly, umbilical hernia, microphthalmia, coloboma, and cataract. Syn., *Bartholin-Patau syndrome; trisomy D syndrome.*

Ullrich's *s.* Cranial deformities with a broad nose and small jaw, skeletal deformities of the vertebrae and extremities, visceral degeneration, and bilateral anophthalmus or microphthalmus.

Usher's *s.* Pigmentary degeneration of the retina associated with deafness.

uveo-meningitic *s.* Acute bilateral uveitis associated with meningitis, of undertermined etiology. Syn., *Rubino-Corrazza syndrome.*

V *s.* Exotropia in which the deviation increases as the eyes rotate straight upward, or esotropia in which the deviation increases as the eyes rotate straight downward. Cf. *A syndrome.* Syn., *V phenomenon.*

vascular encephalotrigeminal *s.* Sturge-Weber syndrome.

vascular neuro-oculo-cutaneous *s.* Sturge-Weber syndrome.

vitreous *s.* Prolapse of the vitreous into the anterior chamber following rupture of the hyaloid face, occurring weeks or months after apparently uncomplicated intracapsular cataract extraction. Subsequent changes include the formation of strandlike adhesions to the operative wound and to the retina, iris, and ciliary body, and macular degeneration, pain, and photophobia. Syn., *Irvine's syndrome.*

Vogt-Koyanagi *s.* Bilateral uveitis, alopecia, poliosis, vitiligo, and deafness, of undetermined etiology.

Waardenburg's *s.* Blepharophimosis, lateral displacement of the medial canthi and the lacrimal puncta, hyperplasia of the root of the nose and the medial eyebrows, pigment anomalies, such as heterochromia iridis and a white forelock, and congenital deafness or deaf-mutism, occurring as a dominant hereditary trait. Syn., *van der Hoeve-Halbertsma-Waardenburg syndrome; interoculo-irido-dermato-auditive syndrome.*

Waldenström's *s.* A pronounced increase of gamma globulin in the blood associated with normocytic anemia, recurrent purpura, and, usually, accompanying ocular signs of sharply reduced central vision with normal peripheral vision, due to retinal edema, hemorrhages, retinal detachment, and occasionally papilledema. Syn., *macroglobulinemia; hyperglobulinemic purpura.*

Wallenberg's *s.* Vertigo, nausea, vomiting, difficulty in swallowing and speaking, nystagmus, ipsilateral ataxia of the limbs, loss of pain and temperature sensibility ipsilaterally of the face and contralaterally of the body, and ipsilateral miosis, ptosis, and enophthalmos, due to occlusion of the posterior inferior cerebellar artery.

Weber's *s.* Homolateral ptosis, dilated and fixed pupil, divergent strabismus, and contralateral hemiplegia of the face and the limbs, due to a lesion in the region of the cerebral peduncles affecting the third cranial nerve. Syn., *Weber's paralysis.*

Weber-Gubler *s.* Millard-Gubler syndrome.

Weil-Marchesani *s.* Marchesani's syndrome.

Werner's *s.* Premature graying and thinning of the hair, scleroderma, especially of the face and the extremities, ulceration of the feet and the legs, bilateral cataracts, hypogonadism, osteoporosis, calcification of peripheral arteries, endocrine dysfunction, and sometimes blue sclerae and keratitis, occurring as a heredofamilial disorder.

Wernicke's *s.* Wernicke's disease.

Weyers-Thier *s.* Oculovertebral dysplasia.

Wilson's s. Wilson's disease.

Wyburn-Mason s. Dilated tortuous and intercommunicating arteries and veins of the retina and midbrain accompanied by facial nevi and mental disorders. Symptoms include hemiplegia, homonymous hemianopsia, ocular paresis, strabismus, ptosis, nystagmus, and facial palsy.

synechia (sih-nek'e-ah). Adhesion of the iris to the cornea or to the capsule of the crystalline lens.

annular s. Posterior synechia of the entire pupillary margin of the iris. Syn., *circular synechia; ring synechia.*

anterior s. Adhesion of the iris to the cornea.

circular s. Annular synechia.

peripheral s. Anterior synechia of the root of the iris.

posterior s. Adhesion of the iris to the capsule of the crystalline lens.

ring s. Annular synechia.

total s. Posterior synechia of the entire iris.

synechotomy (sin"eh-kot'o-me). Surgical division of a synechia, as in cutting the iris free from adhesion to the capsule of the crystalline lens.

synergist (sin'er-jist). See *muscles, synergistic.*

synesthesia (sin"es-the'ze-ah). 1. Concomitant sensation of a sense other than the one being stimulated, such as seeing a color on hearing a sound. 2. Sensation in one part of the body or of an organ, due to stimulation of another part.

synizesis pupillae (sin"ih-ze'sis pu-pil'e). Occlusion or closure of the pupil.

synkinesis, pterygoid-levator (sin-kih-ne'sis). Jaw-winking.

synkinesis, trigeminal-oculomotor (sin-kih-ne'sis). Associated movements between muscles innervated by the trigeminal and oc-

ulomotor nerves, as, for example, jaw-winking.

synophrys (sin-of'ris). Joining of the eyebrows.

synophthalmia (sin"of-thal'me-ah). Cyclopia.

synopsia (sin-op'se-ah). 1. Cyclopia. 2. Synopsy.

synopsy (sin'op-se). A type of synesthesia in which visual sensations are produced by auditory stimulation. See also *color hearing.*

Synoptiscope (sin-op'tih-skōp). A type of major amblyoscope.

synoptophore (sin-op'to-fōr). A type of major amblyoscope.

Synoropticon (sin-or-op'tih-kon). An orthoptic instrument devised by McLaughlin for the treatment of strabismus, consisting essentially of a rectangular box, one square end containing a black field on which is a green disk centered in a complementary-colored, square, red frame. Each target can be independently transilluminated by enclosed light sources and is viewed through complementary red and green filters. See also *synoroptics.*

synoroptics (sin-or-op'tiks). A technique devised by McLaughlin for the orthoptic treatment of strabismus in which the patient views the targets on the Synoropticon through complementary color filters such that the normally deviating eye sees the red square and the fixating eye the central green disk. The targets are illuminated in a prescribed sequence of flash exposures until simultaneous perception and then superimposition are elicited.

synoscope, Terrien's (sin'o-skōp). A hand-held instrument for determining the presence of simultaneous binocular vision, consisting essentially of a bar, one end of which is placed in contact with the bridge of the nose, supporting a vertical median-plane septum at the proximal end, a variable distance, vertical, transverse plate with a square aperture, and a distal pair of vertical, transverse, laterally separable plates in each of which is one half of the letter V.

synthesis, additive (sin'theh-sis). The formation of a color by a mixture of light stimuli of two or more other colors incident on the same area of the retina simultaneously or in rapid succession.

syntonics (sin-ton'iks). A system of corrective procedures in which selected frequencies of the visible spectrum are utilized, usually by means of color filters, with the implication of therapeutic value in the colors themselves.

syntonist (sin'ton-ist). One who practices syntonics.

system. 1. A methodical arrangement of interacting or interdepending parts to subserve a common function. 2. A group of organs serving an over-all biological function, such as the nervous system. 3. Organized ideas, essential principles, or facts arranged in a rational dependence. 4. The body as a functional unit.

boxing s. Boxing method.

C.I.E. co-ordinate s. A graphic system of representing the colors in relation to each other by plotting on a plane co-ordinate scale the proportional values of two of the three primary colors (red, green, and blue) required by a standard observer to match all other colors. The value of the third primary is derived from the fact that the sum of the three is constant

datum s. Datum method.

GOMAC s. GOMAC method.

lens s. A combination of lenses, or lens elements, ordinarily mounted on a common axis, which may be in contact with each other or separated by transparent iso-

tropic media, and which act together to produce an image.

lens s., compound. A lens system having more than two refracting surfaces, i.e., consisting of more than one lens.

lens s., simple. A lens system having only two refracting surfaces, i.e., consisting of only one lens.

Munsell s. A three dimensional, polar, co-ordinate system for cataloging opaque, surface, pigment colors in accordance with three psychophysical attributes called *hue, chroma* (saturation), and *value* (lightness, brightness, or luminance), in which the chroma is represented in equal sensation intervals on a radial scale, hue on a circumferential scale, and value on an axial scale.

optical s. A combination of mirrors, lenses, lens elements, or prisms, ordinarily mounted in a common axis, which may be in contact with each other or separated by transparent isotropic media, and which act together to produce an image.

optical s., achromatic. An optical system designed to minimize chromatic aberration, as represented by its ability to bring the light of two fiducial wavelengths to a common focus.

optical s., afocal. An optical system of zero focal power, such that rays entering parallel emerge parallel.

optical s., aplanatic. An optical system free of both spherical aberration and coma.

optical s., Bouwers'. A catadioptric system consisting of a concave spherical mirror and a diverging meniscus lens having spherical surfaces. The lens, whose convex surface is turned toward the mirror, is located at the center of curvature of the mirror and serves to correct the spherical aberration of the concave mirror.

optical s., centered. Homocentric optical system.

optical s., coaxial. Homocentric optical system.

optical s., concurrent. An optical system in which a displacement of the object along the optical axis results in a displacement of the image in the same direction, characteristic of lens systems.

optical s., contracurrent. An optical system in which a displacement of the object along the optical axis results in a displacement of the image in the opposite direction, characteristic of mirror systems.

optical s., convergent. An optical system which bends incident light rays toward its axis, increasing the curvature of incident wavefronts. Hence, an optical system in which the first principal point is to the right of the primary focal point.

optical s., convergent (dioptric). A convergent optical system employing refracting surfaces.

optical s., convergent (katoptric). A convergent optical system employing reflecting surfaces.

optical s., dioptric. An optical system employing refracting surfaces.

optical s., divergent. An optical system which bends incident light rays away from its axis, decreasing the curvature of incident wavefronts, hence an optical system in which the first principal point is to the left of the primary focal point.

optical s., divergent (dioptric). A divergent optical system employing refracting surfaces.

optical s., divergent (katoptric). A divergent optical system employing reflecting surfaces.

optical s., Gaussian. A method of representing the paraxial properties of compound optical systems in terms of principal points and planes and focal points and planes. The concept of nodal planes and points, sometimes considered in optical systems, was introduced by Moser, but is sometimes alluded to in Gaussian optics.

optical s., hemisymmetric. An optical system consisting of two parts, the second being a magnified mirror image of the first.

optical s., holosymmetric. An optical system consisting of two parts, the second being a mirror image of the first.

optical s., homocentric. An optical system in which the elements are centered on a common axis. Syn., *centered optical system; coaxial optical system.*

optical s., reduced. An optical system in which axial distances are represented by the ratios of the actual distances to the index of refraction of the medium in which they lie.

optical s., schlieren. A combination of light source, lenses, and knife edges arranged so that the interposing of refractive index gradients in the media in the optical path, as by heat, pressure, stress, or tension, produces a change in gradient distribution pattern in the image, used especially to observe air flow as affected by such factors as heat, projectile speed, or turbulence.

optical s., telecentric. An optical system in which either the entrance pupil or the exit pupil is at infinity.

optical s., telescopic. Any optical system which transforms a cylindrical bundle of parallel rays into another cylindrical bundle of parallel rays; an afocal system.

optical s., unreduced. An optical system in which actual distances are designated regardless of the index of refraction of the medium in which they lie.

Ostwald s. A system of specifying surface colors, based on a color match with a hypothetical ideal surface which has either (*a*) a constant value of spectral reflectance for the wavelength band between two spectral complementaries, and another constant value for all wavelengths outside this band, or (*b*) in the case of a wavelength having no spectral complementary, a constant value of spectral reflectance for all wavelengths shorter than this particular wavelength, and another constant value for all longer wavelengths. Underlying this concept of an ideal surface is the basic idea that all surface colors of the same dominant wavelength differ only in the proportions of black, white, and color which they contain, and so can be specified according to these proportions in the equation: $W + B + C = 1$. Hence the variables employed in the system and their correlates in terms of the ideal surface described are: (1) *Ostwald hue,* representative of that portion of the spectrum for which the surface has the higher reflectance value; (2) *full color content,* represented by C in the above equation and specified as the higher reflectance value minus the lower; (3) *white content,* represented by W in the equation, and specified as the lower of the two reflectance values; and (4) *black content,* represented in the equation by B, and specified as the difference between unity and the higher of the two reflectance values. By use of the *Ostwald notation,* these variables are designated for the various *Ostwald tints* and *tones* which comprise the entire array of *Ostwald colors,* consisting of several hundred chromatic and achromatic samples of various mixtures of *semichromes* with black and white.

Ridgway s. A systematic arrangement and notation for naming and specifying colors by reference to the *Ridgway Color Dictionary* (1912 edition) containing 1,113 painted samples. It is widely used for describing colors of flowers, birds, and insects and the arrangement of colors and terminology are similar to the Ostwald system.

Telecon s. A Galilean telescopic system in which the eyepiece is a contact lens of high concave dioptric power and the objective is a wafer of appropriate convex power cemented to the ocular side of a spectacle lens carrier.

von Szily, ring sinus of (fon sil'e). See under *sinus.*

T

T. Abbreviation for (1) *intraocular tension;* (2) *tropia.*

tabes dorsalis (tāb′bēz dor-sa′lis). A degenerative disease of the dorsal columns of the spinal cord, the posterior nerve trunks, and frequently certain cranial nerves, especially the optic nerve, due to neurosyphilis. Ocular symptoms include the Argyll Robertson pupil, absent or diminished pupillary dilation in response to pain, optic atrophy, visual field defects, ptosis, and paralysis of one or more of the extraocular muscles.

table. A collection or an arrangement of related data.

color t. 1. A chromaticity diagram. 2. A systematic arrangement of colors for classification or cataloguing purposes. 3. A pattern or an arrangement of colors for testing color vision.

    color t., Daae's. Seventy colored wool samples in 10 horizontal rows of 7 each, one row of which includes variations of green, another variations of red, and the others, wools of various colors which a color-deficient person may identify as shades of the same color.

    color t., Helmholtz'. 1. Helmholtz' color circle. 2. Helmholtz' color triangle.

    color t., Maxwell's. Maxwell's color triangle.

    color t., Newton's. Newton's color circle.

Donders' t. A table of expected amplitudes of accommodation at different ages, based on Donders' data.

Duane's t. A table, compiled by Duane, indicating maximum, minimum, and average amplitudes of accommodation at different ages.

Neumueller's t's. Tables compiled by Julius Neumueller which indicate the expected lens correction for astigmatism, on the basis of the ophthalmometer finding, after allowing for physiological astigmatism and the effectivity of the spherical component of a lens placed 15 mm. in front of the cornea.

Whitwell's t. A table for indicating the optimal curvatures of the ocular surfaces of the correcting spectacle lenses in anisometropia to minimize aniseikonia.

TABO notation. See under *notation.*

tachistoscope (tah-kis′to-skōp). An instrument which exposes visual stimuli for a brief period of time, usually 1/10 of a second or less.

Tachistoscreener, Roberts (tah-kis′-to-skrēn-er). A visual field screening instrument having a translucent screen from behind which are flashed various patterns of dots of light. A chin rest, occluder, rheostat, rotary switch for target selection, and a flash control device are provided.

tachycardia strumosa exophthalmica (tak″e-kahr′de-ah stroo-mo′sah ek″sof-thal′mih-kah). Excessively rapid heart action in exophthalmic goiter.

Taillefer's valve (tă-yeh-ferz). See under *valve.*

Tait's method (tātz). See under *method.*

Tajiri method (tah-jēr′e). See under *method.*

Takayasu's disease (tah″kah-yah′-suz). Pulseless disease.

Takayasu-Ohnishi disease (tah″-kah-yah′soo-o-nish′e). Pulseless disease.

talantropia (tal″an-tro′pe-ah). Nystagmus.

talbot (tahl′but). A unit of luminous energy. One talbot per sec. = one lumen.

Talbot's (tahl′butz) **bands; effect; law; level.** See under the nouns.

Talbot-Plateau law (tahl′but-plă-to′). See under *law.*

Tamascope (tah′mah-skōp). The trade name for a projector which produces a high contrast magnified image of a contact lens on any smooth vertical surface for the purpose of inspection.

tangent centune (tan′jent sen-tūn). Prism diopter.

tangent screen. See under *screen.*

tape. A narrow strip or band of paper, cloth, metal, etc., usually calibrated.

Holtzer t. An auxiliary tape, 1 m. long, attached to Priestley Smith's tape, extending from beneath the fixating eye to the fixation target, and serving to maintain a constant fixation distance.

Priestley Smith's t. An apparatus for determining the objective angle of strabismus, consisting of two tapes attached to a ring, one being 1 m. in length and the other graduated in centimeters. One end of the meter tape is placed beneath the fixating eye and a light source is placed through the ring on the other end of the tape and positioned in the midplane 1 m. from the subject. A fixation target is moved along the calibrated tape, held perpendicular to the midplane, until the corneal reflex of the light source occupies the same relative position in the deviating eye as originally in the fixating eye, the examiner's eye remaining directly above the light source.

tapetum (tah-pe′tum). Any of certain membranous layers, especially of the choroid and the retina.

cellulosum, t. A type of tapetum lucidum consisting of several layers of highly reflecting endothelial cells in tilelike formation in the choroid of most carnivorous animals, seals, and nocturnal prosimians which gives the pupils a lustrous appearance when illuminated in the dark.

choroidal t. A tapetum lucidum located within the deeper layers of the choroid.

fibrosum, t. A type of tapetum lucidum consisting of wavy, tendinouslike, fibrous tissue in the choroid of most hoofed animals, elephants, whales, some monkeys, and certain fishes, which gives the pupils a lustrous appearance when illuminated in the dark.

guanine t. A type of tapetum lucidum in which guanine crystals are the reflecting medium, found in the choroid of chondrosteans and some teleosts, and in the retina of crocodilians and some teleosts.

lucidum, t. A reflecting structure lying behind the visual receptors, either in the pigmented epithelium of the retina or in the deep layers of the choroid, in the eyes of certain mammals, birds, and fishes which gives a shining appearance to the eyes, as is seen in cats' eyes when illuminated in the dark. It aids vision in dim illumination by reflecting light back through the visual receptors which it has already traversed, thus augmenting the effectiveness of the light stimulating the retina.

nigrum, t. The pigment epithelium layer of the retina.

nonocclusible t. A tapetum lucidum that is not variably obscured by pigment migration, remaining exposed to the same extent in all degrees of illumination.

occlusible t. A tapetum lucidum that is primarily operative in dim light, being obscured in bright light by migrating pigment.

retinal t. A tapetum lucidum in the pigment epithelium of the retina, formed by reflecting crystals such as guanine.

taraxis (tah-rak'sis). 1. Reduced vision resulting from trauma to the eye. *Obs.* 2. Mild conjunctivitis. *Obs.*

target. A pattern or an object of fixation, attention, or observation in vision testing or training.

tarsadenitis (tahrs-ad"e-ni'tis). Inflammation of both the tarsus and the Meibomian glands.

tarsal (tahr'sal). Pertaining to, or situated in, the tarsus.

tarsal arches; cartilage; cyst; glands; plate. See under the nouns.

tarsectomy (tahr-sek'to-me). Surgical removal of a portion of the tarsus.

tarsitis (tahr-si'tis). Inflammation of the tarsus secondary to inflammatory processes originating in the skin and subcutaneous tissues or in the conjunctiva.

necroticans, t. Necrosis of the tarsus with perforations through the conjunctiva and subsequent scarring, due to multiple internal hordeolums occurring simultaneously in crops.

tarso- (tahr'so-). A combining form denoting or pertaining to the tarsus or to the edge of the eyelid.

tarsocheiloplasty (tahr"so-ki'lo-plas"te). Plastic surgery of the eyelid margin.

tarsomalacia (tahr"so-mah-la'she-ah). Softening of the tarsus.

tarso-orbital (tahr"so-ōr'bih-tal). Pertaining to the tarsus and the orbital walls.

tarsophyma (tahr"so-fi'mah). Any tarsal growth or tumor.

tarsoplasia (tahr"so-pla'se-ah). Tarsoplasty.

tarsoplasty (tahr'so-plas"te). Plastic surgery of the eyelid; blepharoplasty.

tarsorrhaphy (tahr-sōr'ah-fe). A surgical operation for shortening or closing the palpebral fissure in which the upper and the lower eyelids are sutured together.

tarsotomy (tahr-sot'o-me). Surgical incision of the tarsus or of the eyelid.

tarsus (tahr'sus). A thin plate of dense fibrous and some elastic tissue in the upper and the lower eyelids, giving them their shape and firmness, located anterior to the palpebral conjunctiva and extending from the orbital septum to the eyelid margin. The tarsus is attached to the lateral and medial walls of the orbit by the lateral and the medial palpebral ligaments and to the superior and the inferior margins of the orbit by the orbital septum. The tarsus in the upper eyelid is larger than in the lower and contains approximately 25 Meibomian glands, while the lower contains approximately 20. Syn., *tarsal cartilage; tarsal plate; tarsus palpebrarum.*

palpebrarum, t. The tarsus.

tattooing, corneal. Surgical embedding of fine particles of metallic salts, such as gold or platinum chlorides, into the subepithelial areas of the cornea, by means of special needles, to color the cornea for therapeutic or cosmetic reasons.

Tay's (tāz) **choroiditis; disease; dots; sign; spot.** See under the nouns.

Taylor reflectometer. See under *re-flectometer.*

Tay-Sachs disease (ta-saks'). See under *disease.*

tears. The salty, slightly alkaline, clear, watery fluid secreted by the lacrimal gland which, together with the secretions of the conjunctival goblet cells, the Meibomian glands, the glands of Zeis, and the accessory lacrimal glands of Krause and Wolfring, serves to keep the conjunctiva and the cornea moist and to facilitate eyelid movement. The fluid contains proteins, urea, sugar, salts, lysozyme, and mucin, and is drained from the eye through the nasolacrimal duct via the lacrimal puncta.

crocodile t's. 1. A spasmodic, copious flow of tears, occurring in facial paralysis, on the tasting or chewing of food. See also *gustolacrimal reflex.* 2. False or affected tears.

technique. See *method* or *test.*

Teichmann's (tīk'mahnz) **lymphatic circle; radial vessels.** See under the nouns.

teichopsia (ti-kop'se-ah). A transient visual sensation of bright shimmering colors, such as the fortification spectrum associated with a scintillating scotoma.

telangiectasis of the retina (tel-an"je-ek'tah-sis). Numerous, small, sharply defined, red globules in a slightly elevated area of the fundus which may become whitish in color due to circulatory disturbance. It consists of groups of dilated capillaries, may be stationary, or progressive (Coats's disease), and is usually unilateral.

Telebinocular (tel"e-bi-nok'u-lar). A trade name for a Brewster-type stereoscope containing 5 D. convex spheroprisms (base-out) for eyepieces.

telecentric (tel"e-sen'trik). Pertaining to an optical system in which either the entrance pupil or the exit pupil is at infinity.

teleceptor (tel"e-sep'tor). Telereceptor.

Telecon system (tel'eh-kon). See under *system.*

teleopsia (tel"e-op'se-ah). A perceptual disturbance characterized by an apparent increase in distances; hence close objects appear to be far away.

telereceptor (tel"e-re-sep'tor). A sensory receptor of stimuli perceptually localized at a distance from the point of reception of the stimulus effect, such as visual or auditory receptors, distinguished from touch or pain receptors. Syn., *teleceptor.*

Telerotor (tel'e-ro-tor). A motor attachment which controls the flash sequence in visual training instruments (especially the Tel-eye-trainer) by means of rotating notched disks whose edges control the light switch.

telescope. An optical instrument for magnifying the apparent size of a distant object, consisting essentially of an objective (a converging lens or mirror) which collects light and forms a real image of the distant object, and an eyepiece which magnifies the image formed by the objective.

astronomical t. A refracting telescope in which both the objective and the eyepiece are converging systems and so placed in relation to each other that the posterior focal point of the objective and the anterior focal point of the eyepiece are coincident, so that the viewed object is seen inverted. Syn., *Kepler telescope.*

Bioptic t. Bioptic telescopic lens. See under *lens.*

Cassegrainian t. A reflecting telescope which has a large, parabolic, concave mirror to collect light from a distant body and **a** small, hyperbolic, convex mirror, located on the optical axis, to transmit the light back through a central hole in the large mirror to the eyepiece or to a photographic plate.

Dutch t. Galilean telescope.

Galilean t. A refracting telescope in which the objective is a large converging lens and the eyepiece is a smaller diverging lens which intercepts the converging rays before they come to a focus. It forms an erect virtual image and is commonly used in opera glasses, low power field glasses, and telescopic spectacles. Syn., *Dutch telescope.*

Gregorian t. A reflecting telescope, having a large concave mirror to collect light from a distant body and a small concave mirror located on the optical axis so that its focus is coincident with the large mirror, which transmits the light back through a hole in the large mirror to the eyepiece.

Hale t. A reflecting telescope which has a large, parabolic, concave mirror to collect light from a distant body and focus it on a point on the axis where the image is directly observed.

Herschelian t. A reflecting telescope in which the parabolic concave mirror is so inclined that the image is formed near one side of the open end of the tube, to be viewed through the eyepiece.

Kepler t. Astronomical telescope.

mercurial t. A reflecting telescope in which light rays are reflected by a basin of mercury either in revolution or at rest.

mirror t., Dixon's. A magnifying telescopic spectacle lens, designed by H. Dixon in 1786, consisting of a concave mirror with a small central aperture, mounted like a spectacle lens, and a small convex mirror anterior to the aperture. The path of light is from the object to the

large mirror, to the small mirror, and through the aperture to the eye.

Newtonian t. A reflecting telescope which has a large, parabolic, concave mirror to collect light from a distant body and a small diagonal plane mirror (or a prism) near the open end of the tube to reflect the light at right angles toward the eyepiece.

reflecting t. A telescope which employs a concave mirror as the objective.

refracting t. A telescope which employs a converging lens as the objective.

Schmidt's t. A reflecting telescope which has a large, spherical, concave mirror to collect light from a distant body, a small, spherical, convex mirror located on the optical axis to transmit the light back through a central hole in the large mirror to the eyepiece, and an optically weak, aspherical lens in the plane of the center of curvature of the large mirror to correct for spherical aberration and coma.

terrestrial t. A telescope having the optical system of an astronomical telescope except that an erecting lens (or lens system) is placed between the objective and the eyepiece to erect the image.

Trioptic t. Trioptic telescopic lens. See under *lens.*

telestereoscope, Helmholtz' (tel″e-ster′e-o-skōp″). An instrument, invented by Helmholtz, to produce exaggerated perception of depth for distant objects. It consists essentially of a long narrow box or tube containing, on one side, two widely separated apertures for collecting light from distant objects, and, on the opposite side, two apertures, separated by an average interpupillary distance, through which the objects are viewed. Light entering through the instrument is reflected in the interior by a system of mirrors or right angle prisms to emerge through the rear apertures into the eyes.

telestereoscopy (tel″e-ster″e-os′kope). Exaggeration of apparent depth relationships by the increased lateral separation of the objectives of a binocular viewing instrument.

teletraumatism, retinal (tel″e-traw′-mah-tizm). Purtscher's disease.

television trainer. See under *trainer.*

Tel-eye-trainer (tel″i-trān′er). A trade name for a Brewster-type stereoscope containing 5.00 D. convex spheroprisms (base-out) for eyepieces, a housing to exclude extraneous light, and a motor attachment to provide variably intermittent illumination of the targets.

Tellais' sign (tel′āz). See under *sign.*

telo-menotaxis (tel-o-men″o-tak′sis). A type of light-compass reaction in which the orientation of movement is governed by directional sensitivities of receptors to light and the ability to select a guiding stimulus with the inhibition of others.

telotaxis (tel″o-tak′sis). A movement of a motile organism directly toward or away from a light source which may be mediated by a single receptor organ having a number of elements spatially distributed, enabling localization of the light source and orientation of the head and body with the light. See also *klinotaxis; menotaxis; mnemotaxis; tropotaxis.*

temperature. The degree or scalar representation of coldness or hotness.

   blackbody t. Radiation temperature.

   brightness t. Luminance temperature.

   color t. The temperature of a complete radiator (blackbody) which yields a chromaticity matching that of a given color sample or source.

   luminance t. The temperature of a complete radiator (blackbody) which has the same luminance for some narrow spectral region (usually at 665 mμ) as that of the source in question. Syn., *brightness temperature.*

   radiation t. The temperature, in degrees Kelvin, of a complete radiator (blackbody) which has the same total radiant emittance as that of the source in question. Syn., *blackbody temperature.*

template (tem′plit). A metal plate cut on one edge to a specific curvature for use as a gauge for the curvature of a lens grinding or polishing tool. Syn., *templet.*

temple. 1. One of a pair of shafts extending backward from the endpieces of a spectacle frame or mounting to rest against the head or the ears for the purpose of holding the frame or mounting in position. 2. The lateral portion of the head above the zygomatic arch, anterior to the ear.

   bent library t. Hollywood temple.

   butt, t. The portion or end of a temple that fastens to the endpiece.

   comfort cable t. A type of riding bow temple whose curl is made of flexible coiled cable.

   gun butt t. Spatula temple.

   Hollywood t. A library temple with a slight downward bend near its posterior end to follow the arc of the sulcus at the top of the base of the pinna, resembling a polo stick. Syn., *bent library temple; polo temple.*

   library t. A temple typically with a continuously tapering size from the small butt end to the vertically wide posterior end, and nearly straight to facilitate easy slipping of the frame on or off the face. It extends to just slightly posterior to the top of the base of the pinna and is commonly used on heavy plastic spectacle frames. Syn., *stub temple.*

paddle t. Spatula temple.

polo t. Hollywood temple.

riding bow t. A temple which has a curved posterior portion designed to follow the posterior contour of the external sulcus at the base of the pinna from the top down to the lobe, originally made of relatively stiff wire.

skull t. Any temple that holds the spectacle frame or mounting primarily by following and resting against the contour of the side of the skull behind the ear, and secondarily by following in part the contour of the sulcus at the base of the pinna.

    skull t., full. A temple having a relatively rigid, posterior portion designed to follow the contour of the external sulcus at the base of the pinna from the top down along an arc of about 75° and thence extending about 2 cm. tangentially downward and curved medially to follow the contour of the mastoid protuberance.

    skull t., semi. A temple having a relatively rigid, posterior portion designed to follow the contour of the external sulcus at the base of the pinna from the top down along an arc of about 40° and thence extending about 2 cm. tangentially downward and curved medially to follow the contour of the skull, barely reaching the top of the mastoid bone.

spatula t. A temple having a posterior portion shaped much like a spatula, a paddle, or a gun butt, designed to rest against the side of the head at the top of the external sulcus at the base of the pinna and extending slightly back and around the contour of the head. Syn., *gun butt temple; paddle temple.*

stub t. Library temple.

templet (tem′plet). A template.

temporal induction. See under *induction.*

tendency, central. The tendency of the data of a frequency distribution to cluster about some value, its position usually being determined by one of the measures of location, as the mean, the median, or the mode.

tendo (ten′do). A tendon.

oculi, t. Medial palpebral ligament.

palpebrarum, t. Medial palpebral ligament

tendon (ten′don). A dense band of fibrous connective tissue constituting the termination of a muscle, usually attaching it to a bone.

ciliary t. An annular tendon adjacent to, and blending with, the scleral spur and the meshwork o. the angle of the anterior chamber, serving as a common origin for the fibers of the ciliary muscle.

lower t. of Lockwood. Lower tendon of Zinn.

lower t. of Zinn. An inferior thickening of the inner surface of the annulus of Zinn, attached to the inferior root of the small wing of the sphenoid bone, which gives origin to the inferior rectus muscle and to portions of the medial and the lateral rectus muscles. Syn., *lower tendon of Lockwood; inferior orbital tendon.*

orbital t., inferior. Lower tendon of Zinn.

orbital t., superior. Upper tendon of Lockwood.

upper t. of Lockwood. A superior thickening of the inner surface of the annulus of Zinn, attached to the body of the sphenoid bone, which gives origin to the superior rectus muscle and to portions of the medial and the lateral rectus muscles. Syn., *superior orbital tendon.*

Zinn, t. of. Annulus of Zinn.

tenebrescence (ten-eh-bres'ens). A decrease in transmittance or increase in absorption of light induced by exposure to it, as in photochromic glass.

tenomyotomy (ten"o-mi-ot'o-me). Incision of a portion of the tendon of an extraocular muscle to weaken its action, in the surgical treatment of strabismus.

Tenon's (te'nonz) **capsule; fascia; membrane; space.** See under the nouns.

tenonitis (ten"on-i'tis). Inflammation of Tenon's capsule or the connective tissue within Tenon's space, occurring in either a purulent or a serous form.

tenonometer (ten"o-nom'eh-ter). Tonometer.

tenontotomy (ten"on-tot'o-me). Tenotomy.

tenoplication (ten"o-pli-ka'shun). A surgical procedure for strabismus to enhance the activity of an extraocular muscle in which the tendon is laid bare, folded forward, and sutured to a denuded sclera at a point nearer the cornea.

tenotomy (ten-ot'o-me). Incision of a tendon, as of an extraocular muscle, in the surgical treatment of strabismus.

central t. Tenotomy in which the central portion of the tendinous insertion is cut, leaving the margins intact.

controlled t. Tenotomy in which sutures are placed through the tendinous insertion before its division and then loosely attached to the sclera and externalized to permit later adjustment of the position of the muscle by loosening or tightening the sutures. Syn., *guarded tenotomy.*

fenestrated t. Tenotomy in which one or more small incisions are made in the tendon, creating openings in it.

free t. Tenotomy in which the entire tendon of the muscle is cut and not surgically reattached.

graduated t. Partial tenotomy.

guarded t. Controlled tenotomy.

marginal t. Tenotomy in which the margins of the tendinous insertion are cut, leaving the central portion intact.

partial t. Incomplete division of a tendon. Syn., *graduated tenotomy.*

tension, intraocular. Ocular tension.

tension, ocular. The resistance of the tunics of the eye to indentation, which depends on the intraocular pressure, the thickness and rigidity of the tunics, the surface area, etc., and which may be estimated digitally or with a tonometer. Abbreviated *T.* Cf. *intraocular pressure.*

tensor choroideae (ten'sor ko-roi'-de-e). Brücke's muscle.

tensor tarsi (ten'sor tar'si). Horner's muscle.

tenthmeter. The ten millionth part of a millimeter, hence equal to 1 A.

teratoma (ter"ah-to'mah). A neoplasm or a tumor in which all three germinal layers are represented and which thus may be composed of skin, hair, teeth, bone, cartilage, muscle, internal organs, etc. It may affect the orbit, the lacrimal gland, etc.

Terrien's (ter'e-enz) **marginal corneal dystrophy; sign; synoscope.** See under the nouns.

Terson's syndrome. See under *syndrome.*

test. 1. A trial or an examination. 2. A task or a series of tasks performed to evaluate ability, quality, strength, etc. 3. Subjection to conditions that show the character of a person or a thing in a certain particular. 4. The equipment or apparatus with which a test is made. For tests not listed here, see under *method.*

Adler's t. A test to distinguish between color blindness and aphasia in which an individual who cannot verbally identify colors is given pairs of colors to match. Aphasia is indicated if he succeeds.

afterimage t. Hering's afterimage test.

afterimage transfer t. Brock's afterimage transfer test.

Albini's E t. A test for determining the visual acuity of children or illiterates in which the subject is given an *E* to hold and orient in the same direction as an indicated *E* on an illiterate *E* chart. Syn., *illiterate E test; rotatable E test.*

alignment t. Rosenbach test.

Ammann's t. Dark filter test.

Amsler-Huber t. A test used to evaluate aqueous humor formation in which fluorescein is injected intravenously and the density of the fluorescein as it arrives in the anterior chamber is determined and plotted as a function of time.

anterior chamber puncture t. Kronfeld's test.

AO H-R-R t. A test for color vision consisting of pseudoisochromatic plates, each containing one or two variously located, geometric figures (circle, cross, or triangle). Four plates are for demonstration, 6 are for screening into red-green-deficient, blue-yellow-deficient, and normal, 10 are for further testing of the red-green-deficient, and 4 are for further testing of the blue-yellow-deficient.

attention span t. A test for determining the amount or complexity of material that can be perceived in a single brief presentation, as with a tachistoscope.

Bach's t. A test for malingering in which the allegedly blind eye fixates the revolving drum of an optokinetoscope, producing nystagmus when vision is present.

Bagolini's striated glass t. A test for visual sensory and motor functioning in which a Bagolini glass is mounted in front of each eye, with the striations oriented 90° apart, while a test target and a light source are viewed. Vision of the test target is relatively unimpaired while the light source appears as two streaks at right angles to each other. The number of streaks perceived (one or two) or the positioning of the two streaks, relative to each other, indicates the state of binocularity.

Bailey's t. A test for determining visual acuity of young children consisting of a series of individual pictures in cutout form, placed near the child, which he attempts to match with identical silhouettes on a chart held at various distances and calibrated to rate the acuity in Snellen fraction values.

Bailliart's dazzling t. A test for treatment amenability of amblyopia in which a bright ophthalmoscope light beam is projected on the macular area for about 15 seconds, and then it is noted whether or not there is a temporary reduction in acuity, how much time is needed for recovery of the former acuity, and whether or not there is a subsequent enhancement of acuity.

bar reading t. A test for the presence of binocular vision in which one or more vertical bars are interposed between the eyes and reading material, such that some portions of the print are excluded to one eye and other portions to the other eye. Perception of all the print without head movement indicates binocular vision. Syn., *Welland's test.*

bead t. A test of color vision in which a set of colored beads are sorted into four groups: red, yellow, green, and blue.

Becker's t. A test for astigmatism in which sets of three parallel lines, each set oriented in a different meridian, are viewed.

Bender's t. A clinical test to evaluate intelligence, emotional stability, school readiness, and visual-motor perception, consisting of nine figures which are presented singly for freely copying on blank paper.

Benton right-left discrimination t. A 32 item performance test (example, touch your right eye with your left hand) designed to assess one's ability to differentiate left from right in terms of lateral parts of his own body and in terms of those of another person facing him.

Berens' Three Character t. A test for binocular vision in which the transilluminated outline of three characters, a red girl, a green elephant, and a white ball on a black background mounted at the head of a flash light, are viewed through complementary-colored red and green filters. The simultaneous perception of all three figures indicates normal binocular vision and the absence of the girl or elephant indicates suppression of one eye.

bichrome t. Duochrome method.

Bielschowsky's afterimage t. Hering's afterimage test.

Bielschowsky's head tilting t. A test for differentiating paralysis of a superior oblique muscle from that of a superior rectus muscle, consisting of forcibly reversing the natural head tilting, i.e., tilting the head toward the side of the palsied muscle. Sharp upward movement of the affected eye indicates paralysis of the superior oblique muscle and no movement, or a downward movement, indicates paralysis of the superior rectus muscle.

Bishop Harman diaphragm t. A test for detecting heterophoria or suppression in which a horizontal row of letters or numbers is viewed through an adjustable aperture which is narrowed until the common binocular field is eliminated and each eye sees an opposite side of the target. Overlapping of the figures indicates esophoria, separation exophoria, one group higher, hyperphoria, and perception of only one side, suppression.

black and red t. A test for malingering in which red and black letters on a white background are viewed while a red filter is before the sound eye, rendering the red letters invisible to this eye. Reading of all the letters indicates vision in the allegedly poor eye.

Blaxter's t. Bulbar pressure test.

Boberg-Ans t. Determination of corneal sensitivity with the Boberg-Ans corneal sensibilitometer (*q.v.*).

Bodal's t. A test for color perception consisting of the sorting of colored blocks.

Boström's t. A test for color vision consisting of 16 pseudoisochromatic plates, 12 containing digits, and 4 blank to detect malingering.

Boström-Kugelberg t. A test for color vision consisting of 20 pseudoisochromatic plates, 15 containing digits, 2 containing winding trails for illiterates, and 3 blank to detect malingering.

box t. A test for determining sighting ocular dominance utilizing a small box, open at both ends, having two vertical rods, one at each end, placed in the center of the open ends. The subject aligns the two rods, one behind the other, while holding the box before himself, and the examiner notes which of the subject's eyes is in line with the vertical rods.

Brock's afterimage transfer t. A test to detect and measure eccentric or anomalous fixation in an amblyopic eye, in cases of normal retinal correspondence, in which only the normal eye is exposed to and fixates a vertical light and is then occluded, while the amblyopic eye fixates a central point on a horizontal scale at at specified distance. The position of the vertical afterimage in relation to the fixated point indicates the angle of eccentric fixation.

Brock's scotoma box t. A test for detecting a central scotoma utilizing two small boxes, one containing a transilluminated red disk with a central black dot and the other containing a spot of light 1 to 5 mm. in diameter. The box with the transilluminated red disk is strapped to the head over the nonamblyopic eye and the head is moved to superimpose the black dot on the spot of light in the other box, which is located variously from 6 in. to 6 ft. in front of the amblyopic eye. Disappearance of the spot of light on superimposition indicates a central scotoma.

Brock's string t. A test to determine binocular fixation in which one end of a string is placed against the bridge of the nose and the other fastened to a light source fixated through red and green filters, one before each eye. The perception of two strings, each the color of the filter of the opposite side, intersecting at the point of fixation, indicates normal binocular fixation. The procedure is also used in training the range of binocular fixation in strabismus.

bulbar compression t. for glaucoma. A provocative test for glaucoma in which a weight of 25 gm. is placed on an anesthetized eye for 2 minutes and tonometry is performed after 5, 15, and 35 minutes.

bulbar pressure t., for glaucoma. A provocative test for glaucoma

in which a pressure of 50 gm. is applied to the eye by an ophthalmodynamometer placed at the site of the insertion of the lateral rectus muscle. Tonometry is performed before the application of pressure (A), and, without removal of the tonometer, 15 seconds (B) and 4 minutes (C) after the application of pressure, and after removal of pressure (D). The percentage that the change in pressure $(B - C)$ is of the initial pressure B, is then calculated by the formula $\dfrac{100(B - C)}{B}$. Values below 30% indicate glaucoma. Syn., *Blaxter's test.*

Burnham-Clark-Munsell color memory t. A test for memory color discrimination for persons with normal color vision, in which 20 colored chips are individually exposed for five seconds and, following a five second waiting period, a selection is made of the one which appears of the same color from among 43 chips mounted in a circle. The chips consist of odd numbered chips from the Farnsworth-Munsell test.

caffeine t. for glaucoma. A provocative test for glaucoma in which ocular tension is measured after 150 cc. of water containing 45 gm. of coffee is drunk. A rise of over 8 mm. Hg in 15 to 60 minutes is considered positive. Syn., *coffee test for glaucoma.*

Cantonnet's t. Determination and measurement of phorias or tropias by means of Cantonnet's diploscope.

card, t. See under *chart.*

Carter's t. A test to determine the thresholds of color perception, in which attempts are made to identify various colored targets viewed in an instrument with a rheostat control for illumination.

catoptric t. A test for the diagnosis of cataract by observing the Purkinje images on the cornea and the lens capsule.

chart, t. See under *chart.*

chi-square t. A test to determine the statistical significance of a discrepancy between an actual and a theoretical distribution.

chromatic t. A test for perceptual ocular dominance, in which a red filter is alternately placed before each of the eyes while a white light is fixated binocularly. The eye with which the light appears reddest is considered the dominant eye.

cobalt blue glass t. A test to determine the refractive state of the eye, in which a spot of white light is viewed through a cobalt lens. A central red spot with a blue halo indicates myopia, a blue spot with a red halo absolute hypermetropia, and a purple spot either emmetropia or facultative hypermetropia. Syn., *Landolt's cobalt blue test.*

Cochet's t. 1. A screening test for the fragility of the corneal epithelium in prospective contact lens wearers, in which a spherical surface having engraved concentric circles and radiating lines is brought to bear on the cornea by means of an adapted Goldmann applanation tonometer. The degree of fluorescein staining as observed with the slit lamp indicates the prognosis. 2. Determination of corneal sensitivity with the Cochet-Bonnet esthesiometer (*q.v.*).

coffee t. for glaucoma. Caffeine test for glaucoma.

Cohn's t. A test for color perception in which attempts are made to identify various colored, embroidered patterns intended to confuse the red-green color blind.

color threshold t. Any color perception test which determines the minimum luminous intensity at which colored lights are correctly identified.

complementary color t. for malingering. A test for malingering in which complementary-colored red and green letters are viewed through complementary-colored red and green filters; the reading of all the letters indicates vision in both eyes.

confrontation t. A test to determine the approximate extent of the visual field in which the subject, with one eye occluded, faces the examiner at a distance of about 2 ft. and fixates the opposite eye of the examiner, while the examiner extends an object beyond the peripheral limit of the visual field of the subject and slowly brings it inward until it is seen.

confrontation field t. for malingering. A test for malingering in which a test object is introduced into the temporal field of the admittedly good eye and moved toward and into the nasal field of that eye. A malingerer, being unaware that the nasal fields overlap, might not admit seeing the object as it passes the median plane.

contrast t. for color blindness. A test for color vision utilizing the principle of simultaneous contrast, e.g., the viewing of gray numbers or letters on a colored background of the same brightness through tissue paper, the letters being invisible to the color blind and appearing tinged with a color complementary to the background to the normal.

convergence t. for ocular dominance. A test to determine motor ocular dominance, in which a fixation object is brought toward the eyes, past the near point of convergence, the eye maintaining fixation being considered the dominant eye.

convex lens t. for malingering. A

test for malingering in which a convex lens of about 2.50 D. is placed before the admittedly good eye while a test card is moved from a position within the focal point of the lens to a position beyond it. The continued reading of the test letters beyond the focal point indicates vision in the supposedly blind eye.

Cords's stereoscopic t. A test for stereoscopic vision in which the attempt is made to align vertically two pointers enclosed in a box and viewed through an aperture, the upper pointer being stationary and the lower manually controlled.

cover t., objective. A test to determine the presence and the type of phoria or strabismus, in which a point is fixated at a given test distance while an opaque cover is placed first before one eye and then the other, and then placed and removed before each eye. Diagnostic data include: the movement of the eye as it is covered, the movement of the eye to assume fixation as the cover is moved to the other eye, and the movement of the two eyes when the cover is removed. Prisms may be used with this test to neutralize eye movement and thus measure the magnitude of the deviation. Syn., *objective screen test.*

cover t., subjective. A test to determine the type of phoria, in which a point is fixated at a given test distance while the eyes are alternately occluded. An apparent lateral movement opposite to the movement of the occluder indicates esophoria, in the same direction of the occluder exophoria, and no apparent movement orthophoria. An apparent downward movement indicates hyperphoria of the eye from which the occluder is moved. Prisms may be placed in front of the eyes

until the movement is eliminated to measure the magnitude of the phoria. Syn., *Duane's parallax test.*

crossed cylinder t. for astigmatism. A clinical test for determining the axis and the amount of astigmatism, in which a crossed cylinder lens is placed before the eye with its axes each 45° away from the axis of a presumed cylinder correction (such as the static retinoscopic finding) which is also before the eye. While letters on a distant test chart are viewed, the crossed cylinder lens is flipped over so that its axes are reversed in position. The position which provides the clearer vision indicates the direction to which the axis of the correcting cylinder should be turned. The setting of the crossed cylinder lens and the axis of the correcting cylinder are varied until vision is equally distorted in both positions, indicating the proper axis of the correcting cylinder. The crossed cylinder lens is then placed with one of its axes coincident with the axis of the correcting cylinder and the flipping of the crossed cylinder is repeated. The position which provides the clearer vision indicates the adjustment of the dioptric power of the correcting cylinder, and the point of equality of vision indicates the proper amount.

crossed cylinder t. (near point). Any of several monocular or binocular clinical tests, usually performed at a 40 cm. fixation distance, in which a test chart containing intersecting, parallel, horizontal, and vertical lines is viewed through the subjective finding and crossed cylinder lenses with axes horizontal and vertical. Spherical lenses are added until the lines on the test chart appear equally black or dark. The finding is compared with findings of other tests to determine the desired near point lens prescription.

cube E t. A cube having a different sized *E* on each of its six sides, used as test targets in the evaluation of visual acuity.

Cuignet's t. 1. The bar reading test as used to detect malingering. 2. Retinoscopy.

Cüppers' bifoveal t. A test for anomalous retinal correspondence in which a light source in the center of a Maddox cross is fixated by one eye while a small ophthalmoscopically projected target is positioned on the fovea of the other. Failure to superimpose the ophthalmoscopic target on the fixated light source indicates anomalous retinal correspondence and the magnitude of the separation is a measure of the angle of anomaly.

Cüppers' neosynoptophore t. A test for either eccentric fixation or anomalous retinal correspondence utilizing the neosynoptophore. Eccentric fixation is indicated if Haidinger's brushes are perceived to be displaced with respect to the fixation dot when both are observed by the amblyopic eye, and anomalous retinal correspondence is indicated if the Haidinger's brushes are displaced with respect to the fixation dot when one eye fixates while the other observes the Haidinger's brushes.

cycloplegic t. Cycloplegic refraction.

dark filter t. A test to differentiate functional amblyopia from organic amblyopia in which visual acuity is measured with and without a neutral density filter. A marked reduction is said to indicate organic amblyopia and a slight reduction or improvement is said to indicate functional amblyopia. Syn., *Am-*

mann's test; neutral density filter test.

dark room t. for glaucoma. A provocative test for glaucoma, in which the patient is placed in complete darkness for one hour. An increase in ocular tension of 10 mm. Hg or more is considered pathological. Syn., *Seidel's test.*

dazzling t. The determination of time required for the recovery of normal acuity following bright ophthalmoscopic illumination of the macula preceded by a period of dark adaptation.

diplopia t. 1. A test for the state of motility of the extraocular muscles in strabismus, in which a light source is fixated in various directions of gaze, in a darkened room, with a red filter before one eye, and sometimes with a green filter before the other, to produce diplopia. The relative separation of the diplopic images is noted, first with one eye fixating and then with the other. 2. A test for suppression, consisting of the determination of the presence or the absence of physiological diplopia.

dissociating t. Any test for measuring a phoria in which fusion is disrupted or made impossible, as by means of a prism.

distortion t. Any test for measuring a phoria in which the stimulus to fusion is eliminated by distorting the retinal image of one eye, as may be done with a Maddox rod.

Dobson's t. A binocular test for constant unilateral suppression, consisting of reading from a book printed with some letters in orange and some in black while one eye views through a filter that renders the orange letters invisible. Reading all the letters indicates no suppression in the uncovered eye.

Dolman's t. 1. A test for sighting ocular dominance, in which the subject sights an object through a pinhole in an opaque card, the eye used to sight being considered dominant. 2. Howard-Dolman test.

Donders' t. A test for color perception consisting of the identification of the colored glass sides of a lantern.

double prism t. 1. A test for malingering in which a double prism is placed before one eye with the seeing of three images indicating vision in the allegedly blind eye. 2. A test for determining the type of phoria, in which a double prism is placed before one eye and a red lens before the other while a small spot of light is fixated, the position of the red image in relation to the double white images indicating the type of phoria. 3. A test for determining the presence of cyclophoria, in which a double prism is placed before one eye while a single horizontal line is fixated, no cyclophoria existing if the resultant three line images are parallel.

drinking t. for glaucoma. Water drinking test for glaucoma.

Driver's t. A test for malingering in which a bar is interposed vertically between the patient's eyes and test letters of various sizes so that it screens the right letters from the left eye and the left letters from the right eye. The reading of all the letters indicates vision in the allegedly blind eye and the size of the letters read indicates the visual acuity.

drop ball t. A test to determine the resistance of a case-hardened lens to breakage by impact, in which a 1.56 oz. steel ball, ⅞ in. in diameter, is dropped perpendicularly onto the front surface of the lens from a distance of 50 in., the lens being supported in a hollow tube by a ⅛ in. rubber washer. A variation of the test calls for a 16 mm. (⅝ in.) steel

ball at a height of 1 m. (39 in.).

dropping t. Hering's drop test.

dry t. for contact lenses. A test for the fit of the corneal section of a fluid scleral contact lens in which the lens is inserted dry, the presence and the size of an air bubble indicating the clearance between the cornea and the lens.

Duane's diplopia t. A test for the state of motility of the extraocular muscles in strabismus, in which a light source on a black screen is fixated in various directions of gaze, in a darkened room, with a red lens before one eye to create diplopia. The patient locates, with a pointer, the position of the diplopic image of the light source for each direction of gaze, first with one eye fixating and then with the other eye fixating.

Duane's parallax t. Subjective cover test.

duction t. 1. Any test in which prism or prism effect is introduced before the eyes to create a vergence demand to a point of blur or diplopia. 2. A test to determine the limits of ocular motility of an eye by moving a fixation target in various directions of gaze with the head held stationary.

Dunnington-Berke t. A test to differentiate between a disturbance in ocular motility due to fibrous adhesions and one due to paralysis, in which forceps are attached to the muscle tendon and traction is exerted in the direction of restricted ocular motility. Easy movement of the eye in this direction indicates paralysis, and considerable resistance indicates fibrous adhesions of the antagonist.

duochrome t. Duochrome method.

duochrome star t. A test to determine the astigmatic and the spherical components of the refractive correction, consisting of an astigmatic dial composed of double stripes, at angles of 60° with each other, superimposed on a half red and half green transilluminated field. The dial is rotated until the border between red and green coincides with one of the principal meridians of the eye.

Dvorine's pseudoisochromatic t. A test for color vision which utilizes pseudoisochromatic plates.

Eames t. A battery of stereograms for the screening of visual acuity, heterophoria, and binocular vision.

Edridge-Green t. A lantern test for color perception in which seven colored filters are mounted on three disks which are rotated in succession or in combination before the aperture. A fourth disk contains a ground glass to represent mist, a ribbed glass to represent rain, and neutral glasses to represent varying intensities of fog. The diaphragm has apertures of different sizes to represent railway signals or ship lights.

electroretinographic glare t. A test for retinal responses to glare in which an electroretinogram is obtained in relation to the application of a high intensity light stimulus (photoflash) in addition to the standard photostimulation.

Evans' t. A test to approximate the visual acuity of infants, in which metal balls of various sizes are moved on a tray by means of a magnet held underneath. The smallest ball which the eyes follow indicates the acuity.

excursion t. A test for ocular motility in which a moving target is fixated in various directions while the head remains motionless. Limitation of ocular movement or overshooting of one eye indicates paralysis or paresis of an extraocular muscle.

extension t. A test for hand domi-

nance devised by Schilder in which, with the eyes closed, the arms are extended horizontally, with the fingers spread, the higher hand being considered dominant. Syn., *Schilder's test.*

Farnsworth D-15 t. Farnsworth dichotomous test.

Farnsworth dichotomous t. A color vision test designed primarily for industrial use to permit detection of workers unable to distinguish colors of industrial color codes. A series of 15 small disks of Munsell 5/2 papers, whose hues appear to comprise a closed circuit of colors (cf. *color circle*) for normal observers, mounted in black plastic caps, must be arranged by the subject into a smooth color series. Score sheets with dots numbered 1 to 15, arranged in a circle, are marked by drawing lines to connect the numbered dots in the order in which the caps were arranged. Normal observers and those with mild color defects make few or no errors and yield generally circular score profiles. Subjects whose score sheets show a crisscrossing of the circle are more severely defective and would be unable to use color codes effectively. The principal direction of the crisscrossing score lines identifies the type of color blindness, e.g., protanopia, deuteranopia, or tritanopia.

Farnsworth-Munsell t. A color vision test consisting of 85 small disks of colored papers selected from the Munsell 100-hue series so that they appear approximately equal in chroma and value but perceptibly different in hue for normal observers. The disks are mounted in black caps and consecutively numbered from 1 to 85. The series is divided into four parts, each in a black tray, with the caps containing the terminal colors for that part mounted at the ends of the tray. The caps are shuffled, and the subject must then arrange them into a smooth color series. Errors are scored as the sum of differences between the number of a cap and the numbers of the two caps adjacent to it and are marked on special polar co-ordinate scoring sheets. The profile of scores on the graph then permits diagnosis of the type and the degree of severity of the color vision defect.

Fink Near-Vision t. A visual acuity test chart calibrated for use at 14 inches and containing continuous sentences with letter sizes designating vision from 20/20 to 20/140.

Firth t. A test for visual acuity consisting of counting the lines on a series of grids, the lines being separated by a different distance in each grid.

flicker fusion t. The determination of the rate of presentation of intermittent, alternate, or discontinuous photic stimuli that just gives rise to a fully uniform and continuous sensation, obliterating the flicker.

fluorescein t. 1. A test for the fit of contact lenses, in which fluorescein is instilled between the eye and the contact lens. Under blue or ultraviolet light illumination the pattern of coloration of the fluorescein indicates the physical fit of the contact lens. 2. The instillation of fluorescein onto the surface of the eye to detect abraded, degenerated, or dying tissue by means of ocular staining.

fly t. A test for gross stereopsis consisting of a vectograph of an enlarged housefly which is viewed through Polaroid filters and appears in marked relief when stereopsis is present.

fogging t. Fogging.

forced duction t. A test for anatomical restriction of motility of an extraocular muscle, in which, under general anesthesia, an attempt is made to passively rotate the eye, by means of a muscle hook or forceps, in the field of action of its antagonist.

Foucault knife-edge t. A test to determine the optical uniformity or equivalency of different portions of a reflecting surface or of different cross-section regions of a refracting system, consisting of a pinhole light source as the object, a movable, across-the-beam, knife edge in the image plane and the pupil of the observer's eye effectively in or near the image plane. The optical variations of the mirror or system thus seen in Maxwellian view appear as variations in brightness patterns.

four color t. Pickford test.

four dot t. Worth's four dot test.

Fridenberg's stigmometric t. A test for visual acuity with the use of Fridenberg's chart.

FRIEND t. A test for binocular vision in which the word FRIEND, printed with letters in alternate complementary red and green colors, is viewed through complementary-colored red and green filters, one before each eye. Simultaneous seeing of all the letters indicates binocular vision. Syn., *Snellen's test.*

Frostig t. A battery of tests of visual perception for evaluating normal and neurologically handicapped children, consisting of five subgroups of tests for eye-motor co-ordination, figure-ground, form constancy, position in space, and spatial relations.

fundus reflex t. Retinoscopy.

Gaviola's caustic t. An adaptation of the Foucault knife-edge test to survey a parabolic mirror using a number of off-axis points to determine the radius of curvature at these points.

Giessen t. A test for anomalous retinal correspondence and the subjective angle in strabismus, in which one eye fixates a light source in the center of a Maddox cross through a red filter after a foveal afterimage has been created by stimulation of the other eye. Failure to superimpose the afterimage on the fixated light source indicates anomalous retinal correspondence, the magnitude of the separation serving as a measure of the angle of anomaly, while the separation of doubled images of the fixation target (one red and one white) serves as a measure of the subjective angle.

gradient t. A test to determine the amount of accommodative convergence associated with a 1.00 D. change in accommodation at a given test distance. It is usually performed clinically by noting the change in phoria induced by adding 1.00 D. convex lenses to the subjective finding, at a 40 cm. test distance.

von Graefe's t. 1. A test for the determination of the type of phoria, in which fusion is made impossible by the placing of a dissociating prism in front of one eye to create diplopia. A rotary prism may be placed in front of the other eye to align the diplopic images and determine the magnitude of the phoria. 2. The past pointing test.

Gray oral reading t. A test for oral reading ability, performed binocularly and with each eye separately, utilizing five sets of cards containing reading material ranging in difficulty from primary to adult levels.

Guibor t. A test for near visual acuity performed with the Guibor chart at a fixation distance of 14 in. and in an illumination of not less than 3 footcandles.

Hall's t. A test to differentiate congenital amblyopia from amblyopia ex anopsia, in which two circular red targets, 5 mm. in diameter and 1½ in. apart, are viewed at a distance of about 25 in. from the eye, with the non-amblyopic eye occluded. Equal brightness of the fixated and the peripheral targets is said to indicate congenital amblyopia, and greater brightness of the peripheral target, amblyopia ex anopsia.

Halldén's t. Halldén's method.

Handy Confirmation t. An assembly of four spherical lenses, +0.50, −0.50, +0.75, and −0.75, mounted on a handle so that each lens can be held individually and conveniently in front of a tentative refractive correction lens for comparison with another of opposite power in the series, the lack of preference indicating the tentative correction to be correct.

Hardy-Rand-Rittler t. AO H-R-R test.

Harlan's t. A test for malingering in which a 6 D. convex lens is placed before the admittedly good eye and a plano lens before the allegedly blind eye, in addition to the correction for ametropia. A reading card is held 6½ in. from the eyes; as the letters are read, it is slowly moved farther away, continued reading of the letters indicating vision in the allegedly blind eye.

Harman's t. Bishop Harman diaphragm test.

Harrington-Flocks t. A screening test to detect defects of the visual field, in which simple, abstract patterns of lines, dots, or crosses are presented tachistoscopically to the fixating eye, the other being occluded. The patterns are printed in fluorescent ink and are visible only when illuminated by a flash of ultraviolet radiation. A black, central, fixation spot is visible in the center of each pattern at all times.

Harris t. of lateral dominance. A group of performance and preference tests for hand, eye, and foot dominance and dexterity, designed for age six or over.

Hartmann t. A test for aberrations in a lens or an optical system, in which a diaphragm containing a series of small holes is placed in contact with the lens or the system, and photographs of a distant light source are taken from a number of positions on both sides of the paraxial focus.

head tilting t. 1. Bielschowsky's head tilting test. 2. Helmholtz' head tilting test.

Helmholtz' head tilting t. Detection and differentiation of palsies of the cyclomotor muscles utilizing Helmholtz' indicator.

Hering's afterimage t. A test to determine the state of retinal correspondence, in which first a vertical light filament is monocularly fixated at its center by one eye, and then a horizontal light filament is monocularly fixated at its center by the other eye, or vice versa. Perception of the afterimages in the form of a cross, regardless of the positions of the eyes, indicates normal retinal correspondence. Syn., *afterimage test; Bielschowsky's afterimage test.*

Hering's drop t. A test of stereoscopic vision consisting of looking through a tube or a box at a horizontal thread and determining whether little balls are dropped in front of or behind the thread.

Hertel's t. A test for color vision utilizing Hertel's plates (*q.v.*).

Hesse's t. A test for malingering, in which strong convex lenses are placed before the eyes, in addition to the correction for ametropia, while distant test letters are viewed. The convex power before the allegedly poorer eye is gradually reduced until the maximum visual acuity is determined.

Hirschberg's t. A test for approximating the objective angle of strabismus, in which the position of the reflex of a fixated light source, in line with the observer's eye, is noted on the cornea of the deviating eye. Syn., *Hirschberg's method.*

hole-in-the-card t. A test for sighting ocular dominance, in which a target is sighted through a hole in a card held in the hands, the eye used for sighting being considered dominant.

hole-in-the-hand t. A test for binocular vision, in which an object is viewed through a tube placed before one eye while a hand is held a few inches before the other eye. Seeing of the object through an apparent hole in the hand indicates binocular vission, and seeing only the object or only the hand indicates its absence.

Holmgren t. A test for color vision consisting of selecting skeins of woolen yarns of various colors, shades, tints, and grays to match three standard test skeins.

homatropine t. for glaucoma. A provocative test for glaucoma in which one drop of a dilute solution of homatropine is instilled into each eye, and tonometry performed each 30 minutes for 2 hours. A rise in ocular tension of 8–11 mm. Hg is considered probably pathological and a greater rise definitely pathological.

Houstoun's t. A test for color vision consisting of the identification of minute spots of color on a microscope slide, or on a gray paper, which are desaturated by transmitted or reflected white light from the surrounding area by setting the microscope out of focus to various degrees.

Howard-Dolman t. A test for depth perception or stereopsis, in which the attempt is made to position a movable vertical rod, by means of a double cord pulley arrangement, to the same distance as a fixed vertical rod. The rods are housed in a rectangular box, are viewed through an aperture in the box from a 20 ft. distance, are black against a white background, and the test score is usually the average error in millimeters for ten trials.

H-R-R t. AO H-R-R test.

Hughes t. Three disk test.

Hunt-Giles t. A test to determine the distance lens correction considered best for daylight vision, consisting of the adding of convex or concave spherical lenses to the correction determined routinely, to obtain maximum acuity for black letters on a transilluminated yellow-green background.

illiterate E t. Albini's E test.

Inter-Society Color Council color aptitude t. A test of color discrimination in which individually dispensed colored chips having small saturation differences for four hues (red, yellow, green, blue) must be quickly and individually matched with one of a series of 50 fixed colored samples mounted on a panel.

Irvine's prism displacement t. A test for the detection of a small angle strabismus, or for plotting the extent of a retinal inhibition or suppression area or of an absolute scotoma, in which prisms are placed momentarily before an eye. Small angle strabismus is indicated if a conjugate movement of the eyes, toward the apex of the prism, is observed when a low power prism is placed before the fixating eye, or if no eye movement is ob-

served when the prism is placed before the deviating eye. The extent of a suppression area in strabismus or of an absolute central scotoma with binocular alignment is measured by momentarily placing prisms of progressively increasing power, in various meridians of orientation, before the deviating or affected eye until diplopia for the fixation target is observed. The area of inhibition in amblyopia ex anopsia is measured by momentarily placing prisms of progressively increasing power, in various meridians of orientation, before the fixating amblyopic eye, the other eye being occluded, until a shift in direction of the fixation target is observed. The degree to which a scotoma approaches the macular area in glaucoma is determined by momentarily placing prisms of progressively increasing power before the glaucomatous eye, the other eye being occluded, such that the image of the fixated target is momentarily shifted toward the scotomatous area, its boundary being indicated when the fixation target disappears.

Ishihara t. A test for color vision which utilizes pseudoisochromatic plates.

Ives's t. The determination of visual acuity by means of the Ives's visual acuity grating.

Jackson's t. A test for malingering, in which two cylindrical lenses, neutralizing each other, are placed before the admittedly good eye and one is rotated to blur vision while test letters are read. Continued reading of the letters indicates vision in the allegedly poor eye.

Jenning's t. A test for color perception, in which standard test skeins of green and rose are matched with green and green confusion colors and rose and rose confusion colors printed on a board. In the center of each color sample is a hole through which a stylus is thrust to register the selection of a matched color by perforating a record sheet placed beneath the board.

jugular compression t. for glaucoma. The lability test for glaucoma, with the exception of the cooling of the hand.

Kestenbaum's limbus t. A test to determine the limits of excursion of the eye in which the positions of the limbus are noted on a transparent millimeter rule as the eye is moved maximally from the straightforward position inward, outward, upward, and downward.

Kestenbaum's outline t. A modification of the confrontation test in which the test object is kept in a plane not more than 2 or 3 cm. from the patient's face so that the outline of a normal visual field will be limited by the facial features.

knife-edge t. Foucault test.

Koster's cocaine t. A test used in congenital ptosis to aid in determining the presence or absence of the levator palpebrae superioris muscle. Complete or almost complete failure of the upper eyelid to elevate upon the administration of cocaine indicates absence of the muscle. Normally cocaine increases contraction of the superior palpebral muscle of Mueller which assists the levator, when present, causing elevation of the upper eyelid.

Krimsky's t. Krimsky's method.

Kronfeld's t. A diagnostic test for glaucoma consisting of paracentesis of the anterior chamber, a rise in ocular tension to 40 mm. Hg, or more, being positive. Syn., *anterior chamber puncture test.*

lability t. for glaucoma. A pro-

vocative test for glaucoma, in which a pressure of 40 to 60 mm. of Hg is applied to the neck with a blood pressure cuff for one minute while one hand is placed in ice water. A rise in ocular tension of more than 8 mm. Hg, or an increase to over 30 mm. Hg, indicates glaucoma. Syn., *pressor-congestion test for glaucoma.*

Lancaster t. A test for the state of motility of the extraocular muscles in strabismus, in which the patient perceptually superimposes two complementary-colored slits of light, one red and one green, projected onto a screen in a darkened room while wearing red and green filters. One projected slit, the fixation target, is controlled by the examiner and is moved to various directions of gaze and the other slit is controlled by the patient. The test is conducted with first one eye fixating and then the other, for each position, and the physical separation of the slits is noted in each instance.

Landolt's broken ring t. A test for visual acuity consisting of locating the gaps in a graduated series of incomplete rings with radial thickness and gap equal to one fifth of their outer diameters. Syn., *Landolt C test.*

Landolt's cobalt blue t. Cobalt blue glass test.

Landolt's projection t. A test for the detection and measurement of false projection with Landolt's projectionometer.

lantern t. Any of several tests for color perception, in which transilluminated, colored glass filters are identified or matched with standard samples, e.g., the Edridge-Green test.

Lazich's t. A test for measuring eccentric fixation, employing two exposed ophthalmoscope bulbs at a distance of one meter, one of which is fixated by the amblyopic eye while the position of the other bulb is adjusted until its corneal reflection in the same eye is so located with respect to the center of the pupil as to correspond symmetrically with the relative position the reflection would have when fixated by the occluded, nonamblyopic eye.

leaf room t. A test utilizing the leaf room (*q.v.*), for demonstrating, detecting, and measuring spatial distortions resulting from aniseikonia.

Leavell t's. A series of tests designed to determine motor-visual directional preferences and their relation to the functioning of the dominant eye, hand, and foot.

light patch t. A test to estimate the magnification required to aid subnormal vision, in which a circular patch of light is projected onto a graduated scale placed one meter from the patient and gradually reduced in size until it no longer appears circular. The size of the spot at this point indicates the size of the lesion, and reference to a special chart indicates the magnification needed.

Linnér's t. A diagnostic test for glaucoma in which the ratio of the coefficient of the facility of aqueous outflow as influenced by pilocarpine, which decreases outflow resistance, to that as influenced by acetazolamide, which increases outflow resistance, is tonographically determined and then compared to the ratio found for a healthy eye.

Livingston binocular gauge t. A test to determine the near point of either convergence or accommodation with the use of Livingston's binocular gauge.

Livingston's phoria t. A test to determine the type and the magnitude of phoria, in which two pairs of complementary-colored red and green slits in an internally illuminated box, one pair oriented vertically and the other horizontally, are viewed through complementary-colored red and green filters. A scale is provided for each pair of slits by which the perceptual displacement is determined.

luster t. 1. A test for sensory fusion, in which a bright light source is placed against the closed eyelid of one eye while the other fixates a black dot on a uniform gray ground. Perception of a red glow over, or mixed with, the gray field indicates binocular vision; perception of either the red glow or the gray field alone indicates suppression. 2. A test for sensory fusion, in which two different surface colors, usually one chromatic and the other achromatic, are viewed in a stereoscope, one color to each eye. Perception of one color as though seen through, or mixed with, the other color indicates binocular vision.

Maddox groove t. 1. A test for measuring a phoria or a heterotropia, in which a Maddox groove is placed in front of one eye while a small light source is fixated. The groove distorts the image of the light source into a streak perpendicular to the axis of the groove, preventing fusion, and its position relative to the fixated source is determined on a tangent scale or estimated with prisms correcting the displacement. 2. A test for cyclophoria, in which a Maddox groove is placed before each eye, each axis oriented in the same meridian, while viewing a spot light source through displacing prisms. Parallelism of the resultant streaks indicates absence of cyclophoria.

Maddox prism t. A test for measuring a phoria or a heterotropia, in which the diplopic images of one eye, created with a Maddox prism, are compared with the position of the single image of the other eye.

Maddox projection t. A test for false projection, in which a black vertical line, about 1 in. long, on a large white card, is monocularly fixated at a 6 in. distance and is located by pointing on the back of the card to its apparent position. An identically located line is on the back of the card, and failure to point to it indicates false projection.

Maddox rod t. The Maddox groove test, except that a Maddox rod is used instead of a groove.

Maddox tangent scale t. 1. A test for the measurement of a phoria or a heterotropia, in which the central light source of a Maddox cross is fixated through a red filter or a Maddox rod before one eye to produce diplopia. 2. A test for determining the objective angle of strabismus, in which the fixating eye moves along the arm of a Maddox cross until the reflex of the central light source appears centered on the cornea of the deviating eye.

Maddox V t. A test, utilizing the Maddox V chart, for determining the axis of astigmatism.

Maddox wing t. A test, utilizing the Maddox wing, to measure a phoria at near.

manoptoscope t. A test for sighting ocular dominance, in which the subject holds the base of a manoptoscope (a hollow truncated cone) against his face, covering both eyes, and views a distant object through the small end of the cone. Only one eye can fixate under this condition, and that eye is considered to be the dominant. Syn., *Parson's test.*

Mark diplopia t. A test for ocular motility consisting of a series of nine stereograms, each having an arrow with a dot above it in one half and an arrow with a dot below it in the other half. Each pair of arrows is positioned so as to provide a stimulus for fixation in a different direction of gaze, with fusion of the arrows, with a dot above and below, indicating normal motility.

Marlow's t. The occlusion of one eye for several days or more to reveal latent heterophoria (especially hyperphoria) or to determine if symptoms are related to binocular vision. Syn., *prolonged occlusion test.*

Massachusetts Vision t. A portable battery of screening tests for visual performance of school children which includes determination of visual acuity, visual acuity through a convex lens, vertical phoria at far, and lateral phorias at both near and far.

massage t. for glaucoma. A provocative test for glaucoma, in which the eyeball is deeply massaged for 1 min., the normal eye losing one third to one half its tension and regaining it in 60 to 70 min., the glaucomatous eye manifesting only a slight reduction in tension, returning to the original tension rapidly, in about 30 min., and then rising above this level with a return to normal in about 90 min.

Mauthner's t. A test for color perception consisting of the identification of colored powders in vials.

Maxwell disk t. A test for color vision, in which a Maxwell disk containing a colored sector on a white ground is rotated at slowly increasing speeds until the color flicker disappears. The slower the speed at which the color disappears, the greater the sensitivity for color.

Meissner's t. A test for torsion of the eyes when fixating a near object, in which a taut vertical thread is placed slightly closer to, or farther from, the eyes than the point of fixation, so as to effect physiological diplopia. The thread is tilted toward or away from the eyes until the diplopic images appear parallel, indicating the type and the amount of torsion.

Meyrowitz' t. A test for color vision employing pseudoisochromatic plates.

Miles A-B-C t. A test for determining the sighting dominant eye, utilizing the V-Scope and a set of cards, each of which has printed on it two round spots which differ from each other in size and shade. The subject is instructed to look through the V-Scope as each target is presented and to report which of the two spots is larger and which is darker, the examiner noting which eye is sighting. A-B-C stands for *area, brightness, comparison.*

Mills's t. A test for motor ocular dominance, in which a target is moved along the median line toward the eyes until the near point of binocular fixation is passed, the eye maintaining fixation being considered dominant.

mirror t. 1. A test for sighting ocular dominance, in which the subject sights his nose within a small circle on a mirror, the eye seeing the nose being the dominant. 2. Hirschberg's test when performed with a retinoscope mirror as the effective light source

mirror-screen t. Travers' test.

Mitchell's stability t. A test for the ability to maintain binocular fixation on a near point target while the lateral overlapping binocular visual fields are being

gradually reduced by a septum moved slowly away from the eyes along a rod in the midplane toward the target.

Mizukawa-Kamada t. A test to measure lacrimal secretion. One end of a scaled strip of filter paper is placed at the inferior lacrimal punctum and the point of absorption is noted at one minute and at five minutes.

mydriasis t. for glaucoma. A provocative test for glaucoma, in which a mydriatic is instilled into the eye and ocular tension is measured at regular intervals. See also *homatropine test for glaucoma.*

Nagel's t. 1. A test for color vision, in which one half of the bipartite field in an anomaloscope is illuminated with a standard yellow, and the other half is matched with the yellow by mixing red and green. Anomalous color vision is indicated by an atypical combination of red and green. 2. A test for color vision utilizing pseudoisochromatic plates.

Nela wools t. A color perception test employing a series of finely graded colored wool skeins to be arranged in triplets with a test skein between each comparison pair, the test score being given in terms of the number of correct distinctions made.

neutral density filter t. Dark filter test.

Newton ring t. A test for the accuracy of curvature of a lens surface in which the pattern of Newton's rings, formed by placing the surface in contact with another surface of known opposite curvature, is observed.

nicotine t. for glaucoma. A test for determining the effectiveness of medical treatment for glaucoma, in which 0.5 ml. of one percent nicotinic acid solution is injected intravenously and tonometry readings are taken at 15,

30, 60, 120, and 180 minute intervals. Readings within normal range and not exceeding preinjection measurement indicate success of medical treatment. Readings above preinjection measurement indicate the need for surgical treatment.

Nucholls' t. A screening test for the measurement of the limits of perception of movement in the lateral peripheral field of vision.

O'Brien t. A series of seven stereograms to be viewed in a stereoscope to detect a central scotoma, and hemianopic and quadrantanopic field defects.

Oliver's t. Any of several early techniques, described by Oliver, for testing the color sense, including a wool skein, color matching test, a colored pellet matching test, and a color wheel technique for mixing the colors in various proportions.

Oppenheim's t. A test for relative hemianopsia, in which test objects are presented simultaneously on either side of a fixated point and then alternately. Perceiving the objects when presented alternately but not when presented simultaneously indicates relative hemianopsia.

optokinetic nystagmus t. 1. A test for simulated or hysterical blindness, in which the patient is asked whether the stripes on the revolving drum of an optokinetoscope are motionless or moving, the manifestation of optokinetic nystagmus being evidence of vision. 2. An objective test for visual acuity, in which the threshold for optokinetic nystagmus is determined, as with an optokinetoscope.

Osterberg bichromatic balance t. A test for determining the spherical and binocularly balanced components of the refractive correction, designed for use with the Rodenstock Rodavist projector, in which polarized targets of figures on red and green backgrounds are viewed through Polaroid filters such that each eye is independently exposed to targets having both red and green backgrounds. Spherical lens power is adjusted before each eye until all of the figures appear equally clear or distinct on both colored backgrounds.

Osterberg coincidence t. A test for measuring heterophoria, designed for use with the Rodenstock Rodavist projector, in which polarized targets of a divided square are viewed through Polaroid filters such that each eye sees one-half of the square. The phoria is determined by the prism power required to align the two halves into a perfect square.

outlying screen deviation t. A test for determining the limits of the field of binocular fixation, in which the subject, with his head held in the straightforward position, fixates a target moved in various directions of gaze until binocular fixation is lost, as revealed by the cover test.

parallax t. 1. A subjective cover test. 2. Determination of the location of an opacity in the eye by the parallactic movement of the opacity in relation to the pupil and the lateral motion of the observer.

Parson's t. Manoptoscope test.

Pascal-Raubitschek t. A test identical to the Raubitschek test except that, in determining the power of the cylinder, the target is usually rotated 35° away from the position at which the lines in the tip of the arrowhead are equal and clearest, and concave cylinder power is then placed before the eye with its axis 20° away from the axis of the ocular astigmatism, toward the meridian of the arrow tip, and increased or decreased until the target lines again appear equally clear at the tip of the arrowhead, the cylinder thus required being the amount necessary to correct the astigmatism. Pascal preferred to rotate the target 40° and the lens 10° for high cylinders, and the target 30° and the lens 30° for low cylinders, the two values of each pair being such that twice the first plus the second equals 90°.

past pointing t. A test for anomalous fixation or for paresis or paralysis of an extraocular muscle, in which an object is fixated by the suspected eye, the other eye being occluded, in various directions of gaze and then localized by pointing to it. Failure to point accurately to the object indicates anomalous fixation, paresis, or paralysis. Syn., *von Graefe's touch test.*

Peckham's blindspot t. A test for eccentric fixation in which the blind spot of Mariotte is plotted for both the normal and amblyopic eyes, an unequal displacement of the blind spots from the fixation target being an indication of eccentric fixation. Syn., *Peckham's method.*

peephole t. for ocular dominance. A test for sighting ocular dominance, in which the patient, without using his hands, sights through a small peephole, such as that of a monocular optical instrument, the eye used being considered dominant.

perilimbal suction cup t. for glaucoma. A test used for evaluating aqueous flow and outflow resistance in the diagnosis of glaucoma, in which the aqueous outflow channels are closed for 15 minutes by a perilimbal suction cup applied under a pressure of 50 mm. Hg. Tonometry is performed before suction, at its termination, and 15 minutes after termination. The rise of pressure

during suction is an indication of the rate of aqueous secretion and the fall of pressure during the 15 minutes after suction is removed is an indication of outflow resistance. Normally, pressure returns to its original level 15 minutes after termination of suction.

Perlia's t. A test for binocular depth perception in which an attempt is made to touch with a small, round, white object a similar object held by the examiner in various positions of binocular gaze. The test is performed without head movement, with white-headed pins at near, or with white balls on three foot sticks at intermediate distances.

Pettit's macula function t. A test used prior to cataract extraction to assist in the determination of macular function. It is performed with an instrument similar to a flashlight, having a central red fixation point of light and 4 surrounding white points of light so separated from the fixation point as to subtend either a one degree or a two degree angle when held 13 inches from the eye. If the 5 points of light cannot be individually resolved, the 4 white targets are shuttered and an accessory light source is used in conjunction with the red fixation target to determine the minimum separation for which the two lights may be distinguished.

phoria t., habitual. Clinical measurement of a phoria through the prescription worn prior to the examination. Cf. *induced phoria test.*

phoria t., induced. Clinical measurement of a phoria through the subjective finding. Cf. *habitual phoria test.*

photostress t. A test to evaluate macular performance, in which the retina is exposed to an intense light of controlled duration and intensity and the time determined at which sufficient visual functioning has recovered to perform a selected visual task. Prolonged recovery indicates macular disease.

physiological diplopia t. for ocular dominance. A test for ocular dominance in which a target is placed between the patient and a distant fixated target to produce crossed physiological diplopia for the nonfixated target, the diplopic image seen more distinctly indicating the dominant eye.

Pickford t. A test to detect red-green and yellow-blue color vision deficiencies, utilizing a specially designed anomaloscope employing colored filters to produce a variable colored stimulus which is to be compared or matched to a standard stimulus. Syn., *four color test.*

Pierce's t. A test for color perception, in which a series of colored disks of finely graded saturation difference are to be placed in the order of their saturation, the result being recorded as the number of misplacements.

pinhole t. The determination of the visual acuity through a pinhole aperture, by means of which the effect of dioptric errors is minimized.

plano-prism t. for malingering. A test for malingering, in which a lens, 6$^\Delta$ base-down in its upper half and plano in its lower half, is placed before the admittedly good eye, the other eye being occluded, while a small spot of light is fixated, such that monocular diplopia results. The allegedly blind eye is then uncovered and, if vision is present, its image will fuse with the lower image of the good eye. The plano-prism lens is lowered, eliminating the lower image of the good eye, and the continuation of diplopia indicates malingering.

pointing t. for ocular dominance. A test for sighting ocular dominance, in which the patient points with the finger, or sights along an object such as a gun, at a designated target, the eye used for pointing or sighting being considered the dominant.

Pola t. An instrument used in refraction and for investigating binocular functions which presents a series of vectograms to be viewed through Polaroid filters for testing heterophoria, fixation disparity, aniseikonia, stereopsis, and visual acuity.

Polaroid t. for malingering. A test for malingering, in which a rotatable polarized disk is viewed through Polaroid filters, such that vision may be blocked from either eye by rotating the disk.

Pray's t. A test, utilizing Pray's astigmatic chart, for estimating the axis of astigmatism.

pressor-congestion t. for glaucoma. Lability test for glaucoma.

Priestley Smith tape t. A test, utilizing Priestley Smith's tape, for determining the objective angle of strabismus

Prince's rule t. A test for determining the near point and the amplitude of accommodation, in which a Prince's rule is held against the lower orbital margin and a test chart is moved along the tape, toward the eye, until a blur is noticed.

Priscol t. for glaucoma. A provocative test for glaucoma, in which 1 ml. of Priscol is injected under the conjunctiva and tonometry is performed each 15 minutes for 1½ hrs. A rise in ocular tension of 11–13 mm. Hg is probably pathological, and a greater rise is considered definitely pathological.

prism t. for malingering. A test for malingering, in which a vertical prism is placed before the admittedly good eye, with its base bisecting the pupil, to produce monocular diplopia. If vision is present in the allegedly blind eye, its image will fuse with one of the images of the other eye. While the target is being viewed, the prism is moved until it is completely over the good eye, and the continuation of diplopia indicates malingering.

prism reflex t. Krimsky's method.

prolonged occlusion t. Marlow's test.

provocative t. for glaucoma. Any diagnostic test for glaucoma which attempts to cause an abnormal elevation of ocular tension, hence, to detect a disturbance in the regulatory mechanism of intraocular pressure.

pseudoisochromatic t. Any test for color vision utilizing pseudoisochromatic plates.

pupillary reaction t. for color blindness. An objective test in which color blindness is indicated, for a portion of the visible spectrum, by an insufficient pupillary constriction on stimulation of the retina with that wavelength.

push-up t. 1. A test for determining the near point of convergence, in which a test target is moved toward the eyes in the midsagittal plane until binocular fixation is lost. 2. A test for determining the near point of accommodation, in which a test target is moved toward the eyes until a beginning blur is noted.

Rabkin t. A test for color vision utilizing Rabkin polychromatic plates (*q.v.*).

railway signal t. A test for color vision, in which standard red and green signal colors are displayed through various sized diaphragms, to simulate various viewing distances, and through five neutral filters of different densities, to simulate varying conditions of visibility from clear atmosphere to heavy fog.

Raubitschek t. A test for determining the axis and the amount of astigmatism with a rotatable target of two parabolic lines in an arrowhead pattern, parallel at one end and each diverging from the other through 90°, used as follows: While the target is viewed through fogging lenses, it is rotated until the lines are equal and clearest at the tip of the arrowhead, 90° from this position being the axis of the concave correcting cylinder; an arbitrarily selected cylinder power, e.g., −1.00 D., is placed before the eye at a specific off-axis amount, e.g., 30°, which will make the target appear to be off axis; the target is rotated until the lines again appear equal and clearest at the arrowhead tip, the amount of this rotation being referred to a prepared table to obtain the cylinder power.

Rayleigh's t. A test for color vision, in which a spectral red and green are mixed to match a spectral yellow. Anomalous color vision is indicated by an atypical combination of red and green.

reading t. for glaucoma. A provocative test for glaucoma, in which fine print is read for 45 min., a rise in ocular tension of 10–15 mm. Hg being considered positive.

red-green t. 1. A test for determining the spherical component of the refractive correction for an eye, in which spherical lenses are placed before the eye until black test targets, one-half on a green background and one-half on a red background, appear equally black or clear. 2. Lancaster test.

Reed-Van Osdal t. A test for sighting ocular dominance, in which an opaque card, with a round hole in its center, is held with both hands and raised to sight a specified distant object through the hole, the eye used for sighting being considered the dominant.

retinal rivalry t. for ocular dominance. A test for ocular dominance, in which retinal rivalry-inducing patterns are viewed, the dominant eye being that whose image predominates in the fluctuations.

Ring Fusion t. A test for binocular vision, in which a projected target of three dots, two red and one green, surrounded by a vertically broken white ring, is viewed through complementary-colored red and green filters, such that one eye sees the two red dots and the white ring and the other eye sees the green dot and the white ring. The perception of the pattern of the original formation indicates normal binocular vision; the three dots and the circle sections, but not in a circular pattern, binocular vision without fusion; and two red dots and a circle section only, or one green dot and a circle section only, suppression of one eye.

ring t. for ocular dominance. A test for sighting ocular dominance, in which a target is sighted through a ring held in the hands, the eye used for sighting being considered the dominant.

Robinson Cohen t. A test for determining the axis and the amount of astigmatism, in which, with a fogging lens before the eye, the crossed lines on a Robinson Cohen slide are rotated to the position at which the blacker line appears blackest, this position being a principal meridian. An alternate method is to rotate the crossed lines until they appear equally black, the principal meridians being located midway between them (45° away). The amount of astigmatism is deter-

mined by equalizing the blackness of the crossed lines, when they are located in the principal meridians, with cylindrical lenses.

Rosenbach t. A test for sighting ocular dominance, in which the patient, with both eyes open, lines up a pencil or a small stick, held at arm's length, with a mark on a distant wall. The eye with which the pencil is aligned is considered to be the dominant. Syn., *alignment test.*

rotatable E t. Albini's E test.

Scheiner's t. A test for determining the monocular near point of accommodation, in which a small target, observed through two laterally separated pinholes placed before the eye, is moved toward the eye until it appears double, the nearest point at which the target can be seen single being the near point.

Schilder's t. Extension test.

Schirmer's t. A test to measure lacrimal secretion, in which one end of a 5 x 25 mm. strip of filter paper is placed in the inner angle of the lower cul-de-sac, over the inferior lacrimal punctum, the moistening of 2 to 3 mm. of the paper per minute being considered normal.

Schmidt-Rimpler t. A test for malingering, in which the patient is instructed to look at his hand; the blind will look directly at it, the simulator will usually look in a different direction.

screen t. A subjective or an objective cover test.

screen comitance t. A diagnostic test for paralysis of the extraocular muscles, in which the primary and the secondary deviations are objectively measured in each of the six cardinal directions of gaze by means of prisms and a cover test. An occluder is placed before one eye, with a prism behind it, while the other eye fixates, and then is moved to occlude the previously fixating eye. Prism power is varied until the uncovered eye makes no fixation movement. The test is then repeated with the other eye fixating.

screen and parallax t. The subjective cover test.

Seidel's t. Dark room test for glaucoma.

shadow t. Retinoscopy.

Shtremel's t. A test for malingering, in which the patient slowly moves his head from one side to the other. In the blind, the eyes move with the head; hence their remaining relatively stationary indicates the presence of vision.

simultaneous prism cover t. A test to determine the angular extent by which the deviating eye in strabismus misses fixation, in which a prism equal in power to the estimated deviation is placed in front of the deviating eye with simultaneous occlusion of the fixating eye. The prism power which neutralizes the movement of the deviating eye upon occlusion of the fixating eye is a measure of the deviation.

Sjögren's hand t. A visual acuity test comprised of seven square cards, each showing a different size black handprint with extended fingers on a white background, representing visual acuities ranging from 20/15 to 20/200 at 20 feet. They may be held with the fingers pointing in any direction, the subject being required to identify their orientation.

Sloan's achromatopsia t. A test to investigate differences in color vision deficiencies in achromatopsia, in which six Munsell colors of high chroma are to be matched to one of a series of 15 grays. Cone and rod monochromats can be distinguished in that their matches agree, respectively, with those computed from photopic and scotopic luminosity functions.

Sloan's color threshold t. A color-naming test in which eight lights simulating aviation signal colors are to be identified when shown at eight intensities ranging from a low value near the chromatic threshold to a maximum 128 times as bright.

Snellen's t. 1. A test for visual acuity utilizing Snellen's test chart. 2. FRIEND test.

Spache binocular reading t. A test to determine the relative participation of each eye in binocular reading, utilizing stereograms containing reading material printed such that some words are seen by both eyes and some by only one eye when viewed in a stereoscope.

Star t. A visual acuity test consisting of a series of Landolt rings arranged in vertical, horizontal, and oblique rows, in a star formation, to detect differences in acuity thresholds as related to the meridional location of the test targets, as may occur in amblyopia ex anopsia.

Stevens' t. A test for measuring a phoria, in which fusion, for a fixated spot source of light, is disrupted by distorting one image with a pinhole disk and a +20.00 D. sphere placed before one eye.

Stilling t. A test for color perception utilizing pseudoisochromatic plates.

STYCAR t's. A series of visual acuity "Screening Tests for Young Children and Retardates," employing selected script letters, capital letters, or small toys which are presented either at 10 feet or at 20 feet and identified by naming, tracing in the air, or matching with key cards or toys close at hand.

Suda ocular compression t. A provocative test for glaucoma, in which 50 gm. pressure is applied to the eye for 10 minutes. A post-compression tension of over 8 mm. Hg indicates glaucoma.

Thibaudet's t. A test for malingering, in which the patient fixates a test chart so constructed that the separations between the component parts of the larger figures subtend smaller visual angles than the separations of the component parts of the smaller figures. Recognition of the details of the larger figures, and not of the smaller, indicates malingering.

Thiel's t. for glaucoma. A provocative test for glaucoma, in which 2.0 gm. of potassium fluorescein is administered orally, the appearance of the dye in the anterior chamber shortly thereafter indicating glaucoma.

Thorington t. A test for the measurement of a near point phoria, in which a calibrated chart, with a light source placed behind an opening corresponding to the zero on the scale, is fixated with a Maddox rod placed in front of one eye. The number through which the streak appears to pass indicates the type and the amount of phoria.

three disk t. A test to differentiate between true and false macular sparing in visual field loss, in which three white disks, each about 10° in diameter and arranged one above the other, are moved from the blind to the seeing portion of the visual field. False macular sparing is indicated by seeing the disks simultaneously and by a shift of the blind spot of Mariotte toward the blind side. True macular sparing is indicated by seeing the central disk before the other two and with no shift of the blind spot of Mariotte. Syn., *Hughes test.*

three needle t. A near point test for stereopsis, in which two fixed vertical rods in the same plane, with a movable one in between, are viewed through slits or small apertures, the observer judging whether the center rod is placed nearer or farther than the others.

tilting plane t. A test for the measurement of aniseikonia, in which a universally rotatable plane surface target is viewed, usually through an aperture, and manually adjusted until it appears to lie in a plane perpendicular to the direction of gaze. A scale attached to the apparatus indicates the error in degrees.

Tokyo Medical College t. A test for color vision consisting of 13 pseudoisochromatic plates divided into four groups. Group I consists of five plates designed to detect deficient red-green color perception of either deutan or protan types, group II of two plates to detect tritan deficiency, group III of three plates to distinguish between deutans and protans, and group IV of three plates to distinguish between three different degrees of red-green color perception deficiency in those who fail group I.

touch t. of von Graefe. Past pointing test.

Travers' t. A test for the determination and the measurement of suppression areas, in which one eye directly fixates a target on a tangent screen, the other eye fixates a light source on another screen placed to the side and perpendicular to the first, perceptually superimposed on the directly fixated screen by means of reflection from a mirror. The field of the directly fixated screen is explored by a test target for any disappearance of the target or the light source. Syn., *mirror-screen test.*

Tschermak's afterimage t. Hering's afterimage test.

Tschermak's congruence t. A test for measuring the subjective angle of strabismus, consisting of the binocular viewing of a small, illuminated, white cross with a vertical red line above the vertical limb, monocularly shielded so as to be seen by one eye, and a vertical green line below the vertical limb, monocularly shielded so as to be seen by the other eye. The localization of the red and green lines in relation to the cross indicates the subjective angle.

Turville's infinity binocular balance t. A test for equalizing the visual acuity of the two eyes, in which a septum is so placed as to allow each eye to see only one half of the test chart, enabling the two halves to be compared in the presence of peripheral fusion. The test may also be used for measuring vertical fixation disparity if the two halves do not appear on the same level.

type, t. See under *type.*

V t. Maddox V test.

Vasculat t. for glaucoma. A provocative test for glaucoma, in which 1 ml. of Vasculat is injected under the conjunctiva and tonometry is performed after 60, 90, and 120 min. A rise in ocular tension of 11–14 mm. Hg is probably pathological, and a greater rise is considered definitely pathological.

Velhagen's t. A test for color vision utilizing Velhagen's plates (*q.v.*).

Verhoeff's t. A test for stereopsis utilizing Verhoeff's stereopter.

walking t. A test for anomalous spatial localization in strabismus, in which, with the normal eye occluded, the subject is asked to walk straight toward a distant object and the path taken is observed.

water drinking t. for glaucoma. A provocative test for glaucoma, in which the patient, after fasting, drinks 1 l. of water, and tonometry is performed every 15 min. for 1 hr. A rise in ocular tension of 9.00 mm. Hg or more, or to 33 mm. Hg or more, indicates glaucoma.

Welland's t. Bar reading test.

Whittington's t. A test for visual acuity, in which a letter E is held by the patient and is oriented in the same directions as varioussized letter E's on a test chart, the letters on the chart being rotatable so that they may be placed in any position.

Wight's t. A variation of the Newton ring test in which the number of rings per unit of diameter is taken to indicate the variance of curvature between the test and standard surfaces.

Wilbrand's t. A diagnostic test used in hemianopsia, in which prisms are suddenly placed before the eyes, while a small spot on a uniform background is fixated, to displace its images onto the blind sides of the retinae. According to Wilbrand, an abrupt refixation movement is diagnostic of a cerebral lesion,

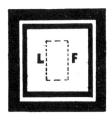

Fig. 40. Turville's infinity binocular balance test. (Left) view of right eye, (center) view of left eye, (right) view with binocular vision. (From *Textbook of Orthoptics,* H. W. Gibson, Hatton Press Ltd., 1955)

while the absence of this movement indicates a lesion in the optic tract.

Williams' lantern t. A test for color perception consisting of the identification of transilluminated colored filters exposed in sequence by means of movable shutters.

Wiltberger's t. A screening test for color perception utilizing six charts, each containing one horizontal and three vertical glossy color strips on a medium gray ground. The color of the afterimage of the horizontal strip, obtained by fixating it for about 20 sec., is compared to the vertical strips, and the one it matches best is said to indicate the type of color vision.

Wirt t. A near point test for the threshold of stereopsis, in which a vectogram consisting essentially of a series of groups of four dots is viewed through Polaroid filters. One dot in each group appears displaced toward the observer, the displacement decreasing with each successive group, and the last group in which it is detected indicates the threshold. Syn., *Wirt stereotest.*

Wood's color aptitude t. A test for color memory, in which a series of colored test patterns are individually viewed and then replaced by a set of four response plates from which one or none is selected as duplicating the same colors as the initial test pattern, regardless of differences in the pattern itself.

Worth's eccentric fixation t. A gross test to detect eccentric fixation, in which angle kappa (lambda) is measured for each eye, a difference between them indicating eccentric fixation.

Worth's four dot t. A test for binocular vision, in which four dots, one white, one red, and two green on a black background, are viewed through complementary red and green colored filters, such that one eye sees the red and the white dot and the other eye sees the two green dots and the white dot. Four dots seen in the pattern of the original formation indicates normal binocular vision, five dots binocular vision without fusion, and two red dots only, or three green dots only, suppression of one eye.

Worth's ivory ball t. A test to measure visual acuity in very young children, in which 5 balls, ranging in size from ½ to 1½ in., are thrown on the floor, one by one, about 6 yds. in front of the child. He is encouraged to retrieve the balls, the smallest which excites his interest providing an estimate of visual acuity.

Worth-Ramstein t. A near point test for binocular vision and fusion consisting of four polarized symbols, a dot, two crosses, and a diamond, colored white, green, and red, which are viewed either through Polaroid filters or through complementary-colored red and green filters. Simultaneous perception of the four symbols in their original formation indicates normal binocular vision. It is one of the tests incorporated in the Freeman Near Vision Unit.

Young's t. A test to determine the state of macular function in an eye affected with cataract, consisting of the viewing of illuminated holes in a disk. The diagnosis is based on the number of holes perceived.

Young's threshold t. A clinical test for the determination of the threshold for light or color, used especially for the early detection of glaucoma. The subject observes gray or colored spots of varying intensities, on white cards bound into five albums, one each for gray, yellow, blue, red, and green. The threshold is indicated by the card on which the spot is first perceived.

Zagora rod t. A test for depth perception, similar to the Howard-Dolman, in which the top movable half of a vertical rod is aligned with the bottom stationary half, such that one continuous rod is perceived, thus involving height as well as depth judgment.

tetartanopia (tě-tahr″tah-no′pe-ah). Tetartanopsia.

tetartanopsia (tě-tahr″tah-nop′se-ah). 1. Homonymous quadrantanopsia. 2. G. E. Mueller's term for a type of blue-yellow blindness, in which there are two neutral points, one in the yellow and one in the blue of the normal spectrum, which appear as white. Both red and green are seen normally and can be differentiated while blue and yellow are confused.

tetrachromatism (tet″rah-kro′mah-tizm). 1. Normal color vision according to the Hering theory of four primary colors. 2. Hering's theory of color vision.

tetranopsia (tet″rah-nop′se-ah). Quadrantanopsia.

tetrastichiasis (tet″rah-stih-ki′ah-sis). An anomalous condition, in which there are four rows of eyelashes on a single eyelid.

thalamus (thal′ah-mus). One of a pair of ovoid masses of gray matter, about 1½ in. long, whose medial surface forms a portion of the lateral walls of the third ventricle in the diencephalon of the forebrain. The anterior extremity forms the posterior boundary of the foramen of Monro and the posterior end, the pulvinar, overhangs the midbrain and continues laterally into the external geniculate body. The internal capsule separates it above and laterally from the lenticular

nucleus. It is a relay station for sensory pathways ending in the cerebral cortex, receives fibers from the cortex, and is connected with the tegmentum and with fibers of the optic tract.

optic t. The thalamus.

thaumatrope (thaw′mah-trōp). A disk having on each face a picture representing a different portion of an object or a scene or a different stage in the movement of an object. When rotated so that both sides are alternately and rapidly viewed, the effect of a whole object or scene, or of a moving object, is obtained.

thelaziasis (the″la-zi′ah-sis). Infestation of the conjunctival sac with the nematode *Thelazia callipaeda.*

theory. 1. The general or abstract principles of a science or an art, as distinguished from the application of that science or art. 2. A general principle or formula, derived from an analysis of related facts to explain a phenomenon, which is generally more plausible than a hypothesis.

Abbe's t. The theory of resolution with coherent illumination, in which the diffracting properties of both the illuminated object and the aperture of the lens are considered to contribute to the form of the image.

active excretory t. Metabolic pump theory.

Adams' t. A theory of color vision, derived from that of Hering, which postulates a receptor system of rods and three types of cones, red, white, and blue. The receptors contain photosensitive pigment of different spectral properties and are associated with ganglion cells whose fibers relay impulses for three opponent color systems, white-black, red-green, and blue-yellow. The rods and white cones synapse directly with white optic nerve fibers and give rise to a sensation of white, the blue and red cones first modulate the response of the white cones by means of assumed lateral connections and then synapse with blue and red optic nerve fibers, respectively. Only an excess of a red or a blue response over a white response can reach the red or blue optic nerve fiber and so produce a red or blue sensation, while a white response in excess of a red or blue response results in a red optic nerve response, the negative of red (green), and a blue optic nerve response, the negative of blue (yellow).

additive t. Young-Helmholtz theory.

aim intent t. Voluntary eye movements do not cause a perception of apparent movement of objects whose images are moving across the retina, as such movement signals are cancelled by central signals from the brain which command the eyes to move. Cf. *inflow theory.* Syn., *outflow theory.*

air t. of space perception. Point theory of space perception.

Allen's t. A theory that every color stimulates all three primary color sensations, thereby causing a sensation of whiteness underlying and inseparable from color, thus explaining achromatic vision at high and low intensities, nonsaturation of colors, contrast, and complementary colors.

alternation of response t. A postulation that uniform continuous response to continuous visual stimulation is effected by groups of parallel circuits activated in a sequential co-ordinated manner, each group going through a cycle of activity and recovery before again responding.

antichromatic t. Hartridge's antichromatic theory.

Arlt's t. The theory that myopia

is caused by pressure of the extraocular muscles in convergence impeding the outflow of blood from the eye through the vortex veins, resulting in congestion and increased intraocular pressure.

Aubert's t. A theory which postulates two pairs of "pure" colors, viz., red and green, yellow and blue, each member of the pair being capable of evoking its appropriate sensation when combined with either or both members of the other pair, but failing to do so if combined with the other member of its own pair.

Bach's t. Lenticular theory for colobomata.

Barnet's t. The theory that color vision is analogous to hearing, in that wavelengths of light may be differentiated similarly to the wavelengths of sound.

Behr's t. The theory that tissue fluid in the optic nerve normally flows from the eye toward the skull because the pressure is normally higher in the eye, and that choked disk results from a reversal of this flow when the pressure in the eye becomes lower than in the skull.

Brücke's t. The theory that the binocular perception of depth is due to continuous motion of the eyes, alternately increasing and decreasing convergence, which integrates successively the different aspects of the two scenes as seen by the two eyes.

Buffon's t. The theory that strabismus is due to reduced vision in one eye and that this eye deviates to avoid the disturbance arising from blurred vision.

capillary attraction t. (of lacrimal flow). The theory that tears are drained by capillary attraction of the canaliculi.

Carmona y Valle's t. The theory that accommodation is accomplished by the compression of the periphery of the crystalline lens by the action of the circular fibers of the ciliary muscle on the fibers of the zonule of Zinn. This compression is said to act on soft peripheral portions of the lens, forcing the central portion of the lens to become more convex.

central dip t. of resolution. The theory that at threshold visual resolution the peaks of the light distributions of two adjacent point targets are separated by an intervening central dip in light distribution of fixed proportion. In the Rayleigh criterion for resolution (*q.v.*), this is about 10% of the peak height.

Chavasse's t. The theory that strabismus is due to interference preventing normal development of the reflex acts involved in binocular vision, or if normally developed, hindering or abolishing them. The interference may be sensory, motor, or central, and congenital or acquired.

Cogan-Kinsey t. Osmotic pump theory.

Cohn's t. The theory that myopia is caused by the effects of excessive accommodation during near work in school.

Collins' t. Vascular theory for colobomata.

compression t. (of lacrimal flow). The theory that tears are drained by the action of the orbicularis oculi muscle on the lacrimal sac in the opening and closing of the eyelids. When the eyelids are closed, the lacrimal sac is compressed, forcing the tears into the lacrimal duct; when the eyelids are opened, the tears are sucked into the lacrimal sac through the canaliculi.

corpuscular t. Newton's theory.

Cramer's t. The theory that the increased convexity of the crystalline lens in accommodation is due to contraction of the iris exerting pressure on the periphery of the

lens and to contraction of the ciliary muscle, which pulls the choroid forward to compress the vitreous against the posterior surface of the lens.

Cüppers' t. The theory that eccentric fixation is due to a preexisting anomalous retinal correspondence in that the shift of the straight-ahead principal visual direction from the central fovea of the deviating amblyopic eye to an extrafoveal area, exhibited under binocular conditions, continues to operate monocularly when the amblyopic eye attempts to fixate; hence monocular fixation is with the retinal site which corresponds directionally to the foveal center of the fixating eye.

Dartnall's t. The theory that the absorption curve of visual purple for low intensities and the absorption curve for bleached visual purple at higher intensities are the physiological correlates of the scotopic and photopic luminosity curves, respectively, and that the displaced luminosity curve in the protan may be accounted for by some abnormality in the environment of the receptor, such as an unusual *pH* value.

decreased tension t. of accommodation. Any theory that accommodation is due to decreased tension of the suspensory ligament on action of the ciliary muscle, as in Helmholtz' theory of accommodation.

dialysation t. The theory that the aqueous humor is a dialysate from the blood of the capillaries of the ciliary body in thermodynamic equilibrium with the blood.

dichromatic t. Any theory which postulates a two component system for the explanation of color vision in dichromatism.

Dieffenbach's t. The theory that strabismus is due to a peripheral disturbance of the extraocular muscles.

distention t. The theory that retinal detachment in high myopia is due to elongation of the anteroposterior axis of the eyeball, assisted by an accompanying hyperemia.

dominator-modulator t. A theory of color vision in which a particular sense cell called the *dominator* is responsible for the brightness aspect of vision, chromatic effects being introduced by other receptors modulating the dominator response.

Donders' t. of accommodation. A maximal contraction of the ciliary muscle is required to produce maximal accommodation at any age, and each fraction of the actual range of accommodation corresponds to an equal fraction of the entire contractibility of the ciliary muscle. Hence, a greater amount of ciliary muscle contraction is required to produce a unit change in accommodation than was required at a younger age or the ability of the ciliary muscle to contract is diminished in some manner. Cf. *Hess's theory.*

Donders' t. of strabismus. The theory, attributed to Donders, that strabismus is due to uncorrected refractive errors, that hypermetropia is the cause of esotropia, and that myopia is the cause of exotropia.

Druault's t. The theory that the vitreous humor is originally mesodermal, derived from ingrowing vessels, and that, as the eye grows, a secondary, ectodermal vitreous is formed from the retinal surface. The secondary vitreous displaces the primary toward the center of the eye and thus forms Cloquet's canal.

Duane's t. The theory that strabismus is caused by excessive or insufficient nerve impulses from a convergence or divergence center in the brain.

duplicity t. The theory that visual sensation stems from two independent receptor systems in the retina, one said to be composed of rods and the other of cones, the former mediating achromatic sensations at very low levels of intensity, the latter mediating vision at higher levels of intensity and capable of distinguishing colors. Syn., *von Kries duplicity theory.*

Ebbecke's t. The theory that the successive reappearances of afterimages with abrupt changes in illuminance levels of the total retina are dependent on the continued effectiveness of the initial stimulus, even for several hours, and the otherwise balanced inhibitory and counterinhibitory mechanisms of local adaptation and simultaneous contrast, respectively.

Edridge-Green t. of color vision. A speculative theory that the cones alone are the visual receptors and that rods merely secrete visual purple which flows via small channels into the fovea, where stimulation by light sets up vibrations which are transmitted via the optic nerve to two independent centers in the brain, a light center and a color center, where perceptual analysis takes place. The light center is supposed to be more primitive, the color center evolving later, with subsequent evolution of subcenters for differentiation of seven specific colors. Color blindness is atavistic, resulting from central failure of development.

Edridge-Green t. of myopia. The theory that myopia is caused by increased intraocular pressure from obstruction of the flow of lymph out of the eye during bending, straining, or lifting.

Einstein's t. The theory that (*a*)

the uniform motion of translation cannot be detected by an observer stationed on the moving system from observations confined to the system, and (*b*) the velocity of light in space is a constant, independent of the relative velocity of the source and the observer.

electromagnetic t. Maxwell's theory.

electrostatic t. The theory that differential permeability of the cornea is due to static electrical charges on its surface which propel appropriately charged ions through its cell membranes.

emission t. Newton's theory.

empiristic t. See *empiricism*.

Enoch's t. The theory that anomalous anatomical composition or disturbed anatomical orientation of the central retinal receptors may be an etiological factor in amblyopia.

evolutionary t. Ladd-Franklin theory.

Exner's t. The theory that the illusion of movement of a stationary object, occurring after prolonged viewing of an object moving in one direction, is due to streams of afterimages.

Fick's t. The theory that protanopia and deuteranopia are due to the absence of either the red- or the green-sensitive photopigments, that in protanopia both the red and the green receptors contain green-photosensitive pigment, and in deuteranopia both the red and the green receptors contain red-photosensitive pigment.

field t. The theory that the neural functions and processes with which the perceptual facts are associated in each case are located in a continuous medium, and that the events in one part of this medium influence the events in other regions in a way that depends directly on the properties of both in their relation to each other.

filtration t. The theory that the formation of aqueous humor is by filtration from the capillaries of the ciliary body which are permeable to crystalloids but not to colloids of the blood plasma; hence, the filtered fluid would be devoid of proteins, whereas crystalloids and other substances would be in the same proportion as in the blood.

Fincham's t. The theory that in accommodation the anterior surface of the crystalline lens assumes a conoidal shape, with increased convexity primarily in the pupillary area, due to the elasticity of the anterior capsule and to the relative thinness of the anterior capsule in the pupillary area, an elaboration of Helmholtz' theory. The reduction of the amplitude of accommodation with age is due to sclerosing of the lens substance, such that it changes less in form for a given pressure of the capsule.

first order t. Theory of Gauss.

Förster's t. The theory that myopia is caused by stretching of the eyeball in excessive convergence, and that its increase can be prevented by the use of full correcting lenses or abducting prisms.

Fourier's t. A theory, developed by the French physicist, Fourier, showing that it is possible to describe any complex periodic wave form as the sum of a specific series of sine and cosine waves. The amplitudes, phases, and frequencies of these waves are a characteristic of the original wave form and constitute a full description of it.

Frieberg's t. The theory that tears are drained by the action on the canaliculi of the opening and closing of the eyelids. When the eyelids are closed, the canaliculi are compressed, forcing the tears into the lacrimal sac; when the eyelids are opened, the tears are sucked into the canaliculi from the conjunctival sac.

fusion faculty t. Worth's theory.

Gauss, t. of. The theory that, for tracing paraxial rays through a lens system, the system may be analyzed in terms of six cardinal planes, two principal planes, two nodal planes, and two focal planes. Syn., *first order theory.*

genetic color t. Ladd-Franklin theory.

Gibson's texture gradient t. of space perception. The theory that all three dimensions are represented on the retina, since distant features of a scene are projected on the retina as smaller than nearby ones, this gradation forming a texture gradient by means of which all features within it are given size and location. Cf. *point theory of space perception.*

Goethe's t. A very subjectively derived explanation of color phenomena tending to relegate colors as phenomenal attributes inherent in the light stimulus or in the substance reflecting or transmitting the light, and hypothesizing the admixture of dark with light as the essential determining factor, with blue and yellow as the extremes on the dark to light scale, whence other colors could also be described as mixtures of these two colors.

Göthlin's t. A theory postulating that the impulse for a given color sensation releases to some extent an inhibition for the complementary color within the same area, to account for the fact that a mixture of two spectral primaries is less saturated than the matching monochromatic hue until spectral primary is added to the latter.

von Graefe's t. The theory that strabismus is due to a congenital or acquired anomaly of the ligament and muscle system of the eye, and that a disturbance in this relationship causes a predominance in one group of muscles or an insufficiency in the antagonistic group.

Granit's t. The theory that the seven relatively narrow, electroretinographic, response curves obtained by Granit, which he called *modulator curves*, might be related to the fibers of the optic nerve in such a way as to constitute three systems of receptors, by virtue of their clustering in three groups corresponding to the three main parts of the spectrum associated with three-receptor theories of color vision.

Harris' t. Metabolic pump theory.

Hartridge's antichromatic t. A postulation to account for the apparent compensation for chromatic aberration of the eye, in which the depressed sensitivity for the blue and yellow fringes of the retinal image is attributed to a neurological mechanism.

Hartridge's t. of color vision. A theory of color vision postulating seven types of receptors, six (orange, yellow, green, blue-green, blue, and blue-violet) having single response curves on the spectral scale and one, crimson, having two, one at each end of the spectral scale. Syn., *polychromatic theory.*

Hartridge's t. of visual acuity. The theory that the resolving power of the retina is facilitated by the ability of each cone to detect gradations of light intensity, not as an all-or-none receptor.

Hasner's t. The theory that myopia is caused by a stretching of the eyeball due to pulling on the posterior pole by the optic nerve.

Hecht's photochemical t. The theory that the action of light on the retinal receptors decomposes a photosensitive substance into two photochemical products which act as catalysts in a secondary reaction which results in nerve impulses.

Hecht's t. of visual acuity. The theory that the increase in visual acuity with increased illumination is due to an increase in the number of retinal receptors activated; that the retinal receptors have varied light thresholds and react individually according to the all-or-none law.

Helmholtz' t. of accommodation. The theory that in accommodation the ciliary muscle contracts, relaxing the tension of the suspensory ligament and allowing the crystalline lens to become more convex, especially its anterior surface, due to its own elasticity. The choroid aids in maintaining the tension of the suspensory ligament on the crystalline lens in its unaccommodated state and the contraction of the ciliary body pulls the choroid forward, releasing the tension. Syn., *decreased tension theory; relaxation theory.*

Helmholtz' t. of color vision. Young-Helmholtz theory.

Helmholtz' empiristic t. See *empiricism.*

Henderson's t. The theory that tension of the suspensory ligament on the crystalline lens is maintained chiefly by the longitudinal and the radial fibers of the ciliary muscle, that the contraction of the circular fibers overcomes this tension and slackens the suspensory ligament in accommodation, that both sympathetic and parasympathetic innervation are involved in accommodation, and that presbyopia is due to sclerosis of the connective tissue of the ciliary body.

Henschen's t. The theory that sensory fusion occurs in the middle stratum of three strata which compose the superficial layer of the area striata, that the fibers from the temporal retina of the eye on the same side terminate in the outer stratum and the fibers from the nasal retina on the opposite side terminate in the inner stratum, and that fibers from the corresponding points of these two strata stimulate the same cell in the middle stratum.

Hering's t. of color vision. The theory that postulates three primary retinal substances, each responsible for one mutually antagonistic pair of color sensations, red-green, yellow-blue, or white-black, and that light falling on the retina, depending on its wavelength composition, causes a breakdown (catabolism) or synthesis (anabolism) of one or more of these substances, causing transmission of one or neither of each pair of sensations to the brain. Syn., *opponent colors theory.*

Hering's nativistic t. See *nativism.*

Hering's t. of retinal projection. The theory that the estimation of distance between points in the field of vision depends on the chord connecting the retinal images of the points and not on the angular distance between them, an explanation of the optical illusion of empty spaces appearing smaller than subdivided spaces.

Hering's t. of stereoscopic vision. The theory that stereoscopic vision is based on retinal disparity and that the appreciation of this disparity is an innate physiological process.

Hess's t. The same amount of ciliary muscle contraction will produce a unit change in accommodation at any age. Cf. *Donders' theory of accommodation.*

van der Hoeve's t. The theory that strabismus is caused by the failure of the summation of all the reflexes affecting the extra-ocular muscles to produce a nearly orthophoric position, the resultant diplopia acting as a stimulus to move the nonfixating eye to a position of greater deviation to facilitate suppression.

Holm's t. The theory that myopia is caused by overgrowth of the eyeball, that the tonus of the ciliary body regulates the growth of the eye, and that the increased innervation from prolonged reading acts as a growth-promoting factor.

Houstoun's t. A theory which postulates two types of cones, a red-green type and a yellow-blue type, each capable of responding to stimulation with two alternative frequencies or modes of electric discharge, each discharge frequency corresponding to its appropriate color sensation, with a third, less clearly postulated system to account for white, gray, and black.

Hubbard-Kropf t. A theory of the nature of *meta*-rhodopsin and its relation to rhodopsin, according to which *meta*-rhodopsin consists of a mixture of thermally stable rhodopsin, thermally stable 9-*cis* rhodopsin, and thermally unstable compounds of opsin with *all-trans* retinene and additional retinene isomers other than 11-*cis* and 9-*cis;* that the absorption of one quantum of light isomerizes the chromophore of either rhodopsin or 9-*cis* rhodopsin to the *all-trans* configuration, but while the *all-trans* retinene is still attached to the opsin, a second quantum of light may cause isomerization to still another configuration. If the new stereoisomer thus formed is either 11-*cis* or 9-*cis*, then rhodopsin or 9-*cis* rhodopsin will be reformed.

Hurvich-Jameson t. A quantified version of the Hering theory of color vision. It postulates a system of three independent photosensitive materials in the retina which mediate between the incident light and the three opponent color neural response systems; it relates the total mechanism to the physical variables of stimulus wavelength and energy levels and to their dependence on adapting and surrounding stimulation.

Huygens' t. The theory that light is propagated through space in waves and that space is filled with a luminiferous ether which penetrates and permeates all matter. The ether is composed of tiny elastic particles whose mutual impacts are transmitted from one to another and act as the vehicle for the light waves. Syn., *undulation theory; wave theory.*

hydraulic t. of accommodation. The theory that the increased convexity of the crystalline lens in accommodation is due to compression of the aqueous humor against its periphery, causing the anterior pole to bulge forward, as a result of contraction of the ciliary muscle compressing the aqueous humor in the posterior chamber, where it is confined by the constricted pupil.

increased tension t. of accommodation. Any theory that accommodation is due to increased tension of the suspensory ligament on action of the ciliary muscle, as in Tscherning's theory of accommodation.

inflow t. Eye movements do not cause a perception of apparent movement of objects whose images are moving across the retina, because such movement signals are cancelled by feedback signals from the extraocular muscles to the brain. Cf. *aim intent theory.*

Ivanoff's t. The theory that night myopia is due to chromatic aberration, the Purkinje phenomenon, and a voluntary effort to accommodate to eliminate spherical aberration.

Ives's t. The theory that flicker or intermittent vision is a perceptual process involving three steps; a reversible photochemical reaction; diffusion of substances formed by the photochemical reaction; and a constant critical value of the rate of change of a transmitted reaction which must be exceeded before the perception of flicker can occur.

Javal's t. The theory that strabismus is caused by a functional anomaly of binocular vision and not by primary involvement of the extraocular muscles.

Kant's nativistic t. See *nativism*.

Keiner's t. The theory that convergent strabismus is due to an inherited retardation of the development of the myelin sheaths of nerve fibers in the visual pathways, thus delaying the acquisition of binocular reflexes.

Keith's t. The theory that myopia is caused by a growth disorder occasioned by the conditions civilization has imposed on man.

Kinsey-Cogan t. Osmotic pump theory.

Koenig's t. The theory of color vision that visual purple is the excitant of the rods at low intensity levels and hence the basis of achromatic vision, that visual yellow, the first product of bleaching of visual purple with higher intensities, is the basis of the blue sensation also carried out by the rods and absent from the fovea, that red and green sensations are accomplished by differential absorption of the pigment cells of the pigment epithelium, dichromatism being due to coincidence of the elementary sensation curves, and that the cones serve only as a dioptric

mechanism to concentrate light on the pigment epithelium.

Kölliker's t. The theory that the cornea is derived entirely from mesodermal tissue which in the embryo migrates between the surface epithelium and the lens vesicle.

von Kries duplicity t. Duplicity theory.

von Kries t. of color vision. The supposition that the sensations of vision may be aroused by two different mechanisms, perhaps operating both in series and in parallel, more or less independent of each other, only one of which has the tripartite structure of the trichromatic system, whereas the other reacts to its stimulus in a simple monotone, wherefore the "colorless sensation has some outstanding physiological significance." Syn., *theory of zones; zonal theory.*

Ladd-Franklin t. A theory of color vision which postulates an evolutionary development of receptor substances from an initial "whiteness" detector, presumed to persist in the rods and the peripheral cones, from which are derived, by molecular change, two paired substances that serve as detectors of blue and yellow, the latter of which is further changed into paired substances that serve to detect red and green, whence mixtures of red and green are perceived as yellow, and mixtures of yellow and blue are perceived as white. Types of color blindness are thus regarded atavistically as incomplete recapitulations of evolutionary development. Syn., *evolutionary theory; genetic color theory; tetrachromatic theory.*

Land's t. A theory for color vision which postulates a series of retinal-cerebral systems (retinexes), each having retinal receptors with the same peak sensitivity to a given band of the spectrum. The retinal receptors for each retinex operate as a cooperative unit, independent of other retinexes, and form, through cerebral liaison, an image corresponding to the optical image on the retina but differing in terms of lightness from the images of the other retinexes. The image of the same object in each retinex has its own rank order in relation to lightness, its rank order being different in each retinex and dependent on the interaction of the spectral absorption curve of the receptors with the spectral absorption curves of all objects in the field of vision. The image from each retinex becomes superimposed, and the comparison of the rank order of lightness for the image of the same object from each retinex results in a designation of color for that object, color being the correlation number for several rank orders of lightness.

Landolt's t. The theory that strabismus is due to the topographical anatomy of the eyes, i.e., to mechanical factors.

Langworthy's t. The theory that the sphincter pupillae muscle acts against a tonal background maintained by the blood volume of the iris and the natural elasticity of its blood vessels, and that, when the sympathetic nervous system is stimulated, the arterioles and the capillaries constrict, forcing out the blood, which reduces the mass of the iris and causes the pupil to dilate.

lattice t. Maurice's theory.

Leber's t. Migration theory.

lenticular t. for colobomata. The theory that a typical coloboma is due to an abnormally large crystalline lens which mechanically prevents closure of the embryonic fissure. Syn., *Bach's theory.*

Levinsohn's t. The theory that myopia is caused by stretching of the eyeball, resulting in increased axial length, from tilting the head forward.

lid closure t. The theory that tears are drained by being forced into the lacrimal puncta by the eyelids on closure.

Lindner t. The theory that myopia is caused by weakening of the choroid and the sclera, due to a transudation of blood elements from the choroidal vessels into the surrounding tissues during near work.

linked-receptor t. of color vision. The theory that there may be a greater number of types of receptors in the retina than there are types of response mechanisms, and that pairs or groups of two or more receptors may be "linked" together to elicit a single type of response, resulting in a polychromatism of the retina with trichromatism of vision.

Lomonosov's t. The theory for color vision postulating three primary types of particles of light consisting of mercury, salt, and sulphur which are responsible for sensations of red, yellow, and blue when stimulating preferentially sensitive particles in the optic nerve which are also composed of mercury, salt, and sulphur, all other colors being a mixture of these three. One of the earliest attempts to explain color vision, advanced by Lomonosov in 1756 and subsequently modified by Young.

Lotze's t. of local signs. The theory that each point on the retina, when stimulated, will give rise to a specific sense of direction, that this is an innate phenomenon not dependent on previous experience.

Luneburg's t. A theory of binocular spatial localization formulated on non-Euclidean, hyperbolic geometry, whence visual space is said to be non-Euclidean in character.

Lythgoe's t. The theory that the increase in visual acuity with increased illumination is due to a decrease in the dimensions of the retinal receptor fields.

Mackenzie's t. The theory that strabismus is due to a functional anomaly of the areas in the brain and the nerves which associate the actions of the extraocular muscles.

Manz's t. Mesoblastic theory for colobomata.

Maurice's t. The theory that corneal transparency is based on the orderly and symmetrical arrangement of the collagen fibrils in the corneal stroma, which are of uniform diameter, arranged in a two-dimensional lattice pattern, of equal spacing, and with the interspaces being less than one wavelength of visible light. Under these conditions, each line of fibrils will correspond to a diffraction grating and interference will suppress the scattering of light in any direction except that of the incident beam. Syn., *lattice theory.*

Maxwell's t. The theory that light consists of electromagnetic waves. Syn., *electromagnetic theory.*

McDougall's t. A color vision theory postulating four mediating systems, corresponding to red, green, blue, and white, each including an appropriate light-sensitive substance at the receptor level and each terminating in one of four appropriate, bilaterally represented, cortical centers, with presumed inhibitory interaction mechanisms between the cortical centers for the three color primaries and with inductive and integrative mechanisms between all four systems at the retinal level.

mesoblastic t. for colobomata. The theory that a typical colo-boma is due to blockage of the fetal fissure by the normally migrating vascular formative mesodermal tissue. Syn., *Manz's theory.*

metabolic pump t. The theory that the normal relative deturgescence or normal water content of the cornea is maintained by the active excretion or "pumping" of tissue fluid and electrolytes from the corneal stroma through the endothelial and epithelial cells, and that this excretion requires cellular energy and is therefore a metabolic process. Syn., *active excretory theory; Harris' theory; Potts-Maurice theory.*

migration t. The theory that sympathetic ophthalmia is caused by migration of the pathogenic agent through the lymph canals of the optic nerve. Syn., *Leber's theory.*

modulation t. for color vision. The theory that color sensation is mediated by variations in the temporal pattern of afferent optic nerve impulses, rather than by types of receptors or by the subdivision of neural pathways.

Morgan's t. of accommodation. The theory that accommodation is due in part to the blood volume of the ciliary body, which affects the pull on the suspensory ligament, and that a decrease in the blood volume of the ciliary body with age produces a decreased response of the ciliary muscle.

Morgan's t. of anomalous correspondence. The theory that anomalous retinal correspondence represents an adaptive adjustment derived from an innervational pattern or position sense of the deviating eye with respect to the other eye, rather than an adaptation of the local direction signs of the retina.

Mueller's t. of color vision. A

theory employing the concept that an equality, a similarity, or a difference in the condition of sensations corresponds to an equality, a similarity, or a difference in the condition of psychophysical processes, and postulating four chromatic retinal substances correlated with red, yellow, green, and blue that are chemically altered by the action of light so as to transmit impulses corresponding to their modifications to cerebral substrata of actual sensations for which there are six basic values (red, yellow, green, blue, white, and black), the resulting sensation being derived from a complex linkage system between the four types of peripheral retinal substances and the six central value processes.

Mueller's t. of strabismus. The theory that strabismus is due to a false or displaced macula in the one eye.

Nagel's empiristic t. See *empiricism.*

nasal aspiration t. The theory that tears are drained by a sucking action created by changes in pressure in the nasal cavity due to breathing.

nativistic t. See *nativism.*

neurogeometric sensory feedback t. The theory that all major characteristics of visual behavior are ascribable not to the receptor, the motor system, or learning, but to the spatial or geometric properties of neural feedback control systems linking the sensory and motor systems of the body

Newman's t. The theory that myopia is caused by the effects of excessive accommodation on the choroid, decreasing its nutrition by pulling and tensing, so that it becomes weakened.

Newton's t. The theory that light consists of a flight of invisible,

rapidly moving particles projected from a light source, the size of the particles varying with the apparent color and moving in a substance called *ether,* which varies in density for different media. Syn., *corpuscular theory; emission theory.*

noise t. The theory for the basis of the brightness difference threshold in which the fluctuations in absorption of quanta per unit area of the retina, corresponding to the background, constitute the noise against which the signal (stimulus) must be detected; hence the number of quanta from the signal, to be detected, must sufficiently exceed that of the background noise.

Norris' t. The theory that myopia is caused by "abuse" of the eyes leading to congestion and softening of the coats of the eyeball so that they stretch under normal intraocular pressure.

opponent colors t. Hering's theory of color vision.

opponent process t. Any theory postulating retinal substances which respond with opposing reactions, such as anabolic and catabolic reactions. See *Hering's theory of color vision* and *Hurvich-Jameson theory.*

osmotic pump t. The theory that the normal relative deturgescence or normal water content of the cornea is maintained by a difference in osmotic pressure between the corneal stroma and the hypertonic tear fluid and aqueous humor which bathe the intact epithelium and endothelium; hence, tissue fluid entering the corneal stroma through the limbal capillaries is continually passed through the endothelium and epithelium. Syn., *Cogan-Kinsey theory.*

Otero's t. The theory that night myopia is due to a combination of the aberrations of the eye (spherical and chromatic) and the posture of the accommodative mechanism at low levels of illumination.

outflow t. Aim intent theory.

Palmer's t. The theory for color vision, advanced by G. Palmer in 1777, that there are three color components in white light, red, yellow, and blue, and three corresponding retinal receptor systems preferentially sensitive to these three colors, that a sensation of white results from uniform agitation of the three systems, and that color sensations result from nonuniform agitation. Total color blindness results from failure of the three systems to respond differentially, and partial color blindness is due to impairment of one or two of the three systems.

Parinaud's t. 1. Two retinae theory. 2. The theory that strabismus is caused by a defect in the brain centers controlling the eyes. 3. The theory that choked disk results from edema of the brain, due to tumor, which spreads through the optic nerve to the papilla.

Petzval t. The theory that for eliminating the curvature of a stigmatic image produced by a system of two thin lenses, in contact or separated, the sum of the product of the refractive indices and the focal lengths of the two lenses must equal zero.

physical t. of color vision. Young-Helmholtz theory of color vision.

Piéron's t. A theory for color vision postulating three types of cone, each containing a single pigment, and a fourth supplementary cone receptor concerned with the reception of luminosity and containing a mixture of the three pigments.

Planck's t. The theory that radiation is intermittent and spasmodic and operates by definite quanta or units of energy in the case of both emission and absorption. Syn., *quantum theory.*

point t. of space perception. The theory that objects are aggregations of points and that all positions in the frontal plane are localized in relation to that of the point of fixation. Cf. *Gibson's texture gradient theory.* Syn., *air theory of space perception.*

Polyak's t. The theory that the receptor mechanism responsible for color perception does not lie in the retinal cones, as they are identical in their chemical properties, morphological structure, and synaptic relationships, and that the synthesis and compounding of colors may involve the bipolar and the ganglion cell layers.

polychromatic t. Hartridge's theory of color vision.

pore t. The theory that the differential permeability of the cornea is due to sievelike pores in the structure of the cornea which permit passage of molecules and ions of limited size.

Posey's t. The theory that myopia is caused by the shape of the skull, which determines the conformation of the orbit and, in turn, the eyeball.

Potts-Maurice t. Active excretory theory.

projecton t. The theory that an object is localized in space along a line representing the pathway of light traveled from the object to the retina and that in binocular fixation an object is localized at the point of intersection of two lines, one to each retina.

psychological t. of color vision. Hering's theory of color vision.

quantum t. Planck's theory.

quantum t. of color vision. Any theory of color vision postulating the quantal energy difference of different wavelengths as the

[751]

initial or fundamental factor in color differentiation.

Rayleigh's t. The theory that an optical system will be free of spherical aberration when the difference between the optical paths of a paraxial ray and a marginal ray leading to a selected focus is less than one-quarter of a wavelength.

relaxation t. of accommodation. Helmholtz' theory of accommodation.

replacement t. Verhoeff's theory.

rivalry t. The theory that single, binocular vision is obtained through rapid, alternate perception of the two monocular images, that each monocular image is periodically suppressed and replaced by the other.

Roaf's t. The theory that color vision is mediated by three types of receptors, one being stimulated by the entire visible spectrum, one by the red end to 490 mμ (blue-green), and one by the red end to 580 mμ (yellow-green). Thus long wavelengths stimulate all three receptor types, medium, two receptor types, and short, one receptor type, the differentiation presumed to be due to color filters in the receptors.

Ronchi's t. The theory that night myopia is due to the chromatic aberration of the eye, the Purkinje phenomenon, and to the action of the pupil when it dilates in low levels of illumination. The dilatation allows the crystalline lens to move forward so that its periphery presses on the iris, forcing the central portion of the lens to bulge and become more convex.

Rydberg's t. The theory of color vision that the outer segment of the cones consists of uniform double layers of protein and lipoid lamellae which act as an interference color filter, and that

each cone will react only to the one, two, or three spectral wavelengths which are able to form standing waves in its protein lamellae. Hence, the thickness of the lamellae must be an integer multiple of the half-wavelengths of these colors.

sac dilation t. The theory that tears are drained by the action of the orbicularis oculi muscle on the lacrimal sac in the opening and closing of the eyelids. When the eyelids are closed, the lacrimal sac expands, sucking in tears, and when the eyelids are opened, the lacrimal sac is compressed, forcing the tears into the lacrimal duct.

Schenck's t. A theory employing the evolutionary concept of development of color vision, largely identical to Ladd-Franklin's, and postulating an original cone substance resembling the rod substance, which underwent a "panchromatization," making it relatively sensitive to long waves, subsequently but independently differentiating into blue and yellow components, with the final stage of differentiation being that of the yellow component into red and green subcomponents, whence types of color blindness were identified categorically with absence of the cone mechanism, failure of pan-chromatization, and/or failure of the yellow cleavage process.

Schmidt-Rimpler t. The theory that choked disk results from congested cerebrospinal fluid in the skull being forced into the intervaginal spaces of the optic nerve, causing edema of the nerve and the papilla.

Schober's t. The theory that the largest portion of night myopia is due to an increase in accommodation caused by the effort to see under low levels of illumination, that under these conditions the dioptric stimulus to accommodation is not adequate to fix its amount.

Schoen's t. The theory that accommodation is due to contraction of the ciliary muscle exerting pressure on the equator of the crystalline lens which causes the surfaces to bulge, increasing the total refractive power of the eye.

Schöler's t. The theory that the vitreous humor is entirely mesodermal in origin and can be considered to be a specialized form of connective tissue.

secretion-diffusion t. The theory that the aqueous humor is formed by secretion from the epithelium of the ciliary body and by diffusion from the blood vessels of the iris.

secretory t. The theory that the aqueous humor is formed by secretion from the epithelium of the ciliary body.

Shaxby's t. A theory postulating that the different quanta of energy contained in the different wavelengths striking the cones are the basis for color differentiation, and not the cone structures or connections themselves (single neural connections of each cone with the brain being assumed).

Sherrington's t. The theory that sensory fusion is the result of a psychic process at some higher brain level, and that the two monocular images are complete and independent sensations until they are united at this level. When the two monocular sensations are alike, the resulting binocular perception does not differ from either; when they are slightly dissimilar, the result is intermediate between the two; and when they differ widely, rivalry results.

siphon t. The theory that tears are drained by a passive flow from the eye into the nose by a siphoning action.

solvent t. The theory that the differential permeability of solutes through the cornea is effected by the cell membranes having the property of dissolving the solutes.

Speciale-Circincione t. The theory that the vitreous humor is derived from the ectoderm of the crystalline lens and the retina.

Steiger's t. The theory that myopia is caused by a chance association of inherited variables, such as the curvature of the anterior surface of the cornea and the axial length of the eye; that all refractive errors are due to normal biologic variations.

Stiles t. A color vision theory based on the assumption of five fundamental receptor mechanisms with specific spectral sensitivities and with the activity of each mechanism related to both test and background wavelength.

Stilling's t. of myopia. The theory that myopia is caused by pressure of the superior oblique muscle on the eyeball in convergence, the pressure varying with the position of the trochlea, resulting in congestion and increased intraocular tension.

Stilling's t. of strabismus. The theory that strabismus is due to the topographical anatomy of the eyes, i.e., to mechanical factors.

Straub's t. The theory that the state of refraction of the eye is caused by the psyche, that those who wish to see well at a distance are emmetropic and those overly attracted to near objects become myopic.

tetrachromatic t. Ladd-Franklin theory.

third-order t. The theory that the deviation of the path of a ray from that prescribed by the theory of Gauss may be expressed mathematically by the Seidel formulae, and that, for a lens to be free of all aberration, all of the formulae would have to be simultaneously and individually equal to zero.

three component t. Young-Helmholtz theory.

Tornatola's t. The theory that the vitreous humor is derived from ectoderm, probably from the retinal layer of the optic cup.

transudation t. The theory that the aqueous humor is formed by a pressure filtration from the blood of the ciliary body and the iris.

trichromatic t. Young-Helmholtz theory.

trireceptor t. Any theory which postulates that color vision is accomplished by means of three kinds of retinal receptors, each mediating one of the three primary hue sensations.

Troland's t. A theory postulating five "molecular resonators" which may be selectively ionized by appropriate wavelengths to give rise to respective sensations of red, green, blue, yellow, and white, for which the positive ions represent the psychophysical correlates, with the further postulation that antagonistic relations between blue and yellow, and between red and green, represent ionization phenomena occurring in a "complementation substance" in the ganglionic retinal cells, while other ion combinations result in fused or additive sensations.

Tscherning's t. The theory that accommodation is due to contraction of the ciliary muscle, which tightens the suspensory ligament and pulls the choroid forward, causing the vitreous humor to exert pressure on the posterior surface of the crystalline lens. Since the periphery of the lens is held taut by the suspensory ligament, the pressure of the vitreous causes the anterior pole of the lens to bulge forward, increasing its convexity. Syn., *increased tension theory*.

Turner's t. The theory that myopia is caused by toxins from a diseased condition of the nose or the throat, producing waterlogging of the choroid and the sclera and an increase in the bulk of the vitreous humor, with a resultant stretching of the eyeball without change in intraocular tension.

two retinae t. The theory that the retina is composed of two distinct neural mechanisms, the rods of the peripheral retina primarily responsible for distinguishing light and dark, concerned with scotopic vision, and the cones of the central retina responsible for distinguishing color and form, concerned with photopic vision. In the evolutionary development of the eye the retinal receptors were capable only of distinguishing light from dark. Later some receptor cells became more complex, and color and form vision became possible, although these cells lost sensitivity to low levels of illumination. Syn., *Parinaud's theory*.

ultrafiltration t. The theory that the formation of aqueous humor is by filtration through the capillary walls, primarily from the capillary bed of the ciliary body.

undulation t. Huygen's theory.

vascular t. for colobomata. The theory that all colobomata are due to failure of formation of blood vessels in the mesoderm surrounding the optic cup which prevents fusion of the embryonic fissure. Syn., *Collins' theory*.

Verhoeff's t. The theory that the single percept arising from binocular vision consists of a constantly changing mosaic containing parts of each monocular image. Syn., *replacement theory*.

Vogt's t. The theory that myopia is caused by overgrowth of the eyeball, that the size of the retina controls the size of the eye, and that in myopia the retina has an excessive inherent growth potential.

Walls's t. A theory postulating that each of three types of color receptors, if isolated, would be capable of invoking a pure hue sensation appropriate to itself, but that each receptor responds to all wavelengths, whence the dominant hue sensation is invoked by the maximally stimulated receptor, while the common response of all three receptors produces a certain degree of desaturation.

wave t. Huygen's theory.

Wiener's t. The theory that myopia is caused by an endocrine disturbance.

Wolfrum's t. The theory that the primary vitreous is the result of the original adhesions between the neural and surface ectoderm in the region of the lens plate, that as these two surfaces separate, protoplasmic processes are pulled out between them and an intermediate substance is formed by interlacing fibrils from this source.

Worth's t. The theory that a fusion faculty or fusion sense controls the position of the eyes for binocular fixation and that the absence or imperfect development of this fusion faculty is the essential cause of strabismus. Syn., *fusion faculty theory.*

Wright's t. A theory that the receptor subdivision responsible for color perception resides in the presumed triplicate neural connection of each cone to three separate nerve pathways by means of three different bipolar cells.

Wundt's t. A theory postulating two relatively independent processes, one, a uniform photochemical process mediating achromatic perception, related to wavelength only as an intensity

function, and the other, a polyform photochemical process mediating the gradations of color perception by changes associated with wavelength variance.

Young's t. of accommodation. The theory that accommodation results from a change in form of the crystalline lens.

Young's t. of color vision. Young-Helmholtz theory.

Young-Helmholtz t. The theory that three different, independent types of receptors or receptor components mediate all color sensations by their individual and combined activities, and that these types correspond to three color primaries. Syn., *additive theory; Helmholtz' theory of color vision; three component theory; trichromatic theory; Young's theory of color vision.*

Zeeman's t. The theory that strabismus is caused by the failure or retardation of normal sequential development of the conditioned reflexes involved in co-ordinated eye movements.

zones, t. of. Von Kries theory of color vision.

thermoluminescence (ther"mo-lu"-mih-nes'ens). The emission of light by a substance when heated, but not incandescent.

theta (θ). The Greek letter used as a symbol for *angle of latitude* in the field of regard. *Fry.*

thiamine (thi'ah-min). Vitamin B_1.

Thibaudet's test (te-bo-dāz'). See under *test.*

thickness. The degree or extent to which something is thick; measurement in the third dimension; the dimension from one surface to its opposite.

apparent t. Reduced thickness.

axial t. Thickness of a lens as measured along the optical axis. Syn., *polar thickness.*

center t. Thickness of a lens either at its optical center or at its geometrical center.

point t. Thickness of a lens expressed in points, 1 point being equal to ⅕ mm.

polar t. Axial thickness.

reduced t. Axial thickness of a lens divided by its index of refraction. Syn., *apparent thickness.*

strap t. The thickness of an ophthalmic lens at the hole or point over which the strap of a rimless mounting fits.

Thiel's test (thēlz). See under *test.*

Thiéry's (tyĕ″rēz′) **figure; visual illusion.** See under the nouns.

Thies's sign (thēs′ez). See under *sign.*

third dimension. The dimension of depth as contrasted to the dimensions of width and length, or the percept of distance away from an observer.

Thollon prism. See under *prism.*

Thomas' chart (tom′as). See under *chart.*

Thompson's circles (tom′sonz). See under *circle.*

Thomsen's disease (tom′senz). See under *disease.*

Thomson's effect (tom′sonz). See under *effect.*

Thorington (thōr′ing-ton) **chart; prism; test.** See under the nouns.

Thorpe contact lens. See under *lens, contact.*

Thouless ratio. See under *ratio.*

threshold. 1. The least stimulus value that will excite a response or a just noticeable difference in response. 2. Statistically, the central tendency in a range of stimulus values at which occurs a transition in a series of sensory judgments. Syn., *limen.*

absolute t. The least stimulus value that will produce a response or cause a transition from no sensation to sensation. Syn., *stimulus threshold.*

achromatic t. Light threshold.

brightness difference t. The smallest difference in luminous intensity that can be perceived as a difference in brightness. Syn., *light difference.*

chromatic t. The minimum intensity of a specified wavelength of light that gives rise to a sensation of color. Syn., *specific threshold.*

color t. Chromatic threshold.

differential t. The smallest difference between two stimuli that for a given individual gives rise to a perceived difference in sensation. Syn., *just noticeable difference.*

discrimination t. The smallest detectable change in a sensory stimulus.

double point t. Two point threshold.

flicker fusion t. Critical fusion frequency.

general t. Light threshold.

light t. The absolute threshold for the perception of light. It varies with the state of dark adaptation, location of the retinal area stimulated, size of the stimulus, spectral composition of the stimulus, etc. Syn., *light minimum; achromatic threshold; general threshold.*

linear t. of distance discrimination. Threshold of stereopsis expressed in terms of the linear difference in distance of the test objects.

movement t. 1. The minimum movement of an object that can be perceived. 2. The maximum speed at which an object moving between two points can be perceived as moving. 3. The minimal conditions necessary for inducing phi movement.

pause t. The shortest time interval between two pulses of light that will provide for the perception of two flashes, or the shortest interruption in otherwise continuous light that can be perceived as such.

photochromatic t. The lowest luminance at which hue is perceived.

relational t. The ratio between two

stimulus values when their difference is just noticeable.

resolution t. The threshold of ability to resolve or perceive separately two small, nearly adjacent objects observed simultaneously; the minimum separable.

specific t. Chromatic threshold.

stereopsis, t. of. The smallest difference between the two binocular parallactic angles subtended at two objects which just gives rise to a perceptible difference in distance of the two objects from the observer; the smallest difference in retinal disparity created by two objects, in space, which gives rise to a just perceptible difference in distance. Syn., *lower threshold of stereopsis; stereoacuity.*

　stereopsis, t. of (lower). Threshold of stereopsis.

　stereopsis, t. of (upper). The largest difference between the two binocular parallactic angles subtended at two objects which gives rise to a perceptible difference in distance of the two objects without producing physiological diplopia; the greatest difference in retinal disparity created by two objects in space which gives rise to a perceptible difference in distance without producing physiological diplopia, i.e., the retinal disparity is within Panum's area.

stimulus t. Absolute threshold.

two point t. The minimum separation at which two points are perceived as two. Syn., *double point threshold.*

thromboangiitis obliterans (throm"-bo-an"je-i'tis ob-lit'er-ans). Buerger's disease.

thrombosis (throm-bo'sis). The formation or presence of a thrombus.

thrombus (throm'bus). A plug or clot in a blood vessel or in the heart, formed by coagulation of the constituents of the blood and

remaining at the site of its formation.

thyrotoxicosis (thi"ro-tok"sih-ko'sis). Graves's disease.

Tibbs binocular trainer. See under *trainer.*

Tiedemann's nerve (te'de-manz). See under *nerve.*

Tillaux, spiral of (te-yo'). See under *spiral.*

Tillyer lens (til'yer). See under *lens.*

tilt, face. Head tilt.

tilt, head. 1. A deviation of the head from its upright position, especially as a clinical symptom. 2. A forward or backward tilt of the head, as distinguished from *shoulder tipping.* Syn., *face tilt.*

time. The period during which a condition, a process, or an action continues or occurs.

accommodation t. The time interval required to change the accommodation from one dioptric level to another. Positive or negative accommodation time relates to increase or decrease of accommodation, respectively.

action t. 1. The time interval required, following the latent period, for a sensation or response to reach its maximum intensity. 2. The minimum duration required of a stimulus to give a maximum effect.

cortical t. The period of time (about 33–35 msec.) between a flash of light and the appearance of the positive electroencephalogram potential.

fixation t. 1. The time required for the eye to change fixation from one point to another. 2. The time during which the eye steadily fixates an object.

fixation response t. The time interval between the onset of an extrafoveal stimulus and the beginning of eye movement to fixate the stimulating target. Syn., *eye reaction time.*

nystagmic t. The time interval between the observed onset of induced nystagmus and the observed termination.

perception t. The critical time interval between the tachistoscopic presentations of two stimuli for which the second stimulus does not act to interfere with the perception of the initial stimulus.

persistence t. 1. The time during which a response continues after termination of the stimulus. 2. The duration of the darkness interval at the critical flicker frequency.

reaction t. The time between the onset of a stimulus and the response.

  reaction t., eye. Fixation response time.

recognition t. The time between the onset of a stimulus and its identification.

regression t. The time, in reading, in which a readjustment fixation is made at the beginning of a new line or in which words previously fixated in the same line are refixated.

retinal t. The period of time (about 25 msec.) between a light flash and the beginning of the b-wave of the electroretinogram.

retino-cortical t. The period of time required for an impulse to travel the entire afferent visual pathway, beginning in the retina and terminating in the visual cortex; the cortical time minus the retinal time.

wearing t. The length of time a contact lens can be worn continuously without discomfort, blurredness, haze, abrasion, edema, injection, or other subjective or objective signs of damage or unfavorable tissue reaction.

tinea favosa (tin′e-ah fa-vo′sah). Favus.

tinea tarsi (tin′e-ah tar′si). Mycotic blepharitis.

tint. 1. A mixture of white with a color, thus the antonym of *shade*. 2. Any color lighter than median gray. 3. A slight coloring; a pale or faint tinge of any hue. 4. A term descriptive of a difference in hue only, as, "A yellower tint of green." 5. To color slightly; to tinge.

Ostwald t's. In the Ostwald color system, mixtures of semichromes with white.

tintometer, Lovibond (tin-tom′eh-ter). An empirical colorimeter in which light from the sample is matched with light passed through a combination of red, yellow, and blue filters that are numbered approximately in proportion to their densities. The color of the sample is then specified (in the Lovibond system) by three numbers representing the sums of all glasses of each of the three colors inserted into the instrument to obtain a match.

tipping, shoulder. A tilting of the head toward one shoulder, especially as a clinical symptom.

tissue. A group of cells of similar structure and their intercellular substance.

border t. of Elschnig. A ring of white fibrous tissue and neuroglia around the optic nerve, separating it from the adjacent sclera and the choroid.

intercalary t. of Elschnig. Connective tissue and neuroglial elements surrounding the central retinal vessels in the lamina cribrosa.

intermediate t. of Kuhnt. A ring or partial ring of glial tissue around the optic nerve and separating it from the adjacent retina.

pore t. of Flocks. Endothelial meshwork of Speakman.

Tolosa-Hunt syndrome. See under *syndrome*.

tone, color. 1. A perceptual attribute of color variously corresponding to hue, color, or lightness. 2. A variation of a color other than a change of hue. 3. In the Ostwald system, the black content of a color.

affective color t. The emotional affective tone associated with the perception of different colors, thought to be a learned response, whence green, e.g., may be a soothing color.

Ostwald color t's. In the Ostwald color system, mixtures of semichromes with black.

tongs, tourmaline. Two plates of tourmaline crystal, mounted parallel to each other on a tonglike handle, providing for variable separation and rotation about a common axis perpendicular to their surfaces, serving as a polarizer and analyzer.

tonicity (to-nis'ih-te). The condition of normal tone or tension of muscles.

tonofibrils (ton'o-fi''brilz). Delicate fibers found in the cytoplasm of epithelial cells, such as those of the cornea.

tonogram (to'no-gram). The recorded changes in tonometer readings obtained during tonography.

Tonographer, Mueller (to-nog'rah-fer). A Mueller Electronic Tonometer coupled to a strip-chart recorder, used in tonography.

tonography (to-nog'rah-fe). The determination of the rate of outflow of aqueous humor under the continuous pressure exerted by the weight of a tonometer over a 4 to 5 min. period, as represented in a series of changes or a continuously recorded change in tonometer readings.

constant pressure t. Tonography in which the intraocular pressure is maintained approximately constant by incremental increases in plunger load corresponding to changes in tonometer readings.

tonometer (to-nom'eh-ter). An instrument for determining ocular tension, usually by measuring the impressibility of the tunics of the eye, so as to evaluate intraocular pressure.

applanation t. A tonometer in which the ocular tension is determined either by the force required to flatten a constant area of the cornea, as with the Goldmann tonometer, or by the area flattened by a constant force, as with the Maklakov tonometer.

Bailliart t. An impression tonometer using a calibrated spring instead of weights, with corneal and scleral direct reading pressure scales and interchangeable footplates for corneal or scleral use.

corneal t. A tonometer applied to the anterior surface of the cornea.

Crescent Electronic t. The trade name for an indentation tonometer of the Schiötz type equipped with a transistorized circuit and an electronic readout, used in tonometry or tonography.

Draeger t. A hand-held applanation tonometer which indicates ocular tension by the force required to applanate a corneal area of constant size and having a counterweight mechanism permitting measurements independent of patient position. It contains a microscope with a built-in scale, a light source to illuminate both the applanated area and the scale, an adjustable support for steadying the instrument against the forehead, and a motor-controlled spring-loaded lever arm for adjusting the force on the plunger.

Durham t. An applanation tonometer which indicates ocular tension by the air pressure required to flatten a fixed small area of the cornea or sclera in the center of an area flattened by the footplate. It consists essentially of a diaphragm-covered flat footplate having a pneumatic sensing nozzle in its center, an air pump, bottled gas, a pneumatic-to-electric transducer, and a combined amplifier and strip recorder.

electronic t. Any tonometer with an electronic readout, usually a meter or strip recorder.

Fick's t. An applanation tonometer in which the area of application is held constant while the pressure is varied.

Gambs t. The trade name for an applanation tonometer of the Goldmann type.

Gradle t. A type of impression tonometer.

Harrington t. A modified Schiötz tonometer with a transparent plastic footplate and a circular dial which magnifies the readings four times that of the Schiötz instrument.

Goldmann's t. An applanation tonometer consisting essentially of a transparent plastic footplate, a pair of juxtaposed prisms with bases in opposite directions, a coil spring and lever system to apply force to the prisms and footplate, and a dial calibrated in centimeters of mercury. The edge of the contact area is rendered visible by the instillation

of fluorescein into the tears and is seen through the prisms and a blue filter, with a slit lamp microscope, as two light green semicircles on a blue ground. Force is varied until the semicircles interlock, so that the inner edge of the upper coincides with the inner edge of the lower.

Husted t. An impression tonometer which evaluates ocular tension through the closed eyelid by determining the compression required on a spring-loaded plunger to produce an indentation of 3.5 mm., a direct reading being obtained from a scale on the spring-enclosing barrel.

impression t. A tonometer which measures the depth of the impression produced by a plunger of small bearing area carrying a known weight. The excursion of the plunger is read from a calibrated scale. Syn., *indentation tonometer.*

indentation t. Impression tonometer.

MacKay-Marg Electronic t. A tonometer having a flat plunger, in the center of the flat footplate of the probe, sensitive to displacements of less than one micron and which measures the ocular tension in the center of a small area of the cornea flattened

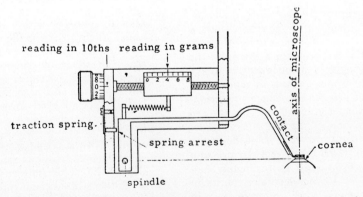

Fig. 41. The Goldmann applanation tonometer. (From *The Glaucomas*, ed. 2, H. Saul Sugar, Hoeber, 1957)

[760]

by the footplate. It electrically records on a scaled strip the counter force required to resist displacement of the plunger, to keep it flush with the footplate, and thus to flatten the corneal area in contact with the plunger.

Maklakov's t. One of a set of five applanation tonometers ranging in weight from five to fifteen grams and consisting of a dumbbell-shaped metal cylinder balanced on the cornea with the aid of a loop on a handle. One end is for the right eye and one for the left, and each end has a flat disk of polished glass which is coated with a dye prior to placement on the cornea. The area of the cornea flattened is indicated by the smallest diameter of the area of dye removed, measured by holding a transparent plastic scale against the end plate and by referring this finding to a table.

McLean t. An indentation tonometer, similar in construction to the Schiötz tonometer, in which a weighted plunger is placed on the cornea and the ocular tension is read directly from an attached scale calibrated in millimeters of mercury.

microtransfiguration t. A tonometer equipped with a clear transparent plastic concave footplate, ten millimeters in diameter and of a radius of curvature of 9½ millimeters, having in its center a clear transparent plastic plunger, 2 millimeters in diameter and of radius of curvature 5 microns less than that of the footplate. When the area of contact of the footplate is between 4 and 6 millimeters, as indicated by fluorescein dye applied to the footplate and exposed to black light, the force against the plunger is electrically measured and recorded from a strain gauge hooked to the plunger.

Mueller Electronic t. The trade name for an indentation tonometer of the Schiötz type equipped with an electronic readout, used principally in tonography.

Schiötz t. An impression corneal tonometer which consists essentially of a footplate, a weighted plunger, and a measuring scale to record the vertical movement of the plunger.

scleral t. An impression tonometer applied to the surface of the sclera.

Souter's t. A tonometer in which the area of application is constant while the pressure is increased until the plunger produces the slightest recognizable indentation of the cornea.

Tonair t. A pneumatic tonometer in which a probe of fixed mass applanates an area of the surface of the cornea or sclera in excess of that of the central plunger of the instrument, and air pressure supplied by a chamber behind the central plunger is increased until the force against the posterior plunger surface just exceeds the force of the eye against its front surface. At this point air escapes from the chamber, resulting in a constant pressure serving as a measure of the ocular tension read from a dial calibrated in millimeters of mercury.

vibration t. See *Vibra-Tonometer.*

Wolfe t. A modified Bailliart tonometer, especially intended for use on the sclera.

tonometry (to-nom'eh-tre). Measurement of ocular tension with a tonometer.

ballistic t. Tonometry in which photographs are made of the oscillations in the recoil of a minute hammer striking the cornea under standard conditions.

digital t. Estimation of the ocular tension by applying light pressure to the eyeball through the upper eyelid with the fingers.

tonotics (to-not′iks). A method of visual training which stresses rotations of the eyes, performed for short periods of time with frequent rest periods.

tonus (to′nus). The slight continuous contraction present in muscles not undergoing active movement.

    ophthalmokinetic t. Tonus imparted to the extraocular muscles by stimuli originating in the semicircular canals of the inner ear.

    ophthalmostatic t. Tonus imparted to the extraocular muscles by stimuli originating from the otoliths in the inner ear.

top, Benham's. A disk, half black and half white, with a number of concentric black arcs on the white sector, which, when rotated, elicits a variety of chromatic color sensations. Syn., *Benham's disk.*

top, Maxwell's color. A device for studying the effects of additive color mixing, consisting of a spinning top with a flat surface on which various colors are placed in sectors.

top, Munsell. A three dimensional representation of colors in the Munsell system in which the series of neutrals, from white through gray to black form the central core, and the various hues are arranged in circles of increasing saturation around the central gray of the same lightness.

Topalanski's sign. See under *sign.*

Topogometer (to-pog′om-eh-ter). A device attached to the front of a keratometer which provides a movable fixation target for measuring corneal curvature at points other than at the line of sight, the displacement of the fixation target from the optical axis of the instrument being indicated by a horizontal and vertical scale.

topometer (to-pom′eh-ter). An instrument for photographing, from both front and side views, the position of a pair of lenses mounted in front of the eyes.

Toposcope (top′o-skōp). An instrument used to measure the curvature characteristics of a contact lens by the use of moiré fringes. The fringes are created by nearly superimposing the reflected or refracted image of a grating upon a second grating attached to a microscope.

Toposcope, Corneal (top′o-skōp). An instrument used to measure corneal curvatures from limbus to limbus by the use of moiré fringes.

topotaxis (top′uh-tak-sis). Directional movements of a motile organism in response to light stimulation. See also *klinotaxis; tropotaxis; telotaxis; menotaxis; mnemotaxis; phototaxis; scototaxis.*

toric (tor′ik). 1. Pertaining to, resembling, or shaped like a surface, or a segment of a surface, described by a circle rotating about a straight line in its own plane, especially about an off-center line. 2. Pertaining to a lens which has one surface with meridians of least and greatest curvature located at right angles to each other. 3. A toric lens.

Tornatola's theory (tōrn″ah-to′lahz). See under *theory.*

toroidal (to-roi′dal). 1. Pertaining to, resembling, or shaped like a surface, or a segment of a surface, described by a circle rotating about a straight line in its own plane, especially about an off-center line. 2. Pertaining to a lens which has one surface with meridians of least and greatest curvature located at right angles to each other.

torpor retinae (tōr′por ret′ih-ne). Lack of response of the retina to stimuli of normal threshold value.

Torres-Ruiz implant; lens. See under *lens.*

torsiometer (tōr"se-om'eh-ter). An instrument for measuring torsion, cycloductions, or cyclophorias.

torsion (tōr'shun). Rotation, or more specifically cyclorotation, of the eye around an anteroposterior axis such as the fixation axis. See also *extorsion; intorsion; dextrotorsion; levotorsion; angle of torsion.*

false t. The apparent cyclorotation associated with a change in direction of regard from the primary position to a tertiary position, which occurs when movement of the eye is analyzed in terms of azimuth and elevation (Helmholtz system) or in terms of longitude and latitude (Fick system). When the movement is analyzed in terms of the rotation of the eye around Listing's axis, no cyclorotation or torsion is found; hence, the cyclorotation found by other means of analysis is called false torsion.

fusional t. Torsion induced by cyclofusional stimuli.

minus t. Torsion in which the upward extension of the vertical retinal meridian rotates temporally from the true vertical.

negative t. Torsion in which the eye rotates in the direction opposite to that of the hands of a watch which it fixates.

plus t. Torsion in which the upward extension of the vertical retinal meridian rotates nasally from the true vertical.

positive t. Torsion in which the eye rotates in the same direction as the hands of a watch which it fixates.

secondary t. False torsion.

true t. Torsion representing an actual rotation of the eye around its line of sight with respect to a given system of axes for specify-

ing eye movements; distinguished from *false torsion.*

tort. In reference to the eye, to rotate about an anteroposterior axis, i.e., to a position of torsion.

torticollis (tōr"tih-kol'is). Head tilting; twisting of the neck, producing an unnatural position of the head.

congenital t. Torticollis present from birth, due to primary contracture of the sternocleidomastoid muscle of one side. It is differentiated from *ocular torticollis* in that it is more pronounced, the head cannot be passively straightened, and conjugate ocular movements are normal.

neurogenic t. Torticollis due to irritation of the spinal accessory nerve.

ocular t. Torticollis which serves to compensate for hyperphoria or for paresis of paralysis of one or more of the vertically acting extraocular muscles. It is differentiated from congenital torticollis in that it is less pronounced, no true contracture of the sternocleidomastoid muscle is present, the head can be passively straightened, and conjugate ocular movements may be abnormal.

tortoise shell. Shell plates from the hawksbill turtle used in the making of spectacle frames.

Touraine-Solente-Golé syndrome. See under *syndrome.*

tourmaline (tōōr'mah-lin, -lēn). A mineral crystal, a silicate of boron and aluminum, which polarizes light by absorbing the ordinary ray and transmitting the extraordinary ray.

Tournay's pupillary reflex (tōōr-nāz'). See under *reflex.*

toxoplasmosis (toks"o-plaz-mo'sis). A disease caused by infection with the protozoan parasite *Toxoplasma* and occurring in a number of forms. The congenital or infantile type, which produces encephalitis, is especially associated with chorioretinitis, appearing bilaterally as deep, heavily pigmented, necrotic lesions affecting both macular and peripheral areas, and with secondary optic nerve atrophy. There is extensive connective tissue proliferation from the lesions, the retina surrounding the lesions remains normal, and the ocular media remain clear.

Toynbee's corpuscle (toin'bēz). Corneal corpuscle.

trabecula (trah-bek'u-lah). A small column, fiber, or bundle of fibers in the framework of an organ.

bridge trabeculae. A fine net of fibrillar tissue spanning the opening of some of the crypts of the iris.

corneoscleral trabeculae. Corneoscleral meshwork.

uveal trabeculae. Uveal meshwork.

trabeculectomy (trah-bek″u-lek'to-me). Surgical removal of a portion of the trabecular meshwork to facilitate aqueous humor outflow in glaucoma.

trabeculodialysis, anterior (trah-bek″u-lo-di-al'ih-sis). A surgical procedure for glaucoma in which the corneoscleral trabeculae are detached from the overlying sclera, allowing free communication of the canal of Schlemm with the anterior chamber.

trabeculotomy (trah-bek″u-lot'o-me). Surgical incision of the trabecular meshwork to create a communication between the anterior chamber and outflow channels, for the treatment of glaucoma.

trachoma (trah-ko'mah). A chronic, contagious, viral infection of the conjunctiva and the cornea characterized by the formation of conjunctival follicles, papillary hypertrophy, pannus, and subsequent cicatrization. The course of the disease may be classified into four stages: (1) Infection of the epithelium of the conjunctiva and the cornea followed by subepithelial infiltration, formation of minute follicles, mild conjunctivitis, and inclusion bodies in epithelial scrapings. (2) Inflammatory reaction in the subepithelial tissues and the tarsal plate with the formation of larger follicles, papillae, and pannus. This stage lasts from several months to several years and mainly affects the upper eyelids, giving them a granular appearance resembling that of a raspberry. (3) Necrosis of subepithelial tissue leading to extensive and deforming cicatrization. (4) Subsidence of the disease with the persistence of scar tissue and the sequellae of ptosis, trichiasis, entropion, symblepharon, corneal opacities, and xerosis of the conjunctiva and the cornea. It responds favorably to sulfanilamide treatment. Syn., *Egyptian conjunctivitis; granular conjunctivitis; Egyptian ophthalmia; granular ophthalmia; military ophthalmia; war ophthalmia.*

Arlt's t. The granular form of trachoma.

trachomatous (trah-ko'mah-tus). Pertaining to, of the nature of, or affected with trachoma.

tracing, ray. Tracing of the paths of selected light rays through a schematic representation of a longitudinal section of an optical system.

tract. 1. A bundle or collection of nerve fibers in the brain or the spinal cord. 2. A system of organs serving a special purpose, such as the digestive tract.

anterior accessory optic t. of Bochenek. A bundle of decussated optic nerve fibers from the retina, found in some subprimates, which originates at the posterior chiasma and courses through the cerebral peduncle to terminate at the subthalamic nucleus. Syn., *anterior accessory optic bundle of Bochenek; anterior accessory fasciculus of Bochenek.*

corticobulbar t. A group of fibers, arising in the motor cortex, which synapse in motor nuclei of the cranial nerves throughout the brain stem and subserve voluntary control of skeletal muscles. The cells of origin are the large pyramidal cells (including the giant cells of Betz) located in the fifth layer of the cerebral cortex. All fibers of the tract pass through the corona radiata, twist their way in such a fashion as to occupy a particular locus in the internal capsule, and then pass downward into the base of the cerebral peduncle, with the individual fibers splitting off at the appropriate level to go to the nuclei of the III, IV, V, VI, VII, IX, X, XI, and XII cranial nerves. Syn., *corticonuclear tract.*

corticomesencephalic t. Voluntary fibers of the corticobulbar tract that arise in the frontal eye field, descend as a portion of the pyramidal system, decussate within the pons, and terminate with the motor nuclei of cranial nerves III, IV, and VI.

corticonuclear t. Corticobulbar tract.

corticotectal t. A group of fibers originating from cell bodies located in the striate, the parastriate, and the peristriate areas of the visual cortex in the occipital lobe. The fibers pass between the pulvinar and the geniculate bodies of the thalamus, course through the brachium of the superior colliculus and synapse in the tectal region of the midbrain with fibers of either the tectobulbar or colliculonuclear tracts to bring im-

pulses ultimately to the nuclei of the extraocular muscles. It also contains fibers from the peristriate area which are involved in the accommodation near pupillary reflex. Syn., *occipitomesencephalic tract.*

Darkschewitsch's t. A bundle of nerve fibers that leave the optic tract, proceed to the habenular ganglion, pass through the posterior commissure, and end in the contralateral oculomotor nucleus. Their use in the indirect or consensual pupillary reflex is not established.

geniculocalcarine t. A group of axons, conveying visual impulses, which arise in the lateral geniculate body and pass out in a fan-shaped manner to terminate in the area striata of the occipital lobe. Syn., *optic radiations of Gratiolet.*

geniculocortical t. Geniculocalcarine tract.

occipitomesencephalic t. Corticotectal tract.

optic t's. The centralward continuation of the optic nerves beyond the optic chiasm, by which the visual impulses travel from the optic chiasm to the brain. From the posterolateral angle of the chiasm, the optic tracts run lateral and backward, each taking the form of a rounded band, running at first between the tuber cinereum and the anterior perforated substance behind which it is continued posteriorly as a flattened band sweeping around the cerebral peduncles in close association with the posterior cerebral artery. Reaching the posterolateral aspect of the optic thalamus, each breaks into two roots: (1) a lateral and larger root which ends in the lateral geniculate body; (2) a medial and smaller root which runs to the lateral geniculate body.

opticotectal t. Nerve fibers from

the optic tract which run to the superior colliculus via the superior brachium.

posterior accessory optic t. of von Gudden. Transverse peduncular tract.

pyramidal t. The corticospinal and corticobulbar tracts.

spinal t. of the trigeminal nerve. A nerve tract located in the medulla and the cervical cord, composed of sensory fibers of the trigeminal nerve which terminate in the nucleus of the spinal tract of the trigeminal nerve, transmitting pain and temperature impulses from the head area.

tectobulbar t. A group of fibers arising from cell bodies located in the superior colliculus of the tectum which cross in the dorsal tegmental decussation and descend to their termination in three locations: (1) the motor nuclei of the lower part of the medulla oblongata; (2) the pontine nuclei; and (3) the reticular formation of the brain stem.

tectopontine t. A group of nerve fibers originating in the superior colliculus, and some in the inferior colliculus, of the tectum which, together with the tectospinal and tectobulbar tracts, crosses in the fountain decussation of Meynert and descends to synapse with pontine nuclei.

tectospinal t. A group of nerve fibers originating in the superior colliculus, and some in the inferior colliculus, of the tectum which, together with the tectobulbar and tectopontine tracts, crosses in the fountain decussation of Meynert and descends to synapse with motor neurons in the spinal cord that supply skeletal muscles. It conveys impulses mediating reflex postural movements in response to auditory and visual stimuli.

transverse peduncular t. A tract,

present in about 30% of humans, which originates from the optic tract, travels transversely over the ventral surface of the cerebral peduncle and enters the midbrain near the exit of the oculomotor nerve. Syn., *posterior accessory optic tract of von Gudden.*

uveal t. The iris, the ciliary body, and the choroid considered collectively.

vestibulo-ocular t. A tract of homolateral and contralateral nerve fibers arising from the vestibular nuclei, which ascends in the medial longitudinal fasciculus to the nuclei of the oculomotor, the trochlear, and the abducens nerves. The tract mediates reflex movements of the head and eyes.

visual t. Visual pathway.

tractus hyaloideus (trak'tus hi″ah-loid'e-us). Membrana plicata of Vogt.

tractus opticus (trak'tus op'tih-kus). Optic tract.

trainer, television. An antisuppression visual training device consisting either of two perpendicularly oriented Polaroid filters or of complementary-colored red and green filters mounted side by side and attached in front of a television screen, such that, when viewed through appropriate filters, a portion of the television picture is visible only to one eye and another portion is visible only to the other eye.

trainer, Tibbs binocular. A visual training instrument consisting of three wood leaves, hinged together at one end as in a book, with a plane mirror on each face of the middle leaf. With the middle leaf held to the nose as a septum, a target placed on the inner face of one outer leaf is seen by one eye by reflection from the mirror and is perceived as though originating on the inner face of the other outer leaf, on which the projected image may be traced, or superimposed or fused with a second target seen directly by the other eye.

Trainer, Van Orden. A visual training device consisting essentially of a target holder mounted at one end of a rod, with trans-illuminated targets, and two pairs of lens cells at the other end, one fixed and one vertically adjustable so that it may be flipped down in front of the fixed cells to vary accommodative demand.

training, visual. The teaching and training process for the improvement of visual perception and/or the co-ordination of the two eyes for efficient and comfortable binocular vision. Cf. *orthoptics.*

diplopia visual t. Visual training to eliminate peripheral suppression by inducing awareness of physiological or pathological diplopia. Syn., *peripheral visual training.*

distance motivation visual t. Visual training to improve distance visual acuity in which test type is brought toward the eyes until it is distinguished, the attempt then being made to continue reading as it is moved back.

peripheral visual t. Diplopia visual training.

plus-acceptance visual t. Visual training to increase negative relative accommodation, positive fusional reserve convergence, or manifest hypermetropia in which the attempt is made to see clearly through increasing amounts of convex lens power introduced binocularly.

pointer visual t. Visual training to improve hand and eye co-ordination and spatial localization, or to eliminate suppression, in which the patient locates objects in a stereogram, a vectogram, or an anaglyph, with pointers.

primary visual t. Visual training of monocular functions.

secondary visual t. Visual training to establish or improve sensory fusion.

specific visual t. 1. Visual training to establish or improve motor fusion. 2. Visual training to establish or improve any specific visual function.

transcurve. The curve on the posterior surface of the transitional zone of a scleral contact lens.

transformation. A shift from one mode of appearance to another, e.g., from film to surface color, brought about by a change in the physical conditions of viewing or by a change in the mental set of the observer.

transillumination (trans"ih-lu"mih-na'shun). Illumination transmitted through a wall, usually translucent, especially to illuminate the interior of a body cavity or organ.

transition. Transitional zone.

translucence (trans-lu'sens). The condition of being translucent; partial transparency.

translucent (trans-lu'sent). Pertaining to a medium which transmits light diffusely so that objects viewed through it are not clearly distinguished; partially transparent.

translucid (trans-lu'sid). Translucent.

transmission. 1. The passing of radiant energy through a medium or space. 2. The ratio of the amount of radiant energy leaving the last surface of an optical system to the amount of radiant energy incident on the first surface.

diffuse t. Transmission in which the emitted light is scattered in all directions.

regular t. Transmission in which the direction of the emitted light bears a definite relationship to the direction of the incident light.

transmissivity (trans″mih-siv′ih-te). The internal transmittance for a unit thickness of a nondiffusing substance.

transmissometer (trans″mih-som′eh-ter). An instrument for measuring transmittance of radiant energy.

transmittance (trans-mit′ans). The ratio of radiant flux transmitted through a body to that incident on it. Syn., *transmission factor.*

diffuse t. The ratio of diffusely transmitted flux leaving a surface or medium to incident flux.

directional t. Transmittance determined in a given direction.

internal t. The ratio of the flux incident on the second surface of a medium to that transmitted by the first.

radiant t. Transmittance.

regular t. The fraction of incident flux transmitted through a medium without being scattered.

spectral t. Transmittance for a specific wavelength of incident flux.

specular t. The proportion of the flux of a collimated beam transmitted through a turbid medium without deviation.

transmittancy (trans-mit′an-se). The ratio of the transmittance of a solution to that of the solvent in equivalent thickness.

transocular (trans-ok′u-lar). Extending across the eyeball.

transparency. 1. The state or quality of being transparent. 2. A picture to be viewed by the aid of light transmitted through it.

transparent. Pertaining to a medium having the property of transmitting light so that objects can be seen through it.

transplantation, cornea (trans-plan-ta′shun). The operation of transplanting healthy corneal tissue to replace opaque or diseased corneal tissue removed from another eye or rotated in the same eye. See *keratoplasty.*

transplantation, vitreous. A surgical procedure for retinal detachment in which donor vitreous is injected into the vitreous chamber.

transpose. To alter or change the mathematical form of representation of the focal properties of an ophthalmic lens, specifically from the sphere-combined-with-minus-cylinder form to the sphere-combined-with-plus-cylinder form, or vice versa.

transposition. The act of transposing. See also *transpose.*

Trantas' dots (tran′tas). See under *dot.*

traumatic (traw-mat′ik). Pertaining to, of, or caused by, an injury.

Travers' test (trav′erz). See under *test.*

Treacher Collins syndrome (trēch′er kol′inz). Mandibulofacial dysostosis.

tree, color. A three dimensional representation of all colors, chromatic and achromatic, in an orderly arrangement according to their hue, value, and chroma (or saturation). The achromatic series of black, grays, and white constitutes the "trunk" or axis of the tree, the various hues are arranged circumferentially around this axis, and chroma or saturation is represented as the radial distance from the axis. See also *color sphere.*

Treleaven's method (tre-lev′ens). See under *method.*

trepanation (trep″ah-na′shun). Trephining.

trephining (tre-fi′ning, -fe′ning). Removal of a circular button or disk of tissue.

corneoscleral t. Trephining at the superior corneolimbal junction into the anterior chamber under a conjunctival flap, followed by an iridectomy at the trephine hole, for glaucoma.

limboscleral t. Trephining at the superior scleral limbal junction into the anterior chamber under a conjunctival flap, followed by an iridectomy at the trephine hole, for glaucoma. Syn., *limbosclerectomy*.

triad (tri'ad). A group of three related symptoms or signs.

   Basedow's t. The three cardinal symptoms of exophalthalmic goiter: exophthalmos, goiter, and tachycardia. Syn., *Merseburg triad*.

   Charcot's t. The three cardinal symptoms of multiple sclerosis: nystagmus, intention tremor, and staccato speech.

   Hutchinson's t. A syndrome found in congenital syphilis consisting of notched teeth (Hutchinson's teeth), interstitial keratitis, and deafness.

   Jacod's t. Total ophthalmoplegia, amaurosis, and trigeminal neuralgia from involvement of cranial nerves two through six by a tumor in the region of the cavernous sinus and the chiasm.

   Merseburg t. Basedow's triad.

trial case; frame; lens. See under the nouns.

triangle, Birren's constant hue. A systematic arrangement of tints and shades of a single hue based on the Ostwald color system; it specifies for each hue sample the percentages of white and of black mixed with the pure color. Thus, the designation 7-57 indicates that this sample is a mixture of 7% white, 57% black, and 36% color.

triangle, color. A chromaticity diagram whose co-ordinates are represented on a triangle with three primary colors assigned to apices, and mixtures of these primaries represented by nonapical points whose positions designate the proportion of each primary in the mixtures.

   Helmholtz' color t. A chromaticity diagram similar to Maxwell's color triangle, but having two real spectral primaries at two of its apices and an imaginary third primary at the other apex, whereby the locus of all spectral colors is represented by a curved line inside the triangle. Syn., *Helmholtz' color table*.

   Koenig's color t. A chromaticity diagram similar in principle to Helmholtz' color triangle, based on measurements of spectral mixtures and employing three imaginary primaries of greater saturation than spectral red, green, and blue.

   Maxwell's color t. A chromaticity diagram whose co-ordinates are represented on an equilateral triangle with three real color primaries assigned to the apices and each mixture of a pair of colors designated by a "center of gravity" point on the line connecting the colors mixed. Since real primaries are employed, many of the spectral and near-spectral colors are represented by extrapolated points outside the triangle. Syn., *Maxwell's color table*.

   Ostwald color t. An arrangement of colors of a single constant Ostwald hue in a triangle with black, white, and an Ostwald semichrome at the corners, and orderly variations of black content, white content, and full color content within the triangle.

   Young's color t. The color triangle as originally conceived by Young, with three primaries represented at the apices and mixtures represented by points within the triangle.

triboluminescence (tri"bo-lu"mihnes'ens). The emission of light by friction.

trichiasis (trih-ki'ah-sis). Inversion of the eyelashes resulting in impingement on the eyeball and subsequent irritation.

trichiniasis (trik"ih-ni'ah-sis). Trichinosis.

trichinosis (trik″ih-no′sis). A disease due to infestation with *Trichinella spiralis* produced by eating undercooked pork containing this nematode parasite, characterized by muscular and abdominal pain, nausea, diarrhea, fever, and stiffness and swelling of the muscles. Eye signs include edema of the eyelids, subconjunctival petechiae, chemosis, and encystment of the larvae in the extraocular muscles causing ocular immobility because of pain on movement. Syn., *trichiniasis.*

trichomegaly (trik″o-meg′ah-le). A condition in which the eyelashes are abnormally long.

trichosis carunculae (trih-ko′sis kah-rung′ku-le). Abnormal growth of hair on the caruncle.

trichromacy (tri-kro′mah-se). Trichromatism.

trichromasy (tri-kro′mah-se). Trichromatism.

trichromat (tri′kro-mat). One having trichromatism.

trichromate (tri′kro-māt). Trichromat.

trichromatic (tri″kro-mat′ik). Requiring the use of three color mixture primaries to match all perceived hues. Syn., *trichromic.*

trichromatism (tri-kro′mah-tizm). Color vision in which mixtures of three independently adjustable primaries (e.g., red, green, and blue) are required to match all perceived hues. Syn., *trichromacy; trichromasy; trichromatopia; trichromatopsia; trichromatic vision.*

  anomalous t. A form of defective color vision in which three primary colors are required for color matching, but the proportions of primaries in the mixture-matches are significantly different from those required in normal trichromatism. It occurs in three forms: *protanomaly, deuteranomaly,* and *tritanomaly.* Syn., *partial dichromatism; anomalous trichromasy;*

anomalous trichromatic vision; color weakness.

  deuteranomalous t. Deuteranomaly.

  protanomalous t. Protanomaly.

  tritanomalous t. Tritanomaly.

trichromatopia (tri″kro-mah-to′pe-ah). Trichromatism.

trichromatopsia (tri″kro-mah-top′se-ah). Trichromatism.

trichromator (tri-kro′ma-tor). A colorimeter which isolates three selected spectral bands and combines them for color-matching investigation.

trichorrhexis nodosa (trik″o-rek′sis no-do′sah). A rare condition, of unknown etiology, in which the hairs show regularly spaced swellings and tend to break at them. It is congenital and may involve the eyelashes as well as the hair of the scalp.

trichromic (tri-kro′mik). Trichromatic.

trident, visual. The collective visual field of birds of prey of approximately 180°, consisting of a central binocular field derived from the common straight-ahead projection of the temporal foveae and two lateral uniocular fields, each associated with a laterally projecting central fovea.

trifocal (tri-fo′kal). See under *lens.*

trigeminus (tri-jem′ih-nus). The trigeminal nerve.

Trioptic lens. See under *lens.*

triplet (trip′let). A combination of three lenses.

  aplanatic t. A microscopic lens consisting of a double convex crown glass lens, cemented between two concave flint glass meniscus lenses, which provides magnification relatively free from chromatic aberration and distortion.

  Hastings′ t. A series of aplanatic triplets of different magnifying powers, designed by C. S. Hastings.

[770]

triplokoria (trip″lo-ko′re-ah). The abnormal condition of three pupils in one eye.

triplopia (trip-lo′pe-ah). The condition in which a single object is perceived as three rather than as one.

triptokoria (trip″to-ko′re-ah). Triplokoria.

tristichia (tris-tik′e-ah). Tristichiasis.

tristichiasis (tris″tih-ki′ah-sis). The anomalous condition of three rows of eyelashes. Syn., *tristichia.*

tritan (tri′tan). One having tritanopia or tritanomaly. Syn., *tritanoid.*

tritanoid (trit″ah-noid′, tri″tah-). 1. One having color vision of the tritanopic or tritanomalous type; a tritanomal or a tritanope. Syn., *tritan.* 2. Of, pertaining to, or having the characteristics of tritanopia or tritanomaly. Syn., *tritanous.*

tritanomal (trit-an′o-mal, tri-tan′-). One having tritanomaly.

tritanomaly (trit″ah-nom′ah-le, tri″tah-). A rare type of defective color vision in which an abnormally large proportion of blue must be mixed with green in order to match a standard blue-green stimulus. Very few cases of tritanomaly have been described, so details of its characteristics are not well known. Syn., *tritanomalous trichromatism.*

tritanope (trit′an-ōp, tri′tan-). One having tritanopia or defective color vision of the tritanopic type.

tritanopia (trit″ah-no′pe-ah, tri″tah-). A form of dichromatism in which all colors can be matched by suitable mixtures of only a red primary and a green (or blue) primary. Brightness (luminosity) of all colors is within normal limits. Sensitivity to differences in hue of blues, blue-greens, and greens is greatly reduced, but discrimination of short wavelength violets appears to be superior to that of normal ob-

servers. A neutral point occurs at about 570 mμ in the spectrum. Acquired tritanopia occurs as the result of retinal disease or detachment. Congenital tritanopia is rare; its incidence is estimated as between 1 in 13,000 and 1 in 65,000, the higher frequency being more probable. The mode of inheritance is not yet known, but is unlike that of the protanoid and deuteranoid defects, although a slight sex difference has been shown. Syn., *blue blindness; blue-yellow blindness; tritanopic vision.*

small-area t. A normal reduction in color discrimination for the blue wavelengths found for color fields of small angular subtense (approximately twenty minutes of arc or less) stimulating the central fovea. Under these stimulus conditions, all colors can be matched by a mixture of two primaries, and purplish blues and greenish yellows are confused with neutral and with each other.

tritanopic (trit″ah-nop′ik, tri″tah-). Pertaining to or having tritanopia.

tritanous (trit′ah-nus, tri′tah-). Tritanoid.

trochlea (trok′le-ah). A ringlike structure of fibrocartilage attached to the trochlear fossa of the frontal bone through which passes the tendon of the superior oblique muscle. It is lined by endothelium and to it is attached the fascial sheath of the muscle.

trochlear (trok′le-ar). Pertaining to the trochlea or the trochlear nerve.

trochlearis (trok″le-a′ris). The superior oblique muscle.

troland (tro′land). A unit of retinal illumination equal to that produced by viewing a surface having a luminance (photometric brightness) of 1 candle per sq. m. through a pupil having an area of 1 sq. mm. Originally called *photon* by Troland and later renamed in his honor to differentiate it from a photon of light energy.

Troland's theory (tro'landz). See under *theory.*

Troncoso (tron-ko'so) **goniolens; contact lens.** See *goniolens, Troncoso.*

tropia (tro'pe-ah). Strabismus.

tropicamide (troh-pik'ah-mīd). A parasympatholytic drug used as a mydriatic and cycloplegic.

tropo-menotaxis (tro"po-men-o-tak'-sis). A type of light-compass reaction in which the orientation of movement is governed primarily by the intensity of the light or by the summated intensities of more than one light. See also *telo-menotaxis.*

tropometer, Steven's (tro-pom'eh-ter). An instrument for measuring the extent of rotation of an eye, consisting essentially of a head rest, a metal box with a circular aperture containing a transparent glass disk with a central fixation dot, a mirror in the box at a 45° angle behind the glass disk, and a telescope viewing system attached to the box. An aerial image of the fixating eye is focused on a graduated disk in the telescope, and the excursions of the eye are measured with the graduations on the disk.

Troposcope (tro'po-skōp). A type of major amblyoscope.

tropotaxis (tro"po-tak'sis). Movement of a motile organism toward or away from light as mediated by two symmetrical light receptors which simultaneously detect differences of light intensities from a single source, thus serving to orient the organism in the proper direction. See also *klinotaxis; telotaxis; menotaxis; mnemotaxis.*

Troutman's air space doublet. See under *doublet.*

Troxler's (troks'lerz) **effect; phenomenon.** See under *phenomenon.*

trueing. The restoring of a desired curvature to a worn lens-grinding tool.

Tru-Scope. The trade name for an instrument that projects either a 12X or a 20X magnified image of a contact lens onto a calibrated viewing screen for the purpose of inspection.

Tschermak's (cher'makz) **diagram; rectangle; test.** See under the nouns.

Tschermak-Seysenegg visual illusion. See under *illusion, visual.*

Tscherning (chern'ing) **ellipse; filters; theory.** See under the nouns.

tube. A hollow cylindrical structure; something resembling a cylindrical structure; something with a tube or tubelike part as its chief feature.

  Bowman's t's. Artifacts in stained corneal sections, originally thought to be spaces between the lamellae of the corneal stroma.

  Gratama's t's. A pseudoscope used in the detection of malingering.

  photoelectric t. A vacuum or gas-filled tube which produces electrical current when radiant energy is received on its sensitive surface (cathode). It may be used with either a galvanometer or an electrometer for photometric measurements.

  photomultiplier t. Photomultiplier.

  Wessely's t's. A device used to detect malingering, consisting essentially of two viewing tubes slightly converged toward each other, through which a distant object is fixated. Physiological diplopia produced by placing an object in front of the tubes indicates vision in both eyes.

tubercle (tu'ber-kl). 1. A small nodule or protuberance. 2. The nodular lesion produced by the tubercle bacillus.

infraoptic t. A roughness on the small wing of the sphenoid bone between the optic foramen and the sphenoidal fissure, to which is attached the lower tendon of Zinn.

lacrimal t. A tubercle on the anterior lacrimal crest where the frontal process of the superior maxillary bone becomes continuous with the lower orbital margin.

lateral orbital t. A small elevation on the orbital surface of the zygomatic bone, just within the outer orbital margin and about 11 mm. below the frontozygomatic suture. It gives attachment to the check ligament of the lateral rectus muscle, the ligament of Lockwood, the lateral palpebral ligament, and the aponeurosis of the levator palpebrae superioris muscle. These combined attachments form the *lateral retinaculum of Hesser.* Syn., *Whitnall's tubercle.*

muscular t. A small bony tubercle, on the small wing of the sphenoid bone below the optic foramen, which frequently marks a point of origin of the extraocular muscles.

Whitnall's t. Lateral orbital tubercle.

zygomatic t. A tubercle on the frontosphenoidal process of the zygomatic bone, beneath the frontozygomatic suture.

tuberous sclerosis (tu'ber-us skle-ro'-sis). Bourneville's disease.

tucking. A surgical procedure for shortening an extraocular muscle for the correction of strabismus, in which a portion of the tendon of the muscle is folded on itself and sutured in position.

tularemia, oculoglandular (too''lah-re'me-ah). Infection with the bacterium *Pasteurella tularensis*, transmitted to humans from rabbits or other rodents, character-ized by acute inflammation and chemosis of the conjunctiva, small, yellow, necrotic ulcers primarily on the tarsal conjunctiva, high fever, headaches, vomiting, and involvement of the parotid, preauricular, submaxillary, and cervical glands.

tunic (tu'nik). A membrane, or a layer of tissue, covering an organ or a part of the body.

fibrous t. of the eye. The outer layer of the eyeball, consisting of the cornea and sclera.

Haller's t. Haller's layer.

nervous t. of the eye. The retina.

vascular t. of the eye. The uvea.

tunica (tu'nih-kah). A tunic.

adnata oculi, t. 1. The bulbar conjunctiva. 2. The conjunctiva.

albuginea oculi, t. The sclera.

chorioidea, t. The choroid.

conjunctiva bulbi, t. The bulbar conjunctiva.

conjunctiva palpebrarum, t. The palpebral conjunctiva.

cornea pellucida, t. The cornea.

dura, t. The sclera.

fibrosa lentis, t. Fibrous tissue surrounding the embryonic crystalline lens.

fibrosa oculi, t. The outer layer of the eyeball, consisting of the cornea and the sclera.

interna oculi, t. The retina.

nervosa oculi t. The retina.

ruyschiana, t. The choriocapillary layer of the choroid.

uvea, t. The uvea.

vasculosa choroideae, t. The uvea.

vasculosa lentis, t. The vascular network surrounding the embryonic crystalline lens, derived anteriorly from branches of the annular vessel and posteriorly from branches of the hyaloid artery. It normally degenerates and disappears prior to birth.

vasculosa lentis, t. persistent. Persistent hyperplastic primary vitreous.

vasculosa oculi, t. The uvea.

vitrea, t. The hyaloid membrane.

Tuohy contact lens (too'e). See under *lens, contact.*

Turay (tu'ra). A trade name for a one-piece bifocal lens.

Türk's line (tĕrks). See under *line.*

turn, face. Head rotation.

turn, head. Head rotation.

Turner's syndrome; theory. See under the nouns.

Turville's test (tur'vilz). See under *test.*

tutamina oculi (tu-tam'ih-nah ok'-u-li). The protective appendages of the eye, as the eyelids, the eyelashes, and the eyebrows.

Twinsite (twin'sīt). A trade name for a one-piece bifocal lens.

Twyman and Green interferometer (twi'man). See under *interferometer.*

tyloma conjunctivae (ti-lo'mah kon"junk-ti've). A localized cornification of the conjunctival epithelium, occurring in xerosis of the conjunctivae. Syn., *keratosis conjunctivae.*

tylosis (ti-lo'sis). Hypertrophic blepharitis.

Tyndall's (tin'dalz) **effect; light; phenomenon.** See under the nouns.

type, case. See under *case.*

type, test. Letters, figures, or characters used in vision testing.

   Bjerrum test t. Black test letters on a gray background used for testing retinal sensitivity in persons suspected of having retinal or optic nerve pathology.

   Jaeger test t. A numbered arrangement of words and phrases in various sizes of ordinary printer's type on a chart, for testing visual acuity at given reading distances.

   Landolt test t. Incomplete rings of various sizes, similar to the letter *C* in appearance, used as test targets for visual acuity, especially in children and illiterates. The width of each ring and the break in its continuity are each one fifth of its over-all diameter. The breaks are placed in different positions with their locations to be identified by the observer, and the identification of breaks subtending 1 minute of arc corresponds to 20/20 vision.

   Pray's test t. Assorted, relatively large letters, each hatched with lines in a given, different meridian, whence the most distinctly seen letter indicates, by the orientation of its hatching lines, the principal meridian of the astigmatism of the viewing eye.

   Snellen test t. A series of letters for testing visual acuity, each so constructed that it can be enclosed in a square five times the thickness of the limbs composing the letter. Each limb, and the separation between, subtends a visual angle of one minute at a specified distance, hence each entire letter subtends a visual angle of 5 minutes at this distance. See also *Snellen fraction.*

   Weiss's test t. Test type arranged so that each type size represents an equal decimal interval of visual acuity from the preceding and following ones, whence the acuity is expressed as .9, .8, etc.

typhloid (tif'loid). Pertaining to or having defective vision.

typhlolexia (tif"lo-lek'se-ah). Word blindness.

typhlology (tif-lol'o-je). The science that deals with blindness; the scientific study of blindness, its causes, effects, etc.

typhlosis (tif-lo'sis). Blindness.

typoscope (ti'po-skōp). A rectangle of dull black material having a central rectangular aperture of a size allowing two or three lines of type to be seen through it when laid against a printed page. It is used by persons having subnormal vision to aid vision by excluding extraneous light reflected from the surface of the paper.

U

U. Symbol for *reduced object vergence.*

U'. Symbol for *reduced image vergence.*

u. Symbol for *object distance.*

u'. Symbol for *image distance.*

Uhthoff's sign (oot'hofs). See under *sign.*

ulcer, corneal (ul'ser). Pathological loss of substance of the surface of the cornea, due to progressive erosion and necrosis of the tissue.

acne rosacea, corneal u. of. A corneal ulcer, either marginal or central, resulting from the rupturing of a vesicle, in rosacea keratitis. It has a tendency to recur, is resistant to treatment, and after repeated attacks the entire cornea may become scarred and vascularized.

ameboid corneal u. Geographic corneal ulcer.

atheromatous corneal u. A rapidly progressing corneal ulcer occurring in an old leucomatous scar which has undergone degeneration. Perforation followed by panophthalmitis often takes place.

catarrhal corneal u. A crescent-shaped ulcer near the limbus associated with catarrhal conjunctivitis. The conjunctiva opposite the ulcer is usually swollen and chemotic, and capillary vascularization often extends from the pericorneal arcades.

chronic serpiginous corneal u. A rodent corneal ulcer.

creeping corneal u. A serpiginous corneal ulcer.

dendritic corneal u. A branching, linear-shaped, corneal ulcer occurring in herpes simplex of the cornea. The ends of the branches are typically club-shaped, it is slow in healing, and is accompanied by pain, lacrimation, and photophobia.

eczematous corneal u. Phlyctenular corneal ulcer.

fascicular corneal u. A corneal ulcer which commences at a phlycten, in phlyctenular keratoconjunctivitis, and creeps toward the central area of the cornea. As the circular edge advances centrally, the peripheral portion is healing, and a straight sheath of blood vessels from the conjunctiva follows in the furrow created by the ulcer. It never perforates, usually remains superficial, and the blood vessels gradually disappear after the ulcer heals.

geographic corneal u. A sharply demarcated, irregularly shaped, superficial corneal ulcer formed in the late stage of herpetic keratitis by loss of the epithelium between the branches of a dendritic ulcer; so named because its outline resembles the map of a continent. Syn., *ameboid corneal ulcer.*

hypopyon corneal u. 1. A serpiginous corneal ulcer. 2. A severe suppurative corneal ulcer accompanied by hypopyon. Syn., *panmural fibrosis.*

indolent corneal u. A shallow, superficial ulcer, usually located centrally in the cornea, occurring in debilitated children. It is unaccompanied by vascularization and infiltration, causes little reaction or few symptoms, and shows little tendency to spread or to heal.

internal corneal u. An ulcer involving the posterior surface of the cornea, usually with loss of the endothelium and Descemet's membrane in the affected area, and typically occurring in association with inflammatory involvement of the cornea or uvea.

marantic corneal u. A superficial corneal ulcer typically of long duration and with a delay in scar formation, occurring with little or no infiltration and in association with metabolic disturbances of the cornea or with chronic debilitating disease.

metaherpetic corneal u. A small, round or oval, superficial, corneal ulcer which follows the healing of a dendritic ulcer.

Mooren's corneal u. Rodent corneal ulcer.

phlyctenular corneal u. A corneal ulcer, resulting from the breakdown of a corneal phlycten, which may heal without leaving an opacity or may progress to a fascicular corneal ulcer. Syn., *eczematous corneal ulcer; scrofulous corneal ulcer.*

pneumococcal corneal u. Serpiginous corneal ulcer.

rodent corneal u. A painful, chronic, superficial ulcer of unknown etiology, occurring in elderly people, which commences near the limbus and may partially or completely surround the cornea and slowly progress centrally until the entire cornea is involved. Its advancing border characteristically has a grayish, crescentic, thickened, overhanging ledge. Syn., *chronic serpiginous corneal ulcer; Mooren's ulcer; ulcus corneae rodens.*

Saemisch's corneal u. Serpiginous corneal ulcer.

scrofulous corneal u. Phlyctenular corneal ulcer.

serpent corneal u. Serpiginous corneal ulcer.

serpiginous corneal u. A severe, disk-shaped, corneal ulcer, caused by the pneumococcus, characterized by a marked tendency to spread in one direction and usually associated with diffuse keratitis, iridocyclitis, and hypopyon. It has a gray sloughing base and a yellow crescentic advancing border, increases rapidly in depth as well as in extent, usually starts with an abrasion, more commonly affects the elderly or the debilitated, and may result in perforation of the cornea. Syn., *creeping corneal ulcer; hypopyon corneal ulcer; pneumococcal corneal ulcer; Saemisch's corneal ulcer; serpent corneal ulcer; ulcus corneae serpens.*

trachomatous corneal u. A superficial indolent ulcer appearing at the advancing margin of a trachomatous pannus.

ulcer, Jacob's (ul'ser). A basal-celled carcinoma or rodent ulcer of the eyelid, typically commencing with a raised nodular border and indurated base, which extends superficially and deeply and erodes the surrounding tissue of the face and the nose.

ulcus (ul'kus). An ulcer.

corneae rodens, u. Rodent corneal ulcer.

corneae serpens, u. Serpiginous corneal ulcer.

eczematosum, u. Phlyctenular corneal ulcer.

ulerythema ophryogenes (u-ler"ih-the'mah of"re-o'jēns). A chronic disease of the skin of the eyebrows marked by redness, hard conical elevations at the base of the hair, and loss of hair.

Ullrich's syndrome. See under *syndrome.*

Ultex (ul'teks). A trade name for a one-piece bifocal or trifocal lens.

ultrasonogram, orbital (ul″trah-son′-o-gram). A composite photograph of the serial recordings of the echoes of ultrasound waves reflected from structures of the eye or orbit occupying successive horizontal planes, primarily to detect and localize tumors.

ultrasonography, orbital (ul″trah-son-og′rah-fe). The production and study of the orbital ultrasonogram.

ultraviolet (ul″trah-vi′o-let). Radiant energy of wavelengths shorter than the violet end of the visible spectrum and longer than the roentgen radiations, usually considered to be wavelengths of from 400 to 200 mμ.

umbilication of the lens (um-bil″-ih-ka′shun). A developmental abnormality of the crystalline lens consisting of a shallow gutter or depression in its posterior surface.

umbo. 1. A rounded protuberance, or the corresponding depression, as, e.g., the central portion of a lenticular lens. 2. The apex or pole of a spherical lens surface. 3. The small central concavity of the foveola.

umbra (um′brah). The part of the shadow of an opaque body receiving no illumination from the source of reference. Cf. *penumbra.*

umbraculum (um-brak′u-lum). A flaplike contractible structure protruding from the iris margin of the hyrax and some cetaceans. It may be extended almost to occlude the pupillary aperture or be retracted to be free of it.

umbrascopy (um-brahs′ko-pe). Retinoscopy.

undercorrection. 1. Ophthalmic lens power less than that required to correct or neutralize a refractive error. 2. An aberration of a lens or an optical system in which the marginal rays intersect the optical axis at a point nearer the lens

than the paraxial rays; the spherical aberration normally present in a lens.

unifocal (u″nih-fo′kal). Pertaining to or having a single focus.

uniform density. See *lens, uniform density.*

unilateral. Affecting, pertaining to, or located in one side or half of the body with reference to the midsagittal plane.

uniocular (u″nih-ok′u-lar). Pertaining to, identified with, having, or performed with one eye. Syn., *monocular.*

unit. 1. A specific amount or quantity used as a standard measurement. 2. A distinct part of an aggregate whole. 3. A single thing or person, or a group regarded as an individual member of an aggregate of groups.

Aloe distance u. A Galilean telescopic system with an adjustable focus, which is hooked over a spectacle lens for distance viewing in subnormal vision, providing 3× magnification.

Aloe reading u. A Galilean telescopic system, providing 2.2× magnification, which is hooked over a spectacle lens for near viewing in subnormal vision.

angstrom u. A unit of wavelength of radiant energy, one unit being equal to one ten-millionth of a millimeter. Symbol: A or Å.

C u. Retinal elements in fish which give rise to graded changes in the resting potential as a function of the wavelength stimulating the retina, being opposite in polarity for red and green and for yellow and blue. Syn., *chromatic unit.*

chromatic u. C unit.

Freeman Near Vision U. A triangular-shaped instrument presenting transilluminated near point test targets on each of its three faces which may be either hand held or attached to a phoropter near point rod. The targets are polarized to permit monocular

testing under binocular conditions
and include a red-green test for
determining and balancing the
near point addition, the Worth-
Ramstein test for checking binocular vision and fusion, a graduated Landolt ring chart, a reading chart, and a heterophoria
test used in conjunction with a
Maddox rod.

Giles-Archer color perception u.
A device for testing color vision
deficiencies and central scotomata, consisting of a lantern with
various size apertures and a series
of color filters.

L u. Retinal elements in fish which
give rise to the same type of
polarity change in the normal
resting potential for all wavelengths, a graded change of potential occurring as a function
of light intensity. Syn., *luminosity unit.*

luminosity u. L unit.

*Osterberg Bino near vision test
u.* A hand-held self-illuminated
device for testing visual acuity
and binocular functioning at various reading distances, with targets mounted in a rotatable
disk so as to be individually exposed, and an attached tape for
measuring the test distance.

Updegrave's method (up'de-grāvz).
See under *method.*

uranin (u'rah-nin). Sodium fluorescein used in dilute solution as
a dye which fluoresces under
black light, for determining the
fit of contact lenses, and for the
detection of external pathology,
such as corneal or conjunctival
abrasions or ulcers, the affected
areas staining a yellow-green.

Ur-O-Vue. A trade name for an instrument used in the inspection
of contact lenses consisting essentially of a self-contained light
source, an optical system providing 14× magnification, and a
viewing screen on which either
the shadow image of the edge

profile or the image of the transilluminated lens itself may be observed.

Usher's syndrome. See under *syndrome.*

uvea (u've-ah). The pigmented vascular coat of the eyeball, consisting of the choroid, the ciliary
body, and the iris, which are continuous with each other.

uveitis (u"ve-i'tis). Inflammation of
the uvea.

anterior u. Iridocyclitis.

atrophic u. A recurring uveitis in
blind degenerated eyes that is
presumed to be due to toxins
liberated by tissue necrosis.

Boeck's sarcoid, u. of. Sarcoidosis
affecting the uveal tract, especially the iris, although it may
also invade the choroid.

Förster's u. Diffuse syphilitic inflammation of the entire uveal
tract.

granulomatous u. Nonpurulent,
endogenous uveitis characterized
by nodular or tuberclelike lesions
on the iris, mutton-fat deposits
on the anterior lens capsule,
marked tendency to the formation of posterior synechia, and
frequently Koeppe nodules. The
onset is insidious rather than
acute, and it may be due to infection with any of a variety of
nonpyogenic agents, as in toxoplasmosis, actinomycosis, sarcoidosis, syphilis, or tuberculosis.

heterochromic u. Heterochromic
cyclitis of Fuchs.

nongranulomatous u. Nonpurulent, endogenous uveitis in which
the onset is usually acute and
marked by ciliary congestion,
photophobia, and lacrimation.
There are no nodules and little
tendency to the formation of
posterior synechia. Aqueous flare
is usually pronounced, small pinpoint deposits are on the posterior surface of the cornea, but
neither mutton-fat deposits nor

Koeppe's nodules are present. It mainly affects the anterior uvea only, is usually of short course with prompt recovery, and is considered due to physical, toxic, or allergic causes.

peripheral u. A form of granulomatous uveitis which commences in the region of the pars plana or ora serrata. It may emanate from inflammation of the ciliary body or of the peripheral choroid, or may result from perivasculitis of the peripheral retinal blood vessels.

phacoanaphylactic u. Inflammation of the uveal tract occurring after extracapsular cataract extraction or a needling operation, presumed to be an allergic reaction to one's own liberated lenticular proteins.

phacolytic u. Uveitis secondary to hypermature cataract and due to permeation of liquefied cortical material through the lens capsule.

phacotoxic u. Inflammation of the uveal tract attributed to toxic reaction to liberated lens proteins following cataract surgery or, in hypermature cataract, to liquefied cortical material which has permeated the lens capsule.

sympathetic u. Sympathetic ophthalmitis.

uveoparotitis (u″ve-o-par″o-ti′tis). Chronic bilateral parotitis, uveitis, fever, and often paralysis of the cranial nerves, especially the seventh, occurring characteristically in young people and considered to be a form of sarcoidosis. The uveitis is generalized and usually includes a nodular iridocyclitis. Other ocular manifestations may include keratitis, optic neuritis, cataract, and glaucoma. The disease is self-limiting, and the only permanent disability is visual impairment. Syn., *Heerfordt's disease; uveoparotid fever; Heerfordt's syndrome.*

uveoscleritis (u″ve-o-skle-ri′tis). Inflammation of both the uvea and the sclera.

V

V. Abbreviation for *vision*.

V.A. Abbreviation for *visual acuity*.

vaccinia, ocular (vak-sin′e-ah). A virus infection with smallpox vaccine which may accidentally occur on the eyelids, the conjunctiva, or the cornea as a result of careless inoculation from a vaccine pustule located elsewhere. On the eyelid, it appears as a pustular eruption which may ulcerate, on the cornea as a marginal infiltration, an interstitial pustule, or a disciform keratitis, and on the conjunctiva as a membranous conjunctivitis with extensive ulceration. The condition is usually accompanied by fever and swelling of the preauricular and the postauricular glands.

vagina (vah-ji′nah). A sheath or sheathlike structure.

bulbi, v. Tenon's capsule.

oculi, v. Tenon's capsule.

nervi optici, vaginae. The sheaths of the optic nerve.

valence (va′lens). The capacity of a visual stimulus to evoke a color sensation, as contrasted with its capacity to evoke brightness.

validity. The extent to which a test measures what it is intended to measure; the relevancy to the task for which a test is proposed as a criterion.

value. 1. The relative worth, importance, or degree of usefulness. 2. Brightness or lightness of a color.

C v. The coefficient of facility of aqueous outflow.

F v. The rate of aqueous outflow.

Munsell v. In the Munsell system, the portion of the notation corresponding to lightness and specified on a scale ranging from 1 (black) to 10 (white). It is approximately equal to the square root of the reflectance expressed in per cent.

nu (ν) v. The reciprocal of the dispersive power of optical glass. Syn., *Abbe's number.* See *optical constringence.*

P_o *v.* The magnitude of the intraocular pressure just prior to tonometric measurement.

P_t *v.* The magnitude of the intraocular pressure during tonometry.

P_v *v.* The average pressure in the small episcleral veins or in the aqueous veins near the limbus.

retinomotor v. A value assigned to a retinal receptor which indicates its angular distance and radial direction from the foveal center, or other point of reference. It provides information as to the angular extent and direction an eye must rotate to assume fixation of an image stimulating the receptor.

target v. The attention-drawing attribute of an object in the field of vision, especially as applied to traffic signs, signals, and markers.

tristimulus v's. The amounts of each of three primaries required to match a color. Symbols: X; Y; Z.

   tristimulus v's., spectral. Tristimulus values, symbols: $\bar{x}(\lambda)$, $\bar{y}(\lambda)$, $\bar{z}(\lambda)$, per unit wavelength interval per unit radiant flux of the colors of the spectrum, adopted by the C.I.E. They are tabulated as functions of wavelength throughout the spectrum and are employed for the evaluation of radiant energy as light. The $\bar{y}$ values are identical with values of spectral luminous efficiency for photopic vision.

valve. A structure for closing an orifice or a passage or for preventing the backward flow of fluid.

Béraud, v. of. Valve of Krause.

Bianchi, v. of. Plica lacrimalis.

Bochdalek, v. of. A fold of mucous membrane at the punctum of the lacrimal canaliculus.

Cruveilhier, v. of. Plica lacrimalis.

Foltz, v. of. A fold of mucous membrane in the vertical portion of the lacrimal canaliculus, near the lacrimal punctum.

Hasner's v. Plica lacrimalis.

Huschke's v. Rosenmueller's valve.

Hyrtl, v. of. A pseudovalve consisting of a fold of mucous membrane between the valves of Krause and Taillefer in the nasolacrimal duct.

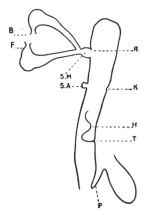

Fig. 42. Valves of nasolacrimal duct: (B) Valve of Bochdalek, (F) Valve of Foltz, (S. M.) Sinus of Maier, (R) Valve of Rosenmueller, (S. A.) Sinus of Arlt, (K) Valve of Krause, (H) Valve of Hyrtl, (T) Valve of Taillefer, (P) Plica lacrimalis. (From *Text-book of Ophthalmology*, Vol. V, Duke-Elder, Henry Kimpton, 1952)

Krause, v. of. A pseudovalve consisting of a fold of mucous membrane at the junction of the lacrimal sac and the nasolacrimal duct. Syn., *valve of Béraud.*

Rosenmueller's v. A crescentic fold in the lacrimal duct near its junction with the lacrimal sac. Syn., *Huschke's valve.*

Taillefer's v. A pseudovalve consisting of a fold of mucous membrane above the plica lacrimalis in the nasolacrimal duct.

Van den Bosch syndrome. See under *syndrome.*

Van den Orden Trainer. See under *trainer.*

Vaquez' disease (vak'āz). See under *disease.*

variability. The property of fluctuation or change, either qualitative or quantitative, possessed by some phenomenon, with reference to certain qualities or characteristics of that phenomenon, variously identified in statistical terminology as scatter, dispersion, deviation, range, or variance.

variable. Any magnitude which has different values under different conditions.

dependent v. A variable whose magnitude may be considered to be influenced by another variable within the same framework of reference, as may be expressed by a mathematical formula or a closed system incorporating the values of both. Cf. *independent variable.*

fundamental v's. 1. A variable which may be represented by an elementary component of a system of parameters. 2. Any of the physiological correlates of the position of the phoria line, the width of each of the pair of adjoining parallelogramlike zones, their height, and their slope, in the geometric representation of the interrelationship of accommodation and convergence on the ordinate and the abscissa, respectively, of a co-ordinate system; clinically designated as the distance phoria, positive and negative fusional convergence, amplitude of accommodation, and the A.C.A. ratio, respectively.

independent v. 1. A variable whose magnitude may be considered to be the determining factor influencing another variable within the same framework of reference, as may be expressed by a mathematical formula or a closed system incorporating the values of both. Cf. *dependent variable.* 2. A variable whose magnitude is unrelated to another given variable of reference.

variance. A statistical designation of the variability of a series of measurements, as the square of the standard deviation or the sum of the squared deviations divided by the number of degrees of freedom. Symbolically,

$$s^2 = \frac{\Sigma x^2}{n-1}$$

where s^2 = variance
Σx^2 = sum of the squared deviations
$n - 1$ = number of degrees of freedom

variation, mean. Average deviation.
varicoblepharon (var″ih-ko-blef′ah-ron). A dilated or varicose vein of the eyelid.
varicula (vah-rik′u-lah). An enlarged and tortuous vein of the conjunctiva.
vasa (vah′sah). Vessels.
hyaloidea propria, v. Branches of the hyaloid artery of the fetal intraocular blood system which fill the vitreous cavity and anastomose with each other and with the posterior tunica vasculosa lentis.
sanguinea retinae, v. The retinal blood vessels.

vorticosa, v. The vortex veins.
vasculosa lentis (vas-ku-lo′sah len′-tis). Tunica vasculosa lentis.
vase, Rubin's. A line drawing which may be perceived either as a vase or as two oppositely oriented human profiles.
vault. The dome-shaped inner surface of the corneal section of a scleral contact lens.
vectogram (vek′to-gram). A polarized stereogram consisting of two photographic images printed on opposite sides of a gelatin film with their axes of polarization at right angles to each other, to be viewed through Polaroid filters so that one image is seen only by one eye while the other is seen only by the other eye. Syn., *vectograph.*
vectograph (vek′to-graf). Vectogram.
Vectoluminator (vek″to-lu′mih-na″-tor). An instrument for transilluminating vectographs to be viewed through Polaroid filters at a near fixation distance.
vector-electronystagmography (vek″tor-e-lek″tro-nis-tag-mog′-rah-fe). See under *electronystagmography.*
vector-electro-oculography (vek″-tor-e-lek″tro-ok″u-log′rah-fe). See under *electro-oculography.*
Vego Graph. The trade name for an instrument that projects a magnified image of a contact lens onto a calibrated viewing screen for the purpose of inspection.
veils, congenital vascular, in the vitreous. Retinoschisis.
veil, prepapillary. Prepapillary membrane.
veil, Sattler's. Mistiness of vision usually accompanied by seeing colored halos around lights, resulting from wearing contact lenses and attributed to corneal edema. Syn., *Fick's phenomenon.*
veiling, dimple. Fogging of vision due to dimpling of the cornea in the pupillary area.

vein. A tubular vessel which conveys blood toward, or to, the heart. Like arteries, the walls of veins are composed of three coats, the tunica adventitia, the tunica media, and the tunica intima, though typically thinner. Many veins also have valves.

angular v. A vein, formed by the junction of the frontal and the supraorbital veins, which courses obliquely downward on the side of the root of the nose, about 8 mm. medial to the inner canthus, to the level of the lower margin of the orbit, where it becomes the anterior facial vein. Its tributaries are an orbital branch, the superior and inferior palpebral veins, the supraorbital vein, and the frontal vein.

annular v. An annular vessel.

aqueous v's. Small vessels which transmit aqueous humor from the canal of Schlemm to episcleral, conjunctival, and subconjunctival veins.

central retinal v. A vein formed by the confluence of the superior and inferior retinal veins at about the level of the lamina cribrosa, lying temporal to the central retinal artery. After running a short course within the optic nerve, it leaves slightly posterior to the entrance of the central retinal artery and empties into the superior ophthalmic vein, the cavernous sinus, or rarely, the inferior ophthalmic vein.

chiasmal v., superior. One of two venous trunks which drain blood from the superior portion of the optic chiasm and empty into the anterior cerebral vein.

chorio-vaginal v's. Veins, lying in a stratum behind the retinal vessels, which drain a large portion of the posterior choroid and leave the eyeball in the region of the optic disk to course into the pia mater of the optic nerve.

ciliary v's., anterior. Veins which drain the anterior portion of the ciliary body, deep and superficial scleral plexuses, anterior conjunctival veins, and episcleral veins to empty into the muscular veins.

ciliary v's., posterior. 1. The vortex veins. 2. A few small veins which occasionally accompany the posterior ciliary arteries and drain the posterior region of the sclera.

cilioretinal v. A rare retinal vein which disappears at the optic disk margin instead of in the central retinal vein and drains into the ciliary system. Syn., *marginal vein.*

conjunctival v's., anterior. Veins which drain capillaries of the bulbar conjunctiva near the limbus and the superficial scleral plexus to empty into the anterior ciliary veins.

conjunctival v's., posterior. Veins which drain capillaries of the nonlimbal bulbar conjunctiva and the fornix to empty into the palpebral veins.

emissary v's. 1. Veins connecting the intracranial venous sinuses and the extracranial veins which function as added drainage channels for the venous blood of the brain, especially if the inner cranial pressure is temporarily increased. As they pass through the cranial wall, they receive tributaries from the diploë. 2. Veins joining the ciliary plexus with the episcleral veins. There are usually four to six in number, arranged circularly and symmetrically between the limbus and the equator.

episcleral v's. Veins which receive blood from the outer layer of the sclera, aqueous humor from the aqueous veins, and empty into the anterior ciliary and vortex veins.

ethmoidal v., anterior. A vein which drains the anterior ethmoidal air cells, the frontal sinus, the nose, and the dura mater, and passes through the anterior ethmoidal canal to empty into the superior ophthalmic vein.

ethmoidal v., posterior. A vein which drains the posterior ethmoidal air cells, the nose, and the dura mater, and passes through the posterior ethmoidal canal to empty into the superior ophthalmic vein.

facial v., anterior. A vein, commencing as a direct continuation of the angular vein at the root of the nose, which runs obliquely downward and backward until it meets the posterior facial vein, near the angle of the mandible, to form the common facial vein.

facial v., common. A vein formed by the confluence of the anterior and posterior facial veins, draining into the internal jugular vein at about the level of the hyoid bone.

facial v., deep. A vein connecting the pterygoid venous plexus and the anterior facial vein, of which it is considered a tributary.

facial v., posterior. A vein formed by the union of the superficial temporal and internal maxillary veins which descends in the substance of the parotid gland and divides into an anterior branch, which joins with the anterior facial vein to form the common facial vein, and a posterior branch, which unites with the posterior auricular vein to form the external jugular vein.

frontal v. A vein originating on the forehead as a venous plexus and communicating with the anterior division of the superficial temporal vein. It descends near the midline of the lower forehead as a single trunk; at the root of the nose it joins the supraorbital vein to form the angular vein.

lacrimal v. A vein which arises from the lacrimal gland, corresponding in its course to the lacrimal artery, and drains into the superior ophthalmic vein.

laminated v. A vein, consisting of a joined episcleral vein and an aqueous vein, in which blood and aqueous humor flow side by side.

marginal v. Cilioretinal vein.

muscular v's. Veins which drain extraocular muscles. Those of the rectus muscles receive the anterior ciliary veins. The upper muscular veins empty into the superior ophthalmic vein and the lower empty into the inferior ophthalmic vein.

nasofrontal v. A vein anastomosing with the angular vein at the orbital margin and emptying into the superior ophthalmic vein.

ophthalmic v., inferior. A vein extending from the anterior facial vein, over the inferior orbital margin, and continuing as a venous network on the floor of the orbit. It runs backward on the inferior rectus, dividing into two branches, one passing through the inferior orbital fissure to join the pterygoid plexus, the other passing through the superior orbital fissure to terminate in the cavernous sinus, usually in common with the superior ophthalmic vein. It receives branches from the inferior rectus and the inferior oblique muscles, the lacrimal sac, the eyelids, and the two inferior vortex veins.

ophthalmic v., superior. The largest orbital vein, formed in the upper part of the medial angle of the orbital margin by a communication with the frontal, the supraorbital, and the angular veins. It runs backward and somewhat laterally to the superior orbital fissure, where it meets the inferior ophthalmic vein and drains into the cavernous sinus. Its tributaries are the anterior ethmoidal, the posterior ethmoidal, the muscular, the lacrimal, the central retinal, the superior vortex, and usually the inferior ophthalmic veins.

optico-ciliary v. An uncommon retinal vein which drains a part of the choroid. It may appear abruptly at or near the disk margin, passing over the disk and draining into the central retinal vein, or it may drain into the central retinal vein behind the lamina cribrosa. Syn., *retinociliary vein.*

palpebral v's. Veins in the upper and lower eyelids, arranged in pretarsal and retrotarsal plexi or in venous arcades, which empty into the angular, the anterior facial, the supraorbital, the superior ophthalmic, the inferior ophthalmic, the lacrimal, and the superficial temporal veins.

papillary v., inferior. A vein formed in the region of the optic disk by the junction of the main retinal veins from the inferior temporal and inferior nasal quadrants and which, by confluence with the superior papillary vein within the optic disk, forms the central retinal vein.

papillary v., superior. A vein formed in the region of the optic disk by the junction of the main retinal veins from the superior temporal and superior nasal quadrants, and which, by confluence with the inferior papillary vein within the optic disk, forms the central retinal vein.

postcentral v. of Kuhnt. A branch of the central retinal vein which extends posteriorly in the center of the optic nerve to the optic foramen.

posterior central v. Postcentral vein of Kuhnt.

preinfundibular v. A semicircular venous arch on the inferior surface of the optic chiasm which courses anteriorly around the infundibulum, interconnects with the superior plexus of the optic chiasm, and empties into the basal veins.

recipient v. An episcleral vein which joins with an aqueous vein to form a laminary vein.

retino-ciliary v. Optico-ciliary vein.

supraorbital v. A vein which communicates with the superficial temporal vein and courses along the superior orbital margin to join the frontal vein at the medial angle of the orbit to form the angular vein. It sends a branch through the supraorbital notch to the superior ophthalmic vein.

Vesalius, v. of. An emissary vein which passes through the foramen of Vesalius, medial to the foramen ovale in the great wing of the sphenoid bone, and forms a communication between the pterygoid plexus and the cavernous sinus.

vortex v's. Four, or more, veins formed by the confluence of four large whorls of veins in the choroid which drain blood from the iris, the ciliary body, and all of the choroid and leave the eyeball via canals in the sclera. They emerge slightly posterior to the equator of the eyeball and the superior and inferior veins drain into the superior and inferior ophthalmic veins, respectively. Syn., *vasa vorticosa; posterior ciliary veins; venae vorticosae.*

Velhagen's charts; plates; test. See under the nouns.

velonoskiascopy (ve″lo-no-ski-as′ko-pe). A subjective method of determining ametropia, in which a very thin rod, held near to the eye, is moved across the pupil while a distant, small, light source is fixated. In myopia the perceived shadow of the rod will appear to move with the rod, in hypermetropia opposite to the movement of the rod, and in emmetropia no shadow is seen.

vena. A vein.

venting. Providing for or effecting the circulation of tear fluid under a contact lens by virtue of its design in relation to its riding position and movements.

aperture v. Venting facilitated by one or more fenestrations in a contact lens.

chamfer v. Venting facilitated by one or more grooves or channels on the posterior surface of the contact lens.

primary v. Venting facilitated by the design and selection of the conventional variables of the contact lens, such as base curve radius, peripheral curve radii, optical zone diameter, and size and shape of the lens.

secondary v. Venting facilitated by techniques employed in addition to those of primary venting, as, for example, apertures, grooves, ballasts, or truncations.

ventricle, optic (ven′trih-kl). The cavity of the optic vesicle.

vergence (ver′jens). 1. A disjunctive rotational movement of the eyes such that the points of reference on the globes move in opposite directions, as in convergence, cyclovergence, or sursumvergence. 2. The dioptric or wavefront characteristic of a bundle of light rays, as when emanating from a point source (divergence) or directed toward a real image point (convergence).

fusional v. A vergence movement of the eye occurring as a response to disparate or unfused binocular stimuli, or the range or extent of such movement with respect to given conditions of reference.

　fusional v., reserve. Fusional vergence in excess of that required for the fixation distance, clinically measured by vergence-inducing prisms from the fusional demand point to the limit of clear, single, binocular vision.

image v. The vergence of the light leaving an optical surface, ex-pressed in terms of the curvature of the wavefront, usually in diopters.

　image v., reduced. The reciprocal of the reduced image distance, hence the index of refraction of the image medium divided by the image distance. It is conventionally designated by the symbol U′.

object v. The vergence of the light entering an optical surface, expressed in terms of the curvature of the wavefront, usually in diopters.

　object v., reduced. The reciprocal of the reduced object distance, hence the index of refraction of the object medium divided by the object distance. It is conventionally designated by the symbol U.

relative v. Fusional vergence measured and/or specified with reference to the position of the eyes corresponding to the normal fusional demand for a given testing distance. Its extent is clinically determined by the amount of vergence-inducing prism effect through which single, binocular vision can be maintained.

tonic v. The continuous vergence response maintained by the extraocular muscle tonus, hence absent in paralysis and in death and diminished during sleep or narcosis; the amount of vergence in effect when fixating a distant object with accommodational and fusional impulses absent.

vergens (ver′jenz). Vergence.

deorsum, v. Deorsumvergence.

sursum, v. Sursumvergence.

verger, Maddox prism (ver′jer). A pair of prisms of equal power, mounted in a frame so that one prism is before each eye, to rotate in opposite directions by equal amounts to give variable prismatic effect over a range from zero to the sum of the prism powers.

Verhoeff's (ver'hefz) **chart; circle; membrane; rings; test; theory; stereopter.** See under the nouns.

version (ver'zhun). A conjugate movement of the eyes such that their meridians or lines of reference move in the same direction.

vertex (ver'teks). 1. The point of intersection of the principal axis with a reflecting or refracting surface. 2. A point of reference on the surface of a lens used in specifying the distance of the surface from another optical element in the system, ordinarily a point centered in the lens aperture.

vertex depth; distance; focal length; power; refraction. See under the nouns.

vertigo (ver'tih-go, ver-ti'go). The sensation that one is revolving in space or that fixed objects in space are revolving about one.

epidemic paralyzing v. Gerlier's disease.

ocular v. Vertigo attributed to an ocular or oculomotor disorder.

Vertometer (ver-tom'eh-ter). A trade name for an instrument which determines the vertex refractive power, the cylinder axis, the op-tical center, and the prismatic effect of ophthalmic lenses.

vesicle (ves'ih-kl). 1. A small bladder or sac containing fluid. 2. A small blister. 3. A small cavity.

Greeff's v's. Collections of protein-rich fluid beneath the ciliary epithelium, associated with the production of plasmoid intraocular fluid.

lens v. A hollow spherical body of a single row of cells, formed by invagination of the lens plate into the optic cup, after formation of the lens pit, at about the fourth week of embryonic life; the forerunner of the adult crystalline lens.

optic v. One of a pair of ventrolateral, hollow, evaginations of the neural ectoderm of the forebrain, derived from the optic pits after closure of the embryonic neural groove, which subsequently invaginate to form the optic cups. Syn., *primary optic vesicle.*

optic v., secondary. Optic cup.

vessel. A canal or tube containing and conveying blood or lymph.

annular v. An embryonic vessel

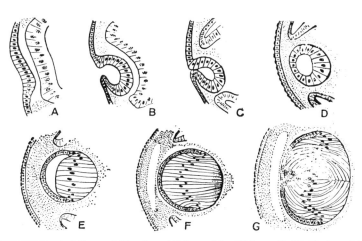

Fig. 43. Development of the crystalline lens: (A) Lens plate, (B) Lens pit, (C) Closing of lens pit, (D) Lens vesicle, (E) Elongation of posterior cells of lens vesicle, (F) Complete filling of cavity of lens vesicle, (G) Formation of lens sutures. (From *The Development of the Human Eye,* Ida Mann, British Medical Association, 1950)

appearing at about the fourth week which circles the edge of the optic cup and branches to form the anterior portion of the tunica vasculosa lentis, variously considered to be an artery and a vein.

lymphatic v's., posttarsal. A plexus of lymphatic vessels, located in the palpebral conjunctiva of the eyelid posterior to the tarsus, which communicate with pretarsal lymphatic vessels through the tarsus. They drain the conjunctival and the Meibomian glands and empty into the submaxillary lymph nodes.

lymphatic v's., pretarsal. A plexus of lymphatic vessels, located in the eyelid anterior to the tarsus, which communicate with the posttarsal lymphatic vessels through the tarsus. They drain the skin and adjacent structures and empty into the preauricular and parotid lymph nodes.

radial v's. of Teichmann. Radial lymphatic vessels in the region of the limbus which receive from the lymphatic circle of Teichmann and drain into larger subconjunctival lymphatic vessels.

sentinel v's. Dilated and tortuous episcleral vessels representing a neovascularization in response to an underlying choroidal tumor.

v.f. Abbreviation for *visual field.*

Vibrating Localizer. A visual training instrument designed by Bangerter to teach spatial localization with the assistance of auditory clues, in the preliminary treatment of amblyopia ex anopsia. It is hand-held against a screen and creates a buzzing sound and vibration which is localized and touched from the opposite side of the screen. A light source in the instrument is added to the stimulus when the site of sound and vibration has been successfully localized, and finally only the light source is presented.

Vibra-Tonometer. A tonometer which electronically modifies the force of a driven plunger until it is in equilibrium with the counter force of the elastic recoil of the tissue of the cornea, this equalizing force being recorded on a milliammeter.

Vicq d'Azyr's band (vik daz-arz'). Line of Gennari.

Vieth-Mueller (vēth-mūl'er) **circle; horopter.** See under the nouns.

view. 1. That which may be seen, usually implying an extent of delineation; the sight presented to the eye. 2. The act of seeing. 3. A sketch, a picture, or other artificial reproduction of a scene. 4. To see.

Maxwellian v. The appearance of a lens or a lens aperture filled with light of uniform intensity, obtained when the light is focused at the entrance pupil of the observing eye. Under these conditions the amount of light entering the eye is not affected by the size of the pupil.

viewing, eccentric. Fixation with an off-center retinal site and with the subjective awareness that the eye is not aimed directly at the target, as may occur with an absolute central scotoma.

vignetting (vin-yet'ing). 1. A graduated reduction in illumination at the edges of an image due to a series of stops in the lens system selectively blocking obliquely incident light. 2. The photographic process of gradually blending the picture with the surrounding ground.

Vincent's sign (vin'sents). Argyll Robertson pupil.

violet. 1. The hue attribute of visual sensations typically evoked by stimulation of the normal human eye with radiation of wavelengths of the visible spectrum shorter than 450 mμ. 2. Any hue predominantly similar to that of the typical violet.

visual v. Porphyropsin.

Virchow's corpuscle (fẽr'kōz). A corneal corpuscle.

visibility. 1. The degree, state, or quality of being visible. 2. The range of vision for objects under existing conditions of atmosphere, light, etc. 3. Luminosity. 4. The degree of clearness of the atmosphere as represented on a meteorological scale.

visibility coefficient; curve; factor; meter. See under the nouns.

visible. Capable of being perceived or distinguished through the sense of vision.

visie (vis'ih, ve'zih). 1. A careful look, as when aiming or aligning. 2. The front sight of a gun or of a similar aiming system.

visile (viz'il). 1. Of or pertaining to vision; readily recalling visual impressions. 2. A visile person; one who visualizes readily.

vision. 1. The special sense by which objects, their form, color, position, etc., in the external environment are perceived, the exciting stimulus being light from the objects striking the retina of the eye; the act, function, process, or power of seeing; sight. 2. That which is seen. 3. To look at; to see. 4. A visual hallucination. 5. The quality of seeing; visual acuity.

achromatic v. Total color blindness.

after v. See *aftervision.*

alternating v. Vision considered as a process in which the impulses from each eye are alternately inhibited or suppressed while the impulses from the other eye are utilized.

ambiocular v. Vision as obtained in ambiocular strabismus.

arhythmic v. Vision equally suited for both high and low levels of illumination, as in most teleost fishes, frogs, crocodiles, ungulates,

or wolves. See also *crepuscular, diurnal,* and *nocturnal vision.*

averted v. Observation of a target with peripheral vision.

bifoveal v. Binocular vision involving the foveas of both eyes.

binocular v. 1. Vision in which both eyes contribute toward producing a single fused percept. 2. Vision occurring as a co-ordinated, integrated, or simultaneous function of both eyes.

    binocular v., grades of. Degrees of fusion. See under *fusion.*

    binocular v., single. Vision in which both eyes contribute toward producing a single fused percept.

black v. A perversion of vision in which objects appear blackish, or darker than normal, as may occur in bromide intoxication.

blue v. Cyanopsia.

central v. Foveal or macular vision. Syn., *direct vision.*

chromatic v. 1. Vision in which the color sense is present, as distinguished from *achromatic vision.* 2. Chromatopsia.

color v. Chromatic vision.

cone v. Vision or vision attributes identified with cone function. Cf. *duplicity theory; photopic vision.*

crepuscular v. Vision suited only for twilight levels of illumination, as is said to occur in some snakes. See also *arhythmic, diurnal,* and *nocturnal vision.*

cyclopean v. Binocular vision regarded or schematically represented in terms of the hypothetical cyclopean eye.

daylight v. Photopic vision.

deuteranomalous v. Deuteranomaly.

deuteranopic v. Deuteranopia.

dichromatic v. Dichromatism.

direct v. Central vision.

distance v. Vision or visual acuity for objects at distances representing reasonably approximate dioptric equivalents of infinity, the distance of 20 ft. or 6 m. being commonly accepted for clinical purposes.

distance of distinct v. See under *distance.*

diurnal v. 1. Vision especially suited for daylight, occurring in animals whose retinae predominately or entirely contain cone cells, as in lizards, birds, and squirrels. See also *arhythmic, crepuscular,* and *nocturnal vision.* 2. Photopic vision.

double v. Diplopia.

eccentric v. Peripheral vision.

entoptic v. Illusory perception of images or patterns in the external visual field, derived from sensory stimulation by shadows or other optical effects of structures or objects inside the eye, or induced by nonphotic disturbances of the receptor system.

extrafoveal v. 1. Vision resulting from stimulation of the retina, exclusive of the fovea; peripheral vision. 2. Macular vision, other than foveal.

field of v. See under *field.*

fogged v. 1. Vision artificially blurred, generally by the use of convex lenses in excess of the power required for best vision. 2. Vision hazed by an affection of the ocular media.

form v. Perception of shape or contour.

foveal v. Vision resulting from stimulation of the fovea.

green v. Chloropsia.

gun barrel v. Tunnel vision.

halo v. Vision in which colored or luminous rings are perceived around lights.

haploscopic v. Vision as obtained by presenting separate fields of view to the two eyes so that they may be seen as a single, superimposed, integrated, or fused field.

indirect v. Peripheral vision.

industrial v. The branch of visual care identified or concerned with visual problems of industrially

classified occupational groups, involving evaluation of visual ability, prescribing corrective lenses and protective ocular devices, and determining the optimum environment for visual efficiency.

intermittent v. 1. Vision resulting from intermittent stimulation, as from a series of light pulses. 2. Vision in which objects alternately appear and disappear, as may occur in intermittent suppression or when an absolute threshold is approached.

iridescent v. Vision in which colors are perceived around the borders of an image. Syn., *rainbow vision.*

macular v. Vision resulting from stimulation of receptors in the region of the macula lutea.

mesopic v. Vision said to be intermediate or transitional between photopic and scotopic vision, identified with levels of illumination approximately between 0.001 and 10 cd./m². Syn., *mesopia; twilight vision.*

mobile v. Lawson's term for vision occurring just before, and just after, the blackout period of a blink, i.e., as the upper eyelid moves across the pupil. Cf. *static vision.*

monochromatic v. Monochromatism.

monocular v. Vision or visual acuity as a function of one eye only or of each eye separately.

motorist v. The branch of visual care identified or concerned with visual problems of automobile drivers, driver licensing, and vehicle and highway design.

multiple v. Vision in which more than one image of a single object is perceived. Syn., *polyopia.*

naked v. Visual acuity as measured without an ophthalmic lens or any other corrective device before the eye; unaided visual acuity.

near v. Vision or visual acuity for objects at distances corresponding to the normal reading distance, clinical standards varying from about 13 to 16 in., usually specified from the spectacle plane.

night v. 1. Scotopic vision. 2. Vision which improves in dim light; day blindness.

nocturnal v. 1. Vision especially suited for low levels of illumination, as at night, occurring in animals whose retinae predominately or entirely contain rod cells, such as in cats, alligators, and rats. Cf. *arhythmic, crepuscular,* and *diurnal vision.* 2. Scotopic vision.

null, v. Vision characterized by unawareness of abnormal scotomata in the visual field. Cf. *vision obscure.*

obscure, v. Vision characterized by awareness of abnormal scotomata present in the visual field. Cf. *vision null.*

oscillating v. Vision in which objects appear to swing back and forth. Syn., *oscillopsia.*

panoramic v. Vision as obtained in animals whose eyes are so laterally located or divergently oriented as to make their monocular fields complementary and continuous, with a minimum of overlapping.

paracentral v. Vision resulting from stimulation of the retina immediately surrounding or near the fovea or the macula.

parafoveal v. Vision resulting from stimulation of the retina immediately surrounding or near the fovea.

peripheral v. 1. Vision resulting from stimulation of the retina exclusive of the fovea or the macula. Syn., *eccentric vision; indirect vision.* 2. Vision resulting from stimulation of receptors at or near the periphery of the retina.

persistent v. Aftervision.

photopic v. Vision attributed to cone function, normally identified with higher levels of illumination, approximately 10 cd./m². or more, and characterized by the ability to discriminate colors and small detail. Syn., *photopia; daylight vision.*

Pick's v's. Visual hallucinations or visual space distortions resulting from a lesion involving the medial longitudinal fasciculus.

protanomalous v. Protanomaly.

pseudoscopic v. Vision in reverse stereoscopic relief or as obtained with a pseudoscope.

rainbow v. Iridescent vision.

range of v. 1. The linear distance from far to near through which objects can be seen. 2. The angular extent of the visual field. 3. The range of illumination through which vision is possible.

recurrent v. Perception of the series of negative and positive afterimages after the exciting stimulus has terminated.

red v. Erythropsia.

rod v. Vision or vision attributes identified with rod function. Cf. *scotopic vision; duplicity theory.*

scotopic v. Vision attributed to rod function, normally identified with levels of illumination below approximately 0.001 cd./m²., characterized by the lack of ability to discriminate colors and small detail, and effective primarily in the detection of movement and low luminous intensities. Syn., *scotopia; night vision.*

shaft v. Tunnel vision.

simultaneous v. Binocular vision.

solid v. Vision characterized by the perception of relief or depth.

speed of v. See under *speed.*

static v. Lawson's term for vision occurring during the interblink period. Cf. *mobile vision.*

stereoscopic v. Stereopsis.

subnormal v. Vision considered to be inferior to normal vision, as represented by accepted standards of acuity, field of vision, or motility, and uncorrectable by conventional lenses, or the branch of visual care identified with its correction or rehabilitation by special aids or techniques. Cf. *blindness.*

telescopic v. Tunnel vision.

tetartanopic v. Tetartanopsia.

tetrachromatic v. Tetrachromatism.

training, v. See under *training.*

traveling v. Subnormal vision of a level sufficient to permit walking about without guidance.

trichromatic v. Trichromatism.

   trichromatic v., anomalous. Anomalous trichromatism.

tritanomalous v. Anomalous trichromatism.

tritanopic v. Tritanopia.

tubular v. Tunnel vision.

tunnel v. 1. Vision in which the visual field is concentrically contracted and constant in diameter irrespective of the testing distance, as if looking through a tube, usually attributed to hysteria or malingering. Syn., *gun barrel vision; shaft vision; telescopic vision; tubular vision.* 2. Vision in which the visual field is severely contracted.

twilight v. Mesopic vision.

violet v. A perversion of vision in which objects appear violet, sometimes occurring as a consequence of toxic amblyopia.

white v. A perversion of vision in which objects appear whitish, as covered with snow, as may occur in digitalis intoxication.

yellow v. Xanthopsia.

Vision Tester, Titmus. A visual screening instrument containing targets for measuring visual acuity, phorias, fusion, stereopsis, and color perception. It consists essentially of a Brewster-type stereoscope, an internally illuminated rotating drum for holding up to 12 targets, and an adjustment to simulate either a near or a far testing distance.

visionics (vizh″e-on′iks). The study of aiding vision with electronic devices.

visual. Pertaining to vision.

visual achievement; acuity; **agnosia;** agraphia; amnesia; analysis; angle; aphasia; apparatus; apraxia; autokinesis; **reflex arc;** axis; cells; centers; concession; cone; cortex; direction; discrimination; dominance; efficiency; fibers; field; green; laterality; line; memory; pathway; plane; point; projection; purple; red; skill; space; tract; training; violet; white; yellow. See under the nouns.

Visual Stimulator. A trade name for a visual testing apparatus which provides binocular or monocular light stimuli with variations in light intensity, spectral distribution, flicker frequency, and duration of single light pulses.

visualization. The act or the faculty of forming a mental visual image of an object not present to the eyes, or the image itself.

visualize. To form a mental visual image of an object not present to the eyes.

visualness. The visual aspect or attribute of a percept not initiated by the visual mechanism, as, e.g., the visually identified attribute of a tactually sensed object, brought about by experience and association.

visuo- (vizh′u-o-). A combining form denoting *vision.*

visuoauditory (vizh″u-o-aw′dih-tōr″e). Both visual and auditory; pertaining to seeing and hearing.

visuognosis (vizh″u-og-no′sis). Recognition and interpretation of visual stimuli.

visuometer (vizh″u-om′eh-ter). An instrument designed by Smee to measure the separation of the lines of sight by the separation of a pair of parallel cylindrical apertures through each of which a distant object appears centered by each of the two eyes, respectively.

visuopsychic (vizh″u-o-si′kik). Pertaining to the visual association areas of the occipital cortex, Brodmann's areas 18 and 19.

visuosensory (vizh″u-o-sen′sor-e). Pertaining to the visual sensory area of the occipital cortex, Brodmann's area 17.

visus (vi′sus). Vision.

brevior, v. Myopic vision.

coloratus, v. Chromatopsia.

debilitas, v. Asthenopia.

decoloratus, v. Achromatopsia.

defiguratus, v. Distorted vision.

dimidiatus, v. Hemianopsia.

duplicatus, v. Diplopia.

muscarum, v. Vision in which spots are seen before the eyes.

reticulatus, v. Vision in which the field appears sievelike, due to scotomata.

senilis, v. Presbyopia.

triplex, v. Triplopia.

Visuscope (vizh′u-skōp). An instrument designed to determine the type of monocular fixation in amblyopia, consisting essentially of an ophthalmoscope adapted with a small, central, opaque, fixation target which projects a shadow onto the retina, the position of the shadow in relation to the fovea indicating the type of fixation.

visuum (vizh′u-um). The two eyes, their extrinsic muscles and other contents of the orbits, the nerves, the pathways, and the visual cortex, considered collectively. Syn., *visual apparatus.*

vitamin A. A fat-soluble vitamin found in fish liver oils, liver, eggs, milk and milk products, and in some vegetables and fruits. Deficiency in the diet causes inadequate production and regeneration of rhodopsin, resulting in night blindness, and disturbed metabolism of epithelial tissue, resulting in keratomalacia, xerophthalmia, and lessened resistance to infection through epithelial surfaces.

vitamin B$_1$. A water-soluble vitamin present in small quantities in most edible plant and animal tissues and more abundantly in milk, yeast, unrefined cereal grains, liver, heart, kidney, and pork. It is necessary in carbohydrate metabolism, and a deficiency in the diet results in peripheral neuropathy, such as beriberi with the accompanying eye signs of nystagmus, ptosis, extraocular muscle paresis, corneal dystrophy, and optic atrophy. Its deficiency is considered a primary cause of nutritional amblyopia. Syn., *aneurine; thiamine.*

vitamin B$_6$. Pyridoxine.

vitamin B$_{12}$. Cyanocobalamin.

vitamin C. Ascorbic acid.

vitamin D. A group of fat-soluble vitamins involved in the absorption of phosphates and calcium salts from the alimentary canal to increase the supply of calcium and phosphorus in the blood for producing and maintaining bone and teeth structure. It is found in fish liver oils, to a lesser extent in milk, eggs, and butter, and is produced by the action of ultraviolet radiation on foods containing sterols, or of sunlight on the body. Deficiency in the diet in children results in rickets and, in adults, osteomalacia, either of which may have associated cataract. Excessive therapeutic doses may impair renal function and produce metastatic calcifications with involvement of the conjunctiva, cornea, and sclera.

vitamin G. Riboflavin.

vitiligo (vit″ih-li′go). A disease of the skin characterized by patches of depigmentation of various sizes and shapes.

v. of the choroid. Absence of pigment in the choroid with the choroidal circulation and underlying sclera being easily visible.

iridis, v. The condition of small, white, depigmented areas on the iris.

vitrein (vit're-in). A residual protein of the collagen-gelatin type in the vitreous humor, which partially accounts for the gel state of the vitreous body. Syn., *vitrosin.*

vitrella (vih-trel'ah). A specialized cell in the compound eyes of arthropods which secretes the crystalline cone of the ommatidium. Syn., *retinophore.*

vitreocapsulitis (vit"re-o-kap"su-li'-tis). Hyalitis.

vitreous (vit're-us). The vitreous humor or body.

anterior v. Fibrillar protoplasmic adhesions between the lens vesicle and the surface ectoderm of the 12 mm. human embryo. It loses its connection with the lens vesicle in the 13–14 mm. stage and soon disappears.

body, v. See under *body.*

chamber, v. See under *chamber.*

detached v. Vitreous separated from its normal attachments, due to shrinkage from degenerative or inflammatory conditions, trauma, myopia, or senility.

fluid v. Vitreous which is liquefied due to inflammatory or degenerative conditions of the eye. Ophthalmoscopically visible opacities are usually an accompaniment. See also *synchysis.*

humor, v. See under *humor.*

hyaloidean v. Primary vitreous.

membrane, v. See under *membrane.*

persistent hyperplastic primary v. A congenital condition occurring in full term infants characterized by a fibroplastic retrolental mass formed by a persistent primary vitreous and remnants of the hyaloid vascular system and tunica vasculosa lentis. It is usually unilateral, occurs in a microphthalmic eye, and distinguishing features include a white pupil, shallow anterior chamber, elongated ciliary processes, visible blood vessels in the iris, a partially or totally absorbed crystalline lens, and retinal detachment due to adhesions.

primary v. The first vitreous formed in the embryo, consisting of a mass of fibrils between the inner wall of the optic cup and the lens vesicle, derived from neuroectoderm (optic cup), surface ectoderm (lens vesicle), and mesoderm. It becomes vascularized by the hyaloid artery and its branches (vasa hyaloidea propria), and its development ends with the appearance of the hyaline capsule of the crystalline lens at about the 13 mm. stage. As the secondary vitreous develops, a line of condensation between it and the primary vitreous forms the walls of the hyaloid canal to which the primary vitreous is restricted. Syn., *hyaloidean vitreous.*

secondary v. Avascular vitreous formed around the primary vitreous in the embryo from the 13

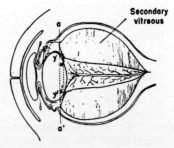

Fig. 44. Diagram of the secondary vitreous around the primary vitreous. xx' marks the site of the arcuate line; yy' marks the site of Egger's line, and aa' indicates the peripheral boundary of the secondary vitreous. (From *Embryology of the Human Eye,* A. N. Barber, C. V. Mosby, 1955)

mm. stage to the 65–70 mm. stage. It consists of a mass of densely packed, fine fibrils derived from the inner layer of the optic cup (neuroectoderm), although there may be a few fibrils derived from the lens vesicle in its central portion.

tertiary v. Vitreous fibrils derived from the neuroepithelium at the margin of the optic cup in the region of the ciliary body, commencing at the 65–70 mm. stage of the embryo and giving rise to the zonule of Zinn.

vitreum (vit're-um). The vitreous humor.

vitric (vit'rik). Pertaining to or appearing like glass.

vitrics (vit'riks). The study of glass and glass manufacture.

vitrina (vih-tri'nah). The vitreous humor.

oculi, v. The vitreous humor.

vitritis (vit-ri'tis). Hyalitis.

vitrosin (vit'ro-sin). Vitrein.

Vogt's (fōgts) **cataract; floury cornea; mosaic degeneration; limbus girdle; lucid interval; subluxated lens; line; membrana plicata; sign; keratoconus stripes; theory.** See under the nouns.

Vogt-Koyanagi syndrome (fōgt-ko-yah-nah'ge). See under *syndrome.*

Vogt-Spielmeyer disease (fōgt-spēl'ma-er). Batten-Mayou disease.

Voight effect (voit). Magnetic double refraction.

Volk conoid lens. See under *lens.*

Volkmann's (fōlk'mahnz) **center of rotation; disks.** See under the nouns.

vortex, lens. The configuration formed by the elongated extensions of the cells of the subcapsular epithelium of the crystalline lens which arc anteriorly from the region of the equator.

Vossius (vos'e-us) **ring cataract; ring opacity; ring.** See *cataract, Vossius ring.*

V-Scope. A truncated paper cone, so folded that it must be pressed between the two hands to keep it open, used for determining sighting dominance by sighting through it at a target. See also *Miles's A-B-C test.*

Vu-Tach. A trade name for a near point tachistoscope with six exposure speeds from 1/100 to 1.0 second, used to improve speed and span of comprehension in reading

W

Waardenburg's syndrome (vahr'-
den-burgz). See under *syndrome*.

Wachendorf's membrane (vahk'en-
dorfs). The pupillary membrane.

Wadsworth (wahds'wurth) **mirror;
prism.** See under the nouns.

wafer. A very thin meniscus lens designed to be cemented to a larger
lens to form a bifocal lens.

Wald cycle (wahld). See under
cycle.

Waldenström's syndrome (vahl'den-
stremz). See under *syndrome*.

Waldeyer's gland (vahl'di-erz). See
under *gland*.

Walker's (wok'erz) **chart; color
disk.** See under the nouns.

Wallace chart (wol'is). See under
chart.

Wallach's rings. See under *ring*.

Wallenberg's syndrome (vahl'en-
bergz). See under *syndrome*.

walleye. Leukoma of the cornea.

walleyed. Having divergent strabismus.

Walls's theory (wawlz'ez). See under *theory*.

Walser shell. See under *shell*.

wand, Branchaud. A hand-held device for testing and training pursuit fixation movements consisting essentially of a miniature
neon lamp, flickering at a rate
of 120 times per second, mounted
at one end of a 14″ black plastic
rod which houses an electrical
connection to the lamp. Deviations from accurate fixational pursuit are indicated when the subject detects flicker.

Wartenberg's sign (wor'ten-bergz).
See under *sign*.

warts, Hassall-Henle. Hassall-Henle
bodies.

warts, Henle's. Hassall-Henle bodies.

waterfall, James's. A device for
creating a waterfall visual illusion, consisting of a pattern of
alternate black and white, horizontal, parallel stripes which may
be moved continuously in one
direction against a stationary
background of the same pattern.

wave. A periodic or systematic fluctuation, modulation, pulsation, or
undulation, or one of a series of
such variations.

A w. Alpha rhythm.

a w. A small negative dip in the
electroretinogram following the
latent period, after the onset of
the stimulus.

alpha w. Alpha rhythm.

amplitude, w. See under *amplitude*.

b w. A tall postive wave of brief
duration in the electroretinogram
immediately following the *a*
wave.

c w. A relatively long, slowly rising wave in the electroretinogram
immediately following the *b*
wave.

d w. A small positive hump in the
electroretinogram, higher than
the *c* wave, which follows the latent period at the cessation of the
stimulus.

electromagnetic w. A wave produced by the oscillation of an
electric charge, characterized by
a varying electric field at right
angles to the direction of propagation and a varying magnetic
field at right angles to both.

frequency, w. See under *frequency.*

light *w.* 1. In the wave theory of light propagation, a single pulse or disturbance in a space of one wavelength of the advance of the disturbance in a medium. 2. A wave of radiant energy, between approximately 380 and 760 mμ, that gives rise to visual sensation on stimulating the retina.

 light w's., coherent. Light waves having a constant phase difference, as when derived from the same source.

 light w., intensity of. The amount of energy, as represented in a light wave, that flows per second across a unit area perpendicular to the direction of propagation, directly proportional to the product of the velocity and the square of the amplitude.

 light w., noncoherent. Concurrent light waves not having a constant phase difference, as when derived from different sources.

 light w., phase of. See under *phase.*

 light w., plane. A light wave having a plane wavefront.

 light w., secondary. A light wave generated by the oscillations of the bound charges of an atom or a molecule induced by incident light waves.

 light w., spherical. A light wave having a spherical wavefront.

longitudinal w. A wave in which the direction of vibration is parallel to its direction of propagation, e.g., a sound wave.

number, w. See under *number.*

surface, w. A wavefront.

transverse w. A wave in which the direction of vibration is perpendicular to its direction of propagation, e.g., a light wave.

wavefront. An imaginary surface representing the locus of points in wave motion for which, at a given instant, the phase is the same.

 strip division of w. The subdivision of a wavefront into strips of infinitesimal width, parallel to the slit source, for the theoretical analysis of the diffractional contribution of each portion.

wavelength. The distance in the line of advance of a wave from any one point to the next point at which, at the same instant, the phase is the same.

 complementary w. A complementary color designated in terms of its dominant wavelength.

 dominant w. The spectral wavelength which, on proper mixing with white, will match a given sample of color.

wavelet. In the wave theory of light propagation, one of the infinitesimal component wave elements considered to originate at any point on a wavefront, integrating with its fellow wavelets from all other points on the same wavefront to constitute a further advanced wavefront.

weakness, color. Defectivity of color vision characterized by a diminished sensitivity to color or lowered ability to discriminate small differences in hue; usually considered synonymous with *anomalous trichromatism.*

web, terminal. A thin cytoplasmic structure, just anterior to and lining the posterior cellular membrane (the posterior limit) of the corneal mesothelium.

Weber's (va'berz) **law; phenomenon.** See under the nouns.

Weber's (web'erz) **paralysis; sign; symptom; syndrome.** See under the nouns.

Weber-Fechner law (va'ber-fek'ner). See under *law.*

Weber-Gubler syndrome (web'er-goōb'ler). See under *syndrome.*

Wedensky inhibition. See under *inhibition.*

wedge, optical. A gradient filter.

weeping. 1. Excessive lacrimation. 2. Exuding fluid, as from a raw surface.

primary w. Lacrimation due to direct stimulation or irritation of the lacrimal gland.

psychic w. Lacrimation associated with emotional states or physical pain.

reflex w. Weeping in response to neurogenic stimulation, as irritation of the cornea or the conjunctiva, glare, vomiting, etc.

Weil's disease (vīlz). See under *disease*.

Weil-Marchesani syndrome. See under *syndrome*.

Weiss's (vīsz'ez) **reflex; sign; test type.** See under the nouns.

Welland's test (wel'andz). Bar reading test.

Werner's syndrome (ver'nerz). See under *syndrome*.

Wernicke's (ver-nih-kēz) **aphasia; disease; triangular field; prism; pupillary reaction; pupillary reflex; sign; symptom; syndrome.** See under the nouns.

Wessely's tubes (ves'lēz). See under *tube*.

Westphal, pseudosclerosis of (vest'fahl). Wilson's disease.

Westphal's sign (vest'fahlz). See under *sign*.

Westphal-Piltz (vest'fahl-piltz) **phenomenon; reaction; reflex.** Orbicularis pupillary reflex.

Weyers-Thier syndrome. Oculovertebral dysplasia.

Weymouth-Anderson hypothesis (wa'muth-an'der-sen). See under *hypothesis*.

Wheatstone stereoscope (whēt'stōn). See under *stereoscope*.

wheel, color. Color circle.

white. 1. An achromatic color of maximum lightness or minimum darkness representing one limit of the series of grays; the complement or opposite of *black*. 2. The attribute of visual sensations typically evoked by stimulation of the normal human eye by a mixture of radiant energy of different wavelengths approximating in physiological action that which is characteristic of daylight. The ideal white is obtained when a normally illuminated surface reflects all the light incident on it.

visual w. Leukopsin.

White's absorption cell. See under *cell, absorption*.

whiteness. 1. A positive perceptual attribute of any surface or part thereof which has higher reflectance than its surroundings, whiteness being induced by the dimmer surround. 2. The degree of approach to that extreme or limit of the series of grays known as *white*. 3. Suggesting *white*, e.g., the tint of a color.

Whitnall's (hwit'nalz) **ciliary mass; tubercle.** See under the nouns.

Whittington's (hwit'ing-tons) **stereoscope; test.** See under the nouns.

Whitwell's table. See under *table*.

Whytt's reflex (hwits). See under *reflex*.

Widesite (wīd'sīt). 1. A trade name for a series of corrected curve lenses. 2. A trade name for a series of fused bifocal lenses.

Widmark's conjunctivitis (wid'mahrks). See under *conjunctivitis*.

Wieger's ligament (ve'gerz). Hyaloideo-capsular ligament.

Wien's law (vēnz). See under *law*.

Wiener's theory (wēn'erz). See under *theory*.

Wight's test. See under *test*.

Wilbrand's (vil'brahntz) **exhaustion visual field; phenomenon; test.** See under the nouns.

Wilder's sign (wil'derz). See under *sign*.

Williams' refractometer; test. See under the nouns.

Willis' circle (wil'is). See under *circle*.

Wils-Edge. See *mounting, Wils-Edge*.

Wilson's (wil'sunz) **disease; phenomenon; phorometer.** See under the nouns.

Wiltberger's (wilt'ber-gerz). See under *test*.

window. An opening for the admission of light or air.

entrance w. Entrance port.

exit w. Exit port.

Hering w. A device to demonstrate color contrast, consisting essentially of a black shutter with two openings, one containing a white ground glass, the other a colored glass. Shadows formed on a white surface by a black rod in the beams from the two openings are compared. See also *colored shadow experiment.*

wing, Maddox. A hand-held instrument for measuring a phoria at near, consisting of a target containing an intersecting vertical and horizontal tangent scale, a horizontal arrow pointing to the left and a finger pointing upward, a septum, and two slit apertures, one for each eye. In viewing the target one eye sees the arrow and the finger, the other sees the tangent scale, and the numbers, to which the finger and the arrow appear to point, indicate the magnitude of the vertical and horizontal components of the phoria.

wink. To momentarily close the eyelids, especially of only one eye; the act itself.

winking. The brief closing of the eyelids, especially of one eye. Cf. *blinking.*

jaw w. See under *jaw-winking.*

pterygoid w. Paradoxical movements of the upper eyelids occurring in association with movements of the muscles of mastication; a rare congenital anomaly.

rectus muscle w. Paradoxical movements of the upper eyelids occurring in association with movement of a rectus muscle; a rare congenital anomaly.

Winslow's stars (wins'lōz). See under *stars*.

Wirt stereotest; test. See under *test*.

wl. Abbreviation for *wavelength.*

Wolfe tonometer (woolf). See under *tonometer.*

Wolfring's gland (vōlf'ringz). See under *glands.*

Wolfrum's theory (volf'rumz). See under *theory.*

Wollaston's (wool'as-tonz) **doublet; lens; loupe; polarizer; prism.** See under the nouns.

Wood's filter; glass; light; sign; test. See under the nouns.

word blindness. Alexia.

Worst's goniotomy lens. See under *lens.*

Worth's (worths) **amblyoscope; deviometer; test; theory.** See under the nouns.

Worth-Ramstein test. See under *test.*

Wratten filters (rat'en). See under *filter.*

Wright's (rīts) **colorimeter; theory.** See under the nouns.

Wrisberg, intermediate nerve of (ris'berg). See under *nerve.*

writing, mirror. Writing which appears normal when viewed in a mirror, or the act of writing in this manner. Syn., *retrography.*

Wundt's (voondts) **experiment; figure; visual illusion; theory.** See under the nouns.

Wundt-Lamanski law (voondt-lahman'ske). See under *law.*

Wyburn-Mason syndrome. See under *syndrome.*

X

x. Abbreviation for *axis* in an astigmatic lens formula.

xanthelasma (zan″thel-az′mah). A condition characterized by the presence of rounded or oval, dull yellow, slightly elevated, flat plaques containing foam cells, in the skin of the eyelids. The lesions are usually located near the inner canthi and usually commence on the upper eyelid. It is benign and chronic, occurs primarily in the elderly, and most frequently affects females. Syn., *xanthelasma palpebrarum; xanthoma palpebrarum.*

xanthocyanopia (zan″tho-si″ah-no′-pe-ah). Xanthocyanopsia.

xanthocyanopsia (zan″tho-si″ah-nop′se-ah). Anomalous color vision in which yellow and blue are distinguished, but not red or green.

xanthocyanopsy (zan″tho-si″ah-nop′-se). Xanthocyanopsia.

xanthogranuloma, ocular juvenile (zan″tho-gran″u-lo′mah). Intraocular nevoxanthoendothelioma.

xanthokyanopy (zan″tho-ki-an′o-pe). Xanthocyanopsia.

xanthoma palpebrarum (zan-tho′-mah). Xanthelasma.

xanthomatosis (zan″tho-mah-to′sis). A systemic disorder of fat metabolism characterized by the formation of lipoid tumors in bone, skin, internal organs, etc.

corneae, x. Dystrophia adiposa corneae.

essential hyperlipemic x. Essential familial hyperlipemia.

lentis, x. A rare, late, degenerative change in cataract due to fatty impregnation of the crystalline lens.

xanthophane (zan′tho-fān). A yellow pigment in the retinal receptor cells of some animals.

xanthophose (zan′tho-fōz). A subjective sensation of yellow light or color.

xanthophyll (zan′tho-fil). A yellow photopigment found in plants, a carotenoid of the formula $C_{40}H_{54}(OH)_2$, its chemical derivatives being active in photosynthesis of plant metabolism.

xanthopsia (zan-thop′se-ah). A condition in which all objects appear tinged with yellow, as may occur in picric acid or santonin poisoning and jaundice. Syn., *yellow vision.*

xanthopsin (zan-thop′sin). An intermediate product of the decomposition of rhodopsin on exposure to light, following the breakdown of transient orange and prior to the formation of retinene. Syn., *indicator yellow; visual yellow.*

xenophthalmia (zen″of-thal′me-ah). Conjunctivitis due to trauma or to a foreign body.

xeroderma pigmentosum (ze″ro-der′mah pig-men-to′sum). A progressive pigmentary degeneration of the skin, frequently familial, marked in the first years of life by the appearance of small telangiectases and freckles, particularly in areas exposed to sunlight. Later atrophic patches appear, followed by warty growths, ulcerations, and carcinoma. It frequently affects the eye, and. when involving the conjunctiva, characteristically is manifested as nodules similar to phlyctenules or pingueculae, at the limbus, which ulcerate. Exposure keratitis is common as a result of shrinkage and contracture of the skin of the eyelid margins. Syn., *angioma pigmentosum atrophicum; atrophoderma pigmentosum; Kaposi's disease; melanosis lenticularis progressiva.*

xeroma (ze-ro'mah). Xerosis of the conjunctiva.

xerophthalmia (ze"rof-thal'me-ah). Xerosis of the conjunctiva.

xerosis of the conjunctiva (ze-ro'-sis). A dry, thickened, degenerative condition of the conjunctiva due to failure of its own secretory activity. It commences with localized, lusterless, dry patches which may increase in size and number and coalesce with accompanying opacification, kera-

tinization, and wrinkles. It may be due to local disease, trauma, systemic nutritional disturbance, or exposure. Syn., *conjunctivitis arida; ophthalmoxerosis; scheroma; xeroma; xerophthalmia.*

epithelial x. of the conjunctiva. Xerosis of the conjunctiva initially confined to the epithelial layers, due to a systemic nutritional disturbance such as vitamin A deficiency. Accompanying symptoms may be keratomalacia or night blindness.

parenchymatous x. of the conjunctiva. Xerosis of the conjunctiva affecting all its layers, occurring as a sequel to trauma or local disease, such as pemphigus, trachoma, membranous conjunctivitis, etc.

superficial x. of the conjunctiva. Epithelial xerosis of the conjunctiva.

Y

yellow. 1. The normal visual sensory hue correlate of wavelengths of approximately 578 mμ, or any hue predominantly similar, located between red and green on the spectral scale, classified as one of the psychologically unique colors, and occurring as a complement of blue. 2. Any substance or pigment of yellow color.

indicator y. Lythgoe's term for an intermediate product in the breakdown of rhodopsin, thought to be *xanthopsin*.

sighted, y. Said to display an abnormally high color sensitivity to yellow or a tendency to see all objects tinged with yellow.

spot, y. Macula lutea.

visual y. Xanthopsin.

Young's experiment; optometer; test; theory; color triangle. See under the nouns.

Young-Helmholtz theory (yung-helm'hōltz). See under *theory*.

Z

Zagora rod test (zah-gōr′ah). See under *test*.

Zeeman's (za′mahnz) **effect; theory.** See under the nouns.

Zeis's gland (zīs′ez). See under *gland*.

Zelex. A trade name for a molding compound used in taking eye impressions in the fitting of impression contact lenses.

Zenger prism. See under *prism*.

Zeune's law (zu′nēz). See under *law*.

Ziegler prism scale (zēg′ler). See under *scale*.

Zinn's (zinz) **annulus; artery; circle; corona; ligament; membrane; tendon; zone; zonule.** See under the nouns.

zoetrope (zo′eh-trōp). A hollow cylinder containing on its inside surface a series of pictures representing the successive stages in the movement of objects or persons. The pictures are viewed through slits in the cylinder, while it is rapidly revolving, so that each picture is seen individually and instantaneously and the effect of animation is obtained.

Zöllner's (zel′nerz) **figure; visual illusion; lines.** See under the nouns.

zona (zo′nah). A zone.

  ciliaris, z. The ciliary zone.

  ophthalmica, z. Herpes zoster ophthalmicus.

zone. An arbitrarily or differentially delimited area or region.

  capillary z. of the choroid. Choriocapillaris.

  chromatic z's. Color zones.

  ciliary z. The peripheral region of the anterior surface of the iris located between the root of the iris and the collarette. It has been divided by Fuchs into an inner smooth area, a middle furrowed area, and a marginal cribriform area next to the ciliary body. Syn., *greater ring of the iris; greater ring of Merkel.*

  color z's. Regions of the visual field differentiated according to chromatic response, usually determined by means of the perimeter with various color targets.

  comfort, z. of. Area of comfort.

  crystalline lens, z's. of the. The embryonic nucleus, the fetal nucleus, the infantile nucleus, the adult nucleus, and the cortex of the crystalline lens.

  discontinuity, z's of. Zones of varying optical density in the crystalline lens or cornea, as seen in slit lamp biomicroscopy.

  equidistant z. The zone in space between the anterior and posterior limits of the apparent frontoparallel plane horopter. Anteroposterior displacement of a nonfixated target within this space will still be judged as lying in the same plane as the fixation target, hence the displacement is less than the threshold of stereopsis.

  Fresnel's z. Half-period zone.

  half-period z. Any one of a series of concentric zones on a wavefront of monochromatic light whose successive contingent borders are each one-half wavelength farther or nearer from a given point of reference exterior to the wavefront surface and in its advancing path. Syn., *Fresnel's zone.*

interpalpebral z. The portion of the cornea and the sclera not covered when the eyelids are opened.

marginal z. of the optic cup. Marginal layer of the optic cup.

nuclear z. The region of the crystalline lens containing an aggregation of nuclei of cells of the anterior epithelium located beneath the anterior capsule.

optical z. of contact lens. The central, optically useful, portion of a contact lens which corresponds to the area occupied by the base curve.

optical z. of cornea. The central third of the cornea.

plateaus and furrows, z. of. The zone of the conjunctiva containing Stieda's plateaus and Stieda's grooves.

pupillary z. The central region of the anterior surface of the iris located between the collarette and the pupillary margin. Syn., *lesser ring of the iris; lesser ring of Merkel.*

retinal z's. Regions of the retina corresponding to those of the visual field, which are differentiated according to chromatic response or other function.

single clear binocular vision, z. of. In the graphic representation of the functional relationships between accommodation and convergence on a co-ordinate system, the region enclosed by the extremes of accommodation and convergence that can be elicited while maintaining binocular fusion and clear retinal imagery. Clinically, these extremes or limits may be determined haploscopically, or by varying com-

binations of binocular fixation distance, binocularly added concave or convex lenses, and base-in or base-out prism until blurredness or diplopia is reported.

specular reflection, z. of. In slit lamp biomicroscopy, a surface area at which specular reflection occurs, appearing as a dazzling light reflex with irregularities or defects in the surface appearing as dark areas in the bright region.

trabecular z. Trabecular band.

transitional z. The annular portion of a scleral contact lens which joins the corneal section with the scleral section. Syn., *transition.*

Zinn, z. of. Zonule of Zinn.

zonule (zŏn'ūl). A little zone.

Zinn, z. of. The suspensory apparatus of the crystalline lens consisting of a series of noncellular extensions which originate in the orbiculus ciliaris and the corona ciliaris of the ciliary body and insert into the capsule of the lens at and near its equator. The tension of these fibers varies with the state of contraction of the ciliary muscle and thus determines the degree of convexity of the lens. Syn., *suspensory ligament.*

zonulolysis (zōn-u-lo-li'sis). Dissolving of the fibers of the zonule of Zinn by an enzyme instilled into the aqueous humor to facilitate surgical removal of the crystalline lens.

zonulotomy (zōn″u-lot'o-me). Surgical division of the zonule of Zinn.

zoster ophthalmicus (zos'ter ofthal'mih-kus). Herpes zoster ophthalmicus.

zylonite (zi'lo-nīt). A cellulose nitrate thermoplastic material used in spectacle frames.